INTERNATIONAL INDEX
TO
RECORDED POETRY

INTERNATIONAL
INDEX
TO
RECORDED
POETRY

Compiled by

HERBERT H. HOFFMAN

RITA LUDWIG HOFFMAN

New York

THE H. W. WILSON COMPANY

Library of Congress Cataloging in Publication Data

Hoffman, Herbert H.
    International index to recorded poetry.

    Discography: p.
      1. Poetry—Indexes.   2. Poetry—Discography.
I. Hoffman, Rita L.   II. Title.
PN1022.H63   983   011'.38   83–16659
ISBN 0-8242-0682-7

International Standard Book Number 0-8242-0682-7

PRINTED IN THE UNITED STATES OF AMERICA

CONTENTS

Preface   vii

List of Recordings Analyzed   xi

Author Index   1

Title Index   261

First Line Index   361

Reader Index   503

Register of Poets by Language of Composition   517

PREFACE

Intended for librarians, teachers, students of language and literature, and everyone who enjoys the spoken arts, this book is a guide to the world's poetry on recordings. It identifies and indexes—by author, title, first line, and reader—the contents of more than 1,700 recordings issued up through 1981 in the United States and abroad: some 15,000 poems by approximately 2,300 authors, read in upwards of twenty languages on phonodiscs, tapes, audio cassettes, film strips, and video cassettes. Many of these recordings are available commercially, and those that are not can still be found in large library collections (see note at beginning of List of Recordings Analyzed, page xi).

The *Index* is focused on recited poetry, and we have made a special effort to locate recordings of poets reading from their own works. Recordings of verse drama and of poetry set to music are not generally covered here.

The International Index to Recorded Poetry is divided into six sections. The first section is a List of Recordings Analyzed, grouped by manufacturer. The manufacturer's name and address (where known) are given first, then the recordings issued on that label are listed. For the purposes of this index, each recording has been assigned a code number, which appears in the left margin of the list. Thus, the Caedmon section of the list begins:

> CAED   Caedmon, 1995 Broadway, New York,
> NY 10023, USA
> 1   J. R. R. TOLKIEN SOUNDBOOK. Readers: The
> author and Christopher Tolkien. Caedmon
> SBR 101 (4 pd) or SBC 101 (4 ac)

The CAED prefix will be used for all Caedmon recordings analyzed; the Tolkien record will be referred to by its recording code number, CAED 1, in subsequent sections of the book.

The second section, the Author Index, is the main part of the work. It is arranged alphabetically by name. The date of the author's birth and the language of composition appear on the same line as the author's name. Titles and first lines of poems by that author are then listed in alphabetical order (disregarding initial articles in the nominative case). If a poem is untitled, it is alphabetized by its first line; otherwise the first line follows the title. Titles are printed in SMALL CAPITALS, first lines in "Upper and lower case" type with quotation marks. Works of unknown authorship are filed under the headings **Anonymous, Bible,** and **Children's Verses and Nursery Rhymes.** The code numbers in the righthand margin indicate the recordings of each poem and refer the user back to the List of Recordings Analyzed.

Wherever possible, we have analyzed the actual recording. In doubtful cases (and there were some of these—record labels may be garbled, the sound may be distorted, whole tracks on cassettes may turn out to be blank), we have checked titles and first lines against printed sources. We have also used printed sources to verify titles and first lines whenever we have had to work from a producer's description rather than the recording itself.

Bilingual recordings and recordings of translations are identified, in the Author Index, by a note before the recording code. The titles and first lines of translations are given in the translated form, if that is the only version recorded; occasionally,

because of practical exigencies, we have given the title in the original language. In either case, a note preceding the recording code will identify any recording that is *not* in the original language. Transliterated material is presented according to the system used on the actual recording or its accompanying literature; in a few instances we have had to rely on our own phonetic transcriptions.

A sample entry in the Author Index reads:

> **Villon, François. 1431. in French.**
> BALLADE DES PENDUS. "Frères humains qui
> après nous vivez" ADES 53, CBS 1,
> DOVER 4, FOLKW 84, GMS 8, HACH 1,
> HACH 7, HACH 54, PENN 2, PERIOD 2
> _____, exc. "La pluye nous a debuez et lavez"
> French and English LEARNC 2
> RONDEAU. ADES 53; English EAV 22

This entry indicates that Francois Villon was born in 1431 and wrote in French; that there are ten recordings of his BALLADE DES PENDUS in the original French; that one section of the BALLADE is the subject of a bilingual recording; and that his RONDEAU is read in French on ADES 53 and in an English translation on EAV 22.

The third and fourth sections of this work are the Title and First Line indexes. These are arranged alphabetically, and references are to authors. Since first lines usually follow titles in the Author Index, someone tracing a poem by the first line alone may have to check a number of entries under the author's name.

The Reader Index, the fifth section, lists all the performers who can be heard on the recordings—the poets themselves, professional actors, and scholars. References are to the recording, as listed in the first section of the book. *Recordings of poets reading from their own works are identified by the prefix "a/" before the recording code.*

The final section of this work is a Register of Poets by Language of Composition. We have used broad language designations only, and have not attempted to differentiate among the various forms—historical, ethnic, regional, and literary—of each language. Thus, William Dunbar and Sonia Sanchez are both registered under the heading "English," though he was a fifteenth-century Scot and she is a contemporary Black American.

When we began this project four years ago, we intended to analyze and index *all* electronic recordings of poetry issued through 1980, anywhere, in any language. But the sheer amount of material that exists or has existed, the fugitive nature of much of it, the difficulty of accurate transcription, and the absence of any central bibliographic clearinghouse have combined to impose practical limits upon our undertaking. In *East Coker*, T. S. Eliot described poetry as "a raid on the inarticulate;" this volume represents a raid on the impossible. Nevertheless, we are pleased to have gone this far toward our goal, and we will welcome additions and corrections to the *Index*. We hope that our book will serve not only as an aid in locating recordings of particular works but also as an introduction to the range and diversity of the world's recorded poetry.

Many friendly people have helped to make this index. The compilers want to thank especially Anna Lesser of Orange, CA (Yiddish); Ulla Persson of Santa Ana, CA (Swedish); Nicolas Michalopoulos of Aachen, Germany (Greek); Zuzana Nagy of Harvard University, Cambridge, MA (Czech); Marianna D. Birnbaum of the University

of California, Los Angeles (Hungarian); and Stratis Haviaras of Harvard University, Cambridge, MA (Italian). Norris Smith of The H. W. Wilson Company seined the entire manuscript for big errors as well as for the rich plankton of small inaccuracies and missing details.

From among the producers of recorded poetry who have sent catalogs, lists of contents, recordings, and other helpful materials, the compilers must single out three that have gone far out of their way: Alan Austin of the Watershed Foundation, Washington, D.C.; Jeffrey Norton Publishers, Inc., New York; and Folkways Records, New York.

Two nationwide distributors of spoken literature of all genres and in all languages deserve special mention for their generous assistance: Goldsmith's Audio Visuals of Great Neck, NY, and Vincent R. Tortora of Applause Productions, Inc., Port Washington, NY.

The compilers also want to acknowledge the help of all the nameless library stack workers who reshelved thousands of poetry books consulted for correct titles, first lines, spelling of names, and so forth, especially at the University of California in Irvine, Riverside, Los Angeles, San Diego, and Santa Barbara; at Long Beach State University; and the Los Angeles and New York Public Libraries.

H. H. H.
R. L. H.

LIST OF RECORDINGS ANALYZED

The recordings indexed in this book are listed below by manufacturer and will be referred to in subsequent sections of the book by the code number found in the left margin of the list. The recording code number is a combination of a capital-letter prefix derived from the manufacturer's name (for instance, ACAD for Academie du disques de poésie) and an arabic numeral, which has been assigned to the specific recording (ACAD 1 for the disc POÈMES DIT PAR L'AUTEUR).

The entry for each recording includes the following information: title of recording, name of reader (if that is not evident from the title), manufacturer's serial number, and type of format. Most recordings are phonodiscs; if the format is not specified, the recording is a disc. The following abbreviations are used:

pd phonodisc
ac audio cassette
fs film strip
at audio tape
vc video cassette

Where the language of the recording is not immediately obvious, we have included a note of clarification, but it should be remembered that most poetry is recorded in the language in which it was written.

A word about availability. The larger companies that specialize in spoken arts materials keep most of their stock "in print"; this is by no means the case with the smaller firms. These are often short-lived, underfinanced companies that appear, issue a few recordings, and then go out of business. Some are absorbed by larger concerns—the entire recording industry has a tendency toward conglomeration. When a company ceases to exist, its unsold stock may be bought, relabeled, and sold under another name. Master tapes, from which commercial recordings are made, are particularly valuable assets which often pass to new owners once the original company has been dissolved. (See, for example, the Carillon Yale Poets series, which has already outlasted two owners.)

Advances in technology complicate the "in print" picture, for old material may be reissued in a new format. Many masters for 78 rpm recordings were combined (and occasionally rearranged) to produce early long-playing records; now discs are being converted to cassettes.

Under the circumstances, it is difficult to apply the terms "available" and "not available" with certainty. We have tried to find addresses for all manufacturers of the recordings indexed here; the phrase "current address unknown" implies that the company has changed ownership or gone out of business. The recordings issued on such elusive labels are not likely to be available through ordinary commercial channels, at least not in their original form, and must be tracked down in other ways.

For the person who simply wants to listen to a particular recording, library collections and the resources of the interlibrary loan system are the obvious choices. These collections contain most of the recordings listed here.

A person who wants to purchase an "out of print" recording faces a more arduous search, through secondhand stores, specialty shops, and even garage sales. In the

United States, there are several shops devoted to rare and discontinued records—principally musical, of course, but including recordings of poetry. Some of these firms are:

Dayton's, 824 Broadway, New York, NY 10003
Gryphon Record Shop, 606 Amsterdam Avenue, New York, NY 10024
The Magic Flute, 510½ Frederick Street, San Francisco, CA 94117

Secondhand bookstores are another possible source, and advertisements placed in *Gramophone* magazine and in *Fanfare* may net out-of-the-way items.

Recordings produced abroad are hard to obtain because most foreign manufacturers will not fill individual orders from the United States. A letter to the manufacturer may elicit the name of a U.S. distributor for that label, or an order may be placed through a dealer who specializes in imports, such as Applause Productions (85 Longview Road, Port Washington, NY, 11050). Foreign-language bookstores sometimes carry imported recordings: Macondo Books (221 West 14th Street, New York, NY, 10011) is a good source for Latin American poetry.

The Library of Congress is the repository of a vast amount of recorded material in English and other languages. The recordings listed below under LIBC (Library of Congress heading) are those the Library has made available in quantity, on a commercial basis. The Library can also supply copies of its archival tapes—requests for information about this service should be directed to the Recorded Sound Section. As tapes of archival material made on request require special attention, they are more expensive than the mass-produced recordings listed here.

ACAD   Academie du disque de poesie. Current address unknown.
1   POÈMES DITS PAR L'AUTEUR. Reader: Martin Saint-René, pseud. Académie du disque de poésie, AC-8-13-MAR

ACTIV   Activity Records, Stanley Bowmar Co., 4 Broadway, Valhalla, NY 10595, USA
1   POETRY, LIKE IT OR NOT. Reader: Terry Borton. Activity Records AR 5.

ADES   Disques Ades SA, 54 Rue St. Lazare, 75009 Paris, France
1   POÈTES D'AUJOURD'HUI: PAUL VERLAINE. Reader: François Perier. ADES P 37 LA 4001
2   DANIEL GELIN RÉCITE RENÉ GUY CADOU. ADES LA 4002
3   BAUDELAIRE. Reader: Jean Desailly. ADES P37 LA 4003
4   APOLLINAIRE. Reader: Jacque Duby. VEGA P 37 A 4004
5   GERARD DE NERVAL. Reader: Jean Vilar. ADES P 37 LA 4006
6   JEAN COCTEAU. Reader: Jean Mercure. VEGA P 37 A 4007
7   VICTOR HUGO. Reader: Maurice Teynac. ADES P 37 LA 4008
8   POÈTES D'AUJOURD'HUI: ARAGON. Reader: Jean-Louis Barrault. ADES P 37 LA 4009
9   CLAUDE LAYDU RÉCITE ALFRED DE MUSSET. ADES LA 4010

10   MARIA CASARES DIT SONNET ETC. BY GARCIA LORCA. In French. ADES LA 4011
11   PIERRE VANECK RÉCITE CHARLES PEGUY. ADES LA 4012
12   JEAN NEGRONI RÉCITE FRANCIS JAMMES. ADES LA 4013
13   CLAUDE NOLLIER RÉCITE PAUL CLAUDEL. ADES LA 4016
14   JEAN VILAR RÉCITE PAUL VALERY. ADES LA 4017
15   JEAN-PIERRE AUMONT RÉCITE FRANCIS CARCO. ADES LA 4020
16   FRANÇOIS MAURIAC: POÈMES. Readers: Jean-Louis Barrault and others. ADES LA 4022
17   GEORGES AMINEL RÉCITE LEOPOLDE SEDAR SENGHOR. ADES LA 4024
18   RENÉ LEFEVRE RÉCITE JULES LAFORGUE. ADES LA 4025
19   CLAUDE NOLLIER RÉCITE MARIE NOËL. ADES LA 4027
20   JEAN-LOUIS JEMMA RÉCITE MAURICE FOMBEURE. ADES LA 4028
21   COMTE DE LAUTRÉAMONT. Reader: Mouloudji. ADES LA 4029
22   JEHAN RICTUS: POÈMES. Reader: Jacques Duby. ADES LA 4030
23   JULES SUPERVIELLE: POÈMES. Reader: M. Bouquet. ADES LA 4031
24   PIERRE BRASSEUR DIT PERET. ADES LA 4035
25   MICHEL BOUQUET RÉCITE PHILIPPE SOUPAULT. ADES LA 4036

26 FRANÇOIS MAISTRE RÉCITE TRISTAN TZARA. ADES LA 4037
27 LAURENT TERZIEFF RÉCITE POÈMES PAR PIERRE SEGHERS. ADES LA 4038
28 ANDRÉ REYBAZ DIT PIERRE DE RONSARD. ADES LA 6002
29 ANDRÉ CHENIER: LA JEUNE TARENTINE, etc. Reader: Jean Bolo. ADES LA 6003
30 GUILLAUME APOLLINAIRE. Readers: Denis Manuel and others. ADES 7.018 (2 pd) & 7.019
31 GIDE. Readers: Jean Amrouche and others. ADES 7.032 & 7.033 (2 pd)
32 CHARLES PEGUY. Readers: Madeleine Renaud, Alain Cuny, Claude Nollier, Pierre Vaneck. ADES 10.033
33 MILOSZ. Reader: Laurent Terzieff. ADES 10.034
34 DIS-MOI BLAISE. Readers: Simone Valere and others. ADES 10.035
35 RENÉ DE OBALDIA. Reader: Madeleine Renaud. ADES 10.036
36 ARAGON/ÉLUARD. Reader: Jean-Louis Barrault. ADES 10.041
37 BAUDELAIRE & NERVAL. Reader: Jean Desailly. ADES 10.042
38 APOLLINAIRE: LES COLCHIQUES, etc. Readers: Jacques Duby and others. ADES 10.043
39 HUGO/LAMARTINE. Reader: Georges Wilson. ADES 10.044
40 MICHAUX & PERET. Reader: Michel Bouquet. ADES 10.045
41 MUSSET—VIGNY. Readers: Francis Huster, Michel Vitold. ADES 10.046
42 CHAR & PERSE. Readers: L. Terzieff, J. Vilar. ADES 10.047
43 RIMBAUD & VERLAINE. Readers: Sacha Pitoeff, Roger Coggio, François Perier, Charles Dullin, Denis Manuel. ADES 10.048
44 PREVERT—QUENEAU. Read by authors. ADES 10.049
45 GARCIA LORCA/DESNOS. Readers: Maria Casares and others. In French. ADES 10.050
46 VALÉRY/MALLARMÉ. Readers: Pierre Bertin, Jean Vilar. ADES 10.051
47 BRETON & TZARA. Reader: Roger Blin. ADES 10.052
48 POÉSIE: LES ROMANTIQUES. ADES 13.020
49 POÉSIE: LES MAUDITS. ADES 13.021
50 POÉSIE: XXe SIÈCLE. Readers: Alain Cuny, Jacques Duby, Daniel Gélin, René Lefèvre, Jean Negroni, Jean-Pierre Aumont, Charles Dullin. ADES 13.022
51 POÉSIE: XXe SIÈCLE. Readers: Madeleine Renaud, Claude Nollier, Jean-Louis Barrault, Pierre Vaneck, Alain Cuny, Denis Manuel, Jean Negroni. ADES 13.023
52 POÉSIE: XXe SIÈCLE, LES SURREALISTS. Readers: Gérard Philipe, Roger Blin, François Maistre, Jean-Louis Barrault, Michel Bouquet, Pierre Brasseur. ADES 13.024
53 RONSARD/VILLON. Reader: André Reybaz. ADES 13.047
54 LES POÈTES EN FRANCE. ADES 19.009 and 19.010 (2 pd)
55 LA RÉSISTANCE, SES CHANTS ET SES POÈTES.
Readers: François Chaumette, Suzanne Flon, Michel Lonsdale, Denis Manuel, Emmanuele Riva, Laurent Terzieff. ADES 21.001 and 21.002 (2 pd)
56 BORIS VIAN. Reader: Jean Rochefort. ADES 23.001 (3 pd)

AGE Arthur G. Evans, 460 Arroyo Parkway, Pasadena, CA 91101, USA
1 CASEY AT THE BAT: ERNEST LAWRENCE THAYER. AGE, OXT (16mm film)
2 THE CREATION: JAMES WELDON JOHNSON. Readers: Margaret O'Brien, Raymond St. Jacques. AGE, OXT (16mm film)
3 MENDING WALL, by Robert Frost. Reader: Leonard Nemoy. AGE, PARMT (16mm film)
4 EDGAR ALLAN POE. Reader: Lorne Greene. AGE, PARMT (16mm film)

AGENTV Agency for Instructional TV, Box A, Bloomington, IN 47401, USA
1 POETRY ALIVE: FROM THE FANTASIES OF A NOT-SO-YOUNG-ANYMORE SCHOOL TEACHER, by E. T. Johnston. Read by author. Agency for Instructional TV, 1 (v.c.)
2 POETRY ALIVE: WHO SAID TODAY'S KIDS DON'T HAVE FEELINGS? By E. T. Johnston. Read by author. Agency for Instructional TV, 2 (v.c.)
3 POETRY ALIVE: WE DON'T DO NOTHIN' IN HERE! By E. T. Johnston. Read by author. Agency for Instructional TV, 3 (v.c.)
4 POETRY ALIVE: THEY WORRY ABOUT ME, by E. T. Johnston. Read by author. Agency for Instructional TV, 4 (v.c.)
5 POETRY ALIVE: SO—WHAT HAPPENED TO YOU? By E. T. Johnston. Read by author. Agency for Instructional TV, 5 (v.c.)

AGUIL Discos Aguilar, Juan Bravo, 38, Madrid, Spain
1 ME LLAMO GABRIEL CELAYA. Read by author. AGUILAR MLL 001
2 ME LLAMO LUIS FELIPE VIVANCO. Read by author. AGUILAR MLL 005
3 DOCE POETAS EN SUS VOCES. AGUILAR GPE 10 100
4 POESÍA DE AMOR EN CASTELLANO. Readers: José Maria Rodero and others. AGUILAR GPE 10 101
5 POESÍA DE DIOS. Readers: Ana Maria Noé, Fernando Fernan Gomez, Agustin Gonzalez. AGUILAR GPE 10 102
6 POESÍA DE ESPAÑA. Readers: Fernando Fernan Gomez and others. AGUILAR GPE 10,103 and 10,104 (2 pd)
7 ROMANCERO ESPANOL I. Readers: Fernando Fernan Gomez and others. Aguilar GPE 10,107
8 POESÍAS EN LENGUA CASTELLANA. Readers: Ana Maria Noé, María Luisa Ponte, Berta Riaza. AGUILAR GPE 10 111
9 POESÍA ARGENTINA DE TODOS LOS TIEMPOS. Readers: Alfredo Alcon and others. AGUILAR GPE 10 113
10 DOCE POETAS EN SUS VOCES, 2a serie. AGUILAR GPE 10 114

AGUIL (continued)

11 POESÍAS DE GARCIA LORCA. Readers: Berta Riaza and others. AGUILAR GPE 12 100

12 POESÍAS DE JUAN RAMON JIMÉNEZ. Readers: Berta Riaza and others. AGUILAR GPE 12 106

13 POESÍAS DE RUBEN DARIO. Readers: Fernando Fernan Gomez and others. AGUILAR GPE 12 108

14 POETES CATALANS CONTEMPORANS. Readers: Nuria Espert, Josep-Miquel Velloso. AGUILAR GPE 10 112

15 POESÍAS DE MIGUEL DE UNAMUNO. Readers: Fernando Fernan Gomez, Ana Maria Noé. AGUILAR GPE 12 109

16 POESÍA DE ANTONIO MACHADO. Readers: Ana Maria Noé, Fernando Fernan Gomez, Agustin Gonzalez. AGUILAR GPE 12 101

17 ROMANCERO ESPANOL, II. Readers: Fernando Fernan Gomez and others. AGUILAR GPE 10 108

18 POESÍA DE GUSTAVO ADOLFO BECQUER. Readers: Fernando Fernan Gomez, Agustin Gonzalez. AGUILAR GPE 12 107

AMAD Amadeo Oesterreichische Schallplatten GmbH, Mariahilfer Guertel 32, A 1060 Vienna, Austria

1 AMERIKABALLADE: HELMUT PAULUS. Reader: Klaus Kinski. AMADEO AVRS 1023

2 DA WÖG DURI'S LÖBN: HANS SCHATZDORFER. Read by the author. AMADEO AVRS 1074

3 DIE WEISE VON LIEBE UND TOD DES CORNETS CHRISTOPH RILKE: R. M. RILKE: Reader: Fred Liewehr. Austria Vanguard AVRS 2003-X

4 SILVESTER SKURILLO, AND OTHERS: WILHELM RUDNIGGER. Read by the author. AMADEO AVRS 14128

5 ANTON WILDGANS: GEDICHTE. Read by author. AMADEO AVRS 14129

ANGEL Capitol Records Inc., 1750 North Vine St., Hollywood, CA 90028, USA

1 HOMAGE TO DYLAN THOMAS. ANGEL RG 29

2 FOUR QUARTETS, by T. S. Eliot. Read by author. ANGEL 45012

APPL Applause Recordings, Vincent R. Tortora, 85 Longview Rd., Port Washington, NY 11050, USA

1 EZRA POUND AT SPOLETO. Read by author. Applause SP 411 M

2 AMERICAN POETS AT SPOLETO: ALLEN GINSBERG and others. Read by authors. Applause SP 412 M

3 ENGLISH POETS AT SPOLETO. Read by authors. Applause SP 413 M

4 ITALIAN POETS AT SPOLETO. Read by authors. Applause SP 414

5 SPANISH POETS AT SPOLETO: Rafael Alberti and others. Read by authors. Applause SP 415 MA

6 SPANISH POETS AT SPOLETO. Read by authors. Applause SP 415 MB

7 RALPH WALDO EMERSON. Applause L 1165 (2 pd/ac)

8 POE: CELEBRATED POEMS. Reader: Basil Rathbone. Applause CM 1377 (2 pd)

9 GEORGE STARBUCK, SELECTIONS. Read by author. Applause CM 1444

10 TENNYSON. AN 1890 RECORDING OF MAUD read by author. Other readers: John Gielgud and others. Applause CM 1471

11 ROBERT PENN WARREN, SELECTIONS. Read by author. Applause CM 1517

12 VERNON WATKINS, SELECTIONS. Read by author. Applause CM 1521

13 EARLY ENGLISH POETRY, BEOWULF, AND CANTERBURY TALES. In modern English. Applause E 2401 A (1 tape)

14 A TREASURY OF POE. Readers: A. Scourby, H. Hatfield. Applause S 1382 B (10 pd)

ARGO Argo Records, Spoken Word Division, c/o Decca Records (U.K.), 50 New Bond Street, London W1Y 9HA, England Retail outlets that will fill orders from abroad include Direction, 97-99 Dean St., Oxford St., London W1, England, and Freese Verlag, Potsdamer Strasse 16, 1000 Berlin, 45 West Germany.

1 POEMS BY GERARD MANLEY HOPKINS AND JOHN KEATS. Reader: Margaret Rawlings. Argo RG 13

2 ANTHOLOGY OF SPOKEN POETRY: DONNE AND WORDSWORTH. Reader: Christopher Hassall. Argo RG 24

3 POETRY AND JAZZ IN CONCERT. Readers: R. Adrian Mitchell and others. Argo DA 26 (ZTA 513)

4 POETRY AND JAZZ IN CONCERT. Readers: Jeremy Robson and others. Argo DA 27 (ZTA 514)

5 RIME OF THE ANCIENT MARINER, by Coleridge. Readers: Richard Burton, John Neville, Robert Hardy. Argo RG 41

6 RICHARD BURTON READS FIFTEEN POEMS BY DYLAN THOMAS. Argo RG 43

7 OLD POSSUM'S BOOK OF PRACTICAL CATS, BY T. S. ELIOT. Read by author. Argo RG 116 (SW 504)

8 JOHN MASEFIELD, O. M., READS A FOX'S DAY, A SPECIAL ADAPTATION OF REYNARD THE FOX. Argo RG 224 (PLP 1066)

9 MORTE D'ARTHUR. Adapted from Sir Thomas Malory. Argo RG 227 - 229 (3 pd)

10 JOHN MASEFIELD, O. M., READS THE FORTUNE OF THE SEA, THE WANDERER'S IMAGE. Argo RG 230 (PLP 1068)

11 A HISTORICAL ANTHOLOGY OF AMERICAN POETRY FROM ITS INCEPTION TO POETS BORN BEFORE 1900 (I). Reader: Robert Beloof. Argo 245

12 A HISTORICAL ANTHOLOGY OF AMERICAN POETRY FROM ITS INCEPTION TO POETS BORN BEFORE 1900 (II). Reader: Robert Beloof. Argo 246

13 SHAKESPEARE: THE SONNETS. Readers: George Rylands, John Barton, Tony Church, Tony White, Anthony Jacobs, Gary Watson, Richard Marquand, David Gibson. Argo ZPR 254/6 (3 pd)

14 SHAKESPEARE: VENUS AND ADONIS. Readers: Peter Orr, Michael Hordern, Irene Worth, George Rylands, Ian Lang. Argo ZPR 257/8 (A 4250; OSA 1250; ARG 2427) (2 pd)

15 SHAKESPEARE: RAPE OF LUCRECE. Readers: Tony Church, Peggy Ashcroft, Peter Holmes. Argo ZPR 259/260 (2 pd)

16 POETRY INTERNATIONAL '69. Argo MPR 262/263 (2 pd)

17 BEYOND THE BLUES: AMERICAN NEGRO POETRY. Readers: Brock Peters, Vinette Carroll, Gordon Heath, Cleo Laine. Argo RG 338 (PLP 1071)

18 BYRON: DON JUAN. Reader: Richard Johnson. Argo RG 374

19 JOHN DONNE. Readers: Richard Johnson and others. Argo RG 403

20 MILTON: PARADISE LOST. Argo RG 431-32, 463-64, 508-9 (6 pd)

21 COLERIDGE. Readers: Yvonne Bonnamy, Richard Burton, William Devlin, John Neville, Robert Hardy. Argo 438

22 DYLAN THOMAS: POEMS. Reader: Richard Burton. Argo SW 503

23 THE PRE-RAPHAELITES. Argo RG 534

24 EMLYN WILLIAMS AS DYLAN THOMAS: A BOY GROWING UP. Argo RG 547

25 PROLOGUE TO CANTERBURY TALES, CHAUCER. Reader: Nevill Coghill. In Middle English. Argo PLP 1001

26 NUN'S PRIEST'S TALE, CHAUCER. Reader: Nevill Coghill. In Middle English. Argo PLP 1002

27 CHAUCER: TROILUS AND CRISEYDE. Readers: Gary Watson, Prunella Scales, Derek Brewer, Richard Marquand, Peter Orr. In Middle English. Argo ZPL 1003/4 (2 pd)

28 VISIONS FROM PIERS PLOWMAN. Readers: Richard Pasco and others. In modern English. Argo ZPL 1005/6 (2 pd)

29 HENRYSON AND DUNBAR. Readers: Freda Dowie, Duncan McIntyre. Argo PLP 1007

30 SKELTON AND EARLY LYRICS. Readers: David King and others. Argo ZPL 1008

31 ELIZABETHAN AND JACOBEAN LYRIC POETRY. Readers: Peggy Ashcroft and others. Argo PLP 1009 (RG 484)

32 ELIZABETHAN SONNETEERS AND SPENSER. Readers: Richard Johnson, Ian Holm and others. Argo PLP 1010

33 SPENSER: FAERIE QUEENE. Readers: Tony Church, William Squire and others. Argo PLP 1011

34 LOVE POEMS BY JOHN DONNE. Readers: Richard Johnson and others. Argo PLP 1012

35 CAMPION—JONSON—HERRICK. Reader: Peggy Ashcroft. Argo PLP 1013

36 THE ENGLISH POETS FROM CHAUCER TO YEATS: THE METAPHYSICAL POETS. Reader: Tony Church and others. Argo PLP 1014

37 THE METAPHYSICAL POETS, SECULAR. Readers: John Stride, Yvonne Bonnamy and others. Argo PLP 1015

38 JOHN MILTON: SHORTER POEMS. Readers: William Devlin and others. Argo PLP 1016

39 MILTON: PARADISE LOST, BOOK I COMPLETE. Readers: Tony Church and others. Argo PLP 1017

40 MILTON: PARADISE LOST, BOOK II. Readers: Tony Church and others. Argo PLP 1018

41 MILTON: PARADISE LOST, BOOKS III, IV. Readers: Tony Church and others. Argo PLP 1019

42 MILTON: PARADISE LOST, BOOKS V, VI. Readers: Tony Church and others. Argo PLP 1020

43 MILTON: PARADISE LOST, BOOKS VII, IX. Readers: Tony Church and others. Argo PLP 1021

44 MILTON: PARADISE LOST, BOOKS IX, X, XII Readers: Tony Church and others. Argo PLP 1022

45 MILTON: PARADISE REGAINED, BOOKS I, II, III, IV. Readers: Denis McCarthy and others. Argo PLP 1023

46 JOHN DRYDEN: POEMS. Readers: William Devlin and others. Argo ZPL 1027

47 RESTORATION AND AUGUSTAN VERSE. Readers: Richard Bebb and others. Argo PLP 1028

48 ALEXANDER POPE: POEMS. Readers: Max Adrian and others. Argo PLP 1029 (343)

49 ALEXANDER POPE: THE RAPE OF THE LOCK, COMPLETE. Readers: George Rylands and others. Argo PLP 1030

50 POEMS BY GRAY AND COLLINS. Readers: Richard Bebb and others. Argo PLP 1031

51 JOHNSON, GOLDSMITH, COWPER. Reader: John Neville. Argo PLP 1032

52 GEORGE CRABBE: POEMS. Readers: Ian Holm and others. Argo PLP 1033

53 ROBERT BURNS: POEMS. Reader: Julian Glover. Argo PLP 1034

54 WILLIAM BLAKE: POEMS. Reader: Alan Bates. Argo PLP 1035 (428)

55 WORDSWORTH: POEMS, VOL. 1. Readers: Tony Church and others. Argo PLP 1036

56 WORDSWORTH: POEMS, VOL. 2. Readers: Alan Bates and others. Argo PLP 1037

57 WORDSWORTH: THE PRELUDE. Readers: Peter Orr and others. Argo PLP 1038

58 SAMUEL TAYLOR COLERIDGE: POEMS. Readers: Yvonne Bonnamy and others. Argo PLP 1039

59 LORD BYRON: POEMS. Reader: Peter Orr. Argo PLP 1040

60 LORD BYRON: DON JUAN. Readers: Richard Johnson and others. Argo PLP 1041

61 PERCY BYSSHE SHELLEY: POEMS. Reader: Richard Marquand. Argo PLP 1042

62 JOHN KEATS: POEMS. Readers: Tony Church and others. Argo PLP 1043

63 EARLY VICTORIAN POETRY. Readers: Gary Watson and others. Argo PLP 1044

64 ALFRED, LORD TENNYSON: POEMS, VOL. 1. Readers: Tony Church and others. Argo PLP 1045

65 ALFRED, LORD TENNYSON: POEMS, VOL. 2. Readers: Frank Duncan and others. Argo PLP 1046

66 ROBERT BROWNING: POEMS, VOL. 1. Readers: Alan Bates and others. Argo PLP 1047

67 ROBERT BROWNING: POEMS, VOL. 2. Readers: Gary Watson and others. Argo PLP 1048

68 ARNOLD, CLOUGH, AND FITZGERALD. Reader: Ian Holm. Argo PLP 1049

69 THE ENGLISH POETS FROM CHAUCER TO YEATS: THE PRE-RAPHAELITES. Reader: Gary Watson. Argo PLP 1050

ARGO (continued)

70 GERARD MANLEY HOPKINS: POEMS. Reader: Barbara Jefford. Argo PLP 1051

70A LATE VICTORIAN POETRY. Reader: Frank Duncan. Argo PLP 1052

71 THOMAS HARDY: POEMS, VOL. 1. Readers: Ian Holm and others. Argo PLP 1053

72 THOMAS HARDY: POEMS, VOL. 2. Reader: Ian Holm. Argo PLP 1054

73 RUDYARD KIPLING: POEMS. Reader: Richard Johnson. Argo PLP 1055

74 WILLIAM BUTLER YEATS: POEMS. Reader: Arthur O'Sullivan. Argo PLP 1056 (RG 449)

75 BEOWULF. Readers: Kevin Crossley-Holland and others. In modern English. Argo ZPL 1057

76 THE BATTLE OF MALDON AND OTHER OLD ENGLISH POEMS. Readers: Frank Duncan and others. Argo ZPL 1058

77 ROBERT DONAT READS SELECTED POETRY. Argo PLP 1059

78 HOMAGE TO DYLAN THOMAS. Reader: Louis MacNeice. Argo PLP 1060

79 STEPHEN SPENDER: POEMS. Read by author. Argo PLP 1061

80 WYSTAN HUGH AUDEN: POEMS. Read by author. Argo PLP 1062

81 ROBERT GRAVES: POEMS. Read by author. Argo PLP 1063

82 ROBERT DONAT READS FAVORITE POEMS AT HOME. Argo PLP 1064

83 LOUIS MACNEICE: POEMS. Read by author. Argo PLP 1065

84 JOHN BETJEMAN: POEMS. Read by author. Argo PLP 1067

85 THE FORTUNE OF THE SEA: POEMS BY JOHN MASEFIELD. Read by author. Argo PLP 1068

86 SUMMONED BY BELLS, BY JOHN BETJEMAN. Read by author. Argo PLP 1069

87 HUBERT GREGG AS JEROME K. JEROME. Argo PLP 1070

88 NOW WHAT IS LOVE? Readers: Max Adrian and others. Argo PLP 1073

89 WHAT PASSING BELL. Reader: Jill Balcon. Argo PLP 1074

90 WILFRED OWEN: POETRY AND LETTERS. Readers: Richard Johnson and others. Argo PLP 1075

91 THE POET SPEAKS, v.1. JAMES REEVES AND OTHERS. Argo PLP 1081 (RG 451)

92 THE POET SPEAKS, v.2. NORMAN NICHOLSON AND OTHERS. Argo PLP 1082 (RG 452)

93 THE POET SPEAKS, v.3. JOHN HEATH-STUBBS AND OTHERS. Argo PLP 1083

94 THE POET SPEAKS, v.4. TONY CONNOR AND OTHERS. Argo PLP 1084 (RG 454)

95 THE POET SPEAKS, v.5. TED HUGHES AND OTHERS. Argo PLP 1085 (RG 455)

96 THE POET SPEAKS, v.6. JOHN ARDEN AND OTHERS. Argo PLP 1086 (RG 456)

97 THE POET SPEAKS, v.7. JOHN BETJEMAN AND OTHERS. Argo PLP 1087 (RG 517)

98 THE POET SPEAKS, v.8. PHILIP LARKIN AND OTHERS. Argo PLP 1088 (RG 518)

99 THE POET SPEAKS, v.9. HUGH MACDIARMID AND OTHERS. Argo PLP 1089 (RG 519)

100 THE POET SPEAKS, v.10. EDMUND BLUNDEN AND OTHERS. Argo PLP 1090 (RG 520)

101 DAVID JONES—POEMS. Read by author. Argo PLP 1093

102 T. S. ELIOT: POEMS. Reader: Robert Speaight. Argo PLP 1108

103 T. S. ELIOT: FOUR QUARTETS. Reader: Robert Speaight. Argo PLP 1109

104 EDWARD BRATHWAITE—THE RIGHTS OF PASSAGE. Read by author. Argo PLP 1110/1111 (2 pd)

105 HILAIRE BELLOC: POEMS. Reader: Robert Speaight. Argo PLP 1118

106 POEMS BY EDWARD MORGAN FORSTER. Read by author. Argo PLP 1152

107 THE GEORGICS, BY VIRGIL. Reader: Cecil Day Lewis. Argo PLP 1153

108 PEOPLE PAST AND PRESENT: EDWARD LEAR. Reader: Charles Lewsen. Argo ZPL 1163

109 PEOPLE PAST AND PRESENT: THOMAS HARDY. Readers: Jill Balcon and others. Argo ZPL 1164

110 PEOPLE PAST AND PRESENT: JOHN CLARE. Reader: Edward Woodward. Argo ZPL 1166

111 PEOPLE PAST AND PRESENT: JOHN DONNE. Reader: Carleton Hobbs. Argo ZPL 1167

112 EDWARD BRATHWAITE: MASKS. Read by author. Argo PLP 1183

113 EDWARD BRATHWAITE: ISLANDS. Read by author. Argo PLP 1184/5 (2 pd)

114 BRITISH POETRY OF OUR TIME: T. S. ELIOT. Reader: Alec Guinness. Argo PLP 1206/7 (2 pd), SAY 25 (ac)

115 EUROPA AND THE BULL: W. R. RODGERS. Read by author. Argo XWN 18151

116 THE MIND OF EMILY DICKINSON. Reader: Glenda Jackson. Argo ZSW 600/601 (2 pd)

117 THE WORLD OF DYLAN THOMAS. Reader: Emlyn Williams. Argo PA 166

118 WORLD OF CHILDREN. Readers: Peter Ustinov, Tony Church. Argo SPA 200

119 WILL IT BE SO AGAIN. Reader: Robert Hardy. Argo ZPR 261

120 CONSORT OF MUSICKE. Reader: Bale. Argo SOL 328

121 BETJEMAN: POETRY. Read by author. Argo PA 339

123 BELLOC: CAUTIONARY TALES. Reader: Peter Ustinov. Argo SW 506

125 SENSE AND NONSENSE. Reader: Peggy Ashcroft. Argo ZSW 532

126 ROBERT SOUTHWELL: POETRY. Reader: William Squire. Argo ZRG 550

127 MANXMAN: THOMAS EDWARD BROWN AND OTHERS. Read by the authors. Argo ZSW 556

128 BUTTERFLY BALL AND THE GRASSHOPPER'S FEAST, by William Roscoe with additions by William Plomer. Readers: Judi Dench, Michael Hordern. Argo ZSW 557/8 (2 pd)

129 FACADE, BY EDITH SITWELL. Read by author. Argo ECS 560

130 WHEN WE WERE VERY YOUNG, by A. A. Milne. Reader: Norman Shelley. Argo ZSW 568

131 NOW WE ARE SIX, by A. A. Milne. Reader: Norman Shelley. Argo ZSW 569

132 LATER THAN LAUGHARNE. Read by the author, Aeronwy Thomas-Ellis. Argo ZSW 578

133 LAURIE LEE: POETRY. Read by author. Argo ZSW 593/4/5 (3 pd)

134 STEVIE SMITH: POETRY. Reader: Glenda Jackson. Argo ZSW 608

135 FACADE, BY EDITH SITWELL. Readers: Peggy Ashcroft and others. Argo ZRG 649

136 LO, COUNTRY SPORTS. Reader: John Neville. Argo ZRG 658

137 BETJEMAN: POETRY. Reader: Richard Burton. Argo ZDSW 714

138 ENGLISH POETS—MILTON. Argo PLP 1024/5 (2 pd)

139 BARROW POETS. Argo PLP 1072

140 POETS OF WALES: DANNIE ABSE. Read by the author. Argo PLP 1155

141 POETS OF WALES. Read by the author, Raymond Garlick. Argo PLP 1156

142 POETS OF WALES: DAVID JONES. Read by author. Argo PLP 1180

143 EVENING WITH SYBIL THORNDIKE. Argo ZPL 1186

144 BRITISH POETS OF OUR TIME: C. DAY LEWIS. Read by author. Argo PLP 1187

145 THE STONES REMEMBER: BRYN GRIFFITHS. Read by the author. Argo PLP 1189

146 BRITISH POETS OF OUR TIME. Read by authors Roger McGough and others. Argo ZPL 1190

147 BRITISH POETS OF OUR TIME. Read by authors Norman Nicholson and others. Argo PLP 1191

148 POETS OF WALES: EDWARD THOMAS. Read by the author. Argo ZPL 1192

149 BRITISH POETS OF OUR TIME: W. H. AUDEN. Read by the author. Argo PLP 1193

150 BRITISH POETS OF OUR TIME: ADRIAN HENRI AND HUGO WILLIAMS. Read by the authors. Argo PLP 1194

151 SO LATE INTO THE NIGHT: BYRON. Argo ZPL 1195

152 POETS OF WALES: GILLIAN CLARK. Read by author. Argo PLP 1201

153 BRITISH POETS OF OUR TIME: THOM GUNN. Read by the author. Argo PLP 1203

154 BRITISH POETS OF OUR TIME: PETER REDGROVE AND OTHERS. Read by the authors. Argo PLP 1204

155 BRITISH POETS OF OUR TIME: ROY FULLER AND OTHERS. Read by the authors. Argo PLP 1205

156 CANTERBURY TALES: CHAUCER. In Middle English. Argo ZPL 1211

157 CANTERBURY TALES, CHAUCER. Readers: P. Scales, R. Bebb. In Middle English. Argo ZPL 1212/13 (2 pd)

158 HERE IS WALES. Reader: Richard Burton. Argo DPA 3025/6 (2 pd)

ARIZ Arizona State Univ., Central Arizona Film Coop., Tempe, AZ 85281, USA

 1 FOCUS ON PAUL REVERE: LONGFELLOW. Ariz. State U. (16mm film)

 2 NAMING OF PARTS: HENRY REED. Ariz. State U. (16mm film)

ASCH Asch Records c/o Folkways Records, 43 West 61st St., New York, NY 10023, USA

 1 THE WOOD BURNS RED. Read by author, Roberta Goldstein. Folkways AH 9709

ATHENA Ariola-Eurodisc GmbH, Steinhauserstr. 3, D-8000 Munich 80, West Germany

 1 DEUTSCHE BALLADEN. Reader: Horst Caspar. Athena 53022G

 2 LYRIK: GERHART HAUPTMANN. Readers: Gisela Mattishent and others. Athena 56015B (pd 45rpm)

 3 KLEINE KOSTBARKEITEN. Readers: Paul Henckels and others. Athena 56017C (pd 45rpm)

 4 DICHTER UNBEKANNT. Reader: Matthias Wiemann. Athena 56019C

 5 GELIEBTE MUTTER: DROSTE-HULSHOFF. Readers: Tilla Durieux and others. Athena 56023 (pd 45rpm)

 6 ABENDS WENN ICH SCHLAFEN GEH. Reader: Matthias Wiemann. Athena 56098 (pd 45 rpm)

 7 RINGS UM RUHET DIE STADT: LYRIK UND MUSIK DER ROMANTIK. Reader: Heinz Schimmelpfennig. Athena 56104C

 8 GEDICHTE VON SCHILLER. Reader: Ernst Deutsch. Athena 56141C

 9 GEDICHTE VON EICHENDORFF. Reader: Matthias Wiemann. Athena 56176C (pd 45rpm)

 10 EWALD BALSER SPRICHT GEDICHTE VON GOETHE. Athena 56185C

 11 FÜR KINDER UND KENNER. Reader: Matthias Wiemann. Athena 56186B (pd 45rpm)

 12 ICH BIN EIN GAST AUF ERDEN: PAULUS GERHARDT. Reader: Matthias Wiemann. Athena 56187C

 13 DER STROM DER NEBEN MIR VERRAUSCHTE: AUGUST GRAF VON PLATEN UND FRIEDRICH RÜCKERT. Reader: Matthias Wiemann. Athena 56188C (pd 45rpm)

 14 KÄTHE GOLD SPRICHT GEDICHTE: STORM. Athena 56196C

AUDIA Audio Arts, Inc., 5617 Melrose Av., Los Angeles, CA 90038, USA

 1 19TH CENTURY ENGLISH POETS. Readers: Alexander Scourby and others. Audio Arts AA 3306

 2 19TH CENTURY AMERICAN POETS. Readers: Alexander Scourby and others. Audio Arts AA 3307

AUDIBK Audio Book Co., 301 Pasadena Av., South Pasadena, CA 91030, USA

 1 COMPLETE SONNETS OF WILLIAM SHAKESPEARE. Reader: Ronald Colman. Audio Books AB 3021-3026 (3 pd)

AUDIBT Audio Books/Talking Books, St. Joseph, MI 49085, USA

 1 A CHILD'S GARDEN OF VERSES: STEVENSON. Reader: Elinor Gene Hoffman. Audio Book/Talking Book AB 10007/8 (pd 16 2/3 rpm)

AUDIL Audio Lingual Education Press, 22 Vernon Rd., East Northport, NY 11731, USA

AUDIL (continued)
1 READINGS FROM LOVE POETRY OF DANTE. Audio Lingual (2 pd)
2 READINGS FROM LA GINESTRA: LEOPARDI. Audio Lingual (2 ac)
3 READINGS FROM POETRY OF MICHELANGELO. Audio Lingual (2 pd)

AUDIOT Audio-Text Cassettes, Center for Cassette Studies, 8110 Webb Av., North Hollywood, CA 91605, USA
1 A GWENDOLYN BROOKS TREASURY. Read by author. Center for Cass. Stud. 5314 (ac)
2 SYLVIA PLATH: POET IN RAGE, I. Center for Cass. Stud. 27543 (ac)
3 SYLVIA PLATH: POET IN RAGE, II. Reader: Elizabeth Hardwick. Center for Cass. Stud. 27544 (ac)
4 POESÍA NAHUATL. Center for Cass. Stud. 28603 (ac)
5 W. H. AUDEN: THE MODERN BARD. Center for Cass. Stud. 30261 (ac)
6 ALURISTA: POET DE AZTLAN. Center for Cass. Stud. 35314
7 THE POETRY OF JESSE WILLS. Center for Cass. Stud. 39001 (ac)

BABB Babbitt Film Specialties, PO Box 10, Park Forest, IL 60466, USA
1 ANTONIO MACHADO: CANTOR DE SORIA. Babbitt (16mm film)
2 JUAN RAMON JIMÉNEZ Y SU MOGUER. Babbitt (16mm film)

BANKST Bank Street College of Education, 610 West 112th St. New York, NY 10025, USA
1 A CHILD'S GARDEN OF VERSES, by R. L. Stevenson. Reader: Robert Goulet. Bank Street (16mm film)

BBC British Broadcasting Co., 630 Fifth Av., New York, NY 10020, USA
1 UNDER A BRIGHT HEAVEN: VERNON WATKINS. BBC-TV (16mm film)
2 EZRA POUND: STUDY OF A POET. Read by author. BBC (16mm film)

BIGSUR Big Sur Recordings, PO Box 91, Big Sur, CA 93920, USA
1 THE POETRY OF MADNESS. Reader: Allen Ginsberg. Big Sur 1030 (2 at)
2 EVE MERRIAM READS HER POETRY. Big Sur 1891 (at)
3 ON ROBINSON JEFFERS. Reader: Robert Brophy. Big Sur 5020 (at)
4 POETRY OF THE EARTH: BROTHER ANTONINUS AND ROBINSON JEFFERS. Reader: William Everson (Brother Antoninus). Big Sur 5090 (at)
5 THE POETRY OF ROBINSON JEFFERS. Readers: Rex Campbell and others. Big Sur 5170 (2 at)

BLACKF Black Forum. Current address unknown.
1 BLACK SPIRITS—FESTIVAL OF NEW BLACK POETS. Black Forum B-456-L

BLACKS Black Sparrow Press, Box 3993, Santa Barbara, CA 93105, USA
1 CODE OF FLAG BEHAVIOR: DAVID ANTIN. Read by author. Black Sparrow Press (at)

BOS Steven Bosustow Prod., 1649 11th St., Santa Monica, CA 90404, USA
1 JUST LIKE YOU: EUGENE OSBORN SMITH. Read by author. Bosustow Prod. (16mm film)

BOWMAR Bowmar/Noble Publishers, Inc., 4563 Colorado Bl., Los Angeles, CA 90039, USA
1 POEMS FOR THE VERY YOUNG. Bowmar LP 063 (CL-16)

BRITAM British and American Recordings. Current address unknown. Recordings may have passed to Argo.
1 LONDON LIBRARY OF RECORDED ENGLISH, BKS. 1-3. Britam XTV 23862/67 (3 pd)
2 LONDON LIBRARY OF RECORDED ENGLISH, BK. 5, 16TH & 17TH CENTURY LYRICS. Readers: V. C. Clinton-Baddeley and others. Mfgrs. code unknown
3 LONDON LIBRARY OF RECORDED ENGLISH, BK. 6, 18TH & 19TH CENTURY. Reader: V. C. Clingon-Baddeley. Britam LL 1006
4 CANTERBURY TALES: CHAUCER. Reader: Nevil Coghill. In modern English. Sp. Word XTV-23513-20 (2 pd)

BROADR Broadside Records, Broadside/Crummell Press, 74 Glendale Av., Highland Park, MI 48203, USA
1 THE ORIGINAL READ-IN FOR PEACE IN VIETNAM. Read by authors Galway Kinnell and others. Broadside Records BR 452
2 NEW JAZZ POETS. Broadside Records BR 461
3 POEMS FOR PEACE. Reader: Ann Charters. Broadside Records BR 465
4 JOHN BEECHER: TO LIVE AND DIE IN DIXIE. Read by author. Broadside Records BR 470

BROADV Broadside Voices, Broadside/Crummell Press, 74 Glendale Av., Highland Park, MI 48203, USA
1 BLACK MAN LISTEN: MARVIN X. Read by author. Broadside Voices (at)
2 BLACK WISDOM: FRENCHY JOLENE HODGES. Read by author. Broadside Voices (at)
3 CITIES BURNING: DUDLEY RANDALL. Read by author. Broadside Voices (at)
4 DON'T CRY, SCREAM: DON L. LEE. Read by author. Broadside Voices (at)
5 FAMILY PICTURES: GWENDOLYN BROOKS. Read by author. Broadside Voices (at)
6 HOMECOMING: SONIA SANCHEZ. Read by author. Broadside Voices (at)
7 HOME IS WHERE THE SOUL IS: JON ECKELS. Read by author. Broadside Voices (at)
8 MOVING DEEP: STEPHANY. Read by author. Broadside Voices (at)
9 MY BLACKNESS IS THE BEAUTY OF THIS LAND: LANCE JEFFERS. Read by author. Broadside Voices (at)
10 PANTHER MAN: JAMES A. EMANUEL. Read by author. Broadside Voices (at)
11 POEM COUNTERPOEM: MARGARET DANNER AND DUDLEY RANDALL. Read by authors. Broadside Voices (at)
12 POEMS FROM PRISON: ETHERIDGE KNIGHT. Read by author. Broadside Voices (at)

13 PROPHETS FOR A NEW DAY: MARGARET WALK-ER. Read by author. Broadside Voices (at)

14 SPIRITS UNCHAINED: KGOSITSILE. Read by author. Broadside Voices (at)

15 THE ROCKS CRY OUT: BEATRICE MURPHY AND OTHERS. Read by Beatrice Murphy and others. Broadside Voices (at)

16 TREEHOUSE AND OTHER POEMS: JAMES A. EMANUEL. Read by author. Broadside Voices (at)

17 WE A BADDDDD PEOPLE: SONIA SANCHEZ. Read by author. Broadside Voices (at)

18 WE WALK THE WAY OF THE NEW WORLD: DON L. LEE. Read by author. Broadside Voices (at)

CAED Caedmon, 1995 Broadway, New York, NY 10023, USA

1 J. R. R. TOLKIEN SOUNDBOOK. Readers: The author and Christopher Tolkien. Caedmon SBR 101 (4 pd) or SBC 101 (4 ac)

2 DYLAN THOMAS SOUNDBOOK. Read by author. Caedmon SBR 102 (4 pd) or SBC 102 (4 ac)

3 OGDEN NASH SOUNDBOOK. Read by author. Caedmon SBR 105 (4 pd) or SBC 105 (4 ac)

4 EDGAR ALLAN POE SOUNDBOOK. Readers: Basil Rathbone and Vincent Price. Caedmon SBR 106 (4 pd) or SBC 106 (4 ac)

5 VENUS AND ADONIS AND A LOVER'S COMPLAINT: SHAKESPEARE. Readers: Claire Bloom and Max Adrian. Caedmon SRS 240 (2 pd) or CDL5 240 (2 ac)

6 SONNETS: SHAKESPEARE. Reader: John Gielgud. Caedmon SRS 241 (2 pd) or CDL5 (2 ac)

7 DYLAN THOMAS READING A CHILD'S CHRISTMAS IN WALES AND OTHER POEMS. Caedmon TC 1002 (pd) or CP 1002 (ac)

8 DYLAN THOMAS READING AND DEATH SHALL HAVE NO DOMINION AND OTHER POEMS. Caedmon TC 1018 (pd) or CP 1018 (ac)

9 DYLAN THOMAS READING OVER SIR JOHN'S HILL AND OTHER POEMS. Caedmon SWC 1043 (ac)

10 DYLAN THOMAS READING A VISIT TO AMERICA AND POEMS BY OTHERS. Caedmon SWC 1061 (ac)

11 DYLAN THOMAS READING QUITE EARLY ONE MORNING AND OTHER POEMS. Caedmon TC 1132 (pd) or CDL5 1132 (ac)

12 TENNESSEE WILLIAMS READING FROM HIS WORKS. Caedmon SWC 1005 (ac)

13 PARDONER'S TALE AND NUN'S PRIEST'S TALE: CHAUCER. Reader: Robert Ross. In Middle English. Caedmon SWC 1008 (ac)

14 ARCHIBALD MACLEISH READS HIS POETRY. Caedmon SWC 1009 (ac)

15 OSBERT SITWELL READING HIS POETRY. Caedmon SWC 1013 (ac)

16 OGDEN NASH READS OGDEN NASH. Caedmon TC 1015 (pd) or CDL5 1015 (ac)

17 EDITH SITWELL READING HER POEMS. Caedmon SWC 1016 (ac)

18 E. E. CUMMINGS READING HIS POETRY. Caedmon TC 1017 (pd) or CDL5 1017 (ac)

19 W. H. AUDEN READING. Caedmon SWC 1019 (ac)

20 HEARING POETRY: CHAUCER TO MILTON. Readers: Hurd Hatfield and others. Caedmon SWC 1021 (ac)

21 HEARING POETRY: DRYDEN TO BROWNING. Readers: Hurd Hatfield and others. Caedmon SWC 1022 (ac)

22 FITZGERALD: THE RUBAIYAT (4th translation) / ARNOLD: SOHRAB AND RUSTUM. Reader: Alfred Drake. Caedmon SWC 1023 (ac)

23 POETRY OF EDNA ST. VINCENT MILLAY. Reader: Judith Anderson. Caedmon SWC 1024 (ac)

24 MARIANNE MOORE READING HER POEMS AND FABLES FROM LA FONTAINE. Caedmon SWC 1025 (ac)

25 THE POETRY OF WORDSWORTH. Reader: Cedric Hardwicke. Caedmon SWC 1026 (ac)

26 EDGAR ALLAN POE: THE RAVEN AND OTHER WORKS. Reader: Basil Rathbone. Caedmon TC 1028 (pd) or CDL5 1028 (ac)

27 LES FLEURS DU MAL: BAUDELAIRE. Readers: Eva Le Gallienne and Louis Jourdan. In French. Caedmon SWC 1029 (ac)

28 GOLDEN TREASURY OF GREEK POETRY AND PROSE. Reader: Pearl C. Wilson. In Ancient Greek. Caedmon SWC 1034 (ac)

29 WHITMAN: LEAVES OF GRASS: I HEAR AMERICA SINGING. Reader: Ed Begley. Caedmon SWC 1037 (ac)

30 WHITMAN: LEAVES OF GRASS: SONG OF THE OPEN ROAD. Reader: Ed Begley. Caedmon SWC 1154 (ac)

31 CONRAD AIKEN READING HIS OWN POEMS. Caedmon SWC 1039 (ac)

32 VACHEL LINDSAY READING THE CONGO, CHINESE NIGHTINGALE AND OTHER POEMS. Caedmon SWC 1041 (ac)

33 POETRY OF BYRON. Reader: Tyrone Power. Caedmon SWC 1042 (ac)

34 T. S. ELIOT READING THE LOVE SONG OF J. ALFRED PRUFROCK AND OTHER POEMS. Caedmon TC 1045 (pd) or CDL5 1045 (ac)

35 WALTER DE LA MARE SPEAKING AND READING. Caedmon SWC 1046 (ac)

36 WILLIAM CARLOS WILLIAMS READS HIS POETRY. Caedmon SWC 1047 (ac)

37 THE POETRY OF BROWNING. Reader: James Mason. Caedmon SWC 1048 (ac)

38 METAPHYSICAL POETRY OF THE 17TH CENTURY. Readers: Cedric Hardwicke and Robert Newton. Caedmon SWC 1049 (ac)

39 GERTRUDE STEIN READS FROM HER WORKS. Caedmon TC 1050 (pd) or CDL5 1050 (ac)

40 PSALMS AND THE TALE OF DAVID. Reader: Judith Anderson. Caedmon SWC 1053 (ac)

41 THE POETRY OF SHELLEY. Reader: Vincent Price. Caedmon SWC 1059 (ac)

42 ROBERT FROST READS THE ROAD NOT TAKEN AND OTHER POEMS. Caedmon TC 1060 (pd) or CDL5 1060 (ac)

43 ROBERT GRAVES READS FROM HIS POETRY AND THE WHITE GODDESS. Caedmon SWC 1066 (ac)

44 POESIA Y DRAMA DE LORCA. Readers: Maria Douglas and Raul Dantes. In Spanish. Caedmon SWC 1067 (ac)

45 WALLACE STEVENS READING HIS POEMS. Caedmon SWC 1068 (ac)

CAED (continued)

46 SONNETS FROM THE PORTUGUESE: ELIZABETH BARRETT BROWNING. Readers: Katharine Cornell and Anthony Quayle. Caedmon SWC 1071 (ac)

47 GERMAN LYRIC POETRY. Reader: Lotte Lehmann. In German. Caedmon SWC 1072 (ac)

48 THE PIED PIPER: BROWNING / THE HUNTING OF THE SNARK: CARROLL. Reader: Boris Karloff. With music. Caedmon CDL5 1075 (ac only)

49 A CHILD'S GARDEN OF VERSES: STEVENSON. Reader: Judith Anderson. Caedmon TC 1077 (pd) or CDL5 1077 (ac)

50 NONSENSE VERSE OF CARROLL AND LEAR. Readers: Beatrice Lillie and others. Caedmon TC 1078 (pd) or CDL5 1078 (ac)

51 JUAN RAMÓN JIMÉNEZ READING HIS OWN POEMS. Caedmon SWC 1079 (ac)

52 THE POETRY OF TENNYSON. Readers: Sybil Thorndike and Lewis Casson. Caedmon SWC 1080 (ac)

53 POETRY OF WILLIAM BUTLER YEATS. Readers: Siobhan McKenna and Cyril Cusack. Caedmon TC 1081 (pd) or CDL5 1081 (ac)

54 JEAN COCTEAU READING HIS OWN WORKS. In French. Caedmon SWC 1083 (ac)

55 STEPHEN SPENDER READING HIS POETRY. Caedmon SWC 1084 (ac)

56 THE SONG OF SONGS AND THE LETTERS OF HELOISE AND ABELARD. Readers: Claire Bloom and others. Caedmon SWC 1085 (ac)

57 POETRY OF KEATS. Reader: Ralph Richardson. Caedmon TC 1087 (pd) or CDL5 1087 (ac)

58 MOTHER GOOSE. Readers: Cyril Ritchard and others. With music. Caedmon TC 1091 (pd) or CDL5 1091 (ac)

59 THE POETRY OF COLERIDGE. Reader: Ralph Richardson. Caedmon SWC 1092 (ac)

60 PARADISE LOST: MILTON. Reader: Anthony Quayle. Caedmon TC 1093 (2 pd)

61 NOEL COWARD READING HIS POEMS / G. B. SHAW: THE APPLECART INTERLUDE. Readers: Noel Coward and Margaret Leighton. Caedmon SWC 1094 (ac)

62 THE POETRY OF WILLIAM BLAKE. Reader: Ralph Richardson. Caedmon SWC 1101 (ac)

63 THE WIFE OF BATH: CHAUCER. Reader: Peggy Ashcroft. In modern English. Caedmon SWC 1102 (ac)

64 THE POETRY OF ROBERT BURNS AND SCOTTISH BORDER BALLADS. Readers: Frederick Worlock and C.R.M. Brookes. Caedmon SWC 1103 (ac)

65 THE BAB BALLADS: W. S. GILBERT / CAUTIONARY VERSES: BELLOC. Readers: Stanley Holloway and Joyce Grenfell. Caedmon CDL5 1104 (ac only)

66 THE BEST LOVED POEMS OF LONGFELLOW. Reader: Hal Holbrook. Caedmon SWC 1107 (ac)

67 CHAUCER: THE CANTERBURY TALES: THE PARDONER'S TALE AND THE NUN'S PRIEST'S TALE. Reader: Robert Ross. In Middle English.

Caedmon SWC 1008 (ac)

68 THE POETRY OF GERARD MANLEY HOPKINS. Reader: Cyril Cusack. Caedmon SWC 1111 (ac)

69 POEMS AND LETTERS OF EMILY DICKINSON. Reader: Julie Harris. Caedmon TC 1119 (pd) or CDL5 1119 (ac)

70 EZRA POUND READING HIS POETRY. Reissued with additions as CAED 84. Caedmon TC 1122 (pd)

71 EDNA ST. VINCENT MILLAY READING HER POETRY. Caedmon TC 1123 (pd only)

72 CARL SANDBURG'S POEMS FOR CHILDREN. Read by author. Caedmon TC 1124 (pd) or CDL5 1124 (ac)

73 THE POETRY OF JOHN DRYDEN. Reader: Paul Scofield. Caedmon SWC 1125 (ac)

74 THE FAERIE QUEENE AND EPITHALAMION: SPENSER. Reader: Micheal MacLiammoir. Caedmon SWC 1126 (ac)

75 POETRY OF RAINER MARIA RILKE. Reader: Lotte Lehmann. In German. Caedmon SWC 1128 (ac)

76 CHAUCER: THE CANTERBURY TALES: THE MILLER'S TALE AND THE PARDONER'S TALE. Readers: Micheal MacLiammoir and Stanley Holloway. In modern English. Caedmon SWC 1130 (ac)

77 THE POETRY OF THOMAS HARDY. Reader: Richard Burton. Caedmon SWC 1140 (ac)

78 LOVE POEMS OF JOHN DONNE. Reader: Richard Burton. Caedmon TC 1141 (pd) or CDL5 1141 (ac)

79 JOHN MASEFIELD READING SEAFEVER AND OTHER POEMS. Caedmon SWC 1147 (ac)

80 CARL SANDBURG READING COOL TOMBS AND OTHER POEMS. Caedmon SWC 1150 (ac)

81 CHAUCER: THE CANTERBURY TALES: THE PARSON'S TALE. Reader: J. B. Bessinger Jr. In Middle English. Caedmon TC 1151 (pd) or CDL5 1151 (ac)

82 SPOON RIVER ANTHOLOGY: EDGAR LEE MASTERS. Reader: Julie Harris. Caedmon SWC 1152 (ac)

83 YEVTUSHENKO READS BABII YAR AND OTHER POEMS. Read by the author in Russian and Alan Bates in English. Caedmon SWC 1153 (ac)

84 EZRA POUND READING HIS POETRY. Caedmon SWC 2088 (2 ac)

85 DISCOVERING RHYTHM AND RHYME IN POETRY. Readers: Julie Harris and David Wayne. Caedmon TC 1156 (pd) or CDL5 1156 (ac)

86 AN EVENING WITH DYLAN THOMAS READING HIS OWN WORK AND POEMS OF OTHERS. Caedmon TC 1157 (pd) or CDL5 1157 (ac)

87 BEOWULF AND OTHER POETRY IN OLD ENGLISH. Reader: J. B. Bessinger Jr. Caedmon SWC 1161 (ac)

88 THE RAPE OF THE LOCK AND OTHER POEMS: POPE. Reader: Michael Redgrave. Caedmon SWC 1171 (ac)

89 ODE ON SOLITUDE AND OTHER WORKS: POPE. Readers: Claire Bloom and Max Adrian. Caedmon SWC 1311 (ac)

90 EVANGELINE: LONGFELLOW. Reader: Hal Holbrook. Caedmon SWC 1179 (ac)

91 GAWAIN AND THE GREEN KNIGHT AND THE

PEARL. Readers: J. B. Bessinger Jr. and Marie Borroff. In Middle English. Caedmon SWC 1192 (ac)

92 GUNGA DIN AND OTHER POEMS: KIPLING. Readers: Boris Karloff and others. Caedmon SWC 1193 (ac)

93 THE FALL OF THE HOUSE OF USHER AND OTHER WORKS: POE. Reader: Basil Rathbone. Caedmon SWC 1195 (ac)

94 THE ILIAD: HOMER. Reader: Anthony Quayle. In English. Caedmon SWC 1196 (ac)

96 MY LAST DUCHESS AND OTHER POEMS: ROBERT BROWNING. Reader: James Mason. Caedmon SWC 1201 (ac)

97 A. E. HOUSMAN: A SHROPSHIRE LAD AND OTHER POETRY. Reader: James Mason. Caedmon TC 1203 (pd) or CDL5 1203 (ac)

98 AMERICAN PATRIOTISM IN POEMS AND PROSE. Readers: Julie Harris and others. Caedmon CDL5 1204 (ac only)

99 THE POETRY OF HART CRANE. Reader: Tennessee Williams. Caedmon SWC 1206 (ac)

100 FAVORITE AMERICAN POEMS. Reader: Ed Begley. Caedmon SWC 1207 (ac)

101 PABLO NERUDA READING HIS POETRY. In Spanish. Caedmon SWC 1215 (ac)

102 POETRY OF VACHEL LINDSAY. Reader: Nicholas Cave Lindsay. Caedmon SWC 1216 (ac)

103 THE POETRY OF ROBERT W. SERVICE. Reader: Ed Begley. Caedmon TC 1218 (pd) or CDL5 1218 (ac)

104 CHAUCER: THE CANTERBURY TALES: THE MILLER'S TALE AND THE REEVE'S TALE. Reader: J. B. Bessinger Jr. In Middle English. Caedmon SWC 1223 (ac)

105 CHAUCER: THE PARLIAMENT OF FOWLS AND SIX LYRIC POEMS. Reader: J. B. Bessinger Jr. In Middle English. Caedmon SWC 1226 (ac)

106 J.R.R. TOLKIEN: POEMS AND SONGS OF MIDDLE EARTH. Read and sung by J.R.R. Tolkien and William Elvin. Music by Donald Swann. Caedmon TC 1231 (pd) or CP 1231 (ac)

107 THE POETRY OF PASTERNAK. Readers: Yevgeny Yevtushenko and Morris Carnovsky. In Russian and English. Caedmon SWC 1232 (ac)

108 CROSSING BROOKLYN FERRY AND OTHER POEMS: WALT WHITMAN. Reader: Ed Begley. Caedmon SWC 1233 (ac)

109 A GATHERING OF GREAT POETRY FOR CHILDREN, KINDERGARTEN AND UP. Readers: Julie Harris and others. CDL5 1235 (ac only)

110 A GATHERING OF GREAT POETRY FOR CHILDREN, SECOND GRADE AND UP. Readers: Julie Harris and others. Caedmon CDL5 1236 (ac only)

111 A GATHERING OF GREAT POETRY FOR CHILDREN, THIRD GRADE AND UP. Readers: Julie Harris and others. Caedmon CDL5 1237 (ac only)

112 A GATHERING OF GREAT POETRY FOR CHILDREN, FOURTH GRADE AND UP. Readers: Julie Harris and others. Caedmon CDL5 1238 (ac only)

113 RICHARD EBERHART READING HIS POETRY. Caedmon SWC 1243 (ac)

114 GWENDOLYN BROOKS READING HER POETRY. Caedmon SWC 1244 (ac)

115 RICHARD WILBUR READING HIS POETRY. Caedmon SWC 1248 (ac)

116 SELECTIONS FROM THE BHAGAVAD-GITA, THE SONG OF GOD. Reader: Zia Mohyeddin. In English. Caedmon SWC 1249 (ac)

117 CARL SANDBURG READING FOG AND OTHER POEMS. Caedmon TC 1253 (pd) or CDL5 1253 (ac)

118 THE POETRY OF JOHN MILTON. Reader: Anthony Quayle. Caedmon SWC 1259 (ac)

119 THE SAVAGERY OF LOVE: BROTHER ANTONINUS READS HIS POETRY. Caedmon SWC 1260 (ac)

120 THE POETRY OF LANGSTON HUGHES. Readers: Ruby Dee and Ossie Davis. Caedmon TC 1272 (pd) or CDL5 1272 (ac)

121 THE POETRY OF GEORGE SEFERIS READ IN GREEK BY THE AUTHOR AND IN ENGLISH BY THE TRANSLATOR, EDMUND KEELEY. Caedmon SWC 1277 (ac)

122 IN COUNTRY HEAVEN—THE EVOLUTION OF A POEM: DYLAN THOMAS. Read by the author and others. Caedmon SWC 1281 (ac)

123 PARENTS KEEP OUT: OGDEN NASH. Read by author. Caedmon TC 1282 (pd) or CDL5 1282 (ac)

124 TENNYSON: IDYLLS OF THE KING: GERAINT AND ENID. Reader: Anthony Quayle. Caedmon SWC 1285 (ac)

125 THE PURLOINED LETTER AND OTHER WORKS: POE. Reader: Anthony Quayle. Caedmon TC 1288 (pd) or CDL5 1288 (ac)

126 DYLAN THOMAS READS A PERSONAL ANTHOLOGY. Caedmon SWC 1294 (ac)

127 W. S. MERWIN READING HIS POETRY. Caedmon SWC 1295 (ac)

128 CLASSICS OF LATIN POETRY AND PROSE. Readers: James Hynd and others. In Latin. Caedmon SWC 1296 (ac)

129 POETRY OF ROBINSON JEFFERS. Reader: Judith Anderson. Caedmon SWC 1297 (ac)

130 WYNKEN, BLYNKEN, AND NOD AND OTHER POEMS: EUGENE FIELD. Reader: Julie Harris. Caedmon TC 1298 (pd) or CDL5 1298 (ac)

131 BRIAN PATTEN READING HIS POETRY. Caedmon SWC 1300 (ac)

132 CLASSICS OF ENGLISH POETRY FOR THE ELEMENTARY CURRICULUM. Readers: Katharine Cornell and others. Caedmon CDL5 1301 (ac only)

133 OLD IRONSIDES AND OTHER POEMS: OLIVER WENDELL HOLMES. Reader: Ed Begley. Caedmon SWC 1302 (ac)

134 REFLECTIONS ON A WICKED WORLD: OGDEN NASH. Read by author. Caedmon SWC 1307 (ac)

135 THE BAREFOOT BOY AND OTHER POEMS: JOHN GREENLEAF WHITTIER. Reader: Ed Begley. Caedmon SWC 1308 (ac)

136 POEMS FROM BLACK AFRICA. Reader: James Earl Jones. With music. Caedmon SWC 1315 (ac)

137 THE POETRY OF CHRISTIAN MORGENSTERN. Reader: Ogden Nash. In English. Caedmon CDL5 1316 (ac only)

CAED (continued)

138 CHRISTMAS WITH OGDEN NASH. Read by author. Caedmon SWC 1323 (ac)

139 T. S. ELIOT READING THE WASTE LAND AND OTHER POEMS. Caedmon TC 1326 (pd) or CDL5 1326 (ac)

140 JAMES DICKEY READS HIS POETRY AND PROSE. Caedmon SWC 1333 (ac)

141 THE POETRY OF STEPHEN VINCENT BENET. Read by the author and Joseph Wiseman. Caedmon SWC 1337 (ac)

142 CATCH A LITTLE RHYME! POEMS FOR ACTIVITY TIME: EVE MERRIAM. Read by the author. Caedmon TC 1339 (pd) or CDL5 1339 (ac)

143 JAMES JOYCE READS JAMES JOYCE (FROM ULYSSES AND FINNEGAN'S WAKE). Also, Cyril Cusack reads Joyce poems. Caedmon TC 1340 (pd) or CDL5 1340 (ac)

144 DYLAN THOMAS READING FROM HIS WORK AND THE WORKS OF SEAN O'CASEY AND DJUNA BARNES. Caedmon SWC 1342 (ac)

145 DYLAN THOMAS AND EDITH SITWELL READ AND DISCUSS HER POETRY. Caedmon SWC 1343 (ac)

146 THEODORE ROETHKE READS HIS POETRY. Caedmon SWC 1351 (ac)

147 DYLAN THOMAS READS THE POETRY OF WILLIAM BUTLER YEATS AND OTHERS. Caedmon SWC 1353 (ac)

148 WHEN WE WERE VERY YOUNG: A. A. MILNE. Reader: Judith Anderson. Caedmon TC 1356 (pd) or CP 1356 (ac)

149 THE POETRY OF RALPH WALDO EMERSON. Reader: Archibald MacLeish. Caedmon SWC 1359 (ac)

150 RANDALL JARRELL READS AND DISCUSSES HIS POEMS AGAINST WAR. Caedmon SWC 1363 (ac)

151 HANS CHRISTIAN ANDERSEN: HIS POEMS AND THE STORY OF HIS LIFE. Reader: Siobhan McKenna. Caedmon SWC 1366 (ac)

152 MALORY: MORTE D'ARTHUR: LAUNCELOT AND GUENEVER. Reader: Siobhan McKenna. Caedmon SWC 1374 (ac)

153 POETS OF THE WEST INDIES READING THEIR OWN WORKS. Readers: Derek Walcott and others. Caedmon SWC 1379 (ac)

154 POEMS BY A LITTLE GIRL: HILDA CONKLING. Read by author. Caedmon CDL5 1387 (ac only)

155 TOUGH POEMS FOR TOUGH PEOPLE. Readers: Ruby Dee and others. Caedmon SWC 1396 (ac)

156 POETRY OF COUNTEE CULLEN. Readers: Ruby Dee and Ossie Davis. Caedmon SWC 1400 (ac)

157 POETRY OF BENÉT. Reader: Joseph Wiseman. Caedmon SWC 1401 (ac)

158 BERRIGAN RAPS: DANIEL BERRIGAN. Caedmon SWC 1402 (ac)

159 FOUR QUARTETS: T. S. ELIOT. Read by the author. Caedmon TC 1403 (pd) or CDL5 1403 (ac)

160 EARTH DAY (THOREAU, EMERSON, KEATS AND OTHERS). Reader: Stacy Keach. With music. Caedmon SWC 1430 (ac)

161 ANNE SEXTON READS HER POETRY. Caedmon SWC 1441 (ac)

162 THE BALLAD OF READING GAOL: WILDE. Reader: James Mason. Caedmon SWC 1473 (ac)

163 THE WHITE MAN'S BURDEN AND OTHER POEMS: KIPLING. Reader: Anthony Quayle. Caedmon SWC 1481 (ac)

164 SILVER PENNIES (INTRODUCTORY POETRY FOR CHILDREN). Readers: Claire Bloom and Cyril Ritchard. Caedmon CDL5 1495 (ac only)

165 THE POETRY AND VOICE OF MAY SWENSON. Caedmon SWC 1500 (ac)

166 THE POETRY AND VOICE OF MARILYN HACKER. Caedmon SWC 1501 (ac)

167 THE POETRY AND VOICE OF GALWAY KINNELL. Caedmon SWC 1502 (ac)

168 THE POETRY AND VOICE OF PHILIP LEVINE. Caedmon SWC 1503 (ac)

169 MORE SILVER PENNIES. Readers: Claire Bloom and Cyril Ritchard. Caedmon CDL5 1511 (ac only)

170 ROBERT FROST IN RECITAL. Caedmon TC 1523 (pd) or CDL5 1523 (ac)

171 ALLIGATOR PIE AND OTHER POEMS: DENNIS LEE. Read by the author. With music. Caedmon TC 1530 (pd) or CP 1530 (ac)

172 THE POETRY AND VOICE OF TED HUGHES. Caedmon SWC 1535 (ac)

173 THE POETRY AND VOICE OF MURIEL RUKEYSER. Caedmon SWC 1536 (ac)

174 THE POETRY AND VOICE OF MARGARET ATWOOD. Caedmon SWC 1537 (ac)

175 THE POETRY AND VOICE OF JAMES WRIGHT. Caedmon SWC 1538 (ac)

176 THE LOST ZOO: COUNTEE CULLEN. Reader: Ruby Dee. Caedmon TC 1539 (pd) or CDL5 1539 (ac)

177 SYLVIA PLATH READING HER POETRY. Caedmon TC 1544 (pd) or CDL5 1544 (ac)

178 SIR JOHN BETJEMAN READING HIS POETRY. Caedmon TC 1557 (pd) or CDL5 1557 (ac)

179 SELECTED POETRY OF ALGERNON CHARLES SWINBURNE. Reader: James Mason. Caedmon SWC 1560 (ac)

180 ROBERT LOWELL: A READING. Caedmon TC 1569 (pd) or CDL5 1569 (ac)

181 HOW DID I GET TO BE FORTY AND OTHER ATROCITIES: JUDITH VIORST. Read by the author. Caedmon TC 1586 (pd) or CDL5 1586 (ac)

182 UNDER MILK WOOD: DYLAN THOMAS. Read by author and others. Caedmon TC 2005 (2 pd) or CDL5 2005 (2 ac)

183 THE CAEDMON TREASURY OF MODERN POETS READING THEIR OWN POETRY. Caedmon TC 2006 (2 pd) or CDL5 2006 (2 ac)

184 MILTON'S PARADISE LOST. Reader: Anthony Quayle. Caedmon TC 2008; on Caedmon TC 1093 (2 pd) with other material

185 GREAT AMERICAN POETRY. Readers: Eddie Albert and others. Caedmon SWC 2009 (2 ac)

186 PALGRAVE'S GOLDEN TREASURY OF ENGLISH POETRY. Readers: Claire Bloom and others. Caedmon SWC 2011 (2 ac)

187 DYLAN THOMAS READING HIS POETRY. Caedmon TC 2014 (2 pd) or CDL5 2014 (2 ac)

188 TENNYSON: IDYLLS OF THE KING: LANCELOT AND ELAINE AND THE PASSING OF ARTHUR.

Reader: Basil Rathbone. Caedmon SWC 2022 (2 ac)

189 THE PEOPLE, YES: CARL SANDBURG. Read by the author. Caedmon SWC 2023 (2 ac)

190 EMILY DICKINSON: A SELF-PORTRAIT. Reader: Julie Harris. Caedmon TC 2026 (2 pd) or CDL5 2026 (2 ac)

191 SAMSON AGONISTES: MILTON. Reader: Michael Redgrave. Caedmon SWC 2028 (2 ac)

192 PARADISE LOST: MILTON. Reader: Anthony Quayle. Caedmon TC 2034; on Caedmon TC 1093 (2 pd) with other material

193 CLASSICAL RUSSIAN POETRY. Readers: Yevgeny Yevtushenko and Morris Carnovsky. In Russian and English. Caedmon SWC 2036 (2 ac)

194 WALT WHITMAN: EYE WITNESS TO THE CIVIL WAR. Reader: Ed Begley. Caedmon SWC 2040 (2 ac)

195 CLASSICS OF AMERICAN POETRY FOR THE ELEMENTARY CURRICULUM. Readers: Hal Holbrook and others. Caedmon CDL5 2041 (2 ac)

196 JAMES AGEE: A PORTRAIT. Read by the author and Father James Flye. Caedmon SWC 2042 (2 ac)

197 THE SONG OF ROLAND. Reader: Anthony Quayle. In English. Caedmon SWC 2059 (2 ac)

198 E. E. CUMMINGS READS HIS COLLECTED POETRY 1920-1940 AND PROSE. Caedmon SWC 2080 (2 ac)

199 E. E. CUMMINGS READS HIS COLLECTED POETRY 1943-1958. Caedmon TC 2081 (2 pd) or CDL5 2081 (2 ac)

200 HOMER: THE ODYSSEY: BOOKS 9-12. Reader: Anthony Quayle. In English. Caedmon TC 3001 (3 pd) or CDL5 3001 (3 ac)

201 VICTORIAN POETRY. Readers: Max Adrian and others. Caedmon SWC 3004 (3 ac)

202 ENGLISH ROMANTIC POETRY. Readers: Claire Bloom and others. Caedmon TC 3005 (3 pd) or CDL5 3005 (3 ac)

203 EIGHTEENTH-CENTURY POETRY AND DRAMA. Readers: Max Adrian and others. Caedmon SWC 4002 (4 ac)

205 SELECTED POETRY OF CATULLUS. Reader: James Mason. In English. Caedmon TC 1611 (pd) or CDL5 1611 (ac)

206 SELECTIONS FROM CROW AND WODWO: TED HUGHES. Read by the author. Caedmon TC 1628 (pd) or CDL5 1628 (ac)

207 POETRY AND REFLECTIONS: LANGSTON HUGHES. Read by the author. Caedmon TC 1640 (pd) or CDL5 1640 (ac)

208 DANTE: THE DIVINE COMEDY: INFERNO CANTOS 1-6. Reader: Ian Richardson. In English. Caedmon TC 1632 (pd) or CDL5 1632 (ac)

CAPITOL Capitol Records Inc., 1750 North Vine St., Hollywood, CA 90028, USA

1 THE STORY-TELLER. Reader: Charles Laughton. Capitol TBO-1650

CARIL Carillon, New Haven, CT, USA
Carillon (now defunct) issued the original Yale Poets series of 22 records. The entire series was then reissued by Decca (U.S.) and, upon the dissolution of that company, became the property of CMS Records

(q.v.). Several discs were reissued by CMS.

1 ALLEN TATE READS HIS WORKS. Carillon YP 300; Decca (U.S.) DL 9130

2 STANLEY KUNITZ READS HIS OWN POETRY. Carillon YP 302; Decca (U.S.) DL 9131

3 DUDLEY FITTS READS FROM HIS OWN WORKS. Carillon YP 303; Decca (U.S.) DL 9138; CMS 675

4 GEORGE STARBUCK READS HIS OWN WORK. Carillon YP 304; Decca (U.S.) DL 9137; CMS 676

5 LOUIS SIMPSON READS HIS OWN WORK. Carillon YP 305; Decca (U.S.) DL 9146

6 JOHN CROWE RANSOM READS HIS WORKS. Carillon YP 306; Decca (U.S.) DL 9147

7 LOUISE BOGAN READS HER WORKS. Carillon YP 308; Decca (U.S.) DL 9132

8 YVOR WINTERS READS HIS WORKS. Carillon YP 309; Decca (U.S.) DL 9136

9 LEE ANDERSON READS. Carillon YP 310; Decca (U.S.) DL 9133

10 MARIANNE MOORE READS HER WORKS. Carillon YP 312; Decca (U.S.) DL 9135; CMS 678

11 RICHARD EBERHART READS HIS OWN WORKS. Carillon YP 314; Decca (U.S.) DL 9145

12 THEODORE WEISS READS FROM HIS OWN WORKS. Carillon YP 315; Decca (U.S.) DL 9144; CMS 680

13 JOHN HOLLANDER READS FROM HIS OWN WORKS. Carillon YP 316; Decca (U.S.) DL 9143

14 VERNON WATKINS READS HIS OWN WORKS. Carillon YP 317; Decca (U.S.) DL 9142; CMS 681

15 LOUIS MACNEICE READS FROM HIS OWN WORKS. Carillon YP 318; Decca (U.S.) DL 9141

16 C. DAY LEWIS READS FROM HIS OWN WORKS. Carillon YP 319; Decca (U.S.) DL 9139

17 ROBERT FROST READS HIS OWN WORKS. Carillon YP 320; Decca (U.S.) DL 9127

18 WINFIELD TOWNLEY SCOTT READS HIS OWN WORK. Carillon YP 321; Decca (U.S.) DL 9140

19 CONRAD AIKEN READS FROM HIS OWN WORKS. Carillon YP 307; Decca (U.S.) DL 9128; CMS 677

20 ROBERT LOWELL READS FROM HIS WORKS. Carillon YP 301; Decca (U.S.) DL 9129

21 ROBERT PENN WARREN READS HIS POETRY. Carillon YP 313; Decca (U.S.) DL 9148; CMS 679

22 R. P. BLACKMUR READS FROM HIS OWN WORKS. Carillon YP 311; Decca (U.S.) DL 9134

CASSC Cassette Curriculum, Everett/Edwards, Inc., PO Box 1060, Deland, FL 32720, USA

1A THE WORKS OF ROBERT PENN WARREN. Reader: James A. Grimshaw. Cassette Curriculum 76

1 GEORGE HITCHCOCK READS HIS POETRY. Cassette Curriculum 151

2 GUY OWEN READS HIS POETRY. Cassette Curriculum 152

3 DIANE WAKOSKI READS HER WORK. Cassette Curriculum 153

4 ROBERT BLY READS HIS POETRY. Cassette Curriculum 154

CASSC (continued)

5 DARWIN TURNER READS HIS WORK. Cassette Curriculum 155

6 JOHN MEADE HAINES READS HIS WORK. Cassette Curriculum 156

7 JESSE STUART READS HIS WORK. Cassette Curriculum 158

8 ALLEN GINSBERG READS HIS WORK. Cassette Curriculum 161

9 ROBERT CREELEY READS HIS WORK. Cassette Curriculum 162

10 WM. E. TAYLOR READS HIS WORK. Cassette Curriculum 163

11 LAWRENCE FERLINGHETTI READS HIS WORK. Cassette Curriculum 164

12 JOHN CIARDI READS HIS WORK. Cassette Curriculum 165

12A POETRY OF WM. CARLOS WILLIAMS. Reader: Linda Wagner. Cassette Curriculum 808

12B WORKS OF PHILLIS WHEATLEY. Reader: Houston A. Baker, Jr. Cassette Curriculum 1425

12C SIR GAWAIN AND THE GREEN KNIGHT. Reader: Stephen Medcalf. Cassette Curriculum 3004

12D THE SONNETS: WORDSWORTH. Reader: Stephen Prickett. Cassette Curriculum 3501

12E THE PRELUDE: WORDSWORTH. Reader: Stephen Prickett. Cassette Curriculum 3502

12F ODE: INTIMATIONS OF IMMORTALITY: WORDSWORTH. Reader: Stephen Prickett. Cassette Curriculum 3503

12G TINTERN ABBEY: WORDSWORTH. Reader: Stephen Prickett. Cassette Curriculum 3504

13 MARGE PIERCY READS HER WORK. Cassette Curriculum 5526

CBC Canadian Broadcasting Corp., PO Box 500, Terminal A, Toronto, Ont., Canada

1 A. M. KLEIN: THE POET AS LANDSCAPE. Reader: Earl Pennington. CBC (16mm film)

CBS CBS Disques, 1-3 rue de Chateau, Paris, France

1 FLORILÈGE POÉTIQUE. Reader: Jean-Marc Tennberg. CBS 88036

CENTCA Center for Cassette Studies, Audio-Text Cassettes, 8110 Webb Av., North Hollywood, CA 91605, USA

1 PHILIP WHALEN AND GARY SYNDER, TWO MODERN SAN FRANCISCO POETS DISCUSS AND READ FROM THEIR WORKS. Center for Cassette Studies 020-10154

CETRA Fonit-Cetra SpA, Via G. Meda 45, 20141 Milano, Italy

1 ORLANDO FURIOSO: ARIOSTO. Readers: Giorgio Albertazzi and others. Cetra CLC 0839 - 0845 (7 pd)

2 POETRY OF GIOSUE CARDUCCI. Readers: Ruggero Ruggeri and others. In Italian. Cetra CLC 0833

3 DIVINA COMMEDIA: DANTE. Readers: Arnaldo Foa and others. In Italian. Cetra MS 17 (CL 0402; CLC 0803-0808, 0811-0822) (18 pd)

4 EDUARDO DE FILIPPO—POESIE. Read by author. Cetra CL 0429 (2 pd)

5 UGO FOSCOLO—SONETTI. Readers: Vittorio Gassman and others. Cetra CLC 0946

6 FIORETTI: SAN FRANCESCO D'ASSISI. Reader: Nando Gazzolo. Cetra LPZ 2026

7 GUIDO GOZZANO—POESIE. Readers: Giancarlo Sbragia and others. Cetra CLC 0836

8 GIACOMO LEOPARDI—POESIE. Readers: Arnoldo Foa and others. Cetra CLC 0828 - 0830 (3 pd)

9 GIACOMO LEOPARDI & A. MANZONI—POESIE. Readers: Giorgio Albertazzi and others. Cetra LPZ 2049

10 EUGENIO MONTALE—POESIE. Readers: Vittorio Gassman and others. Cetra LPZ 2034

11 ALDO PALAZZESCHI—POESIE. Reader: Paolo Poli. Cetra LPZ 2039

12 GIUSEPPE PARRINI & UGO FOSCOLO—POESIE. Readers: Paolo Poli and others. Cetra LPZ 2048

13 GIOVANNI PASCOLI—POESIE. Readers: Vittorio Gassman and others. Cetra CLC 0834

14 FRANCESCO PETRARCA—POESIE. Readers: Giorgio Albertazzi and others. Cetra CLC 0847

15 LA NOMINA DE CAPPELLAN: CARLO PORTA. Reader: Franca Valeri. Cetra CL 0404

16 UMBERTO SABA READS FROM HIS POETRY. In Italian. Cetra LPZ 2061

17 GIUSEPPE UNGARETTI—POESIE. Read by the author and others. Cetra LL 3001

18 POESIA LATINA. Reader: Arnoldo Foa. Cetra LL 1001 - 1003 (3 pd)

19 IL DUECENTO. Readers: Giorgio Albertazzi and others. Cetra LPZ 2041

20 DANTE—PETRARCA. Readers: Giorgio Albertazzi and others. Cetra LPZ 2042

21 IL QUATTROCENTO. Readers: Giorgio Albertazzi and others. Cetra LPZ 2043

22 ARIOSTO—TASSO. Readers: Giorgio Albertazzi and others. Cetra LPZ 2045

23 IL CINQUECENTO. Readers: Giorgio Albertazzi and others. Cetra LPZ 2044

24 IL SEICENTO. Readers: Giorgio Albertazzi and others. Cetra LPZ 2046

25 IL SETTECENTO. Readers: Giorgio Albertazzi and others. Cetra LPZ 2047

26 POESIA DEL RISORGIMENTO. Readers: Arnoldo Foa and others. Cetra CLC 0849

27 L'OTTOCENTO. Readers: Giorgio Albertazzi and others. Cetra LPZ 2050

28 FINE OTTOCENTO. Readers: Giorgio Albertazzi and others. Cetra LPZ 2051

29 POESIE NAPOLETANE. Readers: Nino Taranto and others. Cetra LPQ 09049-09050 (2 pd)

30 ROMA NELLA VOCE DEI SUOI POETI. Readers: Paolo Stoppa and others. Cetra CLC 0848

31 CONCERTO DI POESIA—AUTORI SICILIANI. Reader: Massimo Mollica. Cetra LPZ 2053

32 POESIE D'AMORE: SALVATORE DI GIACOMO. Reader: Achille Millo. Cetra LPZ 2074

33 POESIE DI RAFFAELE VIVIANI. Reader: Achille Millo. Cetra LPZ 2073

34 IGNAZIO BUTTITTA—POETA. Readers: Sergio Colomba and others. Cetra LPZ 2069

35 BIAGIO MARIN—POETA. Readers: Sergio Colomba and others. Cetra LPZ 2068

36 LIBRO D'AMORE. Reader: Pamela Villoresi. Cetra LPZ 2067

37 TOTO'. Read by author. Cetra SP 1455

38 GIUSEPPE UNGARETTI—POESIE. Reader: Giancarlo Sbragia. Cetra CL 0526

39 CESARE PAVESE—POESIE. Reader: Vittorio

Gassman. Cetra CL 0497

40 SALVATORE QUASIMODO—POESIE. Reader: Neda Naldi. Cetra CL 0450

.41 CESARE PAVESE—POESIE. Readers: Diana Torrieri and others. Cetra CL 0432

42 GIUSEPPE UNGARETTI—POESIE. Read by author. Cetra CL 0430

43 ANTOLOGIA DI MODERNI. Reader: Vittorio Gassman. Cetra CL 0426

44 FILASTROCCHE IN CIELO E IN TERRA: GIANNI RODARI. Readers: Carmen Scarpitta and others. Cetra LPZ 2060

45 UN NUOVO GIORNO: MARIA CARLI. Reader: Lilla Brignone. Cetra LPZ 2056

46 IL NOVECENTO. Readers: Giorgio Albertazzi and others. Cetra LPZ 2052

47 A MILANO CON CARLO PORTA. Reader: Franco Parenti. Cetra LPZ 2029

48 EDUARDO LEGGE NAPOLI, 2. Reader: Eduardo de Filippo. Cetra CLC 0851

49 EDUARDO LEGGE NAPOLI. Reader: Eduardo de Filippo. Cetra CLC 0838

50 POESIE DI TOTO' DETTE DA TOTO'. Readers: C. Gelli and others. Cetra LPP 99

51 ALBERTO BEVILACQUA: L'INDIGNAZIONE. Readers: Lilla Brignone and others. Cetra LPZ 2059

CHILDC Children's Classics on Tape, 6722 Bostwick Drive, Springfield, VA 22151, USA

1 PAUL REVERE'S RIDE: LONGFELLOW. Children's Classics 130 (ac)

CHRIST Christophorus-Verlag Herder GmbH, Hermann Herderstr. 4, D-7800 Freiburg i.B., West Germany

2 WERNER BERGENGRÜN: GEDICHTE. Read by author. Christophorus CLX 72 112

3 CARL ZUCKMAYER: GEDICHTE. Read by author. Christophorus CLX 73 307

4 VOR LAUTER LICHT ERGLANZT DAS LAND. Readers: Gert Westphal and others. Christophorus CLP 73 320

5 LEG DEINEN SCHATTEN AUF DIE SONNENUHREN. Readers: Gert Westphal and others. Christophorus CLP 73 321

6 NUN RIESELN WEISSE FLOCKEN UNSRE SCHRITTE EIN. Readers: Gert Westphal and others. Christophorus CLP 73 322

7 NUN WACHSEN DER ERDE DIE GROSSEN FLÜGEL. Reader: Gert Westphal and others. Christophorus CLP 73 323

8 WALTHER VON DER VOGELWEIDE. Reader: Friedrich von Bülow. Christophorus CLX 75 430

9 ANNETTE VON DROSTE-HÜLSHOFF. Reader: Maria Ott. Christophorus CLX 75 431

10 DER MENSCH: HÖLDERLIN. Reader: Rolf Henniger. Christophorus CLX 75 432

11 DER MOND IN DER DEUTSCHEN DICHTUNG. Readers: Rolf Henniger and others. Christophorus CLX 75 434

12 EDUARD MÖRIKE. Reader: Elfriede Kuzmany. Christophorus CLX 75 436

13 FRÜHE ZEUGNISSE DEUTSCHER DICHTUNG. Reader: Friedrich von Bülow. Christophorus CLX 75 437

14 ANDREAS GRYPHIUS: GEDICHTE. Reader:

Werner Hinz. Christophorus CLX 75 438

15 DEUTSCHE BALLADEN VON BÜRGER BIS BRECHT. Reader: Gert Westphal. Christophorus CLX 75 439

16 DICHTER UND WELTRAUM VON GRYPHIUS BIS JEAN PAUL. Readers: Eduard Marks and others. Christophorus CLX 75 440

17 MITTELALTERLICHE DICHTUNG VOM TODE. Readers: Manfred Schradi and others. Christophorus CLX 75 442

18 DIE PASSION IN DER DEUTSCHEN DICHTUNG. Readers: Friedrich von Bülow and others. Christophorus CLX 75 446

19 DAS GEDICHT UND SEINE VERTONUNG. Readers: Maria Ott and others. Christophorus CLX 75 447

20 W. VON ESCHENBACH: PARZIVAL. Readers: Friedrich von Bülow and others. Christophorus CLX 75 448

21 GEDANKENLYRIK—SCHILLER. Reader: Gert Westphal. Christophorus CLX 75 450

22 DEUTSCHE ODEN VON WECKHERLIN BIS KROLOW. Readers: Peter Lühr and others. Christophorus CLX 75 451

23 DEUTSCHE MUNDARTEN. Reader: Wilhelm Menzel. Christophorus CLX 75 453

24 STEFAN GEORGE UND HUGO VON HOFMANNSTHAL. Readers: Peter Arens and others. Christophorus CLX 75 456

25 DIE ELEGIE. Readers: Peter Arens and others. Christophorus CLX 75 457

26 GOETHES ALTERSLYRIK. Reader: Wilhelm Borchert. Christophorus CLX 75 460

27 ROMANTISCHE LYRIK. Reader: Klausjürgen Wussow. Christophorus CLX 75 461

28 VERKLÄRTER HERBST. Reader: Gert Westphal. Christophorus CLX 75 462

29 PSALM UND ANTIPSALM. Reader: Maria Ott. Christophorus CLX 75 463

30 DICHTER UND VATERLAND. Readers: Gert Westphal and others. Christophorus CLX 75 464

31 MARIE LUISE KASCHNITZ: GEDICHTE. Read by author. Christophorus CLX 75 517

CLADD Claddagh Records. Current address unknown.

1 AUSTIN CLARKE READS HIS OWN POETRY. Claddagh LP 33

CMS CMS Records Inc., 12 Warren St., New York, NY 10007, USA
For the Yale Poets series, see Carillon.

1 THE PRISON DIARY: HO CHI MINH. Reader: Martin Donegan. CMS 109

2 POETRY PROGRAM FOR CHILDREN, 1. Reader: Elinor Basescu. CMS 506

3 POETRY PROGRAM FOR CHILDREN, 2. Reader: Elinor Basescu. CMS 526

4 POETRY PROGRAM FOR CHILDREN, 3. Reader: Elinor Basescu. CMS 530

5 SELECTIONS FROM SPANISH POETRY. Reader: Seymour Resnick. In Spanish and English. CMS 510

6 RUSSIAN POETRY AND PROSE. Reader: Marshall Shatz. In English and Russian. CMS 511

7 ALASTAIR REID: ODDMENTS, INKLINGS, OMENS. Read by author. CMS 522

CMS (continued)

8   JOHN UPDIKE READING FROM HIS WORKS. CMS 523

9   THE RUBAIYAT OF OMAR KHAYYAM. Reader: Khigh Dhiegh. (complete) CMS 527

10 STAR SPANGLED BANNER AND OTHER FAMOUS AMERICAN DOCUMENTS. Reader: Martin Donegan. CMS 532

10A SHAKESPEARE—GREAT SONNETS AND SOLILO-QUIES. Reader: David Allen. CMS 541

11 NO MAN IS AN ISLAND AND OTHER GREAT PO-EMS. Reader: David Allen. CMS 542

12 GREAT POEMS OF THE ENGLISH LANGUAGE, 1. Reader: David Allen. CMS 544

13 GREAT POEMS OF THE ENGLISH LANGUAGE, 2. Reader: David Allen. CMS 545

14 GREAT POEMS OF THE ENGLISH LANGUAGE, 3. Reader: David Allen. CMS 546

15 THE BROWNINGS. Readers: Esther Benson and others. CMS 576

16 SHORT STORIES OF E. A. POE AND SELECTED PO-EMS. Reader: Martin Donegan. CMS 592/2

17 AENEID (Book 2 complete). Readers: L. A. Mo-ritz and others. In Latin. CMS 597/2

18 ROBERT BURNS IN POETRY, SONG, AND PROSE. Reader: Arnold Johnston. CMS 614

19 ILIAD: HOMER (excerpts). Reader: Robert Fitz-gerald. In English. CMS 674/2

20 WALT WHITMAN: LEAVES OF GRASS. Reader: David Allen. CMS 543

COLPIX Colpix Records. Current address un-known.

1   A LITTLE TREASURY OF TWENTIETH CENTURY AMERICAN POETRY. Colpix PS 1001

COLUMB Columbia, CBS Records Group, 51 West 52nd St., New York, NY 10019, USA

1   A PICNIC CANTATA; JAMES MARCUS SCHUYLER. With music by Paul Bowles. Columbia ML 5068

2   JOHN BROWN'S BODY: BENET. Readers: Ty-rone Power and others. Columbia SL-181 (2 pd)

3   EXCERPT FROM A POET'S NOTEBOOK: SITWELL. Read by author Edith Sitwell. Columbia DSL 190 (ML 4759; LP14387-8)

4   SHAKESPEARE'S AGES OF MAN, 1. Reader: John Gielgud. Columbia CSP 91-A-02055 (pd) or PT 11460 (ac); rerecorded for Caedmon on Caedmon SRS 200 (2 pd) or CP 200 (2 ac)

5   SHAKESPEARE'S AGES OF MAN, 2. Reader: John Gielgud. Columbia CSP 91-A-02057 (pd) or PT 11460 (ac); rerecorded for Caedmon on Caedmon SRS 200 (2 pd) or CP 200 (2 ac)

6   AMERICA THE BEAUTIFUL. Reader: Vincent Price. Columbia CSP 91-A-02013 (ML 5668) (pd) or PT 11455 (ac)

7   FACADE: EDITH SITWELL. Read by author. With music by Walton. Columbia ML 2047; reissued with CARNIVAL OF THE ANI-MALS on Columbia Odyssey Y-32359

8   PLEASURE DOME. Readings by Auden, E. Bishop, Cummings, Eliot, M. Moore, Nash, D. Thomas, W. C. Williams. CBS 91-A-02049 (ML 4259)

9   SAINT-SAËNS; CARNIVAL OF THE ANIMALS. VERSES BY OGDEN NASH. Reader: Noel Cow-ard. Columbia ML 4355; reissued with FACADE on Columbia Odyssey Y-32359

10 AN EVENING OF ELIZABETHAN VERSE AND ITS MUSIC. Reader: W. H. Auden. With Green-berg, Pro Musica. Columbia ML 5051

11 A ROUND OF POEMS. Reader: Lloyd Franken-berg. Columbia ML 5148

12 LOVE RESPELT, OLD AND NEW POEMS BY ROB-ERT GRAVES. Read by author. Columbia OL 6400

13 ANTIWORLDS: THE POETRY OF ANDREI VOZ-NESENSKY. Read by author and others. In Russian and English. Columbia OL 6590

14 YEVTUSHENKO IN READINGS FROM HIS NEW YORK AND SAN FRANCISCO POETRY CONCERTS. Columbia S 31344

15 BRECHT ON BRECHT. Readers: Lotte Lenya and others. In English. Columbia OL 5831

COR Coronet, 65 East South Water St., Chica-go, IL 60601, USA

1   SPOON RIVER ANTHOLOGY (selections). Coronet M 0193 (2 ac and 2 fs)

CREAT Creative Visuals, Gamco Industries, Inc., PO Box 1911, Big Spring, TX 79720, USA

1   READING AND LISTENING TO POETRY. Cre-ative Visuals 808.1 BO-SR (ac, 14 transp.)

CROWN Crown Publishers Inc., One Park Av., New York, NY 10016, USA

1   LIVING LITERATURE: THE SONNETS OF SHAKE-SPEARE. Reader: Ronald Colman. Crown (4 pd)

DANA Dana Productions, 6249 Babcock Av., North Hollywood, CA 91606, USA

1   NO MAN IS AN ISLAND: DONNE. Reader: Orson Welles. Dana (film)

DAV Davidson Films Inc., 3701 Buchanan St., San Francisco, CA 94123, USA

1   NOAH'S JOURNEY: GEORGE MACBETH. Reader: Godfrey Cambridge. Davidson Films (16 mm film)

DECCA Decca Records (U.K.), 50 New Bond Street, London WIY 9HA, England

1   KURT TUCHOLSKY: ABENDS NACH SECHS. Read-ers: Martin Held and others. Decca SDSC 13.907

2   FACE IS FAMILIAR: OGDEN NASH. Read by au-thor. Decca 342 (23267) (3 pd)

3   THE CHILDREN'S HOUR: LONGFELLOW. Read-er: Donald Crisp. Decca A-434

4   OUR COMMON HERITAGE. Reader: Walter Huston. Decca A-536 (6 pd, 78rpm)

5   THE PEOPLE YES: SANDBURG. Read by author. Decca DL 5135(A-273)

6   SANDBURG READS SANDBURG. Decca DL 7541

7   ABRAHAM LINCOLN. Reader: Walter Huston. Decca DL 8515

8   ROBERT FROST READS THE POEMS OF ROBERT FROST. Decca 9033 (DL 79033)

9   CARL SANDBURG READS THE POEMS OF CARL SANDBURG. Decca 9039

10 PARNASSUS: FAMOUS POEMS THAT TELL GREAT STORIES. Readers: R. E. Johnson and others. Decca DL 9040. See also LIST 21

11 PARNASSUS: A TREASURY OF THE SPOKEN WORD. THE FUNMAKERS. Readers: Arnold Moss and others. Decca DL 9042. See also LIST 22

12 PARNASSUS: THE HEART SPEAKS—LYRICS OF

LOVE. Readers: Arnold Moss and others. Decca DL 9043

13 PARNASSUS: THE HEROIC SOUL. POEMS OF PATRIOTISM. Readers: R. E. Johnson and others. Decca DL 9044. See also LIST 23

DEUTGR Deutsche Grammophon GmbH, PO Box 301240, D-2000 Hamburg 36, West Germany
Deutsche Grammophon, division of Polygram Classics Inc., 137 West 55th St., New York, NY 10019, USA

1 WALDEINSAMKEIT: HEINE. Reader: Oskar Werner. DG 34 008 (pd, 45rpm)

2 DICHTUNG AFRIKANISCHER VÖLKER. Reader: Klaus Kinski. DG 34 016 (pd, 45rpm)

3 DEM UNBEKANNTEN GOTT: NIETZSCHE. Reader: Klaus Kinski. DG 34 027

4 ROMANTISCHE GEDICHTE. Reader: Will Quadflieg. DG 34 028

5 FERNÖSTLICHE DICHTUNG. Reader: Anna Dammann. DG 34 040

6 GEDICHTE VON F. HÖLDERLIN. Reader: Will Quadflieg. DG 34 041

7 GEDICHTE VON GOETHE. Reader: Will Quadflieg. DG 34 042 (2571-035)

8 WILHELM BUSCH: DU SIEHST DIE WESTE, NICHT DAS HERZ. Reader: Günther Lüders. DG 34 048

9 WALTHER MEHRING: GEDICHTE. Read by the author. DG 34 065

10 OSKAR WERNER SPRICHT: EDUARD MÖRIKE. DG 40 007 (2571-034)

11 MARIA BECKER SPRICHT: ELSE LASKER-SCHÜLER. DG 40 008

12 KÄTHE GOLD SPRICHT: MARCELINE DESBORDES-VALMORE. In German. DG 40 009

13 DEUTSCHE LYRIK DES ROKOKO. Reader: Ernst Ginsburg. DG 41 002

14 GEDICHTE. PROSA: GOTTFRIED BENN. Read by author. DG LPS 41 003

15 DAS LIED VON DER GLOCKE: SCHILLER. Readers: Walter Franck and others. DG 42 001

16 MATHIAS WIEMANN SPRICHT GOTTFRIED KELLER. DG 42 006

17 DIE WEISE VON LIEBE UND TOD DES CORNETS CHR. RILKE, UND FRÜHE GEDICHTE: RILKE. Reader: Will Quadflieg. DG 42 009

18 GOTTFRIED BENN: GEDICHTE UND PROSA. Read by author. DG 42 023

19 BALLADEN: SCHILLER. Readers: Maria Becker and others. DG 43 007

20 JUGENDLYRIK UND BALLADEN: GOETHE. Readers: Will Quadflieg and others. DG 43 008

21 ÜBER ALLEN GIPFELN: GOETHE. Reader: Will Quadflieg. DG 43 030

22 HÖLDERLIN: IHR WANDELT DROBEN IM LICHT. Reader: Will Quadflieg. DG 43 031

23 BRECHT: GEDICHTE UND PROSA, 1. Reader: Helene Weigel. DG 43 052 (2571-033)

24 BRECHT: GEDICHTE UND PROSA, 2. Reader: Helene Weigel. DG 43 075 (2571-033)

25 DIE WEISE VON LIEBE UND TOD DES CORNETS CHRISTOPH RILKE: RILKE. Reader: Will Quadflieg. DG 43 080

26 FONTANE: JA, DAS MÖCHT' ICH NOCH ERLEBEN. Reader: O. E. Hasse. DG 44 003

27 TUCHO, TIGER, PANTHER & CO.: TUCHOLSKY. Reader: Ursula Herking. DG 44 016

28 LEGENDEN, LIEDER UND BALLADEN: BRECHT. Reader: Ernst Busch. DG 44 028

29 O. E. HASSE SPRICHT: GOETHE. DG 140 010

30 IN MEMORIAM. DIE STIMME VON ERNST GINSBERG. DG 140 025

31 HEITERER HEINRICH HEINE. Reader: Martin Held. DG 140 029

32 GISELA MAY SINGT TUCHOLSKY. DG 144 030

33 GISELA MAY SINGT ERICH KÄSTNER. DG 144 032

34 SONGS, GEDICHTE UND GESCHICHTEN: BRECHT. Reader: Wolf Kaiser. DG 144 034

35 SONGS MIT GISELA MAY: BRECHT. DG 144 035

36 BITTERSÜSS AUS DEUTSCHER FEDER. DG 168 085

37 EIN BERTOLT BRECHT ABEND MIT THERESE GIEHSE, 1. DG 168 093

38 EIN BERTOLT BRECHT ABEND MIT THERESE GIEHSE, 2. DG 168 094

39 INGEBORG BACHMANN: GEDICHTE. Reader: Marianne Hoppe. DG 2570 002

40 KARLHEINZ BÖHM LIEST RAINER MARIA RILKE. DG 2570 005

40A IN DIESEM LANDE LEBEN WIR. DG 2570 203

41 GEDICHTE: HÖLDERLIN UND RILKE. Reader: Will Quadflieg. DG 2571 002

42 HERMANN HESSE: TRACTAT VOM STEPPENWOLF. Reader: Gert Westphal. DG 2571 009

43 GEDICHTE UND ERZÄHLUNGEN. Reader: Marie Luise Kaschnitz. DG 2571 015

44 EUGEN ROTH LIEST EUGEN ROTH. GÜNTHER LÜDERS LIEST WILHELM BUSCH. DG 2571 29

45 MATHIAS WIEMANN LIEST GEDICHTE, MÄRCHEN, PROSA. DG 2575 001

46 REINEKE FUCHS: GOETHE. Reader: Erich Ponto. DG 2752 001

47 ODYSEE: HOMER. Reader: Mathias Wiemann. In German. DG 2752 003 (2 pd)

48 GOTTFRIED BENN LIEST EIGENE WERKE. DG 2757 001 (2 pd)

DISC Discurio. Current address unknown.
1 PASTERNAK SPEAKS. Discurio

DOVER Dover Publications Inc., 180 Varick St., New York, NY 10014, USA
1 INVITATION TO GERMAN POETRY. Reader: Lotte Lenya. In German. Dover IPG 1 and 2

2 INVITATION TO SPANISH POETRY. Reader: Eugenio Florit. In Spanish. Dover IP 9894

3 INVITATION TO ITALIAN POETRY. Reader: Luciano Rebay. In Italian. Dover 99893-2

4 INVITATION TO FRENCH POETRY. Reader: Michel Moinot. In French. Dover 99895-5

EAV Educational Audio Visual Inc., Pleasantville, NY 10570, USA
1 THE RIME OF THE ANCIENT MARINER. Eav A2RF 0380 (pd with fs)

2 GOD'S TROMBONES: JAMES WELDON JOHNSON. Read by author. Eav A5R 0440

3 THE TIME, LIFE AND WORKS OF CHAUCER. Eav A6RF 0205 (pd with fs)

4 CHAUCER'S CANTERBURY PILGRIMS. Eav A9RF 0233 (pd with fs)

5 BEOWULF and CHAUCER. Readers: Helge Kökeritz and others. Eav A9T 0395 (7414) (at)

6 ANTHOLOGY OF ENGLISH AND AMERICAN PO-

EAV (continued)

ETRY, 1. Readers: Nancy Marchand and others. Eav A9R 0931 (7413-1)

7 ANTHOLOGY OF ENGLISH AND AMERICAN PO-ETRY, 2. Readers: Nancy Marchand and others. Eav A9R 0932 (7413-2)

8 ANTHOLOGY OF ENGLISH AND AMERICAN PO-ETRY, 3. Readers: David Hooks and others. Eav A9R 0933 (7413-3)

9 ANTHOLOGY OF ENGLISH AND AMERICAN PO-ETRY, 4. Readers: David Hooks and others. Eav A9R 0934 (LE 7525)

10 ANTHOLOGY OF ENGLISH AND AMERICAN PO-ETRY, 5. Readers: Nancy Marchand and others. Eav A9R 0935 (7413-5)

11 A THOUSAND YEARS OF ENGLISH PRONUNCIA-TION. Reader: Helge Kökeritz. Eav A9RR 0937 (2 pd)

12 EARLY ENGLISH BALLADS. Readers: Richard Hampton and others. Eav A9R 0962 (7269-1)

13 POEMS BY ROBERT BURNS AND SCOTTISH BOR-DER BALLADS. Readers: Gordon Jackson and others. Eav A9R 0963

14 AMERICAN POETRY TO 1900, 1. Readers: David Allen and others. Eav A9RR 0964 (2 pd)

15 AMERICAN POETRY TO 1900, 2. Reader: Robert Burns and others. Eav A9RR 0965 (2 pd)

16 THE NEW BLACK POETRY. Eav IRR 136

17 COLLECTION OF POETRY. Eav FSC 483 (ac with fs)

18 KEATS/ SHELLEY. Reader: Theodore Marcuse. Eav LE 7505 (A9R 0926)

19 EDGAR ALLEN POE. Reader: David Hooks. Eav A9R 0927 (LE 7600)

20 FAMOUS AMERICAN STORY POEMS, 1. Readers: John Randolph and others. Eav A9RR 0936 (LE 7610)

21 FAMOUS AMERICAN STORY POEMS, 2. Readers: John Randolph and others. Eav LE 7615 (7299-1)

22 FORMS OF POETRY. Readers: David Allen and others. EavA9RR 0938 (LE 7620)

23 SEVEN OLD ENGLISH POEMS. Reader: John C. Pope. In Old English. Eav A5RB 0148 (LE 7645)

EBEC Encyclopedia Britannica, Educational Corp., 425 North Michigan Av., Chicago, IL 60611, USA

1 THE LADY OF SHALOTT: TENNYSON. Enc. Brit. (16mm film)

2 FOG: SANDBURG. Enc. Brit. (16mm film)

3 JAMES DICKEY: LORD LET ME DIE BUT NOT DIE OUT. Read by author. Enc. Brit. (16mm film)

EDUC Educational Dimensions. Current address unknown.

1 THE POETRY OF ROBERT FROST. Ed. Dimensions 714 (2 ac with fs)

EMC EMC CORP., 180 East Sixth St., Saint Paul, MN 55101, USA

1 THE SEASONS OF VERGIL. EMC DTH 400 (at)

2 POETRY OF WALT WHITMAN. Reader: David Allen. EMC HT 3307/08 (at)

3 AN ANTHOLOGY OF ROBERT BURNS. Reader: Douglas Campbell. EMC HR 3309 (at)

4 THE GLORY AND THE TORMENT: GERARD MAN-LEY HOPKINS. Reader: Douglas Campbell. EMC HT 3310

5 A SUMMER IN THE STOMACH: DONALD HALL. Read by author. EMC HR 3325

6 CREATIVE WRITING: THE WHOLE KIT AND CABOODLE, 1. EMC ELC 251 102 (ac)

7 CREATIVE WRITING: THE WHOLE KIT AND CABOODLE, 2. EMC ELC 152 103 (ac)

ENGL English Classics. Current address unknown.

1 NUN'S PRIEST'S TALE: CHAUCER. Reader: Kemp Malone. In Middle English. Engl. Classics XTV 17216-7

EPIU EPIU. Current address unknown.

1 ITALIAN POETS READING THEIR OWN POETRY. In Italian. EPIU 6000–B (originally a 45 rpm pd; reissued on long-play)

EVERG Evergreen Records, Dimitri Music Co., 7859 Bastille Pl., Severn, MD 21144, USA

1 SAN FRANCISCO POETS. EVR 1

FANT FANTASY, 10th and Parker Sts., Berkeley, CA 94710, USA

1 POETRY READINGS IN THE CELLAR. Fantasy 7002

2 TENTATIVE DESCRIPTION OF A DINNER: LAW-RENCE FERLINGHETTI. Read by author. Fantasy 7004

3 HOWL AND OTHER POEMS: GINSBERG. Read by author. Fantasy 7006

FFHS Films for the Humanities, PO Box 2053, Princeton, NJ 08540, USA

1 OCTAVIO PAZ. Read by author. Films for the Humanities (16mm film)

FIDIAS Orfeo Importing Co., 356 South Goodman St., Rochester, NY 14607, USA

1 EL MODERNISMO. Readers: Manuel Dicenta and others. In Spanish. Orfeo F 010

2 POESÍA FEMENINA. In Spanish. Orfeo F 017

3 VERSOS Y COPLAS: POESÍA HISPANOAMERICANA Readers: Carmen Bernardos and others. In Spanish. Orfeo F 032

FISCH Fischer Verlag, Geleitsstrasse 25, Postfach 700480, D-6000 Frankfurt am Main 70, West Germany

1 GEDICHTE VON FRANZ WERFEL. In German. Fischer Vlg.

FML Film Maker's Library, 133 East 58th St., Suite 703a, New York, NY 10022, USA

1 BY DAYLIGHT AND IN DREAMS: JOHN HALL WHEELOCK. Read by author. Film Maker's (16mm film)

FOLKW Folkways Records, 43 West 61st St., New York, NY 10023, USA

1 ANTHOLOGY OF NEGRO POETS. Readers: Langston Hughes and others. Folkways 9791 (pd)

2 LES PÂQUES À NEW YORK: BLAISE CENDRARS. Reader: J.-H. Lévesque. In French. Folkways 9595 (pd)

3 THE INFERNO: DANTE. Reader: John Ciardi. In English. Folkways 9871 (pd)

4 SONG OF HIAWATHA: LONGFELLOW. Reader: Harry Fleetwood. Folkways 9730 (pd)

5   THE DREAM KEEPER: LANGSTON HUGHES. Read by the author. Folkways 7104 (pd)

6   AN ANTHOLOGY OF NEGRO POETRY FOR YOUNG PEOPLE. Reader: Arna Bontemps. Folkways 7114 (pd)

8   POETRY IN THE ROUND: A POETRY WORKSHOP. GEORGE ABBE READS HIS POEMS. Folkways 9164 (pd)

9   EVANGELINE: LONGFELLOW. Reader: Harry Fleetwood. Folkways 9502 (pd)

10 MEDIEVAL ROMANCE POETRY. Reader: Mario Pei. In original and English. Folkways 9578 (2 pd)

11 POEMS OF FEDERICO GARCIA LORCA. Reader: Jorge Juan Rodriguez. In Spanish. Folkways 9580 (pd)

12 LA CHANSON DE ROLAND. Readers: Montreal "Proscenium Studio" directed by Lucie de Vienne. In 12th century French. Folkways 9587 (2 pd)

13 POÉMONTAGES: PETITE ANTHOLOGIE DE LA POÉSIE FRANÇAISE MODERNE. Reader: Jacques-Henry Lévesque. In French. Folkways 9595 (2 pd)

14 AARON KRAMER READS HIS SERENADE AND OTHER WORKS BY NEW YORK POETS. Folkways 9703 (pd)

15 THE POEMS OF NORMAN ROSTEN. Read by the author. Folkways 9704 (pd)

16 BOSS SOUL: SARAH WEBSTER FABIO. Read by the author. With drum talk and rhythms. Folkways 9710 (pd)

17 SOUL AIN'T: SOUL IS: SARAH WEBSTER FABIO. Read by the author. Folkways 9711 (pd)

18 JUJUS: ALCHEMY OF THE BLUES: SARAH WEBSTER FABIO. Read by the author. With music. Folkways 9714 (pd)

19 SELECTED POEMS OF KENNETH PATCHEN. Read by the author. Folkways 9717 (pd)

20 KENNETH PATCHEN READS WITH JAZZ IN CANADA. With the Alan Neil Quartet. Folkways 9718 (pd)

21 OF POETRY AND POWER: POEMS OCCASIONED BY THE PRESIDENCY AND BY THE DEATH OF JOHN F. KENNEDY. Readers: Irene Dailey and Martin Donegan. Folkways 9721 (2 pd)

22 ROBERT FRANCIS READS HIS POEMS. Folkways 9729 (pd)

24 DERRY DOWN DERRY: ROBERT FROST. Reader: Lesley Frost. Folkways 9733 (pd)

25 ANTHOLOGY OF CONTEMPORARY AMERICAN POETRY. Reader: George Abbe. Folkways 9735 (pd)

26 WORDS FOR THE WIND: SELECTIONS FROM THE POETRY OF THEODORE ROETHKE. Read by the author. Folkways 9736 (pd)

27 PADRAIC COLUM READING FROM HIS IRISH TALES AND POEMS. Folkways 9737 (pd)

28 CHARLES OLSON READS FROM MAXIMUS POEMS IV, V, VI. Folkways 9738 (pd)

29 STEPHEN CRANE: SELECTIONS FROM PROSE AND POETRY. Reader: Jared Reed. Folkways 9745 (pd)

31 JEAN SHEPHERD READS POEMS OF ROBERT SERVICE. Folkways 9754 (pd)

32 RALPH WALDO EMERSON: FROM THE ESSAYS, POETRY, AND JOURNALS. Reader: David Cort. Folkways 9758 (pd)

33 ROBINSON JEFFERS: ROAN STALLION. Reader: Marian Seldes. Folkways 9766 (pd)

34 TOWER BEYOND TRAGEDY: ROBINSON JEFFERS. Reader: Marian Seldes. Folkways 9767 (pd)

35 REPORT TO THE STOCKHOLDERS AND OTHER POEMS: JOHN BEECHER. Read by the author. Folkways 9779 (pd)

36 AS IF: SELECTED POEMS OF JOHN CIARDI. Read by the author. Folkways 9780 (pd)

37 COLLECTED AND NEW POEMS: MARK VAN DOREN. Read by the author. Folkways 9782 (pd)

38 SWEET THUNDER: BLACK POETRY BY NANCY LORRAINE DUPREE. Read by the author. Folkways 9787 (pd)

39 GOD'S TROMBONES: JAMES WELDON JOHNSON. Reader: Boyce Bond. With music. Folkways 9788 (pd)

40 POEMS: STERLING ALLEN BROWN AND LANGSTON HUGHES. Read by the authors. Folkways 9790 (pd)

41 ANTHOLOGY OF NEGRO POETS IN THE USA— 200 YEARS. Reader: Arna Bontemps. Folkways 9792 (pd)

42 SONIA SANCHEZ: A SUN LADY FOR ALL SEASONS READS HER POETRY. Folkways 9793 (pd)

43 16 POEMS OF STERLING A. BROWN. Read by the author. Folkways 9794 (pd)

44 THE POETRY OF MARGARET WALKER. Read by the author. Folkways 9795 (pd)

45 MARGARET WALKER ALEXANDER READS POEMS OF PAUL LAURANCE DUNBAR, JAMES WELDON JOHNSON, AND LANGSTON HUGHES. Folkways 9796 (pd)

46 MARGARET WALKER READS POEMS BY LANGSTON HUGHES AND MARGARET WALKER. Folkways 9797 (pd)

47 FEELINGS OF LOVE NOT YET EXPRESSED: AN ALBUM OF POETRY BY THE NEW BLACK WOMEN IN POETRY. Readers: Amirh Bahati and others. Folkways 9799 (pd)

48 A READING OF PRIMITIVE AND ARCHAIC POETRY. Readers: Jerome Rothenberg and others. Folkways 9801 (pd)

49 SIX MONTREAL POETS READ THEIR OWN WORKS (Leonard Cohen, Louis Dudek, A. M. Klein, Irving Layton, F. R. Scott, A. J. M. Smith). Folkways 9805 (pd)

50 SIX TORONTO POETS READ THEIR OWN WORKS (Margaret Avison, Jay Macpherson, James Reaney, W. W. Eustage Rosa, Raymond Souster, Anne Wilkinson). Folkways 9806 (pd)

51 THE POEMS OF RUPERT BROOKE. Reader: Richard Waring. Folkways 9818 (pd)

52 IRISH TRADITION: O'CONNOR, YEATS, SYNGE, AND OTHERS. Reader: Frank O'Connor. Folkways 9825 (pd)

52A THE WESTERN HUDSON SHORE, TO THE GREAT FRIENDS IN LIFETIME: JOHN MASEFIELD. Read by the author. Folkways 9843 (pd)

53 EARLY ENGLISH POETRY. Reader: Charles W. Dunn. In Old and Middle English. Folkways 9851 (pd)

FOLKW (continued)

54 LYRICS FROM THE OLD ENGLISH. Readers: Burton Raffel and Robert P. Creed. In Old and modern English. Folkways 9858 (pd)

55 SAN JUAN DE LA CRUZ: POESÍAS. POEMS OF ST. JOHN OF THE CROSS. Reader: Khigh Dhiegh. In English. Folkways 9865 (pd)

56 POEMS BY HEINRICH HEINE. Reader: Claire Luce. In English. Folkways 9867 (pd)

57 YEVTUSHENKO: ZIMA JUNCTION. Read by Milt Commons and Jere Jacob. In English. Folkways 9868 (pd)

58 THE POETRY OF YEVTUSHENKO. Readers: Milt Commons and Jere Jacob. In English. Folkways 9869 (pd)

59 POEMS AND LETTERS OF ROBERT BURNS. Reader: Maxwell John Dunbar. Folkways 9877 (pd)

59A ANTHOLOGY OF 20TH CENTURY ENGLISH POETRY III. Readers: Kingsley Amis and others. Folkways 9879 (pd)

60 CONVERSATION PIECES: KEATS, PLOMER, HOUSEMAN AND OTHERS. Readers: Jill Balcon and others. Folkways 9880 (pd)

61 EARLY ENGLISH BALLADS. Reader: Kathleen Danson Read. Folkways 9881 (pd)

62 ENGLISH LYRIC POEMS AND BALLADS. Reader: Kathleen Danson Read. Folkways 9882 (pd)

63 ENGLISH ROMANTIC POETRY. Reader: John S. Martin. Folkways 9883 (pd)

64 ANTHOLOGY OF 20TH CENTURY ENGLISH POETRY I. Readers: C. Day Lewis and others. Folkways 9886 (pd)

65 ANTHOLOGY OF 20TH CENTURY ENGLISH POETRY II. Readers: John Betjeman and others. Folkways 9887 (pd)

65A CONTEMPORARY ENGLISH LITERATURE, 1. Readers: Robert Graves and others. Folkways 9888 (pd)

66 CONTEMPORARY ENGLISH LITERATURE, 2: POETRY AND PROSE READ BY THE AUTHORS — LAURIE LEE, CHRISTOPHER LOGUE, C. NORTHCOTE PARKINSON. Folkways 9889 (pd)

67 ANTHOLOGY OF ENGLISH VERSE, 1. Readers: V. C. Clinton-Baddeley and others. Folkways 9891 (pd)

68 ANTHOLOGY OF ENGLISH VERSE, 2. Readers: C. Day Lewis and others. Folkways 9892 (pd)

69 CHRISTIAN POETRY AND PROSE. Reader: Alec Guiness. Folkways 9893 (pd)

70 VOIX DE 8 POÈTES DU CANADA (Hébert and others). In French. Folkways 9905 (pd)

71 MODERN BRAZILIAN POETRY. Reader: Cassiano Nunes. In Portuguese. Folkways 9914 (pd)

72 MODERN PORTUGUESE POETRY. Reader: Jose Rodrigues Miguéis. In Portuguese. Folkways 9915 (pd)

73 POETRY OF FRIEDRICH VON SCHILLER. Reader: Klaus Kinski. Folkways 9916 (pd)

74 THE GERMAN BALLAD: BÜRGER, GOETHE, SCHILLER. Readers: Eric W. Bauer and Brigitt Schaidnagl. In German. Folkways 9918 (pd)

75 READINGS FROM THE RAMAYANA. Reader: S. R. Ranganathan. In Sanskrit. Folkways 9920 (pd)

76 CHINESE POEMS OF THE TANG AND SUNG DYNASTIES. Reader: Lo Kung-Yuan. In Northern Chinese. Folkways 9921 (pd)

77 THE PERSIAN EPIC: SHAH NAMEH — THE BOOK OF KINGS BY ABOL MANSUR FERDOVCI. Reader: Shah-Keh Agajanian. In Persian. Folkways 9923 (pd)

78 POÉSIE DE LA NEGRITUDE: LEON DAMAS READS SELECTED POEMS. In French. Folkways 9924 (pd)

79 RECITAL POETICO: NINE SPANISH POETS (Chocano, Darío, Ibarbourou, Jiménez, Garcia Lorca, Mistral, Nervo, Storni, Valencia). Reader: Catalina Levinton. In Spanish. Folkways 9925 (pd)

80 LATIN-AMERICAN POETS. ANTOLOGIA ORAL; POESIA HISPANOAMERICANA DEL SIGLO XX. Reader: Octavio Corvalan. In Spanish. Folkways 9926 (pd)

81 EL GAUCHO MARTIN FIERRO: JOSÉ HERNANDEZ. Reader: Roberto Garcia Pinto. In Spanish. Folkways 9927 (pd)

82 SAN JUAN DE LA CRUZ: POESÍAS. Reader: José Crespo. In Spanish. Folkways 9932 (pd)

83 FRENCH AFRICAN POEMS. Reader: Paul Mankin. In French. Folkways 9933 (pd)

84 SIX CENTURIES OF RECITED FRENCH: RUTEBOEUF TO VOLTAIRE. Readers: Lucie de Vienne and Henri Barras. Folkways 9934 (pd)

85 THE BIBLE IN FRENCH: EXCERPTS FROM PSALMS, PROVERBS, ECCLESIASTES. Reader: Armand Begué. Folkways 9935 (pd)

86 19TH CENTURY FRENCH POETRY. Reader: Paul Mankin. In French. Folkways 9936 (pd)

87 BLAISE CENDRARS: PROSE DU TRANSSIBERIEN ET DE LA PETITE JEANNE DE FRANCE. Reader: Jacques-Henry Lévesque. In French. Folkways 9940 (pd)

88 20TH CENTURY FRENCH POETRY. Reader: Paul Mankin. Folkways 9943 (pd)

89 L'HONNEUR DES POÈTES: FOUR FRENCH RESISTANCE WRITERS — ARAGON, CAMUS, ÉLUARD, MAURIAC. In French. Folkways 9944 (pd)

90 JEWISH CLASSICAL LITERATURE. Reader: Chaim Ostrowsky. In Yiddish. Folkways 9945 (pd)

91 THE POETRY OF ABRAHAM SUTZKEVER, THE VILNO POET. Read by the author. In Yiddish. Folkways 9947 (pd)

92 MARC CHAGALL — A POEM BY AARON KURTZ. Read by author. In Yiddish. Folkways 9949 (pd)

93 READINGS FROM THE WORKS OF TARAS SHEVCHENKO. Readers: Natalia Uzhvy and others. In Ukrainian. Folkways 9952 (pd)

94 RUSSIAN POETRY AND PROSE. Reader: Vladimir Markov. In Russian. Folkways 9961 (pd)

95 MODERN SOVIET POETRY AND HUMOR. Reader: Alexander Demidov. In Russian. Folkways 9962 (pd)

96 VIRGIL AND HORACE. Reader: Mario Pei. In Church Latin. Folkways 9964 (pd)

97 ITALIAN CLASSICS READ IN ITALIAN: DANTE, MANZONI AND OTHERS. Reader: Mario Palladini. Folkways 9965 (pd)

98 ROMAN LOVE POETRY. Reader: J. F. C. Rich-

ards. In Latin. Folkways 9967 (pd)

99 18 ODES OF QUINTUS HORATIUS FLACCUS. Reader: John F. C. Richards. In Latin. Folkways 9968 (pd)

100 VIRGIL: THE AENEID, BOOKS I, II, IV, VI. Reader: J. F. C. Richards. In Latin. Folkways 9969 (pd)

101 OVID: SELECTIONS FROM METAMORPHOSES AND THE ART OF LOVE. Reader: J. F. C. Richards. In Latin. Folkways 9970 (pd)

102 VIRGIL: THE AENEID, SELECTIONS FROM BOOKS I, II, IV, VI, IX, XII. Reader: Moses Hadas. In English. Folkways 9973 (pd)

103 DANTE: LA DIVINA COMMEDIA — INFERNO. Reader: Enrico de Negri. In Italian. Folkways 9977 (pd)

104 ANCIENT GREEK POETRY. Reader: J. F. C. Richards. In Greek. Folkways 9984 (pd)

105 HOMER: THE ILIAD AND THE ODYSSEY, SELECTIONS. Reader: J. F. C. Richards. In Greek. Folkways 9985 (pd)

106 BENTLEY ON BRECHT: SONGS AND POEMS. Reader: Eric Bentley. In English. With music. Folkways 5434 (pd)

107 KENNETH PATCHEN READS HIS LOVE POEMS. Folkways 9719 (pd)

108 LEGACIES: THE POETRY OF NIKKI GIOVANNI. Read by the author. Folkways 9798 (pd)

109 COTTON CANDY ON A RAINY DAY: NIKKI GIOVANNI. Read by the author. Folkways 9756 (pd)

110 STORIES AND POEMS OF NEW GUINEA. Reader: Bernard Barshay. In English. Folkways 9786 (pd)

111 ZEN POEMS. Read by the translator, Lucien Stryk. In English. Folkways 9855 (pd)

112 LOOSE JOINTS: PEDRO PIETRI. Read by the author. Folkways 9722 (pd)

FREED Edward Freed, 3651 Lavell Dr., Los Angeles, CA 90065, USA

1 READIN'S FROM RILEY. Reader: Edward Freed. Freed WR 4766

GAZ Sonet Grammofon AB, Box 1205, Atlasvaegen 1, S-18123 Lindingoe, Sweden

1 NILS FERLIN LÄSER EGNA DIKTER, 1. In Swedish. GMG-1220

2 NILS FERLIN LÄSER EGNA DIKTER, 2. In Swedish. GMG-1234

GIORNO Giorno Poetry Systems Records, 222 Bowery, New York, NY 10012, USA

1 JOHN GIORNO AND ANNE WALDMAN. Read by the authors. Giorno GPS-010-011 (2 pd)

GMS Goldsmith Audio Visuals Music Shop, Inc., c/o Applause Recordings, Vincent R. Tortora, 85 Longview Rd., Port Washington, NY 11050, USA

1 PAUL GÉRALDY: TOI ET MOI. Read by author. GMS FLD 6

2 PAUL VALÉRY: LE CIMETIÈRE MARIN. Readers: Servais and others. GMS FLD 81

3 ARTHUR RIMBAUD: LE BATEAU IVRE. Reader: Jean Deschamps. GMS LAE 3321

4 AMOURS: LOUIS ARAGON. Read by author. GMS LDY 6002

5 PAUL ELUARD: LA VOIX DE PAUL ELUARD. Read by author. GMS LDX 6033

6 A TREASURY OF FRENCH POETRY. Reader: Ruth Mandel. In French. GMS-D-7000

7 FRENCH POETRY. Reader: Jeanne Varney Pleasants. In French. GMS-D-7013

8 LES PLUS BEAUX POÈMES DE LA LANGUE FRANÇAISE, 1. Readers: Gérard Philipe and others. GMS-D-7065

9 LES PLUS BEAUX POÈMES DE LA LANGUE FRANÇAISE, 2. Readers: Gérard Philipe and others. GMS-D-7066

10 JEAN COCTEAU VOUS PARLE. In French. GMS-D-7084

11 EICHENDORFF: POEMS. Reader: Peter Lühr. In German. GMS-DISC-7l24

12 JACQUES PRÉVERT LIT SES POÈMES. GMS-D-7126

13 EXPOSICION DE POESIA LATINO-AMERICANA: VICENTE HUIDOBRO AND OTHERS. GMS 7174

14 POESÍA DE RAFAEL DE LEON. Reader: José Luis. GMS SEDL 19.080 (pd 45rpm)

15 ROMANCES: LITERATURA ESPAÑOLA. In Spanish. GMS P 33.155

16 SIGLO XVI Y XVII: LIRICOS GARCILASO DE LA VEGA AND OTHERS. In Spanish. GMS P 33.156

17 SAGARRA RECITA SAGARRA. GMS 95.0.007 (pd 45rpm)

18 POESÍA : RAFAEL DE LEON. Reader: Nati Mistral. GMS 95.0.012

GOLDOW Golden Owl Publishing Co., Box 462, Yorktown Heights, NY 10598, USA

1 CASEY AT THE BAT: THAYER. Golden Owl 42

GRAM Grammofon AB Electra, PO Box 1178, 17123 Solna 1, Sweden

1 LÄNGTAN HETER VAR ARVEDEL. Reader: Signe Hasso. Grammofon TRS 11073

2 SWEDISH POETRY. Reader: Maria Schildknecht-Wahlgren. In Swedish. Grammofon TRS 11078

3 LEVANDA SVENSK LYRIK: NORDENFLYCHT AND OTHERS. Readers: Barbro Hiort af Ornäs and others. Grammofon TR 11096

4 SVENSKA DIKTARRÖSTER: BERGMAN AND OTHERS. Read by the authors. Grammofon LT 33111

5 SVENSKA DIKTARRÖSTER: LAGERKVIST AND OTHERS. Read by the authors. Grammofon LT 33112

6 SVENSKA DIKTARRÖSTER: BLOMBERG AND OTHERS. Read by the authors. Grammofon LT 33113

7 SVENSKA DIKTARRÖSTER: LO-JOHANSSON AND OTHERS. Read by the authors. Grammofon LT 33114

8 SVENSKA DIKTARRÖSTER: LUNDKVIST AND OTHERS. Read by the authors. Grammofon LT 33116

9 SVENSKA DIKTARRÖSTER: HEDBERG AND OTHERS. Read by the authors. Grammofon LT 33119

10 SVENSKA DIKTARRÖSTER: KARLFELDT AND OTHERS. Read by the authors. Grammofon LT 33120

GRYPH Gryphon Records, Collectors' Guild, 507 Fifth Av., New York, NY 10017, USA

1 POETRY OF JOHN W. CLARK. Read by author. Gryphon GR 901

GRYPH (continued)

2 ALLAN DOWLING: POEMS. Read by author. Gryphon GR 905

3 BREATHING OF FIRST THINGS: HY SOBILOFF. Read by author. Gryphon GR 907

HACH Hachette, 79 Blvd. St. Germain, 75006 Paris, France

1 LE GRAND TESTAMENT: FRANÇOIS VILLON. Readers: Jean Deschamps and others. Hachette 190 E 859

2 POÈMES II: HUGO. Readers: Jean Davy and others. Hachette 190 E 868

3 CHANSON DE ROLAND (RONCEVAUX). In French. Hachette 270 E 047

4 BESTIAIRE POÉTIQUE. Hachette 270 E 815

5 LA BATAILLE DE QADECH. Reader: Jean Deschamps. Hachette 270 E 832

6 VISAGES DE MUSSET. Reader: Pierre Vaneck. Hachette 320 E 058

7 LE MOYEN AGE. Hachette 320 E 810

8 LA RENAISSANCE: BELLAY AND OTHERS. In French. Hachette 320 E 811

9 DIX-SEPTIÈME SIÈCLE. Hachette 320 E 812

10 DIX HUITIEME SIÈCLE ET PRÉROMANTIQUES. Hachette 320 E 813

11 GRANDS ROMANTIQUES. Hachette 320 E 814

12 ROMANTIQUES ET PARNASSE. Hachette 320 E 815

13 LES SYMBOLISTES. Hachette 320 E 816

14 POÈTES D'HIER. Hachette 320 E 817

15 VISAGES DE LAMARTINE. Reader: Raymond Rouleau. Hachette 320 E 846

16 CHARLES PÉGUY AND OTHERS. Readers: Jean Deschamps and others. In French. Hachette 320 E 868

17 PAUL ÉLUARD. Readers: Jean Topart and others. Hachette 320 E 870

18 PAUL VALÉRY. Readers: Marguerite Perrin and others. Hachette 320 E 884

19 POÈMES DE GUILLAUME APOLLINAIRE. Readers: Jean-Paul Moulinot and others. Hachette 320 E 889

20 VISAGES DE BAUDELAIRE. Reader: Pierre Blanchar. Hachette 320 E 891

21 ODES ET BALLADES: HUGO. Reader: Jean Deschamps. Hachette 320 E 892

22 PERSE: ELOGES. Readers: Jean-Louis Jemma and others. Hachette 320 E 897

23 VIGNY: POÈMES ANTIQUES ET MODERNES. Readers: Michel Bouquet and others. Hachette 320 E 908

24 BATEAU IVRE: RIMBAUD AND OTHERS. Reader: Jean Deschamps. Hachette LAE 3321

HARB Harcourt Brace / HARBRACE, H B J Bookstore, 1255 5th Ave., San Diego, CA 92101, USA School orders to: School Department, Harcourt Brace Jovanovich, Saddle Brook Industrial Park, Saddle Brook, NJ 07662, USA

1 LANGUAGE FOR DAILY USE: POETRY, 1. Harbrace PR 1

2 LANGUAGE FOR DAILY USE: POETRY, 2. Harbrace PR 2

3 LANGUAGE FOR DAILY USE: POETRY, 3. Harbrace PR 3

4 LANGUAGE FOR DAILY USE: POETRY, 4. Harbrace PR 4

5 LANGUAGE FOR DAILY USE: POETRY, 5. Harbrace PR 5

6 LANGUAGE FOR DAILY USE: POETRY, 6. Harbrace PR 6

HARC Harcourt Brace, H B J Bookstore, 1255 5th Ave., San Diego, CA 92101, USA School orders to: School Department, Harcourt Brace Jovanovich, Saddle Brook Industrial Park, Saddle Brook, NJ 07662, USA

1 ADVENTURES IN AMERICAN LITERATURE, 1. Harcourt 1

2 ADVENTURES IN AMERICAN LITERATURE, 2. Harcourt 2

3 ADVENTURES IN AMERICAN LITERATURE, 3. Harcourt 3

4 MANY VOICES: ADVENTURE IN APPRECIATION. Readers: Nash, Cummings, and others. Harcourt 4 A/B

HARPV Harvard University Press, Poet's Voice, 79 Garden St., Cambridge, MA 02138, USA

1 EZRA POUND AND T. S. ELIOT. Read by the authors. Harvard Poets Voice 1 (ac)

2 MARIANNE MOORE AND W. C. WILLIAMS. Read by the authors. Harvard Poets Voice 2 (ac)

3 WALLACE STEVENS AND ROBERT FROST. Read by the authors. Harvard Poets Voice 3 (ac)

4 W. H. AUDEN, ROBINSON JEFFERS, AND THEODORE ROETHKE. Read by the authors. Harvard Poets Voice 4 (ac)

5 RANDALL JARRELL AND JOHN BERRYMAN. Read by the authors. Harvard Poets Voice 5 (ac)

6 ROBERT LOWELL AND SYLVIA PLATH. Read by the authors. Harvard Poets Voice 6 (ac)

HARVOC Harvard Vocarium Records, Harvard University, Cambridge, MA 02138, USA

1 THE PARDONER'S TALE: CHAUCER. Reader: Fred Norris Robinson. Vocarium L 990 (pd 78rpm)

2 GERONTION: ELIOT. Read by author. Vocarium P 991 (pd 78rpm)

3 POEMS: GERARD MANLEY HOPKINS. Reader: Robert Speaight. Vocarium L 1000/1001 (pd 78rpm)

4 DIVINE POEMS: DONNE. Reader: Robert Speaight. Vocarium L 1004/5 (pd 78rpm)

5 POEMS: BLAKE. Reader: Robert Speaight. Vocarium L 1008/9 (pd 78rpm)

6 GEORGE HERBERT AND HENRY KING. Reader: Robert Speaight. Vocarium P 1010/1

7 POEMS: YEATS. Reader: Robert Speaight. Vocarium L 1012/13

8 POEMS: ROBERT SILLIMAN HILLYER. Read by author. Vocarium P 1022/27 (3 pd 78rpm)

9 POEMS: THEODORE SPENCER. Read by author. Vocarium P-1032/33 (pd 78rpm)

10 ROBINSON JEFFERS READING HIS OWN POEMS. Vocarium P 1050/1 (pd 78rpm)

11 THE TRAVELLER, SONNETS: AUDEN. Read by author. Vocarium P-1052 (pd 78rpm)

12 ROBERT PENN WARREN READING FROM HIS SELECTED POEMS. Vocarium P-1088/89 (pd 78 rpm)

13 POEMS: HORACE GREGORY. Read by author. Vocarium P-1102/05 (2 pd 78rpm)

14 JOHN MALCOLM BRINNIN READS POEMS. Vocarium P-1110/1 (pd 78rpm)

15 PRUFROCK: T. S. ELIOT. Read by author. Vocarium P-1200/1 (pd 78rpm)

16 MAGI: T. S. ELIOT. Read by author. Vocarium P-1202/3 (pd 78rpm)

17 TRIUMPHAL MARCH: T. S. ELIOT. Read by author. Vocarium P-1204/5 (pd 78rpm)

17A T. S. ELIOT. Read by author. Vocarium L-6002/3 (pd 78rpm)

18 WILLIAM ALFRED READING HIS OWN POEMS. Vocarium SP 45083 (pd 78rpm)

HBCF Halas & Batchelor, 317 Kean St., Aldwich, London WC2, England

1 PAINTER AND POET. Readers: Michael Redgrave and others. Halas & Batchelor (16mm film)

HELV Helvern Press, 835 Medea Way, Denver, CO 80209, USA

1 BRIGHT HORIZONS: HELEN L. MARSHALL. Read by author. Helvern (ac)

2 CLOSE TO THE HEART: HELEN L. MARSHALL. Read by author. Helvern (ac)

3 DARE TO BE HAPPY: HELEN L. MARSHALL. Read by author. Helvern (ac)

4 AIM FOR A STAR: HELEN L. MARSHALL. Read by author. Helvern (ac)

5 HOLD TO YOUR DREAM: HELEN L. MARSHALL. Read by author. Helvern (ac)

6 GIFT OF WONDER: HELEN L. MARSHALL. Read by author. Helvern (ac)

7 WALK THE WORLD PROUDLY: HELEN L. MARSHALL. Read by author. Helvern (ac)

8 QUIET POWER: HELEN L. MARSHALL. Read by author. Helvern (ac)

9 LEAVE A TOUCH OF GLORY: HELEN L. MARSHALL. Read by author. Helvern (ac)

HOLT Holt, Rinehart and Winston, 383 Madison Av., New York, NY 10017, USA

1 POESÍA HISPANICA, UNOS MOMENTOS LIRICOS. Readers: Maria Brenes and others. Holt 31803-1385

HOUGHT Houghton-Mifflin, 2 Park St., Boston, MA 02107, USA

1 DISCOVERING LITERATURE. Reader: Claire Bloom. Houghton 2-26218

2 EXPLORING LITERATURE. Readers: Claire Bloom and others. Houghton 2-26248

3 VALUES IN LITERATURE. Readers: Robert Frost and others. Houghton 2-26409

4 INSIGHTS INTO LITERATURE. Readers: Julie Harris and others. Houghton 2-26429

5 AMERICAN LITERATURE. Readers: E. E. Cummings and others. Houghton 2-26449

IDIOM Idiom Records. Current address unknown.

1 AUSTIN WARREN READING EMILY DICKINSON AND OTHERS. Idiom EI-LQL-12958

IFB International Film Bureau, 332 South Michigan Av., Chicago, IL 60604, USA

1 BROOMS OF MEXICO: ALVIN GORDON. Read by author. Intern. Film (16mm film)

IMP Imperial Educational Resources Inc., 19 Marble Av., Pleasantville, NY 10570, USA

1 ENGLISH POETRY. Imperial Ed. Res. W3KL 71000 (8 ac)

2 TENNYSON'S IDYLLS OF THE KING. Imperial Educ Res. W3RG 90300 (4 ac with fs)

INSTPR Instituto de Cultura Puertorriqueña, Apdo 4184, San Juan, PR

1 POESIA PUERTORRIQUEÑA. Reader: Maricusa Ornes. Inst. de Cultura Puertorriqueña

2 LA VOZ POETICA DE JOSÉ DE DIEGO. Inst. de Cultura Puertorriqueña

JNP Jeffrey Norton Publishers Inc., 145 East 49 St., New York, NY 10017, USA

1 MARIANNE MOORE READS HER POETRY. JNP 23044 (ac)

2 U. S. SENATOR EUGENE J. MCCARTHY READS HIS POETRY. JNP 23046 (ac)

3 POET'S SATURDAY NIGHT: MALCOLM COWLEY. Read by author. JNP 23048 (ac)

4 ROBERT FROST READS HIS POEMS. JNP 23066 (ac)

5 BYRON'S RHETORIC: SELECTED READINGS. Reader: G. Wilson Knight. JNP 23068

6 PROSE AND POETRY: STEPHEN SPENDER. Read by author. JNP 23083 (ac)

7 EDITH SITWELL READS HER POETRY. JNP 23084 (ac)

8 SOUND AND SENSE IN POETRY. Reader: G. B. Harrison. JNP 23153 (ac)

9 THE POETRY OF DANNIE ABSE. Read by author. JNP 23156 (ac)

10 THE POETRY OF JOHN ASHBERY. Read by author. JNP 23157 (ac)

11 THE POETRY OF W. H. AUDEN, 1. Read by author. JNP 23158 (ac)

12 THE POETRY OF ROBERT BRAGG. Read by author. JNP 23160 (ac)

13 MODERN GREEK POETRY. Reader: Kimon Friar. JNP 23163 (ac)

14 THE POETRY OF ISABELLA GARDNER, 1964. Read by author. JNP 23164 (ac)

15 THE POETRY OF ISABELLA GARDNER, 1967. Read by author. JNP 23165 (ac)

16 THE POETRY OF JEAN GARRIGUE. Read by author. JNP 23166 (ac)

17 THE POETRY OF RICHARD GELLER. Read by author. JNP 23167 (ac)

18 THE POETRY OF MICHAEL GOLDMAN. Read by author. JNP 23168 (ac)

19 THE POETRY OF DONALD HALL. Read by author. JNP 23169 (ac)

20 THE POETRY OF MICHAEL HAMBURGER. Read by author. JNP 23170 (ac)

21 THE POETRY OF SAMUEL HAZO. Read by author. JNP 23171 (ac)

22 THE POETRY OF DARYL HINE. Read by author. JNP 23172 (ac)

23 THE POETRY OF RICHARD HOWARD. Read by author. JNP 23273 (ac)

24 THE POETRY OF JOHN HOLLANDER. Read by author. JNP 23174 (ac)

25 THE POETRY OF BARBARA HOWES. Read by author. JNP 23175 (ac)

26 THE POETRY OF ROBERT HUFF. Read by author. JNP 23176 (ac)

27 THE POETRY OF DAN JACOBSON. Read by author. JNP 23177 (ac)

28 THE POETRY OF RANDALL JARRELL. Read by author. JNP 23178 (ac)

29 THE POETRY OF GALWAY KINNELL. Read by author. JNP 23179 (ac)

JNP (continued)

30 THE POETRY OF DENISE LEVERTOV. Read by author. JNP 23183 (ac)

31 THE POETRY OF C. DAY LEWIS. Read by author. JNP 23184 (ac)

32 THE POETRY OF LAURENCE LIEBERMAN. Read by author. JNP 23185 (ac)

33 THE POETRY OF ROBERT LOWELL. Read by author. JNP 23187 (ac)

34 THE POETRY OF GEORGE MACBETH. Read by author. JNP 23188 (ac)

35 THE POETRY OF HUGH MACDIARMID. Read by author. JNP 23189 (ac)

36 THE POETRY OF HUGH MACDIARMID IN SCOTS. Read by author. JNP 23190 (ac)

37 THE POETRY OF JACK MARSHALL. Read by author. JNP 23191 (ac)

38 THE POETRY OF HOWARD MOSS. Read by author. JNP 23192 (ac)

39 THE POETRY OF STANLEY MOSS. Read by author. JNP 23193 (ac)

40 THE POETRY OF HOWARD NEMEROV, 1. Read by author. JNP 23194 (ac)

41 THE POETRY OF HOWARD NEMEROV, 2. Read by author. JNP 23195 (ac)

42 THE POETRY OF GEORGE OPPEN. Read by author. JNP 23196 (ac)

43 THE POETRY OF SHREELA RAY. Read by author. JNP 23201 (ac)

44 THE POETRY OF F. D. REEVE. Read by author. JNP 23202 (ac)

45 THE POETRY OF ADRIANNE RICH. Read by author. JNP 23203 (ac)

46 THE POETRY OF PAUL ROCHE. Read by author. JNP 23204 (ac)

47 THE POETRY OF THEODORE ROETHKE. Read by author. JNP 23205 (ac)

48 POETRY OF RAPHAEL RUDNICK. Read by author. JNP 23206 (ac)

49 THE POETRY OF MURIEL RUKEYSER, 1. Read by author. JNP 23207 (ac)

50 THE POETRY OF MURIEL RUKEYSER, 2. Read by author. JNP 23208 (ac)

51 THE POETRY OF DENNIS SCHMITZ. Read by author. JNP 23210 (ac)

52 THE POETRY OF WINFIELD TOWNLEY SCOTT. Read by author. JNP 23211 (ac)

53 THE POETRY OF ANNE SEXTON. Read by author. JNP 23212 (ac)

54 THE POETRY OF WILLIAM JAY SMITH. Read by author. JNP 23214 (ac)

55 THE POETRY OF STEPHEN SPENDER. Read by author. JNP 23215 (ac)

56 THE POETRY OF ALLEN TATE, 1. Read by author. JNP 23219 (ac)

57 THE POETRY OF ALLEN TATE, 2. Read by author. JNP 23220 (ac)

58 THE POETRY OF JAMES TATE. Read by author. JNP 23221 (ac)

59 THE POETRY OF TONY TOWLE. Read by author. JNP 23223 (ac)

60 THE POETRY OF LOUIS UNTERMEYER. Read by author. JNP 23224 (ac)

61 THE PROSE AND POETRY OF JOHN UPDIKE. Read by author. JNP 23225 (ac)

62 JOHN WAIN READS CONTEMPORARY ENGLISH POETRY. JNP 23228 (ac)

63 THE POETRY OF JOHN WAIN. Read by author. JNP 23229 (ac)

64 THE POETRY OF RICHARD WEBER. Read by author. JNP 23230 (ac)

65 THE POETRY OF JOHN HALL WHEELOCK. Read by author. JNP 23235 (ac)

66 THE POETRY OF JOHN WIENERS. Read by author. JNP 23236 (ac)

67 THE POETRY OF MILLER WILLIAMS. Read by author. JNP 23237 (ac)

68 THE POETRY OF MAY SWENSON. Read by author. JNP 23239 (ac)

69 THE POETRY OF BEN BELITT. Read by author. JNP 23240 (ac)

70 THE POETRY OF WENDELL BERRY. Read by author. JNP 23241 (ac)

71 THE POETRY OF ROBERT BLY. Read by author. JNP 23242 (ac)

72 THE POETRY OF PHILIP BOOTH. Read by author. JNP 23243 (ac)

73 THE POETRY OF JOHN MALCOLM BRINNIN. Read by author. JNP 23244 (ac)

74 THE POETRY OF MICHAEL DENNIS BROWNE. Read by author. JNP 23245 (ac)

75 THE POETRY OF MELVILLE CANE. Read by author. JNP 23248 (ac)

76 THE POETRY OF JOHN CHEEVER. Read by author. JNP 23249 (ac)

77 THE POETRY OF JOHN CIARDI. Read by author. JNP 23250 (ac)

78 THE POETRY OF ROBERT CREELEY. Read by author. JNP 23251 (ac)

79 THE POETRY OF EDWARD DAHLBERG. Read by author. JNP 23252 (ac)

80 THE POETRY OF WILLIAM DICKEY. Read by author. JNP 23256 (ac)

81 POETRY AND PROSE OF LOREN EISLEY. Read by author. JNP 23257 (ac)

82 THE POETRY OF GEORGE P. ELLIOTT. Read by author. JNP 23258 (ac)

83 THE POETRY OF JAMES T. FARRELL. Read by author. JNP 23259 (ac)

84 THE POETRY OF IRVING FELDMAN. Read by author. JNP 23260 (ac)

85 THE POETRY OF DONALD FINKEL. Read by author. JNP 23261 (ac)

86 THE POETRY OF KATHLEEN FRASER. Read by author. JNP 23262 (ac)

87 BROWNING AS A PAINTER: MY LAST DUCHESS. Reader: Gilbert Highet. JNP 23292 B (ac)

88 PROPAGANDA AND POETRY: BALLADS OF ANCIENT ROME. Reader: Gilbert Highet. JNP 23293 (ac)

89 KICKING HIS MOTHER: W. H. AUDEN. Reader Gilbert Highet. JNP 23298 (ac)

90 THE HARP THAT ONCE: MODERN IRISH POETRY Reader: Gilbert Highet. JNP 23300 (ac)

91 AN INDEPENDENT AMERICAN: WHITMAN Reader: Gilbert Highet. JNP 23303 (ac)

92 AN UNFINISHED POEM: ELIOT'S CORIOLAN Reader: Gilbert Highet. JNP 23304 (ac)

93 THE EPIC OF CRIME. Reader: Gilbert Highet JNP 23311 B (ac)

94 A LITTLE LATIN LYRIC. Reader: Gilbert Highet. JNP 23312 A (ac)

95 A RECITAL OF ANCIENT GREEK POETRY. Reader: Stephen G. Daitz. In Greek and En

glish. JNP 23601/4 (4 ac)

96   JOHN DOS PASSOS READS HIS POETRY. JNP 23045 (ac)

JUG   Juggernaut Records. Current address unknown.

1   RIGHT ON! THE LAST POETS. Read by the authors. Juggernaut LP-8802

JUP   Jupiter Records. Current address unknown.

1   JUPITER ANTHOLOGY OF 20TH CENTURY ENGLISH POETRY. Reader: Jill Balcon. Jupiter JUR 00A2

KIWI   Kiwi Records, 182 Wakefield St., Wellington, New Zealand

1   ALLEN CURNOW READS LANDFALL IN UNKNOWN SEAS. Kiwi SLD-2

2   POEMS BY ALISTAIR CAMPBELL. Read by author. Kiwi SLD-13

3   MAUI'S FAREWELL BY DORA SOMERVILLE. Reader: Inia Te Wiata. Kiwi SLD-15

4   DENIS GLOVER READS A SELECTION OF HIS OWN VERSE. Kiwi SLD-28

5   HONE TUWHARE READS A SELECTION OF HIS OWN VERSE. Kiwi SLD-43

LEARNC   Learning Corp. of America, 1350 Av. of the Americas, New York, NY 10019, USA

1   ROMANTICISM: REVOLT OF THE SPIRIT. Learn. Corp. EG 505 (film)

2   THE MIDDLE AGES. Learn. Corp. EG 506 (film)

3   THE SONNETS: SHAKESPEARE. Learn. Corp. EG 721 (film)

4   THE POEM AS IMAGERY. Learn. Corp. EG 741 (film)

5   THE POEM AS ALLEGORY. Learn. Corp. EG 742 (film)

6   THE POEM AS A PERSONAL STATEMENT. Learn. Corp. EG 743 (film)

7   THE POEM AS SOCIAL COMMENT. Learn. Corp. EG 744 (film)

8   THE POEM AS SYMBOLISM. Learn. Corp. EG 752 (film)

9   THE POEM AS EVOCATION. Learn. Corp. EG 753 (film)

10   THE POEM AS IRONY. Learn. Corp. EG 754 (film)

LEARNS   Learning Systems Corp., 60 Connolly Parkway, Hamden, CT 06514, USA

1   SELECTED POETRY. Reader: Cynthia L. Whitaker. Learn. Syst. C-4112 (ac)

2   SELECTED POEMS. Learn. Syst. C-4118 (ac)

LIBC   Library of Congress, Recorded Sound Section, Washington, DC 20540, USA Recordings on phonodiscs; cassettes upon request. Taped recordings of archival material are also available.

1   NATIONAL POETRY FESTIVAL, 1962. 51 poets reading own works. LC 3868, 3869, 3870 (3 tapes each)

2   TWENTIETH CENTURY POETRY: KATHERINE GARRISON CHAPIN. Read by author. LC P1 (78rpm); available on long-play LC PL 1 with other material

3   TWENTIETH CENTURY POETRY IN ENGLISH: CHAPIN, VAN DOREN, AUDEN, AND EBERHART. Read by authors. LC PL 1

4   TWENTIETH CENTURY POETRY: VAN DOREN. Read by author. LC P2 (78rpm); available on long-play LC PL 1 with other material

5   TWENTIETH CENTURY POETRY IN ENGLISH: BOGAN, ENGLE, MARIANNE MOORE, AND ALLEN TATE. Read by authors. LC PL 2

6   TWENTIETH CENTURY POETRY: AUDEN. Read by author. LC P3 (78rpm); available on long-play LC PL 1 with other material

7   T. S. ELIOT READING HIS OWN POETRY. LC PL 3

8   TWENTIETH CENTURY POETRY: EBERHART. Read by author. LC P4 (78rpm); available on long-play LC PL 1 with other material

9   POETRY RECITAL: WARREN, FLETCHER, BRINNIN, AND W. C. WILLIAMS. Read by authors. LC PL 4

10   TWENTIETH CENTURY POETRY: BOGAN. Read by author. LC P5 (78rpm); available on long-play LC PL 2 with other material

11   TWENTIETH CENTURY POETRY IN ENGLISH: CUMMINGS, JEFFERS, SPENCER, AND RANSOM. Read by authors. LC PL 5

12   TWENTIETH CENTURY POETRY: PAUL ENGLE. Read by author. LC P6 (78rpm); available on long-play LC PL 2 with other material

13   ROBERT FROST READING HIS OWN POEMS. LC PL 6

14   POETRY READING: MARIANNE MOORE. Read by author. LC P7 (78rpm); available on long-play LC PL 2 with other material

15   TWENTIETH CENTURY POETRY IN ENGLISH: WILLIAM MEREDITH, WINTERS, JARRELL AND KARL SHAPIRO. Read by authors. LC PL 7

16   POETRY READING: ALLEN TATE. Read by author. LC P8 (78rpm); available on long-play LC PL 2 with other material

17   TWENTIETH CENTURY POETRY IN ENGLISH: READ, PUTNAM, BERRYMAN, GREGORY. Read by authors. LC PL 8

18   POETRY RECITAL: JOHN GOULD FLETCHER. LC P9 (78rpm); available on long-play LC PL 4 with other material

19   TWENTIETH CENTURY POETRY IN ENGLISH: SCHWARTZ, BLACKMUR, SPENDER, AND BISHOP. Read by authors. LC PL 9

20   POETRY RECITAL: JOHN MALCOLM BRINNIN. LC P10 (78rpm); available on long-play LC PL 4 with other material

21   TWENTIETH CENTURY POETRY IN ENGLISH: ROETHKE, BYNNER, FITZGERALD, AND ZATURENSKA. Read by authors. LC PL 10

22   THE WASTE LAND: T. S. ELIOT (1). Read by author. LC P11 (78rpm); available on long-play LC PL 3 with other material

23   TWENTIETH CENTURY POETRY IN ENGLISH: ROBERT LOWELL, AIKEN, EMPSON, AND MACLEISH. Read by authors. LC PL 11

24   THE WASTE LAND: T. S. ELIOT (2). Read by author. LC P12 (78rpm); available on long-play on LC PL 3 with other material

25   TWENTIETH CENTURY POETRY IN ENGLISH: RUKEYSER, BAKER, LEONIE ADAMS, AND JANET LEWIS. Read by authors. LC PL 12

26   THE WASTE LAND: T. S. ELIOT (3). Read by author. LC P13 (78rpm); available on long-play on LC PL 3 with other material

LIBC (continued)

28   ASH WEDNESDAY (1): T. S. ELIOT. Read by author. LC P14 (78rpm); available on long-play on LC PL 3 with other material

29   ASH WEDNESDAY (2) AND LANDSCAPES: T. S. ELIOT. Read by author. LC P15 (78rpm); available on long-play LC PL 3 with other material

30   POETRY READING: WILLIAM CARLOS WILLIAMS. LC P16 (78rpm); available on long-play LC PL 4 with other material

31   WALT WHITMAN SPEAKS FOR HIMSELF. Reader: Arnold Moss. LC PL 16/17 (2 pd)

32   POETRY RECITAL: ROBERT PENN WARREN. LC P17 (78 rpm); available on long-play LC PL 4 with other material

33   POETRY RECITAL: E. E. CUMMINGS. LC P18 (78 rpm); available on long-play LC PL 5 with other material

34   POETRY RECITAL : ROBINSON JEFFERS. LC P19 (78rpm); available on long-play LC PL 5 with other material

35   POETRY RECITAL: THEODORE SPENCER. LC P20 (78 rpm); available on long-play LC PL 5 with other material

36   AN ALBUM OF MODERN POETRY: AN ANTHOLOGY READ BY POETS. PART 1. Part of a 3-disc set; 46 poets all told. LC PL 20

37   POETRY RECITAL: JOHN CROWE RANSOM. LC P21 (78 rpm); available on long-play LC PL 5 with other material

38   AN ALBUM OF MODERN POETRY: AN ANTHOLOGY READ BY POETS. PART 2. LC PL 21

39   POETRY RECITAL: WILLIAM MEREDITH. LC P22 (78 rpm); available on long-play LC PL 7 with other material

40   AN ALBUM OF MODERN POETRY: AN ANTHOLOGY READ BY POETS. PART 3. LC PL 22

41   POETRY RECITAL: YVOR WINTERS. LC P23 (78 rpm); available on long-play LC PL 7 with other material

42   TWENTIETH CENTURY POETRY IN ENGLISH: STEPHEN VINCENT BENÉT AND EDWIN MUIR. Read by authors. LC PL 23

43   POETRY RECITAL: RANDALL JARRELL. LC P24 (78 rpm); available on long-play LC PL 7 with other material

44   TWENTIETH CENTURY POETRY IN ENGLISH: JOHN PEALE BISHOP AND MAXWELL BODENHEIM. Read by authors. LC PL 24

45   POETRY RECITAL: KARL SHAPIRO. LC P25 (78rpm); available on long-play LC PL 7 with other material

46   TWENTIETH CENTURY POETRY IN ENGLISH: ROBERT HILLYER AND JOHN HALL WHEELOCK. Read by authors. LC PL 25

47   POETRY RECITAL: ROBERT FROST. LC P26 (78rpm); available on long-play LC PL 6 with other material

48   TWENTIETH CENTURY POETRY IN ENGLISH: I. A. RICHARDS AND OSCAR WILLIAMS. LC PL 26

49   POETRY RECITAL: ROBERT FROST. LC P27 (78rpm); available on long-play LC PL 6 with other material

50   TWENTIETH CENTURY POETRY IN ENGLISH: JOHN CIARDI AND W. D. SNODGRASS. Read by authors. LC PL 27

51   POETRY RECITAL: ROBERT FROST. LC P28 (78 rpm); available on long-play LC PL 6 with other material

52   TWENTIETH CENTURY POETRY IN ENGLISH: DANIEL G. HOFFMAN AND NED O'GORMAN. Read by authors. LC PL 28

53   POETRY RECORDING: ROBERT FROST. LC P29 (78rpm); available on long-play LC PL 6 with other material

54   NINE PULITZER PRIZE POETS READ THEIR OWN POEMS (Dugan, Kunitz, McGinley, MacLeish, Roethke, Snodgrass, Viereck, Warren, Wilbur). LC PL 29

55   POETRY RECITAL: ROBERT FROST. LC P30 (78 rpm); available on long-play LC PL 6 with other material.

56   POETRY RECITAL: HERBERT READ. LC P31 (78rpm); available on long-play LC PL 8 with other material

57   POETRY RECITAL: PHELPS PUTNAM. LC P32 (78rpm); available on long-play LC PL 8 with other material

58   POETRY RECITAL: JOHN BERRYMAN. LC P33 (78rpm); available on long-play LC PL 8 with other material

59   POETRY RECITAL: HORACE GREGORY. LC P34 (78rpm); available on long-play LC PL 8 with other material

60   POETRY RECITAL: JANET LEWIS. LC P35 (78 rpm); available on long-play LC PL 12 with other material

61   POETRY RECITAL: RICHARD BLACKMUR. LC P36 (78 rpm); available on long-play LC PL 9 with other material

62   POETRY RECITAL: STEPHEN SPENDER. LC P37 (78 rpm); available on long-play LC PL 9 with other material

63   POETRY RECITAL: ELIZABETH BISHOP. LC P38 (78 rpm); available on long-play LC PL 9 with other material

64   POETRY RECITAL: THEODORE ROETHKE. LC P39 (78 rpm); available on long-play LC PL 10 with other material

65   POETRY RECITAL: WITTER BYNNER. LC P40 (78 rpm); available on long-play LC PL 10 with other material

66   POETRY RECITAL: ROBERT FITZGERALD. LC P41 (78 rpm); available on long-play LC PL 10 with other material

67   POETRY RECITAL: MARYA ZATURENSKA. LC P42 (78rpm); available on long-play LC PL 10 with other material

68   RECORDING OF POETRY: ROBERT LOWELL. LC P43 (78rpm); available on long-play LC PL 11 with other material

69   TWENTIETH CENTURY POETRY IN ENGLISH: CONRAD AIKEN. Read by author. LC P44 (78 rpm); available on long-play on LC PL 11 with other material

70   POETRY RECITAL: WILLIAM EMPSON. LC P45 (78 rpm); available on long-play LC PL 11 with other material

71   POETRY RECITAL: ARCHIBALD MACLEISH. LC P46 (78 rpm); available on long-play LC PL 11 with other material

72   POETRY RECITAL: MURIEL RUKEYSER. LC P47 (78rpm); available on long-play LC PL 12 with other material

73   POETRY RECITAL: HOWARD BAKER. LC P48

(78rpm); available on long-play LC PL 12 with other material

74   TWENTIETH CENTURY POETRY IN ENGLISH: LEONIE ADAMS. Read by author. LC P49 (78 rpm); available on long-play LC PL 12 with other material

75   POETRY RECITAL: DELMORE SCHWARTZ. LC P50 (78 rpm); available on long-play LC PL 9 with other material

78   PEDRO SALINAS: EL CONTEMPLADO. Read by author. LC HPL 1

76   TWO COLOMBIAN POETS: CARRANZA AND PARDO GARCIA. Read by authors. LC HPL 3

77   GABRIELA MISTRAL READING HER OWN POETRY. LC HPL 2

78   WILLIAM JAY SMITH READING HIS POEMS FOR CHILDREN. LC PL 30-31

LION   Lion, Engel Marketing, 1745 North Campbell, Tucson, AZ 85719, USA

1   A FESTIVAL OF CHRISTMAS. Reader: Jim Ameche. Lion

2   LION LIBRARY OF POETRY. Reader: Jim Ameche. Lion (4 ac)

LIST   Listening Library, 1 Park Av., Old Greenwich, CT 06870, USA

1   TREASURY OF GREAT POETRY, 1. Readers: Alexander Scourby and others. Listening Lib. CXL 510/1 (ac)

2   TREASURY OF GREAT POETRY, 2. Readers: Alexander Scourby and others. Listening Lib. CXL 510/2 (ac)

3   TREASURY OF GREAT POETRY, 3. Readers: Alexander Scourby and others. Listening Lib. CXL 510/3 (ac)

4   LIVING PROSE AND POETRY SERIES. Listening Lib. CX 21-16 (6 ac)

5   COURTSHIP OF MILES STANDISH: LONGFELLOW. Reader: Richard Pyatt. Listening Lib. CXL 322/23

6   EDGAR ALLAN POE. Reader: Ed Blake. Listening Lib. CXL 514 (6 ac)

7   A KIPLING COLLECTION. Reader: Noel Leslie. Listening Lib. A 1625 (2 pd 16rpm)

8   A POE COLLECTION. Reader: Ed Blake. Listening Lib. A 1636 (pd 16rpm)

9   SHAKESPEARE: SONNETS. Reader: Ronald Colman. Listening Lib. A 1637 (pd 16rpm)

10   THE ENGLISH ROMANTIC POETS. Reader: Bramwell Fletcher. Listening Lib. CX 305 (ac)

11   19TH CENTURY ENGLISH POETS. Reader: Alexander Scourby. Listening Lib. CX 306 (ac)

12   19TH CENTURY AMERICAN POETS. Reader: Alexander Scourby. Listening Lib. CX 307 (ac)

13   AN ALBUM OF MODERN POETRY, I. Listening Lib. CX 308 (ac)

14   AN ALBUM OF MODERN POETRY, II. Listening Lib. CX 309 (ac)

15   AN ALBUM OF MODERN POETRY, III. Listening Lib. CX 310 (ac)

16   THE HOOSIER POET: J. W. RILEY. Reader: Robert Donley. Listening Lib. CX 325 (ac)

17   WHITTIER: SNOWBOUND, AND OTHERS. Reader: Richard Pyatt. Listening Lib. CX 326 (ac)

18   SARA TEASDALE. Reader: Esther Benson. Listening Lib. CX 337 (ac)

19   POEMS OF SUSPENSE AND HORROR. Readers: Patrick Horgan and others. Listening Lib. CX 363 (ac)

20   THE RIME OF THE ANCIENT MARINER: COLERIDGE. Reader: Christopher Plummer. Listening Lib. CX 399 (ac)

21   FAMOUS POEMS THAT TELL GREAT STORIES. Readers: Frederic March and others. Listening Lib. CX 772 (ac). See also DECCA 10

22   THE FUNMAKERS. Readers: Arnold Moss and others. Listening Lib. CX 773 (ac). See also DECCA 11

23   THE HEROIC SOUL: POEMS OF PATRIOTISM. Readers: Arnold Moss and others. Listening Lib. CX 774 (ac). See also DECCA 13

LITAR   Literarisches Archiv. Current address unknown.

1   GEDICHTE: KÄSTNER. Read by author. In German. Lit. Archiv

LIVLAN   Living Language Course, One Park Av., New York, NY 10003, USA

1   TREASURY OF THE WORLD'S BEST LOVED POEMS Reader: Marvin Miller. Living Lang. (4 pd)

LONDON   London Records Inc., c/o Argo-Spoken Word, Decca (U.K.), 50 New Bond Street, London WIY 9HA, England

1   POETRY READINGS BY PEGGY ASHCROFT. London Records 5253

2   ROBERT LOUIS STEVENSON ALBUM. Reader: Laurence Olivier. London Records 5425

LONGM   Longman Group, Ltd., Longman House, Burnt Mill, Harlow, Essex, England Longman Inc., 19 West 44th St., New York, NY 10036, USA

1   THE ENGLISH POETS. Longman EP 1-13 (13 ac)

LUCHT   Luchterhand Verlag, Heddesdorfer Strasse 31, Postfach 1780, D-5450 Neuwied 1, West Germany

1   PHONETISCHE POESIE: MON. Read by the author. Luchterhand F 60 379

MARV   Marvell Press. Current address unknown.

1   A SEQUENCE FOR FRANCIS PARKMAN: DONALD DAVIE. Read by author. Marvell LB1-2

MELOD   Melodiya, 24 Tverskoi Blvd. Moscow K-9, USSR

1   EVGENII ONEGIN: PUSHKIN. Reader: Yakov Smolensky. In Russian. Melodia (5 pd)

2   STIKHI I PESNI EVGENIYA EVTUSHENKO. Read by author. In Russian. Melodia 28073/74

MERC   Mercury Records, Phonogram Inc., 810 Seventh Av., New York, NY 10019, USA

1   AD NAUSEAM, OR DEATH AT FUN CITY: PAUL ROCHE. Read by author. Mercury

MGM   Polydor, 810 Seventh Av., New York, NY 10019, USA

1   THE WEARY BLUES: LANGSTON HUGHES. Polydor E 3697

MIAMI   Miami Records, 2819 NW 7th Av., Miami, FL 33127, USA

1   POETAS COLOMBIANOS. Reader: Juan Peñalver Laserna. Miami LD 1252

MIAMI (continued)

2 POETAS LATINOAMERICANAS. Reader: Juan Peñalver Laserna. Miami LD 1256

MICHM Michigan Media TV, 400 Fourth St., Ann Arbor, MI 48109, USA

1 ROBERT FROST AT 88. Michigan Media 8401 (16mm film)

2 TAO-CHI: POET-PAINTER OF OLD CHINA. Michigan Media 8624 (vc)

3 PARLIAMENT OF FOWLS. Michigan Media 8639 (vc)

4 ALAN PATON: A PROFILE. Michigan Media 8837 (vc)

5 FOR THIS WORLD'S LOVING: BONARO OVERSTREET. Michigan Media 8848 (vc)

6 THE PAINTERS AND THE POETS OF MALAYSIA. Michigan Media 9551 (vc)

7 TAGORE, POET OF INDIA. Michigan Media 9565 (vc)

8 POETS TALKING: DONALD HALL. Michigan Media 9712 (vc)

9 POETS TALKING: GALWAY KINNELL. Michigan Media 9713 (vc)

10 POETS TALKING: GREGORY ORR. Michigan Media 9714 (vc)

11 POETS TALKING: CAROLYN KIZER. Michigan Media 9715 (vc)

12 POETS TALKING: ROBERT BLY. Michigan Media 9716 (vc)

13 POETS TALKING: LOUIS SIMPSON. Michigan Media 9717 (vc)

14 POETS TALKING: MARVIN BELL. Michigan Media 9718 (vc)

15 POETS TALKING: JEROME ROTHENBERG. Michigan Media 9719 (vc)

16 POETS TALKING: WENDELL BERRY. Michigan Media 9720 (vc)

17 POETS TALKING: LARRY FAGIN. Michigan Media 9721 (vc)

18 POETS TALKING. W. S. MERWIN. Michigan Media 9722 (vc)

19 POETS TALKING: ROBERT HAYDEN. Michigan Media 9723 (vc)

20 POETS TALKING: HOWARD NORMAN. Michigan Media 9724 (vc)

21 POETS TALKING: LAWRENCE RAAB. Michigan Media 9725 (vc)

22 POETS TALKING: JOYCE PESEROFF. Michigan Media 9726 (vc)

23 THE PURITAN POET: MILTON. Michigan Media 9941 (vc)

MILLER Miller Brody, 400 Hahn Bl., Westminster, MD 21157, USA

1 EDWARD FIELD. Read by author. Miller Brody (ac)

2 G. D. ODEN. Read by author. Miller Brody (ac)

3 MAY SWENSON. Read by author. Miller Brody (ac)

MINU University of Minnesota, AV Library, Minneapolis, MN 55414, USA

1 THE HIGHWAYMAN: NOYES. Reader: John Carradine. U. of MN (16mm film)

MK MK Records, Moscow, USSR. Current address unknown.

1 M. LERMONTOV: VERSES; PUSHKIN: VERSES. Readers: V. Aksenov and others. MK 4124/5

MONIT Monitor Records, Moscow, USSR. Current address unknown.

1 SIMONOV. Read by author. Monitor MR 108

2 THE VOICES OF YEVTUSHENKO AND VOZNESENSKY. Monitor 113

MUSENG Musical Engineering Association. Current address unknown.

1 HAIKU. Readers: Sumire Jacobs and others. Mus. Engineering MEA/LP 1001

2 ZEN AND SENRYN POEMS. Readers: Sumira Hasegawa Jacobs and others. In Japanese. Mus. Engineering MEA/LP 1002

NACTE National Council of Teachers of English, 1111 Kenyon Rd., Urbana, IL 61801, USA

1 ROBERT FROST READING HIS POETRY. Natl Council (4 pd 78rpm)

2 VERGIL: AENEID. Reader: Harry Morgan Ayres. In Latin. Natl Council (manufacturer's number unknown)

3 ROBERT FROST READING HIS POETRY. Natl Council LP 1

4 ROBERT FROST READING HIS POEMS. Natl Council LP 2 (D9-CC-1661/2)

5 PROLOGUE TO CANTERBURY TALES. Reader: Harry Morgan Ayres. Natl Council D9-CB-1915 (pd 78rpm)

6 VACHEL LINDSAY: THE CONGO. Read by author. Natl Council D9-CB-1917/8 (pd 78rpm)

7 EMILY DICKINSON. Reader: Lucyle Hook. Natl Council RL 20-5

8 W. H. AUDEN READING POEMS. Natl Council 23/4 (82109R) (pd 78rpm)

9 MARK VAN DOREN READING HIS POEMS. Natl Council 41/42 (pd 78rpm)

10 STEPHEN VINCENT BENET READING POEMS. Natl Council 43/44 (pd 78rpm)

11 ALLEN TATE READING HIS POEMS. Natl Council 53/54 (pd 78rpm)

12 WILLIAM ROSE BENÉT. Read by author. Natl Council 57 (pd 78rpm)

13 ROBERT FROST READING MENDING WALL. Natl Council G-110/111 M (pd 78rpm)

14 TWELVE CONTEMPORARY POETS. Natl Council 868N-8519

15 ARCHIBALD MACLEISH READING HIS FRESCOES FOR MR. ROCKEFELLER'S CITY. Natl Council 8040/2 (3 pd 78rpm)

16 THE SECRET HEART: ROBERT P. TRISTRAM COFFIN. Read by author. Natl Council 79202 R (pd 78rpm)

17 VACHEL LINDSAY READING HIS POEMS. Natl Council 80209 R (4pd 78rpm)

NAITV National Instructional TV, Box A, Bloomington, IN 47401, USA

1 SYLVESTER AND THE MAGIC PEBBLE. Reader: Ann McGregor. Natl Instr TV pbp 101 (vc)

2 BEDTIME FOR FRANCES. Reader: Ann McGregor. Natl Instr TV pbp 103 (vc)

3 MIGHTY HUNTERS. Reader: Ann McGregor. Natl Instr TV pbp 201 (vc)

4 MICE ARE NICE. Reader: Ann McGregor. Natl Instr TV pbp 203 (vc)

5 LOVABLE LYLE. Reader: Ann McGregor. Natl Instr TV pbp 301 (vc)

6 FRIENDS. Reader: Ann McGregor. Natl Instr TV pbp 302 (vc)

NBC National Broadcasting Co., 30 Rockefeller Plaza, New York, NY 10020, USA

1 YEVTUSHENKO INTERVIEW. NBC (16mm film)

2 ROBERT FROST. Reading by author. NBC (16mm film)

NESKE Verlag Gunther Neske, PO Box 7240, D-7417 Pfullingen, West Germany

1 LYRIK DER ZEIT, I: BACHMAN. Read by author. In German. Neske

2 LYRIK DER ZEIT, II: ARP. Read by author. In German. Neske

NET National Educational Television, Inc., Indiana University, Bloomington, IN 47401, USA

1 ALLEN GINSBERG AND LAWRENCE FERLING-HETTI. Readings by authors. Natl Ed TV (16mm film)

2 ANNE SEXTON. Reading by author. Natl Ed TV (16mm film)

3 STEPHEN SPENDER. Reading by author. Natl Ed TV (16mm film)

4 ROBINSON JEFFERS: GIVE YOUR HEART TO THE HAWKS. Reading by author. Natl Ed TV (16mm film)

5 ROBERT DUNCAN AND JOHN WIENERS. Readings by authors. Natl Ed TV (16mm film)

6 ROBERT CREELEY. Reading by author. Natl Ed TV (16mm film)

7 RICHARD WILBUR AND ROBERT LOWELL. Readings by authors. Natl Ed TV (16mm film)

8 RICHARD WILBUR. Reading by author. Natl Ed TV (16mm film)

9 PHILIP WHALEN AND GARY SNYDER. Natl Ed TV (16mm film)

10 OGDEN NASH. Reading by author. Natl Ed TV (16mm film)

11 LOUIS ZUKOFSKY. Reading by author. Natl Ed TV (16mm film)

12 LEOPOLD SEDAR SENGHOR. Reading by author. Natl Ed TV (16mm film)

13 JOHN CROWE RANSOM. Reading by author. Natl Ed TV (16mm film)

14 IN SEARCH OF HART CRANE. Reader: Gary Merrill. Natl Ed TV (16mm film)

15 GWENDOLYN BROOKS. Reading by author. Natl Ed TV (16mm film)

16 FRANK O'HARA AND ED SANDERS. Readings by authors. Natl Ed TV (16mm film)

17 AN ESSAY ON WILLIAM BLAKE. Natl Ed TV (16mm film)

18 DENISE LEVERTOV AND CHARLES OLSON. Reading by authors. Natl Ed TV (16mm film)

NFBC National Film Board of Canada, 1251 Av. of the Americas, New York, NY 10020, USA

1 MORNING ON THE LIÉVRE: ARCHIBALD LAMP-MAN. Natl Film Bd (16mm film)

NIKTOM Niktom Records. Current address unknown.

1 LIKE A RIPPLE ON A POND: NIKKI GIOVANNI. Read by author. Niktom Records NK 4200

ORTH Orthological Institute. Current address unknown.

1 JAMES JOYCE. Read by author. Ortholog Inst (pd 78rpm)

OUTL Outlets Records, 48 Smithfield Sq., Belfast, Northern Ireland

1 CITY AND WESTERN: JAMES STEWART ALEXANDER SIMMONS. Outlets Records

OXF Oxford Films, Inc. Current address unknown.

1 JAMES WELDON JOHNSON. Oxf Films (16mm film)

PATHE Pathé Marconi EMI, 36 Rue Pierret, 92200 Neuilly-sur-Seine, France

1 LES RÊVES DU JEUNE HUGO. Pathe

PATHN Pathe News Inc., 250 West 57th St., New York, NY 10019, USA

1 OLD IRONSIDES: HOLMES. Pathe News (16mm film)

PATHW Pathways of Sound, 6 Craigie Circle, Cambridge, MA 02138, USA

1 THE ELEPHANT'S CHILD. Reader: Carl de Suze. Pathways POS 1021

2 THE PICKETY FENCE: DAVID MCCORD. Read by author. Pathways POS 1042

PENN Pennsylvania State Univ., AV Services, University Park, PA 16802, USA

1 ALIVE AND KICKING: BRITISH POET BRIAN PATTEN. Read by author. Penn. State U. (16mm film)

2 FRANÇOIS VILLON. Reader: George Brassens. In French. Penn. State U. (16mm film)

PERC Perception Records. Current address unknown.

1 BLACK IVORY: WANDA ROBINSON. Read by author. Perception PLP 18

PERIOD Everest Recording Group, 2020 Av. of the Stars, Century City, CA 90067, USA

1 POEMS OF VERLAINE AND OTHERS. Readers: James Lewis and others. Period FRL 1524

2 AN ANTHOLOGY OF FRENCH POETRY. Readers: Linette Fischer and others. In French. Period FRL 1522

3 JEAN COCTEAU, HIS WORK AND VOICE. Read by author. Period FRL 1530

PHIL Philips/Phonogram BV, Catharina van Renneslaan 10, 1217 CX Hilversum, Netherlands

1 JEAN COCTEAU, TEXTE INÉDIT. In French. Philips A 76.715 R

PLEI Disques Pleiade, 8 rue de Berri, 75008 Paris, France

1 LES PLUS BELLES FABLES DE LA FONTAINE. In French. Pleiade 3051-54 (4pd)

POETAS Los Poetas, Distex SA, Buenos Aires, Argentina

1 GARCIA LORCA RECITADO POR MARGARITA XIRGU. Los Poetas LPLP 1

2 GARCIA LORCA RECITADO POR RAFAEL ALBERTI. Los Poetas LPLP 2

POETRY Poetry Records, 475 Fifth Av., New York, NY 10017, USA

1 SIXTEEN SONNETS: SHAKESPEARE. Reader: David Allen. Poetry Records PR 201

POETRY (continued)

2 NO SINGLE THING ABIDES. Reader: David Allen. Poetry Records PR 202

3 LEAVES OF GRASS. Poetry Records PR 300

POLYDR Polydor Intl GmbH, PO Box 132266, D-2000 Hamburg 13, West Germany

1 DYLAN THOMAS: FIFTEEN POEMS. Reader: Richard Burton. Polydor

2 CHARLES BAUDELAIRE: AUSWAHL. Reader: Pierre Blanchar. Polydor 1373 S

POLYGL Polyglot. Current address unknown.

1 RIMBAUD: LE BATEAU IVRE. Polyglot

2 SHAKESPEARE: SONNETS. Readers: Claire Bloom and others. Polyglot

POSEID Poseidon. c/o Crystal Record Co., 2235 Willida Lane, Sedro Woolley, WA 98284, USA

1 POETS READ THEIR POETRY: GALWAY KINNELL AND OTHERS. Poseidon 1003

PRENT Prentice Hall Media Inc. These recordings are now owned and distributed by Clearvue Incorporated, 6666 Oliphant Av., Chicago, IL 60631, USA

1 BLACK POEMS, BLACK IMAGES. KHC 323 (kit: 6 pd, ac, fs)

2 MAN AND EARTH: THE POET'S VIEW. KHC 456 (kit: 2 pd, ac, fs)

3 POETRY: COMMITMENT AND ALIENATION. KHC 740 (2 ac)

PREST Prestige, 10th and Parker Sts., Berkeley, CA 94710, USA

1 NORMAN MAILER READS. Prestige PRST 782

PROTHM Prothman Assoc. Inc., 650 Thomas Av., Baldwin, NY 11510, USA

1 ELEGY WRITTEN IN A COUNTRY CHURCHYARD: GRAY. Prothman IEV 1 (study tape)

2 EVE OF ST. AGNES: KEATS. Prothman IEV 2 (study tape)

3 THE ANCIENT MARINER: COLERIDGE. Prothman IEV 3 (study tape)

4 PETER GRIMES: CRABBE. Prothman IEV 4 (study tape)

5 THE POETRY OF WILFRED OWEN. Prothman IEV 5 (study tape)

6 POETRY OF THE TWO ELIZABETHS: LOVE. Prothman T 101 (ac)

7 POETRY OF THE TWO ELIZABETHS: VIOLENCE. Prothman T 113 (ac)

8 POETRY OF THE TWO ELIZABETHS: DISCOVERY. Prothman T 122 (ac)

9 THE PIED PIPER OF HAMELIN: BROWNING. Prothman AVP 403 (ac)

10 JOHN GILPIN: WILLIAM COWPER. Prothman AVP 407 (study tape)

11 SIR PATRICK SPENS. Prothman AVP 408 (ac)

12 THE CHILDREN'S CRUSADE: PHILIP LEVINE. Prothman AVP 411 (ac)

13 BALAAM BY KEBLE, AND FLOOD BY HEATH-STUBBS. Prothman AVP 412 (ac)

14 THE HIGHWAYMAN: NOYES. Prothman AVP 413 (ac)

PYR Pyramid Film Productions, PO Box 1048, Santa Monica, CA 90406, USA

1 EMILY DICKINSON: A CERTAIN SLANT OF LIGHT. Reader: Julie Harris. M/S Prod. (16mm film)

RCA RCA Records, 1133 Av. Americas, New York, NY 10036, USA

1 A PERSONAL CHOICE. Reader: Alec Guinness. RCA VDM 102

2 PROGRAM OF POEMS BY EDITH SITWELL. Readers: John Gielgud and others. RCA VDS 106

3 EVERYBODY KNOWS THE TROUBLE I'VE SEEN: OGDEN NASH. Read by author. RCA VDM 114

4 AN ANTHOLOGY OF ENGLISH LYRIC VERSE. Reader: Cornelia Otis Skinner. RCA CAL 190

4A MINE EYES HAVE SEEN THE GLORY: HELEN HAYES. RCA M 909-1/4 (78rpm)

5 WALT WHITMAN. Reader: Ralph Bellamy. RCA M 955 (4pd 78rpm)

6 DOROTHY PARKER: POEMS. Reader: Ilka Chase. RCA M 971 (11-8605/6) (2 pd 78rpm)

7 EDNA ST. VINCENT MILLAY: POEMS. RCA LCT 1147

8 POETS' GOLD, 1. Reader: Helen Hayes. RCA LM 1812

9 POETS' GOLD, 2. Readers: Raymond Massey and others. RCA LM 1813

10 POETS' GOLD, 3. Readers: Archibald MacLeish and others. RCA LM 1883

11 FOUR QUARTETS: ELIOT. Read by author. RCA C3598-3603 (6pd 78rpm)

REX Rex, Australia. Current address unknown.

1 RUBAIYAT OF OMAR KHAYYAM. Readers: Frank Semple and others. Rex RA 2012

SBARB Santa Barbara Museum of Art, 1130 State St., Santa Barbara, CA 93101, USA

1 READINGS OF POETRY: DYLAN THOMAS, APRIL 1950. Read by author. Santa Barbara Mus.

SCHOL Scholastic Audio-Visual, 906 Sylvan Av., Englewood Cliffs, NJ 07632, USA

1 TODAY'S POETS, 1. Scholastic FS 11001

2 TODAY'S POETS, 2. Scholastic FS 11002

3 TODAY'S POETS, 3. Scholastic FS 11003

4 TODAY'S POETS, 4. Scholastic FS 11004

5 TODAY'S POETS, 5. Readers: Robert Bly and others. Scholastic FS 11005

6 SOUND OF WORLD POETRY: COPPOLA. Scholastic FS 11006

7 REFLECTIONS ON A GIFT OF WATERMELON PICKLE. Reader: Paul Hecht. Scholastic FS 11007

8 POEMS AND BALLADS. Readers: Donald Hall and others. Scholastic FS 11008

SCOT Scottish Records. Current address unknown.

1 POEMS OF ROBERT BURNS. Reader: Harold Weightman. Scottish Records SR 124

2 ROBERT BURNS READ BY JEAN TAYLOR SMITH. Scottish Records SR 1252 (pd 78rpm)

SERAPH Seraphim/Capitol, c/o Capitol Records Inc., 1750 North Vine St., Hollywood, CA 90028, USA

1 PRACTICAL CATS: ELIOT; AND SHAKESPEAREAN SONNETS. Readers: Robert Donat and Edith Evans. With music by Alan Rawsthorne. Seraphim 60042; reissued on Angel 37972 (Capitol Records)

SERIF   Serif Records, Clarke & Way. Current address unknown.

1   GENE DERWOOD READING FROM HER OWN POETRY. Serif Records 1001

SINGER   L. W. Singer Co. Current address unknown.

1   PROSE AND POETRY ENRICHMENT RECORDS, 1. Readers: Howard Lindsay and others. Singer

2   PROSE AND POETRY ENRICHMENT RECORDS, 2. Reader: Raymond Massey. Singer

3   PROSE AND POETRY ENRICHMENT RECORDS, 3. Readers: Ogden Nash and others. Singer

4   PROSE AND POETRY ENRICHMENT RECORDS, 4. Readers: Ralph Bellamy and others. Singer

5   PROSE AND POETRY ENRICHMENT RECORDS, 5. Readers: Julie Harris and others. Singer

6   PROSE AND POETRY ENRICHMENT RECORDS, 6. Readers: Charles Dunn and others. Singer

SMC   Spanish Music Center, 319 West 48th St., New York, NY 10036, USA

1   DE CORAZÓN A CORAZÓN: RECITAL POETICO. Reader: Ernesto Hoffman Llevano. Span. Music SMC 1001

2   RIMAS AMOROSAS: BECQUER. Reader: E. Hoffman Llevano. Span. Music SMC 1007

3   PANORAMA POETICO ESPAÑOL. Reader: Carola Yonmar. Span. Music SMC 1009

4   FEDERICO GARCIA LORCA, 2. Reader: Carola Yonmar. Span. Music SMC 1010

5   PANORAMA POETICO ANDALUZ. Reader: Carola Yonmar. Span. Music SMC 1011

6   PANORAMA POETICO HISPANOAMERICANO. Reader: Carola Yonmar. Span. Music SMC 1012

7   MUJER. POETRY FOR ALL AGES. Reader: Carola Yonmar. In Spanish. Span. Music SMC 1013

8   LITERATURA COLOMBIANA. Reader: Andres Berger-Kiss. Span. Music SMC 1014

9   PUERTO RICO: SELECCIONES POETICAS. Reader: Rafael Bartolomei. Span. Music SMC 1036

10   POEMAS DEL CANTE JONDO: GARCIA LORCA. Sung by Enrique Montoy. Span. Music SMC 1037

11   ANTOLOGIA POETICA: GARCIA LORCA. Reader: José Jorda. Span. Music SMC 1060

12   FILOSOFIA Y MISTICA DEL DOLOR Y DE LA MUERTE: ISIDORO MARTINEZ ALONSO. Reader: Angel Morillo. Span. Music SMC 1062

13   POESIA CUBANA. Reader: Oscar Fernandez de la Vega. Span. Mus. SMC 1081

14   PLATERO Y YO: JIMENEZ. Reader: Ricardo Fabregues. Span. Music SMC 1091

15   LITERATURA HISPANICA. Reader: Ricardo Fabregues. Span. Music SMC 1092

16   PARA AMANTES. Reader: Ricardo Fabregues. Span. Music SMC 1093

17   POEMAS DE AMOR Y DE TOROS. Reader: Ricardo Fabregues. Span. Music SMC 1094

18   MARTIN FIERRO: HERNANDEZ. Reader: Acides Dorado. Span. Music SMC 1095

19   PERFILES DE AMERICA: LITERATURA CUBANA. Span. Music SMC 1078

SPA   SPA Records. Current address unknown.

1   TWO ODES OF JOHN KEATS. Reader: Vincent Price. SPA Records SPA-1

SPOA   Spoken Arts Inc., 310 North Av., New Rochelle, NY 10801, USA

1   ROBERT BURNS. Reader: Ann Moray. SA 754

2   A CHILD'S GARDEN OF VERSES: STEVENSON. Reader: Basil Langton. SA 904/5 (2pd)

5   THE GOLDEN TREASURY OF GERMAN VERSE. Reader: Heinrich Schnitzler. In German. SA 701

6   IRISH VERSE. Reader: Padraic Colum. SA 706

7   IRISH VERSE AND BALLADS. Reader: Siobhan McKenna. SA 707

8   GOLDEN TREASURY OF JOHN BETJEMAN. Read by author. SA 710

9   GOLDEN TREASURY OF FRENCH VERSE. Reader: Jean Vilar. In French. SA 711

10   GOLDEN TREASURY OF CATHOLIC VERSE. Readers: Josephine Callan and others. SA 712

11   AN INFORMAL HOUR WITH DOROTHY PARKER. Read by author. SA 726

12   ANTHONY QUAYLE READING SONNETS FROM SHAKESPEARE AND OTHERS. SA 729

13   THE GEORGICS OF VIRGIL. In Latin. SA 733

14   T. S. ELIOT: WASTELAND. Reader: Robert Speaight. SA 734

15   GENE DERWOOD: POEMS. Readers: Joseph Bennet and others. SA 736

16   BRIAN MERRIMAN: THE MIDNIGHT COURT. Readers: Siobhan McKenna and others. SA 742

17   THE POEMS OF JAMES STEPHENS. Read by author. SA 744

18   LENORE MARSHALL READS HER POETRY. SA 746

19   THE POEMS OF RICHARD WILBUR. Read by the author. SA 747

20   IRELAND FREE: MICHEAL MACLIAMMOIR. SA 749

21   LENNOX ROBINSON PRESENTS WILLIAM BUTLER YEATS. SA 752

22   THE POEMS OF WILLIAM BUTLER YEATS READ BY THE AUTHOR AND OTHERS. SA 753

— 23   JOHN MASEFIELD: OSSIAN. Read by author. SA 755

24   BORIS PASTERNAK: POEMS. Reader: Tatiana Probers. In Russian. SA 756

25   T. S. ELIOT READS OLD POSSUM'S BOOK OF PRACTICAL CATS. SA 758

26   POEMS OF EMILY DICKINSON. Reader: Nancy Wickwire. SA 761

27   GOLDEN TREASURY OF NERVAL AND OTHERS. Readers: Jean Vilar and others. In French. SA 764

28   FOUR QUARTETS: ELIOT. Reader: Robert Speaight. SA 765

29   GOLDEN TREASURY OF MILTON AND OTHERS. Reader: Hilton Edwards. SA 768

30   GOLDEN TREASURY OF ITALIAN VERSE. In Italian. SA 771

31   GOLDEN TREASURY OF AMERICAN VERSE. Readers: Alexander Scourby and others. SA 772

32   GOLDEN TREASURY OF APOLLINAIRE. Readers: Jacques Duby and others. In French. SA 801

SPOA (continued)

33 THE POEMS OF WILLIAM BLAKE AND OTHERS. Reader: Robert Speaight. SA 814

34 THE LOVE POEMS OF LAWRENCE DURRELL. Read by author. SA 818

35 THE GOLDEN TREASURY OF CHILDREN'S VERSE, I. Read by Jill Balcon and others. SA 820

36 GOLDEN TREASURY OF FRENCH LITERATURE. Reader: Jean-Gabriel Gaussens. In French. SA 822

37 GOLDEN TREASURY OF SPANISH POETRY. Readers: Ricardo and Eugenio Florit. In Spanish. SA 829

38 THE ILIAD AND THE ODYSSEY OF HOMER: PART 1. Reader: Ennis Rees. In English. SA 833

39 GOLDEN TREASURY OF SPANISH-AMERICAN VERSE. Reader: Manuel Durán. In Spanish. SA 839

40 RALPH WALDO EMERSON: POEMS. Reader: Kenneth S. Lynn. SA 842

41 ROBERT DONAT READS FAVORITE POEMS. SA 848

42 TREASURY OF TENNYSON. Reader: Robert Speaight. SA 858

43 TREASURY OF JOHN DONNE. Readers: Robert Speaight and others. SA 859

44 TREASURY OF WILLIAM WORDSWORTH. Reader: Robert Speaight. SA 860

45 TREASURY OF ROBERT BROWNING. Reader: Robert Speaight. SA 861

46 TREASURY OF JOHN DRYDEN. Reader: Robert Speaight. SA 866

47 TREASURY OF JOHN MILTON. Readers: Robert Speaight and others. SA 867

48 TREASURY OF JOHN KEATS. Reader: Robert Speaight. SA 868

49 FABLES DE LA FONTAINE, 1. Reader: Georges Riquier. In French. SA 895

50 ELIZABETHAN LOVE POEMS. Readers: Robert Speaight and others. SA 896

51 TREASURY OF LONGFELLOW. Reader: Donald Hall. SA 898

52 LOLITA AND POEMS: VLADIMIR NABOKOV. SA 902

54 TREASURY OF WALT WHITMAN: LEAVES OF GRASS, 1. Reader: Alexander Scourby. SA 907

55 THE TREASURY OF GEORGE GORDON, LORD BYRON. Reader: Peter Orr. SA 908

56 FABLES DE LA FONTAINE, 2. Reader: Georges Riquier. In French. SA 909

57 THE RIME OF THE ANCIENT MARINER AND OTHERS. Readers: Christopher Casson and others. SA 910

58 TREASURY OF ANDRÉ MAUROIS. Read by author. In French. SA 911/2

59 GOLDEN TREASURY OF MODERN SPANISH VERSE. Reader: Eugenio Florit. In Spanish. SA 913

60 BEOWULF READ IN OLD ENGLISH. Readers: Norman Davis and others. SA 918

61 SELECTIONS FROM THE CANTERBURY TALES. Readers: Nevill Coghill and others. In Middle English. SA 919

62 PAUL CLAUDEL AND OTHERS. Readers: Claude Nollier and others. In French. SA 923

63 ILIAD: HOMER Readers: Michael Redgrave and others. In English. SA 926

64 TREASURY OF OLIVER GOLDSMITH AND OTHERS. Reader: Christopher Casson. SA 927

65 ANTHOLOGY OF TENNYSON AND BROWNING. Readers: Cecil Bellamy and others. SA 934

66 SHAKESPEARE: THE RAPE OF LUCRECE. SA 943

67 HERE TODAY: POEMS OF 45 CONTEMPORARY AUTHORS, 1. Readers: Angela Baddeley and others. SA 944

68 HERE TODAY: POEMS OF 45 CONTEMPORARY AUTHORS, 2. Readers: Angela Baddeley and others. SA 945

69 WALT WHITMAN: LEAVES OF GRASS. Reader: Alexander Scourby. SA 946

70 SELECTED POEMS BY STEPHEN SPENDER. Read by author. SA 953

71 THE STRANGEST EVERYTHING: JOHN CIARDI, 1. Read by author. SA 956

72 THE STRANGEST EVERYTHING: JOHN CIARDI, 2. Read by author. SA 957

73 THE RAPE OF THE LOCK: POPE. Reader: Robert Speaight. SA 961

74 TREASURY OF ALEXANDER POPE. Reader: Robert Speaight. SA 962

75 ANTHOLOGY OF 19TH CENTURY AMERICAN POETRY. Reader: Kenneth S. Lynn. SA 963

76 THE ILIAD AND THE ODYSSEY OF HOMER: PART 2. Reader: Ennis Rees. In English. SA 983

77 THE RUBAIYAT OF OMAR KHAYYAM. Robert Speaight reads Fitzgerald's tr.; Robert Graves reads his own tr. SA 965

78 SONNETS FROM THE PORTUGUESE: ELIZABETH BROWNING. Reader: Penelope Lee. SA 973

79 TREASURY OF MATTHEW ARNOLD. Reader: Robert Speaight. SA 974

80 SOHRAB AND RUSTUM: ARNOLD. Reader: Peter Orr. SA 975

81 THE POEMS OF JAMES DICKEY. Read by author. SA 984

82 POETS FOR PEACE. Read by authors. SA 990

83 POETRY OF THE 16TH CENTURY. Readers: Peter Orr and others. SA 993

84 POETRY OF THE EARLY 17TH CENTURY. Readers: David King and others. SA 994

85 SELECTED POEMS: AUDEN. Read by author. SA 999-HS

86 THE RUBAIYAT OF OMAR KHAYYAM. (tr. by Graves.) SA 1010

87 EDGAR ALLAN POE: THE RAVEN AND OTHERS. Reader: Hurd Hatfield. SA 1023

88 BLACK SCENE IN PROSE AND POETRY (1). Reader: Vinie Burrows. SA 1030

89 BLACK SCENE IN PROSE AND POETRY (2). Reader: Vinie Burrows. SA 1031

90 SA TREASURY OF 100 MODERN AMERICAN POETS, 1. SA 1040

91 SA TREASURY OF 100 MODERN AMERICAN POETS, 2. SA 1041

92 SA TREASURY OF 100 MODERN AMERICAN POETS, 3. SA 1042

93 SA TREASURY OF 100 MODERN AMERICAN POETS 4. SA 1043

94 SA TREASURY OF 100 MODERN AMERICAN POETS 5. SA 1044

95 SA TREASURY OF 100 MODERN AMERICAN POETS 6. SA 1045

96 SA TREASURY OF 100 MODERN AMERICAN POETS, 7. SA 1046
97 SA TREASURY OF 100 MODERN AMERICAN POETS, 8. SA 1047
98 SA TREASURY OF 100 MODERN AMERICAN POETS, 9. SA 1048
99 SA TREASURY OF 100 MODERN AMERICAN POETS, 10. SA 1049
100 SA TREASURY OF 100 MODERN AMERICAN POETS, 11. SA 1050
101 SA TREASURY OF 100 MODERN AMERICAN POETS, 12. SA 1051
102 SA TREASURY OF 100 MODERN AMERICAN POETS, 13. SA 1052
103 SA TREASURY OF 100 MODERN AMERICAN POETS, 14. SA 1053
104 SA TREASURY OF 100 MODERN AMERICAN POETS, 15. SA 1054
105 SA TREASURY OF 100 MODERN AMERICAN POETS, 16. SA 1055
106 SA TREASURY OF 100 MODERN AMERICAN POETS, 17. SA 1056
107 SA TREASURY OF 100 MODERN AMERICAN POETS, 18. SA 1057
108 LANGSTON HUGHES READS. SA 1064
109 PABLO NERUDA READS HIS POEMS IN SPANISH. SA 1114
110 EZRA POUND READING HIS TRANSLATIONS OF THE CONFUCIAN ODES. SA 1098
111 SONNETS OF SHAKESPEARE. Reader: Robert Speaight. SA 947-949 (3 pd)
112 A CHILD'S GARDEN OF VERSES: STEVENSON. Readers: Nancy Wickwire and others. SA 904/5 (2 pd)
113 POEMS OF D. H. LAWRENCE. SA 1062
114 POETRY OF WILLIAM BLAKE. SA 1061
115 POEMS OF YEATS. Reader: Lennox Robinson. SA 751
116 POEMS AND SONGS FOR YOUNGER CHILDREN: LEAR AND OTHERS. Readers: Cecil Bellamy and others. SA 1060
117 ANTHOLOGY OF POETS FOR CHILDREN. Readers: Cecil Bellamy and others. SA 977
119 THE DREAM AWAKE: OWEN DODSON. SA 1095
120 OFFERED BY OWNER: LYN LIFSHIN READING HER POEMS. SA NSD 703
121 TREASURY OF PERCY BYSSHE SHELLEY. Readers: Robert Speaight and others. SA 869
122 VENUS AND ADONIS: SHAKESPEARE. Readers: Robert Speaight and others. SA 942
123 TREASURY OF 19TH CENTURY ENGLISH POETS. Readers: Robert Speaight and others. SA 7012
124 SELECTED SONNETS OF SHAKESPEARE. Reader: Robert Speaight. SA 8006
125 SELECTIONS FROM FRENCH LITERATURE. Reader: J. Provost. SA 985
126 ANTHOLOGY OF GERMAN POETRY. Reader: A. Rothschild. SA 998
127 TREASURY OF HEINRICH HEINE. Reader: A. L. Klein. SA 1152
128 THE PSALMS IN HEBREW AND ENGLISH. Readers: Morris Carnovsky and others. SA 776
129 THE SONG OF SONGS. Readers: Carol Veazie and others. In Hebrew and English. SA 777
130 ABBA EBAN READS THE PSALMS AND ECCLESIASTES. In Hebrew and English. SA 757
131 TREASURY OF NURSERY RHYMES. Reader: Christopher Casson. SA 857 and 885 (2 pd)
132 TREASURY OF LEWIS CARROLL. Reader: Christopher Casson. SA 897
133 SOUNDS AND SWEET AIRS: SONGS OF SHAKESPEARE. Readers: Christopher Casson and others. SA 900
134 FEAR OF FLYING AND POEMS: ERICA JONG. Read by the author. SA 1140

SPOWRD Spoken Word (Argo), c/o Decca Records (U.K.), 50 New Bond Street, London WIY 9HA, England
1 THE DESERTED ALTAR AND OTHER POEMS: POSNER. Read by author. Sp. Word SW 110
2 DECLENSION: GREGOR. Read by author. Sp. Word SW 111
3 A MASK FOR JANUS AND OTHER POEMS: MERWIN. Read by author. Sp. Word SW 122
4 FABLES. Read by author Paul Roche. Sp. Word SW 129
5 CAUTIONARY VERSES: BELLOC. Reader: Peter Ustinov. Sp. Word SW 506

STANFD Stanford University, Program for Recording in Sound, 150 Encina Commons, Stanford, CA 94305, USA
1 ADRIENNE RICH READING AT STANFORD. Stanford CFS 331
2 DONALD DAVIE READING AT STANFORD. Stanford P-1974-CFS 3647

STANY Stanyan Records, 8440 Santa Monica Bl., Los Angeles, CA 90069, USA
1 THE BODY ELECTRIC: WHITMAN. Stanyan DSQ 4012

STERL Sterling Educational Films, 241 East 34th St., New York, NY 10016, USA
1 CASEY AT THE BAT: THAYER. Sterling (16mm film)
2 A CHILD'S GARDEN OF VERSES: STEVENSON. Sterling (16mm film)
3 HAILSTONES AND HALIBUT BONES: MARY O'NEILL. Sterling (16mm film)

SUHRK Suhrkamp Verlag, Lindenstr., Suhrkamp Haus, 6 Frankfurt, West Germany
1 HERMANN BROCH LIEST. In German. Suhrkamp
2 HANS MAGNUS ENZENSBERGER LIEST. In German. Suhrkamp
3 HERMANN HESSE LIEST GEDICHTE. In German. Suhrkamp
4 ÜBER DAS GLÜCK: HESSE. Read by author. Suhrkamp
5 NELLY SACHS LIEST GEDICHTE. In German. Suhrkamp
6 PAUL CELAN LIEST GEDICHTE. In German. Suhrkamp 3-518-0950702
7 GÜNTER EICH LIEST GEDICHTE. In German. Suhrkamp 3-518-09512-9
8 HERMANN KASACK LIEST GEDICHTE. In German. Suhrkamp 3-518-09514-5
9 KROLOW LIEST AUS SEINEN GEDICHTEN. Suhrkamp 3-518-09515-3

SUPER Superscope Library of the Spoken Word. Current address unknown.
1 THIS LUNATIC WORLD: RUBAIYAT. Superscope I-171 (ac)

TAPES Tapes for Readers, 5078 Fulton St. NW, Washington, DC 20016, USA

1 MAYA ANGELOU READS. Tapes for Readers (ac)

2 LITTLE LAMB: BLAKE, AND OTHERS. Readers: Allen Ginsberg and others. Tapes for Readers BB-C-851 (ac)

3 ROBERT HAYDEN COMMENTS AND READS SHORT SELECTIONS. Tapes for Readers BB-C-852 (ac)

4 JOSEPHINE JACOBSON COMMENTS AND READS. Tapes for Readers BB-C-853 (ac)

5 PABLO NERUDA DISCUSSES POETRY AND READS BRIEF EXCERPTS. Tapes for Readers BB-C-855 (ac)

6 ANNE SEXTON INTERVIEW WITH READINGS. Tapes for Readers BB-C-857 (ac)

7 ANDREI VOZNESENSKY READS IN RUSSIAN. Tapes for Readers BB-C-858 (ac)

8 THE GIFT OUTRIGHT: FROST. Reader: R. H. Winnick. Tapes for Readers BB-C-859 (ac)

9 RICHARD EBERHART READS THE GROUNDHOG. Tapes for Readers BB-C-860 (ac)

10 LAWRENCE FERLINGHETTI READS POEMS. Tapes for Readers BB-C-861 (ac)

11 DANIEL HALPERN READS I AM A DANCER AND OTHERS. Tapes for Readers BB-C-862 (ac)

12 STANLEY KUNITZ READS WAR AGAINST THE TREES AND OTHERS. Tapes for Readers BB-C-863 (ac)

13 HOWARD NEMEROV READS SEVERAL POEMS. Tapes for Readers BB-C-864 (ac)

TELEF Teldec Telefunken, Decca Schallplatten GmbH, Heussweg 25, D-2000 Hamburg 19, West Germany

1 CLAUDIUS UND HÖLDERLIN. Reader: Matthias Wiemann. Telefunken (manufacturer's number unknown)

2 EIN DICHTERPORTRAIT: HEINE. Reader: Martin Held. Telefunken LT 6620 (LP 038 474/5)

3 GALGENLIEDER: MORGENSTERN. Reader: Günther Lüders. Telefunken PLB 6223

4 BALLADEN UND GEDICHTE: GOETHE (1). Reader: Walter Franck. Telefunken TSF 13001 (pd 45rpm)

5 BALLADEN UND GEDICHTE: GOETHE (2). Reader: Walter Franck. Telefunken TSF 13005 (pd 45rpm)

6 SAG ATOME, SAGE STÄUBCHEN: GEDICHTE VON BUSCH. Reader: Eduard Marks. Telefunken TSF 13002 (pd 45rpm)

TEMPO Tempo Inc., 1900 West 47th Pl. Mission, KS 66205, USA

1 DON BLANDING READS POEMS. Tempo TT 2200

TENNY Thomas Tenny Records. Current address unknown.

1 SCOTS BORDER BALLADS. Reader: George S. Emmerson. Tenny TG 1001

THEAL Theatre Alumni Association, State University of New York. Current address unknown.

1 EXQUISITE YELLOW. Reader: Agnes Futterer. Theatre Alumni

2 FORMS OF POETRY. Reader: Agnes Futterer. Theatre Alumni

3 READINGS FROM SHAKESPEARE AND NASH. Reader: Agnes Futterer. Theatre Alumni

TROPIC Tropical Music Inc., PO Box 1494 Honolulu, Hawaii 96806, USA

1 POETAS ESPAÑOLES DE GARCIA LORCA A NUESTROS DIAS. Reader: Juan Peñalver Laserna. Tropical LD 1231

UA United Artists, EMI America Records Inc., 6920 Sunset Bl., Los Angeles, CA 90028, USA

1 GOD'S TROMBONES. Reader: Harold Scott. United Artists UAL 4039

2 POETRY OF THE BLACK MAN. Readers: Sidney Poitier and others. United Artists UAS 6693

UARIZ University of Arizona Press, 1615 East Speedway Blvd., Tucson, AZ 85719, USA

1 SPOKEN ANTHOLOGY OF AMERICAN LITERATURE. Readers: Priscilla Manspeaker and others. Univ. of Ariz. 4454 (6 pd)

UARIZM Univ. of Arizona, Div. of Media and Instructional Services, Tucson, AZ 85706, USA

1 PAUL REVERE'S RIDE: LONGFELLOW. Univ. of Ariz. Media (16mm film)

UCAL Extension Media Center, Univ. of California, Berkeley, CA 94720, USA

1 ROBERTO VARGAS, CHICANO POET. Read by author. UC Media AT 179 (ac)

2 LYNN SUKENICK READS HER POETRY. UC Media AT 183 (ac)

3 POETRY FOR AN ISLAND: GINSBERG AND MCCLURE. Read by authors. UC Media AT 176 (ac)

4 POETRY FOR AN ISLAND: SNYDER AND SAKAKI. Read by authors. UC Media AT 175 (ac)

UCALI University of California, Irvine, CA 92717, USA

1 SELECTED POEMS BY ERNEST M. ROBSON. Read by author. UC Irvine PS 3568.0318 A6 1970 (ac)

UCALM Extension Media Center, University of California, 2223 Fulton St., Berkeley, CA 94720, USA

1 IN A DARK TIME: ROETHKE. Read by author. UC Media (16mm film)

2 WHOLLY COMMUNION: GINSBERG AND OTHERS. Read by authors. UC Media (16mm film)

UCOL Univ. of Colorado, Educational Media Ctr., Boulder, CO 80309, USA

1 THE DEACON'S MASTERPIECE: HOLMES. U. of Colorado Media (16mm film)

2 POEMS OF TENNYSON AND BROWNING. U. of Colorado Media (16mm film)

3 POEMS OF WALT WHITMAN. U. of Colorado Media (16mm film)

4 POEMS OF LEWIS CARROLL. U. of Colorado Media (16mm film)

VAN Vanguard Recording Society Inc., 71 West 23rd Street, New York, NY 10010, USA

1 POEMS AND STORIES: POE. Reader: Nelson Olmsted. Vanguard VRS 9046

2 LAMENT ON THE DEATH OF A BULLFIGHTER:

LORCA. Reader: Germaine Montero. Vanguard VRS 9055 (6535E)

3 BAPTISM: A JOURNEY THROUGH OUR TIME. Reader: Joan Baez. Vanguard VSD 79275

VERVE Verve Records, c/o PolyGram Classics Inc., 137 West 55th St., New York, NY 10019, USA

1 POETRY FOR THE BEAT GENERATION: KEROUAC. Read by author. Verve MG-V-15005

2 READINGS FROM WALT WHITMAN. Verve FV 9750

3 SONGS OF INNOCENCE AND EXPERIENCE: BLAKE. Reader: Allen Ginsberg. Verve FTS 3083 (69B1/004A)

VOIX La Voix de l'Auteur. Current address unknown.

1 TOI ET MOI: GÉRALDY. Read by author. LVA 4

2 VOUS ET MOI: GÉRALDY. Read by author. LVA 16

2A PAUL GÉRALDY. Read by author. LVA 18

3 POÈMES: JACQUES PRÉVERT. Read by author. LVA 34

4 LAWRENCE DURRELL READING FROM GRECIAN ECHOES. LVA 1003/4

WAGENB Verlag Klaus Wagenbach, Bamberger Strasse 6, Postfach 1409, D-1000 Berlin 30, West Germany

1 JOHANNES BOBROWSKI LIEST GEDICHTE UND PROSA. In German. Wagenbach T75/654-655

WARNER Warner Bros. Records Inc., 3300 Warner Blvd., Burbank, CA 91510, USA

1 THE DAYS OF WILFRED OWEN. Reader: Richard Burton. Warner Bros. B 1635

WATSHD Poets' Audio Center, Watershed Foundation, PO Box 50145, Washington, DC 20004, USA

1 ANDREA WYATT AND OTHERS. Black Box 1 (ac)

2 DUDLEY RANDALL AND OTHERS. Black Box 2 (ac)

3 SONIA SANCHEZ AND ROBERT BLY. Black Box 3 (ac)

4 WILLIAM TALEN AND OTHERS. Black Box 4 (ac)

5 PAUL VIOLI AND OTHERS. Black Box 5 (ac)

6 MURIEL RUKEYSER AND JULIUS LESTER. Black Box 6 (ac)

7 AHMOS ZU-BOLTON AND OTHERS. Black Box 7 (ac)

8 THE WASHINGTON SOUND: LOVE AND DEATH IN DEMON CITY. Black Box 8 (ac)

9 JUDITH JOHNSON SHERWIN AND OTHERS. Black Box 9 (ac)

10 OTIS BROWN AND OTHERS. Black Box 11 (ac)

11 AUDRE LORDE AND OTHERS. Black Box 12 (ac)

12 THULANI NKABINDE DAVIS AND OTHERS. Black Box 13-14 (2 ac)

13 BREATHING SPACE/77. Black Box 15 (ac)

14 JOHN LOGAN AND OTHERS. Black Box 16 (ac)

15 FOR THE STOMACH: POEMS 1975: ROBERT BLY. Read by the author. Watershed C-101 (ac)

16 AN EAR TO THE EARTH: CAROLYN KIZER. Read by the author. Watershed C-103 (ac)

17 AT THE CORE: MARGE PIERCY. Read by the author. Watershed C-104 (ac)

18 JUST BEFORE THE GATES: MURIEL RUKEYSER. Read by the author. Watershed C-105 (ac)

19 PROGRESS REPORT: MAXINE KUMIN. Read by the author. Watershed C-106 (ac)

20 SELECTED POEMS: SONIA SANCHEZ. Read by the author. Watershed C-107 (ac)

21 POEMS AND SONGS: JULIUS LESTER. Read by the author. Watershed C-108 (ac)

22 THE SELF AND THE MULBERRY TREE: MARVIN BELL. Read by the author. Watershed C-109 (ac)

24 HEAR ME: PHILIP LEVINE. Read by the author. Watershed C-111 (ac)

25 SELECTED POEMS: JOSEPHINE JACOBSEN. Read by the author. Watershed C-112 (ac)

26 THE TOWN SCOLD: JUDITH JOHNSON SHERWIN. Read by the author and others. Watershed C-113 (ac)

27 HOW THE DEAD COUNT: JUDITH JOHNSON SHERWIN. Read by the author. Watershed C-114 (ac)

28 THE PLACE FOR KEEPING: LUCILLE CLIFTON. Read by the author. Watershed C-115 (ac)

29 A WHITTEMORE MISCELLANY: REED WHITTEMORE. Read by the author. Watershed C-116 (ac)

30 EXISTING LIGHT: MADELINE DeFREES. Read by the author. Watershed C-117 (ac)

32 ONLY THE DREAMER CAN CHANGE THE DREAM: JOHN LOGAN. Read by the author. Watershed C-118 (ac)

33 HIGH DARK: ANN DARR. Read by the author. Watershed C-120 (ac)

34 DADDY!: CHASEN GAVER. Read by the author. Watershed C-122 (ac)

35 SAY IT: ROLAND FLINT. Read by the author. Watershed C-123 (ac)

36 A PERFORMANCE AT HOG THEATER: RUSSELL EDSON. Watershed C-124 (ac)

37 SELF-EMPLOYED: DAVID IGNATOW. Read by the author. Watershed C-125 (ac)

38 FULL MOON, FLOOD MOON: THEODORE ENSLIN. Read by the author. Watershed C-126 (ac)

39 SCHOOL FOR DARK THOUGHTS: CHARLES SIMIC. Read by the author. Watershed C-127 (ac)

40 A SELECTION: WILLIAM BRONK. Read by the author. Watershed C-128 (ac)

41 A READING IN HAVANA: NICHOLAS GUILLEN. Read by the author. In Spanish. Watershed C-129 (ac)

42 JAZZ IN PRAISE OF THE LORD: OWEN DODSON. Read by the author. Watershed C-131 (ac)

43 RARE MEAT: KENWARD ELMSLIE. Read by the author. Watershed C-132 (ac)

44 WANDERER: CHESTER KALLMAN. Read by the author. Watershed C-133 (ac)

45 A SWORD IN A CLOUD OF LIGHT: KENNETH REXROTH. Reader: Kenneth Rexroth. Watershed C-134 (ac)

46 NOTHING BUT COLOR: AI. Read by the author. Watershed C-152 (ac)

47 TO LET IN THE LIGHT: DAISY ALDAN. Read by the author. Watershed C-147 (ac)

48 BOTH OF US TOGETHER, EACH OF US APART: YEHUDA AMICHAI. Read by the author. In English and Hebrew. Watershed C-151 (ac)

49 IF I YES: OLGA BROUMAS. Read by the author. Watershed C-148 (ac)

WATSHD (continued)

50   TERRA NOVA: JESSICA TARAHATA HAGEDORN.
     Read by the author. Watershed C-146 (ac)

51   I WANT TO TELL YOU: KATHLEEN SPIVACK.
     Read by the author. Watershed C-149 (ac)

52   ELECTION DAY: GEORGE STARBUCK. Read by
     the author. Watershed C-150 (ac)

53   THE PRINCIPLE OF FIT, 2: DAVID ANTIN. Impro-
     vised in performance by author. Water-
     shed WTC-145 (ac)

54   AN OCCASIONAL SUITE: DEIDRA BALDWIN.
     Read by the author. Watershed C-141 (ac)

55   TRAFFIC AU BOUT DU TEMPS: ANDREI CODRE-
     SCU. In English. Watershed C-138 (ac)

56   NO BELLS TO BELIEVE: RICHARD HUGO. Read
     by the author. Watershed C-130 (ac)

57   FOR SOMEBODY TO START SINGING: JUNE JOR-
     DAN. Read by the author. With music by
     Bernice Reagon. Watershed C-144 (ac)

58   INTRICATE LIVES: SHIRLEY KAUFMAN. Read by
     the author. Watershed C-140 (ac)

59   MY LITTLE SISTER AND OTHER POEMS: ABBA
     KOVNER. Read in Hebrew by the author, in
     English by Shirley Kaufman. Watershed
     C-143 (ac)

60   GETTING IN TOUCH WITH REALITY: LOU LIP-
     SITZ. Read by author. Watershed C-135 (ac)

61   BLUE STREAK: HEATHER MCHUGH. Read by
     the author. Watershed C-142 (ac)

62   TRANSFORMATIONS: DAN PAGIS. In Hebrew
     and English. Watershed C-139 (ac)

63   AN OLD NICKEL AND DIME STORE: DAVID RAY.
     Read by the author. Watershed C-136 (ac)

64   THINGS THAT I DO IN THE DARK AND OTHER
     POEMS: JUNE JORDAN. Read by the author.
     Watershed C-563 (ac)

WESTNG Westinghouse Learning Corpora-
     tion. Current address unknown.

1   W. H. AUDEN READS. West. Learning 11-8100
     (2 at)

2   LEE ANDERSON. West. Learning 11-8114 (2
     ac)

WOMAUD Women's Audio Exchange. Current
     address unknown.

1   OFFERED BY OWNER: LYN LIFSHIN. Read by
     author. Women's Audio Exch.

WORLDP World Pacific Records. Current ad-
     dress unknown.

1   POETRY AND JAZZ. Readers: John Carradine
     and others. World Pacific 878 (WP 1409)

AUTHOR INDEX

References Are to Recordings

Abbe, George. 1911. in English.
THE ANIMAL. "That March had a neck like an animal" FOLKW 8
BLUEBERRY GIRL. "The air grieved and the island" FOLKW 8
THE BOOK. "I came to the margin of yesterday" FOLKW 8
CHANGED. "I saw a man turned into money" FOLKW 8
THE EXPIATION. "Where I lectured, the platform was ankle-deep in water" FOLKW 8
A FAT MAN DIES. "I heard a woman soft with fat" FOLKW 8
THE FIRST DREAM: THE GARAGE. "I kept telephoning the repairman at the garage" FOLKW 8
FROM THE MOTIONLESS TWIG. "The wisdom I learned from the motionless twig" FOLKW 8
THE GIANTS. "There was a town without roof tops" FOLKW 8
THE HAND-CAR. "Down railroad track" FOLKW 8
HORIZON THONG. "Go back now, pause to mark that hill town" FOLKW 8
I SAW AN ARMY. "I saw an army coming against the sun" FOLKW 8
THE ICEHOUSE. "I came through sun" FOLKW 8
THE INVADERS. "The birches slash at the shadow" FOLKW 8
LAST PATCH OF SNOW. "I'm not sure why I touched it" FOLKW 8
THE LONE, IMMORTAL CAR. "Take, now, the lone, immortal car" FOLKW 8
NEW YORK CITY. "Flying in plane's rib" FOLKW 8
THIRST, AND A DOG RUNNING. "Open the pure door of that summer air" FOLKW 8
TRAFFIC QUINCE. "When you see the traffic light" FOLKW 8
UNDERGROUND. "I entered a subway at bleeding noon" FOLKW 8
THE VIOLATION. "Hard by my window, under the frost" FOLKW 8

Abrams, Robert. in English.
CIRCLES IN THE SAND. "Some day I shall die" ARGO 17

Abril, Xavier. 1903. in Spanish.
ELEGÍA A LA MUJER INVENTADA. "Una mujer o su sombra de hiedra" FOLKW 80

Abse, Dannie. 1923. in English.
THE ABANDONED, exc. "Dear God, in the end you had to go" ARGO 3
AFTER A DEPARTURE. "Intimate god of stations" ARGO 140
ALBERT. "Albert loved dogs mostly, though this was absurd" ARGO 140
DUALITY. "Twice upon a time" ARGO 140
ELEGY FOR DYLAN THOMAS. "All down the valleys they are talking" ARGO 140
EPITHALAMION. "Singing today I married my white girl" ARGO 3
THE GAME. "Follow the crowds to where the turnstiles click" ARGO 140
THE GRAND VIEW. "Mystics, in their far, erotic stance" ARGO 100
IN LLANDOUGH HOSPITAL. "To hasten night would be humane" ARGO 140
INTERVIEW WITH A SPIRIT HEALER. "Smiling, he says no man should fear the tomb" ARGO 140
LETTER TO ALEX COMFORT. "Alex, perhaps a colour of which neither of us had" ARGO 140
MISS BOOK WORLD. "We, the judges, a literary lot" ARGO 140
MYSTERIES. "At night, I do not know who I am" ARGO 140
NOT ALDESTROP. "Not Aldestrop, no—besides the name" ARGO 100
ODD. "In front of our house in Golders Green" ARGO 3
OLFACTORY PURSUITS. "Often, unobserved, I smell my own hand" ARGO 140
100 HATS. "To balance one hundred hats on my head" ARGO 140
RETURN TO CARDIFF. "Hometown; well, most admit an affection for a city" ARGO 140
SUNDAY EVENING. "Loved not for themselves, those tenors" ARGO 3
TWO SMALL STONES. "After the therapy of the grave ritual" ARGO 140
TWO VOICES. "To own nothing, but to be" ARGO 140
VICTIM OF AULIS. "A multitude of masts in the harbour" ARGO 3
Poetry* JNP 9

Abu-l-Hasan al-Husri, El Ciego. in Spanish.
EL LUTO EN AL-ANDALUS. "Si es el blanco el color" AGUIL 6

Achillini, Claudio. 1574. in Italian.
Poetry* CETRA 24

Acosta, Agustín. 1886. in Spanish.
DECIMA. "Gallarda, hermosa, triunfal" SMC 13
MI CAMISA. "Esta blanca camisa que mi madre ha zurcido" SMC 13

Adams, Leonie. 1899. in English.
ALAS, KIND ELEMENT. "Then I was sealed, and like the wintering tree" LIBC 1
BELL TOWER. "I have seen, desolate one, the voice has its tower" LIBC 1, SPOA 96
COUNTRY SUMMER. "Now the rich cherry, whose sleek wood" LIBC 25, LIBC 40, LIBC 74, SPOA 96
DEATH AND THE LADY. "Death to the lady said" LIBC 1
THE FONT IN THE FOREST. "Before remembrance we moved here, withheld" LIBC 1
GRAPES MAKING. "Noon sun beats down the leaf; the noon" LIBC 1, LIBC 25, LIBC 74, SPOA 96

* Recording not available for analysis

1

Adams, Leonie (continued)

LIGHT AT EQUINOX. "A realm is here of masquing light"   SPOA 96
LULLABY. "Hush, lullay/ Your treasures all"
                        LIBC 25, LIBC 74, SPOA 96
THE MOUNT. "No, I have tempered haste"
                                    LIBC 25, LIBC 74
THE RUNNER WITH THE LOTS. "We listen, wind from where"   LIBC 25, LIBC 74
SUNDOWN. "This is the time lean woods shall spend"   LIBC 25, SPOA 96
TIME AND SPIRIT. "Spirit going with me here"
                                                LIBC 1
TO THE SUN DIAL.   EAV 14
WORDS FOR THE RAKER OF LEAVES. "Birds are of passage now"   LIBC 1
Poetry*   LIST 15

Addamo, Giuseppe. in Italian.
SICILIA 1973.   CETRA 31

Addison, Joseph. 1672. in English.
HYMN. "The spacious firmament on high"
                        ARGO 47, CAED 203, RCA 4

Agathias. 6th c. A.D. in Greek.
ON TROY FALLEN. "O City, where are the once proud walls, the temples" English CARIL 3

Agee, James. 1909. in English.
DELINQUENT. "Neat in their niches with retroussé faces"   CAED 196
A LULLABY. "Sleep, child, lie quiet, let be"
                                            CAED 196
RAPID TRANSIT.   CAED 196
SONNET. "Now on the world and on my life as well"   CAED 196
THEME WITH VARIATIONS. "Night stands up the east"   CAED 196

Agnello, Giuseppe. in Italian.
SERE D'INVERNO.   CETRA 31

Aguirre, Guillermo. in Spanish.
EL BRINDIS DEL BOHEMIO. "En torno de una mesa"   SMC 1

Agustini, Delmira. 1886. in Spanish.
DESDE LEJOS. "En el silencio siento pasar hora tras hora"   HOLT 1
LO INEFABLE. "Yo muero extrañamente . . . No me mata la vida"   FIDIAS 3, FOLKW 80

Ai (Florence Anthony). 1947. in English.
FATHER AND SON. "The Man: The priest and the old woman"   WATSHD 9
HE KEPT ON BURNING. "In the cafe, the chandelier hangs from the ceiling"   WATSHD 9
JERICHO. "The question mark in my belly kicks me"   WATSHD 9
THE KID. "My sister rubs the doll's face in mud"
                                            WATSHD 9
LESSON LESSON. "I draw a circle on a paper bag"
                                            WATSHD 9
THE RAVINE. "I wake, sweating, reach for your rosary and drop it"   WATSHD 9
Poetry*   WATSHD 46

Aiken, Conrad Potter. 1889. in English.
BLUES FOR RUBY MATRIX. "Where's Ruby, where has she gone this evening?"   CAED 31
THE CICADA. "Views the phenomenal world as a congeries"   CARIL 19
THE FLUTEPLAYERS. "Excellent o excellent in morning sunlight"   CARIL 19

LANDSCAPE WEST OF EDEN, PT. 1. "It was a deck, the prow of a ship, uplifted"   CARIL 19
———, PT. 11. "And then the minstrel fellow, whom I hated"   CARIL 19
———, PT. 19. "Between the snow and summer, I heard Adam's anger"   CARIL 19
A LETTER FROM LI PO, I. "Fanfare of northwest wind, a bluejay wind"   CAED 31
———, II. "And yet not love, not only love. Not caritas"   CAED 31
———, III. "Sole pride and loneliness: it is the state"   CAED 31
MAYFLOWER. "Listen: the ancient voices hail us from the farther shore"   CARIL 19
THE ORCHARD. "Taking our time by the compass"   CARIL 19
THE POET IN GRANADA. "Chickweed, gorse, pink cistus; and the white cistus with furry leaves"
                                            CARIL 19
PRELUDES FOR MEMNON, I. "Winter for a moment takes the mind; the snow"   SPOA 93
———, III. "Sleep and between the closed eyelids of sleep"   LIBC 23, LIBC 69
———, XIV. "You went to the verge, you say, and come back safely?" LIBC 23, LIBC 69
———, XIX. "Watch long enough, and you will see the leaf"   LIBC 23, LIBC 69
———, XXIX. "What shall we do —what ʰhall we think—what shall we say"   LIBC 23, LIBC 69
———, LVI. "Rimbaud and Verlaine, precious pair of poets"   LIBC 36
———, LXIII. "Thus systole addressed diastole"
                                    LIBC 23, LIBC 69
PROEM TO THE KID. "Where now he roves, by wood or swamp whatever"   CARIL 19
THE ROOM. "Through that window—all else being extinct"   LIBC 36
SEA HOLLY. "Begotten by the meeting of rock with rock"   SPOA 93
TETELESTAI. "How shall we praise the magnificence of the dead"   CAED 183
THE THINGS. "The house in Broad Street, red brick with nine rooms"   CARIL 19
TIME IN THE ROCK, 22. "If man, that angel of bright consciousness"   CAED 31, SPOA 93
———, 25. "The picture world, that falls apart, and leaves"   CAED 31
Poetry*   LIST 13

Akhmatova, Anna. 1888. in Russian.
PUSHKIN. "Kto znaet, chto takoe slava"
                                            CAED 193
VECHEROM. "Zvenela musyka v sadu"
                                            CAED 193

Alakoye, Adesanya. in English.
"After that"   WATSHD 8
BILLIE'S BLUES.   WATSHD 4
BLUES POEMS.   WATSHD 4
ESHU. "You beat a rock till it bleeds"
                                            WATSHD 8
I WILL GLORIFY THIS WOMAN.   WATSHD 4
UPSOUTH. "I came upsouth"   WATSHD 8

Alberti, Rafael. 1902. in Spanish.
A 'NIEBLA', MI PERRO. " 'Niebla', tu no comprendes: lo cantan tus orejas"   AGUIL 10
EL ÁNGEL BUENO. "Vino el que yo quería"
                                            DOVER 2

---

* Recording not available for analysis

LOS ÁNGELES BÉLICOS. "Viento contra viento"
APPL 5
LOS ÁNGELES DE LA PRISA. "Espíritus de seis alas"
APPL 5
LOS ÁNGELES MUERTOS. "Buscad, buscadlos"
SPOA 59.
LOS DOS ÁNGELES. "Ángel de luz, ardiendo"
AGUIL 10
EL ESPEJO Y EL TIRANO. "En verdad: este espejo"
APPL 5
MARINERO EN TIERRA, exc.   TROPIC 1
MUJER. "Mujer! En un silencio que me sabrá"
SMC 1
EL NIÑO DE LA PALMA. "¡Qué revuelo! / Aire que
al toro"   AGUIL 6
LOS OJOS DE PICASSO. "Siempre es todo ojos"
APPL 5
LA PUTANA ANDALUSA. "Señora, la conosco,
donde vive"   APPL 5
RETORNOS DEL AMOR EN LOS BALCONES. "A llega-
do ese tiempo en que los años"   APPL 5
SALAS DE LOS INFANTES. "Arriba, trabajadores"
HOLT 1
"Si mi voz muriera en tierra"   AGUIL 10,
HOLT 1
Alcaeus. 7th c. B.C. in Greek.
"Asynnetémi tón anemón stasin," exc.
FOLKW 104; Greek and English JNP 95
Alcamo, Ciullo d'. 12th c. A.D. in Italian.
CONTRASTO, exc. "Rosa fresca aulentissima"
FOLKW 10
Poetry*   CETRA 19
Alcántara, Manuel. 1928. in Spanish.
CARNET DE IDENTIDAD. "Nadie avisó. Más tarde
o más temprano"   AGUIL 3
NOTICIAS DE ULTIMA HORA. "Ha sido detenido en
París un turista"   AGUIL 3
EL POETA CANTA POR SOLEARES LA RESURRECCIÓN
DE LA CARNE. "Cuando termine la muerte"
AGUIL 3
SONETO PARA PEDIR POR LOS AMIGOS MUERTOS.
"Yo los llevaba dentro. Los tenía" AGUIL 3
Alcázar, Baltasar del. 1530. in Spanish.
TRES COSAS. "Tres cosas me tienen preso"
SPOA 37
Alcman. 7th c. B.C. in Greek.
PARTHENIA, 26. "Ou ē eti, parthenikai meli-
garyēs ierophōnoi"   FOLKW 104
———, 36. "Eudoisin d'oreōn koryphai to kai
pharagges"   FOLKW 104, JNP 95
Alcover i Maspons, Joan. 1854. in Catalan.
RECORD DE SOLLER. "Amic, teixiu aquesta visio
de la infantesa"   AGUIL 14
Aldan, Daisy. 1923. in English.
Poetry*   WATSHD 47
Aldis, Dorothy. 1896. in English.
EVERYBODY SAYS. "Everybody says I look just
like my mother"   HARB 1
THE GRASSHOPPERS. "High up over the top of
feathery grasses"   BOWMAR 1
WHAT AM I? "They chose me from my brothers"
HARB 1
Aleardi, Count Aleardo. 1812. in Italian.
Poetry*   CETRA 27
Alegría, José S. in Spanish.
VERDAD HISTORICA.   INSTPR 1

Aleixandre, Vicente. 1898. in Spanish
CIUDAD DEL PARAISO. "Siempre te ven mis ojos,
ciudad de mis días marinos"   HOLT 1
EN LA PLAZA. "Hermoso es, hermosamente hu-
milde y confiante"   AGUIL 3
MANO ENTREGADA. "Pero otro día toco tu mano.
Mano tibia"   SPOA 59
EL NIÑO MURIO. "¿Quién sufre? Pasé de prisa"
AGUIL 3
SE QUERIAN. "Se querían/ sufrían por la luz"
TROPIC 1
EL ULTIMO AMOR. "Amor mío, amor mío"
AGUIL 4
EL VISITANTE. "Aquí también entré, en esta
casa"   DOVER 2
Alexander, Floyce. 1938. in English.
LOS ANGELES.   CAED 155
Alexander, Margaret Walker. See **Walker, Marga-
ret.**
Alexander, William. See **Stirling, Earl of.**
Alfieri, Count Vittorio. 1749. in Italian.
Poetry*   CETRA 25
Alfred, William. 1922. in English.
Poetry*   HARVOC 18
Allen, Marie Louise. in English.
MY ZIPPER SUIT. "My zipper suit is bunny
brown"   HARB 1
Allen, Samuel. 1917. in English.
A MOMENT PLEASE. "When I gaze at the sun"
ARGO 17
TO SATCH. (AMERICAN GOTHIC) "Sometimes I feel
like I will never stop"   ARGO 17
Poetry*   PRENT 1
Allingham, William. 1824. in English.
THE FAIRIES, exc. "Up the airy mountain"
CMS 3
A MEMORY. "Four ducks on a pond"   CMS 2,
JNP 90
A SWING SONG. "Swing, swing, sing, sing"
CAED 109, CMS 3, HARB 2
Allmers, Hermann. 1821. in German.
Poetry*   CHRIST 4
Alonso, Dámaso. 1898. in Spanish.
CALLE DE ARRABAL. "Se me quedó en lo hondo"
SPOA 59
CIENCIA DE AMOR. "No sé. Sólo me llega en el
venero"   AGUIL 4, HOLT 1
LOS CONTADORES DE ESTRELLAS. "Yo estoy can-
sando"   DOVER 2
HOMBRE Y DIOS. "Hombre es amor. Hombre es
un haz, un centro"   AGUIL 5
LA INJUSTICIA. "¿De qué sima te yergues, som-
bra negra?"   AGUIL 3
INSOMNIO. "Madrid es una ciudad de más de un
millón de cadáveres"   AGUIL 3
MONSTRUOS. "Todos los días rezo esta oración"
TROPIC 1
SEGUNDA PALINODIA: LA SANGRE. "He viajado por
la mitad del mundo"   AGUIL 3
SEGUNDO COMENTARIO. "Creación tiene un
polo: hombre se llama"   AGUIL 5
Alston, Gary. in English.
EUTHANASIA/LORTONMANIA. "Cracking chicken
bones"   WATSHD 8

* Recording not available for analysis

Alurista (Alberto Balthasar Urista). 1947. in English and Spanish.
ANTS, ANTS CRAWLING. "Anthills climb through corridors" AUDIOT 6
"Can this really be the end" AUDIOT 6
DANZA LEONINA. "Zipping through concrete telarañas" AUDIOT 6
"Death riding on a soda cracker" AUDIOT 6
"Down walled alleys marked" AUDIOT 6
HOT HUESOS. "Hot huesos/and war pending" AUDIOT 6
"I can see reality" AUDIOT 6
"Let yourself be sidetracked" AUDIOT 6
"Mis ojos hinchados/flooded with lágrimas" AUDIOT 6
"Must be the season of the witch" AUDIOT 6
"Los nopales con espinas carnes" AUDIOT 6
"Out of the alley our soul awaits us" AUDIOT 6
"Tal vez en el amanecer" AUDIOT 6
"We walk on pebbled streets" AUDIOT 6
"What's happening/Mr. Jones" AUDIOT 6
Álvarez Gato, Juan. 1433. in Spanish.
"Venida es venida/ al mundo la vida" AGUIL 5
Amichai, Yehuda. 1924. in Hebrew.
Poetry* English and Hebrew WATSHD 48
Amini, Johari. 1935. in English.
BLACK EXPRESSIONS. "The catalogue could have told you" WATSHD 2
A FOLK FABLE FOR MY PEOPLE. BLACKF 1
A HIP TALE IN THE DEATH-STYLE. "You were a God once" WATSHD 2
MONOLOG: ON THE CREATORS. "I could have been" WATSHD 2
TRANSITION. "The stomach pains" WATSHD 2
Amis, Kingsley. 1922. in English.
AUTOBIOGRAPHICAL FRAGMENT. "When I lived down in Devonshire" SPOA 67
NOCTURNE. "Under the winter street lamps near the bus stop" FOLKW 59A
A SONG OF EXPERIENCE. "A quiet start/the tavern" FOLKW 59A
Ammianus. ca. 120. in Greek.
EPITAPH OF NEARCHOS. "Rest lightly O Earth upon this wretched Nearchos" English CARIL 3
Ammonides. in Greek.
SECRET WEAPON. "Send Antipatra naked to meet the Parthian cavalry" English CARIL 3
Anacreon. ca. 550 B.C. in Greek.
EIS EROTA. "Eros pot' en ródoisin" CAED 28
"Pole threkie, ti de me loxon ommasin blepousa" Greek and English JNP 95
"Polioi me hemin ede" Greek and English JNP 95
"Sphaire deute me porphyree" Greek and English JNP 95
Andersen, Hans Christian. 1805. in Danish.
AGNETES VUGGEVISE. "Sol deroppe ganger under lide" CAED 151
THE BOGEYMAN HAS DONE IT. English CAED 151
BURY ME THERE. "Dandse, dandse Dukke min" CAED 151

DANMARK MIT FAEDRELAND. "I Danmark er jeg født" CAED 151
DET ER LIV AT REISE. "Foraars-Taagerne sig haeve" CAED 151
ET DIGT OM KONERNE. "En Kurvemager havde gjort" CAED 151
EN DIGTERS SIDSTE SANG. "Løft mig kun bort, Du staerke Død" CAED 151
FARVEL TIL ITALIEN. "Jeg saae det Land, hvis Luft har himmelsk Lyst" CAED 151
FORAARSSANG. "End ligger Jorden i Sneens Svøb" CAED 151
"Gaaer Du paa Glatiis og falder min Ven" CAED 151
HJERTETS MELODIER. "To brune Øine jeg nylig saae" CAED 151
HVAD JEG ELSKER. "Jeg elsker Havet, naar det stormer vildt" CAED 151
HYTTEN. "Hvor Bolgen høit mod Kysten slaaer" CAED 151
I CARTAGENA. II. "Se dansde med Castagnetter" CAED 151
KJØBENHAVN. "Kjøbenhavn, du livsglade By" CAED 151
KOMMER ALDRIG IGJEN. "Alt farer hem som Vinden" CAED 151
KONEN MED AEGGENE. "Der var en Kone paa Landet" CAED 151
LITTLE COTTAGE. "I hytten hos min Moder" CAED 151
LIV VEL, JENNY LIND. CAED 151
THE MERRY NIGHT OF HALLOWEEN. English CAED 151
OCTOBER, exc. "Storken er reist til fremmed land" CAED 151
ODENSE, exc. "Du Kjaere, gamle Fødeby" CAED 151
POESIEN. "Der er et herligt Land" CAED 151
"Skyd frem, Skovmaerke" CAED 151
Anderson, Beth. in English.
IF I WERE A POET. WATSHD 13
Anderson, Charles. in English.
"Blow, man, blow" ARGO 17
Anderson, Doug. in English.
THERE WILL BE NO REVOLUTION. "Skipping by the pretty" WATSHD 1
Anderson, Lee. in English.
NAG'S HEAD: THE PAINTED DESERT. WESTNG 2, CARIL 9
NEW YEAR'S EVE. WESTNG 2, CARIL 9
POTOSI. WESTNG 2, CARIL 9
SUSQUEHANNA. WESTNG 2, CARIL 9
Andrade, Carlos Drummond de. See **Drummond de Andrade, Carlos.**
Andrade, Mario de. 1893. in Portuguese.
COCO DO MAJOR. "O major Venâncio da Silva" FOLKW 71
TESTAMENTO. "Quando en morrer quero ficar" FOLKW 71
Andrade, Olegario Victor. 1841. in Spanish.
LA VUELTO AL HOGAR. "Todo está como era entonces" AGUIL 9
Andrea da Barberino. 1370. in Italian.
Poetry* CETRA 19
Andrews, Bruce. 1948. in English.
AGAIN, AROUND THE PHOSPORUS. "At the bend" WATSHD 2

* Recording not available for analysis

SEND THE TROOPS OVER. "In any short burst"
WATSHD 2
VOWELS, exc. WATSHD 13
WORKER'S DETROIT. "Fastening cables"
WATSHD 2

Angelou, Maya. 1928. in English.
AND STILL I RISE. TAPES 1

Angiolieri, Cecco. 1250. in Italian.
"S'i fosse foco, arderei 'l mondo" DOVER 3,
SPOA 30
Poetry* CETRA 19

Annunzio, Gabriele d'. See D'Annunzio, Gabriele.

Anonymous. See also **Bible and Pseudepigraphia; Children's Verses and Nursery Rhymes**

Anonymous—African languages
Congo
PADDLING SONG. English CAED 136
Ethiopia
TROUSERS OF WIND. English CAED 136
Gabon
"Elephant hunter, take your bow"
English FOLKW 48
"The fish does . . . HIP"
English FOLKW 48
LAMENT. "The animal runs, it passes"
English FOLKW 48
THE LITTLE BIRD. English CAED 136
Ghana
FOOLISH CHILD. English CAED 136
PRAYER FOR EVERY DAY.
English CAED 136
Liberia
NANA KRU. CAED 136
Malagasy
HALF SIGH. English CAED 136
Nigeria
O LAMB GIVE ME MY SALT.
English CAED 136
Southern Africa
ABSENT LOVER. English CAED 136
KEEP IT DARK. English CAED 136
KING OF THE ZULUS. English CAED 136
PASS OFFICE SONG. English CAED 136
SHAKA. English CAED 136
SIX TO SIX. English CAED 136
Swahili
"Hapana jiti, pumbavu, ya pita la mnazi"
SCHOL 6
"Kwa heri, bwana, kwa heri" SCHOL 6
"Masikini bibi yangu kasafiri na waarabu"
SCHOL 6
"Mkofu wangu mwembamba wa kufitia
jehazi" SCHOL 6
Yoruba
"He is firm and strong"
English FOLKW 48

Anonymous—American Indian languages
Algonquin
THE STARS. "For we are the stars, for we
sing" English FOLKW 48
Chippewa
ARROW SONG. "Its head/ is red"
English FOLKW 48
BUTTERFLY SONG. "In the coming heat"
English FOLKW 48

DEATH SONG. "Is there anyone who would
weep" English FOLKW 48
LOVE SONG. "A loon I thought it was"
English FOLKW 48
Eskimo
"The gull, it is said" English FOLKW 48
Fox
LAMENTATION. "It is he, it is he"
English FOLKW 48
Nahuatl
CHICHIMECAS. Nahuatl, Spanish, and
English AUDIOT 4
EL PINTOR. Nahuatl, Spanish, and
English AUDIOT 4
EL SABIO. Nahuatl, Spanish, and
English AUDIOT 4
THE FLIGHT OF QUETZALCOATL. "Then the
time came for Quetzalcoatl too"
English FOLKW 48
FOR TLACAHUEPAN. "The field where the
hero's" English FOLKW 48
PRINCIPIO DEL SENORIO CHICHIMECA.
Nahuatl, Spanish, and
English AUDIOT 4
Navajo
NAVAJO PRAYER. "Restore all for me in
beauty" English CAED 160
THE WAR GOD'S HORSE SONG. "I am the Tur-
quoise Woman's son"
English FOLKW 48
Papago
DEATH SONG. "In the great night my heart
will go out" English FOLKW 48
Peruvian
AYACUCHO DANCE SONG. "Wake up, wom-
an" English FOLKW 48
Uitoto
MYTH. "A phantasm, nothing else existed in
the beginning" English FOLKW 48
Winnebago
"When hare heard of death, he started for
his lodge" English FOLKW 48

Anonymous—Asian languages. See also **Anony-
mous—Sanskrit.**
BAUMBESCHNEIDUNG. German DEUTGR 5
BOOK OF CHANGES. "The Creative is heav-
en" English FOLKW 48
FLUSS IM SCHNEE. German DEUTGR 5
FREMDE. German DEUTGR 5
GWEI YWAN. "Gwei jung shan fu bu jr chou"
FOLKW 76
HAIKU. Japanese and English MUSENG 1
HEIMLICHER BRIEF. German DEUTGR 5
HIGH PERFECT WISDOM. "Ma/ ga/ he/ nja/
pa/ ra/ mi/ thah" APPL 2
HIMMEL UND ERDE. German DEUTGR 5
IN DEINEM SCHAFPELZ.
German DEUTGR 5
DIE JUNGE FRAU. German DEUTGR 5
DER MILDE SUDWIND. German DEUTGR 5
MINISTER OF WAR. English VAN 3
MINYO. "Mukashi mishi yume" SCHOL 6
O LEBENS NEIGE. German DEUTGR 5
REGEN. German DEUTGR 5
SENRYU POEMS. Japanese and
English MUSENG 2
THRONREDE DES JUNGEN KAISERS.
German DEUTGR 5

* Recording not available for analysis

Anonymous—East Asian languages (continued)

UM MITTERNACHT.   German DEUTGR 5
ZEN POEMS.   Japanese and
English MUSENG 2;
English FOLKW 111

Anonymous—Australasian languages
Australian

THE BLOWFLY. "Oh, the blowfly is whining
there"   English FOLKW 48
"The ring-neck parrots"
English FOLKW 48
"She has gone from us; never as she was
will she return"   English FOLKW 48

Maori

CREATION OF LIGHT. "From the conception
the increase"   English FOLKW 48

Anonymous—Basque

ALTABISKARCO CANTUA, exc.   FOLKW 10

Anonymous—Egyptian

LA BATAILLE DE QADECH. French HACH 5
"Behold, my name stinks"
English FOLKW 48

Anonymous—English
Old English

ABRAHAM AND ISAAC. "Thá thaes rinces se
ríca ongann"   FOLKW 54
THE BATTLE OF BRUNANBURH. "Her Aedel-
stan cyning, eorla dryhten.   CAED 87,
EAV 23, LIST 1, SINGER 6
THE BATTLE OF MALDON. " . . . brocen
wurde/ Het tha hyssa hwone"
ARGO 76, EAV 23
———. "Da gyt on orde stod Eadweard se
langa"   FOLKW 53
BEOWULF, exc. "Aefter dham wordym
wyrm yree cwom"   CAED 87, EAV 5,
EAV 11, FOLKW 53, SPOA 60;
Modern English APPL 13, ARGO 75,
SINGER 6, SCHOL 6
———. "Bīowulf máthelode—hē ofer
benne spraec"   FOLKW 53
———. "Com on wanre niht"   CAED 87
———. "Him tha gegiredan Geata leode"
CAED 87
———. "Hwaet, we Gar-Dena in gear-
dagum"   CAED 87
———. "Thaet fram ham gefraegn Hige-
laces thegn"   CAED 87
CHARM.   ARGO 76
DEOR. "Weland him be wearnum wraeces
cunnode"   EAV 23
THE DREAM OF THE ROOD. "Hwaet, ic swefna
cyst secgan wille"   ARGO 76,
CAED 87, EAV 23
THE HUSBAND'S MESSAGE. "Nu ic onsundran
the secgan wille"   FOLKW 54
RIDDLES. BELLOWS.   ARGO 76
———. BOOKWORM.   ARGO 76
———. COAT OF MAIL.   ARGO 76
———. HORN.   ARGO 76
———. JAY. "Ic thurh múth sprece mani-
gum reordum"   FOLKW 54
———. MEAD.   ARGO 76
———. MOON AND SUN. "Ic wiht zeseah

wundorlícé"   ARGO 76, FOLKW 54
———. ONION.   ARGO 76
———. OYSTER.   ARGO 76
———. REED.   ARGO 76
———. A SHIP. "Is thes middan-yeard mis-
senlícúm"   FOLKW 54
———. STORM. "Hwelc is haeleda thaes
horse"   FOLKW 54
———. SWAN. "Hraezl min swigath thanne
ic hrusan trede"   ARGO 76,
FOLKW 54
———. WINE. "Hraezl is min hasu-fag,
hyrste beorhte"   FOLKW 54
THE RUIN. "Wraettlic is thes weall-stan"
FOLKW 54
THE SEAFARER. "Maeg ic be me sylfum
sodgied wrecan" FOLKW 53, EAV 23;
Modern English HARPV 1
THE WANDERER. "Oft him an-haya are ge-
bideth" ARGO 76, CAED 87, EAV 23
A WIFE'S LAMENT.   CAED 87
WULF AND EADWACER. "Leodum is minum
swelce him man lac ziefe" FOLKW 54,
LIST 1

Middle English

"Adam lay i-bounded"   ARGO 30
CUCKOO SONG. "Sumer is icumen in"
ARGO 76, EAV 11, LIST 1, SERIF 1,
SINGER 6
HOW DEATH COMES. "Wanne mine eyhnen
misten"   LONGM 1
THE PEARL, exc. "Perle, plesaunte to
prynces paye"   CAED 91
SIR GAWAIN AND THE GREEN KNIGHT, exc.
CASSC 12C, EAV 11
——— "Ful erly bifore de day folk vpry-
sen"   CAED 91
——— "Thay bozen bi bonkkez ther bozez
ar bare"   FOLKW 53

Modern English

ABDUL A-BUL-BUL A-MIR. "The sons of the
Prophet are brave men and bold"
DECCA 11
AGAINST PLATONICK LOVE. "'Tis true, fair
Celia, that by thee I live"   ARGO 47
ALL'S WELL THAT ENDS WELL. FOLKW 68
THE ANIMAL FAIR. "I went to the animal
fair"   CREAT 1
"As I was going down the stair"   CMS 2
THE BAILIFF'S DAUGHTER OF ISLINGTON.
EAV 12
BARBARA ALLEN. "'Twas early in the month
of May"   LION 2, SPOA 117
THE BATTLE OF OTTERBOURNE.   TENNY 1
BEDBUG.   FOLKW 6
THE BLUETAIL FLY. "When I was young I
used to wait"   SCHOL 8
BONNIE GEORGE CAMPBELL. "High upon
Highlands and way upon Tay" EAV 13
BONNY BARBARA ALLEN. "It was in about the
Martinmas time" FOLKW 61, LIST 1,
SINGER 6
THE BROWN GIRL. "I am as brown as brown
can be"   SPOA 35
"By-low, my babe"   IMP 1

---

* Recording not available for analysis

"Can she excuse my wrongs?" EAV 12

CASEY JONES. "Come, all you rounders, if you want to hear" CAED 195, COLUMB 6, SCHOL 8

CAUTIOUS CROW. "A cautious crow clings to a bare bough" HARB 4

THE CHERRY TREE CAROL. "Joseph was an old man" EAV 12, FOLKW 69, LION 1, LIST 1, THEAL 1

CHEVY CHASE. "Lord Percy of Northumberland" FOLKW 61

CHRIST CALLS MAN HOME. ARGO 30

CLERK SAUNDERS. "Clarke Saunders and may Margret" CAED 64, RCA 1, TENNY 1

CLEVER TOM CLINCH. EAV 12

THE CORPUS CHRISTI CAROL. "Lully, lulley, lully, lulley" LONGM 1

"Dear if you change I'll never choose again" SPOA 50

DEBATE OF THE BODY AND THE SOUL. HARVOC 1

DEFORMED PRIEST'S EPITAPH. "Beneath this yew the shadow of a shade" ARGO 82

THE DEMON LOVER. "O where hae ye been, my long, long love" LONGM 1

DID YOU FEED MY COW. FOLKW 6

"Do not, oh, do not prize thy beauty" ARGO 31

THE DOUGLAS TRAGEDY. HOUGHT 1

EDWARD, EDWARD. "Quhy dois your brand sae drop wi' bluid" CAED 64, TENNY 1

THE ELEPHANT AND THE FLEA. "Way down south where bananas grow" CREAT 1

EPITAPH: DOR. "Beneath this place in paper case a pretty dormouse lies" ARGO 82

FAIR ANNIE. TENNY 1

FAIR MARGARET AND SWEET WILLIAM. EAV 12

THE FARMER'S CURST WIFE. "There was an old farmer in Sussex did dwell" FOLKW 61

"Fine knacks for Ladies, cheap, choice, brave and new" LONGM 1

"The first Nowell" LION 1

"Flora gave me fairest flowers" COLUMB 10

FORTUNE, MY FOE. EAV 12

"Gaze not on swans, in whose soft breast" ARGO 47

GEORDIE. EAV 12

GET UP AND BAR THE DOOR. "It fell about the Martinmas time" CAED 64, CMS 2, EAV 13, FOLKW 61, HOUGHT 4, IMP 1

"God rest you merry, gentlemen" LION 1

THE GOLDEN VANITY. HOUGHT 2

GREENSLEEVES. "Alas, my love, you do me wrong" EAV 12

"The groves of Blarney, they are so charming" FOLKW 27

THE GUEST. "Yet if his majesty, our Sovereign Lord" ARGO 30, LONGM 1

"I cannot eat but little meat" ARGO 30

I FELL INTO A BOX OF EGGS. CAED 109

I KNOW MY LOVE. "I know my love by his way of walking" SPOA 7

"I know where I'm going" ARGO 88A, CAED 112

I MUST GO WALK THE WOOD WALKING ALONE. ARGO 30

"I saw my lady weep" ARGO 31, COLUMB 10

"I sing of a maiden" ARGO 30, ARGO 82, COLUMB 9, FOLKW 69, SPOA 41

I WANT TO BE MARRIED AND CANNOT TELL HOW. "To the field I carried my milking pail" SPOA 7

"I will give my love an apple" CAED 112

"I'm a 'round-town gent" FOLKW 6

"In darkness let me dwell" COLUMB 10

JOHN HENRY. "When John Henry was nothin' but a baby" CAED 195, EAV 20, EAV 21

KING JOHN AND THE ABBOT OF CANTERBURY. "An ancient story I will tell you anon" RCA 1

KINMONT WILLIE. TENNY 1

LADY ISABEL AND THE ELF-KNIGHT. "Fair Lady Isabel sits in her bower sewing" FOLKW 61

THE LAILY WORM AND THE MACHREL OF THE SEA. "I was but seven year auld" LONGM 1

THE LAMENT OF THE BORDER WIDOW. "My love he built me a bonny bower" CAED 64

"Lavender's blue, dilly dilly [var. diddle, diddle]" CAED 58, CAED 109

"Let's away with study" LEARNC 2

LIMERICKS HARC 4

———. "A diner while dining at Crewe" HARB 3

———. "There once was a boy of Bagdad" HARB 3

LITTLE MUSGRAVE AND LADY BARNARD. COLUMB 11

"Load of hay, load of hay" CAED 85

LONDON SAD LONDON. "What wants thee, that thou art in this sad taking?" ARGO 47

LONDON'S WELCOME. ARGO 77

LORD RANDAL. "O where ha you been, Lord Randal, my son" BRITAM 1, FOLKW 61, HARC 4, HOUGHT 4

LORD RONALD. EAV 12

"Love me little, love me long" DECCA 12, SPOA 50

"A lovely church, a home for God" FOLKW 52

A LYKE-WAKE DIRGE. "This ae nighte, this ae nighte" BRITAM 1, LONGM 1

THE MAGICIAN AND THE BARON'S DAUGHTER. ARGO 30

THE MAIDEN LAY IN THE WILDS. "Maiden in the mor lay" LONGM 1

MARY COMPLAINS TO OTHER MOTHERS. ARGO 30

MOY CASTLE. "There are seven men in Moy Castle" CMS 4

* Recording not available for analysis

Anonymous—English (continued)

"My grief on the sea"   FOLKW 52
"My love in her attire"   ARGO 31,
                                  SPOA 83
MY LOVE IS LIKE THE SUN. "The winter is past
  and the summer comes at last"
                                  SPOA 6
"Never trouble trouble"   CAED 85
A NEW YEAR CAROL. "Here we bring new
  water from the well so clear"
                                  LONGM 1
THE NIGHTINGALE.   LIST 1
O DEATH. "O Death, rock me to sleep"
                                  SPOA 83
THE OLD BATTALION.   ARGO 89
OLD BLUE. "I had a dog and his name was
  Blue"   SCHOL 8
AN OLD WOMAN.   CAED 109
OMAR REPENTANT.   REX 1
ON THE TOMBS IN WESTMINSTER ABBEY. "Mor-
  talim, behold and fear"   ARGO 31
ONE AND HIS MISTRESS A-DYING. "Shall we
  die, both thou and I"   ARGO 47
OUR GOODMAN. "Hame came our good-
  man"   FOLKW 61
PHILLADA FLOUTS ME. "O what a plague is
  Love"   POLYGL 2, SPOA 12
"Pleasure it is"   ARGO 30
RABBITS. "The rabbit has a charming face"
                                  CAPITOL 1
A RIDDLE.   SINGER 6
RIDDLES WISELY EXPOUNDED.   EAV 13
THE RIDDLING KNIGHT.   EAV 12
ROBIN GOODFELLOW, PT. 2. "And can the
  physician make sick men well?"
                          POLYGL 2, SPOA 12
ROBIN HOOD'S GOLDEN PRIZE. "I have heard
  talk of bold Robin Hood"   EAV 12,
                                  FOLKW 61
SAINT STEPHEN AND HEROD. "Saint Stephen
  was clerk in King Herod's hall"
                                  FOLKW 61
THE SCHOLAR AND THE CAT. "Each of us pur-
  sues his trade"   FOLKW 52
THE SCHOLAR COMPLAINS.   ARGO 30
SIR PATRICK SPENS. "The king sits in Dum-
  ferling Toune" BRITAM 1, CAED 64,
  COLUMB 9, EAV 13, PROTHM 11,
                                  TENNY 1
A SONG IN HIS LADY'S ABSENCE.   ARGO 30
THE STREETS OF LAREDO. "As I walked out in
  the streets of Laredo"   HOUGHT 2
"Sweet honey-sucking bees"
                                  COLUMB 10
"Sweet Kate of late"   COLUMB 10
SWEET WILLIAM'S GHOST. "There came a
  ghost to Margret's door"   FOLKW 61
TAKING OFF. "The airplane taxies down the
  field"   HARB 1
"Tan ta ra cries Mars"   COLUMB 10
"There is a lady sweet and kind"
                          POLYGL 2, SPOA 12
"There was once a king of York"
                                  CAED 111
THOMAS RYMER. "True Thomas lay o'er yon
  grassy bank"   CAED 64, EAV 13,
                          EAV 22, TENNY 1

THE THREE RAVENS. "There were three ravens sat on a tree" EAV 12, FOLKW 61
TOM O'BEDLAM'S SONG. "From the hag and
  hungry goblin"   ARGO 31
THE TWA CORBIES. "As I was walking all
  alane"   CAED 64, EAV 13, TENNY 1
THE TWA SISTERS. "There were two sisters
  sat in a bower"   COLUMB 9
THE UNQUIET GRAVE. "The wind doth blow
  to-day, my love" EAV 12, FOLKW 60,
                                  FOLKW 61
WALK WITH ME MY BELOVED. "I would I were
  on yonder hill"   SPOA 7
THE WEARIN' OF THE GREEN. "Oh, Paddy
  dear, and did ye hear the news that's
  goin' round?"   CAED 95, THEAL 1
"Weep you no more, sad fountains"
          ARGO 31, SPOA 35, SPOA 83
THE WELLS OF JESUS' WOUNDS.   ARGO 30
"Westron winde, when will thou blow"
                                  LONGM 1
WHAT IF A DAY.   EAV 12
WHEN THE KING ENJOYS HIS OWN AGAIN.
                                  EAV 12
"Who shall have my faire lady?"
                                  CAED 17
THE WIFE OF USHER'S WELL. "There lived a
  wife at Usher's Well"   CAED 64,
  EAV 13, FOLKW 61, TENNY 1
THE WOMAN OF THREE COWS. "O woman of
  three cows, agra"   SPOA 7
"Women are best when they are pressed"
                                  SPOA 50
WONDERS. "Thule, the period of cosmogra-
  phy"   ARGO 31, LONGM 1
THE WRAGGLE-TAGGLE GYPSIES. "There were
  three gypsies a-come to the door"
                                  CAED 110
YANKEE DOODLE. "Fath'r and I went down
  to camp"   CAED 98
YOUNG BEICHAN.   EAV 13
YOUNG HUNTING.   EAV 12

Anonymous—French

BALLADE DE MARGUERITE. "I am weary of lying
  within the chase"   English EAV 22
LA CHANSON DE ROLAND, exc. "Carles li reis, nos-
  tre emperere magnes"   FOLKW 10,
  FOLKW 12, HACH 3; English CAED 197,
                                  LEARNC 2
LA COMPLAINTE DU ROI RENAUD. "Le Roi Renaud
  de gai"   CBS 1
LE DIT DES PEINTRES. "Bonnes gens, je puis tes-
  moignier"   FOLKW 84
GATHER YE ROSEBUDS, exc. "Woman should gath-
  er roses ere"   English LEARNC 2
THE GOBLIN. "A Goblin lives in our house"
                          English CREAT 1
"Je fuyais l'amour"   HACH 9
ROCHERS INACCESSIBLES   HACH 10

Anonymous—German

"Abends wenn ich schlafen geh" ATHENA 6
"Ach wär mein Lieb ein Brünnlein kalt"
                                  ATHENA 4
AN EINEN BOTEN. "Wenn du zu mei'm Schatzel
  kommst"   SPOA 5

BAMBURGER HANDSCHRIFT. "Brumans est mors" CHRIST 17

BASLER HANDSCHRIFT. "Wêne Herzen, wênent Ougen" CHRIST 18

"Bleib noch mein lieb Gespiel" ATHENA 4

"Es war einmal ein Zimmergesell" ATHENA 4

HANDSCHRIFT. "Ich weiss mir einen meien" CHRIST 18

HARFENKLANG UND SAITENSPIEL. DEUTGR 45

"Hätt ich sieben Wünsch" DEUTGR 45

DAS HILDEBRANDSLIED. CHRIST 13

"Ich schlaf, ich wach" ATHENA 4

IN MEINEM BETT. ATHENA 4

DAS LIED VOM HEILIGEN GEORG. CHRIST 13

"Liegst du schon in sanfter Ruh" ATHENA 4

MEIN. "Du bist mein, ich bin dein" SPOA 5

"Morgen muss ich fort von hier" ATHENA 4

SCHLESISCHE MUNDART, exc. CHRIST 23

EIN SEEKADETT AN SEINE STIEFMUTTER, 1915. ATHENA 5

STRASSBURGER HANDSCHRIFT. "Nü denchent, wib unde man" CHRIST 17

VATER UNSER: HELIAND. CHRIST 13

VON DER ZERSTÖRUNG JERUSALEMS UND DEM JÜNGSTEN GERICHT: HELIAND. CHRIST 13

"Wenn ich ein Vöglein wär" ATHENA 4

DAS WESSOBRUNNER GEBET. CHRIST 13

"Will ich in mein Gärtlein gehn" ATHENA 11

"Willst du dein Herz mir schenken" ATHENA 4, DEUTGR 45

ZWEITER MERSEBURGER ZAUBERSPRUCH. CHRIST 13

Anonymous—Greek

EPITAPH OF A NICENE ACTOR. "Philistion of Nikaia lies here, whose laughter" English CARIL 3

EPITAPH OF A SAILOR. English CARIL 3

EPITAPH OF A YOUNG MAN. "Hail me Diogenes underground, O Stranger, and pass by" English CARIL 3

EPITAPH OF DIONYSIOS OF TARSOS. "At sixty I, Dionysios of Tarsos, lie here" English CARIL 3

EPITAPH OF SEIKILOS. "Hoson zes phainou, meden holos sy lypu" Greek and English JNP 95

Anonymous—Japanese. See Anonymous—Asian languages

Anonymous—Sanskrit

BHAGAVAD GITA, exc. English CAED 116

_____. "Arjuna uvàca: sthitaprajñasya kā bhāsā samādhisthasya keśava" FOLKW 75

CHHANDOGYA UPANISHAD, exc. "In the beginning" English FOLKW 48

RAMAYANA. YUDHAKANDA. "Evam bahu vidhām cintām cintayitvā mahā matihi" FOLKW 75

RIGVEDA. TO THE GOD OF FIRE AS A HORSE. English FOLKW 48

Anonymous—Spanish

A BASILIO. MIAMI 1

"Á casa va el caballero" SMC 3

A CRISTO CRUCIFICADO. "No me mueve, mi Dios" HOLT 1

A MI CIUDAD NATIVA. MIAMI 1

A SATÁN. MIAMI 1

"Al alba venid, buen amigo" AGUIL 4

LA AMIGA DE BERNAL FRANCES. "Sola me estoy en mi cama" AGUIL 7

AMOR MAS PODEROSO QUE LA MUERTE. "Conde Niño por amores" AGUIL 4

BALLADS OF BERNALDO DEL CARPIO. FOLKW 10

CAMPESINA. MIAMI 1

CANCION DE UNA GENTIL DAMA Y UN RUSTICO PASTOR. "Pastor, que estas en el campo" AGUIL 17

EL CANTAR DE MÍO CID, exc. CMS 5, FOLKW 10

_____."El campeador adeliñó a su posada" DOVER 2

_____."Mio Cid movió de Bivar" AGUIL 6

EL CONDE ARNALDOS. "Quien hubiese tal ventura" AGUIL 7, CMS 5, DOVER 2, GMS 15, HOLT 1, SPOA 37

DO NOT LOOK AT ME. Spanish and English CMS 5

EL ENAMORADO Y LA MUERTE. "Un sueño soñaba anoche" HOLT 1

LOS INFANTES DE LARA. "Muy grand era el lamentar" GMS 15

LA JURA EN SANTA GADEA. "En Santa Gadea de Burgos" AGUIL 7, SMC 3

LA MISA DE AMOR. "Mañanita de San Juan" AGUIL 4, HOLT 1, SMC 3

"Los mozos de Monleón" AGUIL 6

MUCHACHAS DE PROVINCIA. MIAMI 1

MUERTE DE DURANDARTE. "Oh, Belerma! Oh, Belerma!" AGUIL 7

EL PASTOR DESESPERADO. "Por aquel liron arriba" AGUIL 17

LOS PEREGRINITOS. "Hacía Roma caminan dos peregrinos" · SMC 3

ROMANCE ANTIGUO VERDADERO DE ALORA, LA BIEN CERCADA. "Alora, la bien cercada" AGUIL 17

ROMANCE DE ABENÁMAR Y EL REY DON JUAN. "Abenámar, Abenámar" AGUIL 17, DOVER 2

ROMANCE DE COMO MUDARRA GONZALEZ MATÓ A RUY VELAZQUEZ, TIÓ DE LOS SIETE INFANTES DE LARA. "A casa va Don Rodrigo" AGUIL 17

ROMANCE DE DON BUESO. "Lunes era, lunes" AGUIL 17

ROMANCE DE FONTE-FRIDA Y CON AMOR. "Fontefrida, fonte-frida" AGUIL 7, SPOA 37

ROMANCE DE GERINELDO Y LA INFANTA. "Gerineldo, Gerineldo" AGUIL 7

ROMANCE DE LA INFANTINA. "De Francia partió la niña" SMC 3

ROMANCE DE LA LINDA ALBA. "Ay, cuan linda que eres, Alba" AGUIL 17

ROMANCE DE LA LOBA PARDA. "Estando yo en la mi choza" AGUIL 17

ROMANCE DE LA PENITENCIA DEL REY RODRIGO. "Después que el rey don Rodrigo" AGUIL 7

ROMANCE DE UN GALAN DE ESTA VILLA. "¡Ay! Un Galan de esta villa" SMC 3

ROMANCE DE UNA FATAL OCASIÓN. "Por aquellos prados verdes" AGUIL 7, SMC 3

ROMANCE DEL PRISIONERO. "Por el mes era de Mayo" GMS 15

* Recording not available for analysis

Anonymous—Spanish (continued)

ROMANCE DEL PRISIONERO. "Que por mayo era,
por mayo"   AGUIL 7
Spanish and English CMS 5

ROMANCE DEL RETO DE DIEGO ORDÓÑEZ. "Ya
cabalga Diego Ordóñez"   AGUIL 7

ROMANCE DEL REY MORO QUE PERDIÓ ALHAMBRA.
"Paseabase el rey moro por la ciudad de
Granada"   AGUIL 6, SMC 3, SPOA 37

ROMANCE DEL VENENO DE MORIANA. "Madrugada
Don Alonso"   AGUIL 17

ROMANCE EN QUE DOÑA URRACA RECUERDA CUAN-
DO EL CID SE CRIABA CON ELLA EN SU PALACIO
DE ZAMORA. "Afuera, afuera, Rodrigo"
AGUIL 7

ROSAFLORIDA. "En Castilla está un castillo"
AGUIL 7

SE MURIÓ CASIMIRO.   MIAMI 1

SERENATA.   MIAMI 1

SIN APRENDER EL ALFABETO.   MIAMI 1

LA TRAICIÓN DEL CONDE DON JULIAN. "En Ceupta esta don Julian"   AGUIL 6

"Tres Morillas me enamoran"   CMS 5

VERSOS PARA TI.   MIAMI 1

ZULEMA. "Aquel valeroso Moro"   GMS 15

Ansen, Alan. 1922. in English.

THE DEATH OF NEARCHUS, A THRENODY IN THE
FORM OF A PASTORAL DIALOGUE. "Melampsus:
This death is timely"   FOLKW 21

Anthony, Florence. See Ai.

Antin, David. 1932. in English.

THE BLACK PLAGUE, exc. "Veins that are extensible and expansible"   BROADR 3

CODE OF FLAG BEHAVIOR, exc.   BLACKS 1

Poetry*   WATSHD 53

Antipater of Sidon. in Greek.

PRIAPOS OF THE HARBOR. "Now Spring returning
beckons the little boats" English CARIL 3

THE SIDON GIRLS! THE SIDON GIRLS! "O scaly-
backed Lykaimis"   English CARIL 3

Antoninus, Brother (William Everson). 1912. in
English.

THE AFTERGLOW OF THE ROSE. "As what goes
out"   CAED 119

"The face I know"   CAED 119

"From the rock untombed"   CAED 119

IMMORTAL STRANGENESS. "Spring. And the vanquishing"   CAED 119

MISSA DEFUNCTORUM. "The preacher's coagulated rhetoric"   SPOA 99

MISSA SANCTORUM. "The sensuality of women at
Mass: that deceptive"   SPOA 99

ORIGINAL SIN. "And the heart"   SPOA 99

OUT OF THE ASH. "Solstice of the dark, the absolute"   EVERG 1

THE RAGING OF THE ROSE. "And the rose/rages"
CAED 119

THE ROSE OF SOLITUDE. "Her heart a bruise on
the Christ-flesh suffered out of locked agonies
of rebirth"   CAED 119

THE SOUTH COAST. "Salt creek mouths unflushed
by the sea"   EVERG 1

THE WAY OF LIFE AND THE WAY OF DEATH. "Mexico: and a wind on the mesa"   CAED 119

Poetry*   BIGSUR 4

Apollinaire, Guillaume. 1880. in French.

L'ADIEU. "J'ai cueilli ce brin de bruyère"
ADES 30, ADES 38

L'ADIEU DU CAVALIER. "Ah Dieu! que la guerre
est jolie"   ADES 30

A LA SANTÉ. "Avant d'entrer dans ma cellule"
ADES 30, ADES 38, CBS 1

ALLONS PLUS VITE. "Et le soir vient et les lys
meurent"   HACH 19

ANNIE. "Sur la côte du Texas"   ADES 30

AUTOMNE. "Dans le brouillard s'en vont un paysan cagneux"   ADES 30, HACH 19

LA BLANCHE NEIGE. "Les anges les anges dans le
ciel"   ADES 54

LA BOUCLE RETROUVÉE. "Il retrouve dans sa
mémoire"   HACH 19

LA CARPE. "Dans vos viviers, dans vos étangs"
HACH 19

C'EST LOU QU'ON LA NOMMAIT. "Il est des loups de
toute sorte" ADES 30, ADES 38, ADES 54,
HACH 19

LA CHANSON DU MAL-AIMÉ. "Un soir de demi-
brume à Londres"   ADES 30, ADES 38,
HACH 14, HACH 19

CHANT DE L'HORIZON EN CHAMPAGNE. "Boyaux et
rumeur de canon"   HACH 19

LE CHAT. "Je souhaite dans ma maison"
HACH 19

LE CIEL EST ÉTOILÉ. "Le ciel est étoilé par les
obus des Boches"   HACH 19

LA CLEF. "Pour te guider ô toi que j'aime"
ADES 30

LES CLOCHES. "Mon beau tzigane mon amant"
CAED 204

LES COLCHIQUES. "Le pré est vénéneux mais jolí
en automne"   ADES 4, ADES 38, SPOA 9,
SPOA 32, DOVER 4

CORS DE CHASSE. "Notre histoire est noble et tragique"   ADES 4, ADES 38, SPOA 32

CRÉPUSCULE. "Frolée par les ombres des morts"
ADES 30

"Dans le crépuscule fané"   HACH 19

DANS LE JARDIN D'ANNA. "Certes si nous avions
vécu en l'an dix-sept cent soixante"
HACH 19

L'ÉCREVISSE. "Incertitude, ômes délices"
HACH 19

L'EMIGRANT DE LANDOR ROAD. "Le chapeau à la
main il entra du pied droit"   ADES 4,
ADES 30, ADES 38, SPOA 32

FÊTE. "Feu d'artifice en acier"   ADES 4,
ADES 38

IL ÉTAIT UNE FOIS. "Il était une fois en Bohême
un poète"   HACH 19

IL Y A. "Il y a un vaisseau qui a emporté ma
bien-aimée"   ADES 30

JE DONNE A MON ESPOIR. "Je donne a mon espoir
ces perreries"   HACH 19

LA JOLIE ROUSSE. "Me voici devant tous un
homme plein de sens"   ADES 4,
FOLKW 88, SPOA 32

LIENS. "Cordes faites de cris"   FOLKW 13

MARIE. "Vous y dansiez petite fille" ADES 30,
ADES 38, ADES 54

MARIZIBILL. "Dans la Haute-Rue à Cologne"
ADES 30

---

* Recording not available for analysis

MOURMELON-LE-GRAND. "Ma Lou je coucherai ce soir dans les tranchées" HACH 19

NUIT RHÉNANE. "Mon verre est plein d'un vin trembleur comme une flamme" HACH 19

"O ma jeunesse abandonnée" ADES 4, ADES 30, ADES 38, HACH 19, SPOA 32

LA PAON. "En faisant la roue, cet oiseau" CAED 204

LA PETITE AUTO. "Le 31 du mois d'Août 1914" ADES 30, ADES 38

LE PONT MIRABEAU. "Sous le pont Mirabeau coule la Seine" ADES 4, ADES 30, ADES 38, CBS 1, FOLKW 88, HACH 14, HACH 19, SPOA 9, SPOA 32

LA PUCE. "Puces, amie, amantes même" HACH 19

ROSE GUERRIÈRE. "L'air est plein d'un terrible alcool" HACH 19

LES SAISONS. "C'était un temps béni nous étions sur les plages" ADES 30

SALTIMBANQUES. "Dans la plaine les baladins" ADES 30, HACH 19

LE SERPENT. "Tu t'acharnes sur la beauté" CAED 204

SI JE MOURAIS LÀ-BAS. "Si je mourais là-bas sur le front de l'armée" ADES 4, ADES 30, ADES 38, HACH 14, HACH 19

TE SOUVIENS-TU MON LOU. "Te souviens-tu mon Lou de ce panier d'oranges" HACH 19

TRISTESSE D'UNE ÉTOILE. "Une belle Minerve est l'enfant de ma tête" HACH 19

VEILLE. "Mon cher André Rouveyre" ADES 30

ZONE. "A la fin tu es las de ce monde ancien" ADES 30

Poetry* ADES 50

Appleton, Peter. 1925. in English.
THE RESPONSIBILITY. "I am the man who gives the word" PROTHM 7

Aragon, Louis. 1897. in French.
UN AIR EMBAUMÉ. "Les fruits à la saveur de sable" ADES 8, ADES 36, ADES 52, SPOA 32

LES AMANTS SÉPARÉS. "Comme des sourds-muets parlant dans une gare" ADES 8, ADES 38, SPOA 32

AMOUR D'ELSA. "Jaloux des gouttes de pluie" ADES 8, ADES 36, GMS 4, SPOA 32

BALLADE DE CELUI QUI CHANTA DANS LES SUP-PLICES. "Et s'il était à refaire" ADES 55, FOLKW 89

LE CRI DU BUTOR. "Maintenant que la jeunesse s'éteint" ADES 8, ADES 36, SPOA 32

ELSA AU MIROIR. GMS 4

GLOIRE AU MAQUIS. "Ceux qui n'ont pas voulu se rendre" FOLKW 89

IL N'Y A PAS D'AMOUR HEUREUX. "Rien n'est jamais acquis à l'homme ni sa force" ADES 8, ADES 36, ADES 54

JE VOUS SALUE, MA FRANCE. "Je vous salue, ma France, arrachée aux fantômes" FOLKW 88, FOLKW 89

LES LILAS ET LES ROSES. "O mois des floraisons mois des metamorphoses" FOLKW 13, GMS 4, DOVER 4

PARIS. GMS 4

LE PAYSAN DE PARIS CHANTE. ADES 8, ADES 36, ADES 52

POÉME DE CAPE ET D'ÉPÉE. "Les chevaliers de l'ouragan s'accrochent aux volets des boutiques" ADES 8, ADES 36, ADES 52, SPOA 32

POUR UN CHANT NATIONAL. ADES 55

PRAGUE. ADES 36

RICHARD II QUARANTE. "La patrie est comme une barque" ADES 8, ADES 36, GMS 4, SPOA 32

LA ROSE ET LE RESEDA. "Celui qui croyait" ADES 55, CBS 1, GMS 4

X . . . FRANCAIS. ADES 55

LES YEUX D'ELSA. GMS 4

ZONE LIBRE. "Fading de la tristesse oubli" FOLKW 88

Arana, Felipe. in Spanish.
TIERRA AMARGA. "Encorvado día tras día, sobre la rústica azada" SMC 9

Arboleda, Julio. in Spanish.
RETRATO, exc. MIAMI 1

Archilochos. 7th c. B.C. in Greek.
"Thyme, thym' amekhanoisi kedesin kykomene" Greek and English JNP 95

Arden, J.E.M. See **Conquest, Robert.**

Arden, John. 1930. in English.
HERE I COME. "John paddles up and down" ARGO 96

JOHNNY FINN. "Johnny Finn rode out one day" SPOA 67

THE LOBSTER POT. "Who can tell how the lobster got" SPOA 67

Arderiu, Clementina. in Catalan.
NIT DE PRIMAVERA. "Aire de maig, no dignis res" AGUIL 14

Aridjis, Homero. 1940. in Spanish.
GRECIA. "Otro viento roza, otra agua lava" APPL 5

"Virgen hincada impieza a ser visible" APPL 5

Ariosto, Lodovico. 1474. in Italian.
ORLANDO FURIOSO, CANTO XXIII, exc. "Pel bosco errò tutta la notte il Conte" DOVER 3, SPOA 30

———, exc. CETRA 1, CETRA 22

Poetry* CETRA 23

Arnault, Antoine Vincent. 1766. in French.
LA FEUILLE. PATHE 1

Arnez, Nancy Levi. 1928. in English.
BIRMINGHAM. "A storm rushed in his eye" BROADV 15

A BROWN CHILD'S PRAYER. "A child stepped into the sunshine today" BROADV 15

DISCORD. "Cracked chessmen lying on" BROADV 15

KEEP PUSHING. "We are farmers" BROADV 15

LAID OFF BLUES. "Ghetto's the talk this year" BROADV 15

THE MASK. "Ease a mask from out of space" BROADV 15

NEBULOUS. "Down, down, down." BROADV 15

NEW LOVE. "What stopped the ticking of the clock?" BROADV 15

PLEA. "For my own part" BROADV 15

* Recording not available for analysis

Arnez, Nancy Levi (continued)

POVERTY BLUES. "Gonna give a baby a home"
. BROADV 15
STOOD UP. "I dressed all up for freedom"
BROADV 15
"To be black in America"   BROADV 15
WHAT DEEPER SIN. "A larger sin could not obtain"   BROADV 15
WHAT IS A NEGRO. "Blood flows and mingles"
BROADV 15
WHY DON'T YOU LOVE US? "We gave you food we did not want"   BROADV 15

Arnold, Matthew. 1822. in English.
DOVER BEACH. "The sea is calm tonight"
AUDIA 1, BRITAM 3, CAED 186,
CAED 201, CMS 12, COLUMB 11,
EAV 10, LIST 3, SPOA 79, THEAL 3,
LONGM 1.
THE FORSAKEN MERMAN. "Come, dear children, let us away"   DECCA 4, FOLKW 62
GROWING OLD. "What is it to grow old?"
ARGO 68, LONGM 1
THE LAST WORD. "Creep into thy narrow bed"
ARGO 68, CMS 14
MEMORIAL VERSES. "Goethe in Weimar sleeps, and Greece"   ARGO 68
PALLADIUM. "Set where the upper streams of Simois flow"   ARGO 68
POOR MATTHIAS. "Poor Matthias! Wouldst thou have"   ARGO 68, CAED 201
REQUIESCAT. "Strew on her roses, roses"
CMS 14
RUGBY CHAPEL. "Coldly, sadly descends"
SPOA 79
THE SCHOLAR GIPSY. "Go, for they call you, shepherd, from the hill"   ARGO 68, SPOA 79
SHAKESPEARE. "Others abide our question. Thou art free"   SPOA 79
SOHRAB AND RUSTUM. "And the first grey of morning fill'd the east"   CAED 22,
SPOA 80
———, exc. "So, on the bloody sand Sohrab lay dead"   ARGO 68, LONGM 1
A SUMMER NIGHT. "In the deserted, moonblanch'd street"   SPOA 79, LION 2
TO MARGUERITE. "We were apart; yet, day by day"   ARGO 68
Poetry*   LIST 11, PRENT 3, SPOA 123

Arouet, François Marie. See **Voltaire.**

Arp, Hans. 1887. in German.
WIR ALLE SAUMEN. "Als ich dich zum letzten Male sah"   CHRIST 11
Poetry*   NESKE 2

Arras-Caeta, Juan Julio. in Spanish.
TESTAMENT.   German DEUTGR 2

Arrieta, Rafael Alberto. 1889. in Spanish.
LIED. "Eramos tres hermanas. Dijo una"
AGUIL 9

Arriví, Francisco. in Spanish.
DESDE EL SILENCIO QUE PUDIERA SER INSTPR 1

Artale, Giuseppe. 1628. in Italian.
Poetry*   CETRA 24

Arvers, Felix. 1806. in French.
MON AME A SON SECRET.   ADES 54
SONNET.   HACH 12

Ascasubi, Hilario. 1807. in Spanish.
LA INDIADA, exc. "Siempre al ponerse en camino"   AGUIL 9

Ashbery, John. 1927. in English.
A LAST WORLD. "These wonderful things were planted"   SPOA 106
SOME TREES. "These are amazing" SPOA 106
"They dream only of America"   SPOA 106
THOUGHTS OF A YOUNG GIRL. "It is such a beautiful day I had to write you a letter"
SPOA 106
Poetry*   JNP 10

Asplund, Karl. 1890. in Swedish.
BUKETTER. "Det spelar mjukt omkring mitt hjärta"   GRAM 5
JAPANSKT SKADESPEL "Scenfonden/ a japanskt"
GRAM 5
KARTAN. "En skolflicka sitter och ritar"
GRAM 5
EN LITEN ATENARE. "Det gassar av vårsol på gravgatans vårdar"   GRAM 5
MINIATYRER. "Leu är luften. Fåglar kvittra"
GRAM 5
SKOGSKÄLLA. "Min barndoms skog" GRAM 5
VÅGORNA. "Silkesblå, Tyrrkenska vågar hag jar setti glitter bära"   GRAM 5

Atwood, Margaret. 1939. in English.
THE ANIMALS IN THAT COUNTRY. "In that country the animals"   CAED 174
"At first I was given centuries"   CAED 174
AT THE TOURIST CENTER IN BOSTON. "There is my country under glass"   CAED 174
BOOK OF ANCESTORS. "Book of Ancestors: these brutal, with curled"   CAED 174
CYCLOPS. "You, going along the path"
CAED 174
DREAMS OF THE ANIMALS. "Mostly the animals dream"   CAED 174
A FOUNDLING. "He left himself on my doorstep"
CAED 174
GAME AFTER SUPPER. "This is before electricity"
CAED 174
GIRL AND HORSE, 1928. "You are younger than I am, you are"   CAED 174
THE LANDLADY. "This is the law of the landlady"
CAED 174
LATE AUGUST. "This is the plum season, the nights"   CAED 174
MIDWINTER, PRESOLSTICE. "The cold rises around"   CAED 174
"My beautiful wooden leader"   CAED 174
PROGRESSIVE INSANITIES OF A PIONEER. "He stood, a point"   LEARNC 4
ROOMING HOUSE, WINTER. "Catprints, dogprints, marks"   CAED 174
6 A.M., BOSTON, SUMMER SUBLET.   CAED 174
THE SMALL CABIN. "The house we built gradually"   CAED 174
THERE IS ONLY ONE OF EVERYTHING. "Not a tree but the tree"   CAED 174
THEY ARE HOSTILE NATIONS. "In view of the fading animals"   CAED 174
THEY EAT OUT. "In restaurants we argue"
CAED 174
"They were all inaccurate"   CAED 174
TRICKS WITH MIRRORS. "It's no coincidence"
CAED 174

* Recording not available for analysis

"We are hard on each other" CAED 174
YOU ARE HAPPY. "The water turns" CAED 174
"You fit into me" CAED 174
"You refuse to own/yourself" CAED 174
YOUNGER SISTER, GOING SWIMMING. "Beside this lake" CAED 174

Aubert, Alvin. 1930. in English.
BAPTISM. "Ancestral pearls so deep" WATSHD 4
DIZ ON T.V. "In color soft" WATSHD 4
FEELING THROUGH. "Through the open porch window" WATSHD 4
FOUR DAY CREEPER. "Who is that nude dude" WATSHD 4
HOW IT'S DONE. "Palm the head just so" WATSHD 4
NAT TURNER IN THE CLEARING. "Ashes, Lord, but warm still from the fire" WATSHD 4
ONE MORE TIME. "You should have stopped them" WATSHD 4
THE OPPOSITE OF GREEN. "The white neighbor lady" WATSHD 4
SPRING, 1937. "The full moon" WATSHD 4

Aubigné, Theodore-Agrippa d'. 1552. in French.
L'HYVER, exc. "Mes volages humeurs plus ster-iles que belles" HACH 8
JUGEMENT. PERIOD 2
"O France désolée" GMS 8
LE PRINTEMPS, exc. ADES 54
LES TRAGIQUES: VENGEANCES. PERIOD 2
"Vous qui pillez l'email de ces couleurs" ADES 54

Auden, Wystan Hugh. 1907. in English.
AFTER READING OF A CHILD'S GUIDE TO MODERN PHYSICS. "If all a top physicist knows" ARGO 16, SPOA 85, SPOA 98
THE ALIENS. "Wide though the interrupt be that divides us" WESTNG 1, ARGO 149
AS HE IS. "Wrapped in a yielding air, beside" CAED 19
"As I walked out one evening" CAED 10, CAED 19, CAED 86, HARPV 4, HARVOC 11
AUGUST 1968. "The ogre does what ogres can" WESTNG 1, ARGO 149
THE CAPITAL. "Quarter of pleasures where the rich are always waiting" CAED 19
CASINO. "Only their hands are living, to the wheel" NACTE 8
CATTIVO TEMPO. "Sirocco brings the minor devils" SPOA 85
THE CAVE OF MAKING. "For this and for all enclo-sures like it the archetype" SPOA 85, WESTNG 1
CIRCE. "Her telepathic station transmits thought-waves" WESTNG 1
THE COMMON LIFE. "A living room, the catholic area you" WESTNG 1
A CURSE. "Dark was the day when diesel" ARGO 149
DOGGEREL BY A SENIOR CITIZEN. HARPV 4
"Doom is dark and deeper than any sea-dingle" ARGO 80, ARGO 97, SPOA 85
ELEGY FOR J.F.K. "Why then? Why there?" FOLKW 21
EPISTLE TO A GODSON. "Dear Philip: thank God for boozey godfathers" ARGO 16

EULOGY. "In our beginning/was a snuffling life without" WESTNG 1
THE EXILES. "What siren zooming is sounding our coming" HARPV 4
THE FALL OF ROME. "The piers are pummeled by the waves" ARGO 149
FIRST THINGS FIRST. "Woken, I lay in the arms of my own warmth and listened" ARGO 80
FLEET VISIT. "The sailors come ashore" AUDIOT 5, SPOA 85
FORTY YEARS ON. "Except where blast-furnaces and generating stations" WESTNG 1
FRIDAY'S CHILD. "He told us we were free to choose" WESTNG 1
THE HARD QUESTION OR WHAT DO YOU THINK? "To ask the hard question is simple" ARGO 80, ARGO 97
HEARING OF HARVESTS, ROTTING IN THE VALLEY. "Hearing of harvests, rotting in the valley" RCA 1
HOMAGE TO CLIO. "Our hill has made its submis-sion" ARGO 80
HORAE CANONICAE, I. PRIME. "Simultaneously, as soundlessly" COLUMB 8
———, III. SEXT. "You need not see what" ARGO 80
———, IV. NONES. "What we know to be not" ARGO 80
———, V. VESPERS. "If the hill overlooking our city has always been known as Adam's grave" ARGO 80, SPOA 85
———, VI. COMPLINE. "Now, as desire and the things desired cease to require attention" ARGO 80
THE HOSPITAL. HARPV 4
IF I COULD TELL YOU. "Time will say nothing but I told you so" FOLKW 65, JUP 1, SPOA 85, SPOA 98
IN DUE SEASON. "Springtime, Summer and Fall: days to behold a world" ARGO 149
IN MEMORY OF W.B. YEATS. "He disappeared in the dead of winter" CAED 19, CAED 183, NACTE 8
IN PRAISE OF LIMESTONE. "If it form the one landscape that we the inconstant ones" CAED 19
ISLANDS. "Old saints on millstones float with cats" CAED 19
JOSEPH WEINHEBER (1892-1945). "Reaching my gate, a narrow lane" ARGO 16, ARGO 149
"Jumbled in the common box" CAED 19, SPOA 85, ARGO 149
"Lady, weeping at the crossroads" ARGO 80, ARGO 97
LAKES. "A lake allows an average father, walk-ing slowly" AUDIOT 5, CAED 19, CAED 86
LAW LIKE LOVE. "Law, say the gardeners, is the sun" NACTE 8
LEGEND. "Enter with him" SPOA 85
METALOGUE TO THE MAGIC FLUTE. "Relax, Mae-stro. Put your baton down" ARGO 80
MOON LANDING. "It's natural the boys should whoop it up for" HARPV 4, WESTNG 1
THE MORE LOVING ONE. "Looking up at the stars, I know quite well" ARGO 80, ARGO 97

* Recording not available for analysis

Auden, Wystan Hugh (continued)

MOUNTAINS. "I know a retired dentist who only paints mountains"   CAED 19

MUNDUS ET INFANS. "Kicking his mother until she let go of his soul"   JNP 89

MUSÉE DES BEAUX ARTS. "About suffering they were never wrong"   FOLKW 65, JUP 1, LIBC 3, LIBC 6, LIBC 38, RCA 10

NATURAL LINGUISTICS.   HARPV 4, ARGO 149

A NEW YEAR GREETING. "On this day tradition allots"   ARGO 16, WESTNG 1, ARGO 149

NIGHT MAIL. "This is the Night Mail crossing the border"   FOLKW 68

NOCTURNE. "Make this night loveable"
                                        ARGO 149

"Now the leaves are falling fast"   HARPV 4, SPOA 85

"O what is that sound which so thrills the ear" COLUMB 8, FOLKW 60, HOUGHT 4, PROTHM 14

"O where are you going? said Reader to Rider" SCHOL 8, SPOA 85, SPOA 98

ON THE CIRCUIT. "Among pelagian travelers"
                    ARGO 16, SPOA 85, ARGO 149

PLAINS. "I can imagine quite easily ending up"
                                        CAED 19

PRECIOUS FIVE. "Be patient, solemn nose"
                                        CAED 19

PROLOGUE AT SIXTY. "Dark-green upon distant heights"   ARGO 149

REFUGEE BLUES. "Say this city has ten million souls"   LIBC 3, LIBC 6

RIVER PROFILE. "Out of a bellicose fore-time, thundering"   SPOA 85, SPOA 98, WESTNG 1

SCHOOLCHILDREN. "Here are all the captivities"
                                        CAED 19

THE SEA AND THE MIRROR, exc. ALONSO TO FERDINAND. "Dear Son, when the warm multitudes cry" ARGO 80, LIBC 3, LIBC 6, SPOA 85, ARGO 149

———, exc. "At Dirty Dick's and Sloppy Joe's"
                    CAED 10, CAED 86

———, exc. MIRANDA'S SONG. "My dear one is mine as mirrors are lonely"   ARGO 149, CAED 19

———, exc. "Sing, Ariel, sing"   CAED 19

SECONDARY EPIC. "No, Virgil, no/not even the first"   WESTNG 1

"Seen when night is silent"   CAED 19

SEPTEMBER 1, 1939. "I sit in one of the dives"
                                        CAED 147

THE SHIELD OF ACHILLES. "She looked over his shoulder"   HARPV 4, JNP 89, SPOA 85, WESTNG 1

SONG OF THE DEVIL.   ARGO 149

SONG OF THE OGRES. "Little fellow, you're amusing"   ARGO 16, ARGO 149

SONNET XVII. "They are and suffer; that is all they do"   HARVOC 11

———XVIII.   HARPV 4

———XXI. "The life of man is never quite completed"   HARVOC 11

——— XXVII. "Wandering lost upon the mountains of our choice"   HARVOC 11

SPRING IN WARTIME. "O season of repetition" HARPV 4, HARVOC 11

STREAMS. "Dear water, clear water, playful in all your streams"   AUDIOT 5, CAED 19

TALKING TO MYSELF. "Spring this year in Austria started off benign"   ARGO 149

THANK YOU, FOG.   ARGO 149

THANKSGIVING FOR A HABITAT, exc.   HARPV 4

THE TRAVELLER. "Holding the distance up before his face"   HARPV 4, HARVOC 11

THE TRUEST POETRY IS THE MOST FEIGNING. "By all means sing of love, but if you do"
                                        AUDIOT 5

UNDER WHICH LYRE. "Ares at last has quit the field"   WESTNG 1

THE UNKNOWN CITIZEN. "He was found by the Bureau of Statistics to be"   LIBC 38

UNPREDICTABLE BUT PROVIDENTIAL. "Spring with its thrusting leaves"   ARGO 149

A WALK AFTER DARK. "A cloudless night like this"
                    ARGO 80, HARPV 4, SPOA 85

"When rites and melodies begin"   SPOA 85, ARGO 149

WINDS. "Deep below our violences"
                    AUDIOT 5, CAED 19

WOODS. "Sylvan meant savage in those primal woods"   AUDIOT 5, CAED 19

Poetry*   JNP 11, LIST 14, PRENT 3

Austin, Mary. 1868. in English.

GRIZZLY BEAR. "If you ever, ever, ever meet a grizzly bear"   CAED 109

Austin, William. in English.

A LULLABY.   LION 1

Averitt, Eleanor. in English.

NOVEMBER DAY.   SCHOL 7

Avison, Margaret. 1918. in English.

NOT THE SWEET CICELY OF GERARDE'S HERBAL. "Myrrh, bitter myrrh, diagonal"
                                        FOLKW 50

OUR WORKING DAY MAY BE MENACED. "From this orange-pippery"   FOLKW 50

TENNIS. "Service is joy, to see or swing"
                                        FOLKW 50

A YOUNG WOMAN TALKING TO A YOUNG MAN, THE NIGHT THEY BECOME ENGAGED, exc. "In the glassed porch"   FOLKW 50

Bachmann, Ingeborg. 1926. in German.

AN DIE SONNE. "Schöner als der beachtliche Mond"   NESKE 1

BLEIB. "Die Fahrten gehn zu Ende"
                                        NESKE 1

ERKLAR MIR LIEBE. "Dein Hut lüftet sich leis"
                                        NESKE 1

EXIL. "Ein Toter bin ich"   NESKE 1

FRÜHER MITTAG. "Still grünt die Linde"
                                        NESKE 1

DIE GESTUNDETE ZEIT. "Es kommen härtere Tage"   NESKE 1

DIE GROSSE FRACHT. "Die grosse Fracht des Sommers"   NESKE 1

DAS SPIEL IST AUS. "Mein lieber Bruder"
                                        NESKE 1

VIER SPÄTE GEDICHTE.   DEUTGR 39

"Wenn einer fort geht"   NESKE 1

---

* Recording not available for analysis

Bacmeister, Rhoda W. 1893. in English.
GALOSHES. "Susie's galoshes make splishes and sploshes"   CREAT 1, HARB 1
Bacon, Josephine Daskam. 1876. in English.
THE SLEEPY SONG. "As soon as the fire burns red and low"   CAED 164
Bagg, Robert. 1935. in English.
Poetry*   JNP 12
Bahati, Amirh. in English.
CREATION.   FOLKW 47
I AM AMIRH BAHATI.   FOLKW 47
THE MEETING.   FOLKW 47
THEN, I REMEMBERED.   FOLKW 47
WARMTH.   FOLKW 47
Bai Jyu Yi. 772 A.D. in Chinese.
CHANG HEN GE. "Han hwang chung se sz ching gwo"   FOLKW 76
GUNG TSZ. "Lei jui lwo jui meng bu cheng"   FOLKW 76
WEN CHUNG. "Wen chung ji ji ye myan myan"   FOLKW 76
WEN LYOU SHR JYOU. "Lyu yi syin pei jyou"   FOLKW 76
Baïf, Antoine de. 1532. in French.
PSAUME 121. "Sur le haut mont, ça et la regardant"   PERIOD 2
Baker, Howard. 1905. in English.
ODE TO THE SEA. "O first created and creating source"   LIBC 25, LIBC 73
Baker, Karle Wilson. 1878. in English.
DAYS. "Some days my thoughts are just cocoons"   CAED 169
Balbuena, Bernardo de. 1561. in Spanish.
LA GRANDEZA MEXICANA, , exc. "Los claros rayos de Faeronte altivo"   SPOA 39
Balde, Jakob. 1604. in German.
DEM STOIKER CHRISTOPH IMMOLA   CHRIST 22
Baldwin, Deirdra. in English.
FAMILY PORTRAIT. "She is dozing" WATSHD 9
HOMAGE . . . OLDER WOMAN. "I went East"   WATSHD 9
THE PROCESS. "I enter your room"   WATSHD 9
Poetry*   WATSHD 54
Baldwin, Michael. 1930. in English.
DEATH ON A LIVE WIRE. "Treading afield I saw afar"   ARGO 96, SPOA 68
THE HOUSEWIFE. "My love could come home early"   SPOA 67
SOCIAL STUDY. "While my mother ate her heart out"   SPOA 67
Ballagas, Emilio. 1910. in Spanish.
FUENTE COLONIAL. "No lloréis más, delfines de la fuente"   SMC 13
Balthasa, Martin. in English.
LOVELY BED. "Oh! There you lie motionless"   FOLKW 110
Banchs, Enrique. 1888. in Spanish.
BALBUCEO. "Triste está la casa nuestra"   FOLKW 80
Bandeira, Manuel. 1886. in Portuguese.
CANÇÂO DO VENTO E DA MINHA VIDA. "O vento varria as fôlhas"   FOLKW 71
ESTRELA DA MANHÂ. "En quero a estrêla da manhâ"   FOLKW 71
ULTIMA CANÇÂO DO BECO. "Beco que cantei num dístico"   FOLKW 71

Bangs, John Kendrick. 1862. in English.
THE LITTLE ELF. "I met a little elf-man once"   CAED 164
Banville, Théodore de. 1823. in French.
"Oh! Quand la mort que rien ne saurait apaiser"   ADES 54
LE SAUT DU TREMPLIN. "Clown admirable, en vérité"   GMS 9
Baraka, Imamu Amiri. 1934. in English.
BLACK FIRE, exc. "The black artist"   BROADV 4
A HISTORY POEM.   BLACKF 1
Barba Jacob, Porfirio. 1883. in Spanish.
BALADA DE LA LOCA ALEGRIA. "Mi vaso lleno; el vino del Anahuac"   SMC 8
CANCION DE LA VIDA PROFUNDA. "Hay días en que somos tan moviles"   SMC 1
PARABOLA DEL RETORNO. "Señora, buenos días; señor, muy buenos días"   SMC 8
Barbera, Renzino. in Italian.
UN GIOVANE SICILIANO.   CETRA 31
Barbieri, Vicente. 1903. in Spanish.
RETABLO DE LA FÁBULA. "La fábula escondida"   AGUIL 9
Barker, Eric Wilson. in English.
EASTER PRAYER.   PROTHM 8
Barker, George. 1913. in English.
GALWAY BAY. "With the gulls' hysteria above me"   FOLKW 65, JUP 1
THE GOLDEN CHAINS, 1. "I stare into"   ARGO 100
————, 2. "The seraph ascends"   ARGO 100
————, 3. "The golden episodes are"   ARGO 100
————, 4. "The clock is banging"   ARGO 100
————, 5. "The lyre hums and sighs"   ARGO 100
————, 6. "When the intellect walks"   ARGO 100
————, 7. "What mind has made that voyage"   ARGO 100
————, 9. "When the babe in the cradle"   ARGO 100
————, 10. "The statues do not"   ARGO 100
NEWS OF THE WORLD, I. "Cold shuttered loveless star, skulker in clouds"   CAED 147, LIBC 38
————, II. "In the first year of the last disgrace"   LIBC 38
————, III. "Let her lie naked here, my hand resting"   LIBC 38
SONNET: TO MY MOTHER. "Most near, most dear, most loved and most far"   LIBC 38
THERE IS NO SKY.   ARGO 100
THREE MEMORIAL SONNETS FOR TWO YOUNG SEAMEN. "For two young seamen lost overboard"   LIBC 38
Barker, Richard. in English.
NIGHT OF THE PRESIDENT'S FUNERAL. "Sixty thousand faces go dark on the Strip"   FOLKW 21
Barnes, Barnabe. 1569. in English.
"A blast of wind, a momentary breath"   ARGO 32
Barnes, William. 1801. in English.
LINDEN LEA.   ARGO 139

* Recording not available for analysis

Barnfield, Richard. 1574. in English.
A COMPARISON OF THE LIFE OF MAN. "Man's life is well compared to a feast" PROTHM 8, SPOA 83
THE NIGHTINGAL. "As it fell upon a day" CAED 186
TO HIS FRIEND MASTER R. L. "If music and sweet poetry agree" ARGO 32
Barrows, Marjorie. in English.
CRICKET. "And when the rain had gone away" BOWMAR 1
Baruch, Dorothy Walter. in English.
"Funny the way different cars start" HARB 2
Bashford, H. H. in English.
PARLIAMENT HILL. "Have you seen the lights of London, how they twinkle, twinkle, twinkle" CAED 164
Bass, George Houston. in English.
LIFE CYCLE IN THE DELTA. SPOA 88
Basso, Andrea del. in Italian.
Poetry* CETRA 21.
Bates, Katherine Lee. 1859. in English.
AMERICA THE BEAUTIFUL. "O beautiful for spacious skies" CAED 98, COLUMB 6
Baudelaire, Charles. 1821. in French.
A UNE PASSANTE. "La rue assourdissante autour de moi hurlait" CAED 27
L'ALBATROS. "Souvent, pour s'amuser, les hommes d'équipage" GMS 6, CAED 204.
ALCHIMIE DE LA DOULEUR. "L'un t'éclaire avec son ardeur" CAED 27
L'AMOUR DU MENSONGE. "Quand je te vois passer, ô ma chère indolente" ADES 3 ADES 37, ADES 48, CAED 27
L'AMOUR ET LE CRÂNE VIEUX CUL-DE-LAMPE. "L'amour est assis sur le crâne" CAED 27
ANYWHERE OUT OF THE WORLD. "Cette vie est un hôpital où chaque malade" HACH 20
ASSOMONS LES PAUVRES. "Pendant quinze jours je m'étais confiné dans ma chambre" HACH 20
AU LECTEUR. "La sottise, l'erreur, le péché, la lésine" CAED 27, FOLKW 86, HACH 20, POLYDR 2
LE BALCON. "Mère des souvenirs, maîtresse des maîtresses" HACH 12, HACH 20
LE BEAU NAVIRE. "Je veux te raconter, ô molle enchanteresse" ADES 3, ADES 37, SPOA 27
LA BEAUTE. "Je suis belle, ô mortels! comme un rêve de pierre" ADES 37, ADES 48, ADES 54
LES BIJOUX. "La très-chère était nue, et, connaissant mon coeur" ADES 3, ADES 37, ADES 49, SPOA 27
BRUMES ET PLUIES. "Ô fins d'automne, hivers, printemps trempés de boue" CAED 27
CAUSERIE. "Vous êtes un beau ciel d'automne clair et rose" CAED 27
LA CHAMBRE DOUBLE. "Une chambre qui ressemble à une rêverie" HACH 20
LE CHAT. GMS 6
LES CHATS. "Les amoureux fervents et les savants austères" CAED 27
LA CHEVELURE. "O Toison, moutonnant jusque sur l'encolure" ADES 3, ADES 37, ADES 49, SPOA 9, SPOA 27

LA CLOCHE FELEE. "Il est amer est doux, pendant les nuits d'hiver" ADES 32, CAED 27
CONFESSION. "Une fois, une seule, aimable et douce femme" CAED 27
CONFITEOR DE L'ARTISTE. "Que les fins de journées d'automne" HACH 20
CORRESPONDANCES. "La nature est un temple où de vivants piliers" ADES 37, ADES 48, ADES 54, FOLKW 13, FOLKW 86, HACH 20, POLYDR 2, SCHOL 6
LE COUCHER DU SOLEIL ROMANTIQUE. "Que le soleil est beau quand tout frais il se lève" CAED 27
LE CRÉPUSCULE DU MATIN. "La diane chantait dans les cours des casernes" CAED 27 FOLKW 86
LE CRÉPUSCULE DU SOIR. "Voici le soir charmant, ami du criminel" CAED 27, HACH 20
LE CYGNE. "Andromaque, je pense à vous!" CAED 27, FOLKW 86
LA DESTRUCTION. "Sans cesse à mes côtés s'agite le Démon" CAED 27
ÉLÉVATION. "Au-dessus des étangs, au-dessus des vallées" CAED 27, HACH 20, POLYDR 2
ENIVREZ-VOUS. "Il faut être toujours ivre" HACH 12, HACH 20
L'ENNEMI. "Ma jeunesse ne fut qu'un ténébreux orage" ADES 3, ADES 37, HACH 20, POLYDR 2, SPOA 109
ÉPIGRAPHE POUR UN LIVRE CONDAMNÉ. "Lecteur paisible et bucolique" CAED 27
L'ETRANGER. "Qui aimes-tu le mieux" CBS 1
LES FENÊTRES. "Celui qui regarde du dehors à travers une fenêtre" HACH 20
LA FIN DE LA JOURNÉE. "Sous une lumière blafarde" CAED 27, HACH 20
LA GÉANTE. "Du temps que la nature en sa verve puissante" ADES 3, ADES 37, SPOA 27
HARMONIE DU SOIR. "Voici venir les temps où vibrant sur sa tige" ADES 32, CAED 27, HACH 12, HACH 20, POLYDR 2
LES HIBOUX. "Sous les ifs noirs qui les abritent" CAED 27
L'HORLOGE. "Horloge! dieu sinistre, effrayant, impassible" CAED 27
HYMNE. "À la très chère, à la très belle" CAED 27, CAED 204
L'IDÉAL. "Ce ne seront jamais ces beautés de vignettes" CAED 27
INCOMPATIBILITÉ. "Tout la-haut, tout là-haut loin de la route sûre" GMS 6
L'INVITATION AU VOYAGE. "Mon enfant, ma soeur" ADES 3, ADES 37, ADES 49, FOLKW 86, HACH 12, HACH 20, POLYDR 2, SPOA 20
LE JET D'EAU. "Tes beaux yeux sont las, pauvre amante" CAED 27
LE LÉTHÉ. "Viens sur mon coeur, âme cruelle et sourde" CAED 27
MADRIGAL TRISTE. "Que m'importe que tu sois sage?" CAED 27
LE MAUVAIS VITRIER. "Il y a des natures purement contemplatives" HACH 20
MOESTA ET ERRABUNDA. "Dis-moi, ton coeur par fois s'envole-t-il, Agathe" HACH 20

* Recording not available for analysis

LA MORT DES AMANTS. "Nous aurons des lits pleins d'odeurs légères" ADES 3, ADES 37, ADES 49, CAED 27

LA MUSE MALADE. "Ma pauvre muse, hélas! qu'as-tu donc ce matin?" CAED 27

LA MUSIQUE. "La musique souvent me prend comme une mer" SPOA 36

OBSESSION. "Grand bois, vous m'effrayez comme des cathédrales" CAED 27

LE PARFUM. "Lecteur, as-tu quelque fois respiré" CAED 27

PARFUM EXOTIQUE. "Quand, les deux yeux fermés, en un soir chaud" CAED 27

PAYSAGE. "Je veux, pour composer chastement mes églogues" HACH 20

LE PORTRAIT. "La maladie et la mort font des cendres" CAED 27

RECUEILLEMENT. "Sois sage, ô ma douleur, et tiens-toi plus tranquille" ADES 32, ADES 37, ADES 48, ADES 54, CAED 27, FOLKW 86, GMS 9, HACH 12, HACH 20, POLYDR 2, SPOA 9

RENIEMENT DE SAINT PIERRE. "Qu'est-ce que Dieu fait donc de ce flot d'anathèmes" ADES 37

RÉVÉRSIBILITE. "Ange plein de gaieté, connaissez-vous l'angoisse" CAED 27, HACH 12, HACH 20, POLYDR 2

SPLEEN ET IDEAL, XXXIX. "Je te donne ces vers afin que si mon nom" CAED 27, GMS 6

———, LXXVI. "J'ai plus de souvenirs que si j'avais mille ans" CAED 27

———, LXXVII. "Je suis comme le roi d'un pays pluvieux" CAED 27, DOVER 4

———, LXXVIII. "Quand le ciel bas et lourd pèse comme un couvercle" CAED 27

LE VAMPIRE. "Toi qui, comme un coup de couteau" HACH 20, POLYDR 2

LA VIE ANTERIEURE. "J'ai longtemps habité sous de vastes portiques" CAED 27, HACH 12, HACH 20, POLYDR 2, DOVER 4.

LE VIN DE L'ASSASSIN. "Ma femme est morte, je suis libre" CBS 1

LE VIN DES AMANTS. "Aujourd'hui l'espace est splendide" HACH 20

LE VOYAGE, VIII. "Ô Mort, vieux capitaine, il est temps!" CAED 27

Poetry* SPOA 125

Baybars, Taner. in English.

GOING HOME TO MEET MYSELF. "Heads or tails? Heads, home" ARGO 96

Beasley, Joshua, Jr. in English.

THIS IS A BLACK ROOM. CAED 155

Beaubien, Michael. in English.

HOME: A REDEFINITION. "Walter Rodney going back" WATSHD 8

Becker, John. in English.

FEATHER OR FUR. "When you watch for feather or fur" HARB 3

Becquer, Gustavo Adolfo. 1836. in Spanish.

AMOR ETERNO. "Podrá nublarse el sol eternamente" AGUIL 18.

RIMAS. 1. "Yo sé un himno gigante" DOVER 2, SMC 2, AGUIL 18

———. 2. "Saeta que voladora cruza" SMC 2, AGUIL 18

———. 4. "No digáis que agotado su tesoro" SMC 2, AGUIL 18

———. 5. "Espíritu sin nombre" AGUIL 18

———. 7. "Del salón en el ángulo oscuro" SMC 2, AGUIL 18; Spanish and English CMS 5

———. 8. "Cuando miro el azul horizonte perderse" SMC 2, AGUIL 18

———. 9. "Besa al aura que gime blandamente" AGUIL 4, AGUIL 18

———. 10. "Los invisibles atomos del aire" AGUIL 4, DOVER 2, HOLT 1, SMC 2, AGUIL 18

———. 11. "Yo soy ardiente, yo soy morena" SMC 2, AGUIL 18; Spanish and English CMS 5

———. 12. "Porque son niña tus ojos/verdes" SMC 2

———. 13. "Tu pupila es azul" SMC 2

———. 14. "Te vi un punto" SMC 2, AGUIL 18

———. 16. "Si al mecer las azules campanillas" SMC 2, AGUIL 18

———. 17. "Hoy la tierra y los cielos me sonríen" SMC 2, AGUIL 18

———. 18. "Fatigada del baile, encendido el color" SMC 2, AGUIL 18

———. 19. "Cuando sobre el pecho" SMC 2

———. 20. "Sabe si alguna vez sus labios rojos/quema" SMC 2, AGUIL 18

———. 21. "¿Qué es poesía? dices mientras clavas" SCHOL 6, SMC 2, AGUIL 18; Spanish and English CMS 5

———. 22. "Cómo vive esa rosa" SMC 2, AGUIL 18

———. 23. "Por una mirada, un mundo" SMC 2, AGUIL 18

———. 24. "Dos rojas lenguas de fuego" SMC 2, AGUIL 18

———. 25. "Cuando en la noche te envuelven" SMC 2

———. 26. "Voy contra mi interés al confesarlo" AGUIL 18

———. 27. "Despierta, tiemblo al mirarte" SMC 2

———. 28. "Cuando entre la sombra" SMC 2, AGUIL 18

———. 29. "Sobre la falda tenía el libro abierto" SMC 2

———. 30. "Asomaba a sus ojos una lágrima" SMC 2, AGUIL 18

———. 31. "Nuestra pasión fué un trágico sainete" SMC 2, AGUIL 18

———. 33. "Es questión de palabras" SMC 2

———. 34. "Cruza callada, y son sus movimientos" SMC 2

———. 35. "No me admiró tu olvido" SMC 2, AGUIL 18

———. 36. "Si de nuestros agravios" SMC 2

———. 37. "Antes que tú me moriré" SMC 2, AGUIL 18

———. 38. "Los suspiros son aire" SMC 2, AGUIL 18

———. 39. "A qué me lo decís" SMC 2, AGUIL 18

———. 40. "Su mano entre mis manos" SMC 2

* Recording not available for analysis

Becquer, Gustavo Adolfo (continued)

_____. 41. "Tu eras el huracán"   SMC 2, AGUIL 18

_____. 42. "Cuando me lo contaron"   SMC 2, AGUIL 18

_____. 43. "Dejé la luz a un lado, y en el borde"   AGUIL 18

_____. 44. "Como en un libro abierto"   SMC 2, AGUIL 18

_____. 45. "En la clave del arco mal seguro"   SMC 2

_____. 46. "Me ha herido recatándose en las sombras"   AGUIL 18

_____. 47. "Yo me he asomado"   SMC 2

_____. 48. "Como se arranca el hierro"   SMC 2, AGUIL 18

_____. 49. "Alguna vez la encuentro"   SMC 2

_____. 50. "Lo que el salvaje que con torpe mano"   SMC 2, AGUIL 18

_____. 51. "De lo poco de la vida"   SMC 2

_____. 52. "Olas gigantes que os rompéis bramando"   AGUIL 4, HOLT 1, AGUIL 18

_____. 53. "Volverán las oscuras golondrinas"   AGUIL 4, SCHOL 6, SMC 2, AGUIL 18

_____. 54. "Cuando volvemos las fugaces"   SMC 2, AGUIL 18

_____. 55. "Entre el discorde estruendo"   SMC 2

_____. 56. "Hoy, como ayer, mañana como hoy"   SMC 2, AGUIL 18

_____. 59. "Yo sé cuál el objeto de tus suspiros es"   SMC 2

_____. 60. "Mi vida es un erïal"   AGUIL 18

_____. 61. "Al ver mis horas de fiebre"   SMC 2, AGUIL 18

_____. 62. "Primero es un albor trémulco"   SMC 2, AGUIL 18

_____. 65. "Llegó la noche y no encontré un asilo"   AGUIL 18

_____. 66. "De dónde vengo—el más horrible áspero"   DOVER 2, SMC 2, AGUIL 18

_____. 68. "No se lo que he soñado"   SMC 2, AGUIL 18

_____. 69. "Al brillar un relámpago"   SMC 2

_____. 72. "Las ondas tienen vaga armonía"   AGUIL 18

_____. 73. "Cerraron sus ojos que aun tenía abiertos"   SMC 2

_____. 77. "Dices que tienes corazón"   SMC 2

_____. 80. "Es un sueño la vida"   SMC 2

_____. 81. "Podra nublarse el sol eternamente"   SMC 2

_____. 85. "Para que los leas con tus ojos"   SMC 2

Beddoes, Thomas Lovell. 1803. in English.

DREAM-PEDLARY. "If there were dreams to sell"   CMS 13

LOVE-IN-IDLENESS. "He: Shall I be your first love, lady shall I be your first?"   CAED 202

THE PHANTOM-WOOER. "A ghost that loved a lady fair"   CAED 202

SONG.   CAED 202

Bede, Venerable. 673. in Old English.

DEATH SONG. "For thaem nead-foera naeniz wyrtheth"   FOLKW 54

Bédier, Joseph. 1864. in French.

PETIT CRU.   HACH 4

Beecher, John. 1904. in English.

AN AIR THAT KILLS. "Times were worse then"   FOLKW 35

ALTOGETHER SINGING. "Dream of people altogether singing"   FOLKW 35

AZTEC FIGURINE. "Ray-hee-nah! Ya voy, senora! All day on the double with her mop"   FOLKW 35

BEAUFORT TIDES. "Low tide. The scavenging gulls"   FOLKW 35

BESTRIDE THE NARROW WORLD. "We dangled them upon the edge a week"   BROADR 4

BODEGA HEAD. "On these miles of sand the cold sea beats"   FOLKW 35

CHAINY. "The field boss claimed his privilege. Her knife"   BROADR 4

THE CONVICT MINES. "You sho' God bettah dig yo' task lessen"   BROADR 4

A DOG'S LIFE AND SOME OTHERS. "Jack was the smartest dog in town, or so I thought"   FOLKW 35

ENGAGEMENT AT THE SALT FORK. "Like tumbleweeds before the wind we moved"   FOLKW 35

ENSLEY, ALABAMA: 1932. "The mills are down"   FOLKW 35

THE FACE YOU HAVE SEEN. "April has come"   FOLKW 35

FIRE BY NIGHT. "When the burnt black bodies of the homeless"   FOLKW 35

FREE WORLD NOTES. "Lowdown white sonofabitch"   BROADR 4

GOOD SAMARITAN. "The Negro walked his shoes out looking for work"   FOLKW 35

HOMAGE TO A SUBVERSIVE. "Soon, Henry David, wind will fill the land"   FOLKW 35

THE HONEY WAGON MAN. "Gre't God! Yond' come de honey wagon man!"   FOLKW 35

A HUMBLE PETITION TO THE PRESIDENT OF HARVARD. "I am, sir, so to speak, a Harvard man"   BROADR 4

IF I FORGET THEE O BIRMINGHAM. "Like Florence from your mountain"   BROADR 4

IN EGYPT LAND. "It was Alabama, 1932"   BROADR 4

"Old man John the melter"   FOLKW 35

REPORT TO THE STOCKHOLDERS. "He fell off his crane"   FOLKW 35

RUN OF THE MINE. "I went into tight places for them (he said)"   FOLKW 35

SCREENED. "Most mornings you will find him"   FOLKW 35

THE SEARCH FOR TRUTH. "Do I have freedom here"   BROADR 4

SILENT IN DARIEN. "He glimpses through dividing wire gold thighs"   BROADR 4

TO LIVE AND DIE IN DIXIE. "Our gang/laid for the kids"   BROADR 4

UNDESIRABLES. "The lifted lamp is guttering, near spent"   BROADR 4

A VETERAN'S DAY OF RECOLLECTION. "We'd liberated Naples and the Wops"   BROADR 4

VEX NOT THIS GHOST. "Deep in the moss-draped woods you come upon it"   FOLKW 35

* Recording not available for analysis

WISDOM OF THE ABBOT MACARIUS I. "Said he: I can no longer sanction"   BROADR 4

Beer, Patricia. 1924. in English.
BALLAD OF THE RED-HEADED MAN. "When I was sixteen and as smooth as a bee"   ARGO 96

Beerbohm, Max. 1872. in English.
CHARACTERS OF SHAKESPEARE. "Charles Lamb and Samuel Taylor C."   THEAL 1

Behn, Aphra. 1640. in English.
LOVE ARM'D. "Love in fantastic triumph sate"   ARGO 47

Behn, Harry. 1898. in English.
ADVENTURE. "It's not very far to the edge of town"   BOWMAR 1
HALLOWE'EN. "Tonight is the night when dead leaves fly"   HARB 3
THE KITE. "How bright on the blue"   HARB 5

Belitt, Ben. 1911. in English.
Poetry*   JNP 69

Bell, Marvin. 1937. in English.
ACCEPTANCE SPEECH. "My friends/I am amazed"   WATSHD 10
AMERICAN POETS. "Vision doesn't mean anything real"   WATSHD 22
A BIOGRAPHY. "Poetry cripples. Tempus fugit"   WATSHD 22
CONSTANT FEELINGS. "Some acts I could never, not"   WATSHD 22
THE DAILY GRIND. "How to account—if you can't"   WATSHD 22
THE DELICATE BIRD WHO IS FLYING UP OUR ASSES. "The delicate bird who flies up your asses"   WATSHD 22
GEMWOOD. "In the shoppes"   WATSHD 10
GETTING LOST IN NAZI GERMANY. "You do not move about, but try"   WATSHD 22
THE HOLE IN THE SEA. "It's there/in the hole"   WATSHD 22
HOMAGE TO THE RUNNER. "The form of this 'sport' is pain"   WATSHD 22
HONI SOIT QUI MAL Y PENSE. "Metaphysical, not pornographic"   WATSHD 22
IN THE HOME. "Nothing in thick clothes is"   WATSHD 22
"The Israeli Navy/ sailing"   WATSHD 22
OBSESSIVE. "It could be a clip, it could be a comb"   WATSHD 22
PUT BACK THE DARK. "Let's not stop in cold, in drought"   WATSHD 22
SONG: THE ORGANIC YEARS. "Love, if nothing solid rises like wood"   WATSHD 22
STUDY GUIDE FOR THE ODYSSEY. "Briefly, in ten years"   WATSHD 10
TO DOROTHY. "You are not beautiful, exactly"   WATSHD 10
TO NO ONE IN PARTICULAR. "Whether you sing or scream"   WATSHD 10
TREETOPS. "My father moves through the South hunting duck"   WATSHD 22
TRINKET. "I love watching the water"   WATSHD 10
WE HAVE KNOWN. "We have known such joy as a child knows"   WATSHD 22
WHAT LASTS. "So help me, Love, you and I"   WATSHD 22
WHAT SONGS THE SOLDIERS SANG. "Those with few images, lyrics"   WATSHD 22

WHATEVER WE WERE GOING TO TELL EACH OTHER WON'T MEAN AS MUCH. "You were brushing your hair"   WATSHD 10
YOUR SHAKESPEARE. "If I am sentenced not to talk to you"   WATSHD 22
Poetry*   MICHM 14

Bellamy, Francis. 1886. in English.
THE PLEDGE OF ALLEGIANCE. "I pledge allegiance"   CAED 98

Bellay, Joachim du. See **Du Bellay, Joachim.**

Belleau, Remi. 1528. in French.
AVRIL. "Avril, l'honneur et des bois"   PERIOD 2

Belli, Giuseppe Gioacchino. 1791. in Italian.
L'AFFARE DER FRITTO. "Ho dda ricurre? a cchi? ffamme er zervizzio"   CETRA 30
L'AMORE DE LI MORTI. "A sto paese tutti li penzieri"   CETRA 30
LA BBONA FAMIJJA. "Mi'nonna a un' or de notte che voie ttota"   CETRA 30
CHI CCERCA TROVA. "Se le vvorzuta lui: dunque su danno"   CETRA 30
CHI VA A LA NOTTE, VA A LA MORTE. "Come so lle dizgrazzie! Ecco l'istoria"   CETRA 30
LE CHIAMATA DELL'APPIGGIONANTE. "Sora sabbella.-Ée.-ssora sabbella"   CETRA 30
ER CIMITERIO DE LA MORTE. "Come tornai de la Madon-dell'-Orto"   CETRA 30
LA CRATURA IN FASSCIOLA. "Bbella cratura! E cche ccose? Un maschietto"   CETRA 30
ER CUSTITUTO. "Chi ssiete?- Un omo. - Come vi chiamate?"   CETRA 30
LE DIMANNE A TTESTA PER ARIA. "Quanno loro s'incontreno, Bbeatrisce"   CETRA 30
LE DONNE A MMESSA. "Sposa, è bbona la messa?"   CETRA 30
LA FAMIJJA POVERELLA. "Quiete, crature mie, stateve quiete"   CETRA 30
ER FIJJO D'ORO. "Che ttalento de fijjo! Uh bbenedetto"   CETRA 30
ER GIRO DE LE PIZZICARIE. "De le pizzicarie che ttutte fanno"   CETRA 30
LA GIUSTIZZIA AR POPOLO. "Disce ch'er monno e bbello perch'e vvario"   CETRA 30
L'ILLUMINAZIONE DE LA CUPPOLA. "Tutti li forestieri, oggni nazzione"   CETRA 30
L'INCONTRO DE DU' COMMARE. "Oh, addio, commare: indove vai de cqua?"   CETRA 30
ER MARITO PASCIOCCONE. "Si mme vo bbene? povero cammillo!"   CETRA 30
ER MERCATO DE PIAZZA NAVONA. "Cher mercordi a mmercato, ggente mie"   CETRA 30
ER MISERERE DE LA SITTIMANA SANTA. "Tutti l'ingresi de Piazza de Spaggna"   CETRA 30
LA MOJJE GGELOSA. "Io ve dico accusi cche nun zo ttonta"   CETRA 30
LA MORMORAZZIONE. "Avete inteso cos'ha ddeto er frate"   CETRA 30
LA MORTE DE TUTA. "Povera fijja mia! Una regazza"   CETRA 30
LI MORTI DE ROMA. "Cuell morti che ssò dde mezza tacca"   CETRA 30
LI PERICOLI DER TEMPORALE. "Santus Deo, Santusfòrtisi, che scrocchio"   CETRA 30
PIAZZA NAVONA. "Se p̀ ffregà Ppiazza Navona mia"   CETRA 30

* Recording not available for analysis

Belli, Giuseppe Gioacchino (continued)

LE SCIARLETTE DE LA COMMARE. "Dico, diteme
un pò, ssora commare"   CETRA 30
LA STAGGIONACCIA. "Zitto, don Fabbio mio, pe
ccanità!"   CETRA 30
ER TEMPO BBONO. "Una ggiornata come stammatina"   CETRA 30
LA TOLETTA DE LA PADRONA. "Li congressi de lei
co Ppetronilla"   CETRA 30
Poetry*   CETRA 27

Bello, Andrés. 1781. in Spanish.
A LA NAVE. "Qué nuevo esperanzas" FIDIAS 3
LA AGRICULTURA DE LA ZONA TORRIDA. "Salve,
fecunda zona"   SPOA 39

Belloc, Hilaire. 1870. in English.
ABOUT JOHN, WHO LOST A FORTUNE BY THROWING
STONES. "John Vavassour/De Quentin Jones"
CAED 65, SPOWRD 5, ARGO 123
ALGERNON, WHO PLAYED WITH A LOADED GUN,
AND, ON MISSING HIS SISTER, WAS REPRIMANDED
BY HIS FATHER. "Young Algernon, the Doc-
tor's son"   CAED 65, SPOWRD 5,
ARGO 123
CHARLES AUGUSTUS FORTESCUE, WHO ALWAYS DID
WHAT WAS RIGHT, AND SO ACCUMULATED AN IM-
MENSE FORTUNE. "The nicest child I ever
knew" CAED 65, SPOWRD 5, ARGO 123
COURTESY. "Of courtesy, it is much less"
SPOA 10
DUNCTON HILL.   ARGO 105
THE EARLY MORNING. "The moon on the one
hand, the dawn on the other"   HARB 3
THE EXAMPLE. "John Henderson, an unbeliev-
er"   CAED 65
FRANKLYN HYDE WHO CAROUSED IN THE DIRT AND
WAS CORRECTED BY HIS UNCLE. "His Uncle
came on Franklyn Hyde"   SPOWRD 5,
ARGO 123
THE FROG. "Be kind and tender to the frog"
HARB 5
THE GARDEN PARTY. "The rich arrived in pairs"
CAED 65
GEORGE, WHO PLAYED WITH A DANGEROUS TOY,
AND SUFFERED A CATASTROPHE OF CONSIDERA-
BLE DIMENSIONS. "When George's Grand-
mamma was told"   CAED 65, HARB 5,
SPOWRD 5, ARGO 123
GODOLPHIN HORNE, WHO WAS CURSED WITH THE
SIN OF PRIDE, AND BECAME A BOOT-BLACK.
"Godolphin Horne was nobly born"
CAED 65, SPOWRD 5, ARGO 123
HA'NACKER MILL. "Sally is gone that was so kind-
ly"   ARGO 105
HENRY KING, WHO CHEWED BITS OF STRING, AND
WAS CUT OFF IN DREADFUL AGONIES. "The chief
defect of Henry King"   CAED 65,
SPOWRD 5, ARGO 123
HEROIC POEM IN PRAISE OF WINE. "To exalt, en-
throne, establish and defend"   ARGO 105
HILDEBRAND, WHO WAS FRIGHTENED BY A PASSING
MOTOR, AND WAS BROUGHT TO REASON. "Oh,
Murder! What was that, Papa!" ARGO 123
"It freezes—all across a soundless sky"
BRITAM 1
JACK AND HIS PONY, TOM. "Jack had a little pony
Tom"   CAED 65

JIM, WHO RAN AWAY FROM HIS NURSE AND WAS
EATEN BY A LION. "There was a boy whose
name was Jim"   ARGO 105, CAED 65,
SPOWRD 5, ARGO 118, ARGO 123
LINES TO A DON. "Remote and ineffectual Don"
ARGO 105, SPOA 10
A LITTLE SERVANT MAID. "There was a Queen of
England"   RCA 10
LORD LUNDY (SECOND CANTO). "It happened to
Lord Lundy then" CAED 65, SPOWRD 5
LORD LUNDY, WHO WAS TOO FREELY MOVED TO
TEARS, AND THEREBY RUINED HIS POLITICAL CA-
REER. "Lord Lundy from his earliest years"
CAED 65, ARGO 123
MARIA, WHO MADE FACES AND A DEPLORABLE MAR-
RIAGE. "Maria loved to pull a face"
ARGO 105, CAED 65
MATILDA, WHO TOLD LIES, AND WAS BURNED TO
DEATH. "Matilda told such dreadful lies"
ARGO 105, CAED 65, FOLKW 68,
SPOWRD 5, ARGO 118, ARGO 123,
ARGO 125
THE MICROBE. "The Microbe is so very small"
ARGO 118
MY OWN COUNTRY. "I shall go without compan-
ions"   ARGO 105
NOEL. "On a winter's night long time ago"
ARGO 82, SPOA 41
ON FOOD. "Alas! What various tastes in food"
ARGO 105
OUR LORD AND OUR LADY. "They warned our
Lady for the Child"   SPOA 10
REBECCA WHO SLAMMED DOORS FOR FUN AND PER-
ISHED MISERABLY. "A trick that everyone ab-
hors"   SCHOL 7, SPOWRD 5, ARGO 123
A REPROOF OF GLUTTONY. "The Elephant will eat
of hay"   ARGO 105, SPOWRD 5,
ARGO 123
SARAH BING, WHO COULD NOT READ AND WAS
TOSSED INTO A THORNY HEDGE BY A BULL.
"Some years ago you heard me sing"
ARGO 105, CAED 65
SONNET 19. "We will not whisper, we have
found the place"   RCA 10
THE SOUTH COUNTRY. "When I am living in the
Midlands"   ARGO 105
TARANTELLA. "Do you remember an Inn/
Miranda"   ARGO 105, BRITAM 1, RCA 1,
SPOA 10
TO DIVES. "Dives, when you and I go down to
Hell"   ARGO 105, SPOA 10
TOM, AND HIS PONY, JACK. "Tom had a little pony
Jack"   CAED 65

Bembo, Pietro. 1470. in Italian.
Poetry*   CETRA 23

Ben-Chorin, Schalom. in German.
MEINER MUTTER.   ATHENA 5

Ben Safar Al-Marini. in Spanish.
EL VALLE DE ALMERÍA. "Valle de Almería"
AGUIL 6

Benavente, Jacinto. 1866. in Spanish.
EL MEETING DE LA HUMANIDAD. "En el meeting
de la Humanidad milliones de hombres gritan lo mismo"   SMC 3

Benedikt, Michael. 1935. in English.
AIR. "Air, air, you are the distantmost thing I
know"   SCHOL 5

* Recording not available for analysis

THE CITIES. "Tired of poultry, the experimental chemist"   SCHOL 5
COIFFURE. "Hair! It was hair"   SCHOL 5
THE EUROPEAN SHOE. "The European shoe is constructed of grass and reed"   SCHOL 5
THE EYE. "The narcissist's eye is black, fringed with white and covered with tempting salad leaves"   SCHOL 5
IN LOVE WITH YOU. "Would you mind revealing to me exactly what is your symbol, a tendril?"
                                         SCHOL 5
"Inside the mystery"   SCHOL 5
"Pink buds, pink buds ah look"   SCHOL 5
SOME LITANIES. "Was the arrangement made between the two couples legal?" SCHOL 5
"The wings of the nose"   SCHOL 5

Benét, Rosemary Carr. 1898. in English.
NANCY HANKS. "If Nancy Hanks/came back as a ghost"   DECCA 4, DECCA 7, DECCA 10,
                            HARB 6, HARC 3
SOUTHERN SHIPS AND SETTLERS. "O, where are you going, 'Goodspeed' and 'Discovery' "
                                          HARC 3

Benét, Stephen Vincent. 1898. in English.
AMERICAN NAMES. "I have fallen in love with American names"   CAED 141
THE BALLAD OF MARCO POLO.   HOUGHT 4
THE BALLAD OF WILLIAM SYCAMORE. "My Father, he was a mountaineer"   CAED 141,
            LIBC 42, NACTE 10, SINGER 5
DANIEL BOONE. "When Daniel Boone goes by, at night"   CAED 141
DIFFERENCE. "My mind's a map. A mad sea-captain drew it"   CAED 157
DO YOU REMEMBER, SPRINGFIELD? "The Illinois earth is black"   CAED 141
DULCE REDENTEM. "The bee, he has white honey"   CAED 141
JOHN BROWN'S BODY, exc.   CAED 141,
                           LIBC 42, SPOA 88
———. THE DEATH OF STONEWALL JACKSON.
                           CAED 141, LIBC 42
———. GENERAL LEE.   HOUGHT 3
———. PORTRAIT OF A SOUTHERN LADY.
                                  NACTE 10
JOHN JAMES AUDUBON. "Some men live for warlike deeds"   CAED 141
LITANY FOR DICTATORSHIPS. "For all those beaten, for the broken heads"   CAED 141,
                           LIBC 42, SPOA 95
METROPOLITAN NIGHTMARE. "It rained quite a lot, that spring"   CAED 157
MINOR LITANY. "This being a time confused and with few clear stars"   CAED 141
THE MOUNTAIN WHIPPOORWILL. "Up in the mountains, it's lonesome all the time"
                           CAED 141, SINGER 3
NIGHTMARE AT NOON. "There are no trenches dug in the park"   CAED 157
NIGHTMARE FOR FUTURE REFERENCE. "That was the second year of the Third World War"
                                   CAED 157
NIGHTMARE NUMBER THREE. "We have expected everything but revolt"   CAED 141
NIGHTMARE, WITH ANGELS. "An angel came to me and stood by my bedside"   CAED 157

NOTES TO BE LEFT IN A CORNERSTONE. "This is for you who are to come, with Time"
                                   CAED 157
ODE TO WALT WHITMAN. "Now comes Fourth Month and the early buds on the tree"
                                   CAED 157
SHORT ODE. "It is time to speak of these"
                                   CAED 157
SPARROW. "Lord may I be"   SPOA 95
THOMAS JEFFERSON. "Thomas Jefferson/what do you say"   CAED 157, SINGER 4
WESTERN WAGONS. "They went with axe and rifle"   CAED 141, HARB 4

Benét, William Rose. 1886. in English.
THE DUST WHICH IS GOD, exc.   NACTE 12
THE FALCONER OF GOD. "I flung my soul to the air like a falcon flying"   NACTE 12
JESSE JAMES. "Jesse James was a two-gun man"
                           COLUMB 6, SPOA 92
THE SKATER OF GHOST LAKE. "Ghost Lake's a dark lake, a deep lake and cold"   SINGER 3
THE WHALE. "Rain, with a silver flail"
                                     SPOA 92

Benitez, Osorio, see **Barba Jacob, Porfirio.**
Benn, Gottfried. 1886. in German.
ABSCHIED. "Du füllst mich an wie Blut die frische Wunde"   DEUTGR 48
ANEMONE. "Erschütterer—Anemone"
                                  DEUTGR 48
ASTERN. "Astern—schwälende Tage"
                                  DEUTGR 48
AUS FERNEN, AUS REICHEN. "Was dann nach jener Stunde"   DEUTGR 14, DEUTGR 18,
                                  DEUTGR 48
BILDER. "Siehst du auf Bildern in den Galerien"
       DEUTGR 14, DEUTGR 18, DEUTGR 48
DANN—. "Wenn ein Gesicht, das man als Junges kannte"   DEUTGR 48
DENK DER VERGEBLICHEN. "Wenn ein Verzweifeln"   DEUTGR 48
DENNOCH DIE SCHWERTER HALTEN. "Der soziologische Nenner"   DEUTGR 14,
                                  DEUTGR 48
DER DUNKLE. "Ach, gäb er mir zurück die alte Trauer"   DEUTGR 48
DU MUSST DIR ALLES GEBEN. "Gib in dein Glück, dein Sterben"   DEUTGR 48
"Du übersiehst dich nicht mehr"
                                  DEUTGR 48
"Einsamer nie als im August"   DEUTGR 14,
                    DEUTGR 18, DEUTGR 48
EINST. "Einst, wenn der Winter begann"
                                  DEUTGR 48
EPILOG 1949. "Die trunkenen Fluten fallen"
                    DEUTGR 14, DEUTGR 48
DAS GANZE. "Im Taumel war ein Teil, ein Teil in Tränen"   DEUTGR 14, DEUTGR 48
GEDICHTE. "Im Namen dessen, der die Stunden spendet"   DEUTGR 14
JENA. "Jena vor uns im lieblichen Tale"
                                  DEUTGR 48
KEINER WEINE.   DEUTGR 48
DER KNABENCHOR. "So sprach das Fleisch zu allen Zeiten"   DEUTGR 48
"Kommt, reden wir zusammen"
                                  DEUTGR 48

* Recording not available for analysis

Benn, Gottfried (continued)

"Lebe wohl/farewell"   DEUTGR 14,
        DEUTGR 18, DEUTGR 48
MÄRZ. BRIEF NACH MERAN. "Blüht nicht zu früh,
    ach blüht erst, wenn ich komme"
        DEUTGR 48
MELANCHOLIE. "Wenn man von Faltern liest,
    von Schilf und Immen"   DEUTGR 48
NEBEL.   DEUTGR 48
NUR ZWEI DINGE. "Durch so viel Formen gesch-
    ritten"   DEUTGR 14, DEUTGR 48
REISEN. "Meinen Sie Zürich zum Beispiel"
        DEUTGR 14, DEUTGR 48
SATZBAU. "Alle haben den Himmel, die Liebe
    und das Grab"   DEUTGR 48
"Sieh die Sterne, die Fänge"   DEUTGR 48
TEIL-TEILS. "In meinem Elternhaus hingen
    keine Gainsboroughs"   DEUTGR 48
DAS UNAUFHÖRLICHE: SOPRANSOLO, exc. "Es trägt
    die Nacht/das Ende"   DEUTGR 14,
        DEUTGR 18, DEUTGR 48
"Wer allein ist, ist auch im Geheimnis"
    DEUTGR 14, DEUTGR 18, DEUTGR 48
WORTE. "Allein: du mit den Worten"
    DEUTGR 14, DEUTGR 18, DEUTGR 48
"Zerstörungen"   DEUTGR 48
"Die Züge deiner, die dem Blut verschworen"
        DEUTGR 48

Bennett, Bob. in English.
Poetry*   PRENT 1
Bennett, Joseph. 1922. in English.
TO ELIZA, DUCHESS OF DORSET.   LIBC 40
Poetry*   LIST 15
Bennett, Rowena. in English.
SMOKE ANIMALS. "Out of the factory chimney
    tall"   HARB 1
THE WITCH OF WILLOBY WOOD. "There once was
    a witch of Willoby"   HARB 4
Benserade, Isaac de. 1612. in French.
JOB. "Job, de mille tourments atteint"
        HACH 9
Béranger, Pierre Jean. 1780. in French.
MON HABIT. "Sois-moi fidèle, ô pauvre habit que
    j'aime"   PATHE 1
Berchet, Giovanni. 1783. in Italian.
ALL' ARMI ALL' ARMI. "Su, figli d'Italia"
        CETRA 26
IL GIURAMENTO DI PONTIDA.   CETRA 26
Bergé, Carol. 1928. in English.
PAVANE FOR THE WHITE QUEEN, THE LOVED WIFE
    FALLING SLOWLY AWAKE. "Not as the word
    death"   FOLKW 21
Bergengren, Ralph. in English.
THE WORM. "When the earth is turned in
    spring"   BOWMAR 1
Bergengruen, Werner. 1892. in German.
ABEND NACH DEM GEWITTER. "Noch stockt im
    Haus die Schwüle"   CHRIST 2
DERENGEL SPRICHT. "Gehorche. Was für ein
    Lohn dir bereitet?"   CHRIST 2
GEGEN DIE UNGEDULD. "Fahr aus, du heftiger
    Geist"   DEUTGR 45
IM SINKENDEN JAHR. "Manchmal streift dich
    kühl ein Hauch"   CHRIST 2
LEBEN EINES MANNES. "Gestern fuhr ich Fische
    fangen"   CHRIST 2

DIE MÜHLE. "Es rinnen die Wasser vom Bühle"
        CHRIST 2
SOMMER. "Atme, Seele, erhöhter"   CHRIST 2
SPATHERBST. "Das Jahr wird gross, die Erde
    weit"   CHRIST 2
UM FRIEDEN. "Wir haben so lange Krieg gese-
    hen"   DEUTGR 45
UM STARKUNG UND UNVERLOSCHBARKEIT DER
    SONNE. "Was machen wir immer und heuer?"
        DEUTGR 45
UM VIELERLEI GUTE GABEN. "Ich rufe dich an, Al-
    lewelt"   DEUTGR 45
DIE UNSICHTBAREN. "Rüste abendlich die
    Schale"   CHRIST 2
Berger, Art. in English.
LIFE HAS NO DIMENSION. "The eagle drizzle"
        BROADR 3
MARCH ON THE DELTA. "One more march"
        BROADR 2
Berger-Kiss, Andrés. in Spanish.
CANTO A LA TIERRA. "Mi hogar es la tierra"
        SMC 8
LOS HERIDOS. "Vedlos pasar a través de los en-
    sangrentados años"   SMC 8
Bergman, Alexander F. 1912. in English.
JERICHO. "We cannot be kept within the walls"
        FOLKW 14
LAMENT. "In this time of the year when leaves
    fall"   FOLKW 14
LETTER. "I hope he doesn't see me walking past
    his bed"   FOLKW 14
WARSONG. "Under the palaces, the marble and
    granite"   FOLKW 14
Bergman, Bo. 1869. in Swedish.
DE GAMLA. "Jag ser dem i hucklen och hattar"
        GRAM 2
FRIHETSORDET. "Stormen har slunyat den fly-
    gande"   GRAM 4
HJÄRTAT. "Hjärtat skall gro av drömmar"
        GRAM 1
IRRBLOSSET OCH ÄLVAN. "I livet har jag irrat"
        GRAM 4
MÄNNISKORNAS ÖGON. "Klara skola människor-
    nas ögon vara"   GRAM 4
MÅNSKEN PÅ STRÖMMEN. "Som klippt i sotat pap-
    per"   GRAM 4
MARIONETTERNA. "Det sitter en herre i himlens
    sal"   GRAM 4
STOCKHOLM. "Än rullar bruset under dina bå-
    gar"   GRAM 4
TILL EN KONSTNÄR. "Jag säger dig: du måste van-
    dra vida"   GRAM 4
UNDER VINTERGATAN. "Högt i det höga slår"
        GRAM 4
Berkeley, George. 1685. in English.
VERSES ON THE PROSPECT OF PLANTING ARTS AND
    LEARNING IN AMERICA. "The Muse, disgusted
    at an age and clime"   CAED 203
Bernard, Roger. in French.
LES PARTS SEMBLABLES.   ADES 55
Bernárdez, Francisco Luis. 1900. in Spanish.
ESTAR ENAMORADO. "Estar enamorado amigos
    es"   SMC 1
ORACIÓN POR EL ALMA DE UN NIÑO MONTAÑES
    "Perdónalo, Señor, era inocente" FIDIAS 3
SONETOS NOCTURNOS I. "Lejos está la luz que yo
    tenía"   AGUIL 9

* Recording not available for analysis

———, II. "De quien es esta voz que va conmigo" AGUIL 9

Bernhard, Thomas. 1931. in English.
PSALM. CHRIST 29

Berni, Francesco. 1497. in Italian.
"Chiome d'argento fine, irte ed attorte"
DOVER 3
Poetry* CETRA 23

Bernstein, Charles. in English.
MYLMYLMY. "My pillow, my shirt"
WATSHD 11

Berrigan, Daniel. 1921. in English.
FALSE GODS, REAL MEN. "Our family moved in 25
years from Acceptable Ethnic" CAED 158
FISH. "A freak's eye" SPOA 82
A SERMON FROM THE UNDERGROUND. CAED 158
TRIAL POEMS I: WINGS. "In Baltimore as we flew
in for trial" CAED 158
——— II: THE MARSHAL. "The marshal is taking
my measure" CAED 158

Berry, Wendell. 1934. in English.
Poetry* JNP 70, MICHM 16

Berryman, John. 1914. in English.
THE BALL POEM. "What is the boy now, who has
lost his ball" LIBC 17
CANTO AMOR. "Dream in a dream the heavy
soul somewhere" LIBC 17
DREAM SONGS, 1. "Huffy Henry hid the day"
APPL 2, HARPV 5
———, 3. A STIMULANT FOR AN OLD BEAST.
"Acacia, burnt myrrh, velvet, pricky stings"
HARPV 5
———, 4. "Filling her compact and delicious
body" LIBC 1, SPOA 101
———, 5. "Henry sats in de bar & was odd"
APPL 2, HARPV 5
———, 8. "The weather was fine. They took
away his teeth" APPL 2, HARPV 5
———, 14. "Life, friends, is boring we must not
say so" APPL 2
———, 16. "Henry's pelt was put on sundry
walls" APPL 2, LIBC 1, SPOA 101
———, 17. "Muttered Henry: Lord of matter,
thus" APPL 2, HARPV 5
———, 22. "I am the little man who smokes and
smokes" HARPV 5, LIBC 1, SPOA 101
———, 23. THE LAY OF IKE. HARPV 5, LIBC 1
———, 27. "The greens of the Ganges delta foliate" HARPV 5, LIBC 1
———, 29. "There sat down, once, a thing on
Henry's heart" HARPV 5, LIBC 1,
SPOA 101
———, 34. "My mother has your rifle"
HARPV 5
———, 36. "The high ones die, die. They die"
HARPV 5
———, 48. "He yelled at me in Greek"
HARPV 5
———, 53. "He lay in the middle of the world,
and twitcht" HARPV 5
———, 55. "Peter's not friendly. He gives me
sideways looks" HARPV 5
———, 67. "I don't operate often. When I do"
HARPV 5
———, 69. "Love her he doesn't but the thought
he puts" HARPV 5

———, 71. "Spellbound held subtle Henry all
his four" HARPV 5
———, 75. "Turning it over, considering like a
madman" HARPV 5, SCHOL 2, SPOA 101
———, 77. "Seedy Henry rose up shy in de
world" APPL 2, HARPV 5
FORMAL ELEGY. "A hurdle of water, and O these
waters are cold" FOLKW 21
THE LIGHTNING. "Sick with the lightning lay my
sister-in-law" LIBC 17
WINTER LANDSCAPE. "The three men coming
down the winter hill" LIBC 17

Bertrand de Born. 1140. in Provençal.
EPIGRAM. "Engles, de flors faitz capelh"
FOLKW 10

Bervoets, Marguerite. in French.
LETTRE. ADES 55

Betjeman, John. 1906. in English.
ANGLO-CATHOLIC CONGRESSES. "We, who re-
member Faith, the grey-headed ones"
CAED 178
THE ARREST OF OSCAR WILDE. "He sipped at a
weak hock and seltzer" ARGO 84
THE ATTEMPT. "I love your brown curls"
ARGO 84
A BAY IN ANGLESEY. "The sleepy sound of a tea-
time tide" CAED 178
BEFORE THE ANAESTHETIC. "Intolerably sad, pro-
found" ARGO 97, ARGO 121
BESIDE THE SEASIDE. "Green shutters, shut your
shutters" SPOA 8
BUSINESS WOMEN. "From the geyser ventilators
autumn winds are blowing down" SPOA 8
CAPRICE. "I sat only two tables off from the one
I was sacked at" CAED 178
CHRISTMAS. "The bells of waiting Advent ring"
ARGO 82, FOLKW 69, SPOA 41
"The Church's restoration in 1883"
FOLKW 65
CORNWALL IN ADOLESCENCE. "The Arrol-John-
ston spun him down to Slough" ARGO 121.
CORNWALL IN CHILDHOOD. "Come, Hygiene,
goddess of the growing boy" ARGO 121
DAWN OF GUILT. "My dear deaf old father, how
I loved him then" ARGO 121
DEAR OLD VILLAGE. "The dear old village! Lin-
lan-lone the bells" ARGO 121
DEATH AT LEAMINGTON. "She died in the up-
stairs bedroom" ARGO 77
DEVONSHIRE STREET W 1. "The heavy mahogany
door with its wrought iron screen"
ARGO 84, ARGO 121
DIARY OF A CHURCHMOUSE. "Here among long-
discarded cassocks" ARGO 84
DISCOVERING POETRY, exc. PROTHM 8
EUNICE. "With her latest roses happily encum-
bered" ARGO 84, ARGO 121
FALSE SECURITY. "I remember the dread"
SPOA 8
FELIXSTOWE. "With one consuming roar along
the shingle" ARGO 121
FIVE O'CLOCK SHADOW. "This is the time of day
when we in the men's ward" CAED 178
GOOD-BYE. "Some days before death"
CAED 178
GREAT CENTRAL RAILWAY. "Unmitigated Eng-
land" CAED 178

* Recording not available for analysis

Betjeman, John (continued)

GREENAWAY. "I know so well this turfy mile"
CAED 178

HARROW-ON-THE-HILL. "When melancholy Autumn comes to Wembley"   ARGO 84,
CAED 178, ARGO 121

HARVEST HYMN. "We spray the fields and scatter"   CAED 178

THE HEART OF THOMAS HARDY. "The heart of Thomas Hardy flew out of Stinsford churchyard"   ARGO 84

HENLEY-ON-THAMES. "I see the winding water make"   ARGO 84, ARGO 121

THE HON. SEC. "The flag that hung half-mast today"   CAED 178

HOUSE OF REST. "Now all the world she knew is dead"   SPOA 8

HUNTER TRIALS. "It's awf'lly bad luck on Diana"
CAED 178, SPOA 8, ARGO 137

I. M. WALTER RAMSDEN. "Dr. Ramsden cannot read the Times obituary to-day, He's dead"
ARGO 121, ARGO 84, ARGO 137

IN A BATH TEASHOP. "Let us not speak, for the love we bear one another"   ARGO 84

"In the public gardens"   ARGO 84

INDOOR GAMES NEAR NEWBURY. "In among the silver birches"   ARGO 121

IN WESTMINSTER ABBEY. "Let me take this other glove off"   THEAL 1

IRELAND'S OWN. "In the Churchyard of Bromham the yews intertwine"   CAED 178

THE IRISH UNIONIST'S FAREWELL TO GRETA HELLSTROM IN 1922. "Golden haired and golden hearted"   ARGO 84

THE LAST OF HER ORDER.   ARGO 84

LATE-FLOWERING LUST. "My head is bald, my breath is bad"   ARGO 97, ARGO 121

THE LICORICE FIELDS AT PONTREFACT. "In the licorice fields at Pontrefact my love and I did meet"   SPOA 8

A LINCOLNSHIRE CHURCH. "Greyly tremendous the thunder"   ARGO 84, ARGO 121

MATLOCK BATH. "From Matlock Bath's half-timbered station"   ARGO 84, CAED 178,
ARGO 121

MEDITATION ON THE A30. "A man on his own in a car"   CAED 178

THE METROPOLITAN RAILWAY. "Early Electric! With what radiant hope"   ARGO 97,
ARGO 121

MIDDLESEX. "Gaily into Ruislip Gardens"
ARGO 84

NORFOLK. "How did the devil come"   SPOA 8

NORTH COAST RECOLLECTIONS. "No people on the golf courses"   SPOA 8

THE OLYMPIC GIRL. "The sort of girl I like to see"
FOLKW 65; JUP 1

THE OPENING WORLD. "Balkan Sobranies in a wooden box"   ARGO 121

OUR PADRE. "Our padre is an old sky pilot"
ARGO 121

POTPOURRI FROM A SURREY GARDEN. "Miles of pram in the wind and Pam in the gorse track"   ARGO 84

REMORSE. "The lungs draw in the air and rattle it out again"   SPOA 8

REPROOF DESERVED, OR AFTER THE LECTURE. "When I saw the Grapefruit drying"
CAED 178, SPOA 8

A RUSSELL FLINT. "I could not speak for amazement at your beauty"   CAED 178

SEASIDE GOLF. "How straight it flew, how long it flew"   SPOA 8

A SHROPSHIRE LAD. "The gas was on in the Institute"   ARGO 97

A SUBALTERN'S LOVE SONG. "Miss J. Hunter Dunn, Miss J. Hunter Dunn"   CAED 178
SPOA 8

SUMMONED BY BELLS, exc.   ARGO 86
CAED 178

SUN AND FUN, SONG OF A NIGHT-CLUB PROPRIETRESS. "I walked into the nightclub in the morning"   CAED 178, SPOA 8

SUNDAY IN IRELAND. "Bells are booming down the bohreens"   SPOA 8

TO MY SON AGED EIGHT.   CAED 86

TREBETHERICK. "We used to picnic where the thrift"   ARGO 84

TREGARDOCK. "A mist from the moor arose"
CAED 178

UPPER LAM BOURNE. "Up the ash-tree climbs the ivy"   ARGO 84

WANTAGE BELLS. "Now with the bells through the apple bloom"   ARGO 84

YOUTH AND AGE ON BEAULIEU RIVER, HANTS. "Early sun on Beaulieu water"   CAED 178
SPOA 8

Poetry*   PROTHM 6

Betteloni, Vittorio. 1840. in Italian.
Poetry*   CETRA 27

Bevilacqua, Alberto. 1934. in Italian.
UN' ALTRA PIETA.   CETRA 51
I BAMBINI DI AKYAB.   CETRA 51
CÒSI IL PARMA.   CETRA 51
DOPO LA FUCILAZIONE DI UN RIBELDE DI AKYAB.
CETRA 51
E DUNQUE ECCOMI.   CETRA 51
E IL SOLE PROSCIUGÒ LE ORE DELL' INFANZIA.
CETRA 51
E' IN QUESTA PIETRA.   CETRA 51
E' QUESTO IL PRIMO LAGER.   CETRA 51
GIUSEPPINA CANTADORI.   CETRA 51
IN LIMITE UMANO.   CETRA 51
LITANIA ALLE PORTE DI LEOPOLDVILLE.
CETRA 51
MATERNA.   CETRA 51
LA MORTE ALGERINA.   CETRA 51
NATA E LA STORIA.   CETRA 51
PAGINA DI UN VANGELO NAUTICO.   CETRA 51
PARLIAMONE.   CETRA 51
PENSANDO AL LUOGO DELL' ORIGINE DA UN LUOGO DEL MONDO.   CETRA 51
QUANDO LA NOTTE.   CETRA 51
QUESTI MIEI ANNI SESSANTA.   CETRA 51
QUI LA PIETRA.   CETRA 51
S'ACCORDIA LA GIORNATA.   CETRA 51
SALVEZZA DALLA BAIA DI LUANDA.   CETRA 51
SUICIDO.   CETRA 51

Bevington, Helen. 1906. in English.
A BOWL OF OCTOBER. "October is a breakfast food"   HARB 6

* Recording not available for analysis

Beyer, Evelyn. 1907. in English.
JUMP OR JIGGLE. "Frogs jump, caterpillers hump"   CREAT 1, HARB 2
Bhartrihari. 7th c. in Sanskrit.
Poetry, in Swedish translation*   GRAM 1
Bibbs, Hart Leroi. in English.
SIX: SUNDAY.   EAV 16
Bible and Pseudepigrapha
BOOK OF ENOCH. "And I commanded in the very lowest"   FOLKW 48
PSALM 8.   English CAED 40; French FOLKW 85
———— 21.   French FOLKW 85
———— 22.   French FOLKW 85
———— 23.   English ARGO 11, CAED 40, HOUGHT 1, SINGER 6; German SPOA 5
———— 81.   French FOLKW 85
———— 84.   English CAED 40
———— 88.   English CAED 40
———— 90.   English SCHOL 6; German SPOA 5
———— 91.   English CAED 40
———— 93.   English HOUGHT 4
———— 100.   English CAED 40, HOUGHT 3
———— 102.   German CHRIST 29
———— 103.   French FOLKW 85
———— 104.   English CAPITOL 1
———— 107.   English HARC 4
———— 121.   English CAED 40, HOUGHT 2; French PERIOD 2
———— 123.   English CAED 40
———— 130.   English CAED 40
———— 143.   French FOLKW 85
———— 146 (Douay 145).   French DOVER 4, HACH 9, PERIOD 2
———— 149.   English CAED 40
———— 150.   English CAED 40
Psalms*   Hebrew and English SPOA 128; SPOA 130
SAMUEL, exc. "When David heard that Absalom was slain"   COLUMB 10
THE SONG OF SONGS, exc. "For, lo, the winter is past"   English CAED 56, CAED 160, CMS 4; Hebrew and English SPOA 129
Bickerstaffe, Isaac. 1735. in English.
LOVE IN A VILLAGE. "There was a jolly miller once"   CAED 203
Bienek, Horst. 1930. in German.
ANWEISUNG FUR ZEITUNGSLESER. "Prüft jedes Wort"   DEUTGR 40A
LERN VON DEN WOMBATS.   DEUTGR 40A
Binyon, Laurence. 1869. in English.
Poetry*   PROTHM 7
Birney, Earle. 1904. in English.
THE EBB BEGINS FROM DREAM. "The stars like stranded starfish pale and die" LEARNC 5
Bishop, Elizabeth. 1911. in English.
ANAPHORA. "Each day with so much ceremony"   COLUMB 8
AT THE FISHHOUSES. "Although it is a cold evening"   LIBC 19, LIBC 63
FAUSTINA, OR, ROCK ROSES. "Tended by Faustina/ yes in a crazy house"   LIBC 19, LIBC 63
THE FISH. "I caught a tremendous fish"
            COLUMB 8, HOUGHT 3, SPOA 99
THE IMAGINARY ICEBERG. "We'd rather have the iceberg"   SPOA 99

JERONIMO'S HOUSE. "My house, my fairy palace is"   LIBC 19, LIBC 63
LATE AIR. "From a magician's midnight sleeve"   COLUMB 8
VARICK STREET. "At night the factories struggle awake"   SPOA 99
VISITS TO ST. ELIZABETH'S. "This is the house of Bedlam"   SPOA 99
Bishop, John Peale. 1892. in English.
BEYOND CONNECTICUT, BEYOND THE SEA. "When I look into my son's eyes I see"   LIBC 44
ENCOUNTER. "In the rags of a wind" LIBC 44
MOVING LANDSCAPE WITH FALLING RAIN. "Woodlands are lost upon a haze"   LIBC 44
PERSPECTIVES ARE PRECIPICES. "Sister Anne, Sister Anne"   LIBC 44
THE RETURN. "Night and we heard heavy and cadenced hoofbeats"   LIBC 44
RETURN TO CONNECTICUT. "Fall, and we came to the rock-bleached pasture"   LIBC 44
THAT SUMMER'S END. "The yellow wallpaper and the polished floor"   LIBC 44
WINTER PRINT. "Snow in Connecticut is thatched"   LIBC 44
Bishop, Morris. 1893. in English.
OZYMANDIAS REVISITED. "I met a traveller from an antique land"   HOUGHT 4
Blackburn, Paul. 1926. in English.
DECEMBER 6TH AND 7TH. "The news keeps squirting in from all over"   BROADR 3
IS ANY COHERENCE WORTH THE CELEBRATION. "Is any coherence"   BROADR 3
LISTENING TO SONNY ROLLINS AT THE FIVE-SPOT. "There will be many other nights"
                                BROADR 2
Blackburn, Thomas. 1916. in English.
THE CITIZENS. "After the marsh was drained and its vast monsters"   SPOA 68
HOSPITAL FOR DEFECTIVES. "By your unnumbered charities"   FOLKW 59A
THE JUDAS TREE. "Listen, the hounds of the judge and priest"   ARGO 93
MARK. "The fallen city rides from the dark"
                                 ARGO 93
A SMELL OF BURNING. "After the savage hysterical episode so common with us"
                                FOLKW 59A
TREWARMETT. "Darkness, feathers are shed"
                                 ARGO 93
Blackman, Gary. in English.
THE DJ POEM. "Hey, right on"   WATSHD 14
Blackmur, Richard P. 1904. in English.
ALL'S THE FOUL FRIEND'S. "Now in the fond unhappiness of sleep"   CARIL 22
THE DEAD RIDE FAST. "Nobody ever galloped on this road"   LIBC 1
ELEGY OF FIVE. "When I lay sick and like to die"   CARIL 22
"I knew a bear once ate a man named Virtue"   LIBC 1
ITHYPHALLICS. "Surely we hear thunder"
                                CARIL 22
JORDAN'S DELIGHT. "What is that island"
                                CARIL 22
JUDAS PRIEST. "Come, let us gather up"
                                CARIL 22

———————————————————————
* Recording not available for analysis

Blackmur, Richard P. (continued)

MICHING MALLECHO. "Hopping, half flying" CARIL 22
MISSA VOCIS. "Priests not only" CARIL 22
MR. VIRTUE AND THE THREE BEARS. "We handle our time" CARIL 22
OCTOBER FROST. "The comfortable noise long reading makes" CARIL 22, LIBC 1
PETIT MANAN POINT. "At last from the third mile" CARIL 22
PHASELLUS ILLE. "This little boat you see, my friends, has not" LIBC 61
THE RAPE OF EUROPA. "This age it is the same, with less remembered" LIBC 1
SEA-ODALISQUE. "East of the eastern ledge a hundred yards" LIBC 1
THE SECOND WORLD. "Who that has sailed" CARIL 22
SUNT LACRIMAE RERUM. "I cross" CARIL 22
THREE POEMS FROM A TEXT—ISAIAH LXI: 1-3. I. BEAUTY FOR ASHES. "All day I trespassed on my friend's new death" CARIL 22, LIBC 19, LIBC 61
———. II. THE OIL OF JOY FOR MOURNING. "Him whom the old joy fell over" CARIL 22, LIBC 19, LIBC 61
———. III. A GARMENT OF PRAISE FOR THE SPIRIT OF HEAVINESS. "How may I see the triune man at once?" CARIL 22, LIBC 19, LIBC 61
THRENOS. "Among the grave" CARIL 22
UNA VITA NUOVA. "That crazy wretch got up" CARIL 22

Blair, Robert. in English.
THE GRAVE, exc. CAED 203

Blake, William. 1757. in English.
AUGURIES OF INNOCENCE "To see a world in a grain of sand" BRITAM 3, CAED 62
THE BOOK OF THEL. "The daughters of the Seraphim led round their sunny flocks" SPOA 33
THE BUILDINGS OF TIME. ARGO 54
THE CRYSTAL CABINET. "The maiden caught me in the wild" ARGO 54, CAED 62
ETERNITY. "He who binds to himself a joy" ARGO 54
THE EVERLASTING GOSPEL, exc. "The Vision of Christ that thou dost see" HARVOC 5, LONGM 1
THE FRENCH REVOLUTION, exc. "The dead brood over Europe" SPOA 33
GATES OF PARADISE. EPILOGUE. "Truly, my Satan" ARGO 54, LONGM 1
"I asked a thief to steal me a peach" ARGO 54, CAED 62
"I laid me down upon a bank" ARGO 54
"I saw a chapel all of gold" ARGO 54, CAED 62
LOVE'S SECRET. "Never seek to tell thy love" ARGO 54, CMS 13, LIST 2, SPOA 33, LION 2
THE MENTAL TRAVELLER. "I travelled through a land of men" CAED 62
MILTON. PREFACE ("JERUSALEM"). "And did those feet in ancient time" ARGO 54, BRITAM 1, CAED 62, JNP 8, SPOA 33

———. exc. "England, Awake! awake! awake!" FOLKW 67
———. THE WINEPRESS OF LOS, "But the winepress of Los is eastward" ARGO 54
"Mock on, mock on Voltaire, Rousseau" ARGO 54, CAED 62
MORNING. "To find the Western path" ARGO 54
"My silks and fine array" LIST 2, LIST 10
"Oh, I say, you, Joe" CAED 62
THE QUESTION ANSWERED. "What is it men in women do require" ARGO 54
REEDS OF INNOCENCE. EAV 7
SOFT SNOW. "I walked abroad in a snowy day" ARGO 54
SONG: "How sweet I roam'd from field to field" ARGO 54, DECCA 12, LIST 2, LIST 10
SONG: "Whether on Ida's shady brow" ARGO 54, CAED 62
SONGS OF EXPERIENCE. THE ANGEL. "I dreamt a dream! What can it mean?" CAED 62
———. THE CHIMNEY SWEEPER. "A little black thing among the snow" ARGO 54
———. THE CLOD AND THE PEBBLE. "Love seeketh not itself to please" ARGO 54, CMS 13, CAED 62, CAED 202
———. A DIVINE IMAGE. "Cruelty has a human heart" ARGO 54, CAED 62
———. EARTH'S ANSWER. "Earth raised up her head" ARGO 54, CAED 62
———. THE FLY. "Little fly/Thy summer's play" CAED 62, VERVE 3
———. THE GARDEN OF LOVE. "I went to the garden of love" ARGO 88A, ARGO 54, CAED 21, CAED 62, VERVE 3
———. THE HUMAN ABSTRACT. "Pity would be no more" ARGO 54
———. INFANT SORROW. "My mother groaned, my father wept" ARGO 54, CAED 62
———. INTRODUCTION. "Hear the voice of the Bard" ARGO 54, CAED 21, CAED 62, CAED 202, HARVOC 5
———. A LITTLE BOY LOST. "Nought loves another as itself" ARGO 54, CAED 62
———. THE LITTLE GIRL FOUND. "All the night in woe" CAED 62
———. THE LITTLE GIRL LOST. "In futurity/I prophesy" CAED 62
———. LONDON. "I wander through each charter'd street" ARGO 54, CAED 62, LEARNC 1, VAN 3
———. MY PRETTY ROSE TREE. "A flower was offered to me" CAED 62
———. A POISON TREE. "I was angry with my friend" ARGO 54, CAED 21, CAED 62, CAED 202, IMP 1, LONGM 1
———. THE SCHOOLBOY. "I love to rise in a summer morn" CAED 62, VERVE 3
———. THE SICK ROSE. "O Rose, thou art sick" ARGO 54, CAED 62, LONGM 1, VERVE 3
———. THE SUNFLOWER. "Ah, Sunflower, weary of time" ARGO 54, CAED 62, JNP 8, VERVE 3

* Recording not available for analysis

———. THE TIGER. "Tiger, tiger, burning bright"   ARGO 54, BRITAM 1, CAED 21, CAED 62, CAED 111, CAED 202, CMS 12, EAV 7, LIST 2, LIST 10, RCA 4, RCA 8, SINGER 6, SPOA 33, SPOA 117

SONGS OF INNOCENCE. THE BLOSSOM. "Merry, merry sparrow"   CAED 62, VERVE 3

———. THE CHIMNEY SWEEPER. "When my mother died I was very young"   ARGO 54, CAED 62, CAED 202, VERVE 3

———. A CRADLE SONG. "Sweet dreams, form a shade"   EAV 22, VERVE 3

———. THE DIVINE IMAGE. "To Mercy, Pity, Peace, and Love"   ARGO 54, CAED 62, VERVE 3

———. A DREAM. "Once a dream did weave a shade"   ARGO 54, VERVE 3

———. THE ECHOING GREEN. "The sun does arise"   CAED 62, VERVE 3

———. HOLY THURSDAY. "'Twas on a holy Thursday, their innocent faces clean"   ARGO 54, CAED 62, VERVE 3

———. INFANT JOY. "I have no name"   CAED 62, CAED 202, VERVE 3

———. THE LAMB. "Little lamb, who made thee"   CAED 21, CAED 62, CAED 202, EAV 7, LIST 2, LIST 10, RCA 8, SPOA 117, SINGER 6, SPOA 33, TAPES 2, THEAL 3, VERVE 3

———. LAUGHING SONG. "When the green woods laugh with the voice of joy"   VERVE 3

———. THE LITTLE BLACK BOY. "My mother bore me in the southern wild"   ARGO 54, CAED 62, CAED 202, SPOA 33, THEAL 2, VERVE 3

———. THE LITTLE BOY FOUND. "The little boy lost in the lonely fen"   ARGO 54, CAED 21, CAED 62, CAED 202, VERVE 3

———. THE LITTLE BOY LOST. "Father, father, where are you going"   ARGO 54, CAED 21, CAED 62, CAED 202, VERVE 3

———. NIGHT. "The sun descending in the West"   ARGO 54, CAED 62, RCA 1

———. NURSE'S SONG. "When the voices of children are heard on the green"   LONGM 1, ARGO 54, CAED 62, CAED 85, LONDON 1, VERVE 3

———. ON ANOTHER'S SORROW. "Can I see another's woe"   ARGO 54, CAED 62, VERVE 3

———. THE PIPER. "Piping down the valleys wild"   ARGO 54, CAED 21, CAED 62, CAED 202, LIST 10, RCA 4, SPOA 33

———. THE SHEPHERD. "How sweet is the shepherd's sweet lot"   ARGO 54, CAED 62, CAED 202, VERVE 3

———. SPRING. "Sound the flute"   CAED 62, CAED 109, VERVE 3

TO THE DEISTS. "I saw a monk of Charlemagne"   ARGO 54

TO THE MUSES. "Whether on Ida's shady brow"   ARGO 54, CAED 62

THE VOICE OF THE ANCIENT BARD. "Youth of delight! come hither"   ARGO 54, CAED 62, VERVE 3

Poetry*   SPOA 114, NET 17

Blanco, Andrés Eloy. 1897. in Spanish.

REGRESO AL MAR. "Siempre es el mar donde mejor se quiere"   FOLKW 80

LAS UVAS DEL TIEMPO. "Madre: Esta noche se nos muere un año"   SMC 1

Blanding, Don. 1894. in English.

ALOHA OE. "It's more than just an easy word for casual good-bye"   TEMPO 1

BABY STREET. "I walk quite slowly down Baby Street"   TEMPO 1

DREAMER. "I don't suppose I'll ever see"   TEMPO 1

DRIFTER. "I am bloodbrother of all drifting things"   TEMPO 1

DRIFTWOOD. "Never a tide"   TEMPO 1

FOOTSTEPS. "A winding Honolulu street"   TEMPO 1

GOLD. "My treasure chest is filled with gold"   TEMPO 1

LEAVES FROM MY GRASS HOUSE. "My grass-house stands by the open sea"   TEMPO 1

NAMES ARE SHIPS. "Names! The lure in names of places"   TEMPO 1

SOME LINES SCRAWLED ON THE DOOR OF VAGABOND'S HOUSE. "West of the sunset stands my house"   TEMPO 1

VAGABOND'S HOUSE. "When I have a house . . . as I sometime may"   TEMPO 1

VAGABOND'S ROAD. PREFACE. "Not for all the lonely winding road that leads across the hill"   TEMPO 1

Blok, Aleksandr Aleksandrovich. 1880. in Russian.

DVENADTSAT. "Tshernyi vecher"   Russian and English CAED 193

GARMONIKA, GARMONIKA. "Garmonika, garmonika"   FOLKW 94

NA POLE KULIKOVOM. "Reka raskinulas. Techet, grustit lenivo"   FOLKW 94

NEZNAKOMKA. "Po vecheram nad restoranami"   FOLKW 94; Russian and English CAED 193

Blomberg, Erik. 1894. in Swedish.

DÖDENS ÄNGEL. "Evige, du som ruvar"   GRAM 6

EN MODER. "Först skymningen, då allt blir stumt"   GRAM 6

FÅNGEN. "Det dagas redan"   GRAM 6

DEN FANGNE GUDEN. "Hur fåfängt till himlen vi ropa: 'O Herre, befria oss"   GRAM 6

DEN FÖRTRAMPADE. "Ja trampa, trampa på mig"   GRAM 6

DEN GÖMDA DALEN, exc. "Du skapade mig av luft och ler"   GRAM 6

MÄNNISKANS HEM. "Nu är det natt över jorden"   GRAM 6

RÅDJUR I EN PARK. "Jag älskar de små bräckliga rådjuren där de dansa förbi"   GRAM 6

SKAPAREN. "Som människan måste du sträcka"   GRAM 6

SNÖBLOMMOR. "I dag är luften blå"   GRAM 6

VIOLONCELLEN. "Då bomblarmet tystnat"   GRAM 6

* Recording not available for analysis

Blunden, Edmund. 1896. in English.

THE AUTHOR'S LAST WORD TO HIS STUDENTS. "Forgive what I, adventuring highest themes"
ARGO 100

FOREFATHERS. "Here they went with smock and crook" ARGO 100, BRITAM 1, FOLKW 68

THE MIDNIGHT SKATERS. "The hop-poles stand in cones" FOLKW 65, JUP 1

Blunt, Wilfrid Scawen. 1840. in English.

LAUGHTER AND DEATH. "There is no laughter in the natural world" CMS 14

Bly, Robert. 1926. in English.

AFTER LONG BUSYNESS. "I start out for a walk"
WATSHD 3

AFTER THE INDUSTRIAL REVOLUTION, ALL THINGS HAPPEN AT ONCE. "Now we enter a strange world, where the Hessian Christmas"
WATSHD 3

AT NIGHT. "Everyday I want so much to see"
WATSHD 3

AWAKENING. "We are approaching sleep: the chestnut blossoms in the mind" SCHOL 5

A BUSY MAN SPEAKS. "Not to the mother of solitude will I give myself" SPOA 105,
CASSC 4

CLIMBING MT. VISION WITH MY LITTLE BOY. "We started up" WATSHD 3

CONDITION OF THE WORKING CLASSES, 1960.
SPOA 105

COUNTING SMALL-BONED BODIES. "Let's count the bodies over again" ARGO 16,
CAED 155, SCHOL 5, WATSHD 3,
CASSC 4

THE DEAD SEAL NEAR MCCLURE'S BEACH. "Walking north toward the point, I came upon a dead seal" EMC 7, WATSHD 3

DRIVING THROUGH MINNESOTA DURING THE HANOI BOMBINGS. "We drive between lakes just turning green" SCHOL 5

DRIVING THROUGH OHIO. "We slept that night in Delaware, Ohio" NACTE 14, SCHOL 5

DRIVING TO TOWN LATE TO MAIL A LETTER. "It is a cold and snowy night. The main street is deserted" SCHOL 5

DRIVING TOWARD THE LAC QUI PARLE RIVER. "I am driving; it is dusk; Minnesota" SCHOL 5,
WATSHD 3

HATRED OF MEN WITH BLACK HAIR. "I hear voices praising Tshombe, and the Portuguese"
SCHOL 5, WATSHD 3, CASSC 4

"Inside this clay jug" WATSHD 3

LETTER FROM A GIRL. "Dear Father, I am saying good bye" WATSHD 3

LOVE POEM. "When we are in love, we love the grass" SCHOL 5

THE MAN WHOM THE SEA KEPT AWAKE. "I have heard the sea upon the troubled rocks"
SPOA 105

"My poetry resembles the bread of Egypt"
WATSHD 3

ON A MOONLIT ROAD IN THE NORTH WOODS. "I sit on the forest road" WATSHD 3

A PLACE PREPARED. "I want what is inside you"
WATSHD 3

POEM IN THREE PARTS. "Oh, on an early morning I think I shall live for ever!" NACTE 14,
WATSHD 3, CASSC 4

SEPTEMBER NIGHT WITH AN OLD HORSE.
NACTE 14

SIX WINTER PRIVACY POEMS. "About four, a few flakes" WATSHD 3, CASSC 4

SNOW BANKS, NORTH OF THE HOUSE. "Those great sweeps of snow" WATSHD 3

SNOWFALL IN THE AFTERNOON. "The grass half-covered with snow" CASSC 4, SPOA 105

"Student, do the simple purification"
WATSHD 3

SUFI SONG. "And when I" WATSHD 3

TAKING THE HANDS. "Taking the hands of someone you love" SCHOL 5, CASSC 4

THE TEETH-MOTHER NAKED AT LAST. "Massive engines lift beautifully from the deck"
WATSHD 3

THINKING OF THE AUTUMN FIELDS. "Already autumn begins" WATSHD 3

THREE KINDS OF PLEASURES. "Sometimes, riding in a car, in Wisconsin" SCHOL 5

TONGUES WHIRLING. "You open your mouth, I put my tongue in" ARGO 16

TURTLE CLIMBING FROM A ROCK. "How shiny the turtle is" WATSHD 3

UNANSWERED LETTERS. "The sun comes in through shutters" WATSHD 3

WAKING FROM AN AFTERNOON SLEEP. "I slowly came down from the mountains of sleep"
SCHOL 5

WATCHING TELEVISION. "Sounds are heard too high for ears" SCHOL 5

WATER UNDER THE EARTH. "O, yes, I love you, book of my confessions" WATSHD 3

WHERE WE MUST LOOK FOR HELP. "The dove returns" CASSC 4

Poetry* JNP 71, MICHM 12, WATSHD 15

Bobrowski, Johannes. 1917. in German.

AN KLOPSTOCK. "Wenn ich das Wirkliche nicht"
WAGENB 1

AN NELLY SACHS. "Höhlen, das Waldgetier"
CHRIST 29

BEGEGNUNG. "Vom ueberhängenden Baum"
WAGENB 1

ERFAHRUNG. "Zeichen/Kreuz und Fische"
WAGENB 1

IM STROM. "Mit den Flössen hinab"
WAGENB 1

KALMUS. "Mit Regensegeln umher/fliegt ein Geheul" WAGENB 1

DER LETTISCHE HERBST. "Das Tollkirschendickicht/ist geöffnet" WAGENB 1

SCHATTENLAND. "Die Raschelstimmen/Blätter, Vögel" WAGENB 1

SPRACHE. "Der Baum/grösser als die Nacht"
WAGENB 1

DIE WOLGASTADTE. "Der Mauerstrich/Türme."
WAGENB 1

Boccaccio, Giovanni. 1313. in Italian.

"Io mi son giovinetta, e volentieri"
DOVER 3

Bodenheim, Maxwell. 1892. in English.

CHINESE GIFTS, I–III. "Your soul began to dance"
LIBC 44

DEAD LAD. LIBC 44

FANTASY. "Geography locates actual mountains" LIBC 44

---

* Recording not available for analysis

FINALITIES. PART VI. "Dead men sit down beside the telephone"   LIBC 44
INSANITY. "Like a vivid hyperbole"   LIBC 44
POEM TO NEGROES AND WHITES.   LIBC 44
SINCERELY YOURS, CULTURE. FIFTH SONNET. "The clock struck three, the rooming house was filled"   FOLKW 14
A SISTER WRITES. "But yesterday, I heard his bantering"   LIBC 44
SMALL TOWN. "The town-hall clock seems to possess"   LIBC 44
SOLDIER'S STAND. "Suppose we say that God is naked hope"   LIBC 44
SONNET. "The simple words and gestures"
                                          LIBC 44
SPRING, 1943. "Peeking, dotting, skeining"
                                        FOLKW 14
TO A ROSE. "Red rose, the crude, flat revelry has died"   LIBC 44
Bogan, Louise. 1897. in English.
THE ALCHEMIST. "I burned my life, that I might find"   CARIL 7, LIBC 5, LIBC 10
BAROQUE COMMENT. "From loud sound and still chance"   SPOA 95
COME, SLEEP. "The bee's fixed hexagon"
                                          CARIL 7
THE CROSSED APPLE. "I've come to give you fruit from out my orchard"   CARIL 7
THE DAEMON. "Must I tell again"   LIBC 5,
                                 LIBC 10, SPOA 95
DIVISION. "Long days and changing weather"
                                          CARIL 7
THE DREAM. "O God, in the dream the terrible horse began"   CARIL 7, LIBC 40
FRIEND'S WEATHER. "O embittered joy"
                                          CARIL 7
"Henceforth from the mind"   CARIL ,
                          LIBC 5, LIBC 10, SPOA 95
ITALIAN MORNING. "Half circle's come before we know"   SPOA 95
JULY DAWN. "It was a waning crescent"
                                          CARIL 7
KEPT. "Time for the wood, the clay" CARIL 7
LAST HILL IN A VISTA. "Come, let us tell the weeds in ditches"   LIBC 5, LIBC 10
M. SINGING. "Now, innocent, within the deep"
                                          CARIL 7
MAN ALONE. "It is yourself you seek" CARIL 7
MARCH TWILIGHT. "This light is loss backward; delight by hurt and by bias gained"
                                          CARIL 7
THE MARK. "Where should he seek, to go away"
                                          LIBC 10
MEDUSA. "I had come to the house, in a cave of trees"   CARIL 7
THE MEETING. "For years I thought I knew, at the bottom of the dream"   CARIL 7
"Men loved wholly beyond wisdom"
                                          CARIL 7
OLD COUNTRYSIDE. "Beyond the hour we counted rain that fell"   CARIL 7, LIBC 1
PUTTING TO SEA. "Who, in the dark, has cast the harbor-chain"   CARIL 7
THE ROMANTIC. "Admit the ruse to fix and name her chaste"   CARIL 7
THE SLEEPING FURY. "You are here now"
                          CARIL 7, LIBC 5, LIBC 10

SONG FOR A LYRE. "The landscape where I lie"
                                          SPOA 95
SONG FOR THE LAST ACT. "Now that I have your face by heart, I look"   CARIL 7, RCA 10
SPIRIT'S SONG. "How well you served me above ground"   CARIL 7
STATUE AND BIRDS. "Here, in the withered arbor, like the arrested wind"   CARIL 7
SUMMER WISH. "That cry's from the first cuckoo of the year"   CARIL 7
TO AN ARTIST, TO TAKE HEART. "Slipping in blood, by his own hand, through pride" SPOA 82
TO MY BROTHER (KILLED HAUMONT WOOD, OCTOBER 1918). "O you so long dead"   SPOA 95
VARIATION ON A SENTENCE. "Of white and tawny, black as ink"   CARIL 7
WOMEN. "Women have no wilderness in them"
                                          CARIL 7
THE YOUNG MAGE. "The young mage said"
                                          CARIL 7
Poetry*   LIST 15, SPOA 82
Boiardo, Matteo Maria, Count of Scandiano. 1434. in Italian.
Poetry*   CETRA 21
Boileau-Despréaux, Nicolas. 1636. in French.
"Voici les lieux charmants"   ADES 54
Bolton, Edmund. 1575. in English.
A CANZON PASTORAL. "Alas, what pleasure, now the pleasant spring"   ARGO 136
A CAROL.   LION 1
Bond, Julian. 1940. in English.
THE BISHOP OF ATLANTA: RAY CHARLES.
                                         SCHOL 8
"I, too, hear America singing"   ARGO 17
LOOK AT THAT GAL.   FOLKW 7
Bonnefoy, Yves. 1923. in French.
"Aube, filles des larmes, rétablis"   DOVER 4
ICI, TOUJOURS ICI. "Ici, dans le lieu clair"
                                         DOVER 4
Bontemps, Arna. 1902. in English.
A BLACK MAN TALKS OF REAPING. "I have sown beside all waters in my day"   FOLKW 41
DARK GIRL. "Easy on your drums"   FOLKW 6
THE DAY-BREAKERS. "We are not come to wage a strife"   FOLKW 6, FOLKW 41
MIRACLES. "Doubt no longer miracles"
                                 FOLKW 6, FOLKW 41
NOCTURNE AT BETHESDA. "I thought I saw an angel flying low"   FOLKW 41
A NOTE OF HUMILITY. "When all our hopes are sown on stony ground"   FOLKW 41
THE RETURN. "Once more, listening to the wind and rain"   FOLKW 41
SOUTHERN MANSION. "Poplars are standing there still as death"   FOLKW 41
Booth, Philip. 1925. in English.
THE ANCHOR. "The wind submerges this house"
                                         SPOA 104
CLEANING OUT THE GARAGE. "Hooks, screw-eyes and screws; the walls"   SCHOL 4
CROSSING. "STOP LOOK LISTEN"   SCHOL 7
THE DANCER. "The Dancer mended sheep and tended fences"   SCHOL 4
EGO. "When I was on Night Line" SCHOL 4
FIRST LESSON. "Lie back, daughter, let your head"   SCHOL 4

* Recording not available for analysis

Booth, Philip (continued)

THE ISLANDERS. "Winters when we set our traps
offshore"   SPOA 104
MAINE. "When old cars get retired they go to
Maine"   SCHOL 4, SPOA 104
THE OWL. "I thought he'd gone, that owl"
                                         SCHOL 4
PROPELLER. "Caged lightly by two-by-fours,
rigged flat"   SCHOL 4
SABLE ISLAND. "You wouldn't want to go there.
Sand is all there is"   SPOA 104
TENANTS HARBOR. "Listen, the tide has turned"
                                         SCHOL 4
THANKSGIVING 1963. "She walks a beach assault-
ed by the sea"   FOLKW 21
THAT CLEAR FIRST MORNING. "That clear first
morning after"   SCHOL 4
WAS A MAN. "Was a man, was a twofaced man"
                                         SCHOL 4
Poetry*   JNP 72
Bopp, Raul. 1898. in Portuguese.
FAVELA. "Meio dia/O môrro coxo"
                                        FOLKW 71
Borchers, Elisabeth. in German.
JAHRLICH, IM SOMMER. "Die heiteren Hügel"
                                       DEUTGR 40A
WIEDERSEHN NACH LANGERER ZEIT. "Komm. Ruh
dich aus"   DEUTGR 40A
ZWEI SCHNELLE TODE. "Wie war das"
                                       DEUTGR 40A
Borchert, Wolfgang. 1921. in German.
DER MOND LÜGT. "Der Mond malt ein groteskes
Muster an die Wand"   CHRIST 11
Borges, Jorge Luis. 1900. in Spanish.
LA FUNDACION MITOLÓGICA DE BUENOS AIRES. "Y
fue por este río de suenera y de barro"
                                         AGUIL 9
LA GUITARRA. "He mirado la pampa"
                                        FOLKW 80
Born, Bertrand de. See **Bertrand de Born.**
Born, Nicolas. in German.
ENTSORGT. "So wird der Schrecken ohne Ende
langsam"   DEUTGR 40A
IM ZUG ATHEN—PATRAS. "Kahle Felsschädel,
helle Augen"   DEUTGR 40A
Borton, Terry. ca. 1930. in English.
SPIDER, BUILD YOUR CASTLE. "What do you spin
you ugly brute"   ACTIV 1
Bosi, Carlo Alberto. 1813. in Italian.
ADDIO MIA BELLA ADDIO.   CETRA 26
Botero, Juan José. in Spanish.
QUIERO SER GATO. "Si Dios dijera: 'ven acá Juan-
cho, díme qué quieres'"   SMC 8
Botto, António. 1902. in Portuguese.
CANÇAO. "A terra floresce"   FOLKW 72
OUTRA CANÇÃO. "Se passares pelo adro"
                                        FOLKW 72
Bourdillon, Francis William. 1852. in English.
"The night has a thousand eyes"   DECCA 12
Bousoño, Carlos. 1923. in Spanish.
ESPAÑA EN EL SUEÑO. "Desde aquí yo contem-
plo, tendido, sin memoria"   HOLT 1
PERO COMO DECIRTELO. "Pero como decirtelo si
eres"   AGUIL 10
PRECIO DE LA VERDAD. "En el desván antiguo de
raída memoria"   AGUIL 10

TRES POEMAS SOBRE LA MUERTE. "Hay veces que
los hombres tristemente"   SPOA 59
Bovio, Libero. 1883. in Italian.
ARIETTA 'E NU CORE CUNTENTO. "No, nun vurria
muri"   CETRA 29
LA FORZA DEL DESTINO.   CETRA 29
GENTILHOMMERIE. "Noi siamo canoscenti di fa-
miglia"   CETRA 29
'O MBRIACO. "Tu vi' che faccia allera tene ò
muorto"   CETRA 29
'A SCIENZA. "Che v'aggia di', mio caro?"
                                        CETRA 29
Boyden, Polly Chase. in English.
MUD. "Mud is very nice to feel"   HARB 2
Brackett, Kate. in English.
SOMETHING HAS TO BURN.   FOLKW 25
Bradstreet, Anne. 1612. in English.
CONTEMPLATIONS, exc. "Some time now past in
the autumned tide"   CAED 185, EAV 14
TO MY DEAR AND LOVING HUSBAND. "If ever two
were one, then surely we"   CAED 185
UPON THE BURNING OF OUR HOUSE. "In silent
night when rest I took"   HOUGHT 5
Bragg, Robert. in English.
Poetry*   JNP 12
Braithwaite, William Stanley. 1878. in English.
THE WATCHERS.   HOUGHT 2
Brathwaite, Edward. 1930. in English.
ALL GOD'S CHILDREN. "They call me Uncle"
                                        ARGO 104
ANCESTORS. "Every Friday morning my grand-
father left"   ARGO 16
ARRIVAL. "His first feet arrived and stumbled
over stone"   ARGO 112
BEGINNING: TIZZIC. "An' then there was Tizzic"
                                        ARGO 113
BREAD.   CAED 153
THE CABIN. "Under the burnt out green"
                                        ARGO 104
CALYPSO. "The stone had skidded arc'd and
bloomed"   ARGO 104
CROSSING THE RIVER BOSOMPRA. "So crossing the
river"   ARGO 112
DIDN'T HE RAMBLE. "So to New York London"
                                        ARGO 104
THE DUST. "Evenin' Miss Evvy Miss Maisie,
Miss"   ARGO 104
THE EMIGRANTS. "So you have seen them"
                                        ARGO 104
EPILOGUE. "So drum skin whip lash master
sun's"   ARGO 104
FOLKWAYS. "I am a fuck-ing negro, man hole in
my head"   ARGO 104
FRANCINA. "In the park that was once green"
                                        CAED 153
THE JOURNEYS. "E-/gypt/in Af/rica"
                                        ARGO 104
LIBATION: PRELUDE. "Out/of this/bright/Sun"
                                        ARGO 112
LIMBO: THE CRACKED MOTHER. "My mother said
I'd be alone"   ARGO 113
LIMITS: THE FOREST. "Like walls the forest stops
us"   ARGO 112
MAMMON. "So in this tilted alleyway"
                                        ARGO 104
NEW WORLD A-COMIN'. "Helpless like this leader-
less like this"   ARGO 104

* Recording not available for analysis

O DREAMS O DESTINATIONS. "But I returned to find Jack"   ARGO 104
PATH-FINDERS. "Summon now the kings of the forest"   ARGO 112
POSSESSION: CORAL. "A yellow mote of sand dreams in the polyp's eye"   ARGO 113
POSTLUDE: HOME. "Where then is the nigger's home"   ARGO 104
REBELLION: WAKE. "Ship/house on the water"   ARGO 113
THE RETURN. "The New Ships: 'Takoradi was hot' "   ARGO 112
SOUTH. "But today I recapture the islands"   ARGO 104
THE SPADES: PRELUDE. "Memories are smoke/ lips we can't kiss"   ARGO 104
TOM. "So many seeds the cotton breeds"   ARGO 104
THE TWIST. "In a little shanty town"   ARGO 104
WINGS OF THE DOVE. "Brother Man the Rasta man"   ARGO 104
WORK SONGS AND BLUES: PRELUDE. "Drum skin whip/lash master sun's"   ARGO 104
Braun, Henry. 1930. in English.
THESE DAYS. "These days the sunlight almost seems total"   CAED 155
Braxton, Jodi. in English.
BLACK SHEBA. "Who is this woman"   WATSHD 4
DO YOU KNOW JESUS. "You sweet black semitic"   WATSHD 4
MISS MAME. "No straight lines but drooping"   WATSHD 4
OF MARYLAND. "Big old houses"   WATSHD 4
THE PALACE AT 4 A.M. "I live in a house"   WATSHD 4
PASSING TIME. "I was passing time"   WATSHD 4
PEGASUS. "Where is my Pegasus"   WATSHD 4
RISING. "Bring me some news"   WATSHD 4
WHATEVER HAPPENED TO BLACK AMERICA? OR: THE SETZUAN INVISIBILITY BLACK AND BLUE. "Whatever happened to black America?"
                                                                          WATSHD 4
Brecht, Bertolt. 1898. in German.
AN DEN SCHWANKENDEN. "Du sagst: Es steht schlecht um unsere Sache"   DEUTGR 24
AN DIE NACHGEBORENEN. "Wiklich, ich lebe in finsteren Zeiten"   DEUTGR 24,
                                                                          DEUTGR 38
AN MEINE LANDSLEUTE. "Ihr, die ihr überlebtet in gestorbenen Städten"   DEUTGR 24,
                                                     DEUTGR 38, FOLKW 106
AUF EINEN CHINESISCHEN TEEWURZELLÖWEN. "Die Schlechten fürchten deine Klaue"
                                                                          DEUTGR 38
DER AUFHALTSAME AUFSTIEG DES ARTURO UI: EPILOG. "Ihr aber lernet, wie man sieht statt stiert"   DEUTGR 38
THE BALLAD OF MARIE SANDERS.
                                      English FOLKW 106
BALLAD OF SEXUAL SUBMISSIVENESS.
                                      English FOLKW 106
BALLADE, IN DER MACHEATH JEDERMANN ABBITTE LEISTET. "Ihr Menschenbrüder, die ihr nach uns lebt"   DEUTGR 34

DIE BALLADE VOM ANGENEHMEN LEBEN. "Da preisst man uns das Leben grosser Geister"   DEUTGR 34
BALLADE VOM PFUND. "Als unser Herr auf Erden"   DEUTGR 37
BALLADE VOM WEIB UND DEM SOLDATEN. "Das Schiessgewehr schiesst, und das Spiessmesser spiesst"   CHRIST 15, DEUTG 28,
                                        DEUTG 35, FOLKW 106
BALLADE VON DEN SELBSTHELFERN. "Noch sitzen sie rauchend da"   DEUTGR 35
BERICHT ÜBER DEN TOD EINES GENOSSEN. "Aber als er zur Wand ging, um erschossen zu werden"   DEUTGR 35
DER BLUMENGARTEN. "Am See, tief zwischen Tann and Liberpappel"   DEUTGR 38
"Da das Instrument verstimmt ist"
                                      DEUTGR 38
DES FELDPREDIGERS GESPRÄCHE UEBER KRIEG UND FRIEDEN.   DEUTGR 34
DEUTSCHES MISERERE. "Eines schönen Tages befahlen uns unsere Obern"   DEUTGR 38
DEUTSCHLAND. "O Deutschland, bleiche Mutter"   DEUTGR 30
DEUTSCHLAND. "In Sturmesnacht, in dunkler Nacht"   DEUTGR 24
EASTER SUNDAY, 1935.   English FOLKW 106
ERINNERUNG AN DIE MARIE A. "An jenem Tag im blauen Mond September"   DOVER 1,
                                               FOLKW 106
DIE FRAGE, OB ES EINEN GOTT GIBT.
                                      DEUTGR 34
FRAGEN EINES LESENDEN ARBEITERS. "Wer baute das siebentorige Theben?"   DEUTGR 37
                                                 SPOA 5
DAS FRÜHJAHR. "Das Frühjahr kommt"
                                      DEUTGR 35
GEGEN VERFÜHRUNG. "Lasst euch nicht verführen"   DEUTGR 28
GESANG VON DER FRAU. "Abends am Fluss in dem dunklen Herz der Gesträucher"
                                      DEUTGR 34
GESANG VON EINER GELIEBTEN. "Ich weiss es, Geliebte: jetzt fallen mir die Haare aus"
                                      DEUTGR 34
GLEICHNIS DES BUDDHA VOM BRENNENDEN HAUS. "Gothama, der Buddha, lehrte"
                                      DEUTGR 23
DAS GLEICHNIS DES MENENIUS AGRIPPA.
                                      DEUTGR 34
DIE GUTE NACHT. "Der Tag, vor dem der grosse Christ"   DEUTGR 37
HERRN K'S LIEBLINGSTIER, IX 35.   DEUTGR 34
HOLLYWOOD. "Jeden Morgen, mein Brot zu verdienen"   DEUTGR 37
HYMN OF THE GREAT BAAL.
                                      English FOLKW 106
ICH, DER ÜBERLEBENDE. "Ich weiss natürlich einzig durch Glück"   DEUTGR 38
KEINER ODER ALLE. "Sklave, wer wird dich befreien?"   FOLKW 106
KINDERKREUZZUG. "In Polen, im Jahr Neununddreissig"   DEUTGR 24, DEUTGR 38
DIE KRÜCKEN. "Sieben Jahre wollt kein Schnitt mir glücken"   DEUTGR 38
KUPPELLIED. "Ach, man sagt, des roten Mondes Anblick"   DEUTGR 35

* Recording not available for analysis

Brecht, Bertolt (continued)

LEGENDE DER DIRNE EVELYN ROE. "Als der Frühling kam und das Meer war blau" DEUTGR 35

LEGENDE VOM TOTEN SOLDATEN. "Und als der Krieg im vierten Lenz" DEUTGR 28, FOLKW 106

LEGENDE VON DER ENTSTEHUNG DES BUCHES TAO-TEKING AUF DEM WEG DES LAOTSE IN DIE EMIGRATION. "Als er Siebzig war und war gebrechlich" DEUTGR 23, DEUTGR 37

DIE LIEBENDEN. "Sieh jene Kraniche in grossem Bogen" DEUTGR 23

DAS LIED DER EISENBAHNTRUPPE VON FORT DONALD. "Die Männer von Fort Donald—hohé!" DEUTGR 35

LIED DER MÜDEN EMPÖRER (PHILOSOPHISCHES TANZLIED) "Wer immer seinen Schuh gespart" DEUTGR 35

DAS LIED VOM EXTRA. "Père Joseph hat kein Dach überm Kopfe" DEUTGR 34

DAS LIED VOM KLASSENFEIND. "Als ich klein war, ging ich zur Schule" DEUTGR 24

LIED VON DER VERDERBTEN UNSCHULD BEIM WÄSCHEFALTEN. "Was meine Mutter mir sagte" DEUTGR 35

DAS LIED VON DER WOLKE DER NACHT. "Mein Herz ist trüb wie die Wolke der Nacht" DEUTGR 35

LIED VON EINER DEUTSCHEN MUTTER. "Mein Sohn, ich hab dir die Stiefel" DEUTGR 35, DEUTGR 38, FOLKW 106

LIED VON MEINER MUTTER. "Ich erinnere mich thres Gesichts nicht mehr" DEUTGR 37

LITURGIE VOM HAUCH. "Einst kam ein altes Weib einher" DEUTGR 37

A MAN'S A MAN. English FOLKW 106

MARIA. "Die Nacht ihrer ersten Geburt war" DEUTGR 37

DIE MASKE DES BOSEN. "An meiner Wand hängt ein japanisches Holzwerk" DEUTGR 37

"Mein Bruder war ein Flieger" DEUTGR 37

MEINER MUTTER. "Als sie nun aus war, liess man in Erde sie" DEUTGR 37

MODERNE LEGENDE. "Als der Abend übers Schlachtfeld wehte" DEUTGR 28

MONOLOG DER ANTIGONE DES SOPHOKLES. "Schwester, Ismene, Zwillingsreis" DEUTGR 23

MORGENDLICHE REDE AN DEN BAUM GRIEHN. "Griehn, ich muss Sie um Entschuldigung bitten" DEUTGR 34, DEUTGR 37

DIE MORITAT VON MACKIE MESSER. "Und der Haifisch, der hat Zähne" DEUTGR 34, FOLKW 106

MÜHSAL DER BESTEN. DEUTGR 34

MUTTER BEIMLEN. "Mutter Beimlen hat ein Holzbein" DEUTGR 35, DEUTGR 37

NACH DEM TODE MEINER MITARBEITERIN M.S. "Im neunten Jahr der Flucht vor Hitler" DEUTGR 37

DER NEUE KANONEN-SONG. "Fritz war SA und Karl war Partei" DEUTGR 34

DIE NIEDERKUNFT DER GROSSEN BABEL. "Als ihre schwere Stunde gekommen war" DEUTGR 37

1940. "Mit Furcht/Erwarten" DEUTGR 37

1940: VI ÖDER DIE ANTWORT. "Mein junger Sohr öder fragt mich" DEUTGR 34

O FALLADAH, DIE DU HANGEST! "Ich zog meine Fuhre trotz meiner Schwäche" DEUTGR 35

ORGE'S HYMN. English FOLKW 106

DER PFLAUMENBAUM. "Im Hofe steht ein Pflaumenbaum" DEUTGR 37

DER RADWECHSEL. "Ich sitze am Strassenrand" DEUTGR 38

DER RAUCH. "Das kleine Haus unter Bäumer am See" DEUTGR 38

RÜCKKEHR. "Die Vaterstadt, wie find ich sie doch" DEUTGR 38

RUF AUS DER GRUFT. "Nun hört die Stimme, die um Mitleid ruft" DEUTGR 34

DER SCHNEIDER VON ULM. "Bischof, ich kann flie gen" DEUTGR 37

SONG OF MOTHER COURAGE. English FOLKW 106

SUPPLY AND DEMAND. English FOLKW 106

TANNEN. "In der Frühe/sind die Tannen kupf ern" DEUTGR 38

DIE TEPPICHWEBER VON KUJAN-BULAK EHREN LEN IN. "Oftmals wurde geehrt und ausgiebig" DEUTGR 24

THAT'S HOW IT SHOULD BE. English FOLKW 106

TO THE LITTLE RADIO. English FOLKW 106

UNTERSUCHUNG, OB DER MENSCH DEM MENSCHEN HILFT. "Einer von uns ist über das Meer gefahren und" DEUTGR 37

VERGNÜGEN. "Der erste Blick aus dem Fenster am Morgen" DEUTGR 34, DEUTGR 38

VISION IN WEISS. "Nachts erwache ich schweiss gebadet am Husten" DEUTGR 34

A VISIT TO THE EXILED POETS. English FOLKW 106

VOM ARMEN B.B. "Ich, Bertolt Brecht, bin aus den schwarzen Wäldern" DEUTGR 23 DEUTGR 37, FOLKW 106

VOM ERTRUNKENEN MÄDCHEN. "Als sie ertrunken war und hinunterschwamm" DEUTGR 23, DEUTGR 35, DEUTGR 37

VOM KIND, DAS SICH NICHT WASCHEN WOLLTE. "Es war einmal ein Kind/Das wollte sich nicht waschen" DEUTGR 37

VOM SCHWIMMEN IN SEEN UND FLÜSSEN. "Im blei chen Sommer wenn die Winde oben" DEUTGR 37

VOM SPRENGEN DES GARTENS. "O Sprengen des Gartens, das Grün zu ermutigen" DEUTGR 37

VON DER FREUNDLICHKEIT DER WELT. "Auf die Erde voller kaltem Wind" DOVER 1

DAS WASCHEN. "Als ich dir vor Jahren zeigte" DEUTGR 38

DAS WIEDERSEHEN. DEUTGR 34

WO SOLL DAS HIN? "Grossvater Stöffel/Isst den Brotaufstrich mit dem Löffel" DEUTGR 37

DER WOLF IST ZUM HUHN GEKOMMEN. "Der Wol ist zum Huhn gekommen" DEUTGR 37

ZEITUNGSLESEN BEIM TEEKOCHEN. "Frühmorgens lese ich in der Zeitung von epochalen Plänen" DEUTGR 37

* Recording not available for analysis

"Zu Potsdam unter den Eichen"
                     DEUTGR 35
DER ZWECKDIENER.   DEUTGR 34
Poetry*   COLUMB 15
Brentano, Clemens. 1778. in German.
ABENDSTÄNDCHEN. "Hör, es klagt die Flöte
   wieder"   CHRIST 27
"Säusle liebe Myrte"   DEUTGR 4
SCHWANENLIED. "Wenn die Augen brechen"
                     DEUTGR 4
"Sprich aus der Ferne"   DEUTGR 4
"Was reif in diesen Zeilen steht"
                     ATHENA 11
WIDMUNG.   CHRIST 27
"Wie in Gewölben von Smaragd"
                     DEUTGR 4
WIEGENLIED/LURELAY. "Singet leise, leise, leise"
   ATHENA 6, CHRIST 27, DEUTGR 45,
                     SPOA 126
Breton, André. 1896. in French.
L'AIR DE L'EAU. "A ta place je me méfierais du
   chevalier de paille"   ADES 52
"Au beau demi-jour"   ADES 47
COURS—LES TOUTES.   ADES 47
GUERRE. "Je regarde la Bête pendant qu'elle se
   lèche"   ADES 47
SUR LA ROUTE DE SAN ROMANO. "Dites-moi ou
   s'arrêtera la flamme"   ADES 47
L'UNION LIBRE. "Ma femme à la chevelure de
   feu de bois"   ADES 47, ADES 52
VIGILANCE. "A Paris la tour Saint-Jacques chan-
   celante"   ADES 47, ADES 52
Breton, Nicholas. 1551. in English.
NOW FOR THE DELIGHT OF YOUR EYE. ARGO 120
SHEPHERD AND SHEPHERDESS. "Who can live in
   heart so glad"   ARGO 120
A SWEET LULLABY. "Come little babe, come, silly
   soul"   ARGO 31
Bridges, Robert. 1841. in English.
LONDON SNOW. "When men were all asleep the
   snow came flying" ARGO 70A, CAED 201,
                     HOUGHT 4
NIGHTINGALES. "Beautiful must be the moun-
   tains whence ye come"   ARGO 82,
                     SPOA 41
A PASSER-BY. "Whither, O splendid ship, thy
   white sails crowding"   ARGO 70A
TRIOLET. "When first we met, we did not guess"
                     EAV 22
Brierre, Jean-François. 1909. in French.
BLACK SOUL. "Cinq siecles vous ont vus les
   armes a la main"   FOLKW 83
Brinnin, John Malcolm. 1916. in English.
AMERICAN PLAN. "The antique Indian should be
   Henry James"   SPOA 102
CRADLE SONG OF OEDIPUS THE KING. "Who is my
   shepherd, that I shall not want" SPOA 102
EVERY EARTHLY CREATURE. "The shifty limpet on
   his rocky shore"   HARVOC 14
FOR MY PUPILS IN THE WAR YEARS. "To come to a
   congress of books when thoughtless death"
                   HARVOC 14
HEAVY, HEAVY, HEAVY. "Who winds the clumsy
   flower-clock now, I wonder" SPOA 102
LITTLE ELEGY FOR GERTRUDE STEIN. "Pass gently,
   pigeons on the grass"   SPOA 102

LOVE IN PARTICULAR. "When the orchard that
   clings to the terrace is boxed for the winter"
               LIBC 9, LIBC 20
NUNS AT EVE. "On St. Martin's evening green"
                   SPOA 102
ROWING IN LINCOLN PARK. "You are, in 1925, my
   father"   HARVOC 14
A SALIENT OF WAR. "In time's unconscious shad-
   ow and return"   HARVOC 14
SECOND SIGHT.   LIBC 9, LIBC 20
VIEWS OF THE FAVORITE COLLEGES. "Approach-
   ing by the gate (class of '79, all dead)
               LIBC 9, LIBC 20
Poetry*   JNP 73
Britting, Georg. 1891. in German.
Poetry*   CHRIST 7
Broch, Hermann. 1886. in German.
Poetry*   SUHRK 1
Brock, Edwin. in English.
A MOMENT OF RESPECT. "Two things I remember
   about my grandfather"   LONDON 2,
                     SPOA 67
Brockes, Berthold Heinrich. 1680. in German.
DAS FIRMAMENT. "Als jüngst mein Auge sich in
   die sapphirne Tiefe"   CHRIST 16
Bronk, William. 1918. in English.
Poetry*   WATSHD 40
Brontë, Anne. 1820. in English.
IF THIS BE ALL.   ARGO 63
Brontë, Charlotte. 1816. in English.
MEMENTOS, exc.   ARGO 63
STANZAS. "If thou be in a lonely place"
                 CAED 201
Brontë, Emily. 1818. in English.
DEATH. "Death, that struck when I was most
   confiding"   ARGO 63
LAST LINES. "No coward soul is mine"
            ARGO 63, CAED 199
"Often rebuked, yet always back returning"
                 ARGO 63
THE PRISONER, exc. "Still let my tyrants know"
            ARGO 63, CAED 199
REMEMBRANCE. "Cold in the earth—and the
   deep snow piled above thee" ARGO 63,
                   CAED 199
THE VISIONARY. "Silent is the house: all are laid
   asleep"   SPOA 35
Brooke, 1st Baron. See Greville, Fulke.
Brooke, Rupert. 1887. in English.
"Blow out, you bugles, over the rich Dead!"
                 FOLKW 51
THE CALL. "Out of the nothingness of sleep"
                 FOLKW 51
A CHANNEL PASSAGE. "The damned ship lurched
   and slithered"   FOLKW 51
THE DEAD. "These hearts were woven of human
   joys and cares"   FOLKW 51
DESERTION. "So light we were, so right we
   were"   FOLKW 51
DINING-ROOM TEA. "When you were there, and
   you, and you"   FOLKW 51
THE GREAT LOVER. "I have been so great a lover:
   filled my days"   FOLKW 51
HEAVEN. "Fish (fly-replete, in depth of June)"
                 FOLKW 51
THE HILL. "Breathless, we flung us on the windy
   hill"   ARGO 77

* Recording not available for analysis

Brooke, Rupert (continued)

JEALOUSY. "When I see you, who were so wise
and cool"   FOLKW 51
KINDLINESS. "When love has changed to kindliness—"   FOLKW 51
THE OLD VICARAGE, GRANTCHESTER. "Just now
the lilac is in bloom"   FOLKW 51
PINE-TREES AND THE SKY: EVENING. "I'd watched
the sorrow of the evening sky" FOLKW 51
SAFETY. "Dear! of all happy in the hour, most
blest"   FOLKW 51
THE SOLDIER. "If I should die, think only this of
me"   FOLKW 51, RCA 4
SONNET. "I said I splendidly loved you; it's not
true"   ARGO 93, FOLKW 51
THERE'S WISDOM IN WOMEN. "Oh love is fair, and
love is rare"   FOLKW 51
THE VOICE. "Safe in the magic of my words"
                                   FOLKW 51

Brooks, Gwendolyn. 1917. in English.
"About aloneness and loneliness I have said"
                                     AUDIT 1
THE ASSASSINATION OF JOHN F. KENNEDY. "I hear
things crying in the world"   FOLKW 21
THE BALLAD OF RUDOLPH REED. "Rudolph Reed
was oaken"   AUDIT 1, LIBC 1, SPOA 102
THE BEAN EATERS. "They eat beans mostly, this
old yellow pair"   CAED 114
BEVERLY HILLS, CHICAGO. "The dry brown
coughing beneath their feet"   AUDIT 1,
                                   FOLKW 1
CHARLES.   CAED 110
THE CHICAGO DEFENDER SENDS A MAN TO LITTLE
ROCK, FALL 1957. "In Little Rock the people
bear"   ARGO 17
THE CHILDREN OF THE POOR. "People who have
no children can be hard"   CAED 114,
                            LIBC 1, SPOA 102
THE CHILDREN OF THE POOR, SONNET NO. 2. "What
shall I give my children"   AUDIT 1,
                                   FOLKW 1
"Do not be afraid of no"   CAED 114
GANG GIRLS. "Gang girls are sweet exotics"
                                   CAED 114
GARBAGEMAN: THE MAN WITH THE ORDERLY MIND.
"What do you think of us in fussy endeavor"
                                   CAED 114
THE GHOST AT THE QUINCY CLUB. "All filmy down
the drifts"   CAED 114
KID BRUIN. "I rode into the golden yell"
                                   CAED 114
KITCHENETTE BUILDING. "We are things of dry
hours and the involuntary plan" AUDIT 1,
     CAED 114, FOLKW 1, LIBC 1, SPOA 102
LEAVES FROM A LOOSE-LEAF WAR DIARY. "You
need the untranslatable ice to watch"
                                   CAED 114
THE LIFE OF LINCOLN WEST. "Ugliest little boy"
                                   BROADV 5
LOVE YOU RIGHT BACK.   BROADV 5
"The lovers of the poor/arrive. The Ladies"
                                   CAED 114
MALCOLM X. "Original/Ragged-round"
                                   CAED 155
A MAN OF THE MIDDLE CLASS. "I'm what has gone
out blithely and with noise"   CAED 114

MATTHEW COLE. "Here are the facts"
                                   CAED 114
THE MOTHER. "Abortions will not let you forget"
                                   CAED 114
MY LITTLE 'BOUT-TOWN GAL. "My little 'bout-
town gal has gone"   CAED 114
NORA. "I was not sleeping when Brother said"
                                     LIBC 1
OBITUARY FOR A LIVING LADY. "My friend was de-
cently wild"   CAED 114
OF DE WITT WILLIAMS ON HIS WAY TO LINCOLN
CEMETERY. "He was born in Alabama"
                                     AUDIT 1
OLD LAUGHTER. "The men and women long ago
in Africa"   FOLKW 1, HOUGHT 2
OLD MARY. "My last defense"   CAED 114
THE PARENTS: PEOPLE LIKE OUR MARRIAGE MAXIE
AND ANDREW. "Clogged and soft and sloppy
eyes"   CAED 114
THE PREACHER RUMINATES BEHIND THE SERMON.
"I think it must be lonely to be God"
              FOLKW 1, LIBC 1, SPOA 102
THE PROGRESS. "And still we wear our uniforms,
follow"   LIBC 1
PYGMIES ARE PYGMIES STILL, THOUGH PERCHT ON
ALPS. "But can see better there, and laughing
there"   CAED 114
QUEEN OF THE BLUES. "Mame was singing"
                                   CAED 114
RIOT. "John Cabot, out of Wilma, once a Wy-
cliffe"   CAED 114
THE RITES FOR COUSIN VIT. "Carried her unpro-
testing out the door"   CAED 114
SADIE AND MAUD. "Maud went to college"
                                   CAED 114
THE SERMON ON THE WARPLAND. "And several
strengths from drowsiness campaigned"
                       CAED 114, CAED 155
A SONG IN THE FRONT YARD. "I stayed in the front
yard all my life"   FOLKW 1
SONG: THE REV. MUBUGWU DICKINSON RUMINATES
BEHIND THE SERMON. "If possible"
                                   BROADV 5
SPEECH TO THE YOUNG, SPEECH TO THE PROGRESS-
TOWARD. "Say to them"   BROADV 5
THE SUNDAYS OF SATIN-LEGS SMITH. "Inamorates,
with an approbation"   CAED 114
THE VACANT LOT. "Mrs. Coley's three-flat brick"
                                   CAED 114
THE WALL. "A drumdrumdrum/Humbly we
come"   CAED 114
WE REAL COOL, OR THE POOL PLAYERS, SEVEN AT
THE GOLDEN SHOVEL. "We real cool. We"
                    CAED 155, LIBC 1, SPOA 102
WEAPONED WOMAN. "Well, life has been a
baffled vehicle"   CAED 114
WHEN YOU HAVE FORGOTTEN SUNDAY. "And when
you have forgotten the bright bedclothes on
a Wednesday and a Saturday"   UA 2
WOMEN IN LOVE: ESTIMABLE MABLE. BROADV 5
YOUNG AFRICANS. "Of the furious" BROADV 5
YOUNG HEROES I. TO KEORAPETSE KGOSITSILE. "He
is very busy with his looking." BROADV 5
_____ II. TO DON AT SALAAM. "I like to see you
lean back in your chair"   BROADV 5
_____ III. WALTER BRADFORD. "Just as you think
you're 'better now' "   BROADV 5

* Recording not available for analysis

Poetry*   PRENT 1, NET 15
Brooks, Phillips. in English.
"O little town of Bethlehem"   LION 1
Broughton, James. in English.
BRIDGE TO THE INNERMOST FOREST. "I could not match the labels"   EVERG 1
THE MADMAN'S HOUSE. "Slippers he made me"   EVERG 1
Broumas, Olga. in English.
Poetry*   WATSHD 49
Brown, George Mackay. 1921. in English.
THE SEVEN HOUSES: IN MEMORY OF JOHN F. KENNEDY. "Man, you are at the first door"   ARGO 96
Brown, Hubert "Rap" Geroid. 1943. in English.
Poetry*   PRENT 1
Brown, Otis. in English.
BB. "Big Bad"   WATSHD 10
"Body shop"   WATSHD 10
HARDLY "A day"   WATSHD 10
LIGHT AS A FEATHER, MAMA. "You, you, you come on"   WATSHD 10
"A son can make a father"   WATSHD 10
STRANDED. "Stranded was written"   WATSHD 10
"Zabeeba"   WATSHD 10
Brown, Rosalie Gertrude Moore. See **Moore, Rosalie.**
Brown, Sterling A. 1901. in English.
AFTER WINTER. "He snuggles his fingers"   ARGO 79, FOLKW 43
BALLAD OF BIG BOY. "Lemme be wid Casey Jones"   ARGO 79
BREAK OF DAY. "Big Jess fired on the Alabama Central"   FOLKW 40
CHILDREN'S CHILDREN. "When they hear/these songs"   FOLKW 43
CONJURED. "She done put her little hands"   ARGO 79
LONG GONE. "I like your kind of loving"   FOLKW 1
MA RAINEY. "When Ma Rainey comes to town"   ARGO 17, ARGO 79, FOLKW 1
MR. SAMUEL AND SAM. "Mister Samuel, he belong to Rotary"   ARGO 79
OLD KING COTTON. "Ole King Cotton/Ole Man Cotton"   FOLKW 40
OLD LEM. "I talked to old Lem"   ARGO 79, FOLKW 40
PARISH DOCTOR. "They come to him for subscriptions"   FOLKW 43
PUTTIN' ON DOG. "Look at old Scrappy, puttin' on dog"   FOLKW 40
SAM SMILEY. "The whites had taught him how to rip"   FOLKW 43
SHARECROPPERS. "When they rode up at first dark and called his name"   FOLKW 40
SISTER LOU. "Honey/When de man"   FOLKW 6, FOLKW 41
SLIM GREER. "Listen to the tale"   ARGO 79
SLIM IN ATLANTA. "Down in Atlanta"   ARGO 79
SLIM IN HELL. "Slim Greer went to heaven"   ARGO 79, FOLKW 40
SLIM LANDS A JOB. "Poppa Greer happened"   ARGO 79

SPORTING BEASLEY. "Good glory, give a look at Sporting Beasley"   FOLKW 43
UNCLE JOE.   FOLKW 43
Poetry*   PRENT 1
Brown, Thomas Edward. 1830. in English.
BELLA GORRY, exc.   ARGO 127
BETSY LEE, exc.   ARGO 127, ARGO 139
THE CHRISTENING, exc.   ARGO 127
CLIFTON. "I'm here at Clifton, grinding at the mill"   ARGO 127
THE DHOON. "Leap from the crags, brave boy"   ARGO 127
THE DOCTOR, exc.   ARGO 127
IN THE COACH, 3. "Yes, comin' home from the North Sea fishin' we were, past John o' Groat's"   ARGO 127
KITTY OF THE SHERRACH VANE. "And she pressed her hands against my lips"   ARGO 127
ST. BEE'S HEAD. "I have seen cliffs that met the ocean foe"   ARGO 127
THE SCHOOLMASTERS, exc.   ARGO 127
TOMMY BIG-EYES, exc.   ARGO 127
Brown, William. in English.
HALLELUJAH CORNER. "Cimbals clash"   ARGO 17
"Saturday night in Harlem"   ARGO 17
Browne, Michael Dennis. 1940. in English.
PARANOIA. "When you drive on the freeway, cars follow you"   EMC 7
Poetry*   JNP 74
Browne, William. 1591. in English.
ON THE COUNTESS DOWAGER OF PEMBROKE. "Underneath this sable Herse"   CAED 38
THE SIREN'S SONG. "Steer hither, steer your winged pines"   ARGO 31
SONG. "For her gait, if she be walking"   CAED 38
Browning, Elizabeth Barrett. 1806. in English.
AURORA LEIGH, BOOK V, exc.   ARGO 63
THE CRY OF THE CHILDREN, exc.   ARGO 63
GRIEF. "I tell you, hopeless grief is passionless"   CMS 13
A MUSICAL INSTRUMENT. "What was he doing, the great god Pan"   EAV 10, RCA 4
SONNETS FROM THE PORTUGUESE, 1. "I thought once how Theocritus had sung"   AUDIA 1, CAED 46, CAED 201, CMS 12, LIST 3, SPOA 78
_____, 2. "But only thee in all God's universe"   CAED 46, SPOA 78
_____, 3. "Unlike are we, unlike, O princely heart"   SPOA 78
_____, 4. "Thou hast thy calling to some palace-floor"   SPOA 78
_____, 5. "I lift my heavy heart up solemnly"   CAED 46, SPOA 78
_____, 6. "Go from me. Yet I feel that I shall stand"   AUDIA 1, CAED 46, CAED 201, LIST 3, SPOA 78
_____, 7. "The face of all the world is changed, I think"   AUDIA 1, CAED 46, SPOA 78
_____, 8. "What can I give thee back, O liberal"   CAED 46, SPOA 78
_____, 9. "Can it be right to give what I can give"   SPOA 78
_____, 10. "Yet love, mere love, is beautiful indeed"   CAED 46, SPOA 78

* Recording not available for analysis

Browning, Elizabeth Barrett (continued)

———, 11. "And therefore if to love can be desert"   SPOA 78

———, 12. "Indeed this very love which is my boast"   SPOA 78

———, 13. "And wilt thou have me fashion into speech"   SPOA 78

———, 14. "If thou must love me, let it be for nought"   CAED 46, CAED 201, DECCA 12, EAV 10, SPOA 78

———, 15. "Accuse me not, beseech thee, that I wear"   SPOA 78

———, 16. "And yet because thou overcomest so"   CAED 46, SPOA 78

———, 17. "My poet, thou canst touch on all the notes"   SPOA 78

———, 18. "I never gave a lock of hair away"   CAED 46, SPOA 78

———, 19. "The soul's Rialto hath its merchandise"   SPOA 78

———, 20. "Beloved, my beloved, when I think"   CAED 46, SPOA 78

———, 21. "Say over again, and yet once over again"   CAED 46, SPOA 78

———, 22. "When our two souls stand up erect and strong"   CAED 46, CAED 201, SPOA 78

———, 23. "Is it indeed so? If I lay here dead"   CAED 46, SPOA 78

———, 24. "Let the world's sharpness like a clasping knife"   SPOA 78

———, 25. "A heavy heart, Beloved, have I borne"   SPOA 78

———, 26. "I lived with visions for my company"   CAED 46, SPOA 78

———, 27. "My own Beloved, who hast lifted me"   SPOA 78

———, 28. "My letters! All dead paper- mute and white"   CAED 46, CAED 201, SPOA 78

———, 29. "I think of thee—my thoughts do twine and bud"   SPOA 78

———, 30. "I see thine image through my tears to-night"   SPOA 78

———, 31. "Thou comest!—all is said without a word"   CAED 201, SPOA 78

———, 32. "The first time that the sun rose on thine oath"   CAED 201, SPOA 78

———, 33. "Yes, call me by my pet name! Let me hear"   CAED 46, SPOA 78

———, 34. "With the same heart I said, I'll answer three"   SPOA 78

———, 35. "If I leave all for thee, wilt thou exchange"   CAED 201, SPOA 78

———, 36. "When we met first and loved, I did not build"   SPOA 78

———, 37. "Pardon, oh, pardon, that my soul should make"   SPOA 78

———, 38. "First time he kissed me, he but only kissed"   CAED 46, CAED 201, SPOA 78

———, 39. "Because thou hast the power and own'st the grace"   SPOA 78

———, 40. "Oh, yes! They love through all this world of ours"   SPOA 78

———, 41. "I thank all who have loved me in their hearts"   SPOA 78

———, 42. "My future will not copy fair my past"   SPOA 78

———, 43. "How do I love thee? Let me count the ways"   AUDIA 1, CAED 46, CAED 132, CAED 201, DECCA 12, LIST 3, LIVLAN 1, THEAL 3, SPOA 78, LION 2

———, 44. "Beloved, thou hast brought me many flowers"   CAED 46, SPOA 78
Poetry*   CMS 15, LIST 11, SPOA 123

Browning, Robert. 1812. in English.

ABT VOGLER. "Would that the structure brave, the manifold music I build"   ARGO 67

AFTER. "Take the cloak from his face, and at first"   ARGO 66

ANDREA DEL SARTO. "But do not let us quarrel any more"   CAED 37

ANY WIFE TO ANY HUSBAND. "My love, this is the bitterest, that thou"   CAED 201

BISHOP BLOUGRAM'S APOLOGY, exc. "No more wine? then we'll push back chairs and talk"   ARGO 66

THE BISHOP ORDERS HIS TOMB AT SAINT PRAXED'S CHURCH. "Vanity, saith the preacher, vanity!"   ARGO 66, CAED 37, SPOA 45

BOOT AND SADDLE. "Boot, saddle, to horse, and away"   SPOA 65

CALIBAN UPON SETEBOS, exc. "Setebos, Setebos, and Setebos"   LONGM 1

CHILDE ROLAND TO THE DARK TOWER CAME. "My first thought was he lied in every word"   CAED 96

CONFESSIONS. "What is the buzzing in my ears"   ARGO 88A, ARGO 66

DE GUSTIBUS. "Your ghost will walk, you lover of trees"   ARGO 66

A FACE. "If one could have that little head of hers"   ARGO 67

FRA LIPPO LIPPI. "I am poor brother Lippo, by your leave"   CAED 37, SPOA 45

GIVE A ROUSE. "King Charles, and who'll do him right now?"   SPOA 65

A GRAMMARIAN'S FUNERAL. "Let us begin and carry up this corpse"   ARGO 67

HOME-THOUGHTS, FROM ABROAD. "Oh, to be in England" ARGO 66, CAED 96, CAED 201, EAV 10, SPOA 45, THEAL 2

HOW THEY BROUGHT THE GOOD NEWS FROM GHENT TO AIX. "I sprang to the stirrup, and Joris, and he"   BRITAM 1, CAED 96, CAED 132, EAV 10, FOLKW 68, HOUGHT 2, SINGER 1, SPOA 65

INCIDENT OF THE FRENCH CAMP. "You know, we French stormed Ratisbon"   CAED 132, CAED 201, DECCA 10, HOUGHT 1, LIST 3, LIST 21, SPOA 65 UCOL 1

INSTANS TYRANNUS. "Of the million or two, more or less"   ARGO 67

JOHANNES AGRICOLA IN MEDITATION. "There's heaven above, and night by night"   ARGO 66

LIFE IN A LOVE. "Escape me?/Never—Beloved!"   ARGO 66

A LIGHT WOMAN. "So far as our story approaches the end"   ARGO 67

A LIKENESS. "Some people hang portraits up"   ARGO 67

* Recording not available for analysis

THE LOST LEADER. "Just for a handful of silver he left us"   ARGO 66, AUDIA 1, CAED 96, CAED 201, LIST 3

THE LOST MISTRESS. "All's over then: does truth sound bitter"   ARGO 66

LOVE AMONG THE RUINS. "Where the quiet-colored end of evening smiles"   ARGO 67

LOVE IN A LIFE. "Room after room/I hunt the house through"   ARGO 66, COLUMB 11

MEETING AT NIGHT. "The gray sea and the long black land"   ARGO 66, LION 2, CMS 14, RCA 4, SPOA 45, ARGO 143,

MEMORABILIA. "Ah, did you once see Shelley plain"   ARGO 66, CAED 96

MY LAST DUCHESS. "That's my last duchess painted on the wall"   ARGO 66, AUDIA 1, BRITAM 3, CAED 21, CAED 96, CAED 132, CMS 12, DECCA 10, EAV 10, JNP 8, JNP 87, LIST 2, LIST 3, LIST 4, SINGER 6, TEMPO 1, THEAL 2, LONGM 1

ONE WAY OF LOVE. "All June I bound the rose in sheaves"   ARGO 67

PARTING AT MORNING. "Round the cape of a sudden came the sea"   ARGO 66, SPOA 45, ARGO 143

THE PATRIOT. "It was roses, roses all the way"   ARGO 66

PAULINE, exc. "And my choice fell"   ARGO 66

THE PIED PIPER OF HAMELIN. "Hamelin Town's in Brunswick"   CAED 48, CAED 85, DECCA 11, FOLKW 62, LIST 22, LONDON 1, PROTHM 9, SINGER 1, SPOA 65, SPOWRD 5, ARGO 123

———, exc. "Rats!/They fought the dogs"   CMS 4

PIPPA PASSES, exc. SONG. "The year's at the Spring"   CAED 96, LIST 3

PORPHYRIA'S LOVER. "The rain set early in tonight"   ARGO 67, CAED 96

PROSPICE. "Fear death?—to feel the fog in my throat"   ARGO 67, CAED 96, CMS 14, SPOA 45

RABBI BEN EZRA. "Grow old along with me!"   CAED 96

———, exc.   ARGO 66

THE RING AND THE BOOK, exc. "First of the first, such I pronounce Pompilia"   ARGO 82, SPOA 41

———, exc. "Do you see this Ring?"   ARGO 67

A SERENADE AT THE VILLA. "That was I, you heard last night"   SPOA 45

SOLILOQUY OF THE SPANISH CLOISTER. "Gr-r-r—there go, my heart's abhorrence!"   CAED 96, JNP 87

SONG.   AUDIA 1

A TOCCATA OF GALUPPI'S. "Oh, Galuppi, Baldassaro, this is very sad to find"   ARGO 66, RCA 1, LONGM 1

TWO IN THE CAMPAGNA. "I wonder do you feel to-day"   ARGO 66, SPOA 45

UP AT A VILLA, DOWN IN THE CITY. "Had I but plenty of money"   ARGO 67

YOUTH AND ART. "It once might have been, once only"   ARGO 143

Poetry*   CMS 15, LIST 11, SPOA 123

Bruchac, Joseph. 1942. in English.

AND STILL YOU ASK ME WHY. "I am looking for a place"   WATSHD 2

CLEVELAND NINE.   WATSHD 2

WHERE DO YOU GO? "They pilled the dam"   WATSHD 2

Brukner, Ira. in English.

HOT FLASH NUMBER ONE. "A contact lens falls"   WATSHD 8

Brull, Mariano. 1891. in Spanish.

EL NIÑO Y LA LUNA. "La luna y el niño juegan"   SMC 13

Bruni, Atilio. in Italian.

Poetry*   SMC 16

Bryant, F. J., Jr. 1942. in English.

THE LANGUAGES WE ARE.   EAV 16

Bryant, William Cullen. 1794. in English.

THE DEATH OF LINCOLN. "Oh, slow to smite and swift to spare"   EAV 14

A FOREST HYMN. "The groves were God's first temples"   EAV 15

"I broke the spell that held me long"   EAV 15

"O Fairest of the rural maids"   EAV 14

THE PRAIRIES. "These are the gardens of the Desert, these"   ARGO 11, CAED 185

SONG OF MARION'S MEN. "Our band is few but true and tried"   DECCA 13, SINGER 2

THANATOPSIS. "To him who in the love of Nature holds"   AUDIA 2, EAV 14, HOUGHT 5, LIST 3

TO A WATERFOWL. "Whither, midst falling dew"   AUDIA 2, EAV 9, EAV 15, LIST 3, SINGER 5, SPOA 31

TO THE FRINGED GENTIAN. "Thou blossom bright with autumn dew"   EAV 14

Poetry*   LIST 12

Buesa, José Angel. in Spanish.

CARTA A USTED. "Según dicen, ya usted tiene otro amante"   SMC 7

ELEGÍA PARA TI Y PARA MI. "Yo seguiré soñando mientras pasa la vida"   SMC 7

POEMA DE LA DESPEDIDA. "Te digo adios y acaso te quiero todavia"   SMC 1

Bulwer-Lytton, Edward Robert, 1st Earl of Lytton (Owen Meredith). 1831. in English.

Poetry*   HBCF 1

Bunner, Henry Cuyler. in English.

ONE-TWO-THREE. "It was an old, old, old, old lady"   CMS 2

Bunting, Basil. 1900. in English.

"Let them remember Samangan, the bridge and tower"   ARGO 97

"Mesh cast for Mackerel"   ARGO 97

Bunyan, John. 1628. in English.

SONG OF THE SHEPHERD IN THE VALLEY OF HUMILIATION. "He that is down needs fear no fall"   ARGO 47, BRITAM 2

Buonarroti, Michelangelo. See Michelangelo.

Burchiello (Domenico di Giovanni). 1404. in Italian.

Poetry*   CETRA 21

Burger, Gottfried August. 1747. in German.

AN DIE MENSCHENGESICHTER. "Ich habe was Liebes, das hab ich so lieb"   DEUTGR 13

DER BAUER. "Wer bist du, Fürst, dass ohne Scheu"   DOVER 1

* Recording not available for analysis

Burger, Gottfried August (continued)

LENORE. "Lenore fuhr ums Morgenrot"
                    CHRIST 15, FOLKW 74
Burgos, Julia de. in Spanish.
CAMPO.   INSTPR 1
Burke, Kenneth. 1897. in English.
ALKY, ME LOVE. "Spirit of Alcohol"   JNP 3
UNEASY THOUGHT OF PEACE. "In our street/we lie
late"   JNP 3
Burns, Robert. 1759. in English.
ADDRESS TO A TOOTH-ACHE. "My curse upon your
venom'd stang"   ARGO 53
ADDRESS TO AN ILLEGITIMATE CHILD. "Thou's
welcome, wean, mishanter fa' me"
                            FOLKW 59
ADDRESS TO THE UNCO GUID, OR THE RIGIDLY
RIGHTEOUS. "O ye wha are sae guid yoursel"
            ARGO 53, EMC 3, FOLKW 59
AULD LANG SYNE. "Should auld acquaintance be
forgot"   ARGO 53, CAED 64, CAED 202
THE BANKS O'DOON. "Ye banks and braes o'bonie
Doon"   ARGO 53, CAED 64, CAED 202,
                    EAV 13, LIST 2, LIST 10
_____, exc.   SPOA 1
BONNIE DOON. "Ye flowery banks o' bonnie
Doon"   CMS 18
BONNIE LESLEY. "O saw ye bonnie Lesley"
                    ARGO 53, BRITAM 1
THE BRAW WOOER.   CMS 18
THE COTTER'S SATURDAY NIGHT, exc. "My lov'd,
my honor'd, much respected friend!"
                            ARGO 53
THE DEIL'S AWA' WI' THE EXCISEMAN. "The deil
cam fiddling through the town"   CMS 18
DUNCAN GRAY. "Duncan Gray cam here to woo"
                            EMC 3
EPISTLE TO A YOUNG FRIEND. "I lang hae thought,
my youthfu' friend"   ARGO 53
EPISTLE TO JAMES SMITH. "Dear Smith, the slee'-
est, paukie thief"   EMC 3
FAREWELL TO NANCY. "Ae fond kiss, and then we
sever"   DECCA 12, EAV 13, FOLKW 59
"First when Maggy was my care"
                            FOLKW 59
"Flow gently, sweet Afton, among thy green
braes"   EAV 7, EAV 13, EMC 3, LIST 2,
                    LIST 10, LION 2
FOR THE SAKE OF SOMEBODY. "My heart is sair—I
dare na tell"   ARGO 53
GREEN GROW THE RASHES. "There's nought but
care on ev'ry han' "   ARGO 53, CMS 18,
                    EMC 3, FOLKW 59
HIGHLAND MARY. "Ye banks, and braes, and
streams around"   ARGO 53, CAED 186,
                            FOLKW 59
HOLY WILLIE'S PRAYER, exc. "O Thou that in the
Heavens does dwell"   ARGO 53, CMS 18
"I hae a wife o'my ain"   CMS 18
I'M O'ER YOUNG TO MARRY YET. "I'm o'er young,
I'm o'er young"   ARGO 53
"Jamie, come try me"   ARGO 53
JOHN ANDERSON MY JO. "John Anderson my jo,
John"   ARGO 53, CAED 64, CAED 202,
                    EAV 7, EAV 13 EMC 3
THE JOLLY BEGGARS. "A fig for those by law pro-
tected"   LONGM 1

THE LEA-RIG. "When o'er the hill the eastern
star"   CMS 18
THE LOVELY LASS O'INVERNESS. "The lovely lass of
Inverness"   ARGO 53
A MAN'S A MAN FOR A' THAT. "Is there for honest
poverty" ARGO 53, CAED 64, CAED 202,
            CMS 18, EMC 3, FOLKW 59, LIST 2
MARY MORISON. "O Mary, at thy window be"
            ARGO 53, CAED 64, EAV 13, EMC 3
MY BONNIE MARY. "Go, fetch to me a pint
o'wine"   ARGO 53
"My heart's in the Highlands, my heart is not
here"   BRITAM 3, EAV 7, HARC 3
MY JEAN. "Of a' the airts the wind can blaw"
                    EMC 3, HOUGHT 3
MY WIFE'S A WANTON WEE THING. "I never saw a
fairer"   ARGO 53
"O, whistle and I'll come to Ye my Lad"
                    ARGO 53, LONGM 1
ON JOHN BUSHBY. "Here lies John Bushby, hon-
est man"   FOLKW 59
OPEN THE DOOR TO ME, OH. "O, open the door
some pity to shew"   ARGO 53
A RED, RED ROSE. "My love is like a red, red rose"
            ARGO 53, BRITAM 1, CAED 186,
        CAED 203, CMS 18, DECCA 12, EAV 22,
            EMC 3, LIST 2, LIST 10, LION 2
THE RIGS O' BARLEY. "It was upon a Lammas
night"   FOLKW 59
ROBERT BRUCE'S MARCH TO BANNOCKBURN. "Scots,
wha hae wi' Wallace bled"   ARGO 53,
            CMS 18, EMC 3, FOLKW 59
SCOTCH DRINK, exc. "Let other poets raise a
fracas"   ARGO 53
THE SELKIRK GRACE. "Some hae meat and canna
eat"   FOLKW 59
"The simple Bard, unbroken by rules of art"
                            FOLKW 59
SUCH A PARCEL OF ROGUES IN A NATION. "Fare-
weel to a' our Scottish fame"   FOLKW 59
TAM GLEN. "My heart is a breaking, dear tittie"
                            ARGO 53
TAM O'SHANTER: A TALE. "When chapman billies
leave the street"   CAED 64, EAV 13,
                    EMC 3, FOLKW 59
"There's a youth in this city, it were a great
pity"   ARGO 53
"Thou hast left me ever, Jamie"   ARGO 53
TIBBIE DUNBAR. "O, wilt thou go wi'me"
                            FOLKW 59
TO A HAGGIS. "Fair fa' your honest, sonsie face"
                            FOLKW 59
TO A LOUSE, ON SEEING ONE ON A LADY'S BONNET
AT CHURCH. "Ha! whare ye gaun, ye crowlin
ferlie"   ARGO 53, CAED 64, CAED 202,
            CMS 18, EAV 13, EMC 3, FOLKW 59
TO A MOUSE, ON TURNING HER UP IN HER NEST.
"Wee, sleekit, cow'rin', tim'rous beastie"
    ARGO 53, CAED 64, CAED 202, CMS 18,
            EAV 13, EMC 3, FOLKW 59, LIST 2,
                LIST 4, LIST 10, LIVLAN 1,
THE TREE OF LIBERTY, exc. "Heard ye o' the Tree
o' France"   ARGO 53
"What can a young lassie"   ARGO 53
WILLIE BREWED A PECK O'MAUT. "O, Willie
brew'd a peck o'maut"   EMC 3

---

* Recording not available for analysis

WILLIE WASTLE. "Willie Wastle dwalt on Tweed"   CAED 64, CAED 202, CMS 18
Poetry*   EAV 7, SCOT 1, SCOT 2
Burr, Amelia Josephine. in English.
NIGHT MAGIC. "The apples falling from the tree"   CAED 164
RAIN IN THE NIGHT. "Raining, raining"   CAED 164, CREAT 1
Burr, Gray. 1919. in English.
A DEATH BEFORE KILLING. "Raw ulcers and his aspirin signify"   FOLKW 21
Busch, Wilhelm. 1832. in German.
DIE AFFEN. "Der Bauer sprach zu seinem Jungen"   DEUTGR 8, DEUTGR 40
"Der alte Förster Püsterich"   TELEF 6
DIE ALTE SORGE. "Er kriegte Geld. Die Sorge wich"   DEUTGR 8, DEUTGR 40
AN DIE MUTTER.   TELEF 6
AUF WIEDERSEHEN. "Ich schnürte meinen Ranzen"   DEUTGR 8, DEUTGR 40
BESCHRÄNKT. "Halt dein Röslein nur im Zügel"   DEUTGR 8, DEUTGR 40, TELEF 6
BEWAFFNETER FRIEDE. "Ganz unverhofft an einem Hügel"   DEUTGR 8, DEUTGR 40
BÖS UND GUT. "Wie kam ich nur aus jenem Frieden"   DEUTGR 8, DEUTGR 40
BUCH DES LEBENS. "Hass, als minus und vergebens"   DEUTGR 8, DEUTGR 40
DANEBEN. "Stoffel hackte mit dem Beile"   DEUTGR 8, DEUTGR 40
DER EINSAME. "Wer einsam ist, der hat es gut"   TELEF 6
"Die erste alte Tante sprach"   DEUTGR 30
"Es flog einmal ein muntres Fliegel"   DEUTGR 30
DER GECK.   TELEF 6
"Gestern war in meiner Mütze"   TELEF 6
GLÜCKSPILZ. "Geborn ward er ohne Wehen"   DEUTGR 8, DEUTGR 40
GRÜNDER. "Geschäftig sind die Menschenkinder"   DEUTGR 8, DEUTGR 40
GRÜNDLICHE HEILUNG. "Es sass der fromme Meister"   DEUTGR 8, DEUTGR 40
DIE KLEINSTEN. "Sag Atome, sage Stäubchen"   TELEF 6
DER KNOTEN. "Als ich in Jugendtagen"   DEUTGR 30
LEIDER. "So ist's in alter Zeit gewesen"   DEUTGR 8, DEUTGR 40
NOCH ZWEI. "Durch das Feld ging die Familie"   DEUTGR 8, DEUTGR 40
PFANNKUCHEN UND SALAT. "Von Fruchtomletts, da mag berichten"   TELEF 6
PST. "Es gibt ja leider Sachen und Geschichten"   DEUTGR 8, DEUTGR 40, TELEF 6
REUE. "Die Tugend will nicht immer passen"   DEUTGR 8, DEUTGR 40
DIE SCHÄNDLICHE. "Sie ist ein reizendes Geschöpfchen"   DEUTGR 8, DEUTGR 40
SCHEIN UND SEIN. Mein Kind, es sind allhier die Dinge"   DEUTGR 8, DEUTGR 40
"Sehr tadelnswert ist unser Tun"   DEUTGR 8, DEUTGR 40
"Die Selbstkritik hat viel für sich"   TELEF 6
"Selig sind die Auserwählten"   DEUTGR 30
"Sie hat nichts und du desgleichen"   DEUTGR 8

"Sie stritten sich beim Wein herum"   DEUTGR 8, DEUTGR 40
DIE TUTE. "Wenn die Tante Adelheid"   DEUTGR 8, DEUTGR 40
DER UNDANKBARE. "Einen Menschen names Meier"   TELEF 6
"Wer möchte diesen Erdenball"   DEUTGR 30
"Wirklich, er war unentbehrlich"   DEUTGR 8, DEUTGR 40
Buson, Yosa. 1716. in Japanese.
HAZE. "Morning haze:/as in a painting"   English HARB 6
Butcher, Grace. in English.
ASSIGNMENT. "Hey Mom!"   EMC 7
Butler, Celia. in English.
SPLISH, SPLOSH, SPLATTER. "Raindrops falling, all around"   HARB 1
Butler, Samuel. 1612. in English.
HUDIBRAS, exc. "For his religion it was fit"   LONGM 1
Butler, William. in English.
NOVEMBER 25, 1963. "Drums, drums, I too am dead"   FOLKW 21
Buttitta, Ignazio. in Italian.
A LI MATRI DI LI CARUSI.   CETRA 34
ARSURA D'AMMURI.   CETRA 34
COMPAGNI DI VIAGGIO.   CETRA 31
LAMENTU PI LA MORTI DI TURIDDU CARNIVALI.   CETRA 34
U LETTU. "U lettu e un piattu"   CETRA 34
LINGUA E DIALETTU. "Un populu"   CETRA 34
NCUNTRAVU U SIGNURI. "Do pa strata"   CETRA 34
NON SUGNU PUETA. "Non pozzu chianciri"   CETRA 34
L'OCCHI DI L'OMU. "Quannu passanu li fimmini"   CETRA 34
PARRU CU TIA.   CETRA 34
LA PEDDI NOVA.   CETRA 34
LU PICCIRIDDU E LU MBRIACU.   CETRA 34
U RANCURI. "Chi mi cuntati"   CETRA 34
Buxton, John. 1912. in English.
THE SQUIRREL. "Whisky, frisky"   CAED 109
Buzzati, Dino. 1906. in Italian.
CONIGLI SOTTO LA LUNA.   EPIU 1
Bynner, Witter. 1881. in English.
AGAINST THE COLD. SONNET 14.   LIBC 21, LIBC 65
_____ SONNET 18.   LIBC 21, LIBC 65
_____ SONNET 20. "Autumn is only winter in disguise"   LIBC 21, LIBC 65
D.H. LAWRENCE. "Prowling in a corridor"   SPOA 91
A DANCE FOR RAIN. "You may never see rain, unless you see"   LIBC 21, LIBC 65
EPITHALAMIUM AND ELEGY. "My single constancy is love of life"   SPOA 91
A FARMER REMEMBERS LINCOLN. "Lincoln?-/ Well, I was in the old Second Maine"   HARC 3, HOUGHT 3
A THRUSH IN THE MOONLIGHT. "In came the moon and covered me with wonder"   LIBC 21, LIBC 65
Byrne, Bonifacio. 1861. in Spanish.
MI BANDERA. "Al volver de distante ribera"   SMC 13

* Recording not available for analysis

Byron, George Gordon, Lord. 1788. in English.

BEPPO, exc. " 'Tis known, at least it should be, that throughout"   ARGO 59

CHILDE HAROLD'S PILGRIMAGE, exc.   CAED 202

———. CANTO 2, exc.   ARGO 151

———. CANTO 3, exc. "And Harold stands upon this place of skulls"   CAED 33

———. "Is thy face like thy mother's, my fair child"   EAV 22

———. "Sky, mountains, river, winds, lake, lightnings! ye"   JNP 18

———. WATERLOO. "There was a sound of revelry by night"   ARGO 59, EAV 8, SPOA 55

———. CANTO 4, exc. "And thou, who never yet of human wrong"   JNP 18

———. "I stood in Venice on the Bridge of Sighs"   ARGO 59, LONGM 1

———. "Roll on, thou deep and dark blue ocean —roll!"   HOUGHT 1, IMP 1, SINGER 6

———. "There is a pleasure in the pathless woods"   CAED 33, SPOA 55

THE DESTRUCTION OF SENNACHERIB. "The Assyrian came down like the wolf on the fold"
EAV 8, JNP 18, LIST 2, LIST 10, LIVLAN 1, SPOA 55

DON JUAN, exc.   ARGO 139

———. CANTO 1, exc. "Happy the nations of the moral north"   CAED 21

———. "I want a hero: an uncommon want"
ARGO 18, ARGO 59, ARGO 60

———. "If ever I shall condescend to prose"
LONGM 1

———. "It was upon a day, a summer's day"
SPOA 55

———. "Such love is innocent and may exist"
ARGO 60

———. "Young Juan now was sixteen years of age"   CAED 33

———. CANTO 2, exc.   ARGO 151

———. "But to our tale, the Donna Inez sent"
ARGO 18

———. "I said that Juan had been sent to Cadiz"   ARGO 60

———. "They were alone, but not alone as they"   LONGM 1

———. CANTO 3, exc. "The Isles of Greece, the Isles of Greece"   ARGO 59, ARGO 151

———. CANTO 13, exc. "Steel barons, molten the next generation"   LONGM 1

ELEGY ON THYRZA. "And thou art dead, as young and fair"   JNP 18

FARE THEE WELL. "Fare thee well! and if for ever"   CAED 202

ON THIS DAY I COMPLETE MY THIRTY-SIXTH YEAR. " 'Tis time this heart should be unmoved"
CAED 33, JNP 18

THE PRISONER OF CHILLON. "My hair is grey, but not with years"   SPOA 55

THE SEA.   CMS 12

"She walks in beauty, like the night"
ARGO 59, CAED 33, CAED 186, CAED 202, CMS 13, DECCA 12, LION 2, EAV 22, LIST 2, ARGO 151

SONNET TO THE PRINCE REGENT ON THE REPEAL OF LORD EDWARD FITZGERALD'S FORFEITURE. "To be the father of the fatherless"   JNP 18

STANZAS FOR MUSIC. "There be none of beauty's daughters"   DECCA 12

STANZAS FOR MUSIC. "There's not a joy the world can give like that it takes away"   SPOA 55

STANZAS WRITTEN ON THE ROAD BETWEEN FLORENCE AND PISA. "Oh, talk not to me of a name great in story"   SPOA 55, DECCA 12, EAV 8

" 'Tis time this heart should be unmoved"
ARGO 59

THE VISION OF BELSHAZZAR. "The king was on his throne"   EAV 8

THE VISION OF JUDGEMENT. "Saint Peter sat by the celestial gate"   ARGO 59

WE'LL GO NO MORE A-ROVING. "So, we'll go no more a-roving"   LION 2, ARGO 59, BRITAM 3, CAED 202, EAV 8, RCA 4, ARGO 151

"When a man has no freedom to fight for at home"   IMP 1, ARGO 151

"When we two parted in silence and tears"
CMA 13, DECCA 12, LIST 2, LIST 10, SPOA 55, LION 2

Poetry*   JNP 5, SPOA 123

Cabrisas, Hilarión. in Spanish.

LA PLEGARIA DEL PEREGRINO ABSURDO. "¡Madre India! Madre mía"   SMC 6

Cadilla, Carmen Alicia. in Spanish.

NANA AL LUCERO DEL ALBA.   INSTPR 1

Cadou, René Guy. 1920. in French.

LE CHANT DE SOLITUDE. "Laissez venir a moi tous les chevaux toutes les femmes et les bêtes bannies"   ADES 2

"Derrière les rideaux et l'épaisseur du temps"   ADES 2

"Devant cet abre immense et calme"
ADES 2

L'HOMME AU KÉPI DE GARDE-CHASSE. "Qu'est-ce que je suis moi Pacifique Liotrot"   ADES 2

"Je t'attendais ainsi qu'on attend les navires"   ADES 2

LETTRE À PIERRE YVERNAULT, CURÉ DE CHAMPAGNE. "Cher ami! sans doute etes-vous comme moi dans un village"   ADES 2

"Pourquoi n'allez-vous pas à Paris?"   ADES 2

SANS SAVOIR QUE LA NUIT. "Quand les soirs sont plus courts et que le ciel est comme"
ADES 2

LA SOIRÉE DE DÉCEMBRE. "Amis pleins de rumeurs ou êtes-vous ce soir"   ADES 2

SYMPHONIE DE PRINTEMPS. "O vieilles pluies souvenez-vous d'Augustin Meaulnes"   ADES 2

Poetry*   ADES 50

Caedmon. Ca. 670. in Old English.

"Nú wé sculon herian Heofon-ríces Weard"
CAED 87, EAV 23, FOLKW 53; Old and Modern English FOLKW 54; Modern English ARGO 76

Calderón de la Barca, Pedro. 1600. in Spanish.

LA VIDA ES SUENO, exc. "¡Ay, misero de mi! Ay, infelice"   SMC 15; English CMS 5

———. "Ay misero de mi vida"   SMC 3

———. "Es verdad; pues reprimamos"
HOLT 1

SONETO. "Éstas, que fueron pompa y alegría"
HOLT 1

---

* Recording not available for analysis

Calverly, Charles Stewart. 1831. in English.
BALLAD. LION 2
COMPANIONS. A TALE OF A GRANDFATHER. "I know
not of what we ponder'd" LION 2
LOVE. "Canst thou love me, lady?"
DECCA 11
Camilleri, Andrea. in Italian.
UN UOMO CHE SPACCA LE PIETRE. CETRA 31
Camino Galicia, León Felipe. 1884. in Spanish.
COMO TU. "Así es mi vida" DOVER 2,
HOLT 1
COMO UN PULGON. "Yo no puedo tener un verso
dulce" AGUIL 10
PRECEPTIVA POETICA. "Pesia/tristeza"
AGUIL 10
TAL VEZ ME LLAME JONAS. "Yo no soy nadie"
SPOA 59
Camões, Luis de. 1524. in Portuguese.
LAMENT. "Alma minha gentil, que te partiste"
FOLKW 10
Campana, Dino. 1885. in Italian.
Poetry* CETRA 28
Campanella, Tommaso. 1568. in Italian.
Poetry* CETRA 24.
Campanile, Alfonso. in Italian.
SON FIORITI CAMPANI E CAMPANELLI. CETRA 31
Campbell, Alistair. 1925. in English.
ELEGY. "Storn. Storm in the trees" KIWI 2
THE RETURN. "And again I see the long pouring
headland" KIWI 2
Campbell, Joseph. in English.
"I will go with my father a-plowing"
HOUGHT 1
Campbell, Roy. 1901. in English.
TRAVELLING IN GREECE, exc. ARGO 119
Campbell, Thomas. 1777. in English.
LORD ULLIN'S DAUGHTER. "A chieftain to the
Highlands bound" EAV 8
Campion, Thomas. 1567. in English.
ADVICE TO A GIRL. "Never love unless you can"
ARGO 35, SPOA 50
CORRINA. "When to her lute Corrina sings"
LIST 1
"A cypress curtain of the night is spread"
SPOA 50
FIRST LOVE. "Silly boy, 'tis full moon yet"
ARGO 35
"Follow your saint, follow with accents sweet"
ARGO 35
"Followe thy faire sunne, unhappy shaddowe"
SPOA 50
"Give beauty all her right" ARGO 35
"Kind are her answers" ARGO 35,
ARGO 139
"My sweetest Lesbia, let us live and love"
ARGO 35, BRITAM 1, SPOA 50, SPOA 83,
LION 2
"Never weather-beaten sail more willing bent
to shore" ARGO 35, LONGM 1
"Now winter nights enlarge" ARGO 35,
SPOA 50
"Rose-cheekt Laura, come" LIST 1
"Sleep, angry beauty, sleep, and fear not me"
ARGO 35
"So sweet is thy discourse to me" ARGO 35
"There is a garden in her face" ARGO 35,
LIST 1, SPOA 83

"Thinkst thou to seduce me then" ARGO 35
"Thou art not fair, for all thy red and white"
ARGO 35
"Though you are yoong and I am olde"
ARGO 35, SPOA 83
"Though your strangenesse frets my hart"
COLUMB 10
"Thrice tosse these oaken ashes in the ayre"
SPOA 50, LION 2
"Turn all thy thoughts to eyes" ARGO 35
"When thou must home to shades of under-
ground" ARGO 35, BRITAM 2, SPOA 50
Campoamor, Ramon de. 1817. in Spanish.
EL PEOR DE LOS MUNDOS. "Escribe un pensador"
Spanish and English CMS 5
EL TREN EXPRESO. "Mi carta, que es feliz, pues
va a buscaros" AGUIL 4
Cane, Melville. in English.
FOG, THE MAGICIAN. "Wrapped in a cloak"
HARC 2
Poetry* JNP 75
Capdevila, Arturo. 1889. in Spanish.
CONFESIÓN. "Donde la infancia al fin sus juegos
deja" AGUIL 9
EN VANO. "Cuánto verso de amor, cantado en
vano" FOLKW 80
MELPOMENE. MIAMI 2
Capurro, Giovanni. 1859. in Italian.
'O FISCO. CETRA 29
STORIA SACRA. CETRA 29
Carco, Francis. 1886. in French.
L'AMANT SURPRIS. "Lestement, l'amant de
Madama grimpa" ADES 15
LES AMIES. "Léa, qui fut assassinée" ADES 15
DANSE. "Sarah, voluptueuse et rousse"
ADES 15
"Le doux caboulot" ADES 15
ENFANCE. "Les persiennes ouvraient sur le
grand jardin clair" ADES 15
LES FILLES DE LA NUIT. "Ce morne soir de pluit
et de neige fondue" ADES 15
L'HEURE DU POÈTE. "La fillette aux violettes"
ADES 15
IL PLEUT. "Il pleut - c'est merveilleux. Je
t'aime" ADES 15
MONTMARTRE. "Montmartre a connu d'autres
jeux" ADES 15
NUITS D'HIVER. "Nuits d'hiver! quel bastringue
allume" ADES 15
RETRAITE. "Le gazon râpé de la berge"
ADES 15
TE VOILA. "Contre le ciel trop blanc, trop vide"
ADES 15
Poetry* ADES 50
Cardarelli, Vincenzo. 1887. in Italian.
Poetry* CETRA 46
Carducci, Giosuè. 1835. in Italian.
ALLA STAZIONE IN UNA MATTINA D'AUTUNNO. "Oh
quei fanali come s'inseguono" SPOA 30
IL BOVE. "T'amo, o pio bove; e mite un sen-
timento" CETRA 2
LA CHIESA DI POLENTA. "Agile e solo vien di colle
in colle" CETRA 2
DAVANTI SAN GUIDO. "I cipressi che a Bólgheri
alti e schetti" CETRA 2
FAIDA DI COMUNE. "Manda a Cuosa in val di
Serchio" CETRA 2

* Recording not available for analysis

Carducci, Giosuè (continued)

FUNERE MERSIT ACERBO. "O tu che dormi là su la fiorita"   CETRA 2

MEZZOGIOMO ALPINO. "Nel gran cerchio de l'alpi, su'l granito"   CETRA 2

IL PARLAMENTO. "Sta Federico imperatore in Como"   CETRA 2

PER LA MORTE DI NAPOLEONE EUGENIO. "Questo la inconscia zagaglia barbara"   CETRA 2

PIANTO ANTICO. "L'albero a cui tendevi"
                                                         CETRA 2

QUI REGNA AMORE. "Ove sei? de'sereni occhi ridenti"   CETRA 2

SAN MARTINO. "La nebbia a gl'irti colli"
                                                         CETRA 2

SANTA MARIA DEGLI ANGELI. "Frate Francesco, quanto d'aere abbraccia"   CETRA 2

SERENATA. "Le stelle che viaggiano su l'mare"
                                                         CETRA 2

SOGNO D'ESTATE. "Tra le battaglie, Omero"
                                                         CETRA 2

TRAVERSANDO LA MAREMMA TOSCANA. "Dolce paese, onde portai conforme"   CETRA 2

VIRGILIO. "Come, quando su' campi arsi la pia"
                                                         CETRA 2

Poetry*   CETRA 28

Carew, Thomas. 1595. in English.

BEAUTY THREATENED. "Know, Celia, since thou art so proud"   ARGO 37

A DEPOSITION FROM LOVE. "I was foretold your rebel sex"   ARGO 37

ETERNITY OF LOVE PROTESTED. "How ill does he deserve a lover's name"   ARGO 37

MEDIOCRITY IN LOVE REJECTED. "Give me more love, or more disdain"   ARGO 37

SONG. "Ask me no more where Jove bestows"
                                                ARGO 37, LION 2

THE SPRING. "Now that the winter's gone"
                                                         IMP 1

TO A LADY THAT DESIRED I WOULD LOVE HER. "Now you have freely given me leave to love"   ARGO 37

TO MY INCONSTANT MISTRESS. "When thou, poor excommunicate"   ARGO 37

THE TRUE BEAUTY.   DECCA 12

Carey, Henry. 1687. in English.

SALLY IN OUR ALLEY. "Of all the girls that are so smart"   EAV 7, CAED 203

Carner i Puig-Oriol, Josep. 1884. in Catalan.

L'ESCARRASSADA. "Oh dona que fas via només per corriol"   AGUIL 14

Carney, Julia A. Fletcher. 1823. in English.

LITTLE THINGS. "Little drops of water"
                                                         CAED 85

Carossa, Hans. 1878. in German.
Poetry*   CHRIST 6

Carranza, Eduardo. 1915. in Spanish.

LOS ÁNGELES.   LIBC 76

DÍA LEJANO.   LIBC 76

DOMINGO. "Un domingo sin ti, de ti perdido"
                                                        FOLKW 80

ES AMOR.   LIBC 76

ES EL TIEMPO.   LIBC 76

ES MELANCOLÍA.   LIBC 76

EL EXTRANJERO.   LIBC 76

HACIA LA SOLEDAD.   LIBC 76

INTERIOR.   LIBC 76

KASIDA DEL VINO.   LIBC 76

Carrasco, Benitez. in Spanish.
Poetry*   SMC 16, SMC 17

Carrera Andrade, Jorge. 1903. in Spanish.

LA ALQUIMIA VITAL. "Un viejo vive en mi fabricando mi muerte"   GMS 13

BIOGRAFÍA PARA USO DE LOS PÁJAROS. "Naci en el siglo de la defunción de la rosa"   GMS 13

CORTE DE CEBADA. "En un cuerno vacío de toro"   FOLKW 80

LA VIDA PERFECTA. "Conejo: hermano timido, mi maestro"   GMS 13

Carroll, Lewis. 1832. in English.

ALICE'S ADVENTURES IN WONDERLAND, exc. "Beautiful soup, so rich and green"
                                     CAED 50, CMS 3, SPOA 132

————. "They told me you had been to her"   LONGM 1

———— "'Tis the voice of the lobster: I heard him declare"   CAED 50, SPOA 132

———— "Will you walk a little faster"
                                                CAED 50, EAV 17

———— "You are old, Father William, the young man said" CAED 50, ARGO 123, MCGH 2, LION 2, ARGO 118, DECCA 11, FOLKW 68, SPOWRD 5, THEAL 3, SPOA 132

THE HUNTING OF THE SNARK. "Just the place for a snark! the Bellman cried"   CAED 48, CAED 201, PATHW 1, SPOA 132

————. "They roused him with muffins, they roused him with ice"   LION 2

JABBERWOCKY. "'Twas brillig, and the slithy toves" CAED 50, HOUGHT 4, LIVLAN 1, PATHW 1, RCA 8, SPOA 132

SYLVIE AND BRUNO, exc. "He thought he saw a Buffalo"   ARGO 125, MCGH 2

————. "He thought he saw an elephant"
                                                CAED 50, SPOA 132

————. "Little birds are dining"   CAED 50

THROUGH THE LOOKING GLASS, exc. "A boat beneath a sunny sky"   LION 2

————. "Child of the pure unclouded brow"
                                                         LION 2

————. "I'll tell thee everything I can"
                                     CAED 50, CMS 4, SPOA 132

————. "In winter, when the fields are white"
                                     CAED 50, CMS 3, SPOA 132

————. THE WALRUS AND THE CARPENTER. "The sun was shining on the sea"   MCGH 2, CAED 50, DECCA 11, HARB 4, LIST 22, ARGO 123, LION 2, PATHW 1, SPOA 35, SPOWRD 5, SPOA 132

Poetry*   SPOA 116

Carryl, Charles Edward. in English.

COMPLAINT OF THE CAMEL.   CAED 85

ROBINSON CRUSOE'S STORY.   THEAL 2

Carryl, Guy Wetmore. 1873. in English.

THE EMBARRASSING EPISODE OF LITTLE MISS MUFFET. "Little Miss Muffet discovered a tuffet" HARB 6

THE SYCOPHANTIC FOX AND THE GULLIBLE RAVEN. "A raven sat upon a tree"   THEAL 3

Carter, Connie. in English.
"If I lived on the land"   WATSHD 8

---

* Recording not available for analysis

POEM-DITTY FOR TAJ MAHAL. "Taj Mahal, where you come from"   WATSHD 8

Cartwright, William. 1611. in English.
NO PLATONIQUE LOVE. "Tell me no more of minds embracing minds"   CAED 38

Carvajal, Juan F. 1914. in Spanish.
"Esa tu voz serena, tu voz hecha a la ausencia"   SMC 13

Cary, Patrick. fl. 1651. in English.
TRIOLET. "Worldly designs, fears, hopes, farewell"   EAV 22
Poetry*   EAV 7

Casa, Giovanni della. 1503. in Italian.
Poetry*   CETRA 23

Casal, Julian del. 1863. in Spanish.
A MI MADRE. "No fuiste una mujer, sino una santa"   SMC 13
EN EL CAMPO. "Tengo el impuro amor de las ciudades"   SPOA 39

Casona, Alejandro. in Spanish.
EL MILAGRO PEQUEÑO. "Aquella pobre niña que aùn no tenía senos"   SMC 6

Casson, John. in English.
ARK ROYAL 1940.
NIGHT AT SEA AFTER FLYING.
SUNSET FROM A PRISON CAMP.   ARGO 143

Cassou, Jean. in French.
"La plaie que, depuis"   ADES 55

Castro, Eugénio de. 1869. in Portuguese.
SALOME. "Grácil, curvada sobre os feixes"
SONETO. "Acorda cedo como os passarinhos"   FOLKW 72

Castro, Rosalía de. 1837. in Spanish.
A LAS ORILLAS DEL SAR. "En los ecos de órgano, o en el rumor del viento"   AGUIL 8
——— "Pensamiento de alas negras"   FIDIAS 2
LAS CAMPANAS. "Yo las amo, yo las oigo"   DOVER 2
"Dicen que no hablan las plantas, ni las fuentes, ni los pájaros"   HOLT 1
"En los ecos del órgano, o en el rumor del viento"   SPOA 37
"Era apacible el día"   HOLT 1
UNA MANCHA SOMBRIA. "Una mancha sombría y extensa"   FIDIAS 2
UN MANSO RIO. "Un manso rio, una vereda estrecha"   SMC 3
TRISTES RECORDOS. "Un-ha tarde alá en Castilla"   AGUIL 6
VOLVED. "Volved, que os aseguro"   FIDIAS 1

Castro Saavedra, Carlos. in Spanish.
CANCION DEL AMOR HERIDO.   MIAMI 1

Cattafi, Bartolo. in Italian.
ME NE VADO.   CETRA 31

Cattonar, Joanna. in English.
BLACK CLOUDS. "Black clouds on a black mountain"   WATSHD 11
INLAND, A THOUSAND MILES. "Because you are standing"   WATSHD 11
MOVING DAY. "This room is breaking apart"   WATSHD 11
PLAINSONG. "The mind's paying"   WATSHD 11

Catullus, Gaius Valerius. 84 BC. in Latin.
CARMINA. 1. "Qui dono lepidum novum libellum"   CAED 205.

——— 2. "Passer, deliciae meae puellae"   CAED 128, CAED 205
——— 3. "Lugete, o veneres cupidinesque"   CAED 128, CAED 205, FOLKW 98
——— 4. "Phasellus ille, quem uidetis, hospites"   CAED 205
——— 5. "Vivamus, mea Lesbia, atque amemus"   CAED 128, CAED 205, FOLKW 98; English ARGO 35, SPOA 50, SPOA 83
——— 6. "Flavi, delicias tuas Catullo"   CAED 205
——— 7. "Quaeris, quot mihi basiationes"   CAED 128, CAED 205, FOLKW 98
——— 8. "Miser Catulle, desinas ineptire"   CAED 128, CAED 205, FOLKW 98
——— 10. "Varus me meus ad suos amores"   CAED 128
——— 11. "Nec meum respectet, ut ante, amorem"   CAED 205, FOLKW 98
——— 13. "Cenabis bene, mi Fabulle, apud me"   CAED 205, FOLKW 98
——— 14. "Nei te plus oculis meis amarem"   CAED 205
——— 14b. "Si qui forte mearum ineptiarum"   CAED 205
——— 15. "Commendo tibi me ac meos amores"   CAED 205
——— 16. "Pedicabo ego vos et irrumabo"   CAED 205
——— 21. "Aureli, pater esuritionum"   CAED 205
——— 22. "Suffenus iste, Vare, quem probe nosti"   CAED 205
——— 23. "Furei, cui neque sernos est neque arca"   CAED 205
——— 26. "Furi, uillula nostra bon ad Austri"   CAED 205
——— 30. "Alfene immemor atque unanimis false sodalibus"   CAED 205
——— 31. "Paene insularum, Sirmio, insularumque"   CAED 205
——— 32. "Amabo, mea dulcis Ipsithilla"   CAED 205
——— 33. "O Furum optime balneariorum"   CAED 205
——— 34. "Dianae sumus in fide" CAED 205
——— 35. "Poetate tenero, meo sodali"   CAED 205
——— 37. "Salax taberna nosque contubernales"   CAED 205
——— 43. "Salve, nec minimo puella naso"   CAED 205
——— 48. "Mellitos oculos tuos, Inventi"   CAED 205
——— 49. "Disetissime Romuli nepotum"   CAED 205
——— 50. "Hesterno, Licini, die otiosi"   CAED 205
——— 51. "Ille mi par esse deo videtur"   CAED 128, CAED 205, FOLKW 98
——— 56. "O rem ridiculam, Cato, et iocosam"   CAED 205
——— 58. "Caeli, Lesbia nostra, Lesbia illa"   CAED 205
——— 61. "Collis o Heliconiei"   CAED 205
——— 69. "Noli admirari, quare tibi femina nulla"   CAED 205

* Recording not available for analysis

Catullus, Gaius Valerius (continued)

———. 70. "Nulli se dicit mulier mea nubere malle"   FOLKW 98,
SPOA 100 (with English trans.)

———. 72. "Dicebas quondam solum te nosse Catullum"   CAED 205, FOLKW 98

———. 73. "Desine de quoquam quisquam bene velle mereri"   CAED 205

———. 75. "Huc est mens deducta tua, mea Lesbia, culpa"   CAED 205, FOLKW 98

———. 76. "Siqua recordanti benefacta priora voluptas"   CAED 205, FOLKW 98

———. 79. "Lesbius est pulcer. quid ni? quem Lesbia malit"   CAED 205

———. 83. "Lesbia mi praesente viro mala plurima dicit"   CAED 205

———. 85. "Odi et amo. Quare id faciam, fortasse requiris"   CAED 128, CAED 205, FOLKW 98

———. 86. "Quintia formosast multis; mihi candida, longa"   FOLKW 98

———. 87. "Nulla potest mulier tantum se dicere amatam"   CAED 205

———. 92. "Lesbia mi dicit semper male nec tacet umquam"   CAED 205, FOLKW 98

———. 98. "In te, si in quemquam, dici pote putide Victi"   CAED 205

———. 101. "Multas per gentes et multa per aequora uectus"   CAED 128, CAED 205

———. 106. "Cum puero bello praecocem qui videt isse"   CAED 205

———. 107. "Si quoi quid cupido optantique optigit umquam"   CAED 205

———. 109. "Iucundum, mea vita, mihi propones amorem"   CAED 205, FOLKW 98
Poetry*   CETRA 18

Causley, Charles. 1917. in English.
AT THE BRITISH WAR CEMETERY, BAYEUX. "I walked where in their talking graves"   ARGO 98
THE BALLAD OF BILLY OF NOSEY BENT. "When I was born"   FOLKW 59 A
BALLAD OF THE FIVE CONTINENTS. "In blue Bristol city at tall tide I wandered"   ARGO 98
CHILD'S SONG. "Christopher Beer/used to live here"   FOLKW 59 A
"I am the great sun but you do not see me"   ARGO 98
INNOCENT'S SONG. "Who's that knocking on the window"   ARGO 98
MY FRIEND, MALONEY. "My friend Maloney, eighteen"   SPOA 67
NURSERY RHYME OF INNOCENCE AND EXPERIENCE. "I had a silver penny/and an apricot tree"   SPOA 67
SONG OF THE DYING GUNNER A.A.1. "Oh mother my mouth is full of stars"   ARGO 119
TIMOTHY WINTERS. "Timothy Winters comes to school"   SPOA 67

Cavafy, Constantine. 1863. in Greek.
THE DANGERS. "Said Myrthius, a student come from Syria to Alexandria"   English JNP 13
ONE OF THE JEWS.   English JNP 13
WAITING FOR THE BARBARIANS. "What are we waiting for, all crowded in the forum"
English FOLKW 60

Cavalcanti, Guido. 1255. in Italian.
"In un boschetto trova' pasturella" DOVER
"Perch'i' no spero di tornar giammai"
SPOA 3
Poetry*   CETRA 19, CETRA 3

Cavalieri, Grace. in English.
THE AFTERWARD KISS. "Insist upon a star"
WATSHD
ELLSWORTH AVENUE. "It started with a bad taste"   WATSHD
THE GOOD LIFE. "Things are getting simpler"
WATSHD
THE ORPHANAGE. "Down the brick divided street"   WATSHD

Cavestany, Juan. in Spanish.
GITANA Y MARE. "¡Señorito! ¡Señorito! Mayo ofensa no cabe"   SMC

Caxton, William. 1421. in English.
ENEYDOS.   EAV 1

Cayrol, Jean. in French.
DORMEZ-VOUS?   ADES 5
ECRIT SUR LE MUR.   ADES 5

Celan, Paul. 1920. in German.
PSALM. "Niemand knetet uns wieder aus Erde und Lehm"   CHRIST 1
SCHWANENGEFAHR. "Lappentaucher"
English WATSHD 1
SPÄT UND TIEF. "Boshaft wie goldene Rede beginnt diese Nacht"   CHRIST 1
STIMMEN. "Stimmen, ins Grün"
English WATSHD 1
Poetry*   NESKE 2, SUHRK

Celaya, Gabriel. 1911. in Spanish.
A SANCHO PANZA. "Sancho-bueno, Sancho-arcilla"   AGUIL
A VUESTRO SERVICIO. "Me acercaba hasta e puerto"   AGUIL
LA ARCILLA QUE PALPO Y BESO. "Iberia, barro de Espana"   AGUIL
AVISO. "La ciudad es de goma lisa y negra"
AGUIL
BUENOS DIAS. "Son las diez de la mañana"
AGUIL
MATINAL. "Un hombre, los caminos" AGUIL
MOMENTOS FELICES. "Cuando llueve, y revis mis papeles"   AGUIL
"Nadie es nadie"   AGUIL
LA POESIA ES UN ARMA CARGADA DE FUTURO "Quando ya nada se espera personalment exaltante"   AGUIL

Celi, Maria Celeste. in Italian.
SE GUARDO CRISTO IN CROCE.   CETRA 3

Cendrars, Blaise. 1887. in French.
L'ABSOUTE AVAIT ÉTÉ DONNÉE.   ADES 3
AU LENDEMAIN D'UNE CRUE.   ADES 3
AU MOMENT OÚ L'ON AFFICHAIT.   ADES 3
AUJOURD'HUI, J'AI QUARANTE ANS.   ADES 3
LES BOUBOUS. "Oh ces négresses que l'on ren contre"   ADES 3
CENDRARS EST UN OBSÉDÉ.   ADES 3
C'EST LE PARADIS TERRESTRE.   ADES 3
LE CRI LE PLUS AFFREUX.   ADES 3
DIEU, QU'IL EST DIFFICILE.   ADES 3
EN 1915 . . .   ADES 3
"En ce temps-la j'étais en mon adolescence"
ADES 34, FOLKW 8
LES FRONTIÈRES.   ADES 3

———

* Recording not available for analysis

HOMMAGE A GUILLAUME APOLLINAIRE. "Le pain
lève" ADES 34
J'AI FAIT MES PLUS BEAUX POÈMES. ADES 34
J'AI TRENTE ANS. ADES 34
JE ME SOUVIENS D' AVOIR LU. ADES 34
JE SUIS EN ROUTE. ADES 34
"Je voudrais tant t'aimer que tes deux seins en
pleurent" ADES 34
MA VIE DURANT. ADES 34
MAINTENANT IL SE TROUVERA. ADES 34
LA NUIT, LES RUES DE NEW YORK. ADES 34
O MON AMOUR! ADES 34
LES PÂQUES A NEW YORK. "Seigneur, c'est au-
jourd'hui le jour de votre Nom"
FOLKW 2, FOLKW 13
———, exc. "Seigneur, l'aube a glissé froide
comme un suaire" ADES 34
LA PARESSE. ADES 34
UN PARFUM ÉMANAIT D'ELLE. ADES 34
PARTIR. PRENDRE LA ROUTE. ADES 34
QUELLE CHOSE ÉTONNANTE QUE LA LECTURE.
ADES 34
RIJ ÉTAIT UNE POUFFIASSE. ADES 34
"Les sirènes miaulent et se taisent" ADES 34
TU AS TELLEMENT AIGUISÉ. ADES 34
TU ES PLUS BELLE QUE LE CIEL ET LA MER. "Quand
tu aimes il faut partir" ADES 34
"Une deux une deux" ADES 34
LE VENTRE DE MA MÈRE. "C'est mon premier
domicile" ADES 34, FOLKW 13

Cernuda, Luis. 1904. in Spanish.
"Donde habite el olvido" DOVER 2
TIERRA NATIVA. "Es la luz misma, la que abrió
mis ojos" SPOA 59

Cervantes Saavedra, Miguel de. 1547. in Spanish.
AL TUMULTO DEL REY FELIPE II EN SEVILLA. "Voto
a Dios que me espanta esta grandeza"
AGUIL 6
DIALOGO ENTRE BABIECA Y ROCINANTE. "Cómo
estáis, Rocinante, tan delgado" AGUIL 6
LA GITANILLA. "Cuando Preciosa el panderete
toca" SPOA 37
LETRILLA. "Madre, la mi madre, guardas me
poneis" SMC 3
OVILLEJOS. "¿Quien menoscaba mis bienes?"
AGUIL 4, SMC 15
QUIÉN DEJARÁ. "Quién dejará, del verde prado
umbroso" SPOA 37

Césaire, Aimé. 1913. in French.
CAHIER D'UN RETOUR AU PAYS NATAL, exc.
"Gonflement aux quatre coins"
LA FEMME ET LA FLAMME. "Un morceau de lu-
mière qui descend la source d'un regard"
NEGRITUDE. "Ceux qui n'ont inventé ni la
poudre ni la boussole" FOLKW 83

Cesarotti, Melchiorre. 1730. in Italian.
Poetry* CETRA 25

Cetina, Gutierre de. 1520. in Spanish.
MADRIGAL. "Ojos claros, serenos" AGUIL 4,
DOVER 2; Spanish and English CMS 5

Chamisso, Adelbert von. 1781. in German.
DAS SCHLOSS BONCOURT. "Ich träum als Kind
mich zurücke" DOVER 1
DIE SONNE BRINGT ES AN DEN TAG. "Gemächlich
in der Werkstatt sass" ATHENA 1

Chamizo, Luis. in Spanish.
LA NACENCIA. "Bruño los recios nubarrones pardos" SMC 1

Champourcin, Ernestina de. in Spanish.
ENTREGA. "Iré a tus manos, limpia, indemne, sin
memoria" AGUIL 8

Chapin, Katherine Garrison. 1890. in English.
AT STONEHENGE. "Here are the wise men
baffled, here is a much" LIBC 1
AUTUMN SONG, PROVENCE. LIBC 2, LIBC 3
CHRISTMAS EVE. "A winter sun turned the
mountains red" LIBC 1
DUST. "A spirit is coming across the valley"
LIBC 2, LIBC 3
GIRL IN THE SUN. "Here on smooth white sand,
by blue water" LIBC 2, LIBC 3
THE GREAT ROSE. "Once under the great rose
window I knelt alone" LIBC 2, LIBC 3
INVOCATION. "Song!/Rise as bright" LIBC 2,
LIBC 3
LOVE POEM IN AN OCCUPIED COUNTRY. "More
alone than survivors on a storm-wracked is-
land" LIBC 1
MORNING SONG. "Walking toward the moun-
tain" LIBC 2, LIBC 3
NIGHT SONG. "This is no night to sleep, the
dark" LIBC 1
THE SAVAGE FLUTES. "The savage flutes of disas-
ter" LIBC 1
THIS LONELY LIGHT. "This illumined wonder"
LIBC 2, LIBC 3
TOO SOON THE SHADOW. "Stay on your out-
stretched wing O sweet, O lovely time"
LIBC 2, LIBC 3

Chapman, J. Alexander. in English.
CHRISTUS NATUS EST. "Christus natus est, the
cock crowed" ARGO 82, SPOA 41

Char, René. 1907. in French.
A . . . "Tu es mon amour depuis tant s'années"
ADES 42
AFFRES, DÉTONATION, SILENCE. "Le moulin du
Calavon" ADES 42
L'AMOUREUSE EN SÉCRET. "Elle a mis le couvert"
ADES 42
L'ARTISANAT FURIEUX. "La roulotte rouge au
bord du clou" ADES 42
BIEN ÉGAUX. "Je suis épris de ce morceau ten-
dre" ADES 42
COMMUNE PRÉSENCE. "Eclaireur comme tu sur-
viens tard" ADES 42
DÉCLARER SON NOM. "J'avais dix ans" ADES 42
INVITATION. "J'appelle les amours qui roués"
ADES 42
J'AI ÉTRANGLÉ MON FRÈRE. ADES 42
POÈTES. "La tristesse des illettrés dans les
ténèbres des bouteilles" ADES 42
REDONNEZ-LEUR. "Redonnez-leur ce qui n'est
plus présent en eux" ADES 42
REMISE. "Laissez filer les guides, maintenant
c'est la plaine" ADES 42
LE SOLEIL DE LA NUIT. ADES 42
LA SORGUE. "Riviere trop tôt partie, d'une traite
sans compagnon" ADES 42

Charles II, King of England. 1630. in English.
SONG. "I pass all my hours in a shady old grove"
ARGO 47

* Recording not available for analysis

Charles D'Orleans. 1391. in French.

BALLADE SUR LA PAIX. "Priez pour paix, doulce
vierge Marie"   FOLKW 84
"Cuer, qu'est-ce là?—Ce sommes-nous voz
yeux"   FOLKW 84
"Dedans mon livre de pensee"   PERIOD 2
"Dieu, qu'il la fait bon regarder"   GMS 7,
                                    SPOA 9
EN FAITES-VOUS DOUTE.   HACH 7
"En la forest d'ennuyeuse Tristesse"
                                 FOLKW 84
EN VERRAI-JE JAMAIS LA FIN.   HACH 7
"Monstrez les moy ces poures yeulx"
                                 FOLKW 84
"Petit mercier! petit pannier!"   FOLKW 84
"Qui? quoy? comment? à qui? pourquoy?"
                                 FOLKW 84
SUR LE MORT DE SA DAME.   HACH 7
"Le temps a laissé son manteau"   ADES 54,
          DOVER 4, FOLKW 84, HACH 7,
                        PERIOD 2, SPOA 36
"Yver, vous n'estes qu'un villain" ADES 54,
                       FOLKW 84, SPOA 9

Chartier, Alain. 1390. in French.

LA BELLE DAME SANS MERCI. "Nagueres chevauchant pensoye"   FOLKW 84

Chaucer, Geoffrey. 1340. in Middle English.

CANTERBURY TALES. GENERAL PROLOGUE, exc. "A
clerk ther was of Oxenford also"   EAV 5
_____. "A knyght ther was and that a worthy
man"   Modern English IMP 1
_____. "The millere was a stout carl for the
nones"   HARB 6
_____. "This pardoner hadde heer as yelow as
wax"   LONGM 1
_____. "Whan that Aprill with his shoures
soote"   ARGO 25, CAED 81, EAV 5,
          EAV 11, LIST 1, LONGM 1, SPOA 61;
          Modern and Middle English EAV 4;
       Modern English BRITAM 4, NACTE 5
_____. THE MAN OF LAW'S PREAMBLE AND TALE,
exc. "O hateful harm! condicion of poverte"
                 Modern English BRITAM 4
_____. THE MANCIPLE'S TALE. "Whan Phebus
dwelled heere in this world adoun"
                 Modern English BRITAM 4
_____. THE MILLER'S TALE. "Whilom ther was
dwellynge at Oxenford"   CAED 104,
                 Modern English CAED 76
_____. THE MONK'S TALE. "I wol biwaille, in
manere of tragedie"
                 Modern English SPOWRD 6
_____. THE NUN'S PRIEST'S TALE. "A povre
widwe, somdel stope in age"   ARGO 26,
          CAED 13, CAED 67, ENGL 1;
       Modern English BRITAM 4, NACTE 5
_____. THE PARDONER'S PROLOGUE. "Lordynges,
quod he, in Chirches whan I preche"
          CAED 13; Modern English CAED 76
_____. THE PARDONER'S TALE. "In Flandres why-
lom was a companye"   ARGO 156,
          CAED 13, CAED 67, SPOA 61;
                 Modern English CAED 76
_____, exc. "Thise ryotoures three, of which I
telle"   LONGM 1
_____, exc.   HARVOC 1

_____. THE PARSON'S PROLOGUE. "By that the
maunciple hadde his tale al ended"
                                  CAED 81
_____. THE PRIORESS'S TALE. "O Lord, oure
Lord, thy name how mervaillous"   EAV 5
_____. THE REEVE'S TALE. "At Trumpyngtoun
nat fer from Cantebrigge"   CAED 104
                 Modern English BRITAM 4
_____. THE WIFE OF BATH'S PROLOGUE. "Experi-
ence, though noon auctoritee"   EAV 5
                 Modern English CAED 63
_____. THE WIFE OF BATH'S TALE. "In th'olde
dayes of the King Arthour"   ARGO 157,
                 EAV 3, FOLKW 53
                 Modern English CAED 63
_____, exc.   APPL 13, LIST 4,
          SPOA 60, Modern English SINGER 6
COMPLAINT TO HIS EMPTY PURSE. "To you, my
purs, and to noon other wight" CAED 105,
                 Modern English LEARNC 2
LACK OF STEADFASTNESS. "Sometyme the worlde
was so stedfast and stable"   CAED 105
THE LEGEND OF GOOD WOMEN: PROLOGUE. "A
thousand tymes have I herd men telle"
                                  CAED 20
MERCILESS BEAUTY. "Your eyen two wol slee me
sodeinly"   CAED 105,
                 Modern English EAV 22
THE PARLIAMENT OF FOWLS. "The lif so short, the
craft so long to lerne"   CAED 105
_____, exc.   MICHM 3
TO HIS SCRIBE ADAM. "Adam scrivain, if evere it
thee bifalle"   CAED 105
TO ROSAMOND. "Madame, ye been of alle
beautee shrine"   CAED 105
TROILUS AND CRYSEIDE, exc. "And therwithal he
henge adoun the hede"   EAV 11
_____. "The double sorowe of Troylus to tel-
len"   ARGO 27, EAV 5
_____. THE LOVE UNFEIGNED. "O yonge fresshe
folke, he or she"   Modern English EAV 22
TRUTH. "Flee from the press, and dwelle with
sothfastnesse"   LIST 1

Chen Dau. 841. in Chinese.

LUNG SYI SYING. "Shr sau syung nu bu gu shen"
                                 FOLKW 76

Chénier, André. 1762. in French.

CAMILLE. "Ah! portons dans les bois ma triste
inquiétude"   ADES 29
"Comme un dernier rayon, comme un dernier
zéphyr"   ADES 29, ADES 48, ADES 54,
                                  HACH 10
FANNY. "Précurseurs de l'automne, ô fruits"
                                  ADES 29
LA FLUTE. "Toujours ce souvenir m'attendrit et
me touche"   GMS 7
LA JEUNE CAPTIVE. "L'épi naissant mûrit de la
faux respecté"   ADES 29, HACH 10,
                                   SPOA 9
LA JEUNE TARENTINE. "Pleurez, doux alcyons, ô
vous, oiseaux sacrés"   ADES 29, GMS 8,
                                  HACH 10
ODE.   ADES 29
"Quand au mouton bêlant la sombre boucher-
ie"   DOVER 4
"Salut, ô belle nuit"   HACH 10

* Recording not available for analysis

Cherrier, Claude. 1660. in French.
DESCRIPTION CHIMÉRIQUE D'UN ÊTRE DE RAISON, FABRIQUÉ DE PIÈCES RAPPORTÉES, HABILLÉ D'UNE ÉTOFFE A DOUBLE SENS, LEQUEL FUT CONSTRUIT PAR UNE ASSEMBLÉE D'EQUIVOQUES, ASSISTÉES DE GÉNIE BURLESQUE. "Il a un corps de garde" FOLKW 84

Chester, Laura. 1949. in English.
FOR THE LOVE OF THE LAMB LION-LION. "Emergency evening" WATSHD 9
MY PLEASURE. "Walk down Chinatown" WATSHD 14

Chesterton, Frances. in English.
"How far is it to Bethlehem?" FOLKW 62

Chesterton, Gilbert Keith. 1874. in English.
THE HOUSE OF CHRISTMAS. "There fared a mother driven forth" SPOA 10
LEPANTO. "White founts falling in the courts of the sun" SPOA 10
THE TRUTH OF CHRISTMAS. "Even such am I; within whose thoughts resides" SPOA 10

Chettle, Henry. in English.
DAMELUS' SONG TO HIS DIAPHENIA. "Diaphenia, like the daffadowndilly" ARGO 31

Chiabrera, Gabriello. 1552. in Italian.
Poetry* CETRA 24

Child, Lydia Maria. in English.
THANKSGIVING DAY. COLUMB 6

Children's Verses and Nursery Rhymes
"A was an archer, who shot at a frog" CAED 58
"Anna Elise, she jumped with surprise" CAED 58
"Baa, Baa, Black Sheep" CAED 58
"Betty Botter bought some butter" CAED 58, CAED 85, CMS 3
"Bobby Shafto's gone to sea" SPOA 131
BRIAN O'LINN. "Brian O'Linn was a gentleman born" SPOA 7
BUMPETY BUMP. CAED 58
"Cackle, cackle, Mother Goose" CAED 58
"A cat came fiddling out of a barn" CAED 58
THE CHICKENS. "Said the first little chicken with a queer little squirm" BOWMAR 1
"Curly-Locks! Curly-Locks! Wilt thou be mine?" CAED 58
"Dame, get up and bake your pies" CAED 85
DEATH AND BURIAL OF COCK ROBIN. "Who killed Cock Robin?" CAED 58, CAED 85, SPOA 131
THE DERBY RAM. "There was a ram in Derby-town" CAED 85
"Ding, dong, bell" CAED 58
DR. FELL. "I do not like thee, Dr. Fell" CAED 58
"Dr. Foster went to Glo'ster" CREAT 11
"Early to bed" CAED 85
"Eenie, meenie, miney, mo" CAED 85
"Engine, engine, number nine" CAED 85
FISH POND. CAED 58
FOL-DE-ROL AND RIDDLE-MA-REE. CAED 85
"For want of a nail the shoe was lost" CAED 58
THE FOX AND THE GOOSE. CAED 58

THE FROG AND THE MOUSE. "There was a frog lived in a well" CAED 58, CAED 85
THE FUNNY OLD MAN AND HIS WIFE. "Once upon a time, in a little wee house" CMS 3
"Georgey Porgey" CAED 58
"Go to bed first" CAED 58
THE GRENADIER. CAED 58
"Hector Protector was dressed all in green" CAED 58
HENNY-PENNY. CAED 85
HERE'S TO YOU AND YOURS. CAED 110
"Hey! Diddle, Diddle" CAED 58
THE HOUSE THAT JACK BUILT. "This is the house that Jack built" CAED 58
"How do you do?" CAED 109
"How much wood would a woodchuck chuck" CMS 4
"Humpty Dumpty sat on a wall" CAED 58, SPOA 131
"Hush little baby" CAED 109
"I asked my mother for fifty cents" CMS 2
"I had a little pony" CAED 58
"I love little pussy, her coat is so warm" CAED 58, HARB 3
I SAW A PEACOCK WITH A FIERY TAIL. CAED 110
"Ibbity, bibbity, sibbity, sab" CAED 85
"Icker-backer/ soda-cracker" CAED 85
"If all the seas were one sea" CAED 58, CAED 109
"If you should meet a crocodile" CAED 109
"If you sneeze on a Monday, you sneeze for danger" CAED 85
"Jack and Gye" CAED 58
"Jack and Jill went up the hill" CAED 58, CREAT 1
"Jack be nimble" SPOA 131
"Jack Sprat" CAED 58
"Jerry Hall/he is so small" CAED 58
THE KANGAROO. CAED 109
"The King was in his counting house" CREAT 1
A KITE. "I often sit and wish that I" CMS 3
"Lady Bird, Lady Bird" CAED 58, SPOA 117
LITTLE BO-PEEP. "Little Bo-Peep has lost her sheep" CAED 58, HARB 1
"Little Boy Blue come blow your horn" CAED 58
THE LITTLE BOY WITH THE LONG NAME. CAED 85
LITTLE HEN. CREAT 1
"Little Jack Horner sat in a corner" CAED 58, SPOA 131
LITTLE JUMPING JOAN. "Here am I, little jumping Joan" CAED 58
LITTLE MAN AND LITTLE MAID. CAED 58
"Little Miss Muffett/ sat on a tuffet" CAED 58, CREAT 1, HARB 1, SPOA 131
LITTLE PIGS. CREAT 1
"Little Robin Redbreast" SPOA 131
"Little Tommy Tucker" CAED 58
"London Bridge is broken down" CAED 58
"Mary had a little lamb" CAED 58
MEET-ON-THE-ROAD. CAED 110
MERRY MAN OF PARIS. CREAT 1
"Mr. East gave a feast" CAED 58
MR. NOBODY. "I know a funny little man" CMS 3

* Recording not available for analysis

Children's Verses and Nursery Rhymes (continued)

"Monday's child is fair of face"   SPOA 131
"The north wind doth blow"   CAED 58,
                                CMS 3
"Now I lay me down to sleep"   SPOA 131
"O where have you been, Billy Boy?"
                               CAED 85
"Old King Cole"   CAED 58, HARB 1,
                              SPOA 131
"Old Mother Hubbard"   CAED 58
"Old woman, old woman, shall we go ashear-
ing"   CAED 58, CMS 2
"One, two/buckle my shoe"   CAED 85
"One, two, three, four, five"   CAED 110
"One, two, three, four, five, six, seven"
                               CAED 85
"Pat-a-cake, pat-a-cake" CAED 58, CAED 85
"Pease-porridge hot"   CAED 58
"Peter Piper picked a peck of pickled peppers"
                         CAED 58, CMS 3
"Pussy-cat, pussy-cat, where have you been"
                         CAED 58, CREAT 1
"Rain, rain, go away"   CAED 85
RIDE A COCK HORSE. "Ride a cock-horse to Ban-
bury Cross"   CAED 58, CAED 85
A RIDDLE.   CAED 58
"Rub-a-dub-dub"   CAED 58
A SAD, SAD STORY. "Three children sliding on the
ice"   CAED 58
THE SECRET. "We have a secret, just we three"
                                CMS 3
SILLY BILLY.   CAED 85
SIMPLE SIMON. "Simple Simon met a pieman
going to the fair"   LEARNS 1
"Sing a song of sixpence"   SPOA 131
STAR LIGHT. "Star light, star bright"   CMS 3,
                              SPOA 131
THE STORE OF MINIKIN AND MANIKIN. CAED 85
"There was a crooked man and he went a
crooked mile"   CAED 58
"There was a little girl and she had a little curl"
                         CAED 58, CAED 85
THERE WAS A LITTLE MAN.   CAED 58
"There was a little woman"   COLUMB 11
"There was an old woman/ and nothing she
had"   CAED 58
"There was an old woman, and what do you
think?"   CAED 58
"There was an old woman tossed up in a bas-
ket"   CAED 58, LEARNS 1
"There was an old woman who lived in a shoe"
                               CAED 58
"Thirty days hath September"   CAED 58,
                            CAED 85, CMS 2
"This is the key of the kingdom"   CMS 3
"This little piggy went to market" CAED 85
"Three blind mice, see how they run"
                               CAED 58
"Three wise men of Gotham"   SPOA 131
"A tisket, a tasket"   CAED 85
"Tom, Tom, the piper's son"   CAED 58
THE WEE WEE MAN. "As I was walking all alone"
                          CAED 64, EAV 13
"Wee Willie Winkie runs through the town"
                               CAED 58

"What are little boys made of, made of"
                               CAED 58
"What are little girls made of, made of"
                               CAED 58
"When I was a little boy I lived by myself"
                               CAED 85

Chiurazzi, Raffaele. 1875. in Italian.
COSCE ARGENTE. "Cosce 'argiento è tantillo"
                             CETRA 29
Chlebnikov, Velemir. 1885. in Russian.
ORA SMETIS.   LUCHT 1
Chopin, Henri. 1922. in English.
DELFT.   LUCHT 1
Christine de Pisan. 1364. in French.
BALLADES, 3. "Seulette suis, et seulette veuil es-
tre"   FOLKW 84, HACH 7
RONDEL. "Je chante par couverture"
                              FOLKW 84
Church, Richard. 1893. in English.
HAYS WHARF. "Who hasn't heard of London
Bridge"   FOLKW 65, JUP 1
Chute, Marchette. 1909. in English.
DRINKING FOUNTAIN. "When I climb up to get a
drink"   HARB 1
MY DOG. "His nose is short and scrubby"
                               HARB 1
Ciardi, John. 1916. in English.
ABOUT CROWS.   HOUGHT 2
AFTER A NIGHT THAT CAME TO NOTHING. "They're
twittering again, my day-starters and anoth-
er"   SPOA 72
AT A CONCERT OF MUSIC, REMEMBERING THE DEAD
IN KOREA. "Consider says the music how man
is an age"   FOLKW 36
AT MY FATHER'S GRAVE. "A leaf is not too little"
                                SPOA 71
A BALLAD OF TELEOLOGIES. "Says ego's ape shak-
ing its tree"   SPOA 71
BEDLAM REVISITED. "Nobody told me anything
much"   SPOA 102
BOY. "He is in his room sulked shut"
                                SPOA 71
THE CATALPA. "The catalpa's white week is end-
ing there"   SPOA 72
CHOICES. "Joyce says he chooses poverty"
                                SPOA 72
COMING HOME ON THE 5:22. "A prosperous well
tailored"   SPOA 71
A CROW'S LONG SCRATCH OF SOUND. "A crow's
long scratch of sound"   SPOA 72
DAEMONS. "I pass enough savages on the street"
                                SPOA 71
DAYS. "Something in the wild cherry"
                               FOLKW 36
DOCTOR FAUSTUS. "Gnostic Faustus, Sapphic,
sophic"   FOLKW 36
THE DOLLS. "Night after night forever the dolls
lay stiff"   SPOA 102
AN EDGE, A TWILIGHT, A PLOVER. "I had left my-
self on the beach like a towel" SPOA 71
ELEGY. "Some gone like boys to school wearing
their badges"   FOLKW 36, LIBC 50
ELEGY FOR G. B. SHAW. "Administrators of
minutes into hours" FOLKW 36, LIBS 50,
                              SPOA 102
ELEGY FOR SANDRO. "Read down into the dead
and close"   FOLKW 36

* Recording not available for analysis

ELEGY JUST IN CASE. "Here lie Ciardi's pearly bones"   FOLKW 36

EPITHALAMIUM AT SAINT MICHAEL'S CEMETERY. "My father lay fifty years in St. Michael's bed"   SPOA 71

AN EVENING OF THE PRIVATE EYE. "I live, therefore I love, said the Excerpt-Lifter"   SPOA 72

FLOWERING QUINCE. "This devils me: uneasy ease"   FOLKW 36, LIBC 50

THE FORMALITIES. "On September 2, 1945, the battleship"   SPOA 72

I MARRY YOU. "Men marry what they need"   FOLKW 36, FOLKW 67

IN THE WITCH-HUNTING SEASON. "I tell you, don't trust the living. Their eyes"   FOLKW 36

INCIDENT. "Not that it matters. Or not much, and not"   SPOA 71

KRISTOFFER SECOND. "Kristoffer the Second, by Grace of God"   FOLKW 36

THE LAMB. "A month before Easter"   FOLKW 36

LETTER TO A MIDNIGHT. "You will tire of many acceptances"   SPOA 71

L'INGLESE. "Walpole, traveling in the Alps"   SPOA 72

THE LONGEST WAY IS BACK. "The longest way is back. Lazarus learned"   SPOA 71

A MAGUS. "A missionary from the Mau Mau told me"   SPOA 72

A MASQUE FOR BUCKINGHAM. "Here's to the bodies from which we come"   SPOA 72

MEASUREMENTS. "I've zeroed an altimeter on the floor"   FOLKW 36

NEW YEAR'S EVE. "The age is running out. I guess I feel"   SPOA 72

NOTES ON THE PSALMIST. "What is man? the Psalmist cried"   SPOA 72

ON AN ECDYSIAST. "She stripped herself of all"   SPOA 72

ON BEING. "Ann says she trusts me"   SPOA 72

ON LEAVING THE PARTY AFTER HAVING BEEN POSSIBLY BRILLIANT FOR CERTAINLY TOO LONG. "While the magician"   SPOA 72

ON LOOKING EAST TO THE SEA WITH A SUNSET BEHIND ME. "In a detachment cool as the glint of light"   FOLKW 36, LIBC 50

ON THE POET AS A DAMNED POOR THING. "I adored her and she giggled and I adored her"   SPOA 72

ON THE POET AS A MARIONETTE. "A comic in a mashed hat, eating"   SPOA 72

ONE DAY. "One day in a rush of dogwood all the world married"   SPOA 71

PARENTHOOD. "My son was insolent to me"   SPOA 72

PLEASE!   CAED 109

POEMS FROM ITALY. "Nona Domenica Garnaro sits in the sun"   LIBC 50

PROJECT FOR A CLIFF-FACE. "Before I die, said the self-riddling stonecutter"   SPOA 72

THE SEA SHINES. "The sea shines. Wind-raked, the waters run light"   SPOA 102

SMALL ELEGY. "I saw a bird pasted to muck"   SPOA 72

SNOWY HERON.   FOLKW 67

SOME SORT OF GAME. "Toy-maker Ptolemy"   SPOA 72

SUNDAY MORNING. "I light a cigarette, my dead mouth steaming"   FOLKW 36

SUNSET AND AFTER. "This easy-gone world now —that one cloud it sets to"   SPOA 71

TALKING MYSELF TO SLEEP AT ONE MORE HILTON. "I have a country but no town"   SPOA 71

TEMPTATION.   LIBC 50

A THOUGHT ABOUT SHEIK BEDREDDIN. "I read in a tattered book about Sheik Bedreddin"   FOLKW 36

THOUGHTS ON LOOKING INTO A THICKET. "And stay away from the cellar door"   FOLKW 36

THREE VIEWS OF A MOTHER. "Good soul, my mother holds my daughter"   FOLKW 36, LIBC 50

TO JUDITH. I. "Men marry what they need. I marry you"   FOLKW 36, FOLKW 67

———. II. "My dear, darkened in sleep, turned from the moon"   FOLKW 36

———. III. "Sometimes the foundering fury that directs"   FOLKW 36

———. IV. "I look through my dead friend's eyes"   FOLKW 36

———. V. "The deaths about you when you stir in sleep"   FOLKW 36

TO SOMATICA TO SAY NOTHING, AND NOT "NO". "Avoid dialogue, Somatica. What you are"   SPOA 72

TWO LECTURES AND A FEW FLOURISHES. "Pico della Mirandola, when he was nineteen"   SPOA 71

V. J. DAY. "On the tallest day in time the dead came back"   SPOA 102

WAS A MAN. "Ted Roethke was a tearing man"   SPOA 71

THE WEEK THAT WAS. "The pet shops were advertising"   SPOA 72

WHY DON'T YOU WRITE FOR ME? "For you, or of you? It can't be"   SPOA 71

Poetry*   CASSC 12, JNP 77

Ciconi, Teobaldo. 1824. in Italian.
PASSA LA RONDA.   CETRA 26

Cino Da Pistoia. 1270. in Italian.
Poetry*   CETRA 36

Clare, John. 1793. in English.
AUTUMN.   ARGO 137

CLOCK-A-CLAY. "In the cowslip pips I lie"   FOLKW 67, LONGM 1

EMMONSAIL'S HEATH IN WINTER. "I love to see the old heath's withered brake"   LONGM 1

FIRST LOVE. "I ne'er was struck before that hour"   ARGO 63

I AM. "I am—yet what I am none cares or knows"   ARGO 63, CAED 202, CMS 13, LONGM 1

AN INVITE TO ETERNITY. "Wilt thou go with me sweet maid"   ARGO 63

LOVE LIVES BEYOND THE TOMB. "Love lives beyond the tomb"   ARGO 63

ON A LANE IN SPRING. "A little lane—the brook runs close"   FOLKW 67

* Recording not available for analysis

Clare, John (continued)

SCHOOLBOYS IN WINTER. "The schoolboys still
their morning rambles take" COLUMB 11
SUMMER EVENING. "The sinking sun is taking
leave"   BRITAM 1
SUMMER IMAGES. "Now swarthy summer, by
rude health embrowned"   ARGO 63
THE WIND THAT SHAKES THE RUSHES.   LION 2
Poetry*   ARGO 110

Clark, China. in English.
THE BLACK MESSIAH.   FOLKW 47
BROWN SUGAR. "Let me announce myself"
                              FOLKW 47
THE DANCE OF FOREVER.   FOLKW 47
MOTION.   FOLKW 47
PECAN PIE.   FOLKW 47
PRAYIN' AND MAKIN' LOVE.   FOLKW 47
SUNSHINE.   FOLKW 47

Clark, David Ridgley. 1920. in English.
PINNACLE.   FOLKW 25

Clark, Gillian. 1937. in English.
HARVEST AT MYNACHLOG.   ARGO 152
LUNCHTIME LECTURE. "And this, from the sec-
ond or third millennium"   ARGO 152
SUNDIAL. "Owain was ill today. In the night"
                              ARGO 152

Clark, John W. 1907. in English.
AND NOW I.   GRYPH 1
THE BEACH WATCHERS.   GRYPH 1
BEYOND THE SEA.   GRYPH 1
BLACK AND WHITE.   GRYPH 1
THE CLOUDS.   GRYPH 1
COCKTAIL LOUNGE.   GRYPH 1
COLD.   GRYPH 1
DEAD POET.   GRYPH 1
THE DESCENT.   GRYPH 1
THE DREAMER.   GRYPH 1
THE FUTURE.   GRYPH 1
GOD'S OWN.   GRYPH 1
HER EYES EXCHANGE.   GRYPH 1
IN TURN.   GRYPH 1
THE LAST YEAR.   GRYPH 1
THE LION TAMER.   GRYPH 1
LOOK BACK.   GRYPH 1
MISERERE.   GRYPH 1
ON THE SAND.   GRYPH 1
OUTWARD.   GRYPH 1
SLEEP AWAKE.   GRYPH 1
SPACE PORT.   GRYPH 1
THE TIGER.   GRYPH 1
TOMB OF MARIE ANDERSON.   GRYPH 1
A VERY CONFUSING DAY.   GRYPH 1
THE VIEW.   GRYPH 1
THE WHEEL.   GRYPH 1
WHERE HAS THE WIND GONE.   GRYPH 1
WHY DOES THE FLY.   GRYPH 1

Clarke, Austin. 1896. in English.
BEYOND THE PALE, exc.   CLADD 1
CELIBACY. "On a brown isle of Lough Corrib"
                              ARGO 16
HER VOICE COULD NOT BE SOFTER. "Suddenly in
the dark wood"   ARGO 99
IRISH-AMERICAN VISITOR. "Up in the clouds, a
blessed dot"   ARGO 99
MABEL KELLY. "Lucky the husband" ARGO 99

MARRIAGE. "Parents are sinful now, for they
must whisper"   ARGO 99
PEGGY BROWNE. "The dark-haired girl, who
holds my thought entirely"   ARGO 10
PILGRIMAGE. "When the far south glittered"
                              ARGO 10
THE STRAYING STUDENT. "On a holy day when
sails were blowing"   ARGO 10
SUMMER LIGHTNING. "The heavens opened
With a scream"   ARGO 99
TENEBRAE. "This is the hour that we must
mourn"   ARGO 99
WANDERING MEN. "When sudden night had
trapped the wood"   ARGO 99

Claudel, Paul. 1868. in French.
CANTIQUE DU RHÔNE. "Laeta.—Qu'il est beau, le
navire noir que le vent"   ADES 13
                              SPOA 62
CHANSON D'AUTOMNE. "Dans la lumière
éclatante d'automne" ADES 13, ADES 54
                              SPOA 62
CHEMIN DE LA CROIX (ONZIÈME STATION). "Voic
l'aire où le grain de froment céleste est ég
rugé"   ADES 13, SPOA 62
"Derriere moi la plaine"   DOVER
L'ESPRIT ET L'EAU. "Après le long silence fu
mant"   ADES 13, HACH 14, SPOA 62
INTROIT. "Une fois de plus l'exil" ADES 1
VERS D'EXIL. "Paul, il nous faut partir pour un
départ plus beau"   ADES 13, SPOA 62
LA VIERGE A MIDI. "Il est midi. Je vois l'église
ouverte"   FOLKW 1
Poetry*   ADES 5

Claudius, Matthias. 1740. in German.
ABENDLIED. "Der Mond ist aufgegangen"
              DOVER 1, SPOA 5, TELEF
AN FRAU REBEKKA. "Ich habe Dich geliebet und
ich will Dich lieben"   TELEF
AUF DEN TOD DER KAISERIN. "Sie machte Fried
en! Das ist mein Gedicht"   TELEF
KRIEGSLIED. "'S ist Krieg! 's Krieg! O Gott Enge
wehre, Und rede Du darein!"   TELEF
DER MENSCH. "Empfangen und genähret"
                      SPOA 5, TELEF
DIE MUTTER BEI DER WIEGE. "Schlaf, süsse
Knabe, süss und mild"   ATHENA
OSTERLIED. "Das Grab ist leer, das Grab ist leer"
                              CHRIST 18
TÄGLICH ZU SINGEN. "Ich danke Gott und freue
mich"   TELEF
DER TOD UND DAS MÄDCHEN. "Vorüber, ach
vorüber geh, wilder Knochenmann!"
                              DOVER
WIEGENLIED, BEI MONDSCHEIN ZU SINGEN. "S
schlafe nun, du Kleine"   CHRIST 11
                              TELEF
Poetry*   CHRIST 4, CHRIST 6

Clay, Buriel. in English.
DEPRIVED. "The sweet solid smell"
                              WATSHD
STOLEN EXPRESSIONS. "If de blues was whiskey"
                              WATSHD

Cleanthes. 330 B.C. in Greek.
"Agoy de m', o Zeu, kai sy g he pepromene"
                              FOLKW 104

---

* Recording not available for analysis

Clifton, Lucille. 1936. in English.

ADMONITIONS. "Boys, I don't promise you"
WATSHD 5

IN SALEM. "Weird sister/the Black witches"
WATSHD 5

"In the inner city"   WATSHD 5

THE LOST BABY POEM. "The time i dropped your
almost body down"   WATSHD 5

"The thirty eighth year"   WATSHD 5

UNTITLED: BENEDICTION.   WATSHD 2

UNTITLED: ON NAMES.   WATSHD 2

Poetry*   WATSHD 28

Cloakley, William Leo. in English.

INSECTS.   CAED 155

Clough, Arthur Hugh. 1819. in English.

AMOURS DE VOYAGE, exc. "I am in love, mean-
time, you think"   LONGM 1

———. "Over the great windy waters, and
over the clear-crested summits" ARGO 68

———. "So, I have seen a man killed"
LONGM 1

"It fortifies my soul to know"   ARGO 68

THE LATEST DECALOGUE. "Thou shalt have one
God only"   ARGO 68, BRITAM 3,
CAED 201, THEAL 1, LONGM 1

"Say not the struggle naught availeth"
ARGO 68, AUDIA 1, LIST 3, LONGM 1

THE SHADOW. "I dreamed a dream: I dreamt
that I espied"   ARGO 68

SPECTATOR AB EXTRA. "As I sat in the cafe I said
to myself"   RCA 1

Poetry*   LIST 11

Coatsworth, Elizabeth. 1893. in English.

THE BAD KITTENS. "You may call, you may call"
HARB 3

THE BARN. "I am tired of this barn! said the colt"
HARB 5

DARK KINGDOM.   CAED 110

THE MOUSE COMPLAINS. "I heard a mouse"
SCHOL 8

THE RABBIT'S SONG OUTSIDE THE TAVERN. "We
who play under the pines"   BOWMAR 1

SNOW. "A snow can come as quietly" HARB 3

SUMMER RAIN. "What could be lovelier than to
hear"   HARB 5

"Swift things are beautiful"   HARB 6,
SCHOL 7

Cobbing, Bob. 1920. in English.

DREI STÜCKE AUS ABC.   LUCHT 1

Cocteau, Jean. 1889. in French.

LES ALLIANCES. "Ce sont les anges qui préparent"   ADES 6

UN AMI DORT. "Tes mains jonchant les draps"
CAED 54, PHIL 1

L' ANGE HEURTEBISE. "L'ange Heurtebise, sur les
gradins"   CAED 54

LES ANGES MALADROITES. "Les anges maladroits
vous imitent"   FOLKW 13

BATTERIE. "Soleil, je t'adore comme les sauvages"   ADES 6, SPOA 32

"Les cheveux gris, quand jeunesse les porte"
ADES 6, SPOA 32

CONSEIL DE TOUTE IMPORTANCE. "Une ange ne
doit pas parler"   ADES 6

"De tous les partis"   ADES 6

LA DIFFICULTÉ D'ÊTRE, exc.   GMS 10

"Franchement, je croyais qu'amour, en poésie"
CAED 54

"Hélas! vais-je a présent me plaindre dans ces
stances"   CAED 54

HOMMAGE A MANOLETE. "Autre ni fut, autre titre
de noblesse"   CAED 54

HOMMAGE A PICASSO.   ADES 6

"J'ai peine à soutenir le poids d'or des musées"
CAED 54

"Je n'aime pas dormir quand ta figure habite"
ADES 6, CAED 54, SPOA 32

"Je veux tout oublier, et cet ange cornu"
CAED 54

"Lit d'amour"   ADES 6, SPOA 32

"Lorsque nous seront tous deux sous la terre"
CAED 54

"Mauvaise compagne, espèce de morte"
ADES 6, CAED 54, SPOA 32

LE MENTEUR. "Je voudrais dire la verité"
CBS 1

"Mon ange, vois, je te loue"   CAED 54

"Muses, pardonnez-moi"   ADES 6

"Muses qui ne songez à plaire ou à déplaire"
ADES 6, SPOA 32

"Les muses sont de feux, de cristaux, comme un
lustre"   CAED 54

"Ne m'interrogez pas. Interrogez ces filles"
CAED 54

"Notre entrelacs d'amour à des lettres ressemble"   CAED 54

LE PAQUET ROUGE. "Mon sang est devenu de
l'encre"   ADES 6, CAED 54, SPOA 32

PAR LUI-MÊME. "Accidents du mystère et fautes
de calcul"   ADES 6, SPOA 32

"Rien ne m'effraye plus que la fausse accalmie"
ADES 6, SPOA 32

"Les soeurs, comme un cheval, nous savent la
main mordre"   CAED 54

LES VOLEURS D'ENFANTS. "Presque nue et soudain sortie"   ADES 6, CAED 54

Poetry*   PERIOD 3

Codax, Martin. in Portuguese.

CANTIGA. "Ondas do mar de Vigo"
FOLKW 10

Codrescu, Andrei. 1946. in English.

Poetry*   WATSHD 55

Coffin, Robert Peter Tristram. 1892. in English.

ALEXANDER GRAHAM BELL DID NOT INVENT THE
TELEPHONE. "Alexander Graham Bell"
SPOA 94

THE FOG. "He knew how Roman legions
looked"   NACTE 16

THE LADY OF THE TOMAHAWK. "Hannah was a
lady"   SINGER 5

LANTERN IN THE SNOW. "This thing is beautiful, I
know"   NACTE 16, SPOA 94

LULLABY FOR PEREGRINE. "Hush! new baby, bob-
cats creep"   HOUGHT 2

THE ROCKER. "When Tom Bailey wants to rest"
SPOA 94

ROXINEY BOODY. "When Fall winds began to
blow"   SPOA 94

THE SECRET HEART. "Across the years he could
recall"   NACTE 16, SINGER 3

TREE SLEEPING. "When I was small and trees
were high"   CAED 111

* Recording not available for analysis

Cohen, Leonard. 1934. in English.

ELEGY. "Do not look for him"FOLKW 49

FOR WILF AND HIS HOUSE. "When young the Christians told me"FOLKW 49

POEM. "I heard of a man"FOLKW 49

THE SPARROWS. "Catching winter in their carved nostrils"FOLKW 49

LES VIEUX. "Northeastern lunch"FOLKW 49

WARNING. "If your neighbour disappears"FOLKW 49

Cohn, Marianne. in French.

JE TRAHIRAI DEMAIN.ADES 55

Colbert, Alison. in English.

THE AIR DOES NOT TOUCH US. "Something about standing"WATSHD 4

"He said he was leaving for Phoenix"WATSHD 4

"I slept in the light"WATSHD 4

LET THE CIRCLE BE UNBROKEN. "I came to your house"WATSHD 4

THE LITERARY PARTY. "This is my nutcracker"WATSHD 4

"Looking for my brother under the ground"WATSHD 4

THE MIRACULOUS TRANSFORMATION. "I was looking for the"WATSHD 4

SECOND DAY OF DEATH. "In the sunlit room"WATSHD 4

WALKER EVANS. "Walker Evans, 65 years old"WATSHD 4

"Will it sell"WATSHD 4

WOMEN WHO WRITE IN THEIR BLOOD. "We are sorority"WATSHD 4

Coleridge, Mary Elizabeth. 1861. in English.

"Egypt's might is tumbled down"ARGO 70A

UNWELCOME. "We were young, we were merry, we were very very wise"ARGO 70A

Coleridge, Samuel Taylor. 1772. in English.

CHRISTABEL, exc. " 'Tis the middle of night by the castle clock"ARGO 21, ARGO 58

A CHRISTMAS CAROL. "The shepherds went their hasty way"LION 1

DEJECTION: AN ODE. "Well! If the Bard was weather-wise, who made"ARGO 21, ARGO 58, CAED 59, LIST 20

———, exc. "My genial spirits fail"LONGM 1

FRAGMENT OF AN ODE TO MAIA. "Mother of Hermes! and still youthful Maia!"FOLKW 63

FROST AT MIDNIGHT. "The frost performs its secret ministry"ARGO 21, ARGO 58, CAED 59, FOLKW 63, LIST 20, SPOA 57

KUBLA KHAN. "In Xanadu did Kubla Khan"ARGO 21, ARGO 58, BRITAM 1, CAED 59, CAED 186, CAED 202, CMS 12, EAV 7, FOLKW 63, IMP 1, LIST 2, LIST 10, LIST 20, SPOA 35, SPOA 57, LONGM 1

LINES ADDED TO SCHILLER'S WALLENSTEIN. "The intelligible forms of ancient poets"ARGO 21

THE PAINS OF SLEEP. "Ere on my bed my limbs I lay"ARGO 21, ARGO 58

THE RIME OF THE ANCIENT MARINER. "It is an ancient Mariner"ARGO 5, ARGO 21, ARGO 58, CAED 59, CAED 132, CAED 202, EAV 1, LIST 20, PROTHM 3, RCA 8, SPOA 57

———, exc.CAED 21, EAV 22

THIS LIME-TREE BOWER MY PRISON. "Well, they are gone, and here must I remain"CAED 59

TIME, REAL AND IMAGINARY. "On the wide level of a mountain's head"SPOA 57

YOUTH AND AGE. "Verse, a breeze mid blossoms straying"SPOA 57

Poetry*SPOA 123

Collier, Tom. in English.

TRUE MYTHS. "How deeply must we plunge"WATSHD 7

Collins, Leslie M. in English.

SOLILOQUI. "I am an American, yes, an American"ARGO 17

STEVEDORE. "The enigmatic moon has at long last died"ARGO 17

Collins, William. 1721. in English.

CYMBELINE: DIRGE FOR FIDELE. "To fair Fidele's grassy tomb"ARGO 50, ARGO 82

ODE ON THE POPULAR SUPERSTITIONS OF THE HIGHLANDS, exc.ARGO 50

ODE TO EVENING. "If ought of oaten stop, or pastoral song"ARGO 50, CAED 203, SPOA 64

ODE TO SIMPLICITY. "O thou by nature taught"SPOA 64

ODE WRITTEN IN THE BEGINNING OF THE YEAR 1746.ARGO 50

THE PASSIONS: AN ODE FOR MUSIC. "When music, Heav'nly Maid, was young"ARGO 50, SPOA 64

Collymore, Frank. in English.

LULLABY. "Darkness broods on earth and air"CAED 153

ON THE KITE.CAED 153

VOICI LA PLUME DE MON ONCLE. "In a couple of weeks' time school will reopen"CAED 153

Colonna, Vittoria. 1492. in Italian.

Poetry*CETRA 23

Colum, Padraic. 1881. in English.

THE BIRD OF JESUS. "It was pure indeed"FOLKW 27

BIRD OF PARADISE. "With sapphire for her crown"FOLKW 27

CONDORS FLYING. "We watched the condors winging toward the moon"FOLKW 27

A CRADLE SONG. "O men from the fields"SPOA 7

HONEY-SELLER. "Down a street that once I lived in"FOLKW 27

THE LITTLE MOUSE.CAED 109

MAY DAY. "May day! Surpassing time!"FOLKW 27

AN OLD SONG RE-SUNG. "As I went down through Dublin city"FOLWK 27

AN OLD WOMAN OF THE ROADS. "Oh, to have a little house"CAED 169, FOLKW 27, HARB 5, HARC 3

REMINISCENCE II. "I saw the wind to-day"FOLKW 27

---

* Recording not available for analysis

REMINISCENCE X. "At the fore of the year, and on Candlemas Day"   FOLKW 27

WILD ASS. "The Wild Ass lounges, legs struck out"   FOLKW 27

YOUNG GIRL: ANNAM. "I am a young girl"   CAED 112

Compiuta Donzella, La. See **Donzella, La Compiuta.**

Conde, Carmen. in Spanish.

"Conozco un silencio nuevo"   AGUIL 10

"Cuando de perdí lloraban"   AGUIL 10

"La herida tiene parpados que crujen duramente"   AGUIL 10

LLANTO POR ABEL. "Negro cuajar de mi entraña"   AGUIL 8

PRIMER AMOR. "Qué sorpresa tu cuerpo, qué inefable vehemencia"   FIDIAS 2

TORO EN GUADARRAMA. "Porque tú eres lo que comes, pisas"   AGUIL 8

Confucius. 550 B.C. in Chinese.

ODES, exc.   English SPOA 110

Congreve, William. 1670. in English.

AMORET. "Fair Amoret is gone astray"   CAED 203

THE MOURNING BRIDE, exc. "Music hath charms to soothe the savage breast"   CAED 203

Conkling, Hilda. 1910. in English.

ABOUT ANIMALS. "Animals are my friends and my kin"   CAED 154

ABOUT MY DREAMS. "Now the flowers are all folded"   CAED 154

ADVENTURE. "I went slowly through the wood of shadows"   BOWMAR 1, CAED 154

THE APPLE-JELLY-FISH TREE. "Down in the depths of the sea"   CAED 154

AUGUST AFTERNOON. "Sea-blue of gentian"   CAED 154

BUTTERFLY. "As I walked through my garden"   CAED 154

BUTTERFLY ADVENTURE. "I saw a butterfly"   CAED 154

THE CELLAR. "I love my queer cellar with its dusty smell"   CMS 2

CHICKADEE. "The chickadee in the appletree"   CAED 154

COZY SONG. "Cozy we sit/a cricket and I"   CAED 154

DANDELION. "O little soldier with the golden helmet"   CAED 110, CAED 154, HARB 2

THE DEW-LIGHT. "The Dew-man comes over the mountains"   CAED 154

ELSA. "My sister stood on a hilltop"   CAED 154

ENVOY. "If I am happy, and you"   CAED 154

FAIRIES. "I cannot see fairies"   CAED 164

FIELD MOUSE. "Little brown field mouse"   CAED 154

FIRST SONGS. "Rosy plum-tree, think of me"   CAED 154

FOR YOU, MOTHER. "I have a dream for you, Mother"   CAED 154

GEOGRAPHY. "I can tell balsam trees"   CAED 154

GIFT. "This is mint and here are three pinks"   CAED 154

HILLS. "The hills are going somewhere"   CAED 154, CMS 2

I AM. "I am willowy boughs"   CAED 154

I KEEP WONDERING. "I saw a mountain"   CAED 154

I LIVE IN A COTTAGE. "There's a little cottage"   CAED 154

I SHALL COME BACK. "I shall be coming back to you"   CAED 154

I WENT TO SEA. "I went to sea in a glass-bottomed boat"   CAED 154

IF I COULD TELL YOU THE WAY. "Down through the forest"   CAED 154

LITTLE PAPOOSE. "Little Papoose/Swing high in the branches"   CAED 154

THE LITTLE SNAIL. "I saw a snail come down the garden walk"   BOWMAR 1, CAED 109, CAED 154, HARB 2

THE LONESOME GREEN APPLE. "There was a little green apple"   CAED 154

MARY COBWEB. "She was not exactly a doll"   CAED 154

THE MILKY WAY. "Down the highroad of the Milky Way"   CAED 154

MOON DOVES. "The moon has a dove-cote safe and small"   CAED 154

MOON SONG. "There is a star that runs very fast"   CAED 154, CAED 164

MORNING. "There is a brook I must hear"   CAED 154

MOUSE. "Little mouse in gray velvet"   CAED 154

MUSHROOM SONG. "Oh little mushrooms with brown faces"   CAED 154

NEVER-KNOWN. "The chickadee taught me this river"   CAED 154

THE OLD BRASS POT. "The old brass pot in the corner"   CAED 154

THE OLD BRIDGE. "The old bridge has a wrinkled face"   CAED 154, CAED 164, HARB 5

PIGEONS JUST AWAKE. "As the sun rose"   CAED 154, CMS 2, HARB 5

POEMS. "I know how poems come"   CAED 154, CMS 2

THE RED MOON COMES OUT IN THE NIGHT.   CAED 109

RED ROOSTER. "Red Rooster in your gray coop"   CAED 154

ROSE-MOSS. "Little Rose-Moss beside the stone"   CAED 154

SILVERHORN. "It is out in the mountains"   CAED 154

SUMMER-DAY SONG. "Wild birds fly over me"   CAED 154

TIME. "Time is a harp"   CAED 154

TREE-TOAD. "Tree-Toad is a small gray person"   CAED 154

VELVETS. "This pansy has a thinking face"   CAED 154

VERMONT HILLS. "The Vermont hills curve"   CAED 154

WATER. "The world turns softly"   CAED 109, CAED 154, HARB 4

WET DAY. "Rain-drops slanted down"   CAED 154

Connor, Tony. 1930. in English.

APPROACHING BOLTON.   ARGO 147

A CHILD HALF ASLEEP. "Stealthily parting the small-hours silence"   ARGO 147

* Recording not available for analysis

Connor, Tony (continued)

CHILDREN'S GAMES. "Papu, Tariq, Oguchi, Paulo"   ARGO 147

COMMUNITY SINGING. "Grandad Connor toiled at the forge"   ARGO 147

THE CROFT. "The croft, shadowed between houses"   ARGO 94, ARGO 147

ELEGY FOR ALFRED HUBBARD. "Hubbard is dead, the old plumber"   ARGO 94, ARGO 147, SPOA 67

AN EMPTY HOUSE. "Doors bolted; windows dirt-bleared"   ARGO 147

IN OAK TERRACE.   ARGO 147

THE LOOK OF LOVE. "Beleaguered by passions, as by thunder"   ARGO 94

MRS. ROOT. "Busybody, nosey-parker"   ARGO 94, ARGO 147

PORTO VENERI. "One midnight, glittering-eyed, in restless silence"   ARGO 147

SAYING IT. "Questions of tact are uppermost"   ARGO 147

TO HIS WIFE.   ARGO 147

WINTER WALK. "Take the street where the cinders crunch"   ARGO 147

Conquest, Robert. 1917. in English.

REVUE BAR STRIP. "Undepilated beauty stands"   PROTHM 8

Constable, Henry. 1562. in English.

IF THIS BE LOVE. "To live in Hell, and heaven to behold"   ARGO 32

Copeland, Josephine. in English.

THE ZULU KING; NEW ORLEANS. "The Zulu King arrived"   FOLKW 6

Coplen, Grace Wilson. in English.

FIREFLIES. "I like to chase the fire flies"   BOWMAR 1

Coppée, François. 1842. in French.

STATUE D'HOMME D'ÉTAT.   CAED 202

Corazzini, Sergio. 1886. in Italian.

Poetry*   CETRA 28

Corbet, Richard. 1582. in English.

TO HIS SON, VINCENT. "What I shall leave thee none can tell"   IMP 1

Corbière, "Tristan" (Édouard-Joachim). 1845. in French.

LE MOUSSE.   CAED 204

LE PARDON DE SAINTE-ANNE-LA-PALUD, exc. "Bénite est l'infertile plage"   HACH 13

Corke, Hilary. 1921. in English.

THE EARLY DROWNED. "Great while I lay at mercy of the sea"   ARGO 97

Corneille, Pierre. 1606. in French.

PSYCHE.   ADES 54

STANCES À LA MARQUISE. "Marquise, si mon visage"   ADES 54, HACH 9

STANCES DE POLYCEUCTE. "Source délicieuse, en misères"   HACH 9

Corner, Philip. in English.

PEACE, BE STILL. "Our words go slowly out"   WATSHD 13

Coronado, Carolina. 1823. in Spanish.

A UNA ESTRELLA. "Chispa de luz, que, fija en lo infinito"   FIDIAS 2

"LA LUZ DEL DÍA SE APAGA"   AGUIL 8

SONETO. "¡Oh, cuán te adoro! Con la luz del día"   AGUIL 8

Corretjer, Juan Antonio. in Spanish.

DECIMAS DEL POEMA EL LENERO.   INSTPR 1

Corsaro, Antonio. in Italian.

GROTTE DI ULISSE.   CETRA 31

Corso, Gregory. 1930. in English.

LINES WRITTEN NOV. 22, 23—1963. "Ah, the Disney dinosaur's light laughter"   FOLKW 21

MAN. "The good scope of him is history, old and ironic"   APPL 2

PHAESTOS. "Phaestos is a village with 25 families"   APPL 2

REFLECTIONS IN A GREEN ARENA. "Where marble stood and fell"   APPL 2

WRITTEN ON FINDING AN UNMARKED GRAVE. "Children, Children, don't you know"   APPL 2

Poetry*   UCALM 2

Costa i Llobera, Miquel. 1854. in Catalan.

EL PI DE FORMENTOR. "Mon cor estima un arbre! Més vell que l'olivera"   AGUIL 14

Cotton, Charles. 1630. in English.

EVENING QUATRAINS. "The day's grown old, the fainting sun"   SPOA 84, LONGM 1

THE RETIREMENT. "Farewell thou busie World"   ARGO 47

Couto, Ribeiro. 1898. in Portuguese.

CAIS DO PAQUETÁ. "Lusitana melodia"   FOLKW 71

ELEGIA. "Que quer o vento?"   FOLKW 71

Coward, Noel. 1899. in English.

THE BOY ACTOR. "I can remember. I can remember"   CAED 61

DO I BELIEVE? "Do I believe in God?"   CAED 61

HONEYMOON. "They were married"   CAED 61

A LADY AT A PARTY.   CAED 61

LETTER FROM THE SEASIDE, 1880. "Dearest Mama"   CAED 61

MRS. MALLORY. "Mrs. Mallory went to a psychiatrist"   CAED 61

1901. "When Queen Victoria died"   CAED 61

NOTHING IS LOST. "Deep in our subconscious, we are told"   CAED 61

OPERA NOTES. "I feel inclined to send a teenyweeny"   CAED 61

A QUESTION OF VALUES. "Christopher Marlowe or Francis Bacon"   CAED 61

Cowley, Abraham. 1618. in English.

BEAUTY. "Beauty, thou wild fantastick Ape"   CAED 38

THE CHANGE. "Love in her sunny eyes does basking play"   ARGO 37

ODE UPON DOCTOR HARVEY. "Coy Nature, which remain'd"   CAED 38

Cowley, Malcolm. 1898. in English.

BLUE JUNIATA: BONES OF A HOUSE. "Farm houses curl like horns of plenty, hide"   JNP 3, SPOA 95

BOY IN SUNLIGHT. "The boy having fished alone"   JNP 3

COMMEMORATIVE BRONZE. "Every man his own Robespierre"   JNP 3

THE FLOWER AND THE LEAF. "All of an age, all heretics"   JNP 3

MINE NUMBER 6. "They scoured the hill with steel"   JNP 3

MY LAND.   JNP 3

---

* Recording not available for analysis

PINEY WOODS. "Teeth on the saw"   SPOA 95
POEM IN A TIME OF CRISIS. "—jumped over the quick brown fox"   SPOA 95
THE PYRE. "Strangers were buying the house"   JNP 3
THE ROCKING CHAIRS. "At seven o'clock"   JNP 3, SPOA 95
TOWERS OF SONG. "Out of an empty sky the dust of hours"   JNP 3
THE URN. "Wanderers outside the gates, in hollow"   SPOA 95
VALUTA. "Following the dollar, ah"   JNP 3
VOICES FROM HOME: 1923. "Fresh from the factory"   JNP 3
WINTER TENEMENT. "When everything but love was spent"   JNP 3

Cowper, William. 1731. in English.
THE CASTAWAY. "Obscurest night involv'd the sky"   ARGO 51, LONGM 1
THE DIVERTING HISTORY OF JOHN GILPIN. "John Gilpin was a citizen"   PROTHM 10
EPITAPH ON A HARE. "Here lies, whom hound did ne'er pursue"   ARGO 51
ON THE LOSS OF THE ROYAL GEORGE. "Toll for the brave"   ARGO 51, IMP 1
ON THE RECEIPT OF MY MOTHER'S PICTURE OUT OF NORFOLK. "Oh that those lips had language"   ARGO 51
THE POPLAR FIELD. "The poplars are felled, farewell to the shade"   ARGO 51, CAED 203
THE TASK, BK. 1, exc. "How oft upon yon eminence our pace"   ARGO 51
———, BK. 2, exc. "England, with all thy faults, I love thee still"   ARGO 51
TO MARY. "The twentieth year is well-nigh past"   ARGO 51, EAV 7
VERSES SUPPOSED TO BE WRITTEN BY ALEXANDER SELKIRK. "I am monarch of all I survey"   ARGO 51

Cox, Kenyon. in English.
THE OCTOPUSSYCAT. "I love Octopussy, his arms are so long"   HARB 3

Crabbe, George. 1754. in English.
THE BOROUGH. PETER GRIMES, exc. "Old Peter Grimes made fishing his employ"   ARGO 52, PROTHM 4
———. THE PLAYERS, exc. "Children of thespis, welcome; knights before your scenes"   ARGO 52
MARRIAGE RING. "The ring so worn, as you behold"   ARGO 52
THE PARISH REGISTER, II, exc. "Love, that impatient guide—too proud to think"   ARGO 52
SIR EUSTACE GREY, exc. "Then those ill-favored ones"   ARGO 52
TALES OF THE HALL: ADVENTURES OF RICHARD, exc.   ARGO 52
"Theirs is yon house"   LONGM 1
"Up yonder hill"   LONGM 1
THE VILLAGE, exc. "Anon, a figure enters"   LONGM 1
———. "Lo! Where the heath"   LONGM 1
———. "The village life, and every care that reigns"   ARGO 52
"The whistling boy that holds the plough"   IMP 1

Crane, Hart. 1899. in English.
AT MELVILLE'S TOMB. "Often beneath the wave"   ARGO 12
THE BROKEN TOWER. "The bell-rope that gathers God at dawn"   CAED 99
CUTTY SARK. "I met a man in South Street, tall"   CAED 99
EMBLEMS OF CONDUCT. "By a peninsula the wanderer sat"   ARGO 12
ETERNITY. "After it was over, though still gusting balefully"   CAED 99
THE HURRICANE. "Lo, Lord, Thou ridest!"   CAED 99
ISLAND QUARRY. "Square sheets-they saw the marble into"   ARGO 12
LEGEND. "As silent as a mirror is believed"   CAED 99
MY GRANDMOTHER'S LOVE LETTERS. "There are no stars"   CAED 99
O CARIB ISLE! "The tarantula rattling at the lily's foot"   CAED 99
THE PHANTOM BARK. "So dream thy sails, O phantom bark"   CAED 99
POWHATAN'S DAUGHTER. INDIANA. "The morning-glory, climbing"   CAED 99
———. THE DANCE. "The swift red flesh, a winter king"   CAED 99
———. THE HARBOR DAWN. "Insistently through sleep"   CAED 99
PRAISE FOR AN URN. "It was a kind and northern face"   CAED 99
RECITATIVE. "Regard the capture here, O Janus-faced"   ARGO 12
ROYAL PALM. "Green rustlings, more than regal charities"   CAED 99
SOUTHERN CROSS. "I wanted you, nameless Woman of the South"   CAED 99
TO BROOKLYN BRIDGE. "How many downs, chill from his"   CAED 99
VOYAGES, 2. "And yet this great wink of eternity"   JNP 3
———, 3. "Infinite consanguinity it bears"   CAED 99
———, 5. "Meticulous, past midnight in clear rime"   CAED 99
Poetry*   NET 4

Crane, Stephen. 1871. in English.
THE BLACK RIDERS, exc. "Tell brave deeds of war"   FOLKW 29
———, exc.   ARGO 12
WAR IS KIND, exc. "A man said to the universe"   ARGO 12
———, exc. "Ay, workman, make me a dream"   FOLKW 29
———, exc. "Do not weep, maiden, for war is kind"   FOLKW 29, HOUGHT 5
———, exc.   CAED 185

Crashaw, Richard. 1612. in English.
THE FLAMING HEART, exc. "O Heart! the equal poise of love's both parts"   LONGM 1
——— "Well-meaning readers! you that come as friends"   CAED 38
A HYMN TO THE NAME AND HONOUR OF THE ADMIRABLE SAINT TERESA. "Love, thou art absolute, sole Lord"   FOLKW 69
SHEPHERD'S HYMN. "Gloomy night embraced the place"   LIST 2

* Recording not available for analysis

Crashaw, Richard (continued)

UPON THE BLEEDING CRUCIFIX.   LIST 2
WISHES TO HIS SUPPOSED MISTRESS. "Whoe'er she
be"   CAED 186

Creeley, Robert. 1926. in English.
THE BALL GAME. "The one damn time (7th in-
ning)"   SCHOL 3
THE CARNIVAL. "Whereas the man who hits"
                                   NACTE 14
THE CRACKS. "Don't step"   SCHOL 3
THE DOOR FOR ROBERT DUNCAN. "It is hard going
to the door"   SCHOL 3
THE FINGER. "Either in or out of the mind"
                                   SPOA 105
THE FIRST TIME.   NET 6
FOR LOVE. "Yesterday I wanted to" SPOA 105
A FORM OF WOMEN. "I have come far enough"
                                   SCHOL 3
THE INVOICE. "I once wrote a letter as follows"
                                   SCHOL 3
"Love comes quietly"   SPOA 105
THE NAME. "Be natural"   NACTE 14,
                                   SCHOL 3
NAUGHTY BOY. "When he brings home a whale"
                                   SCHOL 3
LA NOCHE.   NET 6
OH NO. "If you wander far enough" SCHOL 3
A PLACE. "The wetness of that street, the light"
                                   NET 6
A REASON. "Each gesture"   SCHOL 3
THE RESCUE. "The man sits in a timelessness"
                                   NACTE 14
SOME PLACE. "I resolved it, I"   NET 6
SONG. "What do you want, love"   SPOA 105
A TALLY. "A tally of forces, consequent"
                                   SCHOL 3
THE WIFE. "I know two women"   SCHOL 3
WORDS. "You are always"   SCHOL 3
Poetry*   CASSC 9, JNP 78

Cremer, Victoriano. in Spanish.
MUJER REDONDA. "Hasta los niños la miraban
cuando"   AGUIL 10, TROPIC 1

Cremona, Antonio. in Italian.
OCCHI APERTI.   CETRA 31

Crichton Smith, Iain. See **Smith, Iain Crichton.**

Crimi, Nino. in Italian.
IL RITORNO.   CETRA 31

Cros, Charles. 1842. in French.
MONOLOGUE DE L' AMOUR MATERNAL.
                                   CAED 204

Crouch, Stanley. in English.
A DEATH REQUEST.   BLACKF 1
PIMP'S LAST MACK.   BLACKF 1

Cruz, Juan de la. See **Juan de la Cruz.**
Cruz, Juana Inés de la. See **Juana Inés de la Cruz.**

Cuadra, Pablo Antonio. 1912. in Spanish.
EL MENDIGO. "Su mano era la última embajada"
                                   SMC 6

Cuestas, Katherine L. in English.
POEM. "One day a long time ago"   ARGO 17

Cullen, Countee. 1903. in English.
AND LEO LION'S LINES. "Please bear in mind my
royal descent"   CAED 176
AND THIS FROM BRUIN BEAR. "As I must have
honey"   CAED 176

THE BLACK CHRIST. "Glory and my country's
shame"   CAED 156
BROWN BOY AND GIRL UNDER THE MISTLETOE. "As
surely as I hold your hand in mine"
                                   FOLKW 6
CHRISTOPHER CAT.   CAED 176
EPITAPH FOR A POET. "I have wrapped my
dreams in a silken cloth"   CAED 156,
                       FOLKW 6, FOLKW 41, VAN 3
FIRST CAME L. E. PHANT'S LETTER. "Dear Noah:
Please save me a spot"   CAED 176
FOR A LADY I KNOW. "She even thinks that up in
heaven"   FOLKW 6, FOLKW 41
FOR MY GRANDMOTHER. "This lovely flower fell
so seed"   FOLKW 6
FOR PAUL LAURENCE DUNBAR. "Born of the sor-
rowful of heart"   CAED 156
FROM THE DARK TOWER. "We shall not always
plant while others reap"   FOLKW 41
THE HA-HA-HA. "Oh, merry, merry, merry, mer-
ry"   CAED 176
HERITAGE. "What is Africa to me" CAED 156,
                    FOLKW 1, UARIZ 1, SPOA 97
THE HOODINKUS-WITH-THE-DOUBLE-HEAD, OR JUST
HOODINKUS. "How often have you heard it
said"   CAED 176
INCIDENT. "Once riding in old Baltimore"
                       ARGO 17, CAED 156
KARENGE YA MARENGE. "Wherein are words sub-
lime or noble"   CAED 156
NEXT FROM THE BEES. "Dear Noah: A rumor"
                                   CAED 176
PAGAN PRAYER. "Not for myself I make this
prayer"   CAED 156
PROLOGUE. "You've heard, no doubt, of the
Dinosaur"   CAED 176
RED. "She went to buy a brand new hat"
                                   FOLKW 6
SATURDAY'S CHILD. "Some are teethed on a sil-
ver spoon"   CAED 156, FOLKW 41
SCOTTSBORO, TOO, IS WORTH ITS SONG. "I said/now
will the poets sing"   CAED 156
SIMON THE CYRENIAN SPEAKS. "He never spoke a
word to me"   CAED 156
THE-SNAKE-THAT-WALKED-UPON-HIS-TAIL. "How
envied, how admired a male"   CAED 176
THE SQUILILILIGEE. "He was the gentlest crea-
ture made"   CAED 176
TABLEAU. "Locked arm in arm they cross the
way"   CAED 156
THEN CAME ATOM'S ANSWER. "Dear Noah: to lend
a flavor"   CAED 176
TO CERTAIN CRITICS. "Then call me traitor if you
must"   CAED 156
TO JOHN KEATS, POET AT SPRINGTIME. "I cannot
hold my peace, John Keats"   UA 2
THE UNKNOWN COLOR. "I've often heard my
mother say"   FOLKW 6
THE WAKEUPWORLD. "This was the song of the
Wakeupworld"   CAED 176
YET DO I MARVEL. "I doubt not God is good, well
meaning, kind"   CAED 156, FOLKW 41
                                   UA 2
YOUTH SINGS A SONG OF ROSEBUDS. "Since men
grow diffident at last"   FOLKW 41
Poetry*   EAV 2, PRENT 1

---

* Recording not available for analysis

Cultrera, Giuseppe. in Italian.
   FORSE L'ULTIMA VOLTA.   CETRA 31
Cummings, E. E. 1894. in English.
   "all ignorance toboggans into know"
                      CAED 199
   "All in green went my love riding"   VAN 3
   &: SEVEN POEMS, III. "spring is like a perhaps
     hand"   CAED 198, COLUMB 8
   "anyone lived in a pretty how town"
                CAED 198, HOUGHT 5
   "as freedom is a breakfastfood"   CAED 198
   "because you take life in your stride (instead)"
                CAED 199, SPOA 94
   "both eaching come ghostlike"   CAED 199
   "but also dying"   CAED 199
   CHANSONS INNOCENTES. "in Just-/spring"
                CAED 198, SCHOL 7
   ————. "Little tree/little silent"   CAED 198
   "crazy jay blue)"   CAED 199, SPOA 94
   "darling! because my blood can sing"
                      CAED 199
   "dominic has/a doll"   CAED 199, SPOA 94
   "dying is fine but death"   CAED 18
   "except in your/honour"   CAED 199,
                        LIBC 40
   FOUR, VII. "since feeling is first"   CAED 198
   "the great advantage of being alive"
                      CAED 199
   LA GUERRE. "O sweet spontaneous"
                      CAED 198
   ————. "the bigness of cannon"   UARIZ 1
   "handsome and clever and he went cruising"
                      CAED 199
   HATE BLOWS A BUBBLE OF DESPAIR INTO.
                      CAED 18
   HELLO IS WHAT A MIRROR SAYS.   CAED 18
   "how generous is that himself the sun"
                      CAED 199
   "i am a little church (no great cathedral)"
                      CAED 199
   "i carry your heart with me (i carry it in"
                      CAED 199
   "i love you much (most beautiful darling"
                      CAED 199
   I SAY NO WORLD.   CAED 18
   I THANK YOU GOD FOR MOST THIS AMAZING.
              CAED 18, CAED 112
   "if everything happens that can't be done"
                      CAED 199
   "if i/or anybody don't"   CAED 198
   "in time of daffodils (who know"   CAED 199
   "in time's a noble mercy of proportion"
                      CAED 199
   "it was a goodly co"   CAED 199
   "jake hates/all the girls (the"   CAED 199
   "joyful your complete fearless and pure love"
                      CAED 199
   "kumrads die because they're told"
                      CAED 198
   "-laughing to find"   CAED 199
   "let's, from some loud unworld's most rightful
     wrong"   CAED 199
   LIFE IS MORE TRUE THAN REASON WILL DECEIVE.
                      CAED 18
   "the little horse is newly"   CAED 199
   "luminous tendril of celestial wish"
                      CAED 199

   "maggie and milly and molly and may"
         CAED 199, HOUGHT 4, SPOA 94
   "may my heart always be open to little"
                      CAED 198
   "The moon looked into my window" RCA 1
   "my father moved through dooms of love"
         CAED 198, LIBC 11, LIBC 33
   "neither awake"   CAED 199
   "no time ago"   CAED 199
   "nobody loses all the time"   CAED 198
   "noone and a star stand, am to am"
                      CAED 199
   NOTHING FALSE AND POSSIBLE IS LOVE.
                      CAED 18
   "now air is air and thing is thing: no bliss"
                CAED 199, SPOA 94
   "now all the fingers of this tree (darling) have
     hands"   CAED 199
   "now (more near ourselves than we)"
                      CAED 199
   "o by the by"   CAED 18, CAED 110
   "o the sun comes up, up, up"   RCA 1
   "(of Ever-Ever Land i speak"   CAED 198
   "(once like a spark)"   CAED 199
   ONE, XXVII: MEMORABILIA. "stop look &/listen
     Venezia"   CAED 198
   ————, XXV III. "a man who had fallen among
     thieves"   CAED 198
   ONE'S NOT HALF TWO. IT'S TWO ARE HALVES OF ONE.
                      CAED 18
   "open his head, baby"   CAED 199
   "out of the lie of no"   CAED 199
   "over us if (as what was dusk becomes"
                      CAED 199
   "pity this busy monster, manunkind"
              CAED 199, COLUMB 8
   PLATO TOLD HIM.   LIBC 11, LIBC 33
   POEM, OR BEAUTY HURTS MR. VINAL. "take it from
     me kiddo"   UARIZ 1
   "a politician is an arse upon"   CAED 199
   PORTRAITS, VIII. "Buffalo Bill's/defunct/"
                      CAED 198
   POST IMPRESSIONS, XII. "suppose/life is an old
     man"   CAED 198
   "proud of his scientific attitude"   CAED 198
   "purer than purest pure"   CAED 199
   "rain or hail/ sam done"   CAED 199,
              COLUMB 8, LIBC 40
   "a salesman is an it that stinks Excuse"
                      CAED 199
   "she being Brand"   CAED 198
   "so many selves (so many fiends and gods"
                      CAED 199
   "So shy shy shy (and with a"   CAED 199,
                      SPOA 94
   "stand with your lover on the ending earth"
                      CAED 199
   "sweet spring is your time"   CAED 18,
                CAED 183, RCA 1
   "swim so now million many worlds in each"
                      CAED 199
   THANKSGIVING (1956). "a monstering horror swal-
     lows"   CAED 199
   "that melancholy"   CAED 199
   "this is a rubbish of human rind" CAED 199
   "this (let's remember) day died again and"
                      CAED 199

* Recording not available for analysis

Cummings, E. E (continued)

"this little bride & groom"   COLUMB 8
"this mind made war"   CAED 198
TRUE LOVERS IN EACH HAPPENING OF THEIR
    HEARTS.   CAED 18
TWO, X. "my sweet old etcetera"   CAED 198
————, III. "next to of course god america i"
          CAED 198
"unlove's the heaveless hall and homeless
    home"   CAED 199
W(VIVA), XXX. "i sing of Olaf glad and big"
          CAED 198
————, XLII. "if there are any heavens my
    mother will (all by herself) have"
          CAED 198
————, LVII. "somewhere i have never trav-
    elled, gladly beyond"   CAED 198
"what a proud dreamhorse pulling (smooth-
    loomingly)"   CAED 198
"what freedom's not some under's mere
    above"   CAED 198
"what Got him was nothing"   CAED 199,
          SPOA 94
"what if a much of a which of a wind"
          CAED 18, CAED 183, HOUGHT 5
"whatever's merely wilful"   CAED 199
"when faces called flowers float out of the
    ground"   CAED 18, RCA 1
WHEN GOD DECIDED TO INVENT.   CAED 18
"when serpents bargain for the right to
    squirm"   CAED 18, CAED 199
who (is? are) who. "or who and who)"
          CAED 199
"who sharpens every dull"   CAED 199
WHO WERE SO DARK OF HEART THEY MIGHT NOT
    SPEAK.   CAED 18
"whose are these (wraith a clinging with a
    wraith)"   CAED 199
"why must itself up every of a park"
          CAED 18
YES IS A PLEASANT COUNTRY.   CAED 18
ygUDuh.   CAED 199
"you no / tice"   CAED 199
"you shall above all things be glad and young"
          UARIZ 1
Poetry*   LIST 15, PRENT 3
Cuney, Waring. 1906. in English.
CHARLES PARKER. "Listen! This here's what
    Charlie did to the blues"   ARGO 17
MY LORD, WHAT A MORNING. "Oh, my Lord"
          ARGO 17
NO IMAGES. "She does not know her beauty"
          FOLKW 6, FOLKW 41
TROUBLED JESUS. "Ma Jesus/was a troubled
    man"   FOLKW 6
Poetry*   EAV 2
Cunningham, Allan. 1784. in English.
A WET SHEET AND A FLOWING SEA.   EAV 8
Cunningham, James Vincent. 1911. in English.
AT THE TRACK. "I had gone broke"   SPOA 99
AUGUST HAIL. "In late summer the wild geese"
          SPOA 99
CAREER. "Career was feminine, resourceful,
    clever"   SPOA 99
EPIGRAM. "And what is love? Misunderstanding,
    pain"   LIBC 1

EPIGRAM. "Friend, on this scaffold Thomas Mor‹
    lies dead"   LIBC
EPIGRAM. "I write you in my need"   LIBC
EPIGRAM. "Lady, of anonymous flesh and face
          LIBC
EPIGRAM. "Lip was a man who used his head'
          LIBC
EPIGRAMS: A JOURNAL, XI. "When shall I be with
    out regret"   LIBC
EPITAPH. "Here lies my wife"   SPOA 9❬
HYCIATHE - THE QUALITY OF BEING THIS. "Evil ❬
    any"   SPOA 9❬
"In the thirtieth year of life"   SPOA 9❬
MEDITATION ON A MEMOIR. "Who knows h❬
    will?"   SPOA 9❬
MIRAMAR BEACH. "The night is still"   SPOA 9❬
SOFT. "Soft found a way to damn me"
          SPOA 9❬
TO MY WIFE. "And does the heart grow old? Yo❬
    know"   LIBC
TO THE READER. "Time will assuage"   LIBC
THE TOURIST. "On either side of the white line'
          SPOA 9❬
THE TRUE RELIGION. "The New Religion is th❬
    True"   LIBC
Cuomo, George. 1929. in English.
THE MAN OF MY DREAMS. "The wild man that la❬
    night"   FOLKW 2
Curnow, Allen. in English.
Poetry*   KIWI
Curran, John P. in English.
LET US BE MERRY BEFORE WE GO. "If sadly think
    ing"   SPOA ❬
Curtwright, Wesley. in English.
HEART OF THE WOODS.   FOLKW ❬
Curzio, Guglielmo lo. See **Lo Curzio, Guglielm❬**

Dahlberg, Edward. in English.
Poetry*   JNP 7❬
Daly, Thomas Augustine. 1871. in English.
LEETLA GIORGIO WASHEENTON. "You know w'a
    for ees school keep out"   DECCA 1❬
          LIST 2
MIA CARLOTTA. "Giuseppe, da barber, ees grea
    ta for mash"   THEAL
Damas, Léon G. 1912. in French.
A LA MEMOIRE DE GEORGE MISAINE. "Accoudés a❬
    désir de la avec elle insatisfait" FOLKW 7❬
"Against our love"
          French and English WATSHD 1
COCU ET CONTENT. "Ma femme m'avait bie❬
    dit"   French and English WATSHD 1
"Elle s'en vint"   FOLKW 7❬
          French and English WATSHD 1
EN FILE INDIENNE. "Et les abots"
          French and English WATSHD 1
ET VOICI. "Et voici que/pour toi" FOLKW 7❬
"Foi de marron"   FOLKW 7❬
HOQUET.   French and English WATSHD 1
IL EST DES NUITS. "Il est des nuits sans nom"
          FOLKW 7❬
"Il ne pouvait venir"   FOLKW 7❬
"Il n'est pas le midi qui tienne"   FOLKW 7❬
"Ils sont venus ce soir"
          French and English WATSHD 1
"Je ne sais en vérité"   FOLKW 7❬
"Malgré les sarcasmes des uns"   FOLKW 7❬

* Recording not available for analysis

POUR SUR. French and English WATSHD 11
SAVOIR-VIVRE. On ne bâille pas chez moi"
FOLKW 78
SCHWARZE PUPPEN. German DEUTGR 2
SHINE "Avec d'autres/ des alentours"
FOLKW 78
SI SOUVENT. "Si souvent mon sentiment de race
m'effraie" FOLKW 78
SOLDE. "J'ai l'impression d'etre ridicule"
French and English WATSHD 11
"Toute a ce besoin d'évasion" FOLKW 78
"Tu étais au bar" FOLKW 78
"Tu m'as dit" FOLKW 78
LE VENT. "Sur l'océan/ nuit noire"
FOLKW 78
"Vous dont les ricanement" FOLKW 78
Dana, Richard Henry. 1787. in English.
IMMORTALITY. EAV 15
Daniel, Arnaud. 12th c. in Provencal.
LO FERM VOLER. "Lo ferm voler qu'el cor m'in-
tra" FOLKW 10
Daniel, Samuel. 1562. in English.
"Care-charmer sleep, son of the sable night"
ARGO 32, SPOA 83
TO DELIA, IX. "If this be love, to draw a weary
breath" ARGO 32
_____, XXIII. "Time, cruel time, come and sub-
due that brow" ARGO 32
ULYSSES AND THE SIREN. "Come, worthy Greek,
Ulysses, come" SPOA 50
"When men shall find thy flower, thy glory,
pass" ARGO 32
Danner, Margaret. 1915. in English.
AND THROUGH THE CARIBBEAN SEA. "We, like
shades" BROADV 11
BEAUTIFUL? YOU ARE THE MOST. "If to do is to be,
take this lovely cat here" BROADV 11
BELLE ISLE. "Are these millions of white velvety
petalled bells" BROADV 11
GOODBYE DAVID TAMUNDOEMI WEST. "When you
were here in wonderful Detroit"
BROADV 11
I'LL WALK THE TIGHTROPE. "I'll walk the
tightrope that's been stretched for me"
ARGO 17, BROADV 11
PASSIVE RESISTANCE. "And to this man who
turned the other cheek" BROADV 11
THE PATRIARCH. "I saw him bearded, framed in
a modern setting" BROADV 11
A SPARROW IS A BIRD. "Why would a robin think
that a sparrow" BROADV 11
THIS IS AN AFRICAN WORM. "This is an African
worm" BROADV 11
TO A NIGERIAN STUDENT OF METALLURGY. "Page
one and I enter a land" BROADV 11
D'Annunzio, Gabriele. 1863. in Italian.
I PASTORI. "Settembre, andiamo. È tempo di
migrare" SPOA 30
LA PIOGGIA NEL PINETO. "Taci. Su le soglie"
DOVER 3
Poetry* CETRA 28
Dante Alighieri. 1265. in Italian.
DIVINA COMMEDIA (complete). CETRA 3
_____. INFERNO. CANTO 1. "Nel mezzo del cam-
min di nostra vita" FOLKW 103;
English CAED 208, FOLKW 3

_____. CANTO 2. "Lo giorno se n'andava, e
l'aere bruno" FOLKW 103;
English CAED 208, FOLKW 3
_____. CANTO 3. "Per me si va nella città do-
lente" FOLKW 103, SCHOL 6;
English CAED 208, FOLKW 3
_____. CANTO 4. "Ruppemi l'alto sonno nella
testa" FOLKW 103; English CAED 208,
FOLKW 3
_____. CANTO 5. "Così discesi dal cerchio
primaio" FOLKW 97, FOLKW 103;
English CAED 208, FOLKW 3
_____, exc. "I' cominciai: Poeta, volentieri"
DOVER 3; English CAED 208
_____, exc. "Noi leggiavamo un giorno per
diletto" SPOA 30; English CAED 208
_____. CANTO 6. "Al tornar de la mente, che si
chiuse" FOLKW 103; English CAED 208,
FOLKW 3
_____. CANTO 7. "Papè Satàn, papè Satàn
aleppe" FOLKW 103; English FOLKW 3
_____. CANTO 8. "Io dico, seguitando, ch'assai
prima" FOLKW 103; English FOLKW 3
_____. CANTO 33. "La bocca sollevò dal fiero
pasto" FOLKW 97
_____, exc. "Breve pertugio dentro dalla
muda" SPOA 30
_____. PARADISO. CANTO 33. "Vergine Madre,
figlia del tuo Figlio" CETRA 3, FOLKW 97
RIME, 15. "Guido I'vorrei che tu e Lapo ed Io"
SPOA 30
RIME, exc. CETRA 20
SESTINA I. "Al poco giorno, ed al gran cerchio
d'ombra" English EAV 22
SONETO XVII. "Tanto gentile e tanto onesta
pare" DOVER 3, SPOA 30;
English LEARNC 2
LA VITA NUOVA, exc. CETRA 20
Poetry* AUDIL 1, CETRA 36
Danton, Georges Jacques. 1759. in French.
APPEL AUX ARMES. PATHE 1
D'Aquino, Rinaldo. See Rinaldo d'Aquino.
D'Arcy, Hugh Antoine. 1843. in English.
THE FACE UPON THE FLOOR. " 'Twas a balmy sum-
mer evening, and a goodly crowd was there"
CAED 100
Darío, Rubén. 1867. in Spanish.
A MARGARITA DEBAYLE. "Margarita, está linda la
mar" AGUIL 13, FOLKW 79
A ROOSEVELT. "Es la voz de la Biblia, o verso de
Walt Whitman" AGUIL 13, MIAMI 2
AL REY OSCAR. "Así, Sire, en el aire de la
Francia" HOLT 1
ANTONIO MACHADO. "Misterioso y silencioso"
AGUIL 13
CANCIÓN DE OTOÑO EN PRIMAVERA. "Juventud,
divino tesoro" AGUIL 4
CANTOS DE VIDA Y ESPERANZA. "Yo soy aquel que
ayer no más decía" AGUIL 13
LA CARTUJA. MIAMI 2
DE INVIERNO. "En invernales horas, mirad a
Carolina" AGUIL 13
EHEU. "Aquí, junto al mar latino" AGUIL 13
LO FATAL. "Dichoso el árbol, que es apenas sen-
sitivo" CAED 77, HOLT 1, MIAMI 2,
SPOA 39

* Recording not available for analysis

Darío, Rubén (continued)

LETANIAS DE NUESTRO SEÑOR DON QUIJOTE. "Rey de los hidalgos, señor de los tristes"
AGUIL 13

MARCHA TRIUNFAL. "Ya viene el cortejo"
SMC 1

MARGARITA. "Recuerdas que querías ser una Margarita?"   AGUIL 13

LOS MOTIVOS DEL LOBO. "El varón que tiene corazón de lis"   AGUIL 13, FIDIAS 1,
MIAMI 2, SMC 6

POESÍA CASTELLANA. "Dulce como la miel de los panales"   FIDIAS 3

SONATINA. "La princesa esta triste"   SMC 1

UN SONETO A CERVANTES. "Horas de pesadumbre y de tristeza"   HOLT 1

VERLAINE. "Padre y maestro mágico, liróforo celeste"   AGUIL 13

Darr, Ann. 1920. in English.

ADVICE I WISH SOMEONE HAD GIVEN ME. "Be strange if it is necessary, be quiet"
WATSHD 33

BROTHER. "Brother is such a solid word"
WATSHD 33

CLEARED FOR APPROACH, CLEARED FOR LANDING. "If you draw the vectors"   WATSHD 8

DEAR OEDIPUS. "And so deciding everything has been done"   WATSHD 33

DR. LEVINSON'S OFFICE DISAPPEARED SHE SAID. "Dr. Levinson's office disappeared, she said"
WATSHD 33

EAST OF OMAHA. "My gentle father led me by the hand"   WATSHD 33

GATHER MY WINGS. "There is a part of me that looks"   WATSHD 33

THE GIFT. "Daughter, this small stiletto which I found"   WATSHD 33

HANGAR NINE. "Place your name in a time capsule"   WATSHD 33

I REMEMBER. "I was alone over desert flying"
WATSHD 33

LOVE IS. "A flock of birds, soaring, twisting, turning"   WATSHD 33

THE MYTH OF A WOMAN'S FIST. "The myth about a woman's fist"   WATSHD 33

NO RIGHT. "What can I do to feel close to you?"
WATSHD 33

ONLY IN MADNESS. "Only in madness would we conceive"   WATSHD 33

OSMOSIS. "Osmosis is the process"
WATSHD 33

REPLY TO AN ACCUSATION. "I am not Medea"
WATSHD 33

ROBERT FROST DIED THIS MORNING. "Look this way"   WATSHD 33

ST. ANN'S GUT. "Once at St. Ann's gut"
WATSHD 33

SELF EXPRESSION.   WATSHD 33

SEND A BIOGRAPHICAL NOTE. "I have published poems"   WATSHD 33

THE SERENE GREEN WORM. "The serene green worm eating the green"   WATSHD 33

STYX. "Come on get in, he says, but"
WATSHD 33

33 1/3. "Your voice is coming trippingly"
WATSHD 33

THE WOODEN CARDINAL. "They tell me there are red birds"   WATSHD 33

Darragh, Martina. in English.
"And the babies screamed"   WATSHD 2

AT THE MED-SCHOOL PARTY. "It was a room full of would-be doctors"   WATSHD 2

"Grammar from out west"   WATSHD 2

A KISS FROM A BROTHER. "The lavender stars"
WATSHD 2

Dauthendey, Max. 1867. in German.
Poetry*   CHRIST 5

Davenant, Sir William. 1606. in English.
SONG. "O thou that sleep'st like pig in straw"
COLUMB 11

Davidson, Donald. 1893. in English.
CORYMBA. "Corymba has bound no snood"
SPOA 94

JOE CLISBY'S SONG. "What did my old song say?"
SPOA 94

ON A REPLICA OF THE PARTHENON. "Why do they come?"   SPOA 94

RANDALL, MY SON. "Randall, my son, before you came just now"   SPOA 94

A TOUCH OF SNOW. "Cold showers, drumming fit to wake"   SPOA 94

Davie, Donald. 1922. in English.
BOUGAINVILLE. "All the soft runs of it, the tin white gashes"   MARV 1

CREON'S MOUSE. "Creon, I think, could never kill a mouse"   STANFD 2

DEMI-EXILE HOWTH. "Daisy and dandelion speedwell"   STANFD 2

EZRA POUND IN PISA. "Excellence is sparse"
STANFD 2

FRONTENAC. "In what was wilderness as inviolate then"   MARV 1

HEART BEATS. "If music be the muses' paragon"
STANFD 2

IOWA. "The blanched tree livid behind"
STANFD 2

THE JESUITS IN NORTH AMERICA. "Cure and pastor, dead"   MARV 1

KILLALA. "Forlorn indeed Hope on these shores"   STANFD 2

LASALLE. "Lasalle who, for no sordid end pressing to"   MARV 1

A LETTER TO CURTIS BRADFORD. "Curtis, you've been American too long"   MARV 1

THE LIFE OF SERVICE. "Service, or Latin sorbus"
STANFD 2

MEETING OF CULTURES. "Iced with a vanilla"
STANFD 2

METALS. "Behind the hills, from the city of an Etruscan"   STANFD 2

MONTCALM. "In Candiac by Nimes in Languedoc"   MARV 1

THE MUSHROOM GATHERERS. "Strange walkers See their"   STANFD 2

THE NORTH SEA. "North Sea, Protestant Sea"
STANFD 2

OUT OF EAST ANGLIA. "Pacific: in Russian as"
STANFD 2

PONTIAC. "Pontiac fire Detroit"   MARV 1

REMEMBERING THE THIRTIES. "Hearing one saga we enact"   STANFD 2

RODEZ. "Northward I came, and knocked in the coated wall"   STANFD 2

---

* Recording not available for analysis

TIME PASSING, BELOVED. "Time passing, and the memories" STANFD 2

TO A BROTHER IN THE MYSTERY, CIRCA 1290. "The world of God has turned its two stone faces" FOLKW 59A, STANFD 2

TO CERTAIN ENGLISH POETS. "My dears, don't I know?" STANFD 2

THE WIND AT PENISTONE. "The wind meets me at Penistone" STANFD 2

A WINTER LANDSCAPE NEAR ELY. "It is not life being short" STANFD 2

WOODPIGEONS AT RAHENY. "One simple and effective rhyme" STANFD 2

ZIP. "I'd have the silence like a heavy chock" STANFD 2

Davies, John, of Herford. 1565. in English.

HOMELY MEATS. "If there were, oh! an Helles-pond of cream" ARGO 32

"It is as true as strange, else trial feigns" ARGO 32

Davies, Mary Carolyn. in English.

AFTER ALL AND AFTER ALL. "Dreaming of a Prince" CAED 169

"The day before April" CAED 164

Davies, William Henry. 1871. in English.

CHILD LOVERS. "Six summers old was she, and when she came" CAED 126

EARLY MORN. "When I did wake this morn from sleep" BRITAM 1

AN INTRODUCTION TO THOMAS HARDY. CAED 86

THE KINGFISHER. "It was the Rainbow gave thee birth" BRITAM 1, FOLKW 64

LEISURE. "What is this life if, full of care" FOLKW 64, HOUGHT 3

ONE POET VISITS ANOTHER. "His car was worth a thousand pounds and more" CAED 86

SHEEP. "When I was once in Baltimore" FOLKW 64

A WOMAN'S HISTORY. "When Mary Price was five years old" CAED 147

Dávila, José Antonio. 1899. in Spanish.

BIBLICA. "El tiempo había volado como las golondrinas" SMC 9

CARTA DE RECOMENDACIÓN. "Señor, en breve llegará a tu cielo una tímida y dulce viejecita" INSTPR 1, SMC 9

YERBA MORA. INSTPR 1

Dávila, Virgilio. 1869. in Spanish.

ELEGIA DE REYES. INSTPR 1

Dávila Semprit, José. See Semprit, José Davila.

Davis, Fannie Stearns. in English.

EVENING SONG. "Little child, good child, go to sleep" CAED 164

MOON FOLLY. "I will go up the mountain after the Moon" CAED 164

Davis, Gloria. in English.

TO EGYPT. EAV 16

Davis, Thomas. in English.

THE BATTLE EVE OF THE IRISH BRIGADE. SPOA 6

Davis, Thulami Nkabinde. in English.

MAGNOLIA. "My house is barren" WATSHD 12

"One who so hated the war" WATSHD 12

ROGUE AND JAR 4 27 77. "The iron man sat" WATSHD 12

ZOOM! THE COMMODORES. "I once drove to At-lantic City" WATSHD 12

Davison, Frances. in English.

SWEET, IF YOU LIKE AND LOVE ME STILL. COLUMB 10

Davison, Peter. 1928. in English.

ARTEMIS. "See how this girl, trim" SPOA 106

LUNCH AT THE COQ D'OR. "The place is called the Golden Cock" SPOA 106

NOT FORGOTTEN. A. WATCHING HER GO. "Drawn by her mumbled entreaties" SPOA 106

———. B. DREAM. "I stood alone at a funeral" SPOA 106

———. C. REALITY. "Have I no right" SPOA 106

———. D. SELF-DEFENSE. "I came to hold her hand" SPOA 106

———. E. AFTERMATH. "The world now has a grey look to it" SPOA 106

PLAUSIBLE MAN. "A plausible man keeps us from feeling uneasy" SPOA 106

Day Lewis, Cecil. 1904. in English.

AIRMEN BROADCAST ARGO 119

"Beauty's end is in sight" ARGO 144

BIRTHDAY POEM FOR THOMAS HARDY. "Is it birth-day weather for you, dear soul?" FOLKW 65, JUP 1

THE CHRISTMAS TREE. "Put out the lights now" ARGO 91, CARIL 16, ARGO 144

THE COMMITTEE. "So the committee met again, and again" CARIL 16

THE CONFLICT. "I sang as one" CARIL 16

DEPARTURE IN THE DARK. "Nothing so sharply re-minds a man he is mortal" ARGO 144

DERELICT. "The soil, flinty at best, grew sour" ARGO 144

THE ECSTATIC. ARGO 144

ELEGY FOR A WOMAN UNKNOWN. "At her charmed height of summer" ARGO 144

AN EPISODE. ARGO 144

A FAILURE. "The soil was deep and the field well-sited" CARIL 16, ARGO 144

FINAL INSTRUCTIONS. "For sacrifice, there are certain principles" ARGO 144

FLIGHT TO ITALY. "The winged bull trundles to the wired perimeter" ARGO 91

THE FOX. "Look, its a fox" ARGO 91, ARGO 144

FROM FEATHERS TO IRON, 5. "Beauty's end is in sight" CARIL 16

———, 19. "Do not expect again a Phoenix hour" CARIL 16

THE GATE. "In the foreground, clots of cream-white flowers" CARIL 16, FOLKW 1A

A HARD FROST. "A frost came in the night" FOLKW 65, JUP 1

HORNPIPE. "Now the peak of summer's past, the sky" CARIL 16

HOW THE FULL-THROATED DAFFODILS. ARGO 144

IN ME TWO WORLDS. "In me two worlds at war" CARIL 16

THE INNOCENT. "A forward child, a sullen boy" CARIL 16

JIG. "That winter love spoke and we raised no objection" CARIL 16

LEARNING TO TALK. "See this one, tiptoe on" ARGO 144

* Recording not available for analysis

Day Lewis, Cecil (continued)

A LETTER FROM ROME. "We have been here three days"   CARIL 16

LOVE AND PITY. "Love without pity is a child's hand reaching"   CARIL 16

THE MAGNETIC MOUNTAIN, 2. "But two there are, shadow us everywhere"   CARIL 16

———, 5. "Let us be off! Our steam"   CARIL 16

———, 6. "Nearing again the legendary isle"   CARIL 16

MAPLE AND SUMACH. "Maple and sumach down"   FOLKW 65, JUP 1

MOODS OF LOVE, exc. "Inert, blanched, naked, at the gale's last gasp"   CARIL 16

THE NEUROTIC. "The spring came round, and still he was not dead"   CARIL 16

O DREAMS, O DESTINATIONS, 3. "That was the fatal move"   CARIL 16

———, 9. "To travel like a bird"   CARIL 16

ON NOT SAYING EVERYTHING. "This tree outside my window here"   ARGO 144

PASSAGE FROM CHILDHOOD. "His earliest memory, the mood"   CARIL 16

PEGASUS. "It was there on the hillside, no tall travellers story"   ARGO 144

THE REBUKE. "Down in the lost and April days"   ARGO 144

REST FROM LOVING. "Rest from loving and be living"   CARIL 16

THE ROOM.   ARGO 144

SHEEPDOG TRIAL IN HYDE PARK. "A shepherd stands at one end of the arena" CARIL 16, FOLKW 65A, SPOA 67

STAND-TO.   ARGO 119

TRANSITIONAL POEM, 5. "My love is a tower"   CARIL 16, ARGO 144

———, 15. "Desire is a witch"   CARIL 16

———, 27. "With me, my lover makes"   CARIL 16, ARGO 144

VIEW FROM AN UPPER WINDOW. "From where I am sitting"   FOLKW 65A

WILL IT BE SO AGAIN.   ARGO 119

"You that love England, who have an ear for her music"   ARGO 144

Poetry*   JNP 31

De Frees, Madeline. 1919. in English.

ALADDIN LAMP. "With luck and the slow hand"   WATSHD 10

THE OLD WOMAN. "At parties I want to get even"   WATSHD 10

THE PATCHED EYE. "Looks into its crater"   WATSHD 10

PICKING YOUNG BERRIES ON MR. HARVEY'S LAND. "Five hours"   WATSHD 10

Poetry*   WATSHD 30

De la Mare, Walter. 1873. in English.

ALL THAT'S PAST. "Very old are the woods"   ARGO 77, BRITAM 1, CAED 35, FOLKW 64

ANOTHER SPRING. "What though the first pure snowdrop"   BRITAM 1

AT THE KEYHOLE. "Grill me some bones, said the cobbler"   CAED 147

AWAY. "There is no sorrow"   CAED 35

THE BARDS. "My aged friend, Miss Wilkinson"   CAED 10

BEFORE DAWN. "Dim-berried is the mistletoe"   ARGO 82, SPOA 41

THE DOORS.   CAED 109

ENGLAND. "No lovelier hills than thine have laid"   CAED 35

FARE WELL. "When I lie where shades of darkness"   CAED 35

FIVE EYES. "In Hans' old mill his three black cats"   FOLKW 67

HERE I SIT. "Here I sit and glad I am"   CAED 35

HIDE AND SEEK. "Hide and seek, says the wind"   CAED 110

IN A LIBRARY. "Would—would that there were"   CAED 35

THE LISTENERS. "Is there anybody there?"   CMS 12, LIST 4, SINGER 6, THEAL 3

A LITTLE ABOUT WITCHES.   CAED 35

THE LITTLE GREEN ORCHARD. "Some one is always sitting there"   CAED 109

MARTHA. "Once . . . once upon a time"   BOWMAR 1, FOLKW 62

MUSIC. "When music sounds, gone is the earth I know"   CAED 35

OFF THE GROUND. "Three jolly farmers"   BRITAM 1, FOLKW 67

OLD SHELLOVER. "Come! said Old Shellover"   FOLKW 60

THE OWL. "The door-bell jangled in evening's peace"   FOLKW 64

PEACE. "A heart to be at peace with"   CAED 35

THE PRINCESS.   CAED 35

QUACK! "The Duck is whiter than whey is"   CAED 110

THE RAILWAY JUNCTION. "From here through tunnelled gloom the track"   BRITAM 1, CAED 35, FOLKW 64

SAM. "When Sam goes back in memory"   BRITAM 1, FOLKW 68

THE SCRIBE. "What lovely things thy hand hath made"   CAED 35

SILVER. "Slowly, silently, now the moon"   FOLKW 64, HARB 5, HARC 3, HOUGHT 3

THE SNOWFLAKE. "Before I melt/come look at me"   CAED 110

SOME ONE. "Someone came knocking at my wee, small door"   CAED 109, CAED 147, HARB 3

SONG OF ENCHANTMENT. "A song of enchantment I sang me there"   BRITAM 1

SONG OF THE MAD PRINCE. "Who said, 'Peacock Pie'?"   FOLKW 64

TARTARY. "If I were Lord of Tartary"   CAED 169

TIRED TIM. "Poor tired Tim! It's sad for him"   HARC 4

TO A CANDLE. "Burn stilly, thou; and come with me"   CAED 35

THE VEIL. "I think and think; yet still I fail"   CAED 35

De Lisle, Charles Marie René, Leconte. See **Leconte de Lisle, Charles Marie René.**

* Recording not available for analysis

De Loach, Allen. 1939. in English.
I AM A MULTITUDE. "In this life of unholy wars"
BROADR 2
De Regniers, Beatrice Schenk. in English.
"Keep a poem in your pocket"   HARB 3
Dehmel, Richard. 1863. in German.
DER ARBEITSMANN. "Wir habe ein Bett, wir
haben ein Kind"   DOVER 1
Poetry*   CHRIST 4
Dehn, Paul. 1912. in English.
SWEET WAR MAN.   ARGO 119
Dei-Anang, Michael. 1909. in English.
MY AFRICA.   CAED 136
Dekker, Thomas. 1570. in English.
CRADLE SONG. "Golden slumbers kisse your
eyes"   CAED 109, SPOA 35
PATIENT GRISSELL: THE BASKETMAKER'S SONG. "Art
thou poore, yet hast thou golden slumbers"
CAED 20
Delegall, Walter. in English.
ELEGY FOR A LADY. "Bare and bow your Chris-
tian heads"   ARGO 17
Della Casa, Giovanni. See **Casa, Giovanni della.**
Dempster, Roland Tombekai. in English.
AFRICA'S PLEA.   CAED 136
Den Boer, James. 1937. in English.
THE CHILD IS FRIGHTENED BY BOOKS. "My books
are dreams"   WATSHD 2
THE LAST BOOK. "The last book sighed and lay
down"   WATSHD 2
THE WHISKEY BOOK. "The whiskey book is
round"   WATSHD 2
Denby, Edwin. in English.
FIRST WARM DAYS.   LIBC 40
Poetry*   LIST 15
Derwood, Gene. 1909. in English.
AFTER READING ST. JOHN THE DIVINE. "Moon's
glow by sevenfold multiplied, turned red"
COLPIX 1, SERIF 1, SPOA 15
BIRD, BIRD. "Age after age our bird through in-
cense flies"   SERIF 1, SPOA 15
CAMEL. "Wild white camel, camel wild, what
behind"   SPOA 15
ELEGY ON GORDON BARBER, LAMENTABLY
DROWNED IN HIS EIGHTEENTH YEAR. "When in
the mirror of a permanent tear" LIBC 38,
SERIF 1, SPOA 15
IN COMMON. "Here am I, this carrot eating"
SPOA 15
THE INNOCENT. "Beautiful always the littoral
line"   SERIF 1, SPOA 15
THE LAST POEM "Let men keep from me"
SPOA 15
MADRIGAL.   SPOA 15
N. B. SYMMETRIANS. "We the symmetrians seek
justice here"   COLPIX 1, SERIF 1,
SPOA 15
THE POOL. "Derwood perceives thee in still un-
worded mood"   SPOA 15
PORISM. "The convoluted consonance of all"
SPOA 15
RE-SINGING LOVE, exc. 8. "Let be my cinerary
monument"   SPOA 15
_____ 9. "What artist's steady hand"
SPOA 15
RIDES. "So we ride, and ride through milked
heaven"   SPOA 15

SHELTER. "While people for what can satisfy
their wants"   SPOA 15
SPRING AIR. "In blows the loitering air of
spring"   SPOA 15
STAR. "Star, star shining bright"   SPOA 15
TO GEORGE BARKER. "O, who will speak from a
womb or cloud; and cloud"   SPOA 15
WAR'S CLOWN: IN THE PROSCENIUM. "The night,
too long illumined, comes a stranger"
COLPIX 1, SERIF 1, SPOA 15
WITH GOD CONVERSING. "Red paths that wander
through the gray, and cells"   LIBC 38,
SERIF 1, SPOA 15
Derzhavin, G.R. 1743. in Russian.
RUSSKIE DEVUSHKI. "Zrel li ty, pevets ty drevnii"
CMS 6
Desangiers. in French.
PARIS À 5 HEURES DU MATIN.   PATHE 1
LA TABLE.   PATHE 1
Desbordes-Valmore, Marceline. 1786. in French.
AN JENE, DIE WEINEN.   German DEUTGR 12
LA COURONNE EFFEUILLÉE. "J'irai, j'irai porter
mon couronne effeuillée"   HACH 10
LA FLEUR RENVOYÉE. "Adieu, douce pensée"
CAED 204
L'ISOLEMENT. "Quoi! ce n'est plus pour lui"
HACH 10
QU'EN AVEZ-VOUS FAIT. "Vous aviez mon coeur"
HACH 10
LES ROSES DE SAADI. "J'ai voulu ce matin te rap-
porter des roses"   ADES 54, HACH 10
SOUVENIR. "Quand il pâlit un soir, et que sa voix
tremblante"   ADES 54
UM DAS KIND EINZUSCHLÄFERN.
German DEUTGR 12
DIE VERZEIHUNG.   German DEUTGR 12
Deschamps, Eustache. 1340. in French.
AUTRE BALLADE, SUR LES DIFFERENTES MANIÈRES
DE RIRE. "Avoir ne puis trop grant merenco-
lie"   FOLKW 84
BALLADE CONTRE LA GUERRE. "J'ay les estas de ce
monde advisez"   FOLKW 84
BON AN, BON JOUR.   HACH 7
REMÈDIE CONTRE L'EMPEDIMIE. "Prent plain un
grant panier de vent"   FOLKW 84
SUR LA TRISTESSE DE CE TEMPS.   HACH 7
VIRELAI. "Sui-je, sui-je, sui-je belle?"
FOLKW 84
Desnos, Robert. 1900. in French.
L'ALLIGATOR. "Sur les bords du Mississippi"
HACH 4
L'ANÉMONE QUI RÉGNAIT SUR LA MER.   ADES 45
APPARITION. "Né de la boue, jailli au ciel"
FOLKW 13
AU TEMPS DES DONJONS.   ADES 45
LE CIMETIÈRE. "Ici sera ma tombe, et pas ail-
leurs"   ADES 45
COUPLETS DE LA RUE ST-MARTIN. "Je n'aime plus
la rue Saint-Martin"   ADES 55
LE DERNIER POÈME. "J'ai rêvé tellement fort de
toi"   ADES 45
L'ÉPITAPHE. "J'ai vécu dans ces temps et depuis
mille années"   ADES 45
LES GORGES FROIDES. "A la poste d'hier tu télé-
graphieras"   ADES 45
LE LÉOPARD. "Si tu vas dans le bois" HACH 4
LA MÉNAGERIE DE TRISTAN.   ADES 45

* Recording not available for analysis

Desnos, Robert (continued)

P'OASIS. "Nous sommes les pensées" ADES 45
LES QUATRES SANS-COU. "Ils étaient quatre qui n'avaient plus de tête" ADES 45
SOL DE COMPIÈGNE. ADES 45
LE VEILLEUR DU PONT-AU-CHANGE. "Je suis le veilleur" ADES 55
LA VILLE DE DON JUAN. "Clopin-clopant s'en allaient des aveugles" ADES 45

Desportes, Philippe. 1546. in French.
"Ceux qui liront ces vers qu'en pleurant j'ay chantez" ADES 54
PLAINTE, exc. "La terre, naguères glacée" HACH 8

Deutsch, Babette. 1895. in English.
CEZANNE. "Air. Energy. Light. A birth of joy" LIBC 1
DAMNATION. "Hell is not far below" LIBC 1
FIREWORKS. SCHOL 7
HOMAGE TO JOHN SKELTON. "Your name is Parrot" SPOA 95
HOMAGE TO PAUL KLEE. "Itiskit, Itasket" SPOA 95
LIZARD AT POMPEII. "Little finger of fiery green, it" LIBC 1
THE POEM. "The painter of Dante's awful ferry-ride" LIBC 1
SMALL COLORED BOY IN THE SUBWAY. "A slight-boned animal, young. What jungle fruit" LIBC 1
STRANGER THAN THE WORST. "London Bridge was built in a foggy century" SPOA 95

Devaul, Diane. in English.
A BIRTHDAY PRESENT. "Midday found me barely" WATSHD 7
END OR BEGINNING. "Monday calls me on Friday" WATSHD 7
LEGACY RECLAIMED. "There is a place" WATSHD 7
SPRING. "I want you" WATSHD 7
WORDPLAY. "No, you can't go" WATSHD 7

Deveaux, Alexis. 1948. in English.
EIGHTH AVENUE SONATA. "The solution will come" WATSHD 10
MASSISSI. WATSHD 10
THE ORACLE OF THE ZEBRA. "He was what his Mamma called" WATSHD 10
THE SISTERS. "And Tabu" WATSHD 10

Devereux, Robert. See Essex, Earl of.

Di Giacomo, Salvatore. 1860. in Italian.
A SAN FRANCISCO. "Vuie ccà!" CETRA 29
AMMORE ABBASATO. "Vuie comm' a ll uva 'e contratiempo site" CETRA 32
ARILLO, ANIMALUCCIO CANTATORE. "Arillo animaluccio cantatore" CETRA 32
"Avite maie liggiuto quacche cosa" CETRA 32
BONGIORNO, RO'! "Rosa, si chiove ancora" CETRA 32
BUONO NATALE! "Teresi, buono Natale!" CETRA 32
CATENA. "Catena, ca mme tiene ncatenato" CETRA 32
'A CHITARRA. "'E sta vecchia chitarra frangese" CETRA 32

COMME VA? "Comme va, comme va" CETRA 49
CUNTRORA. "Sto menato ncopp' 'o lietto" CETRA 32
D' 'A 'O QUARTO PIANO. "Giacchi te cucche ampresso" CETRA 32, CETRA 48
DINT' 'A VILLA. "Mare, liscio e turchino" CETRA 32
DINT' 'O CIARDINO. "A vi lla; vestuta rosa" CETRA 32
DINT' 'O SUONO. "Tu duorme, io te guardo" CETRA 32
DISPIETTO. "Doppo tre mmise ll' aggio vista aiere" CETRA 32
DONN' AMALIA 'A SPERANZELLA. "Donn' Amalia 'a speranzella" CETRA 32
DOPPO N' ANNO. "'O nniro 'e ll uocchie mieie bella, vuie site" CETRA 32
'E CECATE 'E CARAVAGGIO. "Dimme na cosa. T'allicuoroe tu" CETRA 29, CETRA 49
'E MATINA, PE TULETO. "Sola mo te ne vaie, povera Rosa" CETRA 32
'E RIMPETTO. "L' oto iuorno c' 'o sciato facette" CETRA 32
'E TTREZZE 'E CARULINA. "Oi petteno, che piet tene" CETRA 32
LASSAMO FA' DIO. "'A dummeneca 'e Pasca" CETRA 49
LETTERA AMIROSA. "Ve voglio fa' na lettera a ll'ingrese" CETRA 29, CETRA 32 CETRA 48
LETTERA MALINCONICA. "Luntana staie. Natale sta venenno" CETRA 32
'A MAMMA. "Vvie c'ancora tenite" CETRA 29
MARZO. "Marzo: mi poco chiove" CETRA 32 CETRA 48
NA TAVERNELLA. "Maggio. Na tavernella" CETRA 32
NCOPP' 'E CCHIANCHE. "Ncopp' 'e chianche, 'int 'a na chianca" CETRA 32
LL' ORTENZIE. "St' ortenzie ca tenite 'int 'a sta testa" CETRA 32, CETRA 49
PAROLE D'AMMORE SCUNTENTO. "Nu' scennere p 'a Posta! Nun te ferme lla nnanze! CETRA 32
PE LA VIA. "Nu cane sperzo pe mmiezo Tuleto" CETRA 32
PIANEFFORTE 'E NOTTE. "Nu pianefforte 'e notte" CETRA 32, CETRA 49
PRIMAVERA. "Guarda: e celeste 'a chella parte 'o cielo" CETRA 32
"Quanno stammo vicine" CETRA 32
'A SENZITIVA. "Carme, nun fa' 'a superba" CETRA 32
"Si dummeneca e bontiempo" CETRA 32
TUTTO SE SCORDA. "Tutto, tutto se scorda" CETRA 32
'O VI' 'LLOCO. CETRA 49
'O VICO D' 'E SUSPIRE. "'A cchiu meglia farenara" CETRA 32
VOCCA ADDUROSA. "Vocca addurosa e fresca" CETRA 32
VURRIA. "Vurria c' uno, int' o' suonno, me pug nesse" CETRA 32
"Vurria scrivere nu libbro" CETRA 32 CETRA 48

* Recording not available for analysis

Di Tarsia, Galeazzo. in Italian.
Poetry* CETRA 23
Dibdin, Thomas. 1771. in English.
THE SAILOR'S CONSOLATION. HBCF 1
Dicenta, Joaquin. in Spanish.
PASTORAL. "Es la hora agonizante" SMC 3
Poetry* SMC 16
Dicker, Harold. in English.
THE MOUTH IS A ZOO. "Peace the politician predicted" BROADR 3
THE PRIZE OF WAR IS ALWAYS. "That war is an emotional release" BROADR 3
Dickey, James. 1923. in English.
A BIRTH. "Inventing a story with grass" SPOA 81
THE CELEBRATION. "All wheels, a man breathed fire" CAED 140
CHERRYLOG ROAD. "Off Highway 106" SPOA 81
DIABETES. "One night I thirsted like a prince" CAED 140
ENCOUNTER IN THE CAGE COUNTRY. "What I was would not work for them all" CAED 140
FALLING. "The states when they black out and lie there" CAED 140
THE FIREBOMBING. "Homeowners unite" SPOA 81
"Fog envelops the animals" SPOA 81
FOR THE LAST WOLVERINE. "They will soon be down to one" CAED 140, EBEC 3
THE HEAVEN OF ANIMALS. "Here they are. The soft eyes open" SPOA 81, SPOA 104
THE HOSPITAL WINDOW. "I have just come down from my father" SPOA 81, SPOA 104
HUNTING CIVIL WAR RELICS AT NIMBLEWILL CREEK. "As he moves the mine detector a few inches over the ground" CAED 140
IN THE MOUNTAIN TENT. "I am hearing the shape of the rain" SPOA 81, SPOA 104
IN THE TREE HOUSE AT NIGHT. "And now the green household is dark" CAED 140
THE LIFEGUARD. "In a stable of boats I lie still" SPOA 81, SPOA 104
LOOKING FOR THE BUCKHEAD BOYS. EBEC 3
MERCY. "Ah, this night" CAED 140
MESSAGES, I. BUTTERFLIES. "Over and around, grass banked and packed short" CAED 140
———, II. GIVING A SON TO THE SEA. "Gentle blondness and the moray eel" CAED 140
ON THE HILL BELOW THE LIGHTHOUSE. "Now I can be sure" SPOA 81
THE PERFORMANCE. "The last time I saw Donald Armstrong" SPOA 81
THE SCARRED GIRL. "All glass may yet behold" CAED 140
THE SHEEP CHILD. "Farm boys wild to couple" SPOA 81
SUN. "O Lord, it was all night" SPOA 81
TO HIS CHILDREN IN DARKNESS. "You hear my step" SPOA 81
Dickey, William. 1928. in English.
Poetry* JNP 80
Dickinson, Emily. 1830. in English.
"After great pain, a formal feeling comes" ARGO 11, CAED 69, SPOA 26, SPOA 31
"Ample make this bed" UARIZ 1
"Answer July" CAED 110
"Arcturus is his other name" CAED 111
"As by the dead we love to sit" CAED 111
"As imperceptibly as grief" SPOA 26
"At least to pray is left, is left" SPOA 26
"Because I could not stop for death" CAED 69, EAV 14, HOUGHT 5, SPOA 26, THEAL 2, UARIZ 1
"Before I got my eye put out" CAED 69, SPOA 26
"Besides the autumn poets sing" CAED 69
"A bird came down the walk" CAED 69, CAED 112, COLUMB 11, EAV 15
"Bring me the sunset in a cup" EAV 26, SPOA 26
"The bustle in a house the morning after death" SPOA 26, SPOA 31
"A clock stopped" SPOA 26
"Doubt me! My dim companion" CMS 14
"Each life converges to some centre" SPOA 26
"Elysium is as far as to the very nearest room" EAV 14, SPOA 26, SPOA 31, UARIZ 1
"Further in summer than the birds" SPOA 26
"God made a little gentian" UARIZ 1
"The heart asks pleasure first" CAED 69, EAV 15
"Heart! We will forget him" SPOA 26
"Hope is the thing with feathers" CAED 69, CAED 185, CMS 12, EAV 14
"How happy is the little stone" CAED 111
"I asked no other thing, no other was denied" SPOA 26, SPOA 31
"I cannot live with you" ARGO 11, CAED 69, SPOA 26
"I cautious scanned my little life" CAED 69, CAED 190
"I died for beauty, but was scarce" CAED 69, CAED 185, SPOA 26, THEAL 3
"I dreaded that first robin so" EAV 14
"I dwell in possibility" CAED 69
"I felt a funeral in my brain" CAED 69
"I had no time to hate" EAV 15
"I have no life but this" CAED 190
"I heard a fly buzz when I died" ARGO 11, CAED 69
"I know a place where summer strives" ARGO 11
"I know some lonely houses off the road" CAED 111
"I like to see it lap the miles" CAED 69, HOUGHT 5, SPOA 26, SPOA 31
"I lost a world the other day" CAED 160
"I never lost as much but twice" CAED 69
"I never saw a moor, I never saw the sea" AUDIA 2, CAED 69, CMS 12, EAV 14, LIST 3, LIST 4, SINGER 2, SPOA 26, SPOA 31, UARIZ 1
"I reason, earth is short" ARGO 11, CAED 69, CAED 185
"I taste a liquor never brewed" CAED 69, SPOA 26, UARIZ 1
"I years had been from home" CAED 69
"If I can stop one heart from breaking" CAED 190
"If you were coming in the fall" CAED 69, HOUGHT 5

* Recording not available for analysis

Dickinson, Emily (continued)

"I'll tell you how the Sun rose"   CAED 69,
        CAED 112, CAED 185, HOUGHT 3,
                                    UARIZ 1
"I'm nobody! Who are you"   CAED 69,
        CAED 185, EAV 14, SPOA 26, SPOA 31,
                                    UARIZ 1
"It sifts from leaden sieves"   SPOA 26
"It struck me—every day"   CAED 111
"Just lost, when I was saved"   SPOA 26
"The lilac is an ancient shrub"   CAED 190
"A little madness in the Spring"   SPOA 26
"Love is anterior to life"   CAED 69
MORNING. "Will there really be a morning?"
                                    CMS 4
"The mountains grow unnoticed"   AUDIA 2,
                                    LIST 3
"The mushroom is the elf of plants"
                                    SPOA 26
"My life closed twice before its close"
        AUDIA 2, CAED 69, CAED 185, CMS 14,
                LIST 3, SINGER 5, SPOA 26
"My river runs to thee"   CAED 69
"A narrow fellow in the grass"   CAED 69,
        CAED 195, HOUGHT 4, LIST 3, SPOA 26
"Nature the gentlest mother is"   SPOA 26
"The nearest dream recedes unrealized"
                                    SPOA 26
"Of all the sounds despatched abroad"
        CAED 111, SPOA 26, SPOA 31
"Pain has an element of blank"   CAED 69
"Remorse is memory awake"   CAED 111
"The robin is a Gabriel"   SPOA 26
"The robin is the one"   CAED 190
"A route of evanescence with a revolving
        wheel"   SPOA 26, SPOA 31
"Safe in their alabaster chambers"   CAED 69,
                        CAED 185, SPOA 26
"The sky is low, the clouds are mean"
                        CAED 69, UARIZ 1
"Some keep the Sabbath going to Church"
                        CAED 190, SPOA 26
"The soul selects her own society"   AUDIA 2,
                CAED 69, CAED 185, CMS 12,
        HOUGHT 5, LIST 3, SINGER 5, UARIZ 1
"The spider holds a silver ball"   CAED 111
"Split the lark and you'll find the music"
                                    SPOA 26
"Success is counted sweetest"   SPOA 26
"Superiority to fate"   CAED 190, UARIZ 1
"Tell all the truth but tell it slant"
                                    CAED 111
"There came a wind like a bugle"   CAED 69
"There is no frigate like a book to take us lands
        away"   AUDIA 2, EAV 15, LIST 3,
                        SPOA 26, SPOA 31
"There is no silence in the earth"   CAED 190
"There's a certain slant of light"   ARGO 11,
                                    CAED 69
"These are the days when birds come back"
                                    SPOA 26
"This is my letter to the world"   CAED 69,
        CAED 190, HOUGHT 5, SPOA 26
"This quiet dust was gentlemen and ladies"
                                    SPOA 26
"A thought went up my mind today"   CMS 4

"Through the strait pass of suffering"
                                    SPOA 26
"Title divine is mine"   CAED 111
"To fight aloud is very brave"   CAED 69
"To make a prairie it takes a clover and one
        bee"   CAED 69, CAED 190
"A toad can die of light"   CAED 69
"Twas like a Maelstrom with a notch"
                                    ARGO 11
"We grow accustomed to the dark"
                                    ARGO 11
"What soft, cherubic creatures"   CAED 69
"Who robbed the woods"   CAED 160
"You cannot make remembrance grow"
                                    CAED 111
Poetry*   IDIOM 1, LIST 12, NACTE 7,
                        ARGO 116, PYR 1

Dickinson, Patric. 1914. in English.
LINCOLN CATHEDRAL. "Midnight, and twelve
        dark doves"   ARGO 97
SONG. "When you are young"   ARGO 97
THIS COLD UNIVERSE. "These stars and planets"
                                    ARGO 97

Diego, Eliseo. 1920. in Spanish.
UN SORBO DE CAFÉ. "Un sorbo de café a la ma-
        drugada"   SMC 13

Diego, Gerardo. 1896. in Spanish.
EL CIPRÉS DE SILOS. "Enhiesto surtidor de som-
        bra y sueño"   HOLT 1, SPOA 59
"Dicen que ya estoy maduro"   TROPIC 1
EMILIA. "La adelantada fuiste tú en la tierra"
                                    AGUIL 3
INSOMNIO. "Tú y tu desnudo sueño. No lo sabes"
                                    AGUIL 4
REVELACIÓN. "Era en Numancia, al tiempo que
        declina"   HOLT 1
VERONICAS GITANAS. "Lenta, olorosa, redonda"
                                    AGUIL 3

Diego, José de. 1868. in Spanish.
LAURA. "Laura mía: Ya sé que no lo eres"
                                    SMC 9
SUEÑOS Y VOLANTINES. "El Cerro de las Animas
        benditas"   INSTPR 1
Poetry*   INSTPR 2

Díez-Canedo, Enrique. 1879. in Spanish.
"Han venido los Húngaros, hermana"
                                    FIDIAS 1

Diogenes Laertius. 3rd century A.D. in Greek.
TAUROMANCY AT MEMPHIS.   English CARIL 3

Diop, David. 1927. in French.
A UNE DANSEUSE NOIRE. Négresse ma chaude ru-
        meur d'Afrique"   FOLKW 83
AUPRÈS DE TOI. "Auprès de toi j'ai retrouvé mon
        nom"   FOLKW 83
LISTEN COMRADES, exc. "To the keen clamor of
        the Negro"   English BROADV 4
RAMA KAM. "Me plaît ton regard de fauve"
                                    FOLKW 83
LE TEMPS DU MARTYRE. "Le blanc a tué mon
        père"   German DEUTGR 2

Diouara, Bouna Boukary. in French.
LE ROCHER EN FEUILLES. A ceux qui sont lavés de
        pluie"   FOLKW 83

Dlugos, Tim. in English.
AMERICAN BASEBALL. "It's for real, not for prac-
        tice"   WATSHD 8

---

* Recording not available for analysis

ANOTHER STANZA FOR MARTINA. "Half of the flags are at half mast"   WATSHD 8
AS IT IS. "The poems, leaving"   WATSHD 8
GREAT BOOKS OF THE 1950'S. "I was a communist for the FBI"   WATSHD 8
JOHN TONGUE. "Tongue in the city"
                                      WATSHD 8
SOUNDING BACK. "Always an animal"
                                      WATSHD 8

Dobell, Sydney. 1824. in English.
THE ORPHAN'S SONG. "I had a little bird"
                          LONDON 1, SPOA 35

Dobson, Henry Austin. 1840. in English.
IN AFTER DAYS. "In after days when grasses high"   EAV 22
A KISS. "Rose kissed me today"   EAV 22
URCEUS EXIT. "I intended an ode"   EAV 22

Dodgson, Charles Lutwidge. See Carroll, Lewis.

Dodson, Owen. 1914. in English.
BLACK MOTHER PRAYING. "My Great God, you been a tenderness to me through the thick and through the thin"   SPOA 82,
                      SPOA 101, WATSHD 42
THE CONFESSION STONE. "Oh my boy: Jesus"
                                      ARGO 17
THE DREAM AWAKE.   SPOA 119
JONATHAN'S SONG: A NEGRO SAW THE JEWISH PAG-
  EANT. "We will never die"   WATSHD 42
JUBILEE.   WATSHD 42
ONE DAY. "This is a joy of a day"   SPOA 101
THE REUNION. "I love the apple sweetness of the air"   SPOA 101

Dodson-Letourneau, Gayle. in English.
THE CALL. "I call you to collect"   WATSHD 5
CAMEL'S GARDEN. "Three boulders like camels' humps"   WATSHD 5
IT'S TIME. "This stringy lump"   WATSHD 5
PIECING TOGETHER "He drove to see"
                                      WATSHD 5

Domenico di Giovanni. See Burchiello.

Domett, Alfred. 1811. in English.
A CHRISTMAS HYMN. "It was the calm and silent night"   LION 1

Domínguez Alba, Bernardo. 1904. in Spanish.
GUITARRA DECAPITADA.   GMS 13
MI DOBLE MALO SE MUERE.   GMS 13

Donaldson, June. in English.
AUTOBIOGRAPHY. "Can you imagine me"
                                      WATSHD 8

Donne, John. 1573. in English.
AIRE AND ANGELS. "Twice or thrice had I loved thee"   ARGO 19
THE ANNIVERSARIE. "All Kings, and all their fa-
  vorites"   ARGO 2, ARGO 19, CAED 78,
            POLYGL 2, SPOA 12, SPOA 43
THE APPARITION. "When by thy scorne, O mur-
  dresse, I am dead"   ARGO 19, CAED 78,
            POLYGL 2, SPOA 12, SPOA 43
"At the round earth's imagin'd corners, blow"
      ARGO 2, ARGO 36, JNP 8, SPOA 43,
                                   ARGO 137
THE AUTUMNALL. "No Spring, nor Summer Beauty hath such grace"   SPOA 43
THE BAITE. "Come live with mee, and bee my love"   CAED 20, BRITAM 2

"Batter my heart, three-person'd God, for you"
      ARGO 2, ARGO 36, HARVOC 4, JNP 8,
                        LIST 1, SPOA 43
BREAK OF DAY.   LIST 1, LONDON 1
THE BROKEN HEART. "He is starke mad, who ever sayes"   SPOA 43
THE COMPARISON. "As the sweet sweat of roses in a still"   CAED 78
THE CANONIZATION. "For Godsake hold your tongue"   ARGO 2, ARGO 19, CAED 78,
                                       JNP 8
THE CURSE. "Who ever guesses, thinks, or dreams he knowes"   ARGO 19, CAED 78
"Death be not proud, though some have called thee"   ARGO 2, ARGO 36, BRITAM 2,
            CAED 20, CMS 12, IMP 1, LIST 1,
            SPOA 43, THEAL 2, ARGO 137
THE DREAME. "Deare Love, for nothing lesse than thee"   ARGO 19
ELEGIE. "Natures lay Ideot, I taught thee to love"   CAED 78
THE EXPIRATION. "So, so, breake off this last la-
  menting kisse"   COLUMB 10
THE EXTASIE. "Where, like a pillow on a bed"
                ARGO 2, ARGO 19, CAED 78
A FEAVER. "Oh doe not die, for I shall hate"
                                      CAED 78
THE FLEA. "Marke but this flea, and marke in this"   ARGO 19, CAED 78, LONGM 1
THE FUNERALL. "Who ever comes to shroud me, do not harme"   ARGO 2, ARGO 19,
                        CAED 78, SPOA 43
GOOD FRIDAY 1613. "Let mans soul be a spheare"
                        ARGO 2, ARGO 36
THE GOOD-MORROW. "I wonder by my troth, what thou, and I"   ARGO 2, ARGO 19,
            CAED 78, CAED 186, LION 2,
          HARVOC 4, JNP 8, ARGO 137
HIS PICTURE. "Here take my picture, though I bid farewell"   ARGO 19
HOLY SONNET 17. "Since she whom I lov'd hath payd her last debt"   LONGM 1
A HYMNE TO CHRIST. "In what torne ship soever I embarke"   ARGO 36, ARGO 137,
                                   HARVOC 4
HYMNE TO GOD MY GOD, IN MY SICKNESSE. "Since I am comming to that Holy roome"
      ARGO 36, POLYGL 2, SPOA 12, SPOA 43
A HYMNE TO GOD THE FATHER. "Wilt thou forgive that sinne where I begunne"   ARGO 2,
            ARGO 36, HARVOC 4, SPOA 43
"I am a little world made cunningly"
                                      ARGO 36
THE INDIFFERENT. "I can love both faire and browne"   ARGO 19
JEALOSIE. "Fond woman which would'st have thy husband die"   ARGO 19, CAED 78
THE LEGACIE. "When I dyed last, and, Deare, I dye"   CAED 78, SPOA 43
LOVES ALCHYMIE. "Some that have deeper digg'd loves myne"   ARGO 19, SPOA 43
LOVES DEITIE. "I long to talke with some old lovers ghost"   ARGO 19, SPOA 43
LOVES INFINITENESS. "If yet I have not all thy love"   ARGO 19
LOVES PROGRESS. "Whoever loves, if he do not propose"   SPOA 43

* Recording not available for analysis

Donne, John (continued)

A NOCTURNALL UPON S. LUCIES DAY. "Tis the yeares midnight, and it is the dayes"
    ARGO 19, CAED 78, SPOA 84

"O, might those sighes and teares returne againe"   ARGO 36

ON HIS MISTRIS. "By our first strange and fatall interview"   SPOA 43

PERFUME, exc. "Thy little brethren, which like Faery Sprights"   LONGM 1

THE RELIQUE. "When my grave is broke up againe" ARGO 19, CAED 78, HARVOC 4,
    SPOA 43

"Show me deare Christ, thy spouse so bright and deare"   ARGO 36

SONG.   EAV 6

SONG. "Goe, and catche a falling starre"
    ARGO 19, CAED 78, CAED 186, CMS 13,
    HARVOC 4, IMP 1, JNP 8, LIST 1,
    POLYGL 2, SPOA 12, SPOA 43,
    ARGO 137

SONG. "Sweetest love, I do not goe"
    CAED 78, COLUMB 11

"Spit in my face, you Jewes, and pierce my side"   ARGO 36, SPOA 84

THE SUNNE RISING. "Busie old foole, unruly Sunne"   ARGO 2, ARGO 19, CAED 78,
    LIST 1, POLYGL 2, SPOA 12, SPOA 43

"This is my play's last scene; here heavens appoint"   ARGO 36

"Thou hast made me, and shall thy worke decay?"   ARGO 2, ARGO 36, SPOA 84

TO HIS MISTRIS GOING TO BED. "Come, Madame, come, all rest my powers defie"
    ARGO 88A, ARGO 19, PROTHM 8,
    SPOA 43

THE TRIPLE FOOLE. "I am two fooles, I know"
    CAED 78

TWICKENHAM GARDENS. "Blasted with sighs, and surrounded with teares"   ARGO 2,
    ARGO 19

THE UNDERTAKING. "I have done one braver thing"   ARGO 19

A VALEDICTION: FORBIDDING MOURNING. "As virtuous men passe mildly away" ARGO 19,
    CAED 78

A VALEDICTION: OF WEAPING. "Let me powre forth"   ARGO 19

"What if this present were the worlds last night"   ARGO 36, SPOA 84

WOMANS CONSTANCY. "Now thou hast lov'd me one whole day"   ARGO 19

Poetry*   ARGO 111, EAV 11, PRENT 3,
    PROTHM 6

Donzella, La Compiuta. ca. 1250. in Italian.
"A la stagion che il mondo foglia e fiora"
    DOVER 3

Doolittle, Hilda. (H.D.) 1886. in English.
HELEN IN EGYPT. "Few were the words we said"
    SPOA 92

SHELTERED GARDEN. "I have had enough. I gasp for breath"   RCA 10

Dorn, Alfred. in English.
SNOWFLAKE.   FOLKW 25

Dorset, Earl of. See Sackville, Charles.

Dos Passos, John. 1896. in English.
Poetry*   JNP 96

Dotti, Bartolomeo. 1651. in Italian.
Poetry*   CETRA 24

Douglas, Keith. 1920. in English.
ARISTOCRATS.

HOW TO KILL. "Under the parabola of a ball"
    ARGO 119

Douglas, Sharon. in English.
INSTANT CHOCOLATE. "You know I almost forgot"   WATSHD 8

Douglas, William. 1672. in English.
ANNIE LAURIE.   EAV 7

Dowling, Allan. 1903. in English.
ACCEPTANCE OF AUTUMN. "No longer to hate the autumn, no longer"   GRYPH 2

AFTER 2000 YEARS. "How fiercely we must struggle to remain"   GRYPH 2

THE BACK COUNTRY. "Brazil is in the mind, enormous, dim"   GRYPH 2

THE BALLAD OF DESPAIR. "It were better the world were peopled"   GRYPH 2

THE DEAD THIEF. "When Jesus hung upon the cross"   GRYPH 2

A DEVIL'S PRAYER. "The devil in heaven made me wise"   GRYPH 2

THE DREAMER'S EPILOGUE. "Now that the curtain is about to fall"   GRYPH 2

EPIGRAM. "Beware in the beginning! having once left the shore"   GRYPH 2

THE FLAME. "Once in a vision"   GRYPH 2

FROM THE GRANDE CORNICHE. "Beyond the seasons of the sun"   GRYPH 2

GETHSEMANE. "In a garden called Gethsemane, in Palestine"   GRYPH 2

THE ISLAND OF BIRDS. "Long long ago there was an island set"   GRYPH 2

THE LAKE OF ANNECY. "To Lisa in a letter once I wrote"   GRYPH 2

THE LAST ADAM. "In the late and lovely evening of the world"   GRYPH 2

MEMORY OF WINTER MAGIC. "In winter, when the branches of the trees"   GRYPH 2

THE MIMOSA. "I walked out on a winter's day"
    GRYPH 2

THE MIRACLE. "When, in the dawn of love and my desire"   GRYPH 2

THE NEEDLE POINT OF NOW. "When this perishable body ceases"   GRYPH 2

NO ARK, NO ARARAT. "The sullen building up of pain"   GRYPH 2

REGRET. "If Art and Joy go hand in hand"
    GRYPH 2

A SAD JINGLE. "The lights are electric"
    GRYPH 2

A SENSE OF THE MOMENT. "When I remember what I must forget"   GRYPH 2

THE SHEPHERD BOY. "A shepherd boy comes down from the hill"   GRYPH 2

A SONG OF LONGING. "A man may long for love and long for art"   GRYPH 2

THE SONG OF THE TIRED MEN. "Beauty has drifted"   GRYPH 2

TO PRAISE DELIGHT. "In spite of all the solemnhearted fools"   GRYPH 2

TRUST. "God grant me that at last I reach my goal"   GRYPH 2

---

* Recording not available for analysis

LA VITA NUOVA. "I am in Dante's city, quite alone" GRYPH 2

THE WHITE STARS. "The white stars laboring above the world" GRYPH 2

Dowson, Ernest. 1867. in English.

EXTREME UNCTION. "Upon the eyes, the lips, the feet" LONGM 1

NON SUM QUALIS ERAM BONAE SUB REGNO CYNA-RAE. "Last night, ah yesternight, betwixt her lips and mine" ARGO 70A, ARGO 137, LONGM 1

VILLANELLE OF HIS LADY'S TREASURES. "I took her dainty eyes, as well" EAV 22

VITAE SUMMA BREVIS SPEM NOS VETAT INCOHARE LONGAM. "They are not long, the weeping and the laughter" LONGM 1

Dragonette, Ree. in English.

VALLEY OF SHADOWS, exc. "Moon Cat, my nettle dancer" BROADR 2

Drake, Joseph Rodman. 1795. in English.

THE AMERICAN FLAG. "When freedom from her mountain" DECCA 4, EAV 14

THE ELFIN SONG. EAV 14

Drake, Leah Bodine. in English.

PRECARIOUS GROUND. "On the volcanic hill" FOLKW 25

Drayton, Michael. 1563. in English.

AGINCOURT. "Fair stood the wind for France" IMP 1

"Clear had the day been from the dawn" SPOA 50

IDEA. XX. "An evil spirit, your beauty haunts me still" ARGO 32

LOVE'S FAREWELL. EAV 6

NYMPHIDIA, exc. ARGO 31

THE PARTING. "Since there's no help, come let us kiss and part" ARGO 32, POLYGL 2, RCA 4, SPOA 12, SPOA 50

"So well I love thee" SPOA 83

SONNET. "How many paltry, foolish, painted things" ARGO 32

TO THE VIRGINIAN VOYAGE. "You brave heroic minds" PROTHM 8

UPON A BANK WITH ROSES. COLUMB 10

Poetry* PROTHM 6

Dreyer, Lynn. in English.

DEAR CRAIG. "I'm not the junkie" WATSHD 14

DEAR DANNY. "I'm not sure about the paper" WATSHD 14

Drinkwater, John. 1882. in English.

THE CROWNING OF DREAMING JOHN. "Seven days he travelled" FOLKW 62

WASHING. "What is all this washing about" HARB 2

Droste-Hülshoff, Annette von. 1797. in German.

DIE ÄCHZENDE KREATUR. "An einem Tag, wo feucht der Wind" CHRIST 9

AM DRITTEN SONNTAGE NACH OSTERN. "Ich seh dich nicht" CHRIST 9

AM GRÜNDONNERSTAGE. "O Wundernacht, ich grüsse" CHRIST 18

AN MEINE MUTTER. "So gern hätt ich ein schönes Lied gemacht" ATHENA 5

BRENNENDE LIEBE. "Und willst du wissen, warum" CHRIST 9

DURCHWACHTE NACHT. "Wie sank die Sonne glüh und schwer" CHRIST 9

DAS HIRTENFEUER. "Dunkel, dunkel im Moor" CHRIST 9

MONDEAUFGANG. "An des Balkones Gitter lehnte ich" CHRIST 11

DAS ÖDE HAUS. "Tief ab im Tobel liegt ein Haus" CHRIST 9

DIE SCHENKE AM SEE. "Ist's nicht ein heitrer Ort" CHRIST 9

DIE VERGELTUNG. "Der Kapitän steht an der Spiere" ATHENA 1

WASSER. "Alles still ringsum" CHRIST 9

DER WEIHER. "Er liegt so still im Morgenlicht" DOVER 1

Drummond, William. in English.

JOHNNY COURTEAU. THEAL 1

Drummond de Andrade, Carlos. 1902. in Portuguese.

CASTIDADE. "O perdido caminho, a perdida estrêla" FOLKW 71

O ELEFANTE. "Fabrico um elefante" FOLKW 71

LEMBRANCA DO MUNDO ANTIGO. "Clara passeava no jardim com as crianças" FOLKW 71

Drummond of Hawthornden, William. 1585. in English.

MADRIGAL: THIS LIFE. "This life, which seems so fair" ARGO 35

"Sleepe, silence child" ARGO 32

Dryden, John. 1631. in English.

ABSALOM AND ACHITOPHEL, exc. EAV 6

———. "In pious times, ere priestcraft did begin" CAED 73, SPOA 46

———. "Of these the false Achitophel was first" CAED 21, LONGM 1

———. "Such were the tools; but a while hydra more" LONGM 1

ALEXANDER'S FEAST. "Twas at the royal feast, for Persia won" CAED 73, EAV 6, SPOA 46

ANNUS MIRABILIS, exc. "The diligence of trades and noiseful gain" LONGM 1

THE CONQUEST OF GRANADA, exc. "Beneath a myrtle shade" CAED 73

———. SONG. "How unhappy a lover am I" SPOA 46

AN EVENING'S LOVE. "When first our poet set himself to write" CAED 73, SPOA 46

THE HIND AND THE PANTHER, exc. "A milk white hind" SPOA 46

MACFLECKNOE. "All human things are subject to decay" IMP 1, LONGM 1

THE MAN OF MODE: EPILOGUE. "Most modern wits such monstrous fools have shown" CAED 73

SONG. "I feed a flame within" CAED 73

SONG. "Whilst Alexis lay press'd" CAED 73

A SONG FOR SAINT CECILIA'S DAY. "From harmony, from heavenly harmony" CAED 186, LIST 2, SPOA 46

TO THE MEMORY OF MR. OLDHAM. "Farewell, too little, and too lately known" CAED 73, LONGM 1

TYRANNIC LOVE: EPILOGUE. "Hold! are you mad?" CAED 21

"What flocks of critics hover here today" SPOA 46

* Recording not available for analysis

Dryden, John (continued)

Poetry* ARGO 46

Du Bellay, Joachim. 1525. in French.

À VENUS. "Ayant après long desir" DOVER 4
prits, et vous Umbres poudreuses"
PERIOD 2

COMPLAINTE DU DÉSESPÉRE, exc. "Qui prêtera la
parole" HACH 8

D'UN VANNEUR DU BLE AUX VENTS. "A vous troppe
legere" HACH 8

LOUANGES D'ANJOU, exc. HACH 8

L'OLIVE: SONNET 32. "Tout ce qu'ici la nature environne" HACH 8

———83. "Déja la nuit en son parc amassoit"
HACH 8, PERIOD 2

———113. "Si nostre vie est moins qu'une journée" ADES 54

LES REGRETS: SONNET 6. "Las! où est maintenant
ce mépris de Fortune?" HACH 8

———9. "France, mère des arts, des armes et
des loix" HACH 8, PERIOD 2

———31. "Heureux qui, comme Ulysse, a fait
un bon voyage" CAED 170, CAED 204,
GMS 7, GMS 8, HACH 8, PERIOD 2,
SPOA 9, SPOA 36

Du Fu. 712. in Chinese.

CHWUN WANG. "Gwo pwo shan he dzai"
FOLKW 76

CHYANG TSWUN. "Jeng rung chr yun syi"
FOLKW 76

DZENG WEI BA CHU SHR. "Ren sheng bu syang
jyan" FOLKW 76

JU FENG SYING. "Jyun bu jyan" FOLKW 76

MAU WU WEI CHYOU FENG SWO PWO GE. "Ba ywe
chyou gau feng nu hau" FOLKW 76

Du Mu. 803. in Chinese.

BWO CHIN HWAI. "Yan lung han shwei ywe lung
sha" FOLKW 76

DZENG BYE. "Dwo ching chywe dz dzung wu
ching" FOLKW 76

PAK CHUN HUAI. "Yin loong hrurn suy ye loong
sa" SCHOL 6

Ducasse, Isidore. See **Lautréamont, Comte de.**

Duchamp, Marcel. 1887. in French.

LA MARIÉE MISE À NU PAR SES CÉLIBATAIRES, MÊME,
exc. "Moules mâliques" FOLKW 13

Dudek, Louis. 1918. in English.

A CRACKER JACK. "If you and I ceased to exist,
my Dear" FOLKW 49

ETERNAL FORM. "The single power, working
alone" FOLKW 49

LINE AND FORM. "The great orchestrating principle of gravity" FOLKW 49

POEM 19 FROM EUROPE. "The commotion of these
waves" FOLKW 49

POEM 95 FROM EUROPE. "The sea retains such images" FOLKW 49

THE POMEGRANATE. "The jewelled mine of the
pomegranate" FOLKW 49

TO AN UNKNOWN IN A RESTAURANT. "Thank you
for sitting" FOLKW 49

Dufrêne, François. in French.

CRIRYTHME. "Avril déjá" LUCHT 1

Dugan, Alan. 1923. in English.

LOVE SONG: I AND THOU. "Nothing is plumb, level
or square" LIBC 54

MORNING SONG. "Look, it's morning, and a little
water" LIBC 54

NOTES TOWARD A SPRING OFFENSIVE. "I will begin
in May" LIBC 54

PHILODENDRON. "The person of this plant with
heart-shaped leaves" LIBC 54

Dunbar, Paul Laurence. 1872. in English.

AN ANTE-BELLUM SERMON. "We is gathahed
hyeah, my brothahs" FOLKW 45, UA 2

AT CANDLE LIGHTIN' TIME. "When I come in f'om
de co'n-fiel' aftah wo'kin' ha'd all day"
UA 2

COMPENSATION. "Because I had loved so deeply" FOLKW 41

A COQUETTE CONQUERED. "Yes, my ha't's ez ha'd
ez stone" FOLKW 45, THEAL 1

DAWN. "An angel robed in spotless white"
FOLKW 6, FOLKW 41

THE DEBT. "This is the debt I pay" UA 2

"Ere Sleep comes down to soothe the weary
eyes" UA 2

IN THE MORNING. "'Lias! 'Lias! Bless de Lawd"
FOLKW 45

"Little brown baby with sparkling eyes"
FOLKW 41

THE PARTY. "Dey had a gread big pahty down to
Tom's de othah night" FOLKW 45,
SPOA 88

"We wear the mask that grins and lies"
FOLKW 7, UA 2

WHEN DEY 'LISTED COLORED SOLDIERS. "Dey was
talkin' in de cabin, dey was talkin' in de hall"
FOLKW 45

WHEN MALINDY SINGS. "G'way an' quit dat
noise" FOLKW 45, UA 2

Poetry* EAV 2, PRENT 1

Dunbar, William. 1460. in English.

LAMENT FOR THE MAKARIS. "I that in heill wes
and gladnes" ARGO 29, ARGO 137

OF LIFE. "What is this life" ARGO 29

ON HIS HEID-AKE. ARGO 29

TO A LADY. "Sweit rois of vertew and gentilnes"
ARGO 29

TO THE CITY OF LONDON. "London, thou art of
towns" ARGO 29

Duncan, Robert Edward. 1919. in English.

THE ARCHITECTURE. "It must have recesses"
NET 5

THE FEAR THAT PRECEDES. EVERG 1

THE STRUCTURE OF RIME, exc. EVERG 1

"This place, rumored to have been Sodom,
might have been" EVERG 1

Dunlop, William. in English.

CAT. "Nine days old" SPOA 67

LANDSCAPE AS WEREWOLF. "Near here the last
grey wolf in England" SPOA 68

Dupree, Nancy Lorraine. 1940. in English.

BATS AND BUTTERFLIES. "Seems like to me there
be two kinds of people in this world"
FOLKW 38

THE BROTHERS. "I believed it, y'all"
FOLKW 38

FIRST LOVE. "Love makes the world go round"
FOLKW 38

* Recording not available for analysis

HAPPY 4TH OF JULY, Y'ALL. "Ring, you bells"
FOLKW 38
HERD RUNNERS. "You hip to Herd Runners?"
FOLKW 38
LET ME. "I want to be a circle around you"
FOLKW 38
MY PEOPLE IS. "My people is ignorant . . . selfish
. . . and . . . cruel"   FOLKW 38
NEW LOW. "Every morning when I wake up"
FOLKW 38
SELF-LOVE. "Wanna see a miracle?"
FOLKW 38
Durem, Ray. in English.
"Now, all you children"   ARGO 17
D'Urfey, Thomas. 1653. in English.
THE BULLY (with John Wilmot). "Room, room
for a blade of the town"   ARGO 47
"I'll sail upon the dog-star"   CAED 111
Durrell, Lawrence. 1912. in English.
ALEXANDRIA. "To the lucky now who have lov-
ers"   SPOA 34
AT ALEXANDRIA. "Wind among prisons"
SPOA 34
AT RHODES. "Anonymous hand records"
SPOA 34
BALLAD OF PSYCHOANALYSIS. "She dreams she is
chased"   SPOA 34
A BALLAD OF THE GOOD LORD NELSON. "The Good
Lord Nelson had a swollen gland"
SPOA 34
BALLAD OF THE OEDIPUS COMPLEX. "From Tra-
vancore to Tripoli"   SPOA 34
BITTER LEMONS. "In an island bitter lemons"
SPOA 34
BY THE LAKE. "If seen by many minds at once"
SPOA 34
CONAN IN EXILE. "Three women have stepped
at my books"   SPOA 34
CRADLE SONG. "Curled like a hoop in sleep"
SPOA 34
EPISODE. "I should set about memorizing this
little room"   SPOA 34
FREEDOM. "O freedom which to every man en-
tire"   SPOA 34
"Heloise and Abelard, nature's great herma-
phrodites"   SPOA 34
HOW TO BUY A HOUSE.   VOIX 4
IN ATHENS. "At last with four"   SPOA 34
IN BEIRUT. "After twenty years another meet-
ing"   SPOA 34
IN BRITAIN. "When they brought on the sleep-
ing child"   SPOA 34
IN CAIRO. "God, Sir, when you draw off those"
SPOA 34
IN PARIS. "In youth the decimal days"
SPOA 34
IN PATMOS. "Quiet room, four candles"
SPOA 34
IN RHODES. "From intellect's grosser denomina-
tions"   SPOA 34
IN RHODES. "Incision of a comb in hair"
SPOA 34
IN RIO. "And so at last good bye"   SPOA 34
JOHN DONNE. "From the dark viands of the
Church"   SPOA 34
LA ROCHEFOUCAULD. "A penny for your
thoughts"   SPOA 34

LEVANT. "Gum, oats, and syrup the Arabians
bore"   SPOA 34
NEMEA. "A song in the valley of Nemea"
FOLKW 65, JUP 1
POGGIO. "The rubber penis, the wig, the false
breasts"   SPOA 34
A PORTRAIT OF THEODORA. "I recall her by a
freckle"   SPOA 34
PROSPERO'S CELL.   VOIX 4
REFLECTIONS ON A MARINE VENUS.   VOIX 4
SONG FOR ZARATHUSTRA. "The Saltimbanc is
coming, the acrobat, the acrobat" SPOA 34
TO PING-KU, ASLEEP. "You sleeping child asleep"
SPOA 34
WATER MUSIC. "Wrap your sulky beauty up"
SPOA 34
Durston, Georgia Roberts. in English.
THE WOLF. "When the pale moon hides"
BOWMAR 1
Dwight, Timothy. in English.
GREENFIELD HILL, II. THE FLOURISHING VILLAGE.
"Fair Verna! loveliest village of the west"
EAV 15
Dyer, Sir Edward. 1543. in English.
A MODEST LOVE. "The lowest trees have tops,
the ant her gall"   ARGO 31, BRITAM 2,
LION 2
"My mind to me a kingdom is"   IMP 1,
LIST 1

Earley, Jackey. in English.
ONE THOUSAND NINE HUNDRED AND SIXTY EIGHT
WINTERS.   BLACKF 1
Eastman, Max. 1883. in English.
AT THE AQUARIUM. "Serene the silver fishes
glide"   SPOA 91
EPITAPH. "Now life has had her fill of me"
SPOA 91
TOO MANY PEOPLE. "Too many people on the
earth"   SPOA 91
Eberhart, Richard. 1904. in English.
AM I MY NEIGHBOR'S KEEPER? "The poetry of
tragedy is never dead"   CAED 113
THE BOOK OF NATURE. "As I was reading the
book of nature"   CARIL 11
THE CANCER CELLS. "Today I saw a picture of
the cancer cells"   CAED 113, CARIL 11,
NACTE 14
COUSIN FLORENCE. "There it is, a block of leap-
ing marble"   CARIL 11
DAM NECK, VIRGINIA. "Anti-aircraft seen from a
certain distance"   CARIL 11, LIBC 3,
LIBC 8
DREAM JOURNEY OF THE HEAD AND HEART. "My
head, so rarely rent"   LIBC 1
THE DRY ROT. "The fine powder of the dry rot"
CARIL 11
EQUIVALENCE OF GNATS AND MICE. "As a pillar of
gnats, moving up and down"   SPOA 97
THE EXPLORER ON MAIN STREET. "You will see
this big-jawed man walking up and down"
CAED 113
FOR A LAMB. "I saw on the slant hill a putrid
lamb"   CAED 113, CARIL 11, COLPIX 1,
SPOA 97

* Recording not available for analysis

Eberhart, Richard (continued)

THE FURY OF AERIAL BOMBARDMENT. "You would think the fury of aerial bombardment" CAED 113, CARIL 11, COLPIX 1, LIBC 3, LIBC 8, SPOA 82

THE GESTURE. "From the drama of horror and despair" LIBC 1

"Go to the shine that's on a tree" CAED 113, CARIL 11

GREAT PRAISES. "Great praises of the summer come" CARIL 11

THE GROUNDHOG. "In June, amid the golden fields" CAED 113, CAED 183, LIBC 3, LIBC 8, LIBC 38, TAPES 9

HALF-RENT MAN. "Haunts me the lugubrious shape" CARIL 11

THE HARD STRUCTURE OF THE WORLD. "Is made up of reservoirs" CARIL 11

HARDENING INTO PRINT. "To catch the meaning out of the air" CAED 113

HARK BACK. "To have stepped lightly among European marbles" LIBC 1

THE HORSE CHESTNUT TREE. "Boys in sporadic but tenacious droves" CAED 113, CARIL 11, FOLKW 25, LIBC 38

THE HUMAN BEING IS A LONELY CREATURE. "It is borne in upon me that pain" SPOA 97

"I walked out to the graveyard to see the dead" CAED 113, CARIL 11

THE IDES OF MARCH. "As I was riding through New England" CAED 113

"If I could only live at the pitch that is near madness" CAED 113, CARIL 11, COLPIX 1, NACTE 14, RCA 10

THE ILLUSION OF ETERNITY. "Things of this world" CAED 113

THE INCOMPARABLE LIGHT. "The light beyond compare is the light I saw" CAED 113

INDIAN PIPE. "Searching once I found a flower" CARIL 11

LA CROSSE AT NINETY MILES AN HOUR. "Better to be the rock above the river" CAED 113

A MAINE ROUSTABOUT. HE WAS THERE AS THE YACHTS WENT BY. "Percy is my name; my accent is good" CAED 113

"Man's greed and envy are so great" NACTE 14

MARRAKECH. "The dance begins with the sun descending" CAED 113

THE MASTERY. "The mysteries beyond our sight" CAED 113

A MEDITATION. "Now you are holding my skull in your hand" CAED 113

MEDITATION TWO. "Style is the perfection of a point of view" LIBC 1

A NEW ENGLAND BACHELOR. "My death was arranged by special plan in heaven" CAED 113

A NEW ENGLAND VIEW: MY REPORT. "The men of Vermont" LIBC 1

NEW HAMPSHIRE, FEBRUARY. "Nature had made them hide in crevices" CAED 113, CARIL 11

NOTHING BUT CHANGE. "We saw nothing but change in all the ways we went" CAED 113, CARIL 11

"Now is the air made of chiming balls" LIBC 3, LIBC 8

THE OAK. "Some sway for long and then decline" SPOA 97

ON A SQUIRREL CROSSING THE ROAD IN AUTUMN IN NEW ENGLAND. "It is what he does not know" CAED 113, CARIL 11, COLPIX 1

ON RETURNING TO ALOKE IN SPRING. "When the new frogs in their exuberant arrivals" CAED 113

ONLY IN THE DREAM. "Only in the dream that is like sleep" CARIL 11

THE PLACE. "Eventually one finds" CAED 113

RAINSCAPES, HYDRANGEAS, ROSES, AND SINGING BIRDS. "Rain thunderstorms over the Potomac" LIBC 1

RUMINATION. "When I can hold a stone within my hand" CAED 113

THE RUSH. "When the wind is stirring in the evening" LIBC 1

SEA BURIAL FROM THE CRUISER REVE. "She is now water and air" CAED 113

SEA-HAWK. "The six-foot nest of the sea hawk" CAED 113, CARIL 11

SEALS, TERNS, TIME. "The seals at play off Western Isle" CAED 113, CARIL 11, SPOA 97

A SHIP BURNING AND A COMET ALL IN ONE DAY. "When the tide was out" CARIL 11, SPOA 97

THE SOUL LONGS TO RETURN WHENCE IT CAME. "I drove up to the graveyard, which" CARIL 11

THE SPIRIT OF POETRY SPEAKS. "Each man must suffer his fate" FOLKW 21

SPRING MOUNTAIN CLIMB. "Till thinking had worn out my enterprise" SPOA 97

THE TOBACCONIST OF EIGHTH STREET. "I·saw a querulous old man, the tobacconist of Eighth Street" CARIL 11

THE VERBALIST OF SUMMER. "The verbalist, with colours at his hand" CARIL 11

WAR AND POETRY. CARIL 11

A WEDDING ON CAPE ROSIER. "Today there is another marriage" CAED 113

THE WISDOM OF INSECURITY. "The endless part of disintegration" CARIL 11

WORDS. "First a word was fuzzy, and was nothing" CARIL 11

Poetry* LIST 14

Eckels, Jon. in English.

AGITATE. "Let us not wait" BROADV 7

AND WE HID. "Staring at me, from across the room" BROADV 7

BLACK IS. "Black does not mean" BROADV 7

DATE WITH APOLLO 8. "The moon is here" BROADV 7

HELL, MARY. "Hell, Mary/ Bell Jones" BROADV 7

HOME IS WHERE THE SOUL IS. "I have never seen Africa" BROADV 7

IN MEMORY OF MARCUS. "A land wild with" BROADV 7

IT AND THEM. "In the beginning it traversed the seas and the" BROADV 7

MAGIC WORDS TO RUN (AND RUIN) THE WORLD BY. "Law and order" BROADV 7

MY POLICY. "My people had" BROADV 7

* Recording not available for analysis

NEW BREED OF CAT. "My Daddy was a Cat"
BROADV 7
THE NEW FOX. "I know/ a nice" BROADV 7
A RESPONSIBLE NEEGROW LEADER (WHITE APPOINT-
ED) TALKS ABOUT THE GOOD OLD DAYS IN L. A.
"Dere wa' no Black Power" BROADV 7
TO A VIRGIN. "The erect hardness" BROADV 7
TOGETHER AGAIN. "Ever lastingly" BROADV 7
WHAT PUEBLO MEANS TO ME. BROADV 7
WHITE COLLAR JOB. "Willie works" BROADV 7

Edfelt, Johannes. in Swedish.
ETT AR NÖDVÄNDIGT. "Ett är nödvändigt: att fär-
das mot Brunnar" GRAM 6
FÖRBJUDEN MUSIK. "Der borde väl vara under-
bart" GRAM 6
KONTRAPUNKT. "Detta är evigt; bäckens sång"
GRAM 6
SÅNG I PIREUS. "Ni dricka, Lykabettos' träd, den
sista klungen" GRAM 6
SE MÄNNISKEN. "Mannishospillra, hur kan du
blomma" GRAM 6
SONATIN. "Det klingar i hans grånande liv"
GRAM 6

Edgardh, B. in Swedish.
HUR MÅNGA VÅGOR. GRAM 1

Edman, Irwin. in English.
ON HEARING FRENCH CHILDREN SPEAK FRENCH.
HARC 4

Edson, Russell. in English.
THE GROSS SITUATION. "A very gross gentleman"
WATSHD 14
THE MAN WITH THE ELEGANT FEET. "A man who
decided" WATSHD 14
THE PROSTHETIC DUCK. "A beloved duck gets
cooked" WATSHD 14
THE RUINED ECLAIR. "A man, having to do with"
WATSHD 14
THE SARDINE CAN DORMITORY. "A man opened a
can of sardines" WATSHD 14
WHAT ELSE, BUT FOR LOVE. "An old woman had
fallen in love" WATSHD 14
Poetry* WATSHD 36

Edwardes, Richard. ca. 1523. in English.
AMANTIUM IRAE. "In going to my naked bed as
one that would have slept" ARGO 30
WESTERN WIND. ARGO 30

Edwards, Harry. 1855. in English.
Poetry* PRENT 1

Ehrmann, Max. 1872. in English.
DESIDERATA. "Go placidly amid the noise and
haste" CAED 160

Eich, Günther. 1907. in German.
BELAGERÜNG. "Vögel die um Futter kommen"
NESKE 1
BOTSCHAFTEN. "Nachrichten die für mich be-
stimmt sind" NESKE 1
D-ZUG MUNCHEN-FRANKFURT. "Die Donaubrücke
von Ingolstadt" NESKE 1
EINSICHT. "Alle wissen, dass Mexiko ein erfun-
denes Land ist" NESKE 1
ENDE AUGUST. "Mit weissen Bäuchen hängen
die toten Fische" NESKE 1
ENDE EINES SOMMERS. "Wer möchte leben"
NESKE 1
FRAGMENT, DEM MOND GEWIDMET. "Von Kaffee
und von Träumen lieg ich wach"
CHRIST 11

HERRENCHIEMSEE. "All ihr herbstlich Fliegen-
den" NESKE 1
HIMBEERRANKEN. "Der Wald hinter den Ge-
danken" NESKE 1
IM SONNENLICHT. "Die Sonne, wie sie mir zu-
fällt" NESKE 1
IN ANDEREN SPRACHEN. "Wenn der Elstern Flug
mich befragte" NESKE 1
KURZ VOR DEM REGEN. "Gleich wird es regnen"
NESKE 1
MIRJAM. "Im Pavillon wo Mirjam war"
NESKE 1
TAGE MIT HÄHERN. "Der Häher wirft mir die
blaue Feder" NESKE 1
TAUBEN. "Taubenflug über die Äcker hin"
NESKE 1
WEG ZUM BAHNHOF. "Noch schweigt die Fabrik"
NESKE 1
WESTWIND. "Vorhergesagter Wind" NESKE 1
Poetry* SUHRK 7

Eichendorff, Joseph von. 1788. in German.
ABSCHIED. "O Täler weit, o Höhen"
ATHENA 9
DAS ALTER. "Hoch mit den Wolken geht der
Vögel Reise" ATHENA 9
DER EINSIEDLER. "Komm, Trost der Welt, du
stille Nacht" ATHENA 7, CHRIST 27,
SPOA 126
FRISCHE FAHRT. "Laue Luft kommt blau gefloss-
en" SPOA 5
HERMANNS ENKEL. "Altdeutsch! Altdeutsch?—
Nun, das ist" CHRIST 27
DER KEHRAUS. "Es fiedeln die Geigen"
ATHENA 9
MONDNACHT. "Es war, als hätt' der Himmel"
DOVER 1, SPOA 126
DER MORGEN. "Fliegt der erste Morgenstrahl"
ATHENA 9
DIE NACHTBLUME. "Nacht ist wie ein stilles
Meer" ATHENA 7
DIE NACHTIGALLEN. "Möcht wissen, was sie
schlagen" CHRIST 27
DER PILGER. "Man setzt uns auf die Schwelle"
ATHENA 9
SANGERFAHRT. "Kühlrauschend unterm hellen"
ATHENA 9, DEUTGR 4
SCHÖNE FREMDE. "Es rauschen die Wipfel und
schauern" SPOA 5
SEHNSUCHT. "Es schienen so golden die Sterne"
CHRIST 27
SPRUCH. "Bau nur auf Weltgunst recht"
CHRIST 27
DER STILLE FREIER. "Mond, der Hirt, lenkt seine
Herde" CHRIST 27
DER STILLE GRUND. "Der Mondenschein verwir-
ret" CHRIST 27
TODESLUST. "Bevor er in die blaue Flut gesunk-
en" ATHENA 9
DER VERSPÄTETE WANDERER. "Wo aber werd ich
sein im kunftigen Lenze?" ATHENA 9
WÜNSCHELRUTE. "Schläft ein Lied in allen Din-
gen" ATHENA 9
DAS ZERBROCHENE RINGLEIN. "In einem kühlen
Grunde" ATHENA 9, SPOA 126
DIE ZWEI GESELLEN. "Es zogen zwei rüst'ge Ge-
sellen" ATHENA 9

* Recording not available for analysis

Eichendorff, Joseph von (continued)

ZWIELICHT. "Dämmerung will die Flügel spreiten"   ATHENA 9
Poetry*   CHRIST 6, GMS 11
Eiseley, Loren. 1907. in English.
Poetry*   JNP 81
Eizmendi, Ignacio de. in Basque.
"Arrantzaleak, gaur kanturako"   AGUIL 6
Ekelöf, Gunnar. 1907. in Swedish.
"Det finns nagonting som ingenstans passar"
                                         GRAM 8
ELEGI. "Jag vände mig bort och allt förändrades"   GRAM 8
FAUN. "Mig är given"   GRAM 8
PANTHOIDENS SÅNG. "För att utröna hur"
                                         GRAM 8
SÅNG FÖR ATT DÖVA S MÄRTAN. "Gå till stranden, mumlande i vinden"   GRAM 1
El Ciego. See **Abu-l-Hasan al-Husri.**
El Muhajir. See **Marvin X.**
Elgström, Anna Lenah. 1884. in Swedish.
BARA BORJAN.   GRAM 10
Eliot, George (Mary Anne Evans). 1819. in English.
"O may I join the choir invisible" CAED 201
Eliot, Thomas Stearns. 1888. in English.
ASH WEDNESDAY. "Because I do not hope to turn again"   ARGO 102, CAED 34, LIBC 7,
                              LIBC 28, LIBC 29
CAPE ANN. "O quick quick quick, quick hear"
                                       CAED 139
"Clear the air! Clean the sky! Wash the wind!"
                                       CAED 160
CORIOLAN: DIFFICULTIES OF A STATESMAN. "Cry, what shall I cry" CAED 139, HARVOC 17,
                                     HARVOC 17A
_____. TRIUMPHAL MARCH. "Stone, bronze, stone, steel, stone, oak leaves, horses' heels"
          CAED 34, HARVOC 17, HARVOC 17A,
                                        JNP 92
LA FIGLIA CHE PIANGE. "Stand on the highest pavement"   CAED 139
FOUR QUARTETS. BURNT NORTON. "Time present and time past"   ANGEL 2, ARGO 103,
        ARGO 114, CAED 159, RCA 11, SPOA 28
FRAGMENT OF AN AGON. "I'll carry you off"
                          HARPV 1, HARVOC 17A
GERONTION. "Here I am, an old man in a dry month"   HARPV 1, HARVOC 2,
                          HARVOC 17A, LIBC 36
THE HIPPOPOTAMUS. "The broad-backed hippopotamus"   ARGO 114
THE HOLLOW MEN. "We are the hollow men"
          ARGO 102, CAED 139, HARPV 1,
                        HARVOC 1A, HARVOC 2
IT IS NOT WE ALONE.   CAED 160
JOURNEY OF THE MAGI. "A cold coming we had of it"   ARGO 82, ARGO 114, CAED 139,
        FOLKW 65, FOLKW 69, HARPV 1,
        HARVOC 16, HARVOC 17A, JUP 1,
        LIBC 36, PROTHM 8, SPOA 41
LINES TO A YORKSHIRE TERRIER. "In a brown field stood a tree"   RCA 10

THE LOVE SONG OF J. ALFRED PRUFROCK. "Let us go then, you and I"   ARGO 102,
        ARGO 114, CAED 34, HARPV 1,
        HARVOC 1A, HARVOC 15, HOUGHT 5
_____, exc. "The yellow fog that rubs its back upon the window-panes"   CAED 110
MARINA. "What seas what shores what grey rocks and what island"   CAED 34
MR. ELIOT'S SUNDAY MORNING SERVICE. "Polyphiloprogenitive the sapient sutlers of the Lord"   CAED 34
MORNING AT THE WINDOW. "They are rattling breakfast"   CAED 139
NEW HAMPSHIRE. "Children's voices in the orchard"   ARGO 114, CAED 139, LIBC 7,
                                        LIBC 29
"O light invisible, we praise thee"   CAED 34
OLD POSSUM'S BOOK OF PRACTICAL CATS.
                              ARGO 7, SPOA 25
_____. THE AD-DRESSING OF CATS. "You've read of several kinds of cat" ARGO 7, SPOA 25
_____. BUSTOPHER JONES: THE CAT ABOUT TOWN. "Bustopher Jones is not skin and bones"
                      ARGO 7, SERAPH 1, SPOA 25
_____. GROWLTIGER'S LAST STAND. "Growltiger was a Bravocat, who lived upon a barge"
                              ARGO 7, SPOA 25
_____. GUS, THE THEATRE CAT. "Gus is the cat at the Theatre Door"   ARGO 7, ARGO 82,
        ARGO 114, SERAPH 1, SPOA 25,
                                        SPOA 41
_____. MACAVITY: THE MYSTERY CAT. "Macavity's a Mystery Cat: he's called the Hidden Paw"
        ARGO 7, CAED 139, SPOA 25, SPOA 93
_____. MR. MISTOFFELEES. "You ought to know Mr. Mistoffelees"   ARGO 7, SPOA 25
_____. MORGAN: THE COMMISSIONAIRE CAT. "I once was a pilot"   ARGO 7, SPOA 25,
                                        SPOA 93
_____. MUNGOJERRIE AND RUMPELTEAZER. "Mungojerry and Rumpelteazer were a very notorious couple of cats"   ARGO 7,
                                       SPOA 25
_____. THE NAMING OF CATS. "The naming of cats is a difficult matter"   ARGO 7,
                             SERAPH 1, SPOA 25
_____. OF THE AWFUL BATTLE OF THE PEKES AND THE POLLICLES. "The Pekes and the Pollicles, everyone knows"   ARGO 7, SPOA 25
_____. OLD DEUTERONOMY. "Old Deuteronomy's lived a long time"   ARGO 7,
                             SERAPH 1, SPOA 25
_____. THE OLD GUMBIE CAT. "I have a Gumbie Cat in mind, her name is Jennyanydots"
                 ARGO 7, SERAPH 1, SPOA 25
_____. THE RUM TUM TUGGER. "The Rum Tum Tugger is a curious cat" ARGO 7, LIST 4,
                             SINGER 1, SPOA 25
_____. SKIMBLESHANKS: THE RAILWAY CAT. "There's a whisper down the line at 11:39"
                      ARGO 7, SPOA 25, SPOA 93
_____. THE SONG OF THE JELLICLES. "Jellicle cats come out to-night" ARGO 7, CAED 139,
                                       SPOA 25
PORTRAIT OF A LADY. "Among the smoke and fog of a December afternoon"   CAED 34

* Recording not available for analysis

PRELUDES. I. "The winter evening settles down"
ARGO 114, CAED 34, CAED 111, HARPV 1

RANNOCH BY GLENCOE. "Here the crow starves"
CAED 139

A SONG FOR SIMEON. "Lord, the Roman hyacinths are blooming in bowls and"
CAED 34, FOLKW 65, HARPV 1, HARVOC 16, HARVOC 17A, JUP 1

SWEENEY AMONG THE NIGHTINGALES. "Apeneck Sweeney spreads his knees" ARGO 114, CAED 139, HARPV 1, LIBC 7, LIBC 29

USK. "Do not suddenly break the branch or"
CAED 139

VIRGINIA. "Red river, red river" CAED 139, LIBC 7, LIBC 29

THE WASTE LAND.

———. I. THE BURIAL OF THE DEAD. "April is the cruellest month, breeding" ARGO 102, ARGO 114, CAED 139, CAED 183, JNP 92, LIBC 7, LIBC 22, SPOA 14

———. II. A GAME OF CHESS. "The chair she sat in, like a burnished throne" ARGO 114, COLUMB 8, LIBC 7, LIBC 22

———. III. THE FIRE SERMON. "The river's tent is broken; the last fingers of leaf" ARGO 114, LIBC 7, LIBC 24

———. IV. DEATH BY WATER. "Phlebas the Phoenician, a fortnight dead" ARGO 114, LIBC 7, LIBC 24

———. V. WHAT THE THUNDER SAID. "After the torch light red on sweaty faces"
ARGO 114, LIBC 7, LIBC 26

WHISPERS OF IMMORTALITY. "Webster was much possessed by death" CAED 139
Poetry*   LIST 13

Elizabeth I, Queen of England. 1533. in English.
YOUTH AND CUPID. "When I was fair and young"
ARGO 31

Elliot, Ebenezer. in English.
THE PEOPLE'S ANTHEM.   DECCA 13

Elliott, George P. 1918. in English.
Poetry*   JNP 82

Elmslie, Kenward. 1929. in English.
AT THE CONTROLS. "Though I'm not a woman"
WATSHD 4

GIRL MACHINE. "My nerves my nerves I'm going mad"   WATSHD 4

LONG HAUL. "A remote male"   WATSHD 4

OFFICIAL SERUMS. "Any impartial study"
WATSHD 4

SIN IN THE HINTERLANDS. "Congratulations, fingerprint man"   WATSHD 4
Poetry*   WATSHD 43

Éluard, Paul. 1895. in French.
A L'ENDROIT. "Venant du dedans" FOLKW 89

L'ABSENCE. "Je te parle à travers les villes"
HACH 17

L'AMOUREUSE. "Elle est debout sur mes paupières" ADES 36, FOLKW 13, HACH 17, SPOA 32

ANNEAU DE PAIX. "J'ai passé les portes du froid"
HACH 17

LES ARMES DE LA DOULEUR. "On l'avait durement traité"   FOLKW 89

AU NOM DU FRONT PARFAIT. "Au nom du front parfait profond"   HACH 17

"Au premier mot limpide"   DOVER 4
AUJOURD'HUI.   GMS 5
AVIS. "La nuit que précéda sa mort"   GMS 5, HACH 17

LES BELLES BALANCES DE L'ENNEMI. "Des saluts font justice de la dignité"   FOLKW 89

BONNE JUSTICE. "C'est la chaude loi des hommes"   ADES 36

CELLE DE TOUJOURS, TOUTE. "Si je vous dis: 'j'ai tout abandonné' "   FOLKW 88

LE CHATEAU DES PAUVRES. "La vérité fait notre joie écoute-moi"   HACH 17

LE 5e POÈME VISIBLE. "Je vis dans les images innombrables des saison" GMS 5, HACH 17

COURAGE. "Paris a froid Paris a faim"
FOLKW 88, FOLKW 89, GMS 5

LA COURBE DE TES YEUX. "La courbe de tes yeux fait le tour de mon coeur"   HACH 17

COUVRE-FEU. "Que voulez-vous la porte était gardée" ADES 36, ADES 55, HACH 17, SPOA 32

DIMANCHE APRÈS-MIDI. "S'enlaçaient les domaines voûtés d'une aurore grise dans un pays gris" ADES 36, ADES 52, SPOA 32

LE DIT DE LA FORCE DE L'AMOUR. "Entre tous mes tourments entre la mort et moi"   GMS 5

DOMINIQUE AUJOURD'HUI PRESENTE. "Toutes les choses au hasard"   GMS 5, HACH 17

D'UN ET DE DEUX, DE TOUS.   GMS 5

ECRIRE, DESSINER, INSCRIRE. "J'ai rêvé du printemps le printemps a noirci"   HACH 17

L'EXTASE. "Je suis devant ce paysage féminin"
HACH 17

FRESQUES. "Jetais celui qui se promène"
HACH 17

HIER IL Y A TRES LONGTEMPS. "Hier il y a très longtemps"   HACH 17

L'HONNEUR DES POÈTES. "Whitman animé par son peuple"   ADES 55, FOLKW 89

INTIMES, exc. "Je n'ai envie que de t'aimer"
HACH 17

———, exc. "Tu glisses dans le lit"
FOLKW 88

INVOCATION. "Entre en moi toi ma multitude"
HACH 17

J'AI EU LONGTEMPS. "J'ai eu longtemps un visage inutile"   HACH 17

JE NE SUIS PAS SEUL. "Chargée/De fruits légers aux lèvres"   ADES 36, SPOA 32

JE T'AI IMAGINÉE.   GMS 5

JE TE L'AI DIT. "Je te l'ai dit pour les nuages"
ADES 36, ADES 52

LIBERTÉ. "Sur mes cahiers d'écolier"
ADES 36, ADES 55, GMS 5, HACH 17, SPOA 32

LA LIBERTÉ CONQUISE. "Je vois brûler l'eau pure et l'herbe du matin"   HACH 17

LA MORT, L'AMOUR, LA VIE. "J'ai cru pouvoir briser la profondeur l'immensité"   GMS 5, HACH 17

NOTRE MOUVEMENT. "Nous vivont dans l'oubli de nos métamorphoses"   HACH 17

NOTRE VIE. "Notre vie tu l'as faite elle est ensevelie"   ADES 36, ADES 54, SPOA 32

NUITS PARTAGÉES. "Au terme d'un long voyage"
ADES 36, ADES 52

* Recording not available for analysis

Éluard, Paul (continued)

LE PHENIX. "Je suis le dernier sur la route"
    ADES 36, ADES 52, HACH 17, DOVER 4
POÈME PERPÉTUEL. "De l'oeil du doigt j'étudie
    des sourires"   FOLKW 88
LA POÉSIE DOIT AVOIR POUR BUT LA VÉRITÉ PRA-
    TIQUE. "Si je vous dis que le soleil dans le
    forêt"   ADES 36
POÉSIE ININTERROMPUE. "Nue effacée ensom-
    meillée"   ADES 36, ADES 52
_____, exc. "Hier, c'est la jeunesse"
                                                    SPOA 32
POUR VIVRE ICI. "Je fis un feu, l'azur m'ayant
    abandonne" ADES 36, ADES 52, SPOA 32
PRINTEMPS. "Il y a sur la plage quelques flaques
    d'eau"   ADES 36
SANS AGE. "Nous approchons"   HACH 17
LES SEPT POÈMES D'AMOUR EN GUERRE. "Le coin
    du coeur, disait-il gentiment"   FOLKW 89
TOUT DIRE. "Le tout est de tout dire et je
    manque de mots"   HACH 17
LA VICTOIRE DE GUERNICA. "Beau monde des
    masures"   HACH 17

Emanuel, James A. 1921. in English.

AFTER THE ACCIDENT. "Tomorrow we'll find
    much to do"   BROADV 16
AFTER THE RECORD IS BROKEN. "My mind slips
    back"   BROADV 16
ANIMAL TRICKS. "Yesterday read something
    new"   BROADV 10
AT BAY. "My sirens"   BROADV 16
BETWEEN MOUTHFULS. "Things I'd rather die"
                                         BROADV 10
BLACK ECHO. "over-/ cunh-/ unh- /um"
                                         BROADV 10
BLACK HUMOR IN FRANCE: FOR ETHA. "Outshout-
    ing bathwater"   BROADV 10
BLACK MAN, 13TH FLOOR. "Hotel Ameridemo-
    cratogrando"   BROADV 10
BLACK POET ON THE FIRING RANGE. "Cantcha pull
    that trigger"   BROADV 10
CAT ON A TREE. "Big icy fists of sullen snow"
                                         BROADV 10
CHRIST, ONE MORNING. "Jesus saves. Him"
                                         BROADV 10
A CLOWN AT TEN. "We should have guessed"
                                         BROADV 16
CROSSOVER: FOR RFK. "Come on, Senator"
                                         BROADV 10
EMMETT TILL. "I hear a whistling"
                                         BROADV 16
FISHERMEN. "When three, he fished these lakes"
                                         BROADV 16
FLIRTATION. "If you should meet September"
                                         BROADV 10
FOR MALCOLM, U.S.A. "Thus, black javelin"
                                         BROADV 16
FOR "MR. DUDLEY", A BLACK SPY. "Harlem dud"
                                         BROADV 10
FOR THE 4TH GRADE, PROSPECT SCHOOL: HOW I
    BECAME A POET. "My kite broke loose"
                                         BROADV 10
FOURTEEN. "Something is breaking loose"
                                         BROADV 10
FREEDOM RIDER: WASHOUT. "The first blow hurt"
                                         BROADV 16

FURNACE IN MAY. "Never saw them burn"
                                         BROADV 10
GET UP, BLUES.   BROADV 16
"I wish I had a red balloon"   BROADV 16
ITEM: BLACK MEN THINKING. "Sprang at my
    throat"   BROADV 10
LINES FOR RICHARD WRIGHT. "White man with
    hateless home to share"   BROADV 10
NEGRITUDE. "Black is the first nail I ever
    stepped on"   BROADV 16
THE NEGRO. "Never saw him"   BROADV 16
A NEGRO AUTHOR. "I wrote something black to-
    day"   BROADV 16
NIGHTMARE. "From deep sleep"   BROADV 16
OLD BLACK MAN SAY. "They say 'Son'"
                                         BROADV 10
PANTHER MAN. "Wouldn't think" BROADV 10
SCHOOL FOR COPS. "Machine it seemed said"
                                         BROADV 10
SIXTEEN, YEAH. "Practices brutality closing
    doors"   BROADV 10
A SMALL DISCOVERY. "Father"   BROADV 16
SONG FOR SOMETHING PRETTY. "Thinking of
    something pretty"   BROADV 16
STOP LIGHT IN HARLEM. "Don't look at ME"
                                         BROADV 16
TIME IS THE GIFT. "Flesh speaks" BROADV 16
TO HARLEM: NOTE ON LANGSTON HUGHES. "He
    meant to pass"   BROADV 10
TO THE NEGRO CHILDREN OF MOUNT VERNON.
    "Understand what I have done"
                                         BROADV 16
THE TREEHOUSE. "To every man"
                                         BROADV 16
A VIEW FROM THE WHITE HELMET. "A glittering
    thing"   BROADV 16
THE VOYAGE OF JIMMY POO. "A soapship went a-
    rocking"   BROADV 16
WEDDING PROCESSION, FROM A WINDOW. "To-
    gether, we looked down"   BROADV 16
"Where will their names go down?"
                                         BROADV 16
WHITE POWER STRUCTURE. "What are the
    negroes saying?"   BROADV 16
WHITEY, BABY. "whatCHU care" BROADV 10
THE YOUNG ONES, FLIP SIDE. "In tight pants, tight
    skirts"   BROADV 16

Emerson, Ralph Waldo. 1803. in English.

BACCHUS. "Bring me wine, but wine which
    never grew"   CAED 149
BRAHMA. "If the red slayer think he slays"
    ARGO 1, CAED 149, CAED 185, CMS 13,
                               EAV 9, SPOA 40
COMPENSATION. "Why should I keep holiday"
                                         SPOA 40
CONCORD HYMN. "By the rude bridge that
    arched the flood"   AUDIA 2, CAED 98,
    CAED 149, CAED 195, DECCA 4, EAV 9,
    HOUGHT 2, LIST 3, RCA 8, SINGER 5,
                            SPOA 40, SPOA 75
DAYS. "Daughters of time, the hypocritic days"
    ARGO 11, CAED 149, CMS 12
                          FOLKW 32, SPOA 40
DIRGE. "I reached the middle of the mount"
                                            EAV 14

EACH AND ALL. "Little thinks, in the field, yon red-cloaked clown" CAED 149, HOUGHT 5, SPOA 40, SPOA 75

FABLE. "The mountain and the squirrel" CMS 13, EAV 9

FORBEARANCE. "Hast thou named all the birds without a gun?" EAV 14, SPOA 40

FRAGMENTS. "Of all wit's uses" CAED 149

GIVE ALL TO LOVE. "Give all to love" CAED 149, FOLKW 32, SPOA 40

HAMATREYA. "Bulkeley, Hunt, Willard, Hosmer, Meriam, Flint" CAED 149, CAED 185, SPOA 40

IS THIS BEAUTY TO PERISH. FOLKW 32

LIFE, exc. "Of all wit's uses the main one" SPOA 40

MERLIN. I. "Thy trivial harp will never please" CAED 149

———. II. "The rhyme of the poet" CAED 149

MUSIC. "Let me go where'er I will" CAED 149, SPOA 40

ODE INSCRIBED TO W. H. CHANNING. "Though loath to grieve" ARGO 11, CAED 149, EAV 15, FOLKW 32

THE PROBLEM. "I like a church; I like a cowl" CAED 149

THE RHODORA. "In May, when sea-winds pierced our solitudes" AUDIA 2, CAED 149, EAV 9, EAV 14, HOUGHT 5, LIST 3, SPOA 40

THE SNOW STORM. "Announced by all the trumpets of the sky" CAED 149, CAED 185, EAV 14, FOLKW 32, SPOA 40

TERMINUS. "It is time to be old" CAED 149, CAED 185, FOLKW 32, SPOA 40

THRENODY, exc. "The South-wind brings" CAED 149, SPOA 40

TWO RIVERS. "Thy summer voice, Musketaquit" CAED 149, EAV 14

URIEL. "It fell in the ancient periods" EAV 14, SPOA 40, SPOA 75

VOLUNTARIES. III. "In an age of fogs and toys" SPOA 40

Poetry* APPL 7, LIST 12

Emmanuel, Pierre. in French.
LE ROULEMENT DES ROUES. ADES 55

Empson, William. 1906. in English.
BACCHUS. "The laughing god born of a startling answer" LIBC 23

JUST A SMACK AT AUDEN. "Waiting for the end, boys, waiting for the end" LIBC 23

LEGAL FICTION. "Law makes long spokes of the short stakes of men" ARGO 97, LIBC 38

MISSING DATES. "Slowly the poison the whole blood stream" LIBC 23

TO AN OLD LADY. "Ripeness is all; her in her cooling planet" ARGO 97, LIBC 23

Engle, Paul. 1908. in English.
AMERICAN CHILD, exc. "Hallowe'en. She dressed up in a sheet" LIBC 1

———, exc. "The picture was a young man" SPOA 99

BEASTS. "That was a shocking day" SPOA 99

COLETTE. "Person, woman, child" SPOA 99

CORN, exc. "Too many years, from a vague evening valley" LIBC 5, LIBC 12

THE COUNT DUKE OF OLIVARES: VELASQUEZ. "This is the sort of face that sheep" LIBC 1

THE ENGLISH DANDY AT THE MOULIN ROUGE: TOULOUSE-LAUTREC. "The horse-faced dandy" LINC 1

FISHERMEN. "So in the end he who had seined rivers" LIBC 5, LIBC 12

FOSSIL. "We walked in that green field" LIBC 1

PAIR. "Nothing can live alone" LIBC 5, LIBC 12

RALPH WALDO EMERSON. "First American mature mind" LIBC 5, LIBC 12

SELF-PORTRAIT: VINCENT VAN GOGH. "The paint explodes into a face" LIBC 1

TO PRAISE A POET: ROBERT FROST. "You give this man the sort of praise" SPOA 99

VENUS AND THE LUTE PLAYER. "Far in the background a blue mountain waits" LIBC 1

WEST OF MIDNIGHT. "Five hours west of midnight" LIBC 5, LIBC 12

THE WORD AND THE POET. I. "Verse is not written, it is bled" LIBC 1

YOU CAN'T BE WISE. "Denied, she screamed in rage, and ran away" SPOA 99

Ennis, Julian. 1915. in English.
BLACKBOARD JUNGLE. "Smith is dead, Sir! Killed yesterday" ARGO 93

COLD STORAGE. "Headless and hard as bricks" ARGO 93

ELEGY ON TWO PETS. "I bought him for one and six-pence" ARGO 93

HOUSE PROUD. "I shall depart hence, seal up my dwelling" ARGO 93

ROAD CASUALTY. "If it's squashed red I swerve to the other side" ARGO 93

WIRE-DANCER. "He is well balanced and steady going" ARGO 93

Ennius. 239 B.C. in Latin.
Poetry* CETRA 18

Enright, D. J. 1920. in English.
THE BLACK COUNTRY. "But it is not black, they will tell you, any longer" SPOA 68

FIRST DEATH. PROTHM 8

THE NOODLE VENDOR'S FLUTE. "In a real city, from a real house" FOLKW 66

Enslin, Theodore. 1925. in English.
OPUS ZERO NUMBER ZERO, exc. "Love gets in the cracks" WATSHD 14

A PLACING IN THIS ROOM. "It is a terrible distinction" WATSHD 14

RANGER, BOOK 4, exc. "Is this all of it" WATSHD 14

THINGS DIE OUT. "Things die out" WATSHD 14

Poetry* WATSHD 38

Enzensberger, Hans Magnus. 1929. in German.
Poetry* SUHRK 2

Ercilla, Alonso de. 1534. in Spanish.
LA ARAUCANA, CANTO 2, exc. "Ya la rosada aurora comenzaba" SPOA 39

Escriva, Juan. in Spanish.
WELCOME DEATH. English and Spanish CMS 5

Escudero, Gonzalo. 1887. in Spanish.
ZOO. "Sol, inventario de color" FOLKW 80

Esenin, Sergei. See Yessenin, Sergei.

* Recording not available for analysis

Espada Rodriguez, José. in Spanish.
   CAMPESINA. "Quisiera para ti ser crepúsculo
      mananero"   SMC 9
Espanca, Florbela. 1894. in Portuguese.
   A UMA RAPARIGA. "Abre os olhos e encara a vida"
                                              FOLKW 72
   ALMA PERDIDA. "Toda esta noite o rouxinol cho-
      rou"   FOLKW 72
Espina, Concha. in Spanish.
   LEJOS. "Entre la noche que está dormida"
                                              FIDIAS 2
Espriu, Salvador. 1913. in Catalan.
   "No convé que dignem el nom"   AGUIL 14
   "De vegades és necessari i forçog" AGUIL 14
Espronceda, José de. 1803. in Spanish.
   A UNA ESTRELLA, exc. "Quién eres tú, Lucero
      misterioso"   DOVER 2
   CANCIÓN DEL PIRATA. "Con diez cañones por
      banda"   HOLT 1;
                        English and Spanish CMS 5
   CANTO A TERESA. "Por qué volvéis a la memoria
      mía"   HOLT 1
   EL ESTUDIANTE DE SALAMANCA. "Está la noche
      serena"   SPOA 37
Essex, Earl of (Robert Devereux). 1567. in Eng-
   lish.
   ORACLE FROM A DEVICE.   ARGO 77
Etherege, Sir George. 1635. in English.
   SONG. "If she be not as kind as fair"
                                              ARGO 47
   TO A LADY, ASKING HOW LONG HE WOULD LOVE
   HER. "It is not, Celia, in our power"
                                              ARGO 47
Evans, Abbie Huston. 1881. in English.
   THE FUNDAMENT IS SHIFTED. "The call is for be-
      lief"   SPOA 82
Evans, Liz. in English.
   MARY LINCOLN TAKING LEAVE. "Mister Lincoln
      and his lady"   WATSHD 8
   TO AN UNDECLARED LOVER. "Now I can tell you"
                                             WATSHD 8
   A WOMAN AFTER CHAGALL. "The bride is upside
      down"   WATSHD 8
Evans, Mari. in English.
   STATUS SYMBOL.   SPOA 89
   WHEN IN ROME.   ARGO 17
   Poetry*   PRENT 1
Evans, Mary Anne. See Eliot, George.
Everson, William. See Antoninus, Brother.

Fabio, Cyril Leslie III. in English.
   SOLEMNLY MINE. "Solemnly mine, Universal
      Man"   FOLKW 18
Fabio, Sarah Webster. 1928. in English.
   AFTER BIRMINGHAM, THEY MARCH FOR MARTIN LU-
      THER KING. "They mark time, now, with
      blunt booms"   FOLKW 16
   BLACK BACK. "Back Home again Black back"
                                             FOLKW 16
   BLACK WORLD. "Louis, Louis, Louis, Louis, you
      gotta go right now"   FOLKW 17
   BOSS SOUL. "Is for-real love, hate" FOLKW 16
   BRONZEVILLE BREAKTHROUGH. "Real. Cool. The
      Real thing We are"   FOLKW 17
   CHROMO. "Color it blue funk"   FOLKW 18
   CROSS-FIRE. "Bombs of Birmingham that broke
      those small Black bodies"   FOLKW 17

DIALOGUE BETWEEN TWO MESSENGERS OF PEACE.
   "It is your voice that whispers" FOLKW 17
   "Don't bother up my fungi an Calalu"
                                             FOLKW 16
ECHO OF RAIN. "The rain falls fast pattering"
                                             FOLKW 17
A FIVE-YEAR OLD SCREAM BREAKING THROUGH THE
   NIGHT. "Screamer from way back you and
   Lynn and his horn"   FOLKW 17
FOR MY PEOPLE, A JUBILEE FOR MARGARET WALKER.
   "Something all our own"   FOLKW 17
   "Glimpses of an Image"   FOLKW 16
THE HURT OF IT ALL. "Ain't nobody heard me
   singing sweet songs lately"   FOLKW 17
   "I would be for you rain"   FOLKW 17
IF WE COME LIKE SOFT RAIN. "If we come like soft
   rain"   FOLKW 18
JUJU FOR GRANDMA. "Grandma's talk was Black
   talk"   FOLKW 18, WATSHD 5
JUJU FOR RAY CHARLES ALCHEMY OF THE BLUES.
   "Cry, or Baby, don't you cry"   FOLKW 18
JUJU FOR THE HAND THAT ROCKS THE CRADLE.
   "Baby, last night when you called me"
                                             FOLKW 18
A LESSON TWICE LEARNED NEVER TO BE FORGOT-
   TEN. "John, John, See, see the ceremony's on"
                                             FOLKW 16
A MOVER. "Moving in an earthy way like clover"
                                             FOLKW 16
MY OWN THING. "Like this hand-sized bit of
   driftwood"   FOLKW 17
NINA GIVING MR. BACKLASH THE BLUES. "Gonna
   leave ya', Mr. Backlash"   FOLKW 17
ONCE MORE, THE SWEET SONGS. "Sweet songs, you
   said, were gonna come"   FOLKW 18
PANTHER CAGED. "Caged—within the prisons of
   our lust"   FOLKW 16
RAINBOW SIGNS. "They will appear in the moist
   air"   FOLKW 16
   "Sassafras toned, my grandma sat"
                                             FOLKW 17
SOUL AIN'T: SOUL IS. "Soul ain't nothing but the
   blues"   FOLKW 17
SOUL THROUGH A LICKING STICK. "My black Ma
   sure knows her thing"   FOLKW 16
STILL, A RED HOT AXE. "My Man, yo' axe still"
                                             FOLKW 18
TO TURN FROM LOVE. "No, I cannot turn from
   love"   FOLKW 17
WORK IT OUT. "Gig away Shindig, U.S.A."
                                             FOLKW 16

Faerstein, Chana. in English.
   BULLETIN. "Is dead. Is dead. How all the radios'
                                             FOLKW 21

Fagin, Larry. in English.
   Poetry by Fagin*   MICHM 17
Farahani. in Swahili.
   "Zamani nikipendeza kamma ani la tambun"
                                             SCHOL 6
Fargue, Leon Paul. 1878. in French.
   NOCTURNE. "Un long bras timbre d'or glisse du
      haut des arbres"   FOLKW 1
Farinella, Mario. in Italian.
   L'AMORE TI HA PORTATO OMBRA.   CETRA 3
Farjeon, Eleanor. 1881. in English.
   BEDTIME. "Five minutes, five minutes more
      please!"   NAITV

A CATCHING SONG. CAED 109
CHRISTMAS. ARGO 125
THE ELM-TREE. "One November morning clean and cold" CAED 110
FOR SNOW. CAED 109
GOING INTO DREAM. "Where are you going, child" CAED 110
IT WAS LONG AGO. CAED 110
A KITTEN. "He's nothing much but fur" CREAT 1, HARB 3
NEW CLOTHES AND OLD. CAED 109
"The night will never stay" CMS 2, HARB 4
NINE RED HORSEMEN. "I saw nine red horsemen ride over the Plain" CAED 110
POETRY. "What is poetry? Who knows?" CMS 2
ROBIN-RUN-BY-THE-WALL. CAED 110
SOME TIME. CAED 109
Farrar, John. 1896. in English.
CHANTICLEER. "High and proud on the barnyard fence" BOWMAR 1
A COMPARISON. "Apple blossoms look like snow" HARB 5
THRENODY, exc. "I fly my kite across the hill" HARB 1
Farrell, James T. 1904. in English.
Poetry* JNP 83
Farren, Robert. 1909. in English.
THE PETS. "Colm had a cat/ and a wren/ and a fly" JNP 90
Fauset, Jessie R. 1884. in English.
Poetry* PRENT 1
Feldman, Irving. 1928. in English.
Poetry* JNP 84
Feliciano Mendoza, Esther. See Mendoza, Esther Feliciano.
Ferdovci (Abol Mansur). in Persian.
SHAH NAMEH, exc. "Mahmud! if fear of man hath never awed" English FOLKW 77
Ferguson, Samuel. in English.
DARK DARK HEAD. "Put your head darling darling" SPOA 6
THE FAIRY THORN TREE. "Get up, Oh Anna dear" SPOA 6
Ferlin, Nils Johan Einar. 1898. in Swedish.
ALLTMER SOM IOR. "Jag blir alltmer som lor" GAZ 2
"Andersson tippade fel" GAZ 1
BESYNNERLIG. "For sånt som var stort i byn" GAZ 2 .
BRÅDSKA. "Ett ärende hit, ett ärende dit" GAZ 1
CIRKUS. "Jag lärde mig gå på händer" GAZ 1
DJURGÅRDSMÄSSA. "Bror Andersson går framåt med" GAZ 1
DRÖMMAR, DÅRE. "Drömmare, dåre - din vaggas fe" GAZ 1
"Du har tappat ditt ord" GAZ 2
EN INNEBOENDE. "B-rr, jar är som en inneboende" GAZ 1, GAZ 2
EN VALSMELODI. "Dagen är släckt" GAZ 2
EN VANDRINGSMAN. "Det säjs, att han vida i världen" GAZ 2
ETT BREV. "Nu går jag har alltså och svälter" GAZ 1
ETT MINNE (VINGA FYR). "Skimrande vitt som det vitaste" GAZ 1

FÅFÄNGLIGHET. "Jag har klättrat på önskningens stege" GAZ 2
FRU SORG. "Vem motte du vid grinden" GAZ 1
GATUBILD. "En disponent i pilsnerdricka" GAZ 1, GAZ 2
GETSEMANE. "Han var en så liten ock klen artist" GAZ 2
"Gudarna väcktes" GAZ 2
I LIVETS VILLERVALLA. "I livets villervalla" GAZ 2
INNAN DITT RIKE BLEV KARTLAGT. "Det var bara tokar" GAZ 2
INTE ENS DET FÖRFLUTNA. "Någon rider i natter" GAZ 2
"Inte ens en grå liten fågel" GAZ 2
JAG KUNDE JU VARA. "En luffare är jag - vad mera" GAZ 1, GAZ 2
"Jag mötte" GAZ 2
JUDAS ISKARIOT. "Vi vet allihop, hur det hände" GAZ 2
"Kejsarens papegoja" GAZ 2
KNORR. "Moses dröjer pa Sinai" GAZ 1, GAZ 2
KONDITIONALIS. "Din väg gick bittert allen" GAZ 1
LÖPSEDEL. "Så här är det en som förskingrat" GAZ 2
LUGNT. "Nu Guder i huset en vinterdag" GAZ 2
"Månen är hygglig och lyser" GAZ 1
"Maten var bra" GAZ 2
"Med många kulörta lyktor" GAZ 2
"Men går jag over ängarna" GAZ 1
NATTKVARTER. "Nar kroppens krematorium" GAZ 2
OMHÖLJD AV SITT EGET SILENTIUM. "I vimmel och" GAZ 2
PÅR HÅLL. "Polisen sa: Var bor ni" GAZ 2
POSTE RESTANTE. "Jag ringde en vän" GAZ 2
SANCTA SIMPLICITAS. "En kättare jag ar" GAZ 1, GAZ 2
SEANS. "Sakta från drunknande världa" GAZ 2
SKARE. "Min rädslas stackars hare" GAZ 1
STJÄRNORNA KVITTAR DET LIKA. "Vem kan inte räkna" GAZ 1
STÖRRE OCH MINDRE. "Vi uppstäckte mer och mer" GAZ 2
TIO RATTFARDIGA. "Har star de nu pampiga vardiga" GAZ 1
Ferlinghetti, Lawrence. 1920. in English.
AUTOBIOGRAPHY. "I am leading a quiet life" FANT 1
CRUCIFIXION. FANT 2
DOG. "The dog trots freely in the street" EVERG 1, FANT 2, WORLDP 1, NET 1
GOYA IN AMERICA. "In Goya's greatest scenes we seem to see" FANT 2
JUNKMAN'S OBBLIGATO. "Let's go/come on" FANT 1
KAFKA'S CASTLE. "Kafka's castle stands above the world" FANT 2
LOVE COMES HARDER TO THE AGED. FANT 2
MARC CHAGALL AND HIS HORSE. FANT 2
MUSEUM OF OBJECTS DEPICTING THE HISTORY OF MY RACE. FANT 2

* Recording not available for analysis

Ferlinghetti, Lawrence (continued)

"The Pennycandystore Beyond the El" FANT 2
THE POET AS AN ACROBAT. FANT 2
THE POET'S EYE. FANT 2
SAROLLA'S WOMEN IN THEIR PICTURE HATS. "Sarolla's women in their picture hats" FANT 2
SEE IT WAS LIKE THIS. "See/it was like this when" FANT 2
THE SITUATION IN THE WEST. "Dreaming of utopias" NET 1
THE STATUE OF ST. FRANCIS. FANT 1
TENTATIVE DESCRIPTION OF A DINNER TO PROMOTE THE IMPEACHMENT OF PRESIDENT EISENHOWER. "After it became obvious that the strange rain would never stop" FANT 2
THOUGHTS TO A CONCERTO OF TELEMANN. "The curious upward stumbling motion" SPOA 103
TRUTH IS NOT THE SECRET OF A FEW. "Truth is not the secret of a few" FANT 2
WILLIAM BUTLER YEATS ON THE THIRD AVENUE EL. FANT 2
"The world is a beautiful place" FANT 2
Poetry* CASSC 11, PRENT 2, TAPES 10, UCALM 2

Fernandez Moreno, Baldomero. 1886. in Spanish.
SEGUIDILLAS PERSONALES. "Yo me lancé a la vida" AGUIL 9
Poetry* SMC 16

Ferreira, Ascenso. 1895. in Portuguese.
TREM DE ALAGOAS. "O sino bate" FOLKW 71

Ferron, Marcelle. in French.
Poetry* FOLKW 70

Fet, A. A. 1820. in Russian.
"Siyala noch'" CMS 6

Field, Edward. 1924. in English.
Poetry* MILLER 1

Field, Eugene. 1850. in English.
BALLAD OF THE JELLY-CAKE. "A little boy whose name was Tim" CAED 130
THE BUGABOO. "There was a wonderful bugaboo" CAED 130
CONTENTMENT. "Happy the man that when his day is done" CAED 130
COQUETRY. "Tiddle-de-dumpty, tiddle-de-dee" CAED 130
THE CRICKET'S SONG. "When all around from out of the ground" CAED 130
THE DISMAL DOLE OF THE DOODLEDOO. "A Bingo bird once nestled her nest" CAED 130
THE DUEL. "The gingham dog and the calico cat" CAED 130, CMS 3, LEARNS 1
THE EXPLORER'S WOOING. "Oh, come with me to the arctic sea" CAED 130
EXTINCT MONSTERS. "Oh, had I lived in the good old days" CAED 130
THE FATE OF THE FLIMFLAM. "A Flimflam flopped from a fillamaloo" CAED 130
THE FLY-AWAY HORSE. "Oh, a wonderful horse is the fly-away horse" CAED 130
GANDERFEATHER'S GIFT. "I was just a little thing" CAED 130
GOLD AND LOVE FOR DEARIE. "Out on the mountain" CAED 130

KRINKEN. "Krinken was a little child" CAED 130
LITTLE BLUE PIGEON. "Sleep, little pigeon, and fold your wings" CAED 130
LITTLE BOY BLUE. "The little toy dog is covered with dust" CAED 130, RCA 8
A LULLABY. "The stars are twinkling in the skies" CAED 130
THE PRINCESS MING. "There was a princess by the name of Tsing" CAED 130
THE ROCK-A-BY LADY. "The Rock-a-By Lady from Hushaby Street" CAED 130
"Shuffle-shoon and Amber-locks" CAED 130
THE SHUT-EYE TRAIN. "Come, my little one, with me!" CAED 130
SUGAR PLUM TREE. "Have you ever heard of the Sugar Plum Tree" CAED 130, LEARNS 1
THE TWO LITTLE SKEEZUCKS. "There were two little skeezucks" CAED 130
WYNKEN, BLYNKEN, AND NOD. "Wynken, Blynken, and Nod one night" CAED 130

Field, Rachel. 1894. in English.
THE HILLS. "Sometimes I think the hills" HARB 6
IF ONCE YOU HAVE SLEPT ON AN ISLAND. SINGER 1
SKYSCRAPERS. "Do skyscrapers ever grow tired" HARB 1
SOMETHING TOLD THE WILD GEESE. CAED 110

Fields, Julia. 1938. in English.
MADNESS ONE MONDAY EVENING. "Late that mad Monday" ARGO 1

Figuera, Angela. in Spanish.
CARTA ABIERTA. "Jesus de Nazaret" SPOA 59
MUJER. "Cuán vanamente, cuán ligeramente" AGUIL 8
LA ROSA INCOMODA. "A esto nada menos hemo llegado" AGUIL 8

Figueroa, John. 1936. in English.
AT HOME THE GREEN REMAINS. CAED 153
MAURICIO IS DEAD. CAED 153
ON SEEING THE REFLECTION OF NOTRE DAME IN THE SEINE. "A man builds better than he knows" CAED 153
PORTRAIT OF A WOMAN. CAED 153

Filippo, Eduardo de. 1900. in Italian.
L'AMMORE CHED'E? "Scusate, sapite l'ammore ched'e?" CETRA 4, CETRA 48
FINA E LENTA. "Spaparanze sti llastre'e stu balcone" CETRA 4, CETRA 49
"Io vulesse truva pace" CETRA 49
O MUNNO D' 'E PPAROLE. "Si t' 'o ddico nun me cride" CETRA 4, CETRA 49
NUN ME GUARDATE. "Ve voglio di na cosa" CETRA 4, CETRA 48
'A PAURA MIA. "Tengo nemice? Faccio 'o paro sparo" CETRA 4, CETRA 48
'O RAGGIO 'E SOLE. "E na tristezza chesta casa mia" CETRA 48
'O RRAU. "'O rrau ca me piace a me" CETRA 49
SI T'O SSAPESSE DICERE. "Ah . . . si putesse dicere" CETRA 4, CETRA 48
STAMATTINA. "Me so scetato tant' 'e buonu more" CETRA 4, CETRA 48
STATTE ATTIENTO. "Quann' ammore se ne trase CETRA 4, CETRA 48

* Recording not available for analysis

"Tre ppiccerille"   CETRA 4, CETRA 49
VINCENZO DE PRETORE. "De Pretore Vincenzo
    s'arrangiava"   CETRA 4, CETRA 48,
                                             CETRA 49
Finch, Anne, Countess of Winchilsea. 1661. in
    English.
A NOCTURNAL REVERIE.   CAED 203
THE PETITION FOR AN ABSOLUTE RETREAT. "Give
    me, O indulgent fate"   IMP 1
THE TREE. "Fair tree! for thy delightful shade"
                                           ARGO 47
Finch, Francis. 1827. in English.
NATHAN HALE. "To drum-beat and heart-beat"
                                         DECCA 13
Finkel, Donald. 1929. in English.
HUNTING SONG.   SCHOL 7
Poetry*   JNP 85
Fiore, Francesco. 1889. in Italian.
'O PULLASTO. "Ogne matina, Giacomo Fulliere"
                                         CETRA 29
Fisher, Aileen. 1906. in English.
LITTLE TALK. "Don't you think its probable"
                                          HARB 2
THE PACKAGE. "There's a package, there's a
    package"   HARB 1
A PICNIC. "We had a picnic, we had buns"
                                          HARB 1
Fitts, Dudley. 1903. in English.
ELEGY ON HERAKLEITOS.   CARIL 3
THE LITURGY OF SMALL SUSAN.   CARIL 3
PRERAPHAELITE ENCOUNTER WITH YOUR GRANDFA-
    THER.   CARIL 3
PRIAM.   CARIL 3
Fitzgerald, Robert. 1910. in English.
CELESTINE. "The mother fragrant in her dust"
                                  LIBC 21, LIBC 66
DE ORBE NOVO. "A sumptuous moss hoods the
    skull"   LIBC 21, LIBC 66
Fitzsimmons, Tom. 1926. in English.
THE HOUSE OF MY FRIEND, A VOICEWEAVE. "Long,
    long, long"   WATSHD 12
Flanders, Jane. in English.
EXPECTATIONS. "I was expecting Lauren Bacall"
HEADS. "She laughed when they cut off"
                                       WATSHD 8
WALKING THROUGH WAYNESBORO. "I am walking
    down the aisle"   WATSHD 8
YOU GOTTA BE TALKED TO, ANNE. "You gotta be
    talked to, Anne"   WATSHD 8
Flecker, James Elroy. 1884. in English.
THE OLD SHIPS. "I have seen old ships sail like
    swans"   FOLKW 64
SANTORIN. "Who are you, sea lady"
                                       FOLKW 60
YASMIN: A GHAZEL. "How splendid in the morn-
    ing glows the lily"   ARGO 137
Fleming, Paul. 1609. in German.
AN DEUTSCHLAND. "Ja Mutter es ist wahr"
                                        CHRIST 30
AN DIE WUNDEN DES HERRN. "Ihr Zuflucht mein-
    er Angst"   CHRIST 18
MAHNUNG. "Sei dennoch unverzagt"   SPOA 5
ODE.   CHRIST 22
WIE ER WOLLE GEKÜSSET SEIN. "Nirgends hin als
    auf den Mund"   SPOA 126

Fletcher, John. 1579. in English.
CARE-CHARMING SLEEP. "Care-charming sleep,
    thou easer of all woes"   SPOA 84
ORPHEUS WITH HIS LUTE. "Orpheus with his lute
    made trees"   FOLKW 68
THE RIVER GOD. "I am this fountain's God"
                                           IMP 1
SONG IN THE WOOD.   CAED 111
Fletcher, John Gould. 1886. in English.
CLIPPER SHIPS. "Beautiful as a tiered cloud"
                                  LIBC 9, LIBC 18
LINCOLN. "Like a gaunt scraggly pine"
                                        CAED 169
Poetry*   PROTHM 6
Fletcher, Phineas. 1582. in English.
HYMN. "Drop, drop. Slow tears"   SPOA 84
Flint, Roland. in English.
INDIANS ARE BAD DRINKERS. "The drug man in
    the new hat"   WATSHD 8
MADRECITA. "When I am dead"   WATSHD 8
POEM BEGINNING AND ENDING, OH. "Oh it was
    beautiful"   WATSHD 8
SAY IT. "Having lent my apartment"
                                       WATSHD 8
Poetry*   WATSHD 35
Flores, Blanca. in Spanish.
Poetry*   SMC 16
Flórez, Julio. in Spanish.
MIS FLORES NEGRAS.   MIAMI 1
Florit, Eugenio. 1903. in Spanish.
A LA MARIPOSA MUERTA. "Tu júbilo, en el vuelo"
                                       FOLKW 80
LA COMPAÑERA. "A veces se la encuentra"
                                          HOLT 1
MARTIRIO DE SAN SEBASTIAN. "Sí, venid a mis
    brazos"   SMC 13
Foix, J. V. 1894. in Catalan.
VAIG ARRIBAR EN AQUELL POBLE. "Com se diu
    aquest poble"   AGUIL 14
Foleti, Adebayo. in English.
INDEPENDENCE.   CAED 136
Folgore da San Gimignano. 14th c. in Italian.
Poetry*   CETRA 19
Follen, Eliza Lee. 1787. in English.
THREE LITTLE KITTENS. "Three little kittens lost
    their mittens"   CAED 58, HARB 1
Fombeure, Maurice. 1906. in French.
ARBRE. "Voici la nuit qui m'éteint, me traverse"
                                        ADES 20
"Batelier de la Loire"   ADES 20
CHEVAUX DES BOIS, CHEVAUX DE MON ENFANCE.
    "Chevaux de bois, bêtes d'apocalypse"
                                        ADES 20
D'UNE AUBE ÉTRANGE. "L'aube point avant que
    passent"   ADES 20
ILS S'EN VONT AUX VEILLÉES. "A grandes ped-
    zouillées"   ADES 20
JUGEMENT DERNIER. "Je l'emporte avec moi de
    mes amours"   ADES 20
MARINE. "J'ai vu par trois fois la mer violette"
                                        ADES 20
NAÏF. "Je stipule/ dit le roi"   ADES 20
PAYSAGE URBAINS. "Au coin de la rue des Ursin"
                                        ADES 20
PLUIE DU SOIR. "Le grand-pere est à la fenêtre"
                                        ADES 20

* Recording not available for analysis

Fombeure, Maurice (continued)

PREUILLY-SUR-CLAISE. "Allons loin de la ville lasse"   ADES 20
QUEL EST CE COEUR? "Quel est ce coeur qui me parle a l'oreille"   ADES 20
LE RETOUR DU SERGENT. "Le sergent s'en revient de guerre"   ADES 20
SOLITUDE. "Je marche sans arrêt"   ADES 20

Fombona-Pachano, Jacinto. 1901. in Spanish.
MI AMÉRICA, LA DULCE. "Tú venías vestida de guitarras y pájaros"   FOLKW 80

Fondane, Benjamin. in French.
C'EST À VOUS QUE JE PARLE.   ADES 55

Fontaine, Pierre. in French.
MON COEUR PLEURE.   HACH 7

Fontane, Theodor. 1819. in German.
ABER ES BLEIBT AUF DEM ALTEN FLECK. "Wie konnt' ich das tun, wie konnt' ich das sagen"   DEUTGR 26
ABER WIR LASSEN ES ANDERE MACHEN. "Ein Chinese ('s sind schon an 200 Jahr)"
                                                      DEUTGR 26
DIE ALTEN UND DIE JUNGEN. "Unverständlich sind uns die Jungen"   DEUTGR 26
AUSGANG. "Immer enger leise leise"
                                                      DEUTGR 26
DIE BRÜCK AM TAY. "Wann treffen wir drei wieder zusamm"   CHRIST 15
ES KRIBBELT UND WIBBELT WEITER. "Die Flut steigt bis an den Ararat"   DEUTGR 26
DIE FRAGE BLEIBT. "Halte dich still, halte dich stumm"   DEUTGR 26
FRÜHLING. "Nun ist er endlich kommen doch"
                                                      DEUTGR 26
"Herr von Ribbeck auf Ribbeck im Havelland"
                                                      DEUTGR 26
HEUTE FRÜH IM GARTEN.   DEUTGR 26
JA, DAS MÖCHT' ICH NOCH ERLEBEN. "Eigentlich ist mir alles gleich"   DEUTGR 26
JOHN MAYNARD. "John Maynard!/Wer ist John Maynard?"   DEUTGR 26
LEBENSWEGE. "Fünfzig Jahre werden es ehstens sein"   DEUTGR 26
"O trübe diese Tage nicht"   DEUTGR 26
RANGSTREITIGKEITEN. "In einem Lumpenkasten"   DEUTGR 26
SO UND NICHT ANDERS. "Die Menschen kümmerten mich nicht viel"   DEUTGR 26
SPRUCH."Wen hast du dir auserlesen"
                                                      DEUTGR 26
UND ALLES OHNE LIEBE. "Die Mutter spricht: Lieb Else mein"   DEUTGR 26
UNTER EIN BILDNIS ADOLF MENZELS. "Gaben, wer hätte sie nicht? Talente-"   DEUTGR 26
WURZELS. "Wurzel, wir wollen nun an die See"
                                                      DEUTGR 26

Fontanella, Girolamo. 1612. in Italian.
Poetry*   CETRA 24

Ford, John. 1586. in English.
THE BROKEN HEART, exc. "Sure, if we were all Sirens"   LONGM 1

Ford, M. Lucille. in English.
TRAFFIC LIGHTS. "Red lights mean danger"
                                                      HARB 1

Forster, Edward Morgan. 1879. in English.
Poetry*   ARGO 106

Fort, Paul. 1872. in French.
LES BALAINES. "Du temps qu'on allait encore aux baleines"   CBS 1
COMPLAINTE DU PETIT CHEVAL BLANC. "Le petit cheval dans le mauvais temps"   HACH 4
LA GRENOUILLE BLEUE.   HACH 4
LA RONDE. "Si toutes les filles du monde"
                                         FOLKW 13, CAED 204

Foscolo, Ugo. 1778. in Italian.
A FRANCESCO SAVERIO FABRE.   CETRA 5
A VENEZIA. "O di mille tiranni, a cui rapina"
                                                      CETRA 5
A VICENZO MONTI. "Se fra' pochi mortali a cui negli anni"   CETRA 5
A ZACINTO. "Né più mai toccherò le sacre sponde"   CETRA 5, CETRA 12
ALLA MUSA. "Pur tu copia versavi alma di canto"
                                    CETRA 5, CETRA 12
ALLA SERA. "Forse perchè della fatal quiete"
                          DOVER 3, SPOA 30, CETRA 12
ALLA SUA DONNA LONTANA.   CETRA 5
DEI SEPOLCRI, exc.   CETRA 5
_____. "A egregie cose il forte animo"
                                                      SPOA 30
_____. "All' ombra de' cipressi" FOLKW 97
DI SE STESSO. "Che stai? gia il secol l'orma"
                                                      CETRA 5
IN MORTE DEL FRATELLO GIOVANNI. "Un di', s'io non andrò sempre fuggendo"   CETRA 5
                               CETRA 12, DOVER 3
IN MORTE DEL PADRE. "Perché, o mie luci, l'angoscioso pianto"   CETRA 5
IL PROPRIO RITRATTO. "Solcata ho fronte, occh incavati"   CETRA 5

Foss, Sam Walter. 1858. in English.
THE HOUSE BY THE SIDE OF THE ROAD. "These are hermit souls that live withdrawn"
                   CAED 100, CAED 195, COLUMB 6

Fourest, Georges. in French.
LE CID. "Le palais de Gormaz, comte et gobernador"   CBS 1

Fox, Charles. in English.
EARTHSHIP. "You've been away a long time"
JA. "Screaming loose"   WATSHD 5
"Manhood-human sculptured"   WATSHD 5
ONE-EYED NIGHT. "The moon reads what she writes"   WATSHD 5
RAPE IN THE MIND CAVE. "Adrift on green water"
                                                      WATSHD 5
RAVEN ON THE MOON. "Her shadow melts on the street"   WATSHD 5
RELATIONSHIP POEM. "Manhood is a glasshouse"
                                                      WATSHD 5
RITUAL. "He and she have been" WATSHD 5
STEPMOTHER COUNTRY BLUES. "Sculptured rock with windows"   WATSHD 5

Fox, George. in English.
THE COUNTY OF MAYO. "On the deck of Patrick Lynch's boat"   SPOA 6

Fox, Siv Cedering. 1939. in English.
ARCHITECTURE IN WHITE. "I construct white rooms"   WATSHD 1
MAD WOMAN. "I have done with the devil"
                                                      WATSHD 1

Francesco da Barberino. 1264. in Italian.
Poetry*   CETRA 19

---

* Recording not available for analysis

ancis of Assisi, Saint (San Francesco d'Assisi). 1186. in Italian.
CANTICLE OF THE SUN, exc. "Praise be to Thee, my Lord, with all Thy creatures" English LEARNC 2
CANTICO DELLE CREATURE. "Altissimu, omnipotente, bon Signore" DOVER 3; Italian and English FOLKW 10, SPOA 30, CETRA 6
FIORETTI, exc. CETRA 6
PRAYER. ARGO 82
PRAYER. "Lord make me a channel of thy peace" English SPOA 41
Poetry* CETRA 19
ancis, Robert. 1901. in English.
THE BASE STEALER. "Poised between going on and back, pulled" FOLKW 22, SCHOL 7
BLOOD STAINS. "Blood stains how to remove from cotton" FOLKW 22
BLUEJAY. "So bandit-eyed, so undovelike a bird" FOLKW 22
BOY RIDING FORWARD BACKWARD. "Presto, pronto! Two boys, two horses" SCHOL 1
THE BULLDOZER. "Bulls by day" FOLKW 22
BURIAL. "Aloft, lightly on finger tips" FOLKW 22
CATCH. "Two boys uncoached are tossing a poem together" CAED 111
CATS. "Cats walk neatly" FOLKW 22
CHIMAPHILA, 1972. "How easily I could have missed you" FOLKW 22
CITY. "In the scare city" FOLKW 22
COIN DIVER (FUNCHAL). "He takes it first with his eye like a sparrow hawk" FOLKW 22, SCHOL 1
COME. "As you are (said Death)" FOLKW 22
CROMWELL. "After the celebrated carved misericords" FOLKW 22
CYPRESSES. "At noon they talk of evening and at evening" FOLKW 22
DECEMBER. "Dim afternoon December afternoon" FOLKW 22
DOLPHIN. "In mythology the restraint shown by dolphins" FOLKW 22
EAGLE PLAIN. "The American eagle is not aware he is" FOLKW 22, SCHOL 1
EDITH SITWELL ASSUMES THE ROLE OF LUNA, OR IF YOU KNOW WHAT I MEAN SAID THE MOON. "Who (said the Moon)" FOLKW 22
EPITAPH: BUTCHER. "Falleth the rain, falleth the leaf" FOLKW 22
EPITAPH: DIPLOMAT. "Here lies a diplomat, alas" FOLKW 22
EPITAPH: EVERYMAN. "Preacher or lecher, saint or not" FOLKW 22
EPITAPH: FISHERMAN. "Now comes the fisherman to terms" FOLKW 22
EPITAPH: OLD LADY PATRIOT. "How calm she lies in death, how calm" FOLKW 22
EPITAPH: PREACHER. "He called on God to smite the foe" FOLKW 22
EPITAPH: THE FURRED LADY. "What can this careful lady think" FOLKW 22
EPITAPH: THE PROUD AND PASSIONATE MAN. "Stiff both in passion and in pride" FOLKW 22
EPITAPH: TOMB OF A WELL-KNOWN SOLDIER. "Here lies the military mind" FOLKW 22

EPITAPH: UNDERTAKER. "The man who yesterday was seen" FOLKW 22
FARM BOY AFTER SUMMER. "A seated statue of himself he seems" SCHOL 1
A FEAR. "Against a falling snow" FOLKW 22
GOING TO THE FUNERAL. "Death hushes all the bigwigs the big shots" FOLKW 22
GOLD. "Suddenly all the gold I ever wanted" FOLKW 22, SCHOL 1
THE HALF TWIST "What the camera did" FOLKW 22
A HEALTH TO EARTH. "A health to earth and her magnificent digestion" FOLKW 22
HIS RUNNING MY RUNNING. "Mid-autumn late autumn" FOLKW 22
HISTORY. "History to the historians" FOLKW 22
HOGWASH. "The tongue that mothered such a metaphor" FOLKW 22
LIGHT CASUALTIES. "Light things falling- I think of rain" FOLKW 22
LIKE GHOSTS OF EAGLES. "The Indians have mostly gone" FOLKW 22
THE MOUNTAIN. "The mountain does not move" FOLKW 22
"The mouse whose name is time" CAED 110, FOLKW 22
NIGHT TRAIN. "Across the dim frozen fields of night" CAED 110
O WORLD OF TOMS. "O world of toms—tomfools, Tom Peppers" SCHOL 1
OLD MAN'S CONFESSION OF FAITH. "The blowing wind I let it blow" FOLKW 22
ON A THEME BY FROST. "Amherst never had a witch" FOLKW 22
THE ORB WEAVER. "Here is the spinner, the orb weaver" SCHOL 1
OVERHEARING TWO ON A COLD SUNDAY MORNING. "We left our husbands sleeping" FOLKW 22
PAPER MEN TO AIR HOPES AND FEARS. "The first speaker said" FOLKW 22, SCHOL 1
THE PEACOCK. "The over-ornate can be a burden" FOLKW 22
PICASSO AND MATISSE (CIRCA 1950) "At Vallauris and Vence, Picasso and Matisse" FOLKW 22
PITCHER. "His art is eccentricity, his aim" FOLKW 22, SCHOL 1
THE POPE. "The Pope in Rome" FOLKW 22
RETROSPECT. "Yes, I was one of them. And what a cast" FOLKW 22
THE RIGHTEOUS. "After the saturation bombing divine" FOLKW 22
SAILBOAT, YOUR SECRET. "Sailboat, your secret. With what dove-and-serpent" SCHOL 1
SILENT POEM. "Backroad leafmold stonewall chipmunk" FOLKW 22
SNOWSPELL. "Look, it is falling a little" FOLKW 22
SUMMONS. "Keep me from going to sleep too soon" FOLKW 22, SCHOL 1, SCHOL 7
SUSPENSION. "Where bees bowing from flower to flower" FOLKW 22
THREE OLD LADIES AND THREE SPRING BULBS. "I wouldn't be buried in anything but black" FOLKW 22

* Recording not available for analysis

Francis, Robert (continued)

TRADE. "The little man with the long nose"
FOLKW 22

WHEN I COME. "Once more the old year peters out"
FOLKW 22

WHILE I SLEPT. "While I slept, while I slept and the night grew colder"
FOLKW 22

Franks, David. in English.
PAY ATTENTION. "I try to live for the moment"
WATSHD 10

Fraser, G. S. 1915. in English.
INSTEAD OF AN ELEGY. "Bullets blot out the Life-Time smile"
FOLKW 21

Fraser, Kathleen. in English.
THE STORY OF EMMA SLIDE. "Emma Slide, I'm a slide"
WATSHD 10
Poetry*
JNP 86

Freeman, C. in English.
Poetry*
PRENT 1

Freivalds, Karl. in English.
A PRESENCE IN THINGS. "There's a wild promise"
WATSHD 8
TO THE SUMMER CITY. "Of all the corners"
WATSHD 8

Fremantle, Anne. 1910. in English.
NO MINDLESS ESCALATION. "We shall give this undeclared war"
SPOA 82

Frenaud, André. in French.
BRANDEBOURG.
ADES 55

Freneau, Philip. 1752. in English.
THE INDIAN BURYING GROUND. "In spite of all the learned have said"   ARGO 11, CAED 185, EAV 7, EAV 14

ON RETIREMENT. "A hermit's house beside a stream"
EAV 14

ON THE DEATH OF DR. BENJAMIN FRANKLIN. "Thus, some tall tree that long hath stood"
HOUGHT 5

TO THE MEMORY OF THE BRAVE AMERICANS. "At Eutaw Springs the valiant died"   EAV 15

THE WILD HONEYSUCKLE. "Fair flower, that dost so comely grow"
EAV 15
Poetry*
EAV 8

Freni, Melo. in Italian.
FIERA DEL SUD.
CETRA 31

Frescobaldi, Dino. 1271. in Italian.
Poetry*
CETRA 36

Frey, Friedrich Hermann. See **Greif, Martin.**

Fröding, Gustaf. 1860. in Swedish.
"Si drömmaren kommer där"
GRAM 1

Froissart, Jean. 1333. in French.
RONDEAU. "My heart enjoys the fragrance of the rose"
English EAV 22

Frost, Frances M. in English.
FATHER.
SINGER 2
THE LITTLE WHISTLER. "My mother whistled softly"
HARB 1
MOTHER.
SINGER 2
NIGHT OF WIND. "How lost is the little fox at the borders of night"
HARB 6
NIGHT PLANE. "The midnight plane with its riding lights"
HARB 2

Frost, Richard. in English.
ON NOT WRITING AN ELEGY. "My friend told me about kids in a coffee house"   FOLKW 21

Frost, Robert. 1874. in English.
ACCIDENTALLY ON PURPOSE. "The universe is but the fling of things"
HARPV 3

ACQUAINTED WITH THE NIGHT. "I have been one acquainted with the night"   CAED 42, CAED 112, LIBC 13, LIBC 53

AFTER APPLE-PICKING. "My long two-pointed ladder's sticking through a tree"   CAED 42, CAED 183, FOLKW 24, NACTE 4

THE AIM WAS SONG. "Before man came to blow it right"
CAED 170

AMERICA IS HARD TO SEE. "Columbus may have worked the wind"
CAED 170

AWAY! "Now I out walking"   CARIL 17, LIBC 36

BIRCHES. "When I see birches bend to left and right"   CAED 42, CAED 110, CAED 183, CAED 195, DECCA 8, FOLKW 24, HARPV 3, HOUGHT 4, NACTE 1, NACTE 3, NACTE 13

BLUEBERRIES. "You ought to have seen what I saw on my way"   FOLKW 24, SINGER 3

BOND AND FREE. "Love has earth to which she clings"
HARPV 3

THE BONFIRE. "Oh, let's go up the hill and scare ourselves"
FOLKW 24

A CABIN IN THE CLEARING. "I don't believe the sleepers"
CAED 170

A CASE FOR JEFFERSON. "Hamson loves my country too"
CAED 170

CHOOSE SOMETHING LIKE A STAR. "O Star (the first one in sight)"   CAED 42, DECCA 8, LIBC 13, LIBC 53

CLEAR AND COLDER. "Wind the season-climate mixer"
FOLKW 24

CLOSED FOR GOOD. "They come not back with steed"   CAED 170, DECCA 8

COME IN. "As I came to the edge of the woods"
CAED 170, DECCA 8, LIBC 13, LIBC 49

A CONSIDERABLE SPECK. "A speck that would have been beneath my sight"   CAED 42, DECCA 8, HARPV 3, LIBC 13, LIBC 53

THE COURAGE TO BE NEW. "I hear the world reciting"
CARIL 17

THE COW IN APPLE TIME. "Something inspires the only cow of late"
FOLKW 24

THE DEATH OF THE HIRED MAN. "Mary sat musing on the lamp-flame at the table"   CAED 42, DECCA 8, HOUGHT 5, NACTE 1, NACTE 3, SINGER 5

DEPARTMENTAL. "An ant on the table cloth"
CAED 42, DECCA 8, LIBC 13, LIBC 53

DESERT PLACES. "Snow falling and night falling fast, oh, fast"   CAED 170, CARIL 17, NACTE 4

DESIGN. "I found a dimpled spider, fat and white"
CARIL 17

DIRECTIVE. "Back out of all this now too much for us"   LIBC 13, LIBC 36, SPOA 9

DOES NO ONE AT ALL EVER FEEL THIS WAY IN THE LEAST? "O ocean sea for all your being vast"
CAED 17

A DRUMLIN WOODCHUCK. "One thing has a shelving bank"   CAED 170, DECCA 8, LIBC 13, LIBC 53, NBC

---

* Recording not available for analysis

DUST OF SNOW. "The way a crow" FOLKW 24, HARC 2, NACTE 1, NACTE 4, NACTE 13, SINGER 2

ETHEREALIZING. "A theory if you hold it hard enough" CAED 42, HARPV 3

EVENING IN A SUGAR ORCHARD. "From where I lingered" FOLKW 24

FIRE AND ICE. "Some say the world will end in fire" BRITAM 1, CAED 170, DECCA 8, EDUC 1, NACTE 1, NACTE 4, UARIZ 1

FIREFLIES IN THE GARDEN. "Here come real stars to fill the upper skies" FOLKW 24

FOR JOHN F. KENNEDY HIS INAUGURATION. "Summoning artists to participate" FOLKW 21

FORGIVE, OH LORD. "Forgive, oh Lord, my little jokes on thee" CARIL 17

GATHERING LEAVES. "Spades take up leaves" FOLKW 24

THE GIFT OUTRIGHT. "The land was ours before we were the land's" CAED 170, CARIL 17, DECCA 8, FOLKW 21, HARPV 3, LIBC 13, LIBC 55, SINGER 3, TAPES 8

GOOD-BY AND KEEP COLD. "This saying good-by on the edge of the dark" FOLKW 24, UARIZ 1

HAPPINESS MAKES UP IN HEIGHT FOR WHAT IT LACKS IN LENGTH. "Oh stormy, stormy world" CAED 42, DECCA 8

THE HARDSHIP OF ACCOUNTING. "Never ask of money spent" CAED 170

A HUNDRED COLLARS, exc. "What I like best's the lay of different farms" EDUC 1

HYLA BROOK. "By June our brook's run out of song and speed" FOLKW 24

IT IS ALMOST THE YEAR 2000. "To start the world of gold" CAED 170, DECCA 8

THE LAST WORD OF A BLUEBIRD (AS TOLD TO A CHILD) "As I went out a crow" FOLKW 24

A LEAF-TREADER. "I have been treading on leaves all day" EDUC 1

THE LINE-GANG. "Here come the line-gang pioneering by" CARIL 17

LINES WRITTEN IN DEJECTION ON THE EVE OF GREAT SUCCESS. "I once had a cow that jumped over the moon" HARPV 3

A LONE STRIKE. "The swinging mill bell changed its rate" DECCA 8

A MASQUE OF REASON, exc. CAED 170

MENDING WALL. "Something there is that doesn't love a wall" CAED 42, DECCA 8, EDUC 1, FOLKW 24, HOUGHT 5, NACTE 1, NACTE 4, NACTE 13, AGE 3

THE MOST OF IT. "He thought he kept the universe alone" CARIL 17, LIBC 13, SPOA 90

THE MOUNTAIN. "The mountain held the town as in a shadow" LIBC 13, LIBC 49, SPOA 90

MOWING. "There was never a sound beside the wood but one" CAED 42, FOLKW 24, LIBC 13, LIBC 51, NACTE 4

_____, exc. EDUC 1

MY NOVEMBER GUEST. "My sorrow, when she's here with me" CAED 42

THE NEED OF BEING VERSED IN COUNTRY THINGS. "The house had gone to bring again" CAED 170, CARIL 17

NEITHER OUT FAR NOR IN DEEP. "The people along the sand" CARIL 17, HARPV 3, NACTE 1, NACTE 4

NEVER AGAIN WOULD BIRDS' SONG BE THE SAME. CARIL 17

"No holy wars for them" CARIL 17

NOT QUITE SOCIAL. "Some of you will be glad I did what I did" CAED 170

NOTHING GOLD CAN STAY. "Nature's first green is gold" FOLKW 24, NACTE 4

THE OBJECTION TO BEING STEPPED ON. "At the end of the row" CARIL 17, HARPV 3, LIBC 36

OCTOBER. "O hushed October morning mild" FOLKW 24, EDUC 1

AN OLD MAN'S WINTER NIGHT. "All out of doors looked darkly in at him" CAED 170, CARIL 17, LIBC 13, LIBC 51, SPOA 90

ON LOOKING UP BY CHANCE AT THE CONSTELLATIONS. "You'll wait a long, long time for anything much" CAED 170, LIBC 13, LIBC 55, SPOA 90

ONCE BY THE PACIFIC. "The shattered water made a misty din" CAED 170, DECCA 8

ONE MORE BREVITY. "I opened the door so my last look" CAED 42, HARPV 3

ONE STEP BACKWARD TAKEN. "Not only sands and gravel" CAED 42, DECCA 8, LIBC 13, LIBC 55, NACTE 4

THE ONSET. "Always the same, when on a fated night" CARIL 17, FOLKW 24, NACTE 3

THE OVEN BIRD. "There is a singer everyone has heard" CAED 170, CARIL 17

THE PASTURE. "I'm going out to clean the pasture spring" CAED 42, CAED 109, CAED 169, EDUC 1, FOLKW 24, LIBC 13, LIBC 51, NACTE 4, SINGER 1

THE PEACEFUL SHEPHERD. "If heaven were to do again" NACTE 4

A PECK OF GOLD. "Dust always blowing about" NACTE 1, NACTE 3

A PRAYER IN SPRING. "Oh, give us pleasure in the flowers today" EDUC 1, FOLKW 24

PROVIDE, PROVIDE. "The witch that came (the withered hag)" CAED 42, DECCA 8, LIBC 13, LIBC 51

THE QUEST OF THE PURPLE-FRINGED. "I felt the chill of the meadow underfoot" FOLKW 24

A RECORD STRIDE. "In a Vermont bedroom closet" FOLKW 24

RELUCTANCE. "Out through the fields and the woods" CAED 42, LIBC 13, LIBC 51, NACTE 3

REVELATION. "We make ourselves a place apart" HARPV 3

THE ROAD NOT TAKEN. "Two roads diverged in a yellow wood" BRITAM 1, CAED 42, EDUC 1, HARC 4, HOUGHT 4, LIBC 36, NACTE 1, NACTE 3, SINGER 4

A ROADSIDE STAND. "The little old house was out with a little new shed" CARIL 17

ROSE POGONIAS. "A saturated meadow" EDUC 1, FOLKW 24

* Recording not available for analysis

Frost, Robert (continued)

THE RUNAWAY. "Once when the snow of the year was beginning to fall" CAED 170, DECCA 8, FOLKW 24, LIBC 13, LIBC 53, LIST 4, NACTE 1, NACTE 3, SINGER 1, SPOA 75, THEAL 3, UARIZ 1

SAND DUNES. "Sea waves are green and wet" HARPV 3

THE SECRET SITS. "We dance around in a ring and suppose" CAED 170, CARIL 17

THE SILKEN TENT. "She is as in a field a silken tent" CARIL 17

A SOLDIER. "He is that fallen lance that lies as hurled" CAED 170, DECCA 8, HARPV 3, LIBC 13, LIBC 55

THE SOUND OF TREES. "I wonder about the trees" CARIL 17

SPRING POOLS. "These pools that, though in forests, still reflect" CAED 170, CARIL 17, DECCA 8, EDUC 1, FOLKW 24

THE STAR-SPLITTER. "You know Orion always comes up sideways" CARIL 17

STOPPING BY WOODS ON A SNOWY EVENING. "Whose woods these are I think I know" BRITAM 1, CAED 170, DECCA 8, EDUC 1, FOLKW 24, HARC 2, LIBC 13, LIBC 36, LIBC 51, NACTE 1, NACTE 3, NACTE 13, THEAL 3, NBC 2

STORM FEAR. "When the wind works against us in the dark" FOLKW 24

TREE AT MY WINDOW. "Tree at my window, window tree" BRITAM 1, CAED 42, HARPV 3, NACTE 4

TRIPLE BRONZE. "The Infinite's being is wide" CARIL 17

THE TUFT OF FLOWERS. "I went to turn the grass once after one" CAED 42, FOLKW 24, HOUGHT 3, NACTE 1, NACTE 4

TWO TRAMPS IN MUD TIME. "Out of the mud two strangers came" CAED 170, DECCA 8, HARPV 3, NACTE 1, NACTE 4

———, exc. "You know how it is with an April day" EDUC 1

WEST-RUNNING BROOK. "Fred, where is north?" CAED 42

THE WHITE-TAILED HORNET. "The white-tailed hornet lives in a balloon" NACTE 4

WHY WAIT FOR SCIENCE. "Sarcastic Science, she would like to know" CAED 42, DECCA 8, HARPV 3, LIBC 13, LIBC 53

THE WITCH OF COOS. "I stayed the night for shelter at a farm" CAED 42, LIBC 13, LIBC 47

THE WOOD-PILE. "Out walking in the frozen swamp one gray day" CARIL 17

A YOUNG BIRCH. "The birch begins to crack its outer sheath" CARIL 17

Poetry* JNP 4, LIST 13, MICHM 1, PRENT 2

Frugoni, Francesco Fulvio. 1620. in Italian.
Poetry* CETRA 25

Fry, Harvey. in English.
MORE TO COME. "Winds changing their clothes" WATSHD 8

PART SONG. "Cuttin' mustard" WATSHD 8

THUMBS RULE. "The old gnome" WATSHD 8

Fuertes, Gloria. 1917. in Spanish.
FICHA INGRESO HOSPITAL GENERAL. "Nombre: Antonio Martín Cruz" AGUIL 3

LABRADOR. "Labrador/ ya eres más de la tierra" AGUIL 3

LAS TRES TONTAS. "Por el pueblo ceniza" AGUIL 3

PUESTO DEL RASTRO. "Hornillos eléctricos, brocados, bombillas" AGUIL 3

VENTANAS PINTADAS. "Vivía en una casa" AGUIL 3

Fuld, Nancy. in English.
"Leaves crumple slowly" HARB 3

Fuller, John. in English.
AN EXCHANGE BETWEEN THE FINGERS AND THE TOES. "Fingers. Cramped, you are hardly anything" ARGO 96

Fuller, Roy. 1912. in English.
AMATEUR FILM-MAKING. "A cold, still afternoon: mist gathered under" ARGO 155

THE EMOTION OF FICTION. "Reading a book of tales" ARGO 155

AN ENGLISH EXPLORER. ARGO 155

THE FAMILY CAT. "This cat was bought upon the day" FOLKW 65, JUP 1

FAMILY MATTERS. ARGO 155

THE FINAL WAR. ARGO 155

FLORESTAN TO LEONORA. "Our shadows fall beyond the empty cage" ARGO 98

THE GIRAFFES. "I think before they saw me the giraffes" ARGO 155

IN MEMORY OF MY CAT DOMINO. ARGO 155

MEDITATION. "Now the ambassadors have gone, refusing" LIBC 38

THE MIDDLE OF A WAR. "My photograph already looks historic" ARGO 155

OBITUARY OF R. FULLER. "We note the death, with small regret" ARGO 155

TRANSLATION. "Now that the Barbarians have got as far as Picra" FOLKW 65, JUP 1

YMCA WRITING ROOM. "A map of the world is on the wall" ARGO 155

Poetry* LIST 14

Fuller, Stephany Jean Dawson. See **Stephany.**

Furse, Jill. in English.
CAROL. "Beyond this room daylight is brief" ARGO 82, SPOA 41

Fusinato, Arnaldo. 1817. in Italian.
L'ADDIO A VENEZIA. "E fosco l'aere" CETRA 26

Fyleman, Rose. in English.
THE BIRTHDAY CHILD. "Everything's been different all the day" HARB 1

THE CHILD NEXT DOOR. "The child next door has a wreath" CAED 164

"The Fairies have never a penny to spend" CAED 164

THE GOBLIN. "A Goblin lives in our house" CREAT 1

HAVE YOU WATCHED THE FAIRIES. "Have you watched the fairies when the rain is done" CAED 164

OCTOBER. "The summer is over, the trees are all bare" HARB 4

THE SPRING. "A little mountain spring I found" HARB 4

* Recording not available for analysis

Gabriel y Galán, José María. 1870. in Spanish.
DEL VIEJO EL CONSEJO. "Deja la charla consuelo"
SMC 3

Galdieri, Rocco. 1877. in Italian.
'O CECATO ALLERO. CERTA 29
DUMMENECA. "I' mo, trasenno p' a porta"
CETRA 29
E PE'ME. CETRA 48
LL' OMMO 'E NIENTE. CETRA 29
'A PACE D' 'A CASA. CETRA 29, CETRA 48
'O PREVETE. CETRA 48
SCIAGURATELLA. CETRA 48
SIGNURELLA. CETRA 48

Gale, Norman. in English.
BARTHOLOMEW. "Bartholomew is very sweet"
CAED 164

Gallagher, F. O'Neill. in English.
THE ALL ALONE TREE. "There is a tree that is growing alone" BOWMAR 1

Gallagher, Tess. in English.
THE ABSENCE. "I am writing this out of vengeance" WATSHD 11
THE COATS. "They made you complicated"
WATSHD 11
DISAPPEARANCES IN THE GUARDED SECTOR. "When we stopped" WATSHD 11
LOVE POEM. "I have had to write this down"
WATSHD 11

Gambara, Veronica. 1485. in Italian.
Poetry* CETRA 23

Gan, Peter (Richard Möring). 1894. in German.
PREISLIED AUF EINE SEIFENBLASE. CHRIST 29

Gaos, Vicente. 1919. in Spanish.
EN EL ZOOLOGICO. "Esta mañana he estado en el Zoologico con mi hija" HOLT 1

Garcia Lorca, Federico. 1899. in Spanish.
A IRENE GARCIA. "En el soto" POETAS 2
ADELINA DEL PASEO. "La mar no tiene naranjas"
POETAS 2
AGOSTO. "Agosto/ Contraponientes"
POETAS 2
AIRE DE NOCTURNO. "Tengo mucho miedo/ de las hojas muertas" CAED 44, SMC 4
AL OÍDO DE UNA MUCHACHA. "No quise"
POETAS 2
ALMA AUSENTE. "No te conoce el toro" SMC 4
"Arbolé, arbolé" FOLKW 11, POETAS 2
AY. "El grito deja en el viento" AGUIL 11
BAILA. "La Carmen está bailando" POETAS 2
BAILE POR FARRUCA. SMC 10
BALADA DE UN DIA DE JULIO. "Esquilones de plata llevan los bueyes" SMC 4
BALADA DEL AGUA DEL MAR. "El mar/ sonríe"
POETAS 2
BALADA INTERIOR. "El corazon que tenía en la escuela" SMC 4
BALADA TRISTE. "Mi corazon es una mariposa"
SMC 4
BALADILLA DE LOS TRES RIOS. "El río Guadalquivir" AGUIL 6, AGUIL 11, FOLKW 11, POETAS 2
BODAS DE SANGRE, exc. "Nana, niño, nana"
POETAS 2
BURLA DE DON PEDRO A CABALLO. "Por una vereda/ venía Don Pedro" CAED 44, SMC 4
CANCIÓN. French ADES 10, ADES 45

CANCIÓN CHINA EN EUROPA. "La señorita/ del abanico" AGUIL 11, POETAS 2
CANCIÓN DE BELISA. "Por las orillas del rio"
POETAS 2, VAN 2
CANCIÓN DE JINETE. "Córdoba/ Lejana y sola"
AGUIL 11, CAED 44, FOLKW 11, POETAS 2; French ADES 10, ADES 45
CANCIÓN TONTA. "Mamá/ Yo quiero ser de plata" AGUIL 11, POETAS 2
CANTES DE CÁDIZ. "¡Ole! Viva Cadiz" SMC 10
CANTES DE HUELVA. "Toro negro, toro bravo"
SMC 10
LA CASADA INFIEL. "Y que yo me la llevé a río"
FOLKW 11, POETAS 1, SMC 4, TROPIC 1, VAN 2
CASIDA DE LA ROSA. "La Rosa/ no buscaba"
POETAS 2
CASIDA DE LAS PALOMAS OSCURAS. "Por las ramas del laurel" POETAS 2
CASIDA DE LOS RAMOS. "Por las arboledas del Tamarit" AGUIL 11
CASIDA DEL HERIDO POR EL AGUA. "Quiero bajar al pozo" POETAS 2
CASIDA DEL LLANTO. "He cerrado mibalcon"
SPOA 59, VAN 3
CIUDAD SIN SUEÑO. "No duerme nadie por el cielo" CAED 44
LOS CUATRO MULEROS. "La otra tarde en la Ribera" SMC 10
CUERPO PRESENTE. "La piedra es una frente donde los sueños" SMC 4
DE OTRO MODO. "La hoguera pone al campo"
AGUIL 11, POETAS 2
DESEO. "Sólo tu corazón caliente" SMC 4
DESPEDIDA. "Si muero/ dejad el balcón abierto"
AGUIL 11, POETAS 2
"Despierte la novia" VAN 2
DESPOSORIO. "Tirad ese anillo" AGUIL 11
DOÑA ROSITA LA SOLTERA, exc. "Cuando se abre en la mañana" POETAS 2
———. "Granada, calle de Elvira" POETAS 2
EN EL INSTITUTO Y EN LA UNIVERSIDAD. "La primera vez" POETAS 2
ENCINA. "Bajo tu casta sombra, encina vieja"
CAED 44
LOS ENCUENTROS DE UN CARACOL AVENTURERO. "Hay dulzura infantil" CAED 44, SMC 4
ES VERDAD. "Ay, qué trabajo me cuesta"
AGUIL 4, POETAS 2
ESTE ES EL PRÓLOGO. "Dejaría en este libro"
FOLKW 11
GACELA DE LA HUIDA. "Me he perdido muchas veces" AGUIL 11
GACELA DEL MERCADO MATUTINO. "Por el arco de Elvira" AGUIL 11, POETAS 2
GACELA DEL NIÑO MUERTO. "Todas las tardes en Granada" AGUIL 11
GALÁN. "Galán/ galancillo" POETAS 2
GRÁFICO DE LA PETENERA. "Bordón/ En la torre"
FOLKW 11
EL GRITO. "La elipse de un grito" VAN 2
GRITO HACÍA ROMA. "Manzanas levemente heridas" FOLKW 11
LA GUITARRA. "Empieza el llanto de la guitarra"
POETAS 2, SMC 4, SMC 10, VAN 2

* Recording not available for analysis

Garcia Lorca, Federico (continued)

LA GUITARRA. "Sigue guitarra tocando"
SMC 10

HORA DE ESTRELLAS. "El silencio redondo de la noche"   CAED 44

"El lagarto esta llorando"   POETAS 2

EL LAGARTO VIEJO. "En la angosta senda he visto"   SMC 4

LAMENTACION DE LA MUERTE. "Sobre el cielo negro"   SMC 4

LLANTO POR IGNACIO SÁNCHEZ MEJÍAS. "A las cinco de la tarde" AGUIL 11, FOLKW 11, FOLKW 79, HOLT 1, POETAS 1, SMC 11, VAN 2

LA LOLA. "Bajo el naranjo lava"   POETAS 2

LA LUNA Y LA MUERTE. "La luna tiene dientes de marfil"   SMC 4

MADRIGAL. "Yo te miré a los ojos"   SMC 4

MAÑANA. "Y la canción del agua"   CAED 44

MARIANA PINEDA, I., exc. "En la corrida más grande"   POETAS 2

———— II., exc. "Torrijos, el general"
POETAS 2

MARTIRIO DE SANTA OLALLA. "Por la calle brinca y corre"   POETAS 1

MEMENTO. "Gran Serrano"   SMC 10

MEMENTO. "Cuando yo me muera" AGUIL 11 French ADES 10, ADES 45

"Mi niña se fue a la mar"   POETAS 2

LA MONJA GITANA. "Silencio de cal y mirto"
FOLKW 11, POETAS 1

LAS MORILLAS DE JAÉN. "Tres moricas me enamoran"   VAN 2

MUERTE DE ANTOÑITO EL CAMBORIO. "Voces de muerte sonaron"   FOLKW 11, POETAS 1, VAN 2

MUERTE DE LA PETENERA. "En la casa blanca muere"   POETAS 2

MUERTO DE AMOR. "Qué es aquello que reluce" French ADES 10, ADES 45, CAED 44, FOLKW 11, POETAS 1

NARCISO. "Niño. Que te vas a caer al río"
CAED 44

NIÑA AHOGADA EN EL POZO. "Las estatuas sufren por los ojos con la oscuridad de los ataúdes"
AGUIL 11

NOVIEMBRE. "Todos los ojos estaban abiertos"
SMC 4

ODA A WALT WHITMAN. "Por el East River y el Bronx"   CAED 44, FOLKW 11

PAISAJE. "El campo/ de olivos"   FOLKW 11

PAISAJE. "Las estrellas apagadas llenan de ceníza"   SMC 4

EL PASO DE LA SIGUIRIYA. "Entre mariposas negras"   POETAS 2

PEQUEÑO VALS VIENÉS. "En Viena hay diez muchachas"   CAED 44

POEMA DE LA SAETE. "Los arqueros oscuros"
AGUIL 11

POEMA DE LA SOLEA. "Tierra seca/ tierra quieta"
AGUIL 11, POETAS 2

PRECIOSA Y EL AIRE. "Su luna de pergamino"
FOLKW 11, POETAS 1, SMC 11, TROPIC 1

PRENDIMIENTO DE ANTOÑITO EL CAMBORIO EN EL CAMINO DE SEVILLA. "Antonio Torres Heredia"   AGUIL 11, CAED 44, FOLKW 11, POETAS 1, SMC 11, VAN 2

EL PRESENTIMIENTO. "El presentimiento es la senda del alma"   SMC 4

PUEBLO. "Sobre el monte pelado"   AGUIL 11

QUE BONITA ES MI NIÑA. "Ayer tarde yo cantaba"
SMC 10

REMANSILLO. "Me miré en tus ojos"
POETAS 2

REMANSO. "Ya viene la noche"   POETAS 2

REYERTA. "En la mitad del barranco"
FOLKW 11, POETAS 1, SMC 11

ROMANCE DE DON PEDRO Á CABALLO. "Por una vereda"   FOLKW 11

ROMANCE DE LA GUARDIA CIVIL ESPANOLA. "Los caballos negros son"   FOLKW 11, POETAS 1, VAN 2

ROMANCE DE LA LUNA LUNA. "La luna vino a la fragua"   CAED 44, DOVER 2, FOLKW 11, HOLT 1, POETAS 1, SMC 11

ROMANCE DE LA PENA NEGRA. "Las piquetas de los gallos"   CAED 44, FOLKW 11, POETAS 1, SMC 4, VAN 3

ROMANCE DEL EMPLAZADO. "Mi soledad sin descanso" CAED 44, FOLKW 11, POETAS 1, SMC 4

ROMANCE SONÁMBULO. "Verde que te quiero verde" CAED 44, FOLKW 11, POETAS 1, SMC 11, SPOA 59, TROPIC 1

SAETE. "Cristo moreno"   FOLKW 11

SAN GABRIEL. "Un bello niño de junco"
FOLKW 11, POETAS 1

SAN MIGUEL, GRANADA. "Se ven desde las barandas"   FOLKW 11

SAN RAFAEL, CÓRDOBA. "Coches cerrados llegaban"   FOLKW 11

LA SANGRE DERRAMADA. "Que no quiero verla"
SMC 11

SEGUNDA LUGUNA. "Bajo el agua"   FOLKW 11

LAS SEIS CUERDAS. "Ti-ri-ti-ri, Ay!"   SMC 10

SEVILLA. "Sevilla es una torre"   AGUIL 11

EL SILENCIO. "Oye, hijo mío, el silencio"
VAN 2

LA SOLEA. "Vestida con mantos negros"
SMC 10

LA SOMBRA DE MI ALMA. "La sombra de mi alma huye por un ocaso"   CAED 44, SMC 4

SORPRESA. "Muerte se quedó en la calle"
POETAS 2

SONETO.   French ADES 10

SONETO. "Tengo miedo a perder la maravilla"
French ADES 45, AGUIL 11

SUEÑO. "Iba yo montado sobre un macho cabrío"   SMC 4

SUEÑO. "Mi corazón reposa junto á la fuente fria"   POETAS 2

SUSTO EN EL COMEDOR. "Eras rosa" POETAS 2

TARDE. "Tarde lluviosa en gris"   SMC

THAMÁR Y AMNÓN. "La luna gira en el cielo" French ADES 10, ADES 45, FOLKW 11, SMC

LAS TRES HOJAS. "Debajo de la hoja"   VAN

TRES RIOS. "El río Guadalquivir va"   SMC 10

* Recording not available for analysis

TRES ROMANCES HISTÓRICOS. I. PANORAMA DE MÉRI-
DA. "Por la calle brinca y corre"
                                    FOLKW 11
————. II. EL MARTIRIO. "Flora desnuda se sube"
                                    FOLKW 11
————. III. INFIERNO Y GLORIA. "Nieve ondulada
reposa"   FOLKW 11
VALS EN LAS RAMAS. "Cayó una hoja"
                                    CAED 44
VERLAINE. "La canción/ que nunca dire"
                       French ADES 10, ADES 45
VOISINE, AVEC UN COUTEAU.   French ADES 10,
                                    ADES 45
ZAPATEADO.   SMC 10
ZAPATERA. "La señora Zapatera"   VAN 2
LA ZAPATERA PRODIGIOSA, ACTO 2, exc. "Caballos
de emperadora"   POETAS 2
ZORONGO. "Las manos de mi cariño"   SMC 10
ZORONGO GITANO. "La luna es un pozo chico"
                                    SMC 10

García Nieto, José. 1914. in Spanish.
DIÓS EN LA TARDE. "Como cuando era niño, Dios
parece"   AGUIL 3
EL HACEDOR. "Entra en la playa de oro el mar y
llena"   AGUIL 3
LA PARTIDA. "Contigo, mano a mano. Y no reti-
ro"   AGUIL 3
TODAVIA EN SILENCIO. "Te han nacido los ojos"
                                    AGUIL 3

García Tudurí, Mercedes. 1903. in Spanish.
SINTESIS. "Palma: mástil de amarre" SMC 13

Gardner, Isabella Stewart. 1915. in English.
SUMMER REMEMBERED. "Sounds sum and sum-
mon the remembering summers"   EMC 7
Poetry*   JNP 14, JNP 15

Garelick, Barry. in English.
Poetry*   WATSHD 14

Garfinkel, Pat. in English.
NIGHT SOUND. "I woke from the warm"
                                    WATSHD 8
PALM-READING. "In the transparency of this
hand"   WATSHD 8
QUEEN OF HAIR. "You are the Queen of Hair"
                                    WATSHD 8

Garland, Hamlin. 1860. in English.
DO YOU FEAR THE WIND. "Do you fear the force
of the wind"   CAED 169

Garlick, Raymond. 1926. in English.
ACADEMIC OVERTURE.   ARGO 141
AGINCOURT.   ARGO 141
ANCESTORS.   ARGO 141
AUGUST COUNTRY.   ARGO 141
CAPITALS.   ARGO 141
DIRECTIONS FOR VISITORS.   ARGO 141
EXPLANATORY NOTE.   ARGO 141
IEUAN AP HYWEL SWRDWAL.   ARGO 141
THE IMMORTALS.   ARGO 141
JUDGEMENT DAY.   ARGO 141
MATTERS ARISING. "No doubt what you say is
right"   ARGO 141
NOTE ON THE ILIAD. "Why are epics"
                                    ARGO 141
RECONCILIATION.   ARGO 141
SAUNDERS LEWIS AT NEWTOWN.   ARGO 141
SHALOM.   ARGO 141
SPORTING PRINT.   ARGO 141

STILL LIFE. "A piece of forest"   ARGO 141
TENBY. "In winter"   SPOA 68
TRAETH LLANSTEFFAN.   ARGO 141
VIEW FROM LLANSTEFFAN.   ARGO 141
WATERLOO. "Waterloo? We went once"
                                    ARGO 141

Garnier, Robert. 1534. in French.
ÉLEGIE SUR LA MORT DE RONSARD, exc. "Que ne
ressemblons-nous aux vagueuses rivières"
                                    PERIOD 2

Garrigue, Jean. 1914. in English.
CATCH WHAT YOU CAN. "The thing to do is to try
for that sweet skin"   SPOA 101
FOREST. "There is the star bloom of the moss"
                                    LIBC 40
"I sought from love what no love gives"
                                    SPOA 101
INVITATION TO A HAY. "A settlement of love is
what I'd risk"   SPOA 101
NOTES FROM UNDERGROUND. "That's enough I
said to the"   SPOA 101
THE STRANGER. "Now upon this piteous year"
                                    LIBC 40
Poetry*   JNP 16, LIST 15

Gascoigne, George. 1525. in English.
A FAREWELL. "And if I did, what then?"
                                    SPOA 50

Gascoyne, David. 1916. in English.
WINTER GARDEN. "The season's anguish, crashing whirlwind"   HBCF 1

Gasztold, Carmen Bernos de. in French.
THE PRAYER OF THE BUTTERFLY. "Lord!/Where
was I"   English HARB 6
THE PRAYER OF THE DOG. "Lord/I keep watch"
                            English HARB 6
THE PRAYER OF THE LITTLE DUCKS. "Dear God/
give us a flood"   English HARB 6

Gatto, Alfonso. 1909. in Italian.
A UNO STRANIERO. "Se voi sapeste, l'Italia"
                                    APPL 4
UN ALBA AL DUOMO DI ANCONA. "Fu allo svegliar-
mi dal sonno con l'aria di vivere" APPL 4
ALLA MIA TERRA. "Io so che nulla potra"
                                    APPL 4
AMORE DELLA VITA. "Io vedo i grandi alberi
della sera"   APPL 4
ANNIVERSARIO. "Io ricordo quei giorni: nell' ig-
noto"   APPL 4
DOMANI. "Che senso, dimmi, ha il numero degli
anni"   APPL 4
FORSE MI LASCERÁ DEL TUO BEL VOLTO. "Forse mi
lascera"   APPL 4
UNA NOTTE. "Questa, delle mie mani, della
voce"   APPL 4
POTREBBERO DIRTI MORTA. "I tuoi occhi son
come la giovinezza"   APPL 4
RICORDAMI COSI. "Mi chiedi come ho potuto
vivere pensando sempre alla morte"
                                    APPL 4
SERA DI PUGLIA. "Il bimbo d'afa che la mosca
nera"   APPL 4
"Torneranno le sere"   APPL 4
VIVI. "Una casa da nulla, ma ragazza alle per-
siane"   APPL 4
Poetry*   CETRA 46

* Recording not available for analysis

Gautier, Théophile. 1811. in French.
A ZURBARAN. "Moines de Zurbaran, blancs char-
treux"   ADES 54
CARMEN. "Carmen est maigre- un trait de bis-
tre"   CAED 204
DANS LA SIERRA.   CAED 204
PAYSAGE NOCTURNE.   GMS 6
Gaver, Chasen. in English.
AH-WHOO-AH. "Ah-whoo-ah"   WATSHD 34
AU REVOIR. "Good bye"   WATSHD 34
LA BOHÈME. "Attention, attention"
                                          WATSHD 34
D. C. HEAT. "Hotsa"   WATSHD 14,
                                          WATSHD 34
DADDY! "Di-da-di-da, Daddy"   WATSHD 34
DIANA ROSS DOES NOT SING IN THIS MOVIE. "Diana
Ross Diana yes does not sing"
                                          WATSHD 34
DISCO. "Pu another nickel in"   WATSHD 14,
                                          WATSHD 34
DO YOU DELIVER. "Hello, I'd like to place my or-
der"   WATSHD 34
THE EGO MEDIATES. "I'm hot"   WATSHD 34
GIRLS KNOW HOW TO LOSE. "Girls know how to
lose alright"   WATSHD 34
"Give the dancers castanets"   WATSHD 14
IMP/ERFECT. "Watch, she said"   WATSHD 34
ITALY. "All roads lead to Sicily" WATSHD 34
LACED WITH CHASEN. "A man helped me choose
it"   WATSHD 34
LIFE UNDER MY UMBRELLA. "The fleece of the
sacrificed lamb"   WATSHD 34
LITTLE SISTER BIG. "Some times you know"
                                          WATSHD 34
MA' CHEER. "Shum, shum, bang, bang"
                                          WATSHD 34
MAN AS (EVERYTHING BUT) MAN. "Man as gift, man
as lift"   WATSHD 14, WATSHD 34
MY NEW YORK STARS. "My New York stars can't
help it"   WATSHD 8, WATSHD 34
NOW THAT A. LOOKS LIKE AN ARTIST. "Now that A.
looks like an artist"   WATSHD 8
PERFORMANCE POETS. "Jingle cell, jingle cell"
                                          WATSHD 34
PHILADELPHIA. "My face has not been washed"
                                          WATSHD 34
RAMA RAMA. "Memorize the rhythms"
                                          WATSHD 34
RECENT WHITE HOUSE TOUR. "We enter the
Roosevelt room"   WATSHD 34
SONIDO RICO. "In the land of nunca nunca"
                                          WATSHD 34
SOUNDS. "Zzzip"   WATSHD 34
STRAIGHT TO HELL. "Face to face"
                                          WATSHD 34
WHO. "And all along the avenues"
                     WATSHD 14, WATSHD 34
WHO AM I? "Sex. I am the unlicked spickum"
                                          WATSHD 34
"Yousa yousa"   WATSHD 34
Gay, John. 1688. in English.
ACIS AND GALATEA, AIR. "Love in her eyes sits
playing"   ARGO 47, CAED 203
———, AIR. "O ruddier than the cherry"
                                          CAED 203
BEGGAR'S OPERA. AIR XXXV. "How happy could I
be"   CAED 203

HIS OWN EPITAPH. "Life is a jest; and all thing
show it"   CAED 20
MR. POPE'S WELCOME FROM GREECE. "Long has
thou, friend! been absent from thy soil"
                                          ARGO 4
POLLY. AIR XXIII. "Sleep, O sleep" CAED 20
WHAT D'YE CALL IT, BALLAD. "'Twas when th
seas were roaring"   CAED 20
Gay, Zhenya. 1906. in English.
"Night things are soft and loud"   HARB
Gee, Lethonia. in English.
Poetry*   PRENT
Geijer, Erik Gustaf. 1783. in Swedish.
DEN LILLA KOLARGOSSEN. "I skogen vid mila
sitter far"   GRAM
Geller, Richard. in English.
Poetry*   JNP 1
Gellert, Christian Fürchtegott. 1715. in Germa
EHSTANDSSEGEN.   ATHENA
Gemmingen, Eberhard Friedrich von. 1726. i
German.
DAS SCHWEIGEN. "Ernsthafte Gottheit, heilige
Schweigen"   DEUTGR 1
Genser, Cynthia. 1950. in English.
CLUB 82: LISA. "They're dancing" WATSHD
DEUTERONOMY AND THE SIX O'CLOCK KID.
                                          WATSHD 1
FOR THE GREEKS. "Me too, I'm crying for th
Greeks"   WATSHD 1
O MIAMI. "O Miami, I remember you"
                                          WATSHD
SHOWDOWN. "Retain logos"   WATSHD
George, Stefan. 1868. in German.
DU SCHLANK UND REIN WIE EINE FLAMME. "D
schlank und rein wie eine Flamme"
                         CHRIST 24, DOVER
"Gemahnt dich noch das schöne Bildnis des
en"   CHRIST 2
DER HERR DER INSEL. "Die Fischer überliefern
                                          DOVER
Der Hügel wo wir wandeln liegt im Schatten
                                          CHRIST 2
"Komm in den todgesagten Park und schau'
                                          DOVER
"Nun lass mich rufen über die verschneiten
Gefilde"   CHRIST 2
DIE TOTE STADT. "Die weite Bucht erfüllt de
neue Hafen"   CHRIST 2
DIE UNTERGEHENDEN. "Sie rühmen sich ihre
dreifachen Verderbtheit"   CHRIST 2
WIR SCHREITEN AUF UND AB. "Wir schreiten a
und ab im reichen Flitter"   CHRIST 2
Poetry*   CHRIST
Geraldy, Paul. 1885. in French.
ABAT-JOUR. "Tu demandes pourquoi je reste sar
rien dire"   GMS
APAISEMENT. "Cherie, on s'est encore tres m
quittes"   GMS
AVEU. "Je sais qu'irritable, exigeant et morose
                                          GMS
BRUIT DE VOIX. "Tu as eu tort! Tu as eu tort!
te repète"   GMS
CHANCE. "Et pourtant, nous pouvions ne jama
nous connaitre"   GMS
DUALISME. "Chérie, explique-moi pourquoi"
                                          GMS

* Recording not available for analysis

EXPANSION. "Ah! je vous aime! je vous aime!"
GMS 1

FINALE. "Alors, adieu. Tu n'oublies rien"
GMS 1

LETTRE. "Ah! ma chérie, que ce sera long! Tout un mois" GMS 1

PIANO. "Mon amour, j'ai fait pout toi" GMS 1

SAGESSE. "Ne soyons pas trop exigeants"
GMS 1

STEREOSCOPE. "Je ne veux les voir. Emporte ces clichés" GMS 1

TOI ET MOI (exc.) GMS 1, VOIX 1

TRISTESSE. "Ton passé! car tu as un passé, toi aussi" GMS 1

VOUS QUI PASSEZ. VOIX 2A

Poetry* VOIX 2

Gerhardt, Paul. 1607. in German.
"Geh' aus mein Herz und suche Freud'"
ATHENA 12

"Ich bin ein Gast auf Erden" ATHENA 12

"Nun lasst uns gehn und treten"
ATHENA 12

"Nun ruhen alle Wälder" ATHENA 12

PASSIONSLIED. "O Haupt voll Blut und Wunden" CHRIST 18

TROSTGESANG. "Noch dennoch musst du drum nicht ganz" ATHENA 12

Poetry* CHRIST 4

Ghose, Zulfikar. 1935. in English.
COMING TO ENGLAND. "My father moved out"
SPOA 68

Giacomo, Salvatore di. See **Di Giacomo, Salvatore.**

Giàcomo da Lentini. 12th c. in Italian.
Poetry* CETRA 19

Gianni degli Alfani. 1271. in Italian.
Poetry* CETRA 19, CETRA 36

Gibson, Margaret. 1944. in English.
THE GARDEN. "Snow seeds the air"
WATSHD 5

Gibson, Wilfred. 1878. in English.
FLANNAN ISLE. "Though three men dwell on Flannan Isle" SINGER 3

NORTHUMBRIAN DUET. ARGO 139

THE PARROTS. "Somewhere, somewhere I've seen" CAED 111

Gide, André. 1869. in French.
POLITIQUE. ADES 31

PORTRAITS. ADES 31

LE SCANDALE. ADES 31

Giguere, Roland. 1929. in French.
LES HEURES LENTES. "On tourne pesamment la tête" FOLKW 70

MORNE GLEBE. "Air aigu des soirs de hurlement" FOLKW 70

LA NUIT HUMILIÉE. "Il fait jour sans nuage cette fois" FOLKW 70

ROSES ET RONCES. "Rosace rosace les roses"
FOLKW 70

Gilbert, Celia. in English.
THE BIRD. "It was a bird" WATSHD 7

BIRTHDAY POEM. "Alone now, and most certainly" WATSHD 7

THE GOD IN US WISHES TO LIVE. "Beautiful goldfish" WATSHD 7

LIFE AND DEATH OF HERO STICK. "God he had gone off" WATSHD 7

MADAME CARNELIA DOES SOLEMNLY SWEAR TO FULFILL EVERY CLAIM SHE MAKES. "Madame Carnelia in the dark room" WATSHD 7

WE ARE. "You are/ the kitchen sink"
WATSHD 7

Gilbert, Dorothy. in English.
AT THE BROOKLYN DOCKS NOVEMBER 23, 1963. "In the morning air, the freighter Havskar"
FOLKW 21

Gilbert, Nicolas-Joseph. 1751. in French.
ADIEUX À LA VIE. SPOA 88

Gilbert, Sir William Schwenck. 1836. in English.
THE APE AND THE LADY. CAED 65

BABETTE'S LOVE. "Babette she was a fisher gal"
CAED 65

BEN ALLAH ACHMET, OR THE FATAL TUM. "I once did know a Turkish man" CAED 65

GENERAL JOHN. "The bravest names for fire and flames" DECCA 11

H.M.S. PINAFORE. SONG. "When I was a lad"
LIST 22

IOLANTHE, exc. "When you're lying awake with a dismal headache" LONGM 1

LITTLE BILLEE. ARGO 125

THE MIKADO. SONG: I'VE GOT A LITTLE LIST. "As some day it may happen that a victim must be found" HARC 2

PETER THE WAG. "Policeman Peter forth I drag"
CAED 65

PHRENOLOGY. "Come, collar this bad man"
CAED 65

THE PIRATES OF PENZANCE. THE POLICEMAN'S SONG. "When a felon's not engaged in his employment" HARC 2

THE SENSATION CAPTAIN. "No nobler captain ever trod" CAED 65

THE YARN OF THE 'NANCY BELL'. "Twas on the shores that round our coast" CAED 65, FOLKW 67

THE YEOMEN OF THE GUARD. SONG. "I have a song to sing" CMS 4

Gill, John. in English.
AT NINETY-TWO. "At ninety-two he weakened a bit" WATSHD 2

BEFORE THE THAW. "Have you seen me at all"
WATSHD 2

HYMN TO WINTER SPARROWS. "May your body lice" WATSHD 2

IN THE BIG WORLD. "In the big world this is of no consequence" WATSHD 2

Ginsberg, Allen. 1926. in English.
AMERICA. "America I've given you all and now"
FANT 3

AUTO POESY TO NEBRASKA. "Turn right next corner" BROADR 3

CAFE IN WARSAW. "These spectres resting on plastic stools" APPL 2

CIA DOPE CALYPSO. "In nineteen hundred and forty five" WATSHD 11

DON'T GROW OLD. "O poet, poetry is fine old subject" WATSHD 11

EUROPE, EUROPE. FANT 3

FATHER DEATH BLUES. "Hey, Father Death"
WATSHD 11

FIRST PARTY AT KEN KESEY'S WITH HELL'S ANGELS. "Cool black night thru the red woods"
APPL 2

* Recording not available for analysis

Ginsberg, Allen (continued)

FOOTNOTE TO HOWL.   FANT 3
THE GURU. "I can't find anyone to show me"
                                     NET 1
HOWL. PART 1. "I saw the best minds of my gen-
    eration"   EVERG 1, FANT 3
_____. exc.   NET 1
IN BACK OF THE REAL.   FANT 3
JULY 9, 1976, ON ARRIVING HOME. "Near the scrap-
    yard"   WATSHD 11
KADDISH. "Strange now to think of you, gone
    without corsets"   FANT 3
LAY DOWN. "Lay down"   WATSHD 11
MESSAGE II. "Long since the years"   APPL 2
NEW YORK TO SAN FRAN. "And the place bobs"
                                     NET 1
PORTLAND COLISEUM. "A brown piano in dia-
    mond"   APPL 2
QUESTION OF FREEDOM.   COLUMB 14
SMALL SPOLETO MANTRA. "Since poetry is made
    of language, let's make language move"
                                     APPL 2
STRANGE NEW COTTAGE IN BERKELEY.   FANT 3
THE SUNFLOWER SUTRA. "I walked on the banks
    of the tincan banana dock"   FANT 3
A SUPERMARKET IN CALIFORNIA. "What thoughts I
    have"   FANT 3
TO THE BODY. "Enthroned in plastic, shrouded
    in wool"   APPL 2
TRANSCRIPTION OF ORGAN MUSIC.   FANT 3
UPTOWN NEW YORK CITY. "Yellow-lit Budweiser
    signs over oaken bars" APPL 2, SPOA 105
WHO TO BE KIND TO. "Be kind to your self, it is
    only one and perishable"   APPL 2,
                             SPOA 105, NET 1
Poetry*   BIGSUR 1, CASSC 8, PRENT 3,
                         UCAL 3, UCALM 2

Giorno, John. 1936. in English.
EVERYONE IS A COMPLETE DISAPPOINTMENT.
                                   GIORNO 1

Gioseffi, Daniela. 1941. in English.
EGGS. "Eggs that come from chickens"
                                  WATSHD 4
PEACE PROSPECT. "Too many people scribbling"
                                  WATSHD 4
THE VASES OF WOMBS. "For a long time"
                                  WATSHD 4

Giovanni, Domenico di. See Burchiello.
Giovanni, Nikki. 1943. in English.
ADULTHOOD II. "There is always something"
                                 FOLKW 109
AFRICA II. "Africa is a young man bathing"
                                  NIKTOM 1
AGE. "We tend to fear old age"   FOLKW 109
ALWAYS THERE ARE THE CHILDREN. "And always
    there are the children"   FOLKW 108
BEAUTIFUL BLACK MAN. "I want to say"
                                 FOLKW 108
BECAUSE. "I wrote a poem"   FOLKW 109
THE BEEP BEEP POEM. "I should write a poem"
                                 FOLKW 109
BEING AND NOTHINGNESS. "I haven't done any-
    thing"   FOLKW 109
BOXES. "I am in a box"   FOLKW 109
CATEGORIES. "Sometimes you hear a question"
                                 FOLKW 108

CHOICES. "If I can't do"   FOLKW 109
COMMUNICATION. "If music is the universal lan-
    guage"   NIKTOM 1
CONVERSATION. "Yeah, she said, my man's gone
    too"   FOLKW 108, NIKTOM 1
COTTON CANDY ON A RAINY DAY. "Don't look
    now"   FOLKW 109
CRUTCHES. "It's not the crutches we decry"
                                 FOLKW 109
THE DECEMBER OF MY SPRINGS. "In the Decem-
    ber of my Springs"   FOLKW 108
DREAMS. "In my younger years"   FOLKW 108
"Everytime it rains"   FOLKW 108
FASCINATIONS. "Finding myself still fascinated"
                                 FOLKW 109
FORCED RETIREMENT. "All problems being"
                                 FOLKW 109
THE GENI IN THE JAR. "Take a note"
                                 FOLKW 108
GUS. "He always had pretty legs"
                                 FOLKW 109
HABITS. "I haven't written a poem in so long"
                                 FOLKW 109
HOUSECLEANING. "I always liked housecleaning"
                                 FOLKW 108
"How do you write a poem"   FOLKW 108
INTROSPECTION. "She didn't like to think in ab-
    stracts"   FOLKW 109
LEGACIES. "Her Grandmother called her"
                       FOLKW 108, NIKTOM 1
LIFE CYCLES. "She realized"   FOLKW 109
THE LIFE I LED. "I know my upper arms"
                                 FOLKW 108
LIKE A RIPPLE IN A POND.   NIKTOM 1
MAKE UP. "We make up our faces"
                                 FOLKW 109
THE MOON SHINES DOWN. "The moon shines
    down"   FOLKW 109
MOTHERS. "The last time I was home"
                       FOLKW 108, NIKTOM 1
MOTHER'S HABITS. "I have all my mother's hab-
    its"   FOLKW 108
MY HOUSE. "I only want to"   NIKTOM 1
THE NEW YORKERS. "In front of the bank build-
    ing"   FOLKW 109
NIKKI ROSA. "Childhood remembrances"
                                 FOLKW 108
ONCE A LADY TOLD ME. "Like my mother"
                                 FOLKW 108
PATIENCE. "There are sounds"   FOLKW 109
PHOTOGRAPHY. "The eye we are told"
                                 FOLKW 108
POEM. "I have considered"   FOLKW 108
A POEM FOR ED AND ARCHIE. "I dreamed of you
    last night"   FOLKW 108
POEM (FOR EMA). "Though I do wonder"
                                 FOLKW 108
POEM (FOR NINA). "We are all imprisoned"
                                 FOLKW 108
A POEM OF FRIENDSHIP. "We are not lovers"
                                 FOLKW 108
A POEM OFF CENTER. "How do poets write"
                                 FOLKW 108
PRISON POEM.   NIKTOM
A RESPONSE. "You say I'm as cold"
                                 FOLKW 108

THE ROSE BUSH. "I know I haven't grown but" FOLKW 109

SCRAPBOOKS. "It's funny that smells and sound return" FOLKW 108, NIKTOM 1

SPACE. "A flying saucer landed" FOLKW 109

A STATEMENT ON CONSERVATION. "Scarcity in oil and gas" FOLKW 109

STRAIGHT TALK. "I'm giving up" NIKTOM 1

THAT DAY. "If you've got the key" FOLKW 109

THEIR FATHERS. "I will be bitter" FOLKW 109

TURNING (I NEED A BETTER TITLE). "She often wondered why people spoke" FOLKW 109

WINTER. "Frogs burrow the mud" FOLKW 109

THE WINTER STORM. "Somewhere there was a piano playing" FOLKW 109

WOMAN. "She wanted to be a blade" FOLKW 109

"The women gather" FOLKW 108

"The world is not a pleasant place to be" FOLKW 108

YOU ARE THERE. "I shall save my poems" FOLKW 109

Girondo, Oliverio. 1891. in Spanish.

VISITA. "No estoy/ No la conosco" AGUIL 9

Gitlin, Todd. 1943. in English.

ALIENS. "Reminder: January is the month" WATSHD 1

SLOW SONG IN THE DARK. "Who now is watching" WATSHD 1

Gittings, Robert. 1911. in English.

A DAUGHTER. PROTHM 8

SENILE. PROTHM 8

Giusti, Giuseppe. 1809. in Italian.

BRINDISI DI GIRELLA. "Girella (emerito" CETRA 26

IL DELENDA DA CARTAGO. "E perche paga Vostra Signoria" CETRA 26

IL RE TRAVICELLO "Al Re Travicello" CETRA 26

SANT' AMBROGIO. "Vostra Eccellenza che mi sta in cagnesco" CETRA 26

Poetry* CETRA 27

Giustinàn, Leonardo. 1388. in Italian.

Poetry* CETRA 21

Glaze, Andrew. 1920. in English.

BOOK BURIAL. POSEID 1

EARL. "He was twenty. He was half crazy" POSEID 1

GEORGE WASHINGTON'S MUD. "It's a great comfort to know" POSEID 1

I WANT TO HAVE BEEN THE SHAMAN. POSEID 1

JOY GOES DEEP. POSEID 1

NEW MAN. "I'm going to be a new man at once next year" POSEID 1

SUM. POSEID 1

THE TRASH DRAGON OF SHENSI. POSEID 1

WHAT'S THAT YOU SAY, CESAR? POSEID 1

ZEPPELIN. "Some one has built a dirigible in my parlor" POSEID 1

Gleason, Maud. in English.

"A spark in the sun" HARB 3

"How cool cut hay smells" HARB 3

"Over the meadows" HARB 3

"We rode into the fog" HARB 3

Gleim, Johann Wilhelm Ludwig. 1719. in German.

AN DEN MOND. "Du schienest, sagt man, lieber Mond" CHRIST 11

Glover, Denis. 1912. in English.

ARAWATA BILL. KIWI 4

MICK STIMSON. KIWI 4

SINGS HARRY. KIWI 4

Göckingk, Leopold Friedrich Günther von. 1748. in German.

ALS DER ERSTE SCHNEE FIEL. "Gleich einem König" DEUTGR 13

AN MEINE FREUNDE. "Hört ihr einst, ich sei gestorben" DEUTGR 13

JUGEND-ERINNERUNGEN. "O du Garten, wo als Knaben" DEUTGR 13

Godoy, Tamara. in Spanish.

COPAIA PU, exc. "Ven, levantate hija, dijo mi viejo padre" APPL 6

CORAZON, VIEJO INDIO. "Corazon, viejo Indio ya no estes" APPL 6

"Eres de un material al que nadie poso nombre" APPL 6

MONUMENTO MORTUORIO A LA MUERTE DE NACI-NICMED. "Nacinicmed ha muerto—ha muerto" APPL 6

NADIE ES TANTO TU. "Nadie es tanto tu, nadie, cuando me amas" APPL 6

Goethe, Johann Wolfgang von. 1749. in German.

AM BRUNNEN. DEUTGR 12

AN BELINDEN. "Warum ziehst du mich unwiderstehlich" DEUTGR 21

AN CHARLOTTE VON STEIN. DEUTGR 21

AN DEN ABEND. CHRIST 11

AN DEN MOND. "Füllest wieder Busch und Tal" ATHENA 10, DEUTGR 7, DEUTGR 21, SPOA 5, TELEF 4

AN SCHWAGER KRONOS. "Spute dich, Kronos" DEUTGR 20

AUF DEM SEE. "Und frische Nahrung, neues Blut" ATHENA 10, DEUTGR 7, DEUTGR 21

AUSSÖHNUNG. "Die Leidenschaft bringt Leiden" CHRIST 26, DEUTGR 21

BEHERZIGUNG. "Feiger Gedanken" SPOA 5

BEI BETRACHTUNG VON SCHILLERS SCHÄDEL. "Im ernsten Beinhaus wars wo ich beschaute" CHRIST 26

DIE BRAUT VON KORINTH. "Nach Korinthus von Athen" FOLKW 74

DER BRÄUTIGAM. "Um Mitternacht, ich schlief, im Busen wachte" CHRIST 26

CHINESISCH-DEUTSCHE TAGES-UND JAHRESZEITEN. "Sag', was könnt' uns Mandarinen" CHRIST 26

DAUER IM WECHSEL. "Hielte diesen frühen Segen" DEUTGR 7

DEM AUFGEHENDEN VOLLMOND. "Willst du mein sogleich verlassen" CHRIST 11, CHRIST 26

EINS UND ALLES. "Im Grenzenlosen sich zu finden" CHRIST 26

ELEGIE. "Was soll ich nun vom Widersehen hoffen" CHRIST 26, DEUTGR 21

DER ERLKÖNIG. "Wer reitet so spät durch Nacht und Wind" ATHENA 1, DEUTGR 20, FOLKW 74, SPOA 5, SPOA 126

* Recording not available for analysis

Goethe, Johann Wolfgang von (continued)

EUPHROSYNE. "Auch von des höchsten Gebirgs beeisten zackigen Gipfeln" CHRIST 25

DER FISCHER. "Das Wasser rauscht', das Wasser schwoll" DEUTGR 20, FOLKW 74, SPOA 126

"Früh, wenn Tal, Gebirg und Garten" CHRIST 26

GANYMED. "Wie im Morgenglanze du rings mich anglühst" CAED 47, DEUTGR 20

GEFUNDEN. "Ich ging im Walde so für mich hin" ATHENA 10, DOVER 1

"Geh! gehorche meinem Winken" DEUTGR 7

GEHEIMES. "Über meines Liebchens Äugeln" CAED 47

GEISTES GRUSS. "Hoch auf dem alten Turme steht" DEUTGR 20

GESANG DER GEISTER ÜBER DEN WASSERN. "Des Menschen Seele" ATHENA 10, DEUTGR 7, DEUTGR 21, DOVER 1

GEWOHNT, GETAN. "Ich habe geliebet; nun lieb ich erst recht" DEUTGR 7

DER GOTT UND DIE BAJADERE. "Mahadöh, der Herr der Erde" CHRIST 22, TELEF 4

DAS GÖTTLICHE. "Edel sei der Mensch" ATHENA 10, DEUTGR 21

GRENZEN DER MENSCHHEIT. "Wenn der uralte" ATHENA 10, DEUTGR 21

GRETCHENS LIED. "Meine Ruh ist hin" SPOA 126

HARZREISE IM WINTER. "Dem Geier gleich" DEUTGR 21

HEIDENRÖSLEIN. "Sah' ein Knab' ein Röslein stehn" SPOA 5

HERBSTGEFÜHL. "Fetter grüne, du Laub" DEUTGR 21

HOCHZEITSLIED. "Wir singen und sagen vom Grafen so gern" DEUTGR 20

JÄGERS ABENDLIED. "Im Felde schleich ich still und wild" DEUTGR 7, DEUTGR 21

KLÄRCHENS LIED. "Freudvoll und leidvoll" SPOA 126

DER KÖNIG IN THULE. "Es war ein König in Thule" CHRIST 15, DEUTGR 20, FOLKW 74, SPOA 5; French GMS 6

KÜNSTLERS ABENDLIED. "O dass die innre Schöpfungskraft" DEUTGR 21

MAHOMETS-GESANG. "Seht den Felsenquell" DEUTGR 20

MAILIED. "Wie herrlich leuchtet" DEUTGR 20, SCHOL 6, SPOA 126

MIGNONS LIED. "Kennst du das Land wo die Zitronen blühn" CAED 47, CHRIST 19, DEUTGR 22, SPOA 126

MIT EINEM GEMALTEN BANDE. "Kleine Blumen, kleine Blätter" DEUTGR 20

NACHTGESANG. "O gieb, vom weichen Pfühle" ATHENA 10

NÄHE DES GELIEBTEN. "Ich denke Dein, wenn mir der Sonne Schimmer" DEUTGR 7

"Natur und Kunst, sie scheinen sich zu fliehen" ATHENA 10

NEUE LIEBE, NEUES LEBEN. "Herz, mein Herz, was soll das geben" DEUTGR 7, DEUTGR 21

PARABASE. "Freudig war, vor vielen Jahren" ATHENA 10

PARABEL. "In einer Stadt, wo Parität" DEUTGR 7

PROMETHEUS. "Bedecke deinen Himmel, Zeus, mit Wolkendunst" DEUTGR 20, TELEF 5

RASTLOSE LIEBE. "Dem Schnee, dem Regen" DEUTGR 21

REINEKE FUCHS, exc. DEUTGR 46

RETTUNG. "Mein Mädgen ward mir ungetreu" TELEF 4

RÖMISCHE ELEGIEN.

———. I. "Saget, Steine, mir an" DEUTGR 21

———. II. "Ehret, wen ihr auch wollt" DEUTGR 21

———. III. "Lass Dich, Geliebte, nicht reun" DEUTGR 21

———. V. "Froh empfind ich mich nun auf klassischem Boden" DEUTGR 21 DOVER 1

———. IX. "Herbstlich leuchtet die Flamme vom ländlich gesilligen Herde" DEUTGR 21

———. XVII. "Manche Töne sind mir Verdruss" DEUTGR 21

"Sag' ich's euch, geliebte Bäume" DEUTGR 7

DER SÄNGER. "Was hör' ich draussen vor dem Tor" DEUTGR 20

DER SCHÄFER. "Es war ein fauler Schäfer" CAED 47, TELEF 5

DER SCHATZGRÄBER. "Arm am Beutel, krank am Herzen" TELEF 5

SEEFAHRT. "Taglang nachtlang stand mein Schiff befrachtet" DEUTGR 21

SEHNSUCHT. "Dies wird die letzte Trän' nicht sein" DEUTGR 7

SELIGE SEHNSUCHT. "Sagt es niemand, nur den Weisen" ATHENA 10, SCHOL 6

DER TOTENTANZ. "Der Türmer, der schaut zu Mitten der Nacht" CHRIST 22, FOLKW 74, TELEF 4

TRILOGIE DER LEIDENSCHFT. I. AN WERTER. "Noch einmal wagst du, vielbeweinter Schatten" CHRIST 26, DEUTGR 21

URFAUST MONOLOG. "Hab nun, ach, die Philosophie" ATHENA 1

VERMÄCHTNIS. "Kein Wesen kann zu Nichts zerfallen" CHRIST 26

DIE WANDELNDE GLOCKE. "Es war ein Kind, das wollte nie" FOLKW 74

WANDERERS NACHTLIED. 1. "Über allen Gipfeln ist Ruh" ATHENA 6, ATHENA 10, DEUTGR 7, DEUTGR 21, SPOA 5, SPOA 126; English HARB 2

———. 2. "Der du von dem Himmel bist" ATHENA 6, ATHENA 10, CAED 47, DEUTGR 7, DEUTGR 21

"Wenn im Unendlichen dasselbe" DEUTGR 7

WILLKOMMEN UND ABSCHIED. "Es schlug mein Herz, geschwind zu Pferde" DEUTGR 20, SPOA 5

WIRKUNG IN DIE FERNE. "Die Königin steht im hohen Saal" ATHENA 3, DEUTGR 20, TELEF 5

* Recording not available for analysis

WONNE DER WEHMUT. "Trocknet nicht, trocknet
nicht" DEUTGR 21
DER ZAUBERLEHRLING. "Hat der alte Hexenme-
ister" FOLKW 74, SPOA 126
ZU DEN LEIDEN DES JUNGEN WERTHER. "Jeder Jün-
gling sehnt sich so zu lieben" DEUTGR 21
ZUEIGNUNG. "Der Morgen kam; es scheuchten
seine Tritte" DEUTGR 20
ZWIEGESPRÄCHE. ATHENA 3
ZWINGER. DEUTGR 12
Gogarty, Oliver St. John. 1878. in English.
O BOYS! O BOYS! "O Boys! the times I've seen"
RCA 10
Gogol, Nikolai Vasilyevich. 1809. in Russian.
RUS'. "Rus'! Rus'! Vizhu tebya" CMS 6
Gold, Edward. in English.
AN OWL. "He tried to hide" WATSHD 1
STEADY STATE. "First there was the event"
WATSHD 1
Goldfarb, Sidney. in English.
KNOW HOW. "I want/ to do it" CAED 155
Goldman, Michael. 1936. in English.
THE SPONTANEOUS MAN, THE GIFTED ASSASSIN.
"The spontaneous man, the gifted assassin"
FOLKW 21
Poetry* JNP 18
Goldsmith, Oliver. 1728. in English.
THE DESERTED VILLAGE. "Sweet Auburn! loveli-
est village of the plain" BRITAM 1, LIST 2
————, exc. "In all my wanderings round this
world of care" ARGO 51
————, exc. CAED 203, EAV 7, SPOA 64
ELEGY ON THE DEATH OF A MAD DOG. "Good peo-
ple all, of every sort" DECCA 11,
SPOA 64, ARGO 125
RETALIATION, exc. "Here lies our good Ed-
mund" ARGO 51
SHE STOOPS TO CONQUER, exc. "Let school-mas-
ters puzzle their brain" CAED 203
THE TRAVELLER, exc. "Remote, unfriended,
melancholy, slow" ARGO 51, CAED 203
(Exc.)
THE VICAR OF WAKEFIELD, exc. "When lovely
woman stoops to folly" CAED 186,
CAED 203, CMS 13, LIST 2, SPOA 64
THE VILLAGE SCHOOLMASTER. "Beside yon strag-
gling fence that skirts the way" IMP 1
Goldstein, Roberta. 1918. in English.
AM I MY BROTHER'S KEEPER? "How could I know
his blood ran red" ASCH 1
THE AUGUST OF MY LOVE. "Brawny smithy at the
forge" ASCH 1
THE BURNING CANVAS. "The poppy flames leap
high" ASCH 1
THE DRUMS OF JUSTICE. "How can we learn not
to hate" ASCH 1
ELECTRA MOURNS. "The re-lipped maples still
stand tall" ASCH 1
EVEN THOUGH YOU LIE WITH LAUGHTER. "Glass
slippers danced throughout the year"
ASCH 1
GINA. "Gina knew he loved her even"
ASCH 1
THE GREEN WOMAN. "You called her a raceless
woman" ASCH 1
I WILL PURSUE. "I have pursued You in vaulted
cathedrals" ASCH 1

IN MEMORIAM JOHN FITZGERALD KENNEDY 1917-
1963 PROFILE WRITTEN IN BLOOD. "The empty
saddle and muffled drums" ASCH 1
LINES TO MY DAUGHTER. "You are the priestess of
a templed world" ASCH 1
THE MAID AND THE FLAME. "Languishing in the
dank dark dungeon" ASCH 1
MEA CULPA, MEA CULPA. "Four little girls in their
Sunday best" ASCH 1
MORNING AND EVENING STARS. "Man becomes
Emperor at daybreak" ASCH 1
NOT IN VAIN. "They tore down my doll house"
ASCH 1
RANDOM HARVEST. "Words can be arrows"
ASCH 1
SAMSON AND DELILAH. "The morning is a man's
select domain" ASCH 1
SCARLET SEAS. "There is a scarlet sea that
churns" ASCH 1
SEALED IN HISTORY. "Death magnifies the face of
a hero" ASCH 1
SILENCE AND TEARS. "Sound no bells for ghostly
glory" ASCH 1
SNOW SORCERY. "An endless mat of white vel-
vet" ASCH 1
TATTERED DREAMS. "Where have they fled"
ASCH 1
A TEEN-AGER ASKS WHY. "Man lives by faith and
not by bread alone" ASCH 1
TO MY PATRICIAN MOTHER. "I will not praise you
in the laurel way" ASCH 1
TO YOU WHO SAYS THERE IS NO GOD. "To whom are
you talking" ASCH 1
THE WALL OF DESTINY. "The copper gong of the
mid-east sun" ASCH 1
WHEN DRAGONS LIE SLAIN. "The winds brush
pine against the pane" ASCH 1
WHEN OBOES PLAY. "I see your shadow in the
lilac mist" ASCH 1
WHEN TIME STOOD STILL. "The town clock of
Hiroshima was a usual sort of clock"
ASCH 1
THE WOOD BURNS RED. "The wood burns red on
the hearth" ASCH 1
Goll, Yvan. 1891. in German.
DIE ASCHENHÜTTE. "Wir hatten kein Haus"
English and German WATSHD 2
ELEGIE DES ARMEN ICH. "Was tatest du"
English and German WATSHD 2
"In jeder Amsel hab ich dich geliebt"
English and German WATSHD 2
DIE MÜHLE DES TODES. "Unter dem Gips meiner
Gegenwart"
English and German WATSHD 2
DER REGENPALAST. "Ich hab dir einen Regen-
palast" English and German WATSHD 2
DAS WÜSTENHAUPT. "Ich ballte"
English and German WATSHD 2
Gombauld, Jean Ogier de. 1570. in French.
SONNET CHRETIEN. PERIOD 2
Gómez de Avellaneda, Gertrudis. 1814. in Span-
ish.
A EL. "Era la edad lisonjera" AGUIL 8
A UN NIÑO DORMIDO. "Duerme tranquilo, ino-
cente" FIDIAS 2
AL PARTIR. "Perla del mar! Estrella de Oc-
cidente!" SMC 13, SPOA 39

* Recording not available for analysis

Gómez de Avellaneda, Gertrudis (continued)

SOLEDAD DE ALMA. "La flor delicada, que apenas existe"   FIDIAS 2

Góngora, Luis de Argote y. 1561. in Spanish.
A CÓRDOBA. "Oh excelso muro, oh torres coronadas"   HOLT 1
AL NACIMIENTO DE CRISTO NUESTRO SEÑOR. "Caído se le ha un clavel"   AGUIL 5
DINEROS SON CALIDAD. "Dineros son calidad (Verdad)"   SMC 3
"La dulce boca, que a gustar convida"   AGUIL 4
"En los piñares de Júcar"   SPOA 37
EL FORZADO.   GMS 16
HERMANA MARICA. "Hermana Marica, mañana que es fiesta"   SMC 3
LET ME GO WARM.   English CMS 5
MADRIGAL. "De la florida falda"   DOVER 2
LA MAS BELLA NIÑA.   English CMS 5
MIENTRAS POR COMPETIR. "Mientras por competir con tu cabello"   SPOA 37
ROMANCILLO. "Las flores de romero, niña Isabel"   DOVER 2

González, Ángel. 1925. in Spanish.
INTRODUCCIÓN A UNAS FABULAS PARA ANIMALES. "Durante muchos siglos"   AGUIL 10
"Para que you me llame Angel González"   AGUIL 10

González-Martínez, Enrique. 1871. in Spanish.
TUÉRCELE EL CUELLO AL CISNE. "Tuércele el cuello al cisne de engañoso plumaje"   FOLKW 80, HOLT 1

Goodman, Godfrey. 16th c. in English.
THE LITTLE CHIRPING BIRDS.   ARGO 120

Goodman, Paul. 1911. in English.
WATERS AND SKIES. "Waters and skies, hours and seas"   SPOA 82

Goodsir Smith, Sydney. See **Smith, Sydney Goodsir.**

Googe, Barnabe. 1504. in English.
GOING TOWARDS SPAIN. "Farewell, theu fertyll soyle, that Brutus fyrst out founde"   LONGM 1

Gordon, Alvin J. 1912. in English.
THE GIRL CHILD'S SONG.   IFB 1
THE GUITAR MAKER'S SONG.   IFB 1
THE OLD MAN'S SONG.   IFB 1
THE OLD WOMAN'S SONG.   IFB 1
THE YOUNG GIRL'S SONG.   IFB 1
THE YOUNG MAN'S SONG.   IFB 1

Gori, Mario. in Italian.
UN GARO FANO ROSSO.   CETRA 31

Gourmont, Remy de. 1858. in French.
JEANNE. "Bergère née en Lorraine"   FOLKW 13

Govoni, Corrado. 1884. in Italian.
Poetry*   CETRA 28

Gozzano, Guido. 1883. in Italian.
ACHERONTIA ATROPOS. "D'estate, in un sentiero"   CETRA 7
L'AMICA DI NONNA SPERANZA. "Loreto impagliato ed il busto d'Alfieri, di Napoleone"   CETRA 7
UNA RISORTA. "Chiesi di voi: nessuno"   CETRA 7

LA SIGNORINA FELICITA OVVERO LA FELICITA. "Signorina Felicita, a quest'ora"   CETRA 7
Poetry*   CETRA 28

Gozzi, Count Carlo. 1720. in Italian.
Poetry*   CETRA 25

Graham, D. L. in English.
Poetry*   PRENT 1

Graham, James. See **Montrose, 1st Marquess of.**

Graham, William Sydney. 1918. in English.
THE BEAST IN THE SPACE. "Shut up. Shut up. There's nobody here"   ARGO 100
THE CONSTRUCTED SPACE. "Meanwhile surely there must be something to say"   ARGO 100

Gramigna, Giuliano. in Italian.
GLI ANNI MILITARI.   EPIU 1

Grandbois, Alain. 1900. in French.
L'ETOILE POURPRE. "C'etait l'ombre aux pas de velours"   FOLKW 70
O TOURMENTS. "O tourments plus forts de n'être qu'une seule apparence"   FOLKW 70
LE SONGE. "J'ai dormi d'amour"   FOLKW 70

Grant, Carolyn Hart. in English.
FIREFLIES. "Little lamps of the dusk" HARB 2

Grass, Günter. 1927. in German.
Poetry*   NESKE 2

Graves, Robert. 1895. in English.
ABOVE THE EDGE OF DOOM. "Bats at play taunt us with 'guess how many'"   COLUMB 12
ALL I TELL YOU FROM MY HEART. "I begged my love to wait a bit"   COLUMB 12
ALLIE. "Allie, call the birds in"   CAED 43, CAED 110
AMBIENCE. "The nymph of the forest, only in whose honour"   COLUMB 12
ANGRY SAMSON. "Are they blind, the Lords of Gaza"   CAED 43
ANY HONEST HOUSEWIFE. "Any honest housewife could sort them out"   CAED 43
AROUND THE MOUNTAIN. "Some of you may know, others perhaps can guess" ARGO 81
AT BEST, POETS. "Woman with her forest, moons, flowers"   COLUMB 12
THE BARDS. "The bards falter in shame, their running verse"   ARGO 81
BATXOCA. "Firm-lipped, high-bosomed slender Queen"   COLUMB 12
THE BEACH. "Louder than gulls the little children scream"   ARGO 81
BEAUTY IN TROUBLE. "Beauty in trouble flees to the good angel"   ARGO 81
BETWEEN HYSSOP AND AXE. "To know our destiny is to know the horror"   COLUMB 12
BIRD OF PARADISE. "At sunset only to his true love"   COLUMB 12
BLACK. "Black drinks the sun and draws all colours to it"   COLUMB 12
THE BLACK GODDESS. "Silence, words into foolishness fading"   COLUMB 12
THE BLUE-FLY. "Five summer days, five summer nights"   CAED 43
CAT-GODDESSES. "A perverse habit of cat-goddesses"   CAED 43
CHANGE. "This year she has changed greatly"   COLUMB 12
THE CHINK. "A sunbeam on the well-waxed oak"   FOLKW 65, JUP 1

---

* Recording not available for analysis

CHRISTMAS ROBIN. "The snows of February had buried Christmas" ARGO 81

THE CLOAK. "Into exile with only a few shirts" CAED 43

CONJUNCTION. "What happens afterwards, none need enquire" COLUMB 12

THE COOL WEB. "Children are dumb to say how hot the day is" CAED 43

THE CORAL POOL. "It was a hippocamp addressed her darling" ARGO 81

THE CUIRASSIER OF THE FRONTIER. "Goths, Vandals, Huns" ARGO 81

DARIEN. "It is a poet's privilege and fate" ARGO 81

DAWN BOMBARDMENT. "Guns from the sea open against us" ARGO 81

DAZZLE OF DARKNESS. "The flame guttered, flared" COLUMB 12

THE DEATH ROOM. "Look forward, truant, to your second childhood" CAED 43

DELIVERANCE. "Lying disembodied under the trees" COLUMB 12

THE DEVIL'S ADVICE TO STORY-TELLERS. "Lest men suspect your tale to be untrue" ARGO 81, ARGO 97

DOUBLE BASS. "He coils so close about his double-bass" COLUMB 12

1805. "At/ Viscount Nelson's lavish funeral" FOLKW 65, JUP 1

ENDLESS PAVEMENT. "In passage along an endless, eventless pavement" COLUMB 12

EVERYWHERE IS HERE. "By this exchange of eyes, this encirclement" COLUMB 12

EXPECT NOTHING. "Give, ask for nothing, hope for nothing" COLUMB 12

THE FACE IN THE MIRROR. "Grey haunted eyes, absent-mindedly glaring" ARGO 81

THE FALLEN TOWER OF SILOAM. "Should the building totter" CAED 43

FLYING CROOKED. "The butterfly, a cabbage-white" CAED 43

FOOD OF THE DEAD. "Blush as you stroke the curves—chin, lips and brow" COLUMB 12

FORBIDDEN WORDS. "There are some words carry a curse" ARGO 81

THE FOREBODING. "Looking by chance in at the open window" CAED 43

FRIDAY NIGHT. "Love, the sole Goddess fit for swearing by" ARGO 81

FRIGHTENED MEN. "We were not ever of their feline race" ARGO 81

THE FROG AND THE GOLDEN BALL. "She let her golden ball fall down the well" COLUMB 12

FULL MOON. "As I walked out that sultry night" ARGO 81

THE GENERAL ELLIOT. "He fell in victory's fierce pursuit" FOLKW 68

GOLD AND MALACHITE. "After the hour of illumination" COLUMB 12

GRATITUDE FOR A NIGHTMARE. "His appearances are incalculable" ARGO 81

THE GREEN CASTLE. "The first heaven is a flowery plain" COLUMB 12

GROTESQUES. I. "My Chinese uncle, gouty, deaf, half-blinded" ARGO 81

———. II. "The Lion-faced boy at the fair" ARGO 97

———. III. "Dr. Newman with the crooked pince-nez" ARGO 97

THE HALLS OF BEDLAM. "Forewarned of madness" ARGO 81

THE HAUNTED HOUSE. "Come, surly fellow, come: a song" CAED 43

HENRY AND MARY. "Henry was a young king" CAED 109

THE HIDDEN GARDEN. "Nor can ambition make this garden theirs" COLUMB 12

THE HILLS OF MAY. "Walking with a virgin heart" CAED 43

I WILL WRITE. "He had done for her all that a man could" COLUMB 12

I'M THROUGH WITH YOU FOREVER. "The oddest, surely, of odd tales" FOLKW 65A

THE IMPOSSIBLE. "Dear love, since the impossible proves" COLUMB 12

IN PROCESSION. "Often, half-way to sleep" CAED 43

IN THE WILDERNESS. "He, of his gentleness" FOLKW 65A

IN TIME. "In time all undertakings are made good" COLUMB 12

IRON PALACE. "We stood together, side by side, rooted" COLUMB 12

IT WAS ALL VERY TIDY. "When I reached his place" ARGO 81

A JEALOUS MAN. "To be homeless is a pride" CAED 43

JOHN SKELTON. "What could be dafter" LONGM 1

JUDGEMENT OF PARIS. "What if Prince Paris, after taking thought" COLUMB 12

LANGUAGE OF THE SEASON. "Living among orchards, we are ruled" ARGO 81

A LAST POEM. "A 1st poem, and a very last" COLUMB 12

THE LEAP. "Forget the rest: my heart is true" COLUMB 12

LEAVING THE REST UNSAID. "Finis, apparent on an earlier page" CAED 43

THE LEGS. "There was this road" CAED 111, LIBC 36

LIKE SNOW. "She, then, like snow in a dark night" CAED 43

A LOVE STORY. "The full moon easterly rising, furious" CAED 43

LOVE WITHOUT HOPE. "Love without hope, as when the young bird-catcher" CAED 42

A MEASURE OF CASUALNESS. "Too fierce the candlelight" COLUMB 12

THE MEETING. "We two elementals woman and man" COLUMB 12

LA MEJICANA. "Perfect beneath an eight-rayed sun you lie" COLUMB 12

MIKE AND MANDY. FOLKW 65A

MY NAME AND I. "The impartial law enrolled a name" CAED 43

THE NAKED AND THE NUDE. "For me, the naked and the nude" ARGO 81, LIBC 36

NOT TO SLEEP. "Not to sleep all the night long for pure joy" COLUMB 12

NOTHING NOW ASTONISHES. "A month of vigilance draws to its close" COLUMB 12

* Recording not available for analysis

Graves, Robert (continued)

OGRES AND PYGMIES. "Those famous men of old,
the Ogres"   CAED 43

THE OLEASTER. "Each night for seven nights
beyond the gulf"   COLUMB 12

ON DWELLING. "Coutesies of good-morning and
good-evening"   ARGO 81

ON PORTENTS. "If strange things happen where
she is"   ARGO 81

OUTLAWS. "Owls—they whinny down the
night"   CAED 43

THE PERSIAN VERSION. "Truth-loving Persians do
not dwell upon"   ARGO 81

THE PRESENCE. "Why say death? Death is nei-
ther harsh nor kind"   CAED 43

PROMETHEUS. "Close bound in a familiar bed"
                                                             ARGO 81

SHE IS NO LIAR. "She is no liar, yet she will wash
away"   COLUMB 12

SIROCCO AT DEYA. "How most unnatural-seem-
ing, yet how proper"   CAED 43

A SLICE OF WEDDING CAKE. "Why have such
scores of lovely, gifted girls"   ARGO 81,
                                                             ARGO 139

THE SNAP-COMB WILDERNESS. "Magic is tangled
in a woman's hair"   COLUMB 12

SON ALTESSE. "Alone, you are no more than
many another"   COLUMB 12

SONG. LIST BOY. "Let me tell you the story of
how I began"   FOLKW 65A

SONG OF CONTRARIETY. "Far away is close at
hand"   CAED 43

SONG. THE FAR SIDE OF YOUR MOON. "The far side
of your moon is black"   COLUMB 12

THE SURVIVOR. "To die with a forlorn hope, but
soon to be raised"   CAED 43, FOLKW 65,
                                                             JUP 1

THESEUS AND ARIADNE. "High on his figured
couch beyond the waves"   CAED 43

THIEF.   ARGO 81

THIS HOLY MONTH. "The demon who throughout
our late"   COLUMB 12

THOSE WHO CAME SHORT. "Those who came short
of love for me or you"   COLUMB 12

THE THREE-FACED. "Who calls her two-faced?
Faces, she has three"   COLUMB 12

THROUGH NIGHTMARE. "Never be disenchanted
of that place"   RCA 1

TIME. "The vague sea thuds against the marble
cliffs"   CAED 43

"To bring the dead to life"   CAED 43

TO JUAN AT THE WINTER SOLSTICE. "There is one
story and one story only"   CAED 43,
                                                             CAED 183

TO WALK ON HILLS. "To walk on hills is to em-
ploy legs"   ARGO 81

TOMORROW'S ENVY OF TODAY. "Historians may
scorn the close engagement"   COLUMB 12

THE TRAVELLER'S CURSE AFTER MISDIRECTION.
"May they wander stage by stage"
                                          CAED 86, FOLKW 65A

THE TROLL'S NOSEGAY. "A simple nosegay! was
that much to ask?"   FOLKW 65A

TRUDGE, BODY! "Trudge, body, and climb,
trudge and climb"   ARGO 81

TRUE JOY. "Whoever has drowned and awhile
entered"   COLUMB 12

THE UNDEAD. "To be the only woman alive in a
vast hive"   COLUMB 12

THE VILLAGERS AND DEATH. "The Rector's pallid
neighbour"   ARGO 81

THE VISITATION. "Drowsing in my chair of dis-
belief"   PROTHM 8

THE VOW. "No vow once sworn may ever be an-
nulled"   COLUMB 12

WARNING TO CHILDREN. "Children, if you dare
to think"   CAED 43, CAED 112

THE WEDDING. "When down I went to the rust-
red quarry"   COLUMB 12

WELSH INCIDENT. "But that was nothing to what
things came out"   ARGO 81, ARGO 97,
                                          FOLKW 60, ARGO 137

WHAT DID I DREAM. "What did I dream? I do not
know"   CAED 43

WHAT WILL BE, IS. "Manifest reason glared at you
and me"   COLUMB 12

WHOLE LOVE. "Every choice is always the
wrong choice"   COLUMB 12

WILD CYCLAMEN. "What can I do for you? she
asked gently"   COLUMB 12

WILLIAM BRAZIER. "At the end of Tarriers' Lane,
which was the street"   ARGO 81

YOUR PRIVATE WAY. "Whether it was your way of
walking"   ARGO 81

Poetry*   LIST 13

Gray, Thomas. 1716. in English.

ELEGY WRITTEN IN A COUNTRY CHURCHYARD. "The
curfew tolls the knell of parting day"
                      ARGO 50, BRITAM 3, CAED 162
                      CAED 203, LIST 2, POETRY 2
                      PROTHM 1, RCA 9, SPOA 64, THEAL 2

HYMN TO ADVERSITY. "Daughter of Jove, relent-
less Power"   SPOA 64

ODE ON A DISTANT PROSPECT OF ETON COLLEGE.
"Ye distant spires"   ARGO 50

———, exc. "Alas, regardless of their doom"
                                                             LONGM 1

ODE ON THE DEATH OF A FAVORITE CAT, DROWNED
IN A TUB OF GOLDFISHES. "'Twas on a lofty
vase's side"   ARGO 50, CAED 186, EAV 7
                                          SPOA 64, SPOA 117

ODE ON THE PLEASURE ARISING FROM VICISSITUDE.
"Now the golden Morn aloft"   ARGO 50

ON LORD HOLLAND'S SEAT.   ARGO 50

SONNET ON THE DEATH OF RICHARD WEST. "In
vain to me the smiling mornings shine"
                                                             IMP 1

Green, Kate. in English.
MIGRATION. "I wake"   EMC 1

Green, Mary McBride. in English.
AEROPLANE. "There's a humming in the sky"
                                                             HARB 2

Greenaway, Kate. 1846. in English.
LITTLE WIND. "Little wind, blow on the hill-
top"   CAED 108

Greene, Robert. 1558. in English.
THE SHEPHERD'S WIFE'S SONG. "Ah, what is love!
It is a pretty thing"   IMP 1, SPOA 50

Greenham, Peter. 1926. in English.
PIN POINT PUFF.   LUCHT 1

---

* Recording not available for analysis

Greenwald, Roger. in English.
BLOW-UP. "Let me twist your arm"
WATSHD 8
FUNNELS. "I no longer build in stone"
WATSHD 8
NOTE ON LEAVING. "I have picked long enough"
WATSHD 8
A PIANIST'S ASYLUM. "Though he never played for faces"
WATSHD 8
SURVIVORS. "The best do not always make it"
WATSHD 8
Gregor, Arthur. 1923. in English.
AT KOVALAM. "Again I was caught by it"
SPOWRD 2
THE CHASE. "In search through gardens, woods"
SPOWRD 2
DECLENSIONS OF A REFRAIN. "More or less of a relative gesture"
SPOWRD 2
THE FACT THAT ONE IS. "I have seen strange things"
SPOWRD 2
THE FUNERAL TRANSPORT BURNS AT SEA. "Because all desecration in this life"
SPOWRD 2
THE GOLD OF GOLD. "The ax that threatens"
SPOWRD 2
IT IS A WORLD OF ROCKS.
SPOWRD 2
MISCALCULATIONS. "Divinities are apt to be"
SPOWRD 2
OCTAVIAN SHOOTING TARGETS. "The top hat French poodle"
SPOWRD 2
OUR BEING IS AN IMPERCEPTIBLE WIND. "I decry lack of absorption"
SPOWRD 2
POEM. "Venice at night"
SPOWRD 2
SIENA. "As if pictured in a children's book"
SPOWRD 2
SINGING.
SPOWRD 2
SONG. "There, by the flower vendor's stand"
SPOWRD 2
A THOUGHT. "The tragic, I would always shun"
SPOWRD 2
TO CREATE THE POEM. "To create the poem"
SPOWRD 2
WASTING ARCHITECTURE. "Now that your parcel lies unwrapped"
SPOWRD 2
WHEN A BOAT DRAWS NEAR. "When a boat draws near"
SPOWRD 2
THE WINGBEAT. "The bird. The bird moving"
SPOWRD 2
Gregory, Carole. in English.
Poetry*
PRENT 1
Gregory, Horace. 1898. in English.
CHORUS FOR SURVIVAL: POEM 14. "The voyage crossed, the firmament one star" LIBC 17,
LIBC 59
FORTUNE FOR MIRABEL. "Tell, tell our fortune, Mirabel"
LIBC 17
OPERA, OPERA. "What work is that?" LIBC 17,
LIBC 59
Poetry*
HARVOC 13
Greif, Martin (Friedrich Hermann Frey). 1839. in German.
Poetry*
CHRIST 4
Grenfell, Julian. in English.
LETTER TO HIS MOTHER.
ARGO 89
Greville, Fulke, 1st Baron Brooke. 1554. in English.
"Fie, foolish Earth, think'st thou the Heaven wants glory"
ARGO 32

Gridley, Gordon. in English.
THE HERO. "Young Jimmy Stone"
SPOA 67
Grieve, Christopher Murray. See **MacDiarmid, Hugh.**
Griffin, Gerald. 1803. in English.
EILEEN AROON. "When, like the early rose"
SPOA 6
Griffiths, Bryn. in English.
BECAUSE OF FLOWERS.
ARGO 145
THE DARK CONVOYS.
ARGO 145
DEATH AT PALLE.
ARGO 145
GHOST OF SILENCE.
ARGO 145
HEY SAILOR!
ARGO 145
PENTRE IFAN. "The trees crouch uphill towards the ridgecrest"
ARGO 145
THE STONES REMEMBER. "Only the stones remember"
ARGO 145
TALLEY ABBEY.
ARGO 145
VOYAGE.
ARGO 145
Grigson, Geoffrey Edward Harvey. 1905. in English.
ABOUT OWLS.
ARGO 100
HOLLOWED STONE. "Looked for the hollowed stone"
ARGO 100
TO THE NECKAR.
ARGO 100
Grimké, Angelina. 1805. in English.
THE BLACK FINGER. "I have just seen a beautiful thing"
FOLKW 41
Gryphius, Andreas. 1616. in German.
ABEND. "Der schnelle Tag ist hin; die Nacht schwingt ihre Fahn" ATHENA 6,
DEUTGR 45, SPOA 5
AN DIE STERNE. "Ihr lichter, die ich nicht auf Erden satt kann schuen" CHRIST 14
ANDENKEN EINES AUF DER SEE AUSGESTANDENEN GEFAHRLICHEN STURMES. "O Gott! was rauhe Noth! Wie schaumt die schwarze See"
CHRIST 14
AUF DEN SONNTAG DES GUTTHÄTIGEN WANDER-MANNS. "Wie kan ich, herr! dein lob vermehren"
CHRIST 14
AUF DEN SONNTAG DES VOR UNS SORGENDEN SCHÖPFERS. "Weg welt! weg traurig-seyn! weg teuffel, fleisch und zagen" CHRIST 14
AUF DIE GEBURT SEINES ÄLTESTEN SOHNES CHRISTIANI. "Willkommen süsses kind! der mutter höchste lust" CHRIST 14
AUF SEINEN GEBURTSTAG. "Dass du den bau gemacht, den bau der schönen Welt"
CHRIST 14
DOMINE, MINOR SUM CUNCTIS MISERATIONIBUS TUIS! "Lass alles trauren seyn! hör auf, mein hertz, zu klagen" CHRIST 14
DOMINUS DE ME COGITAT. "In meiner ersten blüt, im frühling zarter tage" CHRIST 14
EITELKEIT DER WELT. "Du siehst, wohin du siehst, nur Eitelkeit auf Erden"
CHRIST 14, SPOA 5
MENSCHLICHES ELENDE. "Was sind wir Menschen doch" DOVER 1
MORGEN. "Die ewig-helle schar wil nun ihr licht verschliessen" CHRIST 14
QUANTAS OSTENDISTI MIHI TRIBULATIONES. "Reiss erde! reis entzwey! ihr berge brecht und decket" CHRIST 14
RUHE DES GEMÜTHES. "Wie selig ist der hohe Geist zu schätzen" CHRIST 14

* Recording not available for analysis

Gryphius, Andreas (continued)

SCHLUSS DES 1650STEN JAHRES. "Nach leiden, leid
und ach und letzt ergrimmten nöthen"
                                        CHRIST 14
THRÄNEN IN GROSSER HUNGERSNOT. "So muss
dein fluch den himmel schliessen"
                                        CHRIST 14
ÜBER DIE GEBURT UNSERES HERRN. "Wilkommen
süsse Nacht"   CHRIST 14
ÜBER DIE NACHT MEINER GEBURT. "Die erden lag
verhüllt"   CHRIST 14
ÜBER NICOLAUS COPERNICI BILD. "Du dreymall
weiser Geist"   CHRIST 16
ÜBERSCHRIFT AN DEM TEMPEL DER STERBLIGKEIT.
"Ihr irrt"   CHRIST 14
VANITAS! VANITATUM VANITAS! "Die herrligkeit
der erden"   CHRIST 14

Guest, Barbara. 1920. in English.
VERBA IN MEMORIAM. "How to speak of it"
                                        FOLKW 21

Guest, Edgar. 1881. in English.
HOME. "It takes a heap o' livin' in a house t'make
it home"   CAED 100
IT COULDN'T BE DONE.   CAED 100

Guggenmos, Josef. in German.
AUSFLUG. "Sieben Kleine Bären" ATHENA 11
DAS FISCHLEIN IM WEIHER. "Weisst du, was das
Fischlein im Weiher macht" ATHENA 11
HANS SECHZEHNENDER. "Ein Hirsch sass am
Waldrand"   ATHENA 11
ICH HABE VERLOREN MEINEN HUT. ATHENA 11
IM RINGSPIEL.   ATHENA 11
"Tief, tief im tiefsten Tannenwald"
                                       ATHENA 11
TREIB DU ES NICHT AUCH.   ATHENA 11
"Was denkt di Maus am Donnerstag"
                                       ATHENA 11
WENN DAS KIND TROTZIG IST. "Der Wächter auf
dem Turme"   ATHENA 11

Guido delle Colonne. 13th c. in Italian.
Poetry*   CETRA 19
Guillaume de Machaut. See **Machaut, Guillaume
de.**
Guillén, Jorge. 1893. in Spanish.
ADEMAS. "Jubilo al sol"   SPOA 59
LA AFIRMACIÓN HUMANA. "En torno el crimen
absoluto"   AGUIL 10
LOS AIRES.   TROPIC 1
LAS DOCE EN EL RELOJ. "Dije: todo ya pleno"
                                        AGUIL 10
LOS NOMBRES. "Albor. El horizonte"
                                        DOVER 2
RIO. "Que serena va el agua"   HOLT 1
Guillén, Nicolás. 1904. in Spanish.
BALADA DE LOS DOS ABUELOS. "Sombras que sólo
yo veo"   Spanish and English WATSHD 7
GUITARRA. "Tendida en la madrugada"
                                        SMC 13
EL HAMBRE. "Ésta es el hambre. Un animal"
            Spanish and English WATSHD 7
MULATA. "Ya yo me enteré, mulata"
            Spanish and English WATSHD 7
LA SED. "Esponja de agua dulce"
            Spanish and English WATSHD 7
SENSEMAYA. "Mayombe—bombe—mayombé!"
            Spanish and English WATSHD 7

VELORIO DE PAPÁ MONTERO. "Quemaste la ma-
drugada"   FOLKW 80
Poetry*   WATSHD 41
Guillevic, Eugène. 1907. in French.
DEUX CHANSONS.   ADES 55
Guinicelli, Guido. 1240. in Italian.
Poetry*   CETRA 19, CETRA 36
Güiraldes, Ricardo. 1892. in Spanish.
MI CABALLO. "Es un flete criollo, violento y
amontonado"   AGUIL 9
Guiterman, Arthur. 1871. in English.
ANCIENT HISTORY.   SCHOL 7
APOLOGY. "Perhaps I made a slight mistake"
                                        EAV 22
HABITS OF THE HIPPOPOTAMUS.   HOUGHT 3
THE YOUNG WASHINGTON. "Tie the moccasin"
                                        HARC 4
Gullberg, Hjalmar. 1898. in Swedish.
FÖRKLÄDD GUD.   GRAM 6
HÄNRYCKNING. "Dä skall ej vär jordiska bekam-
er"   GRAM 6
DEN HELIGA NATTEN, exc. "Vi kunde inte sova"
KYSSANDE VIND.   GRAM 6
SJON.   GRAM 6
Gunderson, Keith Robert. 1935. in English.
THE BEAUTIFUL TIGER. "Parting of grasses"
                                        EMC 7
Gunn, Thom. 1929. in English.
THE ALLEGORY OF THE WOLF BOY. "The causes are
in Time"   ARGO 95
THE ANNIHILATION OF NOTHING. "Nothing re-
mained: Nothing, the wanton name"
                                        FOLKW 59A
AUTUMN CHAPTER IN A NOVEL. "Through woods,
Mme Une Telle, a trifle ill"   ARGO 153
THE BOOK OF THE DEAD. "The blood began to
waste into the clods"   ARGO 95
THE BYRNIES. "The heroes paused upon the
plain"   ARGO 153
CONSIDERING THE SNAIL. "The snail pushes
through a green"   ARGO 95, ARGO 153
ELEGY ON THE DUST. "The upper slopes are
busy"   ARGO 95
EPITAPH FOR ANTO SCHMIDT. "The Schmidts
obeyed and marched on Poland" ARGO 95
FAIR IN THE WOODS. "The woodsmen blow their
horns, and close the day"   ARGO 153
THE FEEL OF HANDS. "The hands explore tenta-
tively"   ARGO 153
FLYING ABOVE CALIFORNIA. "Spread beneath me
it lies—lean upland"   ARGO 153
FROM THE WAVE. "It mounts at sea, a concave
wall"   ARGO 153
THE GODDESS. "When eyeless fish meet her on"
                                ARGO 153
GRASSES. "Laurel and eucalyptus, dry sharp
smells"   ARGO 153
IN SANTA MARIA DEL POPOLO. "Waiting for when
the sun an hour or less"   ARGO 153
INCIDENT ON A JOURNEY. "One night I reached a
cave: I slept, my head"   ARGO 153
INNOCENCE. "He ran the course and as he ran he
grew"   FOLKW 59A, ARGO 153
JESUS AND HIS MOTHER. "My only son, more
God's than mine"   ARGO 153
A MAP OF THE CITY. "I stand upon a hill and see"
                                ARGO 95

---

* Recording not available for analysis

THE MESSENGER. "Is this man turning angel as he stares"   ARGO 153

MISANTHROPOS 9. "A serving man. Curled my hair"   ARGO 95

MOLY. "Nightmare of beasthood, snorting, how to wake"   ARGO 153

MY SAD CAPTAINS. "One by one they appear in"   ARGO 153

PIERCE STREET. "Nobody home. Long threads of sunlight slant"   ARGO 153

RITES OF PASSAGE. "Something is taking place"   ARGO 153

THE SECRET SNARER. "Over the ankles in snow"   SPOA 68, ARGO 153

THE SILVER AGE. "Do not enquire from the centurion nodding"   ARGO 153

SUNLIGHT. "Some things, by their affinity light's token"   ARGO 153

THOUGHTS ON UNPACKING. "Unpacking in the raw new rooms"   ARGO 95

TO HIS CYNICAL MISTRESS. "And love is then no more than a compromise"   ARGO 153

TOUCH. "You are already asleep"   ARGO 153

THE UNSETTLED MOTORCYCLIST'S VISION OF HIS DEATH. "Across the open countryside into the walls of rain"   ARGO 95

THE VALUE OF GOLD. "The hairs turn gold upon my thigh"   ARGO 153

VOX HUMANA. "Being without quality"   ARGO 153

WORDS. "The shadow of a pine-branch quivered"   ARGO 153

THE WOUND.   PROTHM 7, ARGO 153

Günther, Christian. 1695. in German.
STUDENTENLIED. "Brüder lasst uns lustig sein"   SPOA 5

Gutiérrez, Juan Maria. 1809. in Spanish.
ENDECHA DEL GAUCHO. "Mi caballo era mi vida"   AGUIL 9

Gutiérrez Nájera, Manuel. 1859. in Spanish.
PARA ENTONCES. "Quiero morir cuando decline el día"   HOLT 1, SPOA 39

Guyot de Dijon. in French.
CHANTERAI POUR MON COURAGE.   HACH 7

H.D. See Doolittle, Hilda.

Hacker, Marilyn. 1942. in English.
THE ART OF THE NOVEL. "The afternoon breaks from a pale"   CAED 166

BEFORE THE WAR. "We are asleep under mirrors. What do I"   CAED 166

CITIES. "Wrapped in thick sweaters in the high cold noon"   CAED 166

CONTE.   CAED 166

THE DARK TWIN. "Turning in the brain, to wake"   CAED 166

ELEGY—FOR JANIS JOPLIN. "Crying from exile, I"   CAED 166

EXILES. "Her brown falcon perches above the sink"   CAED 166

FOR ELEKTRA. "My father dies again in dreams, a twin"   CAED 166

GEOGRAPHER. "I have nothing to give you but these days"   CAED 166

THE NAVIGATORS. "Between us on our wide bed we cuddle"   CAED 166

NIGHTSONG. "A plant will draw back vision to its source"   CAED 166

PRESENTATION PIECE. "About the skull of the beloved"   CAED 166

THE SEA COMING INDOORS. "The war is far away, sweet"   CAED 166

SOMEWHERE IN A TURRET. "Somewhere in a turret in time"   CAED 166

Hadrian, Emperor of Rome. 76 A.D. in Latin.
Poetry*   CETRA 18

Hafiz (Shams ad-Din Muhammad). 13th c. in Persian.
GHAZAL 115. "Yusofe gom gaeshte baz ayaed be kaenahn"   SCHOL 6

Hagedorn, Friedrich von. 1708. in German.
DER MORGEN. "Uns lockt die Morgenröte"   DEUTGR 13

Hagedorn, Jessica Tarahata. See Tarahata, Jessica

Hagelstange, Rudolf. 1912. in German.
DAS ZEICHEN DER AUFERSTANDENEN.
                                   CHRIST 18

Haines, John. 1924. in English.
Poetry*   CASSC 6

Hale, Edward Everett. 1822. in English.
BALLAD OF BUNKER HILL.   DECCA 13, LIST 23

Hall, Donald. 1928. in English.
THE ADULTS. "Lady, what are you laughing at?"   SCHOL 1

AFTERNOON. "My mouse, my girl in gray"   SCHOL 1

AN AIRSTRIP IN ESSEX, 1960. "It is a lost road into the air"   SCHOL

AT 35.   EMC 5

CHRISTMAS EVE IN WHITNEYVILLE. "December, and the closing of the year"   EMC 5, SPOA 106

COLD WATER.   EMC 5

COPS AND ROBBERS. "You play the cop, and I'm the robber"   SCHOL 1

THE DUMP. "The trolley has stopped long since"   SPOA 106

THE FARM. "Standing on top of the hay"   EMC 5

GOLD. "Pale gold of the walls, gold"   SPOA 106

IN A KITCHEN IN AN OLD HOUSE. "In the kitchen of the old house, late"   EMC 5

IUVENES DUM SUMUS. "Bowing he asks her the favor"   SCHOL 1

THE JEALOUS LOVERS. "When he lies in the night away from her"   NACTE 14, SCHOL 1

THE LONE RANGER. "Anarchic badlands spread without road"   NACTE 14, SCHOL 1

THE MAN IN THE DEAD MACHINE. "High on a slope in New Guinea"   SPOA 106

MY SON, THE EXECUTIONER. "My son, my executioner"   EMC 5

NEW HAMPSHIRE (SEASONS). "October wind"   EMC 5

THE OLD PILOT'S DEATH. "He discovers himself on an old airfield"   SCHOL 1

RECLINING FIGURE. "Then the knee of the wave"   SPOA 106

RESIDENTIAL STREETS. "Up and down the small streets"   SCHOL 1

SELF-PORTRAIT AS A BEAR. "Here is a fat animal, a bear"   EMC 5, NACTE 14, SCHOL 1

* Recording not available for analysis

Hall, Donald (continued)

THE SLEEPING GIANT. "The whole day long, under the walking sun"   SCHOL 1, SCHOL 8
SPIDER HEAD. "The spider glints"   FOLKW 21
Poetry*   JNP 19, MICHM 8

Halleck, Fitz-Greene. in English.
ON THE DEATH OF JOSEPH RODMAN DRAKE. "Green be the turf above thee"   EAV 14

Halley, Anne. in English.
AUTOGRAPH BOOK–PROPHECY.   CAED 155
"Each day I must relearn"   CAED 155

Hallström, Per. 1866. in Swedish.
FLYTTFÅGLARNA. "När sjön står mörk med fläckar"   GRAM 9

Halpern, Daniel. 1945. in English.
I AM A DANCER.   TAPES 11

Hamburger, Michael. 1938. in English.
Poetry*   JNP 20

Handy, W. C. 1873. in English.
Poetry*   LIST 11

Hannan, Greg. in English.
ARROWHEADS. "Arrowheads are instinctive"
                                  WATSHD 9
EASTER. "To have no excuse"   WATSHD 9
THE NIGHT CLERK. "The wind has picked up"
                                  WATSHD 9
THERE GOES THE ROOF. "People make mistakes"
                                  WATSHD 9
THE WALK. "Just as your eyes"   WATSHD 9

Hans, Marcie. in English.
HOW MANY 'ERS' ARE YOU.   NAITV 1

Haraucourt, Edmond. 1856. in French.
RONDEL DE L'ADIEU.   HACH 14

Hardenberg, Friedrich von. See Novalis.

Hardy, Thomas. 1840. in English.
AFTER A JOURNEY. "Hereto I come to view a voiceless ghost"   ARGO 71, CAED 77
AFTER THE CLUB DANCE. "Black'on frowns east on Maidon"   CAED 77
AFTER THE FAIR. "The singers are gone from the Cornmarketplace"   CAED 77
AFTERWARDS. "When the present has latched its postern"   ARGO 72
AN ANCIENT TO ANCIENTS. "Where once we danced, where once we sang"   ARGO 72, FOLKW 64
AT A LUNAR ECLIPSE. "Thy shadow, Earth, from Pole to Central Sea"   BRITAM 1, FOLKW 64
AT CASTLE BOTEREL. "As I drive to the junction of lane and highway"   ARGO 71, ARGO 88A, CAED 77, LONGM 1
AT THE DRAPER'S. "It's the townfolks' cheery compliment"   ARGO 72
AT THE PYRAMID OF CESTIUS. "Who, then, was Cestius"   ARGO 71
AT THE RAILWAY STATION, UPWAY. "There is not much that I can do"   ARGO 72
AT THE WORD "FAREWELL". "She looked like a bird"   ARGO 72
AUTUMN IN KING'S HINTOCK PARK. "Here by the baring bough raking up leaves" ARGO 71
THE BALLAD SINGER. "Sing, ballad singer, raise a hearty tune"   CAED 77

BEENY CLIFF. "O the opal and the sapphire o that wandering western sea"   ARGO 7
BEYOND THE LAST LAMP. "While rain, with eve in partnership"   CAED 7
THE BLINDED BIRD. "So zestfully canst thou sing"   ARGO 7
A BROKEN APPOINTMENT. "You did not come"
                                  CAED 1(
CHANNEL FIRING. "That night your great guns unawares"   CAED 7
THE CHOIRMASTER'S BURIAL. "He often would ask us"   ARGO 7
THE CHRISTENING. "Whose child is this they bring"   ARGO 7
THE CONVERGENCE OF THE TWAIN. "In a solitude of the sea"   ARGO 7
THE DARKLING THRUSH. "I leant upon a coppice gate"   ARGO 71, AUDIA 1, BRITAM 1
                  CAED 201, CMS 14 LIST
THE DYNASTS, exc.   ARGO 7
FORMER BEAUTIES. "These market-dames, mid aged"   CAED 7
GOD-FORGOTTEN. "I towered far, and lo!"
                                  ARGO 7
GOD'S EDUCATION. "I saw him steal the ligh away"   ARGO 7
THE GOING. "Why did you give no hint tha night"   ARGO 7
GREAT THINGS. "Sweet cyder is a great thing"
                       ARGO 71, CAED 7
HAP. "If but some vengeful god would call to me"   THEAL
THE HARBOUR BRIDGE. "From here, the quay one looks above to mark"   LONGM
THE HAUNTER. "He does not think that I haun here nightly"   ARGO 7
HE ABJURES LOVE. "At last I put off love"
                                  ARGO 7
HE REVISITS HIS FIRST SCHOOL. "I should not have shown"   ARGO 7
HEREDITY. "I am the family face"   ARGO 7
I FOUND HER OUT THERE. "I found her out there on a slope few see"   ARGO 71, CAED 7
I LOOK INTO MY GLASS. "I look into my Glass/ and view"   ARGO 7
"I said to Love"   ARGO 7
THE IMPERCIPIENT. "That with this bright believing band"   ARGO 7
IN A WOOD. "Pale beech and pine so blue"
                       ARGO 71, CAED 20
IN CHURCH. "And now to God the Father, he ends"   ARGO 72, LONGM
IN DEATH DIVIDED. "I shall not here, with those whom"   CAED 1(
IN TENEBRIS. I. "Wintertime nighs"   CAED 7
IN THE BRITISH MUSEUM. "What do you see"
                                  ARGO 7
IN THE MOONLIGHT. "O lonely workman, stand ing there"   ARGO 7
IN THE NIGHT SHE CAME. "I told her when I lef one day"   ARGO 7
IN THE OLD THEATRE, FIESOLE. "I traced the cir cus"   ARGO 7
IN THE SERVANTS' QUARTERS. "Man, you too aren't you"   CAED 7
IN THE STUDY. "He enters, and mute on the edge"   CAED 7

* Recording not available for analysis

IN TIME OF THE BREAKING OF THE NATIONS. "Only a man harrowing clocks"   ARGO 72

THE INQUIRY. "And are ye one of Hermitage"   CAED 77

LAUSANNE—IN GIBBON'S OLD GARDEN. "A spirit seems to pass"   ARGO 71

LET ME ENJOY. "Let me enjoy the earth no less"   CAED 77

LIDDELL AND SCOTT—ON THE COMPLETION OF THEIR LEXICON. "Well, though it seems"   FOLKW 60

LINES TO A MOVEMENT IN MOZART'S E-FLAT SYMPHONY. "Show me again the tune"   ARGO 71

LOST LOVE. "I play my sweet old airs"   ARGO 71

THE MAN HE KILLED. "Had he and I but met"   HOUGHT 3

THE MARKET-GIRL. "Nobody took any notice of her"   CAED 77

MEN WHO MARCH AWAY. "What of the faith and fire"   ARGO 71, ARGO 89

MIDNIGHT ON THE GREAT WESTERN. "In the third-class"   ARGO 71

MY SPIRIT WILL NOT HAUNT THE MOUND. "My spirit will not haunt the mound"   ARGO 71

NEW YEAR'S EVE. "I have finished another year, said God"   ARGO 71

"Not only I"   ARGO 72

OLD FURNITURE. "I know not how it may be with others"   CAED 77

ON THE DEPARTURE PLATFORM. "We kissed at the barrier"   ARGO 72

OUTSIDE THE WINDOW. "My stick, he says, and turns"   ARGO 72

THE OXEN. "Christmas Eve and twelve of the clock"   ARGO 72, ARGO 82, SPOA 41

THE PHANTOM HORSEWOMAN. "Queer are the ways of a man I know"   ARGO 71, CAED 77

THE PINE PLANTERS. "We work here together"   ARGO 72

THE PLACE ON THE MAP. "I look upon the map"   ARGO 72

REMINISCENCES OF A DANCING MAN. "Who now remembers"   CAED 77

THE RESPECTABLE BURGHER ON THE HIGHER CRITICISM. "Since Reverend Doctors now declare"   ARGO 71

THE RIVAL. "I determined to find out whose it was"   ARGO 71

ROME. "We walked where Victor Jove was shrined awhile"   ARGO 71

THE RUINED MAID. "O 'Melia, my dear, this does everything crown"   CAED 86, FOLKW 60

SHE CHARGED ME. "She charged me with having said this"   CAED 77

SHE OPENED THE DOOR. "She opened the door of the West to me"   ARGO 71

SHE, TO HIM. I. "When you shall see me in the toils"   ARGO 71

SHUT OUT THAT MOON. "Close up the casement, draw the blind"   ARGO 72, CAED 77, FOLKW 64

SNOW IN THE SUBURBS. "Every branch big with it"   ARGO 71

SO VARIOUS. "You may have met a man—quite young"   ARGO 72

THE SOULS OF THE SLAIN. "The thick lids if night closed"   CAED 77

THE SUNSHADE. "Ah—it's the skeleton of a lady's sunshade"   CAED 77

SURVIEW. "A cry from the green-grained sticks"   ARGO 71

TESS'S LAMENT. "I would that folk forgot me quite"   ARGO 71

THROWING A TREE. "The two executioners stalk along"   ARGO 71

TIMING HER. "Lalage's coming"   CAED 77

TO LIZBIE BROWNE. "Dear Lizbie Brown"   CAED 10, CAED 86

TO MEET, OR OTHERWISE. "Whether to sally and see thee"   ARGO 72

TO THE MOON. "What have you looked at, Moon"   ARGO 71, FOLKW 60

A TRAMPWOMAN'S TRAGEDY. "From Wynard's Gap the livelong day"   ARGO 72

THE TRESSES. "When the air was damp"   ARGO 72

UNDER THE WATERFALL. "Whenever I plunge my arm"   ARGO 71

THE VOICE. "Woman much missed, how you call to me"   ARGO 71, CAED 77

WEATHERS. "This is the weather the cuckoo likes"   BRITAM 1, CAED 77, FOLKW 67

WESSEX HEIGHTS. "There are some heights in Wessex"   CAED 77, CAED 201

WHERE THE PICNIC WAS. "Where we made the fire"   ARGO 71

WHISPERED AT THE CHURCH-OPENING. "In the brand-new pulpit the bishop stands"   ARGO 72

WHY DO I. "Why do I go on doing these things"   ARGO 72

A WIFE AND ANOTHER. "War ends, and he's returning"   ARGO 88A

THE YOUTH WHO CARRIED A LIGHT. "I saw him pass as the new day dawned"   ARGO 72

ZERMATT: TO THE MATTERHORN. "Thirty-two years since"   CAED 201

Poetry*   ARGO 109

Harkness, Edward. 1947. in English.

FIFTH GRADE SCAR. "Jimmy D. Martin had this fountain pen"   WATSHD 12

LETTER FROM DANNY. "Nothing's left"   WATSHD 12

"The man in the recreation room"   WATSHD 12

THE NIGHT BENNY KID PARET WAS KILLED ON TV. "Again the sky has gone to seed"   WATSHD 12

NUMBER 7 AGAIN. "You turn yourself in"   WATSHD 12

SITTING DOWN. "Outside it is April"   WATSHD 12

Harnett, Michael. in English.

THEY DRAG ME RAW. "They drag me raw on a gravel track"   ARGO 96

Harper, Michael S. 1938. in English.

ALONE. "A friend told me"   WATSHD 9

BIAFRA BLUES. "Another Brother gone"   WATSHD 9

BROTHER JOHN. "Black man"   WATSHD 9

* Recording not available for analysis

Harper, Michael S. (continued)

DEAR JOHN, DEAR COLTRANE. "A love supreme"
WATSHD 9
DEATHWATCH. "Twitching in the cactus hospital gown" WATSHD 9
FOR BUD. "Could it be Bud" WATSHD 9
A MOTHER SPEAKS—THE ALGIERS MOTEL INCIDENT, DETROIT. "It's too dark to see black"
WATSHD 9

Harriman, John. in English.
POEM FOR ADOLF EICHMANN. "Your lips pressed together" BROADR 2

Hart, Howard. in English.
TO JACKIE IN JAIL. BROADR 2

Harte, Bret. 1836. in English.
JOHN BURNS AT GETTYSBURG. "Have you heard the story that gossips tell" EAV 20, EAV 21
SOCIETY UPON THE STANISLAUS. "I reside at Table Mountain" EAV 20, EAV 21

Harteis, Richard. in English.
A FAREWELL DRINK FOR B. L. "First they sliced off the left" WATSHD 9
GLADYS. "I used to have a dressing room"
WATSHD 9
THE LIVE MANNEQUIN AT RANDOLPH'S. "I have to eat" WATSHD 9

Hasso, Signe. in Swedish.
DÄR BOR EN KONUNG. GRAM 1
DEN ENSAMMA DROMMEN. GRAM 1
INLEDNING. GRAM 1
OM KÄRLEKEN DU FINNER. GRAM 1
SJÖNG BÄCKEN. GRAM 1
EN SNÄCKA I SANDEN. GRAM 1

Hauptmann, Gerhart. 1862. in German.
"Du weisst nicht" ATHENA 2
"Durchdrungen von Pein" ATHENA 2
"Elf Schläge dröhnt zu mir herab"
ATHENA 2
"Es stieg ein Morgen herauf" ATHENA 2
"Süsse Luft und zartes Werden" ATHENA 2
"Verhör ich Hauch und Klang" ATHENA 2
DIE WEIHE. ATHENA 2

Haushofer, Albrecht. in German.
DER VATER. "Ein tiefes Märchen aus dem Morgenland" DOVER 1

Hausmann, Manfred. 1898. in German.
Poetry* CHRIST 6

Hausmann, Raoul. 1886. in German.
LAUTGEDICHT. LUCHT 1

Hawker, Stephen. 1803. in English.
A RAPTURE ON THE CORNISH HILLS. "I stood at the foot of Rocky Carradon" FOLKW 60

Hay, John. 1915. in English.
JIM BLUDSO. "Wall, no! I can't tell whar he lives"
EAV 21
LITTLE BREECHES. "I don't go much on religion"
EAV 20, EAV 21

Hay, Sara Henderson. 1906. in English.
THE BUILDERS. "I told them a thousand times"
SCHOL 7
FOR A DEAD KITTEN. "Put the rubber mouse away" SCHOL 7

Hayden, Robert E. 1913. in English.
APPROXIMATIONS. "In dead of winter"
SCHOL 4

THE BALLAD OF SUE ELLEN WESTERFIELD. "Sh
grew up in bedeviled Southern wilderness
SCHOL
THE BURLY FADING ONE. "The burly fading on
beside the engine" SCHOL
THE DIVER. "Sank through easeful" ARGO 8
EL-HAIJ MALIK EL-SHABAZZ (MALCOLM X) "The ic
evil that struck his father down" SCHOL
FREDERICK DOUGLASS. "When it is finally our
this freedom" FOLKW 4
FULL MOON. "No longer throne of a goddess t
whom we pray" ARGO 1
HOMAGE TO THE EMPRESS OF THE BLUES. "Becaus
there was a man somewhere in a candystrip
silk shirt" SCHOL
KID. "He is found with the homeless dogs"
SCHOL
MOURNING POEM FOR THE QUEEN OF SUNDA
"Lord's lost him his mockingbird"
SCHOL
NIGHT, DEATH, MISSISSIPPI. "A quavering cry"
SCHOL
O DAEDALUS, FLY AWAY HOME. "Drifting night i
the Georgia pines" SCHOL
RUNAGATE, RUNAGATE. "Runs falls rises stumble
on from darkness into darkness" SPOA 8
SOLEDAD. "Naked, he lies in the blinded room
SCHOL
SUMMERTIME AND THE LIVING. "Nobody plante
roses" SCHOL
THOSE WINTER SUNDAYS. "Sundays too my fathe
got up early" SCHOL
THE WHIPPING. "The old woman across th
way" SCHOL
Poetry* EAV 2, JNP 21, MICHM 1
PRENT 1, TAPES

Hayes, Donald Jeffrey. in English.
POET. "No rock along the road but knows"
FOLKW 4

Hazel, Robert. in English.
GUARD OF HONOR. "Leave the flattering libra
ies" FOLKW 2

Hazo, Samuel. in English
Poetry* JNP 2

Hazze, Z. in Swedish.
BIÅST PRINSEN. GRAM 1

He Jr Jang. 659. in Chinese.
HWEI SYANG OU SHU. "Shan syan li syang lan d
hwei" FOLKW 7

Heaney, Seamus. 1939. in English.
DEATH OF A NATURALIST. "All year the flax-da
festered in his heart" ARGO 9
FOLLOWER. "My father worked with a hors
plough" ARGO 9
POEM FOR MARIE. "Love, I shall perfect for yo
the child" ARGO 9
POOR WOMEN IN A CITY CHURCH. "The small wa
candles melt to light" ARGO 9
ST. FRANCIS AND THE BIRDS. "When Franc
preached love to the birds" ARGO 9

Heath, Gordon. in English.
"Do not mistake me" ARGO 1
"There is no other time for us" ARGO 1

Heath-Stubbs, John. 1918. in English.
BRYANT PARK, NEW YORK. "Adjacent to the publi
library" FOLKW 59

---

* Recording not available for analysis

EPITAPH FOR THAIS. "Traveler! Under this stone" ARGO 93

THE HISTORY OF THE FLOOD. "Bang bang bang" PROTHM 13, SPOA 67

IN EVERY SENSE OF THE WORD. "When my heart was young" ARGO 93

MAY-FLY. "Under the willow whose roots are shallow" ARGO 93

MOZART AND SALIERI. "Salieri encountered Mozart" ARGO 93

"Poetry is a formality" ARGO 93

SONG OF THE DEATH-WATCH BEETLE. "Here come I, the Death-Watch Beetle, chewing away at the great cathedral" ARGO 93

THE TIMELESS NIGHTINGALE. "A nightingale sat perched" ARGO 93

TITUS AND BERENICE. "Turn to me in the darkness" FOLKW 59A

THE TORTOISE. "Always to be at home" ARGO 93

TO EDMUND BLUNDEN ON HIS SIXTIETH BIRTHDAY. "Thysis, or Meliboeus, or old Damoetas" ARGO 93

Hebbel, Friedrich. 1813. in German.
Poetry* CHRIST 4

Heber, Reginald. 1783. in English.
"The brightest and best of the sons of the morning" LION 1

Hébert, Anne. 1916. in French.
LA FILLE MAIGRE. "Je suis une fille maigre" FOLKW 70

"Il y a certainement quelqu'un" FOLKW 70

LES PETITES VILLES. "Je te donnerai de petites villes" FOLKW 70

LE TOMBEAU DES ROIS. "J'ai mon coeur au poing" FOLKW 70

VIE DE CHATEAU. "C'est un château d'ancêtres" FOLKW 70

Hecht, Anthony. 1923. in English.
THE DOVER BITCH. "So there stood Matthew Arnold and this girl" SPOA 104

A HILL. "In Italy, where this sort of thing can occur" SPOA 104

A LETTER. "I have been wondering" SPOA 104

THE VOW. "In the third month, a sudden flow of blood" SPOA 104

Hedberg, Tor. 1862. in Swedish.
SEPTEMBER. GRAM 9

STOCKHOLM. GRAM 9

DET SUSAR GENOM TRADEN. GRAM 9

Hegarty, Teddy. in English.
"You and me walked long" WATSHD 8

Heidenstam, Verner von. 1859. in Swedish.
ALDERDOMEN. GRAM 9

HIMMLADROTTNINGENS BILD I HEDA. "Atta hundra julenätter" GRAM 9

VID VÄGENS SLUT. "Vis, o människa, det blir du först" GRAM 9

Heine, Heinrich. 1797. in German.
ABENDDÄMMERUNG. "Am blassen Meeresstrande" ATHENA 7

"Aber einst wird kommen der Tag" TELEF 2

"Ah, I long for tears returning" English FOLKW 56

"Ah, the world is so fair and the heaven so blue" English FOLKW 56

"Alles geben die Götter, die unendlichen" DEUTGR 7, DEUTGR 21

"Allnächtlich im Traume seh ich dich" CAED 47, TELEF 2

ALTE ROSE. DEUTGR 29

"Die alten bösen Lieder" CAED 47, TELEF 2

"Am leuchtenden Sommermorgen geh ich im Garten herum" CAED 47

AN MEINE MUTTER. "Ich bin's gewohnt, den Kopf recht hoch zu tragen" SPOA 5, TELEF 2

"Anfangs wollt ich fast verzagen" DEUTGR 31; English FOLKW 56

ANGELIQUE. 4. "Ich halte ihr die Augen zu" DEUTGR 29

———. 7. "Ja freilich du bist mein Ideal" DEUTGR 29

DER ASRA. "Täglich ging die wonderschöne Sultanstochter" SPOA 126

"Auf Flügeln des Gesanges" CHRIST 27, DEUTGR 10

"Auf meiner Herzliebsten Äugelein" TELEF 2

"Aus alten Märchen winkt es" CHRIST 47

"Aus meinen grossen Schmerzen" TELEF 2

"Aus meinen Tränen spriessen" CAED 47, TELEF 2

"Autumn mists, cold dreams are filling" English FOLKW 56

BEGEGNUNG. "Wohl unter der Linde erklingt die Musik" DEUTGR 29

BELSATZAR. "Die Mitternacht zog näher schon" SPOA 126

DER BRAVE MANN. ATHENA 3

CLARISSE. 1. "Meinen schönsten Liebesantrag" DEUTGR 29

"Death brings the end; and though I do dread it" English FOLKW 56

"Death, it is but the long, cool night" English FOLKW 56

DIANA. "Diese schönen Gliedermassen" DEUTGR 29

DICHTERLIEBE. "Im wunderschoenen Monat Mai" CAED 47, DOVER 1, TELEF 2; English FOLKW 56

"Did not my pallid face betray" English FOLKW 56

"Don't send me off, now that your thirst" English FOLKW 56

"Du bist wie eine Blume" SPOA 5

"Du liebst mich nicht, du liebst mich nicht" DEUTGR 31, TELEF 2

ENTARTUNG. DEUTGR 29

"Es stehen unbeweglich" TELEF 2

"Es war ein alter König" SPOA 5

"Every morn I send you violets" English FOLKW 56

"Das Fräulein stand am Meere" DEUTGR 31

"Fürchte nichts, geliebte Seele" DEUTGR 31

GIB HER DIE LARV'. "Gib her die Larv', ich will mich jetzt maskieren" DEUTGR 29, DEUTGR 31

GUTER RAT. DEUTGR 29

* Recording not available for analysis

Heine, Heinrich (continued)

DIE HARZREISE, exc. "Schwarze Röcke, seidne
Strümpfe"   DEUTGR 31, TELEF 2
"Have you really grown to hate me"
                              English FOLKW 56
"He who for the first time loves"
                              English FOLKW 56
"Heart, my heart . . . let naught o'ercome you"
                              English FOLKW 56
DAS HOHELIED. "Des Weibes Leib ist ein Ge-
dicht"   DEUTGR 31
"Hör ich das Liedchen klingen"   CAED 47
"I am helpless. You defeat me"
                              English FOLKW 56
"I pace the greenwood, bitter"
                              English FOLKW 56
"Ich grolle nicht, und wenn das Herz auch
bricht"   CAED 47
"Ich hab im Traum geweinet"   CAED 47;
                              English FOLKW 56
"Ich habe in der tat"   TELEF 2
"Ich lache ob den abgeschmackten Laffen"
                                    DEUTGR 31
"Ich rief den Teufel und er kam"
                                    DEUTGR 29
ICH TANZ NICHT MIT. "Ich tanz nicht mit, ich
räuchre nicht den Klötzen"   DEUTGR 31
"Ich wandelte unter Bäumen"   DEUTGR 29
"Ich will meine Seele tauchen"   CAED 47
"Ich wollte meine Lieder"   DOVER 1
"Im lieben Deutschland daheime"   TELEF 2
"Im Rhein, im heiligen Strome"   CAED 47
"In memory many pictures"
                              English FOLKW 56
"Das ist ein Flöten und Geigen"   CAED 47;
                              English FOLKW 56
"It was in July that I lost you"
                              English FOLKW 56
JETZT WOHIN? "Jetzt wohin? Der dumme Fuss"
                              DEUTGR 31, TELEF 2
"Ein Jüngling liebt ein Mädchen"   CAED 47,
              DEUTGR 29, DEUTGR 31, TELEF 2
KÖNIG DAVID. "Lächelnd scheidet der Despot"
                                      TELEF 2
LAMENTATIONEN. "Das Glück ist eine leichte
Dirne"   TELEF 2
"Lehn deine Wang an meine Wang"
                      DEUTGR 1, DEUTGR 10
"Leise zieht durch mein Gemüt"   SPOA 126
DIE LIEBE.   ATHENA 3
LIEBESLIEDER. 52. "Es kommt der Lenz mit dem
Hochzeitgeschenk"   DEUTGR 29
"Lonely now, I pour my sadness"
                              English FOLKW 56
DIE LORELEI. "Ich weiss nicht was soll es be-
deuten"   CHRIST 27, DEUTGR 31,
                                    SPOA 126
LYRISCHES INTERMEZZO, exc. "Es fällt ein Stern
herunter"   TELEF 2; English FOLKW 56
"Man glaubt, dass ich mich gräme"
                      DEUTGR 1, DEUTGR 10
"Manch Bild vergessner Zeiten"   CHRIST 27
"Mein Kind, wir waren Kinder"   ATHENA 3,
                      DEUTGR 29, DEUTGR 31
"Mein susses Lieb, wenn du im Grab"
              TELEF 2; English FOLKW 56

MEIN TAG WAR HEITER. "Mein Tag war heiter,
glücklich meine Nacht"   SPOA 5
MELODIE.   CHRIST 11
"Mir träumt' ich bin der liebe Gott"
                                    ATHENA 3
"Mir träumte wieder der alte Traum"
              DEUTGR 1, DEUTGR 10, DEUTGR 31,
                                      TELEF 2
MIT DUMMEN MÄDCHEN. "Mit dummen Mäd-
chen, hab' ich gedacht"   DOVER 1
"My love, lay your hand on my heart in its
gloom"   English FOLKW 56
DIE NORDSEE. "Ich liebe das Meer"   TELEF 2
"Now the night grows deeper, stronger"
                              English FOLKW 56
"Oh, what lies there are in kisses"
                              English FOLKW 56
"Oh, why are all the roses so pale"
                              English FOLKW 56
DER RITTER TANNHÄUSER. "Ihr guten Christen
lasst euch nicht"   DEUTGR 31
"Die Rose, die Lilie, die Taube, die Sonne"
                                      CAED 47
RÜCKSCHAU. "Ich habe gerochen alle Gerüche"
                            DEUTGR 31, TELEF 2
SALON, exc.   CHRIST 30
DER SCHELM VON BERGEN. "Im Schloss zu Düs-
seldorf"   TELEF 2
SERAPHINE. 12. "Wie schändlich du gehandelt"
                                    DEUTGR 29
"Shadow-love and shadow-kisses"
                              English FOLKW 56
"Sie sassen und tranken am Teetisch"
              DEUTGR 29, DEUTGR 31, TELEF 2
"So hast du ganz und gar vergessen"
                              FOLKW 56, TELEF 2
"Stars with fair and golden ray"
                              English FOLKW 56
"Stars with golden feet are walking"
                              English FOLKW 56
"The sweet desires blossom"
                              English FOLKW 56
"Tag und Nacht hab ich gedichtet"   TELEF 2
"These gray clouds, so thickly strewn"
                              English FOLKW 56
"They buried him at the crossroads"
                              English FOLKW 56
"They're having a party this evening"
                              English FOLKW 56
"Too late, your sighs and smiles of promise"
                              English FOLKW 56
TRAGÖDIE. "Entflieh mit mir und sei mein
Weib"   DEUTGR 1, DEUTGR 10
"Und bist du erst mein ehlich Weib"
                      ATHENA 3, DEUTGR 31
"Und wüsstens die Blumen, die kleinen"
                            CAED 47, FOLKW 56
UNTERGANG DER SONNE. "Die schöne Sonne"
                                    CHRIST 27
WALDEINSAMKEIT. "Ich hab in meinen Jugendta-
gen"   DEUTGR 1, DEUTGR 10
"Was ist Traum? Was ist Tod?"   TELEF 2
"We stood upon a corner, where"
                              English FOLKW 56
DIE WEBER. "Im düstern Auge keine Träne"
                                    SPOA 126

---

* Recording not available for analysis

"Die Welt ist dumm, die Welt ist blind"
DEUTGR 31, TELEF 2,
English FOLKW 56
WELTLAUF. "Hat man viel, so wird man bald"
TELEF 2
"Wenn ich beseligt von schönen Küssen"
DEUTGR 31
"Wenn ich in deine Augen seh"   CAED 47,
TELEF 2
"Wenn zwei voneinander scheiden"
TELEF 2; English FOLKW 56
"Werdet nur nicht ungeduldig"
English FOLKW 56
"What drives you out in this night of spring"
English FOLKW 56
"When I lie down for comfort"
English FOLKW 56
"Why does this lonely tear-drop"
English FOLKW 56
"Wie kannst du ruhig schlafen"   DEUTGR 1,
DEUTGR 10
"Wir fuhren allein im dunkeln"   DEUTGR 31
"Wir haben viel füreinander gefühlt"
DEUTGR 29, TELEF 2;
English FOLKW 56
"With kisses my lips were wounded by you"
English FOLKW 56
YOLANTE UND MARIE, 2. "In welche soll ich mich
verlieben"   DEUTGR 29
"Zu Aachen, im alten Dome liegt"
DEUTGR 31
Poetry*   SPOA 126, SPOA 127 X
Heissenbüttel, Helmut. in German.
EINST. "Die Melodie der Einundzwanzigjährig-
keit"   NESKE 1
KOMBINATION IV. "Gefangen in der Falle der
Verbindlichkeiten"   NESKE 1
LEHRGEDICHT UBER GESCHICHTE 1954. "Die
Ereignisse und das Nichtereignete"
NESKE 1
"Schwarze Wand"   NESKE 1
TOPOGRAPHIEN. I. "Atemlos überqueren die Vö-
gel"   NESKE 1
_____. II. "Zeit. Vorzeit"   NESKE 1
_____. III. "Unaufhörlich begegnen sich"
NESKE 1
_____. IV. "Tage abziehen"   NESKE 1
_____. V. "Inhaltlose Sätze"   NESKE 1
UNTERGANGSSTRASSEN. "Untergangsstrassen zu
überqueren"   NESKE 1
WENN IMMER SINN HAT. "Herabgebeugt über
sich selbst"   NESKE 1
Helton, Roy. in English.
OLD CHRISTMAS.   HOUGHT 4
Hemans, Felicia Dorothea. 1793. in English.
LANDING OF THE PILGRIM FATHERS. "The break-
ing waves dashed high"   COLUMB 6,
DECCA 4, DECCA 13, HARC 4, LIST 23,
SINGER 2
Hemmer, Jarl. 1893. in Swedish.
"Varför vaxa alla dessa blommor"   GRAM 1
Henault, Gilles. 1920. in French.
CHANSON DU GRAND ECHANSON. "Voice pour toi,
figure close"   FOLKW 70
FEU SUR LA BETE-ANGOISE. "L'attente d'un beau
jour"   FOLKW 70

MIROIR TRANSPARENT. "L'amour est plus simple
qu'on le dit"   FOLKW 70
VOICI VENIR TEMPS. "Je suis de ceux qui accep-
tent"   FOLKW 70
Henderson, David. 1942. in English.
BOPPIN.   BLACKF 1
ELVIN JONES GRETCH FREAK (COLTRANE AT THE
HALF NOTE). "Gretch love/gretch hate"
BROADR 2
Henderson, Hamish. in English.
THE FLYING O'LIFE AND DAITH. "Quo Life, the
warld is mine"   ARGO 96
Henley, William Ernest. 1849. in English.
BALLADE OF ANTIQUE DANCES. "Before the town
has lost its wits"   EAV 22
INVICTUS. "Out of the night that covers me"
AUDIA 1, CAED 100, CAED 201, LIST 3
"Madam Life's a piece in bloom" LONGM 1
Poetry*   LIST 11
Henri, Adrian. 1932. in English.
AUTOBIOGRAPHY.   ARGO 150
EPILOGUE. "Autumn and leaves swirl at the
roadside"   ARGO 150
GALACTIC LOVE POEM. "Universes away from
you"   ARGO 150
IN THE MIDNIGHT HOUR. "When we meet"
PROTHM 8
LOVE FROM ARTHUR RAINBOW.   ARGO 150
LOVE IS. "Love is feeling cold in the back of
vans"   ARGO 150, PROTHM 6
NIGHTSONG.   ARGO 150
TONIGHT AT NOON. "Tonight at noon"
ARGO 150
TWO LULLABIES. "Here is a poem written on the
clouds for you"   ARGO 150
WHO.   ARGO 150
WITHOUT YOU. "Without you every morning
would be like going back to work after a holi-
day"   ARGO 150
Henry VIII, King of England. 1509. in English.
"Green groweth the holly"   IMP 1
Henryson, Robert. in Middle English.
THE TESTAMENT OF CRESSEID.   ARGO 29
Herbert, George. 1593. in English.
AFFLICTION.   ARGO 36
THE AGONIE. "Philosophers have measur'd
mountains"   ARGO 36
BITTER-SWEET. "Ah my deare angrie Lord"
ARGO 36
THE COLLAR. "I struck the board, and cry'd 'No
more'"   ARGO 36 BRITAM 2, CAED 20,
IDIOM 1, JNP 8, SPOA 84, THEAL 3
CONSCIENCE. "Peace pratler, do not loure"
ARGO 36
DEATH.   PROTHM 8
DIALOGUE. "Sweetest Savior, if my soul"
ARGO 126
DISCIPLINE.   SPOA 84
EASTER. "Rise heart: thy Lord is risen"
ARGO 36
EASTER WINGS. "Lord, who createdst man in
wealth"   PROTHM 8
THE ELIXIR.   IDIOM 1
EVENSONG.   IDIOM 1
THE FLOWER. "How fresh, O Lord, how sweet
and clean"   IDIOM 1, LONGM 1

* Recording not available for analysis

Herbert, George (continued)

HOPE. "I gave to hope a watch of mine"
                                CAED 38

JORDAN. "Who sayes that fistions onely and false
   hair"   CAED 38

LOVE. "Love bade me welcome: yet my soul"
   ARGO 36 BRITAM 2, CAED 38,
   HARVOC 6, SPOA 84, LONGM 1

MAN. "My God, I heard this day"   CAED 38

MISERIE. "Lord, let the Angels praise thy name"
                                CAED 38

MORTIFICATION. "How soon doth man decay"
                                ARGO 36

PEACE.   HARVOC 6, SPOA 84

THE PEARL. "I know the wayes of learning"
                                LONGM 1

PRAYER. "Prayer, the Churche's banquet"
                           CAED 38, IDIOM 1

THE PULLEY. "When God at first made man"
   ARGO 36, BRITAM 2, CAED 38, IDIOM 1,
   LONGM 1

REDEMPTION. "Having been tenant long to a
   rich Lord"   LONGM 1

SIGHS AND GRONES. "O do not use me"
                                CAED 38

SIN   IDIOM 1

VERTUE. "Sweet day, so cool, so calm, so bright"
   ARGO 36, COLUMB 11, IDIOM 1,
   SPOA 84

"When first my lines of heav'nly joyes made
   mention"   LONGM 1
Poetry*   EAV 6, EAV 11

Herburger, Günter. in German.
EHEGEDICHT. "Geliebt haben wir uns"
                              DEUTGR 40A

UNSERE WIRTSCHAFT. "Im Radio höre ich türkisch"   DEUTGR 40A

Heredia, José-Maria de. 1842. in French.
LES CONQUÉRANTS. "Comme un vol de gerfauts
   hors du charnier natal"   ADES 54, GMS 9,
   SPOA 36

ÉPITAPHE D'UNE SAUTERELLE.   HACH 12
L'OUBLI.   CAED 204

Heredia y Campuzano, José María de. 1803. in
   Spanish.
EN EL TEOCALI DE CHOLULA. "Cuánto es bella la
   tierra"   FIDIAS 3

ODA AL NIAGARA. "Dadme mi lira, dádmela, que
   siento"   SMC 13 SPOA 39

Herford, Oliver. in English.
THE ELF AND THE DORMOUSE. "Under a toadstool
   crept a wee Elf"   CAED 164, CREAT 1

THE MILK JUG. "The Gentle Milk Jug, blue and
   white"   HARB 5

STAIRS. "Here's to the man who invented stairs"
                                HARB 6

Hernández, José. 1834. in Spanish.
MARTÍN FIERRO, exc. "Aquí me pongo a cantar"
   AGUIL 9, FIDIAS 3, FOLKW 81, SMC 18,
   SPOA 39

———. "Atención pido al silencio"   SMC 18

———. "De carta de mas me via"
                               FOLKW 81

———. "Esto conto Picardia y despues guardo
   silencio"   SMC 18

———. "Monté y me encomendé a Dios"
                                SMC 18

———. "Un padre que da consejos"
                          FOLKW 81, SMC 18

———. "Sin saber que hacer de mi"   SMC 18

———. "Tuve en mi pago en un tiempo"
                               FOLKW 81

———. "Vamos dentrando recien"
                               FOLKW 81

———. "Volví al cabo de tres años"   SMC 18

———. "Y apenas la madrugada"   FOLKW 81

———. "Ya veo que somos los dos"
                               FOLKW 81

LA VUELTA DE MARTIN FIERRO, exc. "Anque el
   gajo se parece"   FOLKW 81

———. "Después. a los cuatro vientos"
                               FOLKW 81

———. "Lo que les voy a decir"   FOLKW 81

———. "Me llevó consigo un viejo"
                               FOLKW 81

———. "Siempre andaba retobado"
                               FOLKW 81

Hernández, José P. H. in Spanish.
"Si Dios algun día cegara toda fuente de luz"
                          INSTPR 1, SMC 9

Hernández, Miguel. 1910. in Spanish.
ELEJIA A RAMON SIJE.   TROPIC 1
EL HERIDO. "Por los campos luchados"
                                SPOA 59

ME TIRASTE UN LIMÓN. "Me tiraste un limon, y
   tan amargo"   AGUIL 4

SONETO FINAL. "Por desplumar arcángeles glaciales"   AGUIL 4

"Te dormiste, niño mio?"   HOLT 1

EL TREN DE LOS HERIDOS. "Silencio que naufraga
   en el silencio"   DOVER 2

"Yo se que ver y oír a un triste enfada"
                                AGUIL 4

Hernández Cruz, Victor. 1949. in English.
URBAN DREAM.   EAV 16
Poetry*   PRENT 1

Hernton, Calvin C. 1934. in English.
JITTERBUGGING IN THE STREETS. "There will be
   no Holyman crying out this year"
                         BROADR 2, SPOA 89

Herrera y Reissig, Julio. 1875. in Spanish.
JULIO. "Flota sobre el esplín de la campaña"
                                SPOA 39

Herrick, Robert. 1591. in English.
CEREMONIES FOR CHRISTMAS. "Come bring with
   a noise"   LION 1

CHERRIE-RIPE. "Cherrie-ripe, ripe, ripe, I cry"
                                SPOA 84

CORINNA'S GOING A-MAYING. "Get up, get up for
   shame, the blooming morne"   ARGO 35,
   LONDON 1

DELIGHT IN DISORDER. "A sweet disorder in the
   dresse"   ARGO 35

GRACE FOR A CHILD. "Here a little child I stand"
                          ARGO 35, SPOA 84

HAPPINESS TO HOSPITALITY. "First, may the hand
   of bounty"   ARGO 35

HIS LITANY TO THE HOLY SPIRIT. "In the houre of
   my distresse"   ARGO 35, SPOA 84

HIS WINDING-SHEET. "Come thou, who art the
   Wine, and wit"   ARGO 35

---

* Recording not available for analysis

LOVERS HOW THEY COME AND PART. "A Gyges
  Ring they beare"   ARGO 35
LYRIC FOR LEGACIES. "Gold I've none, for use or
  show"   ARGO 35
AN ODE FOR BEN JONSON. "Here lyes Jonson with
  the rest"   ARGO 35
TO APOLLO. "Thou mighty Lord and master of
  the Lyre"   BRITAM 1
TO DAFFODILS. "Faire Daffadills, we weep to
  see"   ARGO 35, BRITAM 2, FOLKW 68,
                                     SPOA 84
TO DAISIES, NOT TO SHUT SO SOON. "Shut not so
  soon"   LONGM 1
TO DIANEME. "I'le to thee a simnell bring"
                                     ARGO 35
TO ELECTRA. "Love love begets, then never be"
                                     ARGO 35
TO MEADOWS. "Ye have been fresh and green"
                                     ARGO 35
TO MUSIC, TO BECALM HIS FEVER. "Charm me as-
  leep, and melt me so"   ARGO 35
TO THE VIRGINS, TO MAKE MUCH OF TIME. "Gather
  ye Rosebuds while ye may"   ARGO 35,
        ARGO 88A, BRITAM 2, CAED 186,
  CMS 13, DECCA 12, SINGER 6, SPOA 84
TO VIOLETS. "Welcome Maids of Honour"
                                     ARGO 35
UPON HIS DEPARTURE HENCE. "Thus I/Passe by"
                                     ARGO 35
UPON JULIA'S CLOTHES. "When as in silks my
  Julia goes"   ARGO 35
UPON LOVE. "Love brought me to a silent
  grove"   IMP 1
Poetry*   EAV 11, PROTHM 6
errmann-Neisse, Max. in German.
ICH MÖCHTE HEIM.   CHRIST 30
erschberger, Ruth. 1917. in English.
THE HURON.   LIBC 40
IN PANELLED ROOMS.   LIBC 40
Poetry*   LIST 15
ershenson, Miriam. in English.
HUSBANDS AND WIVES.   SCHOL 7
esse, Hermann. 1877. in German.
BALLADE VOM KLASSIKER. "Früher schon zum
  Klassiker berufen"   DEUTGR 42
EIN BRIEF. "Mein hochgeehrter Herr von
  Klein"   DEUTGR 42
"Der Hummer liebte die Languste"
                                   DEUTGR 42
ICH LIEBE FRAUEN. "Ich liebe Frauen, die vor
  tausend Jahren"   DOVER 1
PFEIFEN. "Klavier und Geige, die ich wahrlich
  schätze"   DEUTGR 42
WALLFAHRER-LIED. "Die Woge wogt, es wallt die
  Quelle"   DEUTGR 42
Poetry*   CHRIST 4, CHRIST 6, SUHRK 3,
                                     SUHRK 4
ey, Wilhelm. 1789. in German.
"Weisst du, wieviel Sternlein stehen"
                                   ATHENA 11
eywood, Thomas. in English.
"Pack, clouds, away, and welcome day"
                                     SPOA 50
ickey Pellizzoni, Margarita. in Spanish.
ROMANCE. "Aprended, flores, de mi"
                                     FIDIAS 2

Hierro, José. 1922. in Spanish.
EL INDIFERENTE. "Ahora seremos felices"
                                     AGUIL 3
REQUIEM. "Manuel del Río, natural" AGUIL 3
TERCERA FÁBULA. "Todo lo puede el viento: va/
  y viene"   HOLT 1
Hill, Geoffrey. 1932. in English.
THE ASSISI FRAGMENTS. "Lion and lioness, the
  mild"   ARGO 98
CANTICLE FOR GOOD FRIDAY. "The cross stag-
  gered him"   ARGO 98
IN MEMORY OF JANE FRASER. "When snow like
  sheep lay in the fields"   SPOA 67
IN PIAM MEMORIAM. "Created purely from glass"
                                     ARGO 98
LITTLE APOCALYPSE. "Abrupt tempter; close
  enough to survive"   ARGO 98
TO THE (SUPPOSED) PATRON. "Prodigal of loves"
                                     ARGO 98
Hill-Abu-Isak, Elton. in English.
THEME BROWN GIRL.   CAED 155
Hillary, Richard. 1919. in English.
ACTION.   ARGO 119
TARFSIDE.   ARGO 119
Hillyer, Robert Silliman. 1895. in English.
ASSASSINATION. "Do you not find something
  very strange"   HARVOC 8
BANDUSIA.   HARVOC 8
BARCAROLLE. "The long stems of the waterli-
  lies"   LIBC 46
THE CARDINAL FLOWER. "Cold and amber"
                                     LIBC 46
THE CAVE.   HARVOC 8
CLEAR MELODY.   HARVOC 8
FAMILIAR FACES, LONG DEPARTED. "Where are
  the dear domestics, white and black"
                                     LIBC 46
FOLK SONG.   LIBC 46
"He who in Spring's rebirth has put his trust"
                                   HARVOC 8
HOME PORT. "Have the boats all come home
  yet"   LIBC 46
IN THE TIDAL MARSHES. "White above the after-
  flare"   LIBC 46
IN TIME OF MISTRUST, exc. "It was the morning
  after the great wind"   HARVOC 8
INTERVAL.   HARVOC 8
LIGHT SNOWFALL.   HARVOC 8
MOO. "Summer is over, the old cow said"
                                   HARVOC 8
OVERHEARD. "The windswept beach was emp-
  ty"   HARVOC 8
OVERTURE. "This record played in the room has
  lost all the music"   LIBC 46
PASTORAL. 2. "So soft in the hemlock wood"
                                   HARVOC 8
_____. 6. "Piping Anne and husky Paul"
                                   HARVOC 8
THE RELIC. "A murmuring in empty shells"
                                     LIBC 46
REPARTEE. "As one who bears beneath his
  neighbor's roof"   HARVOC 8
THE RUINED CASTLE OF MANORBIER.   LIBC 46
SONG. "Verse is a turning"   HARVOC 8
VISITANTS IN A COUNTRY HOUSE AT NIGHT. "My
  ears are alert"   HARVOC 8
WITH SIMPLE WORDS.   HARVOC 8

* Recording not available for analysis

Hine, Daryl. 1936. in English.
Poetry*   JNP 22
Hines, Carl Wendell. in English.
JAZZ POEM.   SPOA 89
Hinton, Robert. in English.
THE DEAD WAGON. "The dirty white van"
                                             WATSHD 8
FIRST-BORN SON. "The forces of liberation"
                                             WATSHD 8
FOR EL-HAJJ MALIK EL-SHABAZZ.   WATSHD 8
TEN CENTS WORTH OF BALONEY.   WATSHD 8
Hippius, Zanaída. 1869. in Russian.
"Iznemogayu ot ustalosti"   CMS 6
Hitchcock, George. 1914. in English.
MR. KENNEDY PROPOSES TO PACIFY THE CARIB-
BEANS. "Recalling the manicured nails on the
mandolin"   FOLKW 21
Poetry*   CASSC 1
Ho Chi Minh. 1890. in Vietnamese.
PRISON DIARY, exc.   English CMS 1
Hobbs, Suzanne. in English.
LETTING SALLY GO. "They name this pain"
                                             WATSHD 12
THE MAN IN THE MIRROR IN A ROOM LIT BY ONE
LAMP. "Lazarus, I bring you lilies"
                                             WATSHD 12
POEM IN THREE VOICES BY ANY OTHER NAME. "It
might have been"   WATSHD 12
SALLY CHISOLM PLAYING LOVE IN THE AFTERNOON.
"Sometimes Billy rides in"   WATSHD 12
SALLY CHISOLM THINKING BACK. "Last time I saw
him he was leaving"   WATSHD 12
Hodges, Frenchy Jolene. in English.
BLACK HAIKU. "The light inside" BROADV 2
A BLACK MEMORIAL DAY. "See America first"
                                             BROADV 2
BLACK WISDOM. "Dilemma"   BROADV 2
DREAMS, COMMON SENSE AND STUFF. "I have a
dream"   BROADV 2
ELEGY WRITTEN IN AMERICA. "Born down in
Georgia"   BROADV 2
THE GRASSHOPPER WORLD. "The grasshopper
world"   BROADV 2
THE HILLS. "The hills are calling" BROADV 2
IN FRONT OF FIFTH AVENUE LIBRARY ON THE STEPS.
"In front of Fifth Avenue"   BROADV 2
INNOCENT QUESTION. "And bless Uncle Jim"
                                             BROADV 2
INVITATION. "Swift little thought" BROADV 2
LISTEN, I'SE TALKIN' TO YOU, LAWD. "Lawd, hab
mussy"   BROADV 2
ON DREAMS. "Brothers"   BROADV 2
SHATTERED DREAMS. "When you told of Paul"
                                             BROADV 2
STEREO ABSTRACT. "I went out in the world"
                                             BROADV 2
SUPER THOUGHT. "If I could bend each yester-
day"   BROADV 2
SYNCOPATING RHYTHM. "Syncopating rhythm,
please echo home to me"   BROADV 2
A TALISMAN. "And what do I have"
                                             BROADV 2
TO REGGIE. "One day and a sleep ago"
                                             BROADV 2
UNENCOURAGED LINGERING. "I've got to go
now"   BROADV 2

WHAT IT MEANS TO BE AN "N". "When you got up
in the morning"   BROADV 2
WHEN. "When I wake up"   BROADV 2
Hodgson, Ralph. 1871. in English.
EVE. "Tumbling in twenty rings" FOLKW 67
GYPSY GIRL. "Come, try your skill, kind gentle-
men"   BRITAM 1
Hoey, Edwin A. in English.
FOUL SHOT.   SCHOL 7
Hoffenstein, Samuel. in English.
BREATHES THERE A MAN.   LIST 23
Hoffman, Daniel G. 1923. in English.
"An antelope of canteloupe"   LIBC 52
"An Armada of thirty whales"   LIBC 52
THE EVERLASTING.   LIBC 52
EXPLORATION. "I am who the trail took"
                                             LIBC 52
THE HERMIT OF CAPE ROSIER. "The Hermit of
Cape Rosier has three houses"   LIBC 52
"I dreamt my love a-dying lay"   LIBC 52
IN THE BEGINNING. "On the jetty, our fingers
shading"   LIBC 52
ISLANDS. "Springtide noon's low-watermark"
                                             LIBC 52
LOBSTERPOT LABYRINTHS. "Lobsterpot laby-
rinths wait. A porridge"   LIBC 52
A RAINRIDE. "If sky is water then this train"
                                             LIBC 52
SCHOLIAST/ICONOCLAST. "You are absolutely for
the relative"   LIBC 52
"The seals in Penobscot Bay"   LIBC 52
THAT THE PEAR DELIGHTS ME NOW. "That the
pear's boughs"   LIBC 52
"The voice of the woodthrush played at half
speed"   LIBC 52
Hoffman Llevano, Ernesto. in Spanish.
POEMA DEL HIJO. "Hijo de mi tristeza, de mi
desesperanza"   SMC 1
Hoffmann, Heinrich. 1809. in German.
STRUWWELPETER, exc.   ARGO 143
Hofmannsthal, Hugo von. 1874. in German.
BALLADE DES ÄUSSEREN LEBENS. "Und Kinder
wachsen auf mit tiefen Augen"
                               CHRIST 24, SPOA 8
DIE BEIDEN. "Sie trug den Becher in der Hand"
                                             DOVER 1
SCHONE SPRACHE.   CHRIST 24
TERZINEN, I - IV. "Noch spür ich ihren Atem"
                                             CHRIST 24
VORFRÜHLING. "Es läuft der Frühlingswind"
                                             SPOA 8
Poetry*   CHRIST
Hogg, James. 1770. in English.
A BOY'S SONG.   BRITAM 3
Holbrook, David. 1923. in English.
CARDONESS CASTLE. "The keeper stopped the
mower"   ARGO 90
Hölderlin, Friedrich. 1770. in German.
ABBITTE. "Heilig Wesen! gestört hab' ich die gol-
dene"   DEUTGR 22, DEUTGR 4
ABENDPHANTASIE. "Vor seiner Hütte ruhig im
Schatten sitzt der Pflüger"   DEUTGR 22
                                             DEUTGR 4
DER ABSCHIED. "Trennen wollten wir uns?"
                               CHRIST 22, DEUTGR 2

* Recording not available for analysis

AN DIE JUNGEN DICHTER. "Liebe Brüder! es reift unsere Kunst vielleicht" DEUTGR 22, DEUTGR 41
AN DIE NATUR. "Da ich noch um deinen Schleier spielte" DEUTGR 22, DEUTGR 41
AN DIE PARZEN. "Nur einen Sommer gönnt, ihr Gewaltigen" DEUTGR 6 DEUTGR 22, DEUTGR 41, SPOA 5, TELEF 1
AN DIOTIMA. DEUTGR 22, TELEF 1
ANDENKEN. "Der Nordost wehet" TELEF 1
BROT UND WEIN. "Rings um ruhet die Stadt" ATHENA 7, TELEF 1
DIE BÜCHER DER ZEITEN. "Herr! Herr!" CHRIST 10
DICHTERBERUF. "Des Ganges Ufer horten des Freudengotts" CHRIST 10
DICHTERMUT. "Sind denn dir nicht verwandt alle Lebendigen" DEUTGR 22
EHMALS UND JETZT. "In jüngern Tagen war ich des Morgens froh" DEUTGR 22, DEUTGR 41
DIE EICHBÄUME. "Aus den Gärten komm ich zu euch" DEUTGR 6, DEUTGR 22
DER FRIEDEN. "Wie wenn die alten Wasser, die" DEUTGR 22, TELEF 1
GEBET FÜR DIE UNHEILBAREN. "Eil o zaudernde Zeit" DEUTGR 22
GEH' UNTER, SCHÖNE SONNE. "Geh unter, schöne Sonne, sie achteten" DEUTGR 6, DEUTGR 22
GESANG DES DEUTSCHEN. "O Heilig Herz der Völker, O Vaterland" CHRIST 30
DER GOTT DER JUGEND. "Gehn dir im Dämmerlichte" DEUTGR 22, DEUTGR 41
DIE GOTTER. "Du stiller Aether! immer bewahrst du schon" DEUTGR 22, DEUTGR 41
GUTER RAT. "Hast du Verstand und ein Herz" DEUTGR 22, DEUTGR 41
HÄLFTE DES LEBENS. "Mit gelben Birnen hanget" CHRIST 10, SPOA 5
HEIDELBERG. "Lange lieb ich dich schon" DEUTGR 22, DEUTGR 41
DIE HEIMAT. "Froh kehrt der Schiffer heim an den stillen Strom" DEUTGR 6
HYPERIONS SCHICKSALSLIED. "Ihr wandelt droben im Licht" DEUTGR 6, DEUTGR 22, DOVER 1
DIE JUGEND. TELEF 1
DER JUNGLING AN DIE KLUGEN RATGEBER. "Ich sollte ruhn? Ich soll die Liebe zwingen?" DEUTGR 6, DEUTGR 22, DEUTGR 41
DIE KÜRZE. "Warum bist du so kurz? liebst du, wie vormals denn" DEUTGR 22, DEUTGR 41
LEBENSLAUF. "Grössers wolltest auch du" CHRIST 10, DEUTGR 22
DIE LIEBE. "Wenn ihre Freunde vergesst, wenn ihr die Euern all" DEUTGR 6, DEUTGR 22, DEUTGR 41, TELEF 1
MEIN EIGENTUM. "In seiner Fülle ruhet der Herbsttag" DEUTGR 22
MENONS KLAGEN UM DIOTIMA. "Täglich geh' ich heraus" DEUTGR 45
DER MENSCH. CHRIST 10
MENSCHENBEIFALL. "Ist nicht heilig mein Herz" DEUTGR 22, DEUTGR 41

DER NECKAR. "In deinen Tälern wachte mein Herz mir auf" CHRIST 10
RÜCKKEHR IN DIE HEIMAT. "Ihr milden Lüfte" CHRIST 22
SOKRATES UND ALKIBIADES. "Warum huldigest du, heiliger Sokrates" DEUTGR 22, DEUTGR 41
SONNENUNTERGANG. "Wo bist du? trunken dämmert die Seele mir" DEUTGR 22, DEUTGR 41
SOPHOKLES. "Viele versuchten umsonst das Freudigste freudig zu sagen" DEUTGR 22
TROST. DEUTGR 6, DEUTGR 22, DEUTGR 41
DER ZEITGEIST. "Zu lang schon waltest über dem Haupte mir" DEUTGR 22
DER ZÜRNENDE DICHTER. "Fürchtet den Dichter nicht, wenn er edel zürnet" DEUTGR 22
Holland, Bill. in English.
GOT TO GET YOU OFF MY MIND. "Stripped of your matter" WATSHD 4
Holland, Josiah Gilbert. in English.
GOD GIVE US MEN. DECCA 13
Hollander, John. 1929. in English.
ARISTOTLE TO PHYLLIS. "This chair I trusted, lass" CARIL 13
BY THE SEA. "The dark, gray receding tide uncovers" CARIL 13
CANZONA: A PARTING ON SHIPBOARD. "A bright jeweled beetle" CARIL 13
DIGGING IT OUT. "The icicle finger of death, aimed" SPOA 107
THE FABLE OF THE BEARS IN WINTER. "I once saw weeping" CARIL 13
FOR BOTH OF YOU, THE DIVORCE BEING FINAL. "We cannot celebrate with doleful music" CARIL 13
THE GREAT BEAR. "Even on clear nights, lead the most supple children" CARIL 13
HEAT OF SNOW. "When she, laughing, plastered a snowball" CARIL 13
JEFFERSON VALLEY. "The tops of the spruces here" CARIL 13
THE LADY'S-MAID'S SONG. "When Adam found his rib was gone" SPOA 107
LATE AUGUST ON THE LIDO. "To lie on these beaches for another summer" CARIL 13
A LION NAMED PASSION. "Hungering on the gray plain of its birth" CARIL 13
A NEW LEAF. "Manhattan, this hospital" SPOA 107
OFF MARBLEHEAD. "A woeful silence, following in our wash" CARIL 13
ON THE SAND BAR. CARIL 13
OVERCAST. "Bare alder and twiggy locust on our hill" CARIL 13
RACE ROCK LIGHT. "Over sparkling and green water" CARIL 13
THE SUNDIAL. "When in the festival of August heat" CARIL 13
A THEORY OF MEASURE. "We draw our own dimensions" CARIL 13
A THEORY OF WAVES. "Having no surface of its own" CARIL 13
UNDER CANCER. "On the memorial building's" SPOA 107
"When all of them ran off" CARIL 13

* Recording not available for analysis

Hollander, John (continued)

THE WHOLE STORY.   CARIL 13
Poetry*   JNP 24
Höllerer, Walter. in German.
Poetry*   NESKE 2
Hollo, Anselm. 1934. in English.
UNTIL DEATH DO US PART. "To think of them"
                                           FOLKW 21
Holman, Felice. 1919. in English.
PROTEST.   EAV 17
Holman, M. Carl. in English.
DEBATE OF DARK BROTHERS.   UA 2
Holmes, John. 1904. in English.
ALL'S WELL THAT ENDS.   SPOA 97
AUCTION.   CAED 111
CARRY ME BACK. "The big blue-jean, the sum-
mer-bored boy next door"   SPOA 97
THE FEAR OF DYING. "All men know it, the
young"   SPOA 97
Holmes, Oliver Wendell. 1809. in English.
BALLAD OF THE BOSTON TEA PARTY. "No! never
such a draught was poured"   DECCA 13,
                                            LIST 23
BALLAD OF THE OYSTERMAN. "It was a tall young
oysterman"   CAED 133, EAV 20
BILL AND JOE. "Come, dear old comrade, you
and I"   CAED 133
BROTHER JONATHAN'S LAMENT FOR SISTER CARO-
LINE. "She has gone, she has left us in passion
and pride"   CAED 133
CACOETHES SCRIBENDI. "If all the trees in all the
woods"   EAV 15
THE CAMBRIDGE CHURCHYARD. "Our ancient
church!"   CAED 133
THE CHAMBERED NAUTILUS. "This is the ship of
pearl, which, poets feign"   CAED 133,
EAV 14, HOUGHT 5, SPOA 31, SPOA 75,
                                            UCOL 1
CONTENTMENT. "Little I ask; my wants are few"
                              CAED 133, EAV 15
THE DEACON'S MASTERPIECE. "Have you heard of
the wonderful one-hoss shay"   CAED 133,
CAED 185, CAED 195, EAV 20, RCA 8
EPILOGUE TO THE BREAKFAST-TABLE SERIES. "A
crazy bookcase, placed before" CAED 133
GOD SAVE THE FLAG. "Washed in the blood of the
brave"   CAED 133
GRANDMOTHER'S STORY OF BUNKER-HILL BATTLE.
"'T is like stirring living embers when, at
eighty one remembers"   CAED 133
THE HEIGHT OF THE RIDICULOUS. "I wrote some
lines once on a time"   SPOA 31, SPOA 75
THE LAST LEAF. "I saw him once before"
AUDIA 2, CAED 133, EAV 14, LIST 3
THE LIVING TEMPLE. "Not in the world of light
alone"   CAED 133
MY AUNT. "My aunt! my dear unmarried aunt"
                                            EAV 15
OLD IRONSIDES. "Ay, tear her tattered ensign
down"   CAED 98 CAED 133, CAED 185,
CAED 195, DECCA 4, DECCA 13,
EAV 20, HARC 2, HOUGHT 5, LIST 4,
LIST 23, SINGER 2, PATHN 1
VERSES FOR AFTER-DINNER. "I was thinking last
night"   CAED 133
Poetry*   LIST 12

Hölty, Ludwig Heinrich Christopher. 1748. in
German.
AUFMUNTERUNG ZUR FREUDE. "Wer wollte sich
mit Grillen plagen"   DEUTGR 13, SPOA 5
LEBENSPFLICHTEN. "Rosen auf den Weg ges-
treut"   DOVER 1
DIE LIEBE. "Eine Schale des Harms, eine der
Freuden wog"   CHRIST 22
DIE MAINACHT. "Wenn der silberne Mond
durch die Gesträucher blickt"   ATHENA 7,
                                           CHRIST 11
VERMÄCHTNIS. "Ihr Freunde hänget, wann ich
gestorben bin"   DEUTGR 13
Holub, Miroslav. 1923. in Czech.
KAPRÁL, KTERÝ PROBODL ARCHIMEDA. "Smělým
zásahem"   Czech and English ARGO 16
V MIKROSKOPU. "I tady jsou krajiny snící"
                    Czech and English ARGO 16
VYNÁLEZY. "Moudří mužové v bílých   togách
předstupují" Czech and English ARGO 16
Holz, Arno. 1863. in German.
MONDNACHT IM SOMMER.   CHRIST 11
Homer. 9th c. B.C. in Greek.
ILIAD, exc. "Eute pur aidelon epiphlegei aspe-
ton hylen"   SCHOL 6
———. "He ra gyne tamie, o d'apessyto doma-
tos Hektor"   FOLKW 105;
                    Greek and English JNP 95
———. "Hos ara phonesas apebe pros makron
Olympon"   FOLKW 105;
                    Greek and English JNP 95
———. "Menin aeide, Thea, Peleiadeo Ak-
hileos"   CAED 28;
                    Greek and English JNP 95
———. "Nos phamene kai kerdosyne hegesat'
Athene"   Greek and English JNP 95
———. "Zeus de heon pros doma Theoi d'hama
pantes anestan" Greek and English JNP 95
ODYSSEY, exc. "Ai d'ote de potamoio roon peri-
kalle ikonto"   FOLKW 105
———. "Andra moi ennepe, Mousa, polypro-
pon, hos mala polla"   CAED 28;
                    Greek and English JNP 95
———. "Autar ego dikha pantas euknemidas
etairous"   FOLKW 105
———. "Autar epei tarpesan edetyos ede pote-
tos"   CAED 28
———. "Autar Odyssea megaletora fo en
foiko"   Greek and English JNP 95
———. "He d'anemon hos pnoie epessyt
demnia koures"   CAED 28
———. "Egno de psyche me podokeos Aiaki
dao"   CAED 28
———. "Emos d erigeneia phane rododaktylo
Eos"   FOLKW 105
———. He men ar os eipous apebe glaukopi
Athene"   FOLKW 105
———. "Hos eipon Thamnon hypedyseto dio
Odysseus"   Greek and English JNP 9
———. "Hos phamene psykhe men ebe domo
Aidos eiso"   FOLKW 10
———. "Kyklops, te, pie foinon, epei phage
andromea krea" Greek and English JNP 9
———. "Ton o harameibomenos prosepl
polymetis Odysseus"
                    Greek and English JNP

---

* Recording not available for analysis

Poetry* HOUGHT 3;
German DEUTGR 47; English CAED 94,
CAED 200, CMS 19, SPOA 38, SPOA 63,
SPOA 76

Honig, Edwin. 1919. in English.
THE GAZABOS. LIBC 40
Poetry* LIST 15

Hood, Thomas. 1799. in English.
BRIDGE OF SIGHS. "One more unfortunate"
DECCA 10, EAV 9, LIST 21
I REMEMBER, I REMEMBER. CAED 100,
CAED 111
NO! [NOVEMBER] "No sun—no moon!"
CAED 110
RUTH. "She stood breast-high amid the corn"
DECCA 12
SILENCE. "There is a silence where hath been no
sound" CAED 202, CMS 12
SONG OF THE SHIRT. "With fingers weary and
worn" EAV 9
SONNET. CAED 202
SONNET TO VAUXHALL. "The cold transparent
ham is on my fork" LONGM 1
THE TIME OF ROSES. CMS 13

Hopkins, Gerard Manley. 1844. in English.
"As king-fishers catch fire, dragonflies draw
flame" ARGO 70
BINSEY POPLARS. "My aspens dear, whose airy
cages quelled" ARGO 70, HARVOC 3,
SPOA 33
THE BROTHERS. "How lovely the elder bro-
ther's" CAED 68
THE CAGED SKYLARK. "As a dare-gale skylark
scanted in a dull cage" ARGO 70, EMC 4
THE CANDLE INDOORS. "Some candle clear burns
somewhere I come by" ARGO 70
CARRION COMFORT. "Not, I'll not, carrion com-
fort, Despair, not feast on thee" ARGO 70,
CAED 68, EMC 4, SPOA 33
EPITHALAMION, exc. "Hark, hearer, hear what I
do; lend a thought now, make believe"
EMC 4
FELIX RANDAL. "Felix Randal the farrier, O is he
dead then? my duty all ended" ARGO 70,
CAED 68, EMC 4, HARVOC 3, SPOA 33
GOD'S GRANDEUR. "The world is charged with
the grandeur of God" ARGO 70,
CAED 68, EMC 4, HARVOC 3,
LONGM 1, SPOA 33, THEAL 2
THE HABIT OF PERFECTION. "Elected Silence,
sing to me" ARGO 70, CAED 68,
LONGM 1, SPOA 33
HEAVEN–HAVEN: A NUN TAKES THE VEIL. "I have
desired to go" CAED 68, SPOA 33
HENRY PURCELL. "Have fair fallen, O fair, fair
have fallen, so dear" ARGO 70
HURRAHING IN HARVEST. "Summer ends now;
now, barbarous in beauty, the stooks rise"
ARGO 70, CAED 68, EMC 4, SPOA 33
"I wake and feel the fell of dark, not day"
ARGO 70, CAED 68, EMC 4, HARVOC 3,
LONGM 1, SPOA 33
INVERSNAID. "This darksome burn, horseback
brown" SPOA 33

THE LEADEN ECHO AND THE GOLDEN ECHO. "How
to keep—is there any any, is there none such,
nowhere known some, bow or brooch"
ARGO 70, ARGO 137, ARGO 143,
CAED 68, CAED 126, RCA 1, SPOA 33
THE MAY MAGNIFICAT. "May is Mary's month,
and I" ARGO 70
"My own heart let me have more pity on"
CAED 68, EMC 4
NO WORST, THERE IS NONE. "No worst, there is
none. Pitched past pitch of grief"
ARGO 70, CAED 68, EMC 4 SPOA 33,
LONGM 1
PATIENCE, HARD THING! "Patience, hard thing!
the hard thing but to pray" CAED 68,
EMC 4
PEACE. "When will you ever, Peace, wild wood-
dove, shy wings shut" ARGO 70, EMC 4
PIED BEAUTY. "Glory be to God for dappled
things" ARGO 70, AUDIA 1, BRITAM 1,
CAED 68, CAED 111, CMS 14, EMC 4,
HARVOC 3, JNP 8, LIST 3, LONGM 1,
SPOA 33
THE SEA AND THE SKYLARK. "On ear and ear two
noises too" EMC 4
SPELT FROM SIBYL'S LEAVES. "Earnest, earthless,
equal, attuneable, vaulty, voluminous, stu-
pendous" ARGO 70
SPRING. "Nothing is so beautiful as Spring"
EMC 4, SPOA 33
SPRING AND FALL: TO A YOUNG CHILD. "Margaret,
are you grieving" ARGO 70, CAED 69,
CAED 201, HARVOC 3, LONGM 1
THE STARLIGHT NIGHT. "Look at the stars"
CAED 68, CMS 14
THAT NATURE IS A HERACLITEAN FIRE AND OF THE
COMFORT OF THE RESURRECTION. "Cloud-puff-
ball, torn tufts, tossed pillows" CAED 68,
EMC 4
"Thee, God, I come from, to thee I go"
EMC 4
"Thou art indeed just, Lord, if I contend"
ARGO 70, CAED 68, EMC 4, SPOA 33
TO ROBERT BRIDGES. "The fine delight that fa-
thers thought" ARGO 70, SPOA 33
THE WINDHOVER: TO CHRIST OUR LORD. "I caught
this morning morning's minion, kingdom of
daylight's dauphin" ARGO 70, CAED 68,
CAED 201, CMS 12, EMC 4, HARVOC 3,
LONGM 1, SPOA 33
THE WRECK OF THE DEUTSCHLAND. "Thou master-
ing me" ARGO 70, CAED 68
———, exc. "She drove in the dark to leeward"
LONGM 1
Poetry* ARGO 1, LIST 11, PRENT 2,
PRENT 3

Hopkinson, Francis. 1737. in English.
AMERICAN INDEPENDENCE. DECCA 13
THE BATTLE OF THE KEGS. "Gallants attend and
hear" EAV 14

Hopkinson, Joseph. 1770. in English.
HAIL COLUMBIA. "Hail! Columbia, happy land"
DECCA 4, EAV 14

Horace (Quintus Horatius Flaccus). 65 B.C. in Lat-
in.
CARMINA. I. 1. "Maecenas atavis edite"
FOLKW 96

* Recording not available for analysis

Horace (Quintus Horatius Flaccus) (continued)

———— 4. "Solvitur acris hiems grata vice veris et favoni"   CAED 128, FOLKW 99

———— 5. "Quis multa gracilis to puer in rosa"   CAED 128, JNP 94

———— 9. "Vides ut alta stet nive candidum"   CAED 128, FOLKW 96, FOLKW 99

———— 11. "Tu ne quaesieris, scire nefas, quem mihi, quem tibi"   CAED 128, FOLKW 99

———— 14. "O navis, referent"   FOLKW 96

———— 16. "O matre pulchra filia pulchrior"   FOLKW 99

———— 17. "Velox amoenum saepe lucretilem"   FOLKW 99

———— 22. "Integer vitae"   FOLKW 96

———— 37. "Nunc est bibendum, nunc pede libero"   CAED 128

———— 38. "Persicos odi, puer, apparatus"   FOLKW 99

CARMINA. II. 2. "Nullus argento color est avaris"   FOLKW 99

———— 3. "Aequam memento rebus in arduis"   FOLKW 99

———— 7. "O saepe mecum tempus in ultimum"   FOLKW 99

———— 10. "Rectius vives, Licini, neque altum"   FOLKW 99

———— 14. "Eheu fugaces, Postume, Postume"   FOLKW 96, FOLKW 99

———— 16. "Otium divos rogat in parenti"   FOLKW 99

CARMINA. III. 13. "O fons bandusiae splendidior vitro"   FOLKW 99

———— 16. "Inclusam Danaen turris aenea"   FOLKW 99

———— 21. "O nata mecum consule Manlio"   FOLKW 99

———— 30. "Exegi monumentum aere perennius"   CAED 128, FOLKW 96

CARMINA. IV. 7. "Diffugere nives, dedeunt iam gramina campis"   FOLKW 99

———— 9. "Ne forte credas interitura quae"   FOLKW 99

———— 12. "Iam veris comites, quae mare temperant"   FOLKW 99

Poetry*   CETRA 18, JNP 94

Horne, Frank. 1900. in English.

TO JAMES. "Do you remember how you won your last race"   FOLKW 6, FOLKW 41

Poetry*   PRENT 1

Housman, Alfred Edward. 1859. in English.

"Along the field as we came by"   CAED 97

"As through the wild green hills of Wyre"   CAED 97

"Be still, my soul, be still; the arms you bear are brittle"   ARGO 1A

BREDON HILL. "In summertime on Bredon"   CAED 97

THE CARPENTER'S SON. "Here the hangman stops his cart"   CAED 97

"The chestnut casts his flambeaux, and the flowers"   ARGO 70A

CLUNTON AND CLUNBURY. "In valleys of springs of rivers"   CAED 97

"Could man be drunk forever"   ARGO 1A

"Crossing alone the nighted ferry"   ARGO 1A, LONGM 1

THE CULPRIT. "The night my father got me"   CAED 97, CMS 14

THE DESERTER. "What sound awakened me, I wonder"   FOLKW 6

EIGHT O'CLOCK. "He stood, and heard the steeple"   ARGO 1A CAED 97, HOUGHT 4

1887. "From Clee to heaven the beacon burns"   CAED 97

EPITAPH ON AN ARMY OF MERCENARIES. "These, in the day when heaven was falling"   ARGO 1A

FANCY'S KNELL. "When lads were home from labor"   ARGO 1A, BRITAM 1, CAED 97

"Farewell to barn and stack and tree"   CAED 97

THE FIRST OF MAY. "The orchards half the way"   CAED 97

FROM FAR, FROM EVE AND MORNING.   ARGO 77

"Good creatures, do you love your lives"   CAED 97

"Here dead lie we because we did not choose"   CAED 97

"I did not lose my heart in summer's even"   CAED 97

"I hoed and trenched and weeded"   ARGO 70A, CAED 97

"If it chance your eye offend you"   CAED 97

"In my own shire, if I was sad"   CAED 97

"In valleys green and still"   LONGM 1

"Into my heart an air that kills"   ARGO 70A

"Is my team ploughing"   CAED 97, CMS 14

"The lads in their hundreds to Ludlow come in for the fair"   ARGO 70A, CAED 97

"The laws of God, the laws of man"   CAED 97

"Loitering with a vacant eye"   CAED 97

"Loveliest of trees, the cherry now"   AUDIA 1, BRITAM 1, CAED 97, CMS 14 FOLKW 67, LIST 3, LIST 4, SINGER 6 THEAL 2

MERCENARY SOLDIERS.   CAED 196

MY BROTHER BERT.   ARGO 118

THE NEW MISTRESS. "O, sick I am to see you, will you never let me be"   CAED 97

"The night is freezing fast"   ARGO 70A

"Oh see how thick the goldcup flowers"   CAED 97, ARGO 139

"Oh, when I was in love with you"   CAED 97, DECCA 12

"On forelands high in heaven"   CAED 97

"On moonlit heath and lonesome bank"   CAED 97

"On the idle hill of summer"   ARGO 70A

"On Wenlock edge the wood's in trouble"   ARGO 70A, ARGO 77, BRITAM 1 CAED 97, CAED 201, LONGM 1

"Others, I am not the first"   ARGO 70A

PARTA QUIES. "Good-night; ensured release"   ARGO 1A, CAED 97

THE RECRUIT. "Leave your home behind, lad"   CAED 97

"Shot? So quick, so clean an ending"   CAED 97

"Stone, steel, dominions pass"   CAED 97

"Tarry, delight; so seldom met"   ARGO 70A

———

* Recording not available for analysis

"Tell me not here, it needs not saying"
        ARGO 70A, BRITAM 1, CAED 97,
                                FOLKW 64, JNP 62
"Terence, this is stupid stuff"   CAED 97
"This time of year a twelvemonth past"
                                        CAED 97
TO AN ATHLETE DYING YOUNG. "The time you
        won your town the race"   CAED 97,
                                        CAED 201
"Twice a week the winter thorough"
                                        CAED 97
"We'll to the woods no more"   CAED 97
"When first my way to fair I took" CAED 97
"When I was one-and-twenty"   AUDIA 1,
        CAED 97, DECCA 12, HOUGHT 4,
                                        LIST 3
"When I watch the living meet"   CAED 97
"When smoke stood up from Ludlow"
                        CAED 97, FOLKW 60
"White in the Moon the long road lies"
                                        DECCA 12
"The winds out of the West land blow"
                        CAED 97, DECCA 12
"With rue my heart is laden"   AUDIA 1,
        CAED 97, HARC 4, LIST 3
Poetry*   LIST 11
oward, Henry. See Surrey, Earl of.
oward, Lee. in English.
AND SOME CHILDREN COST AN ARM AND A LEG NOT
        TO MENTION THE REST OF YOUR LIFE. "I remem-
        ber the very day"   WATSHD 12
GRANNY. "Granny had a two-fisted approach"
                                        WATSHD 12
NO ONE IS EVER AT THE WHEEL. "She is afraid of
        tornadoes"   WATSHD 12
THE RAPE OF DONA. "We had always lived"
                                        WATSHD 12
oward, Richard. in English.
DRAMATIC MONOLOGUES, exc.   JNP 23
oward, Winifred. in English.
FAIRY WINGS. "Through the windmills fairies
        weave"   BOWMAR 1
owe, Julia Ward. 1819. in English.
BATTLE HYMN OF THE REPUBLIC. "Mine eyes have
        seen the glory of the coming of the Lord"
        CAED 98, DECCA 13, EAV 10, LIST 23,
                                RCA 4, RCA 9
owells, Mildred. in English.
GOING TOO FAR. "A woman who lived in Hol-
        land of old"   HARB 3
owes, Barbara. 1914. in English.
CITY AFTERNOON. "Far, far down"   SPOA 100
COQ DE COMBAT. "There Jack-cock struts"
                                        SPOA 100
THE CRITIC. "Ugolino takes his rest"
                                        SPOA 100
DEAD TOUCAN—GUADALOUPE. "Down like the
        oval fall"   SPOA 100
EARLY SUPPER. "Laughter of children brings"
                                        SPOA 100
LANDSCAPE: DEER SEASON. "Snorting his pleasure
        in the dying sun"   SPOA 100
ON A BOUGAINVILLEA VINE AT THE SUMMER PAL-
        ACE. "Under the sovereign crests of dead vol-
        canoes"   SPOA 100
TO W. H. AUDEN ON HIS 50TH BIRTHDAY. "Books col-
        lide"   SPOA 100

THE TRIUMPH OF DEATH. "Illusion forms before
        us like a grove"   SPOA 100
VIET NAPALM. "To save face we bomb"
                                        SPOA 82
Poetry*   JNP 25
Howitt, Mary. in English.
THE FAIRIES OF THE CALDON LOW. "And where
        have you been, my Mary"   CMS 4
Hoyt, Helen. in English.
ELLIS PARK. "Little park that I pass through"
                                        CAED 169
Huch, Ricarda. 1864. in German.
HEIMKEHR. "Ja, ich kam zurück"   CHRIST 22
Huchel, Peter. 1903. in German.
PSALM. "Dass aus dem Samen des Menschen"
                                        CHRIST 29
Huff, Barbara A. in English.
THE LIBRARY. "It looks like any building"
                                        HARB 2
Huff, Robert. 1924. in English.
Poetry*   JNP 26
Hughes, Langston. 1902. in English.
AFRICAN DANCE. "The low beatings of the tom-
        toms"   FOLKW 5
AFRO-AMERICAN FRAGMENT. "So long"
                                        SPOA 108
ALABAMA EARTH. "Deep in Alabama earth"
                                        FOLKW 6
ALBERTA K. JOHNSON.   SPOA 89
AMERICAN HEARTBREAK. "I am the American
        heartbreak"   LIBC 1 SPOA 108
APRIL RAIN SONG. "Let the rain kiss you"
                        FOLKW 5, HARB 2
AS I GREW OLDER. "It was a long time ago"
                                        FOLKW 5
AUNT SUE'S STORIES. "Aunt Sue has a head full of
        stories"   CAED 120 FOLKW 5
BABY. "Albert/Hey, Albert"   FOLKW 5
BAD LUCK CARD. "Cause you don't love me"
                                        SPOA 108
BAD MORNING. "Here I sit"   SPOA 108
BALLAD OF THE LANDLORD. "Landlord, land-
        lord"   CAED 120, FOLKW 46
BLUES AT DAWN. "I don't dare start thinking"
                                        UA 2
BOMBINGS IN DIXIE. "It's not enough to mourn"
                                        CAED 120
BORDER LINE. "I used to wonder"   LIBC 1,
                                        SPOA 108
BOUND NO'TH BLUES. "Goin' down de road,
        Lawd"   FOLKW 7, SPOA 108
THE CAT AND THE SAXOPHONE (2 A.M.). "Every-
        body"   FOLKW 45
CHRIST IN ALABAMA. "Christ is a nigger"
                                        CAED 120
CITY. "In the morning the city spreads its
        wings"   HARB 2
COULD BE. "Could be Hasting Street"
                                        SPOA 108
CROSS. "My old man's a white old man"
                                        FOLKW 45
CROWNS AND GARLANDS. "Make a garland of
        Leontynes"   CAED 120
CULTURAL EXCHANGE. "In the quarter of the
        negroes"   LIBC 1 SPOA 96, CAED 207
DAYBREAK IN ALABAMA. "When I get to be a
        composer"   CAED 120 WORLDP 1

* Recording not available for analysis

Hughes, Langston (continued)

DEAD IN THERE. "Sometimes"   CAED 120

DEFERRED. "This year, maybe, do you think"
                                    CAED 120

DEMOCRACY. "Democracy will not come"
                                    SPOA 108

DREAM BOOGIE. "Tinkling trebel"   CAED 120
                                    SPOA 108

DREAM DUST. "Gather out of star-dust"
                                    CAED 120

THE DREAM KEEPERS. "Leave me all of your
   dreams"   FOLKW 5 WORLDP 1

DREAM VARIATION. "To fling my arms wide"
                    FOLKW 5, SPOA 108

DREAMS. "Hold fast to dreams"   FOLKW 5,
                    FOLKW 6, SCHOL 7

DRESSED UP. "I had ma clothes cleaned"
                                    FOLKW 5

FEET O' JESUS. "At de feet o' Jesus" FOLKW 5,
                                    SPOA 108

FINAL CALL. "Send for the Pied Piper and let
   him pipe the rats away"   CAED 120

FLATTED FIFTH. "Little cullud boys with beards"
                                    SPOA 108

FLORIDA ROAD WORKERS. "Hey, Buddy"
                                    FOLKW 6

FREDERICK DOUGLASS: 1817–1895. "Douglass was
   someone who"   CAED 120

GENIUS CHILD. "This is a song for the genius
   child"   SPOA 108

GRADUATION. "Cinnamon and rayon"
                                    SPOA 108

HARLEM. "What happens to a dream deferred"
                    FOLKW 46, SPOA 108

HAVANA DREAMS. "The dream is a cocktail at
   Sloppy Joe's"   FOLKW 41

HEAVEN. "Heaven is/ the place where"
                                    CAED 120

HOMESICK BLUES. "The railroad bridge's"
                                    FOLKW 5

I TOO. "I too sing America"   CAED 120,
                    FOLKW 1, FOLKW 5, UA 2

IMPASSE. "I could tell you"   CAED 120

"In time of silver rain"   CAED 120,
                                    FOLKW 6

JUDGMENT DAY. "They put ma body in de
   ground"   SPOA 108

JUKE BOX LOVE SONG. "I could take the Harlem
   night"   CAED 120

KU KLUX. "They took me out"   SPOA 108,
                                    CAED 207

"Let America be America again"   SPOA 89

LIFE IS FINE. "I went down to the river"
                    CAED 120, SPOA 108

LINCOLN MONUMENT: WASHINGTON. "Let's go see
   Old Abe"   FOLKW 5

LINCOLN THEATRE. "The head of Lincoln looks
   down from the wall"   CAED 120

LITTLE LYRIC (OF GREAT IMPORTANCE). "I wish the
   rent"   SPOA 108

LITTLE OLD LETTER. "It was yesterday morning"
                                    CAED 120

LONG TRIP. "The sea is a wilderness of waves"
                                    FOLKW 5

LONG VIEW: NEGRO. "Emancipation: 1865"
                                    CAED 120

LYNCHBAUM.   German DEUTGR

MA LORD. "Ma Lord ain't no stuck-up man"
                    FOLKW 5, FOLKW

MADAM AND HER MADAM. "I worked for a wom
   an"   CAED 120, FOLKW 4

MADAM AND HER MIGHT-HAVE-BEEN. "I had tw
   husbands"   FOLKW 4

MADAM AND THE CENSUS MAN. "The census man
                    CAED 120, FOLKW 4

MADAM AND THE CHARITY CHILD. "Once I adop
   ed"   FOLKW 4

MADAM AND THE FORTUNE TELLER. "Fortune tel
   er looked in my hand"   FOLKW 4

MADAM AND THE MINISTER. "Reverend Butl
   came by"   FOLKW 4

MADAM AND THE NUMBER WRITER. "Number ru
   ner"   FOLKW 4

MADAM AND THE PHONE BILL. "You say I O.K.ec
                    CAED 120, FOLKW 4

MADAM AND THE RENT MAN. "The rent ma
   knocked"   CAED 120, FOLKW 4

MADAM AND THE WRONG VISITOR. "A ma
   knocked three times"   FOLKW 4

MADAM'S CALLING CARD. "I had some car
   printed"   FOLKW 46, LIBC

MADAM'S PAST HISTORY. "My name is Johnson
                                    FOLKW 4

ME AND THE MULE. "My old mule"   CAED 12

MERRY-GO-ROUND. "Where is the Jim Crow se
   tion"   LIBC 1, SPOA 96, CAED 20

MEXICAN MARKET WOMAN. "This ancient hag"
                                    FOLKW

MIDNIGHT RAFFLE. "I put my nickel"
                                    SPOA 10

MIDWINTER BLUES. "In the middle of the wi
   ter"   CAED 12

MILITANT. "Let all who will"   CAED 12

MISS BLUES'ES CHILD. "If the blues would let m
                                    SPOA 10

MOTHER IN WARTIME. "As if it were some not
   thing"   CAED 12

MOTHER TO SON. "Well, son, I'll tell you"
           FOLKW 5, FOLKW 45, HOUGHT
                    SCHOL 8, SPOA 108, UA

MOTTO. "I play it cool"   CAED 12
                                    SPOA 10

NEGRO. "I am a negro"   LIBC 1, SPOA 9
                                    SPOA 10

NEGRO DANCERS. "Me an' ma baby's"
                                    FOLKW

NEGRO SERVANT. "All day subdued, polite"
                                    CAED 1

THE NEGRO SPEAKS OF RIVERS. "I have known ri
   ers"   CAED 120, CAED 195, FOLKW
           FOLKW 5, HOUGHT 1, LIBC
           SPOA 96, SPOA 108, CAED 2

NIGHT AND MORN. "Sun's a settin' " FOLKW
                                    WORLDP

NIGHT: FOUR SONGS. "Night of the two moons
                                    CAED 1

NO REGRETS. "Out of love"   SPOA 1

NOT A MOVIE. "Well, they rocked him with roa
   apples"   CAED 1

ODE TO DINAH. "In the quarter of the negroe
                                    CAED 1

ONE-WAY TICKET. "I pick up my life"
                    SPOA 108, CAED 2

* Recording not available for analysis

PARADE. "Seven ladies"   CAED 120

PARISIAN BEGGAR WOMAN. "Once you were young"   FOLKW 5

POEM. "I loved my friend"   CAED 112

POEM. "We have tomorrow"   LIBC 1, SPOA 96

PRAYER. "Gather up"   SPOA 108

PRAYER. "I ask you this"   FOLKW 5

PRAYER MEETING. "Glory! Halleluiah!"   FOLKW 5

PUZZLED. "Here on the edge of hell"   CAED 120, CAED 207

QUESTION AND ANSWER. "Durban, Birmingham"   CAED 120

REFUGE IN AMERICA. "There are words like freedom"   CAED 120, SPOA 108

ROLAND HAYES BEATEN (GEORGIA: 1942). "Negroes/ sweet"   SPOA 108

SAILOR. "He sat upon the rolling deck"   FOLKW 5

SAN FRANCISCO CITY: SAN FRANCISCO. FOLKW 6

SEA CALM. "How still"   CAED 109

SEASCAPE. "Off the coast of Ireland"   FOLKW 5

SILHOUETTE. "Southern gentle lady"   SPOA 108

SINNER. "Have mercy, Lord"   SPOA 108

THE SNAIL. "Little snail, Dreaming you go"   CAED 120, FOLKW 6

SONG FOR A DARK GIRL. "Way down South in Dixie"   CAED 120, FOLKW 41, SPOA 108

SONG FOR BILLIE HOLLIDAY. "What can purge my heart"   CAED 120

SOUTHERN MAMMY SINGS. "Miss Gardner's in her garden"   CAED 120, CAED 207

STILL HERE. "I been scared and battered"   CAED 120, LIBC 1, SPOA 96

SUICIDE'S NOTE. "The calm"   SPOA 108

TOMORROW.   SPOA 108

TOO BLUE. "I got those sad old weary blues"   CAED 120, SCHOL 7

TRUMPET PLAYER. "The Negro with the trumpet"   ARGO 17, CAED 207

VARI-COLORED SONG. "If I had a heart of gold"   CAED 120

WATER-FRONT STREETS. "The spring is not so beautiful there"   FOLKW 5

THE WEARY BLUES. "Droning a drowsy syncopated tune"   FOLKW 5, SPOA 108

WHEN SUE WEARS RED. "When Susanna Jones wears red"   ARGO 17, CAED 120, FOLKW 5

WHO BUT THE LORD. "I looked and I saw"   CAED 120

WIDE RIVER. "Ma baby lives across de river"   FOLKW 5

WINTER SWEETNESS. "This little house is sugar"   FOLKW 6

WITHOUT BENEFIT OF DECLARATION. "Listen here, Joe"   CAED 120

YOUTH. "We have tomorrow"   FOLKW 6

Poetry*   EAV 2, MGM 1, PRENT 1, PRENT 2

Iughes, Ted. 1930. in English.

APPLE TRAGEDY. "So on the seventh day"   CAED 206

BOWLED OVER. "By kiss of death, bullet on brow"   ARGO 95

A CHILDISH PRANK. "Man's and woman's bodies lay without souls"   CAED 206

COLLISION WITH THE EARTH. "Collision with the earth has finally come"   CAED 172

THE CONTENDER. "There was this man and he was the strongest"   CAED 206

CROW AND MAMA. "When Crow cried his mother's ear"   CAED 206

CROW HEARS FATE KNOCK ON THE DOOR. "Crow looked at the world, mountainously heaped"   CAED 206

CROW PAINTS HIMSELF INTO A CHINESE MURAL. "The grass camps in its tussock"   CAED 206

CROW'S ELEPHANT TOTEM SONG. "Once upon a time"   CAED 206

CROW'S FALL. "When Crow was white he decided the sun was too white"   CAED 206

CROW'S FIRST LESSON. "God tried to teach Crow how to talk"   CAED 206

THE DEAD MAN LIES. "The dead man lies"   CAED 172

EVERY DAY OF THE WORLD. "Every day of the world"   CAED 172

FULL MOON AND LITTLE FRIEDA. "A cool small evening shrunk to a dog bark and the clank of a bucket"   ARGO 95, CAED 206

GNAT-PSALM. "When the gnats dance at evening"   CAED 206

GOG. "I woke to a shout: 'I am Alpha and Omega'"   ARGO 95, CAED 206

THE GREEN WOLF. "Your neighbor moves less and less, attempts less"   CAED 206

HAWK ROOSTING. "I sit in the top"   CAED 172

HEPTONSTALL. "Black village of gravestones"   CAED 206

HER HUSBAND. "Comes home dull with coal-dust deliberately"   ARGO 95, CAED 206

HIS LEGS RAN ABOUT. "Till they tangled and seemed to trip"   CAED 172

A HORRIBLE RELIGIOUS ERROR. "When the serpent emerged, earth-bowel brown"   CAED 206

HOW WATER BEGAN TO PLAY. "Water wanted to live"   CAED 206

THE HOWLING OF WOLVES. "Is without world"   CAED 206

ICECRUST AND SNOWFLAKE. "A polished glancing. A bluefrost-bright dawn"   CAED 172

THE JAGUAR. "The apes yawn and adore their fleas in the sun"   CAED 172

KREUTZER SONATA. "Now you have stabbed her good"   CAED 206

THE LOVEPET. "Was it an animal was it a bird?"   CAED 206

LOVESONG. "He loved her and she loved him"   CAED 206

MAYDAY ON HOLDERNESS. "This evening motherly summer"   CAED 172

MOUNTAINS. "I am a fly if these are not stones"   ARGO 95

NOTES FOR A LITTLE PLAY. "First—the sun coming closer, growing by the minute"   CAED 206

* Recording not available for analysis

Hughes, Ted (continued)

ONCE I SAID LIGHTLY. "Once I said lightly"
CAED 172
AN OTTER. "Underwater eyes, an eel's"
CAED 172
OUT. "My father sat in his chair recovering"
ARGO 95, CAED 206
PIBROCH. "The sea cries with its meaningless
voice"   CAED 206
PIKE. "Pike, three inches long; perfect"
CAED 172
A PRIMROSE PETAL'S EDGE. "A primrose petal's
edge"   CAED 172
THE RETIRED COLONEL. "Who lived at the end of
our street"   CAED 172
THE SEA GRIEVES. "The sea grieves"
CAED 172
SECOND GLANCE AT A JAGUAR. "Skinful of bowls,
he bowls them"   CAED 206
SHEEP, exc.   CAED 172
SIX YOUNG MEN. "The celluloid of a photograph
holds them well"   CAED 172
SONG FOR A PHALLUS. "There was a boy was
Oedipus"   CAED 206
STILL LIFE. "Outcrop stone is miserly"
ARGO 95
SUNSTROKE. "Frightening the blood in its tun-
nel"   CAED 172
THEOLOGY. "No, the serpent did not"
CAED 206
THIS IS THE MANEATER'S SKULL. "This is the
maneater's"   CAED 172
THISTLES. "Against the rubber tongues of cows
and hoeing hands of men"   CAED 206
THE THOUGHT-FOX. "I imagine this midnight
moment's forest"   CAED 172, LIBC 40
VIEW OF A PIG. "The pig lay on the barrow"
CAED 172, SPOA 67
THE WARRIORS OF THE NORTH. "Bringing their
frozen swords, their salt-bleached eyes, their
salt-bleached hair"   ARGO 95
WAVING GOODBYE. "Waving goodbye from your
banked hospital bed"   CAED 172
"What will you make of half a man"
CAED 172
"When the still-soft eyelid"   CAED 172
WODWO. "What am I? Nosing here, turning
leaves over"   ARGO 95
Poetry*   LIST 15

Hugo, Richard F. 1923. in English.
KENNEDY UCCISO. "Don't scream at me you God
damn' wops"   FOLKW 21
Poetry*   WATSHD 56

Hugo, Victor. 1802. in French.
A L'HOMME QUI A LIVRÉ UNE FEMME. "O Honte! ce
n'est pas seulement cette femme"   ADES 7
A MA FILLE, ADELE.   CAED 204
A VILLEQUIER. "Maintenant que Paris, ses pavés
et ses marbres"   HACH 11, HACH 21
"Apres la bataille"   HACH 2
AU BORD DE LA MER. "La nuit vient. Vénus
brille"   ADES 39
AVE, DEA; MORITURUS TE SALUTAT. "La mort et la
beauté sont deux choses profondes"
ADES 7, ADES 48, ADES 54

BOOZ ENDORMI, exc. "Booz c'était couché de
fatigue accablé"   ADES 7, ADES 54
FOLKW 86
———. "Pendant qu'il sommeillait, Ruth, une
Moabite"   SPOA 9
———, exc.   ADES 39, ADES 48, GMS 9
LA CAMPAGNE DE RUSSIE. "Il neigeait. On était
vaincu par sa conquête"   ADES 39
HACH 21, SPOA 30
CE QUE DIT LA BOUCHE D'OMBRE. "L'Homme en
songeant descend au gouffre universel"
ADES 39
CHANT DU BOL DE PUNCH. "Je suis la flamme
breue"   ADES 7
LES CHANTS DU CRÉPUSCULE. XXV. "Puisque j'a
mis ma lèvre à ta coupe encor pleine"
HACH 11
LA CONSCIENCE.   HACH 2
LES CONTEMPLATIONS. VII. "Elle était pâle, e
pourtant rose"   GMS 6
DEMAIN, DÈS L'AUBE. "Demain, dès l'aube, à
l'heure où blanchit la campagne"
ADES 39, FOLKW 86, GMS 6
ELLE.   ADES 48, DOVER 4
L'ENFANT GREC. "Les turques ont passé la"
PATHE 1
FABLE OU HISTOIRE. "Un jour, maigre et sentan
un royal appétit"   ADES 39
LES FEUILLES D'AUTOMNE, exc. "Ce siècle avai
deux ans! Rome remplaçait Sparte"
ADES 39, HACH 2
———, exc. "Ô mes letters d'amours, de vertu
de jeunesse"   ADES 39
FONCTION DU POÈTE. "Pourquoi t'exiler, ô po
ète"   ADES 54, HACH 21
HYMNE. "Ceux qui pieusement sont morts pou
la patrie"   PATHE 1
JE CONTRAINS TOUTE SÈVE.   ADES 39
"Jeanne était au pain sec dans le cabinet noir"
HACH 2
JEUNE FILLE, L'AMOUR.   CAED 20
"J'eus un rève: le mur des siècles m'apparut"
ADES 39
MON ENFANCE. "J'ai des rêves de guerre en mo
âme"   HACH 21
LA MORT D'UN CHIEN.   HACH 2
NUITS DE JUIN. "L'été, lorsque le jour a fin"
DOVER 4
ODE A LA COLONNE. "A, Quand il"   PATHE 1
"Oh! Je fus comme fou dans le premier mo
ment"   HACH 21
LA PETITE INFANTE DE CASTILLE, exc.   GMS 6
LE PEUPLE ÉTAIT DEBOUT.   HACH 21
PREMIER JANVIER. "Enfants, on vous dira plu
tard que le grand-pere"   HACH 2
"Puisque mai tout en fleurs dans les prés nou
reclame"   ADES 7, ADES 48
RENCONTRE. "Après avoir donné son aumône u
plus jeune"   ADES 39
LA ROSE DE L'INFANTE. "Elle est toute petite"
HACH 2
LE SACRE DE LA FEMME. I. "L'aurore apparaissait"
ADES 7
LA SAISON DES SEMAILLES. "C'est le moment cré
pusculaire"   ADES 54, HACH 2, SPOA 9
"Sonnez, sonnez toujours, clairons de l
pensés"   HACH 21

* Recording not available for analysis

TRISTESSE D'OLYMPIO. "Les champs n'étaient point noirs, les cieux n'étaient pas mornes" HACH 11, HACH 21

LA VACHE. "Devant la blanche ferme où parfois vers midi" HACH 2

VIEILLE CHANSON DU JEUNE TEMPS. "Je ne songeais pas à Rose" ADES 7, ADES 54

"Viens! Une flûte invisible" HACH 2

Poetry* HACH 17

Huidobro, Vicente. 1893. in Spanish.
EN. "El corazón del pájaro" FOLKW 80
RUY DÍAZ PARTE A LA GUERRA. GMS 13

Humphreys, Emyr. 1919. in English.
DREAM FOR A SOLDIER. ARGO 152
A ROMAN DREAM. ARGO 152
TWENTY-FOUR PAIRS OF SOCKS. ARGO 152

Humphries, Rolfe. 1894. in English.
FROM THE NORTH TERRACE. HOUGHT 2

Hunt, (James Henry) Leigh. 1784. in English.
ABOU BEN ADHEM. "Abou ben Adhem (may his tribe increase)" CAED 162, DECCA 10, EAV 8, LIST 21

DIALOGUE BETWEEN A MAN AND A FISH. "You strange, astonished looking anglefaced" FOLKW 60

THE NILE. "It flows through old hushed Egypt" CAED 202

RONDEAU. "Jenny kissed me when we met" CAED 202, DECCA 12, LION 2

Hurtado de Mendoza, Diego. 1364. in Spanish.
COSANTE. "Á aquel árbol que mueve la foxa" DOVER 2

Ibarbourou, Juana de. 1895. in Spanish.
LA CUNA. "Si yo supiera de que selva vino" GMS 13

"He bebido del chorro cándido de la fuente" AGUIL 8

LA HIGUERA. "Porque es áspera y fea" FIDIAS 2, GMS 13, HOLT 1

IMPLACABLE. "Y te dí el olor de todas mis dalias" SMC 7

LA INQUIETUD FUGAZ. "He mordido manzanas y he besado tus labios" FOLKW 79

NOCHE DE LLUVIA. "Llueve . . . , espera, no te duermas" FOLKW 80

OLOR FRUTAL. "Con membrillos maduros" GMS 13

LA PEQUEÑA LLAMA. "Yo siento por la luz un amor de salvaje" HOLT 1

SALVAJE. "Bebo el agua clara y limpia del arroyo" FIDIAS 2

Ignatow, David. 1914. in English.
ALL QUIET. "How come nobody is being bombed today" SCHOL 3

APPLE WATCHER. "Rose is my apple watcher" SCHOL 3

THE BAGEL. "I stopped to pick up the bagel" SCHOL 3

BEFORE THE SABBATH. "The man is gone on a Friday" FOLKW 21

BOTHERING ME AT LAST. "Where is my mother" SCHOL 3

THE DEBATE. "This man brings me stones" SCHOL 3

EMERGENCY CLINIC. "Come in with your stab wound" SCHOL 3

GET THE GASWORKS. "Get the gasworks into a poem" SCHOL 3

HOW COME? "I'm in New York covered by a layer of soap" SCHOL 3

MOVING PICTURE. "When two take gas" SCHOL 3

NICE GUY. "I had a friend and he died, me" SCHOL 3

PLAYFULLY. "Lovely death of the horse" SCHOL 3

RESCUE THE DEAD. "Finally, to forego love is to kiss a leaf" SCHOL 3

THE SKY IS BLUE. "Put things in their place" SCHOL 3

SOLDIER. "In his hands, the submachine gun is excited" SCHOL 3

TO NOWHERE. "I carry my keys like a weapon" SCHOL 3

TWO FRIENDS. "I have something to tell you" SCHOL 3

Poetry* WATSHD 37

Inman, Will. 1923. in English.
JACQUELINE. "And when she strides" FOLKW 21

KAURI. "Kauri is a Hindi word" BROADR 2

Ipagongnaik, Nende. in English.
PAPUA NEW GUINEA. "Progressing land of peace and freedom" FOLKW 110

Iriarte, Tomás de. 1750. in Spanish.
THE ASS AND THE FLUTE. Spanish and English CMS 5

Isaacs, Jorge. in Spanish.
LA TUMBA DE BELISARIO. MIAMI 1

Isgrò, Emilio. in Italian.
PRODUCE ARANCE. CETRA 31

Ivo, Ledo. 1924. in Portuguese.
A LAGARTIXA. "Da meninice lembro apenas" FOLKW 71

Jackson, Gerald. in English.
POEM TO AMERICANS. "I watched the road" BROADR 2

Jackson, Kathryn. in English.
NOONDAY SUN. "Oh I've ridden plenty of horses" HARB 4

Jacob, Max. 1876. in French.
AMOUR DU PROCHAIN. "Qui a vu le crapaud traverser" ADES 55

CONFESSION DE L'AUTEUR: SON PORTRAIT EN CRABE. "Comme une cathédrale il est cravaté d'ombre" ADES 38

GLOIRE, CAMBRIOLAGE OU RÉVOLUTION. ADES 38

LA GUERRE. ADES 38

IL SE PEUT. ADES 38

LE KAMICHI. "L'échafaud, c'est la guillotine" FOLKW 13

LA LETTRE IMAGINAIRE. "Non, Marcel, non, tout est fini" CBS 1

LETTRES. ADES 55

LUEURS DANS LES TÉNÈBRES. ADES 38

LUNE COULEUR DE SANG. "Tristesse d'eau, Vierge qui pâme" ADES 38, ADES 54

MILLE REGRETS. ADES 38

POUR LES ENFANTS ET POUR LES RAFFINÉS. ADES 38

LA SALTIMBANQUE EN WAGON DE 3e CLASSE. "La saltimbanque! la saltimbanque" ADES 38

* Recording not available for analysis

Jacob, Max (continued)

VILLONELLE.   ADES 38
Poetry*   ADES 50, ADES 51

Jacob, Violet. in English.
TAM I' THE KIRK. "O Jean, my Jean, when the bell"   BRITAM 1

Jacobi, Johann Georg. 1740. in German.
AN DIE NACHT. "Bist du nicht mehr dem Sänger hold?"   DEUTGR 13

Jacobs, Leland B. 1907. in English.
TAILS. "Some tails wiggle"   CREAT 1

Jacobsen, Ethel. in English.
DID YOU EVER. "Did you ever, ever, ever"   HARB 1

Jacobsen, Josephine. 1908. in English.
Poetry*   TAPES 4, WATSHD 25

Jacobson, Dan. 1929. in English.
Poetry*   JNP 27

Jaffe, Dan. 1933. in English.
THE FORECAST.   SCHOL 7

Jaffe, Ellen. in English.
VIET NAM . . . AUGUST 11, 1966.   PROTHM 7

Jaimes Freyre, Ricardo. 1868. in Spanish.
LO FUGAZ. "La rosa temblorosa"   HOLT 1

James I, King of Scotland. 1394. in English.
THE KINGIS QUAIR, exc.   ARGO 30

Jammes, Francis. 1868. in French.
AVEC TON PARAPLUIE BLEU ET TES BREBIS. "Avec ton parapluie bleu et tes brebis sales"   ADES 54
ÉLÉGIE QUATORZIÈME. "Mon amour, disais-tu"   ADES 12
FINALE.   ADES 12
J'AIME L'ÂNE. "J'aime l'âne si doux"   HACH 4
J'ALLAIS DANS LE VERGER. "J'allais dans le verger où les framboises au soleil"   ADES 12
LA JEUNE FILLE. "La Jeune fille est blanche"   ADES 12
LES MYSTÈRES DOULOUREUX. "Par le petit garcon qui meurt près de sa mère"   ADES 12
PRIÈRE POUR ALLER AU PARADIS AVEC LES ÂNES. "Lorsqu'il faudra aller vers vous, ô mon Dieu, faites"   ADES 12, HACH 14; English LIBC 54, SPOA 19
PRIÈRE POUR AVOIR UNE FEMME SIMPLE. "Mon Dieu, faites que celle qui pourra être ma femme"   ADES 12
QU'EST-CE QUE LE BONHEUR? "Qu'est-ce que le bonheur? Peut-être un vallon bleu"   ADES 12
LA SALLE A MANGER. "Il y a une armoire à peine luisante"   FOLKW 13
TU SERAS NUE. "Tu seras nue dans le salon aux vieilles choses"   ADES 12
LA VALLÉE. "La vallée d'Alméria"   ADES 12
LE VILLAGE À MIDI. "Le village a midi. La mouche d'or bourdonne"   ADES 54
Poetry*   ADES 50, ADES 51

Jandl, Ernst. 1925. in German.
IM REICH DER TOTEN.   LUCHT 1

Jang Ji. 756 A.D. in Chinese.
FENG CHAU YE BWO. "Ywe lwo wu ti shwang mau tyan"   FOLKW 76

Jarrell, Randall. 1914. in English.
A CAMP IN THE PRUSSIAN FOREST. "I walk beside the prisoners to the road"   HARP 5
CINDERELLA. "Her imaginary playmate was a grown-up"   LIBC 1, SPOA 101
THE DEATH OF THE BALL TURRET GUNNER. "From my mother's sleep I fell into the State"   CAED 150, CAED 155
EIGHTH AIR FORCE. "If, in an odd angle of the hutment"   CAED 150, LIBC 1
GUNNER. "Did they send me away from my cat"   HARPV 5
IN MONTECITO.   HARPV 5
LADY BATES. "The lightning of a summer"   LIBC 15, LIBC 43
THE LINES. "After the centers' naked files, the basic line"   CAED 150, HARPV 5
LOSSES. "It was not dying: everybody died"   LIBC 1
A LULLABY. "For wars his life and half a world away"   CAED 150
MAIL CALL. "The letters always just evade the hand"   CAED 150
NEXT DAY.   HARPV 5
THE PLAYER PIANO.   HARPV 5
THE PRINCE. "After the door shuts and the foot steps die"   HARPV 5
STALAG LUFT. "In the yard, by the house"   LIBC 15, LIBC 43
THREE BILLS.   HARPV 5
A WARD IN THE STATES. "The ward is barred with moonlight"   HARPV 5
THE WOMAN AT THE WASHINGTON ZOO. The sari go by me from the embassies"   LIBC 1 SPOA 10
Poetry*   JNP 2

Jarry, Alfred. 1873. in French.
LE BAIN DU ROI. "Rampant d'argent sur un champ de sinople, dragon"   FOLKW 1

Jaszi, Jean. in English.
FIGHT. "Cat and I"   HARB

Jeffers, Lance. 1919. in English.
THE AFROAMERICAN FACE. "The black face ha greater weight"   BROADV
BLACK MAN IN A NEW DAY. "The lungs that sculp tured slave songs"   BROADV
BLACK SOUL OF THE LAND. "I saw an old blac man walk down the road"   BROADV
CHILDREN AND A FETUS. "So to these tulip buds   BROADV
CRUELTY. "There is an arctic icefloe in the human soul"   BROADV
A DARK AND SUDDEN BEAUTY. "Dark and sudde beauty"   WATSHD
DEATH OF AMERICA. "The table on which m earthenware rests its feet"   BROADV
HOMECOMING. "Seamstress of my night's swee lace"   BROADV
HOW MANY WHITENESSES. "How many white nesses"   WATSHD
HUMAN LIFE. "Human life is like a black and leg less beggar stumping"   BROADV
HUMILIATION. "The train drives down the can yon walls"   BROADV
'I REPENT' SHOULD BE. "I repent should be"   WATSHD

I SING MY PEOPLE. "I sing the endless cartracks in my flesh that must be ripped up" BROADV 9

I WAIT. "I wait for the white light" WATSHD 7

LET MY LAST BREATH BE IMMORTAL SANDALS: FOR MY CHILDREN. "Let me die with the memory of their love songs" BROADV 9

MAN WITH A FURNACE IN HIS MIND. "From the ocean filled with sand inside of me" BROADV 9

"My blackness is the beauty of this land" BROADV 9

MY FATHER (HENRY NELSON) "My father lies in his grave" WATSHD 7

MY GIRL IN A GEORGIA TOWN. "If my soul be empty, if my soul be fettered" BROADV 9

NAT. "His knotty hand trembled" WATSHD 7

THE NIGHT RAINS HOT TAR. "The night rains hot tar into my throat" BROADV 9

NO ONE ELSE. "No one else can hum the mutter of my silence" BROADV 9

"O Africa where I bake my bread" WATSHD 7

ON LISTENING TO THE SPIRITUALS. "When a master lived" WATSHD 7

POETRY. "Poetry the strong-backed wrathy whore whose" BROADV 9

PRAYER. "Their madness can never be my god" WATSHD 7

PRISON. "And where my prison walls squatted down upon" BROADV 9

THE ROCKS MY PEOPLE THREW. "The rocks my people threw in Birmingham" BROADV 9

SO DEEP IN RIVERS OF THAT STROMSBERG TIME. "The locks of sleep overflow upon my lap" BROADV 9

THE SONG. "When I was a janitor's stepson among the wealthy whites" BROADV 9

A STRANGE BLACK WOMAN SPEAKS OF CHEYNEY. "I know Cheyney as if he were conceived within my womb" BROADV 9

TEARSPLOTCHES FOR MY CHILDREN. "Tearsplotches for my children will turn no muscle red" BROADV 9

THE UNKNOWN. "A river of slush runs down through my heart" BROADV 9

VIETNAM: I NEED MORE THAN THIS CRUST OF SALT. "I need more than this crust of salt upon my eye" BROADV 9

WHAT BLACK I. "If leaves shaking the wind" WATSHD 7

WHEN I KNOW THE POWER OF MY BLACK HAND. "I do not know the power" WATSHD 7

WHEN SHE SPOKE OF GOD. "Mrs. Williams' face was pleading when she spoke of her God to me" BROADV 9

Poetry* PRENT 1

ffers, Robinson. 1887. in English.

ANTE MORTEM. "It is likely enough that lions and scorpions" CAED 129

APOLOGY FOR BAD DREAMS. "In the purple light, heavy with redwood, the slopes drop seaward" CAED 129

AVE CAESAR. "No bitterness: our ancestors did it" CAED 129

THE BEAKS OF EAGLES. "An eagle's nest on the head of an old redwood on one of the precipice-footed ridges" LIBC 11, LIBC 34

THE BEAUTY OF THINGS. "To feel and speak the astonishing beauty of things—earth, stone, and water" CAED 129, RCA 10

THE BED BY THE WINDOW. "I chose the bed downstairs by the sea-window" CAED 129

BIRTH-DUES. "Joy is a trick in the air" CAED 129

THE BLOODY SIRE. HARPV 4, HARVOC 10, LIBC 36

BOATS IN A FOG. "Sports and gallantries, the stage, the arts, the antics of dancers" CAED 129

THE CONDOR. HOUGHT 2

DIVINELY SUPERFLUOUS BEAUTY. "The storm-dances of gulls, the barking game of seals" CAED 129

GRANITE AND CYPRESS. "White-maned, wide-throated, the heavy-shouldered children of the wind" CAED 129

THE HOUSE DOG'S GRAVE. "I've changed my ways a little" CAED 129

HUNGERFIELD, exc. "It is no good, Una has died and I" CAED 129

HURT HAWKS, I. "The broken pillar of the wings" CAED 129, HOUGHT 5, SPOA 93

————, II. "I'd sooner, except the penalties, kill a man than a hawk" CAED 129, SPOA 93

LOVE THE WILD SWAN. "I hate my verses, every line" CAED 129

THE LOW SKY. "No vulture is here, hardly a hawk" SPOA 93

NATURAL MUSIC. "The old voice of the ocean" HARPV 4, HARVOC 10

NIGHT. "The ebb slips from the rock, the sunken" CAED 129, SPOA 93

NOVEMBER SURF. "Some lucky day each November great waves awake and are drawn" CAED 129

NOW RETURNED HOME. "Beyond the narrows of the Inner Hebrides" SPOA 93

O, LOVELY ROCK. "We stayed the night in the pathless gorge" BIGSUR 4, LIBC 11, LIBC 34

THE OLD STONEMASON. "Stones that rolled in the sea" CAED 129

OSSIAN'S GRAVE. "Steep up in Lubitavish townland stands" LIBC 11, LIBC 34

PHENOMENA. "Great-enough both accepts and subdues" CAED 129

POST MORTEM. "Happy people die whole, they are all dissolved in a moment" CAED 129

REARMAMENT. "These grand and fatal movements toward death" CAED 129

RETURN BIRTHDAY. ARGO 12

THE ROAN STALLION. "The dog barked; then the woman stood in the doorway" FOLKW 33

ROCK AND HAWK. "Here is a symbol in which" CAED 129

SCIENCE. "Man, introverted man, having crossed" BIGSUR 4, CAED 129

SHANE O'NEILL'S CAIRN. "When you and I on the Palos Verdes cliff" SPOA 93

* Recording not available for analysis

Jeffers, Robinson (continued)

SHINE, PERISHING REPUBLIC. "While this America settles in the mould of its vulgarity, heavily thickening to empire"   CAED 129
SUICIDE'S STONE. "Peace is the heir of dead desire"   HARPV 4, HARVOC 10
SUMMER HOLIDAY. "When the sun shouts and people abound"   CAED 129, HOUGHT 5
THEIR BEAUTY HAS MORE MEANING. "Yesterday morning enormous the moon hung low on the ocean"   CAED 129
TO THE STONE-CUTTERS. "Stone-cutters fighting time with marble, you foredefeated"
                    CAED 129, HARPV 4, HARVOC 10
TOWER BEYOND TRAGEDY. "You'd never have thought the Queen was Helen's sister"
                    FOLKW 34, HARPV 4
THE TRUCE AND THE PEACE. VII. "Peace now for every fury has had her day"   HARPV 4, HARVOC 10
WATCH THE LIGHTS FADE.   HARPV 4, HARVOC 10
WISE MEN IN THEIR BAD HOURS. "Wise men in their bad hours have envied"   HARPV 4, HARVOC 10
THE WOMEN AT POINT SUR. XII. "Here were new idols again"   CAED 129
Poetry*   BIGSUR 3, ISU 1, NET 4, BIGSUR 5, LIST 13

Jeffries, Christine F. in English.
ZEBEDEE, THE ZEBRA. "Zebedee, the Zebra, lived in a zoo"   HARB 2

Jennings, Elizabeth. 1926. in English.
CARAVAGGIO'S NARCISSUS IN ROME. "Look at yourself, the shine, the sheer"   PROTHM 8
FOR A CHILD BORN DEAD. "What ceremony can we fit"   FOLKW 59A, FOLKW 65A
FOUNTAIN.   FOLKW 65A
HARVEST AND CONSECRATION. "After the heaped piles"   ARGO 94
HOSPITAL. "Observe the hours which seem to stand"   ARGO 94
IN A FOREIGN CITY.   FOLKW 65A
MY GRANDMOTHER. "She kept an antique shop"   ARGO 94
PATIENTS IN A PUBLIC WARD. "Like children now, bed close to bed"   ARGO 94
SAN PAOLO FUORI LE MURE.   FOLKW 65A
THE SHOT. "The bullet shot me and I lay"
                    FOLKW 59A, FOLKW 65A
TWO DEATHS. "It was only a film"   ARGO 94
Poetry*   PROTHM 6

Jennison, Lucia. 1850. in English.
"I'm apt to be surly getting up early"
                    HARC 4

Jerome, Jerome K. 1859. in English.
Poetry*   ARGO 87

Jimason, Joanne. in English.
BITCHES' BREW. "Says I be's so crazy"
                    WATSHD 7
DARKNESS AND A BLUES LADY. "There are holes in her walls"   WATSHD 7
ELECTRIC LADY BLUES. "Blues coming in all over me"   WATSHD 7
THERE ARE POETS. "There are poets"
                    WATSHD 7

Jiménez, Juan Ramon. 1881. in Spanish.
Á LA POESÍA. "Si: en tu cerca ruin, que desor dena"   CAED 5
"Á la puente del amor"   AGUIL 1
Á MI ALMA. "Siempre tienes la rama preparada"
                    CAED 5
AL MAR ANOCHECIDO. "Si su belleza en mí mori pudiera"   CAED 5
AL SONETO CON MI ALMA. "Como en el ala el inf nito vuelo"   CAED 5
ALAMO BLANCO. "Arriba canta el pajaro"
                    SMC 1
"Alrededor de la copa"   AGUIL 1
AMISTAD. "Nos entendemos bien"   SMC 1
ANGELUS. "Mira, Platero, qué de rosas"
                    SMC 1
"Ante mí estás, si"   AGUIL 1
ARIA OTOÑAL. "Río de cristal, dormido"
                    HOLT
AURORAS DE MOGUER. "Los alamos de plata"
                    AGUIL 1
BALADA DE PRIMAVERA. "El amor se va por l campos"   SMC 1
EL BORRIQUETE. "Puse en el borriquete"
                    SMC 1
CARTA REVIVIDA A GEORGINA HUBNER. "El cons del Peru"   AGUIL 1
"Cierra, cierra la puerta"   AGUIL 1
CON LA CRUZ DEL SUR. "La Cruz del Sur se ech en una nube"   CAED 5
CON LA FLOR MÁS ALTA. "Perdida en la noche"
                    CAED 5
"Con lilas llenas de agua"   AGUIL 1
CONCIENCIA PLENA. "Tú me llevas, concienc plena deseante Diós"   CAED 5
CONFUSION DE LA ROSA ELLA. "Quien fuera n me vió, me vió su sombra"   CAED 5
CORPUS. "Entrando por la calle"   SMC 1
CRIATURA AFORTUNADA. "Cantando vas, riend por el agua"   CAED 5
CUANDO YO ERA NIÑODIOS. "Cuando yo era niñ diós"   AGUIL 1
DARBÓN. "Darbón, el médico de Platero"
                    SMC 1
"El dormir es como un puente"   AGUIL 1
ESPACIO. "Tu forma se deshizo. Deshiciste forma"   CAED 5
LA ESTRELLA VENIDA. "En el naranjo está la e trella"   AGUIL 1
LA FLOR DEL CAMINO. "Qué pura Platero"
                    SMC 1
FLOR QUE VUELVE. "Igual, la flor retorna"
                    CAED 51, SPOA
GOLONDRINAS. "Ahí la tienes ya, Platero"
                    SMC 1
HADO ESPAÑOL DE LA BELLEZA. "Te veo mientr pasas"   CAED 5
LOS HUNGAROS. "Míralos, Platero, tirados todo su largor"   SMC 1
IDILIO DE ABRIL. "Los niños han ido con Plat ro"   SMC 1
EL JARDÍN. "Era—no, no era así—de otra ma era"   AGUIL 1
LA LLUVIA HA CESADO; HUELE. "La lluvia ha ces do"   AGUIL 1
"Lo recuerdo, de pronto"   AGUIL 1

* Recording not available for analysis

MADRUGADA. "Vamos llegando en el tren"
AGUIL 12
"Mariposa de luz" AGUIL 12
EL MAS FIEL. "Cantaron los gallos tristes"
AGUIL 12
"Me adelanté el corazón" AGUIL 12
MIRLO FIEL. "Cuando el mirlo, en lo verde
nuevo, un día" CAED 51
MOGUER MÍO. "Buenas tardes, Moguer mio"
AGUIL 12
LA MUERTE. "Encontré a Platero echado en su
cama" SMC 14
NAVIDAD. "La candela en el campo" SMC 14
NIÑOS. "Bajo la higuera aun" AGUIL 12
EL NOMBRE CONSEGUIDO DE LOS NOMBRES. "Si yo,
por ti, he creado un mundo para ti"
CAED 51
LA NOVIA. "El claro viento del mar" SMC 14
EL NUEVO MAR. "Para olvidarme de porque he
venido" AGUIL 12
OCTUBRE. "A traves de la paz del agua pura"
AGUIL 12, SPOA 59
EL OTOÑADO. "Estoy completo de naturaleza"
CAED 51
PAISAJE DEL CORAZÓN. "A qué qieres que te ha-
ble" AGUIL 4, AGUIL 12
PAISAJE GRANA. "La cumbre. Ahí está el ocaso"
SMC 14
EL PAN. "Te he dicho, Platero, que el alma"
SMC 14
PARAÍSO. "Como en la noche, el aire ve su
fuente" CAED 151
PASEO. "Por los hondos caminos" SMC 14
PLATERO. "Platero es pequeño, peludo"
SMC 14
EL POETA A CABALLO. "Qué tranquilidad violeta"
AGUIL 12
EL POZO. "¡El pozo! ¡Platero!" SMC 14
LA PRIMAVERA. "¡Ay! Qué relumbres y olores"
SMC 14
PRIMAVERA AMARILLA. "Abril venía, lleno"
DOVER 2
LA PUA. "Entrando en la dehesa de los caballos"
SMC 14
QUÉ GOCE TRISTE ESTE. "Qué goce triste este de
hacer todas las cosas" SMC 1
RENACERÉ YO. "Renaceré yo piedra"
AGUIL 12
RETORNO. "Veníamos los dos, cargados"
SMC 14
RETORNO FUGAZ. "Cómo era, Diós mio, cómo
era" AGUIL 4 CAED 51
LOS REYES MAGOS. "Qué ilusión, esta noche"
SMC 14
ROSAS DE SEPTIEMBRE. "El agua lava la hiedra"
SMC 15
SER EN FLOR. "Lo he visto en el frío"
CAED 51
"Si vas de prisa" AGUIL 12
SITIO PERPETUO. "Aquel purpúreo monte, que
tenía" CAED 51
"Solo el olor de unas flores" SMC 15
"Solo lo hiciste un momento" AGUIL 12
SOY ANIMAL DE FONDO. "En el fondo de aire
(dije) estoy" CAED 51
"Soy como un niño distraído" AGUIL 12

TAL COMO ESTABAS. "En el recuerdo estás tal
como estabas" CAED 51
LA TRASPARENCIA, DIÓS, LA TRASPARENCIA. "Diós
del venir, te siento entre mis manos"
AGUIL 12, CAED 51
TÚ. "Pasan todas, verdes, granas" AGUIL 12
"Tu me mirarás llorando" AGUIL 12
EL VIAJE DEFINITIVO. "Y yo me iré. Y se queda-
rán los pájaros cantando" HOLT 1
VIENTO DE AMOR. "Por la cima del árbol iré"
AGUIL 12
"Vino, primero, pura" AGUIL 12
"Yo dije que me gustaba" AGUIL 12
"Yo no soy yo" AGUIL 12
Poetry* BABB 2
Joans, Ted. 1928. in English.
WHY TRY. ARGO 17
Poetry* PRENT 1
Jodelle, Etienne. 1532. in French.
AUX CENDRES DE CLAUDE COLET, exc. "Si ma
voix, que me doit bientot pousser au nom-
bre" PERIOD 2
Joglar Cacho, Manuel. in Spanish.
AQUÍ CERCA PODRIA ESTAR EL CIELO. INSTPR 1
Johnson, B.S. 1933. in English.
SONG OF THE WAGONDRIVER. "My first love was
the ten ton truck" SPOA 67
Johnson, Fenton. 1888. in English.
AUNT JANE BROWN. FOLKW 6
THE BANJO PLAYER. "There is music in me"
FOLKW 6, FOLKW 41
RULERS PHILADELPHIA. FOLKW 6
SCARLET WOMAN. "Once I was good like the Vir-
gin Mary" SPOA 88
Poetry* PRENT 1
Johnson, Georgia Douglas. in English.
MY LITTLE DREAMS. "I'm folding up my little
dreams" FOLKW 6, FOLKW 41
Johnson, Helene. in English.
THE ROAD. "Ah, little road, all whirry in the
breeze" FOLKW 41
Johnson, James Weldon. 1871. in English.
THE CREATION. "And God stepped out of space"
DECCA 10, EAV 2, FOLKW 39,
FOLKW 41, HOUGHT 3, SPOA 90, UA 1,
UA 2, UARIZ 1, OXF 1, AGE 2
THE CRUCIFIXION. "Jesus, my gentle Jesus"
UA 1
GO DOWN DEATH. A FUNERAL SERMON. "Weep not,
weep not" EAV 2, FOLKW 39,
FOLKW 45, UA 1
THE JUDGEMENT DAY. "In that great day"
FOLKW 39 FOLKW 45, UA 1
LET MY PEOPLE GO. "And God called Moses from
the burning bush" CAED 195, FOLKW 39,
HOUGHT 1
LIFT EVERY VOICE. "Lift every voice and sing"
CAED 98, UA 2
LISTEN LORD. "O Lord, we come this morning"
EAV 2, FOLKW 39, FOLKW 45, UA 1
NOAH BUILT THE ARK. "In the cool of the day"
FOLKW 39, UA 1
THE PRODIGAL SON. "Young man" EAV 2,
FOLKW 39, FOLKW 45, UA 1
Poetry* PRENT 1
Johnson, Joe. 1940. in English.
"If I ride this train" BROADR 2

* Recording not available for analysis

Johnson, Joe (continued)

POEM FOR FRANCES P. "Frances P. was on the
  roof"   WATSHD 4

Johnson, Lenore. in English.
  FRAGMENT: THE PRIDE OF MAN.   BROADR 1

Johnson, Lionel. 1867. in English.
  BAGLEY WOOD. "The night is full of stars, full of
  magnificence"   ARGO 70A

Johnson, Robert. in English.
  Poetry*   SPOA 116

Johnson, Samuel. 1709. in English.
  LONDON, exc. "London! the needy villain's gen'-
  ral home"   ARGO 51
  ───── "Tho' grief and fondness in my breast
  rebel"   CAED 203
  ON THE DEATH OF DR. ROBERT LEVET. "Con-
  demn'd to hope's delusive mine"
                                 LONGM 1
  PROLOGUE SPOKEN BY MR. GARRICK. "When
  Learning's triumph her barb'rous foes"
                                 ARGO 51
  A SHORT SONG OF CONGRATULATION. "Long-ex-
  pected one and twenty"   ARGO 51,
                                 CAED 203
  THE VANITY OF HUMAN WISHES, exc. "When first
  the college rolls receive his name"
                                 ARGO 51

Johnson, Tom. in English.
  GDBA.   WATSHD 13
  GLABL AP.   WATSHD 13
  LOLMO.   WATSHD 13
  TOMO LASTA.   WATSHD 13
  VZH.   WATSHD 13
  WOLO YOLO.   WATSHD 13

Johnston, Ellen Turlinton. 1929. in English.
  ALL I NEED. "Magnolia"   AGENTV 2
  AND SO I PASSED. "A girl—quiet, skinny, small"
                                 AGENTV 3
  THE AWAKENING. "We had this talent show"
                                 AGENTV 1
  DO YOU REMEMBER ME, BERNICE GRENADINE? "Do
  you remember me, Miss Grenadine"
                                 AGENTV 5
  DON'T BLOW YOUR MEAN. "Before I went into the
  Blackboard Jungle"   AGENTV 5
  EXPEDIENCY. "The first time that" AGENTV 5
  EXTRA-CREDIT (OR IT'S TOO LATE, JOHN) "It comes
  that time again"   AGENTV 3
  THE FALL. "I felt really good today"
                                 AGENTV 1
  FROM MY HOMEROOM TO ME: THE LINE. "Our lady
  wanted to lead a line"   AGENTV 4
  FROM THE FANTASIES OF A NOT-SO-YOUNG-ANY-
  MORE SCHOOL TEACHER. "There's a lot of
  things I've done"   AGENTV 1
  HANDLE WITH CARE. "Yesterday"   AGENTV 4
  HERO. "A golden bronze zig-zag" AGENTV 3
  IT WAS HERE NOT THREE DAYS AGO. "Yesterday I
  went to Ms. B's room"   AGENTV 1
  MIRROR, MIRROR ON THE WALL. "I crown you with
  'A' "   AGENTV 3
  MY LINE. "One day I'm going to lead a line"
                                 AGENTV 4
  MY SPECIAL FRIEND. "I had a special friend in
  study hall"   AGENTV 2

ONE OF THOSE DAYS. "It is one of those days"
                                 AGENTV
OUR 'BELL'. "We used to have a nice bell"
                                 AGENTV
THE SECRET. "The first time I ever saw her"
                                 AGENTV
SO—WHAT HAPPENED TO YOU? "We were watch
  ing a movie in class"   AGENTV
THEY JUST GIVE THE PRIZE FOR YOUR DOOR. "W
  sat there"   AGENTV
THEY WORRY ABOUT ME. "I thought for a lon
  while"   AGENTV
TO OUR YOUNG BUILDERS. "You are the heroes-
  you"   AGENTV
TURN AROUND'S FAIR PLAY. "We watched a fil
  one day"   AGENTV
WE DON'T DO NOTHIN' IN HERE. "Today"
                                 AGENTV
WHAT IS THIS? "What IS this???" AGENTV
WHAT YOUR TEACHER'S MANUAL CAN AND CANNO
  DO FOR YOU. "When I first became a teacher
                                 AGENTV
WHO SAID TODAY'S KIDS DON'T HAVE FEELINGS? ".
  Booster Club person"   AGENTV
WONDERFULNESS. "Bulletin boards are a mus
  you may know"   AGENTV

Johnston, Percy E. in English.
  CANTO 4, SIX CYLINDER OLYMPUS. "I, Bos Tauru
  spatha"   BROADR

Jolobe, James J. R. 1902. in Xhosa.
  ICH WEISS JA.   German DEUTGR

Jones, David. 1895. in English.
  A. A. A. DOMINE DEUS. "I said, Ah! what shall
  write?"   ARGO 14
  THE ANATHEMATA, exc.   ARGO 10
  THE FATIGUE. "Relief details, Halt" ARGO 9
                                 ARGO 14
  THE HUNT. " . . . and the hundreds"
                                 ARGO 10
  IN PARENTHESIS, exc.   ARGO 89, ARGO 10
  MABINOG'S LITURGY. "Two centuries"
                                 ARGO 10
  MIDDLE-SEA AND LEAR-SEA. "Twelve hundre
  years"   ARGO 10
  SHERTHURSDAYE AND VENUS DAY. "He that wa
  her son"   ARGO 10
  THE SLEEPING LORD, exc.   ARGO 14
  THE TRIBUNE'S VISITATION. "Sir! No Sir, yes si
  Middle Watch Relief, sir"   ARGO 14
  THE WALL.   ARGO 14

Jones, Gayl. 1949. in English.
  Poetry*   PRENT

Jones, Glyn. 1905. in English.
  A DRAUGHT OF FISHES.   ARGO 15
  EASTER. "Morning in the honey-months, th
  star"   ARGO 15
  GOODBYE, WHAT WERE YOU. "At the voice of th
  mother on a warm hearth"   ARGO 15
  NANT CERI. "Blessed were those Bowens wh
  saw all this"   ARGO 15
  THE SEAGULL. "Gracing the tide-warmth, th
  seagull"   ARGO 15

Jones, Leroy. See **Baraka, Imamu Amiri.**

Jones, Ted. in English.
  WHY TRY. "And she was brown"   ARGO

* Recording not available for analysis

Jong, Erica. 1946. in English.

THE AGE OF EXPLORATION. "Sailing with your chest" WATSHD 2

THE COMMANDMENTS. "If a women wants to be a poet" SPOA 134

"Dear Colette" SPOA 134

THE EGGPLANT EPITHALAMION. "There are more than a hundred Turkish poems" SPOA 134

THE EVIDENCE. "Evidence of life" WATSHD 2

THE GIRL IN THE MIRROR. "Throwing away my youth" WATSHD 2

HERE COMES. "The silver spoons were warbling" SPOA 134

IN SYLVIA PLATH COUNTRY. "The skin of the sea has nothing to tell me" SPOA 134

"The man under the bed" SPOA 134

MEN. "The impossible man" SPOA 134

NEEDLEPOINT. "Mothers and daughters" SPOA 134

PAPER CUTS. "I have known the imperial powers" SPOA 134, WATSHD 2

PARABLE OF THE FOURPOSTER. "Because she wants to touch him" SPOA 134

THE PURIFICATION. "Because she loved her husband" SPOA 134

THE QUARREL. "It is a rainy night" SPOA 134

17 WARNINGS IN SEARCH OF A FEMINIST POEM. "Beware of the man" SPOA 134, WATSHD 2

THE SHEETS. "We used to meet on this corner" SPOA 134

THE TEACHER. "The teacher stands before the class" SPOA 134

TESTAMENT. "I, Erica Jong" SPOA 134

TO THE ONION. "I am thinking of the onion again" SPOA 134

TO THE READER. "At the point X" EMC 7

Jonson, Ben. 1572. in English.

THE ALCHEMIST, exc. "I will have my beds blown up, not stuffed" LONGM 1

ECHO'S SONG. "Slow, slow, fresh fount, keep time" ARGO 35, LIST 1

EPITAPH ON ELIZABETH, L.H. "Would'st thou heare" ARGO 35

EPITAPH ON SOLOMON PAVY. "Weepe with me all you that read" ARGO 35, SPOA 84

"Fools, they are the only nation" COLUMB 11

"Have you seen but a bright lily grow" ARGO 35

HYMN TO DIANA. "Queene, and Huntresse, chaste and faire" ARGO 35, EAV 6, LIST 1

INVITING A FRIEND TO SUPPER. "Tonight, Grave Sir, both my poor house and I" ARGO 35, SPOA 35

"It was a beauty that I saw" ARGO 35, LIST 1

OAK AND LILY. "It is not growing like a tree" LIST 1

ODE (TO HIMSELF). "Come leave the loathed stage" ARGO 35

ON HIS FIRST SONNE. "Farewell, thou child of my right hand, and joy" ARGO 35

ON MY FIRST DAUGHTER. "Here lies to each her parents' ruth" ARGO 35

THE SATIRIST IS CHARMED BY THE QUEEN. ARGO 77

SIMPLEX MUNDITIIS. "Still to be neat, still to be drest" ARGO 35, IMP 1, JNP 8, LIST 1, SPOA 84

SONG—TO CELIA. "Come my Celia, let us prove" ARGO 35, COLUMB 10, DECCA 12, EAV 6, SPOA 84

THAT WOMEN ARE BUT MENS SHADOWS. "Follow a shadow, it still flies you" ARGO 35

TO CELIA. "Drink to me, only, with thine eyes" ARGO 35, IMP 1, LIST 1, LION 2

THE TRIUMPH OF CHARIS. BRITAM 2

THE WITCHES' CHARM. "The owl is abroad, the bat and the toad" SPOA 50

Poetry* EAV 11

Jordan, June. 1936. in English.

ALL THE WORLD MOVED. "All the world moved next to me strange" EAV 16

GETTIN' DOWN TO GET OVER. "Momma, Momma" WATSHD 5

POEM AGAINST THE STATE (OF THINGS): 1975. "Wherever I go these" WATSHD 5

Poetry* WATSHD 57, WATSHD 64, SPOA 4

Jordan, Norman. 1938. in English.

ABOVE KARMA. BLACKF 1

ALLAH. BLACKF 1

BROTHER, THE STRUGGLE MUST GO ON. BLACKF 1

CLAIRVOYANCE. BLACKF 1

MIND AND SOUL AFTER DARK. BLACKF 1

ONE FOR ALL. BLACKF 1

ONE-EYED CRITICS. BLACKF 1

THE POET THE DREAMER. BLACKF 1

POPSICLE COLD. BLACKF 1

Poetry* PRENT 1

Joselow, Beth. in English.

THE APRIL WARS, exc. "In the last days" WATSHD 11

GYPSIES 1–4. "I don't remember enough" WATSHD 11

MARS. "We wanted Mars" WATSHD 11

WITHOUT WINDOWS. "Dark men awash on the lawn" WATSHD 11

Joseph, Steven M. 1938. in English.

Poetry* PRENT 1

Joyce, James. 1882. in English.

ALONE. "The moon's greygolden meshes make" CAED 143

BAHNHOFSTRASSE. "The eyes that mock me sign the day" CAED 143

CHAMBER MUSIC. "All day I hear the noise of waters" HARB 5, HOUGHT 3

ECCE PUER. "Of the dark past" CAED 143, VAN 3

FLOOD. "Goldbrown upon the sated flood" CAED 143

A FLOWER GIVEN TO MY DAUGHTER. "Frail the white rose and frail are" CAED 143

I HEAR AN ARMY. "I hear an army charging upon the land" SPOA 7

A MEMORY OF THE PLAYERS IN A MIRROR AT MIDNIGHT. "They mouth love's language. Gnash" CAED 143

NIGHTPIECE. "Gaunt in gloom" CAED 143

ON THE BEACH AT FONTANA. "Wind whines and whines the shingle" CAED 143, SPOA 8

A PRAYER. "Again!" CAED 143

* Recording not available for analysis

Joyce, James (continued)

SHE WEEPS OVER RAHOON. "Rain on Rahoon falls softly, softly falling"   CAED 143, SPOA 7

SIMPLES. "Of cool and sweet dew and radiance mild"   CAED 143

THIS HEART THAT FLUTTERS. "This heart that flutters near my heart"   SPOA 6

TILLY. "He travels after a winter sun"   CAED 143

TUTTO E SCIOLTO. "A birdless heaven, seadusk, one lone star"   CAED 143

WATCHING THE NEEDLEBOATS AT SAN SABBA. "I heard their young hearts crying"   CAED 143

Ju Ching Yu. 825 A.D. in Chinese.

JIN SHR SHANG JANG SCHWEI BU. "Dung fang dzwo ye ting hung ju"   FOLKW 76

Juan de la Cruz. 1542. in Spanish.

A LO DIVINO. "Tras de un amoroso lance" FOLKW 82; English FOLKW 55

CANCIÓN DE CRISTO Y EL ALMA. "Un pastorcico solo está penado"   FOLKW 82; English FOLKW 55

CANCIONES DEL ALMA EN LA INTIMA COMUNICA-CIÓN DE UNIÓN DE AMOR DE DIÓS. "Oh llama de amor viva"   FOLKW 82; English FOLKW 55

CANCIONES ENTRE EL ALMA Y EL ESPOSO. "A donde te escondiste"   AGUIL 5, FOLKW 82; English FOLKW 55

CANTAR DEL ALMA QUE SE HUELGA DE CONOSCER A DIÓS POR FE. "Que bien sé yo la fonte que mana y corre"   FOLKW 82; English FOLKW 55

COPLAS DEL ALMA QUE PENA POR VER A DIÓS. "Vivo sin vivir en mí"   FOLKW 82; English FOLKW 55

COPLAS SOBRE UN ÉXTASIS DE ALTA CONTEMPLA-CIÓN. "Éntreme donde no supe" FOLKW 82; English FOLKW 55

GLOSA A LO DIVINO. "Por toda la hermosura" FOLKW 82; English FOLKW 55

———. "Sin arrimo y con arrimo" FOLKW 82; English FOLKW 55

NOCHE OSCURA DEL ALMA. "En una noche oscura"   AGUIL 5, DOVER 2, FOLKW 82, HOLT 1, SMC 3; English FOLKW 55

OTRO POR 'SUPER FLUMINA BABYLONIS'. "Encima de las corrientes"   FOLKW 82; English FOLKW 55

ROMANCE I. SOBRE EL EVANGELIO 'IN PRINCIPIO ERAT VERBUM'. "En el principio moraba" FOLKW 82; English FOLKW 55

——— II. DE LA COMUNICACIÓN DE LAS TRES PER-SONAS. "En aquel amor inmenso" FOLKW 82; English FOLKW 55

——— III. DE LA CREACIÓN. "Una esposa que te ame"   FOLKW 82; English FOLKW 55

——— IV. "Hágese, pues, dijo el Padre" FOLKW 82; English FOLKW 55

——— V. "Con esta buena esperanza" FOLKW 82; English FOLKW 55

——— VI. "En aquestos y otros ruegos" FOLKW 82; English FOLKW 55

——— VII. PROSIGUE LA ENCARNACIÓN. "Ya que el tiempo era llegado"   FOLKW 82; English FOLKW 55

——— VIII. PROSIGUE LA ENCARNACIÓN. "Entonces llamó un arcángel"   FOLKW 82; English FOLKW 55

——— IX. DEL NACIMIENTO. "Ya que era llegado el tiempo"   FOLKW 82; English FOLKW 55

SUMA DE LA PERFECCIÓN. "Olvido de lo criado" FOLKW 82; English FOLKW 55

Juana Inés de la Cruz. 1648. in Spanish.

REDONDILLAS. "Este amoroso tormento" SPOA 39

——— "Hombres necios que acusais" AGUIL 8, FIDIAS 2, SMC 6

SONETO. "Detente, sombra de mi bien esquivo" SPOA 39

SONETO. "Este, que ves, engaño colorido" HOLT 1

Junqueiro, Guerra. 1850. in Portuguese.

PRESTITO FUNEBRE. "Que alegrias virgens, campesinas, fremem"   FOLKW 72

Justice, Donald. 1925. in English.

HERE IN KATMANDU. "We have climbed the mountain"   FOLKW 25

THE STRAY DOG.   FOLKW 25

THE SUMMER HOUSE.   FOLKW 25

Juvenal (Decimus Junius Juvenalis). 55 A.D. in Latin.

"In Saturn's reign, at nature's early birth" English SPOA 46

Poetry*   CETRA 18

Jya Dau. 779 A.D. in Chinese.

SYUN YIN JE BY YU. "Sung sya wen tung dz" FOLKW 76

Jyang Jye. 1275. in Chinese.

YU MEI REN. "Shan nyan ting yu ge lou shang" FOLKW 76

Kali. in English.

BLACK IS.   BLACKF 1

CIRCLES.   BLACKF 1

LADYBIRD.   BLACKF 1

NIGGER, DO YOU.   BLACKF 1

THIS LITTLE LIGHT OF MINE.   BLACKF 1

WHAT'S HAPPENING TO THE HEROES.   BLACKF 1

Kallimachos. 330 B.C. in Greek.

EPITAPH OF CHARIDAS OF KYRENE. "And does Charidas sleep there"   English CARIL 3

TIMON THE MISANTHROPE. "Timon, since you are dead"   English CARIL 3

Kallman, Chester. 1921. in English.

Poetry*   WATSHD 44

Karamzin, N. M. 1766. in Russian.

VOLGA. "Reka svyashchenneishaya v mire" CMS 6

Karlfeldt, Erik Axel. 1864. in Swedish.

ELIE HIMMELSFÄRD. "Här åker sankt Elia upp till himmelens land"   GRAM 9

HÖSTPSALM. "Jag såg en rosenbuske stänkt med blod"   GRAM 9

I JUDA STRÄDER. "Hur präktigt leva vi i Juda städer"   GRAM 9

"Längtan heter min arvedel"   GRAM 1

SUB LUNA. "Sub luna amo"   GRAM 9

---

* Recording not available for analysis

TRÄSLOTTET. "Uret slår med hammaren"
GRAM 10

Kasack, Hermann. 1896. in German.
Poetry* SUHRK 8

Kaschnitz, Marie Luise. in German.
AHASVER. "In London sah ich den, der sterben
wollte" CHRIST 31
AUF DER ERDE. DEUTGR 43
BRÄUTIGAM FROSCHKÖNIG. "Wie hässlich ist"
CHRIST 31
EIN GEDICHT. "Ein Gedicht, aus Worten ge-
macht" DEUTGR 43
GENAZZANO. "Genazzano am Abend"
DEUTGR 43
HERBST IM BREISGAU. "Zeit ist zu gehen in das
Haus" CHRIST 31
HIROSHIMA. "Der den Tod auf Hiroshima warf"
DEUTGR 43
INTERVIEW. "Wenn er kommt, der Besucher"
DEUTGR 43
JUNI. "Uber den Tod geht nichts"
DEUTGR 43
DIE KINDER DIESER WELT. "Die Kinder dieser
Welt hab ich" DEUTGR 43
LANGE SCHATTEN. DEUTGR 43
DER LEUCHTTURM. "Wer weiss ob diese Alten
auf der Insel" CHRIST 31
MORGEN. DEUTGR 43
NICHT GESAGT. "Nicht gesagt" CHRIST 31
OSTIA ANTICA. "Durch die Tore: niemand"
DEUTGR 43
TORRE SAN LORENZO "Der Winterstrand ist
leer" DEUTGR 43
VORSTADT. "Nur noch zwei Bäume"
DEUTGR 43

Kästner, Erich. 1899. in German.
ANSPRACHE EINER BARDAME. "Der zweite Herr
von links" DEUTGR 33
CHOR DER GIRLS. "Wir konnen bloss in Reih und
Glied" DEUTGR 33
DIE DAME SCHREIBT DER DAME. DEUTGR 33
DIE ENTWICKLUNG DER MENSCHHEIT. "Einst
haben die Kerls auf Bäumen gehockt"
DOVER 1
FANTASIE VON ÜBERMORGEN. "Und als der
nächste Krieg begann" DEUTGR 33
GANZ BESONDERS FEINE DAMEN. "Sie tragen die
Büsten und Nasen" DEUTGR 36, LITAR 1
DER HANDSTAND AUF DER LORELEI. "Die Lorelei
bekannt als Fee und Felsen" DEUTGR 36,
LITAR 1
HÖHERE TÖCHTER IM GESPRACH. "Die Eine sitzt
Die Andre liegt" DEUTGR 33
KENNST DU DAS LAND, WO DIE KANONEN BLÜHEN?
"Kennst du das Land wo die Kanonen blü-
hen?" DEUTGR 33
KLASSENZUSAMMENKUNFT. "Sie trafen sich, wie
ehemals" DEUTGR 33
KOPERNIKANISCHE CHARAKTERE GESUCHT. "Wenn
der Mensch aufrichtig bedächte"
DEUTGR 33
EIN KUBIKKILOMETER GENÜGT. "Ein Mathematik-
er hat behauptet" DEUTGR 36, LITAR 1
DAS LEBEN OHNE ZEITVERLUST. DEUTGR 33
DAS LIED, GENANNT 'ZUR SELBEN STUNDE'.
DEUTGR 33

DAS LIED VOM KLEINEN MANN. "Ich kann, im
Kino" DEUTGR 33
MATHILDE, ABER EINGERAHMT. "Es lebe das
Grossreinemachen" DEUTGR 36, LITAR 1
DIE MAULWÜRFE. "Als sie, krank von den letzten
Kriegen" DEUTGR 36, LITAR 1
MODERNES MÄRCHEN. "Sie waren so sehr inei-
nander verliebt" DEUTGR 33
EINE MUTTER ZIEHT BILANZ. "Mein Sohn schreibt
mir so gut wie gar nicht mehr"
DEUTGR 33
SACHLICHE ROMANZE. "Als sie einander acht
Jahre kannten" DEUTGR 36, LITAR 1
STILLER BESUCH. "Jüngst war seine Mutter zu
Besuch" DEUTGR 36, LITAR 1

Katzman, Allen. 1937. in English.
ELEGY. "Sometimes I go about the street"
BROADR 3
POEMS FROM OKLAHOMA. "I sing a song"
BROADR 3
"Who is Bernice" BROADR 2

Kaufman, Bob. 1925. in English.
BENEDICTION. SPOA 89

Kaufman, Shirley. 1923. in English.
LOOKING AT HENRY MOORE'S ELEPHANT SKULL
ETCHINGS IN JERUSALEM DURING THE WAR. "It
wants to be somewhere else" WATSHD 10
LOVING. "There is a tiny wind" WATSHD 10
THE MOUNTAIN. "In the morning I am alone"
WATSHD 10
TAKE ANYTHING. "At the end of summer"
WATSHD 10
Poetry* WATSHD 58

Kavanagh, P. J. 1931. in English.
BEGGAR AT VILLA D'ESTE. "No legs—I must sit
still" APPL 3
"Curled in your night dress on the beach"
APPL 3
IMITATIONS OF UNREALITY. "A square skulled
moonfaced" APPL 3
IN THE RUBBER DINGHY. "In the rubber dinghy
on the lake" APPL 3
MOVING. "There is a perfect socket in the cen-
ter" APPL 3
ON THE WAY TO THE DEPOT. "It is a pleasant
night" APPL 3
PERFECTION ISN'T LIKE A PERFECT STORY. "I think
of the time" APPL 3
SEPTEMBER. "Cold light of the moon" APPL 3
SURVIVING. "I am, O I am sick of grief"
APPL 3
WHEREVER YOU ARE. APPL 3
YEATS' TOWER. "The rain is the same" APPL 3

Keats, John. 1795. in English.
LA BELLE DAME SANS MERCI. "O what can ail
thee, knight-at-arms" ARGO 62, ARGO 82,
BRITAM 1, CAED 57, CAED 160,
CAED 186, CAED 202, EAV 18,
FOLKW 60, LEARNC 1, SPOA 29,
SPOA 35, SPOA 41, SPOA 48, THEAL 2
BRIGHT STAR. "Bright star! Would I were stead-
fast as Thou art" ARGO 62, ARGO 82,
CAED 57, CAED 186, CAED 202,
LIST 10, SPOA 41, LION 2
ENDYMION, exc. "A thing of beauty is a joy for
ever" ARGO 62, CMS 13, EAV 8,
FOLKW 62

* Recording not available for analysis

Keats, John (continued)

THE EVE OF ST. AGNES. "St. Agnes' Eve—ah, bitter chill it was"   ARGO 62, CAED 57, EAV 22, PROTHM 2, SPOA 48

FALL OF HYPERION, exc. "Then to the west I look'd, and saw far off"   ARGO 62

HYMN TO PAN. "O Hearkener to the loud-clapping shears"   CAED 57

HYPERION. "Deep in the shady sadness of a vale"   ARGO 62, IMP 1

"I had a dove, and the sweet dove died"   SPOA 48

I STOOD TIP-TOE UPON A LITTLE HILL, exc. "I stood tip-toe upon a little hill"   ARGO 62

LINES ON THE MERMAID TAVERN. "Souls of poets dead and gone"   CAED 57, CAED 186, CAED 202

MEG MERRILIES. "Old Meg she was a gypsy"   BRITAM 1, FOLKW 62, FOLKW 67

ODE ON A GRECIAN URN. "Thou still unravish'd bride of quietness"   ARGO 62, ARGO 77, BRITAM 1, CAED 21, CAED 52, CAED 202, CMS 13, EAV 8, EAV 18, LIST 10, LONDON 1, RCA 4, RCA 9, SPA 1, SPOA 48

ODE ON MELANCHOLY. "No, no! go not to Lethe, neither twist"   ARGO 62, ARGO 82, CAED 52, CAED 202, EAV 18, SPOA 41, SPOA 48

ODE TO A NIGHTINGALE. "My heart aches, and a drowsy numbness"   ARGO 62, ARGO 77, CAED 15, CAED 57, CAED 186, CAED 202, EAV 8, EAV 18, LONDON 1, SPOA 29, SPOA 48

ODE TO AUTUMN. "Season of mists and mellow fruitfulness"   ARGO 62, ARGO 82, CAED 57, CAED 202, CMS 12, COLUMB 11, SPOA 29, SPOA 35, SPOA 41, SPOA 48, LONGM 1

ODE TO PSYCHE. "Goddess! hear these tuneless numbers, wrung"   SPOA 48

ON FIRST LOOKING INTO CHAPMAN'S HOMER. "Much have I travell'd in the realms of gold"   ARGO 62, BRITAM 1, CAED 52, CAED 186, CAED 202, CMS 13, EAV 18, EAV 22, HOUGHT 3, IMP 1, LIST 2, LIST 10, RCA 9, SPOA 29, SPOA 48

ON SEEING THE ELGIN MARBLES. "My spirit is too weak"   RCA 9

ON THE GRASSHOPPER AND CRICKET. "The poetry of earth is never dead"   HOUGHT 2, SINGER 2

ON THE SEA. "It keeps eternal whisperings around"   ARGO 62

A SONG ABOUT MYSELF. "There was a naughty boy"   CAED 52, CAED 202, EAV 18, ARGO 125

SONNET. "Keen, fitful gusts are whispering here and there"   CAED 57, CAED 202

SONNET. "To one who has been long in city pent"   EAV 18

SONNET. "When I have fears that I may cease to be"   ARGO 62, ARGO 77, CAED 57, CAED 186, CAED 202, EAV 18, LONDON 1, POETRY 2, SPOA 29, SPOA 48

STANZAS. "In a drear-nighted December"   EAV 2

"This living hand, now warm and capable"   ARGO 6

TO SLEEP. "O soft embalmer of the still mid night"   CAED 202, SPOA 48, LONGM Poetry*   ARGO 1, SPOA 116, SPOA 12

Keble, John. in English.
BALAAM.   PROTHM 1

Keeler, Charles Augustus. in English.
A LESSON. "Tell me, little spider"   HARB

Kefasdotter, M. in Swedish.
OBUNDEN SJÄL.   GRAM
SÄRTINGEN.   GRAM

Kell, Richard. 1927. in English.
PIGEONS. "They paddle with staccato feet"   SPOA 6

Keller, Gottfried. 1819. in German.
ABENDLIED. "Augen, meine lieben Fensterlein"   DEUTGR 16, DEUTGR 4

DIE KLEINE PASSION. "Der sonnige Duft, Sep temberluft"   DEUTGR 1

SPIELMANNSLIED. "Im Frührot stand der Mor genstern"   DEUTGR 1

EIN TAGEWERK. "Vom Lager stand ich mit der Frühlicht auf"   DEUTGR 1

DER TAUGENICHTS. "Die ersten Veilchen ware schon"   DEUTGR 1

EIN WALDLIED. "Arm in Arm und Kron' a Krone steht der Eichenwald verschlungen"   DEUTGR 1

WINTERNACHT. "Nicht ein Flügelschlag gin durch die Welt"   DEUTGR 1

DIE ZEIT GEHT NICHT. "Die Zeit geht nicht, si stehet still"   DEUTGR 16, DEUTGR 4
Poetry*   CHRIST

Keller, Helen. 1880. in English.
THREE DAYS TO SEE.   HARC

Kellgren, Johan Henrik. 1751. in Swedish.
DEN NYA SKAPELSEN. "Du, som av shönhet oc behagen"   GRAM

Kelly, Robert. 1935. in English.
THE ALCHEMIST. "The origin, far side of th lake"   SPOA 10

FINDING THE MEASURE (PREFIX) "Finding th measure"   SPOA 10

POEM FOR EASTER. "All women are beautiful"   SPOA 10

SONNET 7. "Even with the least we know"   SPOA 10

Kendrick, Delores. in English.
INQUIRY. "In the room"   WATSHD
MAGNIFICAT. "Her back arched like"   WATSHD

RITE FOR THE CITY, exc. "I have broken my fast   WATSHD

THEY HAD NO POETS. "And I saw the poets"   WATSHD

Kennedy, Marian. in English.
BAKESHOP WINDOW. "When I go downtown"   HARB

Kennedy, X. J. 1929. in English.
DOWN IN DALLAS. "Down in Dallas, down i Dallas"   FOLKW 2

Kern, Bliem. in English.
BETWEEN.   WATSHD 1
BOTH.   WATSHD 1

---

* Recording not available for analysis

CLOCK.	WATSHD 13
HORNS.	WATSHD 13
IPITS.	WATSHD 13
JEALOUSY.	WATSHD 13
LEMONS.	WATSHD 13
MAGWEBA.	WATSHD 13
OUT.	WATSHD 13
TOAST.	WATSHD 13

Kerouac, Jack. 1922. in English.
LUCIEN MIDNIGHT: THE SOUNDS OF THE UNIVERSE IN MY WINDOW. "Friday afternoon in the universe"   VERVE 1
SAN FRANCISCO BLUES, exc. "San Francisco, San Francisco, you're a muttering bum"
          VERVE 1

Kersh, Gerald. 1911. in English.
A SOLDIER—HIS PRAYER.   ARGO 119

Ketchum, Arthur. in English.
THE SPIRIT OF THE BIRCH. "I am the dancer of the wood"   CAED 169

Key, Francis Scott. 1779. in English.
THE STAR-SPANGLED BANNER. "O say, can you see"   CAED 98, CMS 10, COLUMB 6, DECCA 4, DECCA 13, HARVOC 17

Keyes, Sidney. in English.
WAR POET.   PROTHM 7
WILLIAM WORDSWORTH. "No room for mourning: he's gone out"   FOLKW 65, JUP 1

Kgositsile, Keorapetse. 1938. in English.
BROTHER MALCOLM'S ECHO. "Translated furies sing"   BROADV 14
ELEGY FOR DAVID DIOP. "He who thinks immortality"   BROADV 14
FOR LEROI JONES, APRIL, 1965.   BROADV 14
FOR SPELLMAN AT SPELMAN.   BROADV 14
I AM MUSIC PEOPLE.   BROADV 14
IVORY MASKS IN ORBIT. "These new lights"
          BROADV 14
LUMUMBA SECTION. "Searching past what we see and hear"   BROADV 14
MANDELA'S SERMON. "Blessed are the dehumanized"   BROADV 14
MY NAME IS AFRIKA. "All things come to pass"
          BROADV 14
ORIGINS. "Deep in your cheeks"   BROADV 14
SONG FOR AIMÉ CÉSAIRE.   BROADV 14
SPIRITS UNCHAINED. "Rhythm it is we"
          BROADV 14
TO FANON. "Tears"   BROADV 14
TO GLORIA.   BROADV 14
WHEN BROWN IS BLACK. "Are you not the light"
          BROADV 14

Khalil, Amma. in English.
INTERFACE. "Back to back"   WATSHD 8
ISLE OF LOVE. "The words of love"
          WATSHD 8
RETAKE. "From the shadows I am returning"
          WATSHD 8

Khayyam, Omar. See **Omar Khayyam.**

Kilmer, Aline. in English.
SONG AGAINST CHILDREN. "O the barberry bright"   CAED 164

Kilmer, Joyce. in English.
THE HOUSE WITH NOBODY IN IT. "Whenever I walk to Suffern along the Erie track"
          CAED 169

TREES. "I think that I shall never see"
          CAED 100, COLUMB 6

King, Henry. 1592. in English.
A CONTEMPLATION UPON FLOWERS. "Brave flowers, that I could gallant it like you"
          SPOA 35
EXEQUY ON HIS WIFE, exc.   HARVOC 6, ARGO 137
LIKE THE FALLING OF A STARRE.   SPOA 84
SONNET. "Tell me no more how fair she is"
          ARGO 37
Poetry*   PROTHM 6

Kingsley, Charles. 1819. in English.
"When all the world is young, lad"
          CAED 201

Kinnell, Galway. 1927. in English.
ANOTHER NIGHT IN THE RUINS. "In the evening haze"   SPOA 105
THE AVENUE BEARING THE INITIAL OF CHRIST INTO THE NEW WORLD, exc. "In the pushcart market, on Sunday"   SCHOL 5
———. "The fishmarket closed, the fishes gone into flesh"   SCHOL 5
THE BEAR. "In late winter"   POSEID 1, SCHOL 5, SPOA 105
THE CALL ACROSS THE VALLEY OF NOT-KNOWING. "In the red house sinking down"
          CAED 167
THE DEAD SHALL BE RAISED IN INCORRUPTIBLE. "A piece of flesh gives off smoke in the fields"
          CAED 167
DEAR STRANGER EXTANT IN MEMORY BY THE BLUE JUNIATA. "Having given up on the desk man passed out under his clock"   CAED 167
FIRST SONG. "Then it was dusk in Illinois, the small boy"   CAED 111, SCHOL 5
THE FLY.   NACTE 14
THE HEN FLOWER. "Sprawled on our faces in the spring nights"   CAED 167, POSEID 1
HOW MANY NIGHTS.   NACTE 14
IN THE HOTEL OF LOST LIGHT. "In the left hand sank the drunk smelling of autopsies died in"
          CAED 167
LAST SONGS.   NACTE 14
LASTNESS. "The skinny waterfalls, footpaths wandering out of heaven"   CAED 167, POSEID 1
LITTLE SLEEP'S-HEAD SPROUTING HAIR IN THE MOONLIGHT. "When I sleepwalk into your room"   CAED 167, POSEID 1
THE PATH AMONG THE STONES. "On the path winding upward"   CAED 167
THE PORCUPINE. "Fatted"   SCHOL 5, SPOA 82
THE SHOES OF WANDERING. "Squatting at the rack in the store of the Salvation Army"
          CAED 167
TO CHRIST OUR LORD.   FOLKW 25
UNDER THE MAUD MOON. "On the path, by this wet site of old fires."   CAED 167, POSEID 1
VAPOR TRAIL REFLECTED IN A FROG POND. "The old watch"   BROADR 1, SPOA 105
Poetry*   JNP 29, MICHM 9

Kinsella, Thomas. 1928. in English.
AT THE HEART.   ARGO 94
A COUNTRY WALK. "Sick of the piercing company of women"   ARGO 94

          * Recording not available for analysis

Kinsella, Thomas (continued)

COVER HER FACE. "They dither softly at her bedroom door"   ARGO 94

MIRROR IN FEBRUARY. "The day dawns with scent of must and rain"   ARGO 94

AN OLD ATHEIST PAUSES BY THE SEA. "I choose at random, knowing less and less"   ARGO 94

SEVENTEENTH CENTURY LANDSCAPE NEAR BALLYFERRITER.   ARGO 94

Kipling, Rudyard. 1865. in English.

THE AMERICAN REBELLION (PT. 2) AFTER. "The snow lies thick on Valley Forge"
                                                FOLKW 67

THE APPEAL. "If I have given you delight"
                                                ARGO 73

THE BALLAD OF EAST AND WEST. "Oh, East is East, and West is West, and never the twain shall meet"   CAED 92, HOUGHT 3, LIST 7

THE BETROTHED. "Open the old cigar-box, get me a Cuba stout"   CAED 163

BOOTS. "We're foot-slog-slog-slog-sloggin' over Africa"   CAED 85, CAED 163

BROWN BESS. "In the days of lace-ruffles, perukes and brocade"   ARGO 73

CELLS. "I've a head like a concertina"
                                                ARGO 73

CHAPTER HEADING FROM THE JUNGLE BOOK. "Now Chil the Kite brings home the night"
                                                CAED 163

A CHARM. "Take of English earth as much"
                                                ARGO 73

"Cities and thrones and powers"   ARGO 73

THE CRAFTSMAN. "Once after long drawn revel"
                                                FOLKW 64

DANE-GELD. "It is always a temptation to an armed and agile nation"   ARGO 73

DANNY DEEVER. "What are the bugles blowin' for?"   ARGO 73, CAED 92, HOUGHT 4, LIST 7, LONGM 1

THE DAWN WIND. "At two o'clock in the morning"   ARGO 73

THE DISCIPLE. "He that hath a gospel"
                                                ARGO 73

THE DUTCH IN THE MEDWAY. "If wars were won by feasting"   ARGO 73

THE 'EATHEN. "The 'eathen in 'is blindness bows down to wood and stone"   ARGO 73

THE FEMALE OF THE SPECIES. "When the Himalayan peasant meets the he-bear in his pride"   CAED 163

"FUZZY-WUZZY". "We've fought with many men acrost the seas"   CAED 92

GENTLEMEN-RANGERS. "To the legion of the lost ones, to the cohort of the damned"
                                                CAED 163

GUNGA DIN. "You may talk o' gin and beer"
        CAED 92, CAED 132, DECCA 10, LIST 7, LIST 21

THE HOLY WAR. "A tinker out of Bedford"
                                                ARGO 73

THE HYAENAS. "After the burial-parties leave"
                                                ARGO 73

IF—. "If you can keep your head when all about you"   CAED 92, SINGER 2

IN THE NEOLITHIC AGE. "In the neolithic age savage warfare did I wage"   CAED 163

JAMES I. "The child of Mary Queen of Scots"
                                                ARGO 73

THE LADIES. "I've taken my fun where I've found it"   CAED 92, CAED 163

THE LAW OF THE JUNGLE. "Now this is the law of the jungle—as old and as true as the sky"
                        CAED 92, CAED 132, RCA 8

MANDALAY. "By the old Moulmein Pagoda, lookin' eastward to the sea"   AUDIA 1,
        CAED 92, DECCA 10, LIST 21, SINGER 6

MINE SWEEPERS. "Dawn off the Foreland—the young flood making"   ARGO 73

MOTHER O' MINE. "If I were hanged on the highest hill"   CAED 163

"Non Nobis Domine"   ARGO 73

OUTSONG IN THE JUNGLE. "For the sake of him who showed"   CAED 163

THE PIRATES IN ENGLAND. "When Rome was rotten—ripe to her fall"   ARGO 73

PRELUDE TO THE DEPARTMENTAL DITTIES. "I have eaten your bread and salt"   CAED 163

PUCK'S SONG. "See you the ferny ride that steals"   ARGO 73

RECESSIONAL. "God of our fathers, known of old"   ARGO 73, AUDIA 1, CAED 92,
        CAED 201, LIST 3, LIST 7, RCA 9

THE RIVER'S TALE. "Twenty bridges from Tower to Kew"   ARGO 73

THE ROMAN CENTURION'S SONG. "Legate, I had the news last night—my cohort ordered home"   ARGO 73

ROMULUS & REMUS. "Oh little did the Wolf-Child care"   ARGO 73

THE RUNES ON WIELAND'S SWORD. "A smith makes me"   LONGM 1

A ST. HELENA LULLABY. "How far is St. Helena from a little child at play?"   ARGO 73

THE SEAL'S LULLABY. "Oh hush thee, my baby, the night is behind us"   HARB 5

THE SECRET OF THE MACHINES. "We were taken from the ore-bed and the mine"   ARGO 73

A SERVANT WHEN HE REIGNETH. "Three things make earth unquiet"   ARGO 73

SESTINA OF THE TRAMP-ROYAL. "Speakin' in general, I 'ave tried 'em all"   EAV 22

A SMUGGLER'S SONG. "If you wake at midnight, and hear a horse's feet"   ARGO 73

THE SONG OF THE DEAD, II. "We have fed our sea for a thousand years"   CAED 92

SONG OF THE GALLEY-SLAVES. "We pulled for you when the wind was against us and the sails were low"   CAED 92

THE STORM CONE. "This is the midnight—let no star"   ARGO 73

THE STRANGER. "The stranger within my gate"
                                                ARGO 73

"There was a young boy of Quebec" EAV 22

TO THOMAS ATKINS. "I have made for you a song"   CAED 92

TOMLINSON. "Now Tomlinson gave up the ghost in his house in Berkeley Square"   RCA 9

TOMMY. "I went into a public-'ouse to get a pint o'beer"   CAED 92

THE VAMPIRE. "A fool there was and he made his prayer"   CAED 163

---

* Recording not available for analysis

THE WAY THROUGH THE WOODS. "They shut the road through the woods"   ARGO 73, ARGO 82, CAED 92, SPOA 41
WHEN EARTH'S LAST PICTURE IS PAINTED. "When Earth's last picture is painted and the tubes are twisted and dried"   CAED 163
"When 'Omer smote 'is blooming lyre"   ARGO 73
THE WHITE MAN'S BURDEN. "Take up the white man's burden"   CAED 92, CAED 163, CAED 201
Poetry*   LIST 11
Kirkup, James. 1927. in English.
THE LONELY SCARECROW. "My poor old bones (I have only two)"   HARB 3
Kirsanov, Simeon. 1906. in Russian.
ETOT MIR. "Stchaste—Bit"   MONITR 1
NE PO POSLOVITSE. "Esli slovo vret v glaza"   MONITR 1
Kirsch, Sarah. in German.
IM SOMMER. "Dünnbesiedelt das Land"   DEUTGR 1A
DIE LUFT RIECHT SCHON NACH SCHNEE. "Die Luft riecht schon nach Schnee, mein Geliebter"   DEUTGR 1A
NEBEL.   DEUTGR 1A
Kizer, Carolyn. 1925. in English.
THE APOSTATE. "I, Hypocrite Harry, that Hamburg handkisser"   WATSHD 16
BY THE RIVERSIDE. "Once I lived at a Riverside"   WATSHD 16
THE DEATH OF A PUBLIC SERVANT. "This is a day when good men die from windows"   WATSHD 16
THE FIRST OF JUNE AGAIN. "Dateline Saigon: Marines wait in the rain"   WATSHD 16
FOR MY DAUGHTER. "It was lingering summer"   WATSHD 16
FOR SAPPHO AFTER SAPPHO. "And you say"   WATSHD 16
FROM TU FU TO LI PO. "My Lord, how beautifully you write"   WATSHD 16
THE GREAT BLUE HERON. "As I wandered on the beach"   WATSHD 16
HOW IT PASSES. "Tomorrow I begin to cook"   WATSHD 16
LOVE SONG. "O to fall easily, easily, easily in love"   NACTE 14
A MUSE OF WATER. "We who must act as handmaidens"   WATSHD 16
MY HOME TOWN. "When I go home"   WATSHD 16
MY SISTER'S LETTER. "Your letter wrecks my day"   WATSHD 16
OCTOBER, 1973. "Last night I dreamed"   WATSHD 16
PLAINT OF THE POET IN AN IGNORANT AGE. "I would I had a flower-boy"   NACTE 14
POEM. "In the first stanza"   WATSHD 16
PROFESSIONAL POET. "A last word"   WATSHD 16
SEMELE RECYCLED. "After you left me forever"   WATSHD 16
TYING ONE ON IN VIENNA. "I have been, faithfully, to the 39 birthplaces of Beethoven"   WATSHD 16
Poetry*   MICHM 11

Klaj, Johann. 1616. in German.
ANAKREONTISCHE ODE.   CHRIST 22
Klappert, Peter. 1942. in English.
THE HYPOTHETICAL DREAM. "I am afraid of what will happen"   WATSHD 4
THE PRISONER: AFTER A STATUE BY MICHELANGELO. "Blind as stone"   WATSHD 4
RSVP. "When the exposition open"   WATSHD 4
THE TRAPPER. "I am digging a pit"   WATSHD 4
Klein, Abraham Moses. 1909. in English.
FOR THE SISTERS OF THE HOTEL DIEU. "In pairs as if to illustrate their Sisterhood"   FOLKW 49
MONTREAL. "O City metropole, isle riverain"   FOLKW 49
PLUMAGED PROXY. "O Rooster, circled over my brother's head"   FOLKW 49
POLITICAL MEETING. "On the school platform, draping the folding seats"   FOLKW 49
PSALM XXII. "O sign and wonder of the barnyard"   FOLKW 49
THE ROCKING CHAIR. "It seconds the crickets"   FOLKW 49
Poetry*   CBC 1
Klingsor, Tristan. 1874. in French.
SUR LE PONT.   CAED 204
Klopstock, Friedrich Gottlieb. 1724. in German.
DIE FRÜHEN GRÄBER. "Willkommen, o silberner Mond"   CHRIST 11
DIE FRÜHLINGSFEIER. "Nicht in den Ozean der Welten alle"   CHRIST 16
DIE KÜNFTIGE GELIEBTE. "Dir nur, liebendes Herz, euch, meine vertraulichsten Tränen"   CHRIST 25
DAS ROSENBAND. Im Frühlingsschatten fand ich sie"   DOVER 1
DER ZÜRCHERSEE. "Schön ist Mutter Natur, deiner Erfindung Pracht"   CHRIST 22
Knight, Etheridge. 1931. in English.
APOLOGY FOR APOSTASY. "Soft songs, like birds"   BROADV 12
AS YOU LEAVE ME "Shiny record albums scattered over"   BROADV 12
BEWARE. "The Mississippi cop"   BROADV 12
CELL SONG. "Night music slanted"   BROADV 12
CRAZY PIGEON. "Crazy pigeon strutting outside my cell"   BROADV 12
FOR LANGSTON HUGHES. "Gone. Gone"   BROADV 12
FOR MALCOLM, A YEAR AFTER. "Compose for Red a proper"   BROADV 12
FOR P.F.C. JOE ROGERS. "Now the moon mocks full"   BROADV 12
HAIKU. "Eastern guard tower"   BROADV 12
HARD ROCK RETURNS TO PRISON FROM THE HOSPITAL FOR THE CRIMINAL INSANE. "Hard Rock was known not to take shit"   BROADV 12, WATSHD 1
"He sees thru stone"   BROADV 12, WATSHD 1
HERE WE IS, Y'ALL. "Well, Niggers, here we is"   WATSHD 1
THE IDEA OF ANCESTRY. "Taped to the wall of my cell are 47 pictures: 47 black"   BROADV 12, CAED 155

* Recording not available for analysis

Knight, Etheridge (continued)

"It was a funky deal"　　　　　BROADV 12
A LOVE POEM. "I do not expect the spirit of Penelope"　　　　　BROADV 12
A NICKLE BET. "Be slow. Fold the daily news"　　　　　BROADV 12
ON UNIVERSALISM. "I see no single thread"　　　　　BROADV 12
PEACE. "Hound dog sits his tail"　BROADV 12
POEM OF ATTRITION. "I do not know if the color of the day"　　　　　WATSHD 1
PORTRAIT OF MALCOLM X. "He has the sign"　　　　　BROADV 12
THE SUN CAME. "The sun came, Miss Brooks"　　　　　BROADV 12
SWEETHEARTS IN A MULBERRY TREE. "I shimmied with Bea"　　　　　BROADV 12
TO DINAH WASHINGTON. "I have heard your voice floating, royal and real" BROADV 12
TO GWENDOLYN BROOKS. "O Courier on Pegasus"　　　　　BROADV 12
TO MAKE A POEM IN PRISON. "It is hard"　　　　　BROADV 12
2 POEMS FOR BLACK RELOCATION CENTER. "Flukum couldn't stand the strain. Flukum"　　　　　BROADV 12
THE VIOLENT SPACE. "Exchange in greed the ungraceful signs. Thrust"　BROADV 12
"The warden said to me the other day"　　　　　BROADV 12
A WATTS MOTHER MOURNS WHILE BOILING BEANS. "The blooming flower of my life is roaming"　　　　　WATSHD 1

Knight, John. in English.
AND BECAUSE. "And because we listened"　　　　　SPOA 68

Komey, Ellis Ayitey. in English.
THE DAMAGE YOU HAVE DONE.　CAED 136

Kops, Bernard. 1926. in English.
"Peach, plum or apricot"　　　SPOA 68
SKY MAN. "My God, I'm dead"　SPOA 67

Korolenko, V. G. 1853. in Russian.
OGNI. "Kak-to davno, temnym osennim vecherom"　　　　　CMS 6

Kostelanetz, Richard. 1940. in English.
THE DECLARATION OF INDEPENDENCE.　　　　　WATSHD 13

Kovner, Abba. in Hebrew.
Poetry*　　　　　WATSHD 59

Kraft, W. in German.
DIE RUHE.　　　　　CHRIST 22

Kramer, Aaron. 1921. in English.
BOARDWALK BLUES. "I've got a hunger, don't know where"　　　FOLKW 14
CHAINS. "I took a walk through the streets of my town"　　　　FOLKW 14
HALLOWEEN. "Forgive me, dear, if I did not gasp"　　　　　FOLKW 14
IN THE LUNCH WAGON. "There is no cafeteria in Hell"　　　　　FOLKW 14
THE LOVERS. "In the solitary places"　　　　　FOLKW 14
NOCTURNE. "With what amazing wand, oh night"　　　　　FOLKW 14
AN OLD MATTRESS IN THE LOTS. "Far off where most people pass"　FOLKW 14

THE ROCKABYE LOVE. "Rockabye love on the fire-escape"　　　　FOLKW 14
RUSH HOUR. "Too late to kiss my wife goodbye"　　　　　FOLKW 14
SADIE: A SERENADE. "Sadie, Sadie—the men have all gone"　　　FOLKW 14
SERENADE. "Home to your eyes" FOLKW 14
SONG OF NEW YORK. "New York! proudly I breathe its magic name"　FOLKW 14
TRAIN SONG. "Rain in the shoe, cold in the lung"　　　　　FOLKW 14
TREATMENT. "Fix our firm in the back of your brain"　　　　　FOLKW 14
UNEMPLOYED SONG. "Last month I worked in a hell-hole shop"　　FOLKW 14
WORK DAY. "I've been working arms and back all day"　　　　FOLKW 14

Kresh, Dave. in English.
IN BEBOP NIGHTS. "There is nothing like it now"　　　　　WATSHD 8
JANE. "While the other kids on the block were reading"　　　　WATSHD 8
TURN OFF, OR USE OPENER. "It is the height of high summer"　WATSHD 8

Krolow, Karl. 1915. in German.
AM SEE. "Gehen wir Steine mit kühlen Gesichtern"　　　　　NESKE 1
AUF VERLORENEM POSTEN. "I Habe die Vernunft nach ihm ausgeschickt"　NESKE 1
DIE ERINNERUNG. "Die Erinnerung ist eine weibliche Statue"　NESKE 1
DIE ERSCHEINUNG. "Ihr Gesicht ist leicht"　　　　　NESKE 1
JEMAND. "Jemand schüttet Licht aus dem Fenster"　　　　NESKE 1
DIE ODE 1950.　　　　　CHRIST 22
WAHRNEHMUNG. "Er wirft ein Auge auf die Viertelstunde"　　NESKE 1
DER WIND IM ZIMMER. "Unter Gelächter und Türenschlagen"　NESKE 1
ZIEMLICH VIEL. "Ziemlich viel Glück gehört dazu"　　　　NESKE 1
Poetry*　　　　　SUHRK 9

Krows, Jane W. in English.
WORLD OF SOUND. "I went to the city and what did I hear?"　HARB 1

Krucenych, Aleksei. 1886. in Ukrainian.
DYR BU SCYL.　　　　　LUCHT 1
IKE MINA NI.　　　　　LUCHT 1
SIEG ÜBER DIE SONNE, exc. FLIEGERLIED.　　　　　LUCHT 1
ZOK ZOK ZOK.　　　　　LUCHT 1

Krüger, Michael. in German.
GEDICHTE ÜBER EINEN SPAZIERGANG AM STAUSEE UND ÜBER GEDICHTE.　DEUTGR 40A
WIE ES SO GEHT.　　　　DEUTGR 40A

Krüss, James. in German.
DIE GESCHICHTE VON FRAU MARA UND IHREM SOHN VUK.　　　　　ATHENA 5

Kuhlmann, Quirinius. 1651. in German.
DER 64. KUHLPSALM.　　　CHRIST 29
ÜBER DEN TRÄNENWÜRDIGEN TOD DES SOHNES GOTTES, JESUS.　CHRIST 18

Kuhn, Friedrich Adolf. 1774. in German.
DAS GEDICHT. "Tönte dir der liebliche Gesang"　　　　　DEUTGR 13

---

* Recording not available for analysis

Kumin, Maxine. 1925. in English.
BODY AND SOUL, A MEDITATION. "Mornings after leg lifts"   WATSHD 19
EXTRAPOLATIONS FROM HENRY MANLEY'S PIE PLANT. "The stalks are thick"   WATSHD 19
HELLO, HELLO HENRY. "My neighbor in the country, Henry Manley"   WATSHD 19
HENRY MANLEY LIVING ALONE KEEPS TIME. "Sundowning, the doctor calls it" WATSHD 19
THE JESUS INFECTION. "Jesus is with me on the Blue Grass Parkway going east-bound"
                                                  WATSHD 19
THE MICROSCOPE.   SCHOL 7
MY FATHER'S NECKTIES. "Last night my color-blind"   WATSHD 19
PROGRESS REPORT. "The middle age you wouldn't wait"   WATSHD 19
PURGATORY. "And suppose the darlings"
                                                  WATSHD 19
THE RETRIEVAL SYSTEM. "It begins with my dog"
                                                  WATSHD 19
SONG FOR SEVEN PARTS OF THE BODY. "This one"
                                                  WATSHD 19
SPLITTING WOOD AT SIX ABOVE. "I open a tree"
                                                  WATSHD 19
SUNBATHING ON A ROOFTOP IN BERKELEY. "Eleven palm tree"   WATSHD 19
Kunert, Günter. in German.
FRÜHTER MORGEN.   DEUTGR 40A
GEDICHTE.   DEUTGR 40A
Kunitz, Stanley. 1905. in English.
AFTER THE LAST DYNASTY. "Reading in Li Po"
                                                     LIBC 1
AMBERGRIS. "This body, tapped of every drop of breath"   CARIL 2
APPROACH OF AUTUMN. "The early violets we saw together"   CARIL 2
THE APPROACH TO THEBES. "In the zero of the night, in the lipping hour"   CARIL 2
BENEDICTION. "God banish from your house"
                                                   CARIL 2
BY LAMPLIGHT. "Welcome, eccentric life"
                                         CARIL 2, LIBC 1
CARELESS LOVE. "Who have been lonely once"
                                                   CARIL 2
THE CHILD NEXT DOOR.   LIBC 54
A CHOICE OF WEAPONS. "Reviewing me without undue elation"   SPOA 98
THE CLASS WILL COME TO ORDER. "O tell me all about Anna Livia!"   CARIL 2
THE DARK AND THE FAIR. "A roaring company that festive night"   LIBC 1
THE DAUGHTERS OF THE HORSELEECH. "The daughters of the horseleech crying 'Give! Give!'"   BROADR 1
DECIDUOUS BRANCH. "Winter, that coils in the thickets now"   CARIL 2
THE DRAGON FLY. "Fallen, so freshly fallen"
                                                   SPOA 98
END OF SUMMER. "An agitation of the air"
                                         CARIL 2, LIBC 54
FATHER AND SON. "Now in the suburbs and the falling light"   CARIL 2, SPOA 82
FOR THE WORD IS FLESH. "O ruined father dead, long sweetly rotten"   CARIL 2
GEOMETRY OF MOODS. "Concentrical, the universe and I"   SPOA 98

GREEN WAYS. "Let me not say it, let me not reveal"   CARIL 2
GULL'S CRY.   LIBC 54
THE MOUND-BUILDERS. "Let the old poets jig on Penn"   LIBC 1
MY SURGEONS. "My surgeons are a savage band"
                                                   CARIL 2
NIGHT LETTER. "The urgent letter that I try to write"   CARIL 2
OPEN THE GATES. "Within the city of the burning cloud"   CARIL 2
REVOLVING MEDITATION. "How much I disapprove of it"   CARIL 2
ROVER. "How shall I keep this violence in"
                                                   CARIL 2
THE SCIENCE OF THE NIGHT. "I touch you in the night, whose gift was you"   CARIL 2,
                                                   LIBC 40
THE SCOURGE. "My heart felt need to die"
                                                   CARIL 2
"So intricately is this world resolved"
                                                   SPOA 98
A SPARK OF LAUREL. "This man, this poet, said"
                                                   CARIL 2
THE SUMMING-UP. "When young I scribbled, boasting, on my wall"   LIBC 1
THE THIEF. "In a Roman tram, where the famous Roman mob"   CARIL 2, LIBC 54
THE THING THAT EATS THE HEART. "The thing that eats the heart comes wild with years"
                                         CARIL 2, LIBC 1
THE TUTORED CHILD. "Your mother, whom the mirror-world has claimed"   SPOA 98
VITA NUOVA. "I abdicate my daily self that bled"
                                                   CARIL 2
THE WALTZER IN THE HOUSE. "A sweet, a delicate white mouse"   SPOA 98
WAR AGAINST THE TREES. "The man who sold his lawn to standard oil"   TAPES 12
THE WAY DOWN. "Time swings her burning hands"   CARIL 2
Poetry*   LIST 15
Kunze, Reiner. in German.
ABBITTE NACH DER REISE.   DEUTGR 40A
MÖGLICHKEIT, EINEN SINN ZU FINDEN.
                                   DEUTGR 40A
TAGEBUCHBLATT '74.   DEUTGR 40A
Kurtz, Aaron. in Yiddish.
MARC CHAGALL. "Ich vill eich da tzellin a mietza"   FOLKW 92
Kyd, Thomas. 1558. in English.
Poetry*   PROTHM 7

La Farge, Peter. in English.
AUTUMN, 1964. "Sitting here in the night with"
                                                 BROADR 2
THE SENECAS.   SCHOL 8
La Fontaine, Jean de. 1621. in French.
L'ALOUETTE ET SES PETITS AVEC LE MAITRE D'UN CHAMP. "Les alouettes font leur nid"
                                                     PLEI 1
L'AMOUR ET LA FOLIE. "Tout est mystère dans l'amour"   CBS 1
L'ÂNE CHARGÉ D'EPONGES ET L'ÂNE CHARGÉ DE SEL. "Un ânier, son sceptre à la main"
                                                     PLEI 1

* Recording not available for analysis

La Fontaine, Jean de (continued)

L'ÂNE ET LE PETIT CHIEN. "Ne forçont point notre talent" PLEI 1

L'ÂNE ET SES MÂITRES. "L'Âne d'un jardinier se plaignoit au Destin" PLEI 1

L'ÂNE PORTANT LES RELIQUES. "Un Baudet chargé de reliques" PLEI 1

L'ÂNE VETU DE LA PEAU DU LION. "De la peau du Lion l'Âne s'étant vêtu" PLEI 1

LES ANIMAUX MALADES DE LA PESTE. "Un mal qui répand la terreur" PLEI 1, SPOA 9, SPOA 56

L'ASTROLOGUE QUI SE LAISSE TOMBER DANS UN PUITS. "Un astrologue un jour se laissa choir" PLEI 1

L'AVARE QUI A PERDU SON TRÉSOR. "L'usage seulement fait la possession" PLEI 1

LA BELETTE ENTRÉE DANS UN GRENIER. "Damoiselle Belette, au corps long et flouet" PLEI 1

LA BESACE. "Jupiter dit un jour: 'Que tout ce qui respire" PLEI 1

LE BÛCHERON ET MERCURE. "Votre goût a servi de règle à mon ouvrage" PLEI 1

LE CERF SE VOYANT DANS L'EAU. "Dans le cristal d'une fontaine" PLEI 1

LE CHARTIER EMBOURBÉ. "Le Phaéton d'une voiture à foin" PLEI 1

LE CHAT ET UN VIEUX RAT. "J'ai lu chez un conteur de fables" PLEI 1

LE CHAT, LA BELETTE ET LE PETIT LAPIN. "Du palais d'un jeune lapin" PLEI 1, SPOA 36, SPOA 49

LA CHAUVE-SOURIS ET LES DEUX BELETTES. "Une chauve-souris donna tête baissée" PLEI 1

LE CHÊNE ET LE ROSEAU. "Le Chêne, un jour, dit au Roseau" ADES 54, PLEI 1, SPOA 49

LE CHEVAL ET LE LOUP. "Un certain Loup, dans la saison" PLEI 1

LE CHIEN QUI LÂCHE SA PROIE POUR L'OMBRE. "Chacun se trompe ici-bas" PLEI 1

LA CIGALE ET LA FOURMI. "La cigale, ayant chanté tout l'été" GMS 6, PLEI 1, SPOA 49, CAED 204

LE COCHE ET LA MOUCHE. "Dans un chemin montant, sablonneux, malaisé" PLEI 1, SPOA 56

LE COCHET, LE CHAT ET LE SOURICEAU. "Un souriceau tout jeune, et qui n'avait rien vu" PLEI 1, SPOA 56

LA COLOMBE ET LA FOURMI. "Il faut, autant qu'on peut, obliger tout le monde" PLEI 1, SPOA 49

LE CONSEIL TENU PAR LES RATS. "Un chat, nommé Rodilardus" PLEI 1

LE COQ ET LA PERLE. "Un jour un coq détourna" PLEI 1

LE COQ ET LE RENARD. "Sur la branche d'un arbre était en sentinelle" PLEI 1, SPOA 49

LE CORBEAU ET LE RENARD. "Maître Corbeau, sur un arbre perché" GMS 6, PLEI 1, SPOA 49

LES DEUX AMIS. "Deux vrais amis vivaient au Monomotapa" SPOA 56

LES DEUX MULETS. "Deux Mulets cheminoient, l'un d'avoine chargé" PLEI 1

LES DEUX PIGEONS. "Deux pigeons s'aimaient d'amour tendre" GMS 8, PLEI 1, SPOA 56

L'ENFANT ET LE MÂITRE D'ECOLE. "Dans ce récit je prétends faire voir" PLEI 1

LA FILLE. "Certaine Fille, un peu trop fiere" PLEI 1

LA FORTUNE ET LE JEUNE ENFANT. "Sur le bord d'un puits très-profond" PLEI 1

LE GEAI PARÉ DES PLUMES DU PAON. "Un paon muoit: un Geai prit son plumage" PLEI 1

LA GÉNISSE, LA CHÈVRE ET LA BREBIS EN SOCIÉTÉ AVEC LE LION. "La génisse, la chèvre, et leur soeur la brebis" PLEI 1

LE GLAND ET LA CITROUILLE. "Dieu fait bien ce qu'il fait. Sans en charcher la preuve" PLEI 1

LA GRENOUILLE ET LE RAT. "Tel, comme dit Merlin, cuide engeigner autrui" PLEI 1

LA GRENOUILLE QUI VEUT SE FAIRE AUSSI GROSSE QUE LE BOEUF. "Une grenouille vit un boeuf" GMS 6, PLEI 1, SPOA 49

LES GRENOUILLES QUI DEMANDENT UN ROI. "Les Grenouilles se lassant" PLEI 1

LE HÉRON. "Un jour, sur ses long pied, allait je ne sais où" PLEI 1, SPOA 56

L'HIRONDELLE ET LES PETITS OISEAUX. "Une hirondelle en ses voyages" PLEI 1

L'HUÎTRE ET LES PLAIDEURS. "Un jour deux Pèlerins sur sable rencontrent" PLEI 1

LA JEUNE VEUVE. "La perte d'un époux ne va point sans soupirs" CBS 1, PLEI 1, SPOA 56

LE LABOUREUR ET SES ENFANTS. "Un riche laboureur, sentant sa mort prochaine" GMS 6, PLEI 1

LA LAITIÈRE ET LE POT AU LAIT. "Perrette, sur sa tête ayant un pot au lait" PLEI 1, SPOA 56

LA LICE ET SA COMPAGNE. "Une lice étant sur son terme" PLEI 1

LE LIÈVRE ET LA PERDRIX. "Il ne se faut jamais moquer des misérables" PLEI 1

LE LIÈVRE ET LA TORTUE. "Rien ne sert de courir; il faut partir à point" PLEI 1, SPOA 56

LE LIÈVRE ET LES GRENOUILLES. "Un lièvre en son gîte songeoit" PLEI 1

LE LION DEVENU VIEUX. "Le lion, terreur des forêts" PLEI 1

LE LION ET LE MOUCHERON. "Va-t'en, chétif insecte, excrément de la terre" PLEI 1, SPOA 49

LE LION ET LE RAT. "Il faut, autant qu'on peut, obliger tout le monde" PLEI 1, SPOA 49

LE LOUP DEVENU BERGER. "Un loup, qui commençoit d'avoir petite part" PLEI 1

LE LOUP ET LA CIGOGNE. "Les loups mangent gloutonnement" PLEI 1, SPOA 49

LE LOUP ET L'AGNEAU. "La raison du plus fort est toujours la meilleure" GMS 6, PLEI 1, SPOA 49

LE LOUP ET LE CHIEN. "Un loup n'avait que les os et la peau" PLEI 1, SPOA 49

LE LOUP, LA CHÈVRE ET LE CHEVREAU. "La Bique, allant remplir sa traînante mamelle" PLEI 1

LE LOUP, LA MÈRE ET L'ENFANT. "Un villageois avoit a l'écart son logis" PLEI 1

* Recording not available for analysis

LES LOUPS ET LES BREBIS. "Apres mille ans et plus de guerre déclarée" PLEI 1, SPOA 49

LES MEMBRES ET L'ESTOMAC. "Je devois par la royauté" PLEI 1

LE MEUNIER, SON FILS ET L'ÂNE. "L'invention des arts étant un droit d'aînesse" PLEI 1, SPOA 49

LA MORT ET LE BÛCHERON. "Un pauvre Bûcheron, tout couvert de ramée" PLEI 1

LE MULET SE VANTANT DE SA GÉNÉALOGIE. "Le Mulet d'un prélat se piquoit de noblesse" PLEI 1

L'OEIL DU MAÎTRE. "Un cerf s'étant sauvé dans une étable à boeufs" PLEI 1

L'OISEAU BLESSÉ D'UNE FLÈCHE. "Mortellement atteint d'une flèche empennée" PLEI 1

L'OURS ET L'AMATEUR DE JARDINS. "Certain ours montagnard, ours à demi léché" PLEI 1

L'OURS ET LES DEUX COMPAGNONS. "Deux Compagnons, pressés d'argent" PLEI 1

PARAPHRASE DU DIES IRAE, exc. HACH 9

LE PÂTRE ET LE LION. "Les fables ne sont pas ce qu'elles semblet être" SPOA 49, SPOA 56

LE PAYSAN DU DANUBE. "Il ne faut point juger des gens sur l'apparence" PLEI 1

LE PETIT POISSON ET LE PÊCHEUR. "Petit poisson deviendra grand" PLEI 1, SPOA 49

PHOEBUS ET BORÉE. "Borée et le Soleil virent un voyageur" PLEI 1

LE POT DE TERRE ET LE POT DE FER. "Le pot de fer proposa" PLEAI 1, SPOA 49

LA POULE AUX OEUFS D'OR. "L'avarice perd tout en voulant tout gagner" PLEI 1

LE RAT DE VILLE ET LE RAT DES CHAMPS. "Autrefois le rat de ville" PLEI 1, SPOA 49

LE RENARD AYANT LA QUEUE COUPÉE. "Un vieux Renard, mais des plus fins" PLEI 1

LE RENARD ET LA CIGOGNE. "Compère le Renard se mit un jour en frais" PLEI 1, SPOA 49

LE RENARD ET LE BOUC. "Capitaine Renard alloit de compagnie" PLEI 1

LE RENARD ET LE BUSTE. "Les grands, pour la plupart, sont masques de théatre" PLEI 1

LE RENARD ET LES RAISINS. "Certain Renard gascon, d'autres disent normand" PLEI 1, SPOA 49

LE SATYRE ET LE PASSANT. "Au fond d'un antre sauvage" PLEI 1

LE SAVETIER ET LE FINANCIER. "Un savetier chantait du matin jusqu'au soir" PLEI 1, SPOA 56, DOVER 4

LE SONGE D'UN HABITANT DU MOGOL. "Jadis certain Mogol vit en songe un Vizir" HACH 9

LA TORTUE ET LES DEUX CANARDS. "Une tortue étoit, a la tête légère" PLEI 1

LE VIEILLARD ET L'ÂNE. "Un vieillard sur son âne apercut, en passant" PLEI 1

LE VIEILLARD ET LES TROIS JEUNES HOMMES. "Un octogenaire plantoit" PLEI 1

LA VIEILLE ET LES DEUX SERVANTES. "Il étoit une Vieille ayant deux chambrieres" PLEI 1

LE VILLAGEOIS ET LE SERPENT. "Ésope conte qu'un Manant" PLEI 1

LES VOLEURS ET L'ÂNE. "Pour un âne enleve deux voleurs se battoient" PLEI 1

Poetry* SPOA 125

La Motte-Fouqué, Friedrich, Freiherr de. 1777. in German.

"Ich hatt ein süsses Leben" DEUTGR 4

Labé, Louise. 1525. in French.

"Apres qu'un tems la gresle et le tonnerre" German DEUTGR 12

"Je vis, ie meurs: ie me brule et me noye" ADES 54, GMS 8; German DEUTGR 12

"Oh si i'estois en ce beau sein rauie" German DEUTGR 12

SONNET 8. PERIOD 2

SONNET 24. "Ne reprenez, Dames, si i'ay ayme" DOVER 4; German DEUTGR 12

"Tant que mes yeux" HACH 8

Laepa, L. in English.

EXPATRIATES. "If you go away" FOLKW 110

LIBERATION FOR WOMEN. "A prisoner I was" FOLKW 110

Laforgue, Jules. 1860. in French.

AVANT-DERNIER MOT. "L'Espace?" ADES 18

AVERTISSEMENT. "Mon père (un dur par timidité)" ADES 18

COMPLAINTE DE LA LUNE EN PROVINCE. "Ah! la belle pleine Lune" ADES 18

COMPLAINTE DE L'OUBLI DES MORTS. "Mesdames et Messieurs" SPOA 9

COMPLAINTE DU PAUVRE JEUNE HOMME. "Quand ce jeune homm' rentra chez lui" ADES 18

COMPLAINTE DU ROI DE THULÉ. "Il était un roi du Thulé" ADES 18

COMPLAINTE SUR CERTAINS ENNUIS. "Un couchant des Cosmogonies" ADES 18, FOLKW 13

DIMANCHES. CAED 204

L'HIVER QUI VIENT. "Blocus sentimental! Messageries du Levant" ADES 18

L'IMPOSSIBLE. "Je puis mourir ce soir! Averses, vents, soleil" HACH 13

LOCUTIONS DES PIERROTS.
"Encore un livre; ô nostalgies" ADES 18
"Les main dans les poches" ADES 18
. . . others HACH 13

SOIR DE CARNAVAL. "Paris chahute au gaz. L'hologe comme un glas" HACH 13

Poetry* ADES 50

Lagerkvist, Pär. 1891. in Swedish.

"Det är vackrast när det skymmer" GRAM 5

"Det kom ett brev am sommarsäd" GRAM 5

DRÖMMAR ÅRO VÅRA TANKAR. GRAM 1

"Engång blir allting stilla" GRAM 5

HOPPETS FACKLA. "Tänd hoppets fackla i kvävande kväll" GRAM 1

"Jag vet att bortom det jag dunkelt anar" GRAM 5

"Livet tar sitt barn till sig" GRAM 5

LIVSBÅTEN. "Snart ar du död och vet ej att du glider" GRAM 5

"Nu löser solen sitt blonda hår" GRAM 5

"O människa, du brun där stjärnar speglas" GRAM 5

"Tillfällig som en vallmo, som vecket i en vandrandes kläder" GRAM 5

TORSO. GRAM 5

"Vam gick förbi min barndoms fönster" GRAM 5

VÅRT ENDA HEM AR KARLEKEN. GRAM 5

* Recording not available for analysis

Lagerlöf, Selma. 1858. in Swedish.
BROLLOPSMARSCHEN. GRAM 9
DEN HELIGA NATTEN. GRAM 9

Lahui, Jack. in English.
TO HER MAJESTY (ELIZABETH II). "When I heard you were coming" FOLKW 110

Lair, Clara. in English.
NOCTURNA 27. INSTPR 1

Lally, Michael. 1942. in English.
THE FAT MAN. "The fat man who owns the carnival" WATSHD 2
GETTING WHAT WE WANT. "In the doorways" WATSHD 2
TIME TO GO OUT. "I strap on my holster" WATSHD 2
THE WHOLE NEIGHBORHOOD. "Marilyn Monroe, everybody" WATSHD 2

Lamartine, Alphonse de. 1790. in French.
L'AUTOMNE. "Salut! bois couronnés d'un reste de verdure!" ADES 48
LA CLOCHE DU VILLAGE, exc. "Ne t'étonne pas, enfant, si ma pensée" DOVER 4
LE CRUCIFIX. "Toi que j'ai recueilli sur sa bouche expirante" HACH 15
LE DÉSERT OU L'IMMATÉRIALITÉ DE DIEU. ADES 39
GETHSEMANI, exc. "Je fus dès la mamelle un homme de douleur" HACH 11
L'ISOLEMENT. "Souvent sur la montagne, a l'ombre du vieux chêne" ADES 39, ADES 54, HACH 15
LE LAC. "Ainsi toujours poussés vers de nouveau rivages" ADES 39, ADES 48, ADES 54, FOLKW 86, GMS 7, GMS 8, HACH 11, HACH 15, PATHE 1, SPOA 9
MILLY OU LA TERRE NATALE. "Pourquoi le prononcer ce nom de la patrie" HACH 15
Ô MON CHIEN. ADES 39
ODE SUR LES REVOLUTIONS. "Peuple! des crimes de tes pères" ADES 54
LE PAPILLON. "Naitre avec le printemps, mourir avec les roses" ADES 39
PENSÉE DES MORTS. "Voilà les feulles sans sève" ADES 39
POUR-QUOI MON ÂME EST-ELLE TRISTE? "Pourquoi gémis-tu sans cesse" ADES 39
PREMIER REGRET, exc. HACH 11
LE SOIR. "Le soir ramène le silence" SPOA 36
LE VALLON. "Mon coeur, lassé de tout, même de l'espérance" ADES 48, PATHE 1
VERS SUR UN ALBUM. "Le livre de la vie est le livre supreme" ADES 39
LA VIGNE ET LA MAISON. "Quel fardeau te pèse, ô mon âme!" ADES 39
VOILA LE BLANC RUSTIQUE. ADES 39

Lamb, Charles. 1775. in English.
A BACHELOR'S COMPLAINT. ARGO 88A
THE OLD FAMILIAR FACES. EAV 7
ON AN INFANT DYING AS SOON AS BORN. LIVLAN 1

Lampman, Archibald. 1861. in English.
MORNING ON THE LIEVRE. NFBC 1

Landor, Walter Savage. 1775. in English.
CORINNA TO TANAGRA, exc. CAED 202
"From you, Ianthe, little troubles pass" IMP 1

ON HIS SEVENTY-FIRST BIRTHDAY. "The day returns, my natal day" EAV 8
PERICLES AND ASPASIA, exc. CAED 202
ROSE AYLMER. "Ah what avails the sceptred race" EAV 8
SWEET WAS THE SONG. "Sweet was the song that youth sang once" CAED 202
Poetry* PRENT 3

Lang, Andrew. 1844. in English.
BALLADE OF CHRISTMAS GHOSTS. "Between the moonlight and the fire" EAV 22

Langland, Joseph. 1917. in English.
ROCKY MOUNTAIN SNOWSTORM. "Loined in lean wind" SCHOL 1
SACRIFICE OF A GUNNYSACK OF CATS. "The quick small bubbles popping the gunnysack" SCHOL 1
SACRIFICE OF A RAINBOW TROUT. "Suddenly, from the rocky spring" SCHOL 1
SACRIFICE OF GOPHERS AND WOODCHUCKS. "When I was a young one" SCHOL 1
SACRIFICE OF MY DOG, REX. "When my dog came whimpering out of the hayfields" SCHOL 1
SACRIFICE OF THE GOLDEN OWL. "We strung our Wyandotte rooster, dead on a post" SCHOL 1
SONG WITH BELLS. "Once in childhood's rainwater wells" SCHOL 1
WAR. "When my young brother was killed" SCHOL 1

Langland, William. 1330. in Middle English.
PIERS PLOWMAN, exc. "In a somer sesoun whanne softe was the sonne" EAV 11; Modern English ARGO 28

Lanier, Sidney. 1842. in English.
A BALLAD OF TREES AND THE MASTER. "Into the woods my Master went" CMS 14, EAV 22
THE MARSHES OF GLYNN. "Glooms of the live-oaks, beautiful braided and woven" CAED 185
THE REVENGE OF HAMISH. "It was three slim does and a ten-tined buck" EAV 15
SONG OF THE CHATTA HOOCHEE. "Out of the hills of Habersham" EAV 15, HOUGHT 5

Lanusse, Armand. in English.
EPIGRAM. UA 2

Lapalma, Marina. in English.
CAFE. "They are getting up from the table" WATSHD 14

Lapo Gianni. 1270. in Italian.
Poetry* CETRA 36

Lapointe, Paul-Marie. 1929. in French.
COMME ON L'AVAIT ESPERE. "Rien/ ni fleuve ni mysique" FOLKW 70
"Corps tendre et blond" FOLKW 70
"Nous sommes installés sous le tonerre" FOLKW 70
"Soyez tristes/ pleurez dans la lutte" FOLKW 70

Larbaud, V. 1881. in French.
ALMA PERDIDA. "De la digestion qui se fait apaisement" FOLKW 13

Larkin, Philip. 1922. in English.
AN ARUNDEL TOMB. "Side by side, their faces blurred" FOLKW 59A
COMING. "On longer evenings, light chill and yellow" ARGO 9

---

* Recording not available for analysis

DAYS. "What are days for" ARGO 98, JNP 62
DOCKERY AND SON. "Dockery was junior to you" ARGO 98
FOR SYDNEY BRADSHAW. "That note you hold" JNP 62
I REMEMBER, I REMEMBER. "Coming up England by a different line" SPOA 68
MR. BLEANEY. "This was Mr. Bleaney's room. He stayed" FOLKW 59A
NOTHING TO BE SAID. "For nations vague as weed" ARGO 98
SELF'S THE MAN. "Oh, no one can deny" JNP 62
SUNNY PRESTATYN. "Come to Sunny Prestatyn" JNP 62
WANTS. "Beyond all this the wish to be alone" ARGO 98

Lasker-Schüler, Else. 1876. in German.
EIN ALTER TIBETTEPPICH. "Deine Seele, die die meine" DEUTGR 11
AN MEIN KIND. "Immer wieder wirst du mir" DEUTGR 11
AUS DER FERNE. "Die Welt, aus der ich lange mich" DEUTGR 11
ES KOMMT DER ABEND. "Es kommt der Abend und ich" CHRIST 30
GEBET. DEUTGR 11
EIN LIEBESLIED. DEUTGR 11
MEIN BLAUES KLAVIER. "Ich habe zu Hause ein blaues" DEUTGR 11
DIE VERSCHEUCHTE. "Es ist der Tag im Nebel" DEUTGR 11
VERSÖHNUNG. "Es wird ein grosser stern in meinen Schoss fallen" DEUTGR 11
VOLLMOND. "Leise schwimmt der Mond durch mein Blut" CHRIST 11

Lasnier, Rina. 1915. in French.
AU BORD DE L'EAU. "Je serai à genoux dans ma robe comme l'eau" FOLKW 70
ENSEMBLE. "Par le seul désir de durer ensemble" FOLKW 70
JOIE DE L'AMOUR OBSCUR. "Moi, naïve, cachée à la niche" FOLKW 70
MARIE MAGDELEINE. "Si vous cherchez une lanterne sourde" FOLKW 70
L'OMBRE ROUGE. "N'entre pas à l'ómbre de mon ombre gisante" FOLKW 70

Last Poets, The. in English.
ALLEY. JUG 1
AND SEE HER IMAGE IN THE RIVER. BLACKF 1
BEEN DONE ALREADY. JUG 1
BLACK WOMAN. JUG 1
DIE NIGGA. JUG 1
HEY NOW. JUG 1
INTO THE STREETS. JUG 1
JAMES BROWN. JUG 1
JAZZ. JUG 1
JIBARO—MY PRETTY NIGGER. JUG 1
THE LIBRARY. JUG 1
LITTLE WILLIE ARMSTRONG JONES. JUG 1
POETRY IS BLACK. JUG 1
PUERTO RICAN RHYTHMS. JUG 1
RIFLE PRAYER. JUG 1
THE SHALIMAR. JUG 1
SONG OF DITTA, PART 2. BLACKF 1
TELL ME BROTHER. JUG 1
TODAY IS A KILLER. JUG 1

Laudon, Alice. in English.
SPACE PILOT. "I'm a space pilot" HARB 2
Laura, Victoria. in Spanish.
EN SECRETO. "Ven, acércate más, bebe en mi boca" SMC 7
Lautréamont, Comte de (Isidore Ducasse). 1846. in French.
APOSTROPHES A L'OCEAN, exc. HACH 13
LES CHANTS DE MALDOROR. "Vieil ocean, ta forme" ADES 21, ADES 54, FOLKW 13
CHAQUE NUIT, A L'HEURE OU LE SOMMEIL. ADES 21, ADES 49
LES MAGASINS DE LA RUE. ADES 21
LE VAUTOUR DES AGNEAUX. ADES 21, ADES 49
Lavant, Christine. 1915. in German.
BEI DIR UND DER DREIFALTIGKEIT. CHRIST 29
Lavin, Stuart. in English.
CAMBODIAN SPRING. "Confucian" WATSHD 5
Lawrence, D. H. 1885. in English.
THE MESS OF LOVE. "We've made a great mess of love" ARGO 88A
PIANO. "Softly, in the dusk, a woman is singing to me" FOLKW 64
THE SHIP OF DEATH. "Now it is autumn and the falling fruit" CAED 126
SNAKE. "A snake came to my water-trough" BRITAM 1, FOLKW 64
TO WOMEN AS FAR AS I'M CONCERNED. "The feelings I don't have I don't have" ARGO 88A
WHALES, WEEP NOT. "They say the sea is cold, but the sea contains" CAED 147
THE YOUNG WIFE. "The pain of loving you" ARGO 88A
Poetry* SPOA 113
Layton, Irving. 1912. in English.
THE BIRTH OF TRAGEDY. "And me happiest when I compose" FOLKW 49
THE BULL CALF. "The thing could barely stand yet taken" FOLKW 49
THE COLD GREEN ELEMENT. "At the end of the garden walk" FOLKW 49
THE FERTILE MUCK. "There are brightest apples on those trees" FOLKW 49
THE IMPROVED BINOCULARS. "Below me the city was in flames" FOLKW 49
MAXIE. "Son, braggart and thrasher" FOLKW 49
TO A VERY OLD WOMAN. "Old woman, your face is a halo of praise" LEARNC 6
Lazarus, Emma. 1849. in English.
THE NEW COLOSSUS. "Not like the brazen giant of Greek fame" CAED 98, CAED 195, COLUMB 6
Le Gallienne, Richard. in English.
"I meant to do my work today" CAED 164, CMS 3
Leadbelly (Huddie Ledbetter). 1888. in English Poetry* PRENT 1
Leal, Gomes. 1848. in Portuguese.
A SENHORA DUQUESA DE BRABANTE. "Tem um legue de plumas gloriosas" FOLKW 72
NO CALVÁRIO. "Maria, com seus olhos magoados" FOLKW 72
Lear, Edward. 1812. in English.
THE AKOND OF SWAT. "Is he tall or short, or dark or fair" CMS 2
THE BEARDED MAN. HARC 4

* Recording not available for analysis

Lear, Edward (continued)

THE BROOM, THE SHOVEL, THE POKER AND THE
TONGS.   LONDON 1
BY WAY OF PREFACE. "How pleasant to know Mr.
Lear"   CAED 50, ARGO 125 LONDON 1,
LONGM 1
CALICO PIE.   FOLKW 67
THE COURTSHIP OF THE YONGHY-BONGHY-BO. "On
the Coast of Coromandel"   CMS 4
DAY OF THESE DAYS.   ARGO 139
THE DONG WITH A LUMINOUS NOSE. "When awful
darkness and silence reign"   CAED 50,
CAED 201
THE DUCK AND THE KANGAROO. "Said the duck to
the kangaroo"   CAED 50, CMS 3
INCIDENTS IN THE LIFE OF MY UNCLE ARLY.
LONDON 1
THE JUMBLIES. "They went to sea in a sieve, they
did"   CAED 50, CMS 3, SPOA 35,
THEAL 1, LION 2
"Mr. and Mrs. Discobolos"   CAED 50
THE NEW VESTMENTS. "There lived an old man
in the Kingdom of Tess"   ARGO 125
THE OWL AND THE PUSSY-CAT. "The owl and the
pussy-cat went to sea"   CAED 50,
CAED 85, CAED 109, CAED 132,
DECCA 11, FOLKW 67, LIST 22, LION 2,
RCA 8, THEAL 2, SPOA 117
"The Pobble who has no toes"   CAED 50,
CAED 85, CMS 2
THE QUANGLE WANGLE'S HAT. "On the top of the
Crumpetty Tree"   ARGO 118
"There was a young lady of Parma"
CAED 50
"There was a young lady of Sweden"
EAV 22
"There was a young lady who said, why"
CMS 4
"There was a young lady whose bonnet"
CAED 50
"There was a young lady whose chin"
CAED 50
"There was a young lady whose eyes"
CAED 50
"There was a young person of Smyrna"
CAED 50, EAV 22
"There was an old lady whose folly"
CAED 50
"There was an old man in a tree"   CAED 50,
CMS 2
"There was an old man of Dunluce"
CAED 50
"There was an old man of the Nile"
CAED 50
"There was an old man of Thermopylae"
CAED 50
"There was an old man of Whitehaven"
CAED 50
"There was an old man on some rocks"
CAED 50
"There was an old man who said, Hush"
CAED 50
"There was an old man who said, Well"
CAED 50
"There was an old man with a gong"
CAED 50

"There was an old person of Bow"   CAED 50
"There was an old person of Crowle"
CAED 50
"There was an old person of Dutton"
CAED 50
"There was an old person of Sark" CAED 50
THE TWO OLD BACHELORS. "Two old bachelors
were living in one house"   CAED 50
Poetry*   ARGO 108, SPOA 116
Lechlitner, Ruth. in English.
KANSAS BOY.   SCHOL 7
Leconte de Lisle, Charles Marie René. 1818. in
French.
L'ASTRE ROUGE. Sur les Continents morts, les
houles léthargiques"   ADES 54, SPOA 9
MIDI. "Midi, roi des étés, épandu sur la pleine"
GMS 7, GMS 9
Ledbetter, Huddie. See **Leadbelly.**
Ledwidge, Francis. in English.
THE FIND. "I took a reed and blew a tune"
CAED 164
THE SHADOW PEOPLE. "Old lame Bridget doesn't
hear"   CAED 164
Lee, Dennis. 1939. in English.
ALLIGATOR EMILY.   CAED 171
ALLIGATOR PIE. 1.   CAED 171
_____. 2.   CAED 171
_____. 3   CAED 171
BATH SONG. "A biscuit, a basket"   CAED 171
BEING FIVE. "I'm not exactly big" CAED 171
THE BIG MOLICE PAN AND THE BERTIE DUMB. 1.
CAED 171
_____. 2.   CAED 171
BILLY BATTER.   CAED 171
BLOODY BILL. "You say you want to fight me"
CAED 171
BOUNCING SONG. "Hambone, Jawbone"
CAED 171
BUMP ON YOUR THUMB.   CAED 171
THE COMING OF TEDDY BEARS. "The air is quiet"
CAED 171
THE FISHES OF KEMPENFELT BAY.   CAED 171
THE FRIENDS.   CAED 171
GARBAGE DELIGHT. "Now, I'm not the one"
CAED 171
HALF WAY DRESSED. "I sometimes sit"
CAED 171
HIGGLEDY PIGGLEDY.   CAED 171
I EAT KIDS YUM YUM. "A child went out one day"
CAED 171
IN KAMLOOPS.   CAED 171
INSPECTOR DOGBONE GETS HIS MAN. "Inspector
Dogbone"   CAED 171
MR. HOOBODY.   CAED 171
THE MOON. "I see the moon"   CAED 171
MUMBO, JUMBO.   CAED 171
ON TUESDAYS I POLISH MY UNCLE.   CAED 171
PETER WAS A PILOT. "Peter was a pilot"
CAED 171
THE QUESTION.   CAED 171
RATTLESNAKE SKIPPING SONG.   CAED 171
THE SITTER AND THE BUTTER AND THE BETTER BAT-
TER FRITTER.   CAED 171
SKYSCRAPER. 1.   CAED 171
_____. 2.   CAED 171
SMELLY FRED. "A sort of beetle-bug is crawling"
CAED 171

---

* Recording not available for analysis

THE SPECIAL PERSON.   CAED 171
SUZY GREW A MOUSTACHE. "Suzy grew a mous-
    tache"   CAED 171
TONGUE TWISTER. "Someday I'll go to Win-
    nipeg"   CAED 171
TRICKING.   CAED 171
WELLINGTON THE SKELETON.   CAED 171
WINDSHIELD WIPERS.   CAED 171
Lee, Don L. 1942. in English.
AFTER HER MAN HAD LEFT HER FOR THE SIXTH TIME
    THAT YEAR. "she stood nakedly"
                                       BROADV 18
ASSASSINATION. "it was wild"   BROADV 4
BIG MOMMA. "finally retired"   BROADV 18
BLACK SKETCHES. "I / was five"   BROADV 4
BLACKGIRL LEARNING. "She couldn't quote
    french poetry"   BROADV 4
BLACKMUSIC/ A BEGINNING. "pharoah sanders"
                                       BROADV 4
BLACKRUNNERS/ BLACKMEN. "U beat them"
                                       BROADV 4
BLACKWOMAN. "blackwoman:/ is an"
                                       BROADV 4
BLACKWOMAN. "Will define herself"
                                       BROADV 4
BUT HE WAS COOL. "super-cool"   BROADV 4
CHANGE IS NOT ALWAYS PROGRESS. "Africa/ don't
    let them"   BROADV 18
COMMUNICATION IN WHI-TE. "Dee dee dee dee
    dee wee"   BROADV 4
DON'T CRY, SCREAM. "into the sixties"
                                       BROADV 4
FOR BLACK PEOPLE. "In the beginning"
                                       BROADV 18
FROM A BLACK PERSPECTIVE. "Wallace for presi-
    dent"   BROADV 4
GWENDOLYN BROOKS. "She doesn't wear"
                     BROADV 4, CAED 114
HERO. "Little willie" BROADV 4, CAED 155
HISTORY OF THE POET AS A WHORE. "Yeats in
    brown-tone"   BROADV 4
JUDY—ONE. "She's the camera's" BROADV 18
KNOCKING DONKEY FLEAS OFF A POET FROM THE
    SOUTHSIDE OF CHI. "a worldman"
                                       BROADV 18
LISTEN COMRADES, exc.   BROADV 4
A LONELINESS.   BROADV 18
MALCOLM SPOKE/ WHO LISTENED. "he didn't say"
                                       BROADV 4
MAN THINKING ABOUT WOMAN. "Some thing is
    lost in me"   BROADV 18
A MESSAGE ALL BLACKPEOPLE CAN DIG. "We are
    going to do it"   BROADV 4
MIXED SKETCHES. "U feel that way some times"
                                       BROADV 18
MOVE UN-NOTICED TO BE NOTICED: A NATIONHOOD
POEM. "move, into our own, not theirs"
                                       BROADV 18
NIGERIAN UNITY/ OR LITTLE NIGGERS KILLING LIT-
    TLE NIGGERS. "Suppose those" BROADV 4
ON SEEING DIANA GO MADDDDDDD. "a dog lover"
                                       BROADV 18
ONE SIDED SHOOT.   BROADV 18
A POEM FOR A POET. "read yr/ exile"
                                       BROADV 18
A POEM FOR NEGRO INTELLECTUALS. "&/ black-
    woman be ahead"   BROADV 4

A POEM LOOKING FOR A READER. "black is not"
                                       BROADV 4
A POEM TO COMPLEMENT OTHER POEMS.
    "Change/ like if you were a match"
                     BROADV 4, CAED 155
RE-ACT FOR ACTION. "re-act to animals"
                                       EAV 16
REFLECTIONS ON A LOST LOVE. "back in chi"
                                       BROADV 4
THE REVOLUTIONARY SCREW. "brothers"
                                       BROADV 4
SEE SAMMY RUN IN THE WRONG DIRECTION. "we
    know others"   BROADV 18
SUN HOUSE.   BROADV 18
THE THIRD WORLD BOND. "They were"
                                       BROADV 4
THE WAY OF LIFE, exc.   BROADV 4
WE WALK THE WAY OF THE NEW WORLD. "we run
    the dangercourse"   BROADV 18
Poetry*   PRENT 1
Lee, Laurie. 1913. in English.
THE ABANDONED SHADE. "Walking the aban-
    doned shade of childhood habitations"
                     FOLKW 65, JUP 1
APPLES. "Behold the apple's rounded worlds"
                                       ARGO 4
APRIL RISE. "If ever I saw a blessing in the air"
           ARGO 4, ARGO 98, FOLKW 66
BOY ON ICE. "O river, green and still"
                                       FOLKW 66
DAY OF THESE DAYS. "Such a morning it is when
    love"   ARGO 4, ARGO 98, FOLKW 65,
                                       JUP 1
FIRST LOVE. "That was her beginning"
                                       ARGO 4
HOME FROM ABROAD. "Far-fetched with tales of
    other worlds and ways"   FOLKW 66
JUNIPER. "Juniper holds to the moon a girl ador-
    ing"   ARGO 4
THE LONG WAR. "Less passionate, the long war
    throws"   ARGO 4
MAN ON THE OTHER SIDE.   FOLKW 66
STORK IN JEREZ. "White-arched in loops of si-
    lence"   ARGO 4
SUMMER MILK MAID. "The girl's far treble, muted
    to the heat"   ARGO 4, ARGO 98
TOWN OWL. "On eves of cold, when slow coal
    fires"   FOLKW 66
Lee-Hamilton, Eugene. 1845. in English.
LUCCA SIGNORELLI TO HIS SON. "They brought
    thy body back to me quite dead"
                                       LONGM 1
Léger, Alexis St.-Léger. See **Perse, St.-John.**
Lehmann. in German.
DEUTSCHE ZEIT 1947.   CHRIST 30
Lemaitre, Maurice. 1926. in French.
LETTRE ROCK.   LUCHT 1
Lenau, Nikolaus. 1802. in German.
AM GRABE HÖLTYS. "Hölty! dein Freund, der
    Frühling, ist gekommen"   CHRIST 22
KOMMEN UND SCHEIDEN. "So oft sie kam, erschi-
    en mir die Gestalt"   DOVER 1
SCHILFLIEDER, exc. "Auf geheimem Waldesp-
    fade"   DOVER 1
WINTERNACHT. "Vor Kälte ist die Luft erstarrt"
                                       CHRIST 11
Poetry*   CHRIST 5

* Recording not available for analysis

Lenngren, Anna Maria. 1755. in Swedish.
GREVINNANS BESÖK. "Bevars vilket fläng både ute och innan"   GRAM 3
Lenz, Jakob Michael Reinhold. 1751. in German.
"Wo bist du itzt"   DOVER 1
León, Fray Luis de. 1527. in Spanish.
BENEDICE ANIMA MEA.   IMP 2
NOCHE SERENA. "Morada de grandeza"   SPOA 37
ODA A FRANCISCO SALINAS. "El aire se serena"   DOVER 2, GMS 16
ON LEAVING PRISON
                    Spanish and English CMS 5
VIDA RETIRADA. "Que descansada vida"   GMS 16, HOLT 1
León, Rafael de. in Spanish.
AUTO DE FÉ. "Esta noche de agosto he quemado tus cartas"   SMC 7
BALADILLA DE LOS TRES PUÑALES. "He comprado tres puñales"   SMC 7
ENCUENTRO. "Me tropecé contigo en primavera"   SMC 5
ESCOMBRO. "¿Cómo me quieres, dime?"   SMC 5
KASIDA DE LA VOZ. "Cuando me llamas, toda la casa huele a pregon de naranjas"   SMC 5
KASIDA DE LAS MANOS. "Como una rosa, como una almendra"   SMC 7
KASIDA DE LOS OJOS. "Cuando iba por el zoco murmuraron"   SMC 7
MUERTA DE AMOR. "No lo sabe mi brazo"   SMC 7
PAVANA ANDALUZA DE TU CALLE SIN SALIDA. "En tu calle sin salida"   GMS 14
PENA Y ALEGRIÁ DEL AMOR.   GMS 14
PROFECÍA. "Me lo contaron ayer"   GMS 18
ROMANCE DE LA LIRIO.   GMS 18
SOLTERA. "Mi prima Matilde"   GMS 18
Poetry*   SMC 16, SMC 17
Leonidas the Alexandrian. 1st century A.D. in Greek.
COMPENSATION. "Simelos the harper played a night-long recital"   English CARIL 3
Leopardi, Giacomo. 1798. in Italian.
A SÈ STESSO. "Or poserai per sempre"   CETRA 8, SPOA 30
A SILVIA. "Silvia, rimembri ancora"   CETRA 8
AD ANGELO MAI. "Italo ardito, a che giammai non posi"   CETRA 8
ALLA LUNA. "O graziosa luna, io mi rammento"   CETRA 8
ALLA SUA DONNA. "Cara beltá che amore"   CETRA 8
ALL'ITALIA. "O patria mia, vedo le mura e gli archi"   CETRA 8
AMORE E MORTE. "Fratelli, a un tempo stesso, Amore e Morte"   CETRA 8
BRUTO MINORE. "Poi che divelta, nella tracia polve"   CETRA 8
CANTO NOTTURNO DI UN PASTORE ERRANTE DELL-'ASIA. "Che fai tu, Luna, in ciel?"   CETRA 8
CANTI, exc.   CETRA 9
LA GINESTRA. "Qui su l'arida schiena"   CETRA 8; AUDIL 2 (exc.)
L'INFINITO. "Sempre caro mi fu quest'ermo colle"   CETRA 8, DOVER 3, SPOA 30

NELLE NOZZE DELLA SORELLA PAOLINA. "Poi che del patrio nido"   CETRA 8
IL PASSERO SOLITARIO. "D'in su la vetta della torre antica"   CETRA 8
IL PENSIERO DOMINANTE. "Dolcissimo, possente"   CETRA 8
IL PRIMO AMORE. "Tornami a mente il di che la bataaglia"   CETRA 8
LA QUIETE DOPO LA TEMPESTA. "Passata è la tempesta"   CETRA 8, DOVER 3
LE RICORDANZE. "Vaghe stelle dell' Orsa, io non credea"   CETRA 8
IL SABATO DE VILLAGGIO. "La donzelletta vien dalla campagna"   CETRA 8
LA SERA DEL DI DÌ FESTA. "Dolce e chiara è la notte e senza vento"   CETRA 8
IL SOGNO. "Era il mattino, e tra le chiuse imposte"   CETRA 8
IL TRAMONTO DELLA LUNA. "Quale in notte solinga"   CETRA 8
ULTIMO CANTO DI SAFFO. "Vile, o natura, e grave ospite"   CETRA 8
LA VITA SOLITARIA. "La mattutina pioggia, allor che"   CETRA 8
Lermontov, Mikhail. 1814. in Russian.
BALLADA.   MK 1
BALLADA. "Nad morem krasavitsa-deva sidit"   MK 1
BLAGODARNOST'. "Za vse, za vse tebya blagodaryu ya"   CAED 193
DUMA. "Pechal'no ya glyazhu na nashe pokolenye"   CAED 193
"Est' rechi"   MK 1
"Kak nebesa, tvoi vsor blistaet"   MK 1
MOLITVA. "Ne obvinyai menya, vsesil'nyi"   CMS 6
NADEZHDA. "Est' ptichka raya u menya"   MK 1
NEZABUDKA. "V starinny gody lyudi byli"   MK 1
POTOK. "Istochnik strasti est' vo mne"   MK 1
PREDSKAZANIYE. "Nastanyet god, Rossii chernyi god"   CMS 6
ROMANS.   MK 1
SHCHERBATOVOI. "Poveryu l'ya chtob vy khoteli"   MK 1
ZAVESHANIE. "Est' mesto: bliz tropy glukhoi"   English CAED 193
ZHELANIE.   MK 1
Leslie, Cy. in English.
ON RIOTS.   EAV 16
Lessing, Gotthold Ephraim. 1729. in German.
DIE EHELICHE LIEBE. "Klorinde starb; sechs Wochen drauf"   ATHENA 3
FAUSTIN. "Faustin, der ganze funfzehn Jahr"   ATHENA 3
NIX BODENSTROM. "Nix Bodenstrom, ein Schiffer, nahm"   ATHENA 3
Lester, Julius. 1939. in English.
A FISH. "A fish comes up for food"   WATSHD 6
FLIES. "Once inside"   WATSHD 6
FOR JOAN. "The revolution does not begin"   WATSHD 6
HAIKU 2   WATSHD 6
HAIKU 18 "Living upstream"   WATSHD 6

* Recording not available for analysis

HAIKU 19 "The man who tried to kill himself"
WATSHD 6
HAIKU 55 "Her smile comes" WATSHD 6
HAIKU 59 "In summer make love" WATSHD 6
I CARRIED HER. "I carried her through the cold"
WATSHD 6
KANSAS AUGUST, 1973. "It could not be"
WATSHD 6
THE MUD OF VIET NAM. "The mud of Viet Nam"
WATSHD 6
ST. JOSEPH ABBEY VIGILS. "The darkness consumes even" WATSHD 6
SONG: I'M GOING HOME. "My mother prayed"
WATSHD 6
SONG: MAYBE THE LAST TIME. "Maybe the last time" WATSHD 6
SONG: NOBODY'S FAULT BUT MINE. "Nobody's fault" WATSHD 6
SONG: WADE IN THE WATER. "Wade in the water"
WATSHD 6
SONG: WATCH THE SEAGULLS FLYING. "Watch the seagulls" WATSHD 6
SONG: WORRIED BLUES. "Yeah some folks tell me" WATSHD 6
STOCKHOLM, MAY. "First light comes at 3 A.M."
WATSHD 6
SUMMER, 1975. "Even the aspen leaves"
WATSHD 6
TEMPLE. "O God, is it wrong" WATSHD 6
WHEN I LEFT. "When I left her, the roosters"
WATSHD 6
Poetry* WATSHD 21

_esto, Julio. in Spanish.
LAS ABANDONADAS. "Como me dan pena las abandonadas" SMC 6

_evendosky, Charles. 1936. in English.
BOOM TOWN, WYOMING. "Long hair Nam vets"
WATSHD 10
BUY ME. "I want to be a postage stamp"
WATSHD 10
DRIVING THROUGH NEBRASKA. "Monday, Tuesday" WATSHD 10
TO MARIA MONTESSORI. "Dear Ms. Montessori, I love you" WATSHD 10

_evertov, Denise. 1923. in English.
THE ACHE OF THE MARRIAGE. "The ache of the marriage" SPOA 104
ADVENT 1966. "Because in Viet Nam the vision of a Burning Babe" SCHOL 3
THE DEAD. "Earnestly I looked" SCHOL 3
GONE AWAY. "When my body leaves me"
SCHOL 3
THE JACOB'S LADDER. "The stairway is not a thing of gleaming strands" SPOA 104
LIFE AT WAR. "The disasters numb within us"
NET 18
LIVING. "The fire in leaf and grass"CAED 155
LOOKING-GLASS. "I slide my face along to the mirror" SCHOL 3
LOSING TRACK. NET 18
LUXURY. "To go by the asters" SPOA 104
MERRITT PARKWAY. "As if it were" SCHOL 3
A MUSIC. "Melody moving downstream"
SCHOL 3
THE RAINWALKERS. "An old man whose black face" SCHOL 3

THE SAGE. "The cat is eating the roses"
SCHOL 3
THE SECRET. "Two girls discover" SCHOL 3
A SOLITUDE. "A blind man. I can stare at him"
SCHOL 3, SPOA 104
SONG FOR A DARK VOICE. "My black sun, my Odessa sunflower" SPOA 104
SONG FOR ISHTAR. "The moon is a sow"
SPOA 104, NET 18
TO THE SNAKE. "Green snake, when I hung you round my neck" SCHOL 3
THE TULIPS. "Red tulips living into their death"
SPOA 104
TWO ANGELS. NET 18
WE ARE THE HUMANS. BROADR 1
WHAT WERE THEY LIKE? "1) Did the people of Viet Nam" CAED 155
THE WHIRLWIND. "The doors keep rattling—I"
SCHOL 3
Poetry* JNP 30

Levi, Peter. 1931. in English.
THE FOX-COLORED PHEASANT. "The foxcolored pheasant" SPOA 68
IN MIDWINTER A WOOD WAS. "In midwinter a wood was" SPOA 68

Levine, Philip. 1928. in English.
THE ANGELS OF DETROIT. "I could hear them in fever" WATSHD 24
ASK THE ROSES. "Snow fell forward forever"
WATSHD 24
ASKING. "Once in the beginning"
WATSHD 12, WATSHD 24
AT THE FILLMORE. "The music was going on"
CAED 168
BABY VILLON. "He tells me in Bangkok he's robbed" CAED 168
BLASTING FROM HEAVEN. CAED 168
BREATH. "Who has the humming" CAED 168
THE CHILDREN'S CRUSADE. "Crossbow wanted a child" PROTHM 12
CLOUDS. CAED 168
CRY FOR NOTHING. "Make the stream"
WATSHD 24
DARK HEAD. "Wakened suddenly by my own"
WATSHD 12, WATSHD 24
FOR FRAN. "She packs the flower beds with leaves" WATSHD 24
FOR THE POETS OF CHILE WHO DIED WITH THEIR COUNTRY. CAED 168
FRANCISCO, I'LL BRING YOU RED CARNATIONS. "Here in the great cemetery"
WATSHD 24
GRANDMOTHER IN HEAVEN. "Darkness gathering in the branches" CAED 168
HEAR ME. "I watch the filthy light"
WATSHD 24
HEAVEN. "If you were twenty-seven"
CAED 168
HOLDING ON. CAED 168
THE HORSE. CAED 168
A LATE ANSWER. "Beyond that stand of firs"
WATSHD 24
THE LIFE AHEAD. "I wakened, still a child"
WATSHD 12, WATSHD 24
THE MIDGET. "In this cafe Durruti"
WATSHD 24

* Recording not available for analysis

Levine, Philip (continued)

MY SON AND I. "In a coffee house at 3 A.M."
WATSHD 24

A NEW DAY. "The headlights fading out at dawn"   CAED 168

NEW SEASON. "My son and I go walking"
WATSHD 24

NO ONE REMEMBERS. "A soft wind"
WATSHD 24

ON THE EDGE. "My name is Edgar Poe and I was born"   CAED 168

ON THE MURDER OF LIEUTENANT JOSE DEL CASTIL-LO BY THE FALANGIST BRAVO MARTINEZ, JULY 12TH, 1936.   CAED 168

PEACE. "Our words go slowly out"
WATSHD 12, WATSHD 24

THE POEM CIRCLING HAMTRAMCK, MICHIGAN ALL NIGHT IN SEARCH OF YOU. "He hasn't gone to work"   CAED 168

SALAMI. "Stomach of goat, crushed"
CAED 168

SATURDAY SWEEPING. "Saturday sweeping/with an old broom"   CAED 168

THEY FEED THEY LION. "Out of burlap sacks, out of bearing butter"   CAED 168

TO MY GOD IN HIS SICKNESS. "A boy is as old as the stars"   CAED 168

TO P.L., 1916-1937. "Gray earth peeping through snow"   CAED 168

TOWARD HOME. "The years are turning"
WATSHD 12, WATSHD 24

UNCLE. "I remember the forehead born"
WATSHD 24

WAKING AN ANGEL. "Sparrows quarreled outside our window"   WATSHD 24

ZAYDEE. "Why does the sea burn? Why do the hills cry?"   CAED 168

Lewis, Alun. 1915. in English.
ALL DAY IT HAS RAINED.   ARGO 119
BATTLE SCHOOL.   ARGO 119
SACCO WRITES TO HIS SON.   CAED 126
SONG.   CAED 86

Lewis, C. Day. see **Day Lewis, Cecil.**

Lewis, Janet. 1899. in English.
BABY GOAT. "New-born, gilded with blood"
LIBC 25, LIBC 60

COUNTRY BURIAL. "After the words of the mag-nificence and doom"   LIBC 25

GIRL HELP. "Mild and slow and young"
LIBC 25

GOING HOME FROM THE PARTY. "I heard the far lowing"   LIBC 25

A LULLABY. "Lullee, lullay"   LIBC 25

OLD LOVE. "Love that is rooted deep"
LIBC 25

ON AN OLD WOMAN DYING. "Something was marred in making at her birth"   LIBC 25

REMEMBERED MORNING. "The axe rings in the wood"   LIBC 25

WINTER GARDEN. "Child, dream of a pome-granate tree"   LIBC 25

Lewis, Richard. 1935. in English.
THERE WAS A LITTLE BOY.   CAED 109

Lezama Lima, José. 1912. in Spanish.
"Una oscura pradera me convida"   SMC 13

Li Bai (Li Po). 701. in Chinese.
CHANG GAN SYING. "Chye fa chu fu e"
FOLKW 7

THE EXILE'S LETTER. "To So-Kin of Rakuyo, an cient friend, Chancellor of Gen"
English CAED 8

YE SEE. "Chwang chyan ming ywe gwang"
FOLKW 76, SCHOL

Li Ching Jau. 1084. in Chinese.
DZWEI HWA YIN. "Bwo wu nung yun chou yun jou"   FOLKW 7

Li Yu. 936. in Chinese.
SYANG JYAN HWAN. "Wu yan du shang syi lou"
FOLKW 7

Liddy, James. 1934. in English.
PATRICK KAVANAGH'S DUBLIN. "We travel t Dublin's white streets"   ARGO 9

Lieberman, Elias. 1883. in English.
I AM AN AMERICAN.   CAED 9

Lieberman, Laurence. 1935. in English.
Poetry*   JNP 3

Lifshin, Lynn. in English.
AFTER THE VISIT. "Flat blue hills" WOMAUD

ANOTHER UNCLE. "Another uncle"
WOMAUD

ARIZONA RUINS. "Past Mogollon River"
WOMAUD

BERYL. "My father in his"   WOMAUD

CAT CALLAHAN. "Being fat until" WOMAUD

CUCUMBERS. "The more you"   WOMAUD

DIAMOND RING. "Paying for half of it"
WOMAUD

DIVORCE DUMPLINGS. "Take whatever you've"
WOMAUD

FAT. "Some of it i've"   WOMAUD

FAT THIGHS & 30 DOLLAR EYES. "Black at th roots"   WOMAUD

HYPNOSIS POEM. "Maybe we're both"
WOMAUD

IN SPITE OF HIS DANGLING PRONOUN. "He wa really her favorite"   WOMAUD

IN THE OLD HOUSE PLYMOUTH. "A closet of"
WOMAUD

JOHN B. STETSON. "Wanting to cure"
WOMAUD

LEMOND WIND. "All day"   WOMAUD

MAMA. "I read love with"   WOMAUD

THE MAN IN THE BOILER ROOM IS. "Drilling litt holes"   WOMAUD

THE MOLE UNDER MY EYE. "I didn't always have
WOMAUD

MY MOTHER AND I WERE. "The closest but we"
WOMAUD

MY MOTHER AND THE BED. "No not that wa she'd"   WOMAUD

THE NO MORE APOLOGIZING THE NO MORE LITTL LAUGHING BLUES. "Apologizing for going to
WOMAUD

THE OLD HOUSE: PLYMOUTH. "9 children in the
WOMAUD

ORALS. "Half of them"   WOMAUD

PH.D. PANCAKES ENGLISH STYLE. "Take someboo who"   WOMAUD

PHOTOGRAPH. "My father sister and"
WOMAUD

PLYMOUTH WOMEN. "The winters seem darke here"   WOMAUD

* Recording not available for analysis

THE READING. "Someone's already"
WOMAUD 1

TENTACLES, LEAVES. "He saw my"
WOMAUD 1

WOMEN: EARLY PLYMOUTH. "Borning room hot"
WOMAUD 1

YOU UNDERSTAND THE REQUIREMENTS. "We are"
WOMAUD 1

Poetry*   SPOA 120

iliencron, Detley von. 1844. in German.

DIE MUSIK KOMMT. "Klingling, Bumbum und
Tschingdada"   DOVER 1

SEHNSUCHT. "Ich ging den Weg entlang"
CHRIST 19

WER WEISS WO. "Auf Blut und Leichen, Schutt
und Qualm"   DOVER 1

ima, Jorge de. 1893. in Portuguese.

SONETO. "Vinte séculos de revoluçâo"
FOLKW 71

"Vago espaço de natal"   FOLKW 71

inde, Otto zur. 1873. in German.

VORSTADT.   CHRIST 11

indegren, Erik. 1910. in Swedish.

DOENDE GLADIATOR. "Vem rände dig på livet
med sin treudd"   GRAM 8

GAMMAL INDIAN. "Ja, jag minns min ungdom"
GRAM 8

HAMLETS HIMMELSFARD. "När livets skrift blev
ett med dödens drömmar"   GRAM 8

KOSMISK MODER.   GRAM 8

MANNEN UTAN VÄG, exc.   GRAM 8

PASTORALSVIT, exc.   GRAM 8

indorm, Erik. 1889. in Swedish.

EN DÖD ARBETARHUSTRU. "Ej längre med tillbringaren du går sa rädd att spilla"
GRAM 10

JORDSKEPPET. "Fram glider genom rymden den
gamla skutan Jord"   GRAM 10

VÄCKELSE. "Jag kan ej se hur människorna ga"
GRAM 1

indqvist, Ebba. in Swedish.

FISKARE KOMMA HEM FRÅN SHETLAND. "De kom
på natten, då alla sov"   GRAM 2

FISKLAGE: SAMHÄLLET. "Har ligger samhället"
GRAM 2

indsay, Lady Anne. 1750. in English.

AULD ROBIN GRAY.   EAV 7

indsay, Vachel. 1879. in English.

ABRAHAM LINCOLN WALKS AT MIDNIGHT. "It is
portentous, and a thing of state"
CAED 102, DECCA 4, DECCA 7,
HOUGHT 2, SINGER 5

THE BLACKSMITH'S SERENADE. "John Littlehouse
the redhead was a large ruddy man"
CAED 102

THE BRONCHO THAT WOULD NOT BE BROKEN. "A
little colt-broncho, loaned to the farm"
HARC 4, HOUGHT 1

THE CHINESE NIGHTINGALE. "How, how, he said,
Friend Chang, I said"   CAED 32,
NACTE 17

THE CONGO. "Fat black bucks in a wine-barrel
room"   CAED 32, CAED 102, NACTE 6,
NACTE 17

DANIEL. "Darius the Mede was a king and a
wonder"   CAED 102

THE DRUNKARD'S FUNERAL. "Yes, said the sister
with a little pinched face"   CAED 102

THE EAGLE THAT IS FORGOTTEN. "Sleep softly
. . . eagle forgotten . . . under the stone"
CAED 102

THE FLOWER-FED BUFFALOES. "The flower-fed
buffaloes of the spring"   CAED 32,
CAED 102, CAED 111, NACTE 17

GENERAL WILLIAM BOOTH ENTERS INTO HEAVEN.
"Booth led boldly with his big bass drum"
ACTIV 1, CAED 32, HOUGHT 5,
NACTE 17

THE GHOSTS OF THE BUFFALOES. "Last night at
black midnight I woke with a cry"
CAED 102

THE HAUGHTY SNAIL-KING. "Twelve snails went
walking after night"   CAED 111

THE KALLYOPE YELL. "Proud men" CAED 102,
HARC 3

THE LEADEN-EYED. "Let not young souls be
smothered"   ACTIV 1

THE LION. "The lion, the lion, he dwells in the
waste"   CAED 102, HARC 4

THE LITTLE TURTLE. "There was a little turtle"
CAED 109, CAED 164, CREAT 1

"The moon's the north wind's cooky"
CAED 32, CAED 102, HARC 4,
NACTE 17

"The mouse that gnawed the oak-tree down"
CAED 102

THE MYSTERIOUS CAT. "I saw a proud, mysterious
cat"   CAED 32, CAED 164, NACTE 17

THE POTATOES' DANCE. "Down cellar, said the
cricket"   CAED 102, CAED 164

THE SEA SERPENT CHANTEY. "There's a snake on
the western wave"   CAED 102

SIMON LEGREE. "Legree's big house was white
and green"   ACTIV 1, CAED 102

THE SORCERESS. "I asked her, Is Aladdin's lamp
hidden anywhere?"   CAED 102

TWO OLD CROWS. "Two old crows sat on a fence
rail"   ACTIV 1, CAED 102

WHAT THE HYENA SAID. "The moon is but a gold-
en skull"   CAED 102

YET GENTLE WILL THE GRIFFIN BE. "The moon? It
is a griffin's egg"   CAED 164

Link, Lenore M. in English.

HOLDING HANDS. "Elephants walking along the
trails"   BOWMAR 1, HARB 1

Liost, Guerau de. 1878. in Catalan.

ODA AL PIADOS BARO PERFET. "Sortosa la nissaga
que te un baro perfet!"   AGUIL 14

Lipsitz, Lou. in English.

SKINNY POEM.   CAED 155

Poetry*   WATSHD 60

Lipton, Lawrence. 1898. in English.

NIGHT SONG FOR THE SLEEPLESS. "In Africa a million drums beat endlessly"   WORLDP 1

Lisboa, Henriqueta. in Portuguese.

RESTAURADORA. "A morte é limpa"
FOLKW 71

Lisboa, Irene. 1892. in Portuguese.

OUTRO PEQUENO POEMA MENTAL. "Cai um pás-
aro do ar, devagar, muito devagar"
FOLKW 72

PEQUENO POEMA MENTAL. "Quem não sai da sua
casa"   FOLKW 72

* Recording not available for analysis

Lloréns Torres, Luís. 1878. in Spanish.
BOLIVAR. "Político, militar, héroe, orador y poeta"   HOLT 1
CANCIÓN DE LAS ANTILLAS. "Somos islas! Islas verdes"   SMC 9
CHEFA.   INSTPR 1
MUJER PUERTORRIQUEÑA. "Mujer de la tierra mía"   SMC 9
PARIO LA LUNA.   INSTPR 1
EL PATITO FEO.   INSTPR 1
TROVA GUAJIRA. "Cuba es verde en la hoja verde"   SMC 9
EL VALLE DE COLLORES. "Cuando salí de Collores"   SMC 9

Lo Curzio, Guglielmo. 1894. in Italian.
UOMINI   CETRA 31

Lobo, Eugenio Gerardo. in Spanish.
ILUSIONES DE QUIEN VA A LAS INDIAS A HACER FORTUNA. "Y válgame Díos, el tesoro"
                                          AGUIL 6

Lockwood, Annea. in English.
MALAMAN.   WATSHD 13

Lodge, Thomas. 1558. in English.
CORYDON'S SONG. "A blythe and bonny country lasse"   ARGO 136
ROSALIND'S MADRIGAL. "Love in my bosom like a bee"   ARGO 31, SPOA 50

Loerke, Oskar. 1884. in German.
OHNE FALSCHE ZEUGEN. "Das Mondlicht räumt den Alltag aus"   CHRIST 11

Logan, John. 1923. in English.
THE BROTHERS: TWO SALTIMBANQUES. "Two boys stand at the end of the full train"
                                          SCHOL 5
ELEGY FOR DYLAN THOMAS. "In the Welsh town"
                                          WATSHD 14
LINES FOR AN UNKNOWN LOVER. "I desire to hold in my heart"   WATSHD 14
NEW YORK SCENE: MAY 1958. "It is just getting dark as the rain stops"   SCHOL 5
THE PICNIC. "It is the picnic with Ruth in the Spring"   SCHOL 5
THE PREPARATION.   FOLKW 25
PROTEST AFTER A DREAM. "You tell me, for I"
                                          SCHOL 5
SONG ON THE DREAD OF A CHILL SPRING. "I thought"   SCHOL 5
Poetry*   WATSHD 32

Logue, Christopher. 1926. in English.
GREAT MEN IN THE MORNING.   FOLKW 66
I WAS BORN ON A BOARD.   ARGO 100
AN IRISHMAN TO HIS RAT.   FOLKW 66
ONE FOR MISS BLIGH.   FOLKW 66
THE SONG OF THE IMPERIAL CARRION. "Not long ago"   FOLKW 66
SONNET.   FOLKW 66

Lo-Johansson, Ivar. 1901. in Swedish.
KLOCKNYCKELN.   GRAM 7

Lombardi, Eliodoro. in Italian.
SCESI A MARSALA.   CETRA 26

Longfellow, Henry Wadsworth. 1807. in English.
THE ARROW AND THE SONG. "I shot an arrow into the air"   CAED 66, CMS 4, LEARNS 2,
                                          LION 2
THE ARSENAL AT SPRINGFIELD. "This is the Arsenal. From floor to ceiling"   EAV 15,
                                HOUGHT 5, SPOA 51

THE BRIDGE. "I stood on the bridge at midnight"   LION 2
THE BUILDING OF THE SHIP. "Build me straight, o worthy Master"   CAED 66, CAED 98,
                                DECCA 13, EAV 15
CHAUCER. "An old man in a lodge within a park"
                                COLUMB 11, SPOA 51
THE CHILDREN'S HOUR. "Between the dark and the daylight"   CAED 66, CAED 185,
       CAED 195, DECCA 3, DECCA 12, EAV 9,
                                SINGER 1, LION 2
CHIMES. "Sweet chimes! that in the loneliness of night"   EAV 14
CHRISTMAS BELLS. "I heard the bells on Christmas Day"   LION 1
THE COURTSHIP OF MILES STANDISH. PART 3. "So the strong will prevailed, and Alden went on his errand"   CAED 66
_____, exc.   LIST 5
CURFEW. "Solemnly, mournfully"   LION 2
THE DAY IS DONE. "The day is done, and the darkness"   AUDIA 2, CMS 13, EAV 9,
       HOUGHT 5, LIST 3, LIVLAN 1, RCA 8,
       SPOA 31, SPOA 51, SPOA 75, LION 2
DIVINA COMMEDIA. "Oft have I seen at some cathedral door"   SPOA 51
A DUTCH PICTURE. "Simon Danz has come home again"   EAV 15, HARC 3
EVANGELINE. "This is the forest primeval"
                                          FOLKW 9
_____. exc.   CAED 90, EAV 15, EAV 22,
                                HOUGHT 2, SPOA 51
THE FIRE OF DRIFT-WOOD. "We sat within the farm-house old"   LION 2
THE GOLDEN MILE STONE. "Leafless are the trees; their purple branches"   LION 2
HYMN TO THE NIGHT. "I heard the trailing garments of the night"   AUDIA 2, EAV 14,
                   LIST 3, SPOA 51, SPOA 75
THE JEWISH CEMETERY AT NEWPORT. "How strange it seems! These Hebrews in their graves"   CAED 66, SPOA 51
KEATS. "The young Endymion sleeps Endymion's sleep"   SPOA 51
MEZZO CAMMIN. "Half of my life is gone, and I have let"   CAED 66
MILTON. "I pace the sounding sea-beach and behold"   SPOA 51
MY LOST YOUTH. "Often I think of the beautiful town"   EAV 14, LION 2, SPOA 51
NATURE. "As a fond mother, when the day is o'er"   ARGO 11, EAV 14
PAUL REVERE'S RIDE. "Listen, my children, and you shall hear"   CAED 66, CAED 98
       CAED 195, CHILDC 1, COLUMB 6
   DECCA 4, DECCA 10, EAV 20, EAV 21
   HARC 2, HOUGHT 1, LIST 4, UARIZM 1
   LIST 21, RCA 8, SINGER 1, ARIZ
A PSALM OF LIFE. "Tell me not, in mournful numbers"   CAED 6
RAIN IN SUMMER. "How beautiful is the rain"
                                          CMS
THE RAINY DAY. "The day is cold, and dark, and dreary"   LION
SHAKESPEARE. "A vision as of crowded cit streets"   SPOA

---

* Recording not available for analysis

THE SHIP OF STATE. "Sail on, o ship of state"
SPOA 51, SPOA 75
THE SKELETON IN ARMOR. "Speak! speak! thou
fearful guest"   CAED 66, CAED 185,
SINGER 3
THE SONG OF HIAWATHA. III. Hiawatha's Child-
hood, exc. "By the shores of Gitche Gumee/
By the shining Big-Sea-Water/Stood the wig-
wam"   CAED 66, CMS 4, FOLKW 4,
FOLKW 23
_____. VII. Hiawatha's Sailing, exc. "Give me of
your bark, O Birch-tree"   FOLKW 4,
FOLKW 23
_____. IX. Hiawatha and the Pearl-Feather,
exc. "On the shores of Gitche Gumee/Of the
shining Big-Sea-Water/Stood Nokomis"
FOLKW 4, FOLKW 23
_____. x. Hiawatha's Wooing, exc. "As unto the
bow the cord is"   CAED 185, FOLKW 4,
FOLKW 23
_____. XVII. The Hunting of Pan-Puk-Keewis,
exc. "Full of wrath was Hiawatha"
FOLKW 4, FOLKW 23
_____. XXII. Hiawatha's Departure, exc. "By
the shores of Gitche Gumee/By the shining
Big-Sea-Water/At the doorway of his wig-
wam"   FOLKW 4, FOLKW 23
_____, exc.   SINGER 1
THE SPANISH JEW'S TALE. "Rabbi Ben Levi, on the
Sabbath"   EAV 9
TALES OF A WAYSIDE INN, exc.   CAED 98
THE THREE KINGS. "Three Kings came riding
from far away"   LION 1
"The tide rises, the tide falls"   ARGO 11,
AUDIA 2, EAV 14, HOUGHT 4, LIST 3
VILLAGE BLACKSMITH. "Under a spreading
chestnut-tree"   CAED 66, CAED 195,
COLUMB 6, EAV 9
THE WRECK OF THE HESPERUS. "It was the schoon-
er Hesperus"   CAED 66, CAED 195,
EAV 9, EAV 21, EAV 22, LION 2
Poetry*   LIST 12, SPOA 116
_ope de Vega. See Vega Carpio, Lope de.
_ópez, Luis Carlos. 1883. in Spanish.
CAMPESINA, NO DEJES. "Campesina, no dejes de
acudir"   SMC 8
CIELO Y MAR. "Cielo y mar, cielo y mar"
SMC 8
MUCHACHAS SOLTERONAS. "Muchachas sol-
teronas de provincia"   FOLKW 80
SEPELIO. "Cuantas mujeres, cuando muera"
MIAMI 1
_ópez De Mendoza, Inigo. See Santillana,
Marques de.
_ópez, Pico, Josep Maria. in Catalan.
D'UN XIPRER. "Ta vida és un desitg d'agilitat"
AGUIL 14
_ópez Silva. in Spanish.
Poetry*   SMC 16
_ópez Suria, Violeta. in Spanish.
ALGO DEBI DECIRTE.   INSTPR 1
_ora-Totino, Arrigo. 1928. in French.
PHONÈMES STRUCTURES, TEXTE 4.   LUCHT 1
_orca. See Garcia Lorca, Federico.
_orde, Audre. 1934. in English.
BLACK STUDIES. "A chill wind sweeps"
WATSHD 11

FOR ANNE, DEAD. "Hidden in a forest of ques-
tions"   WATSHD 11
FOR MY SISTER, HARRIET. "Harriet, there was al-
ways"   WATSHD 11
LOVE POEM. "Speak, earth, and bless me"
WATSHD 11
MEET. "Woman, when we left"   WATSHD 11
Poetry*   PRENT 1
Lovelace, Earl. 1935. in English.
THE WINE OF ASTONISHMENT, exc. "And so this
Sunday"   WATSHD 7
Lovelace, Richard. 1618. in English.
LA BELLA BONA ROBA. "I cannot tell who loves
the skeleton"   LONGM 1
GRATIANA DAUNCING AND SINGING. "See! with
what constant Motion"   ARGO 37
LUCASTA. "Lucasta frown and let me die"
LIST 4
THE SCRUTINIE. "Why should you sweare I am
forsworn"   ARGO 37
TO ALTHEA FROM PRISON. "When love with un-
confined wings"   ARGO 37, CAED 38,
CAED 186, EAV 6, LIST 2, SPOA 84,
LION 2
TO LUCASTA GOING BEYOND THE SEAS. "If to be
absent were to be"   ARGO 37, CAED 186,
LIST 2, SINGER 6
TO LUCASTA ON GOING TO THE WARRES. "Tell me
not (Sweet) I am unkinde"   ARGO 37,
EAV 6, LIST 2, SINGER 6
Loveman, Robert. in English.
APRIL RAIN. "It isn't raining rain to me"
HARB 4
Lover, Samuel. in English.
ASK AND HAVE.   DECCA 12
Lowbury, Edward. 1913. in English.
THE HUNTSMAN. "Caguar hunted the lion
through bush and forest"   ARGO 92
NOTHING. "Her sixth midsummer eve keeps
Ruth awake"   ARGO 92
SURGERY OF A BURN. "Cathedral silence and the
light flooding a square of skin"   ARGO 92
TIME FOR SALE. "Through the narrow streets all
day"   ARGO 92
Lowell, Amy. 1874. in English.
FRINGED GENTIANS. "Near where I live there is
a lake"   CAED 164
NIGHT CLOUDS. "The white mares of the moon
rush along the sky"   HARB 6
TRADES.   LIST 4, SINGER 2
Lowell, James Russell. 1819. in English.
ALADDIN. "When I was a beggarly boy"
EAV 14
THE COURTIN' "God makes sech nights, all white
an' still"   EAV 20, SPOA 31, SPOA 75
A FABLE FOR CRITICS.   EAV 15
THE FIRST SNOWFALL. "The snow had begun in
the gloaming"   CAED 100
LINCOLN.   EAV 14
SHE CAME AND WENT. "As a twig trembles, which
a bird"   EAV 10, LIST 3
THE VISION OF SIR LAUNFAL. PRELUDE.   EAV 10
_____. JUNE. "And what is so rare as a day in
June"   HOUGHT 5
_____, exc. "Not only in our infancy"
CMS 14
_____, exc. "Not what we give"   HARB 3

* Recording not available for analysis

Lowell, James Russell (continued)

————, exc.   EAV 14, SINGER 4
WASHINGTON. "Soldier and statesman, rarest
    unison"   DECCA 13
WHAT MR. ROBINSON THINKS. "Guvener B. is a
    sensible man"   EAV 20
Poetry*   EAV 10
Lowell, Robert. 1917. in English.
BETWEEN THE PORCH AND THE ALTAR. "Meeting
    his mother makes him lose ten years"
                                    LIBC 23, LIBC 68
BRINGING A TURTLE HOME.   HARPV 6
CAROLINE. 4. MARRIAGE. "I think of you every
    minute of the day"   CAED 180
CENTRAL PARK.   HARPV 6
CHARLES THE FIFTH AND THE PEASANT. "Elected
    Kaiser, burgher and a knight"   SPOA 102
CHRISTMAS EVE UNDER HOOKER'S STATUE. "To-
    night a blackout. Twenty years ago"
                        COLPIX 1, LIBC 23, LIBC 68
COMMANDER LOWELL. "There were no undesira-
    bles or girls in my set"   CARIL 20
DEATH OF THE SHERIFF. Part I. "We park and
    stare. A full sky of the stars"   LIBC 23,
                                          LIBC 68
THE DRUNKEN FISHERMAN. "Wallowing in this
    bloody sty"   COLPIX 1
DUNBARTON. "My Grandfather found"
                                          CARIL 20
DURING FEVER. "All night the crib creaks"
                                          CARIL 20
EPILOGUE. "Those blessed structures, plot and
    rhyme"   CAED 180
THE EXILE'S RETURN. "There mounts in squalls a
    sort of rusty mire"   CAED 180, LIBC 33
EYE AND TOOTH. "My whole eye was sunset red"
                                          CAED 180
FALL, 1961. "Back and forth, back and forth"
                                          NET 7
FALLING ASLEEP OVER THE AENEID. "The sun is
    blue"   SPOA 102
FATHER'S BEDROOM. "In my Father's bedroom"
                                          CARIL 20
THE FLAW. "A seal swims like a poodle"
                                          NET 7
FOR GEORGE SANTAYANA (1863–1952) "In the hey-
    days of forty-five"   COLPIX 1, SPOA 102
FOR JOHN BERRYMAN.   HARPV 6
FOR SALE. "Poor sheepish plaything"
                                          CARIL 20
GRANDPARENTS. "They're altogether other-
    worldly now"   CARIL 20
HOME AFTER THREE MONTHS AWAY. "Gone now
    the baby's nurse"   CARIL 20
HOMECOMING. "What was is . . . since 1930"
                                          CAED 180
JEAN STAFFORD. "Towmahss Mahnn: that's how
    you say it"   CAED 180
MAN AND WIFE. "Tamed by Miltown, we lie on
    Mother's bed"   CARIL 20
THE MARCH, I AND II.   HARPV 6
MEMORIES OF WEST STREET AND LEPKE. "Only
    teaching on Tuesdays, book-worming"
                        CAED 180, DECCA 15, HARPV 6
MERMAID. "One wondered who would see and
    date you next"   CAED 180

MR. EDWARDS AND THE SPIDER.   HARPV 6
MY LAST AFTERNOON WITH UNCLE DEVEREUX WINS-
    LOW. "I won't go with you. I want to stay with
    Grandpa!"   CARIL 20
THE OLD FLAME. "My old flame, my wife"
                                          CAED 180
THE OPPOSITE HOUSE. "All day the opposite
    house"   NET 7
PIGEONS. "The same old flights"   SPOA 102
POEM, 1961.   BROADR 1
THE QUAKER GRAVEYARD IN NANTUCKET. "A
    brackish reach"   CARIL 20
READING MYSELF. "Like thousands, I took just
    pride"   CAED 180
RETURNING TURTLE.   HARPV 6
ROBERT FROST. "Robert Frost at midnight, the
    audience gone"   CAED 180
SAILING HOME FROM RAPALLO. "Your nurse could
    only speak Italian"   CARIL 20
SKUNK HOUR. "Nautilus Island's hermit"
                                CAED 180, CARIL 20
SOFT WOOD. "Sometimes I have supposed seals"
                                          NET 7
STALIN. "Winds on the stems make them creak
    like things of man"   CAED 180
TERMINAL DAYS AT BEVERLY. "At Beverly Farms
    a portly uncomfortable boulder" CARIL 20
TO FRANK PARKER.   HARPV 6
TO SPEAK OF WOE THAT IS IN MARRIAGE. "The hot
    night makes us keep our bedroom windows
    open"   CARIL 20
WAKING IN THE BLUE. "The night attendant, a B.
    U. sophomore"   CARIL 20
WATER 1948. "Stonington: each morning boat-
    loads of hands"   SPOA 82, NET 7
WHERE THE RAINBOW ENDS. "I saw the sky de-
    scending, black and white"   LIBC 40
WILLIAM CARLOS WILLIAMS. "Who loved more?
    William Carlos Williams"   CAED 180
Poetry*   JNP 33, LIST 15
Lowenfels, Walter. 1897. in English.
"All our valises are packed"   BROADR 3
Loynaz, Dulce María. 1903. in Spanish.
VIAJERO. "Yo soy como el viajero"   SMC 13
Lu Lwun. in Chinese.
SAI SYA CHYU. "Ywe hei yan fei gan"
                                          FOLKW 76
Lubrano, Giacomo. 1619. in Italian.
Poetry*   CETRA 24
Lucanus, Marcus Annaeus. 39 A.D. in Latin.
Poetry*   CETRA 18
Lucian of Samosata. in Greek.
MEDITATION ON BEAVERS. "O lovely Whiskers, O
    inspirational mop!"   English CARIL 3
Lucie-Smith, Edward. 1933. in English.
THE LESSON. "Your father's gone, my bald head-
    master said"   FOLKW 59A
ON LOOKING AT STUBBS ANATOMY OF THE HORSE
    "In Lincolnshire"   FOLKW 59A
Lucilius, Gaius. 180 B.C. in Latin.
ON APIS THE PRIZEFIGHTER. "To Apis the boxer"
                                English CARIL 3
ON HERMOGENES THE PHYSICIAN. "Diophantos
    went to bed"   English CARIL 3
A VALENTINE FOR A LADY. "Darling, at the
    beautician's you buy"   English CARIL 3
Poetry*   CETRA 18

* Recording not available for analysis

ucini, Gian Pietro. 1867. in Italian.
Poetry*   CETRA 27
ucretius Carus, Titus. 99 B.C. in Latin.
DE RERUM NATURA, exc. AGAINST THE FEAR OF
DEATH. "What has this Bugbear Death to
frighten man"   English SPOA 46
_____, exc. "No single thing abides"
English POETRY 2
Poetry*   CETRA 18
ugones, Leopoldo. 1874. in Spanish.
EL CANTO DE LA ANGUSTIA. "Yo andaba solo y callado"   SMC 1
SALMO PLUVIAL. "Érase una caverna de agua
sombría el cielo"   AGUIL 9, FOLKW 80
ugones, Ricardo. in Spanish.
LA PALMERA. "Al llegar la hora esperada"
FIDIAS 3
uis, Leopoldo de. 1918. in Spanish.
PATRIA DE CADA DÍA. "Cada uno en el rumor de
sus talleres"   HOLT 1
una, José Carlos de. in Spanish.
EL PIYAYO. "No conocéis al Piyayo?"   SMC 5
undkvist, Artur. in Swedish.
KÄRLEK TILL TRÄ. "Kräver det skarpaste stål,
säger snickaren"   GRAM 8
LIV SOM GRÄS. "Och gräset vandranda över
världen"   GRAM 8
METEOREN TALAR. "Jag har det våldsamma ned-
slagets ansikte"   GRAM 8
SKATAN. "Mit blåsiga lynnes fågel"   GRAM 8
TVINGA MIG INTE. "Att förneka"   GRAM 8
urie, Toby. 1925. in English.
DUET. "Have I ever told you"   WATSHD 4
SOUND HAPPENING FOR TWO. "B—B—mmm"
WATSHD 4
TWO ONE-WORD POEMS. "In no sense"
WATSHD 4
uther, Martin. 1483. in German.
GEBET VOR DER MARTER CHRISTI.   CHRIST 18
DER 102. PSALM. "Ein Gebet des Elenden, so er
betrübt ist"   CHRIST 29
utzky, A. in Yiddish.
CHASSIDIM. "A braeta hussick kine ane ora zol
im nit shotten"   FOLKW 90
uzi, Mario. 1914. in Italian.
DAL FONDO DELLE CAMPAGNE, exc. DALLA TORRE
"Questa terra grigia lisciata dal vento"
APPL 4
_____. IL DURO FILAMENTO. "Passa sotto la nos-
tra casa qualche volta"   APPL 4
_____. QUANTA VITA. "Quanta vita, si leva una
voce alta di bambino"   APPL 4
NEL MAGMA, exc. PRESSO IL BISENZO. "La nebbia
ghiacciata affumica la gora della concia"
APPL 4
ONORE DEL VERO, exc. NEL L'IMMINENZA DI QUAR-
ANT' ANNI. "Il pensiero m' insegne in questo
borgo"   APPL 4
Poetry*   CETRA 46
vly, John. 1554. in English.
CARDS AND KISSES. "Cupid and my Campaspe
played"   CAED 186, RCA 4
you Dzung, Ywan. 773. in Chinese.
JYANG SYWE. "Chyan shan nyan fei jywe"
FOLKW 76
you Yung. 1034. in Chinese.
YU LIN LING. "Han chan chi chye" FOLKW 76

Macaulay, Thomas Babington. 1800. in English.
THE BATTLE OF LAKE REGILLUS, exc. "Hermini-
us!"   JNP 88
_____, exc. "Ho, trumpets"   JNP 88
HORATIUS, exc. "Lars Porsena of Clusium"
JNP 88
_____, exc. "Then out spake brave Horatius"
JNP 88
THE PROPHECY OF CAPYS. "Now slain is King
Amulius"   JNP 88
VIRGINIA. "Ye good men of the Commons"
JNP 88
MacBeth, George. 1932. in English.
THE ABSENTEES. "When Egil Skallagrimsson"
FOLKW 59A
THE DRAWER. "Their belongings were buried
side by side"   ARGO 96, SPOA 67
THE MINER'S HELMET. "My father wore it work-
ing coal at Shotts"   FOLKW 59A
NOAH'S JOURNEY. "Oak/is the keel"   DAV 1
REPORT TO THE DIRECTOR.   PROTHM 7
Poetry*   JNP 34
MacCaig, Norman. 1910. in English.
ASSISI. "The dwarf with his hands on back-
wards"   ARGO 99
SMUGGLER. "Watch him when he opens"
ARGO 99
YOU WENT AWAY. "Suddenly, in my world of
you"   ARGO 99
McCarthy, Agnes. in English.
CAT DREAM. "Asleep on a mat"   HARB 1
JOHNNY APPLESEED. "If someone asked me why
I left"   BARD 2
McCarthy, Eugene J. in English.
Poetry*   JNP 2
McClure, Michael. 1932. in English.
CAT'S AIR: THE.   EVERG 1
NIGHT WORDS: THE RAVISHING.   EVERG 1
Poetry*   UCAL 3
McCord, David. 1897. in English.
CROWS. "I like to walk"   SCHOL 7
"Daedalus, stay away from my transom"
THEAL 1
THE FROST PANE.   CAED 109
THE PICKETY FENCE.   PATHW 2
"This is my rock"   CAED 110
McCrae, John. 1872. in English.
IN FLANDERS FIELDS. "In Flanders fields the pop-
pies blow"   CAED 100, CAED 195,
EAV 22, HARC 4
McCrimmon, Dan. 1872. in English.
LEGEND OF THE WASHEEN. "In the remainder"
WATSHD 1
MacDiarmid, Hugh (Christopher Murray
Grieve). 1892. in English.
AT THE CENOTAPH. "Are the living so much use"
ARGO 99
THE BONNIE LOWE. "Aboun the snaw-white
channel"   ARGO 99
CORONACH FOR THE END OF THE WORLD. "Mony a
piper has played himsel"   ARGO 99
FIRST LOVE. "I have been in this garden of un-
ripe fruit"   ARGO 99
THE GRAVE OF ALL MANKIND. "Shudderin' thistle,
gi'e owre, gi'e owre"   ARGO 99

* Recording not available for analysis

MacDiarmid, Hugh (continued)

IN THE CHILDRENS HOSPITAL. "Now let the legless boy show the great lady"   ARGO 99
O WHA'S THE BRIDE. "O wha's the bride that cairries the bunch"   ARGO 99
SKALD'S DEATH. "I have known all the storms that roll"   ARGO 99
THE THISTLE AS A SPIDER'S WEB. "Omsk and the Calton"   ARGO 99
UNDER THE GREENWOOD TREE. "A sodger laddie's socht a hoose"   ARGO 99
WHEESHT, WHEESHT. "Wheesht, wheesht, my foolish hert"   ARGO 99
Poetry*   JNP 35, JNP 36

MacDonagh, Thomas. in English.
JOHN-JOHN. "I dreamt last night of you, John-John"   SPOA 6

McFarlane, Basil. in English.
HIMMELFAHRT.   German DEUTGR 2
NIMM DIESEN TAG.   German DEUTGR 2

McGahey, Jeanne. in English.
OREGON WINTER.   SCHOL 7

McGinley, Phyllis. 1905. in English.
THE CONQUERORS. "It seems vainglorious and proud"   HOUGHT 4
THE DAY AFTER SUNDAY. "Always on Monday, God's in the morning papers"   LIBC 54
IN PRAISE OF DIVERSITY. "Since this ingenious earth began"   THEAL 1
A KIND OF LOVE LETTER TO NEW YORK. "Love is a mischief"   THEAL 2
NOT WRITTEN ON A DAMP VERANDA. "Do they need any rain"   RCA 10
POOR TIMING. "I sing Saint Valentine, his day"   HOUGHT 5
PORTRAIT OF A GIRL WITH COMIC BOOK. "Thirteen's no age at all. Thirteen is nothing"   LIBC 54
REFLECTIONS AT DAWN. "I wish I owned a Dior dress"   THEAL 1
REFLECTIONS DENTAL. "How pure, how beautiful, how fine"   HARC 4, SCHOL 7
SIMEON STYLITES. "On top of a pillar Simeon sat"   LIBC 54
THE TEMPTATIONS OF SAINT ANTHONY. "Off in the wilderness bare and level"   LIBC 54

McGough, Roger. in English.
ASSASSIN.   ARGO 146
A CAT, A HORSE AND THE SUN.   ARGO 146
COUSIN DAISY.   ARGO 146
COUSIN FIONA.   ARGO 146
CRUSADER.   ARGO 146
DREAMPOEM. "In a corner of my bedroom"   ARGO 146
EX ART STUDENT.   ARGO 146
GEORGE AND THE DRAGONFLY.   ARGO 146
HEAD INJURY.   ARGO 146
HUMDINGER.   ARGO 146
THE IDENTIFICATION.   ARGO 146
INTRODUCTORY POEM.   ARGO 146
LET ME DIE A YOUNGMAN'S DEATH. "Let me die a youngman's death"   ARGO 146
MY BUSSEDUCTRESS.   ARGO 146
MY CAT AND I.   ARGO 146
NINE TO FIVE.   ARGO 146
PANTOMIME POEM.   ARGO 146

PICTURE.   ARGO 146
SLEEP.   ARGO 146
SNIPERS.   ARGO 146
SOIL.   ARGO 146
STINK.   ARGO 146
STORM.   ARGO 146
THE STRANGER.   PROTHM
TRAIN CRASH.   ARGO 146

Machado, Antonio. 1875. in Spanish.
Á DON FRANCISCO GINER DE LOS RIOS. "Como se fue el maestro"   AGUIL 1
Á JOSÉ MARIA PALACIO. "Palacio, buen amigo"   SPOA 5
Á UN OLMO SECO. "Al, olmo viejo, hendido por el rayo"   AGUIL 1
AL MAESTRO AZORIN POR SU LIBRO 'CASTILLA'. "La venta de Cidones está en la carretera"   AGUIL 1
"Allá, en las tierras altas"   HOLT
"Anoche cuando dormía"   AGUIL 16
    HOLT 1, SPOA 5
APUNTES. II. "Sobre el olivar"   AGUIL 1
_____. III. "Por un ventanal"   AGUIL 1
_____. IV. "Sobre el olivar"   AGUIL 1
_____. V. "Dondequiera vaya"   AGUIL 1
"Ayer soñé que veía"   AGUIL 1
CAMPOS DE SORIA. "Es la tierra de Soria árida y fría"   AGUIL 1
COPLAS MUNDANAS. "Poeta ayer, hoy triste pobre"   FIDIAS
"Desgarrada la nube; el arco iris"   AGUIL 1
"¿Dices que nada se crea?"   AGUIL 1
"En Santo Domingo"   AGUIL 1
EN TREN. "Yo, para todo viaje"   AGUIL 1
"Eres tú, Guadarrama, viejo amigo"   AGUIL 1
UNA ESPAÑA JOVEN. "Fue un tiempo de mentir de infamia"   AGUIL 1
"He vuelto a ver"   SPOA 5
"Hoy buscaras en vano"   AGUIL 1
"Llamo mi corazón, un claro día"   AGUIL 1
EL MAÑANA EFÍMERO. "La España de charanga pandereta"   AGUIL 1
¿MI AMOR? ... RECUERDAS, DIME. "¿Mi amor?"   AGUIL 1
"Moneda que está en la mano"   AGUIL 1
"Oh Guadalquivir!"   AGUIL 1
POEMA DE UN DIA. "Heme aquí ya, profesor"   AGUIL 1
"Poned atención"   AGUIL 1
"La primavera besaba"   AGUIL 1
"La primavera ha venido"   AGUIL 1
RECUERDO INFANTIL. "Una tarde parda y fría"   AGUIL 1
RETRATO. "Mi infancia son recuerdos de un patio de Sevilla"   AGUIL 1
"Señor, ya me arrancaste lo que yo más quería"   AGUIL 1
"Soria fría, Soria pura"   AGUIL 1
"Todo pasa y todo queda"   AGUIL 1
"Y podrás conocerte, recordando"   AGUIL 1
"Ya hay un español que quiere"   AGUIL 1
"Yo voy soñando caminos"   AGUIL
    AGUIL 16, DOVER 2, HOLT 1, SMC
Poetry*   AGUIL 16, BABB

* Recording not available for analysis

Machado, Manuel. 1874. in Spanish.

Á JUAN RAMON JIMÉNEZ. "Era una noche del mes de mayo"   SMC 15

ADELFOS. "Yo soy como las gentes que a mi tierra vinieron"   SMC 3

ANDALUCÍA. "Cádiz, salada claridad . . . Granada"   AGUIL 6

CANTARES. "Vino, sentimiento, guitarra y poesía"   SMC 5

CASTILLA. "El ciego sol se estrella" FIDIAS 1, HOLT 1

FELIPE IV. "Nadie más cortesano ni pulido" HOLT 1

"Una noche de verano"   SMC 15

PARABOLA. "Era un niño que soñaba un caballo de cartón"   SMC 15

PROVERBIOS Y CANTARES. "El que espera desespera"   SMC 15

Machaut, Guillaume de. 1300. in French.

DE TOUTES FLEURES.   HACH 7

Macheral, Leopoldo. 1900. in Spanish.

ENVIO. "José del Sur, cunado sin ribera" AGUIL 9

McHugh, Heather. 1948. in English.

Poetry*   WATSHD 61

McKay, Claude. 1891. in English.

AFTER THE WINTER. "Some day, when trees have shed their leaves"   FOLKW 6

AMERICA. "Although she feeds me bread of bitterness"   German DEUTGR 2

FLAME-HEART. "So much have I forgotten in ten years"   FOLKW 41

HOME THOUGHTS. "Oh something just now must be happening there"   FOLKW 6

IF WE MUST DIE. "If we must die, let it not be like hogs"   FOLKW 1

NORTH AND SOUTH. "O sweet are tropic lands for waking dreams"   FOLKW 6

ST. ISAAC'S CHURCH, LENINGRAD. "Bow down my soul in worship"   FOLKW 1

THE SPANISH NEEDLE. "Lovely dainty Spanish needle"   FOLKW 6

SPRING IN NEW HAMPSHIRE. "Too green the springing April grass"   FOLKW 6

THE TROPICS IN NEW YORK. "Bananas ripe and green"   FOLKW 1, FOLKW 6

Poetry*   PRENT 1

Mackin, Sharon. in English.

BECAUSE I HAVE NOT LOVED YOU. "We have ridden out the waves"   WATSHD 8

PSALM. "The raging river has ripped sleep" WATSHD 8

McKnight, Jo Anne. in English.

ELEMENTAL ENTRY—SEA.   FOLKW 47

ELEMENTAL ENTRY—SUN.   FOLKW 47

A GIFT OF LOVE.   FOLKW 47

I'M LOVE.   FOLKW 47

MacLeish, Archibald. 1892. in English.

ACTFIVE, exc. "The flesh that once sang" LIBC 23, LIBC 71

_____ a) THE STAGE ALL BLOOD. "Whereat the King unthroned, the God"   CAED 14

_____ b) THE MASQUE OF MUMMERS. "The corse is taken off: the scene"   CAED 14

_____ c) THE SHAPE OF FLESH AND BONE. "The lights come up. A painted door" CAED 14, LIBC 23, LIBC 71

L'AN TRENTIESME DE MON EAGE. "And I have come upon this place" CAED 14, LIBC 54

ARS POETICA. "A poem should be palpable and mute"   LIBC 54

BACKGROUND WITH REVOLUTIONARIES. "When they're shunting the cars on the Katy a mile off" NACTE 15

BERNAL DIAZ, PREFACE TO HIS BOOK. "That which I have myself seen and the fighting" CAED 14, LIBC 23

BURYING GROUND BY THE TIES. "Ayee! Ai! This is heavy earth on our shoulders" NACTE 15

CALYPSO'S ISLAND. "I know very well, goddess, she is not beautiful"   CAED 14

THE CAT IN THE WOOD. "The cat in the wood cried farewell"   CAED 14

CONQUISTADOR.   LIBC 23, LIBC 71

DOVER BEACH—A NOTE TO THAT POEM. "The wave withdrawing"   NACTE 15

EMPIRE BUILDERS. "This is the making of America in five panels"   NACTE 15

THE END OF THE WORLD. "Quite unexpectedly as Vasserot"   LIBC 36

EPISTLE TO BE LEFT IN THE EARTH. "It is colder now; there are many stars" CAED 14, CAED 183, LIBC 23 LIBC 71

EZRY. "Maybe you ranted in the grove" CAED 14

GEOGRAPHY OF THIS TIME. "What is required of us"   SPOA 94

IMMORTAL HELIX. "Hereunder Jacob Schmidt who, man and bones"   CAED 14

LANDSCAPE AS A NUDE. "She lies on her left side her flank golden"   NACTE 15

THE LEARNED MEN. "Whose minds like horse or ox"   CAED 14

A MAN'S WORK. "An apple-tree, a cedar and an oak"   CAED 14

NOT MARBLE NOR THE GILDED MONUMENTS. "The praisers of women in their proud and beautiful poems"   CAED 14

OIL PAINTING OF THE ARTIST AS THE ARTIST. "The plump Mr. Pl'f is washing his hands of America"   NACTE 15

THE OLD MAN TO THE LIZARD. "Lizard, lover of heat, of high"   CAED 14

POEM IN PROSE. "This poem is for my wife" LIBC 54

POLE STAR. "When the wheel of light is turned" SPOA 94

THE RENOVATED TEMPLE. "Ma'am, you should see your house"   CAED 14

THE SILENT SLAIN. "We too, we too, descending once again"   CAED 14

THE 6TH BOOK OF CONQUISTADOR, PART I. "So did we pray: and took arms: and we marched: and"   CAED 14

THE SPANISH LIE. "This will be answered" SPOA 94

THEORY OF POETRY. "Know the world by heart" RCA 10

THEY COME NO MORE, THOSE WORDS, THOSE FINCHES. "Oh when you're young"   CAED 14

THE TOO-LATE BORN.   LIBC 23, LIBC 71

THE TWO PRIESTS. "Man in the West" SPOA 94

WHAT ANY LOVER LEARNS. "Water is heavy silver over stone"   CAED 14

* Recording not available for analysis

MacLeish, Archibald (continued)

WILDWEST. "There were none of my blood in this battle"   NACTE 15

WINTER IS ANOTHER COUNTRY. "If the autumn would end"   CAED 14

WORDS IN TIME. "Bewildered with the broken tongue"   SPOA 94

YEARS OF THE DOG. "Before, though, Paris was wonderful"   CAED 14

YOU, ANDREW MARVELL. "And here face down beneath the sun"   ARGO 12, LIBC 54
Poetry*   LIST 13

McLeod, Irene Rutherford. in English.

LONE DOG. "I'm a lean dog, a keen dog, a wild dog, and lone"   CAED 169, HARC 3

Mac Low, Jackson. 1922. in English.

SPEECH, 9 AUG 61. "If I were to speak"
BROADR 3

THIRTY-FIRST LIGHT POEM: FOR THE CENTRAL REGIONS OF THE SUN. "The sun has to solve"
WATSHD 2

A WORD EVENT FOR BICI FORBES ON THE BOOK TITLE LUCY CHURCH AMIABLY.   WATSHD 13

MacManus, Seumas. 1869. in English.

LULLABY. "Softly now"   SPOA 6

MacNeice, Louis. 1907. in English.

APPLE BLOSSOM. "The first blossom was the best blossom"   ARGO 83, CARIL 15

AUTUMN JOURNAL, exc. "Close and slow, summer is ending in Hampshire"   CARIL 15

THE BACK AGAIN. "Back for his holiday from across"   ARGO 83

BAGPIPE MUSIC. "It's no go the merrygoround"
ARGO 83, CARIL 15

THE BRANDY GLASS. "Only let it form within his hands"   CARIL 15

THE BRITISH MUSEUM READING ROOM. "Under the hive-like dome the stooping haunted readers"   ARGO 83, CARIL 15

BROTHER FIRE. "When our brother fire was having his dog's day"   ARGO 83, CARIL 15

CARRICKFERGUS. "I was born in Belfast"
ARGO 83, ARGO 99

CHRISTINA. "It all began so easy"   ARGO 83, CARIL 15

CONVERSATION. "Ordinary people are peculiar too"   ARGO 83, CARIL 15, FOLKW 65, JUP 1

THE CYCLIST. "Freewheeling down the escarpment past"   ARGO 83

THE DEATH OF A CAT.   CARIL 15

DEATH OF AN OLD LADY. "At five in the morning"
ARGO 83

DUBLIN. "Grey brick upon brick"   ARGO 83, CARIL 15

EVENING IN CONNECTICUT. "Equipoise: becalmed"   CARIL 15

EXTRACT FROM AUTUMN SEQUEL.   ARGO 83

FROM A HAND OF SNAPS.   CARIL 15

THE GONE TOMORROW. "Two years high by the world wide"   ARGO 83

INVOCATION. "Dolphin plunge, fountain play"
ARGO 83

THE LEFT BEHIND. "Peering into your stout you see"   ARGO 83

THE LIBERTINE.   CAED 147

MEETING POINT. "Time was away and somewhere else"   ARGO 83, ARGO 99, CARIL 15

THE MERMAN. "The merman under the plough"
ARGO 83

A NOVELETTE.   CAED 147

THE NURSE.   ARGO 83

NUTS IN MAY. "May come up with bird-din"
ARGO 83, CARIL 15

PRAYER BEFORE BIRTH. "I am not yet born; O hear me"   ARGO 83, ARGO 99, PROTHM 7

PROGNOSIS. "Good-bye, Winter"   ARGO 83, CARIL 15

REFUGEES. "With prune-dark eyes, thick lips, jostling"   CAED 183

REQUIEM CANTO.   ARGO 78

RITES OF WAR. "So, Fortinbras; Alas is now the keyword here"   ARGO 83

SELVA OSCURA. "A house can be haunted by those who were never there"   ARGO 83, ARGO 99

THE SLOW STARTER. "A watched clock never moves"   SPOA 67

"The sunlight on the garden"   ARGO 83, CARIL 15

LES SYLPHIDES. "Life in a day: he took his girl"
CARIL 15

A TOAST. "The slurred and drawled and crooning sounds"   ARGO 83

THE TRUISMS. "His father gave him a box of truisms"   ARGO 83

TURFSTACKS. "Among these turf-stacks"
CAED 183

VISITATIONS, IV, OR THE MUSE. "The gull hundreds of miles below him"   CARIL 15

McNeill, Anthony. 1941. in English.

BLACK SPACE.   CAED 153

ODE TO BROTHER JOE.   CAED 153

MacPherson, Jay. 1931. in English.

ABOMINABLE SNOWMAN. "The guardian stalking his eternal snows"   FOLKW 50

BOOK. "Dear Reader, not your fellow flesh and blood"   FOLKW 50

A BOOK OF RIDDLES. "Go take the world my dearest wish"   FOLKW 50

CORAL. "A living tree that harbours"
FOLKW 50

EGG. "Reader, in your hand you hold"
FOLKW 50

THE FISHERMAN. "The world was first a private park"   FOLKW 50

LUNG-FISH. "The seas where once I swam as slick as herring"   FOLKW 50

MANDRAKE. "The fall from man engenders me"
FOLKW 50

MERMAID. "The fish-tailed lady offering her breast"   FOLKW 50

PHOENIX. "If I am that bird, then I am alone"
FOLKW 50

READER. "My old shape-changer, who will be"
FOLKW 50

RETINA. "The struggler in the net"
FOLKW 50

STORM. "That strong creature"   FOLKW 50

SUN AND MOON. "A strong man"   FOLKW 50

---

* Recording not available for analysis

WHALE. "Art thou the first of creatures, that Leviathan"   FOLKW 50
MacSweeney, Margaret Phyllis. in English.
CARMEL POINT.   SCHOL 7
Maeterlinck, Maurice. 1862. in French.
J'AI MARCHÉ TRENTE ANS, MES SOEURS. "J'ai cherché trente ans, mes soeurs"   FOLKW 13
Magee, John Gillespie, Jr. in English.
HIGH FLIGHT.   SINGER 3, ARGO 143
Mahony, Francis. in English.
THE BELLS OF SHANDON. "With deep affection and recollection"   SPOA 6
Mailer, Norman. 1923. in English.
CATNIP FOR THE KIDDIES. "Does the football team"   PREST 1
ELEGANCE.   PREST 1
RAINY AFTERNOON WITH THE WIFE. "Gray/without grace"   PREST 1
TESTAMENTS. "I never/scored"   PREST 1
TIMING. "Listen/my love"   PREST 1
TO THE GHOST OF HIS LATE HIGHNESS THE SENATOR.
                                       PREST 1
TOGETHERNESS. "My flesh must smell like an old tire"   PREST 1
Maison-Noire. in French.
"Peu vous importe"   ADES 55
Major, Clarence. 1936. in English.
AIR. "Breathing the breath. clearance. the air"
                                       CAED 155
KITCHEN CHAIR POEM NO. 5.   BLACKF 1
THE RASPBERRY TRAGEDY. "A raspberry ribbon"
                                       WATSHD 4
THE WAY THE ROUNDNESS FEEL. "Your fingers cruise"   WATSHD 4
Malam, Charles. in English.
STEAM SHOVEL.   SCHOL 7
Malanga, Gerard. in English.
DEVOTION—FOR KAREN. "Words simply given"
                                       WATSHD 9
HE WENT OUT QUIETLY. "He is not with us anymore"   WATSHD 9
A MEETING IN N'HAMPTON. "We create the place"   WATSHD 9
THE RELATIONSHIP. "What I know"
                                       WATSHD 9
TALKING. "I have felt utter loneliness"
                                       WATSHD 9
Malcolm X (Malcolm Little). 1925. in English.
Poetry*   PRENT 1
Malevic, Kazimir. 1878. in Russian.
LAUTGEDICHT.   German LUCHT 1
Malherbe, François de. 1558. in French.
AUX OMBRES DE DAMON, exc.   PERIOD 2
CONSOLATION A M. DU PERIER, exc.   GMS 8,
                            HACH 9, PERIOD 2
DESSEIN DE QUITTER UNE DAME QUI NE LE CONTENTOIT QUE DE PROMESSE. "Beauté, mon beau soucy, de qui l'ame incertaine"   SPOA 9
LES LARMES DE SAINT-PIERRE, exc. "Ce n'est pas en mes vers qu'une amante abusée"
                                       HACH 9
PARAPHRASE DU PSAUME 145. "N'esperons plus, mon ame, aux promesses du monde"
                            HACH 9, PERIOD 2
PRIERE POUR LE ROI ALLANT EN LIMOUSIN, exc. "O Dieu, dont les bontez de nos larmes touchees"   HACH 9

Mallarmé, Stéphane. 1842. in French.
APPARITION. "La lune s'attristait"   ADES 46,
        CBS 1, FOLKW 13, GMS 7, HACH 13,
                                       DOVER 4
L'APRÈS-MIDI D'UN FAUNE.   ADES 46, ADES 54
AU SEUL SOUCI DE VOYAGER.   ADES 46
L'AZUR.   ADES 46
BRISE MARINE. "La chair est triste, hélas! et j'ai lu tous les livres"   ADES 46, ADES 54,
                FOLKW 86, GMS 9, HACH 13,
                            PERIOD 1, SPOA 9
LA CHEVELURE.   ADES 46
"Une dentelle s'abolit"   PERIOD 1
DON DU POÈME. "Je t'apporte l'enfant d'une nuit d'Idumée"   PERIOD 1
ÉVENTAIL DE MLLE MALLARME.   HACH 13
HÉRODIADE. II. SCENE. "O miroir"   PERIOD 1
————. III. CANTIQUE DE SAINT JEAN. "Le soleil"
                                       PERIOD 1
IMITATION DU PSAUME "LAUDA ANIMA". "N'esperons plus, mon ame, aux promesses du monde"   DOVER 4
LAS DE L'AMER REPOS. "Las de l'amer repos où ma paresse offence"   PERIOD 1
RONDEL.   ADES 46
"Surgi de la croupe et du bond"   ADES 46,
                                       PERIOD 1
TOAST FUNÈBRE, exc. "Magnifique, total et solitaire"   ADES 46, PERIOD 1
LE TOMBEAU D'EDGAR POE. "Tel qu'en lui-meme enfin l'éternité le change"   ADES 46,
                                       PERIOD 1
TOMBEAU DE VERLAINE, exc. "Qui cherche, parcourant le solitaire bond"   PERIOD 1
LA VIERGE, LE VIVACE ET LE BEL AUJOURD'HUI. "La vierge, le vivace et le bel aujourd'hui"
        ADES 46, FOLKW 86, HACH 13,
                                       PERIOD 1
Malmberg, Bertil. 1889. in Swedish.
AFTONRODNAD, exc. "Hur obevekligt våra timslag falla"   GRAM 4
DÅRARNA. "Jag vet ej vad de känna, vilke ting"
"Drag mig ur rummets skugga"   GRAM 4
Mandarà, Emanuele. in Italian.
SCHIARITA.   CETRA 31
Mandel, Oscar. 1926. in English.
WE WHO DO NOT GRIEVE IN SILENCE. "First came the special issues of the magazines"
                                       FOLKW 21
Manent, Maria. 1898. in Catalan.
"L'acacia plena de lluna"   AGUIL 14
Mangan, James Clarence. 1803. in English.
DARK ROSALEEN. "Oh my dark Rosaleen"
                                       SPOA 6
TWENTY GOLDEN YEARS AGO. "Oh, the rain, the weary, dreary rain"   FOLKW 52
Manilius. 20 A.D. in Latin.
Poetry*   CETRA 18
Manrique, Jorge. 1440. in Spanish.
"Con dolorido cuidado"   DOVER 2
COPLAS POR LA MUERTE DE SU PADRE. "Recuerde el alma dormida"   CMS 5, HOLT 1,
                            SMC 15, SPOA 37
"No tardes, muerte, que muero"   DOVER 2
SIN DIÓS Y SIN VOS Y MI. "Yo soy quien libre me vi"   AGUIL 4

* Recording not available for analysis

Mansfield, Katherine. 1888. in English.
LITTLE BROTHER'S SECRET. "When my birthday was coming"   HARB 4
Mantero, Manuel. in Spanish.
ENCUENTRO DE LUIS CERNUDA CON VERLAINE Y EL DEMONIO. "Por una senda llena de amatistas y gotas"   AGUIL 10
Manzoni, Alessandro. 1785. in Italian.
ADELCHI, exc.   CETRA 9
IL CINQUE MAGGIO. "Ei fu. Siccome immobile"   FOLKW 97, CETRA 9
INNI SACRI, exc.   CETRA 9
Maragall, Joan. 1860. in Catalan.
CANT ESPIRITUAL. "Si el món ja és tan formós, Senyor, si es mira"   AGUIL 14
HIMNE IBERIC. "¡Cantàbria!, som tos braus mariners"   AGUIL 6
Marcello, Joseph. in English.
TODAY'S THE ONLY DAY OF MY LIFE.   EAV 17
Marcus, Adrianne. 1935. in English.
THE FIRST TIME. "In the close breathing"   WATSHD 2
LADY, SISTER. "Lady, sister, it is cold"   WATSHD 2
SEQUENCE. "I know the probable"   WATSHD 2
STANDING IN MY LIGHT. "Turncoat sleep is quick"   WATSHD 2
WHOSE DINOSAURS ARE NUMBERED? "What is alive crawls"   WATSHD 2
Marguerite de Navarre. 1492. in French.
"Elle m'a dit"   PERIOD 2
Mariah, Paul. 1937. in English.
AN APPARITION. "There is this black pauper's suit"   WATSHD 5
DARING TO LIVE FOR THE IMPOSSIBLE. "I saw her lift herself"   WATSHD 5
EVEN IN SLEEP. "Asleep the spider bites"   WATSHD 5
FROM BOTH SIDES. "Love, I have seen you from both sides"   WATSHD 5
JANIS (TO THE 4TH POWER). "The most precious thing at first"   WATSHD 5
WALLS BREATHE. "It was so quiet you could hear"   WATSHD 5
Marin, Biagio. in Italian.
BREVE ISTAE DE SAN MARTIN.   CETRA 35
LE CAMPANE DE GRAVO.   CETRA 35
CIÀ COLA 'L MAR INTORNO.   CETRA 35
CÔ SARÉ MORTO.   CETRA 35
UN DIO GRANDO, SOLAR.   CETRA 35
EL FARO.   CETRA 35
FELISSE MORO.   CETRA 35
GNO FIGIO XE 'NDAO IN GUERA.   CETRA 35
LA GNO ZENTE.   CETRA 35
ME VEDO UN BASTIMENTO IN MESA RADA.   CETRA 35
MEGIO 'L SILENSIO.   CETRA 35
LA MORTE. "L'asfalto negro cala dentro un' aria"   CETRA 35
NEGRA TU GERI E RISSA.   CETRA 35
NO MÉ MAI BUO 'NA MARE.   CETRA 35
OH ZENTE DE L'INFANZIA.   CETRA 35
PAESE MASSA STRETO.   CETRA 35
PAESE MIO.   CETRA 35
PESCAURI.   CETRA 35
QUANDO 'L CANEO RINFRESCA.   CETRA 35

"Quanto più moro"   CETRA 35
TE CARESSO I GENUCI.   CETRA 35
TE PIASEVA, MARIA.   CETRA 35
"T'hé levao ogni fogia"   CETRA 35
TU GERI L'ORTO CHE NISSUN CULTIVA.   CETRA 35
TU GERI ZA VECIA.   CETRA 35
TU SA DUTA DE SAL E DE SALMASTRO.   CETRA 35
VECIO CORCAL SUL FAR DE LA FOSA.   CETRA 35
Marino, Giambattista. 1569. in Italian.
BELLA SCHIAVA. "Nera sì, ma se'bella, o di Natura"   DOVER 3
Poetry*   CETRA 24
Markham, Edwin Charles. 1852. in English.
THE DAY AND THE WORK.   SINGER 1
LINCOLN, THE MAN OF THE PEOPLE, exc. "The color of the ground was in him, the red earth"   DECCA 4, DECCA 7
THE MAN WITH THE HOE. "Bowed by the weight of centuries"   AUDIA 2, CAED 100, CAED 195, CMS 12, EAV 10, HOUGHT 5, LIST 3
THE RIGHT KIND OF PEOPLE.   HOUGHT 4
VICTORY IN DEFEAT.   SINGER 2
Poetry*   LIST 12
Marlowe, Christopher. 1564. in English.
DIDO, exc. "Dido that hath store of plums"   CAED 110
DOCTOR FAUSTUS, exc. "Ah Faustus"   LONGM 1
HERO AND LEANDER. "On Hellespont guilty of true-loves' blood"   PROTHM 8
THE PASSIONATE SHEPHERD TO HIS LOVE. "Come, live with me and be my love"   ARGO 31, ARGO 137, CAED 186, CMS 13, DECCA 12, EAV 6, FOLKW 60, IMP 1, LIST 1, LIVLAN 1, POLYGL 2, SPOA 12, SPOA 50
WHO EVER LOVED.   DECCA 12
Poetry*   PROTHM 6
Mármol, José. 1817. in Spanish.
CANTOS DEL PEREGRINO AL BRASIL—LA MUJER BRASILEÑA. "Mujeres de tez morena"   SPOA 39
Marot, Clément. 1495. in French.
L'ADIEU AUX DAMES. "Adieu Paris, la bonne ville"   GMS 8
CHANT DE MAY ET DE VERTU. "Voulentiers en ce moys icy"   HACH 8
DE LA JEUNE DAME QUI A VIEIL MARY. "En languissant, et en grefve tristesse"   DOVER 4
DE SA GRANDE AMIE.   CAED 204
DE SOY MESME. "Plus ne suis ce que j'ai été"   ADES 54, HACH 8, PERIOD 2
"Dedans Paris, ville jolie" ADES 54, HACH 8
LE PARLEMENT.   HACH 8
Marques, Oswaldino. 1916. in Portuguese.
CANTIGA. "Nas Hébridas nâo nasci en"   FOLKW 71
ESTUDO NO. 2. "Me deleito na espuma dos salsos temporais"   FOLKW 71
Marquis, Don. 1878. in English.
ARCHY IS SHOCKED. "speaking of shocking things"   ACTIV 1
THE COMING OF ARCHIE.   SCHOL 8
THE DISSIPATED HORNET. "well boss i had a"   ACTIV 1

* Recording not available for analysis

A HOT-WEATHER SONG. "I feel so exceedingly lazy"   HARB 6
THE LESSON OF THE MOTH. "i was talking to a moth"   ACTIV 1
SOME NATURAL HISTORY. "the patagonian"   ARGO 118
A SPIDER AND A FLY. "i heard a spider"   ACTIV 1

Marriott, Jack. in English.
STREET SCENE. "Housewives stand at their door-steps"   SPOA 68

Marshall, Helen Lowrie. 1904. in English.
ANOTHER YEAR. "I swear, the way time passes"   HELV 9
ARRIVING—NOT LEAVING. "My dearest ones, don't grieve for me"   HELV 9
AN ARTIST'S PRAYER. "Dear God and Ruler of all time"   HELV 9
BABY SISTER. "What good's a baby sister"   HELV 9
BACK HOME. "Strange, isn't it—of all the places"   HELV 6
BE FRIENDS WITH YOURSELF. "Stand back and take a good look"   HELV 6
BEST FOR ME. "How often I've been put to test"   HELV 6
BEYOND. "Beyond the reach of reason"   HELV 9
A BIT OF ETERNITY. "I saw a butterfly today"   HELV 9
BLESS THIS LITTLE CHAPEL. "Bless this little chapel, Lord"   HELV 6
A CANDLE OF UNDERSTANDING. "There is so much of darkness"   HELV 9
THE CHALLENGE OF OUR DOUBTS. "We ought not be alarmed if doubts"   HELV 6
COMES TWILIGHT NOW. "Comes twilight now, of all the day the best"   HELV 6
CORNER CUPBOARD. "When I was just a little girl"   HELV 6
THE CROSSROADS. "You met at the crossroads"   HELV 9
CRYSTAL MOMENTS. "Crystal moments, yours and mine"   HELV 9
A CUSHIONING OF PRAYER. "Prayer fits into any little corner of the day"   HELV 6
ENCHANTED LAND. "Keep a little wonder"   HELV 6
ENTER SINGING. "Each morning a new play be-gins"   HELV 9
EYES OF UNDERSTANDING. "Let me see life through a thousand eyes"   HELV 9
FAITH IN YOURSELF. "Does the task ahead seem much too hard"   HELV 9
FALLEN IDOL. "So your idol of gold"   HELV 6
FELLOWSHIP. "Fellowship's a maker of friend-ships"   HELV 9
FIRST FROST. "Isn't it odd the memories"   HELV 6
FRIENDS WITH GOD. "He never speaks with loud"   HELV 9
FROM GOD'S LOVE. "This love that joins today"   HELV 9
A GARDENER SEES. "Oh a gardener's eyes"   HELV 9
THE GIFT OF WONDER. "As daily now man con-quers space"   HELV 6

GLORY FOREVER. "What a grand old world we live in"   HELV 6
GRANDMA'S GUMPTION. "Everyone has her down days"   HELV 9
GREATER THE SOUL. "I looke upon a mountain high"   HELV 6
HAVE I, TODAY. "I look back on this day"   HELV 9
THE HEART KNOWS. "The French have a saying"   HELV 6
A HEAVEN BELOW. "Let there be goodness"   HELV 9
HEAVEN ON EARTH. "Heaven's not a fenced-off place"   HELV 9
HILLS ARE FOR CLIMBING. "Hills are for climbing, ask any small boy"   HELV 9
HIS GIFTS. "Into every soul is born"   HELV 9
HOLD FAST A DREAM. "Hold fast a dream. On this careening earth"   HELV 6
HOME AGAIN. "The house was fast asleep"   HELV 6
I AM NOT BLIND. "You say that I've gone blind"   HELV 9
I CANNOT TEACH YOU. "I cannot teach you, though the years"   HELV 6
I OWE EVERY MAN. "I owe every man, he proudly said"   HELV 9
I WILL NOT FALL. "It may not make it across the sea"   HELV 6
I WISH YOU HAPPINESS. "I wish you happiness, God's gift"   HELV 6
I'M GLAD. "I'm glad the great Creator"   HELV 6
THE IMPORTANT THING "It's nice to be impor-tant"   HELV 6
IN CASE A TREE GROWS THERE. "We used to have"   HELV 6
INSPIRATION IN DESPAIR. "There is an inspira-tion"   HELV 6
IT'S CONTAGIOUS. "Cheer is a contagious thing"   HELV 6
KING'S – X. "Remember how we used to call"   HELV 6
LEAVE A TOUCH OF GLORY. "Have you watched the sun"   HELV 9
LEFT-OVER LAUGHTER. "I love you most, I think"   HELV 6
LET'S GO. "Why is it that a steering wheel"   HELV 6
LIFE MEETS YOU. "Enter into the game of life"   HELV 9
THE LONG-HAIRED MALE OF THE SPECIES. "I be-lieve in evolution"   HELV 6
LOVE SPEAKS. "Love speaks in such a silent voice"   HELV 6
LOVE THIS LAND. "Love this land—it's mighty mountains"   HELV 9
A LOVELY TIME TO WALK. "He who trod the coun-try roads"   HELV 9
MAKE IT RADIANT. "Make it radiant, this day"   HELV 9
MAKE WAY! "Remove the barriers"   HELV 6
MAN ABOVE THE MOUNTAINS. "A mountain tower-ing to the skies"   HELV 9
MAY-DAY. "When I was small, I lived in a town"   HELV 9
"May his hand be on your shoulder" HELV 6

* Recording not available for analysis

Marshall, Helen Lowrie (continued)

MEADOW LARK. "Was there ever a sound more brimming with cheer"   HELV 9

MEMORIAL DAY. "Our fathers sacrificed so much"   HELV 9

MEMORY. "Isn't memory wonderful, though?"   HELV 9

MOUNTAIN BEAUTY. "The air is crisp and fresh and clean"   HELV 9

NEW FRIEND. "There's a special little halo"   HELV 9

NEW MORNINGS. "New mornings, each a precious gift"   HELV 9

THE OLD CHURCH BELL. "I remember so well"   HELV 6

OUTREACH OF PRAYER. "A prayer is a way of lifting ourselves"   HELV 9

THE PEOPLE GROWER. "He has a sort of green thumb"   HELV 6

PICK YOURSELF A STAR. "So you've a dream"   HELV 6

A POCKET OF SMILES. "Each morning pack a pocket of smiles"   HELV 9

POSSESSED OF A DREAM. "A dream isn't really something you have"   HELV 6

POWER TO LIFT. "If God has given you the special power"   HELV 6

PRAYER OF TRUST. "Lord, let me not be guilty"   HELV 9

RAGAMUFFIN DAY. "Today was a ragamuffin day"   HELV 6

THE REASON WHY. "I've a halo to live up to"   HELV 6

REBUILDING FOR CHRIST. "Our Church now rebuilds"   HELV 9

RESEARCH SCIENTIST. "This is the road"   HELV 9

RESULTS IN REVERSE. "A fact which may seem strange to you"   HELV 9

THE ROAD TO SUCCESS. "The road to success has many a turn"   HELV 9

SECRET FORMULA. "Sometimes seeds sown in seasons"   HELV 9

SEPTEMBER HILLS. "Have you seen the hills in September"   HELV 6

SHIFTING SANDS. "Are the sands of your young son's values"   HELV 6

SIMPLICITY OF PRAYER. "Prayer is such a simple thing"   HELV 9

SMALL-TOWN, USA. "Have you paid a visit recently"   HELV 6

SOMEHOW I KNOW. "I have never seen the whole sea"   HELV 6

SOMETHING TO LIVE FOR. "Something to live for, this the need"   HELV 6

THE SOUND OF LAUGHTER. "God must receive so many solemn prayers"   HELV 6

STAND TALL. "Stand tall, reach high" HELV 6

THE STAR OF CASTLE ROCK. "Long years ago in Bethlehem"   HELV 9

STATION LOVE. "I believe love travels"   HELV 6

SYMPHONY OF BEAUTY. "No lovelier time"   HELV 9

THANK HEAVEN FOR THE WEATHER. "Thank heaven for the weather"   HELV 6

THANK YOU. "Must I say only "Thank You"?"   HELV

THANKSGIVING DAY. "This is the time"   HELV

THIS IS THE ROAD. "This is the road the Master took"   HELV

TIMBERLAND STILLNESS. "Have you known"   HELV

TO GOD WITH LOVE. "We've all known that special lift"   HELV

TO IRENE. "The glow of friendliness" HELV

TO ONE NO LONGER HERE. "I never think of he without a smile"   HELV

TO SAVE A ROSE. "If we can, in our living"   HELV

TODAY IS ENOUGH. "Why are we here?"   HELV

UNLESS A LOVE BE FREE. "Love cannot be held in bonds"   HELV

WAGONFUL OF WALNUTS. "Along about this time of year"   HELV

WALK IN THE WOODS. "Walk carefully"   HELV

WASTE NOT, WANT NOT. "Waste not, want not the quaint old phrase"   HELV

"We ought to have a glory"   HELV

WEDDING DAY. "This love of ours"   HELV

WEST WIND GOSSIP. "What's happening to the westward"   HELV

WHEN DO WE EAT? "My bride's in the kitchen"   HELV

WHEN YOU DREAM. "When you dream, may the dream be worthy"   HELV

WHERE ONCE HER LILACS GREW. "Spring slipped in through the garden gate"   HELV

WHO DO YOU WORK FOR? "Who do you work for? Myself, he said"   HELV

A WORD OF PRAISE. "I spoke a word of praise today"   HELV

Poetry*   HELV 1, HELV 2, HELV 3, HELV 4, HELV 5, HELV 7, HELV

Marshall, Jack. 1937. in English.

ELEGY FOR THE NEW YEAR. "Dulled by the new all day I keep behind"   FOLKW 2

Poetry*   JNP 3

Marshall, Lenore G. 1897. in English.

ARGUMENT ON IMMORTALITY. "Though we are atoms"   SPOA 1

AS THOUGH FROM LOVE. "Out of the matrix"   SPOA 18, SPOA 9

AUTUMN HILLTOP.   SPOA 1

CRICKET SONG.   SPOA 1

GOGGLEHEAD. "I was the first to see the gogglehead"   SPOA 1

HOW WILL YOU SHOW IT. "Painter, the mountain rims the mesa"   SPOA 1

INTERLOPER. "All interlopers in antiquity"   SPOA 1

INVENTED A PERSON. "Invented a person named I"   SPOA 18, SPOA 9

LATEST WILL. "I, of the city and state of do declare"   SPOA 9

LOVE POEM. "Here where you never have been you walk"   SPOA 1

MEXICAN NIGHT. "On the million Mexican mountains"   SPOA 1

---

* Recording not available for analysis

A MOTHER THINKS OF HER CHILD. "Over him like a tent"   SPOA 18
NO BOUNDARY.   SPOA 18
OTHER KNOWLEDGE. "Nothing is strange to them"   SPOA 18
RELATIVITY. "My great stone house sways to and fro"   SPOA 18
RESPITE. "Spring is your season. Where you are"   SPOA 18
THE RETURN. "In the night, in thick dark of midnight"   SPOA 18
RUMOR. "Not of new earth and not of new men"   SPOA 18
SHADOW AND ANSWER. "What color is the shadow"   SPOA 95
SHADOW PLAY.   SPOA 18
SHELL SONG. "Under my shell"   SPOA 18
STILL LIFE.   SPOA 18
THIS TWENTIETH-CENTURY MIND. "This twentieth-century mind"   SPOA 18
THOUGH I AM FALSE.   SPOA 18
TO A HOUSE BEING BUILT. "Each stone and cornice calls"   SPOA 18
TWO POEMS IN ONE. "Being ourselves is less than love"   SPOA 18
WHILE READING HISTORY. "Among Florentine cinquecentists taste in manuscripts"
                                          SPOA 18

Martí, José. 1853. in Spanish.
ARBOL DE MI ALMA. "Como un ave que cruza el aire claro"   SMC 13
CRIN HIRSUTA.   SMC 19
"¿Del tirano? Del tirano"   SMC 19
DOS PATRIAS. "Dos patrias tengo yo: Cuba y la noche"   SPOA 39
"En ti encerré mis horas de alegría"   SMC 19
GUANTÁNAMERA. "Yo soy un hombre sincero"
                                          SMC 19
MI CABALLERO. "Por las mañanas"   SMC 13
"Mi reyecillo"   SMC 19
MI VERSO. "Si ves un monte de espumas"
                               FIDIAS 3, SMC 19
"¡Penas! Quién osa decir . . . "   SMC 19
"Quiero a la sombra de un ala"   SMC 19
LA ROSA BLANCA. "Cultivo una rosa blanca"
                               FIDIAS 3, SMC 19
SOBRE MI HOMBRO. "Ved: sentado lo llevo"
                                          SPOA 39
SUEÑO CON CLAUSTROS DE MARMOL.   SMC 19
SUEÑO DESPIERTO. "Yo sueño con los ojos"
                                          SPOA 39
VERSOS SENCILLOS. "Cultivo una rosa blanca"
                                          HOLT 1
"Vierte, corazón, tu pena"   SMC 19
"Yo pienso cuando me alegro"   SMC 19
"Yo quiero salir del mundo"   SMC 19
YUGO Y ESTRELLA.   SMC 19

Martial (Marcus Valerius Martialis). 40 A.D. in Latin.
Poetry*   CETRA 18; English CARIL 3

Martínez Alonso, Isidoro. in Spanish.
EL ARBOL ALTO. "Sencilla semilla: Tú tendrás mañana una lírica cabellera obscura"
                                          SMC 12
EL BESO DE LA LUNA. "En mi fuente consagrada a Diana"   SMC 12

CORAZON DE NARDO. "Había antes vírgenes novias"   SMC 12
LA DANZA DEL VIENTO. "Terpsicore es Eolo"
                                          SMC 12
EL DIA DE PLATA. "Comiezan los días lánguidos"
                                          SMC 12
LA ESCALINATA DE PIEDRAS. "Los niños, qué alegres juegan"   SMC 12
FILOSOFÍA DE LA MUERTE. "Muerto, quiénes besarán mis sienes?"   SMC 12
FILOSOFÍA DEL DOLOR. "Alza, humano, la frente abatida"   SMC 12
LA GRACIA DE LAS COSAS. "Dadme, oh números, vuestra armonía pitagórica"   SMC 12
JUEGOS CONSIGO MISMO. "Juega el amor con sus besos"   SMC 12
LA LLUVIA METAFISICA. "Oh cristalina cabellera"
                                          SMC 12
LA LUZ EN EL ALMA. "El amor es tener, noche y día"   SMC 12
LA MISA BLANCA. "Todo el jardín en una quietud de éxtasis"   SMC 12
MISTICA DE LA MUERTE. "La muerte, para el alma, es vida"   SMC 12
MISTICA DEL DOLOR. "Ama, hermano, el dolor"
                                          SMC 12
LA NIÑA CONFITADA. "La sorprendí una tarde saboreando"   SMC 12
LA NIÑA ILUSIONADA. "Benilde, esta noche tienes"   SMC 12
LA NORIA AZUL. "La mula y la noria"   SMC 12
EL PÁJARO ESCONDIDO. "Una tarde, comenzamos a oír la melodía de un pájaro ideal"
                                          SMC 12
EL PÁJARO Y LA ROSA. "La rosa le dijo al pájaro"
                                          SMC 12
PANOPTES. "Las flores no son ciegas"   SMC 12
LA PUERTA ABIERTA. "El miedo es una puerta abierta"   SMC 12
LA ROSA DE CRISTAL. "Yo os prefiero maravillosas rosas rojas"   SMC 12
LAS ROSAS ESCARMENTADAS. "Yo tengo en mi jardín aquel rosal"   SMC 12
LOS SENTIDOS FANTASMAGORICOS. "Cuando digo rosas, se perfume el aire"   SMC 12
EL TRIGO QUE NO SE SIEGA. "Trigales del corazón"   SMC 12
LA VID VIRGEN. "Todo el astío, el policrono sol"
                                          SMC 12
LA VISITA INEFABLE. "Ya llegas, Oh dulce Primavera"   SMC 12

Martínez Capó, Juan. in Spanish.
VOZ A MI PADRE, LEJOS.   INSTPR 1

Martínez Estrada, Ezequiel. 1895. in Spanish.
PENA. "Este hastío, esta pena o esta melancolía"
                                          AGUIL 9

Martínez Sierra, Gregorio. in Spanish.
UNA VIDA DE MUJER. "En pocos versos váis a saber"   SMC 7

Martinson, Harry. 1904. in Swedish.
BARNDOMSLANDSKAP. "Åren skymma bort varanda"   GRAM 7
ENBUSKEN. "Tyst står han vid stenen"
                                          GRAM 7
FLYGARDIKT. "På väven Asien vi sågo ner"
                                          GRAM 7
I SOLEN. "Biet mot solen den sköna" GRAM 1

* Recording not available for analysis

Martinson, Harry (continued)

LI TI'S RÅD. "Äger du tvenne slantar sade Li Ti
på en resa"   GRAM 1
ÖPPEN KUST. "Sjösorlen hugga byigt i bankarna"
                                               GRAM 7
OROANDE INBLICK. "När larven ur trädet till
puppning"   GRAM 7
RESANS SLUT. "Många som varit på bio tala"
                                               GRAM 7
SNÅLEN.   GRAM 7
Martynov, Leonid N. 1905. in Russian.
"Khochetsa/sosredototchitsya"   MONITR 1
"Kto dal tebe soviet, zakontchiv stchet pobed"
                                            MONITR 1
SHAG. "Sdelan shag"   MONITR 1
Marvell, Andrew. 1621. in English.
THE BERMUDAS. "Where the remote Bermudas
ride"   ARGO 37, BRITAM 2
THE DEFINITION OF LOVE. "My love is of a birth
as rare"   ARGO 37, LIST 2, SPOA 84
THE GARDEN. "How vainly men themselves
amaze"   ARGO 37, CAED 38
THE HORATIAN ODE. "The forward youth that
would appear"   ARGO 37
THE MOWER TO THE GLO-WORMS. "Ye living lamps
by whose dear light"   ARGO 37
THE NYMPH COMPLAINING FOR THE DEATH OF HER
FAWN. "The wanton Troopers riding by"
                                       ARGO 37
THE PICTURE OF LITTLE T. C. IN A PROSPECT OF
FLOWERS. "See with what simplicity"
                                       ARGO 37
TO HIS COY MISTRESS. "Had we but World
enough, and Time" ARGO 37, BRITAM 2,
        CAED 38, CMS 12, JNP 8, LION 2,
     LIST 2, SPOA 84, THEAL 3, LONGM 1
UPON APPLETON HOUSE, exc. "Within this sober
frame expect"   ARGO 37
Marvin X. in English.
BIGGER THOMAS LIVES! "You know what Bigger
Thomas did"   BROADV 1
DID YOU VOTE NIGGER. "Did u vote, nigger"
                                       BROADV 1
ELIJAH. "Elijah"   BROADV 1
EXILED. "I have run"   BROADV 1
HEAVEN IS A CONDITION OF LIFE. "Black woman"
                                       BROADV 1
THE ORIGIN OF BLACKNESS. "Sudan la al lawn"
                                       BROADV 1
THE PEOPLE'S CHILD. "I am"   BROADV 1
SURVIVAL LESSON 1. "When you enter"
                                       BROADV 1
TILL THE SUN GOES DOWN. "Malika"
                                       BROADV 1
TOMMY SMITH POEM.   BROADV 1
THE WINTER SOLDIER. "The snow"   BROADV 1
Masefield, John. 1878. in English.
CAPTAIN STRATTON'S FANCY. "Oh some are fond
of red wine, and some are fond of white"
                                       CAED 79
CARGOES. "Quinquireme of Nineveh"
                             CAED 79, HOUGHT 3
C. L. M. "In the dark womb where I began"
                                       CAED 79
A CREED. "I held that when a person dies"
                                       CAED 79

THE DOWNLAND. "Night is on the downland, o
the lonely moorland"   CAED 7
THE EVERLASTING MERCY, exc. CONCLUSIO
"How swift the summer grows"   CAED 7
_____. SAUL KANE'S OUTBURST. "I opened wi
dow wide"   CAED 7
FORTUNE OF THE SEA, exc.   ARGO 1
"Four bells were struck, the watch was calle
on deck"   ARGO 8
GOOD FRIDAY, exc. "Only a penny, a penny"
                                       CAED 7
THE GREAT EASTERN.   ARGO 8
HERE IN THE SELF.   CMS 1
LOLLINGDON DOWNS. II. "O wretched man, tha
for a little mile"   CAED 7
_____. V. "I could not sleep for thinking of th
sky"   CAED 79, CAED 11
_____. VI. "How did the nothing come, ho
did these fires"   CAED 7
_____. VII. "It may be so; but let the unknow
be"   CAED 7
MOTHER CAREY.   FOLKW 6
ON EASTNOR KNOLL. "Silent are the woods, an
the dim green boughs are"   CAED 11
THE PASSING STRANGE. "Out of the earth to re
or range"   CAED 7
A POEM ABOUT FRANCIS DRAKE.   ARGO 8
REYNARD THE FOX, exc. "The meet was at Th
Cock and Pye"   ARGO 8, BRITAM
THE RIDER AT THE GATE. "A windy night w
blowing on Rome"   CAED 7
ROADWAYS.   HOUGHT 2, SINGER
ROUNDING THE HORN. "Then came the cry
Call all hands on deck"   EAV 2
SALT WATER BALLADS, exc.   ARGO 14
SEAFEVER. "I must go down to the seas again, t
the lonely sea and the sky"   CAED 7
              CAED 169, HARB 5, HARC
     HOUGHT 4, RCA 4, SINGER 4, THEAL
THE SETTING OF THE WINDCOCK. "The dust la
white upon the chisel marks"   FOLKW 6
THE SONGS OF THE MERCHANTS.   ARGO 8
SPANISH WATERS. "Spanish waters, Spanish w
ters you are ringing in my ears"   CAED 7
THE STORY OF OSSIAN. "All this began becaus
Finn wished to wed"   SPOA 2
TO THE GREAT FRIENDS IN LIFETIME.
                                       FOLKW 59
TWO STORIES.   ARGO 8
THE WANDERER'S IMAGE: A POEM ABOUT OLD SHIF
                             ARGO 10, ARGO 8
THE WEST WIND. "It's a warm wind, the we
wind, full of birds' cries"   CAED 7
THE WESTERN HUDSON SHORE (THE PALISADES).
                                       FOLKW 59
THE WIDOW IN THE BYE STREET, exc. "Singing he
crazy song the mother goes"   CAED 7
THE WILD DUCKS. "Twilight. Red in the west"
                                       CAED 7
Mason, Chris. in English.
CLIFF NOTES. "Housekeeper assistant"
                                       WATSHD 1
GASOLINA SESTINA. "Bill's timely Amoco"
                                       WATSHD 1
Masson, Loys. in French.
POÈME POUR PAULA.   ADES 5

* Recording not available for analysis

Masters, Edgar Lee. 1868. in English.

ACHILLES DEATHERIDGE. HOUGHT 1

A. D. BLOOD. "If you in the village think that my work was a good one" CAED 82

ALBERT SCHIRDING. "Jonas Keene thought his lot a hard one" CAED 82

ANDY, THE NIGHT-WATCH. "In my Spanish cloak" CAED 82

ANNE RUTLEDGE. "Out of me unworthy and un-known" COR 1, LIBC 40, SPOA 90

ANTHONY FINDLAY. "Both for the country and for the man" CAED 82

BARNEY HAINSFEATHER. "If the excursion train to Peoria" COR 1

BATTERTON DOBYNS. "Did my widow flit about" CAED 82

BENJAMIN PANTIER. "Together in this grave lie Benjamin Pantier, attorney at law" COR 1

BERT KESSLER. "I winged my bird" CAED 82

BUTCH WELDY. "After I got religion and steadied down" CAED 82

CHARLIE FRENCH. "Did you ever find out" CAED 82

CHASE HENRY. "In life I was the town drunkard" COR 1

CLARENCE FAWCETT. "The sudden death of Eugene Carman" CAED 82

COONEY POTTER. "I inherited forty acres from my father" COR 1

DAISY FRASER. "Did you ever hear of Editor Whedon" CAED 82

DANIEL M'CUMBER. "When I went to the city, Mary McNeely" CAED 82

DIPPOLD THE OPTICIAN. "What do you see now?" CAED 82

DOCTOR MEYERS. "No other man, unless it was Doc Hill" COR 1

DORA WILLIAMS. "When Reuben Pantier ran away and threw me" CAED 82

EDMUND POLLARD. "I would I had thrust" SPOA 90

ELSA WERTMAN. "I was a peasant girl from Germany" CAED 82, RCA 10

EMILY SPARKS. "Where is my boy, my boy" CAED 82, SPOA 90

EUGENE CARMAN. "Rhodes' slave! Selling shoes and gingham" CAED 82

FELIX SCHMIDT. "It was only a little house of two rooms" CAED 82

FIDDLER JONES. "The earth keeps some vibration going" CAED 82, HOUGHT 5

FLOSSIE CABANIS. "From Bindle's opera house in the village" CAED 82

FRANK DRUMMER. "Out of a cell into this darkened space" CAED 82

FRANKLIN JONES. "If I could have lived another year" CAED 82

HAMILTON GREENE. "I was the only child of Frances Harris of Virginia" CAED 82

HARE DRUMMER. "Do the boys and girls still go to Siever's" CAED 82, SPOA 90

HARMON WHITNEY. "Out of the lights and roar of cities" CAED 82

HAROLD ARNETT. "I leaned against the mantel, sick, sick" CAED 82

HARRY WILMANS. "I was just turned twenty-one" CAED 82

THE HILL. "Where are Elmer, Herman, Bert, Tom and Charley" COR 1, HOUGHT 5

HOD PUTT. "Here I lie close to the grave" COR 1

JACK MCGUIRE. "They would have lynched me" CAED 82

JAMES GARBER. "Do you remember, passer-by, the path" CAED 82

JOHN HANCOCK OTIS. "As to democracy, fellow-citizens" CAED 82

JONAS KEENE. "Why did Albert Schirding kill himself" CAED 82

JUDGE SELAH LIVELY. "Suppose you stood just five feet two" CAED 82

JUDGE SOMERS. "How does it happen, tell me" COR 1

JUSTICE ARNETT. "Tis true, fellow citizens" CAED 82

KNOWLT HOHEIMER. "I was the first fruits of the battle of Missionary Ridge" COR 1

LUCINDA MATLOCK. "I went to the dances at Chandlerville" COR 1, HOUGHT 5, LIBC 40, SPOA 90

LUCIUS ATHERTON. "When my moustache curled" COR 1

LYDIA HUMPHREY. "Back and forth, back and forth, to and from the church" COR 1

MARGARET FULLER SLACK. "I would have been as great as George Eliot" COR 1

MARIE BATESON. "You observe the carven hand" COR 1

MINERVA JONES. "I am Minerva, the village poetess" COR 1

MRS. BENJAMIN PANTIER. "I know that he told that I snared his soul" COR 1

MRS. CHARLES BLISS. "Reverend Wiley advised me not to divorce him" COR 1

MRS. GEORGE REECE. "To this generation I would say" CAED 82

MRS. MEYERS. "He protested all his life long" COR 1

MRS. PURKAPILE. "He ran away and was gone for a year" CAED 82

NELLIE CLARK. "I was only eight years old" CAED 82

OLLIE MCGEE. "Have you seen walking through the village" COR 1

PAULINE BARRETT. "Almost the shell of a woman after the surgeon's knife" COR 1

PENNIWIT, THE ARTIST. "I lost my patronage in Spoon River" CAED 82

PERCY BYSSHE SHELLEY. "My father who owned the wagon-shop" COR 1

PETER ZOLL. "My thanks, friends of the County Scientific Association" CAED 82

PETIT, THE POET. "Seeds in a dry pod, tick, tick, tick" COR 1

REUBEN PANTIER. "Well, Emily Sparks, your prayers were not wasted" SPOA 90

REV. LEMUEL WILEY. "I preached four thousand sermons" COR 1

ROGER HESTON. "Oh many times did Ernest Hyde and I" CAED 82

ROSCOE PURKAPILE. "She loved me. Oh! how she loved me" CAED 82

ROY BUTLER. "If the learned Supreme Court of Illinois" CAED 82

* Recording not available for analysis

Masters, Edgar Lee (continued)

SEREPTA MASON. "My life's blossom might have bloomed on all sides"   COR 1

STATE'S ATTORNEY FALLAS. "I, the scourge-wielder, balance-wrecker"   CAED 82

TOM MERRITT. "At first I suspected something"   CAED 82

(TOMBSTONE) "Good friends, let's to the fields"   COR 1

THE TOWN MARSHAL. "The Prohibitionists made me Town Marshal"   CAED 82

THE VILLAGE ATHEIST. "Ye young debaters over the doctrine"   COR 1

WILLIAM AND EMILY. "There is something about Death"   COR 1

WILLIE METCALF. "I was Willie Metcalf"   CAED 82

YEE BOW. "They got me into the Sunday-school"   COR 1

Poetry*   LIST 15

Masters, Marcia. in English.
THE COUNTESS OF PERSHING SQUARE.   FOLKW 25
NIGHTFALL.   FOLKW 25

Mata, Pedro. in Spanish.
PANDERETA. "Que beban otros las burbujas"   SMC 5
VAS A VENIR. "Vas a venir, con que ilusión"   SMC 7

Materdona, Gian Francesco Maia. in Italian.
Poetry*   CETRA 24

Mathias, Roland. 1915. in English.
ABSALOM IN THE TREE. "Hey, friend, I have been here a long time"   ARGO 152
CHINON. "The lizards on the wall move"   ARGO 152
DEPARTURE IN MIDDLE AGE. "The hedges are dazed as cock-crow, heaps of leaves"   ARGO 152
NEW LEASE. "It's a dead house, he said. Done for"   ARGO 152
"They have not survived"   ARGO 152

Matiabe, Aruru. in English.
PAST AND PRESENT. "As I sit in despair"   FOLKW 110

Matos Paoli, Francisco. in Spanish.
ENTRE TANTA PRESENCIA DE MUERTOS.   INSTPR 1

Mauriac, François. 1885. in French.
ATYS À CYBÈLE. "La chair encore endormie"   ADES 16, SPOA 62
ATYS CHRÉTIEN. "Mais un dernier venu se coucha"   ADES 16, SPOA 62
ATYS EST CHANGÉ EN PIN. "Trop longtemps j'ai souffert de denouer l'entreinte"   ADES 16, SPOA 62
CYBÈLE ATTEND SON HEURE. "Il faut fermer les yeux, Cybèle"   ADES 16, SPOA 62
PLAINTES DE CYBÈLE. "Ton rire jaillissait, vif entre les eaux vives"   ADES 16, SPOA 62
RENONCEMENT. "Mon corps etait léger au jour naissant des rues"   ADES 16, SPOA 62
SOMMEIL D'ATYS. "Il dort. Je forcerai les dieux même à se taire"   ADES 16, SPOA 62
Poetry*   ADES 51

Maurois, André. 1885. in French.
Poetry*   SPOA 58

Maximianus of Etruria. 6th c. A.D. in Latin.
Poetry*   CETRA 18

Mayakovsky, Vladimir Vladimirovich. 1893. in Russian.
KHOROSHEYE OTNOSHENIYE K LOSHADYAM. "Bili kopyta"   FOLKW 94
OBLAKO V SHTANAKH. "Vashu mysl'"   CAED 193
OTNOSHENIYE K BARYSHNE. "Etot vecher reshal"   FOLKW 94
PASPORT.   FOLKW 95

Mayer, Beatrice. in English.
THE OLD WOMAN IN THE BOMBED CHURCH.   ARGO 143

Maynard, François. 1582. in French.
UNE BELLE VIEILLE, exc.   HACH 9, PERIOD 2

Mayo, E. L. 1904. in English.
WAGON TRAIN.   FOLKW 25

Mazzini, Giuseppe. 1805. in Italian.
L'ADDIO ALLE ALPE.   CETRA 26

Meckel, Christoph. 1935. in German.
ES IST DER WIND AUF DEN BRÜCKEN.   DEUTGR 40A
LANDSCHAFTEN, DIE SIE DURCHFAHREN.   DEUTGR 40A

Medici, Lorenzo de'. 1449. in Italian.
TRIONFO DI BACCO E DI ARIANNA, exc. "Quant'è bella giovinezza"   DOVER 3
Poetry*   CETRA 21

Mehring, Walther. 1896. in German.
AUFTAKT. "Hier steht ein Mann und singt ein Lied"   DEUTGR 9
HEIMAT BERLIN. "Die Linden lang, galopp, galopp"   DEUTGR 9, DEUTGR 36
DIE KLEINEN HOTELS. "Vom Bahnhof angeschwemmt"   DEUTGR 9 DEUTGR 36
MARSEILLE. "Bon jour, Marseille, am Mittelmeer"   DEUTGR 9, DEUTGR 36
ZIEHENDE SCHAFHERDE. "Die Schafe ziehn wie Poeten frisiert"   DEUTGR 9
ZU BEIDEN SEITEN DES ATLANTIK.   DEUTGR 9

Meigs, Mildred Plew. in English.
THE PIRATE DON DURK OF DOWDEE. "Ho, for the Pirate Don Durk of Dowdee"   HARB 6

Meireles, Cecilia. 1901. in Portuguese.
ESTRÊLA. "Quem vin aquêle que se inclinou sôbre palavras trêmulas"   FOLKW 71
EXPLICAÇÃO. "O pensamento é triste; o amor"   FOLKW 71
MOTIVO. "En canto porque o instante existe"   FOLKW 71

Meleager (Meleagros). 60 B.C. in Greek.
HIS EPITAPH. "Quietly O Stranger pass by"   English CARIL 3
PRAYER BEFORE DEATH. "My nurse was the island of Tyre: the land of my birth"   English CARIL 3
STEPHANOS, exc. "O stephanos peri krati marainetai Eliodoras"   FOLKW 104
TO LYKAINIS; A METAPHOR. "Tell her this, Dorkas"   English CARIL 3

Melendez Valdes, Juan. 1756. in Spanish.
EL AMOR MARIPOSA. "Viendo el Amor un dia"   SPOA 37

---

* Recording not available for analysis

Melk, Heinrich von. in German.
"Nu ginc dar, wîp wolgetân" CHRIST 17
Melo Neto, João Cabral de. 1920. in Portuguese.
PREGÃO TURÍSTICO DO RECIFE. "Aqui o mar é uma montanha" FOLKW 71
VALE DO CAPIBARIBE. "Vale do . . . " FOLKW 71
Meltzer, David. 1937. in English.
BLUE RAGS. "Talk of elegance" WATSHD 12
Melville, Herman. 1819. in English.
BILLY IN THE DARBIES. "Good of the Chaplain to enter Lone Bay" CAED 185
THE MALDIVE SHARK. "About the Shark, phlegmatical one" CAED 185
THE MARCH INTO VIRGINIA (JULY 1861). "Did all the lets and bars appear" CMS 14
MISGIVINGS 1860. "When ocean-clouds over inland hills" HOUGHT 5
SHILOH, A REQUIEM. "Skimming lightly, wheeling still" HOUGHT 5
Mendes, Murilo. 1902. in Portuguese.
AMOR-VIDA. "Vivi entre os homens" FOLKW 71
POEMA DO FANÁTICO. "Nâo bebo álcool, nâo tomo ópio nem éter" FOLKW 71
Mendive, Rafael María de. 1821. in Spanish.
LA GOTA DEL ROCÍO. "Cuán bella en la pluma sedosa de un ave" SMC 13
Mendoza, Esther Feliciano. in Spanish.
DECIMA A AGUADILLA. "Aguadilla, cielo y mar, capullo de sol" SMC 9
ESTA NOCHE. INSTPR 1
Mendoza, Fray Iñigo. 1422. in Spanish.
VITA CRISTI. COPLA 101, exc. "Heres niño y as amor" AGUIL 5
Menéndez y Pelayo, Marcelino. 1856. in Spanish.
EPÍSTOLA A HORACIO. "Cuánta imagen fugaz y halagadora" FIDIAS 1
Meng Hau Ran (Men Hao-Jan). 689. in Chinese.
CHWUN SYAU. "Chwun myan bu jywe syan" FOLKW 76
Mercantini, Luigi. 1821. in Italian.
L'INNO DI GARIBALDI. "Si scopron le tombe" CETRA 26
LA SPIGOLATRICE DI SAPRI. "Eran trecento, eran giovani e forti" CETRA 26
Meredith, George. 1828. in English.
BATTLE WAGON. "I see you standing out from the mind's" LIBC 15, LIBC 39
CARRIER. LIBC 15
DIRGE IN WOODS. "A wind sways the pines" SPOA 35
LOVE IN THE VALLEY, exc. "Under yonder beech-tree single on the green-sward" ARGO 63
MELAMPUS. "With love exceeding a simple love of the things" CAED 201
MODERN LOVE. 1. "By this he knew she wept with waking eyes" ARGO 63
———. 2. "It ended, and the morrow brought the task" ARGO 63
———. 3. "This was the woman; what now of the man" ARGO 63
———. 4. "All other joy of life he strove to warm" ARGO 63
———. 7. "She issues radiant from her dressing room" ARGO 63

———. 10. "But where began the change; and what's my crime" ARGO 63
———. 11. "Out in the yellow meadows, where the bee" ARGO 63
———. 13. "I play for seasons, not eternities" ARGO 63
———. 21. "We three are on the cedar-shadowed lawn" ARGO 63
———. 23. "'Tis Christmas weather, and a country house" ARGO 63
———. 25. "You like not that French novel? Tell me why" ARGO 63
———. 30. "What are we first? First, animals; and next" ARGO 63
———. 34. "Madam would speak with me" LONGM 1
———. 43. "Mark where the pressing wind shoots javelin-like" ARGO 63
———. 47. "We saw the swallows gathering in the sky" ARGO 63
———. 48. "Their sense is with their senses all mixed in" ARGO 63
———. 49. "He found her by the ocean's moaning verge" ARGO 63
———. 50. "Thus piteously love closed what he begat" ARGO 63
STRING QUARTET. LIBC 15
TRANSPORT. LIBC 15
Meredith, Owen. See **Bulwer-Lytton, Edward Robert.**
Meredith, William. 1919. in English.
BATTLEWAGON. "I see you standing out from the mind's roadstead" LIBC 15, LIBC 39
CARRIER. "She troubles the waters, and they part and close" LIBC 15, LIBC 39
FOR GUILLAUME APOLLINAIRE. "The day is colorless like Swiss characters in a novel" LIBC 1, SPOA 103
MY ACTS. "The acts of my life swarm down the street like Puerto Rican kids" SPOA 103
THE OPEN SEA. "We say the sea is lonely; better say" LIBC 1, SPOA 103
ROOTS. "Mrs. Leamington stood on a cloud" LIBC 1, SPOA 103
STRING QUARTET. "How learn our way among these mazy strings" LIBC 15, LIBC 39
TRANSPORT. "Now seven days from land the gulls still wheel" LIBC 15, LIBC 39
Merriam, Eve. 1916. in English.
ALLIGATOR ON THE ESCALATOR. "Through the revolving door" CAED 142
BACKWARDS. CAED 142
BAM, BAM, BAM. CAED 142
CATCH A LITTLE RHYME! CAED 142
CHEERS. SCHOL 7
HOW TO EAT A POEM. CAED 111, SCHOL 7
INSIDE THE ZOO. CAED 142
KITTENS. CAED 142
MANNERS. CAED 142
A MATTER OF TASTE. CAED 142
MEAN SONG. CAED 142
METAPHOR. CAED 110
MR. TALL AND MR. SMALL. CAED 142
THE MOTORBOAT SONG. CAED 142
NIGHT SONG. CAED 142
OLLIE'S POLLY. CAED 142
ON OUR WAY. CAED 142

* Recording not available for analysis

Merriam, Eve (continued)

A RHYME IS A JUMP ROPE.	CAED 142
A ROUND. "Spaghetti"	CAED 142
SATELLITE, SATELLITE.	CAED 142
TOASTER TIME.	CAED 142
WHAT IN THE WORLD (RIDDLES).	CAED 142
A YELL FOR YELLOW.	CAED 142
Poetry*	BIGSUR 2

Merrill, James. 1926. in English.

ANNIE HILL'S GRAVE. "Amen. The casket like a spaceship" SPOA 105

THE CURRENT. "Down the dawn brown river" SPOA 105

TIME. "Ever that Everest" SPOA 105

WATCHING THE DANCE. A. BALANCHINE. "Poor savage doubting" SPOA 105

WATCHING THE DANCE. B. DISCOTHEQUE. "Having survived entirely your own youth" SPOA 105

Merriman, Brian. 1740. in Gaelic.

CÚIRT AN MHEADHON OIDHCHE. English SPOA 16

Merwin, W. S. 1927. in English.

ANABASIS. SPOWRD 3

BALLAD OF JOHN CABLE AND THREE GENTLEMEN. "He that had come that morning" SPOWRD 3

BANISHMENT IN WINTER. CAED 127

BEGINNING. "The moon drops one or two feathers into the field" CAED 127

THE BIRDS ON THE MORNING OF GOING. "If I can say yes I" CAED 127

BLIND WILLIAM'S SONG. "Stand from my shadow where it goes" SPOWRD 3

BREAD AND BUTTER. "I keep finding this letter" CAED 127

THE BRIDGES. "Nothing but me is moving" CAED 127

BURNING THE CAT. NACTE 14

CANCIÓN Y GLOSA. "Among the almond trees" SPOWRD 3

CAROL OF THE THREE KINGS. "How long ago we dreamed" SPOWRD 3

THE COLD BEFORE THE MOONRISE. "It is too simple to turn to the sound" CAED 127

DICTUM: FOR A MASQUE OF DELUGE. "There will be the cough before the silence, then" SPOWRD 3

THE DIFFERENT STARS. "I could never have come to the present without you" CAED 127

THE DRUNK IN THE FURNACE. "For a good decade" CAED 127

DUSK IN WINTER. "The sun sets in the cold without friends" CAED 127

EPITAPH ON CERTAIN SCHISMATICS. "These were they whom the body could not please" SPOWRD 3

THE EYES OF THE DROWNED WATCH KEELS GOING OVER. NACTE 14

FLY. "I have been cruel to a fat pigeon" CAED 127

FOR A DISSOLVING MUSIC. "What shall be seen" SPOWRD 3

FOR THE ANNIVERSARY OF MY DEATH. "Every year without knowing it I have passed the day" CAED 127

THE GARDENS OF ZUÑI. "The one-armed explorer" CAED 127

HALF ROUNDEL. "I make no prayer" SPOWRD 3

HERONS. "As I was dreaming between hills" SPOWRD 3

HOW WE ARE SPARED. "At midsummer before dawn" CAED 127

THE LAST ONE. "Well they'd made up their minds to be everywhere because why not" CAED 127

LEMUEL'S BLESSING. "You that know the way" CAED 127

LEVIATHAN. "This is the black sea-brute bulling through wave-wrack" LIBC 40

LOW FIELDS AND LIGHT. "I think it is in Virginia, that place" CAED 127

MENG TZU'S SONG. "The sparrows gleaming gutters" SPOWRD 3

THE MOUNTAIN. "Only on the rarest occasions, when the blue air" CAED 127

MY FRIENDS. "My friends without shields" CAED 127

THE NAILS. "I gave you sorrow" CAED 127

NOAH'S RAVEN. "Why should I have returned" CAED 127

ODYSSEUS. "Always the setting forth was the same" CAED 127

OVER THE BIER OF THE WORLDING. "My friends what can I say" SPOWRD 3

THE PIPER. "It is twenty years" CAED 127

THE PORT. "The river is slow" CAED 127

PROVISION. "All morning with dry instruments" CAED 127

RIME OF THE PALMERS. "Where, and in the morning" SPOWRD 3

THE RIVER OF BEES. "In a dream I returned to the river of bees" CAED 127

THE ROOM. "I think all this is somewhere in myself" CAED 127

THE SAINT OF THE UPLANDS. "Their prayers still swarm" CAED 127

SAINT SEBASTIAN. LIBC 40

SESTINA. "Where I came by torchlight there is dawn-song" SPOWRD 3

THE SIGNALS. "When the ox-horn sounds in the buried hills" CAED 127

SONG. SPOWRD 3

THE STATION. "Two boards with a token roof, backed" CAED 127

TEACHERS. "Pain is in this dark room like many speakers" CAED 127

VARIATION ON A LINE BY EMERSON. "In May, when sea-winds pierced our solitudes" SPOWRD 3

WHEN YOU GO AWAY. "When you go away the wind clicks around to the north" CAED 127

Poetry* LIST 15, MICHM 18

Mesa, E. de. in Spanish.

AUTOSEMBLANZA. "Al amanecer sería" FIDIAS 1

CAMINERA. "Sol de medio día. Castilla se abrasa" FIDIAS 1

Messimanus. in Latin.

Poetry* CETRA 18

---

* Recording not available for analysis

Metastasio (Pietro Antonio Domenico Bonaventura Trapassi). 1698. in Italian.
Poetry*   CETRA 25
Meyer, Augusto. 1902. in Portuguese.
ORAÇÃO AO NEGRINHO DO PASTOREIO. "Negrinho do Pastoreio"   FOLKW 71
Meyer, Conrad Ferdinand. 1825. in German.
MIT ZWEI WORTEN. "Am Gestade Palästinas, auf und nieder, Tag und Nacht"   CHRIST 15
NACHTGERÄUSCHE. "Melde mir die Nachtgeräusche, Muse"   ATHENA 7
DER RÖMISCHE BRUNNEN. "Aufsteigt der Strahl und fallend giesst"   DOVER 1
Meyer, June. See Jordan, June.
Meynell, Alice. 1847. in English.
THE RAINY SUMMER. "There's much afoot in heaven"   CAED 111
THE SHEPHERDESS. "She walks—the lady of my delight"   BRITAM 1
Michelangelo Buonarroti. 1475. in Italian.
A GIOVANNI DA PISTOIA QUANDO L'AUTORE DIPINGEVA LA VOLTA DELLA SISTINA, 1509. "I'ho già fatto un gozzo in questo stento" DOVER 3
"Non ha l'ottimo artista alcun concetto"
                                           SPOA 30
"O nott', O dolce tempo, benchè Nero"
                                           SPOA 30
"Veggio nel tuo bel viso, Signor mio"
                                           DOVER 3
Poetry*   AUDIL 3, CETRA 23
Michaux, Henri. 1899. in French.
CONTRE! "Je vous construirai une ville"
                                           ADES 40
"Dans la nuit"   ADES 40
EMPORTEZ-MOI. "Emportez-moi dans une caravelle"   ADES 40, ADES 54
LE GRAND COMBAT. "Il l'emparouille et l'endosque"   ADES 40
UN HOMME PAISIBLE. "Etendant les mains"
                                   ADES 40, CBS 1
"Mais toi, quand viendras-tu?"   ADES 40
MES OCCUPATIONS. "Je peux rarement voire"
                                           ADES 40
NAUSÉE OU C'EST LA MORT QUI VIENT? "Rends-toi, mon coeur"   ADES 40
REPOS DANS LE MALHEUR. "Le Malheur, mon grand laboureur"   ADES 40
LE VIDE. "Il y souffle un vent terrible"
                                           FOLKW 13
Michie, James. in English.
AT ANY RATE. "He's dead, they shouted"
                                           SPOA 68
DOOLEY IS A TRAITOR. "So then you won't fight"   SPOA 68
Middleton, Christopher. 1926. in English.
DANGERS OF WAKING. "Waking has dangers where children"   ARGO 96
Middleton, Thomas. 1570. in English.
A CHASTE MAID IN CHEAPSIDE, exc. "The founder's come to town"   LONGM 1
Miegel, Agnes. 1879. in German.
DIE MÄR VOM RITTER MANUEL. "Das ist die Mär vom Ritter Manuel"   CHRIST 15
Poetry*   CHRIST 7
Milanés, José Jacinto. 1814. in Spanish.
INVIERNO EN CUBA. "Benigno alumbra el sol; suelto va el río"   SMC 13

Miles, Josephine. 1911. in English.
BELIEF. "Mother said to call her if the H bomb exploded"   SCHOL 2
BLOOM. "The steamfitter comes home in a pink cloud plainly"   SCHOL 2
CONJURE. "I was sitting in what that afternoon I thought to be"   SCHOL 2
DAVID. "Goliath stood up clear in the assumption of status"   SCHOL 2
THE DISTURBED. "They drummed salvation in the darker districts"   SCHOL 2
DRIVER SAYING. "Lady hold your horses, sit down in your seat"   SCHOL 2
EXPECTATION. "Four hundred children expect from one another"   NACTE 14
FRONTIER. "Daniel Boone stepped up to a window"   FOLKW 21
GOVERNMENT INJUNCTION RESTRAINING HARLEM COSMETIC CO. "They say La Jac Brite Pink Skin Bleach avails not"   SCHOL 2
HERALD. "Delivers papers to the doors of sleep"   SCHOL 2
IDEA OF JOY. "The idea of joy, abruptly"
                                           NACTE 14
KIND. "When I think of my kindness which is tentative and quiet"   NACTE 14
MAXIM. "It is said that certain orientational concepts of an"   SCHOL 2
MESSAGE. "Into the side aisle seats flicker the pony tails"   EVERG 1, SCHOL 2
MIDWEEK. "Plentiful people went to the cadillac drawing"   SCHOL 2
ORDERLY. "Hysteric sparks of self in the ward of night"   EVERG 1
PROJECT.   EVERG 1
REASON. "Said, Pull her up a bit will you, Mac, I want to unload"   SCHOL 2
RECEPTION. "When fate from its plane stepped down"   EVERG 1
RIDE. "It's not my world I grant, but I make it"   SCHOL 2
SALE. "Went into a shoestore to buy a pair of shoes"   SCHOL 2
$7.50. "I cannot tell you what a bargain this is"   SCHOL 2
STATUTE. "The way I would look at the world the house"   NACTE 14
THREE STAGES. "When a city undergoes disaster, it moves as a mass"   SCHOL 2
Millay, Edna St. Vincent. 1892. in English.
THE ANGUISH. "I would to God I were quenched and fed"   CAED 23, CAED 71, RCA 7
ASSAULT. "I had forgotten how the frogs must sound"   CAED 23
THE BALLAD OF THE HARP-WEAVER. "Son, said my mother"   CAED 71, HOUGHT 1, RCA 7, RCA 9, SINGER 3
BIOLOGICALLY SPEAKING.   RCA 7
THE BUCK IN THE SNOW.   HOUGHT 3
CAP D'ANTIBES. "The storm is over, and the land has forgotten the storm; the trees are still"   CAED 23
CHILDHOOD IS THE KINGDOM WHERE NOBODY DIES. "Childhood is not from birth to a certain age and at a certain age"   CAED 71
CITY TREES. "The trees along this city street"
                                           CAED 23

* Recording not available for analysis

Millay, Edna St. Vincent (continued)

COUNTING-OUT RHYME. "Silver bark of beech, and sallow"   CAED 109
THE CURSE. "Oh, lay my ashes on the wind"
                                     CAED 23
ELEGY. "Let them bury your big eyes"
                              CAED 71, RCA 7
"Euclid alone has looked on beauty bare"
                                     CMS 12
EXILED. "Searching my heart for its true sorrow"   CAED 71
THE FAWN.   SINGER 1
FOR PAO-CHIN, A BOATMAN ON THE YELLOW SEA.
"Where is he now, in his soiled shirt reeking of garlick"   CAED 71, RCA 7
FROM A VERY LITTLE SPHINX. I. "Come along in then, little girl"   CAED 110
GOD'S WORLD. "O world, I cannot hold thee close enough"   CAED 71
I MUST NOT DIE OF PITY. "I must not die of pity, I must live"   CAED 71
LAMENT.   HOUGHT 5
MORITURUS. "If I could have"   CAED 23
NEW ENGLAND SPRING, 1942. "The rush of rain against the glass"   CAED 23
NOT IN A SILVER CASKET. "Not in a silver casket cool with pearls"   CAED 71
"Oh, sleep forever in the Latmian cave"
                           CAED 71, LIBC 36
THE PARSI WOMAN. "Beautiful Parsi woman in your pale silk veil"   CAED 23
THE PLUM GATHERER. "The angry nettle and the mild"   CAED 23
PORTRAIT BY A NEIGHBOR. "Before she has her floor swept"   CAED 71, CAED 169,
                              HOUGHT 4, RCA 7
RECUERDO. "We were very tired, we were very merry"   CAED 71, LIBC 36, LIST 4,
          RCA 4, RCA 7, SINGER 5, THEAL 2
RENASCENCE. "All I could see from where I stood"   CAED 23, CAED 71, RCA 7
THE RETURN FROM TOWN. "As I sat down by Saddle Stream"   CAED 71
SONNET. 1. "Thou art not lovelier than lilacs, no"   CAED 23
_____ 3. "Mindful of you the sodden earth in spring"   CAED 23
_____ 4. "Not in this chamber only at my birth"   CAED 23
_____ 10. "Oh, think not I am faithful to a vow"   CAED 23
_____ 11. "I shall forget you presently, my dear"   CAED 71
_____ 20. "Let you not say of me when I am old"   CAED 23
_____ 27. "I know I am but summer to your heart"   CAED 23
_____ 71. "This beast that rends me in the sight of all"   CAED 71
_____ 96. "Moon, that against the lintel of the west"   CAED 23
_____ 99. "Love is not all: it is not meat nor drink"   CAED 23, CAED 71, LIBC 36,
                                     RCA 7
_____ 117. "Now by the path I climbed, I journey back"   CAED 23

_____ 123. "Where can the heart be hidden in the ground"   CAED 23, CAED 71
_____ 173. "Now sits the autumn cricket in the grass"   CAED 23
_____ 178. "What rider spurs him from the darkening east"   CAED 23
SORROWFUL DREAMS REMEMBERED. "Sorrowful dreams remembered after waking"
                              CAED 71, RCA 7
SPRING. "To what purpose, April, do you return again"   CAED 23, HOUGHT 5
THE SPRING AND THE FALL. "In the spring of the year, in the spring of the year" CAED 71,
                                  HOUGHT 5
TO THE MAID OF ORLEANS. "Joan, Joan, can you be"   CAED 71, RCA 7
TRAVEL. "The railroad track is miles away"
                              CAED 71, RCA 7
WILD SWANS. "I looked in my heart while the wild swans went over"   CAED 23
Miller, Arthur. in English.
WHAT BLOOD-RED LAW. "What blood-red law"
                                  SPOA 82

Miller, E. Ethelbert. in English.
THE GHOSTSELF OF THE DEAD LECTURER. "The ghostself slips out of the past" WATSHD 5
THE LAND OF SMILES. "I cross the ocean of skeletons"   WATSHD 5
Miller, Joaquin (Cincinnatus Hiner Miller). 1841. in English.
COLUMBUS. "Behind him lay the gray Azores"
                    DECCA 4, HARB 5, SINGER 2
KIT CARSON'S RIDE. "Run? Now you bet you; I rather guess so"   CAED 185
Miller, Mary Britton. 1883. in English.
CAT. "The black cat yawns"   HARB 2
Miller, May. in English.
THE ACQUITTAL. "Now I am freed from the stockade"   WATSHD 8
CALVARY WAY. "How did you feel, Mary"
                                  ARGO 17
FOR A YOUNG FRIEND SEEKING IDENTITY. "I have lost"   WATSHD 5
HISTORY. "Pale as cold moons"   WATSHD 5
Millevoye, Charles-Hubert. 1782. in French.
LE POÈTE MOURANT. "Le poète chantait: de sa lampe fidèle"   HACH 10
Mills, Barriss. 1912. in English.
GONE FOREVER.   SCHOL 7
Milne, Alan Alexander. 1882. in English.
AT THE ZOO. "There are lions and roaring tigers"   CAED 148
BEFORE TEA. "Emmeline"   CAED 148
BINKER. "Binker—what I call him—is a secret of my own"   CAED 148
BUCKINGHAM PALACE. "They're changing the guard at Buckingham Palace" CAED 148
THE CHARCOAL-BURNER. "The charcoal-burner has tales to tell"   CAED 148
CRADLE SONG. "O Timothy Tim"   CAED 148
DISOBEDIENCE. "James James"   CAED 148
THE EMPEROR'S RHYME. "The King of Peru"
                                  CAED 148
THE END. "When I was one"   CAED 148
FORGIVEN. "I found a little beetle, so that Beetle was his name"   CAED 148

* Recording not available for analysis

THE FOUR FRIENDS. "Ernest was an elephant"
CAED 148
FURRY BEAR. "If I was a bear" CAED 109,
CAED 148
THE GOOD LITTLE GIRL. "It's funny how often
they say to me, Jane" CAED 148
HOPPITY. "Christopher Robin goes"
CAED 148
IF I WERE KING. "I often wish I were a King"
CAED 148
THE INVADERS. "In careless patches through the
wood" CAED 148
THE ISLAND. "If I had a ship" CAED 110,
CAED 148
JOURNEY'S END. "Christopher, Christopher,
where are you going" CAED 148
KING JOHN'S CHRISTMAS. "King John was not a
good man" CAED 148
THE KING'S BREAKFAST. "The King asked/ The
Queen" CAED 148
KNIGHT-IN-ARMOUR. "Whenever I am a shining
knight" CAED 148
KNIGHTS AND LADIES. "There is in my old pic-
ture-book" CAED 148
THE LITTLE BLACK HEN. "Berryman and Baxter"
CAED 148
MISSING. "Has anybody seen my mouse"
CAED 148
THE OLD SAILOR. "There was once an old sailor"
CAED 148
POLITENESS. "If people ask me" CAED 148
PUPPY AND I. "I met a man as I went walking"
CAED 148
RICE PUDDING. "What is the matter with Mary
Jane" CAED 148
SNEEZLES. "Christopher Robin/ Had wheezles"
CAED 148
SOLITUDE. "I have a house where I go"
CAED 148
SPRING MORNING. "Where am I going? I don't
quite know" CAED 109, CAED 148
SWING SONG. "Here I go up in my swing"
CAED 148
TEDDY BEAR. "A bear, however hard he tries"
CAED 148
THE THREE FOXES. "Once upon a time there
were three little foxes" CAED 148
TWINKLETOES. "When the sun/ shines"
CAED 109
US TWO. "Wherever I am, there's always Pooh"
CAED 148
VESPERS. "Little boy kneels at the foot of the
bed" CAED 148
WATER-LILIES. "Where the water-lilies go to and
fro" CAED 148
WIND ON THE HILL. "No one can tell me"
CAED 148
Poetry* ARGO 130, ARGO 131
Milosz, Oscar. 1877. in French.
LA BERLINE ARRÊTÉE DANS LA NUIT. "En attend-
ant les clefs" ADES 33
CANTIQUE DU PRINTEMPS. "Le printemps est
revenu de ses lointaines voyages" ADES 33
"Et surtout que Demain n'apprenne pas"
ADES 33
"Grincement doux et rouillé d'une berline"
ADES 33

KAROMAMA. "Mes pensées sont à toi"
ADES 33
LE PONT. "Les feuilles mortes tombent dans
l'air dormant" ADES 33
"Quand elle viendra" ADES 33
"Une rose pour l'amante" ADES 33
SYMPHONIE DE SEPTEMBRE. "Soyez la bienve-
nue" ADES 33
"Tous les morts sont ivres" ADES 33
Milton, John. 1608. in English.
L'ALLEGRO. "Hence, loathèd Melancholy"
ARGO 38, CAED 118, CAED 186,
SPOA 29, SPOA 47
_____, exc. "Haste thee, Nymph, and bring
with thee" LIST 2
ARCADES, exc. "O'er the smooth enamelled
green" LIST 2
AT A SOLEMN MUSIC. "Blest pair of sirens, pledges
of heaven's joy" ARGO 38, LIST 2,
SPOA 29, SPOA 47
COMUS, exc. "Sweet Echo, sweetest nymph that
liv'st unseen" LIST 2
_____, exc. "To the ocean now I fly"
CAED 118
_____, exc. SPOA 47, ARGO 138
LYCIDAS. "Yet once more, O ye laurels, and once
more" ARGO 38, CAED 20, CAED 118,
SPOA 47
_____, exc. "Weep no more, woeful shep-
herds" EAV 11
_____, exc. EAV 6
ON SHAKESPEARE. "What needs my Shakespeare
for his honored bones" CAED 118,
CMS 13, SPOA 47
ON THE MORNING OF CHRIST'S NATIVITY. "This is
the month, and this the happy morn"
ARGO 38, CAED 118, SPOA 47,
ARGO 126
ON TIME. "Fly, envious time, till thou run out
thy race" ARGO 38
PARADISE LOST. BOOK 1, exc. "He spake: and to
confirm his words, out flew" CAED 126
_____ "If thou beest he—but O how fall'n!
how chang'd" LONGM 1
_____ "Is this the Region, this the soil, the
clime" CAED 126
_____ "Of Man's first disobedience, and the
fruit" ARGO 20, ARGO 39, CAED 60,
CAED 184, EAV 11, SPOA 47, LONGM 1
_____ "Princes, Potentates" CAED 126
_____ "But now at last the sacred influence"
ARGO 40
_____ BOOK 2, exc. "Dear Daughter, since thou
claim'st me for thy Sire" CAED 126
_____ "He ceas'd, and next him Moloc, Scep-
ter'd King" CAED 126
_____ "High on a throne of royal state, which
far" ARGO 20, ARGO 40, CAED 192
_____ "Into this wild abyss the wary Fiend"
ARGO 40
_____ "Meanwhile the Adversary of God and
man" ARGO 40
_____ "T'whom Satan turning boldly, thus. Ye
Powers" CAED 126
_____ "Whence and what art thou, execrable
shape" CAED 126

* Recording not available for analysis

Milton, John (continued)

———— BOOK 3, exc. "Hail, holy light, offspring of Heav'n first-born" ARGO 20, ARGO 41, CAED 192, JNP 8, LONGM 1

———— BOOK 4, exc. "But mark what I agreed thee now: Avaunt" ARGO 41

———— "Hail, wedded Love, mysterious law, true source" ARGO 41

———— "O for that warning voice, which he who saw" ARGO 20, ARGO 41, CAED 60, CAED 184

———— "So promised he, and Uriel to his charge" ARGO 41

———— "While thus he spake, th' Angelic squadron bright" LONGM 1

———— BOOK 5, exc. "Now Morn her rosy steps in th' eastern clime" ARGO 20, ARGO 42

———— "Now when ambrosial night, with clouds exhaled" ARGO 42

———— "O alienate from God, O Spirit accurst" ARGO 42

———— "On to their morning's rural work they haste" ARGO 42

———— "Thus when with meats and drinks they had sufficed" ARGO 42

———— BOOK 6, exc. "All night the dreadless angel unpursued" ARGO 20, ARGO 42

———— "And now all heav'n/Had gone to wrack" ARGO 42

———— "He said, and on his son with rays direct" ARGO 42

———— "So spake the Son, and into terror changed" ARGO 42

———— BOOK 7, exc. "Descend from heav'n, Urania, by that name" ARGO 20, ARGO 43

———— BOOK 9, exc. "No more of talk where God or angel guest" ARGO 20, ARGO 43

———— "Thus Eve with count'nance blithe her story told" ARGO 20, ARGO 44

———— BOOK 10, exc. "Meanwhile the heinous and despiteful act" ARGO 20, ARGO 44

———— "O miserable of happy! Is this the end" ARGO 44

———— "Thus Adam to himself lamented loud" ARGO 44

———— BOOK 12, exc. "O prophet of glad tidings, finisher" ARGO 20, ARGO 44

———— "This having learnt, thou hast attained" LONGM 1

PARADISE REGAINED. BOOK 1, exc. "I who erewhile the happy garden sung" ARGO 45

———— "Meanwhile the Son of God, who yet some days" ARGO 45

———— "So spake our Morning Star then in his rise" ARGO 45

———— BOOK 2, exc. "Where will this end? Four times ten days I have passed" ARGO 45

———— BOOK 3, exc. "All things are best fulfilled in their due time" ARGO 45

———— BOOK 4, exc. "Look once more, ere we leave this specular mount" ARGO 45

———— "Perplexed and troubled at his bad success" ARGO 45

———— "Then hear, O son of David, virgin-born" ARGO 45

IL PENSEROSO. "Hence, vain deluding joys" ARGO 38, CAED 118, CAED 186, SPOA 29, SPOA 47

SAMSON AGONISTES, exc. "A little onward lend thy guiding hand" CAED 118, CAED 191

———— "Oh how comely it is, and how reviving" LIST 2

SONNETS. 7. "How soon hath Time, the subtle thief of youth" ARGO 38, CAED 118

———— 8. WHEN THE ASSAULT WAS INTENDED TO THE CITY. "Captain or Colonel, or knight in arms" ARGO 38

———— 13. TO MY FRIEND, MR. HENRY LAWES, ON HIS AIRS. "Harry, whose tuneful and well-measur'd song" ARGO 38

———— 15. ON THE LORD GENERAL FAIRFAX AT THE SIEGE OF COLCHESTER. "Fairfax, whose name in arms through Europe rings" ARGO 38

———— 16. TO THE LORD GENERAL CROMWELL. "Cromwell, our chief of men, who through a cloud" ARGO 38, IMP 1

———— 18. ON THE LATE MASSACRE IN PIEDMONT. "Avenge, O Lord, thy slaughter'd saints, whose bones" ARGO 38, SPOA 29

———— 19. "When I consider how my light is spent" ARGO 38, BRITAM 1, CAED 118, CAED 186, CMS 12, EAV 6, EAV 22, IMP 1, LIST 2, RCA 4, SINGER 6, SPOA 29, SPOA 35, SPOA 47, THEAL 3

———— 20. "Lawrence, of virtuous father virtuous son" ARGO 38

———— 21. "Cyriack, whose grandsire on the royal bench" ARGO 38

———— 22. TO MR. CYRIACK SKINNER UPON HIS BLINDNESS. "Cyriack, this three years' day these eyes, though clear" ARGO 38

———— 23. "Methought I saw my late espoused saint" ARGO 38, EAV 11, SPOA 47

Poetry* BRITAM 2, EAV 6, MICHM 23

Mimnermus of Colophon. 7th century B.C. in Greek.

"Helios men gar ponon ellakhen emata panta" CAED 28

"Tis de bios, ti de terpnon ater khryses Aphrodites" FOLKW 104, JNP 95

Mir, Marjorie. in English.

FOUR DAYS IN NOVEMBER. "In late autumn sun" FOLKW 21

Mistral, Gabriela. 1889. in Spanish.

APEGADO A MI. "Velloncito de mi carne" LIBC 77

ARRULLO PATAGÓN. "Nacieron esta noche" LIBC 77

BALADA. "El pasó con otra" AGUIL 8

BENDICIONES. I. "Bendita mi lengua sea" LIBC 77

———— II. "Bendita seas andando" LIBC 77

LA CAJITA DE OLINALÁ. "Cajita mía" LIBC 77

CANCIÓN QUECHUA. "Donde fue Tihuantisuyo" LIBC 77

LA CASA. "La mesa, hijo, está tendida" LINC 77

EL CORRO LUMINOSO. "Corro de las niñas" FIDIAS 2

DIOS LO QUIERE. "La tierra se hace madrasta" FOLKW 79

DORMIDA. "Meciendo, mi carne" LIBC 77

———

* Recording not available for analysis

ENCARGOS. "Le he rogado al almud de trigo"
LIBC 77
HOMBRECITO. "Madre, cuando sea grande"
FIDIAS 2
INTERROGACIONES. "Cómo quedan, señor"
SMC 6
LA MANCA. "Que mi delito lo cogió una almeja"
LIBC 77
MECIENDO. "El mar sus millares de olas mece"
FIDIAS 2, SMC 15, LIBC 77
MIEDO. "Yo no quiero que a mi niña"
LIBC 77
EL NIÑO SOLO. "Como escuchase un llanto, me
paré en el repecho"   FIDIAS 3, SMC 15
NOCTURNO. "Padre nuestro, que estás en los
cielos"   FIDIAS 2
"País de la ausencia"   LIBC 77
UNA PALABRA. "Yo tengo una palabra en la gar-
ganta"   LIBC 77
RECADO A LOLITA ARRIAGA EN MEXICO. "Lolita
Arriaga, de vejez divina"   LIBC 77
RONDA DE LA CEIBA ECUATORIANA. "En el mundo
está la luz"   LIBC 77
RONDA DE SEGADORES. "Columpiamos el santo"
LIBC 77
EL RUEGO. "Señor, tú sabes cómo, con encen-
dido brío"   FOLKW 80, SMC 1
SONETO DE LA MUERTE. "Del nicho helado en
que los hombres te pusieron"   SMC 15
SUEÑO GRANDE. "A niño tan dormido"
LIBC 77
YO NO TENGO SOLEDAD. "En la noche desam-
paro"   SMC 15

Mitchell, Adrian. 1932. in English.
A CHILD IS SINGING. "A child singing"
SPOA 68
THE DUST. "Singing, as she always must"
ARGO 96
NOSTALGIA—NOW THREEPENCE OFF. "Where are
they now, the heroes"   ARGO 3
PAL. "My bird had a grin like a water melon"
ARGO 3
TIME AND MOTION STUDY. "Slow down the film.
You see that bit"   ARGO 3
VETERAN WITH A HEAD WOUND. "Nothing to show
for it at first"   ARGO 3

Mitchell, Julian. 1935. in English.
HOLIDAY. "When the boys came out of school"
SPOA 68
LAMENT FOR THE COWBOY LIFE. "Where the trails
met"   SPOA 68

Mitchell, Lucy Sprague. in English.
"The house of the mouse"   BOWMAR 1,
HARB 4
"It is raining"   HARB 3

Mitchell, Ruth Comfort. in English.
THE VINEGAR MAN. "The crazy old Vinegar Man
is dead"   CAED 169

Modisane, Bloke. in English.
BLUE BLACK; BLACK BLUES.   CAED 136

Molière, (Jean-Baptiste Poquelin). 1622. in
French.
SONNET D'ORONTE.   HACH 9

Molinari, Ricardo E. 1898. in Spanish.
"El aire desdeñoso"   AGUIL 9

Mon, Franz. 1926. in German.
ERGE EREKT.   LUCHT 1

Monkhouse, Cosmo. 1840. in English.
"There was a young lady of Niger"   EAV 22,
HARB 3
"There was a young lady of Wilts" EAV 22

Monro, Harold. in English.
OVERHEARD ON A SALTMARSH. "Nymph, nymph,
what are your beads"   CAED 164

Montale, Eugenio. 1896. in Italian.
L'ANGUILLA. "L'anguilla, la sirena" DOVER 3
LA CASA DEI DOGANIERI. "Tu non ricordi la casa
dei doganieri"   DOVER 3
CASA SUL MARE. "Il viaggio finisce qui"
CETRA 10
"Ciò che di me sapeste"   CETRA 10
DORA MARCUS. "Fu dove il ponte di legno"
CETRA 10
FALSETTO. "Esterina, i vent'anni ti minacciano"
CETRA 10
"Forse un mattino andando in un'aria de vetro"
CETRA 10
"Meriggiare pallido e assorto"   CETRA 10,
DOVER 3
"Non chiederci la parola che squadri da ogni
lato"   CETRA 10
IL PIRLA.   CETRA 10
LA PRIMAVERA.   EPIU 1
IL RONDONE.   CETRA 10
IL SOGNO DEL PRIGIONERO. "Albe e notti qui
variano per pochi segni"   CETRA 10
"Valmorbia, discarrevano il tuo fondo"
CETRA 10
Poetry*   CETRA 43, CETRA 46

Monti, Vincenzo. 1754. in Italian.
Poetry*   CETRA 27

Montrose, 1st Marquess of (James Graham). 1612.
in English.
"My dear and only. Love, pray"   ARGO 37

Monvel, Mario. in Spanish.
EL ODIO. "Te odio. Lo digo con la unción
enorme"   SMC 7

Moore, Amus. in English.
HIP MEN.   BLACKF 1

Moore, Clement Clarke. 1779. in English.
A VISIT FROM ST. NICHOLAS. "'Twas the night
before Christmas, when all through the
house"   DECCA 11, LION 1

Moore, Honor. 1945. in English.
FIRST TIME, 1950. "In the back bedroom laughing"   WATSHD 14
HOTEL BREAKFAST. "I want no sexual, announces
he"   WATSHD 14

Moore, Marianne. 1887. in English.
THE ARCTIC OX (OR GOAT). "To wear the arctic
fox"   CARIL 10
ARMOUR'S UNDERMINING MODESTY. "At first I
thought a pest"   CAED 24, JNP 1
BIRD-WITTED. "With innocent wide penguin
eyes, three"   CARIL 10
A CARRIAGE FROM SWEDEN. "They say there is a
sweeter air"   CAED 24, HARPV 2, JNP 1
EFFORTS OF AFFECTION. "Genesis tells us of Ju-
bal"   CARIL 10
AN EGYPTIAN PULLED GLASS BOTTLE IN THE SHAPE
OF A FISH.   ARGO 12
A FACE. "I am not treacherous, callous, jealous"
CAED 24, JNP 1

* Recording not available for analysis

Moore, Marianne (continued)

THE FISH. "Wade/ through black jade"
CAED 24

THE FRIGATE PELICAN. "Rapidly cruising or lying on the air there is a bird"   CARIL 10

GRANITE AND STEEL (BROOKLYN BRIDGE). "Enfranchising cable"   SCHOL 8

A GRAVE. "Man looking into the sea"
ARGO 12

HE DIGESTETH HARDE YRON. "Although the aepyornis"   HARPV 2

IN DISTRUST OF MERITS. "Strengthened to live, strengthened to die for"   COLUMB 8,
JNP 1, SPOA 93

IN LIEU OF THE LYRE. "One debarred from enrollment"   HARPV 2

IN THIS AGE OF HARD TRYING NONCHALANCE IS GOOD AND. "In this age of hard trying nonchalance is good and/really, it is not the"
CARIL 10

A JELLYFISH. "Visible, invisible"   CARIL 10

THE LABORS OF HERCULES.   JNP 1

LEONARDO DA VINCI'S. "Saint Jerome and his lion"   CARIL 10, HARPV 2

MELCHIOR VULPIUS. "A Contrapuntalist—composer of chorales"   CARIL 10

THE MIND IS AN ENCHANTING THING. "Is an enchanted thing"   CAED 24, HARPV 2

NEVERTHELESS. "You've seen a strawberry"
CAED 24, UARIZ 1

NINE NECTARINES. "Arranged by two's as peaches are"   CAED 24, JNP 1

O TO BE A DRAGON. "If I, like Solomon"
CARIL 10

THE PANGOLIN. "Another armored animal—scale"   CARIL 10

THE PLUMED BASILISK. "In blazing driftwood"
CARIL 10

POETRY. "I, too, dislike it: there are things that are important beyond all this fiddle"
ARGO 12, UARIZ 1

PROPRIETY. "Is some such word"   CAED 24

RIGORISTS. "We saw reindeer"   CAED 24,
LIBC 5, LIBC 14, JNP 1

SAINT NICHOLAS. "Might I, if you can find it, be given"   CARIL 10

SILENCE. "Self reliance"   ARGO 12, JNP 1

SPENSER'S IRELAND. "Has not altered"
CAED 24, LIBC 5, LIBC 14, LIBC 36

TELL ME, TELL ME. "Where might there be a refuge for me"   HARPV 2

TO A CHAMELEON. "Hid by the august foliage and fruit"   CARIL 10, JNP 1

TO A GIRAFFE. "When plagued by the psychological"   HARPV 2

TO A SNAIL. "If compression is the first grace of style"   HARPV 2

TO A STEAM ROLLER. "The illustration"
CAED 24

VIRGINIA BRITANNIA, exc. "Pale sand edges England's Old"   LIBC 5, LIBC 14

VORACITIES AND VERITIES SOMETIMES ARE INTERACTING. "I don't like diamonds"
CARIL 10, SPOA 93

W. S. LANDOR. *"There/* is someone"   HARPV 2

WHAT ARE YEARS. "What is our innocence"
CAED 24, JNP 1, CAED 183, HARPV 2

WHEN I BUY PICTURES. "Or what is closer to the truth"   JNP 1

THE WOLF AND THE STORK. "Wolves can outeat anyone"   SPOA 93

THE WOODS AND THE WOODMAN. "A woodman chanced to split the ax-haft"   SPOA 93

THE WOOD-WEASEL. "Emerges daintily, the skunk"   CAED 24

Poetry*   LIST 13

Moore, Merrill. 1903. in English.

THE BOOK OF HOW. "After the stars were all hung"   SPOA 97

ENTHUSIASM. "When he returned"   SPOA 97

HOW SHE RESOLVED TO ACT. "I shall be careful to say nothing at all"   SPOA 97

THE NOISE THAT TIME MAKES. "The noise that time makes in passing by"   LIBC 38,
SPOA 97

OLD MEN AND OLD WOMEN GOING HOME ON THE STREET CAR. "Carrying their packages of groceries in particular"   SPOA 97

ON THE GRAND TOUR 1638–1639. "Milton said, I saw the golden chain"   SPOA 97

Poetry*   LIST 14

Moore, Rosalie. 1910. in English.

CATALOGUE.   SCHOL 7

FEAR BY HANGING. "What a battle it did make"
WATSHD 12

LETTER TO BELDEN. "In Saint Louis"
WATSHD 12

VALLEY OF LOIRE. "Reclimbing the plateau"
WATSHD 12

Moore, Thomas. 1779. in English.

"At the mid-hour of night"   SPOA 6

"Believe me if all those endearing young charms"   DECCA 12

CHILD'S SONG.   CAED 202

"The harp that once through Tara's halls"
CAED 202, EAV 8, SPOA 6

"The time I've lost in wooing"   DECCA 12

Moraes, Dom. 1938. in English.

CRAXTON. "Sunlight daubs my eyes"
ARGO 98

JASON. "I was the captain of my ship"
ARGO 98

Morais, Vinicius de. 1913. in Portuguese.

O FALSO MENDIGO. "Minha mãe, manda comprar um quilo"   FOLKW 71

Morales, Jorge L. in Spanish.

CANTO A PUERTO RICO. "Cómo te miro isla"
SMC 9

Moratin, Nicolas Fernandez de. 1737. in Spanish.

EPIGRAM.   Spanish and English CMS 3

Mordaunt, Charles, Earl of Peterborough. 1658. in English.

CHLOE. "I said to my Heart, between sleeping and waking"   ARGO 4

Moréas, Jean (Pappadiamantopoulos). 1856. in French.

FEUILLES D'AUTOMNE.   HACH 1

UNE JEUNE FILLE PARLE.   HACH 1

STANCES. "Ne dites pas: la vie est un joyeux festin"   CAED 204, FOLKW 1

Morel, François. in French

Poetry*   FOLKW 7

* Recording not available for analysis

oreno, Baldomero Fernandez. See **Fernandez Moreno, Baldomero.**

organ, John. in English.
THE SECOND COMING. "I see you"   BROADR 2

organ, Karen. in English.
BILLIONS, ZILLIONS. "Creepin', crawlin' through the night"   WATSHD 8
THE TRUTH ABOUT LITTLE RED RIDING HOOD. "Little Red Riding Hood"   WATSHD 8

organ, Robin. 1941. in English.
THE INVISIBLE WOMAN.   CAED 155

organstern, Christian. 1871. in German.
DER AESTHET. "Wenn ich sitze, will ich nicht"   English CAED 137
DAS AESTHETISCHE WIESEL. "Ein Wiesel"   DEUTGR 29, TELEF 3; English CAED 137
ANTO-LOGY. "Of yore, on earth was dominant"   English CAED 137
"Auf dem Fliegenplaneten"   English CAED 137
DIE BEHÖRDE. "Korf erhält vom Polizeibüro"   TELEF 3; English CAED 137
DIE BEIDEN ESEL. "Ein finstrer Esel sprach einmal"   TELEF 3; English CAED 137
BILDER. "Bilder, die man aufhängt umgekehrt"   English CAED 137
BIM, BAM, BUM. "Ein Glockenton fliegt durch die Nacht"   TELEF 3; English CAED 137
BONA FIDE. "Palmström geht durch eine fremde Stadt"   TELEF 3
DIE BRILLE. "Korf liest gerne schnell und viel"   TELEF 3; English CAED 137
BUNDESLIED DER GALGENBRÜDER. "O schauerliche Lebenswirr"   DEUTGR 29
DAS BUTTERBROTPAPIER. "Ein Butterbrotpapier im Wald"   DEUTGR 29, TELEF 3
CECILY. "For Cecily, the first concern and bother"   English CAED 137
THE CULTURE-INSPIRING PEN. "You are a cultured citizen"   English CAED 137
DENKMALSWUNSCH. "Setze mir ein Denkmal, cher"   English CAED 137
DER EINGEBUNDENE KORF. "Korf lässt sich in einem Folianten einbinden"   English CAED 137
DAS EINHORN. "Das Einhorn lebt von Ort zu Ort"   English CAED 137
EXLIBRIS. "Ein Anonymus aus Tibris"   English CAED 137
GALGENBERG. "Blödem Volke unverständlich"   TELEF 3
GALGENBRUDERS LIED AN SOPHIE, DIE HENKERSMAID. "Sophie, mein Henkersmädel"   DEUTGR 29; English CAED 137
GALGENKINDES WIEGENLIED. "Schlaf, Kindlein, schlaf"   DEUTGR 29
DAS GEBET. "Die Rehlein beten zur Nacht"   TELEF 3; English CAED 137
GEBURTSAKT DER PHILOSOPHIE. "Erschrocken staunt der Heide Schaf mich an"   English CAED 137
GESPENST. "Es gibt ein Gespenst"   TELEF 3
GESPRÄCH EINER HAUSSCHNECKE MIT SICH SELBST. "Soll i aus meim Hause raus?"   English CAED 137

DER GINGGANZ. "Ein Stiefel wandern und sein Knecht"   English CAED 137
DER GLAUBE. "Eines Tags bei Kohlhasficht"   English CAED 137
GLEICHNIS. "Palmström schwankt als wie ein Zweig im Wind"   English CAED 137
GOLCH AND FLUBIS. "Golch and Flubis, these are two"   English CAED 137
DAS GROSSE LALULA. "Kroklokwafzi? Semememi!"   DEUTGR 29
HIMMEL UND ERDE. "Der Nachtwindhund weint wie ein Kind"   TELEF 3
DAS HUHN. "In der Bahnhofshalle, nicht für es gebäut"   TELEF 3; English CAED 137
"Im Reich der Interpunktionen"   TELEF 3; English CAED 137
IM TIERKOSTÜM. "Palmström liebt es, Tiere nachzuahmen"   English CAED 137
KM 21. "Ein Rabe sass auf einem Meilenstein"   TELEF 3
DAS KNIE. "Ein Knie geht einsam durch die Welt"   DEUTGR 29; English CAED 137
DER KORBSTUHL. "Was ich am Tage stumm gedacht"   English CAED 137
"Korf erfindet eine Art von Witzen"   TELEF 3; English CAED 137
DIE KORFSCHE UHR. "Korf erfindet eine Uhr"   English CAED 137
KRONPRÄTENDENTEN. "Ich bin der Graf von Reaumur"   TELEF 3
DIE KUGELN. "Palmström nimmt Papier aus seinem Schube"   DEUTGR 29; English LIBC 1
DIE LÄMMERWOLKE. "Es blökt eine Lämmerwolke"   DEUTGR 29
LÄRMSCHUTZ. "Palmström liebt, sich in Geräusch zu wickeln"   English CAED 137
DER LATTENZAUN. "Es war einmal ein Lattenzaun"   DEUTGR 29, TELEF 3; English CAED 137
LEBENS-LAUF. "Ein Mann verfolgte einen andern"   TELEF 3
DER LEU. "Auf einem Wandkalenderblatt"   TELEF 3; English CAED 137
DIE LUFT. "Die Luft war einst dem Sterben nah"   English CAED 137
DIE MAUSEFALLE. "Palmström hat nicht Speck im Haus"   DEUTGR 29
DIE MITTAGSZEITUNG. "Korf erfindet eine Mittagszeitung"   DEUTGR 29, TELEF 3
DAS MONDSCHAF. "Das Mondschaf steht auf weiter Flur"   English CAED 137
MONDENDINGE. "Dinge gehen vor im Mond"   DEUTGR 29
MOPSENLEBEN. "Es sitzen Möpse gern auf Mauerrecken"   TELEF 3
MÖWENLIED. "Die Möwen sehen alle aus"   DEUTGR 29, TELEF 3
MUHME KUNKEL. "Palma Kunkel ist mit Palm verwandt"   English CAED 137
NACH NORDEN. "Palmström ist nervös geworden"   TELEF 3
DIE NÄHE. "Die Nähe ging verträumt umher"   DEUTGR 29
DAS NASOBEM. "Auf seinen Nasen schreitet"   DEUTGR 29; English CAED 137

* Recording not available for analysis

Morgenstern, Christian (continued)

NATURE SPECTACLE. "A dog"
English CAED 137
NEIN! "Pfeift der Sturm?" TELEF 3;
English CAED 137
PALMSTROEM ADDRESSING A NIGHTINGALE THAT
DID NOT LET HIM SLEEP. "Can't you turn your-
self into a fish" English CAED 137, LIBC 1
PALMSTROM. "Palmström steht an einem
Teiche" TELEF 3; English CAED 137,
LIBC 1
PALMSTRÖM LOBT. "Palmström lobt das
schlechte wetter sehr" TELEF 3
PALMSTRÖMS UHR. "Palmströms Uhr ist andrer
Art" English CAED 137
DER PAPAGEI. "Palma Kunkels Papagei"
English CAED 137
DAS PERLHUHN. "Das Perlhuhn zählt: eins, zwei,
drei, vier" English CAED 137
DAS POLIZEIPFERD. "Palmström führt ein Poli-
zeipferd vor" English CAED 137
DIE PROBE. "Zu einem seltsamen Versuch"
TELEF 3; English CAED 137
PROFESSOR PALMSTRÖM. "Irgendwo im Lande
gibt es meist" TELEF 3
"Der Rabe Ralf" TELEF 3
DER SCHAUKELSTUHL AUF DER VERLASSENEN TE-
RASSE. "Ich bin ein einsamer Schaukelstuhl"
TELEF 3; English CAED 137
SCHICKSAL. "Der Wolke Zickzackzunge
spricht" English CAED 137
DIE SCHILDKRÖKRÖTE. "Ich bin nun tausend
Jahre alt" English CAED 137
DER SCHNUPFEN. "Ein Schnupfen hockt auf der
Terasse" English CAED 137
DER SEUFZER. "Ein Seufzer lief Schlittschuh auf
nächtlichem Eis" TELEF 3
DER SPERLING UND DAS KÄNGURUH. "In seinem
Zaun das Känguruh" English CAED 137
DER STEINOCHS. "Der Steinochs schüttelt
stumm sein Haupt" TELEF 3
DIE TAGNACHTUHR. "Korf erfindet eine Tag-
nachtlampe" English CAED 137
DER TANZ. "Ein Vierviertelschwein und eine
Auftakteule" TELEF 3
DIE TAPETENBLUME. "Tapetenblume bin ich
fein" DEUTGR 29, TELEF 3;
English CAED 137
DER TRAUM DER MAGD. "Am morgen spricht die
Magd ganz wild" English CAED 137
DER TRÄUMER. "Palmström stellt ein Bündel
Kerzen" English CAED 137
DIE UNMÖGLICHE TATSACHE. "Palmström, etwas
schon an Jahren" DEUTGR 29, TELEF 3;
English CAED 137
UNTER ZEITEN. "Das Perfekt und das Imper-
fekt" English CAED 137
VENUS-PALMSTRÖM-ANADYOMENE. "Palmström
wünscht sich manchmal aufzulösen"
English CAED 137
VICE VERSA. "Ein Hase sitzt auf einer Wiese"
TELEF 3; English CAED 137
VOM ZEITUNGLESEN. "Korf trifft oft Bekannte,
die voll von Sorgen" English CAED 137
DER VORGESCHLAFENE HEILSCHLAF. "Palmström
schläft vor zwölf Experten" TELEF 3

DIE WAAGE. "Korfen glückt die Konstruierur
einer" English CAED 1:
DAS WASSER. "Ohne Wort, ohne Wort"
English CAED 1:
DIE WEGGEWORFENE FLINTE. "Palmström find‹
eines Abends" TELEF
English CAED 1:
DER WERWOLF. "Ein Werwolf eines Nachts en
wich" DOVER 1, TELEF
WEST-ÖSTLICH. "Als er dies v. Korf erzählt"
TELEF
WIE SICH DAS GALGENKIND DIE MONATSNAME
MERKT. "Jaguar" English CAED 1:
DIE ZWEI WURZELN. "Zwei Tannenwurzeln gr‹
und alt" English CAED 1:
DER ZWÖLF-ELF. "Der Zwölf-Elf hebt die linl
hand" TELEF
Poetry* CHRIST 5, CHRIST
Mörike, Eduard. 1804. in German.
AN DIE GELIEBTE. "Wenn ich, von deinem A
schaun tief gestillt" DEUTGR
AN EINE ÄOLSHARFE. "Angelehnt an die Efe‹
wand" CHRIST
BEGEGNUNG. "Was doch heut Nacht ein Stur‹
gewesen" CAED 47, DEUTGR
DENK ES, O SEELE. "Ein Tännlein grünet wo"
CHRIST
ER ISTS. "Frühling lässt sein blaues Band"
SPOA 1:
ERINNA AN SAPPHO. "Vielfach sind zum Had‹
die Pfade, heisst ein" CHRIST
GEBET. "Herr! Schicke, was du willt"
CAED ‹
DER GENESENE AN DIE HOFFNUNG. "Tödli‹
graute mir der Morgen" CAED 4
DEUTGR
IDYLLE AM BODENSEE. "Tone, des Schiffman‹
Sohn" CHRIST
IM FRÜHLING. "Hier lieg' ich auf dem Frühlin
shügel" CAED 47, CHRIST
IN DER FRÜHE. "Kein Schlaf noch kühlt das Au‹
mir" SPOA
JOHANN KEPLER. "Gestern, als ich vom nächt
chen Lager den Stern mir im Osten"
CHRIST :
KARWOCHE. "O Woche, Zeugin heiliger Besc
werde" CHRIST
NACHTS. "Horch! auf der Erde feuchte‹
Grunde gelegen" CHRIST
NEUE LIEBE. "Kann auch ein Mensch des an
ern auf der Erde" CHRIST
NIMMERSATTE LIEBE. "So ist die Lieb'! So ist ‹
Lieb'!" CAED ‹
PEREGRINA I. "Der Spiegel dieser treue‹
braunen Augen" CAED 47, DEUTGR
SCHÖNES GEMUT. "Wieviel Herrliches auch ‹
Natur" CHRIST
EIN STÜNDLEIN WOHL VOR TAG. "Derweil i‹
schlafend lag" CHRIST
TROST. "Ja, mein Glück, das lang gewohnte"
DEUTGR
UM MITTERNACHT. "Gelassen stieg die Nacht a‹
Land" ATHENA 6, DEUTGR
DEUTGR ‹
VERBORGENHEIT. "Lass, o Welt, o lass mich sei‹
CAED ‹

* Recording not available for analysis

DAS VERLASSENE MÄGDLEIN. "Früh wann die Hähne krähn"   CHRIST 12, DOVER 1, SPOA 5
WO FIND' ICH TROST. "Eine Liebe kenn' ich, die ist treu"   CHRIST 12
Poetry*   CHRIST 7

Möring, Richard. See **Gan, Peter.**

Morley, Christopher. 1890. in English.
ANIMAL CRACKERS. "Animal crackers, and cocoa to drink"   CAED 164
SMELLS. "Why is it that the poets tell"   HARB 5

Morra, Isabella de. 1520. in Italian.
Poetry*   CETRA 23

Morris, George Pope. 1802. in English.
NEAR THE LAKE. "Near the lake where drooped the willow"   EAV 15
"Woodman, spare that tree"   CAED 100, EAV 15

Morris, James. in English.
THE BLUES. "These are the blues"   ARGO 17

Morris, Mervyn. in English.
LITERARY EVENING JAMAICA. "In a dusty old crumbling building just fit for rats"   CAED 153
TO AN EXPATRIATE FRIEND.   CAED 153
VALLEY PRINCE.   CAED 153

Morris, William. 1834. in English.
EARTHLY PARADISE: PROLOGUE. "Of heaven or Hell"   ARGO 69
IN PRISON. "Wearily, drearily"   ARGO 69
INSCRIPTION FOR A BED AT KELMSCOTT MANOR. "The wind's on the wold"   BRITAM 1
THE MESSAGE OF THE MARCH WIND, exc. "Fair now is the spring-tide, now earth lies beholding"   ARGO 69
OUTLANDERS, WHENCE COME YE, LAST?   LION 1
SHAMEFUL DEATH. "There were four of us about that bed"   ARGO 69, BRITAM 1
SUMMER DAWN. "Pray but one prayer for me 'twixt thy closed lips"   ARGO 69
Poetry*   ARGO 23

Morrow, Charles. in English.
SUNCHANT.   WATSHD 13

Morton, David. in English.
TRAVELLER'S REPORT.   FOLKW 25

Moss, Howard. 1922. in English.
THE FALL. "Where are you going that I want to go"   SPOA 103
IF YOU CAN. "Countryman, tell me if you can"   SPOA 103
SANDS. "Dry. The wind is parched by the wind"   SPOA 103
TOURISTS. "Cramped like sardines on the Queens"   SPOA 103
TRACTION. "His brother said that pain was what he knew"   FOLKW 21
WATER ISLAND. "Finally, from your house, there is no view"   SPOA 103
Poetry*   JNP 38

Moss, Stanley. 1925. in English.
Poetry*   JNP 39

Mostar, Hermann. in German.
IN DIESEM SINN, DEIN ONKEL FRANZ, exc. "Mein lieber Neffe. Ich erfahre"   DEUTGR 36

Motte-Fouqué, Friedrich de La. See **La Motte-Fouqué, Friedrich, Freiherr de.**

Mountzoures, H. L. in English.
THREE NIGHTS OF MOURNING: JOHN F. KENNEDY. "The sea begins, far out beyond the light"   FOLKW 21

Muir, Edwin. 1887. in English.
ADAM'S DREAM. "They say the first dream Adam our father had"   LIBC 42
THE ANIMALS. "They do not live in the world"   LIBC 42
THE CONFIRMATION. "Yes, yours, my love, is the right human face"   LIBC 42
THE DESOLATIONS. "The desolations are not the sorrows' kin"   ARGO 100
THE HORSES. "Barely a twelvemonth after"   FOLKW 64
HORSES. "Those lumbering horses in the steady plough"   LIBC 42
IN LOVE FOR LONG. "I've been in love for long"   LIBC 36, LIBC 42
THE LATE WASP. "You that through all the dying summer"   LIBC 42
ONE FOOT IN EDEN. "One foot in Eden still, I stand"   LIBC 42
THE RIDER VICTORY.   LIBC 36
TELEMACHOS REMEMBERS. "Twenty years, every day"   LIBC 42
TO ANN SCOTT-MONCRIEFF (1914–1943). "Dear Ann, wherever you are"   LIBC 42
TOY HORSE. "See him, the gentle Bible beast"   LIBC 42
THE TWO BROTHERS. "Last night I watched my brothers play"   ARGO 100
Poetry*   LIST 13

Müller, Wilhelm. 1794. in German.
DER LINDENBAUM. "Am Brunnen vor dem Tore"   SPOA 126
DIE WINTERREISE. "Fremd bin ich eingezogen"   CAED 47

Munday, Anthony. 1560. in English.
FEDELE'S SONG. "I serve a mistress whiter than the snow"   ARGO 31

Munkittrick, Richard Kendall. in English.
UNSATISFIED YEARNING.   SCHOL 7

Muñoz Marín, Luis. in Spanish.
YO SOY TU FLAUTA. "Arbol: yo soy tu flauta"   SMC 6

Muñoz Rivera, Luis. in Spanish.
PARENTESIS.   INSTPR 1

Mura, Ettore de. in Italian.
'O CUNTO 'E LL'OVE. "Tutt' e pulle d' 'o cumpare"   CETRA 29

Murciano, Carlos. 1931. in Spanish.
18 DE NOVIEMBRE. "Ellos son enemigos del silencio"   AGUIL 3
EL RELOJ. "Esto de no ser más que tiempo espanta"   AGUIL 3
REQUIEM POR UN HOMBRE. "Hoy se ha acabado Andrés. Vivía era"   AGUIL 3
EL SUICIDA. "Iba saliendo al campo, a la esperanza"   AGUIL 3

Murolo, Ernesto. 1876. in Italian.
IN LICENZA. "Schiattarella Pasquale"   CETRA 29
'O MIERCURI D' 'A MADONNA O CARMENE. "Chiove"   CETRA 29

Muroti, Manuel. in Spanish.
EL DUELO. "¿Cómo fue Señora?"   SMC 6

* Recording not available for analysis

Murphy, Beatrice. 1908. in English.
DEADLINES FOR MIRACLES. "Please send me a
    miracle"   BROADV 15
THE DEMONSTRATORS. "And how will future his-
    tory"   BROADV 15
DISCLAIMER. "Mine is no Southern tradition"
                                BROADV 15
EVEN AMONG THIEVES. "I could forgive you"
                                BROADV 15
NEGRO CHOIR. "Sing your song to Jesus"
                                BROADV 15
OBITUARY. "The assassin dealt America"
                                BROADV 15
PLEDGE OF ALLEGIANCE. "I will walk all day with
    you"   BROADV 15
SIGNS.   FOLKW 6
THEY SAY. "They say: Black women are primi-
    tive"   BROADV 15
TO ANY NEGRO YOUTH. "I am the Uncle Tom"
                                BROADV 15
W A C. "There's nothing quite so beautiful"
                                BROADV 15
WE ARE NOT ALONE. "Mama! Mama! Tell me"
                                BROADV 15
Musset, Alfred de. 1856. in French.
À GEORGE SAND. I. "Te voilà revenu, dans mes
    nuits étoilées"   ADES 9, ADES 48
À GEORGE SAND. III. "Puisque votre moulin
    tourne avec tous les vents"   ADES 54
À GEORGE SAND. V. "Il faudra bien t'y faire à
    cette solitude"   ADES 9
À GEORGE SAND. VII. "Porte ta vie ailleurs, ô toi
    qui fus ma vie"   ADES 9
À JULIE. "On me demande, par les rues"
                            ADES 48, ADES 54
À NINON. "Si je vous le disais pourtant"
                            ADES 9, HACH 12
ANGE ÉTERNEL DES NUITS HEUREUSES.   ADES 9
BALLADE À LA LUNE. "C'était, dans la nuit
    brune"   ADES 9, ADES 48
LA CHANSON DE FORTUNIO. "Si vous croyez que
    je vais dire"   ADES 9, ADES 41, SPOA 36
ELÉGIE.   ADES 41
L'ETOILE DU SOIR.   ADES 48
"J'ai dit à mon coeur"   HACH 12
NAMOUNA. "Le sofa sur lequel Hassan était
    couché"   ADES 41
LA NUIT D'AOÛT. "Depuis que le soleil, dans
    l'horizon immense"   ADES 41, HACH 12
LA NUIT DE DÉCEMBRE. "Du temps que j'étais
    écolier"   ADES 41, HACH 12
LA NUIT DE MAI. "Poëte, prends ton luth et me
    donne un baiser"   ADES 9, ADES 48,
                                    GMS 9
Ô CIEL! JE VOUS REVOIS MADAME.   ADES 9
LE RIDEAU DE MA VOISINE.   ADES 41
ROLLA. "Regrettez-vous le temps où le ciel sur
    la terre"   ADES 41
UNE SOIRÉE PERDUE. "J'étais seul, l'autre soir, au
    Théâtre-Français"   ADES 41
SONNET.   ADES 9, ADES 41
SOUVENIR, exc. "J'espérais bien pleurer, mais je
    croyais souffrir"   HACH 12
SURE UNE MORTE. "Elle était belle, si la Nuit"
                                    DOVER 4
TRISTESSE. "J'ai perdu ma force et ma vie"
        CAED 204, GMS 7, HACH 12, SPOA 9

Poetry*   HACH 6
Myers, Neil. in English.
KENNEDY POEM. "The shot, the horse"
                                    FOLKW 21

Nabokov, Vladimir. 1899. in English.
THE BALLAD OF LONGWOOD GLEN. "That Sunday
    morning, at half past ten"   SPOA 52
A DISCOVERY. "I found it in a legendary land"
                                    SPOA 52
AN EVENING OF RUSSIAN POETRY. "The subject
    chosen for tonight's discussion" SPOA 52
LINES WRITTEN IN OREGON. "Esmeralda! Now we
    rest"   SPOA 52
ON TRANSLATING "EUGENE ONEGIN". "What is
    translation? On a platter"   SPOA 52
RAIN. "How mobile is the bed on these"
                                    SPOA 52
THE SWIFT.   SPOA 52
Nalé-Roxlo, Conrado. 1898. in Spanish.
CANCIÓN DE GUIA. "Hay que andar por el mun-
    do"   AGUIL 9
LO IMPREVISTO. "Señor, nunca me des lo que te
    pida"   FOLKW 80
Namatianus, Rutilius Claudius. 400 A.D. in Latin.
Poetry*   CETRA 18
Napier, Winston. in English.
CYCLE NUMBER ONE. "Hear laughs and cries"
                                    WATSHD 8
THE DANCER. "She flies"   WATSHD 8
Nash, Ogden. 1902. in English.
THE ABSENTEES. "I'd ride a cock horse to Ban-
    bury Cross"   CAED 123
ADMONITORY LINES FOR THE BIRTHDAY OF AN
    OVERENERGETIC CONTEMPORARY. "Lord, the
    calendar is droll"   CAED 134
ADVENTURES OF ISABEL. "Isabel met an enor-
    mous bear"   CAED 123, THEAL 3
AFTER THE CHRISTENING. "Come along, every-
    body, see the pretty baby"   CAED 123
ALL GOOD AMERICANS GO TO LAROUSSE, OR, I DON'T
    PRETEND TO BE MOLIÈRE THAN THOU. "I reckon
    it is nearly fifty years to the day"
                                    CAED 134
ALLOW ME, MADAM, BUT IT WON'T HELP. "Adorable
    is an adjective"   ARGO 16, CAED 16,
                                    COLUMB 8
ALL'S BRILLIG IN TIN PAN ALLEY. I. I SAW EUTERPE
    KISSING SANTA CLAUS. "Thomas Lovell
    Beddoes inquired, If there were dreams to
    sell, what would you buy?"   RCA 3
ALL'S BRILLIG IN TIN PAN ALLEY. II. GOOD NIGHT,
    SWEET MIND. "May I remark, at the risk of
    being called an egghead or New Dealer"
                                    RCA 3
AN UNTOLD ADVENTURE OF SANTA CLAUS.
                                    CAED 138
ANYBODY FOR MONEY. "Consider the banker"
                                    RCA 3
THE AQUARIUM. "Some fish are minnows"
                                    COLUMB 9
ARABIAN DANCE.   CAED 138
AS I WAS SAYING TO ST. PAUL JUST THE OTHER DAY.
    "Opsimathy, says my dictionary, opsimathy is
    learning acquired late"   RCA 3
THE ASP. "Whenever I behold an asp"
                                    CAED 134

* Recording not available for analysis

AVANT GUARD.   RCA 3

THE AXOLOTL. "I've never met an axolotl"
                                CAED 123, RCA 3

BANKERS ARE JUST LIKE ANYBODY ELSE, EXCEPT
RICHER. "This is the song to celebrate banks"
                                CAED 16, DECCA 2

BEEP, BEEP. "When comes my second child-
hood"   ARGO 16

A BEGINNER'S GUIDE TO THE OCEAN. "Let us now
consider the ocean"   CAED 16

THE BIRDS. "Puccini was Latin, and Wagner
Teutonic"   COLUMB 9

THE BOY WHO LAUGHED AT SANTA CLAUS. "In Baltimore there lived a boy"   CAED 123,
                                                CAED 138

BRIEF LIVES IN NOT SO BRIEF. "John Aubrey had a
nose for news"   LIBC 1, RCA 3

THE BUSES HEADED FOR SCRANTON. "The buses
headed for Scranton travel in pairs"
                                CAED 123, RCA 3

THE CALF. "The calf is born with prospects
grim"   CAED 123

THE CAMEL. "The camel has a single hump"
                                                CAED 123

THE CANARY. "The song of canaries"
                                                CAED 123

THE CANTALOUPE. "One cantaloupe is ripe and
lush"   CAED 123

THE CARAJOU AND THE KINCAJOU. "They tell me
of a distant zoo"   CAED 123, RCA 3

CARNIVAL OF THE ANIMALS. GRAND FINALE. "Now
we reach the grand finale"   COLUMB 9

CARNIVAL OF THE ANIMALS. INTRODUCTION. "Camille St. Saens was racked with pains"
                                                COLUMB 9

A CAROL FOR CHILDREN. "God rest you merry,
Innocents"   CAED 138

CAT NAPS ARE TOO GOOD FOR CATS. "Oh, early
every afternoon"   CAED 134

THE CATERPILLAR. "I find among the poems of
Schiller"   CAED 123

A CAUTION TO EVERYBODY. "Consider the auk"
                                COLPIX 1, RCA 3

CELERY. "Celery, raw"   CAED 123

THE CENTIPEDE. "I objurgate the centipede"
                                                CAED 123

CHILDREN'S PARTY. "May I join you in the dog
house, Rover?"   CAED 123, THEAL 1

A CHILD'S GUIDE TO PARENTS. "Children, I crave
your kind forbearance"   CAED 123

CHINESE DANCE.   CAED 138

THE CHRISTMAS THAT ALMOST WASN'T.
                                                CAED 138

COCKS AND HENS. "The rooster is a roistering
hoodlum"   COLUMB 9

COME, COME, KEROUAC, MY GENERATION IS BEATER
THAN YOURS. "My dictionary defines progress
as an advance toward perfection"   RCA 3

THE COMMON COLD. "Go hang yourself, you old
M.D."   DECCA 2

THE COW. "The cow is of the bovine ilk"
                                CAED 123, HARC 2

THE CRICKET. "I love to hear a cricket in my
house"   CAED 134

CROSSING THE BORDER. "Senescence begins"
                                CAED 134, RCA 3

THE CUCKOO IN THE WOODS. "Cuckoos lead
Bohemian lives"   COLUMB 9

THE DARKEST HALF HOUR, OR, TOO EARLY IS THE
TIME FOR ALL GOOD GUESTS TO COME TO THE AID
OF THE PARTY. "They are ready for their
party"   CAED 134

THE DOG. "The truth I do not stretch or shove"
                                                CAED 123

"Don't be cross, Amanda"   CAED 123

DON'T GRIN, OR YOU'LL HAVE TO BEAR IT. "It is better in the long run to posses an abcess or a
tumor"   CAED 16

DON'T LOOK NOW, BUT THERE'S SOMETHING BEHIND
THE CURTAIN. "Life is more exciting for
greenhorns than for tired-eyed old fogies"
                                                RCA 3

THE DROP OF A HAT. "Darling, what is that"
                                                DECCA 2

THE DUCK. "Behold the duck"   CAED 123,
                                HARC 2, SINGER 4

THE EEL. "I don't mind eels"   CAED 123

ELEPHANTS. "Elephants are useful friends"
                                                COLUMB 9

EPISTLE.   LIST 4

EPISTLE TO THE OLYMPIANS. "Dear Parents, I
write you this letter"   SINGER 1

THE EVENING OUT. "You have your hat and coat
on and she says she will be right down"
                                                CAED 16

EVERYBODY TELLS ME EVERYTHING. "I find it very
difficult to enthuse"   RCA 3

EXIT, PURSUED BY A BEAR. "Chipmunk chewing
the Chippendale"   CAED 134, RCA 3

EXPERIMENT DEGUSTATORY. "A gourmet challenged me to eat"   CAED 123

THE FIREFLY. "The firefly's flame"   CAED 123

THE FLUTES.   CAED 138

THE FLY. "God in his wisdom made the fly"
                                                CAED 123

FOR A GOOD DOG. "My little dog ten years ago"
                                                RCA 3

FT. WORTH. "A chuckling tycoon of Fort Worth"
                                                RCA 3

THE FOSSILS. "At midnight in the museum hall"
                                                COLUMB 9

FOUR LIMICKS. "A cook named McMurray"
                                                CAED 134

_____ "An old person of Troy"   CAED 134

_____ "Three young Tennesseans"
                                                CAED 134

_____ "Two nudists of Dover"   CAED 134

THE GANDER. "Be careful not to cross the gander"   CAED 123

GEDDONDILLO. "The sharrot scudders nights in
the quastron now"   CAED 16

THE GERM. "A mighty creature is the germ"
                                                CAED 123

GOOD-BYE, OLD YEAR, YOU OAF, OR, WHY DON'T
THEY PAY THE BONUS? "Many of the three hundred and sixty-five days of the year are fol-
lowed by dreadful nights but one night is by
far, oh yes, by far the worst"   CAED 16

GOODY FOR OUR SIDE AND YOUR SIDE TOO. "Foreigners are people somewhere else"
                                                SINGER 3

GRANDPA IS ASHAMED. "A child need not be very
clever"   CAED 123

* Recording not available for analysis

Nash, Ogden (continued)

THE GUPPY. "Whales have calves" CAED 123, HARC 2

THE HIPPOPOTAMUS. "Behold the hippopotamus" CAED 123

HOW CAN ECHO ANSWER WHAT ECHO CANNOT HEAR? "Why shouldn't I laud my love?" CAED 134, RCA 3

HOW DO YOU SAY 'HA-HA' IN FRENCH. "There are several people who I can claim I am glad I am not, without being accused of pride and effrontery" CAED 16

HOW TO BE MARRIED WITHOUT A SPOUSE, OR MR. KIPLING, WHAT HAVE YOU DONE WITH MRS. HAUKSBEE? "Do any of you old fogies remember Mrs. Hauksbee?" RCA 3

THE HUNTER. "The hunter crouches in his blind" CAED 123, COLUMB 8, RCA 3

THE HUSBAND'S COMMENT. DECCA 2

I DO, I WILL, I HAVE. "How wise I am to have instructed the Butler" ARGO 16, CAED 16, LIBC 1, SPOA 97, ARGO 139

I DON'T MEAN US, EXCEPT OCCASIONALLY. "I know a man who when he bares his breast to life it comes back to him all covered with welts" CAED 16

I HAVE IT ON GOOD AUTHORITY. "There are two kinds of people who blow through life like a breeze" DECCA 2

I KNOW EXACTLY WHO DROPPED THE OVERALLS IN MRS. MURPHY'S CHOWDER. "I know a man named Mr. Nagle" RCA 3

I NEVER EVEN SUGGESTED IT. "I know lots of men who are in love and lots of men who are married" LIBC 38, RCA 3

I REMEMBER YULE. "I guess I am just an old fogey" CAED 16, CAED 138

I WILL ARISE AND GO NOW. "In far Tibet" CAED 123, COLPIX 1, RCA 3

IF HE WERE ALIVE TODAY, MAYHAP, MR. MORGAN WOULD SIT ON THE MIDGET'S LAP. "When comes my second childhood" CAED 134

ILL MET BY FLUORESCENCE. "I know a dance, a perilous dance" ARGO 16, RCA 3

I'M A PLEASURE TO SHOP FOR. "Mine is a dauntless spirit, meaning a spirit that is hard to daunt" CAED 138

THE INDIVIDUALIST. "Once there was a man named Jarvis Gravel" DECCA 2

AN INTRODUCTION TO DOGS. "The dog is man's best friend" CAED 123

INTROSPECTIVE REFLECTION. "I would live all my life in nonchalance and insouciance" COLUMB 8

ISN'T NATURE WONDERFUL. DECCA 2

JACK DO-GOOD-FOR-NOTHING, A CURSORY NURSERY TALE FOR TOT-BAITERS. "Once there was a kindhearted lad named Jack Do-Good-for-Nothing" CAED 134

THE JELLYFISH. "Who wants my jellyfish?" CAED 123, HARC 2

JOHN PEEL—SHAKE HANDS WITH 37 MAMAS. "Oh, blithe it is to bless the hounds" RCA 3

JUST KEEP QUIET AND NOBODY WILL NOTICE. "There is one thing that ought to be taught in all colleges" DECCA 2

KANGAROOS. "The kangaroo can jump incredible" COLUMB 9

KIND OF AN ODE TO DUTY. "O Duty" CAED 16

KINDLY UNHITCH THAT STAR, BUDDY. "I hardly suppose I know anybody who wouldn't rather be a success" HOUGHT 5

THE KITTEN. "The trouble with a kitten is that" CAED 123, HARC 2

LADY OF NATCHEZ. RCA 3

THE LAMB. "Little gamboling lamb" CAED 123

LAMENTS FOR A DYING LANGUAGE. "In the nice-minded Department of Prunes and Prisms" LIBC 1

LAMENTS FOR A DYING LANGUAGE. "What's the monster of this week" CAED 134

LINE TO BE EMBROIDERED ON A BIB, OR, THE CHILD IS FATHER OF THE MAN, BUT NOT FOR QUITE A WHILE. "So Thomas Edison" CAED 134

LINES TO A WORLD-FAMOUS POET WHO FAILED TO COMPLETE A WORLD-FAMOUS POEM, OR, COME CLEAN, MR. GUEST! "Oft when I am sitting without anything to read waiting for a train in a depot" RCA 10

THE LION. "Oh, weep for Mr. and Mrs. Bryan" HARC 2

LOOK WHAT YOU DID, CHRISTOPHER. "In fourteen hundred and ninety-two" SINGER 5

A MAN CAN COMPLAIN, CAN'T HE. "Pallid and moonlike" RCA 3

MS FOUND UNDER A SERVIETTE IN A LOVELY HOME. "Dear Cousin Nancy" RCA 1

MEDUSA AND THE MOT JUSTE. "Once there was a Greek divinity of the sea named Ceto" CAED 16, RCA 3

THE MIRACULOUS COUNT-DOWN. "Let me tell you of Dr. Faustus Foster" CAED 138

MR. BETT'S MIND A KINGDOM IS. "Do you know my friend Mr. Betts?" CAED 16

THE MULES. "In the world of mules" COLUMB 9

MY CHILD IS PHLEGMATIC—ANXIOUS PARENT. "Anxious Parent, I guess you have just never been around" CAED 123, CAED 134

NO DOCTORS TODAY, THANK YOU. "They tell me that euphoria is the feeling of feeling wonderful" ARGO 16

NUTCRACKER SUITE. CAED 138

THE NYMPH AND THE SHEPHERD, OR, SHE WENT THAT-A-WAY. "Few things are less endearing than a personal comparison" CAED 134, RCA 3

O TEMPORA, OH-OH. "The sober journal that I read" RCA 3

THE OCTOPUS. "Tell me, O Octopus, I begs" CAED 123

OH, PLEASE DON'T GET UP. "There is one form of life to which I unconditionally surrender" COLPIX 1

ONE THIRD OF A CALENDAR. "In January everything freezes" DECCA 2

ONE WESTERN, TO GO. "I know a lady, name of Blanche" CAED 134

THE OUTCOME OF MR. MCLEOD'S GRATITUDE "When Thanksgiving came twice, who walked so proud" COLUMB 8

THE PANTHER. "The panther is like a leopard" CAED 123

THE PARENT. "Children aren't happy with nothing to ignore" CAED 134

PEDIATRIC REFLECTIONS. "Many an infant that screams like a calliope" CAED 123

PEEKABOO, I ALMOST SEE YOU. "Middle-aged life is merry, and I love to lead it" SPOA 97

THE PERFECT HUSBAND. "He tells you when you've got on too much lipstick" COLUMB 8, RCA 3

THE PIANISTS. "Some claim that pianists are human" COLUMB 9

PIANO TUNER, UNTUNE ME THAT TUNE. "I regret that before people can be reformed they have to be sinners" CAED 16, SPOA 97

THE PIG. "The pig, if I am not mistaken" CAED 123

THE PIONEER. "I seek in anonymity's cloister" CAED 134

THE PIZZA. "Look at itsy-bitsy Mitzi" CAED 134

PLEASE PASS THE BISCUIT. "I have a little dog" CAED 123

THE POLTERGUEST, MY POLTERGUEST. "I've put Miss Hopper upon the train" CAED 16

THE PORCUPINE. "Any hound a porcupine nudges" HARC 2

PORTRAIT OF THE ARTIST AS A PREMATURE OLD MAN. "It is common knowledge to every schoolboy and even every Bachelor of Arts" CAED 16, LIBC 38

A POTTED WATCH NEVER BOILS, OR, MAYBE THAT'S WHAT THEY'VE BEEN TRYING TO PROVE. "You blow yourself to a handsome watch" CAED 134

THE POULTRIES. "Let's think of eggs" CAED 123

A PRINCESS. "A princess who lived near a bog" RCA 3

THE PRIVATE DINING ROOM. "Miss Rafferty wore taffeta" ARGO 16, COLPIX 1, LIBC 1, SPOA 97

THE PURIST. "I give you now Professor Twist" ARGO 16, CAED 123, RCA 3, SINGER 4

THE RABBITS. "Here's a verse about rabbits" CAED 123

REFLECTION ON A WICKED WORLD. "Purity" CAED 134

REFLECTION ON BABIES. "A bit of talcum" CAED 123

REFLECTIONS ON ICE-BREAKING. "Candy" CAED 134

REFLECTIONS ON INGENUITY. "Here's a good rule of thumb" CAED 134

THE RHINOCEROS. "The Rhino is a homely beast" CAED 123, HARC 2, THEAL 3

RODENT. "A handsome young rodent named Gratian" RCA 3

ROLL ON, THOU DEEP AND DARK BLUE SYLLABLES, ROLL ON. "Like Stephen Vincent Benet, I have fallen in love" CAED 134

ROYAL MARCH OF THE LIONS. "The lion is the king of beasts" COLUMB 9

RUSSIAN DANCE. CAED 138

SAMSON AGONISTES. "I test my bath before I sit" ARGO 16, RCA 3

THE SEA-GULL. "Hark to the whimper of the sea-gull" CAED 123, LIBC 38

SEASIDE SERENADE. "It begins when you smell a funny smell" DECCA 2

THE SHORT ORDER COCKTAIL, OR, ONE COOK TO TAKE OUT. "Once there was a couple named Mr. and Mrs. Plackett" CAED 134

THE SHREW. "Strange as it seems, the smallest mammal" CAED 123

THE SHRIMP. "A shrimp who sought his lady shrimp" CAED 123, LIBC 1

THE SKINK. "Let us do justice to the skink" CAED 123

SO I RESIGNED FROM THE CHUCHIN CHOWDER AND MARCHING CLUB. "The thing about which I know the least" RCA 3

SO PENSEROSO. "Come, megrims, mollygrubs and colly wobbles" ARGO 16, COLUMB 8, RCA 3

THE SOLITUDE OF MR. POWERS. "Once there was a lonely man named Mr. Powers" CAED 134

SONG FOR A TEMPERATURE OF A HUNDRED AND ONE. "Of all God's creatures give me man" CAED 16

SONG OF THE OPEN ROAD. "I think that I shall never see" CAED 134

SOPRANO. "A thrifty soprano of Hingham" RCA 3

SPRING COMES TO MURRAY HILL. "I sit in an office at 244 Madison Avenue" CAED 16

SPRING SONG. "Listen, buds, it's March twenty-first" CAED 16

THE SQUIRREL. "A squirrel to some is a squirrel" CAED 123

THE STILLY NIGHT: A SOPORIFIC REFLECTION. "There is one source of marital discord so delicate that" CAED 134, RCA 3

THE STRANGE CASE OF MR. DONNYBROOK'S BOREDOM. "Once upon a time there was a man named Mr. Donnybrook" CAED 123

THE STRANGE CASE OF MR. ORMANTUDE'S BRIDE. "Once there was a bridegroom named Mr. Ormantude whose intentions were hard to disparage" CAED 16

THE STRANGE CASE OF MRS. MOODUS'S SECOND HONEYMOON (OR, HOW TO UNOBSTREPERIZE A HUSBAND). "Once there was a man named Mr. Rory Moodus" ARGO 16, CAED 134

THE STRANGE CASE OF THE CAUTIOUS MOTORIST. "Have you read the biography of Mr. Schwellenbach?" CAED 123, SPOA 97

THE STRANGE CASE OF THE ENTOMOLOGIST'S HEART. "Consider the case of Mr. Suggs" RCA 3

THE STRANGE CASE OF THE IRKSOME PRUDE. "Once upon a time there was a young man named Harold Scrutiny" CAED 134

SUGARPLUM DANCE. CAED 138

THE SUNSET YEARS OF SAMUEL SHY. "Master I may be" CAED 134

THE SWAN. "The swan can swim while sitting down" COLUMB 9

TABOO TO BOOT. "One bliss for which" CAED 123

THE TALE OF CUSTARD THE DRAGON. "Belinda lived in a little white house" THEAL 1

* Recording not available for analysis

Nash, Ogden (continued)

THE TERMITE. "Some primal termite knocked on wood" CAED 123

THE TERRIBLE PEOPLE. "People who have what they want are very fond of telling" CAED 16, RCA 3

THAT REMINDS ME. "Just imagine yourself seated on a shadowy terrace" CAED 16

THOUGHTS THOUGHT AFTER A BRIDGE PARTY. "All women are pets" CAED 16

THOUGHTS THOUGHT WHILE WAITING FOR A PRONOUNCEMENT FROM A DOCTOR, AN EDITOR, A BIG EXECUTIVE, THE DEPARTMENT OF INTERNAL REVENUE OR ANY OTHER MOMENTOUS PRONOUNCER. "Is time on my hands? Yes it is, it is on my hands and my face and my torso and my tendons of Achilles" RCA 3

TRAVELER'S REST. "I know a renegade hotel" DECCA 2

TRY IT SUNS. AND HOLS.—IT'S CLOSED THEN. "I know a little restaurant" RCA 3

TUNE FOR AN ILL-TEMPERED CLAVICORD. "Oh, once there lived in Kankakee" COLPIX 1, LIBC 1, RCA 3, SPOA 97

THE TURKEY. "There is nothing more perky" CAED 123

THE TURTLE. "The turtle lives 'twixt plated decks" CAED 123

TURTLES. "Come crown my brow with leaves of myrtle" COLUMB 9

TWEEDLE DEE AND TWEEDLE DOOM. "Said the undertaker to the overtaker" RCA 3

TWO AND ONE ARE A PROBLEM. "Dear Miss Dix, I am a young man of half-past thirty-seven" DECCA 2

UMPIRE. "There once was an umpire whose vision" RCA 3

UNFORTUNATELY, IT'S THE ONLY GAME IN TOWN. "Often I think that this shoddy world would be more nifty" CAED 134, RCA 3

VERY FUNNY, VERY FUNNY. "In this foolish world there is nothing more numerous" CAED 134

VERY LIKE A WHALE. "One thing that literature would be greatly the better for" HOUGHT 4

THE WALTZ OF THE FLOWERS. CAED 138

WATCHMAN, WHAT OF THE FIRST FIRST LADY. "Everybody can tell you the date of George Washington's birth" CAED 16

WE WOULD REFER YOU TO OUR SERVICE DEPARTMENT IF WE HAD ONE. "It fills me with elation" SPOA 97

WE'RE FINE, JUST FINE. "Some people slowly acquire a healthy glowing complexion" ARGO 16

WHAT, NO SHEEP? "I don't need no sleepin' medicine" CAED 134, LIBC 1, RCA 3

WHAT TO DO UNTIL THE DOCTOR GOES, OR IT'S TOMORROW THAN YOU THINK. "Oh hand me down my old cigar with its Havana wrapper and its filling of cubeb" CAED 16

WHILE HOMER NODDED: A FOOTNOTE TO THE ILIAD. "In the days when the hollow ships of the well-greaved" CAED 134

WILD JACKASS. "Have you ever harked to t jackass wild" COLUMB

WILL CONSIDER SITUATION. "These here a words of radical advice for a young man" SINGER

A WORD TO HUSBANDS. "To keep your marria brimming" CAED 134, RCA

YOU AND ME AND P. B. SHELLEY. "What is life? L is stepping down a step or sitting on a cha ARGO 16, CAED

YOU'LL DRINK YOUR ORANGE JUICE AND LIKE "There is a Cyprus Citrus surplus" ARGO 16, RCA

Poetry* CAED 3, LIST 14, NET

Nashe, Thomas. 1567. in English.

AUTUMN. "Autumn hath all the summer's fru ful treasure" IMF

IN PLAGUE TIME. "Adieu, farewell earth's blis ARGO 31, BRITAM 2, POLYGL 2, SPOA SPOA 83, LONGM

"Spring, the sweet spring" CAED 1 IMP 1, ARGO 1

Nasibu. in Swahili.

"Bwana wangu kajisafiria" SCHOL

Nathan, R. 1894. in English.

DUNKIRK. SINGER

Neal, Larry. 1937. in English.

HOLY DAYS. BLACKF

Nekrasov, Nikolay Alekseyevich. 1821. in R sian.

PESNAYA UBOGOGO STRANNIKA. "Ya lugami idu veter svishschet v lugakh" FOLKW

Nemerov, Howard. in English.

BOOM. "Here at the Vespasian" JNP 4 JNP

DANDELIONS. "These golden heads, these co mon suns" COLPIX

DIALOGUE. "O father, answer me" SPOA 1

THE FALL. "It is the old man" JNP 40, JNP

FALL SONG. COLPIX

"From Molekolole" JNP 40, JNP

THE GOOSE FISH. "On the long shore, lit by t moon" IMP 2, SPOA 1

I ONLY AM ESCAPED ALONE TO TELL THEE. "I t you that I see her still" COLPIX

LIFE CYCLE OF COMMON MAN. "Roughly figure this man of moderate habits" FOLKW JNP 40, JNP

LION AND HONEYCOMB. "He didn't want to do JNP 40, JNP

LOVE. "A sandwich and a beer" JNP 4 JNP

MAKE BIG MONEY AT HOME—WRITE POEMS IN SPA TIME. "Oliver wanted to write about realit JNP 40, JNP

METAMORPHOSES ACCORDING TO STEINBE "These people with their illegible diploma JNP 40, JNP

MOMENT. "Now starflake frozen" JNP 4 JNP

"Now it is night" JNP 40, JNP

PRIMER OF THE DAILY ROUND. "A peels an appl JNP 40, JNP

THE QUARRY. "The place is forgotten now: wh I was a child" SPOA 1

SANTA CLAUS. "Somewhere in his travels" JNP 40, JNP 41, LIBC

---

* Recording not available for analysis

THE STATUES IN PUBLIC GARDENS. "Alone at the end of green alleys"   JNP 40, JNP 41

STORM WINDOWS. "People are putting up storm windows"   COLPIX 1

TO CLIO, MUSE OF HISTROY, ON LEARNING THAT THE ETRUSCAN WARRIOR IN THE METROPOLITAN MUSEUM OF ART HAS PROVED A MODERN FORGERY. "One more casualty"   JNP 40, JNP 41, LIBC 40

"To go low, to be as nothing" JNP 40, JNP 41

TO THE BLEEDING HEARTS ASSOCIATION OF AMERICAN NOVELISTS. "My grownups told me when I started out"   JNP 40, JNP 41

TO THE MANNEQUINS. "Adorable images"   JNP 40, JNP 41, LIBC 40

TRUTH. "Around, above my bed, the pitch-dark fly"   SPOA 103

THE VACUUM. "The house is so quiet now"   SPOA 103

Poetry*   LIST 15, TAPES 13

Nerman, Ture. in Swedish.

GOKKVALL.   GRAM 10
PINGSTFORMIDDAG.   GRAM 10
TILL EN LITEN KVINNA.   GRAM 10
TVA SKARGARDSVISOR.   GRAM 10
DEN VACKRASTE VISAN.   GRAM 10

Neruda, Pablo. 1904. in Spanish.

ADIÓS. "Desde el fondo de tí y arrodillado"   SMC 1

ALTURAS DE MACCHU PICCHU, exc. "Del aire al aire, como una red vacía"   CAED 101, SMC 15

———. IV. "La poderosa muerte me invitó"   SPOA 109

———. VI. "Entonces en la escala de la tierra"   SPOA 109

———. VIII. "Sube conmigo, amor americano"   SPOA

———. IX. "Águila sideral, viña de bruma"   SPOA 109

———. XI. "A través del confuso esplendor"   SPOA 109

———. XII. "Sube a nacer conmigo, hermano"   SPOA 109

ARTE POÉTICA. "Entre sombra y espacio, entre guarniciones y doncellas"   CAED 101

BARCAROLA. "Si solamente me tocaras el corazon"   SPOA 109

LA CIUDAD. "Y cuando en el palacio"   English and Spanish WATSHD 1

UN DÍA SOBRESALE. "De lo sonoro"   SPOA 109

EHRENBURG. "Cuantos perros hirsutos"   English and Spanish WATSHD 1

ENTRADA A LA MADERA. "Con mi razón apenas, con mis dedos".   SPOA 109

FÁBULA DE LA SIRENA Y LOS BORRACHOS. "Todos estos señores estaban dentro"   CAED 101

LOS FRUTOS. "Dulces olivas verdes de Frascati"   English and Spanish WATSHD 1

MADRIGAL ESCRITO EN INVIERNO. "En el fondo de mar profundo"   SPOA 109

NO HAY OLVIDO. "Si me preguntais"   SPOA 109

ODA A LOS CALCETINES. "Me trajo Maru Mori"   CAED 101

ODA A UNAS FLORES AMARILLAS. "Contra el azul moviendo sus azules"   HOLT 1

PALABRAS A EUROPA. "Yo, Americano, de las tierras pobres"   English and Spanish WATSHD 1

PICASSO. "En Vallauris en cada casa"   English and Spanish WATSHD 1

POEMA 15. "Me gustas cuando callas, porque estás como ausente"   FOLKW 80

POEMA 20. "Puedo escribir los versos más tristes"   ÁGUIL 4, MIAMI 2, SMC 6

RESIDENCIA EN LA TIERRA, exc.   English and Spanish SPOA 109

SOLO EL HOMBRE. "Yo atravese las hostiles"   English and Spanish WATSHD 1

SOLO LA MUERTE. "Hay cementerios solos"   CAED 101, SPOA 109

EL SUR DEL OCEANO. "De consumida sal y garganta en peligro"   SPOA 109

TANGO DEL VIUDO. "A Malina"   SPOA 109

TENEIS QUE OIRME. "Yo fui cantando errante"   Spanish and English WATSHD 1

TESTAMENTO DE OTONO. "Entre morir y no morir"   CAED 101

LAS UVAS DE EUROPA, exc.   English and Spanish WATSHD 1

Poetry*   TAPES 5

Nerval, Gerard de. 1808. in French.

ARTÉMIS. "La Treizième revient . . . C'est encore la première"   ADES 5, ADES 37

CHOEUR DES GNOMES. "Les petites gnomes chantent"   ADES 5, ADES 37, SPOA 27

LES CYDALISES. "Où sont nos amoureuses"   ADES 5, ADES 37, SPOA 27

DELFICA. "La connais-tu, Dafné, cette ancienne romance"   DOVER 4

EL DESDICHADO. "Je suis le ténébreux,—le veuf, —l'inconsolé"   ADES 5, ADES 37, ADES 49, ADES 54, FOLKW 86, GMS 8, HACH 11, SPOA 9, SPOA 27

ÉPITAPHE. "Il a vécu tantôt gai comme un sansonnet"   ADES 3, ADES 5, ADES 49, HACH 11

FANTAISIE. "Il est un air pour qui je donnerais"   ADES 5, ADES 37, ADES 49, HACH 11

LES FILLES DU FEU, exc.   ADES 37, ADES 48

NI BONJOUR NI BONSOIR. "Ne kaliméra, ne hóra kalí"   HACH 11

LE POINT NOIR. "Quiconque a regardé le soleil fixement"   ADES 5, ADES 37, ADES 49, SPOA 27

LE RÊVE EST UNE SECONDE VIE.   ADES 5, ADES 37, SPOA 27

LE ROI DE THULE. "Il était un roi de Thulé"   GMS 6

TROISIÈME CHÂTEAU. "Château de cartes, château de Bohême"   ADES 5, ADES 37, SPOA 27

VERS DORÉS. "Homme, libre penseur! te crois-tu seul pensant"   ADES 5, ADES 37, FOLKW 13, CAED 204

Nervo, Amado. 1870. in Spanish.

EL DÍA QUE ME QUIERAS. "El día que me quieras tendrá más luz que junio"   MIAMI 2, SMC 1

A KEMPIS. "Hay muchos años que busco el yermo"   FIDIAS 3, HOLT 1

¿LLORAR? ¿POR QUE? "Éste es el libro de mi dolor"   FOLKW 79

* Recording not available for analysis

Nervo, Amado (continued)

OFERTORIO. "Dios mío, yo te ofresco mi dolor"
FOLKW 79

Nesbit, Edith. 1858. in English.
BABY SEED SONG. "Little brown brother, oh! little brown brother"CAED 164
THE SINGING OF THE MAGNIFICAT. "In midst of wide green pasture lands"FOLKW 62

Newman, Cardinal John Henry. 1801. in English.
THE PILLAR OF CLOUD. "Lead, Kindly Light, amid the encircling gloom"CAED 201

Newton, Mary Leslie. in English.
QUEEN ANNE'S LACE. "Queen Anne, Queen Anne, has washed her lace"CAED 164

Nicholson, Norman. 1914. in English.
BOND STREET. "Bond Street, I said, Now where the Devil's that?"ARGO 92
CLEATOR MOOR. "From one shaft at Cleator Moor"ARGO 92
GATHERING STICKS ON SUNDAY. "If the man in the moon"ARGO 92
"Have you been to London"ARGO 147
MILLOM OLD QUARRY. "They dug ten streets from that there hole, he said"ARGO 92, ARGO 147
NICHOLSON, SUDDENLY. "So Norman Nicholson is dead!"ARGO 147
THE POT GERANIUM. "Green slated gables clasp the stem of the hill"ARGO 92, ARGO 147
RISING FIVE. "I'm rising five, he said, not four"
ARGO 92, SPOA 68, ARGO 147
WEEDS.ARGO 147
THE WHISPERER. "For twenty months I whispered"ARGO 147
WINDSCALE. "The toadstool towers infest the shore"ARGO 147

Nicol, Abioseh. 1924. in English.
THE MEANING OF AFRICA.CAED 136

Nicolardi, Edoardo. 1878. in Italian.
'O NONNO.CETRA 29
TESTAMENTO.CETRA 29

Nietzsche, Friedrich Wilhelm. 1844. in German.
AN DEN MISTRAL. "Mistral-Wind, du Wolken-Jäger"DEUTGR 3
ANTWORT.DEUTGR 3
DEM UNBEKANNTEN GOTT. "Wer wärmt mich, wer liebt mich noch?"DEUTGR 3
ECCE HOMO. "Ja! Ich weiss, woher ich stamme"
DEUTGR 3
DER GEHEIMNISVOLLE NACHEN. "Gestern nachts, als alles schlief"DEUTGR 3
NACH NEUEN MEEREN. "Dorthin—will ich; und ich traue"DEUTGR 3
NIEDERGANG. "Er sinkt, er fällt jetzt-höhnt ihr hin und wieder"DEUTGR 3
OHNE NEID. "Ja, neidlos blickt er: und ihr ehrt ihn drum"DEUTGR 3
VEREINSAMT. "Die Krähen schrein"
DEUTGR 3, DOVER 1
DER WANDERER. "Kein Pfad mehr! Abgrund rings und Totenstille"DEUTGR 3
ZIGEUNERSPRUCH.DEUTGR 3
Poetry*ATHENA 6

Nikarchos. ca. 50 A.D. in Greek.
"Fortunatus the portrait-painter got twenty sons"English CARIL 3

VALENTINE FOR A POPULAR TENOR. "Fatal, fatal is the song of the dire night-raven"
English CARIL 3

Nims, John Frederick. 1913. in English.
CATULLUS POEM 70. "Well, Catullus, so you knew"SPOA 100
DAWN SONG. "Dearest, sleep"SPOA 100
LOVE POEM. "My clumsiest"SPOA 100
THE YOUNG IONIA. "If you could come on the late train"SPOA 100

Nina Siciliana. 13th c. in Italian.
Poetry*CETRA 36

Noailles, Comtesse Mathieu de. 1876. in French.
LE FAUNE.HACH 14
JEUNESSE. "Pourtant tu t'en iras un jour de moi, Jeunesse"HACH 14
LES REGRETS. "Allez, je veux rester seule avec les tombeaux"HACH 14

Nobre, António. 1867. in Portuguese.
MEMORIA. "Ora isto, senhores, deu-se em Trás-os-Montes"FOLKW 72
TELEGRAFO. "Nâo repararam nunca? Pela aldeida"FOLKW 72

Noël, Marie. 1883. in French.
ACCUSATION.ADES 19
CHANSON.ADES 19
CRÉPUSCULE.ADES 19
DANS LA CHAMBRE ARRIVAIENT LES JOURS.
ADES 19
ECOLIÈRE.ADES 19
LA MORTE ET SES MAINS TRISTES.ADES 19
Poetry*ADES 5

Noll, Bink. 1927. in English.
QUAKER HERO, BURNING. "He erupts from our soil"SPOA 8

Nordenflycht, Hedvig Charlotta. 1718. in Swedish.
OVER EN HYACINT. "Du rara ört, som ei din like"
GRAM

Norman, Howard. in English.
Poetry*MICHM 2

Norris, Leslie. 1921. in English.
AUTUMN ELEGY. "September. The small summer hangs its suns"ARGO 14
BURNING THE BRACKEN.ARGO 14
CARDIGAN BAY. "The buzzard hung crossed"
ARGO 14
EARLY FROST. "We were warned about frost, y all day the summer"ARGO 1
A GIRL'S SONG. "Early one morning as I went o walking"ARGO 1
JULY 7TH.ARGO 1
MOUNTAINS, POLECATS, PHEASANTS.ARGO 1
RANSOM. "What the white ransoms did was wipe away"ARGO 1
SHADOWS.ARGO 1
SKULLS. "Last night the snow came"
ARGO 1
STONES. "On the flat of the earth lie"
ARGO 1
WATER. "On hot summer mornings my aunt glasses"ARGO 1

Novak, Ladislav. 1925. in Czech.
LA STRUCTURE PHONÉTIQUE DE LA LANG TCHÈQUE.LUCHT

* Recording not available for analysis

Novalis (Baron Friedrich von Hardenberg). 1772. in German.
AN ADOLF SELMNITZ. "Was passt, das muss sich ründen" DEUTGR 4
"Gottlob, dass ich auf Erden bin" CHRIST 27
HYMNEN AN DIE NACHT, exc. "Hinüber wall ich" DOVER 1, CHRIST 16
DIE LIEDER DES BERGMANNS. "Der ist der Herr der Erde" DEUTGR 4
"Wenn alle untreu werden" DEUTGR 4
"Wenn ich ihn nur habe" CHRIST 27
"Wenn in bangen trüben Stunden" CHRIST 27
"Wenn nicht mehr Zahlen und Figuren" CHRIST 27

Novo, Salvador. 1904. in Spanish.
LA POESÍA. "Para escribir poemas" FOLKW 80

Nowlan, Alden. 1933. in English.
THE BEGGARS OF DUBLIN. "I'd rather beggars made me happy" LEARNC 10

Noyes, Alfred. 1880. in English.
DADDY FELL INTO THE POND. "Everyone grumbled. The sky was grey" HARB 4
THE HIGHWAYMAN. "The wind was a torrent of darkness" CAED 132, DECCA 10, FOLKW 62, HARC 1, HOUGHT 3, LIST 19, LIST 21, LIVLAN 1, PROTHM 14, SINGER 2, MINU 1
THE MOON IS UP. SINGER 1
SHERWOOD. "Sherwood in the twilight, is Robin Hood awake?" CAED 169, FOLKW 62, SINGER 1

Nunes, Cassiano. 1921. in Portuguese.
ENSINANDO UM PÁSSARO A CANTAR. "O que tu cantas, pássaro" FOLKW 71
HARLEM BLUES. "Oh! noites do Harlem" FOLKW 71
NO QUINTANA'S BAR. "Num bar fechado ha' muitos, muitos" FOLKW 71

Nuñez, Rafael. in Spanish.
TODAVÍA, exc. MIAMI 1

Obaldia, René de. in French.
A FORCE CE N'EST PLUS MAMAN. "Maman est actrice" ADES 35
ADORATION DE L'INDEX. ADES 35
ANTOINETTE ET MOI. ADES 35
LE BALLON. ADES 35
CERCLE VICIEUX. ADES 35
CHEZ MOIS. "Chez moi, dit la petite fille" ADES 35
CONFESSIONS. ADES 35
COQ AU VIN. ADES 35
LE COURANT D'AIR. ADES 35
COURT CIRCUIT. ADES 35
LES CUISSES DE COLETTE. ADES 35
DANS LE SAC. ADES 35
DEPUIS LE TEMPS QU'IL Y A DES GUERRES. ADES 35
DITES! DITES! "Ah, dites, dites" ADES 35
DOULEUR QUANTITATIVE. ADES 35
L'ESPRIT DE FAMILLE. "Dans le ventre de maman" ADES 35
LES FEMMES DE MON GENOU. ADES 35
FÊTE NUPTIALE. ADES 35
LE GRAND SOMMEIL. ADES 35
INTIMITÉ. "L'âne gris de ma tante" ADES 35
LES JUMEAUX DE LA NUIT. ADES 35
LA JUMENT DU CAPITAINE. ADES 35
MA CONCIERGE DETESTE LES MONGOLS. "Chacque fois qu'un" CBS 1
LE MATRIOTE. ADES 35
ODEUR DE SAINTETÉ. ADES 35
PETITE RITOURNELLE IMPÉRIALE. "Napoléon à Sainte-Hélène" ADES 35
QUE CELUI QUI A DES OREILLES. ADES 35
LA RUE OBALDIA. ADES 35
LA SOLOGNE. "Vivement mes dix ans" ADES 35
TEINTURERIE. ADES 35
VESPASIEN. "Vespasien/Empereur romain" ADES 35
LE ZIZI PERPÉTUEL. "Mon petit frère a un zizi" ADES 35

Obligado, Pedro Miguel. in Spanish.
BALADA DE LA ESPERANZA. "Debes dormir, bella esperanza" FIDIAS 3

Obligado, Rafael. 1851. in Spanish.
EL ALMA DEL PAYADOR. "Cuando la tarde se inclina" AGUIL 9 FIDIAS 3

O'Connell, Richard. in English.
NEKROS. "It slouched at the window changing" FOLKW 21

Oden, G. D. in English.
Poetry* MILLER 2

O'Gorman, Ned. 1929. in English.
THE BURNING BUSH. "This was a caustic bush" LIBC 52
EPITHALAMION. "Bastioned with light, dear body and brave heart" LIBC 52
I AM A FALCON HOODED. "I am a falcon hooded, on God's wrist" LIBC 52
ON SAINT THERESA'S DIFFICULTY IN KEEPING HER FEET ON THE GROUND. "She would not leap for joy" LIBC 52
ON SILENCE. "Silence is the pulling in of nets" LIBC 52
A RECTIFICATION OF THE LYRIC. "I know they say it is music" LIBC 52
"The rose and the body of the rose" LIBC 52
THE TENT, THE SONG, THE SIGN, THE ELEMENT. "In God's tent the sun" LIBC 52
THE TREE HOUSE. "All starts in the air where the first" LIBC 52
TOWARD A LANGUAGE OF THE INEFFABLE. "The mind reigns in its ruddy element" LIBC 52
TWO POEMS ON THE CREATION OF A STATUE OF A MAENAD. "I am freewheeling. The unslung hoop" LIBC 52
THE VIRGIN'S HOUSE. "This is a well guarded place" LIBC 52
WAR. "The horse left its footprint" SPOA 82
"Webbed, yellow-billed and aquamarine" LIBC 52

O'Hara, Frank. 1926. in English.
THE DAY LADY DIED. "It is 12:20 in New York a Friday" NET 16
HAVING A COKE WITH YOU. "Is even more fun" NET 16
SONG. NET 16
TO THE FILM INDUSTRY IN CRISIS. "Not you, lean quarterlies and swarthy periodicals" NET 16

* Recording not available for analysis

Oldmixon, John. 1673. in English.
"Prithee, Chloe, not so fast"   ARGO 47
Oldys, William. 1687. in English.
THE FLY. "Busy, curious, thirsty fly" SPOA 117
Olfers-Batocki, Erminia von. in Low German.
ANNE JRENZSTEEN.   CHRIST 23
DE FASTELDANZ.   CHRIST 23
GANGELLEED TOER AUSSTIED.   CHRIST 23
HEEJAUST.   CHRIST 23
KRIEZERSCH OM'T LEEWE BROT.   CHRIST 23
MIEN TOHUUSKE.   CHRIST 23
WONDER.   CHRIST 23
Olmedo, José Joaquín de. 1780. in Spanish.
LA VICTORIA DE JUNIN: CANTO A BOLIVAR. "El
trueno horrendo que en fragor reviente"
SPOA 39
Olson, Charles. 1910. in English.
ABSOLUTENESS.   FOLKW 28
"After the storm was over"   FOLKW 28
ALL MY LIFE I'VE HEARD ABOUT MANY. "He went to
Spain"   FOLKW 28
ANACOLUTHIC AND DRAG.   FOLKW 28
BETWEEN CRUISER AND PLATO.   FOLKW 28
BOHLIN 1. "Fr Cape Sable into the stream in"
FOLKW 28
BOHLIN 2. "Bohlin"   FOLKW 28
CASHES. "I tell you it's cruel"   FOLKW 28
CHOCKABLOCK. "Once a man was traveling"
FOLKW 28
CHRONICLES I. "As Zeus sent Hermes"
FOLKW 28
CHRONICLES II. "Taurus"   FOLKW 28
"The coast goes from Hurrian"   FOLKW 28
THE CORMORANT AND SPINDLE.   FOLKKW 28
THE DIFFERENCE OF A WILD THING. FOLKW 28
THE FRONTLET. "Into the light"   FOLKW 28
"Further completion of Plat"   FOLKW 28
GRAVELY HILL.   FOLKW 28
GULF OF MAINE. "Altham says"   FOLKW 28
HER STERN LIKE A BOX.   FOLKW 28
"I am the gold machine"   FOLKW 28
"I, John Watts"   FOLKW 28
"I swung out, at eight or ten"   FOLKW 28
"In the harbour"   FOLKW 28
"Into the stream or entrance"   FOLKW 28
"J.W. (from the Danelaw) says"   FOLKW 28
"John Watts took"   FOLKW 28
KENT CIRCLE SONG. "At my Aunt Vandla's"
FOLKW 28
LETTER 27 MAXIMUS TO DOGTOWN.   NET 18
THE LIBRARIAN. "The landscape (the landscape!)
again: Gloucester"   NET 18
MAXIMUS FROM DOGTOWN—II. "The Sea—turn yr
Back on"   FOLKW 28
MAXIMUS POEM—JULY 24, 1968.   FOLKW 28
MAYAN LETTER #5. "Yr letter! How it spotted it-
self"   FOLKW 28
MAYAN LETTER #7. "(Marsden Hartley's eyes—as
Stein's eyes"   FOLKW 28
MAYAN LETTER #13. "What continues to hold
me"   FOLKW 28
NOT THE ITALIAN METHOD.   FOLKW 28
"Older than Byblos"   FOLKW 28
"People want delivery"   FOLKW 28
PIGGY-BACK POEM.   FOLKW 28
SEQUENTIOR. "Smallmans definitely there 1721"
FOLKW 28

"Tesserae commisure"   FOLKW 28
THIRD LETTER ON GEORGES. "In this place is a
poem"   FOLKW 28
"To enter into their bodies"   FOLKW 28
TO TRAVEL TYPHON. "To travel Typhon from the
old holdings"   FOLKW 28
UNTITLED MAXIMUS POEM (from mss).
FOLKW 28
"Up the steps, along the porch" FOLKW 28
VEDA UPANISHAD EDDA THAN. "Wrote my first
poem"   FOLKW 28
Omar Khayyam. 1214. in Persian.
RUBAIYAT. "Wake! For the sun, who scatter'd
into flight" English CAED 22, CAED 201
CMS 9, LION 2, LIVLAN 1, RCA 9
REX 1, SPOA 77, SUPER 1
———, exc.   English ARGO 68, BRITAM 3
SPOA 86
SI TU ES MALHEUREUX. "Tu es malheureux?"
French CBS 1
O'Neill, Catherine. in English.
COWBOY'S LOVE SONG. "Imagine his lassoed
walk"   WATSHD 8
FIELD TRIP. "Dan the botanist walks"
WATSHD 8
WINTER SUNSET ROCK CREEK CEMETERY. "I follow
a map"   WATSHD 8
O'Neill, Mary L. 1908. in English.
HAILSTONES AND HALIBUT BONES, exc. STERL 1
Opitz, Martin. 1597. in German.
ELEGIE.   CHRIST 25
Oppen, George. 1908. in English.
Poetry*   JNP 42
Oppenheimer, Joel. 1930. in English.
AFRICAN MEMORIES. "They are fighting, she"
BROADR 1
READING-IN.   BROADR 1
Oquendo de Amat, Carlos. 1909. in Spanish.
MADRE. "Tu nombre viene lento como las músi
cas humildes"   FOLKW 86
O'Reilly, John Boyle. in English.
A WHITE ROSE. "The red rose whispers of pas
sion"   SPOA 1
Orinda. See **Philips, Katharine.**
Orlovsky, Peter. 1933. in English.
JUNE 20, 1961, TANGIERS. "The cleanest place to
bring your baby"   BROADR 1
Ormond, John. 1923. in English.
AFTER A DEATH.   ARGO 14
THE AMBUSH.   ARGO 14
ANCIENT MONUMENTS. "They bide their time of
serpentine"   ARGO 14
AT HIS FATHER'S GRAVE. "Here lies a shoe-maker
whose knife and hammer"   ARGO 14
CATHEDRAL BUILDERS. "They climbed on
sketchy ladders towards God"   ARGO 14
DESIGN FOR A TOMB.   ARGO 14
JOHNNY RANDALL.   ARGO 14
THE KEY. "Its teeth worked doubtfully"
ARGO 14
MY GRANDFATHER AND HIS APPLE-TREE. "Life
sometimes held such sweetness for him"
ARGO 14
ORGANIST.   ARGO 14
SALMON. "The river sucks them home"
ARGO 14

* Recording not available for analysis

Orr, Gregory. in English.
Poetry* MICHM 10
O'Shaughnessy, Arthur William Edgar. 1844. in English.
ODE. "We are the music makers" HARC 4
Osorio Benitez, Miguel Angel. See Barba Jacob, Porfirio.
Ossiannilsson, K. G. 1875. in Swedish.
BISMARCK. GRAM 10
SKÅ NINGAR. GRAM 10
Österling, Anders. 1884. in Swedish.
ALES STENAR. "Där kusten stupar mellan hav och himmel" GRAM 4
HON SOM SKÅR BRODET. GRAM 4
I PAVIJONGEN. GRAM 4
LANTLIG KYRKOGÅRG PSALMODIKON. "Konvolvelns lätta blomsterrevor hanga" GRAM 4
VIPOR I SKYMNINGEN. GRAM 4
Ostroff, Anthony. 1923. in English.
INTIMATE PARTY IN GUADALAJARA, DEC. 1963. "Jorge Hernadez, architect" FOLKW 21
O'Sullivan, Seumas. in English.
LAMENT FOR SEAN MACDERMOTT. "They have slain you, Sean MacDermott" SPOA 6
Otero, Blas de. 1916. in Spanish.
A LA INMENSA MAYORÍA. "Aquí tenéis, en canto y alma, al hombre" AGUIL 6, HOLT 1
GRITANDO NO MORIR. "Quiero vivir, vivir, vivir" SPOA 59
JUICIO FINAL. "Yo, pecador, artista del pecado" TROPIC 1
Overstreet, Bonaro W. in English.
Poetry* MICHM 5
Ovid (Publius Ovidius Naso). 43 B.C. in Latin.
AMORES. 13. "Iam super oceanum venit a seniore marito" FOLKW 98
_____. 16. "Pars me Sulmo tenet Paeligni tertia ruris" FOLKW 98
ARTIS AMATORIAE.
_____. LIBER 1, exc. "Principio quod amare velis" FOLKW 101
_____. LIBER 2, exc. "Sit procul omne nefas" FOLKW 101
_____. LIBER 3, exc. "Sit tibi Callimchi, sit Coi nota poetae" FOLKW 101
METAMORPHOSES. LIBER 1, exc. "Primus amor Phoebi Daphne Peneia" FOLKW 101
_____. LIBER 3, exc. "Ergo ubi Narcissum per devia rura" FOLKW 101
Poetry* CETRA 18
Owen, Guy. in English.
Poetry* CASSC 2
Owen, Wilfred. 1893. in English.
ANTHEM FOR DOOMED YOUTH. "What passing-bells for these who die as cattle?" ARGO 90, PROTHM 5, WARNER 1
APOLOGIA PRO POEMATE MEO. "I, too, saw God through mud" ARGO 90, PROTHM 5, WARNER 1
ARMS AND THE BOY. "Let the boy try along this bayonet-blade" ARGO 89, ARGO 90, FOLKW 65, JUP 1, WARNER 1
ASLEEP. "Under his helmet, up against his pack" PROTHM 5, WARNER 1
AT A CALVARY NEAR THE ANCRE. "One ever hangs where shelled roads part" ARGO 90, WARNER 1

LE CHRISTIANISME. "So the church Christ was hit and buried" WARNER 1
CONSCIOUS. "His fingers wake, and flutter, up the bed" PROTHM 5, WARNER 1
DISABLED. "He sat in a wheeled chair, waiting for dark" PROTHM 5
DULCE ET DECORUM EST. "Bent double, like old beggars under sacks" ARGO 89, PROTHM 5, WARNER 1
EXPOSURE. "Our brains ache, in the merciless iced east winds that knive us" PROTHM 5
FROM MY DIARY, JULY 1914. "Leaves" PROTHM 5
FUTILITY. "Move him into the sun" ARGO 82, ARGO 90, PROTHM 5, SPOA 41, WARNER 1
GREATER LOVE. "Red lips are not so red" ARGO 82, SPOA 41, WARNER 1
INSENSIBILITY. "Happy are men who yet before they are killed" PROTHM 5
THE KIND GHOSTS. "She sleeps on soft, last breaths; but no ghost looms" PROTHM 5
THE LAST LAUGH. "O Jesus Christ! I'm hit, he said; and died" WARNER 1
THE LETTER. "With B. E. F. June 10. Dear Wife" PROTHM 5
MENTAL CASES. "Who are these? Why sit they here in twilight?" PROTHM 5
MINERS. "There was a whispering in my hearth" PROTHM 5
THE NEXT WAR. "Out there, we've walked quite friendly up to Death" WARNER 1
THE PARABLE OF THE OLD MAN AND THE YOUNG. "So Abram rose, and clave the wood, and went" ARGO 89, ARGO 90, VAN 3
THE SEND-OFF. "Down the close, darkening lanes they sang their way" ARGO 90, PROTHM 5, WARNER 1
THE SENTRY. "We'd found an old Boche dug-out and he knew" ARGO 90, PROTHM 5, WARNER 1
THE SHOW. "My soul looked down from a vague height, with Death" PROTHM 5, WARNER 1
SOLDIER'S DREAM. "I dreamed kind Jesus fouled the big-gun gears" ARGO 90, WARNER 1
SONNET: ON SEEING A PIECE OF OUR ARTILLERY BROUGHT INTO ACTION. "Be slowly lifted up, thou long black arm" ARGO 90, WARNER 1
SPRING OFFENSIVE. "Halted against the shade of a last hill" ARGO 77, ARGO 90, PROTHM 5
STRANGE MEETING. "It seemed that out of battle I escaped" ARGO 90, CAED 126, PROTHM 5, SCHOL 5, WARNER 1
THE UNRETURNING. "Suddenly night crushed out the day and hurled" PROTHM 5
WILD WITH ALL REGRETS. "My arms have mutinied against me, brutes" PROTHM 5
Poetry* PROTHM 7
Oxford, Earl of (Edward de Vere). 1550. in English.
A CHOICE. "Were I a king, I could command content" ARGO 35

* Recording not available for analysis

Ozick, Cynthia. 1928. in English.
FOOTNOTE TO LORD ACTON. "While in the Convention they were nominating the next president" FOLKW 21

Pacheco, José Emilio. in Spanish.
DESCRIPCIÓN DE UN NAUFRAGIO EN ULTRAMAR. "Pertenezco a una era fugitiva" APPL 6
EL REPOSO DEL FUEGO. "Brusco olor del azufre" APPL 6

Pack, Robert. 1929. in English.
ADAM ON HIS WAY HOME. "By the wayside, the crows sat on a cross" SPOA 107
THE BOAT. "I dressed my father in his little clothes" SPOA 107
DROWNING. "Screams kicking stretched lungs out" SPOA 107
THE FAITHFUL LOVER. SPOA 107
THE SHOOTING. "I shot an otter because I had a gun" SPOA 107

Page, William Tyler. in English.
THE AMERICAN'S CREED. CAED 98

Pagis, Dan. in Hebrew.
Poetry* Hebrew and English WATSHD 62

Palazzeschi, Aldo. 1885. in Italian.
ANCHE LA MORTE AMA LA VITA. CETRA 11
UNA CASINA DI CRISTALLO. "Non sogno piu castelli rovinati" CETRA 11
CHI SONO? "Son forse un poeta? No, certo" CETRA 11
I FIORI. "Non so perchi quella sera" CETRA 11
LASCIATEMI DIVERTIRE. "Tri, tri, tri" CETRA 11
LA MATRIGNA. "Noi siamo a pregarvi, signora matrigna" CETRA 11
LA MORTE DI COBO. "Cobo e morto, e non gli possono" CETRA 11
IL PASSO DELLE NAZARENE. "Nazarene bianche, Nazarene nere" CETRA 11
REGINA CARLOTTA. "La gente s accalca" CETRA 11
SEGIO CORAZZINI, exc. CETRA 11
SOLE. "Vorrei girar la spagna" CETRA 11
VISITA ALLA CONTESSA EVA PIZZARDINI BA. "Buonasera contessa" CETRA 11
Poetry* CETRA 28, CETRA 43

Palés Matos, Luís. 1898. in Portuguese.
BUSQUEDA ASESINA. INSTPR 1
CANCIÓN FESTIVA PARA SER LLORADA. "Cubañáñigo y bachata" GMS 13
DANZA NEGRA. "Calabó y bambú" HOLT 1
HOY ME HE ECHADO A REÍR. "Hoy me he echado a reír al salir de mi casa" FOLKW 80
LAGARITO VERDE. "El Condesito de la Limonada" INSTPR 1
PUERTA AL TIEMPO EN TRES VOCES. INSTPR 1
TAMBORES. GMS 13
TEN CON TEN. "Estáis en pirata y negro" SMC 9

Palladas. ca. 400. in Greek.
COUPLET. "To the man who has married an ugly wife" English CARIL 3
MEDITATION. "Praise, of course, is best" English CARIL 3

Palma, Ricardo. in Spanish.
ZAPE, GATA! "A la muchacha de major talle" FIDIAS 3

Panero, Leopoldo. 1909. in Spanish.
EN LAS MANOS DE DIOS. "Alli estará también la castañera" AGUIL 3
HIJO MÍO. "Desde mi vieja orilla, desde la fe que siento" AGUIL 3

Pardo Garcia, German. in Spanish.
CLAMOR ANTE EDGAR POE. LIBC 76
DESNUDEZ. LIBC 76
LOS DIÁLOGOS. LIBC 76
ESPÍRITU DE KEATS. LIBC 76
FIDELIDAD. LIBC 76
HONDA AMISTAD. LIBC 76
LA LUZ ES ALIMENTO. LIBC 76
SIGNO DE ESPAÑA. LIBC 76

Parini, Giuseppe. 1729. in Italian.
GIORNO, exc. CETRA 12
ODI, exc. CETRA 12

Parker, Dorothy. 1893. in English.
AFTERNOON. "When I am old and comforted" RCA 6, SPOA 11, SPOA 9
THE BURNED CHILD. "Love has had his way with me" RCA 6, SPOA 1
DAY DREAMS. RCA 6
DILEMMA. "If I were mild, and I were sweet" SPOA 1
THE EVENING PRIMROSE. "You know the bloom unearthly white" SPOA 1
A FAIRLY SAD TALE. "I think that I shall neve know" SPOA 1
THE FALSE FRIENDS. "They laid their hands upo my head" SPOA 1
FOR AN UNKNOWN LADY. "Lady, if you'd slumbe sound" SPOA 11, SPOA 9
INSCRIPTION FOR THE CEILING OF A BEDROOM "Daily dawns another day" SPOA 1, SPOA 9
INVENTORY. "Four be the things I am wiser know" RCA
THE LADY'S REWARD. "Lady, lady, never start" SPOA 11, SPOA 9
LIGHT OF LOVE. "Joy stayed with me a night" RCA
THE LITTLE OLD LADY IN LAVENDER SILK. "I w seventy-seven come August" RCA, SPOA
LOVE SONG. "My own dear love, he is strong ar bold" THEAL
THE MAID-SERVANT AT THE INN. "It's queer, s said, I see the light" RCA
MEN. "They hail you as their morning star" SINGER 5, SPOA 11, SPOA
NEWS ITEM. "Men seldom make passes" RCA
ONE PERFECT ROSE. "A single flow'r he sent n since we met" HOUGHT 4, SPOA, SPOA
PARABLE FOR A CERTAIN VIRGIN. "Oh, pond friend, the porcupine" RCA 6, SPOA
PLEA. "Secrets, you said, would hold us t apart" SPOA
RECURRENCE. "We shall have our little day" SPOA
THE RED DRESS. "I always saw, I always said" SPOA

* Recording not available for analysis

RESUME. "Razors pain you" RCA 6, SCHOL 7, SPOA 11, SPOA 94

THE SATIN DRESS. "Needle, needle, dip and dart" SPOA 11, SPOA 94

THE SECOND OLDEST STORY. "Go I must along my ways" RCA 6

SENTIMENT. RCA 6

SONG OF PERFECT PROPRIETY. "Oh, I should like to ride the seas" THEAL 1

STORY. "And if he's gone away, said she" SPOA 11

SURPRISE. "My heart went fluttering with fear" RCA 6

THEY PART. "And if, my friend, you'd have it end" SPOA 11

THE THIN EDGE. "With you, my heart is quiet here" RCA 6

TO NEWCASTLE. "I met a man the other day" SPOA 11

TOMBSTONES IN THE STARLIGHT. "His little trills and chirpings were his best" RCA 6, SPOA 11, SPOA 94

TWO-VOLUME NOVEL. "The sun's gone dim, and" RCA 6

THE VETERAN. "When I was young and bold and strong" SPOA 11

WAR SONG. "Soldier, in a curious land" SPOA 11

arkes, Francis Ernest Kobina. in English.
THREE PHASES OF AFRICA. CAED 136

arny, Évariste-Désiré de. 1753. in French.
ELEGIE, exc. "Oui, sans regret, du flambeau de mes jours" HACH 10

ascarella, Cesare. 1858. in Italian.
VILLA GLORIA. CETRA 30

ascoaes, Teixeira de. 1877. in Portuguese.
ELEGIA DO AMOR. "Lembras-te, me amor" FOLKW 72

ascoli, Giovanni. 1855. in Italian.
ADDIO! "Dunque, rondini rondini, addio!" CETRA 13

ALLORA. "Allora . . . in un tempo assai lunge" CETRA 13

L'AQUILONE. "C' è qualcosa di nuovo oggi nel sole" CETRA 13

BENEDIZIONE. CETRA 13

LA CAVALLA STORNA. CETRA 13

LA GATTA. "Era una gatta, assai trita" CETRA 13

I GATTICI. "E vi rivedo, o gattici d'argento" CETRA 13

IL GELSOMINO NOTTURNO. "E' s'aprono i fiori notturni" CETRA 13

GESÙ. CETRA 13

LONTANA. CETRA 13

LA MIA SERA. "Il giorno fu pieno di lampi" CETRA 13

IL NAUFRAGO. "Il mare, al buio, fu cattivo" CETRA 13

NEL CARCERE DI GINEVRA. CETRA 13

L'ORA DI BARGA. "Al mio cantuccio, donde non sento" CETRA 13, SPOA 30

PIANO E MONTE. "Il disco, grandissimo, pende" CETRA 13

LA PICCOZZA. CETRA 13

LA QUERCIA CADUTA. "Dov' era l'ombra, or sé la quercia spande" CETRA 13

ROMAGNA. "Sempre un villagio, sempre una campagna" CETRA 13

STOPPIA. "Dov'è, campo, il brusío della maretta" CETRA 13

VALENTINO. "Oh! Valentino vestito di nuovo" CETRA 13

LA VOCE. "C'è una voce nella mia vita" CETRA 13

X AGOSTO. "San Lorenzo, io lo so perché tanto" CETRA 13

Poetry* CETRA 28

Passerat, Jean. 1534. in French.
VILLANELLE. "I have long lost my turtle-doo" English EAV 22

Pastan, Linda. 1932. in English.
LEAVING HOME. "I take a giant step north" WATSHD 5

21ST ANNIVERSARY. "Last week someone said" WATSHD 5

Pasternak, Boris Leonidovich. 1890. in Russian.
AVGUST. "Kak obeshchalo, ne obmanyvaya" SPOA 24

BELAYA NOCH'. "Mne dalekoe vremya mereshchitsya" SPOA 24

CHUDO. "On shel iz vifanii v erusalim" SPOA 24

DRUGI. "Il' ya ne znayu, chto b potemkitychas" English and Russian CAED 107

DURNYE DNI. "Kogda na poslednei nedele" SPOA 24

GAMLET. "Gul zatikh ya vyshel na rodmostki" SPOA 24

GEFSIMANSKII SAD. "Mertsan'em zvezd dalekikh bezrazlichno" SPOA 24

IZ POEMY. "Ya tozhe lyubil, i dykhan'e" English and Russian CAED 107

KHMEL. "Pod rakitoi, obvitoi plyoshchom" SPOA 24

LEITENANT SHMIDT, exc. "Naprasno v gody khaosa" English and Russian CAED 107

LETO V GORODE. "Razgovory vpolgolosa" SPOA 24

MAGDALINA I. "Chut' noch', moi demon tut kak tut" SPOA 24

MAGDALINA II. "U lyudei pred prazdnikom uborka" SPOA 24

NA RANNIKH POEZDAKH. "Mne po dushe stroptivyi norov" English and Russian CAED 107

NA STRASTNOI. "Escche krugom nochnaya mgla" SPOA 24

"O, znaya by ya, chto tak byvaet" English and Russian CAED 107

OB'YASNENIE. "Zhizn' vernulas' tak zhe besprichinno" SPOA 24

OSEN'. "Ty raspugal moikh tovarok" English and Russian CAED 107

OSEN'. "Ya dal raz'ekhat'sya domashnim" SPOA 24

RASSVET. "Ty znachil vso v moei sud'be" SPOA 24

RAZLUKA. "S poroga smotrit chelovek" SPOA 24

"Royal' drozhashchii penu s gub oblizhet" English and Russian CAED 107

ROZHDESTVENSKAY A ZVEZDA. "Stoyala zima" SPOA 24

* Recording not available for analysis

Pasternak, Boris Leonidovich (continued)

SVAD'BA. "Peresekshi krai dvora"   SPOA 24
SVIDANIE. "Zasypet chet dorogi"   SPOA 24
VETER. "Ya konchilsya, a ty zhiva"   SPOA 24;
English and Russian CAED 107
VYSOKAYA BOLEZN'. "Mne stydno i den' oto dnya
studnei"   English and Russian CAED 107
ZEMLYA. "V Moskovskie osobnyaki"   SPOA 24
ZIMNYAYA NOCH'. "Melo, melo po vsei zemle"
SPOA 24; English and Russian CAED 107
Poetry*   DISC 1

Patchen, Kenneth. 1911. in English.
"And what with the blunders"   FOLKW 19
"As frothing wounds of roses"   FOLKW 107
"As we are so wonderfully done with each oth-
er"   FOLKW 107
"Be music, night"   FOLKW 19
THE CHARACTER OF LOVE SEEN AS A SEARCH FOR
THE LOST. "You, the women; I the man"
FOLKW 107
CREATION. "Wherever the dead are"
FOLKW 107
AN EASY DECISION. "I had finished my dinner"
CAED 111
THE EVERLASTING CONTENDERS. "Of the beast
. . . an angel"   FOLKW 19
FALL OF THE EVENING STAR. "Speak softly; sun
going down"   FOLKW 107
"For losing her love"   FOLKW 107
FOR MIRIAM, exc. "As beautiful as the hands"
FOLKW 107
_____. "Do I not deal with angels"
FOLKW 107
_____. "Little birds sit on your shoulders"
FOLKW 107
_____. "The sea is awash with roses"
FOLKW 107
THE FOX. "Because the snow is deep"
FOLKW 19
"From my high love"   FOLKW 107
THE GREAT BIRDS. "A gentle wind blows"
FOLKW 107
HURRAH FOR ANYTHING. "There is a place"
SPOA 99
"In order to apply for the position"
FOLKW 19, SPOA 99
A LAMENT FOR THE UNLASTING JOYS.
FOLKW 107
THE LIONS OF THE FIRE. "The lions of the fire
shall have their hunting in this black land"
FOLKW 19
THE MAGICAL MOUSE.   CAED 109
THE MAN WITH THE GOLDEN ADAM'S APPLE.
"There were four crates of chickens"
FOLKW 19
NICE DAY FOR A LYNCHING. "The bloodhounds
look like sad old judges"   CAED 155,
FOLKW 19
"O fiery river"   FOLKW 25
"O my darling troubles heaven"
FOLKW 107
"O my love"   FOLKW 107
"O now the drenched land wakes"
FOLKW 107
"O she is as lovely-often"   FOLKW 107

THE ORANGE BEARS. "The orange bears with soft
friendly eyes"   FOLKW 19
THE ORIGIN OF BASEBALL. "Someone had been
walking in and out"   FOLKW 19
PASTORAL. "The dove walks with sticky feet"
FOLKW 19
THE REASON FOR SKYLARKS. "It was nearly morn-
ing when the giant"   FOLKW 19
RED WINE AND YELLOW HAIR. "Ah that the world
could use a dream or a flame cold"
FOLKW 19
RELIGION IS THAT I LOVE YOU. "As time will turn
FOLKW 107
SHE HAD CONCEALED HIM. "Going to bed"
FOLKW 107
"The snow is deep on the ground"
FOLKW 107
SO BE IT. "There are no rooms here"
FOLKW 19
"Soon it will be showtime again" FOLKW 19
SUNDAY, APRIL 8. "With this rose I thee world"
SPOA 99
THE STATE OF THE NATION. "Understand that
they were just inside the door" FOLKW 19
23 STREET RUNS INTO HEAVEN. "You stand near
the window"   FOLKW 19, FOLKW 107
"We go out together"   FOLKW 107
WHERE SHALL WE WALK. "Because, straying
through the wine garden"   FOLKW 19
WHILE THE SUN STILL SPENDS HIS FABULOUS
MONEY.   FOLKW 107
"The wolf of winter"   FOLKW 19
"You know you're all nuts, boobs, scamps
frauds"   SPOA 99
Poetry*   FOLKW 2

Patmore, Coventry. 1823. in English.
A FAREWELL. "With all my will, but much
against my heart"   CAED 20
THE TOYS. "My little son, who looked from
thoughtful eyes"   ARGO 77, LONGM

Paton, Alan. 1903. in English.
Poetry*   MICHM

Patten, Bryan. 1946. in English.
ALBATROSS RAMBLE. "I woke this morning to
find an albatross staring at me" ARGO 14
AVOIDING THE DOORS.   ARGO 14
A CREATURE TO TELL THE TIME BY. "I created for
myself"   CAED 13
DOUBT SHALL NOT MAKE AN END OF YOU. "Doubt
shall not make an end of you" CAED 13
EARLY IN THE EVENING. "I met her early in the
evening"   ARGO 14
IN THE DYING OF ANYTHING. "Speaking only that
our words might bend grasses" CAED 13
INTERRUPTION AT THE OPERA HOUSE. "At the very
beginning of an important symphony"
ARGO 14
JANUARY GLADSONG.   CAED 13
LITTLE JOHNNY'S CONFESSION. "This morning
being rather young and foolish" CAED 13
LITTLE JOHNNY'S FINAL LETTER. "Mother, I won't
be home this evening, so"   CAED 13
MAKING A CALL. "Alone in a red phonebooth"
CAED 13
MAUD. "Maud, where are you, Maud"
CAED 13
"The morning's got a sleep head" ARGO 14

* Recording not available for analysis

THE NECESSARY SLAUGHTER. "There was a bird come recently. When I went into my room" CAED 131

NOTE TO A HURRYING MAN. "All day I sit here doing nothing but" CAED 131

NOW WE WILL EITHER SLEEP, LIE STILL, OR DRESS AGAIN. "Evening and the sun warming the bird" CAED 131

OLD CROCK. "I am the very last astronaut, listen" CAED 131

PARK POEM. "See how the lake, less active now, is silent" CAED 131

PARTY NOTES. "The young pop-singers, newly mystical" CAED 131

PARTY PIECE. "He said: Let's stay here" CAED 131

PORTRAIT OF A YOUNG GIRL RAPED AT A SUBURBAN PARTY. "And after this quick bash in the dark" CAED 131

THE PROJECTIONIST'S NIGHTMARE. CAED 131

THE PROPHET'S GOOD IDEA. "A new prophet appeared recently: was first seen" ARGO 146, CAED 131

RAUIN INTO MY MIRROR HAS WALKED. CAED 131

THE RIGHT MASK. "One night a poem came to a poet" ARGO 146

SCHOOLBOY. "Before playtime let us consider the possibilities" CAED 131

A SMALL DRAGON. "I've found a small dragon in the wood shed" CAED 131

SOMEWHERE BETWEEN HEAVEN AND WOOL-WORTH'S "She keeps kingfishers in their cages" CAED 131

SPRING SONG. CAED 131

A TALK WITH A WOOD. "Moving through you one evening" CAED 131

THE TELEPHONISTS. "He dreams" CAED 131

A THEME FOR VARIOUS MURDERS. "She walks alone by the river" CAED 131

THROUGH THE TALL GRASS IN YOUR HEAD. "Through the tall grass in your head" CAED 131

TOWARDS EVENING AND TIRED OF THE PLACE. "Time to uproot again" ARGO 146

TRAVELLING BETWEEN PLACES. CAED 131

UNISONG. CAED 131

WINTER SONG. CAED 131

"You come to me quiet as rain not yet fallen" CAED 131

YOU GO INTO TOWN. "When she has gone you go into town" ARGO 146

Poetry* PROTHM 6, PENN 1

Patterson, Raymond R. in English.
WHEN I AWOKE. CAED 155
Poetry* PRENT 1

Paulus, Helmut. in German.
AMERIKABALLADE, exc. AMAD 1

Paulus, Silentiarius. 6th cent. in Greek.
A GENERAL EPITAPH. "My name is—What does it matter?" English CARIL 3

Pavese, Cesare. 1908. in Italian.
Poetry* CETRA 46

Payne, John Howard. 1791. in English.
HOME, SWEET HOME. "Mid pleasures and palaces though we may roam" CAED 100

Paz, Octavio. 1914. in Spanish.
AQUÍ. "Mis pasos en esta calle" APPL 6

MADRUGADA. "Rapidas manos frias" APPL 6

MADURAI. "En el bar del British club" APPL 6

NOCHE DE RESURRECCIONES, I. "Blanda invasión de alas es la noche" FOLKW 80

PRESENTE. "Sobre la reverberación de la pared" APPL 6

VIENTO ENTERO. "El presente es perpetuo, los nontes" APPL 6
Poetry* FFHS 1

Peacock, Thomas Love. 1785. in English.
SONG. CAED 202

THE WAR SONG OF DINAS VAWR. "The mountain sheep are sweeter" BRITAM 1

THE WISE MEN OF GOTHAM. "Seamen three! What men be ye?" BRITAM 1, FOLKW 67

Peake, Mervyn. 1911. in English.
HAD EACH A VOICE. ARGO 119

Pearse, Padraic H. in English.
THE FOOL. "Since the wise men have not spoken I speak" SPOA 20

"I am Ireland" SPOA 20

LULLABY OF A WOMAN OF THE MOUNTAINS. "Little gold head, my houses" CAED 110

THE REBEL. "I am come of the seed of the people" SPOA 20

RENUNCIATION. "Naked I saw thee" SPOA 20

Pedroni, José. 1899. in Spanish.
MATERNIDAD. "Desde que sé, oh amiga" SMC 6

MUJER. "Mujer, nunca me olvido" AGUIL 9

Peele, George. 1558. in English.
THE BATTLE OF ALCAZAR, exc. ARGO 77

DAVID AND BETHSABA, exc. PROTHM 7

————. BETHSABA'S SONG. "Hot sun, cool fire, tempered with sweet air" ARGO 31

THE KING OF PORTUGAL DESCRIBES HER STATE. ARGO 77

LOVE. "What thing is love? For sure love is a thing" ARGO 31, SPOA 83

THE OLD KNIGHT. "His golden locks time hath to silver turned" ARGO 31, BRITAM 2, IMP 1, POLYGL 2, SPOA 12, SPOA 50

Péguy, Charles. 1873. in French.
ADIEUX À LA MEUSE. HACH 14

CHATEAUX DE LOIRE. "Le long du coteau courbe et des nobles vallées" ADES 11, ADES 32

COEUR. ADES 11, ADES 32, ADES 54

DEVANT LES ACCIDENTS DE LA GLOIRE TEMPORELLE. ADES 32

EVE. "O mère ensevelie hors du premier jardin" ADES 11, ADES 32

HEUREUX CEUX QUI SONT MORTS, exc. HACH 14

LE MYSTÈRE DES SAINTS-INNOCENTS, exc. "Je suis, dit Dieu, Maître des Trois Vertus" ADES 32

LA NUIT. ADES 11

PARIS, DOUBLE GALÈRE. "Depuis le Point-du-Jour jusqu'aux cèdres bibliques" ADES 11, ADES 32

PIERRE. ADES 32

LE PORCHE DE LA DEUXIÈME VERTU, exc. "La foi que j'aime le mieux, dit Dieu, c'est l'espérance" ADES 32

* Recording not available for analysis

Péguy, Charles (continued)

PRÉSENTATION DE LA BEAUCE À NOTRE-DAME DE CHARTRES. "Étoile de la mer, voici la lourde" ADES 11, FOLKW 88, HACH 14, SPOA 36
PRIÈRE DE REPORT. "Nous avons gouverné de si vastes royaumes" ADES 11
QUATRAINS, exc. "Les quatre Cardinales" ADES 32
LA TAPISSERIE DE SAINTE-GENEVIÈVE. "Comme elle avait gardé les moutons à Nanterre" ADES 11, ADES 32
Poetry* ADES 51, HACH 16
Pemán, José María. 1897. in Spanish.
BALADA DE LOS ANSARES. "La moza y la madre" SMC 3
FERIA DE ABRIL EN JEREZ. "Y es que Andalucía" GMS 14, SMC 5
EL VIATICO. "Enjamas podre olvidarlo" SMC 3
Peñalver, Juan. in Spanish.
POEMA DE LA GUERRA DE ESPAÑA. TROPIC 1
Penna, Sandro. 1906. in Italian.
Poetry* CETRA 46
Peterborough, Earl of. See **Mordaunt, Charles.**
Péres Marchand, Lilianne. in Spanish.
SARTA DE VOCES PERDIDAS. INSTPR 1
Péret, Benjamin. 1899. in French.
ALLO. "Mon avion en flammes mon château inondé de vin du Rhin" ADES 24, ADES 40, ADES 52
ÇA CONTINUE. "La vieille valise la chaussette et l'endive" ADES 24, ADES 40, ADES 52
HYMNE DES ANCIENS COMBATTANTES PATRIOTES. "Regardez comme je suis beau" ADES 24, ADES 40
LOUIS XVI S'EN VA À LA GUILLOTINE. "Pue, pue, pue" ADES 24, ADES 40, ADES 52
PAIN RASSIS. "Après avoir réfléchi profondément a l'origine des glands" ADES 24, ADES 40
QUI EST-CE. "J'appelle tabac ce que est oreille" ADES 24, ADES 40, ADES 52
6 FÉVRIER. "Vive le 6 février" ADES 24, ADES 40
"Soleil route usée pierres frémissantes" ADES 24, ADES 40
Peretz, J. L. in Yiddish.
THE MAGICIAN. "In a volina schtatel arine is amule gakimmen a kinsenmache" FOLKW 90
Pérez, Ana Maria. in Spanish.
LA MUERTE DEL AMOR. "Más profunda que todos los abismos" SMC 7
Pérez de Zambrana, Luisa. 1835. in Spanish.
DULZURA DE LA MELANCOLÍA. "Es tan dulce mirar cómo derrama" SMC 13
Périn, René. 1774. in French.
AUBE. HACH 4
Pers, Ciro di. 1599. in Italian.
Poetry* CETRA 24
Perse, Saint-John (Alexis Saint-Léger Léger). 1887. in French.
AMERS, exc. "Amour, amour, qui tiens si hout le cri de ma naissance, qu'il est" FOLKW 88
_____. "Car tu nous reviendras, présence" ADES 42, SPOA 62

_____. "Et c'est la mer qui vint à nous sur les degrés de pierre du drame" HACH 22
_____. "Et vous, Mers, qui lisiez dans de plus vastes songes" ADES 42, HACH 22, SPOA 62
_____. "Étroits sont les vaisseaux, étroite notre couche" FOLKW 88
ANABASE, exc. "Il naissait un poulain sous les feuilles de bronze" ADES 42, SPOA 62
_____. "Nous n'habiterons pas toujours ces terres jaunes, notre délice" ADES 42, HACH 22, SPOA 62
CHRONIQUES. "Grand age, nous voice" DOVER 4
ELOGES, exc. "A présent laissez-moi, je vais seul" HACH 22
_____. "Ô! J'ai lieu de louer" HACH 22
EXIL, exc. "Comme celui qui se dévêt à la vue" HACH 22
_____. "Portes ouvertes sur les sables, porte ouvertes sur l'exil" ADES 42, HACH 22, SPOA 62
_____. "Syntaxe de l'éclair" HACH 22
_____. "Toujours il y eut cette clameur, toujours il y eut cette splendeur" HACH 22
LA GLOIRE DES ROIS. AMITIÉ DU PRINCE. "Assis à l'ombre sur son seuil" HACH 22
NEIGES. "Ce n'était pas assez que tant de mers" HACH 22
PLUIES, exc. "Innombrables sont nos voies" HACH 22
_____. "Soeurs des guerriers d'Assur" HACH 22
VENTS, exc. "Ivre, plus ivre, disais-tu" HACH 22
_____. "Telle est l'instance extrême ou le poète a témoigne" HACH 42, SPOA 62
Persius (Aulus Persius Flaccus). 34 A.D. in Latin
Poetry* CETRA 18
Peseroff, Joyce. in English.
Poetry* MICHM 2
Pessanha, Camilo. 1867. in Portuguese.
AO LONGE, OS BARCOS DE FLORES. "Só, incessante um som de flauta chora" FOLKW 7
SONETO. "Floriram por engano as rosas bravas" FOLKW 7
SONETO. "Quem poluín, quem rasgon os men lençois de linho" FOLKW 7
Pessoa, Fernando. 1888. in Portuguese.
AUTOPSICOGRAFIA. "O poeta é um fingidor" FOLKW 7
"Ela canta, pobre ceifeira" FOLKW 7
O MENINO DE SUA MÂE. "No plaino abandonado" FOLKW 7
ODE (RICARDO REIS). "Nâo só quem nos odeia ou nos inveja" FOLKW 7
OUTRA ODE (RICARDO REIS). "Nâo sei se e amo que tens, ou amor que finges" FOLKW 7
Pestel, Thomas. in English.
PSALM FOR CHRISTMAS DAY. LION
Petrarca, Francesco (Petrarch). 1304. in Italian.
"Alma felice, che sovente torni" CETRA 1
"Amor ed io si pien di meraviglia" CETRA 1
CANZONIERI, exc. CETRA 2
"Chiare, fresche e dolci acque" CETRA 14, SPOA 3

---

* Recording not available for analysis

"Di pensier in pensier, di monte in monte"
CETRA 14
"Erano i capei d'oro all'aura sparsi"
CETRA 14
GIROVAGO. "In nessuna parte"   CETRA 17
"Io son sí stanco sotto 'l fascio antico"
CETRA 14
"Levommi il mio pensier in parte ov'era"
CETRA 14
MY GALY. "My galy charged with forgetfullness"
English SPOA 83
"Né mai pietosa madre al caro figlio"
CETRA 14
"Nova angeletta sovra l'ale accorta" SPOA 30
"O mameretta, che già fosti un porto"
CETRA 14
"Or che 'l ciel e la terra e l' vento tace"
DOVER 3
"Padre del ciel dopo i perdutti giorni"
CETRA 14
"Quand'io mi volgo indietro a mirar gli anni"
CETRA 14
"Quanto più m'avvicino"   CETRA 14
"Quel rossigniuol che si soave piagne"
CETRA 14
"Quel vago impallidir, che 'l dolce riso"
CETRA 14
"Ripensando a quel ch'oggi il ciel onora"
CETRA 14
"S'amor non è, che dunque è quel ch'io sento?"
CETRA 14
"Se lamentar augelli, o verdi fronde"
CETRA 14
"Sento l'aura mia antica e i dolci colli"
CETRA 14
"Solo e pensoso i piú deserti campi"
DOVER 3, SPOA 30
"Tennemi amor anni vent'uno ardendo"
CETRA 14
"Tutta la mia fiorita e verde etade"
CETRA 14
"Vago augelletto, che cantando vai"
CETRA 14
"Valle che de' lamenti miei se' piena"
CETRA 14
"La vita fugge e non s'arresta un'ora"
CETRA 14

haedrus. 1st c. A.D. in Latin.
Poetry*   CETRA 18

hilips, Katharine. 1631. in English.
TO MY EXCELLENT LUCASIA, ON OUR FRIENDSHIP. "I
did not live until this time"   ARGO 37

hilodemos the Epicurean. ca. 110 A.D. in Greek.
REMONSTRANCE. "So I am your 'darling girl'"
English CARIL 3

cabia, Francis. 1878. in French.
LES PERLES AUX POURCEAUX. "J'interroge le
Sphynx"   FOLKW 13

card, Barbara. 1917. in English.
THE SWORD IN THE STONE.   HOUGHT 1

ccolo, Lucio. 1903. in Italian.
LA STRADA FUORI PORTA.   CETRA 18

edra-Bueno, Andrés de. 1903. in Spanish.
SONETO DE EPOCA. "A dónde ir? Cada órbita se
cierra"   SMC 13

Piercy, Marge. 1936. in English.
THE AIM: THE MAGICIAN. "Fusion is miracle"
WATSHD 1
AT THE CORE. "Quiet setting the rough hairy
roots"   WATSHD 17
ATHENA IN THE FRONT LINES.   WATSHD 17
BEAUTY I WOULD SUFFER FOR.   WATSHD 17
CARD MOST HOPED FOR/MOST FEARED: THE JUDGE-
MENT. "I call on the dead"   WATSHD 1
CONCERNING THE MATHEMATICIAN. "In the living
room you are someplace else"
WATSHD 17
THE CONSUMER. "My eyes catch and stick"
WATSHD 17
THE DEVELOPMENT. "The bull dozers come,
they rip"   WATSHD 17
THE FRIEND. "We sat across the table"
WATSHD 17
HIGH FREQUENCY. "They say that trees scream"
WATSHD 17
THE HOMELY WAR. "Wrote two letters while
rain"   WATSHD 17
THE HOUSE, THE ENVIRONMENT: THE EMPEROR. "In
the house of power"   WATSHD 1
I AM A LIGHT YOU COULD READ BY. "A flame from
each"   WATSHD 17
THE INFLUENCE COMING: SEVEN OF PENTACLES.
"Under a sky the color of pea soup"
WATSHD 1
THE INFLUENCE PASSING: KNIGHT OF SWORDS. "I
was a weapon"   WATSHD 1
LIVING IN THE OPEN. "People ask questions"
WATSHD 17
THE MATTER: THE TOWER STRUCK BY LIGHTNING.
"All my life I have been a prisoner"
WATSHD 1
METAMORPHOSIS INTO BUREAUCRAT.   CAED 155
PHYLLIS WOUNDED. "To fight history as it carries
us"   WATSHD 17
PREVIOUS CONDITION. EIGHT OF SWORDS. "Bound,
blinded, stymied"   WATSHD 1
QUERENT'S ATTITUDE: THREE OF CUPS. "A poem is
a dancing"   WATSHD 1
RAPE POEM. "There is no difference between
being raped"   WATSHD 17
RIVER ROAD, HIGH TOSS. "In the reeds the blue"
WATSHD 17
THE ROAD BEHIND THE LAST DUNE. "Mostly you
don't see the ocean"   WATSHD 17
THE ROOT CANAL.   WATSHD 17
THE SIGNIFICATOR: QUEEN OF PENTACLES. "This is
my deck I unwrap"   WATSHD 1
THAT WHICH CROSSES: NINE OF CUPS. "Not fat, not
gross, just well fed"   WATSHD 1
TO BE OF USE. "The people I love best"
WATSHD 17
TO THE PAY TOILET. "You strop my anger, espe-
cially"   WATSHD 17
THE TOKEN WOMAN. "The token woman gleams
like a gold molar in a toothless mouth"
WATSHD 17
A WORK OF ARTIFICE. "The bonsai tree"
WATSHD 17
Poetry*   CASSC 13

* Recording not available for analysis

Pierpont, John. 1785. in English.
WARREN'S ADDRESS AT BUNKER HILL. "Stand! the ground's your own, my braves!" DECCA 4, EAV 14

Pietri, Pedro. 1943. in English.
HOW DO YOUR EGGS WANT YOU. "At the age of empty spaces" FOLKW 112
1 A. M. AT ALL TIMES. "We went to where the mountains" FOLKW 112
PUERTO RICAN OBITUARY. "They worked" FOLKW 112
SUICIDE NOTE FROM A COCKROACH IN A LOW INCOME HOUSING PROJECT. "I hate the world" FOLKW 112
TELEPHONE BOOTH. NUMBER 23. "The next time" FOLKW 112
_____ NUMBER 102. "You and your bottle" FOLKW 112
_____ NUMBER 190. "This is a true story" FOLKW 112
_____ NUMBER 535. "When you receive this letter" FOLKW 112
_____ NUMBER 580. "I will not be over" FOLKW 112
_____ NUMBER 722. "I came over" FOLKW 112
_____ NUMBER 801. "No, of course not" FOLKW 112
_____ NUMBER 905 1/2. "Woke up this morning" FOLKW 112
TO GET DRUNK YOU HAVE TO DRINK. "Unseen faces keep appearing" FOLKW 112
WARNING. "The Surgeon General has determined" FOLKW 112

Pilinszky, Janos. 1921. in Hungarian.
HARBACH 1944. "Újra és úira öket látom" English and Hungarian ARGO 16
RAVENSBRŮCKI PASSIÓ. "Kilép a többiek Közül" English and Hungarian ARGO 16
SZERELEM SIVATAGA. English and Hungarian ARGO 16
ZSOLTÁR. English and Hungarian ARGO 16

Pilon, Jean-Guy. 1930. in French.
INVENTAIRE. "J'établirai pour toi l'inventaire" FOLKW 70
LEGENDE DE LA CHAIR. "Il te faut la nuit pour ramener" FOLKW 70
LE LIEN DE LA TERRE. "Multiples visages d'un même rêve" FOLKW 70
LIVRE DE MON BORD. "L'appel obscur est venu jusqu'à nous par les voix" FOLKW 70
RECONNAISSANCE DES BORNES. "J'attendrai jusqu'à l'aube" FOLKW 70
VISAGES DE LA TERRE. "Visages de la terre, quand j'aurai dit vos" FOLKW 70

Pinar, Florencia. in Spanish.
CANCIÓN. "Es la voz de mi canción" AGUIL 8

Pindar. 522 B. C. in Greek.
"Epameroi ti de tis; ti d ou tis; skias onar" FOLKW 104
"Kaphision hydaton" Greek and English JNP 95
"Philophron hesykhia dikas" Greek and English JNP 95

Pines, Paul. in English.
CANADIAN JAZZ. "Everyone's kissing John Tank" WATSHD 10

LAST CALL AT THE TIN PALACE. "Granada falling at my feet" WATSHD 10
LIVING HIGH OFF NICKELS AND DIMES. "Friday night at the Tin Palace" WATSHD 10

Pinkney, Edward Coote. 1802. in English.
A SERENADE. "Look out upon the stars, my love" EAV 14
VOTIVE SONG. "I burn no incense, hang no wreath" EAV 14

Piontek, Heinz. in German.
DER JÜNGER. "Klingt der Palasthof" CHRIST 18
VERGÄNGLICHE PSALMEN. "Unter der Mövenschwinge des Morgens ist meine Zuflucht" CHRIST 29

Piron, Alexis. 1689. in French.
MON EPITAPHE. CAED 204

Pisan, Christine de. See Christine de Pisan.

Pitter, Ruth. 1897. in English.
A DREAM. "This is a strange twilit country, but full of peace" ARGO 96

Planz, Allen. 1937. in English.
HEAT WAVE—A DISCONTINUOUS POEM. BROADR 3

Platen-Hallermünde, August Graf von. 1796. in German.
DAS GRAB IM BUSENTO. "Nächtlich am Busento lispeln" DOVER
"Die Liebe hat gelogen" ATHENA 1
DIE NACHT. "Die Nacht bedeckt mit schwarzen Schild die Erde" CHRIST 2
"Der Strom der neben mir verrauschte, wo is er nun?" ATHENA 1
"Vergebt, dass alle meine Lieder klagen" ATHENA 1
"Wem das Leben leid ist" ATHENA 1
"Wer in der Brust ein wachsendes Verlangen" ATHENA 1
"Wer Schönheit angeschaut mit Augen" ATHENA 1
"Wer wusste je das Leben recht zu fassen" ATHENA 1
"Wie rafft ich mich auf in der Nacht" ATHENA 1

Plath, Sylvia. 1932. in English.
ALL THE DEAD DEARS. "Rigged poker-stiff on her back" HARPV
THE APPLICANT. "First, are you our sort of person" AUDIOT 3, SPOA 10
THE BEGGARS OF BENIDORM MARKET. "Nightf cold eye" CAED 1
BERCK-PLAGE. "This is the sea, then, this gre abeyance" CAED 1
BLACK ROOK IN RAINY WEATHER. "On the st twig up there" HARPV
THE BULL OF BENDYLAW. "The black bull b lowed" HARPV
CANDLES. "They are the last romantics, the candles" CAED 1
CHILD'S PARK STONES. "In sunless air und pines" CAED 1
DADDY. "You do not do, you do not do" ARGO 95, AUDIOT
"The day she visited the disecting room" AUDIOT
DEPARTURE. "The figs on the fig tree in t yard" HARPV

* Recording not available for analysis

THE DISQUIETING MUSES. "Mother, mother, what illbred aunt" CAED 177

EDGE. "The woman is perfected" AUDIOT 3

FEVER 103 DEGREES. "Pure? What does it mean" ARGO 95, AUDIOT 2

FROG AUTUMN. "Summer grows old, cold blooded mother" HARPV 6

FULL FATHOM FIVE. "Old man, you surface seldom" HARPV 6

THE GHOST'S LEAVETAKING. "Enter the chilly no-man's land of about" CAED 177

THE GORING. "Arena dust rusted by four bulls' blood" CAED 177

THE HERMIT AT OUTERMOST HOUSE. "Sky and sea, horizon-hinged HARPV 6

"I shall never get you together entirely" AUDIOT 2

I WANT, I WANT. "Open-mouthed, the baby god" HARPV 6

"In Breughel's panorama of smoke and slaughter" AUDIOT 2

THE LADY AND THE EARTHENWARE HEAD. "Fired in sanguined clay" CAED 177

LADY LAZARUS. "I have done it again" ARGO 95, AUDIOT 3, SPOA 107

LEAVING EARLY. "Lady your room is lousy with flowers" CAED 177

LORELEI. "It is no night to drown in" HARPV 6

MARY'S SONG. "The Sunday lamb cracks in its fat" AUDIOT 2

MAUDLIN. "Mud-mattressed under the sign of the hag" HARPV 6

MEDUSA. "Off that land spit of tony mouth plugs" SPOA 107

MOONRISE. "Grub-white mulberries redden among leaves" HARPV 6

MORNING SONG. "Love set you going like a fat gold watch" AUDIOT 2

MUSHROOMS. "Overnight, very" CAED 177

MUSSEL HUNTER AT ROCK HARBOR. "I came before the" HARPV 6

NOVEMBER GRAVEYARD. "The scene stands stubborn: skinflint trees" CAED 177

ON THE DECLINE OF ORACLES. "My father kept a speckled" CAED 177

ON THE DIFFICULTY OF CONJURING UP A DRYAD. "Ravening" CAED 177

OUIJA. "It is a chilly god, a god of shades" CAED 177

PARLIAMENT HILL FIELDS. "On this bald hill the new year hones its edge" CAED 177

A PLETHORA OF DRYADS. "Hearing a white saint rave" CAED 177

POINT SHIRLEY. "From Watertown Hill to the brick prison" HARPV 6

POPPIES IN JULY. "Little poppies, little hell flames" AUDIOT 2

SCULPTOR. "To his house the bodiless" CAED 177

SNAKE-CHARMER. "As the gods began one world, and man another" HARPV 6

SOW. "God knows how our neighbour managed" HARPV 6

"Spaces in darkness" AUDIOT 2

SPINSTER. "Now this particular girl" CAED 177

STINGS. "Bare-handed, I hand the combs" AUDIOT 2

THE STONES. "This is the city where men are mended" CAED 177

STOP DEAD. "A squeal of brakes" SPOA 107

THE SURGEON AT TWO A.M. "The white light is artificial, and hygienic as heaven" CAED 177

TOTEM. "The engine is killing the track" AUDIOT 2

WATERCOLOR OF GRANCHESTER MEADOWS. "There, spring" HARPV 6

Plato. 427 B.C. in Greek.
"Asteras eisathreis aster emos" FOLKW 104

DEDICATION OF A MIRROR. "I Lais whose laughter was scornful in Hellas" English CARIL 3

Pleshette, Ann. 1950. in English.
"The ice has melted" HARB 3

Plomer, William. 1903. in English.
AT THE SUPERMARKET. "Fitting a thin glove over a dry hand" ARGO 91

BAMBOO: A BALLAD FOR TWO VOICES. "However dry and windless" FOLKW 60

THE LAST TRAIN. "Suddenly awake at two, and aware of the disintegration" ARGO 91

LIME-FLOWER TEA. "The esplanade empty, closed at this time" ARGO 91

Plunkett, Joseph Mary. 1887. in English and Gaelic.
"I see his blood upon the Rose" English and Gaelic JNP 90

Poe, Edgar Allan. 1809. in English.
ALONE. "From childhood's hour I have not been" CAED 26, HOUGHT 5, SPOA 87

ANNABEL LEE. "It was many and many a year ago" AGE 4, AUDIA 2, CAED 26, CAED 195, CMS 13, DECCA 10, EAV 10, EAV 14, EAV 19, HARC 4, HOUGHT 5, LION 2, LIST 4, LIST 6, LIST 21, SINGER 3, SPOA 87, VAN 1

THE BELLS. "Hear the sledges with the bells" CAED 93, EAV 15, EAV 19, HARB 6, LIST 6, LIST 8, LIST 19, SPOA 87, VAN 1

THE CITY IN THE SEA. "Lo! Death has reared himself a throne" CAED 26, EAV 14, EAV 19, LIST 3, SPOA 87

THE CONQUEROR WORM. "Lo! 'tis a gala night" CMS 16, EAV 20, SPOA 87

A DREAM WITHIN A DREAM. "Take this kiss upon the brow" CAED 125, CMS 16, SPOA 87

DREAMLAND. "By a route obscure and lonely" CMS 16, EAV 19, SPOA 87

DREAMS. "Oh! that my young life were a lasting dream" CMS 16

ELDORADO. "Gaily bedight" CAED 26, CAED 195, CMS 16, EAV 14, EAV 19, HOUGHT 1, SPOA 87

EULALIE. "I dwelt alone" SPOA 87

EVENING STAR. "'Twas noontide of summer" CMS 16, SPOA 87

FOR ANNIE. "Thank Heaven! the crisis" SPOA 87

THE HAUNTED PALACE. "In the greenest of our valleys" EAV 15, EAV 19, SPOA 87

ISRAFEL. "And the angel Israfel, whose heart-strings" EAV 15, EAV 19, EAV 20, SPOA 87

* Recording not available for analysis

Poe, Edgar Allan (continued)

THE LAKE. "In youth's spring, it was my lot"
CMS 16

LENORE. "Ah, broken is the golden bowl! the spirit flown forever!"   EAV 19, SPOA 87, VAN 1

THE RAVEN. "Once upon a midnight dreary"
CAED 26, EAV 19, HOUGHT 3, LIST 6, LIST 8, LIST 19, RCA 9, SPOA 31, SPOA 75, SPOA 87, UARIZ 1, VAN 1

ROMANCE. "Romance, who loves to nod and sing"   SPOA 87

THE SLEEPER. "At midnight in the month of moon"   EAV 19, SPOA 87

SONG. "I saw thee on thy bridal day" CMS 16

SONNET: SILENCE. "There are some qualities— some incorporate things"   SPOA 87

SPIRITS OF THE DEAD. "Thy soul shall find itself alone"   CMS 16

TO_____ "I heed not that my earthly lot"
SPOA 87

TO_____ "Not long ago, the writer of these lines"   CAED 26

TO_____ "The bowers whereat, in dreams, I see"   SPOA 87

TO HELEN. "Helen, thy beauty is to me"
ARGO 11, AUDIA 2, DECCA 12, EAV 10, EAV 14, EAV 19, LIST 3, SINGER 5, SPOA 31, SPOA 75, SPOA 87, UARIZ 1, VAN 1

TO ONE IN PARADISE. "Thou wast that all to me, love"   EAV 19

TO SCIENCE. "Science, true daughter of all time thou art"   EAV 19, SPOA 87

TO THE RIVER. "Fair river! in thy bright, clear flow"   SPOA 87

ULALUME. "The skies they were ashen and so- ber"   CAED 125, EAV 19, LIST 6, LIST 8, LIST 19, SPOA 87, VAN 1

THE VALLEY OF UNREST. "Once it smiled a silent dell"   CAED 125, SPOA 87

Poetry* AGE 4, APPL 8, APPL 14, CAED 4, LIST 12

Polak, Maralyn. in English.

BILL WAGNER'S BONES. "They built Bill Wagner's bones"   WATSHD 4

CRAZY. "I am not always this crazy"
WATSHD 4

FIFTH ANNIVERSARY. "You are a fat Jack Sprat"
WATSHD 4

THE OPPOSITE SIDE OF THE DEATH COIN IS LOVE. "Getting from here"   WATSHD 4

TO AUNT GERTRUDE, WHOM I NEVER MET. "The weather never changes"   WATSHD 4

TO FEEL WHAT WAS HAPPENING. "This woman sandpapered"   WATSHD 4

THE TROUBLE WITH DANCING. "Why I don't dance"   WATSHD 4

THE YOUNG WOMEN. "All the young women"
WATSHD 4

Poliziano, Angelo. 1454. in Italian.
"Ben venga Maggio"   DOVER 3

I'MI TROVAI, FANCIULLE. "I'mi trovai, fanciulle, un bel mattino"   SPOA 30

Poetry*   CETRA 21

Pols, Edward. 1919. in English.
"A tumult of images insist"   FOLKW 21

Pombo, Rafael. 1833. in Spanish.
LA POBRE VIEJECITA.   MIAMI 1

EL RENACUAJO PASEADOR. "El hijo de la rana, Rinrin Renacuajo"   SMC 8

Pommy Vega, Janine. 1942. in English.
BARD OWL. "Almost like tears"   WATSHD 14

THE MERCHANT POET. "I hawk my wares"
WATSHD 14

PANAMA AIRPORT. "Desolation sits in a fluores- cent airport"   WATSHD 14

Popa, Vasko. 1922. in Serbian.
IURKE. "Iedni odgrizu drugima"
Serbian and English ARGO 16

KLINA. "Iedan bude klin drugi kleshta"
Serbian and English ARGO 16

PEPELA. "Iedni su noei drugi svezde"
Serbian and English ARGO 16

POSLE IGRE. "Naizad se ruke ukhvate za trbukh"   Serbian and English ARGO 16

PRE IGRE. "Zazhmuri se na iedno oko"
Serbian and English ARGO 16

SVADBE. "Svako svuche svoiu kozhu"
Serbian and English ARGO 16

ZAVODNIKA. "Iedan miluie nogu stolitse"
Serbian and English ARGO 16

Pope, Alexander. 1688. in English.
THE DUNCIAD, exc. "In vain, in vain—the all- composing hour"   LONGM 1

_____ "Next bidding all draw near on bended knees"   ARGO 48

_____ "Oh Muse! relate (for you can tel alone)"   CAED 88

_____ "The quaking mind, that closed an oped no more"   ARGO 48

ELEGY TO THE MEMORY OF AN UNFORTUNATE LADY "What beck'ning ghost along the moonligh shade"   ARGO 48, SPOA 7

ELOISA TO ABELARD. "In these deep solitude and awful cells"   CAED 89, CAED 203 SPOA 7

EPILOGUE TO THE SATIRES. DIALOGUE 2. "Ask yo what provocation I have had?"   ARGO 4

EPISTLE I: TO LORD COBHAM, exc. "In vain th sage, with retrospective eye"   ARGO 4

EPISTLE II: TO A LADY, exc. "Nothing so true a what you once let fall"   ARGO 48 CAED 8

_____ "Yet Chloe sure was form'd without spot"   ARGO 48, THEAL

_____ "In men we various ruling passio find"   ARGO 4

EPISTLE IV. TO THE EARL OF BURLINGTON, exc. "A Timon's villa let us pass a day"   ARGO 4

EPISTLE TO DR. ARBUTHNOT. "Shut, shut the doo good John! fatigued, I said"   ARGO 4 CAED 88, SPOA 7

_____ "Peace to all such! but were there or whose fires"   ARGO 4

_____ "Let Sporus tremble"   ARGO 4

AN ESSAY ON CRITICISM, exc. "A little learning a dangerous thing"   ARGO 48, CAED 2 CMS 13, JMP

_____ exc. "But most by numbers judge poet's song"   ARGO 48, EAV 1 LONGM

---

* Recording not available for analysis

_____, exc. "Of all the causes which conspire to blind"   CAED 89

_____, exc.   BRITAM 3, CAED 203, LIST 2, SPOA 74

AN ESSAY ON MAN. EPISTLE 1, exc. "Lust, thro' some certain strainers well refin'd"   ARGO 48

_____. EPISTLE 2, exc. "Know then thyself, presume not God to scan"   ARGO 48, CAED 88

_____. exc.   LIST 2, SINGER 6

A FAREWELL TO LONDON. "Dear, damn'd distracting town"   ARGO 48

IMITATIONS. SECOND EPISTLE, SECOND BOOK OF HORACE, exc.   ARGO 48

ODE ON SOLITUDE. "Happy the man, whose wish and care"   CAED 89, CAED 203, LIVLAN 1

ON A CERTAIN LADY AT COURT. "I know the thing that's most uncommon"   ARGO 48

THE RAPE OF THE LOCK. "What dire offence from am'rous causes springs"   ARGO 49

_____, exc.   CAED 88, EAV 11, SPOA 73

_____, exc. "Close by those meads for ever crown'd with flow'rs"   LONGM 1

THE UNIVERSAL PRAYER. "Father of all! in every age"   EAV 6

WINDSOR FOREST. "Thy forest, Windsor! and thy green retreats"   ARGO 48

Pope, Jessie. in English.
NOISE. "I like noise"   HARB 4

Poquelin, Jean-Baptiste. See Molière.

Porta, Carlo. 1775. in Italian.
CATOLEGH, APOSTOLEGH E ROMAN.   CETRA 47
COSS'EL VOEUR EZZELENZA CHE RESPONDA.
                                                CETRA 47
DESCRAZZI DE GIOVANNIN BONGEE.   CETRA 47
MENEGHIN BIROEU DI EX MONEGH.   CETRA 47
LA NINETTA DEL VERZEE.   CETRA 47
LA NOMINA DE CAPPELLAN. "A la marchesa Paola Travasta"   CETRA 15
PARACAR CHE SCAPPEE DE LOMBARDIA.
                                                CETRA 47
QUAND VEDESSEV ON PUBBLEGH FUNZIONARI.
                                                CETRA 47
Poetry*   CETRA 27

Portela, C. in Spanish.
Poetry*   SMC 17

Porter, Bern. 1911. in English.
BAGS. "The Glad food storage bags"
                                               WATSHD 4
GEORGE. "1. George—"   WATSHD 4
AN INDEX OF FIRST LINES. "Wash the dishes"
                                               WATSHD 4
PLAY. "Linger, finger, rub, rub, stroke"
                                               WATSHD 4
WOOD. "Wooden particle board"   WATSHD 4

Porter, Peter. 1929. in English.
BEAST AND THE BEAUTY. "His fear never loud in daylight"   ARGO 95
CLAIRVOYANT.   ARGO 154
THE DUST. "How many divisions has the dust"
                                                ARGO 154
EUROPE. "Breathe honey looking south, the mind land over"   ARGO 154
FOSSIL GATHERING. "Armed with hammers, we move along the cliff"   ARGO 154

FROGS AT LAGO DI BOLSENA. "Having come down and run the car into sand"   ARGO 154
GENIUS LOCI.   ARGO 154
HAPPENING AT SORDID CREEK. "I chose the blonde from the Chemist's, thirty-six"
                                                ARGO 95
HOMILY IN THE ENGLISH READING ROOM.
                                                ARGO 154
THE LAST OF ENGLAND. "It's quiet here among the haunted tenses"   ARGO 154
THE LAST OF THE DINOSAURS.   ARGO 154
MADE IN HEAVEN. "From Heals and Harrods come her lovely bridegrooms"   ARGO 95
MORT AUX CHATS.   ARGO 154
THE PETER PORTER SONG BOOK. I.   ARGO 154
PRINT/OUT: APOCALYPSE. "When the army of ecologists"   ARGO 154
THE SADNESS OF CREATURES. "We live in a third floor flat"   ARGO 154
THE SANATORIUM.   ARGO 154
SEX AND THE OVER FORTIES. "It's too good for them"   ARGO 154
SOMME AND FLANDERS. "Who am I to speak up for the long dead"   FOLKW 59A
WHAT A LYING LOT THE WRITERS ARE. "To put it all down I take my pencil up"   FOLKW 59A
WHITE WEDDING.   ARGO 154
WHO GETS THE POPE'S NOSE? "It is so tiring having to look after the works of God"   ARGO 95, ARGO 154
YOUR ATTENTION PLEASE. "Your attention"
                                   PROTHM 8, SPOA 68

Porter, William N. in English.
PLUM BLOSSOM. "So sweet the plum trees smell"
                                                HARB 6

Posner, David. in English.
THE CITY. "From street to street I often watch the night"   SPOWRD 1
THE DESERTED ALTAR. "Horseman you come to bring us peace"   SPOWRD 1
THE FLOWER. "How do you bloom, young flower"   SPOWRD 1
THE HAND AND THE BOWL. "In the land of Bow and Meissen"   SPOWRD 1
HENRIETTE AT THE GUITAR. "I have heard the singing ghost"   SPOWRD 1
IN MEMORY OF ANDREW HILLS. "What loving shall she try in heaven"   SPOWRD 1
OF PROMISED LANDS. "The book of the marvels of the world"   SPOWRD 1
THE POET. "What has the traveller to say about our dream"   SPOWRD 1
THE TEMPLE. "Tall heart, thin house"
                                                SPOWRD 1

Poulsson, Anne Emilie. in English.
JUDGING BY APPEARANCES. "An old Jack-o-Lantern lay on the ground"   HARB 1

Pound, Ezra. 1885. in English.
CANTICO DEL SOLE. "The thought of what America would be like"   CAED 70, CAED 84, HARPV 1
CANTOS. 1. "And then went down to the ship"
                                   CAED 70, CAED 84
_____. 3. "I sat on the Dogana's steps"
                                   APPL 1, SPOA 92
_____. 4. "Palace in smoky light"   CAED 70, CAED 84

* Recording not available for analysis

Pound, Ezra (continued)

_____ 16. "And before hell mouth"   APPL 1

_____ 17. "So that the vines burst from my
fingers"   HARPV 1

_____ 36. "A Lady asks me I speak in season"
                            CAED 70, CAED 84

_____ 38. "An' that year Metevsky went over
to America del Sud"   SPOA 92

_____ 45. "With Usura" CAED 84, HARPV 1

_____ 49. "For the seven lakes, and by no
man"   APPL 1

_____ 51. "Shines"   CAED 84

_____ 76. "Both eyes, (the loss of) and to find
someone"   CAED 84

_____ 81. "Zeus lies in Ceres bosom"
                                       APPL 1

_____ 84. "8th October: Si tuit li dolh elh plor
Angold"   CAED 70, CAED 84

_____ 92. "And from this Mount were blown
the seed"   APPL 1

_____ 99. "Till the blue grass turn yellow"
                                      CAED 84

_____ 106. "And was her daughter like that"
                            APPL 1, SPOA 92

_____ 115. "Scientists are in terror"   APPL 1

ENVOI, 1919. "Go, dumb-born book" ARGO 12,
                                      HARPV 1

THE GYPSY.   CAED 84

HOMAGE TO SEXTUS PROPERTIUS. "When, when,
and whenever death"   HARPV 1

HUGH SELWYN MAUBERLEY. "For three years, out
of key with his time" ARGO 12, CAED 70,
                             CAED 84, HARPV 1

MAUBERLEY. "Turned from the eau-forte"
                                      HARPV 1

MEDITATIO.   SCHOL 7

MOEURS CONTEMPORAINES. "(Mr. Styrax), Mr.
Hecatomb Styrax, the owner of a large estate
and of large muscles" CAED 70, CAED 84,
                                     CAED 183

ODE POUR L'ELECTION DE SON SEPULCHRE, II, IV, V.
                                      ARGO 12

THE SEAFARER. "May I for my own self song's
truth reckon"   HARPV 1

SESTINA: ALTAFORTE.   HARPV 1

"Siena mi fe: disfecemi Maremma" ARGO 12
Poetry*   BBC 2, SPOA 118

Poveda, José Manuel. 1888. in Spanish.
SOL DE LOS HUMILDES. "Todo el barrio pobro"
                                       SMC 13

Prados, Emilio. 1899. in Spanish.
PÁGINA FIEL . . . , NOSTALGIA. "Lejano mar,
conoces tu misterios?"   DOVER 2
PUÑAL DE LUZ. "Este cuerpo que Diós pone en
mis brazos"   SPOA 59

Praed, Winthrop Mackworth. 1802. in English.
GOOD-NIGHT TO THE SEASON, exc. "Good-night to
the Season! 'tis over"   LONGM 1

Praga, Emilio. 1839. in Italian.
Poetry*   CETRA 27

Prefontaine, Yves. 1937. in French.
MIRAGE. "Les lunes brouillées coulent au bout
de mes doigts"   FOLKW 70
"Ombres très écloses et lointaines"
                                     FOLKW 70

TERRE D'ALERTE. "Une âpreté de fougère cerne
de cruautè"   FOLKW 70

Press, John. 1920. in English.
AFTER LE NOZZE DI FIGARO. "It did not last.
Before the year was out"   ARGO 93
ATHENIAN MORNING. "No day has ever risen like
this day"   ARGO 93
FAREWELL. "Mary, daughter of King James I"
                                      ARGO 93
THE LONG DAYS. "The long days of my child-
hood"   ARGO 93
THE SEAGULL. "The gull in full perfection rides
the storm"   ARGO 93
WINTER LANDSCAPE, GREECE. "Here as I pause
and stay motionless and alone" ARGO 93

Preston, George Nelson. in English.
ASIAN NIGGER. "Runs like an ostrich"
                                     BROADR 2

Prévert, Jacques. 1900. in French.
AU JARDIN DES MISÈRES.   GMS 12
BARBARA. "Rappelle-toi Barbara"   ADES 44,
                             FOLKW 88, GMS 12
LES BELLES FAMILLES. "Louis I"   ADES 44
BRANLE-BAS DE COMBAT. "C'est la nuit"
                                       VOIX 3
CABLE CONFIDENTIEL.   GMS 12
CHANSON DANS LE SANG. "Il y a de grandes
flaques de sang sur le monde"   ADES 44,
                                       VAN 3
CHANSON DES SARDINIÈRES. "Tournez tournez"
                                       GMS 12
CHANT SONG. "Moon lune/ chant song"
                                       GMS 12
CHARADE. "Faites-moi rire, bouffon" ADES 44
CHEZ LA FLEURISTE. "Un homme entre chez une
fleuriste"   ADES 44
LE COMBAT AVEC L'ANGE. "N'y va pas" GMS 12
COMPLAINTE DE VINCENT. "À Arles où roule le
Rhône"   GMS 12
LE CONCERT N'A PAS ÉTÉ REUSSI. "Compagnons
des mauvais jours"   ADES 44
CORTÈGE. "Un vieillard en or avec une montre
en deuil"   VOIX 3
DANS LE BAS-FOND.   GMS 12
DIMANCHE. "Entre les rangées d'arbres de
l'avenne des Gobelins"   GMS 12
DÎNER DE TÊTE.   ADES 44
LE DIVIN MÉLODRAME.   VOIX 3
ECLAIRCIES.   VOIX 3
L'ÉCOLE DES BEAUX-ARTS. "Dans une boîte de
paille"   GMS 12
EN FAMILLE. "La mère est seule dans la maison"
                                       VOIX 3
ENCORE UNE FOIS SUR LE FLEUVE.   VOIX 3
L'ENFANCE.   ADES 44
LES ENFANTS EXIGEANTS. "Pères"   ADES 44
ÉTRANGES ÉTRANGERS.   GMS 12
FAMILIALE. "La mère fait du tricot"
                             CAED 204, CBS 1
FÊTE. "Dans les grands eaux de ma mère"
                                       GMS 12
LE FILS DU GRAND ROSEAU. "Je suis né un soir où
on ne m'attendait pas"   VOIX 3
FOUS DE MISÈRE.   GMS 12
FRONTIÈRES. "Votre nom?"   ADES 44
LA GRASSE MATINÉE. "Il est terrible" ADES 44,
                                       CBS 1

HOMMAGE AU LIT. "Jamais il n'est dit"
ADES 44
IL FAUT PASSER LE TEMPS. ADES 44
IL NE FAUT PAS. "Il ne faut pas laisser les intellectuels jouer avec les allumettes" GMS 12
J'AI TOUJOURS ÉTÉ INTACT DE DIEU. ADES 44
LE JARDIN. "Des milliers et des milliers d'années" GMS 12
"Je suis comme je suis" FOLKW 88
LE MIROIR BRISÉ. "Le petit homme qui chantait sans cesse" ADES 44, VOIX 3
LES MYSTÈRES DE SAINT-PHILIPPE DU ROULE.
ADES 44
PARIS AT NIGHT. "Trois allumettes une à une allumées dans la nuit" VOIX 3
PATER NOSTER. "Notre Père qui êtes aux cieux"
ADES 44, VOIX 3
PLACE DU CARROUSEL. "Place du Carrousel"
GMS 12, VOIX 3
POUR RIRE EN SOCIÉTÉ. "Le dompteur a mis sa tête" GMS 12
QUELQU'UN. "Un homme sort de chez lui"
ADES 44, FOLKW 13
RIEN À CRAINDRE. "Ne craignez rien"
ADES 44
RITOURNELLE. GMS 12
SANGUINE. "La fermeture éclair a glissé sur tes reins" ADES 44, VOIX 3
LE TEMPS PERDU. "Devant la porte de l'usine"
GMS 12
VRAIMENT. "Un vieillard hurle à la mort"
GMS 12
Prince, F. T. 1912. in English.
SOLDIERS BATHING. "The sea at evening moves across the sand" ARGO 119
Prior, Matthew. 1664. in English.
A BETTER ANSWER, OR ANSWER TO CHLOE JEALOUS. "Dear Chloe, how blubbered in that pretty face" ARGO 47
CUPID'S MISTAKE. CAED 203
THE LADY WHO OFFERS HER LOOKING-GLASS TO VENUS. "Venus, take my votive glass"
ARGO 47
A LETTER TO THE HONORABLE LADY MISS MARGARET CAVENDISH HOLLES HARLEY WHEN A CHILD. "My noble, lovely, little Peggy" ARGO 47
A LOVER'S ANGER. "As Chloe came into the room" ARGO 47
ON MY BIRTHDAY. "I, my dear, was born to-day"
ARGO 47
SONG. "The merchant, to secure his treasure"
ARGO 47
TO A CHILD OF QUALITY. "Lords, knights, and squires, the numerous band" ARGO 47
Pritchard, Norman Henry. 1939. in English.
GYRE'S GALAX. "Sound variegated through beneath lit" BROADR 2
Propertius, Sextus. 50 B. C. in Latin.
"Cynthia prima suis miserum me cepit ocellis"
FOLKW 98
"Qualis Thesea iacuit cedente carina"
FOLKW 98
"Sunt aliquid Manes: letum non omnia finit"
FOLKW 98
Poetry* CETRA 18

Prothro, Nancy. in English.
IT WAS A SUMMER. "It was a summer"
WATSHD 8
RUBY. "Ruby. short mother" WATSHD 8
THE THIN AIR. "I have heard molecules"
WATSHD 8
Ptolemaios the Astronomer. ca. 100. in Greek.
INSCRIPTION FOR THE TOMB OF TIMON. "Ask neither my name nor my country, passer-by"
English CARIL 3
STAR-GAZING. "That I am mortal I know and do confess" English CARIL 3
Pucci, Antonio. 1310. in Italian.
Poetry* CETRA 19
Pulci, Luigi. 1432. in Italian.
Poetry* CETRA 21
Purdy, Al. 1918. in English.
ROBLIN'S MILLS. "The mill was torn down last year" LEARNC 9
Purens, Ilmars. in English.
LADIES. "I long for the small fur"
WATSHD 12
TRUCK ODE. "My friend with beautiful hair"
WATSHD 12
Pushkin, Aleksandr Sergeevich. 1799. in Russian.
ARION. MK 1
CHAADAEVU. "Lyubvi, nadezhdy, tikhnoi slavy"
CAED 193
EVGENII ONEGIN, exc. "Ne vos legordi"
MELOD 1
19 OKTYABRYA. "Ronyaet les bagryanii svoi ubor" MK 1
NYANE. "Podruga dnei moikh surovykh"
CMS 6
OSEN' MK 1
VOZROZHDENIE. "Khudozhnik-varvar kist'yu sonnoi" CAED 193
"Ya vas lyubil: lyubov' eshche byt' mozhet"
CAED 193
ZAKLINANIYE. "O, yesli pravda, chto v nochï"
FOLKW 94
ZIMNI VECHER. "Burya Mgloyu Nebo Kroyet"
SCHOL 6
ZOLOTO I BULAT. "Vse moe,—skazalo zlato"
CMS 6
Putnam, Phelps. in English.
BALLAD OF A STRANGE THING. LIBC 17,
LIBC 57
Pyle, Katherine. in English.
THE SEA PRINCESS. "In a garden of shining seaweed" BOWMAR 1, HARB 5

Quarles, Francis. 1592. in English.
A GOOD NIGHT. "Close now thine eyes, and rest secure" ARGO 36
ON ZACHEUS. "Methinks I see, with what a busie haste" ARGO 36
Quart, Pere. 1899. in Catalan.
LA CROADA. "Quan s'acosta l'hora" AGUIL 14
Quasha, George. in English.
SOMAPOETICS, exc. WATSHD 13
Quasimodo, Salvatore. 1901. in Italian.
ALLA NUOVA LUNA. "In principio Dio creo il cielo" Italian and Swedish GRAM 1
ANTICO INVIERNO. "Desiderio delle tue mani chiare" DOVER 3

* Recording not available for analysis

Quasimodo, Salvatore (continued)

LETTERA ALLA MADRE. "Mater dulcissima, ora
scendono"   CETRA 31
UNA RIPOSTA DAL VOL.   EPIU 1
UOMO DEL MIO TEMPO. "Sei ancora quella della
pietra e della fionda"   DOVER 3
Poetry*   CETRA 43, CETRA 46

Queneau, Raymond. 1903. in French.
CE SOIR. "Ce soir"   ADES 44
LES CHIENS D'ASNIÈRES. "On enterre les chiens"
                                             ADES 44
JE CRAINS PAS ÇA TELLEMENT. "Je crains pas ça
tellement"   ADES 44
CYGNES. "Quand Un fit l'amour avec Zero"
                                             ADES 44
UN ENFANT A DIT. "Un enfant a dit"   ADES 44
L'EXPLICATION DES MÉTAPHORES. "Loin du
temps, de l'espace"   ADES 44
JE NAQUIS AU HAVRE.   ADES 44
MARINE. "Les poissons ont de si jolies têtes"
                                             ADES 44
SAINT-OUEN'S BLUES. "Un arbre sans une bran-
che"   ADES 44
SI TU T'IMAGINES. "Si tu t'imagines"   ADES 44
TOUT EST CRU. "Tout est cru, tout est vert"
                                             ADES 44
TRAINS DANS LA BANLIEUE OUEST. "Le train court
on ne sait où"   ADES 44

Quental, Antero de. 1842. in Portuguese.
NA MÃO DE DEUS. "Na mão de Deus, na sua mão
direita"   FOLKW 72
NOCTURNO. "Espírito que passas, quando o vento"   FOLKW 72
TORMENTO DO IDEAL. "Conheci a Beleza que
não morre"   All on: FOLKW 72

Quevedo y Villegas, Francisco de. 1580. in Span-
ish.
A UNA NARIZ. "Érase un hombre a una nariz
pegado"   DOVER 2
"Adán en paraíso, vos en huerto"   AGUIL 5
AMOR CONSTANTE MAS ALLA DE LA MUERTE. "Cer-
rar podrá mis ojos la postrera"   AGUIL 4,
                                           DOVER 2
CÓMO DE ENTRE MIS MANOS. "Cómo de entre mis
manos te resbalas"   SPOA 37
CONTRA LA DUREZA DEL CORAZON DEL HOMBRE.
                                           AGUIL 5
MEMORIA INMORTAL DE DON PEDRO GIRON, DUQUE
DE OSUNA. "Faltar pudo su patria al grande
Osuna"   AGUIL 6
"Miré los muros de la patria mía"   AGUIL 6,
                                           HOLT 1
PODEROSO CABALLERO ES DON DINERO. "Madre,
yo al oro me humillo"   CMS 5, HOLT 1,
                                           SPOA 37
SONETO DE LA MUERTE DE CRISTO.   AGUIL 5

Quiller-Couch, Arthur Thomas. 1863. in English.
UPON ECKINGTON BRIDGE.   ARGO 77

Quintana, Manuel José. in Spanish.
A ESPAÑA, DESPUES DE LA REVOLUCION DE MARZO.
"Qué era, decidme, la nación que un día"
                                           AGUIL 6

Quintana, Mário. 1906. in Portuguese.
SONÊTO. "Este silêncio á feito de agonias"
                                          FOLKW 71

Raab, Lawrence. 1946. in English.
Poetry*   MICHM 2?

Racan, Honorat de Bueil, Seigneur de. 1589. in
French.
LE BONHEUR DE LA VIE CHAMPETRE, exc.
                                           HACH 9

Racine, Jean. 1639. in French.
PLAINTE D'UN CHRÉTIEN. "Mon Dieu, quelle
guerre cruelle"   ADES 5?

Raftery, Antoine. 1784. in Gaelic.
THE COUNTY OF MAYO. "Now with the coming in
of the Spring"   English BRITAM 1
                    Gaelic and English SPOA ?
I AM RAFTERY. "I am Raftery the poet, full o
hope and love"   English SPOA 6
                    Gaelic and English SPOA ?

Rago, Henry. 1915. in English.
THE PROMISING. "Swift/ Signatures of the shore"
                                           LIBC ?
A SKY OF LATE SUMMER. "The fountains of fire"
                                           LIBC ?

Railes, Vilota. in English.
GROWING UP.   CREAT ?

Raimbaut de Vaqueiras. 12th c. in Provençal.
POLYGLOT POEM. "Eras quan vey verdeyar"
                                          FOLKW 1?
TENZO. "Domna, tant vos ai preiada"
                                          FOLKW 1?

Raimon. in Catalan.
"Al vent"   AGUIL 1?
CANÇO DE LES MANS. "De l'home mire"
                                           AGUIL 1?
D'UN TEMPS, D'UN PAIS. "D'un temps que serà e
nostre"   AGUIL 1?

Raine, Kathleen. 1908. in English.
THE ETERNAL CHILD. "A little child enters by a
secret door"   ARGO 9?
STATUES. "They more than we are what we are"
                                           ARGO 9?

Raine, Stephen. in English.
Poetry*   ARGO 9?

Raleigh, Sir Walter. 1522. in English.
ALL THE WORLD'S A STAGE. "What is our life? A
play of passion"   ARGO 31, COLUMB 10
                                           SPOA 8?
"As you came from the Holy Land" SPOA 5?
THE BOOK OF THE OCEAN'S LOVE TO CYNTHIA, exc
                                           ARGO 7?
HIS EPITAPH. "Even such is time, that takes in
trust"   LIST 1, SPOA 8?
THE LIE. "Go, Soul, the body's guest"
                    ARGO 31, COLUMB 11, SPOA 83
                                           LONGM
"Like to a Hermite poore in place obscure"
                                           SPOA 8?
A LOVER'S COMPLAINT.   BRITAM ?
NOW WHAT IS LOVE? "Now what is love, I pray
thee tell"   ARGO 88?
THE NYMPH'S REPLY TO THE SHEPHERD. "If all the
world and love were young"   CMS 13
          FOLKW 60, IMP 1, LIST 1, SPOA 50
                                           ARGO 13
THE PASSIONATE MAN'S PILGRIMAGE. "Give me
my scallop-shell of quiet"   ARGO 31
          LIST 1, POLYGL 2, SPOA 12, SPOA 83
                                           ARGO 13
SIR WALTER PLEADS IN PERSON.   ARGO 7?

---

* Recording not available for analysis

ambler, Karl Wilhelm. 1725. in German.
AN DEN FRIEDEN. "Wo bist du hingeflohn, geliebter Friede?"   DEUTGR 13
andall, Dudley. 1914. in English.
ANALYSANDS. "Sipping whiskey and gin"
                                          BROADV 3
AUGURY FOR AN INFANT. "Venita, you have come
   to us"   BROADV 3
BALLAD OF BIRMINGHAM. "Mother dear, may I go
   downtown"   BROADV 3, BROADV 11
BELLE ISLE. "When leaves were the color of
   sun"   BROADV 11
BLACK POET, WHITE CRITIC. "A critic advises"
                                          BROADV 3
BOOKER T. AND W. E. B. "It seems to me," said
   Booker T."   BROADV 11, SPOA 88
A DIFFERENT IMAGE. "The age/ requires"
                                          BROADV 3
DRESSED ALL IN PINK. "It was a wet and cloudy
   day"   BROADV 3
FOR MARGARET DANNER. "Courage banners"
                                         BROADV 11
GEORGE. "When I was a boy desiring the title of
   man"   BROADV 11
"Hail, Dionysos"   BROADV 3
THE IDIOT. "That cop was powerful mean"
                                          BROADV 3
LEGACY: MY SOUTH. "What desperate nightmare"   BROADV 11
THE MELTING POT. "There is a magic melting
   pot"   BROADV 3
MEMORIAL WREATH. "In this green month when
   resurrected"   BROADV 11
A NET OF SMOKE. "A net of smoke"
                                          WATSHD 2
OLD WITHERINGTON. "Old Witherington had
   drunk too much again"   BROADV 3
PRIMITIVES. "Paintings with stiff"   BROADV 3
THE RITE. "Now you must die, the young one
   said"   BROADV 3
ROSES AND REVOLUTIONS. "Musing on roses and
   revolutions"   BROADV 3
SANCTUARY. "This is the time of the whirlwind"
                                          WATSHD 2
THE SOUTHERN ROAD. "There the black river,
   boundary to hell"   BROADV 11
SOUVENIRS. "My love has left me has gone from
   me"   BROADV 11
THIS BAPTISM OF FIRE. "The shouts shrink"
                                          WATSHD 2
THE TROUBLE WITH INTELLECTUALS. "The intellectuals talked"   WATSHD 2
YOUR HANDS. "Your hands woke"   WATSHD 2
ands, William Brightly. 1823. in English.
"Godfrey Gordon Gustavus Gore"   CMS 3
THE WONDERFUL WORLD. "Great wide beautiful
   wonderful world"   HARB 4
ansom, John Crowe. 1888. in English.
ADDRESS TO THE SCHOLARS OF NEW ENGLAND.
   "When Sarah Pierrepont let her spirit rage"
                                          CARIL 6
ANTIQUE HARVESTERS. "Tawny are the leaves
   turned but they still hold"   CARIL 6
BELLS FOR JOHN WHITESIDE'S DAUGHTER. "There
   was such speed in her little body"
      ARGO 12, CARIL 6, LIBC 11, LIBC 37,
                           LIST 4, SINGER 5

BLUE GIRLS. "Twirling your blue skirts, travelling the sward"   ARGO 12
CAPTAIN CARPENTER. "Captain Carpenter rose
   up in his prime"   CARIL 6, LIBC 11,
                  LIBC 36, LIBC 37, SPOA 93
DEAD BOY. "The little cousin is dead, by foul
   subtraction"   CARIL 6
THE EQUILIBRISTS. "Full of her long white arms
   and milky skin"   ARGO 12, CARIL 6
GOOD SHIPS. "Fleet ships encountering on the
   high seas"   CARIL 6
HERE LIES A LADY. "Here lies a lady of beauty
   and high degree"   CARIL 6, LIBC 11,
                          LIBC 37, SPOA 93
JANET WAKING. "Beautifully Janet slept"
                           LIBC 11, LIBC 37
JUDITH OF BETHULIA. "Beautiful as the flying legend of some leopard"   CARIL 6
LADY LOST. "This morning, flew up the lane"
                                          CARIL 6
OUR TWO WORTHIES. "All the here and all the
   there"   CARIL 6
PAINTED HEAD. "By dark severance the apparition head"   CARIL 6
PIAZZA PIECE. "I am a gentleman in a dustcoat
   trying"   CARIL 6
PRELUDE TO AN EVENING. "Do not enforce the
   tired wolf "   LIBC 1, SPOA 93
SPECTRAL LOVERS. "By night they haunted a
   thicket of April mist"   CARIL 6
SURVEY OF LITERATURE. "In all the good Greek of
   Plato"   CARIL 6
WHAT DUCKS REQUIRE. "Ducks require no ship
   and sail"   CARIL 6
Poetry*   LIST 13, NET 13
Raper, Michele. in English.
MORNING GLORY. "My father would begin each
   day"   SPOA 67
SUNDAY MORNING IN THE NORTH. "Because of
   sunlight"   SPOA 68
Rashidd, Amir. in English.
ECLIPSE.   EAV 16
Rasof, Henry. in English.
HONEY HONEY. "Nee, nee, nee, nee"
                                         WATSHD 11
IT IS.   WATSHD 13
MIAMI MAYA. "A my a my a my"   WATSHD 11
SHORT POEM.   WATSHD 13
WICHITA FALLS I. "Wichita-ta, which which"
                          WATSHD 11, WATSHD 13
Rasul, Sha'ir. in English.
ALAFIA. "Alafia flames, rising"   WATSHD 1
LEFT THE BROTHER DEAD. "Body going to wax
   form"   WATSHD 1
THIS POEM GETS LOCKED UP. "This poem gets
   locked up"   WATSHD 1
THE WARDENS. "The jails are filling up"
                                         WATSHD 1
WHAT IT WAS, IS. "What it was, is" WATSHD 1
Ray, David. 1932. in English.
Poetry*   WATSHD 63
Ray, Shreela. in English.
Poetry*   JNP 43
Read, Herbert. in English.
THE BOY IN THE BARN.   CAED 111
THE BROWN BOOK OF THE HITLER TERROR. "In
   Bednib's shop I picked up a book" LIBC 1

* Recording not available for analysis

Read, Herbert (continued)

THE HEART CONSCRIPTED. "Lorca was killed, singing" LIBC 1
TO A CONSCRIPT OF 1940. "A soldier passed me in the freshly fallen snow" ARGO 96, ARGO 119
————, exc. "But you, my brother and my ghost, if you can go" LIBC 1
A WORLD WITHIN A WAR. LIBC 17, LIBC 56

Read, Thomas Buchanan. 1822. in English.
SHERIDAN'S RIDE. "Up from the South, at break of day" DECCA 4, EAV 10, EAV 15
VALLEY FORGE. DECCA 13

Reale, Basilio. in Italian.
LA CORRENTE VIVA. CETRA 31

Reaney, James. 1926. in English.
THE BEAUTY OF MISS BEATTY. "The beauty of Miss Beatty" FOLKW 50
THE CROW. "A fool once caught a crow" FOLKW 50
DARK LAGOON. "Here lies the newborn child" FOLKW 50
THE HEART AND THE SUN. "Come to me!" cried the Heart to the Star" FOLKW 50
THE KATZENJAMMER KIDS. "With porcupine locks" FOLKW 50
KLAXON. "All day cars mooed and shrieked" FOLKW 50
LAKE SUPERIOR. "I am Lake Superior" FOLKW 50
THREE DEADLY SINS. "Pink protrusion, pachyderm pork crystal" FOLKW 50

Rebora, Clemente. 1885. in Italian.
Poetry* CETRA 28, CETRA 43

Rector, Liam. in English.
BANK ROBBERY. "He goes nuts" WATSHD 12
THE CARPENTER. "Dwelling in dimensions of four" WATSHD 12
AN ORIGIN OF ART. "Modigliani's paintings are being shipped" WATSHD 12

Redgrove, Peter. 1932. in English.
THE ARCHAEOLOGIST. "So I take one of those thin plates" ARGO 94, ARGO 154
AT THE EDGE OF THE WOOD. "First, boys out of school went out of their way home" ARGO 94, ARGO 154
CHRISTIANA. "That day in the interpreter's house. ARGO 154
FOR NO GOOD REASON. "I walk on the wasteground for no good reason" ARGO 94, ARGO 154
FROM THE REFLECTIONS OF MR. GLASS. "White globe of rain, we are caught" ARGO 154
GHOSTS. "The terrace is said to be haunted" ARGO 154
THE HALF-SCISSOR. "Humming water holds the high stars" ARGO 154
THE HEIR. "No here I am, drinking in the tall old house, alone" ARGO 154
THE IDEA OF ENTROPY AT MAENPORTH BEACH. "A boggy wood as full of springs as trees" ARGO 154
IN CASE OF ATOMIC ATTACK. ARGO 94, ARGO 154

MINERALS OF CORNWALL STONES OF CORNWAL "Splinters of information, stones of inform tion" ARGO 15
A PHILOSOPHY IN WELSHESE. "The summe before last I saw my vision" ARGO 15
THE PLAY. ARGO 9
SAM'S CALL. "My uncle Sam Lines alwa seemed" ARGO 15
THE SECRETARY. "At work his arms wave like windmill" ARGO 9
THE STRONGHOLD. "We had a fine place t come" ARGO 9

Redi, Francesco. 1626. in Italian.
Poetry* CETRA 2

Redmond, Eugene. 1937. in English.
GODS IN VIETNAM. "Mechanical/ Oracles" EAV 1

Reecher, Edward. in English.
REVOLUTION'S CRADLE SONG. SPOA 8

Reed, Henry. 1914. in English.
CHARD WITLOW (MR. T.S. ELIOT'S SUNDAY EVENIN BROADCAST) POSTSCRIPT. "As we get older w do not get any younger" CAED 1
JUDGING DISTANCES. ARGO 139, LIBC 3
NAMING OF PARTS. "To-day we have naming parts" ARGO 119, ARIZ 2, CAED 1 FOLKW 65, JUP 1, LIBC 36, SINGER
Poetry* LIST 1

Reed, Ishmael. 1938. in English.
BETTY'S BALL BLUES. "Betty took" WATSHD
BLACK COOK. "He frightens all the witches" WATSHD
THE JACKAL HEADED COWBOY. "We will swi from giant cables" BROADR
THE WARDROBE MASTER OF PARADISE. WATSHD

Reese, Lizette Woodworth. in English.
A LITTLE SONG OF LIFE. "Glad that I live am I CAED 1(

Reeve, F. D. 1928. in English.
Poetry* JNP 4

Reeves, James. 1909. in English.
BEECH LEAVES. "In autumn down the beec wood path" HARB
THE GRASSHOPPER AND THE BIRD. CAED 1(
HONEYSUCKLE SMELL. "What brings the se wind so far ashore" ARGO 9
LEAVING TOWN. "It was impossible to leave t town" SPOA (
MUSIC IN THE WOOD. "Music there would be" ARGO 9
OLD AND YOUNG. "Let the old inherit moo light" ARGO 9
SLOWLY. CAED 1
THE STONE GENTLEMAN. "Let us move the sto gentleman to the toadstool wood" ARGO 9
THIS IS YOUR ELEGY. "This is your elegy, the gr sea grieving" ARGO 9
WHAT KIND OF MUSIC. "What kind of music do Tom like best" HARB

Rega Molina, Horacio. 1899. in Spanish.
A MUCHOS. "Déjame así. Mi corazón no pide" AGUIL

Régnier, Henri de. 1864. in French.
EXPERIENCE. HACH
STANCES. ADES

* Recording not available for analysis

Reid, Alastair. 1926. in English.

CALENTURE. "He never lives to tell"   CMS 7

CASA. "However gracefully"   CMS 7

CAT-FAITH. "As a cat, caught by the door opening"   CMS 7

DISGUISES. "My selves, my presences"   CMS 7

FOR HER SAKE. "Her world is all aware. She reads"   CMS 7

FOR RING GIVERS. "Given the gift of a ring"   CMS 7

A GAME OF GLASS. "I do not believe this room"   CMS 7

GHOST. "Never to see ghosts? Then to be"   CMS 7

GHOSTS' STORIES. "That bull-necked blotch-faced farmer"   CMS 7

GROWING, FLYING, HAPPENING. "Say the soft bird's name, but do not be surprised"   CMS 7

IN MEMORY OF MY UNCLE TIMOTHY. "His name, they told me afterwards, was Able"   CMS 7

A LESSON FOR BEAUTIFUL WOMEN. "Gazing and gazing in the glass"   CMS 7

A NOTE FROM THE COAST. "This coast's not/ easy"   CMS 7

ODDMENTS, INKLINGS, OMENS, MOMENTS. "Oddments, as when/ you see"   CMS 7

THE O-FILLER. "One noon in the library, I watched a man"   CMS 7

OLD PAINTER TO YOUNG MODEL. "If, when the paint has dried"   CMS 7

PIGEONS. "On the crooked arm of Columbus, on his cloak"   CMS 7

SMALL SAD SONG. "I am a lady"   CMS 7

SPAIN, MORNING. "Up early, out of a dream"   CMS 7

SPEAKING A FOREIGN LANGUAGE. "How clumsy on the tongue"   CMS 7

THE SYNTAX OF SEASONS. "Autumn was adjectival, I recall"   CMS 7

THE TALE THE HERMIT TOLD. "It was one afternoon when I was young"   CMS 7

THAT DYING. "As often as not, on fair days"   FOLKW 21

WAS, IS, WILL BE. "It was to have been"   CMS 7

WHAT'S WHAT. "Most people know"   · CMS 7

WHO AM I? "Could it have been mine"   CMS 7

Retamar, Roberto Fernández. 1930. in Spanish.

EL OTRO. "Nosotros, los sobrevivientes"   SMC 13

Reverdy, Paul. 1889. in French.

TARD DANS LA NUIT. "La couleur que décompose la nuit"   FOLKW 13

Rexroth, Kenneth. 1905. in English.

ANOTHER SPRING. "The seasons revolve and the years change"   LIBC 1, SPOA 98

AN EASY SONG. "It's rained every day since you"   LIBC 1, SPOA 98

MAY DAY. "Once more it is early summer"   LIBC 1, SPOA 98

NORETORP-NORETSYH.   EVERG 1

A SWORD IN A CLOUD OF LIGHT. "Your hand in mine, we walk out"   LIBC 1, SPOA 98

THIS NIGHT ONLY. "Moonlight now on Malibu"   LIBC 1, SPOA 98

THOU SHALT NOT KILL. "They are murdering all the young men"   FANT 1

Poetry*   WATSHD 45

Reyes, Alfonso. 1889. in Spanish.

ESTA NECESIDAD. "Esta necesidad de sacrificio"   FOLKW 80

Reyes Fuentes, Maria de los. in Spanish.

COLUMNAS ROTAS. "Cuánto se ha roto, Dios. Tú que lo sabes"   FIDIAS 2

Reynolds, Malvina. in English.

THE EMPEROR'S NIGHTINGALE.   EAV 17

Riba Bracóns, Carles. 1897. in Catalan.

"Gloria de Salamina vermella en el mar de l'aurora"   AGUIL 14

Ribera Chevremont, Evaristo. 1896. in Spanish.

ISLA Y MAR.   INSTPR 1

LOS SONETOS DE LA SOLEDAD, 3. "Aquí es el canto de agua ya escondida"   HOLT 1

LA TIERRA Y EL SUEÑO.   INSTPR 1

Ricardo, Cassiano. 1895. in Portuguese.

O ANJO REBELDE. "Senhor, a estrêla que me destinaste"   FOLKW 71

O BANQUETE. "Em meu quarto, o sile"   FOLKW 71

Rich, Adrienne. 1929. in English.

THE AFTERWAKE. "Nursing your nerves"   SCHOL 4

AUTUMN SEQUENCE. "An old shoe, an old pot, and old skin"   SCHOL 4

BREAKFAST IN A BOWLING ALLEY IN UTICA, NEW YORK.   SCHOL 4

BURNING ONESELF IN. "We can look into the stove tonight"   STANFD 1

CHARLESTON IN THE EIGHTEEN-SIXTIES. "He seized me by the waist and kissed my throat"   SCHOL 4

DIDACTIC POEM.   STANFD 1

DIVING INTO THE WRECK. "First having read the book of myths"   STANFD 1

FOR A RUSSIAN POET. "Everywhere, snow is falling. Your bandaged foot"   SCHOL 4

THE FOURTH MONTH OF THE LANDSCAPE ARCHITECT. "It is asleep in my body"   STANFD 1

GHOST OF A CHANCE. "You see a man"   SCHOL 4, SPOA 106

I DREAM I'M THE DEATH OF ORPHEUS. "I am walking rapidly through striations of light and dark thrown under an arcade"   STANFD 1

IN THE EVENING. "Three hours chain-smoking words"   STANFD 1

IN THE WOODS. "Difficult ordinary happiness"   SPOA 106

INCIPIENCE. "To live, to lie awake"   STANFD 1

LIKE THIS TOGETHER. "Wind rocks the car"   SCHOL 4

MERCED. "Fantasies of old age"   STANFD 1

MOURNING PICTURE. "They have carried the mahogany chair and the cane rocker out under the lilac bush"   SPOA 106

NOVELLA. "Two people in a room, speaking harshly"   SCHOL 4

PASSING ON. "The landlord's hammer in the yard"   SCHOL 4

PEELING ONIONS. "Only to have a grief"   SCHOL 4, SPOA 106

THE PHENOMENOLOGY OF ANGER. "The freedom of the wholly mad"   STANFD 1

* Recording not available for analysis

Rich, Adrienne (continued)

A PRIMARY GROUND. "And this is how you live: a woman"   STANFD 1
THE ROOFWALKER. "Over the half finished houses"   SPOA 106
THE STRANGER. "Looking as I've looked before, straight down the heart"   STANFD 1
TRANSLATIONS. "You show me the poems of some woman"   STANFD 1
UNWRITTEN NOVEL.   STANFD 1
WAKING IN THE DARK. "The thing that arrests me is"   STANFD 1
Poetry*   JNP 45

Richards, Frank. 1875. in English.
CHRISTMAS 1914.   ARGO 89

Richards, I. A. 1893. in English.
BIRTHDAY THOUGHTS. IV. "Surely this day"   LIBC 48
BUT STILL DESIRE AND WILL. "Legs be still"   LIBC 48
COURT OF APPEAL. "Nature is better dressed than man"   LIBC 48
HARVARD YARD IN APRIL: APRIL IN HARVARD YARD. "To and fro"   LIBC 48
LIGHTING FIRES IN SNOW. "Tread out a marble hollow"   LIBC 48
REFLECTIONS II, CONTENT. "Content? Content. Let be what will"   LIBC 48
SEAFARING I, COMB AND GLASS. "Uphill all the way"   LIBC 48
THE SOLITARY DAFFODIL. "From committee-doodled day"   LIBC 48
TO BE. "Still missing it though"   LIBC 48
TO DUMB FORGETFULNESS. "Forget, forget . . . Forget what you forget"   LIBC 48
THE YEARLING SWIFT. "Bygones, begone! They trouble me"   LIBC 48

Richards, Laura E. in English.
THE CAVE-BOY. "I dreamed I was a cave-boy"   HARB 2
THE MONKEYS AND THE CROCODILE. "Five little monkeys"   NAITV 5

Rictus, Jehan. 1867. in French.
BERCEUSE POUR UN PAS-DE-CHANCE.   ADES 22
LES PETITES BARAQUES.   ADES 22
Poetry*   ADES 50

Ridruejo, Dionisio. 1912. in Spanish.
AMOR. "Bajo la sola estrella te he encontrado"   AGUIL 10
"Llevamos—tiene dos asas"   AGUIL 10
MENSAJE A AZORIN, EN SU GENERACION. "Eran jóvenes: avanzaron"   AGUIL 6
PAYESES. "Comen su pan cuando lo sudan"   AGUIL 10
LA TARDE RESPONDIA. "La tarde respondia/ a las viñas"   AGUIL 4

Riggs, Katherine Dixon. in English.
MOCKERY. "Happened that the moon was up before I went to bed"   CAED 164

Riley, James Whitcomb. 1849. in English.
THE BEAR STORY. "W'y wunst they wuz"   FREED 1
THE BUMBLE BEE. "You better not fool with a bumblebee"   FREED 1
A CANARY ON THE FARM. "Folks has be'n to town"   FREED 1

EXTREMES. "A little boy once played so loud"   CMS 3
GRIGGSBY'S STATION. "Pap's got his patent-right"   FREED 1
AN IMPROMPTU FAIRY TALE. "Wunst upon a time"   FREED 1
KNEE-DEEP IN JUNE. "Tell you what I like best"   FREED 1
LITTLE ORPHANT ANNIE. "Little Orphant Annie's come to our house to stay"   FREED 1,
                                                          HARC 4
OLD WINTERS ON THE FARM. "I have jest about decided"   FREED 1
OUT TO OLD AUNT MARY'S. "Wasn't it pleasant, o brother"   FREED 1
THE PET COON. "Noey Bixler ketched him"   FREED 1
THE RAGGEDY MAN. "O the Raggedy Man! He works fer Pa"   FREED 1
A SEA-SONG FROM THE SHORE. "Hail, ho! Sail, ho"   HARB 2
WHAT SMITH KNEW ABOUT FARMING. "There wasn't two"   FREED 1
WHEN THE FROST IS ON THE PUNKIN. "When the frost is on the punkin and the fodder's in the shock"   FREED 1
Poetry*   LIST 16

Rilke, Rainer Maria. 1875. in German.
ABSCHIED. "Wie hab ich das gefühlt was Abschied heisst"   CHRIST 28
AUSGESETZT AUF DEN BERGEN DES HERZENS. "Ausgesetzt auf den Bergen des Herzens. Siehe, wie klein dort"   CHRIST 28
BLAUE HORTENSIE. "So wie das letzte Grün in Farbentiegeln"   CHRIST 28
DER BLINDE KNABE.   DEUTGR 25
THE BLIND MAN'S SONG. "I am blind, you out there. That is a curse"   English LIBC 1
UN CYGNE. "Un cygne avance sur l'eau" [composed in French]   CAED 204
LA DORMEUSE. "Figure de femme, sur son sommeil" [composed in French]   CAED 204
ERSTE DUINESER ELEGIE. "Wer, wenn ich schriebe, hörte mich denn aus der Engel"   CHRIST 25
HERBST. "Die Blätter fallen, fallen wie von weit"   SPOA 5
"Ich fürchte mich so vor der Menschen Wort"   SPOA 5
"Ich lebe mein Leben in wachsenden Ringen"   CAED 47
"Jetzt reifen schon die roten Berberitzen"   CHRIST 28
JUDENFRIEDHOF.   DEUTGR 25
DAS KARUSSELL. "Mit einem Dach und seinem Schatten dreht"   CHRIST 28, DEUTGR 17,
                                                          DEUTGR 25
KINDHEIT. "Darinnt der Schule lange Angst"   DEUTGR 17, DEUTGR 25
DIE KIRCHE VON NAGO.   DEUTGR 25
DER KNABE. "Ich möchte einer werden so wie die"   DEUTGR 17
DAS MARIENLEBEN, exc. "O was muss es die Engel gekostet haben"   CAED 75
_____. "Seht auf, ihr Männer. Männer dort am Feuer"   DEUTGR 17
DIE NACHT.   DEUTGR 25

---

* Recording not available for analysis

DER NARR.   DEUTGR 25
ORPHEUS, EURYDIKE, HERMES. "Das war der Seel-
    en wunderliches Bergwerk"   CHRIST 28
DER PANTHER. "Sein Blick ist im Vorübergehn
    der Stäbe"   CHRIST 28, DEUTGR 17,
                                         DEUTGR 25
RUHMEN, DAS IST'S! "Rühmen, das ist's. Ein zum
    Rühmen Bestellter"   CHRIST 28
DER SCHAUENDE. "Ich sehe den Bäumen die
    Stürme an"   DEUTGR 17
SPANISCHE TÄNZERIN. "Wie in der Hand ein
    Schwefelzündholz"   DOVER 1
"Wandelt sich rasch auch die Welt"
                                         CHRIST 28
"Was wirst du tun, Gott, wenn ich sterbe?"
                                         CHRIST 28
DIE WEISE VON LIEBE UND TOD DES CORNETS CHRIS-
    TOPH RILKE. "Reiten, reiten, reiten, durch
    den Tag, durch die Nacht, durch den Tag"
    AMAD 3, CAED 75, DEUTGR 17
Poetry*   CHRIST 5, DEUTGR 40, PRENT 2
Rimbaud, Arthur. 1854. in French.
ALCHIMIE DU VERBE (HISTOIRE D'UNE DE MES FO-
    LIES). "A moi. L'histoire d'une de mes folies"
                              ADES 43, SPOA 27
APRES LE DÉLUGE. "Aussitôt que l'idée du Dé-
    luge se fut rassise"   ADES 43, ADES 49,
                              FOLKW 13, SPOA 27
AUBE. "J'ai embrassé l'aube d'été"   ADES 43,
                                         FOLKW 86
BAL DES PENDUS. "Au gibet noir, manchot aima-
    ble"   GMS 3, HACH 24, POLYGL 1
LE BATEAU IVRE, exc. "Comme je descendais des
    Fleuves impassibles"   ADES 43, ADES 49,
    FOLKW 86, GMS 3, GMS 7, GMS 9,
    HACH 13, PERIOD 1, POLYGL 1,
                              SPOA 9, SPOA 27
BONNE PENSÉE DU MATIN. "A quatre heures du
    matin, l'été"   ADES 43
CHANSON DE LA PLUS HAUTE TOUR. "Oisive jeu-
    nesse"   HACH 13, PERIOD 1
LES CHERCHEUSES DE POUX. "Quand le front de
    l'enfant, plein de rouges tourmentes"
    ADES 43, ADES 49, ADES 54 PERIOD 1
DÉPART. "Assez vu. La vision s'est rencontrée à
    tous les airs"   DOVER 4
LE DORMEUR DU VAL. "C'est un trou de verdure
    où chante une rivière"   ADES 43,
                              ADES 49, CAED 204
L'ÉTERNITÉ. "Elle est retrouvée"   PERIOD 1
EVIL.   English VAN 3
FÊTES DE LA FAIM. "Ma faim, Anne, Anne"
                                         PERIOD 1
"Loin des oiseaux des troupeaux des vil-
    lageoises"   PERIOD 1
MA BOHÈME. "Je m'en allais, les poings dans mes
    poches crevées"   ADES 43, ADES 49,
    ADES 54, GMS 3, POLYGL 1, SPOA 36,
                                         DOVER 4
MATINÉE D'IVRESSE.   HACH 13
MAUVAIS SANG. "J'ai de mes ancêtres gaulois"
                              ADES 43, SPOA 27
OPHELIE. "Sur l'onde calme et noire où dorment
    les étoiles"   GMS 3, HACH 24, POLYGL 1
LES POÈTES DE SEPT ANS. "Et la Mère, fermant le
    livre du devoir"   PERIOD 1

ROMAN. "On n'est pas sérieux quand on a dix-
    sept ans"   ADES 54, SPOA 9
ROYAUTÉ. "Un beau matin"   ADES 43,
                                         SPOA 27
SAISON EN ENFER, exc. "O saisons, o châteaux"
    ADES 43, ADES 49, PERIOD 1
LES SOEURS DE CHARITÉ. "Le jeune homme dont
    l'oeil est brillant, la peau brune"
                                         PERIOD 1
VOYELLES. "A noir, E blanc, I rouge, U vert, O
    bleu: voyelles"   ADES 43, ADES 49,
    ADES 54, FOLKW 86, PERIOD 1,
                                         SPOA 27
Rinaldo d'Aquino. 13th c. in Italian.
Poetry*   CETRA 19
Risi, Nelo. in Italian.
DENTRO LA SOSTANZA, exc.   APPL 4
PENSIERI ELEMENTARI, exc.   APPL 4
POLSO TESO, exc.   APPL 4
Ritsos, Yannis. 1909. in Greek.
EPITAPHIOS, exc. "Ye mu, splachno tou splach-
    nou mu karthula tis karthias mu"
                                         ARGO 16
Rive, Richard. 1931. in English.
WHERE THE RAINBOW ENDS.   CAED 136
Roach, Eric. in English.
CARIBBEAN CALYPSO. "Roads were rougher in
    their island kingdom"   CAED 153
Roberts, Elizabeth Maddox. 1886. in English.
FIREFLY. "A little light is going by"
                                         CAED 109
THE HENS. "The night was coming very fast"
                                         CAED 164
THE RABBIT. "When they said the time to hide
    was mine"   CAED 109
STRANGE TREE. "Away beyond the Jarboe
    house"   CAED 164, HARB 5
WATER NOISES. "When I am playing by myself"
                                         CAED 164
Robinson, Edwin Arlington. 1869. in English.
AARON STARK. "Withal a meagre man was Aaron
    Stark"   HOUGHT 4
CLIFF KLINGENHAGEN. "Cliff Klingenhagen had
    me in to dine"   HOUGHT 5
EROS TYRANNOS. "She fears him, and will always
    ask"   ARGO 12
THE HOUSE ON THE HILL. "They are all gone
    away"   CMS 4
LOST ANCHORS. "Like a dry fish flung far from
    shore"   ARGO 12
THE MILL. "The miller's wife had waited long"
                                         HOUGHT 5
MINIVER CHEEVEY. "Miniver Cheevey, child of
    scorn"   CMS 12, HOUGHT 5, RCA 10,
                                         THEAL 1
RICHARD CORY. "Whenever Richard Cory went
    down town"   RCA 10, SINGER 4,
                                         THEAL 3
THE SHEAVES. "Where long the shadows of the
    wind had rolled"   ARGO 12
Robinson, Wanda. in English.
A BLACK ORIENTED LOVE POEM, THE FIRST TIME I
    SAW LONELINESS.   PERC 1
CELEBRATION, COMPROMISE.   PERC 1
THE FINAL HOUR.   PERC 1
GOOD THINGS COME.   PERC 1
THE GREAT AMERICAN PASSTIME.   PERC 1

* Recording not available for analysis

Robinson, Wanda (continued)

INSTANT REPLAY.	PERC 1
JOHN HARVEY'S BLUES.	PERC 1
THE MEETING PLACE.	PERC 1
PARTING IS SUCH.	PERC 1
READ STREET FESTIVAL.	PERC 1
TRAGEDY NO. 456.	PERC 1
THE TROUBLE WITH DREAMS / GROOVING.	
	PERC 1
A WORD TO THE WISE.	PERC 1

Robison, Margaret. in English.

BREAKWATER. "On a wide sandy beach"
                                    WATSHD 12
THE CHILD. "They came in with a bulldozer"
                                    WATSHD 12
MY SISTER'S BIRTH. "Dear God, don't let Mother
die"   WATSHD 12
SATURDAY NIGHT. "Miss Mabel"   WATSHD 12
A TRUNK, A WOODEN BOX TIED WITH TWINE. "His
long hair tangled"   WATSHD 12

Robson, Ernest M. 1902. in English.

HYMN TO THE RAT RACE. "Will they castrate"
                                    UCALI 1
"The steeps that onset"   UCALI 1
STONY RIVER. "Under the veil"   UCALI 1

Robson, Jeremy. 1939. in English.

APPROACHING MOUNT CARMEL. "Many had come
before"   ARGO 4
BIOGRAPHY. "They chose pale green" ARGO 4
A FACE IN THE CROWD. "I looked for you in a
crowd"   ARGO 4
LADIES, BEWARE THE POETS. "They will seek you
out, seducing you with words"   ARGO 4
LETTER TO ALGIERS. "No word. And to be frank,
your silence swallowed"   ARGO 4
THE MIDNIGHT SCENE. "Slowly they approach"
                                    ARGO 4
S. O. S.   ARGO 4
WHILE TROOPS MOVED IN. "While troops moved
in to Berlin last night"   ARGO 4
WINTER FEARS. "Shadows of a winter afternoon"
                                    ARGO 4

Roche, Paul. 1928. in English.

THE ANT AND THE GRASSHOPPER.	SPOWRD 4
THE ARCHBISHOP AND THE PUMPKIN.	
	SPOWRD 4
THE BARE-BOTTOMED BABOON.	SPOWRD 4
THE BOURGEOIS BUTTERFLY.	SPOWRD 4
THE BRIDE AND THE LORRY.	SPOWRD 4
THE CAPITALIST FLEA.	SPOWRD 4
THE COMMUNIST FLY.	SPOWRD 4
THE CONCEITED DRAGON.	SPOWRD 4
THE DEPERSONALISED DONKEY.	SPOWRD 4
THE ENLIGHTENED SNAKE.	SPOWRD 4
THE FABLE TO END FABLES.	SPOWRD 4
THE FLY AND THE FLY-PAPER.	SPOWRD 4
THE FROG WHO WOULD AWOOING GO.	
	SPOWRD 4
THE GRATEFUL HUMMINGBIRD.	SPOWRD 4
THE GRUMBLING OLD MAN.	SPOWRD 4
THE LAMP AND THE CANDLE.	SPOWRD 4
THE LION AND THE SHEEP.	SPOWRD 4
THE MAMMON OF INIQUITY.	SPOWRD 4
THE MONKEYS AND THE SUNDIAL.	SPOWRD 4
THE MUCK-BEETLE'S SON.	SPOWRD 4
A PIECE OF NONSENSE.	SPOWRD 4

THE PIG AND THE PLUM TREE.	SPOWRD 4
THE ROSE AND THE DELILAH.	SPOWRD 4
THE SELF-PROTECTING RABBITS.	SPOWRD 4
THE SILVER CUFF AND THE ENCYCLOPAEDIA OF	
KNOWLEDGE.	SPOWRD 4
THE TWO HEARTS.	SPOWRD 4
THE TWO VULTURES.	SPOWRD 4
THE UPSTART DECKCHAIR.	SPOWRD 4
THE VAINGLORIOUS SPARROW.	SPOWRD 4
Poetry*	JNP 46, MERC 1

Rochester, Earl of (John Wilmot). 1647. in English.

AFTER DEATH, NOTHING IS. "After death, nothing
is, and nothing, death"   LONGM 1
THE BULLY (with Thomas D'Urfey). "Room,
room for a blade of the town"   ARGO 47
LOVE AND LIFE. "All my past life is mine no
more"   ARGO 47, LONGM 1
RETURN. "Absent from thee, I languish still"
                                    ARGO 47
A SATIRE AGAINST MANKIND, exc.   ARGO 47
TO A LADY IN A LETTER. "Such perfect bliss, fair
Cloris, we"   LONGM 1
UPON NOTHING. "Nothing! Thou elder brother
ev'n to shade"   IMP 1

Rodari, Gianni. in Italian.

L'ACCENTO SULL'A.	CETRA 44
ARMI DELL' ALLEGRIA.	CETRA 44
L'ASCENSORE.	CETRA 44
IL BASTIMENTO.	CETRA 44
IL CALAMAIO.	CETRA 44
IL CASO DI UNA PARENTESI.	CETRA 44
IL CAVALIERE TONTO.	CETRA 44
IL CIELO È DI TUTTI.	CETRA 44
COMO NEL COMÒ.	CETRA 44
IL DITTATORE.	CETRA 44
LE FAVOLE A ROVESCIO.	CETRA 44
'FERRAGOSTO.	CETRA 44
FILASTROCCA DRONTOLONA.	CETRA 44
FILASTROCCA IMPERTINENTE.	CETRA 44
LA GALERIA.	CETRA 44
IL GATTO INVERNO.	CETRA 44
IL GIOCO DEI 'SE'.	CETRA 44
GIOVANNINO PERDIGIORNO.	CETRA 44
IN FILA INDIANA.	CETRA 44
INVENZIONE DEI FRANCOBOLLI.	CETRA 44
IO VORREI.	CETRA 44
LAGO DI GARDA.	CETRA 44
LA LUNA AL GUINZAGLIO.	CETRA 44
LA LUNA BAMBINA.	CETRA 44
IL MALATINO.	CETRA 44
LA MIA MUCCA.	CETRA 44
L'OMINO DELLA GRU.	CETRA 44
LA PAROLA PALAZZO.	CETRA 44
IL PRINCIPE SPIEDATO.	CETRA 44
QUANTI PESCI CI SONO NEL MARE?	CETRA 44
IL RAGIONIERE A DONDOLO.	CETRA 44
IL SATELITE FILOMENA.	CETRA 44
LA SCUOLA DEI GRANDI.	CETRA 44
UN SIGNORE CON TRE CAPPELLI.	CETRA 44
UN TALE DI MACERATA.	CETRA 44
I TRE DOTTORI DI SALAMANCA.	CETRA 44
IL TRENO DEI BAMBINI.	CETRA 44
IL TRIONFO DELLO ZERO.	CETRA 44
L'UOMO DI NEVE.	CETRA 44
IL VESTITO DI ARLECCHINO.	CETRA 44

---

* Recording not available for analysis

Rodgers, W. R. 1909. in English.

BEAGLES. "Over rock and wrinkled ground"
FOLKW 65, JUP 1

CAROL. "Deep in the fading leaves of night"
FOLKW 65, JUP 1

DIRECTIONS TO A REBEL. "Keep away from roads' webs"
LIBC 40

EUROPA AND THE BULL. "Naked they came, a giggling corps of girls"
ARGO 115

EXPRESS. "As the through-train of words with white-hot whistle"
ARGO 92

FOUR POEMS FOR EASTER. "His breath came in threads"
ARGO 92

———. "Now was the world's back broken"
ARGO 92

———. "They took him out to die" ARGO 92

———. "This was a rough death" ARGO 92

A LAST WORD FOR LOUIS MACNEICE. "Only a green hill"
ARGO 92

LENT. "Mary Magdalene, that easy woman"
ARGO 115, CAED 86

NEITHER HERE NOR THERE. "In that land all is, and nothing's ought"
LIBC 40

SPRING DANCE. "Late, late. But lift now the diffident fiddle and fill"
ARGO 115

THE SWAN. "Bottomed by tugging combs of water"
ARGO 115

Poetry*
LIST 15

Roethke, Theodore. 1908. in English.

ACADEMIC. "The stethoscope tells what everyone fears"
CAED 146

ALL THE EARTH, ALL THE AIR. "I stand with standing stone"
FOLKW 26

THE BAT. "By day the bat is cousin to the mouse" CAED 110, CAED 146, SCHOL 7

BIG WIND. "Where were the greenhouses going"
CAED 146, SPOA 98

BRING THE DAY! "Bees and lilies there were"
FOLKW 26

CUTTINGS (LATER). "This urge, wrestle, resurrection of dry sticks"
CAED 146

THE CYCLE. "Dark water underground"
CAED 146, LIBC 54

THE DECISION. "What shakes the eye but the invisible"
CAED 146

DINKY. "O what's the weather in a beard?"
CAED 146, FOLKW 26

THE DONKEY. "I had a donkey, that was all right"
CAED 146

THE DREAM. "I met her as a blossom on a stem"
FOLKW 26

THE DYING MAN. THE EXULTING, THEY SING, THEY SING.
CAED 146

ELEGY. "Should every creature be as I have been"
CAED 146

ELEGY FOR JANE. "I remember the neckcurls, limp and damp as tendrils.
CAED 146, FOLKW 26, LIBC 40, SPOA 98

THE FAR FIELD, exc. "I dream of journeys repeatedly"
CAED 146

———. "Until the headlights darken"
CAED 146

FOUR FOR SIR JOHN DAVIES. "Is that dance slowing in the mind of man"
CAED 146, FOLKW 26

FRAU BAUMAN, FRAU SCHMIDT, AND FRAU SCHWARTZE. "Gone the three ancient ladies"
CAED 146

GIVE WAY, YE GATES. "Believe me, knot of gristle, I bleed like a tree"
CAED 146, FOLKW 26

THE HAPPY THREE. "Inside, my darling wife"
CAED 146

THE HERON. "The heron stands in water where the swamp"
CAED 112

I KNEW A WOMAN. "I knew a woman, lovely in her bones"
CAED 146, FOLKW 26, LIBC 40, SPOA 98

I NEED, I NEED. "A deep dish. Lumps in it"
FOLKW 26

IN A DARK TIME. "In a dark time, the eye begins to see"
CAED 146

IN EVENING AIR. "A dark theme keeps me here"
CAED 146

INTERLUDE. "The element of air was out of hand"
LIBC 54

THE LADY AND THE BEAR. "A Lady came to a Bear by a stream" CAED 110, FOLKW 26, SPOA 98

THE LONG ALLEY. "A river glides out of the grass"
FOLKW 26, HARPV 4

THE LOST SON. 1. THE FLIGHT. "At Woodlawn I heard the dead cry"
CAED 146, FOLKW 26, LIBC 21, LIBC 64

———. 2. THE PIT. "Where do the roots go"
CAED 146, FOLKW 26, LIBC 21, LIBC 64

———. 3. THE GIBBER. "At the wood's mouth"
CAED 146, FOLKW 26, LIBC 21, LIBC 64

———. 4. THE RETURN. "The way to the boiler was dark"
CAED 146, FOLKW 26, LIBC 21, LIBC 64

———. 5. "It was beginning winter."
CAED 146, FOLKW 26, LIBC 21, LIBC 64

LOVE'S PROGRESS. "The possibles we dare"
FOLKW 26

MEMORY. "In the slow world of dream"
FOLKW 26

MID-COUNTRY BLOW. "All night and all day the wind roared in the trees"
CAED 111

MY PAPA'S WALTZ. "The whiskey on your breath"
CAED 146, FOLKW 26, LIBC 54, SPOA 98

NIGHT CROW. "When I saw that clumsy crow"
SPOA 98

NIGHT JOURNEY. "Now as the train bears west"
HOUGHT 2

OPEN HOUSE. "My secrets cry aloud"
CAED 146

THE OTHER. "What is she, while I live?"
FOLKW 26

PICKLE BELT. "The fruit rolled by all day"
CAED 146

THE PURE FURY. "Stupor of knowledge lacking inwardness"
FOLKW 26

THE RENEWAL. "What glories would we?"
FOLKW 26

REPLY TO A LADY EDITOR. "Sweet Alice S. Morris, I am pleased, of course"
FOLKW 26

THE RETURN. "I circled on leather paws"
FOLKW 25

* Recording not available for analysis

Roethke, Theodore (continued)

A ROUSE FOR STEVENS. "Wallace Stevens, what's he done?" FOLKW 26

THE SENSUALISTS. "There is no place to turn, she said" FOLKW 26

THE SHAPE OF THE FIRE. "What's this? A dish for fat lips" HARPV 4

SHE. "I think the dead are tender" FOLKW 26

THE SHIMMER OF EVIL. "The weather wept, and all the trees bent down" LIBC 40, SPOA 98

THE SLOTH. "In moving-slow he has no peer" CAED 146, FOLKW 26

SONG FOR THE SQUEEZE-BOX. "It wasn't Ernest; it wasn't Scott" FOLKW 26

THE SURLY ONE. "When true love broke my heart in half" FOLKW 26

THE SWAN. "I study out a dark similitude" FOLKW 26

THE VOICE. "One feather is a bird" FOLKW 26

THE WAKING. "I wake to sleep, and take my waking slow" CAED 146, FOLKW 26, SINGER 5

THE WALKING. "I strolled across" LIST 4

THE WRAITH. "Incomprehensible gaiety and dread" FOLKW 25

VERNAL SENTIMENT. "Though the crocuses poke up their heads in the usual places" CAED 146, LIBC 54

WHERE KNOCK IS OPEN WIDE. "A kitten can" CAED 146

WORDS FOR THE WIND. "Love, love, a lily's my care" CAED 146, FOLKW 26

Poetry* JNP 47, LIST 15, UCALM 1

Rogers, Samuel. 1763. in English.

A WISH. "Mine be a cot beside the hill" CAED 186

Rollinat, Maurice. 1846. in French.

LA BICHE BRAME. GMS 6, HACH 4

Romains, Jules. 1885. in French.

"Je sors de ma maison" FOLKW 13

Ronsard, Pierre de. 1524. in French.

À HÉLÈNE. GMS 7

À SON ÂME. "Amelette Ronsardette" ADES 28, ADES 53

À UNE JEUNE MORTE. GMS 8

AMOURS DE CASSANDRE. 66. "Ciel, air et vents, plains et monts découvers" HACH 8

———. 96. "Pren ceste rose aimable comme toy" ADES 28, ADES 53

AMOURS DE MARIE. "Comme on voit sur la branche" PERIOD 2

———. "Je vous envoie un bouquet que ma main" PERIOD 2

LES AMOURS DIVERSES, exc. "Plus estroit que la vigne à l'ormeau se marie" ADES 28, ADES 53

CHANSON. "Quand a beau Printemps je vois" FOLKW 84

CONTRE LES BÛCHERONS DE LA FORET DE GASTINE. "Ecoute, bûcheron, arrête un peu le bras" FOLKW 84

DERNIER VERS—SONNET I. "Je n'ay plus que les os" PERIOD 2

ÉLÉGIE 24, exc. "Forêt, haute maison des o1 seaux bocagers" PERIOD

"Fay refraischir mon vin de sorte" DOVER

HYMNE DE LA MORT, exc. "Que ta puissance, Mort, est grande et admirable" PERIOD

"Marie, levez-vous, ma jeune paresseuse" ADES 28, ADES 5

ODE. "Mignonne, allons voir si la rose" ADES 28, ADES 53, FOLKW 84, HACH 8 PERIOD 2, SPOA 9, SPOA 3

ODE. "O Fontaine Bellerie" ADES 2 ADES 53, HACH

ODE. "Quand je suis vingt ou trente mois" HACH

ODE À CASSANDRE. CAED 204, GMS

ODE À SA MAISTRESSE. "Quand au temple nou serons" CBS

SONNETS. "L'An se rajeunissoit en sa verde jou vence" HACH

———. "Il faut laisser maisons et vergers et jar dins" ADES 28, ADES 53, HACH

———. "Je n'ay plus que les os, un squelette j semble" ADES 54, PERIOD

———. "Je vous enjoye un bouquet, que m main" HACH 8, DOVER

———. "Meschantes nuicts d'hyver" ADES 5

———. "Quand vous serez bien vieille, au soi à la chandelle" ADES 28, ADES 5 HACH 8, PERIOD 2, SPOA

SONNETS POUR HELENE. I. "Le premier jour d may, Hélène, je vous jure" ADES 5

———. VI. "Tu es seule mon coeur, mon sang e ma Déesse" ADES 5

———. VIII. "Je plante en ta faveur cest arbr de Cybelle" ADES 2

———. XVIII. "Cruelle, il suffisoit de m'avoi pouldroyé" ADES 5

———. XXIV. "Amour, je pren congé de ta mer teuse escole" ADES 5

SUR LA MORT DE MARIE, IV. "Comme on voit sur l branche au mois de may la rose" ADES 28 ADES 53, ADES 54, HACH

Ronsisvalle, Vanni. in Italian.

GUARDIA IN MARE. CETRA 3

Rook, Alan. 1909. in English.

DUNKIRK PIER. ARGO 11

Rosales, Luis. 1910. in Spanish.

AUTOBIOGRAFIA. "Como el náufrago metódic que cóntase las olas que le bastan para morir AGUIL

CRECIENDO HACIA LA TIERRA. "Cuando llegue l noche y sea la sombra un báculo" AGUIL

TU, SI LOS LLAMARÁS. "Tienen nombre, Señor son los que sufren" AGUIL

Y ESCRIBIR LO SILENCIO SOBRE EL AGUA. "No sé s es sombra en el cristal, si es solo" AGUIL

Roscoe, William. 1753. in English.

THE BUTTERFLY BALL AND THE GRASSHOPPER FEAST. ARGO 12

Roseliep, Raymond. 1917. in English.

FOR JOHN KENNEDY, JR. "Stand at attention" FOLKW 2

Rosenberg, Isaac. in English.

DEAD MAN'S DUMP. ARGO 8

---

* Recording not available for analysis

Rosenfeld, Morris. 1862. in English.
THE GHETTO TREE. "In New York's teeming ghetto"   FOLKW 14
MY CAMPING GROUND. "Don't seek me where the myrtles bloom"   FOLKW 14
MY LITTLE SON. "I have a son, a little son"   FOLKW 14
THE TEARDROP MILLIONAIRE. "It's not a tuning fork of gold"   FOLKW 14

Ross, Muriel Sipe. in English.
GOOD MORNING. "One day I saw a downy duck"   HARB 1

Ross, W. W. Eustace. 1894. in English.
CATACOMBS. "Dwelling in a cavern, deep"   FOLKW 50
COTTON MATHER. "The devil lives"   FOLKW 50
THE CREEK. "The creek, shining"   FOLKW 50
THE FISH. "A fish dripping"   CAED 110
GERARD DE NERVAL. "Calypso held him in her cave"   FOLKW 50
NOX. "I am the daughter of Chaos, older far"   FOLKW 50
PLUNGING INTO. "Plunging into/ the shining water"   FOLKW 50
THE SAWS WERE SHRIEKING. "The saws were shrieking"   FOLKW 50
THE SNAKE TRYING. "The snake trying/ to escape"   FOLKW 50
THE SPRING. "We hear the spring from far across the lake"   FOLKW 50
THE WALK. "He walked through the woods"   FOLKW 50
WHITE WATER-LILY. "The lily with its cup, intense"   FOLKW 50

Rossetti, Christina. 1830. in English.
A BETTER RESURRECTION. "I have no wit, no words, no tears"   ARGO 69
A BIRTHDAY. "My heart is like a singing bird"   DECCA 12, HOUGHT 4, LION 2
BIRD OR BEAST. "Did any bird come flying"   ARGO 69
THE BOURNE. "Underneath the growing grass"   ARGO 69
THE CATERPILLAR. "Brown and furry"   CAED 110, CREAT 1, HARB 2
CHRISTMAS CAROL. "In the bleak midwinter"   LION 1
THE CITY MOUSE AND THE COUNTRY MOUSE. "The city mouse lives in a house"   NAITV 4
CLOUDS. "White sheep, white sheep"   CMS 3
ECHO. "Come to me in the silence of the night"   ARGO 69, CAED 201
EVE. "While I sit at the door"   ARGO 69
"Ferry me across the water"   CAED 110
THE HEART KNOWETH ITS OWN BITTERNESS. "When all the overwork of life is finished"   ARGO 69
"If all were rain and never sun"   CMS 3
IN AN ARTIST'S STUDIO. "One face looks out from all his canvasses"   ARGO 69
MEMORY. "I nursed it in my bosom while it lived"   ARGO 69, CAED 201
MONNA INNOMINATA, exc. "Come back to me, who wait and watch for you"   CAED 201

REMEMBER. "Remember me when I am gone away"   ARGO 69, CAED 201, CMS 14, DECCA 12, LION 2, THEAL 3
REST. "O Earth, lie heavily upon her eyes"   CAED 201
SLEEPING AT LAST. "Sleeping at last, the trouble and tumult over"   AUDIA 1, LIST 3
SONG. "When I am dead, my dearest"   ARGO 88A, ATHENA 6, AUDIA 1, CAED 201, CMS 14, LIST 3, LION 2
TWICE. "I took my heart in my hand"   ARGO 69
UP-HILL. "Does the road wind up-hill all the way" AUDIA 1, CAED 201, LIST 3, RCA 4
WHAT IS PINK. "What is pink? a rose is pink"   CMS 2
THE WIND. "Who has seen the wind"   CMS 2, HARB 5
Poetry*   ARGO 23

Rossetti, Dante Gabriel. 1828. in English.
AUTUMN SONG. "Know'st thou not at the fall of the leaf"   CMS 14
BARREN SPRING. "Once more the changed year's turning wheel returns"   ARGO 69, CAED 201
THE BLESSED DAMOZEL, exc. "The blessed damozel leaned out"   ARGO 69
THE CHOICE. "Eat thou and drink; to-morrow thou shalt die"   ARGO 69
THE DARK GLASS. "Not I myself know all my love for thee"   CMS 14
MY SISTER'S SLEEP. "She fell asleep on Christmas Eve"   ARGO 69
THE ORCHARD PIT. "Piled deep below the screening apple-branch"   LONGM 1
THE SEA-LIMITS. "Consider the sea's listless chime"   ARGO 69
SILENT NOON. "Your hands lie open in the long fresh grass"   LION 2
SUDDEN LIGHT. "I have been here before"   ARGO 69
A SUPERSCRIPTION. "Look in my face; my name is Might-have-been"   ARGO 69
"There's a combative artist named Whistler"   EAV 22
WITHOUT HER. "What of her glass without her? The blank gray"   CAED 201
THE WOODSPURGE. "The wind flapped loose, the wind was still"   ARGO 69, CAED 201
Poetry*   ARGO 23, LIST 11

Rossman, Michael. in English.
COUNT YOUR KIN. "Well I tell you"   WATSHD 1
LULLABY. "Things might be lazy" WATSHD 1
VERTIGO. "So the touch"   WATSHD 1

Rosten, Norman. 1914. in English.
IN GUERNICA.   VAN 3
Poetry*   FOLKW 15

Roth, Dan. in English.
WAR.   SCHOL 7

Roth, Eugen. 1895. in German.
ABGESANG. "Ein lied gibts von Herrn Urian"   DEUTGR 44
AHNUNGSLOS. "Ein Mensch hört staunend und empört"   DEUTGR 44
DAS FERNGESPRÄCH. "Ein Mensch spricht fern, geraume Zeit"   DEUTGR 36, DEUTGR 44

---

* Recording not available for analysis

Roth, Eugen (continued)

FÜR UNGEÜBTE. "Ein Mensch, der voller Neid vernimmt" DEUTGR 44
DAS HAUS. "Ein Mensch erblickt ein neider-regend" DEUTGR 44
DAS HILFSBUCH. "Ein Mensch nichts wissend von Mormone" DEUTGR 36, DEUTGR 44
DAS KURSBUCH. "Ein Mensch ist der Bewun-drung voll" DEUTGR 44
LEIDER. "Ein Mensch, kein Freund der raschen Tat" DEUTGR 44
DER LEISE NACHBAR. "Ein Mensch für seinen Nachbarn schwärmt" DEUTGR 44
LETZTE ENTSCHEIDUNG. DEUTGR 44
METAPHYSISCHES. "Ein Mensch erträumt, was er wohl täte" DEUTGR 44
NUR. "Ein Mensch der, sagen wir, als Christ" DEUTGR 36, DEUTGR 44
EIN REISEERLEBNIS. "Ein Mensch der kürzlich ganz privat spazieren gehn in München tat" DEUTGR 36, DEUTGR 44
SO UND SO. DEUTGR 44
UNERWÜNSCHTE BELEHRUNG. "Ein Mensch dem's ziemlich dreckig geht" DEUTGR 36, DEUTGR 44
DER UNSCHLÜSSIGE. "Ein Mensch zum Bahnhof dauerlaufend" DEUTGR 36, DEUTGR 44
DIE VERGESSLICHEN. DEUTGR 44
ZWISCHEN DEN ZEITEN. "Ein Mensch lebt noch mit letzter List" DEUTGR 36, DEUTGR 44

Rothenberg, Jerome G. 1931. in English.
CORTÈGE. "The drums have entered my heart" FOLKW 21
POLAND/1931: FIRST SEQUENCE. "A gallery of Jews love" WATSHD 1
Poetry* MICHM 15

Royde-Smith, Naomi Gwladys. 1875. in English.
HORSE. "I know two things about the horse" CAPITOL 1

Rubadiri, James D. in English.
A NEGRO LABORER IN LIVERPOOL. PROTHM 7
STANLEY MEETS MUTESA. CAED 136

Rückert, Friedrich. 1788. in German.
"Aus der Jugendzeit, aus der Jugendzeit" ATHENA 13
"Chidher, der ewig junge, sprach" ATHENA 13
"Du bist mein Mond, und ich bin deine Erde" ATHENA 13
"Du meine Seele, du mein Herz" ATHENA 13
GOTT ÜBERALL. ATHENA 13
KEHR' EIN BEI MIR! "Du bist die Ruh'" DOVER 1

Rudnick, Raphael. 1933. in English.
Poetry* JNP 48

Rudnigger, Wilhelm. 1921. in German.
SILVESTER SKURILLO, exc. AMADEO 4

Rufinus. in Greek.
TO MELITE. "Melite, your eyes are Hera's" English CARIL 3

Rühm, Gerhard. 1930. in German.
KOMPLEX 10. LUCHT 1
ZENSURIERTE REDE. LUCHT 1

Rühmkorf, Peter. 1929. in German.
ALLEIN IST NICHT GENUG. DEUTGR 40A
REISENDER. "Melk-Sankt Pölten-Wien" DEUTGR 40A

Ruiz, Juan, Archipreste de Hita. 1280. in Spanish.
LIBRO DE BUEN AMOR. "Chica es la calandria" CMS 5, DOVER 2

Rukeyser, Muriel. 1913. in English.
AIR. "Flowers of air" SPOA 100
AJANTA. "Came in my full youth to the midnight cave" LIBC 25, LIBC 72
ARE YOU BORN. "A man riding on the meaning of rivers" CAED 173
BALLAD OF ORANGE AND GRAPE. "After you finish your work" CAED 173, WATSHD 6
BURNING THE DREAMS. "On a spring morning of young wood, green wood" CAED 173
COLUMBUS. "Inner greet. Greenberg said it" CAED 173
THE CONJUGATION OF THE PARAMECIUM. "The species is continued" WATSHD 6
THE DAM. "All power is saved, having no end" CAED 173
DELTA POEMS. "Among leaf green this morn-ing" WATSHD 6
DESPISALS. "In the human cities, never again to" CAED 173
DOUBLE ODE. "Wine and oil" WATSHD 6
DREAM DRUMMING. "I braced the drum to my arm, a flat drum and began to play" CAED 173, WATSHD 6
ELEGY AND JOY, X. "We tell beginnings" SPOA 100
EYES OF THE NIGHT-TIME. LIBC 36
FLYING TO HANOI. "I thought I was going to the poets" WATSHD 6
HE HAD A QUALITY OF GROWTH. "No one ever walking this our only earth, various, very clouded" CAED 173
HOW WE DID IT. "We all travelled into that big room" CAED 173
IN OUR TIME. "In our period, they say there is free speech" CAED 173, SPOA 100
ISLANDS. "O for God's sake" WATSHD 6
IT IS THERE. "Yes it is there" WATSHD 6
KÄTHE KOLLWITZ. "Hauled between wars, my life time" WATSHD 6
LETTER TO THE FRONT. VII. "To be a Jew in the twentieth century" CAED 173
LOOKING AT EACH OTHER. "Yes, we were looking at each other" CAED 173, WATSHD 6
MOTHER AS PITCHFORK. "Woman seen as a slen-der instrument" CAED 173
NIGHT FEEDING. "Deeper than sleep but not so deep as death" CAED 173
NINE POEMS FOR THE UNBORN CHILD. "The child-less years alone without a home" CAED 173
ORPHEUS. "The mountaintop stands in silence a minute after murder" CAED 173
THE OVERTHROW OF ONE O'CLOCK AT NIGHT IS MY CONCERN. "That's this moment" SPOA 100
PAINTERS. "In the cave" WATSHD 6
POEM. "I lived in the first century of world wars" CAED 173, SPOA 100, WATSHD 6

---

* Recording not available for analysis

THE POEM AS MASK. "When I wrote of the women in their dances and wildness, it was a mask" CAED 173, WATSHD 6
READING TIME: 1 MINUTE 26 SECONDS. "The fear of poetry" SPOA 100
RUNE. "The word in the bread feeds me" CAED 173
ST. ROACH. "For that I never knew you I only learned to dread you" CAED 173
SONG. CAED 173
SONG. "A voice flew out of the river as morning flew" LIBC 1, SPOA 100
SONG. "Lying in daylight" WATSHD 6
THE SPEED OF DARKNESS. "Whoever despises the clitoris despises the penis" CAED 173, WATSHD 6
THEN. "When I am dead, even then" CAED 173, WATSHD 6
THIS MORNING. "Waking this morning" CAED 155, CAED 173, WATSHD 6
THIS OUR ONLY EARTH. CAED 173
UNTITLED. "Poem, white page" WATSHD 6
WAITING FOR ICARUS. "He said he would be back" WATSHD 6
WATERLILY FIRE, exc. "Girl grown woman fire mother of fire" LIBC 1
WATERLILY FIRE—FRAGILE. "I think of the image brought into my room" CAED 173
WATERLILY FIRE—THE LONG BODY. "This journey is exploring us. Where the child stood" CAED 173
WHAT DO WE SEE? "When they're decent about women" WATSHD 6
WOMAN AS MARKET. "What was it" WATSHD 6
Poetry* JNP 49, JNP 50, LIST 13, WATSHD 18
Runeberg, Johan Ludvig. 1804. in Swedish.
BONDEN PAAVO. GRAM 3
DEN ENDA STUNDEN. "Allena var jag" GRAM 3
FLICKAN KOM IFRÄN SIN ALSKLINGS MÖTE. GRAM 3
Russell, Sidney King. in English.
DUST. SCHOL 7
Russo, Ferdinando. 1866. in Italian.
'O CHIANCHIERE. CETRA 29
IL CICERONE. CETRA 29
'O DENTISTA. CETRA 29
'O LUCIANO D' 'O RRE. "Io mo so bbiecchio" CETRA 29
'O SVENIMENTO. CETRA 29
Ruteboeuf. 1230. in French.
LA COMPLAINTE RUTEBOEUF. "Ne convient pas que vous raconte" ADES 54, FOLKW 84
LE DIT DES RIBAUDS DE GRÈVE. "Ribaut, or estes vos a point" HACH 7
LE MARIAGE RUTEBOEUF. "En l'an de l'Incarnacion" HACH 7
LA MORT RUTEBOEUF. "Lessier m'estuet le rimoier" HACH 7
Rydberg, Viktor. 1828. in Swedish.
JUNGFRU MARIA I ROSENGÅRD. "Maria drömmer i rosengård" GRAM 3
LÄNGTAN. "Han längtar, längtar och anar" GRAM 3
Ryleyev, K. F. in Russian.
GRAZHDANIN. "Ya l' budu v rokovoe vremya" CMS 6

Saavedra, Angel de (Duque de Rivas). 1791. in Spanish.
A LAS ESTRELLAS. "Oh, refulgentes astros! cuya lumbre" SPOA 37
Saba, Umberto. 1883. in Italian.
AL LETTORE. "Se leggi questi versi e se in profondo" CETRA 16
AMORE. "Questa mattina, e come li portavo" CETRA 16
CANARINA AZZURA. "Meravigliosa canarina azzura" CETRA 16
DIVERTIMENTO. "Con voi nella mia vecchia casa entrava" CETRA 16
LE DONNE. "Le donne/ mie di casa" CETRA 16
I LIBRI. "I libri che ti rendo, amico" CETRA 16
MOMENTO. "Gli ucelli alla finestra" CETRA 16
NOSTALGIA. "Con occhi intenti seguono ogni mossa" CETRA 16
PALLA D'ORO. "Con ali tese e il becco aperto e volte" CETRA 16
PRETESTO. "C'è tanto miglio alla finestra" CETRA 16
QUASI UNA MORALITÀ. "Piú non mi temono i passeri" CETRA 16
RICHIAMO. "Perchè, gentile creatura mi strazi" CETRA 16
RISVEGLIO. "Rissano tutto il giorno; a notte dormono" CETRA 16
SOMIGLIANZA. "Fra te e la canarrina azzurra sono" CETRA 16
UCCELLO DI GABBIA. "Tenorino di grazia egli le strofe" CETRA 16
Poetry* CETRA 46
Sabat-Ercasty, Carlos. 1887. in Spanish.
LOS ADIOSES, XVI. "Del alba a la mañana, de la tarde al ocaso" FOLKW 80
Sá-Carneiro, Mario de. 1890. in Portuguese.
CARANGUEJOLA. "Ah, que me metam entre cobertores" FOLKW 72
FIM. "Quando en morrer batam em latas" FOLKW 72
Sacchetti, Franco. 1335. in Italian.
"Passando con pensier per un boschetto" DOVER 3
Poetry* CETRA 19
Sachs, Nelly. 1891. in German.
O THE CHIMNEYS. "On the ingeniously devised habitations of death" English SPOA 82
Poetry* SUHRK 5
Sackville, Charles, Earl of Dorset. 1638. in English.
SONGS. "Dorinda's sparkling wit and eyes" ARGO 47
——. "To all you ladies now at land" ARGO 47
Sagarra, Josep Maria de. 1894. in Catalan.
BALADA DELS TRES FADRINS. "Són tres fadrins que han vingut a la vila" GMS 17
CANÇÓ DE LA FRANCISQUETA. GMS 17
CANÇÓ DE PASSAR CANTANT. GMS 17
CANÇÓ DE TAVERNA. GMS 17
CANÇÓ DEL CAPVESPRE. "Hi ha una vela enllà del mar" GMS 17
EL CEMENTIRI DELS MARINERS. "Quan la passada del vent afina" AGUIL 14

* Recording not available for analysis

Sagarra, Josep Maria de (continued)

VINYES VERDES. "Vinyes verdes vora el mar"
GMS 17

Saint-Amant, Marc-Antoine Gérard de. 1594. in French.
LE PARESSEUX. "Accable de paresse et de melan-
cholie"   DOVER 4
LA SOLITUDE.   PERIOD 2

Saint-Exupéry, Antoine de. 1900. in French.
GEBET DER EINSAMKEIT. German DEUTGR 10
HYMNE AN DIE NACHT.   German DEUTGR 10
HYMNE AUF DIE STILLE. German DEUTGR 10

Saint-René, Martin. in French.
Poetry*   ACAD 1

Sainte-Beuve, Charles Auguste. 1804. in French.
LA SUIVANTE D'EMMA. "Emma, vous fûtes belle,
et depuis Champmêlé"   PATHE 1

Saitta, Antonio. in Italian.
NON FOSSI MAI STATO.   CETRA 31

Sakaki, Nanao. in English.
Poetry*   UCAL 4

Sala, Alberto. in Italian.
SEMPRE PIU DIFFICILE.   EPIU 1

Salinas, Juan. 1559. in Spanish.
ROMANCE DE ENDECHAS. "La moza gallega que
está en la posada"   SMC 3

Salinas, Pedro. 1892. in Spanish.
AY! CUANTAS COSAS PERDIDAS. "Ay! Cuantas cosas
perdidas"   SPOA 59
CANCIÓN DE CUNA. "Como me duermes al niño"
HOLT 1, TROPIC 1
"La luz lo malo que tiene"   AGUIL 4
MUERTES. "Primero te olvidé en tu voz"
DOVER 2
"Las oyes cómo piden realidades?"
AGUIL 10
"Que cuerpos leves, sutiles!" AGUIL 10
TEMA CON VARIACIONES. "De mirarte tanto y
tanto"   LIBC 78

Salvat-Papasseit, Joan. 1894. in Catalan.
L'OFICI QUE MES M'AGRADA. "Hi ha oficis que son
bons perque son de bon vivre" AGUIL 14

Samain, Albert. 1859. in French.
L'INFANTE.   GMS 9
PROMENADE À L'ÉTANG.   HACH 13

Sanchez, Sonia. 1934. in English.
AFTER THE FIFTH DAY. "After the fifth day"
WATSHD 3
"—answer to yo/ question"   FOLKW 42,
WATSHD 3
A BALLAD FOR STIRLING STREET. "Jest finished
readen"   BROADV 17
BLACK MAGIC. "Magic/ my man"   BROADV 6
FOLKW 42
A BLACK WOMAN SPEAKS. "I am deep"
FOLKW 42
A BLACK WOMAN SPEAKS. "We are songs yet un-
sung"   FOLKW 42
BLK CHANT. "We programmed fo death"
BROADV 17
BLK RHETORIC. "Who's gonna make all"
BROADV 17
BLK WOOOOOMEN CHANT. "We stand befo u"
BROADV 17, FOLKW 42
A CHANT FOR YOUNG BROTHAS & SISTUHS. "Yall out
there looooken so cooool"   BROADV 17

CHANGE US. "An u got a"   BROADV 17
CITY SONGS. "Dope pushers dope pushers"
FOLKW 42
A COLTRANE POEM. "My favorite things is u
blowen"   BROADV 17
"The cracker is not to be played with"
BROADV 17, FOLKW 42
DEFINITION FOR BLK/ CHILDREN. "A policeman"
BROADV 6
DEPRESSION. "I have gone into my eyes"
WATSHD 3
DON'T WANNA BE. "Don't wanna be no pimp"
FOLKW 42
FATHER & DAUGHTER.   WATSHD 3
THE FINAL SOLUTION. "The leaders speak"
BROADV 6
FOR MY CHILDREN. "Morani and Mungu"
FOLKW 42
FOR OUR LADY. "Yeh. Billie if someone"
BROADV 17
FOR UNBORN MALCOLMS. "Git the word out"
BROADV 6
FORMULA. "To live"   WATSHD 3
HAIKUS. "Did you ever cry"   WATSHD 3
_____. "I am sad"   WATSHD 3
_____. "If I had known"   WATSHD 3
_____. "Was it yesterday . . . ?" WATSHD 3
HOMECOMING. "I have been a"   BROADV 6
HOSPITAL POEM. "They have sed"
BROADV 17
I HAVE WALKED A LONG TIME. "I have walked a
long time"   WATSHD 3
I WAAAAAANNT TO KNOW; I NEEEEEDS TO KNOW.
"What happens after"   FOLKW 42
"Ima talken bout the Nation of Islam"
FOLKW 42
IN THE BEGINNING. "In the beginning/there was
no end"   WATSHD 3
IN THE COURTROOM. "And they were mostly all
blk"   BROADV 17
INDIANAPOLIS/ SUMMER 1969 POEM. "Like/ I
mean"   BROADV 17
IT'S A NEW DAY. "We gon be"   FOLKW 42,
WATSHD 3
LAST POEM IM GONNA WRITE BOUT US. "Some
times I drem bout u & me" BROADV 17
LET US BEGIN THE REAL WORK. "Let us begin the
real work now"   BROADV 17
LIBERATION/ POEM. "Blues ain't culture"
BROADV 17, FOLKW 42, WATSHD 3
LIFE POEM. "Shall I die shall I die"
BROADV 17
LISTEN TO BIG BLACK AT S. F. STATE. "No mo meet-
ings"   BROADV 17, FOLKW 42
LISTENING TO JIMMY GARRISON. "Who you be"
WATSHD 3
MALCOLM. "Do not speak to me of martyrdom"
BROADV 6
MEMORIAL. "The supremes done gone"
BROADV 6
A NEEDED POEM FOR MY SALVATION. "Am gonna
take me seriously"   BROADV 17,
FOLKW 42, WATSHD 3
NIGGER. "Nigger,/ that word"   BROADV 6
NOW POEM. "Don't let them die out"
BROADV 17

* Recording not available for analysis

OBSERVATION. "And what of the old"
WATSHD 3

OLD WORDS. "We are the dead ones"
WATSHD 3

ON SEEING PHAROAH SANDERS BLOWING. "Listen/ listen" BROADV 6

ON WATCHING A WORLD SERIES GAME. "O say can you see" BROADV 17

PAST. "Come into black geography"
WATSHD 3

PERSONAL LETTER NO. 2. "I speak skimpily to/ you" BROADV 6

PERSONAL LETTER NO. 3. "Nothing will keep"
BROADV 17, WATSHD 3

POEM. "Look at me 8th/ grade" BROADV 6

POEM AT THIRTY. "It is midnight" BROADV 6

POEM FOR ETHERIDGE. "Stone/ cold"
BROADV 17, FOLKW 42

A POEM FOR MY FATHER. "How sad it must be"
BROADV 17

A POEM FOR NINA SIMONE TO PUT SOME MUSIC ON AND BLOW OUR NIGGUH MINDS. "Yeh yeh yeh yeh yeh yeh yeh yeh yeh taught them to wear big naturals" BROADV 17

POEM NO. 3. "I gather up" WATSHD 3

POEM NO. 7. "When he came home"
WATSHD 3

POEM NO. 8. "I've been a woman" WATSHD 3

POEM NO. 9. "The rains" WATSHD 3

POEM NO. 12. "When I am woman, then I shall be wife of your eyes" WATSHD 3

POEM NO. 13. "Brother as-Salaam-Alaikum"
WATSHD 3

PRELUDE TO NOTHING. "I am trying to drain my mind" WATSHD 3

QUEENS OF THE UNIVERSE. "Sister I saw it today"
WATSHD 3

QUESTIONS. 1. "Blk people" BROADV 17

_____. 2. "Why they closing down Alcatraz"
BROADV 17

RIGHT ON: WHITE AMERICA. 1. "It is quite"
BROADV 17

_____. 2. "White America is saying"
BROADV 17

_____. 3. "This country might have"
BROADV 17

_____. 4. "Hear ye! Hear ye!" BROADV 17

SEQUENCES. "Today I am tired" WATSHD 3

SHORT POEM. "My old man" BROADV 6

SMALL COMMENT. "The nature of the beast is the" BROADV 6

SO THIS IS OUR REVOLUTION. "Niggahs with naturals" BROADV 17, FOLKW 42

SUMMARY. "No sleep tonight" BROADV 6

SUMMER WORDS OF A SISTUH ADDICT. "The first day I shot dope" BROADV 17, FOLKW 42, WATSHD 3

SUMMERTIME T. V. "Little Anthony and the imperials" BROADV 17, WATSHD 3

SUNDAY EVENING AT GWEN'S. "And we came that sun day" BROADV 17

TCB. "White motha fucka" BROADV 17

TELEVISION/ POEM. "How many of u niggers watched" BROADV 17

10:15 A. M.—APRIL 27, 1969 POEM. "And every thing" BROADV 17

THERE ARE BLK PURITANS. "There are blk puritans among us" BROADV 17

TO A JEALOUS CAT. "My man/ don't try none of your jealous" BROADV 6, FOLKW 42

TO ALL BROTHERS. "Yeah/ they/ hang you up"
BROADV 6

TO ALL SISTERS. "Hurt/ u worried"
BROADV 6

TO ANITA. "High/ yellow" FOLKW 42, WATSHD 3

TO BLK/ RECORD/ BUYERS. "Don't play me no"
BROADV 6

TO CHUCK. "I'm gonna write me" BROADV 6

TO MORANI/MUNGU. "As-Salaam-Alaikum my black" FOLKW 42

TO YOU/ WHO ALMOST TURNED ME ON. "Yeah./ my man" WATSHD 3

221-1424 (SAN FRANCISCO SUICIDE NUMBER). "Hello" BROADV 17

WE A BADDDDD PEOPLE. "I mean we bees real"
BROADV 17

WE CAN BE. "We can be anything we want"
FOLKW 42

WED POEM BEFORE THANKSGIVING. "Where to go when" BROADV 17

"Welcome home, my prince" FOLKW 42, WATSHD 3

WHEN WE COME. "When we come riden our green horses" FOLKW 42

WHY I DONT GET HIGH ON SHIT. "Cuz it says"
BROADV 17

Poetry* WATSHD 20

Sancho I, King of Portugal. in Portuguese.
"Se Deus me leixe de vos bem aver"
FOLKW 10

Sandburg, Carl. 1878. in English.

THE ABRACADABRA BOYS. "The abracadabra boys —have they been in the stacks" CAED 72

ANYWHERE AND EVERYWHERE. "There are people so near nothing" CAED 72

ARITHMETIC. "Arithmetic is where numbers fly like pigeons in and out of your head"
CAED 72, LIST 4, SCHOL 8, SINGER 1

BABY SONG OF THE FOUR WINDS. "Let me be your baby, south wind" CAED 117, SPOA 90

BILBEA. "Bilbea, I was in Babylon on Saturday night" DECCA 6, DECCA 9, SPOA 90

BOXES AND BAGS. "The bigger the box the more it holds" CAED 72

BRIGHT CONVERSATIONS WITH SAINT-EX. "There is a desperate loveliness to be seen"
CAED 117

BROKEN-FACE GARGOYLES. "All I can give you is broken-face gargoyles" CAED 117

BUFFALO DUSK. "The buffaloes are gone"
CAED 72

CAHOOTS. "Play it across the table" CAED 80

CHANGING LIGHT WINDS. "Changing light winds/ blew" CAED 72, CAED 110

CHEAP BLUE. "Hill blue among the leaves in summer" DECCA 6

CHICAGO. "Hog butcher for the world"
COLUMB 6, LIST 4, SINGER 5, UARIZ 1

CHICAGO BOY BABY. "The baby picked from an ash barrel" SPOA 90

CHICAGO POET. "I saluted a nobody"
CAED 72

* Recording not available for analysis

Sandburg, Carl (continued)

CHILD. "The young child, Christ, is straight and wise"   CAED 117

COOL TOMBS. "When Abraham Lincoln was shoveled into the tombs"   CAED 80, DECCA 6, DECCA 9

CORNUCOPIA. "The naked cornucopia of autumn fields"   CAED 117

A COUPLE. "He was in Cincinnati, she in Burlington"   CAED 117

CROSSED NUMBERS. "Delphiniums are born" CAED 72

DOORS. "An open door says, Come in" CAED 72, CAED 109

DUST. "Here is dust remember it was a rose" CAED 72

EARLY MORN. "The holy moon, a canoe, a silver papoose canoe, sails in the Indian west" CAED 72

EVENING WATERFALL. "What was the name you called me?"   CAED 72

EXPLANATIONS OF LOVE. "There is a place where love begins"   CAED 80, CAED 117

FACE. "I would beat out your face in brass" CAED 80

FAR ROCKAWAY NIGHT TILL MORNING. "What can we say of the night?"   CAED 117

FATHER AND SON.   DECCA 6, DECCA 9

THE FIREBORN ARE AT HOME IN FIRE. "Luck is a star"   CAED 80

FIRE-LOGS. "Nancy Hanks dreams by the fire" DECCA 6, DECCA 9

FLASH CRIMSON. "I shall cry God to give me a broken foot"   CAED 117

FOG. "The fog comes on little cat feet" CAED 117, CAED 164, CAED 195, EBEC 2, UARIZ 1

FOOLISH ABOUT WINDOWS. "I was foolish about windows"   CAED 72

FOR YOU. "The peace of great doors be for you" DECCA 6

FOUR PRELUDES ON PLAYTHINGS OF THE WIND. "The woman named to-morrow" CAED 80, HOUGHT 5

FRANÇOIS VILLON FORGOTTEN. "The women of the city where I was forgotten"   CAED 80

GONE. "Everybody loved Chick Lorimer in our town"   CAED 80

GRASS. "Pile the bodies high at Austerlitz and Waterloo"   DECCA 6, DECCA 9, RCA 4

HARMONICA HUMDRUMS. "And so the days pass" CAED 72

HOW MUCH? "How much do you love me, a million bushels?"   CAED 117, SPOA 90

I AM THE PEOPLE. "I am the People—the mob—the crowd"   CAED 72

IN TALL GRASS. "Bees and a honeycomb in the dried head of a horse in a pasture corner" CAED 80, DECCA 6, DECCA 9

IS THERE ANY EASY ROAD TO FREEDOM? "A relentless man loved France"   CAED 117

JAZZ FANTASIA. "Drum on your drums, batter on your banjoes"   CAED 72, HOUGHT 3

LIGHT AND MOONBELLS. "They could bend low" CAED 117

LIMITED. "I am riding on a limited express, on of the crack trains of the nation"   LIST SINGER

LITTLE CANDLE. "Light may be had for noth ing"   CAED 72, CAED 11

"Little girl, be careful what you say" CAED 7

LOCALITIES. "Wagon Wheel Gap is a place never saw"   SCHOL

LOSERS. "If I should pass the tomb of Jonah" CAED 11

LOST. "Desolate and lone"   HARB

LOVE LETTER TO HANS CHRISTIAN ANDERSEN. "Th kitchen chair speaks to the bread knife" CAED 7

MAG. "I wish to God I never saw you, Mag" CAED 8

THE MAN WITH THE BROKEN FINGERS. "The ma with the broken fingers throws a shadow" CAED 11

MAYBE. "Maybe he believes me, maybe not" CAED 7

MEADOW IN SUMMER. "Life is just a bowl of che ries"   CAED 7

MILK-WHITE MOON. "Milk-white moon, put th cows to sleep"   CAED 72, CAED 10

MR. ATTILA. "They made a myth of you, profe sor"   CAED 117, SPOA 9

MYSTERIOUS BIOGRAPHY. "Christofo Colomb was a hungry man"   CAED 7

NEW SONG FOR INDIANA OPHELIAS. "Twist you fingers, cheery"   CAED 7

NIGHT BELLS. "Two bells six bells two bells si bells"   CAED 72, CAED 111, CAED 11

NIGHT STUFF. "Listen a while, the moon is lovely woman"   CAED 8

NUMBER MAN. "He was born to wonder abou numbers"   CAED 7

OMAHA. "Red barns and red heifers spot th green"   CAED 11

ON A FLIMMERING FLOOM YOU SHALL RIDE. "No body noogers the shaff of a sloo" CAED 11

OUR HELLS. "Milton unlocked hell for us" CAED 7

OVER THE BRIDGE.   DECCA

PAPER I. "Paper is two kinds, to write on, t wrap with"   CAED 7

PAPER II. "I write what I know on one side the paper"   CAED 7

THE PEOPLE, YES, exc. "We'll see what we'll see DECCA 5, SPOA 9

PHIZZOG. "This face you got"   CAED 7 SCHOL

PRAIRIE WATERS BY NIGHT. "Chatter of birds tw by two"   CAED 8

PRAYERS OF STEEL. "Lay me on an anvil, O God CAED 80, DECCA 9, HOUGHT SINGER

PRECIOUS MOMENTS. "Bright vocabularies ar transient as rainbows"   CAED 11

PRIMER LESSON. "Look out how you use prou words"   CAED 72, DECCA 6, DECCA

PSALM OF THOSE WHO GO OFF BEFORE DAYLIGH "The policeman buys shoes slow and careful CAED 8

---

* Recording not available for analysis

RIVER MOON. "The double moon, one on the high backdrop of the West"   CAED 117

SEA CHEST. "There was a woman loved a man"   CAED 80

SEA-WASH. "The sea-wash never ends"   CAED 117, SPOA 90

SEVENTEEN MONTHS. "This girl speaks five words"   CAED 72

SKY PIECES. "Proudly the fedoras march on the heads of the somewhat careless men"   CAED 80

SKY TALK. "Wool white horses and their heads sag and roll"   CAED 72

SLEEP IMPRESSION. "The dark blue wind of early autumn"   CAED 72

SMALL HOMES. "The green bug sleeps in the white lily ear"   CAED 72

SNATCH OF SLIPHORN JAZZ. "Are you happy? It's the only way to be, kid"   CAED 72, HARC 2

SOUTHERN PACIFIC. "Huntington sleeps in a house six feet long"   CAED 80, DECCA 6, DECCA 9

SPECIAL STARLIGHT. "The creator of night and of birth"   CAED 117

STORMS BEGIN FAR BACK. "You can't have a slam offhand"   CAED 80

SWEEPING WENDY: A STUDY IN FUGUE. "Wendy put her black eyes on me"   CAED 72

"They all want to play Hamlet"   CAED 80

THIS STREET NEVER SLEEPS. "At the corner"   CAED 72

TWO MOON FANTASIES. "She bade the moon stand still"   CAED 72

UNDER A TELEPHONE POLE. "I am a copper wire slung in the air"   HOUGHT 2

THE UNKNOWN WAR. "Be calm, collected, easy"   CAED 80

UPSTREAM. "The strong men keep coming on"   CAED 117, DECCA 6, DECCA 9

WALL SHADOWS. "These walls they knew those shadows"   CAED 72

WE HAVE GONE THROUGH GREAT ROOMS TO-GETHER. "And when on the dark steel came the roads"   CAED 117

WE MUST BE POLITE: LESSONS FOR CHILDREN ON HOW TO BEHAVE UNDER PECULIAR CIRCUM-STANCES. "If we meet a gorilla/ what shall we do?"   CAED 72

WHEN DEATH CAME APRIL TWELVE, 1945. "Can a bell ring in the heart"   CAED 117

WHITE ASH. "There is a woman on Michigan Boulevard keeps a parrot and goldfish and two white mice"   CAED 80

WILDERNESS. "There is a wolf in me"   CAED 117, DECCA 6, SPOA 90

THE WIND ON THE WAY. "Every day is the last day"   CAED 72

WIND SONG. "Long ago I learned how to sleep"   CAED 117, HARC 3

WINDY CITY, exc. "Put the city up; tear the city down"   DECCA 6, DECCA 9

_____. "The lean hands of wagon men"   CAED 80

WORMS AND WIND. "Worms would rather be worms"   CAED 72

YOUNG SEA. "The sea is never still"   CAED 72

Sanders, Ed. 1939. in English.
PEACE FREAK POEM. "Young Consuela"   BROADV 3
Poetry*   NET 16

Sansores, Rosario. in Spanish.
TU NADA MAS. "En esta soledad que me acom-paña"   SMC 7

Santa Clara, Abraham a. 1644. in German.
DIE UNGLEICHEN EHELEUT.   ATHENA 3

Santayana, George. 1863. in English.
ODE.   CAED 201

Santillana, Marqués de. 1398. in Spanish.
SERRANA. "Después que nací"   AGUIL 4
SERRANILLA. "Moza tan fermosa non ví en la frontera"   CMS 5, DOVER 2, HOLT 1, SMC 3
SERRANILLA DE BORES. "Moçuela de Bores"   SPOA 37

Santos Chocano, José. 1875. in Spanish.
EL AMOR DE LAS SELVAS.   MIAMI 2
NOSTALGIA. "Hace ya dos años"   HOLT 1
¡QUIÉN SABE! "Indio que asomas a la puerta"   FOLKW 79
EL SALMO DE LAS CUMBRES. "Silencio y paz"   FIDIAS 3

Sappho. 7th c. B.C. in Greek.
" . . . Apy Sardion"   Greek and English JNP 95
"Dedyke men a selanna"   FOLKW 104; Greek and English JNP 95
"Epaman men ego sethen atthi, palai pota"   Greek and English JNP 95
"Hoi men ippeon stroton, hoi de pesdon"   Greek and English JNP 95
"Oion to glykymalon ereuthetai akro ep' ysdo"   FOLKW 104; Greek and English JNP 95
"Phainetai moi kenos isos theoisin"   FOLKW 104; Greek and English JNP 95
"Poikilothron athanat' Aphrodita"   CAED 28; Greek and English JNP 95

Sarett, Lew. 1888. in English.
FOUR LITTLE FOXES.   CAED 112

Sargent, William D. in English.
WIND-WOLVES. "Do you hear the cry as the pack goes by"   HARB 5

Sassoon, Siegfried. 1886. in English.
AT THE GRAVE OF HENRY VAUGHN. "Above the voiceful windings of a river"   FOLKW 64
THE DEATH BED. "He drowsed and was aware of silence"   ARGO 77
THE GENERAL. "Good morning; good morning! The General said"   ARGO 89
GLORY OF WOMEN. "You love us when we're heroes"   ARGO 89
ON PASSING THE NEW MENIN GATE. "Who will re-member"   ARGO 89
SONG-BOOKS OF THE WAR. "In fifty years, when peace"   ARGO 89
SURVIVORS. "No doubt they'll soon get well"   ARGO 89

Sawyer, Mark. 1895. in English.
KITE DAYS. "A kite, a sky, and good firm breeze"   HARB 4

Saxe, John G. in English.
A BLIND MAN AND THE ELEPHANT. "It was six men of Indostan"   EAV 21, HARC 4

* Recording not available for analysis

Saxe, John G (continued)

MY FAMILIAR. "Again I hear that creaking step"
  EAV 21

Sbarbaro, Camillo. 1888. in Italian.
  Poetry*   CETRA 28

Scannell, Vernon. 1922. in English.
  ACT OF LOVE. "This is not the man that women
    choose"   ARGO 155
  AUTOBIOGRAPHICAL NOTE. "Beeston, the place,
    near Nottingham"   SPOA 68
  BATTLEFIELDS. "Tonight in the pub I talked with
    Ernie Jones"   ARGO 155
  BESIDE THE SEA.   ARGO 155
  A CASE OF MURDER. "They should not have left
    him there alone"   ARGO 155
  CIGARETTE.   ARGO 155
  DEAD DOG. "One day I found a lost dog"
    FOLKW 59A
  FIRST FIGHT. "Tonight, then, is the night"
    SPOA 67
  THE GREAT WAR.   ARGO 155
  I'M COVERED NOW. "What would happen to your
    lady wife"   ARGO 155
  THE JEALOUS WIFE. "Like a private eye she
    searches"   ARGO 155
  THE RIVALS. "All, all of them wanted her"
    ARGO 155
  SIX REASONS FOR DRINKING. "It relaxes me, he
    said"   ARGO 155
  THE SOLDIER'S DREAM. "After the late shouts, the
    silences"   ARGO 155
  THE TELEPHONE NUMBER. "Searching for a lost
    address I find"   FOLKW 59A
  TIME FOR A QUICK ONE. "Noon holds the city
    back"   ARGO 155
  WALKING WOUNDED. "A mammoth morning
    moved grey flanks and groaned"
    ARGO 155
  THE WIDOW'S COMPLAINT. "You left as you so
    often left before"   ARGO 155
  Poetry*   PROTHM 6

Scève, Maurice. 1510. in French.
  L'AUBE ÉTEIGNAIT ÉTOILES. "L'Aulbe estaingnoit
    Estoilles a Foison."   HACH 8
  DELIE, exc. "Quand l'oeil aux champs est d'es-
    clairs esblouy"   DOVER 4

Schaeffer, Albrecht. 1885. in German.
  DIE GEFANGENEN (NACH DEM 126. PSALM)
    CHRIST 29

Scharpenberg, Margot. in German.
  DAMALS WAR ES MEIN MOND.   CHRIST 11

Schatzdorfer, Hans. in German.
  DA WÖG DURI'S LÖBN, exc.   AMAD 2

Scheffel, Joseph Viktor von. 1826. in German.
  ALTASSYRISCH. "Im Schwarzen Walfisch zu Aska-
    lon"   DOVER 1

Scheffler, Johann. 1624. in German.
  DIE LIEBE AM KREUZ.   CHRIST 18

Schiller, Friedrich von. 1759. in German.
  DER ABEND. "Die Sonne zeight, vollendend
    gleich dem Helden"   CHRIST 22
  AN DIE FREUNDE. "Liebe Freunde, es gab
    schönre Zeiten"   ATHENA 8, CHRIST 21,
    SPOA 5
  DIE BÜRGSCHAFT. "Zu Dionys, dem Tyrannen,
    schlich"   DEUTGR 19, FOLKW 73

CASSANDRA. "Freude war in Trojas Hallen"
  DEUTGR 1
EPIGRAMME.   CHRIST 2
DIE ERWARTUNG. "Hör' ich das Pförtchen nich
  gehen?"   DEUTGR 1
DAS GLÜCK. "Selig, welchen die Götter, di
  gnädigen, vor der Geburt schon liebten"
  CHRIST 21, DEUTGR 1
DIE GRÖSSE DER WELT. "Die der schaffende Geis
  einst aus dem Chaos schlug"   CHRIST 1
DER HANDSCHUH. "Vor seinem Löwengarten"
  DOVER 1, FOLKW 7
HOFFNUNG. "Es reden und träumen die Mensc
  hen viel"   DEUTGR 15, DEUTGR 3
  FOLKW 7
DER KAMPF MIT DEM DRACHEN. "Was rennt da
  Volk, was wälzt sich dort"   FOLKW 7
DIE KRANICHE DES IBYKUS. "Zum Kampf de
  Wangen und Gesänge"   DEUTGR 19
  FOLKW 7
DAS LIED VON DER GLOCKE. "Fest gemauert i
  der Erden"   DEUTGR 1
DIE MACHT DES GESANGES. "Ein Regenstrom au
  Felsenrissen"   CHRIST 2
DAS MÄDCHEN AUS DER FREMDE. "In einem Ta
  bei armen Hirten"   FOLKW 7
NANIE. "Auch das Schöne muss sterben! Da
  Mensch und Götter bezwingen"
  CHRIST 2
PEGASUS IM JOCHE. "Auf einem Pferdemarkt–
  vielleicht zu Haymarket"   DEUTGR 1
DER PILGRIM. "Noch in meines Lebens Lenze
  CHRIST 2
POESIE DES LEBENS. "Wer möchte sich an Scha
  tenbildern weiden"   CHRIST 2
PUNSCHLIED. "Vier Elemente, Innig gesellt"
  DEUTGR 1
DER RING DES POLYKRATES. "Er stand auf seine
  Daches Zinnen"   ATHENA 8, FOLKW 7
RITTER TOGGENBURG. "Ritter, treue Schweste
  liebe"   DEUTGR 1
DIE SÄNGER DER VORWELT. "Sagt, wo sind di
  Vortrefflichen hin"   DEUTGR 1
  DEUTGR 3
SPRÜCHE DES KONFUZIUS. "Dreifach ist de
  Schritt der Zeit"   CHRIST 2
DER TANZ. "Siehe wie schwebenden Schritts i
  Wellenschwung sich die Paare drehen"
  CHRIST 2
DER TAUCHER. "Wer wagt es, Rittersmann ode
  Knapp"   ATHENA 1, DEUTGR 1
  FOLKW 7
DIE TEILUNG DER ERDE. "Nehmt hin die Wel
  rief Zeus von seinen Höhen"   ATHENA
  ATHENA 8, DEUTGR 15, DEUTGR 3
  FOLKW 73, SPOA
DAS VERSCHLEIERTE BILD ZU SAIS. "Ein Jünglin
  den des Wissens heisser Durst"
  DEUTGR 1
DIE WORTE DES GLAUBENS. "Drei Worte nen
  ich euch, inhaltschwer"   CHRIST 2
  DEUTGR 1
DIE WORTE DES WAHNS. "Drei Worte hört ma
  bedeutungsschwer"   CHRIST 2

Schlegel, Friedrich. 1767. in German.
  IM WALDE. "Windes Rauschen, Gottes Flügel"
    CHRIST 2

---

* Recording not available for analysis

Schmidt, Augusto Frederico. 1906. in Portuguese.
SONÊTO DE LUCIANO. "Seu olhar se fechou para
    êste mundo"   FOLKW 71
Schmitz, Dennis. 1937. in English.
CANDLEFISH. "Indians used to burn their
    greasy"   WATSHD 1
LIFE OF THE LOCKSMITH. "When you retired"
                                                   WATSHD 1
Poetry*   JNP 51
Schröder, Rudolf Alexander. 1878. in German.
DEUTSCHE ODE, 7. "Armselig Volk, was häufet
    ihr Schätze"   CHRIST 22
Poetry*   CHRIST 4 CHRIST 6
Schubart, Christian Friedrich Daniel. 1739. in
    German.
GELLERTS GRABSCHRIFT. "Hier liegt—steh, Wan-
    derer, und schau"   DEUTGR 13
NACH DEM 90. PSALM.   CHRIST 29
Schuyler, James Marcus. 1923. in English.
Poetry*   COLUMB 1
Schwartz, Delmore. 1913. in English.
AT A SOLEMN MUSICK. "Let the musicians begin"
                                          LIBC 1, SPOA 100
THE BALLAD OF THE CHILDREN OF THE CZAR. "The
    children of the Czar"   LIBC 1, SPOA 100
DARKLING SUMMER, OMINOUS DUSK, RUMOROUS
    RAIN. "A tattering of rain and then the reign"
                                                   LIBC 1
GENESIS, exc. "Manic-depressive Lincoln, na-
    tional hero"   LIBC 19
_____, exc. "Me next to sleep, all that is left of
    Eden"   LIBC 75
IN THE GREEN MORNING, NOW, ONCE MORE. "In
    the green morning, before"   LIBC 1
LINCOLN.   LIBC 19, LIBC 75
THE REPETITIVE HEART. Part 9. "The heavy bear
    who goes with me"   LIBC 19, LIBC 40
STARLIGHT LIKE INTUITION PIERCED THE TWELVE.
    "Starlight like intuition pierced the twelve"
                                                   LIBC 19
SWIFT. "What shall Presto do for pretty prattle"
                                          LIBC 1, SPOA 100
Schwerner, Armand. 1927. in English.
THE EMPTYING. "All that's left is pattern"
                                                   BROADR 3
Schwitters, Kurt. 1887. in German.
SOONATE IN UURLAUTEN, exc.   LUCHT 1
Scott, Dennis. in English.
FARMERS' NOTEBOOK. "The canes burn. I show
    you"   CAED 153
FISHERMAN. "The scales like metal flint his feet"
                                                   CAED 153
FOR THE LAST TIME, FIRE. "That August the birds
    kept away"   CAED 153
UNCLE TIME. "Uncle Time is a ole, ole man"
                                                   CAED 153
Scott, F. R. 1899. in English.
THE BIRD. "Fluffed and still as snow the white"
                                                   FOLKW 49
BONNE ENTENTE. "The advantages of living
    with two cultures"   FOLKW 49
CARING. "Caring is loving, motionless"
                                                   FOLKW 49
CONFLICT. "When I see the falling bombs"
                                                   FOLKW 49
THE EXAMINER. "The routine trickery of the ex-
    amination"   LEARNC 7

LAKESHORE. "The lake is sharp along the shore"
                                                   FOLKW 49
A LANGUAGE OF FLESH AND OF ROSES. "Now there
    are pre-words"   FOLKW 49
LAURENTIAN SHIELD. "Hidden in wonder and
    snow"   FOLKW 49
MEMORY. "Tight skin called Face is drawn"
                                                   FOLKW 49
SURFACES. "This rock-bound river, ever flow-
    ing"   FOLKW 49
WILL TO WIN. "Your tall French legs, my V for
    victory"   FOLKW 49
Scott, Sir Walter. 1771. in English.
THE BLACK KNIGHT AND WAMBA. "Anna-Marie,
    Love, up is the sun"   CAED 202
BORDER SONG. "March, march, Ettrick and
    Teviotdale"   HOUGHT 1
CORONACH. "He is gone on the mountain"
                                                   CAED 202
JOCK OF HAZELDEAN. "Why weep ye by the tide,
    ladie"   BRITAM 1, FOLKW 68
THE LAY OF THE LAST MINSTREL, exc. "Breathes
    there a man with soul so dead"   CAED 98,
        CAED 132, DECCA 13, EAV 8, IMP 1
_____, exc. "The feast was over in Branksome
    tower"   CAED 96
MARMION. LOCHINVAR. "O, young Lochinvar is
    come out of the west"   CAED 132,
    DECCA 10, EAV 8, HARC 2, HOUGHT 1,
                                                   LIST 21
"Pibroch of Donuil Dhu"   BRITAM 1
ROKEBY. ALLEN-A-DALE. "Allen-a-Dale has no
    fagot for burning"   HARC 3
ROSABELLE. "O listen, listen, ladies gay"
                                                   FOLKW 62
"Soldier, rest! Thy warfare o'er"   IMP 1
Scott, Winfield Townley. 1910. in English.
A AND B AND THE MIRROR. "You there—I here—
    triangled with the mirror"   CARIL 18
BLUE SLEIGH. "Blue-Sleigh that fifty winters
    gone"   CARIL 18
CODICIL FOR PVT. JOHN HOGG'S WILL. "Gray and
    blue, the boy ghosts with guns are in the
    spring woods"   CARIL 18
COLERIDGE. "Old father, blessed ghost, mari-
    ner"   CARIL 18, SPOA 99
COME GREEN AGAIN. "If what heals can bless"
                                                   CARIL 18
COMMUNICATION ESTABLISHED. "Asleep in the
    night I dreamed that you owed me a letter"
                                                   CARIL 18
DEAD LEAVES OUT OF PLACE. "If I return to walk
    these woods"   CARIL 18, SPOA 99
FROM CHIRICO TO CHARON. "Vacancies of Chirico
    Square repeated as far as Charon's River"
                                                   CARIL 18
LANDSCAPE AS METAL AND FLOWERS. "All over
    America railroads ride through roses"
                                                   CARIL 18
THE LAST ONE. "Now all that name are gone"
                                                   SPOA 99
A LICK AND A PROMISE.   CARIL 18
THE LONG PARTY. "Identification had to be by
    mask"   SPOA 99
THE MAN AT MIDCENTURY. "We cannot guess
    how long he'll wait"   CARIL 18, SPOA 99

* Recording not available for analysis

Scott, Winfield Townley (continued)

MAY 1506. "I do not want your praises later on"
CARIL 18

MEMENTO. "This is a rocksaw seacoast"
CARIL 18

MR. WHITTIER. "It is so much easier to forget than to have been Mr. Whittier"
CARIL 18

THE MOTHER. "Bowed down she turned but halfway up the stairs" CARIL 18, SPOA 99

PHELPS PUTNAM. "He twirled his tabled high-ball"   CARIL 18

POSTSCRIPT.   CARIL 18

PVT. JOHN HOGG. "In the war—oh, not the last war nor the one before"   CARIL 18

TO ALL OBJECTIVISTS. "Beyond O'Ryan's bar in the dirty river"   CARIL 18

THE U. S. SAILOR WITH THE JAPANESE SKULL. "Bald-bare, lone-bare, and ivory yellow: skull"
CARIL 18

WE ARE SO FOND OF ONE ANOTHER, BECAUSE OUR AILMENTS ARE THE SAME. "There are no girls among us now with small high breasts"
CARIL 18

WE'LL ALL FEEL GAY. "Even along the railway platform it was spring"   CARIL 18

WHAT I ASSEMBLED AND DISSEMBLED. "What I assembled and dissemble"   CARIL 18

THE WRONG IS MIXED. "Can cockcrow fix a land-scape"   CARIL 18

Poetry*   JNP 52

Sedley, Sir Charles. 1639. in English.

TO CELIA. "Not, Celia, that I juster am"
ARGO 47

Seferis, George (Sephariados). 1900. in Greek.

ANOIKSE M. KH. "Pali me ten anoxe"
CAED 121

EPIKALEO TOI TEN THEON. "Ladi sta mele"
CAED 121

EROTIKOS, PART 4. "Dyo phidia horaia khi alar-gina"   CAED 121

———, PART 5. "Pou pege he mera he dikope pou eikhe to panta allaxei"   CAED 121

HELENE. "T'aedonia de o'aphenoume na koime-theis stis Platres"   CAED 121

KIKHLE. "Ta spitia pou eikha mou ta peran"
CAED 121

LEPTOMEREIES STEN KYPRO. "He mikre koukou-bagia eitane panta ekei"   CAED 121

MNEME, A'. "Ki ego sta kheria mono m'henakala-mi"   CAED 121

TRIZONIA. "To spiti gemise trizonia"
CAED 121

Seghers, Pierre. 1906. in French.

AUTOMNE.   ADES 27

LE BEAU TRAVAIL. "J'ai chanté mes amours sur de grands chevaux noirs"   ADES 55

LA FÊTE.   ADES 27

UNE FILLE DE FEU.   ADES 55

IROQUOISES. "Ni chien ni chat sans oiseaux ni poissons"   ADES 27

LE MONSIEUR. "Le monsieur ne demande pas l'aumône"   ADES 27

L'OISEAU-LYRE. "Sur les ailes de l'oiseau-lyre je n'ai jamais rencontré"   ADES 27

LE PIPELINE DE BASSORAH. "Ceux qui sont morts pour rien ne reviendront jamais dans cet em-pire"   ADES 27

PORTRAITS.   ADES 27

QUAND LE SOLEIL. "Quand le soleil visite les sou-terrains de la nuit"   ADES 27

RACINES. "Qui parlait de linceul?"   ADES 27

"La rivière de ton dos"   ADES 27

TZIGANES. "Le coeur est fait de mille cordes"
ADES 27

VIVRE SE CONJUGUE AU PRESENT. "Celui qui vit de souvenirs"   ADES 27

Selander, Sten. 1891. in Swedish.

EN DAG, exc.   GRAM 5

SOMMARNATTEN.   GRAM 5

TRÄDTOPPARNA.   GRAM 5

Semprit, José Davila. in Spanish.

TRANSFORMACIÓN. "Cuando suceda el cambio que el mundo llama muerte"   SMC 9

Senghor, Léopolde Sedar. 1906. in French.

À NEW-YORK. "New York! D'abord j'ai été con-fondu par ta beauté"   ADES 17

L'ABSENCE. "C'est le temps de partir"
ADES 17

CAMP 1940. "Saccagé le jardin des fiançailles"
ADES 17

CE COIR SOPÉ.   ADES 17

CHANT DU FEU. "Feu que les hommes regardent dans la nuit, dans la nuit profonde"
FOLKW 83

FEMME NOIRE. "Femme nue, femme noire"
ADES 17, BROADV 18, FOLKW 83

IN MEMORIAM. "C'est Dimanche"   ADES 17

JOAL. "Joal/ Je me rappelle"   ADES 17

LE KAYA-MAGAN.   ADES 17

MEDITERRANÉE. "Et je redis ton nom: Dyallo"
FOLKW 83

Poetry*   NET 12

Sereni, Vittorio. 1913. in Italian.

E ANCORA D'UNA TENDA S'AGITA. "E ancora"
EPIU 1

IL MURO.   APPL 4

IL PIATTO PIANGE.   APPL 4

LA PIETÁ.   APPL 4

UN POSTO DI VACANZA.   APPL 4

LA SPIAGGIA.   APPL 4

Poetry*   CETRA 46

Serraillier, Ian. 1912. in English.

THE TICKLE RHYME.   CAED 109

Service, Robert William. 1874. in English.

AMBITION. "They brought the mighty chief to town"   FOLKW 31

THE BALDNESS OF CHEWED-EAR. "When Chewed-ear Jenkins got hitched up"   FOLKW 31

THE BALLAD OF HARD-LUCK HENRY. "Now wouldn't you expect to find a man an awful crank"   FOLKW 31

THE BALLAD OF PIOUS PETE. "I tried to refine that neighbor of mine, honest to God, I did"
CAED 103, FOLKW 31

THE CALL OF THE WILD. "Have you gazed on naked grandeur where there's nothing else to gaze on"   CAED 103

CLANCY OF THE MOUNTED POLICE. "In the little Crimson Manual it's written plain and clear"
CAED 103

* Recording not available for analysis

THE CREMATION OF SAM MCGEE. "There are strange things done in the midnight sun" CAED 103, FOLKW 31, LIST 4, SINGER 3

THE LAW OF THE YUKON. "This is the law of the Yukon, and ever she makes it plain" CAED 103

THE LOW-DOWN WHITE. "This is the pay-day up at the mines" FOLKW 31

THE MEN THAT DON'T FIT IN. "There's a race of men that don't fit in" CAED 103

THE PARSON'S SON. "This is the song of the parson's son" FOLKW 31

THE PINES. "We sleep in the sleep of ages" FOLKW 31

THE RHYME OF THE REMITTANCE MAN. "There's a four-pronged buck a-swinging in the shadow of my cabin" CAED 103

THE SCEPTIC. "My Father Christmas passed away" FOLKW 31

THE SHOOTING OF DAN MCGREW. "A bunch of the boys were whooping it up in the Malamute Saloon" CAED 103, FOLKW 31

THE SPELL OF THE YUKON. "I wanted the gold, and I sought it" CEAD 100, CAED 103

THE TRAIL OF NINETY-EIGHT. "Gold! We leapt from our benches. Gold! We sprang from our stools" CAED 103

Setoun, Gabriel. in English.

JACK FROST. "The door was shut as doors should be" HARB 2

Sexton, Anne. 1928. in English.

THE ABORTION. CAED 155

THE ADDICT. NET 2

THE AMBITION BIRD. "So it is come to this" CAED 161

DIVORCE: THY NAME IS WOMAN. "I am divorcing Daddy" CAED 161

THE FARMER'S WIFE. "From hodge porridge of their country" SPOA 106

FUNNEL. "The family story tells" SPOA 106

THE FURY OF COCKS. "There they are, drooping over the breakfast plates" CAED 161

THE FURY OF OVERSHOES. "They sit in a row outside the Kindergarten" CAED 161

GODS. "Miss Sexton went out looking for the Gods" CAED 161

HER KIND. "I have gone out" CAED 161, NET 2

JESUS COOKS. "Jesus saw the multitudes were hungry" CAED 161

JESUS WALKING. "When Jesus walked into the wilderness" CAED 161

LETTER WRITTEN ON A FERRY WHILE CROSSING LONG ISLAND SOUND. "I am surprised to see that the ocean is still going on" CAED 161

LITTLE GIRL, MY STRING BEAN, MY LOVELY WOMAN. "My daughter at eleven, almost twelve" CAED 161, NET 2

THE LITTLE PEASANT. "Oh how the women" CAED 161

LIVE. NET 2

MAKING A LIVING. "Jonah made his living inside the belly" CAED 161

MUSIC SWIMS BACK TO ME. "Wait, Mister. Which way is home?" CAED 161

THE PLAY. "I am the only actor" CAED 161

RIDING THE ELEVATOR INTO THE SKY. "As the fireman said" CAED 161

RINGING THE BELLS. "And this is the way they ring the bells" CAED 161, NET 2

ROWING. "A story, a story!" CAED 161

THE ROWING ENDETH. "I'm mooring my rowboat" CAED 161

SELF IN 1958. "What is reality" CAED 161, NET 2

THE STARRY NIGHT. "That does not keep me from having a terrible need of shall I say the word" CAED 161

THOSE TIMES. NET 2

THE TOUCH. "For months my hands had been sealed off" CAED 161

THE TRUTH THE DEAD KNOW. "Gone, I say, and walk from Church" CAED 161, SPOA 106

UNKNOWN GIRL IN THE MATERNITY WARD. "Child, the current" SPOA 106

US. "I was wrapped in black" CAED 161

WITH MERCY FOR THE GREEDY. "Concerning your letter in which you ask me" CAED 161

YOUNG. "A thousand doors ago" NET 2

Poetry* JNP 53, TAPES 6

Shakespeare, William. 1564. in English.

AS YOU LIKE IT, exc. AGES OF MAN. "All the world's a stage" COLUMB 4, COLUMB 5, HOUGHT 2, SINGER 6

_____. "Blow, blow thou winter wind" EAV 6, LIST 1

_____. "It was a lover and his lass" CAED 186, LIST 1, POLYGL 2

_____. "Under the Greenwood Tree" EAV 6, HARC 2

CYMBELINE, exc. "Fear no more the heat o'the sun" CAED 186, LION 2, LIST 1, POLYGL 2, SPOA 12, SPOA 35, SPOA 41

_____. "Hark, hark the lark" EAV 6

HAMLET, exc. "And will a' not come again" LIST 1

_____. "Some say that ever 'gainst that season comes" ARGO 82, SPOA 41

_____. "To be, or not to be: that is the question" SINGER 6

HENRY V, exc. "Now entertain conjecture of a time" LONGM 1

HENRY VI, PART 3, exc. "Oh God! methinks it were a happy life"

LOVE'S LABOR'S LOST, exc. "When daisies pied and violets blue" LIST 1

_____. "When icicles hang by the wall" ARGO 82, CAED 186, CMS 2, POLYGL 2, SPOA 41

MEASURE FOR MEASURE, exc. "Be absolute for death" LONGM 1

THE MERCHANT OF VENICE, exc. "The quality of mercy is not strained" JNP 8

MIDSUMMER NIGHT'S DREAM, exc. "Ill met by moonlight, proud Titania" SPOA 35

_____. "You spotted snakes with double tongue" CAED 111

MUCH ADO ABOUT NOTHING, exc. "Sigh no more ladies, sigh no more" LION 2

RAPE OF LUCRECE, exc. "From the besieged Ardea all in post" ARGO 15, SPOA 66

SONNETS—COMPLETE. ARGO 13, AUDIBK 1, CROWN 1, LIST 9, SPOA 111

* Recording not available for analysis

Shakespeare, William (continued)

SONNETS—SELECTED

———. 1. "From fairest creatures we desire increase" CAED 6, LIST 1

———. 2. "When forty winters shall besiege thy brow" CAED 6, SERAPH 1, SPOA 12

———. 3. "Look in thy glass, and tell the face thou viewest" CAED 6, CMS 10A, LEARNC 3, POETRY 1

———. 4. "Unthrifty loveliness, why dost thou spend" CAED 6

———. 5. "Those hours, that with gentle work did frame" CAED 6

———. 6. "Then let not winter's ragged hand deface" CAED 6

———. 7. "Lo in the orient when the gracious light" CAED 6

———. 8. "Music to hear, why hears't thou music sadly?" CAED 6, CMS 10A, POETRY 1, SERAPH 1

———. 9. "Is it for fear to wet a widow's eye" CAED 6

———. 10. "For shame! deny that thou bear'st love to any" CAED 6

———. 11. "As fast as thou shalt wane, so fast thou grow'st" CAED 6

———. 12. "When I do count the clock that tells the time" CAED 6, SPOA 12; German DEUTGR 30

———. 13. "O! that you were yourself; but, love, you are" CAED 6

———. 14. "Not from the stars do I my judgment pluck" CAED 6, SPOA 12

———. 15. "When I consider everything that grows" CAED 6, CMS 10A, IMP 1, POETRY 1, SERAPH 1

———. 16. "But wherefore do not you a mightier way" CAED 6

———. 17. "Who will believe my verse in time to come" CAED 6

———. 18. "Shall I compare thee to a summer's day" BRITAM 1, CAED 6, CAED 186, CMS 10A, COLUMB 11, LION 2, LIST 1, LONDON 1, POETRY 1, POLYGL 2, SERAPH 1, SPOA 12, THEAL 2; German DEUTGR 30

———. 19. "Devouring time, blunt thou the lion's paws" CAED 6, CMS 10A, POETRY 1, SPOA 12

———. 20. "A woman's face with Nature's own hand painted" CAED 6

———. 21. "So is it not with me as with that Muse." Complete sets only.

———. 22. "My glass shall not persuade me I am old" CAED 6

———. 23. "As an unperfect actor on the stage" CAED 6, SERAPH 1

———. 24. "Mine eye hath play'd the painter and hath stell'd" CAED 6

———. 25. "Let those who are in favour with their stars" CAED 6

———. 26. "Lord of my love, to whom in vassalage" CAED 6

———. 27. "Weary with toil, I haste me to my bed" CAED 6, SERAPH 1

———. 28. "How can I then return in happy plight" CAED 6

———. 29. "When, in disgrace with fortune and men's eyes" BRITAM 2, CAED 6, CAED 186, CMS 10A, EAV 22, IMP 1, LION 2, LIST 1, POETRY 1, POLYGL 2, SERAPH 1, SPOA 12, THEAL 2

———. 30. "When to the sessions of sweet silent thought" CAED 6, CAED 20, CAED 186, CMS 10A, LION 2, POETRY 1, POLYGL 2, SPOA 12

———. 31. "Thy bosom is endeared with all hearts" CAED 6

———. 32. "If thou survive my well-contented day" CAED 6

———. 33. "Full many a glorious morning have I seen" CAED 6, CMS 3, LONDON 1, SERAPH 1, SPOA 12

———. 34. "Why didst thou promise such a beauteous day" CAED 6, LONDON 1, SPOA 12

———. 35. "No more be griev'd at which thou hast done" CAED 6

———. 36. "Take all my loves, my love, yes, take them all" CAED 6

———. 37. "Those pretty wrongs that liberty commits" CAED 6

———. 38. "That thou hast her, it is not all my grief" CAED 6, LEARNC 3; German DEUTGR 30

———. 39. "Let me confess that we two must be twain" CAED 6

———. 40. "As a decrepit father takes delight" CAED 6

———. 41. "How can my muse want subject to invest" CAED 6

———. 42. "O how thy worth with manners may I sing." See Sonnets—Complete.

———. 43. "When most I wink, then do mine eyes best see." See Sonnets—Complete.

———. 44. "If the dull substance of my flesh were thought" CAED 6

———. 45. "The other two, slight air and purging fire." See Sonnets—Complete.

———. 46. "Mine eye and heart are at a mortal war" CAED 6

———. 47. "Betwixt mine eye and heart a league is took" CAED 6

———. 48. "How careful was I, when I took my way" CAED 6

———. 49. "Against that time, if ever that time come" CAED 6, SPOA 12

———. 50. "How heavy do I journey on the way" CAED 6, CMS 10A, POETRY

———. 51. "Thus can my love excuse the slow offence" CAED 6

———. 52. "So am I as the rich, whose blessed key" CAED 6, SERAPH

———. 53. "What is your substance, whereof are you made" CAED

———. 54. "O! how much more doth beauty beauteous seem" CAED

———. 55. "Not marble, nor the gilded monuments" CAED 6, CMS 10A, LION POETRY 1, SPOA 12 German DEUTGR 3

———

* Recording not available for analysis

———. 56. "Sweet love, renew thy force; be it not said" CAED 6, SERAPH 1

———. 57. "Being your slave, what should I do but tend" CAED 6, LION 2, SERAPH 1

———. 58. "That God forbid that made me first your slave" CAED 6

———. 59. "Is it thy will thy image should keep open" CAED 6, LONDON 1, SERAPH 1

———. 60. "Sin of self-love possesseth all mine eye" CAED 6

———. 61. "Against my love shall be, as I am now" CAED 6

———. 62. "When I have seen by Time's fell hand defaced" CAED 6, CMS 10A, LION 2, POETRY 1

———. 63. "Since brass, nor stone, nor earth, nor boundless sea" CAED 6, CMS 10A, POETRY 1

———. 64. "If there be nothing new, but that which is." See Sonnets—Complete.

———. 65. "Like as the waves make towards the pebbled shore" CAED 6

———. 66. "Tir'd with all these, for restful death I cry" CAED 6, CAED 186, LION 2, POLYGL 2, SERAPH 1, SPOA 12; German DEUTGR 30

———. 67. "Ah wherefore with infection should he live." See Sonnets—Complete.

———. 68. "Thus is his cheek the map of days out worn." See Sonnets—Complete.

———. 69. "Those parts of thee that the world's eye doth view" CAED 6

———. 70. "That thou art blam'd shall not be thy defect." See Sonnets—Complete.

———. 71. "They that have power to hurt and will do none" CAED 6, LIST 1, SERAPH 1

———. 72. "How sweet and lovely dost thou make the shame" CAED 6

———. 73. "Some say thy fault is youth, some wantonness" CAED 6

———. 74. "Or shall I live your epitaph to make." See Sonnets—Complete.

———. 75. "No longer mourn for me when I am dead" CAED 6, CMS 13, EAV 11, IMP 1, LEARNC 6, LION 2, SPOA 12

———. 76. "O lest the the world should task you to recite." See Sonnets—Complete.

———. 77. "That time of year thou mayst in me behold" CAED 6, CAED 186, CMS 10A, LION 2, POETRY 1, POLYGL 2, SERAPH 1, SPOA 12

———. 78. "But be contented: when that fell arrest" CAED 6

———. 79. "Why is my verse so barren of new pride" CAED 6

———. 80. "So are you to my thoughts as food to life" CAED 6

———. 81. "Thy glass will show thee how thy beauties wear." See Sonnets—Complete.

———. 82. "So oft have I invok'd thee for my Muse." See Sonnets—Complete.

———. 83. "Whilst I alone did call upon thy aid" CAED 6

———. 84. "O! how I faint when I of you do write" CAED 6

———. 85. "I grant thou wert not married to my Muse." See Sonnets—Complete.

———. 86. "I never saw that you did painting need." See Sonnets—Complete.

———. 87. "Who is it that says most? which can say more" SPOA 12

———. 88. "My tongue-tied Muse in manners holds her still." See Sonnets—Complete.

———. 89. "Was it the proud full sail of his great verse" CAED 6

———. 90. "Farewell! thou art too dear for my possessing" CAED 6, CAED 186, CMS 12, POLYGL 2, SPOA 12; German DEUTGR 30

———. 91. "When thou shalt be dispos'd to set me light" SPOA 12

———. 92. "Say that thou didst forsake me for some fault." See Sonnets—Complete.

———. 93. "Then hate me when thou wilt; if ever, now" CAED 6, CMS 10A, LION 2, POETRY 1

———. 94. "Some glory in their birth, some in their skill" CAED 6, SERAPH 1, SPOA 12

———. 95. "But do thy worst to steal thyself away" CAED 6

———. 96. "So shall I live, supposing thou art true" CAED 6

———. 97. "How like a winter hath my absence been" CAED 6, CAED 186, LEARNC 3, POLYGL 2, SERAPH 1, SPOA 12

———. 98. "From you have I been absent in the spring" BRITAM 2, CAED 6

———. 99. "The forward violet thus did I chide" CAED 6

———. 100. "Where art thou, Muse, that thou forget'st so long" CAED 6

———. 101. "O truant Muse, what shall be thy amends." See Sonnets—Complete.

———. 102. "My love is strengthened though more weak in seeming." See Sonnets—Complete.

———. 103. "Alack! what poverty my Muse brings forth" CAED 6

———. 104. "To me, fair friend, you never can be old" CAED 6, CMS 10A, LEARNC 3, POETRY 1, SERAPH 1

———. 105. "Let not my love be call'd idolatry" CAED 6

———. 106. "When in the chronicle of wasted time" CAED 6, CAED 186, LION 2, LIST 1, POLYGL 2, SERAPH 1, SPOA 12

———. 107. "Not mine own fears, nor the prophetic soul" CAED 6

———. 108. "What's in the brain, that ink may character" CAED 6

———. 109. "Those lines that I before have writ do lie" CAED 6

———. 110. "Let me not to the marriage of true minds" BRITAM 2, CAED 6, CMS 10A, COLUMB 11, EAV 22, LION 2, LIST 1, POETRY 1, SERAPH 1, SPOA 12, THEAL 3

———. 111. "Since I left you, mine eye is in my mind" CAED 6

———. 112. "Or whether doth my mind, being crown'd with you." See Sonnets—Complete.

———. 113. "O! never say I was false of heart" CAED 6

* Recording not available for analysis

Shakespeare, William (continued)

———. 114. "Alas! 'tis true, I have gone here and there" CAED 6

———. 115. "O! for my sake do you with Fortune chide" CAED 6

———. 116. "Your love and pity doth th' impression fill" CAED 6

———. 117. "Accuse me thus: that I have scanted all" CAED 6

———. 118. "Like as, to make our appetites more keen." See Sonnets—Complete.

———. 119. "What potions have I drunk of Siren tears" CAED 6

———. 120. "That you were once unkind befriends me now" CAED 6

———. 121. " 'Tis better to be vile than vile esteemed." See Sonnets—Complete.

———. 122. "Thy gift, thy tables, are within my brain." See Sonnets—Complete.

———. 123. "No, Time, thou shalt not boast that I do change" CAED 6

———. 124. "If my dear love were but the child of state." See Sonnets—Complete.

———. 125. "Were't aught to me I bore the canopy." See Sonnets—Complete.

———. 126. "O thou, my lovely boy, who in thy power" CAED 6

———. 127. "In the old age black was not counted fair" CAED 6

———. 128. "How oft, when thou my music, music play'st" CAED 6

———. 129. "My mistress' eyes are nothing like the sun" CAED 6, CMS 10A, LEARNC 3, POETRY 1, SPOA 12

———. 130. "Thou art as tyrannous, so as thou art" CAED 6

———. 131. "O! from what power hast this powerful might" CAED 6

———. 132. "Thine eyes I love, and they, as pitying me" CAED 6

———. 133. "O me! What eyes hath Love put in my head." See Sonnets—Complete.

———. 134. "Thou blind fool, Love, what dost thou to mine eyes" CAED 6

———. 135. "O call me not to justify the wrong." See Sonnets—Complete.

———. 136. "Be wise as thou art cruel; do not press" CAED 6

———. 137. "In faith, I do not love thee with mine eyes" CAED 6

———. 138. "Love is my sin, and thy dear virtue hate" CAED 6

———. 139. "Canst thou, O cruel! say I love thee not." See Sonnets—Complete.

———. 140. "Lo, as a careful housewife runs to catch" CAED 6

———. 141. "Whoever hath her wish, thou hast thy Will" CAED 6

———. 142. "If thy soul check thee that I come so near." See Sonnets—Complete.

———. 143. "Those lips that love's own hand did make" LEARNC 3

———. 144. "Love is too young to know what conscience is" CAED 6

———. 145. "When my love swears that she is made of truth" CAED 6, LEARNC 3 LION 2, SPOA 1?

———. 146. "Two loves I have, of comfort and despair" CAED 6, COLUMB 11 LEARNC 3, SPOA 1?

———. 147. "Beshrew that heart that makes my heart to groan" CAED ?

———. 148. "So, now I have confess'd that he is thine." See Sonnets—Complete.

———. 149. "In loving thee thou know'st I am forsworn" CAED ?

———. 150. "My love is as a fever, longing still" CAED 6; German DEUTGR 3?

———. 151. "Th'expense of spirit in a waste of shame" CAED 6, LEARNC 3, LIST ? SPOA 1?

———. 152. "Poor soul, the centre of my sinful earth" CAED ?

———. 153. "Cupid laid by his brand and fell asleep." See Sonnets—Complete.

———. 154. "The little love-god lying once asleep." See Sonnets—Complete.

THE TEMPEST, exc. "Full fathom five thy father lies" LION 2, LIST 1, RCA

———. "Ye elves of hills, brooks, standing lakes and groves" LONGM

TWELFTH NIGHT, exc. "O Mistress mine, where are you roaming" CAED 186, EAV 6 LION 2, LIST 1, POLYGL ?

———. "Come away, come away, death" LION ?

THE TWO GENTLEMEN OF VERONA, exc. "Who is Sylvia? what is she" DECCA 12, LIST

VENUS AND ADONIS, exc. "Even as the sun with purple colour'd face" ARGO 14, CAED ? Poetry* PRENT 2, SPOA 122, SPOA 13?

Shange, Ntozake. 1948. in English.
"Chicago and San Francisco and you and me" WATSHD 1?

FAYE. "She left the front gate open" WATSHD 1

THE RESURRECTION OF THE DAUGHTER. "The family had been ill" WATSHD 1?

WHERE THE MISSISSIPPI MEETS THE AMAZON. "You fill me up so much" WATSHD 1?

Shannon, Monica. in English.
ONLY MY OPINION. "Is a caterpillar ticklish" HARB ?

Shapiro, Harvey. 1924. in English.
NATIONAL COLD STORAGE COMPANY. "The National Cold Storage Company contains" FOLKW 2

Shapiro, Karl. 1913. in English.
AUTO WRECK. "Its quick soft silver bell beating beating" SINGER ?

ELEGY FOR A DEAD SOLDIER. "A white sheet on the tailgate of a truck" LIBC 15, LIBC 4?

THE FIGUREHEAD. "Watching my paralytic friend" SPOA 10?

"A gas station in the playground of kings" LIBC

THE INTERLUDE. "Much of transfiguration that we hear" FOLKW 2?

THE KISS. "The first kiss was with stumbling fingertips" SPOA 10?

---

* Recording not available for analysis

LOVE FOR A HAND. "Two hands lie still, the hairy and the white"   SPOA 100
"Office love, love of money and fight"
                                      LIBC 1
THE RECOGNITION OF EVE. "Whatever it was she had so fiercely fought"   SPOA 100
THE SICKNESS OF ADAM. "In the beginning, at every step, he turned"   SPOA 100
"There's a Parthenon in Nashville large as life"
                                      LIBC 1
"Waiting in front of the columnar high school"
                                      LIBC 1
"What kind of notation is in my Time file for my life"   LIBC 1

Shaw, Frances. in English.
"Who loves the rain"   CAED 169

Shelley, Percy Bysshe. 1792. in English.
ADONAIS, exc. "I weep for Adonais he is dead"
      ARGO 61, ARGO 77, CAED 41, LIST 2,
                                      SPOA 121
———, exc. "The one remains, the many change and pass"   CAED 21
THE BOAT ON THE SERCHIO, exc. "Our boat is a-sleep on Serchio's stream"   LONGM 1
CHARLES I, exc. "A widow bird sate mourning"
                                      ARGO 61
THE CLOUD, exc.   HARC 2, SPOA 121
EPIPSYCHIDION, exc. "I never was attached to that great sect"   ARGO 61
HELLAS: FINAL CHORUS. "The world's great age begins anew"   ARGO 61, IMP 1, LIST 2
HYMN TO INTELLECTUAL BEAUTY. "The awful shadow of some unseen power"   CAED 41,
                                      EAV 18
INDIAN SERENADE. "I arise from dreams of thee"
      ARGO 61, CAED 202, SPOA 29
LINES. "When the lamp is shattered"
      ARGO 61, CMS 12
LOVE'S PHILOSOPHY. "The fountains mingle with the river"   ARGO 61, EAV 18, SPOA 29
THE MASK OF ANARCHY, exc. "As I lay asleep in Italy"   LONGM 1
THE MOON. "And like a dying lady, lean and pale"   IMP 1
ODE TO THE WEST WIND. "O wild West Wind, thou breath of Autumn's being"   ARGO 61,
      BRITAM 3, CAED 41, CAED 202,
      EAV 18, LIST 2, LIST 10, SPOA 29,
                      SPOA 121, THEAL 2
OZYMANDIAS. "I met a traveller from an antique land"   ARGO 61, CAED 41, EAV 8,
      EAV 18, FOLKW 68, HOUGHT 4, LIST 2,
      LIST 10, POETRY 2, SPOA 29, SPOA 121
PROMETHEUS UNBOUND, exc. "Gentleness, Virtue, Wisdom, and Endurance"   ARGO 61
———, exc. "My soul is an enchanted boat"
                                      CAED 41
———, exc. "On a poet's lips I slept"
                                      ARGO 61
STANZAS, APRIL 1, 1814. "Away! the moor is dark beneath the moon"   ARGO 61
STANZAS WRITTEN IN DEJECTION NEAR NAPLES, exc. "Alas! I have nor hope nor health"
                                      LONGM 1
SUMMER AND WINTER. "It was a bright and cheerful afternoon"   EAV 18

TO——. "Music, when soft voices die"
      ARGO 61, CAED 41, CAED 202, CMS 13
TO——. "One word is too often profaned"
                                      CMS 13
TO A SKYLARK. "Hail to thee, blithe Spirit"
      CAED 41, CAED 186, EAV 8, EAV 18,
      EAV 22, LIST 2, LIST 10, SPOA 29,
                                      SPOA 121
TO JANE: THE INVITATION. "Best and brightest, come away"   LONDON 1
TO JANE: THE RECOLLECTION. "Now the last day of many days"   ARGO 61
TO NIGHT. "Swiftly walk o'er the western wave"
      ARGO 61, CAED 186, EAV 18, RCA 4,
                                      SPOA 121
WITH A GUITAR, TO JANE. "Ariel to Miranda: Take"   CAED 41
Poetry*   SPOA 123

Sheridan, Richard Brinsley. 1751. in English.
"Here's to the maiden of bashful fifteen"
                      CAED 202, HOUGHT 4

Sherman, Guy. ca. 1950. in English.
ANTHILL. "Ants keep busy. Makes you dizzy"
                                      HARB 2

Sherwin, Judith Johnson. 1936. in English.
THE ALARM. "The hands lie low"   WATSHD 9
ANALYSIS. "Says she doesn't like the way"
                                      WATSHD 26
ARGUMENT ONE. "Now put me near your chess pieces"   WATSHD 26
ARGUMENT TWO: MIRRORS. "Yes, these are love poems"   WATSHD 26
ASPEN LEAVES. "We lay on a grid of rock"
                                      WATSHD 26
THE BLOB SPEAKS TO ITS MOTHER. "Just to have held"   WATSHD 9
A GENTLE HEART. I. "Stone walls are nothing"
                      WATSHD 12, WATSHD 26
———. II. "A lady walks down a road bed"
                                      WATSHD 26
———. III. "It seems I've got it all"
                                      WATSHD 26
GIFT. "This is a pig woman"   WATSHD 26
HAPPY JACK COMES HOME. "Such jolly nights, my old friend"   WATSHD 9
HARVEST HOME. "When they crack the sound barrier"   WATSHD 26
LA DOLCE VITA IN BRUSSELS. "Paper profits"
                                      WATSHD 26
MORNING LIGHT. "This is a place"   WATSHD 9
NOON. "You, flat yellow light"   WATSHD 26
PLOTTING THE CHANGE OF WORLD. "From sweet and stern"   WATSHD 9
THE POINT OF THE SILVER SCREWDRIVER. "Love came to me"   WATSHD 9
RELIC. "Here I am, great big dinosaur lady"
                      WATSHD 12, WATSHD 26
RENEGADE. "Tell me all I want"
                      WATSHD 12, WATSHD 26
RUNES FOR A BAD DAY. "The maidens came when I"   WATSHD 26
SHAKE. "Shake, shake"   WATSHD 26
SONNET. "Again I won't do what you want"
                                      WATSHD 26
SONNET ON WOMEN'S BUSINESS.   WATSHD 9
SOON BE OVER. "Where did you go"
                                      WATSHD 26

* Recording not available for analysis

Sherwin, Judith Johnson (continued)

SUMMER, THE HAY FEVER. "Summer, the hay fever in the air"   WATSHD 26
THE TOWN SCOLD AT THE DUCKING POND. "When the good"   WATSHD 26
WITH A SILVER COMB. "I'm too clever to say it"   WATSHD 26
YOURS. "Yours exasperate"   WATSHD 9
Poetry*   WATSHD 27

Shevchenko, Taras. ca. 1810. in Russian.

DUMI MOYI. "Dumi moyi, dumi moyi"   FOLKW 93
"I veris va na chuzhyni"   FOLKW 93
"I zolotoyi i dorohoyi"   FOLKW 93
KATERINA, exc. "Krichat sovi, spit dibrova"   FOLKW 93
MENI ODNAKOVO. "Meni odnakovo, chi budu"
"Meni trinadtsyati minalo"   FOLKW 93
MENI ZDAYETSYA. "Meni zdayetsya, ya ne znayu"   FOLKW 93
"Minayut dni, minayut nochi"   FOLKW 93
"Postavlyu khatu i kimnatu"   FOLKW 93
SVITE YASNY. "Svite yasny, svite yasny"   FOLKW 93
TECHE VODA. "Teche voda v sine more"   FOLKW 93
"Yakbi vi znali panichi"   FOLKW 93

Shirley, James. 1596. in English.

DEATH THE LEVELLER. "The glories of our blood and state"   ARGO 35, BRITAM 1, CMS 13, SPOA 50

Shiva. in English.

CHANCE IS THE GOD OF DEATH. "We are waiting"   WATSHD 2
CHICAGO. "Hey, he sort of like Chicago"   WATSHD 2
IMPROVISATION: ON AUTHORITY. "This is for reference purposes"   WATSHD 2
WHERE ARE WE? "Where are we?"   WATSHD 2

Shpunt, Lori. in English.

BIRTHDAY POEM. "The party hats perch like"   WATSHD 8
CHANGING THE WORLD. "The secret word for change is hurt"   WATSHD 8
HOW TO MAKE IT THROUGH THE NIGHT. "Because they may"   WATSHD 8

Sidney, Sir Philip. 1554. in English.

ARCADIAN DUOLOGUE. "My true love hath my heart and I have his"   BRITAM 2, LIST 1
ASTROPHEL AND STELLA, exc. "Because I breathe not love to every one"   LIST 1
_____. "Loving in truth and fain in verse my love to show"   ARGO 32, JNP 8, LIST 1
_____. "With how sad steps, O Moon, thou climb'st the skies"   ARGO 32, BRITAM 2, LONGM 1, SPOA 50, SPOA 83
_____. "Come sleep, o sleep, the certain knot of peace"   ARGO 32, LONGM 1
_____. "Having this day my horse, my hand, my lance"   ARGO 32
_____. "Highway, since you my chief Parnassus be"   ARGO 32
_____. "Leave me, o Love, which reachest but to dust"   ARGO 32
_____. "No more, my dear, no more these counsels try"   ARGO 32

_____. "Thou blind man's mark, thou fool's self-chosen snare"   ARGO 32
TRUE LOVE. "My true love hath my heart and I have his"   ARGO 31, POLYGL 2, SPOA 12, SPOA 50

Siewertz, Sigfrid. 1882. in Swedish.

FIKTIONSVARLDEN.   GRAM 4
FORSTA STROVTÅGEN.   GRAM 4

Silkin, Jon. 1930. in English.

ASLEEP. "Today, I want to speak of human agony"   ARGO 98
BOWL. "The beggar's bowl is formed from hands"   ARGO 98
DEATH OF A SON WHO DIED IN A MENTAL HOSPITAL AGED 1. "Something has ceased to come along with me"   ARGO 98
SNOW DROP. "The blanched melted snows"   ARGO 98
THE STRAWBERRY PLANT. "The rootless strawberry plant"   ARGO 98
TO MY FRIENDS. "It does not matter she never knew"   ARGO 98

Sill, Edward Rowland. in English.

THE FOOL'S PRAYER.   EAV 15
OPPORTUNITY.   EAV 15, HOUGHT 4

Sillitoe, Alan. 1928. in English.

CAR FIGHTS CAT. "In a London crescent"   SPOA 67
Poetry*   PROTHM 6

Silva, José Asunción. 1865. in Spanish.

LOS MADEROS DE SAN JUAN. "Y aserrín, aserrán"   FIDIAS 3
NOCTURNO. "Una noche, una noche toda llena de murmullos"   HOLT 1, MIAMI 1, SMC 6, SPOA 39

Simic, Charles. 1938. in English.

INNER MAN. "It isn't the body"   EMC 7
STONE. "Go inside a stone"   EMC 7
Poetry*   WATSHD 39

Simmons, Judy. 1944. in English.

ALABAMA. "Back in back of the back country"   WATSHD 1
DEATH OF DUCKS. "I wish you happy death of ducks"   WATSHD 1
JUDITH'S BLUES. "Get it on"   WATSHD 1
NEW YORK. "Gravely like a priest"   WATSHD 1
TO SWINEHERDS. "Now I am only aggravated"   WATSHD 1

Simmons, James Stewart Alexander. in English.
Poetry*   OUTL 1

Simonides. in Greek.

"Hellenon promakhountes Athenaioi Marathoni"   Greek and English JNP 9

Simonov, Konstantin M. 1915. in Russian.

"Byl u menya khoroshi drug"   MONITR 1
DOM V VYAZME. "Ya pomnyu v vyazme starim dom"   MONITR 1
"Druzhba nastoyashchaya ne staritsya"   MONITR 1
"Ne serdites—k luchemu"   MONITR 1
OTKRITOE PISMO. "Ya vas obyasan izvestit"   MONITR 1
"Ti pomnish, Alyosha, dorogi smolenshchini"   MONITR 1
"Umer drug u menya vot kakaya beda"   MONITR 1

---

* Recording not available for analysis

"Yesli bog nas svoim mogushchestvom"
                       MONITR 1
"Zhdi menya, i ya vernus"   MONITR 1
Simpson, Louis. 1923. in English.
AEGEAN. "Where only flowers fret"   CARIL 5
AN AMERICAN IN THE THIEVES' MARKET. "In Italy
   the dead have all the passion"   CARIL 5,
                          SCHOL 1
THE ASH AND THE OAK. "When men discovered
   freedom first"   CARIL 5, SCHOL 1
THE BATTLE. "Helmet and rifle, pack and over-
   coat"   CARIL 5, SCHOL 1
BIRCH. "Birch tree, you remind me"
                        SPOA 104
BLACK KETTLE RAISES THE STARS AND STRIPES.
   "Nits make lice, said Chivington"
                        SCHOL 1
BROOKLYN FLATS.   CARIL 5
THE DEATH OF LOVE.   CARIL 5
"Early in the morning" CARIL 5, SCHOL 1
THE GREEN SHEPHERD. "Here sit a shepherd and
   a shepherdess"   CARIL 5
THE HEROES. "I dreamed of war-heroes, of
   wounded war-heroes" CARIL 5, SCHOL 1
HOT NIGHT ON WATER STREET. "A hot midsum-
   mer night on Water Street"   CARIL 5,
                        SCHOL 1
"I dreamed that in a city dark as Paris"
                        CARIL 5
THE INNER PART. "When they had won the war"
                        SCHOL 1
INVITATION TO A QUIET LIFE.   CARIL 5
LANDSCAPE FROM A TRAIN.   CARIL 5
LAZARUS CONVALESCENT.   CARIL 5
A LION IN THE WIND.   CARIL 5
THE LOVER'S GHOST. "I fear the headless man"
                        CARIL 5
"The man who married Magdalene"
             CARIL 5, SPOA 104
MEMORIES OF A LOST WAR. "The guns know what
   is what, but underneath"   CARIL 5
"My father in the night commanding no"
                        SPOA 104
ORPHEUS IN AMERICA. "Here are your meadows,
   Love, as wide as heaven"   CARIL 5
ORPHEUS IN THE UNDERWORLD. "Night, dark
   night, night of my distress"   CARIL 5
THE SHADOW-HUNTER. "The man points, and the
   child"   SCHOL 1
THE SILENT GENERATION. "When Hitler was the
   devil"   SPOA 104
THE SILENT LOVER. "She sighs. What shall I say?"
                        SPOA 104
SLEEPING BEAUTY.   CARIL 5
STUMPFOOT ON 42ND STREET. "A Negro sprouts
   from the pavement like an asparagus"
                        SCHOL 1
SUMMER STORM. "In that so sudden summer
   storm they tried"   CARIL 5
THERE IS. "Look! From my window there's a
   view"   SPOA 104
TO THE WESTERN WORLD. "A siren sang, and
   Europe turned away"   CARIL 5
THE TRUE WEATHER FOR WOMEN. "Young women
   in their April moodiness"   CARIL 5
WINTER.   CARIL 5

A WOMAN TOO WELL REMEMBERED. "Having put
   on new fashions, she demands"   CARIL 5
Poetry*   MICHM 13
Sinán, Rogelio. See **Domínguez Alba, Bernardo.**
Sitwell, Edith. 1887. in English.
THE BEE ORACLES, I: THE BEE-KEEPER. "In the
   plain of the world's dust like a great sea"
               CAED 17, CAED 145
BLACK MRS. BEHEMOTH. "In a room of the pal-
   ace"   COLUMB 7
THE CANTICLE OF THE ROSE. "The rose upon the
   wall"   CAED 17, CAED 145, COLUMB 3
COLONEL FANTOCK. "Thus spoke the lady un-
   derneath the tree"   RCA 2
COUNTRY DANCE. "That hobnailed goblin, the
   bob-tailed Hob"   COLUMB 7
DIDO'S SONG. "My Sun of Death is to the deep,
   reversedly"   CAED 17
DIRGE FOR THE NEW SUNRISE. "Bound to my
   heart as Ixion to the wheel"   ARGO 119,
          COLUMB 3, FOLKW 65A, RCA 2
EURIDICE. "Fires on the hearth! Fires in the
   heavens! Fires in the hearts of men!"
                        RCA 2
FACADE, exc.   ARGO 129, ARGO 135
_____. BY THE LAKE. "Across the flat and the
   pastel snow"   COLUMB 7, RCA 2
_____. EN FAMILLE. "In the early springtime
   after their tea"   COLUMB 7, RCA 2
_____. HORNPIPE. "Sailors come, to the drum"
                 COLUMB 7, RCA 2
_____. I DO LIKE TO BE BESIDE THE SEASIDE.
   "When/ Don/ Pasquito"   COLUMB 7,
                  RCA 1, RCA 2
_____. LULLABY FOR JUMBO. "Jumbo asleep!"
                 COLUMB 7, RCA 2
_____. SCOTCH RHAPSODY. "Do not take a bath
   in the Jordan, Gordon"   COLUMB 7,
       FOLKW 64, FOLKW 65A, RCA 2
_____. TRIO FOR TWO CATS AND A TROMBONE.
   "Long steel grass" CAED 17, COLUMB 7,
                        RCA 2
_____. WALTZ. "Daisy and Lily, lazy and silly"
                 COLUMB 7, RCA 2
_____. "The wind's bastinado"   CAED 17
FOUR IN THE MORNING. "Cried the navy-blue
   ghost"   COLUMB 7
FOX TROT. "Old/ Sir/ Faulk"   COLUMB 7
GARDENERS AND ASTRONOMERS. "Where the
   green airs seem fanning palms and the green
   psalms"   CAED 17
"Green flows the river of Lethe-O"
                        CAED 17
HARVEST. "I, an old woman whose heart is like
   the Sun"   CAED 145, COLUMB 3
HEART AND MIND. "Said the lion to the lioness"
         CAED 145, FOLKW 65A, RCA 2
HOW MANY HEAVENS.   FOLKW 69
JODELLING SONG. "We bear velvet cream"
                      COLUMB 7
"The King of China's daughter" CAED 110
LULLABY. "Though the world has slipped and
   gone"   COLUMB 3, FOLKW 65A
"Madame mouse trots"   CAED 109
THE MAN FROM A FAR COUNTRY. "Rose and Alice"
                      COLUMB 7

* Recording not available for analysis

Sitwell, Edith (continued)

MARINER MAN. "What are you staring at, mariner-man"   COLUMB 7

MOST LOVELY SHADE. "Most lovely Dark, my Ethiopia born"   CAED 17, FOLKW 64

NURSERY RHYME. "Said King Pompey the emperor's ape"   CAED 17

AN OLD WOMAN. "I, an old woman in the light of the sun"   CAED 17

ON THE VANITY OF HUMAN ASPIRATIONS. "In the time of King James I"   RCA 2

POLKA. "Tra la la la—See me dance the polka"   COLUMB 7, RCA 1

POPULAR SONG. "Lily O'Grady"   COLUMB 7

"The Queen Bee sighed"   RCA 2

THE QUEEN OF SCOTLAND'S REPLY TO A REPROOF FROM JOHN KNOX. "Said the bitter Man of Thorns to me, the White-Rose-Tree"
                    CAED 17

SAILOR, WHAT OF THE ISLES? "Sailor, what of the isles"   CAED 17

SERENADE: ANY MAN TO ANY WOMAN. "Dark angel who art clear and straight"   CAED 17

THE SHADOW OF CAIN. "Under great yellow flags and banners of the ancient cold"
                    CAED 145

SIR BEELZEBUB. "When/ Sir/ Beelzebub called for his syllabub"   COLUMB 7, FOLKW 64

THE SLEEPING BEAUTY, NO. 8. "In the great gardens after bright spring rain"   RCA 2

A SLEEPY TUNE. "I was a Gold Man—now I lie under the earth"   COLUMB 3

SOMETHING LIES BEYOND THE SCENE. "Something lies beyond the scene, the encore de chine, marine, obscene horizon"   COLUMB 7

SONG. "Where is all the bright company gone"
                    CAED 17

SONG OF QUEEN ANNE BOLEYN AT COCKCROW. "As I lay in my love's low bed"   CAED 17

SPINNING SONG. "The miller's daughter"
                    CAED 17

"Still falls the rain"   ARGO 119, CAED 145,
                CAED 183, COLUMB 3, RCA 2

STREET SONG. "Love my heart for an hour, but my bone for a day"   CAED 17

A SYLPH'S SONG. "The cornucopia of Ceres"
                    CAED 17

TATTERED SERENADE: BEGGAR TO SHADOW, II. "In the summer, when no one is cold"
                    CAED 17

"Through gilded trellises"   COLUMB 7

THE TWO LOVES, exc.   CAED 145

"Who shall have my fair lady"   CAED 17

THE YOUTH WITH THE RED-GOLD HAIR. "The gold-armored ghost from the Roman road"
                    CAED 17

Poetry*   JNP 7

Sitwell, Osbert. 1892. in English.

AUTUMN. "The moth hums under the beams"
                    CAED 15

DANSE MACABRE. "The Countess Clondyke"
                    CAED 15

ELEGY FOR MR. GOODBEARE. "Do you remember Mr. Goodbeare"   CAED 15

FOOL'S SONG I. "Yesterday is my To-morrow"
                    CAED 15

FOX TROT. "The navy at Ezion-Geba"
                    CAED 15

THE GREAT NEMO. "The gypsy, the Great Nemo"
                    CAED 15

JOURNALIST'S SONG. "Who will buy my pretty wares"   CAED 15

LOCAL PRESS. "Mr. Timberley, the Editor of the Tidesend Courier"   CAED 15

LOUSY PETER. "Lousy Peter's terror was the Workhouse"   CAED 15

MARY-ANNE. "Mary-Anne/ Wise, simple old woman"   CAED 15

MISS LOPEZ. "What erratic wind from Andalusia"   CAED 15

MR. HAROLD COLBERT. "For over ninety years"
                    CAED 15

MR. NUTCH. "Mr. Nutch/ Brown-bearded bear"
                    CAED 15

MRS. BUSK. "On dull mornings"   CAED 15

MRS. CHIVERS. "Ethereal Ethel—Mrs. Chivers"
                    CAED 15

MRS. FROSSART. "Pale, flat-faced Mrs. Frossart"
                    CAED 15

MRS. GRANDESTIN. "Mrs. Grandestin, with grouse-coloured hair"   CAED 15

MRS. HUMBLEBY. "Clumsy Mrs. Humbleby"
                    CAED 15

MRS. LIVERSEDGE. "Mrs. Liversedge, shivering in her furs"   CAED 15

MRS. NUTCH. "Deep in the summer wood"
                    CAED 15

MRS. SOUTHERN'S ENEMY. "Oh, would that the cruel daylight, too"   CAED 15

MUNICIPAL IDYLL: A DIALOGUE. "They stood, side by side, in an idle moment"   CAED 15

OSMUND TOULMIN. "The name of Osmund Toulmin, the Gentleman-Jockey"   CAED 15

OUT OF THE FLAME. "From my high window"
                    CAED 15

PREFACE. "Before the dawning of the death-day"   CAED 15

SPRING MORNING. "Not so fine"   CAED 15

SUMMER. "Sun dissolves to recreate"
                    CAED 15

THE THREE MISS COLTRUMS. "Three large balloons in a dog-cart"   CAED 15

WINTER. "Rime lies crisp upon the ground"
                    CAED 15

WINTER THE HUNTSMAN. "Through his iron glades"   CAED 15

Skellings, Edmund. 1932. in English.

ULTRA-RED: AN ELECTRONIC LOVE POEM. "Ul-ul-ul-tra-tra"   WATSHD 1

Skelton, John. 1460. in English.

CALLIOPE.   ARGO 30

COLIN CLOUT, exc. "What can it avayle"
                    ARGO 30

MAGNIFICENCE. "Unto this process briefly compiled"   LONGM 1

THE MANNER OF THE WORLD NOWADAYS.
                    ARGO 30

"My darlyng Dere, my Daysy floure"
                    ARGO 30

PHILIP SPARROW, exc. "Pla ce bo"   ARGO 30

_____. "It had a velvet cap"   LONGM 1

SPEAK, PARROT, exc. "So many moral matters and so little used"   LONGM 1

---

* Recording not available for analysis

TO MISTRESS ANNE.   ARGO 30
TO MISTRESS ISABEL PENNELL. "By Saint Mary,
   my lady"   ARGO 30
TO MISTRESS MARGARET HUSSEY. "Merry Marga-
   ret"   ARGO 30, LONGM 1
THE TUNNING OF ELINOUR RUMMING. "When she
   goeth out"   LONGM 1
UPON A DEEDMANS HED. "Youre ugly tokyn"
                                            ARGO 30
WHY COME YE NOT TO COURT.   ARGO 30
"Woefully arrayed" (at.)   LONGM 1
Skelton, Robin. 1925. in English.
THE DAY LARRY WAS STRETCHED.   SPOA 68
Sklarew, Myra. in English.
FROM THE BACKYARD OF THE DIASPORA. "So I say
   that we are enclosed"   WATSHD 8
LETTING THE PLANTS DIE. "This one's gone to
   straw"   WATSHD 8
THE REASON I CAN'T INVITE YOU IN FOR A DRINK. "I
   been thinking"   WATSHD 8
WALKING INTO FIRE. "There is a legend"
                                           WATSHD 8
Skratz, G. P. in English.
ARTICHOKE. "Artichoke spaghetti"
                                           WATSHD 9
Slutsky, Boris A. 1919. in Russian.
MEDNIE DENGI.   MONITR 1
PISARYA.   MONITR 1
ZOOPARK NOCHIU.   MONITR 1
Smart, Christopher. 1722. in English.
JUBILATE AGNO, exc. "For I will consider my cat
   Jeoffrey"   LONGM 1
"Let Achsah rejoice with the pigeon"
                                           LONGM 1
SONG TO DAVID.   ARGO 50
Smith, A. J. M. 1902. in English.
THE ARCHER. "Bend back thy bow, O Archer,
   till the string"   FOLKW 49
BUSINESS AS USUAL. "Across the craggy indigo"
                                           FOLKW 49
FEAR AS NORMAL. "But gently clank? The clank
   has grown"   FOLKW 49
A HYACINTH FOR EDITH. "Now that the ashen
   rain of gummy April"   FOLKW 49
LIKE AN OLD KING IN A PARABLE. "A bitter king in
   anger to be gone"   FOLKW 49
MY DEATH. "I carry my Death within me"
                                           FOLKW 49
NOCTAMBULE. "Under the flag of this pneumatic
   moon"   FOLKW 49
THE PLOT AGAINST PROTEUS. "This is a theme for
   muted coronets"   FOLKW 49
SONNET. "How all men wrongly death to digni-
   fy"   FOLKW 49
Smith, Eugene Osborn. in English.
JUST LIKE YOU.   BOS 1
Smith, Iain Crichton. 1928. in English.
GIRL WITH ORANGE SUNSHADE.   ARGO 99
OLD WOMAN.   ARGO 99
Smith, Ken. 1938. in English.
FOSSIL. "Made stone, cleft, shape and shell of a
   thing"   ARGO 98
GRASS. "Grass erupts slowly, locking the soil in
   frail roots"   ARGO 98
Smith, Samuel Francis. 1808. in English.
AMERICA. "My country, 'tis of thee"
                                 CAED 98, DECCA 4

Smith, Stevie. 1902. in English.
AH, WILL THE SAVIOUR. "The cross"   ARGO 92
"Away, melancholy"   ARGO 134
THE BISHOPS OF THE CHURCH OF ENGLAND. "I ad-
   mire the Bishops of the Church of England"
                                     ARGO 134
THE BOAT. "The boat that took my love away"
                                     ARGO 134
THE CASTLE. "I married the Earl of Egremont"
                                     ARGO 134
THE CELTIC FRINGE. "Kathleen ni Houlihan"
                                     ARGO 134
CHRISTMAS. "A child is born, they cry, a child"
                                     ARGO 134
COME DEATH. "I feel ill. What can the matter
   be"   ARGO 134
CONVICTION, 1-4. "Christ died for God and me"
                                     ARGO 134
"Do take Muriel out"   ARGO 134
FAFNIR AND THE KNIGHT. "In the quiet waters of
   the forest pool"   ARGO 92, ARGO 134
FISH, FISH. "Look, man, look"   ARGO 134
FREDDY. "Nobody knows what I feel about
   Freddy"   ARGO 134
FROM THE COUNTY LUNATIC ASYLUM. "The people
   say that spiritism is a joke and a swizz"
                                     ARGO 134
THE GALLOPING CAT. "Oh I am a cat that likes
   to"   ARGO 134
GIRLS. "Girls! although I am a woman"
                                     ARGO 134
GOD SPEAKS. "I made man with too many faults.
   Yet I love him"   ARGO 134
THE GRANGE. "Oh there hasn't been much
   change"   ARGO 134
GRAVE BY A HOLM-OAK. "You lie there, Anna"
                                     ARGO 134
LA GRETCHEN DE NOS JOURS. "O Queen of Heav-
   en have pity on me"   ARGO 134
HAROLD'S LEAP. "Harold, are you asleep"
                            ARGO 134, SPOA 67
HER-ZIE. "What's wrong with you-zie"
                                     ARGO 134
HOW SLOWLY TIME LENGTHENS. "How slowly
   time lengthens from a hated event"
                                     ARGO 134
I WAS SO FULL. "I was so full of love and joy"
                                     ARGO 134
I WISH. "Oh I wish that there were some wing,
   some wing"   ARGO 134
INFANT. "It was a cynical babe"   ARGO 134
INFELICE. "Walking swiftly with a dreadful
   duchess"   ARGO 134
MURDER. "Farewell for ever, well for ever fare"
                                     ARGO 134
THE MURDERER. "My true love breathed her lat-
   est breath"   ARGO 134
NOT WAVING BUT DROWNING. "Nobody heard
   him, the dead man"   ARGO 134
OBLIVION. "It was a human face in my oblivion"
                                     ARGO 134
"Oh Christianity, Christianity"   ARGO 92,
                                     ARGO 134
ONE OF MANY. "You are only one of many"
                            ARGO 92, ARGO 134
OUR OFFICE CAT. "Our office cat is a happy cat"
                                     ARGO 134

* Recording not available for analysis

Smith, Stevie (continued)

PAPA LOVE BABY. "My mother was a romantic girl"   ARGO 134
PEARL.   ARGO 134
PROGRESSION. "I fell in love with Major Spruce"   ARGO 134
THE REASON. "My life is vile"   ARGO 134
THE REPENTANCE OF LADY T. "I look in the glass, whose face do I see"   ARGO 92
THE RIVER DEBEN. "All the waters of the river Deben"   ARGO 134
THE RIVER GOD. "I may be smelly and I may be old"   ARGO 134
SCORPION. "This night shall thy soul be required of thee"   ARGO 134
SEA-WIDOW. "How fares it with you, Mrs. Cooper my bride?"   ARGO 134
THE SINGING CAT. "It was a little captive cat"   ARGO 134
THE SONGSTER. "Miss Pauncefort sang at the top of her voice"   ARGO 134
THE STROKE. "I was a beautiful plant"   ARGO 134
SUNT LEONES. "The lions who ate the Christians on the sands of the arena"   ARGO 134
"Tender only to one"   ARGO 134
TENUOUS AND PRECARIOUS. "Tenuous and precarious were my guardians"   ARGO 92
THIS ENGLISHWOMAN. "This Englishwoman is so refined"   ARGO 134
THOUGHTS ABOUT THE PERSON FROM PORLOCK. "Coleridge received the person from Porlock"   ARGO 92, ARGO 134
VALUABLE. "All these illegitimate babies"   ARGO 134
VENUS WHEN YOUNG CHOOSING DEATH. "I stood knee-deep in the sea"   ARGO 134
THE WEDDING PHOTOGRAPH. "Good Bye, Harry, I must"   ARGO 92
WHEN WALKING. "A talented old gentleman painting a hedge"   ARGO 134
YES, I KNOW. "That pale face stretches across the centuries"   ARGO 134

Smith, Sydney Goodsir. 1915. in English.

EXILE. "I saw my luve in black velvet"   ARGO 99
THE GRACE OF GOD AND THE METH-DRINKER. "There ye gang"   ARGO 99
HAMEWITH. "Man at the end"   ARGO 99
LARGO. "Ae boat anerlie nou"   ARGO 99
THE REID REID ROSE. "It is wi luve"   ARGO 99
SIMMER NICHTSANG. "The nicht is far spent"   ARGO 99
THE WINTER O THE HERT. "O, the rain that rains upo the toun"   ARGO 99

Smith, Welton. in English.

Poetry*   PRENT 1

Smith, William Jay. 1918. in English.

AMERICAN PRIMITIVE. "Look at him there in his stovepipe hat"   SPOA 102
THE CLOSING OF THE RODEO. "The lariat snaps"   SPOA 102
CUPIDON. "To love is to give"   SPOA 102
DEAD SNAKE.   FOLKW 25
DEATH OF A JAZZ MUSICIAN. "I dreamed that when I died"   SPOA 102

LIGHT.   FOLKW 25
THE LOVERS. "Above through lunar woods"   SPOA 102
MOLE. "Jiminy Jiminy Jokebox! Wheatcakes! Crumbs!   HARB 6
MORNING AT ARNHEM. "From the cassowary's beak"   SPOA 102
A PAVANE FOR THE NURSERY. "Now touch the air softly"   SPOA 102
THE PEACOCK OF JAVA. "I thought of the mariners"   SPOA 102
PIDGIN PINCH. "Joe, you big shot"   SPOA 102
THE TOASTER. "A silver-scaled dragon with jaws flaming red"   HARB 3
VISION AT TWILIGHT.   FOLKW 25
THE WOOING LADY. "Once upon the earth"   SPOA 102
Poetry*   JNP 54, LIBC 78

Snodgrass, W. DeWitt. 1926. in English.

AFTER EXPERIENCE TAUGHT ME. "After experience taught me that all the ordinary"   SPOA 82
APRIL INVENTORY. "The green catalpa tree has turned"   LIBC 50
"Child of my winter born"   LIBC 54
THE EXAMINATION. "Under the thick beams of that swirly smoking light"   LIBC 1
A FLAT ONE. "Old Fritz, on this rotating bed"   SPOA 104
"Late April and you are three"   LIBC 54
THE LOVERS GO FLY A KITE. "What's up, today, with our lovers"   LIBC 1
LYING AWAKE. "This moth caught in the room tonight"   LIBC 50, SPOA 104
MONET: LES NYMPHÉAS. "The eyelids glowing, some chill"   LIBC 1
THE OPERATION.   LIBC 50
RETURNED TO FRISCO, 1946.   LIBC 50
SEEING YOU HAVE A WOMAN.   LIBC 50
SEPTEMBER IN THE PARK.   LIBC 50
"Sweet Beast, I have gone prowling" LIBC 54
THESE TREES STAND. "These trees stand very tall under the heavens"   LIBC 50
"The vicious winter finally yields" LIBC 54

Snoilsky, Carl. 1841. in Swedish.

GAMMALT PORSLIN. "En kung: Sachsen samlade porslin"   GRAM 3
NOLI ME TANGERE. "Jag torgfor ej mitt hjartas lust och kval"   GRAM 3
TATTERSKAN.   GRAM 2

Snyder, Gary. 1930. in English.

ABOVE PIUTE VALLEY. "We finished clearing the last section of trail"   CENTCA 1, NET 9
AN AUTUMN MORNING IN SHÔKOKUJI. "Last night watching the Pleiades"   NACTE 14
BURNING.   SCHOL 4
A CABIN IN MARIN COUNTY. "Sun breaks over the eucalyptus"   CENTCA 1
HAY FOR THE HORSES. "He had driven"   CENTCA 1, NET 9, SCHOL 4
HOP, SKIP, AND JUMP.   NACTE 14, SCHOL 4
HUNTING.   SCHOL 4
KYOTE: MARCH.   SCHOL 4
THE MARKET. "Heart of the city"   CENTCA 1
                                     NET 9

---

* Recording not available for analysis

MID-AUGUST AT SOURDOUGH MOUNTAIN LOOKOUT. "Down valley a smoke haze"   SCHOL 4

OIL. "Soft rainsqualls on the swells"   NACTE 14

PIUTE CREEK. "One granite ridge"   SCHOL 4

7. IV. 64.   SCHOL 4

THE SPRING. "Beating asphalt into highway potholes"   SCHOL 4

TWELVE HOURS OUT OF NEW YORK AFTER TWENTY-FIVE DAYS AT SEA.   SCHOL 4

THE USES OF LIGHT. "It warms my bones"   EMC 7

VAPOR TRAILS. "Twin streaks twice higher than cumulus"   SCHOL 4

YASE: SEPTEMBER. "Old Mrs. Kawatata"   SCHOL 4

Poetry*   UCAL 4

Sobecks, Elaine. in English.

DOODLE-DEE-DO, FIND ME A FRIEND.   NAITV 6

Sobiloff, Hy. 1912. in English.

AIRSHIP. "I slept in a sleepy field"   SPOA 100

"Am I too old to play with blocks"   GRYPH 3

ANNUAL SEARCH. "The annual search for love began"   GRYPH 3

BLIND BOY IN NASSAU. "He became blind earlier than any of us"   GRYPH 3

BOY CHILD. "A boy child buried the bird"   GRYPH 3

A CHILD AND THE COCONUT HEAD. "There in the sand grew a coconut face"   GRYPH 3

THE CHILD'S SIGHT. "The child's wisdom is in saying"   GRYPH 3

CHRISTMAS POEM. "A child sits near a fireplace"   SPOA 100

DANCE OUTSIDE MY SHOES. "Your love has lived in you long"   GRYPH 3

ELEGY TO MY DEAD COUSIN. "My cousin Sara Preblod and I"   GRYPH 3

EXPLORATION OF A CHILD—HOW IT EXPLORES ITSELF AND WHY. "Is that a fly"   GRYPH 3

THE GANG. "I came to grief and grips with a gang"   GRYPH 3

HANS CHRISTIAN ANDERSEN IN CENTRAL PARK. "O Statue"   SPOA 100

HORSE LANGUAGE. "The language of those horses"   GRYPH 3

I AM OLDER NOW. "Howard you are twenty-five now and I am fifty"   GRYPH 3

A JAMAICAN CHILD. "It has been so long"   GRYPH 3

JUMP ROPE. "I look too often at my feet when I jump rope"   GRYPH 3

THE KITE THE CHILD AND THE SHOE. "Speak to me child as you fly your kite in your child-filled shoes"   GRYPH 3

MY MOTHER'S TABLE. "My mother's table"   SPOA 100

MY UNCLE'S DERBY. "I almost lost my favorite uncle"   GRYPH 3

THE PIMPLY WOLF. "The pimply wolf who is shorter than I"   GRYPH 3

PITTSBURGH. "Near the roadbrim"   SPOA 100

ROVER. "Speak to me child as I speak to myself"   GRYPH 3

THE SCARECROW. "In some things I am a child's size"   GRYPH 3

THE SCHOOLMASTER. "This was the first time"   SPOA 100

SCIENCE OBESE. "Logic is peculiar feel"   GRYPH 3

SHORT HATE. "They hated me because I was short"   GRYPH 3

SOUL'S RHYME. "Plunder throws angels into serfdom"   GRYPH 3

SPEAK TO ME CHILD AS I SPEAK TO MYSELF. "Speak to me child speak to me"   GRYPH 3

STAFFORD IS NOW FIVE YEARS OLD. "I wondered as a dream will what Stafford could see"   GRYPH 3

THEY BOTH LOVE ME. "My mother baked the bread"   GRYPH 3

A TONGUE'S TICKLE. "A tongue's tickle is tickling inside me"   GRYPH 3

THE TWO-DOLLAR BILL. "I was six when my mother first trusted me with a two-dollar bill"   GRYPH 3

WEATHER WISDOM. "There is wisdom in this weather"   GRYPH 3

"Who will I be like"   GRYPH 3

"Your beauty is more than beauty now"   GRYPH 3

Södergran, E. in Swedish.

LANDET SOM ICKE AR.   GRAM 1

Solomon, Marvin. in English.

SONNET FOR JOHN-JOHN. "My father died in nineteen thirty-four"   FOLKW 21

Somerville, Dora. in English.

MAUI'S FAREWELL.   KIWI 3

Sondé, Susan. in English.

FROM THE FIFTIES. "Child, even the buds"   WATSHD 5

POEM & INVOCATION. "On behalf of poets everywhere"   WATSHD 5

SINCERELY YOURS. "Dear Friend, how can you"   WATSHD 5

Sorley, Charles Hamilton. in English.

SONNET.   ARGO 89

Soupault, Philippe. 1897. in French.

ARTICLES DE SPORT. "Courageux comme un timbre-poste"   ADES 25

BIEN AIMÉE.   ADES 25

LA BOUÉE. "Foutez-moi à la mer"   ADES 25

CHANSONS DU BOUT DU QUAI. "Les filles de Gentilly"   ADES 25, ADES 52

LE CRI ET LES CENDRES. "Les cendres du soleil et les notes d'étoiles"   ADES 25, ADES 52

FLEUVE. "Couloir longitudinal des grands bâtiments souterrains"   ADES 25

HORIZON. "Toute la ville est entrée dans ma chambre"   ADES 25

JE RENTRE. "Mon chapeau se cabosse"   ADES 25

LES MAINS JOINTES. "Dans le ciel fument de grands vaisseaux"   ADES 25, ADES 52

NE RETOURNER PAS LA TÊTE. "Etends les bras"   ADES 25

QUAND ON REGARDE UNE MONTRE. "Je n'ai pas fini d'espérer"   ADES 25

RONDE. "Quel est celui d'entre vous"   ADES 25

ROUTE. "J'aperçus le souvenir de ta voix se percher"   ADES 25, ADES 52

* Recording not available for analysis

Soupault, Philippe (continued)

SWANEE. "Mes mains tremblent comme celles d'un brave garçon d'alcoolique"   FOLKW 13

VOUS QUI DORMEZ. "A l'ouest vous dormez encore"   ADES 25, ADES 52

Souster, Raymond. 1921. in English.

THE AMUSEMENT PARK. "What fascinated in childhood seems trivial"   FOLKW 50

BRIDGE OVER THE DON. "Why does your loneliness surge up"   FOLKW 50

THE CHILD'S UMBRELLA. "What's it like to be homeless"   FOLKW 50

THE CREEPER ALONG THE HOUSE WALL. "Did I think it somehow sucked"   FOLKW 50

DARK ANGEL. "Talk about the grace of your bullfighters"   FOLKW 50

DOWNTOWN CORNER NEWS-STAND. "It will need all of death"   FOLKW 50

FLIGHT OF THE ROLLER-COASTER. "Once more round should do it"   FOLKW 50

THE FULL GOSPEL MISSION. "A big old family bible"   FOLKW 50

HAPPY BIRTHDAY. "Thirty-seven today"   FOLKW 50

JOHN STREET. "I can't decide which will outlive each other"   LEARNC 8

THE QUARRY. "The terrified look"   FOLKW 50

THE RAINBOW. "Red blue green of it"   FOLKW 50

REBIRTH. "When your hair turns gray"   FOLKW 50

THE SELLER OF ROSES. "Has a perpetual cold"   FOLKW 50

THE SIX QUART BASKET. "The six quart basket/one side gone"   FOLKW 50

THE SLEEPER. "Yes, she's quiet now"   FOLKW 50

THE SWING. "If you swing hard enough"   FOLKW 50

THE TOP HAT. "Whether it's just a gag or the old geezer's"   FOLKW 50

THE URGE. "Spring drives them eagerly out into the street"   FOLKW 50

THE WRECKERS. "Five men pushing over part of a wall"   LEARNC 8

WRECKING BALL. "The wrecking-ball"   LEARNC 8

Southey, Robert. 1774. in English.

THE BATTLE OF BLENHEIM. "It was a summer evening"   EAV 7, RCA 9

INCHCAPE ROCK. "No stir in the air, no stir in the sea"   EAV 8, PROTHM 11, SINGER 1

Southwell, Robert. 1561. in English.

THE BURNING BABE. "As I in hoary winter's night"   PROTHM 8, ARGO 126

Soynar, Dulce Maria. in Spanish.
Poetry*   SMC 16

Spacks, Barry. 1931. in English.

BY THIS TO REMEMBER. "By this to remember, this spring again"   FOLKW 21

Spatling, Neil. in English.
Poetry*   PROTHM 6

Spee von Langenfeld, Friedrich. 1591. in German.

TRAUR-GESANG VON DER NOT CHRISTI AM ÖLBERG IN DEM GARTEN. "Bei stiller Nacht zur ersten Wacht"   CHRIST 18

Spellman, A. B. 1935. in English.
TOMORROW THE HEROES.   CAED 155

Spencer, Theodore. 1902. in English.

AFTERWARDS.   HARVOC 9

A CIRCLE.   HARVOC 9

THE CIRCUS.   HARVOC 9

THE DAY.   LIBC 11, LIBC 35

ENLISTMENT. "We cannot know our world"   SPOA 97

ESCAPIST'S SONG. "The first woman I loved"   SPOA 97

THE INFLATABLE GLOBE. "When the allegorical man came calling"   LIBC 11, LIBC 35, LIBC 38, SPOA 97

A KIND OF PROGRESSION.   HARVOC 9

LESSON IN NATURAL HISTORY. "The ripples spread through"   SPOA 97

A NARRATIVE.   LIBC 11, LIBC 35

OLD MAN'S SONG.   HARVOC 9

THE PHOENIX.   LIBC 11, LIBC 35

POLITICAL SONG.   HARVOC 9

A RELIGIOUS QUESTION.   HARVOC 9

THEME SONG. "The cup whose shape is sound"   SPOA 97

TRUTH.   HARVOC 9

VERSIONS OF THE SAME THING.   HARVOC 9

THE WIDOW.   HARVOC 9

Poetry*   LIST 14

Spender, Stephen. 1909. in English.

BAGATELLE. "You lay so quiet at your end of the room"   APPL 3

BEETHOVEN'S DEATH MASK. "I imagine him still with heavy brow"   ARGO 79, CAED 55

THE DOUBLE SHAME. "You must live through the time when everything hurts"   CAED 55, SPOA 70

DYLAN THOMAS, NOVEMBER 1953. "In November of Catherine wheels and rockets"   CAED 55

EARTH-TREADING STARS THAT MAKE DARK HEAVEN LIGHT. "How can they call this dark when stars"   ARGO 97, JNP 55, SPOA 70

ELEGY FOR MARGARET, exc.   ARGO 79

———. I. "Darling of our hearts, drowning"   CAED 55

———. IV. "Already you are beginning to become"   CAED 55

———. VI. "Dearest and nearest brother"   CAED 55

AN ELEMENTARY SCHOOL CLASS ROOM IN A SLUM. "Far far from gusty waves these childrens' faces"   ARGO 79, LIBC 19, LIBC 62, SPOA 70

THE EXPRESS. "After the first powerful, plain manifest"   APPL 3, ARGO 79, CAED 55, HOUGHT 4, SPOA 70

FOUR SHORT POEMS ABOUT CHILDREN.   ARGO 79

THE GENEROUS DAYS. "His are the generous days"   JNP 55

THE HAWK.   ARGO 79

"He will watch the hawk with an indifferent eye"   CAED 55

---

* Recording not available for analysis

HÖLDERLIN'S OLD AGE. "When I was young I woke gladly in the morning"   CAED 55

"An 'I' can never be a great man" ARGO 79, CAED 55, LIBC 19, LIBC 62

ICE. "She came in from the snowing air"   CAED 55

IF IT WERE NOT. "If it were not for that lean executioner"   APPL 3, JNP 55, SPOA 70

IN ATTICA. "Again, again, I see this form repeated"   FOLKW 65, JUP 1, SPOA 70

JUDAS ISCARIOT. "The eyes of twenty centuries"   PROTHM 7

THE LANDSCAPE NEAR AN AERODROME. "More beautiful and soft than any moth"   ARGO 79, LIBC 19, LIBC 62, SPOA 70

MEMENTO. "Remember the blackness of that flesh"   CAED 55

"My parents kept me from children who were rough"   ARGO 79, CAED 55, CAED 111

NOCTURNE. "Their six-weeks-old daughter lies"   SPOA 70

NOT PALACES. "Not palaces, an era's crown"   SPOA 70

"Not to you I sighed, no not a word"   ARGO 79

ONE MORE NEW BOTCHED BEGINNING. "Their voices heard, I stumble suddenly"   JNP 55, SPOA 70

THE PRISONERS. "Far far the least of all, in want"   ARGO 79, SPOA 70

PRONOUNS OF THIS TIME, exc. "In the middle of a war"   JNP 55

THE PYLONS. "The secret of these hills was stone, and cottages"   LIBC 19, LIBC 62

THE ROOM ABOVE THE SQUARE. "The light in the window seemed perpetual"   CAED 55

SEASCAPE. "There are some days the happy ocean lies"   ARGO 97, CAED 55, CAED 183

SONG.   ARGO 79

SONG. "Stranger, you who hide my love"   CAED 55, SPOA 70

SOUVENIR DE LONDRES. "My parents quarrel in the neighbour room"   SPOA 70

"A stopwatch and an ordnance map"   CAED 55, LIBC 19, LIBC 62, SPOA 70

SUBJECT, OBJECT, SENTENCE. "A subject thought: because he had a verb."   JNP 55, SPOA 70

THOUGHTS DURING AN AIR RAID. "Of course, the entire effort is to put oneself"   CAED 55, SPOA 70

TO MY DAUGHTER. "Bright clasp of her whole hand around my finger"   APPL 3, ARGO 97, CAED 55, SPOA 70

THE TRULY GREAT. "I think continually of those who were truly great"   APPL 3, ARGO 79, CAED 183, LIBC 19, LIBC 38, LIBC 62

TWO ARMIES. "Deep in the winter plain two armies"   CAED 55

ULTIMA RATIO REGUM. "The guns spell money's ultimate reason"   FOLKW 65, JUP 1, LIBC 38, SPOA 70

THE WAR GOD. "Why cannot the one good"   ARGO 119, SPOA 70

"What I expected was/ Thunder" ARGO 79, CAED 55

"Who live under the shadow of war"   ARGO 79, CAED 55

WORD. "The word bites like a fish"   APPL 3, ARGO 79, CAED 55

Poetry*   JNP 6, LIST 14, PRENT 3, NET 3

Spenser, Edmund. 1552. in English.

AMORETTI. 30. "My love is like to ice, and I to fire"   IMP 1, LIST 1

_____. 37. "What guile is this, that those her golden tresses"   IMP 1

_____. 54. "Of this world's theatre in which we stay"   ARGO 33

_____. 55. "So oft as I her beauty do behold"   LIST 1

_____. 63. "After long storms and tempests' sad assay"   SPOA 83

_____. 67. "Like as a huntsman after weary chase"   EAV 11, IMP 1, LIST 1

_____. 68. "Most glorious lord of life, that on this day"   SPOA 83

_____. 70. "Fresh spring, the herald of loves mighty king"   CAED 20

_____. 75. "One day I wrote her name upon the strand"   POLYGL 2, SPOA 12, SPOA 83

DIDO MY DEAR, ALAS, IS DEAD. "Up then, Melpomene, thou mournfulst Muse of mine"   COLUMB 10

EPITHALAMION. "Ye learned sisters, which have oftentimes"   ARGO 32, CAED 74, EAV 11

THE FAERIE QUEENE. BOOK 1, exc. "A gentle knight was pricking on the plaine"   ARGO 33

_____. "He there does now enjoy eternal rest"   BRITAM 2

_____. BOOK 2, exc. "And is there care in heaven? and is there love"   ARGO 33

_____. "Eftsoones they heard a most melodious sound"   ARGO 33, LONGM 1

_____. BOOK 3, exc. "O hatefull hellish snake! what furie furst"   CAED 74

_____. "Tho, when as chearelesse night ycovered had"   CAED 74

_____. BOOK 4, exc. "Into the inmost Temple thus I came"   ARGO 33

_____. BOOK 6, exc. "But Meliboee (so hight that good old man)"   ARGO 33

_____. "The waies, through which my weary steps I guyde"   ARGO 33

_____. BOOK 7, exc. "Ah! whither doost thou now, thou greater Muse"   ARGO 33

_____. "And after these, there came the day"   LONGM 1

_____. "What man that sees the ever-whirling wheele"   ARGO 33

_____. "When I bethinke me on that speech whyleare"   ARGO 33

AN HYMNE IN HONOUR OF BEAUTIE, exc. "Ah whither, Love, wilt thou now carrie mee?"   ARGO 32

PROTHALAMIUM. "Calm was the day, and through the trembling air"   IMP 1, SPOA 50

Speyer, Leonora. in English.

MEASURE ME SKY.   CAED 110

Spicer, Jack. 1925. in English.

THE DANCING APE.   EVERG 1

PSYCHOANALYSIS: AN ELEGY.   EVERG 1

* Recording not available for analysis

Spicer, Jack (continued)

THE SONG OF THE BIRD IN THE LOINS. EVERG 1

Spivack, Kathleen. 1938. in English.
Poetry*   WATSHD 51

Sponde, Jean de. 1557. in French.
CHANSON.   CAED 204
SONNET.   PERIOD

Stadler, Ernst. 1883. in German.
Poetry*   CHRIST 6

Stafford, William E. in English.
AT A TENTH GRADE PARTY. "The only relics left are those long"   SCHOL 2
BROTHER. "It's cold where Bob is"   SCHOL 2
THE FARM ON THE GREAT PLAINS. "A telephone line goes cold"   SCHOL 2
FIFTEEN. "South of the bridge on Seventeenth"   SCHOL 2
HOLDING THE SKY. "We saw a town by the track in Colorado"   SCHOL 2
HOMECOMING. "Under my hat I custom you intricate, Ella"   SCHOL 2
IN THE MUSEUM.   NACTE 14
MONUMENTS FOR A FRIENDLY GIRL.   SCHOL 2
THE MUSEUM AT TILLAMOOK. "Still faces on the wall: that look"   SCHOL 2
PASSING REMARK. "In scenery I like flat country"   SCHOL 2
SOME SHADOWS. "You would not want too reserved a speaker"   SCHOL 2
THE STAR IN THE HILLS. "A star hit in the hills behind our house"   NACTE 14, SCHOL 2
THAT WEATHER. "Our boy was a child when the good"   SCHOL 2
THINGS WE DID THAT MEANT SOMETHING.   NACTE 14
TRAVELING THROUGH THE DARK. "Traveling through the dark I found a deer"   SCHOL 2
WATCHING THE JET PLANES DIVE.   SCHOL 8
WITH ONE LAUNCHED LOOK. "The cheetah levels at one far deer"   SCHOL 2

Stagnelius, Erik Johan. 1793. in Swedish.
AMANDA. "I blomman, i solen"   GRAM 3
ENDYMION. "Skön, med lågande hy och slutna ögon"   GRAM 3
NÄCKEN. "Kvällens gullmoln fåstet kransa"   GRAM 3

Stallworthy, Jon. 1935. in English.
A LETTER FROM BERLIN. "My dear, today a letter from Berlin"   ARGO 98

Stampa, Gaspara. 1523. in Italian.
Poetry*   CETRA 23

Stanley, Thomas. 1625. in English.
LA BELLE CONFIDENTE. "You earthly souls that court a wanton flame"   ARGO 37
EXPECTATION. "Chide, chide no more away"   ARGO 37
THE REPULSE. "Not that by this disdain"   ARGO 37

Starbuck, George. 1931. in English.
AB OVO. "Beak gumming my entrails"   CARIL 4
AMONG THOSE KNOWN TO HAVE BEEN SUSPECTED IN THIS CONNECTION. "They hold a committee today"   CARIL 4

AUTUMN PROGRESS REPORT. "Becalmed in old Back Bay's dead water"   CARIL 4
BONE THOUGHTS ON A DRY DAY. "Walking to the museum over the outer drive"   CARIL 4
CAPE COD AUTUMN. "Deep as Manhattan's earth the billion-dollar"   CARIL 4
COMMUNICATION TO THE CITY FATHERS OF BOSTON. "Dear Sirs: is it not time we formed a Boston"   CARIL 4
DIABOLIST. "Through water his own waterfall"   CARIL 4
ELEGY. "O lovers cold on mountain drives"   CARIL 4
FABLE FOR FLIPPED LID. "There was a rat who, whatever he did"   CARIL 4
IF SATURDAY. "Four easy hours from San Francisco, yes"   CARIL 4
NEW STRAIN. "You should see these musical mice"   CARIL 4
NEW YEAR: VIEW WEST OVER SORROW.   CARIL 4
ON FIRST LOOKING ON BLODGETT'S KEAT'S CHAPMAN'S HOMER. "Mellifluous as bees, these brittle men"   CARIL 4
OUTBREAK OF SPRING. "Stirring porchpots up with green-fingered witchcraft"   CARIL 4
POEMS FROM A FIRST YEAR IN BOSTON. "Boston, Lord God, the ocean never to windward"   CARIL 4
A TAPESTRY FOR BAYEUX. "Over the seaworthy cavalry arches"   CARIL 4
TECHNOLOGIES. "On Commonwealth, on Marlborough"   CARIL 4
THREE DREAMS ON A WARM SABBATH. "The heavy sabbath breasted Persian rugs"   CARIL 4
TO HIS CHI MISTRESS. "It's spring. The city, wrapped"   CARIL 4
WAR STORY. "The 4th of July he stormed a nest"   CARIL 4
WORSHIP. "Lofting fungoes at the rose"   CARIL 4
Poetry*   APPL 9, WATSHD 52

Statius, Publius Papinius. 45 A.D. in Latin.
Poetry*   CETRA 18

Stefanile, Felix. 1920. in English.
THE AFTERNOON AS AN ARIA. "The afternoon was an aria from Verdi"   FOLKW 25
A LATE ELEGY FOR A BASEBALL PLAYER. "He was all back"   FOLKW 25

Steffens, Lincoln. 1866. in English.
A MISERABLE MERRY CHRISTMAS.   HARC 1

Stein, Charles. in English.
EASTER.   WATSHD 13

Stein, Gertrude. 1874. in English.
"I like what I like when I do not worry"   CAED 112
IF I TOLD HIM: A COMPLETED PORTRAIT OF PICASSO. "If I told him would he like it"   CAED 39, CAED 183
MATISSE. "One was quite certain"   SPOA 90
A PORTRAIT OF CHRISTIAN BERARD, A PAINTER. "Eating is her subject"   SPOA 90
A PORTRAIT OF T. S. ELIOT. "On the 15th of November"   SPOA 90
SACRED EMILY, exc. "Compose compose beds"   UARIZ 1
SHE BOWED TO HER BROTHER. "The story of how she bowed"   SPOA 90

* Recording not available for analysis

A VALENTINE TO SHERWOOD ANDERSON. "I knew too that through them I knew" CAED 39

Stephany (Stephany Jean Dawson Fuller). 1947. in English.

APRIL.	BROADV 8
AT SOME POINT PAST ECSTASY.	BROADV 8
BECAUSE I HAVE WANDERED LONG.	BROADV 8
THE BIRDS ARE NO MORE.	BROADV 8
CLAD IN GARMENTS NOW.	BROADV 8
DESCRIBE NICELY THE.	BROADV 8
DISSATISFACTION STRETCHES INTO PAIN.	
	BROADV 8
DRAGGING BEHIND ME.	BROADV 8
ESTRANGED FROM DYING LEAVES.	BROADV 8
GROWN TO YOU AT LAST.	BROADV 8
HOW FIRM AND SWIFT.	BROADV 8
I HAVE SPENT MY LIFE.	BROADV 8
IN THE SILENCE.	BROADV 8
IN VAST COMPLEXITY THE ORDER LIES.	
	BROADV 8
IT IS AGAIN.	BROADV 8
IT IS THE SAFETY.	BROADV 8
KNEELING TO THE.	BROADV 8
LET APRIL COME.	BROADV 8
LET FALL THE GLOWING VEILS.	BROADV 8
LET ME BE HELD WHEN THE LONGING COMES.	
	BROADV 8
MOVING DEEP, exc.	BROADV
MY LOVE WHEN THIS IS PAST.	BROADV 8
MY SEASONS ARE THE LEAVES.	BROADV 8
REALITY SHIFTED.	BROADV 8
THAT I AM YOURS.	BROADV 8
THAT WE HEAD TOWARDS.	BROADV 8
THIS IS BEGINNING.	BROADV 8
WHAT IS KNOWN.	BROADV 8
WHAT MARKED THE RIVER'S FLOW.	BROADV 8
WHO COLLECTS THE PAIN.	BROADV 8
WHO IS NOT A STRANGER STILL.	BROADV 8
YOU ARE INSTANTLY ENFOLDED.	BROADV 8

Stephens, James. 1882. in English.

CADENCE. "See the lightning leaping in the sky" SPOA 17

THE CANAL BANK. "I know a girl, and the girl knows me" SPOA 17

THE CENTAURS. CAED 111

CHECK. "The night was creeping on the ground" CAED 110, CAED 164, HARB 4

THE COOLIN. "Come with me, under my coat" SPOA 6, SPOA 17

THE DAISIES. "In the scented bud of the morning" SPOA 17

DANNY MURPHY. "He was as old as old can be" SPOA 17

EILEEN, DIARMUID AND TEIG. "Be kind unto these three, Oh King" SPOA 17

THE FIFTEEN ACRES. BRITAM 1, FOLKW 67

GEOFFREY KEATING. "Oh, woman, full of wiliness" SPOA 17

A GLASS OF BEER. "The lanky hank of a she in the inn over there" ARGO 139, CAED 86, SPOA 6, SPOA 7, SPOA 17

THE GOAT PATHS. "The crooked paths go every way" HARC 3, SINGER 1, SPOA 6, SPOA 17

GREEN WEEDS. "To be not jealous, give not love" SPOA 17

"I without bite or sup" SPOA 17

IN THE ORCHARD. "There was a giant by the orchard wall" CAED 111

IN THE POPPY FIELD. "Mad Patsy said, he said to me" SPOA 17

LESBIA. "Sweet and delicate and rare" SPOA 17

LITTLE THINGS. "Little things that run" CAED 112, SPOA 17

THE MAIN-DEEP. "The long rolling steady pouring" SPOA 17

THE MARKET. "A man came to me at the fair" SPOA 17

MARY HYNES. "She is the sky of the sun" SPOA 17

"The mountains stand" SPOA 17

NANCY WALSH. "It is not on her gown she fears to tread" SPOA 17

OULD SNARLY-GOB. "There was a little fire in the grate" SPOA 17

THE PIT OF BLISS. "When I was young I dared to sing" SPOA 17

THE RIVALS. "I heard a bird at dawn" CAED 164

THE SHELL. "And then I pressed the shell close to my ear" HOUGHT 4, SPOA 17

THE SNARE. "I hear a sudden cry of pain" CAED 110, HARB 3, SPOA 17

TO THE QUEEN OF THE BEES. "Bee, tell me, whence do you come" SPOA 17

THE WHITE WINDOW. "The moon comes every night to peep" HARB 1

WHY CROOKED THOMAS CAM WAS GRUMPY. "If I were rich, what would I do?" SPOA 17

Stern, Sholom. in Yiddish.

ALEPH BEIZ. "Fa brent der shule oif es is shoyne kinde" FOLKW 90

Sterns, Monroe. in English.

KNITTING. CREAT 1

Stevens, Wallace. 1879. in English.

THE AURORAS OF AUTUMN. HARPV 3

BANTAMS IN PINE-WOODS. "Chieftain Iffucan of Azcan" SPOA 91

CREDENCES OF SUMMER. "Now is midsummer come" CAED 45

DOMINATION OF BLACK. "At night, by the fire" ARGO 12

FABLIAU OF FLORIDA. "Barque of phosphor" SPOA 91

FINAL SOLILOQUI OF THE INTERIOR PARAMOUR. "Light the first light of evening, as in a room" CAED 45

THE IDEA OF ORDER AT KEY WEST. "She sang beyond the genius of the sea" CAED 45, CAED 183

IMAGO. "Who can pick up the weight of Britain" SPOA 91

IN THE ELEMENT OF ANTAGONISMS. "If it is a world without a genius" CAED 45

INDIAN RIVER. "The trade-wind jingles the rings in the nets" SPOA 91

INFANTA MARINA. "Her terrace was the sand" SPOA 91

LARGE RED MAN READING. "There were ghosts that returned to earth to hear his phrases" CAED 45

---

* Recording not available for analysis

Stevens, Wallace (continued)

LESS AND LESS HUMAN, O SAVAGE SPIRIT. "If there must be a god in the house, must be" SPOA 91

LOOKING ACROSS THE FIELDS AND WATCHING THE BIRDS FLY. "Among the more irritating minor ideas" CAED 45

THE MAN WITH THE BLUE GUITAR. "The man bent over his guitar" UARIZ 1

MOUNTAINS COVERED WITH CATS. "The sea is full of fishes in shoals" LIBC 36

NOMAD EXQUISITE. "As the immense dew of Florida" SPOA 91

NOT IDEAS ABOUT THE THING BUT THE THING ITSELF. HARPV 3

THE NOVEL. "The crows are flying above the foyer of summer" SPOA 91

PETER QUINCE AT THE CLAVIER. "Just as my fingers on these keys" RCA 10

THE PLAIN SENSE OF THINGS. "After the leaves have fallen, we return" ARGO 12

PLOUGHING ON SUNDAY. "The white cock's tail" ARGO 139

THE POEM THAT TOOK THE PLACE OF A MOUNTAIN. "There it was, word for word" CAED 45

PROLOGUES TO WHAT IS POSSIBLE. II. "The metaphor stirred his fear" CAED 45

PUELLA PARVULA. "Every thread of summer is at last unwoven" CAED 45

THE SNOW MAN. "One must have a mind of winter" ARGO 12

SO-AND-SO RECLINING ON HER COUCH. "On her side, reclining on her elbow" LIBC 36

THIS SOLITUDE OF CATARACTS. "He never felt twice the same about the flecked river" CAED 45

TO AN OLD PHILOSOPHER IN ROME. "On the threshold of heaven, the figures in the street" CAED 45

TO THE ONE OF FICTIVE MUSIC. HARPV 3

TWO ILLUSTRATIONS THAT THE WORLD IS WHAT YOU MAKE IT. I. THE CONSTANT DISQUISITION OF THE WIND. "The sky seemed so small that winter day" CAED 45

_____. II. THE WORLD IS LARGER IN SUMMER. "He left half a shoulder and half a head" CAED 45

VACANCY IN THE PARK. "March . . . Someone has walked across the snow" CAED 45

THE VIRGIN CARRYING A LANTERN. "There are no bears among the roses" ARGO 12
Poetry* LIST 13, PRENT 3

Stevens, Wendy. in English.

THE HYMNS MY MOTHER SANG. "Hymns to the tune" WATSHD 8

THIS SONG IS TO YOUR DEATH. "You know I must admit" WATSHD 8

Stevenson, Robert Louis. 1850. in English.

AT THE SEASIDE. "When I was down beside the sea" AUDIBT 1, CREAT 1, SPOA 112

AUNTIE'S SKIRTS. "Whenever Auntie moves around" AUDIBT 1

AUTUMN FIRES. "In the other gardens" AUDIBT 1, CAED 49

BED IN SUMMER. "In winter I get up at night" AUDIBT 1, CMS 3, SPOA 112

BLOCK CITY. "What are you able to build with your blocks?" AUDIBT 1, CAED 49, CMS 3

THE CELESTIAL SURGEON. "If I have faltered more or less" ARGO 70A, AUDIA 1, LIST 3

THE COW. "The friendly cow all red and white" AUDIBT 1, HARB 5

THE DUMB SOLDIER. "When the grass was closely mown" AUDIBT 1, CAED 49

ESCAPE AT BEDTIME. "The lights from the parlour and kitchen shone out" AUDIBT 1, CAED 49

FAIRY BREAD. "Come up here, O dusty feet" AUDIBT 1, CAED 49

FAREWELL TO THE FARM. "The coach is at the door at last" AUDIBT 1, CAED 49

THE FLOWERS. "All the names I know from nurse" AUDIBT 1, CAED 49

FOREIGN CHILDREN. "Little Indian, Sioux or Crow" AUDIBT 1, CAED 49

FOREIGN LANDS. "Up into the cherry tree who should climb but little me" AUDIBT 1, LEARNS 2

FROM A RAILWAY CARRIAGE. "Faster than fairies, faster than witches" AUDIBT 1, CAED 49

THE GARDENER. "The gardener does not love to talk" AUDIBT 1

GOOD AND BAD CHILDREN. "Children you are very little and your bones are very brittle" AUDIBT 1, RCA 8

A GOOD BOY. "I woke before the morning" AUDIBT 1

A GOOD PLAY. "We built a ship upon the stairs" AUDIBT 1, CAED 49

HAPPY THOUGHT. "The world is so full of a number of things" AUDIBT 1, CAED 49, RCA 8

THE HAYLOFT. "Through all the pleasant meadow-side" AUDIBT 1

HISTORICAL ASSOCIATIONS. "Dear Uncle Jim, this garden ground" CAED 49

THE HOUSE BEAUTIFUL. "A naked house, a naked moor" ARGO 70A

THE LAMPLIGHTER. "My tea is nearly ready and the sun has left the sky" AUDIBT 1

THE LAND OF COUNTERPANE. "When I was sick and lay abed" AUDIBT 1, CAED 49, LEARNS 2, RCA 8, SPOA 112

THE LAND OF NOD. "From breakfast on through all the day" AUDIBT 1, CAED 49, SPOA 112

THE LAND OF STORY-BOOKS. "At evening when the lamp is lit" AUDIBT 1

THE LITTLE LAND. "When at home alone I sit" AUDIBT 1, CAED 49, SPOA 112

LOOKING FORWARD. "When I am grown to man's estate" AUDIBT 1, CAED 49

LOOKING-GLASS RIVER. "Smooth it slides upon its travel" CAED 49

MARCHING SONG. "Bring the comb and play upon it" AUDIBT 1, CAED 49

THE MOON. "The moon has a face like the clock in the hall" AUDIBT 1, CAED 49

MY BED IS A BOAT. "My bed is like a little boat" AUDIBT 1, CAED 49

* Recording not available for analysis

MY KINGDOM. "Down by a shining water well"
        AUDIBT 1, CAED 49
MY SHADOW. "I have a little shadow that goes in
    and out with me"   AUDIBT 1, CAED 49,
        CMS 2, LEARNS 1, RCA 8
MY SHIP AND I. "O it's I that am the captain of a
    tidy little ship"   AUDIBT 1, SPOA 112
MY TREASURES. "These nuts, that I keep in the
    back of the nest"   AUDIBT 1
NEST EGGS. "Birds all the sunny day"
        AUDIBT 1, CAED 49
NIGHT AND DAY. "When the golden day is done"
        CAED 49
NORTHWEST PASSAGE. "When the bright lamp is
    carried in"   CAED 49
ON HIS PITIABLE TRANSFORMATION. "I who was
    young so long"   ARGO 70A
PICTURE BOOKS IN WINTER. "Summer fading,
    winter comes"   AUDIBT 1
PIRATE STORY. "Three of us afloat in the mead-
    ow by the swing"   AUDIBT 1
RAIN. "The rain is raining all around"
    AUDIBT 1, CAED 49, HARB 1, SPOA 112
REQUIEM. "Under the wide and starry sky"
    ARGO 70A, AUDIA 1, CAED 201, LIST 3,
        LIVLAN 1
SINGING. "Of speckled eggs the birdie sings"
        AUDIBT 1
SUMMER SUN. "Great is the sun, and wide he
    goes"   AUDIBT 1, CAED 49
THE SUN'S TRAVELS. "The sun is not a-bed when
    I"   AUDIBT 1
THE SWING. "How do you like to go up in a
    swing"   AUDIBT 1, CAED 49, CREAT 1
SYSTEM. "Every night my prayers I say"
        AUDIBT 1
A THOUGHT. "It is very nice to think"
        AUDIBT 1, CAED 49, SPOA 112
TIME TO RISE. "A birdie with a yellow bill"
        AUDIBT 1, CREAT 1
TO ANY READER. "As from the house your
    mother sees"   AUDIBT 1, CAED 49
TO MINNIE. "The red room with the giant bed"
        CAED 49
TO MY NAME-CHILD. "Some day soon this rhym-
    ing volume, if you learn with proper speed"
        CAED 49
TRAVEL. "I should like to rise and go"
        AUDIBT 1
THE UNSEEN PLAYMATE. "When children are
    playing alone on the green"   AUDIBT 1,
        CAED 49, SPOA 112
THE VAGABOND. "Give to me the life I love"
        CAED 201
WHERE GO THE BOATS. "Dark brown is the river,
    golden is the sand" AUDIBT 1, LEARNS 2,
        SPOA 112
WHOLE DUTY OF CHILDREN. "A child should al-
    ways say what's true"   AUDIBT 1,
        CAED 49, RCA 8
THE WIND. "I saw you toss the kites on high"
    AUDIBT 1, CAED 49, CMS 3, HARB 4,
        LEARNS 1
WINDY NIGHTS. "Whenever the moon and stars
    are set"   AUDIBT 1, CAED 49
YOUNG NIGHT-THOUGHT. "All night long and
    every night"   AUDIBT 1, CAED 49

Poetry*   BANKST 1, LIST 11, LONDON 2,
        SPOA 2, SPOA 112, STERL 2
Stirling, Earl of (William Alexander). 1567. in
    English.
"Let others of the world's decaying tell"
        ARGO 32
Stolberg, Friedrich Leopold von. 1750. in Ger-
    man.
AN DEN ABENDSTERN. "Ehmals winktest du mir,
    Führer des schweigenden"   CHRIST 22
DEUTSCHLANDS BERUF.   CHRIST 30
DER MOND. "Der Mond, der uns so freundlich
    scheint"   DEUTGR 13
Stone, Ronald. in English.
LADY DAY SPRING-TONED.   BROADR 2
Stone, Ruth. 1915. in English.
IN AN IRIDESCENT TIME. "My mother, when
    young, scrubbed laundry in a tub"
        SPOA 101
IN THE MADNESS OF AGE. "She, in the drapery of
    shadows"   SPOA 101
LOVE'S RELATIVE. "The couple who remain in
    bed"   SPOA 101
THE MAGNET. "I loved my lord, my black haired
    lord"   SPOA 101
VERNAL EQUINOX. "Daughters in the wind bois-
    terous roughing"   SPOA 101
Stoneham, Gillian. in English.
MOTHER AND CHILD.   PROTHM 7
Storm, Theodor. 1817. in German.
ABSEITS. "Es ist so still: die Heide liegt"
        ATHENA 14
APRIL. "Das ist die Drossel die da schlägt"
        ATHENA 14
ELIZABETH. "Meine Mutter hat's gewollt"
        ATHENA 14
HERBST.   ATHENA 14
IM VOLKSTON.   ATHENA 14
KOMM, LASS UNS SPIELEN. "Wie bald des Som-
    mers holdes Fest verging!"   ATHENA 14
MEERESSTRAND. "Ans Haff nun fliegt die Möve"
        ATHENA 14
DIE NACHTIGALL. "Das macht, es hat die Nach-
    tigall"   ATHENA 14
"Schliesse mir die Augen beide"
        ATHENA 14
DIE STADT. "Am grauen Strand, am grauen
    Meer"   ATHENA 14, SPOA 5
VERIRRT. "Ein Vöglein singt so süsse"
        ATHENA 14
WEIHNACHTSLIED. "Vom Himmel in die tiefsten
    Klüfte"   ATHENA 14

DIE ZEIT IST HIN. "Die Zeit ist hin; du löst dich
    unbewusst"   ATHENA 14
Poetry*   CHRIST 4
Storni, Alfonsina. 1892. in Spanish.
CAPRICHO. "Escrútame los ojos"   SMC 7
LA CAPRICIA PERDIDA. "Se me vá de los dedos"
        SMC 7
CARTA LÍRICA A OTRA MUJER. "Vuestro nombre no
    sé"   SMC 7
DOLOR. "Quisiera esta tarde divina de octubre"
        FOLKW 79
ENCUENTRO. "Lo encontré en una esquina"
        SMC 7

* Recording not available for analysis

Storni, Alfonsina (continued)

FIERO AMOR. "Oh, fiero amor, llegaste como la
  mariposa"   AGUIL 9
HOMBRE PEQUEÑITO. "Hombre pequeñito, hom-
  bre pequeñito"   FOLKW 80, SMC 7
EL LLAMADO. "Es noche, tal silencio"
                                    FIDIAS 2
RUEDA. "La casta y honda amiga me dice sus
  razones"   SMC 7
SILENCIO. "Un día estaré muerta, blanca como
  la nieve"   AGUIL 8
TU ME QUIERES BLANCA. "Tu me quieres alba, me
  quieres de espuma"   SMC 7
TU Y YO. "Mi casa está llena de mirtos"
                                    FIDIAS 2
VIAJE FINIDO. "Qué hacen tus ojos largos"
                                      SMC 7

Strand, Mark. 1934. in English.
KEEPING THINGS WHOLE. "In a field"
                                    SPOA 107
THE LAST BUS—RIO DE JANEIRO. "It is dark"
                                    SPOA 107
THE MARRIAGE. "The wind comes from opposite
  poles"   SPOA 107
MY LIFE. "The huge doll of my body"
                                    SPOA 107
THE TUNNEL. "A man has been standing"
                                    SPOA 107

Strode, William. ca. 1600. in English.
ON WESTWALL DOWNES. "When Westwall
  Downes I gan to tread"   CAED 38

Stryk, Lucien. 1924. in English.
AWAKENING. "Shoichi brushed the black"
                                   FOLKW 111
BURNING ONESELF TO DEATH. "That was the best
  moment of the monk's life"   FOLKW 111
CAMEL. "The camel's humps"   FOLKW 111
THE DUCKPOND. "Crocus, daffodil"
                                   FOLKW 111
FISH. "I hold a newspaper, reading"
                                   FOLKW 111
FLIGHT OF THE SPARROW. "Sparrow dives from
  roof to ground"   FOLKW 111
SHELL. "Nothing, nothing at all is born"
                                   FOLKW 111
TIME. "Time like a lake breeze" FOLKW 111
WHAT IS MOVING. "When I turned to look back"
                                   FOLKW 111
ZEN: THE ROCKS OF SESSHU. "What do they think
  of"   FOLKW 111

Stuart, Jesse. in English.
Poetry*   CASSC 7

Su Shih. in Chinese.
SUY TIO GOR TAU. "Ming yuet gkay see y'ow"
                                     SCHOL 6

Suckling, Sir John. 1609. in English.
BALLAD ON A WEDDING. "I tell thee, Dick, where
  I have been"   ARGO 88A
THE CONSTANT LOVER. "Out upon it, I have
  loved"   ARGO 37, CAED 186, EAV 6,
        LIST 2, SPOA 84, DECCA 12, LION 2
SONNET. "Oh for some honest lover's ghost"
                                     ARGO 37
SONG. SEND ME BACK MY HEART. "I prithee send
  me back my heart" DECCA 12, THEAL 3
TRUTH IN LOVE. "Of thee kind boy" ARGO 37

"Why so pale and wan, fond lover"
  ARGO 37, CAED 38, DECCA 12, EAV 6,
        RCA 4, SPOA 84, SPOA 90

Sukenick, Lynn. in English.
"As woman says you look young"   UCAL 2
BEATRICE REMEMBERS. "Her ivory fan opening"
                                   WATSHD 11
HIS ANGERS. "When he thought a love"
                                   WATSHD 11
HOUDINI, exc. "Hidden all over the world"
                                     UCAL 2
HOUDINI RESTORES SAMSON'S SIGHT. "Like cures
  like. Homeopathic"   WATSHD 11
HOW IT WENT. "I like the part of you"
                                   WATSHD 11
"I put on my dream suit"   UCAL 2
MEAN ANNUAL RAINFALL. "Inch by inch"
                                     UCAL 2
PARTING AGAIN. "Begin by parting your hair"
                                     UCAL 2
POINT. "One is a point"   UCAL 2
PORTRAITS. "We prepare ourselves for mirrors"
                                     UCAL 2

Sully-Prudhomme, René-François-Armand. 1839.
  in French.
LE VASE BRISÉ. "Le vase où meurt cette verveine"
LES YEUX. "Bleus ou noirs, tous aimés, tous
  beaux"   HACH 12

Sulpicia. 25 B. C. in Latin.
TIBULLI LIBER. III. 14. "Invisus natalis adest, qui
  rure molesto"   FOLKW 98
———. 17. "Estne tibi, Cerinthe, tuae pia cura
  puellae"   FOLKW 98

Sulpicius Severus. 365 A.D. in Latin.
Poetry*   CETRA 18

Summers, Hal. in English.
OUT OF SCHOOL.   CAED 112
THE RESCUE.   CAED 112
ROBIN. "With a bonfire throat"   SPOA 67

Summers, Hollis. 1916. in English.
COLORED CLAY HORSE WITH WINGS. "Yawning,
  the girl in the Metepec tourist trap says 5
  pesos"   SPOA 101
FEMALE, MALE, AND BOTH. "Little Bo Peep waits
  for her sheep"   SPOA 101
ON ACCEPTING THE GOLD WATCH. "I have admired the marks of many men" SPOA 101
ONCE UPON A TIME. "Christian, Socialist, he undone"   SPOA 101
THE SEPTEMBER AFTERNOON TREES. "We know of
  course the world will last"   SPOA 101
VALENTINE. "She is like pearls, of course"
                                   SPOA 101

Supervielle, Jules. 1884. in French.
À MOI-MÊME.   ADES 23
LES AMIS INCONNUS. "Il vous naît un poisson que
  se met a tourner"   ADES 23
CE PUR ENFANT. "Ce pur enfant, rose de chas-
  teté"   FOLKW 88
COEUR. "Il ne sait pas mon nom"   ADES 23
LE CORPS. "Ici l'univers est à l'abri dans la pro-
  fonde température de l'homme" ADES 23
"Dans la forêt sans heures"   DOVER 4
DIEU PENSE À L'HOMME. "Il faudra bien qu'il me
  ressemble"   FOLKW 88

---

* Recording not available for analysis

LE HORS VENU. "D'où venez-vous ainsi couvert de précipices" ADES 23
JE ME SOUVIENS. ADES 23
MONTEVIDEO. "Je naissais, et par la fenêtre" ADES 23
MOUVEMENT. "Ce cheval qui tourne la tête" ADES 23
OUBLIEUSE MÉMOIRE. ADES 23
PLEIN CIEL. "J'avais un cheval" HACH 4
LES POISSONS. "Mémoire des poissons dans les criques profondes" ADES 23
PROPHÉTIE. "Un jour la Terre ne sera" FOLKW 88
LE REGRET DE LA TERRE. "Un jour, quand nous diron: c'était le temps du soleil" ADES 23
RÉVEIL. Le monde me quitte, ce tapis, ce livre" DOVER 4

Surrey, Earl of (Henry Howard). 1517. in English.
BRITTLE BEAUTY. "Brittle beauty, that nature made so frail" LONGM 1
MARTIAL. "My friend, the things that do attain" IMP 1
NIGHT. "Alas! so all things now do hold their peace" ARGO 32, SPOA 83
PRISONED IN WINDSOR, HE RECOUNTETH HIS PLEASURE THERE PASSED. "So cruel prison" IMP 1
THE SOOTE SEASON. "The soote season, that bud and bloom forth bringes" LONGM 1
TO HIS LADY. "Set me whereas the sun doth parch the green" ARGO 32, SPOA 83
WYATT RESTETH HERE. "Wyatt resteth here, that quick could never rest" LONGM 1

Sutheim, Susan. in English.
FOR WITCHES. CAED 155

Sutzkever, Abraham. in Yiddish.
A WAGON OF SHOES. "Dei rader, yugen, yugen, vus brengen zei mit zich" FOLKW 91
AT THE MEMORIAL IN YAD MORDECAI. "Atzined ven mir schtellen die toita Denkmall" FOLKW 91
DEI BLYENA PLATEN FUN ROMES DRUKEREI. "Mir Lubben vie finga gestreckter" FOLKW 91
DEER AT THE DEAD SEA. "Hershen bein yom tov der zun Fagang" FOLKW 91
IN SINAI DESERT. "Die Trayeer die benken dicker oif mein vay" FOLKW 91
PETITIONS ON THE GRAVE OF RABBI SIMEON YECHOI. "Oif mit zaver Schtayner blau" FOLKW 91
PLAYTHINGS. "Deine speilsteig mine Kind—alt zei tyre" FOLKW 91
SO SHOULD YOU SPEAK TO THE ORPHAN. "En a zoi solst du reddin tzum yusen" FOLKW 91
THE SCHOOLTEACHER MIRA. "Mit lattes oif leber tze schnitten" FOLKW 91
THE SNOWS OF MOUNT HERMON. "May ka mish schomer lon" FOLKW 91
THE WELL OF PROPHECY. "Fa plantered in zamsicha flachan" FOLKW 91
WERE I NOT WITH YOU. "Ven ich volt nit zein mit dere by nandt" FOLKW 91
YIDDISCHE GASS. "Bist nicht fagangen—Dein pustkeit is feil" FOLKW 91

Svetlov, Mikhail A. 1903. in Russian.
BASNYA. "Bilo tak—legendi govoryat" MONITR 1
SOBATCHKA. "Letit sobatchka po vselennoi" MONITR 1

UKAZANIE. "Ukazanie prishlo na zare" MONITR 1

Sward, Robert. 1933. in English.
CELEBRATION. "Outside, the snow on a low" FOLKW 21
DEC. '63. "The talk is of Johnson and a Congress" FOLKW 21
INVOCATION: TO THE MUSE. "Oh Muse, lady" WATSHD 2
POEM. "The rocks dark, green as leaves" FOLKW 21
POEM FOR A NEW YORK FOUNDATION STONE. "Here people laying a foundation" WATSHD 2
READING BUBER. "Words escape me, I face a loss" FOLKW 21
SURPRISE ATTACK. "What does it mean" WATSHD 2
THAT IT THAT THING LIGHT. "Night, light and the night, light" FOLKW 21
TITLES. "How you title poems" WATSHD 2

Swenson, May. 1927. in English.
AFTER THE DENTIST. "My left upper" SCHOL 2
ALMANAC. "The hammer struck my nail" SPOA 103
BISON CROSSING NEAR MT. RUSHMORE. "There is our herd of cars stopped" CAED 165
BLEEDING. "Stop bleeding said the knife" CAED 165
THE BLINDMAN. "The blindman placed" SCHOL 2
THE BLUE BOTTLE. "Go to the other shore and return" CAED 165
BY MORNING. "Some for everyone" SCHOL 2
CAT AND THE WEATHER. "Cat takes a look at the weather" SCHOL 2
CAUSE AND EFFECT. "Am I the bullet/ or the target" CAED 165
THE CENTAUR. "The summer that I was ten" SCHOL 2
"The DNA molecule" CAED 165
EARLY MORNING: CAPE COD. "We wake to double blue" SCHOL 2
FOUNTAINS OF AIX. "Beards of water some of them have" CAED 165, SPOA 103
FRONTISPIECE. "In this book I see your face" SPOA 103
HORSES IN CENTRAL PARK. "Colors of horses like leaves or stone" SCHOL 2
HOW EVERYTHING HAPPENS (BASED ON A STUDY OF THE WAVE) "When nothing is happening, something is stacking up to happen" CAED 165
HOW TO BE OLD. "It is easy to be young" SPOA 103
IN NAVAJOLAND. "Eye dazzlers the Indians weave" CAED 165
THE KEY TO EVERYTHING. "Is there anything I can do" CAED 165, SPOA 103
THE LIGHTNING. "The lightning waked me. It slid under" CAED 165
LION. FOLKW 25
A LOAF OF TIME. "A loaf of time round and thick" SPOA 103
NAKED IN BORNEO. "They wear air/ or water like a skin" CAED 165

* Recording not available for analysis

Swenson, May (continued)

ORBITER 5 SHOWS HOW EARTH LOOKS FROM THE MOON. "There's a woman in the earth, sitting on"   CAED 165

ORDER OF DIET. "Salt of the soil and liquor of the rock"   SCHOL 2

OUT OF THE SEA, EARLY. "A bloody egg yolk. A blind hole"   CAED 165

OVERBOARD. "What throws you out is what drags you in"   CAED 165

PIGEON WOMAN. "Slate, or dirty-marble-colored"   SCHOL 2

"The pure suit of happiness"   CAED 165

THE RED BIRD TAPESTRY.   NACTE 14

SOUTHBOUND ON THE FREEWAY. "A tourist came in from Orbitville"   SCHOL 2, SCHOL 7

SPEED. "In 200 miles/ a tender painting"   CAED 165

STONE GULLETS. "Stone gullets among"   CAED 165

SURVEY OF THE WHOLE. "World's lopsided/ that's its trouble"   CAED 165

THINGS IN COMMON. "We have a good relationship, the elevator boy and I"   SCHOL 2

TRANCE. "Out of an hour I built a hut"   CAED 165

"Unconscious came a beauty wrist"   CAED 165

UNTITLED. "I will be earth you be the flower"   CAED 165

THE WATCH. "When I took my watch to the watchfixer"   CAED 165

WHILE SITTING IN THE TUILERIES AND FACING THE SLANTING SUN. "There is the line"   CAED 165

WORKING ON WALL STREET.   NACTE 14

Poetry*   JNP 68, MILLER 3

Swift, Jonathan. 1667. in English.

BIRTHDAY POEM TO ESTHER JOHNSON. "All travellers at first incline"   LONGM 1

MARKET WOMEN'S CRIES. "Come, buy my fine wares"   SPOA 6

STELLA'S BIRTHDAY.   CAED 203

TO THEIR EXCELLENCIES THE LORDS JUSTICES OF IRELAND, THE HUMBLE PETITION OF FRANCES HARRIS.   CAED 203

VERSES ON THE DEATH OF DR. SWIFT, exc. "As Rochefoucault his Maxims drew"   BRITAM 3

———. "Behold the fatal day arrive"   LONGM 1

Swinburne, Algernon. 1837. in English.

ATALANTA IN CALYDON, exc. "Before the beginning of years"   CAED 179, JNP 8

———. "Maiden, and mistress of the months and stars"   ARGO 69

———. "When the hounds of Spring are on Winter's traces"   ARGO 69, CMS 14, JNP 8

A BALLAD OF DREAMLAND. "I hid my heart in a nest of roses"   CAED 179

A BALLAD OF FRANCOIS VILLON. "Bird of the bitter bright grey golden morn"   CAED 201, EAV 22

A CHILD'S LAUGHTER. "All the bells of heaven may ring"   CAED 179, RCA 8

ENVOI. "Fly, white butterflies, out to sea"   CAED 110

EROTION. "Sweet for a little even to fear, and sweet"   CAED 179

A FORSAKEN GARDEN. "In a coign of the cliff between lowland and highland"   CAED 179

THE GARDEN OF PROSERPINE, exc. "Here, where the world is quiet"   ARGO 69, AUDIA 1   CAED 179, EAV 22, LIST 3, LONGM 1

HENDECASYLLABICS. "In the month of the long decline of roses"   LONGM 1

IN MEMORY OF BARRY CORNWALL. "In the garden of death, where the singers"   CAED 179

IN MEMORY OF WALTER SAVAGE LANDOR. "Back to the flowertown, side by side"   CAED 179

THE INTERPRETERS. "Days dawn on us that make amends for many Sometimes"   CAED 201

ITYLUS. "Swallow, my sister, O sister swallow"   CAED 179

JOHN WEBSTER. "Thunder: the flesh quails, and the soul bows down"   COLUMB 11

A LYRIC.   CAED 179

A MATCH. "If love were what the rose is"   CAED 179

THE ROUNDEL. "A roundel is wrought as a ring or a star-bright sphere"   EAV 22

SAPPHICS. "All the night sleep came not upon my eyelids"   CAED 179

SESTINA. "I saw my soul at rest upon a day"   EAV 22

SEVEN YEARS OLD. "Seven white roses on one tree"   CAED 179

WHITE BUTTERFLIES, exc. "Fly, white butterflies out to sea"   HARB 2

Poetry*   ARGO 23, LIST 11

Sylvain, André. in French.

CHANT PROFANE POUR DES TEMPS INQUIÉTS.   ADES 55

Symons, Arthur. 1865. in English.

AT DIEPPE: GREY AND GREEN. "The grey-green stretch of sandy grass"   LONGM 1

NERVES. "The modern malady of love is nerves"   LONGM 1

A ROUNDEL OF REST. "If rest is sweet at shut of day"   EAV 22

WANDERER'S SONG. "I have had enough of women, and enough of love"   CAED 201

WHITE HELIOTROPE. "The feverish room and that white bed"   LONGM 1

Tabb, John Bannister. in English.

A BUNCH OF ROSES. "The rosy mouth and rosy toe"   CAED 16

Tagore, Rabindranath. 1861. in Bengali.

PAPER BOATS. "Day by day I float my paper boats"   English BOWMAR 1, CAED 16

URSPRUNGET.   Swedish GRAM 2

Poetry*   MICHM 1

Talbot, Ethel. in English.

CRAB APPLE. "I dreamed the fairies wanted me"   BOWMAR 3

Talen, William. in English.

AMERICAN TRADITIONAL CHANT. "Let nasty hab its let me out"   WATSHD 4

AURORA AND THE TRUCKER. "The H-O-U-R hours"   WATSHD 4

MOUNTAIN MAN. "Talk about beauty"   WATSHD 4

* Recording not available for analysis

WALTER SULLIVAN OF THE NEW YORK TIMES. "The most elaborate"   WATSHD 4

Tao-Chi (Tao-Yuan-Ming). 365 A. D. in Chinese.
Poetry*   MICHM 2

Tarahata, Jessica. in English.
Poetry*   WATSHD 50

Tardieu, Jean. in French.
ORADOUR.   ADES 55

Tasso, Torquato. 1544. in Italian.
"Un' ape esser vorrei"   DOVER 3
"Écco mormorar l'onde"   DOVER 3,
                                            SPOA 30
GERUSALEMME LIBERATA, exc.   CETRA 22
———. "Amico, hai vinto: io ti perdon . . . ;
perdona"   SPOA 30
"O via piu bianca e fredda"   SPOA 30
"Qual rugiada o qual pianto"   DOVER 3,
                                            SPOA 30
RIME, exc.   CETRA 22
"Tacciono i bischi e i fiumi"   DOVER 3

Tassoni, Alessandro. 1565. in Italian.
Poetry*   CETRA 24

Tate, Allen. 1899. in English.
AENEAS AT WASHINGTON. "I myself saw furious with blood"   CARIL 1
THE BURIED LAKE. "Lady of light, I would admit a dream"   CARIL 1
THE CROSS. "There is a place that some men know"   CARIL 1, NACTE 11
DEATH OF LITTLE BOYS. "When little boys grow patient at last, weary"   CARIL 1, JNP 3
EMBLEMS. "Maryland, Virginia, Caroline"
                               NACTE 11, SPOA 96
LAST DAYS OF ALICE. "Alice grown lazy, mammoth but not fat"   CARIL 1
THE MEANING OF DEATH. "I rise, gentlemen, it is the pleasant hour"   CARIL 1
THE MEANING OF LIFE. "Think about it at will: there is that"   CARIL 1
THE MEDITERRANEAN. "Where we went in the boat was a long bay" CARIL 1, COLPIX 1,
                                            NACTE 11
MOTHER AND SON. "Now all day long the man who is not dead"   CARIL 1
ODE TO OUR YOUNG PROCONSULS OF THE AIR.
                               LIBC 5, LIBC 16
ODE TO THE CONFEDERATE DEAD. "Row after row with strict impunity" CARIL 1, COLPIX 1,
                               LIBC 5, LIBC 16
RECORDS. I. A DREAM. "At nine years a sickly boy lay down"   LIBC 5, LIBC 16
———. II. A VISION. "At twenty years the strong boy walked alone"   LIBC 5, LIBC 16
SEASONS OF THE SOUL. 1. SUMMER. "Summer, this is our flesh"   CARIL 1
———. 2. AUTUMN. "It had an autumn smell"
                                            CARIL 1
———. 3. WINTER. "Goddness sea-born and bright"   CARIL 1
———. 4. SPRING. "Irritable spring, infuse"
                                            CARIL 1
SONNETS AT CHRISTMAS. "This is the day His hour of life draws near"   LIBC 5, LIBC 16,
                                            LIBC 38
———. "Ah Christ I love you rings to the wild sky"   LIBC 5, LIBC 16, LIBC 38

THE SUBWAY. "Dark accurate plunger down the successive knell"   NACTE 11
THE SWIMMERS. "Kentucky water, clear springs: a boy fleeing" CARIL 1, LIBC 1, SPOA 96
WINTER MASK. "Towards nightfall when the wind"   CARIL 1, SPOA 96
THE WOLVES. "There are wolves in the next room waiting"   CARIL 1, COLPIX 1,
                                            LIBC 1
Poetry*   JNP 56, JNP 57, LIST 14

Tate, James. 1943. in English.
ABSENCES. "When did you begin your guest"
                                            WATSHD 1
SUCCESS COMES TO COW CREEK. "I sit on the tracks"   CAED 155
Poetry*   JNP 58

Taylor, Ann and Jane. 1782 and 1783. in English.
THE STAR. "Twinkle, twinkle, little star"
                                            CAED 58

Taylor, Edward. 1645. in English.
GOD'S DETERMINATIONS. PREFACE, exc. "Upon what base was fixed the lath, wherein"
                     CAED 185, EAV 15, HOUGHT 5
HUSWIFERY. "Make me, O Lord, thy spinning wheele compleate"   ARGO 11, CAED 185,
                                            EAV 15
MEDITATION 6   HOUGHT 5

Taylor, Rex. 1921. in English.
THE POSTER. "Why do they pose"   SPOA 68

Taylor, William E. 1920. in English.
Poetry*   CASSC 10

Teasdale, Sara. 1884. in English.
BARTER. "Life has loveliness to sell"
                                            CAED 169
THE COIN. "Into my heart's treasury"
                                            CAED 169
FEBRUARY TWILIGHT. "I stood beside a hill"
                                            HARB 2
THE LONG HILL. "I must have passed the crest a while ago"   HOUGHT 5
NIGHT, or IT IS NOT FAR. "Stars over snow"
                                            SINGER 2
STARS. "Alone in the night"   CAED 164
Poetry*   LIST 18

Tegner, Esaias. 1782. in Swedish.
DET EVIGA. "Vål formar den starke med svårdet sin värld"   GRAM 3

Tejada, José Luis. in Spanish.
EL RETROCESO DE LA PRIMAVERA. "Achanta marzo al ave que aún se duele"
¿TAMBIÉN ME AÑORAS TU? "¿De veras tú también . . . ?"
VAYA POR DÍOS. "Bueno que está contigo, Padre, Hermano"   AGUIL 10

Tennyson, Alfred Lord. 1809. in English.
BREAK, BREAK, BREAK   ARGO 64, AUDIA 1,
   BRITAM 3, DECCA 12, EAV 9, LIST 3,
                                            THEAL 3
THE BROOK. "Here by this brook we parted, I to the East"   FOLKW 67, SPOA 65
THE CHARGE OF THE LIGHT BRIGADE. "Half a league, half a league"   ARGO 65,
   CAED 132, DECCA 10, EAV 9, HARB 5,
   HARC 2, HOUGHT 2, LIST 21, SPOA 42,
                                            UCAL 2

* Recording not available for analysis

Tennyson, Alfred Lord (continued)

CROSSING THE BAR. "Sunset and evening star"
ARGO 64, AUDIA 1, CAED 52, EAV 9,
LIST 3, RCA 4

THE DAISY. "O Love, what hours were thine and
mine"   ARGO 65

THE DYING SWAN. "The plain was grassy, wild
and bare"   ARGO 65

THE EAGLE. "He clasps the crag with crooked
hands"   ARGO 65, AUDIA 1, LIST 3

ENOCH ARDEN, exc.   ARGO 65

A FAREWELL. "Flow down, cold rivulet, to the
sea"   ARGO 65

FRATER AVE ATQUE VALE. "Row us out from
Desenzano, to your Sirmione row"
ARGO 65

IDYLLS OF THE KING, exc.   ARGO 65

———. THE COMING OF ARTHUR, exc. "Leodogran
the king of Cameliard"   IMP 1

———. "Yet Merlin thro' his craft"   IMP 1

———. GARETH AND LYNETTE, exc. "The last tall
son of Lot and Bellicent"   HOUGHT 4,
SINGER 4

———. GERAINT AND ENID, exc. "O purblind
race of miserable men"   CAED 124

———. GUINEVERE, exc.   ARGO 65

———. LANCELOT AND ELAINE, exc. "Elaine the
faire, Elaine the loveable"   CAED 188

———. MERLIN AND VIVIEN, exc.   ARGO 65

———. THE PASSING OF ARTHUR, exc. "And slowly
answered Arthur from the barge"   EAV 22
LONGM 1

———. "That story which the bold Sir Bedivere"   CAED 188, IMP 1

———. "Then spake King Arthur to Sir Bedivere"   IMP 1

IN MEMORIAM, exc.   CAED 201

———. "Be near me when the light is low"
CAED 52

———. "Calm is the morn without a sound"
CAED 52

———. "Dark house by which once more I
stand"   CAED 52, THEAL 2, LONGM 1

———. "Fair ship, that from the Italian shore"
CAED 52

———. "From art, from nature, from the
schools"   ARGO 64

———. "How pure at heart and sound in head"
ARGO 64

———. "I cannot see the features right"
CAED 64

———. "Now fades the last long streak of snow"
ARGO 64

———. "Oh yet we trust that somehow good"
CAED 186, THEAL 2

———. "Old yew, which graspest at the stones"
ARGO 64

———. "One writes, that other friends remain"
CAED 52

———. "Ring out, wild bells, to the wild sky"
AUDIA 1, BRITAM 3, CAED 52, CAED 201,
LIST 3

———. "Strong Son of God, immortal love"
AUDIA 1, LIST 3

———. "To sleep I give my powers away"
CAED 52

———. "Unwatch'd the garden bough shall
sway"   ARGO 64

IN THE GARDEN AT SWAINSTON. "Nightingales
warbled without"   ARGO 65

IN THE VALLEY OF CAUTERETZ. "All along the valley"   ARGO 65

LADY CLARE. "Lord Ronald courted Lady
Clare"   CMS 2

THE LADY OF SHALOTT. "On either side the river
lie"   ARGO 65, BRITAM 1, CAED 52,
EBEC 1, FOLKW 68, SINGER 3, SPOA 65

LOCKSLEY HALL, exc. "Make me feel the wild
pulsation"   EAV 9

THE LOTUS-EATERS, exc.   CAED 201

———. "Courage! he said, and pointed toward
the land"   ARGO 64, SPOA 42

———. "There is sweet music here that softer
falls"   CAED 186, JNP 8

MARIANA. "With blackest moss the flower-plots"
ARGO 64, CAED 201, LONGM 1

MAUD, exc.   APPL 10

———. "Cold and clear-cut face, why come you
so cruelly meek"   ARGO 64

———. "Come into the garden, Maud"
SPOA 65

———. "I have led her home, my love, my only
friend"   ARGO 64

———. "Long have I sigh'd for a calm; God
grant I may find it at last"   ARGO 64

———. "A million emeralds break from the
ruby-budded lime"   ARGO 64

———. "O, let the solid ground"   ARGO 64

———. "O, that 't were possible"   ARGO 64

———. "See what a lovely shell"   ARGO 64

———. "She came to the village church"
ARGO 64

———. "Sick, am I sick of a jealous dread?"
ARGO 64

———. "A voice by the cedar tree"
ARGO 64

MERLIN AND THE GLEAM. "O Young Mariner"
CAED 52

THE MERMAID. "Who would be"   FOLKW 62

MILTON—ALCAICS. "O Mighty-mouth'd inventor
of harmonies"   ARGO 65

MORTE D'ARTHUR. "So all day long the noise of
battle roll'd"   ARGO 64

———, exc. "And answer made King Arthur,
breathing hard"   CAED 52

THE OWL. "When cats run home and light is
come"   ARGO 65, CMS 4

THE PRINCESS, exc. "Come down, O Maid, from
yonder mountain height"   ARGO 64
LONGM 1

———. "Now sleeps the crimson petal, now the
white"   ARGO 64, CAED 52, LIST 3,
LONDON 1, SPOA 35, SPOA 42, SPOA 65

———. "O swallow, swallow flying, flying
south"   SPOA 65

———. "Sweet and low, sweet and low"
CAED 85, EAV 9

———. "The splendour falls on castle walls"
ARGO 64, BRITAM 1, CMS 13, FOLKW 68,
LIST 3, SPOA 42

---

* Recording not available for analysis

_____. "Tears, idle tears, I know not what they mean"   CAED 52, CAED 186, COLUMB 11, EAV 9, LIST 3, SPOA 42, SPOA 65, THEAL 2

THE REVENGE. "At Flores in the Azores Sir Richard Grenville lay"   CAED 52

THE SAILOR BOY. "He rose at dawn and, fired with hope"   ARGO 65

SIR GALAHAD. "My good blade carves the casques of men"   SPOA 65

SONG. "A spirit haunts the year's last hours"   ARGO 64

TITHONUS. "The woods decay, the woods decay and fall"   ARGO 65

TO E. FITZGERALD. "Old Fitz, who from your suburb grange"   ARGO 65

TO E. L., ON HIS TRAVELS IN GREECE. "Illyrian woodlands, echoing falls"   ARGO 65

TO VIRGIL. "Roman Virgil, thou that singest"   ARGO 65

ULYSSES. "It little profits that an idle king"   ARGO 64, CAED 52, SINGER 6, SPOA 42

THE VISION OF SIN, exc.   ARGO 65

VOYAGE OF MAELDUNE. "And we came to the isle of flowers"   CAED 160

Poetry*   APPL 10, EAV 9, LIST 11, SPOA 123

Teresa de Avila Saint (Teresa de Jesus). 1515. in Spanish.

"Nada te turbe"   Spanish and English CMS 5

VERSOS. "Vivo sin vivir en mí"   AGUIL 5, AGUIL 8

Terrazas, Francisco de. 1525. in Spanish.

SONETO. "Dejad las hebras de oro ensortijado"   SPOA 39

Terry, Lucy. fl. 1746. in English.

BAR'S FIGHT, AUGUST 28, 1746. "August 'twas, the twenty-fifth"   FOLKW 41

Tessimond, A. S. J. 1902. in English.

MIDDLE AGED CONVERSATION. "Are you sad to think how often"   FOLKW 60

TALK IN THE NIGHT. "Why are you sighing?"   FOLKW 60

Thackeray, William Makepeace. 1811. in English.

THE BALLAD OF BOUILLABAISSE, exc.   CAED 201

Thayer, Ernest L. in English.

CASEY AT THE BAT. "It looked extremely rocky for the Mudville nine that day"   AGE 1, CAED 100, CAED 195, COLUMB 6, DECCA 11, EAV 20, EAV 21, GOLDOW 1, LIST 22, STERL 1

Thenior, Ralph. in German.

APRIK. MARM. "In Sutterlinschrift auf dem Glas"   DEUTGR 40A

DICHTER. "Rasche Spiegelung im Schaufenster"   DEUTGR 40A

EINFACHE DINGE. "Jeden Tag geschehen einfache Dinge"   DEUTGR 40A

Theobaldy, Jürgen. in German.

ICH WEISS ES WIRD EINE ANDERE ZEIT KOMMEN. "Es wäre schön könnte ich den ganzen Tag"   DEUTGR 40A

NASSE ERDE. "Heute abend, wenn die Strassen"   DEUTGR 40A

Thibaut de Champagne. 1201. in French.

"Pour mal temps ni pour gelée"   HACH 7

Thich Nhat Hanh. in Vietnamese.

"Säng naỹ thí'u dây"   Vietnamese and English SPOA 82

Thomas, Dylan. 1914. in English.

AFTER THE FUNERAL. "After the funeral, mule praises, brays"   CAED 9, CAED 187

ALTARWISE BY OWL LIGHT, exc. "Altarwise by owl-light in the halfway house"   CAED 187

AMONG THOSE KILLED IN THE DAWN RAID. "When the morning was waking over the war"   ARGO 124, CAED 187

"And death shall have no dominion"   ARGO 6, ARGO 22, ARGO 117, CAED 8, CAED 187, POLYDR 1

AUTHOR'S PROLOGUE. "This day winding down now"   CAED 187

BALLAD OF THE LONG-LEGGED BAIT. "The bows glided down and the coast"   ARGO 6, ARGO 22, CAED 7, CAED 187, POLYDR 1

BEFORE I KNOCKED. "Before I knocked and flesh let enter"   ARGO 6, ARGO 22, POLYDR 1

CEREMONY AFTER A FIRE RAID. "Myselves/ The grievers"   CAED 7, CAED 187

DEATHS AND ENTRANCES. "On almost the incendiary eve"   ARGO 6, ARGO 22, POLYDR 1

"Do not go gentle into that good night"   ARGO 6, ARGO 22, ARGO 117, CAED 7, CAED 187, FOLKW 65, JUP 1, POLYDR 1

ELEGY. "Too proud to die, broken and blind he died"   ARGO 137

"Especially when the October wind"   CAED 144

FERN HILL. "Now as I was young and easy under the apple boughs"   ARGO 6, ARGO 22, ARGO 78, ARGO 117, CAED 7, CAED 112, CAED 183, CAED 187, POLYDR 1

"The force that through the green fuse drives the flower"   ARGO 6, ARGO 22, POLYDR 1

THE HAND THAT SIGNED THE PAPER. "The hand that signed the paper felled a city"   ARGO 22, CAED 187, FOLKW 65, JUP 1, POLYDR 1

"The hunchback in the park"   ARGO 6, ARGO 22, ARGO 78, ARGO 117, CAED 9, CAED 187, POLYDR 1

I SEE THE BOYS OF SUMMER. "I see the boys of summer in their ruin"   ARGO 6, ARGO 22, POLYDR 1

"If I were tickled by the rub of love"   CAED 8, CAED 187

"If my head hurt a hair's foot"   CAED 86, CAED 187

IN COUNTRY HEAVEN. "Always when he, in country heaven"   CAED 122

IN COUNTRY SLEEP. "Never and never my girl riding far and near"   CAED 9, CAED 122, CAED 187

"In my craft and sullen art"   ARGO 6, ARGO 22, ARGO 117, ARGO 158, CAED 86, CAED 187, COLUMB 8, POLYDR 1, WORLDP 1

* Recording not available for analysis

Thomas, Dylan (continued)

IN THE WHITE GIANT'S THIGH. "Through throats
where many rivers meet the curlews cry"
CAED 7, CAED 122, CAED 187
LAMENT. "When I was a windy boy and a bit"
ARGO 6, ARGO 22, CAED 8, CAED 187,
POLYDR 1, RCA 10, WORLDP 1
LIE STILL, SLEEP BECALMED. "Lie still, sleep be-
calmed, sufferer with the wound"
ARGO 6, ARGO 22, POLYDR 1
"Light breaks where no sun shines" CAED 9,
CAED 187
LOVE IN THE ASYLUM. "A stranger has come to
share my room in the house not right in the
head"   CAED 187
ON THE MARRIAGE OF A VIRGIN. "Waking alone in
the multitude of loves"   CAED 9,
CAED 187
OVER SIR JOHN'S HILL. "Over Sir John's Hill the
hawk on fire hangs still"   CAED 9,
CAED 122, CAED 187
POEM IN OCTOBER. "It was my thirtieth year to
heaven"   ARGO 6, ARGO 22, ARGO 78,
ARGO 117, CAED 86, CAED 187,
COLUMB 8, POLYDR 1
POEM ON HIS BIRTHDAY. "In the mustardseed
sun"   CAED 8, CAED 187
A REFUSAL TO MOURN THE DEATH BY FIRE, OF A
CHILD IN LONDON. "Never until the mankind
making"   ARGO 119, CAED 8, CAED 183

SHOULD LANTERNS SHINE. "Should lanterns shine
the holy face"   CAED 8, CAED 187
THERE WAS A SAVIOUR. "There was a saviour
rarer than radium"   CAED 8, CAED 187
THIS SIDE OF TRUTH. "This side of truth you may
not see"   CAED 86, CAED 187
"The tombstone told when she died"
CAED 187
UNDER MILK WOOD. "To begin at the beginning"
CAED 182
A WINTER'S TALE. "It is a winter's tale that the
snow blind twilight ferries over the lakes"
ARGO 6, ARGO 22, CAED 8, CAED 187,
POLYDR 1
Poetry*   ANGEL 1, ARGO 24, CAED 2,
PRENT 3, SBARB 1
Thomas, Edward. 1878. in English.
ADLESTROP. "Yes, I remember Adlestrop"
ARGO 96, ARGO 137, ARGO 148
AS THE TEAM'S HEAD BRASS. "As the team's head
brass flashed out on the turn"   ARGO 148
ASPENS. "All day and night, save winter, every
weather"   ARGO 148
BEAUTY. "What does it mean? Tired, angry, and
ill at ease"   ARGO 148
BLAKE RELATES THE FLOWER.   ARGO 148
THE CHERRY TREES. "The cherry trees bend over
and are shedding"   ARGO 148
THE CHILD ON THE CLIFFS. "Mother, the root of
this little yellow flower"   CAED 126
COCK CROW. "Out of the wood of thoughts that
grows by night"   ARGO 148
THE COMBE. "The combe was ever dark, ancient
and dark"   ARGO 148
THE COUNTRYMAN IS DYING OUT.   ARGO 148

A DREAM. "Over known fields with an old friend
in dream"   ARGO 148
FOR THESE. "An acre of land between the shore
and the hills"   ARGO 148
THE GALLOWS. "There was a weasel lived in the
sun"   FOLKW 64
HELEN. "And you, Helen, what should I give
you"   ARGO 148
"If I should ever by chance grow rich"
BRITAM 1
IN MEMORIAM.   ARGO 148
IT RAINS. "It rains and nothing stirs within the
fence"   ARGO 148
THE LAST SHEAF, exc.   ARGO 148
LIBERTY. "The last light has gone out of the
world except"   ARGO 148
LIGHTS OUT. "I have come to the borders of
sleep"   ARGO 148, BRITAM 1
THE LONG SMALL ROOM.   ARGO 148
THE NEW HOUSE. "Now first, as I shut the door"
ARGO 148
NO ONE SO MUCH AS YOU.   ARGO 148
OCTOBER. "The green elm with the one great
bough of gold"   ARGO 148
OLD MAN. "Old Man, or Lad's-love—in the
name there's nothing"   ARGO 148
LONGM 1
OUT IN THE DARK. "Out in the dark over the
snow"   ARGO 148
THE OWL. "Downhill I came, hungry, and yet
not starved"   ARGO 148, CAED 10
THE PATH. "Running along a bank, a parapet"
ARGO 148
ROADS. "I love roads"   ARGO 148
THE SEDGE-WARBLERS. "This beauty makes me
dream there was a time"   ARGO 148
SNOW. "In the gloom of whiteness"
ARGO 148
SOWING. "It was a perfect day"   ARGO 148
TALL NETTLES. "Tall nettles cover up, as they
have done"   ARGO 148
THERE WAS A TIME. "There was a time when this
poor frame was whole"   ARGO 148
TWO PEWITS. "Under the after-sunset sky"
ARGO 148
WE WERE ALONE.   ARGO 148
THE WORD. "There are so many things I have
forgot"   ARGO 148
WORDS. "Out of us all that make rhymes"
ARGO 148, BRITAM 1
Thomas, H. Carey. in English.
DIE TAM-TAMS KLOPFEN NICHT MEHR.
German DEUTGR 2
Thomas, Jill. in English.
THE ACT OF DEATH.   PROTHM 7
"Brain smashed, skull splintered"
PROTHM 7
Thomas, Lorenzo. 1944. in English.
NOT THAT HURRIED GRIEF. "You were only a
graying face in the newspaper"
FOLKW 2
Thomas, Martha B. in English.
THE CHIRRUPY CRICKET. "There's a chirrupy
cricket as guest in my room"   HARB 2
Thomas, Ronald Stuart. 1913. in English.
ABERSOCH. "There was that headland"
SPOA 68

---

* Recording not available for analysis

CYNDDYLAN ON A TRACTOR. "Ah you should see Cynddylan on a tractor"   SPOA 67
HERE.   PROTHM 8
THE LAST OF THE PEASANTRY. "What does he know, moving through the fields"   ARGO 97
THE LONELY FARMER. "Poor hill farmer astray in the grass"   ARGO 137
NO THROUGH ROAD. "All in vain. I will cease now my long absorption with the plow"   ARGO 97
PISCES. "Who said to the trout"   ARGO 97
PRIEST AND PEASANT. "You are ill, Davies, ill in mind"   ARGO 137
THE WELSH HILL COUNTRY. "Too far for you to see"   ARGO 97
Thomas-Ellis, Aeronwy. in English.
CHINESE DOLL.   ARGO 132
FOUNTAIN: BRIDGES.   ARGO 132
LATER THAN LAUGHARNE.   ARGO 132
LILIES.   ARGO 132
PEACOCKS: NON ACTION.   ARGO 132
THE PINE.   ARGO 132
RETURN VISIT TO LAUGHARNE.   ARGO 132
RIPPLE.   ARGO 132
SPIDER.   ARGO 132
Thompson, Francis. 1859. in English.
ARAB LOVE SONG.   SPOA 10
DAISY. "Where the thistle lifts a purple crown"   SPOA 10
THE HOUND OF HEAVEN. "I fled him, down the nights and down the days"   ARGO 70A, ARGO 137, CAED 162, CAED 201, CMS 14, JNP 8, LIST 3, SPOA 10
THE KINGDOM OF GOD, or IN NO STRANGE LAND. "O world invisible, we view thee"   ARGO 70A, SPOA 10
TO A SNOWFLAKE. "What heart could have thought you?"   SPOA 10
Thompson, John. in English.
A LOVE FOR PATSY.   LIBC 40
Poetry*   LIST 15
Thompson, W. H. in English.
THE HIGH TIDE AT GETTYSBURG. "A cloud possessed the hollow field"   EAV 20
Thomson, James. 1700. in English.
CASTLE INDOLENCE, exc. "O mortal man, who livest here by toil"   ARGO 50
THE CITY OF DREADFUL NIGHT, exc.   ARGO 70A, CAED 201
THE SEASONS, exc. "Along the blushing borders"   ARGO 50
_____. "Thro the hush'd air"   ARGO 50
VERSES OCCASIONED ON THE DEATH OF MR. AIKMAN. "As those we love decay, we die in part"   ARGO 50
Thoreau, Henry David. 1817. in English.
"Any fool can make a rule"   ARGO 6
GREAT FRIEND. "I walk in nature still alone"   ARGO 6
"I'm contented you should stay"   ARGO 6
INSPIRATION. "Whate'er we leave to God, God does"   EAV 14
"Men say they know many things"   ARGO 6
Thwaite, Anthony. 1930. in English.
DISTURBANCES. "After the darkness has come"   SPOA 68

HEDGEHOG. "Twitching the leaves"   SPOA 67
MR. COOPER. "Two nights in Manchester, nothing much to do"   ARGO 96
Tibullus, Albius. 48 B. C. in Latin.
CORPUS TIBULLIANUM, exc. "Divitias alius fulvo sibi congerat auro"   FOLKW 98
_____. "Quis fuit, horrendos primus qui protulit enses"   FOLKW 98
Tichborne, Chidiock. 1558. in English.
WRITTEN ON THE EVE OF HIS EXECUTION. "My prime of youth is but a frost of cares"   CMS 13, POETRY 2, SPOA 83
Tieck, Ludwig. 1773. in German.
AN NOVALIS. "Wer in den Blumen, Wäldern, Bergesreihen"   CHRIST 27
ERKENNEN.   CHRIST 27
EINE STIMME.   CHRIST 27
Tiedge, Christopher August. 1752. in German.
ELEGIE AUF DEM SCHLACHTFELD BEI KUNERSDORF. "Nacht umfängt den Wald, von jenen Hügeln"   DEUTGR 13
DER FRIEDLICHE LÖWE. "Ein Löwe der sich weit umhergetrieben"   DEUTGR 13
Timrod, Henry. 1828. in English.
ODE TO THE CONFEDERATE DEAD. "Sleep sweetly in your humble graves"   HOUGHT 5
Tippett, James S. in English.
CIRCUS PARADE. "Here it comes, here it comes"   BOWMAR 1
THE PARK. "I'm glad that I"   HARB 4
SLEET STORM. "Tic-tic-tic"   HARB 3
Tirolien, Guy. 1917. in French.
JE NE VEUX PLUS ALLER A LEUR ECOLE. "Seigneur, je suis très fatigué"   FOLKW 83
Tobias, John. in English.
REFLECTIONS ON A GIFT OF WATERMELON PICKLE RECEIVED FROM A FRIEND CALLED FELICITY.   SCHOL 7
Todi, Jacopone de la. 1230. in Italian.
Poetry*   CETRA 19
Toleau, Gwen. in English.
THE BREEZE. "If you are lonely"   FOLKW 110
Toledo, Lillian. in Spanish.
HASTIO. "Yo no sé si te quise"   SMC 7
Tolkien, John Ronald Reuel. 1892. in English.
THE ADVENTURES OF TOM BOMBADIL. "Little Tom Bombadil was a merry fellow"   CAED 1, CAED 106
ERRANTRY. "There was a merry passenger"   CAED 1, CAED 106
THE HOARD. "When the moon was new and the sun young"   CAED 1, CAED 106
LORD OF THE RINGS, exc. "A Elbereth Gilthoniel"   CAED 1, CAED 106
THE MAN IN THE MOON CAME DOWN TOO SOON. "The man in the moon had silver shoon"   CAED 1, CAED 106
THE MEWLIPS. "The shadows where the Mewlips dwell"   CAED 1, CAED 106
MIDDLE EARTH, exc.   CAED 1
PERRY-THE-WINKLE. "The lonely troll he sat on a stone"   CAED 1, CAED 106
THE SEA-BELL. "I walked by the sea, and there came to me"   CAED 1, CAED 106
Tomlinson, Charles. 1927. in English.
AT DELFT. "The clocks begin, civilly simultaneous"   ARGO 98

* Recording not available for analysis

Tomlinson, Charles (continued)

AT WELLS: POLYPHONY. "The unmoving vault"
ARGO 98

CÉZANNE AT AIX. "And the mountain: each day"
APPL 3

THE DOOR. "Too little has been said of the door"
APPL 3

FAREWELL TO VAN GOGH. "The quiet deepens"
APPL 3

THE HAND AT CALLOW HILL FARM. "Silence. The
man defined" ARGO 98

IDYL, WASHINGTON SQ. S. F. "A door: per l'universo, is what it says" APPL 3

MR. BRODSKY. "I heard/ before, of an/ American" APPL 3

OXEN PLOUGHING AT FIESOLE. "The heads impenetrable, and the slow bulk soundless"
APPL 3

PARING THE APPLE. "There are portraits and still
lives" APPL 3

THE PICTURE OF J. T. IN A PROSPECT OF STONE.
"What should one wish a child" APPL 3

TRAMONTANA AT LERICI. "Today, should you let
fall a glass it would" APPL 3

WORDS FOR THE MADRIGALIST. "Look with the
ears, said Horacio Vecchi" APPL 3

Tommaseo, Niccolò (Tomašić). 1802. in Italian.
Poetry* CETRA 27

Tonks, Rosemary. in English.
BADLY CHOSEN LOVER. "Criminal! You took a
great piece of my life" ARGO 96

Toomer, Jean. 1894. in English.
SONG OF THE SON. "Pour O pour that parting
soul in song" FOLKW 41

Torello, Barbara. in Italian.
Poetry* CETRA 23

Torres, César G. in Spanish.
JÍBARA DEL GANDUBÁN. "Jibara del Ganduban,
toda fresca" SMC 9

Torres, Luís Lloréns. See **Lloréns Torres, Luís.**

Torres Bodet, Jaime. 1902. in Spanish.
DANZA. "Llama que por morir mas pronto se
levanta" FOLKW 80
Poetry* SMC 16

Torres y Villarroel, Diego. in Spanish.
CONFUSION Y VICIOS DE LA CORTE. "Mulas, médicos, sastres y letrados" AGUIL 6

Torrisi, Fiore. in Italian.
QUESTO FIORE E DEL TEMPO. CETRA 31

Totò. in Italian.
L'ACQUAIOLA. CETRA 50
LA CONSEGNA. CETRA 50
FELICITA. CETRA 50
LA FILOSOFIA DEL CORNUTO. CETRA 50
'A LIVELLA. CETRA 29, CETRA 37
LUDOVICO E SARCHIAPONE. CETRA 50
PASQUALE. CETRA 37
'A PASSIONE MIA ERANO 'E RROSE. CETRA 50
SE IO FOSSI 'N AUCIELLO STATUETTE. CETRA 50

Toulet, Paul-Jean. 1867. in French.
ROMANCE SANS MUSIQUE. "Dans Arles, où sont les
Aliscamps" HACH 14

Toure, Aski Mohammad. in English.
NOTES FROM A GUERRILLA DIARY. BLACKF 1

Tourneur, Cyril. 1575. in English.
THE REVENGER'S TRAGEDY, exc. "And now me-
thinks I could e'en chide myself"
LONGM 1

Towle, Tony. 1939. in English.
Poetry* JNP 59

Traherne, Thomas. 1637. in English.
THE CITY, exc. "What sculptures here among
God's works" JNP 90
"If I delight my God, my king" JNP 90
THE SALUTATION. "These little limbs"
ARGO 36, SPOA 35, LONGM 1
SHADOWS IN THE WATER. "In unexperienc'd in-
fancy" CAED 38
"That light, that sight, that thought" JNP 90

Trakl, Georg. 1887. in German.
ABENDLAND. "Mond, als träte ein Totes"
CHRIST 11
ABENDLÄNDISCHES LIED. "O der Seele näch-
tlicher Fluegelschlag CHRIST 25
ABENDLIED. "Am Abend, wenn wir auf dunklen
Pfaden gehn" CHRIST 28
CONFITEOR. "Die bunten Bilder, die das Leben
malt" DEUTGR 10
CRUCIFIXUS. "Er ist der Gott, vor dem die
Armen knien" CHRIST 18, DEUTGR 10
DE PROFUNDIS. "Es ist ein Stoppelfeld, in das ein
schwarzer Regen fällt" CHRIST 28
GESANG DES ABGESCHIEDENEN. "Voll Harmonien
ist der Flug der Vögel" CHRIST 28
GESANG ZUR NACHT, I - XII. "Vom Schatten eines
Hauchs geboren" DEUTGR 10
GRODEK. "Am Abend tönen die herbstlichen
Wälder" CHRIST 28
IN EIN ALTES STAMMBUCH. "Immer wieder kehrst
du Melancholie" DEUTGR 10
DIE JUNGE MAGD. "Oft am Brunnen, wenn es
dämmert" DEUTGR 10
KASPAR HAUSER LIED. "Er wahrlich liebte die
Sonne, die purpurn den Hügel ninabstieg"
CHRIST 28
NACHTLIED. "Des Unbewegten Odem - Ein
Tiergesicht" CHRIST 28
PASSION. "Wenn silbern Orpheus die Laute
rührt" CHRIST 28
PSALM. CHRIST 29
TRÜBSINN. "In schenken träumend oft am Nach-
mittag" CHRIST 28
UNTERGANG. "Über den weissen Weiher"
CHRIST 28
VERFALL. "Am Abend, wenn die Glocken Fried-
en läuten" CHRIST 28
VERKLÄRTER HERBST. "Gewaltig endet so das
Jahr" CHRIST 28
EIN WINTERABEND. "Wenn der Schnee ans Fen-
ster fällt" CHRIST 28
ZIGEUNER. "Die Sehnsucht glüht in ihrem näch-
tigen Blick" CHRIST 18, DEUTGR 10
Poetry* CHRIST 5, CHRIST 6

Trapassi, Pietro. See **Metastasio.**

Treece, Henry. 1912. in English.
CONQUEROR. "By sundown we came to a hidden
valley" SPOA 67
THE MAGIC WOOD. "The wood is full of shining
eyes" VAN 3
OH, LITTLE CHILD. "See how the flower"
VAN 3

* Recording not available for analysis

WHO MURDERED THE MINUTES. "Who murdered the minutes" VAN 3
Treitel, Margot. in English.
BETWEEN THE WARS. "Always between two wars" WATSHD 14
EATING APPLES, exc. "I get big with child in Africa" WATSHD 14
LUNCH IN THE LAND OF PLENTY. "How long it took" WATSHD 14
THE SILENT GENERATION. "Long flat years of listening" WATSHD 14
WAITING FOR THE BOMB: N. Y., 1960. "Gladly we expected it to drop" WATSHD 14
WHY WE NEED EXPERTS IN OUR LIVES. "At fifteen, the expert" WATSHD 14
Tripp, John. 1927. in English.
LINCOLN 1301. ARGO 152
ON MY FORTIETH BIRTHDAY. "When I was forty the stocktaker came" ARGO 152
SOLILOQUY. ARGO 152
Tristan l'Hermite (François l'Hermite). 1602. in French.
LE PROMENOIR DES DEUX AMANTS, exc. HACH 9, PERIOD 2
Tropp, Gloria. in English.
POEM TO ERNIE HENRY. "Paint my crib a" BROADR 2
Tropp, Steven. in English. (With Howard Hart)
TO JACKIE IN JAIL. "Your hands are envelopes" BROADR 2
Troupe, Quincy. in English.
POEM FOR OLD BLACK LADIES WHO STAND ON BUS-STOP CORNERS. "Blue black" WATSHD 5
THESE DAYS. "A crossfertilization of blood" WATSHD 5
Poetry* PRENT 1
Trumbull, John. in English.
THE LIBERTY POLE. EAV 15
Tucholsky, Kurt. 1890. in German.
AN DIE BERLINERIN. "Mädchen, kein Casanova" DEUTGR 27
AUGEN IN DER GROSSSTADT. "Wenn du zur Arbeit gehest" DEUTGR 32
DIE BARFRAU. DEUTGR 27
DIE DAME MIT'N AVEC. "Alle könn sie mir, könn sie mir" DEUTGR 27
DISKRETION. "Dass Josefine eine schiefe Nase hat" DECCA 1
EHEKRACH. "Ja—!/ Nein—!" DECCA 1
FRAGE. "Es laufen vor Premieren" DEUTGR 27
DER GRABEN. "Mutter, wozu hast du deinen aufgezogen?" DEUTGR 32
DAS IDEAL. "Ja, das möchste" DECCA 1
IDEAL UND WIRKLICHKEIT. "In stiller Nacht und monogamen Betten" DECCA 1, DEUTGR 27
JAPANLIED. DEUTGR 32
KRIEG DEM KRIEGE. "Sie lagen vier Jahre in Schützengraben" DEUTGR 32
DAS LÄCHELN DER MONA LISA. "Ich kann den Blick nicht von dir wenden" DEUTGR 32
LAMENTO. "Der deutsche Mann" DEUTGR 27, DEUTGR 32
DAS LEIBREGIMENT. DEUTGR 32
DAS LIED VON DER GLEICHGÜLTIGKEIT. "Eine Hur steht unter der Laterne" DEUTGR 27

MALWINE. "Ich hab mich deinetwegen" DEUTGR 27
DAS MITGLIED. "In mein' Verein bin ich hineingetreten" DEUTGR 27
MUTTERNS HÄNDE. "Hast uns Stulln jeschnitten" ATHENA 5, DEUTGR 27
DIE NACHFOLGERIN "Ich hab meinen ersten Mann gesehn" DEUTGR 32
NUR DAS. DEUTGR 27
PARK MONCEAU. "Hier ist es hübsch. Hier kann ich ruhig träumen" DEUTGR 27
ROTE MELODIE. "Ich bin allein" DEUTGR 32
SCHIFF AHOI! DEUTGR 27
SIE ZU IHM. "Ich hab dir alles hingegeben" DEUTGR 32
STOSSSEUFZER EINER DAME IN BEWEGTER NACHT. DEUTGR 27
WAS IST IM INNERN EINER ZWIEBEL. "Nun nimmt wohl bald der Bauer Geld aus der Schatulle" DEUTGR 27
WENN EENA DOT IS. "Wenn eena dot is kriste'n Schreck" DEUTGR 32
WENN EENA JEBORN WIRD. "Nu liechste da, du kleene Kröte" DEUTGR 32
Poetry* JNP 39
Tuckerman, Frederick Goddard. 1821. in English.
SONNET. ARGO 11
Tullos, Rod. in English.
FINDING THE MASCULINE PRINCIPLE IN BABYSHIT. "Four hours cleaning" WATSHD 7
HER BLACK PLASTIC NAMETAG SAID 'HELENE'. "Oh Helene" WATSHD 7
INSTEAD OF A GIFT. "It is a farce that steals" WATSHD 7
OLD SON OF A BITCH DEATH HOTEL. "An old woman grinds corn" WATSHD 7
OVERPRODUCTION OF CORN. "In March, unharvested corn" WATSHD 7
TELEGRAM FROM PARANOIA. "Eyes awaken" WATSHD 7
31ST OF JANUARY, 1974. "For the second time" WATSHD 7
A YOUNG WOMAN SITTING UP AT MIDNIGHT. "And now she said" WATSHD 7
Tul'si Das. 16th century. in Hindi.
RAMAYANA, exc. "Dhahe Mahidhar Sikhar Kotinh Bibidh Bidhi Gola Chale" SCHOL 6
———. "Priya Bachan Mridu Sunat Nripu Chityan Ankhi Udhari" SCHOL 6
Tunkeler, Der. in Yiddish.
JEWS CHANTING. "Tzwai yidden sitzen en zingen—einer ayst commet Moishe Hatzkul in der anderer ayst commet Mortrer Laibisch" FOLKW 90
Turco, Lewis. 1934. in English.
AN IMMIGRANT BALLAD. FOLKW 25
Turgenev, Ivan Sergeyevich. 1818. in Russian.
NISHCHIJ. "Ya prokhodil na ulitse" CMS 6
SOBAKA. "Nas dvoe v komnate" CMS 6
SON. "Davnen'ko ne byval v storone rodnoi" CMS 6
Turner, David. in English.
Poetry* CASSC 5
Turner, Nancy Byrd. in English.
THE LITTLE ROAD. "A little road was straying" HARB 4

---

* Recording not available for analysis

Turner, Nancy Byrd (continued)

OLD QUIN QUEERIBUS. "Old Quin Queeribus he
loved his garden so"   CREAT 1, HARB 3
Turner, Walter James. in English.
ROMANCE. "When I was but 13 or so"   RCA 1
TALKING WITH SOLDIERS. "The mind of the peo-
ple is like mud"   FOLKW 65
Tuwhare, Hone. in English.
Poetry*   KIWI 5
Tyard, Pontus de. 1521. in French.
PÈRE DU DOUX REPOS.   ADES 54
Tymnes. in Greek.
EPITAPH OF A MALTESE WATCH-DOG. "Beneath me
(says the stone) lies the white dog from Meli-
ta"   English CARIL 3
Tyutchev, Fedor Ivanovich. 1803. in Russian.
NE RASSUZHDAY. "Ne rassuzhday, ne khlopochi"
FOLKW 94
ONA SIDELA NA POLU.   CAED 193
POSLEDNIY KATAKLIZM.   CAED 193
ROSSIYA. "Umom Rossiyu ne ponyat'"
CAED 193, CMS 6
RUSSKOY SHENSHCHINE. "Vdali ot solutsa i priro-
dy"   FOLKW 94
SILENTIUM. "Molchi, skryvaisya i tai"   CMS 6
Tzara, Tristan. 1896. in French.
LES CLOCHES SONNENT SANS RAISON.   ADES 26,
ADES 47, ADES 52
LA FACE INTERIEURE. "Dur paves des rues
mettez des pas d'acier"   ADES 26,
ADES 47
LA GRANDE COMPLAINTE DE MON OBSCURITÉ
TROIS. "Chez nous les fleurs des pendules s'al-
lument et les plumes encerclent la clarte"
ADES 26, ADES 47, ADES 52
LE PUISATIER DES REGARDS. "Seul dans une âme
ample j'ai vu se perdre"   ADES 26,
ADES 47
SANS COUP FÉRIR. "Ne tirez pas sur le pianiste"
ADES 26, ADES 47
SUR UNE RIDE DU SOLEIL. "Noyez matins les soifs
les muscles et les fruits"   ADES 26,
ADES 47, FOLKW 13
LE TEMPS DETRUIT. "Qu'il parle encore que dit-il
la derobée des vagues"   ADES 26,
ADES 47
VOLT. "Les tours penchées les cieux obliques"
ADES 26, ADES 47, ADES 52
Tzvetaeva, Marina. 1892. in Russian.
TOSKA PO RODINE.   CAED 193

Uccello, Antonino. 1922. in Italian.
NOTTE DELL' ASCENSIONE.   CETRA 31
Uchoita, J. A. in Spanish.
Poetry*   SMC 16
Uhland, Ludwig. 1787. in German.
DER WIRTIN TÖCHTERLEIN. "Es zogen drei Burs-
che wohl über den Rhein"   DOVER 1
FRÜHLINGSGLAUBE. "Die linden Lüfte sind er-
wacht"   CHRIST 27
Poetry*   CHRIST 7
Ullman, Gustaf. in Swedish.
UR STRIDEN, exc.   GRAM 2
Unamuno, Miguel de. 1864. in Spanish.
"Á un hijo de españoles arropamos"
AGUIL 15

"Ahora que voy tocando ya la cumbre"
AGUIL 1
CASTILLA. "Tú me levantas, tierra de Castilla"
DOVER
"La Catedral de Barcelona dice"   AGUIL 1
EL CRISTO DE VELAZQUEZ, exc. "¿En qué piensa
Tú, muerto, Cristo mío?"   AGUIL 5
SPOA 5
_____. "No me verá dentro de poco el mundo
AGUIL
_____. "Tú que callas, oh Cristo! para oírnos
AGUIL
EL CRISTO YACENTE DE SANTA CLARA. "Este e
aquel convento de Franciscas"   AGUIL 1
"Cuál de vosotros, olas de consuelo"
AGUIL 1
DENSO, DENSO. "Mira, amigo, cuando libres"
AGUIL 1
DULCE SILENCIOSO PENSAMIENTO. "En el fondo
las risas de mis hijos"   AGUIL 1
ELEGÍA EN LA MUERTE DE UN PERRO. "La quietu
sujetó con recia mano"   AGUIL 1
EN UN CEMENTERIO DE LUGAR CASTELLANO. "Co
ral de muertos, entre pobres tapias"
FIDIAS 1, SPOA 5
"España! Á alzar su voz nadie se atreve"
AGUIL 1
FRAGMENTO VII DE EL CRISTO DE VELÁZQUE
"Con aquellos sus ojos que probaron"
AGUIL 1
"Hoy te goce, Bilbao"   AGUIL 1
¡LIBERTATE, SEÑOR! "Dime tú que quiero"
AGUIL 1
"Lo que sufres, mi pobre España, es como"
AGUIL 1
"Oh, mi pueblo castizo, el del mañana"
AGUIL 1
¿QUÉ ES TU VIDA, ALMA MÍA? "¿Qué es tu vida
alma mía? ¿cuál tu pago?"   AGUIL 13
HOLT
SALAMANCA. "Alto soto de torres, que, al po
nerse"   AGUIL
SALMO III. "Oh, Señor, Tú que sufres del mur
do"   AGUIL 1
"El tiempo se ablandó"   AGUIL 1
"Tú me levantas, tierra de Castilla"
AGUIL 1
LA VIDA DE LA MUERTE. "Oir llover no mas, ser
tirme vivo"   SMC
"Ya sé lo que es el porvenir: la espera"
AGUIL 1
Ungaretti, Giuseppe. 1888. in Italian.
ALLA NOIA. "Quiete, quando risorse in un
trama"   CETRA 1
AMSTERDAM, MARZO 1933.   CETRA 1
APOCALISSI, exc. "Da una finestra trapeland
luce"   CETRA 3
APOCALYPSE.   APPL
CAINO. "Corre sopra le sabbie favolose"
CETRA 38, CETRA 17, CETRA 4
LA CONCHIGLIA. "A conchiglia del buio"
CETRA 1
DEFUNTI SU MONTAGNE. "Poche cose mi restan
visibili"   CETRA 17, CETRA 4
IL DOLORE, exc.   APPL
DONO. "Ora domi, cuore inquieto" CETRA 1

* Recording not available for analysis

DOVE LA LUCE. "Come allodola ondosa"
                                    CETRA 17
DUNJA. "Si volge verso l'est l'ultimo amore"
                                    CETRA 17
È DIETRO. "E dietro le casipole il porticciuolo"
                            CETRA 17, CETRA 42
"Fa dolce e forse qui vicino passi" CETRA 38
FINE DI CRONO. "L'ora impaurita"   CETRA 17
I FIUMI. "Mi tengo a quest' albero mutilato"
                            CETRA 17, CETRA 38
GIORNO PER GIORNO. "Mai, non saprete mai
   come m'illumina"   CETRA 17
INNO ALLA MORTE. "Amore, mio giovine em-
   blema" CETRA 17, CETRA 38, CETRA 42
IL LAMPO DELLA BOCCA. "Migliaia d'uomini
   prima di me"   CETRA 17
LUCCA. "A casa mia in Egitto"   CETRA 17,
                                    CETRA 38
LA MADRE. "E il cuore quando d'un ultimo bat-
   tito"   CETRA 17, CETRA 38, CETRA 42
LA MORTE MEDITATA. "Hai chiuso gli occhi"
                            CETRA 17, CETRA 42
NON GRIDATE PIU. "Cessate d'uccidere i morti"
                            CETRA 17, CETRA 38
"Non piu furori reca a me l'estate"
                                    CETRA 38
IL PORTO SEPOLTO. "Via arriva il poeta"
                                    CETRA 17
LA PREGHIERA. "Come dolce prima dell'uomo"
                                    CETRA 17
SEGRETO DEL POETA. "Solo ho amica la notte"
                            CETRA 17, CETRA 42
SENZA PIÙ PESO. "Per un Iddio che rida come un
   bimbo" CETRA 17, CETRA 42, DOVER 3
SONO UNA CREATURA. "Come questa pietra"
                    CETRA 17, CETRA 38, CETRA 42
"Sotto la scure il disilluso ramo" CETRA 38
STELLA. "Stella, mia unica stella" CETRA 17
IL TACCUINO DEL VECCHIO, exc.   CETRA 17,
                                    APPL 4
TU TI SPEZZASTI. "I molti, immani, sparsi, grigi
   sassi"   DOVER 3, CETRA 17, CETRA 38
ULTIMO QUARTO. "Luna, piuma di cielo"
                                    CETRA 17
VARIAZIONI SU NULLA. "Quel nonnulla di sabbia
   che trasorre"   CETRA 17
VEGLIA. "Un' intera nottata"   DOVER 3
Poetry*   CETRA 43, CETRA 46
Untermeyer, Louis. 1885. in English.
ALMOST. "My sweetheart has beneficent arms"
                                    SPOA 91
AT THE BOTTOM OF THE WELL. "Something be-
   fell"   LIBC 1
CALIBAN IN THE COAL MINES. "God, we don't like
   to complain"   SPOA 91
COAL FIRE. "And once, in some swamp forest
   these"   LIBC 1
EDGAR A. GUEST CONSIDERS THE GOOD OLD WOMAN
   WHO LIVED IN A SHOE AND THE GOOD OLD
   TRUTHS SIMULTANEOUSLY. "It takes a heap
   o'children to make a home that's true"
                                    LIBC 1
FOOD AND DRINK. "Why has our poetry es-
   chewed"   LIBC 1
HANDS. "Strange how this smooth and supple
   joint"   SPOA 91

IRONY. "Why are the things that have no death"
                                    SPOA 91
LONG FEUD. "Where, without bloodshed, can
   there be"   LIBC 1
ON THE BIRTH OF A CHILD.   BROADR 1
PRAYER. "God, though this life is but a race"
                                    SPOA 91
QUESTIONS AT NIGHT. "Why is the sky"
                        BOWMAR 1, NAITV 2
SONG TOURNAMENT: NEW STYLE. "Rain, said the
   first, as it falls in Venice" LIBC 1, SPOA 91
THE WISE WOMAN. "His eyes grow hot"
                                    SPOA 91
Poetry*   JNP 60
Updike, John. 1932. in English.
EARTHWORM. "We pattern our heavens"
                                    CMS 8
FEBRUARY 22ND. "Three boys, American, in dun-
   garees"   SPOA 107
FLIRT. "The flirt is an antelope of flame"
                                    CMS 8
MAPLES IN A SPRUCE FOREST.   CMS 8
MOBILE OF BIRDS. "There is something"
                                    CMS 8
DIE NEUEN HEILIGEN. "Kierkegaard, a/ cripple"
                                    SPOA 107
LES SAINTS NOUVEAUX. "Proust, doing penance"
                                    SPOA 107
THE SENSUALIST. "Come Capsicum, cast off"
                                    SPOA 107
THE STUNT FLYER. "I come into my dim bed-
   room"   SPOA 107
SUMMER: WEST SIDE. "When on the coral-red
   steps of old brownstones"   SPOA 107
TELEPHONE POLES. "They have been with us a
   long time"   CMS 8
TIME'S FOOL. "Frederick Alexander Pott"
                                    SPOA 107
TO AN USHERETTE. "Ah, come with me"
                                    SPOA 107
Poetry*   JNP 61
Urrutia, Francisco A. in Spanish.
Poetry*   SMC 17
Uschold, Maud E. in English.
MOONLIGHT. "Like a white cat moonlight peers"
                                    HARB 3

Valdés, Gabriel de la Concepción. 1809. in Span-
   ish.
PLEGARIA A DIÓS. "Sér de inmensa bondad, Diós
   poderoso"   SMC 13
Valencia, Guillermo. 1873. in Spanish.
JUDITH Y HOLOFERNES. "Blancos senos, redondos
   y desnudos, que al paso"   SPOA 39
PALÉMON EL ESTILITA. "Palémon el Estilita,
   sucesor del viejo Antonio"   FOLKW 79
Valerio, Xandro. in Spanish.
Poetry*   SMC 16
Valerius (Caius Valerius Flaccus). 50 A.D. in Latin.
Poetry*   CETRA 18
Valéry, Paul. 1871. in French.
L'ABEILLE. "Quelle, et si fine, et si mortelle"
                                    DOVER 4
LE BOIS AMICAL. "Nous avons pensé des choses
   pures"   HACH 14, HACH 18
CHANSON À PART.   ADES 14, ADES 46,
                                    SPOA 62

* Recording not available for analysis

Valéry, Paul (continued)

LE CIMETIÈRE MARIN. "Ce toit tranquille, où marchent des colombes" ADES 14, ADES 46, FOLKW 88, GMS 2, HACH 14, HACH 18, SPOA 62
ÉTÉ. ADES 14, ADES 46
LA FILEUSE. "Assise, la fileuse au bleu de la croi- sée" ADES 54, FOLKW 88, HACH 18, SPOA 9
L'INSINUANT. "O Courbes, méandre" FOLKW 13
LA JEUNE PARQUE, exc. "Qui pleure là, sinon le vent simple, à cette heure" HACH 18
NARCISSE PARLE, exc. "O frères! tristes lys, je lan- guis de beauté" ADES 14, ADES 46, GMS 2, HACH 14, HACH 18
PALME. "De sa grâce redoutable" FOLKW 88
LES PAS. "Tes pas, enfants de mon silence" HACH 14, HACH 18
LE VIN PERDU. "J'ai quelque jour, dans l'Ocean" ADES 14, ADES 46, DOVER 4, SPOA 62
Valle Caviedes, Juán del. 1652. in Spanish.
SONETO. "Para ser caballero de accidentes" SPOA 39
Valle Inclan, Ramón del. in Spanish.
GARROTE VIL. "¡Tan, tan, tan! canta el martillo" FIDIAS 1
Vallejo, César. 1895. in Spanish.
LOS HERALDOS NEGROS. "Hay golpes en la vida tan fuertes" SMC 6
TRILCE. XXVIII. "He almorzado solo ahora, y no he tenido madre" FOLKW 80
Valmiki. in Sanskrit.
RAMAYANA, exc. "Evam bahu vidham cintam cintayitva maha matihi" FOLKW 75
Valverde, José Maria. in Spanish.
DE UNA VIDA DE SANTO. "Sobre su nombre y nacimiento" AGUIL 10
HUERTO DE LOS OLIVAS. AGUIL 5
LA MAÑANA. "En la mañana, en su fino y mojado aire" AGUIL 10
VOCES Y ACOMPAÑAMIENTOS PARA SAN MATEO. AGUIL 5
Van Doren, Mark. 1894. in English.
AFTER DRY WEATHER. "If the people under that portico" FOLKW 37
ALWAYS EVENING. "You eyes, forever west of afternoon" NACTE 9
THE BIRD DESIRE. "I took my gun" FOLKW 37
BORN BROTHERS. "Equality is absolute or no" FOLKW 37
THE CHILD AT WINTER SUNSET. "The child at win- ter sunset" FOLKW 37
CIVIL WAR. "The country is no country I have seen" FOLKW 37, LIBC 3, LIBC 4
THE DEEPEST DREAM. "The deepest dream is of mad governors" FOLKW 37
DIALOGUE IN DECEMBER. "In so much dark no light is little" FOLKW 37
DUNCE SONGS. 1. "Where is the bell, the horn" FOLKW 37, SPOA 94
_____. 2. "If rain rose" FOLKW 37, SPOA 94
_____. 3. "Some day" FOLKW 37, LIBC 1, SPOA 82, SPOA 94
_____. 4. "Then I'll be four-footed" FOLKW 37, LIBC 1, SPOA 94

_____. 5. "I have no enemy" FOLKW 3 LIBC 1, SPOA 82, SPOA 9
_____. 6. "Her hand in my hand" FOLKW 37, LIBC 1, SPOA 9
_____. 7. "If I had a wife" FOLKW 3 LIBC 1, SPOA 9
_____. 8. "Pepper and salt" FOLKW 3 LIBC 1, SPOA 9
_____. 9. "Love me little, love me long" FOLKW 37, LIBC 1, SPOA 9
EPITAPH. "Let this be true, that I have loved FOLKW 3
FAMILY PRIME. "Our golden age was then, whe lamp and rug" FOLKW 3
FAREWELL AND THANKSGIVING. "Whatever have left unsaid" FOLKW 3
THE FIRST SNOW OF THE YEAR. "The old man, li tening to the careful" FOLKW 3
FORMER BARN LOT. "Once there was a fenc here" HOUGHT
GET UP, I SAY. "Get up, I say, and see them" SPOA 9
THE GOD OF GALAXIES. "The god of galaxies ha more to govern" FOLKW 3
GOOD NIGHT. "This moonlight lies" FOLKW 3
HE LOVES ME. "That God should love me is mor wonderful" FOLKW 3
HE'S COMING. "He's coming. He just called. Sai he was coming" FOLKW 3
HOMER, SIDNEY, PHILO. "Homer, Sidney, Phil strung along the Wabash" FOLKW 3
INVINCIBLE. "Rain, that wets powder" LIBC 3, LIBC
LIKE SON. "Your stillness here at evening, wit the shade" NACTE
MEMORIAL. "If nothing else let this poor pape say" NACTE
MEN DO NOT LEAVE THINGS SO. "The small min of birds" SPOA 9
MORNING WORSHIP. "I wake and hear it raining FOLKW 37, LIBC 1, SPOA 9
MY POOR LOVE. "Keep up your humming, we wind, and your silly songs" FOLKW 3
O WORLD. "O world, my friend, my foe" FOLKW 3
THE PLAGUE. "Little boy, what ails me, that yo walk" FOLKW 3
POSY GOD. "Wherever a still apron" NACTE
PROPHET. "He did not say anything utterl strange" FOLKW 3
RETURN TO RITUAL. "The mother of life indulge all our wandering" LIBC 3, LIBC
SCHOOLROOM GOD. "Knowledge here will ove grow" NACTE
THE SIGN IN THE SKY. "Look, he said aloud" FOLKW 3
SIMPLE BEAST. "With rope, knife, guns, bra knucks, and bloody laws" NACTE
THE SINGLE HERO. "This man kept courag when the map of fear" LIBC 3, LIBC
SLEEP, GRANDMOTHER. "Sleep, grandmothe sleep" FOLKW 3
SOFT, SOFT, SOFT. "Soft, soft, soft is her gazing FOLKW 3

* Recording not available for analysis

SPRING THUNDER. "Listen. The wind is still"
                                    HOUGHT 5
THE STORY-TELLER. "He talked, and as he
talked"   CAED 111, HOUGHT 5
THIS AMBER SUNSTREAM. "This amber sunstream,
with an hour to live"   FOLKW 37, LIBC 1
TO A CHILD WITH EYES. "Footprints now on
bread or cake"   FOLKW 37
TRAVELLING STORM. "The sky above us here is
open again"   CAED 109
XXVIII. "Never to be renewed or to increase"
                                  FOLKW 37
UNDERSONG. "In wonderment I walk to music
pouring"   FOLKW 37
THE UNKNOWN ARMY. "We are the civil fathers,
the poor necessary"   LIBC 3, LIBC 4
UNRESPONSIVE. "I love you as a bee loves"
                                  FOLKW 37
WHEN THE WIND ENDS. "When the wind ends it
is too much to hope"   FOLKW 37
WOMAN FEW OF WORDS. "Lady, excellently brief"
                                  FOLKW 37

Van Dyke, Henry. 1928. in English.
AMERICA FOR ME.   COLUMB 6

Vann'anto. in Italian.
LA LETTERA DELLA MAMMA.   CETRA 31

Vargas, Roberto. in English and Spanish.
BONES OF MY FATHER. "Y que me sirvan"
                        UCAL 1, WATSHD 9
CANTO PA BERKELEY. "Camino no se por que"
                                    UCAL 1
CARTA LLANTO PA LORCA. "Federico, on the grey
ledges"   WATSHD 5
ELEGY PA GRINGOLANDIA. "It seems just the
other day"   WATSHD 5, UCAL 1
FLORES.   UCAL 1
GUATEMALA. "Roman Catholic priest"
                                  WATSHD 9
HENRIQUE. "Henrique walked back to his room"
                                    UCAL 1
"I have loved, te quiero"   UCAL 1
MARIPOSA. "Tomorrow I will not love you"
                        UCAL 1, WATSHD 5
"Oye"   UCAL 1

Vaughan, H. A. in English.
THE CONVICT.   CAED 153
FOR CERTAIN DEMAGOGUES. "We love the peo-
ple, sir. You do?"   CAED 153
REVELATION. "Turn sideways now and let them
see"   CAED 153
TUDOR STREET SHOP GIRL. "You, too, seek beauty.
Past the unlovely smells"   CAED 153

Vaughan, Henry. 1621. in English.
ASCENSION-HYMN. "Dust and clay"   ARGO 36
CORRUPTION. "Sure, it was so. Man in those early
days"   ARGO 36
MAN. "Weighing the stedfastness and state"
                                   CAED 38
THE MORNING-WATCH. "O Joyes! Infinite sweet-
ness! with what flowres"   ARGO 36
THE NIGHT.   FOLKW 69
PEACE. "My soul, there is a countrie"
                        ARGO 36, LONGM 1
QUICKNESS. "False life! a foil and no more,
when"   ARGO 36

THE RETREATE. "Happy those early dayes! when
I"   ARGO 36, BRITAM 2, CAED 38,
                LIST 2, LONGM 1, SPOA 84
SILENCE AND STEALTH OF DAYES. "Silence and
stealth of dayes! 'tis now"   ARGO 36
"They are all gone into the world of light"
                         LONGM 1, SPOA 84
THE WORLD. "I saw Eternity the other night"
        ARGO 36, CAED 38, LIST 2, LONGM 1,
                                   SPOA 84

Vega, Garcilaso de la. 1503. in Spanish.
A LA FLOR DE GNIDO.   GMS 16
"Cuando contemplo el cielo"   SPOA 37
SONETO. 5. "Escrito está en mi alma"
                         AGUIL 4, DOVER 2
_____. 10. "Oh dulces prendas, por mi mal hal-
ladas"   CMS 5, DOVER 2, SPOA 37
_____. 23. "En tanto que de rosa y azucena"
                         HOLT 1, SPOA 37

Vega, Oscar Fernández de la. 1914. in Spanish.
MENSAJE Á CUBA. "¡Cuba! ¡Patria!"   SMC 13

Vega Carpio, Lope de. 1562. in Spanish.
"A mis soledades voy"   HOLT 1
CANCIÓN. "Cuando la noche oscura" SPOA 37
CANCIÓN. "Ni temo al poderoso"   SPOA 37
CANCIÓN. "Oh libertad preciosa"   SPOA 37
CANTARCILLO DE LA VIRGEN. "Pues andáis en las
palmas"   SPOA 37
ES LA MUJER. "Es la mujer del hombre lo mas
bueno"   SMC 3
"Madre, unos ojuelos vi"   AGUIL 4
PASTOR QUE CON TUS SILBOS. "Pastor que con tus
silbos amorosos"   SPOA 37
POEM.   Spanish and English CMS 5
"Que de noche le matarón"   HOLT 1
SONETO 18. "¿Qué tengo yo que mi amistad
procuras?"   AGUIL 5, DOVER 2, HOLT 1
SONETO A CRISTO NUESTRO SENOR. TEMORES EN EL
FAVOR. "Cuando en mis manos, Rey eterno, os
miro"   AGUIL 5
VARIOS EFECTOS DEL AMOR. "Desmayarse,
atreverse, estar furioso"   AGUIL 4,
                                   DOVER 2

Venevitinov, D. V. 1805. in Russian.
RODINA. "Priroda nasha, tachno, merzost' "
                                    CMS 6

Vennberg, Karl. in Swedish.
ATT LEVA.   GRAM 8
DU MÅSTE VÄRJA DITT LIV.   GRAM 8
REQUIEM, exc.   GRAM 8
SMYCKA MIN MORGON.   GRAM 8
SNART FORBI.   GRAM 8
VÅRBRACKNING.   GRAM 8

Verdaguer, Jacint. 1845. in Catalan.
A LA PLANA DE VIC. "Niuada de calandries, poetes de ma terra"   AGUIL 14

Verde, Cesário. 1855. in Portuguese.
AVÈ-MARIAS. "Nas nossas ruas, ao anoitecer"
                                  FOLKW 72
DE TARDE. "Naguele pic-nic de burguesas"
                                  FOLKW 72

Vere, Edward de. See **Oxford, Earl of.**

Verhaeren, Émile. 1855. in French.
JE T'APPORTE, CE SOIR.   HACH 14
LORSQUE TU FERMERAS.   CAED 204
LE MOULIN. "Le moulin tourne au fond du soir"
                                  FOLKW 13

* Recording not available for analysis

Verlaine, Paul-Marie. 1844. in French.

ARIETTES OUBLIÉES. "Il pleure dans mon coeur"
ADES 1, ADES 43, ADES 49, FOLKW 86,
GMS 7, HACH 13, PERIOD 1, SCHOL 6

ART POÉTIQUE. "De la musique avant toute
chose"   FOLKW 86

CHANSON D'AUTOMNE. "Les sanglots longs"
ADES 1, ADES 43, ADES 49, FOLKW 13,
GMS 7, SPOA 27

"Les chères mains qui furent miennes"
ADES 1, ADES 43, PERIOD 1

"Le ciel est, par-dessus le toit"   ADES 1,
ADES 43, ADES 49

CLAIR DE LUNE. "Votre âme est un paysage choisi"   ADES 1, ADES 43, FOLKW 86,
HACH 13, SPOA 9, SPOA 27

COLLOQUE SENTIMENTAL. "Dans le vieux parc
solitaire et glacé"   ADES 1, ADES 43,
FOLKW 86, GMS 7, GMS 9, PERIOD 1,
SPOA 27, SPOA 36

CRÉPUSCULE DU SOIR MYSTIQUE. "Le Souvenir
avec le Crépuscule"   PERIOD 1

CRIMEN AMORIS. "Dans un palais, soie et or, dans
Ecbatane"   PERIOD 1

"Dans l'interminable/ ennui de la plaine"
ADES 1, ADES 43, SPOA 27

"L'échelonnement des haies"   DOVER 4

"Écoutez la chanson bien douce"   ADES 1,
ADES 43, HACH 13, SPOA 27

EN SOURDINE. "Calmes dans le demi-jour"
CAED 204, DOVER 4

L'ESPOIR LUIT. "L'espoir luit comme un brin de
paille"   ADES 1, ADES 43, PERIOD 1,
SPOA 27

LES FAUX BEAUX JOURS. "Les faux beaux jours ont
lui tout le jour"   ADES 1, ADES 43,
SPOA 27

GREEN.   HACH 13

IMPRESSION FAUSSE. "Dame souris trotte"
ADES 43, GMS 6, HACH 4

"Je suis venu, calme orphelin"   ADES 1,
ADES 43, CBS 1

KALÉIDOSCOPE. "Dans une rue, au coeur d'une
ville de rêve"   PERIOD 1

LA LUNE BLANCHE.   CAED 204, HACH 13

MANDOLINE. "Les donneurs de sérénades"
PERIOD 1

MON DIEU M'A DIT: MON FILS, IL FAUT M'AIMER.
GMS 7

MON REVE FAMILIER. "Je fais souvent ce rêve
étrange et pénétrant"   ADES 1, ADES 43,
ADES 49, ADES 54, HACH 13, SPOA 9,
SPOA 27

NEVERMORE. "Souvenir, souvenir, que me veux-
tu?"   ADES 1, ADES 43, SPOA 27

PANTOMIME. "Pierrot qui n'a rien d'un Clitandre"   SPOA 9

PROMENADE SENTIMENTALE. "Le couchant dardait ses rayons suprêmes"   ADES 1,
ADES 43, SPOA 27

SEIGNEUR, J'AI PEUR. "Mon ame a moi tressaille
toute"   PERIOD 1

SOLEILS COUCHANTS.   HACH 13

SPLEEN, exc.   ADES 43

STREETS. I.   ADES 43, ADES 49, ADES 54,
HACH 13

Very, Jones. in English.
THE DEAD.   ARGO 11

Vesey, Paul. See Allen, Samuel.

Vian, Boris. 1920. in French.
L' ARRACHE-COEUR.   ADES 56
CHANSON DE LANCELOT.   ADES 56
DERNIÈRE VALSE.   ADES 56
LE DÉSERTEUR.   ADES 56
LES FRÈRES.   ADES 56
JE VOUDRAIS PAS CREVER.   ADES 56
UN JOUR.   ADES 56
PARIS, LE 15 DÉCEMBRE 1999.   ADES 56
VALSE DINGUE.   ADES 56

Viau, Théophile de. 1590. in French.
LETTRE A SON FRERE, exc.   PERIOD 2
LA MAISON DE SYLVIE, exc.   PERIOD 2
LE MATIN. "L'Aurore sur le front du jour"
GMS 6, HACH 9

Vicens, Nimia. in Spanish.
PLEGARIA DESDE LA TERRA.   INSTPR 1

Vicente, Gil. 1465. in Spanish.
"Dicen que me case yo"   SMC 3
"Muy graciosa es la doncella"   CMS 5,
HOLT 1

Victor, Florence. in English.
BERLIN CRISIS. "The dentist drilled for two-and-
one-half hours"   FOLKW 21

Victoria, Laura. in Spanish.
NOCTURNO. "Escucha, tengo miedo"   SMC 7

Viereck, Peter. 1916. in English.
CHILDHOOD. "You cannot bear this silent heav-
enly sadness"   SPOA 102
HOMECOMING. "My seven sons came back from
Indonesia"   SPOA 102
OBSESSED BY HER BEAUTY. "Kind as noon, calm of
unfalling petals"   LIBC 54
POET. "The night he died, earth's images all
came"   SPOA 102
WHICH OF US TWO. "When both are strong with
tenderness too wild"   LIBC 54

Vigny, Alfred de. 1797. in French.
LE BAIN. "C'était pas d'une source à l'onde pure
et sombre"   ADES 41
LA BOUTEILLE À LA MER. "Courage, o faible enfant, de qui ma solitude"   ADES 41,
ADES 54
CHANT DE SUZANNE AU BAIN. "De l'époux bien-
aimé n'entends-je pas la voix"   HACH 11
LA COLÈRE DE SAMSON. "Le désert est muet, la
tente est solitaire"   FOLKW 86
LE COR. "J'aime le son du Cor, le soir, au fond
des bois"   ADES 41, CAED 204, GMA 6
_____, exc. "Éva, j'aimerai tout dans les choses
créés"   DOVER 4
LA FEMME ADULTÈRE. "Mon lit est parfumé
d'aloès et de myrrhe"   ADES 41
LA FRÉGATE 'LA SÉRIEUSE', exc. "Qu'elle étai
belle, ma Frégate"   HACH 23
LA MAISON DU BERGER, exc. "Elle me dit: Je sui
l'impossible théâtre"   SPOA 9
_____. "Si ton coeur, gémissant du poids de
notre vie"   ADES 23, ADES 48, HACH 1
MOÏSE. "Le soleil prolongeait sur la cime de
tentes"   ADES 48, GMS 7, HACH 2
LA MORT DU LOUP. "Les nuages couraient sur la
lune enflammée"   ADES 41, ADES 54
GMS

---

* Recording not available for analysis

PÁLEUR. "Lorsque sur ton beau front riait l'adolescence" ADES 41
LE REPOS. "Une fois, par malheur, si vous avez pris terre" ADES 41
Villaespesa, Francisco. in Spanish.
LAS FUENTES DE GRANADA. "Granada, Granada, de tu poderío" SMC 5
Villalón, Fernando. in Spanish.
LA SAETA. "Quejidos en la noche" SMC 5
Villaroel, Calogero. in Italian.
ALL' ANTICA. CETRA 31
Villaroel, Giuseppe. 1889. in Italian.
MI DISTACCO DA TE STANCO D'AMORE.
CETRA 31
Villegas, Esteban Manuel de. 1589. in Spanish.
AL CÉFIRO. "Dulce vecino de la verde selva" SPOA 37
Villon, François. 1431. in French.
BALLADE. "Je meurs de seuf auprès de la fontaine" FOLKW 84
BALLADE DES DAMES DU TEMPS JADIS. "Dictes moy ou, n'en quel pays" ADES 53, ADES 54, GMS 7, HACH 1, HACH 7, PENN 2, SPOA 9; English CAED 115
BALLADE DES FEMMES DE PARIS. ADES 53
BALLADE DES MENUS PROPOS. "Je congnois bien mouches en let" FOLKW 84
BALLADE DES PENDUS. "Frères humains qui après nous vivez" ADES 53, CBS 1, DOVER 4, FOLKW 84, GMS 8, HACH 1, HACH 7, HACH 54, PENN 2, PERIOD 2
———, exc. "La pluye nous a debuez et lavez" French and English LEARNC 2
BALLADE QUE FIST VILLON A LA REQUESTE DE SA MÈRE POUR PRIER NOSTRE DAME. "Dame du ciel, regente terrienne" FOLKW 84, HACH 1, HACH 7, PERIOD 2
CHANSON. ADES 53
LE DÉBAT DU CUER ET DU CORPS DE VILLON EN FORME DE BALLADE. "Qu'est ce que j'ay!—Ce suis je—Qui?—Ton cuer" FOLKW 84, PENN 2
L'EPITAPHE EN FORME DE BALLADE. See BALLADE DES PENDUS.
LE GRAND TESTAMENT, exc. PENN 2, PERIOD 2
———. "Je plains le temps de ma jeunesse" HACH 1
LE LAIS. ADES 53
LAY OU PLUSTOST RONDEAU. "Mort, j'appelle de ta rigueur" ADES 53, FOLKW 84, HACH 1, HACH 7
LE PETIT TESTAMENT, exc. ADES 53, PENN 2
LES REGRETS DE VILLON, exc. HACH 7
RONDEAU. ADES 53; English EAV 22
ʻioli, Paul. 1944. in English.
EXACTA. "And they're off" WATSHD 5
ʻiorst, Judith. in English.
ADULT EDUCATION. "I have grown to understand that" CAED 181
ALONE. "Alone I could own both sides of the double bed" CAED 181
AMONG OTHER THOUGHTS ON OUR WEDDING ANNIVERSARY. "Over the years" CAED 181
ANTI-HEROINE. "I'd planned to be Heathcliff's Cathy, Lady Brett" CAED 181

THE GOOD DAUGHTER. "She's been a good daughter, my cousin Elaine" CAED 181
THE GOURMET. CAED 181
THE HONEYMOON IS OVER. CAED 181
INFIDELITY. CAED 181
IT'S HARD TO BE HIP OVER THIRTY. CAED 181
MARRIED IS BETTER. CAED 181
MID-LIFE CRISIS. "What am I doing with a mid-life crisis?" CAED 181
NICE BABY. CAED 181
NO MORE BABIES. "The sterilizer's up for grabs" CAED 181
NOTHING BUT THE TRUTH. "I made him swear he'd always tell me nothing but the truth" CAED 181
OPEN HOUSE. "Everyone is coming to our party" CAED 181
SECRET MEETINGS. "Ellie and Marvin" CAED 181
SELF-IMPROVEMENT PROGRAM. "I've finished six pillows in needle point" CAED 181
THE SENSUOUS WOMAN. "I'm giving up nice and becoming a sensuous woman" CAED 181
SEX IS NOT SO SEXY ANYMORE. CAED 181
TRUE LOVE. CAED 181
THE TRUTH. "The truth is" CAED 181
WHERE IS IT WRITTEN? CAED 181
THE WHOLE TRUTH. "He always called her honey and" CAED 181
A WOMEN'S LIBERATION MOVEMENT WOMAN.
CAED 181
Virgil (Publius Vergilius Maro). 70 B.C. in Latin.
AENEID, exc. NACTE 2
———. I, exc. "Arma virumque cano, Troiae qui primus ab oris" FOLKW 100; English FOLKW 102
———. "Hic templum Iunoni ingens Sidonia Dido" FOLKW 100
———. "Olli subridens hominum sator atque deorum" FOLKW 100
———. II Complete. English CMS 17
———. II, exc. "Conticuere omnes intentique ora tenebant" FOLKW 96, FOLKW 100
———. "Dividimus muros et moenia pandimus urbis" FOLKW 100
———. "Non tibi Tyndaridis facies invisa Lacaenae" FOLKW 100
———. "Primus ibi ante omnis, magna comitante" FOLKW 100
———. "Quaerenti et tectis urbis sine fine furenti" FOLKW 100
———. "Quis cladem illius noctis, quis funera fando" FOLKW 100
———. IV, exc. "At regina dolos (quis fallere possit amantem?)" CAED 128, FOLKW 100
———. "Dixerat ille Iovis monitis immota tenebat" FOLKW 100
———. VI, exc. FOLKW 96
———. "Illae antem, paribus quas fulgere cernis in armis" FOLKW 100
———. "Inter quas Phoenissa recens a volnere Dido" FOLKW 100
———. "Portitor has horrendus aquas et flumina servat" FOLKW 100
———. "Tum pater Anchises: animae, quibus altera fato" FOLKW 100

* Recording not available for analysis

Virgil (Publius Vergilius Maro) (continued)

_____. "Venisti tandem, tuaque exspectata
  parenti"   SCHOL 6
GEORGICS, exc. SPOA 13; English ARGO 107,
                                      ARGO 144
Poetry*   CETRA 18, EMC 1
Vittorelli, Iacopo. 1749. in Italian.
Poetry*   CETRA 25
Vittorini, Elio. in Italian.
AUTOBIOGRAFIA IN TEMPO DI GUERRE.   EPIU 1
Vivanco, Luis Felipe. 1907. in Spanish.
"Cada vez mas aparte"   AGUIL 2
CONFIANZA. "Ante la mentira"   AGUIL 2
"Contigo, Tierra de España"   AGUIL 3,
                                       AGUIL 6
CRIATURA DESDE GREDOS,exc. "Lo ajeno al alma"
                                       AGUIL 2
LARGAS LADERAS ARIDAS. "Subir a otro país más
  abierto y más llano"   AGUIL 3
MEMORIA DE LA PLATA. "Si la nieve me ordena"
                                       AGUIL 2
EL OTOÑO, exc. "No le nombramos nunca"
                                       AGUIL 2
"Que bien se lo que quiero"   AGUIL 2
Viviani, Raffaele. in Italian.
'O CANTO D' 'O MANGANIELLO.   CETRA 33
'A CANZONE D' 'A FATICA.   CETRA 33
'A CARAVANA.   CETRA 33
'A CARTA 'E VISITA.   CETRA 33
CORO 'E CAMPAGNUOLE.   CETRA 33
'E CCOSE 'MPRUVVISATE.   CETRA 33
'E ZINGARE.   CETRA 33
EROISMO.   CETRA 29, CETRA 33
FACIMMECE 'A CROCE.   CETRA 33
FATICANNO SOTT' 'E SCHIZZE.   CETRA 33
FRAVECATURE.   CETRA 33
GNASTILLO.   CETRA 33
GUAGLIONE.   CETRA 33
GUERRA E PACE.   CETRA 33
IO QUANNO SENTO 'E DI.   CETRA 33
'A LEGGE.   CETRA 33
'A MANO D'OPERA.   CETRA 33
MAST'ERICO.   CETRA 29
'NGIULINA.   CETRA 33
OJE NINNO.   CETRA 33
OMBRE E ADDORE.   CETRA 33
'O PESCE NICOLO.   CETRA 33
PISCATURE.   CETRA 33
PRIMITIV AMENTE. "Me ne vogl'i a campa
  'mmienzo a 'na terra"   CETRA 29,
                                       CETRA 33
QUANT' AUCIELLE.   CETRA 33
'O RAGGIO 'E SOLE.   CETRA 33
O' SCUPATORE.   CETRA 33
SI OVERO MORE 'O CUORPO.   CETRA 33
SOTTO 'A NU LAMPIONE.   CETRA 29
VEGLIA.   CETRA 33
Vocos-Lescano, Jorge. 1924. in Spanish.
SONETO. "Y qué fuerza de Dios, qué ardiente y
  pura"   FOLKW 80
Vogel, Jakob. in German.
RÖMISCH-DEUTSCHER TON.   CHRIST 30
Vogeler, Sara. in English.
A CHRISTMAS STORY.   WATSHD 10
GUTTERS.   WATSHD 10

Voiture, Vincent. 1598. in French.
À URANIE.   HACH
RONDEAU. "You bid me try" English EAV
Voltaire (François Marie Arouet). 1694.
  French.
EPITAPHE DE MME DU CHATELET.   CAED 2(
ÉPITRE À LA MARQUISE DE CHATELET, exc. "Die
  parle, et le chaos se dissipe à sa voix"
                          CAED 204, FOLKW
POÈME SUR LE DÉSASTRE DE LISBONNE. "O ma
  heureux mortels! O terre déplorable"
                                       ADES
SI VOUS VOULEZ QUE J'AIME ENCORE.   ADES
LES 'VOUS' ET LES 'TU'. "Philis, qu'est devenu
  temps"   DOVER
Poetry*   SPOA 1
Voznesensky, Andrei. 1933. in Russian.
AKHILLESOVO SERDTSE."V dni neslykhanno bo
  vyye"   Russian and English COLUMB
ANTIMIRY. "Zhivet u nas sosed bukashkin"
                                       MONITR
            Russian and English COLUMB
GOIYA. "Ya—Goiya"   MONITR
            Russian and English COLUMB
LOBNAYA BALLADA. "Iz velichestvom para
  vlechsya"
            Russian and English COLUMB
MOTOGONKI PO VERTIKAL 'NOI STENE. "Zavora
  hivaya, Manezha"
            Russian and English COLUMB
NOCHNOY AEROPORT V NYU-IORKE. "Avtoportr
  moi, retorta neona"   MONITR
            Russian and English COLUMB
OSEN' V SIGULDE. "Svisayu s vagonnoi plos
  chadki"   MONITR
            Russian and English COLUMB
PARABOLICHESKAYA BALLADA. "Sud'ba, kak rak
  ta letit po parabole"   MONITR
            Russian and English COLUMB
POYUT NEGRY. "My/ Tamtamy"   MONITR
POZHAR V ARKHITEKTURNOM INSTITUTE. "Pozh
  v Arkhitekturnom!" Russian and English
                                   COLUMB
SIBIRSKIYE BANI. "Bani! Bani! Dveri-khlop"
                                       MONITR
SIDISH' BEREMENNAYA. "Sidish', blednaya"
                                       MONITR
TUMANNYI ULITSA. "Tumannyi prigorod, k
  turman" Russian and English COLUMB
YOU LIVE WITH YOUR AUNT. Ty s tekoi zhivesh
            Russian and English COLUMB
ZAMERLI. "Zavedi mne ladoni za plechi"
            Russian and English COLUMB
Poetry*   TAPES 7, UCALM
Vree, Paul de. 1909. in Flemish.
APRIL BIJ SNEEUW.   LUCHT
Vring, Georg von der. 1889. in German.
NACHTLIED.   ATHENA
Vyazemsky, P. A. 1792. in Russian.
ZIMA. "Zdravstvui, v belom sarafane"   CMS

Wagoner, David. 1926. in English.
AFTER CONSULTING MY YELLOW PAGES.
                                       SCHOL
BUMS AT BREAKFAST. "Daily, the bums sat do
  to eat in our kitchen"   SPOA 1(

---

* Recording not available for analysis

THE CIRCUIT. "My circuit-riding great-grandfather" SCHOL 2, SPOA 105

COME BEFORE HIS COUNTENANCE WITH A JOYFUL LEAPING. "Swivelling flat-soled on the dirt but ready to bound in arches" SPOA 105

EVERY GOOD BOY DOES FINE. SCHOL 2

THE FRUIT OF THE TREE. "With a wall and a ditch between us, I watched the gate-legged dromedary" SPOA 105

THE HOLD-UP. SCHOL 2

HOUSE HUNTING. "The wind has twisted the roof from an old house" SPOA 105

LEAVING SOMETHING BEHIND. SCHOL 2

SONG TO ACCOMPANY THE BEARER OF BAD NEWS. SCHOL 2

A VALEDICTORY TO STANDARD OIL OF INDIANA. SCHOL 2

THE WORDS. SCHOL 2

WORKING AGAINST TIME. SCHOL 2

Wain, John. 1925. in English.

ANECDOTE OF 2 AM. "Why was she lost? my darling said aloud" ARGO 100

AU JARDIN DES PLANTES. "The gorilla lay on his back" SPOA 68

REASON FOR NOT WRITING ORTHODOX NATURE POETRY. "The January sky is deep and calm" ARGO 100

TIME WAS. "A mind ago I took the stones for clay" FOLKW 59A

WILDTRACK, exc. "Engrave the snowflake" ARGO 100

Poetry* JNP 62, JNP 63

Wakoski, Diane. 1937. in English.

THE MECHANIC. "Most men use" EMC 7

Poetry* CASSC 3

Walcott, Derek. 1930. in English.

AIR. "The unheard, omnivorous" ARGO 16

BLUES. "Those five or six young guys" ARGO 16

A CHANGE OF SKIN. "The fog, a sheepdog circling, bared" ARGO 16

THE GLORY TRUMPETER. "Old Eddie's face, wrinkled with river lights" CAED 153

GOD REST YE MERRY GENTLEMEN. "Splitting from Jack Delaney's, Sheridan Square" CAED 153

THE GULF. "The airport coffee tastes less of America" ARGO 16

A LETTER FROM BROOKLYN. "An old lady writes me in a spidery style" CAED 153

MASS MAN. "Through a great lion's head clouded by mange" CAED 153

THE TRAIN. "On one hand, harrowed England" ARGO 16

Waldman, Anne. 1945. in English.

Poetry* GIORNO 1

Walker, Margaret. 1915. in English.

AMOS. "Amos is a Shepherd of suffering sheep" BROADV 13

AMOS (POSTSCRIPT) "From Montgomery to Memphis he marches" BROADV 13

AT THE LINCOLN MONUMENT IN WASHINGTON AUGUST 28, 1963. "There they stand together, like Moses standing with Aaron" BROADV 13

BAD-MAN STAGOLEE. "That Stagolee was an all-right lad" FOLKW 1, FOLKW 46

A BALLAD FOR PHILLIS WHEATLEY. "Pretty little black girl" FOLKW 44

THE BALLAD OF THE FREE. "Bold Nat Turner by the blood of God" BROADV 13, FOLKW 44

BALLAD OF THE HOPPY-TOAD. "Ain't been on Market Street for nothing" BROADV 13, FOLKW 44

BIG JOHN HENRY. "This here's a tale of a sho-nuff man" FOLKW 1, FOLKW 46

BIRMINGHAM. "With the last whippoorwill call of evening" BROADV 13

DARK BLOOD. "There were bizarre beginnings in old lands for the making of me" FOLKW 46

DELTA. "I am a child of the valley" FOLKW 46

ELEGY. "Strange summer sun shines round our globe of circumstance" BROADV 13

EPITAPH FOR MY FATHER. "Jamaica is an Island full of Bays" FOLKW 44

FOR ANDY GOODMAN—MICHAEL SCHWERNER—AND JAMES CHANEY. "Three faces/ mirrored" BROADV 13

FOR MALCOLM X. "All you violated ones with gentle hearts" BROADV 13

FOR MY PEOPLE. "For my people everywhere singing their slave songs repeatedly" FOLKW 1, FOLKW 44

GIRL HELD WITHOUT BAIL. "I like it here just fine" BROADV 13

"Gus, the lineman" FOLKW 46

HARRIET TUBMAN. "Dark is the face of Harriet" FOLKW 44

HOSEA. "Hear this prayer from a Plaquemines jail" BROADV 13

"How many silent centuries sleep in my sultry veins" BROADV 13

ISAIAH. "Isaiah was a man of the court" BROADV 13

JACKSON, MISSISSIPPI. "City of tense and stricken faces" BROADV 13, FOLKW 44

JEREMIAH. "Jeremiah, prophet of Jerusalem" BROADV 13

JOEL. "Joel, that young prophet-son of Pethuel" BROADV 13

KISSIE LEE. "Toughest gal I ever did see" FOLKW 1, FOLKW 46

"Long John Nelson and Sweetie Pie" FOLKW 46

MICAH. "Micah was a young man of the people" BROADV 13

NOW. "Time to wipe away the slime" BROADV 13

OCTOBER JOURNEY. "Traveler take heed for journeys undertaken in the dark of the year" ARGO 17

OLD MOLLEY MEANS. "Old Molley Means was a hag and a witch" FOLKW 1, FOLKW 46

"Oxford is a legend" BROADV 13

POPPA CHICKEN. "Poppa was a sugah daddy" FOLKW 46

PROPHETS FOR A NEW DAY. "As the word came to prophets of old" BROADV 13

SIT-INS. "You were our first brave ones to defy their dissonance of hate" BROADV 13

* Recording not available for analysis

Walker, Margaret (continued)

SORROW HOME. "My roots are deep in southern life; deeper than John Brown" FOLKW 46

SOUTHERN SONG. "I want my body bathed again by southern suns" FOLKW 46

STREET DEMONSTRATION. "We're hoping to be arrested" BROADV 13

TEACHER. "The teacher was a bad man" FOLKW 46

TWO-GUN BUSTER AND TRIGGER SLIM. "Two-Gun Buster was a railroad han'" FOLKW 46

WE HAVE BEEN BELIEVERS. "We have been believers believing in the black gods of an old land" FOLKW 44

YALLUH HAMMUH. "Old Yalluh Hammuh were a guy" FOLKW 46
Poetry* EAV 2

Wallace, Rudy. in English.

FUNERAL. "You head" WATSHD 10

HERE NOW. "Ju ju metamorphosis" WATSHD 10

MOTHER NATURE'S SON. "Shach, shach, maka" WATSHD 10

WITHOUT WORDS. "Let me talk to you" WATSHD 10

Waller, Edmund. 1606. in English.
"Go, lovely rose" ARGO 37, CAED 186, CMS 13, EAV 22, SPOA 84

ON A GIRDLE. "That which her slender waist confined" LION 2

Wallin, Johan Olaf. 1779. in Swedish.
VAR AR EN VAN. GRAM 3

Walsh, William. 1663. in English.
RIVALS. "Of all the torments, all the cares" ARGO 47, BRITAM 2

Walters, Bryan. in English.

ALL THAT REMAINS. ARGO 145
BLIND JOHN. ARGO 145
THE BONKS. ARGO 145
CITY IN TERROR. ARGO 145
THE FAREWELL. ARGO 145
FIGHT THE GOOD ... ARGO 145
FROM A FEAR OF THE DARK. ARGO 132
I ASK YOU. ARGO 145
IN THIS YOUR COUNTRY SLEEP. ARGO 132
INCIDENT. ARGO 145
A MOUSE IN THE HOUSE OF NORMAN MACCAIG. ARGO 132
ON WENLOCK EDGE. ARGO 145
RHIANNON. ARGO 145
SONG OF THE EARTH. ARGO 145
STONES. ARGO 145
TELL ME, IF YOU KNOW. ARGO 132
TO MAKE YOU THINK. ARGO 132
TROUBLE IN A TAVERN. ARGO 145
TRUTH. ARGO 145
WAVES: PLUSCULUS. ARGO 132
THE WILD ANCESTRAL CROW. ARGO 145
THE WIND. ARGO 145
WOMAN WITH A PRAM. ARGO 145

Walther von der Vogelweide. 1160. in Middle High German.
"Allerêst lebe ich mir werde'" CHRIST 8

ELEGIE. "O weh, ihr langen Jahre, wohin entschwandet ihr?"
Modern German SPOA 5

"Frô welt, ir sult dem wirte sagen" CHRIST 8

"Ich hân min lehen, al die werlt, ich han min lehen" CHRIST 8

"Ich hôrte ein wazzer diezen" CHRIST 8

"Ich sach mit minen ougen" CHRIST 8

"Ich sâz uf einem steine" CHRIST 8

"Ir reinen wip, ir werden man" CHRIST 8

"Ir sult sprechen willekomen" CHRIST 8

"Nemt frowe disen kranz" CHRIST 8

"Owê war sint verswunden alliu miniu jar" CHRIST 8

"So die bluomen ûz dem grase dringent" CHRIST 8

"Uns hât der winter geschât über al" CHRIST 8

"Unter den Linden" CHRIST 8; Modern German DOVER 1

"Von Rôme vogt, von pülle künec" CHRIST 8

Wang Han. 710. in Chinese.
LYANG JOU TSZ. "Pu tan mei jyou ye gwang bei" FOLKW 76

Wang Jyan. 751. in Chinese.
SYIN JYA NYANG. "San r ru chu sya" FOLKW 76

Wang Wei. 699. in Chinese.
DZA SHR. "Jyun dz gu syang lai" FOLKW 76

Wanley, Nathaniel. in English.
ROYALL PRESENTS. "The off'rings of the Easterne kings of old" ARGO 47

Ward, Jerry. in English.
AN ANGER AS MEMORY. "Rich real moss mingled earth" WATSHD 5

CRUCIFIXION. "Passion has three acts" WATSHD 5

DUES. "I plays a mean guitar" WATSHD 5

TRUEBLOOD. "Trueblood, he never heard of incest" WATSHD 5

Warren, Robert Penn. 1905. in English.
AFTER NIGHT FLIGHT SON REACHES BEDSIDE OF ALREADY UNCONSCIOUS FATHER, WHOSE RIGHT HAND LIFTS IN A SPASMODIC GESTURE, AS THOUGH TRYING TO MAKE CONTACT: 1955. "In Time's concatenation and" CARIL 2

ARROGANT LAW. "Have you crouched with rifle in woods in Autumn" CARIL 2

BEAR TRACK PLANTATION. "Two things a man built for, killing and you-know-what" CARIL 2

BEARDED OAKS. "The oaks, how subtle and marine" LIBC 54, SPOA 9

THE CHILD NEXT DOOR. LIBC 5

CLEARLY ABOUT YOU. "Whoever you are, this poem is clearly about you" CARIL 2

COUNTRY BURYING (1919). "A thousand times you've seen that scene" CARIL 2

A DEAD LANGUAGE: CIRCA 1885. "Father dead land lost, Stepmother haggard with kids" CARIL 2

DEBATE: QUESTION, QUARRY, DREAM. "Asking what, asking what?—all a boy's afternoon" CARIL 2

DRAGON COUNTRY: TO JACOB BOEHME. "This is the dragon's country, and these his own streams" CARIL 2

---

* Recording not available for analysis

FOUNDING FATHERS. "They were human, they suffered, wore long black coat and gold watch chain" CARIL 21

FOX-FIRE: 1956. "Years later, I find the old grammar, yellowed. Night" CARIL 21

THE GARDEN. "How kind, how secret, now the sun" CARIL 21

GULL'S CRY. LIBC 53

HARVARD '61: BATTLE FATIGUE. "I didn't mind dying—it wasn't that at all" CARIL 21

"In the turpitude of time" CARIL 21

THE LETTER ABOUT MONEY. "Having accepted the trust so many years back" CARIL 21

MEXICO IS A FOREIGN COUNTRY. 1. "Butterflies, over the map of Mexico" HARVOC 12

———. 4. "The mango on the mango tree" HARVOC 12

MONOLOGUE AT MIDNIGHT. "Among the pines we ran and called" HARVOC 12

ORIGINAL SIN. "Nodding, its great head rattling like a gourd" CARIL 21

PURSUIT. LIBC 9, LIBC 32

TERROR. "Not picnics or pageants or improbable" COLPIX 1, LIBC 9, LIBC 32, SPOA 98

TIBERIUS ON CAPRI. "All is nothing, nothing all" CARIL 21

TO A LITTLE GIRL, ONE YEAR OLD, IN RUINED FORTRESS, exc. "To a place of ruined stone we brought you" LIBC 54

A VISION. "Out of the woods where pollen is a powder of gold" CARIL 21

Poetry* APPL 11, CASSC A

Warton, Joseph. 1722. in English.

THE ENTHUSIAST, exc. "Ye green-rob'd Dryads, oft at dusky eve" ARGO 50, CAED 203

Warton, Thomas (the elder). 1688. in English.

RETIREMENT, AN ODE, exc. "On beds of daisies idly laid" CAED 203

Warton, Thomas (the younger). 1728. in English.

VERSES ON SIR JOSHUA REYNOLD'S PAINTED WINDOW. "Ah, stay thy treacherous hand, forbear to trace" ARGO 50

Watkins, Vernon P. 1906. in English.

BALLAD OF CULVER'S HOLE. "What feet are heard about these rocks" ARGO 92, CARIL 14

BALLAD OF THE ROUGH SEA. "I like the smell of the wind, the sniff" CARIL 14

THE BROKEN SEA, exc. "My lamp that was lit every night has burnt a hole in the shade" CARIL 14

BURIED LIGHT. "What are the light and wind to me" ARGO 92

THE COLLIER. "When I was born on Amman hill" CAED 126

DISCOVERIES. "The poles are flying where the two eyes set" LIBC 37, LIBC 38

ELEGY ON THE HEROINE OF CHILDHOOD. "Who flung this world? What gangs proclaimed a truce?" CARIL 14

GREAT NIGHTS RETURNING. "Great nights returning, midnight's constellations" ARGO 92

THE HEALING OF THE LEPER. "O, have you seen the leper healed" LIBC 37, LIBC 38

THE HERON. "The cloud-backed Heron will not move" FOLKW 65, JUP 1

MOONRISE. "Dew is falling now, the daylight is spent" ARGO 92

MUSIC OF COLOURS, WHITE BLOSSOM. "White blossom, white, white shell; the Nazarene" CARIL 14

ODE TO SWANSEA. "Bright town, tossed by waves of time" CARIL 14

PEACE IN THE WELSH HILLS. "Calm in the landscape when the storm has passed" CARIL 14

SEMELE. "I saw you come in a swan's shape" CARIL 14

THE SPRING. "Dark the words break" CARIL 14

SWEDENBORG'S SKULL. "Note this survivor, bearing the mark of the violator" CARIL 14

TALIESIN AND THE SPRING OF VISION. "I tread the sand at the sea's edge, sand of the hour-glass" CARIL 14

"Touch with your fingers" ARGO 92

THE TRIBUTARY SEASONS. "I can discern at last how grew" CARIL 14

Poetry* APPL 12, BBC 1, LIST 14

Watson, Robert. in English.

LINES FOR A PRESIDENT. "You could not stop the snow" FOLKW 21

Watts, Isaac. in English.

THE SLUGGARD. CAED 203

Watts-Dunton, Theodore. 1832. in English.

WASSAIL CHORUS AT THE MERMAID TAVERN. "Christmas knows a merry, merry place" ARGO 83, SPOA 41

Webb, Harri. 1920. in English.

DUFFRYN WOODS. "In perfect equipoise a moment" ARGO 152

EPIL Y FILIAST. "Already something of a stranger now" ARGO 152

ISRAEL. "Listen, Wales. Here was a people" ARGO 152

Weber, Richard. in English.

THE HUNT. "Out of the old cold dark" SPOA 68

Poetry* JNP 64

Weber, Ron. in English.

THE HUNT. "You stalk it patiently" WATSHD 8

NOTICE OF EVICTION. "I have locked myself out" WATSHD 8

"When fame arrives in a limousine" WATSHD 8

Webster, H. in English.

STREET GANG. "Everywhere they are waiting" SPOA 68

Webster, John. 1580. in English.

THE DEVIL'S LAWCASE, exc. NETS TO CATCH THE WIND. "All the flowers of the spring" ARGO 31, LIST 1

THE WHITE DEVIL, exc. CORNELIA'S SONG. "Call for the Robin-Red-Breast and the wren" ARGO 35

———. "My soule, like to a ship" LIST 1

Weckherlin, Georg Rudolf. 1584. in German.

KLAG. CHRIST 22

DER 90 PSALM. CHRIST 29

Wedekind, Frank. 1864. in German.

AUF EIGENEN FÜSSEN—DONNERWETTER! "In der Jugend frühster Pracht" DEUTGR 29

* Recording not available for analysis

Wedekind, Frank (continued)

CHRISTINE. "Bessern soll ich mich?—O Himmel"   DEUTGR 29

ERDGEIST. "Greife wacker nach der Sünde"
                                                DEUTGR 29

GRAND ÉCART (TANZLIED) "Sind die Muskeln straff gespannt"   DEUTGR 29

DIE HUNDE (ELEGIE) "Es waren einmal zwei Hunde"   DEUTGR 29

LIEBESANTRAG. "Lass uns mit dem Feuer spielen"   DEUTGR 29

MEIN LIESCHEN. "Mein Lieschen trägt keine Hosen"   DEUTGR 29

MORGENSTIMMUNG. "Leise schleich ich wie auf Eiern"   DEUTGR 29

DER TANTENMÖRDER. "Ich hab meine Tante geschlachtet"   DEUTGR 29

VERGÄNGLICHKEIT. "Streck deine Beine, mein hübscher Genoss"   DEUTGR 29

Wei Jwang. 855. in Chinese.

NYU GWAN DZ. "Dz wo ye ye ban" FOLKW 76

Weinheber, Josef. 1892. in German.

AN DEN MOND. "Du mir am Himmel"
                                                ATHENA 6

WIEGENLIED.   CHRIST 11

Poetry*   CHRIST 4

Weiss, Theodore Russell. 1916. in English.

A CANTICLE. "And, Silence, matter still"
                                                CARIL 12

THE CHANGE. "The change is too complete"
                                                CARIL 12

A COMMONPLACE. "As the silly shepherds"
                                                CARIL 12

THE DANCE CALLED DAVID. "How could I know"
                                                CARIL 12

AN EGYPTIAN PASSAGE. "Beside me she sat, hand hooked and hovering"   CARIL 12

THE FIRE AT ALEXANDRIA. "Imagine it! A Sophocles, complete"   CARIL 12

THE GOTHIC TALE. "Framed by our window, skaters, winding"   CARIL 12

HOMECOMING. "Like that old timer who has kept by me"   CARIL 12

THE HOOK. "The student, lost in raucousness"
                                                CARIL 12

HOUSE OF FIRE. "To burn is surely bad, to be"
                                                CARIL 12

A LESSER PROPHET. "And here the sun began once more"   CARIL 12

PANORAMIC SUE.   CARIL 12

A SUM OF DESTRUCTIONS.   CARIL 12

TO PENNY WHEN SHE COMES OF READING AGE. "Her eyes are full of winding distance"
                                                CARIL 12

A TRIP THROUGH YUCATAN. "You have, in a sense"
                                                CARIL 12

Weissenburg, Otto von. in German.

MARIA MAGDALENA AM GRABE DES HEILANDS.
                                                CHRIST 13

VATER UNSER.   CHRIST 13

Welles, Winifred. 1893. in English.

GREEN MOTH. "The night the green moth came for me"   BOWMAR 1

QUESTIONS FOR A NEW MOON. "Is it Cinderella's slipper"   HARB 4

STOCKING FAIRY. "In the hole of a heel of an ol brown stocking"   CMS

A TREE AT DUSK. "With secrets in their eyes, th blue-winged hours"   CAED 16

Wellman, John. in English.

BATRACHOMYOMACHIA. "That part of the coun try"   WATSHD 1

A CLASSICAL LOCATION. "Her motion was clar ty"   WATSHD 1

A FAREWELL TO MAGIC. "Triple sphere of fo fire"   WATSHD 1

FOR THE SAKE OF SOME BEING. "We live here t gether"   WATSHD 1

MANTICES.   WATSHD 1

SECRET EXPEDITION TO THE SOUTH. "I want to se the world"   WATSHD 1

Wen Ting-Yueh. in Chinese.

KANG LAU GEE. "Yo lo hrurn"   SCHOL

Werfel, Franz. 1890. in German.

AN DEN LESER. "Mein einziger Wunsch ist, Di oh Mensch"   DOVER

ELTERNLIED. "Kinder laufen fort"   FISCH

LÄCHELN ATMEN SCHREITEN. "Schöpfe du, trag du, halte"   FISCH

DER SCHÖNE STRAHLENDE MENSCH SPRICHT. "Di Freunde, die mit mir sich unterhalten"
                                                FISCH

DER WANDERNDE KNIET. "Gib nur, dass ich wein en kann"   FISCH

West, Graeme. in English.

LETTER TO HIS MOTHER.   ARGO 8

Weston, Mildred. in English.

CENTRAL PARK TOURNEY.   SCHOL

Wevill, David. 1937. in English.

THE FOX AT ARLES.   ARGO 9

Whalen, Philip. 1923. in English.

BIG HIGH SONG FOR SOMEBODY. "F/ Train/ abs lutely stoned"   WORLDP

HOMAGE TO ROBERT CREELEY. "What I thought
                                                EVERG

HOMAGE TO RODIN. "Thinker/ in the classic"
                                        CENTCA 1, NET

THE ROAD-RUNNER. "Thin long bird"
                                                EVERG

SMALL TANTRIC SERMON. "The release itself"
                                                EVERG

Whan Chei. 740. in Chinese.

STONE FISH LAKE. "I loved you dearly, Ston Fish Lake"   English ARGO 82; SPOA 4

Wheatley, Phillis. 1753. in English.

HIS EXCELLENCY GENERAL WASHINGTON. "Cele tial choir, enthron'd in realms" FOLKW 4

Poetry*   CASSC 12

Wheelock, John Hall. 1886. in English.

AFTERNOON: AMAGANSETT BEACH, exc.

_____. "Glory—glory to God in the highest— and on earth Glory"   LIBC 4

_____. "Sea-wind and the sea's irregula rhythm"   LIBC 4

THE BIG I. "A bird with a big eye"   SPOA 8

BONAC. "This is enchanted country, lies under spell"   LIBC 4

DIALECTICS OF FLIGHT. "To get off the groun has always been difficult"   LIBC 4
                                                LIBC 4

THE DIVINE INSECT. "Already it's late summe Sun-bathers go"   SPOA 9

---

* Recording not available for analysis

THE FISH-HAWK. "On the large highway of the ample air that flows"   LIBC 45, LIBC 46

THE GARDENER. "Father, whom I knew well for forty years"   LIBC 46

THE HERRING-GULL. "Run seaward, launch upon the air, and sound your desolate cry"   LIBC 45, LIBC 46

THE HOUSE IN THE GREEN WELL. "You came to it through wild country"   SPOA 92

IT IS FINISHED. "There was a trampling of horses from Calvary"   LIBC 45, LIBC 46

MEDITATION. "I live in an old house on a dark star"   LIBC 45, LIBC 46

WOOD-THRUSH. "Behind the wild bird's throat"   LIBC 45

Poetry*   FML 1, JNP 65

Whistler, Laurence. 1912. in English.

FLOWERS FOR HER GRAVE. "The common places of the string"   ARGO 93

A FORM OF EPITAPH. "Name in block letters"   ARGO 93

THE GUEST. "Bill the pillows plump as mushrooms"   ARGO 93

NOW THERE IS ONLY FOLLOWING. "Now there is only following to be done"   ARGO 93

Whitbread, Thomas. 1931. in English.

NOVEMBER 25, 1963. "The assassination of the President"   FOLKW 21

White, Elwyn B. 1899. in English.

DISTURBERS OF THE PEACE. "The cows lie sweetly by the pond"   RCA 10

SPRINGTIME CROSSTOWN EPISODE IN FOUR-TIME. "As I was crossing Chatham Bar"   RCA 10

VILLAGE REVISITED. "In the days of my youth, in the days of my youth"   RCA 10

Whitman, Walt. 1819. in English.

AUTUMN RIVULETS, exc. "I was looking a long while for intentions"   RCA 5

_____. "Miracles/ why, who makes much of a miracle" CAED 112, EAV 15, HOUGHT 5, SINGER 5, SPOA 31, UCOL 3

_____. "O Star of France"   RCA 5

_____. PASSAGE TO INDIA. "Singing my days"   RCA 5

_____. "There was a child went forth every day"   ARGO 11, RCA 8, LIBC 31

_____. TO A FOIL'D EUROPEAN REVOLUTIONAIRE. "Courage, yet, my brother or my sister"   RCA 5

_____. "The past and present wilts"   LIBC 31

_____. "Thou, America"   LIBC 31

BIRDS OF PASSAGE, exc. A BROADWAY PAGEANT. "Over the Western sea hither from Niphon come"   RCA 5

_____. FRANCE. "O Liberty! O mate for me!"   DECCA 13, RCA 5

_____. "Pioneers! O Pioneers!"   CAED 108

BY BLUE ONTARIO'S SHORE, exc. "By blue Ontario's shore" CAED 108, CMS 14, LIBC 31, RCA 5, SINGER 1

BY THE ROADSIDE, exc. A BOSTON BALLAD. "To get betimes in Boston town I rose this morning early"   JNP 91

_____. EUROPE. "Suddenly out of its stale and drowsy lair, the lair of slaves"   RCA 5

_____. "When I heard the learn'd astronomer"   CAED 29, CAED 185, EMC 2, HOUGHT 3, POETRY 3, LION 2, UCOL 3

CALAMUS, exc. "For you, O Democracy"   RCA 5

_____. "I hear it was charged against me that I sought to destroy institutions"   SPOA 69

_____. "I saw in Louisiana a live-oak growing"   LIBC 31, SPOA 31, SPOA 69, SPOA 75

_____. "No labor-saving machine"   CAED 108, LIBC 31

CHILDREN OF ADAM, exc. "From pent-up aching rivers"   SPOA 54

_____. "The full spread pride of man"   STANY 1

_____. "I knew a man a common farmer"   CAED 108, SPOA 54, STANY 1

_____. "The love of the body of man"   STANY 1

_____. "A man's body at auction"   STANY 1

_____. "Oh, my body! I dare not desert"   STANY 1

_____. "This is the female form"   STANY 1

_____. "A woman waits for me"   STANY 1

_____. "A woman's body at auction, she too is not herself, she is the teeming mother of mothers"   SPOA 54

CROSSING BROOKLYN FERRY, exc. "Flood-tide below me! I see you face to face"   CAED 108

DAREST THOU NOW O SOUL. "Darest thou now o soul walk out with me"   SPOA 31

DRUM TAPS, exc.   LIBC 31

_____. "A march in the ranks hard-prest and the road unknown"   CAED 29, CAED 194

_____. "A sight in camp in the daybreak gray and dim"   CAED 194

_____. "An army corps on the march"   CAED 194

_____. "As toilsome I wander'd Virginia's woods to the music of rustling leaves"   CMS 14, SPOA 31

_____. "Beat! Beat! drums—blow! bugles! blow"   CAED 194, EMC 2, LIBC 31, RCA 4

_____. "Bivouac on a mountain side"   CAED 194

_____. "By the bivouac's fitful flame"   CAED 194

_____. "Cavalry crossing a ford" CAED 194, HOUGHT 4

_____. "Come up from the fields, Father"   SPOA 31, SPOA 75

_____. "Eighteen sixty-one"   CAED 194, LIBC 31

_____. "Ethiopia saluting the colors"   CAED 194

_____. "From Paumanok starting I fly like a bird"   CAED 194

_____. "Give me the splendid silent sun with all his beams full dazzling"   CAED 29, EAV 14, SPOA 69

_____. "Lo, Victress on the peaks"   CAED 194

_____. "Long, too long America" CAED 194, RCA 5

* Recording not available for analysis

Whitman, Walt (continued)

———. "Not youth pertains to me"
CAED 194

———. "O tan-faced prairie-boy" CAED 194

———. "Race of veterans—race of victors!"
CAED 194

———. "Reconciliation/ word over all"
HOUGHT 5

———. TO A CERTAIN CIVILIAN. "Did you ask dulcet rhymes from me?"   RCA 5

———. "Vigil strange I kept on the field one night"   CAED 194, EMC 2, LIBC 31, POETRY 3, RCA 5

———. "World take good notice, silver stars fading"   CAED 194

———. THE WOUND DRESSER. "An old man bending I come among new faces"   LIBC 31, SPOA 69

———. "Year that trembled and reel'd beneath me"   CAED 194

FROM NOON TO STARRY NIGHT, exc. A CLEAR MIDNIGHT. "This is thy hour O Soul"
CAED 108

———. MANNAHATTA. "I was asking for something specific"   EAV 15

———. "The old face of the mother of many children"   CAED 29

———. OLD WAR DREAMS. "In Midnight sleep of many a face"   CAED 194

———. TO A LOCOMOTIVE IN WINTER. "Thee for my recitative"   CAED 29, EAV 22, HOUGHT 5

GOOD-BYE MY FANCY, exc. "Good-bye, my fancy/ Farewell"   CAED 29, EMC 2, LIBC 31, POETRY 3, SPOA 31, SPOA 75

HALCYON DAYS. "Not from successful love alone"   LION 2

"I saw the vision of armies"   VAN 3

INSCRIPTIONS, exc.   LIBC 31

———. I HEAR AMERICA SINGING. "I hear America singing"   CAED 29, CAED 195, DECCA 13, EAV 10, EAV 14, EMC 2, HOUGHT 2, LIBC 31, POETRY 3, SPOA 31, SPOA 69, SPOA 75, UCOL 3

———. "One's-self I sing, a simple separate person"   EMC 2, POETRY 3

———. "Poets to come! Orators, singers, musicians to come"   EMC 2, POETRY 3, WORLDP 1

"I sit and look out upon all the sorrows of the world"   LION 2

"It is enough to touch anyone"   STANY 1

MEMORIES OF PRESIDENT LINCOLN, exc.
LIBC 31

———. "Hush'd be the camps today"
CAED 194, EMC 2, POETRY 3, SPOA 69

———. O CAPTAIN! MY CAPTAIN! "O Captain! My Captain! our fearful trip is done"
AUDIA 2, CAED 30, CAED 194, CAED 195, COLUMB 6, DECCA 4, DECCA 7, DECCA 13, EAV 15, HARC 2, HOUGHT 1, LIST 3, LIST 23, RCA 8, SPOA 69, UCOL 3

———. "This dust was once the man"
CAED 194, SPOA 69

———. WHEN LILACS LAST IN THE DOORYARD BLOOMED. "When lilacs last in the dooryard bloomed"   CAED 30, CAED 194, DECCA 13, EAV 10, HARB 6, LIBC 31, LIST 23, POETRY 3, SPOA 69, THEAL 3, UARIZ 1

———, exc. "Lo, body and soul—this land"
CAED 160

NAKED SWIMMERS AND HORSEMEN.   STANY 1

"On the beach at night"   LION 2

"Once I pass'd through a populous city imprinting my brain for future"   LION 2

RECONCILIATION. "Word over all, beautiful as the shy"   LION 2

THE SACRED ONES.   STANY 1

SALUT AU MONDE, exc "O take my hand Walt Whitman"   LIBC 31

SANDS AT SEVENTY, exc. ABRAHAM LINCOLN. "Today from each and all"   CAED 194

———. "Thanks in old age—thanks ere I go"
LIBC 31

SEA-DRIFT, exc. "After the sea-ship, after the whistling winds"   CAED 108

———. "On the beach at night"   LIBC 31

OUT OF THE CRADLE ENDLESSLY ROCKING. "Out of the cradle endlessly rocking"   CAED 29, CMS 12, EMC 2, LIVLAN 1, POETRY 3, SPOA 54

———. "Patrolling Barnegat/ wild, wild the storm"   HOUGHT 3

———. TO THE MAN-OF-WAR BIRD. "Thou who hast slept all night upon the storm" RCA 5

———. "The world below the brine"
CAED 108

THE SLEEPERS, exc.   SPOA 69

———. "The sleepers are very beautiful as they lie unclothed"   CAED 29

SONG OF MYSELF, exc.   AUDIA 2, EAV 14, LIBC 31, LION 2

———. "A child said, What is the grass"
ARGO 11, CAED 29, CAED 185, EMC 2, HOUGHT 5, LIST 3

———. "Have you reckoned a thousand acres much?"   POETRY 3

———. "I am the poet of the body"   LIST 3

———. "I believe a leaf of grass is no less than the journey-work of the stars"   LIST 3
RCA 5

———. "I believe in you my soul, the other I am must not abase itself to you"   ARGO 11

———. I CELEBRATE MYSELF. "I celebrate myself, and I sing myself"   ARGO 11, CAED 29, LIST 3, POETRY 3

———. "I have heard what the talkers are talking"   POETRY 3

———. "I think I could turn and live with animals, they are so placid and self-contain'd"   CAED 29, CMS 14, RCA 5, SCHOL 8

———. "Now I will do nothing but listen"
CAED 108

———. "The spotted hawk swoops by and accuses me, he complains of my gab and my loitering"   CAED 29

———. "Twenty-eight young men bathe by the shore"   CAED 30

———. "Who goes there? hankering, gross, mystical, nude"   CAED 29

* Recording not available for analysis

SONG OF THE BROAD-AXE, exc. "I see the European headsman"   LIBC 31
————. "What do you think endures?"
                                        LIBC 31
SONG OF THE EXPOSITION, exc.   LIBC 31
SONG OF THE OPEN ROAD, exc. "Afoot and light-hearted I take to the open road"
                                CAED 30, RCA 5
A SONG OF THE ROLLING EARTH, exc. "A song of the rolling earth, and of words according"
                                       CAED 108
————, "Youth, day, old age, and night"
                                      HOUGHT 4
SONGS OF PARTING, exc.   LIBC 31
————. "Now finale to the shore" CAED 108
————. SO LONG. "To conclude, I announce what comes after me"   RCA 5
————. "Years of the modern! years of the unperform'd"   RCA 5, LIBC 31
WHISPERS OF HEAVENLY DEATH, exc. "A noiseless patient spider I marked" EAV 15, EAV 22, LION 2, SPOA 31
————. "The last invocation/ at the last, tenderly"   EAV 14, EMC 2, POETRY 3
Poetry*   CMS 20, EAV 10, PRENT 2, SPOA 116, VERVE 2

Whittemore, Reed. 1919. in English.
A DAY WITH LITERATURE.   NACTE 14
THE HIGH SCHOOL BAND. "On warm days in September the high school band"   SCHOL 8
THE POPULAR MAGAZINES. "The popular magazines line the shelves of the drugstores"
                                      NACTE 14
Poetry*   WATSHD 29

Whittier, John Greenleaf. 1807. in English.
ALL'S WELL. "The clouds which rise with thunder"   SPOA 31
BARBARA FRIETCHIE. "Up from the meadows rich with corn"   CAED 98, CAED 135, CAED 185, CAED 195, DECCA 4, DECCA 13, EAV 9, LIBC 23, RCA 8, SPOA 53, SPOA 75
THE BAREFOOT BOY. "Blessings on thee, little man" CAED 135, CAED 195, COLUMB 6, EAV 14, SPOA 53, SPOA 75
THE DEAD SHIP OF HARPSWELL. "What flecks the outer gray beyond"   SPOA 53
THE ETERNAL GOODNESS. "O Friends! with whom my feet have trod"   SPOA 53
ICHABOD. "So fallen, so lost! the light withdrawn"   EAV 14, SPOA 53
LAUS DEO. "It is done"   SPOA 53
MAUDE MULLER. "Maude Muller on a summer's day"   CAED 135, EAV 20, SPOA 53
RESPONSE. "Beside that milestone where the level sun"   EAV 15
SKIPPER IRESON'S RIDE. "Of all the rides since the birth of time"   CAED 135, EAV 20, SPOA 53, SPOA 75
SNOWBOUND, exc. "The sun that brief December day" ARGO 11, AUDIA 2, CAED 135, CAED 185, CAED 195, EAV 14, HOUGHT 5, LIST 3, LIST 17, SPOA 53
————. THE HEARTH FIRE.   HARC 2
SUNSET ON THE BEARCAMP. "A gold fringe on the purpling hem"   EAV 15

TELLING THE BEES. "Here is the place"
                        CAED 135, EAV 15, SPOA 53
TO OLIVER WENDELL HOLMES 8TH MO. 29TH, 1892. "Among the thousands who, with hail and cheer"   SPOA 53
THE TRAILING ARBUTUS. "I wandered lonely where the pine-trees made"   EAV 14
Poetry*   EAV 9, LIST 12, LIST 17
Widdemer, Margaret. 1895. in English.
THE FAITHLESS FLOWERS. "I went this morning down to where the Johnny-Jump-Ups grow"
                                       CAED 164
Wieners, John. 1934. in English.
COCAINE.   NET 5
A POEM FOR PAINTERS. "Our age bereft of nobility"   NET 5
Poetry*   JNP 66
Wilbur, Richard. 1921. in English.
ADVICE TO A PROPHET. "When you come, as you soon must, to the streets of our city"
                        CAED 115, LIBC 40, NET 7
AFTER THE LAST BULLETINS. "After the last bulletins the windows darken"   CAED 115, SPOA 19
ALL THESE BIRDS. "Agreed that all these birds"   CAED 115
ALTITUDES. "Look up into the dome"
                           CAED 115, SPOA 19
APOLOGY. "A word sticks in the wind's throat"
                                       CAED 115
THE ASPEN AND THE STREAM. "Beholding element, in whose pure eye"   CAED 115
BALLADE FOR THE DUKE OF ORLEANS. "Flailed from the heart of water in a bow"
                                       CAED 115
A BAROQUE WALL-FOUNTAIN IN THE VILLA SCIARRA. "Under the bronze crown"   CAED 115, LIBC 1, SPOA 19
THE BEACON. "Founded on rock and facing the night-fouled sea"   SPOA 19
A BLACK NOVEMBER TURKEY. "Nine white chickens come"   SPOA 19
COMPLAINT. "Why is it that whenever I talk with the duchess"   CAED 115
DIGGING FOR CHINA. "Far enough down is China, somebody said"   SPOA 19, SPOA 103
DRIFTWOOD. "In greenwoods once these relics must have known"   FOLKW 25
FOR THE NEW RAILWAY STATION IN ROME. "Those who said God is praised"   SPOA 19, SPOA 103
A GRASSHOPPER. "But for a brief"   CAED 115
JOHN CHRYSOSTOM. "He who had gone a beast"   SPOA 19
JUGGLER. "A ball will bounce, but less and less"
                                       LIBC 40
JUNK. "An axe angles"   LIBC 1
THE LILACS. "Those laden lilacs"   CAED 115
LOOKING INTO HISTORY. "Five soldiers fixed by Mathew Brady's eye" SPOA 19, SPOA 103
LOVE CALLS US TO THE THINGS OF THIS WORLD. "The eyes open to a cry of pulleys"
            CAED 115, CAED 183, LIBC 54, NET 7, SPOA 19, SPOA 103
LOVES OF THE PUPPETS.   SPOA 19

* Recording not available for analysis

Wilbur, Richard (continued)

MERLIN ENTHRALLED. "In a while they rose and went out aimlessly riding" CAED 115, SPOA 19

THE MILL. "The spoiling daylight inched along the bar-top" SPOA 19

MIND. "Mind in its purest play is like some bat" CAED 115, SPOA 103, SPOA 115

MUSEUM PIECE. "The good grey guardians of art" SPOA 19, SPOA 103

ON THE MARGINAL WAY. "Another cove of shale" CAED 115, NET 7, SPOA 82

PANGLOSS'S SONG: A COMIC-OPERA LYRIC. "Dear boy, you will not hear me speak" CAED 115

THE PARDON. "My dog lay dead five days without a grave" SCHOL 8, SPOA 19

THE PROOF. "Shall I love God for causing me to be?" CAED 115

RUNNING. "What are we playing? Was it prisoner's base?" CAED 115

SEED LEAVES. "Here is something stubborn comes" CAED 115

SHAME. "It is a cramped little state with no foreign policy" CAED 115

SHE. "What was her beauty in our first estate" CAED 115

SOMEONE TALKING TO HIMSELF. "Even when first her face" CAED 115

SONNET. "The winter deepening, the hay all in" CAED 115, SPOA 19

STILL, CITIZEN SPARROW. "Still, citizen sparrow, this vulture which you call" SPOA 19

TWO QUATRAINS FOR FIRST FROST. "Hot summer has exhausted her intent" CAED 115

TWO VOICES IN A MEADOW. "Anonymous as cherubs" CAED 115, LIBC 1, SPOA 19, SPOA 103

THE UNDEAD. "Even as children they were late sleepers" CAED 115

UNDER CYGNUS. "Who says I shall not straighten till I bend" CAED 115

VILLON: BALLADE OF THE LADIES OF TIME PAST. "O tell me where, in lands or seas" CAED 115

A VOICE FROM UNDER THE TABLE. "How shall the wine be drunk, or the woman known?" SPOA 19

WALKING TO SLEEP. "As a queen sits down, knowing that a chair will be there" CAED 115

WINTER SPRING. "A script of trees before the hill" HOUGHT 5

A WOOD. "Some would distinguish nothing here but oaks" CAED 115

YEAR'S END. "Now winter downs the dying of the year" FOLKW 25, HOUGHT 5, SPOA 19

Poetry* LIST 15, NET 8

Wilde, Oscar. 1854. in English.

THE BALLAD OF READING GAOL. "In Reading gaol by Reading town" ARGO 70A, ARGO 85, CAED 162, CAED 201, LIST 3, LIVLAN 1, REX 1

PAN. "O Goat-foot God of Arcady" EAV 22

Wildgans, Anton. 1881. in German.

Poetry* AMAD 5

Wilkinson, Anne. 1910. in English.

IN PRAISE OF BURTON. "Devil, being slender spirit" FOLKW 5

LENS. "The poet's daily chore" FOLKW 5

NATURE BE DAMNED. "Pray where would lamb and lion be" FOLKW 5

NOEL. "She sought a blessing in the snow" FOLKW 5

PENELOPE. "The turf she strokes above h head" FOLKW 5

THE PRESSURE OF NIGHT. "The pressure of nigh is on her" FOLKW 5

TIGERS KNOW FROM BIRTH. "My bones predic the striking hour of thunder" FOLKW 5

Williams, Gwyn. 1904. in English.

COLD FRONT. "Doom of hesitant Septembe weighs" ARGO 15

CWM YR EGLWYS. ARGO 15

INNS OF LOVE. "You are my Anchor and m Ship" ARGO 15

SAINT URSULA OF LLANGWYRFON. "Picked offhan by the angels to demonstrate" ARGO 15

SKULL OF THE WORLD. ARGO 15

SONG FOR CARMARTHEN. "A doxy is my newe dear" ARGO 15

VIEW FROM THE BORDER. ARGO 15

Williams, Hugo. 1942. in English.

ABORIGINE SKETCHES. "The black men han their shadows" ARGO 15

AT THE END OF THE WORLD. ARGO 15

BABYLON. ARGO 15

BEDROOM OF MUSIC. "The mirror waits on us" ARGO 15

BEGINNING TO GO. "I watch your complicate face" ARGO 15

THE BRINK. ARGO 15

THE BUTCHER. "The butcher carves veal for us ARGO 15

CATCH. "Low stars, high boats" ARGO 15

CATS AND CLOCKS. ARGO 15

CHERRY BLOSSOM. "Delicate red flames" ARGO 15

THE CHERRY TREE. ARGO 15

CLOUDS. "They say the clouds are men an women" ARGO 15

DELPHI. "Light is present in this valley" ARGO 15

THE DISEASE. "The earth breathes fire" ARGO 15

THE ELEPHANT IS OVERTURNED. "The elephant overturned" ARGO 15

HEMLOCK. "I have drawn up" ARGO 15

IN EGYPT. "Torquoise wings on Diamond Ha bour Road" ARGO 15

LOW TIDE. "Up there" ARGO 15

THE MEETING. ARGO 15

MURPHY. ARGO 15

THE NESTLING. "Bird who stoops on my sleep ARGO 15

THE NORTH. "Water turns back" ARGO 15

A PRAYER. ARGO 15

PRAYER WHILE SLEEPING. "Brave blanket cove ing me" ARGO 15

THE PRISONER. "I hold in me the body of a man ARGO 15

REMEMBERING DOWNWARDS. ARGO 15

* Recording not available for analysis

A REVOLVING STAGE. "Gold on the doorstep, whose steps" ARGO 150

RIPPLE. ARGO 150

SONNY JIM CROWNED. "The haemophiliac boy king" ARGO 150

THE STAGE IS UNLIT. "I come back late at night from your room" ARGO 150

SUGAR DADDY. "You do not look like me. I'm glad" ARGO 150

TAVISTOCK SQUARE. "The Hiroshima silver birch 1963" ARGO 150

TRUCE. "Each dawn might be winter again" ARGO 150

THE WEDDING FRAME. "Her veil blows across his face" ARGO 150

Williams, Jonathan. 1929. in English.

DAVENPORT GAP. "The tulip poplar is not a poplar" FOLKW 21

Williams, Miller. 1930. in English.

AND THEN. "Your toothbrush won't remember" WATSHD 2

FOR BECKY. "Whose tongues are twisted" WATSHD 2

THE NEIGHBOR. "No one knows" WATSHD 2

PROBLEMS IN THE SPACE-TIME CONTINUUM. "If in the future" WATSHD 2

Poetry* JNP 67

Williams, Oscar. 1900. in English.

THE BORROWER OF SALT. "The man who saw the light hanging on the tall end" LIBC 1, LIBC 48

BY FIAT OF ADORATION. LIBC 48

THE CHILDREN'S PLAYGROUND. "This is the children's playground" SPOA 96

I SING AN OLD SONG. "I sing an old song" SPOA 96

JUDAS. LIBC 48

THE LAST SUPPER. "Apostles of the hidden sun" LIBC 1, LIBC 48

THE LEG IN THE SUBWAY. LIBC 38, LIBC 48

THE MAN COMING TOWARD YOU. "The man coming toward you" LIBC 48, SPOA 96

THE MAN IN THAT AIRPLANE. LIBC 48

THE MIRAGE. "I lived a life without love, and saw the being" LIBC 48

SHOPPING FOR MEAT IN WINTER. "What lewd, naked and revolting shape is this" LIBC 1, LIBC 48

TENT. LIBC 48

A TOTAL REVOLUTION. "I advocate a total revolution" LIBC 1

WHY THE SEA IS SALT. "We are affrighted now to think we fear" LIBC 1, SPOA 96

Williams, Otis. in English.

FOR CANNONBALL ADDERLY. "It was in far away Japan" WATSHD 8

Williams, Tennessee. 1914. in English.

CRIED THE FOX. "I run, cried the fox, in circles." CAED 12

THE EYES. "The eyes are last to go out" CAED 12

GOLD-TOOTH BLUES. "Now there's many fool things a woman will do" CAED 12

HEAVENLY GRASS. "My feet took a walk in heavenly grass" CAED 12

KITCHEN-DOOR BLUES. "My old lady died of a common cold" CAED 12

LITTLE HORSE. "Mignon he was or mignonette" CAED 12

MY LITTLE ONE. "My little one whose tongue is dumb" CAED 12

THE SUMMER BELVEDERE. "Such icy wounds the city people bear" CAED 12

WHICH IS MY LITTLE BOY. "Which is my little boy, which is he" CAED 12

Williams, William Carlos. 1883 in English.

AT THE BAR. HARPV 2

BETWEEN WALLS. "The back wings" CAED 36

THE BIRTH OF VENUS. HARPV 2

THE BOTTICELLIAN TREES. "The alphabet of/ the trees" CAED 36, COLPIX 1

THE BULL. "It is in captivity" COLUMB 8

BURNING THE CHRISTMAS GREENS. "Their time past" COLPIX 1, HARPV 2

THE CATHOLIC BELLS. "Tho' I'm no Catholic" CAED 36

THE COLD NIGHT. "It is cold. The white moon" SPOA 91

COMPLAINT. "They call me and I go" SPOA 91

THE DANCE. "In Breughel's great picture, The Kermess" COLPIX 1, COLUMB 8

DEDICATION FOR A PLOT OF GROUND. "This plot of ground" SPOA 91

DESCENT. "The descent beckons as the ascent beckoned" CAED 36

FERTILE. HARPV 2

FISH. "It is the whales that drive" CAED 36

FLOWERS BY THE SEA. "When over the flowery, sharp pasture's" CAED 36, HARPV 2

FOR ELEANOR AND BILL MONAHAN. "Mother of God! Our Lady!" CAED 36

EL HOMBRE. "It's a strange courage you give me" ARGO 12, COLUMB 8

THE HOST. "According to their need, this tall Negro Evangelist" CAED 36

THE HOUNDED LOVERS. "Where shall we go?" SPOA 91

THE HURRICANE. HARPV 2

IN SISTERLY FASHION. "The ugly woman clutched her lover" CAED 36, SPOA 91

IT IS A LIVING CORAL. "A trouble" LIBC 9, LIBC 30

LEAR. "When the world takes over for us" COLUMB 8

LIGHTHEARTED WILLIAM. "Lighthearted William twirled" CAED 111, LIBC 9, LIBC 30

THE LION. "Traffic, the lion, the sophisticate" HARPV 2

NANTUCKET. "Flowers through the window" HOUGHT 5

ON GAY WALLPAPER. "The green-blue ground" CAED 36, HARPV 2

THE ORCHESTRA. "The precise counterpart of a cacophony of bird calls" CAED 36

PATERSON. "Death will be too late to bring us aid" UARIZ 1

———. THE FALLS. "What common language to unravel" SPOA 91

PEACE ON EARTH. LIBC 9, LIBC 30

PERFECTION. HARPV 2

PICTURE OF A NUDE IN A MACHINE SHOP. HARPV 2

* Recording not available for analysis

Williams, William Carlos (continued)

POEM. "As the cat climbed over the top"
                                    CAED 109, COLUMB 8
PORTRAIT OF A WOMAN IN BED. "There's my
    things"   SPOA 91
PRELUDE TO WINTER. "The moth under the
    eaves"   ARGO 12
PRIMROSE. "Yellow, yellow, yellow, yellow"
                                    CAED 36, SPOA 91
QUEEN-ANN'S LACE. "Her body is not so white
    as"   LIBC 9, LIBC 30
THE RED LILY. "To the bob-white's call"
                                              CAED 36
THE RED WHEELBARROW. "So much depends"
                                    COLPIX 1, HOUGHT 5
THE SEAFARER. "The sea will wash in".
                                              CAED 183
SMELL! "Oh strong-ridged and deeply hol-
    lowed"   CAED 36, HARPV 2
SONNET: 1909. "Alone today I mounted the steep
    hill"   SPOA 91
SPRING AND ALL. "By the road to the contagious
    hospital"   HARPV 2, LIBC 9, LIBC 30
SPRING STRAINS. "In a tissue-thin monotone of
    blue-grey buds"   SPOA 91
SYMPATHETIC PORTRAIT OF A CHILD. "The mur-
    derer's little daughter"   SPOA 91
THIS IS JUST TO SAY. "I have eaten"   SCHOL 7,
                                               HARPV 2
TO DAPHNE AND VIRGINIA. "The smell of the
    heath is box wood"   CAED 36
TO ELSIE. "The pure products of America"
                                              CAED 36
TO GREET A LETTER CARRIER.   HARPV 2
TRACT. "I will teach you my townspeople"
                                             WORLDP 1
VENUS OVER THE DESERT.   HARPV 2
VIRTUE.   HARPV 2
THE VISIT. "I have committed many errors"
                                               HARPV 2
WORK IN PROGRESS, exc. "Of Asphodel, that
    greeny flower"   CAED 36
THE WORLD NARROWED TO A POINT. "Liquor and
    love"   SPOA 91
THE YACHTS. "The yachts contend in a sea
    which the land partly encloses"   ARGO 12,
    CAED 36, HARPV 2, LIBC 9, LIBC 30,
                                               LIBC 36
THE YELLOW FLOWER. "What can I say, because
    talk I must"   CAED 36
THE YOUNG HOUSEWIFE. "At 10 AM the young
    housewife moves about in negligee"
                                             COLUMB 8
YOUNG SYCAMORE. "I must tell you/ this young
    tree"   WORLDP 1
Poetry*   LIST 13, CASSC 12A, SMC 13
Wills, Jesse. in English.
Poetry*   AUDIOT 7
Wilmot, John. See **Rochester, Earl of.**
Wilson, Patrice. in English.
THE ANGEL: EASTER 1975. "Nobody wonders
    about the angel"   WATSHD 8
THE CHIMNEY-TOP CHILD. "Light is a memory"
                                             WATSHD 8
FADE-OUT. "They used to tell him"
                                             WATSHD 8

KINDA BLUE. "Pappa used to play"
                                             WATSHD 8
SISTER, THERE ARE MONSTERS. "They tell me"
                                             WATSHD 8
Winch, Terence. 1945. in English.
HONKY TONK. "The nose sat down next to me"
                                             WATSHD 8
I AM DRESSED AS A GONDOLIER. "Around 1968
    this woman"   WATSHD 8
Winchilsea, Countess of. See **Finch, Anne.**
Winters, Yvor. 1900. in English.
AT THE SAN FRANCISCO AIRPORT. "This is the ter-
    minal: the light"   CARIL 8
BEFORE DISASTER. "Evening traffic homeward
    burns"   SPOA 96
THE CALIFORNIA OAKS. "Spreading and low, un-
    watered, concentrated" CARIL 8, LIBC 15,
                                               LIBC 41
THE COLD. "Frigidity the hesitant"   CARIL 8
THE FALL OF LEAVES. "The green has suddenly"
                                               CARIL 8
INSCRIPTION FOR A GRAVEYARD. "When men are
    laid away"   CARIL 8
JOHN SUTTER. "I was the patriarch of the shining
    land"   LIBC 15, LIBC 41, SPOA 96
THE MANZANITA. "Under the forest, where the
    day is dark"   CARIL 8
MUCH IN LITTLE. "Amid the iris and the rose"
                                               CARIL 8
THE OLD AGE OF THESEUS. "He gathered Phae-
    dra, hard with childhood, small"   CARIL 8
ON A VIEW OF PASADENA FROM THE HILLS. "From
    the high terrace porch I watch the dawn"
                                               CARIL 8
ON TEACHING THE YOUNG. "The young are quick
    of speech"   CARIL 8
ON THE PORTRAIT OF A SCHOLAR OF THE ITALIAN
    RENAISSANCE. "The color, quick in fluid oil"
                                               CARIL 8
ORPHEUS (IN MEMORY OF HART CRANE) "Climbing
    from the Lethal dead"   SPOA 96
A PRAYER FOR MY SON. "Eternal Spirit, you"
                                               CARIL 8
QUOD TEGIT OMMA. "Earth darkens and is bead-
    ed"   CARIL 8
SIR GAWAINE AND THE GREEN KNIGHT. "Reptilian
    green the wrinkled throat"   CARIL 8,
                                    LIBC 15, LIBC 41
THE SLOW PACIFIC SWELL. "Far out of sight forev-
    er stands the sea"   CARIL 8
A SPRING SERPENT. "The little snake now
    grieves"   CARIL 8
A SUMMER COMMENTARY. "When I was young"
                                               SPOA 96
SUMMER NOON: 1941. "With visionary care"
                                               CARIL 8
TIME AND THE GARDEN. "The spring has dark-
    ened with activity"   LIBC 15, LIBC 41,
                                               SPOA 96
TO A MILITARY RIFLE 1942. "The time come round
    again"   CARIL 8
TO THE HOLY SPIRIT. "Immeasurable haze"
                                               CARIL 8
TO THE MOON. "Goddess of poetry"   SPOA 96
A VISION. "Years had elapsed; the long room
    was the same"   CARIL 8

---

* Recording not available for analysis

Wither, George. 1588. in English.
THE MANLY HEART.   DECCA 12
"Shall I, wasting in despair"   ARGO 35,
                                               IMP 1
Wolfe, Humbert. in English.
THE BLACKBIRD. "In the far corner"
                                           CAED 110
Wolfram von Eschenbach. 1170. in Middle High
    German.
PARZIVAL. BUCH 9, exc. "Tuot ûf. Wem? wer sît
    ir?"   CHRIST 20
Wood, Marguerite. in English.
HE BURNED HIS SOUL'S COAT.   PROTHM 7
Woodworth, Samuel. 1785. in English.
THE BUCKET. "How dear to this heart are the
    scenes of my childhood"   CAED 100,
                                              EAV 14
Wordsworth, William. 1770. in English.
THE DAFFODILS. "I wandered lonely as a cloud"
    ARGO 2, ARGO 55, CAED 21, CAED 186,
    CAED 202, EAV 7, EAV 22, FOLKW 63,
    FOLKW 67, HARC 2, LION 2, LIST 2,
                      LIST 10, SPOA 35, SPOA 44
ELEGIAC STANZAS SUGGESTED BY A PICTURE OF
    PEELE CASTLE, IN A STORM, PAINTED BY SIR
    GEORGE BEAUMONT. "I was thy neighbour
    once, thou rugged pile"   ARGO 55
THE EXCURSION. BOOK 1, exc. "Which, if with
    truth it correspond, and sink"   ARGO 56
EXPOSTULATION AND REPLY. "Why, William on
    that old grey stone"   ARGO 55
EXTEMPORE EFFUSION ON THE DEATH OF JAMES
    HOGG. "When first, descending from the
    moorlands"   ARGO 56
"Great men have been among us"
                                           FOLKW 63
"I have travelled among unknown men"
    ARGO 55, CAED 25, LION 2
INSIDE OF KINGS CHAPEL, CAMBRIDGE. "Tax not
    the royal Saint with vain expense"
                                           ARGO 56
INTIMATIONS OF IMMORTALITY FROM RECOLLEC-
    TIONS OF EARLY CHILDHOOD. "There was a
    time when meadow, grove, and stream"
                                           ARGO 2
_____, exc. "Our birth is but a sleep" JNP 88
_____, exc.   ARGO 77, CAED 25,
                        CASSC 12F, EAV 7, LION 2
"It is a beauteous evening, calm and free"
    ARGO 55, CAED 25, CAED 202
IT IS NOT TO BE THOUGH OF, WRITTEN IN LONDON,
    1802. "It is not to be thought of that the flood"
    ARGO 2, ARGO 56, SPOA 44
LINES COMPOSED A FEW MILES ABOVE TINTERN AB-
    BEY. "Five years have past; five summers,
    with the length"   ARGO 55, CASSC 12G,
            CAED 25, CAED 202, LEARNC 1,
                        SINGER 6, SPOA 44
_____. exc. "And now, with gleams of half-ex-
    tinguished thought"   JNP 8
_____. exc. "For I have learned" LONGM 1
LINES WRITTEN IN EARLY SPRING. "I heard a thou-
    sand blended notes"   ARGO 2, ARGO 55
LONDON, 1802 [ENGLAND, 1802]. "O Friend! I
    know not which way I must look"
                        ARGO 2, ARGO 56, CAED 186,
                            HARVOC 5, SPOA 44

"Most sweet it is with unuplifted eyes"
                                           SPOA 44
"My heart leaps up when I behold"
    ARGO 55, CAED 25, EAV 7, LIST 2,
                                           LIST 10
"Nuns fret not at their convent's narrow room"
                                           CAED 25
ODE TO DUTY. "Stern daughter of the voice of
    God"   ARGO 56
ON THE EXTINCTION OF THE VENETIAN REPUBLIC.
    "Once did she hold the gorgeous east in fee"
    ARGO 56, IMP 1, LION 2, SPOA 44
ON WESTMINSTER BRIDGE. "Earth has not any-
    thing to show more fair"   ARGO 2,
            ARGO 55, ARGO 82, BRITAM 3,
    CAED 25, CAED 186, CAED 202, EAV 7,
    FOLKW 63, LION 2, LIST 2, LIST 10,
                                           SPOA 41
PERSONAL TALK, 4 SONNETS. "I am not one who
    much or oft delight"   ARGO 56
A POET'S EPITAPH, exc. "Art thou a statist in the
    van"   ARGO 55
_____. "He is retired as noontide dew"
                                           LONGM 1
THE PRELUDE. exc.   CASSC 12E
_____. 1, exc. "Fair seed-time had my soul, and
    I grew up"   ARGO 57
_____. "Oh, many a time have I, a Five-Year's
    Child"   CAED 25
_____. "One summer evening (led by her) I
    found"   CAED 21
_____. 2, exc. "Many are our joys/ in youth"
                                           ARGO 57
_____. 3, exc. "It was a dreary morning when
    the wheels"   ARGO 57
_____. 5, exc. "There was a boy: ye knew him
    well, ye cliffs"   ARGO 2, ARGO 55
_____. "When I was seated in a rocky cave"
                                           CAED 25
_____. 6, exc. "All winter long, whenever free
    to choose"   ARGO 57
_____. THE SIMPLON PASS. "Vallombrosa! I
    longed in thy shadiest wood"   ARGO 55
_____. 7, exc. "O Friend! one feeling was there
    which belong'd"   ARGO 57
_____. 10, exc. "Having two natures in me, joy
    the one"   ARGO 57
_____. "This was the time in which enflam'd
    with hope"   ARGO 57
_____. 12, exc. "There are in our existence
    spots of time"   ARGO 57
_____. 11, exc. "But from these bitter truths I
    must return"   ARGO 57
_____. "In November days"   CAED 25
_____. "Praise to the end"   LONGM 1
RESOLUTION AND INDEPENDENCE. "There was a
    roaring in the wind all night"   ARGO 56
THE REVERIE OF POOR SUSAN. "At the corner of
    Wood Street, when daylight appears"
                        BRITAM 1, SPOA 44
THE RIVER DUDDON: AFTERTHOUGHT. "The Min-
    strels played their Christmas tune"
                                           ARGO 55
RUTH, exc. "When Ruth was left half desolate"
                                           ARGO 55

* Recording not available for analysis

Wordsworth, William (continued)

"She dwelt among the untrodden ways"
ARGO 55, BRITAM 1, CAED 186,
CMS 13, DECCA 12, EAV 22, LION 2,
SPOA 44, THEAL 3

"She was a phantom of delight"   ARGO 56,
CAED 186, CAED 202, CMS 12,
DECCA 12, SPOA 44

"A slumber did my spirit seal"   ARGO 55,
CAED 186, CAED 202, FOLKW 63,
LION 2, SPOA 44

THE SOLITARY REAPER. "Behold her, single in the
field"   ARGO 2, ARGO 56, BRITAM 1,
CAED 25, CAED 202, FOLKW 68,
LION 2, LONGM 1, RCA 4, SPOA 44

SONNETS, exc.   CASSC 12D

STEPPING WESTWARD. "What, you are stepping
westward?"   ARGO 55

"Strange fits of passion have I known"
ARGO 55, CAED 15, FOLKW 63, LIST 2

SURPRISED BY JOY. "Surprised by joy—impatient
as the wind"   ARGO 2, ARGO 56

THE TABLES TURNED. "Up! Up! my friend, and
quit your books"   ARGO 2, ARGO 55

THOUGHT OF A BRITON ON THE SUBJUGATION OF
SWITZERLAND. "Two voices are there: one is of
the sea"   ARGO 56

"Three years she grew in sun and shower"
ARGO 55, FOLKW 63, SPOA 44

"Tis said that some have died for love"
SPOA 44

TO A SKYLARK. "Up with me! Up with me into
the clouds"   LIST 2, LIST 10

TO H. C., SIX YEARS OLD. "O Thou! whose fancies
from afar are brought"   ARGO 55

TO MILTON. "Milton, thou shouldst be living at
this hour"   ARGO 2, LION 2, LIST 2,
SPOA 44

TO SLEEP. "A flock of sheep that leisurely pass
by"   SPOA 44

TO THE CUCKOO. "O blithe new-comer! I have
heard"   ARGO 55

TO TOUSSAINT L'OUVERTURE. "Toussaint, the
most unhappy man of men"   ARGO 56,
IMP 1, SPOA 44

"When I have borne in memory what has
tamed"   SPOA 44

"The world is too much with us"   ARGO 2,
ARGO 56, BRITAM 1, CAED 25,
CAED 186, CAED 202, CMS 12, EAV 7,
FOLKW 63, LION 2, LIST 2, LIST 10,
RCA 4, THEAL 2

YEW-TREES. "There is a yew-tree, pride of Lorton Vale"   ARGO 55

Poetry*   PRENT 2, SPOA 123

Work, Henry Clay. 1832. in English.

GRANDFATHER'S CLOCK. "My grandfather's clock
was too large for the shelf"   CAED 100

Wotton, Sir Henry. 1568. in English.

CHARACTER OF A HAPPY LIFE. "How happy is he
born and taught"   LIST 1

ON A BANK AS I SAT A-FISHING.   SPOA 50

ON HIS MISTRESS, THE QUEEN OF BOHEMIA. "You
meaner beauties of the night"   SPOA 50

Wright, Charles. 1935. in English.

NOVEMBER 22, 1963. "Morning; the slow rising o
a cold sun"   FOLKW 2.

YELLOW. "Yellow is for regret, the distal, th
second hand"   EMC

Wright, James. 1927. in English.

AS I STEP OVER A PUDDLE AT THE END OF WINTER
I THINK OF AN ANCIENT CHINESE GOVERNOR
"Po Chu-i, balding old politician"
CAED 17!

AT THOMAS HARDY'S BIRTHPLACE. "The nurse car
ried him up the stair"   CAED 17!

AUTUMN BEGINS IN MARTINS FERRY, OHIO. "In th
Shreve High football stadium" CAED 175
SCHOL

BEFORE A CASHIER'S WINDOW. "The beautifu
cashier's white face has risen once more"
CAED 175, SCHOL

THE BEST DAYS. "First, the two men stand pon
dering"   CAED 17!

A BLESSING. "Just off the highway to Rochester
Minnesota"   CAED 175, SCHOL

A CENTENARY ODE. "I had nothing to do with it
I was not here"   CAED 17!

CITY OF EVENINGS.   CAED 17!

DEPRESSED BY A BOOK OF BAD POETRY, I WALK TO
WARD AN UNUSED PASTURE AND INVITE THE IN
SECTS TO JOIN ME. "Relieved I let the boo
fall"   SPOA 10(

DOG IN A CORNFIELD. "Fallow between th
horny trees"   SPOA 10(

THE FIRST DAYS. "The first thing I saw in th
morning"   CAED 17!

FROM A BUS WINDOW IN CENTRAL OHIO JUS
BEFORE A THUNDER SHOWER. "Cribs loade
with roughage"   SPOA 10(

GAMBLING IN STATELINE, NEVADA. "The grea
cracked shadow of the Sierra Nevada"
SCHOL

HOOK. "I was only a young man"   CAED 17!

LIFTING ILLEGAL NETS BY FLASHLIGHT. "The car
are secrets"   CAED 17!

"The lights in the hallway"   CAED 17!

LYING IN A HAMMOCK AT WILLIAM DUFFY'S FARM IN
PINE ISLAND, MINNESOTA. "Over my head,
see the bronze butterfly"   CAED 175
EMC (

MILKWEED. "While I stood here, in the open, los
in myself"   CAED 17!

MINERS. "The police are probing tonight"
SPOA 10(

THE MINNEAPOLIS POEM. "I wonder how man
old men last winter"   CAED 17!

MUTTERINGS OVER THE CRIB OF A DEAF CHILD
"How will he hear the bell at school"
SCHOL

MY GRANDMOTHER'S GHOST. "She skimmed th
yellow water like a moth"   CAED 17!

NAMES IN MONTERCHI: TO RACHEL.   CAED 17!

NORTHERN PIKE. "All right. Try this"
CAED 17!

A NOTE LEFT IN JIMMY LEONARD'S SHACK.
SCHOL

AN OFFERING FOR MR. BLUEHART. "That was
place, when I was young"   SCHOL

---

* Recording not available for analysis

A POEM WRITTEN UNDER AN ARCHWAY IN A DISCON-
TINUED RAILROAD STATION, FARGO, NORTH
DAKOTA.   SCHOL 3
POEMS TO A BROWN CRICKET. "I woke/ just about
daybreak"   CAED 175
RAIN. "It is the sinking of things"   SPOA 106
RIP. "It can't be the passing of time that casts"
                                      SCHOL 3
SAINT JUDAS. "When I went out to kill myself, I
caught"   CAED 175
THE SILENT ANGEL.   CAED 175
SPARROWS IN A HILLSIDE DRIFT.   FOLKW 25
SPRING IMAGES. "Two athletes"   SCHOL 3
STAGES ON A JOURNEY WESTWARD. "I began in
Ohio"   CAED 175
TO THE EVENING STAR. "Under the water tower
at the edge of town"   CAED 175
TODAY I WAS HAPPY, SO I MADE THIS POEM. "As the
plump squirrel scampers"   SPOA 106
TROUBLE. "Leering across Pearl Street"
                                      CAED 175
TWO HORSES PLAYING IN THE ORCHARD. "Too
soon, too soon, a man will come"
                                      SPOA 106
TWO POEMS ABOUT PRESIDENT HARDING. "In Mari-
on, the honey locust trees are falling"
                                      CAED 175
YOUTH. "Strange bird"   SCHOL 3
Poetry*   LIST 15
Wright, Judith. 1915. in English.
LYREBIRDS. "Over the west side of this moun-
tain"   CAED 112
Wright, Richard. in English.
BETWEEN THE WORLD AND ME.   SPOA 89
Wright, Robert. in English.
Poetry*   PRENT 1
Wyatt, Andrea. in English.
F-STOP/ DIANE ARBUS. "Over and over she said,
there's no time"   WATSHD 1
Wyatt, Sir Thomas. 1503. in English.
APPEAL. "And wilt thou leave me thus"
                             ARGO 35, SPOA 83
FAREWELL. "What should I saye"   ARGO 35,
                                      SPOA 83
THE HIND. "Whoso list to hunt"   LIST 1
I AM AS I AM. "I am as I am and so will be"
                                      SPOA 83
MY GALY. "My galy charged with forgetfullness"
                                      SPOA 83
MY LUTE. "My lute awake! performe the last"
                    EAV 11, LONGM 1, SPOA 83
OF THE MEAN AND SURE ESTATE. "My mother's
maids when they do sew and spin"   IMP 1
"Ons in your grace I know I was"   LONGM 1
REMEMBRANCE. "They flee from me, that some-
time did me seek"   ARGO 35, CAED 186,
                            LONGM 1, SPOA 83
STEADFASTNESS. "Forget not yet the tried in-
tent"   ARGO 35, SPOA 83
"Stond whoso list upon the slipper toppe"
                                      LONGM 1
SUPPLICATION. "Hear my prayer, O Lord"
                                      DECCA 12
VARIUM ET MUTABILE. "Is it possible" ARGO 35
"Who lyst his welthe and eas retayne"
                                      LONGM 1

Wycherley, William. 1640. in English.
TO HIS MISTRESS. A SONG. "O hate me not for my
grey hair"   ARGO 47
Wylie, Elinor. 1885. in English.
AUGUST. "Why should this Negro insolently
stride"   ARGO 12
PRETTY WORDS. "Poets make pets of pretty, doc-
ile words"   HARB 6, HOUGHT 4
VELVET SHOES. "Let us walk in the white snow"
      CAED 169, CMS 4, HARB 6, HOUGHT 5,
                                      SINGER 4
Wynne, Annette. in English.
"I keep three wishes ready"   BOWMAR 1
INDIAN CHILDREN.   NAITV 3
LITTLE FOLKS IN THE GRASS. "In the grass"
                                      CAED 164
"A wish is quite a tiny thing"   CAED 164

X, Malcolm. See Malcolm X.
X, Marvin. See Marvin X.
Xenophanes. 556 B.C. in Greek.
"All ei kheiras ekhon ge boes th' hippoi t'
ethelontes"   Greek and English JNP 95

Yeats, William Butler. 1865. in English.
AN ACRE OF GRASS. "Picture and book remains"
                                      ARGO 74
AFTER LONG SILENCE. "Speech after long si-
lence; it is right"   FOLKW 64, SPOA 22
AMONG SCHOOL CHILDREN. "I walk through the
long schoolroom questioning"   LONGM 1
THE BALLAD OF FATHER GILLIGAN. "The old
priest Peter Gilligan" SPOA 21, THEAL 2
THE BALLAD OF MOLL MAGEE. "Come round me,
little childer"   SPOA 7, SPOA 21
BEFORE THE WORLD WAS MADE. "If I make the
lashes dark"   SPOA 7
BROKEN DREAMS "There is grey in your hair"
                            CAED 53, SPOA 22
BROWN PENNY. "I whispered, I am too young"
                                      SPOA 7
BYZANTIUM. "The unpurged images of day
recede"   ARGO 74, CAED 53
THE CAP AND BELLS. "The jester walked in the
garden"   SPOA 7, SPOA 21
THE CAT AND THE MOON. "The cat went here and
there"   CAED 53
THE CHAMBERMAID'S TWO SONGS. "How came this
ranger"   CAED 53
THE CIRCUS ANIMALS' DESERTION. "I sought a
theme and sought for it in vain" ARGO 74,
                                      CAED 147
A COAT. "I made my song a coat"   SPOA 22
THE COLD HEAVEN. "Suddenly I saw the cold
and rook-delighting heaven"   ARGO 74
COOLE PARK AND BALLYLEE. "Under my window-
ledge the waters race"   ARGO 74,
                            SPOA 21, SPOA 22
———, exc. "Another emblem there! That
stormy white"   CAED 183
COOLE PARK, 1929. "I meditate upon a swallow's
flight"   HARVOC 7
A CRAZED GIRL. "That crazed girl improvising
her music"   CAED 53
THE CRAZED MOON. "Crazed through much
child-bearing"   CAED 53

* Recording not available for analysis

Yeats, William Butler (continued)

CRAZY JANE AND JACK THE JOURNEYMAN. "I know, although when looks meet"   ARGO 74, CAED 53

CRAZY JANE AND THE BISHOP. "Bring me to the blasted oak"   CAED 53

CRAZY JANE GROWN OLD LOOKS AT THE DANCERS. "I found that ivory image there" CAED 53

CRAZY JANE ON GOD. "That lover of a night"   ARGO 74, CAED 53

CRAZY JANE ON THE DAY OF JUDGEMENT. "Love is all"   CAED 53

CRAZY JANE ON THE MOUNTAIN. "I am tired of cursing the Bishop"   CAED 53

CRAZY JANE REPROVED. "I care not what the sailors say"   CAED 53

CRAZY JANE TALKS WITH THE BISHOP. "I met the Bishop on the road"   ARGO 74, CAED 53

CUCHULAIN COMFORTED. "A man that had six mortal wounds, a man"   CAED 53

DEATH.   HARVOC 7

THE DELPHIC ORACLE UPON PLOTINUS. "Behold that great Plotinus swim"   ARGO 74

A DIALOGUE OF SELF AND SOUL. "My soul: I summon to the winding ancient stair"   ARGO 74, CAED 53, CAED 147

DOWN BY THE SALLEY GARDENS. "Down by the salley gardens my love and I did meet"   SPOA 21

A DRINKING SONG. "Wine comes in at the mouth"   SPOA 7

EASTER 1916. "I have met them at close of day"   ARGO 74, SPOA 20, SPOA 21

"The fascination of what's difficult" ARGO 74

THE FIDDLER OF DOONEY. "When I play on my fiddle in Dooney"   ARGO 74, FOLKW 67, RCA 9, SPOA 21

FIRST LOVE. "Though nurtured like the sailing moon"   CAED 53

THE FOLLY OF BEING COMFORTED. "One that is ever kind said yesterday"   ARGO 74

FOR ANNE GREGORY. "Never shall a young man"   ARGO 74, CAED 147

THE FOUR AGES OF MAN. "He with body waged a fight"   SPOA 7

GIRL'S SONG. "I went out alone"   CAED 53, SPOA 7

THE HAPPY TOWNLAND. "There's many a strong farmer"   SPOA 21

HE REPROVES THE CURLEW. "O curlew, cry no more in the air"   SPOA 7, SPOA 22

HE THINKS OF HIS PAST GREATNESS WHEN A PART OF THE CONSTELLATIONS OF HEAVEN. "I have drunk ale from the country of the young"   SPOA 22

HE WISHES FOR THE CLOTHS OF HEAVEN. "Had I the heavens' embroidered cloths" SPOA 7, SPOA 22

HER ANXIETY. "Earth in beauty dressed"   SPOA 22

HUMAN DIGNITY. "Like the moon her kindness is"   CAED 53

"I am of Ireland"   ARGO 74, SPOA 22

IMITATED FROM THE JAPANESE. "A most astonishing thing"   BRITAM 1

IN MEMORY OF EVA GORE-BOOTH AND CON MAR KIEWICZ. "The light of evening"   HARVOC 7, SPOA 2

IN MEMORY OF MAJOR ROBERT GREGORY. "Now that we're almost settled in our house"   ARGO 7

IN TARA'S HALLS. "A man I praise that once in Tara's Halls"   CAED 8

AN IRISH AIRMAN FORESEES HIS DEATH. SPOA 2

JOHN KINSELLA'S LAMENT FOR MRS. MARY MOORE "A bloody and a sudden end"   CAED 126 ARGO 13

THE LADY'S THREE SONGS. "I turn round"   CAED 5

THE LAKE ISLE OF INNISFREE. "I will rise and go now, and go to Innisfree"   AUDIA 1 CAED 53, CAED 111, CAED 183, LIST 3 RCA 9, SPOA 21, SPOA 2

THE LAMENTATION OF THE OLD PENSIONER. "Although I shelter from the rain"   ARGO 7

LAPIS LAZULI. "I have heard that hysterica women say"   CAED 53, CAED 8

A LAST CONFESSION. "What lively lad most plea sured me"   ARGO 88A, ARGO 74 CAED 5

LEDA AND THE SWAN. "A sudden blow: the grea wings beating still"   ARGO 74, CAED 53 CAED 147

THE LONG-LEGGED FLY. "That civilisation may not sink"   CAED 147

THE LOVER MOURNS FOR THE LOSS OF LOVE. "Pale brows, still hands and dim hair"   SPOA 22

THE LOVER PLEADS WITH HIS FRIEND FOR OLD FRIENDS. "Though you are in your shining days"   ARGO 74

THE LOVER'S SONG. "Bird sighs for the air"   CAED 53

MAD AS THE MIST AND SNOW. "Bolt and bar the shutter"   ARGO 74, BRITAM 1

THE MASK. "Put off that mask of burning gold"   SPOA 22

THE MERMAID. "A mermaid found a swimming lad"   CAED 53, SPOA 7

THE MUNICIPAL GALLERY REVISITED. "Around me the images of thirty years"   ARGO 74

MY PAISTIN FINN. "My Paistin Finn is my sole desire"   CAED 53

NEWS FOR THE DELPHIC ORACLE. "There all the golden codgers lay"   CAED 53

NO SECOND TROY. "Why should I blame her that she filled my days"   ARGO 74, CAED 53

O DO NOT LOVE TOO LONG. "Sweetheart, do not love too long"   SPOA 7

OEDIPUS AT COLONUS, exc. "Endure what life God gives and ask no longer span"   CAED 147, SPOA 21

ON A POLITICAL PRISONER.   SPOA 21

THE PEOPLE. "What have I earned for all that work, I said"   SPOA 22

A PRAYER FOR MY DAUGHTER. "Once more the storm is howling, and half hid" FOLKW 52

RED HANRAHAN'S SONG ABOUT IRELAND. "The old brown thorn trees break in two high over Cummen Strand"   SPOA 20, SPOA 21

THE ROSE OF THE WORLD. "Who dreamed that beauty passes like a dream"   SPOA 22

* Recording not available for analysis

THE ROSE TREE. "O words are lightly spoken"
ARGO 74, SPOA 20, SPOA 21
SAILING TO BYZANTIUM. "That is no country for
old men. The young" ARGO 74, CAED 53,
CMS 14, HARVOC 7
THE SCHOLARS. "Bald heads forgetful of their
sins" ARGO 74
THE SECOND COMING. "Turning and turning in
the widening gyre" ARGO 74, CAED 53,
CMS 14, FOLKW 64
SEPTEMBER 1913. "What need you, being come
to sense" ARGO 74, SPOA 21
SOLOMON AND THE WITCH. "And thus declared
that Arab lady" CAED 147
THE SONG OF THE HAPPY SHEPHERD. "The woods
of Arcady are dead" SPOA 7
THE SONG OF THE OLD MOTHER. "I rise in the
dawn, and I kneel and blow" CAED 183,
SPOA 22
THE SONG OF WANDERING AENGUS. "I went out to
the hazel wood" CAED 53, CAED 112,
CMS 12, SPOA 7, SPOA 22
THE STATUES. "Pythagoras planned it. Why did
the people stare?" SPOA 22
THE STOLEN CHILD. "Where dips the rocky high-
land" SPOA 7, SPOA 21
SWIFT'S EPITAPH. "Swift has sailed into his rest"
ARGO 74
THAT THE NIGHT COME. "She lived in storm and
strife" ARGO 74
THOSE DANCING DAYS ARE GONE. "Come, let me
sing into your ear" CAED 53
A THOUGHT FROM PROPERTIUS. "She might, so
noble from head" SPOA 22
THE THREE BUSHES. "Said lady once to lover"
CAED 86, CAED 147
THREE THINGS. "O cruel Death, give three
things back" CAED 147, SPOA 7
TO A CHILD DANCING IN THE WIND. "Dance there
upon the shore" ARGO 74
TO A FRIEND WHOSE WORK HAS COME TO NOTHING.
"Now all the truth is out" SPOA 21
TO IRELAND IN THE COMING TIMES. "Know, that I
would accounted be" SPOA 21, SPOA 22
TO THE ROSE UPON THE ROOD OF TIME. "Red Rose,
proud Rose, sad Rose of all my days"
SPOA 22
TWO SONGS FROM A PLAY. I. "I saw a staring virgin
stand" ARGO 74, HARVOC 7
———. II. "In pity for man's darkening
thought" ARGO 74
UNDER BEN BULBEN, exc. "Irish poets, learn your
trade" ARGO 74
———, exc. "Under bare Ben Bulben's head"
ARGO 74
———, exc. SPOA 21, SPOA 22
VACILLATION III. "Get all the gold and silver
that you can" HARVOC 7
———. IV. "My fiftieth year had come and
gone" HARVOC 7
WHEN YOU ARE OLD. "When you are old and grey
and full of sleep" ARGO 88A, RCA 9
"Why should not old men be mad" CAED 53
THE WILD OLD WICKED MAN. "Because I am mad
about women" CAED 53

THE WILD SWANS AT COOLE. "The trees are in
their autumn beauty" AUDIA 1, ARGO 74,
CAED 53, FOLKW 64, LIST 3, SPOA 7
YOUNG MAN'S SONG. "She will change, I cried"
CAED 53
Poetry* LIST 11, PRENT 3, SPOA 115
Yessenin, Sergei. 1895. in Russian.
DO SVIDANYA. CAED 193
FLOWERS. English FOLKW 95
GODY MOLODYE. CAED 193
HOMECOMING. English FOLKW 95
VSE ZHIVOE. CAED 193
Yevtushekno, Yevgeny. 1933. in Russian.
AMERIKANSKII SOLOVEI. "V stranye perlona i
dakrona" CAED 83
BABII YAR. "Nad Babim Yarom pamyatnikov
net" CAED 83, MONITR 2; English and
Russian COLUMB 14; English FOLKW 58
BABUSHKI. "Prostim otsov ustaluyu nebrezh-
nost'" MELOD 2
BIRTHDAY. "Mother, let me congratulate you"
English FOLKW 58
BOMBAMI PO BALALAIKAM. "Vnov', vnov', vnov'"
COLUMB 14
COLORS. "When your face"
English FOLKW 58, VAN 3
COMPANION. "She was sitting on the rough em-
bankment" English FOLKW 58
DA I NET. "Ya, kak poezd"
Russian and English COLUMB 14
ENCOUNTER. "We were sitting about taking
coffee" English FOLKW 58
FREEDOM TO KILL.
Russian and English COLUMB 14
GENTLENESS. "This can't go on"
English FOLKW 58
GRAD V KHARKOVE "V grade Khar'kove-grad"
MONITR 2
I POTOM. "A shto potom?" MONITR 2
IN A STEELWORKER'S HOME.
Russian and English COLUMB 14
IN GEORGIA. "I loafed about at leisure munching
pears" English FOLKW 58
KAR'ERA. "Tverdili pastyri shto vreden"
CAED 83
KNIGHTS. "They have remained unaltered like
nature" English FOLKW 58
KOSHUETI. "I am inside the church of Koshueti"
English FOLKW 58
KRADENYE YABLOKI. "Krenilis' ot shtorma zabo-
ry" MELOD 2
LATER. "Oh what a sobering"
English FOLKW 58
LIES. "Telling lies to the young is wrong"
English FOLKW 58
LYUDI. "Lyudei neinteresnyki v mire net"
MELOD 2; English FOLKW 58
MOSKVA TOVARNAYA. "Studentu khotshetsya"
CAED 83, MONITR 2
MURDER. "I can recall that distant valley"
English FOLKW 58
NASLEDNIKI STALINA. "Vezmolstvoval marmor"
MONITR 2
ON A BICYCLE. "Under the dawn I wake to my
two-wheel friend" English FOLKW 58
"Okno vykhodit v belye derev'ya" CAED 83,
MONITR 2; English FOLKW 58

* Recording not available for analysis

Yevtushekno, Yevgeny (continued)

PARTY CARD. "A shot-up forest full of black holes"   English FOLKW 58
PROCESSION WITH THE MADONNA.
                Russian and English COLUMB 14
PROLOG. "Ya rasnyi"   CAED 83
"Prosnutsya bylo, kak prisnitsya"
                English FOLKW 58
RAKETY I TELEGI. "Telegu obizhat' ne nado"
                CAED 83
"The salty spray glistens on the fence"
                English MELOD 2
"Sosulek tonkii zvon"   MONITR 2
TALK. "You're a brave man, they tell me"
                English FOLKW 58
VISIT. "Going to Zima Junction, quiet place"
                English FOLKW 58
WAKING. "Waking then was like dreaming"
                English FOLKW 58
WAITING. "My love will come"
                English FOLKW 58
WEDDINGS. "Those weddings in wartime! The deceiving comfort"   English FOLKW 58
ZAKLINANIYE. "Vesennei noch'yu dumai obo mne"   MELOD 2, MONITR 2
ZAVIST. "Zaviduyu ya"   CAED 83
ZHENSHCHINA I MORE. "Nad morem/ molnii"
                CAED 83, MONITR 2
Poetry*   FOLKW 57, NBC 1
Yorck, Ruth Landshoff. 1909. in English.
I M J F K. "We may stop worrying" FOLKW 21
Young, Andrew. 1885. in English.
THE BURNT LEAVES. "They have been burning leaves"   FOLKW 64
CUCKOOS. "When coltsfoot withers and begins to wear"   FOLKW 64
IN THE FALLOW FIELD. "I went down on my hands and knees"   FOLKW 64
LAST SNOW. "Although the snow still lingers"
                ARGO 100
THE MEN. "I sat to listen to each sound"
                FOLKW 64
ON MIDDLETON EDGE. "If this life-saving rock should fail"   FOLKW 64
PASSING THE GRAVEYARD. "I see you did not try to save"   CAED 86
A PROSPECT OF DEATH. "If it should come to this"
                FOLKW 64
THE SECRET WOOD.   ARGO 100
THE STARS.   ARGO 100
A WINDY DAY. "This wind brings all dead things to life"   CAED 111
WOOD AND HILL. "Nowhere is one alone"
                FOLKW 64
Young, Bartholomew. ca. 1577. in English.
THE SHEPHERD, ARSILIUS', REPLY.   ARGO 136
Young, David. in English.
A FAR-OFF WAR.   CAED 155
SUMMER.   CAED 155
Young, Francis Brett. in English.
BÊTE HUMAINE. "Riding through Ruwu swamp, about sunrise"   CAED 112
Young, Marguerite. in English.
DIDACTIC BOMB AGAINST WAR. "In pathos of distance"   SPOA 82
Ywan Jen. 779. in Chinese.
CHYAN BEI HWAI. "Sye gung dzwei syan pyan

* Recording not available for analysis

lyan nyu"   FOLKW 76

Zardoya, Concha. in Spanish.
LLANTO DE UN PAJARO POR EL POETA MUERTO. "Un puro cuerpo, tierra"   FIDIAS 2
Zaturenska, Marya. 1902. in English.
AFTER SAINT THERESA. "Let nothing disturb you"
                LIBC 21, LIBC 67
THE CASTAWAYS. "No matter where they lived the same dream came" LIBC 21, LIBC 67
FALLING TEARS, AWAKENING HEAVENS. LIBC 21, LIBC 67
FOR THE SEASONS. "Burning with heat and cold"
                LIBC 21, LIBC 67
SNOWSTORM IN JANUARY. "Calm is the season, cold and clear the air" LIBC 21, LIBC 67
WATER AND SHADOW. "By the long flow of green and silver water"   LIBC 21, LIBC 67
Zenea, Juan Clemente. 1832. in Spanish.
RECUERDO. "Cuando emigran las aves en bandadas"   SMC 13
Zhukovsky, V. A. 1783. in Russian.
19 MARTA 1823. "Ty predo mnoyu"   CMS 6
Zogarrio, Giuseppe. in Italian.
IL GIORNO DEI POETI.   CETRA 31
Zorrilla, José. 1817. in Spanish.
ORIENTAL. "Corriendo va por la vega" SMC 3,
                SPOA 37
Zorilla de San Martin, Juan. in Spanish.
TABARE. "Ahogada por las sombras" FIDIAS 3
Zu-Bolton, Ahmos. 1948. in English.
THE FOOL.   WATSHD 4
HOMELESS. "I am a stranger"   WATSHD 4
QUICKTALES OF A BLIND PAINTER. "This is how the blind sees"   WATSHD 4
SPACEDREAM STRUGGLE. "It has been a long day"
                WATSHD 4
Zuckmayer, Carl. 1896. in German.
DER CELLOSPIELER AUS THÜRINGEN. "Herr, lass mich musizieren"   CHRIST 3
COGNAC IM FRÜHLING. "Ich bin im braunen Cognac-See ertrunken"   CHRIST 3
EINE HULDIGUNG AN MAINZ.   CHRIST 3
KLEINE STROPHEN VON DER UNSTERBLICHKEIT. "Dauer, Zeit und Raum"   CHRIST 3
MARSCHLIED. "Ich will es öfter sagen"
                CHRIST 3
MEIN TOD—EIN FROMMER WUNSCH. "Ich werde einmal plötzlich auf die Nase fallen"
                CHRIST 3
DIE MUTTER. "Im Walde säugt ein Reh"
                CHRIST 3
RINDERLEGENDE. "Die Rinder sind vom Schöpfer ausersehen"   CHRIST 3
ÜBER DIE PFERDE. "Über die Pferde hat der Herr die himmlische Satteldecke ausgebreitet.   CHRIST 3
WEIHNACHTSLIED. "Frost klirre Glas!"
                CHRIST 3
WIEGENLIED AN DER BERGSTRASSE. "Tropf, tropf, tau"   CHRIST 3
DIE WÖLFE. "Mit wildem Geripp, mit harten mageren Flanken"   CHRIST 3
Poetry*   CHRIST 7
Zukofsky, Louis. 1904. in English.
A (SECTION NINE).   NET 11
BOTTOM ON SHAKESPEARE.   NET 11

TITLE INDEX

References Are to Authors

A . . . —*Char*
A [SECTION NINE]—*Zukofsky*
A. A. A. DOMINE DEUS—*Jones, David*
A AND B AND THE MIRROR—*Scott, Winfield Townley*
Á BASILIO—*Anonymous–Spanish*
À CASSANDRE—*Ronsard*
A CÓRDOBA—*Góngora*
Á CRISTO CRUCIFICADO—*Anonymous–Spanish*
A. D. BLOOD—*Masters, Edgar Lee*
Á DON FRANCISCO GINER DE LOS RÍOS—*Machado, Antonio*
Á EL—*Gómez de Avellaneda*
Á ESPAÑA, DESPUES DE LA REVOLUCIÓN DE MARZO—*Quintana, Manuel José*
À FORCE CE N'EST PLUS MAMAN—*Obaldia*
Á FRANCESCO SAVERIO FABRE—*Foscolo*
À GEORGE SAND—*Musset*
A GIOVANNI DA PISTOIA QUANDO L'AUTORE DIPINGEVA LA VOLTA DELLA SISTINA—*Michelangelo*
À HÉLÈNE—*Ronsard*
Á IRENE GARCÍA—*Garcia Lorca*
Á JOSÉ MARIA PALACIO—*Machado, Antonio*
Á JUAN RAMÓN JIMÉNEZ—*Machado, Manuel*
À JULIE—*Musset*
À KEMPIS—*Nervo*
Á LA FLOR DE GNIDO—*Vega, Garcilaso de la*
Á LA INMENSA MAYORIA—*Otero*
Á LA MARIPOSA MUERTA—*Florit*
À LA MÉMOIRE DE GEORGE MISAINE—*Damas*
Á LA NAVE—*Bello*
Á LA PLANA DE VIC—*Verdaguer*
Á LA POESÍA—*Jiménez*
À LA SANTÉ—*Apollinaire*
A LAGARTIXA—*Ivo*
Á LAS ESTRELLAS—*Saavedra*
Á LAS ORILLAS DEL SAR—*Castro, Rosalía de*
À L'ENDROIT—*Éluard*
À L'HOMME QUI A LIVRÉ UNE FEMME—*Hugo, Victor*
A LI MATRI DI LI CARUSI—*Buttitta*
A LO DIVINO—*Juan de la Cruz*
À MA FILLE, ADÈLE—*Hugo, Victor*
Á MARGARITA DEBAYLE—*Darío*
Á MI ALMA—*Jiménez*
Á MI CIUDAD NATIVA—*Anonymous–Spanish*
Á MI MADRE—*Casal*
À MOI-MÊME—*Supervielle*

Á MUCHOS—*Rega Molina*
À NEW-YORK—*Senghor*
A NIEBLA, MI PERRO—*Alberti*
À NINON—*Musset*
A ROOSEVELT—*Darío*
A SAN FRANCISCO—*Di Giacomo*
Á SANCHO PANZA—*Celaya*
Á SATÁN—*Anonymous–Spanish*
A SÈ STESSO—*Leopardi*
A SENHORA DUQUESA DE BRABANTE—*Leal*
A SILVIA—*Leopardi*
À SON ÂME—*Ronsard*
A SZERELEM SIVATAGA—*Pilinszky*
A UMA RAPARIGA—*Espanca*
Á UN NIÑO DORMIDO—*Gómez de Avellaneda*
Á UN OLMO SECO—*Machado, Antonio*
Á UNA ESTRELLA—*Coronado*
Á UNA ESTRELLA—*Espronceda*
Á UNA NARIZ—*Quevedo y Villegas*
À UNE DANSEUSE NOIRE—*Diop*
À UNE JEUNE MORTE—*Ronsard*
À UNE PASSANTE—*Baudelaire*
A UNO STRANIERO—*Gatto*
À URANIE—*Voiture*
A VENEZIA—*Foscolo*
À VENUS—*Du Bellay*
A VINCENZO MONTI—*Foscolo*
Á VUESTRO SERVICIO—*Celaya*
A ZACINTO—*Foscolo*
A ZURBARÁN—*Gautier*
AARON STARK—*Robinson, Edwin Arlington*
AB OVO—*Starbuck*
LAS ABANDONADAS—*Lesto*
THE ABANDONED—*Abse*
THE ABANDONED SHADE—*Lee, Laurie*
ABAT-JOUR—*Geraldy*
ABBITTE—*Hölderlin*
ABBITTE NACH DER REISE—*Kunze*
ABDUL A-BUL-BUL A-MIR—*Anonymous—English–Modern English*
L'ABEILLE—*Valéry*
ABEND—*Gryphius*
ABEND—*Schiller*
ABEND NACH DEM GEWITTER—*Bergengruen*
ABENDDÄMMERUNG—*Heine*
ABENDLAND—*Trakl*
ABENDLÄNDISCHES LIED—*Trakl*
ABENDLIED—*Claudius*
ABENDLIED—*Keller, Gottfried*
ABENDLIED—*Trakl*
ABENDPHANTASIE—*Hölderlin*
ABENDSTÄNDCHEN—*Brentano*
ABER ES BLEIBT AUF DEM ALTEN FLECK—*Fontane*

ABER WIR LASSEN ES ANDERE MACHEN—*Fontane*
ABERSOCH—*Thomas, Ronald Stuart*
ABGESANG—*Roth, Eugen*
ABOMINABLE SNOWMAN—*MacPherson*
ABORIGINE SKETCHES—*Williams, Hugo*
THE ABORTION—*Sexton*
ABOU BEN ADHEM—*Hunt*
ABOUT ANIMALS—*Conkling*
ABOUT CROWS—*Ciardi*
ABOUT JOHN, WHO LOST A FORTUNE BY THROWING STONES—*Belloc*
ABOUT MY DREAMS—*Conkling*
ABOUT OWLS—*Grigson*
ABOVE KARMA—*Jordan, Norman*
ABOVE PIUTE VALLEY—*Snyder*
ABOVE THE EDGE OF DOOM—*Graves*
THE ABRACADABRA BOYS—*Sandburg*
ABRAHAM AND ISAAC—*Anonymous–English–Old English*
ABRAHAM LINCOLN—*Whitman*
ABRAHAM LINCOLN WALKS AT MIDNIGHT—*Lindsay, Vachel*
ABSALOM AND ACHITOPHEL—*Dryden*
ABSALOM IN THE TREE—*Mathias*
ABSCHIED—*Benn*
ABSCHIED—*Eichendorff*
ABSCHIED—*Hölderlin*
ABSCHIED—*Rilke*
ABSEITS—*Storm*
ABSENCE—*Éluard*
ABSENCE—*Gallagher, Tess*
ABSENCE—*Senghor*
ABSENCES—*Tate, James*
ABSENT LOVER—*Anonymous–African languages–Southern Africa*
THE ABSENTEES—*MacBeth*
THE ABSENTEES—*Nash*
ABSOLUTENESS—*Olson*
L'ABSOUTE AVAIT ÉTÉ DONNÉE—*Cendrars*
ABT VOGLER—*Browning, Robert*
ACADEMIC—*Roethke*
ACADEMIC OVERTURE—*Garlick*
L'ACCENTO SULL'A—*Rodari*
ACCEPTANCE OF AUTUMN—*Dowling*
ACCEPTANCE SPEECH—*Bell*
ACCIDENTALLY ON PURPOSE—*Frost, Robert*
ACCUSATION—*Noël*
THE ACHE OF MARRIAGE—*Levertov*

ACHERONTIA ATROPOS—*Gozzano*

ACHILLES DEATHERIDGE—
Masters, Edgar Lee

1886—*Benn*

DIE ÄCHZENDE KREATUR—
Droste-Hülshoff

ACIS AND GALATEA—*Gay, John*

ACQUAINTED WITH THE NIGHT—
Frost, Robert

L'ACQUAIOLA—*Totò*

THE ACQUITTAL—*Miller, May*

AN ACRE OF GRASS—*Yeats*

THE ACT OF DEATH—*Thomas, Jill*

ACT OF LOVE—*Scannell*

ACTFIVE—*MacLeish*

ACTION—*Hillary*

AD ANGELO MAI—*Leopardi*

THE AD-DRESSING OF CATS—*Eliot,
Thomas Stearns*

ADAM ON HIS WAY HOME—*Pack*

ADAM'S DREAM—*Muir*

THE ADDICT—*Sexton*

ADDIO!—*Pascoli*

L'ADDIO A VENEZIA—*Fusinato*

L'ADDIO ALLE ALPE—*Mazzini*

ADDIO MIA BELLA ADDIO—*Bosi*

ADDRESS TO A TOOTH-ACHE—
Burns

ADDRESS TO AN ILLEGITIMATE
CHILD—*Burns*

ADDRESS TO THE SCHOLARS OF
NEW ENGLAND—*Ransom*

ADDRESS TO THE UNCO GUID, OR
THE RIGIDLY RIGHTEOUS—
Burns

ADELCHI—*Manzoni*

ADELFOS—*Machado, Manuel*

ADELINA DE PASEO—*Garcia
Lorca*

ADEMÁS—*Guillén, Jorge*

L'ADIEU—*Apollinaire*

L'ADIEU AUX DAMES—*Marot*

L'ADIEU DU CAVALIER—
Apollinaire

ADIEUX À LA MEUSE—*Péguy*

ADIEUX À LA VIE—*Gilbert,
Nicolas-Joseph*

ADIÓS—*Neruda*

LOS ADIOSES—*Sabat-Ercasty*

ADLESTROP—*Thomas, Edward*

ADMONITIONS—*Clifton*

ADMONITORY LINES FOR THE
BIRTHDAY OF AN
OVER-ENERGETIC
CONTEMPORARY—*Nash*

ADONAIS—*Shelley*

ADORATION DE L'INDEX—
Obaldia

ADULT EDUCATION—*Viorst*

ADULTHOOD—*Giovanni*

THE ADULTS—*Hall*

ADVENT 1966—*Levertov*

ADVENTURE—*Behn, Harry*

ADVENTURE—*Conkling*

ADVENTURES OF ISABEL—*Nash*

ADVENTURES OF RICHARD—
Crabbe

THE ADVENTURES OF TOM
BOMBADIL—*Tolkien*

ADVICE I WISH SOMEONE HAD
GIVEN ME—*Darr*

ADVICE TO A GIRL—*Campion*

ADVICE TO A PROPHET—*Wilbur*

AEGEAN—*Simpson*

AENEAS AT WASHINGTON—*Tate,
Allen*

AENEID—*Virgil*

AEROPLANE—*Green, Mary
McBride*

DER AESTHET—*Morgenstern*

DAS AESTHETISCHE WIESEL—
Morgenstern

L'AFFARE DER FRITTO—*Belli*

DIE AFFEN—*Busch*

AFFLICTION—*Herbert*

AFFRES, DÉTONATION, SILENCE—
Char

LA AFIRMACION HUMANA—
Guillén, Jorge

AFRICA—*Giovanni*

AFRICAN DANCE—*Hughes,
Langston*

AFRICAN MEMORIES—
Oppenheimer

AFRICA'S PLEA—*Dempster*

AFRO-AMERICAN FRAGMENT—
Hughes, Langston

THE AFROAMERICAN FACE—
Jeffers, Lance

AFTER—*Browning, Robert*

AFTER A DEATH—*Ormond*

AFTER A DEPARTURE—*Abse*

AFTER A JOURNEY—*Hardy*

AFTER A NIGHT THAT CAME TO
NOTHING—*Ciardi*

AFTER ALL AND AFTER ALL—
Davies, Mary Carolyn

AFTER APPLE-PICKING—*Frost,
Robert*

AFTER BIRMINGHAM, THEY MARCH
FOR MARTIN LUTHER KING—
Fabio, Sarah Webster

AFTER CONSULTING MY YELLOW
PAGES—*Wagoner*

AFTER DEATH, NOTHING IS—
Rochester, Earl of

AFTER DRY WEATHER—*Van
Doren*

AFTER EXPERIENCE TAUGHT ME—
Snodgrass

AFTER HER MAN HAD LEFT HER
FOR THE SIXTH TIME THAT YEAR
—*Lee, Don L.*

AFTER LE NOZZE DI FIGARO—
Press

AFTER LONG BUSYNESS—*Bly*

AFTER LONG SILENCE—*Yeats*

AFTER NIGHT FLIGHT SON
REACHES BEDSIDE OF ALREADY
UNCONSCIOUS FATHER—
Warren

AFTER READING OF A CHILD'S
GUIDE TO MODERN PHYSICS—
Auden

AFTER READING ST. JOHN THE
DIVINE—*Derwood*

AFTER SAINT THERESA—
Zaturenska

AFTER THAT—*Alakoye*

AFTER THE ACCIDENT—*Emanuel*

AFTER THE CHRISTENING—*Nash*

AFTER THE CLUB DANCE—*Hardy*

AFTER THE DENTIST—*Swenson*

AFTER THE FAIR—*Hardy*

AFTER THE FIFTH DAY—*Sanchez*

AFTER THE FUNERAL—*Thomas,
Dylan*

AFTER THE INDUSTRIAL
REVOLUTION, ALL THINGS
HAPPEN AT ONCE—*Bly*

AFTER THE LAST BULLETINS—
Wilbur

AFTER THE LAST DYNASTY—
Kunitz

AFTER THE RECORD IS BROKEN—
Emanuel

AFTER THE VISIT—*Lifshin*

AFTER 2000 YEARS—*Dowling*

AFTER THE WINTER—*McKay*

AFTER WINTER—*Brown,
Sterling A.*

THE AFTERGLOW OF THE ROSE—
Antoninus

AFTERMATH—*Davison, Peter*

AFTERNOON—*Hall*

AFTERNOON—*Parker*

AFTERNOON: AMAGANSETT BEACH
—*Wheelock*

THE AFTERNOON AS AN ARIA—
Stefanile

THE AFTERWAKE—*Rich*

THE AFTERWARD KISS—*Cavalieri*

AFTERWARDS—*Hardy*

AFTERWARDS—*Spencer*

AFTONRODNAD—*Malmberg*

AGAIN, AROUND THE PHOSPHORUS
—*Andrews*

AGAINST OUR LOVE—*Damas*

AGAINST PLATONICK LOVE—
*Anonymous–English–
Modern English*

AGAINST THE COLD—*Bynner*

AGAINST THE FEAR OF DEATH—
Lucretius Carus

AGE—*Giovanni*

THE AGE OF EXPLORATION—*Jong*

AGES OF MAN—*Shakespeare*

AGINCOURT—*Drayton*

AGINCOURT—*Garlick*

AGITATE—*Eckels*

AGNETES VUGGEVISE—*Andersen*

THE AGONIE—*Herbert*

AGOSTO—*Garcia Lorca*

LA AGRICULTURA DE LA ZONA
TÓRRIDA—*Bello*

AH-WHOO-AH—*Gaver*

AH, WILL THE SAVIOUR—*Smith,
Stevie*

AHASVER—*Kaschnitz*

AHNUNGSLOS—*Roth, Eugen*

THE AIM: THE MAGICIAN—*Piercy*

THE AIM WAS SONG—*Frost, Robert*
AIR—*Benedikt*
AIR—*Major*
AIR—*Rukeyser*
AIR—*Walcott*
L'AIR DE L'EAU—*Breton, André*
THE AIR DOES NOT TOUCH US—*Colbert*
UN AIR EMBAUMÉ—*Aragon*
AN AIR THAT KILLS—*Beecher*
AIRE AND ANGELS—*Donne*
AIRE NOCTURNO—*Garcia Lorca*
LOS AIRES—*Guillén, Jorge*
AIRMEN BROADCAST—*Day Lewis*
AIRSHIP—*Sobiloff*
AN AIRSTRIP IN ESSEX, 1960—*Hall*
AJANTA—*Rukeyser*
AKHILLESOVO SERDTSE—*Voznesensky*
THE AKOND OF SWAT—*Lear*
AL CÉFIRO—*Villegas*
AL LETTORE—*Saba*
AL MAESTRO AZORIN POR SU LIBRO CASTILLA—*Machado, Antonio*
AL MAR ANOCHECIDO—*Jiménez*
AL NACIMIENTO DE CRISTO NUESTRO SEÑOR—*Góngora*
AL PARTIR—*Gómez de Avellaneda*
AL OÍDO DE UNA MUCHACHA—*Garcia Lorca*
AL REY OSCAR—*Darío*
AL SONETO CON MI ALMA—*Jiménez*
AL TUMULTO DEL REY FELIPE II EN SEVILLA—*Cervantes Saavedra*
ALABAMA—*Simmons, Judy*
ALABAMA EARTH—*Hughes, Langston*
ALADDIN—*Lowell, James Russell*
ALADDIN'S LAMP—*De Frees*
ALAFIA—*Rasul*
ALAMO BLANCO—*Jiménez*
THE ALARM—*Sherwin*
ALAS, KIND ELEMENT—*Adams*
IN ALBA AL DUOMO DI ANCONA—*Gatto*
L'ALBATROS—*Baudelaire*
ALBATROSS RAMBLE—*Patten*
ALBERT—*Abse*
ALBERT SCHIRDING—*Masters, Edgar Lee*
ALBERTA K JOHNSON—*Hughes, Langston*
THE ALCHEMIST—*Bogan*
THE ALCHEMIST—*Jonson*
THE ALCHEMIST—*Kelly*
ALCHIMIE DE LA DOULEUR—*Baudelaire*
ALCHIMIE DU VERBE—*Rimbaud*
ALDERDOMEN—*Heidenstam*
ALEPH BEIZ—*Stern*
ALLES STENAR—*Österling*

ALEXANDER GRAHAM BELL DID NOT INVENT THE TELEPHONE—*Coffin*
ALEXANDER'S FEAST—*Dryden*
ALEXANDRIA—*Durrell*
ALGERNON, WHO PLAYED WITH A LOADED GUN, AND, ON MISSING HIS SISTER, WAS REPRIMANDED BY HIS FATHER—*Belloc*
ALGO DEBI DECIRTE—*López Suria*
ALICE'S ADVENTURES IN WONDERLAND—*Carroll*
ALIENS—*Auden*
ALIENS—*Gitlin*
ALKY—*Burke*
THE ALL ALONE TREE—*Gallagher, F. O'Neill*
ALL' ANTICA—*Villaroel, Calogero*
ALL' ARMI ALL' ARMI—*Berchet*
ALL DAY IT HAS RAINED—*Lewis, Alun*
ALL FOR LOVE—*Byron*
ALL GOD'S CHILLUN—*Brathwaite*
ALL GOOD AMERICANS GO TO LAROUSSE—*Nash*
ALL I NEEDED—*Johnston, Ellen Turlington*
ALL I TELL YOU FROM MY HEART—*Graves*
ALL' ITALIA—*Leopardi*
ALL MY LIFE I'VE HEARD ABOUT MANY—*Olson*
ALL QUIET—*Ignatow*
ALL THAT REMAINS—*Walters*
ALL THAT'S PAST—*De la Mare*
ALL THE DEAD DEARS—*Plath*
ALL THE EARTH, ALL THE AIR—*Roethke*
ALL THE WORLD MOVED—*Jordan, June*
ALL THE WORLD'S A STAGE—*Raleigh;* see also *Shakespeare*
ALL THESE BIRDS—*Wilbur*
ALLA LUNA—*Leopardi*
ALLA MIA TERRA—*Gatto*
ALLA MUSA—*Foscolo*
ALLA NOIA—*Ungaretti*
ALLA NUOVA LUNA—*Quasimodo*
ALLA SERA—*Foscolo*
ALLA STAZIONE IN UNA MATTINA D'AUTUNNO—*Carducci*
ALLA SUA DONNA—*Leopardi*
ALLA SUA DONNA LONTANA—*Foscolo*
ALLAH—*Jordan, Norman*
THE ALLEGORY OF THE WOLF BOY—*Gunn*
L'ALLEGRO—*Milton*
ALLEIN IST NICHT GENUG—*Rühmkorf*
ALLEN-A-DALE—*Scott, Sir Walter*
ALLEY—*Last Poets*
LES ALLIANCES—*Cocteau*
ALLIE—*Graves*
L'ALLIGATOR—*Desnos*

ALLIGATOR EMILY—*Lee, Dennis*
ALLIGATOR ON THE ESCALATOR—*Merriam*
ALLIGATOR PIE—*Lee, Dennis*
ALLO—*Péret*
ALLONS PLUS VITE—*Apollinaire*
ALLORA—*Pascoli*
ALLOW ME, MADAM, BUT IT WON'T HELP—*Nash*
ALL'S BRILLIG IN TIN PAN ALLEY—*Nash*
ALL'S THE FOUL FIEND'S—*Blackmur*
ALL'S WELL—*Whittier*
ALL'S WELL THAT ENDS—*Holmes, John*
ALL'S WELL THAT ENDS WELL—*Anonymous–English–Modern English*
ALLTMER SOM IOR—*Ferlin*
ALMA AUSENTE—*Garcia Lorca*
EL ALMA DEL PAYADOR—*Obligado, Rafael*
ALMA PERDIDA—*Espanca*
ALMA PERDIDA—*Larbaud*
ALMANAC—*Swenson*
ALMOST—*Untermeyer*
ALOHA OE—*Blanding*
ALONE—*Harper*
ALONE—*Joyce*
ALONE—*Poe*
ALONE—*Viorst*
ALONSO TO FERDINAND—*Auden*
L'ALOUETTE ET SES PETITS AVEC LE MAÎTRE D'UN CHAMP—*La Fontaine*
LA ALQUIMÍA VITAL—*Carrera Andrade*
ALS DER ERSTE SCHNEE FIEL—*Göckingk*
ALTABISKARCO CANTUA—*Anonymous–Basque*
ALTARWISE BY OWL LIGHT—*Thomas, Dylan*
ALTASSYRISCH—*Scheffel*
ALTE ROSE—*Heine*
DIE ALTE SORGE—*Busch*
DIE ALTEN UND DIE JUNGEN—*Fontane*
DAS ALTER—*Eichendorff*
EIN ALTER TIBETTEPPICH—*Lasker-Schüler*
ALTITUDES—*Wilbur*
ALTOGETHER SINGING—*Beecher*
UN'ALTRA PIETÀ—*Bevilacqua*
ALTURAS DE MACCHU PICCHU—*Neruda*
ALWAYS EVENING—*Van Doren*
ALWAYS THERE ARE THE CHILDREN—*Giovanni*
AM BRUNNEN—*Goethe*
AM DRITTEN SONNTAGE NACH OSTERN—*Droste-Hülshoff*
AM GRABE HÖLTYS—*Lenau*
AM GRÜNDONNERSTAGE—*Droste-Hülshoff*

AM I MY BROTHER'S KEEPER?—
  Goldstein
AM I MY NEIGHBOR'S KEEPER?—
  Eberhart
AMANDA—Stagnelius
L'AMANT SURPRIS—Carco
AMANTIUM IRAE—Edwardes
LES AMANTS SÉPARÉS—Aragon
AMATEUR FILM-MAKING—Fuller,
  Roy
AMBERGRIS—Kunitz
AMBIENCE—Graves
AMBITION—Service
THE AMBITION BIRD—Sexton
THE AMBUSH—Ormond
AMERICA—Ginsberg
AMERICA—Smith, Samuel
  Francis
AMERICA FOR ME—Van Dyke
AMERICA IS HARD TO SEE—Frost,
  Robert
AMERICA THE BEAUTIFUL—Bates
AMERICAN BASEBALL—Dlugos
AMERICAN CHILD—Engle
THE AMERICAN CREED—Page
THE AMERICAN FLAG—Drake,
  Joseph Rodman
AMERICAN GOTHIC—Allen,
  Samuel
AMERICAN HEARTBRBREAK—
  Hughes, Langston
AN AMERICAN IN THE THIEVES'
  MARKET—Simpson
AMERICAN INDEPENDENCE—
  Hopkinson, Francis
AMERICAN NAMES—Benét,
  Stephen Vincent
AMERICAN PLAN—Brinnin
AMERICAN POETS—Bell
AMERICAN PRIMITIVE—Smith,
  William Jay
THE AMERICAN REBELLION—
  Kipling
AMERICAN TRADITIONAL CHANT—
  Talen
AMERIKA—McKay
AMERIKABALLADE—Paulus
AMERIKANSKII SOLOVEI—
  Yevtushenko
AMERS—Perse
UN AMI DORT—Cocteau
L'AMICA DI NONNA SPERANZA—
  Gozzano
LES AMIES—Carco
LA AMIGA DE BERNAL FRANCES—
  Anonymous–Spanish
LES AMIS INCONNUS—Supervielle
AMISTAD—Jiménez
AMMORE ABBASATO—Di Giacomo
L'AMMORE CHED'È?—Filippo
AMONG OTHER THOUGHTS ON OUR
  WEDDING ANNIVERSARY—
  Viorst
AMONG SCHOOL CHILDREN—Yeats
AMONG THOSE KILLED IN THE
  DAWN RAID—Thomas, Dylan
AMOR—Ridruejo

AMOR CONSTANTE MAS ALLA DE
  LA MUERTE—Quevedo y
  Villegas
EL AMOR DE LAS SELVAS—Santos
  Chocano
AMOR ETERNO—Becquer
EL AMOR MARIPOSA—Melendez
  Valdes
AMOR MAS PODEROSO QUE LA
  MUERTE—Anonymous–Span-
  ish
AMOR-VIDA—Mendes
AMORE—Saba
L'AMORE DE LI MORTI—Belli
AMORE DELLA VITA—Gatto
AMORE E MORTE—Leopardi
L'AMORE TI HA PORTATO OMBRA—
  Farinella
AMORES—Ovid
AMORET—Congreve
AMORETTI—Spenser
AMOS—Walker
AMOUR D'ELSA—Aragon
L'AMOUR DU MENSONGE—
  Baudelaire
AMOUR DU PROCHAIN—Jacob,
  Max
L'AMOUR ET LA FOLIE—La
  Fontaine
L'AMOUR ET LE CRÂNE VIEUX
  CUL-DE-LAMPE—Baudelaire
L'AMOUREUSE—Éluard
L'AMOUREUSE EN SÉCRET—Char
AMOURS DE CASSANDRE—Ronsard
AMOURS DE MARIE—Ronsard
AMOURS DE VOYAGE—Clough
LES AMOURS DIVERSES—Ronsard
AMSTERDAM—Ungaretti
THE AMUSEMENT PARK—Souster
AN ADOLF SELMNITZ—Novalis
AN BELINDEN—Goethe
AN CHARLOTTE VOM STEIN—
  Goethe
AN DEN ABEND—Goethe
AN DEN ABENDSTERN—Stolberg
AN DEN FRIEDEN—Rambler
AN DEN LESER—Werfel
AN DEN MISTRAL—Nietzsche
AN DEN MOND—Gleim
AN DEN MOND—Goethe
AN DEN MOND—Weinheber
AN DEN SCHWANKENDEN—Brecht
AN DEUTSCHLAND—Fleming
AN DIE BERLINERIN—Tucholsky
AN DIE FREUNDE—Schiller
AN DIE GELIEBTE—Mörike
AN DIE JUNGEN DICHTER—
  Hölderlin
AN DIE MENSCHENGESICHTER—
  Bürger
AN DIE MUTTER—Busch
AN DIE NACHGEBORENEN—Brecht
AN DIE NACHT—Jacobi
AN DIE NATUR—Hölderlin
AN DIE PARZEN—Hölderlin
AN DIE SONNE—Bachmann
AN DIE STERNE—Gryphius

AN DIE WUNDEN DES HERRN—
  Fleming
AN DIOTIMA—Hölderlin
AN EINE ÄOLSHARFE—Mörike
AN EINEN BOTEN—
  Anonymous–German
AN FRAU REBEKKA—Claudius
AN JENE, DIE WEINEN—
  Desbordes-Valmore
AN KLOPSTOCK—Bobrowski
AN MEIN KIND—Lasker-Schüler
AN MEINE FREUNDE—Göckingk
AN MEINE LANDSLEUTE—Brecht
AN MEINE MUTTER—
  Droste-Hülshoff
AN MEINE MUTTER—Heine
AN NELLY SACHS—Bobrowski
AN NOVALIS—Tieck
AN SCHWAGER KRONOS—Goethe
L'AN TRENTIESME DE MON EAGE—
  MacLeish
ANABASE—Perse
ANABASIS—Merwin
ANACOLUTHIC AND DRAG—Olson
ANAKREONTISCHE ODE—Klaj
ANALYSANDS—Randall
ANALYSIS—Orr
ANAPHORA—Bishop, Elizabeth
THE ANATHEMATA—Jones, David
ANCESTORS—Brathwaite
ANCESTORS—Garlick
ANCHE LA MORTE AMA LA VITA—
  Palazzeschi
THE ANCHOR—Booth
ANCIENT HISTORY—Guiterman
ANCIENT MONUMENTS—Ormond
AN ANCIENT TO ANCIENTS—
  Hardy
AND BECAUSE—Knight, John
AND LEO LION'S LINES—Cullen
AND NOW I—Clark, John W.
AND SEE HER IMAGE IN THE RIVER
  —Last Poets
&: SEVEN POEMS—Cummings
AND SO I PASSED—Johnston,
  Ellen Turlington
AND SOME CHILDREN COST AN
  ARM AND A LEG NOT TO
  MENTION THE REST OF YOUR
  LIFE—Howard, Lee
AND STILL I RISE—Angelou
AND STILL YOU ASK ME WHY—
  Bruchac
AND THE BABIES SCREAMED—
  Darragh
AND THEN—Williams, Miller
AND THIS FROM BRUIN BEAR—
  Cullen
AND THROUGH THE CARIBBEAN
  SEA—Danner
AND WE HID—Eckels
ANDALUCÍA—Machado, Manuel
ANDENKEN—Hölderlin
ANDENKEN EINES AUF DER SEE
  AUSGESTANDENEN
  GEFÄHRLICHEN STURMES—
  Gryphius

ANDREA DEL SARTO—*Browning, Robert*
ANDY, THE NIGHT-WATCH—*Masters, Edgar Lee*
L'ÂNE CHARGÉ D'ÉPONGES ET L'ÂNE CHARGÉ DE SEL—*La Fontaine*
L'ÂNE ET LE PETIT CHIEN—*La Fontaine*
L'ÂNE ET SES MAÎTRES—*La Fontaine*
L'ÂNE PORTANT LES RELIQUES—*La Fontaine*
L'ÂNE VÊTU DE LA PEAU DU LION—*La Fontaine*
ANECDOTE OF 2 AM—*Wain*
ANEMONE—*Benn*
L'ANÉMONE QUI RÉGNAIT SUR LA MER—*Desnos*
ANGE ÉTERNEL DES NUITS HEUREUSES—*Musset*
L'ANGE HEURTEBISE—*Cocteau*
THE ANGEL—*Blake*
EL ANGEL BUENO—*Alberti*
THE ANGEL: EASTER 1975—*Wilson, Patrice*
LOS ÁNGELES—*Carranza*
LOS ANGELES BELICOS—*Alberti*
LOS ÁNGELES DE LA PRISA—*Alberti*
LOS ÁNGELES MUERTOS—*Alberti*
ANGELIQUE—*Heine*
THE ANGELS OF DETROIT—*Levine*
ANGELUS—*Jiménez*
AN ANGER AS MEMORY—*Ward*
LES ANGES MALADROITS—*Cocteau*
ANGLO-CATHOLIC CONGRESSES—*Betjeman*
ANGRY SAMSON—*Graves*
L'ANGUILLA—*Montale*
THE ANGUISH—*Millay*
THE ANIMAL—*Abbe*
ANIMAL CRACKERS—*Morley*
THE ANIMAL FAIR—*Anonymous–English–Modern English*
ANIMAL TRICKS—*Emanuel*
THE ANIMALS—*Muir*
THE ANIMALS IN THAT COUNTRY—*Atwood*
LES ANIMAUX MALADES DE LA PESTE—*La Fontaine*
O ANJO REBELDE—*Ricardo*
ANNABEL LEE—*Poe*
ANNE JRENZSTEEN—*Olfers-Batocki*
ANNE RUTLEDGE—*Masters, Edgar Lee*
ANNEAU DE PAIX—*Éluard*
GLI ANNI MILITARI—*Gramigna*
ANNIE—*Apollinaire*
ANNIE HILL'S GRAVE—*Merrill*
ANNIE LAURIE—*Douglas, William*
THE ANNIHILATION OF NOTHING—*Gunn*
THE ANNIVERSARIE—*Donne*

ANNIVERSARIO—*Gatto*
ANNUAL SEARCH—*Sobiloff*
ANNUS MIRABILIS—*Dryden*
ANOIKSE M. KH—*Seferis*
ANOTHER NIGHT IN THE RUINS—*Kinnell*
ANOTHER SPRING—*De la Mare*
ANOTHER SPRING—*Rexroth*
ANOTHER STANZA FOR MARTINA—*Dlugos*
ANOTHER UNCLE—*Lifshin*
ANOTHER YEAR—*Marshall, Helen Lowrie*
ANSPRACHE EINER BARDAME—*Kästner*
THE ANT AND THE GRASSHOPPER—*Roche*
AN ANTE-BELLUM SERMON—*Dunbar, Paul Laurence*
ANTE MORTEM—*Jeffers, Robinson*
ANTHEM FOR DOOMED YOUTH—*Owen, Wilfred*
ANTHILL—*Sherman*
ANTHONY FINDLAY—*Masters, Edgar Lee*
ANTI-HEROINE—*Viorst*
ANTICO INVERNO—*Quasimodo*
ANTIMIRY—*Voznezensky*
ANTIQUE HARVESTERS—*Ransom*
LES ANTIQUES DE ROME—*Du Bellay*
ANTOINETTE ET MOI—*Obaldia*
ANTO-LOGY—*Morgenstern*
ANTONIO MACHADO—*Darío*
ANTS, ANTS CRAWLING—*Alurista*
ANTWORT—*Nietzsche*
ANWEISUNG FÜR ZEITUNGSLESER—*Bienek*
ANY HONEST HOUSEWIFE—*Graves*
ANY WIFE TO ANY HUSBAND—*Browning, Robert*
ANYBODY FOR MONEY—*Nash*
ANYWHERE AND EVERYWHERE—*Sandburg*
ANYWHERE OUT OF THE WORLD—*Baudelaire*
AO LONGE, OS BARCOS DE FLORES—*Pessanha*
APAISEMENT—*Geraldy*
THE APE AND THE LADY—*Gilbert, Sir William Schwenck*
APEGADO A MÍ—*Mistral*
APOCALISSI—*Ungaretti*
APOLOGIA PRO POEMATE MEO—*Owen, Wilfred*
APOLOGY—*Guiterman*
APOLOGY—*Wilbur*
APOLOGY FOR APOSTASY—*Knight, Etheridge*
APOLOGY FOR BAD DREAMS—*Jeffers, Robinson*
THE APOSTATE—*Kizer*
APOSTROPHES À L'OCÉAN—*Ducasse*
APPARITION—*Desnos*
APPARITION—*Donne*
APPARITION—*Mallarmé*

APPARITION—*Mariah*
THE APPEAL—*Kipling*
THE APPEAL—*Wyatt, Sir Thomas*
APPEL AUX ARMES—*Danton*
APPLE BLOSSOM—*MacNeice*
THE APPLE-JELLY-FISH TREE—*Conkling*
APPLE TRAGEDY—*Hughes, Ted*
APPLE WATCHER—*Ignatow*
APPLES—*Lee, Laurie*
THE APPLICANT—*Plath*
APPROACH OF AUTUMN—*Kunitz*
THE APPROACH TO THEBES—*Kunitz*
APPROACHING BOLTON—*Connor*
APPROACHING MOUNT CARMEL—*Robson, Jeremy*
APPROXIMATIONS—*Hayden*
APRES LE DÉLUGE—*Rimbaud*
L'APRÈS-MIDI D'UN FAUNE—*Mallarmé*
APRIK. MARM—*Thenior*
APRIL—*Stephany*
APRIL—*Storm*
APRIL BIJ SNEEUW—*Vree*
APRIL INVENTORY—*Snodgrass*
APRIL RAIN—*Loveman*
APRIL RAIN SONG—*Hughes, Langston*
APRIL RISE—*Lee, Laurie*
THE APRIL WARS—*Joselow*
APUNTES—*Machado, Antonio*
THE AQUARIUM—*Nash*
AQUI—*Paz*
AQUI CERCA PODRÍA ESTAR EL CIELO—*Joglar Cacho*
L'AQUILONE—*Pascoli*
ARAB LOVE SONG—*Thompson, Francis*
ARABIAN DANCE—*Nash*
LA ARAUCANA—*Ercilla*
ARAWATA BILL—*Glover*
DER ARBEITSMANN—*Dehmel*
EL ARBOL ALTO—*Martinez Alonso*
ARBOL DE MI ALMA—*Martí*
ARBRES—*Fombeure*
ARCADES—*Milton*
ARCADIAN DUOLOGUE—*Sidney*
THE ARCHAEOLOGIST—*Redgrove*
THE ARCHBISHOP AND THE PUMPKIN—*Roche*
THE ARCHER—*Smith, A. J. M.*
THE ARCHITECTURE—*Duncan*
ARCHITECTURE IN WHITE—*Fox, Siv Cedering*
ARCHY IS SHOCKED—*Marquis*
LA ARCILLA QUE PALPO Y BESO—*Celaya*
THE ARCTIC OX—*Moore, Marianne*
ARE YOU BORN?—*Rukeyser*
ARGUMENT ON IMMORTALITY—*Marshall, Lenore G.*
ARGUMENT ONE—*Sherwin*
ARGUMENT TWO: MIRRORS—*Sherwin*

ARIA OTOÑAL—*Jiménez*
ARIETTA 'E NU CORE CUNTENTO—
Bovio
ARIETTES OUBLIÉES—*Verlaine*
ARILLO, ANIMALUCCIO CANTATORE
—*Di Giacomo*
ARION—*Pushkin*
ARISTOCRATS—*Douglas, Keith*
ARISTOTLE TO PHYLLIS—
Hollander
ARITHMETIC—*Sandburg*
ARIZONA RUINS—*Lifshin*
ARK ROYAL 1940—*Casson*
LES ARMES DE LA DOULEUR—
Éluard
ARMI DELL' ALLEGRIA—*Rodari*
ARMOR'S UNDERMINING MODESTY
—*Moore, Marianne*
ARMS AND THE BOY—*Owen,*
Wilfred
AROUND THE MOUNTAIN—*Graves*
L'ARRACHE-COEUR—*Vian*
ARRANTZALEAK—*Eizmendi*
THE ARREST OF OSCAR WILDE—
Betjeman
ARRIVAL—*Brathwaite*
ARRIVING—NOT LEAVING—
Marshall, Helen Lowrie
ARROGANT LAW—*Warren*
THE ARROW AND THE SONG—
Longfellow
ARROW SONG—
Anonymous–American
Indian languages–Chippewa
ARROWHEADS—*Hannan*
ARRULLO PATAGÓN—*Mistral*
ARS POETICA—*MacLeish*
THE ARSENAL AT SPRINGFIELD—
Longfellow
ARSURA D'AMMURI—*Buttitta*
THE ART OF THE NOVEL—*Hacker*
ART POÉTIQUE—*Verlaine*
ARTE POÉTICA—*Neruda*
ARTEMIS—*Davison, Peter*
ARTEMIS—*Nerval*
ARTICHOKE—*Skratz*
ARTICLES DE SPORT—*Soupault*
ARTIS AMATORIAE—*Ovid*
L'ARTISANAT FURIEUX—*Char*
AN ARTIST'S PRAYER—*Marshall,*
Helen Lowrie
AN ARUNDEL TOMB—*Larkin*
AS HE IS—*Auden*
AS I GREW OLDER—*Hughes,*
Langston
AS I STEP OVER A PUDDLE—
Wright, James
AS I WAS SAYING TO ST. PAUL JUST
THE OTHER DAY—*Nash*
AS IT IS—*Dlugos*
AS THE TEAM'S HEAD BRASS—
Thomas, Edward
AS THOUGH FROM LOVE—
Marshall, Lenore G.
AS YOU LEAVE ME—*Knight,*
Etheridge
AS YOU LIKE IT—*Shakespeare*

ASCENSION-HYMN— *Vaughan,*
Henry
L'ASCENSORE—*Rodari*
DIE ASCHENHÜTTE—*Goll*
THE ASH AND THE OAK—*Simpson*
ASH WEDNESDAY—*Eliot, Thomas*
Stearns
ASIAN NIGGER—*Preston*
ASK AND HAVE—*Lover*
ASK THE ROSES—*Levine*
ASKING—*Levine*
ASLEEP—*Owen, Wilfred*
ASLEEP—*Silkin*
THE ASP—*Nash*
THE ASPEN AND THE STREAM—
Wilbur
ASPEN LEAVES—*Sherwin*
ASPENS—*Thomas, Edward*
DER ASRA—*Heine*
THE ASS AND THE FLUTE—*Iriarte*
ASSASSIN—*McGough*
ASSASSINATION—*Hillyer*
ASSASSINATION—*Lee, Don L.*
THE ASSASSINATION OF JOHN F.
KENNEDY—*Brooks,*
Gwendolyn
ASSAULT—*Millay*
ASSIGNMENT—*Butcher*
ASSISI—*MacCaig*
THE ASSISI FRAGMENTS—*Hill*
ASSOMONS LES PAUVRES—
Baudelaire
ASTERN—*Benn*
L'ASTRE ROUGE—*Leconte de*
Lisle
L'ASTROLOGUE QUI SE LAISSE
TOMBER DANS UN PUITS—*La*
Fontaine
ASTROPHEL AND STELLA—*Sidney*
ASYNNETEMI TON ANEMON—
Alcaeus
AT A CALVARY NEAR THE ANCRE—
Owen, Wilfred
AT A CONCERT OF MUSIC,
REMEMBERING THE DEAD IN
KOREA—*Ciardi*
AT A LUNAR ECLIPSE—*Hardy*
AT A SOLEMN MUSIC—*Milton*
AT A SOLEMN MUSICK—*Schwartz*
AT A TENTH GRADE PARTY—
Stafford
AT ALEXANDRIA—*Durrell*
AT ANY RATE—*Michie*
AT BAY—*Emanuel*
AT BEST, POETS—*Graves*
AT CANDLE LIGHTIN' TIME—
Dunbar, Paul Laurence
AT CASTLE BOTEREL—*Hardy*
AT DELFT—*Tomlinson*
AT DIEPPE: GREY AND GREEN—
Symons
AT HIS FATHER'S GRAVE—*Ormond*
AT HOME THE GREEN REMAINS—
Figueroa
AT KOVALAM—*Gregor*
AT MELVILLE'S TOMB—*Crane,*
Hart

AT MY FATHER'S GRAVE—*Ciardi*
AT NIGHT—*Bly*
AT NINETY-TWO—*Gill*
AT RHODES—*Durrell*
AT SOME POINT PAST ECSTASY—
Stephany
AT STONEHENGE—*Chapin*
AT THE AQUARIUM—*Eastman*
AT THE BAR—*Williams, William*
Carlos
AT THE BOTTOM OF THE WELL—
Untermeyer
AT THE BRITISH WAR CEMETERY,
BAYEUX—*Causley*
AT THE BROOKLYN DOCKS
NOVEMBER 23, 1963—*Gilbert,*
Dorothy
AT THE CENOTAPH—*MacDiarmid*
AT THE CONTROLS—*Elmslie*
AT THE CORE—*Piercy*
AT THE DRAPER'S—*Hardy*
AT THE EDGE OF THE WOOD—
Redgrove
AT THE END OF THE WORLD—
Williams, Hugo
AT THE FILLMORE—*Levine*
AT THE FISHHOUSES—*Bishop,*
Elizabeth
AT THE GRAVE OF HENRY VAUGHN
—*Sassoon*
AT THE HEART—*Kinsella*
AT THE KEYHOLE—*De la Mare*
AT THE LINCOLN MONUMENT IN
WASHINGTON, AUGUST 28, 1963—
Walker
AT THE MED-SCHOOL PARTY—
Darragh
AT THE MEMORIAL IN YAD
MORDECAI—*Sutzkever*
AT THE PYRAMID OF CESTIUS—
Hardy
AT THE RAILWAY STATION, UPWAY
—*Hardy*
AT THE SAN FRANCISCO AIRPORT—
Winters
AT THE SEASIDE—*Stevenson*
AT THE SUPERMARKET—*Plomer*
AT THE TOURIST CENTER IN
BOSTON—*Atwood*
AT THE TRACK—*Cunningham,*
James Vincent
AT THE WORD "FAREWELL"—
Hardy
AT THE ZOO—*Milne*
AT 35—*Hall*
AT THOMAS HARDY'S BIRTHPLACE
—*Wright, James*
AT WELLS: POLYPHONY—
Tomlinson
ATALANTA IN CALYDON—
Swinburne
ATHENA IN THE FRONT LINES—
Piercy
ATHENIAN MORNING—*Press*
ATT LEVA—*Vennberg*
THE ATTEMPT—*Betjeman*
ATYS À CYBÈLE—*Mauriac*

ATYS CHRÉTIEN—*Mauriac*
ATYS EST CHANGÉ EN PIN—
Mauriac
AU BEAU DEMI-JOUR—*Breton,*
André
AU BORD DE LA MER—*Hugo,*
Victor
AU BORD DE L'EAU—*Lasnier*
AU JARDIN DES MISÈRES—*Prévert*
AU JARDIN DES PLANTES—*Wain*
AU LECTEUR—*Baudelaire*
AU LENDEMAIN D'UNE CRUE—
Cendrars
AU MOMENT OÙ L'ON AFFICHAIT—
Cendrars
AU NOM DU FRONT PARFAIT—
Éluard
AU REVOIR—*Gaver*
AU SEUL SOUCI DE VOYAGER—
Mallarmé
AU TEMPS DES DONJONS—*Desnos*
AUBE—*Périn*
AUBE—*Rimbaud*
L'AUBE ÉTEIGNAIT ÉTOILES—*Scève*
AUCTION—*Holmes, John*
AUF DEM SEE—*Goethe*
AUF DEN KLEINEN RADIOAPPARAT
—*Brecht*
AUF DEN SONNTAG DES
GUTTHÄTIGEN WANDERMANNS
—*Gryphius*
AUF DEN SONNTAG DES VOR UNS
SORGENDEN SCHÖPFERS—
Gryphius
AUF DEN TOD DER KAISERIN—
Claudius
AUF DER ERDE—*Kaschnitz*
AUF DIE GEBURT SEINES ÄLTESTEN
SOHNES CHRISTIAN—*Gryphius*
AUF EIGENEN
FÜSSEN—DONNERWETTER—
Wedekind
AUF EINEN CHINESISCHEN
TEEWURZELLÖWEN—*Brecht*
AUF SEINEN GEBURTSTAG—
Gryphius
AUF VERLORENEM POSTEN—
Krolow
AUF WIEDERSEHEN—*Busch*
DER AUFHALTSAME AUFSTIEG DES
ARTURO UI: EPILOG—*Brecht*
AUFMUNTERUNG ZUR FREUDE—
Hölty
AUFTAKT—*Mehring*
AUGEN IN DER GROSSSTADT—
Tucholsky
AUGURIES OF INNOCENCE—*Blake*
AUGURY FOR AN INFANT—*Randall*
AUGUST—*Wylie*
AUGUST AFTERNOON—*Conkling*
AUGUST COUNTRY—*Garlick*
AUGUST HAIL—*Cunningham,*
James Vincent
AUGUST 1968—*Auden*
THE AUGUST OF MY LOVE—
Goldstein
AUJOURD'HUI—*Éluard*

AUJOURD'HUI, J'AI QUARANTE ANS
—*Cendrars*
AULD LANG SYNE—*Burns*
AULD ROBIN GRAY—*Lindsay,*
Lady Anne
AUNT JANE BROWN—*Johnson,*
Fenton
AUNT SUE'S STORY—*Hughes,*
Langston
AUNTIE'S SKIRTS—*Stevenson*
AUPRES DE TOI—*Diop*
AURORA AND THE TRUCKER—
Talen
AURORA LEIGH—*Browning,*
Elizabeth Barrett
AURORAS—*Jiménez*
AURORAS DE MOGUER—*Jiménez*
THE AURORAS OF AUTUMN—
Stevens, Wallace
AUS DER FERNE—*Lasker-Schüler*
AUS FERNEN, AUS REICHEN—*Benn*
AUSFLUG—*Guggenmos*
AUSGANG—*Fontane*
AUSGESETZT AUF DEN BERGEN DES
HERZENS—*Rilke*
AUSSÖHNUNG—*Goethe*
THE AUTHOR'S LAST WORDS TO HIS
STUDENTS—*Blunden*
AUTHOR'S PROLOGUE—*Thomas,*
Dylan
AUTO DE FÉ—*León, Rafael de*
AUTO POESY TO NEBRASKA—
Ginsberg
AUTO WRECK—*Shapiro, Karl*
AUTOBIOGRAFIA—*Rosales*
AUTOBIOGRAFIA IN TEMPO DI
GUERRE—*Vittorini*
AUTOBIOGRAPHICAL FRAGMENT—
Amis
AUTOBIOGRAPHICAL NOTE—
Scannell
AUTOBIOGRAPHY—*Donaldson*
AUTOBIOGRAPHY—*Ferlinghetti*
AUTOBIOGRAPHY—*Henri*
AUTOGRAPH BOOK-PROPHECY—
Halley
AUTOMNE—*Apollinaire*
AUTOMNE—*Lamartine*
AUTOMNE—*Seghers*
AUTOPSICOGRAFIA—*Pessoa*
AUTOSEMBLANZA—*Mesa*
AUTRE BALLADE, SUR LES
DIFFÉRENTES MANIÈRES DE RIRE
—*Deschamps*
AUTUMN—*Clare*
AUTUMN—*Nashe*
AUTUMN—*Sitwell, Osbert*
AUTUMN—*Tate, Allen*
AUTUMN BEGINS IN MARTINS
FERRY, OHIO—*Wright, James*
AUTUMN CHAPTER IN A NOVEL—
Gunn
AUTUMN ELEGY—*Norris*
AUTUMN FIRES—*Stevenson*
AUTUMN HILLTOP—*Marshall,*
Lenore G.

AUTUMN IN KING'S HINTOCK PARK
—*Hardy*
AUTUMN JOURNAL—*MacNeice*
AN AUTUMN MORNING IN
SHÔKOKU-JI—*Snyder*
AUTUMN, 1964—*La Farge*
AUTUMN: PROGRESS REPORT—
Starbuck
AUTUMN RIVULETS—*Whitman*
AUTUMN SEQUENCE—*Rich*
AUTUMN SONG—*Rossetti, Dante*
Gabriel
AUTUMN SONG, PROVENCE—
Chapin
THE AUTUMNALL—*Donne*
AUX CENDRES DE CLAUDE COLET
—*Jodelle*
AUX OMBRES DE DAMON—
Malherbe
AVANT-DERNIER MOT—*Laforgue*
AVANT GUARD—*Nash*
L'AVARE QUI A PERDU SON TRÉSOR
—*La Fontaine*
AVE CAESAR—*Jeffers, Robinson*
AVE, DEA MORITURUS TE SALUTAT
—*Hugo, Victor*
AVE-MARIAS—*Verde*
AVEC TON PARAPLUIE BLEU ET TES
BREBIS—*Jammes*
THE AVENUE BEARING THE INITIAL
OF CHRIST INTO THE NEW
WORLD—*Kinnell*
AVERTISSEMENT—*Laforgue*
AVEU—*Geraldy*
AVGUST—*Pasternak*
AVIS—*Éluard*
AVISO—*Celaya*
AVOIDING THE DOORS—*Patten*
AVRIL—*Belleau*
AWAKENING—*Bly*
AWAKENING—*Johnston, Ellen*
Turlington
AWAKENING—*Stryk*
AWAY—*De la Mare*
AWAY—*Frost, Robert*
THE AXOLOTL—*Nash*
AY!—*Garcia Lorca*
¡AY! CUANTAS COSAS PERDIDAS—
Salinas, Pedro
AYACUCHO DANCE SONG—
Anonymous–American
Indian languages–Peruvian
AZTEC FIGURINE—*Beecher*
L'AZUR—*Mallarmé*

BABETTE'S LOVE—*Gilbert, Sir*
William Schwenck
BABII YAR—*Yevtushenko*
BABUSHKI—*Yevtushenko*
BABY—*Hughes, Langston*
BABY GOAT—*Lewis, Janet*
BABY SEED SONG—*Nesbit*
BABY SISTER—*Marshall, Helen*
Lowrie
BABY SONG OF THE FOUR WINDS—
Sandburg
BABY STREET—*Blanding*

BABY VILLON—*Levine*
BABYLON—*Williams, Hugo*
BACCHUS—*Emerson*
BACCHUS—*Empson*
A BACHELOR'S COMPLAINT—
 Lamb
THE BACK AGAIN—*MacNeice*
THE BACK COUNTRY—*Dowling*
BACK HOME—*Marshall, Helen
 Lowrie*
BACKGROUND WITH
 REVOLUTIONARIES—*MacLeish*
BACKWARDS—*Merriam*
THE BAD KITTENS—*Coatsworth*
BAD LUCK CARD—*Hughes,
 Langston*
BAD-MAN STAGOLEE—*Walker*
BAD MORNING—*Hughes,
 Langston*
BADLY CHOSEN LOVER—*Tonks*
BAGATELLE—*Spender*
THE BAGEL—*Ignatow*
BAGLEY WOOD—*Johnson, Lionel*
BAGPIPE MUSIC—*MacNeice*
BAGS—*Porter, Bern*
BAHNHOFSTRASSE—*Joyce*
BAILA—*Garcia Lorca*
BAILE POR FARRUCA—*Garcia
 Lorca*
THE BAILIFF'S DAUGHTER OF
 ISLINGTON—*Anonymous–
 English—Modern English*
LE BAIN—*Vigny*
LE BAIN DU ROI—*Jarry*
THE BAITE—*Donne*
BAKESHOP WINDOW—*Kennedy,
 Marian*
BAL DES PENDUS—*Rimbaud*
BALAAM—*Keble*
BALADA—*Mistral*
BALADA DE LA ESPERANZA—
 Obligado, Pedro Miguel
BALADA DE LA LOCA ALEGRÍA—
 Barba Jacob
BALADA DE LOS ANSARES—*Pemán*
BALADA DE LOS DOS ABUELOS—
 Guillén, Nicolás
BALADA DE PRIMAVERA—*Jiménez*
BALADA DE UN DÍA DE JULIO—
 Garcia Lorca
BALADA DEL AGUA DEL MAR—
 Garcia Lorca
BALADA DELS TRES FADRINS—
 Sagarra
BALADA INTERIOR—*Garcia Lorca*
BALADA TRISTE—*Garcia Lorca*
BALADILLA DE LOS TRES PUÑALES
 —*León, Rafael de*
BALADILLA DE LOS TRES RÍOS—
 Garcia Lorca
LES BALAINES—*Fort*
BALBUCEO—*Banchs*
LE BALCON—*Baudelaire*
THE BALDNESS OF CHEWED-EAR—
 Service
THE BALL GAME—*Creeley*
THE BALL POEM—*Berryman*

BALLAD—*Calverley*
A BALLAD FOR PHILLIS WHEATLEY
 —*Walker*
A BALLAD FOR STIRLING STREET—
 Sanchez
BALLAD OF A STRANGE THING—
 Putnam
BALLAD OF BIG BOY—*Brown,
 Sterling A.*
THE BALLAD OF BILLY OF NOSEY
 BENT—*Causley*
BALLAD OF BIRMINGHAM—
 Randall
THE BALLAD OF BOUILLABAISSE—
 Thackeray
BALLAD OF BUNKER HILL—*Hale*
BALLAD OF CULVER'S HOLE—
 Watkins
THE BALLAD OF DESPAIR—
 Dowling
A BALLAD OF DREAMLAND—
 Swinburne
THE BALLAD OF EAST AND WEST—
 Kipling
THE BALLAD OF FATHER GILLIGAN
 —*Yeats*
A BALLAD OF FRANCOIS VILLON—
 Swinburne
THE BALLAD OF HARD-LUCK
 HENRY—*Service*
BALLAD OF JOHN CABLE AND
 THREE GENTLEMEN—*Merwin*
THE BALLAD OF LONGWOOD GLEN
 —*Nabokov*
THE BALLAD OF MARCO POLO—
 Benét, Stephen Vincent
THE BALLAD OF MARIE SANDERS—
 Brecht
THE BALLAD OF MOLL MAGEE—
 Yeats
BALLAD OF ORANGE AND GRAPE—
 Rukeyser
THE BALLAD OF PIOUS PETE—
 Service
BALLAD OF PSYCHOANALYSIS—
 Durrell
THE BALLAD OF READING GAOL—
 Wilde
THE BALLAD OF RUDOLPH REED—
 Brooks, Gwendolyn
BALLAD OF SEXUAL
 SUBMISSIVENESS—*Brecht*
THE BALLAD OF SUE ELLEN
 WESTERFIELD—*Hayden*
A BALLAD OF TELEOLOGIES—
 Ciardi
BALLAD OF THE BOSTON TEA
 PARTY—*Holmes, Oliver
 Wendell*
THE BALLAD OF THE CHILDREN OF
 THE CZAR—*Schwartz*
BALLAD OF THE FIVE CONTINENTS
 —*Causley*
THE BALLAD OF THE FREE—
 Walker
A BALLAD OF THE GOOD LORD
 NELSON—*Durrell*

THE BALLAD OF THE HARP-WEAVER
 —*Millay*
BALLAD OF THE HOPPY-TOAD—
 Walker
BALLAD OF THE JELLY-CAKE—
 Field, Eugene
BALLAD OF THE LANDLORD—
 Hughes, Langston
BALLAD OF THE LONG-LEGGED
 BAIT—*Thomas, Dylan*
BALLAD OF THE OEDIPUS COMPLEX
 —*Durrell*
BALLAD OF THE OYSTERMAN—
 Holmes, Oliver Wendell
BALLAD OF THE RED-HEADED MAN
 —*Beer*
BALLAD OF THE ROUGH SEA—
 Watkins
A BALLAD OF THE TREES AND THE
 MASTER—*Lanier*
THE BALLAD OF WILLIAM
 SYCAMORE—*Benét, Stephen
 Vincent*
BALLAD ON A WEDDING—
 Suckling
THE BALLAD SINGER—*Hardy*
BALLADA—*Lermontov*
BALLADA—*Lermontov*
BALLADE—*Villon*
BALLADE À LA LUNE—*Musset*
BALLADE CONTRE LA GUERRE—
 Deschamps
BALLADE DE CELUI QUI CHANTA
 DANS LES SUPPLICES—*Aragon*
BALLADE DE MARGUERITE—
 Anonymous–French
BALLADE DES ÄUSSEREN LEBENS—
 Hofmannsthal
BALLADE DES DAMES DU TEMPS
 JADIS—*Villon*
BALLADE DES FEMMES DE PARIS—
 Villon
BALLADE DES MENUS PROPOS—
 Villon
BALLADE DES PENDUS—*Villon*
BALLADE FOR THE DUKE OF
 ORLÉANS—*Wilbur*
BALLADE, IN DER MACHEATH
 JEDERMANN ABBITTE LEISTET—
 Brecht
BALLADE OF ANTIQUE DANCES—
 Henley, William Ernest
BALLADE OF CHRISTMAS GHOSTS—
 Lang
BALLADE QUE FIST VILLON A LA
 REQUESTE DE SA MÈRE POUR
 PRIER NOSTRE DAME—*Villon*
BALLADE SUR LA PAIX—*Charles
 d'Orleans*
BALLADE VOM KLASSIKER—*Hesse*
BALLADE VOM PFUND—*Brecht*
BALLADE VOM WEIB UND DEM
 SOLDATEN—*Brecht*
DIE BALLADE VON ANGENEHMEN
 LEBEN—*Brecht*
BALLADE VON DEN
 SELBSTHELFERN—*Brecht*

BALLADES—*Pisan*
BALLADES OF BERNALDO DEL
  CARPIO—*Anonymous–Spanish*
LE BALLON—*Obaldia*
BAM, BAM, BAM—*Merriam*
BAMBINI DI AKYAB—*Bevilacqua*
BAMBOO: A BALLAD FOR TWO
  VOICES—*Plomer*
HAMBURGER HANDSCHRIFT—
  Anonymous–German
BANDUSIA—*Hillyer*
BANISHMENT IN WINTER—*Merwin*
THE BANJO PLAYER—*Johnson,
  Fenton*
BANK ROBBERY—*Rector*
BANKERS ARE JUST LIKE ANYBODY
  ELSE, EXCEPT RICHER—*Nash*
THE BANKS O' DOON—*Burns*
O BANQUETE—*Ricardo*
BANTAMS IN PINE-WOODS—
  Stevens, Wallace
BAPTISM—*Aubert*
BARA BORJAN—*Elgström*
BARBARA—*Prévert*
BARBARA ALLEN—
  *Anonymous–English–
  Modern English*
BARBARA FRIETCHIE—*Whittier*
BARCAROLA—*Neruda*
BARCAROLLE—*Hillyer*
BARD OWL—*Pommy Vega,
  Janine*
THE BARDS—*De la Mare*
THE BARDS—*Graves*
THE BARE-BOTTOMED BABOON—
  Roche
THE BAREFOOT BOY—*Whittier*
DIE BARFRAU—*Tucholsky*
THE BARN—*Coatsworth*
BARNDOMSLANDSKAP—*Martinson*
BARNEY HAINSFEATHER—*Masters,
  Edgar Lee*
BAROQUE COMMENT—*Bogan*
A BAROQUE WALL-FOUNTAIN IN
  THE VILLA SCIARRA—*Wilbur*
BARREN SPRING—*Rossetti, Dante
  Gabriel*
BAR'S FIGHT, AUGUST 28, 1746—
  Terry
BARTER—*Teasdale*
BARTHOLOMEW—*Gale*
THE BASE STEALER—*Francis*
BASLER HANDSCHRIFT—
  Anonymous–German
BASNYA—*Svetlov*
IL BASTIMENTO—*Rodari*
THE BAT—*Roethke*
LA BATAILLE DE QADECH—
  Anonymous–Egyptian
LE BATEAU IVRE—*Rimbaud*
BATH SONG—*Lee, Dennis*
BATRACHOMYOMACHIA—*Well-
  man*
BATS AND BUTTERFLIES—*Dupree*
BATTERIE—*Cocteau*
BATTERTON DOBYNS—*Masters,
  Edgar Lee*

THE BATTLE—*Simpson*
THE BATTLE EVE OF THE IRISH
  BRIGADE—*Davis, Thomas*
BATTLE FIELDS—*Scannell*
BATTLE HYMN OF THE REPUBLIC—
  Howe
THE BATTLE OF ALCAZAR—*Peele*
THE BATTLE OF BLENHEIM—
  Southey
THE BATTLE OF BRUNANBURH—
  *Anonymous–English—Old
  English*
THE BATTLE OF THE KEGS—
  Hopkinson, Francis
THE BATTLE OF THE LAKE
  REGILLUS—*Macaulay*
THE BATTLE OF MALDON—
  *Anonymous–English—Old
  English*
THE BATTLE OF OTTERBOURNE—
  *Anonymous–English—
  Modern English*
BATTLE SCHOOL—*Lewis, Alun*
BATTLE WAGON—*Meredith,
  George*
BATXOCA—*Graves*
DER BAUER—*Bürger*
BAUMBESCHNEIDUNG—*Anony-
  mous–Asian languages*
A BAY IN ANGLESEY—*Betjeman*
BB—*Brown, Otis*
LA BBONA FAMIJJA—*Belli*
BE FRIENDS WITH YOURSELF—
  Marshall, Helen Lowrie
THE BEACH—*Graves*
THE BEACH WATCHERS—*Clark,
  John W.*
THE BEACON—*Wilbur*
BEAGLES—*Rodgers*
THE BEAKS OF EAGLES—*Jeffers,
  Robinson*
THE BEAN EATERS—*Brooks,
  Gwendolyn*
THE BEAR—*Kinnell*
THE BEAR STORY—*Riley*
BEAR TRACK PLANTATION—
  Warren
THE BEARDED MAN—*Lear*
BEARDED OAKS—*Warren*
BEAST AND THE BEAUTY—*Porter,
  Peter*
THE BEAST IN THE SPACE—
  Graham, William Sydney
BEASTS—*Engle*
BEATRICE REMEMBERS—*Sukenick*
LE BEAU NAVIRE—*Baudelaire*
LE BEAU TRAVAIL—*Seghers*
BEAUFORT TIDES—*Beecher*
LA BEAUTÉ—*Baudelaire*
BEAUTIFUL BLACK MAN—
  Giovanni
THE BEAUTIFUL TIGER—
  Gunderson
BEAUTIFUL YOU ARE THE MOST—
  Danner
BEAUTY—*Cowley, Abraham*
BEAUTY—*Thomas, Edward*

BEAUTY FOR ASHES—*Blackmur*
BEAUTY I WOULD SUFFER FOR—
  Piercy
BEAUTY IN TROUBLE—*Graves*
THE BEAUTY OF MISS BEATTY—
  Reaney
THE BEAUTY OF THINGS—*Jeffers,
  Robinson*
BEAUTY THREATENED—*Carew*
BECAUSE—*Giovanni*
BECAUSE I HAVE NOT LOVED YOU
  —*Mackin*
BECAUSE I HAVE WANDERED LONG
  —*Stephany*
BECAUSE OF FLOWERS—*Griffiths*
THE BED BY THE WINDOW—
  Jeffers, Robinson
BED IN SUMMER—*Stevenson*
BEDBUG—*Anonymous–English
  —Modern English*
BEDLAM REVISITED—*Ciardi*
BEDROOM OF MUSIC—*Williams,
  Hugo*
BEDTIME—*Farjeon*
THE BEE ORACLES—*Sitwell,
  Edith*
BEECH LEAVES—*Reeves*
BEEN DONE ALREADY—*Last Poets*
BEENY CLIFF—*Hardy*
BEEP, BEEP—*Nash*
THE BEEP BEEP POEM—*Giovanni*
BEETHOVEN'S DEATH MASK—
  Spender
BEFORE A CASHIER'S WINDOW—
  Wright, James
BEFORE DAWN—*De la Mare*
BEFORE DISASTER—*Winters*
BEFORE I KNOCKED—*Thomas,
  Dylan*
BEFORE TEA—*Milne*
BEFORE THE ANAESTHETIC—
  Betjeman
BEFORE THE SABBATH—*Ignatow*
BEFORE THE THAW—*Gill*
BEFORE THE WAR—*Hacker*
BEFORE THE WORLD WAS MADE—
  Yeats
BEGEGNUNG—*Bobrowski*
BEGEGNUNG—*Heine*
BEGEGNUNG—*Mörike*
BEGGAR AT VILLA D'ESTE—
  Kavanagh
THE BEGGARS OF BENIDORM
  MARKET—*Plath*
THE BEGGARS OF DUBLIN—
  Nowlan
BEGGAR'S OPERA—*Gay, John*
A BEGINNER'S GUIDE TO THE
  OCEANS—*Nash*
BEGINNING—*Merwin*
BEGINNING: TIZZIC—*Brathwaite*
BEGINNING TO GO—*Williams,
  Hugo*
BEHERZIGUNG—*Goethe*
DIE BEHÖRDE—*Morgenstern*
BEI BETRACHTUNG VON SCHILLERS
  SCHÄDEL—*Goethe*

BEI DIR UND DER DREIFALTIGKEIT —*Lavant*
DIE BEIDEN—*Hofmannsthal*
DIE BEIDEN ESEL—*Morgenstern*
BEING AND NOTHINGNESS—*Giovanni*
BEING FIVE—*Lee, Dennis*
BELAGERUNG—*Eich*
BELAYA NOCH'—*Pasternak*
LA BELETTE ENTRÉE DANS UN GRENIER—*La Fontaine*
BELIEF—*Miles*
BELL TOWER—*Adams*
LA BELLA BONA ROBA—*Lovelace, Richard*
BELLA GORRY—*Brown, Thomas Edward*
BELLA SCHIAVA—*Marino*
LA BELLE CONFIDENTE—*Stanley*
LA BELLE DAME SANS MERCI—*Chartier*
LA BELLE DAME SANS MERCI—*Keats*
BELLE ISLE—*Danner*
BELLE ISLE—*Randall*
UNE BELLE VIEILLE—*Maynard*
LES BELLES BALANCES DE L'ENNEMI—*Éluard*
LES BELLES FAMILLES—*Prévert*
BELLOWS—*Anonymous–English —Old English*
THE BELLS—*Poe*
BELLS FOR JOHN WHITESIDE'S DAUGHTER—*Ransom*
THE BELLS OF SHANDON—*Mahony*
BELSATZAR—*Heine*
BEN ALLAH ACHMET—*Gilbert, Sir William Schwenck*
BENDICIONES—*Mistral*
BENEDICE ANIMA MEA—*León, Fray Luis de*
BENEDICTION—*Kaufman, Bob*
BENEDICTION—*Kunitz*
BENEDIZIONE—*Pascoli*
BENJAMIN PANTIER—*Masters, Edgar Lee*
BEOWULF—*Anonymous–English —Old English*
BEPPO—*Byron*
BERCEUSE POUR UN PAS-DE-CHANCE—*Rictus*
BERCK-PLAGE—*Plath*
BERICHT ÜBER DEN TOD EINES GENOSSEN—*Brecht*
BERLIN CRISIS—*Victor*
LA BERLINE ARRÊTÉE DANS LA NUIT—*Milosz*
THE BERMUDAS—*Marvell*
BERNAL DIAZ, PREFACE TO HIS BOOK—*MacLeish*
BERT KESSLER—*Masters, Edgar Lee*
BERYL—*Lifshin*
LA BESACE—*La Fontaine*
BESCHRÄNKT—*Busch*
BESIDE THE SEA—*Scannell*

BESIDE THE SEASIDE—*Betjeman*
EL BESO DE LA LUNA—*Martinez Alonso*
THE BEST DAYS—*Wright, James*
BEST FOR ME—*Marshall, Helen Lowrie*
BESTRIDE THE NARROW WORLD—*Beecher*
BESYNNERLIG—*Ferlin*
BÊTE HUMAINE—*Young, Francis Brett*
BETHSABE'S SONG—*Peele*
THE BETROTHED—*Kipling*
BETSY LEE—*Brown, Thomas Edward*
A BETTER ANSWER—*Prior*
A BETTER RESURRECTION—*Rossetti, Christina*
BETTY'S BALL BLUES—*Reed, Ishmael*
BETWEEN—*Kern*
BETWEEN CRUISER AND PLATO—*Olson*
BETWEEN HYSSOP AND AXE—*Graves*
BETWEEN MOUTHFULS—*Emanuel*
BETWEEN THE PORCH AND THE ALTAR—*Lowell, Robert*
BETWEEN THE WARS—*Treitel*
BETWEEN THE WORLD AND ME—*Wright, Richard*
BETWEEN WALLS—*Williams, William Carlos*
BEVERLY HILLS, CHICAGO—*Brooks, Gwendolyn*
BEWAFFNETER FRIEDE—*Busch*
BEWARE—*Knight, Etheridge*
BEYOND—*Marshall, Helen Lowrie*
BEYOND CONNECTICUT, BEYOND THE SEA—*Bishop, John Peale*
BEYOND THE LAST LAMP—*Hardy*
BEYOND THE PALE—*Clarke*
BEYOND THE SEA—*Clark, John W.*
BHAGAVAD GITA—*Anonymous–Sanskrit*
BIAFRA BLUES—*Harper*
BIÅST PRINSEN—*Hazze*
BIBLICA—*Dávila, José Antonio*
LA BICHE BRAME—*Rollinat*
BIEN AIMÉE—*Soupault*
BIEN ÉGAUX—*Char*
BIG HIGH SONG FOR SOMEBODY—*Whalen*
THE BIG I—*Wheelock*
BIG JOHN HENRY—*Walker*
THE BIG MOLICE PAN AND THE BERTIE DUMB—*Lee, Dennis*
BIG MOMMA—*Lee, Don L.*
BIG WIND—*Roethke*
BIGGER THOMAS LIVES—*Marvin X*
LES BIJOUX—*Baudelaire*
BILBEA—*Sandburg*
BILDER—*Benn*
BILDER—*Morgenstern*

BILL AND JOE—*Holmes, Oliver Wendell*
BILL WAGNER'S BONES—*Polak*
BILLIE'S BLUES—*Alakoye*
BILLIONS, ZILLIONS—*Morgan, Karen*
BILLY BATTER—*Lee, Dennis*
BILLY IN THE DARBIES—*Melville*
BIM, BAM, BUM—*Morgenstern*
BINKER—*Milne*
BINSEY POPLARS—*Hopkins*
BIOGRAFÍA PARA USO DE LOS PÁJAROS—*Carrera Andrade*
BIOGRAPHY—*Bell*
BIOGRAPHY—*Robson, Jeremy*
BIOLOGICALLY SPEAKING—*Millay*
BIRCH—*Simpson*
BIRCHES—*Frost, Robert*
THE BIRD—*Gilbert, Celia*
THE BIRD—*Scott, F. R.*
BIRD, BIRD—*Derwood*
THE BIRD DESIRE—*Van Doren*
THE BIRD OF JESUS—*Colum*
BIRD OF PARADISE—*Colum*
BIRD OF PARADISE—*Graves*
BIRD OR BEAST?—*Rossetti, Christina*
BIRD-WITTED—*Moore, Marianne*
THE BIRDS—*Nash*
THE BIRDS ARE NO MORE—*Stephany*
BIRDS OF PASSAGE—*Whitman*
THE BIRDS ON THE MORNING OF GOING—*Merwin*
BIRMINGHAM—*Arnez*
BIRMINGHAM—*Walker*
A BIRTH—*Dickey, James*
THE BIRTH OF TRAGEDY—*Layton*
THE BIRTH OF VENUS—*Williams, William Carlos*
A BIRTHDAY—*Rossetti, Christina*
BIRTHDAY—*Yevtushenko*
THE BIRTHDAY CHILD—*Fyleman*
BIRTHDAY POEM—*Gilbert, Celia*
BIRTHDAY POEM—*Shpunt*
BIRTHDAY POEM—*Swift*
BIRTHDAY POEM FOR THOMAS HARDY—*Day Lewis*
A BIRTHDAY PRESENT—*Devaul*
BIRTHDAY THOUGHTS—*Richards, I. A.*
BIRTH-DUES—*Jeffers, Robinson*
BISHOP BLOUGRAM'S APOLOGY—*Browning, Robert*
THE BISHOP OF ATLANTA: RAY CHARLES—*Bond*
THE BISHOP ORDERS HIS TOMB AT SAINT PRAXED'S CHURCH—*Browning, Robert*
THE BISHOPS OF THE CHURCH OF ENGLAND—*Smith, Stevie*
BISMARCK—*Ossiannilsson*
BISON CROSSING NEAR MT. RUSHMORE—*Swenson*
A BIT OF ETERNITY—*Marshall, Helen Lowrie*
BITCHES' BREW—*Jimason*

BITTER LEMONS—*Durrell*
BITTER-SWEET—*Herbert*
BLACK—*Graves*
BLACK AND WHITE—*Clark, J. W.*
BLACK BACK—*Fabio, Sarah Webster*
THE BLACK CHRIST—*Cullen*
BLACK CLOUDS—*Cattonar*
BLACK COCK—*Reed, Ishmael*
THE BLACK COUNTRY—*Enright*
BLACK ECHO—*Emanuel*
BLACK EXPRESSIONS—*Amini*
THE BLACK FINGER—*Grimké*
BLACK FIRE—*Baraka*
THE BLACK GODDESS—*Graves*
BLACK HAIKU—*Hodges*
BLACK HUMOR IN FRANCE—*Emanuel*
BLACK IS—*Eckels*
BLACK IS—*Kali*
BLACK KETTLE RAISES THE STARS AND STRIPES—*Simpson*
THE BLACK KNIGHT AND WAMBA—*Scott, Sir Walter*
BLACK MAGIC—*Sanchez*
BLACK MAN IN A NEW DAY—*Jeffers, Lance*
A BLACK MAN TALKS OF REAPING—*Bontemps*
BLACK MAN, 13TH FLOOR—*Emanuel*
A BLACK MEMORIAL DAY—*Hodges*
THE BLACK MESSIAH—*Clark, China*
BLACK MOTHER PRAYING—*Dodson*
BLACK MRS. BEHEMOTH—*Sitwell, Edith*
A BLACK NOVEMBER TURKEY—*Wilbur*
A BLACK ORIENTED LOVE POEM, THE FIRST TIME I SAW LONELINESS—*Robinson, Wanda*
THE BLACK PLAGUE—*Antin*
BLACK POET ON THE FIRING RANGE—*Emanuel*
BLACK POET, WHITE CRITIC—*Randall*
THE BLACK RIDERS—*Crane, Stephen*
BLACK ROOK IN RAINY WEATHER—*Plath*
BLACK SHEBA—*Braxton*
BLACK SKETCHES—*Lee, Don L.*
BLACK SOUL—*Brierre*
BLACK SOUL OF THE LAND—*Jeffers, Lance*
BLACK SPACE—*McNeill*
BLACK STUDIES—*Lorde*
BLACK WISDOM—*Hodges*
BLACK WOMAN—*Last Poets*
A BLACK WOMAN SPEAKS—*Sanchez*
BLACK WORLD—*Fabio, Sarah Webster*
THE BLACKBIRD—*Wolfe*

BLACKBOARD JUNGLE—*Ennis*
BLACKGIRL LEARNING—*Lee, Don L.*
BLACKMUSIC/ A BEGINNING—*Lee, Don L.*
BLACKRUNNERS/ BLACKMEN—*Lee, Don L.*
THE BLACKSMITH'S SERENADE—*Lindsay, Vachel*
BLACKWOMAN—*Lee, Don L.*
BLAGODARNOST'—*Lermontov*
BLAKE RELATES THE FLOWER—*Thomas, Edward*
LA BLANCHE NEIGE—*Apollinaire*
BLASTING FROM HEAVEN—*Levine*
BLAUE HORTENSIE—*Rilke*
BLEEDING—*Swenson*
BLEIB—*Bachmann*
BLESS THIS LITTLE CHAPEL—*Marshall, Helen Lowrie*
THE BLESSED DAMOZEL—*Rossetti, Dante Gabriel*
A BLESSING—*Wright, James*
BLIND BOY IN NASSAU—*Sobiloff*
BLIND JOHN—*Walters*
A BLIND MAN AND THE ELEPHANT—*Saxe*
THE BLIND MAN'S SONG—*Rilke*
BLIND WILLIAM'S SONG—*Merwin*
DER BLINDE KNABE—*Rilke*
THE BLINDED BIRD—*Hardy*
THE BLINDMAN—*Swenson*
BLK CHANT—*Sanchez*
BLK RHETORIC—*Sanchez*
BLK WOOOOOMEN CHANT—*Sanchez*
THE BLOB SPEAKS TO ITS MOTHER—*Sherwin*
BLOCK CITY—*Stevenson*
BLOOD STAINS—*Francis*
BLOODY BILL—*Lee, Dennis*
THE BLOODY SIRE—*Jeffers, Robinson*
BLOOM—*Miles*
THE BLOSSOM—*Blake*
THE BLOWFLY—*Anonymous–Australasian languages–Australian*
BLOW-UP—*Greenwald*
BLUE BLACK; BLACK BLUES—*Modisane*
THE BLUE BOTTLE—*Swenson*
THE BLUE-FLY—*Graves*
BLUE GIRLS—*Ransom*
BLUE JUNIATA: BONES OF A HOUSE—*Cowley, Malcolm*
BLUE RAGS—*Meltzer*
BLUE SLEIGH—*Scott, Winfield Townley*
BLUEBERRIES—*Frost, Robert*
BLUEBERRY GIRL—*Abbe*
BLUEJAY—*Francis*
BLUES—*Morris, James*
BLUES—*Walcott*
BLUES AT DAWN—*Hughes, Langston*
BLUES FOR RUBY MATRIX—*Aiken*

BLUES POEM—*Alakoye*
THE BLUETAIL FLY—*Anonymous–English—Modern English*
DER BLUMENGARTEN—*Brecht*
DEI BLYENA PLATEN FUN ROMES DRUKEREI—*Sutzkever*
BOARDWALK BLUES—*Kramer*
THE BOAT—*Pack*
THE BOAT—*Smith, Stevie*
THE BOAT ON THE SERCHIO—*Shelley*
BOATS IN A FOG—*Jeffers, Robinson*
BODAS DE SANGRE—*Garcia Lorca*
BODEGA HEAD—*Beecher*
BODY AND SOUL, A MEDITATION—*Kumin*
BODY SHOP—*Brown, Otis*
THE BOGEYMAN HAS DONE IT—*Andersen*
LA BOHÈME—*Gaver*
BOHLIN—*Olson*
LE BOIS AMICAL—*Valéry*
BOLÍVAR—*Lloréns Torres*
BOMBAMI PO BALALAIKAM—*Yevtushenko*
BOMBINGS IN DIXIE—*Hughes, Langston*
BON AN, BON JOUR—*Deschamps*
BON CONSEIL AUX AMANTS—*Hugo, Victor*
BONA FIDE—*Morgenstern*
BONAC—*Wheelock*
BOND AND FREE—*Frost, Robert*
BOND STREET—*Nicholson*
BONDEN PAAVO—*Runeberg*
BONE THOUGHTS ON A DRY DAY—*Starbuck*
BONES OF MY FATHER—*Vargas*
THE BONFIRE—*Frost, Robert*
BONGIORNO, RO'—*Di Giacomo*
BONHEUR DE LA VIE—*Racan*
THE BONKS—*Walters*
BONNE ENTENTE—*Scott, F. R.*
BONNE JUSTICE—*Éluard*
BONNE PENSÉE DU MATIN—*Rimbaud*
BONNIE DOON—*Burns*
BONNIE GEORGE CAMPBELL—*Anonymous–English—Modern English*
BONNIE LESLEY—*Burns*
THE BONNIE LOWE—*MacDiarmid*
BONNY BARBARA ALLEN—*Anonymous–English—Modern English*
BOOK—*Abbe*
BOOK—*MacPherson*
BOOK BURIAL—*Glaze*
BOOK OF ANCESTORS—*Atwood*
BOOK OF CHANGES—*Anonymous–Asian languages*
BOOK OF ENOCH—*Bible and Pseudepigrapha*

THE BOOK OF HOW—*Moore, Merrill*

THE BOOK OF NATURE—*Eberhart*

A BOOK OF RIDDLES—*MacPherson*

THE BOOK OF THE DEAD—*Gunn*

THE BOOK OF THE OCEAN'S LOVE TO CYNTHIA—*Raleigh*

THE BOOK OF THEL—*Blake*

BOOKER T. AND W.E.B.—*Randall*

BOOKWORM—*Anonymous–English—Old English*

BOOM—*Nemerov*

BOOM TOWN, WYOMING—*Levendosky*

BOOT AND SADDLE—*Browning, Robert*

BOOTS—*Kipling*

BOOZ ENDORMI—*Hugo, Victor*

BOPPIN—*Henderson, David*

BORDER LINE—*Hughes, Langston*

BORDER SONG—*Scott, Sir Walter*

BORN BROTHERS—*Van Doren*

THE BOROUGH—*Crabbe*

EL BORRIQUETE—*Jiménez*

THE BORROWER OF SALT—*Williams, Oscar*

BÖS UND GUT—*Busch*

BOSS SOUL—*Fabio, Sarah Webster*

A BOSTON BALLAD—*Whitman*

BOTH—*Kern*

BOTHERING ME AT LAST—*Ignatow*

BOTSCHAFTEN DES REGENS—*Eich*

THE BOTTICELLIAN TREES—*Williams, William Carlos*

BOTTOM ON SHAKESPEARE—*Zukofsky*

LES BOUBOUS—*Cendrars*

LA BOUCLE RETROUVÉE—*Apollinaire*

LA BOUEE—*Soupault*

BOUGAINVILLE—*Davie*

BOUNCING SONG—*Lee, Dennis*

BOUND NO'TH BLUES—*Hughes, Langston*

THE BOURGEOIS BUTTERFLY—*Roche*

THE BOURNE—*Rossetti, Christina*

LA BOUTEILLE À LA MER—*Vigny*

IL BOVE—*Carducci*

BOWL—*Silkin*

A BOWL OF OCTOBER—*Bevington*

BOWLED OVER—*Hughes, Ted*

BOXES—*Giovanni*

BOXES AND BAGS—*Sandburg*

BOY—*Ciardi*

THE BOY ACTOR—*Coward*

BOY CHILD—*Sobiloff*

BOY IN SUNLIGHT—*Cowley, Malcolm*

THE BOY IN THE BARN—*Read, Herbert*

BOY ON ICE—*Lee, Laurie*

BOY RIDING FORWARD BACKWARD—*Francis*

THE BOY WHO LAUGHED AT SANTA CLAUS—*Nash*

A BOY'S SONG—*Hogg*

BRÅDSKA—*Ferlin*

BRAHMA—*Emerson*

BRANDEBOURG—*Frenaud*

THE BRANDY GLASS—*MacNeice*

BRANLE-BAS DE COMBAT—*Prévert, Jacques*

DIE BRAUT VON KORINTH—*Goethe*

DER BRÄUTIGAM—*Goethe*

BRÄUTIGAM FROSCHKONIG—*Kaschnitz*

DER BRAVE MANN—*Heine*

THE BRAW WOOER—*Burns*

BREAD—*Brathwaite*

BREAD AND BUTTER—*Merwin*

BREAK, BREAK, BREAK—*Tennyson*

BREAK OF DAY—*Brown, Sterling A.*

BREAK OF DAY—*Donne*

BREAKFAST IN A BOWLING ALLEY IN UTICA, NEW YORK—*Rich, Adrienne*

BREAKWATER—*Robison*

BREATH—*Levine*

BREATHES THERE A MAN—*Hoffenstein*

BREDON HILL—*Housman*

THE BREEZE—*Toleau*

BRENNENDE LIEBE—*Droste-Hülshoff*

ETT BREV—*Ferlin*

BREVE ISTAE DE SAN MARTIN—*Marin*

BRIAN O'LINN—*Children's Verses and Nursery Rhymes*

THE BRIDGE—*Longfellow*

THE BRIDGE AND THE LORRY—*Roche*

BRIDGE OF SIGHS—*Hood*

BRIDGE OVER THE DON—*Souster*

BRIDGE TO THE INNERMOST FOREST—*Broughton*

THE BRIDGES—*Merwin*

EIN BRIEF—*Hesse*

BRIEF LIVES IN NOT SO BRIEF—*Nash*

BRIGHT CONVERSATIONS WITH SAINT-EX—*Sandburg*

BRIGHT STAR!—*Keats*

DIE BRILLE—*Morgenstern*

EL BRINDIS DEL BOHEMIO—*Aguirre*

BRINDISI DI GIRELLA—*Giusti*

BRING THE DAY!—*Roethke*

BRINGING A TURTLE HOME—*Lowell, Robert*

THE BRINK—*Williams, Hugo*

BRISE MARINE—*Mallarmé*

THE BRITISH MUSEUM READING ROOM—*MacNeice*

BRITTLE BEAUTY—*Surrey*

A BROADWAY PAGEANT—*Whitman*

A BROKEN APPOINTMENT—*Hardy*

BROKEN DREAMS—*Yeats*

BROKEN-FACE GARGOYLES—*Sandburg*

THE BROKEN HEART—*Donne*

THE BROKEN HEART—*Ford, John*

THE BROKEN SEA—*Watkins*

THE BROKEN TOWER—*Crane, Hart*

BROLLOPSMARSCHEN—*Lagerlöf*

THE BRONCHO THAT WOULD NOT BE BROKEN—*Lindsay, Vachel*

BRONZEVILLE BREAKTHROUGH—*Fabio, Sarah Webster*

THE BROOK—*Tennyson*

BROOKLYN FLATS—*Simpson*

THE BROOM, THE SHOVEL, THE POKER AND THE TONGS—*Lear*

BROT UND WEIN—*Hölderlin*

BROTHER—*Darr*

BROTHER—*Stafford*

BROTHER FIRE—*MacNeice*

BROTHER JOHN—*Harper*

BROTHER JONATHAN'S LAMENT—*Holmes, Oliver Wendell*

BROTHER MALCOLM'S ECHO—*Kgositsile*

BROTHER, THE STRUGGLE MUST—*Jordan, Norman*

THE BROTHERS—*Dupree*

THE BROTHERS—*Hopkins*

THE BROTHERS: TWO SALTIMBANQUES—*Logan*

BROWN BESS—*Kipling*

THE BROWN BOOK OF THE HITLER TERROR—*Read, Herbert*

BROWN BOY AND GIRL UNDER THE MISTLETOE—*Cullen*

A BROWN CHILD'S PRAYER—*Arnez*

THE BROWN GIRL—*Anonymous–English–Modern English*

BROWN PENNY—*Yeats*

BROWN SUGAR—*Clark, China*

DIE BRÜCK AM TAY—*Fontane*

BRUIT DE VOIX—*Geraldy*

BRUMES ET PLUIES—*Baudelaire*

BRUTO MINORE—*Leopardi*

BRYANT PARK, NEW YORK—*Heath-Stubbs*

BUCH DES LEBENS—*Busch*

DIE BUCHER DER ZEITEN—*Hölderlin*

LE BÛCHERON ET MERCURE—*La Fontaine*

THE BUCK IN THE SNOW—*Millay*

THE BUCKET—*Woodworth*

BUCKINGHAM PALACE—*Milne*

BUENOS DÍAS—*Celaya*

BUFFALO DUSK—*Sandburg*

THE BUGABOO—*Field, Eugene*

THE BUILDERS—*Hay, Sara Henderson*

THE BUILDING OF THE SHIP—*Longfellow*

THE BUILDINGS OF TIME—*Blake*

BUKETTER—*Asplund*

THE BULL—*Williams, William Carlos*

THE BULL CALF—*Layton*

THE BULL OF BENDYLAW—*Plath*
THE BULLDOZER—*Francis*
BULLETIN—*Faerstein*
THE BULLY—*Rochester, Earl of*
THE BUMBLE BEE—*Riley*
BUMP ON THUMB—*Lee, Dennis*
BUMPETY BUMP—*Children's Verses and Nursery Rhymes*
BUMS AT BREAKFAST— *Wagoner*
A BUNCH OF ROSES—*Tabb*
BUNDESLIED DER GALGENBRÜDER —*Morgenstern*
BUONO NATALE!—*Di Giacomo*
THE BÜRGSCHAFT—*Schiller*
BURIAL—*Francis*
THE BURIED LAKE—*Tate, Allen*
BURIED LIGHT— *Watkins*
BURLA DE DON PEDRO A CABALLO —*Garcia Lorca*
THE BURLY FADING ONE—*Hayden*
THE BURNED CHILD—*Parker*
BURNING—*Snyder*
THE BURNING BABE—*Southwell*
THE BURNING BUSH—*O'Gorman*
THE BURNING CANVAS—*Goldstein*
BURNING ONESELF IN—*Rich*
BURNING ONESELF TO DEATH— *Stryk*
BURNING THE BRACKEN—*Norris*
BURNING THE CAT—*Merwin*
BURNING THE CHRISTMAS GREENS — *Williams, William Carlos*
BURNING THE DREAMS—*Rukeyser*
THE BURNT LEAVES— *Young, Andrew*
BURNT NORTON—*Eliot, Thomas Stearns*
BURY ME THERE—*Andersen*
BURYING GROUND BY THE TIES— *MacLeish*
THE BUSES HEADED FOR SCRANTON —*Nash*
BUSINESS AS USUAL—*Smith, A. J. M.*
BUSINESS WOMEN—*Betjeman*
BUSQUEDA ASESINA—*Palés Matos*
BUSTOPHER JONES: THE CAT ABOUT TOWN—*Eliot, Thomas Stearns*
BUSY MAN SPEAKS—*Bly*
BUT HE WAS COOL—*Lee, Don L.*
BUT STILL DESIRE AND WILL— *Richards, I. A.*
BUTCH WELDY—*Masters, Edgar Lee*
THE BUTCHER— *Williams, Hugo*
AS BUTTERBROTPAPIER— *Morgenstern*
BUTTERFLIES—*Dickey, James*
BUTTERFLY—*Conkling*
BUTTERFLY ADVENTURE— *Conkling*
THE BUTTERFLY BALL AND THE GRASSHOPPER'S FEAST—*Roscoe*
BUTTERFLY SONG— *Anonymous–American Indian languages–Chippewa*

BUY ME—*Levendosky*
BWO CHIN HWAI—*Du Mu*
BY BLUE ONTARIO'S SHORE— *Whitman*
BY FIAT OF ADORATION— *Williams, Oscar*
BY LAMPLIGHT—*Kunitz*
BY MORNING—*Swenson*
BY THE LAKE—*Durrell*
BY THE LAKE—*Sitwell, Edith*
BY THE RIVERSIDE—*Kizer*
BY THE ROADSIDE— *Whitman*
BY THE SEA—*Hollander*
BY THIS TO REMEMBER—*Spacks*
BY WAY OF PREFACE—*Lear*
THE BYRNIES—*Gunn*
BYZANTIUM—*Yeats*

C. L. M.—*Masefield*
ÇA CONTINUE—*Péret*
THE CABIN—*Brathwaite*
A CABIN IN MARIN COUNTY— *Snyder*
A CABIN IN THE CLEARING—*Frost, Robert*
CABLE CONFIDENTIAL—*Prévert*
CACOETHES SCRIBENDI—*Holmes, Oliver Wendell*
CADENCE—*Stephens*
CAEDMON'S HYMN—*Caedmon*
CAFE—*Lapalma*
CAFE IN WARSAW—*Ginsberg*
THE CAGED SKYLARK—*Hopkins*
CAHIER D'UN RETOUR AU PAYS NATAL—*Césaire*
CAHOOTS—*Sandburg*
CAINO—*Ungaretti*
CAIS DO PAQUETÁ—*Couto*
LA CAJITA DE OLINALÁ—*Mistral*
IL CALAMAIO—*Rodari*
CALAMUS— *Whitman*
CALENTURE—*Reid*
THE CALF—*Nash*
CALIBAN IN THE COAL MINES— *Untermeyer*
CALIBAN UPON SETEBOS— *Browning, Robert*
CALICO PIE—*Lear*
THE CALIFORNIA OAKS— *Winters*
THE CALL—*Brooke*
THE CALL—*Dodson-Letourneau, Gayle*
THE CALL ACROSS THE VALLEY OF NOT-KNOWING—*Kinnell*
THE CALL OF THE WILD—*Service*
CALLE DE ARRABAL—*Alonso*
CALLIOPE—*Skelton, John*
CALVARY WAY—*Miller, May*
CALYPSO—*Brathwaite*
CALYPSO'S ISLAND—*MacLeish*
CAMBODIAN SPRING—*Lavin*
THE CAMBRIDGE CHURCHYARD— *Holmes, Oliver Wendell*
THE CAMEL—*Derwood*
THE CAMEL—*Nash*
THE CAMEL—*Stryk*

CAMEL'S GARDEN— *Dodson-Letourneau, Gayle*
CAMILLE—*Chénier*
CAMINERA—*Mesa*
CAMP 1940—*Senghor*
A CAMP IN THE PRUSSIAN FOREST —*Jarrell*
LA CAMPAGNE DE RUSSIE—*Hugo, Victor*
LAS CAMPANAS—*Castro, Rosalía de*
LE CAMPANE DE GRAVO—*Marin*
CAMPESINA—*Anonymous–Spanish*
CAMPESINA—*Espada Rodriguez*
CAMPESINA, NO DEJES—*López*
CAMPO—*Burgos*
CAMPOS DE SORIA—*Machado, Antonio*
CANADIAN JAZZ—*Pines*
THE CANAL BANK—*Stephens*
CANARINA AZZURA—*Saba*
THE CANARY—*Nash*
A CANARY ON THE FARM—*Riley*
CANÇÃO—*Botto*
CANÇÃO DO VENTO E DA MINHA VIDA—*Bandeira*
THE CANCER CELLS—*Eberhart*
CANCIÓN—*Garcia Lorca*
CANCIÓN—*Pinar*
CANCIÓN—*Vega Carpio*
CANCIÓN CHINA EN EUROPA— *Garcia Lorca*
CANCIÓN DE BELISA—*Garcia Lorca*
CANCIÓN DE CRISTO Y EL ALMA— *Juan de la Cruz*
CANCIÓN DE CUNA—*Salinas, Pedro*
CANCIÓN DE GUIA—*Nalé-Roxlo*
CANCIÓN DE JINETE—*Garcia Lorca*
CANCIÓN DE LA VIDA PROFUNDA —*Barba Jacob*
CANCIÓN DE LAS ANTILLAS— *Lloréns Torres*
CANCIÓN DE OTOÑO EN PRIMAVERA—*Darío*
CANCIÓN DE UNA GENTIL DAMA Y UN RUSTICO PASTOR— *Anonymous–Spanish*
CANCIÓN DEL AMOR—*Castro Saavedra*
CANCIÓN DEL PIRATA— *Espronceda*
CANCIÓN FESTIVA PARA SER LLORADA—*Palés Matos*
CANCIÓN QUECHUA—*Mistral*
CANCIÓN TONTA— *Garcia Lorca*
CANCIÓN Y GLOSA—*Merwin*
CANCIONES DEL ALMA EN LA INTIMA COMUNICACIÓN DE UNIÓN DE AMOR DE DÍOS—*Juan de la Cruz*
CANCIONES ENTRE EL ALMA Y EL ESPOSO—*Juan de la Cruz*

CANÇÓ DE LA FRANCISQUETA—
   Sagarra
CANÇÓ DE LES MANS—*Raimon*
CANÇÓ DE PASSAR CANTANT—
   Sagarra
CANÇÓ DE TAVERNA—*Sagarra*
CANÇÓ DEL CAPVESPRE—*Sagarra*
THE CANDLE INDOORS—*Hopkins*
A CANDLE OF UNDERSTANDING—
   Marshall, Helen Lowrie
CANDLEFISH—*Schmitz*
CANDLES—*Plath*
THE CANONIZATION—*Donne*
CANT ESPIRITUAL—*Maragall*
THE CANTALOUPE—*Nash*
CANTARCILLO DE LA VIRGEN—
   Vega Carpio
EL CANTAR DE MÍO CID—
   Anonymous–Spanish
CANTAR DEL ALMA QUE SE
   HUELGA DE CONOSCER Á DÍOS
   POR FÉ—*Juan de la Cruz*
CANTARES—*Machado, Manuel*
CANTERBURY TALES—*Chaucer*
CANTES DE CÁDIZ—*Garcia Lorca*
CANTES DE HUELVA—*Garcia
   Lorca*
CANTI—*Leopardi*
A CANTICLE—*Weiss*
CANTICLE FOR GOOD FRIDAY—
   Hill
THE CANTICLE OF THE ROSE—
   Sitwell, Edith
CANTICLE OF THE SUN—*Francis
   of Assisi*
CANTICO DEL SOLE—*Pound*
CANTICO DELLE CREATURE—
   Francis of Assisi
CANTIGA—*Codax*
CANTIGA—*Marques*
CANTIQUE DE SAINT JEAN—
   Mallarmé
CANTIQUE DU PRINTEMPS—*Milosz*
CANTIQUE DU RHÔNE—*Claudel*
CANTO Á LA TIERRA—*Berger-Kiss*
CANTO Á PUERTO RICO—*Morales*
CANTO Á TERESA—*Espronceda*
CANTO AMOR—*Berryman*
'O CANTO D' 'O MANGANIELLO—
   Viviani
EL CANTO DE LA ANGUSTÍA—
   Lugones, Leopoldo
CANTO 4, SIX CYLINDER OLYMPUS
   —*Johnston, Percy E.*
CANTO NOTTURNO DI UN PASTORE
   ERRANTE DELL' ASIA—*Leopardi*
CANTO PA BERKELEY—*Vargas*
CANTOS—*Pound*
CANTOS DE VIDA Y ESPERANZA—
   Darío
CANTOS DEL PEREGRINO AL
   BRASIL—LA MUJER BRASILEÑA—
   Mármol
A CANZON PASTORAL—*Tao-Chi*
CANZONA: A PARTING ON
   SHIPBOARD—*Hollander*

'A CANZONE D' 'A FATICA—
   Viviani
CANZONIERI—*Petrarca*
THE CAP AND BELLS—*Yeats*
CAP D'ANTIBES—*Millay*
CAPE ANN—*Eliot, Thomas
   Stearns*
CAPE COD AUTUMN—*Starbuck*
THE CAPITAL—*Auden*
THE CAPITALIST FLEA—*Roche*
CAPITALS—*Garlick*
CAPRICE—*Betjeman*
CAPRICHO—*Storni*
LA CAPRICIA PERDIDA—*Storni*
CAPTAIN CARPENTER—*Ransom*
CAPTAIN STRATTON'S FANCY—
   Masefield
CAR FIGHTS CAT—*Sillitoe*
CARANGUEJOLA—*Sá-Carneiro*
CARAVAGGIO'S 'NARCISSUS' IN
   ROME—*Jennings*
'A CARAVANA—*Viviani*
THE CARCAJOU AND THE KINCAJOU
   —*Nash*
CARD MOST HOPED FOR/ MOST
   FEARED: THE JUDGEMENT—
   Piercy
CARDIGAN BAY—*Norris*
THE CARDINAL FLOWER—*Hillyer*
CARDONESS CASTLE—*Holbrook*
CARDS AND KISSES—*Lyly*
CARE-CHARMING SLEEP—*Fletcher,
   John*
CAREER—*Cunningham, James
   Vincent*
CARELESS LOVE—*Kunitz*
CARGOES—*Masefield*
CARIBBEAN CALYPSO—*Roach*
CARING—*Scott, F. R.*
CARMEL POINT—*MacSweeney*
CARMEN—*Gautier*
CARMINA—*Catullus*
CARMINA—*Horace*
CARNET DE IDENTIDAD—
   Alcántara
THE CARNIVAL—*Creeley*
CARNIVAL OF THE ANIMALS—
   Nash
CAROL—*Bolton*
CAROL—*Furse*
CAROL—*Rodgers*
A CAROL FOR CHILDREN—*Nash*
CAROL OF THE THREE KINGS—
   Merwin
CAROLINE—*Lowell, Robert*
LA CARPE—*Apollinaire*
THE CARPENTER—*Rector*
THE CARPENTER'S SON—*Housman*
A CARRIAGE FROM SWEDEN—
   Moore, Marianne
CARRICKFERGUS—*MacNeice*
CARRIER—*Meredith, George*
CARRION COMFORT—*Hopkins*
CARRY ME BACK—*Holmes, John*
CARTA A USTED—*Buesa*
CARTA ABIERTA—*Figuera*

CARTA DE RECOMENDACION—
   Dávila, José Antonio
'A CARTA 'E VISITA—*Viviani*
CARTA EN LOS CIELOS DE LIMA—
   Jiménez
CARTA LÍRICA A OTRA MUJER—
   Storni
CARTA/LLANTO PA LORCA—
   Vargas
CARTA REVIVIDA A GEORGINA
   HUBNER—*Jiménez*
LA CARTUJA—*Darío*
CASA—*Mistral*
CASA—*Reid*
LA CASA DEI DOGANIERI—
   Montale
CASA SUL MARE—*Montale*
LA CASADA INFIEL—*Garcia Lorca*
A CASE FOR JEFFERSON—*Frost,
   Robert*
A CASE OF MURDER—*Scannell*
CASEY AT THE BAT—*Thayer*
CASEY JONES—
   *Anonymous–English–
   Modern English*
CASHES—*Olson*
CASIDA DE LA ROSA—*Garcia
   Lorca*
CASIDA DE LAS PALOMAS OSCURAS
   —*Garcia Lorca*
CASIDA DE LOS RAMOS—*Garcia
   Lorca*
CASIDA DEL HERIDO POR EL AGUA
   —*Garcia Lorca*
CASIDA DEL LLANTO—*Garcia
   Lorca*
UNA CASINA DI CRISTALLO—
   Palazzeschi
CASINO—*Auden*
IL CASO DI UNA PARENTESI—
   Rodari
CASSANDRA—*Schiller*
THE CASTAWAY—*Cowper*
THE CASTAWAYS—*Zaturenska*
CASTIDADE—*Drummond de
   Andrade*
CASTILLA—*Machado, Manuel*
CASTILLA—*Unamuno*
THE CASTLE—*Smith, Stevie*
CASTLE INDOLENCE—*Thomson*
CAT—*Dunlop*
CAT—*Miller, Mary Britton*
A CAT, A HORSE AND THE SUN—
   McGough
THE CAT AND THE MOON—*Yeats*
THE CAT AND THE SAXOPHONE—
   Hughes, Langston
CAT AND THE WEATHER—
   Swenson
CAT CALLAHAN—*Lifshin*
CAT DREAM—*McCarthy, Agnes*
CAT-FAITH—*Reid*
CAT-GODDESSES—*Graves*
THE CAT IN THE WOOD—
   MacLeish
CAT NAPS ARE TOO GOOD FOR
   CATS—*Nash*

AT ON A TREE—*Emanuel*
ATACOMBS—*Ross, W. W.*
  Eustace
ATALOGUE—*Moore, Rosalie*
HE CATALPA—*Ciardi*
ATCH—*Francis*
ATCH—*Williams, Hugo*
ATCH A LITTLE RHYME—
  Merriam
ATCH WHAT YOU CAN—*Garrigue*
CATCHING SONG—*Farjeon*
ATEGORIES—*Giovanni*
ATENA—*Di Giacomo*
HE CATERPILLAR—*Nash*
HE CATERPILLAR—*Rossetti,*
  Christina
ATHEDRAL BUILDERS—*Ormond*
HE CATHOLIC BELLS—*Williams,*
  William Carlos
ATNIP FOR THE KIDDIES—*Mailer*
ATOLEGH, APOSTOLEGH E ROMAN
  —*Porta*
ATS—*Francis*
AT'S AIR: THE—*McClure*
ATS AND CLOCKS—*Williams,*
  Hugo
ATTIVO TEMPO—*Auden*
ATULLUS POEM LXX—*Nims*
AUSE AND EFFECT—*Swenson*
AUSERIE—*Baudelaire*
CAUTION TO EVERYBODY—*Nash*
AUTIOUS CROW—
  Anonymous–English–
  Modern English
L CAVALIERE TONTO—*Rodari*
A CAVALLA STORNA—*Pascoli*
HE CAVE—*Hillyer*
HE CAVE-BOY—*Richards, Laura*
  E.
HE CAVE OF MAKING—*Auden*
CCOSE 'MPRUVVISATE—*Viviani*
E COIR SOPÉ—*Senghor*
E PUR ENFANT—*Supervielle*
E QUE DIT LA BOUCHE D'OMBRE
  —*Hugo, Victor*
E SOIR—*Queneau*
O CECATO ALLERO—*Galdieri*
ECILY—*Morgenstern*
ELEBRATION—*Dickey, James*
ELEBRATION—*Sward*
ELEBRATION, COMPROMISE—
  Robinson, Wanda
ELERY—*Nash*
HE CELESTIAL SURGEON—
  Stevenson
ELESTINE—*Fitzgerald*
ELIBACY—*Clarke*
ELL SONG—*Knight, Etheridge*
HE CELLAR—*Conkling*
ELLE DE TOUJOURS, TOUTE—
  Éluard
ER CELLOSPIELER AUS
  THÜRINGEN—*Zuckmayer*
ELLS—*Kipling*
HE CELTIC FRINGE—*Smith,*
  Stevie

EL CEMENTIRI DELS MARINERS—
  Sagarra
CENDRARS EST UN OBSÉDÉ—
  Cendrars
THE CENTAUR—*Swenson*
THE CENTAURS—*Stephens*
A CENTENARY ODE—*Wright,*
  James
THE CENTIPEDE—*Nash*
CENTRAL PARK—*Lowell, Robert*
CENTRAL PARK TOURNEY—*Weston*
CERCLE VICIEUX—*Obaldia*
CEREMONIES FOR CHRISTMAS—
  Herrick
CEREMONY AFTER A FIRE RAID—
  Thomas, Dylan
LE CERF SE VOYANT DANS L'EAU—
  La Fontaine
C'EST À VOUS QUE JE PARLE—
  Fondane
C'EST LE PARADIS TERRESTRE—
  Cendrars
C'EST LOU QU'ON LA NOMMAIT—
  Apollinaire
CÉZANNE—*Deutsch*
CÉZANNE AT AIX—*Tomlinson*
CHAADAEVU—*Pushkin*
CHAINS—*Kramer*
CHAINY—*Beecher*
THE CHALLENGE OF OUR DOUBTS
  —*Marshall, Helen Lowrie*
CHAMBER MUSIC, 35—*Joyce*
THE CHAMBERED NAUTILUS—
  Holmes, Oliver Wendell
THE CHAMBERMAID'S TWO SONGS
  —*Yeats*
LA CHAMBRE DOUBLE—
  Baudelaire
CHANCE—*Geraldy*
CHANCE IS THE GOD OF DEATH—
  Shiva
CHANG GAN SYING—*Li Bai*
CHANG HEN GE—*Bai Jyu Yi*
CHANGE—*Cowley, Abraham*
CHANGE—*Graves*
CHANGE—*Weiss*
CHANGE IS NOT ALWAYS PROGRESS
  —*Lee, Don L.*
A CHANGE OF SKIN—*Walcott*
CHANGE US—*Sanchez*
CHANGED—*Abbe*
CHANGING LIGHT WINDS—
  Sandburg
CHANGING THE WORLD—*Shpunt*
CHANNEL FIRING—*Hardy*
A CHANNEL PASSAGE—*Brooke*
CHANSON—*Noël*
CHANSON—*Ronsard*
CHANSON—*Sponde*
CHANSON—*Villon*
CHANSON À PART—*Valéry*
CHANSON DANS LE SANG—*Prévert*
CHANSON D'AUTOMNE—*Claudel*
CHANSON D'AUTOMNE—*Verlaine*
LA CHANSON DE FORTUNIO—
  Musset

CHANSON DE LA PLUS HAUTE TOUR
  —*Rimbaud*
CHANSON DE LANCELOT—*Vian*
LA CHANSON DE ROLAND—
  Anonymous–French
CHANSON DES SARDINIÈRES—
  Prévert
CHANSON DU GRAND ECHANSON—
  Henault
LA CHANSON DU MAL-AIMÉ—
  Apollinaire
CHANSONS DU BOUT DU QUAI—
  Soupault
CHANSONS INNOCENTES—
  Cummings
CHANT DE L'HORIZON EN
  CHAMPAGNE—*Apollinaire*
CHANT DE MAY ET DE VERTU—
  Marot
LE CHANT DE SOLITUDE—*Cadou*
CHANT DE SUZANNE AU BAIN—
  Vigny
CHANT DU BOL DE PUNCH—*Hugo,*
  Victor
CHANT DU FEU—*Senghor*
A CHANT FOR YOUNG BROTHAS
  AND SISTUHS—*Sanchez*
CHANT PROFANE POUR DES TEMPS
  INQUIÉTS—*Sylvain*
CHANT SONG—*Prévert*
CHANTERAI POUR MON COURAGE—
  Guyot de Dijon
CHANTICLEER—*Farrar*
LES CHANTS DE MALDOROR—
  Ducasse
LES CHANTS DU CRÉPUSCULE—
  Hugo, Victor
CHAPTER HEADING FROM THE
  JUNGLE BOOKS—*Kipling*
CHAQUE NUIT, À L'HEURE OÙ LE
  SOMMEIL—*Ducasse*
CHARACTER OF A HAPPY LIFE—
  Wotton
THE CHARACTER OF LOVE SEEN AS
  A SEARCH FOR THE LOST—
  Patchen
CHARACTERS OF SHAKESPEARE—
  Beerbohm
CHARADE—*Prévert*
THE CHARCOAL-BURNER—*Milne*
CHARD WITLOW—*Reed, Henry*
THE CHARGE OF THE LIGHT
  BRIGADE—*Tennyson*
CHARLES—*Brooks, Gwendolyn*
CHARLES AUGUSTUS FORTESCUE,
  WHO ALWAYS DID WHAT WAS
  RIGHT—*Belloc*
CHARLES I—*Shelley*
CHARLES PARKER—*Cuney*
CHARLES THE FIFTH AND THE
  PEASANT—*Lowell, Robert*
CHARLESTON IN THE
  EIGHTEEN-SIXTIES—*Rich*
CHARLIE FRENCH—*Masters,*
  Edgar Lee
CHARM—*Anonymous–English–*
  Old English

A CHARM—*Kipling*

LE CHARTIER EMBOURBÉ—*La Fontaine*

THE CHASE—*Gregor*

CHASE HENRY—*Masters, Edgar Lee*

CHASSIDIM—*Lutzky*

A CHASTE MAID IN CHEAPSIDE—*Middleton, Thomas*

LE CHAT—*Apollinaire*

LE CHAT—*Baudelaire*

LE CHAT ET UN VIEUX RAT—*La Fontaine*

LE CHAT, LA BELETTE ET LE PETIT LAPIN—*La Fontaine*

LE CHÂTEAU DES PAUVRES—*Éluard*

CHÂTEAUX DE LOIRE—*Péguy*

LES CHATS—*Baudelaire*

CHAUCER—*Longfellow*

LA CHAUVE-SOURIS ET LES DEUX BELETTES—*La Fontaine*

CHEAP BLUE—*Sandburg*

CHECK—*Stephens*

CHEERS—*Merriam*

CHEFA—*Lloréns Torres*

CHEMIN DE LA CROIX—*Claudel*

LE CHÊNE ET LE ROSEAU—*La Fontaine*

LES CHERCHEUSES DE POUX—*Rimbaud*

CHERRIE-RIPE—*Herrick*

CHERRY BLOSSOM—*Williams, Hugo*

THE CHERRY TREE—*Williams, Hugo*

THE CHERRY TREE CAROL—*Anonymous–English–Modern English*

THE CHERRY TREES—*Thomas, Edward*

CHERRYLOG ROAD—*Dickey, James*

LE CHEVAL ET LE LOUP—*La Fontaine*

CHEVAUX DES BOIS—*Fombeure*

LA CHEVELURE—*Baudelaire*

LA CHEVELURE—*Mallarmé*

CHEVY CHASE—*Anonymous–English–Modern English*

CHEZ LA FLEURISTE—*Prévert*

CHEZ MOI—*Obaldia*

CHHANDOGYA UPANISHAD—*Anonymous–Sanskrit*

CHI CCERCA TROVA—*Belli*

CHI SONO?—*Palazzeschi*

CHI VA A LA NOTTE, VA A LA MORTE—*Belli*

LE CHIAMATE DELL'APPIGGIONANTE—*Belli*

'O CHIANCHIERE—*Russo*

CHICAGO—*Sandburg*

CHICAGO—*Shiva*

CHICAGO AND SAN FRANCISCO AND YOU AND ME—*Shange*

CHICAGO BOY BABY—*Sandburg*

THE CHICAGO "DEFENDER" SENDS A MAN TO LITTLE ROCK—*Brooks, Gwendolyn*

CHICAGO POET—*Sandburg*

CHICHIMECAS—*Anonymous–American Indian languages–Nahuatl*

CHICKADEE—*Conkling*

THE CHICKENS—*Children's Verses and Nursery Rhymes*

LE CHIEN QUI LÂCHE SA PROIE POUR L'OMBRE—*La Fontaine*

LES CHIENS D'ASNIÈRES—*Queneau*

LA CHIESA DI POLENTA—*Carducci*

CHILD—*Robison*

CHILD—*Sandburg*

A CHILD AND THE COCONUT HEAD—*Sobiloff*

THE CHILD AT WINTER SUNSET—*Van Doren*

A CHILD HALF-ASLEEP—*Connor*

THE CHILD IS FRIGHTENED BY BOOKS—*Den Boer*

A CHILD IS SINGING—*Mitchell, Adrian*

CHILD LOVERS—*Davies, William Henry*

THE CHILD NEXT DOOR—*Fyleman*

THE CHILD NEXT DOOR—*Kunitz*

THE CHILD NEXT DOOR—*Warren*

THE CHILD ON THE CLIFFS—*Thomas, Edward*

CHILDE HAROLD'S PILGRIMAGE—*Byron*

CHILDE ROLAND TO THE DARK TOWER CAME—*Browning, Robert*

CHILDHOOD—*Viereck*

CHILDHOOD IS THE KINGDOM WHERE NOBODY DIES—*Millay*

A CHILDISH PRANK—*Hughes, Ted*

CHILDREN AND A FETUS—*Jeffers, Lance*

CHILDREN OF ADAM—*Whitman*

CHILDREN OF THE POOR—*Brooks, Gwendolyn*

CHILDREN'S CHILDREN—*Brown, Sterling A.*

THE CHILDREN'S CRUSADE—*Levine*

CHILDREN'S GAMES—*Connor*

THE CHILDREN'S HOUR—*Longfellow*

CHILDREN'S PARTY—*Nash*

THE CHILDREN'S PLAYGROUND—*Williams, Oscar*

CHILD'S GARDEN OF VERSES—*Stevenson*

A CHILD'S GUIDE TO PARENTS—*Nash*

A CHILD'S LAUGHTER—*Swinburne*

CHILD'S PARK STONES—*Plath*

THE CHILD'S SIGHT—*Sobiloff*

CHILD'S SONG—*Causley*

CHILD'S SONG—*Moore, Thomas*

THE CHILD'S UMBRELLA—*Souster*

CHIMAPHILA, 1972—*Francis*

CHIMES—*Longfellow*

THE CHIMNEY SWEEPER—*Blake*

THE CHIMNEY-TOP CHILD—*Wilson*

CHINESE DANCE—*Nash*

CHINESE DOLL—*Thomas-Ellis*

CHINESE GIFTS—*Bodenheim*

THE CHINESE NIGHTINGALE—*Lindsay, Vachel*

CHINESISCH-DEUTSCHE TAGES-UND JAHRESZEITEN—*Goethe*

THE CHINK—*Graves*

CHINON—*Mathias*

THE CHIRRUPY CRICKET—*Thomas, Martha B.*

'A CHITARRA—*Di Giacomo*

CHLOE—*Mordaunt*

CHOCKABLOCK—*Olson*

CHOEUR DES GNOMES—*Nerval*

CHOICE—*Oxford*

CHOICE—*Rossetti, Dante Gabriel*

CHOICE OF WEAPONS—*Kunitz*

CHOICES—*Ciardi*

CHOICES—*Giovanni*

THE CHOIRMASTER'S BURIAL—*Hardy*

CHOOSE SOMETHING LIKE A STAR—*Frost, Robert*

CHOR DER GIRLS—*Kästner*

CHORUS FOR SURVIVAL: POEM 14—*Gregory, Horace*

CHRIST CALLS MAN HOME—*Anonymous–English–Modern English*

CHRIST IN ALABAMA—*Hughes, Langston*

CHRIST, ONE MORNING—*Emanuel*

CHRISTABEL—*Coleridge, Samuel Taylor*

THE CHRISTENING—*Brown, Thomas Edward*

THE CHRISTENING—*Hardy*

CHRISTIANA—*Redgrove*

LE CHRISTIANISME—*Owen, Wilfred*

CHRISTINA—*MacNeice*

CHRISTINE—*Wedekind*

CHRISTMAS—*Betjeman*

CHRISTMAS—*Farjeon*

CHRISTMAS—*Smith, Stevie*

CHRISTMAS BELLS—*Longfellow*

A CHRISTMAS CAROL—*Coleridge, Samuel Taylor*

A CHRISTMAS CAROL—*Rossetti, Christina*

CHRISTMAS EVE—*Chapin*

CHRISTMAS EVE IN WHITNEYVILLE—*Hall*

CHRISTMAS EVE UNDER HOOKER'S STATUE—*Lowell, Robert*

A CHRISTMAS HYMN—*Domett*

CHRISTMAS 1914—*Richards, Frank*

CHRISTMAS POEM—*Sobiloff*
CHRISTMAS ROBIN—*Graves*
A CHRISTMAS STORY— *Vogeler*
THE CHRISTMAS THAT ALMOST WASN'T—*Nash*
THE CHRISTMAS TREE—*Day Lewis*
CHRISTOPHER CAT—*Cullen*
CHRISTUS NATUS EST—*Chapman*
CHROMO—*Fabio, Sarah Webster*
CHRONICLES—*Olson*
CHRONIQUE 8—*Perse*
CHUDO—*Pasternak*
CHWUN SYAU—*Meng Hau Ran*
CHWUN WANG—*Du Fu*
CHYAN BEI HWAI—*Ywan Jen*
CHYANG TSWUN—*Du Fu*
CIA DOPE CALYPSO—*Ginsberg*
CIÀCOLA 'L MAR INTORNO AL DOSSO—*Marin*
THE CICADA—*Aiken*
IL CICERONE—*Russo*
LE CID—*Fourest*
LE CIEL EST ÉTOILÉ—*Apollinaire*
IL CIELO È DI TUTTI—*Rodari*
CIELO Y MAR—*López*
CIENCIA DE AMOR—*Alonso*
LA CIGALE ET LA FOURMI—*La Fontaine*
CIGARETTE—*Scannell*
LE CIMETIÈRE—*Desnos*
LE CIMETIÈRE MARIN— *Valéry*
IL CIMITERIO DE LA MORTE—*Belli*
CINDERELLA—*Jarrell*
IL CINQUE MAGGIO—*Manzoni*
LE 5e POÈME VISIBLE—*Éluard*
IL CIPRÉS DE SILOS—*Diego, Gerardo*
CIRCE—*Auden*
A CIRCLE—*Spencer*
CIRCLES—*Kali*
CIRCLES IN THE SAND—*Abrams*
THE CIRCUIT—*Wagoner*
THE CIRCUS—*Spencer*
THE CIRCUS ANIMALS' DESERTION — *Yeats*
CIRCUS PARADE—*Tippett*
CIRKUS—*Ferlin*
CITIES—*Benedikt*
CITIES—*Hacker*
THE CITIZENS—*Blackburn, Thomas*
CITY—*Francis*
CITY—*Hughes, Langston*
CITY—*Posner*
CITY—*Traherne*
CITY AFTERNOON—*Howes*
CITY IN TERROR—*Walters*
THE CITY IN THE SEA—*Poe*
THE CITY MOUSE AND THE COUNTRY MOUSE—*Rossetti, Christina*
THE CITY OF DREADFUL NIGHT—*Thomson*
CITY OF EVENINGS— *Wright, James*

CITY SONGS—*Sanchez*
CITY TREES—*Millay*
CIUDA—*Neruda*
CIUDAD DEL PARAÍSO—*Aleixandre*
CIUDAD SIN SUEÑO—*Garcia Lorca*
CIVIL WAR— *Van Doren*
CLAD IN GARMENTS NOW—*Stephany*
CLAIR DE LUNE—*Verlaine*
CLAIRVOYANCE—*Jordan, Norman*
CLAIRVOYANT—*Porter, Peter*
CLAMOR ANTE EDGAR POE—*Pardo Garcia*
CLANCY OF THE MOUNTED POLICE —*Service*
CLARENCE FAWCETT—*Masters, Edgar Lee*
CLARISSE—*Heine*
THE CLASS WILL COME TO ORDER —*Kunitz*
A CLASSICAL LOCATION—*Wellman*
CLEANING OUT THE GARAGE—*Booth*
CLEAR AND COLDER—*Frost, Robert*
CLEAR MELODY—*Hillyer*
A CLEAR MIDNIGHT— *Whitman*
CLEAR THE AIR! CLEAN THE SKY! WASH THE WIND!—*Eliot, Thomas Stearns*
CLEARED FOR APPROACH, CLEARED FOR LANDING—*Darr*
CLEARLY ABOUT YOU— *Warren*
CLEATOR MOOR—*Nicholson*
LA CLEF—*Apollinaire*
CLERK SAUNDERS—*Anonymous–English–Modern English*
CLEVELAND NINE—*Bruchac*
CLEVER TOM CLINCH—*Anonymous–English–Modern English*
CLIFF KLINGENHAGEN—*Robinson, Edwin Arlington*
CLIFF NOTES—*Mason*
CLIFTON—*Brown, Thomas Edward*
CLIMBING MT. VISION WITH MY LITTLE BOY—*Bly*
CLIPPER SHIPS—*Fletcher, John Gould*
THE CLOAK—*Graves*
LA CLOCHE DU VILLAGE—*Lamartine*
LA CLOCHE FÊLÉE—*Baudelaire*
LES CLOCHES—*Apollinaire*
LES CLOCHES SONNENT SANS RAISON—*Tzara*
CLOCK—*Kern*
CLOCK-A-CLAY—*Clare*
THE CLOD AND THE PEBBLE—*Blake*

CLOSED FOR GOOD—*Frost, Robert*
THE CLOSING OF THE RODEO—*Smith, William Jay*
THE CLOUD—*Shelley*
CLOUDS—*Clark, John W.*
CLOUDS—*Levine*
CLOUDS—*Rossetti, Christina*
CLOUDS—*Williams, Hugo*
A CLOWN AT TEN—*Emanuel*
CLUB 82: LISA—*Genser*
CLUNTON AND CLUNBURY—*Housman*
CÔ SARÉ MORTO—*Marin*
COAL FIRE—*Untermeyer*
COALITION: RHYMES WITH REVOLUTION—*Gaver*
A COAT—*Yeats*
COAT OF MAIL—*Anonymous–English—Old English*
THE COATS—*Gallagher, Tess*
COCAINE—*Wieners*
LE COCHE ET LA MOUCHE—*La Fontaine*
LE COCHET, LE CHAT ET LE SOURICEAU—*La Fontaine*
COCK CROW—*Thomas, Edward*
COCKS AND HENS—*Nash*
COCKTAIL LOUNGE—*Clark, John W.*
CÔCO DO MAJOR—*Andrade, Mario de*
COCU ET CONTENT—*Damas*
CODE OF FLAG BEHAVIOR—*Antin*
CODICIL FOR PVT. JOHN HOGG'S WILL—*Scott, Winfield Townley*
COEUR—*Péguy*
COEUR—*Supervielle*
COGNAC IM FRÜHLING—*Zuckmayer*
COIFFURE—*Benedikt*
THE COIN—*Teasdale*
COIN DIVER (FUNCHAL)—*Francis*
LES COLCHIQUES—*Apollinaire*
COLD—*Clark, John W.*
COLD— *Winters*
THE COLD BEFORE THE MOONRISE —*Merwin*
COLD FRONT— *Williams, Gwyn*
THE COLD GREEN ELEMENT—*Layton*
THE COLD HEAVEN— *Yeats*
THE COLD NIGHT— *Williams, William Carlos*
COLD STORAGE—*Ennis*
COLD WATER—*Hall*
LA COLÈRE DE SAMSON— *Vigny*
COLERIDGE—*Scott, Winfield Townley*
COLETTE—*Engle*
COLIN CLOUT—*Skelton, John*
THE COLLAR—*Herbert*
THE COLLIER—*Watkins*
COLLISION WITH THE EARTH—*Hughes, Ted*

COLLOQUE SENTIMENTAL—
  Verlaine
LA COLOMBE ET LA FOURMI—*La
  Fontaine*
COLONEL FANTOCK—*Sitwell,
  Edith*
COLORED CLAY HORSE WITH
  WINGS—*Summers, Hollis*
COLORS—*Yevtushenko*
A COLTRANE POEM—*Sanchez*
COLUMBUS—*Miller, Joaquin*
COLUMBUS—*Rukeyser*
COLUMNAS ROTAS—*Reyes
  Fuentes*
COMB AND GLASS—*Richards,
  I. A.*
LE COMBAT AVEC L'ANGE—
  Prévert
THE COMBE—*Thomas, Edward*
COME—*Francis*
COME BEFORE HIS COUNTENANCE
  WITH A JOYFUL LEAPING—
  Wagoner
COME, COME, KEROUAC, MY
  GENERATION IS BEATER THAN
  YOURS—*Nash*
COME DEATH—*Smith, Stevie*
COME GREEN AGAIN—*Scott,
  Winfield Townley*
COME IN—*Frost, Robert*
COME, SLEEP—*Bogan*
COMES TWILIGHT NOW—
  Marshall, Helen Lowrie
COMING—*Larkin*
COMING HOME ON THE 5:22—
  Ciardi
THE COMING OF ARCHIE—
  Marquis
THE COMING OF ARTHUR—
  Tennyson
THE COMING OF TEDDY BEARS—
  Lee, Dennis
COMING TO ENGLAND—*Ghose*
COMMANDER LOWELL—*Lowell,
  Robert*
THE COMMANDMENTS—*Jong*
COMME ON L'AVAIT ESPÉRÉ—
  Lapointe
COMME VA?—*Di Giacomo*
COMMEMORATIVE BRONZE—
  Cowley, Malcolm
THE COMMITTEE—*Day Lewis*
THE COMMON COLD—*Nash*
THE COMMON LIFE—*Auden*
A COMMONPLACE—*Weiss*
COMMUNE PRÉSENCE—*Char*
COMMUNICATION—*Giovanni*
COMMUNICATION ESTABLISHED—
  Scott, Winfield Townley
COMMUNICATION IN WHITE—*Lee,
  Don L.*
COMMUNICATION TO THE CITY
  FATHERS OF BOSTON—*Starbuck*
THE COMMUNIST FLY—*Roche*
COMMUNITY SINGING—*Connor*
CÓMO DE ENTRE MIS MANOS—
  Quevedo y Villegas
COMO NEL COMÒ—*Rodari*

COMO TÚ—*Camino Galicia*
COMO UN PULGON—*Camino
  Galicia*
COMPAGNI DI VIAGGIO—*Buttitta*
LA COMPAÑERA—*Florit*
COMPANION—*Yevtushenko*
COMPANIONS: A TALE OF A
  GRANDFATHER—*Calverley*
COMPARISON—*Donne*
COMPARISON—*Farrar*
A COMPARISON OF THE LIFE OF A
  MAN—*Barnfield*
COMPENSATION—*Dunbar, Paul
  Laurence*
COMPENSATION—*Emerson*
COMPENSATION—*Leonidas the
  Alexandrian*
COMPLAINT—*Wilbur*
COMPLAINT—*Williams, William
  Carlos*
COMPLAINT OF THE CAMEL—
  Carryl, Charles Edward
COMPLAINT TO HIS EMPTY PURSE—
  Chaucer
COMPLAINTE DE LA LUNE EN
  PROVINCE—*Laforgue*
COMPLAINTE DE L'OUBLI DES
  MORTS—*Laforgue*
COMPLAINTE DE VINCENT—
  Prévert
COMPLAINTE DU DÉSESPÉRÉ—*Du
  Bellay*
COMPLAINTE DU PAUVRE JEUNE
  HOMME—*Laforgue*
COMPLAINTE DU PETIT CHEVAL
  BLANC—*Fort*
COMPLAINTE DU ROI DE THULÉ—
  Laforgue
LA COMPLAINTE DU ROI RENAULD
  —*Anonymous-French*
LA COMPLAINTE RUTEBOEUF—
  Ruteboeuf
COMPLAINTE SUR CERTAINS
  ENNUIS—*Laforgue*
COMPLINE—*Auden*
COMPOSED ON WESTMINSTER
  BRIDGE—*Wordsworth*
COMUS—*Milton*
CON LA CRUZ DEL SUR—*Jiménez*
CON LA FLOR MÁS ALTA—*Jiménez*
CONAN IN EXILE—*Durrell*
THE CONCEITED DRAGON—*Roche*
CONCERNING THE
  MATHEMATICIAN—*Piercy*
LE CONCERT N'A PAS ÉTÉ RÉUSSI—
  Prévert
LA CONCHIGLIA—*Ungaretti*
CONCIENCIA PLENA—*Jiménez*
CONCORD HYMN—*Emerson*
EL CONDE ARNALDOS—
  Anonymous-Spanish
CONDITION OF THE WORKING
  CLASSES, 1960—*Bly*
THE CONDOR—*Jeffers, Robinson*
CONDORS FLYING—*Colum*
CONFESIÓN—*Capdevila*
CONFESSION—*Baudelaire*

CONFESSION DE L'AUTEUR, SON
  PORTRAIT EN CRABE—*Jacob,
  Max*
THE CONFESSION STONE—*Dodson*
CONFESSIONS—*Browning, Robert*
CONFESSIONS—*Obaldia*
CONFIANZA—*Vivanco*
THE CONFIRMATION—*Muir*
CONFITEOR—*Trakl*
CONFITEOR DE L'ARTISTE—
  Baudelaire
CONFLICT—*Day Lewis*
CONFLICT—*Scott, F. R.*
THE CONFLICT—*Vaughan, H. A.*
CONFUSIÓN DE LA ROSA ELLA—
  Jiménez
CONFUSIÓN Y VICIOS DE LA CORTE
  —*Torres y Villaroel*
THE CONGO—*Lindsay, Vachel*
CONIGLI SOTTO LA LUNA—
  Buzzati
THE CONJUGATION OF THE
  PARAMECIUM—*Rukeyser*
CONJUNCTION—*Graves*
CONJURE—*Miles*
CONJURED—*Brown, Sterling A.*
LES CONQUÉRANTS—*Heredia*
CONQUEROR—*Treece*
THE CONQUEROR WORM—*Poe*
THE CONQUERORS—*McGinley*
THE CONQUEST OF GRANADA—
  Dryden
CONQUISTADOR—*MacLeish*
CONSCIENCE—*Herbert*
CONSCIENCE—*Hugo, Victor*
CONSCIOUS—*Owen, Wilfred*
LA CONSEGNA—*Totò*
CONSEIL DE TOUTE IMPORTANCE
  —*Cocteau*
LE CONSEIL TENU PAR LES RATS—
  La Fontaine
A CONSIDERABLE SPECK—*Frost,
  Robert*
CONSIDERING THE SNAIL—*Gunn*
CONSOLATION À M. DU PÉRIER—
  Malherbe
CONSTANCY—*Suckling*
THE CONSTANT DISQUISITION OF
  THE WIND—*Stevens, Wallace*
CONSTANT FEELINGS—*Bell*
THE CONSTANT LOVER—*Suckling*
THE CONSTRUCTED SPACE—
  Graham, William Sydney
THE CONSUMER—*Piercy*
LOS CONTADORES DE ESTRELLAS—
  Alonso
CONTE—*Hacker*
A CONTEMPLATION UPON FLOWER
  —*King*
CONTEMPLATIONS—*Bradstreet*
CONTEMPLATIONS—*Hugo, Victor*
THE CONTENDER—*Hughes, Ted*
CONTENT—*Richards, I. A.*
CONTENTMENT—*Field, Eugene*
CONTENTMENT—*Holmes, Oliver
  Wendell*

CONTRA LA DUREZA DEL CORAZON DEL HOMBRE—*Quevedo y Villegas*
CONTRASTO—*Alcamo*
CONTRE!—*Michaux*
CONTRE LES BÛCHERONS DE LA FORÊT DE GASTINE—*Ronsard*
THE CONVERGENCE OF THE TWAIN—*Hardy*
CONVERSATION—*Giovanni*
CONVERSATION—*MacNeice*
THE CONVICT MINES—*Beecher*
CONVICTION—*Smith, Stevie*
COOL TOMBS—*Sandburg*
THE COOL WEB—*Graves*
COOLE PARK AND BALLYLEE—*Yeats*
COOLE PARK, 1929—*Yeats*
THE COOLIN—*Stephens*
COONEY POTTER—*Masters, Edgar Lee*
COPLAS DEL ALMA QUE PENA POR VER A DIÓS—*Juan de la Cruz*
COPLAS MUNDANAS—*Machado, Antonio*
COPLAS POR LA MUERTE DE SU PADRE—*Manrique*
COPLAS SOBRE UN ÉXTASIS DE ALTA CONTEMPLACIÓN—*Juan de la Cruz*
COPS AND ROBBERS—*Hall*
COQ AU VIN—*Obaldia*
COQ DE COMBAT—*Howes*
LE COQ ET LA PERLE—*La Fontaine*
LE COQ ET LE RENARD—*La Fontaine*
COQUETRY—*Field, Eugene*
A COQUETTE CONQUERED—*Dunbar, Paul Laurence*
LE COR—*Vigny*
CORAL—*MacPherson*
THE CORAL POOL—*Graves*
CORAZON DE NARDO—*Martinez Alonso*
CORAZON, VIEJO INDIO—*Godoy*
LE CORBEAU ET LE RENARD—*La Fontaine*
CORINNA TO TANAGRA—*Landor*
CORINNA'S GOING A-MAYING—*Herrick*
CORIOLAN—*Eliot, Thomas Stearns*
THE CORMORANT AND SPINDLE—*Olson*
CORN—*Engle*
CORNELIA'S SONG—*Webster, John*
CORNER CUPBOARD—*Marshall, Helen Lowrie*
CORNUCOPIA—*Sandburg*
CORNWALL IN ADOLESCENCE—*Betjeman*
CORNWALL IN CHILDHOOD—*Betjeman*
CORO 'E CAMPAGNUOLE—*Viviani*
CORONACH—*Scott, Sir Walter*

CORONACH FOR THE END OF THE WORLD—*MacDiarmid*
THE CORPORAL WHO KILLED ARCHIMEDES—*Holub*
LE CORPS—*Supervielle*
CORPUS—*Jiménez*
THE CORPUS CHRISTI CAROL—*Anonymous–English–Modern English*
CORPUS TIBULLIANUM—*Tibullus*
LA CORRENTE VIVA—*Reale*
CORRESPONDANCES—*Baudelaire*
CORRINA—*Campion*
EL CORRO LUMINOSO—*Mistral*
CORRUPTION—*Vaughan, Henry*
CORS DE CHASSE—*Apollinaire*
CORTE DE CEBADA—*Carrera Andrade*
CORTÈGE—*Prévert*
CORTÈGE—*Rothenberg*
CORYDON'S SONG—*Lodge*
CORYMBA—*Davidson*
COSANTE—*Hurtado de Mendoza*
COSCE 'ARGIENTE—*Chiurazzi*
COSÌ IL PARMA—*Bevilacqua*
COSS'EL VOEUR EZZELENDZA CHE RESPONDA—*Porta*
THE COTTER'S SATURDAY NIGHT—*Burns*
COTTON CANDY ON A RAINY DAY—*Giovanni*
COTTON MATHER—*Ross, W. W. Eustace*
LE COUCHER DU SOLEIL ROMANTIQUE—*Baudelaire*
COULD BE—*Hughes, Langston*
THE COUNT DUKE OF OLIVARES: VELASQUEZ—*Engle*
COUNT YOUR KIN—*Rossman*
THE COUNTESS OF PERSHING SQUARE—*Masters, Marcia*
COUNTING-OUT RHYME—*Millay*
COUNTING SMALL-BONED BODIES—*Bly*
COUNTRY BURIAL—*Lewis, Janet*
COUNTRY BURYING (1919)—*Warren*
COUNTRY DANCE—*Sitwell, Edith*
COUNTRY SUMMER—*Adams*
A COUNTRY WALK—*Kinsella*
THE COUNTRYMAN IS DYING OUT—*Thomas, Edward*
THE COUNTY OF MAYO—*Fox, George*
THE COUNTY OF MAYO—*Raftery*
A COUPLE—*Sandburg*
COUPLET—*Palladas*
COUPLETS DE LA RUE ST.-MARTIN—*Desnos*
COURAGE—*Éluard*
THE COURAGE TO BE NEW—*Frost, Robert*
LE COURANT D'AIR—*Obaldia*
LA COURBE DE TES YEUX—*Éluard*
LA COURONNE EFFEUILLÉE—*Desbordes-Valmore*
COURS—LES TOUTES—*Breton, André*

COURT CIRCUIT—*Obaldia*
COURT OF APPEAL—*Richards, I. A.*
COURTESY—*Belloc*
THE COURTIN'—*Lowell, James Russell*
THE COURTSHIP OF MILES STANDISH—*Longfellow*
THE COURTSHIP OF THE YONGHY-BONGHY-BO—*Lear*
COUSIN DAISY—*McGough*
COUSIN FIONA—*McGough*
COUSIN FLORENCE—*Eberhart*
COUVRE-FEU—*Éluard*
COVER HER FACE—*Kinsella*
THE COW—*Nash*
THE COW—*Stevenson*
THE COW IN APPLE TIME—*Frost, Robert*
COWBOY'S LOVE SONG—*O'Neill, Catherine*
COZY SONG—*Conkling*
CRAB APPLE—*Talbot*
A CRACKER JACK—*Dudek*
THE CRACKS—*Creeley*
CRADLE SONG—*Blake*
CRADLE SONG—*Colum*
CRADLE SONG—*Dekker*
CRADLE SONG—*Durrell*
CRADLE SONG—*Milne*
CRADLE SONG OF OEDIPUS REX—*Brinnin*
THE CRAFTSMAN—*Kipling*
LA CRATURA IN FASSCIOLA—*Belli*
CRAXTON—*Moraes*
A CRAZED GIRL—*Yeats*
THE CRAZED MOON—*Yeats*
CRAZY—*Polak*
CRAZY JANE AND JACK THE JOURNEYMAN—*Yeats*
CRAZY JANE AND THE BISHOP—*Yeats*
CRAZY JANE GROWN OLD LOOKS AT THE DANCERS—*Yeats*
CRAZY JANE ON GOD—*Yeats*
CRAZY JANE ON THE DAY OF JUDGEMENT—*Yeats*
CRAZY JANE ON THE MOUNTAIN—*Yeats*
CRAZY JANE REPROVED—*Yeats*
CRAZY JANE TALKS WITH THE BISHOP—*Yeats*
CRAZY PIGEON—*Knight, Etheridge*
CREATION—*Bahati*
CREATION—*Johnson, James Weldon*
CREATION—*Patchen*
CREATION OF LIGHT—*Anonymous–Australasian languages–Maori*
A CREATURE TO TELL THE TIME BY—*Patten*
CRECIENDO HACIA LA TIERRA—*Rosales*
CREDENCES OF SUMMER—*Stevens, Wallace*

A CREED—*Masefield*
THE CREEK—*Ross, W. W. Eustace*
THE CREEPER ALONG THE HOUSE WALL—*Souster*
THE CREMATION OF SAM MCGEE—*Service*
CREON'S MOUSE—*Davie*
CRÉPUSCULE—*Apollinaire*
CRÉPUSCULE—*Noël*
LE CRÉPUSCULE DU MATIN—*Baudelaire*
LE CRÉPUSCULE DU SOIR—*Baudelaire*
CRÉPUSCULE DU SOIR MYSTIQUE—*Verlaine*
LE CRI DU BUTOR—*Aragon*
LE CRI ET LES CENDRES—*Soupault*
LE CRI LE PLUS AFFREUX—*Cendrars*
CRIATURA AFORTUNADA—*Jiménez*
CRIATURA DESDE GREDOS—*Vivanco*
CRICKET—*Barrows*
CRICKET—*Nash*
CRICKET SONG—*Marshall, Lenore G.*
THE CRICKET'S SONG—*Field, Eugene*
CRIED THE FOX—*Williams, Tennessee*
CRIMEN AMORIS—*Verlaine*
CRIN HIRSUTA—*Martí*
CRIRYTHME—*Dufrêne*
EL CRISTO DE VELAZQUEZ—*Unamuno*
EL CRISTO YACENTE DE SANTA CLARA—*Unamuno*
THE CRITIC—*Howes*
LA CROADA—*Quart*
CROMWELL—*Francis*
CROSS—*Hughes, Langston*
CROSS—*Tate, Allen*
CROSS-FIRE—*Fabio, Sarah Webster*
THE CROSSED APPLE—*Bogan*
CROSSED NUMBERS—*Sandburg*
CROSSING—*Booth*
CROSSING BROOKLYN FERRY—*Whitman*
CROSSING THE BAR—*Tennyson*
CROSSING THE BORDER—*Nash*
CROSSING THE RIVER—*Brathwaite*
CROSSOVER: FOR RFK—*Emanuel*
THE CROSSROADS—*Marshall, Helen Lowrie*
THE CROW—*Reaney*
CROW AND MAMA—*Hughes, Ted*
CROW HEARS FATE KNOCK ON THE DOOR—*Hughes, Ted*
CROW PAINTS HIMSELF INTO A CHINESE MURAL—*Hughes, Ted*
THE CROWNING OF DREAMING JOHN—*Drinkwater*
CROWNS AND GARLANDS—*Hughes, Langston*

CROWS—*McCord*
CROW'S ELEPHANT TOTEM SONG—*Hughes, Ted*
CROW'S FALL—*Hughes, Ted*
CROW'S FIRST LESSON—*Hughes, Ted*
A CROW'S LONG SCRATCH OF SOUND—*Ciardi*
LE CRUCIFIX—*Lamartine*
CRUCIFIXION—*Ferlinghetti*
CRUCIFIXION—*Johnson, James Weldon*
CRUCIFIXION—*Ward*
CRUCIFIXUS—*Trakl*
CRUELTY—*Jeffers, Lance*
CRUSADER—*McGough*
CRUTCHES—*Giovanni*
CRY FOR NOTHING—*Levine*
THE CRY OF THE CHILDREN—*Browning, Elizabeth Barrett*
THE CRYSTAL CABINET—*Blake*
CRYSTAL MOMENTS—*Marshall, Helen Lowrie*
CUANDO YO ERA NINODIÓS—*Jiménez*
LOS CUATRO MULEROS—*Garcia Lorca*
CUCHULAIN COMFORTED—*Yeats*
THE CUCKOO IN THE WOODS—*Nash*
CUCKOO SONG—*Anonymous–English–Middle English*
CUCKOOS—*Young, Andrew*
CUCUMBERS—*Lifshin*
CUERPO PRESENTE—*Garcia Lorca*
THE CUIRASSIER OF THE FRONTIER—*Graves*
CÚIRT AN MHEADHOIN—*Merriman*
LES CUISSES DE COLETTE—*Obaldia*
THE CULPRIT—*Housman*
CULTURAL EXCHANGE—*Hughes, Langston*
THE CULTURE-INSPIRING PEN—*Morgenstern*
LA CUNA—*Ibarbourou*
'O CUNTO 'E LL'OVE—*Mura*
CUNTRORA—*Di Giacomo*
CUPID AND CAMPASPE—*Lyly*
CUPIDON—*Smith, William Jay*
CUPID'S MISTAKE—*Prior*
CURFEW—*Longfellow*
THE CURRENT—*Merrill*
CURSE—*Auden*
CURSE—*Donne*
CURSE—*Millay*
A CUSHIONING OF PRAYER—*Marshall, Helen Lowrie*
ER CUSTITUTO—*Belli*
CUTTINGS—*Roethke*
CUTTY SARK—*Crane, Hart*
CWM YR EGLWYS—*Williams, Gwyn*

CYBÈLE ATTEND SON HEURE—*Mauriac*
THE CYCLE—*Roethke*
CYCLE NUMBER ONE—*Napier*
THE CYCLIST—*MacNeice*
CYCLOPS—*Atwood*
LES CYDALISES—*Nerval*
CYGNE—*Baudelaire*
CYGNE—*Rilke*
CYGNES—*Queneau*
CYMBELINE—*Shakespeare*
CYMBELINE: DIRGE FOR FIDELE—*Collins, William*
CYNARA—*Dowson*
CYNDDYLAN ON A TRACTOR—*Thomas, Ronald Stuart*
CYPRESSES—*Francis*

D' 'A 'O QUARTO PIANO—*Di Giacomo*
D. C. HEAT—*Gaver*
D. H. LAWRENCE—*Bynner*
D-ZUG MÜNCHEN-FRANKFURT—*Eich*
DA I NET—*Yevtushenko*
DADDY—*Gaver*
DADDY—*Plath*
DADDY FELL INTO THE POND—*Noyes*
THE DAEMON—*Bogan*
DAEMONS—*Ciardi*
THE DAFFODILS—*Wordsworth*
EN DAG—*Selander*
THE DAILY GRIND—*Bell*
THE DAISIES—*Stephens*
DAISY—*Tennyson*
DAISY—*Thompson, Francis*
DAISY FRASER—*Masters, Edgar Lee*
DAL FONDO DELLE CAMPAGNE—*Luzi*
DALLA TORRE—*Luzi*
THE DAM—*Rukeyser*
DAM NECK, VIRGINIA—*Eberhart*
THE DAMAGE YOU HAVE DONE—*Komey*
DAMALS WAR ES MEIN MOND—*Scharpenberg*
DIE DAME MIT'N AVEC—*Tucholsky*
DIE DAME SCHREIBT DER DAME—*Kästner*
DAMELUS' SONG TO HIS DIAPHENIA—*Chettle*
DAMNATION—*Deutsch*
DANCE—*Andersen*
THE DANCE—*Crane, Hart*
DANCE—*Williams, William Carlos*
THE DANCE CALLED DAVID—*Weiss*
A DANCE FOR RAIN—*Bynner*
THE DANCE OF FOREVER—*Clark, China*
DANCE OUTSIDE MY SHOES—*Sobiloff*
THE DANCER—*Booth*

THE DANCER—*Napier*
THE DANCING APE—*Spicer*
DANDELION—*Conkling*
DANDELIONS—*Nemerov*
DANE-GELD—*Kipling*
DANEBEN—*Busch*
THE DANGERS—*Cavafy*
DANGERS OF WAKING—
    Middleton, Christopher
DANIEL—*Lindsay, Vachel*
DANIEL BOONE—*Benét, Stephen
    Vincent*
DANIEL M'CUMBER—*Masters,
    Edgar Lee*
DANMARK MIT FAEDRELAND—
    Andersen
DANN—*Benn*
DANNY DEEVER—*Kipling*
DANNY MURPHY—*Stephens*
DANS LA CHAMBRE ARRIVAIENT
    LES JOURS—*Noël*
DANS LA SIERRA—*Gautier*
DANS LE JARDIN D'ANNA—
    Apollinaire
DANS LE SAC—*Obaldia*
DANS LES BAS-FONDS—*Prévert*
DANSE—*Carco*
DANSE MACABRE—*Sitwell, Osbert*
DANZA—*Torres Bodet*
LA DANZA DEL VIENTO—*Martinez
    Alonso*
DANZA LEONINA—*Alurista*
DANZA NEGRA—*Palés Matos*
DAR BOR EN KONUNG—*Hasso*
DÅRARNA—*Malmberg*
DARBON—*Jiménez*
DAREST THOU NOW O SOUL—
    Whitman
DARIEN—*Graves*
DARING TO LIVE FOR THE
    IMPOSSIBLE—*Mariah*
A DARK AND SUDDEN BEAUTY—
    Jeffers, Lance
THE DARK AND THE FAIR—*Kunitz*
DARK ANGEL—*Souster*
DARK BLOOD—*Walker*
THE DARK CONVOYS—*Griffiths*
DARK DARK HEAD—*Ferguson*
DARK GIRL—*Bontemps*
THE DARK GLASS—*Rossetti,
    Dante Gabriel*
DARK HEAD—*Levine*
DARK LAGOON—*Reaney*
DARK ROSALEEN—*Mangan*
THE DARK TWIN—*Hacker*
THE DARKEST HALF HOUR—*Nash*
DARKLING SUMMER, OMINOUS
    DUSK, RUMOROUS RAIN—
    Schwartz
THE DARKLING THRUSH—*Hardy*
DARKNESS AND A BLUES LADY—
    Jimason
DATE WITH APOLLO—*Eckels*
DAUER IM WECHSEL—*Goethe*
A DAUGHTER—*Gittings*
THE DAUGHTERS OF THE
    HORSELEECH—*Kunitz*

DAVANTI SAN GUIDO—*Carducci*
DAVENPORT GAP—*Williams,
    Jonathan*
DAVID—*Miles*
DAVID AND BETHSABA—*Peele*
DAWN—*Dunbar, Paul Laurence*
DAWN BOMBARDMENT—*Graves*
DAWN OF GUILT—*Betjeman*
DAWN SONG—*Nims*
THE DAWN WIND—*Kipling*
THE DAY—*Spencer*
THE DAY AFTER SUNDAY—
    McGinley
THE DAY AND THE WORK—
    Markham
THE DAY-BREAKERS—*Bontemps*
DAY DREAMS—*Parker*
THE DAY IS DONE—*Longfellow*
THE DAY LADY DIED—*O'Hara*
THE DAY LARRY WAS STRETCHED—
    Skelton, Robin
DAY OF THESE DAYS—*Lear*
DAY OF THESE DAYS—*Lee, Laurie*
A DAY WITH LITERATURE—
    Whittemore
DAYBREAK IN ALABAMA—*Hughes,
    Langston*
DAYS—*Baker, Karle Wilson*
DAYS—*Ciardi*
DAYS—*Emerson*
DAYS—*Larkin*
DAZZLE OF DARKNESS—*Graves*
DE GUSTIBUS—*Browning, Robert*
DE INVIERNO—*Darío*
DE LA COMMUNICACÍON DE LAS
    TRES PERSONAS—*Juan de la
    Cruz*
DE LA CREACÍON—*Juan de la
    Cruz*
DE LA JEUNE DAME QUI A VIEIL
    MARY—*Marot*
DE ORBE NOVO—*Fitzgerald*
DE OTRO MODO—*Garcia Lorca*
DE PROFUNDIS—*Trakl*
DE RERUM NATURA—*Lucretius
    Carus*
DE SA GRANDE AMIE—*Marot*
DE SOY MESME—*Marot*
DE TARDE—*Verde*
DE TOUTES FLEURES—*Machaut*
DE UNA VIDA DE SANTO—
    Valverde
THE DEACON'S MASTERPIECE—
    Holmes, Oliver Wendell
THE DEAD—*Brooke*
THE DEAD—*Levertov*
THE DEAD—*Very*
DEAD BOY—*Ransom*
DEAD DOG—*Scannell*
DEAD IN THERE—*Hughes,
    Langston*
DEAD LAD—*Bodenheim*
A DEAD LANGUAGE: CIRCA 1885—
    Warren
DEAD LEAVES OUT OF PLACE—
    Scott, Winfield Townley

THE DEAD MAN LIES—*Hughes,
    Ted*
DEAD MAN'S DUMP—*Rosenberg*
DEAD POET—*Clark, John W.*
THE DEAD RIDE FAST—*Blackmur*
THE DEAD SEAL NEAR MCCLURE'S
    BEACH—*Bly*
THE DEAD SHALL BE RAISED
    INCORRUPTIBLE—*Kinnell*
THE DEAD SHIP OF HARPSWELL—
    Whittier
DEAD SNAKE—*Smith, William
    Jay*
THE DEAD THIEF—*Dowling*
DEAD TOUCAN—GUADALOUPE—
    Howes
THE DEAD WAGON—*Hinton*
DEADLINES FOR MIRACLES—
    Murphy
DEAR CRAIG—*Dreyer*
DEAR DANNY—*Dreyer*
DEAR JOHN, DEAR COLTRANE—
    Harper
DEAR OEDIPUS—*Darr*
DEAR OLD VILLAGE—*Betjeman*
DEAR STRANGER EXTANT IN
    MEMORY BY THE BLUE JUNIATA
    —*Kinnell*
DEATH—*Brontë, Emily*
DEATH—*Herbert*
DEATH—*Yeats*
DEATH AND BURIAL OF COCK
    ROBIN—*Children's Verses and
    Nursery Rhymes*
DEATH AND THE LADY—*Adams*
DEATH AT LEAMINGTON—
    Betjeman
DEATH AT PALLE—*Griffiths*
THE DEATH BED—*Sassoon*
A DEATH BEFORE KILLING—*Burr,
    Gray*
THE DEATH OF A CAT—*MacNeice*
DEATH OF A JAZZ MUSICIAN—
    Smith, William Jay
DEATH OF A NATURALIST—
    Heaney
THE DEATH OF A PUBLIC SERVANT
    —*Kizer*
DEATH OF A SON WHO DIED IN A
    MENTAL HOSPITAL, AGED 1—
    Silkin
DEATH OF AMERICA—*Jeffers,
    Lance*
DEATH OF AN OLD LADY—
    MacNeice
DEATH OF DUCKS—*Simmons,
    Judy*
THE DEATH OF LINCOLN—*Bryant,
    William Cullen*
THE DEATH OF LITTLE BOYS—
    Tate, Allen
THE DEATH OF LOVE—*Simpson*
THE DEATH OF NEARCHUS—*Ansen*
THE DEATH OF STONEWALL
    JACKSON—*Benét, Stephen
    Vincent*

THE DEATH OF THE BALL TURRET GUNNER—*Jarrell*

THE DEATH OF THE HIRED MAN—*Frost, Robert*

DEATH OF THE SHERIFF—*Lowell, Robert*

DEATH ON A LIVE WIRE—*Baldwin, Michael*

A DEATH REQUEST—*Crouch*

THE DEATH ROOM—*Graves*

DEATH SONG—*Anonymous-American Indian languages-Chippewa*

DEATH SONG—*Anonymous-American Indian languages-Papago*

DEATH SONG—*Bede*

DEATH THE LEVELLER—*Shirley*

DEATH WATCH—*Harper*

DEATHS AND ENTRANCES—*Thomas, Dylan*

LE DEBAT DU CUER ET DU CORPS DE VILLON—*Villon*

THE DEBATE—*Ignatow*

DEBATE OF DARK BROTHERS—*Holman, M. Carl*

DEBATE OF THE BODY AND THE SOUL—*Anonymous-English—Modern English*

DEBATE: QUESTION, QUARRY, DREAM—*Warren*

19 MARTA 1823—*Zhukovsky*

19 OKTYABRYA—*Pushkin*

THE DEBT—*Dunbar, Paul Laurence*

DEC. '63—*Sward*

DECEMBER—*Francis*

THE DECEMBER OF MY SPRINGS—*Giovanni*

DECEMBER 6TH AND 7TH—*Blackburn, Paul*

DECIDUOUS BRANCH—*Kunitz*

DECIMA—*Acosta*

DECIMA Á AGUADILLA—*Mendoza, Esther Feliciano*

DECIMAS DEL POEMA EL LEÑERO—*Corretjer*

THE DECISION—*Roethke*

THE DECLARATION OF INDEPENDENCE—*Kostelanetz*

DÉCLARER SON NOM—*Char*

DECLENSIONS OF A REFRAIN—*Gregor*

DEDICATION FOR A PLOT OF GROUND—*Williams, William Carlos*

DEDICATION OF A MIRROR—*Plato*

DEEPEST DREAM—*Van Doren*

DEER AT THE DEAD SEA—*Sutzkever*

DEFERRED—*Hughes, Langston*

DEFINITION FOR BLK/CHILDREN—*Sanchez*

THE DEFINITION OF LOVE—*Marvell*

DEFORMED PRIEST'S EPITAPH—*Anonymous-English—Modern English*

DEFUNTI SU MONTAGNE—*Ungaretti*

DEI SEPOLCRI—*Foscolo*

THE DEIL'S AWA' WI' THE EXCISEMAN—*Burns*

DEJECTION: AN ODE—*Coleridge, Samuel Taylor*

DEL NACIMIENTO—*Juan de la Cruz*

DEL VIEJO EL CONSEJO—*Gabriel y Galán*

IL DELENDA CARTAGO—*Giusti*

DELFICA—*Nerval*

DELFT—*Chopin*

THE DELICATE BIRD WHO IS FLYING UP OUR ASSES—*Bell*

DÉLIE—*Scève*

DELIGHT IN DISORDER—*Herrick*

DELINQUENT—*Agee*

DELIVERANCE—*Graves*

DELPHI—*Williams, Hugo*

THE DELPHIC ORACLE UPON PLOTINUS—*Yeats*

DELTA—*Walker*

DELTA POEMS—*Rukeyser*

DEM AUFGEHENDEN VOLLMOND—*Goethe*

DEM STOIKER CHRISTOPH IMMOLA—*Balde*

DEM UNBEKANNTEN GOTT—*Nietzsche*

DEMAIN, DÈS L'AUBE—*Hugo, Victor*

DEMI-EXILE HOWTH—*Davie*

DEMOCRACY—*Hughes, Langston*

THE DEMON LOVER—*Anonymous-English—Modern English*

THE DEMONSTRATORS—*Murphy*

DENK DER VERGEBLICHEN—*Benn*

DENK ES, O SEELE—*Mörike*

DENKMALSWUNSCH—*Morgenstern*

DENNOCH DIE SCHWERTER HALTEN—*Benn*

DENSO, DENSO—*Unamuno*

'O DENTISTA—*Russo*

DENTRO LA SOSTANZA—*Risi*

DEOR—*Anonymous-English—Old English*

DÉPART—*Rimbaud*

DEPARTMENTAL—*Frost, Robert*

DEPARTURE—*Plath*

DEPARTURE IN MIDDLE AGE—*Mathias*

DEPARTURE IN THE DARK—*Day Lewis*

THE DEPERSONALISED DONKEY—*Roche*

A DEPOSITION FROM LOVE—*Carew*

DEPRESSED BY A BOOK OF BAD POETRY, I WALK TOWARD AN UNUSED PASTURE—*Wright, James*

DEPRESSION—*Sanchez*

DEPRIVED—*Clay*

DEPUIS LE TEMPS QU'IL Y A DES GUERRES—*Obaldia*

DER WIRTIN TÖCHTERLEIN—*Uhland*

THE DERBY RAM—*Children's Verses and Nursery Rhymes*

DERELICT—*Day Lewis*

LE DERNIER POÈME—*Desnos*

DERNIER VERS—*Ronsard*

DERNIÈRE VALSE—*Vian*

DES FELDPREDIGERS GESPRÄCHE ÜBER KRIEG UND FRIEDEN—*Brecht*

DESCENT—*Williams, William Carlos*

DESCENT—*Clark, John W.*

DESCRIBE NICELY THE—*Stephany*

DESCRIPCIÓN DE UN NAUFRAGO EN ULTRAMAR—*Pacheco*

DESCRIPTION CHIMÉRIQUE D'UN ÊTRE DE RAISON, FABRIQUÉ DE PIÈCES RAPPORTÉES—*Cherrier*

DESDE EL SILENCIO QUE PUDIERA SER—*Arriví*

DESDE LEJOS—*Agustini*

EL DESDICHADO—*Nerval*

DESEO—*Garcia Lorca*

LE DÉSERT OU L'IMMATÉRIALITÉ DE DIEU—*Lamartine*

DESERT PLACES—*Frost, Robert*

THE DESERTED ALTAR—*Posner*

DESERTED VILLAGE—*Goldsmith*

THE DESERTER—*Housman*

LE DÉSERTEUR—*Vian*

DESERTION—*Brooke*

DESGRAZZI DE GIOVANNIN BONGEE—*Porta*

DESIDERATA—*Ehrmann*

DESIGN—*Frost, Robert*

DESIGN FOR A TOMB—*Ormond*

DESNUDEZ—*Pardo Garcia*

THE DESOLATIONS—*Muir*

DESPEDIDA—*Garcia Lorca*

DESPISALS—*Rukeyser*

DESPOSORIO—*Garcia Lorca*

DESSEIN DE QUITTER UNE DAME QUI NE LE CONTENTOIT QUE DE PROMESSE—*Malherbe*

LA DESTRUCTION—*Baudelaire*

THE DESTRUCTION OF SENNACHERIB—*Byron*

DET ER LIV AT REISE—*Andersen*

DET SUSAR GENOM TRÄDEN—*Hedberg*

DEUTERONOMY AND THE SIX O'CLOCK KID—*Genser*

DEUTSCHE ODE—*Schröder*

DEUTSCHE ZEIT 1947—*Lehmann*

DEUTSCHES MISERERE—*Brecht*

DEUTSCHLAND—*Brecht*

DEUTSCHLANDS BERUF—*Stolberg*

LES DEUX AMIS—*La Fontaine*
DEUX CHANSONS—*Guillevic*
LES DEUX MULETS—*La Fontaine*
LES DEUX PIGEONS—*La Fontaine*
DEVANT LES ACCIDENTS DE LA
  GLOIRE TEMPORELLE—*Péguy*
THE DEVELOPMENT—*Piercy*
THE DEVIL'S ADVICE TO
  STORY-TELLERS—*Graves*
THE DEVIL'S LAWCASE—*Webster,
  John*
A DEVIL'S PRAYER—*Dowling*
DEVONSHIRE STREET W. 1—
  Betjeman
DEVOTION-FOR KAREN—*Malanga*
THE DEW-LIGHT—*Conkling*
THE DHOON—*Brown, Thomas
  Edward*
DI SE STESSO—*Foscolo*
EL DÍA DE PLATA—*Martinez
  Alonso*
DÍA LEJANO—*Carranza*
EL DÍA QUE ME QUIERAS—*Nervo*
DIABETES—*Dickey, James*
DIABOLIST—*Starbuck*
DIALECTICS OF FLIGHT—
  Wheelock
DIALOGO ENTRE BABIECA Y
  ROCINANTE—*Cervantes
  Saavedra*
LOS DIALOGOS—*Pardo Garcia*
DIALOGUE—*Herbert*
DIALOGUE—*Nemerov*
DIALOGUE BETWEEN A MAN AND A
  FISH—*Hunt*
DIALOGUE BETWEEN TWO
  MESSENGERS OF PEACE—*Fabio,
  Sarah Webster*
DIALOGUE IN DECEMBER—*Van
  Doren*
A DIALOGUE OF SELF AND SOUL—
  Yeats
DIAMOND RING—*Lifshin*
DIANA—*Heine*
DIANA ROSS DOES NOT SING IN
  THIS MOVIE—*Gaver*
DIARY OF A CHURCHMOUSE—
  Betjeman
DICEN QUE ESTOY MADURO—
  Diego, Gerardo
DICEN QUE NO HABLAN—*Castro,
  Rosalía de*
DICHTER—*Thenior*
DICHTERBERUF—*Hölderlin*
DICHTERMUT—*Hölderlin*
DICTUM: FOR A MASQUE OF
  DELUGE—*Merwin*
DID YOU EVER—*Jacobsen, Ethel*
DID YOU FEED MY COW—
  *Anonymous–English—
  Modern English*
DID YOU VOTE NIGGER—*Marvin
  X*
DIDACTIC BOMB AGAINST WAR—
  Young, Marguerite
DIDACTIC POEM—*Rich*
DIDN'T HE RAMBLE—*Brathwaite*

DIDO—*Marlowe*
DIDO MY DEAR, ALAS, IS DEAD—
  Spenser
DIDO'S SONG—*Sitwell, Edith*
THE DIFFERENCE OF A WILD
  THING—*Olson*
LA DIFFICULTÉ D'ÊTRE—*Cocteau*
DIE NIGGA—*Last Poets*
DIEU PENSE À L'HOMME—
  Supervielle
DIEU, QU'IL EST DIFFICILE—
  Cendrars
DIFFERENCE—*Benét, Stephen
  Vincent*
DIFFERENT IMAGE—*Randall*
THE DIFFERENT STARS—*Merwin*
DIGGING FOR CHINA—*Wilbur*
DIGGING IT OUT—*Hollander*
ET DIGT OM KONERNE—*Andersen*
EN DIGTERS SIDSTE SANG—
  Andersen
DILEMMA—*Parker*
DILLY DILLY—*Children's Verses
  and Nursery Rhymes*
DIMANCHE—*Prévert*
DIMANCHE APRÈS-MIDI—*Éluard*
DIMANCHES—*Laforgue*
LE DIMANNE ATTESTA PER ARIA—
  Belli
DÎNER DE TÊTE—*Prévert*
DINEROS SON CALIDAD—*Góngora*
DINING-ROOM TEA—*Brooke*
DINKY—*Roethke*
DINT' 'A VILLA—*Di Giacomo*
DINT' 'O CIARDINO—*Di Giacomo*
DINT' 'O SUONNO—*Di Giacomo*
UN DIO GRANDO, SOLAR—*Marin*
DIÓS EN LA TARDE—*Garcia Nieto*
DIÓS LO QUIERE—*Mistral*
DIPPOLD THE OPTICIAN—*Masters,
  Edgar Lee*
DIRECTIONS FOR VISITORS—
  Garlick
DIRECTIONS TO A REBEL—
  Rodgers
DIRECTIVE—*Frost, Robert*
DIRGE—*Emerson*
DIRGE FOR FIDELE—*Collins,
  William*
DIRGE FOR THE NEW SUNRISE—
  Sitwell, Edith
DIRGE IN WOODS—*Meredith,
  George*
DISABLED—*Owen, Wilfred*
DISAPPEARANCES IN THE GUARDED
  SECTOR—*Gallagher, Tess*
THE DISCIPLE—*Kipling*
DISCIPLINE—*Herbert*
DISCLAIMER—*Murphy*
DISCO—*Gaver*
DISCORD—*Arnez*
DISCOVERIES—*Watkins*
DISCOVERING POETRY—*Betjeman*
A DISCOVERY—*Nabokov*
THE DISEASE—*Williams, Hugo*
DISGUISES—*Reid*
DISKRETION—*Tucholsky*

THE DISMAL DOLE OF THE
  DOODLEDOO—*Field, Eugene*
DISOBEDIENCE—*Milne*
DISPIETTO—*Di Giacomo*
THE DISQUIETING MUSES—*Plath*
DISSATISFACTION STRETCHES INTO
  PAIN—*Stephany*
THE DISSIPATED HORNET—
  Marquis
DISTURBANCES—*Thwaite*
THE DISTURBED—*Miles*
DISTURBERS OF THE PEACE—
  White
LE DIT DE LA FORCE DE L'AMOUR
  —*Éluard*
LE DIT DES PEINTRES—
  Anonymous–French
LE DIT DES RIBAUDS DE GRÈVE—
  Ruteboeuf
IL DITTATORE—*Rodari*
DITES! DITES!—*Obaldia*
THE DIVER—*Hayden*
DIVERTIMENTO—*Saba*
THE DIVERTING HISTORY OF JOHN
  GILPIN—*Cowper*
LE DIVIN MÉLODRAME—*Prévert*
DIVINA COMMEDIA—*Longfellow*
A DIVINE IMAGE—*Blake*
THE DIVINE INSECT—*Wheelock*
DIVINELY SUPERFLUOUS BEAUTY—
  Jeffers, Robinson
DIVING INTO THE WRECK—*Rich*
DIVISION—*Bogan*
DIVORCE DUMPLINGS—*Lifshin*
DIVORCE: THY NAME IS WOMAN—
  Sexton
DIZ ON T. V.—*Aubert*
THE DJ POEM—*Blackman*
DJURGÅRDSMÄSSA—*Ferlin*
DO I BELIEVE?—*Coward*
DO NOT LOOK AT ME—
  Anonymous–Spanish
DO SVIDANYA—*Yessenin*
DO YOU DELIVER—*Gaver*
DO YOU FEAR THE WIND—
  Garland
DO YOU KNOW JESUS—*Braxton*
DO YOU REMEMBER ME, BERNICE
  GRENADINE?—*Johnston, Ellen
  Turlington*
DO YOU REMEMBER, SPRINGFIELD?
  —*Benét, Stephen Vincent*
LAS DOCE EN EL RELOJ—*Guillén,
  Jorge*
DOCKERY AND SON—*Larkin*
THE DOCTOR—*Brown, Thomas
  Edward*
DOCTOR FAUSTUS—*Ciardi*
DOCTOR FAUSTUS—*Marlowe*
DR. FELL—*Children's Verses
  and Nursery Rhymes*
DR. LEVINSON'S OFFICE
  DISAPPEARED, SHE SAID—*Darr*
DOCTOR MEYERS—*Masters,
  Edgar Lee*
EN DÖD ARBETARHUSTRU—
  Lindorm

DÖDENS ÄNGEL—*Blomberg*

DOENDE GLADIATOR—*Lindegren*

DOES NO ONE AT ALL EVER FEEL THIS WAY IN THE LEAST?—*Frost, Robert*

DOG—*Ferlinghetti*

DOG—*Nash*

DOG IN A CORNFIELD— *Wright, James*

DOGGEREL BY A SENIOR CITIZEN—*Auden*

A DOG'S LIFE AND SOME OTHERS—*Beecher*

LA DOLCE VITA IN BRUSSELS—*Sherwin*

THE DOLLS—*Ciardi*

DOLOR—*Storni*

IL DOLORE—*Ungaretti*

DOLPHIN—*Francis*

DOM V VYAZME—*Simonov*

DOMANI—*Gatto*

DOMINATION OF BLACK—*Stevens, Wallace*

DOMINE, MINOR SUM CUNCTIS MISERA TIONIBUS TUIS—*Gryphius*

DOMINGO—*Carranza*

DOMINIQUE AUJOURD'HUI PRESENTE—*Éluard*

DOMINUS DE ME CIGITAT—*Gryphius*

DON DU POÈME—*Mallarmé*

DON JUAN—*Byron*

DOÑA ROSITA LA SOLTERA—*Garcia Lorca*

THE DONG WITH A LUMINOUS NOSE—*Lear*

THE DONKEY—*Roethke*

DONN' AMALIA 'A SPERANZELLA—*Di Giacomo*

LE DONNE—*Saba*

LE DONNE A MMESSA—*Belli*

DONO—*Ungaretti*

DON'T BLOW YOUR MEAN—*Johnston, Ellen Turlington*

DON'T CRY, SCREAM—*Lee, Don L.*

DON'T GRIN, OR YOU'LL HAVE TO BEAR IT—*Nash*

DON'T GROW OLD—*Ginsberg*

DON'T LOOK NOW, BUT THERE'S SOMETHING BEHIND THE CURTAIN—*Nash*

DON'T WANNA BE—*Sanchez*

DOODLE-DEE-DO, FIND ME A FRIEND—*Sobecks*

DOOLEY IS A TRAITOR—*Michie*

DOOMED GENERATIONS—*Brecht*

THE DOOR—*Tomlinson*

THE DOOR FOR ROBERT DUNCAN—*Creeley*

DOORS—*De la Mare*

DOORS—*Sandburg*

DOPO LA FUCILAZIONE DE UN RIBELLE DI AKYAB—*Bevilacqua*

DOPPO N' ANNO—*Di Giacomo*

DORA MARCUS—*Montale*

DORA WILLIAMS—*Masters, Edgar Lee*

LE DORMEUR DU VAL—*Rimbaud*

LA DORMEUSE—*Rilke*

DORMEZ-VOUS—*Cayrol*

DORMIDA—*Mistral*

LOS DOS ANGELES—*Alberti*

DOS PATRIAS—*Martí*

DOUBLE BASS—*Graves*

DOUBLE ODE—*Rukeyser*

THE DOUBLE SHAME—*Spender*

DOUBT SHALL NOT MAKE AN END OF YOU—*Patten*

THE DOUGLAS TRAGEDY—*Anonymous–English—Modern English*

DOULEUR QUANTITATIVE—*Obaldia*

DOVE LA LUCE—*Ungaretti*

DOVER BEACH—*Arnold*

DOVER BEACH–A NOTE TO THAT POEM—*MacLeish*

THE DOVER BITCH—*Hecht*

DOWN BY THE SALLEY GARDENS—*Yeats*

DOWN IN DALLAS—*Kennedy, X. J.*

THE DOWNLAND—*Masefield*

DOWNTOWN CORNER NEWS-STAND—*Souster*

DRAGGING BEHIND ME—*Stephany*

DRAGON COUNTRY: TO JACOB BOEHME—*Warren*

THE DRAGON FLY—*Kunitz*

DRAMATIC MONOLOGUES—*Howard, Richard*

A DRAUGHT OF FISHES—*Jones, Glyn*

THE DRAWER—*MacBeth*

DREAM—*Blake*

DREAM—*Bogan*

DREAM—*Davison, Peter*

DREAM—*Pitter*

DREAM—*Roethke*

A DREAM—*Tate, Allen*

DREAM—*Thomas, Edward*

THE DREAM AWAKE—*Dodson*

DREAM BOOGIE—*Hughes, Langston*

DREAM DRUMMING—*Rukeyser*

DREAM DUST—*Hughes, Langston*

DREAM FOR A SOLDIER—*Humphreys*

DREAM JOURNEY OF THE HEAD AND HEART—*Eberhart*

THE DREAM KEEPERS—*Hughes, Langston*

DREAM-LAND—*Poe*

THE DREAM OF THE ROOD—*Anonymous–English—Old English*

DREAM-PEDLARY—*Beddoes*

DREAM SONGS—*Berryman*

DREAM VARIATIONS—*Hughes, Langston*

A DREAM WITHIN A DREAM—*Poe*

THE DREAME—*Donne*

DREAMER—*Blanding*

DREAMER—*Clark, John W.*

THE DREAMER'S EPILOGUE—*Dowling*

DREAMPOEM—*McGough*

DREAMS—*Giovanni*

DREAMS—*Hughes, Langston*

DREAMS—*Poe*

DREAMS, COMMON SENSE AND STUFF—*Hodges*

DREAMS OF THE ANIMALS—*Atwood*

DREI STÜCKE AUS ABC—*Cobbing*

DRESSED ALL IN PINK—*Randall*

DRESSED UP—*Hughes, Langston*

DRIFTER—*Blanding*

DRIFTWOOD—*Blanding*

DRIFTWOOD—*Wilbur*

DRINKING FOUNTAIN—*Chute*

A DRINKING SONG—*Yeats*

DRIVER SAYING—*Miles*

DRIVING THROUGH MINNESOTA DURING THE HANOI BOMBINGS—*Bly*

DRIVING THROUGH NEBRASKA—*Levendosky*

DRIVING THROUGH OHIO—*Bly*

DRIVING TO TOWN LATE TO MAIL A LETTER—*Bly*

DRIVING TOWARD THE LAC QUI PARLE RIVER—*Bly*

DRÖMMAR ÅRO VÅRA TANKAR—*Lagerkvist*

DRÖMMAR, DÅRE—*Ferlin*

THE DROP OF A HAT—*Nash*

DROWNING—*Pack*

DRUGI—*Pasternak*

DRUM-TAPS—*Whitman*

A DRUMLIN WOODCHUCK—*Frost, Robert*

THE DRUMS OF JUSTICE—*Goldstein*

THE DRUNK IN THE FURNACE—*Merwin*

THE DRUNKARD'S FUNERAL—*Lindsay, Vachel*

THE DRUNKEN FISHERMAN—*Lowell, Robert*

THE DRY ROT—*Eberhart*

THE DRY SALVAGES—*Eliot, Thomas Stearns*

DU MÅSTE VÄRJA DITT LIV—*Vennberg*

DU MUSST DIR ALLES GEBEN—*Benn*

DU SCHLANK UND REIN WIE EINE FLAMME—*George*

DUALISME—*Geraldy*

DUALITY—*Abse*

DUBLIN—*MacNeice*

THE DUCK—*Nash*

THE DUCK AND THE KANGAROO—*Lear*

THE DUCKPOND—*Stryk*

THE DUEL—*Field, Eugene*

EL DUELO—*Muroti*

DUES—*Ward*
DUET—*Lurie*
DUFFRYN WOODS—*Webb*
DULCE ET DECORUM EST—*Owen, Wilfred*
DULCE RIDENTEM—*Benét, Stephen Vincent*
DULCE SILENCIOSO PENSAMIENTO —*Unamuno*
DULZURA DE LA MELANCOLÍA— *Pérez de Zambrana*
DUMA—*Lermontov*
THE DUMB SOLDIER—*Stevenson*
DUMI MOYI—*Shevchenko*
DUMMENECA—*Galdieri*
THE DUMP—*Hall*
D'UN ET DE DEUX, DE TOUS— *Éluard*
D'UN TEMPS, D'UN PAIS—*Raimon*
D'UN VANNEUR DE BLÉ AUX VENTS —*Du Bellay*
D'UN XIPRER—*López Pico*
DUNBARTON—*Lowell, Robert*
DUNCAN GRAY—*Burns*
DUNCE SONGS—*Van Doren*
THE DUNCIAD—*Pope, Alexander*
DUNCTON HILL—*Belloc*
D'UNE AUBE ÉTRANGE—*Fombeure*
DUNJA—*Ungaretti*
DUNKIRK—*Nathan*
DUNKIRK PIER—*Rook*
DER DUNKLE—*Benn*
DURCHWACHTE NACHT— *Droste-Hülshoff*
DURING FEVER—*Lowell, Robert*
DURNYE DNI—*Pasternak*
IL DURO FILAMENTO—*Luzi*
DUSK IN WINTER—*Merwin*
DUST—*Brathwaite*
DUST—*Chapin*
DUST—*Mitchell, Adrian*
DUST—*Porter, Peter*
DUST—*Russell*
DUST—*Sandburg*
DUST OF SNOW—*Frost, Robert*
THE DUST WHICH IS GOD—*Benét, William Rose*
THE DUTCH IN THE MEDWAY— *Kipling*
A DUTCH PICTURE—*Longfellow*
DVENADTSAT—*Blok*
THE DYING MAN—*Roethke*
THE DYING SWAN—*Tennyson*
DYLAN THOMAS, NOVEMBER 1953— *Spender*
THE DYNASTS—*Hardy*
DYR BU SCYL—*Krucenych*
DZA SHR—*Wang Wei*
DZENG BYE—*Du Mu*
DZENG WEI BA CHU SHR—*Du Fu*
DZWEI HWA YIN—*Li Ching Jau*

E ANCORA D'UNA TENDA S'AGITA— *Sereni*
'E CECATE 'E CARAVAGGIO—*Di Giacomo*
E DIETRO—*Ungaretti*

E DUNQUE ECCOMI—*Bevilacqua*
E IL SOLE PROSCIUGO LE ORE DELL' INFANZIA—*Bevilacqua*
E' IN QUESTA PIETRA—*Bevilacqua*
E PE' ME—*Galdieri*
E' QUESTO IL PRIMO LAGER— *Bevilacqua*
'E RIMPETTO—*Di Giacomo*
'E TTREZZE 'E CARULINA—*Di Giacomo*
EACH AND ALL—*Emerson*
THE EAGLE—*Tennyson*
EAGLE PLAIN—*Francis*
THE EAGLE THAT IS FORGOTTEN— *Lindsay, Vachel*
EARL—*Glaze*
THE EARLY DROWNED—*Corke*
EARLY FROST—*Norris*
EARLY IN THE EVENING—*Patten*
EARLY MOON—*Sandburg*
EARLY MORN—*Davies, William Henry*
EARLY MORNING—*Belloc*
EARLY MORNING: CAPE COD— *Swenson*
EARLY SUPPER—*Howes*
EARTH-TREADING STARS THAT MAKE DARK HEAVEN LIGHT— *Spender*
EARTHLY PARADISE: PROLOGUE— *Morris, William*
EARTH'S ANSWER—*Blake*
EARTHSHIP—*Fox, Charles*
EARTHWORM—*Updike*
EAST COKER—*Eliot, Thomas Stearns*
EAST OF OMAHA—*Darr*
EASTER—*Hannan*
EASTER—*Herbert*
EASTER—*Jones, Glyn*
EASTER—*Stein, Charles*
EASTER 1916—*Yeats*
EASTER PRAYER—*Barker, Eric Wilson*
EASTER SUNDAY, 1935—*Brecht*
EASTER WINGS—*Herbert*
AN EASY DECISION—*Patchen*
AN EASY SONG—*Rexroth*
THE 'EATHEN—*Kipling*
EATING APPLES—*Treitel*
THE EBB BEGINS FROM DREAM— *Birney*
ECCE HOMO—*Nietzsche*
ECCE PUER—*Joyce*
ECHO—*Rossetti, Christina*
ECHO OF RAIN—*Fabio, Sarah Webster*
THE ECHOING GREEN—*Blake*
ECHO'S SONG—*Jonson*
ÉCLAIRCIES—*Prévert*
ECLIPSE—*Rashidd*
L'ÉCOLE DES BEAUX-ARTS— *Prévert*
ÉCOLIÈRE—*Noël*
L'ÉCREVISSE—*Apollinaire*
ÉCRIRE, DESSINER, INSCRIRE— *Éluard*

ÉCRIT SUR LE MUR—*Cayrol*
THE ECSTATIC—*Day Lewis*
EDGAR A. GUEST CONSIDERS THE GOOD 'OLD WOMAN WHO LIVED IN A SHOE'—*Untermeyer*
EDGE—*Plath*
AN EDGE, A TWILIGHT, A PLOVER— *Ciardi*
EDITH SITWELL ASSUMES THE ROLE OF LUNA—*Francis*
EDMUND POLLARD—*Masters, Edgar Lee*
EDWARD, EDWARD— *Anonymous–English– Modern English*
THE EEL—*Nash*
EFFORTS OF AFFECTION—*Moore, Marianne*
EGG—*MacPherson*
THE EGGPLANT EPITHALAMION— *Jong*
EGGS—*Gioseffi*
EGO—*Booth*
THE EGO MEDIATES—*Gaver*
AN EGYPTIAN PASSAGE—*Weiss*
AN EGYPTIAN PULLED GLASS BOTTLE IN THE SHAPE OF A FISH —*Moore, Marianne*
EHEGEDICHT—*Turner, David*
EHEKRACH—*Tucholsky*
DIE EHELICHE LIEBE—*Lessing*
EHEU1—*Darío*
EHMALS UND JETZT—*Hölderlin*
EHRENBURG—*Neruda*
EHSTANDSSEGEN—*Gellert*
DIE EICHBÄUME—*Hölderlin*
EIGHT O'CLOCK—*Housman*
1805—*Graves*
1887—*Housman*
EIGHTH AIR FORCE—*Jarrell*
EIGHTH AVENUE SONATA— *Deveaux*
EILEEN AROON—*Griffin*
EILEEN, DIARMUID AND TEIG— *Stephens*
EINFACHE DINGE—*Thenior*
DER EINGEBUNDENE KORF— *Morgenstern*
DAS EINHORN—*Morgenstern*
EINS UND ALLES—*Goethe*
DER EINSAME—*Busch*
EINSICHT—*Eich*
DER EINSIEDLER—*Eichendorff*
EINST—*Benn*
EINST—*Heissenbüttel*
EIS EROTA—*Anacreon*
EITELKEIT DER WELT—*Gryphius*
ELDORADO—*Poe*
ELECTRA MOURNS—*Goldstein*
ELECTRIC LADY BLUES—*Jimason*
O ELEFANTE—*Drummond de Andrade*
ELEGANCE—*Mailer*
ELEGI—*Ekelöf*
ELEGÍA—*Couto*
ELEGÍA A LA MUJER INVENTADA— *Abril*

ELEGÍA DE REYES—*Dávila,
Virgilio*
ELEGÍA DO AMOR—*Pascoaes*
ELEGÍA EN LA MUERTE DE UN
PERRO—*Unamuno*
ELECÍA PARA TI Y PARA MI—*Buesa*
ELEGIAC STANZAS SUGGESTED BY A
PICTURE OF PEELE CASTLE—
Wordsworth
ELEGIE—*Donne*
ELEGIE—*Goethe*
ÉLÉGIE—*Musset*
ELEGIE—*Opitz*
ÉLÉGIE—*Parny*
ELEGIE—*Walther von der
Vogelweide*
ELEGIE AUF DEM SCHLACHTFELDE
BEI KUNERSDORF—*Tiedge*
ELEGIE DES ARMEN ICH—*Goll*
ÉLÉGIE QUATORZIÈME—*Jammes*
ÉLÉGIE SUR LA MORT DE RONSARD
—*Garnier*
ÉLÉGIE 24—*Ronsard*
ELEGY—*Campbell, Alistair*
ELEGY—*Ciardi*
ELEGY—*Cohen*
ELEGY—*Katzman*
ELEGY—*Millay*
ELEGY—*Roethke*
ELEGY—*Starbuck*
ELEGY—*Thomas, Dylan*
ELEGY—*Walker*
ELEGY AND JOY—*Rukeyser*
ELEGY FOR A DEAD SOLDIER—
Shapiro, Karl
ELEGY FOR A LADY—*Delegall*
ELEGY FOR A WOMAN UNKNOWN—
Day Lewis
ELEGY FOR ALFRED HUBBARD—
Connor
ELEGY FOR DAVID DIOP—
Kgositsile
ELEGY FOR DYLAN THOMAS—*Abse*
ELEGY FOR DYLAN THOMAS—
Logan
ELEGY FOR G. B. SHAW—*Ciardi*
ELEGY FOR J. F. K.—*Auden*
ELEGY FOR JANE—*Roethke*
ELEGY FOR JANIS JOPLIN—*Hacker*
ELEGY FOR MARGARET—*Spender*
ELEGY FOR MR. GOODBEARE—
Sitwell, Osbert
ELEGY FOR SAPPHO—*Ciardi*
ELEGY FOR THE NEW YEAR—
Marshall, Jack
ELEGY FOR WILLIAM HUBBARD—
Connor
ELEGY JUST IN CASE—*Ciardi*
ELEGY OF FIVE—*Blackmur*
ELEGY ON GORDON BARBER—
Derwood
ELEGY ON HERAKLEITOS—*Fitts*
ELEGY ON THE DEATH OF A MAD
DOG—*Goldsmith*
ELEGY ON THE DUST—*Gunn*
ELEGY ON THE HEROINE OF
CHILDHOOD—*Watkins*

ELEGY ON THYRZA—*Byron*
ELEGY ON TWO PETS—*Ennis*
ELEGY PA GRINGOLANDIA—
Vargas
ELEGY TO A LADY—*Delegall*
ELEGY TO MY DEAD COUSIN—
Sobiloff
ELEGY TO THE MEMORY OF AN
UNFORTUNATE LADY—*Pope,
Alexander*
ELEGY WRITTEN IN A COUNTRY
CHURCHYARD—*Gray*
ELEGY WRITTEN IN AMERICA—
Hodges
ELEJIA A RAMON SIJE—
Hernández, Miguel
ELEMENTAL ENTRY—*McKnight*
ELEMENTAL ENTRY-SUN—
McKnight
ELEMENTARY SCHOOL CLASSROOM
IN A SLUM—*Spender*
THE ELEPHANT AND THE FLEA—
*Anonymous–English–
Modern English*
THE ELEPHANT IS OVERTURNED—
Williams, Hugo
ELEPHANTS—*Nash*
ÉLÉVATION—*Baudelaire*
THE ELF AND THE DORMOUSE—
Herford
THE ELFIN SONG—*Drake, Joseph
Rodman*
EL-HAIJ MALIK EL-SHABAZZ—
Hayden
ELIE HIMMELSFÄRD—*Karlfeldt*
ELIJAH—*Marvin X*
ELISABETH—*Storm*
THE ELIXIR—*Herbert*
ELLE—*Hugo, Victor*
ELLIS PARK—*Hoyt*
ELLSWORTH AVENUE—*Cavalieri*
THE ELM-TREE—*Farjeon*
ÉLOGES—*Perse*
ELOISA TO ABELARD—*Pope,
Alexander*
ELSA—*Conkling*
ELSA AU MIROIR—*Aragon*
ELSA WERTMAN—*Masters, Edgar
Lee*
ELTERNLIED—*Werfel*
ELVIN JONES GRETCH FREAK—
Henderson, David
THE EMBARRASING EPISODE OF
LITTLE MISS MUFFET—*Carryl,
Guy Wetmore*
EMBLEMS—*Tate, Allen*
EMBLEMS OF CONDUCT—*Crane,
Hart*
EMERGENCY CLINIC—*Ignatow*
L'ÉMIGRANT DE LANDOR ROAD—
Apollinaire
THE EMIGRANTS—*Brathwaite*
EMILIA—*Diego, Gerardo*
EMILY SPARKS—*Masters, Edgar
Lee*
EMMETT TILL—*Emanuel*

EMMONSAIL'S HEATH IN WINTER—
Clare
THE EMOTION OF FICTION—
Fuller, Roy
THE EMPEROR'S NIGHTINGALE—
Reynolds
THE EMPEROR'S RHYME—*Milne*
EMPIRE BUILDERS—*MacLeish*
EMPORTEZ-MOI—*Michaux*
AN EMPTY HOUSE—*Connor*
THE EMPTYING—*Schwerner*
EN—*Huidobro*
EN 1915—*Cendrars*
EN EL CAMPO—*Casal*
EN EL INSTITUTO Y EN LA
UNIVERSIDAD—*Garcia Lorca*
EN EL TEOCALI DE CHOLULA—
Heredia y Campuzano
EN EL ZOOLOGICO—*Gaos*
EN FAITES-VOUS DOUTE—*Charles
d'Orleans*
EN FAMILLE—*Prévert*
EN FAMILLE—*Sitwell, Edith*
EN FILE INDIENNE—*Damas*
EN LA PLAZA—*Aleixandre*
EN LAS MANOS DE DIÓS—*Panero*
EN SECRETO—*Laura*
EN SOURDINE—*Verlaine*
EN TREN—*Machado, Antonio*
EN UN CEMENTERIO DE LUGAR
CASTELLANO—*Unamuno*
EN VANO—*Capdevila*
EN VERRAI-JE JAMAIS LA FIN—
Charles d'Orleans
EL ENAMORADO Y LA MUERTE—
Anonymous–Spanish
ENBUSKEN—*Martinson*
ENCARGOS—*Mistral*
ENCHANTED LAND—*Marshall,
Helen Lowrie*
ENCINA—*Garcia Lorca*
ENCORE UNE FOIS SUR LE FLEUVE
—*Prévert*
ENCOUNTER—*Bishop, John Peale*
ENCOUNTER—*Yevtushenko*
ENCOUNTER IN THE CAGE
COUNTRY—*Dickey, James*
ENCUENTRO—*León, Rafael de*
ENCUENTRO—*Storni*
ENCUENTRO DE LUIS CERNUDA
CON VERLAINE Y EL DEMONIO—
Mantero
LOS ENCUENTROS DE UN CARACOL
AVENTURERO—*Garcia Lorca*
THE END—*Milne*
END OF SUMMER—*Kunitz*
THE END OF THE WORLD—
MacLeish
END OR BEGINNING—*Devaul*
DEN ENDA STUNDEN—*Runeberg*
ENDE AUGUST—*Eich*
ENDE EINES SOMMERS—*Eich*
ENDECHA DEL GAUCHO—
Gutierrez
ENDLESS PAVEMENT—*Graves*
ENDYMION—*Keats*
ENDYMION—*Stagnelius*

ENEYDOS—*Caxton*
ENFANCE—*Carco*
L'ENFANCE—*Prévert*
UN ENFANT A DIT—*Queneau*
L'ENFANT ET LE MAÎTRE D'ÉCOLE
    —*La Fontaine*
L'ENFANT GREC—*Hugo, Victor*
LES ENFANTS EXIGEANTS—*Prévert*
ENGAGEMENT AT THE SALT FORK
    —*Beecher*
DER ENGEL SPRICHT—
    Bergengruen
ENGLAND—*De la Mare*
ENGLAND, 1802—*Wordsworth*
THE ENGLISH DANDY AT THE
    MOULIN ROUGE:
    TOULOUSE-LAUTREC—*Engle*
AN ENGLISH EXPLORER—*Fuller,*
    Roy
ENIVREZ-VOUS—*Baudelaire*
THE ENLIGHTENED SNAKE—*Roche*
ENLISTMENT—*Spencer*
L'ENNEMI—*Baudelaire*
ENOCH ARDEN—*Tennyson*
DEN ENSAMMA DROMMEN—*Hasso*
ENSEMBLE—*Lasnier*
ENSINANDO UM PASSARO A CANTAR
    —*Nunes*
ENSLEY, ALABAMA: 1932—*Beecher*
ENTARTUNG—*Heine*
ENTER SINGING—*Marshall,*
    Helen Lowrie
ENTHUSIASM—*Moore, Merrill*
ENTHUSIAST—*Warton, Joseph*
ENTRADA A LA MADERA—*Neruda*
ENTRE TANTA PRESENCIA DE
    MUERTOS—*Matos Paoli*
ENTREGA—*Champourcin*
ENTSORGT—*Born, Nicolas*
DIE ENTWICKLUNG DER
    MENSCHHEIT—*Kästner*
ENVIO—*Macheral*
ENVOI—*Swinburne*
ENVOI, 1919—*Pound*
ENVOY—*Conkling*
ENVOY TO SCOGAN—*Chaucer*
EPIGRAM—*Bertrand de Born*
EPIGRAM—*Cunningham, James*
    Vincent
EPIGRAM—*Dowling*
EPIGRAM—*Lanusse*
EPIGRAM—*Moratin*
EPIGRAMME—*Schiller*
EPIGRAMS: A JOURNAL—
    Cunningham, James Vincent
ÉPIGRAPHE POUR UN LIVRE
    CONDAMNÉ—*Baudelaire*
EPIKALEO TOI TEN THEON—
    Seferis
EPIL Y FILIAST—*Webb*
EPILOG 1949—*Benn*
EPILOGUE—*Brathwaite*
EPILOGUE—*Henri*
EPILOGUE—*Lowell, Robert*
EPILOGUE TO THE
    BREAKFAST-TABLE SERIES—
    Holmes, Oliver Wendell

EPILOGUE TO THE SATIRES,
    DIALOGUE—*Pope, Alexander*
EPIPSYCHIDION—*Shelley*
AN EPISODE—*Day Lewis*
EPISODE—*Durrell*
EPISTLE—*Nash*
EPISTLE TO A GODSON—*Auden*
EPISTLE TO A LADY—*Pope,*
    Alexander
EPISTLE TO A YOUNG FRIEND—
    Burns
EPISTLE TO BE LEFT IN THE EARTH
    —*MacLeish*
EPISTLE TO DR. ARBUTHNOT—
    Pope, Alexander
EPISTLE TO JAMES SMITH—*Burns*
EPISTLE TO LORD COBHAM—*Pope,*
    Alexander
EPISTLE TO THE EARL OF
    BURLINGTON—*Pope,*
    Alexander
EPISTLE TO THE OLYMPIANS—
    Nash
EPÍSTOLA A HORACIO—*Menendez*
    y Pelayo
EPITAPH—*Cunningham, James*
    Vincent
EPITAPH—*Eastman*
EPITAPH—*Van Doren*
EPITAPH: BUTCHER—*Francis*
EPITAPH: DIPLOMATS—*Francis*
EPITAPH: DOR—
    Anonymous-English—
    Modern English
EPITAPH: EVERYMAN—*Francis*
EPITAPH: FISHERMAN—*Francis*
EPITAPH FOR A POET—*Cullen*
EPITAPH FOR ANTON SCHMIDT—
    Gunn
EPITAPH FOR MY FATHER—*Walker*
EPITAPH FOR THAIS—
    Heath-Stubbs
EPITAPH OF A MALTESE
    WATCH-DOG—*Tymnes*
EPITAPH OF A NICENE ACTOR—
    Anonymous-Greek
EPITAPH OF A SAILOR—
    Anonymous-Greek
EPITAPH OF A YOUNG MAN—
    Anonymous-Greek
EPITAPH OF CHARIDAS OF KYRENE
    —*Kallimachos*
EPITAPH OF DIONYSIOS OF TARSOS
    —*Anonymous-Greek*
EPITAPH OF NEARCHOS—
    Ammianus
EPITAPH OF SEIKILOS—
    Anonymous-Greek
EPITAPH: OLD LADY PATRIOT—
    Francis
EPITAPH ON A HARE—*Cowper*
EPITAPH ON AN ARMY OF
    MERCENARIES—*Housman*
EPITAPH ON CERTAIN SCHISMATICS
    —*Merwin*
EPITAPH ON ELIZABETH, L. H.—
    Jonson

EPITAPH ON SOLOMON PAVY—
    Jonson
EPITAPH: PREACHER—*Francis*
EPITAPH: THE FURRED LADY—
    Francis
EPITAPH: THE PROUD AND
    PASSIONATE MAN—*Francis*
EPITAPH: TOMB OF A WELL-KNOWN
    SOLDIER—*Francis*
EPITAPH: UNDERTAKER—*Francis*
ÉPITAPHE—*Desnos*
ÉPITAPHE—*Nerval*
ÉPITAPHE DE MME DU CHÂTELET
    —*Voltaire*
ÉPITAPHE D'UNE SAUTERELLE—
    Heredia
ÉPITAPHE EN FORME DE BALLADE
    QUE FEIT VILLON POUR LUY ET
    SES COMPAIGNONS—*Villon*
EPITAPHIOS—*Ritsos*
EPITHALAMION—*Abse*
EPITHALAMION—*Hopkins*
EPITHALAMION—*O'Gorman*
EPITHALAMION—*Spenser*
EPITHALAMIUM AND ELEGY—
    Bynner
EPITHALAMIUM AT SAINT
    MICHAEL'S CEMETERY—*Ciardi*
ÉPITRE A LA MARQUISE DE
    CHÂTELET—*Voltaire*
EQUILIBRISTS—*Ransom*
EQUIVALENCE OF GNATS AND
    MICE—*Eberhart*
ER ISTS—*Mörike*
ERDGEIST—*Wedekind*
ERFAHRUNG—*Bobrowski*
ERGE EREKT—*Mon*
ERINNA AN SAPPHO—*Mörike*
DIE ERINNERUNG—*Krolow*
ERINNERUNG AN DIE MARIE A—
    Brecht
ERKENNEN—*Tieck*
ERKLÄR MIR LIEBE—*Bachmann*
DER ERLKÖNIG—*Goethe*
EROISMO—*Viviani*
EROS TYRANNOS—*Robinson,*
    Edwin Arlington
EROTIKOS—*Seferis*
EROTION—*Swinburne*
ERRANTRY—*Tolkien*
DIE ERSCHEINUNG—*Krolow*
ERSTE DUINESER ELEGIE—*Rilke*
DIE ERWARTUNG—*Schiller*
ES AMOR—*Carranza*
ES EL TIEMPO—*Carranza*
ES IST DER WIND AUF DEN
    BRÜCKEN—*Meckel*
ES KOMMT DER ABEND—
    Lasker-Schüler
ES KRIBBELT UND WIBBELT WEITER
    —*Fontane*
ES LA MUJER—*Vega Carpio*
ES MELANCOLÍA—*Carranza*
ES VERDAD—*Garcia Lorca*
LA ESCALINATA DE PIEDRAS—
    Martinez Alonso
ESCAPE AT BED TIME—*Stevenson*

ESCAPIST SONG—*Spencer*
L'ESCARRASSADA—*Carner I
    Puig-Oriol*
ESCOMBRO—*León, Rafael de*
ESHU—*Alakoye*
ESPACIO—*Jiménez*
ESPAÑA EN EL SUEÑO—*Bousoño*
UNA ESPAÑA JOVEN—*Machado,
    Antonio*
EL ESPEJO Y EL TIRANO—*Alberti*
ESPÍRITU DE KEATS—*Pardo
    Garcia*
L'ESPOIR LUIT—*Verlaine*
L'ESPRIT DE FAMILLE—*Obaldia*
L'ESPRIT ET L'EAU—*Claudel*
AN ESSAY ON CRITICISM—*Pope,
    Alexander*
AN ESSAY ON MAN—*Pope,
    Alexander*
ESTA NECESIDAD—*Reyes*
ESTA NOCHE—*Mendoza, Esther
    Feliciano*
ESTAR ENAMORADO—*Bernárdez*
ESTE ES EL PRÓLOGO—*Garcia
    Lorca*
ESTRANGED FROM DYING LEAVES
    —*Stephany*
ESTRÊLA—*Meireles*
ESTRÊLA DA MANHÂ—*Bandeira*
LA ESTRELLA VENIDA—*Jiménez*
EL ESTUDIANTE DE SALAMANCA—
    Espronceda
ESTUDO NO. 2—*Marques*
ET VOICI—*Damas*
ETERNAL CHILD—*Raine*
ETERNAL FORM—*Dudek*
THE ETERNAL GOODNESS—
    Whittier
ÉTÉ—*Valéry*
L'ÉTERNITÉ—*Rimbaud*
ETERNITY—*Blake*
ETERNITY—*Crane, Hart*
ETERNITY OF LOVE PROTESTED—
    Carew
ETHEREALIZING—*Frost, Robert*
L'ETOILE DU SOIR—*Musset*
ETOILE POURPRE—*Grandbois*
ETOT MIR—*Kirsanov*
L'ÉTRANGER—*Baudelaire*
ÉTRANGES ÉTRANGERS—*Prévert*
ETT ÄR NÖDVÄNDIGT—*Edfelt*
ETT MINNE—*Ferlin*
EUGENE CARMAN—*Masters,
    Edgar Lee*
EULALIE—*Poe*
EULOGY—*Auden*
EUNICE—*Betjeman*
EUPHROSYNE—*Goethe*
EUROPA AND THE BULL—*Rodgers*
EUROPE—*Porter, Peter*
EUROPE—*Whitman*
EUROPE, EUROPE—*Ginsberg*
THE EUROPEAN SHOE—*Benedikt*
EURYDICE—*Sitwell, Edith*
EUTHANASIA/LORTONMANIA—
    Alston
EVANGELINE—*Longfellow*

EVE—*Hodgson*
EVE—*Péguy*
EVE—*Rossetti, Christina*
EVE OF ST. AGNES—*Keats*
EVEN AMONG THIEVES—*Murphy*
EVEN IN SLEEP—*Mariah*
EVEN THOUGH YOU LIE WITH
    LAUGHTER—*Goldstein*
EVENING—*Cotton*
EVENING IN A SUGAR ORCHARD—
    Frost, Robert
EVENING IN CONNECTICUT—
    MacNeice
AN EVENING OF RUSSIAN POETRY—
    Nabokov
AN EVENING OF THE PRIVATE EYE
    —*Ciardi*
THE EVENING OUT—*Nash*
THE EVENING PRIMROSE—*Parker*
EVENING QUATRAINS—*Cotton*
EVENING SONG—*Davis, Fannie
    Stearns*
EVENING STAR—*Poe*
EVENING WATERFALL—*Sandburg*
AN EVENING'S LOVE: PROLOGUE—
    Dryden
EVENSONG—*Herbert*
ÉVENTAIL DE MLLE MALLARME—
    Mallarmé
THE EVERLASTING—*Hoffman*
THE EVERLASTING CONTENDERS—
    Patchen
THE EVERLASTING MERCY—
    Masefield
EVERY DAY OF THE WORLD—
    Hughes, Ted
EVERY EARTHLY CREATURE—
    Brinnin
EVERY GOOD BOY DOES FINE—
    Wagoner
EVERYBODY SAYS—*Aldis*
EVERYBODY TELLS ME
    EVERYTHING—*Nash*
EVERYONE IS A COMPLETE
    DISAPPOINTMENT—*Giorno*
EVERYWHERE IS HERE—*Graves*
EVGENII ONEGIN—*Pushkin*
THE EVIDENCE—*Jong*
DET EVIGA—*Tegner*
EVIL—*Rimbaud*
EX ART STUDENT—*McGough*
EX LIBRIS—*Morgenstern*
EXACTA—*Violi*
THE EXAMINATION—*Snodgrass*
THE EXAMINER—*Scott, F. R.*
THE EXAMPLE—*Belloc*
AN EXCHANGE BETWEEN THE
    FINGERS AND THE TOES—
    Fuller, John
THE EXCURSION—*Wordsworth*
EXEQUY ON HIS WIFE—*King*
EXIL—*Bachmann*
EXIL—*Perse*
EXILE—*Smith, Sydney Goodsir*
EXILED—*Marvin X*
EXILED—*Millay*
THE EXILES—*Auden*

EXILES—*Hacker*
THE EXILE'S LETTER—*Li Bai*
THE EXILE'S RETURN—*Lowell,
    Robert*
EXIT, PURSUED BY A BEAR—*Nash*
EXPANSION—*Geraldy*
EXPATRIATES—*Laepa*
EXPECT NOTHING—*Graves*
EXPECTATION—*Miles*
EXPECTATION—*Stanley*
EXPECTATIONS—*Flanders*
EXPEDIENCY—*Johnston, Ellen
    Turlington*
EXPÉRIENCE—*Régnier*
EXPERIMENT DEGUSTATORY—
    Nash
THE EXPIATION—*Abbe*
THE EXPIRATION—*Donne*
EXPLANATIONS OF LOVE—
    Sandburg
EXPLANATORY NOTE—*Garlick*
EXPLICAÇÃO—*Meireles*
L'EXPLICATION DES MÉTAPHORES
    —*Queneau*
EXPLORATION—*Hoffman*
EXPLORATION OF A CHILD—HOW
    IT EXPLORES ITSELF AND WHY—
    Sobiloff
THE EXPLORER ON MAIN STREET—
    Eberhart
THE EXPLORER'S WOOING—*Field,
    Eugene*
EXPOSTULATION AND REPLY—
    Wordsworth
EXPOSURE—*Owen, Wilfred*
EXPRESS—*Rodgers*
EXPRESS—*Spender*
L'EXTASE—*Éluard*
THE EXTASIE—*Donne*
EXTEMPORE EFFUSION ON THE
    DEATH OF JAMES HOGG—
    Wordsworth
EXTINCT MONSTERS—*Field,
    Eugene*
EXTRA-CREDIT (OR IT'S TOO LATE,
    JOHN)—*Johnston, Ellen
    Turlington*
EXTRACT FROM AUTUMN SEQUEL—
    MacNeice
EL EXTRANJERO—*Carranza*
EXTRAPOLATIONS FROM HENRY
    MANLEY'S PIE PLANT—*Kumin*
EXTREME UNCTION—*Dowson*
EXTREMES—*Riley*
THE EYE—*Benedikt*
EYE AND TOOTH—*Lowell, Robert*
THE EYES—*Williams, Tennessee*
THE EYES OF THE DROWNED
    WATCH KEELS GOING OVER—
    Merwin
EYES OF THE NIGHT-TIME—
    Rukeyser
EYES OF UNDERSTANDING—
    Marshall, Helen Lowrie
EZRA POUND IN PISA—*Davie*
EZRY—*MacLeish*

F-STOP/DIANE ARBUS—*Wyatt, Andrea*
FABLE—*Emerson*
A FABLE FOR CRITICS—*Lowell, James Russell*
FABLE FOR FLIPPED LID—*Starbuck*
THE FABLE OF THE BEARS IN WINTER—*Hollander*
FABLE OU HISTOIRE—*Hugo, Victor*
THE FABLE TO END FABLES—*Roche*
FABLIAU OF FLORIDA—*Stevens, Wallace*
FÁBULA DE LA SIRENA Y LOS BORRACHOS—*Neruda*
FAÇADE—*Sitwell, Edith*
FACE—*Browning, Robert*
FACE—*Moore, Marianne*
FACE—*Sandburg*
A FACE IN THE CROWD—*Robson, Jeremy*
THE FACE IN THE MIRROR—*Graves*
LA FACE INTÉRIEURE—*Tzara*
THE FACE UPON THE FLOOR—*D'Arcy*
THE FACE YOU HAVE SEEN—*Beecher*
FACIMMECE 'A CROCE—*Viviani*
THE FACT THAT ONE IS—*Gregor*
FADE-OUT—*Wilson*
THE FAERIE QUEENE—*Spenser*
FAFÄNGLIGHET—*Ferlin*
FAFNIR AND THE KNIGHT—*Smith, Stevie*
FAIDA DI COMUNE—*Carducci*
A FAILURE—*Day Lewis*
FAIR ANNIE—*Anonymous–English–Modern English*
FAIR IN THE WOODS—*Gunn*
FAIR MARGARET AND SWEET WILLIAM—*Anonymous–English–Modern English*
THE FAIRIES—*Allingham*
THE FAIRIES—*Conkling*
THE FAIRIES OF THE CALDON LOW—*Howitt*
A FAIRLY SAD TALE—*Parker*
FAIRY BREAD—*Stevenson*
THE FAIRY THORN TREE—*Ferguson*
FAIRY WINGS—*Howard, Winifred*
FAITH IN YOURSELF—*Marshall, Helen Lowrie*
THE FAITHFUL LOVER—*Pack*
THE FAITHLESS FLOWERS—*Widdemer*
THE FALCONER OF GOD—*Benét, William Rose*
THE FALL—*Johnston, Ellen Turlington*
THE FALL—*Moss, Howard*
THE FALL—*Nemerov*
FALL, 1961—*Lowell, Robert*

FALL OF HYPERION—*Keats*
THE FALL OF LEAVES—*Winters*
THE FALL OF ROME—*Auden*
FALL OF THE EVENING STAR—*Patchen*
FALL SONG—*Nemerov*
FALLEN IDOL—*Marshall, Helen Lowrie*
THE FALLEN TOWER OF SILOAM—*Graves*
FALLING—*Dickey, James*
FALLING ASLEEP OVER THE AENEID—*Lowell, Robert*
FALLING TEARS, AWAKENING HEAVENS—*Zaturenska*
THE FALSE FRIENDS—*Parker*
FALSE GODS, REAL MEN—*Berrigan*
FALSE SECURITY—*Betjeman*
FALSETTO—*Montale*
O FALSO MENDIGO—*Morais*
LA FAMIJJA POVERELLA—*Belli*
FAMILIALE—*Prévert*
FAMILIAR FACES, LONG DEPARTED—*Hillyer*
THE FAMILY CAT—*Fuller, Roy*
FAMILY MATTERS—*Fuller, Roy*
FAMILY PORTRAIT—*Baldwin, Deirdra*
FAMILY PRIME—*Van Doren*
FANCY'S KNELL—*Housman*
FÅNGEN—*Blomberg*
DEN FÅNGNE GUDEN—*Blomberg*
FANNY—*Chénier*
FANTAISIE—*Nerval*
FANTASIE VON ÜBERMORGEN—*Kästner*
FANTASY—*Bodenheim*
THE FAR FIELD—*Roethke*
FAR ROCKAWAY NIGHT TILL MORNING—*Sandburg*
FARE THEE WELL—*Byron*
FARE WELL—*De la Mare*
A FAREWELL—*Gascoigne*
A FAREWELL—*Patmore*
A FAREWELL—*Press*
A FAREWELL—*Tennyson*
A FAREWELL—*Walters*
A FAREWELL—*Wyatt, Sir Thomas*
FAREWELL AND THANKSGIVING—*Van Doren*
A FAREWELL DRINK FOR B. L.—*Harteis*
A FAREWELL TO LONDON—*Pope, Alexander*
A FAREWELL TO MAGIC—*Wellman*
FAREWELL TO NANCY—*Burns*
FAREWELL TO THE FARM—*Stevenson*
FAREWELL TO VAN GOGH—*Tomlinson*
THE FARM—*Hall*
FARM BOY AFTER SUMMER—*Francis*
THE FARM ON THE GREAT PLAINS—*Stafford*

A FARMER REMEMBERS LINCOLN—*Bynner*
THE FARMER'S CURST WIFE—*Anonymous–English–Modern English*
FARMERS' NOTEBOOK—*Scott, Dennis*
THE FARMER'S WIFE—*Sexton*
EL FARO—*Marin*
A FAR-OFF WAR—*Young, David*
FARVEL 'TIL ITALIEN—*Andersen*
FASCINATION—*Giovanni*
DE FASTELDANZ—*Olfers-Batocki*
FAT—*Lifshin*
THE FAT MAN—*Lally*
A FAT MAN DIES—*Abbe*
FAT THIGHS AND 30 DOLLAR EYES—*Lifshin*
LO FATAL—*Darío*
THE FATE OF THE FLIMFLAM—*Field, Eugene*
FATHER—*Frost, Frances M.*
FATHER AND DAUGHTER—*Sanchez*
FATHER AND SON—*Ai*
FATHER AND SON—*Kunitz*
FATHER AND SON—*Sandburg*
FATHER DEATH BLUES—*Ginsberg*
FATHER'S BEDROOM—*Lowell, Robert*
FATICANNO SOTT' 'E SGHIZZE—*Viviani*
THE FATIGUE—*Jones, David*
FAUN—*Ekelöf*
LE FAUNE—*Noailles*
FAUSTIN—*Lessing*
FAUSTINA—*Bishop, Elizabeth*
LES FAUX BEAUX JOURS—*Verlaine*
FAVELA—*Bopp*
LE FAVOLE A ROVESCIO—*Rodari*
THE FAWN—*Millay*
FAYE—*Shange*
FEAR—*Francis*
FEAR AS NORMAL—*Smith, A. J. M.*
FEAR BY HANGING—*Moore, Rosalie*
THE FEAR OF DYING—*Holmes, John*
THE FEAR THAT PRECEDES—*Duncan*
FEATHER OR FUR—*Becker*
A FEAVER—*Donne*
FEBRUARY 22nd—*Updike*
FEBRUARY TWILIGHT—*Teasdale*
FEDELE'S SONG—*Munday*
THE FEEL OF HANDS—*Gunn*
FEELING THROUGH—*Aubert*
FEET O' JESUS—*Hughes, Langston*
FELICITÀ—*Totò*
FELIPE—*Machado, Manuel*
FELISSE MORO—*Marin*
FELIX RANDAL—*Hopkins*
FELIX SCHMIDT—*Masters, Edgar Lee*
FELIXSTOWE—*Betjeman*

FELLOWSHIP—*Marshall, Helen Lowrie*
FEMALE, MALE AND BOTH—*Summers, Hollis*
THE FEMALE OF THE SPECIES—*Kipling*
LA FEMME ADULTÈRE—*Vigny*
LA FEMME ET LA FLAMME—*Césaire*
FEMME NOIRE—*Senghor*
LES FEMMES DE MON GENOU—*Obaldia*
LES FENÊTRES—*Baudelaire*
FENG CHAU YE BWO—*Jang Ji*
FERIA DE ABRIL EN JEREZ—*Pemán*
LO FERM VOLER—*Daniel, Arnaud*
FERN HILL—*Thomas, Dylan*
DAS FERNGESPRÄCH—*Roth, Eugen*
FERRAGOSTO—*Rodari*
FERTILE—*Williams, William Carlos*
THE FERTILE MUCK—*Layton*
FÊTE—*Apollinaire*
FÊTE—*Prévert*
FÊTE—*Seghers*
FÊTE NUPTIALE—*Obaldia*
FÊTES DE LA FAIM—*Rimbaud*
FEU SUR LA BÊTE-ANGOISSE—*Henault*
LA FEUILLE—*Arnault*
LES FEUILLES D'AUTOMNE—*Hugo, Victor*
LES FEUILLES D'AUTOMNE—*Moréas*
FEVER 103 DEGREES—*Plath*
FICHA INGRESO HOSPITAL GENERAL—*Fuertes*
FIDDLER JONES—*Masters, Edgar Lee*
THE FIDDLER OF DOONEY—*Yeats*
FIDELIDAD—*Pardo Garcia*
FIELD MOUSE—*Conkling*
FIELD TRIP—*O'Neill, Catherine*
FIERA DEL SUD—*Freni*
FIERO AMOR—*Storni*
FIFTEEN—*Stafford*
THE FIFTEEN ACRES—*Stephens*
FIFTH ANNIVERSARY—*Polak*
FIFTH GRADE SCAR—*Harkness*
FIGHT—*Jaszi*
FIGHT THE GOOD—*Middleton, Thomas*
LA FIGLIA CHE PIANGE—*Eliot, Thomas Stearns*
THE FIGUREHEAD—*Shapiro, Karl*
ER FIJJO D'ORO—*Belli*
FIKTIONSVARLDEN—*Siewertz*
FILASTROCCA BRONTOLONA—*Rodari*
FILASTROCCA IMPERTINENTE—*Rodari*
LA FILEUSE—*Valéry*
LA FILLE—*La Fontaine*
UNE FILLE DE FEU—*Seghers*
LA FILLE MAIGRE—*Hébert*

LES FILLES DE LA NUIT—*Carco*
LES FILLES DU FEU—*Nerval*
FILOSOFÍA DE LA MUERTE—*Martinez Alonso*
LA FILOSOFIA DEL CORNUTO—*Totò*
FILOSOFÍA DEL DOLOR—*Martinez Alonso*
LE FILS DU GRAND ROSEAU—*Prévert*
FIM—*Sá-Carneiro*
LA FIN DE LA JOURNÉE—*Baudelaire*
FINA E LENTA—*Filippo*
FINAL CALL—*Hughes, Langston*
THE FINAL HOUR—*Robinson, Wanda*
FINAL INSTRUCTIONS—*Day Lewis*
FINAL SOLILOQUY OF THE INTERIOR PARAMOUR—*Stevens, Wallace*
THE FINAL SOLUTION—*Sanchez*
THE FINAL WAR—*Fuller, Roy*
FINALE—*Geraldy*
FINALE—*Jammes*
FINALITIES—*Bodenheim*
THE FIND—*Ledwidge*
FINDING THE MASCULINE PRINCIPLE IN BABYSHIT—*Tullos*
FINDING THE MEASURE—*Kelly*
FINE DI CRONO—*Ungaretti*
THE FINGER—*Creeley*
FIORETTI—*Francis of Assisi*
I FIORI—*Palazzeschi*
FIRE AND ICE—*Frost, Robert*
THE FIRE AT ALEXANDRIA—*Weiss*
FIRE BY NIGHT—*Beecher*
FIRE LOGS—*Sandburg*
THE FIRE OF DRIFT-WOOD—*Longfellow*
THE FIREBOMBING—*Dickey, James*
THE FIREBORN ARE AT HOME IN FIRE—*Sandburg*
FIREFLIES—*Coplen*
FIREFLIES—*Grant*
FIREFLIES IN THE GARDEN—*Frost, Robert*
THE FIREFLY—*Nash*
THE FIREFLY—*Roberts*
FIREWORKS—*Deutsch*
DAS FIRMAMENT—*Brockes*
FIRST-BORN SON—*Hinton*
FIRST CAME L. E. PHANT'S LETTER—*Cullen*
THE FIRST DAYS—*Wright, James*
FIRST DEATH—*Enright*
THE FIRST DREAM: THE GARAGE—*Abbe*
FIRST FIGHT—*Scannell*
FIRST FROST—*Marshall, Helen Lowrie*
FIRST LESSON—*Booth*
FIRST LOVE—*Campion*
FIRST LOVE—*Clare*
FIRST LOVE—*Dupree*
FIRST LOVE—*Lee, Laurie*

FIRST LOVE—*MacDiarmid*
FIRST LOVE—*Yeats*
THE FIRST OF JUNE AGAIN—*Kizer*
THE FIRST OF MAY—*Housman*
FIRST PARTY AT KEN KESEY'S WITH HELL'S ANGELS—*Ginsberg*
THE FIRST SNOW OF THE YEAR—*Van Doren*
THE FIRST SNOWFALL—*Lowell, James Russell*
FIRST SONG—*Kinnell*
FIRST SONGS—*Conkling*
FIRST THINGS FIRST—*Auden*
THE FIRST TIME—*Creeley*
THE FIRST TIME—*Marcus*
FIRST TIME, 1950—*Moore, Honor*
FIRST WARM DAYS—*Denby*
DER FISCHER—*Goethe*
O FISCO—*Capurro*
FISH—*Berrigan*
FISH—*Lester*
FISH—*Moore, Marianne*
FISH—*Ross, W. W. Eustace*
FISH—*Stryk*
FISH—*Williams, William Carlos*
FISH, FISH—*Smith, Stevie*
THE FISH-HAWK—*Wheelock*
FISH POND—*Children's Verses and Nursery Rhymes*
FISHERMAN—*Engle*
FISHERMAN—*MacPherson*
FISHERMAN—*Scott, Dennis*
FISHERMEN—*Emanuel*
THE FISHES OF KEMPENFELT BAY—*Lee, Dennis*
FISKARE KOMMA HEM FRÅN SHETLAND—*Lindqvist*
FISKLÄGE: SAMHÄLLET—*Lindqvist*
I FIUMI—*Ungaretti*
FIVE EYES—*De la Mare*
FIVE O'CLOCK—*Betjeman*
A FIVE-YEAR-OLD SCREAM BREAKING THROUGH THE NIGHT—*Fabio, Sarah Webster*
THE FLAME—*Dowling*
FLAME-HEART—*McKay*
THE FLAMING HEART—*Crashaw*
FLANNAN ISLE—*Gibson, Wilfred*
FLASH CRIMSON—*Sandburg*
A FLAT ONE—*Snodgrass*
FLATTED FIFTH—*Hughes, Langston*
THE FLAW—*Lowell, Robert*
THE FLEA—*Donne*
FLEET VISIT—*Auden*
LA FLEUR RENVOYÉE—*Desbordes-Valmore*
FLEUVE—*Soupault*
FLICKAN KOM IFRÅN SIN ALSKLINGS MOTE—*Runeberg*
FLIES—*Lester*
THE FLIGHT—*Roethke*
THE FLIGHT OF QUETZALCOATL—*Anonymous–American Indian languages–Nahuatl*
FLIGHT OF THE ROLLER-COASTER—*Souster*

FLIGHT OF THE SPARROW—*Stryk*

FLIGHT TO ITALY—*Day Lewis*

FLIRT—*Updike*

FLIRTATION—*Emanuel*

FLOOD—*Joyce*

LA FLOR DEL CAMINO—*Jiménez*

FLOR QUE VUELVE—*Jiménez*

FLORES—*Vargas*

FLORESTAN—*Fuller, Roy*

FLORIDA ROAD WORKERS—
Hughes, Langston

FLOSSIE CABANIS—*Masters,
Edgar Lee*

THE FLOURISHING VILLAGE—
Dwight

THE FLOWER—*Herbert*

THE FLOWER—*Posner*

THE FLOWER AND THE LEAF—
Cowley, Malcolm

THE FLOWER-FED BUFFALOES—
Lindsay, Vachel

A FLOWER GIVEN TO MY
DAUGHTER—*Joyce*

FLOWERING QUINCE—*Ciardi*

FLOWERS—*Stevenson*

FLOWERS—*Yessenin*

FLOWERS BY THE SEA—*Williams,
William Carlos*

FLOWERS FOR HER GRAVE—
Whistler

FLUSS IM SCHNEE—
Anonymous–Asian languages

LA FLÛTE—*Chénier*

THE FLUTEPLAYERS—*Aiken*

THE FLUTES—*Nash*

FLY—*Blake*

FLY—*Kinnell*

FLY—*Merwin*

FLY—*Nash*

FLY—*Oldys*

THE FLY AND THE FLY-PAPER—
Roche

THE FLY-AWAY HORSE—*Field,
Eugene*

FLYGARDIKT—*Martinson*

FLYING ABOVE CALIFORNIA—
Gunn

FLYING CROOKED—*Graves*

FLYING TO HANOI—*Rukeyser*

FLYTING O' LIFE AND DAITH—
Henderson, Hamish

FLYTTFÅGLARNA—*Hallström*

FOG—*Coffin*

FOG—*Sandburg*

FOG, THE MAGICIAN—*Cane*

FOL-DE-ROL AND RIDDLE-MA-REE
—*Children's Verses and
Nursery Rhymes*

A FOLK FABLE FOR MY PEOPLE—
Amini

FOLK SONG—*Hillyer*

FOLKWAYS—*Brathwaite*

FOLLOWER—*Heaney*

THE FOLLY OF BEING COMFORTED
—*Yeats*

FONCTION DU POETE—*Hugo,
Victor*

THE FONT IN THE FOREST—
Adams

FOOD AND DRINK—*Untermeyer*

FOOD OF THE DEAD—*Graves*

THE FOOL—*Pearse*

THE FOOL—*Zu-Bolton*

FOOLISH ABOUT WINDOWS—
Sandburg

FOOLISH CHILD—
*Anonymous–African
languages–Ghana*

THE FOOL'S PRAYER—*Sill*

FOOL'S SONG—*Sitwell, Osbert*

FOOLS, THEY ARE THE ONLY
NATION—*Jonson*

FOOTNOTE TO HOWL—*Ginsberg*

FOOTNOTE TO LORD ACTON—
Ozick

FOOTSTEPS—*Blanding*

FOR A CHILD BORN DEAD—
Jennings

FOR A DEAD KITTEN—*Hay, Sara
Henderson*

FOR A DISSOLVING MUSIC—
Merwin

FOR A GOOD DOG—*Nash*

FOR A LADY I KNOW—*Cullen*

FOR A LAMB—*Eberhart*

FOR A RUSSIAN POET—*Rich*

FOR A YOUNG FRIEND SEEKING
IDENTITY—*Miller, May*

FOR AN UNKNOWN LADY—*Parker*

FOR ANDY GOODMAN—MICHAEL
SCHWERNER—AND JAMES
CHANEY—*Walker*

FOR ANNE, DEAD—*Lorde*

FOR ANNE GREGORY—*Yeats*

FOR ANNIE—*Poe*

FOR BECKY—*Williams, Miller*

FOR BLACK PEOPLE—*Lee, Don L.*

FOR BOTH OF YOU, THE DIVORCE
BEING FINAL—*Hollander*

FOR BUD—*Harper*

FOR CANNONBALL ADDERLY—
Williams, Otis

FOR CERTAIN DEMAGOGUES—
Vaughan, H. A.

FOR ELEANOR AND BILL MONAHAN
—*Williams, William Carlos*

FOR ELEKTRA—*Hacker*

FOR EL-HAJJ MALIK EL-SHABAZZ—
Hinton

FOR FRAN—*Levine*

FOR GEORGE SANTAYANA—
Lowell, Robert

FOR GUILLAUME APOLLINAIRE—
Meredith, William

FOR HER SAKE—*Reid*

FOR JOAN—*Lester*

FOR JOHN BERRYMAN—*Lowell,
Robert*

FOR JOHN F. KENNEDY HIS
INAUGURATION—*Frost, Robert*

FOR JOHN KENNEDY, JR.—*Roseliep*

FOR LANGSTON HUGHES—*Knight,
Etheridge*

FOR LEROI JONES, APRIL, 1965—
Kgositsile

FOR LOVE—*Creeley*

FOR MALCOLM, A YEAR AFTER—
Knight, Etheridge

FOR MALCOLM, U. S. A.—*Emanuel*

FOR MALCOLM X—*Walker*

FOR MARGARET DANNER—
Randall

FOR MIRIAM—*Patchen*

FOR "MR. DUDLEY", A BLACK SPY—
Emanuel

FOR MY CHILDREN—*Sanchez*

FOR MY DAUGHTER—*Kizer*

FOR MY GRANDMOTHER—*Cullen*

FOR MY PEOPLE—*Walker*

FOR MY PEOPLE, A JUBILEE—
Fabio, Sarah Webster

FOR MY PUPILS IN THE WAR YEARS
—*Brinnin*

FOR MY SISTER, HARRIET—*Lorde*

FOR NO GOOD REASON—*Redgrove*

FOR OUR LADY—*Sanchez*

FOR P. F. C. JOE ROGERS—*Knight,
Etheridge*

FOR PAO-CHIN, A BOATMAN ON
THE YELLOW SEA—*Millay*

FOR PAUL LAURENCE DUNBAR—
Cullen

FOR RING GIVERS—*Reid*

FOR SALE—*Lowell, Robert*

FOR SAPPHO AFTER SAPPHO—
Kizer

FOR SNOW—*Farjeon*

FOR SPELLMAN AT SPELMAN—
Kgositsile

FOR SYDNEY BRADSHAW—*Larkin*

FOR THE ANNIVERSARY OF MY
DEATH—*Merwin*

FOR THE 4TH GRADE, PROSPECT
SCHOOL: HOW I BECAME A POET
—*Emanuel*

FOR THE GREEKS—*Genser*

FOR THE LAST TIME, FIRE—*Scott,
Dennis*

FOR THE LAST WOLVERINE—
Dickey, James

FOR THE LOVE OF THE LAMB
LION-LION—*Chester*

FOR THE NEW RAILWAY STATION IN
ROME—*Wilbur*

FOR THE POETS OF CHILE WHO
DIED WITH THEIR COUNTRY—
Levine

FOR THE SAKE OF SOME BEING—
Wellman

FOR THE SAKE OF SOMEBODY—
Burns

FOR THE SEASONS—*Zaturenska*

FOR THE SISTERS OF THE HÔTEL
DIEU—*Klein*

FOR THE WORD IS FLESH—*Kunitz*

FOR THESE—*Thomas, Edward*

FOR TLACAHUEPAN—
  *Anonymous–American
  Indian languages–Nahuatl*
FOR UNBORN MALCOLMS—
  Sanchez
FOR WILF AND HIS HOUSE—*Cohen*
FOR WITCHES—*Sutheim*
FOR YOU—*Sandburg*
FOR YOU, MOTHER—*Conkling*
FORAARSSANG—*Andersen*
FORBEARANCE—*Emerson*
FORBIDDEN WORDS—*Graves*
FÖRBJUDEN MUSIK—*Edfelt*
FORCED RETIREMENT—*Giovanni*
THE FOREBODING—*Graves*
THE FORECAST—*Jaffe, Dan*
FOREFATHERS—*Blunden*
FOREIGN CHILDREN—*Stevenson*
FOREIGN LANDS—*Stevenson*
FOREST—*Garrigue*
A FOREST HYMN—*Bryant,
  William Cullen*
FORGIVE, OH LORD—*Frost,
  Robert*
FORGIVEN—*Milne*
FÖRKLADD GUD—*Gullberg*
A FORM OF EPITAPH—*Whistler*
A FORM OF WOMEN—*Creeley*
FORMAL ELEGY—*Berryman*
THE FORMALITIES—*Ciardi*
FORMER BARN LOT—*Van Doren*
FORMER BEAUTIES—*Hardy*
FORMULA—*Sanchez*
A FORSAKEN GARDEN—
  Swinburne
THE FORSAKEN MERMAN—*Arnold*
FORSE L'ULTIMA VOLTA—*Cultrera*
FORSE MI LASCERÁ DEL TUO BEL
  VOLTO—*Gatto*
FORSTA STROVTÅGEN—*Siewertz*
DEN FÖRTRAMPADE—*Blomberg*
LA FORTUNE ET LE JEUNE ENFANT
  —*La Fontaine*
FORTUNE FOR MIRABEL—*Gregory,
  Horace*
FORTUNE, MY FOE—
  *Anonymous–English—
  Modern English*
FORTUNE OF THE SEA—*Masefield*
FORTY YEARS ON—*Auden*
LA FORZA DEL DESTINO—*Bovio*
EL FORZADO—*Góngora*
FOSSIL—*Engle*
FOSSIL—*Smith, Ken*
FOSSIL GATHERING—*Porter, Peter*
THE FOSSILS—*Nash*
FOUL SHOT—*Hoey*
FOUNDING FATHERS—*Warren*
A FOUNDLING—*Atwood*
FOUNTAIN—*Jennings*
FOUNTAIN: BRIDGES—
  Thomas-Ellis
FOUNTAINS OF AIX—*Swenson*
FOUR—*Cummings*
THE FOUR AGES OF MAN—*Yeats*
FOUR DAY CREEPER—*Aubert*
FOUR DAYS IN NOVEMBER—*Mir*

FOUR FOR SIR JOHN DAVIES—
  Roethke
THE FOUR FRIENDS—*Milne*
FOUR IN THE MORNING—*Sitwell,
  Edith*
FOUR LIMICKS—*Nash*
FOUR LITTLE FOXES—*Sarett*
FOUR POEMS FOR EASTER—
  Rodgers
FOUR PRELUDES ON PLAYTHINGS
  OF THE WIND—*Sandburg*
FOUR QUARTETS—*Eliot, Thomas
  Stearns*
FOUR SHORT POEMS ABOUT
  CHILDREN—*Spender*
FOURTEEN—*Emanuel*
THE FOURTH MONTH OF THE
  LANDSCAPE ARCHITECT—*Rich*
FOUS DE MISÈRE—*Prévert*
THE FOX—*Day Lewis*
THE FOX—*Patchen*
THE FOX AND THE GOOSE—
  *Children's Verses and
  Nursery Rhymes*
THE FOX AT ARLES—*Wevill*
THE FOX-COLORED PHEASANT—
  Levi
FOX-FIRE, 1956—*Warren*
FOX TROT—*Sitwell, Edith*
FOX TROT—*Sitwell, Osbert*
FRA LIPPO LIPPI—*Browning,
  Robert*
FRAGE—*Tucholsky*
DIE FRAGE BLEIBT—*Fontane*
DIE FRAGE, OB ES EINEN GOTT
  GIBT—*Brecht*
FRAGEN EINES LESENDEN
  ARBEITERS—*Brecht*
FRAGMENT, DEM MOND GEWIDMET
  —*Eich*
FRAGMENT OF AN AGON—*Eliot,
  Thomas Stearns*
FRAGMENT OF AN ODE TO MAIA—
  Coleridge, Samuel Taylor
FRAGMENT: THE PRIDE OF MAN—
  Johnson, Lenore
FRAGMENTO VII DE EL CRISTO DE
  VELÁZQUEZ—*Unamuno*
FRAGMENTS—*Emerson*
FRANCE—*Whitman*
FRANCINA—*Brathwaite*
FRANCISCO, I'LL BRING YOU RED
  CARNATIONS—*Levine*
FRANÇOIS VILLON FORGOTTEN—
  Sandburg
FRANK DRUMMER—*Masters,
  Edgar Lee*
FRANKLIN JONES—*Masters,
  Edgar Lee*
FRANKLYN HYDE WHO CAROUSED
  IN THE DIRT AND WAS
  CORRECTED BY HIS UNCLE—
  Belloc
FRATER AVE ATQUE VALE—
  Tennyson

FRAU BAUMAN, FRAU SCHMIDT,
  AND FRAU SCHWARTZE—
  Roethke
FRAVECATURE—*Viviani*
FREDDY—*Smith, Stevie*
FREDERICK DOUGLASS—*Hayden*
FREDERICK DOUGLASS: 1817–1895—
  Hughes, Langston
FREE WORLD NOTES—*Beecher*
FREEDOM—*Durrell*
FREEDOM RIDER: WASHOUT—
  Emanuel
FREEDOM TO KILL—*Yevtushenko*
LA FREGATE "LA SERIEUSE"—
  Vigny
FREMDE—*Anonymous–Asian
  languages*
THE FRENCH REVOLUTION—*Blake*
LES FRÈRES—*Vian*
FRESQUES—*Éluard*
FRIDAY NIGHT—*Graves*
FRIDAY'S CHILD—*Auden*
DER FRIEDEN—*Hölderlin*
DER FRIEDLICHE LÖWE—*Tiedge*
THE FRIEND—*Piercy*
THE FRIENDS—*Lee, Dennis*
FRIEND'S WEATHER—*Bogan*
FRIENDS WITH GOD—*Marshall,
  Helen Lowrie*
THE FRIGATE PELICAN—*Moore,
  Marianne*
FRIGHTENED MEN—*Graves*
FRIHETSORDET—*Bergman, Bo*
FRINGED GENTIANS—*Lowell,
  Amy*
FRISCHE FAHRT—*Eichendorff*
FRÔ WELT, IR SULT DEM WIRTE
  SAGEN—*Walther von der
  Vogelweide*
THE FROG—*Belloc*
THE FROG AND THE GOLDEN BALL
  —*Graves*
THE FROG AND THE MOUSE—
  *Children's Verses and
  Nursery Rhymes*
FROG AUTUMN—*Plath*
THE FROG WHO WOULD AWOOING
  GO—*Roche*
FROGS AT LAGO DI BOLSENA—
  Porter, Peter
FROM A BLACK PERSPECTIVE—*Lee,
  Don L.*
FROM A BUS WINDOW IN CENTRAL
  OHIO JUST BEFORE A THUNDER
  SHOWER—*Wright, James*
FROM A FEAR OF THE DARK—
  Walters
FROM A HAND OF SNAPS—
  MacNeice
FROM A RAILWAY CARRIAGE—
  Stevenson
FROM A VERY LITTLE SPHINX—
  Millay
FROM BOTH SIDES—*Mariah*
FROM CHIRICO TO CHARON—
  Scott, Winfield Townley

FROM FAR, FROM EVE AND MORNING—*Housman*
FROM FEATHERS TO IRON—*Day Lewis*
FROM GOD'S LOVE—*Marshall, Helen Lowrie*
FROM MY DIARY, JULY 1914—*Owen, Wilfred*
FROM MY HOMEROOM TO ME: THE LINE—*Johnston, Ellen Turlington*
FROM NOON TO STARRY NIGHT—*Whitman*
FROM THE BACKYARD OF THE DIASPORA—*Sklarew*
FROM THE COUNTY LUNATIC ASYLUM—*Smith, Stevie*
FROM THE DARK TOWER—*Cullen*
FROM THE FANTASIES OF A NOT-SO-YOUNG-ANYMORE SCHOOL TEACHER—*Johnston, Ellen Turlington*
FROM THE FIFTIES—*Sondé*
FROM THE GRANDE CORNICHE—*Dowling*
FROM THE MOTIONLESS TWIG—*Abbe*
FROM THE NORTH TERRACE—*Humphries*
FROM THE REFLECTIONS OF MR. GLASS—*Redgrove*
FROM THE WAVE—*Gunn*
FROM TU FU TO LI PO—*Kizer*
FRONTENAC—*Davie*
FRONTIER—*Miles*
FRONTIÈRES—*Cendrars*
FRONTIÈRES—*Prévert*
FRONTISPIECE—*Swenson*
FRONTLET—*Olson*
FROST AT MIDNIGHT—*Coleridge, Samuel Taylor*
THE FROST PANE—*McCord*
FRU SORG—*Ferlin*
DIE FRÜHEN GRÄBER—*Klopstock*
FRÜHER MITTAG—*Bachmann*
FRÜHER MORGEN—*Kunert*
DAS FRÜHJAHR—*Brecht*
FRÜHLING—*Fontane*
DIE FRÜHLINGSFEIER—*Klopstock*
FRÜHLINGSGLAUBE—*Uhland*
THE FRUIT OF THE TREE—*Wagoner*
LOS FRUTOS—*Neruda*
FT. WORTH—*Nash*
FUENTE COLONIAL—*Ballagas*
LAS FUENTES DE GRANADA—*Villaespesa*
LO FUGAZ—*Jaimes Freyre*
FULL FATHOM FIVE—*Plath*
THE FULL GOSPEL MISSION—*Souster*
FULL MOON—*Graves*
FULL MOON—*Hayden*
FULL MOON AND LITTLE FRIEDA—*Hughes, Ted*
LA FUNDACIÓN MITOLÓGICA DE BUENOS AIRES—*Borges*

THE FUNDAMENT IS SHIFTED—*Evans, Abbie Huston*
FUNERAL—*Wallace*
THE FUNERAL TRANSPORT BURNS AT SEA—*Gregor*
THE FUNERALL—*Donne*
FUNERE MERSIT ACERBO—*Carducci*
FUNNEL—*Sexton*
FUNNELS—*Greenwald*
THE FUNNY OLD MAN AND HIS WIFE—*Children's Verses and Nursery Rhymes*
FÜR UNGEÜBTE—*Roth, Eugen*
FURNACE IN MAY—*Emanuel*
FURRY BEAR—*Milne*
FURY OF AERIAL BOMBARDMENT—*Eberhart*
THE FURY OF COCKS—*Sexton*
THE FURY OF OVERSHOES—*Sexton*
FUTILITY—*Owen, Wilfred*
THE FUTURE—*Clark, John W.*
FUZZY-WUZZY—*Kipling*

G D B A—*Johnson, Tom*
GACELA DE LA HUIDA—*Garcia Lorca*
GACELA DEL MERCADO MATUTINO—*Garcia Lorca*
GACELA DEL NIÑO MUERTO—*Garcia Lorca*
GALACTIC LOVE POEM—*Henri*
GALAN—*Garcia Lorca*
LA GALERIA—*Rodari*
GALGENBERG—*Morgenstern*
GALGENBRUDERS LIED AN SOPHIE, DIE HENKERSMAID—*Morgenstern*
GALGENKINDES WIEGENLIED—*Morgenstern*
THE GALLOPING CAT—*Smith, Stevie*
THE GALLOWS—*Thomas, Edward*
GALOSHES—*Bacmeister*
GALWAY BAY—*Barker, George*
GAMBLING IN STATELINE NEVADA—*Wright, James*
THE GAME—*Abse*
GAME AFTER SUPPER—*Atwood*
A GAME OF GLASS—*Reid*
DE GAMLA—*Bergman, Bo*
GAMLET—*Pasternak*
GAMMAL INDIAN—*Lindegren*
GAMMALT PORSLIN—*Snoilsky*
THE GANDER—*Nash*
GANDERFEATHER'S GIFT—*Field, Eugene*
THE GANG—*Sobiloff*
GANG GIRLS—*Brooks, Gwendolyn*
GANGELLEED TOER AUSSTIED—*Olfers-Batocki*
GANYMED—*Goethe*
GANZ BESONDERS FEINE DAMEN—*Kästner*
DAS GANZE—*Benn*
GARBAGE DELIGHT—*Lee, Dennis*

GARBAGEMAN: THE MAN WITH THE ORDERLY MIND—*Brooks, Gwendolyn*
THE GARDEN—*Gibson, Margaret*
THE GARDEN—*Marvell*
THE GARDEN—*Warren*
THE GARDEN OF LOVE—*Blake*
THE GARDEN OF PROSERPINE—*Swinburne*
THE GARDEN PARTY—*Belloc*
THE GARDENER—*Stevenson*
THE GARDENER—*Wheelock*
A GARDENER SEES—*Marshall, Helen Lowrie*
GARDENERS AND ASTRONOMERS—*Sitwell, Edith*
THE GARDENS OF ZUÑI—*Merwin*
GARETH AND LYNNETTE—*Tennyson*
A GARMENT OF PRAISE FOR THE SPIRIT OF HEAVINESS—*Blackmur*
GARMONIKA, GARMONIKA—*Blok*
UN GAROFANO ROSSO—*Gori*
GARROTE VIL—*Valle Inclan*
GASOLINA SESTINA—*Mason*
THE GATE—*Day Lewis*
GATES OF PARADISE—*Blake*
GATHER MY WINGS—*Darr*
GATHER YE ROSEBUDS—*Anonymous-French*
GATHERING LEAVES—*Frost, Robert*
GATHERING STICKS ON SUNDAY—*Nicholson*
LA GATTA—*Pascoli*
I GATTICI—*Pascoli*
IL GATTO INVERNO—*Rodari*
GATUBILD—*Ferlin*
THE GAZABOS—*Honig*
LE GEAI PARÉ DES PLUMES DU PAON—*La Fontaine*
LA GÉANTE—*Baudelaire*
GEBET—*Lasker-Schüler*
GEBET—*Morgenstern*
GEBET—*Mörike*
GEBET DER EINSAMKEIT—*Saint-Exupéry*
GEBET FUR DIE UNHEILBAREN—*Hölderlin*
GEBET VOR DER MARTER CHRISTI—*Luther*
GEBURTSAKT DER PHILOSOPHIE—*Morgenstern*
DER GECK—*Busch*
GEDDONDILLO—*Nash*
GEDICHT—*Kaschnitz*
GEDICHT—*Kuhn*
GEDICHTE—*Benn*
GEDICHTE—*Kunert*
GEDICHTE ÜBER EINEN SPAZIERGANG AM STAUSEE UND ÜBER GEDICHTE—*Krüger*
DIE GEFANGENEN—*Schaeffer*
GEFSIMANSKII SAD—*Pasternak*
GEFUNDEN—*Goethe*

GEGEN DIE UNGEDULD—
  Bergengruen
GEGEN VERFUHRUNG—*Brecht*
GEH' UNTER, SCHÖNE SONNE—
  Hölderlin
GEHEIMES—*Goethe*
DER GEHEIMNISVOLLE NACHEN—
  Nietzsche
GEISTES GRUSS—*Goethe*
GELLERTS GRABSCHRIFT—
  Schubart
IL GELSOMINO NOTTURNO—
  Pascoli
GEMWOOD—*Bell*
GENAZZANO—*Kaschnitz*
THE GENERAL—*Sassoon*
THE GENERAL ELLIOT—*Graves*
A GENERAL EPITAPH—*Paulus
  Silentiarius*
GENERAL JOHN—*Gilbert, Sir
  William Schwenck*
GENERAL LEE—*Benét, Stephen
  Vincent*
GENERAL WILLIAM BOOTH ENTERS
  INTO HEAVEN—*Lindsay,
  Vachel*
THE GENEROUS DAYS—*Spender*
DER GENESENE AN DIE HOFFNUNG
  —*Mörike*
GENESIS—*Schwartz*
THE GENI IN THE JAR—*Giovanni*
LA GÉNISSE, LA CHÈVRE ET LA
  BREBIS EN SOCIÉTÉ AVEC LE
  LION—*La Fontaine*
GENIUS CHILD—*Hughes,
  Langston*
GENIUS LOCI—*Porter, Peter*
GENTILHOMMERIE—*Bovio*
A GENTLE HEART—*Sherwin*
GENTLEMEN-RANKERS—*Kipling*
GENTLENESS—*Yevtushenko*
GEOFFREY KEATING—*Stephens*
GEOGRAPHER—*Hacker*
GEOGRAPHY—*Conkling*
GEOGRAPHY OF THIS TIME—
  MacLeish
GEOMETRY OF MOODS—*Kunitz*
GEORDIE—*Anonymous-English-
  -Modern English*
GEORGE—*Porter, Bern*
GEORGE—*Randall*
GEORGE AND THE DRAGONFLY—
  McGough
GEORGE WASHINGTON'S MUD—
  Glaze
GEORGE, WHO PLAYED WITH A
  DANGEROUS TOY—*Belloc*
GEORGICS—*Virgil*
GERAINT AND ENID—*Tennyson*
GÉRARD DE NERVAL—*Ross, W.
  W. Eustace*
THE GERM—*Nash*
GERONTION—*Eliot, T. S.*
GERUSALEMME LIBERATA—*Tasso*
GESANG DER GEISTER ÜBER DEN
  WASSERN—*Goethe*

GESANG DES ABGESCHIEDENEN—
  Trakl
GESANG DES DEUTSCHEN—
  Hölderlin
GESANG VON DER FRAU—*Brecht*
GESANG VON EINER GELIEBTEN—
  Brecht
GESANG ZUR NACHT—*Trakl*
DIE GESCHICHTE VON FRAU MARA
  UND IHREM SOHN VUK—*Krüss*
GESPENST—*Morgenstern*
GESPRÄCH EINER HAUSSCHNECKE
  MIT SICH SELBST—*Morgenstern*
DIE GESTUNDETE ZEIT—
  Bachmann
THE GESTURE—*Eberhart*
GESÙ—*Pascoli*
GET THE GASWORKS—*Ignatow*
GET UP AND BAR THE DOOR—
  *Anonymous-English—
  Modern English*
GET UP BLUES—*Emanuel*
GET UP, I SAY—*Van Doren*
GETHSEMANE—*Dowling*
GETHSÉMANI—*Lamartine*
GETSÉMANE—*Ferlin*
GETTIN' DOWN TO GET OVER—
  Jordan, June
GETTING LOST IN NAZI GERMANY
  —*Bell*
GETTING WHAT WE WANT—*Lally*
GEWOHNT, GETAN—*Goethe*
GHAZAL 115—*Hafiz*
THE GHETTO TREE—*Rosenfeld*
GHOST—*Reid*
THE GHOST AT THE QUINCY CLUB
  —*Brooks, Gwendolyn*
GHOST OF A CHANCE—*Rich*
GHOST OF SILENCE—*Griffiths*
GHOSTS—*Redgrove*
THE GHOST'S LEAVETAKING—
  Plath
THE GHOSTS OF THE BUFFALOES—
  Lindsay, Vachel
GHOSTS' STORIES—*Reid*
THE GHOSTSELF OF THE DEAD
  LECTURER—*Miller, E.
  Ethelbert*
THE GIANTS—*Abbe*
GIB HER DIE LARV'—*Heine*
THE GIBBER—*Roethke*
GIFT—*Conkling*
GIFT—*Darr*
GIFT—*Sherwin*
A GIFT OF LOVE—*McKnight*
THE GIFT OF WONDER—*Marshall,
  Helen Lowrie*
THE GIFT OUTRIGHT—*Frost,
  Robert*
GINA—*Goldstein*
LA GINESTRA—*Leopardi*
DER GINGGANZ—*Morgenstern*
IL GIOCO DEI "SE"—*Rodari*
GIORNO—*Parini*
IL GIORNO DEI POETI—*Zogarrio*
GIORNO PER GIORNO—*Ungaretti*
UN GIOVANE SICILIANO—*Barbera*

GIOVANNINO PERDIGIORNO—
  Rodari
THE GIRAFFES—*Fuller, Roy*
GIRL AND HORSE, 1928—*Atwood*
THE GIRL CHILD'S SONG—*Gordon*
GIRL HELD WITHOUT BAIL—
  Walker
GIRL HELP—*Lewis, Janet*
THE GIRL IN THE MIRROR—*Jong*
GIRL IN THE SUN—*Chapin*
GIRL MACHINE—*Elmslie*
GIRL WITH ORANGE SUNSHADE—
  Smith, Iain Chrichton
GIRLS—*Smith, Stevie*
GIRLS KNOW HOW TO LOSE—
  Gaver
GIRL'S SONG—*Norris*
A GIRL'S SONG—*Yeats*
GIRO DE LE PIZZICARIE—*Belli*
GIROVAGO—*Ungaretti*
GITANA Y MARE—*Cavestany*
LA GITANILLA—*Cervantes
  Saavedra*
IL GIURAMENTO DI PONTIDA—
  Berchet
GIUSEPPINA CANTADORI—
  Bevilacqua
LA GIUSTIZIA AR POPOLO—*Belli*
GIVE A ROUSE—*Browning,
  Robert*
GIVE ALL TO LOVE—*Emerson*
GIVE THE DANCERS CASTANETS—
  Gaver
GIVE WAY, YE GATES—*Roethke*
GIVING A SON TO THE SEA—
  Dickey, James
GLABL AP—*Johnson, Tom*
GLADYS—*Harteis*
LE GLAND ET LA CITROUILLE—*La
  Fontaine*
A GLASS OF BEER—*Stephens*
DER GLAUBE—*Morgenstern*
GLEICHNIS—*Morgenstern*
GLEICHNIS DES BUDDHA VOM
  BRENNENDEN HAUS—*Brecht*
DAS GLEICHNIS DES MENENIUS
  AGRIPPA—*Brecht*
GLOIRE AU MAQUIS—*Aragon*
GLOIRE, CAMBRIOLAGE OU
  RÉVOLUTION—*Jacob, Max*
LA GLOIRE DES ROIS—*Perse*
GLORY FOREVER—*Marshall,
  Helen Lowrie*
GLORY OF WOMEN—*Sassoon*
THE GLORY TRUMPETER—*Walcott*
GLOSA A LO DIVINO—*Juan de la
  Cruz*
DAS GLÜCK—*Schiller*
GLÜCKSPILZ—*Busch*
GNASTILLO—*Viviani*
GNAT-PSALM—*Hughes, Ted*
GNO FIGIO XE 'NDAO IN GUERA—
  Marin
LA GNO ZENTE—*Marin*
GO DOWN DEATH—*Johnson,
  James Weldon*
THE GOAT PATHS—*Stephens*

THE GOBLIN—*Fyleman*
GOD-FORGOTTEN—*Hardy*
GOD GIVE US MEN—*Holland, Josiah Gilbert*
THE GOD IN US WISHES TO LIVE—*Gilbert, Celia*
THE GOD OF GALAXIES—*Van Doren*
GOD REST YE MERRY GENTLEMEN—*Walcott*
GOD SAVE THE FLAG—*Holmes, Oliver Wendell*
GOD SPEAKS—*Smith, Stevie*
THE GODDESS—*Gunn*
GODOLPHIN HORNE, WHO WAS CURSED WITH THE SIN OF PRIDE—*Belloc*
GODS—*Sexton*
GOD'S DETERMINATION. PREFACE—*Taylor, Edward*
GOD'S EDUCATION—*Hardy*
GOD'S GRANDEUR—*Hopkins*
GODS IN VIETNAM—*Redmond*
GOD'S OWN—*Clark, John W.*
GOD'S WORLD—*Millay*
GODY MOLODYE—*Yessenin*
GOG—*Hughes, Ted*
GOGGLEHEAD—*Marshall, Lenore G.*
THE GOING—*Hardy*
GOING HOME FROM THE PARTY—*Lewis, Janet*
GOING HOME TO MEET MYSELF—*Baybars*
GOING INTO DREAM—*Farjeon*
GOING TO THE FUNERAL—*Francis*
GOING TOO FAR—*Howells*
GOING TOWARDS SPAIN—*Googe*
GOIYA—*Voznezensky*
GOKKVALL—*Nerman*
GOLCH AND FLUBIS—*Morgenstern*
GOLD—*Blanding*
GOLD—*Francis*
GOLD—*Hall*
GOLD AND LOVE FOR DEARIE—*Field, Eugene*
GOLD AND MALACHITE—*Graves*
THE GOLD OF GOLD—*Gregor*
GOLD-TOOTH BLUES—*Williams, Tennessee*
THE GOLDEN CHAINS—*Barker, George*
THE GOLDEN MILESTONE—*Longfellow*
THE GOLDEN VANITY—*Anonymous–English–Modern English*
GOLONDRINAS—*Jiménez*
DEN GÖMDA DALEN—*Blomberg*
GONE—*Sandburg*
GONE AWAY—*Levertov*
GONE FOREVER—*Mills*
THE GONE TOMORROW—*MacNeice*
GOOD AND BAD CHILDREN—*Stevenson*

A GOOD BOY—*Stevenson*
GOOD-BY AND KEEP COLD—*Frost, Robert*
GOOD-BYE—*Betjeman*
GOOD-BYE MY FANCY—*Whitman*
GOOD-BYE, OLD YEAR, YOU OAF—*Nash*
THE GOOD DAUGHTER—*Viorst*
GOOD FRIDAY—*Masefield*
GOOD FRIDAY 1613—*Donne*
THE GOOD LIFE—*Cavalieri*
THE GOOD LITTLE GIRL—*Milne*
GOOD MORNING—*Ross, Muriel Sipe*
THE GOOD-MORROW—*Donne*
GOOD NIGHT—*Van Doren*
GOOD NIGHT—*Quarles*
GOOD NIGHT TO THE SEASON—*Praed*
A GOOD PLAY—*Stevenson*
GOOD SAMARITAN—*Beecher*
GOOD SHIPS—*Ransom*
GOOD THINGS COME—*Robinson, Wanda*
GOODBY DAVID TAMUNDOEMI WEST—*Danner*
GOODBYE, WHAT WERE YOU—*Jones, Glyn*
GOODY FOR OUR SIDE AND YOUR SIDE TOO—*Nash*
THE GOOSE FISH—*Nemerov*
LES GORGES FROIDES—*Desnos*
THE GORING—*Plath*
GOT TO GET YOU OFF MY MIND—*Holland, Bill*
LA GOTA DEL ROCÍO—*Mendive*
THE GOTHIC TALE—*Weiss*
DER GOTT DER JUGEND—*Hölderlin*
GOTT ÜBERALL—*Rückert*
DER GOTT UND DIE BAJADERE—*Goethe*
DIE GÖTTER—*Hölderlin*
DAS GÖTTLICHE—*Goethe*
THE GOURMET—*Viorst*
GOVERNMENT INJUNCTION RESTRAINING HARLEM COSMETIC CO—*Miles*
GOYA IN AMERICA—*Ferlinghetti*
DAS GRAB IM BUSENTO—*Platen-Hallermünde*
DER GRABEN—*Tucholsky*
GRACE FOR A CHILD—*Herrick*
THE GRACE OF GOD AND THE METH-DRINKER—*Smith, Sydney Goodsir*
LA GRACIA DE LAS COSAS—*Martinez Alonso*
GRAD V KHARKOVE—*Yevtushenko*
GRADUATION—*Hughes, Langston*
GRÁFICO—*Garcia Lorca*
GRAMMAR FROM OUT WEST—*Darragh*
A GRAMMARIAN'S FUNERAL—*Browning, Robert*
LE GRAND COMBAT—*Michaux*

GRAND ÉCART—*Wedekind*
LE GRAND SOMMEIL—*Obaldia*
LE GRAND TESTAMENT—*Villon*
THE GRAND VIEW—*Abse*
LA GRANDE COMPLAINTE DE MON OBSCURITÉ TROIS—*Tzara*
LA GRANDEZA MEXICANA—*Balbuena*
GRANDFATHER'S CLOCK—*Work*
GRANDMA'S GUMPTION—*Marshall, Helen Lowrie*
GRANDMOTHER IN HEAVEN—*Levine*
GRANDMOTHER'S STORY OF BUNKER-HILL BATTLE—*Holmes, Oliver Wendell*
GRANDPA IS ASHAMED—*Nash*
GRANDPARENTS—*Lowell, Robert*
THE GRANGE—*Smith, Stevie*
GRANITE AND CYPRESS—*Jeffers, Robinson*
GRANITE AND STEEL—*Moore, Marianne*
GRANNY—*Howard, Lee*
GRAPES MAKING—*Adams*
GRASS—*Sandburg*
GRASS—*Smith, Ken*
LA GRASSE MATINÉE—*Prévert*
GRASSES—*Gunn*
A GRASSHOPPER—*Wilbur*
THE GRASSHOPPER AND THE BIRD—*Reeves*
THE GRASSHOPPER WORLD—*Hodges*
THE GRASSHOPPERS—*Aldis*
THE GRATEFUL HUMMINGBIRD—*Roche*
GRATIANA DAUNCING AND SINGING—*Lovelace, Richard*
GRATITUDE FOR A NIGHTMARE—*Graves*
A GRAVE—*Blair*
A GRAVE—*Moore, Marianne*
GRAVE BY A HOLM-OAK—*Smith, Stevie*
THE GRAVE OF ALL MANKIND—*MacDiarmid*
GRAVELY HILL—*Olson*
GRAZHDANIN—*Ryleyev*
THE GREAT AMERICAN PASSTIME—*Robinson, Wanda*
THE GREAT BEAR—*Hollander*
THE GREAT BIRDS—*Patchen*
THE GREAT BLUE HERON—*Kizer*
GREAT BOOKS OF THE 1950'S—*Dlugos*
GREAT CENTRAL RAILWAY—*Betjeman*
THE GREAT EASTERN—*Masefield*
GREAT FRIEND—*Thoreau*
THE GREAT LOVER—*Brooke*
GREAT MEN IN THE MORNING—*Logue*
THE GREAT NEMO—*Sitwell, Osbert*
GREAT NIGHTS RETURNING—*Watkins*

GREAT PRAISES—*Eberhart*
THE GREAT ROSE—*Chapin*
GREAT THINGS—*Hardy*
THE GREAT WAR—*Scannell*
GREATER LOVE—*Owen, Wilfred*
GREATER THE SOUL—*Marshall, Helen Lowrie*
GRECIA—*Aridjis*
GREEN—*Verlaine*
THE GREEN CASTLE—*Graves*
GREEN GROW THE RASHES—*Burns*
GREEN MOTH—*Welles*
THE GREEN SHEPHERD—*Simpson*
GREEN WAYS—*Kunitz*
GREEN WEEDS—*Stephens*
THE GREEN WOLF—*Hughes, Ted*
THE GREEN WOMAN—*Goldstein*
GREENAWAY—*Betjeman*
GREENFIELD HILL—*Dwight*
GREENSLEEVES—*Anonymous–English—Modern English*
THE GRENADIER—*Children's Verses and Nursery Rhymes*
LA GRENOUILLE BLEUE—*Fort*
LA GRENOUILLE ET LE RAT—*La Fontaine*
LA GRENOUILLE QUI VEUT SE FAIRE AUSSI GROSSE QUE LE BOEUF—*La Fontaine*
LES GRENOUILLES QUI DEMANDENT UN ROI—*La Fontaine*
GRENZEN DER MENSCHHEIT—*Goethe*
LA GRETCHEN DE NOS JOURS—*Smith, Stevie*
GRETCHENS LIED—*Goethe*
GREVINNANS BESÖK—*Lenngren*
GRIEF—*Browning, Elizabeth Barrett*
GRIGGSBY'S STATION—*Riley*
GRITANDO NO MORIR—*Otero*
EL GRITO—*Garcia Lorca*
GRITO HACIA ROMA—*Garcia Lorca*
GRIZZLY BEAR—*Austin, Mary*
GRODEK—*Trakl*
THE GROSS SITUATION—*Edson*
DIE GRÖSSE DER WELT—*Schiller*
DIE GROSSE FRACHT—*Bachmann*
DAS GROSSE LALULA—*Morgenstern*
GROTESQUES—*Graves*
GROTTE DI ULISSE—*Corsaro*
THE GROUNDHOG—*Eberhart*
GROWING, FLYING, HAPPENING—*Reid*
GROWING OLD—*Arnold*
GROWING UP—*Railes*
GROWLTIGER'S LAST STAND—*Eliot, Thomas Stearns*
GROWN TO YOU AT LAST—*Stephany*
THE GRUMBLING OLD MAN—*Roche*
GRÜNDER—*Busch*
GRÜNDLICHE HEILUNG—*Busch*

GUAGLIONE—*Viviani*
GUANTÁNAMERA—*Martí*
GUARD OF HONOR—*Hazel*
GUARDIA IN MARE—*Ronsisvalle*
GUATEMALA—*Vargas*
GUERRA E PACE—*Viviani*
LA GUERRE—*Breton, André*
LA GUERRE—*Cummings*
LA GUERRE—*Jacob, Max*
THE GUEST—*Anonymous–English—Modern English*
THE GUEST—*Whistler*
GUINEVERE—*Tennyson*
THE GUITAR MAKER'S SONG—*Gordon*
GUITARRA—*Borges*
GUITARRA—*Garcia Lorca*
GUITARRA—*Guillén, Nicolás*
GUITARRA DECAPITADA—*Domínguez Alba*
THE GULF—*Walcott*
GULF OF MAINE—*Olson*
GULL'S CRY—*Kunitz*
GULL'S CRY—*Warren*
GUNG TSZ—*Bai Jyu Yi*
GUNGA DIN—*Kipling*
GUNNER—*Jarrell*
THE GUPPY—*Nash*
THE GURU—*Ginsberg*
GUS—*Giovanni*
GUS, THE THEATRE CAT—*Eliot, Thomas Stearns*
DIE GUTE NACHT—*Brecht*
GUTER RAT—*Heine*
GUTER RAT—*Hölderlin*
GUTTERS—*Vogeler*
GWEI YWAN—*Anonymous–Asian languages*
GWENDOLYN BROOKS—*Lee, Don*
GYPSIES—*Joselow*
THE GYPSY—*Pound*
GYPSY GIRL—*Hodgson*
GYRE'S GALAX—*Pritchard*

H.M.S. PINAFORE—*Gilbert, Sir William Schwenck*
THE HA-HA-HA—*Cullen*
THE HABIT OF PERFECTION—*Hopkins*
HABITS—*Giovanni*
HABITS OF THE HIPPOPOTAMUS—*Guiterman*
EL HACEDOR—*Garcia Nieto*
HACIA LA SOLEDAD—*Carranza*
HAD EACH A VOICE—*Peake*
HADO ESPANOL DE LA BELLEZA—*Jiménez*
HAIKU—*Anonymous–Asian languages*
HAIKU—*Knight, Etheridge*
HAIKU—*Lester*
HAIKU—*Sanchez*
HAIL COLUMBIA—*Hopkinson, Joseph*
HAILSTONES AND HALIBUT BONES—*O'Neill, Mary L.*

HALCYON DAYS—*Whitman*
HALF-BENT MAN—*Eberhart*
HALF ROUNDEL—*Merwin*
THE HALF-SCISSOR—*Redgrove*
HALF SIGH—*Anonymous–African languages–Malagasy*
HALF TWIST—*Francis*
HALF WAY DRESSED—*Lee, Dennis*
HÄLFTE DES LEBENS—*Hölderlin*
HALLELUJAH CORNER—*Brown, William*
HALLOWEEN—*Behn, Harry*
HALLOWEEN—*Kramer*
THE HALLS OF BEDLAM—*Graves*
HAMATREYA—*Emerson*
EL HAMBRE—*Guillén, Nicolás*
HAMEWITH—*Smith, Sydney Goodsir*
HAMILTON GREENE—*Masters, Edgar Lee*
HAMLET—*Shakespeare*
HAMLETS HIMMELSFÄRD—*Lindegren*
HA'NACKER MILL—*Belloc*
THE HAND AND THE BOWL—*Posner*
THE HAND AT CALLOW HILL FARM—*Tomlinson*
THE HAND-CAR—*Abbe*
THE HAND THAT SIGNED THE PAPER—*Thomas, Dylan*
HANDLE WITH CARE—*Johnston, Ellen Turlington*
HANDS—*Untermeyer*
HANDSCHRIFT—*Anonymous–German*
DER HANDSCHUH—*Schiller*
DER HANDSTAND AUF DER LORELEI—*Kästner*
HANGAR NINE—*Darr*
HANRYCKNING—*Gullberg*
HANS CHRISTIAN ANDERSEN IN CENTRAL PARK—*Sobiloff*
HANS SECHZEHNENDER—*Guggenmos*
HAP—*Hardy*
HAPPENING AT SORDID CREEK—*Porter, Peter*
HAPPINESS MAKES UP IN HEIGHT FOR WHAT IT LACKS IN LENGTH—*Frost, Robert*
HAPPINESS TO HOSPITALITY—*Herrick*
HAPPY BIRTHDAY—*Souster*
HAPPY 4TH OF JULY, Y'ALL—*Dupree*
HAPPY JACK COMES HOME—*Sherwin*
HAPPY THOUGHT—*Stevenson*
THE HAPPY THREE—*Roethke*
THE HAPPY TOWNLAND—*Yeats*
HARBACH 1944—*Pilinszky*
THE HARBOR DAWN—*Crane, Hart*
THE HARBOUR BRIDGE—*Hardy*
A HARD FROST—*Day Lewis*
THE HARD QUESTION—*Auden*

HARD ROCK RETURNS TO PRISON FROM THE HOSPITAL FOR THE CRIMINAL INSANE—*Knight, Etheridge*

THE HARD STRUCTURE OF THE WORLD—*Eberhart*

HARDENING INTO PRINT—*Eberhart*

HARDLY—*Brown, Otis*

THE HARDSHIP OF ACCOUNTING—*Frost, Robert*

HARE DRUMMER—*Masters, Edgar Lee*

HARFENKLANG UND SAITENSPIEL—*Anonymous–German*

HARK BACK—*Eberhart*

HARLEM—*Hughes, Langston*

HARLEM BLUES—*Nunes*

HARMON WHITNEY—*Masters, Edgar Lee*

HARMONICA HUMDRUMS—*Sandburg*

HARMONIE DU SOIR—*Baudelaire*

HAROLD ARNETT—*Masters, Edgar Lee*

HARRIET TUBMAN—*Walker*

HARROW-ON-THE-HILL—*Betjeman*

HARRY WILMANS—*Masters, Edgar Lee*

HARVARD '61: BATTLE FATIGUE—*Warren*

HARVARD YARD IN APRIL—*Richards, I. A.*

HARVEST—*Sitwell, Edith*

HARVEST AND CONSECRATION—*Jennings*

HARVEST AT MYNACHLOG—*Clark, Gillian*

HARVEST HOME—*Sherwin*

HARVEST HYMN—*Betjeman*

DIE HARZREISE—*Heine*

HARZREISE IM WINTER—*Goethe*

HASTIO—*Toledo*

HATE BLOWS A BUBBLE OF DESPAIR INTO—*Cummings*

HATRED OF MEN WITH BLACK HAIR—*Bly*

DER HAUCH DER AHNEN—*Escudero1*

THE HAUGHTY SNAIL-KING—*Lindsay, Vachel*

THE HAUNTED HOUSE—*Graves*

THE HAUNTED PALACE—*Poe*

THE HAUNTER—*Hardy*

DAS HAUS—*Roth, Eugen*

HAVANA DREAMS—*Hughes, Langston*

HAVE I, TODAY—*Marshall, Helen Lowrie*

HAVE YOU WATCHED THE FAIRIES—*Fyleman*

HAVING A COKE WITH YOU—*O'Hara*

THE HAWK—*Spender*

HAWK ROOSTING—*Hughes, Ted*

HAY FOR THE HORSES—*Snyder*

THE HAYLOFT—*Stevenson*

HAYS WHARF—*Church*

HAZE—*Buson*

HE ABJURES LOVE—*Hardy*

HE BURNED HIS SOUL'S COAT—*Wood*

HE DIGESTETH HARDE YRON—*Moore, Marianne*

HE HAD A QUALITY OF GROWTH—*Rukeyser*

HE KEPT ON BURNING—*Ai*

HE LOVES ME—*Van Doren*

HE REPROVES THE CURLEW—*Yeats*

HE REVISITS HIS FIRST SCHOOL—*Hardy*

HE SAID HE WAS LEAVING FOR PHOENIX—*Colbert*

HE THINKS OF HIS PAST GREATNESS WHEN A PART OF THE CONSTELLATIONS OF HEAVEN—*Yeats*

HE WENT OUT QUIETLY—*Malanga*

HE WISHES FOR THE CLOTHS OF HEAVEN—*Yeats*

HEAD INJURY—*McGough*

HEADS—*Flanders*

THE HEALING OF THE LEPER—*Watkins*

A HEALTH TO THE EARTH—*Francis*

HEAR ME—*Levine*

HEART AND MIND—*Sitwell, Edith*

THE HEART AND THE SUN—*Reaney*

HEART BEATS—*Davie*

THE HEART CONSCRIPTED—*Read, Herbert*

THE HEART KNOWETH ITS OWN BITTERNESS—*Rossetti, Christina*

THE HEART KNOWS—*Marshall, Helen Lowrie*

HEART OF THE WOODS—*Curtwright*

THE HEART OF THOMAS HARDY—*Betjeman*

HEAT OF SNOW—*Hollander*

HEAT WAVE—A DISCONTINUOUS POEM—*Planz*

HEAVEN—*Brooke*

HEAVEN—*Hughes, Langston*

HEAVEN—*Levine*

A HEAVEN BELOW—*Marshall, Helen Lowrie*

HEAVEN-HAVEN: A NUN TAKES THE VEIL—*Hopkins*

HEAVEN IS A CONDITION OF LIFE—*Marvin X*

THE HEAVEN OF ANIMALS—*Dickey, James*

HEAVEN ON EARTH—*Marshall, Helen Lowrie*

HEAVENLY GRASS—*Williams, Tennessee*

HEAVY, HEAVY, HEAVY—*Brinnin*

HEDGEHOG—*Thwaite*

HEEJAUST—*Olfers-Batocki*

HEIDELBERG—*Hölderlin*

HEIDENRÖSLEIN—*Goethe*

THE HEIGHT OF THE RIDICULOUS—*Holmes, Oliver Wendell*

DIE HEIMAT—*Hölderlin*

HEIMAT BERLIN—*Mehring*

HEIMKEHR—*Huch*

HEIMLICHER BRIEF—*Anonymous–Asian languages*

THE HEIR—*Redgrove*

HELEN—*Thomas, Edward*

HELEN IN EGYPT—*Doolittle*

HELENE—*Seferis*

DEN HELIGA NATTEN—*Gullberg*

DEN HELIGA NATTEN—*Lagerlöf*

HELL, MARY—*Eckels*

HELLAS: FINAL CHORUS—*Shelley*

HELLO, HELLO HENRY—*Kumin*

HELLO IS WHAT A MIRROR SAYS—*Cummings*

HEMLOCK—*Williams, Hugo*

THE HEN FLOWER—*Kinnell*

HENDECASYLLABICS—*Swinburne*

HENLEY-ON-THAMES—*Betjeman*

HENNY-PENNY—*Children's Verses and Nursery Rhymes*

HENRIETTE AT THE GUITAR—*Posner*

HENRIQUE—*Vargas*

HENRY AND MARY—*Graves*

HENRY KING, WHO CHEWED BITS OF STRING—*Belloc*

HENRY MANLEY LIVING ALONE KEEPS TIME—*Kumin*

HENRY PURCELL—*Hopkins*

HENRY VI—*Shakespeare*

THE HENS—*Roberts*

HEPTONSTALL—*Hughes, Ted*

HER ANXIETY—*Yeats*

HER BLACK PLASTIC NAMETAG SAID "HELENE"—*Tullos*

HER EYES EXCHANGE—*Clark, John W.*

HER HUSBAND—*Hughes, Ted*

HER KIND—*Sexton*

HER STERN LIKE A BOX—*Olson*

HER VOICE COULD NOT BE SOFTER—*Clarke*

HER-ZIE—*Smith, Stevie*

HERALD—*Miles*

LOS HERALDOS NEGROS—*Vallejo*

HERBST—*Rilke*

HERBST—*Storm*

HERBST IM BREISGAU—*Kaschnitz*

HERBSTGEFÜHL—*Goethe*

HERD RUNNERS—*Dupree*

HERE—*Thomas, Ronald Stuart*

HERE COMES—*Jong*

HERE I COME—*Arden*

HERE I SIT—*De la Mare*

HERE IN KATMANDU—*Justice*

HERE IN THE SELF—*Masefield*

HERE LIES A LADY—*Ransom*

HERE NOW—*Wallace*

HERE WE IS, Y'ALL—*Knight, Etheridge*

HEREDITY—*Hardy*

HERE'S TO YOU AND YOURS—
*Children's Verses and
Nursery Rhymes*
EL HERIDO—*Hernández, Miguel*
LOS HERIDOS—*Berger-Kiss*
HERITAGE—*Cullen*
HERMANA MARICA—*Góngora*
HERMANNS ENKEL—*Eichendorff*
THE HERMIT AT OUTERMOST HOUSE
—*Plath*
THE HERMIT OF CAPE ROSIER—
Hoffman
HERO—*Gridley*
HERO—*Johnston, Ellen
Turlington*
HERO—*Lee, Don L.*
HERO AND LEANDER—*Marlowe*
HÉRODIADE—*Mallarmé*
THE HEROES—*Simpson*
HEROIC POEM IN PRAISE OF WINE
—*Belloc*
LE HÉRON—*La Fontaine*
THE HERON—*Roethke*
THE HERON—*Watkins*
HERONS—*Merwin*
DER HERR DER INSEL—*George*
HERRENCHIEMSEE—*Eich*
THE HERRING-GULL—*Wheelock*
HERRN K'S LIEBLINGSTIER—*Brecht*
HE'S COMING—*Van Doren*
L'HEURE DU POÈTE—*Carco*
LES HEURES LENTES—*Giguere*
HEUREUX CEUX QUI SONT MORTS—
Péguy
HEUTE FRÜH IM GARTEN—
Fontane
HEY NOW—*Last Poets*
HEY SAILOR!—*Griffiths*
HIAWATHA—*Longfellow*
LES HIBOUX—*Baudelaire*
THE HIDDEN GARDEN—*Graves*
HIDE AND SEEK—*De la Mare*
HIER IL Y A TRÈS LONGTEMPS—
Éluard
HIGGLEDY PIGGLEDY—*Lee,
Dennis*
HIGH FLIGHT—*Magee*
HIGH FREQUENCY—*Piercy*
HIGH PERFECT WISDOM—
Anonymous–Asian languages
THE HIGH SCHOOL BAND—
Whittemore
THE HIGH TIDE AT GETTYSBURG—
Thompson, W. H.
HIGHLAND MARY—*Burns*
THE HIGHWAYMAN—*Noyes*
LA HIGUERA—*Ibarbourou*
HIJO MÍO—*Panero*
HILDEBRAND, WHO WAS
FRIGHTENED BY A PASSING
MOTOR—*Belloc*
DAS HILDEBRANDSLIED—
Anonymous–German
DAS HILFSBUCH—*Roth, Eugen*
THE HILL—*Brooke*
THE HILL—*Hecht*

THE HILL—*Masters, Edgar Lee*
HILLS—*Conkling*
HILLS—*Field, Rachel*
HILLS—*Hodges*
HILLS ARE FOR CLIMBING—
Marshall, Helen Lowrie
THE HILLS OF MAY—*Graves*
HIMBEERRANKEN—*Eich*
HIMLADROTTNINGENS BILD I HEDA
—*Heidenstam*
HIMMEL UND ERDE—
Anonymous–Asian languages
HIMMEL UND ERDE—*Morgenstern*
HIMMELFAHRT—*McFarlane*
HIMNE IBERIC—*Maragall*
THE HIND—*Wyatt, Sir Thomas*
THE HIND AND THE PANTHER—
Dryden
HIP MEN—*Moore, Amus*
A HIP TALE IN THE DEATH-STYLE—
Amini
THE HIPPOPOTAMUS—*Eliot,
Thomas Stearns*
THE HIPPOPOTAMUS—*Nash*
L'HIRONDELLE ET LES PETITS
OISEAUX—*La Fontaine*
HIROSHIMA—*Kaschnitz*
DAS HIRTENFEUER—
Droste-Hülshoff
HIS ANGERS—*Sukenick*
HIS EPITAPH—*Meleager*
HIS EPITAPH—*Raleigh*
HIS EXCELLENCY GENERAL
WASHINGTON—*Wheatley*
HIS GIFTS—*Marshall, Helen
Lowrie*
HIS LEGS RAN ABOUT—*Hughes,
Ted*
HIS LITANY TO THE HOLY SPIRIT—
Herrick
HIS OWN EPITAPH—*Gay, John*
HIS PICTURE—*Donne*
HIS RUNNING MY RUNNING—
Francis
HIS WINDING-SHEET—*Herrick*
HISTORICAL ASSOCIATIONS—
Stevenson
HISTORY—*Francis*
HISTORY—*Miller, May*
THE HISTORY OF THE FLOOD—
Heath-Stubbs
HISTORY OF THE POET AS A WHORE
—*Lee, Don L.*
A HISTORY POEM—*Baraka*
L'HIVER QUI VIENT—*Laforgue*
HJÄRTAT—*Bergman, Bo*
HJERTETS MELODIER—*Andersen*
THE HOARD—*Tolkien*
HOCHZEITLIED—*Goethe*
HOD PUTT—*Masters, Edgar Lee*
HOFFNUNG—*Schiller*
HOGWASH—*Francis*
DAS HOHELIED—*Heine*
HÖHERE TÖCHTER IM GESPRÄCH—
Kästner

HOLD FAST A DREAM—*Marshall,
Helen Lowrie*
THE HOLD-UP—*Wagoner*
HÖLDERLIN'S OLD AGE—*Spender*
HOLDING HANDS—*Link*
HOLDING ON—*Levine*
HOLDING THE SKY—*Stafford*
THE HOLE IN THE SEA—*Bell*
HOLIDAY—*Mitchell, Julian*
THE HOLLOW MEN—*Eliot,
Thomas Stearns*
HOLLOWED STONE—*Grigson*
HOLLYWOOD—*Brecht*
HOLY DAYS—*Neal*
HOLY SONNETS—*Donne*
HOLY THURSDAY—*Blake*
THE HOLY WAR—*Kipling*
HOLY WILLIE'S PRAYER—*Burns*
HOMAGE . . . OLDER WOMAN—
Baldwin, Deirdra
HOMAGE TO A SUBVERSIVE—
Beecher
HOMAGE TO CLIO—*Auden*
HOMAGE TO JOHN SKELTON—
Deutsch
HOMAGE TO PAUL KLEE—*Deutsch*
HOMAGE TO ROBERT CREELEY—
Whalen
HOMAGE TO RODIN—*Whalen*
HOMAGE TO SEXTUS PROPERTIUS—
Pound
HOMAGE TO THE EMPRESS OF THE
BLUES—*Hayden*
HOMAGE TO THE RUNNER—*Bell*
HOMBRE—*Williams, William
Carlos*
HOMBRE PEQUEÑITO—*Storni*
HOMBRE Y DIÓS—*Alonso*
HOMBRECITO—*Mistral*
HOME—*Guest, Edgar*
HOME: A REDEFINITION—
Beaubien
HOME AFTER THREE MONTHS AWAY
—*Lowell, Robert*
HOME AGAIN—*Marshall, Helen
Lowrie*
HOME FROM ABROAD—*Lee,
Laurie*
HOME IS WHERE THE SOUL IS—
Eckels
HOME PORT—*Hillyer*
HOME, SWEET HOME—*Payne*
HOME THOUGHTS—*McKay*
HOME-THOUGHTS, FROM ABROAD—
Browning, Robert
HOMECOMING—*Jeffers, Lance*
HOMECOMING—*Lowell, Robert*
HOMECOMING—*Sanchez*
HOMECOMING—*Stafford*
HOMECOMING—*Viereck*
HOMECOMING—*Weiss*
HOMECOMING—*Yessenin*
HOMELESS—*Zu-Bolton*
HOMELY MEATS—*Davies, John, of
Hereford*
THE HOMELY WAR—*Piercy*

HOMER, SIDNEY, PHILO— *Van Doren*

HOMESICK BLUES— *Hughes, Langston*

HOMILY IN THE ENGLISH READING ROOMS— *Porter, Peter*

HOMMAGE À GUILLAUME APOLLINAIRE— *Cendrars*

HOMMAGE À MANOLETE— *Cocteau*

HOMMAGE À PICASSO— *Cocteau*

HOMMAGE AU LIT— *Prévert*

L'HOMME AU KÉPI DE GARDE-CHASSE— *Cadou*

UN HOMME PAISIBLE— *Michaux*

THE HON. SEC— *Betjeman*

HON SOM SKÅR BRODET— *Österling*

HONDA AMISTAD— *Pardo Garcia*

HONEY HONEY— *Rasof*

HONEY-SELLER— *Colum*

THE HONEY WAGON MAN— *Beecher*

HONEYMOON— *Coward*

THE HONEYMOON IS OVER— *Viorst*

HONEYSUCKLE SMELL— *Reeves*

HONI SOIT QUI MAL Y PENSE— *Bell*

HONKY TONK— *Winch*

L'HONNEUR DES POETES— *Éluard*

THE HOODINKUS-WITH-THE-DOUBLE-HEAD— *Cullen*

HOOK— *Weiss*

HOOK— *Wright, James*

HOP, SKIP, AND JUMP— *Snyder*

HOPE— *Herbert*

HOPPETS FACKLA— *Lagerkvist*

HOPPITY— *Milne*

HOQUET— *Damas*

HORA DE ESTRELLAS— *Garcia Lorca*

HORAE CANONICAE— *Auden*

THE HORATIAN ODE— *Marvell*

HORATIUS— *Macaulay*

HORIZON— *Soupault*

HORIZON THONG— *Abbe*

L'HORLOGE— *Baudelaire*

HORN— *Anonymous–English– Old English*

HORNPIPE— *Day Lewis*

HORNPIPE— *Sitwell, Edith*

HORNS— *Kern*

HORRIBLE RELIGIOUS ERROR— *Hughes, Ted*

LE HORS VENU— *Supervielle*

HORSE— *Levine*

HORSE— *Royde-Smith*

THE HORSE CHESTNUT TREE— *Eberhart*

HORSE LANGUAGE— *Sobiloff*

HORSES— *Muir*

HORSES IN CENTRAL PARK— *Swenson*

HOSEA— *Walker*

THE HOSPITAL— *Auden*

THE HOSPITAL— *Jennings*

HOSPITAL FOR DEFECTIVES— *Blackburn, Thomas*

HOSPITAL POEM— *Sanchez*

THE HOSPITAL WINDOW— *Dickey, James*

THE HOST— *Williams, William Carlos*

HÖSTPSALM— *Karlfeldt*

HOT FLASH NUMBER ONE— *Brukner*

HOT HUESOS— *Alurista*

HOT NIGHT ON WATER STREET— *Simpson*

A HOT-WEATHER SONG— *Marquis*

HOTEL BREAKFAST— *Moore, Honor*

HOUDINI— *Sukenick*

HOUDINI RESTORES SAMSON'S SIGHT— *Sukenick*

THE HOUND OF HEAVEN— *Thompson, Francis*

THE HOUNDED LOVERS— *Williams, William Carlos*

THE HOUSE BEAUTIFUL— *Stevenson*

THE HOUSE BY THE SIDE OF THE ROAD— *Foss*

THE HOUSE DOG'S GRAVE— *Jeffers, Robinson*

HOUSE HUNTING— *Wagoner*

THE HOUSE IN THE GREEN WELL— *Wheelock*

THE HOUSE OF CHRISTMAS— *Chesterton, Gilbert Keith*

HOUSE OF FIRE— *Weiss*

THE HOUSE OF MY FRIEND, A VOICEWEAVE— *Fitzsimmons*

HOUSE OF REST— *Betjeman*

THE HOUSE ON THE HILL— *Robinson, Edwin Arlington*

HOUSE PROUD— *Ennis*

THE HOUSE THAT JACK BUILT— *Children's Verses and Nursery Rhymes*

THE HOUSE, THE ENVIRONMENT: THE EMPEROR— *Piercy*

THE HOUSE WITH NOBODY IN IT— *Kilmer, Joyce*

HOUSECLEANING— *Giovanni*

THE HOUSEWIFE— *Baldwin, Michael*

HOW CAN ECHO ANSWER WHAT ECHO CANNOT HEAR?— *Nash*

HOW COME?— *Ignatow*

HOW DEATH COMES— *Anonymous–English–Middle English*

HOW DO YOU SAY "HA-HA" IN FRENCH— *Nash*

HOW DO YOUR EGGS WANT YOU?— *Pietri*

HOW EVERYTHING HAPPENS— *Swenson*

HOW FIRM AND SWIFT— *Stephany*

HOW IT PASSES— *Kizer*

HOW IT WENT— *Sukenick*

HOW IT'S DONE— *Aubert*

HOW MANY 'ERS' ARE YOU— *Hans*

HOW MANY HEAVENS— *Sitwell, Edith*

HOW MANY NIGHTS— *Kinnell*

HOW MANY WHITENESSES— *Jeffers, Lance*

HOW MUCH?— *Sandburg*

HOW SHE RESOLVED TO ACT— *Moore, Merrill*

HOW SLOWLY TIME LENGTHENS— *Smith, Stevie*

HOW THE FULL-THROATED DAFFODILS— *Day Lewis*

HOW THEY BROUGHT THE GOOD NEWS FROM GHENT TO AIX— *Browning, Robert*

HOW TO BE MARRIED WITHOUT A SPOUSE— *Nash*

HOW TO BE OLD— *Swenson*

HOW TO BUY A HOUSE— *Durrell*

HOW TO EAT A POEM— *Merriam*

HOW TO KILL— *Douglas, Keith*

HOW TO MAKE IT THROUGH THE NIGHT— *Shpunt*

HOW WATER BEGAN TO PLAY— *Hughes, Ted*

HOW WE ARE SPARED— *Merwin*

HOW WE DID IT— *Rukeyser*

HOW WILL YOU SHOW IT— *Marshall, Lenore G.*

HOWL— *Ginsberg*

THE HOWLING OF WOLVES— *Hughes, Ted*

HOY ME HE ECHADO A REÍR— *Palés Matos*

HUDIBRAS— *Butler, Samuel*

HUELE— *Jiménez*

HUERTO DE LOS OLIVAS— *Valverde*

HUGH SELWYN MAUBERLEY— *Pound*

DAS HUHN— *Morgenstern*

L'HUÎTRE ET LES PLAIDEURS— *La Fontaine*

EINE HULDIGUNG AN MAINZ— *Zuckmayer*

THE HUMAN ABSTRACT— *Blake*

THE HUMAN BEING IS A LONELY CREATURE— *Eberhart*

HUMAN DIGNITY— *Yeats*

HUMAN LIFE— *Jeffers, Lance*

A HUMBLE PETITION TO THE PRESIDENT OF HARVARD— *Beecher*

HUMDINGER— *McGough*

HUMILIATION— *Jeffers, Lance*

DIE HUNDE— *Wedekind*

DER 102. PSALM— *Luther*

A HUNDRED COLLARS— *Frost, Robert*

LOS HUNGAROS— *Jiménez*

HUNGERFIELD— *Jeffers, Robinson*

THE HUNT— *Jones, David*

THE HUNT— *Weber, Richard*

THE HUNT— *Weber, Ron*

THE HUNTER— *Nash*

HUNTER TRIALS— *Betjeman*

HUNTING— *Snyder*

HUNTING CIVIL WAR RELICS AT NIMBLEWILL CREEK—*Dickey, James*

THE HUNTING OF THE SNARK—*Carroll*

HUNTING SONG—*Finkel*

THE HUNTSMAN—*Lowbury*

HUR MÅNGA VÅGOR—*Edgardh*

THE HURON—*Herschberger*

HURRAH FOR ANYTHING—*Patchen*

HURRAHING IN HARVEST—*Hopkins*

THE HURRICANE—*Crane, Hart*

THE HURRICANE—*Williams, William Carlos*

HURT HAWKS—*Jeffers, Robinson*

THE HURT OF IT ALL—*Fabio, Sarah Webster*

HUSBANDS AND WIVES—*Hershenson*

THE HUSBAND'S COMMENT—*Nash*

THE HUSBAND'S MESSAGE—*Anonymous–English—Old English*

HUSWIFERY—*Taylor, Edward*

HVAD JEG ELSKER—*Andersen*

HWEI SYANG OU SHU—*He Jr Jang*

HYACINTH FOR EDITH—*Smith, A. J. M.*

THE HYAENAS—*Kipling*

HYCIATHE—*Cunningham, James Vincent*

HYLA BROOK—*Frost, Robert*

HYMN—*Addison*

HYMN—*Fletcher, Phineas*

HYMN OF THE GREAT BAAL—*Brecht*

HYMN TO ADVERSITY—*Gray*

HYMN TO DIANA—*Jonson*

HYMN TO INTELLECTUAL BEAUTY—*Shelley*

HYMN TO PAN—*Keats*

A HYMN TO THE NAME AND HONOUR OF THE ADMIRABLE SAINT TERESA—*Crashaw*

HYMN TO THE NIGHT—*Longfellow*

HYMN TO THE RAT RACE—*Robson, Ernest M.*

HYMN TO WINTER SPARROWS—*Gill*

HYMNE—*Baudelaire*

HYMNE—*Hugo, Victor*

HYMNE AN DIE NACHT—*Saint-Exupéry*

HYMNE AUF DIE STILLE—*Saint-Exupéry*

HYMNE DE LA MORT—*Ronsard*

HYMNE DES ANCIENS COMBATTANTS PATRIOTES—*Péret*

HYMNE IN HONOR OF BEAUTIE—*Spenser*

A HYMNE TO CHRIST—*Donne*

HYMNE TO GOD MY GOD, IN MY SICKNESSE—*Donne*

A HYMNE TO GOD THE FATHER—*Donne*

HYMNEN AN DIE NACHT—*Novalis*

THE HYMNS MY MOTHER SANG—*Stevens, Wendy*

HYPERION—*Keats*

HYPERIONS SCHICKSALSLIED—*Hölderlin*

HYPNOSIS POEM—*Lifshin*

THE HYPOTHETICAL DREAM—*Klappert*

HYTTEN—*Andersen*

L'HYVER—*Aubigné*

I AM—*Clare*

I AM—*Conkling*

I AM A DANCER—*Halpern*

I AM A FALCON HOODED—*O'Gorman*

I AM A LIGHT YOU COULD READ BY—*Piercy*

I AM A MULTITUDE—*De Loach*

I AM AMIRH BAHATI—*Bahati*

I AM AN AMERICAN—*Lieberman, Elias*

I AM AS I AM—*Wyatt, Sir Thomas*

I AM DRESSED AS A GONDOLIER—*Winch*

I AM MUSIC PEOPLE—*Kgositsile*

I AM NOT BLIND—*Marshall, Helen Lowrie*

I AM OLDER NOW—*Sobiloff*

I AM RAFTERY—*Raftery*

I AM THE PEOPLE—*Sandburg*

I ASK YOU—*Walters*

I CANNOT TEACH YOU—*Marshall, Helen Lowrie*

I CARRIED HER—*Lester*

I CARTAGENA II—*Andersen*

I CELEBRATE MYSELF—*Whitman*

I DO, I WILL, I HAVE—*Nash*

I DO LIKE TO BE BESIDE THE SEASIDE—*Sitwell, Edith*

I DON'T MEAN US, EXCEPT OCCASIONALLY—*Nash*

I DREAM I'M THE DREAM OF ORPHEUS—*Rich*

I EAT KIDS YUM YUM—*Lee, Dennis*

I FELL INTO A BOX OF EGGS—*Anonymous–English—Modern English*

I FOUND HER OUT THERE—*Hardy*

I HAVE IT ON GOOD AUTHORITY—*Nash*

I HAVE SPENT MY LIFE—*Stephany*

I HAVE WALKED A LONG TIME—*Sanchez*

I HEAR AMERICA SINGING—*Whitman*

I HEAR AN ARMY—*Joyce*

I JUDA STÄDER—*Karlfeldt*

I LIVE IN A COTTAGE—*Conkling*

I LIVETS VILLERVALLA—*Ferlin*

I LOOK INTO MY GLASS—*Hardy*

I KEEP WONDERING—*Conkling*

I KNEW A WOMAN—*Roethke*

I KNOW EXACTLY WHO DROPPED THE OVERALLS IN MRS. MURPHY'S CHOWDER—*Nash*

I KNOW MY LOVE—*Anonymous–English—Modern English*

I M J F K—*Yorck*

I. M. WALTER RAMSDEN—*Betjeman*

I MARRY YOU—*Ciardi*

I' MI TROVAI, FANCIULLE—*Poliziano*

I MUST GO WALK THE WOOD WALKING ALONE—*Anonymous–English—Modern English*

I MUST NOT DIE OF PITY—*Millay*

I NEED, I NEED—*Roethke*

I NEVER EVEN SUGGESTED IT—*Nash*

I ONLY AM ESCAPED ALONE TO TELL THEE—*Nemerov*

I OWE EVERY MAN—*Marshall, Helen Lowrie*

I PAVIJONGEN—*Österling*

I POTOM—*Yevtushenko*

I REMEMBER—*Darr*

I REMEMBER, I REMEMBER—*Hood*

I REMEMBER, I REMEMBER—*Larkin*

I REMEMBER YULE—*Nash*

I SAW A PEACOCK WITH A FIERY TAIL—*Children's Verses and Nursery Rhymes*

I SAW AN ARMY—*Abbe*

I SAY NO WORLD—*Cummings*

I SEE THE BOYS OF SUMMER—*Thomas, Dylan*

I SHALL COME BACK—*Conkling*

I SING AN OLD SONG—*Williams, Oscar*

I SING MY PEOPLE—*Jeffers, Lance*

I SLEPT IN THE LIGHT—*Colbert*

I SOLEN—*Martinson*

I STOOD TIP-TOE UPON A LITTLE HILL—*Keats*

I THANK YOU GOD FOR MOST HIS AMAZING—*Cummings*

I TOO—*Hughes, Langston*

I, TOO, HEAR AMERICA SINGING—*Bond*

I WAAAAAANNT TO KNOW: I NEEEEEDS TO KNOW—*Sanchez*

I WAIT—*Jeffers, Lance*

I WANT, I WANT—*Plath*

I WANT TO BE MARRIED AND CANNOT TELL HOW—*Anonymous–English—Modern English*

I WANT TO HAVE BEEN THE SHAMAN—*Glaze*

I WAS BORN ON A BOARD—*Logue*

I WAS SO FULL—*Smith, Stevie*

I WENT TO SEA—*Conkling*

I WILL ARISE AND GO NOW—*Nash*

I WILL GLORIFY THIS WOMAN—*Alakoye*

WILL NOT FALL—*Marshall, Helen Lowrie*
WILL PURSUE—*Goldstein*
WILL WRITE—*Graves*
WISH—*Smith, Stevie*
WISH YOU HAPPINESS—*Marshall, Helen Lowrie*
ICE—*Spender*
ICECRUST AND SNOWFLAKE—*Hughes, Ted*
THE ICEHOUSE—*Abbe*
ICH, DER ÜBERLEBENDE—*Brecht*
ICH HABE VERLOREN MEINEN MUT—*Guggenmos*
ICH HATT EIN SÜSSES LEBEN—*La Motte-Foqué*
ICH LIEBE FRAUEN—*Hesse*
ICH MÖCHTE HEIM—*Herrmann-Neisse*
ICH TANZ NICHT MIT—*Heine*
ICH WEISS ES WIRD EINE ANDERE ZEIT KOMMEN—*Theobaldy*
ICH WEISS JA—*Jolobe*
ICHABOD—*Whittier*
ICI, TOUJOURS ICI—*Bonnefoy*
IDEA—*Drayton*
IDEA OF ANCESTRY—*Knight, Etheridge*
THE IDEA OF ENTROPY AT MAENPORTH BEACH—*Redgrove*
IDEA OF JOY—*Miles*
THE IDEA OF ORDER AT KEY WEST—*Stevens, Wallace*
DAS IDEAL—*Tucholsky*
L'IDÉAL—*Baudelaire*
IDEAL UND WIRKLICHKEIT—*Tucholsky*
THE IDENTIFICATION—*McGough*
THE IDES OF MARCH—*Eberhart*
IDILIO DE ABRIL—*Jiménez*
THE IDIOT—*Randall*
IDYL, WASHINGTON SQ. S. F.—*Tomlinson*
IDYLLE AM BODENSEE—*Mörike*
IDYLLS OF THE KING—*Tennyson*
IEUAN AP HYWEL SWRDWAL—*Garlick*
IF—*Kipling*
IF HE WERE ALIVE TODAY, MAYHAP, MR. MORGAN WOULD SIT ON THE MIDGET'S LAP—*Nash*
IF I COULD TELL YOU—*Auden*
IF I COULD TELL YOU THE WAY—*Conkling*
IF I FORGET THEE O BIRMINGHAM—*Beecher*
IF I LIVED ON THE LAND—*Carter*
IF I TOLD HIM: A COMPLETED PORTRAIT OF PICASSO—*Stein, Gertrude*
IF I WERE A POET—*Anderson, Beth*
IF I WERE KING—*Foscolo*
IF IT WERE NOT—*Spender*
IF ONCE YOU HAVE SLEPT ON AN ISLAND—*Field, Rachel*
IF SATURDAY—*Starbuck*

IF THIS BE ALL—*Brontë, Anne*
IF THIS BE LOVE—*Constable*
IF WE COME LIKE SOFT RAIN—*Fabio, Sarah Webster*
IF WE MUST DIE—*McKay*
IF YOU CAN—*Moss, Howard*
IKE MINA NI—*Krucenych*
IL EST DES NUITS—*Damas*
IL ÉTAIT UNE FOIS—*Apollinaire*
IL FAUT PASSER LE TEMPS—*Prévert*
IL NE FAUT PAS—*Prévert*
IL N'Y A PAS D'AMOUR HEUREUX—*Aragon*
IL PLEUT—*Carco*
IL SE PEUT—*Jacob, Max*
IL Y A—*Apollinaire*
ILIAD—*Homer*
ILL MET BY FLUORESCENCE—*Nash*
I'LL WALK THE TIGHTROPE—*Danner*
L'ILLUMINAZIONE DE LA CUPPOLA—*Belli*
THE ILLUSION OF ETERNITY—*Eberhart*
ILS S'EN VONT AUX VEILLÉES—*Fombeure*
ILS SONT VENUS CE SOIR—*Damas*
ILUSIONES DE QUIEN VA A LAS INDIAS A HACER FORTUNA—*Lobo*
I'M A PLEASURE TO SHOP FOR—*Nash*
I'M COVERED NOW—*Scannell*
IM FRÜHLING—*Mörike*
I'M GLAD—*Marshall, Helen Lowrie*
I'M LOVE—*McKnight*
I'M O'ER YOUNG TO MARRY YET—*Burns*
IM REICH DER TOTEN—*Jandl*
IM RINGELSPIEL—*Guggenmos*
IM SINKENDEN JAHR—*Bergengruen*
IM SOMMER—*Kirsch*
IM SONNENLICHT—*Eich*
IM STROM—*Bobrowski*
I'M THROUGH WITH YOU FOREVER—*Graves*
IM TIERKOSTÜM—*Morgenstern*
IM VOLKSTON—*Storm*
IM WALDE—*Schlegel*
IM ZUG ATHEN-PATRAS—*Born*
THE IMAGINARY ICEBERG—*Bishop, Elizabeth*
IMAGO—*Stevens, Wallace*
IMITATED FROM THE JAPANESE—*Yeats*
IMITATION DU PSAUME "LAUDA ANIMA"—*Malherbe*
IMITATIONS—*Pope, Alexander*
AN IMMIGRANT BALLAD—*Turco*
IMMORTAL HELIX—*MacLeish*
IMMORTAL STRANGENESS—*Antoninus*
IMMORTALITY—*Dana*
THE IMMORTALS—*Garlick*

IMP/ERFECT—*Gaver*
IMPASSE—*Hughes, Langston*
THE IMPERCIPIENT—*Hardy*
IMPLACABLE—*Ibarbourou*
THE IMPORTANT THING—*Marshall, Helen Lowrie*
THE IMPOSSIBLE—*Graves*
THE IMPOSSIBLE—*Laforgue*
IMPRESSION FAUSSE—*Verlaine*
LO IMPREVISTO—*Nalé-Roxlo*
AN IMPROMPTU FAIRY TALE—*Riley*
THE IMPROVED BINOCULARS—*Layton*
IMPROVISATION: ON AUTHORITY—*Shiva*
IN A BATH TEASHOP—*Betjeman*
IN A DARK TIME—*Roethke*
IN A FOREIGN CITY—*Jennings*
IN A KITCHEN IN AN OLD HOUSE—*Hall*
IN A LIBRARY—*De la Mare*
IN A STEELWORKER'S HOME—*Yevtushenko*
IN A WOOD—*Hardy*
IN AFTER DAYS—*Dobson*
IN AN ARTIST'S STUDIO—*Rossetti, Christina*
IN AN IRIDESCENT TIME—*Stone, Ruth*
IN ANDEREN SPRACHEN—*Eich*
IN ATHENS—*Durrell*
IN ATTICA—*Spender*
IN BACK OF THE REAL—*Ginsberg*
IN BEBOP NIGHTS—*Kresh*
IN BEIRUT—*Durrell*
IN BRITAIN—*Durrell*
IN CAIRO—*Durrell*
IN CASE A TREE GROWS THERE—*Marshall, Helen Lowrie*
IN CASE OF ATOMIC ATTACK—*Redgrove*
IN CHURCH—*Hardy*
IN COMMON—*Derwood*
IN COUNTRY HEAVEN—*Thomas, Dylan*
IN COUNTRY SLEEP—*Thomas, Dylan*
IN DEATH DIVIDED—*Hardy*
IN DEINEM SCHAFFPELZ—*Anonymous–Asian languages*
IN DER FRÜHE—*Mörike*
IN DIESEM SINN, DEIN ONKEL FRANZ—*Mostar*
IN DISTRUST OF MERITS—*Moore, Marianne*
IN DUE SEASON—*Auden*
IN EGYPT—*Williams, Hugo*
IN EGYPT LAND—*Beecher*
IN EIN ALTES STAMMBUCH—*Trakl*
IN EVENING AIR—*Roethke*
IN EVERY SENSE OF THE WORD—*Heath-Stubbs*
IN FILA INDIANA—*Rodari*
IN FLANDERS FIELDS—*McCrae*

IN FRONT OF FIFTH AVENUE
  LIBRARY ON THE STEPS—
  Hodges
IN GEORGIA— *Yevtushenko*
IN GUERNICA—*Rosten*
IN JEDER AMSEL HABE ICH DICH
  GELIEBT— *Goll*
IN KAMLOOPS—*Lee, Dennis*
IN LICENZA—*Murolo*
IN LIEU OF THE LYRE—*Moore,
  Marianne*
IN LIMITE UMANO—*Bevilacqua*
IN LLANDOUGH HOSPITAL—*Abse*
IN LOVE FOR LONG—*Muir*
IN LOVE WITH YOU—*Benedikt*
IN ME TWO WORLDS—*Day Lewis*
IN MEINEM BETT—
  Anonymous-German
IN MEMORIAM—*Senghor*
IN MEMORIAM—*Thomas, Edward*
IN MEMORIAM A. H. H.—*Tennyson*
IN MEMORIAM JOHN FITZGERALD
  KENNEDY 1917-1963 PROFILE
  WRITTEN IN BLOOD—*Goldstein*
IN MEMORY OF ANDREW HILLS—
  Posner
IN MEMORY OF BARRY CORNWALL
  —*Swinburne*
IN MEMORY OF EVA GORE-BOOTH
  AND CON MARKIEWICZ—*Yeats*
IN MEMORY OF JANE FRASER—*Hill*
IN MEMORY OF MAJOR ROBERT
  GREGORY— *Yeats*
IN MEMORY OF MARCUS—*Eckels*
IN MEMORY OF MY CAT DOMINO—
  Fuller, Roy
IN MEMORY OF MY UNCLE
  TIMOTHY—*Reid*
IN MEMORY OF W. B. YEATS—
  Auden
IN MEMORY OF WALTER SAVAGE
  LANDOR—*Swinburne*
IN MIDWINTER A WOOD WAS—
  Levi
IN MONTECITO—*Jarrell*
IN MORTE DEL FRATELLO
  GIOVANNI—*Foscolo*
IN MORTE DEL PADRE—*Foscolo*
IN NAVAJOLAND—*Swenson*
IN NO STRANGE LAND—
  Thompson, Francis
IN OAK TERRACE—*Connor*
IN OUR TIME—*Rukeyser*
IN PANELLED ROOMS—
  Herschberger
IN PARENTHESIS—*Jones, David*
IN PARIS—*Durrell*
IN PATMOS—*Durrell*
IN PIAM MEMORIAM—*Hill*
IN PLAGUE TIME—*Nashe*
IN PRAISE OF BURTON—
  Wilkinson
IN PRAISE OF DIVERSITY—
  McGinley
IN PRAISE OF LIMESTONE—*Auden*
IN PRISON— *Morris, William*
IN PROCESSION—*Graves*

IN RHODES—*Durrell*
IN RIO—*Durrell*
IN SALEM—*Clifton*
IN SANTA MARIA DEL POPOLO—
  Gunn
IN SINAI DESERT—*Sutzkever*
IN SISTERLY FASHION— *Williams,
  William Carlos*
IN SPITE OF HIS DANGLING
  PRONOUN—*Lifshin*
IN SYLVIA PLATH COUNTRY—*Jong*
IN TALL GRASS—*Sandburg*
IN TARA'S HALLS— *Yeats*
IN TENEBRIS—*Hardy*
IN THE BEGINNING—*Hoffman*
IN THE BEGINNING—*Sanchez*
IN THE BIG WORLD—*Gill*
IN THE BRITISH MUSEUM—*Hardy*
IN THE CHILDREN'S HOSPITAL—
  MacDiarmid
IN THE COACH—*Brown, Thomas
  Edward*
IN THE COURTROOM—*Sanchez*
IN THE DYING OF ANYTHING—
  Patten
IN THE ELEMENT OF ANTAGONISMS
  —*Stevens, Wallace*
IN THE EVENING—*Rich*
IN THE FALLOW FIELD— *Young,
  Andrew*
IN THE GARDEN AT SWAINSTON—
  Tennyson
IN THE GREEN MORNING, NOW,
  ONCE MORE—*Schwartz*
IN THE HOME—*Bell*
IN THE HOTEL OF LOST LIGHT—
  Kinnell
IN THE LUNCH WAGON—*Kramer*
IN THE MADNESS OF AGE—*Stone,
  Ruth*
IN THE MIDNIGHT HOUR—*Henri,
  Adrian*
IN THE MOONLIGHT—*Hardy*
IN THE MORNING—*Dunbar, Paul
  Laurence*
IN THE MOUNTAIN TENT—*Dickey,
  James*
IN THE MUSEUM—*Stafford*
IN THE NEOLITHIC AGE—*Kipling*
IN THE NIGHT SHE CAME—*Hardy*
IN THE OLD HOUSE PLYMOUTH—
  Lifshin
IN THE OLD THEATRE, FIESOLE—
  Hardy
IN THE ORCHARD—*Stephens*
IN THE POPPY FIELD—*Stephens*
IN THE RUBBER DINGY—
  Kavanagh
IN THE SERVANTS' QUARTERS—
  Hardy
IN THE SILENCE—*Stephany*
IN THE STUDY—*Hardy*
IN THE TIDAL MARSHES—*Hillyer*
IN THE TREE HOUSE AT NIGHT—
  Dickey, James
IN THE VALLEY OF CAUTERETZ—
  Tennyson

IN THE WHITE GIANT'S THIGH—
  Thomas, Dylan
IN THE WILDERNESS—*Graves*
IN THE WITCH-HUNTING SEASON—
  Ciardi
IN THE WOODS—*Rich*
IN THIS AGE OF HARD TRYING—
  Moore, Marianne
IN THIS TREACHEROUS WORLD—
  Campoamor
IN THIS YOUR COUNTRY SLEEP—
  Walters
IN TIME— *Graves*
IN TIME OF MISTRUST—*Hillyer*
IN TIME OF PESTILENCE—*Nashe*
IN TIME OF "THE BREAKING OF TH
  NATIONS"—*Hardy*
IN TURN—*Clark, John W.*
IN VAST COMPLEXITY THE ORDER
  LIES—*Stephany*
IN WESTMINSTER ABBEY—
  Betjeman
INCHCAPE ROCK—*Southey*
INCIDENT—*Ciardi*
INCIDENT—*Cullen*
INCIDENT— *Walters*
INCIDENT OF THE FRENCH CAMP—
  Browning, Robert
INCIDENT ON A JOURNEY—*Gunn*
INCIDENTS IN THE LIFE OF MY
  UNCLE ARLY—*Lear*
INCIPIENCE—*Rich*
THE INCOMPARABLE LIGHT—
  Eberhart
INCOMPATIBILITÉ—*Baudelaire*
L'INCONTRO DE DU' COMMARE—
  Belli
INDEPENDENCE—*Foleti*
AN INDEX OF FIRST LINES—*Porte
  Bern*
LA INDIADA—*Ascasubi*
THE INDIAN BURYING GROUND—
  Freneau
INDIAN CHILDREN— *Wynne*
INDIAN PIPE—*Eberhart*
INDIAN RIVER—*Stevens, Wallac*
INDIAN SERENADE—*Shelley*
INDIANA—*Crane, Hart*
INDIANAPOLIS/SUMMER 1969 POEM
  —*Sanchez*
INDIANS ARE BAD DRINKERS—
  Flint
EL INDIFERENTE—*Hierro*
THE INDIFFERENT—*Donne*
THE INDIVIDUALIST—*Nash*
INDOOR GAMES NEAR NEWBURY—
  Betjeman
LO INEFABLE—*Agustini*
INFANT—*Smith, Stevie*
INFANT JOY—*Blake*
INFANT SORROW—*Blake*
INFANTA MARINA—*Stevens,
  Wallace*
L'INFANTE—*Samain*
LOS INFANTES DE LARA—
  Anonymous-Spanish
INFELICE—*Smith, Stevie*

INFERNO—*Dante Alighieri*
INFIDELITY—*Viorst*
INFIERNO Y GLORIA—*Garcia Lorca*
L'INFINITO—*Leopardi*
THE INFLATABLE GLOBE—*Spencer*
THE INFLUENCE COMING: SEVEN OF PENTACLES—*Piercy*
THE INFLUENCE PASSING: KNIGHT OF SWORDS—*Piercy*
INGLESE—*Ciardi*
LA INJUSTICIA—*Alonso*
INLAND, A THOUSAND MILES—*Cattonar*
INLEDNING—*Hasso*
INNAN DIT RIKE BLEV KARTLAGT—*Ferlin*
IN INNEBOENDE—*Ferlin*
INNER MAN—*Simic*
THE INNER PART—*Simpson*
INNI SACRI—*Petrarca*
INNO ALLA MORTE—*Ungaretti*
INNO DI GARIBALDI—*Mercantini*
INNOCENCE—*Gunn*
THE INNOCENT—*Day Lewis*
THE INNOCENT—*Derwood*
INNOCENT QUESTION—*Hodges*
INNOCENT'S SONG—*Causley*
INNS OF LOVE—*Williams, Gwyn*
LA INQUIETUD FUGAZ—*Ibarbourou*
THE INQUIRY—*Hardy*
THE INQUIRY—*Kendrick*
INSANITY—*Bodenheim*
INSCRIPTION FOR A BED AT KELMSCOTT MANOR—*Morris, William*
INSCRIPTION FOR A GRAVEYARD—*Winters*
INSCRIPTION FOR THE CEILING OF A BEDROOM—*Parker*
INSCRIPTION FOR THE TOMB OF TIMON—*Ptolemaios the Astronomer*
INSCRIPTIONS—*Whitman*
INSECTS—*Coakley*
INSENSIBILITY—*Owen, Wilfred*
INSIDE OF KING'S CHAPEL, CAMBRIDGE—*Wordsworth*
INSIDE THE ZOO—*Merriam*
INSIDE THIS CLAY JUG—*Bly*
INSINUANT—*Valéry*
INSPECTOR DOGBONE GETS HIS MAN—*Lee, Dennis*
INSPIRATION—*Thoreau*
INSPIRATION IN DESPAIR—*Marshall, Helen Lowrie*
INSOMNIO—*Alonso*
INSOMNIO—*Diego, Gerardo*
INSTANS TYRANNUS—*Browning, Robert*
INSTANT CHOCOLATE—*Douglas, Sharon*
INSTANT REPLAY—*Robinson, Wanda*
INSTEAD OF A GIFT—*Tullos*

INSTEAD OF AN ELEGY—*Fraser, G. S.*
INTE ENS DET FÖRFLUTNA—*Ferlin*
INTERFACE—*Khalil*
INTERIOR—*Carranza*
INTERLOPER—*Marshall, Lenore G.*
INTERLUDE—*Roethke*
INTERLUDE—*Shapiro, Karl*
THE INTERPRETERS—*Swinburne*
INTERROGACIONES—*Mistral*
INTERRUPTION AT THE OPERA HOUSE—*Patten*
INTERVAL—*Hillyer*
INTERVIEW—*Kaschnitz*
INTERVIEW WITH A SPIRIT HEALER—*Abse*
INTIMATE PARTY IN GUADALAJARA, DEC. 1963—*Ostroff*
INTIMATIONS OF IMMORTALITY FROM RECOLLECTIONS OF EARLY CHILDHOOD—*Wordsworth*
INTIMATIONS OF UNREALITY—*Kavanagh*
INTIMES—*Éluard*
INTIMITÉ—*Obaldia*
INTO THE STREETS—*Last Poets*
INTRODUCCÍON A UNAS FABULAS PARA ANIMALES—*González*
INTRODUCTION—*Blake*
AN INTRODUCTION TO DOGS—*Nash*
AN INTRODUCTION TO THOMAS HARDY—*Davies, William Henry*
INTRODUCTORY POEM—*McGough*
INTROIT—*Claudel*
INTROSPECTION—*Giovanni*
INTROSPECTIVE REFLECTION—*Nash*
INVADERS—*Abbe*
INVADERS—*Milne*
INVENTAIRE—*Pilon*
INVENTED A PERSON—*Marshall, Lenore G.*
INVENTIONS—*Holub*
INVENTORY—*Parker*
INVENZIONE DEI FRANCOBOLLI—*Rodari*
INVERSNAID—*Hopkins*
INVICTUS—*Henley, William Ernest*
INVIERNO EN CUBA—*Milanés*
INVINCIBLE—*Van Doren*
THE INVISIBLE WOMAN—*Morgan, Robin*
INVITATION—*Char*
INVITATION—*Hodges*
L'INVITATION AU VOYAGE—*Baudelaire*
INVITATION TO A HAY—*Garrigue*
INVITATION TO A QUIET LIFE—*Simpson*
AN INVITE TO ETERNITY—*Clare*
INVITING A FRIEND TO SUPPER—*Jonson*

INVOCATION—*Chapin*
INVOCATION—*Éluard*
INVOCATION—*MacNeice*
INVOCATION: TO THE MUSE—*Sward*
THE INVOICE—*Creeley*
IO QUANNO SENTO 'E DI—*Viviani*
IO VORREI—*Rodari*
IOLANTHE—*Gilbert, Sir William Schwenck*
IOWA—*Davie*
IPITS—*Kern*
IRELAND'S OWN—*Betjeman*
AN IRISH AIRMAN FORESEES HIS DEATH—*Yeats*
IRISH-AMERICAN VISITOR—*Clarke*
THE IRISH UNIONIST'S FAREWELL TO GRETA HELLSTROM IN 1922—*Betjeman*
AN IRISHMAN TO HIS RAT—*Logue*
IRON PALACE—*Graves*
IRONY—*Untermeyer*
IROQUOISES—*Seghers*
IRRBLOSSET OCH ÄLVAN—*Bergman, Bo*
IS ANY COHERENCE WORTH THE CELEBRATION—*Blackburn, Paul*
IS THERE ANY EASY ROAD TO FREEDOM?—*Sandburg*
IS THIS BEAUTY TO PERISH—*Emerson*
ISAIAH—*Walker*
ISLA Y MAR—*Ribera Chevremont*
THE ISLAND—*Milne*
THE ISLAND OF BIRDS—*Dowling*
ISLAND QUARRY—*Crane, Hart*
THE ISLANDERS—*Booth*
ISLANDS—*Auden*
ISLANDS—*Hoffman*
ISLANDS—*Rukeyser*
ISLE OF LOVE—*Khalil*
ISN'T NATURE WONDERFUL—*Nash*
ISOLATION—*Arnold*
L'ISOLEMENT—*Desbordes-Valmore*
L'ISOLEMENT—*Lamartine*
ISRAEL—*Webb*
ISRAFEL—*Poe*
IT AND THEM—*Eckels*
IT COULDN'T BE DONE—*Guest, Edgar*
IT IS—*Rasof*
IT IS A LIVING CORAL—*Williams, William Carlos*
IT IS A WORLD OF ROCKS—*Gregor*
IT IS AGAIN—*Stephany*
IT IS ALMOST THE YEAR 2000—*Frost, Robert*
IT IS FINISHED—*Wheelock*
IT IS NOT TO BE THOUGHT OF, WRITTEN IN LONDON, 1802—*Wordsworth*
IT IS NOT WE ALONE—*Eliot, Thomas Stearns*
IT IS THE SAFETY—*Stephany*
IT IS THERE—*Rukeyser*

IT RAINS—*Thomas, Edward*
IT WAS A SUMMER—*Prothro*
IT WAS ALL VERY TIDY—*Graves*
IT WAS HERE NOT THREE DAYS AGO
—*Johnston, Ellen Turlington*
IT WAS LONG AGO—*Farjeon*
ITALIAN MORNING—*Bogan*
ITALY—*Gaver*
ITEM: BLACK MEN THINKING—
Emanuel
ITHYPHALLICS—*Blackmur*
IT'S A NEW DAY—*Sanchez*
IT'S CONTAGIOUS—*Marshall,
Helen Lowrie*
IT'S HARD TO BE HIP OVER THIRTY
—*Viorst*
IT'S TIME—*Dodson-Letourneau,
Gayle*
ITYLUS—*Swinburne*
IURKE—*Popa*
IUVENES DUM SUMUS—*Hall*
I'VE GOT A LITTLE LIST—*Gilbert,
Sir William Schwenck*
IVORY MASKS IN ORBIT—*Kgositsile*
IZ POEMY—*Pasternak*

JA—*Fox, Charles*
JA, DAS MÖCHT' ICH NOCH
ERLEBEN—*Fontane*
JABBERWOCKY—*Carroll*
JACK AND HIS PONY, TOM—*Belloc*
JACK DO-GOOD-FOR-NOTHING—
Nash
JACK FROST—*Setoun*
JACK MCGUIRE—*Masters, Edgar
Lee*
THE JACKALHEADED COWBOY—
Reed, Ishmael
JACKSON, MISSISSIPPI—*Walker*
THE JACOB'S LADDER—*Levertov*
JACQUELINE—*Inman*
JAG KUNDE JU VARA—*Ferlin*
JÄGERS ABENDLIED—*Goethe*
THE JAGUAR—*Hughes, Ted*
JÄHRLICH, IM SOMMER—*Borchers*
J'AI ÉTRANGLÉ MON FRÈRE—*Char*
J'AI EU LONGTEMPS—*Éluard*
J'AI FAIT MES PLUS BEAUX POÈMES
—*Cendrars*
J'AI MARCHÉ TRENTE ANS, MES
SOEURS—*Maeterlinck*
J'AI TOUJOURS ÉTÉ INTACT DE DIEU
—*Prévert*
J'AI TRENTE ANS—*Cendrars*
J'AIME L' ÂNE—*Jammes*
J'ALLAIS DANS LE VERGER—
Jammes
A JAMAICAN CHILD—*Sobiloff*
JAMES BROWN—*Last Poets*
JAMES I—*Kipling*
JAMES GARBER—*Masters, Edgar
Lee*
JANE—*Kresh*
JANET WAKING—*Ransom*
JANIS (TO THE 4TH POWER)—
Mariah
JANUARY GLADSONG—*Patten*

JAPANLIED—*Tucholsky*
JAPANSKT SKÅDESPEL—*Asplund*
EL JARDÍN—*Jiménez*
LE JARDIN—*Prévert*
JASON—*Moraes*
JAY—*Anonymous–English—Old
English*
JAZZ—*Last Poets*
JAZZ FANTASIA—*Sandburg*
JAZZ POEM—*Hines*
JE CONTRAINS TOUTE SÈVE—
Hugo, Victor
JE CRAINS PAS ÇA TELLEMENT—
Queneau
JE DONNE À MON ESPOIR—
Apollinaire
JE ME SOUVIENS—*Supervielle*
JE ME SOUVIENS D'AVOIR LU—
Cendrars
JE NAQUIS AU HAVRE—*Queneau*
JE NE SUIS PAS SEUL—*Éluard*
JE NE VEUX PLUS ALLER À LEUR
ÉCOLE—*Tirolien*
JE RENTRE—*Abril*
JE SUIS EN ROUTE—*Cendrars*
JE T'AI IMAGINÉ—*Éluard*
JE T'APPORTE, CE SOIR—
Verhaeren
JE TE L'AI DIT—*Éluard*
JE TRAHIRAI DEMAIN—*Cohn,
Marianne*
JE VOUDRAIS PAS CREVER—*Vian*
JE VOUS SALUE, MA FRANCE—
Aragon
JEALOSIE—*Donne*
JEALOUS LOVERS—*Hall*
JEALOUS MAN—*Graves*
THE JEALOUS WIFE—*Scannell,
Vernon*
JEALOUSY—*Brooke*
JEALOUSY—*Kern*
JEAN STAFFORD—*Lowell, Robert*
JEANNE—*Gourmont*
JEFFERSON VALLEY—*Hollander*
THE JELLYFISH—*Moore,
Marianne*
THE JELLYFISH—*Nash*
JEMAND—*Krolow*
JENA—*Benn*
JEREMIAH—*Walker*
JERICHO—*Ai*
JERICHO—*Bergman,
Alexander F.*
JERONIMO'S HOUSE—*Bishop,
Elizabeth*
JERUSALEM—*Blake*
JESSE JAMES—*Benét, William
Rose*
THE JESUITS IN NORTH AMERICA—
Davie
JESUS AND HIS MOTHER—*Gunn*
JESUS COOKS—*Sexton*
THE JESUS INFECTION—*Kumin*
JESUS WALKING—*Sexton*
LE JET D'EAU—*Baudelaire*
JETZT WOHIN?—*Heine*
LA JEUNE CAPTIVE—*Chénier*

LA JEUNE FILLE—*Jammes*
JEUNE FILLE, L'AMOUR—*Hugo,
Victor*
UNE JEUNE FILLE PARLE—*Moréas*
LA JEUNE PARQUE—*Valéry*
LA JEUNE TARENTINE—*Chénier*
LA JEUNE VEUVE—*La Fontaine*
JEUNESSE—*Noailles*
THE JEWISH CEMETERY AT
NEWPORT—*Longfellow*
JEWS CHANTING—*Tunkeler*
JIBARA DEL GANDUBAN—*Torres*
JIBARO—MY PRETTY NIGGER—*Las
Poets*
JIG—*Day Lewis*
JIM BLUDSO—*Hay, John*
JIM, WHO RAN AWAY FROM HIS
NURSE AND WAS EATEN BY A
LION—*Belloc*
JIN SHR SHANG JANG SCHWEI BU—
Ju Ching Yu
JITTERBUGGING IN THE STREETS—
Hernton
JOAL—*Senghor*
JOB—*Benserade*
JOCK OF HAZELDEAN—*Scott, Sir
Walter*
JODELLING SONG—*Sitwell, Edith*
JOE CLISBY'S SONG—*Davidson*
JOEL—*Walker*
JOHANN KEPLER—*Mörike*
JOHANNES AGRICOLA IN
MEDITATION—*Browning,
Robert*
JOHN ANDERSON MY JO—*Burns*
JOHN B. STETSON—*Lifshin*
JOHN BROWN'S BODY—*Benét,
Stephen Vincent*
JOHN BURNS AT GETTYSBURG—
Harte
JOHN CHRYSOSTOM—*Wilbur*
JOHN DONNE—*Durrell*
JOHN HANCOCK OTIS—*Masters,
Edgar Lee*
JOHN HARVEY'S BLUES—*Robinson,
Wanda*
JOHN HENRY—
*Anonymous–English—
Modern English*
JOHN JAMES AUDUBON—*Benét,
Stephen Vincent*
JOHN-JOHN—*MacDonagh*
JOHN KINSELLA'S LAMENT FOR
MRS. MARY MOORE—*Yeats*
JOHN MAYNARD—*Fontane*
JOHN PEEL—SHAKE HANDS WITH 3
MAMAS—*Nash*
JOHN SKELTON—*Graves*
JOHN STREET—*Souster*
JOHN SUTTER—*Winters*
JOHN TONGUE—*Dlugos*
JOHN WEBSTER—*Swinburne*
JOHNNY APPLESEED—*McCarthy,
Agnes*
JOHNNY COURTEAU—*Drummond*
JOHNNY FINN—*Arden*
JOHNNY RANDALL—*Ormond*

JOIE DE L'AMOUR OBSCUR—
  Lasnier
LA JOLIE ROUSSE—*Apollinaire*
THE JOLLY BEGGARS—*Burns*
JONAS KEENE—*Masters, Edgar
  Lee*
JONATHAN'S SONG: A NEGRO SAW
  THE JEWISH PAGEANT—*Dodson*
JORDAN—*Herbert*
JORDAN'S DELIGHT—*Blackmur*
JORDSKEPPET—*Lindorm*
JOSEPH WEINHEBER (1892–1945)—
  Auden
JOURNALIST'S SONG—*Sitwell,
  Osbert*
JOURNEY OF THE MAGI—*Eliot,
  Thomas Stearns*
THE JOURNEYS—*Brathwaite*
JOURNEY'S END—*Milne*
JOY GOES DEEP—*Glaze*
JU FENG SYING—*Du Fu*
JUBILATE AGNO—*Smart*
JUBILEE—*Dodson*
JUDAS—*Williams, Oscar*
JUDAS ISCARIOT—*Spender*
JUDAS ISKARIOT—*Ferlin*
JUDAS PRIEST—*Blackmur*
JUDAS TREE—*Blackburn, Thomas*
JUDENFRIEDHOF—*Rilke*
JUDGE SELAH LIVELY—*Masters,
  Edgar Lee*
JUDGE SOMERS—*Masters, Edgar
  Lee*
JUDGEMENT DAY—*Garlick*
JUDGEMENT DAY—*Johnson,
  James Weldon*
THE JUDGEMENT OF PARIS—
  Graves
JUDGING BY APPEARANCES—
  Poulsson
JUDGING DISTANCES—*Reed,
  Henry*
JUDGMENT DAY—*Hughes,
  Langston*
JUDITH OF BETHULIA—*Ransom*
JUDITH Y HOLOFERNES—*Valencia*
JUDITH'S BLUES—*Simmons, Judy*
JUDY—ONE—*Lee, Don L.*
JUEGOS CONSIGO MISMO—
  Martinez Alonso
JUGEMENT—*Aubigné*
JUGEMENT DERNIER—*Fombeure*
DIE JUGEND—*Hölderlin*
JUGEND-ERINNERUNGEN—*Göck-
  ingk*
JUGGLER—*Wilbur*
JUICIO FINAL—*Otero*
JUJU FOR GRANDMA—*Fabio,
  Sarah Webster*
JUJU FOR RAY CHARLES ALCHEMY
  OF THE BLUES—*Fabio, Sarah
  Webster*
JUJU FOR THE HAND THAT ROCKS
  THE CRADLE/THAT ROCKS THE
  BOAT—*Fabio, Sarah Webster*
JUKE BOX LOVE SONG—*Hughes,
  Langston*

JULIO—*Herrera y Reissig*
JULY DAWN—*Bogan*
JULY 9, 1976, ON ARRIVING HOME—
  Ginsberg
JULY 7TH—*Norris*
THE JUMBLIES—*Lear*
LES JUMEAUX DE LA NUIT—
  Obaldia
LA JUMENT DU CAPITAINE—
  Obaldia
JUMP OR JIGGLE—*Beyer*
JUMP ROPE—*Sobiloff*
JUNE 20, 1961, TANGIERS—
  Orlovsky
DIE JUNGE FRAU—
  Anonymous–Asian languages
DIE JUNGE MAGD—*Trakl*
DER JÜNGER—*Piontek*
JUNGFRU MARIA I ROSENGÅRD—
  Rydberg
DER JÜNGLING AN DIE KLUGEN
  RATGEBER—*Hölderlin*
JUNI—*Kaschnitz*
JUNIPER—*Lee, Laurie*
JUNK—*Wilbur*
JUNKMAN'S OBBLIGATO—
  Ferlinghetti
LA JURA EN SANTA GADEA—
  Anonymous–Spanish
JUST A SMACK AT AUDEN—
  Empson
JUST KEEP QUIET AND NOBODY
  WILL NOTICE—*Nash*
JUST LIKE YOU—*Smith, Eugene
  Osborn*
JUSTICE ARNETT—*Masters, Edgar
  Lee*
JYANG SYWE—*Lyou Dzung Ywan*

KADDISH—*Ginsberg*
KAFKA'S CASTLE—*Ferlinghetti*
KALEIDOSCOPE—*Verlaine*
KALLYOPE YELL—*Lindsay,
  Vachel*
KALMUS—*Bobrowski*
KAMICHI—*Jacob, Max*
KAMPF MIT DEM DRACHEN—
  Schiller
KANG LAU GEE—*Wen Ting-Yueh*
THE KANGAROO—*Children's
  Verses and Nursery Rhymes*
KANGAROOS—*Nash*
KANSAS AUGUST, 1973—*Lester*
KANSAS BOY—*Lechlitner*
KARENGE YA MARENGE—*Cullen,
  Countee*
KAR'ERA—*Yevtushenko*
KARLEK TILL TRA—*Lundkvist*
KAROMAMA—*Milosz*
KARTAN—*Asplund*
KARUSSELL—*Rilke*
KARWOCHE—*Mörike*
KASIDA DE LA VOZ—*León, Rafael
  de*
KASIDA DE LAS MANOS—*León,
  Rafael de*

KASIDA DE LOS OJOS—*León,
  Rafael de*
KASIDA DEL VINO—*Carranza*
KASPAR HAUSERLIED—*Trakl*
KATERINA—*Shevchenko*
KÄTHE KOLLWITZ—*Rukeyser*
KATZENJAMMER KIDS—*Reaney*
KAURI—*Inman*
KAYA-MAGAN—*Senghor*
KEATS—*Longfellow*
KEEP IT DARK—
  *Anonymous–African
  languages–Southern Africa*
KEEP PUSHING—*Arnez*
KEEPING THINGS WHOLE—*Strand*
KEHR' EIN BEI MIR—*Rückert*
KEHRAUS—*Eichendorff*
KEINER ODER ALLE—*Brecht*
KEINER WEINE—*Benn*
KENNEDY POEM—*Myers*
KENNEDY UCCISO—*Hugo,
  Richard F.*
KENNST DU DAS LAND WO DIE
  KANONEN BLUHEN—*Kästner*
KENT CIRCLE SONG—*Olson*
KEPT—*Bogan*
THE KEY—*Ormond*
THE KEY TO EVERYTHING—
  Swenson
KHMEL'—*Pasternak*
KHOROSHEYE OTNOSHENIYE K
  LOSHADYAM—*Mayakovsky*
KID—*Ai*
KID—*Hayden*
KID BRUIN—*Brooks, Gwendolyn*
KIKHLE—*Seferis*
KILLALA—*Davie*
KIND—*Miles*
KIND GHOSTS—*Owen, Wilfred*
KIND OF AN ODE TO DUTY—*Nash*
KIND OF LOVE LETTER TO NEW
  YORK—*McGinley*
KIND OF PROGRESSION—*Spencer*
KINDA BLUE—*Wilson*
DIE KINDER DIESER WELT—
  Kaschnitz
KINDERKREUZZUG—*Brecht*
KINDHEIT—*Rilke*
KINDLINESS—*Brooke*
KINDLY UNHITCH THAT STAR,
  BUDDY—*Nash*
KING HENRY V—*Shakespeare*
KING JOHN AND THE ABBOT OF
  CANTERBURY—*Anonymous–En-
  glish–Modern English*
KING JOHN'S CHRISTMAS—*Milne*
KING OF PORTUGAL DESCRIBES
  HER STATE—*Peele*
KING OF THE ZULUS—
  *Anonymous–African
  languages–Southern Africa*
THE KINGDOM OF GOD—
  Thompson, Francis
THE KINGFISHER—*Davies,
  William Henry*
THE KINGIS QUAIR—*James I,
  King of Scotland*

THE KING'S BREAKFAST—*Milne*
KING'S-X—*Marshall, Helen Lowrie*
KINMONT WILLIE—*Anonymous–English– Modern English*
DIE KIRCHE VON NAGO—*Rilke*
A KISS—*Dobson*
A KISS—*Shapiro, Karl*
A KISS FROM A BROTHER— *Darragh*
KISSIE LEE—*Walker*
KIT CARSON'S RIDE—*Miller, Joaquin*
KITCHEN CHAIR POEM NO.5— *Major*
KITCHEN-DOOR BLUES—*Williams, Tennessee*
KITCHENETTE BUILDING—*Brooks, Gwendolyn*
KITE—*Behn, Harry*
A KITE—*Children's Verses and Nursery Rhymes*
KITE DAYS—*Sawyer*
THE KITE THE CHILD AND THE SHOE—*Sobiloff*
KITTEN—*Farjeon*
THE KITTEN—*Nash*
KITTENS—*Merriam*
KITTY OF THE SHERRACH VANE— *Brown, Thomas Edward*
KJØBENHAVN—*Andersen*
KLAG—*Weckherlin*
KLÄRCHENS LIED—*Goethe*
KLASSENZUSAMMENKUNFT—*Kästner*
KLAXON—*Reaney*
DIE KLEINE PASSION—*Keller, Gottfried*
KLEINE STROPHEN VON DER UNSTERBLICHKEIT—*Zuckmayer*
DIE KLEINEN HOTELS—*Mehring*
DIE KLEINSTEN—*Busch*
KLINA—*Popa*
KLOCKNYCKELN—*Lo-Johansson*
KM 21—*Morgenstern*
DER KNABE—*Rilke*
DER KNABENCHOR—*Benn*
KNEE-DEEP IN JUNE—*Riley*
KNEELING TO THE—*Stephany*
DAS KNIE—*Morgenstern*
KNIGHT-IN-ARMOUR—*Milne*
KNIGHTS—*Yevtushenko*
KNIGHTS AND LADIES—*Milne*
KNITTING—*Sterns*
KNOCKING DONKEY FLEAS OFF A POET FROM THE SOUTHSIDE OF CHI—*Lee, Don L.*
KNORR—*Ferlin*
DER KNOTEN—*Busch*
KNOW HOW—*Goldfarb*
KNOWLT HOHEIMER—*Masters, Edgar Lee*
KOMBINATION IV—*Heissenbüttel*
KOMM, LASS UNS SPIELEN— *Storm*
KOMMEN UND SCHEIDEN—*Lenau*

KOMMER ALDRIG IGJEN— *Andersen*
KOMPLEX 10—*Rühm*
KONDITIONALIS—*Ferlin*
KONEN MED AEGGENE—*Andersen*
KÖNIG DAVID—*Heine*
DER KÖNIG IN THULE—*Goethe*
KONTRAPUNKT—*Edfelt*
KOPERNIKANISCHE CHARAKTERE GESUCHT—*Kästner*
DER KORBSTUHL—*Morgenstern*
DIE KORFSCHE UHR—*Morgenstern*
KOSHUETI—*Yevtushenko*
KOSMIK MODER—*Lindegren*
DIE KRANICHE DES IBYKUS— *Schiller*
KREUTZER SONATA—*Hughes, Ted*
KRIEG DEM KRIEGE—*Tucholsky*
KRIEGSLIED—*Claudius*
KRIEZERSCH—*Olfers-Batocki*
KRINKEN—*Field, Eugene*
KRISTOFFER SECOND—*Ciardi*
KRONPRÄTENDENTEN—*Morgenstern*
DIE KRÜCKEN—*Brecht*
KU KLUX KLAN—*Hughes, Langston*
EIN KUBIKKILOMETER GENÜGT— *Kästner*
KUBLA KHAN—*Coleridge, S. T.*
DIE KUGELN—*Morgenstern*
DIE KÜNFTIGE GELIEBTE— *Klopstock*
KÜNSTLERS ABENDLIED—*Goethe*
KUPPELLIED—*Brecht*
DAS KURSBUCH—*Roth, Eugen*
KURZ VOR DEM REGEN—*Eich*
DIE KÜRZE—*Hölderlin*
KYOTE: MARCH—*Snyder*
KYSSANDE VIND—*Gullberg*

LA CROSSE AT NINETY MILES AN HOUR—*Eberhart*
THE LABORS OF HERCULES— *Moore, Marianne*
LE LABOUREUR ET SES ENFANTS— *La Fontaine*
LABRADOR—*Fuertes*
LE LAC—*Lamartine*
LACED WITH CHASEN—*Gaver*
LÄCHELN ATMEN SCHREITEN— *Werfel*
LÄCHELN DER MONA LISA— *Tucholsky*
LACK OF STEADFASTNESS— *Chaucer*
THE LADIES—*Kipling*
LADIES—*Purens*
LADIES, BEWARE THE POETS— *Robson, Jeremy*
THE LADY AND THE BEAR— *Roethke*
THE LADY AND THE EARTHENWARE HEAD—*Plath*
A LADY AT A PARTY—*Coward*
LADY BATES—*Jarrell*
LADY CLARE—*Tennyson*

LADY DAY SPRING-TONED—*Stone, Ronald*
LADY ISABEL AND THE ELF-KNIGHT —*Anonymous–English—Modern English*
LADY LAZARUS—*Plath*
LADY LOST—*Ransom*
LADY OF NATCHEZ—*Nash*
THE LADY OF SHALOTT— *Tennyson*
THE LADY OF THE TOMAHAWK— *Coffin*
LADY, SISTER—*Marcus*
THE LADY WHO OFFERS HER LOOKING-GLASS TO VENUS— *Prior*
LADYBIRD—*Kali*
THE LADY'S REWARD—*Parker*
THE LADY'S THREE SONGS—*Yeats*
THE LADY'S-MAID'S SONG— *Hollander*
LAGARITO VERDE—*Palés Matos*
LAGARTO VIEJO—*Garcia Lorca*
LAGO DI GARDA—*Rodari*
LAID OFF BLUES—*Arnez*
THE LAILY WORM AND THE MACHREL OF THE SEA— *Anonymous–English— Modern English*
LAIS—*Fleming*
LA LAITIÈRE ET LE POT AU LAIT— *La Fontaine*
THE LAKE—*Poe*
LAKE ISLE OF INNISFREE—*Yeats*
THE LAKE OF ANNECY—*Dowling*
LAKE SUPERIOR—*Reaney*
LAKES—*Auden*
LAKESHORE—*Scott, F. R.*
THE LAMB—*Blake*
THE LAMB—*Ciardi*
THE LAMB—*Nash*
LAMENT—*Anonymous–African languages–Gabon*
LAMENT—*Bergman, Alexander F.*
LAMENT—*Camoes*
LAMENT—*Millay*
LAMENT—*Thomas, Dylan*
LAMENT FOR SEAN MACDERMOTT —*O'Sullivan*
LAMENT FOR THE COWBOY LIFE— *Mitchell, Julian*
LAMENT FOR THE MAKARIS— *Dunbar, William*
A LAMENT FOR THE UNLASTING JOYS—*Patchen*
THE LAMENT OF THE BORDER WIDOW—*Anonymous–English —Modern English*
LAMENTACIÓN DE LA MUERTE— *Garcia Lorca*
LAMENTATION—*Anonymous–American Indian languages–Fox*
THE LAMENTATION OF THE OLD PENSIONER—*Yeats*
LAMENTATIONEN—*Heine*
LAMENTO—*Tucholsky*

LAMENTS FOR A DYING LANGUAGE
—*Nash*

LAMENTU PI LA MORTI—*Buttitta*

DIE LÄMMERWOLKE—
Morgenstern

THE LAMP AND THE CANDLE—
Roche

LAMPLIGHTER—*Stevenson*

IL LAMPO DELLA BOCCA—
Ungaretti

LANCELOT AND ELAINE—
Tennyson

THE LAND OF COUNTERPANE—
Stevenson

THE LAND OF NOD—*Stevenson*

THE LAND OF SMILES—*Miller, E.
Ethelbert*

THE LAND OF STORY-BOOKS—
Stevenson

LANDET SOM ICKE AR—*Södergran*

LANDING OF THE PILGRIM
FATHERS—*Hemans*

LANDLADY—*Atwood*

LANDSCAPE AS A NUDE—
MacLeish

LANDSCAPE AS METAL AND
FLOWERS—*Scott, Winfield
Townley*

LANDSCAPE AS WEREWOLF—
Dunlop

LANDSCAPE: DEER SEASON—
Howes

LANDSCAPE FROM A TRAIN—
Simpson

THE LANDSCAPE NEAR AN
AERODROME—*Spender*

LANDSCAPE WEST OF EDEN—
Aiken

LANDSCHAFTEN, DIE SIE
DURCHFAHREN—*Meckel*

LANGE SCHATTEN—*Kaschnitz*

LÄNGTAN—*Rydberg*

A LANGUAGE OF FLESH AND ROSES
—*Scott, F. R.*

LANGUAGE OF THE SEASON—
Graves

THE LANGUAGES WE ARE—*Bryant,
F. J., Jr.*

LANTERN IN THE SNOW—*Coffin*

LANTLIG KYRKOGÅRG
PSALMODIKON—*Österling*

LAPIS LAZULI—*Yeats*

LARGAS LADERAS ARIDAS—
Vivanco

LARGE RED MAN READING—
Stevens, Wallace

LARGO—*Smith, Sydney Goodsir*

LES LARMES DE SAINT-PIERRE—
Malherbe

LÄRMSCHUTZ—*Morgenstern*

LAS DE L'AMER REPOS—*Mallarmé*

ASALLE—*Davie*

ASCIATEMI DIVERTIRE—
Palazzeschi

ASSAMO FA' DIO—*Di Giacomo*

THE LAST ADAM—*Dowling*

THE LAST BOOK—*Den Boer*

THE LAST BUS—RIO DE JANEIRO—
Strand

LAST CALL AT THE TIN PALACE—
Pines

A LAST CONFESSION—*Yeats*

LAST DAYS OF ALICE—*Tate, Allen*

LAST HILL IN A VISTA—*Bogan*

THE LAST LAUGH—*Owen,
Wilfred*

THE LAST LEAF—*Holmes, Oliver
Wendell*

LAST LINES—*Brontë, Emily*

THE LAST OF ENGLAND—*Porter,
Peter*

THE LAST OF HER ORDER—
Betjeman

THE LAST OF THE DINOSAURS—
Porter, Peter

THE LAST OF THE PEASANTRY—
Thomas, Ronald Stuart

THE LAST ONE—*Merwin*

THE LAST ONE—*Scott, Winfield
Townley*

LAST PATCH OF SNOW—*Abbe*

THE LAST POEM—*Derwood*

A LAST POEM—*Graves*

LAST POEM I'M GONNA WRITE
'BOUT US—*Sanchez*

THE LAST SHEAF—*Thomas,
Edward*

LAST SNOW—*Young, Andrew*

LAST SONGS—*Kinnell*

LAST SUPPER—*Williams, Oscar*

THE LAST TRAIN—*Plomer*

THE LAST WORD—*Arnold*

A LAST WORD FOR LOUIS
MACNEICE—*Rodgers*

THE LAST WORD OF A BLUEBIRD—
Frost, Robert

A LAST WORLD—*Ashbery*

THE LAST YEAR—*Clark, John W.*

LASTNESS—*Kinnell*

LATE AIR—*Bishop, Elizabeth*

A LATE ANSWER—*Levine*

LATE AUGUST—*Atwood*

LATE AUGUST ON THE LIDO—
Hollander

A LATE ELEGY FOR A BASEBALL
PLAYER—*Stefanile*

LATE-FLOWERING LUST—
Betjeman

THE LATE WASP—*Muir*

LATER—*Yevtushenko*

LATER THAN LAUGHARNE—
Thomas-Ellis

THE LATEST DECALOGUE—*Clough*

LATEST WILL—*Marshall, L. G.*

DER LATTENZAUN—*Morgenstern*

LAUGHING SONG—*Blake*

LAUGHTER AND DEATH—*Blunt*

LAURA—*Diego, José de*

LAURENTIAN SHIELD—*Scott, F. R.*

LAUS DEO!—*Whittier*

LAUSANNE—IN GIBBON'S OLD
GARDEN—*Hardy*

LAUTGEDICHT—*Hausmann,
Raoul*

LAUTGEDICHT—*Malevic*

LAW LIKE LOVE—*Auden*

THE LAW OF THE JUNGLE—
Kipling

THE LAW OF THE YUKON—*Service*

LAY DOWN—*Ginsberg*

THE LAY OF IKE—*Berryman*

THE LAY OF THE LAST MINSTREL—
Scott, Sir Walter

LAY OU PLUSTOST RONDEAU—
Villon

LAZARUS CONVALESCENT—
Simpson

THE LEA-RIG—*Burns*

THE LEAD—*Graves*

THE LEADEN ECHO AND THE
GOLDEN ECHO—*Hopkins*

THE LEADEN-EYED—*Lindsay,
Vachel*

A LEAF-TREADER—*Frost, Robert*

LEAR—*Williams, William
Carlos*

THE LEARNED MEN—*MacLeish*

LEARNING TO TALK—*Day Lewis*

LEAVE A TOUCH OF GLORY—
Marshall, Helen Lowrie

LEAVES FROM A LOOSE-LEAF WAR
DIARY—*Brooks, Gwendolyn*

LEAVES FROM MY GRASS HOUSE—
Blanding

LEAVING EARLY—*Plath*

LEAVING HOME—*Pastan*

LEAVING SOMETHING BEHIND—
Wagoner

LEAVING THE REST UNSAID—
Graves

LEAVING TOWN—*Reeves*

LEBEN EINES MANNES—
Bergengruen

DAS LEBEN OHNE ZEITVERLUST—
Kästner

LEBENSLAUF—*Hölderlin*

LEBENSLAUF—*Morgenstern*

LEBENSPFLICHTEN—*Hölty*

LEBENSWEGE—*Fontane*

LEDA AND THE SWAN—*Yeats*

LEETLA GIORGIO WASHEENTON—
Daly

THE LEFT BEHIND—*MacNeice*

LEFT-OVER LAUGHTER—*Marshall,
Helen Lowrie*

LEFT THE BROTHER DEAD—*Rasul*

THE LEG IN THE SUBWAY—
Williams, Oscar

THE LEGACIE—*Donne*

LEGACIES—*Giovanni*

LEGACY: MY SOUTH—*Randall*

LEGACY RECLAIMED—*Devaul*

LEGAL FICTION—*Empson*

LEGEND—*Auden*

LEGEND—*Crane, Hart*

THE LEGEND OF GOOD WOMEN—
Chaucer

LEGEND OF THE WASHEEN—
McCrimmon

LEGENDE DE LA CHAIR—*Pilon*

LEGENDE DER DIRNE EVELYN ROE
—*Brecht*
LEGENDE VOM TOTEN SOLDATEN
—*Brecht*
LEGENDE VON DER ENTSTEHUNG
DES BUCHES TAOTEKING AUF
DEM WEG DES LAOTSE—*Brecht*
'A LEGGE—*Viviani*
THE LEGS—*Graves*
LEHRGEDICHT ÜBER GESCHICHTE
—*Heissenbüttel*
LEIBREGIMENT—*Tucholsky*
LEIDER—*Busch*
LEIDER—*Roth, Eugen*
DER LEISE NACHBAR—*Roth,
Eugen*
LEISURE—*Davies, William
Henry*
LEITENANT SHMIDT—*Pasternak*
LEJOS—*Espina*
LEMBRANÇA DO MUNDO ANTIGO—
Drummond de Andrade
LEMOND WIND—*Lifshin*
LEMONS—*Kern*
LEMUEL'S BLESSING—*Merwin*
LENORE—*Bürger*
LENORE—*Poe*
LENS—*Wilkinson*
LENT—*Rodgers*
LEONARDO DA VINCI'S—*Moore,
Marianne*
LE LÉOPARD—*Desnos*
LEPANTO—*Chesterton, Gilbert
Keith*
LEPTOMEREIES—*Seferis*
LERN VON DEN WOMBATS—
Bienek
LESBIA—*Stephens*
LESS AND LESS HUMAN, O SAVAGE
SPIRIT—*Stevens, Wallace*
A LESSER PROPHET—*Weiss*
A LESSON—*Keeler*
THE LESSON—*Lucie-Smith*
LESSON FOR BEAUTIFUL WOMEN—
Reid
LESSON IN NATURAL HISTORY—
Spencer
LESSON LESSON—*Ai*
THE LESSON OF THE MOTH—
Marquis
A LESSON TWICE LEARNED NEVER
TO BE FORGOTTEN—*Fabio,
Sarah Webster*
LET APRIL COME—*Stephany*
LET FALL THE GLOWING VEILS—
Stephany
LET ME—*Dupree*
LET ME BE HELD WHEN THE
LONGING COMES—*Stephany*
LET ME DIE A YOUNGMAN'S DEATH
—*McGough*
LET ME ENJOY—*Hardy*
LET ME GO WARM—*Góngora*
LET MY LAST BREATH BE
IMMORTAL SANDALS FOR MY
CHILDREN—*Jeffers, Lance*

LET MY PEOPLE GO—*Johnson,
James Weldon*
LET NOTHING DISTURB THEE—
Teresa de Avila
LET THE CIRCLE BE UNBROKEN—
Colbert
LET US BE MERRY BEFORE WE GO—
Curran
LET US BEGIN THE REAL WORK—
Sanchez
LETANIAS DE NUESTRO SEÑOR DON
QUIJOTE—*Darío*
LE LÉTHÉ—*Baudelaire*
LETO V GORODE—*Pasternak*
LETRILLA—*Cervantes Saavedra*
LET'S GO!—*Marshall, Helen
Lowrie*
LETTER—*Bergman, Alexander F.*
A LETTER—*Hecht*
THE LETTER—*Owen, Wilfred*
THE LETTER ABOUT MONEY—
Warren
LETTER FROM A GIRL—*Bly*
A LETTER FROM BERLIN—
Stallworthy
A LETTER FROM BROOKLYN—
Walcott
LETTER FROM DANNY—*Harkness*
A LETTER FROM LI PO—*Aiken*
A LETTER FROM ROME—*Day
Lewis*
LETTER FROM THE SEASIDE, 1880—
Coward
LETTER TO A MIDNIGHT—*Ciardi*
LETTER TO ALEX COMFORT—*Abse*
LETTER TO ALGIERS—*Robson,
Jeremy*
LETTER TO BELDEN—*Moore,
Rosalie*
A LETTER TO CURTIS BRADFORD—
Davie
LETTER TO HIS MOTHER—
Grenfell
LETTER TO HIS MOTHER—*West*
LETTER TO THE FRONT, VII—
Rukeyser
LETTER TO THE HONORABLE LADY
MISS MARGARET CAVENDISH
HOLLES HARLEY—*Prior*
LETTER 27 MAXIMUS TO DOGTOWN
—*Olson*
LETTER WRITTEN ON A FERRY
WHILE CROSSING LONG ISLAND
SOUND—*Sexton*
LETTERA A MI ROSA—*Di Giacomo*
LETTERA ALLA MADRE—
Quasimodo
LA LETTERA DELLA MAMMA—
Vann'anto
LETTERA MALINCONICA—*Di
Giacomo*
LETTING SALLY GO—*Hobbs*
LETTING THE PLANTS DIE—
Sklarew
DER LETTISCHE HERBST—
Bobrowski
LETTRE—*Bervoets*

LETTRE—*Geraldy*
LETTRE À PIERRE YVERNAULT,
CURÉ DE CAMPAGNE—*Cadou*
LETTRE À SON FRÈRE—*Viau*
LA LETTRE IMAGINAIRE—*Jacob,
Max*
LETTRE ROCK—*Lemaitre*
LETTRES—*Jacob, Max*
U LETTU—*Buttitta*
LETZTE ENTSCHEIDUNG—*Roth,
Eugen*
DER LEU—*Morgenstern*
DER LEUCHTTURM—*Kaschnitz*
LEVANT—*Durrell*
LEVIATHAN—*Merwin*
LI TI'S RÅD—*Martinson*
LIBATION: PRELUDE—*Brathwaite*
LIBERATION FOR WOMEN—*Laepa*
LIBERATION/POEM—*Sanchez*
LIBERTATE, SEÑOR!—*Unamuno*
LIBERTÉ—*Éluard*
LIBERTÉ CONQUISE—*Éluard*
THE LIBERTINE—*MacNeice*
LIBERTY—*Thomas, Edward*
THE LIBERTY POLE—*Trumbull*
THE LIBRARIAN—*Olson*
THE LIBRARY—*Huff, Barbara A.*
THE LIBRARY—*Last Poets*
I LIBRI—*Saba*
LIBRO DE BUEN AMOR—*Ruiz*
LA LICE ET SA COMPAGNE—*La
Fontaine*
A LICK AND A PROMISE—*Scott,
Winfield Townley*
THE LICORICE FIELDS AT
PONTEFRACT—*Betjeman*
LIDDELL AND SCOTT—ON THE
COMPLETION OF THEIR LEXICON
—*Hardy*
THE LIE—*Raleigh*
LIE STILL, SLEEP BECALMED—
Thomas, Dylan
DIE LIEBE—*Heine*
DIE LIEBE—*Hölderlin*
DIE LIEBE—*Hölty*
DIE LIEBE AM KREUZ—*Scheffler*
DIE LIEBENDEN—*Brecht*
LIEBESANTRAG—*Wedekind*
EIN LIEBESLIED—*Lasker-Schüler*
LIEBESLIEDER, 52—*Heine*
LIED—*Arrieta*
DAS LIED DER EISENBAHNTRUPPE
VON FORT DONALD—*Brecht*
LIED DER MÜDEN EMPORER—
Brecht
LIED DER VERDERBTEN UNSCHULD
BEIM WÄSCHEFALTEN—*Brecht*
DAS LIED GENANNT 'ZUR SELBEN
STUNDE'—*Kästner*
DAS LIED VOM EXTRA—*Brecht*
DAS LIED VOM HEILIGEN GEORG—
Anonymous–German
DAS LIED VOM KLASSENFEIND—
Brecht
DAS LIED VOM KLEINEN MANN—
Kästner

DAS LIED VON DER GLEICH-
GÜLTIGKEIT—*Tucholsky*

DAS LIED VON DER GLOCKE—
Schiller

DAS LIED VON DER WOLKE DER
NACHT—*Brecht*

LIED VON EINER DEUTSCHEN
MUTTER—*Brecht*

LIED VON MEINER MUTTER—
Brecht

DIE LIEDER DES BERGMANNS—
Novalis

LE LIEN DE LA TERRE—*Pilon*

LIENS—*Apollinaire*

LIES—*Yevtushenko*

LE LIÈVRE ET LA PERDRIX—*La
Fontaine*

LE LIÈVRE ET LA TORTUE—*La
Fontaine*

LE LIÈVRE ET LES GRENOUILLES—
La Fontaine

LIFE—*Emerson*

LIFE AHEAD—*Levine*

LIFE AND DEATH OF HERO STICK—
Gilbert, Celia

LIFE AT WAR—*Levertov*

LIFE CYCLE IN THE DELTA—*Bass*

LIFE CYCLE OF COMMON MAN—
Nemerov

LIFE CYCLES—*Giovanni*

LIFE HAS NO DIMENSION—*Berger*

THE LIFE I LED—*Giovanni*

LIFE IN A LOVE—*Browning,
Robert*

LIFE IS FINE—*Hughes, Langston*

LIFE IS MORE TRUE THAN REASON
WILL DECEIVE—*Cummings*

LIFE MEETS YOU—*Marshall,
Helen Lowrie*

THE LIFE OF LINCOLN WEST—
Brooks, Gwendolyn

THE LIFE OF SERVICE—*Davie*

LIFE OF THE LOCKSMITH—
Schmitz

LIFE POEM—*Sanchez*

LIFE UNDER MY UMBRELLA—
Gaver

THE LIFEGUARD—*Dickey, James*

LIFT EVERY VOICE—*Johnson,
James Weldon*

LIFTING ILLEGAL NETS BY
FLASHLIGHT—*Wright, James*

LIGHT—*Smith, William Jay*

LIGHT AND MOONBELLS—
Sandburg

LIGHT AS A FEATHER, MAMA—
Brown, Otis

LIGHT AT EQUINOX—*Adams*

LIGHT CASUALTIES—*Francis*

LIGHT OF LOVE—*Parker*

LIGHT SNOWFALL—*Hillyer*

A LIGHT WOMAN—*Browning,
Robert*

LIGHTHEARTED WILLIAM—
Williams, William Carlos

LIGHTING FIRES IN SNOW—
Richards, I. A.

LIGHTNING—*Berryman*

LIGHTNING—*Swenson*

LIGHTS OUT—*Thomas, Edward*

LIKE A RIPPLE IN A POND—
Giovanni

LIKE AN OLD KING IN A PARABLE
—*Smith, A. J. M.*

LIKE GHOSTS OF EAGLES—*Francis*

LIKE SNOW—*Graves*

LIKE SON—*Van Doren*

LIKE THIS TOGETHER—*Rich*

LIKE TO THE FALLING OF A STONE
—*King*

A LIKENESS—*Browning, Robert*

THE LILACS—*Wilbur*

LES LILAS ET LES ROSES—*Aragon*

LILIES—*Thomas-Ellis*

DEN LILLA KOLARGOSSEN—*Geijer*

LIMBO: THE CRACKED MOTHER—
Brathwaite

LIME-FLOWER TEA—*Plomer*

LIMERICKS—*Anonymous–
English–Modern English*

LIMITED—*Sandburg*

LIMITS: THE FOREST—*Brathwaite*

LINCOLN—*Fletcher, John Gould*

LINCOLN—*Lowell, James Russell*

LINCOLN—*Schwartz*

LINCOLN—*Tripp*

LINCOLN CATHEDRAL—
Dickinson, Patric

LINCOLN MONUMENT:
WASHINGTON—*Hughes,
Langston*

LINCOLN, THE MAN OF THE
PEOPLE—*Markham*

LINCOLN THEATRE—*Hughes,
Langston*

A LINCOLNSHIRE CHURCH—
Betjeman

LINDEN LEA—*Barnes, William*

DER LINDENBAUM—*Müller*

LINE AND FORM—*Dudek*

THE LINE-GANG—*Frost, Robert*

THE LINES—*Jarrell*

LINES—*Shelley*

LINES ADDED TO SCHILLER'S
WALLENSTEIN—*Coleridge,
Samuel Taylor*

LINES COMPOSED A FEW MILES
ABOVE TINTERN ABBEY—
Wordsworth

LINES FOR A PRESIDENT—*Watson*

LINES FOR AN UNKNOWN LOVER—
Logan

LINES FOR RICHARD WRIGHT—
Emanuel

LINES ON THE MERMAID TAVERN—
Keats

LINES TO A DON—*Belloc*

LINES TO A MOVEMENT IN
MOZART'S E-FLAT SYMPHONY—
Hardy

LINES TO A WORLD-FAMOUS POET
WHO FAILED TO COMPLETE A
WORLD-FAMOUS POEM—*Nash*

LINES TO A YORKSHIRE TERRIER—
Eliot, Thomas Stearns

LINES TO BE EMBROIDERED ON A
BIB—*Nash*

LINES TO MY DAUGHTER—
Goldstein

LINES WRITTEN IN DEJECTION ON
THE EVE OF GREAT SUCCESS—
Frost, Robert

LINES WRITTEN IN EARLY SPRING
—*Wordsworth*

LINES WRITTEN IN OREGON—
Nabokov

LINES WRITTEN NOV. 22/23—1963—
Corso

LINGUA E DIALETTU—*Buttitta*

THE LION—*Lindsay, Vachel*

THE LION—*Nash*

LION—*Swenson*

THE LION—*Williams, William
Carlos*

LION AND HONEYCOMB—
Nemerov

THE LION AND THE SHEEP—*Roche*

LE LION DEVENU VIEUX—*La
Fontaine*

LE LION ET LE MOUCHERON—*La
Fontaine*

LE LION ET LE RAT—*La Fontaine*

A LION IN THE WIND—*Simpson*

A LION NAMED PASSION—
Hollander

THE LION TAMER—*Clark, John
W.*

THE LIONS OF FIRE—*Patchen*

LISTEN COMRADES—*Diop*

LISTEN COMRADES—*Lee, Don L.*

LISTEN, I'SE TALKIN' TO YOU, LAWD
—*Hodges*

LISTEN LORD—*Johnson, James
Weldon*

LISTEN TO BIG BLACK AT S. F.
STATE—*Sanchez*

LISTENERS—*De la Mare*

LISTENING TO JIMMY GARRISON—
Sanchez

LISTENING TO SONNY ROLLINS AT
THE FIVE-SPOT—*Blackburn,
Paul*

LITANIA ALLE PORTE DI
LEOPOLDVILLE—*Bevilacqua*

LITANY FOR DICTATORSHIPS—
Benét, Stephen Vincent

EN LITEN ATENARE—*Asplund*

LITERARY EVENING JAMAICA—
Morris, Mervyn

THE LITERARY PARTY—*Colbert*

A LITTLE ABOUT WITCHES—*De la
Mare*

LITTLE APOCALYPSE—*Hill*

LITTLE BILLEE—*Gilbert, Sir
William Schwenck*

THE LITTLE BIRD—
*Anonymous–African
languages–Gabon*

THE LITTLE BLACK BOY—*Blake*

THE LITTLE BLACK HEN—*Milne*

LITTLE BLUE PIGEON—*Field, Eugene*

LITTLE BO-PEEP—*Children's Verses and Nursery Rhymes*

LITTLE BOY BLUE—*Field, Eugene*

THE LITTLE BOY FOUND—*Blake*

A LITTLE BOY LOST—*Blake*

THE LITTLE BOY LOST—*Blake*

THE LITTLE BOY WITH THE LONG NAME—*Children's Verses and Nursery Rhymes*

LITTLE BREECHES—*Hay, John*

LITTLE BROTHER'S SECRET—*Mansfield*

LITTLE CANDLE—*Sandburg*

THE LITTLE CHIRPING BIRDS—*Goodman, Godfrey*

LITTLE COTTAGE—*Andersen*

LITTLE ELEGY FOR GERTRUDE STEIN—*Brinnin*

THE LITTLE ELF—*Bangs*

LITTLE FOLKS IN THE GRASS—*Wynne*

LITTLE GIDDING—*Eliot, Thomas Stearns*

LITTLE GIRL—*Sexton*

THE LITTLE GIRL FOUND—*Blake*

THE LITTLE GIRL LOST—*Blake*

LITTLE GIRL, MY STRING BEAN, MY LOVELY WOMAN—*Sexton*

THE LITTLE GREEN ORCHARD—*De la Mare*

LITTLE HEN—*Children's Verses and Nursery Rhymes*

LITTLE HORSE—*Williams, Tennessee*

LITTLE JOHNNY'S CONFESSION—*Patten*

LITTLE JOHNNY'S FINAL LETTER—*Patten*

LITTLE JUMPING JOAN—*Children's Verses and Nursery Rhymes*

THE LITTLE LAND—*Stevenson*

LITTLE LYRIC (OF GREAT IMPORTANCE)—*Hughes, Langston*

LITTLE MAN AND LITTLE MAID—*Children's Verses and Nursery Rhymes*

THE LITTLE MOUSE—*Colum*

LITTLE MUSGRAVE AND LADY BARNARD—*Anonymous–English–Modern English*

THE LITTLE OLD LADY IN LAVENDER SILK—*Parker*

LITTLE OLD LETTER—*Hughes, Langston*

LITTLE ORPHANT ANNIE—*Riley*

LITTLE PAPOOSE—*Conkling*

THE LITTLE PEASANT—*Sexton*

LITTLE PIGS—*Children's Verses and Nursery Rhymes*

THE LITTLE ROAD—*Turner, Nancy Byrd*

A LITTLE SERVANT MAID—*Belloc*

LITTLE SISTER BIG—*Gaver*

LITTLE SLEEP'S–HEAD SPROUTING HAIR IN THE MOONLIGHT—*Kinnell*

THE LITTLE SNAIL—*Conkling*

A LITTLE SONG OF LIFE—*Reese*

LITTLE TALK—*Fisher*

LITTLE THINGS—*Stephens*

THE LITTLE TURTLE—*Lindsay, Vachel*

THE LITTLE WHISTLER—*Frost, Frances M.*

LITTLE WILLIE ARMSTRONG JONES—*Last Poets*

LITTLE WIND—*Greenaway*

LITURGIE VOM HAUCH—*Brecht*

THE LITURGY OF SMALL SUSAN—*Fitts*

LIV SOM GRÄS—*Lundkvist*

LIV VEL, JENNY LIND—*Andersen*

LIVE—*Sexton*

THE LIVE MANNEQUIN AT RANDOLPH'S—*Harteis*

'A LIVELLA—*Totò*

LIVING—*Levertov*

LIVING HIGH OFF NICKELS AND DIMES—*Pines*

LIVING IN THE OPEN—*Piercy*

THE LIVING TEMPLE—*Holmes, Oliver Wendell*

LIVRE DE MON BORD—*Pilon*

LIVSBÅTEN—*Lagerkvist*

LIZARD AT POMPEII—*Deutsch*

LLAMADO—*Storni*

LLANTO DE UN PÁJARO POR EL POETA MUERTO—*Zardoya*

LLANTO POR ABEL—*Conde*

LLANTO POR IGNACIO SÁNCHEZ MEJÍAS—*Garcia Lorca*

¿LLORAR? ¿POR QUE?—*Nervo*

LA LLUVIA METAFISICA—*Martinez Alonso*

LOAF OF TIME—*Swenson*

LOBNAYA BALLADA—*Voznesensky*

THE LOBSTER POT—*Arden*

LOBSTERPOT LABYRINTHS—*Hoffman*

LOCAL PRESS—*Sitwell, Osbert*

LOCALITIES—*Sandburg*

LOCHINVAR—*Scott, Sir Walter*

LOCKSLEY HALL—*Tennyson*

LOCUTIONS DES PIERROTS—*Laforgue*

LA LOLA—*Garcia Lorca*

LOLLINGDON DOWNS—*Masefield*

LOLMO—*Johnson, Tom*

LONDON—*Blake*

LONDON—*Johnson, Samuel*

LONDON 1802—*Wordsworth*

LONDON SAD LONDON—*Anonymous–English–Modern English*

LONDON SNOW—*Bridges*

LONDON'S WELCOME—*Anonymous–English–Modern English*

LONE DOG—*McLeod*

THE LONE, IMMORTAL CAR—*Abbe*

THE LONE RANGER—*Hall*

A LONE STRIKE—*Frost, Robert*

A LONELINESS—*Lee, Don L.*

THE LONELY FARMER—*Thomas, Ronald Stuart*

THE LONELY SCARECROW—*Kirkup*

THE LONESOME GREEN APPLE—*Conkling*

THE LONG ALLEY—*Roethke*

THE LONG DAYS—*Press*

LONG FEUD—*Untermeyer*

LONG GONE—*Brown, Sterling A*

THE LONG-HAIRED MALE OF THE SPECIES—*Marshall, Helen Lowrie*

LONG HAUL—*Elmslie*

THE LONG HILL—*Teasdale*

LONG JOHN NELSON AND SWEETIE PIE—*Walker*

THE LONG-LEGGED FLY—*Yeats*

THE LONG PARTY—*Scott, Winfield Townley*

THE LONG SMALL ROOM—*Thomas, Edward*

LONG TRIP—*Hughes, Langston*

LONG VIEW: NEGRO—*Hughes, Langston*

THE LONG WAR—*Lee, Laurie*

THE LONGEST WAY IS BACK—*Ciardi*

LONTANA—*Pascoli*

LOOK AT THAT GAL—*Bond*

LOOK BACK—*Clark, John W.*

THE LOOK OF LOVE—*Connor*

LOOK WHAT YOU DID, CHRISTOPHER—*Nash*

LOOKING ACROSS THE FIELDS AND WATCHING THE BIRDS FLY—*Stevens, Wallace*

LOOKING AT EACH OTHER—*Rukeyser*

LOOKING AT HENRY MOORE'S ELEPHANT SKULL ETCHINGS IN JERUSALEM DURING THE WAR—*Kaufman, Shirley*

LOOKING FOR MY BROTHER UNDER THE GROUND—*Colbert*

LOOKING FOR THE BUCKHEAD BOYS—*Dickey, James*

LOOKING FORWARD—*Stevenson*

LOOKING-GLASS—*Levertov*

LOOKING-GLASS RIVER—*Stevenson*

LOOKING INTO A FACE—*Bly*

LOOKING INTO HISTORY—*Wilbur*

LÖPSEDEL—*Ferlin*

LORD LUNDY—*Belloc*

LORD LUNDY, WHO WAS TOO FREELY MOVED TO TEARS—*Belloc*

LORD OF THE RINGS—*Tolkien*

LORD RANDAL—*Anonymous–English–Modern English*

LORD RONALD—
Anonymous–English–
Modern English
LORD ULLIN'S DAUGHTER—
Campbell, Thomas
DIE LORELEI—Heine
LORELEI—Plath
LORSQUE TU FERMERAS—
Verhaeren
LOS ANGELES—Alexander
LOSERS—Sandburg
LOSING TRACK—Levertov
LOSSES—Jarrell
LOST—Sandburg
LOST ANCHORS—Robinson,
Edwin Arlington
THE LOST BABY POEM—Clifton
THE LOST LEADER—Browning,
Robert
LOST LOVE—Hardy
THE LOST MISTRESS—Browning,
Robert
THE LOST SON—Roethke
THE LOTUS-EATERS—Tennyson
LOUANGES D'ANJOU—Du Bellay
LOUIS XVI S'EN VA À LA
GUILLOTINE—Péret
LE LOUP DEVENU BERGER—La
Fontaine
LE LOUP ET LA CICOGNE—La
Fontaine
LE LOUP ET L'AGNEAU—La
Fontaine
LE LOUP ET LE CHIEN—La
Fontaine
LE LOUP, LA CHÈVRE ET LE
CHEVREAU—La Fontaine
LE LOUP, LA MÈRE ET L'ENFANT—
La Fontaine
LES LOUPS ET LES BREBIS—La
Fontaine
LOUSY PETER—Sitwell, Osbert
LOVE—Calverley
LOVE—Herbert
LOVE—Nemerov
LOVE—Peele
LOVE AMONG THE RUINS—
Browning, Robert
LOVE AND LIFE—Rochester, Earl
of
LOVE AND PITY—Day Lewis
LOVE ARM'D—Behn, Aphra
LOVE CALLS US TO THE THINGS OF
THIS WORLD—Wilbur
LOVE COMES HARDER TO THE
AGED—Ferlinghetti
LOVE FOR A HAND—Shapiro,
Karl
A LOVE FOR PATSY—Thompson,
John
LOVE FROM ARTHUR RAINBOW—
Henri
LOVE IN A LIFE—Browning,
Robert
LOVE IN A VILLAGE—Bickerstaffe
LOVE-IN-IDLENESS—Beddoes
LOVE IN PARTICULAR—Brinnin

LOVE IN THE ASYLUM—Thomas,
Dylan
LOVE IN THE VALLEY—Meredith,
George
LOVE IS—Darr
LOVE IS—Henri
LOVE LETTERS TO HANS CHRISTIAN
ANDERSEN—Sandburg
LOVE LIVES BEYOND THE TOMB—
Clare
LOVE POEM—Bly
LOVE POEM—Gallagher, Tess
LOVE POEM—Knight, Etheridge
LOVE POEM—Lorde
LOVE POEM—Marshall,
Lenore G.
LOVE POEM—Nims
LOVE POEM IN AN OCCUPIED
COUNTRY—Chapin
THE LOVE POT—Hughes, Ted
LOVE SONG—
Anonymous–American
Indian languages–Chippewa
LOVE SONG—Hughes, Ted
LOVE SONG—Kizer
LOVE SONG—Parker
LOVE SONG: I AND THOU—Dugan
THE LOVE SONG OF J. ALFRED
PRUFROCK—Eliot, Thomas
Stearns
LOVE SPEAKS—Marshall, Helen
Lowrie
A LOVE STORY—Graves
LOVE THE WILD SWAN—Jeffers,
Robinson
LOVE THIS LAND—Marshall,
Helen Lowrie
THE LOVE UNFEIGNED—Chaucer
LOVE WITHOUT HOPE—Graves
LOVE YOU RIGHT BACK—Brooks,
Gwendolyn
LOVELY BED—Balthasa
THE LOVELY LASS O' INVERNESS—
Burns
A LOVELY TIME TO WALK—
Marshall, Helen Lowrie
THE LOVER MOURNS FOR THE LOSS
OF LOVE—Yeats
THE LOVER PLEADS WITH HIS
FRIEND FOR OLD FRIENDS—
Yeats
THE LOVERS—Kramer
THE LOVERS—Smith, William
Jay
A LOVER'S ANGER—Prior
A LOVER'S COMPLAINT—Raleigh
THE LOVER'S GHOST—Simpson
THE LOVERS GO FLY A KITE—
Snodgrass
LOVERS HOW THEY COME AND
PART—Herrick
THE LOVER'S SONG—Yeats
LOVES ALCHYMIE—Donne
LOVES DUTIE—Donne
LOVE'S FAREWELL—Drayton
LOVES INFINITENESS—Donne

LOVE'S LABOUR'S LOST—
Shakespeare
LOVES OF THE PUPPETS—Wilbur
LOVE'S PHILOSOPHY—Shelley
LOVE'S PROGRESS—Donne
LOVE'S PROGRESS—Roethke
LOVE'S RELATIVE—Stone, Ruth
LOVE'S SECRET—Blake
LOVING—Kaufman, Shirley
LOW FIELDS AND LIGHT—Merwin
THE LOW SKY—Jeffers, Robinson
LOW TIDE—Williams, Hugo
THE LOW-DOWN WHITE—Service
LUCASTA—Lovelace, Richard
LUCCA—Ungaretti
LUCCA SIGNORELLI TO HIS SON—
Lee-Hamilton
'O LUCIANO D' 'O RRE—Russo
LUCIEN MIDNIGHT: THE SOUNDS
OF THE UNIVERSE IN MY
WINDOW—Kerouac
LUCINDA MATLOCK—Masters,
Edgar Lee
LUCIUS ATHERTON—Masters,
Edgar Lee
LUDOVICO E SARCHIAPONE—Totò
LUEURS DANS LES TÉNÈBRES—
Jacob, Max
DIE LUFT—Morgenstern
DIE LUFT RIECHT SCHON NACH
SCHNEE—Kirsch
LUGNT—Ferlin
LULLABY—Adams
A LULLABY—Agee
A LULLABY—Austin, William
LULLABY—Collymore
A LULLABY—Field, Eugene
A LULLABY—Jarrell
A LULLABY—Lewis, Janet
LULLABY—MacManus
LULLABY—Sitwell, Edith
LULLABY—Rossman
LULLABY FOR JUMBO—Sitwell,
Edith
LULLABY FOR PEREGRINE—Coffin
LULLABYE OF A WOMAN OF THE
MOUNTAINS—Pearse
LUMUMBA SECTION—Kgositsile
LA LUNA AL GUINZAGLIO—Rodari
LA LUNA BAMBINA—Rodari
LA LUNA Y LA MUERTE—Garcia
Lorca
LUNCH AT THE COQ D'OR—
Davison, Peter
LUNCH IN THE LAND OF PLENTY—
Treitel
LUNCHTIME LECTURE—Clark,
Gillian
LA LUNE BLANCHE—Verlaine
LUNE COULEUR DE SANG—Jacob,
Max
LUNG-FISH—MacPherson
LUNG SYI SYING—Chen Dau
LUTO EN AL-ANDALUS—
Abu-l-Hasan al-Husri, "el
ciego"
LUXURY—Levertov

LA LUZ EN EL ALMA—*Martinez Alonso*
LA LUZ ES ALIMENTO—*Pardo Garcia*
LYANG JOU TRZ—*Wang Han*
LYCIDAS—*Milton*
LYDIA HUMPHREY—*Masters, Edgar Lee*
LYING AWAKE—*Snodgrass*
LYING IN A HAMMOCK AT WILLIAM DUFFY'S FARM—*Wright, James*
A LYKE-WAKE DIRGE—*Anonymous–English–Modern English*
LYNCHBAUM—*Hughes, Langston*
LYREBIRDS—*Wright, Judith*
A LYRIC—*Swinburne*
LYRIC FOR LEGACIES—*Herrick*
LYRISCHES INTERMEZZO—*Heine*
LYUDI—*Yevtushenko*

M., SINGING—*Bogan*
MA BOHÈME—*Rimbaud*
MA' CHEER—*Gaver*
MA CONCIERGE DETESTE LES MONGOLS—*Obaldia*
MA LORD—*Hughes, Langston*
MA RAINEY—*Brown, Sterling A.*
MA VIE DURANT—*Cendrars*
MABEL KELLY—*Clarke*
MABINOG'S LITURGY—*Jones, David*
MACAVITY: THE MYSTERY CAT—*Eliot, Thomas Stearns*
MAC FLECKNOE—*Dryden*
DIE MACHT DES GESANGES—*Schiller*
MAD AS THE MIST AND SNOW—*Yeats*
MAD WOMAN—*Fox, Siv Cedering*
MADAM AND HER MADAM—*Hughes, Langston*
MADAM AND HER MIGHT-HAVE-BEEN—*Hughes, Langston*
MADAM AND THE CENSUS MAN—*Hughes, Langston*
MADAM AND THE CHARITY CHILD—*Hughes, Langston*
MADAM AND THE FORTUNE TELLER—*Hughes, Langston*
MADAM AND THE MINISTER—*Hughes, Langston*
MADAM AND THE NUMBER WRITER—*Hughes, Langston*
MADAM AND THE PHONE BILL—*Hughes, Langston*
MADAM AND THE RENT MAN—*Hughes, Langston*
MADAM AND THE WRONG VISITOR—*Hughes, Langston*
MADAME CARNELIA DOES SOLEMNLY SWEAR TO FULFILL EVERY CLAIM SHE MAKES—*Gilbert, Celia*
MADAM'S CALLING CARD—*Hughes, Langston*

MADAM'S PAST HISTORY—*Hughes, Langston*
DAS MÄDCHEN AUS DER FREMDE—*Schiller*
MADE IN HEAVEN—*Porter, Peter*
LOS MADEROS DE SAN JUAN—*Silva*
THE MADMAN'S HOUSE—*Broughton*
MADNESS ONE MONDAY EVENING—*Fields*
MADRE—*Oquendo de Amat*
LA MADRE—*Ungaretti*
MADRECITA—*Flint*
MADRIGAL—*Cetina*
MADRIGAL—*Derwood*
MADRIGAL—*Garcia Lorca*
MADRIGAL—*Góngora*
MADRIGAL—*Hernández, José P. H.*
MADRIGAL ESCRITO EN INVIERNO—*Neruda*
MADRIGAL: THIS LIFE—*Drummond of Hawthornden*
MADRIGAL TRISTE—*Baudelaire*
MADRUGADA—*Jiménez*
MADRUGADA—*Paz*
MADURAI—*Paz*
MAG—*Sandburg*
LES MAGASINS DE LA RUE—*Ducasse*
MAGDALINA—*Pasternak*
THE MAGIC WOOD—*Treece*
MAGIC WORDS TO RUN (AND RUIN) THE WORLD BY—*Eckels*
THE MAGICAL MOUSE—*Patchen*
THE MAGICIAN—*Peretz*
THE MAGICIAN AND THE BARON'S DAUGHTER—*Anonymous–English–Modern English*
THE MAGNET—*Stone, Ruth*
THE MAGNETIC MOUNTAIN—*Day Lewis*
MAGNIFICAT—*Kendrick*
MAGNIFICENCE—*Skelton, John*
MAGNOLIA—*Davis, Thulami Nkabinde*
A MAGUS—*Ciardi*
MAGWEBA—*Kern*
MAHNUNG—*Fleming*
MAHOMETS-GESANG—*Goethe*
THE MAID AND THE FLAME—*Goldstein*
THE MAIDEN LAY IN THE WILDS—*Anonymous–English–Modern English*
THE MAID-SERVANT AT THE INN—*Parker*
MAIL CALL—*Jarrell*
MAILIED—*Goethe*
DIE MAINACHT—*Hölty*
THE MAIN-DEEP—*Stephens*
MAINE—*Booth*
A MAINE ROUSTABOUT—*Eberhart*
LES MAINS JOINTES—*Soupault*
MAINTENANT IL SE TROUVERA—*Cendrars*
LA MAISON DE SYLVIE—*Viau*

LA MAISON DU BERGER—*Vigny*
MAKE BIG MONEY AT HOME—WRITE POEMS IN SPARE TIME—*Nemerov*
MAKE IT RADIANT—*Marshall, Helen Lowrie*
MAKE UP—*Giovanni*
MAKE WAY!—*Marshall, Helen Lowrie*
MAKING A CALL—*Patten*
MAKING A LIVING—*Sexton*
MALAMAN—*Lockwood*
IL MALATINO—*Rodari*
MALCOLM—*Sanchez*
MALCOLM SPOKE / WHO LISTENED—*Lee, Don L.*
MALCOLM X—*Brooks, Gwendolyn*
THE MALDIVE SHARK—*Melville*
MALWINE—*Tucholsky*
MAMA—*Lifshin*
MAMMA—*Di Giacomo*
MAMMON—*Brathwaite*
THE MAMMON OF INIQUITY—*Roche*
MAN—*Corso*
MAN—*Herbert*
MAN—*Vaughan, Henry*
MAN ABOVE THE MOUNTAINS—*Marshall, Helen Lowrie*
MAN ALONE—*Bogan*
MAN AND WIFE—*Lowell, Robert*
MAN AS (EVERYTHING BUT) MAN—*Gaver*
THE MAN AT MIDCENTURY—*Scott, Winfield Townley*
A MAN CAN COMPLAIN, CAN'T HE—*Nash*
THE MAN COMING TOWARD YOU—*Williams, Oscar*
THE MAN FROM A FAR COUNTRY—*Sitwell, Edith*
THE MAN HE KILLED—*Hardy*
THE MAN IN THAT AIRPLANE—*Williams, Oscar*
THE MAN IN THE BOILER ROOM IS—*Lifshin*
THE MAN IN THE DEAD MACHINE—*Hall*
THE MAN IN THE MIRROR IN A ROOM LIT BY ONE LAMP—*Hobbs*
THE MAN IN THE MOON CAME DOWN TOO SOON—*Tolkien*
THE MAN IN THE RECREATION ROOM—*Harkness*
THE MAN OF LAW'S PREAMBLE AND TALE—*Chaucer*
THE MAN OF MODE: EPILOGUE—*Dryden*
THE MAN OF MY DREAMS—*Cuomo*
A MAN OF THE MIDDLE CLASS—*Brooks, Gwendolyn*
MAN ON THE OTHER SIDE—*Lee, Laurie*
MAN THINKING ABOUT WOMAN—*Lee, Don L.*

THE MAN WHOM THE SEA KEPT AWAKE—*Bly*
MAN WITH A FURNACE IN HIS HAND—*Jeffers, Lance*
THE MAN WITH THE BLUE GUITAR—*Stevens, Wallace*
THE MAN WITH THE BROKEN FINGERS—*Sandburg*
THE MAN WITH THE ELEGANT FEET —*Edson*
THE MAN WITH THE GOLDEN ADAM'S APPLE—*Patchen*
THE MAN WITH THE HOE—*Markham*
MAÑANA—*Garcia Lorca*
MAÑANA—*Valverde*
EL MAÑANA EFÍMERO—*Machado, Antonio*
LA MANCA—*Mistral*
UNA MANCHA SOMBRIA—*Castro, Rosalía de*
THE MANCIPLE'S TALE—*Chaucer*
MANDALAY—*Kipling*
MANDELA'S SERMON—*Kgositsile*
MANDOLINE—*Verlaine*
MANDRAKE—*MacPherson*
THE MANLY HEART—*Wither*
MANNAHATTA—*Whitman*
MANNEN UTAN VÄG—*Lindegren*
THE MANNER OF THE WORLD NOWADAYS—*Skelton, John*
MANNERS—*Merriam*
MÄNNISKANS HEM—*Blomberg*
MÄNNISKORNAS ÖGON—*Bergman, Bo*
'A MANO D'OPERA— *Viviani*
MANO ENTREGADA—*Aleixandre*
A MAN'S A MAN—*Brecht*
A MAN'S A MAN FOR A' THAT—*Burns*
A MAN'S WORK—*MacLeish*
MÅNSKEN PÅ STRÖMMEN—*Bergman, Bo*
UN MANSO RIO—*Castro, Rosalía de*
MANTICES— *Wellman*
MS FOUND UNDER A SERVIETTE IN A LOVELY HOME—*Nash*
THE MANZANITA— *Winters*
A MAP OF THE CITY—*Gunn*
MAPLE AND SUMAC—*Day Lewis*
MAPLES IN A SPRUCE FOREST—*Updike*
DIE MÄR VOM RITTER MANUEL—*Miegel*
MARC CHAGALL—*Kurtz*
MARC CHAGALL AND HIS HORSE—*Ferlinghetti*
THE MARCH—*Lowell, Robert*
MARCH INTO VIRGINIA (JULY 1861) —*Melville*
MARCH ON THE DELTA—*Berger*
MARCH TWILIGHT—*Bogan*
MARCHA TRIUNFAL—*Darío*
MARCHING SONG—*Stevenson*
MARGARET FULLER SLACK—*Masters, Edgar Lee*

MARGARITA—*Darío*
MARIA—*Brecht*
MARIA MAGDALENA AM GRABE DES HEILANDS— *Weissenburg*
MARIA, WHO MADE FACES AND A DEPLORABLE MARRIAGE—*Belloc*
LE MARIAGE RUTEBOEUF—*Ruteboeuf*
MARIANA—*Tennyson*
MARIANA PINEDA—*Garcia Lorca*
MARIE—*Apollinaire*
MARIE BATESON—*Masters, Edgar Lee*
MARIE MAGDELEINE—*Lasnier*
LA MARIÉE MISE À NU PAR SES CÉLEBATAIRES, MÊME—*Duchamp*
DAS MARIENLEBEN—*Rilke*
MARINA—*Eliot, Thomas Stearns*
MARINE—*Fombeure*
MARINE—*Queneau*
MARINER MAN—*Sitwell, Edith*
MARINERO EN TIERRA—*Alberti*
MARIONETTERNA—*Bergman, Bo*
MARIPOSA—*Vargas*
ER MARITO PASCIOCCONE—*Belli*
MARIZIBILL—*Apollinaire*
MARK—*Blackburn, Thomas*
MARK—*Bogan*
THE MARKET—*Snyder*
THE MARKET—*Stephens*
THE MARKET-GIRL—*Hardy*
MARKET WOMEN'S CRIES—*Swift*
MARMION—*Scott, Sir Walter*
MARRAKECH—*Eberhart*
MARRIAGE—*Clarke*
MARRIAGE—*Strand*
MARRIAGE RING—*Crabbe*
MARRIED IS BETTER— *Viorst*
MARS—*Joselow*
MARSCHLIED—*Zuckmayer*
MARSEILLE—*Mehring*
THE MARSHAL—*Berrigan*
THE MARSHES OF GLYNN—*Lanier*
MARTHA—*De la Mare*
MARTIAL—*Surrey*
MARTÍN FIERRO—*Hernández, José*
EL MARTIRIO—*Garcia Lorca*
MARTIRIO DE SAN SEBASTIAN—*Florit*
MARTIRIO DE SANTA OLALLA—*Garcia Lorca*
MARY-ANNE—*Sitwell, Osbert*
MARY COBWEB—*Conkling*
MARY COMPLAINS TO OTHER MOTHERS—*Anonymous-English—Modern English*
MARY HYNES—*Stephens*
MARY LINCOLN TAKING LEAVE—*Ascasubi*
MARY MORISON—*Burns*
MARY'S SONG—*Plath*
MÄRZ. BRIEF NACH MERAN—*Benn*
MARZO—*Di Giacomo*

LA MÁS BELLA NIÑA—*Góngora*
EL MÁS FIEL—*Jiménez*
MASK—*Arnez*
MASK— *Yeats*
THE MASK OF ANARCHY—*Shelley*
DIE MASKE DES BÖSEN—*Brecht*
A MASQUE FOR BUCKINGHAM—*Ciardi*
THE MASQUE OF MUMMERS—*MacLeish*
A MASQUE OF REASON—*Frost, Robert*
MASS MAN— *Walcott*
MASSISSI—*Deveaux*
MAST'ERICO— *Viviani*
THE MASTERY—*Eberhart*
A MATCH—*Swinburne*
MATERNA—*Bevilacqua*
MATERNIDAD—*Pedroni*
MATHILDE, ABER EINGERAHMT—*Kästner*
MATILDA, WHO TOLD LIES, AND WAS BURNED TO DEATH—*Belloc*
LE MATIN— *Viau*
'E MATINA, PE TULETO—*Di Giacomo*
MATINAL—*Celaya*
MATINÉE D'IVRESSE—*Rimbaud*
MATISSE—*Stein, Gertrude*
MATLOCK BATH—*Betjeman*
LA MATRIGNA—*Palazzeschi*
LE MATRIOTE—*Obaldia*
A MATTER OF TASTE—*Merriam*
THE MATTER: THE TOWER STRUCK BY LIGHTNING—*Piercy*
MATTERS ARISING—*Garlick*
MATTHEW COLE—*Brooks, Gwendolyn*
MAU WU WEI CHYOU FENG SWO PWO GE—*Du Fu*
MAUD—*Patten*
MAUD—*Tennyson*
MAUDE MULLER— *Whittier*
MAUDLIN—*Plath*
MAUI'S FAREWELL—*Somerville*
DIE MAULWÜRFE—*Kästner*
MAURICIO IS DEAD—*Figueroa*
DIE MAUSEFALLE—*Morgenstern*
MAUVAIS SANG—*Rimbaud*
LE MAUVAIS VITRIER—*Baudelaire*
MAXIE—*Layton*
MAXIM—*Miles*
MAXIMUS FROM DOGTOWN—*Olson*
MAXIMUS POEM—JULY 24, 1968—*Olson*
MAY DAY—*Colum*
MAY DAY—*Marshall, Helen Lowrie*
MAY DAY—*Rexroth*
MAY 1506—*Scott, Winfield Townley*
MAY-FLY—*Heath-Stubbs*
THE MAY MAGNIFICAT—*Hopkins*
MAYAN LETTER—*Olson*
MAYBE—*Sandburg*
MAYDAY ON HOLDERNESS—*Hughes, Ted*

MAYFLOWER—*Aiken*
'O MBRIACO—*Bovio*
ME AND THE MULE—*Hughes, Langston*
ME NE VADO—*Cattafi*
ME TIRASTE UN LIMÓN—*Hernández, Miguel*
ME VEDO UN BASTIMENTO IN MESA RADA—*Marin*
MEA CULPA, MEA CULPA—*Goldstein*
MEAD—*Anonymous–English—Old English*
MEADOW IN SUMMER—*Sandburg*
MEADOW LARK—*Marshall, Helen Lowrie*
MEAN ANNUAL RAINFALL—*Sukenick*
MEAN SONG—*Merriam*
THE MEANING OF AFRICA—*Nicol*
THE MEANING OF DEATH—*Tate, Allen*
THE MEANING OF LIFE—*Tate, Allen*
MEASURE FOR MEASURE—*Shakespeare*
MEASURE ME SKY—*Speyer*
A MEASURE OF CASUALNESS—*Graves*
MEASUREMENTS—*Ciardi*
THE MECHANIC—*Wakoski*
MECIENDO—*Mistral*
MEDIOCRITY IN LOVE REJECTED—*Carew*
MEDITATIO—*Pound*
MEDITATION—*Eberhart*
MEDITATION—*Fuller, Roy*
MEDITATION—*Palladas*
MEDITATION—*Taylor, Edward*
MEDITATION—*Wheelock*
MEDITATION ON A MEMOIR—*Cunningham, James Vincent*
MEDITATION ON BEAVERS—*Lucian of Samosata*
MEDITATION ON THE A30—*Betjeman*
MEDITATION TWO—*Eberhart*
THE MEDITERRANEAN—*Tate, Allen*
MEDITERRANÉE—*Senghor*
MEDNIE DENGI—*Slutsky*
MEDUSA—*Bogan*
MEDUSA—*Plath*
MEDUSA AND THE MOT JUSTE—*Nash*
MEERESSTRAND—*Storm*
MEET—*Lorde*
MEET-ON-THE-ROAD—*Coatsworth*
THE MEETING—*Bahati*
THE MEETING—*Bogan*
THE MEETING—*Graves*
THE MEETING—*Williams, Hugo*
MEETING AT NIGHT—*Browning, Robert*
EL MEETING DE LA HUMANIDAD—*Benavente*

A MEETING IN N'HAMPTON—*Malanga*
MEETING OF CULTURES—*Davie*
THE MEETING PLACE—*Robinson, Wanda*
MEETING POINT—*MacNeice*
MEG MERRILIES—*Keats*
MEGIO 'L SILENSIO—*Marin*
MEIN—*Anonymous–German*
MEIN BLAUES KLAVIER—*Lasker-Schüler*
MEIN EIGENTUM—*Hölderlin*
MEIN LIESCHEN—*Wedekind*
MEIN TAG WAR HEITER—*Heine*
MEIN TOD—EIN FROMMER WUNSCH—*Zuckmayer*
MEINER MUTTER—*Ben-Chorin*
MEINER MUTTER—*Brecht*
LA MEJICANA—*Graves*
MELAMPUS—*Meredith, George*
MELANCHOLIE—*Benn*
MELCHIOR VULPIUS—*Moore, Marianne*
MELODIE—*Heine*
MELPOMENE—*Capdevila*
THE MELTING POT—*Randall*
LES MEMBRES ET L'ESTOMAC—*La Fontaine*
MEMENTO—*Garcia Lorca*
MEMENTO—*Scott, Winfield Townley*
MEMENTO—*Spender*
MEMENTOS—*Brontë, Charlotte*
MEMORABILIA—*Browning, Robert*
MEMORIA—*Nobre*
MEMORIA DE LA PLATA—*Vivanco*
MEMORIA INMORTAL DE DON PEDRO GIRON, DUQUE DE OSUNA—*Quevedo y Villegas*
MEMORIAL—*Sanchez*
MEMORIAL—*Van Doren*
MEMORIAL DAY—*Marshall, Helen Lowrie*
MEMORIAL VERSES—*Arnold*
MEMORIAL WREATH—*Randall*
MEMORIES OF A LOST WAR—*Simpson*
MEMORIES OF PRESIDENT LINCOLN—*Whitman*
MEMORIES OF WEST STREET AND LEPKE—*Lowell, Robert*
MEMORY—*Allingham*
MEMORY—*Marshall, Helen Lowrie*
MEMORY—*Roethke*
MEMORY—*Rossetti, Christina*
MEMORY—*Scott, F. R.*
A MEMORY OF THE PLAYERS IN A MIRROR AT MIDNIGHT—*Joyce*
MEMORY OF WINTER MAGIC—*Dowling*
MEN—*Jong*
MEN—*Parker*
MEN—*Young, Andrew*
MEN DO NOT LEAVE THINGS SO—*Van Doren*

THE MEN THAT DON'T FIT IN—*Service*
MEN WHO MARCH AWAY—*Hardy*
LA MÉNAGERIE DE TRISTAN—*Desnos*
EL MENDIGO—*Cuadra*
MENDING WALL—*Frost, Robert*
MENEGHIN BIROEÙ DI EX MONEGH—*Porta*
MENG TZU'S SONG—*Merwin*
MENI ODNAKOVO—*Shevchenko*
MENI ZDAYETSYA—*Shevchenko*
MENONS KLAGEN UM DIOTIMA—*Hölderlin*
MENSAJE A AZORÍN, EN SU GENERACIÓN—*Ridruejo*
MENSAJE Á CUBA—*Vega, Oscar Fernández de la*
DER MENSCH—*Claudius*
DER MENSCH—*Hölderlin*
MENSCHENBEIFALL—*Hölderlin*
MENSCHLICHES ELENDE—*Gryphius*
MENTAL CASES—*Owen, Wilfred*
THE MENTAL TRAVELLER—*Blake*
LE MENTEUR—*Cocteau*
ER MERCATO DE PIAZZA NAVONA—*Belli*
MERCED—*Rich*
MERCENARY SOLDIERS—*Housman*
THE MERCHANT OF VENICE—*Shakespeare*
THE MERCHANT POET—*Pommy Vega, Janine*
MERCILESS BEAUTY—*Chaucer*
MERCY—*Dickey, James*
MERLIN—*Emerson*
MERLIN AND THE GLEAM—*Tennyson*
MERLIN AND VIVIEN—*Tennyson*
MERLIN ENTHRALLED—*Wilbur*
MERMAID—*Lowell, Robert*
MERMAID—*MacPherson*
MERMAID—*Tennyson*
MERMAID—*Yeats*
THE MERMAN—*MacNeice*
MERRITT PARKWAY—*Levertov*
MERRY-GO-ROUND—*Hughes, Langston*
MERRY MAN OF PARIS—*Children's Verses and Nursery Rhymes*
THE MERRY NIGHT OF HALLOWEEN—*Andersen*
MES OCCUPATIONS—*Michaux*
THE MESS OF LOVE—*Lawrence*
MESSAGE—*Ginsberg*
MESSAGE—*Miles*
A MESSAGE ALL BLACKPEOPLE CAN DIG—*Lee, Don L.*
THE MESSAGE OF THE MARCH WIND—*Morris, William*
MESSAGES—*Dickey, James*
THE MESSENGER—*Gunn*
METALOGUE TO THE MAGIC FLUTE—*Auden*
METALS—*Davie*
METAMORPHOSES—*Ovid*

METAMORPHOSES ACCORDING TO STEINBERG—*Nemerov*

METAMORPHOSIS INTO BUREAUCRAT—*Piercy*

METAPHOR—*Merriam*

METAPHYSISCHES—*Roth, Eugen*

METEOREN TALAR—*Lundkvist*

METROPOLITAN NIGHTMARE—*Benét, Stephen Vincent*

THE METROPOLITAN RAILWAY—*Betjeman*

LE MEUNIER, SON FILS ET L'ÂNE—*La Fontaine*

MEWLIPS—*Tolkien*

MEXICAN MARKET WOMAN—*Hughes, Langston*

MEXICAN NIGHT—*Marshall, Lenore G.*

MEXICO IS A FOREIGN COUNTRY—*Warren*

MEZZO CAMMIN—*Longfellow*

MEZZOGIOMO ALPINO—*Carducci*

MI AMÉRICA, LA DULCE—*Fombona-Pachano*

MI AMOR? . . . RECUERDAS, DIME—*Machado, Antonio*

MI BANDERA—*Byrne*

MI CABALLERO—*Martí*

MI CABALLO—*Güiraldes*

MI CAMISA—*Acosta*

MI DISTACCO DA TE STANCO D'AMORE—*Villaroel, Giuseppe*

MI DOBLE MALO SE MUERE—*Domínguez Alba*

MI VERSO—*Martí*

MIA CARLOTTA—*Daly*

LA MIA MUCCA—*Rodari*

LA MIA SERA—*Pascoli*

MIAMI MAYA—*Rasof*

MICAH—*Walker*

MICHING MALLECHO—*Blackmur*

MICK STIMSON—*Glover*

THE MICROBE—*Belloc*

THE MICROSCOPE—*Kumin*

MID-AUGUST AT SOURDOUGH MOUNTAIN LOOKOUT—*Snyder*

MID-COUNTRY BLOW—*Roethke*

MID-LIFE CRISIS—*Viorst*

MIDDLE AGED CONVERSATION—*Tessimond*

MIDDLE EARTH—*Tolkien*

THE MIDDLE OF A WAR—*Fuller, Roy*

MIDDLE-SEA AND LEAR-SEA—*Jones, David*

MIDDLESEX—*Betjeman*

THE MIDGET—*Levine*

MIDI—*Leconte de Lisle*

MIDNIGHT ON THE GREAT WESTERN—*Hardy*

MIDNIGHT RAFFLE—*Hughes, Langston*

THE MIDNIGHT SCENE—*Robson, Jeremy*

THE MIDNIGHT SKATERS—*Blunden*

MIDSUMMER NIGHT'S DREAM—*Shakespeare*

MIDWEEK—*Miles*

MIDWINTER BLUES—*Hughes, Langston*

MIDWINTER, PRESOLSTICE—*Atwood*

MIEDO—*Mistral*

MIEN TOHUUSKE—*Olfers-Batocki*

MIENTRAS POR COMPETIR—*Góngora*

'O MIERCURÌ D' 'A MADONNA—*Murolo*

MIGNON LIED—*Goethe*

MIGRATION—*Green, Kate*

MIKE AND MANDY—*Graves*

EL MILAGRO PEQUEÑO—*Casona*

DER MILDE SÜDWIND—*Anonymous–Asian languages*

MILITANT—*Hughes, Langston*

THE MILK JUG—*Herford*

MILK-WHITE MOON—*Sandburg*

MILKWEED—*Wright, James*

THE MILKY WAY—*Conkling*

THE MILL—*Robinson, Edwin Arlington*

THE MILL—*Wilbur*

MILLE REGRETS—*Jacob, Max*

THE MILLER'S TALE—*Chaucer*

MILLOM OLD QUARRY—*Nicholson*

MILLY OU LA TERRE NATALE—*Lamartine*

MILTON—*Blake*

MILTON—*Longfellow*

MILTON—*Tennyson*

MIMOSA—*Dowling*

MIND—*Wilbur*

MIND AND SOUL AFTER DARK—*Jordan, Norman*

MINE NUMBER 6—*Cowley, Malcolm*

MINE SWEEPER—*Kipling*

MINERALS OF CORNWALL STONES—*Redgrove*

MINERS—*Owen, Wilfred*

MINERS—*Wright, James*

MINER'S HELMET—*MacBeth*

MINERVA JONES—*Masters, Edgar Lee*

MINIATYRER—*Asplund*

MINISTER OF WAR—*Anonymous–Asian languages*

MINIVER CHEEVEY—*Robinson, Edwin Arlington*

THE MINNEAPOLIS POEM—*Wright, James*

MINOR LITANY—*Benét, Stephen Vincent*

MINYO—*Anonymous–Asian languages*

THE MIRACLE—*Dowling*

MIRACLES—*Bontemps*

MIRACLES—*Whitman*

THE MIRACULOUS COUNT-DOWN—*Nash*

THE MIRACULOUS TRANSFORMATION—*Colbert*

MIRAGE—*Prefontaine*

MIRAGE—*Williams, Oscar*

MIRAMAR—*Cunningham, James Vincent*

MIRANDA'S SONG—*Auden*

MIRIAM TAZEWELL—*Ransom*

MIRJAM—*Eich*

MIRLO FIEL—*Jiménez*

LE MIROIR BRISÉ—*Prévert*

MIROIR TRANSPARENT—*Henault*

MIRROR IN FEBRUARY—*Kinsella*

MIRROR, MIRROR ON THE WALL—*Johnston, Ellen Turlington*

MIS FLORES NEGRAS—*Flórez*

LA MISA BLANCA—*Martinez Alonso*

LA MISA DE AMOR—*Anonymous–Spanish*

MISANTHROPOS 9—*Gunn*

A MISERABLE MERRY CHRISTMAS—*Steffens*

MISERERE—*Clark, John W.*

ER MISERERE DE LA SITTIMANA SANTA—*Belli*

MISERIE—*Herbert*

MISCALCULATIONS—*Gregor*

MISGIVINGS 1860—*Melville*

MISS BLUES'ES CHILD—*Hughes, Langston*

MISS BOOK WORLD—*Abse*

MISS LOPEZ—*Sitwell, Osbert*

MISS MAME—*Braxton*

MISSA DEFUNCTORUM—*Antoninus*

MISSA SANCTORUM—*Antoninus*

MISSA VOCIS—*Blackmur*

MISSING—*Milne*

MISSING DATES—*Empson*

MR. ATTILA—*Sandburg*

MR. BETT'S MIND A KINGDOM IS—*Nash*

MR. BLEANEY—*Larkin*

MR. BRODSKY—*Tomlinson*

MR. COOPER—*Thwaite*

MR. EDWARDS AND THE SPIDER—*Lowell, Robert*

MR. ELIOT'S SUNDAY MORNING SERVICE—*Eliot, Thomas Stearns*

MR. HAROLD COLBERT—*Sitwell, Osbert*

MR. HOOBODY—*Lee, Dennis*

MR. KENNEDY PROPOSES TO PACIFY THE CARIBBEANS—*Hitchcock*

MR. MISTOFFELEES—*Eliot, Thomas Stearns*

MR. NOBODY—*Children's Verses and Nursery Rhymes*

MR. NUTCH—*Sitwell, Osbert*

MR. POPE'S WELCOME FROM GREECE—*Gay, John*

MR. SAMUEL AND SAM—*Brown, Sterling A.*

MR. TALL AND MR. SMALL—*Merriam*

MR. VIRTUE AND THE THREE BEARS
    —*Blackmur*
MR. WHITTIER—*Scott, Winfield
    Townley*
MÍSTICA DE LA MUERTE—
    Martinez Alonso
MÍSTICA DEL DOLOR—*Martinez
    Alonso*
MRS. BENJAMIN PANTIER—
    Masters, Edgar Lee
MRS. BUSK—*Sitwell, Osbert*
MRS. CHARLES BLISS—*Masters,
    Edgar Lee*
MRS. CHIVERS—*Sitwell, Osbert*
MRS. FROSSART—*Sitwell, Osbert*
MRS. GEORGE REECE—*Masters,
    Edgar Lee*
MRS. GRANDESTIN—*Sitwell,
    Osbert*
MRS. HUMBLEBY—*Sitwell, Osbert*
MRS. LIVERSEDGE—*Sitwell,
    Osbert*
MRS. MALLORY—*Coward*
MRS. MEYERS—*Masters, Edgar
    Lee*
MRS. NUTCH—*Sitwell, Osbert*
MRS. PURKAPILE—*Masters, Edgar
    Lee*
MRS. ROOT—*Connor*
MRS. SOUTHERN'S ENEMY—*Sitwell,
    Osbert*
MIT DUMMEN MÄDCHEN—*Heine*
MIT EINEM GEMALTEN RANDE—
    Goethe
MIT ZWEI WORTEN—*Meyer,
    Conrad Ferdinand*
DAS MITGLIED—*Tucholsky*
DIE MITTAGSZEITUNG—
    Morgenstern
MIXED SKETCHES—*Lee, Don L.*
MNEME, A'—*Seferis*
MOBILE OF BIRDS—*Updike*
MOCKERY—*Riggs*
EN MODER—*Blomberg*
MODERN LOVE—*Meredith,
    George*
MODERNE LEGENDE—*Brecht*
MODERNES MÄRCHEN—*Kästner*
A MODEST LOVE—*Dyer*
MOESTA ET ERRABUNDA—
    Baudelaire
MOEURS CONTEMPORAINES—
    Pound
MÖGLICHKEIT, EINEN SINN ZU
    FINDEN—*Kunze*
MOGUER MÍO—*Jiménez*
MOÏSE—*Vigny*
LA MOJJE GGELOSA—*Belli*
MOLE—*Smith, William Jay*
THE MOLE UNDER MY EYE—
    Lifshin
MOLITVA—*Lermontov*
MOLY—*Gunn*
MOMENT—*Nemerov*
A MOMENT OF RESPECT—*Brock*
A MOMENT PLEASE—*Allen,
    Samuel*

MOMENTO—*Saba*
MOMENTOS FELICES—*Celaya*
MON ÂME A SON SECRET—*Arvers*
MON COEUR PLEURE—*Fontaine*
MON DIEU M'A DIT: MON FILS IL
    FAUT M'AIMER—*Verlaine*
MON ENFANCE—*Hugo, Victor*
MON ÉPITAPHE—*Piron*
MON HABIT—*Béranger*
MON RÊVE FAMILER—*Verlaine*
DER MOND—*Stolberg*
DER MOND LÜGT—*Borchert*
MONDEAUFGANG—*Droste-Hül-
    shoff*
MONDENDINGE—*Morgenstern*
MONDNACHT—*Eichendorff*
MONDNACHT IM SOMMER—*Holz*
DAS MONDSCHAF—*Morgenstern*
MONET: LES NYMPHÉAS—
    Snodgrass
LA MONJA GITANA—*Garcia Lorca*
THE MONKEYS AND THE
    CROCODILE—*Richards,
    Laura E.*
THE MONKEYS AND THE SUNDIAL
    —*Roche*
THE MONK'S TALE—*Chaucer*
MONNA INNOMINATA—*Rossetti,
    Christina*
MONOLOG DER ANTIGONE DES
    SOPHOKLES—*Brecht*
MONOLOG: ON THE CREATORS—
    Amini
MONÓLOGO DE SEGISMUNDO—
    Calderón de la Barca
MONOLOGUE AT MIDNIGHT—
    Warren
MONOLOGUE DE L'AMOUR
    MATERNAL—*Cros*
LE MONSIEUR—*Seghers*
LOS MONSTRUOS—*Alonso*
MONTCALM—*Davie*
MONTEVIDEO—*Supervielle*
MONTMARTRE—*Carco*
MONTREAL—*Klein*
MONUMENTO MORTUORIO A LA
    MUERTE DE NACINICMED—
    Godoy
MONUMENTS FOR A FRIENDLY GIRL
    —*Stafford*
MOO—*Hillyer*
MOODS OF LOVE—*Day Lewis*
THE MOON—*Lee, Dennis*
THE MOON—*Shelley*
THE MOON—*Stevenson*
MOON AND SUN—
    *Anonymous–English–Old
    English*
MOON DOVES—*Conkling*
MOON FOLLY—*Davis, Fannie
    Stearns*
THE MOON IS UP—*Noyes*
MOON LANDING—*Auden*
THE MOON SHINES DOWN—
    Giovanni
MOON SONG—*Conkling*
MOONLIGHT—*Uschold*

MOONRISE—*Plath*
MOONRISE—*Watkins*
MOPSENLEBEN—*Morgenstern*
THE MORE LOVING ONE—*Auden*
MORE TO COME—*Fry*
MORGAN: THE COMMISSIONAIRE
    CAT—*Eliot, Thomas Stearns*
DER MORGEN—*Eichendorff*
MORGEN—*Gryphius*
DER MORGEN—*Hagedorn*
DER MORGEN—*Kaschnitz*
MORGENDLICHE REDE AN DEN
    BAUM GRIEHN—*Brecht*
MORGENSTIMMUNG—*Wedekind*
LAS MORILLAS DE JAÉN—*Garcia
    Lorca*
DIE MORITAT VON MACKIE MESSER
    —*Brecht*
MORITURUS—*Millay*
LA MORMORAZZIONE—*Belli*
MORNE GLEBE—*Giguere*
MORNING—*Blake*
MORNING—*Conkling*
MORNING—*Dickinson, Emily*
MORNING AND EVENING STARS—
    Goldstein
MORNING AT ARNHEM—*Smith,
    William Jay*
MORNING AT THE WINDOW—*Eliot,
    Thomas Stearns*
MORNING GLORY—*Raper*
MORNING LIGHT—*Sherwin*
MORNING ON THE LIEVRE—
    Lampman
MORNING SONG—*Chapin*
MORNING SONG—*Dugan*
MORNING SONG—*Plath*
THE MORNING-WATCH—*Vaughan,
    Henry*
MORNING WORSHIP—*Van Doren*
MORT AUX CHATS—*Porter, Peter*
LA MORT DES AMANTS—
    Baudelaire
LA MORT DU LOUP—*Vigny*
LA MORT D'UN CHIEN—*Hugo,
    Victor*
LA MORT ET LE BUCHERON—*La
    Fontaine*
MORT J'APPELLE DE TA RIGUEUR—
    Villon
LA MORT, L'AMOUR, LA VIE—
    Éluard
MORT RUTEBOEUF—*Ruteboeuf*
LA MORTE—*Marin*
LA MORTE ALGERINA—*Bevilacqua*
MORTE D'ARTHUR—*Malory*
MORTE D'ARTHUR—*Tennyson*
LA MORTE DE TUTA—*Belli*
LA MORTE DI COBÒ—*Palazzeschi*
LA MORTE ET SES MAINS TRISTES—
    Noël
LA MORTE MEDITATA—*Ungaretti*
LI MORTI DE ROMA—*Belli*
MORTIFICATION—*Herbert*
MOSKVA TOVARNAYA—
    Yevtushenko

MOST LOVELY SHADE—*Sitwell, Edith*

THE MOST OF IT—*Frost, Robert*

THE MOTHER—*Brooks, Gwendolyn*

THE MOTHER—*Frost, Frances M.*

THE MOTHER—*Scott, Winfield Townley*

MOTHER AND CHILD—*Stoneham*

MOTHER AND SON—*Tate, Allen*

MOTHER AS PITCHFORK—*Rukeyser*

MOTHER CAREY—*Masefield*

MOTHER IN WARTIME—*Hughes, Langston*

MOTHER NATURE'S SON—*Wallace*

MOTHER O' MINE—*Kipling*

A MOTHER SPEAKS—THE ALGIERS MOTEL INCIDENT, DETROIT—*Harper*

A MOTHER THINKS OF HER CHILD—*Marshall, Lenore G.*

MOTHER TO SON—*Hughes, Langston*

MOTHERS—*Giovanni*

MOTHER'S HABITS—*Giovanni*

MOTION—*Clark, China*

MOTIVO—*Meireles*

LOS MOTIVOS DEL LOBO—*Darío*

MOTOGONKI PO VERTIKAL'NOI STENE—*Voznesensky*

THE MOTOR-BOAT SONG—*Merriam*

MOTTO—*Hughes, Langston*

LE MOULIN—*Verhaeren*

THE MOUND-BUILDERS—*Kunitz*

THE MOUNT—*Adams*

THE MOUNTAIN—*Francis*

THE MOUNTAIN—*Frost, Robert*

THE MOUNTAIN—*Kaufman, Shirley*

THE MOUNTAIN—*Merwin*

MOUNTAIN BEAUTY—*Marshall, Helen Lowrie*

MOUNTAIN MAN—*Talen*

THE MOUNTAIN WHIPPOORWILL—*Benét, Stephen Vincent*

MOUNTAINS—*Auden*

MOUNTAINS—*Hughes, Ted*

MOUNTAINS COVERED WITH CATS—*Stevens, Wallace*

MOUNTAINS, POLECATS, PHEASANTS—*Norris*

MOURMELON-LE-GRAND—*Apollinaire*

THE MOURNING BRIDE—*Congreve*

MOURNING PICTURE—*Rich*

MOURNING POEM FOR THE QUEEN OF SUNDAY—*Hayden*

MOUSE—*Conkling*

THE MOUSE COMPLAINS—*Coatsworth*

A MOUSE IN THE HOUSE OF NORMAN MACCAIG—*Walters*

LE MOUSSE—*Corbière*

THE MOUTH IS A ZOO—*Dicker*

MOUVEMENT—*Supervielle*

MOVE UN-NOTICED TO BE NOTICED: A NATIONHOOD POEM—*Lee, Don L.*

A MOVER—*Fabio, Sarah Webster*

MOVING—*Kavanagh*

MOVING DAY—*Cattonar*

MOVING DEEP—*Stephany*

MOVING LANDSCAPE WITH FALLING RAIN—*Bishop, John Peale*

MOVING PICTURE—*Ignatow*

MÖWENLIED—*Morgenstern*

THE MOWER TO THE GLO-WORMS—*Marvell*

MOWING—*Frost, Robert*

MOY CASTLE—*Anonymous–English–Modern English*

MOZART AND SALIERI—*Heath-Stubbs*

MS FOUND UNDER A SERVIETTE IN A LOVELY HOME—*Nash*

MUCH ADO ABOUT NOTHING—*Shakespeare*

MUCH IN LITTLE—*Winters*

MUCHACHAS DE PROVINCIA—*Anonymous–Spanish*

MUCHACHAS SOLTERONAS—*López*

THE MUCK-BEETLE'S SON—*Roche*

MUD—*Boyden*

THE MUD OF VIET NAM—*Lester, Julius*

MUERTA DE AMOR—*León, Rafael de*

LA MUERTE—*Jiménez*

MUERTE DE ANTOÑITO EL CAMBORIO—*Garcia Lorca*

MUERTE DE DURANDARTE—*Anonymous–Spanish*

MUERTE DE LA PETENERA—*Garcia Lorca*

LA MUERTE DEL AMOR—*Pérez*

MUERTES—*Salinas, Pedro*

MUERTO DE AMOR—*Garcia Lorca*

DIE MÜHLE—*Bergengruen*

DIE MÜHLE DES TODES—*Goll*

MUHME KUNKEL—*Morgenstern*

MÜHSAL DER BESTEN—*Brecht*

MUJER—*Alberti*

MUJER—*Figuera*

MUJER—*Pedroni*

MUJER PUERTORRIQUEÑA—*Lloréns Torres*

MUJER REDONDA—*Cremer*

MULATA—*Guillén, Nicolás*

THE MULES—*Nash*

LE MULET SE VANTANT DE SA GÉNÉALOGIE—*La Fontaine*

MUMBO, JUMBO—*Lee, Dennis*

MUNDUS ET INFANS—*Auden*

MUNGOJERRIE AND RUMPELTEAZER—*Eliot, Thomas Stearns*

THE MUNICIPAL GALLERY REVISITED—*Yeats*

MUNICIPAL IDYLL: A DIALOGUE—*Sitwell, Osbert*

'O MUNNO D' 'E PPAROLE—*Filippo*

MURDER—*Smith, Stevie*

MURDER—*Yevtushenko*

THE MURDERER—*Smith, Stevie*

IL MURO—*Sereni*

MURPHY—*Williams, Hugo*

LA MUSE MALADE—*Baudelaire*

A MUSE OF WATER—*Kizer*

MUSÉE DES BEAUX ARTS—*Auden*

THE MUSEUM AT TILLAMOOK—*Stafford*

MUSEUM OF OBJECTS DEPICTING THE HISTORY OF MY RACE—*Ferlinghetti*

MUSEUM PIECE—*Wilbur*

THE MUSHROOM GATHERERS—*Davie*

MUSHROOM SONG—*Conkling*

MUSHROOMS—*Plath*

MUSIC—*De la Mare*

MUSIC—*Emerson*

MUSIC—*Levertov*

MUSIC IN THE WOOD—*Reeves*

MUSIC OF COLOURS, WHITE BLOSSOM—*Watkins*

MUSIC SWIMS BACK TO ME—*Sexton*

A MUSICAL INSTRUMENT—*Browning, Elizabeth Barrett*

DIE MUSIK KOMMT—*Liliencron*

LA MUSIQUE—*Baudelaire*

MUSSEL HUNTER AT ROCK HARBOR—*Plath*

DIE MUTTER—*Zuckmayer*

DIE MUTTER BEI DER WIEGE—*Claudius*

MUTTER BEIMLEN—*Brecht*

EINE MUTTER ZIEHT BILANZ—*Kästner*

MUTTERINGS OVER THE CRIB OF A DEAF CHILD—*Wright, James*

MUTTERNS HÄNDE—*Tucholsky*

MY ACTS—*Meredith, William*

MY AFRICA—*Dei-Anang*

MY AUNT—*Holmes, Oliver Wendell*

MY BED IS A BOAT—*Stevenson*

MY BONNIE MARY OR THE SILVER TASSIE—*Burns*

MY BROTHER BERT—*Housman*

MY BUSSEDUCTRESS—*McGough*

MY CAMPING GROUND—*Rosenfeld*

MY CAT AND I—*McGough*

MY CHILD IS PHLEGMATIC—ANXIOUS PARENT—*Nash*

MY DEATH—*Smith, A. J. M.*

MY DOG—*Chute*

MY FAMILIAR—*Saxe*

MY FATHER (HENRY NELSON)—*Jeffers, Lance*

MY FATHER'S NECKTIES—*Kumin*

MY FRIEND, MALONEY—*Causley*

MY FRIENDS—*Merwin*

MY GALY—*Petrarch; Wyatt, Thomas*

MY GIRL IN A GEORGIA TOWN—*Jeffers, Lance*

MY GRANDFATHER AND HIS
APPLE-TREE—*Ormond*
MY GRANDMOTHER—*Jennings*
MY GRANDMOTHER'S GHOST—
Wright, James
MY GRANDMOTHER'S LOVE
LETTERS—*Crane, Hart*
MY HOME TOWN—*Kizer*
MY HOUSE—*Giovanni*
MY JEAN (I LOVE MY JEAN)—*Burns*
MY KINGDOM—*Stevenson*
MY LAND—*Cowley, Malcolm*
MY LAST AFTERNOON WITH UNCLE
DEVEREUX WINSLOW—*Lowell,
Robert*
MY LAST DUCHESS—*Browning,
Robert*
MY LIFE—*Strand*
MY LINE—*Johnston, Ellen
Turlington*
MY LITTLE 'BOUT-TOWN GAL—
Brooks, Gwendolyn
MY LITTLE DREAMS—*Johnson,
Georgia Douglas*
MY LITTLE ONE—*Williams,
Tennessee*
MY LITTLE SON—*Rosenfeld*
MY LORD, WHAT A MORNING—
Cuney
MY LOST YOUTH—*Longfellow*
MY LOVE IS LIKE THE SUN—
*Anonymous–English–
Modern English*
MY LOVE WHEN THIS IS PAST—
Stephany
MY LOVELY WOMAN—*Sexton*
MY LUTE AWAKE—*Wyatt, Sir
Thomas*
MY MOTHER AND I WERE—*Lifshin*
MY MOTHER AND THE BED—
Lifshin
MY MOTHER'S TABLE—*Sobiloff*
MY NAME AND I—*Graves*
MY NAME IS AFRIKA—*Kgositsile*
MY NEW YORK STARS—*Gaver*
MY NOVEMBER GUEST—*Frost,
Robert*
MY OWN COUNTRY—*Belloc*
MY OWN THING—*Fabio, Sarah
Webster*
MY PAISTIN FINN—*Yeats*
MY PAPA'S WALTZ—*Roethke*
MY PEOPLE IS—*Dupree*
MY PLEASURE—*Chester*
MY POETRY RESEMBLES THE BREAD
OF EGYPT—*Bly*
MY POLICY—*Eckels*
MY POOR LOVE—*Van Doren*
MY PRETTY ROSE TREE—*Blake*
MY SAD CAPTAINS—*Gunn*
MY SEASONS ARE THE LEAVES—
Stephany
MY SHADOW—*Stevenson*
MY SHIP AND I—*Stevenson*
MY SISTER'S BIRTH—*Robison*
MY SISTER'S LETTER—*Kizer*

MY SISTER'S SLEEP—*Rossetti,
Dante Gabriel*
MY SON AND I—*Levine*
MY SON, THE EXECUTIONER—*Hall*
MY SPECIAL FRIEND—*Johnston,
Ellen Turlington*
MY SPIRIT WILL NOT HAUNT THE
MOUND—*Hardy*
MY STRING BEAR—*Sexton*
MY SURGEONS—*Kunitz*
MY TREASURES—*Stevenson*
MY UNCLE'S DERBY—*Sobiloff*
MY WIFE'S A WANTON WEE THING
—*Burns*
MY ZIPPER SUIT—*Allen, Marie
Louise*
MYLMYLMY—*Bernstein*
LE MYSTÈRE DES
SAINTS-INNOCENTS—*Péguy*
LES MYSTÈRES DE SAINT-PHILIPPE
DU ROULE—*Prévert*
LES MYSTÈRES DOULOUREUX—
Jammes
MYSTERIES—*Abse*
MYSTERIOUS BIOGRAPHY—
Sandburg
THE MYSTERIOUS CAT—*Lindsay,
Vachel*
MYTH—*Anonymous–American
Indian languages–Uitoto*
THE MYTH OF A WOMAN'S FIST—
Darr

N. B. SYMMETRIANS—*Derwood*
NA MÃO DE DEUS—*Quental*
NA POLE KULIKOVOM—*Blok*
NA RANNIKH POEZDAKH—
Pasternak
NA STRASTNOI—*Pasternak*
NA TAVERNELLA—*Di Giacomo*
LA NACENCIA—*Chamizo*
NACH DEM 90. PSALM—*Schubart*
NACH DEM TODE MEINER
MITARBEITERIN M. S.—*Brecht*
NACH NEUEN MEEREN—
Nietzsche, Friedrich Wilhelm
NACH NORDEN—*Morgenstern*
DIE NACHFOLGERIN—*Tucholsky*
DIE NACHT—
Platen-Hallermünde
DIE NACHT—*Rilke*
DIE NACHTBLUME—*Eichendorff*
NACHTGERÄUSCHE—*Meyer,
Conrad Ferdinand*
NACHTGESANG—*Goethe*
DIE NACHTIGALL—*Storm*
DIE NACHTIGALLEN—*Eichendorff*
NACHTLIED—*Trakl*
NACHTLIED—*Vring*
NACHTS—*Mörike*
NÄCKEN—*Stagnelius*
NADEZHDA—*Lermontov*
NADIE ES TANTO TU—*Godoy*
NAG'S HEAD—*Anderson, Lee*
DIE NÄHE—*Morgenstern*
NÄHE DES GELIEBTEN—*Goethe*
NAÏF—*Fombeure*

THE NAILS—*Merwin*
THE NAKED AND THE NUDE—
Graves
NAKED IN BORNEO—*Swenson*
NAKED SWIMMERS AND HORSEMEN
—*Whitman*
THE NAME—*Creeley*
NAMES ARE SHIPS—*Blanding*
NAMES IN MONTERCHI: TO RACHEL
—*Wright, James*
THE NAMING OF CATS—*Eliot,
Thomas Stearns*
NAMING OF PARTS—*Reed, Henry*
NAMOUNA—*Musset*
NANA AL LUCERO DEL ALBA—
Cadilla
NANA KRU—*Anonymous–African
languages–Liberia*
NANCY HANKS—*Benét, Rosemary
Carr*
NANCY WALSH—*Stephens*
NÄNIE—*Schiller*
NANT CERI—*Jones, Glyn*
NANTUCKET—*Williams, William
Carlos*
NARCISO—*Garcia Lorca*
NARCISSE PARLE—*Valèry*
DER NARR—*Rilke*
A NARRATIVE—*Spencer*
NASLEDNIKI STALINA—
Yevtushenko
DAS NASOBEM—*Morgenstern*
NASSE ERDE—*Theobaldy*
NAT—*Jeffers, Lance*
NAT TURNER IN THE CLEARING—
Aubert
NATA E LA STORIA—*Bevilacqua*
NATHAN HALE—*Finch, Francis*
NATIONAL COLD STORAGE
COMPANY—*Shapiro, Harvey*
NATTKVARTER—*Ferlin*
NATURAL LINGUISTICS—*Auden*
NATURAL MUSIC—*Jeffers,
Robinson*
NATURE—*Longfellow*
NATURE BE DAMNED—*Wilkinson*
NATURE SPECTACLE—
Morgenstern
IL NAUFRAGO LAPICOZZA—
Pascoli
NAUGHTY BOY—*Creeley*
NAUSÉE OU C'EST LA MORT QUI
VIENT?—*Michaux*
NAVAJO PRAYER—
*Anonymous–American
Indian languages–Navajo*
NAVIDAD—*Jiménez*
THE NAVIGATORS—*Hacker*
NCOPP' 'E CCHIANCHE—*Di
Giacomo*
NCUNTRAVO U SIGNURI—*Buttitta*
NE PO POSLOVITSE—*Kirsanov*
NE RASSUZHDAY—*Tyutchev*
NE RETOURNEZ PAS LA TÊTE—
Soupault
NEAR THE LAKE—*Morris, George
Pope*

NEBEL—*Benn*
NEBEL—*Kirsch*
NEBULOUS—*Arnez*
THE NECESSARY SLAUGHTER—*Patten*
DER NECKAR—*Hölderlin*
THE NEED OF BEING VERSED IN COUNTRY THINGS—*Frost, Robert*
A NEEDED POEM FOR MY SALVATION—*Sanchez*
THE NEEDLE POINT OF NOW—*Dowling*
NEEDLEPOINT—*Jong*
NEGRA TO GERI E RISSA—*Marin*
NEGRITUDE—*Césaire*
NEGRITUDE—*Emanuel*
NEGRO—*Emanuel*
NEGRO—*Hughes, Langston*
A NEGRO AUTHOR—*Emanuel*
NEGRO CHOIR—*Murphy*
NEGRO DANCERS—*Hughes, Langston*
A NEGRO LABOURER IN LIVERPOOL—*Rubadiri*
NEGRO SERVANT—*Hughes, Langston*
THE NEGRO SPEAKS OF RIVERS—*Hughes, Langston*
NEIGES—*Perse*
THE NEIGHBOR—*Williams, Miller*
NEIN!—*Morgenstern*
NEITHER HERE NOR THERE—*Rodgers*
NEITHER OUT FAR NOR IN DEEP—*Frost, Robert*
NEKROS—*O'Connell*
NEL CARCERE DI GINEVRA—*Pascoli*
NEL MAGMA—*Luzi*
NELLE NOZZE DELLA SORELLA PAOLINA—*Leopardi*
NELLIE CLARK—*Masters, Edgar Lee*
NEMEA—*Durrell*
NERVES—*Symons*
NEST EGGS—*Stevenson*
THE NESTLING—*Williams, Hugo*
A NET OF SMOKE—*Randall*
NETS TO CATCH THE WIND—*Webster, John*
DER NEUE KANONEN-SONG—*Brecht*
NEUE LIEBE—*Mörike*
NEUE LIEBE, NEUES LEBEN—*Goethe*
DIE NEUEN HEILIGEN—*Updike*
1940—*Hölty*
1940: VI ÖDER DIE ANTWORT—*Brecht*
DER 90. PSALM—*Weckherlin*
THE NEUROTIC—*Day Lewis*
NEVER AGAIN WOULD BIRDS' SONG BE THE SAME—*Frost*
NEVER-KNOWN—*Conkling*
NEVERMORE—*Verlaine*

NEVERTHELESS—*Moore, Marianne*
NEW BREED OF CAT—*Eckels*
NEW CLOTHES AND OLD—*Farjeon*
THE NEW COLOSSUS—*Lazarus*
A NEW DAY—*Levine*
A NEW ENGLAND BACHELOR—*Eberhart*
NEW ENGLAND SPRING, 1942—*Millay*
A NEW ENGLAND VIEW: MY REPORT—*Eberhart*
THE NEW FOX—*Eckels*
NEW FRIENDS—*Marshall, Helen Lowrie*
NEW HAMPSHIRE—*Eliot, Thomas Stearns*
NEW HAMPSHIRE, FEBRUARY—*Eberhart*
NEW HAMPSHIRE (SEASONS)—*Hall*
THE NEW HOUSE—*Thomas, Edward*
A NEW LEAF—*Hollander*
NEW LEASE—*Mathias*
NEW LOVE—*Arnez*
NEW LOW—*Dupree*
NEW MAN—*Glaze*
THE NEW MISTRESS—*Housman*
NEW MORNINGS—*Marshall, Helen Lowrie*
NEW SEASON—*Levine*
NEW SONG FOR INDIANA OPHELIAS—*Sandburg*
NEW STRAIN—*Starbuck*
THE NEW VESTMENTS—*Lear*
NEW WORLD A-COMIN'—*Brathwaite*
A NEW YEAR CAROL—*Anonymous-English-Modern English*
A NEW YEAR GREETING—*Auden*
NEW YEAR: VIEW WEST OVER SORROW—*Starbuck*
NEW YEAR'S EVE—*Anderson, Lee*
NEW YEAR'S EVE—*Ciardi*
NEW YEAR'S EVE—*Hardy*
NEW YORK—*Simmons, Judy*
NEW YORK CITY—*Abbe*
NEW YORK SCENE: MAY 1958—*Logan*
NEW YORK TO SAN FRAN—*Ginsberg*
THE NEW YORKERS—*Giovanni*
NEWS FOR THE DELPHIC ORACLE—*Yeats*
NEWS ITEM—*Parker*
NEWS OF THE WORLD—*Barker, George*
NEXT DAY—*Jarrell*
NEXT FROM THE BEES—*Cullen, Countee*
THE NEXT WAR—*Owen, Wilfred*
NEZABUDKA—*Lermontov*
NEZNAKOMKA—*Blok*
'NGIULINA—*Viviani*
NI BONJOUR NI BONSOIR—*Nerval*
NICE BABY—*Viorst*

NICE DAY FOR A LYNCHING—*Patchen*
NICE GUY—*Ignatow*
NICHOLSON, SUDDENLY—*Nicholson*
NICHT GESAGT—*Kaschnitz*
A NICKLE BET—*Knight, Etheridge*
NIEDERGANG—*Nietzsche*
DIE NIEDERKUNFT DER GROSSEN BABEL—*Brecht*
NIGERIAN UNITY/OR LITTLE NIGGERS KILLING LITTLE NIGGERS—*Lee, Don L.*
NIGGER—*Sanchez*
NIGGER, DO YOU—*Kali*
NIGHT—*Blake*
NIGHT—*Jeffers, Robinson*
NIGHT—*Surrey*
NIGHT—*Vaughan, Henry*
NIGHT AND DAY—*Stevenson*
NIGHT AND MORN—*Hughes, Langston*
NIGHT AT SEA AFTER FLYING—*Casson*
NIGHT BELLS—*Sandburg*
THE NIGHT BENNY KID PARET WAS KILLED ON TV—*Harkness*
THE NIGHT CLERK—*Hannan*
NIGHT CLOUDS—*Lowell, Amy*
NIGHT CROWN—*Roethke*
NIGHT, DEATH, MISSISSIPPI—*Hayden*
NIGHT FEEDING—*Rukeyser*
NIGHT: FOUR SONGS—*Hughes, Langston*
NIGHT JOURNEY—*Roethke*
NIGHT LETTER—*Kunitz*
NIGHT MAGIC—*Burr, Amelia Josephine*
NIGHT MAIL—*Auden*
NIGHT OF THE PRESIDENT'S FUNERAL—*Barker, Richard*
NIGHT OF WIND—*Frost, Frances M.*
NIGHT, OR IT IS NOT SO FAR—*Teasdale*
NIGHT PLANE—*Frost, Frances M.*
THE NIGHT RAINS HOT TAR—*Jeffers, Lance*
NIGHT SONG—*Chapin*
NIGHT SONG—*Lipton*
NIGHT SONG—*Merriam*
NIGHT SOUND—*Garfinkel*
NIGHT STUFF—*Sandburg*
NIGHT TRAIN—*Francis*
NIGHT WORDS: THE RAVISHING—*McClure*
NIGHTFALL—*Masters, Marcia*
THE NIGHTINGAL—*Barnfield*
THE NIGHTINGALE—*Anonymous-English-Modern English*
NIGHTINGALES—*Bridges*
NIGHTMARE—*Emanuel*
NIGHTMARE AT NOON—*Benét, Stephen Vincent*

NIGHTMARE FOR FUTURE REFERENCE—*Benét, Stephen Vincent*
NIGHTMARE NUMBER THREE—*Benét, Stephen Vincent*
NIGHTMARE, WITH ANGELS—*Benét, Stephen Vincent*
NIGHTPIECE—*Joyce*
NIGHTSONG—*Hacker*
NIGHTSONG—*Henri*
NIKKI ROSA—*Giovanni*
THE NILE—*Hunt*
NIMM DIESEN TAG—*McFarlane*
NIMMERSATTE LIEBE—*Mörike*
NIÑA AHOGADA EN EL POZO—*Garcia Lorca*
LA NIÑA CONFITADA—*Martinez Alonso*
NINA GIVING MR. BACKLASH THE BLUES—*Fabio, Sarah Webster*
LA NIÑA ILUSIONADA—*Martinez Alonso*
NINE NECTARINES—*Moore, Marianne*
NINE POEMS FOR THE UNBORN CHILD—*Rukeyser*
NINE RED HORSEMEN—*Farjeon*
NINE TO FIVE—*McGough*
1901—*Coward*
LA NINETTA DEL VERZEE—*Porta*
EL NIÑO DE LA PALMA—*Alberti*
EL NIÑO MURIO—*Aleixandre*
EL NIÑO SOLO—*Mistral*
EL NIÑO Y LA LUNA—*Brull*
NIÑOS—*Jiménez*
NISHCHIJ—*Turgenev*
NIT DE PRIMAVERA—*Arderiu*
NIX BODENSTROM—*Lessing*
NO!—*Hood*
NO ARK, NO ARARAT—*Dowling*
NO BOUNDARY—*Marshall, Lenore G.*
NO CALVÁRIO—*Leal*
NO DOCTORS TODAY, THANK YOU—*Nash*
NO HAY OLVIDO—*Neruda*
NO IMAGES—*Cuney*
NO MÉ MEI BUO 'NA MARE—*Marin*
NO MINDLESS ESCALATION—*Fremantle*
THE NO MORE APOLOGIZING THE NO MORE LITTLE LAUGHING BLUES—*Lifshin*
NO MORE BABIES—*Viorst*
NO ONE ELSE—*Jeffers, Lance*
NO ONE IS EVER AT THE WHEEL—*Howard, Lee*
NO ONE REMEMBERS—*Levine*
NO ONE SO MUCH AS YOU—*Thomas, Edward*
NO PLATONIQUE LOVE—*Cartwright*
NO QUINTANA'S BAR—*Nunes*
NO REGRETS—*Hughes, Langston*
NO RIGHT—*Darr*
NO SECOND TROY—*Yeats*

NO THROUGH ROAD—*Thomas, Ronald Stuart*
NO WORST, THERE IS NONE—*Hopkins*
NOAH BUILT THE ARK—*Johnson, James Weldon*
NOAH'S JOURNEY—*MacBeth*
NOAH'S RAVEN—*Merwin*
NOCH ZWEI—*Busch*
LA NOCHE—*Creeley*
NOCHE DE LLUVIA—*Ibarbourou*
NOCHE DE RESURRECCIONES—*Paz*
NOCHE OSCURA DEL ALMA—*Juan de la Cruz*
NOCHE SERENA—*León, Fray Luis de*
NOCHNOY AEROPORT V NYU-IORKE—*Voznezensky*
NOCTAMBULE—*Smith, A. J. M.*
NOCTURNA 27—*Lair*
A NOCTURNAL REVERIE—*Finch, Anne, Countess of Winchelsea*
A NOCTURNAL UPON S. LUCIES DAY—*Donne*
NOCTURNE—*Amis*
NOCTURNE—*Auden*
NOCTURNE—*Kramer*
NOCTURNE—*Fargue*
NOCTURNE—*Spender*
NOCTURNE AT BETHESDA—*Bontemps*
NOCTURNO—*Mistral*
NOCTURNO—*Quental*
NOCTURNO—*Silva*
NOCTURNO—*Victoria*
NOEL—*Belloc*
NOEL—*Wilkinson*
NOISE—*Pope, Jessie*
THE NOISE THAT TIME MAKES—*Moore, Merrill*
NOLI ME TANGERE—*Snoilsky*
NOMAD EXQUISITE—*Stevens, Wallace*
EL NOMBRE CONSEGUIDO DE LOS NOMBRES—*Jiménez*
LOS NOMBRES—*Guillén, Jorge*
LA NOMINA DE CAPPELLAN—*Porta*
NON FOSSI MAI STATO—*Saitta*
NON GRIDATE PIÙ—*Ungaretti*
NON SUGNU PUETA—*Buttitta*
NON SUM QUALIS ERAM BONAE SUB REGNO CYNARAE—*Dowson*
NONES—*Auden*
'O NONNO—*Nicolardi*
THE NOODLE VENDOR'S FLUTE—*Enright*
NOON—*Sherwin*
NOONDAY SUN—*Jackson, Kathryn*
NORA—*Brooks, Gwendolyn*
THE NORDSEE—*Heine*
NORETORP-NORETSYH—*Rexroth*
NORFOLK—*Betjeman*
LA NORIA AZUL—*Martinez Alonso*

THE NORTH—*Williams, Hugo*
NORTH AND SOUTH—*McKay*
NORTH COAST RECOLLECTIONS—*Betjeman*
THE NORTH SEA—*Davie*
NORTHERN PIKE—*Wright, James*
NORTHUMBRIAN DUET—*Gibson, Wilfred*
NORTHWEST PASSAGE—*Stevenson*
NOSTALGIA—*Saba*
NOSTALGIA—*Santos Chocano*
NOSTALGIA-NOW THREEPENCE OFF—*Mitchell, Adrian*
NOT A MOVIE—*Hughes, Langston*
NOT ALDESTROP—*Abse*
NOT FORGOTTEN—*Davison, Peter*
NOT IDEAS ABOUT THE THING BUT THE THING ITSELF—*Stevens, Wallace*
NOT IN A SILVER CASKET—*Millay*
NOT IN VAIN—*Goldstein*
NOT MARBLE NOR THE GILDED MONUMENTS—*MacLeish*
NOT PALACES—*Spender*
NOT QUITE SOCIAL—*Frost, Robert*
NOT THAT HURRIED GRIEF—*Thomas, Lorenzo*
NOT THE ITALIAN METHOD—*Olson*
NOT THE SWEET CICELY OF GERARDE'S HERBALL—*Avison*
NOT TO SLEEP—*Graves*
NOT WAVING BUT DROWNING—*Smith, Stevie*
NOT YOUTH PERTAINS TO ME—*Whitman*
A NOTE FROM THE COAST—*Reid*
A NOTE LEFT IN JIMMY LEONARD'S SHACK—*Wright, James*
A NOTE OF HUMILITY—*Bontemps*
NOTE ON LEAVING—*Greenwald*
NOTE ON THE ILIAD—*Garlick*
NOTE TO A HURRYING MAN—*Patten*
NOTES FOR A LITTLE PLAY—*Hughes, Ted*
NOTES FROM A GUERRILLA DIARY—*Toure*
NOTES FROM UNDERGROUND—*Garrigue*
NOTES ON THE PSALMIST—*Ciardi*
NOTES TO BE LEFT IN A CORNERSTONE—*Benét, Stephen Vincent*
NOTES TOWARD A SPRING OFFENSIVE—*Dugan*
NOTES WRITTEN ON A DAMP VERANDA—*McGinley*
NOTHING—*Lowbury*
NOTHING BUT CHANGE—*Eberhart*
NOTHING BUT THE TRUTH—*Viorst*
NOTHING FALSE AND POSSIBLE IS LOVE—*Cummings*
NOTHING GOLD CAN STAY—*Frost, Robert*
NOTHING IS LOST—*Coward*

NOTHING NOW ASTONISHES—*Graves*

NOTHING TO BE SAID—*Larkin*

NOTICE OF EVICTION—*Weber, Ron*

NOTICIAS DE ULTIMA HORA—*Alcántara*

NOTRE MOUVEMENT—*Éluard*

NOTRE VIE—*Éluard*

UNA NOTTE—*Gatto*

NOTTE DELL' ASCENSIONE—*Uccello*

THE NOVEL—*Stevens, Wallace*

A NOVELETTE—*MacNeice*

NOVELLA—*Rich*

NOVEMBER DAY—*Averitt*

NOVEMBER SURF—*Jeffers, Robinson*

NOVEMBER 25, 1963—*Butler, William*

NOVEMBER 25, 1963—*Whitbread*

NOVEMBER 22, 1963—*Wright, Charles*

LA NOVIA—*Jiménez*

NOVIEMBRE—*Garcia Lorca*

NOW—*Walker*

NOW, ALL YOU CHILDREN—*Durem*

NOW FOR THE DELIGHT OF YOUR EYE—*Breton, Nicholas*

NOW POEM—*Sanchez*

NOW RETURNED HOME—*Jeffers, Robinson*

NOW THAT A. LOOKS LIKE AN ARTIST—*Gaver*

NOW THERE IS ONLY FOLLOWING —*Whistler*

NOW WE WILL EITHER SLEEP, LIE STILL, OR DRESS AGAIN—*Patten*

NOW WHAT IS LOVE?—*Raleigh*

NOX—*Ross, W. W. Eustace*

EL NUEVO MAR—*Jiménez*

LA NUIT—*Péguy*

LA NUIT D'AOÛT—*Musset*

LA NUIT DE DÉCEMBRE—*Musset*

LA NUIT DE MAI—*Musset*

LA NUIT HUMILIÉE—*Giguere*

LA NUIT, LES RUES DE NEW YORK—*Cendrars*

NUIT RHÉNANE—*Apollinaire*

NUITS DE JUIN—*Hugo, Victor*

NUITS D'HIVER—*Carco*

NUITS PARTAGÉES—*Éluard*

NUMBER MAN—*Sandburg*

NUMBER 7 AGAIN—*Harkness*

NUN ME GUARDATE—*Filippo*

NUNS AT EVE—*Brinnin*

THE NUN'S PRIEST'S TALE—*Chaucer*

NUR—*Roth, Eugen*

NUR DAS—*Tucholsky*

NUR ZWEI DINGE—*Benn*

THE NURSE—*MacNeice*

NURSERY RHYME—*Sitwell, Edith*

NURSERY RHYME OF INNOCENCE AND EXPERIENCE—*Causley*

NURSE'S SONG—*Blake*

NUTCRACKER SUITE—*Nash*

NUTS IN MAY—*MacNeice*

DEN NYA SKAPELSEN—*Kellgren*

NYANE—*Pushkin*

THE NYMPH AND THE SHEPHERD, OR, SHE WENT THAT-A-WAY—*Nash*

THE NYMPH COMPLAINING FOR THE DEATH OF HER FAWN—*Marvell*

NYMPHIDIA—*Drayton*

THE NYMPH'S REPLY TO THE SHEPHERD—*Raleigh*

NYU GWAN DZ—*Wei Jwang*

O BOYS! O BOYS!—*Gogarty*

O BY THE BY—*Cummings*

O CAPTAIN, MY CAPTAIN—*Whitman*

O CARIB ISLE—*Crane, Hart*

O CIEL! JE VOUS REVOIS MADAME—*Musset*

O DAEDALUS, FLY AWAY HOME—*Hayden*

O DEATH—*Anonymous–English–Modern English*

O DO NOT LOVE TOO LONG—*Yeats*

O DREAMS O DESTINATIONS—*Brathwaite*

O DREAMS O DESTINATIONS—*Day Lewis*

O FALLADAH, DIE DU HANGEST—*Brecht*

THE O-FILLER—*Reid*

O LAMB GIVE ME MY SALT—*Anonymous–African languages–Nigeria*

O LEBENS NEIGE—*Anonymous–Asian languages*

OH, LITTLE CHILD—*Treece*

OH, LOVELY ROCK—*Jeffers, Robinson*

O MENINO DE SUA MAE—*Pessoa*

O MIAMI—*Genser*

O MON AMOUR!—*Cendrars*

Ô MON CHIEN—*Lamartine*

O MUNNO D' 'E PPAROLE—*Filippo*

OH NO—*Creeley*

OH, PLEASE DON'T GET UP—*Nash*

O TAN-FACED PRAIRIE-BOY—*Whitman*

O TEMPORA, OH-OH—*Nash*

O THE CHIMNEYS—*Sachs*

O TO BE A DRAGON—*Moore, Marianne*

O TOURMENTS—*Grandbois*

O WHA'S THE BRIDE—*MacDiarmid*

O WORLD—*Van Doren*

O WORLD OF TOMS—*Francis*

THE OAK—*Eberhart*

OAK AND LILY—*Jonson*

OBITUARY—*Murphy*

OBITUARY FOR A LIVING LADY—*Brooks, Gwendolyn*

OBITUARY OF R. FULLER—*Fuller, Roy*

THE OBJECTION TO BEING STEPPED ON—*Frost, Robert*

OBLAKO V SHTANAKH—*Mayakovsky*

OBLIVION—*Smith, Stevie*

OBSERVATION—*Sanchez*

OBSESSED BY HER BEAUTY—*Viereck*

OBSESSION—*Baudelaire*

OBSESSIVE—*Bell*

OBUNDEN SJÄL—*Kefasdotter*

OB'YASNENIE—*Pasternak*

OCCHI APERTI—*Cremona*

L'OCCHI DI L'OMU—*Buttitta*

THE OCEAN—*Byron*

OCTAVIAN SHOOTING TARGETS—*Gregor*

18 DE NOVIEMBRE—*Murciano*

OCTOBER—*Andersen*

OCTOBER—*Frost, Robert*

OCTOBER—*Fyleman*

OCTOBER—*Thomas, Edward*

OCTOBER FROST—*Blackmur*

OCTOBER JOURNEY—*Walker*

OCTOBER, 1973—*Kizer*

THE OCTOPUS—*Nash*

THE OCTOPUSSYCAT—*Cox*

OCTUBRE—*Jiménez*

ODA A FRANCISCO SALINAS—*León, Fray Luis de*

ODA A LOS CALCETINES—*Neruda*

ODA A UNAS FLORES AMARILLAS—*Neruda*

ODA A WALT WHITMAN—*Garcia Lorca*

ODA AL NIÁGARA—*Heredia y Campuzano*

ODA AL PIADOS BARO PERFET—*Liost*

ODD—*Abse*

THE ODD WOMAN—*De Frees*

ODDMENTS, INKLINGS, OMENS, MOMENTS—*Reid*

ODE—*Chénier*

ODE—*Emerson*

ODE—*Fleming*

ODE—*O'Shaughnessy*

ODE—*Ronsard*

ODE—*Santayana*

ODE À CASSANDRE—*Ronsard*

ODE A LA COLONNE—*Hugo, Victor*

ODE À SA MAISTRESSE—*Ronsard*

AN ODE FOR BEN JONSON—*Herrick*

DAS ÖDE HAUS—*Droste-Hülshoff*

ODE INSCRIBED TO W. H. CHANNING—*Emerson*

DIE ODE 1950—*Krolow*

ODE ON A DISTANT PROSPECT OF ETON COLLEGE—*Gray*

ODE ON A GRECIAN URN—*Keats*

ODE ON MELANCHOLY—*Keats*

ODE ON SOLITUDE—*Pope, Alexander*

ODE ON THE DEATH OF A FAVORITE CAT, DROWNED IN A TUB OF GOLDFISHES— *Gray*

ODE ON THE PLEASURE ARISING FROM VICISSITUDES— *Gray*

ODE ON THE POPULAR SUPERSTITIONS OF THE HIGHLANDS— *Collins, William*

ODE POUR L'ELECTION DE SON SEPULCHRE— *Pound*

ODE (RICARDO REIS)— *Pessoa*

ODE SUR LES REVOLUTIONS— *Lamartine*

ODE TO A NIGHTINGALE— *Keats*

ODE TO AUTUMN— *Keats*

ODE TO BROTHER JOE— *McNeill*

ODE TO DINAH— *Hughes, Langston*

ODE TO DUTY— *Wordsworth*

ODE TO EVENING— *Collins, William*

ODE (TO HIMSELF)— *Jonson*

ODE TO OUR YOUNG PROCONSULS OF THE AIR— *Tate, Allen*

ODE TO PSYCHE— *Keats*

ODE TO SIMPLICITY— *Collins, William*

ODE TO SWANSEA— *Watkins*

ODE TO THE CONFEDERATE DEAD — *Timrod*

ODE TO THE CONFEDERATE DEAD — *Tate, Allen*

ODE TO THE SEA— *Baker, Howard*

ODE TO THE WEST WIND— *Shelley*

ODE TO WALT WHITMAN— *Benét, Stephen Vincent*

ODE UPON DOCTOR HARVEY— *Cowley, Abraham*

ODE WRITTEN IN THE BEGINNING OF THE YEAR 1746— *Collins, William*

ODENSE— *Andersen*

ODES— *Confucius*

ODES— *Horace*

ODEUR DE SAINTETÉ— *Obaldia*

ODI— *Parini*

EL ODIO— *Monvel*

ODYSSEUS— *Merwin*

ODYSSEY— *Homer*

OEDIPUS AT COLONUS— *Yeats*

L'OEIL DU MAÎTRE— *La Fontaine*

OF DE WITT WILLIAMS ON HIS WAY TO LINCOLN CEMETERY— *Brooks, Gwendolyn*

OF LYFE— *Dunbar, William*

OF MARYLAND— *Braxton*

OF PROMISED LANDS— *Posner*

OF THE AWFUL BATTLE OF THE PEKES AND THE POLLICLES— *Eliot, Thomas Stearns*

OF THE MEAN AND SURE ESTATE— *Wyatt, Sir Thomas*

OF THEE KIND BOY— *Suckling*

OFERTORIO— *Nervo*

OFF MARBLEHEAD— *Hollander*

OFF THE GROUND— *De la Mare*

AN OFFERING FOR MR. BLUEHART — *Wright, James*

OFFICIAL SERUMS— *Elmslie*

L'OFOCO QUE MES M'AGRADA— *Salvat-Papasseit*

OGNI— *Korolenko*

OGRES AND PYGMIES— *Graves*

OH ZENTE DE L'INFANZIA— *Marin*

OHNE FALSCHE ZEUGEN— *Loerke*

OHNE NEID— *Nietzsche*

OIL— *Snyder*

THE OIL OF JOY FOR MOURNING— *Blackmur*

OIL PAINTING OF THE ARTIST AS THE ARTIST— *MacLeish*

L'OISEAU BLESSÉ D'UNE FLÈCHE— *La Fontaine*

L'OISEAU-LYRE— *Seghers*

OJE NINNO— *Viviani*

LOS OJOS DE PICASSO— *Alberti*

THE OLD AGE OF THESEUS— *Winters*

OLD AND YOUNG— *Reeves*

AN OLD ATHEIST PAUSES BY THE SEA— *Kinsella*

THE OLD BATTALION— *Anonymous–English– Modern English*

OLD BLACK MAN SAY— *Emanuel*

OLD BLUE— *Anonymous–English– Modern English*

THE OLD BRASS POT— *Conkling*

THE OLD BRIDGE— *Conkling*

OLD CHRISTMAS— *Helton*

THE OLD CHURCH BELL— *Marshall, Helen Lowrie*

OLD COUNTRYSIDE— *Bogan*

OLD CROCK— *Patten*

OLD DEUTERONOMY— *Eliot, Thomas Stearns*

THE OLD FAMILIAR FACES— *Lamb*

THE OLD FLAME— *Lowell, Robert*

OLD FURNITURE— *Hardy*

THE OLD GUMBIE CAT— *Eliot, Thomas Stearns*

THE OLD HOUSE: PLYMOUTH— *Lifshin*

OLD IRONSIDES— *Holmes, Oliver Wendell*

OLD KING COTTON— *Brown, Sterling A.*

THE OLD KNIGHT— *Peele*

OLD LAUGHTER— *Brooks, Gwendolyn*

OLD LEM— *Brown, Sterling A.*

OLD LOVE— *Lewis, Janet*

OLD MAN— *Thomas, Edward*

THE OLD MAN TO THE LIZARD— *MacLeish*

OLD MAN'S CONFESSION OF FAITH — *Francis*

THE OLD MAN'S SONG— *Gordon*

OLD MAN'S SONG— *Spencer*

AN OLD MAN'S WINTER NIGHT— *Frost, Robert*

OLD MARY— *Brooks, Gwendolyn*

AN OLD MATTRESS IN THE LOTS— *Kramer*

OLD MEN AND OLD WOMEN GOING HOME ON THE STREET CAR— *Moore, Merrill*

OLD MOLLEY MEANS— *Walker*

OLD PAINTER TO YOUNG MODEL— *Reid*

THE OLD PILOT'S DEATH— *Hall*

OLD POSSUM'S BOOK OF PRACTICAL CATS— *Eliot, Thomas Stearns*

OLD QUIN QUEERIBUS— *Turner, Nancy Byrd*

THE OLD SAILOR— *Milne*

OLD SHELLOVER— *De la Mare*

THE OLD SHIPS— *Flecker*

OLD SON OF A BITCH DEATH HOTEL— *Tullos*

AN OLD SONG RE-SUNG— *Colum*

THE OLD STONEMASON— *Jeffers, Robinson*

THE OLD VICARAGE, GRANTCHESTER— *Brooke*

OLD WAR DREAMS— *Whitman*

OLD WINTERS ON THE FARM— *Riley*

OLD WITHERINGTON— *Randall*

AN OLD WOMAN— *Anonymous–English– Modern English*

AN OLD WOMAN— *Sitwell, Edith*

OLD WOMAN— *Smith, Iain Chrichton*

THE OLD WOMAN IN THE BOMBED CHURCH— *Mayer*

AN OLD WOMAN OF THE ROADS— *Colum*

OLD WOMAN'S SONG— *Gordon*

OLD WORDS— *Sanchez*

THE OLEASTER— *Graves*

OLFACTORY PURSUITS— *Abse*

L'OLIVE— *Du Bellay*

OLLIE McGEE— *Masters, Edgar Lee*

OLLIE'S POLLY— *Merriam*

OLOR FRUTAL— *Ibarbourou*

THE OLYMPIC GIRL— *Betjeman*

OM KÄRLEKEN DU FINNER— *Hasso*

OMAHA— *Sandburg*

OMAR REPENTANT— *Anonymous–English– Modern English*

ÔMBRE E ADDORE— *Viviani*

L'OMBRE ROUGE— *Lasnier*

OMHÖLJD AV SITT EGET SILENTIUM — *Ferlin*

L'OMINO DELLA GRU— *Rodari*

LL'OMMO 'E NIENTE— *Galdieri*

ON A BANK AS I SAT A-FISHING— *Wotton*

ON A BICYCLE— *Yevtushenko*

ON A BOUGAINVILLEA VINE AT THE SUMMER PALACE— *Howes*

ON A CERTAIN LADY AT COURT— *Pope, Alexander*

ON A FLIMMERING FLOOM YOU SHALL RIDE— *Sandburg*

ON A GIRDLE—*Waller*
ON A LANE IN SPRING—*Clare*
ON A MOONLIT ROAD IN THE NORTH WOODS—*Bly*
ON A POLITICAL PRISONER—*Yeats*
ON A REPLICA OF THE PARTHENON—*Davidson*
ON A SQUIRREL CROSSING THE ROAD IN AUTUMN—*Eberhart*
ON A THEME BY FROST—*Francis*
ON A VIEW OF PASADENA FROM THE HILLS—*Winters*
ON ACCEPTING THE GOLD WATCH—*Summers, Hollis*
ON AN ECDYSIAST—*Ciardi*
ON AN INFANT DYING AS SOON AS BORN—*Lamb*
ON AN OLD WOMAN DYING—*Lewis, Janet*
ON ANOTHER'S SORROW—*Blake*
ON APIS THE PRIZEFIGHTER—*Lucilius*
ON BEING—*Ciardi*
ON DREAMS—*Hodges*
ON DWELLING—*Graves*
ON EASTNOR KNOLL—*Masefield*
ON FIRST LOOKING IN ON BLODGETT'S KEATS'S "CHAPMAN'S HOMER"—*Starbuck*
ON FIRST LOOKING INTO CHAPMAN'S HOMER—*Keats*
ON FOOD—*Belloc*
ON GAY WALLPAPER—*Williams, William Carlos*
ON HEARING FRENCH CHILDREN SPEAK FRENCH—*Edman*
ON HERMOGENES THE PHYSICIAN—*Lucilius*
ON HIS FIRST SONNE—*Jonson*
ON HIS HEID-AKE—*Dunbar, William*
ON HIS MISTRESS, THE QUEEN OF BOHEMIA—*Wotton*
ON HIS MISTRIS—*Donne*
ON HIS PITIABLE TRANSFORMATION—*Stevenson*
ON HIS SEVENTY-FIRST BIRTHDAY—*Landor*
ON JOHN BUSHBY—*Burns*
ON LEAVING PRISON—*León, Fray Luis de*
ON LEAVING THE PARTY AFTER HAVING BEEN POSSIBLY BRILLIANT FOR CERTAINLY TOO LONG—*Ciardi*
ON LISTENING TO THE SPIRITUALS—*Jeffers, Lance*
ON LOOKING AT STUBB'S ANATOMY OF THE HORSE—*Lucie-Smith*
ON LOOKING EAST TO THE SEA WITH A SUNSET BEHIND ME—*Ciardi*
ON LOOKING UP BY CHANCE AT THE CONSTELLATIONS—*Frost, Robert*
ON LORD HOLLAND'S SEAT—*Gray*

ON MIDDLETON EDGE—*Young, Andrew*
ON MY BIRTHDAY—*Prior*
ON MY FIRST DAUGHTER—*Jonson*
ON MY FORTIETH BIRTHDAY—*Tripp*
ON NOT SAYING EVERYTHING—*Day Lewis*
ON NOT WRITING AN ELEGY—*Frost, Richard*
ON OUR WAY—*Merriam*
ON PASSING THE NEW MENIN GATE—*Sassoon*
ON PORTENTS—*Graves*
ON RETIREMENT—*Freneau*
ON RETURNING TO A LAKE IN SPRING—*Eberhart*
ON RIOTS—*Leslie*
ON SAINT THERESA'S DIFFICULTY IN KEEPING HER FEET ON THE GROUND—*O'Gorman*
ON SEEING DIANA GO MADDDDDDD—*Lee, Don L.*
ON SEEING PHAROAH SANDERS BLOWING—*Sanchez*
ON SEEING THE ELGIN MARBLES—*Keats*
ON SEEING THE REFLECTION OF NOTRE DAME IN THE SEINE—*Figueroa*
ON SHAKESPEARE—*Milton*
ON SILENCE—*O'Gorman*
ON TEACHING THE YOUNG—*Winters*
ON THE BEACH AT FONTANA—*Joyce*
ON THE BIRTH OF A CHILD—*Untermeyer*
ON THE CIRCUIT—*Auden*
ON THE COUNTESS DOWAGER OF PEMBROKE—*Browne, William*
ON THE DEATH OF DR. BENJAMIN FRANKLIN—*Freneau*
ON THE DEATH OF DR. ROBERT LEVET—*Johnson, Samuel*
ON THE DEATH OF JOSEPH RODMAN DRAKE—*Halleck*
ON THE DECLINE OF ORACLES—*Plath*
ON THE DEPARTURE PLATFORM—*Hardy*
ON THE DIFFICULTY OF CONJURING UP A DRYAD—*Plath*
ON THE EDGE—*Levine*
ON THE EXTINCTION OF THE VENETIAN REPUBLIC—*Wordsworth*
ON THE GRAND TOUR 1638–1639—*Moore, Merrill*
ON THE GRASSHOPPER AND CRICKET—*Keats*
ON THE HILL BELOW THE LIGHTHOUSE—*Dickey, James*
ON THE KITE—*Collymore*
ON THE LATE MASSACRE IN PIEDMONT—*Milton*

ON THE LORD GENERAL FAIRFAX AT THE SIEGE OF COLCHESTER—*Milton*
ON THE LOSS OF THE ROYAL GEORGE—*Cowper*
ON THE MARGINAL WAY—*Wilbur*
ON THE MARRIAGE OF A VIRGIN—*Thomas, Dylan*
ON THE MORNING OF CHRIST'S NATIVITY—*Milton*
ON THE MURDER OF LIEUTENANT JOSE DEL CASTILLO BY THE FALANGIST BRAVO MARTINEZ—*Levine*
ON THE POET AS A DAMNED POOR THING—*Ciardi*
ON THE POET AS A MARIONETTE—*Ciardi*
ON THE PORTRAIT OF A SCHOLAR OF THE ITALIAN RENAISSANCE—*Winters*
ON THE RECEIPT OF MY MOTHER'S PICTURE OUT OF NORFOLK—*Cowper*
ON THE SAND—*Clark, John W.*
ON THE SAND BAR—*Hollander*
ON THE SEA—*Keats*
ON THE TOMBS IN WESTMINSTER ABBEY—*Anonymous–English—Modern English*
ON THE VANITY OF HUMAN ASPIRATIONS—*Sitwell, Edith*
ON THE WAY TO THE DEPOT—*Kavanagh*
ON THIS DAY I COMPLETE MY THIRTY-SIXTH YEAR—*Byron*
ON TIME—*Milton*
ON TRANSLATING "EUGENE ONEGIN"—*Nabokov*
ON TROY FALLEN—*Agathias*
ON TUESDAY I POLISH MY UNCLE—*Lee, Dennis*
ON UNIVERSALISM—*Knight, Etheridge*
ON WATCHING A WORLD SERIES GAME—*Sanchez*
ON WENLOCK EDGE—*Housman*
ON WENLOCK EDGE—*Walters*
ON WESTWALL DOWNES—*Strode*
ON ZACHEUS—*Quarles*
ONCE A LADY TOLD ME—*Giovanni*
ONCE BY THE PACIFIC—*Frost, Robert*
ONCE I SAID LIGHTLY—*Hughes, Ted*
ONCE MORE, THE SWEET SONGS—*Fabio, Sarah Webster*
ONCE UPON A TIME—*Summers, Hollis*
ONE—*Ciardi*
1 A.M. AT ALL TIMES—*Pietri*
ONE AND HIS MISTRESS A-DYING—*Anonymous–English—Modern English*
ONE DAY—*Ciardi*
ONE DAY—*Dodson*

ONE-EYED CRITICS—*Jordan,
Norman*
ONE-EYED NIGHT—*Fox, Charles*
ONE FOOT IN EDEN—*Muir*
ONE FOR ALL—*Jordan, Norman*
100 HATS—*Abse*
ONE MORE BREVITY—*Frost,
Robert*
ONE MORE NEW BOTCHED
BEGINNING—*Spender*
ONE MORE TIME—*Aubert*
ONE OF MANY—*Smith, Stevie*
ONE OF THE JEWS—*Cavafy*
ONE OF THOSE DAYS—*Johnston,
Ellen Turlington*
ONE PERFECT ROSE—*Parker*
ONE POET VISITS ANOTHER—
Davies, William Henry
ONE SIDED SHOOT—*Lee, Don L.*
ONE STEP BACKWARD TAKEN—
Frost, Robert
ONE THIRD OF A CALENDAR—
Nash
ONE THOUSAND NINE HUNDRED
AND SIXTY EIGHT WINTERS—
Earley
ONE-TWO-THREE—*Bunner*
ONE, TWO, THREE, FOUR, FIVE—
Coatsworth
ONE WAY OF LOVE—*Browning,
Robert*
ONE-WAY TICKET—*Hughes,
Langston*
ONE WESTERN, TO GO—*Nash*
ONE'S NOT HALF TWO. IT'S TWO
ARE HALVES OF ONE—
Cummings
ONION—*Anonymous–English—
Old English*
ONLY IN MADNESS—*Darr*
ONLY IN THE DREAM—*Eberhart*
ONLY MY OPINION—*Shannon*
ONORE DEL VERO—*Luzi*
THE ONSET—*Frost, Robert*
OPEN HOUSE—*Roethke*
OPEN HOUSE—*Viorst*
THE OPEN SEA—*Meredith,
William*
OPEN THE DOOR TO ME, OH—
Burns
OPEN THE GATES—*Kunitz*
THE OPENING WORLD—*Betjeman*
OPERA NOTES—*Coward*
OPERA, OPERA—*Gregory, Horace*
THE OPERATION—*Snodgrass*
OPHÉLIE—*Rimbaud*
ÖPPEN KUST—*Martinson*
OPPORTUNITY—*Sill*
THE OPPOSITE HOUSE—*Lowell,
Robert*
THE OPPOSITE OF GREEN—*Aubert*
THE OPPOSITE SIDE OF THE DEATH
COIN IS LOVE—*Polak*
OPUS ZERO NUMBER ZERO—*Enslin*
L'ORA DI BARGA—*Pascoli*
ORA SMETIS—*Chlebnikov*

ORAÇÂO AO NEGRINHO DO
PASTOREIO—*Meyer, Augusto*
ORACIÓN POR EL ALMA DE UN
NIÑO MONTAÑES—*Bernárdez*
ORACLE FROM A DEVICE—*Essex*
THE ORACLE OF THE ZEBRA—
Deveaux
ORADOUR—*Tardieu*
ORALS—*Lifshin*
THE ORANGE BEARS—*Patchen*
THE ORB WEAVER—*Francis*
ORBITER 5 SHOWS HOW EARTH
LOOKS FROM THE MOON—
Swenson
THE ORCHARD—*Aiken*
THE ORCHARD PIT—*Rossetti,
Dante Gabriel*
THE ORCHESTRA—*Williams,
William Carlos*
ORDER OF DIET—*Swenson*
ORDERLY—*Miles*
OREGON WINTER—*McGahey*
ORGANIST—*Ormond*
ORGE'S HYMN—*Brecht*
ORIENTAL—*Zorrilla*
AN ORIGIN OF ART—*Rector*
THE ORIGIN OF BASEBALL—
Patchen
THE ORIGIN OF BLACKNESS—
Marvin X
ORIGINAL SIN—*Antoninus*
ORIGINAL SIN—*Warren*
ORIGINS—*Kgositsile*
ORLANDO FURIOSO—*Ariosto*
OROANDE INBLICK—*Martinson*
THE ORPHANAGE—*Cavalieri*
THE ORPHAN'S SONG—*Dobell*
ORPHEUS—*Rukeyser*
ORPHEUS—*Winters*
ORPHEUS, EURYDIKE, HERMES—
Rilke
ORPHEUS IN AMERICA—*Simpson*
ORPHEUS IN THE UNDERWORLD—
Simpson
ORPHEUS WITH HIS LUTE—
Fletcher, John
LL'ORTENZIE—*Di Giacomo*
OSEN—*Pasternak*
OSEN—*Pushkin*
OSEN V SIGULDE—*Derwood*
OSMOSIS—*Darr*
OSMUND TOULMIN—*Sitwell,
Osbert*
OSSIAN'S GRAVE—*Jeffers,
Robinson*
OSTERLIED—*Claudius*
OSTIA ANTICA—*Kaschnitz*
THE OTHER—*Roethke*
OTHER KNOWLEDGE—*Marshall,
Lenore G.*
OTKRITOE PISMO—*Simonov*
OTNOSHENIYE K BARYSHNE—
Mayakovsky
EL OTOÑADO—*Jiménez*
EL OTOÑO—*Vivanco*
EL OTRO—*Retamar*

OTRO POR 'SUPER FLUMINA
BABYLONIS—*Juan de la Cruz*
AN OTTER—*Hughes, Ted*
L'OUBLI—*Heredia*
OUBLIEUSE MÉMOIRE—
Supervielle
OUIJA—*Plath*
OULD SNARLY-GOB—*Stephens*
OUR BEING IS AN IMPERCEPTIBLE
WIND—*Gregor*
OUR "BELL"—*Johnston, Ellen
Turlington*
OUR GOODMAN—
*Anonymous–English—
Modern English*
OUR HELLS—*Sandburg*
OUR LORD AND OUR LADY—*Belloc*
OUR OFFICE CAT—*Smith, Stevie*
OUR PADRE—*Betjeman*
OUR TWO WORTHIES—*Ransom*
OUR WORKING DAY MAY BE
MENACED—*Avison*
L'OURS ET L'AMATEUR DE JARDINS
—*La Fontaine*
L'OURS ET LES DEUX COMPAGNONS
—*La Fontaine*
OUT—*Hughes, Ted*
OUT—*Kern*
OUT IN THE DARK—*Thomas,
Edward*
OUT OF EAST ANGLIA—*Davie*
OUT OF SCHOOL—*Summers, Hal*
OUT OF THE ASH—*Antoninus*
OUT OF THE CRADLE ENDLESSLY
ROCKING—*Whitman*
OUT OF THE FLAME—*Sitwell,
Osbert*
OUT OF THE SEA, EARLY—*Swenson*
OUT TO OLD AUNT MARY'S—*Riley*
OUTBREAK OF SPRING—*Starbuck*
THE OUTCOME OF MR. MCLEOD'S
GRATITUDE—*Nash*
THE OUTCOME: THE SUN—*Piercy*
OUTLANDERS, WHENCE COME YE,
LAST?—*Morris, William*
OUTLAWS—*Graves*
OUTRA CANÇÂO—*Botto*
OUTRA ODE (RICARDO REIS)—
Pessoa
OUTREACH OF PRAYER—*Marshall,
Helen Lowrie*
OUTRO PEQUENO POEMA MENTAL
—*Lisboa, Irene*
OUTSIDE THE WINDOW—*Hardy*
OUTSONG IN THE JUNGLE—
Kipling
OUTWARD—*Clark, John W.*
THE OVEN BIRD—*Frost, Robert*
OVER EN HYACINT—*Nordenflycht*
OVER THE BIER OF THE WORLDING
—*Merwin*
OVER THE BRIDGE—*Sandburg*
OVERBOARD—*Swenson*
OVERCAST—*Hollander*
OVERHEARD—*Hillyer*
OVERHEARD ON A SALTMARSH—
Monro

OVERHEARING TWO ON A COLD SUNDAY MORNING—*Francis*
OVERPRODUCTION OF CORN—*Tullos*
THE OVERTHROW OF ONE O'CLOCK AT NIGHT—*Rukeyser*
OVERTURE—*Hillyer*
OVILLEJOS—*Cervantes Saavedra*
THE OWL—*Booth*
THE OWL—*De la Mare*
THE OWL—*Gold*
THE OWL—*Tennyson*
THE OWL—*Thomas, Edward*
THE OWL AND THE PUSSY-CAT—*Lear*
THE OXEN—*Hardy*
OXEN PLOUGHING AT FIESOLE—*Tomlinson*
OYSTER—*Anonymous–English–Old English*
OZYMANDIAS—*Shelley*
OZYMANDIAS REVISITED—*Bishop, Morris*

PÅ HÄLL—*Ferlin*
'A PACE D' 'A CASA—*Galdieri*
THE PACKAGE—*Fisher*
PADDLING SONG—*Anonymous–African languages–Congo*
PAESE MASSA STRETO—*Marin*
PAESE MIO—*Marin*
PAGAN PRAYER—*Cullen*
PAGINA DI UN VANGELO NAUTICO—*Bevilacqua*
PAGINA FIEL . . ., NOSTALGIA—*Prados*
PAIN RASSIS—*Péret*
THE PAINS OF SLEEP—*Coleridge, Samuel Taylor*
PAINTED HEAD—*Ransom*
PAINTERS—*Rukeyser*
PAIR—*Engle*
PAISAJE—*Garcia Lorca*
PAISAJE DEL CORAZÓN—*Jiménez*
PAISAJE GRANA—*Jiménez*
EL PÁJARO ESCONDIDO—*Martinez Alonso*
EL PÁJARO Y LA ROSA—*Martinez Alonso*
PAK CHUN HUAI—*Du Mu*
PAL—*Mitchell, Adrian*
UNA PALABRA—*Mistral*
PALABRAS A EUROPA—*Neruda*
THE PALACE AT 4 A. M.—*Braxton*
PALEMON EL ESTILITA—*Valencia*
PÂLEUR—*Vigny*
PALLA D'ORO—*Saba*
PALLADIUM—*Arnold*
PALM-READING—*Garfinkel*
PALME—*Valéry*
LA PALMERA—*Lugones, Ricardo*
PALMSTRÖM—*Morgenstern*
PALMSTRÖM ADDRESSING A NIGHTINGALE THAT DID NOT LET HIM SLEEP—*Morgenstern*
PALMSTRÖM LOBT—*Morgenstern*

PALMSTRÖMS UHR—*Morgenstern*
PAN—*Jiménez*
PAN—*Wilde*
PANAMA AIRPORT—*Pommy Vega, Janine*
PANDERETA—*Mata*
PANGLOSS'S SONG: A COMIC-OPERA LYRIC—*Wilbur*
THE PANGOLIN—*Moore, Marianne*
PANOPTES—*Martinez Alonso*
PANORAMA DE MÉRIDA—*Garcia Lorca*
PANORAMIC SUE—*Weiss*
THE PANTHER—*Nash*
DER PANTHER—*Rilke*
PANTHER CAGED—*Fabio, Sarah Webster*
PANTHER MAN—*Emanuel*
PANTHOIDENS SÅNG—*Ekelöf*
PANTOMIME—*Verlaine*
PANTOMIME POEM—*McGough*
LE PAON—*Apollinaire*
PAPA LOVE BABY—*Smith, Stevie*
DER PAPAGEI—*Morgenstern*
PAPER—*Sandburg*
PAPER BOATS—*Tagore*
PAPER CUTS—*Jong*
PAPER MEN TO AIR HOPES AND FEARS—*Francis*
LE PAPILLON—*Lamartine*
PAPUA NEW GUINEA—*Ipagongnaik*
LES PÂQUES A NEW-YORK—*Cendrars*
LE PAQUET ROUGE—*Cocteau*
PAR LUI-MÊME—*Cocteau*
PARA ENTONCES—*Gutiérrez Nájera*
PARABASE—*Goethe*
PARABEL—*Goethe*
PARABLE FOR A CERTAIN VIRGIN—*Parker*
PARABLE OF THE FOURPOSTER—*Jong*
THE PARABLE OF THE OLD MAN AND THE YOUNG—*Owen, Wilfred*
PARABOLA—*Machado, Manuel*
PARABOLA DEL RETORNO—*Barba Jacob*
PARABOLICHESKAYA BALLADA—*Voznezensky*
PARACAR CHE SCAPPEE DE LOMBARDIA—*Porta*
PARADE—*Hughes, Langston*
PARADISE LOST—*Milton*
PARADISE REGAINED—*Milton*
PARADISO—*Dante Alighieri*
PARAÍSO—*Jiménez*
PARANOIA—*Browne, Michael Dennis*
PARAPHRASE DU DIES IRAE—*La Fontaine*
PARAPHRASE DU PSAUME 145—*Malherbe*
THE PARDON—*Wilbur*

LE PARDON DE SAINTE-ANNE-LA-PALUD—*Corbière*
THE PARDONER'S PROLOGUE—*Chaucer*
THE PARDONER'S TALE—*Chaucer*
THE PARENT—*Nash*
PARENTESIS—*Muñoz Rivera*
PARENTHOOD—*Ciardi*
THE PARENTS: PEOPLE LIKE OUR MARRIAGE MAXIE AND ANDREW—*Brooks, Gwendolyn*
LA PARESSE—*Cendrars*
LE PARESSEUX—*Ronsard*
LE PARFUM—*Baudelaire*
UN PARFUM ÉMANAIT D'ELLE—*Cendrars*
PARFUM EXOTIQUE—*Baudelaire*
PARING THE APPLE—*Tomlinson*
PARIÓ LA LUNA—*Lloréns Torres*
PARIS—*Aragon*
PARIS A 5 HEURES DU MATIN—*Desangiers*
PARIS AT NIGHT—*Prévert*
PARIS, DOUBLE GALÈRE—*Péguy*
PARIS, LE 15 DÉCEMBRE 1999—*Vian*
PARISH DOCTOR—*Brown, Sterling A.*
THE PARISH REGISTER—*Crabbe*
PARISIAN BEGGAR WOMAN—*Hughes, Langston*
THE PARK—*Tippett*
PARK MONCEAU—*Tucholsky*
PARK POEM—*Patten*
IL PARLAMENTO—*Carducci*
LE PARLEMENT—*Marot*
PARLIAMENT HILL—*Bashford*
PARLIAMENT HILL FIELDS—*Plath*
THE PARLIAMENT OF FOWLS—*Chaucer*
PARLIAMONE—*Bevilacqua*
LA PAROLA PALAZZO—*Rodari*
PAROLE D'AMMORE SCUNTENTO—*Di Giacomo*
THE PARROTS—*Gibson, Wilfred*
PARRU CU TIA—*Buttitta*
THE PARSI WOMAN—*Millay*
THE PARSON'S PROLOGUE—*Chaucer*
THE PARSON'S SON—*Service*
PART SONG—*Fry*
PARTA QUIES—*Housman*
PARTHENIA—*Alcman*
LA PARTIDA—*Garcia Nieto*
THE PARTING—*Drayton*
PARTING AGAIN—*Sukenick*
PARTING AT MORNING—*Browning, Robert*
PARTING IS SUCH—*Robinson, Wanda*
PARTIR. PRENDRE LA ROUTE—*Cendrars*
LES PARTS SEMBLABLES—*Bernard*
THE PARTY—*Dunbar, Paul Laurence*
PARTY CARD—*Yevtushenko*

PARTY NOTES—*Patten*
PARTY PIECE—*Patten*
PARZIVAL—*Wolfram von
    Eschenbach*
LES PAS—*Valéry*
PASEO—*Jiménez*
EL PASO DE LA SIGUIRIYA—*Garcia
    Lorca*
PASPORT—*Mayakovsky*
PASQUALE—*Totò*
PASS OFFICE SONG—
    *Anonymous–African
    languages–Southern Africa*
PASSA LA RONDA—*Ciconi*
PASSAGE FROM CHILDHOOD—*Day
    Lewis*
PASSAGE TO INDIA—*Whitman*
A PASSER-BY—*Bridges*
IL PASSERO SOLITARIO—*Leopardi*
THE PASSING OF ARTHUR—
    Tennyson
PASSING ON—*Rich*
PASSING REMARK—*Stafford*
THE PASSING STRANGE—*Masefield*
PASSING THE GRAVEYARD— *Young,
    Andrew*
PASSING TIME—*Braxton*
PASSION—*Trakl*
THE PASSIONATE MAN'S
    PILGRIMAGE—*Raleigh*
THE PASSIONATE SHEPHERD TO HIS
    LOVE—*Marlowe*
'A PASSIONE MIA ERANO 'E RROSE—
    Totò
THE PASSIONS: AN ODE FOR MUSIC
    —*Collins, William*
PASSIONSLIED—*Gerhardt*
PASSIVE RESISTANCE—*Danner*
IL PASSO DELLE NAZARENE—
    Palazzeschi
PAST—*Sanchez*
PAST AND PRESENT—*Matiabe*
EL PASTOR DESESPERADO—
    Anonymous–Spanish
PASTOR QUE CON TUS SILBOS—
    Vega Carpio
PASTORAL—*Dicenta*
PASTORAL—*Hillyer*
PASTORAL—*Patchen*
PASTORALSVIT—*Lindegren*
I PASTORI—*D'Annunzio,
    Gabriele*
THE PASTURE—*Frost, Robert*
THE PATCHED EYE—*De Frees*
PATER NOSTER—*Prévert*
PATERSON— *Williams, William
    Carlos*
PATERSON: THE FALLS— *Williams,
    William Carlos*
THE PATH—*Thomas, Edward*
THE PATH AMONG THE STONES—
    Kinnell
PATH-FINDERS—*Brathwaite*
PATIENCE—*Giovanni*
PATIENCE, HARD THING!—
    Hopkins

PATIENT GRISSELL: THE
    BASKET-MAKER'S SONG—*Dekker*
PATIENTS IN A PUBLIC WARD—
    Jennings
EL PATITO FEO—*Lloréns Torres*
LE PÂTRE ET LE LION—*La
    Fontaine*
PATRIA DE CADA DÍA—*Luis*
THE PATRIARCH—*Danner*
PATRICK KAVANAGH'S DUBLIN—
    Liddy
THE PATRIOT—*Browning, Robert*
PAUL REVERE'S RIDE—*Longfellow*
PAULINE—*Browning, Robert*
PAULINE BARRETT—*Masters,
    Edgar Lee*
'A PAURA MIA—*Filippo*
PAVANA ANDALUZA DE TU CALLE
    SIN SALIDA—*León, Rafael de*
A PAVANE FOR THE NURSERY—
    Smith, William Jay
PAVANE FOR THE WHITE QUEEN,
    THE LOVED WIFE FALLING
    SLOWLY AWAKE—*Bergé*
PAY ATTENTION—*Franks*
PAYESES—*Ridruejo*
PAYSAGE—*Baudelaire*
PAYSAGE NOCTURNE—*Gautier*
PAYSAGES URBAINS—*Fombeure*
LE PAYSAN DE PARIS CHANTE—
    Aragon
LE PAYSAN DU DANUBE—*La
    Fontaine*
PE LA VIA—*Di Giacomo*
PEACE—*De la Mare*
PEACE—*Herbert*
PEACE—*Hopkins*
PEACE—*Knight, Etheridge*
PEACE—*Levine*
PEACE— *Vaughan, Henry*
PEACE, BE STILL—*Corner*
PEACE FREAK POEM—*Sanders*
PEACE IN THE WELSH HILLS—
    Watkins
PEACE ON EARTH— *Williams,
    William Carlos*
PEACE PROSPECT—*Gioseffi*
THE PEACEFUL SHEPHERD—*Frost,
    Robert*
PEACH, PLUM OR APRICOT—*Kops*
THE PEACOCK—*Francis*
THE PEACOCK OF JAVA—*Smith,
    William Jay*
PEACOCKS: NON ACTION—
    Thomas-Ellis
THE PEARL—
    *Anonymous–English—Middle
    English*
THE PEARL—*Herbert*
THE PEARL—*Smith, Stevie*
PECAN PIE—*Clark, China*
A PECK OF GOLD—*Frost, Robert*
LA PEDDI NOVA—*Buttitta*
PEDIATRIC REFLECTIONS—*Nash*
PEEKABOO, I ALMOST SEE YOU—
    Nash
PEELING ONIONS—*Rich*

PEGASUS—*Braxton*
PEGASUS—*Day Lewis*
PEGASUS IM JOCHE—*Schiller*
PEGGY BROWNE—*Clarke*
PENA—*Martinez Estrada*
PENA Y ALEGRÍA DEL AMOR—
    León, Rafael de
PENELOPE—*Wilkinson*
PENNIWIT, THE ARTIST—*Masters,
    Edgar Lee*
PENSADO AL LUOGO DELL'
    ORIGINE DA UN LUOGO DEL
    MONDO—*Bevilacqua*
PENSÉE DES MORTS—*Lamartine*
IL PENSEROSO—*Milton*
PENSIERI ELEMENTARI—*Risi*
IL PENSIERO DOMINANTE—
    Leopardi
PENTRE IFAN—*Griffiths*
THE PEOPLE—*Yeats*
THE PEOPLE GROWER—*Marshall,
    Helen Lowrie*
THE PEOPLE, YES—*Sandburg*
THE PEOPLE'S ANTHEM—*Elliot*
THE PEOPLE'S CHILD—*Marvin X*
PEPELA—*Popa*
LA PEQUEÑA LLAMA—*Ibarbourou*
PEQUEÑO POEMA MENTAL—
    Lisboa, Irene
PEQUEÑO VALS VIENÉS—*Garcia
    Lorca*
PER LA MORTE DI NAPOLEONE
    EUGENIO—*Carducci*
PERCY BYSSHE SHELLEY—*Masters,
    Edgar Lee*
PÈRE DU DOUX REPOS—*Tyard*
PEREGRINA—*Mörike*
LOS PEREGRINITOS—
    Anonymous–Spanish
THE PERFECT HUSBAND—*Nash*
PERFECTION— *Williams,
    William Carlos*
PERFECTION ISN'T LIKE A PERFECT
    STORY—*Kavanagh*
THE PERFORMANCE—*Dickey,
    James*
PERFORMANCE POETS—*Gaver*
THE PERFUME—*Donne*
PERICLES AND ASPASIA—*Landor*
LI PERICOLI DER TEMPORALE—
    Belli
LES PERLES AUX POURCEAUX—
    Picabia
DAS PERLHUHN—*Morgenstern*
PERO COMO DECIRTELO—
    Bousoño
PERRY-THE-WINKLE—*Tolkien*
THE PERSIAN VERSION—*Graves*
PERSONAL LETTER NO. 2—
    Sanchez
PERSONAL LETTER NO. 3—
    Sanchez
PERSONAL TALK—*Wordsworth*
PERSPECTIVES ARE PRECIPICES—
    Bishop, John Peale
PESCAURI—*Marin*
'O PESCE NICOLO— *Viviani*

PESNYA UBOGOGO STRANNIKA—*Nekrasov*
THE PET COON—*Riley*
PETER GRIMES—*Crabbe*
PETER QUINCE AT THE CLAVIER—*Stevens, Wallace*
PETER THE WAG—*Gilbert, Sir William Schwenck*
PETER WAS A PILOT—*Lee, Dennis*
PETER ZOLL—*Masters, Edgar Lee*
PETIT CRU—*Bédier*
PETIT MANAN POINT—*Blackmur*
LE PETIT POISSON ET LE PÊCHEUR—*La Fontaine*
LE PETIT TESTAMENT—*Villon*
PETIT, THE POET—*Masters, Edgar Lee*
LA PETITE AUTO—*Apollinaire*
LA PETITE INFANTE DE CASTILLE—*Hugo, Victor*
PETITE RITOURNELLE IMPÉRIALE—*Obaldia*
LES PETITES BARAQUES—*Rictus*
LES PETITES VILLES—*Hébert*
THE PETITION FOR AN ABSOLUTE RETREAT—*Finch, Anne, Countess of Winchelsea*
PETITIONS ON THE GRAVE OF RABBI SIMEON YECHNOI—*Sutzkever*
THE PETS—*Farren*
LE PEUPLE ÉTAIT DEBOUT—*Hugo, Victor*
PFANNKUCHEN UND SALAT—*Busch*
PFEIFEN—*Hesse*
DER PFLAUMENBAUM—*Brecht*
PH.D. PANCAKES ENGLISH STYLE—*Lifshin*
PHAESTOS—*Corso*
THE PHANTOM BARK—*Crane, Hart*
THE PHANTOM HORSEWOMAN—*Hardy*
THE PHANTOM-WOOER—*Beddoes*
PHASELLUS ILLE—*Blackmur*
PHELPS PUTNAM—*Scott, Winfield Townley*
LE PHENIX—*Éluard*
PHENOMENA—*Jeffers, Robinson*
THE PHENOMENOLOGY OF ANGER—*Rich*
PHILADELPHIA—*Gaver*
PHILIP SPARROW—*Skelton, John*
PHILLADA FLOUTS ME—*Anonymous–English–Modern English*
PHILODENDRON—*Dugan*
A PHILOSOPHY IN WELSHESE—*Redgrove*
PHIZZOG—*Sandburg*
PHOEBUS ET BORÉE—*La Fontaine*
PHOENIX—*MacPherson*
PHOENIX—*Spencer*
PHONÈMES STRUCTURES—*Lora-Totino*

PHOTOGRAPH—*Lifshin*
PHOTOGRAPHY—*Giovanni*
PHRENOLOGY—*Gilbert, Sir William Schwenck*
PHYLLIS WOUNDED—*Piercy*
EL PI DE FORMENTOR—*Costa I Llobera*
PIANEFFORTE 'E NOTTE—*Di Giacomo*
THE PIANISTS—*Nash*
A PIANIST'S ASYLUM—*Greenwald*
PIANO—*Geraldy*
PIANO—*Lawrence*
PIANO E MONTE—*Pascoli*
PIANO TUNER, UNTUNE ME THAT TUNE—*Nash*
PIANTO ANTICO—*Carducci*
IL PIATTO PINAGE—*Sereni*
PIAZZA NAVONA—*Belli*
PIAZZA PIECE—*Ransom*
PIBROCH—*Hughes, Ted*
PICASSO—*Neruda*
PICASSO AND MATISSE—*Francis*
LU PICCIRIDDU E LU MBRIACO—*Buttitta*
LA PICCOZZA—*Pascoli*
PICK YOURSELF A STAR—*Marshall, Helen Lowrie*
THE PICKETY FENCE—*McCord*
PICKING YOUNG BERRIES ON MR. HARVEY'S LAND—*De Frees*
PICKLE BELT—*Roethke*
A PICNIC—*Fisher*
A PICNIC—*Logan*
PICTURE—*McGough*
PICTURE-BOOKS IN WINTER—*Stevenson*
PICTURE OF A NUDE IN A MACHINE SHOP—*Williams, William Carlos*
THE PICTURE OF J. T. IN A PROSPECT OF STONE—*Tomlinson*
THE PICTURE OF LITTLE T. C. IN A PROSPECT OF FLOWERS—*Marvell*
PIDGIN PINCH—*Smith, William Jay*
A PIECE OF NONSENSE—*Roche*
PIECING TOGETHER—*Dodson-Letourneau, Gayle*
PIED BEAUTY—*Hopkins*
THE PIED PIPER OF HAMELIN—*Browning, Robert*
PIERCE STREET—*Gunn*
PIERRE—*Péguy*
PIERS PLOWMAN—*Langland, William*
LA PIETÁ—*Sereni*
THE PIG—*Nash*
THE PIG AND THE PLUM TREE—*Roche*
PIGEON WOMAN—*Swenson*
PIGEONS—*Kell*
PIGEONS—*Lowell, Robert*
PIGEONS—*Reid*
PIGEONS JUST AWAKE—*Conkling*

PIGGY-BACK POEM—*Olson*
PIKE—*Hughes, Ted*
DER PILGER—*Eichendorff*
DER PILGRIM—*Schiller*
PILGRIM FISHHEADS—*Bly*
PILGRIMAGE—*Clarke*
THE PILLAR OF CLOUD—*Newman*
THE PIMPLY WOLF—*Sobiloff*
PIMP'S LAST MACK—*Crouch*
PIN POINT PUFF—*Greenham*
THE PINE—*Thomas-Ellis*
THE PINE PLANTERS—*Hardy*
PINE-TREES AND THE SKY: EVENING—*Brooke*
THE PINES—*Service*
PINEY WOODS—*Cowley, Malcolm*
PINGSTFORMIDDAG—*Nerman*
PINNACLE—*Clark, David Ridgley*
EL PINTOR—*Anonymous–American Indian languages–Nahuatl*
LA PIOGGIA NEL PINETO—*D'Annunzio, Gabriele*
THE PIONEER—*Nash*
LE PIPELINE DE BASSORAH—*Seghers*
THE PIPER—*Blake*
THE PIPER—*Merwin*
PIPPA PASSES, SONG—*Browning, Robert*
THE PIRATE DON DURK OF DOWDEE—*Meigs*
PIRATE STORY—*Stevenson*
THE PIRATES IN ENGLAND—*Kipling*
THE PIRATES OF PENZANCE—*Gilbert, Sir William Schwenck*
IL PIRLA—*Montale*
PISARYA—*Slutsky*
PISCATURE—*Viviani*
PISCES—*Thomas, Ronald Stuart*
THE PIT—*Roethke*
THE PIT OF BLISS—*Stephens*
PITCHER—*Francis*
PITTSBURGH—*Sobiloff*
PIUTE CREEK—*Snyder*
EL PIYAYO—*Luna*
THE PIZZA—*Nash*
THE PLACE—*Creeley*
THE PLACE—*Eberhart*
PLACE DU CARROUSEL—*Prévert*
THE PLACE ON THE MAP—*Hardy*
A PLACE PREPARED—*Bly*
A PLACING IN THIS ROOM—*Enslin*
THE PLAGUE—*Van Doren*
LA PLAIE QUE, DEPUIS—*Cassou*
THE PLAIN SENSE OF THINGS—*Stevens, Wallace*
PLAINS—*Auden*
PLAINSONG—*Cattonar*
PLAINT OF THE POET IN AN IGNORANT AGE—*Kizer*
PLAINTE—*Desportes*
PLAINTE D'UN CHRÉTIEN—*Racine*
PLAINTES DE CYBÈLE—*Mauriac*

PLATERO—*Jiménez*
PLATO TOLD HIM—*Cummings*
PLAUSIBLE MAN—*Davison, Peter*
THE PLAY—*Porter, Bern*
THE PLAY—*Redgrove*
THE PLAY—*Sexton*
THE PLAYER PIANO—*Jarrell*
THE PLAYERS—*Crabbe*
PLAYFULLY—*Ignatow*
PLAYTHINGS—*Sutzkever*
PLEA—*Arnez*
PLEA—*Parker*
PLEASE!—*Ciardi*
PLEASE PASS THE BISCUIT—*Nash*
THE PLEDGE OF ALLEGIANCE—
    Bellamy
THE PLEDGE OF ALLEGIANCE—
    Murphy
PLEGARIA A DIÓS—*Valdés*
LA PLEGARIA DEL PEREGRINO
    ABSURDO—*Cabrisas*
PLEGARIA DESDE LA TIERRA—
    Vicens
PLEIN CIEL—*Supervielle*
A PLETHORA OF DRYADS—*Plath*
THE PLOT AGAINST PROTEUS—
    Smith, A. J. M.
PLOTTING THE CHANGE OF THE
    WORLD—*Sherwin*
PLOUGHING ON SUNDAY—*Stevens,*
    Wallace
PLUIE DU SOIR—*Fombeure*
PLUIES—*Perse*
PLUM BLOSSOM—*Porter,*
    William N.
THE PLUM GATHERER—*Millay*
PLUMAGED PROXY—*Klein*
THE PLUMET BASILISK—*Moore,*
    Marianne
PLUNGING INTO—*Ross, W. W.*
    Eustace
PLYMOUTH WOMEN—*Lifshin*
P'OASIS—*Desnos*
LA POBRE VIEJECITA—*Pombo*
A POCKET OF SMILES—*Marshall,*
    Helen Lowrie
PODEROSO CABALLERO ES DON
    DINERO—*Quevedo y Villegas*
POEM—*Cohen*
POEM—*Cuestas*
POEM—*Deutsch*
POEM—*Giovanni*
POEM—*Gregor*
POEM—*Hughes, Langston*
POEM—*Kizer*
POEM—*Rukeyser*
POEM—*Sanchez*
POEM—*Sward*
POEM—*Vega Carpio*
POEM—*Williams, William*
    Carlos
A POEM ABOUT FRANCIS DRAKE—
    Masefield
POEM AGAINST THE STATE (OF
    THINGS): 1975—*Jordan, June*
POEM AND INVOCATION—*Sondé*
THE POEM AS MASK—*Rukeyser*

POEM AT THIRTY—*Sanchez*
POEM BEGINNING AND ENDING,
    OH—*Flint*
THE POEM CIRCLING HAMTRAMCK,
    MICHIGAN ALL NIGHT IN
    SEARCH OF YOU—*Levine*
POEM-DITTY FOR TAJ MAHAL—
    Carter
POEM FOR A NEW YORK
    FOUNDATION STONE—*Sward*
A POEM FOR A POET—*Lee, Don*
    L.
POEM FOR ADOLF EICHMANN—
    Harriman
POEM FOR EASTER—*Kelly*
A POEM FOR ED AND ARCHIE—
    Giovanni
POEM (FOR EMA)—*Giovanni*
POEM FOR ETHERIDGE—*Sanchez*
POEM FOR FRANCES P—*Johnson,*
    Joe
POEM FOR MARIE—*Heaney*
A POEM FOR MY FATHER—*Sanchez*
A POEM FOR NEGRO
    INTELLECTUALS—*Lee, Don L.*
POEM FOR NINA—*Giovanni*
A POEM FOR NINA SIMONE TO PUT
    SOME MUSIC ON—*Sanchez*
POEM FOR OLD BLACK LADIES
    WHO STAND ON BUS-STOP
    CORNERS—*Troupe*
A POEM FOR PAINTERS—*Wieners*
POEM IN A TIME OF CRISIS—
    Cowley, Malcolm
POEM IN OCTOBER—*Thomas,*
    Dylan
POEM IN PROSE—*MacLeish*
POEM IN THREE PARTS—*Bly*
POEM IN THREE VOICES BY ANY
    OTHER NAME—*Hobbs*
A POEM LOOKING FOR A READER—
    Lee, Don L.
POEM 19 FROM EUROPE—*Dudek*
POEM, 1961—*Lowell, Robert*
POEM 95 FROM EUROPE—*Dudek*
POEM OF ATTRITION—*Knight,*
    Etheridge
A POEM OF FRIENDSHIP—
    Giovanni
A POEM OFF CENTER—*Giovanni*
POEM ON HIS BIRTHDAY—*Thomas,*
    Dylan
POEM, OR BEAUTY HURTS MR.
    VINAL—*Cummings*
THE POEM THAT TOOK THE PLACE
    OF A MOUNTAIN—*Stevens,*
    Wallace
POEM TO AMERICANS—*Jackson,*
    Gerald
A POEM TO COMPLEMENT OTHER
    POEMS—*Lee, Don L.*
POEM TO ERNIE—*Tropp, Gloria*
POEM TO NEGROES AND WHITES—
    Bodenheim

A POEM WRITTEN UNDER AN
    ARCHWAY IN A DISCONTINUED
    RAILROAD STATION, FARGO,
    NORTH DAKOTA—*Wright,*
    James
POEMA—*Neruda*
POEMA DE LA DESPEDIDA—*Buesa*
POEMA DE LA GUERRA DE ESPAÑA
    —*Peñalver*
POEMA DE LA SAETA—*Garcia*
    Lorca
POEMA DE LA SOLEA—*Garcia*
    Lorca
POEMA DE UN DÍA—*Machado,*
    Antonio
POEMA DEL HIJO—*Hoffman*
    Llevano
POEMA DO FANÁTICO—*Mendes*
POÈME DE CAPE ET D'EPÉE—
    Aragon
POÈME PERPETUEL—*Éluard*
POÈME POUR PAULA—*Masson*
POÈME SUR LE DESASTRE DE
    LISBONNE—*Voltaire*
POEMS—*Conkling*
POEMS FROM A FIRST YEAR IN
    BOSTON—*Starbuck*
POEMS FROM ITALY—*Ciardi*
POEMS FROM OKLAHOMA—
    Katzman
POEMS TO A BROWN CRICKET—
    Wright, James
LA POESÍA—*Novo*
POESÍA CASTELLANA—*Darío*
LA POESÍA ES UN ARMA CARGADA
    DE FUTURO—*Celaya*
POESIE DES LEBENS—*Schiller*
LA POÉSIE DOIT AVOIR POUR BUT
    LA VÉRITÉ PRATIQUE—*Éluard*
POÉSIE ININTERROMPUE—*Éluard*
POESIEN—*Andersen*
POET—*Hayes*
POET—*Posner*
POET—*Viereck*
THE POET AS AN ACROBAT—
    Ferlinghetti
THE POET IN GRANADA—*Aiken*
THE POET THE DREAMER—*Jordan,*
    Norman
EL POETA Á CABALLO—*Jiménez*
EL POETA CANTA POR SOLEARES LA
    RESURRECCIÓN DE LA CARNE—
    Alcántara
LE POÈTE MOURANT—*Millevoye*
POÈTES—*Char*
LES POÈTES DE SEPT ANS—
    Rimbaud
POETRY—*Farjeon*
POETRY—*Jeffers, Lance*
POETRY—*Moore, Marianne*
POETRY IS BLACK—*Last Poets*
A POET'S EPITAPH—*Wordsworth*
THE POET'S EYE—*Ferlinghetti*
POGGIO—*Durrell*
POINT—*Sukenick*
LE POINT NOIR—*Nerval*

THE POINT OF THE SILVER SCREWDRIVER—*Sherwin*
POINT SHIRLEY—*Plath*
A POISON TREE—*Blake*
LES POISSONS—*Supervielle*
POLAND/1931: FIRST SEQUENCE—*Rothenberg*
POLE STAR—*MacLeish*
POLITENESS—*Milne*
POLITICAL MEETING—*Klein*
POLITICAL SONG—*Spencer*
POLITIQUE—*Gide*
DAS POLIZEIPFERD—*Morgenstern*
POLKA—*Sitwell, Edith*
POLLY—*Gay, John*
POLSO TESO—*Risi*
THE POLTERGUEST, MY POLTERGUEST—*Nash*
POLYGLOT POEM—*Raimbaut de Vaqueiras*
THE POMEGRANATE—*Dudek*
LE PONT—*Milosz*
LE PONT MIRABEAU—*Apollinaire*
PONTIAC—*Davie*
THE POOL—*Derwood*
POOR MATTHIAS—*Arnold*
POOR TIMING—*McGinley*
POOR WOMEN IN A CITY CHURCH—*Heaney*
THE POPE—*Francis*
THE POPLAR-FIELD—*Cowper*
POPPA CHICKEN—*Walker*
POPPIES IN JULY—*Plath*
POPSICLE COLD—*Jordan, Norman*
THE POPULAR MAGAZINES—*Whittemore*
POPULAR SONG—*Sitwell, Edith*
LE PORCHE DE LA DEUXIÈME VERTU—*Péguy*
THE PORCUPINE—*Kinnell*
THE PORCUPINE—*Nash*
PORISM—*Derwood*
PORPHYRIA'S LOVER—*Browning, Robert*
THE PORT—*Merwin*
PORTLAND COLISEUM—*Ginsberg*
IL PORTO SEPOLTO—*Ungaretti*
PORTO VENERI—*Connor*
LE PORTRAIT—*Baudelaire*
PORTRAIT BY A NEIGHBOR—*Millay*
PORTRAIT OF A GIRL WITH COMIC BOOK—*McGinley*
PORTRAIT OF A LADY—*Eliot, Thomas Stearns*
PORTRAIT OF A SOUTHERN LADY—*Benét, Stephen Vincent*
PORTRAIT OF A WOMAN—*Figueroa*
PORTRAIT OF A WOMAN IN BED—*Williams, William Carlos*
PORTRAIT OF A YOUNG GIRL RAPED AT A SUBURBAN PARTY—*Patten*
A PORTRAIT OF CHRISTIAN BERARD, A PAINTER—*Stein, Gertrude*
PORTRAIT OF MALCOLM X—*Knight, Etheridge*

A PORTRAIT OF T. S. ELIOT—*Stein, Gertrude*
PORTRAIT OF THE ARTIST AS A PREMATURELY OLD MAN—*Nash*
A PORTRAIT OF THEODORA—*Durrell*
PORTRAITS—*Cummings*
PORTRAITS—*Gide*
PORTRAITS—*Seghers*
PORTRAITS—*Sukenick*
POSLE IGRE—*Popa*
POSLEDNIY KATAKLIZM—*Tyutchev*
POSSESSED OF A DREAM—*Marshall, Helen Lowrie*
POSSESSION: CORAL—*Brathwaite*
POST IMPRESSIONS—*Cummings*
POST MORTEM—*Jeffers, Robinson*
POSTE RESTANTE—*Ferlin*
THE POSTER—*Taylor, Rex*
POSTLUDE: HOME—*Brathwaite*
UN POSTO DI VACANZA—*Sereni*
POSTSCRIPT—*Scott, Winfield Townley*
POSY GOD—*Van Doren*
LE POT DE TERRE ET LE POT DE FER—*La Fontaine*
THE POT GERANIUM—*Nicholson*
THE POTATOES' DANCE—*Lindsay, Vachel*
POTOK—*Lermontov*
POTOSI—*Anderson, Lee*
POTPOURRI FROM A SURREY GARDEN—*Betjeman*
POTREBBERO DIRTI MORTA—*Gatto*
A POTTED WATCH NEVER BOILS, OR, MAYBE THAT'S WHAT THEY'VE BEEN TRYING TO PROVE—*Nash*
LA POULE AUX OEUFS D'OR—*La Fontaine*
THE POULTRIES—*Nash*
POUR LES ENFANTS ET POUR LES RAFFINÉS—*Jacob, Max*
POUR MAL TEMPS NI POUR GELÉE—*Thibaut de Champagne*
POUR-QUOI MON ÂME EST-ELLE TRISTE?—*Lamartine*
POUR RIRE EN SOCIÉTÉ—*Prévert*
POUR SUR—*Damas*
POUR UN CHANT NATIONAL—*Aragon*
POUR VIVRE ICI—*Éluard*
POVERTY BLUES—*Arnez*
POWER TO LIFT—*Marshall, Helen Lowrie*
POWHATAN'S DAUGHTER—*Crane, Hart*
POYUT NEGRY—*Voznezensky*
POZHAR V ARKHITEKTURNOM INSTITUTE—*Voznesensky*
EL POZO—*Jiménez*
PRAGUE—*Aragon*
PRAIRIE WATERS BY NIGHT—*Sandburg*
THE PRAIRIES—*Bryant, William Cullen*

PRAISE FOR AN URN—*Crane, Hart*
PRAYER—*Francis of Assisi*
PRAYER—*Herbert*
PRAYER—*Hughes, Langston*
PRAYER—*Jeffers, Lance*
PRAYER—*Joyce*
PRAYER—*Untermeyer*
PRAYER—*Williams, Hugo*
PRAYER BEFORE BIRTH—*MacNeice*
PRAYER BEFORE DEATH—*Meleager*
PRAYER FOR EVERY DAY—*Anonymous–African languages–Ghana*
A PRAYER FOR MY DAUGHTER—*Yeats*
A PRAYER FOR MY SON—*Winters*
A PRAYER IN SPRING—*Frost, Robert*
PRAYER MEETING—*Hughes, Langston*
THE PRAYER OF THE BUTTERFLY—*Gasztold*
THE PRAYER OF THE DOG—*Gasztold*
THE PRAYER OF THE LITTLE DUCKS—*Gasztold*
PRAYER OF TRUST—*Marshall, Helen Lowrie*
PRAYER WHILE SLEEPING—*Williams, Hugo*
PRAYERS OF STEEL—*Sandburg*
PRAYIN' AND MAKIN' LOVE—*Clark, China*
PRE IGRE—*Popa*
THE PREACHER: RUMINATES BEHIND THE SERMON—*Brooks, Gwendolyn*
PRECARIOUS GROUND—*Drake, Leah Bodine*
PRECEPTIVA POETICA—*Camino Galicia*
PRECIO DE LA VERDAD—*Bousoño*
PRECIOSA Y EL AIRE—*Garcia Lorca*
PRECIOUS FIVE—*Auden*
PRECIOUS MOMENTS—*Sandburg*
PREDSKAZANIYE—*Lermontov*
PREFACE—*Sitwell, Osbert*
PREGÃO TURÍSTICO DO RECIFE—*Melo Neto*
LA PREGHIERA—*Ungaretti*
PREISLIED AUF EINE SEIFENBLASE—*Gan*
THE PRELUDE [OR, THE GROWTH OF A POET'S MIND]—*Wordsworth*
PRELUDE TO AN EVENING—*Ransom*
PRELUDE TO NOTHING—*Sanchez*
PRELUDE TO THE DEPARTMENTAL DITTIES—*Kipling*
PRELUDE TO WINTER—*Williams, William Carlos*
PRELUDES—*Eliot, Thomas Stearns*
PRELUDES FOR MEMNON—*Aiken*

PREMIER JANVIER—*Hugo, Victor*
PREMIER REGRET—*Lamartine*
PRENDIMIENTO DE ANTOÑITO EL
  CAMBORIO EN EL CAMINO DE
  SEVILLA—*Chamisso*
THE PREPARATION—*Logan*
PRERAPHAELITE ENCOUNTER WITH
  YOUR GRANDFATHER—*Fitts*
THE PRESENCE—*Graves*
A PRESENCE IN THINGS—
  Freivalds
PRÉSENTATION DE LA BEAUCE Á
  NOTRE-DAME DE CHARTRES—
  Péguy
PRESENTATION PIECE—*Hacker*
PRESENTE—*Paz*
EL PRESENTIMIENTO—*Garcia
  Lorca*
THE PRESSURE OF NIGHT—
  Wilkinson
PRÉSTITO FÚNEBRE—*Junqueiro*
PRETESTO—*Saba*
PRETTY WORDS—*Wylie*
PREUILLY-SUR-CLAISE—*Fombeure*
'O PREVETE—*Caldieri*
PREVIOUS CONDITION: EIGHT OF
  SWORDS—*Piercy*
PRIAM—*Fitts*
PRIAPOS OF THE HARBOR—
  Antipater of Sidon
PRIÈRE DE REPORT—*Péguy*
PRIÈRE POUR ALLER AU PARADIS
  AVEC LES ÂNES—*Jammes*
PRIÈRE POUR AVOIR UNE FEMME
  SIMPLE—*Jammes*
PRIÈRE POUR LE ROI ALLANT EN
  LIMOUSIN—*Malherbe*
PRIEST AND PEASANT—*Thomas,
  Ronald Stuart*
A PRIMARY GROUND—*Rich*
LA PRIMAVERA—*Di Giacomo*
LA PRIMAVERA—*Jiménez*
LA PRIMAVERA—*Montale*
PRIMAVERA AMARILLA—*Jiménez*
PRIME—*Auden*
PRIMER AMOR—*Conde*
PRIMER LESSON—*Sandburg*
PRIMER OF THE DAILY ROUND—
  Nemerov
PRIMITIVAMENTE—*Viviani*
PRIMITIVES—*Randall*
IL PRIMO AMORE—*Leopardi*
PRIMROSE—*Williams, William
  Carlos*
A PRIMROSE PETAL'S EDGE—
  Hughes, Ted
THE PRINCE—*Jarrell*
THE PRINCESS—*De la Mare*
THE PRINCESS—*Nash*
THE PRINCESS—*Tennyson*
THE PRINCESS MING—*Field,
  Eugene*
IL PRINCIPE SPIEDATO—*Rodari*
PRINCIPIO DEL SENORIO
  CHICHIMECA—*Anonymous–
  American Indian
  languages–Nahuatl*

PRINT OUT: APOCALYPSE—*Porter,
  Peter*
PRINTEMPS—*Aubigné*
PRINTEMPS—*Éluard*
THE PRIORESS'S TALE—*Chaucer*
PRISON—*Jeffers, Lance*
PRISON DIARY—*Ho Chi Minh*
PRISON POEM—*Giovanni*
PRISONED IN WINDSOR, HE
  RECOUNTETH HIS PLEASURE
  THERE PASSED—*Surrey*
THE PRISONER—*Brontë, Emily*
THE PRISONER—*Williams, Hugo*
THE PRISONER: AFTER A STATUE BY
  MICHELANGELO—*Klappert*
THE PRISONER OF CHILLON—
  Byron
THE PRISONERS—*Spender*
THE PRIVATE DINING ROOM—
  Nash
PVT. JOHN HOGG—*Scott, Winfield
  Townley*
THE PRIZE OF WAR IS ALWAYS—
  Dicker
DIE PROBE—*Morgenstern*
THE PROBLEM—*Emerson*
PROBLEMS IN THE SPACE-TIME
  CONTINUUM—*Williams, Miller*
THE PROCESS—*Baldwin, Deirdra*
PROCESSION WITH THE MADONNA
  —*Yevtushenko*
THE PRODIGAL SON—*Johnson,
  James Weldon*
PRODUCE ARANCE—*Isgrò*
PROFECÍA—*León, Rafael de*
PROFESSIONAL POET—*Kizer*
PROFESSOR PALMSTRÖM—
  Morgenstern
PROGNOSIS—*MacNeice*
THE PROGRESS—*Brooks,
  Gwendolyn*
PROGRESS REPORT—*Kumin*
PROGRESSION—*Smith, Stevie*
PROGRESSIVE INSANITIES OF A
  PIONEER—*Atwood*
PROJECT—*Miles*
PROJECT FOR A CLIFF-FACE—
  Ciardi
THE PROJECTIONIST'S NIGHTMARE
  —*Patten*
PROLOG—*Yevtushenko*
PROLOGUE—*Cullen*
PROLOGUE AT SIXTY—*Auden*
PROLOGUE SPOKEN BY MR.
  GARRICK—*Johnson, Samuel*
PROLOGUES TO WHAT IS POSSIBLE
  —*Stevens, Wallace*
PROEM TO THE KID—*Aiken*
PROMENADE À L' ÉTANG—*Samain*
PROMENADE SENTIMENTALE—
  Verlaine
LE PROMENOIR DES DEUX AMANTS
  —*Tristan l'Hermite*
PROMETHEUS—*Goethe*
PROMETHEUS—*Graves*
PROMETHEUS UNBOUND—*Shelley*
THE PROMISING—*Rago*

PRONOUNS OF THIS TIME—
  Spender
THE PROOF—*Wilbur*
PROPELLER—*Booth*
THE PROPHECY OF CAPYS—
  Macaulay
PROPHET—*Van Doren*
PROPHÉTIE—*Supervielle*
PROPHETS—*Bruchac*
PROPHETS FOR A NEW DAY—
  Walker
THE PROPHET'S GOOD IDEA—
  Patten
PROPRIETY—*Moore, Marianne*
IL PROPRIO RITRATTO—*Foscolo*
PROSIGUE LA ENCARNACÍON—
  Juan de la Cruz
A PROSPECT OF DEATH—*Young,
  Andrew*
PROSPERO'S CELL—*Durrell*
PROSPICE—*Browning, Robert*
THE PROSTHETIC DUCK—*Edson*
PROTEST—*Holman, Felice*
PROTEST AFTER A DREAM—*Logan*
PROTHALAMIUM—*Spenser*
PROVERBIOS Y CANTARES—
  Machado, Manuel
PROVIDE, PROVIDE—*Frost,
  Robert*
PROVISION—*Merwin*
PSALM—*Bernhard*
PSALM—*Celan*
PSALM—*Huchel*
PSALM—*Klein*
PSALM—*Mackin*
PSALM—*Trakl*
PSALM 8—*Bible and
  Pseudepigrapha*
PSALM 21—*Bible and
  Pseudepigrapha*
PSALM 22—*Bible and
  Pseudepigrapha*
PSALM 23—*Bible and
  Pseudepigrapha*
PSALM 81—*Bible and
  Pseudepigrapha*
PSALM 84—*Bible and
  Pseudepigrapha*
PSALM 88—*Bible and
  Pseudepigrapha*
PSALM 90—*Bible and
  Pseudepigrapha*
PSALM 91—*Bible and
  Pseudepigrapha*
PSALM 93—*Bible and
  Pseudepigrapha*
PSALM 100—*Bible and
  Pseudepigrapha*
PSALM 103—*Bible and
  Pseudepigrapha*
PSALM 104—*Bible and
  Pseudepigrapha*
PSALM 107—*Bible and
  Pseudepigrapha*
PSALM 121—*Bible and
  Pseudepigrapha*

PSALM 123—*Bible and Pseudepigrapha*
PSALM 130—*Bible and Pseudepigrapha*
PSALM 143—*Bible and Pseudepigrapha*
PSALM 149—*Bible and Pseudepigrapha*
PSALM 150—*Bible and Pseudepigrapha*
PSALM FOR CHRISTMAS DAY—*Pestel*
A PSALM OF LIFE—*Longfellow*
PSALM OF THOSE WHO GO OFF BEFORE DAYLIGHT—*Sandburg*
PSAUME 121—*Baïf*
PST—*Busch*
PSYCHÉ—*Corneille*
PSYCHOANALYSIS: AN ELEGY—*Spicer*
LA PUA—*Jiménez*
LA PUCE—*Apollinaire*
PUCK'S SONG—*Kipling*
PUEBLO—*Garcia Lorca*
PUELLA PARVULA—*Stevens, Wallace*
LA PUERTA ABIERTA—*Martinez Alonso*
PUERTA AL TIEMPO EN TRES VOCES—*Palés Matos*
PUERTO RICAN OBITUARY—*Pietri*
PUERTO RICAN RHYTHMS—*Last Poets*
PUESTO DEL RASTRO—*Fuertes*
LE PUISATIER DES REGARDS—*Tzara*
'O PULLASTO—*Fiore*
THE PULLEY—*Herbert*
PUÑAL DE LUZ—*Prados*
PUNSCHLIED—*Schiller*
PUPPY AND I—*Milne*
THE PURE FURY—*Roethke*
PURGATORY—*Kumin*
THE PURIFICATION—*Jong*
THE PURIST—*Nash*
PURSUIT—*Warren*
PUSHKIN—*Akhmatova*
PUT BACK THE DARK—*Bell*
LA PUTANA ANDALUSA—*Alberti*
PUTTIN' ON DOG—*Brown, Sterling A.*
PUTTING TO SEA—*Bogan*
PUZZLED—*Hughes, Langston*
PYGMIES ARE PYGMIES STILL THOUGH PERCHT ON ALPS—*Brooks, Gwendolyn*
THE PYLONS—*Spender*
THE PYRE—*Cowley, Malcolm*

QUACK—*De la Mare*
THE QUAKER GRAVEYARD IN NANTUCKET—*Lowell, Robert*
QUAKER HERO, BURNING—*Noll*
QUAND LE SOLEIL—*Seghers*
QUAND ON REGARDE UNE MONTRE—*Soupault*

QUAND VEDESSEV ON PUBBLEGH FUNZIONARI—*Porta*
QUANDO L CANEO RINFRESCA—*Marin*
QUANDO LA NOTTE—*Bevilacqua*
THE QUANGLE WANGLE'S HAT—*Lear*
QUANT' AUCIELLE—*Viviani*
QUANTA VITA—*Luzi*
QUANTAS OSTENDISTI MIHI TRIBULATIONES—*Gryphius*
QUANTI PESCI CI SONO NEL MARE?—*Rodari*
THE QUARREL—*Jong*
THE QUARRY—*Nemerov*
THE QUARRY—*Souster*
QUASI UNA MORALITÀ—*Saba*
QUATRAINS—*Péguy*
LES QUATRE SANS-COU—*Desnos*
QUE BONITA ES MI NIÑA—*Chamisso*
QUE CELUI QUI A DES OREILLES—*Obaldia*
QUÉ ES TU VIDA, ALMA MÍA—*Unamuno*
QUÉ GOCE TRISTE ESTE—*Jiménez*
QUEEN-ANN'S LACE—*Williams, William Carlos*
QUEEN ANNE'S LACE—*Newton*
QUEEN OF HAIR—*Garfinkel*
THE QUEEN OF SCOTLAND'S REPLY TO A REPROOF FROM JOHN KNOX—*Sitwell, Edith*
QUEEN OF THE BLUES—*Brooks, Gwendolyn*
QUEENS OF THE UNIVERSE—*Sanchez*
QUEL EST CE COEUR?—*Fombeure*
QUELLE CHOSE ETONNANTE QUE LA LECTURE—*Cendrars*
QUELQU'UN—*Prévert*
QU'EN-AVEZ VOUS FAIT—*Desbordes-Valmore*
LA QUERCIA CADUTA—*Pascoli*
QUERENT'S ATTITUDE: THREE OF CUPS—*Piercy*
QU'EST-CE QUE LE BONHEUR—*Jammes*
THE QUEST OF THE PURPLE-FRINGED—*Frost*
QUESTI MIEI ANNI SESSANTA—*Bevilacqua*
QUESTION—*Lee, Dennis*
QUESTION—*Sanchez*
QUESTION AND ANSWER—*Hughes, Langston*
THE QUESTION ANSWERED—*Blake*
QUESTION OF FREEDOM—*Ginsberg*
A QUESTION OF VALUES—*Coward*
QUESTIONS—*Sanchez*
QUESTIONS AT NIGHT—*Untermeyer*
QUESTIONS FOR A NEW MOON—*Welles*
QUESTO FIORE È DEL TEMPO—*Torrisi*

QUI EST-CE—*Péret*
QUI LA PIETRA—*Bevilacqua*
QUI REGNA AMORE—*Carducci*
QUICKNESS—*Vaughan, Henry*
QUICKTALES OF A BLIND PAINTER—*Zu-Bolton*
QUIÉN DEJARÁ—*Cervantes Saavedra*
QUIEN SABE—*Santos Chocano*
QUIERO SER GATO—*Botero*
LA QUIETE DOPO LA TEMPESTA—*Leopardi*
QUOD TEGIT OMMA—*Winters*

R S V P—*Klappert*
RABBI BEN EZRA—*Browning, Robert*
THE RABBIT—*Roberts*
RABBITS—*Anonymous–English—Modern English*
THE RABBITS—*Nash*
THE RABBIT'S SONG OUTSIDE THE TAVERN—*Coatsworth*
RACE OF VETERANS—*Whitman*
RACE ROCK LIGHT—*Hollander*
RACINES—*Seghers*
RÅDJUR I EN PARK—*Blomberg*
DER RADWECHSEL—*Brecht*
RAGAMUFFIN DAY—*Marshall, Helen Lowrie*
THE RAGGEDY MAN—*Riley*
'O RAGGIO 'E SOLE—*Filippo*
'O RAGGIO 'E SOLE—*Viviani*
THE RAGING OF THE ROSE—*Antoninus*
IL RAGIONIERE A DONDOLO—*Rodari*
THE RAILWAY JUNCTION—*De la Mare*
RAIN—*Nabokov*
RAIN—*Stevenson*
RAIN—*Wright, James*
RAIN IN SUMMER—*Longfellow*
RAIN IN THE NIGHT—*Burr, Amelia Josephine*
THE RAINBOW—*Souster*
RAINBOW SIGNS—*Fabio, Sarah Webster*
A RAINRIDE—*Hoffman*
RAINSCAPES, HYDRANGEAS, ROSES, AND SINGING BIRDS—*Eberhart*
THE RAINWALKERS—*Levertov*
RAINY AFTERNOON WITH THE WIFE—*Mailer*
THE RAINY DAY—*Longfellow*
THE RAINY SUMMER—*Meynell*
RAKETY I TELEGI—*Yevtushenko*
RALPH WALDO EMERSON—*Engle*
RAMA KAM—*Diop*
RAMA RAMA—*Gaver*
RAMAYANA—*Tul'si Das*
RAMAYANA—*Valmiki*
U RANCURI—*Buttitta*
RANDALL, MY SON—*Davidson*
RANDOM HARVEST—*Goldstein*
RANGER—*Enslin*
RANGSTREITIGKEITEN—*Fontane*

RANNOCH BY GLENCOE—*Eliot,*
   Thomas Stearns
RANSOM—*Norris*
RAPE IN THE MIND CAVE—*Fox,*
   Charles
THE RAPE OF DONA—*Howard,*
   Lee
THE RAPE OF EUROPA—*Blackmur*
RAPE OF LUCRECE—*Shakespeare*
RAPE OF THE LOCK—*Pope,*
   Alexander
RAPE POEM—*Piercy*
RAPID TRANSIT—*Agee*
A RAPTURE ON THE CORNISH HILLS
   —*Hawker*
THE RASPBERRY TRAGEDY—*Major*
RASSVET—*Pasternak*
RASTLOSE LIEBE—*Goethe*
LE RAT DE VILLE ET LE RAT DES
   CHAMPS—*La Fontaine*
A RATHER PUBLIC STATEMENT—
   Connor
RATTLESNAKE SKIPPING SONG—
   Lee, Dennis
DER RAUCH—*Brecht*
RAUIN INTO MY MIRROR HAS
   WALKED—*Patten*
THE RAVEN—*Poe*
RAVEN ON THE MOON—*Fox,*
   Charles
RAVENSBRÜCKI PASSIÓ—
   Pilinszky
THE RAVINE—*Ai*
RAZLUKA—*Pasternak*
RE-ACT FOR ACTION—*Lee,*
   Don L.
RE-SINGING LOVE—*Derwood*
IL RE TRAVICELLO—*Giusti*
READ STREET FESTIVAL—
   Robinson, Wanda
READER—*MacPherson*
THE READING—*Lifshin*
READING BUBER—*Sward*
READING-IN—*Oppenheimer*
READING MYSELF—*Lowell,*
   Robert
READING TIME: 1 MINUTE 26
   SECONDS—*Rukeyser*
REALITY—*Davison, Peter*
REALITY SHIFTED—*Stephany*
REARMAMENT—*Jeffers, Robinson*
REASON—*Creeley*
REASON—*Miles*
REASON—*Smith, Stevie*
REASON FOR NOT WRITING
   ORTHODOX NATURE POETRY—
   Wain
THE REASON FOR SKYLARKS—
   Patchen
THE REASON I CAN'T INVITE YOU
   IN FOR A DRINK—*Sklarew*
THE REASON WHY—*Marshall,*
   Helen Lowrie
REBECCA WHO SLAMMED DOORS
   FOR FUN AND PERISHED
   MISERABLY—*Belloc*
THE REBEL—*Pearse*

REBELLION: WAKE—*Brathwaite*
REBIRTH—*Souster*
REBUILDING FOR CHRIST—
   Marshall, Helen Lowrie
THE REBUKE—*Day Lewis*
RECADO A LOLITA ARRIAGA EN
   MEXICO—*Mistral*
RECENT WHITE HOUSE TOUR—
   Gaver
RECEPTION—*Miles*
RECESSIONAL—*Kipling*
RECITATIVE—*Crane, Hart*
RECLINING FIGURE—*Hall*
THE RECOGNITION OF EVE—
   Shapiro, Karl
RECONCILIATION—*Garlick*
RECONCILIATION—*Whitman*
RECONNAISSANCE DES BORNES—
   Pilon
RECORD DE SOLLER—*Alcover i*
   Maspons
A RECORD STRIDE—*Frost, Robert*
RECORDS—*Tate, Allen*
THE RECRUIT—*Housman*
A RECTIFICATION OF THE LYRIC—
   O'Gorman
RECUEILLEMENT—*Baudelaire*
RECUERDO—*Millay*
RECUERDO—*Zenea*
RECUERDO INFANTIL—*Machado,*
   Antonio
RECURRENCE—*Parker*
RED—*Cullen*
THE RED BIRD TAPESTRY—
   Swenson
THE RED DRESS—*Parker*
RED HANRAHAN'S SONG ABOUT
   IRELAND—*Yeats*
THE RED LILY—*Williams,*
   William Carlos
THE RED MOON COMES OUT IN THE
   NIGHT—*Conkling*
A RED, RED ROSE—*Burns*
RED ROOSTER—*Conkling*
THE RED WHEELBARROW—
   Williams, William Carlos
RED WINE AND YELLOW HAIR—
   Patchen
REDEMPTION—*Herbert*
REDONDILLAS—*Juana Inés de la*
   Cruz
REDONNEZ-LEUR—*Char*
REED—*Anonymous–English—*
   Old English
REEDS OF INNOCENCE—*Blake*
THE REEVE'S TALE—*Chaucer*
REFLECTION IN A GREEN ARENA—
   Corso
REFLECTION ON A WICKED WORLD
   —*Nash*
REFLECTION ON BABIES—*Nash*
REFLECTIONS—*Richards, I. A.*
REFLECTIONS AT DAWN—
   McGinley
REFLECTIONS DENTAL—
   McGinley

REFLECTIONS ON A GIFT OF
   WATERMELON PICKLE—*Tobias*
REFLECTIONS ON A LOST LOVE—
   Lee, Don L.
REFLECTIONS ON A MARINE VENUS
   —*Durrell*
REFLECTIONS ON ICE-BREAKING—
   Nash
REFLECTIONS ON INGENUITY—
   Nash
REFUGE IN AMERICA—*Hughes,*
   Langston
REFUGEE BLUES—*Auden*
REFUGEES—*MacNeice*
A REFUSAL TO MOURN THE DEATH,
   BY FIRE, OF A CHILD IN LONDON
   —*Thomas, Dylan*
REGEN—*Anonymous–Asian*
   languages
DER REGENPALAST—*Goll*
REGINA CARLOTTA—*Palazzeschi*
REGRESO AL MAR—*Blanco*
REGRET—*Dowling*
LE REGRET DE LA TERRE—
   Supervielle
LES REGRETS—*Du Bellay*
LES REGRETS—*Noailles*
LES REGRETS DE VILLON—*Villon*
THE REID REID ROSE—*Smith,*
   Sydney Goodsir
REINEKE FUCHS—*Goethe*
EIN REISEERLEBNIS—*Roth, Eugen*
REISEN—*Benn*
REISENDER—*Rühmkorf*
THE RELATIONSHIP—*Malanga*
RELATIONSHIP POEM—*Fox,*
   Charles
RELATIVITY—*Marshall,*
   Lenore G.
THE RELIC—*Hillyer*
THE RELIC—*Sherwin*
RELIGION IS THAT I LOVE YOU—
   Patchen
A RELIGIOUS QUESTION—*Spencer*
THE RELIQUE—*Donne*
EL RELOJ—*Murciano*
RELUCTANCE—*Frost, Robert*
REMANSILLO—*Garcia Lorca*
REMANSO—*Garcia Lorca*
REMÈDIE CONTRE L'EMPEDIMENT
   —*Deschamps*
REMEMBER—*Rossetti, Christina*
REMEMBERED MORNING—*Lewis,*
   Janet
REMEMBERING DOWNWARDS—
   Williams, Hugo
REMEMBERING THE THIRTIES—
   Davie
REMEMBRANCE—*Brontë, Emily*
REMEMBRANCE—*Wyatt, Sir*
   Thomas
REMINISCENCE—*Colum*
REMINISCENCES OF A DANCING
   MAN—*Hardy*
REMISE—*Char*
REMONSTRANCE—*Philodemos*
   the Epicurean

REMORSE—*Betjeman*
RENACERÉ YO—*Jiménez*
EL RENACUAJO PASEADOR—
Pombo
LE RENARD AYANT LA QUEUE
COUPÉE—*La Fontaine*
LE RENARD ET LA CIGOGNE—*La
Fontaine*
LE RENARD ET LE BOUC—*La
Fontaine*
LE RENARD ET LE BUSTE—*La
Fontaine*
LE RENARD ET LES RAISINS—*La
Fontaine*
RENASCENCE—*Millay*
RENCONTRE—*Hugo, Victor*
RENEGADE—*Sherwin*
THE RENEWAL—*Roethke*
RENIEMENT DE SAINT PIERRE—
Baudelaire
RENONCEMENT—*Mauriac*
THE RENOVATED TEMPLE—
MacLeish
RENUNCIATION—*Pearse*
REPARTEE—*Hillyer*
THE REPENTANCE OF LADY T—
Smith, Stevie
REPETITIVE HEART—*Schwartz*
REPLY TO A LADY EDITOR—
Roethke
REPLY TO AN ACCUSATION—*Darr*
REPORT TO THE DIRECTOR—
MacBeth
REPORT TO THE STOCKHOLDERS—
Beecher
REPOS DANS LE MALHEUR—
Michaux
EL REPOSO DEL FUEGO—*Pacheco*
REPROOF DESERVED, OR AFTER
THE LECTURE—*Betjeman*
A REPROOF OF GLUTTONY—*Belloc*
THE REPULSE—*Stanley*
REQUIEM—*Hierro*
REQUIEM—*Stevenson*
REQUIEM—*Vennberg*
REQUIEM CANTO—*MacNeice*
REQUIEM POR UN HOMBRE—
Murciano
REQUIESCAT—*Arnold*
RESANS SLUT—*Martinson*
THE RESCUE—*Creeley*
THE RESCUE—*Summers, Hal*
RESCUE THE DEAD—*Ignatow*
RESEARCH SCIENTIST—*Marshall,
Helen Lowrie*
RESIDENCIA EN LA TIERRA—
Neruda
RESIDENTIAL STREETS—*Hall*
RESOLUTION AND INDEPENDENCE
—*Wordsworth*
THE RESPECTABLE BURGHER ON
THE HIGHER CRITICISM—*Hardy*
RESPITE—*Marshall, Lenore G.*
RESPONSE—*Giovanni*
RESPONSE—*Whittier*
THE RESPONSIBILITY—*Appleton*

A RESPONSIBLE NEEGROW LEADER
(WHITE APPOINTED) TALKS
ABOUT THE GOOD OLD DAYS—
Eckels
REST—*Rossetti, Christina*
REST FROM LOVING—*Day Lewis*
RESTAURADORA—*Lisboa,
Henriqueta*
RESULTS IN REVERSE—*Marshall,
Helen Lowrie*
RESUME—*Parker*
THE RESURRECTION OF THE
DAUGHTER—*Shange*
RETABLO DE LA FÁBULA—*Barbieri*
RETAKE—*Khalil*
RETALIATION—*Goldsmith*
RETINA—*MacPherson*
THE RETIRED COLONEL—*Hughes,
Ted*
THE RETIREMENT—*Cotton*
RETIREMENT, AN ODE—*Warton,
Thomas (the Elder)*
RETORNO—*Jiménez*
RETORNO FUGAZ—*Jiménez*
RETORNOS DEL AMOR EN LOS
BALCONES—*Alberti*
LE RETOUR DU SERGENT—
Fombeure
RETRAITE—*Carco*
RETRATO—*Arboleda*
RETRATO—*Machado, Antonio*
THE RETREATE—*Vaughan,
Henry*
THE RETRIEVAL SYSTEM—*Kumin*
EL RETROCESO DE LA PRIMAVERA
—*Tejada*
RETROSPECT—*Francis*
RETTUNG—*Goethe*
THE RETURN—*Bishop, John
Peale*
THE RETURN—*Bontemps*
THE RETURN—*Brathwaite*
THE RETURN—*Campbell, Alistair*
THE RETURN—*Marshall,
Lenore G.*
THE RETURN—*Rochester, Earl of*
THE RETURN—*Roethke*
RETURN BIRTHDAY—*Jeffers,
Robinson*
THE RETURN FROM TOWN—*Millay*
RETURN TO CARDIFF—*Abse*
RETURN TO CONNECTICUT—
Bishop, John Peale
RETURN TO RITUAL—*Van Doren*
RETURN VISIT TO LAUGHARNE—
Thomas-Ellis
RETURNED TO FRISCO, 1946—
Snodgrass
RETURNING TURTLE—*Lowell,
Robert*
REUBEN PANTIER—*Masters,
Edgar Lee*
REUE—*Busch*
THE REUNION—*Dodson*
LE RÊVE EST UNE SECONDE VIE—
Nerval
RÉVEIL—*Supervielle*

REVELACIÓN—*Diego, Gerardo*
REVELATION—*Frost, Robert*
REVELATION—*Vaughan, H. A.*
THE REVENGE—*Tennyson*
THE REVENGE OF HAMISH—*Lanier*
THE REVENGER'S TRAGEDY—
Tourneur
REV. LEMUEL WILEY—*Masters,
Edgar Lee*
THE REVERIE OF POOR SUSAN—
Wordsworth
RÉVERSIBILITÉ—*Baudelaire*
THE REVOLUTIONARY SCREW—
Lee, Don L.
REVOLUTION'S CRADLE SONG—
Reecher
REVOLVING MEDITATION—*Kunitz*
A REVOLVING STAGE—*Williams,
Hugo*
REVUE BAR STRIP—*Conquest*
REYERTA—*Garcia Lorca*
LOS REYES MAGOS—*Jiménez*
REYNARD THE FOX—*Masefield*
RHEINWEINLIED—*Claudius*
RHIANNON—*Walters*
THE RHINOCEROS—*Nash*
THE RHODORA—*Emerson*
A RHYME IS A JUMP ROPE—
Merriam
THE RHYME OF THE REMITTANCE
MAN—*Service*
RICE PUDDING—*Milne*
RICHARD CORY—*Robinson,
Edwin Arlington*
RICHARD II QUARANTE—*Aragon*
RICHIAMO—*Saba*
RICORDAMI COSI—*Gatto*
LE RICORDANZE—*Leopardi*
A RIDDLE—
*Anonymous–English—
Modern English*
A RIDDLE—*Children's Verses
and Nursery Rhymes*
RIDDLE: WHAT AM I?—*Aldis*
RIDDLES—*Anonymous–English
—Old English*
RIDDLES WISELY EXPOUNDED—
*Anonymous–English—
Modern English*
THE RIDDLING KNIGHT—
*Anonymous–English—
Modern English*
RIDE—*Miles*
RIDE A COCK HORSE—*Children's
Verses and Nursery Rhymes*
LE RIDEAU DE MA VOISINE—
Musset
THE RIDER AT THE GATE—
Masefield
THE RIDER VICTORY—*Muir*
RIDES—*Derwood*
RIDING THE ELEVATOR INTO THE
SKY—*Sexton*
RIEN À CRAINDRE—*Prévert*
RIFLE PRAYER—*Last Poets*
THE RIGHT KIND OF PEOPLE—
Markham

THE RIGHT MASK—*Patten*
RIGHT ON: WHITE AMERICA—
   Sanchez
THE RIGHTEOUS—*Francis*
RIGORISTS—*Moore, Marianne*
THE RIGS O' BARLEY—*Burns*
RIGVEDA. TO THE GOD OF FIRE AS
   A HORSE—*Anonymous–
   Sanskrit*
RIJ ÉTAIT UNE POUFFIASSE—
   Cendrars
RIMAS—*Becquer*
RIME—*Dante Alighieri*
RIME—*Tasso*
THE RIME OF THE ANCIENT
   MARINER—*Coleridge, Samuel
   Taylor*
RIME OF THE PALMERS—*Merwin*
RINDERLEGENDE—*Zuckmayer*
THE RING AND THE BOOK—
   Browning, Robert
DER RING DES POLYKRATES—
   Schiller
RINGING THE BELLS—*Sexton*
RÍO—*Guillén, Jorge*
RIOT—*Brooks, Gwendolyn*
RIP—*Wright, James*
RIPPLE—*Thomas-Ellis*
RIPPLE—*Williams, Hugo*
RISING—*Braxton*
RISING FIVE—*Nicholson*
UNA RISORTA—*Gozzano*
UNA RISPOSTA DAL VOL—
   Quasimodo
RISVEGLIO—*Saba*
THE RITE—*Randall*
RITE FOR THE CITY—*Kendrick*
THE RITES FOR COUSIN VIT—
   Brooks, Gwendolyn
RITES OF PASSAGE—*Gunn*
RITES OF WAR—*MacNeice*
IL RITORNO—*Crimi*
RITOURNELLE—*Prévert*
DER RITTER TANNHÄUSER—*Heine*
RITTER TOGGENBURG—*Schiller*
RITUAL—*Fox, Charles*
THE RIVAL—*Hardy*
THE RIVALS—*Scannell*
THE RIVALS—*Stephens*
THE RIVALS—*Walsh*
THE RIVER DEBEN—*Smith, Stevie*
THE RIVER DUDDON:
   AFTERTHOUGHT—*Wordsworth*
THE RIVER GOD—*Fletcher, John*
THE RIVER GOD—*Smith, Stevie*
RIVER MOON—*Sandburg*
THE RIVER OF BEES—*Merwin*
RIVER PROFILE—*Auden*
RIVER ROAD, HIGH TOSS—*Piercy*
THE RIVER'S TALE—*Kipling*
THE ROAD—*Johnson, Helene*
THE ROAD BEHIND THE LAST DUNE
   —*Piercy*
ROAD CASUALTY—*Ennis*
THE ROAD NOT TAKEN—*Frost,
   Robert*
THE ROAD-RUNNER—*Whalen*

THE ROAD TO SUCCESS—*Marshall,
   Helen Lowrie*
ROADS—*Thomas, Edward*
A ROADSIDE STAND—*Frost,
   Robert*
ROADWAYS—*Masefield*
THE ROAN STALLION—*Jeffers,
   Robinson*
ROBERT BRUCE'S MARCH TO
   BANNOCKBURN—*Burns*
ROBERT FROST—*Lowell, Robert*
ROBERT FROST DIED THIS
   MORNING—*Darr*
ROBIN—*Summers, Hal*
ROBIN GOODFELLOW, PT. 2—
   *Anonymous–English–
   Modern English*
ROBIN HOOD'S GOLDEN PRIZE—
   *Anonymous–English–
   Modern English*
ROBIN-RUN-BY-THE-WALL—*Far-
   jeon*
ROBINSON CRUSOE'S STORY—
   Carryl, Charles Edward
ROBLIN'S MILLS—*Purdy*
LA ROCHEFOUCAULD—*Durrell*
LE ROCHER EN FEUILLES—
   Diouara
ROCHERS INACCESSIBLES—
   Anonymous–French
THE ROCK-A-BY LADY—*Field,
   Eugene*
ROCK AND HAWK—*Jeffers,
   Robinson*
THE ROCKABYE LOVE—*Kramer*
THE ROCKER—*Coffin*
THE ROCKING CHAIR—*Klein*
THE ROCKING CHAIRS—*Cowley,
   Malcolm*
THE ROCKS MY PEOPLE THREW—
   Jeffers, Lance
ROCKY MOUNTAIN SNOWSTORM—
   Langland, Joseph
RODENT—*Nash*
RODEZ—*Davie*
RODINA—*Venevitinov*
ROGER HESTON—*Masters, Edgar
   Lee*
ROGUE & JAR 4 27 77—*Davis,
   Thulami Nkabinde*
LE ROI DE THULE—*Nerval*
ROKEBY—*Scott, Sir Walter*
ROLAND HAYES BEATEN (GEORGIA:
   1942)—*Hughes, Langston*
ROLL ON, THOU DEEP AND DARK
   BLUE SYLLABLES, ROLL ON—
   Nash
ROLLA—*Musset*
ROMAGNA—*Pascoli*
ROMAN—*Rimbaud*
THE ROMAN CENTURION'S SONG—
   Kipling
A ROMAN DREAM—*Humphreys*
ROMANCE—*Hickey Pellizzoni*
ROMANCE—*Poe*
ROMANCE—*Turner, Walter
   James*

ROMANCE ANTIGUO VERDADERO
   DE ALORA, LA BIEN CERCADA—
   Anonymous–Spanish
ROMANCE DE ABENÁMAR Y EL REY
   DON JUAN—
   Anonymous–Spanish
ROMANCE DE COMO MUDARRA
   GONZALEZ MATÓ A RUY
   VELASQUEZ, TÍO DE LOS SIETE
   INFANTES DE LARA—
   Anonymous–Spanish
ROMANCE DE DON BUESO—
   Anonymous–Spanish
ROMANCE DE DON PEDRO Á
   CABALLO—*Garcia Lorca*
ROMANCE DE ENDECHAS—
   Salinas, Juan
ROMANCE DE FONTE-FRIDA Y CON
   AMOR—*Anonymous–Spanish*
ROMANCE DE GERINELDO Y LA
   INFANTA—*Anonymous–Span-
   ish*
ROMANCE DE LA GUARDIA CIVIL
   ESPAÑOLA—*Garcia Lorca*
ROMANCE DE LA INFANTINA—
   Anonymous–Spanish
ROMANCE DE LA LINDA ALBA—
   Anonymous–Spanish
ROMANCE DE LA LIRIO—*León,
   Rafael de*
ROMANCE DE LA LOBA PARDA—
   Anonymous–Spanish
ROMANCE DE LA LUNA, LUNA—
   Garcia Lorca
ROMANCE DE LA PENA NEGRA—
   Garcia Lorca
ROMANCE DE LA PENITENCIA DEL
   REY RODRIGO—
   Anonymous–Spanish
ROMANCE DE UN GALAN DE ESTA
   VILLA—*Anonymous–Spanish*
ROMANCE DE UNA FATAL
   OCCASIÓN—*Anonymous–Span
   ish*
ROMANCE DEL EMPLAZADO—
   Garcia Lorca
ROMANCE DEL PRISIONERO—
   Anonymous–Spanish
ROMANCE DEL RETO DE DIEGO
   ORDÓÑEZ—*Anonymous–Span-
   ish*
ROMANCE DEL REY MORO QUE
   PERDIÓ ALHAMBRE—
   Anonymous–Spanish
ROMANCE DEL VENENO DE
   MORIANA—*Anonymous–Span-
   ish*
ROMANCE EN QUE DOÑA URRACA
   RECUERDA CUANDO EL CID SE
   CRIABA CON ELLA EN SU
   PALACIO DE ZAMORA—
   Anonymous–Spanish
ROMANCE SANS MUSIQUE—*Toulet*
ROMANCE SONÁMBULO—*Garcia
   Lorca*
ROMANCES—*Juan de la Cruz*
ROMANCILLO—*Góngora*

ROMANS—*Lermontov*
THE ROMANTIC—*Bogan*
ROME—*Hardy*
RÖMISCH-DEUTSCHER TON—*Vogel*
DER RÖMISCHE BRUNNEN—*Meyer, Conrad Ferdinand*
RÖMISCHE ELEGIEN—*Goethe*
ROMULUS AND REMUS
RONDA DE LA CEIBA ECUATORIANA —*Mistral*
RONDA DE SEGADORES—*Mistral*
LA RONDE—*Fort*
RONDE—*Soupault*
RONDEAU—*Charles d'Orleans*
RONDEAU—*Froissart*
RONDEAU—*Hunt*
RONDEAU—*Villon*
RONDEAU—*Voiture*
RONDEL—*Mallarmé*
RONDEL—*Pisan*
RONDEL DE L'ADIEU—*Haraucourt*
IL RONDONE—*Montale*
THE ROOFWALKER—*Rich*
THE ROOM—*Aiken*
THE ROOM—*Day Lewis*
THE ROOM—*Merwin*
THE ROOM ABOVE THE SQUARE— *Spender*
ROOMING HOUSE, WINTER— *Atwood*
THE ROOT CANAL—*Piercy*
ROOTS—*Meredith, William*
LA ROSA BLANCA—*Martí*
LA ROSA DE CRISTAL—*Martinez Alonso*
LA ROSA INCOMODA—*Figuera*
ROSABELLE—*Scott, Sir Walter*
ROSAFLORIDA—*Anonymous– Spanish*
ROSALIND'S MADRIGAL—*Lodge*
ROSAS DE SEPTIEMBRE—*Jiménez*
LAS ROSAS ESCARMENTADAS— *Martinez Alonso*
ROSCOE PURKAPILE—*Masters, Edgar Lee*
THE ROSE AND THE DELILAH— *Roche*
ROSE AYLMER—*Landor*
THE ROSE BUSH—*Giovanni*
LA ROSE DE L'INFANTE—*Hugo, Victor*
LA ROSE ET LE RESEDA—*Aragon*
ROSE GUERRIÈRE—*Apollinaire*
ROSE-MOSS—*Conkling*
THE ROSE OF SOLITUDE— *Antoninus*
THE ROSE OF THE WORLD—*Yeats*
ROSE POGONIAS—*Frost, Robert*
THE ROSE TREE—*Yeats*
DAS ROSENBAND—*Klopstock*
ROSES AND REVOLUTIONS— *Randall*
LES ROSES DE SAADI— *Desbordes-Valmore*
ROSES ET RONCES—*Giguere*
ROSSIYA—*Tyutchev*
ROTE MELODIE—*Tucholsky*

LE ROULEMENT DES ROUES— *Emmanuel*
A ROUND—*Merriam*
THE ROUNDEL—*Swinburne*
A ROUNDEL OF REST—*Symons*
ROUNDING THE HORN—*Masefield*
A ROUSE FOR STEVENS—*Roethke*
ROUTE—*Soupault*
ROVER—*Kunitz*
ROVER—*Sobiloff*
ROWING—*Sexton*
THE ROWING ENDETH—*Sexton*
ROWING IN LINCOLN PARK— *Brinnin*
ROXINEY BOODY—*Coffin*
ROY BUTLER—*Masters, Edgar Lee*
ROYAL MARCH OF THE LIONS— *Nash*
ROYAL PALM—*Crane, Hart*
ROYALL PRESENTS—*Wanley*
ROYAUTÉ—*Rimbaud*
ROZHDESTVENSKAYA ZVEZDA— *Pasternak*
'O RRAU—*Filippo*
RUBAIYAT—*Omar Khayyam*
RUBY—*Prothro*
RÜCKKEHR—*Brecht*
RÜCKKEHR IN DIE HEIMAT— *Hölderlin*
RÜCKSCHAU—*Heine*
LA RUE OBALDIA—*Obaldia*
RUEDA—*Storni*
EL RUEGO—*Mistral*
RUF AUS DER GRUFT—*Brecht*
RUGBY CHAPEL—*Arnold*
DIE RUHE—*Kraft*
RUHE DES GEMÜTHES—*Gryphius*
RÜHMEN, DAS IST'S—*Rilke*
THE RUIN— *Anonymous–English—Old English*
THE RUINED CASTLE OF MANORBIER—*Hillyer*
THE RUINED ECLAIR—*Edson*
THE RUINED MAID—*Hardy*
RULERS: PHILADELPHIA—*Johnson, Fenton*
RUM TUM TUGGER—*Eliot, Thomas Stearns*
RUMINATION—*Eberhart*
RUMOR—*Marshall, Lenore G.*
RUN OF THE MINE—*Beecher*
RUNAGATE, RUNAGATE—*Hayden*
THE RUNAWAY—*Frost, Robert*
RUNE—*Rukeyser*
RUNES FOR A BAD DAY—*Sherwin*
THE RUNES ON WELAND'S SWORD —*Kipling*
THE RUNNER WITH THE LOTS— *Adams*
RUNNING—*Wilbur*
RUS'—*Gogol*
THE RUSH—*Eberhart*
RUSH HOUR—*Kramer*
A RUSSELL FLINT—*Betjeman*
RUSSIAN DANCE—*Nash*

RUSSKIE DEVUSHKI—*Derzhavin*
RUSSKOY ZHENSHCHINE— *Tyutchev*
RUTH—*Hood*
RUTH—*Wordsworth*
RUY DÍAZ PARTE A LA GUERRA— *Huidobro*

S. O. S.—*Robson, Jeremy*
IL SABATO DE VILLAGGIO— *Leopardi*
EL SABIO— *Anonymous–American Indian languages–Nahuatl*
SABLE ISLAND—*Booth*
SACCO WRITES HIS SON—*Lewis, Alun*
S'ACCORCIA LA GIORNATA— *Bevilacqua*
SACHLICHE ROMANZE—*Kästner*
LE SACRE DE LA FEMME—*Hugo, Victor*
SACRED EMILY—*Stein, Gertrude*
THE SACRED ONES—*Whitman*
SACRIFICE OF A GUNNYSACK OF CATS—*Langland, Joseph*
SACRIFICE OF A RAINBOW TROUT— *Langland, Joseph*
SACRIFICE OF GOPHERS AND WOODCHUCKS—*Langland, Joseph*
SACRIFICE OF MY DOG, REX— *Langland, Joseph*
SACRIFICE OF THE GOLDEN OWL— *Langland, Joseph*
A SAD JINGLE—*Dowling*
A SAD, SAD STORY—*Children's Verses and Nursery Rhymes*
SADIE: A SERENADE—*Fabio, Cyril Leslie III*
SADIE AND MAUD—*Brooks, Gwendolyn*
THE SADNESS OF CREATURES— *Porter, Peter*
SAETA—*Garcia Lorca*
SAETA—*Villalón*
SAFETY—*Brooke*
THE SAGE—*Levertov*
SAGESSE—*Geraldy*
SAI SYA CHYU—*Lu Lwun*
SAILBOAT, YOUR SECRET—*Francis*
SAILING HOME FROM RAPALLO— *Lowell, Robert*
SAILING TO BYZANTIUM—*Yeats*
SAILOR—*Hughes, Langston*
THE SAILOR BOY—*Tennyson*
SAILOR, WHAT OF THE ISLES?— *Sitwell, Edith*
THE SAILOR'S CONSOLATION— *Dibdin*
ST. ANN'S GUT—*Darr*
ST. BEE'S HEAD—*Brown, Thomas Edward*
ST. FRANCIS AND THE BIRDS— *Heaney*
A ST. HELENA LULLABY—*Kipling*

ST. ISAAC'S CHURCH, LENINGRAD—
McKay
ST. JOSEPH ABBEY VIGILS—Lester
SAINT JUDAS—Wright, James
SAINT NICHOLAS—Moore,
Marianne
THE SAINT OF THE UPLANDS—
Merwin
SAINT-OUEN'S BLUES—Queneau
ST. ROACH—Rukeyser
SAINT SEBASTIAN—Merwin
SAINT STEPHEN AND HEROD—
Anonymous–English—
Modern English
SAINT URSULA OF LLANG WYRYFON
—Williams, Gwyn
LES SAINTS NOUVEAUX—Updike
LA SAISON DES SEMAILLES—Hugo,
Victor
SAISON EN ENFER—Rimbaud
LES SAISONS—Apollinaire
SALAMANCA—Unamuno
SALAMI—Levine
SALAS DE LOS INFANTES—
Goldstein
SALE—Miles
A SALIENT OF WAR—Brinnin
LA SALLE À MANGER—Jammes
SALLY CHISOLM PLAYING LOVE IN
THE AFTERNOON—Hobbs
SALLY CHISOLM THINKING BACK—
Hobbs
SALLY IN OUR ALLEY—Carey
SALMO—Unamuno
EL SALMO DE LAS CUMBRES—
Santos Chocano
SALMO PLUVIAL—Lugones,
Leopoldo
SALMON—Ormond
SALOMÉ—Castro, Eugénio de
SALON—Heine
SALT WATER BALLADS—Masefield
LA SALTIMBANQUE EN WAGON DE
3e CLASSE—Jacob, Max
SALTIMBANQUES—Apollinaire
SALUT AU MONDE—Whitman
THE SALUTATION—Traherne
SALVAJE—Ibarbourou
SALVEZZA DALLA BAIA DI LUANDA
—Bevilacqua
SAM—De la Mare
SAM SMILEY—Brown, Sterling A.
SAM'S CALL—Redgrove
SAMSON AGONISTES—Milton
SAMSON AGONISTES—Nash
SAMSON AND DELILAH—
Goldstein
SAMUEL—Bible and
Pseudepigrapha
SAN FRANCISCO BLUES—Kerouac
SAN FRANCISCO CITY: SAN
FRANCISCO—Hughes,
Langston
SAN GABRIEL—Garcia Lorca
SAN MARTINO—Carducci
SAN MIGUEL, GRANADA—Garcia
Lorca

SAN PAOLO FUORI LE MURE—
Jennings
SAN RAFAEL, CÓRDOBA—Garcia
Lorca
THE SANATORIUM—Porter, Peter
SANCTA SIMPLICITAS—Ferlin
SANCTUARY—Randall
SAND DUNES—Frost, Robert
SANDS—Moss, Howard
SANDS AT SEVENTY—Whitman
SÅNG FÖR ATT DÖVA SMÄRTAN—
Ekelöf
SÅNG I PIREUS—Edfelt
DER SÄNGER—Goethe
DIE SÄNGER DER VORWELT—
Schiller
SÄNGERFAHRT—Eichendorff
LA SANGRE—Alonso
LA SANGRE DERRAMADA—Garcia
Lorca
SANGUINE—Prévert
SANS AGE—Éluard
SANS COUP FÉRIR—Tzara
SANS SAVOIR QUE LA NUIT—
Cadou
SANT' AMBROGIO—Giusti
SANTA CLAUS—Nemerov
SANTA MARIA DEGLI ANGELI—
Carducci
SANTORIN—Flecker
SAPPHICS—Swinburne
SARAH BYNG, WHO COULD NOT
READ AND WAS TOSSED INTO A
THORNY HEDGE—Belloc
THE SARDINE CAN DORMITORY—
Edson
SARLINGEN—Kefasdotter
SAROLLA'S WOMEN IN THEIR
PICTURE HATS—Ferlinghetti
SARTA DE VOCES PERDIDAS—Péres
Marchand
IL SATELITE FILOMENA—Rodari
SATELLITE, SATELLITE—Merriam
THE SATIN DRESS—Parker
A SATIRE AGAINST MANKIND—
Rochester, Earl of (Wilmot,
John)
THE SATIRIST IS CHARMED BY THE
QUEEN—Jonson
SATURDAY NIGHT—Robison
SATURDAY NIGHT IN HARLEM—
Brown, William
SATURDAY SWEEPING—Levine
SATURDAY'S CHILD—Cullen
LE SATYRE ET LE PASSANT—La
Fontaine
SATZBAU—Benn
SAUL KANE'S OUTBURST—
Masefield
SAUNDERS LEWIS AT NEWTOWN—
Garlick
LE SAUT DU TREMPLIN—Banville
THE SAVAGE FLUTES—Chapin
LE SAVETIER ET LE FINANCIER—
La Fontaine
SAVOIR-VIVRE—Damas

THE SAWS WERE SHRIEKING—Ross,
W. W. Eustace
SAY IT—Flint
SAYING IT—Connor
LE SCANDALE—Gide
THE SCARECROW—Sobiloff
SCARLET SEAS—Goldstein
SCARLET WOMAN—Johnson,
Fenton
THE SCARRED GIRL—Dickey,
James
SCÈNE—Mallarmé
THE SCEPTIC—Service
SCESI A MARSALA—Lombardi
DER SCHÄFER—Goethe
DIE SCHÄNDLICHE—Busch
SCHATTENLAND—Bobrowski
DER SCHATZGRÄBER—Goethe
DER SCHAUENDE—Rilke
DER SCHAUKELSTUHL—
Morgenstern
SCHEIN UND SEIN—Busch
DER SCHELM VON BERGEN—Heine
DIE SCHENKE AM SEE—
Droste-Hülshoff
SCHIARITA—Mandarà
SCHICKSAL—Morgenstern
SCHIFF AHOI!—Tucholsky
DIE SCHILDKRÖKRÖTE—
Morgenstern
SCHILFLIEDER—Lenau
SCHLESISCHE MUNDART—
Anonymous–German
DAS SCHLOSS BONCOURT—
Chamisso
SCHLUSS DES 1650STEN JAHRES—
Gryphius
DER SCHNEIDER VON ULM—
Brecht
DER SCHNUPFEN—Morgenstern
THE SCHOLAR AND THE CAT—
Anonymous–English—
Modern English
THE SCHOLAR COMPLAINS—
Anonymous–English—
Modern English
THE SCHOLAR GIPSY—Arnold
THE SCHOLARS—Yeats
SCHOLIAST/ICONOCLAST—Hoff-
man
SCHÖNE FREMDE—Eichendorff
SCHÖNE SPRACHE—
Hofmannsthal
DER SCHÖNE STRAHLENDE
MENSCH SPRICHT—Werfel
SCHÖNES GEMÜT—Mörike
SCHOOL FOR COPS—Emanuel
SCHOOL FOR SCANDAL—Sheridan
THE SCHOOLBOY—Blake
SCHOOLBOY—Patten
SCHOOLBOYS IN WINTER—Clare
SCHOOLCHILDREN—Auden
THE SCHOOLMASTER—Sobiloff
THE SCHOOLMASTERS—Brown,
Thomas Edward
SCHOOLROOM GOD—Van Doren

THE SCHOOLTEACHER MIRA—*Sutzkever*

SCHWANEN GEFAHR—*Celan*

SCHWANENLIED—*Brentano*

SCHWARZE PUPPEN—*Damas*

DAS SCHWEIGEN—*Gemmingen*

SCIAGURATELLA—*Galdieri*

LE SCIARLETTE DE LA COMMARE—*Belli*

SCIENCE—*Jeffers, Robinson*

SCIENCE OBESE—*Sobiloff*

THE SCIENCE OF THE NIGHT—*Kunitz*

A SCIENZA—*Bovio*

SCORPION—*Smith, Stevie*

SCOTCH DRINK—*Burns*

SCOTCH RHAPSODY—*Sitwell, Edith*

SCOTTSBORO, TOO, IS WORTH ITS SONG—*Cullen*

THE SCOURGE—*Kunitz*

SCRAPBOOKS—*Giovanni*

SCREENED—*Beecher*

THE SCRIBE—*De la Mare*

THE SCRUTINIE—*Lovelace, Richard*

SCULPTOR—*Plath*

LA SCUOLA DEI GRANDI—*Rodari*

O SCUPATORE—*Viviani*

SE GUARDO CRISTO IN CROCE—*Celi*

SE IO FOSSI 'N AUCIELLO STATUETTE—*Totò*

SE MANNISKEN—*Edfelt*

SE MURIÓ CASIMIRO—*Anonymous-Spanish*

LE QUERIAN—*Aleixandre*

THE SEA—*Byron*

THE SEA AND THE MIRROR—*Auden*

THE SEA AND THE SKYLARK—*Hopkins*

THE SEA-BELL—*Tolkien*

SEA BURIAL FROM THE CRUISER REVE—*Eberhart*

SEA CALM—*Hughes, Langston*

SEA CHEST—*Sandburg*

THE SEA COMING INDOORS—*Hacker*

SEA-DRIFT—*Whitman*

SEA FEVER—*Masefield*

THE SEA GRIEVES—*Hughes, Ted*

THE SEA-GULL—*Nash*

SEA-HAWK—*Eberhart*

SEA HOLLY—*Aiken*

THE SEA-LIMITS—*Rossetti, Dante Gabriel*

SEA-ODALISQUE—*Blackmur*

THE SEA PRINCESS—*Pyle*

THE SEA SERPENT CHANTEY—*Lindsay, Vachel*

THE SEA SHINES—*Ciardi*

A SEA-SONG FROM THE SHORE—*Riley*

SEA-WASH—*Sandburg*

SEA-WINDOW—*Smith, Stevie*

THE SEAFARER—*Anonymous-English—Old English; Pound*

THE SEAFARER—*Williams, William Carlos*

SEAFARING—*Richards, I. A.*

THE SEAGULL—*Jones, Glyn*

THE SEAGULL—*Press*

SEALED IN HISTORY—*Goldstein*

THE SEAL'S LULLABY—*Kipling*

SEALS, TERNS, TIME—*Eberhart*

SEANS—*Ferlin*

THE SEARCH FOR TRUTH—*Beecher*

SEASCAPE—*Hughes, Langston*

SEASCAPE—*Spender*

SEASIDE GOLF—*Betjeman*

SEASIDE SERENADE—*Nash*

THE SEASONS—*Thomson*

SEASONS OF THE SOUL—*Tate, Allen*

DER 64. KUHLPSALM—*Kuhlmann*

THE SECOND COMING—*Morgan, John*

THE SECOND COMING—*Yeats*

SECOND DAY OF DEATH—*Colbert*

SECOND GLANCE AT A JAGUAR—*Hughes, Ted*

THE SECOND OLDEST STORY—*Parker*

SECOND SIGHT—*Brinnin*

THE SECOND WORLD—*Blackmur*

SECONDARY EPIC—*Auden*

THE SECRET—*Children's Verses and Nursery Rhymes*

THE SECRET—*Johnston, Ellen Turlington*

THE SECRET—*Levertov*

SECRET EXPEDITION TO THE SOUTH—*Wellman*

SECRET FORMULA—*Marshall, Helen Lowrie*

THE SECRET HEART—*Coffin*

THE SECRET OF THE MACHINES—*Kipling*

SECRET MEETINGS—*Viorst*

THE SECRET SITS—*Frost, Robert*

THE SECRET SNARER—*Gunn*

SECRET WEAPON—*Ammonides*

THE SECRET WOOD—*Young, Andrew*

THE SECRETARY—*Redgrove*

LA SED—*Guillén, Nicolás*

THE SEDGE-WARBLERS—*Thomas, Edward*

SEE IT WAS LIKE THIS—*Ferlinghetti*

SEE SAMMY RUN IN THE WRONG DIRECTION—*Lee, Don L.*

SEED LEAVES—*Wilbur*

SEEFAHRT—*Goethe*

SEEING YOU HAVE A WOMAN—*Snodgrass*

EIN SEEKADETT AN SEINE STIEFMUTTER, 1915—*Anonymous-German*

SEGRETO DEL POETA—*Ungaretti*

SEGUIDILLAS PERSONALES—*Fernandez Moreno*

SEGUNDA LUGUNA—*Garcia Lorca*

SEGUNDA PALINODIA: LA SANGRE—*Alonso*

SEGUNDO COMENTARIO—*Alonso*

SEHNSUCHT—*Eichendorff*

SEHNSUCHT—*Goethe*

SEHNSUCHT—*Liliencron*

SEIGNEUR, J'AI PEUR—*Verlaine*

LAS SEIS CUERDAS—*Garcia Lorca*

SELF-DEFENSE—*Davison, Peter*

SELF EXPRESSION—*Darr*

SELF-IMPROVEMENT PROGRAM—*Viorst*

SELF IN 1958—*Sexton*

SELF-LOVE—*Dupree*

SELF-PORTRAIT AS A BEAR—*Hall*

SELF-PORTRAIT: VINCENT VAN GOGH—*Engle*

THE SELF-PROTECTING RABBITS—*Roche*

SELF'S THE MAN—*Larkin*

SELIGE SEHNSUCHT—*Goethe*

THE SELKIRK GRACE—*Burns*

THE SELLER OF ROSES—*Souster*

SELVA OSCURA—*MacNeice*

SEMELE—*Watkins*

SEMELE RECYCLED—*Kizer*

SEMPRE PIU DIFFICILE—*Sala*

SEND A BIOGRAPHICAL NOTE—*Darr*

SEND ME BACK MY HEART—*Suckling*

THE SEND-OFF—*Owen, Wilfred*

SEND THE TROOPS OVER—*Andrews*

THE SENECAS—*La Farge*

SENILE—*Gittings*

SENRYU POEMS—*Anonymous-Asian languages*

THE SENSATION CAPTAIN—*Gilbert, Sir William Schwenck*

A SENSE OF THE MOMENT—*Dowling*

SENSEMAYA—*Guillén, Nicolás*

THE SENSUALIST—*Updike*

THE SENSUALISTS—*Roethke*

THE SENSUOUS WOMAN—*Viorst*

LOS SENTIDOS FANTASMAGORICOS—*Martinez Alonso*

SENTIMENT—*Parker*

THE SENTRY—*Owen, Wilfred*

SENZA PIÙ PESO—*Ungaretti*

'A SENZITIVA—*Di Giacomo*

SEPELO—*López*

LES SEPT POÈMES D'AMOUR EN GUERRE—*Éluard*

SEPTEMBER—*Hedberg*

SEPTEMBER—*Kavanagh*

THE SEPTEMBER AFTERNOON TREES—*Summers, Hollis*

SEPTEMBER 1, 1939—*Auden*

SEPTEMBER HILLS—*Marshall, Helen Lowrie*

SEPTEMBER IN THE PARK—
Snodgrass
SEPTEMBER NIGHT WITH AN OLD
HORSE—Bly
SEPTEMBER 1913—Yeats
SEQUENCE—Marcus
SEQUENCES—Sanchez
SEQUENTIOR—Olson
SER EN FLOR—Jiménez
LA SERA DEL DÌ DI FESTA—
Leopardi
SERA DI PUGLIA—Gatto
SERAPHINE—Heine
SERE D'INVERNO—Agnello
SERENADE—Kramer
A SERENADE—Pinkney
SERENADE: ANY MAN TO ANY
WOMAN—Sitwell, Edith
A SERENADE AT THE VILLA—
Browning, Robert
SERENATA—Anonymous–
Spanish
SERENATA—Carducci
SERENATA—Garcia Lorca
THE SERENE GREEN WORM—Darr
SEREPTA MASON—Masters, Edgar
Lee
SERGIO CORAZZINI—Palazzeschi
A SERMON FROM THE
UNDERGROUND—Berrigan
THE SERMON ON THE WARPLAND—
Brooks, Gwendolyn
LE SERPENT—Apollinaire
SERRANA—Santillana
SERRANILLA—Santillana
SERRANILLA DE BORES—
Santillana
A SERVANT WHEN HE REIGNETH—
Kipling
SESTINA—Dante Alighieri
SESTINA—Merwin
SESTINA—Swinburne
SESTINA: ALTAFORTE—Pound
SESTINA OF THE TRAMP-ROYAL—
Kipling
THE SETTING OF WINDCOCK—
Masefield
DER SEUFZER—Morgenstern
SEULETTE SUIS—Christine de
Pisan
7. IV. 64—Snyder
$7.50—Miles
THE SEVEN HOUSES: IN MEMORY OF
JOHN F. KENNEDY—Brown,
George Mackay
SEVEN YEARS OLD—Swinburne
SEVENTEEN MONTHS—Sandburg
17 WARNINGS IN SEARCH OF A
FEMINIST POEM—Jong
SEVENTEENTH CENTURY
LANDSCAPE NEAR
BALLYFERRITER—Kinsella
SEVILLA—Garcia Lorca
SEX AND THE OVER FORTIES—
Porter, Peter
SEX IS NOT SO SEXY ANYMORE—
Viorst

SEXT—Auden
THE SHADOW—Clough
SHADOW AND ANSWER—Marshall,
Lenore G.
THE SHADOW-HUNTER—Simpson
THE SHADOW OF CAIN—Sitwell,
Edith
THE SHADOW PEOPLE—Ledwidge
SHADOW PLAY—Marshall,
Lenore G.
SHADOWS—Norris
SHADOWS IN THE WATER—
Traherne
SHAG—Martynov
SHAH NAMEH—Ferdovci
SHAKA—Anonymous–African
languages–Southern Africa
SHAKE—Sherwin
SHAKESPEARE—Arnold
SHAKESPEARE—Longfellow
THE SHALIMAR—Last Poets
SHALOM—Garlick
SHAME—Wilbur
SHAMEFUL DEATH—Morris,
William
SHANE O'NEILL'S CAIRN—Jeffers,
Robinson
THE SHAPE OF FLESH AND BONE—
MacLeish
THE SHAPE OF THE FIRE—Roethke
SHARECROPPERS—Brown,
Sterling A.
SHATTERED DREAMS—Hodges
SHCHERBATOVOI—Lermontov
SHE—Roethke
SHE—Wilbur
SHE BOWED TO HER BROTHER—
Stein, Gertrude
SHE CAME AND WENT—Lowell,
James Russell
SHE CHARGED ME—Hardy
SHE HAD CONCEALED HIM—
Patchen
SHE IS NO LIAR—Graves
SHE OPENED THE DOOR—Hardy
SHE STOOPS TO CONQUER—
Goldsmith
SHE, TO HIM—Hardy
SHE WEEPS OVER RAHOON—Joyce
THE SHEAVES—Robinson, Edwin
Arlington
SHEEP—Davies, William Henry
SHEEP—Hughes, Ted
THE SHEEP CHILD—Dickey,
James
SHEEPDOG TRIAL IN HYDE PARK—
Day Lewis
THE SHEETS—Jong
THE SHELL—Stephens
SHELL—Stryk
SHELL SONG—Marshall,
Lenore G.
SHELTER—Derwood
SHELTERED GARDEN—Doolittle
THE SHEPHERD—Blake
SHEPHERD AND SHEPHERDESS—
Breton, Nicholas

THE SHEPHERD, ARSILIUS', REPLY—
Young, Bartholomew
THE SHEPHERD BOY—Dowling
THE SHEPHERDESS—Meynell
SHEPHERD'S HYMN—Crashaw
THE SHEPHERD'S WIFE'S SONG—
Greene
SHERIDAN'S RIDE—Read, Thomas
Buchanan
SHERTHURSDAYE AND VENUS DAY
—Jones, David
SHERWOOD—Noyes
THE SHIELD OF ACHILLES—Auden
SHIFTING SANDS—Marshall,
Helen Lowrie
SHILOH, A REQUIEM—Melville
THE SHIMMER OF EVIL—Roethke
SHINE—Damas
SHINE, PERISHING REPUBLIC—
Jeffers, Robinson
A SHIP—
Anonymous–English—Old
English
A SHIP BURNING AND A COMET ALL
IN ONE DAY—Eberhart
THE SHIP OF DEATH—Lawrence
THE SHIP OF STATE—Longfellow
THE SHOES OF WANDERING—
Kinnell
THE SHOOTING—Pack
THE SHOOTING OF DAN MACGREW
—Service
SHOPPING FOR MEAT IN WINTER—
Williams, Oscar
SHORT HATE—Sobiloff
SHORT ODE—Benét, Stephen
Vincent
THE SHORT ORDER COCKTAIL, OR,
ONE COOK TO TAKE OUT—Nash
SHORT POEM—Rasof
SHORT POEM—Sanchez
A SHORT SONG OF
CONGRATULATION—Johnson,
Samuel
THE SHOT—Jennings
SHOULD LANTERNS SHINE—
Thomas, Dylan
THE SHOW—Owen, Wilfred
SHOWDOWN—Genser
THE SHREW—Nash
THE SHRIMP—Nash
A SHROPSHIRE LAD—Betjeman
THE SHUT-EYE TRAIN—Field,
Eugene
SHUT OUT THAT MOON—Hardy
SI JE MOURAIS LÀ-BAS—
Apollinaire
SI OVERO MORE 'O CUORPO—
Viviani
SI SOUVENT—Damas
SI T'O SSAPESSE DICERE—Filippo
SI TU ES MALHEUREUX—Omar
Khayyam
SI TU T'IMAGINES—Queneau
SI VOUS VOULEZ QUE J'AIME
ENCORE—Voltaire
SIBIRSKYIYE BANI—Voznezensky

ICILIA 1973—*Addamo*
HE SICK ROSE—*Blake*
HE SICKNESS OF ADAM—*Shapiro, Karl*
IDISH' BEREMENNAYA—*Voznezensky*
HE SIDON GIRLS! THE SIDON GIRLS!—*Antipater of Sidon*
IE ZU IHM—*Tucholsky*
IEG ÜBER DIE SONNE—*Krucenych*
IENA—*Gregor*
IGHS AND GRONES—*Herbert*
HE SIGN IN THE SKY—*Van Doren*
HE SIGNALS—*Merwin*
HE SIGNIFICATOR: QUEEN OF PENTACLES—*Piercy*
IGNO DE ESPAÑA—*Pardo Garcia*
IN SIGNORE CON TRE CAPPELLI—*Rodari*
A SIGNORINA FELICITA OVVERO LA FELICITA—*Gozzano*
IGNS—*Murphy*
IGNURELLA—*Galdieri*
ILENCE—*Hood*
ILENCE—*Moore, Marianne*
ILENCE—*Poe*
ILENCE AND STEALTH OF DAYES! —*Vaughan, Henry*
ILENCE AND TEARS—*Goldstein*
ILENCIO—*Garcia Lorca*
ILENCIO—*Storni*
HE SILENT ANGEL—*Wright, James*
HE SILENT GENERATION—*Simpson*
HE SILENT GENERATION—*Treitel*
ILENT IN DARIEN—*Beecher*
HE SILENT LOVER—*Simpson*
ILENT NOON—*Rossetti, Dante Gabriel*
ILENT POEM—*Francis*
HE SILENT SLAIN—*MacLeish*
ILENTIUM—*Tyutchev*
ILHOUETTE—*Hughes, Langston*
HE SILKEN TENT—*Frost, Robert*
ILLY BILLY—*Children's Verses and Nursery Rhymes*
ILVER—*De la Mare*
HE SILVER AGE—*Gunn*
HE SILVER CUFF AND THE ENCYCLOPAEDIA OF KNOWLEDGE—*Roche*
ILVERHORN—*Conkling*
ILVESTER SKURILLO—*Rudnigger*
IMEON STYLITES—*McGinley*
IMMER NICHTSANG—*Smith, Sydney Goodsir*
IMON LEGREE—*Lindsay, Vachel*
IMON THE CYRENIAN SPEAKS—*Cullen*
IMPLE BEAST—*Van Doren*
IMPLE SIMON—*Children's Verses and Nursery Rhymes*
IMPLES—*Joyce*
IMPLEX MUNDITIIS—*Jonson*

SIMPLICITY OF PRAYER—*Marshall, Helen Lowrie*
THE SIMPLON PASS—*Wordsworth*
SIN—*Herbert*
SIN APRENDER EL ALFABETO—*Anonymous–Spanish*
SIN DIÓS Y SIN VOS Y MI—*Manrique*
SIN IN THE HINTERLANDS—*Elmslie*
SINCERELY YOURS,—*Sondé*
SINCERELY YOURS, CULTURE—*Bodenheim*
SINGING—*Gregor*
SINGING—*Stevenson*
THE SINGING CAT—*Smith, Stevie*
THE SINGING OF THE MAGNIFICAT—*Nesbit*
THE SINGLE HERO—*Van Doren*
SINGS HARRY—*Glover*
SINNER—*Hughes, Langston*
SINTESIS—*García Tudurí*
SIR BEELZEBUB—*Sitwell, Edith*
SIR EUSTACE GREY—*Crabbe*
SIR GALAHAD—*Tennyson*
SIR GAWAIN AND THE GREEN KNIGHT—*Anonymous–English —Middle English*
SIR GAWAINE AND THE GREEN KNIGHT—*Winters*
SIR PATRICK SPENS—*Anonymous–English– Modern English*
SIR WALTER PLEADS IN PERSON—*Raleigh*
THE SIREN'S SONG—*Browne, William*
SIROCCO AT DEYA—*Graves*
SISTER LOU—*Brown, Sterling A.*
SISTER, THERE ARE MONSTERS—*Wilson*
A SISTER WRITES—*Bodenheim*
THE SISTERLY FASHION—*Williams, William Carlos*
THE SISTERS—*Deveaux*
SIT-INS—*Walker*
SITIO PERPETUO—*Jiménez*
THE SITTER AND THE BUTTER AND THE BETTER BATTER FRITTER—*Lee, Dennis*
SITTING DOWN—*Harkness*
THE SITUATION IN THE WEST—*Ferlinghetti*
6 A.M., BOSTON, SUMMER SUBLET—*Atwood*
6 FÉVRIER—*Péret*
THE SIX QUART BASKET—*Souster*
SIX REASONS FOR DRINKING—*Scannell*
SIX: SUNDAY—*Bibbs*
SIX TO SIX—*Anonymous–African languages–Southern Africa*
SIX WINTER PRIVACY POEMS—*Bly*
SIX YOUNG MEN—*Hughes, Ted*
SIXTEEN, YEAH—*Emanuel*
THE SIXTH BOOK OF CONQUISTADOR—*MacLeish*

SJON—*Gullberg*
SJONG BACKEN—*Hasso*
SKÅ NINGAR—*Ossiannilsson*
SKALD'S DEATH—*MacDiarmid*
SKAPAREN—*Blomberg*
SKARE—*Ferlin*
SKATAN—*Lundkvist*
THE SKATER OF GHOST LAKE—*Benét, William Rose*
THE SKELETON IN ARMOR—*Longfellow*
SKIMBLESHANKS: THE RAILWAY CAT —*Eliot, Thomas Stearns*
THE SKINK—*Nash*
SKINNY POEM—*Lipsitz*
SKIPPER IRESON'S RIDE—*Whittier*
SKOGSKÄLLA—*Asplund*
SKULL OF THE WORLD—*Williams, Gwyn*
SKULLS—*Norris*
SKUNK HOUR—*Lowell, Robert*
THE SKY IS BLUE—*Ignatow*
SKY MAN—*Kops*
SKY OF LATE SUMMER—*Rago*
SKY PIECES—*Sandburg*
SKY TALK—*Sandburg*
SKYSCRAPER—*Lee, Dennis*
SKYSCRAPERS—*Field, Rachel*
SLANTED POETRY STATEMENT—*Gaver*
SLEEP—*McGough*
SLEEP AWAKE—*Clark, John W.*
SLEEP, GRANDMOTHER—*Van Doren*
SLEEP IMPRESSION—*Sandburg*
THE SLEEPER—*Souster*
THE SLEEPER—*Poe*
THE SLEEPERS—*Whitman*
SLEEPING AT LAST—*Rossetti, Christina*
THE SLEEPING BEAUTY—*Simpson*
THE SLEEPING BEAUTY—*Sitwell, Edith*
THE SLEEPING FURY—*Bogan*
THE SLEEPING GIANT—*Hall*
THE SLEEPING LORD—*Jones, David*
THE SLEEPY SONG—*Bacon*
A SLEEPY TUNE—*Sitwell, Edith*
SLEET STORM—*Tippett*
A SLICE OF WEDDING CAKE—*Graves*
SLIM GREER—*Brown, Sterling A.*
SLIM IN ATLANTA—*Brown, Sterling A.*
SLIM IN HELL—*Brown, Sterling A.*
SLIM LANDS A JOB—*Brown, Sterling A.*
THE SLOTH—*Roethke*
THE SLOW PACIFIC SWELL—*Winters*
SLOW SONG IN THE DARK—*Gitlin*
THE SLOW STARTER—*MacNeice*
SLOWLY—*Reeves*
THE SLUGGARD—*Watts*
THE SMALL CABIN—*Atwood*

SMALL COLORED BOY IN THE
    SUBWAY—*Deutsch*
SMALL COMMENT—*Sanchez*
A SMALL DISCOVERY—*Emanuel*
A SMALL DRAGON—*Patten*
SMALL ELEGY—*Ciardi*
SMALL HOMES—*Sandburg*
SMALL SONG—*Reid*
SMALL SPOLETO MANTRA—
    Ginsberg
SMALL TANTRIC SERMON—
    Whalen
SMALL TOWN—*Bodenheim*
SMALL-TOWN, U. S. A.—*Marshall,
    Helen Lowrie*
SMELL!—*Williams, William
    Carlos*
A SMELL OF BURNING—
    Blackburn, Thomas
SMELLS—*Morley*
SMELLY FRED—*Lee, Dennis*
SMOKE ANIMALS—*Bennett,
    Rowena*
SMUGGLER—*MacCaig*
A SMUGGLER'S SONG—*Kipling*
SMYCKA MIN MORGON—*Vennberg*
EN SNÄCKA I SANDEN—*Hasso*
THE SNAIL—*Hughes, Langston*
SNAKE—*Lawrence*
SNAKE-CHARMER—*Plath*
THE SNAKE THAT WALKED UPON
    HIS TAIL—*Cullen*
THE SNAKE TRYING—*Ross, W. W.
    Eustace*
SNÅLEN—*Martinson*
THE SNAP COMB WILDERNESS—
    Graves
THE SNARE—*Stephens*
SNART FORBI—*Vennberg*
SNATCH OF SLIPHORN JAZZ—
    Sandburg
SNEEZLES—*Milne*
SNIPERS—*McGough*
SNÖBLOMMOR—*Blomberg*
SNOW—*Coatsworth*
SNOW—*Thomas, Edward*
SNOW BANKS, NORTH OF THE
    HOUSE—*Bly*
SNOW-BOUND—*Whittier*
SNOW DROP—*Silkin*
SNOW IN THE SUBURBS—*Hardy*
THE SNOW MAN—*Stevens,
    Wallace*
SNOW SORCERY—*Goldstein*
THE SNOW-STORM—*Emerson*
SNOWFALL IN THE AFTERNOON—
    Bly
THE SNOWFLAKE—*De la Mare*
THE SNOWFLAKE—*Dorn*
THE SNOWS OF MOUNT HERMON—
    Sutzkever
SNOWSPELL—*Francis*
SNOWSTORM IN JANUARY—
    Zaturenska
SNOWY HERON—*Ciardi*
SO-AND-SO RECLINING ON HER
    COUCH—*Stevens, Wallace*

SO BE IT—*Patchen*
SO DEEP IN RIVERS OF THAT
    STROMSBERG TIME—*Jeffers,
    Lance*
SO I RESIGNED FROM THE CHUCHIN
    CHOWDER AND MARCHING CLUB
    —*Nash*
SO, PENSEROSO—*Nash*
SO SHOULD YOU SPEAK TO THE
    ORPHAN—*Sutzkever*
SO THIS IS OUR REVOLUTION—
    Sanchez
SO UND NICHT ANDERS—*Fontane*
SO UND SO—*Roth, Eugen*
SO VARIOUS—*Hardy*
SO WELL I LOVE THEE—*Drayton*
SO—WHAT HAPPENED TO YOU?—
    Johnston, Ellen Turlington
SOBAKA—*Turgenev*
SOBATCHKA—*Svetlov*
SOBRE EL EVANGELIO 'IN
    PRINCIPIO ERAT VERBUM'—*Juan
    de la Cruz*
SOBRE MI HOMBRO—*Martí*
SOCIAL STUDY—*Baldwin,
    Michael*
SOCIETY UPON THE STANISLAUS—
    Harte
LES SOEURS DE CHARITÉ—
    Rimbaud
SOFT—*Cunningham, James
    Vincent*
SOFT SNOW—*Blake*
SOFT, SOFT, SOFT—*Van Doren*
SOFT WOOD—*Lowell, Robert*
IL SOGNO—*Leopardi*
IL SOGNO DEL PRIGIONIERO—
    Montale
SOGNO D'ESTATE—*Carducci*
SOHRAB AND RUSTUM—*Arnold*
SOIL—*McGough*
LE SOIR—*Lamartine*
SOIR DE CARNAVAL—*Laforgue*
LA SOIRÉE DE DÉCEMBRE—*Cadou*
UNE SOIRÉE PERDUE—*Musset*
SOKRATES UND ALKIBIADES—
    Hölderlin
SOL DE COMPIÈGNE—*Desnos*
SOL DE LOS HUMILDES—*Poveda*
SOLDE—*Damas*
A SOLDIER—*Brooke*
A SOLDIER—*Frost, Robert*
A SOLDIER—*Ignatow*
A SOLDIER—HIS PRAYER—*Kersh*
SOLDIERS BATHING—*Prince*
THE SOLDIER'S DREAM—*Owen,
    Wilfred*
THE SOLDIER'S DREAM—*Scannell*
SOLDIER'S STAND—*Bodenheim*
SOLE—*Palazzeschi*
LA SOLEA—*Garcia Lorca*
SOLEDAD—*Hayden*
SOLEDAD DE ALMA—*Gómez de
    Avellaneda*
LE SOLEIL DE LA NUIT—*Char*
SOLEILS COUCHANTS—*Verlaine*

SOLEMNLY MINE—*Fabio, Cyril
    Leslie III*
SOLILOQUI—*Collins, Leslie M.*
SOLILOQUY—*Tripp*
SOLILOQUY OF THE SPANISH
    CLOISTER—*Browning, Robert*
THE SOLITARY DAFFODIL—
    Richards, I. A.
THE SOLITARY REAPER—
    Wordsworth
SOLITUDE—*Fombeure*
SOLITUDE—*Levertov*
SOLITUDE—*Milne*
LA SOLITUDE—*Saint-Amant*
THE SOLITUDE OF MR. POWERS—
    Nash
SÓLO EL HOMBRE—*Neruda*
SÓLO LA MUERTE—*Neruda*
LA SOLOGNE—*Obaldia*
SOLOMON AND THE WITCH—*Yeats*
SOLTERA—*León, Rafael de*
SOMAPOETICS—*Quasha*
LA SOMBRA DE MI ALMA—*Garcia
    Lorca*
SOME LINES SCRAWLED ON THE
    DOOR OF VAGABOND'S HOUSE—
    Blanding
SOME LITANIES—*Benedikt*
SOME NATURAL HISTORY—
    Marquis
SOME ONE—*De la Mare*
SOME PLACE—*Creeley*
SOME SHADOWS—*Stafford*
SOME SORT OF GAME—*Ciardi*
SOME TIME—*Farjeon*
SOME TREES—*Ashbery*
SOMEHOW I KNOW—*Marshall,
    Helen Lowrie*
SOMEONE TALKING TO HIMSELF—
    Wilbur
SOMETHING HAS TO BURN—
    Brackett
SOMETHING LIES BEYOND THE
    SCENE—*Sitwell, Edith*
SOMETHING TO LIVE FOR—
    Marshall, Helen Lowrie
SOMETHING TOLD THE WILD
    GEESE—*Field, Rachel*
SOMEWHERE BETWEEN HEAVEN
    AND WOOLWORTH'S—*Patten*
SOMEWHERE IN A TURRET—
    Hacker
SOMIGLIANZE—*Saba*
SOMMARNATTEN—*Selander*
SOMME AND FLANDERS—*Porter,
    Peter*
SOMMEIL D'ATYS—*Mauriac*
SOMMER—*Bergengruen*
SON—*Turgenev*
SON ALTESSE—*Graves*
A SON CAN MAKE A FATHER—
    Brown, Otis
SON FIORITI CAMPANI E
    CAMPANELLI—*Campanile*
SONATIN—*Edfelt*
SONATINA—*Darío*
SONETO—*Calderón de la Barca*

SONETO—*Castro, Eugénio de*
SONETO—*Coronado*
SONETO—*Garcia Lorca*
SONETO—*Juana Inés de la Cruz*
SONETO—*Lima*
SONETO—*Pessanha*
SONETO—*Quintana, Mário*
SONETO—*Terrazas*
SONETO—*Valle Caviedes*
SONETO—*Vocos-Lescano*
SONETO 5—*Vega, Garcilaso de la*
SONETO 10—*Vega, Garcilaso de la*
SONETO 17—*Dante Alighieri*
SONETO 18—*Vega Carpio*
SONETO 23—*Vega, Garcilaso de la*
UN SONETO A CERVANTES—*Darío*
SONETO A CRISTO NUESTRO SEÑOR —*Vega Carpio*
SONETO DE ÉPOCA— *Piedra-Bueno*
SONETO DE LA MUERTE—*Mistral*
SONETO DE LA MUERTE DE CRISTO —*Quevedo y Villegas*
SONÊTO DE LUCIANO—*Schmidt*
SONETO FINAL—*Hernández, Miguel*
SONETO PARA PEDIR POR LOS AMIGOS MUERTOS—*Alcántara*
LOS SONETOS DE LA SOLEDAD— *Ribera Chevremont*
SONETOS NOCTURNOS—*Bernárdez*
SONG—*Beddoes*
SONG—*Blake*
SONG—*Browne, William*
SONG—*Browning, Robert*
SONG—*Carew*
SONG—*Charles II*
SONG—*Creeley*
SONG—*Davenant*
SONG—*Dickinson, Patric*
SONG—*Donne*
SONG—*Dryden*
SONG—*Etherege*
SONG—*Gregor*
SONG—*Hillyer*
SONG—*Jeffers, Lance*
SONG—*Lewis, Alun*
SONG—*Merwin*
SONG—*O'Hara*
SONG—*Peacock*
SONG—*Poe*
SONG—*Prior*
SONG—*Rossetti, Christina*
SONG—*Rukeyser*
SONG—*Sackville*
SONG—*Sitwell, Edith*
SONG—*Spender*
SONG—*Suckling*
SONG—*Tennyson*
SONG—*Walsh*
A SONG ABOUT MYSELF—*Keats*
SONG AGAINST CHILDREN— *Kilmer, Aline*

SONG-BOOKS OF THE WAR— *Sassoon*
SONG FOR A DARK GIRL—*Hughes, Langston*
SONG FOR A DARK VOICE— *Levertov*
SONG FOR A LYRE—*Bogan*
SONG FOR A PHALLUS—*Hughes, Ted*
SONG FOR A TEMPERATURE OF A HUNDRED AND ONE—*Nash*
SONG FOR AIMÉ CÉSAIRE— *Kgositsile*
SONG FOR BILLIE HOLLIDAY— *Hughes, Langston*
SONG FOR CARMARTHEN— *Williams, Gwyn*
SONG FOR ISHTAR—*Levertov*
A SONG FOR SAINT CECILIA'S DAY —*Dryden*
SONG FOR SEVEN PARTS OF THE BODY—*Kumin*
A SONG FOR SIMEON—*Eliot, Thomas Stearns*
SONG FOR SOMETHING PRETTY— *Emanuel*
SONG FOR THE LAST ACT—*Bogan*
SONG FOR THE SQUEEZE-BOX— *Roethke*
SONG FOR ZARATHUSTRA—*Durrell*
SONG FROM A PLAY—*Yeats*
SONG: I'M GOING HOME—*Lester*
A SONG IN HIS LADY'S ABSENCE— *Anonymous–English– Modern English*
A SONG IN THE FRONT YARD— *Brooks, Gwendolyn*
SONG IN THE WOOD—*Fletcher, John*
SONG: LIFT BOY—*Graves*
SONG: MAYBE THE LAST TIME— *Lester*
SONG: NOBODY'S FAULT BUT MINE —*Lester*
SONG OF CONTRARIETY—*Graves*
SONG OF DITTA—*Last Poets*
SONG OF ENCHANTMENT—*De la Mare*
A SONG OF EXPERIENCE—*Amis*
THE SONG OF HIAWATHA— *Longfellow*
A SONG OF LONGING—*Dowling*
SONG OF MARION'S MEN—*Bryant, William Cullen*
SONG OF MOTHER COURAGE— *Brecht*
SONG OF MYSELF—*Whitman*
SONG OF NEW YORK—*Kramer*
SONG OF PERFECT PROPRIETY— *Parker*
SONG OF QUEEN ANNE BOLEYN: AT COCKCROW—*Sitwell, Edith*
THE SONG OF SONGS—*Bible and Pseudepigrapha*
THE SONG OF THE BIRD IN THE LOINS—*Spicer*

SONG OF THE BROAD-AXE— *Whitman*
SONG OF THE CHATTA HOOCHEE— *Lanier*
THE SONG OF THE DEAD—*Kipling*
SONG OF THE DEATH-WATCH BEETLE—*Heath-Stubbs*
SONG OF THE DEVIL—*Auden*
SONG OF THE DYING GUNNER A. A. 1—*Causley*
SONG OF THE EARTH—*Walters*
SONG OF THE EXPOSITION— *Whitman*
SONG OF THE GALLEY SLAVES— *Kipling*
THE SONG OF THE HAPPY SHEPHERD—*Yeats*
THE SONG OF THE IMPERIAL CARRION—*Logue*
THE SONG OF THE JELLICLES— *Eliot, Thomas Stearns*
SONG OF THE MAD PRINCE—*De la Mare*
SONG OF THE OGRES—*Auden*
THE SONG OF THE OLD MOTHER— *Yeats*
SONG OF THE OPEN ROAD— *Whitman*
A SONG OF THE ROLLING EARTH— *Whitman*
SONG OF THE SHEPHERD IN THE VALLEY OF HUMILIATION— *Bunyan*
SONG OF THE SHIRT—*Hood*
SONG OF THE SON—*Toomer*
THE SONG OF THE TIRED MEN— *Dowling*
SONG OF THE WAGON DRIVER— *Johnson, B. S.*
THE SONG OF THE WANDERING AENGUS—*Yeats*
SONG ON THE DREAD OF A CHILL SPRING—*Logan*
SONG: THE FAR SIDE OF YOUR MOON—*Graves*
SONG: THE ORGANIC YEARS—*Bell*
SONG: THE REV. MUBUGWU DICKINSON RUMINATES BEHIND THE SERMON—*Brooks, Gwendolyn*
SONG TO ACCOMPANY THE BEARER OF BAD NEWS—*Wagoner*
SONG TO CELIA—*Jonson*
SONG TO DAVID—*Smart*
SONG TOURNAMENT: NEW STYLE— *Untermeyer*
SONG: WADE IN THE WATER— *Lester*
SONG: WATCH THE SEAGULLS FLYING—*Lester*
SONG: WHILST ALEXIS LAY PRESS'D —*Dryden*
SONG WITH BELLS—*Langland, Joseph*
SONG: WORRIED BLUES—*Lester*
LE SONGE—*Grandbois*

LE SONGE D'UN HABITANT DU
  MOGOL—*La Fontaine*
SONGS OF EXPERIENCE—*Blake*
SONGS OF INNOCENCE—*Blake*
SONGS OF PARTING—*Whitman*
THE SONGS OF THE MERCHANTS—
  Masefield
THE SONGSTER—*Smith, Stevie*
SONIDO RICO—*Gaver*
DIE SONNE BRINGT ES AN DEN TAG
  —*Chamisso*
SONNENUNTERGANG—*Hölderlin*
SONNET—*Agee*
SONNET—*Arvers*
SONNET—*Auden*
SONNET—*Belloc*
SONNET—*Bodenheim*
SONNET—*Brooke*
SONNET—*Drayton*
SONNET—*Du Bellay*
SONNET—*Hood*
SONNET—*Keats*
SONNET—*Kelly*
SONNET—*King*
SONNET—*Labé*
SONNET—*Logue*
SONNET—*Millay*
SONNET—*Milton*
SONNET—*Musset*
SONNET—*Ronsard*
SONNET—*Shakespeare*
SONNET—*Sherwin*
SONNET—*Smith, A. J. M.*
SONNET—*Sorley*
SONNET—*Spenser*
SONNET—*Sponde*
SONNET—*Suckling*
SONNET—*Tuckerman*
SONNET—*Wilbur*
SONNET—*Wordsworth*
SONNET CHRÉTIEN—*Gombauld*
SONNET D'ORONTE—*Molière*
SONNET FOR JOHN-JOHN—
  Solomon
SONNET: 1909—*Williams,*
  William Carlos
SONNET: ON SEEING A PIECE OF
  OUR ARTILLERY BROUGHT INTO
  ACTION—*Owen, Wilfred*
SONNET ON THE DEATH OF
  RICHARD WEST—*Gray*
SONNET ON WOMEN'S BUSINESS—
  Sherwin
SONNET: SILENCE—*Poe*
SONNET TO MY MOTHER—*Barker,*
  George
SONNET TO THE PRINCE REGENT
  ON THE REPEAL OF LORD
  EDWARD FITZGERALD'S
  FORFEITURE—*Byron*
SONNET TO VAUXHALL—*Hood*
SONNETS AT CHRISTMAS—*Tate,*
  Allen
SONNETS FROM THE PORTUGUESE
  —*Browning, Elizabeth*
  Barrett
SONNETS POUR HÉLÈNE—*Ronsard*

SONNY JIM CROWNED—*Williams,*
  Hugo
SONO UNA CREATURA—*Ungaretti*
SOON BE OVER—*Sherwin*
SOONATE IN UURLAUTEN—
  Schwitters
THE SOOTE SEASON—*Surrey*
SOPHOKLES—*Hölderlin*
SOPRANO—*Nash*
UN SORBO DE CAFE—*Diego,*
  Eliseo
THE SORCERESS—*Lindsay,*
  Vachel
LA SORGUE—*Char*
SORPRESA—*Chamisso*
SORROW HOME—*Walker*
SORROWFUL DREAMS REMEMBERED
  —*Millay*
SOTTO 'A NU LAMPIONE—*Viviani*
SOUL AIN'T: SOUL IS—*Fabio,*
  Sarah Webster
THE SOUL LONGS TO RETURN
  WHENCE IT CAME—*Eberhart*
SOUL THROUGH A LICKING STICK—
  Fabio, Sarah Webster
THE SOULS OF THE SLAIN—*Hardy*
SOUL'S RHYME—*Sobiloff*
SOUND HAPPENING FOR TWO—
  Lurie
THE SOUND OF LAUGHTER—
  Marshall, Helen Lowrie
THE SOUND OF TREES—*Frost,*
  Robert
SOUNDING BACK—*Dlugos*
SOUNDS—*Gaver*
SOUTH—*Brathwaite*
THE SOUTH COAST—*Antoninus*
THE SOUTH COUNTRY—*Belloc*
SOUTHBOUND ON THE FREEWAY—
  Swenson
SOUTHERN CROSS—*Crane, Hart*
SOUTHERN MAMMY SINGS—
  Hughes, Langston
SOUTHERN MANSION—*Bontemps*
SOUTHERN PACIFIC—*Sandburg*
THE SOUTHERN ROAD—*Randall*
SOUTHERN SHIPS AND SETTLERS—
  Benét, Rosemary Carr
SOUTHERN SONG—*Walker*
SOUVENIR—*Desbordes-Valmore*
SOUVENIR—*Musset*
SOUVENIR DE LONDRES—*Spender,*
  Stephen
SOUVENIRS—*Randall*
SOW—*Plath*
SOWING—*Thomas, Edward*
SOY ANIMAL DE FONDO—*Jiménez,*
  Juan Ramon
SPACE—*Giovanni*
SPACE PILOT—*Laudon*
SPACE PORT—*Clark, John W.*
SPACEDREAM STRUGGLE—
  Zu-Bolton
THE SPADES: PRELUDE—
  Brathwaite
SPAIN, MORNING—*Reid*
SPANISCHE TÄNZERIN—*Rilke*

THE SPANISH JEW'S TALE—
  Longfellow
THE SPANISH LIE—*MacLeish*
THE SPANISH NEEDLE—*McKay*
SPANISH WATERS—*Masefield*
A SPARK OF LAUREL—*Kunitz*
SPARROW—*Benét, Stephen*
  Vincent
A SPARROW IS A BIRD—*Danner*
THE SPARROWS—*Cohen*
SPARROWS IN A HILLSIDE DRIFT—
  Wright, James
SPÄT UND TIEF—*Celan*
SPÄTHERBST—*Bergengruen*
SPEAK, PARROT—*Skelton, John*
SPEAK TO ME CHILD AS I SPEAK TO
  MYSELF—*Sobiloff*
SPEAKING A FOREIGN LANGUAGE—
  Reid
THE SPECIAL PERSON—*Lee,*
  Dennis
SPECIAL STARLIGHT—*Sandburg*
SPECTATOR AB EXTRA—*Clough*
SPECTRAL LOVERS—*Ransom*
SPEECH, 9 AUG 61—*Mac Low*
SPEECH TO THE YOUNG, SPEECH TO
  THE PROGRESS-TOWARD—
  Brooks, Gwendolyn
SPEED—*Swenson*
THE SPEED OF DARKNESS—
  Rukeyser
THE SPELL OF THE YUKON—
  Service
SPELT FROM SIBYL'S LEAVES—
  Hopkins
SPENSER'S IRELAND—*Moore,*
  Marianne
DER SPERLING UND DAS
  KÄNGURUH—*Morgenstern*
LA SPIAGGIA—*Sereni*
SPIDER—*Thomas-Ellis*
A SPIDER AND A FLY—*Marquis*
SPIDER, BUILD YOUR CASTLE—
  Borton
SPIDER HEAD—*Hall*
DAS SPIEL IST AUS—*Castro,*
  Eugénio de
SPIELMANNSLIED—*Keller,*
  Gottfried
LA SPIGOLATRICE DI SAPRI—
  Mercantini
SPINNING SONG—*Sitwell, Edith*
SPINSTER—*Plath*
THE SPIRIT OF POETRY SPEAKS—
  Eberhart
THE SPIRIT OF THE BIRCH—
  Ketchum
SPIRITS OF THE DEAD—*Poe*
SPIRIT'S SONG—*Bogan*
SPIRITS UNCHAINED—*Kgositsile*
SPIRITUAL DEATH AT 45—*Bly*
SPLEEN—*Verlaine*
SPLEEN ET IDÉAL—*Baudelaire*
SPLISH, SPLOSH, SPLATTER—
  Butler, Celia
SPLITTING WOOD AT SIX ABOVE—
  Kumin

THE SPONTANEOUS MAN, THE GIFTED ASSASSIN—*Goldman*
SPORTING BEASLEY—*Brown, Sterling A.*
SPORTING PRINT—*Garlick*
SPRACHE—*Bobrowski*
THE SPRING—*Blake*
THE SPRING—*Carew*
THE SPRING—*Devaul*
THE SPRING—*Fyleman*
THE SPRING—*Hopkins*
THE SPRING—*Millay*
THE SPRING—*Ross, W. W. Eustace*
THE SPRING—*Snyder*
SPRING—*Tate, Allen*
THE SPRING—*Watkins*
SPRING AIR—*Derwood*
SPRING AND ALL—*Williams, William Carlos*
SPRING AND FALL—*Hopkins*
THE SPRING AND THE FALL—*Millay*
SPRING COMES TO MURRAY HILL—*Nash*
SPRING DANCE—*Rodgers*
SPRING IMAGES—*Wright, James*
SPRING IN NEW HAMPSHIRE—*McKay*
SPRING IN WARTIME—*Auden*
SPRING MORNING—*Milne*
SPRING MORNING—*Sitwell, Osbert*
SPRING MOUNTAIN CLIMB—*Eberhart*
SPRING, 1943—*Bodenheim*
SPRING, 1937—*Aubert*
SPRING OFFENSIVE—*Owen, Wilfred*
SPRING POOLS—*Frost, Robert*
A SPRING SERPENT—*Winters*
SPRING SONG—*Nash*
SPRING SONG—*Patten*
SPRING STRAINS—*Williams, William Carlos*
SPRING THUNDER—*Van Doren*
SPRINGTIME CROSSTOWN EPISODE IN FOUR-TIME—*White*
SPRUCH—*Eichendorff*
SPRUCH—*Fontane*
SPRÜCHE DES KONFUZIUS—*Schiller*
THE SQUILILILIGEE—*Cullen, Countee*
THE SQUIRREL—*Buxton*
THE SQUIRREL—*Nash*
DIE STADT—*Storm*
STAFFORD IS NOW FIVE YEARS OLD—*Sobiloff*
THE STAGE ALL BLOOD—*MacLeish*
THE STAGE IS UNLIT—*Williams, Hugo*
STAGES ON A JOURNEY—*Wright, James*
LA STAGGIONACCIA—*Belli*
STAIRS—*Herford*

STALAG LUFT—*Jarrell*
STALIN—*Lowell, Robert*
STAMMATTINA—*Filippo*
STANCES—*Moréas*
STANCES—*Régnier*
STANCES À LA MARQUISE—*Corneille*
STANCES DE POLYEUCTE—*Corneille*
STAND TALL—*Marshall, Helen Lowrie*
STAND-TO—*Day Lewis*
STANDING IN MY LIGHT—*Marcus*
STANLEY MEETS MUTESA—*Rubadiri*
STANZAS—*Brontë, Charlotte*
STANZAS—*Keats*
STANZAS, APRIL 1, 1814—*Shelley*
STANZAS FOR MUSIC—*Byron*
STANZAS WRITTEN IN DEJECTION NEAR NAPLES—*Shelley*
STANZAS WRITTEN ON THE ROAD BETWEEN FLORENCE AND PISA—*Byron*
STAR—*Derwood*
STAR—*Taylor, Ann and Jane*
STAR-GAZING—*Ptolemaios the Astronomer*
THE STAR IN THE HILLS—*Stafford*
STAR LIGHT—*Children's Verses and Nursery Rhymes*
THE STAR OF CASTLE ROCK—*Marshall, Helen Lowrie*
THE STAR-SPANGLED BANNER—*Key*
THE STAR-SPLITTER—*Frost, Robert*
STARLIGHT LIKE INTUITION PIERCED THE TWELVE—*Schwartz*
THE STARLIGHT NIGHT—*Hopkins*
THE STARRY NIGHT—*Sexton*
THE STARS—*Anonymous–American Indian languages–Algonquin*
THE STARS—*Teasdale*
THE STARS—*Young, Andrew*
THE STATE OF THE NATION—*Patchen*
A STATEMENT ON CONSERVATION—*Giovanni*
STATE'S ATTORNEY FALLAS—*Masters, Edgar Lee*
THE STATION—*Merwin*
STATION LOVE—*Marshall, Helen Lowrie*
STATTE ATTIENTO—*Filippo*
STATUE AND BIRDS—*Bogan*
STATUE D'HOMME D'ÉTAT—*Coppée*
THE STATUE OF ST. FRANCIS—*Ferlinghetti*
THE STATUES—*Raine*
THE STATUES—*Yeats*
THE STATUES IN PUBLIC GARDENS—*Nemerov*
STATUS SYMBOL—*Evans, Mari*

STATUTE—*Miles*
STEADFASTNESS—*Wyatt, Sir Thomas*
STEADY STATE—*Gold*
STEAM SHOVEL—*Malam*
DER STEINOCHS—*Morgenstern*
STELLA—*Ungaretti*
STELLA'S BIRTHDAY—*Swift*
STEPHANOS—*Meleager*
STEPMOTHER COUNTRY BLUES—*Fox, Charles*
STEPPING WESTWARD—*Wordsworth*
STEREO ABSTRACT—*Hodges*
STÉRÉOSCOPE—*Geraldy*
STEVEDORE—*Collins, Leslie M.*
STILL, A RED HOT AXE—*Fabio, Sarah Webster*
STILL, CITIZEN SPARROW—*Wilbur*
STILL HERE—*Hughes, Langston*
STILL LIFE—*Garlick*
STILL LIFE—*Hughes, Ted*
STILL LIFE—*Marshall, Lenore G.*
DER STILLE FREIER—*Eichendorff*
DER STILLE GRUND—*Eichendorff*
STILLER BESUCH—*Kästner*
THE STILLY NIGHT: A SOPORIFIC REFLECTION—*Nash*
EINE STIMME—*Tieck*
STIMMEN—*Celan*
A STIMULANT FOR AN OLD BEAST—*Berryman*
STINGS—*Plath*
STINK—*McGough*
STJÄRNORNA KVITTAR DET LIKA—*Ferlin*
STOCKHOLM—*Bergman, Bo*
STOCKHOLM—*Hedberg*
STOCKHOLM, MAY—*Lester*
STOCKING FAIRY—*Welles*
THE STOLEN CHILD—*Yeats*
STOLEN EXPRESSIONS—*Clay*
STONE—*Simic*
STONE FISH LAKE—*Whan Chei*
THE STONE GENTLEMEN—*Reeves*
STONE GULLETS—*Swenson*
THE STONES—*Norris*
THE STONES—*Plath*
THE STONES—*Walters*
THE STONES REMEMBER—*Griffiths*
STONY RIVER—*Robson, Ernest M.*
STOOD UP—*Arnez*
STOOP IN ROUP—*Fry*
STOP DEAD—*Plath*
STOP LIGHT IN HARLEM—*Emanuel*
STOPPIA—*Pascoli*
STOPPING BY WOODS ON A SNOWY EVENING—*Frost, Robert*
THE STORE OF MINIKIN AND MANIKIN—*Children's Verses and Nursery Rhymes*
STORIA SACRA—*Capurro*
STORK IN JEREZ—*Lee, Laurie*
STORM—*Anonymous–English–Old English*

STORM—*McGough*
STORM—*MacPherson*
STORM CONE—*Kipling*
STORM FEAR—*Frost, Robert*
STORM WINDOWS—*Nemerov*
STORMS BEGIN FAR BACK—
  Sandburg
STÖRRE OCH MINDRE—*Ferlin*
STORY—*Parker*
THE STORY OF EMMA SLIDE—
  Fraser, Kathleen
THE STORY OF OSSIAN—*Masefield*
THE STORY-TELLER— *Van Doren*
STOSSSEUFZER EINER DAME IN
  BEWEGTER NACHT—*Tucholsky*
LA STRADA FUORI PORTA—*Piccolo*
STRAIGHT TALK— *Giovanni*
STRAIGHT TO HELL—*Gaver*
STRANDED—*Brown, Otis*
A STRANGE BLACK WOMAN SPEAKS
  OF CHEYNEY—*Jeffers, Lance*
THE STRANGE CASE OF MR.
  DONNYBROOK'S BOREDOM—
  Nash
THE STRANGE CASE OF MR.
  ORMANTUDE'S BRIDE—*Nash*
THE STRANGE CASE OF MRS.
  MOODUS'S SECOND HONEYMOON
  —*Nash*
THE STRANGE CASE OF THE
  CAUTIOUS MOTORIST—*Nash*
THE STRANGE CASE OF THE
  ENTOMOLOGIST'S HEART—*Nash*
THE STRANGE CASE OF THE
  IRKSOME PRUDE—*Nash*
STRANGE MEETING—*Owen,
  Wilfred*
STRANGE NEW COTTAGE IN
  BERKELEY—*Ginsberg*
STRANGE TREE—*Roberts*
THE STRANGER—*Garrigue*
THE STRANGER—*Kipling*
THE STRANGER—*McGough*
THE STRANGER—*Rich*
STRANGER THAN THE WORST—
  Deutsch
STRASSBURGER HANDSCHRIFT—
  Anonymous–German
THE STRAWBERRY PLANT—*Silkin*
THE STRAY DOG—*Justice*
THE STRAYING STUDENT—*Clarke*
STREAMS—*Auden*
STREET DEMONSTRATION—
  Walker
STREET GANG— *Webster, H.*
STREET SCENE—*Marriott*
STREET SONG—*Sitwell, Edith*
STREETS—*Verlaine*
THE STREETS OF LAREDO—
  *Anonymous–English—
  Modern English*
STRIDEN—*Ullman*
STRING QUARTET—*Meredith,
  George*
THE STROKE—*Smith, Stevie*
STRONGHOLD—*Redgrove*

THE STRUCTURE OF RIME—
  Duncan
LA STRUCTURE PHONÉTIQUE DE LA
  LANGUE TCHEQUE—*Novak*
STRUWWELPETER—*Hoffmann*
STUDENT, DO THE SIMPLE
  PURIFICATION—*Bly*
STUDENTENLIED—*Günther*
STUDY GUIDE FOR THE ODYSSEY—
  Bell
STUMPFOOT ON 42ND STREET—
  Simpson
EIN STÜNDLEIN WOHL VOR TAG—
  Mörike
THE STUNT FLYER—*Updike*
STYX—*Darr*
SUB LUNA—*Karlfeldt*
A SUBALTERN'S LOVE SONG—
  Betjeman
SUBJECT, OBJECT, SENTENCE—
  Spender
THE SUBWAY—*Tate, Allen*
SUCCESS COMES TO COW CREEK—
  Tate, James
SUCH A PARCEL OF ROGUES IN A
  NATION—*Burns*
SUDDEN LIGHT—*Rossetti, Dante
  Gabriel*
SUEÑO—*Garcia Lorca*
SUEÑO CON CLAUSTROS DE
  MARMOL—*Martí*
SUEÑO DESPIERTO—*Martí*
SUEÑO GRANDE—*Mistral*
SUEÑOS Y VOLANTINES—*Diego,
  José de*
SUFI SONG—*Bly*
SUGAR DADDY— *Williams, Hugo*
SUGAR PLUM TREE—*Field,
  Eugene*
SUGARPLUM DANCE—*Nash*
EL SUICIDA—*Murciano*
SUICIDE NOTE FROM A
  COCKROACH IN A LOW INCOME
  HOUSING PROJECT—*Pietri*
SUICIDE'S NOTE—*Hughes,
  Langston*
SUICIDE'S STONE—*Jeffers,
  Robinson*
SUICIDIO—*Bevilacqua*
LA SUIVANTE D'EMMA—
  Sainte-Beuve
SUM—*Glaze*
A SUM OF DESTRUCTIONS— *Weiss*
SUMA DE LA PERFECCIÓN—*Juan
  de la Cruz*
SUMMARY—*Sanchez*
SUMMER—*Sitwell, Osbert*
SUMMER—*Tate, Allen*
SUMMER— *Young, David*
SUMMER AND WINTER—*Shelley*
THE SUMMER BELVEDERE—
  Williams, Tennessee
A SUMMER COMMENTARY—
  Winters
SUMMER DAWN—*Morris, William*
SUMMER-DAY SONG—*Conkling*
SUMMER EVENING—*Clare*

SUMMER HOLIDAY—*Jeffers,
  Robinson*
THE SUMMER HOUSE—*Justice*
SUMMER IMAGES—*Clare*
SUMMER LIGHTNING—*Clarke*
SUMMER: MILK MAID—*Lee, Laurie*
A SUMMER NIGHT—*Arnold*
SUMMER, 1975—*Lester*
SUMMER NOON: 1941— *Winters*
SUMMER RAIN—*Coatsworth*
SUMMER REMEMBERED—*Gardner*
SUMMER STORM—*Simpson*
SUMMER SUN—*Stevenson*
SUMMER, THE HAY FEVER IN THE
  AIR—*Sherwin*
SUMMER: WEST SIDE—*Updike*
SUMMER WISH—*Bogan*
SUMMER WORDS OF A SISTUH
  ADDICT—*Sanchez*
SUMMERTIME AND THE LIVING—
  Hayden
SUMMERTIME T. V.—*Sanchez*
THE SUMMING-UP—*Kunitz*
SUMMONED BY BELLS—*Betjeman*
SUMMONS—*Francis*
SUN—*Dickey, James*
SUN AND FUN, SONG OF A
  NIGHT-CLUB PROPRIETRESS—
  Betjeman
SUN AND MOON—*MacPherson*
THE SUN CAME—*Knight,
  Etheridge*
SUN HOUSE—*Lee, Don L.*
SUNBATHING ON A ROOFTOP IN
  BERKELEY—*Kumin*
SUNCHANT—*Morrow*
SUNDAY, APRIL 8—*Patchen*
SUNDAY EVENING—*Abse*
SUNDAY EVENING AT GWEN'S—
  Sanchez
SUNDAY IN IRELAND—*Betjeman*
SUNDAY MORNING—*Ciardi*
SUNDAY MORNING IN THE NORTH
  —*Raper*
THE SUNDAYS OF SATIN-LEGS
  SMITH—*Brooks, Gwendolyn*
SUNDIAL—*Clark, Gillian*
THE SUNDIAL—*Hollander*
SUNDOWN—*Adams*
THE SUNFLOWER—*Blake*
THE SUNFLOWER SUTRA—
  Ginsberg
SUNLIGHT—*Gunn*
THE SUNNE RISING—*Donne*
SUNNY PRESTATYN—*Larkin*
THE SUN'S TRAVELS—*Stevenson*
SUNSET AND AFTER—*Ciardi*
SUNSET FROM A PRISON CAMP—
  Casson
SUNSET ON THE BEARCAMP—
  Whittier
THE SUNSET YEARS OF SAMUEL SHY
  —*Nash*
THE SUNSHADE—*Hardy*
SUNSHINE—*Clark, China*
SUNSTROKE—*Hughes, Ted*

SUNT LACRIMAE RERUM—*Blackmur*

SUNT LEONES—*Smith, Stevie*

SUPER THOUGHT—*Hodges*

SUPERIORIM TO FATE—*Dickinson, Emily*

A SUPERMARKET IN CALIFORNIA—*Ginsberg*

A SUPERSCRIPTION—*Rossetti, Dante Gabriel*

SUPPLICATION—*Wyatt, Sir Thomas*

SUPPLY AND DEMAND—*Brecht*

EL SUR DEL OCEANO—*Neruda*

SUR LA MORT DE MARIE—*Ronsard*

SUR LA ROUTE DE SAN ROMANO—*Breton, André*

SUR LA TRISTESSE DE CE TEMPS—*Deschamps*

SUR LE MORT DE SA DAME—*Charles d'Orleans*

SUR LE PONT-NEUF—*Klingsor*

SUR UNE MORTE—*Musset*

SUR UNE RIDE DU SOLEIL—*Tzara*

SURFACES—*Scott, F. R.*

THE SURGEON AT TWO A. M.—*Plath*

SURGERY OF A BURN—*Lowbury*

THE SURLY ONE—*Roethke*

SURPRISE—*Parker*

SURPRISE ATTACK—*Sward*

SURPRISED BY JOY—*Wordsworth*

SURVEY OF LITERATURE—*Ransom, John Crowe*

SURVEY OF THE WHOLE—*Swenson*

SURVIEW—*Hardy*

SURVIVAL LESSON—*Marvin X*

SURVIVING—*Kavanagh*

THE SURVIVOR—*Graves*

SURVIVORS—*Greenwald*

SURVIVORS—*Sassoon*

SUSPENSION—*Francis*

SUSQUEHANNA—*Anderson, Lee*

SUSTO EN EL COMEDOR—*Garcia Lorca*

SUY TIO GOR TAU—*Su Shih*

SUZY GREW A MOUSTACHE—*Lee, Dennis*

SVAD'BA—*Pasternak*

SVAD'BE—*Popa*

'O SVENIMENTO—*Russo*

SVIDANIE—*Pasternak*

SVITE YASNY—*Shevchenko*

SWAN—*Anonymous–English– Old English*

THE SWAN—*Nash*

THE SWAN—*Rodgers*

THE SWAN—*Roethke*

SWANEE—*Soupault*

SWEDENBORG'S SKULL—*Watkins*

SWEENEY AMONG THE NIGHTINGALES—*Eliot, Thomas Stearns*

SWEEPING WENDY: A STUDY IN FUGUE—*Sandburg*

SWEET, IF YOU LIKE AND LOVE ME STILL—*Davison, Frances*

A SWEET LULLABY—*Breton, Nicholas*

SWEET WAR MAN—*Dehn*

SWEET WAS THE SONG—*Landor*

SWEET WILLIAM'S GHOST—*Anonymous–English– Modern English*

SWEETHEARTS IN A MULBERRY TREE—*Knight, Etheridge*

THE SWIFT—*Nabokov*

THE SWIFT—*Schwartz*

SWIFT'S EPITAPH—*Yeats*

THE SWIMMERS—*Tate, Allen*

THE SWING—*Souster*

THE SWING—*Stevenson*

A SWING SONG—*Allingham*

A SWING SONG—*Milne*

A SWORD IN A CLOUD OF LIGHT—*Rexroth*

THE SWORD IN THE STONE—*Picard*

SYANG JYAN HWAN—*Li Yu*

THE SYCOPHANTIC FOX AND THE GULLIBLE RAVEN—*Carryl, Guy Wetmore*

SYIN JYA NYANG—*Wang Jyan*

LES SYLPHIDES—*MacNeice*

A SYLPH'S SONG—*Sitwell, Edith*

SYLVIE AND BRUNO—*Carroll*

SYMPATHETIC PORTRAIT OF A CHILD—*Williams, William Carlos*

SYMPHONIE DE PRINTEMPS—*Cadou*

SYMPHONIE DE SEPTEMBRE—*Milosz*

SYMPHONY OF BEAUTY—*Marshall, Helen Lowrie*

SYNCOPATING RHYTHM—*Hodges*

THE SYNTAX OF SEASONS—*Reid*

SYSTEM—*Stevenson*

SYUN YIN JE BU YU—*Jya Dau*

T C B—*Sanchez*

TABARÉ—*Zorilla de san Martin*

LA TABLE—*Desangiers*

TABLEAU—*Cullen*

THE TABLES TURNED—*Wordsworth*

TABOO TO BOOT—*Nash*

IL TACCUINO DEL VECCHIO—*Ungaretti*

TAGE MIT HÄHERN—*Eich*

TAGEBUCHBLATT '74—*Kunze*

EIN TAGEWERK—*Keller, Gottfried*

TÄGLICH ZU SINGEN—*Claudius*

DIE TAGNACHTLAMPE—*Morgenstern*

TAILS—*Jacobs*

TAKE ANYTHING—*Kaufman, Shirley*

TAKING OFF—*Anonymous–English– Modern English*

TAKING THE HANDS—*Bly*

TAL COMO ESTABAS—*Jiménez*

TAL VEZ ME LLAME JONÁS—*Camino Galicia*

UN TALE DI MACERATA—*Rodari*

THE TALE OF CUSTARD THE DRAGON—*Nash*

TALE THE HERMIT TOLD—*Reid*

TALES OF A WAYSIDE INN—*Longfellow*

TALES OF THE HALL—*Crabbe*

TALIESIN AND THE SPRING OF VISION—*Watkins*

A TALISMAN—*Hodges*

TALK—*Yevtushenko*

TALK IN THE NIGHT—*Tessimond*

A TALK WITH A WOOD—*Patten*

TALKING—*Malanga*

TALKING MYSELF TO SLEEP AT ONE MORE HILTON—*Ciardi*

TALKING TO MYSELF—*Auden*

TALKING WITH SOLDIERS—*Turner, Walter James*

TALL NETTLES—*Thomas, Edward*

TALLEY ABBEY—*Griffiths*

A TALLY—*Creeley*

TAM GLEN—*Burns*

TAM I' THE KIRK—*Jacob, Violet*

TAM O' SHANTER—*Burns*

DIE TAM-TAMS KLOPFEN NICHT MEHR—*Thomas, H. Carey*

TAMBIÉN ME AÑORAS TU?—*Tejada*

TAMBORES—*Palés Matos*

TANGO DEL VIUDO—*Neruda*

TANNEN—*Brecht*

DER TANTENMÖRDER—*Wedekind*

DER TANZ—*Morgenstern*

DER TANZ—*Schiller*

A TAPESTRY FOR BAYEUX—*Starbuck*

DIE TAPETENBLUME—*Morgenstern*

LA TAPISSERIE DE SAINTE-GENEVIÈVE—*Péguy*

TARANTELLA—*Belloc*

TARD DANS LA NUIT—*Reverdy*

TARDE—*Garcia Lorca*

LA TARDE RESPONDIA—*Ridruejo*

TARFSIDE—*Hillary*

TARTARY—*De la Mare*

THE TASK—*Cowper*

TATTERED DREAMS—*Goldstein*

TATTERED SERENADE—*Sitwell, Edith*

TATTERSKAN—*Snoilsky*

TAUBEN—*Eich*

DER TAUCHER—*Schiller*

DER TAUGENICHTS—*Keller, Gottfried*

TAUROMANCY AT MEMPHIS—*Diogenes Laertius*

TAVISTOCK SQUARE—*Williams, Hugo*

TE CARESSO I GENUCI—*Marin*

TE PIASEVA, MARIA—*Marin*

TE SOUVIENS-TU MON LOU—*Apollinaire*

TE VOILA—*Carco*

TEACHER—*Jong*
TEACHER—*Walker*
TEACHERS—*Merwin*
THE TEARDROP MILLIONAIRE—
  Rosenfeld
TEARSPLOTCHES FOR MY
  CHILDREN—*Jeffers, Lance*
TECHE VODA—*Shevchenko*
TECHNOLOGIES—*Starbuck*
TEDDY BEAR—*Milne*
A TEEN-AGER ASKS WHY—
  Goldstein
THE TEETH-MOTHER NAKED AT
  LAST—*Bly*
TEILS-TEILS—*Benn*
DIE TEILUNG DER ERDE—*Schiller*
TEINTURERIE—*Obaldia*
TELÉGRAFO—*Nobre*
TELEGRAM FROM PARANOIA—
  Tullos
TELEMACHOS REMEMBERS—*Muir*
TELEPHONE BOOTH NUMBER 23—
  Pietri
TELEPHONE BOOTH NUMBER 102—
  Pietri
TELEPHONE BOOTH NUMBER 190—
  Pietri
TELEPHONE BOOTH NUMBER 535—
  Pietri
TELEPHONE BOOTH NUMBER 580—
  Pietri
TELEPHONE BOOTH NUMBER 722—
  Pietri
TELEPHONE BOOTH NUMBER 801—
  Pietri
TELEPHONE BOOTH NUMBER 905½
  —*Pietri*
THE TELEPHONE NUMBER—
  Scannell
TELEPHONE POLES—*Updike*
THE TELEPHONISTS—*Patten*
TELEVISION POEM—*Sanchez*
TELL ME BROTHER—*Last Poets*
TELL ME, IF YOU KNOW—*Walters*
TELL ME, TELL ME—*Moore,
  Marianne*
TELLING THE BEES—*Whittier*
TEMA CON VARIACIONES—*Salinas,
  Pedro*
THE TEMPEST—*Shakespeare*
TEMPLE—*Lester*
TEMPLE—*Posner*
ER TEMPO BBONO—*Belli*
LE TEMPS DÉTRUIT—*Tzara*
LE TEMPS DU MARTYRE—*Diop*
LE TEMPS PERDU—*Prévert*
TEMPTATION—*Ciardi*
THE TEMPTATIONS OF SAINT
  ANTHONY—*McGinley*
TEN CON TEN—*Palés Matos*
10:15 AM—APRIL 27, 1969 POEM—
  Sanchez
TENANTS HARBOR—*Booth*
TENBY—*Garlick*
TENCENTS WORTH OF BALONEY—
  Hinton
TENEBRAE—*Clarke*

TENEIS QUE OÍRME—*Neruda*
TENNIS—*Avison*
TENT—*Williams, Oscar*
THE TENT, THE SONG, THE SIGN,
  THE ELEMENT—*O'Gorman*
TENTACLES, LEAVES—*Lifshin*
TENTATIVE DESCRIPTION OF A
  DINNER TO PROMOTE THE
  IMPEACHMENT OF PRESIDENT
  EISENHOWER—*Ferlinghetti*
TENUOUS AND PRECARIOUS—
  Smith, Stevie
TENZO—*Raimbaut de Vaqueiras*
DIE TEPPICHWEBER VON
  KUJAN-BULAK EHREN LENIN—
  Brecht
TERCERA FÁBULA—*Hierro*
TERMINAL DAYS AT BEVERLY
  FARMS—*Lowell, Robert*
TERMINUS—*Emerson*
THE TERMITE—*Nash*
TERRE D'ALERTE—*Prefontaine*
THE TERRIBLE PEOPLE—*Nash*
TERROR—*Warren*
THE TERROR OF DEATH—*Keats*
TERZINEN—*Hofmannsthal*
TESS'S LAMENT—*Hardy*
TESTAMENT—*Arras-Caeta*
TESTAMENT—*Jong*
LE TESTAMENT—*Villon*
THE TESTAMENT OF CRESSEID—
  Henryson
TESTAMENTO—*Andrade, Mario
  de*
TESTAMENTO—*Nicolardi*
TESTAMENTO DE OTOÑO—*Neruda*
TESTAMENTS—*Mailer*
TETÉLESTAI—*Aiken*
THAMÁR Y AMNÓN—*Garcia Lorca*
THANATOPSIS—*Bryant, William
  Cullen*
THANK YOU—*Marshall, Helen
  Lowrie*
THANK YOU, FOG—*Auden*
THANKSGIVING—*Cummings*
THANKSGIVING DAY—*Child*
THANKSGIVING DAY—*Marshall,
  Helen Lowrie*
THANKSGIVING FOR A HABITAT—
  Auden
THANKSGIVING 1963—*Booth*
THAT CLEAR FIRST MORNING—
  Booth
THAT DAY—*Giovanni*
THAT DYING—*Reid*
THAT I AM YOURS—*Stephany*
THAT IT THAT THING LIGHT—
  Sward
THAT NATURE IS A HERACLITEAN
  FIRE AND OF THE COMFORT OF
  THE RESURRECTION—*Hopkins*
THAT REMINDS ME—*Nash*
THAT SUMMER'S END—*Bishop,
  John Peale*
THAT THE NIGHT COME—*Yeats*
THAT THE PEAR DELIGHTS ME NOW
  —*Hoffman*

THAT WE HEAD TOWARDS—
  Stephany
THAT WEATHER—*Stafford*
THAT WHICH CROSSES: NINE OF
  CUPS—*Piercy*
THAT WOMEN ARE BUT MEN'S
  SHADOWS—*Jonson*
THAT'S HOW IT SHOULD BE—
  Brecht
THEIR BEAUTY HAS MORE MEANING
  —*Jeffers, Robinson*
THEIR FATHERS—*Giovanni*
THEME BROWN GIRL—
  Hill-Abu-Isak
A THEME FOR VARIOUS MURDERS—
  Patten
THEME SONG—*Spencer*
THEME WITH VARIATIONS—*Agee*
THEN—*Rukeyser*
THEN CAME ATOM'S ANSWER—
  Cullen
THEN, I REMEMBERED—*Bahati*
THEOLOGY—*Hughes, Ted*
A THEORY OF MEASURE—
  Hollander
THEORY OF POETRY—*MacLeish*
A THEORY OF WAVES—*Hollander*
THERE ARE BLK PURITANS—
  Sanchez
THERE ARE POETS—*Jimason*
THERE GOES THE ROOF—*Hannan*
THERE IS—*Simpson*
THERE IS NO SKY—*Barker,
  George*
THERE IS ONLY ONE OF
  EVERYTHING—*Atwood*
THERE WAS A LITTLE BOY—*Lewis,
  Richard*
THERE WAS A LITTLE MAN—
  *Children's Verses and
  Nursery Rhymes*
THERE WAS A SAVIOUR—*Thomas,
  Dylan*
THERE WAS A TIME—*Thomas,
  Edward*
THERE WILL BE NO REVOLUTION—
  Anderson, Doug
THERE'S WISDOM IN WOMEN—
  Brooke
THESE DAYS—*Braun*
THESE DAYS—*Troupe*
THESE TREES STAND—*Snodgrass*
THESEUS AND ARIADNE—*Graves*
THERE ARE HOSTILE NATIONS—
  Atwood
THEY BOTH LOVE ME—*Sobiloff*
THEY COME NO MORE, THOSE
  WORDS, THOSE FINCHES—
  MacLeish
THEY DRAG ME RAW—*Harnett*
THEY EAT OUT—*Atwood*
THEY FEED THEY LION—*Levine*
THEY HAD NO POETS—*Kendrick*
THEY JUST GIVE THE PRIZE FOR
  YOUR DOOR!—*Johnston, Ellen
  Turlington*
THEY PART—*Parker*

THEY SAY—*Murphy*
THEY WORRY ABOUT ME—
Johnston, Ellen Turlington
THE THIEF—*Graves*
THE THIEF—*Kunitz*
THE THIN AIR—*Prothro*
THE THIN EDGE—*Parker*
THE THING THAT EATS THE HEART
—*Kunitz*
THE THINGS—*Aiken*
THINGS DIE OUT—*Enslin*
THINGS IN COMMON—*Swenson*
THINGS WE DID THAT MEANT
SOMETHING—*Stafford*
THINKING OF THE AUTUMN FIELDS
—*Bly*
THIRD LETTER ON GEORGES—
Olson
THE THIRD WORLD BOND—*Lee,
Don L.*
THIRST, AND A DOG RUNNING—
Abbe
THIRTY-FIRST LIGHT POEM—*Mac
Low*
31st OF JANUARY, 1974—*Tullos*
33 1/3—*Darr*
THIS AMBER SUNSTREAM—*Van
Doren*
THIS BAPTISM OF FIRE—*Randall*
THIS COLD UNIVERSE—*Dickinson,
Patric*
THIS ENGLISHWOMAN—*Smith,
Stevie*
THIS HEART THAT FLUTTERS—
Joyce
THIS HOLY MONTH—*Graves*
THIS IS A BLACK ROOM—*Beasley*
THIS IS AN AFRICAN WORM—
Danner
THIS IS BEGINNING—*Stephany*
THIS IS JUST TO SAY—*Williams,
William Carlos*
THIS IS THE MANEATER'S SKULL—
Hughes, Ted
THIS IS THE ROAD—*Marshall,
Helen Lowrie*
THIS IS YOUR ELEGY—*Reeves*
THIS LIME-TREE BOWER MY PRISON
—*Coleridge, Samuel Taylor*
THIS LITTLE LIGHT OF MINE—*Kali*
THIS LONELY LIGHT—*Chapin*
THIS MORNING—*Rukeyser*
THIS NIGHT ONLY—*Rexroth*
THIS OUR ONLY EARTH—*Rukeyser*
THIS POEM GETS LOCKED UP—
Rasul
THIS SIDE OF TRUTH—*Thomas,
Dylan*
THIS SOLITUDE OF CATARACTS—
Stevens, Wallace
THIS SONG IS TO YOUR DEATH—
Stevens, Wendy
THIS STREET NEVER SLEEPS—
Sandburg
THIS TWENTIETH-CENTURY MIND—
Marshall, Lenore G.

THE THISTLE AS A SPIDER'S WEB—
MacDiarmid
THISTLES—*Hughes, Ted*
THOMAS JEFFERSON—*Benét,
Stephen Vincent*
THOMAS RYMER—
*Anonymous–English–
Modern English*
THOSE DANCING DAYS ARE GONE
—*Yeats*
THOSE TIMES—*Sexton*
THOSE WHO CAME SHORT—*Graves*
THOSE WINTER SUNDAYS—*Hayden*
THOU SHALT NOT KILL—*Rexroth*
THOUGH I AM FALSE—*Marshall,
Lenore G.*
A THOUGHT—*Gregor*
A THOUGHT—*Stevenson*
A THOUGHT ABOUT SHEIK
BEDREDDIN—*Ciardi*
THE THOUGHT-FOX—*Hughes, Ted*
A THOUGHT FROM PROPERTIUS—
Yeats
THOUGHT OF A BRITON ON THE
SUBJUGATION OF SWITZERLAND
—*Wordsworth*
THOUGHTS ABOUT THE PERSON
FROM PORLOCK—*Smith, Stevie*
THOUGHTS DURING AN AIR RAID—
Spender
THOUGHTS OF A YOUNG GIRL—
Ashbery
THOUGHTS ON LOOKING INTO A
THICKET—*Ciardi*
THOUGHTS ON UNPACKING—
Gunn
THOUGHTS THOUGHT AFTER A
BRIDGE PARTY—*Nash*
THOUGHTS THOUGHT WHILE
WAITING FOR A
PRONOUNCEMENT—*Nash*
THOUGHTS TO A CONCERTO OF
TELEMANN—*Ferlinghetti*
THRÄNEN IN GROSSER
HUNGERSNOT—*Gryphius*
THREE BILLS—*Jarrell*
THE THREE BUSHES—*Yeats*
THREE DAYS TO SEE—*Keller,
Helen*
THREE DEADLY SINS—*Reaney*
THREE DREAMS ON A WARM
SABBATH—*Starbuck*
THE THREE-FACED—*Graves*
THE THREE FOXES—*Milne*
THREE KINDS OF PLEASURES—*Bly*
THE THREE KINGS—*Longfellow*
THREE LITTLE KITTENS—*Follen*
THREE MEMORIAL SONNETS FOR
TWO YOUNG SEAMEN—*Barker,
George*
THE THREE MISS COLTRUMS—
Sitwell, Osbert
THREE NIGHTS OF MOURNING:
JOHN F. KENNEDY—
Mountzoures
THREE OLD LADIES AND THREE
SPRING BULBS—*Francis*

THREE PHASES OF AFRICA—*Parkes*
THREE POEMS FROM A TEXT—
Blackmur
THREE PRESIDENTS—*Bly*
THE THREE RAVENS—
*Anonymous–English–
Modern English*
THREE STAGES—*Miles*
THREE THINGS—*Yeats*
THREE VIEWS OF A MOTHER—
Ciardi
THRENODY—*Emerson*
THRENODY—*Farrar*
THRENOS—*Blackmur*
THRONREDE DES JUNGEN KAISERS
—*Anonymous–Asian
languages*
THROUGH NIGHTMARE—*Graves*
THROUGH THE LOOKING GLASS—
Carroll
THROUGH THE TALL GRASS IN
YOUR HEAD—*Patten*
THROWING A TREE—*Hardy*
A THRUSH IN THE MOONLIGHT—
Bynner
THUMBS RULE—*Fry*
TIBBIE DUNBAR—*Burns*
TIBERIUS ON CAPRI—*Warren*
TIBULLI LIBER—*Sulpicia*
THE TICKLE RHYME—*Serraillier*
TIERRA AMARGA—*Arana*
TIERRA NATIVE—*Cernuda*
LA TIERRA Y EL SUEÑO—*Ribera
Chevremont*
THE TIGER—*Blake*
THE TIGER—*Clark, John W.*
TIGERS KNOW FROM BIRTH—
Wilkinson
TILL EN KONSTNÄR—*Bergman,
Bo*
TILL EN LITEN KVINNA—*Nerman*
TILL THE SUN GOES DOWN—
Marvin X
TILLY—*Joyce*
TIMBERLAND STILLNESS—
Marshall, Helen Lowrie
TIME—*Conkling*
TIME—*Graves*
TIME—*Merrill*
TIME—*Stryk*
TIME AND MOTION STUDY—
Mitchell, Adrian
TIME AND SPIRIT—*Adams*
TIME AND THE GARDEN—*Winters*
TIME FOR A QUICK ONE—*Scannell*
TIME FOR SALE—*Lowbury*
TIME IN THE ROCK—*Aiken*
TIME IS THE GIFT—*Emanuel*
THE TIME OF ROSES—*Hood*
TIME PASSING, BELOVED—*Davie*
TIME, REAL AND IMAGINARY—
Coleridge, Samuel Taylor
TIME TO GO OUT—*Lally*
TIME TO RISE—*Stevenson*
TIME WAS—*Wain*
THE TIMELESS NIGHTINGALE—
Heath-Stubbs

TIME'S FOOL—*Updike*
TIMING—*Mailer*
TIMING HER—*Hardy*
TIMON THE MISANTHROPE—
    Kallimachos
TIMOTHY WINTERS—*Causley*
TINTERN ABBEY—*Wordsworth*
TIO RÄTTFÄRDIGA—*Ferlin*
TIP-TOE—*Keats*
TIRED TIM—*De la Mare*
TITHONIUS—*Tennyson*
TITLES—*Sward*
TITUS AND BERENICE—
    Heath-Stubbs
TO___—*Poe*
TO___—*Shelley*
TO A BROTHER IN THE MYSTERY,
    CIRCA 1290—*Davie*
TO A CANDLE—*De la Mare*
TO A CERTAIN CIVILIAN—
    Whitman
TO A CHAMELEON—*Moore,
    Marianne*
TO A CHILD DANCING IN THE
    WIND—*Yeats*
TO A CHILD OF QUALITY—*Prior*
TO A CHILD WITH EYES—*Van
    Doren*
TO A CONSCRIPT OF 1940—*Read,
    Herbert*
TO A FOIL'D EUROPEAN
    REVOLUTIONAIRE—*Whitman*
TO A FRIEND WHOSE WORK HAS
    COME TO NOTHING—*Yeats*
TO A GIRAFFE—*Moore, Marianne*
TO A HAGGIS—*Burns*
TO A HOUSE BEING BUILT—
    Marshall, Lenore G.
TO A JEALOUS CAT—*Sanchez*
TO A LADY—*Dunbar, William*
TO A LADY, ASKING HOW LONG HE
    WOULD LOVE HER—*Etherege*
TO A LADY IN A LETTER—
    Rochester, Earl of
TO A LADY THAT DESIRED I WOULD
    LOVE HER—*Carew*
TO A LITTLE GIRL, ONE YEAR OLD,
    IN RUINED FORTRESS—*Warren*
TO A LOCOMOTIVE IN WINTER—
    Whitman
TO A LOUSE, ON SEEING ONE ON A
    LADY'S BONNET AT CHURCH—
    Burns
TO A MILITARY RIFLE 1942—
    Winters
TO A MOUSE, ON TURNING HER UP
    IN HER NEST—*Burns*
TO A NIGERIAN STUDENT OF
    METALLURGY—*Danner*
TO A ROSE—*Bodenheim*
TO A SKYLARK—*Shelley*
TO A SKYLARK—*Wordsworth*
TO A SNAIL—*Moore, Marianne*
TO A SNOWFLAKE—*Thompson,
    Francis*
TO A STEAM ROLLER—*Moore,
    Marianne*

TO A VERY OLD WOMAN—*Layton*
TO A VIRGIN—*Eckels*
TO A WATERFOWL—*Bryant,
    William Cullen*
TO ALL BROTHERS—*Sanchez*
TO ALL OBJECTIVISTS—*Scott,
    Winfield Townley*
TO ALL SISTERS—*Sanchez*
TO ALTHEA FROM PRISON—
    Lovelace, Richard
TO AN ARTIST TO TAKE HEART—
    Bogan
TO AN ATHLETE DYING YOUNG—
    Housman
TO AN EXPATRIATE FRIEND—
    Morris, Mervyn
TO AN OLD LADY—*Empson*
TO AN OLD PHILOSOPHER IN ROME
    —*Stevens, Wallace*
TO AN UNDECLARED LOVER—
    Evans, Liz
TO AN UNKNOWN IN A
    RESTAURANT—*Dudek*
TO AN USHERETTE—*Updike*
TO ANITA—*Sanchez*
TO ANN SCOTT-MONCRIEFF—*Muir*
TO ANY NEGRO YOUTH—*Murphy*
TO ANY READER—*Stevenson*
TO APOLLO—*Herrick*
TO AUNT GERTRUDE, WHOM I
    NEVER MET—*Polak*
TO BE—*Richards, I. A.*
TO BE OF USE—*Piercy*
TO BLK/ RECORD/ BUYERS—
    Sanchez
TO BROOKLYN BRIDGE—*Crane,
    Hart*
TO CELIA—*Jonson*
TO CELIA—*Sedley*
TO CERTAIN CRITICS—*Cullen*
TO CERTAIN ENGLISH POETS—
    Davie
TO CHRIST—*Donne*
TO CHRIST OUR LORD—*Kinnell*
TO CHUCK—*Sanchez*
TO CLIO, MUSE OF HISTORY—
    Nemerov
TO CREATE THE POEM—*Gregor*
TO DAFFODILS—*Herrick*
TO DAISIES, NOT TO SHUT SO SOON
    —*Herrick*
TO DAPHNE AND VIRGINIA—
    Williams, William Carlos
TO DELIA—*Daniel, Samuel*
TO DIANEME—*Herrick*
TO DINAH WASHINGTON—*Knight,
    Etheridge*
TO DIVES—*Belloc*
TO DON AT SALAAM—*Brooks,
    Gwendolyn*
TO DOROTHY—*Bell*
TO DUMB FORGETFULNESS—
    Richards, I. A.
TO E. FITZGERALD—*Tennyson*
TO E. L., ON HIS TRAVELS IN
    GREECE—*Tennyson*

TO EDMUND BLUNDEN ON HIS
    SIXTIETH BIRTHDAY—
    Heath-Stubbs
TO EGYPT—*Davis, Gloria*
TO ELECTRA—*Herrick*
TO ELIZA, DUCHESS OF DORSET—
    Bennett, Joseph
TO ELSIE—*Williams, William
    Carlos*
TO FANON—*Kgositsile*
TO FEEL WHAT WAS HAPPENING—
    Polak
TO FRANK PARKER—*Lowell,
    Robert*
TO GEORGE BARKER—*Derwood*
TO GET DRUNK YOU HAVE TO
    DRINK—*Pietri*
TO GLORIA—*Kgositsile*
TO GOD WITH LOVE—*Marshall,
    Helen Lowrie*
TO GREET A LETTER CARRIER—
    Williams, William Carlos
TO GWENDOLYN BROOKS—
    Knight, Etheridge
TO H. C., SIX YEARS OLD—
    Wordsworth
TO HARLEM: NOTE ON LANGSTON
    HUGHES—*Emanuel*
TO HELEN—*Poe*
TO HER MAJESTY—*Lahui*
TO HIS CHI MISTRESS—*Starbuck*
TO HIS CHILDREN IN DARKNESS—
    Dickey, James
TO HIS COY MISTRESS—*Marvell*
TO HIS CYNICAL MISTRESS—*Gunn*
TO HIS FRIEND MASTER R. L.—
    Barnfield
TO HIS LADY—*Surrey*
TO HIS MISTRESS—*Wycherley*
TO HIS MISTRIS GOING TO BED—
    Donne
TO HIS SCRIBE ADAM—*Chaucer*
TO HIS SON, VINCENT—*Corbet*
TO HIS WIFE—*Connor*
TO IRELAND IN THE COMING TIMES
    —*Yeats*
TO IRENE—*Marshall, Helen
    Lowrie*
TO JACKIE IN JAIL—*Tropp, Steven*
TO JAMES—*Horne*
TO JANE: THE INVITATION—
    Shelley
TO JANE: THE RECOLLECTION—
    Shelley
TO JOHN KEATS, POET AT
    SPRINGTIME—*Cullen*
TO JUAN AT THE WINTER SOLSTICE
    —*Graves*
TO JUDITH—*Ciardi*
TO KEORAPETSE KGOSITSILE—
    Brooks, Gwendolyn
TO LIVE AND DIE IN DIXIE—
    Beecher
TO LIZBIE BROWN—*Hardy*
TO LUCASTA GOING BEYOND THE
    SEAS—*Lovelace, Richard*

TO LUCASTA GOING TO THE WARS
—*Lovelace, Richard*
TO LYKAINIS: A METAPHOR—
Meleager
TO MAKE A POEM IN PRISON—
Knight, Etheridge
TO MAKE YOU THINK— *Walters*
TO MARIA MONTESSORI—
Levendosky
TO MARY—*Cowper*
TO MEADOWS—*Herrick*
TO MEET, OR OTHERWISE—*Hardy*
TO MELITE—*Rufinus Domesticus*
TO MILTON— *Wordsworth*
TO MINNIE—*Stevenson*
TO MR. CYRIACK SKINNER UPON HIS
BLINDNESS—*Milton*
TO MISTRESS ANNE—*Skelton,
John*
TO MISTRESS ISABEL PENNELL—
Skelton, John
TO MISTRESS MARGARET HUSSEY—
Skelton, John
TO MORANI/MUNGU—*Sanchez*
TO MUSIC, TO BECALM HIS FEVER—
Herrick
TO MY BROTHER (KILLED
HAUMONT WOOD, OCTOBER 1918)
—*Bogan*
TO MY DAUGHTER—*Spender*
TO MY DEAR AND LOVING
HUSBAND—*Bradstreet*
TO MY EXCELLENT LUCASIA, ON
OUR FRIENDSHIP—*Philips*
TO MY FRIEND, MR. HENRY LAWES,
ON HIS AIRS—*Milton*
TO MY FRIENDS—*Silkin*
TO MY GOD IN HIS SICKNESS—
Levine
TO MY INCONSTANT MISTRESS—
Carew
TO MY NAME-CHILD—*Stevenson*
TO MY PATRICIAN MOTHER—
Goldstein
TO MY SON AGED EIGHT—
Betjeman
TO MY WIFE—*Cunningham,
James Vincent*
TO NEWCASTLE—*Parker*
TO NIGHT—*Shelley*
TO NO ONE IN PARTICULAR—*Bell*
TO NOWHERE—*Ignatow*
TO OLIVER CROMWELL—*Milton*
TO OLIVER WENDELL HOLMES 8TH
MO. 29TH, 1892— *Whittier*
TO ONE IN PARADISE—*Poe*
TO ONE NO LONGER HERE—
Marshall, Helen Lowrie
TO OUR YOUNG BUILDERS—
Johnston, Ellen Turlington
TO P.L., 1916-1937—*Levine*
TO PENNY WHEN SHE COMES OF
READING AGE— *Weiss*
TO PING-KU, ASLEEP—*Durrell*
TO PRAISE A POET: ROBERT FROST
—*Engle*
TO PRAISE DELIGHT—*Dowling*

TO REGGIE—*Hodges*
TO ROBERT BRIDGES—*Hopkins*
TO ROSAMOND—*Chaucer*
TO SATCH—*Allen, Samuel*
TO SAVE A ROSE—*Marshall,
Helen Lowrie*
TO SCIENCE—*Poe*
TO SLEEP—*Keats*
TO SLEEP— *Wordsworth*
TO SOMATICA TO SAY NOTHING,
AND NOT NO—*Ciardi*
TO SPEAK OF WOE THAT IS IN
MARRIAGE—*Lowell, Robert*
TO SWINEHERDS—*Simmons, Judy*
TO THE BLEEDING HEARTS
ASSOCIATION OF AMERICAN
NOVELISTS—*Nemerov*
TO THE BODY—*Ginsberg*
TO THE CITY OF LONDON—
Dunbar, William
TO THE CUCKOO— *Wordsworth*
TO THE DEISTS—*Blake*
TO THE EVENING STAR— *Wright,
James*
TO THE FILM INDUSTRY IN CRISIS—
O'Hara
TO THE FRINGED GENTIAN—
Bryant, William Cullen
TO THE GHOST OF HIS LATE
HIGHNESS THE SENATOR—
Mailer
TO THE GREAT FRIENDS IN
LIFETIME—*Masefield*
TO THE HOLY SPIRIT— *Winters*
TO THE LITTLE RADIO—*Brecht*
TO THE LORD GENERAL
CROMWELL—*Milton*
TO THE MAID OF ORLEANS—
Millay
TO THE MAN-OF-WAR BIRD—
Whitman
TO THE MANNEQUINS—*Nemerov*
TO THE MEMORY OF MR. OLDHAM
—*Dryden*
TO THE MEMORY OF THE BRAVE
AMERICANS—*Freneau*
TO THE MOON—*Hardy*
TO THE MOON— *Winters*
TO THE MUSES—*Blake*
TO THE NECKAR— *Grigson*
TO THE NEGRO CHILDREN OF
MOUNT VERNON—*Emanuel*
TO THE ONE OF FICTIVE MUSIC—
Stevens, Wallace
TO THE ONION—*Jong*
TO THE PAY TOILET—*Piercy*
TO THE QUEEN OF THE BEES—
Stephens
TO THE READER—*Jong*
TO THE READER—*Cunningham,
James Vincent*
TO THE RIVER—*Poe*
TO THE ROSE UPON THE ROOD OF
TIME—*Yeats*
TO THE SNAKE—*Levertov*
TO THE STONE-CUTTERS—*Jeffers,
Robinson*

TO THE SUMMER CITY—*Freivalds*
TO THE SUN DIAL—*Adams*
TO THE SUPPOSED PATRON—*Hill*
TO THE VIRGINIAN VOYAGE—
Drayton
TO THE VIRGINS, TO MAKE MUCH
OF TIME—*Herrick*
TO THE WESTERN WORLD—
Simpson
TO THEIR EXCELLENCIES THE
LORDS JUSTICES OF IRELAND—
Swift
TO THOMAS ATKINS—*Kipling*
TO TOUSSAINT L'OUVERTURE—
Wordsworth
TO TURN FROM LOVE—*Fabio,
Sarah Webster*
TO VIOLETS—*Herrick*
TO VIRGIL—*Tennyson*
TO W. H. AUDEN ON HIS 50TH
BIRTHDAY—*Howes*
TO WALK ON HILLS—*Graves*
TO WOMEN AS FAR AS I'M
CONCERNED—*Lawrence*
TO YOU/WHO ALMOST TURNED/ME
ON—*Sanchez*
TO YOU WHO SAYS THERE IS NO
GOD—*Goldstein*
A TOAST—*Kern*
A TOAST—*MacNeice*
TOAST FUNÈBRE—*Mallarmé*
THE TOASTER—*Smith, William
Jay*
TOASTER TIME—*Merriam*
THE TOBACCONIST OF EIGHTH
STREET—*Eberhart*
A TOCCATA OF GALUPPI'S—
Browning, Robert
DER TOD UND DAS MÄDCHEN—
Claudius
TODAVÍA—*Nuñez*
TODAVÍA EN SILENCIO—*Garcia
Nieto*
TODAY I WAS HAPPY, SO I MADE
THIS POEM— *Wright, James*
TODAY IS A KILLER—*Last Poets*
TODAY IS ENOUGH—*Marshall,
Helen Lowrie*
TODAY'S THE ONLY DAY OF MY
LIFE—*Marcello*
TODESLUST—*Eichendorff*
TOGETHER AGAIN—*Eckels*
TOGETHERNESS—*Mailer*
TOI ET MOI—*Geraldy*
THE TOKEN WOMAN—*Piercy*
LA TOLETTA DE LA PADRONA—
Belli
TOM—*Brathwaite*
TOM, AND HIS PONY, JACK—*Belloc*
TOM MERRITT—*Masters, Edgar
Lee*
TOM O'BEDLAM'S SONG—
*Anonymous-English—
Modern English*
TOMB OF MARIE ANDERSON—
Clark, John W.

TOMBEAU (DE VERLAINE)—
Mallarmé
LE TOMBEAU D'EDGAR POE—
Mallarmé
LE TOMBEAU DES ROIS—*Hébert*
(TOMBSTONE)—*Masters, Edgar
Lee*
TOMBSTONES IN THE STARLIGHT—
Parker
TOMLINSON—*Kipling*
TOMMY—*Kipling*
TOMMY BIG-EYES—*Brown,
Thomas Edward*
TOMMY SMITH POEM—*Marvin X*
TOMO LASTA—*Johnson, Tom*
TOMORROW—*Hughes, Langston*
TOMORROW THE HEROES—
Spellman
TOMORROW'S ENVY OF TODAY—
Graves
TONGUE TWISTER—*Lee, Dennis*
A TONGUE'S TICKLE—*Sobiloff*
TONGUES WHIRLING—*Bly*
TONIGHT AT NOON—*Henri*
TOO BLUE—*Hughes, Langston*
THE TOO-LATE BORN—*MacLeish*
TOO MANY PEOPLE—*Eastman*
TOO SOON THE SHADOW—*Chapin*
THE TOP HAT—*Souster*
TOPOGRAPHIEN—*Heissenbüttel*
TORMENTO DO IDEAL—*Quental*
TORNERANNO LE SERE—*Gatto*
TORO EN GUADARRAMA—*Conde*
TORRE SAN LORENZO—*Kaschnitz*
TORSO—*Lagerkvist*
THE TORTOISE—*Heath-Stubbs*
LA TORTUE ET LES DEUX CANARDS
—*La Fontaine*
TOSKA PO RODINE—*Tzvetaeva*
A TOTAL REVOLUTION—*Williams,
Oscar*
DIE TOTE STADT—*George*
TOTEM—*Plath*
DER TOTENTANZ—*Goethe*
TOUCH—*Gunn*
TOUCH—*Sexton*
A TOUCH OF SNOW—*Davidson*
THE TOURIST—*Cunningham,
James Vincent*
TOURISTS—*Moss, Howard*
TOUT DIRE—*Éluard*
TOUT EST CRU—*Queneau*
TOWARD A LANGUAGE OF THE
INEFFABLE—*O'Gorman*
TOWARD HOME—*Levine*
TOWARDS EVENING AND TIRED OF
THE PLACE—*Patten*
TOWER BEYOND TRAGEDY—
Jeffers, Robinson
TOWERS OF SONG—*Cowley,
Malcolm*
THE TOWN MARSHAL—*Masters,
Edgar Lee*
TOWN OWL—*Lee, Laurie*
THE TOWN SCOLD AT THE
DUCKING POND—*Sherwin*
TOY HORSE—*Muir*

THE TOYS—*Patmore*
TRACT—*Williams, William
Carlos*
TRACTION—*Moss, Howard*
TRADE—*Francis*
TRADES—*Lowell, Amy*
TRÄDTOPPARNA—*Selander*
TRAETH LLANSTEFFAN—*Garlick*
TRAFFIC LIGHTS—*Ford, M.
Lucille*
TRAFFIC QUINCE—*Abbe*
TRAGEDY NO. 456—*Robinson,
Wanda*
LES TRAGIQUES: VENGEANCES—
Aubigné
TRAGÖDIE—*Heine*
LA TRAICIÓN DEL CONDE DON
JULIAN—*Anonymous–Spanish*
THE TRAIL OF NINETY-EIGHT—
Service
THE TRAILING ARBUTUS—*Whittier*
THE TRAIN—*Walcott*
TRAIN CRASH—*McGough*
TRAIN SONG—*Kramer*
TRAINS DANS LA BANLIEUE OUEST
—*Queneau*
TRAMONTANA AT LERICI—
Tomlinson
IL TRAMONTO DELLA LUNA—
Leopardi
A TRAMPWOMAN'S TRAGEDY—
Hardy
TRANCE—*Swenson*
TRANSCRIPTION OF ORGAN MUSIC
—*Ginsberg*
TRANSFORMACIÓN—*Semprit*
TRANSITION—*Amini*
TRANSITIONAL POEMS—*Day
Lewis*
TRANSLATION—*Fuller, Roy*
TRANSLATIONS—*Rich*
TRANSPORT—*Meredith, George*
THE TRAPPER—*Klappert*
THE TRASH DRAGON OF SHENSI—
Glaze
TRÄSLOTTET—*Karlfeldt*
LA TRASPARENCIA, DIÓS, LA
TRASPARENCIA—*Jiménez*
DER TRAUM DER MAGD—
Morgenstern
DER TRÄUMER—*Morgenstern*
TRAUR-GESANG VON DER NOT
CHRISTI AM ÖLBERG IN DEM
GARTEN—*Spee von
Langenfeld*
TRAVEL—*Millay*
TRAVEL—*Stevenson*
TRAVELER'S REST—*Nash*
TRAVELING THROUGH THE DARK—
Stafford
THE TRAVELLER—*Auden*
THE TRAVELLER—*Goldsmith*
THE TRAVELLER'S CURSE AFTER
MISDIRECTION—*Graves*
TRAVELLER'S REPORT—*Morton*
TRAVELLING BETWEEN PLACES—
Patten

TRAVELLING IN GREECE—
Campbell, Roy
TRAVELLING STORM—*Van Doren*
TRAVERSANDO LA MAREMMA
TOSCANA—*Carducci*
I TRE DOTTORI DI SALAMANCA—
Rodari
TRE PPICCERILLE—*Filippo*
TREATMENT—*Kramer*
TREBETHERICK—*Betjeman*
THE TREE—*Finch, Anne,
Countess of Winchelsea*
A TREE AT DUSK—*Welles*
TREE AT MY WINDOW—*Frost,
Robert*
THE TREE HOUSE—*O'Gorman*
THE TREE OF LIBERTY—*Burns*
TREE-SLEEPING—*Coffin*
TREE-TOAD—*Conkling*
THE TREEHOUSE—*Emanuel*
TREES—*Kilmer, Joyce*
TREETOPS—*Bell*
TREGARDOCK—*Betjeman*
TREIB DU ES NICHT AUCH—
Guggenmos
TREM DE ALAGOAS—*Ferreira*
EL TREN DE LOS HERIDOS—
Hernández, Miguel
EL TREN EXPRESSO—*Campoamor*
IL TRENO DEI BAMBINI—*Rodari*
TRES COSAS—*Alcázar*
LAS TRES HOJAS—*Garcia Lorca*
TRES POEMAS SOBRE LA MUERTE—
Bousoño
TRES RIOS—*Garcia Lorca*
TRES ROMANCES HISTÓRICOS—
Garcia Lorca
LAS TRES TONTAS—*Fuertes*
THE TRESSES—*Hardy*
TREWARMETT—*Blackburn,
Thomas*
TRIAL POEMS—*Berrigan*
THE TRIBUNE'S VISITATION—*Jones,
David*
THE TRIBUTARY SEASONS—
Watkins
TRICKING—*Lee, Dennis*
TRICKS WITH MIRRORS—*Atwood*
EL TRIGO QUE NO SE SIEGA—
Martinez Alonso
TRILCE—*Vallejo*
TRILOGIE DER LEIDENSCHAFT—
Goethe
TRINKET—*Bell*
TRIO FOR TWO CATS AND A
TROMBONE—*Sitwell, Edith*
TRIOLET—*Bridges*
TRIOLET—*Cary*
IL TRIONFO DELLO ZERO—*Rodari*
TRIONFO DI BACCO E DI ARIANNA
—*Medici*
A TRIP THROUGH YUCATAN—*Weiss*
TRIPLE BRONZE—*Frost, Robert*
THE TRIPLE FOOLE—*Donne*
TRISTES RECORDOS—*Castro,
Rosalía de*
TRISTESSE—*Geraldy*

TRISTESSE—*Musset*

TRISTESSE D'OLYMPIO—*Hugo, Victor*

TRISTESSE D'UNE ÉTOILE—*Apollinaire*

THE TRIUMPH OF CHARIS—*Jonson*

THE TRIUMPH OF DEATH—*Howes*

TRIZONIA—*Seferis*

TROILUS & CRISEYDE—*Chaucer*

TROISIÈME CHÂTEAU—*Nerval*

THE TROLL'S NOSEGAY—*Graves*

THE TROPICS IN NEW YORK—*McKay*

TROST—*Hölderlin*

TROST—*Mörike*

TROSTGESANG—*Gerhardt*

TROUBLE—*Wright, James*

TROUBLE IN A TAVERN—*Walters*

THE TROUBLE WITH DANCING—*Polak*

THE TROUBLE WITH DREAMS/GROOVING—*Robinson, Wanda*

THE TROUBLE WITH INTELLECTUALS—*Randall*

TROUBLED JESUS—*Cuney*

TROUSERS OF THE WIND—*Anonymous–African languages–Ethiopian*

TROVA GUAJIRA—*Lloréns Torres*

TRÜBSINN—*Trakl*

TRUCE—*Williams, Hugo*

THE TRUCE AND THE PEACE—*Jeffers, Robinson*

THE TRUCE OF CHRISTMAS—*Chesterton, Gilbert Keith*

TRUCK ODE—*Purens*

TRUDGE, BODY—*Graves*

THE TRUE BEAUTY—*Carew*

TRUE JOY—*Graves*

TRUE LOVE—*Viorst*

TRUE LOVE OR HEART EXCHANGE—*Sidney*

TRUE LOVERS IN EACH HAPPENING OF THEIR HEARTS—*Cummings*

TRUE MYTHS—*Collier*

THE TRUE RELIGION—*Cunningham, James Vincent*

THE TRUE WEATHER FOR WOMEN—*Simpson*

TRUEBLOOD—*Ward*

THE TRUEST POETRY IS THE MOST FEIGNING—*Auden*

THE TRUISMS—*MacNeice*

THE TRULY GREAT—*Spender*

TRUMPET PLAYER—*Hughes, Langston*

A TRUNK, A WOODEN BOX TIED WITH TWINE—*Robison*

TRUST—*Dowling*

TRUTH—*Chaucer*

TRUTH—*Nemerov*

TRUTH—*Spencer*

TRUTH—*Viorst*

TRUTH—*Walters*

THE TRUTH ABOUT LITTLE RED RIDING HOOD—*Morgan, Karen*

TRUTH IN LOVE—*Suckling*

TRUTH IS NOT THE SECRET OF A FEW—*Ferlinghetti*

THE TRUTH THE DEAD KNOW—*Sexton*

TRY IT SUNS. AND HOLS.—IT'S CLOSED THEN—*Nash*

TÚ—*Jiménez*

TU AS TELLEMENT AIGUISÉ—*Cendrars*

TU ES PLUS BELLE QUE LE CIEL ET LA MER—*Cendrars*

TU GERI L'ORTO CHE NISSUN CULTIVA—*Marin*

TU GERI ZA VECIA—*Marin*

TU ME QUIERES BLANCA—*Storni*

TU NADA MAS—*Sansores*

TU SA DUTA DE SAL E DE SALMASTRO—*Marin*

TU SERAS NUE—*Jammes*

TU, SI LOS LLAMARAS—*Rosales*

TU TI SPEZZASTI—*Ungaretti*

TU Y YO—*Storni*

TUDOR STREET SHOP GIRL—*Vaughan, H. A.*

TUÉRCELE EL CUELLO AL CISNE—*González-Martínez*

THE TUFT OF FLOWERS—*Frost, Robert*

THE TULIPS—*Levertov*

TUMANNAYA ULITSA—*Voznesensky*

LA TUMBA DE BELISARIO—*Isaacs*

TUNE FOR AN ILL-TEMPERED CLAVICORD—*Nash*

THE TUNNEL—*Strand*

THE TUNNING OF ELINOUR RUMMING—*Skelton, John*

TURFSTACKS—*MacNeice*

THE TURKEY—*Nash*

TURN AROUND'S FAIR PLAY—*Johnston, Ellen Turlington*

TURN OFF, OR USE OPENER—*Kresh*

TURNING (I NEED A BETTER TITLE)—*Giovanni*

THE TURTLE—*Nash*

TURTLE CLIMBING FROM A ROCK—*Bly*

TURTLES—*Nash*

DIE TUTE—*Busch*

THE TUTORED CHILD—*Kunitz*

TUTTO È SCIOLTO—*Joyce*

TUTTO SE SCORDA—*Di Giacomo*

TVA SKARGARDSVISOR—*Nerman*

TVINGA MIG INTE—*Lundkvist*

THE TWA CORBIES—*Anonymous–English–Modern English*

THE TWA SISTERS—*Anonymous–English–Modern English*

'TWAS LIKE A MAELSTROM—*Dickinson, Emily*

TWEEDLE DEE AND TWEEDLE DOOM—*Nash*

TWELFTH NIGHT—*Shakespeare*

TWELVE HOURS OUT OF NEW YORK AFTER TWENTY-FIVE DAYS AT SEA—*Snyder*

XXVIII—*Van Doren*

21st ANNIVERSARY—*Pastan*

TWENTY-FOUR PAIRS OF SOCKS—*Humphreys*

TWENTY GOLDEN YEARS AGO—*Mangan*

23rd STREET RUNS INTO HEAVEN—*Patchen*

TWICE—*Rossetti, Christina*

TWICKENHAM GARDENS—*Donne*

TWINKLETOES—*Milne*

THE TWIST—*Brathwaite*

TWO—*Cummings*

TWO AND ONE ARE A PROBLEM—*Nash*

TWO ANGELS—*Levertov*

TWO ARMIES—*Spender*

THE TWO BROTHERS—*Muir*

TWO DEATHS—*Jennings*

THE TWO-DOLLAR BILL—*Sobiloff*

TWO FRIENDS—*Ignatow*

THE TWO GENTLEMEN OF VERONA—*Shakespeare*

TWO-GUN BUSTER AND TRIGGER SLIM—*Walker*

THE TWO HEARTS—*Roche*

TWO HORSES PLAYING IN THE ORCHARD—*Wright, James*

TWO ILLUSTRATIONS THAT THE WORLD IS WHAT YOU MAKE OF IT—*Stevens, Wallace*

TWO IN THE CAMPAGNA—*Browning, Robert*

TWO LECTURES AND A FEW FLOURISHES—*Ciardi*

THE TWO LITTLE SKEEZUCKS—*Field, Eugene*

THE TWO LOVES—*Sitwell, Edith*

TWO LULLABIES—*Henri*

TWO MOON FANTASIES—*Sandburg*

THE TWO OLD BACHELORS—*Lear*

TWO OLD CROWS—*Lindsay, Vachel*

TWO ONE-WORD POEMS—*Lurie*

TWO PEWITS—*Thomas, Edward*

TWO POEMS ABOUT PRESIDENT HARDING—*Wright, James*

2 POEMS FOR BLACK RELOCATION CENTERS—*Knight, Etheridge*

TWO POEMS IN ONE—*Marshall, Lenore G.*

TWO POEMS ON THE CREATION OF A STATUE OF A MAENAD—*O'Gorman*

THE TWO PRIESTS—*MacLeish*

TWO QUATRAINS FOR FIRST FROST—*Wilbur*

TWO RIVERS—*Emerson*

TWO SMALL STONES—*Abse*

TWO SONGS FROM A PLAY—*Yeats*

TWO STORIES—*Masefield*

TWO TRAMPS IN MUD TIME—*Frost, Robert*

221-1424—*Sanchez*
TWO VOICES—*Abse*
TWO VOICES IN A MEADOW—
   Wilbur
TWO-VOLUME NOVEL—*Parker*
THE TWO VULTURES—*Roche*
TYING ONE ON IN VIENNA—*Kizer*
TYRANNIC LOVE—*Dryden*
TZIGANES—*Seghers*

THE U. S. SAILOR WITH THE
   JAPANESE SKULL—*Scott,*
   Winfield Townley
ÜBER DEN TRANENWÜRDIGEN TOD
   DES SOHNES GOTTES, JESUS—
   Kuhlmann
ÜBER DIE GEBURT UNSERES HERRN
   —*Gryphius*
ÜBER DIE NACHT MEINER GEBURT
   —*Gryphius*
ÜBER DIE PFERDE—*Zuckmayer*
ÜBER NICOLAUS COPERNICI BILD—
   Gryphius
ÜBERSCHRIFT AN DEM TEMPEL DER
   STERBLIGKEIT—*Gryphius*
UCCELLO DI GABBIA—*Saba*
UKAZANIE—*Svetlov*
ULALUME—*Poe*
ULTIMA CANÇÃO DO BECO—
   Bandeira
ULTIMA RATIO REGUM—*Spender*
EL ULTIMO AMOR—*Aleixandre*
ULTIMO CANTO DI SAFFO—
   Leopardi
ULTIMO QUARTO—*Ungaretti*
ULTRA-RED: AN ELECTRONIC LOVE
   POEM—*Skellings*
ULYSSES—*Tennyson*
ULYSSES AND THE SIREN—*Daniel,*
   Samuel
UM DAS KIND EINZUSCHLÄFERN—
   Desbordes-Valmore
UM FRIEDEN—*Bergengruen*
UM MITTERNACHT—
   Anonymous–Asian languages
UM MITTERNACHT—*Mörike*
UM STÄRKUNG UND
   UNVERLÖSCHBARKEIT—*Bergen-*
   gruen
UM VIELERLEI GUTE GABEN—
   Bergengruen
UMPIRE—*Nash*
UN DÍA SOBRESALE—*Neruda*
UN JOUR—*Vian*
UNANSWERED LETTERS—*Bly*
DAS UNAUFHÖRLICHE—*Benn*
UNCLE—*Levine*
UNCLE JOE—*Brown, Sterling A.*
UNCLE TIME—*Scott, Dennis*
UND ALLES OHNE LIEBE—*Fontane*
DER UNDANKBARE—*Busch*
THE UNDEAD—*Graves*
THE UNDEAD—*Wilbur*
UNDER A TELEPHONE POLE—
   Sandburg
UNDER BEN BULBEN—*Yeats*

UNDER CANCER—*Hollander*
UNDER CYGNUS—*Wilbur*
UNDER MILK WOOD—*Thomas,*
   Dylan
UNDER THE GREENWOOD TREE—
   MacDiarmid
UNDER THE MAUD MOON—
   Kinnell
UNDER THE WATERFALL—*Hardy*
UNDER VINTERGATAN—*Bergman,*
   Bo
UNDER WHICH LYRE—*Auden*
UNDERGROUND—*Abbe*
UNDERSONG—*Van Doren*
THE UNDERTAKING—*Donne*
UNDESIRABLES—*Beecher*
UNEASY THOUGHT OF PEACE—
   Burke
UNEMPLOYED SONG—*Kramer*
UNENCOURAGED LINGERING—
   Hodges
UNERWÜNSCHTE BELEHRUNG—
   Roth, Eugen
UNFORTUNATELY, IT'S THE ONLY
   GAME IN TOWN—*Nash*
DIE UNGLEICHEN EHELEUT—
   Santa Clara
L'UNION LIBRE—*Breton, André*
UNISONG—*Patten*
THE UNIVERSAL PRAYER—*Pope,*
   Alexander
THE UNKNOWN—*Jeffers, Lance*
THE UNKNOWN ARMY—*Van*
   Doren
THE UNKNOWN CITIZEN—*Auden*
THE UNKNOWN COLOR—*Cullen*
UNKNOWN GIRL IN THE
   MATERNITY WARD—*Sexton*
THE UNKNOWN WAR—*Sandburg*
UNLESS A LOVE BE FREE—
   Marshall, Helen Lowrie
DIE UNMÖGLICHE TATSACHE—
   Morgenstern
UNPREDICTABLE BUT
   PROVIDENTIAL—*Auden*
THE UNQUIET GRAVE—
   Anonymous–English—
   Modern English
UNRESPONSIVE—*Van Doren*
THE UNRETURNING—*Owen,*
   Wilfred
UNSATISFIED YEARNING—
   Munkittrick
DER UNSCHLÜSSIGE—*Roth,*
   Eugen
THE UNSEEN PLAYMATE—
   Stevenson
UNSERE WIRTSCHAFT—*Herburger*
THE UNSETTLED MOTORCYCLIST'S
   VISION OF HIS DEATH—*Gunn*
DIE UNSICHTBAREN—
   Bergengruen
UNTER EIN BILDNIS ADOLF
   MENZELS—*Fontane*
UNTER ZEITEN—*Morgenstern*
UNTERGANG—*Trakl*
UNTERGANG DER SONNE—*Heine*

UNTERGANGSSTRASSEN—*Heissen-*
   büttel
DIE UNTERGEHENDEN—*George*
UNTERSUCHUNG, OB DER MENSCH
   DEM MENSCHEN HILFT—*Brecht*
UNTIL DEATH DO US PART—*Hollo*
UNTITLED—*Rukeyser*
UNTITLED—*Swenson*
UNTITLED: BENEDICTION—
   Clifton
UNTITLED MAXIMUS POEM—*Olson*
UNTITLED: ON NAMES—*Clifton*
AN UNTOLD ADVENTURE OF SANTA
   CLAUS—*Nash*
UNWELCOME—*Coleridge, Mary*
   Elizabeth
UNWRITTEN NOVEL—*Rich*
UOMINI—*Lo Curzio*
UN UOMO CHE SPACCA LE PIETRE
   —*Camilleri*
UOMO DEL MIO TEMPO—
   Quasimodo
L'UOMO DI NEVE—*Rodari*
UP AT A VILLA–DOWN IN THE CITY
   —*Browning, Robert*
UP-HILL—*Rossetti, Christina*
UPON A BANK WITH ROSES—
   Drayton
UPON APPLETON HOUSE—*Marvell*
UPON ECKINGTON BRIDGE—
   Quiller-Couch
UPON HIS DEPARTURE HENCE—
   Herrick
UPON JULIA'S CLOTHES—*Herrick*
UPON LOVE—*Herrick*
UPON NOTHING—*Rochester,*
   Earl of
UPON THE BLEEDING CRUCIFIX—
   Crashaw
UPON THE BURNING OF OUR HOUSE
   —*Bradstreet*
UPPER LAMBOURNE—*Betjeman*
UPON A DEEDMANS HED—
   Skelton, John
UPSOUTH—*Alakoye*
THE UPSTART DECKCHAIR—*Roche*
UPSTREAM—*Sandburg*
UPTOWN, NEW YORK—*Ginsberg*
URBAN DREAM—*Hernández Cruz*
URCEUS EXIT—*Dobson*
URFAUST-MONOLOG—*Goethe*
THE URGE—*Souster*
URIEL—*Emerson*
THE URN—*Cowley, Malcolm*
URSPRUNGET—*Tagore*
US—*Sexton*
US TWO—*Milne*
THE USES OF LIGHT—*Snyder*
USK—*Eliot, Thomas Stearns*
LAS UVAS DE EUROPA—*Neruda,*
   Pablo
LAS UVAS DEL TIEMPO—*Blanco,*
   Andrés Eloy

V. J. DAY—*Ciardi*
V MIKROSKOPU—*Holub*

VACANCY IN THE PARK—*Stevens, Wallace*

THE VACANT LOT—*Brooks, Gwendolyn*

LA VACHE—*Hugo, Victor*

VACILLATION— *Yeats*

VÄCKELSE—*Quevedo y Villegas*

DEN VACKRASTE VISAN—*Nerman*

THE VACUUM—*Nemerov*

THE VAGABOND—*Stevenson*

VAGABOND'S HOUSE—*Blanding*

VAGABOND'S ROAD—*Blanding*

VÅGORNA—*Asplund*

VAIG ARRIBAR EN AQUELL POBLE —*Foix*

VAINEMENT—*Prévert*

THE VAINGLORIOUS SPARROW— *Roche*

VALE DO CAPIBARIBE—*Melo Neto*

A VALEDICTION: FORBIDDING MOURNING—*Donne*

A VALEDICTION: OF WEEPING— *Donne*

A VALEDICTORY TO STANDARD OIL OF INDIANA—*Wagoner*

VALENTINE—*Summers, Hollis*

A VALENTINE FOR A LADY— *Lucilius*

VALENTINE FOR A POPULAR TENOR —*Nikarchos*

A VALENTINE TO SHERWOOD ANDERSON—*Stein, Gertrude*

VALENTINO—*Pascoli*

EL VALLE DE ALMERÍA—*Ben Safar Al-Marini*

EL VALLE DE COLLORES—*Lloréns Torres*

LA VALLÉE—*Jammes*

VALLEY FORGE—*Read, Thomas Buchanan*

VALLEY OF LOIRE—*Moore, Rosalie*

VALLEY OF SHADOWS— *Dragonette*

THE VALLEY OF UNREST—*Poe*

VALLEY PRINCE—*Morris, Mervyn*

LE VALLON—*Lamartine*

VALS EN LAS RAMAS—*Garcia Lorca*

VALSE DINGUE— *Vian*

EN VALSMELODI—*Ferlin*

VALUABLE—*Smith, Stevie*

THE VALUE OF GOLD—*Gunn*

VALUTA—*Cowley, Malcolm*

VAMPIRE—*Baudelaire*

VAMPIRE—*Kipling*

EN VANDRINGSMAN—*Ferlin*

VANITAS! VANITATUM VANITAS— *Gryphius*

THE VANITY OF HUMAN WISHES— *Johnson, Samuel*

VAPOR TRAIL REFLECTED IN A FROG POND—*Kinnell*

VAPOR TRAILS—*Snyder*

VAR AR EN VAN— *Wallin*

VÅR BRACKNING— *Vennberg*

VARI-COLORED SONG—*Hughes, Langston*

VARIATION ON A LINE BY EMERSON —*Merwin*

VARIATION ON A SENTENCE— *Bogan*

VARIAZIONI SU NULLA—*Ungaretti*

VARICK STREET—*Bishop, Elizabeth*

VARIOS EFECTOS DEL AMOR— *Vega Carpio*

VARIUM ET MUTABILE— *Wyatt, Sir Thomas*

VÅRT ENDA HEM AR KARLEKEN— *Lagerkvist*

VAS A VENIR—*Mata*

LE VASE BRISÉ— *Sully-Prudhomme*

THE VASES OF WOMBS—*Gioseffi*

DER VATER—*Haushofer*

VATER UNSER— *Weissenburg*

VATER UNSER: HELIAND— *Anonymous–German*

LE VAUTOUR DES AGNEAUX— *Ducasse*

VAYA POR DIÓS—*Tejada*

VECHEROM—*Akhmatova*

VECIO CORCAL SUL FAR DE LA FOSA—*Marin*

VEDA UPANISHAD EDDA THAN— *Olson*

VEGELIA—*Ungaretti*

VEGLIA— *Viviani*

THE VEIL—*De la Mare*

VEILLE—*Apollinaire*

LE VEILLEUR DU PONT-AU-CHANGE —*Desnos*

VELORIO DE PAPA MONTERO— *Guillén, Nicolás*

VELVET SHOES—*Wylie*

VELVETS—*Conkling*

LE VENT—*Damas*

VENTANAS PINTADAS—*Fuertes*

LE VENTRE DE MA MERE— *Cendrars*

VENTS—*Perse*

VENUS AND ADONIS—*Shakespeare*

VENUS AND THE LUTE PLAYER— *Engle*

VENUS OVER THE DESERT— *Williams, William Carlos*

VENUS-PALMSTRÖM-ANADYOMENE —*Morgenstern*

VENUS WHEN YOUNG CHOOSING DEATH—*Smith, Stevie*

VERBA IN MEMORIAM—*Guest, Barbara*

THE VERBALIST OF SUMMER— *Eberhart*

VERBORGENHEIT—*Mörike*

VERDAD HISTORICA—*Alegría*

VEREINSAMT—*Nietzsche*

VERFALL—*Trakl*

VERGÄNGLICHE PSALMEN— *Piontek*

VERGÄNGLICHKEIT— *Wedekind*

DIE VERGELTUNG— *Droste-Hülshoff*

DIE VERGESSLICHEN—*Roth, Eugen*

VERGNÜGEN—*Brecht*

VERIRRT—*Storm*

VERKLÄRTER HERBST—*Trakl*

VERLAINE—*Darío*

VERLAINE—*Garcia Lorca*

DAS VERLASSENE MÄGDLEIN— *Mörike*

VERMÄCHTNIS—*Goethe*

VERMÄCHTNIS—*Hölty*

VERMONT HILLS—*Conkling*

VERNAL EQUINOX—*Stone, Ruth*

VERNAL SENTIMENT—*Roethke*

VERONICAS GITANAS—*Diego, Gerardo*

VERS D'EXIL—*Claudel*

VERS DORÉS—*Nerval*

VERS SUR UN ALBUM—*Lamartine*

DIE VERSCHEUCHTE— *Lasker-Schüler*

DAS VERSCHLEIERTE BILD ZU SAIS —*Schiller*

VERSES FOR AFTER-DINNER— *Holmes, Oliver Wendell*

VERSES OCCASIONED ON THE DEATH OF MR. AIKMAN— *Thomson*

VERSES ON SIR JOSHUA REYNOLD'S PAINTED WINDOW— *Warton, Thomas (the Younger)*

VERSES ON THE DEATH OF DR. SWIFT—*Swift*

VERSES ON THE PROSPECT OF PLANTING ARTS AND LEARNING IN AMERICA—*Berkeley*

VERSES SUPPOSED TO BE WRITTEN BY ALEXANDER SELKIRK— *Cowper*

VERSIONS OF THE SAME THING— *Spencer*

VERSÖHNUNG—*Lasker-Schüler*

VERSOS—*Teresa de Avila*

VERSOS PARA TI— *Anonymous–Spanish*

VERSOS SENCILLOS—*Martí*

DER VERSPATETE WANDERER— *Eichendorff*

VERTIGO—*Rossman*

VERTUE—*Herbert*

A VERY CONFUSING DAY—*Clark, John W.*

VERY FUNNY, VERY FUNNY—*Nash*

VERY LIKE A WHALE—*Nash*

DIE VERZEIHUNG— *Desbordes-Valmore*

VESPASIEN—*Obaldia*

VESPERS—*Auden*

VESPERS—*Milne*

IL VESTITO DI ARLECCHINO— *Rodari*

VETER—*Pasternak*

THE VETERAN—*Parker*

VETERAN WITH A HEAD WOUND— *Mitchell, Adrian*

A VETERAN'S DAY OF
    RECOLLECTION—*Beecher*
VEX NOT THIS GHOST—*Beecher*
'O VI' 'LLOCO—*Di Giacomo*
EL VIAJE DEFINITIVO—*Jiménez*
VIAJE FINIDO—*Storni*
VIAJERO—*Loynaz*
EL VIATICO—*Pemán*
THE VICAR OF WAKEFIELD—
    Goldsmith
VICE VERSA—*Morgenstern*
'O VICO D' 'E SUSPIRE—*Di
    Giacomo*
VICTIM OF AULIS—*Abse*
LA VICTOIRE DE GUERNICA—
    Éluard
LA VICTORIA DE JUNÍN: CANTO A
    BOLIVAR—*Olmedo*
VICTORY IN DEFEAT—*Markham*
VID VÅGENS SLUT—*Heidenstam*
LA VID VIRGEN—*Martinez
    Alonso*
LA VIDA DE LA MUERTE—
    Unamuno
UNA VIDA DE MUJER—*Martínez
    Sierra*
LA VIDA ES SUEÑO—*Calderón de
    la Barca*
LA VIDA PERFECTA—*Carrera
    Andrade*
VIDA RETIRADA—*León, Fray
    Luis de*
LE VIDE—*Michaux*
LA VIE ANTERIEURE—*Baudelaire*
VIE DE CHATEAU—*Hébert*
LE VIEILLARD ET L'ÂNE—*La
    Fontaine*
LE VIEILLARD ET LES TROIS JEUNES
    HOMMES—*La Fontaine*
VIEILLE CHANSON DU JEUNE
    TEMPS—*Hugo, Victor*
LA VIEILEE ET LES DEUX
    SERVANTES—*La Fontaine*
VIENTO DE AMOR—*Jiménez*
VIENTO ENTERO—*Paz*
VIER SPÄTE GEDICHTE—
    Bachmann
LA VIÈRGE A MIDI—*Claudel*
LA VIÈRGE, LE VIVACE ET LE BEL
    AUJOURD'HUI—*Mallarmé*
VIET NAM, AUGUST 11, 1966—*Jaffe,
    Ellen*
VIET NAPALM—*Howes*
VIETNAM: I NEED MORE THAN THIS
    CRUST OF SALT—*Jeffers, Lance*
LES VIEUX—*Cohen*
THE VIEW—*Clark, John W.*
VIEW FROM AN UPPER WINDOW—
    Day Lewis
VIEW FROM LLANSTEFFAN—
    Garlick
VIEW FROM THE BORDER—
    Williams, Gwyn
A VIEW FROM THE WHITE HELMET
    —*Emanuel*
VIEW OF A PIG—*Hughes, Ted*

VIEWS OF THE FAVORITE
    COLLEGES—*Brinnin*
VIGILANCE—*Breton, André*
LA VIGNE ET LA MAISON—
    Lamartine
VILLA GLORIA—*Pascarella*
THE VILLAGE—*Crabbe*
LE VILLAGE À MIDI—*Jammes*
THE VILLAGE ATHEIST—*Masters,
    Edgar Lee*
VILLAGE BLACKSMITH—
    Longfellow
VILLAGE REVISITED—*White*
THE VILLAGE SCHOOLMASTER—
    Goldsmith
LE VILLAGEOIS ET LE SERPENT—
    La Fontaine
THE VILLAGERS AND DEATH—
    Graves
VILLANELLE—*Passerat*
VILLANELLE OF HIS LADY'S
    TREASURES—*Dowson*
LA VILLE DE DON JUAN—*Desnos*
A VILLEQUIER—*Hugo, Victor*
VILLON: BALLADE OF THE LADIES
    OF TIME PAST—*Wilbur*
VILLONELLE—*Jacob, Max*
LE VIN DE L'ASSASSIN—
    Baudelaire
LE VIN DES AMANTS—*Baudelaire*
LE VIN PERDU—*Valéry*
VINCENZO DE PRETORE—*Filippo*
THE VINEGAR MAN—*Mitchell,
    Ruth Comfort*
VINYES VERDES—*Sagarra*
THE VIOLATION—*Abbe*
THE VIOLENT SPACE—*Knight,
    Etheridge*
VIOLONCELLO—*Blomberg*
VIPOR I SKYMNINGEN—*Österling*
VIRELAI—*Deschamps*
VIRGILIO—*Carducci*
THE VIRGIN CARRYING A LANTERN
    —*Stevens, Wallace*
VIRGINIA—*Eliot, Thomas
    Stearns*
VIRGINIA—*Macaulay*
VIRGINIA BRITANNIA—*Moore,
    Marianne*
THE VIRGIN'S HOUSE—*O'Gorman*
VIRTUE—*Williams, William
    Carlos*
VISAGES DE LA TERRE—*Pilon*
A VISION—*Tate, Allen*
A VISION—*Warren*
A VISION—*Winters*
VISION AT TWILIGHT—*Smith,
    William Jay*
VISION IN WEISS—*Brecht*
THE VISION OF BELSHAZZAR—
    Byron
THE VISION OF JUDGEMENT—
    Byron
THE VISION OF SIN—*Tennyson*
THE VISION OF SIR LAUNFAL—
    Lowell, James Russell
THE VISIONARY—*Brontë, Emily*

THE VISIT—*Williams, W. C.*
VISIT—*Yevtushenko*
A VISIT FROM ST. NICHOLAS—
    Moore, Clement Clarke
A VISIT TO THE EXILED POETS—
    Brecht
VISITA—*Girondo*
VISITA ALLA CONTESSA EVA
    PIZZARDINI BA—*Palazzeschi*
LA VISITA INEFABLE—*Martinez
    Alonso*
EL VISITANTE—*Aleixandre*
VISITANTS IN A COUNTRY HOUSE AT
    NIGHT—*Hillyer*
THE VISITATION—*Graves*
VISITATIONS—*MacNeice*
VISITS TO ST. ELIZABETH'S—
    Bishop, Elizabeth
VITA CHRISTI—*Mendoza, Fray
    Iñigo*
UNA VITA NUOVA—*Blackmur*
LA VITA NUOVA—*Dante Alighieri*
LA VITA NUOVA—*Dowling*
VITA NUOVA—*Kunitz*
LA VITA SOLITARIA—*Leopardi*
VITAE SUMMA BREVIS SPEM NOS
    VETAT INCOHARE LONGAM—
    Dowson
VIVI—*Gatto*
VIVRE SE CONJUGUE AU PRESENT—
    Seghers
VOCCA ADDUROSA—*Di Giacomo*
LA VOCE—*Pascoli*
VOCES Y ACOMPAÑAMIENTOS—
    Valverde
THE VOICE—*Brooke*
THE VOICE—*Hardy*
THE VOICE—*Roethke*
A VOICE FROM UNDER THE TABLE
    —*Wilbur*
THE VOICE OF THE ANCIENT BARD
    —*Blake*
VOICES FROM HOME: 1923—
    Cowley, Malcolm
VOICI LA PLUME DE MON ONCLE—
    Collymore
VOICI VENIR TEMPS—*Henault*
VOILÀ LE BANC RUSTIQUE—
    Lamartine
VOISINES, AVEC UN COUTEAU—
    Garcia Lorca
LES VOLEURS D'ENFANTS—
    Cocteau
LES VOLEURS ET L'ÂNE—*La
    Fontaine*
VOLGA—*Karamzin*
VOLLMOND—*Lasker-Schüler*
VOLT—*Tzara*
VOLUNTARIES—*Emerson*
VOLVED!—*Castro, Rosalia de*
VOM ARMEN B. B.—*Brecht*
VOM ERTRUNKENEN MÄDCHEN—
    Brecht
VOM KIND, DAS SICH NICHT
    WASCHEN WOLLTE—*Brecht*
VOM SCHWIMMEN IN SEEN UND
    FLÜSSEN—*Brecht*

VOM SPRENGEN DES GARTENS—
 Brecht
VOM ZEITUNGLESEN—
 Morgenstern
VON DER FREUNDLICHKEIT DER
 WELT—*Brecht*
VON DER ZERSTÖRUNG
 JERUSALEMS UND DEM JÜNGSTEN
 GERICHT: HELIAND—
 Anonymous–German
VORACITIES AND VERITIES
 SOMETIMES ARE INTERACTING—
 Moore, Marianne
VORFRÜHLING—*Hofmannsthal*
DER VORGESCHLAFENE
 HEILSCHLAF—*Morgenstern*
VORRIA—*Di Giacomo*
VORSTADT—*Kaschnitz*
VORSTADT—*Linde*
VOTIVE SONG—*Pinkney*
LES "VOUS" ET LES "TU"—*Voltaire*
VOUS QUI DORMEZ—*Soupault*
VOUS QUI PASSEZ—*Geraldy*
THE VOW—*Graves*
THE VOW—*Hecht*
VOWELS—*Andrews*
VOX HUMANA—*Gunn*
LE VOYAGE—*Baudelaire*
VOYAGE—*Griffiths*
THE VOYAGE OF JIMMY POO—
 Emanuel
VOYAGE OF MAELDUNE—
 Tennyson
VOYAGES—*Crane, Hart*
VOYELLES—*Rimbaud*
VOZ A MI PADRE, LEJOS—*Martínez
 Capó*
VOZROZHDENIE—*Pushkin*
VSE ZHIVOE—*Yessenin*
LA VUELTA AL HOGAR—*Andrade,
 Olegario Victor*
LA VUELTA DE MARTÍN FIERRO—
 Hernández, José
VYNALEZY—*Holub*
VYSOKAYA BOLEZN'—*Pasternak*
VZH—*Johnson, Tom*

W A C—*Murphy*
W. S. LANDOR—*Moore, Marianne*
W (VIVA)—*Cummings*
DIE WAAGE—*Morgenstern*
A WAGON OF SHOES—*Sutzkever*
WAGON TRAIN—*Mayo*
WAGONFUL OF WALNUTS—
 Marshall, Helen Lowrie
WAHRNEHMUNG—*Krolow*
WAITING—*Yevtushenko*
WAITING FOR ICARUS—*Rukeyser*
WAITING FOR THE BARBARIANS—
 Cavafy
WAITING FOR THE BOMB: N. Y., 1960
 —*Treitel*
THE WAKING—*Roethke*
WAKING—*Yevtushenko*
WAKING AN ANGEL—*Levine*
WAKING FROM AN AFTERNOON
 SLEEP—*Bly*

WAKING IN THE BLUE—*Lowell,
 Robert*
WAKING IN THE DARK—*Rich*
WALDEINSAMKEIT—*Heine*
EIN WALDLIED—*Keller,
 Gottfried*
THE WALK—*Hannan*
THE WALK—*Ross, W. W. Eustace*
WALK IN THE WOODS—*Marshall,
 Helen Lowrie*
WALK WITH ME MY BELOVED—
 *Anonymous–English–
 Modern English*
WALKER EVANS—*Colbert*
THE WALKING—*Roethke*
WALKING INTO FIRE—*Sklarew*
WALKING TO SLEEP—*Wilbur*
WALKING WOUNDED—*Scannell*
THE WALL—*Jones, David*
THE WALL OF DESTINY—
 Goldstein
WALL SHADOWS—*Sandburg*
WALLFAHRER-LIED—*Hesse*
WALLS BREATHE—*Mariah*
THE WALRUS AND THE CARPENTER
 —*Carroll*
WALTER BRADFORD—*Brooks,
 Gwendolyn*
WALTER SULLIVAN OF THE NEW
 YORK TIMES—*Talen*
WALTZ—*Sitwell, Edith*
THE WALTZER IN THE HOUSE—
 Kunitz
DIE WANDELNDE GLOCKE—
 Goethe
THE WANDERER—
 *Anonymous–English–Old
 English*
THE WANDERER—*Nietzsche*
THE WANDERER'S IMAGE: A POEM
 ABOUT SHIPS—*Masefield*
WANDERERS NACHTLIED—*Goethe*
WANDERER'S SONG—*Symons*
DER WANDERNDE KNIET—*Werfel*
WANTAGE BELLS—*Betjeman*
WANTS—*Larkin*
WAR—*Langland, Joseph*
WAR—*O'Gorman*
WAR—*Roth, Dan*
WAR AGAINST THE TREES—*Kunitz*
WAR AND POETRY—*Eberhart*
THE WAR GOD'S HORSE SONG—
 *Anonymous–American
 Indian languages–Navajo*
WAR IS KIND—*Crane, Stephen*
WAR POET—*Keyes*
WAR SONG—*Parker*
THE WAR SONG OF DINAS VAWR—
 Peacock
WAR STORY—*Starbuck*
THE WARDENS—*Rasul*
THE WARDROBE MASTER OF
 PARADISE—*Reed, Ishmael*
WARMTH—*Bahati*
WARNING—*Cohen*
WARNING—*Pietri*
WARNING TO CHILDREN—*Graves*

WARREN'S ADDRESS AT BUNKER
 HILL—*Pierpont*
THE WARRIORS OF THE NORTH—
 Hughes, Ted
WAR'S CLOWN: IN THE
 PROSCENIUM—*Derwood*
WARSONG—*Bergman, Alexander
 F.*
WAS A MAN—*Booth*
WAS A MAN—*Ciardi*
WAS, IS, WILL BE—*Reid*
WAS IST IM INNERN EINER ZWIEBEL
 —*Tucholsky*
DAS WASCHEN—*Brecht*
WASHINGTON—*Lowell, James
 Russell*
WASSAIL CHORUS AT THE MERMAID
 TAVERN—*Watts-Dunton*
WASSER—*Droste-Hülshoff*
THE WASTE LAND—*Eliot, Thomas
 Stearns*
WASTE NOT, WANT NOT—
 Marshall, Helen Lowrie
WASTING ARCHITECTURE—*Gregor*
WATCH THE LIGHTS FADE—*Jeffers,
 Robinson*
WATCHING HER GO—*Davison,
 Peter*
WATCHING TELEVISION—*Bly*
WATCHING THE DANCE—*Merrill*
WATCHING THE JET PLANES DIVE
 —*Stafford*
WATCHING THE NEEDLEBOATS AT
 SAN SABBA—*Joyce*
WATCHMAN, WHAT OF THE FIRST
 FIRST LADY—*Nash*
WATER—*Conkling*
WATER—*Norris*
WATER AND SHADOW—
 Zaturenska
WATER-FRONT STREETS—*Hughes,
 Langston*
WATER ISLAND—*Moss, Howard*
WATER-LILIES—*Milne*
WATER MUSIC—*Durrell*
WATER, 1948—*Lowell, Robert*
WATER NOISES—*Roberts*
WATER UNDER THE EARTH—*Bly*
WATERCOLOR OF GRANCHESTER
 MEADOWS—*Plath*
WATERLILY FIRE—*Rukeyser*
WATERLOO—*Byron*
WATERLOO—*Garlick*
WATERS AND SKIES—*Beerbohm*
WAVES: PLUSCULUS—*Walters*
WAVING GOODBYE—*Hughes, Ted*
THE WAY DOWN—*Kunitz*
THE WAY OF LIFE—*Lee, Don L.*
THE WAY OF LIFE AND THE WAY OF
 DEATH—*Antoninus*
THE WAY THE ROUNDNESS FEEL—
 Major
THE WAY THROUGH THE WOODS—
 Kipling
WE A BADDDDD PEOPLE—
 Sanchez
WE ARE—*Gilbert, Celia*

WE ARE NOT ALONE—*Murphy*

WE ARE SO FOND OF ONE
ANOTHER, BECAUSE OUR
AILMENTS ARE THE SAME—
Scott, Winfield Townley

WE ARE THE HUMANS—*Levertov*

WE CAN BE—*Sanchez*

WE DON'T DO NOTHIN' IN HERE—
Johnston, Ellen Turlington

WE HAVE BEEN BELIEVERS—
Walker

WE HAVE GONE THROUGH GREAT
ROOMS TOGETHER—*Sandburg*

WE HAVE KNOWN—*Bell*

WE MUST BE POLITE: LESSONS FOR
CHILDREN HOW TO BEHAVE
UNDER PECULIAR
CIRCUMSTANCES—*Sandburg*

WE REAL COOL—*Brooks,
Gwendolyn*

WE WALK THE WAY OF THE NEW
WORLD—*Lee, Don L.*

WE WERE ALONE—*Thomas,
Edward*

WE WHO DO NOT GRIEVE IN
SILENCE—*Mandel*

WE WOULD REFER YOU TO OUR
SERVICE DEPARTMENT IF WE
HAD ONE—*Nash*

WEAPONED WOMAN—*Brooks,
Gwendolyn*

THE WEARIN' OF THE GREEN—
*Anonymous–English—
Modern English*

THE WEARY BLUES—*Hughes,
Langston*

WEATHER WISDOM—*Sobiloff*

WEATHERS—*Hardy*

WED POEM BEFORE THANKSGIVING
—*Sanchez*

THE WEDDING—*Graves*

WEDDING DAY—*Marshall, H. L.*

THE WEDDING FRAME— *Williams,
Hugo*

A WEDDING ON CAPE ROSIER—
Eberhart

WEDDING PROCESSION, FROM A
WINDOW—*Emanuel*

WEDDINGS—*Yevtushenko*

THE WEE WEE MAN—*Children's
Verses and Nursery Rhymes*

WEEDS—*Nicholson*

THE WEEK THAT WAS—*Ciardi*

WEG ZUM BAHNHOF—*Eich*

DIE WEGGEWORFENE FLINTE—
Morgenstern

DER WEIHER—*Droste-Hülshoff*

WEIHNACHTSLIED—*Storm*

WEIHNACHTSLIED—*Zuckmayer*

DIE WEISE VON LIEBE UND TOD
DES CORNETS CHRISTOPH RILKE
—*Rilke*

WEISST DU, WAS DAS FISCHLEIN IM
WEIHER MACHT—*Guggenmos*

WELCOME DEATH—*Escriva*

WE'LL ALL FEEL GAY—*Scott,
Winfield Townley*

WE'LL GO NO MORE A-ROVING—
Byron

THE WELL OF PROPHECY—
Sutzkever

WELLINGTON THE SKELETON—
Lee, Dennis

THE WELLS OF JESUS' WOUNDS—
*Anonymous–English—
Modern English*

THE WELSH HILL COUNTRY—
Thomas, Ronald Stuart

WELSH INCIDENT—*Graves*

WELTLAUF—*Heine*

WEN CHUNG—*Bai Jyu Yi*

WEN LYOU SHR JYOU—*Bai Jyu Yi*

WENN DAS KIND TROTZIG IST—
Guggenmos

WENN EENA JEBORN WIRD—
Tucholsky

WENN EENA DOT IS—*Tucholsky*

WENN IMMER SINN HAT—
Heissenbüttel

WER WEISS WO—*Liliencron*

WE'RE FINE, JUST FINE—*Nash*

WERE I NOT WITH YOU—*Sutzkever*

DER WERWOLF—*Morgenstern*

WESSEX HEIGHTS—*Hardy*

DAS WESSOBRUNNER GEBET—
Anonymous–German

WEST OF MIDNIGHT—*Engle*

WEST-ÖSTLICH—*Morgenstern*

WEST-RUNNING BROOK—*Frost,
Robert*

THE WEST WIND—*Masefield*

WEST WIND GOSSIP—*Marshall,
Helen Lowrie*

THE WESTERN HUDSON SHORE (THE
PALISADES)—*Masefield*

WESTERN WAGONS—*Benét,
Stephen Vincent*

WESTERN WIND—*Edwardes*

WESTWIND—*Eich*

WET DAY—*Conkling*

WHALE—*Benét, William Rose*

WHALE—*MacPherson*

WHALES, WEEP NOT—*Lawrence*

WHAT A LYING LOT THE WRITERS
ARE—*Porter, Peter*

WHAT AM I?—*Aldis*

WHAT ANY LOVER LEARNS—
MacLeish

WHAT ARE YEARS—*Moore,
Marianne*

WHAT BLOOD-RED LAW—*Miller,
Arthur*

WHAT DEEPER SIN—*Arnez*

WHAT DID I DREAM—*Graves*

WHAT DO WE SEE?—*Rukeyser*

WHAT DUCKS REQUIRE—*Ransom,
John Crowe*

WHAT D'YE CALL IT BALLAD—
Gay, John

WHAT ELSE, BUT FOR LOVE—
Edson

WHAT I ASSEMBLED AND
DISSEMBLED—*Scott, Winfield
Townley*

WHAT IF A DAY—
*Anonymous–English—
Modern English*

WHAT IN THE WORLD—*Merriam*

WHAT IS A NEGRO—*Arnez*

WHAT IS KNOWN—*Stephany*

WHAT IS MOVING—*Stryk*

WHAT IS PINK—*Rossetti,
Christina*

WHAT IS THIS—*Johnston, Ellen
Turlington*

WHAT IT MEANS TO BE AN "N"—
Hodges

WHAT IT WAS, IS—*Rasul*

WHAT KIND OF MUSIC—*Reeves*

WHAT LASTS—*Bell*

WHAT MARKED THE RIVER'S FLOW
—*Stephany*

WHAT MR. ROBINSON THINKS—
Lowell, James Russell

WHAT, NO SHEEP?—*Nash*

WHAT PUEBLO MEANS TO ME—
Eckels

WHAT SMITH KNEW ABOUT
FARMING—*Riley*

WHAT SONGS THE SOLDIERS SANG
—*Bell*

WHAT THE HYENA SAID—*Lindsay,
Vachel*

WHAT TO DO UNTIL THE DOCTOR
GOES, OR IT'S TOMORROW THAN
YOU THINK—*Nash*

WHAT WERE THEY LIKE—*Levertov*

WHAT WILL BE, IS—*Graves*

WHAT YOUR TEACHER'S MANUAL
CAN AND CANNOT DO FOR YOU
—*Johnston, Ellen Turlington*

WHATEVER HAPPENED TO BLACK
AMERICA?—*Braxton*

WHATEVER WE WERE GOING TO
TELL EACH OTHER WON'T MEAN
AS MUCH—*Bell*

WHAT'S HAPPENING TO THE
HEROES—*Kali*

WHAT'S THAT YOU SAY, CESAR?—
Glaze

WHAT'S WHAT—*Reid*

THE WHEEL—*Clark, John W.*

WHEESHT, WHEESHT—
MacDiarmid

WHEN—*Hodges*

WHEN A BOAT DRAWS NEAR—
Gregor

WHEN ASSAULT WAS INTENDED TO
THE CITY—*Milton*

WHEN BROWN IS BLACK—
Kgositsile

WHEN DEATH CAME APRIL
TWELVE, 1945—*Sandburg*

WHEN DEY 'LISTED COLORED
SOLDIERS—*Dunbar, Paul
Laurence*

WHEN DO WE EAT?—*Marshall,
Helen Lowrie*

WHEN DRAGONS LIE SLAIN—
Goldstein

WHEN EARTH'S LAST PICTURE IS PAINTED—*Kipling*

WHEN GOD DECIDED TO INVENT—*Cummings*

WHEN I AWOKE—*Patterson*

WHEN I BUY PICTURES—*Moore, Marianne*

WHEN I COME—*Francis*

WHEN I KNOW THE POWER OF MY BLACK HAND—*Jeffers, Lance*

WHEN I LEFT—*Lester*

WHEN IN ROME—*Evans, Mari*

WHEN LILACS LAST IN THE DOORYARD BLOOMED—*Whitman*

WHEN MALINDY SINGS—*Dunbar, Paul Laurence*

WHEN OBOES PLAY—*Goldstein*

WHEN SHE SPOKE OF GOD—*Jeffers, Lance*

WHEN SUE WEARS RED—*Hughes, Langston*

WHEN THE FROST IS ON THE PUNKIN—*Riley*

WHEN THE KING ENJOYS HIS OWN AGAIN—*Anonymous–English—Modern English*

WHEN THE WIND ENDS—*Van Doren*

WHEN TIME STOOD STILL—*Goldstein*

WHEN WALKING—*Smith, Stevie*

WHEN WELCOME—*Sanchez*

WHEN YOU ARE OLD—*Yeats*

WHEN YOU DREAM—*Marshall, Helen Lowrie*

WHEN YOU GO AWAY—*Merwin*

WHEN YOU HAVE FORGOTTEN SUNDAY—*Brooks, Gwendolyn*

WHERE ARE WE—*Shiva*

WHERE DO YOU GO—*Bruchac*

WHERE GO THE BOATS—*Stevenson*

WHERE HAS THE WIND GONE—*Clark, John W.*

WHERE IS IT WRITTEN—*Viorst*

WHERE KNOCK IS OPEN WIDE—*Roethke*

WHERE ONCE HER LILACS GREW—*Marshall, Helen Lowrie*

WHERE SHALL WE WALK—*Patchen*

WHERE THE MISSISSIPPI MEETS THE AMAZON—*Shange*

WHERE THE PICNIC WAS—*Hardy*

WHERE THE RAINBOW ENDS—*Lowell, Robert*

WHERE THE RAINBOW ENDS—*Rive*

WHERE WE MUST LOOK FOR HELP—*Bly*

WHEREVER YOU ARE—*Kavanagh*

WHICH IS MY LITTLE BOY—*Williams, Tennessee*

WHICH OF US TWO—*Viereck*

WHILE HOMER NODDED: A FOOTNOTE TO THE ILIAD—*Nash*

WHILE I SLEPT—*Francis*

WHILE READING HISTORY—*Marshall, Lenore G.*

WHILE SITTING IN THE TUILERIES AND FACING THE SLANTING SUN—*Swenson*

WHILE THE SUN STILL SPENDS HIS FABULOUS MONEY—*Patchen*

WHILE TROOPS MOVED IN—*Robson, Jeremy*

THE WHIPPING—*Hayden*

THE WHIRLWIND—*Levertov*

THE WHISKEY BOOK—*Den Boer*

WHISPERED AT THE CHURCH-OPENING—*Hardy*

THE WHISPERER—*Nicholson*

WHISPERS OF HEAVENLY DEATH—*Whitman*

WHISPERS OF IMMORTALITY—*Eliot, Thomas Stearns*

WHITE ASH—*Sandburg*

WHITE BUTTERFLIES—*Swinburne*

WHITE COLLAR JOB—*Eckels*

THE WHITE DEVIL—*Webster, John*

WHITE HELIOTROPE—*Symons*

THE WHITE MAN'S BURDEN—*Kipling*

WHITE POWER STRUCTURE—*Emanuel*

A WHITE ROSE—*O'Reilly*

THE WHITE STARS—*Dowling*

WHITE WATER-LILY—*Ross, W. W. Eustace*

WHITE WEDDING—*Porter, Peter*

THE WHITE WINDOW—*Stephens*

WHITEY, BABY—*Emanuel*

WHO—*Gaver*

WHO—*Henri*

WHO AM I?—*Gaver*

WHO AM I?—*Reid*

WHO BUT THE LORD—*Hughes, Langston*

WHO COLLECTS THE PAIN—*Stephany*

WHO DO YOU WORK FOR?—*Marshall, Helen Lowrie*

WHO EVER LOVED—*Marlowe*

WHO GETS THE POPE'S NOSE—*Porter, Peter*

WHO IS NOT A STRANGER STILL—*Stephany*

WHO MURDERED THE MINUTES—*Treece*

WHO SAID TODAY'S KIDS DON'T HAVE FEELINGS—*Johnston, Ellen Turlington*

WHO TO BE KIND TO—*Ginsberg*

WHO WERE SO DARK OF HEART THEY MIGHT NOT SPEAK—*Cummings*

WHOLE DUTY OF CHILDREN—*Stevenson*

WHOLE LOVE—*Graves*

THE WHOLE STORY—*Hollander*

THE WHOLE TRUTH—*Viorst*

WHOSE DINOSAURS ARE NUMBERED?—*Marcus*

WHY COME YE NOT TO COURT?—*Skelton, John*

WHY CROOKED THOMAS CAM WAS GRUMPY—*Stephens*

WHY DO I—*Hardy*

WHY DOES THE FLY—*Clark, John W.*

WHY DON'T YOU LOVE US?—*Arnez*

WHY DON'T YOU WRITE FOR ME?—*Ciardi*

WHY I DON'T GET HIGH ON SHIT—*Sanchez*

WHY THE SEA IS SALT—*Williams, Oscar*

WHY TRY—*Joans*

WHY TRY—*Jones, Ted*

WHY WAIT FOR SCIENCE—*Frost, Robert*

WHY WE NEED EXPERTS IN OUR LIVES—*Treitel*

WICHITA FALLS—*Rasof*

WIDE RIVER—*Hughes, Langston*

WIDMUNG—*Brentano*

THE WIDOW—*Spencer*

THE WIDOW IN THE BYE STREET—*Masefield*

THE WIDOW'S COMPLAINT—*Scannell*

WIE ER WOLLE GEKÜSSET SEIN—*Fleming*

WIE ES SO GEHT—*Krüger*

WIE SICH DAS GALGENKIND DIE MONATSNAMEN MERKT—*Morgenstern*

WIEGENLIED—*Weinheber*

WIEGENLIED AN DER BERGSTRASSE—*Zuckmayer*

WIEGENLIED, BEI MONDSCHEIN ZU SINGEN—*Claudius*

WIEGENLIED/LURELAY—*Brentano*

DAS WIEDERSEHEN—*Brecht*

WIEDERSEHN NACH LANGER ZEIT—*Borchers*

THE WIFE—*Creeley*

A WIFE AND ANOTHER—*Hardy*

THE WIFE OF BATH'S PROLOGUE—*Chaucer*

THE WIFE OF BATH'S TALE—*Chaucer*

THE WIFE OF USHER'S WELL—*Anonymous–English—Modern English*

A WIFE'S LAMENT—*Anonymous–English—Old English*

THE WILD ANCESTRAL CROW—*Walters*

WILD ASS—*Colum*

WILD CYCLAMEN—*Graves*

THE WILD DUCKS—*Masefield*

THE WILD HONEYSUCKLE—*Freneau*

WILD JACKASS—*Nash*

THE WILD OLD WICKED MAN—*Yeats*

WILD SWANS—*Millay*

THE WILD SWANS AT COOLE—
Yeats
WILD WITH ALL REGRETS—Owen,
Wilfred
WILDERNESS—Sandburg
WILDTRACK—Wain
WILDWEST—MacLeish
WILL CONSIDER SITUATION—Nash
WILL IT BE SO AGAIN—Day Lewis
WILL TO WIN—Scott, F. R.
WILLIAM AND EMILY—Masters,
Edgar Lee
WILLIAM BRAZIER—Graves
WILLIAM BUTLER YEATS ON THE
THIRD AVENUE EL—
Ferlinghetti
WILLIAM CARLOS WILLIAMS—
Lowell, Robert
WILLIAM WORDSWORTH—Keyes
WILLIE BREWED A PECK O' MAUT—
Burns
WILLIE METCALF—Masters,
Edgar Lee
WILLIE WASTLE—Burns
WILLKOMMEN UND ABSCHIED—
Goethe
THE WIND—Rossetti, Christina
THE WIND—Walters
DER WIND IM ZIMMER—Krolow
WIND ON THE HILL—Milne
THE WIND ON THE WAY—
Sandburg
WIND SONG—Sandburg
THE WIND THAT SHAKES THE
RUSHES—Clare
WIND-WOLVES—Sargent
THE WINDHOVER: TO CHRIST OUR
LORD—Hopkins
WINDS—Auden
WINDSCALE—Nicholson
WINDSHIELD WIPERS—Lee,
Dennis
WINDSOR FOREST—Pope,
Alexander
THE WINDY CITY—Sandburg
A WINDY DAY—Young, Andrew
WINDY NIGHTS—Stevenson
WINE—Anonymous–Old
English–Riddles
THE WINE OF ASTONISHMENT—
Lovelace, Earl
WINGS—Berrigan
WINGS OF THE DOVE—Brathwaite
WINTER—Giovanni
WINTER—Simpson
WINTER—Sitwell, Osbert
WINTER—Tate, Allen
WINTER FEARS—Robson, Jeremy
WINTER GARDEN—Gascoyne
WINTER GARDEN—Lewis, Janet
WINTER IS ANOTHER COUNTRY—
MacLeish
WINTER LANDSCAPE—Berryman
WINTER LANDSCAPE, GREECE—
Press
WINTER MASK—Tate, Allen

THE WINTER O THE HERT—Smith,
Sydney Goodsir
WINTER PRINT—Bishop, John
Peale
THE WINTER SOLDIER—Marvin X
WINTER SONG—Patten
WINTER SPRING—Wilbur
THE WINTER STORM—Giovanni
WINTER SUNSET ROCK CREEK
CEMETERY—O'Neill,
Catherine
WINTER SWEETNESS—Hughes,
Langston
WINTER TENEMENT—Cowley,
Malcolm
WINTER THE HUNTSMAN—Sitwell,
Osbert
WINTER WALK—Connor
EIN WINTERABEND—Trakl
WINTERNACHT—Keller,
Gottfried
WINTERNACHT—Lenau
DIE WINTERREISE—Müller
WIR ALLE SÄUMEN—Arp
WIR SCHREITEN AUF UND AB—
George
WIRE-DANCER—Ennis
WIRKUNG IN DIE FERNE—Goethe
THE WISDOM OF INSECURITY—
Eberhart
WISDOM OF THE ABBOT MACARIUS I
—Beecher
WISE MEN IN THEIR BAD HOURS—
Jeffers, Robinson
THE WISE MEN OF GOTHAM—
Peacock
THE WISE WOMAN—Untermeyer
A WISH—Rogers
WISHES TO HIS SUPPOSED MISTRESS
—Crashaw
THE WITCH OF WILLOWBY WOOD—
Bennett, Rowena
THE WITCHES' CHARM—Jonson
WITH A GUITAR, TO JANE—Shelley
WITH A SILVER COMB—Sherwin
WITH GOD CONVERSING—
Derwood
WITH MERCY FOR THE GREEDY—
Sexton
WITH ONE LAUNCHED LOOK—
Stafford
WITH SIMPLE WORDS—Hillyer
WITHOUT BENEFIT OF
DECLARATION—Hughes,
Langston
WITHOUT HER—Rossetti, Dante
Gabriel
WITHOUT WINDOWS—Joselow
WITHOUT WORDS—Wallace
WITHOUT YOU—Henri
WO FIND' ICH TROST—Mörike
WO SOLL DAS HIN?—Brecht
WODWO—Hughes, Ted
THE WOLF—Durston
THE WOLF AND THE STORK—
Moore, Marianne

DER WOLF IST ZUM HUHN
GEKOMMEN—Brecht
DIE WÖLFE—Zuckmayer
DIE WOLGASTÄDTE—Bobrowski
WOLO YOLO—Johnson, Tom
THE WOLVES—Tate, Allen
WOMAN—Giovanni
A WOMAN AFTER CHAGALL—
Evans, Liz
WOMAN AS MARKET—Rukeyser
THE WOMAN AT THE WASHINGTON
ZOO—Jarrell
WOMAN FEW OF WORDS—Van
Doren
THE WOMAN OF THREE COWS—
Anonymous–English–
Modern English
WOMAN WITH A PRAM—Walters
WOMANS CONSTANCY—Donne
A WOMAN'S HISTORY—Davies,
William Henry
WOMEN—Bogan
THE WOMEN AT POINT SUR—
Jeffers, Robinson
WOMEN: EARLY PLYMOUTH—
Lifshin
WOMEN IN LOVE: ESTIMABLE
MABLE—Brooks, Gwendolyn
WOMEN WHO WRITE IN THEIR
BLOOD—Colbert
A WOMEN'S LIBERATION
MOVEMENT WOMAN—Viorst
WONDER—Olfers-Batocki
THE WONDERFUL WORLD—Rands
WONDERFULNESS—Johnston,
Ellen Turlington
WONDERS—Anonymous–English
—Modern English
WONNE DER WEHMUT—Goethe
WORD—Spender
WORD—Thomas, Edward
THE WORD AND THE POET—Engle
A WORD EVENT FOR BICI FORBES
ON THE BOOK TITLE LUCY
CHURCH AMIABLY—Mac Low
A WORD OF PRAISE—Marshall,
Helen Lowrie
A WORD TO THE WISE—Robinson,
Wanda
WORDPLAY—Devaul
WORDS—Creeley
WORDS—Eberhart
WORDS—Gunn
WORDS—Thomas, Edward
WORDS—Wagoner
WORDS FOR THE MADRIGALIST—
Tomlinson
WORDS FOR THE RAKER OF LEAVES
—Adams
WORDS FOR THE WIND—Roethke
WORDS IN TIME—MacLeish
WORK DAY—Kramer
WORK IN PROGRESS—Williams,
William Carlos
WORK IT OUT—Fabio, Sarah
Webster
A WORK OF ARTIFICE—Piercy

WORK SONGS AND BLUES: PRELUDE
—Brathwaite
WORKER'S DETROIT—Andrews
WORKING AGAINST TIME—
Wagoner
WORKING ON WALL STREET—
Swenson
THE WORLD—Vaughan, Henry
THE WORLD IS LARGER IN SUMMER
—Stevens, Wallace
THE WORLD NARROWED TO A
POINT—Williams, William
Carlos
WORLD OF SOUND—Krows
A WORLD WITHIN A WAR—Read,
Herbert
THE WORM—Bergengren
WORMS AND WIND—Sandburg
WORSHIP—Starbuck
WORTE—Benn
DIE WORTE DES GLAUBENS—
Schiller
DIE WORTE DES WAHNS—Schiller
WOOD—Porter, Bern
WOOD AND HILL—Young,
Andrew
THE WOOD BURNS RED—
Goldstein
WOOD-THRUSH—Wheelock
THE WOOD-WEASEL—Moore,
Marianne
THE WOODEN CARDINAL—Darr
WOODPIGEONS AT RAHENY—
Davie
WOODS—Auden
THE WOODS AND THE WOODMAN
—Moore, Marianne
THE WOODSPURGE—Rossetti,
Dante Gabriel
THE WOOING LADY—Smith,
William Jay
THE WORLD—Vaughan, Henry
THE WOUND—Gunn
THE WOUND-DRESSER—Whitman
THE WRAGGLE-TAGGLE GYPSIES—
Anonymous–English—
Modern English
THE WRAITH—Roethke
THE WRECK OF THE DEUTSCHLAND
—Hopkins
THE WRECK OF THE HESPERUS—
Longfellow
THE WRECKERS—Souster
WRECKING BALL—Souster
WRITTEN ON FINDING AN
UNMARKED GRAVE—Corso
WRITTEN ON THE EVE OF HIS
EXECUTION—Tichborne
THE WRONG IS MIXED—Scott,
Winfield Townley
WULF AND EADWACER—
Anonymous–English—Old
English
WÜNSCHELRUTE—Eichendorff
WURZELS—Fontane
WAS WÜSTENHAUPT—Goll
WYATT RESTETH HERE—Surrey

WYNKEN, BLYNKEN, AND NOD—
Field, Eugene

X AGOSTO—Pascoli
X . . . FRANÇAIS—Aragon

Y ESCRIBIR LO SILENCIO SOBRE EL
AGUA—Rosales
YMCA WRITING ROOM—Fuller,
Roy
THE YACHT—Williams, William
Carlos
YALLUH HAMMUH—Walker
YANKEE DOODLE—
Anonymous–English—
Modern English
THE YARN OF THE NANCY BELL—
Gilbert, Sir William
Schwenck
YASE: SEPTEMBER—Snyder
YASMIN: A GHAZEL—Flecker
YE SEE—Li Bai
THE YEARLING SWIFT—Richards,
I. A.
YEAR'S END—Wilbur
YEARS OF THE DOG—MacLeish
YEATS TOWER—Kavanagh
YEE BOW—Masters, Edgar Lee
A YELL FOR YELLOW—Merriam
YELLOW—Wright, Charles
THE YELLOW FLOWER—Williams,
William Carlos
THE YEOMEN OF THE GUARD SONG
—Gilbert, Sir William
Schwenck
YERBA MORA—Dávila, José
Antonio
YES, I KNOW—Smith, Stevie
YES IS A PLEASANT COUNTRY—
Cummings
YET DO I MARVEL—Cullen
YET GENTLE WILL THE GRIFFIN BE
—Lindsay, Vachel
YEW-TREES—Wordsworth
YGUDUH—Cummings
YIDDISCHE GASS—Sutzkever
YO SOY TU FLAUTA—Muñoz
Marín
YOLANTE UND MARIE—Heine
YOU AND ME AND P. B. SHELLEY—
Nash
YOU, ANDREW MARVELL—
MacLeish
YOU ARE HAPPY—Atwood
YOU ARE INSTANTLY ENFOLDED—
Stephany
YOU ARE THERE—Giovanni
YOU CAN'T BE WISE—Engle
YOU GO INTO TOWN—Patten
YOU GOTTA BE TALKED TO, ANNE
—Flanders
YOU LIVE WITH YOUR AUNT—
Voznezensky
YOU UNDERSTAND THE
REQUIREMENTS—Lifshin
YOU WENT AWAY—MacCaig

YOU'LL DRINK YOUR ORANGE JUICE
AND LIKE IT—Nash
YOUNG—Sexton
YOUNG AFRICANS—Brooks,
Gwendolyn
YOUNG BEICHAN—
Anonymous–English—
Modern English
A YOUNG BIRCH—Frost, Robert
YOUNG GIRL: ANNAM—Colum
THE YOUNG GIRL'S SONG—Gordon
YOUNG HEROES—Brooks,
Gwendolyn
THE YOUNG HOUSEWIFE—
Williams, William Carlos
YOUNG HUNTING—
Anonymous–English—
Modern English
THE YOUNG IONIA—Nims
YOUNG MAN'S SONG—Gordon
YOUNG MAN'S SONG—Yeats
YOUNG NIGHT-THOUGHT—
Stevenson
THE YOUNG ONES, FLIP SIDE—
Emanuel
YOUNG SEA—Sandburg
YOUNG SYCAMORE—Williams,
William Carlos
THE YOUNG WASHINGTON—
Guiterman
THE YOUNG WIFE—Lawrence
A YOUNG WOMAN SITTING UP AT
MIDNIGHT—Tullos
THE YOUNG WOMEN—Polak
YOUNGER SISTER, GOING
SWIMMING—Atwood
YOUR ATTENTION PLEASE—Porter,
Peter
YOUR HANDS—Randall
YOUR PRIVATE WAYS—Graves
YOUR SHAKESPEARE—Bell
YOURS—Sherwin
YOUTH—Hughes, Langston
YOUTH—Wright, James
YOUTH AND AGE—Coleridge,
Samuel Taylor
YOUTH AND AGE ON BEAULIEU
RIVER, NATS—Betjeman
YOUTH AND ART—Browning,
Robert
YOUTH AND CUPID—Elizabeth I
YOUTH SINGS A SONG OF ROSEBUDS
—Cullen
THE YOUTH WITH THE RED-GOLD
HAIR—Sitwell, Edith
YU LIN LING—Lyou Yung
YU MEI REN—Jyang Jye
YUGO Y ESTRELA—Martí

ZAKLINANIYE—Pushkin
ZAKLINANIYE—Yevtushenko
ZAMERLI—Voznesensky
ZAPATEADO—Garcia Lorca
ZAPATERA—Garcia Lorca
ZAPE, GATA!—Palma
DER ZAUBERLEHRLING—Goethe

ZAVESHANIE—*Lermontov*
ZAVIST'—*Yevtushenko*
ZAVODNIKA—*Popa*
ZAYDEE—*Levine*
ZEBEDEE, THE ZEBRA—*Jeffries, Christine F.*
DAS ZEICHEN DER AUFERSTANDENEN—*Hagelstange*
DIE ZEIT GEHT NICHT—*Keller, Gottfried*
ZEITUNGSLESEN BEIM TEEKOCHEN—*Brecht*
ZEMLYA—*Pasternak*
ZEN POEMS—*Anonymous–Asian languages*
ZEN: THE ROCKS OF SESSHU—*Stryk, Lucien*
ZENSURIERTE REDE—*Rühm*
ZEPPELIN—*Glaze*
DAS ZERBROCHENE RINGLEIN—*Eichendorff*
ZERMATT: TO THE MATTERHORN—*Hardy*

ZHELANIE—*Lermontov*
ZHENSHCHINA I MORE—*Yevtushenko*
ZIEHENDE SCHAFHERDE—*Mehring*
ZIEMLICH VIEL—*Krolow*
ZIGEUNER—*Trakl*
ZIGEUNERSPRUCH—*Nietzsche*
ZIMA—*Vyazemsky*
ZIMNI VECHER—*Pushkin*
ZIMNYAYA NOCH'—*Pasternak*
'E ZINGARE—*Viviani*
ZIP—*Davie*
LE ZIZI PERPÉTUEL—*Obaldia*
ZOK ZOK ZOK—*Krucenych*
ZOLOTO I BULAT—*Pushkin*
ZONE—*Apollinaire*
ZONE LIBRE—*Aragon*
ZOO—*Escudero*
ZOO PARK NOCHIU—*Slutsky*
ZOOM! THE COMMODORES—*Davis, Thulami Nkabinde*
ZORONGO—*Garcia Lorca*
ZORONGO GITANO—*Garcia Lorca*

ZSOLTÁR—*Pilinszky*
ZU BEIDEN SEITEN DES ATLANTIK—*Mehring*
ZU DEN LEIDEN DES JUNGEN WERTHER—*Goethe*
ZUEIGNUNG—*Goethe*
ZULEMA—*Anonymous–Spanish*
THE ZULU KING; NEW ORLEANS—*Copeland*
DER ZWECKDIENER—*Brecht*
DIE ZWEI GESELLEN—*Eichendorff*
ZWEI SCHNELLE TODE—*Borchers*
DIE ZWEI WURZELN—*Morgenstern*
ZWIEGESPRÄCHE—*Goethe*
ZWIELICHT—*Eichendorff*
ZWEITER MERSEBURGER ZAUBERSPRUCH—*Anonymous–German*
ZWINGER—*Goethe*
ZWISCHEN DEN ZEITEN—*Roth, Eugen*
DER ZWÖLF-ELF—*Morgenstern*

A aquel árbol que mueve la foxa—*Hurtado de Mendoza*
À Arles où roule le Rhône—*Prévert*
Á casa va el caballero—*Anonymous-Spanish*
Á casa va Don Rodrigo—*Anonymous-Spanish*
A cchiú meglia farenara—*Di Giacomo*
À ceux qui sont lavés de pluie—*Diouara*
¿A dónde ir? Cada órbita se cierra—*Piedra-Bueno*
A dónde te escondiste—*Juan de la Cruz*
A egregie cose il forte animo accendono—*Foscolo*
A Elbereth Gilthoniel—*Tolkien*
A esto nada menos hemos llegado, amigos—*Figuera*
A grandes pedzouillées—*Fombeure*
À la fin tu es las de ce monde ancien—*Apollinaire*
A la marchesa Paola Travasta—*Porta*
A la muchacha de major talle—*Palma*
À la poste d'hier tu télégraphieras—*Desnos*
A la puente del amor—*Jiménez*
A la stagion che il mondo foglia e fiora—*La Compiuta Donzella*
À la très chère, à la très belle—*Baudelaire*
A las cinco de la tarde—*Garcia Lorca*
A llegado ese tiempo en que los años—*Alberti*
À l'ouest vous dormez encore—*Soupault*
A mis soledades voy—*Vega Carpio*
À moi. L'histoire d'une de mes folies—*Rimbaud*
A my a my a my—*Rasof*
A noir, E blanc, I rouge, U vert, O bleu: voyelles—*Rimbaud*
À Paris la tour Saint-Jacques chancelante—*Breton, André*
A peels an apple—*Nemerov*
A, Quand il—*Hugo, Victor*
À quatre heures du matin, l'été—*Rimbaud*
A qué me lo decís—*Becquer*
¿A qué quieres que te hable?—*Jiménez*
A shto potom? A shto potom?—*Yevtushenko*
A sto paese tutti li penzieri—*Belli*
À ta place je me méfierais du chevalier de paille—*Breton, André*
A través de la paz del agua pura—*Jiménez*
A través del confuso esplendor—*Neruda*
Á un hijo de españoles arropamos—*Unamuno*
A veces se la encuentra—*Florit*
A vi lla; vestuta rosa—*Di Giacomo*
À vous troppe légère—*Du Bellay*
A was an archer, who shot at a frog—*Children's Verses and Nursery Rhymes*
Abenámar, Abenámar—*Anonymous-Spanish*
Abends am Fluss in dem dunklen Herz der Gesträucher—*Brecht*
Abends wenn ich schlafen geh—*Anonymous-German*
Aber als er zur Wand ging um erschossen zu werden—*Brecht*
Aber einst wird kommen der Tag—*Heine*
Abortions will not let you forget—*Brooks, Gwendolyn*
Abou Ben Adhem—may his tribe increase—*Hunt*
Aboun the snaw-white channel—*MacDiarmid*

About aloneness and loneliness I have said—*Brooks, Gwendolyn*
About four, a few flakes—*Bly*
About suffering they were never wrong—*Auden*
About the Shark, phlegmatical one—*Melville*
About the skull of the beloved, filled—*Hacker*
Above the voiceful windings of a river—*Sassoon*
Above through lunar woods—*Smith, William Jay*
The abracadabra boys—have they been in the stacks and cloisters?—*Sandburg*
Abre os olhos e encara a vida! A sina—*Espanca*
Abril venía, lleno—*Jiménez*
Abrupt tempter; close enough to survive—*Hill*
Absent from thee, I languish still—*Rochester, Earl of*
Acacia, burnt myrrh, velvet, pricky stings—*Berryman*
L'acacia plena de lluna—*Manent*
Accablé de paresse et de melancholie—*Saint-Amant*
Accidents du mystère et fautes de calculs—*Cocteau*
According to their need, this tall Negro Evangelist—*Williams, William Carlos*
Accoudés au désir de la, avec elle insatisfait—*Damas*
Accuse me not, beseech thee, that I wear—*Browning, Elizabeth Barrett*
Accuse me thus: that I have scanted all—*Shakespeare*
Ach, gäb er mir zurück die alte Trauer—*Benn*
Ach, man sagt, des roten Mondes Anblick—*Brecht*
Ach wär mein Lieb ein Brünnlein kalt—*Anonymous-German*
Achanta marzo al ave que aún se duele—*Tejada*
The ache of marriage—*Levertov*
Acorda cedo como os passarinhos—*Castro, Eugénio de*
An acre of land between the shore and the hills—*Thomas, Edward*
Across the craggy indigo—*Smith, A. J. M.*
Across the dim frozen fields of night—*Francis*
Across the flat and the pastel snow—*Sitwell, Edith*
Across the open countryside into the walls of rain I ride—*Gunn*
Across the years he could recall—*Coffin*
The acts of my life swarm down the street like Puerto Rican kids—*Meredith, William*
Adam lay i-bounded—*Anonymous-English—Middle English*
Adam scrivain, if evere it thee befalle—*Chaucer*
Adán en paraíso, vos en huerto—*Quevedo y Villegas*
La adelantada fuiste tú en la tierra—*Diego, Gerardo*
Adieu, douce pensée—*Desbordes-Valmore*
Adieu, farewell earth's bliss—*Nashe*
Adieu Paris, la bonne ville—*Marot*
Adjacent to the public library—*Heath-Stubbs*
Administrators of minutes into hours—*Ciardi*

Admit the ruse to fix and name her chaste—
Bogan

Adorable images—Nemerov

Adorable is an adjective—Nash

Adrift on green water—Fox, Charles

The advantages of living with two cultures—
Scott, F. R.

Ae boat anerlie nou—Smith, Sydney Goodsir

Ae fond kiss, and then we sever—Burns

T' aedonia de o' aphenoune na koimetheis stis
Platres—Seferis

Aefter dham wordym wyrm yree cwom—Anonymous-English—Old English

Aequam memento rebus in arduis—Horace

Afoot and light-hearted I take to the open road
—Whitman

Africa/don't let them—Lee, Don L.

Africa is a young man bathing—Giovanni

After death, nothing is, and nothing, death—
Rochester, Earl of

After experience taught me that all the ordinary
—Snodgrass

After great pain, a formal feeling comes—Dickinson, Emily

After I got religion and steadied down—Masters,
Edgar Lee

After it became obvious that the strange rain
would never stop—Ferlinghetti

After it was over, though still gusting balefully
—Crane, Hart

After long storms and tempests' sad assay—Spenser

After that—Alakoye

After the burial-parties leave—Kipling

After the celebrated carved misericords—Francis

After the centers' naked files, the basic line—Jarrell

After the darkness has come—Thwaite

After the door shuts, and the footsteps die—Jarrell

After the fifth day—Sanchez

After the first powerful, plain manifesto—
Spender

After the funeral, mule praises, brays—Thomas,
Dylan

After the heaped piles and the cornsheaves waiting—Jennings

After the hour of illumination, when the tottering
mind—Graves

After the last bulletins the windows darken—Wilbur

After the late shouts, the silence—Scannell

After the leaves have fallen, we return—Stevens,
Wallace

After the marsh was drained and its vast monsters
—Blackburn, Thomas

After the saturation bombing divine—Francis

After the savage hysterical episode so common
with us—Blackburn, Thomas

After the sea-ship, after the whistling winds—
Whitman

After the stars were all hung—Moore, Merrill

After the storm was over—Olson

After the therapy of the grave ritual—Abse

After the torchlight red on sweaty faces—Eliot,
Thomas Stearns

After the words of magnificence and doom—
Lewis, Janet

After twenty years another meeting—Durrell

After you finish your work—Rukeyser

After you left me forever—Kizer

The afternoon breaks from a pale—Hacker

The afternoon was an aria from Verdi—Stefanile

Afuera, afuera, Rodrigo—Anonymous-Spanish

Again, again, I see this form repeated—Spender

Again! / Come, give—Joyce

Again I hear that creaking step—Saxe

Again I was caught by it—Gregor

Again I won't do what you want—Sherwin

Again the sky has gone to seed—Harkness

Against a falling snow—Francis

Against my love shall be, as I am now—Shakespeare

Against our love—Damas

Against that time, if ever that time come—Shakespeare

Against the rubber tongues of cows and hoeing
hands of men—Hughes, Ted

Age after age our bird through incense flies—
Derwood

The age is running out, I guess I feel—Ciardi

The age/ requires this task—Randall

Äger du tvenne slantar, sade Li Ti på en resa—
Martinson

Agile e solo vien di colle in colle—Carducci

An agitation of the air—Kunitz

Agosto/ Contraponientes—Garcia Lorca

Agoy de m', o Zeu, kai sy g he pepromene—
Cleanthes

Agreed that all these birds—Wilbur

El agua lava la hiedra—Jiménez

Aguadilla, cielo y mar, capullo de sol—Mendoza
Esther Feliciano

Águila sideral, viña de bruma—Neruda

Ah, broken is the golden bowl—Poe

Ah Christ I love you rings to the wild sky—Tate
Allen

Ah, come with me—Updike

Ah, did you once see Shelley plain—Browning
Robert

Ah Dieu! que la guerre est jolie—Apollinaire

Ah! dites, dites—Obaldia

Ah Faustus—Marlowe

Ah, I long for tears returning—Heine

Ah—it's the skeleton of a lady's sunshade—Hardy

Ah! je vous aime! je vous aime—Geraldy

Ah! la belle pleine Lune—Laforgue

Ah, little road, all whirry in the breeze—Johnson
Helene

Ah! ma chérie, que ce sera long! Tout un mois
—Geraldy

Ah my deare angrie Lord—Herbert

Ah! portons dans les bois ma triste inquiétude—
Chénier

Ah, que me metam entre cobertores—Sá-Car
neiro

Ah . . . si putesse dicere—Giusti

Ah, stay thy treacherous hand, forbear to trace
—Warton, Thomas (the Younger)

Ah, Sunflower, weary of time—Blake

Ah that the world could use a dream or a flame
cold—Patchen

Ah, the Disney dinosaur's light laughter—Corso

Ah, the world is so fair and heaven so blue—Heine

Ah, this night—*Dickey, James*

Ah what avails the sceptred race—*Landor*

Ah, what is love? It is a pretty thing—*Greene*

Ah wherefore with infection should he live—*Shakespeare*

Ah! whither doost thou now, thou greater Muse—*Spenser*

Ah-whoo-ah—*Gaver*

Ah, you should see Cynddylan on a tractor—*Thomas, Ronald Stuart*

Ahí la tienes ya, Platero—*Jiménez*

Ahogada por las sombras—*Zorilla de san Martin*

Ahora que voy tocando ya la cumbre—*Unamuno*

Ahora seremos felices—*Hierro*

Ai d ote de potamoio roon perikalle ikonto—*Homer*

Ainsi, toujours poussés vers de nouveaux rivages—*Lamartine*

Ain't been on Market Street for nothing—*Walker*

Ain't nobody heard me singing sweet songs lately—*Fabio, Sarah Webster*

Air aigu des soirs de hurlements—*Giguere*

Air, air, you are the distantmost thing I know—*Benedikt*

Air. Energy. Light. A birth of joy—*Deutsch*

L'air est plein d'un terrible alcool—*Apollinaire*

The air grieved and the island—*Abbe*

The air is crisp and fresh and clean—*Marshall, Helen Lowrie*

The air is quiet—*Lee, Dennis*

Aire de maig, no dignis res—*Arderiu*

El aire desdeñoso—*Molinari*

El aire se serena—*León, Fray Luis de*

The airplane taxies down the field—*Anonymous-English—Modern English*

The airport coffee tastes less of America—*Walcott*

Lo ajeno al alma—*Vivanco*

Al alba venid, buen amigo—*Anonymous-Spanish*

Al amanecer sería—*Mesa*

Al brillar un relámpago—*Becquer*

Al llegar la hora esperada—*Lugones, Ricardo*

Al mio cantuccio, donde non sento—*Pascoli*

Al olmo viejo, hendido por el rayo—*Machado, Antonio*

Al poco giorno, ed al gran cerchio d'ombra—*Dante Alighieri*

Al re Travicello—*Giusti*

Al tornar de la mente, che si chiuse—*Dante Alighieri*

Al vent—*Raimon*

Al ver mis horas de fiebre—*Becquer*

Al volver de distante ribera—*Byrne*

Alack! what poverty my muse brings forth—*Shakespeare*

Alafia flames, rising—*Rasul*

Los alamos de plata—*Jiménez*

Alas! I have nor hope nor health—*Shelley*

Alas, my love, you do me wrong—*Anonymous-English—Modern English*

Alas! regardless of their doom—*Gray*

Alas! so all things now do hold their peace—*Surrey*

Alas! 'tis true, I have gone here and there—*Shakespeare*

Alas, what pleasure, now the pleasant spring—*Bolton*

Alas! What various tastes in food—*Belloc*

Albe e notti qui variano per pochi segni—*Montale*

L'albero a cui tendevi—*Carducci*

Albert/ Hey, Albert—*Hughes, Langston*

Albert loved dogs mostly, though this was absurd—*Abse*

Albor. El horizonte—*Guillén, Jorge*

Alex, perhaps a colour of which neither of us had—*Abse*

Alexander Graham Bell—*Coffin*

Alexis lay pressed—*Dryden*

Alfene immemor atque unanimus false sodalibus—*Catullus*

Alguna vez la encuentro—*Becquer*

Alice grown lazy, mammoth but not fat—*Tate, Allen*

All, all of them wanted her—*Scannell*

All along the valley, stream that flashest white—*Tennyson*

All day—*Lifshin*

All day and night, save winter, every weather—*Thomas, Edward*

All day cars mooed and shrieked—*Reaney*

All day I hear the noise of waters—*Joyce*

All day I sit here doing nothing but—*Patten*

All day I trespassed on my friend's new death—*Blackmur*

All day subdued, polite—*Hughes, Langston*

All day the opposite house—*Lowell, Robert*

All down the valleys they are talking—*Abse*

All ei kheiras ekhnon ge boes th' hippoi t' ethelontes—*Xenophanes*

All filmy down she drifts—*Brooks, Gwendolyn*

All glass may yet behold—*Dickey, James*

All human things are subject to decay—*Dryden*

All I can give you is broken-face gargoyles—*Sandburg*

All I could see from where I stood—*Millay*

All ignorance toboggans into know—*Cummings*

All ihr herbstlich Fliegenden—*Eich*

All in green went my love riding—*Cummings*

All in the golden afternoon—*Carroll*

All in vain. I will cease now my long absorption with the plow—*Thomas, Ronald Stuart*

All interlopers in antiquity—*Marshall, Lenore G.*

All is nothing, nothing all—*Warren*

All June I bound the rose in sheaves—*Browning, Robert*

All kings, and all their favorites—*Donne*

All men know it, the young when the enemy in them—*Holmes, John*

All morning with dry instruments—*Merwin*

All my life I have been a prisoner—*Piercy*

All my past life is mine no more—*Rochester, Earl of*

All night and all day the wind roared in the trees—*Roethke*

All night long and every night—*Stevenson*

All night the crib creaks—*Lowell, Robert*

All night the dreadless angel unpursued—*Milton*

All of an age, all heretics—*Cowley, Malcolm*

All' ombra de' cipressi e dentro l'urne—*Foscolo*

All other joy of life he strove to warm—*Meredith, George*

All our valises are packed—*Lowenfels*

All out of doors looked darkly in at him—*Frost, Robert*

All over America railroads ride through roses—
  Scott, Winfield Townley
All power is saved, having no end—*Rukeyser*
All problems being—*Giovanni*
All right. Try this—*Wright, James*
All roads lead to Sicily—*Gaver*
All starts in the air where the first—*O'Gorman*
All that's left is pattern—*Schwerner*
All the bells of heaven may ring—*Swinburne*
All the flowers of the spring—*Webster, John*
All the here and all the there—*Ransom*
All the names I know from nurse—*Stevenson*
All the night in woe—*Blake*
All the night sleep came not upon my eyelids—
  Swinburne
All the soft runs of it, the tin-white gashes—*Davie*
All the waters of the river Deben—*Smith, Stevie*
All the world moved next to me strange—*Jordan,
  June*
All the world's a stage—*Shakespeare*
All the young women—*Polak*
All these illegitimate babies—*Smith, Stevie*
All things are best fulfilled in their due time.—
  Milton
All things come to pass—*Kgositsile*
All this because Finn wished to wed—*Masefield*
All Travellers at first incline—*Swift*
All wheels, a man breathed fire—*Dickey, James*
All winter long, whenever free to choose—
  Wordsworth
All women are beautiful—*Kelly*
All women are pets—*Nash*
All year the flax-dam festered in the heart—
  Heaney
All you violated ones with gentle hearts—*Walker*
Allá, en las tierras altas—*Machado, Antonio*
Alle haben den Himmel, die Liebe und das Grab
  —*Benn*
Alle könn sie mir, könn sie mir, könn sie mir—
  Tucholsky
Alle wissen, dass Mexiko ein erfundenes Land ist
  —*Eich*
Allein: du mit den Worten—*Benn*
Allen-a-Dale has no fagot for burning—*Scott, Sir
  Walter*
Allena var jag—*Runeberg*
Allerêst lebe ich mir werde—*Walther von der Vo-
  gelweide*
Alles geben die Götter die unendlichen—*Goethe*
Alles still ringsum—*Droste-Hülshoff*
Allez, je veux rester seule avec les tombeaux—
  Noailles
Allí estará también la castañera—*Panero*
Allie, call the birds in—*Graves*
Allnächtlich im Traume seh ich dich—*Heine*
Allons loin de la ville lasse—*Fombeure*
Allora . . . in un tempo assai lunge—*Pascoli*
All's over then: does truth sound bitter—*Brown-
  ing, Robert*
Alma felice, che sovente torni—*Petrarca*
Alma minha gentil, que te partiste—*Camoes*
Almost the shell of a woman after the surgeon's
  knife—*Masters, Edgar Lee*
Aloft, lightly on fingertips—*Francis*
Alone at the end of green alleys—*Nemerov*
Alone I could own both sides of the double bed
  —*Viorst*

Alone in a red phone booth escaping down the
  wires from myself—*Patten*
Alone in the night—*Teasdale*
Alone now, and most certainly—*Gilbert, Celia*
Alone today I mounted that steep hill—*Williams,
  William Carlos*
Alone, you are no more than many another—
  Graves
Along about this time of year—*Marshall, Helen
  Lowrie*
Along the blushing borders—*Thomson*
Along the field as we came by—*Housman*
Alora, la bien cercada—*Anonymous–Spanish*
Alors, adieu. Tu n'oublies rien?—*Geraldy*
Les alouettes font leur nid—*La Fontaine*
The alphabet of/ the trees—*Williams, William
  Carlos*
Already autumn begins—*Bly*
Already it's late summer. Sun-bathers go—*Whee-
  lock*
Already something of a stranger now—*Webb*
Already you are beginning to become—*Spender*
Alrededor de la copa—*Jiménez*
Als der Abend übers Schlachtfeld wehte—*Brecht*
Als der Frühling kam und das Meer war blau—
  Brecht
Als er dies v. Korf erzählt—*Morgenstern*
Als er Siebzig war und war gebrechlich—*Brecht*
Als ich dich zum letzten Male sah—*Arp*
Als ich dir vor Jahren zeigte—*Brecht*
Als ich in Jugendtagen—*Busch*
Als ich klein war, ging ich zur Schule—*Brecht*
Als ihre schwere Stunde gekommen war—*Brecht*
Als jüngst mein Auge sich in die Sapphirne Tiefe
  —*Brockes*
Als sie einander acht Jahre kannten—*Kästner*
Als sie ertrunien war und hinunterschwamm—
  Brecht
Als sie, krank von den letzten Kriegen—*Kästner*
Als sie nun aus war, liess man in Erde sie—*Brecht*
Als unser Herr auf Erden—*Brecht*
Alt farer hen som vinden—*Andersen*
Altarwise by owl-light in the halfway house—
  Thomas, Dylan
Altdeutsch!—Altdeutsch?—Nun, das ist—*Eichen-
  dorff*
Der alte Förster Püsterich—*Busch*
Die alten bösen Lieder—*Heine*
Altham says—*Olson*
Although I shelter from the rain—*Yeats*
Although it is a cold evening—*Bishop, Elizabeth*
Although she feeds me bread of bitterness—
  McKay
Although the aepyornis—*Moore, Marianne*
Although the snow still lingers—*Young, Andrew*
Altissimu, omnipotente, bon Signore—*Francis of
  Assisi*
Alto soto de torres, que, al ponerse—*Unamuno*
Always an animal—*Dlugos*
Always between two wars—*Treitel*
Always on Monday, God's in the morning papers
  —*McGinley*
Always the same, when on a fated night—*Frost,
  Robert*
Always the setting forth was the same—*Merwin*
Always to be at home—*Heath-Stubbs*

lways when he, in country heaven—*Thomas, Dylan*

lza, humano, la frente abatida—*Martinez Alonso*

m Abend tönen die herbstlichen Wälder—*Trakl*

m Abend, wenn die Glocken Frieden läuten —*Trakl*

m Abend, wenn wir auf dunklen Pfaden gehn —*Trakl*

m blassen Meeresstrande—*Heine*

m Brunnen vor dem Tore—*Müller*

m Gestade Palästinas, auf und nieder, Tag um Tag—*Meyer, Conrad Ferdinand*

m gonna take me seriously—*Sanchez*

m grauen Strand, am grauen Meer—*Storm*

m I the bullet—*Swenson*

m I too old to play with blocks—*Sobiloff*

m leuchtenden Sommermorgen geh ich im Garten herum—*Heine*

m Morgen spricht die Magd ganz wild—*Morgenstern*

m See, tief zwischen Tann und Silberpappel—*Brecht*

ma, hermano, el dolor—*Martinez Alonso*

mabo, mea dulcis Ipsithilla—*Catullus*

melette Ronsardette—*Ronsard*

men. The casket like a spaceship—*Merrill*

merica I've given you all and now I'm nothing —*Ginsberg*

he American eagle is not aware he is—*Francis*

mherst never had a witch—*Francis*

mic, teixiu aquesta visió de la infantesa—*Alcover i Maspons*

mico, hai vinto: io ti perdon—*Tasso*

mid the iris and the rose—*Winters*

mis pleins de rumeurs où êtes-vous ce soir—*Cadou*

mong Florentine cinquecentists taste in manuscripts—*Marshall, Lenore G.*

mong leaf green this morning—*Rukeyser*

mong pelagian travelers—*Auden*

mong the almond trees—*Merwin*

mong the grave—*Blackmur*

mong the more irritating minor ideas—*Stevens, Wallace*

mong the pines we ran and called—*Warren*

mong the smoke and fog of a December afternoon—*Eliot, Thomas Stearns*

mong the thousands who, with hail and cheer —*Whittier*

mong these turf-stacks—*MacNeice*

mor ed io si pien di meraviglia—*Petrarca*

l amor es tener, noche y día—*Martinez Alonso*

mor mío, amor mío—*Aleixandre*

l amor se va por los campos—*Jiménez*

more, mio giovine emblema—*Ungaretti*

mos is a shepherd of suffering sheep—*Walker*

mour, amour, qui tiens si haut le cri—*Perse*

'amour est assis sur le crâne—*Baudelaire*

'amour est plus simple qu'on le dit—*Henault*

'amour fut de tous temps—*Hugo, Victor*

mour, je pren congé de ta menteuse escole—*Ronsard*

es amoureux fervents et les savants austères—*Baudelaire*

mple make this bed—*Dickinson, Emily*

An des Balkones Gitter lehnte ich—*Droste-Hülshoff*

An einem Tag, wo feucht der Wind—*Droste-Hülshoff*

An jenem Tag im blauen Mond September—*Brecht*

An meiner Wand hängt ein japanisches Holzwerk —*Brecht*

Än rullar bruset under dina bågar—*Bergman, Bo*

L'an se rajeunissoit en sa verde jouvence—*Ronsard*

An' that year Metevsky went over to America del Sud—*Pound*

An' then there was Tizzic—*Barbieri*

An U got a—*Sanchez*

Anarchic badlands spread without a road—*Hall*

Ancestral pearls so deep—*Aubert*

An ancient story I will tell you anon—*Anonymous-English—Modern English*

And after these, there came the Day, and Night —*Spenser*

And after this quick bash in the dark—*Patten*

And again I see the long pouring headland—*Campbell, Alistair*

And all along the avenues—*Gaver*

And always there are the children—*Giovanni*

And answer made King Arthur, breathing hard —*Tennyson*

And are ye one of Hermitage—*Hardy*

And because we listened—*Knight, John*

And before hell mouth—*Pound*

&/blackwoman be ahead—*Lee, Don L.*

And bless Uncle Jim—*Hodges*

And can the physician make sick men well—*Anonymous-English—Modern English*

And death shall have no dominion—*Thomas, Dylan*

And did those feet in ancient time—*Blake*

And does Charidas sleep there in death, O Stone, beneath thee—*Kallimachos*

And does the heart grow old?—*Cunningham, James Vincent*

And every thing—*Sanchez*

And from this Mount were blown the seed—*Pound*

And God called Moses from the burning bush—*Johnson, James Weldon*

And God stepped out on space—*Johnson, James Weldon*

And Harold stands upon this place of skulls—*Byron*

And here face down beneath the sun—*MacLeish*

And here the sun began once more—*Weiss*

And how will future history—*Murphy*

And I commanded in the very lowest—*Bible and Pseudepigrapha*

And I have come upon this place—*MacLeish*

And I saw the poets—*Kendrick*

And if he's gone away, said she—*Parker*

And if I did, what then—*Gascoigne*

And if, my friend, you'd have it end—*Parker*

And is there care in heaven? and is there love —*Spenser*

And it doesn't help—*Damas*

And like a dying lady, lean and pale—*Shelley*

And love is then no more than a compromise—*Gunn*

And me happiest when I compose poems—*Layton*

And my choice fell—*Browning, Robert*

And now all heav'n/Had gone to wrack—*Milton*

And now methinks I could e'en chide myself—*Tourneur*

And now she said—*Tullos*

And now the green household is dark—*Dickey, James*

And now to God the Father, he ends—*Hardy*

And now, with gleam of half-extinguished thought—*Wordsworth*

And once, in some swamp forest these—*Untermeyer*

And several strengths from drowsiness campaigned—*Brooks, Gwendolyn*

And she pressed her hands against my lips—*Brown, Thomas Edward*

And she was brown—*Jones, Ted*

And, Silence, matter still—*Weiss*

And slowly answered Arthur from the barge—*Tennyson*

And so at last good-bye—*Durrell*

And so deciding everything has been done—*Darr*

And so the days pass—*Sandburg*

And so this Sunday—*Lovelace, Earl*

And stay away from the cellar door—*Ciardi*

And still we wear our uniforms—*Brooks, Gwendolyn*

And suppose the darlings—*Kumin*

And tabu—*Deveaux*

And the angel Israfel, whose heart-strings—*Poe*

And the babies screamed—*Darragh*

And the first grey of morning fill'd the east—*Arnold*

And the heart—*Antoninus*

And the hundreds—*Jones, David*

And the mountain: each day—*Tomlinson*

And the plane bobs—*Ginsberg*

And the rose—*Antoninus*

And then I pressed the shell close to my ear—*Stephens*

And then the minstrel fellow, whom I hated—*Aiken*

And then went down to the ship—*Pound*

And therefore if to love can be desert—*Browning, Elizabeth Barrett*

And therwithal he henge adoun the hede—*Chaucer*

And they were mostly all blk—*Sanchez*

And they're off—*Violi*

And this, from the second or third millennium—*Clark, Gillian*

And this is how you live: a woman, children—*Rich*

And this is the way they ring the bells—*Sexton*

And thou art dead, as young and fair—*Byron*

And thou, who never yet of human wrong—*Byron*

And thus declared that Arab lady—*Yeats*

And to this man who turned the other cheek—*Danner*

And was her daughter like that—*Pound*

And what do I have—*Hodges*

And what is love? Misunderstanding, pain—*Cunningham, James Vincent*

And what is so rare as a day in June—*Lowel, James Russell*

And what of the old bearded—*Sanchez*

And what with the blunders—*Patchen*

And we came that Sunday—*Sanchez*

And we came to the Isle of Flowers—*Tennyso*

And when I—*Bly*

And when on the dark steel came the roads—*Sandburg*

And when she strides—*Inman*

And when the rain had gone away—*Barrows*

And when you have forgotten the bright be clothes on a Wednesday and a Saturday—*Brooks, Gwendolyn*

And where have you been, my Mary—*Howitt*

And where my prison walls squatted down upo their haunches—*Jeffers, Lance*

And will a' not come again—*Shakespeare*

And wilt thou have me fashion into speech—*Browning, Elizabeth Barrett*

And wilt thou leave me thus—*Wyatt, Sir Thom*

And yet because thou overcomest so—*Brownin, Elizabeth Barrett*

And yet not love, not only love—*Aiken*

And yet this great wink of eternity—*Crane, Ha*

And you, Helen, what should I give you—*Thomas, Edward*

And you say—*Kizer*

Andersson tippade fel—*Ferlin*

Andra moi ennepe, Mousa, Polypropon, hos ma polla—*Homer*

Androgynous child—*Piercy*

Andromaque, je pense à vous—*Baudelaire*

L'Âne d'un jardinier se plaignoit au Destin—*, Fontaine*

L'âne gris de ma tante—*Obaldia*

Anfangs wollt ich fast verzagen—*Heine*

L'ange Heurtebise, sur les gradins—*Cocteau*

Un ange ne doit pas parler de qui l'occupe—*C teau*

Ange plein de gaieté, connaissez-vous l'angois —*Baudelaire*

An angel came to me and stood by my bedsi —*Benét, Stephen Vincent*

Ángel de Luz, ardiendo—*Alberti*

An angel robed in spotless white—*Dunbar, Pa Laurence*

Angelehnt an die Efeuwand—*Mörike*

Les anges les anges dans le ciel—*Apollinaire*

Les anges maladroits vous imitent, pigeons—*C teau*

The angry nettle and the mild—*Millay*

L'anguilla, la sirena—*Montale*

Un ânier, son sceptre à la main—*La Fontaine*

Animal crackers, and cocoa to drink—*Morley*

The animal runs, it passes—*Anonymous–Afric languages–Gabon*

Animals are my friends and my kin—*Conklin*

Ann says she trusts me—*Ciardi*

Anna Elise, she jumped with surprise—*Ch dren's Verses and Nursery Rhymes*

Anna-Marie, Love, up is the sun—*Scott, Sir W ter*

Announced by all the trumpets of the sky—*Em son*

The annual search for love began—*Sobiloff*

Anoche cuando dormía—*Machado, Antonio*

non, a figure enters—*Crabbe*
nonymous as cherubs—*Wilbur*
nonymous hand records—*Durrell*
in Anonymous aus Tibris—*Morgenstern*
nother armored animal—scale—*Moore, Marianne*
nother brother gone—*Harper*
nother cove of shade—*Wilbur*
nother emblem there—*Yeats*
nother uncle—*Lifshin*
nque el gajo se parece—*Hernández, José*
ns Haff nun fliegt die Möve—*Storm*
nswer July—*Dickinson, Emily*
nswer to yo/ question—*Sanchez*
n ant on the table-cloth—*Frost, Robert*
nte la mentira—*Vivanco*
nte mí estás, si—*Jiménez*
n antelope of canteloupe—*Hoffman*
ntes que tú me moriré—*Becquer*
nthills climb through corridors—*Alurista*
nti-aircraft seen from a certain distance—*Eberhart*
he antique Indian should be Henry James'—*Brinnin*
ntoinette et moi—*Obaldia*
ntonio Torres Heredia—*Garcia Lorca*
nts keep busy. Makes you dizzy—*Sherman*
nxious Parent, I guess you have just never been around—*Nash*
ny fool can make a rule—*Thoreau*
ny honest housewife could sort them out—*Graves*
ny hound a porcupine nudges—*Nash*
ny impartial study—*Elmslie*
nyone lived in a pretty how town—*Cummings*
n' ape esser vorrei—*Tasso*
peneck Sweeney spreads his knees—*Eliot, Thomas Stearns*
he apes yawn and adore their fleas in the sun —*Hughes, Ted*
pologizing for going to—*Lifshin*
'appel obscur est venu jusqu'à nous par les voix —*Pilon*
pple blossoms look like snow—*Farrar*
n apple-tree, a cedar and an oak—*MacLeish*
he apples falling from the tree—*Burr, Amelia Josephine*
pproaching by the gate—*Brinnin*
prended, flores, de mi—*Hickey Pellizzoni*
près avoir donné son aumône au plus jeune—*Hugo, Victor*
près avoir réfléchi profondément à l'origine des glands—*Péret*
près la bataille—*Hugo, Victor*
près le long silence fumant—*Claudel*
près mille ans et plus de guerre déclarée—*La Fontaine*
près qu'un tems la gresle et le tonnerre—*Labé*
ne âpreté de fougère cerné de cruauté—*Prefontaine*
pril has come—*Beecher*
pril is the cruellest month, breeding—*Eliot, Thomas Stearns*
py Sard(ion)—*Sappho*
quel purpúreo monte, que tenía—*Jiménez*
quel valeroso Moro—*Anonymous-Spanish*

Aquella pobre niña que aún no tenía senos—*Casona*
Aquí es el canto de agua ya escondida—*Ribera Chevremont*
Aquí, junto al mar latino—*Darío*
Aquí me pongo a cantar—*Hernández, José*
Aqui o mar é una montanha—*Melo Neto*
Aquí tambien entre, en esta casa—*Aleixandre*
Aquí tenéis, en canto y alma, al hombre—*Otero*
Arbol: yo soy tu flauta—*Muñoz Marín*
Arbolé, arbolé—*Garcia Lorca*
Un arbre sans une branche—*Queneau*
Arcturus is his other name—*Dickinson, Emily*
Are the living so much use—*MacDiarmid*
Are the sands of your young son's values—*Marshall, Helen Lowrie*
Are these millions of white velvety petalled bells —*Danner*
Are they blind, the lords of Gaza—*Graves*
Are you happy? It's the only way to be, kid—*Sandburg*
Are you not the light—*Kgositsile*
Are you sad to think how often—*Tessimond*
Åren skymma bort varanda—*Martinson*
Arena dust rusted by four bulls' blood—*Plath*
Ares at last has quit the field—*Auden*
Ariel to Miranda: take—*Shelley*
Arillo animaluccio cantatore—*Di Giacomo*
Arithmetic is where numbers fly like pigeons in and out of your head—*Sandburg*
Arjuna uvàca: sthitaprajñasya kā bhāsā samādhisthasya keśava—*Anonymous-Sanskrit*
Arm am Beutel, krank am Herzen—*Goethe*
Arm in arm und Kron' an Krone steht der Eichenwald verschlungen—*Keller, Gottfried*
Arma virumque cano, Troiae qui primus ab oris —*Virgil*
An armada of thirty whales—*Hoffman*
Arm'd year—year of struggle—*Whitman*
Armed with hammers, we move along the cliff —*Porter, Peter*
Armselig Volk, was häufet ihr Schätze an—*Schröder*
Around, above my bed, the pitch-dark fly—*Nemerov*
Around me the images of thirty years—*Yeats*
Around 1968 this woman in Queens—*Winch*
Los arqueros oscuros—*Garcia Lorca*
Arranged by two's as peaches are—*Moore, Marianne*
Arrantzaleak, gaur kanturako—*Eizmendi*
Arriba canta el pajaro—*Jiménez*
Arriba, trabajadores—*Alberti*
The Arrol-Johnston spun him down to Slough—*Betjeman*
Arrowheads are instinctive—*Hannan*
Art thou a Statist in the van—*Wordsworth*
Art thou poore, yet hast thou golden slumbers —*Dekker*
Art thou the first of creatures that Leviathan—*MacPherson*
Artichoke spaghetti—*Skratz*
As a cat, caught by the door opening—*Reid*
As a dare-gale skylark scanted in a dull cage—*Hopkins*
As a decrepit father takes delight—*Shakespeare*

As a fond mother, when the day is o'er—*Longfellow*

As a pillar of gnats, moving up and down—*Eberhart*

As a queen sits down, knowing that a chair will be there—*Wilbur*

As a twig trembles, which a bird—*Lowell, James Russell*

As an unperfect actor on the stage—*Shakespeare*

As beautiful as the hands—*Patchen*

As by the dead we love to sit—*Dickinson, Emily*

As Chloe came into the room t'other day—*Prior*

As daily now man conquers space—*Marshall, Helen Lowrie*

As fast as thou shalt wane, so fast thou grow'st —*Shakespeare*

As freedom is a breakfastfood—*Cummings*

As from the house your mother sees—*Stevenson*

As frothing wounds of roses—*Patchen*

As he moves the mine detector a few inches—*Dickey, James*

As I came to the edge of the wood—*Frost, Robert*

As I drive to the junction of lane and highway —*Hardy*

As I in hoary winter's night—*Southwell*

As I lay asleep in Italy—*Shelley*

As I lay in my love's low bed—*Sitwell, Edith*

As I must have honey—*Cullen*

As I sat down by Saddle Stream—*Millay*

As I sat in the cafe I said to myself—*Clough*

As I sit in despair—*Matiabe*

As I walked out in the streets of Laredo—*Anonymous-English—Modern English*

As I walked out one evening—*Auden*

As I walked out that sultry night—*Graves*

As I walked through my garden—*Conkling*

As I wandered on the beach—*Kizer*

As I was crossing Chatham Bar—*White*

As I was dreaming between hills—*Merwin*

As I was going down the stair—*Anonymous-English—Modern English*

As I was reading the book of nature—*Eberhart*

As I was riding through New England—*Eberhart*

As I was walking all alane—*Anonymous-English —Modern English*

As I was walking all alone—*Children's Verses and Nursery Rhymes*

As I went down through Dublin city—*Colum*

As I went out a crow—*Frost, Robert*

As if it were—*Levertov*

As if it were some noble thing—*Hughes, Langston*

As if pictured in a children's book—*Gregor*

As imperceptibly as grief—*Dickinson, Emily*

As it fell upon a day—*Barnfield*

As kingfishers catch fire, dragonflies draw flame —*Hopkins*

As one who bears beneath his neighbor's roof—*Hillyer*

As Rochefoucault his Maxims drew—*Swift*

As-Salaam-Alaikum my black princes—*Sanchez*

As silent as a mirror is believed—*Crane, Hart*

As some day it may happen that a victim must be found—*Gilbert, Sir William Schwenck*

As soon as the fire burns red and low—*Bacon*

As surely as I hold your hand in mine—*Cullen*

As the cat climbed over the top—*Williams, William Carlos*

As the fireman said—*Sexton*

As the gods began one world, and man another —*Plath*

As the immense dew of Florida—*Stevens, Wallace*

As the plump squirrel scampers—*Wright, James*

As the silly shepherds—*Weiss*

As the sun rose—*Conkling*

As the sweet sweat of roses in a still—*Donne*

As the team's head brass flashed out on the turn —*Thomas, Edward*

As the through-train of words with white-hot whistle—*Rodgers*

As the word came to prophets of old—*Walker*

As those we love decay, we die in part—*Thomson*

As through the wild green hills of Wyre—*Housman*

As time will turn—*Patchen*

As to democracy, fellow citizens—*Masters, Edgar Lee*

As toilsome I wander'd Virginia's woods to the music of rustling leaves—*Whitman*

As unto the bow the cord is—*Longfellow*

As virtuous men passe mildly away—*Donne*

As we are so wonderfully done with each other —*Patchen*

As we get older we do not get any younger—*Reed, Henry*

As what goes out—*Antoninus*

As you are (said Death)—*Francis*

As you came from the holy land—*Raleigh*

As Zeus sent Hermes—*Olson*

L'asfalto negro cala dentro un'aria—*Marin*

Ashes, Lord, but warm still—*Aubert*

Así es mi vida—*Camino Galicia*

Así, Sire, en el aire de la Francia nos llega—*Darío*

Ask me no more where Jove bestows—*Carew*

Ask neither my name nor my country, passers-by —*Ptolemaios the Astronomer*

Ask you what provocation I have had?—*Pope, Alexander*

Asking what, asking what?—all a boy's afternoon —*Warren*

Asleep in the night I dreamed that you owed me a letter—*Scott, Winfield Townley*

Asleep on a mat—*McCarthy, Agnes*

Asleep the spider bites—*Mariah*

Asomaba a sus ojos una lagrima—*Becquer*

The assassin dealt America—*Murphy*

The assassination of the President—*Whitbread*

Assez vu. La vision s'est rencontrée à tous les airs —*Rimbaud*

Assis à l'ombre sur son seuil—*Perse*

Assise, la fileuse au bleu de la croisée—*Valéry*

The Assyrian came down like the wolf on the fold —*Byron*

Asteras eisathreis aster emos—*Plato*

Astern—schwälende Tage—*Benn*

Un astrologue un jour se laissa choir—*La Fontaine*

Asynnetemi ton anemon stasin—*Alcaeus*

At Beverly Farms a portly uncomfortable boulder —*Lowell, Robert*

At de feet o' Jesus—*Hughes, Langston*

At Dirty Dick's and Sloppy Joe's—*Auden*

At Eutaw Springs the valiant died—*Freneau*
At evening when the lamp is lit—*Stevenson*
At fifteen, the expert—*Treitel*
At first I suspected something—*Masters, Edgar Lee*
At first I thought a pest—*Moore, Marianne*
At first I was given centuries—*Atwood*
At five in the morning there were grey voices —*MacNeice*
At Flores in the Azores Sir Richard Grenville lay —*Tennyson*
At her charmed height of summer—*Day Lewis*
At last from the third mile—*Blackmur*
At last I put off love—*Hardy*
At last with four—*Durrell*
At least to pray is left, is left—*Dickinson, Emily*
At Memphis the horn'd bull told our friend—*Diogenes Laertius*
At midnight in the month of moon—*Poe*
At midnight in the museum hall—*Nash*
At midsummer before dawn—*Merwin*
At my Aunt Vandla's—*Olson*
At night, by the fire—*Stevens, Wallace*
At night, I do not know who I am—*Abse*
At night the factories struggle awake—*Bishop, Elizabeth*
At nine years a sickly boy lay down—*Tate, Allen*
At ninety-two he weakened a bit—*Gill*
At noon they talk of evening and at evening— *Francis*
At parties I want to get even—*De Frees*
At regina dolos (quis fallere possit amantem?)— *Virgil*
At seven o'clock—*Cowley, Malcolm*
At sixty I, Dionysios of Tarso, lie here—*Anonymous–Greek*
At sunset only to his true love—*Graves*
At 10 AM the young housewife moves about in negligee—*Williams, William Carlos*
At the age of empty spaces—*Pietri*
At the bend—*Andrews*
At the corner—*Sandburg*
At the corner of Wood Street, when daylight appears—*Wordsworth*
At the end of summer—*Kaufman, Shirley*
At the end of Tarriers' Lane, which—*Graves*
At the end of the garden walk—*Layton*
At the end of the row—*Frost, Robert*
At the fore of the year, and on Candlemas Day —*Colum*
At the mid-hour of night—*Moore, Thomas*
At the point X—*Jong*
At the round earth's imagin'd corners, blow— *Donne*
At the very beginning of an important symphony —*Patten*
At the voice of the mother on a warm hearth— *Jones, Glyn*
At the wood's mouth—*Roethke*
At Timon's villa let us pass a day—*Pope, Alexander*
At Trumpyngtoun, nat fer fro Cantebrigge— *Chaucer*
At two o'clock in the morning, if you open your window and listen—*Kipling*
At Vallauris and Vence, Picasso and Matisse— *Francis*

At Viscount Nelson's lavish funeral—*Graves*
At Woodlawn I heard the dead cry—*Roethke*
At work his arms wave like a windmill—*Redgrove*
Atemlos überqueren die Vögel—*Heissenbüttel*
Atención pido al silencio—*Hernández, José*
Atme, Seele, erhöhter—*Bergengruen*
Att förneka—*Lundkvist*
Åtta hundra julenätter—*Heidenstam*
L'attente d'un beau jour—*Henault*
Attention, attention—*Gaver*
Atzined ven mir schtellen die toita denkmall— *Sutzkever*
Au coin de la rue des Ursins—*Fombeure*
Au-dessus des étangs, au-dessus des vallées— *Baudelaire*
Au fond d'un antre sauvage—*La Fontaine*
Au gibet noir, manchot aimable—*Rimbaud*
Au nom du front parfait profond—*Éluard*
Au premier mot limpide—*Éluard*
Au terme d'un long voyage—*Éluard*
Aube, fille des larmes, rétablis—*Bonnefoy*
L'aube point avant que passent—*Fombeure*
Auch das Schöne muss sterben—*Schiller*
Auch von des höchsten Gebirgs beeisten zackingen Gipfeln—*Goethe*
Auf Blut und Leichen, Schutt und Qualen—*Liliencron*
Auf dem Fliegenplaneten—*Morgenstern*
Auf die Erde voller kaltem Wind—*Brecht*
Auf einem Pferdemarkt—vielleicht zu Haymarket—*Schiller*
Auf einem Wandkalenderblatt—*Morgenstern*
Auf Flügeln des Gesanges—*Heine*
Auf geheimem Waldespfade—*Lenau*
Auf meiner Herzliebsten Äugelein—*Heine*
Auf seinen Nasen schreitet—*Morgenstern*
Aufsteigt der Strahl und fallend Giesst—*Meyer, Conrad Ferdinand*
Augen, meine lieben Fensterlein—*Keller, Gottfried*
August 'twas, the twenty-fifth—*Terry*
Aujourd'hui l'espace est splendide—*Baudelaire*
L'Aulbe estaingnoit Estoilles a foison—*Scève*
Aunt Sue has a head full of stories—*Hughes, Langston*
Auprès de toi j'ai retrouvé mon nom—*Diop*
Aureli, pater esuritionum—*Catullus*
L'Aurore sur le front du jour—*Viau*
Aus alten Märchen winkt es—*Heine*
Aus den Gärten komm ich zu euch, ihr Söhne des Berges—*Hölderlin*
Aus der Jugendzeit, aus der Jugendzeit—*Rückert*
Aus meinen grossen Schmerzen—*Heine*
Aus meinen Tränen spriessen—*Heine*
Ausgesetzt auf den Bergen des Herzens. Siehe, wie klein dort—*Rilke*
Aussitôt que l'idée du Déluge se fut rassise—*Rimbaud*
Autar ego dikha pantas euknemidas etairous— *Homer*
Autar epei tarpesan edetyos ede potetos—*Homer*
Autar Odyssea megaletora fo eni foiko—*Homer*
Autrefois le rat de ville—*La Fontaine*
Autumn and leaves swirl at the roadside—*Henri*
Autumn has all the summer's fruitful treasure— *Nashe*
Autumn is only winter in disguise—*Bynner*

Autumn mists, cold dreams are filling—*Heine*
Autumn was adjectival, I recall—*Reid*
Avant d'entrer dans ma cellule—*Apollinaire*
L'avarice perd tout en voulant tout gagner—*La Fontaine*
Avec d'autres /des alentours—*Damas*
Avec ton parapluie bleu et tes brebis sales—*Jammes*
Avenge, O Lord, thy slaughtered saints whose bones—*Milton*
Avete intenso cos'ha ddeto er frate—*Belli*
Avite Maie liggiuto quacche cosa—*Di Giacomo*
Avoid dialogue, Somatica. What you are—*Ciardi*
Avoir ne puis trop grant merencolie—*Deschamps*
Avril déjà—*Dufrêne*
Avril, l'honneur et des bois—*Belleau*
Avtoportret moi, retorta neona—*Voznezensky*
Away beyond the Jarboe house—*Roberts*
Away, melancholy—*Smith, Stevie*
Away! the moor is dark beneath the moon—*Shelley*
The awful shadow of some unseen power—*Shelley*
The ax rings in the wood—*Lewis, Janet*
The ax that threatens—*Gregor*
An axe angles—*Wilbur*
Ay, cuan linda que eres, Alba—*Anonymous-Spanish*
¡Ay! Cuantas cosas perdidas—*Salinas, Pedro*
Ay, misero de mi! Ay, infelice—*Calderón de la Barca*
Ay misero de mi vida—*Calderón de la Barca*
¡Ay! Qué relumbres y olores—*Jiménez*
Ay, qué trabajo me cuesta—*Garcia Lorca*
Ay, tear her tattered ensign down—*Holmes, Oliver Wendell*
¡Ay! Un Galan de esta villa—*Anonymous-Spanish*
Ay, workman, make me a dream—*Crane, Stephen*
Ayant après long désir—*Du Bellay*
Ayee! Ai! This is heavy earth on our shoulders—*MacLeish*
Ayer soñé que veía—*Machado, Antonio*
Ayer tarde yo cantaba—*Garcia Lorca*

B-rr, jag är som en inneboende—*Ferlin*
Ba ywe chyou gau feng nu hau—*Du Fu*
Baa, baa, black sheep—*Children's Verses and Nursery Rhymes*
Babette she was a fisher gal—*Gilbert, Sir William Schwenck*
Baby, last night when you called me—*Fabio, Sarah Webster*
The baby picked from an ash barrel—*Sandburg*
Back and forth, back and forth—*Lowell, Robert*
Back and forth, back and forth, to and from the church—*Masters, Edgar Lee*
Back for his holiday from across the water—*MacNeice*
Back Home again Blackback—*Fabio, Sarah Webster*
Back in back of the back country—*Simmons, Judy*
Back in chi—*Lee, Don L.*
Back out of all this now too much for us—*Frost, Robert*
Back to back—*Khalil*

Back to the flower-town, side by side—*Swinburne*
The back wings—*Williams, William Carlos*
Backroad leafmold stone walls chipmunk—*Francis*
Bajo el agua—*Garcia Lorca*
Bajo el naranjo lava—*Garcia Lorca*
Bajo la higuera, aún—*Jiménez*
Bajo la sola estrella te he encontrado—*Ridruejo*
Bajo tu casta sombra, encina vieja—*Garcia Lorca*
Bald-bare, bone-bare, and ivory yellow—*Scott, Winfield Townley*
Bald heads forgetful of their sins—*Yeats*
Balkan Sobranies in a wooden box—*Betjeman*
A ball will bounce, but less and less—*Wilbur*
Bananas ripe and green—*McKay*
Bang bang bang—*Heath-Stubbs*
Bani! Bani! Dveri-khlop—*Voznezensky*
The bards falter in shame, their running verse—*Graves*
Bare alder and twiggy locust on our hill—*Hollander*
Bare and bow your Christian heads—*Delegall*
Bare-handed, I hand the combs—*Plath*
Barely a twelvemonth after—*Muir*
Barque of phosphor—*Stevens, Wallace*
Bartholomew is very sweet—*Gale*
Bastioned with light, dear body and brave heart—*O'Gorman*
Batelier de la Loire—*Fombeure*
Bats at play taunt us with 'guess how many'—*Graves*
Batter my heart, three-person'd God—*Donne*
Bau nur auf Weltgunst recht—*Eichendorff*
Un Baudet chargé de reliques—*La Fontaine*
Der Bauer sprach zu seinem Jungen—*Busch*
Der Baum / grösser als die Nacht—*Bobrowski*
Bbella cratura! E cche ccos'è?—*Belli*
Bbmmm—*Lurie*
Be absolute for death—*Shakespeare*
Be calm, collected, easy—*Sandburg*
Be careful not to cross the gander—*Nash*
Be kind and tender to the Frog—*Belloc*
Be kind to your self, it is only one and perishable—*Ginsberg*
Be kind unto these three, Oh King—*Stephens*
Be Music, Night—*Patchen*
Be natural—*Creeley*
Be near me when the light is low—*Tennyson*
Be patient, solemn nose—*Auden*
Be slow. Fold the daily news—*Knight, Etheridge*
Be slowly lifted up, thou long black arm—*Owen, Wilfred*
Be still; the arms you bear are brittle—*Housman*
Be strange if it is necessary—*Darr*
Be wise as thou art cruel; do not press—*Shakespeare*
Beak gunning my entrails—*Starbuck*
A bear, however hard he tries—*Milne*
Beards of water some of them have—*Swenson*
Beat! beat! drums!—blow! bugles! blow!—*Whitman*
Beating asphalt into highway potholes—*Snyder*
Un beau matin—*Rimbaud*
Beau monde des masures—*Éluard*
Beauté, mon beau soucy, de qui l'âme incertaine—*Malherbe*
Beautiful always the littoral line—*Derwood*

Beautiful as a tiered cloud—*Fletcher, John Gould*

Beautiful as the flying legend of some leopard —*Ransom*

The beautiful cashier's white face—*Wright, James*

Beautiful goldfish—*Gilbert, Celia*

Beautiful must be the mountains whence ye come —*Bridges*

Beautiful Parsi woman in your pale silk veil—*Millay*

Beautiful soup, so rich and green—*Carroll*

Beautifully Janet slept—*Ransom*

Beauty has drifted—*Dowling*

Beauty in trouble flees to the good angel—*Graves*

The beauty of Miss Beatty—*Reaney*

Beauty, thou wild fantastick Ape—*Cowley, Abraham*

Beauty's end is in sight—*Day Lewis*

Bebo el agua clara y limpia del arroyo—*Ibarbourou*

Becalmed in old Back Bay's dead water sulk—*Starbuck*

Because all desecration in this life—*Gregor*

Because I am mad about women—*Yeats*

Because I breathe not love to Everyone—*Sidney*

Because I could not stop for death—*Dickinson, Emily*

Because I do not hope to turn again—*Eliot, Thomas Stearns*

Because I had loved so deeply—*Dunbar, Paul Laurence*

Because in Viet Nam the vision of a Burning Babe —*Levertov*

Because of sunlight—*Raper*

Because she loved her husband—*Jong*

Because she wants to touch him—*Jong*

Because, straying through the wine garden—*Patchen*

Because the snow is deep—*Patchen*

Because there was a man somewhere in a candy-stripe silk shirt—*Hayden*

Because they may twist your body—*Shpunt*

Because thou hast the power—*Browning, Elizabeth Barrett*

Because you are standing—*Cattonar*

Because you take life in your stride—*Cummings*

Beco que cantei num dístico—*Bandeira*

Bedecke deinen Himmel, Zeus, mit Wolkendunst —*Goethe*

The bee, he has white honey—*Benét, Stephen Vincent*

Bee, tell me, whence do you come?—*Stephens*

Bees and a honeycomb in the dried head of a horse—*Sandburg*

Bees and lilies there were—*Roethke*

The bee's fixed hexagon—*Bogan*

Beeston, the place, near Nottingham—*Scannell*

Before I die (said the self-riddling stone-cutter) —*Ciardi*

Before I got my eye put out—*Dickinson, Emily*

Before I knocked and flesh let enter—*Thomas, Dylan*

Before I melt—*De la Mare*

Before I went into the Blackboard Jungle—*Johnston, Ellen Turlington*

Before man came to blow it right—*Frost, Robert*

Before playtime let us consider—*Patten*

Before remembrance we moved here, withheld —*Adams*

Before she has her floor swept—*Millay*

Before the beginning of years—*Swinburne*

Before the dawning of the death-day—*Sitwell, Osbert*

Before the town has lost its wits—*Henley, William Ernest*

Before, though, Paris was wonderful—*MacLeish*

The beggar's bowl—*Silkin*

Begin by parting your hair.—*Sukenick*

Begotten by the meeting of rock with rock— *Aiken*

Behind him lay the gray Azores—*Miller, Joaquin*

Behind the hills, from the city of an Etruscan gateway—*Davie*

Behind the wild bird's throat—*Wheelock*

Behold her, single in the field—*Wordsworth*

Behold, my name stinks—*Anonymous-Egyptian*

Behold that great Plotinus swim—*Yeats*

Behold the apple's rounded worlds—*Lee, Laurie*

Behold the duck—*Nash*

Behold the fatal Day arrive—*Swift*

Behold the hippopotamus—*Nash*

Beholding element, in whose pure eye—*Wilbur*

Bei stiller Nacht zur ersten Wacht.—*Spee von Langenfeld*

Being fat until—*Lifshin*

Being ourselves is less than love—*Marshall, Lenore G.*

Being without quality—*Gunn*

Being your slave, what should I do but tend— *Shakespeare*

Bekränzt mit Laub den lieben vollen Becher— *Claudius*

Beleaguered by passions, as by thunder—*Connor*

Believe me if all those endearing young charms —*Moore, Thomas*

Believe me, knot of gristle, I bleed like a tree— *Roethke*

Belinda lived in a little white house—*Nash*

The bell-rope that gathers God at dawn—*Crane, Hart*

Une belle Minerve est l'enfant de ma tête—*Apollinaire*

Un bello niño de junco—*Garcia Lorca*

Bells are booming down the bohreens—*Betjeman*

The bells of waiting Advent ring—*Betjeman*

A beloved duck gets cooked—*Edson*

Beloved, my Beloved, when I think—*Browning, Elizabeth Barrett*

Beloved, thou hast brought me many flowers— *Browning, Elizabeth Barrett*

Below me the city was in flames—*Layton*

Ben venga Maggio—*Poliziano*

Bend back thy bow, O Archer, till the string— *Smith, A. J. M.*

Bendita mi lengua sea—*Mistral*

Bendita seas andando—*Mistral*

Beneath a Myrtle shade—*Dryden*

Beneath me (says the stone) lies the white dog from Melita—*Tymnes*

Beneath this place in paper case a pretty dormouse lies—*Anonymous-English—Modern English*

Beneath this yew the shadow of a shade—*Anonymous-English—Modern English*

Benigno alumbra el sol—*Milanés*

Benilde, esta noche tienes—*Martinez Alonso*

Bénite est l'infertile plage—*Corbière*

Bent double, like old beggars under sacks—*Owen, Wilfred*

Bergère née en Lorraine—*Gourmont*

Berryman and Baxter—*Milne*

Besa al aura que gime blandamente—*Becquer*

Beshrew that heart that makes my heart to groan —*Shakespeare*

Beside me she sat, hand hooked and hovering —*Weiss*

Beside that milestone where the level sun—*Whittier*

Beside this lake—*Atwood*

Beside yon straggling fence—*Goldsmith*

Besides the autumn poets sing—*Dickinson, Emily*

Bessern soll ich mich—*Wedekind*

Best and brightest, come away—*Shelley*

The best do not always make it—*Greenwald*

Better to be the rock above the river—*Eberhart*

Betty Botter bought some butter—*Children's Verses and Nursery Rhymes*

Betty took—*Reed, Ishmael*

Between the dark and the daylight—*Longfellow*

Between the moonlight and the fire—*Lang*

Between the snow and summer—*Aiken*

Between us on our wide bed—*Hacker*

Betwixt mine eye and heart a league is took—*Shakespeare*

Bevars vilket fläng både ute och innan—*Lenngren*

Bevor er in die blaue Flut gesunken—*Eichendorff*

Beware in the beginning!—*Dowling*

Beware of the man—*Jong*

Bewildered with the broken tongue—*MacLeish*

Beyond all this the wish to be alone—*Larkin*

Beyond O'Ryan's bar in the dirty river—*Scott, Winfield Townley*

Beyond that stand of firs—*Levine*

Beyond the hour we counted rain that fell—*Bogan*

Beyond the narrows of the Inner Hebrides—*Jeffers, Robinson*

Beyond the reach of reason—*Marshall, Helen Lowrie*

Beyond the seasons of the sun the shiftless waters —*Dowling*

Beyond this room daylight is brief—*Furse*

Biet mot solen den sköna—*Martinson*

Big Bad—*Brown, Otis*

The big blue-jean, the summer-bored boy next door—*Holmes, John*

Big icy fists of sullen snow—*Emanuel*

Big Jess fired on the Alabama Central—*Brown, Sterling A.*

A big old family Bible—*Souster*

Big old houses—*Braxton*

The bigger the box the more it holds—*Sandburg*

The bigness of cannon—*Cummings*

Bilbea, I was in Babylon—*Sandburg*

Bilder, die man aufhängt umgekehrt—*Morgenstern*

Bili koyta—*Mayakovsky*

Bill the pillows plump as mushrooms—*Whistler*

Bill's timely Amoco—*Mason*

Bilo tak-legendi govoryat—*Svetlov*

Il bimbo d'afa che la mosca mera—*Gatto*

A Bingobird once nestled her nest—*Field, Eugene*

Binker—what I call him—*Milne*

Bīowulf mathelode—hē ofer benne spraec—*Anonymous–English—Old English*

La Bique, allant remplir sa traînante mamelle-*La Fontaine*

The birch begins to crack its outer sheath—*Fros Robert*

Birch tree, you remind me—*Simpson*

The birches slash at the shadow—*Abbe*

A bird came down the walk—*Dickinson, Emil*

Bird of the bitter bright grey golden morn-*Swinburne*

Bird sighs for the air—*Yeats*

Bird who stoops on my sleep—*Williams, Hugo*

A bird with a big eye—*Wheelock*

A birdie with a yellow bill—*Stevenson*

A birdless heaven—*Joyce*

Birds all the sunny day—*Stevenson*

Birds are of passage now—*Adams*

Bischof, ich kann fliegen—*Brecht*

A Biscuit, a basket—*Lee, Dennis*

Bist du nicht mehr dem Sänger hold?—*Jacobi*

Bist nicht fagangen—Dein pustkeit is feil—*Sut. kever*

A bit of talcum—*Nash*

A bitter King in anger to be gone—*Smith, A. J. M*

A bitterness ascends from the Gulf—*Bly*

The black artist—*Baraka*

Black at the roots—*Bahati*

The black bull bellowed—*Plath*

The black cat yawns—*Miller, Mary Britton*

Black clouds on a black mountain—*Cattonar*

Black does not mean—*Eckels*

Black drinks the sun and draws all colours to —*Graves*

The black face has greater weight—*Jeffers, Lan*

Black is not—*Lee, Don L.*

Black is the first nail I ever stepped on—*Emanu.*

Black man—*Harper*

The black men hang their shadows—*William Hugo*

A black oriented love poem—*Robinson, Wand*

Black village of gravestones—*Hughes, Ted*

Black woman—*Marvin X*

Black'on frowns east on Maidou—*Hardy*

Blackwoman: / is an—*Lee, Don L.*

Le Blanc a tué mon père—*Diop*

The blanched melted snows—*Silkin*

The blanched tree livid behind—*Davie*

Blancos senos, redondos y desnudos, que al pas —*Valencia*

Blanda invasión de alas es la noche—*Paz*

A blast of wind, a momentary breath—*Barne Barnabe*

Blasted with sighs, and surrounded with tear —*Donne*

Die Blätter fallen, fallen wie von weit—*Rilke*

Bleib noch mein lieb Gespiel—*Anonymous–Ge man*

Bless this little chapel, Lord—*Marshall, Hele Lowrie*

Blessed are the dehumanized—*Kgositsile*

The blessed damozel leaned out—*Rossetti, Dante Gabriel*

Blessed were those Bowers who saw all this—*Jones, Glyn*

Blessings on thee, little man—*Whittier*

Blest pair of Sirens, pledges of heaven's joy—*Milton*

Blind as stone—*Klappert*

A blind man. I can stare at him—*Levertov*

The blindman placed—*Swenson*

Blk people—*Sanchez*

Blocus sentimental!—*Laforgue*

Blödem Volke unverständlich—*Morgenstern*

The blood began to waste into the clouds—*Gunn*

Blood flows and mingles—*Arnez*

The bloodhounds look like sad old judges—*Patchen*

Bloodstains, how to remove from cotton—*Francis*

A bloody and a sudden end—*Yeats*

A bloody eggyolk—*Swenson*

Blow, blow thou winter wind—*Shakespeare*

Blow, man blow—*Anderson, Charles*

Blow out, you bugles, over the rich Dead—*Brooke*

The blowing wind I let it blow—*Francis*

Blue black—*Troupe*

Blue-sleigh that fifty winters gone—*Scott, Winfield Townley*

Blues ain't culture—*Sanchez*

Blues coming in all over me—*Jimason*

Blüht nicht zu früh—*Benn*

Blush as you stroke the curves—*Graves*

A blythe and bonny country lasse—*Lodge*

A boat, beneath a sunny sky—*Carroll*

The boat that took my love away—*Smith, Stevie*

Bobby Shafto's gone to sea—*Children's Verses and Nursery Rhymes*

La bocca sollevò dal fiero pasto—*Dante Alighieri*

Body. Going to wax form—*Rasul*

Body shop—*Brown, Otis*

A boggy wood as full of springs as trees—*Redgrove*

Bohlin—*Olson*

Bold Nat Turner by the blood of God—*Walker*

Bolt and bar the shutter—*Yeats*

Bombs of Birmingham that broke those small Black bodies—*Fabio, Sarah Webster*

Bon jour, Marseille, am Mittelmeer—*Mehring*

Bond Street, I said—*Nicholson*

Bonnes gens, je puis tesmoignier—*Anonymous–French*

The bonsai tree—*Piercy*

Book of Ancestors: these brutal—*Atwood*

The Book of the Marvels of the World—*Birney*

Books collide—*Howes*

A Booster Club person—*Johnston, Ellen Turlington*

Boot, saddle, to horse, and away—*Browning, Robert*

Booth led boldly—*Lindsay, Vachel*

Booz s'était couché de fatigue—*Hugo, Victor*

Der borde väl vara underbart—*Edfelt*

Bordón/ En la torre—*Garcia Lorca*

Borée et le Soleil virent un voyageur—*La Fontaine*

Born down in Georgia—*Hodges*

Born of the sorrowful of heart—*Cullen*

Borning room hot—*Lifshin*

Boshaft wie goldene Rede beginnt diese Nacht—*Celan*

Boston. Lord God, the ocean never to windward—*Starbuck*

Both eaching come ghostlike—*Cummings*

Both eyes, (the loss of)—*Pound*

Both for the country and for the man—*Masters, Edgar Lee*

Bottomed by tugging combs of water—*Rodgers*

Bound, blinded, stymied—*Piercy*

Bound to my heart as Ixion to the wheel—*Sitwell, Edith*

Bow down my soul in worship—*McKay*

Bowed by the weight of centuries—*Markham*

Bowed down she turned but halfway up the stairs—*Scott, Winfield Townley*

The bowers whereat, in dreams I see—*Poe*

Bowing he asks her the favor—*Hall*

The bows glided down, and the coast—*Thomas, Dylan*

A boy child buried the bird—*Sobiloff*

The boy having fished alone—*Cowley, Malcolm*

A boy is as old as the stars—*Levine*

Boyaux et rumeur du canon—*Apollinaire*

Boys, I don't promise you—*Clifton*

Boys in sporadic but tenacious droves—*Eberhart*

A brackish reach of shoal off Madaket—*Lowell, Robert*

A braeta hussick kine ane ora zol im nit shotten—*Lutzky*

Brain smashed, skull splintered—*Thomas, Jill*

Brave blanket covering me—*Williams, Hugo*

Brave flowers, that I could gallant it—*King*

The bravest names for fire and flames—*Gilbert, Sir William Schwenck*

Brawny smithy at the forge—*Goldstein*

Brazil is in the mind, enormous, dim—*Dowling*

Break, break, break / On thy cold gray stones, O sea—*Tennyson*

The breaking waves dashed high—*Hemans*

Breathe honey looking south, the mind land over—*Porter, Peter*

Breathes there a man with soul so dead—*Scott, Sir Walter*

Breathing the breath—*Major*

Breathless, we flung us on the windy hill—*Brooke*

Breve pertugio dentro dalla muda—*Dante Alighieri*

Brian O'Linn was a gentleman born—*Children's Verses and Nursery Rhymes*

The bride is upside down—*Evans, Liz*

Briefly, in ten years what happened—*Bell*

Bright clasp of her whole hand around my finger—*Spender*

A bright jeweled beetle like a clump of fire—*Hollander*

Bright star! Would I were steadfast as Thou art—*Keats*

Bright town, tossed by waves of time—*Watkins*

Bright vocabularies are transient as rainbows—*Sandburg*

The brightest and best of the sons of the morning—*Heber*

Bring me some news—*Braxton*

Bring me the sunset in a cup—*Dickinson, Emily*

Bring me to the blasted oak—*Yeats*

Bring me wine, but wine which never grew—*Emerson*

Bring the comb and play upon it—*Stevenson*

Bringing their frozen swords—*Hughes, Ted*

Brittle beauty, that Nature made so frail—*Surrey*

The broad-backed hippopotamus—*Eliot, Thomas Stearns*

... brocen wurde/Het tha hyssa hwone—*Anonymous-English—Old English*

The broken pillar of the wings—*Jeffers, Robinson*

Bror Andersson gåi framåt med—*Ferlin*

Brother as-Salaam-Alaikum—*Sanchez*

Brother is such a solid word—*Darr*

Brother Man the Rasta man—*Brathwaite*

Brothers—*Hodges*

Brothers—*Lee, Don L.*

Brown and furry—*Rossetti, Christina*

A brown piano in diamond—*Ginsberg*

Brüder lasst uns lustig sein—*Günther*

Brumans est mors—*Anonymous-German*

Bruño los recios nubarrones pardos—*Chamizo*

Brusco olor del azufre, repentino—*Pacheco*

Buenas tardes, Moguer mío—*Jiménez*

Bueno que está contigo, Padre, Hermano—*Tejada*

Buffalo Bill's/ defunct—*Cummings*

The buffaloes are gone—*Sandburg*

Build me straight, O worthy Master—*Longfellow*

Bulkeley, Hunt, Willard, Hosmer, Meriam, Flint—*Emerson*

The bulldozers come, they rip—*Piercy*

The bullet shot me and I lay—*Jennings*

Bulletin boards are a must—*Johnston, Ellen Turlington*

Bullets blot out the Life-Time smile—*Fraser, G. S.*

Bulls by day—*Francis*

A bunch of the boys were whooping it up—*Service*

Die bunten Bilder—*Trakl*

Buona sera contessa—*Palazzeschi*

The burly fading one beside the engine—*Hayden*

Burn stilly, thou—*De la Mare*

Burning with heat and cold—*Zaturenska*

Burya mgloyu nebo kroyet—*Pushkin*

Buscad, buscadlos—*Alberti*

The buses headed for Scranton travel in pairs—*Nash*

Busie old foole, unruly sunne—*Donne*

The bustle in a house the morning after death—*Dickinson, Emily*

Bustopher Jones is not skin and bones—*Eliot, Thomas Stearns*

Busy, curious, thirsty fly—*Oldys*

Busybody, nosey-parker—*Connor*

But also dying—*Cummings*

But be contented: when that fell arrest—*Shakespeare*

But can see better there—*Brooks, Gwendolyn*

But do not let us quarrel—*Browning, Robert*

But do thy worst to steal thyself away—*Shakespeare*

But for a brief—*Wilbur*

But from these bitter truths I must return—*Wordsworth*

But gently clank?—*Smith, A. J. M.*

But I returned to find Jack—*Brathwaite*

But it is not Black, they will tell you—*Enright*

But mark what I agreed thee now—*Milton*

But Meliboee (so hight that good old man)—*Spenser*

But most by numbers judge a poet's song—*Pope, Alexander*

But now at last the sacred influence—*Milton*

But only thee in all God's universe—*Browning, Elizabeth Barrett*

But that was nothing to what things came out—*Graves*

But the wine-press of Los in eastward—*Blake*

But to our tale, the Donna Inez sent—*Byron*

But today I recapture the islands—*Brathwaite*

But two there are, shadow us everywhere—*Day Lewis*

But where began the change—*Meredith, George*

But wherefore do not you a mightier way—*Shakespeare*

But yesterday, I heard his bantering—*Bodenheim*

But you, my brother and my ghost—*Read, Herbert*

The butcher carves veal for us—*Williams, Hugo*

Ein Butterbrotpapier im Wald—*Morgenstern*

The butterfly, a cabbage-white—*Graves*

The Buzzard hung crossed—*Norris*

Bwana wangu kajisafiria—*Nasibu*

Bwo wu nung yun chou yung jou—*Li Ching Jau*

By a peninsula the wanderer sat and sketched—*Crane, Hart*

By a route obscure and lonely—*Poe*

By all means sing of love—*Auden*

By Blue Ontario's shore—*Whitman*

By dark severance the apparition head—*Ransom*

By day the bat is cousin to the mouse—*Roethke*

By June our brook's run out of song—*Frost, Robert*

By kiss of death—*Hughes, Ted*

By-low, my babe—*Anonymous-English—Modern English*

By our first strange and fatall interview—*Donne*

By night they haunted a thicket of April mist—*Ransom*

By Saint Mary, my lady—*Skelton, John*

By sundown we came to a hidden village—*Treece*

By that the maunciple hadde his tale al ended—*Chaucer*

By the bivouac's fitful flame—*Whitman*

By the long flow of green and silver water—*Zaturenska*

By the old Moulmein Pagoda lookin' eastward to the sea—*Kipling*

By the road to the contagious hospital—*Williams, William Carlos*

By the rude bridge that arched the flood—*Emerson*

By the shores of Gitche Gumee—*Longfellow*

By the wayside, three crows sat on a cross—*Pack*

By this exchange of eyes—*Graves*

By this he knew she wept with waking eyes—*Meredith, George*

By this to remember, this spring again—*Spacks*

By your unnumbered charities—*Blackburn, Thomas*

Byl u menya khoroshi drug—*Simonov*

Los caballos negros son—*Garcia Lorca*

Cackle, cackle, Mother Goose—*Children's Verses and Nursery Rhymes*

Cada uno en el rumor de sus talleres—*Luis*

Cada vez mas aparte—*Vivanco*

Cadiz, salada claridad . . . Granada—*Machado, Manuel*

Caeli, Lesbia nostra, Lesbia illa—*Catullus*

Caged lightly by two-by-fours—*Booth*

Caged—within the prisons of our lust—*Fabio, Sarah Webster*

Caguar hunted the lion—*Lowbury*

Cai um pássaro do ar—*Lisboa, Irene*

Caído se le ha un clavel—*Góngora*

Cajita mía—*Mistral*

Calabó y bambú—*Palés Matos*

The calf is born with prospects grim—*Nash*

Call for the Robin-Red-Breast and the Wren—*Webster, John*

The call is for belief—*Evans, A. H.*

The calm / cool face—*Hughes, Langston*

Calm is the landscape when the storm has passed —*Watkins*

Calm is the morn without a sound—*Tennyson*

Calm is the season, cold and clear the air—*Zaturenska*

Calm was the day, and through the trembling air —*Spenser*

Calmes dans le demi-jour—*Verlaine*

Calypso held him in her cave—*Ross, W. W. E.*

Came in my full youth—*Rukeyser*

The camel has a single hump—*Nash*

The camel's humps—*Stryk*

Camille St. Saëns was racked with pains—*Nash*

Camino no se por que—*Vargas*

El campeador adeliñó a su posada—*Anonymous–Spanish*

Campesina, no dejes de acudir al mercado—*López*

El campo / de olivos—*Garcia Lorca*

Can a bell ring in the heart—*Sandburg*

Can cockcrow fix a landscape—*Scott, Winfield Townley*

Can I see another's woe—*Blake*

Can it be right to give what I can give—*Browning, Elizabeth Barrett*

Can she excuse my wrongs—*Anonymous–English–Modern English*

Can this really be the end—*Alurista*

Can you imagine me—*Donaldson*

La canción/ que nunca diré—*Garcia Lorca*

La candela en el campo—*Jiménez*

Candy / is dandy—*Nash*

The canes burn. I show you—*Scott, Dennis*

Canst thou love me, lady?—*Calverley*

Canst thou, o cruel! say I love thee not—*Shakespeare*

Can't you turn yourself into a fish—*Morgenstern*

¡Cantàbria! som tos braus mariners—*Maragall*

Cantando vas, riendo por el agua—*Jiménez*

Cantaron los gallos tristes—*Jiménez*

Cantcha pull that trigger—*Emanuel*

Capitaine Renard alloit de compagnie—*La Fontaine*

Captain Carpenter rose up in his prime—*Ransom*

Captain, or Colonel, of knight in arms—*Milton*

Car tu nous reviendras, présence.—*Perse*

Cara belta che amore—*Leopardi*

Care-charmer sleep, son of the sable night—*Daniel, Samuel*

Care-charming sleep, thou easer of all woes—*Fletcher, John*

Career was feminine, resourceful, clever—*Cunningham, James Vincent*

Caring is loving, motionless—*Scott, F. R.*

Carles li reis, nostre emperere magnes—*Anonymous–French*

Carmè, nun fa' 'a superba—*Di Giacomo*

Carmen est maigre—un trait de bistre—*Gautier*

La Carmen está bailando—*Garcia Lorca*

The carp are secrets—*Wright, James*

Carried her unprotesting out the door—*Brooks, Gwendolyn*

Carrying their packages of groceries in particular —*Moore, Merrill*

Una casa da nulla, ma ragazza alle persiane—*Gatto*

A casa mia in Egitto—*Ungaretti*

La casta y honda amiga me dice sus razones—*Storni*

Cat and I—*Jaszi*

A cat came fiddling out of a barn—*Children's Verses and Nursery Rhymes*

The cat in the wood cried farewell—*MacLeish*

The cat is eating the roses—*Levertov*

Cat takes a look at the weather—*Swenson*

The cat went here and there—*Yeats*

The catalpa's white week is ending there—*Ciardi*

Catching winter in their carved nostrils—*Cohen*

La Catedral de Barcelona dice—*Unamuno*

Catena, ca mme tiene ncatenato—*Di Giacomo*

Cathedral silence and the light flooding a square of skin—*Lowbury*

Catprints, dogprints, marks—*Atwood*

Cats walk neatly—*Francis*

Cause you don't love me—*Hughes, Langston*

The causes are in Time—*Gunn*

A cautious crow clings to a bare bough—*Anonymous–English–Modern English*

Cavalry crossing a ford—*Whitman*

Cayó una hoja—*Garcia Lorca*

Ce cheval qui tourna la tête—*Supervielle*

Ce morne soir de pluie et de neige fondue—*Carco*

Ce ne seront jamais ces beautés de vignettes—*Baudelaire*

Ce n'est pas en mes vers qu'une amante abusée —*Malherbe*

Ce n'était pas assez que tant de mers—*Perse*

Ce pur enfant, rose de chasteté—*Supervielle*

C'è qualcosa di nuovo oggi nel sole—*Pascoli*

Ce siècle avait deux ans—*Hugo, Victor*

Ce soir/ si j'ecrivais—*Queneau*

Ce sont les anges qui préparent—*Cocteau*

C'è tanto miglio alla finestra—*Saba*

Ce toit tranquille, ou marchent des colombes—*Valéry*

C'è una voce nella mia vita—*Pascoli*

Celery, raw—*Nash*

Celestial choir, enthron'd in realms of light—*Wheatley*

The celluloid of a photograph holds them well —*Hughes, Ted*

Celui qui croyait—*Aragon*

Celui qui regarde du dehors—*Baudelaire*

Celui qui vit de souvenirs—*Seghers*

Cenabis bene, mi Fabulle, apud me—*Catullus*

Les cendres du soleil et les notes d'etoiles—*Soupault*

The census man—*Hughes, Langston*

Un cerf s'étant sauvé dans une étable à Boeufs —*La Fontaine*

Cerrar podrá mis ojos la postrera—*Quevedo y Villegas*

Cerraron sus ojos que aun tenía abiertos—*Becquer*

El Cerro de las animas benditas—*Diego, José de*

Un certain loup, dans la saison—*La Fontaine*

Certain ours montagnard, ours à demi léché—*La Fontaine*

Certain Renard gascon, d'autres disent normand —*La Fontaine*

Certaine Fille, un peu trop fière—*La Fontaine*

Certes si nous avions vécu en l'an dix-sept cent soixante—*Apollinaire*

Cessate d'uccidere i morte—*Ungaretti*

C'est Dimanche—*Senghor*

C'est la chaude loi des hommes—*Éluard*

C'est la nuit—*Prévert*

C'est le moment crépusculaire—*Hugo, Victor*

C'est le temps de partir—*Senghor*

C'est mon premier domicile—*Cendrars*

C'est un château d'ancêtres—*Hébert*

C'est un trou de verdure où chante une rivière —*Rimbaud*

C'était, dans la nuit brune—*Musset*

C'était l'ombre aux pas de velours—*Grandbois*

C'était près d'une source—*Vigny*

C'était un temps béni nous étions sur les plages —*Apollinaire*

Cette vie est un hôpital où chaque malade— *Baudelaire*

Ceux qui liront ces vers qu'en pleurant j'ay chantez—*Desportes*

Ceux qui n'ont inventé ni la poudre ni la boussole —*Césaire*

Ceux qui n'ont pas voulu se rendre—*Aragon*

Ceux qui pieusement sont morts pour la patrie —*Hugo, Victor*

Ceux qui sont morts pour rien—*Seghers*

Chacun se trompe ici-bas—*La Fontaine*

La chair encore endormie—*Mauriac*

La chair est triste, hélas!—*Mallarmé*

The chair she sat in, like a burnished throne— *Eliot, Thomas Stearns*

Une chambre qui ressemble à une rêverie— *Baudelaire*

Les champs n'étaient point noirs—*Hugo, Victor*

The change is too complete— *Weiss*

Change/ like if you were a match—*Lee, Don L.*

Changing light winds—*Sandburg*

Le chapeau à la main—*Apollinaire*

Chaque fois qu'on découvert—*Obaldia*

The charcoal-burner has tales to tell—*Milne*

Chargé / De fruits légers—*Éluard*

Charles Lamb and Samuel Taylor C.—*Beerbohm*

Charm me asleep, and melt me so—*Herrick*

Un chat, nommé Rodilardus—*La Fontaine*

Château de cartes, château de Bohême—*Nerval*

Chatter of birds two by two—*Sandburg*

Une chauve-souris donna tête baissée—*La Fontaine*

Che fai tu, luna, in ciel?—*Leopardi*

Che senso, dimmi, ha il numero degli anni— *Gatto*

Che stai? gia il secol l'orma—*Foscolo*

Che v'aggia di', mio caro—*Bovio*

Cheer is a contagious thing—*Marshall, Helen Lowrie*

The cheetah levels at one far deer—*Stafford*

Le Chêne, un jour, dit au Roseau—*La Fontaine*

Cher ami! sans doutes êtes-vous comme moi— *Cadou*

Cher mercordi a mmercato, ggente mie—*Belli*

Les chères mains qui furent miennes—*Verlaine*

Chérie, explique-moi pourquoi—*Geraldy*

Chérie, on s'est encore très mal quittés—*Geraldy*

Cherrie-ripe, ripe, ripe—*Herrick*

The cherry trees bend over and are shedding— *Thomas, Edward*

The chestnut casts his flambeaux, and the flowers —*Housman*

Chettalento de fijjo—*Belli*

Les chevaliers de l'ouragan s'accrochent aux volets des boutiques—*Aragon*

Chevaux de bois, bêtes d'apocalypse,—*Fombeure*

Les cheveux gris, quand jeunesse les porte—*Cocteau*

Chez moi, dit la petite fille—*Obaldia*

Chez nous les fleurs des pendules s'allument— *Tzara*

Chi mi cuntati?—*Buttitta*

Chi ssiete? Un omo—*Belli*

Chiare, fresche e dolci acque—*Petrarca*

Chica es la calandria—*Ruiz*

Chicago and San Francisco and you and me— *Shange*

The chickadee in the appletree—*Conkling*

The chickadee taught me this river—*Conkling*

Chickweed, gorse, pink cistus—*Aiken*

Chide, chide no more away—*Stanley*

Chidher—*Rückert*

The chief defect of Henry King—*Belloc*

Chieftain Iffucan of Azcan—*Stevens, Wallace*

A chieftain to the Highlands bound—*Campbell, Thomas*

Chiesi di voi: nessuno—*Gozzano*

The child at winter sunset—*Van Doren*

Child, dream of a pomegranate tree—*Lewis, Janet*

Child, even the buds—*Sondé*

A child is born, they cry, a child—*Smith, Stevie*

A child need not be very clever—*Nash*

The child next door has a wreath on her hat— *Fyleman*

The child of Mary Queen of Scots—*Kipling*

Child of My Winter born—*Snodgrass*

Child of the pure unclouded brow—*Carroll*

A child said what is the grass—*Whitman*

A child should always say what's true—*Stevenson*

A child singing—*Mitchell, Adrian*

A child sits near a fireplace—*Sobiloff*

A child stepped into the sunshine today—*Arnez*

Child, the current of your breath—*Sexton*

A child went out one day—*Lee, Dennis*

Childhood is not from birth to a certain age— *Millay*

Childhood remembrances—*Giovanni*

The childless years alone without a home— *Rukeyser*

Children are dumb to say how hot the day is—*Graves*

Children aren't happy with nothing to ignore—*Nash*

Children, children, don't you know—*Corso*

Children, I crave your kind forbearance—*Nash*

Children, if you dare to think—*Graves*

The children of the Czar—*Schwartz*

Children of Thespis, welcome—*Crabbe*

Children you are very little and your bones are very brittle—*Stevenson*

Children's voices in the orchard—*Eliot, Thomas Stearns*

The child's wisdom is in saying—*Sobiloff*

A chill wind sweeps—*Lorde*

Ein Chinese ('s sind schon an 200 Jahr)—*Fontane*

Chiome d'argente fine, irte ed attorte—*Berni*

Chiove—*Murolo*

Chipmunk chewing the Chippendale—*Nash*

Chispa de luz, que, fija en lo infinito—*Coronado*

Christ died for God and me—*Smith, Stevie*

Christ is a nigger—*Hughes, Langston*

Christian, Socialist, he undone—*Summers, Hollis*

Christmas Eve and twelve of the clock—*Hardy*

Christmas knows a merry, merry place—*Watts-Dunton*

Christofo Colombo was a hungry man—*Sandburg*

Christopher Beer—*Causley*

Christopher, Christopher, where are you going—*Milne*

Christopher Marlowe or Francis Bacon—*Coward*

Christopher Robin goes/ hoppity—*Milne*

Christopher Robin / Had wheezles—*Milne*

Christus natus est the cock crowed—*Chapman*

A chuckling tycoon of Fort Worth—*Nash*

The Church's restoration in 1883—*Betjeman*

Chut' noch', moi demon tut—*Pasternak*

Chwang chyan ming ywe gwang—*Li Bai*

Chwun myan bu jywe syan—*Meng Hau Ran*

Chyan shan nyan fei jywe—*Lyou Dzung Ywan*

Chye fa chu fu e—*Li Bai*

El ciego sol se estrella—*Machado, Manuel*

Ciel, air et vents—*Ronsard*

Le ciel est étoilé par les obus des Boches—*Apollinaire*

Le ciel est, par-dessus le toit—*Verlaine*

Cielo y mar, cielo y mar—*López*

Cierra, cierra la puerta—*Jiménez*

La cigale, ayant chanté tout l'été—*La Fontaine*

Cinnamon and rayon—*Hughes, Langston*

Cinq siècles vous ont vus les armes à la main—*Brierre*

Ciò che di me sapeste—*Montale*

cepressi che a Bólgheri alti e schetti—*Carducci*

Cities and thrones and powers—*Kipling*

The city mouse lives in a house—*Rossetti, Christina*

City of tense and stricken faces—*Walker*

La ciudad es de goma lisa y negra—*Celaya*

Clara passeava no jardin com as crianças—*Drummond de Andrade*

Clarke Saunders and may Margret—*Anonymous –English–Modern English*

El claro viento del mar—*Jiménez*

Los claros rayos de Faetonte altivo—*Balbuena*

The cleanest place to bring your baby—*Orlovsky*

Clear had the day been from the dawn—*Drayton*

Clear the air! Clean the sky! Wash the wind!—*Eliot, Thomas Stearns*

A clerk ther was of Oxenford also—*Chaucer*

Cliff Klingenhagen had me in to dine—*Robinson, Edwin Arlington*

Climbing from the Lethal dead—*Winters*

The clock is banging—*Barker, George*

A clock stopped—*Dickinson, Emily*

The clock struck three, the rooming house was filled—*Bodenheim*

The clocks begin, civicly simultaneous—*Tomlinson*

Clogged and soft and sloppy eyes—*Brooks, Gwendolyn*

Clopin-clopant s'en allaient des aveugles—*Desnos*

Close and slow, summer is ending in Hampshire—*MacNeice*

Close bound in a familiar bed—*Graves*

Close by those meads for ever crown'd with flow'rs—*Pope, Alexander*

Close now thine eyes, and rest secure—*Quarles*

Close up the casement, draw the blind—*Hardy*

The closest but we—*Lifshin*

A closet of—*Lifshin*

The cloud-backed Heron will not move—*Watkins*

A cloud possessed the hollow field—*Thompson, W. H.*

Cloud-Puffball, torn tufts, tossed pillows—*Hopkins*

The clouds which rise with thunder—*Whittier*

Clown admirable, en vérité!—*Banville*

Clumsy Mrs. Humbleby—*Sitwell, Osbert*

The coach is at the door at last—*Stevenson*

Coalition: rhymes with revolution—*Gaver*

The coast goes from Hurrian—*Olson*

Cobó è morto, e non gli possono—*Palazzeschi*

Coches cerrados llegaban—*Garcia Lorca*

Le coeur est fait de mille cordes—*Seghers*

Le coin du coeur, disait-il gentiment—*Éluard*

Cold and amber—*Hillyer*

Cold and clear-cut face—*Tennyson*

A cold coming we had of it—*Eliot, Thomas Stearns*

Cold in the earth, and the deep snow piled above thee—*Brontë, Emily*

Cold light of the moon over the sleeping sea—*Kavanagh*

The cold rises around—*Atwood*

Cold showers, drumming fit to wake the dead—*Davidson*

Cold shuttered loveless star, skulker in clouds—*Barker, George*

A cold, still afternoon: mist gathered under—*Fuller, Roy*

The cold transparent ham is on my fork—*Hood*

Coldly, sadly descends—*Arnold*

Coleridge received the person from Porlock—*Smith, Stevie*

Collis o Heliconiei—*Catullus*

Collision with the earth has finally come—*Hughes, Ted*

Colm had a cat—*Farren*

Color it blue funk—*Fabio, Sarah Webster*

The color of the ground was in him—*Markham*
The color, quick in fluid oil—*Winters*
Colors of horses like leaves or stone—*Swenson*
Columbus may have worked the wind—*Frost, Robert*
Columpiamos el santo—*Mistral*
Com on wanre niht—*Anonymous–English—Old English*
Com se diu aquest poble—*Foix*
The combe was ever dark, ancient and dark—*Thomas, Edward*
Come all you rounders, if you want to hear—*Anonymous–English—Modern English*
Come allodola ondosa—*Ungaretti*
Come along, everybody—*Nash*
Come along in then, little girl—*Millay*
Come away, come away, Death—*Shakespeare*
Come back to me, who wait and watch for you—*Rossetti, Christina*
Come, bring with a noise—*Herrick*
Come, buy my fine wares—*Swift*
Come capsicum, cast off—*Updike*
Come, collar this bad man—*Gilbert, Sir William Schwenck*
Come crown my brow with leaves of myrtle—*Nash*
Come, dear children, let us away—*Arnold*
Come, dear old comrade, you and I—*Holmes, Oliver Wendell*
Come dolce prima dell'uomo—*Ungaretti*
Come down, O maid, from yonder mountain height—*Tennyson*
Come, Hygiene, goddess of the growing boy—*Betjeman*
Come in with your stab wound up the middle—*Ignatow*
Come into black geography—*Sanchez*
Come into the garden, Maud—*Tennyson*
Come leave the loathed stage—*Jonson*
Come, let me sing into your ear—*Yeats*
Come, let us gather up—*Blackmur*
Come, let us tell the weeds in ditches—*Bogan*
Come little babe, come, silly soul—*Breton, Nicholas*
Come, live with me and be my love—*Marlowe*
Come live with mee, and bee my love—*Donne*
Come, Madam, come all rest my powers defie—*Donne*
Come, megrims, mollygrubs and collywobbles—*Nash*
Come my Celia, let us prove—*Jonson*
Come, my little one, with me—*Field, Eugene*
Come my tan-faced children—*Whitman*
Come on get in, he says, but—*Darr*
Come on, Senator—*Emanuel*
Come, quando su' campi arsi la pia—*Carducci*
Come questa pietra—*Ungaretti*
Come round me, little childer—*Yeats*
Come! said Old Shellover—*De la Mare*
Come, sleep, O sleep, the certain knot of peace—*Sidney*
Come so lle dizgrazzie!—*Belli*
Come, surly fellow, come: a song—*Graves*
Come thou, who art the wine, and wit—*Herrick*
Come to me! cried the Heart to the Star—*Reaney*
Come to me in the silence of the night—*Rossetti, Christina*

Come to the sunny Prestatyn—*Larkin*
Come tornay da la madon-dell-Orto—*Belli*
Come, try your skill, kind gentlemen—*Hodgson*
Come up from the fields, Father—*Whitman*
Come up here, O dusty feet—*Stevenson*
Come with me, under my coat—*Stephens*
Come, worthy Greek, Ulysses, come—*Daniel, Samuel*
Comen su pan cuando lo sudan—*Ridruejo*
Comes home dull with coal-dust deliberately—*Hughes, Ted*
Comes twilight now of all the day the best—*Marshall, Helen Lowrie*
The comfortable noise long reading makes—*Blackmur*
A comic in a mashed hat—*Ciardi*
Comienzan los días lánguidos—*Martinez Alonso*
Coming up England by a different line—*Larkin*
Comme celui qui se dévêt à la vue—*Perse*
Comme des sourds-muets parlant dans une gare—*Aragon*
Comme elle avait gardé les moutons à Nanterre—*Péguy*
Comme je descendais des fleuves impassibles—*Rimbaud*
Comme on voit sur la branche au mois de mai la rose—*Ronsard*
Comme un dernier rayon, comme un dernier zéphyr—*Chénier*
Comme un vol de gerfaut—*Heredia*
Comme une cathédrale il est cravaté d'ombre—*Jacob, Max*
Comme va, comme va—*Di Giacomo*
Commendo tibi me ac meos amores—*Catullus*
The common places of the string I bring—*Whistler*
The commotion of these waves however strong cannot—*Dudek*
Como cuando era niño—*Garcia Nieto*
Cómo de entre mis manos te resbala—*Quevedo y Villegas*
Como el náufrago metódico que contase—*Rosales*
Como en el ala el infinito vuelo—*Jiménez*
Como en la noche, el aire ve su fuente—*Jiménez*
Como en un libro abierto—*Becquer*
Cómo era, Dios mío, cómo era—*Jiménez*
Cómo escuchase un llanto—*Mistral*
Cómo estáis, Rocinante, tan delgado—*Cervantes Saavedra*
¿Cómo fue señora?—*Muroti*
Cómo me dan pena las abandonadas—*Lesto*
Como me duermes al niño—*Salinas, Pedro*
Cómo me quieres, dime—*León, Rafael de*
Cómo quedan, señor—*Mistral*
Como se arranca el hierro—*Becquer*
Como se fue el maestro—*Machado, Antonio*
Como te miro isla—*Morales*
Como un ave que cruza el aire claro—*Martí*
Como una rosa, como una almendra—*León, Rafael de*
Cómo vive esa rosa—*Becquer*
Compagnons des mauvais jours—*Prévert*
Compère le Renard se unit un jour en frais—*La Fontaine*
Compose compose beds—*Stein, Gertrude*

Compose for Red a proper verse—*Knight, Etheridge*
Con ali tese e il becco aperto a volte—*Saba*
Con aquellos sus ojos que probaron—*Unamuno*
Con diez cañones por banda—*Espronceda*
Con dolorido cuidado—*Manrique*
Con esta buena esperanza—*Juan de la Cruz*
Con lilas llenas de agua—*Jiménez*
Con membrillos maduros—*Ibarbourou*
Con mi razon apenas, con mis dedos—*Neruda*
Con occhi intenti seguono ogni mossa—*Saba*
Con voi nella mia vecchia casa entrava—*Saba*
Concentrical, the universe and I—*Kunitz*
Concerning your letter in which you ask me—*Sexton*
A conchiglia del buio—*Ungaretti*
Conde Niño por amores—*Anonymous-Spanish*
Condemn'd to hope delusive mine—*Johnson, Samuel*
El Condesito de la Limonada—*Palés Matos*
Conejo: hermano tímido—*Carrera Andrade*
Confucian—*Lavin*
Congratulations, fingerprint man—*Elmslie*
Li congressi de lei co Ppetronilla—*Belli*
Conheci a Beleza que não morre—*Quental*
Conozco un silencio nuevo—*Conde*
Consider says the music how man is an age—*Ciardi*
Consider the auk—*Nash*
Consider the banker—*Nash*
Consider the case of Mr. Suggs—*Nash*
Consider the sea's listless chime—*Rossetti, Dante Gabriel*
El cónsul de Peru me lo dice—*Jiménez*
A contact lens falls—*Brukner*
Content? Content. Let be what will—*Richards, I. A.*
Conticuere omnes intentique ora tenebant—*Virgil*
Contigo, mano a mano—*Garcia Nieto*
Contigo, tierra de España—*Vivanco*
Contra el azul moviendo sus azules—*Neruda*
A Contrapuntalist—composer of chorales—*Moore, Marianne*
Contre le ciel trop blanc, trop vide—*Carco*
Conversation brings us so close—*Bly*
The convoluted consonance of all—*Derwood*
A cook named McMurray—*Nash*
Cool black night thru the red woods—*Ginsberg*
A cool small evening shrunk to a dog bark and the clank of a bucket—*Hughes, Ted*
The copper gong of the mid-east sun—*Goldstein*
El corazón del pájaro—*Huidobro*
El corazón que tenía en la escuela—*Garcia Lorca*
Corazón, viejo Indio ya no estés—*Godoy*
Cordes faites de cris—*Apollinaire*
Córdoba—*Garcia Lorca*
The cornucopia of Ceres—*Sitwell, Edith*
Corps tendre et blond—*Lapointe*
Corral de muertos, entre pobres tapias—*Unamuno*
Corre sopra le sabbie favolese—*Ungaretti*
Corriendo va por la vega—*Zorrilla*
Corro de las niñas—*Mistral*
The corse is taken off—*MacLeish*
Corymba has bound no snood—*Davidson*
Cosce 'argiento è tantillo—*Chiurazzi*

Così discesi dal cerchio primaio—*Dante Alighieri*
Le couchant dardait ses rayons suprêmes—*Verlaine*
Un couchant des Cosmogonies—*Laforgue*
Could be Hasting Street—*Hughes, Langston*
Could it be Bud—*Harper*
Could it have been mine—*Reid*
Could man be drunk forever—*Housman*
La couleur que décompose la nuit—*Reverdy*
Couloir longitudinal des grands bâtiments souterrains—*Soupault*
The Countess Klondyke—*Sitwell, Osbert*
The country is no country I have seen—*Van Doren*
Countryman, tell me if you can—*Moss, Howard*
The couple who remain in bed—*Stone, Ruth*
Courage banners—*Randall*
Courage! he said, and pointed toward the land—*Tennyson*
Courage, O faible enfant, de qui ma solitude—*Vigny*
Courage yet, my brother or my sister—*Whitman*
Courageux comme un timbre-poste—*Soupault*
La courbe de tes yeux fait le tour de mon coeur—*Éluard*
Courtesies of good-morning and good-evening—*Graves*
The Cow is of the bovine ilk—*Nash*
The cows lie sweetly by the pond—*White*
Coy Nature, (which remain'd, tho aged grown)—*Cowley, Abraham*
Cozy we sit—*Conkling*
Cracked chessmen lying on—*Arnez*
The cracker is not to be played with—*Sanchez*
Cracking chicken bones—*Alston*
Cramped like sardines on the Queens—*Moss, Howard*
Crazed through much child-bearing—*Yeats*
A crazy bookcase, placed before—*Holmes, Oliver Wendell*
Crazy Jay blue—*Cummings*
The crazy old Vinegar Man is dead—*Mitchell, Ruth Comfort*
Crazy pigeon strutting outside my cell—*Knight, Etheridge*
Creación tiene un polo: hombre se llama—*Alonso*
Created purely from glass the saint stands—*Hill*
The creative is heaven—*Anonymous-Asian languages*
The creator of night and of birth—*Sandburg*
The creek shining—*Ross, W. W. Eustace*
Creep into thy narrow bed—*Arnold*
Creepin', crawlin' through the night—*Morgan, Karen*
Creon, I think, could never kill a mouse—*Davie*
Cribs loaded with roughage—*Wright, James*
Cried the navy-blue ghost—*Sitwell, Edith*
Criminal! You took a great piece of my life—*Tonks*
Cristo moreno—*Garcia Lorca*
A critic advises—*Randall*
Crocus, daffodil—*Stryk*
The croft, shadowed between houses—*Connor*
Cromwell, our chief of men—*Milton*
The crooked paths go every way—*Stephens*
The cross begot me on stone—*Smith, Stevie*
A cross fertilization of blood—*Troupe*

The cross staggered him. At the cliff-top—*Hill*
Crossbow wanted a child—*Levine*
Crossing alone the nighted ferry—*Housman*
Crow looked at the world, mountainously heaped
  —*Hughes, Ted*
The crows are flying above the foyer of summer
  —*Stevens, Wallace*
A crow's long scratch of sound—*Ciardi*
Cruelle, il suffisoit de m'avoir pouldroyé—*Ronsard*
Cruelty has a human heart—*Blake*
La Cruz del Sur se echa en una nube—*Jiménez*
Cruza callada, y son sus movimientos—*Becquer*
Cry—*Fabio, Sarah Webster*
A cry from the green-grained sticks of the fire
  —*Hardy*
Cry what shall I cry—*Eliot, Thomas Stearns*
Crying from exile, I—*Hacker*
Crystal moments—yours and mine—*Marshall, Helen Lowrie*
Cuál de vosotras, olas de consuelo—*Unamuno*
Cuán bella en la pluma sedosa de un ave—*Mendive*
Cuán vanamente, cuán ligeramente—*Figuera*
Cuando contemplo el cielo—*Vega, Garcilaso de la*
Cuando digo rosas, se perfuma el aire—*Martinez Alonso*
Cuando el mirlo, en lo verde nuevo un día—*Jiménez*
Cuando emigran las aves en bandadas—*Zenea*
Cuando en la noche te envuelven—*Becquer*
Cuando en mis manos, Rey eterno—*Vega Carpio*
Cuando entre la sombra—*Becquer*
Cuando iba por el zoco murmuraron—*León, Rafael de*
Cuando la noche oscura—*Vega Carpio*
Cuando la tarde se inclina—*Obligado, Rafael*
Cuando llegue la noche y sea la sombra un baculo
  —*Rosales*
Cuando llueve, y reviso mis papeles, y acabo—*Celaya*
Cuando me llamas, toda la casa huele a pregón de
  naranjas—*León, Rafael de*
Cuando me lo contaron—*Becquer*
Cuando miro el azul horizonte perderse—*Becquer*
Cuando Preciosa el panderete toca—*Cervantes Saavedra*
Cuando salí de Collores—*Lloréns Torres*
Cuando se abre en la mañana—*Garcia Lorca*
Cuando sobre el pecho enclinas—*Becquer*
Cuando suceda el cambio que el mundo llama
  muerte—*Semprit*
Cuando te perdí lloraban—*Conde*
Cuando termine la muerte—*Alcántara*
Cuando volvemos las fugaces—*Becquer*
Cuando yo era niñodiós—*Jiménez*
Cuando yo muera—*Garcia Lorca*
Cuánta imagen fugaz y halagadora—*Menendez y Pelayo*
Cuántas mujeres, cuando muera—*López*
Cuánto es bella la tierra que habitaban—*Heredia y Campuzano*
Cuánto se ha roto, Dios—*Reyes Fuentes*
Cuánto verso de amor, cantado en vano—*Capdevila*

Cuántos perros hirsutos—*Neruda*
Cuba es verde en la hoja verde—*Lloréns Torres*
Cuba—ñáñigo y bachata—*Palés Matos*
¡Cuba! ¡Patria!—*Vega, Oscar Fernández de la*
Cuckoos lead Bohemian lives—*Nash*
Cuelli morti che ssò dde mezza tacca—*Belli*
Cuer, qu'est-ce là?—Ce sommes-nous voz yeux
  —*Charles d'Orleans*
Cultivo una rosa blanca—*Martí*
Cum puero bello praeconem qui videt isse—
  Catullus
La cumbre. Ahí está el ocaso—*Jiménez*
The cup whose shape is sound—*Spencer*
Cupid laid by his brand, and fell asleep—*Shakespeare*
Curé and pastor, dead at the one time—*Davie*
The curfew tolls the knell of parting day—*Gray*
The curious upward stumbling motion—*Ferlinghetti*
Curled in your night dress on the beach—*Kavanagh*
Curled like a hoop in sleep—*Durrell*
Curly-Locks! Curly-Locks! Wilt thou be mine—
  Children's Verses and Nursery Rhymes
Curtis, you've been American too long—*Davie*
Cuttin' mustard—*Fry*
Cuz it says—*Sanchez*
Un cygne avance sur l'eau—*Rilke*
Cymbals clash—*Brown, William*
Cynthia prima suis miserum me cepit ocellis—
  Propertius
A cypress curtain of the night is spread—*Campion*
Cyriack, this three years' day these eyes, though
  clear—*Milton*
Cyriack, whose grandsire on the royal bench—
  Milton

Då bomblarmet tystnat—*Blomberg*
Da das Instrument verstimmt ist—*Brecht*
Da gyt on orde stod Eadweard se langa—*Anonymous-English—Old English*
Da ich noch um deinen Schleier spielte—*Hölderlin*
Da meninice lembro apenas—*Ivo*
Da preisst man uns das Leben grosser Geister
  —*Brecht*
Dä skall ej vär jordiska bekamen—*Gullberg*
Da una finestra trapelando luce—*Ungaretti*
Dadme mi lira, dádmela, que siento—*Heredia y Campuzano*
Dadme, oh números, vuestra armonía pitagórica
  —*Martinez Alonso*
Daedalus, stay away from my transom—*McCord*
Dagen är släckt—*Ferlin*
Daily dawns another day—*Parker*
Daily, the bums sat down to eat in our kitchen
  —*Wagoner*
Daisy and dandelion, speedwell, daffodil—*Davie*
Daisy and Lily, lazy and silly—*Sitwell, Edith*
Dame du ciel, régente terrienne—*Villon*
Dame, get up and bake your pies—*Children's Verses and Nursery Rhymes*
Dame souris trotte—*Verlaine*
Dämmerung will die Flügel spreiten—*Eichendorff*

The damned ship lurched and slithered—*Brooke*

Damoiselle Belette, au corps long et flouet—*La Fontaine*

Dan the botanist walks—*O'Neill, Catherine*

The dance begins with the sun descending—*Eberhart*

Dance there upon the shore—*Yeats*

The dancer mended sheep and tended fences—*Booth*

Dandse, dandse Dukke min—*Andersen*

Daniel Boone stepped up to a window—*Miles*

Dans Arles, où sont les Aliscamps—*Toulet*

Dans ce récit je prétends faire voir—*La Fontaine*

Dans la forêt sans heures—*Supervielle*

Dans la Haute-Rue à Cologne—*Apollinaire*

Dans la lumière éclatante d'automne—*Claudel*

Dans la nuit—*Michaux*

Dans la plaine les baladins—*Apollinaire*

Dans le brouillard s'en vont un paysan cagneux—*Apollinaire*

Dans le ciel fument de grands vaisseaux—*Soupault*

Dans le crépuscule fané—*Apollinaire*

Dans le cristal d'une fontaine—*La Fontaine*

Dans le ventre de maman—*Obaldia*

Dans le vieux parc solitaire et glacé—*Verlaine*

Dans les grands eaux de ma mère—*Prévert*

Dans l'interminable ennui de la plaine—*Verlaine*

Dans un chemin montant sablonneux—*La Fontaine*

Dans un palais, soie et or, dans Ecbatane—*Verlaine*

Dans une boîte de paille tressée—*Prévert*

Dans une rue, au coeur d'une ville de rêve—*Verlaine*

Dans vos viviers, dans vos étangs—*Apollinaire*

De dansde med Castagnetter—*Andersen*

Där kusten stupar mellan hav och himmel—*Österling*

Darbón, el médico de Platero—*Jiménez*

Darest thou now O soul walk out with me—*Whitman*

Darius the Mede was a king and a wonder—*Lindsay, Vachel*

Dark accurate plunger down the successive knell—*Tate, Allen*

A dark and sudden beauty—*Jeffers, Lance*

Dark angel who art clear and straight—*Sitwell, Edith*

The dark blue wind of early autumn—*Sandburg*

Dark brown is the river, golden is the sand—*Stevenson*

Dark-green upon distant heights—*Auden*

The dark, grey receding tide uncovers—*Hollander*

The dark-haired girl, who holds my thought entirely—*Clarke*

Dark house, by which once more I stand—*Tennyson*

Dark is the face of Harriet—*Walker*

Dark men awash on the lawn—*Joselow*

Dark the words break—*Watkins*

A dark theme keeps me here—*Roethke*

Dark was the day when diesel—*Auden*

Dark water underground—*Roethke*

Darkness broods on earth and air—*Collymore*

The darkness consumes even the white—*Lester*

Darkness, feathers are shed—*Blackburn, Thomas*

Darkness gathering in the branches—*Levine*

Darling, at the Beautician's you buy—*Lucilius*

Darling! because my blood can sing—*Cummings*

Darling of our hearts, drowning—*Spender*

Darling, what is that—*Nash*

Das ist die Drossel die da schlägt—*Storm*

Das ist die Mäf vom Ritter Manuel—*Miegel*

Das ist ein Flöten und Geigen—*Heine*

Das macht, es hat die Nachtigall—*Storm*

Das war der Seelen wunderliches Bergwerk—*Rilke*

Dass aus dem Samen des Menschen—*Huchel*

Dass du den Bau gemacht, den Bau der schönen Welt—*Gryphius*

Dass Josefine eine schiefe Nase hat—*Tucholsky*

Dateline Saigon: Marines wait in the rain—*Kizer*

Dauer, Zeit und Raum—*Zuckmayer*

Daughter of Jove, relentless Power—*Gray*

Daughter, this small stiletto which I found—*Darr*

Daughters in the wind boisterous roughing—*Stone, Ruth*

The daughters of the horseleech crying Give! Give!—*Kunitz*

The Daughters of the Seraphim—*Blake*

Daughters of time, the hypocritic days—*Emerson*

Davnenko ne byval v storone rodnoi—*Turgenev*

Dawn off the Foreland—the young flood making—*Kipling*

A day—*Brown, Otis*

The day before April—*Davies, Mary Carolyn*

Day by day I float my paper boats—*Tagore*

The day dawns with scent of must and rain—*Kinsella*

The day is cold, and dark, and dreary—*Longfellow*

The day is colorless like Swiss characters in a novel—*Meredith, William*

The day is done, and the darkness—*Longfellow*

A day on many levels—*Sereni*

The day returns, my natal day—*Landor*

The day she visited the dissecting room—*Plath*

Days dawn on us that make amends for many Sometimes—*Swinburne*

The day's grown old, the fainting sun—*Cotton*

De carta de más me vía—*Hernández, José*

De consumida sal y garganta en peligro—*Neruda*

De donde vengo—el más horrible áspero—*Becquer*

De Francia partió la niña—*Anonymous–Spanish*

De kom på natten—*Lindqvist*

De la digestion qui se fait—*Larbaud*

De la florida falda—*Góngora*

De la musique avant toute chose—*Verlaine*

De la peau du Lion l'Âne s'étant vêtu—*La Fontaine*

De le pizzicarie che ttutte fanno—*Belli*

De l'époux bien-aimé n'entends-je pas la voix—*Vigny*

De l'home mire—*Raimon*

De lo poco de la vida—*Becquer*

De lo sonoro—*Neruda*

De l'oeil du doigt j'étudie des sourires—*Éluard*

De mirarte tanto y tanto—*Salinas, Pedro*

De Pretore Vincenzo s'arrangiava—*Filippo*

¿De qué sima te yergues, sombra negra?—*Alonso*

¿De quién es esta voz que va conmigo?—*Bernárdez*

De sa grâce redoutable—*Valéry*

De tous les partis—*Cocteau*

De vegades és necessari i forços—*Espriu*

De veras tú también—*Tejada*

The dead brood over Europe—*Blake*

The dead man lies—*Hughes, Ted*

Dead men sit down beside the telephones—*Bodenheim*

Dear Ann, wherever you are—*Muir*

Dear boy, you will not hear me speak—*Wilbur*

Dear Chloe, how blubbered is that pretty face—*Prior*

Dear Colette—*Jong*

Dear Cousin Nancy—*Nash*

Dear, damn'd distracting town, farewell—*Pope, Alexander*

Dear Daughter, since thou claim'st me for thy Sire—*Milton*

Dear Father, I am saying good-bye—*Bly*

Dear Friend: how can you—*Sondé*

Dear God and Ruler of all time—*Marshall, Helen Lowrie*

Dear God, don't let mother die—*Robison*

Dear God, in the end you had to go—*Abse*

Dear if you change I'll never choose again—*Anonymous–English–Modern English*

Dear Lizbie Brown—*Hardy*

Dear love, since the impossible proves—*Graves*

Dear Miss Dix, I am a young man—*Nash*

Dear Ms. Montessori, I love you—*Levendosky*

Dear Noah: A rumor—*Cullen*

Dear Noah: Please save me a spot—*Cullen*

Dear Noah: to lend a flavor—*Cullen*

Dear! of all happy in the hour, most blest—*Brooke*

The dear old village! Lin-lan-lone the bells—*Betjeman*

Dear Parents, I write you this letter—*Nash*

Dear Philip: thank God for boozey godfathers—*Auden*

Dear Reader, not your fellow flesh and blood—*MacPherson*

Dear Sirs: is it not time we formed a Boston—*Starbuck*

Dear Smith, the slee'est, paukie thief—*Burns*

Dear Son, when the warm multitudes cry—*Auden*

Dear Uncle Jim, this garden ground—*Stevenson*

Dear water, clear water, playful in all your streams—*Auden*

Deare love, for nothing lesse than thee—*Donne*

Dearest and nearest brother—*Spender*

Dearest Mama—*Coward*

Dearest, sleep—*Nims*

Death be not proud, though some have called thee—*Donne*

Death brings the end—*Heine*

Death hushes all the bigwigs—*Francis*

Death, it is but the long, cool night—*Heine*

Death magnifies the face of a hero—*Goldstein*

Death riding on a soda cracker—*Alurista*

Death, that struck when I was most confiding—*Brontë, Emily*

Death to the lady said—*Adams*

Death will be too late to bring us aid—*Williams, William Carlos*

The deaths about you when you stir in sleep—*Ciardi*

Debajo de la hoja—*Garcia Lorca*

Debes dormir, bella esperanza—*Obligado, Pedro Miguel*

December, and the closing of the year—*Hall*

Dedans mon livre de pensée—*Charles d'Orleans*

Dedans Paris, ville jolie—*Marot*

Dedyke men a selanna—*Sappho*

Dee dee dee dee dee wee weeeeeeeee—*Lee, Don L.*

Deep as Manhattan's earth the billion-dollar—*Starbuck*

Deep below our violences—*Auden*

A deep dish. Lumps in it—*Roethke*

Deep in Alabama earth—*Hughes, Langston*

Deep in our subconscious, we are told—*Coward*

Deep in the fading leaves of night—*Rodgers*

Deep in the moss-draped woods you come upon it—*Beecher*

Deep in the shady sadness of a vale—*Keats*

Deep in the summer wood—*Sitwell, Osbert*

Deep in the winter plain two armies—*Spender*

Deep in your cheeks—*Kgositsile*

Deeper than sleep but not so deep as death—*Rukeyser*

The deepest dream is of mad governors—*Van Doren*

The deil cam fiddling through the town—*Burns*

Dein Hut lüftet sich leis—*Bachmann*

Deine Seele, die die meine liebet—*Lasker-Schüler*

Deine speilsteig mine kind—*Sutzkever*

Deja la charla consuelo—*Gabriel y Galán*

Déjà la nuit en son parc amassoit—*Du Bellay*

Dejad las hebras de oro ensortijado—*Terrazas*

Déjame así. Mi corazón no pide—*Rega Molina*

Dejaría en este libro—*Garcia Lorca*

Dejé la luz a un lado—*Becquer*

Del aire al aire, como una red vacía—*Neruda*

Del alba a la mañana, de la tarde al ocaso—*Sabat-Ercasty*

Del nicho helado en que los hombres te pusieron—*Mistral*

Del salón en el ángulo oscuro—*Becquer*

¿Del tirano? Del tirano—*Martí*

The delicate bird who flies up your asses—*Bell*

Delicate red flames—*Williams, Hugo*

Delivers papers to the doors of sleep—*Miles*

Delphiniums are born—*Sandburg*

Dem Geier gleich—*Goethe*

Dem Schnee, dem Regen—*Goethe*

Demain, dès l'aube, à l'heure où blanchit la campagne—*Hugo, Victor*

Democracy will not come—*Hughes, Langston*

The demon who throughout our late estrangement—*Graves*

Denied, she screamed in rage, and ran away—*Engle*

Une dentelle s'abolit—*Mallarmé*

The dentist drilled for two and one-half hours—*Victor*

Depuis le Point-du-Jour jusqu'aux cèdres bibliques—*Péguy*

Depuis que le soleil, dans l'horizon immense—*Musset*

Der den Tod auf Hiroshima warf—*Kaschnitz*

Der deutsche Mann—*Tucholsky*
Der du von dem Himmel bist—*Goethe*
Der er et herligt Land—*Andersen*
Der ist der Herr der Erde—*Novalis*
Der var en Kone paa Landet—*Andersen*
Der Wolke Zickzackzunge spricht—*Morgenstern*
Dere wa' no Black Power—*Eckels*
Derrière les rideaux et l'épaisseur du temps—
  Cadou
Derrière moi la plaine—*Claudel*
Derweil ich schlafend lag—*Mörike*
Derwood perceives thee in still unworded mood
  —*Derwood*
Des Ganges Ufer hörten des Freudengotts—
  Hölderlin
Des Menschen Seele—*Goethe*
Des milliers et des milliers d'armées—*Prévert*
Des saluts font justice de la dignité—*Éluard*
Des Unbewegten Odem—Ein Tiergesicht—
  Trakl
Des Weibes Leib ist ein Gedicht—*Heine*
Descend from heav'n, Urania by that name—*Mil-
  ton*
The descent beckons as the ascent beckoned—
  Williams, William Carlos
Desde aquí yo contemplo, tendido, sin memoria
  —*Bousoño*
Desde el fondo de tí y arrodillado—*Neruda*
Desde mi vieja orilla, desde la fe que siento—
  Panero
Desde que sé, oh amiga—*Pedroni*
Le désert est muet, la tente est solitaire—*Vigny*
Desgarrada la nube; el arco iris—*Machado, An-
  tonio*
Desiderio delle tue mani chiare—*Quasimodo*
Desine de quoquam quisquam bene velle mereri
  —*Catullus*
Desire is a witch—*Day Lewis*
Desmayarse, atreverse, estar furioso—*Vega
  Carpio*
Desolate and lone—*Sandburg*
Desolation sits in a fluorescent airport—*Pommy
  Vega, Janine*
The desolations are not the sorrows' kin—*Muir*
Despierta, tiemblo al mirarte—*Becquer*
Despierte la novia—*Garcia Lorca*
Después, a los cuatro vientos—*Hernández, José*
Después que el rey don Rodrigo—*Anonymous-
  Spanish*
Después que nací—*Santillana*
D'estate, in un sentiero di campagna—*Gozzano*
Det är vackrast när det skymmer—*Lagerkvist*
Det dagas redan—*Blomberg*
Det Finns Någonting som ingenstans passar—
  Ekelöf
Det gassar av vårsol på gravgatans vardar—*As-
  plund*
Det klingar i hans grånande liv—*Edfelt*
Det kom ett brev om sommarsäd—*Lagerkvist*
Det sitter en herre i himlens sal—*Bergman, Bo*
Det var bara tokar och dårar—*Ferlin*
Detente, sombra de mi bien esquivo—*Juana Inés
  de la Cruz*
Detta är evigt—*Edfelt*
Deux Compagnons, pressés d'argent—*La Fon-
  taine*

Deux Mulets cheminoirent, l'un d'avoine chargé
  —*La Fontaine*
Deux pigeons s'aimaient d'amour tendre—*La
  Fontaine*
Deux vrais amis vivaient au Monomotapa—*La
  Fontaine*
Devant cet arbre immense et calme—*Cadou*
Devant la blanche ferme où parfois vers midi—
  Hugo, Victor
Devant la porte de l'usine—*Prévert*
Devil, being slender spirit—*Wilkinson*
The devil in heaven made me wise—*Dowling*
The devil lives—*Ross, W. W. Eustace*
Devouring Time, blunt thou the lion's paws—
  Shakespeare
Dew is falling now, the daylight is spent—*Wat-
  kins*
The Dew-man comes over the mountains—*Con-
  kling*
Dey had a gread big pahty down to Tom's—*Dun-
  bar, Paul Laurence*
Dey was talkin' in de cabin—*Dunbar, Paul Lau-
  rence*
Dhahe Mahidhar Sikhar Kotinh—*Tul'si Das*
Di-da-di-da, Daddy—*Gaver*
Di pensier in pensier, di monte in monte—
  Petrarca
Un día estaré muerta, blanca como la nieve—
  Storni
El día que me quieras tendrá más luz que junio
  —*Nervo*
Diana Ross Diana yes does not sing—*Gaver*
Dianae sumus in fide—*Catullus*
La diane chantait dans les cours des casernes—
  Baudelaire
Diaphenia, like the Daffadowndilly—*Chettle*
Dicebas quondam solum te nosse Catullum—
  Catullus
Dicen que me case yo—*Vicente*
Dicen que no hablan las plantas—*Castro, Rosalía
  de*
¿Dices que nada se crea?—*Machado, Antonio*
Dices que tienes corazón—*Becquer*
Dichoso el árbol, que es apenas sensitivo—*Darío*
Dico, diteme un po', ssora commare—*Belli*
Dictes moy où, n'en quel pays—*Villon*
Did all the lets and bars appear—*Melville*
Did any bird come flying—*Rossetti, Christina*
Did I think it somehow sucked—*Souster*
Did my widow flit about—*Masters, Edgar Lee*
Did not my pallid face betray—*Heine*
Did the people of Viet Nam—*Levertov*
Did they send me away from my cat—*Jarrell*
Did u vote nigger—*Marvin X*
Did you ask dulcet rhymes from me—*Whitman*
Did you ever cry—*Sanchez*
Did you ever, ever, ever—*Jacobsen, Ethel*
Did you ever find out—*Masters, Edgar Lee*
Did you ever hear of Editor Whedon—*Masters,
  Edgar Lee*
Die der schaffende Geist einst aus dem Chaos
  schlug—*Schiller*
Die Linden lang, galopp, galopp—*Mehring*
Dies wird die letzte Trän' nicht sein—*Goethe*
Diese schönen Gliedermassen—*Heine*
Dieu fait bien ce qu'il fait sans en chercher la
  preuve—*La Fontaine*

Dieu parle, et le chaos se dissipe à sa voix—*Voltaire*

Dieu, qu'il la fait bon regarder—*Charles d'Orleans*

Difficult ordinary happiness—*Rich*

Diffugere nives redeunt iam gramina campis—*Horace*

Dije: todo ya pleno—*Guillén, Jorge*

Dilemma—*Hodges*

The diligence of trades and noiseful gain—*Dryden*

Dim afternoon December afternoon—*Francis*

Dim-berried is the mistletoe—*De la Mare*

Dime tú que quiero—*Unamuno*

Dimme na cosa—*Di Giacomo*

D'in sú la vetta della torre antica—*Leopardi*

Din våg gick bittert allen—*Ferlin*

A diner while dining at Crewe—*Anonymous-English—Modern English*

Dineros son calidad (verdad)—*Góngora*

Ding, dong, bell—*Children's Verses and Nursery Rhymes*

Dinge gehen vor im Mond—*Morgenstern*

Diophantos went to bed—*Lucilius*

Diós del venir, te siento entre mis manos—*Jiménez*

Dios mío, yo te ofrezco mi dolor—*Nervo*

Dir nur, liebendes Herz, euch, meine vertraulichsten Tränen—*Klopstock*

The dirty white van—*Hinton*

Dis-moi, ton coeur parfois s'envole-t-il, Agathe—*Baudelaire*

The disasters numb within us—*Levertov*

Disce ch'er mormo è bbello perch'è vvario—*Belli*

Il disco grandissimo, pende—*Pascoli*

Disetissime Romuli nepotum—*Catullus*

En disponent i pilsnerdricker—*Ferlin*

Dites-moi où s'arrêtera la flamme—*Breton, André*

Dives, when you and I go down to Hell—*Belloc*

Dividimus muros et moenia pandimus nobis—*Virgil*

Divinities are apt to be—*Gregor*

Divitias alius fulvo sibi congerat auro—*Tibullus*

Dixerat ille Iovis monitis immota tenebat—*Virgil*

The DNA molecule—*Swenson*

Do any of you old fogies remember Mrs. Hauksbee?—*Nash*

Do I believe in God?—*Coward*

Do I have freedom here—*Beecher*

Do I not deal with angels—*Patchen*

Do not be afraid of no—*Brooks, Gwendolyn*

Do not enforce the tired wolf—*Ransom*

Do not enquire from the centurion—*Gunn*

Do not expect again a Phoenix hour—*Day Lewis*

Do not go gentle into that good night—*Thomas, Dylan*

Do not look for him—*Cohen*

Do not mistake me—*Heath*

Do not, oh, do not prize thy beauty—*Anonymous-English—Modern English*

Do not speak to me of martyrdom—*Sanchez*

Do not suddenly break the branch—*Eliot, Thomas Stearns*

Do not take a bath in Jordan, Gordon—*Sitwell, Edith*

Do not weep, maiden, for war is kind—*Crane, Stephen*

Do pa strata—*Buttitta*

Do skyscrapers ever grow tired—*Field, Rachel*

Do svidanya—*Yessenin*

Do take Muriel out—*Smith, Stevie*

Do the boys and girls still go to Siever's—*Masters, Edgar Lee*

Do they need any rain—*McGinley*

Do ye hear the children weeping—*Browning, Elizabeth Barrett*

Do you fear the force of the wind—*Garland*

Do you hear the cry as the pack goes by—*Sargent*

Do you know my friend Mr. Betts—*Nash*

Do you not find something very strange about him—*Hillyer*

Do you not wish to renounce the devil—*Lanusse*

Do you remember an Inn/ Miranda—*Belloc*

Do you remember how you won your last race—*Horne*

Do you remember me, Miss Grenadine—*Johnston, Ellen Turlington*

Do you remember Mr. Goodbeare, the Carpenter—*Sitwell, Osbert*

Do you remember, passer-by, the path—*Masters, Edgar Lee*

Do you see this ring—*Browning, Robert*

Dockery was junior to you—*Larkin*

Dr. Foster went to Glo'ster—*Children's Verses and Nursery Rhymes*

Dr. Levinson's office disappeared—*Darr*

Dr. Newman with the crooked pince-nez—*Graves*

Dr. Ramsden cannot read the Times—*Betjeman*

Does the football team—*Mailer*

Does the road wind up-hill all the way—*Rossetti, Christina*

Does the task ahead seem much too hard—*Marshall, Helen Lowrie*

The dog barked, then the woman stood in the doorway—*Jeffers, Robinson*

The dog is man's best friend—*Nash*

A dog lover—*Lee, Don L.*

The dog trots freely in the street—*Ferlinghetti*

A dog/ with brown markings—*Morgenstern*

Dolce e chiara è la notte—*Leopardi*

Dolce paese, onde portai conforme—*Carducci*

Dolcissimo, possente—*Leopardi*

Dolphin plunge, fountain play—*MacNeice*

Dominic has/ a doll—*Cummings*

Domna, tant vos ai preiada—*Raimbaut de Vaqueiras*

Le dompteur a mis sa tête—*Prévert*

Die Donaubrücke von Ingolstadt—*Eich*

Donde fue Tihuantisuyo—*Mistral*

Donde hábite el olvido—*Cernuda*

Donde la infancia al fin sus juegos deja—*Capdevila*

Dondequiera vaya—*Machado, Antonio*

Donn' Amalia 'a speranzella—*Di Giacomo*

Le donne/ mie di casa—*Saba*

Les donneurs de sérénades—*Verlaine*

Don't be cross, Amanda—*Nash*

Don't bother up my fungi an calalu—*Fabio, Sarah Webster*

Don't let them die out—*Sanchez*

Don't look at me—*Emanuel*

Don't look now—*Giovanni*

Don't play me no/ righteous bros.—*Sanchez*

Don't scream at me you God damn' wops—*Hugo, Richard F.*

Don't seek me where the myrtles bloom—*Rosenfeld*

Don't send me off, now that your thirst—*Heine*

Don't speak to me in obscurities—*Porter, Bern*

Don't step—*Creeley*

Don't wanna be no pimp—*Sanchez*

Don't you think its probable—*Fisher*

La donzelletta vien dalla campagna—*Leopardi*

Doom is dark and deeper than any sea-dingle—*Auden*

Doom of hesitant September weighs—*Williams, Gwyn*

A door: per l'universo, is what it says—*Tomlinson*

The door was shut as doors should be—*Setoun*

The door-bell jangled in evening's peace—*De la Mare*

Doors bolted; windows dirt-bleared—*Connor*

The doors keep rattling—I—*Levertov*

Dope pushers dope pushers—*Sanchez*

Doppo tre mmise ll'aggio vista aiere—*Di Giacomo*

Dorinda's sparkling wit and eyes—*Sackville*

El dormir es como un puente—*Jiménez*

Dorthin—will ich; und ich traue—*Nietzsche*

Dos patrias tengo yo: Cuba y la noche—*Martí*

Dos rojas lenguas de fuego—*Becquer*

D'où venez-vous ainsi couvert de précipices—*Supervielle*

The double moon, one on the high backdrop of the west—*Sandburg*

The double sorowe of Troylus to tellen—*Chaucer*

Doubt me! My dim companion—*Dickinson, Emily*

Doubt no longer miracles—*Bontemps*

Doubt shall—*Patten*

Douglass was someone who—*Hughes, Langston*

Le doux caboulot—*Carco*

Dov'è campo, il brusio della maretta—*Pascoli*

The dove returns—*Bly*

The dove walks with sticky feet—*Patchen*

Dov'era l'ombra, or sé la quercia spande—*Pascoli*

Down a street that once I lived in—*Colum*

Down by a shining water well—*Stevenson*

Down by the Salley gardens my love and I did meet—*Yeats*

Down cellar, said the cricket—*Lindsay, Vachel*

Down, down, down—*Arnez*

Down in Atlanta—*Brown, Sterling A.*

Down in Dallas, down in Dallas—*Kennedy, X. J.*

Down in the depths of the sea—*Conkling*

Down in the lost and April days—*Day Lewis*

Down like the oval fall of a hammer—*Howes*

Down railroad track—*Abbe*

Down the brick divided street—*Cavalieri*

Down the close, darkening lanes they sang their way—*Owen, Wilfred*

Down the dawn brown river—*Merrill*

Down the highroad of the Milky Way—*Conkling*

Down through the forest to the river—*Conkling*

Down valley a smoke haze—*Snyder*

Down walled alleys marked—*Alurista*

Downhill I came, hungry, and yet not starved—*Thomas, Edward*

A doxy is my newest dear—*Williams, Gwyn*

Drag mig ur rummets skugga—*Malmberg*

Drawn by her mumbled entreaties—*Davison, Peter*

Dream in a dream the heavy soul somewhere—*Berryman*

The dream is a cocktail at Sloppy Joes—*Hughes, Langston*

A dream isn't really something you have—*Marshall, Helen Lowrie*

Dream of people altogether singing—*Beecher*

Dreaming of a prince—*Davies, Mary Carolyn*

Dreaming of Utopias—*Ferlinghetti*

Drei Worte hört man, bedeutungsschwer—*Schiller*

Drei Worte nenn' ich euch, inhaltschwer—*Schiller*

Dreifach ist der Schritt der Zeit—*Schiller*

Drifting night in the Georgia pines—*Hayden*

Drilling little holes—*Lifshin*

Drink to me only with thine eyes—*Jonson*

Drömmare, dåre—din vaggas fe—*Ferlin*

Droning a drowsy syncopated tune—*Hughes, Langston*

Drop, drop. Slow tears—*Fletcher, Phineas*

Drowsing in my chair of disbelief—*Graves*

The drug man in the new hat—*Flint*

Drum on your drums, batter on your banjoes—*Sandburg*

Drum skin whip—*Brathwaite*

Drums, drums, I too am dead—*Butler, William*

The drums have entered my heart—*Rothenberg*

Druzhba nastoyashchaya ne staritsya—*Simonov*

The dry brown coagling beneath their feet—*Brooks, Gwendolyn*

Dry. The wind is parched by the wind—*Moss, Howard*

Du bist die Ruh—*Rückert*

Du bist mein, ich bin dein—*Anonymous–German*

Du bist mein Mond, und ich bin deine Erde—*Rückert*

Du bist wie eine Blume—*Heine*

Du dreymall weiser Geist—*Gryphius*

Du füllst mich an wie Blut die frische Wunde—*Benn*

Du har tappat ditt ord—*Ferlin*

Du kjaere, gamle Fødeby—*Andersen*

Du liebst mich nicht, du liebst mich nicht—*Heine*

Du meine Seele, du mein Herz—*Rückert*

Du mir am Himmel—*Weinheber*

Du palais d'un jeune lapin—*La Fontaine*

Du rara ört, som ej din like—*Nordenflycht*

Du sagst: es steht schlecht um unsere—*Brecht*

Du schienest, sagt man, lieber Mond—*Gleim*

Du schlank und rein wie eine Flamme—*George*

Du siehst, wohin du siehst, nur Eitelkeit auf Erden—*Gryphius*

Du skapade mig av luft och ler—*Blomberg*

Du, som av skönket och behagen—*Kellgren*

Du stiller Aether! immer bewahrst du schoen—*Hölderlin*

Du temps que j'étais écolier—*Musset*

Du temps que la Nature en sa verve puissante—*Baudelaire*

Du temps qu'on allait encore aux baleines—*Fort*

Du übersiehst dich nicht mehr—*Benn*

Du weisst nicht—*Hauptmann*

The Duck is whiter than whey is—*De la Mare*

Ducks require no ship and sail—*Ransom*

Duerme tranquilo, inocente—*Gómez de Avellaneda*

La dulce boca, que a gustar convida—*Góngora*

Dulce como la miel de los panales—*Darío*

Dulce vecino de la verde selva—*Villegas*

Dulces olivas verdes de frascati—*Neruda*

Dulled by the news, all day I keep behind—*Marshall, Jack*

Dumi moyi, dumi moyi—*Shevchenko*

A dummeneca 'e Pasca—*Di Giacomo*

D'un temps que serà el nostre—*Raimon*

Duncan Gray cam here to woo—*Burns*

Dung fang dzwo ye ting hung ju—*Ju Ching Yu*

Dunkel, dunkel im Moor—*Droste-Hülshoff*

Dünn besiedelt das Land—*Kirsch*

Dunque, rondini rondini, adelio—*Pascoli*

Durante muchos siglos—*González*

Durban, Birmingham—*Hughes, Langston*

Durch das Feld ging die Familie—*Busch*

Durch die Tore: niemand—*Kaschnitz*

Durch so viel Formen geschritten—*Benn*

Durchdrungen von Pein—*Hauptmann*

Durs pavés des rues mettez des pas d'acier—*Tzara*

Dust always blowing about the town—*Frost, Robert*

Dust and clay—*Vaughan, Henry*

The dust lay white upon the chisel marks—*Masefield*

The dwarf with his hands on backwards—*MacCaig*

Dwelling in a cavern, deep—*Ross, W. W. Eustace*

Dwelling in dimension of four—*Rector*

Dwo ching chywe dz dzung wu ching—*Du Mu*

Dying is fine but death—*Cummings*

Dyo phidia horaia khi alargina—*Seferis*

Dz wo ye ye ban—*Wei Jwang*

È dietro le casipole il porticciuolo—*Ungaretti*

È fosco l'aere—*Fusinato*

E- / gypt—*Brathwaite*

E il cuore quando d'un ultimo battito—*Ungaretti*

È na tristezza chesta casa mia—*Filippo*

E perchè paga Vostra Signoria—*Giusti*

E' s'aprono i fiori notturni—*Pascoli*

E sta vecchia chitarra frangese—*Di Giacomo*

E vi rivedo, o gattici d'argento—*Pascoli*

Each dawn might be winter again—*Williams, Hugo*

Each day I must relearn—*Halley*

Each day with so much ceremony—*Bishop, Elizabeth*

Each gesture—*Creeley*

Each life converges to some centre—*Dickinson, Emily*

Each man must suffer his fate—*Eberhart*

Each morning a new play begins—*Marshall, Helen Lowrie*

Each morning pack a pocket of smiles—*Marshall, Helen Lowrie*

Each night for seven nights beyond the gulf—*Graves*

Each of us pursues his trade—*Anonymous–English–Modern English*

Each stone and cornice calls—*Marshall, Lenore G.*

The eagle drizzle—*Berger*

An eagle's nest on the head of an old redwood—*Jeffers, Robinson*

Early Electric! With what radiant hope—*Betjeman*

Early in the morning—*Simpson*

Early one morning as I went out walking—*Norris*

Early sun on Beaulieu water—*Betjeman*

Early to bed—*Children's Verses and Nursery Rhymes*

The early violets we saw together—*Kunitz*

Earnest, earthless, equal attunable—*Hopkins*

Earnestly I looked—*Levertov*

The earth breathes fire—*Williams, Hugo*

Earth darkens and is beaded—*Winters*

Earth has not anything to show more fair—*Wordsworth*

Earth in beauty dressed—*Yeats*

The earth keeps some vibration going—*Masters, Edgar Lee*

Earth raised up her head—*Blake*

Ease a mask from out of space—*Arnez*

East of the eastern ledge a hundred yards—*Blackmur*

Eastern guard tower—*Knight, Etheridge*

Easy on your drums—*Bontemps*

Eat thou and drink—*Rossetti, Dante Gabriel*

The 'eathen in 'is blindness bows down to wood an' stone—*Kipling*

Eating is her subject—*Stein, Gertrude*

The ebb slips from the rock—*Jeffers, Robinson*

Ecco mormorar l'onde—*Tasso*

L'échafaud, c'est la guillotine—*Jacob, Max*

L'échelonnement des haies—*Verlaine*

Éclaireur comme tu surviens tard—*Char*

Écoute, bûcheron, arrête un peu le bras—*Ronsard*

Écoutez la chanson bien douce—*Verlaine*

Edel sei der Mensch—*Goethe*

Eenie, meenie, miney, mo—*Children's Verses and Nursery Rhymes*

Eftsoones they heard a most melodious sound—*Spenser*

Eggs that come from chickens—*Gioseffi*

Egno de psyche me podokeos Aiakidao—*Homer*

Egypt's might is tumbled down—*Coleridge, Mary Elizabeth*

Eheu fugaces, postume, postume—*Horace*

Ehmals winktest du mir, Führer des Schweigenden—*Stolberg*

Ehret, wen ihr auch wollt—*Goethe*

Ei fu. Siccome immobile—*Manzoni*

Eigentlich ist mir alles gleich—*Fontane*

8th October: si tuit li dolh elh plor Angold.—*Pound*

Eil o zaudernde Zeit—*Hölderlin*

Eine Liebe kenn' ich, die ist treu—*Mörike*

Die Eine sitzt die Andre liegt—*Kästner*

Einen Menschen namens Meier—*Busch*

Einer von uns ist über das Meer gefahren—*Brecht*

Eines schönen Tages befahlen uns unsere Obern—*Brecht*

Eines Tags bei Kohlhasficht—*Morgenstern*

Das Einhorn lebt von Ort zu Ort—*Morgenstern*

Einsamer nie als im August—*Benn*

Einst haben die Kerls auf Bäumen gehockt—*Kästner*

Einst kam ein altes Weib einher—*Brecht*
Einst, wenn der Winter begann—*Benn*
Either in or out of the mind—*Creeley*
Ej längre med tillbringaren du går—*Lindorm*
Él pasó con otra—*Mistral*
Él que espera desespera—*Machado, Manuel*
Ela canta, pobre ceifeira—*Pessoa*
Elaine the faire, Elaine the loveable—*Tennyson*
Elected Kaiser, burgher and a knight—*Lowell, Robert*
Elected Silence, sing to me—*Hopkins*
The element of air was out of hand—*Roethke*
Elephant hunter, take your bow—*Anonymous–African languages–Gabon*
The elephant is overturned—*Williams, Hugo*
The Elephant will eat of hay—*Belloc*
Elephants are useful friends—*Nash*
Elephants walking along the trails—*Link*
Eleven palm trees—*Kumin*
Elf Schläge dröhnt zu mir herab—*Hauptmann*
Elijah—*Marvin X*
La elipse de un grito—*Garcia Lorca*
Elle a mis le couvert—*Char*
Elle est debout sur mes paupières—*Éluard*
Elle est retrouvée—*Rimbaud*
Elle est toute petite—*Hugo, Victor*
Elle était belle, si la Nuit—*Musset*
Elle était pâle—*Hugo, Victor*
Elle m'a dit—*Marguerite de Navarre*
Elle me dit: je suis l'impossible théâtre—*Vigny*
Elle s'en vint—*Damas*
Ellie and Marvin—*Viorst*
Ellos son enemigos del silencio—*Murciano*
Elysium is as far as to the very nearest room—*Dickinson, Emily*
Em meu quarto, o sile—*Ricardo*
Emancipation: 1865—*Hughes, Langston*
Emergency evening—*Chester*
Emerges daintily, the skunk—*Moore, Marianne*
Emma Slide, I'm a slide—*Fraser, Kathleen*
Emma, vous fûtes belle, et depuis Champmêlé—*Sainte-Beuve*
Emmeline—*Milne*
Emos d erigeneia phane—*Homer*
Empfangen und genähret—*Claudius*
Empieza el llanto de la guitarra—*Garcia Lorca*
Emportez-moi dans une caravelle—*Michaux*
The empty saddle and muffled drums—*Goldstein*
En a zoi solst du reddin—*Sutzkever*
En aquel amor inmenso—*Juan de la Cruz*
En aquestos y otros ruegos—*Juan de la Cruz*
En attendant les clefs—*Milosz*
En Castilla está un castillo—*Anonymous–Spanish*
En ce temps-là j'étais en mon adolescence—*Cendrars*
En Ceupta esta don Julian—*Anonymous–Spanish*
En el bar del British Club—*Paz*
En el cuerno vacío de toro—*Carrera Andrade*
En el desván antiguo de raída memoria—*Bousoño*
En el fondo de aire (dije) estoy—*Jiménez*
En el fondo de mar profundo—*Neruda*
En el fondo, las risas de mis hijos—*Unamuno*
En el meeting de la Humanidad, millones de hombres gritan lo mismo—*Benavente*
En el mundo está la luz—*Mistral*
En el naranjo está la estrella—*Jiménez*

En el principio moraba—*Juan de la Cruz*
En el recuerdo estás tal como estabas—*Jiménez*
En el silencio siento pasar hora tras hora—*Agustini*
En el soto—*Garcia Lorca*
En esta soledad que me acompaña—*Sansores*
En faisant la roue, cet oiseau—*Apollinaire*
En invernales horas, mirad a Carolina—*Darío*
En la angosta senda he visto—*Garcia Lorca*
En la casa blanca muere—*Garcia Lorca*
En la clave del arco mal seguro—*Nerval*
En la corrida más grande—*Garcia Lorca*
En la forest d'ennuyeuse Tristesse—*Charles d'Orleans*
En la mañana, en su fino y mojado/ aire—*Valverde*
En la mitad del barranco—*Garcia Lorca*
En l'an de l'Incarnacion—*Ruteboeuf*
En languissant, et en grefve tristesse—*Marot*
En los ecos de órgano—*Castro, Rosalía de*
En los piñares de Júcar—*Góngora*
En mi fuente consagrada a Diana—*Martinez Alonso*
En pocos versos vais a saber—*Martínez Sierra*
¿En qué piensas tú, muerto, Cristo mío?—*Unamuno*
En quero a estrêla da manhâ—*Bandeira*
En Santa Gadea de Burgos—*Anonymous–Spanish*
En Santo Domingo—*Machado, Antonio*
En tanto que de rosa y azucena—*Vega, Garcilaso de la*
En tí encerré mis horas de alegría—*Martí*
En torno de una mesa de cautina—*Aguirre*
En torno el crimen absoluto—*Guillén, Jorge*
En tu calle sin salida—*León, Rafael de*
En una noche obscura—*Juan de la Cruz*
En Vallaurís en cada casa—*Neruda*
En verdad este espejo—*Alberti*
En Viena hay diez muchachas—*Garcia Lorca*
Encima de las corrientes—*Juan de la Cruz*
Encontré a Platero echado en su cama—*Jiménez*
Encore un livre—*Laforgue*
Encorvado día tras día, sobre la rústica azada—*Arana*
End ligger Jorden i Sneens Svøb—*Andersen*
An endless mat of white velvet—*Goldstein*
The endless part of disintegration—*Eberhart*
Endure what life God gives—*Yeats*
Un enfant a dit—*Queneau*
Enfants, on vous dira plus tard que le grand-père—*Hugo, Victor*
Enfranchising cable—*Moore, Marianne*
Engång blir alting stilla—*Lagerkvist*
Engine, engine, number nine—*Children's Verses and Nursery Rhymes*
The Engine is killing the track—*Plath*
England, Awake!—*Blake*
England, with all thy faults—*Cowper*
Engles, de flors faitz capelh—*Bertrand de Born*
Engrave the snowflake—*Wain*
Enhiesto surtidor de sombra y sueño—*Diego, Gerardo*
The enigmatic moon has at long last died—*Collins, Leslie M.*
Enjamás podré olvidarlo—*Pemán*

Enter into the game of life—*Marshall, Helen Lowrie*

Enter the chilly no-man's land of about—*Plath*

Enter with him—*Auden*

Entflieh mit mir und sei mein Weib—*Heine*

Enthroned in plastic, shrouded in wool—*Ginsberg*

Entonces en la escala de la tierra—*Neruda*

Entonces llamó un archángel—*Juan de la Cruz*

Entra en la playa de oro el mar y llena—*Garcia Nieto*

Entrando en la dehesa de los caballos—*Jiménez*

Entrando por la calle—*Jiménez*

Entre el discorde estruendo—*Becquer*

Entre en moi toi ma multitude—*Éluard*

Entre la noche que está dormida—*Espina*

Entre les rangées d'arbres—*Prévert*

Entre mariposas negras—*Garcia Lorca*

Entre morir y no morir—*Neruda*

Entre sombra y espacio—*Neruda*

Entre tous mes tourments entre la mort et moi —*Éluard*

Éntreme donde no supe—*Juan de la Cruz*

Epaman men ego sethen—*Sappho*

Epameroi ti de tis; ti d ou tis—*Pindar*

L'épi naissant mûrit de la faux respecte—*Chénier*

Equality is absolute or no—*Van Doren*

Equipoise: becalmed—*MacNeice*

Er ist der Gott, vor dem die Armen knien—*Trakl*

Er kriegte Geld. Die Sorge wich—*Busch*

Er liegt so still im Morgenlicht—*Droste-Hülshoff*

Er sinkt, er fällt jetzt-höhnt ihr hin und wieder —*Nietzsche*

Er stand auf seines Daches Zinnen—*Schiller*

Er wahrlich liebte die Sonne—*Trakl*

Er wirft ein Auge auf die Viertelstunde—*Krolow*

Era apacible el día—*Castro, Rosalía de*

Era en Numancia, al tiempo que declina—*Diego, Gerardo*

Era il mattino, e tra le chiuse imposte—*Leopardi*

Era la edad lisonjera—*Gómez de Avellaneda*

Era—no, no era así—*Jiménez*

Era un niño que soñaba un caballo de cartón—*Machado, Manuel*

Era una gatta, assai trita—*Pascoli*

Era una noche del mes de mayo—*Machado, Manuel*

Eramos tres hermanas. Dijo una—*Arrieta*

Eran jóvenes: avanzaron—*Ridruejo*

Eran trecento, eran giovani e forti—*Mercantini*

Erano i capei d'oro all'aura sparsi—*Petrarca*

Eras quan vey verdeyar—*Raimbaut de Vaqueiras*

Eras rosa—*Garcia Lorca*

Érase un hombre a una nariz pegado—*Quevedo y Villegas*

Érase una caverna de agua sombría el cielo—*Lugones, Leopoldo*

Die Erden lag verhüllt—*Gryphius*

Ere on my bed my limbs I lay—*Coleridge, Samuel Taylor*

Ere sleep comes down to soothe the weary eyes —*Dunbar, Paul Laurence*

The erect hardness—*Eckels*

Die Ereignisse und das Nichtereignete—*Heissenbüttel*

Eres de un material al que nadie poso nombre —*Godoy*

Eres tú, Guadarrama, viejo amigo—*Machado, Antonio*

Ergo ubi Narcissum per devia rura vagantem—*Ovid*

Die Erinnerung ist eine weibliche Statue—*Krolow*

Ernest was an Elephant—*Milne*

Ernsthafte Gottheit, heiliges Schweigen—*Gemmingen*

Eros pot' en rodoisin—*Anacreon*

Erschrocken staunt der Heide Schaf mich an—*Morgenstern*

Erschütterer—Anemone—*Benn*

Die erste alte Tante sprach—*Busch*

Der erste Blick aus dem Fenster—*Brecht*

Die ersten Veilchen waren schon—*Keller, Gottfried*

Es blökt eine Lämmerwolke—*Morgenstern*

Es con voz de la Biblia, o verso de Walt Whitman —*Darío*

Es fiedeln die Geigen—*Eichendorff*

Es flog einmal ein muntres Fliegel—*Busch*

Es gibt ein Gespenst—*Morgenstern*

Es gibt ja leider Sachen und Geschichten—*Busch*

Es ist der Tag im Nebel völlig eingehüllt—*Lasker-Schüler*

Es ist ein Stoppelfeld, in das ein schwarzer Regen fällt—*Trakl*

Es ist so still: die Heide liegt—*Storm*

Es kommen härtere Tage—*Bachmann*

Es kommt der Abend und ich tauche in die Sterne —*Lasker-Schüler*

Es kommt der Lenz mit dem Hochzeitgeschenk —*Heine*

Es la hora agonizante—*Dicenta*

Es la luz misma, la que abrió mis ojos—*Cernuda*

Es la mujer del hombre lo más bueno—*Vega Carpio*

Es la tierra de Soria árida y fría—*Machado, Antonio*

Es la voz de mi canción—*Pinar*

Es laufen vor Premieren—*Tucholsky*

Es läuft der Frühlingswind—*Hofmannsthal*

Es lebe das Grossreinemachen—*Kästner*

Es noche, tal silencio—*Storni*

Es questión de palabras—*Becquer*

Es rauschen die Wipfel und schauern—*Eichendorff*

Es reden und träumen die Menschen viel—*Schiller*

Es rinnen die Wasser vom Bühle—*Bergengruen*

Es sass der fromme Meister—*Busch*

Es schienen so golden die Sterne—*Eichendorff*

Es schlug mein Herz, geschwind zu Pferde—*Goethe*

Es sitzen Möpse gern auf Mauerecken—*Morgenstern*

Es stehen unbeweglich—*Heine*

Es stieg ein Morgen herauf—*Hauptmann*

Es tan dulce mirar como derrama—*Pérez de Zambrana*

Es tragt die Nacht—*Benn*

Es un flete criollo, violento y amontonado—*Güiraldes*

Es un sueño la vida—*Becquer*

Es verdad; pues reprimamos—*Calderón de la Barca*

Es war, als hätt' der Himmel—*Eichendorff*
Es war ein alter König—*Heine*
Es war ein fauler Schäfer—*Goethe*
Es war ein Kind, das wollte nie—*Goethe*
Es war ein König in Thule—*Goethe*
Es war einmal ein Kind—*Brecht*
Es war einmal ein Lattenzaun—*Morgenstern*
Es war einmal ein Zimmergesell—*Anonymous–German*
Es wäre schön könnte ich den ganzen Tag—*Theobaldy*
Es waren einmal zwei Hunde—*Wedekind*
Es wird ein grosser Stern in meinen Schoss fallen—*Lasker-Schüler*
Es zogen drei Bursche wohl über den Rhein—*Uhland*
Es zogen zwei rüst'ge Gesellen—*Eichendorff*
Esa tu voz serena, tu voz hecha a la ausencia—*Carvajal*
Escape me? never—*Browning, Robert*
Escribe un pensador: Tengo delante—*Campoamor*
Escrito está en mi alma—*Vega, Garcilaso de la*
Escrútame los ojos—*Storni*
Escucha, tengo miedo—*Victoria*
Eshche krugom nochnaya mgla—*Pasternak*
Esli slovo vret v glaza—*Kirsanov*
Esmeralda! Now we rest—*Nabokov*
Ésope conte qu'un Manant—*La Fontaine*
L'Espace?—Mon coeur—*Laforgue*
¡España! Á alzar su voz nadie se atreve—*Unamuno*
La España de charanga y pandereta—*Machado, Antonio*
Especially when the October wind—*Thomas, Dylan*
Espírito que passas, quando o vento—*Quental*
Espíritu sin nombre—*Becquer*
Espíritus de seis alas—*Alberti*
The esplanade empty, closed at this time—*Plomer*
L'espoir luit comme un brin de paille—*Verlaine*
Esponja de agua dulce—*Guillén, Nicolás*
Una esposa que te ame—*Juan de la Cruz*
Esquilones de plata llevan los bueyes—*Garcia Lorca*
Est' mesto: bliz tropy glukhoi—*Lermontov*
Est' ptichka raya u menya—*Lermontov*
Est' rechi—*Lermontov*
Esta blanca camisa que mi madre ha zurcido—*Acosta*
Ésta es el hambre—*Guillén, Nicolás*
Está la noche serena—*Espronceda*
Esta mañana he estado en el Zoológico con mi hija—*Gaos*
Esta necesidad de sacrificio—*Reyes*
Esta noche de agosto he quemado tus cartas—*León, Rafael de*
Esta noche se nos muere un año—*Blanco*
Estáis en pirata y negro—*Palés Matos*
Estando yo en la mi choza—*Anonymous–Spanish*
Estar enamorado amigos es—*Bernárdez*
Éstas, que fueron pompa y alegría—*Calderón de la Barca*
Las estatuas sufren por los ojos con la oscuridad de los ataudes—*Garcia Lorca*
Este amoroso tormento—*Juana Inés de la Cruz*

Este cuerpo que Diós pone en mis brazos—*Prados*
Éste es aquel convento de Franciscas—*Unamuno*
Éste es el libro de mi dolor—*Nervo*
Este hastío, esta pena o esta melancolía—*Martinez Estrada*
Este, que ves, engaño colorido—*Juana Inés de la Cruz*
Este silêncio e feito de agonias—*Quintana, Mário*
Esterina, i vent'anni ti minacciano—*Montale*
Esto conto Picardia y despues guardo silencio—*Hernández, José*
Esto de no ser más que tiempo espanta—*Murciano*
Estoy complete de naturaleza—*Jiménez*
Las estrellas apagadas llenan de ceniza—*Garcia Lorca*
Estue tibi, Cerinthe, tuae pia cura puellae—*Sulpicia*
Et c'est la Mer qui vint à nous sur les degrés de pierre du drame—*Perse*
Et je redis ton nom: Dyallo—*Senghor*
Et la Mère, fermant le livre du devoir—*Rimbaud*
Et le soir vient et les lys meurent—*Apollinaire*
Et les sabots—*Damas*
Et pourtant, nous pouvions ne jamais nous connaître—*Geraldy*
Et s'il était à refaire—*Aragon*
Et surtout que Demain n'aprenne pas—*Milosz*
Et voici que/ pour toi et moi—*Damas*
Et vous, Mers, qui lisiez dans de plus vastes songes—*Perse*
L'été, lorsque le jour a fui—*Hugo, Victor*
Étendant les mains—*Michaux*
Étends les bras—*Soupault*
Eternal Spirit you—*Winters*
Ethereal Ethel-Mrs. Chivers—*Sitwell, Osbert*
Étoile de la mer, voici la lourde—*Péguy*
Etot vecher reshal—*Mayakovsky*
Étroits sont les vaisseaux, étroite notre conche—*Perse*
Ett är nödvändigt: att färdas mot Brunnar—*Edfelt*
Ett årende hit, ett årende dit—*Ferlin*
Eu canto porque o instante existe—*Meireles*
Euclid alone has looked on beauty bare—*Millay*
Eudosin d oreon koryphai te kai pharagges—*Alcman*
The European shoe is constructed of grass and reed—*Benedikt*
Eute pur aidelon epiphlegei aspeton hulen—*Homer*
Éva, j'aimerai tout dans les choses créées—*Vigny*
Évam bahu vidhām cintām—*Valmiki*
Even along the railway platform it was spring—*Scott, Winfield Townley*
Even as children they were late sleepers—*Wilbur*
Even as the sun with purple colour'd face—*Shakespeare*
Even on clear nights, lead the most supple children—*Hollander*
Even such am I; within whose thoughts resides—*Chesterton, Gilbert Keith*
Even such is time, that takes in trust—*Raleigh*
Even when first her face—*Wilbur*
Even with the least we know—*Kelly*

Evenin' Miss Evvy Miss Maisie, Miss—*Brathwaite*
Evening and the sun warming the bird—*Patten*
Evening traffic homeward burns—*Winters*
Eventually one finds—*Eberhart*
Ever that Everest—*Merrill*
Everlastingly—*Eckels*
Every branch big with it—*Hardy*
Every choice is always the wrong choice—*Graves*
Every day is the last day—*Sandburg*
Every day of the world—*Hughes, Ted*
Every Friday morning my grandfather left—*Brathwaite*
Every man his own Robespierre—*Cowley, Malcolm*
Every morn I send you violets—*Heine*
Every morning when I wake up—*Dupree*
Every night my prayers I say—*Stevenson*
Every thread of summer is at last unwoven—*Stevens, Wallace*
Every year without knowing it I have passed the day—*Merwin*
Everybody—*Hughes, Langston*
Everybody can tell you the date of George Washington's birth—*Nash*
Everybody I want so much to see—*Bly*
Everybody loved Chick Lorimer in our town—*Sandburg*
Everybody says I look just like my mother—*Aldis*
Everyone grumbled. The sky was grey—*Noyes*
Everyone has her down days—*Marshall, Helen Lowrie*
Everyone is coming to our party—*Viorst*
Everyone's kissing John Tank—*Pines*
Everything's been different all the day long—*Fyleman*
Everytime it rains—*Giovanni*
Everywhere snow is falling—*Rich*
Everywhere they are waiting—*Webster, H.*
Evidence of life—*Jong*
Evige, du som ruvar—*Blomberg*
An evil spirit, your beauty haunts me still—*Drayton*
Die ewig-helle schar wil nun ihr licht verschliessen—*Gryphius*
Excellence is sparse—*Davie*
Excellent o excellent in morning sunlight—*Aiken*
Except in your—*Cummings*
Except where blast-furnaces and generating-stations—*Auden*
Exchange in greed the ungraceful signs—*Knight, Etheridge*
Exegi monumentum aere perennius—*Horace*
Th'expense of spirit in a waste of shame—*Shakespeare*
Experience, though noon auctoritee—*Chaucer*
The exulting, they sing they sing—*Roethke*
Eye dazzlers the Indians weave—*Swenson*
The eye we are told—*Giovanni*
The eyelids glowing, some chill morning—*Snodgrass*
The eyes are last to go out—*Williams, Tennessee*
Eyes awaken—*Tullos*
The eyes of twenty centuries—*Spender*
The eyes open to a cry of pulleys—*Wilbur*
The eyes that mock me sign the day—*Joyce*

F/ Train/ absolutely stoned—*Whalen*

Fa brent der shule oif es is shoyne kinde mines a tzoura—*Stern*
Fa dolce e forse qui vicino passi—*Ungaretti*
Fa plantered in zamsicha flachan—*Sutzkever*
Les fables ne sont pas ce qu'elles semblent être—*La Fontaine*
Fabrico um elefante—*Drummond de Andrade*
La fábula escondida—*Barbieri*
The face I know—*Antoninus*
The face of all the world is changed—*Browning, Elizabeth Barrett*
Face to face—*Gaver*
A fact which may seem strange to you—*Marshall, Helen Lowrie*
Fading de la tristesse oubli—*Aragon*
Fahr aus, du heftiger Geist—*Bergengruen*
Die Fahrten gehn zu Ende—*Bachmann*
Fair Amoret is gone astray—*Congreve*
Fair fa' your honest, sonsie face—*Burns*
Fair flower, that dost so comely grow—*Freneau*
Fair Lady Isabel sits in her bower sewing—*Anonymous–English—Modern English*
Fair now is the spring-tide—*Morris, William*
Fair river! in the bright clear flow—*Poe*
Fair seed-time had my soul—*Wordsworth*
Fair ship, that from the Italian shore—*Tennyson*
Fair stood the wind for France—*Drayton*
Fair tree! for thy delightful shade—*Finch, Anne, Countess of Winchelsea*
Fair Verna! loveliest village in the west—*Dwight*
Faire Daffadills, we weep to see—*Herrick*
Fairfax, whose name in arms through Europe sings—*Milton*
The Fairies have never a penny to spend—*Fyleman*
Faites-moi rire, bouffon—*Prévert*
Fall, and we came to the rock-bleached pasture—*Bishop, John Peale*
The fall from man engenders me—*MacPherson*
The fallen city rides from the dark—*Blackburn, Thomas*
Fallen, so freshly fallen—*Kunitz*
Falleth the rain, falleth the leaf—*Francis*
Fallow between the horny trees—*Wright, James*
False life! a foil and no more—*Vaughan, Henry*
Faltar pudo su patria al grande Osuna—*Quevedo y Villegas*
The family had been ill—*Shange*
The family story tells—*Sexton*
Fanfare of northwest wind, a bluejay wind—*Aiken*
Fantasies of old age—*Rich*
Far away is close at hand—*Graves*
Far enough down is China—*Wilbur*
Far, far down—*Howes*
Far far the least of all, in want—*Spender*
Far-fetched with tales of other worlds and ways—*Lee, Laurie*
Far in the background a blue mountain waits—*Engle*
Far off from where most people pass—*Kramer*
Far out of sight forever stands the sea—*Winters*
The far side of your moon is black—*Graves*
Fare thee well! and if for ever—*Byron*
Farewell for ever, well for ever fare—*Smith, Stevie*

Farewell! thou art too dear for my possessing—*Shakespeare*

Farewell thou busie World—*Cotton*

Farewell, thou child of my right hand—*Jonson*

Farewell, thou fertyll soyle, that Brutus fyrst out founde—*Googe*

Farewell to a' our Scottish fame—*Burns*

Farewell to barn and stack and tree—*Housman*

Farewell, too little, and too lately known—*Dryden*

Farm boys wild to couple—*Dickey, James*

Farm houses curl like horns of plenty, hide—*Cowley, Malcolm*

The fascination of what's difficult—*Yeats*

Fastening cables—*Andrews*

Faster than fairies, faster than witches—*Stevenson*

Fat black bucks in a wine-barrel room—*Lindsay, Vachel*

The fat man who owns the carnival—*Lally*

Fatal, fatal is the song of the dire night-raven—*Nikarchos*

Father—*Emanuel*

Father dead, land lost, stepmother haggard with kids—*Warren*

Father, father, where are you going—*Blake*

Father, whom I knew well for forty years—*Wheelock*

Fath'r and I went down to camp—*Anonymous–English—Modern English*

Fatigada del baile, encendido el color—*Becquer*

Fatted/ on herbs—*Kinnell*

Faustin, der ganze funfzehn Jahr—*Lessing*

Les faux beaux jours ont lui tout le jour—*Verlaine*

Fay refraischir mon vin de sorte—*Ronsard*

Fear death? to feel the fog in my throat—*Browning, Robert*

Fear no more the heat o' the sun—*Shakespeare*

The fear of poetry—*Rukeyser*

The feast was over in Branksome tower—*Scott, Sir Walter*

Federico. On the grey ledges—*Vargas*

The feelings I don't have I don't have—*Lawrence*

Feiger Gedanken—*Goethe*

Felix Randal the farrier, O is he dead—*Hopkins*

Fellowship's a maker of friendships—*Marshall, Helen Lowrie*

Femme nue, femme noire—*Senghor*

Lo ferm voler qu'el cor m'intra—*Daniel, Arnaud*

La fermeture éclair a glissé sur tes reins—*Prévert*

Ferry me across the water—*Rossetti, Christina*

Fest gemauert in der Erden—*Schiller*

Fetter grüne, du Laub—*Goethe*

Feu d'artifice en acier—*Apollinaire*

Feu que les hommes regardent dans la nuit—*Senghor*

Les feuilles mortes tombent dans l'air dormant—*Milosz*

The feverish room and that white bed—*Symons*

Few things are less endearing than a personal comparison—*Nash*

Few were the words we said—*Doolittle*

Fie, foolish earth, think'st thou the Heaven wants glory—*Greville*

The field boss claimed his privilege—*Beecher*

The field where the hero's—*Anonymous–American Indian languages–Nahuatl*

A fig for those by law protected—*Burns*

The figs on the fig tree in the yard are green—*Plath*

Figure de femme, sur son sommeil—*Rilke*

Les filles de Gentilly—*Soupault*

La fillette aux violettes—*Carco*

Filling her compact and delicious body—*Berryman*

Finally, from your house, there is no view—*Moss, Howard*

Finally retired—*Lee, Don L.*

Finally, to forgo love is to kiss a leaf—*Ignatow*

Finding myself still fascinated—*Giovanni*

Finding the measure—*Kelly*

The fine delight that fathers thought—*Hopkins*

Fine knacks for Ladies, cheap, choice, brave and new—*Anonymous–English—Modern English*

The fine powder of the dry rot—*Eberhart*

Fingers. Cramped, you are hardly anything—*Fuller, John*

Finis, apparent on an earlier page—*Graves*

Ein finstrer Esel sprach einmal—*Morgenstern*

The fire in leaf and grass—*Levertov*

Fired in sanguined clay—*Plath*

The firefly's flame—*Nash*

Fires on the hearth! Fires in the heavens—*Sitwell, Edith*

Firm-lipped, high-bosomed slender Queen—*Graves*

First a word was fuzzy, and was nothing—*Eberhart*

First American mature mind—*Engle*

First, are you our sort of person—*Plath*

The first blossom was the best blossom—*MacNeice*

The first blow hurt—*Emanuel*

First, boys out of school went out of their way home—*Redgrove*

First came the special issues of the magazines—*Mandel*

The first day i shot dope—*Sanchez*

First having read the book of myths—*Rich*

The first heaven is a flowery plain—*Graves*

The first kiss was with stumbling fingertips—*Shapiro, Karl*

First light comes at 3 AM—*Lester*

First, may the hand of bounty bring—*Herrick*

The first Nowell—*Anonymous–English—Modern English*

First of the first, such I pronounce Pompilia—*Browning, Robert*

The first speaker said—*Francis*

First the fish must be caught—*Carroll*

First–the sun coming closer, growing by the minute—*Hughes, Ted*

First, the two men stand pondering—*Wright, James*

First there was the event—*Gold*

First they sliced off the left—*Harteis*

The first thing I saw in the morning—*Wright, James*

First time he kissed me, he but only kissed—*Browning, Elizabeth Barrett*

The first time I ever saw her—*Johnston, Ellen Turlington*

The first time that I gave a test—*Johnston, Ellen Turlington*

The first time that the sun rose on thine oath—*Browning, Elizabeth Barrett*

First when Maggy was my care—*Burns*

The first woman I loved—*Spencer*

Die Fischer überliefern dass im Süden—*George*

A fish comes up for food—*Lester*

The fish does . . . HIP—*Anonymous–African languages–Gabon*

A fish dripping—*Ross, W. W. Eustace*

Fish (fly-replete, in depth of June)—*Brooke*

The fish wade/through black jade—*Moore, Marianne*

The fish-tailed lady offering her breast—*MacPherson*

The fishmarket closed, the fish gone into flesh—*Kinnell*

Fitting a thin glove over a dry hand—*Plomer*

Five hours—*De Frees*

Five hours west of midnight—*Engle*

Five little monkeys—*Richards, Laura E.*

Five men pushing over part of a wall—*Souster*

Five minutes, five minutes more, please—*Farjeon*

Five soldiers fixed by Mathew Brady's eye—*Wilbur*

Five summer days, five summer nights—*Graves*

Five years have past, five summers—*Wordsworth*

Fix our firm in the back of your brain—*Kramer*

The flag that hung half-mast to-day—*Betjeman*

Flailed from the heart of water in a bow—*Wilbur*

A flame from each finger—*Piercy*

The flame guttered, flared impossibly high—*Graves*

Flat blue hills—*Lifshin*

Flavi, delicias tuas Catullo—*Catullus*

Flee from the press—*Chaucer*

The fleece of the sacrificial lamb—*Gaver*

Fleet ships encountering on the high seas—*Ransom*

Flesh speaks—*Emanuel*

The flesh that once sang—*MacLeish*

Fliegt der erste Morgenstrahl—*Eichendorff*

A Flimflam flopped from a fillamaloo—*Field, Eugene*

The flirt is an antelope of flame—*Updike*

A flock of birds, soaring, twisting, turning—*Darr*

A flock of sheep that leisurely pass by—*Wordsworth*

Flood-tide below me! I see you face to face—*Whitman*

La flor delicada, que apenas existe una aurora—*Gómez de Avellaneda*

Flora desnuda se sube—*Garcia Lorca*

Flora gave me fairest flowers—*Anonymous–English—Modern English*

Las flores de romero, niña Isabel—*Góngora*

Las flores no son ciegas—*Martinez Alonso*

Floriram por engano as rosas bravas—*Pessanha*

Flota sobre el esplín de la campaña—*Herrera y Reissig*

Flow down cold rivulet, to the sea—*Tennyson*

Flow gently, Sweet Afton—*Burns*

The flower-fed buffaloes of the spring—*Lindsay, Vachel*

A flower was offered to me—*Blake*

Flowers of air—*Rukeyser*

Flowers through the window—*Williams, William Carlos*

Fluffed and still as snow, the white—*Scott, F. R.*

Flukum couldn't stand the strain—*Knight, Etheridge*

Die Flut steigt bis an den Ararat—*Fontane*

Fly, envious time, till thou run out thy race—*Milton*

Fly, white butterflies, out to sea—*Swinburne*

Flying in plane's rib—*Abbe*

A flying saucer landed—*Giovanni*

The fog, a sheepdog circling, bared—*Walcott*

The fog comes on little cat feet—*Sandburg*

Fog envelops the animals—*Dickey, James*

Foi de marron—*Damas*

La foi que j'aime le mieux—*Péguy*

Folks has be'n to town—*Riley*

Follow a shadow, it still flies you—*Jonson*

Follow the crowds to where the turnstiles click—*Abse*

Follow your saints, follow with accents sweet—*Campion*

Followe thy faire sunne—*Campion*

Following the dollar, ah—*Cowley, Malcolm*

Fond woman which would'st have thy husband die—*Donne*

Fonte-frida, fonte-frida—*Anonymous–Spanish*

A fool once caught a crow—*Reaney*

A fool there was and he made his prayer—*Kipling*

Footprints now on bread or cake—*Van Doren*

For a good decade—*Merwin*

For a long time—*Gioseffi*

For all those beaten, for the broken heads—*Benét, Stephen Vincent*

För att utröna hur—*Ekelöf*

For Cecily the first concern and bother—*Morgenstern*

For far from gusty waves these children's faces—*Spender*

For Godsake hold your tongue, and let me love—*Donne*

For her gait, if she be walking—*Browne, William*

For his Religion it was fit—*Butler, Samuel*

For I have learned—*Wordsworth*

For I will consider my cat Jeoffry—*Smart*

For, lo, the winter is past—*Bible and Pseudepigrapha*

For losing her love—*Patchen*

For me, the naked and the nude—*Graves*

For months my hands had been sealed off—*Sexton*

For my own part—*Arnez*

For my people everywhere singing their slave songs repeatedly—*Walker*

For nations vague as weed—*Larkin*

For over ninety years—*Sitwell, Osbert*

For sacrifice, there are certain principles—*Day Lewis*

For sånt som var stort i byn—*Ferlin*

For shame! deny that thou bear'st love to any—*Shakespeare*

For thaem nead-foera naeniz wyrtheth—*Bede*

For that I never knew you I only learned to dread you—*Rukeyser*

For the sake of him who showed—*Kipling*

For the second time—*Tullos*

For the seven lakes, and by no man—*Pound*

For the shadows I am returning—*Khalil*

For this and for all enclosures like it the archetype —*Auden*

For three years, out of key with his time—*Pound*

For twenty months I whispered—*Nicholson*

For two young seamen lost overboard—*Barker, George*

For want of a nail the shoe was lost—*Children's Verses and Nursery Rhymes*

For wars his life and half a world away—*Jarrell*

For we are the stars, for we sing—*Anonymous–American Indian languages-Algonquin*

For years I thought I knew, at the bottom of the dream—*Bogan*

For you, O Democracy—*Whitman*

For you, or of you? It can't be—*Ciardi*

Foraars-Taagerne sig haeve—*Andersen*

The Force that through the green fuse drives the flower—*Thomas, Dylan*

The forces of liberation—*Hinton*

Foreigners are people somewhere else—*Nash*

Forêt, haute maison des oiseaux bocagers—*Ronsard*

Forewarned of madness—*Graves*

Forget, forget . . . Forget what you forget—*Richards, I. A.*

Forget not yet the tried intent—*Wyatt, Sir Thomas*

Forget the rest: my heart is true—*Graves*

Forgive me, dear, if I did not gasp—*Kramer*

Forgive, O Lord, my little jokes on thee—*Frost, Robert*

Forgive what I, adventuring highest themes—*Blunden*

Forlorn indeed Hope on these shores—*Davie*

The form of this "sport" is pain—*Bell*

Forse perche della fatal quiete—*Foscolo*

Forse un mattino andando in m'aria di vetro—*Montale*

Först skymningen, då allt blir stumt—*Blomberg*

Fortunatus the portrait-painter got twenty sons —*Nikarchos*

Fortune teller looked in my hand—*Hughes, Langston*

A forward child, a sullen boy—*Day Lewis*

The forward violet thus did I chide—*Shakespeare*

The forward youth that would appear—*Marvell*

Founded on a rock and facing the night-fouled sea—*Wilbur*

The founder's come to town—*Middleton, Thomas*

The fountain of fire—*Rago*

The fountains mingle with the river—*Shelley*

Four be the things I am wiser to know—*Parker*

Four bells were struck—*Masefield*

Four ducks on a pond—*Allingham*

Four easy hours from San Francisco, yes—*Starbuck*

Four hours cleaning the oven—*Tullos*

Four hundred children expect from one another —*Miles*

Four little girls in their Sunday best—*Goldstein*

The 4th of July he stormed a nest—*Starbuck*

Foutez-moi à la mer—*Soupault*

The fox-colored pheasant enjoyed his peace—*Levi*

Fr Cape Sable into a stream in—*Olson*

Fra te e la canarina azzura sono—*Saba*

Frail the white rose and frail are—*Joyce*

Fram glider genom rymden den gamla skutan Jord—*Lindorm*

Framed by our window, skaters, winding—*Weiss*

France, Mère des arts, des armes, et des loix—*Du Bellay*

Frances P. was on the roof—*Johnson, Joe*

Franchement, je croyais qu'amour, en poésie—*Cocteau*

Frate Francesco, quanto d'aere abbraccia—*Carducci*

Fratelli, aun tempo stesso, Amore e Morte—*Leopardi*

Das Fräulein stand am Meere—*Heine*

A freak's eye—*Berrigan*

Fred, where is north—*Frost, Robert*

Frederick Alexander Pott—*Updike*

The freedom of the wholly mad—*Rich*

Freewheeling down the escarpment past the unpassing horse—*MacNeice*

Fremd bin ich eingezogen—*Müller*

The French have a saying—*Marshall, Helen Lowrie*

Frères humains qui après nous vivez—*Villon*

Fresh from the factory—*Cowley, Malcolm*

Fresh Spring, the herald of loves mighty king—*Spenser*

Freude war in Trojas Hallen—*Schiller*

Freudig war, vor vielen Jahren—*Goethe*

Freudvoll und leidvoll—*Goethe*

Die Freunde, die mit mir sich unterhalten—*Werfel*

Friday afternoon in the universe—*Kerouac*

Friday Night at the Tin Palace—*Pines*

Friend, on this scaffold Thomas More lies dead —*Cunningham, James Vincent*

A friend told me—*Harper*

The friendly cow all red and white—*Stevenson*

Frightening the blood in its tunnel—*Hughes, Ted*

Frigidity the hesitant—*Winters*

Fritz war SA und Karl war Partei—*Brecht*

Frô Welt, ir sult dem Wirte sagen—*Walther von der Vogelweide*

Frogs burrow the mud—*Giovanni*

Frogs jump, caterpillars hump—*Beyer*

Froh empfind ich mich nun auf klassischem Boden begeistert—*Goethe*

Froh kehrt der Schiffer heim an den stillen Strom —*Hölderlin*

Frolée par les ombres des morts—*Apollinaire*

From a magician's midnight sleeve—*Bishop, Elizabeth*

From art, from nature, from the schools—*Tennyson*

From Bindle's opera house in the village—*Masters, Edgar Lee*

From breakfast on through all the day—*Stevenson*

From childhood's hour I have not been—*Poe*

From Clee to heaven the beacon burns—*Housman*

From committee-doodled day—*Richards, I. A.*

From deep sleep—*Emanuel*

From fairest creatures we desire increase—*Shakespeare*

From harmony, from heavenly harmony—*Dryden*

From Heals and Harrods come her lovely bride-grooms—*Porter, Peter*

From here, the quay, one looks above to mark—*Hardy*

From here through tunnelled gloom the track—*De la Mare*

From intellect's grosser denominations—*Durrell*

From loud sound and still chance—*Bogan*

From Matlock Bath's half-timbered station—*Betjeman*

From Molekolole—*Nemerov*

From Montgomery to Memphis he marches—*Walker*

From my high love—*Patchen*

From my high window—*Sitwell, Osbert*

From my mother's sleep I fell into the State—*Jarrell*

From one shaft at Cleator Moor—*Nicholson*

From Paumanok starting I fly like a bird—*Whitman*

From pent-up aching rivers—*Whitman*

From street to street I often watch the night—*Posner*

From sweet and stern sleep—*Sherwin*

From the besieged Arden all in post—*Shakespeare*

From the cassowary's beak come streaks of light—*Smith, William Jay*

From the conception the increase—*Anonymous–Australasian languages–Maori*

From the dark Viands of the Church—*Durrell*

From the drama of horror and despair—*Eberhart*

From the geyser ventilators autumn winds are blowing down—*Betjeman*

From the hag and hungry goblin—*Anonymous–English—Modern English*

From the high terrace porch I watch the dawn—*Winters*

From the hodge porridge of their country lust—*Sexton*

From the ocean filled with sand inside of me—*Jeffers, Lance*

From the rock untombed—*Antoninus*

From this orange-pippery—*Avison*

From Travancore to Tripoli—*Durrell*

From Water-Town Hill to the brick prison—*Plath*

From where I am sitting, my windowframe—*Day Lewis*

From where I lingered in a lull in March—*Frost, Robert*

From Wynard's Gap the livelong day—*Hardy*

From you have I been absent in the spring—*Shakespeare*

From you, Ianthe, little troubles pass—*Landor*

A frost came in the night and stole my world—*Day Lewis*

Frost klirre Glas—*Zuckmayer*

The frost performs its secret ministry—*Coleridge, Samuel Taylor*

Früh wann die Hähne krähn—*Mörike*

Früh, wenn Tal, Gebirg und Garten—*Goethe*

Früher schon zum Klassiker berufen—*Hesse*

Das Frühjahr kommt—*Brecht*

Frühling lässt sein blaues Band—*Mörike*

Frühmorgens lese ich in der Zeitung von epochalen Plänen—*Brecht*

The fruit rolled by all day—*Roethke*

Les fruits à la saveur de sable—*Aragon*

Fu allo svegliarmi del sonno con l'aria di vivere—*Gatto*

Fu dove il ponte di legno—*Montale*

Fue un tiempo de mentira de infamía—*Machado, Antonio*

Ful erly bifore de day folk vprysen—*Anonymous–English—Middle English*

Full fathom five thy father lies—*Shakespeare*

Full many a glorious morning have I seen—*Shakespeare*

The full moon—*Aubert*

The full moon easterly rising, furious—*Graves*

Full of her long white arms and milky skin—*Ransom*

Full of wrath was Hiawatha—*Longfellow*

The full spread pride of man—*Whitman*

Füllest wieder Busch und Tal—*Goethe*

Fünfzig Jahre werden es ehestens sein—*Fontane*

Funny the way different cars start—*Baruch*

Fürchte nichts, geliebte Seele—*Heine*

Furei, cui neque sernos est neque area—*Catullus*

Furi, nillula nostra non ad Austri—*Catullus*

Further completion of Plat—*Olson*

Further in summer than the birds—*Dickinson, Emily*

Fusion is miracle—*Piercy*

Gå till stranden, mumlande i vinden—*Ekelöf*

Gaaer Du paa Glatiis og falder min Ven—*Andersen*

Gaben, wer hätte sie nicht?—*Fontane*

Gaily bedight—*Poe*

Gaily into Ruislip Gardens—*Betjeman*

Galán—*Garcia Lorca*

Gallants attend and hear a friend—*Hopkinson, Francis*

Gallarda, hermosa, triunfal—*Acosta*

A gallery of Jews love—*Rothenberg*

Gang girls are sweet exotics—*Brooks, Gwendolyn*

Ganz unverhofft an einem Hügel—*Busch*

The gardener does not love to talk—*Stevenson*

Garmonika, garmonika—*Blok*

A gas station in the playground of kings—*Shapiro, Karl*

The gas was on in the Institute—*Betjeman*

Gather out of star-dust—*Hughes, Langston*

Gather up—*Hughes, Langston*

Gather ye Rose-buds while ye may—*Herrick*

Gaunt in gloom—*Joyce*

Gaze not on swans, in whose soft breast—*Anonymous–English—Modern English*

Gazing and gazing in the glass—*Reid*

Le gazon râpé de la berge—*Carco*

Ein Gebet des Elenden, so er betrübt ist—*Luther*

Geborn ward er ohne Wehen—*Busch*

Ein Gedicht, aus Worten gemacht—*Kaschnitz*

Gefangen in der Falle der Verbindlichkeiten—*Heissenbüttel*

Geh aus mein Herz und suche Freud—*Gerhardt*

Geh! gehorche meinem Winken—*Goethe*

Geh unter, schöne Sonne, sie achteten—*Hölderlin*

Gehen wir Steine mit kühlen Gesichtern—*Krolow*

Gehn dir im Dämmerlichte—*Hölderlin*

Gehorche. Was für ein Lohn dir bereitet?—*Bergengruen*
Dem Geier gleich—*Goethe*
Gelassen stieg die Nacht ans Land—*Mörike*
Geliebt haben wir uns—*Fourest*
Gemächlich in der Werkstatt sass—*Chamisso*
Gemahnt dich noch das schöne Bildnis dessen—*George*
Genazzano am Abend—*Kaschnitz*
Genesis tells us of Jubal and Jabal—*Moore, Marianne*
La génisse, la chèvre, et leur soeur la brebis—*La Fontaine*
La gente s'accalca—*Palazzeschi*
Gentle blondness and the moray eel—*Dickey, James*
A gentle knight was pricking o'er the plaine—*Spenser*
The gentle milk jug blue and white—*Herford*
A gentle wind blows—*Patchen*
Gentleness, Virtue, Wisdom, and Endurance—*Shelley*
Geography locates actual mountains—*Bodenheim*
George—*Porter, Bern*
Georgey, Porgey—*Children's Verses and Nursery Rhymes*
Gerineldo, Gerineldo—*Anonymous-Spanish*
Geschäftig sind die Menschenkinder—*Busch*
Gestern, als ich vom nächtlichen Lager den Stern mir im Osten—*Mörike*
Gestern fuhr ich Fische fangen—*Bergengruen*
Gestern nachts, als alles schlief—*Nietzsche*
Gestern war in meiner Mütze—*Busch*
Get all the gold and silver that you can—*Yeats*
Get it on—*Simmons, Judy*
Get the gasworks into a poem—*Ignatow*
Get up, get up for shame—*Herrick*
Get up, I say, and see them—*Van Doren*
Get up, oh Anna dear—*Ferguson*
Getting from here to there—*Polak*
Gewaltig endet so das Jahr—*Trakl*
Una ggiornata come stammatina—*Belli*
Ghetto's the talk this year—*Arnez*
Ghost Lake's a dark lake, a deep lake—*Benét, William Rose*
A Ghost that loved a lady fair—*Beddoes*
The ghostself slips out of the poet—*Miller, E. Ethelbert*
Giacchi te cucche ampresso—*Di Giacomo*
Gib her die Larv', ich will mich jetzt maskieren—*Heine*
Gib in dein Gluck, dein Sterben—*Benn*
Gib mir, dass ich weinen kann—*Werfel*
Gig away Shindig—*Fabio, Sarah Webster*
Gina knew he loved her even—*Goldstein*
The gingham Dog and the calico Cat—*Field, Eugene*
Il giorno fu pieno di lampi—*Pascoli*
Lo giorno se n'andava, e l'aere bruno—*Dante Alighieri*
Girella (emerito—*Giusti*
Girl grown woman fire mother of fire—*Rukeyser*
A girl—quiet, skinny, small—*Johnston, Ellen Turlington*
Girls! although I am a woman—*Smith, Stevie*

The girl's far treble, muted to the heat—*Lee, Laurie*
Girls know how to lose alright—*Gaver*
Git the word out—*Sanchez*
Giuseppe, da barber, ees greata—*Daly*
Give all to love—*Emerson*
Give, ask for nothing, hope for nothing—*Graves*
Give beauty all her right—*Campion*
Give me more love or more disdain—*Carew*
Give me my scallop-shell of quiet—*Raleigh*
Give me, O indulgent fate—*Finch, Anne, Countess of Winchelsea*
Give me of your bark, O Birch-tree—*Longfellow*
Give me the splendid silent sun with all his beams—*Whitman*
Give the dancers castanets—*Gaver*
Give to me the life I love—*Stevenson*
Given the gift of a ring—*Reid*
The Glad food storage bags—*Porter, Bern*
Glad that I live am I—*Reese*
Gladly we expected it to drop—*Treitel*
Glass slippers danced throughout the year—*Goldstein*
Gleich einem König, der in seine Staaten—*Göckingk*
Gleich wird es regnen—*Eich*
Gli uccelli alla finestra, le persiane—*Saba*
Glimpses of an Image—*Fabio, Sarah Webster*
A glittering thing—*Emanuel*
Ein Glockenton fliegt durch die Nacht—*Morgenstern*
Glooms of the live-oaks, beautiful-braided and woven—*Lanier*
Gloomy night embraced the place—*Crashaw*
Gloria de Salamina vermella en el mar de l'aurora—*Riba Bracóns*
The glories of our blood and state—*Shirley*
Glory be to God for dappled things—*Hopkins*
Glory—glory to God in the highest—*Wheelock*
Glory! Halleluiah—*Hughes, Langston*
The glow of friendliness shone in her face—*Marshall, Helen Lowrie*
Das Glück ist eine leichte Dirne—*Heine*
Gno figio xe 'ndao in guera—*Marin*
Gnostic Faustus, Sapphic, sophic—*Ciardi*
Go back now, pause to mark that hill town—*Abbe*
Go, dumb-born book—*Pound*
Go, fetch to me a pint o' wine—*Burns*
Go, for they call you, shepherd, from the hill—*Arnold*
Go from me. Yet I feel that I shall stand—*Browning, Elizabeth Barrett*
Go hang yourself, you old M.D.—*Nash*
Go I must along my ways—*Parker*
Go inside a stone—*Simic*
Go, lovely rose—*Waller*
Go placidly amid the noise and haste—*Ehrmann*
Go, soul, the body's guest—*Raleigh*
Go take the world my dearest wish—*MacPherson*
Go to bed first—*Children's Verses and Nursery Rhymes*
Go to the other shore and return—*Swenson*
Go to the shine that's on a tree—*Eberhart*
A Goblin lives in our house—*Fyleman*
God banish from your house—*Kunitz*
God give this man eternal rest—*Villon*

God grant me that at last I reach my goal—*Dowling*

God he had gone off—*Gilbert, Celia*

God in his wisdom made the fly—*Nash*

God knows how our neighbour managed to breed —*Plath*

God made a little Gentian—*Dickinson, Emily*

God makes sech nights, all white an' still—*Lowell, James Russell*

God must receive so many solemn prayers—*Marshall, Helen Lowrie*

The god of galaxies has more to govern—*Van Doren*

God of our fathers, known of old—*Kipling*

God rest you merry, gentlemen—*Anonymous–English–Modern English*

God rest you merry, Innocents—*Nash*

God, Sir, when you draw off those—*Durrell*

God, though this life is but a race—*Untermeyer*

God tried to teach Crow how to talk—*Hughes, Ted*

God, we don't like to complain—*Untermeyer*

Goddess! hear these tuneless numbers, wrung— *Keats*

Goddess of poetry—*Winters*

Goddess sea-born and bright—*Tate, Allen*

Godfrey Gordon Gustavus Gore—*Rands*

Godolphin Horne was nobly born—*Belloc*

God's glory and my country's shame—*Cullen*

Goe, and catche a falling starre—*Donne*

Goethe in Weimar sleeps, and Greece—*Arnold*

Goin' down de road, Lawd—*Hughes, Langston*

Going to bed—*Patchen*

Going to Zima Junction, quiet place—*Yevtushenko*

Golch and Flubis, these are two—*Morgenstern*

The gold-armored ghost from the Roman road —*Sitwell, Edith*

A Gold fringe on the purpling hem—*Whittier*

Gold I've none, for use or show—*Herrick*

Gold on the doorstep, whose steps—*Williams, Hugo*

Gold! We leapt from our benches, Gold!—*Service*

Goldbrown upon the sated flood—*Joyce*

A golden bronze zig-zag—*Johnston, Ellen Turlington*

The golden epodes are—*Barker, George*

Golden haired and golden hearted—*Betjeman*

Golden slumbers kisse your eyes—*Dekker*

Goliath stood up clear in the assumption of status —*Miles*

Gone, gone—*Knight, Etheridge*

Gone, I say, and walk from Church—*Sexton*

Gone now the baby's nurse—*Lowell, Robert*

Gone the three ancient ladies—*Roethke*

Gonflement de nuit aux quatre coins—*Césaire*

Gonna give a baby a home—*Arnez*

Gonna leave ya', Mr. Backlash—*Fabio, Sarah Webster*

Goodbye—*Gaver*

Good-bye, my Fancy/ Farewell dear mate, dear love—*Whitman*

Good-bye, Winter—*MacNeice*

Good creatures, do you love your lives—*Housman*

Good friends, let's to the fields—*Masters, Edgar Lee*

Good glory, give a look at sporting Beasley— *Brown, Sterling A.*

The good grey guardians of art—*Wilbur*

The good Lord Nelson had a swollen gland—*Durrell*

Good-morning; good morning! The General said —*Sassoon*

Good-night; ensured release—*Housman*

Good-night to the Season! 'tis over—*Praed*

Good of the Chaplain to enter Lone Bay—*Melville*

Good people all, of every sort—*Goldsmith*

The good scope of him is history, old and ironic —*Corso*

Good soul, my mother holds my daughter— *Ciardi*

The gorilla lay on his back—*Wain*

Gothama, der Buddha, lehrte—*Brecht*

Goths, Vandals, Huns, Isaurian mountaineers— *Graves*

Gottlob, dass ich auf Erden bin—*Novalis*

A gourmet challenged me to eat—*Nash*

Gr-r-r—there go, my heart's abhorrence— *Browning, Robert*

Das Grab ist leer, das Grab ist leer—*Claudius*

Grácil, curvada sobre os feixes—*Castro, Eugénio de*

Gracing the tide-warmth, this seagull—*Jones, Glyn*

Grammar from out West—*Darragh*

Gran Serrano—*Garcia Lorca*

Granada, calle de Elvira—*Garcia Lorca*

Granada falling at my feet—*Pines*

Granada, Granada, de tu poderío—*Villaespesa*

Grand âge, nous voici—*Perse*

Grand bois, vous m'effrayez comme des cathédrales—*Baudelaire*

Le grand-père est à la fenêtre—*Fombeure*

Grandad Connor toiled at the forge—*Connor*

Grandma's talk was Black talk—*Fabio, Sarah Webster*

Les grands, pour la plupart, sont masques de théâtre—*La Fontaine*

Granny had a two-fisted approach—*Howard, Lee*

The grass camps in its tussock—*Hughes, Ted*

Grass erupts slowly, locking the soil in frail roots —*Smith, Ken*

The grass is half-covered with snow—*Bly*

The grasshopper world—*Hodges*

Gravely, like a priest—*Simmons, Judy*

Gray and blue, the boy ghosts with guns are in the spring woods—*Scott, Winfield Townley*

Gray earth peeping through snow—*Levine*

The gray sea and the long black land—*Browning, Robert*

Gray/without grace—*Mailer*

The great advantage of being alive—*Cummings*

The great cracked shadow of the Sierra Nevada —*Wright, James*

Great-enough both accepts and subdues—*Jeffers, Robinson*

Great is the sun, and wide he goes—*Stevenson*

Great men have been among us—*Wordsworth*

Great nights returning, midnight's constellations —*Watkins*

The great orchestrating principle of gravity— *Dudek*

Great praises of the summer come—*Eberhart*

Great while I lay at mercy of the sea—*Corke*

Great wide beautiful wonderful world—*Rands*

Green be the turf above thee—*Halleck*

The green-blue ground—*Williams, William Carlos*

The green bug sleeps in the white lily ear—*Sandburg*

The green catalpa tree has turned—*Snodgrass*

The green elm with the one great bough of gold—*Thomas, Edward*

Green flows the river of Lethe-O—*Sitwell, Edith*

Green groweth the holly—*Henry VIII*

The green has suddenly—*Winters*

Green rustlings, more than regal charities—*Crane, Hart*

Green shutters, shut your shutters—*Betjeman*

Green slated gables—*Nicholson*

Green snake, when I hung you round my neck—*Levertov*

The greens of the Ganges delta foliate—*Berryman*

Greife wacker nach der Sünde—*Wedekind*

Une grenouille vit un boeuf—*La Fontaine*

Les grenouilles se lassant—*La Fontaine*

Gre't God! Yond' come de honey wagon man—*Beecher*

Gretch love—*Henderson, David*

Un greve truono, si ch'io mi riscossi—*Dante Alighieri*

Grey brick upon brick—*MacNeice*

The grey-green stretch of sandy grass—*Symons*

Grey haunted eyes, absent-mindedly glaring—*Graves*

Greyly tremendous the thunder—*Betjeman*

Griehn, ich muss Sie um Entschuldigung bitten—*Brecht*

Grill me some bones, said the Cobbler—*De la Mare*

Grincement doux et rouillé d'une berline—*Milosz*

El grito deja en el viento—*Garcia Lorca*

Die grosse Fracht des Sommers—*Bachmann*

Grössers wolltest auch du, aber die Liebe zwingt—*Hölderlin*

Grossvater Stöffel—*Brecht*

The groves of Blarney, they are so charming—*Anonymous-English—Modern English*

The groves were God's first temples ere man learned—*Bryant, William Cullen*

Grow old along with me—*Browning, Robert*

Growltiger was a Bravo Cat, who lived upon a barge—*Eliot, Thomas Stearns*

Grub-white mulberries redden among leaves—*Plath*

Guarda, è celeste 'a chella parte 'o cielo—*Di Giacomo*

The guardian stalking his eternal snows—*MacPherson*

Gudarna väcktes—*Ferlin*

Guido I' vorrei che tu e lapo ed Io,—*Dante Alighieri*

Gul zatikh ya vyshel na podmostki—*Pasternak*

The gull hundreds of miles below him—*MacNeice*

The gull in full perfection rides the storm—*Press*

The gull, it is said—*Anonymous-American Indian languages-Eskimo*

Gum, oats, and syrup the Arabians bore—*Durrell*

Guns from the sea open against us—*Graves*

The guns know what is what, but underneath—*Simpson*

The guns spell money's ultimate reason—*Spender*

Gus is the Cat at the Theatre Door—*Eliot, Thomas Stearns*

Gus, the lineman—*Walker*

Guvener B. is a sensible man—*Lowell, James Russell*

G'way an' quit dat noise—*Dunbar, Paul Laurence*

Gwei jung shan fu bu jr chou—*Anonymous-Asian languages*

Gwo pwo shan he dzai—*Du Fu*

A gyges Ring they beare about them still—*Herrick*

The gypsy, the Great Nemo—*Sitwell, Osbert*

The H-O-U-R hours—*Talen*

Ha muchos años que busco el yermo—*Nervo*

Ha sido detenido en Paris un turista americano—*Alcántara*

Ha! whare ye gaun, ye crowlin ferlie—*Burns*

Hab nun, ach, die Philosophie—*Goethe*

Había antes vírgenes novias—*Martinez Alonso*

Hace ya dos años—*Santos Chocano*

Hacía Roma caminan dos peregrinos—*Anonymous-Spanish*

Had he and I but met—*Hardy*

Had I but plenty of money, money enough and to spare—*Browning, Robert*

Had I the heavens' embroidered cloths—*Yeats*

Had we but World enough, and Time—*Marvell*

The haemophiliac boy king—*Williams, Hugo*

Hágase, pues, dijo el Padre—*Juan de la Cruz*

Der Häher wirft mir die blaue Feder—*Eich*

Hai chiuso gli occhi—*Ungaretti*

Hail! Columbia, happy land!—*Hopkinson, Joseph*

Hail, Dionysos—*Randall*

Hail, ho! Sail, ho!—*Riley*

Hail, holy light, offspring of Heav'n first-born—*Milton*

Hail me Diogenes underground, O stranger, and pass by—*Anonymous-Greek*

Hail to thee, blithe Spirit—*Shelley*

Hail, wedded Love, mysterious law, true source—*Milton*

Hair! it was hair—*Benedikt*

The hairs turn gold upon my thigh—*Gunn*

Half a league, half a league—*Tennyson*

Half circle's come before we know—*Bogan*

Half of my life is gone, and I have let—*Longfellow*

Half of the flags are at half mast—*Dlugos*

Half of them—*Lifshin*

Hallowe'en. She dressed up in a sheet—*Engle*

Halt dein Röslein nur im Zügel—*Busch*

Halte dich still, halte dich stumm—*Fontane*

Halted against the shade of a last hill—*Owen, Wilfred*

Hambone, Jawbone—*Lee, Dennis*

Hame came our goodman—*Anonymous-English—Modern English*

Hamelin Town's in Brunswick—*Browning, Robert*

The hammer struck my nail—*Swenson*

Han chan chi chye—*Lyou Yung*

Han hwang chung se sz ching gwo—*Bai Jyu Yi*

Han längtar, längtar och anar—*Rydberg*

Han var en så—*Ferlin*

Han venido los Húngaros, hermana—*Díez-Cane-do*

The hand that signed the paper felled a city—*Thomas, Dylan*

The hands explore tentatively—*Gunn*

The hands lie low—*Sherwin*

Handsome and clever and he went cruising—*Cummings*

A handsome young rodent named Gratian—*Nash*

Hannah was a lady—*Coffin*

Hapana jiti, pumbavu, ya pita la mnazi—*Anonymous-African languages-Swahili*

Happened that the moon was up before I went to bed—*Riggs*

Happy are men who yet before they are killed —*Owen, Wilfred*

Happy people die whole, they are all dissolved in a moment—*Jeffers, Robinson*

Happy the man that, when his day is done—*Field, Eugene*

Happy the man, whose wish and care—*Pope, Alexander*

Happy the nations of the moral north—*Byron*

Happy those early dayes! when I—*Vaughan, Henry*

Här åker sankt Elia upp till himmelens land—*Karlfeldt*

Här ligger samhället—*Lindqvist*

Här står de nu pampiga värdiga—*Ferlin*

Hard by my window, under the frost—*Abbe*

Hard Rock was known not to take shit—*Knight, Etheridge*

Hark, hark, the lark—*Shakespeare*

Hark, hearer, hear what I do—*Hopkins*

Hark to the whimper of the sea-gull—*Nash*

Harlem dud—*Emanuel*

The harp that once through Tara's Halls—*Moore, Thomas*

Harriet. There was always—*Lorde*

Harrison loves my country too—*Frost, Robert*

Harry, whose tuneful and well-measur'd song—*Milton*

Has a perpetual cold—*Souster*

Has anybody seen my mouse—*Milne*

Has not altered—*Moore, Marianne*

Ein Hase sitzt auf einer Wiese—*Morgenstern*

Hass, als minus und vergebens—*Busch*

Hast du Verstand und ein Herz—*Hölderlin*

Hast thou named all the birds without a gun?—*Emerson*

Hast uns Stulln jeschnitten—*Tucholsky*

Hasta los niños la miraban cuando—*Cremer*

Haste thee, Nymph, and bring with thee—*Milton*

Hat der alte Hexenmeister—*Goethe*

Hat man viel, so wird man bald—*Heine*

Hätt ich sieben Wünsch—*Anonymous-German*

Hauled between wars, my life time—*Rukeyser*

Haunts me the lugubrious shape—*Eberhart*

Have fair fallen, O fair, fair have fallen, so dear —*Hopkins*

Have I ever told you—*Lurie*

Have I no right—*Davison, Peter*

Have mercy, Lord—*Hughes, Langston*

Have the boats all come home yet?—*Hillyer*

Have you been to London—*Nicholson*

Have you crouched with rifle in woods—*Warren*

Have you ever harked to the jackass—*Nash*

Have you ever heard of the sugar plum tree—*Field, Eugene*

Have you gazed on naked grandeur—*Service*

Have you heard of the wonderful one-hoss shay —*Holmes, Oliver Wendell*

Have you heard the story that gossips tell—*Hart*

Have you known the awesome stillness—*Marshall, Helen Lowrie*

Have you paid a visit recently—*Marshall, Helen Lowrie*

Have you read the biography of Mr. Schwellenbach?—*Nash*

Have you really grown to hate me?—*Heine*

Have you reckoned a thousand acres much?—*Whitman*

Have you seen but a bright lily grow—*Jonson*

Have you seen me at all—*Gill*

Have you seen the hills in September—*Marshall, Helen Lowrie*

Have you seen the lights of London how they twinkle, twinkle, twinkle—*Bashford*

Have you seen walking through the village—*Masters, Edgar Lee*

Have you watched the fairies when the rain is done—*Fyleman*

Have you watched the sun descending—*Marshall, Helen Lowrie*

Having accepted the trust so many years back —*Warren*

Having been tenant long to a rich Lord—*Herbert*

Having come down and run the car into sand—*Porter, Peter*

Having given up on the desk man passed out under his clock—*Kinnell*

Having lent my apartment—*Flint*

Having no surface of its own, the proud—*Hollander*

Having survived entirely your own youth—*Merrill*

Having this day my horse, my hand, my lance —*Sidney*

Having two natures in me, joy the one—*Wordsworth*

Hay cementerios solos—*Neruda*

Hay días en que somos tan móviles—*Barba Jacob*

Hay dulzura infantil—*Garcia Lorca*

Hay golpes en la vida tan fuertes—*Vallejo*

Hay que andar por el mundo—*Nalé-Roxlo*

Hay veces que los hombres tristemente—*Bousoño*

He almorzado solo ahora, y no he tenido madre —*Vallejo*

He always called her honey and—*Viorst*

He always had pretty legs—*Giovanni*

He and she have been—*Fox, Charles*

He bebido del chorro cándido de la fuente—*Ibarbourou*

He became blind earlier than any of us—*Sobiloff*

He called on God to smite the foe—*Francis*

He ceas'd, and next him Moloc, scepter'd King —*Milton*

He cerrado mi balcón—*Garcia Lorca*

He clasps the crag with crooked hands—*Tennyson*

He coils so close about his double-bass—*Graves*

He comprado tres puñales—*León, Rafael de*

He d'anemon hos pnoie epessyto demnia koures —*Homer*

He did not say anything utterly strange—*Van Doren*

He didn't say—*Lee, Don L.*

He didn't want to do it—*Nemerov*

He disappeared in the dead of winter—*Auden*

He discovers himself on an old airfield—*Hall*

He does not think that I haunt here nightly— *Hardy*

He dreams—*Patten*

He drove to see—*Dodson-Letourneau, Gayle*

He drowsed and was aware of silence heaped— *Sassoon*

He enters, and mute on the edge of a chair— *Hardy*

He erupts from our soil—*Noll*

He fell in victory's fierce pursuit—*Graves*

He fell off his crane—*Beecher*

He found her by the ocean's moaning verge— *Meredith, George*

He frightens all the witches—*Reed, Ishmael*

He gathered Phaedra, hard with childhood, small —*Winters*

He glimpses through dividing wire gold thighs —*Beecher*

He goes nuts.—*Rector*

He had done for her all that a man could—*Graves*

He had driven half the night—*Snyder*

He has a sort of green thumb—*Marshall, Helen Lowrie*

He has the sign—*Knight, Etheridge*

He hasn't gone to work—*Levine*

He is firm and strong—*Anonymous-African languages-Yoruba*

He is found with the homeless dogs—*Hayden*

He is gone on the mountain—*Scott, Sir Walter*

He is in his room sulked shut—*Ciardi*

He is not with us any more—*Malanga*

He is retired as noontide dew—*Wordsworth*

He is starke mad, who ever sayes—*Donne*

He is that fallen lance that lies as hurled—*Frost, Robert*

He is very busy with his looking—*Brooks, Gwendolyn*

He is well balanced and steady going—*Ennis*

He knew how Roman legions looked—*Coffin*

He lay in the middle of the world—*Berryman*

He left half a shoulder and half a head—*Stevens, Wallace*

He left himself on my doorstep—*Atwood*

He loved her and she loved him—*Hughes, Ted*

He meant to pass—*Emanuel*

He men ar os eipous apebe glaukopis Athene— *Homer*

He mirado la pampa—*Borges*

He mordido manzanas y he besado tus labios— *Ibarbourou*

He never felt twice the same about the flecked river—*Stevens, Wallace*

He never lives to tell—*Reid*

He never speaks with loud and raucous shout— *Marshall, Helen Lowrie*

He never spoke a word to me—*Cullen*

He, of his gentleness—*Graves*

He often would ask us—*Hardy*

He protested all his life long—*Masters, Edgar Lee*

He ra gyne tamie—*Homer*

He ran away and was gone for a year—*Masters, Edgar Lee*

He ran the course and as he ran he grew—*Gunn*

He rose at dawn and, fired with hope—*Tennyson*

He said, and on his Son with rays direct—*Milton*

He said he would be back—*Rukeyser*

He said: Let's stay here—*Patten*

He sat in a wheeled chair, waiting for dark— *Owen, Wilfred*

He sat upon the rolling deck—*Hughes, Langston*

He saw my—*Lifshin*

He sees thru stone—*Knight, Etheridge*

He seized me by the waist and kissed my throat —*Rich*

He: Shall I be your first love—*Beddoes*

He sipped at a weak hock and seltzer—*Betjeman*

He slapped me all over—*Vogeler*

He snuggles his fingers—*Brown, Sterling A.*

He spake: and to confirm his words—*Milton*

He stood, a point—*Atwood*

He stood, and heard the steeple—*Housman*

He takes it first with his eye like a sparrowhawk —*Francis*

He talked, and as he talked—*Van Doren*

He tells me in Bangkok he's robbed—*Levine*

He tells you when you've got on too much lipstick —*Nash*

He that had come that morning—*Merwin*

He that hath a Gospel—*Kipling*

He that is down needs fear no fall—*Bunyan*

He that was her son—*Jones, David*

He there does now enjoy eternal rest—*Spenser*

He thought he kept the universe alone—*Frost, Robert*

He thought he saw a buffalo—*Carroll*

He thought he saw an Elephant—*Carroll*

He told us we were free to choose—*Auden*

He travels after a winter sun—*Joyce*

He tried to hide—*Gold*

He twirled his tabled highball—*Scott, Winfield Townley*

He viajado por la mitad del mundo—*Alonso*

He vuelto a ver—*Machado, Antonio*

He walked through the woods—*Ross, W. W. Eustace*

He was all back—*Stefanile*

He was as old as old can be—*Stephens*

He was born in Alabama—*Brooks, Gwendolyn*

He was born to wonder about numbers—*Sandburg*

He was found by the Bureau of Statistics to be —*Auden*

He was in Cincinnati, she in Burlington—*Sandburg*

He was really her favorite—*Lifshin*

He was the gentlest creature made—*Cullen*

He was twenty. He was half crazy—*Glaze*

He was what his Mamma called—*Deveaux*

He went to Spain—*Olson*

He who binds to himself a joy—*Blake*

He who for the first time loves—*Heine*

He who had gone a beast—*Wilbur*

He who in Spring's rebirth has put his trust— *Hillyer*

He who thinks immortality—*Kgositsile*
He who trod the country roads—*Marshall, Helen Lowrie*
He will watch the hawk with an indifferent eye —*Spender*
He with body waged a fight—*Yeats*
He yelled at me in Greek—*Berryman*
The head of Lincoln looks down from the wall —*Hughes, Langston*
Headless and hard as bricks—*Ennis*
The headlights fading out at dawn—*Levine*
The heads impenetrable, and the slow bulk soundless—*Tomlinson*
Heads or tails? Heads, home—*Baybars*
A health to earth and her magnificent digestion —*Francis*
Hear laughs and cries—*Napier*
Hear my prayer, O Lord—*Wyatt, Sir Thomas*
Hear the sledges with the bells—*Poe*
Hear the voice of the Bard—*Blake*
Hear this prayer from a Plaquemines jail— *Walker*
Hear ye! Hear ye!—*Sanchez*
Heard ye o'the Tree o' France—*Burns*
Hearing a white saint rave—*Plath*
Hearing of harvests, rotting in the valley—*Auden*
Hearing one saga, we enact the next—*Davie*
The heart asks pleasure first—*Dickinson, Emily*
Heart, my heart . . . let naught o'ercome you— *Heine*
Heart of the city—*Snyder*
The heart of Thomas Hardy flew out of Stinsford churchyard—*Betjeman*
A heart to be at peace with—*De la Mare*
Heart! we will forget him—*Dickinson, Emily*
Heaven is—*Hughes, Langston*
Heaven's not a fenced-off place—*Marshall, Helen Lowrie*
The heavens opened. With a scream—*Clarke*
The heavy bear who goes with me—*Schwartz*
The heavy-breasted Persian rugs—*Starbuck*
A heavy heart, Beloved, have I borne—*Browning, Elizabeth Barrett*
The heavy mahogany door with its wrought iron screen—*Betjeman*
Hector Protector was dressed all in green—*Children's Verses and Nursery Rhymes*
The hedges are dazed as cock-crow, heaps of leaves—*Mathias*
Heil! das schlummernde Gefieder—*Hölderlin*
Heilig Wesen! gestört hab' ich die goldene— *Hölderlin*
Die heiteren Hügel—*Borchers*
Hélas! vais-je à présent me plaindre dans ces stances—*Cocteau*
Helen, thy beauty is to me—*Poe*
Helios men gar ponon ellakhen emata panta— *Mimnermus of Colophon*
Hell is not far below—*Deutsch*
Hell, Mary/ Bell Jones—*Eckels*
Hellenon promakhountes Athenaioi Marathoni —*Simonides*
Hello/ are u the—*Sanchez*
Hello, I'd like to place my order please—*Gaver*
Helmet and rifle, pack and overcoat—*Simpson*
Heloise and Abelard nature's great hermaphrodites—*Durrell*

Héme aquí ya, profesor—*Machado, Antonio*
Hence, loathèd Melancholy—*Milton*
Hence, vain deluding Joys—*Milton*
Henceforth, from the mind—*Bogan*
Henrique walked back to his room—*Vargas*
Henry sats in de bar—*Berryman*
Henry was a young king—*Graves*
Henry's pelt was put on sundry walls—*Berryman*
Her Aedelstan cyning, eorla dryhten—*Anonymous–English—Old English*
Her back arched like—*Kendrick*
Her body is not so white as—*Williams, William Carlos*
Her brown falcon perches above the sink— *Hacker*
Her eyes are full of windy distance—*Weiss*
Her grandmother called her from the playground —*Giovanni*
Her hand in my hand—*Van Doren*
Her heat a bruise on the Christ-flesh suffered out of locked agonies of rebirth—*Antoninus*
Her imaginary playmate was a grown-up—*Jarrell*
Her ivory fan opening—*Sukenick*
Her motion was clarity—*Wellman*
Her shadow melts on a street—*Fox, Charles*
Her sixth midsummer eve keeps Ruth awake— *Lowbury*
Her smile comes—*Lester*
Her Telepathic-Station transmits thought-wave —*Auden*
Her terrace was the sand—*Stevens, Wallace*
Her veil blows across his face—*Williams, Hugo*
Her world is all aware—*Reid*
Herabgebeugt über sich selbst—*Heissenbüttel*
Herbstlich leuchtet die Flamme vom ländlich geselligen Herde—*Goethe*
Here a little child I stand—*Herrick*
Here am I, little jumping Joan—*Children's Verses and Nursery Rhymes*
Here am I, this carrot eating—*Derwood*
Here among long-discarded cassocks—*Betjeman*
Here are all the captivities—*Auden*
Here are the facts—*Brooks, Gwendolyn*
Here are the wise men baffled, here is a mark —*Chapin*
Here are your meadows, Love, as wide as heaven —*Simpson*
Here as I pause and stay motionless and alone —*Press*
Here at the Vespasian—*Nemerov*
Here by the baring bough—*Hardy*
Here by this brook we parted—*Tennyson*
Here come I, the death watch beetle, chewing away at the great cathedral—*Heath-Stubbs*
Here come real stars to fill the upper skies—*Frost, Robert*
Here come the line-gang pioneering by—*Frost, Robert*
Here dead lie we because we did not choose— *Housman*
Here I am, an old man in a dry month—*Eliot, Thomas Stearns*
Here I am, great big dinosaur lady—*Sherwin*
Here I go up in my swing—*Milne*
Here I lie close to the grave—*Masters, Edgar Lee*

Here I sit, and glad am I—*De la Mare*

Here I sit/ with my shoes mismatched—*Hughes, Langston*

Here in the great cemetery—*Levine*

Here, in the withered arbor, like the arrested wind—*Bogan*

Here is a fat animal, a bear—*Hall*

Here is a poem written on the clouds for you—*Henri*

Here is a symbol in which—*Jeffers, Robinson*

Here is dust remember it was a rose—*Sandburg*

Here is the place—*Whittier*

Here is the spinner, the orb weaver—*Francis*

Here it comes, here it comes—*Tippett*

Here lie Ciardi's pearly bones—*Ciardi*

Here lies a diplomat, alas—*Francis*

Here lies a lady of beauty and high degree—*Ransom*

Here lies a shoe-maker whose knife and hammer—*Ormond*

Here lies John Bushby, honest man—*Burns*

Here lies my wife—*Cunningham, James Vincent*

Here lies our good Edmund whose genius was such—*Goldsmith*

Here lies the military mind—*Francis*

Here lies the newborn child—*Reaney*

Here lies to each her parents' ruth—*Jonson*

Here lies, whom hound did ne'er pursue—*Cowper*

Here lyes Jonson with the rest—*Herrick*

Here on smooth white sand, by blue water—*Chapin*

Here on the edge of hell—*Hughes, Langston*

Here. People laying a foundation—*Sward*

Here sit a shepherd and a shepherdess—*Simpson*

Here something stubborn comes—*Wilbur*

Here take my Picture, though I bid farewell—*Donne*

Here the crow starves—*Eliot, Thomas Stearns*

Here the hangman stops his cart—*Housman*

Here they are. The soft eyes open—*Dickey, James*

Here they went with smock and crook—*Blunden*

Here we bring new water from the well so clear—*Anonymous–English—Modern English*

Here were new idols again—*Jeffers, Robinson*

Here, where the world is quiet—*Swinburne*

Here where you never have been you walk—*Marshall, Lenore G.*

Here's a good rule of thumb—*Nash*

Here's a verse about rabbits—*Nash*

Heres niño y as amor—*Mendoza, Fray Iñigo*

Here's to the bodies from which we come—*Ciardi*

Here's to the maiden of bashful fifteen—*Sheridan*

Here's to the man who invented stairs—*Herford*

Here's to you and yours—*Coatsworth*

Hereto I come to view a voiceless ghost—*Hardy*

Hereunder Jacob Schmidt who, man and bones—*MacLeish*

La herida tiene párpados que crujen duramente—*Conde*

Hermana Marica, mañana que es fiesta—*Góngora*

Herminius! I have sought thee—*Macaulay*

The Hermit of Cape Rosier has three houses—*Hoffman*

A Hermit's house beside a stream—*Freneau*

Hermoso es, hermosamente humilde y confiante—*Aleixandre*

The heroes paused upon the plain—*Gunn*

The heron stands in water where the swamp—*Roethke*

Herr! Herr!—*Hölderlin*

Herr, lass mich musizieren—*Zuckmayer*

Herr! Schicke, was du willst—*Mörike*

Herr von Ribbeck auf Ribbeck im Havelland—*Fontane*

Die Herrligkeit der Erden—*Gryphius*

Hershen bein yom tov der zun Fagang—*Sutzkever*

Herz, mein Herz, was soll das geben—*Goethe*

He's coming. He just called. Said he was coming—*Van Doren*

He's dead, they shouted—*Michie*

He's nothing much but fur—*Farjeon*

Hesterno, Licini, die otiosi—*Catullus*

Heudoisin d'oreon koryphai te kai pharagges—*Alcman*

Heureux qui, comme Ulysse, a fait un beau voyage—*Du Bellay*

Heute abend, wenn die Strassen—*Theobaldy*

Hey, Buddy—*Hughes, Langston*

Hey! Diddle, Diddle—*Children's Verses and Nursery Rhymes*

Hey, Father Death—*Ginsberg*

Hey, friend, I have been here a long time—*Mathias*

Hey, he sort of like Chicago—*Shiva*

Hey Mom—*Butcher*

Hey, right on—*Blackman*

Hi ha oficis que són bons perquè són de bon viure—*Salvat-Papasseit*

Hi ha una vela en—*Sagarra*

Hic templum Iunoni ingens Sidonia Dido—*Virgil*

Hid by the august foliage and fruit—*Moore, Marianne*

Hidden all over the world—*Sukenick*

Hidden in a forest of questions—*Lorde*

Hidden in wonder and snow—*Scott, F. R.*

Hide and seek, says the wind—*De la Mare*

Hielte diesen frühen Segen—*Goethe*

Hier, c'est la jeunesse—*Éluard*

Hier il y a très longtemps—*Éluard*

Hier ist es hübsch. Hier kann ich ruhig träumen—*Tucholsky*

Hier lieg' ich auf dem Frühlingshügel—*Mörike*

Hier liegt—steh, Wanderer, und schau—*Schubart*

Hier steht ein Mann und singt ein Lied—*Mehring*

High and proud on the barnyard fence—*Farrar*

High on a slope in New Guinea—*Hall*

High on a throne of royal state, which far—*Milton*

High on his figured couch beyond the waves—*Graves*

The high ones die, die. They die—*Berryman*

High up over the top of feathery grasses—*Aldis*

High upon Highlands and way upon Tay—*Anonymous–English—Modern English*

High/ yellow—*Sanchez*

Highway, since you my chief Parnassus be—*Sidney*

Hijo de mi tristeza, de mi desesperanza—*Hoffman Llevano*

El hijo de rana, Rinrin Renacuajo—*Pombo*

Hill blue among the leaves in summer—*Sandburg*
The hills are calling—*Hodges*
Hills are for climbing: ask any small boy—*Marshall, Helen Lowrie*
The hills are going somewhere—*Conkling*
Him tha gegiredan Gaeta leode—*Anonymous–English—Old English*
Him whom the old joy fell over—*Blackmur*
Hinüber will ich—*Novalis*
Une hirondelle en ses voyages—*La Fontaine*
The Hiroshima silver birch—*Nathan*
Ein Hirsch sass am Waldrand—*Guggenmos*
His appearances are incalculable—*Graves*
His are the generous days—*Spender*
His art is eccentricity, his aim—*Francis*
His breath came in threads—*Rodgers*
His brother said that pain was what he knew—*Moss, Howard*
His car was worth a thousand pounds and more—*Davies, William Henry*
His earliest memory, the mood—*Day Lewis*
His eyes grew hot—*Untermeyer*
His father gave him a box of truisms—*MacNeice*
His fear never loud in daylight—*Porter, Peter*
His fingers wake, and flutter up the bed—*Owen, Wilfred*
His first feet arrived and stumbled over stone—*Brathwaite*
His golden locks time hath to silver turned—*Peele*
His knotty hand trembled—*Jeffers, Lance*
His legs ran about—*Hughes, Ted*
His little trills and chirpings were his best—*Parker*
His long hair tangled—*Robison*
His name, they told me afterwards was Able—*Reid*
His nose is short and scrubby—*Chute*
His Uncle came on Franklin Hyde—*Belloc*
Historians may scorn the close engagement—*Graves*
History to the historians—*Francis*
Hjärtat skal gro av drömmar—*Bergman, Bo*
Ho dda ricurre? a cchi? ffamme er zervizzio—*Belli*
Ho, for the Pirate Don Durk of Dowdee—*Meigs*
Ho, trumpets, sound a war-note—*Macaulay*
Hoch auf dem alten Turme steht—*Goethe*
Hoch mit den Wolken geht der Vögel Reise—*Eichendorff*
Hog Butcher for the World—*Sandburg*
Högt i det höga slår—*Bergman, Bo*
La hoguera pone al campo de la tarde—*Garcia Lorca*
Höhlen, das Waldgetier—*Bobrowski*
Hoi men ippeon stroton hoi de pesdon—*Sappho*
Hold! are you mad?—*Dryden*
Hold fast a dream. On this careening earth—*Marshall, Helen Lowrie*
Hold fast to dreams—*Hughes, Langston*
Holding the distance up before his face—*Auden*
Hölty! dein Freund, der Frühling, ist gekommen—*Lenau*
The holy moon, a canoe—*Sandburg*
Hombre es amor—*Alonso*
Un hombre, los caminos—*Celaya*
Hombre pequeñito, hombre pequeñito—*Storni*

Hombres necios que acusáis—*Juana Inés de la Cruz*
Home to your eyes—*Kramer*
Homeowners unite—*Dickey, James*
Homer, Sidney, Philo, strung along the Wabash—*Van Doren*
Hometown; well, most admit an affection for a city—*Abse*
L'Homme en songeant descend au gouffre universel—*Hugo, Victor*
Un homme entre chez une fleuriste—*Prévert*
Homme, libre penseur! te crois-tu seul pensant—*Nerval*
Un homme sort de chez lui—*Prévert*
Honey/ when de man—*Brown, Sterling A.*
Hooks, screw-eyes, and screws—*Booth*
The hop-poles stand in cones—*Blunden*
Hope is the thing with feathers—*Dickinson, Emily*
Hopping, half flying—*Blackmur*
Hör ich das Liedchen klingen—*Heine*
Hör' ich das Pförtchen nicht gehen?—*Schiller*
Horas de pesadumbre y de tristeza—*Darío*
Horch! auf der Erde feuchtem Grunde gelegen—*Mörike*
Horloge! dieu sinistre—*Baudelaire*
Hornillos eléctricos, brocados, bombillas—*Fuertes*
The horse-faced dandy—*Engle*
The horse left its footprint—*O'Gorman*
Horseman, you come to bring us peace—*Posner*
Hört ihr einst, ich sei gestorben—*Göckingk*
Hos ara phonesas apebe—*Homer*
Hos eipon thamnon hypedyseto—*Homer*
Hos phamene kai kerdosyne—*Homer*
Hos phamene psykhe men ebe domon Aidos eiso—*Homer*
Hoson zes phainou, meden holos sy lypu—*Anonymous–Greek*
Hot huesos/ and war pending—*Alurista*
A hot midsummer night on Water Street—*Simpson*
The hot night makes us keep our bedroom windows open—*Lowell, Robert*
Hot summer has exhausted her intent—*Wilbur*
Hot sun, cool fire, tempered with sweet air—*Peele*
Hotel Ameridemocratogrande—*Emanuel*
Hotsa—*Gaver*
Hound dog sits his tail—*Knight, Etheridge*
A house can be haunted by those who were never there—*MacNeice*
The house had gone to bring again—*Frost, Robert*
The house in Broad Street, red brick—*Aiken*
The house is so quiet now—*Nemerov*
The house of the mouse—*Mitchell, Lucy Sprague*
The house was fast asleep when we returned—*Marshall, Helen Lowrie*
The house we built gradually—*Atwood*
Housekeeper assistant—*Mason*
Housewives stand at their doorsteps—*Marriott*
How all men wrongly death do dignify—*Smith, A. J. M.*
How beautiful is the rain—*Longfellow*
How bright on the blue—*Behn, Harry*
How calm she lies in death, how calm—*Francis*
How came this ranger—*Yeats*
How can I then return—*Shakespeare*

How can my muse want subject to invent—*Shakespeare*

How can they call this dark when stars—*Spender*

How can we learn not to hate the man who shot—*Goldstein*

How careful was I, when I took my way—*Shakespeare*

How clumsy on the tongue these acquired idioms—*Reid*

How come nobody is being bombed today—*Ignatow*

How cool cut hay smells—*Gleason*

How could I know—*Weiss*

How could I know his blood ran red—*Goldstein*

How dear to this heart are the scenes of my childhood—*Woodworth*

How deeply must we plunge—*Collier*

How did the devil come—*Betjeman*

How did the nothing come, how did these fires—*Masefield*

How did you feel, Mary—*Miller, May*

How do I love thee?—*Browning, Elizabeth Barrett*

How do poets write—*Giovanni*

How do you bloom, young flower—*Posner*

How do you do—*Children's Verses and Nursery Rhymes*

How do you like to go up in a swing—*Stevenson*

How do you write a poem—*Giovanni*

How does it happen, tell me—*Masters, Edgar Lee*

How doth the little Crocodile—*Carroll*

How easily I could have missed you—*Francis*

How envied, how admired a male—*Cullen*

How far is it to Bethlehem—*Chesterton, Frances*

How far is St. Helena from a little child at play—*Kipling*

How fares it with you, Mrs. Cooper—*Smith, Stevie*

How fiercely we must struggle to remain—*Dowling*

How fresh, O Lord, how sweet and clean—*Herbert*

How generous is that himself the sun—*Cummings*

How happy could I be with either—*Gay, John*

How happy is he born and taught—*Wotton*

How happy is the little stone—*Dickinson, Emily*

How heavy do I journey on the way—*Shakespeare*

How, how, he said—*Lindsay, Vachel*

How ill doth he deserve a lover's name—*Carew*

How kind, how secret now the sun—*Warren*

How learn our way among these mazy strings—*Meredith, George*

How like a winter hath my absence been—*Shakespeare*

How long ago we dreamed—*Merwin*

How long it took—*Treitel*

How lost is the little fox at the borders of night—*Frost, Frances M.*

How lovely the elder brother's—*Hopkins*

How many dawns, chill from his rippling rest—*Crane, Hart*

How many divisions has the dust—*Porter, Peter*

How many of u niggers watched—*Sanchez*

How many paltry, foolish, painted things—*Drayton*

How many silent centuries sleep in my sultry veins—*Walker*

How many whitenesses—*Jeffers, Lance*

How may I see the triune man at once—*Blackmur*

How mobile is the bed on these—*Nabokov*

How most unnatural-seeming, yet how proper—*Graves*

How much do you love me, a million bushels—*Sandburg*

How much I disapprove of it—*Kunitz*

How much wood would a woodchuck chuck—*Children's Verses and Nursery Rhymes*

How oft upon yon eminence our pace—*Cowper*

How oft, when thou my music, music play'st—*Shakespeare*

How often have you heard it said—*Cullen*

How often I've been put to test—*Marshall, Helen Lowrie*

How pleasant to know Mr. Lear—*Lear*

How pure at heart and sound in head—*Tennyson*

How pure, how beautiful, how fine—*McGinley*

How sad it must be—*Sanchez*

How shall I keep this violence in—*Kunitz*

How shall the wine be drunk, or the woman known—*Wilbur*

How shiny the turtle is—*Bly*

How slowly time lengthens from a hated event—*Smith, Stevie*

How soon doth man decay—*Herbert*

How soon hath Time, the subtle thief of youth—*Milton*

How splendid in the morning glows the lily—*Flecker*

How still/ how strangely still—*Hughes, Langston*

How straight it flew, how long it flew—*Betjeman*

How strange it seems! These Hebrews in their graves—*Longfellow*

How sweet and lovely dost thou make the shame—*Shakespeare*

How sweet I roam'd from field to field—*Blake*

How sweet is the shepherd's sweet lot—*Blake*

How swift the summer grows—*Masefield*

How to account—if you can't—*Bell*

How to keep—is there any any, is there none such—*Hopkins*

How to speak of it—*Guest, Barbara*

How unhappy a lover am I—*Dryden*

How vainly men themselves amaze—*Marvell*

How well you served me above ground—*Bogan*

How will he hear the bell at school—*Wright, James*

How wise I am to have instructed the Butler—*Nash*

How you title poems—*Sward*

Howard you are twenty-five now and I am fifty—*Sobiloff*

However dry and windless—*Plomer*

However gracefully—*Reid*

Howling of wolves/Is without world—*Hughes, Ted*

Hoy buscarás—*Machado, Antonio*

Hoy, como ayer, mañana como hoy—*Becquer*

Hoy la tierra y los cielos me sonríen—*Becquer*

Hoy me he echado a reír al salir de mi casa—*Palés Matos*

Hoy se ha acabado Andrés—*Murciano*

Hoy te goce, Bilbao—*Unamuno*
Hraezl is min hasu-fag, hyrste beorhte—*Anonymous-English—Old English*
Hraezl min swigath thanne ic hrusan trede—*Anonymous-English—Old English*
Hubbard is dead, the old plumber—*Connor*
Huc est mens deducta tua, mea Lesbia, culpa—*Catullus*
Huffy Henry hid the day—*Berryman*
The huge doll of my body—*Strand*
Der Hügel wo wir wandeln—*George*
Human life is like a black and legless beggar stumping—*Jeffers, Lance*
Der Hummer liebte die Languste—*Hesse*
Humming water holds the high stars—*Redgrove*
Humpty Dumpty sat on a wall—*Children's Verses and Nursery Rhymes*
The hunchback in the park—*Thomas, Dylan*
Hungering on the gray plain of its birth—*Hollander*
The hunter crouches in his blind—*Nash*
Huntington sleeps in a house six feet long—*Sandburg*
Hur fåfängt till himlen vi ropa—*Blomberg*
Hur obevekligt våra timslag falla—*Malmberg*
Hur präktigt leva vi i Juda städer—*Karlfeldt*
Eine Hur steht unter der Laterne—*Tucholsky*
A hurdle of water, and O these waters are cold —*Berryman*
Hurt—*Sanchez*
Hush-e-by, Lady, in Alice's lap—*Carroll*
Hush little baby—*Children's Verses and Nursery Rhymes*
Hush, lullay—*Adams*
Hush! new baby, bob-cats creep—*Coffin*
Hush'd be the camps today—*Whitman*
Hvor Bølgen høit mod Kysten slaaer—*Andersen*
Hwaet, ic swefna cyst secgan wille—*Anonymous-English—Old English*
Hwaet, we Gar-Dena in geardagum—*Anonymous-English—Old English*
Hwelc is haeleda thaes horse—*Anonymous-English—Old English*
Hymns to the tune—*Stevens, Wendy*
Hysteric sparks of self in the ward of night—*Miles*

I abdicate my daily self that bled—*Kunitz*
I admire the Bishops of the Church of England —*Smith, Stevie*
I adored her and she giggled and I adored her —*Ciardi*
I advocate a total revolution—*Williams, Oscar*
I almost lost my favorite uncle—*Sobiloff*
I always liked housecleaning—*Giovanni*
I always saw, I always said—*Parker*
I am—*Marvin X*
I am a child of the valley—*Walker*
I am a copper wire slung in the air—*Sandburg*
I am a falcon hooded, on God's wrist—*O'Gorman*
I am a fly if these are not stones—*Hughes, Ted*
I am a fuck-ing negro, man hole in my head—*Brathwaite*
I am a gentleman in a dustcoat trying—*Ransom*
I am a lady—*Reid*
I am a little church—*Cummings*
I am a little world made cunningly—*Donne*
I am a Negro—*Hughes, Langston*

I am a stranger—*Zu-Bolton*
I am a young girl—*Colum*
I am afraid of what will happen—*Klappert*
I am an American, yes, an American—*Collins, Leslie M.*
I am as brown as brown can be—*Anonymous-English—Modern English*
I am as I am and so will be—*Wyatt, Sir Thomas*
I am blind, you out there—*Rilke*
I am bloodbrother of all drifting things—*Blanding*
I am come of the seed of the people—*Pearse*
I am daydreaming at Luino—*Sereni*
I am deep/ black soil—*Sanchez*
I am digging a pit—*Klappert*
I am divorcing Daddy—*Sexton*
I am driving; it is dusk; Minnesota—*Bly*
I am freewheeling. The unslung hoop—*O'Gorman*
I am hearing the shape of the rain—*Dickey, James*
I am helpless. You defeat me—*Heine*
I am in a box—*Giovanni*
I am in Dante's city, quite alone—*Dowling*
I am in love—*Clough*
I am inside the church of Koshueti—*Yevtushenko*
I am Ireland—*Pearse*
I am Lake Superior—*Reaney*
I am leading a quiet life—*Ferlinghetti*
I am looking for a place—*Bruchac*
I am Minerva, the village poetess—*Masters, Edgar Lee*
I am monarch of all I survey—*Cowper*
I am not always this crazy—*Polak*
I am not Medea—*Darr*
I am not one who much or oft delight—*Wordsworth*
I am not treacherous, callous, jealous—*Moore, Marianne*
I am not yet born; O hear me—*MacNeice*
I am, O I am sick of grief—*Kavanagh*
I am of Ireland—*Yeats*
I am poor brother Lippo, by your leave—*Browning, Robert*
I am Raftery the poet, full of hope and love—*Raftery*
I am riding on a limited express—*Sandburg*
I am sad—*Sanchez*
I am, sir, so to speak a Harvard man—*Beecher*
I am surprised to see that the ocean is still going on—*Sexton*
I am the American heartbreak—*Hughes, Langston*
I am the dancer of the wood—*Ketchum*
I am the daughter of Chaos—*Ross, W. W. Eustace*
I am the family face—*Hardy*
I am the gold machine—*Olson*
I am the great sun but you do not see me—*Causley*
I am the little man who smokes and smokes—*Berryman*
I am the man who gives the word—*Appleton*
I am the only actor—*Sexton*
I am the people—the mob—the crowd—*Sandburg*
I am the poet of the body—*Whitman*
I am the Turquoise Woman's son—*Anonymous-American Indian languages–Navajo*

I am the Uncle Tom—*Murphy*
I am the very last astronaut, listen—*Patten*
I am thinking of the onion again—*Jong*
I am this fountain's God—*Fletcher, John*
I am tired of cursing the Bishop—*Yeats*
I am tired of this barn! said the colt—*Coatsworth*
I am trying to drain my mind—*Sanchez*
I am two fooles, I know—*Donne*
I am walking rapidly through striations of light and dark—*Rich*
I am weary of lying within the chase—*Anonymous-French*
I am who the trail took—*Hoffman*
I am willowy boughs—*Conkling*
I am writing this out of vengeance—*Gallagher, Tess*
I am—yet what I am none cares or knows—*Clare*
I, an old woman in the light of the sun—*Sitwell, Edith*
I, an old woman whose heart is like the sun—*Sitwell, Edith*
I arise from dreams of thee—*Shelley*
I ask you this—*Hughes, Langston*
I asked a thief to steal me a peach—*Blake*
I asked her, Is Aladdin's lamp hidden anywhere—*Lindsay, Vachel*
I asked my mother for fifty cents—*Children's Verses and Nursery Rhymes*
I asked no other thing, no other was denied—*Dickinson, Emily*
I began in Ohio—*Wright, James*
I begged my love to wait a bit—*Graves*
I been scared and battered—*Hughes, Langston*
I been thinking of removing the pants—*Sklarew*
I believe a leaf of grass is no less than the journey-work of the stars—*Whitman*
I believe in evolution—*Marshall, Helen Lowrie*
I believe in you my soul—*Whitman*
I believe love travels on the air—*Marshall, Helen Lowrie*
I believed it, Y'all—*Dupree*
I blomman, i solen—*Stagnelius*
I, Bos Taurus spatha—*Johnston, Percy E.*
I bought him for one and sixpence—*Ennis*
I braced the drum to my arm, a flat drum—*Rukeyser*
I broke the spell that held me long—*Bryant, William Cullen*
I burn no incense, hang no wreath—*Pinkney*
I burned my life, that I might find—*Bogan*
I call on the dead—*Piercy*
I call you to collect—*Dodson-Letourneau, Gayle*
I came before the water—*Plath*
I came over—*Pietri*
I came through sun—*Abbe*
I came to grief and grips with a gang—*Sobiloff*
I came to hold her hand—*Davison, Peter*
I came to the margin of yesterday—*Abbe*
I came to your house—*Colbert*
I came upsouth—*Alakoye*
I can discern at last how grew—*Watkins*
I can imagine quite easily ending up—*Auden*
I can love both faire and browne—*Donne*
An "I" can never be a great man—*Spender*
I can recall that distant valley—*Yevtushenko*
I can remember. I can remember—*Coward*
I can see reality—*Alurista*
I can tell balsam trees—*Conkling*

I cannot eat but little meat—*Anonymous-English—Modern English*
I cannot hold my peace, John Keats—*Cullen*
I cannot live with you—*Dickinson, Emily*
I cannot see fairies—*Conkling*
I cannot see the features right—*Tennyson*
I cannot teach you, though the years—*Marshall, Helen Lowrie*
I cannot tell who loves the Skeleton—*Lovelace, Richard*
I cannot tell you what a bargain this is—*Miles*
I can't decide which will outlive each other—*Souster*
I can't find anyone to show me—*Ginsberg*
I care not what the sailors say—*Yeats*
I carried her through the cold—*Lester*
I carry my Death within me—*Smith, A. J. M.*
I carry my keys like a weapon—*Ignatow*
I carry your heart with me—*Cummings*
I caught a tremendous Fish—*Bishop, Elizabeth*
I caught this morning morning's minion, king—*Hopkins*
I cautious scanned my little life—*Dickinson, Emily*
I celebrate myself, and sing myself—*Whitman*
I choose at random, knowing less and less—*Kinsella*
I chose the bed downstairs by the sea-window—*Jeffers, Robinson*
I chose the blonde from the chemist's, thirty-six—*Porter, Peter*
I circled on leather paws—*Roethke*
I come back late at night from your room—*Williams, Hugo*
I come into my dim bedroom—*Updike*
I' cominciai: Poeta, volentieri—*Dante Alighieri*
I construct white rooms—*Fox, Siv Cedering*
I could forgive you—*Murphy*
I could have been—*Amini*
I could hear them in fever—*Levine*
I could never have come to the present without you—*Merwin*
I could not match the labels where the span held the patch—*Broughton*
I could not sleep for thinking of the sky—*Masefield*
I could not speak for amazement at your beauty—*Betjeman*
I could take the Harlem night—*Hughes, Langston*
I could tell you—*Hughes, Langston*
I created for myself—*Patten*
I cross—*Blackmur*
I cross the ocean of skeletons—*Miller, E. Ethelbert*
I crown you with A—*Johnston, Ellen Turlington*
I dag är luften blå—*Blomberg*
I Danmark er jeg født—*Andersen*
I decry lack of absorption, lack of—*Gregor*
I desire to hold in my heart—*Logan*
I despaired at first, declaring same—*Heine*
I determined to find out whose it was—*Hardy*
I did not live until this time—*Philips*
I did not lose my heart in summer's even—*Housman*
I didn't always have—*Lifshin*

I didn't mind dying—it wasn't that at all—*Warren*

I died for beauty, but was scarce—*Dickinson, Emily*

I do not believe this room—*Reid*

I do not expect the spirit of Penelope—*Knight, Etheridge*

I do not intend to contribute—*Connor*

I do not know if the color of the day—*Knight, Etheridge*

I do not know much about Gods—*Eliot, Thomas Stearns*

I do not know the power—*Jeffers, Lance*

I do not like thee, Dr. Fell—*Children's Verses and Nursery Rhymes*

I do not want your praises later on—*Scott, Winfield Townley*

I don't believe the sleepers in this house—*Frost, Robert*

I don't dare start thinking in the morning—*Hughes, Langston*

I don't go much on religion—*Hay, John*

I don't like diamonds—*Moore, Marianne*

I don't mind eels—*Nash*

I don't need no sleepin' medicine—*Nash*

I don't operate often—*Berryman*

I don't remember enough—*Joselow*

I don't suppose I'll ever see—*Blanding*

I doubt not God is good—*Cullen*

I draw a circle on a paperbag—*Ai*

I dreaded that first robin so—*Dickinson, Emily*

I dream of journeys repeatedly—*Roethke*

I dreamed a dream: I dreamt that I espied—*Clough*

I dreamed I was a cave-boy—*Richards, Laura E.*

I dreamed kind Jesus fouled the big-gun gears—*Owen, Wilfred*

I dreamed of war-heroes, of wounded war-heroes—*Simpson*

I dreamed of you last night—*Giovanni*

I dreamed that in a city dark as Paris—*Simpson*

I dreamed the fairies wanted me—*Talbot*

I dreamed to write rich poems to my dear—*Derwood*

I dreamt a dream! What can it mean?—*Blake*

I dreamt last night of you, John-John—*MacDonagh*

I dreamt my love a-dying lay—*Hoffman*

I dreamt that when I died—*Smith, William Jay*

I dressed all up for freedom—*Arnez*

I dressed my father in his little clothes—*Pack*

I drove up to the graveyard, which—*Eberhart*

I dwell in possibility—*Dickinson, Emily*

I dwelt alone—*Poe*

I enter your room—*Baldwin, Deirdra*

I entered a subway at bleeding noon—*Abbe*

I, Erica Jong—*Jong*

I fear the headless man—*Simpson*

I feed a flame within, which so torments me—*Dryden*

I feel ill. What can the matter be—*Smith, Stevie*

I feel inclined to send a teeny-weeny—*Coward*

I feel so exceedingly lazy—*Marquis*

I fell in love with Major Spruce—*Smith, Stevie*

I felt a funeral in my brain—*Dickinson, Emily*

I felt really good today—*Johnston, Ellen Turlington*

I felt the chill of the meadow underfoot—*Frost, Robert*

I find among the poems of Schiller—*Nash*

I find it very difficult to enthuse—*Nash*

I fled Him, down the nights and down the days—*Thompson, Francis*

I flung my soul to the air like a falcon flying—*Benét, William Rose*

I fly my kite across the hill—*Farrar*

I follow a map—*O'Neill, Catherine*

I found a dimpled spider, fat and white—*Frost, Robert*

I found a little beetle, so that Beetle was his name—*Milne*

I found her out there on a slope few see—*Hardy*

I found that ivory image there—*Yeats*

I gather up/ each sound—*Sanchez*

I gave to Hope a watch of mine: but he—*Herbert*

I gave you sorrow—*Merwin*

I get big with child in Africa—*Treitel*

I give you now Professor Twist—*Nash*

I got those sad old weary blues—*Hughes, Langston*

I grant thou wert not married to my Muse—*Shakespeare*

I guess I am just an old fogy—*Nash*

I had a dog and his name was Blue—*Anonymous-English—Modern English*

I had a Donkey, that was all right—*Roethke*

I had a dove, and the sweet dove died—*Keats*

I had a friend and he died, me—*Ignatow*

I had a little bird—*Dobell*

I had a little pony—*Children's Verses and Nursery Rhymes*

I had a silver penny—*Causley*

I had a special friend in study hall—*Johnston, Ellen Turlington*

I had come to the house, in a cave of trees—*Bogan*

I had finished my dinner—*Patchen*

I had forgotten how the frogs must sound—*Millay*

I had gone broke—*Cunningham, James Vincent*

I had left myself on the beach like a towel—*Ciardi*

I had ma clothes cleaned—*Hughes, Langston*

I had no time to hate—*Dickinson, Emily*

I had nothing to do with it. I was not here—*Wright, James*

I had some cards printed—*Hughes, Langston*

I had two husbands—*Hughes, Langston*

I hae a wife o' my ain—*Burns*

I hardly suppose I know anybody who wouldn't rather be a success—*Nash*

I hate my verses, every line, every word—*Jeffers, Robinson*

I hate the world—*Pietri*

I have a country but no town—*Ciardi*

I have a dream—*Hodges*

I have a dream for you, Mother—*Conkling*

I have a Gumbie Cat in mind—*Eliot, Thomas Stearns*

I have a house where I go—*Milne*

I have a little dog—*Nash*

I have a little shadow that goes in and out with me—*Stevenson*

I have a son, a little son—*Rosenfeld*

I have a song to sing—*Gilbert, Sir William Schwenck*

I have admired the marks of many men—*Summers, Hollis*

I have all my mother's habits—*Giovanni*

I have an orchard that hath store of plums—*Marlowe*

I have been a/ way so long—*Sanchez*

I have been cruel to a fat pigeon—*Merwin*

I have been faithfully to the 39 birthplaces of Beethoven—*Kizer*

I have been here before—*Rossetti, Dante Gabriel*

I have been in this garden of unripe fruit—*MacDiarmid*

I have been one acquainted with the night—*Frost, Robert*

I have been so great a lover—*Brooke*

I have been treading on leaves all day until I am autumn-tired—*Frost, Robert*

I have been wondering—*Hecht*

I have broken my fast—*Kendrick*

I have come far enough—*Creeley*

I have come to the borders of sleep—*Thomas, Edward*

I have committed many errors—*Williams, William Carlos*

I have considered—*Giovanni*

I have desired to go—*Hopkins*

I have done it again—*Plath*

I have done one braver thing—*Donne*

I have done with the devil—*Fox, Siv Cedering*

I have drawn up—*Williams, Hugo*

I have drunk ale from the country of the young —*Yeats*

I have eaten—*Williams, William Carlos*

I have eaten your bread and salt—*Kipling*

I have fallen in love with American names—*Benét, Stephen Vincent*

I have felt utter loneliness—*Malanga*

I have finished another year, said God—*Hardy*

I have gone into my eyes—*Sanchez*

I have gone out—*Sexton*

I have grown to understand that—*Viorst*

I have had enough. I gasp for breath—*Doolittle*

I have had enough of women, and enough of love —*Symons*

I have had to write this down—*Gallagher, Tess*

I have heard molecules—*Prothro*

I have heard talk of bold Robin Hood—*Anonymous-English—Modern English*

I have heard that hysterical women say—*Yeats*

I have heard the sea upon the troubled rocks— *Bly*

I have heard the singing ghost—*Posner*

I have heard what the talkers are talking—*Whitman*

I have heard your voice floating, royal and real —*Knight, Etheridge*

I have jest about decided—*Riley*

I have just come down from my father—*Dickey, James*

I have just seen a beautiful thing—*Grimké*

I have known all the storms that roll—*MacDiarmid*

I have known rivers—*Hughes, Langston*

I have known the imperial powers—*Jong*

I have led her home, my love, my only friend —*Tennyson*

I have locked myself out—*Weber, Ron*

I have lost my face—*Miller, May*

I have lost my turtle-doo—*Passerat*

I have loved, te quiero—*Vargas*

I have made for you a song—*Kipling*

I have met them at close of day—*Yeats*

I have never seen Africa—*Eckels*

I have never seen the whole sea—*Marshall, Helen Lowrie*

I have no enemy—*Van Doren*

I have no life but this—*Dickinson, Emily*

I have no name—*Blake*

I have no wit, no words, no tears—*Rossetti, Christina*

I have nothing to give you but these days— *Hacker*

I have picked long enough—*Greenwald*

I have published poems in the Potomac River— *Darr*

I have pursued you in vaulted cathedrals—*Goldstein*

I have run—*Marvin X*

I have seen cliffs that met the ocean foe—*Brown, Thomas Edward*

I have seen, desolate one, the voice has its tower —*Adams*

I have seen old ships—*Flecker*

I have seen strange things—*Gregor*

I have something to tell you—*Ignatow*

I have sown beside all waters in my day—*Bontemps*

I have to eat—*Harteis*

I have walked a long time—*Sanchez*

I have wrapped my dreams in a silken cloth— *Cullen*

I haven't done anything—*Giovanni*

I haven't written a poem in so long—*Giovanni*

I hawk my wares in the marketplace—*Pommy Vega, Janine*

I hear a sudden cry of pain—*Stephens*

I hear a whistling—*Emanuel*

I hear America sing—*Whitman*

I hear an army charging upon the land—*Joyce*

I hear it was charged against me that I sought to destroy institutions—*Whitman*

I hear the world reciting—*Frost, Robert*

I hear things crying in the world—*Brooks, Gwendolyn*

I hear voices praising Tshombe and the Portuguese—*Bly*

I heard a bird at dawn—*Stephens*

I heard a fly buzz when I died—*Dickinson, Emily*

I heard a mouse—*Coatsworth*

I heard a spider—*Marquis*

I heard a thousand blended notes—*Wordsworth*

I heard a woman soft with fat—*Abbe*

I heard/ before, of an/ American—*Tomlinson*

I heard of a man—*Cohen*

I heard the bells on Christmas day—*Longfellow*

I heard the far lowing—*Lewis, Janet*

I heard the trailing garments of the night—*Longfellow*

I heard their young hearts crying—*Joyce*

I heed not that my earthly lot—*Poe*

I held that when a person dies—*Masefield*

I hid my heart in a nest of roses—*Swinburne*
I' ho gia fatto un gozzo—*Michelangelo*
I hoed and trenched and weeded—*Housman*
I hold a newspaper, reading—*Stryk*
I hold in me the body of a man— *Williams, Hugo*
I hope he doesn't see me walking—*Bergman, Alexander F.*
I, Hypocrite Harry, that Hamburg hand-kisser—*Kizer*
I hytten hos min moder—*Andersen*
I imagine him still with heavy brow—*Spender*
I imagine this midnight moment's forest—*Hughes, Ted*
I inherited forty acres from my Father—*Masters, Edgar Lee*
I intended an Ode—*Dobson*
I, John Watts—*Olson*
I keep finding this letter—*Merwin*
I keep three wishes ready— *Wynne*
I kept telephoning the repairman at the garage—*Abbe*
I knew a bear once ate a man named Virtue—*Blackmur*
I knew a man a common farmer— *Whitman*
I knew a woman, lovely in her bones—*Roethke*
I knew too that through them I knew—*Stein, Gertrude*
I know a dance—*Nash*
I know a funny, little man—*Children's Verses and Nursery Rhymes*
I know a girl, and the girl knows me—*Stephens*
I know a lady, name of Blanche—*Nash*
I know a little restaurant—*Nash*
I know a man named Mr. Nagle—*Nash*
I know a man who when he bares his breast—*Nash*
I know / a nice—*Eckels*
I know a place where summer strives—*Dickinson, Emily*
I know a renegade hotel—*Nash*
I know a retired dentist who only paints mountains—*Auden*
I know, although when looks meet— *Yeats*
I know Cheyney as if he were conceived within my womb—*Jeffers, Lance*
I know how poems come—*Conkling*
I know I am but summer to your heart—*Millay*
I know I haven't grown but—*Giovanni*
I know lots of men who are in love—*Nash*
I know my love by his way of walking—*Anonymous–English—Modern English*
I know my upper arms—*Giovanni*
I know not how it may be with others—*Hardy*
I know not of what we ponder'd—*Calverley*
I know so well this turfy mill—*Betjeman*
I know some lonely houses off the road—*Dickinson, Emily*
I know that he told that I snared his soul—*Masters, Edgar Lee*
I know the probable—*Marcus*
I know the thing that's most uncommon—*Pope, Alexander*
I know the wayes of learning—*Herbert*
I know they say it is music—*O'Gorman*
I know two things about the horse—*Royde-Smith*
I know two women—*Creeley*

I know very well, goddess, she is not beautiful—*MacLeish*
I know where I'm going—*Anonymous–English—Modern English*
I laid me down upon a bank—*Blake*
I Lais whose laughter was scornful in Hellas—*Plato*
I lang hae thought, my youthfu' friend—*Burns*
I leaned against the mantel, sick, sick—*Masters, Edgar Lee*
I leant upon a coppice gate—*Hardy*
I lift my heavy heart up solemnly—*Browning, Elizabeth Barrett*
I light a cigarette, my dead mouth steaming—*Ciardi*
I like a church; I like a cowl—*Emerson*
I like it here just fine— *Walker*
I like noise—*Pope, Jessie*
I like the part of you—*Sukenick*
I like the smell of the wind, the sniff— *Watkins*
I like to chase the fireflies—*Coplen*
I like to see it lap the miles—*Dickinson, Emily*
I like to see you lean back in your chair—*Brooks, Gwendolyn*
I like to walk—*McCord*
I like what I like when I do not worry—*Stein, Gertrude*
I live in a house—*Braxton*
I live in an old house on a dark star— *Wheelock*
I live, therefore I love—*Ciardi*
I lived a life without love— *Williams, Oscar*
I lived in the first century of world wars—*Rukeyser*
I lived with visions for my company—*Browning, Elizabeth Barrett*
I livet har jag irrat—*Bergman, Bo*
I livets villevalla—*Ferlin*
I loafed about at leisure— *Yevtushenko*
I long for the small jar—*Purens*
I long to talke with some old lovers ghost—*Donne*
I look back on this day that is gone—*Marshall, Helen Lowrie*
I look in the glass, whose face do I see—*Smith, Stevie*
I look into my glass—*Hardy*
I look through my dead friend's eyes at the house of love—*Ciardi*
I look too often at my feet when I jump rope—*Sobiloff*
I look upon the map that hangs by me—*Hardy*
I looked and I saw—*Hughes, Langston*
I looked for you in a crowd—*Robson, Jeremy*
I looked in my heart while the wild swans went over—*Millay*
I looked upon a mountain high—*Marshall, Helen Lowrie*
I lost a world the other day—*Dickinson, Emily*
I lost my patronage in Spoon River—*Masters, Edgar Lee*
I love America— *Yevtushenko*
I love little pussy, her coat is so warm—*Children's Verses and Nursery Rhymes*
I love my queer cellar with its dusty smell—*Conkling*
I love Octopussy, his arms are so long—*Cox*
I love roads—*Thomas, Edward*
I love the apple sweetness of the air—*Dodson*

I love to hear a cricket in my house—*Nash*
I love to rise in a summer morn—*Blake*
I love to see the old heath's withered brake—*Clare*
I love watching the water—*Bell*
I love you as a bee loves—*Van Doren*
I love you most, I think—*Marshall, Helen Lowrie*
I love you much—*Cummings*
I love your brown curls—*Betjeman*
I loved my friend—*Hughes, Langston*
I loved my lord, my black-haired lord—*Stone, Ruth*
I loved you dearly, Stone Fish Lake—*Whan Chei*
I made him swear he'd always tell me nothing but the truth—*Viorst*
I made Man with too many faults. Yet I love him—*Smith, Stevie*
I made my song a coat—*Yeats*
I make no prayer—*Merwin*
I married the Earl of Egremont—*Smith, Stevie*
I may be smelly and I may be old—*Smith, Stevie*
I mean we bees real—*Sanchez*
I meant to do my work today—*Le Gallienne*
I meditate upon a swallow's flight—*Yeats*
I met a little elf-man, once—*Bangs*
I met a man as I went walking—*Milne*
I met a man in South Street, tall—*Crane, Hart*
I met a man the other day—*Parker*
I met a traveller from an antique land—*Bishop, Morris*
I met a traveller from an antique land—*Shelley*
I met her as a blossom on a stem—*Roethke*
I met her early in the evening—*Patten*
I met the Bishop on the road—*Yeats*
I' mi trovai, fanciulle, un bel mattino—*Poliziano*
I might have been—*Hobbs*
I' mo, trasenno p' 'a porta, aggiú sentuto—*Galdieri*
I must go down to the seas again—*Masefield*
I must have passed the crest a while ago—*Teasdale*
I must not die of pity, I must live—*Millay*
I must tell you—*Williams, William Carlos*
I, my dear, was born to-day—*Prior*
I myself saw furious with blood—*Tate, Allen*
I ne'er was struck before that hour—*Clare*
I never gave a lock of hair away—*Browning, Elizabeth Barrett*
I never lost as much but twice—*Dickinson, Emily*
I never saw a fairer—*Burns*
I never saw a moor, I never saw the sea—*Dickinson, Emily*
I never saw that you did painting need—*Shakespeare*
I never/ scored—*Mailer*
I never think of her without a smile—*Marshall, Helen Lowrie*
I never was attached to that great sect—*Shelley*
I no longer build in stone—*Greenwald*
I nursed it in my bosom while it lived—*Rossetti, Christina*
I objurgate the centipede—*Nash*
I, of the City and State of do declare—*Marshall, Lenore G.*
I often sit and wish that I—*Children's Verses and Nursery Rhymes*
I often wish I were a King—*Milne*

I once did know a Turkish man—*Gilbert, Sir William Schwenck*
I once drove to Atlantic City—*Davis, Thulani Nkabinde*
I once had a cow that jumped over the moon—*Frost, Robert*
I once saw weeping in a wood—*Hollander*
I once wrote a letter as follows—*Creeley*
I only want to—*Giovanni*
I open a tree—*Kumin*
I opened the door so my last look—*Frost, Robert*
I opened window wide—*Masefield*
I owe no man, he proudly said—*Marshall, Helen Lowrie*
I pace the greenwood, bitter—*Heine*
I pace the sounding sea-beach and behold—*Longfellow*
I pass all my hours in a shady old grove—*Charles II*
I pass enough savages on the street—*Ciardi*
I pick up my life—*Hughes, Langston*
I play for seasons, not Eternities—*Meredith, George*
I play it cool—*Hughes, Langston*
I play my sweet old airs—*Hardy*
I plays a mean guitar—*Ward*
I pledge allegiance—*Bellamy*
I preached four thousand sermons—*Masters, Edgar Lee*
I prithee send me back my heart—*Suckling*
I put my nickel—*Hughes, Langston*
I put on my dream suit—*Sukenick*
I reached the middle of the mount—*Emerson*
I read in a tattered book about Sheik Bedreddin—*Ciardi*
I read love with—*Lifshin*
I reason, earth is short—*Dickinson, Emily*
I recall her by a freckle of gold—*Durrell*
I reckon it is nearly fifty years to the day—*Nash*
I regret that before people can be reformed they have to be sinners—*Nash*
I remember, I remember—*Hood*
I remember so well the old church bell—*Marshall, Helen Lowrie*
I remember the dread—*Betjeman*
I remember the forehead born—*Levine*
I remember the neckcurls, limp and damp as tendrils—*Roethke*
I remember the very day—*Howard, Lee*
I repent should be—*Jeffers, Lance*
I reside at Table Mountain—*Harte*
I resolved it, I—*Creeley*
I rise, gentlemen, it is the pleasant hour—*Tate, Allen*
I rise in the dawn, and I kneel and blow—*Yeats*
I rode in the golden yell—*Brooks, Gwendolyn*
I run, cried the fox—*Williams, Tennessee*
I said, Ah! what shall I write—*Jones, David*
I said I splendidly loved you; it's not true—*Brooke*
I said:/ now will the poets sing—*Cullen*
I said that Juan had been sent to Cadiz—*Byron*
I said to love—*Hardy*
I said to my Heart, between sleeping and waking—*Mordaunt*
I saluted a nobody—*Sandburg*
I sang as one—*Day Lewis*
I sat on the Dogana's steps—*Pound*

I sat only two tables off from the one I was sacked at—*Betjeman*

I sat to listen to each sound—*Young, Andrew*

I saw a bird pasted to muck—*Ciardi*

I saw a butterfly—*Conkling*

I saw a butterfly today—*Marshall, Helen Lowrie*

I saw a chapel all of gold—*Blake*

I saw a man turned into money—*Abbe*

I saw a monk of Charlemagne—*Blake*

I saw a mountain—*Conkling*

I saw a peacock with a fiery tail—*Coatsworth*

I saw a proud, mysterious cat—*Lindsay, Vachel*

I saw a querulous old man, the tobacconist of Eighth Street—*Eberhart*

I saw a snail come down the garden wall—*Conkling*

I saw a staring virgin stand—*Yeats*

I saw an army coming against the sun—*Abbe*

I saw an old black man walk down the road—*Jeffers, Lance*

I saw eternity the other night—*Vaughan, Henry*

I saw her lift herself—*Mariah*

I saw him bearded, framed in a modern setting —*Danner*

I saw him once before—*Holmes, Oliver Wendell*

I saw him steal the light away—*Hardy*

I saw in Louisiana a live-oak growing—*Whitman*

I saw my lady weep—*Anonymous-English—Modern English*

I saw my luve in black velvet—*Smith, Sydney Goodsir*

I saw my soul at rest upon a day—*Swinburne*

I saw nine red horsemen ride over the plain—*Farjeon*

I saw on the slant hill a putrid lamb—*Eberhart*

I saw the best minds of my generation destroyed by madness—*Ginsberg*

I saw the sky descending, black and white—*Lowell, Robert*

I saw the vision of armies—*Whitman*

I saw the wind today—*Colum*

I saw thee on thy bridal day—*Poe*

I saw you come in a swan's shape—*Watkins*

I see before me now a traveling army halting—*Whitman*

I see his blood upon the Rose—*Plunkett*

I see no single thread—*Knight, Etheridge*

I see the European headsman—*Whitman*

I see the moon—*Lee, Dennis*

I see the winding water make—*Betjeman*

I see thine image through my tears to-night—*Browning, Elizabeth Barrett*

I see you—*Morgan, John*

I see you did not try to save—*Young, Andrew*

I see you standing out from the mind's roadstead —*Meredith, George*

I see your shadow in the lilac mist—*Goldstein*

I seek in anonymity's cloister—*Nash*

I serve a mistress whiter than the snow—*Munday*

I shall be careful to say nothing at all—*Moore, Merrill*

I shall be coming back to you—*Conkling*

I shall cry God to give me a broken heart—*Sandburg*

I shall depart hence, seal up my dwelling—*Ennis*

I shall forget you presently, my dear—*Millay*

I shall go without companions—*Belloc*

I shall never get you together entirely—*Plath*

I shall rot here, with those whom in their day—*Hardy*

I shall save my poems—*Giovanni*

I shimmied with Bea up a mulberry tree—*Knight, Etheridge*

I shot an arrow into the air—*Longfellow*

I shot an otter because I had a gun—*Pack*

I should like to rise and go—*Stevenson*

I should not have shown—*Hardy*

I should set about memorizing this little room —*Durrell*

I should write a poem—*Giovanni*

I sing a song—*Katzman*

I sing an old song—*Williams, Oscar*

I sing of a maiden—*Anonymous-English—Modern English*

I sing of Olaf glad and big—*Cummings*

I sing Saint Valentine, his day—*McGinley*

I sing the endless cartracks in my flesh that must be ripped up—*Jeffers, Lance*

I sit and look out upon all the sorrows of the world —*Whitman*

I sit in an office at 244 Madison Avenue—*Nash*

I sit in one of the dives—*Auden*

I sit in the top—*Hughes, Ted*

I sit on the forestroad—*Bly*

I sit on the tracks—*Tate, James*

I skogen vid milan sitter far—*Geijer*

I slept in a sleeping field—*Sobiloff*

I slept in the light—*Colbert*

I slide my face along to the mirror—*Levertov*

I slowly came down from the mountains of sleep —*Bly*

I sometimes sit—*Lee, Dennis*

I sought a theme and sought for it in vain—*Yeats*

I sought from love what no love gives—*Garrigue*

I speak skimpily to/ you—*Sanchez*

I spoke a word of praise today—*Marshall, Helen Lowrie*

I sprang to the stirrup, and Joris, and he—*Browning, Robert*

I stand upon a hill and see—*Gunn*

I stand with standing stones—*Roethke*

I stare into—*Barker, George*

I start out for a walk—*Bly*

I stayed in the front yard all my life—*Brooks, Gwendolyn*

I stayed the night for shelter at a farm—*Frost, Robert*

I stood alone at a funeral—*Davison, Peter*

I stood at the foot of rocky Carradon—*Hawker*

I stood beside a hill—*Teasdale*

I stood in Venice on the Bridge of Sighs—*Byron*

I stood knee-deep in the sea—*Smith, Stevie*

I stood on the bridge at midnight—*Longfellow*

I stood tiptoe upon a little hill—*Keats*

I stopped to pick up the bagel—*Ignatow*

I strap on my holster—*Lally*

I strolled across—*Roethke*

I struck the board, and cry'd, No more—*Herbert*

I study out a dark similitude—*Roethke*

I summon to the winding ancient stair—*Yeats*

I swear, the way time passes—*Marshall, Helen Lowrie*

I swung out, at eight or ten—*Olson*

I tady jsou krajiny snící—*Holub*

I take a giant step North—*Pastan*
I talked to old Lem—*Brown, Sterling A.*
I taste a liquor never brewed—*Dickinson, Emily*
I tell thee, Dick, where I have been—*Suckling*
I tell you, don't trust the living. Their eyes—*Ciardi*
I tell you, hopeless grief is passionless—*Browning, Elizabeth Barrett*
I tell you it's cruel—*Olson*
I tell you that I see her still—*Nemerov*
I test my bath before I sit—*Nash*
I thank all who have loved me in their hearts—*Browning, Elizabeth Barrett*
I that in heill wes and gladnes—*Dunbar, William*
I, the scourge-wielder, balance-wrecker—*Masters, Edgar Lee*
I think all this is somewhere in myself—*Merwin*
I think and think; yet still I fail—*De la Mare*
I think before they saw me the giraffes—*Fuller, Roy*
I think continually of those who were truly great—*Spender*
I think I could turn and live with animals, they are so placid—*Whitman*
I think it is in Virginia, that place—*Merwin*
I think it must be lonely to be God—*Brooks, Gwendolyn*
I think of the image brought into my room—*Rukeyser*
I think of the time I was perfectly happy—*Kavanagh*
I think of thee—my thoughts do twine and bud—*Browning, Elizabeth Barrett*
I think of you every minute of the day—*Lowell, Robert*
I think that I shall never know—*Parker*
I think that I shall never see/A billboard—*Nash*
I think that I shall never see/A poem—*Kilmer, Joyce*
I think the dead are tender—*Roethke*
I thought (and before it was too late)—*Logan*
I thought for a long while—*Johnston, Ellen Turlington*
I thought he'd gone, that owl—*Booth*
I thought I saw an angel flying low—*Bontemps*
I thought I was going to the poets—*Rukeyser*
I thought of the mariners—*Smith, William Jay*
I thought once how Theocritus had sung—*Browning, Elizabeth Barrett*
I told her when I left one day—*Hardy*
I told them a thousand times if I told them once—*Hay, Sara Henderson*
I, too, dislike it—*Moore, Marianne*
I too hear America singing—*Bond*
I, too, saw God through mud—*Owen, Wilfred*
I too sing America—*Hughes, Langston*
I took a reed and blew a tune—*Ledwidge*
I took a walk through the streets of my town—*Kramer*
I took her dainty eyes, as well—*Dowson*
I took my gun—*Van Doren*
I took my heart in my hand—*Rossetti, Christina*
I touch you in the night—*Kunitz*
I towered far, and lo—*Hardy*
I traced the circus whose gray stones incline—*Hardy*
I travelled among unknown men—*Wordsworth*

I travelled through a land of men—*Blake*
I tread the sand at the sea's edge—*Watkins*
I tried to refine that neighbor of mine—*Service*
I try to live for the moment—*Franks*
I tuoi occhi son come la giovinezza—*Gatto*
I turn round—*Yeats*
I used to have a dressing room—*Harteis*
I used to wonder—*Hughes, Langston*
I veris va na chuzhyni—*Shevchenko*
I vimmel och—*Ferlin*
I wait for the white light—*Jeffers, Lance*
I wake—*Green, Kate*
I wake and feel the fell of dark, not day—*Hopkins*
I wake and hear it raining—*Van Doren*
I wake, sweating, reach for your rosary and drop it—*Ai*
I wake to sleep, and take my waking slow—*Roethke*
I wakened still a child—*Levine*
I walk beside the prisoners to the road—*Jarrell*
I walk in nature still alone—*Thoreau*
I walk on the waste-ground for no good reason—*Redgrove*
I walk quite slowly down Baby Street—*Blanding*
I walk through the long schoolroom questioning—*Yeats*
I walked abroad in a snowy day—*Blake*
I walked by the sea, and there came to me—*Tolkien*
I walked into the nightclub in the morning—*Betjeman*
I walked on the banks of the tincan banana dock—*Ginsberg*
I walked out on a winter's day—*Dowling*
I walked out to the graveyard—*Eberhart*
I walked where in their talking graves—*Causley*
I wander through each chartered street—*Blake*
I wandered lonely as a cloud—*Wordsworth*
I wandered lonely where the pine-trees made—*Whittier*
I want a hero: an uncommon want—*Byron*
I want my body bathed again by southern suns—*Walker*
I want no sexual, announces he—*Moore, Honor*
I want to be a circle around you—*Dupree*
I want to be a postage stamp—*Levendosky*
I want to be a white horse—*Bly*
I want/ to do it—*Goldfarb*
I want to say—*Giovanni*
I want to see the world—*Wellman*
I want what is inside you—*Bly*
I want you—*Devaul*
I wanted the gold, and I sought it—*Service*
I wanted you, nameless Woman of the South—*Crane, Hart*
I was a beautiful plant—*Smith, Stevie*
I was a communist for the FBI—*Dlugos*
I was a Gold Man—Now I lie under the earth—*Sitwell, Edith*
I was a peasant girl from Germany—*Masters, Edgar Lee*
I was a weapon—*Piercy*
I was angry with my friend—*Blake*
I was asking for something specific—*Whitman*
I was born in Belfast between the mountain and the gantries—*MacNeice*

I was but seven year auld—*Anonymous–English
—Modern English*

I was expecting Lauren Bacall—*Flanders*

I/ was five—*Lee, Don L.*

I was flying alone over desert—*Darr*

I was foolish about windows—*Sandburg*

I was foretold, your rebel sex—*Carew*

I was just a little thing—*Field, Eugene*

I was just turned twenty-one—*Masters, Edgar Lee*

I was looking a long while for intentions—*Whitman*

I was looking for the miraculous transformation
—*Colbert*

I was not sleeping when Brother said—*Brooks,
Gwendolyn*

I was once a pilot—*Eliot, Thomas Stearns*

I was only a young man—*Wright, James*

I was only eight years old—*Masters, Edgar Lee*

I was passing time—*Braxton*

I was seventy-seven, come August—*Parker*

I was sitting in what that afternoon I thought to
be—*Miles*

I was six when my mother first trusted me with a
two-dollar bill—*Sobiloff*

I was so full of love and joy—*Smith, Stevie*

I was talking to a moth—*Marquis*

I was the captain of my ship—*Moraes*

I was the first fruits of the battle of Missionary
Ridge—*Masters, Edgar Lee*

I was the first to see the gogglehead—*Marshall,
Lenore G.*

I was the only child of Frances Harris of Virginia
—*Masters, Edgar Lee*

I was the patriarch of the shining land—*Winters*

I was thinking last night, as I sat in the cars—
Holmes, Oliver Wendell

I was thy neighbour once, thou rugged pile—
Wordsworth

I was Willie Metcalf—*Masters, Edgar Lee*

I was wrapped in black—*Sexton*

I watch the filthy light—*Levine*

I watch your complicated face—*Williams, Hugo*

I watched the road—*Jackson, Gerald*

I weep for Adonais—he is dead—*Shelley*

I went down on my hands and knees—*Young,
Andrew*

I went down to the river—*Hughes, Langston*

I went East, Margaret—*Baldwin, Deirdra*

I went into a public-'ouse to get a pint o' beer
—*Kipling*

I went into tight places for them (he said)—*Beecher*

I went out alone—*Yeats*

I went out in the world—*Hodges*

I went out of the hazel wood—*Yeats*

I went slowly through the wood of shadows—
Conkling

I went this morning down to where the Johnny-
Jump-Ups grow—*Widdemer*

I went to sea in a glass-bottomed boat—*Conkling*

I went to the animal fair—*Anonymous–English—
Modern English*

I went to the city and what did I hear?—*Krows*

I went to the dances at Chandlerville—*Masters,
Edgar Lee*

I went to the Garden of Love—*Blake*

I went to turn the grass once after one—*Frost,
Robert*

I whispered, I am too young—*Yeats*

I who ere while the happy garden sung—*Milton*

I who was young so long—*Stevenson*

I will be bitter—*Giovanni*

I will be earth you be the flower—*Swenson*

I will begin in May, describing—*Dugan*

I will give my love an apple—*Anonymous–English—Modern English*

I will go up the mountain after the Moon—*Davis,
Fannie Stearns*

I will go with my father a-plowing—*Campbell,
Joseph*

I will have my beds blown up, not stuffed—*Jonson*

I will not be over—*Jacobsen, Josephine*

I will not praise you in the laurel way—*Goldstein*

I will rise and go now, and go to Innisfree—*Yeats*

I will teach you my taownspeople—*Williams,
William Carlos*

I will walk all day with you—*Murphy*

I winged my bird—*Masters, Edgar Lee*

I wish I had a red balloon—*Emanuel*

I wish I owned a Dior dress—*McGinley*

I wish the rent—*Hughes, Langston*

I wish to God I never saw you, Mag—*Sandburg*

I wish you happy death of ducks—*Simmons, Judy*

I wish you happiness, God's gift—*Marshall, Helen
Lowrie*

I without bite or sup—*Stephens*

I woke before the morning, I was happy all the
day—*Stevenson*

I woke from the warm—*Garfinkel*

I woke/just about daybreak—*Wright, James*

I woke this morning to find an albatross staring at
me—*Patten*

I woke to a shout: 'I am Alpha and Omega'—
Hughes, Ted

I wol biwaille, in manere of tragedie—*Chaucer*

I wonder about the trees—*Frost, Robert*

I wonder by my troth, what thou and I—*Donne*

I wonder do you feel to-day—*Browning, Robert*

I wonder how many old men last winter—
Wright, James

I wondered as a dream will what Stafford could
see—*Sobiloff*

I won't go with you, I want to stay with Grandpa
—*Lowell, Robert*

I worked for a woman—*Hughes, Langston*

I would be for you rain—*Fabio, Sarah Webster*

I would beat out your face in brass—*Sandburg*

I would have been as great as George Eliot—
Masters, Edgar Lee

I would I had a flower-boy—*Kizer*

I would I had thrust my hands of flesh—*Masters,
Edgar Lee*

I would I were on yonder hill—*Anonymous–English—Modern English*

I would live all my life in nonchalance—*Nash*

I would that folk forgot me quite—*Hardy*

I would to God I were quenched and fed—*Millay*

I wouldn't be buried in anything but black—
Francis

I write you in my need—*Cunningham, James
Vincent*

I write what I know on one side of the paper—
Sandburg

I wrote a poem—*Giovanni*
I wrote some lines once on a time—*Holmes, Oliver Wendell*
I wrote something black today—*Emanuel*
I years had been from home—*Dickinson, Emily*
I zolotoyi i dorohoyi—*Shevchenko*
Iam super oceanum venit a seniore marito—*Ovid*
Iam veris comites, quae mare temperant—*Horace*
Iba saliendo al campo, a la esperanza—*Murciano*
Iba yo montado sobre un macho cabrío—*Garcia Lorca*
Ibbity, bibbity, sibbity, sab—*Children's Verses and Nursery Rhymes*
Iberia, barrio de España—*Celaya*
Ić thurh múth sprece manigum reordum—*Anonymous–English—Old English*
Ić wiht zeseah wundorlícé—*Anonymous–English —Old English*
Ich ballte—*Goll*
Ich, Bertolt Brecht, bin aus den schwarzen Wäldern—*Brecht*
Ich bin allein—*Tucholsky*
Ich bin der Graf von Réaumur—*Morgenstern*
Ich bin ein einsamer Schaukelstuhl—*Morgenstern*
Ich bin ein Gast auf Erden—*Gerhardt*
Ich bin im braunen Cognac-See ertrunken—*Zuckmayer*
Ich bin nun tausend Jahre alt—*Morgenstern*
Ich bin's gewohnt, den Kopf recht hoch zu tragen —*Heine*
Ich danke Gott und freue mich—*Claudius*
Ich denke Dein, wenn mir der Sonne Schimmer —*Goethe*
Ich erinnere mich ihres Gesichts nicht mehr—*Brecht*
Ich fürchte mich so vor der Menschen Wort—*Rilke*
Ich ging den Weg entlang, der einsam lag—*Liliencron*
Ich ging im Walde so für mich hin—*Goethe*
Ich grolle nicht, und wenn das Herz auch bricht —*Heine*
Ich hab dir alles hingegeben—*Tucholsky*
Ich hab dir einen Regenpalast—*Goll*
Ich hab im Traum geweinet—*Heine*
Ich hab in meinen Jugendtagen—*Heine*
Ich hab meine Tante geschlachtet—*Wedekind*
Ich hab meinen ersten Mann gesehn—*Tucholsky*
Ich habe dich geliebt und ich will dich lieben—*Claudius*
Ich habe die Vernunft nach ihm ausgeschickt—*Krolow*
Ich habe geliebt; nun lieb ich erst recht—*Goethe*
Ich habe gerochen alle Gerüche—*Heine*
Ich habe in der Tat—*Heine*
Ich habe mich deinetwegen—*Tucholsky*
Ich habe was Liebes, das hab ich so lieb—*Bürger*
Ich habe zu Hause ein blaues Klavier—*Lasker-Schüler*
Ich halte ihr die Augen zu—*Heine*
Ich hân min lehen—*Walther von der Vogelweide*
Ich hôrte ein Wazzer diezen—*Walther von der Vogelweide*
Ich kann den Blick nicht von dir wenden—*Tucholsky*

Ich kann, im Kino, auf wen immer warten—*Kästner*
Ich lache ob den Abgeschmackten Laffen—*Heine*
Ich lebe mein Leben in wachsenden Ringen—*Rilke*
Ich liebe das Meer—*Heine*
Ich liebe Frauen, die vor tausend Jahren—*Hesse*
Ich möchte einer werden so wie die—*Rilke*
Ich rief den Teufel und er kam—*Heine*
Ich rufe dich an, Allewelt—*Bergengruen*
Ich sach mit minen Ougen—*Walther von der Vogelweide*
Ich sâz uf einem Steine—*Walther von der Vogelweide*
Ich schlaf, ich wach—*Anonymous–German*
Ich schnürte meinen Ranzen—*Busch*
Ich seh dich nicht—*Droste-Hülshoff*
Ich sehe den Bäumen die Stürme an—*Rilke*
Ich sitze am Strassenrand—*Brecht*
Ich sollte ruhn? Ich soll die Liebe swingen—*Hölderlin*
Ich tanz nicht mit, ich räuchre nicht den Klötzen —*Heine*
Ich träum als Kind mich zurücke—*Chamisso*
Ich vill eich da tzellin a mietza—*Kurtz*
Ich wandelte unter Bäumen—*Heine*
Ich weiss es, Geliebte: jetzt fallen mir die Haare aus—*Brecht*
Ich weiss mir einen meien—*Anonymous–German*
Ich weiss natürlich: einzig durch Glück—*Brecht*
Ich weiss nicht, was soll es bedeuten—*Heine*
Ich werde einmal plötzlich auf die Nase fallen —*Zuckmayer*
Ich will es ofter sagen—*Zuckmayer*
Ich will meine Seele tauchen—*Heine*
Ich wollte meine Lieder—*Heine*
Ich zog meine Fuhre trotz meiner Schwäche—*Brecht*
The ice has melted—*Pleshette*
Iced with a vanilla—*Davie*
Ici, dans le lieu clair—*Bonnefoy*
Ici l'univers est à l'abri—*Supervielle*
Ici sera ma tombe, et pas ailleurs—*Desnos*
The icicle finger of death, aimed—*Hollander*
Icker-backer/soda-cracker—*Children's Verses and Nursery Rhymes*
The icy evil that struck his father down—*Hayden*
I'd have the silence like a heavy chock—*Davie*
I'd planned to be Heathcliff's Cathy—*Viorst*
I'd rather beggars made me happy—*Nowlan*
I'd ride a cock horse to Banbury Cross—*Nash*
I'd sooner, except the penalties, kill a man than a hawk—*Jeffers, Robinson*
I'd watched the sorrow of the evening sky—*Brooke*
The idea of joy, abruptly—*Miles*
Identification had to be by mask—*Scott, Winfield Townley*
Ie vis, ie meurs: ie me brule et me noye—*Labé*
Iedan bude klin drugi kleshta—*Popa*
Iedan miluie nogu stolitse—*Popa*
Iedni odgrizu drugima—*Popa*
Iedni su noei drugi zvezde—*Popa*
If a woman wants to be a poet—*Jong*
If all a top physicist knows—*Auden*

If all the seas were one sea—*Children's Verses and Nursery Rhymes*

If all the trees in all the woods were men—*Holmes, Oliver Wendell*

If all the world and love were young—*Raleigh*

If all were rain and never sun—*Rossetti, Christina*

If Art and Joy go hand in hand—*Dowling*

If but some vengeful god would call to me—*Hardy*

If compression is the first grace of style—*Moore, Marianne*

If de blues was whisky—*Clay*

If ever I saw a blessing in the air—*Lee, Laurie*

If ever I should condescend to prose—*Byron*

If ever two were one, then surely we—*Bradstreet*

If everything happens that can't be done—*Cummings*

If God has given you the special power—*Marshall, Helen Lowrie*

If heaven were to do again—*Frost, Robert*

If i/ or anybody don't—*Cummings*

If I am happy, and you—*Conkling*

If I am sentenced not to talk to you—*Bell*

If I am that bird, then I am alone—*MacPherson*

If I can say yes I/ must say—*Merwin*

If I can stop one heart from breaking—*Dickinson, Emily*

If I can't do—*Giovanni*

If I could bend each yesterday—*Hodges*

If I could have—*Millay*

If I could have lived another year—*Masters, Edgar Lee*

If I could only live at the pitch that is near madness—*Eberhart*

If I delight my God, my king—*Traherne*

If I had a heart of gold—*Hughes, Langston*

If I had a ship / I'd sail my ship—*Milne*

If I had a wife—*Van Doren*

If I had known—*Sanchez*

If I have faltered more or less—*Stevenson*

If I have given you delight—*Kipling*

If I leave all for thee, wilt thou exchange—*Browning, Elizabeth Barrett*

If I, like Solomon—*Moore, Marianne*

If I lived on the land—*Carter*

If I make the lashes dark—*Yeats*

If I return to walk these woods—*Scott, Winfield Townley*

If I ride this train—*Johnson, Joe*

If I should die, think only this of me—*Brooke*

If I should ever by chance grow rich—*Thomas, Edward*

If I should pass the tomb of Jonah—*Sandburg*

If I told him, would he like it—*Stein, Gertrude*

If I were a bear—*Milne*

If I were hanged on the highest hill—*Kipling*

If I were Lord of Tartary—*De la Mare*

If I were mild, and I were sweet—*Parker*

If I were rich, what would I do—*Stephens*

If I were tickled by the rub of love—*Thomas, Dylan*

If I were to speak—*Mac Low*

If, in an odd angle of the hutment—*Jarrell*

If in the future—*Williams, Miller*

If it chance your eye offend you—*Housman*

If it form the one landscape that we the inconstant ones—*Auden*

If it is a world without a genius—*Stevens, Wallace*

If it should come to this—*Young, Andrew*

If it were not for that lean executioner—*Spender*

If it's squashed red I swerve to the other side—*Ennis*

If leaves shaking the wind—*Jeffers, Lance*

If love were what the rose is—*Swinburne*

If man that Angel of Bright consciousness—*Aiken*

If music and sweet poetry—*Barnfield*

If music be the muses' paragon—*Davie*

If music is the universal language—*Giovanni*

If my dear love were but the child of state—*Shakespeare*

If my head hurt a hair's foot—*Thomas, Dylan*

If my soul be empty, if my soul be fettered—*Jeffers, Lance*

If Nancy Hanks/ came back as a ghost—*Benét, Rosemary Carr*

If nothing else let this poor paper say—*Van Doren*

If one could have that little head of hers—*Browning, Robert*

If ought of oaten stop, or pastoral song—*Collins, William*

If people ask me/ I always tell them—*Milne*

If possible—*Brooks, Gwendolyn*

If rain rose—*Van Doren*

If rest is sweet at shut of day—*Symons*

If sadly thinking—*Curran*

If seen by many minds at once—*Durrell*

If she be not as kind as fair—*Etherege*

If sky is water then this train—*Hoffman*

If someone asked me why I left—*McCarthy, Agnes*

If strange things happen where she is—*Graves*

If the autumn would end—*MacLeish*

If the blues would let me—*Hughes, Langston*

If the dull substance of my flesh were thought—*Shakespeare*

If the excursion train to Peoria—*Masters, Edgar Lee*

If the hill overlooking our city has always been known as Adam's grave—*Auden*

If the learned Supreme Court of Illinois—*Masters, Edgar Lee*

If the man in the moon—*Nicholson*

If the people under that portico—*Van Doren*

If the red slayer think he slays—*Emerson*

If there are any heavens my mother will (all by herself) have—*Cummings*

If there be nothing new, but that which is—*Shakespeare*

If there must be a god in the house, must be—*Stevens, Wallace*

If there were dreams to sell—*Beddoes*

If there were, Oh! an Hellespont of cream—*Davies, John, of Hereford*

If this be love, to draw a weary breath—*Daniel, Samuel*

If this life-saving rock should fail—*Young, Andrew*

If thou be in a lonely place—*Brontë, Charlotte*

If thou beest he—but O how fall'n! how chang'd—*Milton*

If thou must love me, let it be for nought—*Browning, Elizabeth Barrett*

If thou survive my well-contented day—*Shake-speare*

If thy soul check thee that I come so near—*Shake-speare*

If to be absent were to be—*Lovelace, Richard*

If to do is to be, take this lovely cat, here—*Danner*

If wars were won by feasting—*Kipling*

If we can, in our living day by day—*Marshall, Helen Lowrie*

If we come like soft rain—*Fabio, Sarah Webster*

If we meet a gorilla—*Sandburg*

If we must die, let it not be like hogs—*McKay*

If what heals can bless/ can what blesses heal—*Scott, Winfield Townley*

If, when the paint has dried—*Reid*

If yet I have not all thy love—*Donne*

If you and I ceased to exist, my Dear—*Dudek*

If you are lonely—*Toleau*

If you can keep your head when all about you —*Kipling*

If you could come on the late train—*Nims*

If you draw the vectors—*Darr*

If you ever, ever meet a grizzly bear—*Austin, Mary*

If you go away—*Laepa*

If you in the village think that my work was a good one—*Masters, Edgar Lee*

If you should meet a crocodile—*Children's Verses and Nursery Rhymes*

If you should meet September—*Emanuel*

If you sneeze on a Monday, you sneeze for danger —*Children's Verses and Nursery Rhymes*

If you swing hard enough—*Souster*

If you wake at midnight, and hear a horse's feet —*Kipling*

If you wander far enough—*Creeley*

If you were coming in the Fall—*Dickinson, Emily*

If you were twenty-seven—*Levine*

If your neighbour disappears—*Cohen*

Igual, la flor retorna—*Jiménez*

Ihr aber lernet, wie man sieht statt stiert—*Brecht*

Ihr, die ihr überlebtet in gestorbenen Städten —*Brecht*

Ihr Freunde hänget, wann ich gestorben bin— *Hölty*

Ihr Gesicht ist leicht—*Krolow*

Ihr guten Christen lasst euch nicht—*Heine*

Ihr irr't, indem ihr lebt—*Gryphius*

Ihr lichter, die ich nicht auf Erden satt kan schauen—*Gryphius*

Ihr Menschenbrüder, die ihr nach uns lebt— *Brecht*

Ihr milden Lüfte! Boten Italiens—*Hölderlin*

Ihr wandelt droben im Licht—*Hölderlin*

Ihr Zuflucht meiner Angst, ihr aufgetanen Ritze —*Fleming*

Il a un corps de garde—*Cherrier*

Il a vécu tantôt gai comme un sansonnet—*Nerval*

Il dort. Je forcerai les dieux même à se taire— *Mauriac*

Il est amer et doux, pendant les nuits d'hiver— *Baudelaire*

Il est des Loups de toute sorte—*Apollinaire*

Il est des nuits sans nom—*Damas*

Il est midi. Je vois l'église ouverte—*Claudel*

Il est terrible/ le petit bruit—*Prévert*

Il est un air pour qui je donnerais—*Nerval*

Il était un roi de Thulé—*Laforgue*

Il était une fois en Bohême un poète—*Apollinaire*

Il étoit une Vieille ayant deux chambrières—*La Fontaine*

Il fait jour sans nuage cette fois—*Giguere*

Il faudra bien qu'il me ressemble—*Supervielle*

Il faudra bien t'y faire à cette solitude—*Musset*

Il faut, autant qu'on peut, obliger tout le monde —*La Fontaine*

Il faut être toujours ivre—*Baudelaire*

Il faut fermer les yeux, Cybèle—*Mauriac*

Il faut laisser maisons et vergers et jardins—*Ronsard*

Il l'emparouille et l'endosque contre terre—*Michaux*

Il naissait un poulain sous les feuilles de bronze —*Perse*

Il ne faut pas laisser les intellectuels jouer avec les allumettes—*Prévert*

Il ne faut point juger des gens sur l'apparence —*La Fontaine*

Il ne pouvait venir—*Damas*

Il ne sait pas mon nom—*Supervielle*

Il ne se faut jamais moquer des miserables—*La Fontaine*

Il neigeait. On était vaincu par sa conquête— *Hugo, Victor*

Il n'est pas de midi qui tienne—*Damas*

Il pleure dans mon coeur—*Verlaine*

Il pleut—c'est merveilleux—*Carco*

Il retrouve dans sa mémoire—*Apollinaire*

Il te faut la nuit pour ramener—*Pilon*

Il vous naît un poisson que se met à tourner— *Supervielle*

Il y a certainement quelqu'un—*Hébert*

Il y a de grandes flaques de sang sur le monde —*Prévert*

Il y a des natures purement contemplatives— *Baudelaire*

Il y a sur la plage quelques flaques d'eau—*Éluard*

Il y a un vaisseau qui a emporté ma bien-aimée —*Apollinaire*

Il y a une armoire à peine luisante—*Jammes*

Il y souffle un vent terrible—*Michaux*

Il' ya ne znayu, chto v potemki tychas'—*Pasternak*

I'le to thee a Simnell bring—*Herrick*

I'll carry you off—*Eliot, Thomas Stearns*

Ill met by moonlight, proud Titania—*Shake-speare*

I'll sail upon the Dog-Star—*D'Urfey*

I'll tell thee everything I can—*Carroll*

I'll tell you how the sun rose—*Dickinson, Emily*

I'll walk the tightrope that's been stretched for me—*Danner*

Illae autem, paribus quas fulgere cernis in armis — *Virgil*

Ille mi par esse deo videtur—*Catullus*

The Illinois earth is black—*Benét, Stephen Vincent*

Illusion forms before us like a grove—*Howes*

The illustration/is nothing to you—*Moore, Marianne*

Illyrian woodlands, echoing falls—*Tennyson*

Ils étaient quatre qui n'avaient plus de tête—*Desnos*

Ils sont venus ce soir—*Damas*

I'm a lean dog, a keen dog—*McLeod*

I'm a 'round-town gent—*Anonymous–English—Modern English*

I'm a space pilot—*Laudon*

I'm apt to be surly getting up early—*Jennison*

Im bleichen Sommer, wenn die Winde oben—*Brecht*

I'm contented you should stay—*Thoreau*

Im düstern Auge keine Träne—*Heine*

Im ernsten Beinhaus war's wo ich beschaute—*Goethe*

Im Felde schleich' ich still und wild—*Goethe*

I'm folding up my little dreams—*Johnson, Georgia Douglas*

Im Frühlingsschatten fand ich sie—*Klopstock*

Im Frührot stand der Morgenstern—*Keller, Gottfried*

I'm giving up—*Giovanni*

I'm giving up nice and becoming a sensuous woman—*Viorst*

I'm glad that I—*Tippett*

I'm glad the great Creator—*Marshall, Helen Lowrie*

I'm going out to clean the pasture spring—*Frost, Robert*

I'm going to be a new man at once next year—*Glaze*

I'm gonna write me/ a poem like e. e.—*Sanchez*

Im Grenzenlosen sich zu finden—*Goethe*

I'm here at Clifton, grinding at the mill—*Brown, Thomas Edward*

Im Hofe steht ein Pflaumenbaum—*Brecht*

I'm hot—*Gaver*

I'm in New York covered by a layer of soap foam—*Ignatow*

Im lieben Deutschland daheime—*Heine*

I'm mooring my rowboat—*Sexton*

Im Namen dessen, der die Stunden spendet—*Benn*

Im neunten Jahr der Flucht vor Hitler—*Brecht*

I'm Nobody! Who are you—*Dickinson, Emily*

I'm not exactly big—*Lee, Dennis*

I'm not sure about the paper—*Dreyer*

I'm not sure why I touched it—*Abbe*

I'm not the junkie—*Dreyer*

I'm o'er young, I'm o'er young—*Burns*

Im Pavillon wo Mirjam war—*Eich*

Im Radio höre ich türkisch—*Herburger*

Im Reich der Interpunktionen—*Morgenstern*

Im Rhein, im heiligen Strome—*Heine*

I'm rising five, he said, not four—*Nicholson*

Im Schloss zu Düsseldorf am Rhein—*Heine*

Im Schwarzen Walfisch zu Askalon—*Scheffel*

Im Taumel war ein Teil, ein Teil in Tränen—*Benn*

I'm too clever to say it—*Sherwin*

Im Walde säugt ein Reh—*Zuckmayer*

I'm what has gone out blithely and with noise—*Brooks, Gwendolyn*

Im wunderschönen Monat Mai—*Heine*

Ima Talken bout the Nation of Islam—*Sanchez*

Imagine his lassoed walk—*O'Neill, Catherine*

Imagine it! A Sophocles, complete—*Weiss*

Immeasurable haze—*Winters*

Immer enger, leise, leise—*Fontane*

Immer wieder kehrst du Melancholie—*Trakl*

Immer wider wirst du mir—*Lasker-Schüler*

The impartial Law enrolled a name—*Graves*

The impossible man—*Jong*

The impurged images of day recede—*Yeats*

In a brown field stood a tree—*Eliot, Thomas Stearns*

In a coffee house at 3 A.M.—*Levine*

In a coign of the cliff between lowland and highland—*Swinburne*

In a corner of my bedroom—*McGough*

In a couple of weeks' time school will reopen—*Collymore*

In a dark time, the eye begins to see—*Roethke*

In a detachment cool as the glint of light—*Ciardi*

In a dream I returned to the river of bees—*Merwin*

In a drear-nighted December—*Keats*

In a dusty old crumbling building just fit for rats—*Morris, Mervyn*

In a field—*Strand*

In a garden of shining sea-weed—*Pyle*

In a little shanty town—*Brathwaite*

In a London crescent—*Sillitoe*

In a real city, from a real house—*Enright*

In a Roman tram—*Kunitz*

In a room of the palace—*Sitwell, Edith*

In a small untoppled town of Terebina—*Yevtushenko*

In a solitude of the sea—*Hardy*

In a somer sesoun whanne softe was the sonne—*Langland, William*

In a stable of boats I lie still—*Dickey, James*

In a tissue-thin monotone blue-grey buds—*Williams, William Carlos*

In a Vermont bedroom closet—*Frost, Robert*

In a Volina Schtatel arine is amule—*Peretz*

In a while they rose and went out aimlessly riding—*Wilbur*

In Africa a million drums beat endlessly—*Lipton*

In after days when grasses high—*Dobson*

In all my wanderings round this world of care—*Goldsmith*

In all the good Greek of Plato—*Ransom*

In among the silver birches—*Betjeman*

In an age of fops and toys—*Emerson*

In an island bitter lemons—*Durrell*

In any short burst—*Andrews*

In autumn down the beechwood path—*Reeves*

In Baltimore as we flew in for trial—*Berrigan*

In Baltimore there lived a boy—*Nash*

In Bednib's shop I picked up a book—*Read, Herbert*

In blazing driftwood—*Moore, Marianne*

In blows the loitering air of spring—*Derwood*

In blue Bristol city at tall tide I wandered—*Causley*

In Breughel's great picture, The Kermess—*Williams, William Carlos*

In Breughel's panorama of smoke and slaughter—*Plath*

In came the moon and covered me with wonder—*Bynner*

In Candiac by Nimes in Languedoc—*Davie*

In careless patches through the wood—*Milne*

In color soft—*Aubert*

In darkness let me dwell—*Anonymous–English—Modern English*

In dead of winter—*Hayden*

In deinen Tälern wachte mein Herz mir auf—*Hölderlin*

In der Bahnhofshalle, nicht für es gebäut—*Morgenstern*

In der Frühe/ sind die Tannen kupfern—*Brecht*

In der Jugend frühster Pracht—*Wedekind*

In diesem Lande leben wir—*Kunze*

In einem kühlen Grunde—*Eichendorff*

In einem Lumpenkasten—*Fontane*

In einem Tal bei armen Hirten—*Schiller*

In einer Stadt, wo Parität—*Goethe*

In faith, I do not love thee with mine eyes—*Shakespeare*

In far Tibet—*Nash*

In fifty years, when peace outshines—*Sassoon*

In Flanders fields the poppies blow—*McCrae*

In Flandres whylom was a companye—*Chaucer*

In fourteen hundred and ninety-two—*Nash*

In front of Fifth Avenue—*Hodges*

In front of our house—*Abse*

In front of the bank building—*Giovanni*

In futurity/ I prophesy—*Blake*

In God's tent the sun—*O'Gorman*

In going to my naked bed—*Edwardes*

In Goya's greatest scenes we seem to see—*Ferlinghetti*

In greenwoods once these relics must have known—*Wilbur*

In Hans' old mill his three black cats—*De la Mare*

In his hands, the submachine gun is excited—*Ignatow*

In Italy the dead have all the passion—*Simpson*

In Italy, where this sort of thing can occur—*Hecht*

In January everything freezes—*Nash*

In jeder Amsel habe ich dich geliebt—*Goll*

In June, amid the golden fields—*Eberhart*

In jüngern Tagen war ich des Morgens froh—*Hölderlin*

In Just-/ spring—*Cummings*

In late autumn sun—*Mir*

In late summer the wild geese—*Cunningham, James Vincent*

In late winter/ I sometimes glimpse bits of steam—*Kinnell*

In life I was the town drunkard—*Masters, Edgar Lee*

In Lincolnshire, a village full of tongues—*Lucie-Smith*

In Little Rock the people bear—*Brooks, Gwendolyn*

In London sah ich den, der sterben wollte—*Kaschnitz*

In loving thee thou know'st I am forsworn—*Shakespeare*

In March, unharvested corn—*Tullos*

In Marion, the honey locust trees are falling—*Wright, James*

In May, when sea-winds pierced our solitudes—*Emerson*

In May when sea-winds pierced our solitudes—*Merwin*

In me two worlds at war—*Day Lewis*

In mein' Verein bin ich hineingetreten—*Tucholsky*

In meinem Elternhaus hingen keine Gainsboroughs—*Benn*

In meiner ersten Blüt, im Frühling zarter Tage—*Gryphius*

In memory many pictures—*Heine*

In men we various ruling passions find—*Pope, Alexander*

In Midnight sleep of many a face of anguish—*Whitman*

In midst of wide green pasture lands—*Nesbit*

In midwinter a wood was—*Levi*

In moving-slow he has no Peer—*Roethke*

In my beginning is my end—*Eliot, Thomas Stearns*

In my craft or sullen art—*Thomas, Dylan*

In my Father's Bedroom—*Lowell, Robert*

In my own Shire, if I was sad—*Housman*

In my Spanish cloak—*Masters, Edgar Lee*

In my younger years—*Giovanni*

In mythology the restraint shown by dolphins—*Francis*

In nessuna parte—*Ungaretti*

In New York's teeming ghetto—*Rosenfeld*

In nineteen hundred and forty-five—*Ginsberg*

In no sense—*Lurie*

In November days—*Wordsworth*

In November of Catherine wheels and rockets—*Spender*

In order to apply for the position—*Patchen*

In our beginning—*Auden*

In our period, they say there is free speech—*Rukeyser*

In our street/ we lie late in bed—*Burke*

In pairs as if to illustrate their sisterhood—*Klein*

In passage along an endless, eventless Pavement—*Graves*

In pathos of distance—*Young, Marguerite*

In perfect equipoise a moment—*Webb*

In pious times, ere priestcraft did begin—*Dryden*

In pity for man's darkening thought—*Yeats*

In Polen, im Jahr Neununddreissig—*Brecht*

In principio Dio creó il cielo—*Quasimodo*

In Reading gaol by Reading town—*Wilde*

In restaurants we argue—*Atwood*

In Saint Louis—*Moore, Rosalie*

In Saturn's reign, at nature's early birth—*Juvenal*

In scenery I like flat country—*Stafford*

In Schenken träumend oft am Nachmittag—*Trakl*

In search through gardens, woods—*Gregor*

In seinem Zaun das Känguruh—*Morgenstern*

In seiner Fülle ruhet der Herbsttag nun—*Hölderlin*

In silent night when rest I took—*Bradstreet*

In so much dark no light is little—*Van Doren*

In some things I am a child's size—*Sobiloff*

In spite of all the learned have said—*Freneau*

In spite of all the solemn-hearted fools—*Dowling*

In stiller Nacht und monogamen Betten—*Tucholsky*

In Sturmesnacht, in dunkler Nacht—*Brecht*

In summer make love—*Lester*

In summertime on Bredon the bells they sound so clear—*Housman*

In sunless air under pines—*Plath*

In Sütterlinschrift auf dem glas—*Thenior*

In te, si in quemquam, dici pote, putide Victi—*Catullus*

In the back bedroom laughing—*Moore, Honor*

In the beginning—*Anonymous–Sanskrit*

In the beginning, at every step, he turned—*Shapiro, Karl*

In the beginning it traversed the seas and the —*Eckels*

In the beginning/ state street was dead—*Lee, Don L.*

In the beginning/there was no end—*Sanchez*

In the big world this is of no consequence—*Gill*

In the bleak mid-winter—*Rossetti, Christina*

In the brand-new pulpit the bishop stands—*Hardy*

In the cafe, the chandelier hangs from the ceiling —*Ai*

In the cave—*Rukeyser*

In the churchyard of Bromham the yews intertwine—*Betjeman*

In the close breathing—*Marcus*

In the coming heat—*Anonymous–American Indian languages–Chippewa*

In the cool of the day—*Johnson, James Weldon*

In the cowslip pips I lie—*Clare*

In the dark womb where I began—*Masefield*

In the days of lace-ruffles, perukes and brocade —*Kipling*

In the days of my youth, in the days of my youth — *White*

In the days when the hollow ships of the wellgreaved—*Nash*

In the December of my Springs—*Giovanni*

In the deserted, moon-blanched street—*Arnold*

In the doorways—*Lally*

In the early springtime after their tea—*Sitwell, Edith*

In the evening haze—*Kinnell*

In the far corner— *Wolfe*

In the first stanza—*Kizer*

In the first year of the last disgrace—*Barker, George*

In the foreground, clots of cream-white flowers —*Day Lewis*

In the garden called Gethsemane, in Palestine —*Dowling*

In the garden of death, where the singers—*Swinburne*

In the gloom of whiteness—*Thomas, Edward*

In the grass/ a thousand little people pass—*Wynne*

In the great gardens after bright spring rain—*Sitwell, Edith*

In the great night my heart will go out—*Anonymous–American Indian languages–Papago*

In the green morning, before—*Schwartz*

In the greenest of our valleys—*Poe*

In the harbour—*Olson*

In the heydays of forty-five—*Lowell, Robert*

In the hole of a heel of an old brown stocking — *Welles*

In the houre of my distresse—*Herrick*

In the house of power—*Piercy*

In the human cities, never again to—*Rukeyser*

In the inner city—*Clifton*

In the kitchen of the old house, late—*Hall*

In the land of Bow and Meissen—*Posner*

In the land of nunca nunca—*Gaver*

In the last days of the harbor—*Joselow*

In the late and lovely evening of the world—*Dowling*

In the left hand sank the drunk smelling of autopsies died in—*Kinnell*

In the licorice fields at Pontefract my love and I did meet—*Betjeman*

In the little Crimson Manual it's written plain and clear—*Service*

In the livingroom you are someplace else like a cat—*Piercy*

In the middle of a war—*Spender*

In the middle of the winter—*Hughes, Langston*

In the month of the long decline of roses—*Swinburne*

In the morning air, the freighter Havskar—*Gilbert, Dorothy*

In the morning I am alone—*Kaufman, Shirley*

In the morning the city spreads its wings—*Hughes, Langston*

In the mustardseed sun—*Thomas, Dylan*

In the Neolithic Age savage warfare did I wage —*Kipling*

In the nice-minded Department of Prunes and Prisms—*Nash*

In the night, in thick dark of midnight—*Marshall, Lenore G.*

In the old age black was not counted fair—*Shakespeare*

In the other gardens—*Stevenson*

In the park that was once green—*Brathwaite*

In the plain of the world's dust like a great sea —*Sitwell, Edith*

In the public gardens—*Betjeman*

In the purple light, heavy with redwood, the slopes drop seaward—*Jeffers, Robinson*

In the pushcart market, on Sunday—*Kinnell*

In the quarter of the Negroes—*Hughes, Langston*

In the quiet waters of the forest pool—*Smith, Stevie*

In the rags of a wind—*Bishop, John Peale*

In the red house sinking down—*Kinnell*

In the reeds the blue—*Piercy*

In the remainder—*McCrimmon*

In the room—*Kendrick*

In the rubber dinghy on the lake—*Kavanagh*

In the scare city—*Francis*

In the scented bud of the morning, O—*Stephens*

In the shoppes—*Bell*

In the Shreve High football stadium—*Wright, James*

In the slow world of dream—*Roethke*

In the solitary places—*Kramer*

In the spring of the year, in the spring of the year —*Millay*

In the summer, when no one is cold—*Sitwell, Edith*

In the sunlit room—*Colbert*

In the third-class seat sat the journeying boy—*Hardy*

In the third month, a sudden flow of blood—*Hecht*

In the thirteenth year of life—*Cunningham, James Vincent*

In the time of King James I—*Sitwell, Edith*

In the transparency of this hand—*Garfinkel*

In the turpitude of time— *Warren*

In the war—oh, not the last war nor the one before—*Scott, Winfield Townley*
In the Welsh town—*Logan*
In the world of mules—*Nash*
In the yard, by the house of boxes—*Jarrell*
In the zero of the night, in the lipping hour—*Kunitz*
In that country the animals—*Atwood*
In that great day—*Johnson, James Weldon*
In that land all is, and nothing's ought—*Rodgers*
In that so sudden summer storm they tried—*Simpson*
In these deep solitudes and awful cells—*Pope, Alexander*
In this age of hard trying nonchalance is good and really, it is not the—*Moore, Marianne*
In this book I see your face—*Swenson*
In this café Durruti—*Levine*
In this foolish world there is nothing more numerous—*Nash*
In this green month when resurrected flowers—*Randall*
In this life of unholy wars—*De Loach*
In this place is a poem—*Olson*
In this time of the year when leaves fall—*Bergman, Alexander F.*
In th'olde dayes of the Kyng Arthour—*Chaucer*
In tight pants, tight skirts—*Emanuel*
In time all undertakings are made good—*Graves*
In time of daffodils (who know—*Cummings*
In time of silver rain—*Hughes, Langston*
In time's a noble mercy of proportion—*Cummings*
In Time's concatenation and—*Warren*
In time's unconscious shadow and return—*Brinnin*
In 200 miles—*Swenson*
In un boschetto trova' pasturella—*Cavalcanti*
In unexperienc'd Infancy—*Traherne*
In vain, in vain—the all-composing Hour—*Pope, Alexander*
In vain the sage, with retrospective eye—*Pope, Alexander*
In vain to me the smiling mornings shine—*Gray*
In valleys green and still—*Housman*
In valleys of springs of rivers—*Housman*
In view of the fading animals—*Atwood*
In welche soll ich mich verlieben—*Heine*
In what torne ship soever I embarke—*Donne*
In what was wilderness as inviolate then as in the last—*Davie*
In winter—*Garlick*
In winter I get up at night—*Stevenson*
In winter, when the branches of the trees—*Dowling*
In winter, when the fields are white—*Carroll*
In wonderment I walk to music—*Van Doren*
In Xanadu did Kubla Khan—*Coleridge, Samuel Taylor*
In youth the decimal days—*Durrell*
In youth's spring, it was my lot—*Poe*
Inamorates, with an approbation—*Brooks, Gwendolyn*
Incertitude, ô mes délices—*Apollinaire*
Inch by inch—*Sukenick*
Incision of a comb in hair—*Durrell*
Inclusam Danaen turris aenea—*Horace*

Incomprehensible gaiety and dread—*Roethke*
Indeed this very love which is my boast—*Browning, Elizabeth Barrett*
The Indians have mostly gone—*Francis*
Indians used to burn their greasy—*Schmitz*
Indio que asomas a la puerta—*Santos Chocano*
Inert, blanched, naked, at the gale's last gasp—*Day Lewis*
Infinite consanguinity it bears—*Crane, Hart*
The Infinite's being is wide—*Frost, Robert*
Inhaltlose Sätze—*Heissenbüttel*
Inner greet. Greenberg said it—*Rukeyser*
Innombrables sont nos voies—*Perse*
Inside, my darling wife—*Roethke*
Inside the mystery—*Benedikt*
Inside this clay jug—*Bly*
Insist upon a star—*Cavalieri*
Insistently through sleep—a tide of voices—*Crane, Hart*
Inspector Dogbone—*Lee, Dennis*
Inte ens en grå litenfågel—*Ferlin*
The intellectuals talked—*Randall*
The intelligible forms of ancient poets—*Coleridge, Samuel Taylor*
Inter quas Phoenissa recens a volnere Dido—*Virgil*
Un'intera nottata—*Ungaretti*
Intimate god of stations—*Abse*
Into every soul is born—*Marshall, Helen Lowrie*
Into exile with only a few shirts—*Graves*
Into my heart an air that kills—*Housman*
Into my heart's treasury—*Teasdale*
Into the inmost Temple thus I came—*Spenser*
Into the light—*Olson*
Into the side aisle seats flicker the pony tails—*Miles*
Into the sixties—*Lee, Don L.*
Into the stream or entrance—*Olson*
Into the woods my Master went—*Lanier*
Into this wild abyss the wary Fiend—*Milton*
Intolerably sad, profound—*Betjeman*
Invented a person named I—*Marshall, Lenore G.*
Inventing a story with grass—*Dickey, James*
L'invention des arts étant un droit d'aînesse—*La Fontaine*
Los invisibles átomos del aire—*Becquer*
Invisus natalis adest, qui rure molesto—*Sulpicia*
Io ve dico accusi cche nun zo ttonta—*Belli*
Io dico, seguitando, ch'assai prima—*Dante Alighieri*
Io mi son giovinetta, e volentieri—*Boccaccio*
Io mo so' bbiecchio, tengo sittant anne—*Russo*
Io ricordo quei giorni: nell'ignoto—*Gatto*
Io so che nulla potrá mutare—*Gatto*
Io son sì stanco sotto 'l fascio antico—*Petrarca*
Io vedo i grandi alberi della sera—*Gatto*
Io vulesse truvà pace—*Filippo*
Ir reinen wip, ir werden man—*Walther von der Vogelweide*
Ir sult sprechen willekomen—*Walther von der Vogelweide*
Iré a tus manos, limpia, indemne—*Champourcin*
Irgendwo im Lande gibt es meist—*Morgenstern*
Irish poets, learn your trade—*Yeats*
The iron man sat—*Davis, Thulami Nkabinde*
Irritable spring, infuse—*Tate, Allen*
Is a caterpillar ticklish—*Shannon*

Is an enchanted thing—*Moore, Marianne*
Is any coherence—*Blackburn, Paul*
Is dead. Is dead. How all the radios—*Faerstein*
Is even more fun—*O'Hara*
Is for-real love, hate—*Fabio, Sarah Webster*
Is he tall or short, or dark or fair—*Lear*
Is it birthday weather for you, dear soul—*Day Lewis*
Is it Cinderella's slippers—*Welles*
Is it for fear to wet a widow's eye—*Shakespeare*
Is it indeed so? If I lay here dead—*Browning, Elizabeth Barrett*
Is it possible—*Wyatt, Sir Thomas*
Is it thy will thy image should keep open—*Shakespeare*
Is made up of reservoirs—*Eberhart*
Is my team ploughing—*Housman*
Is some such word—*Moore, Marianne*
Is that a fly—*Sobiloff*
Is that dance slowing in the mind of man—*Roethke*
Is there anybody there? said the traveller—*De la Mare*
Is there anyone who would weep—*Anonymous–American Indian languages–Chippewa*
Is there anything I can do—*Swenson*
Is there for honest poverty—*Burns*
Is thes middan-yeard missenlícúm—*Anonymous–English—Old English*
Is this all of it—*Enslin*
Is this man turning angel as he stares—*Gunn*
Is this the region, this the soil, the clime—*Milton*
Is thy face like thy mother's, my fair child—*Byron*
Is time on my hands? Yes it is—*Nash*
Is without world—*Hughes, Ted*
Isabel met an enormous bear—*Nash*
Isaiah was a man of the court—*Walker*
The Isles of Greece, the Isles of Greece—*Byron*
Isn't it odd the memories—*Marshall, Helen Lowrie*
Isn't memory wonderful, though?—*Marshall, Helen Lowrie*
The Israeli Navy/ sailing—*Bell*
Ist nicht heilig mein Herz, schöneren Lebens voll—*Hölderlin*
Istochnik strasti est' vo mne—*Lermontov*
Ist's nicht ein heitrer Ort, mein junger Freund—*Droste-Hülshoff*
It all began so easy—*MacNeice*
It begins when you smell a funny smell—*Nash*
It begins with my dog—*Kumin*
It can't be the passing of time that casts—*Wright, James*
It comes that time again—*Johnston, Ellen Turlington*
It could be a clip, it could be a comb—*Bell*
It could not be—*Lester*
It did not last. Before the year was out—*Press*
It does not matter she never knew—*Silkin*
It ended, and the morrow brought the task—*Meredith, George*
It fell about the Martinmas time—*Anonymous–English—Modern English*
It fell in the ancient periods—*Emerson*
It fills me with elation—*Nash*
It flows through old hushed Egypt and it sends—*Hunt*

It fortifies my soul to know—*Clough*
It freezes—all across a soundless sky—*Belloc*
It had a velvet cap—*Skelton, John*
It had an autumn smell—*Tate, Allen*
It happened to Lord Lundy then—*Belloc*
It has been a long day—*Zu-Bolton*
It has been so long—*Sobiloff*
It is a beauteous evening, calm and free—*Wordsworth*
It is a chilly god, a god of shades—*Plath*
It is a cold and snowy night. The main street is deserted—*Bly*
It is a cramped little state with no foreign policy—*Wilbur*
It is a farce that steals—*Tullos*
It is a lost road into the air—*Hall*
It is a pleasant night—*Kavanagh*
It is a poet's privilege and fate—*Graves*
It is a rainy night—*Jong*
It is a terrible distinction—*Enslin*
It is always a temptation to an armed and agile nation—*Kipling*
It is an ancient mariner—*Coleridge, Samuel Taylor*
It is as true as strange, else trial feigns—*Davies, John, of Hereford*
It is asleep in my body—*Rich*
It is better in the long run to possess an abcess or a tumor—*Nash*
It is borne in upon me that pain—*Eberhart*
It is cold. The white moon—*Williams, William Carlos*
It is colder now; there are many stars—*MacLeish*
It is common knowledge to every schoolboy and even every Bachelor of Arts—*Nash*
It is dark—*Strand*
It is done!—*Whittier*
It is easy to be young—*Swenson*
It is enough to touch anyone—*Whitman*
It is hard—*Knight, Etheridge*
It is hard going to the door—*Creeley*
It is he, it is he—*Anonymous–American Indian languages–Fox*
It is in captivity—*Williams, William Carlos*
It is just getting dark as the rain stops—*Logan*
It is likely enough that lions and scorpions—*Jeffers, Robinson*
It is midnight—*Sanchez*
It is no good, Una has died and I—*Jeffers, Robinson*
It is no night to drown in—*Plath*
It is not, Celia, in our power—*Etherege*
It is not growing like a tree—*Jonson*
It is not on her gown she fears to tread—*Stephens*
It is not to be thought of that the Flood—*Wordsworth*
It is one of those days—*Johnston, Ellen Turlington*
It is out in the mountains—*Conkling*
It is portentous, and a thing of state—*Lindsay, Vachel*
It is quite/ evident by now—*Sanchez*
It is raining—*Mitchell, Lucy Sprague*
It is said that certain orientational concepts of an—*Miles*
It is so much easier to forget than to have been Mr. Whittier—*Scott, Winfield Townley*

It is so tiring having to look after the works of God
—*Porter, Peter*
It is such a beautiful day I had to write you a letter
—*Ashbery*
It is the height of high summer—*Kresh*
It is the old man—*Nemerov*
It is the picnic with Ruth in the spring—*Logan*
It is the sinking of things—*Wright, James*
It is the whales that drive—*Williams, William Carlos*
It is time so speak of these—*Benét, Stephen Vincent*
It is time to be old—*Emerson*
It is too simple to turn to the sound—*Merwin*
It is true, fellow citizens—*Masters, Edgar Lee*
It is 12:20 in New York a Friday—*O'Hara*
It is twenty years—*Merwin*
It is very nice to think—*Stevenson*
It is what he does not know—*Eberhart*
It is wi luve—*Smith, Sydney Goodsir*
It is your voice that whispers—*Fabio, Sarah Webster*
It is yourself you seek—*Bogan*
It isn't raining rain to me—*Loveman*
It isn't the body—*Simic*
It keeps eternal whisperings around—*Keats*
It little profits that an idle king—*Tennyson*
It looked extremely rocky for the Mudville nine that day—*Thayer*
It looks like any building—*Huff, Barbara A.*
It may be so, but let the unknown be—*Masefield*
It may not make it across the sea—*Marshall, Helen Lowrie*
It mounts at sea, a concave wall—*Gunn*
It must have recesses—*Duncan*
It once might have been, once only—*Browning, Robert*
It rained quite a lot, that spring—*Benét, Stephen Vincent*
It rains and nothing stirs within the fence—*Thomas, Edward*
It relaxes me, he said—*Scannell*
It seconds the crickets of the Province Head—*Klein*
It seemed that out of battle I escaped—*Owen, Wilfred*
It seems I've got it all—*Sherwin*
It seems just the other day—*Vargas*
It seems to me, said Booker T.—*Randall*
It seems vainglorious and proud—*McGinley*
It sifts from leaden sieves—*Dickinson, Emily*
It slouched at the window changing—*O'Connell*
It started with a bad task—*Cavalieri*
It struck me—every day—*Dickinson, Emily*
It takes a heap o'children to make a home that's true—*Untermeyer*
It takes a heap o'livin' in a house t'make it home
—*Guest, Edgar*
It wants to be somewhere else—*Kaufman, Shirley*
It warms my bones—*Snyder*
It was a beauty that I saw—*Jonson*
It was a bird—*Gilbert, Celia*
It was a bright and cheerful afternoon—*Shelley*
It was a cynical babe—*Smith, Stevie*
It was a deck, the prow of a ship, uplifted—*Aiken*

It was a dreary morning when the wheels—*Wordsworth*
It was a funky deal—*Knight, Etheridge*
It was a goodly co—*Cummings*
It was a hippocamp addressed her darling—*Graves*
It was a human face in my oblivion—*Smith, Stevie*
It was a kind and northern face—*Crane, Hart*
It was a little captive cat—*Smith, Stevie*
It was a long time ago—*Hughes, Langston*
It was a lover and his lass—*Shakespeare*
It was a perfect day—*Thomas, Edward*
It was a room full of would-be doctors—*Darragh*
It was a summer—*Prothro*
It was a summer evening—*Southey*
It was a tall young oysterman—*Holmes, Oliver Wendell*
It was a waning crescent—*Bogan*
It was a wet and cloudy day—*Randall*
It was Alabama, 1932—*Beecher*
It was an old, old old, old lady—*Bunner*
It was beginning winter—*Roethke*
It was impossible to leave the town—*Reeves*
It was in about the Martinmas time—*Anonymous –English—Modern English*
It was in far away Japan—*Williams, Otis*
It was in July that I lost you—*Heine*
It was lingering summer—*Kizer*
It was many and many a year ago—*Poe*
It was my thirtieth year to heaven—*Thomas, Dylan*
It was nearly morning when the giant—*Patchen*
It was not dying: everybody died—*Jarrell*
It was one afternoon when I was young—*Reid*
It was only a film—*Jennings*
It was only a little house of two rooms—*Masters, Edgar Lee*
It was pure indeed—*Colum*
It was roses, roses all the way—*Browning, Robert*
It was six men of Indostan—*Saxe*
It was so quiet you could hear—*Mariah*
It was the calm and silent night—*Domett*
It was the morning after the great wind—*Hillyer*
It was the rainbow gave the birth—*Davies, William Henry*
It was the schooner Hesperus—*Longfellow*
It was there on the hillside, no tall traveller's story
—*Day Lewis*
It was three slim does and a ten-tined buck—*Lanier*
It was to have been—*Reid*
It was upon a day, a summer's day—*Byron*
It was upon a Lammas night—*Burns*
It was wild—*Lee, Don L.*
It was yesterday morning—*Hughes, Langston*
It wasn't Ernest; it wasn't Scott—*Roethke*
It were better the world were peopled—*Dowling*
It will need all of death—*Souster*
Italo ardito, a che giammai non posi—*Leopardi*
Itiskit, Itasket—*Deutsch*
It's a dead house, he said. Done for—*Mathias*
It's a great comfort to know this country had a father—*Glaze*
It's a pilgrim village—*Bly*
It's a strange courage you give me—*Williams, William Carlos*

It's a warm wind, the west wind, full of birds' cries —*Masefield*

It's awf'lly bad luck on Diana—*Betjeman*

It's cold where Bob is—*Stafford*

It's for real, not for practice—*Dlugos*

It's funny how often they say to me, Jane—*Milne*

It's funny that smells and sounds return—*Giovanni*

Its head/is red—*Anonymous–American Indian languages–Chippewa*

It's more than just an easy word for casual goodbye—*Blanding*

It's natural the Boys should whoop it up for—*Auden*

It's nice to be important—*Marshall, Helen Lowrie*

It's no coincidence—*Atwood*

It's no go the merrygoround, it's no go the rickshaw—*MacNeice*

It's not a tuning-fork of gold—*Rosenfeld*

It's not enough to mourn—*Hughes, Langston*

It's not my world, I grant, but I make it—*Miles*

It's not the crutches we decry—*Giovanni*

It's not very far to the edge of town—*Behn, Harry*

It's queer, she said, I see the light—*Parker*

Its quick soft silver bell beating—*Shapiro, Karl*

It's quiet here among the haunted tenses—*Porter, Peter*

It's rained every day since you—*Rexroth*

It's spring: the city, wrapped—*Starbuck*

Its teeth worked doubtfully—*Ormond*

It's the townfolk's cheery compliment—*Hardy*

It's there/ in the hole—*Bell*

It's too dark to see black—*Harper*

It's too good for them—*Porter, Peter*

Iucundum, mea vita, mihi propones amorem—*Catullus*

I've a halo to live up to—*Marshall, Helen Lowrie*

I've a head like a concertina—*Kipling*

I've been a woman/ with my legs stretched by the wind—*Sanchez*

I've been in love for long—*Muir*

I've been working arms and back all day—*Kramer*

I've changed my ways a little—*Jeffers, Robinson*

I've come to give you fruit from out my orchard —*Bogan*

I've finished six pillows in needlepoint—*Viorst*

I've found a small dragon in the woodshed—*Patten*

I've got a hunger, don't know where—*Kramer*

I've got to go now—*Hodges*

I've never met an axolotl—*Nash*

I've often heard my mother say—*Cullen*

I've put Miss Hopper upon the train—*Nash*

I've taken my fun where I've found it—*Kipling*

I've zeroed an altimeter on the floor—*Ciardi*

Ivre, plus ivre, disais tu—*Perse*

Iz velichestvom porazvlechsya—*Voznesensky*

Iznemogayu ot ustalosti—*Hippius*

J. W. (from the Danelaw) says—*Olson*

Ja, das möchste—*Tucholsky*

Ja freilich du bist mein Ideal—*Heine*

Ja, ich kam zurück—*Huch*

Ja! Ich weiss, woher ich stamme—*Nietzsche*

Ja, jag minns min ungdom: en låga bland mycket rök—*Lindegren*

Ja, mein Glück, das lang gewohnte—*Mörike*

Ja Mutter, es ist wahr. Ich habe diese Zeit—*Fleming*

Ja, neidlos blickt er: und ihr ehrt ihn drum—*Nietzsche*

Ja—!/ Nein—!—*Tucholsky*

Ja trampa, trampa på mig—*Blomberg*

Jack and Gye—*Children's Verses and Nursery Rhymes*

Jack and Jill went up the hill—*Children's Verses and Nursery Rhymes*

Jack be nimble—*Children's Verses and Nursery Rhymes*

Jack had a little pony Tom—*Belloc*

Jack Sprat—*Children's Verses and Nursery Rhymes*

Jack was the smartest dog in town, or so I thought —*Beecher*

Jadis certain Mogol vit en songe un Vizir—*La Fontaine*

Jag älskar de små bräckliga rådjuren där de dansa förbi—*Blomberg*

Jag blir alltmer som Ior—*Ferlin*

Jag har det våldsamma—*Lundkvist*

Jag har klättrat på önskningens stege—*Ferlin*

Jag kan ej se hur människorna gå—*Lindorm*

Jag lärde mig gå på händer—*Ferlin*

Jag mötte—*Ferlin*

Jag ringde en vän—*Ferlin*

Jag såg en rosenbuske, stänkt med blod—*Karlfeldt*

Jag säger dig: du måste vandra vida—*Bergman, Bo*

Jag ser dem i hucklen och hattar—*Bergman, Bo*

Jag torgför ej mitt hjärtas lust och kval—*Snoilsky*

Jag vände mig bort och allt förändrades—*Ekelöf*

Jag vet att bortrom det jag dunkelt anar—*Lagerkvist*

Jag vet ej vad de kärna, vilka ting—*Malmberg*

Jaguar—*Morgenstern*

Das Jahr wird gross, die Erde weit—*Bergengruen*

J'ai chanté mes amours sur de grands chevaux noirs—*Seghers*

J'ai cherché trente ans, mes soeurs—*Maeterlinck*

J'ai cru pouvoir briser la profondeur l'immensité —*Éluard*

J'ai cueilli ce brin de bruyère—*Apollinaire*

J'ai de mes ancêtres gaulois—*Rimbaud*

J'ai des rêves de guerre en mon âme inquiète—*Hugo, Victor*

J'ai dit à mon coeur—*Musset*

J'ai dormi d'amour—*Grandbois*

J'ai embrassé l'aube d'été—*Rimbaud*

J'ai eu longtemps un visage inutile—*Éluard*

J'ai l'impression d'être ridicule—*Damas*

J'ai longtemps habité sous de vastes portiques—*Baudelaire*

J'ai lu chez un conteur de fables—*La Fontaine*

J'ai mon coeur au poing—*Hébert*

J'ai passé les portes du froid—*Éluard*

J'ai peine à soutenir le poids d'or des musées—*Cocteau*

J'ai perdu ma force et ma vie—*Musset*

J'ai plus de souvenirs que si j'avais mille ans—*Baudelaire*

J'ai, quelque jour, dans l'Océan—*Valéry*
J'ai rêvé du printemps le printemps a noirci—*Éluard*
J'ai rêvé tellement fort de toi—*Desnos*
J'ai vécu dans ces temps et depuis mille années—*Desnos*
J'ai voulu ce matin te rapporter des roses—*Desbordes-Valmore*
J'ai vu par trois fois la mer violette—*Fombeure*
The jails are filling up—*Rasul*
J'aime l'âne si doux—*Jammes*
J'aime le son du Cor, le soir, au fond des bois—*Vigny*
Jake hates/ all the girls—*Cummings*
J'allais dans le verger où les framboises au soleil—*Jammes*
Jaloux des gouttes de pluie—*Aragon*
Jamaica is an Island full of Bays—*Walker*
Jamais il n'est dit—*Prévert*
James James/ Morrison Morrison—*Milne*
Jamie, come try me—*Burns*
The January sky is deep and calm—*Wain*
J'aperçus le souvenir de ta voix se percher—*Soupault*
J'appelle les amours qui roués—*Char*
J'appelle tabac ce qui est oreille—*Péret*
J'attendrai jusqu'à l'aube—*Pilon*
J'avais dix ans—*Char*
J'avais un cheval—*Supervielle*
J'ay les estas de ce monde advisez—*Deschamps*
Je chante par couverture—*Pisan*
Je congnois bien mouches en let—*Villon*
Je crains pas ça tellement—*Queneau*
Je devois par la royauté—*La Fontaine*
Je donne a mon espoir mes yeux ces pierreries—*Apollinaire*
Je fais souvent ce rêve étrange et pénétrant—*Verlaine*
Je fis un feu, l'azur m'ayant abandonné—*Éluard*
Je fus dès la mamelle un homme de douleur—*Lamartine*
Je fuyais l'amour—*Anonymous–French*
Je l'emporte avec moi de mes amours terrestres—*Fombeure*
Je marche sans arrêt—*Fombeure*
Je m'en allais, les poings dans mes poches crevées—*Rimbaud*
Je meurs de seuf auprès de la fontaine—*Villon*
Je n'ai envie que de t'aimer—*Éluard*
Je n'ai pas fini d'espérer—*Soupault*
Je n'aime pas dormir quand ta figure habite—*Cocteau*
Je n'aime plus la rue Saint-Martin—*Desnos*
Je naissais, et par la fenêtre—*Supervielle*
Je n'ay plus que les os, un squelette je semble—*Ronsard*
Je ne sais en vérité—*Damas*
Je ne songeais pas à Rose—*Hugo, Victor*
Je ne veux les voir. Emporte ces clichés—*Geraldy*
Je peux rarement voir—*Michaux*
Je plains le temps de ma jeunesse—*Villon*
Je plante en ta faveur cest arbre de Cybelle—*Ronsard*
Je puis mourir ce soir! Averses vents, soleil—*Laforgue*
Je regarde la Bête pendant qu'elle se lèche—*Breton, André*

Je sais qu'irritable, exigeant et morose—*Geraldy*
Je serai à genoux dans ma robe comme l'eau—*Lasnier*
Je sors de ma maison—*Romains*
Je souhaite dans ma maison—*Apollinaire*
Je stipule/ dit le roi—*Fombeure*
Je suis belle, ô mortels! comme un rêve de pierre—*Baudelaire*
Je suis comme je suis—*Prévert*
Je suis comme le roi d'un pays pluvieux—*Baudelaire*
Je suis de ceux qui acceptent—*Henault*
Je suis devant ce paysage féminin—*Éluard*
Je suis, dit Dieu, Maître des Trois Vertus—*Péguy*
Je suis épris de ce morceau tendre—*Char*
Je suis la flamme bleue—*Hugo, Victor*
Je suis le dernier sur ta route—*Éluard*
Je suis le ténébreux,—le veuf,—l'inconsolé—*Nerval*
Je suis le veilleur de la rue de Flandre—*Desnos*
Je suis né un soir où on ne m'attendait pas—*Prévert*
Je suis une fille maigre—*Hébert*
Je suis venu, calme Orphelin—*Verlaine*
Je t'apporte l'enfant d'une nuit d'Idumée—*Mallarmé*
Je t'attendais ainsi qu'on attend les navires—*Cadou*
Je te donne ces vers afin que si mon nom—*Baudelaire*
Je te donnerai de petites villes—*Hébert*
Je te l'ai dit pour les nuages—*Éluard*
Je te parle à travers les villes—*Éluard*
Je veux, pour composer chastement mes églogues—*Baudelaire*
Je veux te raconter, ô molle enchanteresse—*Baudelaire*
Je veux tout oublier, et cet ange cornu—*Cocteau*
Je vis dans les images innombrables des saisons—*Éluard*
Je vois brûler l'eau pure et l'herbe du matin—*Éluard*
Je voudrai dire la vérité—*Cocteau*
Je voudrais tant t'aimer que tes deux seins en pleurent—*Cendrars*
Je vous construirai une ville—*Michaux*
Je vous envoie un bouquet que ma main—*Ronsard*
Je vous salue, ma France, arrachée aux fantômes—*Aragon*
Jeanne était au pain sec dans le cabinet noir—*Hugo, Victor*
Jeden Morgen, mein Brot zu verdienen—*Brecht*
Jeden Tag geschehen einfache Dinge—*Thenior*
Jeder Jüngling sehnt sich so zu lieben—*Goethe*
Jeg elsker Havet naar det stormer vildt—*Andersen*
Jeg saae det Land, hvis Luft har himmelsk Lyst—*Andersen*
Jellicle cats come out to-night—*Eliot, Thomas Stearns*
Jemand schüttet Licht aus dem Fenster—*Krolow*
Jena vor uns im lieblichen Tale—*Benn*
Jeng rung chr yun syi—*Du Fu*
Jenny kissed me when we met—*Hunt*
Jeremiah, prophet of Jerusalem—*Walker*

Jerry Hall/he is so small—*Children's Verses and Nursery Rhymes*

J'espérais bien pleurer, mais je croyais souffrir—*Musset*

Jesse James was a two-gun man—*Benét, William Rose*

Jest finished readen a book—*Sanchez*

The jester walked in the garden—*Yeats*

Jesús de Nazaret—*Figuera*

Jesus is with me on the Blue Grass Parkway going eastbound—*Kumin*

Jesus, my gentle Jesus—*Johnson, James Weldon*

Jesus saves. Him—*Emanuel*

Jesus saw the multitudes were hungry—*Sexton*

J'établirai pour toi l'inventaire—*Pilon*

J'étais celui qui se promène—*Éluard*

J'étais seul, l'autre soir, au Théâtre-Français—*Musset*

Jetzt reifen schon die roten Berberitzen—*Rilke*

Jetzt wohin? Der dumme Fuss—*Heine*

La jeune fille est blanche—*Jammes*

Le jeune homme dont l'oeil est brillant, la peau brune—*Rimbaud*

J'eus un rêve: le mur des siècles m'apparut—*Hugo, Victor*

The jewelled mine of the pomegranate, whose hexagons—*Dudek*

Jíbara del Gandubán, toda fresca—*Torres*

Jiminy Jiminy Jokebox!—*Smith, William Jay*

Jimmy D. Martin had this fountain pen—*Harkness*

Jingle cell, jingle cell—*Gaver*

J'interroge le Sphynx—*Picabia*

J'irai, j'irai porter ma couronne effeuillée—*Desbordes-Valmore*

Joal/ Je me rappelle—*Senghor*

Joan, Joan, can you be—*Millay*

Job, de mille tourments atteint—*Benserade*

Joe, you big shot—*Smith, William Jay*

Joel, that young prophet-son of Pethuel—*Walker*

John Anderson my jo, John—*Burns*

John Aubrey had a nose for news—*Nash*

John Cabot, out of Wilma, once a Wycliffe—*Brooks, Gwendolyn*

John Gilpin was a citizen—*Cowper*

John Henderson, an unbeliever—*Belloc*

John, John, See, see the ceremony's on—*Fabio, Sarah Webster*

John Littlehouse the redhead was a large ruddy man—*Lindsay, Vachel*

John Maynard!/ Wer ist John Maynard—*Fontane*

John paddles up and down—*Arden*

John Vavassour/ De Quentin Jones—*Belloc*

John Watts took—*Olson*

Johnny Finn rode out one day—*Arden*

Jonah made his living inside the belly—*Sexton*

Jonas Keene thought his lot a hard one—*Masters, Edgar Lee*

Jorge Hernandez, architect—*Ostroff*

José del Sur, cuñado sin ribera—*Macheral*

Joseph was an old man—*Anonymous–English—Modern English*

Un jour, sur ses long pieds, allait je ne sais pas où—*La Fontaine*

Joy is a trick in the air; pleasure is merely contemptible, the dangled—*Jeffers, Robinson*

Joy stayed with me a night—*Parker*

Joyful your complete fearless and pure love—*Cummings*

Ju ju metamorphosis—*Wallace*

Júbilo al sol—*Guillén, Jorge*

Juega el amor con sus besos—*Martinez Alonso*

Jumbled in the common box—*Auden*

Jumbo asleep!/ Gray leaves thick-furred—*Sitwell, Edith*

—Jumped over the quick brown fox—*Cowley, Malcolm*

Ein Jüngling, den des Wissens heisser Durst—*Schiller*

Ein Jüngling liebt ein Mädchen—*Heine*

Jüngst war seine Mutter zu Besuch—*Kästner*

Juniper holds to the moon a girl adoring a bracelet—*Lee, Laurie*

Jupiter dit un jour: Que tout ce qui respire—*La Fontaine*

Just as my fingers on these keys—*Stevens, Wallace*

Just as you think you're "better now"—*Brooks, Gwendolyn*

Just as your eyes—*Hannan*

Just for a handful of silver he left us—*Browning, Robert*

Just imagine yourself seated on a shadowy terrace—*Nash*

Just lost, when I was saved—*Dickinson, Emily*

Just now the lilac is in bloom—*Brooke*

Just off the highway to Rochester, Minnesota—*Wright, James*

Just the place for a Snark! the Bellman cried—*Carroll*

Just to have held one clear memory of shape—*Sherwin*

Juventud, divino tesore—*Darío*

Jyun bu jyan—*Du Fu*

Jyun dz gu syang lai—*Wang Wei*

Kafka's castle stands above the world—*Ferlinghetti*

Kahle Felsschädel, helle Augen—*Born, Nicolas*

Kak nebesa, tvoi vsor blistaet—*Lermontov*

Kak obeshchalo, ne obmanyvaya—*Pasternak*

Kak-to davno, temnym osennim vecherom—*Korolenko*

The kangaroo can jump incredible—*Nash*

Kann auch ein Mensch des andern auf der Erde—*Mörike*

Kaphision Hydaton—*Pindar*

Der Kapitän steht an der Spiere—*Droste-Hülshoff*

Kathleen ni Houlihan—*Smith, Stevie*

En kättare jag är—*Ferlin*

Kauri is a Hindi word—*Inman*

Keen, fitful gusts are whispering here and there—*Keats*

Keep a little wonder—*Marshall, Helen Lowrie*

Keep a poem in your pocket—*De Regniers*

Keep away from roads' webs, they always lead—*Rodgers*

Keep me from going to sleep too soon—*Francis*

Keep up your humming, west wind, and your silly songs—*Van Doren*

The keeper stopped the mower on the lawn—*Holbrook*

Kein Pfad mehr! Abgrund rings und Totenstille
—*Nietzsche*
Kein Schlaf noch kühlt das Auge mir—*Mörike*
Kein Wesen kann zu Nichts zerfallen—*Goethe*
Kejsarens Papegoja—*Ferlin*
Kennst du das Land, wo die Kanonen blühen—
Kästner
Kennst du das Land wo die Zitronen blühn—*Goethe*
Kentucky water, clear springs: a boy fleeing—
Tate, Allen
Khochetsa/ sosredototchitsya—*Martynov*
Khudozhnik—Varvar kist'yu sonnoi—*Pushkin*
Ki ego sta khleria mono m' henakalami—*Seferis*
Kicking his mother until she let go of his soul—
Auden
Kierkegaard, a/ cripple—*Updike*
Kilép a többiek Közül—*Pilinszky*
Kind are her answers—*Campion*
Kind as noon, calm of unfalling petals—*Viereck*
Die Kinder dieser Welt hab ich gesehen—*Kaschnitz*
Kinder laufen fort/ Langher kann's noch garnicht
sein—*Werfel*
The King asked/ the Queen—*Milne*
King Charles, and who'll do him right now?—
Browning, Robert
King John was not a good man—*Milne*
The King of China's daughter—*Sitwell, Edith*
The King of Peru/ who was Emperor too—*Milne*
The king sits in Dumferling Toune—*Anonymous
-English—Modern English*
The King was in his counting house—*Children's
Verses and Nursery Rhymes*
The King was on his throne—*Byron*
The kitchen chair speaks to the bread knife—
Sandburg
A kite, a sky, and good firm breeze—*Sawyer*
A kitten can—*Roethke*
Kjøbenhavn, du livsglade By—*Andersen*
Klara skola människornas ögon vara—*Bergman,
Bo*
Klavier and Geige, die ich wahrlich schätze—
Hesse
Kleine Blumen, kleine Blätter—*Goethe*
Das kleine Haus unter Bäumen am See—*Brecht*
Klingling, Bumbum und Tschingdada—*Liliencron*
Klingt der Palasthof—*Piontek*
Klorinde starb; sechs Wochen drauf—*Lessing*
Ein Knie geht einsam durch die Welt—*Morgenstern*
Know, Celia, since thou art so proud—*Carew*
Know, that I would accounted be—*Yeats*
Know the world by heart—*MacLeish*
Know then thyself, presume not God to scan—
Pope, Alexander
Knowledge here will overgrow—*Van Doren*
Know'st thou not at the fall of the leaf—*Rossetti,
Dante Gabriel*
A Knyght ther was and that a worthy man—
Chaucer
Kogda na poslednei nedele—*Pasternak*
Komm in den todgesagten Park und schau—
George
Komm. Ruh dich aus—*Borchers*

Komm, Trost der Welt, du stille Nacht—*Eichendorff*
Kommt, reden wir zusammen—*Benn*
Die Königin steht im hohen Saal—*Goethe*
Konvolvelns lätta blomsterrevor hänga—*Österling*
Korf erfindet eine Art von Witzen—*Morgenstern*
Korf erfindet eine Mittagszeitung—*Morgenstern*
Korf erfindet eine Tagnachtlampe—*Morgenstern*
Korf erfindet eine Uhr—*Morgenstern*
Korf erhält vom Polizeibüro—*Morgenstern*
Korf lässt sich in einen Folianten einbinden—
Morgenstern
Korf liest gerne schnell und viel—*Morgenstern*
Korf trifft oft Bekannte, die voll von Sorgen—
Morgenstern
Korfen glückt die Konstruierung einer—*Morgenstern*
Die Krähen schrein—*Nietzsche*
Kräver det skarpaste stål, säger snickaren—
Lundkvist
Krenilis' ot shtorma zabory—*Yevtushenko*
Krichat sovi, spit dibrova—*Shevchenko*
Krinken was a little child—*Field, Eugene*
Kristoffer the Second, by Grace of God—*Ciardi*
Krolokwafzi! Semememi!—*Morgenstern*
Kto dal tebe soviet zakontchiv stchet pobed—
Martynov
Kto znaet, chto takoe slava—*Akhmatova*
Kühlrauschend unterm hellen/ tiefblauen Himmelsdom—*Eichendorff*
Kumrads die because they're told—*Cummings*
En kung i Sachsen samlade porslin—*Snoilsky*
En Kurvemager havde gjort—*Andersen*
Kvällens gullmoln fàstet kransa—*Stagnelius*
Kwa heri, bwana, kwa heri—*Anonymous-African
languages-Swahili*
Kyklops, te, pie foinon, epei phages andromea
krea—*Homer*

La connais-tu, Dafné, cette ancienne romance
—*Nerval*
La sorprendí una tarde saboreando—*Martinez
Alonso*
Labrador/ ya eres más de la tierra—*Fuertes*
Lächelnd scheidet der Despot—*Heine*
Ladi sta mele—*Seferis*
The lads in their hundreds to Ludlow come in for
the fair—*Housman*
A lady asks me I speak in season—*Pound*
A Lady came to a Bear by a stream—*Roethke*
Lady Bird, Lady Bird—*Children's Verses and
Nursery Rhymes*
Lady Day Spring-toned—*Stone, Ronald*
Lady, excellently brief—*Van Doren*
Lady hold your horses, sit down in your seat—
Miles
Lady, if you'd slumber sound—*Parker*
Lady, lady, never start—*Parker*
Lady, of anonymous flesh and face—*Cunningham, James Vincent*
Lady of light, I would admit a dream—*Tate, Allen*
Lady, Sister, it is cold—*Marcus*
A lady walks down a road bed—*Sherwin*
Lady, weeping at the crossroads—*Auden*
Lady, what are you laughing at—*Hall*
Lady, your room is lousy with flowers—*Plath*

Laeta.—Qu'il est beau, le navire noir que le vent —*Claudel*

El lagarto está llorando—*Garcia Lorca*

Laissez filer les guides, maintenant c'est la plaine —*Char*

Laissez venir à moi tous les chevaux—*Cadou*

A lake allows an average father, walking slowly —*Auden*

The lake is sharp along the shore—*Scott, F. R.*

Lalage's coming—*Hardy*

The land was ours before we were the land's— *Frost, Robert*

A land wild with—*Eckels*

Landlord, landlord—*Hughes, Langston*

The landlord's hammer in the yard—*Rich*

The landscape (the landscape!) again—*Olson*

The landscape where I lie—*Bogan*

Lange lieb' ich dich schon, möchte dich mir zur Lust—*Hölderlin*

Längtan heter min arvedel—*Karlfeldt*

The language of those horses—*Sobiloff*

Languishing in the dank dark dungeon—*Goldstein*

The lanky hank of a she in the inn over there —*Stephens*

Lappentaucher—*Celan*

A larger sin could not obtain—*Arnez*

The lariat snaps, the cowboy rolls—*Smith, William Jay*

Lars Porsena of Clusium—*Macaulay*

Las de l'amer repos où ma paresse offense—*Mallarmé*

Las! Où est maintenant ce mépris de Fortune— *Du Bellay*

¿Las oyes cómo piden realidades?—*Salinas, Pedro*

Lasalle who, for no sordid end pressing to the waters—*Davie*

Lass alles trauren seyn! hör auf, mein hertz, zu klagen—*Gryphius*

Lass dich, Geliebte, nicht reun—*Goethe*

Lass, o Welt, o lass mich sein—*Mörike*

Lass uns mit dem Feuer spielen—*Wedekind*

Lasst euch nicht verführen—*Brecht*

The last invocation—*Whitman*

The last light has gone out of the world except —*Thomas, Edward*

Last month I worked in a hell-hole shop—*Kramer*

Last night, ah, yesternight, betwixt her lips and mine—*Dowson*

Last night at black midnight I woke with a cry —*Lindsay, Vachel*

Last night I dreamed—*Kizer*

Last night I watched my brothers play—*Muir*

Last night my color blind—*Kumin*

Last night the snow came—*Norris*

Last night watching the Pleiades—*Snyder*

A last Poem, and a very last, and yet another— *Graves*

The last tall son of Lot and Bellicent—*Tennyson*

The last time I saw Donald Armstrong—*Dickey, James*

Last time I saw him he was leaving—*Hobbs*

The last time I was home—*Giovanni*

Last week someone said—*Pastan*

A last word—*Kizer*

Late April and you are there—*Snodgrass*

Late, late. But lift now the diffident fiddle and fill —*Rodgers*

Late that mad Monday evening—*Fields*

Laue Luft kommt blau geflossen—*Eichendorff*

The laughing god born of a startling answer— *Empson*

Laughing to find—*Cummings*

Laughter of children brings—*Howes*

Laura mía: Ya sé que no lo eres—*Diego, José de*

Laurel and eucalyptus, dry sharp smells—*Gunn*

L'aurore apparaissait; quelle aurore? Un abîme —*Hugo, Victor*

The lavender star—*Darragh*

Lavender's blue, dilly dilly—*Anonymous–English—Modern English*

Law and order—*Eckels*

Law makes long spokes of the short stakes of men —*Empson*

Law, say the Gardeners, is the Sun—*Auden*

Lawd, hab mussy—*Hodges*

Lawrence, of virtuous father virtuous son—*Milton*

The laws of God, the laws of Man—*Housman*

Lay down—*Ginsberg*

Lay me on an anvil, O God—*Sandburg*

Lazarus, I bring you lilies—*Hobbs*

Le he rogado al almud de trigo—*Mistral*

Léa, qui fut assassinée—*Carco*

Lead, Kindly light, amid the encircling gloom— *Newman*

The leaders speak/ amerika, land of freedom— *Sanchez*

A leaf is not too little—*Ciardi*

Leafless are the trees—*Longfellow*

The lean hands of wagon men—*Sandburg*

Leap from the crags, brave boy—*Brown, Thomas Edward*

Leave me all of your dreams you dream— *Hughes, Langston*

Leave me, O Love, which reachest but to dust —*Sidney*

Leave the flattering libraries—*Hazel*

Leave your home behind, lad—*Housman*

Leaves crumple slowly—*Fuld*

Leaves/ Murmuring by myriads—*Owen, Wilfred*

Lebe wohl/ farewell—*Benn*

Lecteur, as-tu quelquefois respiré—*Baudelaire*

Lecteur paisible et bucolique—*Baudelaire*

Leering across Pearl Street—*Wright, James*

Legate, I had the news last night—my cohort ordered home—*Kipling*

Legree's big house was white and green—*Lindsay, Vachel*

Legs be still—*Richards, I. A.*

Lehn deine Wang' an meine Wang'—*Heine*

Lei jui lwo jui meg bu cheng—*Bai Jyu Yi*

Die Leidenschaft bringt Leiden—*Goethe*

Leise schleich ich wie auf Eiern—*Wedekind*

Leise schwimmt der Mond durch mein Blut— *Lasker-Schüler*

Leise zieht durch mein Gemüt—*Heine*

Lejano mar, conoces tu misterio—*Prados*

Lejos está la luz que yo tenía—*Bernárdez*

Lembras-te, me amor—*Pascoaes*

Lemme be wid Casey Jones—*Brown, Sterling A.*

Lenore fuhr ums Morgenrot—*Bürger*

Lenta, olorosa, redonda—*Diego, Gerardo*

Leodogran the king of Cameliard—*Tennyson*

Leodum is minum swelce him man lac ziefe—*Anonymous-English—Old English*

Lesbia mi dicit semper male nec tacet umquam—*Catullus*

Lesbia mi praesente viro mala plurima dicit—*Catullus*

Lesbius est pulcer. Quid ni? quem Lesbia malit—*Catullus*

Less passionate, the long war throws its burning thorn—*Lee, Laurie*

Lessier m'estuet le rimoier—*Ruteboeuf*

Lest men suspect your tale to be untrue—*Graves*

Lestement, l'amant de Madama grimpa—*Carco*

Let Achsah rejoice with the pigeon who is an antidote to malignity—*Smart*

Let all who will—*Hughes, Langston*

Let America be America again—*Hughes, Langston*

Let be my cinerary monument—*Derwood*

Let her lie naked here, my hand resting—*Barker, George*

Let mans soule be a Spheare—*Donne*

Let me announce myself—*Clark, China*

Let me be your baby, south wind—*Sandburg*

Let me confess that we two must be twain—*Shakespeare*

Let me die a young man's death—*McGough*

Let me die with the memory of their love songs in my ears—*Jeffers, Lance*

Let me enjoy the earth no less—*Hardy*

Let me go where'er I will—*Emerson*

Let me not say it, let me not reveal—*Kunitz*

Let me not to the marriage of true minds—*Shakespeare*

Let me powre forth—*Donne*

Let me see life through a thousand eyes—*Marshall, Helen Lowrie*

Let me take this other glove off—*Betjeman*

Let me talk to you—*Wallace*

Let me tell you of Dr. Faustus Foster—*Nash*

Let me tell you the story of how I began—*Graves*

Let me twist your arm—*Greenwald*

Let men keep from me—*Derwood*

Let nasty habits let me out—*Talen*

Let not my love be call'd idolatry—*Shakespeare*

Let not young souls be smothered out before—*Lindsay, Vachel*

Let other poets raise a fracas—*Burns*

Let others of the world's decaying tell—*Stirling*

Let schoolmasters puzzle their brain—*Goldsmith*

Let Sporus tremble—What? That thing of silk?—*Pope, Alexander*

Let the boy try along this bayonet-blade—*Owen, Wilfred*

Let the musicians begin—*Schwartz*

Let the old inherit moonlight—*Reeves*

Let the old poets jig on Penn—*Kunitz*

Let the rain kiss you—*Hughes, Langston*

Let the world's sharpness like a clasping knife—*Browning, Elizabeth Barrett*

Let them bury your big eyes—*Millay*

Let them remember Samangan, the bridge and tower—*Bunting*

Let there be goodness and beauty—*Marshall, Helen Lowrie*

Let there be new flowering—*Clifton*

Let this be true, that I have loved—*Van Doren*

Let those who are in favour with their stars—*Shakespeare*

Let us be off! Our steam—*Day Lewis*

Let us begin and carry up this corpse—*Browning, Robert*

Let us begin the real work now—*Sanchez*

Let us do justice to the skink—*Nash*

Let us go then, you and I—*Eliot, Thomas Stearns*

Let us move the stone gentleman to the toadstool wood—*Reeves*

Let us not speak, for the love we bear one another—*Betjeman*

Let us not wait—*Eckels*

Let us now consider the ocean—*Nash*

Let us walk in the white snow—*Wylie*

Let you not say of me when I am old—*Millay*

Let yourself be sidetracked—*Alurista*

Letit sobatchka po vselennoi—*Svetlov*

Let's away with study—*Anonymous-English—Modern English*

Let's count the bodies over again—*Bly*

Let's from some loud unworld's most rightful wrong—*Cummings*

Let's go/come on—*Ferlinghetti*

Let's go see old Abe—*Hughes, Langston*

Let's not stop in cold, in drought—*Bell*

Let's think of eggs—*Nash*

The letters always just evade the hand—*Jarrell*

U lettu è un piattu—*Buttitta*

Leu är Luften. Fåglar kvittra—*Asplund*

Levommi il mio pensier in parte ov'ere—*Petrarca*

'Lias! 'Lias! Bless de Lawd—*Dunbar, Paul Laurence*

I libri che ti rendo, amico—*Saba*

Une lice étant sur son terme—*La Fontaine*

Lie still, sleep becalmed, sufferer with the wound—*Thomas, Dylan*

Liebe Brüder! es reift unsere Kunst vielleicht—*Hölderlin*

Liebe Freunde, es gab schönre Zeiten—*Schiller*

Die Liebe hat gelogen—*Platen-Hallermünde*

Ein Lied gibts von Herrn Urian—*Roth, Eugen*

Liegst du schon in sanfter Ruh—*Anonymous-German*

Un lièvre en son gîte songeoit—*La Fontaine*

The lif so short, the craft so long to lerne—*Chaucer*

Life, Friends, is boring—*Berryman*

Life has loveliness to sell—*Teasdale*

Life in a day: he took his girl to the ballet—*MacNeice*

Life is a jest; and all things show it—*Gay, John*

Life is just a bowl of cherries—*Sandburg*

Life is more exciting for greenhorns than for tired-eyed old fogies—*Nash*

The Life of man is never quite completed—*Auden*

Life sometimes held such sweetness for him—*Ormond*

Lift every voice and sing—*Johnson, James Weldon*

The lifted lamp is guttering, near spent—*Beecher*

The light beyond compare is the light I saw—*Eberhart*

Light breaks where no sun shines—*Thomas, Dylan*

The light in the window seemed perpetual—
Spender
The light inside—*Hodges*
Light is a memory—*Wilson*
Light is present in this valley—*Williams, Hugo*
Light may be had for nothing—*Sandburg*
The light of evening—*Yeats*
Light on my mother's tongue—*Clifton*
Light the first light of evening, as in a room—
Stevens, Wallace
Light things falling—I think of rain—*Francis*
Lighthearted William twirled—*Williams, William Carlos*
The lightning of a summer—*Jarrell*
The lightning waked me. It slid under—*Swenson*
The lights are electric—*Dowling*
The lights come up. A painted door—*MacLeish*
The lights from the parlour and kitchen shone out
—*Stevenson*
The lights in the hallway—*Wright, James*
Like a dogfish flung far from shore—*Robinson, Edwin Arlington*
Like a gaunt, scraggly pine—*Fletcher, John Gould*
Like a private eye she searches—*Scannell*
Like a ripple on a pond—*Giovanni*
Like a vivid hyperbole—*Bodenheim*
Like a white cat moonlight peers—*Uschold*
Like as a huntsman after weary chase—*Spenser*
Like as the waves make towards the pebbled shore—*Shakespeare*
Like as, to make our appetites more keen—
Shakespeare
Like children now, bed close to bed—*Jennings*
Like cures like. Homeopathic—*Sukenick*
Like Florence from your mountain—*Beecher*
Like/ I mean/ don't it all come down—*Sanchez*
Like my mother—*Giovanni*
Like Stephen Vincent Benét, I have fallen in love
—*Nash*
Like that oldtimer who has kept by me—*Weiss*
Like the moon her kindness is—*Yeats*
Like this hand-sized bit of driftwood—*Fabio, Sarah Webster*
Like thousands, I took just pride and more than
just—*Lowell, Robert*
Like to a Hermite poore in place obscure—*Raleigh*
Like tumbleweeds before the wind we moved
—*Beecher*
Like walls the forest stops us—*Brathwaite*
I like your kind of loving—*Brown, Sterling A.*
The lilac is an ancient shrub—*Dickinson, Emily*
Lily O'Grady—*Sitwell, Edith*
The lily with its cup, intense—*Ross, W. W. Eustace*
Lincoln?—/ Well, I was in the old Second Maine
—*Bynner*
Die Linden lang, galopp, galopp—*Mehring*
Die linden Lüfte sind erwacht—*Uhland*
A line in long array where thy wind—*Whitman*
Linger, finger, rub, rub, stroke—*Porter, Bern*
Lion and lioness, the mild—*Hill*
The lion is the king of beasts—*Nash*
Le lion, terreur des forêts—*La Fontaine*
The lion, the lion, he dwells in the waste—*Lindsay, Vachel*

The lions of fire/ shall have their hunting in this
black land—*Patchen*
The lions who ate the Christians on the sands of
the arena—*Smith, Stevie*
Lip was a man who used his head—*Cunningham, James Vincent*
Liquor and love—*Williams, William Carlos*
Listen a while, the moon is a lovely woman—
Sandburg
Listen, buds, it's March twenty-first—*Nash*
Listen here, Joe—*Hughes, Langston*
Listen/ listen/ listen—*Sanchez*
Listen, my children, and you shall hear—*Longfellow*
Listen/ My love—*Mailer*
Listen: the ancient voices hail us from the farther
shore—*Aiken*
Listen, the hounds of the judge and priest—
Blackburn, Thomas
Listen, the tide has turned—*Booth*
Listen. The wind is still—*Van Doren*
Listen! This here's what Charlie did to the blues
—*Cuney*
Listen to the tale/ Of Ole Slim Greer—*Brown, Sterling A.*
Listen, Wales. Here was a people—*Webb*
Lit d'amour—*Cocteau*
Little Anthony and the imperials—*Sanchez*
Little Birds are dining—*Carroll*
Little Birds sit on your shoulders—*Patchen*
A little black thing among the snow—*Blake*
Little Bo-Peep has lost her sheep—*Children's Verses and Nursery Rhymes*
Little Bo Peep waits for her sheep—*Summers, Hollis*
Little Boy Blue come blow your horn—*Children's Verses and Nursery Rhymes*
Little Boy kneels at the foot of the bed—*Milne*
The little boy lost in the lonely fen—*Blake*
A little boy once played so loud—*Riley*
Little boy, what ails me, that you walk—*Van Doren*
A little boy whose name was Tim—*Field, Eugene*
Little brown baby—*Dunbar, Paul Laurence*
Little brown brother, oh! little brown brother—
Nesbit
Little brown fieldmouse—*Conkling*
A little child enters by a secret door—*Raine*
Little Child, Good Child, go to sleep—*Davis, Fannie Stearns*
A little colt—broncho, loaned to the farm—*Lindsay, Vachel*
The little cousin is dead, by foul subtraction—
Ransom
Little cullud boys with beards—*Hughes, Langston*
Little fellow, you're amusing—*Auden*
Little finger of fiery green, it—*Deutsch*
Little fly/ Thy summer's play—*Blake*
Little gamboling lamb—*Nash*
Little girl, be careful what you say—*Sandburg*
Little gold head, my house's candle—*Pearse*
The little horse is newly—*Cummings*
Little I ask; my wants are few—*Holmes, Oliver Wendell*
Little Indian, Sioux or Crow—*Stevenson*

Little Jack Horner sat in a corner—*Children's Verses and Nursery Rhymes*

Little Lamb, who made thee—*Blake*

Little lamps of the dusk—*Grant*

A little lane—the brook runs close beside—*Clare*

A little learning is a dangerous thing—*Pope, Alexander*

A little light is going by—*Roberts*

The little love-god lying once asleep—*Shakespeare*

A little madness in the spring—*Dickinson, Emily*

The little man with the long nose—*Francis*

Little Miss Muffet discovered a tuffet—*Carryl, Guy Wetmore*

Little Miss Muffett/sat on a tuffet—*Children's Verses and Nursery Rhymes*

A little mountain spring I found—*Fyleman*

Little mouse in gray velvet—*Conkling*

The little old house was out with a little new shed—*Frost, Robert*

A little onward lend thy guiding hand—*Milton*

Little Orphant Annie's come to our house to stay—*Riley*

Little Papoose/ Swing high in the branches—*Conkling*

Little Park that I pass through—*Hoyt*

Little poppies, little hell flames—*Plath*

Little Red Riding Hood—*Morgan, Karen*

A little road was straying—*Turner, Nancy Byrd*

Little Robin Redbreast—*Children's Verses and Nursery Rhymes*

Little Rose-Moss beside the stone—*Conkling*

Little snail, Dreaming you go—*Hughes, Langston*

The little snake now grieves—*Winters*

Little things that run—*Stephens*

Little thinks, in the field, yon red-cloaked clown—*Emerson*

Little Tom Bombadil was a merry fellow—*Tolkien*

Little Tommy Tucker—*Children's Verses and Nursery Rhymes*

The little toy dog is covered with dust—*Field, Eugene*

Little tree/ little silent Christmas tree—*Cummings*

Little willie—*Lee, Don L.*

Little wind, blow on the hill-top—*Greenaway*

Livet tar sitt barn till sig—*Lagerkvist*

Living among orchards, we are ruled—*Graves*

A living room, the catholic area you—*Auden*

A living tree that harbours—*MacPherson*

Living upstream—*Lester*

Le livre de la vie est le livre suprême—*Lamartine*

Lizard, lover of heat, of high—*MacLeish*

The lizards on the wall move—*Mathias*

Llama que por morir más pronto se levanta—*Torres Bodet*

Llamo mi corazón, un claro día—*Machado, Antonio*

Llegó la noche y no encontré un asilo—*Becquer*

Llevamos—tiene dos asas—*Ridruejo*

Llueve . . ., espera, no te duermas—*Ibarbourou*

La lluvia ha cesado—*Jiménez*

Lo, as a careful housewife runs to catch—*Shakespeare*

Lo, Body and Soul—this Land—*Whitman*

Lo! Death has reared himself a throne—*Poe*

Lo encontré en una esquina—*Storni*

Lo he visto en el frío—*Jiménez*

Lo in the orient when the gracious light—*Shakespeare*

Lo, Lord, Thou ridest—*Crane, Hart*

Lo que el salvaje que con torpe mano—*Becquer*

Lo que les voy a decir—*Hernández, José*

Lo que sufres, mi pobre España, es como—*Unamuno*

Lo recuerdo, de pronto—*Jiménez*

Lo! 'tis a gala night—*Poe*

Lo, victress on the peaks—*Whitman*

Lo! Where the heath—*Crabbe*

Load of hay, load of hay—*Anonymous–English–Modern English*

A loaf of time round and thick—*Swenson*

Lobsterpot labyrinths wait. A porridge—*Hoffman*

Locked arm in arm they cross the way—*Cullen*

The locks of sleep overflow upon my lap—*Jeffers, Lance*

Løft mig kun bort, Du staerke Død—*Andersen*

Lofting fungoes at the rose—*Starbuck*

Logic is peculiar feel—*Sobiloff*

Loin des oiseaux des troupeaux des villageoises—*Rimbaud*

Loin du temps, de l'espace—*Queneau*

Loined in lean wind—*Langland, Joseph*

Loitering with a vacant eye—*Housman*

Lolita Arriaga, de vejez divina—*Mistral*

London Bridge is broken down—*Children's Verses and Nursery Rhymes*

London Bridge was built in a foggy century—*Deutsch*

London! the needy villain's gen'ral home—*Johnson, Samuel*

London, thou art of towns a-per-se—*Dunbar, William*

Lonely now, I pour my sadness—*Heine*

The lonely troll he sat on a stone—*Tolkien*

Long ago I learned how to sleep—*Sandburg*

Un long bras timbré d'or glisse du haut des arbres—*Fargue*

Long days and changing weather—*Bogan*

The long days of my childhood—*Press*

Le long du coteau courbe et des nobles vallés—*Péguy*

Long-expected one and twenty—*Johnson, Samuel*

Long flat years of listening—*Treitel*

Long hair Nam vets—*Levendosky*

Long hast thou, friend! been absent from thy soil—*Gay, John*

Long have I sigh'd for a calm; God grant I may find it at last—*Tennyson*

Long John Nelson and Sweetie Pie—*Walker*

Long long ago there was an island set—*Dowling*

Long, long, long—*Fitzsimmons*

The long rolling steady pouring—*Stephens*

Long since the years—*Ginsberg*

Long steel grass/ the white soldiers pass—*Sitwell, Edith*

The long stems of the water lilies—*Hillyer*

Long, too long America—*Whitman*

Long years ago in Bethlehem—*Marshall, Helen Lowrie*

The longest way is back. Lazarus learned—*Ciardi*
Look at him there in his stovepipe hat—*Smith, William Jay*
Look at itsy-bitsy Mitzi—*Nash*
Look at me 8th/ grade—*Sanchez*
Look at old Scrappy, puttin' on dog—*Brown, Sterling A.*
Look at the stars! Look, look up at the skies—*Hopkins*
Look at yourself, the shine, the sheer—*Jennings*
Look forward, truant, to your second childhood—*Graves*
Look! From my window there's a view—*Simpson*
Look, he said aloud—*Van Doren*
Look in my face; my name is Might-have-been—*Rossetti, Dante Gabriel*
Look in thy glass, and tell the face thou viewest—*Shakespeare*
Look, it is falling a little—*Francis*
Look, it's a fox—*Day Lewis*
Look, it's morning, and a little water gurgles in the tap—*Dugan*
Look, man, look—*Smith, Stevie*
Look once more, ere we leave this specular mount—*Milton*
Look out how you use proud words—*Sandburg*
Look out upon the stars, my love—*Pinkney*
Look this way, say cheese, say—*Darr*
Look up into the dome—*Wilbur*
Look with the ears, said Horacio Vecchi—*Tomlinson*
Looked for the Hollowed Stone—*Grigson*
Looking as I've looked before, straight down the heart—*Rich*
Looking by chance in at the open window—*Graves*
Looking for my brother under the ground—*Colbert*
Looking up at the stars, I know quite well—*Auden*
Looks into its crater, drawn by a quartz gleam—*De Frees*
A loon I thought it was—*Anonymous-American Indian languages-Chippewa*
Lorca was killed, singing—*Read, Herbert*
Lord, let me not be guilty—*Marshall, Helen Lowrie*
Lord, let the Angels praise thy name—*Herbert*
Lord Lundy from his earliest years—*Belloc*
Lord make me a channel of thy peace—*Francis of Assisi*
Lord, may I be—*Benét, Stephen Vincent*
Lord of my love, to whom in vassalage—*Shakespeare*
Lord Percy of Northumberland—*Anonymous-English—Modern English*
Lord Ronald courted Lady Clare—*Tennyson*
Lord, the calendar is droll—*Nash*
Lord, the Roman hyacinths are blooming in bowls—*Eliot, Thomas Stearns*
Lord, who createdst man in wealth and store—*Herbert*
Lords, knights, and squires, the numerous band—*Prior*
Lord's lost Him His mockingbird—*Hayden*
Lordynges, quod he, in Chirches whan I preche—*Chaucer*

Die Lorelei bekannt als Fee und Felsen—*Kästne*
Loreto impagliato ed il busto d'Alfieri di Napoleone—*Gozzano*
Lorsque nous seront tous deux sous la terre—*Cocteau*
Lorsque sur ton beau front riait l'adolescence—*Vigny*
Lorsqu'il faudra aller vers vous o mon Dieu, faite—*Jammes*
Louder than gulls the little children scream—*Graves*
Louis I/ Louis II—*Prévert*
Louis, Louis, Louis, Louis, you gotta go right now—*Fabio, Sarah Webster*
Un Loup n'avait que les os et la peau—*La Fontaine*
Un Loup, qui commençoit d'avoir petite part—*La Fontaine*
Les loups mangent gloutonnement—*La Fontaine*
Lousy Peter's terror was the Workhouse—*Sitwell, Osbert*
Love bade me welcome: yet my soul drew back—*Herbert*
Love came to me with transistors in his hair—*Sherwin*
Love cannot be held in bonds—*Marshall, Helen Lowrie*
Love comes quietly—*Creeley*
Love gets in the cracks—*Enslin*
Love has earth to which she clings—*Frost, Robert*
Love has had his way with me—*Parker*
Love her he doesn't but the thought he puts—*Berryman*
Love, I shall perfect for you the child—*Heaney*
Love, if nothing solid rises like wood—*Bell*
Love in fantastic triumph sate—*Behn, Aphra*
Love in her eyes sits playing—*Gay, John*
Love in her sunny eyes does basking play—*Cowley, Abraham*
Love in my bosom like a bee—*Lodge*
Love is a mischief—*McGinley*
Love is all—*Yeats*
Love is anterior to life—*Dickinson, Emily*
Love is feeling cold in the back of vans—*Henri*
Love is my sin, and thy dear virtue hate—*Shakespeare*
Love is not all: it is not meat nor drink—*Millay*
Love is too young to know what conscience i—*Shakespeare*
Love, I've seen you from both sides—*Mariah*
Love lives beyond the tomb—*Clare*
Love, love, a lily's my care—*Roethke*
Love love begets, then never be—*Herrick*
Love makes the world go round—*Dupree*
Love me little, love me long/Is the burden of my song—*Anonymous-English—Modern English*
Love me little, love me long/Then we neither can be wrong—*Van Doren*
Love my heart for an hour, but my bone for a day—*Sitwell, Edith*
The love of the body of man—*Whitman*
Love seeketh not itself to please—*Blake*
Love set you going like a fat gold watch—*Plath*
Love speaks in such a silent voice—*Marshall, Helen Lowrie*
A love supreme—*Harper*

Love, that impatient guide—too proud to think—*Crabbe*

Love that is rooted deep—*Lewis, Janet*

Love, the sole Goddess fit for wearing by—*Graves*

Love this Land—its mighty mountains—*Marshall, Helen Lowrie*

Love, thou art absolute, sole Lord—*Crashaw*

Love without hope, as when the young bird-catcher—*Graves*

Love without pity is a child's hand reaching—*Day Lewis*

Loved not for themselves, those tenors—*Abse*

Loveliest of trees, the cherry now—*Housman*

A lovely church, a home for God—*Anonymous–English—Modern English*

Lovely dainty Spanish needle—*McKay*

Lovely death of the horse—*Ignatow*

The lovely lass of Inverness—*Burns*

The Lovers of the poor/ arrive. The ladies—*Brooks, Gwendolyn*

Loving in truth and fain in verse my love to show—*Sidney*

The low beating of the tom-toms—*Hughes, Langston*

Low stars, high boats—*Williams, Hugo*

Low tide. The scavenging gulls—*Beecher*

Lowdown white sonofabitch—*Beecher*

Ein Löwe der sich weit umhergetrieben—*Tiedge*

The lowest trees have tops, the ant her gall—*Dyer*

Lucasta frown and let me die—*Lovelace, Richard*

Lucky is a star—*Sandburg*

Lucky the husband—*Clarke*

En luffare är jag—vad mera—*Ferlin*

Die Luft riecht schon nach Schnee—*Kirsch*

Die Luft war einst dem Sterben nah—*Morgenstern*

Lugete, O veneres cupidinesque—*Catullus*

Lullee, lullay/ I could not love thee more—*Lewis, Janet*

Lully, lulley, lully, lulley—*Anonymous–English—Modern English*

Luminous tendril of celestial wish—*Cummings*

La luna es un pozo chico—*Garcia Lorca*

Luna, piuma di cielo—*Ungaretti*

La luna tiene dientes de marfil—*Garcia Lorca*

La luna vino a la fragua—*Garcia Lorca*

La luna y el niño juegan—*Brull*

La lune s'attristait—*Mallarmé*

Les lunes brouillées coulent au bout de mes doigts—*Prefontaine*

Lunes era, lunes—*Anonymous–Spanish*

The lungs draw in the air and rattle it out again—*Betjeman*

The lungs that sculptured slave songs—*Jeffers, Lance*

Luntana staie. Natale sta venenno—*Di Giacomo*

Lusitana melodia—*Couto*

Lust, thro' some certain strainers well refined—*Pope, Alexander*

La luz del día se apaga—*Coronado*

La luz lo malo que tiene—*Salinas, Pedro*

Lying disembodied under the trees—*Graves*

Lying in daylight—*Rukeyser*

Lyu yi syin pei jyou—*Bai Jyu Yi*

Lyubvi, nadeshdy, tikhoi slavy—*Pushkin*

Lyudei neinteresnykh v mire net—*Yevtushenko*

The lyre hums and sighs—*Barker, George*

Ma baby lives across de river—*Hughes, Langston*

Ma faim, Anne, Anne—*Rimbaud*

Ma femme a la chevelure de feu de bois—*Breton, André*

Ma femme est morte, je suis libre—*Baudelaire*

Ma femme m'avait bien dit—*Damas*

Ma/Ga/he/nja/pa/ra/mi/thah—*Anonymous–Asian languages*

Ma Jesus/ was a troubled man—*Cuney*

Ma jeunesse ne fut qu'un ténébreux orage—*Baudelaire*

Ma Lord ain't no stuck-up man—*Hughes, Langston*

Ma Lou je coucherai ce soir dans les tranchées—*Apollinaire*

Ma pauvre muse, hélas! qu'as-tu donc ce matin—*Baudelaire*

Ma'am, you should see your house—*MacLeish*

Macavity's a Mystery Cat: he's called the Hidden Paw—*Eliot, Thomas Stearns*

Machine it seemed said—*Emanuel*

Mad Patsy said, he said to me—*Stephens*

Madam Carnelia in the dark room the green room—*Gilbert, Celia*

Madam Life's a piece in bloom—*Henley, William Ernest*

Madam would speak with me—*Meredith, George*

Madame Mouse trots—*Sitwell, Edith*

Madame, ye been of alle beautee shrine—*Chaucer*

Mädchen, kein Casanova—*Tucholsky*

Made stone, cleft, shape and shell of a thing—*Smith, Ken*

Madre, cuando sea grande—*Mistral*

Madre: Esta noche se nos muere un año—*Blanco*

¡Madre India! Madre mía—*Cabrisas*

Madre, la mi madre, guardas me poneis—*Cervantes Saavedra*

Madre, unos ojuelos vi—*Vega Carpio*

Madre, yo al oro me humillo—*Quevedo y Villegas*

Madrid es una ciudad de más de un millón de cadáveres—*Alonso*

Madrugada Don Alonso—*Anonymous–Spanish*

Maecenas of royal name—*Horace*

Maeg ic be me sylfum sodgied wrecan—*Anonymous–English—Old English*

Maggie and milly and molly and may—*Cummings*

Maggio. Na tavernella—*Di Giacomo*

Magic is tangled in a woman's hair—*Graves*

Magic/ my man—*Sanchez*

Magnifique, total et solitaire—*Mallarmé*

Magnolia/ Porcelain perfection—*Johnston, Ellen Turlington*

Mahadöh, der Herr der Erde—*Goethe*

Mahmud! if fear of man hath never awed—*Ferdovci*

Mai, non saprete mai come m'illumina—*Ungaretti*

Maiden, and mistress of the months and stars—*Swinburne*

The maiden caught me in the wild—*Blake*

Maiden in the mor lay—*Anonymous–English—Modern English*

The maidens came when I was in my mother's—*Sherwin*

Les mains dans les poches—*Laforgue*

Maintenant que la jeunesse s'éteint—*Aragon*

Maintenant que Paris, ses pavés et ses marbres —*Hugo, Victor*

Mais toi, quand viendras-tu?—*Michaux*

Mais un dernier venu se coucha sur Cybèle—*Mauriac*

Maître Corbeau, sur un arbre perché—*La Fontaine*

Make a garland of Leontynes and Lenas—*Hughes, Langston*

Make it radiant—this day—*Marshall, Helen Lowrie*

Make me feel the wild pulsation—*Tennyson*

Make me, O Lord thy Spinning Wheele complete —*Taylor, Edward*

Make the stream/ on the faces—*Levine*

Make this night loveable—*Auden*

Un mal qui répand la terreur—*La Fontaine*

La Maladie et la Mort font des cendres—*Baudelaire*

Malgré les sarcasmes des uns—*Damas*

Le Malheur, mon grand laboureur—*Michaux*

Malika—*Marvin X*

Mama! Mama! Tell me—*Murphy*

Mamá/ Yo quiero ser de plata—*Garcia Lorca*

Maman est actrice—*Obaldia*

Mame was singing—*Brooks, Gwendolyn*

A mammoth morning moved grey flanks and groaned—*Scannell*

Man as gift, man as lift—*Gaver*

Man at the end—*Smith, Sydney Goodsir*

Man becomes Emperor at daybreak—*Goldstein*

The man bent over his guitar—*Stevens, Wallace*

A man builds better than he knows—*Figueroa*

A man came to me at the fair—*Stephens*

The man coming toward you—*Williams, Oscar*

Man glaubt, dass ich mich gräme—*Heine*

A man has been standing—*Strand*

A man, having to do with—*Edson*

A man helped me choose it—*Gaver*

A man I praise that once in Tara's Halls—*Yeats*

The man in the moon had silver shoon—*Tolkien*

The man in the recreation room—*Harkness*

Man in the West—*MacLeish*

Man, introverted man, having crossed—*Jeffers, Robinson*

The man is gone on a Friday—*Ignatow*

A man knocked three times—*Hughes, Langston*

Man lives by faith and not by bread alone—*Goldstein*

Man looking into the sea—*Moore, Marianne*

A man may long for love, and long for art—*Dowling*

The man of life unblemished ever—*Horace*

A man on his own in a car—*Betjeman*

A man opened a can of sardines—*Edson*

The man points, and the child—*Simpson*

A man riding on the meaning of rivers—*Rukeyser*

A man said to the universe—*Crane, Stephen*

Man setzt uns auf die Schwelle—*Eichendorff*

The man sits in a timelessness—*Creeley*

A man that had six mortal wounds—*Yeats*

The Man: The priest and the old woman—*Ai*

The man under the bed—*Jong*

A man who decided—*Edson*

A man who had fallen among thieves—*Cummings*

The man who married Magdalene—*Simpson*

The man who saw the light hanging on the tall end—*Williams, Oscar*

The man who sold his lawn to standard oil—*Kunitz*

The man who tried to kill himself—*Lester*

The man who yesterday was seen—*Francis*

The man with the broken fingers throws a shadow —*Sandburg*

Man, you are at the first door—*Brown, George Mackay*

Man, you too, aren't you one of these rough followers of the criminal—*Hardy*

Mañanita de San Juan—*Anonymous-Spanish*

Manch Bild vergessner Zeiten—*Heine*

Una mancha sombría y extensa—*Castro, Rosalía de*

Manche Töne sind mir Verdruss, doch bleibt am meisten—*Goethe*

Manchmal streift dich kühl ein Hauch—*Bergengruen*

Manda a Cuosa in val di Serchio—*Carducci*

Månen är hygglig och lyser—*Ferlin*

Många som varit på bio tala—*Martinson*

Manhattan, this hospital—*Hollander*

Manhood—Human sculptured—*Fox, Charles*

Manhood is a glasshouse—*Fox, Charles*

Manic-depressive Lincoln, National hero—*Schwartz*

Manifest reason glared at you and me—*Graves*

Ein Mann verfolgte einen andern—*Morgenstern*

Die Männer von Fort Donald—hohé—*Brecht*

Männishospillra, hur kan du blomma—*Edfelt*

Las manos de mi cariño—*Garcia Lorca*

Man's and woman's bodies lay without souls—*Hughes, Ted*

A man's body at auction—*Whitman*

Man's greed and envy are so great—*Eberhart*

Man's life is well compared to a feast—*Barnfield*

Un manso rio, una vereda estrecha—*Castro, Rosalía de*

Manuel del Río, natural—*Hierro*

Many an infant that screams like a calliope—*Nash*

Many are our joys/ in youth—*Wordsworth*

Many had come before—*Robson, Jeremy*

Many of the three hundred and sixty-five days of the year—*Nash*

Manzanas levemente heridas—*Garcia Lorca*

A map of the world is on the wall: its lying—*Fuller, Roy*

Maple and Sumach down this autumn ride—*Day Lewis*

La mar no tiene naranjas—*Garcia Lorca*

El mar/ sonríe a lo lejos—*Garcia Lorca*

El mar sus millares de olas mece—*Mistral*

A march in the ranks hard-prest and the road unknown—*Whitman*

March, march, Ettrick and Teviotdale—*Scott, Sir Walter*

March . . . Someone has walked across the snow —*Stevens, Wallace*

Mare, al buio, fu cattivo—*Pascoli*

Mare, liscio e turchino—*Di Giacomo*

Margaret, are you grieving—*Hopkins*

Margarita, está linda la mar—*Darío*

Maria, com seus olhos magoados—*Leal*

Maria drömmer i rosengård—*Rydberg*

Maria loved to pull a face—*Belloc*

Marie, levez-vous, ma jeune paresseuse—*Ronsard*

Marilyn Monroe, everybody—*Lally*

Mariposa de luz—*Jiménez*

Mark where the pressing wind shoots javelin-like —*Meredith, George*

Marke but this flea, and marke in this—*Donne*

Marquise, si mon visage—*Corneille*

Marsden Hartley's eyes—as Stein's eyes—*Olson*

The marshal is taking my measure—*Berrigan*

Mary-Anne / Wise, simple old woman—*Sitwell, Osbert*

Mary, daughter of King James I—*Press*

Mary had a little lamb—*Children's Verses and Nursery Rhymes*

Mary Magdalene, that easy woman—*Rodgers*

Mary sat musing on the lamp-flame at the table —*Frost, Robert*

Maryland, Virginia, Caroline—*Tate, Allen*

Marzo: mi poco chivve—*Di Giacomo*

La más bella niña—*Góngora*

Más profunda que todos los abismos—*Pérez*

Masikini bibi yangu kasafiri na waarabu—*Anonymous–African languages-Swahili*

Massissi—*Deveaux*

Massive engines lift beautifully from the deck— *Bly*

Master I may be/ But not of my fate—*Nash*

Maten var bra—*Ferlin*

Mater dulcissima, ora scendono le nebbie— *Quasimodo*

Ein Mathematiker hat behauptet—*Kästner*

Matilda told such dreadful lies—*Belloc*

La mattitina pioggia—*Leopardi*

Maud went to college—*Brooks, Gwendolyn*

Maud, where are you Maud—*Patten*

Maude Muller on a summer's day—*Whittier*

Der Mauerstrich—*Bobrowski*

Mauvaise compagne, espèce de morte—*Cocteau*

Les maux ne savent seuls venir—*Ruteboeuf*

May come up with bird-din—*MacNeice*

May day! Surpassing time—*Colum*

May his hand be on your shoulder—*Marshall, Helen Lowrie*

May I for my own self song's truth reckon— *Pound*

May I join you in the dog house, Rover?—*Nash*

May I remark, at the risk of being called an egghead or New Dealer—*Nash*

May is Mary's month, and I—*Hopkins*

May ka mish schomer lon—*Sutzkever*

May my heart always be open to little—*Cummings*

May they wander stage by stage—*Graves*

May your body lice—*Gill*

Maybe he believes me, maybe not—*Sandburg*

Maybe the last time—*Lester*

Maybe we're both—*Lifshin*

Maybe you ranted in the Grove—*MacLeish*

Mayombe—bombe—mayombe—*Guillén, Nicolás*

Me acercaba hasta el puerto—*Celaya*

Me adelanté el corazón—*Jiménez*

Me an' ma baby's—*Hughes, Langston*

Me deleito na espuma dos salsos temporais— *Marques*

Me gustas cuando callas, porque estás como ausente—*Neruda*

Me ha herido recatándose en las sombras—*Becquer*

Me he perdido muchas veces por el mar—*Garcia Lorca*

Me llevó consigo un viejo—*Hernández, José*

Me lo contaron ayer—*León, Rafael de*

Me miré en tus ojos—*Garcia Lorca*

Me ne vogl'i a campà 'mmienzo a 'na terra— *Viviani*

Me next to sleep, all that is left of Eden— *Schwartz*

Me plaît ton regard de fauve—*Diop*

Me so scetato tant e buonumore—*Filippo*

Me tiraste un limón, y tan amargo—*Hernández, Miguel*

Me too, I'm crying for the Greeks—*Genser*

Me trajo Maru Mori—*Neruda*

Me tropecé contigo en primavera—*León, Rafael de*

Me voici devant tous un homme plein de sens —*Apollinaire*

Meanwhile surely there must be something to say —*Graham, William Sydney*

Meanwhile the Adversary of God and man—*Milton*

Meanwhile the heinous and despiteful act—*Milton*

Meanwhile the Son of God, who yet some days —*Milton*

Mechanical/ Oracles dot the sky—*Redmond*

Meciendo, mi carne—*Mistral*

Med många kulörta lyktor—*Ferlin*

The meet was at the Cock and Pye—*Masefield*

Meeting his mother makes him lose ten years— *Lowell, Robert*

Mein Bruder war ein Flieger—*Brecht*

Mein einziger Wunsch ist, Dir, oh Mensch—*Werfel*

Mein Herz ist trüb wie die Wolke der Nacht— *Brecht*

Mein hochgeehrter Herr von Klein—*Hesse*

Mein junger Sohn fragt mich—*Brecht*

Mein Kind, es sind allhier die Dinge—*Busch*

Mein Kind, wir waren Kinder—*Heine*

Mein lieber Bruder—*Bachmann*

Mein lieber Neffe. Ich erfahre—*Mostar*

Mein Lieschen tragt keine Hosen—*Wedekind*

Mein Mädgen ward mir ungetreu—*Goethe*

Mein Sohn, ich hab dir die Stiefel,—*Brecht*

Mein Sohn schreibt mir so gut wie gar nicht mehr —*Kästner*

Mein süsses Lieb, wenn du im Grab—*Heine*

Mein Tag war heiter, glücklich meine Nacht— *Heine*

Meine Mutter hat's gewollt—*Storm*

Meine Ruh ist hin—*Goethe*

Meinen schönsten Liebesantrag—*Heine*

Meinen Sie Zürich zum Beispiel—*Benn*

Meio dia/ O morro coxo—*Bopp*

Melampsus: This death is timely—*Ansen*

Melde mir die Nachtgeräusche, Muse—*Meyer, Conrad Ferdinand*

Melite, your eyes are Hera's—*Rufinus*

Melk—Sankt Pölten—Wien—*Rühmkorf*

Mellifluous as bees, these brittle men—*Starbuck*

Mellitos oculos tuos, Iuventi—*Catullus*

Melo, melo po vsei zemle—*Pasternak*

Die Melodie der Einundzwanzigjährigkeit—*Heissenbüttel*

Melody moving downstream—*Levertov*

Mémoire des poissons dans les criques profondes—*Supervielle*

Memories are smoke/ lips we can't kiss—*Brathwaite*

Memorize the rhythms—*Gaver*

The men and women long ago in Africa—*Brooks, Gwendolyn*

Men går jag över ängarna—*Ferlin*

Men loved wholly beyond wisdom—*Bogan*

Men marry what they need. I marry you—*Ciardi*

The men of Vermont—*Eberhart*

Men say they know many things—*Thoreau*

Men seldom make passes—*Parker*

Meni odnakovo, chi budu—*Shevchenko*

Meni trinadtsyati minalo—*Shevchenko*

Meni zdayetsya, ya ne znayu—*Shevchenko*

Menin aeide, Thea, Peleiadeo Akhileos—*Homer*

Ein Mensch dem's ziemlich dreckig geht—*Roth, Eugen*

Ein Mensch der kürzlich ganz privat—*Roth, Eugen*

Ein Mensch der, sagen wir, als Christ—*Roth, Eugen*

Ein Mensch, der voller Neid vernimmt—*Roth, Eugen*

Ein Mensch erblickt ein neiderregend—*Roth, Eugen*

Ein Mensch erträumt, was er woht täte—*Roth, Eugen*

Ein Mensch für seinen Nachbarn schwärmt—*Roth, Eugen*

Ein Mensch hört staunend und empört—*Roth, Eugen*

Ein Mensch ist der Bewundrung voll—*Roth, Eugen*

Ein Mensch, kein Freund der raschen Tat—*Roth, Eugen*

Ein Mensch lebt noch mit letzter List—*Roth, Eugen*

Ein Mensch nichts wissend von Mormone—*Roth, Eugen*

Ein Mensch spricht fern, geraume Zeit—*Roth, Eugen*

Ein Mensch zum Bahnhof dauerlaufend—*Roth, Eugen*

Die Menschen kümmerten mich nicht viel—*Fontane*

Meravigliosa canarina azzurra—*Saba*

The merchant, to secure his treasure—*Prior*

Mère des souvenirs, maîtresse des maîtresses—*Baudelaire*

La mère est seule dans la maison—*Prévert*

La mère fait du tricot—*Prévert*

Meriggiare pallido e assorto—*Montale*

A mermaid found a swimming lad—*Yeats*

The merman under the Plough—*MacNeice*

Merry Margaret—*Skelton, John*

Merry, merry sparrow—*Blake*

Mertsan' em zvezd dalekikh bezrazlichno—*Pasternak*

Mes mains tremblent comme celles d'un brave garçon d'alcoolique—*Soupault*

Mes pensées sont à toi—*Milosz*

Mes volages humeurs plus steriles que belles—*Aubigné*

La mesa, hijo, está tendida—*Mistral*

Meschantes nuicts d'hyver, nuicts, filles de Cocyte—*Ronsard*

Mesdames et Messieurs—*Laforgue*

Mesh cast for mackerel—*Bunting*

The metaphor stirred his fear. The object with which he was compared—*Stevens, Wallace*

Metaphysical, not pornographic—*Bell*

Methinks I see, with what a busie haste—*Quarles*

Methought I saw my late espoused Saint—*Milton*

Meticulous, past midnight in clear rime—*Crane, Hart*

Mexico: and a wind on the mesa—*Antoninus*

Mexico is a foreign country—*Warren*

Mi amor? . . . recuerdas, dime—*Machado, Antonio*

Mi caballo era mi vida—*Gutierrez*

Mi carta, que es feliz, pues va a buscaros—*Campoamor*

Mi casa está llena de mirtos—*Storni*

Mi chiedi come ho potuto vivere pensando sempre alla morte—*Gatto*

Mi corazón es una mariposa—*Garcia Lorca*

Mi corazón reposa junto a la fuente fría—*Chamisso*

Mi hogar es la tierra—*Berger-Kiss*

Mi infancia son recuerdos de un patio de Seville—*Machado, Antonio*

Mi niña se fue a la mar—*Garcia Lorca*

Mi nonna a un'or de notte che vvie ttota—*Layton*

Mi prima Matilde—*León, Rafael de*

Mi reyecillo—*Martí*

Mi soledad sin descanso—*Chamisso*

Mi tengo a quest'albero mutilato—*Ungaretti*

Mi vaso lleno; el vino del Anahuac—*Barba Jacob*

Mi vida es un erïal—*Becquer*

Micah was a young man of the people—*Walker*

The microbe is so very small—*Belloc*

Mid-autumn late autumn—*Francis*

Mid pleasures and palaces though we may roam—*Payne*

Midday found me barely—*Devaul*

The middle age you wouldn't wait for—*Kumin*

Middle-aged life is merry, and I love to lead it—*Nash*

Midi, roi des étés, épandu sur la pleine—*Leconte de Lisle*

Midnight, and twelve dark doves—*Dickinson, Patric*

The midnight plane with its riding lights—*Frost, Frances M.*

Midwinter Spring is its own season—*Eliot, Thomas Stearns*

El miedo es una puerta abierta—*Martinez Alonso*

Mientras por competir con tu cabello—*Góngora*

Mig är given—*Ekelöf*

Might I, if you can find it, be given—*Moore, Marianne*

A mighty creature is the germ—*Nash*

Migliaia d'uomini prima di me—*Ungaretti*

Mignon he was or mignonette—*Williams, Tennessee*

Mignonne, allons voir si la rose—*Ronsard*

He mikre koukoubagia eitane panta ekei—*Seferis*

Mild and slow and young—*Lewis, Janet*

Miles of pram in the wind and Pam in the gorse track—*Betjeman*

A milk white Hind, immortal and unchang'd—*Dryden*

Milk-white moon, put the cows to sleep—*Sandburg*

The mill was torn down last year—*Purdy*

The millere was a stout carl for the nones—*Chaucer*

The miller's daughter—*Sitwell, Edith*

The miller's wife had waited long—*Robinson, Edwin Arlington*

A million emeralds break from the ruby-budded lime—*Tennyson*

The mills are down—*Beecher*

Milton said, I saw the golden chain—*Moore, Merrill*

Milton, thou shouldst be living at this hour—*Wordsworth*

Milton unlocked hell for us—*Sandburg*

Min barndoms skog—*Asplund*

Min rädslas stackars hare—*Ferlin*

Minayut dni, minayut nochi—*Shevchenko*

A mind ago I took the stones for clay—*Wain*

Mind in its purest play is like some bat—*Wilbur*

The mind is an enchanting thing/is an enchanted thing—*Moore, Marianne*

The mind of the people is like mud—*Turner, Walter James*

The mind reigns in its ruddy element—*O'Gorman*

Mindful of you the sodden earth in spring—*Millay*

The mind's paying—*Cattonar*

Mine be a cot beside the hill—*Rogers*

Mine eye and heart are at a mortal war—*Shakespeare*

Mine eye hath play'd the painter and hath stell'd—*Shakespeare*

Mine eyes have seen the glory of the coming of the Lord—*Howe*

Mine is a dauntless spirit, meaning a spirit that is hard to daunt—*Nash*

Mine is no Southern tradition—*Murphy*

Ming yuet gkay see y'ow—*Su Shih*

Minha mãe, mada comprar um quilo—*Morais*

Miniver Cheevey, child of scorn—*Robinson, Edwin Arlington*

The Minstrels played their Christmas tune—*Wordsworth*

Mio Cid movió de Bivar—*Anonymous-Spanish*

Mir Lubben vie Finga ge strechter—*Sutzkever*

Mir traumt ich bin der liebe Gott—*Heine*

Mir traumte wieder der alte Traum—*Heine*

Mira, amigo, cuando libres—*Unamuno*

Mira, Platero, qué de rosas—*Jiménez*

Míralos, Platero, tirados en todo su largar—*Jiménez*

Mire los muros de la patria mia—*Quevedo y Villegas*

The mirror waits on us—*Williams, Hugo*

Mis ojos hinchados—*Alurista*

Mis pasos en esta calle—*Paz*

Miser Catulle, desinas ineptire—*Catullus*

Miss Gardner's in her garden—*Hughes, Langston*

Miss J. Hunter Dunn, Miss J. Hunter Dunn—*Betjeman*

Miss Mabel—*Robison*

Miss Pauncefort sang at the top of her voice—*Smith, Stevie*

Miss Rafferty wore taffeta—*Nash*

Miss Sexton went out looking for the Gods—*Sexton*

A missionary from the Mau Mau told me—*Ciardi*

The Mississippi cop—*Knight, Etheridge*

A mist from the moor arose—*Betjeman*

Mr. and Mrs. Discobolus—*Lear*

Mr. East gave a feast—*Children's Verses and Nursery Rhymes*

Mister Lincoln and his lady—*Evans, Liz*

Mr. Nutch/ Brown-bearded bear—*Sitwell, Osbert*

Mister Samuel, he belong to Rotary—*Brown, Sterling A.*

Mr. Styrax, Mr. Hecatomb Styrax, the owner of a large estate and of large muscles—*Pound*

Mr. Timberley, the Editor of the Tidesend Courier—*Sitwell, Osbert*

Misterioso y silencioso—*Darío*

Mistral-Wind, du Wolken-Jäger—*Nietzsche*

Mrs. Coley's three-flat brick—*Brooks, Gwendolyn*

Mrs. Grandestin, with grouse-coloured hair—*Sitwell, Osbert*

Mrs. Leamington stood on a cloud—*Meredith, William*

Mrs. Liversedge, shivering in her furs—*Sitwell, Osbert*

Mrs. Mallory went to a psychiatrist—*Coward*

Mrs. Williams' face was pleading when she spoke of her God to me—*Jeffers, Lance*

Mit den Flössen hinab—*Bobrowski*

Mit dummen Mädchen, hab' ich gedacht—*Heine*

Mit einem Dach und seinem Schatten dreht—*Rilke*

Mit Furcht/ Erwarten—*Brecht*

Mit gelben Birnen hänget—*Hölderlin*

Mit lattes oif leber tze schnitten—*Sutzkever*

Mit Regenselgeln umher—*Bobrowski*

Mit weissen Bäuchen hängen die toten Fische—*Eich*

Mit wildem Geripp, mit harten mageren Flanken—*Zuckmayer*

Mitt blåsiga lynnes fågel—*Lundkvist*

Die Mitternacht zog näher schon—*Heine*

Mkofu wangu mwembamba wa kufitia jehazi—*Anonymous-African languages-Swahili*

Mne dalekoe vremya mereshchitsya—*Pasternak*

Mne po dushe stroptivyi norov—*Pasternak*

Mne stydno i den' oto dnya stydnei—*Pasternak*

Möcht wissen, was sie schlagen—*Eichendorff*

Mock on, mock on, Voltaire, Rousseau—*Blake*

Moçuela de Bores—*Santillana*

The modern malady of love is nerves—*Symons*

Modigliani's paintings are being shipped—*Rector*

Moi, naïve, cachée à la niche des fontaines—*Lasnier*

Moines de Zurbaran, blancs chartreux qui, dans l'ombre—*Gautier*

Molchi, skryvaisya i tai—*Tyutchev*

I molti, immani, sparsi, grigi sassi—*Ungaretti*

Momma Momma Momma—*Jordan, June*
Mon âme à moi tressaille toute—*Verlaine*
Mon amour, disais-tu—*Jammes*
Mon amour, j'ai fait pour toi—*Geraldy*
Mon Ange, vois, je te loue—*Cocteau*
Mon avion en flammes mon château inondé de vin du Rhin—*Péret*
Mon beau tzigane mon amant—*Apollinaire*
Mon chapeau se cabosse—*Soupault*
Mon cher André Rouveyre—*Apollinaire*
Mon coeur, lassé de tout, même de l'espérance —*Lamartine*
Mon cor estima un arbre! Mes vell que l'olivera —*Costa i Llobera*
Mon corps était léger au jour naissant des rues —*Mauriac*
Mon Dieu, faites que celle qui pourra être ma femme—*Jammes*
Mon Dieu, quelle guerre cruelle—*Racine*
Mon enfant, ma soeur—*Baudelaire*
Mon lit est parfumé d'aloès et de myrrhe—*Vigny*
Mon père (un dur par timidité)—*Laforgue*
Mon petit frère a un zizi—*Obaldia*
Mon sang est devenu de l'encre—*Cocteau*
Mon verre est plein d'un vin trembleur comme une flamme—*Apollinaire*
Mond, als träte ein Totes—*Trakl*
Mond, der Hirt, lenkt seine Herde—*Eichendorff*
Der Mond, der uns so freundlich scheint—*Stolberg*
Der Mond ist aufgegangen—*Claudius*
Der Mond malt ein groteskes Muster an die Mauer—*Borchert*
Monday calls me on Friday—*Devaul*
Monday, Tuesday—*Levendosky*
Monday's child is fair of face—*Children's Verses and Nursery Rhymes*
Le Monde me quitte, ce tapis, ce livre—*Supervielle*
Der Mondenschein verwirret—*Eichendorff*
Das Mondlicht räumt den Alltag aus—*Loerke*
Das Mondschaf steht auf weiter Flur—*Morgenstern*
Moneda que está en la mano—*Machado, Antonio*
Le Monsieur ne demande pas l'aumône—*Seghers*
A monstering horror swallows—*Cummings*
Monstrez les moy ces poures yeulx—*Charles d'Orléans*
Monté y me encomendé a Dios—*Hernández, José*
A month before Easter—*Ciardi*
A month of vigilance draws to its close—*Graves*
Montmartre a connu d'autres jeux—*Carco*
Mony a piper has played himsel—*MacDiarmid*
Moon cat, my nettle dancer—*Dragonette*
The moon comes every night to peep—*Stephens*
The moon drops one or two feathers into the field —*Merwin*
The moon has a dove-cote safe and small—*Conkling*
The moon has a face like the clock in the hall —*Stevenson*
The moon is a sow—*Levertov*
The moon is but a golden skull—*Lindsay, Vachel*
The moon is here—*Eckels*
The moon? It is a griffin's egg—*Lindsay, Vachel*
The moon looked into my window—*Cummings*
Moon lune/ chant song—*Prévert*

The moon on the one hand, the dawn on the other—*Belloc*
The moon reads what she writes—*Fox, Charles*
The moon shines down—*Giovanni*
Moon, that against the lintel in the West—*Millay*
Moonlight now on Malibu—*Rexroth*
Moon's glow by seven fold multiplied turned red —*Derwood*
The moon's greygolden meshes make—*Joyce*
The moon's the north wind's cooky—*Lindsay, Vachel*
Morada de grandeza—*León, Fray Luis de*
Morani and mungu—*Sanchez*
Un morceau de lumière qui descend la source d'un regard—*Césaire*
More alone than survivors on a storm-wracked island—*Chapin*
More beautiful and soft than any moth—*Spender*
More or less of a relative gesture—*Gregor*
The more you—*Lifshin*
Der Morgen kam; es scheuchten seine Tritte— *Goethe*
Morgen muss ich fort von hier—*Anonymous-German*
The morning-glory, climbing the morning long —*Crane, Hart*
Morning haze/ as in a painting—*Buson*
Morning in the honey-months, the star—*Jones, Glyn*
The morning is a man's select domain—*Goldstein*
Morning; the slow rising of a cold sun—*Wright, Charles*
Mornings after leg lifts—*Kumin*
The morning's got a sleep head—*Patten*
La mort et la beauté sont deux choses profondes —*Hugo, Victor*
Mort, j'appelle de ta rigueur—*Villon*
Mortalim, behold and fear—*Anonymous-English —Modern English*
A morte é limpa—*Lisboa, Henriqueta*
Mortellement atteint d'une flèche empennée— *La Fontaine*
Moses dröjer pa Sinai—*Ferlin*
A most astonishing thing—*Yeats*
The most elaborate—*Talen*
Most glorious lord of life, that on this day—*Spenser*
Most lovely Dark, my Ethiopia born—*Sitwell, Edith*
Most men use—*Wakoski*
Most modern wits such monstrous fools have shown—*Dryden*
Most mornings you will find him—*Beecher*
Most near, most dear, most loved and most far —*Barker, George*
Most people know—*Reid*
The most precious thing at first—*Mariah*
Most sweet it is with unuplifted eyes—*Wordsworth*
Mostly the animals dream—*Atwood*
Mostly you don't see the ocean—*Piercy*
The moth hums under the beams—*Sitwell, Osbert*
The moth under the eaves—*Williams, William Carlos*
Mother dear, may I go downtown—*Randall*

The mother fragrant in her dust and grace—*Fitzgerald*

Mother, I won't be home this evening, so—*Patten*

Mother, let me congratulate you—*Yevtushenko*

Mother, mother, what illbred aunt—*Plath*

Mother of God, our Lady—*Williams, William Carlos*

Mother of Hermes! and still youthful Maia—*Coleridge, Samuel Taylor*

The mother of life indulges all, our wandering —*Van Doren*

Mother said to call her if the H bomb exploded —*Miles*

Mother, the root of this little yellow flower—*Thomas, Edward*

Mothers and daughters—*Jong*

Moudří mužové v bílých togách předstupují—*Holub*

Moules mâliques—*Duchamp*

Le moulin du Calavon—*Char*

Le moulin tourne au fond du soir—*Verhaeren*

The mountain and the squirrel—*Emerson*

The mountain does not move the mountain is not moved—*Francis*

The mountain held the town as in a shadow—*Frost, Robert*

The mountain sheep are sweeter—*Peacock*

A mountain towering to the skies—*Marshall, Helen Lowrie*

The mountains grow unnoticed—*Dickinson, Emily*

The mountains stand and stare around—*Stephens*

The mountaintop stands in silence a minute after the murder—*Rukeyser*

The mouse that gnawed the oak-tree down—*Lindsay, Vachel*

The mouse whose name is time—*Francis*

Move him into the sun—*Owen, Wilfred*

Move into our own, not theirs—*Lee, Don L.*

Moving in an earthy way like clover—*Fabio, Sarah Webster*

Moving through you one evening—*Patten*

Die Möwen sehen alle aus—*Morgenstern*

La moza gallega que está en la posada—*Salinas, Juan*

Moza tan fermosa non ví en la frontera—*Santillana*

La moza y la madre—*Pemán*

Much have I travell'd in the realms of gold—*Keats*

Much of transfiguration that we hear—*Shapiro, Karl*

Muchachas solteronas de provincia—*López*

Mud is very nice to feel—*Boyden*

Mud-mattressed under the sign of the hag—*Plath*

La muerte, pare el alma, es vida—*Martinez Alonso*

Muerte se quedó en la calle—*Garcia Lorca*

Muerto, quiénes besarán mis sienes—*Martinez Alonso*

Mujer de la tierra mía, Venus y a un tiempo María —*Lloréns Torres*

Mujer! En un silencio que me sabrá—*Alberti*

Mujer, nunca me olvido—*Pedroni*

Una mujer o su sombra de hiedra—*Abril*

Mujeres de tez morena—*Mármol*

Mukashi mishi yume—*Anonymous–East Asian*

La mula y la noria—*Martinez Alonso*

Mulas, médicos, sastres y letrados—*Torres y Villaroel*

Le Mulet d'un prélat se pignoit de noblesse—*La Fontaine*

Multas per gentes et multa per aequora vectus —*Catullus*

Multiples visages d'un même rêve—*Pilon*

A multitude of masts in the harbour—*Abse*

Mungojerrie and Rumpelteazer were a very notorious couple of cats—*Eliot, Thomas Stearns*

The murderer's little daughter—*Williams, William Carlos*

A murmuring in empty shells—*Hillyer*

The Muse, disgusted at an age and clime—*Berkeley*

Muses, pardonnez-moi—*Cocteau*

Muses qui ne songez à plaire ou a déplaire—*Cocteau*

Les muses sont de feux, de cristaux, comme un lustre—*Cocteau*

The mushroom is the elf of plants—*Dickinson, Emily*

Music hath charms to soothe the savage breast —*Congreve*

Music there would be of horns far off—*Reeves*

Music to hear, why hear'st thou music sadly—*Shakespeare*

The music was going on—*Levine*

Music, when soft voices die—*Shelley*

Musing on roses and revolutions—*Randall*

La Musique souvent me prend comme une mer —*Baudelaire*

Must be the season of the witch—*Alurista*

Must I say only Thank you—*Marshall, Helen Lowrie*

Must I tell again—*Bogan*

Mutter Beimlen hat ein Holzbein—*Brecht*

Die Mutter spricht: Lieb Else mein—*Fontane*

Mutter, wozu hast du deinen aufgezogen—*Tucholsky*

Muttered Henry:—Lord of matter—*Berryman*

Muy graciosa es la Doncella—*Vicente*

Muy grand era la lamentar—*Anonymous–Spanish*

My aged friend, Miss Wilkinson—*De la Mare*

My arms have mutinied against me—*Owen, Wilfred*

My aspens dear, whose airy cages quelled—*Hopkins*

My aunt! my dear unmarried aunt—*Holmes, Oliver Wendell*

My beautiful wooden leader—*Atwood*

My bed is like a little boat—*Stevenson*

My bird had a grin like a watermelon—*Mitchell, Adrian*

My black Ma sure knows her thing—*Fabio, Sarah Webster*

My black sun, my Odessa sunflower—*Levertov*

My blackness is the beauty of this land—*Jeffers, Lance*

My bones predict the striking hour of thunder —*Wilkinson*

My books are dreams—*Den Boer*

My bride's in the Kitchen—*Marshall, Helen Lowrie*

My Chinese uncle, gouty, deaf, half-blinded—*Graves*

My circuit-riding great-grandfather—*Wagoner*

My clumsiest—*Nims*

My country, 'tis of thee—*Smith, Samuel Francis*

My cousin Sara Preblod and I—*Sobiloff*

My curse upon your venom'd stang—*Burns*

My Daddy was a Cat—*Eckels*

My Darlyng dere, my daysy floure—*Skelton, John*

My daughter at eleven, almost twelve—*Sexton*

My dear and only love, I pray—*Montrose*

My dear, darkened in sleep, turned from the moon—*Ciardi*

My dear deaf old father how I loved him then—*Betjeman*

My dear one is mine as mirrors are lonely—*Auden*

My dear, today a letter from Berlin—*Stallworthy*

My dearest ones, don't grieve for me—*Marshall, Helen Lowrie*

My dears, don't I know? I esteem you more than you think—*Davie*

My death was arranged by special plans in Heaven—*Eberhart*

My dictionary defines progress as an advance toward perfection—*Nash*

My dog lay dead five days without a grave—*Wilbur*

My ears are alert—*Hillyer*

My eyes catch and stick—*Piercy*

My face has not been washed—*Gaver*

My Father Christmas passed away—*Service*

My father died in nineteen thirty-four—*Solomon*

My father dies again in dreams, a twin—*Hacker*

My father, he was a mountaineer—*Benét, Stephen Vincent*

My father in his—*Lifshin*

My father in the night commanding no—*Simpson*

My father kept a speckled conch—*Plath*

My father lay fifty years in St. Michael's bed—*Ciardi*

My father lies in his grave—*Jeffers, Lance*

My father moved out—*Ghose*

My father moved through dooms of love—*Cummings*

My father moves through the South hunting duck—*Bell*

My father sat in his chair recovering—*Hughes, Ted*

My father sister and—*Lifshin*

My father who owned the wagon-shop—*Masters, Edgar Lee*

My father wore it working coal at Shotts—*MacBeth*

My father worked with a horse-plough—*Heaney*

My father would begin each day—*Raper*

My favorite thing is u blowen—*Sanchez*

My feet took a walk in heavenly grass—*Williams, Tennessee*

My fiftieth year had come and gone—*Yeats*

My first Love was the ten ton truck—*Johnson, B. S.*

My first thought was, he lied in every word—*Browning, Robert*

My flesh must smell like an old tire—*Mailer*

My friend Maloney, eighteen—*Causley*

My friend, the things that do attain—*Surrey*

My friend told me about kids in a coffee house—*Frost, Richard*

My friend was decently wild—*Brooks, Gwendolyn*

My friend with beautiful hair—*Purens*

My friends/ I am amazed—*Bell*

My friends what can I say—*Merwin*

My friends without shields—*Merwin*

My future will not copy fair my past—*Browning, Elizabeth Barrett*

My galy chargèd with forgetfulness—*Wyatt, Sir Thomas*

My genial spirits fail—*Coleridge, Samuel Taylor*

My gentle father led me by the hand—*Darr*

My glass shall not persuade me I am old—*Shakespeare*

My God, I heard this day—*Herbert*

My God, I'm dead—*Kops*

My good blade carves the casques of men—*Tennyson*

My Grandfather found/ his grandchild fogbound—*Lowell, Robert*

My grandfather's clock was too large for the shelf—*Work*

My grass-house stands by the open sea—*Blanding*

My Great God, you been a tenderness to me—*Dodson*

My great stone house sways to and fro—*Marshall, Lenore G.*

My grief on the sea—*Anonymous–English—Modern English*

My grownups told me when I started out—*Nemerov*

My hair is grey, but not with years—*Byron*

My head is bald, my breath is bad—*Betjeman*

My head, so rarely rent—*Eberhart*

My heart aches, and a drowsy numbness—*Keats*

My heart enjoys the fragrance of the rose—*Froissart*

My heart felt need to die—*Kunitz*

My heart is a-breaking, dear tittie—*Burns*

My heart is like a singing bird—*Rossetti, Christina*

My heart is sair—I dare na tell—*Burns*

My heart leaps up when I behold—*Wordsworth*

My heart went fluttering with fear—*Parker*

My heart's in the highlands, my heart is not here—*Burns*

My house is barren—*Davis, Thulami Nkabinde*

My house, my fair palace is—*Bishop, Elizabeth*

My kite broke loose—*Emanuel*

My lamp that was lit every night has burnt a hole in the shade—*Watkins*

My last defense—*Brooks, Gwendolyn*

My left upper—*Swenson*

My letters! all dead paper—mute and white—*Browning, Elizabeth Barrett*

My life closed twice before its close—*Dickinson, Emily*

My life is vile—*Smith, Stevie*

My life's blossom might have bloomed on all sides—*Masters, Edgar Lee*

My little 'bout-town gal has gone—*Brooks, Gwendolyn*

My little dog ten years ago—*Nash*

My little one whose tongue is dumb—*Williams, Tennessee*

My little son, who looked from thoughtful eyes —*Patmore*

My long two-pointed ladder's sticking through a tree—*Frost, Robert*

My Lord, how beautifully you write—*Kizer*

My lov'd, my honor'd, much respected—*Burns*

My love could come home early—*Baldwin, Michael*

My love has left me has gone from me—*Randall*

My love he built me a bonny bower—*Anonymous -English—Modern English*

My love in her attire—*Anonymous-English—Modern English*

My love is a tower—*Day Lewis*

My love is as a fever, longing still—*Shakespeare*

My love is like a red, red rose—*Burns*

My love is like to ice, and I to fire—*Spenser*

My love is of a birth as rare—*Marvell*

My love is strengthened though more weak in seeming—*Shakespeare*

My love, lay your hand on my heart in its gloom —*Heine*

My love, this is the bitterest, that thou—*Browning, Robert*

My love will come—*Yevtushenko*

My lute awake! performe the last—*Wyatt, Sir Thomas*

My man/ don't try none of your jealous—*Sanchez*

My Man, yo' axe still—*Fabio, Sarah Webster*

My mind slips back to lesser men—*Emanuel*

My mind to me a kingdom is—*Dyer*

My Mind's a map—*Benét, Stephen Vincent*

My mistress' eyes are nothing like the sun— *Shakespeare*

My mother baked the bread—*Sobiloff*

My mother bore me in the southern wild—*Blake*

My mother groaned, my father wept—*Blake*

My mother has your rifle—*Berryman*

My mother prayed—*Lester*

My mother said I'd be alone—*Brathwaite*

My mother was a romantic girl—*Smith, Stevie*

My mother, when young, scrubbed laundry in a tub—*Stone, Ruth*

My mother whistled softly—*Frost, Frances M.*

My mother's maids when they do sew and spin —*Wyatt, Sir Thomas*

My mother's table—*Sobiloff*

My mouse, my girl in gray, I speak to her—*Hall*

My name is Edgar Poe and I was born—*Levine*

My name is Elijah—*Bruchac*

My name is Johnson—*Hughes, Langston*

My name is—What does it matter—*Paulus Silentiarius*

My neighbor in the country, Henry Manley— *Kumin*

My nerves my nerves I'm going mad—*Elmslie*

My New York Stars can't help it—*Gaver*

My noble, lovely, little Peggy—*Prior*

My nurse was the island of Tyre: the land of my birth—*Meleager*

My old flame, my wife—*Lowell, Robert*

My old lady died of a common cold—*Williams, Tennessee*

My old man/ tells me i'm—*Sanchez*

My old man's a white old man—*Hughes, Langston*

My old mule—*Hughes, Langston*

My old shape-changer, who will be—*MacPherson*

My only son, more God's than mine—*Gunn*

My own beloved, who hast lifted me—*Browning, Elizabeth Barrett*

My own dear love, he is strong and bold—*Parker*

My own heart let me have more pity on—*Hopkins*

My paistin Finn is my sole desire—*Yeats*

My parents kept me from children who were rough—*Spender*

My parents quarrel in the neighbour room— *Spender*

My people had—*Eckels*

My people is ignorant . . . selfish . . . and . . . cruel —*Dupree*

My photograph already looks historic—*Fuller, Roy*

My pillow, my shirt—*Bernstein*

My poet, thou canst touch on all the notes— *Browning, Elizabeth Barrett*

My poetry resembles the bread of Egypt—*Bly*

My poor old bones (I have only two)—*Kirkup*

My prime of youth is but a frost of cares—*Tichborne*

My river runs to thee—*Dickinson, Emily*

My roots are deep in southern life; deeper than John Brown—*Walker*

My secrets cry aloud—*Roethke*

My selves, my presences—*Reid*

My seven sons came back from Indonesia—*Viereck*

My silks and fine array—*Blake*

My single constancy is love of life—*Bynner*

My sirens—*Emanuel*

My sister rubs the doll's face in mud—*Ai*

My sister stood on a hilltop—*Conkling*

My son, my executioner—*Hall*

My son was insolent to me—*Ciardi*

My Sorrow, when she's here with me—*Frost, Robert*

My soul. I summon to the winding ancient stair —*Yeats*

My soul is an enchanted boat—*Shelley*

My soul looked down from a vague height, with Death—*Owen, Wilfred*

My Soul, there is a Countrie—*Vaughan, Henry*

My soule, like to a ship—*Webster, John*

My spirit is too weak—mortality—*Keats*

My spirit will not haunt the mound—*Hardy*

My stick, he says, and turns in the lane—*Hardy*

My Sun of Death is to the deep, reversedly—*Sitwell, Edith*

My surgeons are a savage band—*Kunitz*

My sweet old etcetera—*Cummings*

My sweetest Lesbia, let us live and love—*Campion*

My sweetheart has beneficent arms—*Untermeyer*

My/ Tamtamy—*Voznezensky*

My tea is nearly ready and the sun has left the sky —*Stevenson*

My thanks, friends of the Country Scientific Association—*Masters, Edgar Lee*

My tongue-tied Muse in manners holds her still —*Shakespeare*

My treasure chest is filled with gold—*Blanding*

My true love breathed her latest breath—*Smith, Stevie*

My true love hath my heart and I have his—*Sidney*

My uncle Sam Lines always seemed—*Redgrove*

My whole eye was sunset red—*Lowell, Robert*

My zipper suit is bunny brown—*Allen, Marie Louise*

Myrrh, bitter myrrh, diagonal—*Avison*

Myselves/ the grievers—*Thomas, Dylan*

The mysteries beyond our sight—*Eberhart*

Mystics, in their far, erotic stance—*Abse*

The myth about a woman's fist—*Darr*

Na mão de Deus, na sua mão direita—*Quental*

Nach Korinthus von Athen gezogen—*Goethe*

Nach leiden, leid und ach und letzt ergrimmten nöthen—*Gryphius*

Nachrichten die für mich bestimmt sind—*Eich*

Die Nacht bedeckt mit schwarzem Schild die Erde—*Platen-Hallermünde*

Die Nacht ihrer ersten Geburt war—*Brecht*

Nacht ist wie ein stilles Meer—*Eichendorff*

Nacht umfängt den Wald. Von jenen Hügeln—*Tiedge*

Nächtlich am Busento lispeln—*Platen-Hallermünde*

Nachts erwache ich schweissgebadet am Husten—*Brecht*

Der Nachtwindhund weint wie ein Kind—*Morgenstern*

Nací en el siglo de la defunción de la rosa—*Carrera Andrade*

Nacieron esta noche—*Mistral*

Nacinicmed ha muerto—ha muerto—*Godoy*

Nad Babim Yarom pamyatnikov net—*Yevtushenko*

Nad morem—*Yevtushenko*

Nad morem krasavitsa-deva sidit—*Lermontov*

Nada te turbe—*Teresa de Avila*

Nadie avisó. Más tarde o más temprano—*Alcántara*

Nadie es nadie—*Celaya*

Nadie es tanto tú, nadie, cuando me amas—*Godoy*

Nadie más cortesano ni pulido—*Machado, Manuel*

Någon rider i natter—*Ferlin*

Naguele pic-nic de burguesas—*Verde*

Nagueres chevauchant pensoye—*Chartier*

Die Nähe ging verträumt umher—*Morgenstern*

Naître avec le printemps, mourir avec les roses—*Lamartine*

Naizad se ruke ukhvate za trbukh—*Popa*

The naked cornucopia of autumn fields—*Sandburg*

Naked, he lies in the blinded room—*Hayden*

A naked house, a naked moor—*Stevenson*

Naked I saw thee—*Pearse*

Naked they came, a giggling corps of girls—*Rodgers*

Name in block letters—*Whistler*

The name of Osmund Toulmin, the Gentleman-Jockey—*Sitwell, Osbert*

Names! The lure in names of places—*Blanding*

The Naming of Cats is a difficult matter—*Eliot, Thomas Stearns*

Nana, niño, nana—*Garcia Lorca*

Nancy Hanks dreams by the fire—*Sandburg*

Nao bebo álcool, não tomo ópio nem éter—*Mendes*

Não repararam nunca? Pela aldeia—*Nobre*

Não sei se e amor que tens—*Pessoa*

Não só quem nos odeia ou nos inveja—*Pessoa*

Nápoléon à Sainte-Hélène—*Obaldia*

Naprasno v gody khaosa—*Pasternak*

När kroppens krematorium—*Ferlin*

När larven ur trädet till puppnong gick ner—*Martinson*

När livets skrift blev ett med dödens drömmar—*Lindegren*

När sjön står mörk med fläckar—*Hallström*

The narcissist's eye is blue, fringed with white—*Benedikt*

A narrow fellow in the grass—*Dickinson, Emily*

Nas dvoe v komnate—*Turgenev*

Nas Hébridas não nasci eu—*Marques*

Nas nossas ruas, ao anoitecer—*Verde*

Nastanyet god, Rossii chernyi god—*Lermontov*

The National Cold Storage Company contains—*Shapiro, Harvey*

Natur und Kunst, sie scheinen sich zu fliehen—*Goethe*

La Nature est un temple où de vivants piliers—*Baudelaire*

Nature had made them hide in crevices—*Eberhart*

Nature is better dressed than man—*Richards, I. A.*

The nature of the beast is the—*Sanchez*

Nature the gentlest mother is—*Dickinson, Emily*

Nature's first green is gold—*Frost, Robert*

Natures lay Ideot, I taught thee to love—*Donne*

Nautilus Island's hermit—*Lowell, Robert*

The navy at Ezion-Geba—*Sitwell, Osbert*

Nazarene bianche, Nazarene nere—*Palazzeschi*

Ncapp' 'e chianche, 'int 'a na chianca—*Di Giacomo*

Ne craignez rien—*Prévert*

Né de la boue, jailli au ciel—*Desnos*

Ne dites pas: la vie est un joyeux festin—*Moréas*

Ne forçons point notre talent—*La Fontaine*

Ne forte credas interitura quae—*Horace*

Ne kaliméra, ne hóra kali—*Nerval*

Né mai pietosa madre al caro figlio—*Petrarca*

Ne m'interrogez pas. Interrogez ces filles—*Cocteau*

Ne obvinyai menya, vsesl'nyi—*Lermontov*

Né più mai toccherò le sacre sponde—*Foscolo*

Ne rassuzhday, ne khlopochi—*Tyutchev*

Ne reprenez, Dames, si j'ay aymé—*Labé*

Ne serdites—k luchemu—*Simonov*

Ne soyons pas trop exigeants—*Geraldy*

Ne t'étonne pas, enfant, si ma pensée—*Lamartine*

Ne tirez pas sur le pianiste—*Tzara*

Ne vos legordi—*Pushkin*

Near here the last grey wolf in England—*Dunlop*

Near the lake where drooped the willow—*Morris, George Pope*

Near the roadbrim—*Sobiloff*

Near the scrapyard—*Ginsberg*

Near where I live there is a lake—*Lowell, Amy*

The nearest dream recedes unrealized—*Dickinson, Emily*

Nearing again the legendary isle—*Day Lewis*

Neat in their niches with retroussé faces—*Agee*

La nebbia a gl'irti colli—*Carducci*

La nebbia ghiacciata affumica la gora della concia —*Luzi*

Nec meum respectet, ut ante, amorem—*Catullus*

Nee nee nee nee—*Rasof*

Needle, needle, dip and dart—*Parker*

Négresse ma chaude rumeur d'Afrique—*Diop*

Negrinho do Pastorcio—*Meyer, Augusto*

Negro cuajar de mi entraña—*Conde*

A negro sprouts from the pavement like an asparagus—*Simpson*

The negro walked his shoes out looking for work —*Beecher*

The negro/ with the trumpet at his lips—*Hughes, Langston*

Negroes/ sweet and docile—*Hughes, Langston*

Nehmt hin die Welt! rief Zeus von seinen Höhen —*Schiller*

Nei te plus oculis meis amarem—*Catullus*

Neither awake—*Cummings*

Nel gran cerchio de l'alpi su'l granito—*Carducci*

Nel mezzo del cammin di nostra vita—*Dante Alighieri*

Nemt, Frowe, disen Kranz—*Walther von der Vogelweide*

N'entre pas à l'ombre de mon ombre gisante—*Lasnier*

Nera si, ma se' bella, o di Natura—*Marino*

N'esperons plus, mon âme, aux promesses du monde—*Malherbe*

A net of smoke—*Randall*

Never a tide goes out to sea—*Blanding*

Never and never my girl riding far and near—*Thomas, Dylan*

Never ask of money spent—*Frost, Robert*

Never be disenchanted of that place—*Graves*

Never love unless you can—*Campion*

Never saw him—*Emanuel*

Never saw them burn—*Emanuel*

Never seek to tell thy love—*Blake*

Never shall a young man—*Yeats*

Never to be renewed or to increase—*Van Doren*

Never to see ghosts? Then to be—*Reid*

Never trouble trouble—*Anonymous-English-Modern English*

Never until the mankind making—*Thomas, Dylan*

Never weather-beaten Sail more willing bent to shore—*Campion*

New-born, gilded with blood—*Lewis, Janet*

A new prophet appeared recently: was first seen —*Patten*

The New Religion is the True—*Cunningham, James Vincent*

New York! D'abord j'ai été confondu par ta beauté—*Senghor*

New York! proudly I breathe its magic name—*Kramer*

The news keeps squirting in from all over—*Blackburn, Paul*

Next bidding all draw near on bended knees—*Pope, Alexander*

The next time—*Pietri*

Next to of course god america i—*Cummings*

Ni chien ni chat sans oiseaux ni poissons—*Seghers*

Ni dricka, Lykabettos' träd, den sista klungen—*Edfelt*

Ni temo al poderoso—*Vega Carpio*

The nicest child I ever knew—*Belloc*

Nicht ein Flügelschlag ging durch die Welt—*Keller, Gottfried*

Nicht gesagt—*Kaschnitz*

Nicht in den Ozean der Welten alle—*Klopstock*

The nicht is far spent—*Smith, Sydney Goodsir*

Niebla, tu no comprendes: lo cantan tus ojos—*Alberti*

Niemand knetet uns wieder aus Erde und Lehm —*Celan*

Nieve ondulada reposa—*Garcia Lorca*

Nigger/ that word—*Sanchez*

Nigguhs with naturals—*Sanchez*

Night after night forever the dolls lay stiff—*Ciardi*

Night and we heard heavy and cadenced hoofbeats—*Bishop, John Peale*

The night attendant, a B. U. sophomore—*Lowell, Robert*

Night, dark night, night of my distress—*Simpson*

The night has a thousand eyes—*Bourdillon*

The night he died, earth's images all came—*Viereck*

The night is freezing fast—*Housman*

The night is full of stars, full of magnificence—*Johnson, Lionel*

Night is on the downland, on the lonely moorland —*Masefield*

The night is still—*Cunningham, James Vincent*

Night, light and the night, light—*Sward*

Night Music Slanted—*Knight, Etheridge*

The night my father got me—*Housman*

Night of the two moons—*Hughes, Langston*

The night rains hot tar into my throat—*Jeffers, Lance*

Night stands up the east—*Agee*

The night the green moth came for me—*Welles*

Night things are soft and loud—*Gay, Zhenya*

The night, too long illumined comes a stranger —*Derwood*

The night was coming very fast—*Roberts*

The night was creeping on the ground—*Stephens*

The night will never stay—*Farjeon*

Nightfall cold eye—*Plath*

A nightingale sat perched upon the trellis—*Heath-Stubbs*

Nightingales warbled without—*Tennyson*

Nightmare of beasthood, snorting, how to wake —*Gunn*

9 children in the—*Lifshin*

Nine days old—*Dunlop*

Nine white chickens come—*Wilbur*

Niño. Que te vas a caer al río—*Garcia Lorca*

A niño tan dormido—*Mistral*

Los niños han ido con Platero—*Jiménez*

Los niños, qué alegres juegan—*Martinez Alonso*

Nirgends hin als auf den Mund—*Fleming*

Nits make lice, said Chivington—*Simpson*

Nivada de calàndries, poetes de ma terra—*Verdaguer*

Nix Bodenstrom, ein Schiffer, nahm—*Lessing*

No bitterness: our ancestors did it—*Jeffers, Robinson*

No conocéis al Piyayo?—*Luna*

No convé que diguem el nom—*Espriu*

No coward soul is mine—*Brontë, Emily*

No day has ever risen like this day—*Press*
No digáis que agotado su tesoro—*Becquer*
No doubt they'll soon get well—*Sassoon*
No doubt what you say is right—*Garlick*
No duerme nadie por el cielo—*Garcia Lorca*
No estoy/ no la conozco—*Girondo*
No fuiste una mujer, sino una santa—*Casal*
No holy wars for them—*Frost, Robert*
No, I cannot turn from love—*Fabio, Sarah Webster*
No, I have tempered haste—*Adams*
No labor-saving machine—*Whitman*
No le nombramos nunca—*Vivanco*
No legs—I must sit still—*Kavanagh*
No lloréis más, delfines de la fuente—*Ballagas*
No lo sabe mi brazo—*León, Rafael de*
No longer mourn for me when I am dead—*Shakespeare*
No longer throne of a goddess to whom we pray —*Hayden*
No longer to hate the autumn, no longer—*Dowling*
No lovelier hills than thine have laid—*De la Mare*
No lovelier time is there than set of sun—*Marshall, Helen Lowrie*
No matter where they lived the same dream came—*Zaturenska*
No me admiró tu olvido—*Becquer*
No me mueve, mi Dios—*Anonymous-Spanish*
No me verá dentro de poco el mundo—*Unamuno*
No mo meetings—*Sanchez*
No more be griev'd at which thou hast done—*Shakespeare*
No more, my dear, no more these counsels try —*Sidney*
No more of talk where God or angel guest—*Milton*
No more wine? then we'll push back chairs and talk—*Browning, Robert*
No! never such a draught was poured—*Holmes, Oliver Wendell*
No, no! go not to Lethe, neither twist—*Keats*
No nobler captain ever trod—*Gilbert, Sir William Schwenck*
No not that way she'd—*Lifshin*
No, nun vurria muri—*Bovio*
No, of cause not—*Pietri*
No one can tell me—*Milne*
No one else can hum the mutter of my silence —*Jeffers, Lance*
No one ever walking this our only earth—*Rukeyser*
No one knows—*Williams, Miller*
No other man, unless it was Doc Hill—*Masters, Edgar Lee*
No people on the golf course—*Betjeman*
No plaino abandonado—*Pessoa*
No quise—*Garcia Lorca*
No rock along the road but knows—*Hayes*
No room for mourning: he's gone out—*Keyes*
No sé lo que he soñado—*Becquer*
No sé si es sombra en el cristal si es solo—*Rosales*
No sé. Sólo me llega en el venero—*Alonso*
No single thing abides—*Lucretius Carus*
No sleep tonight—*Sanchez*
No Spring, nor Summer Beauty hath such grace —*Donne*

No stir in the air, no stir in the sea—*Southey*
No straight lines but drooping—*Braxton*
No sun—no moon!—*Hood, Thomas*
No tardes, muerte, que muero—*Manrique*
No te conoce el toro—*Garcia Lorca*
No, the serpent did not—*Hughes, Ted*
No time ago—*Cummings*
No, Time, thou shalt not boast that I do change —*Shakespeare*
No Virgil, no/ Not even the first of the Romans can learn—*Auden*
No vow once sworn may ever be annulled—*Graves*
No vulture is here, hardly a hawk—*Jeffers, Robinson*
No word. And to be frank, your silence swallowed —*Robson, Jeremy*
No worst, there is none. Pitched past pitch of grief —*Hopkins*
No, you can't go—*Devaul*
Nobody ever galloped on this road—*Blackmur*
Nobody heard him, the dead man—*Smith, Stevie*
Nobody home. Long threads of sunlight slant—*Gunn*
Nobody knows what I feel about Freddy—*Smith, Stevie*
Nobody loses all the time—*Cummings*
Nobody noogers the shaff of a sloo—*Sandburg*
Nobody planted roses, he recalls—*Hayden*
Nobody told me anything much—*Ciardi*
Nobody took any notice of her—*Hardy*
Nobody wonders about the Angel—*Wilson*
Nobody's fault but mine—*Lester*
Noch dennoch musst du drum nicht ganz—*Gerhardt*
Noch einmal wagst du, vielbeweinter Schatten —*Goethe*
Noch in meines Lebens Lenze—*Schiller*
Noch schweigt die Fabrik—*Eich*
Noch sitzen sie rauchend da—*Brecht*
Noch spür ich ihren Atem auf den Wangen—*Hofmannsthal*
Noch stockt im Haus die Schwüle—*Bergengruen*
Una noche de verano—*Machado, Manuel*
Une noche, una noche toda llena de murmullos —*Silva*
Nodding, its great head rattling like a gourd—*Warren*
Noey Bixler ketched him—*Riley*
Noi leggiavamo un giorno per diletto—*Dante Alighieri*
Noi siamo a pregarvi, signora matrigna—*Palazzeschi*
Noi siamo conoscenti di famiglia—*Bovio*
The noise that time makes in passing by—*Moore, Merrill*
A noiseless patient spider I marked—*Whitman*
Noli admirari, quare tibi femina nulla—*Catullus*
Nombre: Antonio Martín Cruz—*Fuertes*
Non chiederci la parola che squadri da ogni lato —*Montale*
Non ha l'ottimo artista alcun concetto—*Michelangelo*
Non, Marcel, non, tout est fini—*Jacob, Max*
Non nobis Domine—*Kipling*
Non più furori reca a me l'estate—*Ungaretti*
Non pozzu chianciri—*Buttitta*

Non so perchí quella sera—*Palazzeschi*
Non sogno piu castelli—*Palazzeschi*
Non tibi Tyndaridis facies invisa Lacaenae—*Virgil*
Nona Domenica Garnaro sits in the sun—*Ciardi*
Noon holds the city back—*Scannell*
Noon sun beats down the leaf; the noon—*Adams*
Noone and a star stand, am to am—*Cummings*
Los nopales con esponas carnes—*Alurista*
Nor can ambition make this garden theirs—*Graves*
Der Nordost wehet—*Hölderlin*
North Sea, Protestant Sea—*Davie*
The north wind doth blow—*Children's Verses and Nursery Rhymes*
Northeastern lunch—*Cohen*
Northward I came, and knocked in the coated wall—*Davie*
Nos entendemos bien—*Jiménez*
The nose sat down next to me—*Winch*
Nosotros, los sobrevivientes—*Retamar*
Not a tree but the tree—*Atwood*
Not Aldestrop, no—besides, the name—*Abse*
Not as the word death—*Bergé*
Not, Celia, that I juster am—*Sedley*
Not fat, not gross, just well fed—*Piercy*
Not for all the lonely winding road that leads across the hill—*Blanding*
Not for myself I make this prayer—*Cullen*
Not from successful love alone—*Whitman*
Not from the stars do I my judgment pluck—*Shakespeare*
Not I myself know all my love for thee—*Rossetti, Dante Gabriel*
Not, I'll not, carrion comfort, Despair, not feast on thee—*Hopkins*
Not in a silver casket cool with pearls—*Millay*
Not in the world of light alone—*Holmes, Oliver Wendell*
Not in this chamber only at my birth—*Millay*
Not like the brazen giant of Greek fame—*Lazarus*
Not long ago—*Logue*
Not long ago, the writer of these lines—*Poe*
Not marble, nor the gilded monuments—*Shakespeare*
Not mine own fears, nor the prophetic soul—*Shakespeare*
Not of new earth and not of new men—*Marshall, Lenore G.*
Not only I—*Hardy*
Not only in our infancy—*Lowell, James Russell*
Not only sands and gravels—*Frost, Robert*
Not palaces, an era's crown—*Spender*
Not picnics or pageants or the improbable—*Warren*
Not so fine—*Sitwell, Osbert*
Not that by this disdain—*Stanley*
Not that it matters, or not much, and not—*Ciardi*
Not to sleep all the night long, for pure Joy—*Graves*
Not to the matter of solitude will I give myself—*Bly*
Not to you I sighed. No not a word—*Spender*
Not what we give, but what we share—*Lowell, James Russell*

Not you, lean quarterlies and swarthy periodicals—*O'Hara*
Not youth pertains to me—*Whitman*
Note this survivor, bearing the mark of the violator—*Watkins*
Nothing but me is moving—*Merwin*
Nothing can live alone—*Engle*
Nothing in thick clothes is—*Bell*
Nothing is plumb, level or square—*Dugan*
Nothing is so beautiful as Spring—*Hopkins*
Nothing is strange to them—*Marshall, Lenore G.*
Nothing, nothing at all is born—*Stryk*
Nothing remained: Nothing, the wanton name—*Gunn*
Nothing so sharply reminds a man he is mortal—*Day Lewis*
Nothing so true as what you once let fall—*Pope, Alexander*
Nothing to show for it at first—*Mitchell, Adrian*
Nothing will keep/ us young—*Sanchez*
Nothing's left—*Harkness*
Notre entrelace d'amour à des lettres ressemble—*Cocteau*
Notre histoire est noble et tragique—*Apollinaire*
Notre Père qui êtes aux cieux—*Prévert*
Notre vie tu l'as faite elle est ensévelie—*Éluard*
Nought loves another as itself—*Blake*
Nous approchons—*Éluard*
Nous aurons des lits pleins d'odeurs légères—*Baudelaire*
Nous avons gouverné de si vastes royaumes—*Péguy*
Nous avons pensé des choses pures—*Valéry*
Nous n'habiterons pas toujours ces terres jaunes, notre délice—*Perse*
Nous sommes installés sous le tonnerre—*Lapointe*
Nous sommes les pensées—*Desnos*
Nous vivons dans l'oubli de nos metamorphoses—*Éluard*
Nova angeletta sovra l'ale accorta—*Petrarca*
Now air is air and thing is thing no bliss—*Cummings*
Now all day long the man who is not dead—*Tate, Allen*
Now all that name are gone—*Scott, Winfield Townley*
Now all the fingers of this tree—*Cummings*
Now all the truth is out—*Yeats*
Now all the world she knew is dead—*Betjeman*
Now all you children—*Durem*
Now, as desire and the things desired cease to require attention—*Auden*
Now as I was young and easy under the apple boughs—*Thomas, Dylan*
Now as the train bears west—*Roethke*
Now by the path I climbed I journey back—*Millay*
Now Chil the Kite brings home the night—*Kipling*
Now comes Fourth Month and the early birds on the trees—*Benét, Stephen Vincent*
Now comes the fisherman to terms—*Francis*
Now entertain conjecture of a time—*Shakespeare*
Now fades the last long streak of snow—*Tennyson*
Now finale to the shore—*Whitman*
Now first, as I shut the door—*Thomas, Edward*

Now here I am, drinking in the tall old house, alone—*Redgrove*
Now I am only aggravated—*Simmons, Judy*
Now I can be sure of my sleep—*Dickey, James*
Now I can tell you—*Evans, Liz*
Now I lay me down to sleep—*Children's Verses and Nursery Rhymes*
Now I out walking—*Frost, Robert*
Now I will do nothing but listen—*Whitman*
Now I'm freed from the stockade—*Miller, May*
Now, I'm not the one—*Lee, Dennis*
Now in the fond unhappiness of sleep—*Blackmur*
Now in the suburbs and the falling light—*Kunitz*
Now, innocent, within the deep—*Bogan*
Now is midsummer come and all fools slaughtered—*Stevens, Wallace*
Now is the air made of chiming balls—*Eberhart*
Now it is autumn and the falling fruit—*Lawrence*
Now it is night—*Nemerov*
Now let the legless boy show the great lady—*MacDiarmid*
Now life has had her fill of me—*Eastman*
Now (more near ourselves than we—*Cummings*
Now Morn her rosy steps in th'eastern clime—*Milton*
Now on the world and on my life as well—*Agee*
Now put me near your chess pieces—*Sherwin*
Now seven days from land the gulls still wheel—*Meredith, George*
Now sits the autumn cricket in the grass—*Millay*
Now slain is King Amulius—*Macaulay*
Now sleeps the crimson petal, now the white—*Tennyson*
Now Spring returning beckons the little boats—*Antipater of Sidon*
Now starflake frozen—*Nemerov*
Now swarthy summer, by rude health embrowned—*Clare*
Now that A. looks like an artist—*Gaver*
Now that I have your face by heart, I look—*Bogan*
Now that the ashen rain of gummy April—*Smith, A. J. M.*
Now that the barbarians have got as far as Picra—*Fuller, Roy*
Now that the curtain is about to fall—*Dowling*
Now that the winter's gone—*Carew*
Now that we're almost settled in our house—*Yeats*
Now that your parcel lies unwrapped—*Gregor*
Now the ambassadors have gone, refusing—*Fuller, Roy*
Now the flowers are all folded—*Conkling*
Now the golden Morn aloft—*Gray*
Now the last day of many days—*Shelley*
Now the leaves are falling fast—*Auden*
Now the moon mocks full and naughty—*Knight, Etheridge*
Now the night grows deeper, stronger—*Heine*
Now the peak of summer's past, the sky is overcast—*Day Lewis*
Now the rich cherry, whose sleek wood—*Adams*
Now there are pre-words—*Scott, F. R.*
Now there is only following to be done—*Whistler*
Now there's many fool things a woman will do—*Williams, Tennessee*
Now this is the law of the jungle—as old and as true as the sky—*Kipling*

Now this particular girl—*Plath*
Now thou hast lov'd me one whole day—*Donne*
Now Tomlinson gave up the ghost in his house in Berkeley Square—*Kipling*
Now touch the air softly—*Smith, William Jay*
Now upon this piteous year—*Garrigue*
Now was the world's back broken—*Rodgers*
Now we enter a strange world—*Bly*
Now we reach the grand finale—*Nash*
Now what is love, I pray thee tell—*Raleigh*
Now when ambrosial night—*Milton*
Now winter downs the dying of the year—*Wilbur*
Now winter nights enlarge—*Campion*
Now with the bells through the apple bloom—*Betjeman*
Now with the coming of the Spring the days will stretch a bit—*Raftery*
Now wouldn't you expect to find a man an awful crank—*Service*
Now you are holding my skull in your hand—*Eberhart*
Now you have freely given me leave to love—*Carew*
Now you have stabbed her good—*Hughes, Ted*
Now you must die, the young one said—*Randall*
Nowhere is one alone—*Young, Andrew*
Noyez matins les soifs les muscles et les fruits—*Tzara*
Nu är det natt över Jorden—*Blomberg*
Nu cane sperzo pe mmiezo Tuleto—*Di Giacomo*
Nü denchent, wib unde man—*Anonymous–German*
Nu går jag här alltså och svalter—*Ferlin*
Nu ginc dar, wîp wolgetân—*Melk*
Nu ic onsundran the secgan wille—*Anonymous–English–Old English*
Nu liechste da, du kleene Kröte—*Tucholsky*
Nu ljuder i huset—en vinterdag—*Ferlin*
Nu löser solen sitt blonda hår—*Lagerkvist*
Nu pianefforte 'e notte—*Di Giacomo*
Nu scennere p' 'a Posta—*Di Giacomo*
Nú wé sculon herian Heofon-ríces Weard—*Caedmon*
Les nuages couraient sur la lune enflammée—*Vigny*
Nue effacée ensommeillée—*Éluard*
Nuestra pasión fue un trágico sainete—*Becquer*
La nuit que précéda sa mort—*Éluard*
La nuit vient. Vénus brille—*Hugo, Victor*
Nuits d'hiver! quel bastringue allume—*Carco*
Nulla potest mulier tantum se dicere amatum—*Catullus*
Nulli se dicit mulier mea nubere malle—*Catullus*
Nullus argento color est avaris—*Horace*
Num bar fechado há muitos, muitos—*Nunes*
Number runner/ come to my door—*Hughes, Langston*
Nun hört die Stimme, die um Mitleid ruft—*Brecht*
Nun ist er endlich kommen doch—*Fontane*
Nun lass mich rufen über die verschneiten/ Gefilde—*George*
Nun last uns gehn und treten—*Gerhardt*
Nun nimmt wohl bald der Bauer Geld aus der Schatulle—*Tucholsky*
Nun ruhen alle Wälder—*Gerhardt*
Nunc est bibendum, nunc pede libero—*Horace*

Nuns fret not at their convent's narrow room—*Wordsworth*

Nur einen Sommer gönnt, ihr Gewaltigen—*Hölderlin*

Nur noch zwei Bäume—*Kaschnitz*

The nurse carried him up the stair—*Wright, James*

Nursing your nerves—*Rich*

N'y va pas/ tout est combiné d'avance—*Prévert*

Nymph, nymph, what are your beads?—*Monro*

The nymph of the forest, only in whose honour—*Graves*

Oh a gardener's eyes are magic eyes—*Marshall, Helen Lowrie*

Oh, a wonderful horse is the Fly-Away Horse—*Field, Eugene*

Oh, addio, commare—*Belli*

O Africa where I bake my bread—*Jeffers, Lance*

O alienate from God, O Spirit accurst—*Milton*

O beautiful for spacious skies—*Bates*

¡Oh, Belerma! Oh, Belerma—*Anonymous-Spanish*

Oh, blithe it is to bless the hounds—*Nash*

O blithe new-comer! I have heard—*Wordsworth*

O Boys! the times I've seen—*Gogarty*

O call not me to justify the wrong—*Shakespeare*

O cameretta, che già fosti un porto—*Petrarca*

O Captain! My Captain! our fearful trip is done—*Whitman*

Oh ces négresses que l'on rencontre—*Cendrars*

Oh Christianity, Christianity—*Smith, Stevie*

O city métropole, isle riverain—*Klein*

O City, where are the once proud walls, the temples—*Agathias*

Oh, come with me to the arctic seas—*Field, Eugene*

O Courbes, méandre—*Valéry*

O Courier on Pegasus—*Knight, Etheridge*

Oh cristalina caballera—*Martinez Alonso*

O cruel Death, give three things back—*Yeats*

Oh, cuán te adoro—*Coronado*

O curlew, cry no more in the air—*Yeats*

O dass die innre Schöpfungskraft—*Goethe*

O death, rock me to sleep—*Anonymous-English—Modern English*

O der Seele nächtlicher Flügelschlag—*Trakl*

O Deutschland, bleiche Mutter—*Brecht*

O di mille tiranni, a cui rapina—*Foscolo*

O Dieu, dont les bontés de nos larmes touchées—*Malherbe*

O do not use me/ After my sinnes—*Herbert*

Oh doe not die, for I shall hate—*Donne*

Oh dona que fas via només per corriol—*Carner i Puig-Oriol*

O du Garten, wo als Knaben—*Göckingk*

Oh dulces prendas, por mi mal halladas—*Vega, Garcilaso de la*

O Duty / why hast thou not the visage of a sweetie or a cutie—*Nash*

Oh, early every afternoon—*Nash*

O Earth, lie heavily upon her eyes—*Rossetti, Christina*

Oh, East is East, and West is West—*Kipling*

O embittered joy—*Bogan*

Oh excelso muro, oh torres coronadas—*Góngora*

O Fairest of the Rural Maids—*Bryant, William Cullen*

O Father, answer me—*Nemerov*

Oh, fiero amor, llegaste como la mariposa—*Storni*

O Fiery River—*Patchen*

Ô fins d'automne, hivers, printemps trempés de boue—*Baudelaire*

O first created and creating source—*Baker, Howard*

O fons bandusiae splendidior vitro—*Horace*

O Fontaine Bellerie—*Ronsard*

O for God's sake—*Rukeyser*

O! for my sake do you with Fortune chide—*Shakespeare*

Oh! for some honest lover's ghost—*Suckling*

O for that warning voice, which he who saw—*Milton*

O France désolée—*Aubigné*

O freedom which to every man entire—*Durrell*

O frères! tristes lys, je languis de beauté—*Valéry*

O Friend! I know not which way I must look—*Wordsworth*

O Friend! one feeling was there which belong'd—*Wordsworth*

O Friends! with whom my feet have trod—*Whittier*

O! from what power hast thou this powerful might—*Shakespeare*

O Furum optime balneariorum—*Catullus*

Oh, Galuppi, Baldassaro, this is very sad to find—*Browning, Robert*

O gieb, vom weichen Pfühle—*Goethe*

Oh, give us pleasure in the flowers today—*Frost, Robert*

O Goat-foot God of Arcady—*Wilde*

O God, in the dream the terrible horse began—*Bogan*

O God, is it wrong—*Lester*

Oh God! methinks it were a happy life—*Shakespeare*

O Gott! was rauhe noth! Wie schaumt die schwartze See—*Gryphius*

O graziosa luna, io mi rammento—*Leopardi*

Oh Guadalquivir!—*Machado, Antonio*

Oh, had I lived in the good old days—*Field, Eugene*

Oh hand me down my old cigar with its Havana wrapper and its filling—*Nash*

O' hate me not for my grey hair—*Wycherley*

O hateful harm! condicion of poverte—*Chaucer*

O hateful hellish snake!—*Spenser*

O Haupt voll Blut und Wunden—*Gerhardt*

O, have you seen the leper healed—*Watkins*

O Hearkener to the loud-clapping shears—*Keats*

O Heart! the equal poise of love's both parts—*Crashaw*

O Heilig Herz der Völker, O Vaterland—*Hölderlin*

O Helene, Allegheny Mountain—*Tullos*

O Honte! ce n'est pas seulement cette femme—*Hugo, Victor*

Oh how comely it is, and how reviving—*Milton*

O! how I faint when I of you do write—*Shakespeare*

O! how much more doth beauty beauteous seem—*Shakespeare*

Oh how the women—*Sexton*

O how thy worth with manners may I sing—*Shakespeare*

Oh hush thee, my baby, the night is behind us—*Kipling*

O hushed October morning mild—*Frost, Robert*

Oh I am a cat that likes to—*Smith, Stevie*

Oh, I say, you, Joe—*Blake*

Oh, I should like to ride the seas—*Parker*

Oh I wish that there were some wing—*Smith, Stevie*

Oh it was beautiful—*Flint*

O it's I that am the captain of a tidy little ship—*Stevenson*

Oh I've ridden plenty of horses—*Jackson, Kathryn*

Ô! j'ai lieu de louer—*Perse*

Oh! je fus comme fou dans le premier moment—*Hugo, Victor*

O Jean, my Jean, when the bell ca's the congregation—*Jacob, Violet*

O Jesus Christ! I'm hit, he said; and died—*Owen, Wilfred*

O Joyes! Infinite sweetnes! with what flowres—*Vaughan, Henry*

Oh, lay my ashes on the wind—*Millay*

O lest the world should task you to recite—*Shakespeare*

O, let the solid ground—*Tennyson*

Oh, let's go up the hill and scare ourselves—*Frost, Robert*

Oh libertad preciosa—*Vega Carpio*

O Liberty! O mate for me—*Whitman*

O light invisible, we praise thee—*Eliot, Thomas Stearns*

O listen, listen, ladies gay—*Scott, Sir Walter*

O, little child, see how the flower—*Treece*

Oh little did the Wolf-Child care—*Kipling*

Oh little mushrooms with brown faces—*Conkling*

O little soldier with the golden helmet—*Conkling*

O Little Town of Bethlehem—*Brooks, Phillips*

Oh llama de amor viva—*De la Mare*

O Lonely workman, standing there—*Hardy*

O Lord, it was all night—*Dickey, James*

O Lord, oure Lord, thy name how merveillous—*Chaucer*

O Lord, we come this morning—*Johnson, James Weldon*

Oh love is fair, and love is rare—*Brooke*

O Love, what hours were thine and mine—*Tennyson*

O lovely Whiskers O inspirational Mop—*Lucian of Samosata*

O lovers cold on mountain drives—*Starbuck*

O ma jeunesse abandonnée—*Apollinaire*

O major Venâncio da Silva—*Andrade, Mario de*

O malheureux mortels! O terre déplorable—*Voltaire*

O Malina—*Neruda*

O Människa, du brum där stjärnor speglas—*Lagerkvist*

Oh, many a time have I, a Five-Year's Child—*Wordsworth*

Oh many times did Ernest Hyde and I—*Masters, Edgar Lee*

O Mary, at thy window be—*Burns*

O matre pulchra filia pulchrior—*Horace*

O may I join the choir invisible—*Eliot, George*

O me! what eyes hath Love put in my head—*Shakespeare*

O 'Melia, my dear, this does everything crown—*Hardy*

O men from the fields—*Colum*

O mère ensevelie hors du premier jardin—*Péguy*

Oh, merry, merry, merry, merry—*Cullen*

Ô mes lettres d'amour, de vertu, de jeunesse—*Hugo, Victor*

Oh, mi pueblo castizo, él de la mañana—*Unamuno*

O Miami, I remember you—*Genser*

O, might those sighes and teares returne againe—*Donne*

O Mighty-mouth'd inventor of harmonies—*Tennyson*

O miro 'e ll uocchie miei—*Di Giacomo*

O miroir—*Mallarmé*

O miserable of happy! Is this the end—*Milton*

O Mistress mine, where are you roaming—*Shakespeare*

O mois des floraisons mois des metamorphoses—*Aragon*

Ô Mort, vieux capitaine, il est temps—*Baudelaire*

O Mortal man, who livest here by toil—*Thomson*

Oh mother my mouth is full of stars—*Causley*

Oh, Murder! What was that, Papa—*Belloc*

Oh Muse, Lady—*Sward*

Oh Muse! relate (for you can tell alone—*Pope, Alexander*

Oh, my body! I dare not desert—*Whitman*

Oh my boy: Jesus—*Dodson*

O my darling troubles heaven—*Patchen*

Oh my dark Rosaleen—*Mangan*

Oh, my Lord what a morning—*Cuney*

O My Love/ the Pretty Towns—*Patchen*

O nata mecum consule Manlio—*Horace*

O! never say that I was false of heart—*Shakespeare*

Oh, no one can deny—*Larkin*

Oh! noites do Harlem—*Nunes*

O nott', o dolce tempo—*Michelangelo*

O Now the Drenched Land Wakes—*Patchen*

O ocean sea for all your being vast—*Frost, Robert*

Oh, on an early morning I think I shall live forever—*Bly*

Oh, once there lived in Kankakee—*Nash*

O, open the door some pity to shew—*Burns*

Oh, Paddy dear, and did ye hear the news that's goin' round—*Anonymous-English—Modern English*

O patria mia, vedo le mura e gli archi—*Leopardi*

O poet, poetry is fine old subject.—*Ginsberg*

Oh, ponder, friend, the porcupine—*Parker*

O prophet of glad tidings, finisher—*Milton*

O purblind race of miserable men—*Tennyson*

Oh! quand la mort que rien ne saurait apaiser—*Banville*

O que tu cantas, pássaro—*Nunes*

O Queen of Heaven have pity on me—*Smith, Stevie*

Oh quei fanali come s'insegnono—*Carducci*

O quick, quick, quick, quick hear—*Eliot, Thomas Stearns*

Oh, refulgentes astros! cuya lumbre—*Saavedra*

O rem ridiculam, Cato, et iocosam—*Catullus*
O river, green and still—*Lee, Laurie*
O Rooster, circled over my brother's head—*Klein*
O Rose, thou art sick—*Blake*
O ruddier than the cherry—*Gay, John*
O ruined father dead, long sweetly rotten—*Kunitz*
O saepe mecum tempus in ultimum—*Horace*
O saisons, o châteaux—*Rimbaud*
O, saw ye bonnie Lesley—*Burns*
O say can you see—*Sanchez*
O say, can you see, by the dawn's early light—*Key*
O scaly-backed Lykainis—*Antipater of Sidon*
O schauerliche Lebenswirrn—*Morgenstern*
O Season of repetition—*Auden*
Oh see how thick the Goldcup flowers—*Housman*
Oh, Señor, Tú que sufres del mundo—*Unamuno*
O she is as lovely—often—*Patchen*
Oh si j'estois en ce beau sein rauie—*Labé*
O sign and wonder of the barnyard—*Klein*
O sino bate—*Ferreira*
Oh, sleep forever in the Latmian cave—*Millay*
Oh, slow to smite and swift to spare—*Bryant, William Cullen*
O soft embalmer of the still midnight—*Keats*
Oh some are fond of red wine—*Masefield*
Oh something just now must be happening there—*McKay*
O Sprengen des Gartens, das Grün zu ermutigen—*Brecht*
O Star of France—*Whitman*
O Star (the fairest one in sight)—*Frost, Robert*
O Statue, stand still—*Sobiloff*
O stephanos peri krati marainetai Eliodoras—*Meleager*
Oh stormy, stormy world—*Frost, Robert*
Oh strong-ridged and deeply hollowed—*Williams, William Carlos*
O Swallow, Swallow, flying, flying south—*Tennyson*
O sweet are tropic lands for waking dreams—*McKay*
O sweet spontaneous—*Cummings*
O take my hand Walt Whitman—*Whitman*
O Täler weit, o Höhen—*Eichendorff*
Oh talk not to me of a name great in story—*Byron*
O Tan-Faced Prairie-Boy—*Whitman*
O tell me all about Anna Livia—*Kunitz*
O tell me where, in lands or seas—*Wilbur*
Oh! that my young life were a lasting dream—*Poe*
O that 't were possible—*Tennyson*
Oh that those lips had language—*Cowper*
O! that you were yourself; but, love, you are—*Shakespeare*
O the barberry bright, the barberry bright—*Kilmer, Aline*
Oh, the blowfly is whining there—*Anonymous–Australasian languages–Australian*
O the opal and the sapphire of that wandering western sea—*Hardy*
O the Raggedy Man! He works for Pa—*Riley*
O, the rain that rains upon the town—*Smith, Sydney Goodsir*
Oh, the rain, the weary, dreary rain—*Mangan*
O the sun comes up, up, up—*Cummings*

Oh there hasn't been much change—*Smith, Stevie*
Oh! There you lie motionless—*Balthasa*
Oh, think not I am faithful to a vow—*Millay*
O thou by nature taught—*Collins, William*
O Thou, my lovely boy, who in thy power—*Shakespeare*
O Thou that in the Heavens doest dwell—*Burns*
O thou that sleep'st like pig in straw—*Davenant*
O Thou! whose fancies from afar are brought—*Wordsworth*
O Timothy Tim/ Has ten pink toes—*Milne*
Oh, to be in England—*Browning, Robert*
O to fall easily, easily, easily in love—*Kizer*
Oh, to have a little house—*Colum*
O Toison, moutonnant jusque sur l'encolure—*Baudelaire*
O tourments plus forts de n'être qu'une seule apparence—*Grandbois*
O truant Muse, what shall be thy amends—*Shakespeare*
O trübe diese Tage nicht—*Fontane*
O tu che dormi là sur la fiorita—*Carducci*
Oh! Valentino vestito di nuovo—*Pascoli*
O via piu bianca e fredda—*Tennyson*
O vieilles pluies souvenez-vous d'Augustin Meaulnes—*Cadou*
O was muss es die Engel gekostet haben—*Rilke*
Oh, weep for Mr. and Mrs. Bryan—*Nash*
O weh, ihr langen Jahre, wohin entschwandet ihr?—*Walther von der Vogelweide*
O wha's the bride that cairries the bunch—*MacDiarmid*
O what a plague is Love—*Anonymous–English–Modern English*
Oh what a sobering—*Yevtushenko*
O what can ail thee, knight-at-arms—*Keats*
O what is that sound—*Auden*
Oh, what lies there are in kisses—*Heine*
O what's the weather in a Beard?—*Roethke*
Oh, when I was in love with you—*Housman*
Oh when you're young—*MacLeish*
O, where are you going, "Goodspeed" and "Discovery"?—*Benét, Rosemary Carr*
O where are you going? said Reader to Rider—*Auden*
O where ha you been, Lord Randal, my son—*Anonymous–English–Modern English*
O where hae ye been, my long, long love—*Anonymous–English–Modern English*
O where have you been, Billy Boy—*Children's Verses and Nursery Rhymes*
O whistle, and I'll come to you, my Lad—*Burns*
O, who will speak from a womb or cloud—*Derwood*
Oh, why are all the roses so pale—*Heine*
O wild West Wind, thou breath of Autumn's being—*Shelley*
O, Willie brew'd a peck o' maut—*Burns*
O, wilt thou go wi' me—*Burns*
O Woche, Zeugin heiliger Beschwerde—*Mörike*
Oh, woman, full of wiliness—*Stephens*
O woman of three cows, agra—*Anonymous–English–Modern English*
O Words are lightly spoken—*Yeats*
O world, I cannot hold thee close enough—*Millay*

O world invisible, we view thee—*Thompson, Francis*

O world, my friend, my foe—*Van Doren*

O world of Toms—tomfools, Tom Peppers—*Francis*

Oh, would that the cruel daylight, too—*Sitwell, Osbert*

O wretched man, that for a little mile—*Masefield*

O Wundernacht, ich grüsse—*Droste-Hülshoff*

O ye wha are sae guid yoursel—*Burns*

O yes, I love you, book of my confessions—*Bly*

Oh, yes! They love through all this world of ours —*Browning, Elizabeth Barrett*

O, yesli pravda, chto v nochi—*Pushkin*

Oh yet we trust that somehow good—*Tennyson*

O yonge fresshe folke, he or she—*Chaucer*

O you so long dead—*Bogan*

O, young Lochinvar is come out of the west—*Scott, Sir Walter*

O Young Mariner—*Tennyson*

O, znaya by ya, chto tak byvaet—*Pasternak*

Oak/ is the keel—*MacBeth*

The oaks, how subtle and marine—*Warren*

Obscurest night involv'd the sky—*Cowper*

Observe the hours which seem to stand—*Jennings*

Och gräset vandranda över världen—*Lundkvist*

October is a breakfast food—*Bevington*

October wind—*Hall*

Un octogénaire plantoit—*La Fontaine*

The oddest, surely, of odd tales—*Graves*

Oddments, as when/ you see through skin—*Reid*

Odi et amo. Quare id faciam—*Catullus*

O'er the smooth enamelled green—*Milton*

Of a' the airts the wind can blow—*Burns*

Of all God's creatures give me man—*Nash*

Of all the blessings which to man—*Cummings*

Of all the causes which conspire to blind—*Pope, Alexander*

Of all the comers—*Freivalds*

Of all the girls that are so smart—*Carey*

Of all the rides since the birth of time—*Whittier*

Of all the sounds despatched abroad—*Dickinson, Emily*

Of all the torments, all the cares—*Walsh*

Of all wit's uses the main one—*Emerson*

Of Asphodel, that greeny flower—*Williams, William Carlos*

Of cool and sweet dew and radiance mild—*Joyce*

Of course, the entire effort is to put oneself—*Spender*

Of courtesy, it is much less—*Belloc*

(of Ever-Ever Land i speak—*Cummings*

Of Heaven or Hell I have no power to sing—*Morris, William*

Of Man's first disobedience, and the fruit—*Milton*

Of speckled eggs the birdie sings—*Stevenson*

Of the beast . . and angel—*Patchen*

Of the dark past—*Joyce*

Of the furious—*Brooks, Gwendolyn*

Of the million or two, more or less—*Browning, Robert*

Of these the false Achitophel was first—*Dryden*

Of this world's theatre in which we stay—*Spenser*

Of white and tawny, black as ink—*Bogan*

Of yore, on earth was dominant—*Morgenstern*

Oft him an-haya are gebideth—*Anonymous–English—Old English*

Oi pètteno, che piéttene—*Di Giacomo*

Oif mit zaver schtayner blau—*Sutzkever*

Oion to glykymalon ereuthetai—*Sappho*

Oir llover no más, sentirme vivo—*Unamuno*

Oisive jeunesse—*Rimbaud*

Ojos claros, serenos—*Cetina*

Okno vykhodit v belye derev'ya—*Yevtushenko*

Olas gigantes que os rompéis bramando—*Becquer*

The old brass pot in the corner—*Conkling*

The old bridge has a wrinkled face—*Conkling*

The old brown thorn trees break in two high over Cummen Strand—*Yeats*

The old crow is getting/ slow—*Ciardi*

Old Deuteronomy's lived a long time—*Eliot, Thomas Stearns*

Old Eddie's face, wrinkled with river lights—*Walcott*

The old face of the mother of many children—*Whitman*

Old father, blessed ghost, mariner—*Scott, Winfield Townley*

Old Fitz, who from your suburb grange—*Tennyson*

Old Fritz, on this rotating bed—*Snodgrass*

The old gnome—*Fry*

An old Jack-o-Lantern lay on the ground—*Poulsson*

Old King Cole—*Children's Verses and Nursery Rhymes*

An old lady writes me in a spidery style—*Walcott*

Old lame Bridget doesn't hear—*Ledwidge*

An old man bending I come among new faces —*Whitman*

An old man in a lodge within a park—*Longfellow*

Old man John the melter—*Beecher*

The old man, listening to the careful—*Van Doren*

Old Man, or Lad's-love—in the name there's nothing—*Thomas, Edward*

An old man whose black face—*Levertov*

Old man, you surface seldom—*Plath*

Old Meg she was a gypsy—*Keats*

Old Molley Means was a hag and a witch—*Walker*

Old Mrs. Kawatata—*Snyder*

Old Mother Hubbard—*Children's Verses and Nursery Rhymes*

An old person of Troy—*Nash*

Old Peter Grimes made fishing his employ—*Crabbe*

The old priest Peter Gilligan—*Yeats*

Old Quin Queeribus he loved his garden so—*Turner, Nancy Byrd*

Old saints on millstones float with cats—*Auden*

An old shoe, an old pot, an old skin—*Rich*

Old/ Sir/ Faulk—*Sitwell, Edith*

The old voice of the ocean, the bird-chatter of little rivers—*Jeffers, Robinson*

The old watch—*Kinnell*

Old Witherington had drunk too much again—*Randall*

The old woman across the way—*Hayden*

An old woman grinds corn—*Tullos*

An old woman had fallen in love—*Edson*

Old woman, old woman, shall we go ashearing —*Children's Verses and Nursery Rhymes*

Old woman, your face is a halo of praise—*Layton*
Old Yalluh Hammuh were a guy—*Walker*
Old yew, which graspest at the stones—*Tennyson*
Older than Byblos—*Olson*
Ole King Cotton/ Ole Man Cotton—*Brown, Sterling A.*
¡Ole! Viva Cadiz—*Garcia Lorca*
Oliver wanted to write about reality—*Nemerov*
Olli subridens hominum sator atque deorum—*Virgil*
Olvido de lo criado—*Juan de la Cruz*
Ombres très écloses et lointaines—*Prefontaine*
Omsk and the Calton turn again to dust—*MacDiarmid*
On a brown isle of Lough Corrib—*Clarke*
On a holy day when sails were blowing—*Clarke*
On a poet's lips I slept—*Shelley*
On a spring morning of young wood, green wood—*Rukeyser*
On a white sandy beach—*Robison*
On a winter's night long time ago—*Belloc*
On almost the incendiary eve—*Thomas, Dylan*
On beds of daisies idly laid—*Warton, Thomas (the Elder)*
On behalf of poets everywhere—*Sondé*
On Commonwealth, on Marlborough—*Starbuck*
On dull mornings—*Sitwell, Osbert*
On ear and ear two noises too old to end—*Hopkins*
On either side of the white line—*Cunningham, James Vincent*
On either side the river lie—*Tennyson*
On enterre les chiens—*Queneau*
On eves of cold, when slow coal fires—*Lee, Laurie*
On forelands high in heaven—*Housman*
On Hellespont guilty of true-loves' blood—*Marlowe*
On her side, reclining on her elbow—*Stevens, Wallace*
On hot summer mornings my aunt set glasses—*Norris*
On l'avait durement traité—*Éluard*
On longer evenings, light chill and yellow—*Larkin*
On me demande, par les rues—*Musset*
On moonlit heath and lonesome bank—*Housman*
On ne bâille pas chez moi—*Damas*
On n'est pas sérieux, quand on a dix-sept ans—*Rimbaud*
On one hand, harrowed England—*Walcott*
On St. Martin's evening green—*Brinnin*
On September 2, 1945, the battleship—*Ciardi*
On shel iz vifanii v erusalim—*Pasternak*
On the beach at night—*Whitman*
On the Coast of Coromandel—*Lear*
On the crooked arm of Columbus—*Reid*
On the deck of Patrick Lynch's boat—*Fox, George*
On the 15th of November—*Stein, Gertrude*
On the flat of the earth lie—*Norris*
On the idle hill of summer—*Housman*
On the ingeniously devised habitations of death—*Sachs*
On the jetty, our fingers shading—*Hoffman*
On the large highway of the ample air that flows—*Wheelock*
On the long shore, lit by the moon—*Nemerov*

On the Memorial building's—*Hollander*
On the million Mexican mountains a heartbeat under—*Marshall, Lenore G.*
On the path, by this wet site of old fires—*Kinnell*
On the path winding upward—*Kinnell*
On the school platform, draping the folding seats—*Klein*
On the shores of Gitche Gumee—*Longfellow*
On the stiff twig up there—*Plath*
On the tallest day in time the dead came back—*Ciardi*
On the threshold of heaven, the figures in the street—*Stevens, Wallace*
On the top of the Crumpetty Tree—*Lear*
On the volcanic hill—*Drake, Leah Bodine*
On the wide level of a mountain's head—*Coleridge, Samuel Taylor*
On these miles of sand—*Beecher*
On this bald hill the new year hones its edge—*Plath*
On to their morning's rural work they haste—*Milton*
On top of a pillar Simeon sat—*McGinley*
On tourne pésamment la tête vers un nouvel horizon—*Giguere*
On warm days in September the high school band—*Whittemore*
On Wenlock Edge the wood's in trouble—*Housman*
Ona sidela na polu—*Tyutchev*
Once a dream did weave a shade—*Blake*
Once a man was travelling—*Olson*
Once after long drawn revel—*Kipling*
Once at St. Ann's Gut—*Darr*
Once did she hold the gorgeous East in fee—*Wordsworth*
Once I adopted—*Hughes, Langston*
Once I lived at a Riverside—*Kizer*
Once I pass'd through a populous city imprinting my brain for future—*Whitman*
Once I said lightly—*Hughes, Ted*
Once I was good like the Virgin Mary—*Johnson, Fenton*
Once in a vision—*Dowling*
Once in childhood's rainwater wells—*Langland, Joseph*
Once in the beginning on last Sunday—*Levine*
Once inside—*Lester*
Once it smiled a silent dell—*Poe*
(once like a spark)—*Cummings*
Once more it is early summer—*Rexroth*
Once more, listening to the wind and rain—*Bontemps*
Once more round should do it—*Souster*
Once more the changed year's turning wheel returns—*Rossetti, Dante Gabriel*
Once more the old year peters out—*Francis*
Once more the storm is howling, and half hid—*Yeats*
Once . . . once upon a time—*De la Mare*
Once riding in old Baltimore—*Cullen*
Once there was a bridegroom named Mr. Ormantude—*Nash*
Once there was a couple named Mr. and Mrs. Plackett—*Nash*
Once there was a fence here—*Van Doren*
Once there was a Greek divinity—*Nash*

Once there was a kindhearted lad—*Nash*

Once there was a lonely man named Mr. Powers —*Nash*

Once there was a man named Jarvis Gravel— *Nash*

Once there was a man named Mr. Rory Moodus —*Nash*

Once under the great rose window I knelt alone —*Chapin*

Once upon a midnight dreary—*Poe*

Once upon a time—*Hughes, Ted*

Once upon a time, in a little wee house—*Children's Verses and Nursery Rhymes*

Once upon a time there was a man named Mr. Donnybrook—*Nash*

Once upon a time there was a young man named Harold Scrutiny—*Nash*

Once upon a time there were three little foxes —*Milne*

Once upon the earth—*Smith, William Jay*

Once when the snow of the year was beginning to fall—*Frost, Robert*

Once you were young—*Hughes, Langston*

Ondas do mar de Vigo—*Codax*

Las ondas tienen vaga armonía—*Becquer*

The one-armed explorer—*Merwin*

One bliss for which—*Nash*

One by one they appear in—*Gunn*

One cantaloupe is ripe and lush—*Nash*

The one damn time—*Creeley*

One day a long time ago—*Cuestas*

One day and a sleep ago—*Hodges*

One day I found a lost dog—*Scannell*

One day I saw a downy duck—*Ross, Muriel Sipe*

One day I wrote her name upon the strand— *Spenser*

One day I'm going to lead a line—*Johnston, Ellen Turlington*

One day in a rush of dogwood all the world married—*Ciardi*

One debarred from enrollment at Harvard— *Moore, Marianne*

One ever hangs where shelled roads part—*Owen, Wilfred*

One face looks out from all his canvasses—*Rossetti, Christina*

One feather is a bird—*Roethke*

One foot in Eden still I stand—*Muir*

One granite ridge—*Snyder*

One is a point—*Sukenick*

One midnight, glittering-eyed, in restless silence —*Connor*

One more casualty—*Nemerov*

One more March—*Berger*

One more unfortunate/ weary breath—*Hood*

One must have a' mind of winter—*Stevens, Wallace*

One night a poem came to a poet—*Patten*

One night I reached a cave—*Gunn*

One night I thirsted like a prince—*Dickey, James*

One noon in the Library, I watched a man—*Reid*

One November morning clean and cold—*Farjeon*

The one remains, the many change and pass— *Shelley*

One single and effective rhyme—*Davie*

One summer evening (led by her)—*Wordsworth*

One that is ever kind said yesterday—*Yeats*

One thing has a shelving bank—*Frost, Robert*

One thing that literature would be greatly the better for—*Nash*

One, two/ buckle my shoe—*Children's Verses and Nursery Rhymes*

One, two, three, four, five—*Children's Verses and Nursery Rhymes*

One, two, three, four, five, six, seven—*Children's Verses and Nursery Rhymes*

One was quite certain—*Stein, Gertrude*

One who so hated the war—*Davis, Thulami Nkabinde*

One wondered who would see—*Lowell, Robert*

One word is too often profaned—*Shelley*

One writes, that other friends remain—*Tennyson*

One's-self I sing, a simple separate person—*Whitman*

Only a green hill, and a man with a spade—*Rodgers*

Only a man harrowing clods—*Hardy*

Only a penny, a penny—*Masefield*

Only in madness would we conceive—*Darr*

Only in the dream that is like sleep—*Eberhart*

Only let it form within his hands once more— *MacNeice*

Only on the rarest occasions, when the blue air —*Merwin*

The only relics left are those long—*Stafford*

Only teaching on Tuesdays, book-worming— *Lowell, Robert*

Only the stones remember—*Griffiths*

Only their hands are living, to the wheel attracted—*Auden*

Only to have a grief—*Rich*

Ons in your grace I knowe I was—*Wyatt, Sir Thomas*

An open door says, Come in—*Sandburg*

Open his head, baby—*Cummings*

Open-mouthed, the baby god—*Plath*

Open the old cigar-box, get me a Cuba stout— *Kipling*

Open the pure door of that summer air—*Abbe*

Opsimathy, says my dictionary—*Nash*

Or che 'l ciel e la terra e l'vento tace—*Petrarca*

Or I shall live your epitaph to make—*Shakespeare*

Or poserai per sempre—*Leopardi*

Or what is closer to the truth—*Moore, Marianne*

Or whether doth my mind, being crown'd with you—*Shakespeare*

Ora dormi, cuore inquièto—*Ungaretti*

L'ora impaurita—*Ungaretti*

Ora isto, senhores, deu-se em Trás-os-Montes— *Nobre*

The orange bears with soft friendly eyes—*Patchen*

The orchards half the way—*Housman*

Ordinary people are peculiar too—*MacNeice*

The origin, far side of the lake—*Kelly*

Original/ Ragged-round—*Brooks, Gwendolyn*

Orpheus with his lute made trees—*Fletcher, John*

Una oscura pradera me convida—*Lezama Lima*

Osmosis is the process—*Darr*

The other two, slight air and purging fire—*Shakespeare*

Others abide our question. Thou art free—*Arnold*

Others, I am not the first—*Housman*

Otium divos rogat in patenti—*Horace*

L'oto iuomo c' 'o sciato facette—*Di Giacomo*

La otra tarde en la Ribera—*Garcia Lorca*

Otro viento roza, otra agua lava—*Aridjis*

Ou e eti, pathenikai meligaryes ierophonoi—*Alcman*

Où sont nos amoureuses—*Nerval*

Oui, sans regret, du flambeau de mes jours—*Parny*

Our age bereft of nobility—*Wieners*

Our ancient church! its lowly tower—*Holmes, Oliver Wendell*

Our band is few but true and tried—*Bryant, William Cullen*

Our birth is but a sleep—*Wordsworth*

Our boat is asleep on Serchio's Stream—*Shelley*

Our Boy was a child when the good—*Stafford*

Our brains ache, in the merciless iced east winds that knive us—*Owen, Wilfred*

Our Church now rebuilds for our Christ—*Marshall, Helen Lowrie*

Our family moved in 25 years from Acceptable Ethnic—*Berrigan*

Our fathers sacrificed so much—*Marshall, Helen Lowrie*

Our gang/ laid for the kids from niggertown—*Beecher*

Our golden age was then, when lamps and rug—*Van Doren*

Our hill has made its submission and the green—*Auden*

Our lady wanted to lead a line—*Johnston, Ellen Turlington*

Our office cat is a happy cat—*Smith, Stevie*

Our padre is an old sky pilot—*Betjeman*

Our shadows fall beyond the empty cage—*Fuller, Roy*

Our words go slowly out—*Corner*

Out in the dark over the snow—*Thomas, Edward*

Out in the yellow meadows, where the bee—*Meredith, George*

Out of a bellicose fore-time, thundering—*Auden*

Out of a cell into this darkened space—*Masters, Edgar Lee*

Out of an empty sky the dust of hours—*Cowley, Malcolm*

Out of an hour I built a hut—*Swenson*

Out of burlap sacks, out of bearing butter—*Levine*

Out of love—*Hughes, Langston*

Out of me unworthy and unknown—*Masters, Edgar Lee*

Out of the cradle endlessly rocking—*Whitman*

Out of the earth to rest or range—*Masefield*

Out of the factory chimney tall—*Bennett, Rowena*

Out of the hills of Habersham—*Lanier*

Out of the lie of no—*Cummings*

Out of the lights and roar of cities—*Masters, Edgar Lee*

Out of the matrix—*Marshall, Lenore G.*

Out of the mud two strangers came—*Frost, Robert*

Out of the night that covers me—*Henley, William Ernest*

Out of the nothingness of sleep—*Brooke*

Out of the old cold dark—*Weber, Richard*

Out of the wood of thoughts that grows by night—*Thomas, Edward*

Out of the woods where pollen is a powder of gold—*Warren*

Out/ of this/ bright/ sun—*Brathwaite*

Out of us all that make rhymes—*Thomas, Edward*

Out on the mountain over the town—*Field, Eugene*

Out the Alley our soul awaits us—*Alurista*

Out there, we've walked quite friendly up to death—*Owen, Wilfred*

Out through the fields and the woods—*Frost, Robert*

Out upon it, I have loved—*Suckling*

Outcrop stone is miserly—*Hughes, Ted*

Outshouting bathwater—*Emanuel*

Outside it is April—*Harkness*

Outside, the snow on a low—*Sward*

Ove sei? de' sereni occhi ridenti—*Carducci*

Over and around, grass banked and packed short—*Dickey, James*

Over & over she said, there's no time—*Wyatt, Andrea*

Over-/ cunh-/ unh-/ um—*Emanuel*

Over him like a tent her prayers—*Marshall, Lenore G.*

Over known fields with an old friend in dream—*Thomas, Edward*

Over my head, I see the bronze butterfly—*Wright, James*

The over-ornate can be a burden—*Francis*

Over rock and wrinkled ground—*Rodgers*

Over Sir John's hill the hawk on fire hangs still—*Thomas, Dylan*

Over sparkling and green water, the lighthouse seems—*Hollander*

Over the ankles in snow—*Gunn*

Over the carnage rose prophetic a voice—*Whitman*

Over the great windy waters, and over the clear-crested summits—*Clough*

Over the half-finished houses—*Rich*

Over the meadows—*Gleason*

Over the seaworthy cavalry arches—*Starbuck*

Over the west side of this mountain—*Wright, Judith*

Over the Western sea hither from Niphon come—*Whitman*

Over the years—*Viorst*

Over us if (as what was dusk becomes—*Cummings*

Overnight, very/ Whitely—*Plath*

Owain was ill today. In the night—*Clark, Gillian*

Owê war sint verswunden alliu miniu jar—*Walther von der Vogelweide*

The owl and the pussy-cat went to sea—*Lear*

The owl is abroad, the bat and the toad—*Jonson*

Owls—they whinny down the night—*Graves*

Oxford is a legend—*Walker*

Oye—*Vargas*

Oye, hijo mío, el silencio—*Garcia Lorca*

På väven Asien vi sågo ner—*Martinson*

Pacific: in Russian as/ in our language—*Davie*

Pack, clouds, away, and welcome day—*Heywood*

Padre del ciel dopo i perdutti giorni—*Petrarca*

Padre nuestro, que estás en los cielos—*Mistral*

Un padre que de consejos—*Hernández, José*
Padre y maestro mágico, liráforo celeste—*Darío*
Paene insularum, Sirmio, insularumque—*Catullus*
Page one and I enter a land—*Danner*
Pain has an element of blank—*Dickinson, Emily*
Pain is in this dark room like many speakers—*Merwin*
Le pain lève—*Cendrars*
The pain of loving you—*Lawrence*
The paint explodes into a face—*Engle*
Paint my crib a—*Tropp, Gloria*
The painter of Dante's awful ferry-ride—*Deutsch*
Painter, the mountain rims the mesa—*Marshall, Lenore G.*
Paintings with stiff—*Randall*
País de la ausencia—*Mistral*
Palace in smoky light—*Pound*
Palacio, buen amigo—*Machado, Antonio*
Le palais de Gormaz, comte et gobernador—*Fourest*
Pale as cold moons—*Miller, May*
Pale beech and pine so blue—*Hardy*
Pale brows, still hands and dim hair—*Yeats*
Pale, flat-faced Mrs. Frossart—*Sitwell, Osbert*
Pale gold of the walls, gold—*Hall*
Pale sand edges England's Old—*Moore, Marianne*
Palemón el Estilita, sucesor del viejo Antonio—*Valencia*
Pali me ten anoixe—*Seferis*
Pâles Esprits, et vous Ombres poudreuses—*Du Bellay*
Pallid and moonlike in the smog—*Nash*
Palm the head just so—*Aubert*
Palma Kunkel ist mit Palm verwandt—*Morgenstern*
Palma Kunkels Papagei—*Morgenstern*
Palma: mástil de amarre—*García Tudurí*
Palmström, etwas schon an Jahren—*Morgenstern*
Palmström findet eines Abends—*Morgenstern*
Palmström führt ein Polizeipferd vor—*Morgenstern*
Palmström geht durch eine fremde Stadt—*Morgenstern*
Palmström hat nicht Speck im Haus—*Morgenstern*
Palmström ist nervös geworden—*Morgenstern*
Palmström liebt es, Tiere nachzuahmen—*Morgenstern*
Palmström liebt, sich in Geräusch zu wickeln—*Morgenstern*
Palmström lobt das schlechte Wetter sehr—*Morgenstern*
Palmström nimmt Papier aus seinem Schube—*Morgenstern*
Palmström schläft vor zwölf Experten—*Morgenstern*
Palmström schwankt als wie ein Zweig im Wind—*Morgenstern*
Palmström steht an einem Teiche—*Morgenstern*
Palmström stellt ein Bündel Kerzen—*Morgenstern*
Palmström wünscht sich manchmal aufzulösen—*Morgenstern*
Palmströms Uhr ist andrer Art—*Morgenstern*
The panther is like a leopard—*Nash*

Un paon muoit: un Geai prit son plumage—*La Fontaine*
Papè Satàn, papè Satàn aleppe—*Dante Alighieri*
Paper is two kinds, to write on, to wrap with—*Sandburg*
Pappa used to play—*Wilson*
Pap's got his patent-right—*Riley*
Papu, Tariq, Oguchi, Paulo—*Connor*
Par le petit garçon qui meurt près de sa mère—*Jammes*
Par le seul désir de durer ensemble—*Lasnier*
Para escribir poemas—*Novo*
Para olvidarme de por que he venido—*Jiménez*
Para que los leas con tus ojos—*Becquer*
Para que yo me llame Angel González—*González*
Para ser caballero de accidentes—*Valle Caviedes*
Pardon, oh, pardon, that my soul should make—*Browning, Elizabeth Barrett*
Parents are sinful now, for they must whisper—*Clarke*
Paris a froid Paris a faim—*Éluard*
Paris chahute au gaz—*Laforgue*
Pars me Sulmo tenet Paeligni tertia ruris—*Ovid*
Parting of grasses—beautiful tiger—flutter of fern—beautiful tiger—*Gunderson*
The party hats perch like—*Shpunt*
Pasan todas, verdes, granas—*Jiménez*
Paseabase el rey moro por la cuidad de Granada—*Anonymous–Spanish*
Pass gently, pigeons on the grass—*Brinnin*
Passa sotto la nostra casa qualche volta—*Luzi*
Passando con pensier per un boschetto—*Sacchetti*
Passata è la tempesta—*Leopardi*
Passer, deliciae meae puellae—*Catullus*
Passion has three acts—*Ward*
The past and the present wilts—*Whitman*
Past Mogollon River—*Lifshin*
Pastor que con tus silbos amorosos—*Vega Carpio*
Pastor, que estas en el campo—*Anonymous–Spanish*
Un pastorcico solo está penado—*Juan de la Cruz*
Pat-a-cake, pat-a-cake—*Children's Verses and Nursery Rhymes*
The patagonian—*Marquis*
Patience, hard thing! the hard thing but to pray—*Hopkins*
La patrie est comme une barque—*Aragon*
Patrolling Barnegat/ wild, wild the storm—*Whitman*
Paul, il nous faut partir pour un départ plus beau—*Claudel*
Un pauvre Bûcheron, tout couvert de ramée—*La Fontaine*
Paying for half of it—*Lifshin*
Peace is the heir of dead desire—*Jeffers, Robinson*
Peace now for every fury has had her day—*Jeffers, Robinson*
The peace of great doors be for you—*Sandburg*
Peace pratler, do not lowre—*Herbert*
Peace the politician predicted—*Dicker*
Peace to all such! but were there one whose fires—*Pope, Alexander*
Peach, plum or apricot—*Kops*
Pease-porridge hot—*Children's Verses and Nursery Rhymes*

Pedicabo ego vos et irrumabo—*Catullus*

Peeking, dotting, skeining—*Bodenheim*

Peering into you stout you see a past of Lazybeds —*MacNeice*

The Pekes and the Pollicles, everyone knows— *Eliot, Thomas Stearns*

Pel bosco errò tutta la notte il Conte—*Ariosto*

¡Penas! Quién osa decir—*Martí*

Pendant qu'il sommeillait Ruth, une Moabite— *Hugo, Victor*

Pendant quinze jours je m'étais confiné dans ma chambre—*Baudelaire*

A penny for your thoughts—*Durrell*

The Pennycandystore Beyond the El—*Ferlinghetti*

O pensamento é triste—*Meireles*

Pensamiento de alas negras—*Castro, Rosalía de*

Il pensiero m'insegne in questo borgo—*Luzi*

The people along the sand—*Frost, Robert*

People are putting up storm windows now— *Nemerov*

People ask questions—*Piercy*

The people I love best—*Piercy*

People make mistakes—*Hannan*

The people say that spiritism is a joke—*Smith, Stevie*

People want delivery—*Olson*

People who have no children can be hard— *Brooks, Gwendolyn*

People who have what they want are very fond of telling—*Nash*

Pepper and salt—*Van Doren*

Per me si va nella città dolente—*Dante Alighieri*

Per un Iddio che rida come un bimbo—*Ungaretti*

Perché, gentile creatura, mi strazi—*Saba*

Perché, o mie luci, l'angoscioso pianto—*Foscolo*

Perch'i no spero di tornar giammai—*Cavalcanti*

Percy is my name; my accent is good—*Eberhart*

Perdida en la noche inmensa—*Jiménez*

O perdido caminho, a perdida estrêla—*Drummond de Andrade*

Perdónalo, Señor, era inocente—*Bernárdez*

Père Joseph hat kein Dach überm Kopfe—*Brecht*

Pères/ regardez-vous à gauche—*Prévert*

Peresekshi krai dvora—*Pasternak*

Perfect beneath an eight-rayed sun you lie— *Graves*

Das Perfekt und das Imperfekt—*Morgenstern*

Perhaps I made a slight mistake—*Guiterman*

Perhaps love of your fair face will leave a breath to me—*Gatto*

Perla del mar! Estrella de Occidente—*Gómez de Avellaneda*

Perle, plesaunte to prynces paye—*Anonymous– English–Middle English*

Das Perlhuhn zählt: eins, zwei, drei, vier—*Morgenstern*

Pero como decirtelo si eres—*Bousoño*

Pero otro día toco tu mano—*Aleixandre*

Perplexed and troubled at his bad success—*Milton*

Perrette, sur sa tête ayant un pot au lait—*La Fontaine*

Persicos odi, puer, apparatus—*Horace*

Les persiennes ouvraient sur le grand jardin clair —*Carco*

The person of this plant with heart-shaped leaves —*Dugan*

Person, woman, child—*Engle*

La perte d'un époux ne va point sans soupirs—*La Fontaine*

Pertenezco a una era fugitiva—*Pacheco*

A perverse habit of cat-goddesses—*Graves*

The pet shops were advertising—*Ciardi*

Peter was a pilot—*Lee, Dennis*

Peter Piper picked a peck of pickled peppers— *Children's Verses and Nursery Rhymes*

Peter's not friendly. He gives me sideways looks —*Berryman*

Le petit cheval le mauvais temps—*Fort*

Le petit homme qui chantait sans cesse—*Prévert*

Petit mercier! petit pannier—*Charles d'Orleans*

Petit poisson deviendra grand—*La Fontaine*

Les petites gnomes chantent—*Nerval*

Petshal'no ya glyazhu na nashe pokolen'e—*Lermontov*

Peu vous importe—*Maison-Noire*

Peuple! des crimes de tes pères—*Lamartine*

Pfeift der Sturm?—*Morgenstern*

Phaestos is a village with 25 families—*Corso*

Le Phaéton d'une voiture à foin—*La Fontaine*

Phainetai moi kenos isos theoisin—*Sappho*

A phantasm, nothing else existed in the beginning —*Anonymous–American Indian languages– Uitoto*

Pharoah Sanders—*Lee, Don L.*

Phasellus ille, quem uidetis, hospites—*Catullus*

Philis, qu'est devenu ce temps—*Voltaire*

Philistion of Nikaia lies here, whose laughter— *Anonymous–Greek*

Philophron hesykhia dikas—*Pindar*

Philosophers have measur'd mountains—*Herbert*

Phlebas the Phoenician, a fortnight dead—*Eliot, Thomas Stearns*

Pibroch of Donuil Dhu—*Scott, Sir Walter*

Picked offhand by the angels to demonstrate— *Williams, Gwyn*

Pico della Mirandola, when he was nineteen— *Ciardi*

Picture and book remain—*Yeats*

The picture was a young man—*Engle*

The picture world, that falls apart and leaves— *Aiken*

A piece of flesh gives off smoke in the fields— *Kinnell*

A piece of forest—*Garlick*

La piedra es una frente donde los sueños—*Garcia Lorca*

Pierrot qui n'a rien d'un Clitandre—*Verlaine*

The piers are pummelled by the waves—*Auden*

The pig, if I am not mistaken—*Nash*

The pig lay on a barrow dead—*Hughes, Ted*

Pike, three inches long, perfect—*Hughes, Ted*

Pile the bodies high at Austerlitz and Waterloo —*Sandburg*

Piled deep below the screening apple-branch— *Rossetti, Dante Gabriel*

The pimply wolf who is shorter than I—*Sobiloff*

Pink buds, pink buds ah look—*Benedikt*

Pink protrusion, pachyderm pork crystal— *Reaney*

Piping Anne and husky Paul—*Hillyer*

Piping down the valleys wild—*Blake*

Las piquetas de los gallos—*Garcia Lorca*
Pity this busy monster, manunkind—*Cummings*
Pity would be no more—*Blake*
Piú non mi temono i passeri Vanno—*Saba*
Pla ce bo/ who is there—*Skelton, John*
Place du Carrousel—*Prévert*
The place is called the Golden Cock—*Davison, Peter*
The place is forgotten now: when I was a child —*Nemerov*
Place your name in a time capsule—*Darr*
The plain was grassy, wild and bare—*Tennyson*
A plant will draw back vision to its source—*Hacker*
Platero es pequeño—*Jiménez*
A plausible man keeps us from feeling uneasy—*Davison, Peter*
Play it across the table—*Sandburg*
Please bear in mind my royal descent—*Cullen*
Please send me a miracle—*Murphy*
Pleasure it is—*Anonymous–English–Modern English*
Plentiful people went to the Cadillac drawing—*Miles*
Pleurez, doux alcyons, ô vous, oiseaux sacrés—*Chénier*
The plump Mr. Pl'f is washing his hands of America—*MacLeish*
Plunder throws angels into serfdom—*Sobiloff*
Plunging into/ the shining water—*Ross, W. W. Eustace*
Plus estroit que la vigne à l'ormeau se marie—*Ronsard*
La pluye nous a buez et lavez—*Villon*
Po Chu-i, balding old politician—*Wright, James*
Po vecheram nad restoranami—*Blok*
The pobble who has no toes—*Lear*
Poche cose mi restano visibili—*Ungaretti*
Pod rakitoi, obvitoi plyoshchom—*Pasternak*
La poderosa muerte me invitó—*Neruda*
Podrá nublarse el sol eternamente—*Becquer*
Podruga dnei moikh surovykh—*Pushkin*
A poem is a dancing—*Piercy*
A poem should be palpable and mute—*MacLeish*
Poem, white page—*Rukeyser*
The poems, leaving—*Dlugos*
Poesía/ tristeza—*Camino Galicia*
Poeta ayer, hoy triste y pobre—*Machado, Antonio*
O poeta é um fingidor—*Pessoa*
Poetate tenero, meo sodali—*Catullus*
Le poète chantait: de sa lampe fidèle—*Millevoye*
Poète, prends ton luth et me donne un baiser—*Musset*
Poetry cripples. Tempus fugit—*Bell*
Poetry is a formality—*Heath-Stubbs*
The poetry of earth is never dead—*Keats*
The poetry of tragedy is never dead—*Eberhart*
Poetry the strong-backed wrathy whose—*Jeffers, Lance*
The poet's daily chore—*Wilkinson*
Poets make pets of pretty, docile words—*Wylie*
Poets to come! Orators, singers, musicians to come—*Whitman*
Poi che del patrio nido—*Leopardi*
Poi che divelta, nella tracia polve—*Leopardi*
Poikilothron athanat' Aphrodita—*Sappho*

Poised between going on and back, pulled—*Francis*
Les poissons ont de si jolies têtes—*Queneau*
Pole threkie, ti de me loxon ommasin blepousa —*Anacreon*
The poles are flying where the two eyes set—*Watkins*
The police are probing tonight—*Wright, James*
The policeman buys shoes slow and careful—*Sandburg*
A policeman/ is a pig—*Sanchez*
Policeman Peter Forth I drag—*Gilbert, Sir William Schwenck*
Polioi men hemin ede—*Anacreon*
Polisen sa: Var bor ni?—*Ferlin*
A polished glancing. A bluefrost-bright dawn—*Hughes, Ted*
A politician is an arse upon—*Cummings*
Político, militar, héroe, orador y poeta—*Lloréns Torres*
Polyphiloprogenitive the sapient—*Eliot, Thomas Stearns*
Poned atención—*Machado, Antonio*
Pontiac fire Detroit—*Davie*
Poor hill farmer astray in the grass—*Thomas, Ronald Stuart*
Poor Matthias! wouldst thou have—*Arnold*
Poor savage doubting—*Merrill*
Poor sheepish plaything—*Lowell, Robert*
Poor soul, the centre of my sinful earth—*Shakespeare*
Poor tired Tim! It's sad for him—*De la Mare*
The Pope in Rome—*Francis*
The poplars are felled, farewell to the shade—*Cowper*
Poplars are standing there still as death—*Bontemps*
Poppa Greer happened/ down Arkansaw way—*Brown, Sterling A.*
Poppa was a sugah daddy—*Walker*
The poppy flames leap high—*Goldstein*
The popular magazines line the shelves of the drugstores—*Whittemore*
Un populu—*Buttitta*
Por aquel liron arriba—*Anonymous–Spanish*
Por aquellos prados verdes—*Anonymous–Spanish*
Por desplumar arcángeles glaciales—*Hernández, Miguel*
Por el arco de Elvira—*Garcia Lorca*
Por el East River y el Bronx—*Garcia Lorca*
Por el mes era de Mayo—*Anonymous–Spanish*
Por el pueblo ceniza—*Fuertes*
Por la calle brinca y corre—*Garcia Lorca*
Por la cima del árbol iré—*Jiménez*
Por las arboledas del Tamarit—*Garcia Lorca*
Por las mañanas—*Martí*
Por las orillas del río—*Garcia Lorca*
Por las ramas del laurel—*Garcia Lorca*
Por los campos luchados—*Hernández, Miguel*
Por los hondos caminos—*Jiménez*
Por qué volvéis a la memoria mía—*Espronceda*
Por toda la hermosura—*Juan de la Cruz*
Por un ventanal—*Machado, Antonio*
Por una mirada, un mundo—*Becquer*

Por una senda llena de amatistas y gotas—*Mantero*

Por una vereda/ venía Don Pedro—*Garcia Lorca*

Porque es áspera y fea—*Ibarbourou*

Porque son niña tus ojos/verdes—*Becquer*

Porque tú eres lo que comes, pisas, ves ante ti —*Conde*

Porte ta vie ailleurs, ô toi qui fus ma vie—*Musset*

Portes ouvertes sur les sables—*Perse*

Portitor has horrendus aquas et flumina servat —*Virgil*

The possibles we dare—*Roethke*

Postavlyu khatu i kimnatu—*Shevchenko*

Le pot de fer proposa—*La Fontaine*

Pou pege he mera he dikope pou eikhe ta panta allaxei—*Seferis*

Pour O pour that parting soul in song—*Toomer*

Pour sur, je n'aurais—*Damas*

Pour te guider ô toi que j'aime—*Apollinaire*

Pour un âne enlevé deux voleurs se battoient—*La Fontaine*

Pourquoi gémis-tu sans cesse—*Lamartine*

Pourquoi le prononcer ce nom de la patrie—*Lamartine*

Pourquoi n'allez-vous pas à Paris—*Cadou*

Pourquoi t'exiler, ô poète—*Hugo, Victor*

Pourtant tu t'en iras un jour de moi, Jeunesse—*Noailles*

Povera fijja mia! Una regazza—*Belli*

Poveryu l'ya, chtob vy khoteli—*Lermontov*

A povre widwe, somdel stope in age—*Chaucer*

Pozhar v Arkhitekturnom!—*Voznesensky*

¡El pozo! Platero—*Jiménez*

Practices brutality closing doors—*Emanuel*

Praise be to Thee, my Lord, with all Thy creatures—*Francis of Assisi*

Praise, of course, is best—*Palladas*

Praise to the end—*Wordsworth*

The praisers of women in their proud and beautiful poems—*MacLeish*

Pray but one prayer for me 'twixt thy closed lips —*Morris, William*

Pray where would lamb and lion be—*Wilkinson*

Prayer fits into any little corner of the day—*Marshall, Helen Lowrie*

A prayer is a way of lifting ourselves—*Marshall, Helen Lowrie*

Prayer is such a simple thing—*Marshall, Helen Lowrie*

Prayer, the Churche's banquet, Angels' age—*Herbert*

Le pré est vénéneux mais joli en automne—*Apollinaire*

Preacher or lecher, saint or sot—*Francis*

The preacher's coagulated rhetoric—*Antoninus*

The precise counterpart of a cacophony of bird calls—*Williams, William Carlos*

Précurseurs de l'automne, ô fruits nés d'une terre —*Chénier*

Le premier jour de May, Hélène, je vous jure—*Ronsard*

Pren ceste rose aimable comme toy—*Ronsard*

Prent plain un grant panier de vent—*Deschamps*

A présent laissez-moi, je vais seul—*Perse*

El presente es perpetuo, los mortes—*Paz*

El presentimiento es la senda del alma—*Garcia Lorca*

Presque nue et soudain sortie—*Cocteau*

The pressure of night is on her—*Wilkinson*

Presto, pronto! Two boys, two horses—*Francis*

Pretty little black girl—*Walker*

The priest and the old woman—*Ai*

Priests not only—*Blackmur*

Priez pour paix, doulce vierge Marie—*Charles d'Orleans*

La primavera besaba—*Machado, Antonio*

La primavera ha venido—*Machado, Antonio*

La primera vez—*Garcia Lorca*

Primero es un albor trémulco—*Becquer*

Primero te olvidé en tu voz—*Salinas, Pedro*

A primrose petal's edge—*Hughes, Ted*

Primus amor Phoebi Daphne Peneia, quem non —*Ovid*

Primus ibi ante omnis, magna comitante—*Virgil*

Princes, Potentates/ Warriors—*Milton*

La princesa està triste—*Darío*

A princess who lived near a bog—*Nash*

Principio quod amare velis, reperire labora—*Ovid*

Le printemps est revenu de ses lointains voyages —*Milosz*

Priroda nasha, tochno, merzost'—*Venevitinov*

A prisoner I was—*Laepa*

Prithee, Chloe, not so fast—*Oldmixon*

Priya Bachan Mridu Sunat Nripu Chityan Ankhi Udhari—*Tul'si Das*

Prodigal of loves and barbecues—*Hill*

Progressing land of peace and freedom—*Ipagongnaik*

The Prohibitionists made me Town Marshal—*Masters, Edgar Lee*

A prosperous well tailored plump—*Ciardi*

Prostim otzov ustalyiu—*Yevtushenko*

Proud men/ Eternally—*Lindsay, Vachel*

Proud of his scientific attitude—*Cummings*

Proud ships, the waves and winds conspire—*Horace*

Proudly the fedoras march on the heads of the somewhat careless men—*Sandburg*

Proust, doing penance—*Updike*

Prowling in a corridor—*Bynner*

Prüft jedes Wort—*Bienek*

Pu tan mei jyou ye gwang bei—*Wang Han*

Puccini was Latin, and Wagner Teutonic—*Nash*

Puces, amie, amantes même—*Apollinaire*

Pue pue pue/ Qu'est-ce qui pue—*Péret*

Puedo escribir los versos más tristes—*Neruda*

Pues andáis en las palmas—*Vega Carpio*

Puisque j'ai mis ma lèvre à ta coupe encor pleine —*Hugo, Victor*

Puisque mai tout en fleurs dans les prés nous réclame—*Hugo, Victor*

Puisque votre moulin tourne avec tous les vents —*Musset*

Pur tu copia versavi alma di canto—*Foscolo*

The pure products of America—*Williams, William Carlos*

The pure suit of happiness—*Swenson*

Pure? What does it mean—*Plath*

Purer than purest pure—*Cummings*

Purity/ is obscurity—*Nash*

Un puro cuerpo, tierra—*Zardoya*

Puse en el borriquete—*Jiménez*

Pussy-cat, pussy-cat, where have you been—*Children's Verses and Nursery Rhymes*

Put another nickel in—*Gaver*

Put off that mask of burning gold—*Yeats*

Put out the lights now—*Day Lewis*

Put the city up; tear the city down—*Sandburg*

Put the rubber mouse away—*Hay, Sara Henderson*

Put things in their place—*Ignatow*

Put your head darling darling—*Ferguson*

Pythagoras planned it. Why did the people stare? —*Yeats*

Quaerenti et tectis urbis sine fine furenti—*Virgil*

Quaeris, quot mihi basiationes—*Catullus*

The quaking mind, that closed and oped no more —*Pope, Alexander*

Qual rugiada o qual pianto—*Tasso*

Quale in notte solinga—*Leopardi*

Qualis Thesea iacuit cedente carina—*Propertius*

The quality of being this or that—*Cunningham, James Vincent*

The quality of mercy is not strained—*Shakespeare*

Quam' ammore se ne trase—*Filippo*

Quan la passada del vent—*Sagarra*

Quan s'acosta l'hora—*Quart*

Quand à beau Printemps je vois—*Ronsard*

Quand au mouton bêlant la sombre boucherie —*Chénier*

Quand au temple nous serons—*Ronsard*

Quand ce jeune homm' rentra chez lui—*Laforgue*

Quand elle viendra—*Milosz*

Quand il pâlit un soir, et que sa voix tremblante —*Desbordes-Valmore*

Quand je suis vingt ou trente mois—*Ronsard*

Quand je te vois passer, ô ma chère indolente —*Baudelaire*

Quand le ciel bas et lourd pèse comme un couvercle—*Baudelaire*

Quand le front de l'enfant, plein de rouges tourmentes—*Rimbaud*

Quand le soleil visite les souterrains de la nuit —*Seghers*

Quand, les deux yeux fermés, en un soir chaud —*Baudelaire*

Quand les soirs sont plus courts et que le ciel est comme—*Cadou*

Quand l'oeil aux champs est d'esclairs esblouy—*Scève*

Quand tu aimes il faut partir—*Cendrars*

Quand Un fit l'amour avec Zéro—*Queneau*

Quand vous serez bien vieille, au soir à la chandelle—*Ronsard*

Quand'io mi volgo indietro a mirar gli anni—*Petrarca*

Quando eu morrer batam em latas—*Sá-Carneiro*

Quando eu morrer quero ficar—*Andrade, Mario de*

Quando ya nada se espera personalmente exaltante—*Celaya*

Quanno loro s'incontreno, Bheatrisce—*Belli*

Quanno stammo vicine—*Di Giacomo*

Quannu passanu li fimmini—*Buttitta*

Quanta vita, si leva una voce alta di bambina—*Luzi*

Quant'è bella giovinezza—*Medici*

Quanto più m'avvicino—*Petrarca*

Quanto più moro—*Marin*

Quarter of pleasures where the rich are always waiting—*Auden*

Les quatre Cardinales—*Péguy*

A quavering cry. Screech-owl—*Hayden*

Que alegrías virgenes, campesinas—*Junqueiro*

Que beban otros las burbujas—*Mata*

Que bien sé lo que quiero—*Vivanco*

Que bien sé yo la fonte que mana y corre—*Juan de la Cruz*

Qué cuerpos leves, sutiles—*Salinas, Pedro*

Qué de noche le mataron—*Vega Carpio*

Qué descansada vida—*León, Fray Luis de*

Qué era, decidme, la nación que un día—*Quintana, Manuel José*

Qué es aquello que reluce—*Garcia Lorca*

¿Qué es poesía?—dices mientras clavas—*Becquer*

¿Qué es tu vida, alma mía? cuál tu pago—*Unamuno*

Qué goce triste este de hacer todas las cosas—*Jiménez*

Qué hacen tus ojos largos—*Storni*

Qué ilusión, esta noche—*Jiménez*

Que le Soleil est beau quand tout frais il se lève —*Baudelaire*

Que les fins de journées d'automne—*Baudelaire*

Que mi dedito lo cogió una almeja—*Mistral*

Que m'importe que tu sois sage—*Baudelaire*

Que ne ressemblons-nous aux vagueuses rivières —*Garnier*

Que no quiero verla—*Garcia Lorca*

Qué nuevas esperanzas—*Bello*

Qué pura Platero—*Jiménez*

Que quer a vento—*Couto*

Qué revuelo—*Alberti*

Qué serena va el agua—*Guillen, Jorge*

Qué sorpresa tu cuerpo, qué inefable vehemencia —*Conde*

Que ta puissance, ô Mort, est grande et admirable —*Ronsard*

Qué tengo yo que amistad procuras—*Vega Carpio*

Qué tranquilidad violeta—*Jiménez*

Que voulez-vous la porte était gardée—*Éluard*

Queen Anne, Queen Anne, has washed her lace —*Newton*

The queen bee sighed—*Sitwell, Edith*

Queene and huntresse chaste and faire—*Jonson*

Queer are the ways of a man I know—*Hardy*

Quejidos en la noche—*Villalón*

Quel est ce coeur qui me parle a l'oreille—*Fombeure*

Quel est celui d'entre vous—*Abril*

Quel fardeau te pèse, ô mon âme—*Lamartine*

Quel nonnulla di sabbia che trasorre—*Ungaretti*

Quel rossigniuol che si soave piagne—*Petrarca*

Quel vago impallidir, che 'l dolce riso—*Petrarca*

Quelle, et si fine, et si mortelle—*Valéry*

Qu'elle était belle, ma Frégate—*Vigny*

Quem nao sai da sua casa—*Lisboa, Irene*

Quem poluíu, quem rasgou os meus lencois de linho—*Pessanha*

Quem viu aquêle que se inclinou sôbre palavras trêmulas—*Meireles*

Quemaste la madrugada—*Guillén, Nicolás*

Qu'est-ce que Dieu fait donc de ce flot d'ana-
thèmes—*Baudelaire*
Qu'est ce que j'ay—*Villon*
Qu'est-ce que je suis moi Pacifique Liotrot—
Cadou
Qu'est-ce que le bonheur? Peut-être un vallon
bleu—*Jammes*
Questa, delle mie mani della voce—*Gatto*
Questa mattina, e come li portavo—*Saba*
Questa terra grigia lisciata del vento—*Luzi*
The question mark in my belly kicks me—*Ai*
Questions of tact are uppermost—*Connor*
Questo la inconscia zagaglia barbara—*Carducci*
Quhy dois your brand sae drop wi' bluid—*Anony-
mous–English—Modern English*
Qui a vu le crapaud traverser une rue—*Jacob,
Max*
Qui aimes-tu le mieux—*Baudelaire*
Qui cherche, parcourant le solitaire bond—*Mal-
larmé*
Qui dono lepidum novum libellum—*Catullus*
Qui parlait de linceul? Le bruissement des eaux
—*Seghers*
Qui pleure là, sinon le vent simple, à cette heure
—*Valéry*
Qui prêtera la parole—*Du Bellay*
Qui? Quoy? comment? à qui? pourquoy?—
Charles d'Orléans
Qui su l'arida schiena—*Leopardi*
The quick small bubbles popping the gunnysack
—*Langland, Joseph*
Quiconque a regardé le soleil fixément—*Nerval*
Quién dejará, del verde prado umbroso—*Cer-
vantes Saavedra*
Quién eres tú, Lucero misterioso—*Espronceda*
Quien fuera no me vio, me vio su sombra—*Ji-
ménez*
Quien hubiese tal ventura—*Anonymous–Spanish*
Quien menoscaba mis bienes—*Cervantes Saave-
dra*
¿Quién sufre? Pasé de prisa—*Aleixandre*
Quiero a la sombra de un ala—*Martí*
Quiero bajar al pozo—*Garcia Lorca*
Quiero morir cuando decline el día—*Gutiérrez
Nájera*
Quiero vivir, vivir, vivir—*Otero*
The quiet deepens—*Tomlinson*
Quiet room, four candles—*Durrell*
Quiet setting the rough hairy roots—*Piercy*
A quiet start/ The tavern, our small party—*Amis*
Quiete, crature mie, stateve quiete—*Belli*
Quiete, quando risorse in una trama—*Ungaretti*
Quietly O Stranger pass by—*Meleager*
La quietúd sujeto con recia mano—*Unamuno*
Qu'il parle encore que dit-il à la dérobée des
vagues—*Tzara*
Quinquireme of Nineveh—*Masefield*
Quintia formosast multis; mihi candida, longa—
Catullus
Quis cladem illius noctis, quis funera fando—*Vir-
gil*
Quis fuit, horrendos primus qui protulit enses—
Tibullus
Quis multa gracilis te puer in rosa—*Horace*
Quisiera esta tarde divina de octubre—*Storni*
Quisiera para ti ser crepúsculo mañanero—*Es-
pada Rodriguez*

Quite unexpectedly as Vasserot—*MacLeish*
Quo Life, the warld is mine—*Henderson, Hamish*
Quoi! ce n'est plus pour lui—*Desbordes-Valmore*

Rabbi Ben Levi, on the Sabbath, read—*Longfel-
low*
The rabbit has a charming face—*Anonymous—
English–Modern English*
Der Rabe Ralf—*Morgenstern*
Ein Rabe sass auf einem Meilenstein—*Morgenst-
ern*
Race of veterans, race of victors—*Whitman*
Dei rader, yugen, yugen, vus brengen zei mit zich
—*Sutzkever*
The raging river has ripped sleep—*Mackin*
The railroad bridges—*Hughes, Langston*
The railroad track is miles away—*Millay*
Rain-drops slanted down—*Conkling*
The rain falls fast pattering—*Fabio, Sarah Web-
ster*
Rain in the shoe, cold in the lung—*Kramer*
The rain is raining all around—*Stevenson*
The rain is the same—*Kavanagh*
Rain on Rahoon falls softly, softly falling—*Joyce*
Rain or hail—*Cummings*
Rain, rain, go away—*Children's Verses and Nurs-
ery Rhymes*
Rain, said the first, as it falls in Venice—*Unter-
meyer*
The rain set early in to-night—*Browning, Robert*
Rain, that wets powder—*Van Doren*
Rain thunderstorms over the Potomac—*Eberhart*
Rain, with a silver flail—*Benét, William Rose*
Raindrops falling, all around—*Butler, Celia*
Raining, raining—*Burr, Amelia Josephine*
The rains/ softly come like the cries of a—*San-
chez*
La raison du plus fort est toujours la meilleure
—*La Fontaine*
Rampart d'argent sur un champ de sinople, drag-
on—*Jarry*
Randall, my son, before you came just now—*Da-
vidson*
Rápidas manos frías—*Paz*
Rapidly cruising or lying on the air there is a bird
—*Moore, Marianne*
Rappelle-toi Barbara—*Prévert*
Die Raschelstimmen/ Blätter, Vögel, drei Wege
—*Bobrowski*
A raspberry ribbon—*Major*
Rats/ They fought the dogs and killed the cats
—*Browning, Robert*
A Raven sat upon a tree—*Carryl, Guy Wetmore*
Ravening through the persistent bric-a-brac—
Plath
Raw ulcers and his aspirin signify—*Burr, Gray*
Ray-hee-nah! Ya voy, señora! All day on the dou-
ble with her mop—*Beecher*
Razgovory vpolgolosa—*Pasternak*
Razors pain you—*Parker*
Reaching my gate, a narrow lane—*Auden*
Re-act to animals—*Lee, Don L.*
Read down into the dead and close—*Ciardi*
Read yr/ exile—*Lee, Don L.*
Reader, in your hand you hold—*MacPherson*
Reading a book of tales—*Fuller, Roy*
Reading in Li Po—*Kunitz*

Real. Cool. The Real thing We are—*Fabio, Sarah Webster*

A realm is here of masquing light—*Adams*

Really, it is not the—*Moore, Marianne*

Recalling the manicured nails on the mandolin —*Hitchcock*

Re-climbing the plateau—*Moore, Rosalie*

Reconciliation/ Word over all—*Whitman*

Rectius vives, Licini, neque altum—*Horace*

The rector's pallid neighbour at the Firs—*Graves*

Recuerdas que querías ser una Margarita—*Darío*

Recuerde el alma dormida—*Manrique*

Red barns and red heifers spot the green—*Sandburg*

Red blue green of it—*Souster*

Red lights mean danger—*Ford, M. Lucille*

The red-lipped maples still stand tall—*Goldstein*

Red lips are not so red—*Owen, Wilfred*

Red paths that wander through the gray and cells —*Derwood*

Red river, red river—*Eliot, Thomas Stearns*

The red room with the giant bed—*Stevenson*

Red rooster in your gray coop—*Conkling*

Red Rose, proud Rose, sad Rose of all my days — *Yeats*

Red rose, the crude, flat revelry has died—*Bodenheim*

The red rose whispers of passion—*O'Reilly*

Red tulips living into their death—*Levertov*

Redonnez-leur ce qui n'est plus présent en eux —*Char*

Regard the capture here, O Janus-faced—*Crane, Hart*

Regardez comme je suis beau—*Péret*

Ein Regenstrom aus Felsenrissen—*Schiller*

Regrettez-vouz le temps où le ciel sur la terre —*Musset*

Die Rehlein beten zur Nacht—*Morgenstern*

Reiss erde! reis entzwey! ihr berge brecht und decket—*Gryphius*

Reiten, reiten, reiten durch den Tag, durch die Nacht, durch den Tag—*Rilke*

Reka rashkinulas! Techet, grustit lenivo—*Blok*

Reka svyashchenneishaya v mire—*Karamzin*

Relax, Maestro. Put your baton down—*Auden*

The release itself—*Whalen*

A relentless man loved France—*Sandburg*

Relief details, Halt—*Jones, David*

Relieved I let the book fall—*Wright, James*

Remember how we used to call—*Marshall, Helen Lowrie*

Remember me when I am gone away—*Rossetti, Christina*

Remember the blackness of that flesh—*Spender*

Reminder. January is the month—*Gitlin*

Remorse is memory awake—*Dickinson, Emily*

Remote and ineffectual Don—*Belloc*

A remote male—*Elmslie*

Remote, unfriended, melancholy, slow—*Goldsmith*

Remove the barriers, clear the road—*Marshall, Helen Lowrie*

Ren sheng bu syang jyan—*Du Fu*

Renaceré yo piedra—*Jiménez*

Rends-toi, mon coeur—*Michaux*

The rent man knocked—*Hughes, Langston*

Reptilian green the wrinkled throat—*Winters*

Rest from loving and be living—*Day Lewis*

Rest lightly O Earth upon this wretched Nearchos —*Ammianus*

Restore all for me in beauty—*Anonymous–American Indian languages–Navajo*

Retain Logos—*Genser*

Reverend Butler came by—*Hughes, Langston*

Reverend Wiley advised me not to divorce him —*Masters, Edgar Lee*

Reviewing me with undue elation—*Kunitz*

The revolution does not begin—*Lester*

Rey de los hidalgos, señor de los tristes—*Darío*

The Rhino is a homely beast—*Nash*

Rhodes' slave! Selling shoes and gingham—*Masters, Edgar Lee*

The rhyme of the poet—*Emerson*

Rhythm it is we—*Kgositsile*

Ribaut, or estes vos a point—*Ruteboeuf*

The rich arrived in pairs—*Belloc*

Rich real moss-mingled earth—*Ward*

Un riche laboureur, sentant sa mort prochaine —*La Fontaine*

Ride a cock-horse to Banbury Cross—*Children's Verses and Nursery Rhymes*

Riding through Ruwu swamp, about sunrise—*Young, Francis Brett*

Rien ne m'effraye plus que la fausse accalmie—*Cocteau*

Rien ne sert de courir; il faut partir à point—*La Fontaine*

Rien n'est jamais acquis à l'homme—*Aragon*

Rien/ ni fleuve ni musique ni bête—*Lapointe*

Rigged poker-stiff on her back—*Plath*

Rimbaud and Verlaine, precious pair of poets—*Aiken*

Rime lies crisp upon the ground—*Sitwell, Osbert*

Die Rinder sind vom Schöpfer ausersehen—*Zuckmayer*

The ring-neck parrots—*Anonymous–Australasian languages–Australian*

Ring out, wild bells, to the wild sky—*Tennyson*

The ring so worn, as you behold—*Crabbe*

Ring, you bell—*Dupree*

Rings um ruhet die Stadt—*Hölderlin*

Río de cristal, dormido—*Jiménez*

El río Guadalquivir va—*Garcia Lorca*

Ripeness is all, her in her cooling planet—*Empson*

Ripensando a quel ch'oggi il ciel onora—*Petrarca*

The ripples spread through silent pool—*Spencer*

Rise heart; thy Lord is risen. Sing his praise—*Herbert*

Rissano tutto il giorno; a notte dormono—*Saba*

Ritter, treue Schwesterliebe—*Schiller*

A river glides out of the grass—*Roethke*

The river is slow—*Merwin*

A river of slush runs down through my heart—*Jeffers, Lance*

The river sucks them home—*Ormond*

The river's tent is broken; the last fingers of leaf —*Eliot, Thomas Stearns*

La rivière de ton dos—*Seghers*

Rivière trop tôt partie, d'une traite sans compagnon—*Char*

The road to success has many a turn—*Marshall, Helen Lowrie*

Roads were rougher in their island kingdom—
Roach
A roaring company that festive night—*Kunitz*
Robert Frost at midnight, the audience gone—
Lowell, Robert
The robin is a Gabriel—*Dickinson, Emily*
The robin is the one—*Dickinson, Emily*
The Rock-a-By Lady from Hushaby Street—
Field, Eugene
Rockabye love on the fire-escape—*Kramer*
The rocks dark, green as leaves—*Sward*
The rocks my people threw in Birmingham—*Jeff-
ers, Lance*
Le Roi Renaud de gai—*Anonymous-French*
Roll on, thou deep and dark blue ocean—roll—
Byron
Roman Catholic priest—*Vargas*
Roman Virgil, thou that singest—*Tennyson*
Romance, who loves to nod and sing—*Poe*
Ronyaet les bagryanii svoi ubor—*Pushkin*
Room after room/ I hunt the house through—
Browning, Robert
Room, room for a blade of the town—*Rochester,
Earl of*
The rooster is a roistering hoodlum—*Nash*
The rootless strawberry plant—*Silkin*
Rosa fresca aulentissima—c'apar inver la state—
Alcamo
La rosa le dijo al pájaro—*Martinez Alonso*
La Rosa/ no buscaba—*Garcia Lorca*
Rosa, si chiove ancora—*Di Giacomo*
La rosa temblorosa—*Jaimes Freyre*
Rosace rosace les roses—*Giguere*
Rose and Alice—*Sitwell, Edith*
The rose and the body of the rose—*O'Gorman*
Rose-cheekt Laura, come—*Campion*
Die Rose, die Lilie, die Taube, die Sonne—*Heine*
Rose is my apple watcher—*Ignatow*
Rose kissed me today—*Dobson*
Une rose pour l'amante—*Milosz*
The rose upon the wall—*Sitwell, Edith*
Rosen auf den Weg gestreut—*Hölty*
The rosy mouth and rosy toe—*Tabb*
Rosy plum-tree, think of me—*Conkling*
Roughly figured, this man of moderate habits—
Nemerov
La roulotte rouge au bord du clou—*Char*
Round the cape of a sudden came the sea—
Browning, Robert
A roundel is wrought as a ring or a star-bright
sphere—*Swinburne*
A route of evanescence with a revolving wheel
—*Dickinson, Emily*
The routine trickery of the examination—*Scott, F.
R.*
Row after row with strict impunity—*Tate, Allen*
Row us out from Desenzano, to your Sirmione
row—*Tennyson*
Royal' drozhanshchii penu s gub oblizhet—*Pas-
ternak*
'O rráu ca me piace a me—*Filippo*
Rub-a-dub-dub—*Children's Verses and Nursery
Rhymes*
The rubber penis, the wig, the false breasts—*Dur-
rell*
Ruby, short mother—*Prothro*
Rudolph Reed was oaken—*Brooks, Gwendolyn*

La rue assourdissante autour de moi—*Baudelaire*
Rühmen, das ist's! Ein zum Rühmen Bestellter
—*Rilke*
Rum Tum Tugger is a curious cat—*Eliot, Thomas
Stearns*
Run? Now you bet you; I rather guess so—*Miller,
Joaquin*
Run seaward, launch upon the air, and sound your
desolate cry—*Wheelock*
Running along a bank, a parapet—*Thomas, Ed-
ward*
Runs falls rises stumbles on from darkness into
darkness—*Hayden*
Runs like an ostrich—*Preston*
Ruppemi l'alto sonno nella testa—*Dante Aligh-
ieri*
Rus' Rus' Vizhu tebya—*Gogol*
The rush of rain against the glass—*Millay*
Rüste abendlich die Schale—*Bergengruen*

S ist Krieg! 's ist Krieg! O Gott Engel wehre—
Claudius
S poroga smotrit chelovek—*Pasternak*
Så här är det en som förskingrat—*Ferlin*
Sabe si alguna vez sus labios rojos/quema—*Bec-
quer*
Saccagé le jardin des fiançailles—*Senghor*
Sadie, Sadie—the men have all gone—*Kramer*
Saete que voladora cruza—*Becquer*
Safe in the magic of my words—*Brooke*
Safe in their alabaster chambers—*Dickinson,
Emily*
Sag Atome, sage Stäubchen—*Busch*
Sag' ich's euch, geliebte Bäume—*Goethe*
Sag', was könnt' uns Mandarinen—*Goethe*
Saget, Steine, mir an, o sprecht, ihr hohen Paläste
—*Goethe*
Sagt es niemand, nur den Weisen—*Goethe*
Sagt, wo sind die Vortrefflichen hin—*Schiller*
Sah ein Knab' ein Röslein stehn—*Goethe*
Said he: I can no longer sanction—*Beecher*
Said King Pompey the emperor's ape—*Sitwell,
Edith*
Said lady once to lover—*Yeats*
Said Myrthius, a student come from Syria—*Cava-
fy*
Said, Pull her up a bit will you, Mac, I want to
unload—*Miles*
Said the bitter Man of Thorns to me, the White-
Rose-Tree—*Sitwell, Edith*
Said the Duck to the Kangaroo—*Lear*
Said the first little chicken with a queer little
squirm—*Children's Verses and Nursery
Rhymes*
Said the lion to the lioness—*Sitwell, Edith*
Said the Undertaker to the Overtaker—*Nash*
Sail on, O Ship of State—*Longfellow*
Sailboat, your secret. With what dove-and-ser-
pent—*Francis*
Sailing into your chest—*Jong*
The sailors come ashore—*Auden*
Sailors come, to the drum—*Sitwell, Edith*
Sailor, what of the isles—*Sitwell, Edith*
St. Agnes' Eve—ah, bitter chill it was—*Keats*
St. Anthony, my father's holy man—*Ciardi*
Saint Jerome and his lion—*Moore, Marianne*
Saint Peter sat by the celestial gate—*Byron*

Saint Stephen was a clerk in King Herod's hall
—*Anonymous–English–Modern English*
Det Säjs, att han vida i världen gick—*Ferlin*
Sakta från drunknande världar—*Ferlin*
Salax taberna nosque contubernales—*Catullus*
Salesman is an it that stinks Excuse—*Cummings*
Salieri encountered Mozart, took him friendly by
the arm—*Heath-Stubbs*
Sally is gone that was so kindly—*Belloc*
Salt creek mouths unflushed by the sea—*Antoninus*
Salt of the soil and liquor of the rock—*Swenson*
The Saltimbanc is coming—*Durrell*
La saltimbanque! la saltimbanque—*Jacob, Max*
The salty spray glistens on the fence—*Yevtushenko*
Salut! bois couronnés d'un reste de verdure!—*Lamartine*
Salut, ô Belle Nuit—*Chénier*
Salve, fecunda zona—*Bello*
Salve, nec minimo puella naso—*Catullus*
The same old flights—*Lowell, Robert*
S'amor non è, che dunque è quel ch'io sento—
Petrarca
San Francisco, San Francisco, you're a muttering
bum—*Kerouac*
San Lorenzo, io lo so perché tanto—*Pascoli*
San r ru chu sya—*Wang Jyan*
Sancho-bueno, Sancho-arcilla, Sancho-pueblo—
Celaya
A sandwich and a beer—*Nemerov*
Säng naý thĭŭ dâ̂y—*Thich Nhat Hanh*
Les sanglots longs—*Verlaine*
Sank through easeful—*Hayden*
Sans cesse à mes côtés s'agite le Démon—*Baudelaire*
Santus Deo, Santus fòrtisi, che scrocchio—*Belli*
Sarah, voluptueuse et rousse—*Carco*
Sarcastic Science, she would like to know—*Frost,
Robert*
The saris go by me from the embassies—*Jarrell*
Sarolla's women in their picture hats—*Ferlinghetti*
Sassafras toned, my grandma sat—*Fabio, Sarah
Webster*
A saturated meadow—*Frost, Robert*
Saturday Night in Harlem is life drilled hollow
—*Brown, William*
Saturday sweeping—*Levine*
Säusle liebe Myrte—*Brentano*
The savage flutes of disaster—*Chapin*
Un savetier chantait du matin jusqu'au soir—*La
Fontaine*
The saws were shrieking—*Ross, W. W. Eustace*
Say not the struggle naught availeth—*Clough*
Say over again, and yet once over again—*Browning, Elizabeth Barrett*
Say that thou didst forsake me for some fault—
Shakespeare
Say the soft bird's name—*Reid*
Say this city has ten million souls—*Auden*
Say to them—*Brooks, Gwendolyn*
Says ego's ape shaking its tree—*Ciardi*
Says I be's so crazy—*Jimason*
Says she doesn't like the way you're always moving the pieces about—*Sherwin*

The scales like metal flint his feet—*Scott, Dennis*
Scarcity in oil and gas—*Giovanni*
The scene stands stubborn: skinflint trees—*Plath*
Scenfonden/ a japanskt—*Asplund*
Die Schafe ziehn wie Poeten frisiert—*Mehring*
Eine Schale des Harms, eine der Freuden wog
—*Hölty*
Schiattarella Pasquale—*Murolo*
Das Schiessgewehr schiesst, und das Spiessmesser
spiesst—*Brecht*
Schlaf, Kindlein, schlaf—*Morgenstern*
Schlaf, süsser Knabe, süss und mild—*Claudius*
Schläft ein Lied in allen Dingen—*Eichendorff*
Die Schlechten fürchten deine Klaue—*Brecht*
Schliesse mir die Augen beide—*Storm*
The Schmidts obeyed and marched on Poland
—*Gunn*
Dem Schnee, dem Regen—*Goethe*
Der schnelle Tag ist hin; die Nacht schwingt ihre
Fahn—*Gryphius*
Ein Schnupfen hockt auf der Terasse—*Morgenstern*
Die schöne Sonne/ ist ruhig hinabgestiegen—
Heine
Schöner als der beachtliche Mond—*Bachmann*
The schoolboys still their morning rambles take
—*Clare*
Schöpfe du, trage du, halte—*Werfel*
Schwarze Röcke, seidne Strümpfe—*Heine*
Schwarze Wand—*Heissenbüttel*
Schwester, Ismene, Zwillingsreis—*Brecht*
Science, true daughter of all time thou art—*Poe*
Scientists are in terror—*Pound*
Scots, wha hae wi' Wallace bled—*Burns*
Screamer, from way back you and Lynn and his
horn—*Fabio, Sarah Webster*
Screaming loose—*Fox, Charles*
Screams kicking stretched lungs out—*Pack*
A script of trees before the hill—*Wilbur*
Sculptured rock with windows—*Fox, Charles*
Scusate, sapite l'ammore ched'è?—*Filippo*
Sdelan shag—*Martynov*
Se Deus me leixe de vos bem aver—*Sancho*
Se fra' pochi mortali a cui negli anni—*Foscolo*
Se lamentar augelli, O verdi fronde—*Petrarca*
Se le vvorzuta lui—*Belli*
Se leggi questi versi e se in profondo—*Saba*
Se me quedó en lo hondo—*Alonso*
Se me vá de los dedos—*Storni*
Se p' ffregà Ppiazza-Navona mia—*Belli*
Se passares pelo adro—*Botto*
Se querian/ sufrían por la luz—*Aleixandre*
Se ven desde las barandas—*Garcia Lorca*
Se voi sapeste, l'Italia—*Gatto*
The sea at evening moves across the sand—*Prince*
The sea begins, far out beyond the light—
Mountzoures
Sea-blue of gentian/ Blackberries—*Conkling*
The sea cries with its meaningless voice—*Hughes,
Ted*
The sea grieves—*Hughes, Ted*
The sea is a wilderness of waves—*Hughes, Langston*
The sea is awash with roses—*Patchen*
The sea is calm tonight—*Arnold*
The sea is full of fishes in shoals—*Stevens, Wallace*
The sea is never still—*Sandburg*

The sea retains such images—*Dudek*

The sea shines. Wind-raked, the waters run light —*Ciardi*

The Sea—turn yr Back on—*Olson*

The sea-wash never ends—*Sandburg*

Sea waves are green and wet—*Frost, Robert*

The sea will wash in—*Williams, William Carlos*

Sea-wind and the sea's irregular rhythm—*Wheelock*

A seal swims like a poodle—*Lowell, Robert*

The seals at play off Western Isle—*Eberhart*

The seals in Penobscot Bay/ hadn't heard of the atom bomb—*Hoffman*

Seamen three! What men be ye?—*Peacock*

Seamstress of my night's sweet lace—*Jeffers, Lance*

Searching for a lost address I find—*Scannell*

Searching my heart for its true sorrow—*Millay*

Searching once I found a flower—*Eberhart*

Searching past what we see and hear—*Kgositsile*

The seas where once I swam as slick as herring —*MacPherson*

Season of mists and mellow fruitfulness—*Keats*

The season's anguish, crashing whirlwind—*Gascoyne*

The seasons revolve and the years change—*Rexroth*

A seated statue of himself he seems—*Francis*

The secret of these hills was stone and cottages —*Spender*

The secret word for change is hurt—*Shpunt*

Secrets, you said, would hold us two apart—*Parker*

See America first—*Hodges*

See him, the gentle Bible beast—*Muir*

See how the flower—*Treece*

See how the lake, less active now, is silent—*Patten*

See how this girl, trim—*Davison, Peter*

See/it was like this when—*Ferlinghetti*

See the lightning leaping in the sky—*Stephens*

See this one, tiptoe on—*Day Lewis*

See what a lovely shell—*Tennyson*

See! with what constant Motion—*Lovelace, Richard*

See with what simplicity—*Marvell*

See you the ferny ride that steals—*Kipling*

Seeds in a dry pod, tick tick tick—*Masters, Edgar Lee*

Seedy Henry rose up shy in de world—*Berryman*

Seems like to me there be two kinds of people in this world—*Dupree*

Seen when night is silent—*Auden*

Según dicen, ya usted tiene otro amante—*Buesa*

Die Sehnsucht glüht in ihrem nächtigen Blick —*Trakl*

Sehr tadelnswert ist unser tun—*Busch*

Seht auf, ihr Männer. Männer dort am Feuer— *Rilke*

Seht den Felsenquell—*Goethe*

Sei ancora quello della pietra e della fionda— *Quasimodo*

Sei dennoch unverzagt! Gib dennoch unverloren —*Fleming*

Seigneur, c'est aujourd'hui le jour de votre Nom —*Cendrars*

Seigneur, je suis très fatigué—*Tirolien*

Seigneur, l'aube a glissé froide comme un suaire —*Cendrars*

Sein Blick ist im Vorübergehn der Stäbe—*Rilke*

Die Selbstkritik hat viel für sich—*Busch*

Self reliance—*Moore, Marianne*

Selig sind die Auserwählten—*Busch*

Selig, welchen die Götter, die gnädigen, vor der Geburt schon liebten—*Schiller*

Sempre caro mi fu quest'ermo colle—*Leopardi*

Sempre un villaggio, sempre una campagna— *Pascoli*

Sencilla semilla: Tú tendrás mañana una lírica cabellera obscura—*Martinez Alonso*

Send Antipatra naked to meet the Parthian cavalry—*Ammonides*

Send for the Pied Piper and let him pipe the rats away—*Hughes, Langston*

Senescence begins/ and middle age ends—*Nash*

Senhor, a estrêla que me destinaste—*Ricardo*

S'enlaçaient les domaines voûtés d'une aurore grise—*Éluard*

Señor, en breve llegará a tu cielo una tímida y dulce viejecita—*Dávila, José Antonio*

Señor, nunca me des lo que te pida—*Nalé-Roxlo*

Señor, tú sabes cómo, con encendido brío—*Mistral*

Señor, ya me arrancaste lo que yo más quería— *Machado, Antonio*

Señora, buenos días; señor, muy buenos días— *Barba Jacob*

Señora, la conosco, donde vive—*Alberti*

La señora Zapatera—*Garcia Lorca*

La señorita/ del abanico—*Garcia Lorca*

Señorito! Señorito! Mayor ofensa no cabe—*Cavestany*

The sensuality of women at Mass: that deceptive —*Antoninus*

Sento l'aura mia antica e i dolci colli—*Petrarca*

September. The small summer hangs its suns— *Norris*

Sér de inmensa bondad, Dios poderoso—*Valdés*

The seraph ascends—*Barker, George*

The serene green worm eating the green—*Darr*

Serene the silver fishes glide—*Eastman*

Le sergent s'en revient de guerre—*Fombeure*

Service is joy, to see or swing—*Avison*

Service, or Latin sorbus, European—*Davie*

A serving man. Curled my hair—*Gunn*

Set me whereas the sun doth parch the green —*Surrey*

Set where the upper streams of Simois flow—*Arnold*

Setebos, Setebos, and Setebos—*Browning, Robert*

Settembre, andiamo. È tempo di migrare—*D'Annunzio, Gabriele*

A settlement of love is what I'd risk—*Garrigue*

Setze mir ein Denkmal, cher—*Morgenstern*

Seu olhar se fechou para êste mundo—*Schmidt*

Ein Seufzer lief Schlittschuh auf nächtlichem Eis —*Morgenstern*

Seul dans une âme ample j'ai vu se perdre—*Tzara*

Seulette suis, et seulette veuil estre—*Pisan*

Seven days he travelled—*Drinkwater*

Seven ladies/ and seventeen gentlemen— *Hughes, Langston*

Seven white roses on one tree—*Swinburne*

Sevilla es una torre—*Garcia Lorca*

Sex. I am the unlicked spickum—*Gaver*

Shack, shack maka—*Wallace*

Shadow-love and shadow-kisses—*Heine*

The shadow of a pine-branch quivered—*Gunn*

Shadows of a winter afternoon—*Robson, Jeremy*

The shadows where the Mewlips dwell—*Tolkien*

Shake, shake—*Sherwin*

Shall I be your first love—*Beddoes*

Shall I compare thee to a summer's day—*Shakespeare*

Shall I die shall I die—*Sanchez*

Shall I love God for causing me to be—*Wilbur*

Shall I, wasting in despair—*Wither*

Shall we die, both thou and I—*Anonymous–English–Modern English*

Shan nyan ting yu ge lou shang—*Jyang Jye*

Shau syan li syang lau da hwei—*He Jr Jang*

The sharrot scudders nights in the quastron now—*Nash*

The shattered water made a misty din—*Frost, Robert*

She bade the moon stand still—*Sandburg*

She being Brand—*Cummings*

She came in from the snowing air—*Spender*

She came to the village church—*Tennyson*

She charged me with having said this and that—*Hardy*

She couldn't quote french poetry—*Lee, Don L.*

She didn't like to think in abstracts—*Giovanni*

She died in the upstairs bedroom—*Betjeman*

She does not know her beauty—*Cuney*

She doesn't wear—*Lee, Don L.*

She done put her little hands—*Brown, Sterling A.*

She dreams she is chased by a black—*Durrell*

She drove in the dark to leeward—*Hopkins*

She dwelt among the untrodden ways—*Wordsworth*

She even thinks that up in heaven—*Cullen*

She fears him, and will always ask—*Robinson, Edwin Arlington*

She fell asleep on Christmas Eve—*Rossetti, Dante Gabriel*

She flies—*Napier*

She grew up in bedeviled southern wilderness—*Hayden*

She has gone from us; never as she was will she return—*Anonymous–Australasian languages–Australian*

She has gone, she has left us in passion and pride—*Holmes, Oliver Wendell*

She, in the drapery of shadow I forgive—*Stone, Ruth*

She is afraid of tornadoes—*Howard, Lee*

She is as in a field a silken tent—*Frost, Robert*

She is dozing—*Baldwin, Deirdra*

She is like pearls, of course—*Summers, Hollis*

She is no liar, yet she will wash away—*Graves*

She is now water and air—*Eberhart*

She is the sky of the sun—*Stephens*

She issues radiant from her dressing-room—*Meredith, George*

She keeps kingfishers in their cages—*Patten*

She kept an antique shop—or it kept her—*Jennings*

She laughed when they cut off—*Flanders*

She left the front gate open—*Shange*

She let her golden ball fall down the well—*Graves*

She lies on her left side her flank golden—*MacLeish*

She lived in storm and strife—*Yeats*

She looked like a bird from a cloud—*Hardy*

She looked over his shoulder—*Auden*

She loved me. Oh! how she loved me—*Masters, Edgar Lee*

She might, so noble from head—*Yeats*

She often wondered why people spoke—*Giovanni*

She opened the door of the West to me—*Hardy*

She packs the flower beds with leaves—*Levine*

She realized—*Giovanni*

She sang beyond the genius of the sea—*Stevens, Wallace*

She sighs. What shall I say—*Simpson*

She skimmed the yellow water like a moth—*Wright, James*

She sleeps on soft, last breaths; but no ghost looms—*Owen, Wilfred*

She sought a blessing in the snow—*Wilkinson*

She stood breast-high amid the corn—*Hood*

She stood nakedly—*Lee, Don L.*

She stripped herself of all—*Ciardi*

She, then, like snow in a dark night—*Graves*

She troubles the waters, and they part and close—*Meredith, George*

She walks a beach assaulted by the sea—*Booth*

She walks alone by the river—*Patten*

She walks in beauty like the night—*Byron*

She walks—the lady of my delight—*Meynell*

She wanted to be a blade—*Giovanni*

She was a phantom of delight—*Wordsworth*

She was not exactly a doll—*Conkling*

She was sitting on the rough embankment—*Yevtushenko*

She went to buy a brand new hat—*Cullen*

She will change, I cried—*Yeats*

She would not leap for joy—*O'Gorman*

A shepherd boy comes down from the hill—*Dowling*

A shepherd stands at one end of the arena—*Day Lewis*

The shepherds went their hasty way—*Coleridge, Samuel Taylor*

Sherwood in the twilight, is Robin Hood awake?—*Noyes*

She's been a good daughter, my cousin Elaine—*Viorst*

She's the camera's—*Lee, Don L.*

The shifty limpet on his rocky shore—*Brinnin*

Shines/ in the mind of heaven—*Pound*

Shiny record albums scattered over—*Knight, Etheridge*

Ship/ house on the water—*Brathwaite*

Shoichi brushed the black—*Stryk*

Shot? So quick, so clean an ending?—*Housman*

The shot, the horse—*Myers*

A shot-up forest full of black holes—*Yevtushenko*

Should auld acquaintance be forgot—*Burns*

Should every creature be as I have been—*Roethke*

Should lanterns shine the holy face—*Thomas, Dylan*

Should the building totter, run for an archway—*Graves*

The shouts shrink—*Randall*
Show me again the time—*Hardy*
Show me deare Christ, thy spouse so bright and cleare—*Donne*
Shr sau syung nu bu gu shen—*Chen Dau*
A shrimp who sought his lady shrimp—*Nash*
Shudderin' thistle, gi'e owre, gi'e owre—*MacDiarmid*
Shuffle-shoon and Amber-locks—*Field, Eugene*
Shum, shum, bang, bang—*Gaver*
Shut not so soon; the dull-ey'd night—*Herrick*
Shut, shut the door, good John—*Pope, Alexander*
Shut up, Shut up. There's nobody here—*Graham, William Sydney*
Si al mecer las azules campanillas—*Becquer*
Si de nuestros agravios—*Becquer*
Si Dios algún día cegara toda fuente de luz—*Hernández, José P. H.*
Si Dios dijera: ven acá Juancho, díme qué quieres—*Botero*
Si drömmaren kommer där—*Fröding*
Si dummeneca è bon tiempo—*Sobecks*
Si el món ja és tan formós, Senyor, si es mira—*Maragall*
Sí: en tu cerca ruín, qué desordena—*Jiménez*
Si es el blanco el color—*Abu-l-Hasan al-Husri, "el ciego"*
S'i fosse foco, arderei 'l mondo—*Angiolieri*
Si je mourais là-bas sur le front de l'armée—*Apollinaire*
Si je vous dis: j'ai tout abandonné—*Éluard*
Si je vous dis que le soleil dans la forêt—*Éluard*
Si je vous le disais pourtant que je vous aime—*Musset*
Si la nieve me ordena—*Vivanco*
Si ma voix, que me doit bientôt pousser au nombre—*Jodelle*
Si me preguntais—*Neruda*
Si mi voz muriera en tierra—*Alberti*
Si mme vo bbene? povero Cammillo—*Belli*
Si muero/ dejad el balcón abierto—*Garcia Lorca*
Si nostre vie est moins qu'une journée—*Du Bellay*
Si percorre il deserto con residui—*Ungaretti*
Si qui forte mearum ineptiarum—*Catullus*
Si quoi quid cupido optantique opigit umquam—*Catullus*
Si scopron le tombe, si levano i morti—*Mercantini*
Si solamente me tocaras el corazón—*Neruda*
Si souvent mon sentiment de race m'effraie—*Damas*
Si su belleza en mí morir pudiera—*Jiménez*
Si t' 'o ddico nun me cride—*Filippo*
Si ton coeur, gémissant du poids de notre vie—*Vigny*
Si toutes les filles du monde—*Fort*
Si tu t'imagines—*Queneau*
Si tu vas dans le bois—*Desnos*
Si vas de prisa—*Jiménez*
Sí, venid a mis brazos, palomitas de hierro—*Florit*
Si ves un monte de espumas—*Martí*
Si volge verso l'est l'ultimo amore—*Ungaretti*
Si vous cherchez une lanterne sourde—*Lasnier*
Si vous croyez que je vais dire—*Musset*
Si yo, por ti, he creado un mundo para ti—*Jiménez*

Si yo supiera de que selva vino—*Ibarbourou*
Sick, am I sick of a jealous dread?—*Tennyson*
Sick of the piercing company of women—*Kinsella*
Sick with the lightning lay my sister-in-law—*Berryman*
Side by side, their faces blurred—*Larkin*
Sidish', blednaya—*Voznezensky*
Sie hat nichts und du desgleichen—*Busch*
Sie ist ein reizendes Geschöpfchen—*Busch*
Sie machte Frieden! Das ist mein Gedicht—*Claudius*
Sie rühmen sich ihrer dreifachen Verderbtheit—*George*
Sie sassen und tranken am Teetisch—*Heine*
Sie stritten sich beim Wein herum—*Busch*
Sie trafen sich, wie ehemals—*Kästner*
Sie tragen die Büsten und Nasen—*Kästner*
Sie trug den Becher in der Hand—*Hofmannsthal*
Sie waren so sehr ineinander verliebt—*Kästner*
Sieben Jahre wollt kein Schritt mir glücken—*Brecht*
Sieben kleine Bären—*Guggenmos*
Sieh die Sterne, die Fänge—*Benn*
Sieh jene Kraniche im grossen Bogen—*Brecht*
Siehe wie schwebenden Schritts im Wellenschwung—*Schiller*
Siehst du auf Bildern in den Galerien—*Benn*
Siempre al ponerse en camino—*Ascasubi*
Siempre andaba retobao—*Hernández, José*
Siempre es el mar donde mejor se quiere—*Blanco*
Siempre es todo ojos—*Alberti*
Siempre te ven mis ojos, ciudad de mis días marinos—*Aleixandre*
Siempre tienes la rama preparada—*Jiménez*
Siena mi fe: disfecemi Maremma—*Pound*
Sigh no more Ladies, sigh no more—*Shakespeare*
Sighed and lay down—*Den Boer*
A sight in camp in the daybreak gray and dim—*Whitman*
Signa recordanti benefacta priora voluptas—*Catullus*
Signe guitarra tocando—*Garcia Lorca*
Signorina Felicità a quest'ora—*Gozzano*
Silence, and stealth of dayes! 'tis now—*Vaughan, Henry*
Silence is the pulling in of nets—*O'Gorman*
Silence. The man defined—*Tomlinson*
Silence, words into foolishness fading—*Graves*
Silencio de cal y mirto—*Garcia Lorca*
Silencio que naufraga en el silencio—*Hernández, Miguel*
El silencio redondo de la noche—*Garcia Lorca*
Silencio y paz—*Santos Chocano*
Silent are the woods, and the dim green boughs are—*Masefield*
Silent is the house: all are laid asleep—*Brontë, Emily*
Silkesblå, Tyrrkenska vågar hag jar sett—*Asplund*
Silly boy, 'tis full moon yet; thy night as day shines clearly—*Campion*
Silver bark of beech, and sallow—*Millay*
A silver-scaled dragon with jaws flaming red—*Smith, William Jay*
The silver spoons were warbling—*Jong*

Silvia, rimembri ancora—*Leopardi*

Simelos the harper played a night-long recital—*Leonidas the Alexandrian*

Simon Danz has come home again—*Longfellow*

The simple Bard, unbroken by rules of art—*Burns*

A simple nosegay! was that much to ask—*Graves*

Simple Simon met a pieman going to the fair—*Children's Verses and Nursery Rhymes*

The simple words and gestures—*Bodenheim*

Simultaneously, as soundlessly—*Auden*

Sin arrimo y con arrimo—*Juan de la Cruz*

Sin of self-love possesseth all mine eye—*Shakespeare*

Sin saber qué hacer de mi—*Hernández, José*

Since brass, nor stone, nor earth, nor boundless sea—*Shakespeare*

Since feeling is first—*Cummings*

Since I am coming to that Holy roome—*Donne*

Since I left you, mine eye is in my mind—*Shakespeare*

Since men grow diffident at last—*Cullen*

Since poetry is made of language, let's make language move—*Ginsberg*

Since Reverend Doctors now declare—*Hardy*

Since she whom I lov'd hath payd her last debt—*Donne*

Since the wise men have not spoken, I speak—*Pearse*

Since there's no help, come let us kiss and part—*Drayton*

Since this ingenious earth began—*McGinley*

Sind denn dir nicht verwandt alle Lebendigen—*Hölderlin*

Sind die Muskeln straff gespannt—*Wedekind*

Sing a song of sixpence—*Children's Verses and Nursery Rhymes*

Sing, Ariel, sing—*Auden*

Sing, ballad singer, raise a hearty tune—*Hardy*

Sing your song to Jesus—*Murphy*

The singers are gone from the Cornmarketplace—*Hardy*

Singet leise, leise, leise—*Brentano*

Singing, as she always must—*Mitchell, Adrian*

Singing her crazy song the mother goes—*Masefield*

Singing my days—*Whitman*

Singing today I married my white girl—*Abse*

A single flow'r he sent me, since we met—*Parker*

The single power, working alone—*Dudek*

The sinking sun is taking leave—*Clare*

Sipping whiskey and gin—*Randall*

Sir! No sir, yes sir, Middle Watch Relief, sir—*Jones, David*

A siren sang, and Europe turned away—*Simpson*

Les sirènes miaulent et se taisent—*Cendrars*

Sirocco brings the minor devils—*Auden*

Sister Anne, Sister Anne—*Bishop, John Peale*

Sister, I saw it today—*Sanchez*

Sit procul omne nefas; ut ameris amabilis esto—*Ovid*

Sit tibi Callimachi, sit Coi nota poetae—*Ovid*

Sitting here in the night with—*La Farge*

Sitting in his dentist's waiting room—*Bly*

The six-foot nest of the sea hawk—*Eberhart*

The six quart basket/ one side gone—*Souster*

Six summers old was she, and when she came—*Davies, William Henry*

Sixty thousand faces go dark on the Strip—*Barker, Richard*

Siyala noch'—*Fet*

Sjösorlen hugga byigt i bankama—*Martinson*

The skies they were ashen and sober—*Poe*

Skimming lightly, wheeling still—*Melville*

Skimrande vitt som det vitaste silver var vattnet—*Ferlin*

The skin of the sea has nothing to tell me—*Jong*

Skinful of bowls, he bowls them—*Hughes, Ted*

The skinny waterfalls, footpaths wandering out of heaven—*Kinnell*

Skipping by the pretty—*Anderson, Doug*

Sklave, wer wird dich befreien—*Brecht*

En skolflicka sitter och ritar—*Asplund*

Skön, med lågande hy och slutna ögon—*Stagnelius*

The sky above us here is open again—*Van Doren*

Sky and sea, horizon-hinged—*Plath*

The sky is low, the clouds are mean—*Dickinson, Emily*

Sky, mountains, river, winds, lake, lightnings!—*Byron*

The sky seemed so small that winter day—*Stevens, Wallace*

Skyd frem, Skovmaerke—*Andersen*

Sleep and between the closed eyelids of sleep—*Aiken*

Sleep, angry beauty, sleep, and fear not me—*Campion*

Sleep, child, lie quiet, let be—*Agee*

Sleep, grandmother, sleep—*Van Doren*

Sleep, little pigeon, and fold your wings—*Field, Eugene*

Sleep, O sleep—*Gay, John*

Sleep softly . . . eagle forgotten—*Lindsay, Vachel*

Sleep sweetly in your humble graves—*Timrod*

Sleepe, silence' Child—*Drummond of Hawthornden*

The sleepers are very beautiful as they lie unclothed—*Whitman*

Sleeping at last, the trouble and tumult over—*Rossetti, Christina*

The sleepy sound of a tea-time tide—*Betjeman*

A slight-boned animal, young. What jungle fruit—*Deutsch*

Slim Greer went to heaven—*Brown, Sterling A.*

Slippers he made me—*Broughton*

Slipping in blood, by his own hand, through pride—*Bogan*

Slow down the film. You see that bit—*Mitchell, Adrian*

Slow, slow, fresh fount, keep time with my salt tears—*Jonson*

Slowly, silently, now the moon—*De la Mare*

Slowly the poison the whole blood stream fills—*Empson*

Slowly they approach—*Robson, Jeremy*

A slumber did my spirit seal—*Wordsworth*

The slurred and drawled and crooning sounds—*MacNeice*

The small minds of birds—*Van Doren*

The small wax candles melt to light—*Heaney*

Smallmans definitely there 1721—*Olson*

The smell of the heath is box wood—*Williams, William Carlos*

Smělým zásahem—*Holub*

Smiling, he says no man should fear the tomb—*Abse*

Smith is dead, Sir! Killed yesterday after school—*Ennis*

A smith makes me—*Kipling*

Smooth it slides upon its travel—*Stevenson*

The snail pushes through a green—*Gunn*

A snake came to my water-trough—*Lawrence*

The snake trying/ to escape—*Ross, W. W. Eustace*

Snart är du död och vet ej att du glider—*Lagerkvist*

Snorting his pleasure in the dying sun—*Howes*

The snow—*Marvin X*

A snow can come as quietly—*Coatsworth*

Snow falling and night falling fast, oh fast—*Frost, Robert*

Snow fell forward forever—*Levine*

The snow had begun in the gloaming—*Lowell, James Russell*

Snow in Connecticut is thatched—*Bishop, John Peale*

The snow is deep on the ground—*Patchen*

The snow lies thick on Valley Forge—*Kipling*

Snow seeds the air—*Gibson, Margaret*

The snows of February had buried Christmas—*Graves*

So Abram rose, and clave the wood—*Owen, Wilfred*

So all day long the noise of battle roll'd—*Tennyson*

So am I as the rich, whose blessed key—*Shakespeare*

So are you to my thoughts as food to life—*Shakespeare*

So bandit-eyed, so undovelike a bird—*Francis*

So crossing the river—*Brathwaite*

So cruel prison—*Surrey*

So did we pray: and took arms—*MacLeish*

So die Bluomen ûz dem Grase dringent—*Walther von der Vogelweide*

So dream thy sails, O phantom bark—*Crane, Hart*

So drum skin whip lash master sun's—*Brathwaite*

So fallen, so lost! the light withdrawn—*Whittier*

So far as our story approaches the end—*Browning, Robert*

So, Fortinbras; Alas is now the keyword here—*MacNeice*

So gern hätt ich ein schönes Lied gemacht—*Droste-Hülshoff*

So hast du ganz und gar vergessen—*Heine*

So help me, Love, you and I—*Bell*

So I am you darling girl—*Philodemos the Epicurean*

So, I have seen a man killed—*Clough*

So I say that we are enclosed—*Sklarew*

So I take one of those thin plates—*Redgrove*

So in the end he who had seined rivers—*Engle*

So in this tilted alleyway—*Brathwaite*

Só, incessante, um som de flauta chora—*Pessanha*

So intricately is this world resolved—*Kunitz*

So is it not with me as with that Muse—*Shakespeare*

So ist die Lieb'! So ist die Lieb'—*Mörike*

So ist's in alter Zeit gewesen—*Busch*

So it is come to this—*Sexton*

So light we were, so right we were—*Brooke*

So long/ so far away—*Hughes, Langston*

So many moral matters, and so little used—*Skelton, John*

So many seeds the cotton breeds—*Brathwaite*

So many selves (so many fiends and gods—*Cummings*

So much depends—*Williams, William Carlos*

So much have I forgotten in ten years—*McKay*

So muss dein Fluch den Himmel schliessen—*Gryphius*

So Norman Nicholson is dead—*Nicholson*

So, now I have confess'd that he is thine—*Shakespeare*

So oft as I her beauty do behold—*Spenser*

So oft have I invok'd thee for my Muse—*Shakespeare*

So oft in the hemlock wood—*Hillyer*

So oft sie kam, erschien mir die Gestalt—*Lenau*

So, on the bloody sand, Sohrab lay dead—*Arnold*

So on the seventh day—*Hughes, Ted*

So promised he, and Uriel to his charge—*Milton*

So schlafe nun, du Kleine—*Claudius*

So shall I live, supposing thou art true—*Shakespeare*

So shy shy shy (and with a—*Cummings*

So, so, breake off this last lamenting kisse—*Donne*

So spake our Morning Star then in his rise—*Milton*

So spake the Son, and into terror changed—*Milton*

So sprach das Fleisch zu allen Zeiten—*Benn*

So sweet is thy discourse to me—*Campion*

So sweet the plum trees smell—*Porter, William*

So that the vines burst from my fingers—*Pound*

So the church Christ was hit and buried—*Owen, Wilfred*

So the Committee met again, and again—*Day Lewis*

So the strong will prevailed, and Alden went on his errand—*Longfellow*

So the touch—*Rossman*

So then you won't fight—*Michie*

So there stood Matthew Arnold and this girl—*Hecht*

So Thomas Edison—*Nash*

So to New York London/ I finally come—*Brathwaite*

So to these tulip buds—*Jeffers, Lance*

So we ride through milked heaven above earth—*Derwood*

So, we'll go no more a-roving—*Byron*

So wie das letzte Grün in Farbentiegeln—*Rilke*

So wird der Schrecken ohne Ende langsam—*Born, Nicolas*

So you have seen them—*Brathwaite*

So your idol of gold—that wondrous one—*Marshall, Helen Lowrie*

So you've a dream—well, so have I—*Marshall, Helen Lowrie*

So zestfully canst thou sing?—*Hardy*

A soapship went a-rocking—*Emanuel*

The sober journal that I read—*Nash*

Sobre el cielo negro—*Garcia Lorca*

Sobre el monte pelado—*Garcia Lorca*

Sobre él, olivar—*Machado, Antonio*

Sobre la falda tenía el libro abierto—*Becquer*

Sobre la reverberación de la pared—*Paz*

Sobre su nombre y nacimiento—*Valverde*

A sodger laddie's socht a hoose—*MacDiarmid*

Les soeurs, comme un cheval, nous savent la main mordre—*Cocteau*

Soeurs des guerriers d'Assur—*Perse*

Le sofa sur lequel Hassan était couché—*Musset*

Soft found a way to damn me—*Cunningham, James Vincent*

Soft rainsqualls on the swells—*Snyder*

Soft, soft, soft is her gazing—*Van Doren*

Soft songs, like birds—*Knight, Etheridge*

A soft wind/ off the stones of the dead—*Levine*

Softly, in the dusk, a woman is singing to me—*Lawrence*

Softly now—*MacManus*

The soil, flinty at best, grew sour—*Day Lewis*

The soil was deep and the field well-sited—*Day Lewis*

Un soir de demi-brume à Londres—*Apollinaire*

Le soir ramène le silence—*Lamartine*

Sois-moi fidèle, ô pauvre habit que j'aime—*Béranger*

Sois sage, ô ma douleur, et tiens-toi plus tranquille—*Baudelaire*

Sol de medio día. Castilla se abrasa—*Mesa*

Sol deroppe ganger under Lide—*Andersen*

Sol, inventario de color—*Escudero*

Sola me estoy en mi cama—*Anonymous-Spanish*

Sola mo te ne vaie, povera Rosa—*Di Giacomo*

Solcata ho fronte, occhi incavati intenti—*Foscolo*

Soldier and statesman, rarest unison—*Lowell, James Russell*

Soldier, in a curious land—*Parker*

A soldier passed me in the freshly-fallen snow—*Read, Herbert*

Soldier, rest! Thy warfare o'er—*Scott, Sir Walter*

Sole pride and loneliness: it is the state—*Aiken*

Soleil, je t'adore comme les sauvages—*Cocteau*

Le soleil prolongeait sur la cime des tentes—*Vigny*

Le soleil que sa halte—*Mallarmé*

Soleil route usée pierres frémissantes—*Péret*

Solemnly mine, Universal man—*Fabio, Cyril Leslie III*

Solemnly, mournfully—*Longfellow*

Soll i aus meim Hause raus?—*Morgenstern*

Solo e pensoso i più deserti campi—*Petrarca*

Solo el olor de unas flores—*Jiménez*

Solo ho amica la notte—*Ungaretti*

Sólo lo hiciste un momento—*Jiménez*

Sólo tu corazón caliente—*Garcia Lorca*

Solstice of the dark, the absolute—*Antoninus*

The solution will come—*Deveaux*

Solvitur acris hiems grata vice veris et favoni—*Horace*

Som klippt i sotat papper—*Bergman, Bo*

Som människan måste du sträcka—*Blomberg*

La sombra de mi alma huye por un ocaso—*Garcia Lorca*

Sombras que sólo yo veo—*Guillén, Nicolás*

Some acts I could never, not—*Bell*

Some are teethed on a silver spoon—*Cullen*

Some candle clear burns somewhere I come by—*Hopkins*

Some claim that pianists are human—*Nash*

Some day I shall die—*Abrams*

Some day soon this rhyming volume, if you learn with proper speed—*Stevenson*

Some day/ when the great clock—*Van Doren*

Some day, when trees have shed their leaves—*McKay*

Some days before death—*Betjeman*

Some days my thoughts are just cocoons—*Baker, Karle Wilson*

Some fish are minnows—*Nash*

Some for everyone—*Swenson*

Some glory in their birth, some in their skill—*Shakespeare*

Some gone like boys to school wearing their badges—*Ciardi*

Some hae meat and canna eat—*Burns*

Some keep the Sabbath going to Church—*Dickinson, Emily*

Some lucky day each November great waves awake and are drawn—*Jeffers, Robinson*

Some men live for warlike deeds—*Benét, Stephen Vincent*

Some of it I've—*Lifshin*

Some of you may know, others perhaps can guess—*Graves*

Some of you will be glad I did what I did—*Frost, Robert*

Some one has built a dirigible in my parlor—*Glaze*

Some one is always sitting there—*De la Mare*

Some people hang portraits up—*Browning, Robert*

Some people slowly acquire a healthy glowing complexion—*Nash*

Some primal termite knocked on wood—*Nash*

Some say that ever 'gainst that season comes—*Shakespeare*

Some say the world will end in fire—*Frost, Robert*

Some say thy fault is youth, some wantonness—*Shakespeare*

Some sway for long and then decline—*Eberhart*

Some tails wiggle—*Jacobs*

Some that have deeper digg'd loves myne than I—*Donne*

Some thing is lost in me—*Lee, Don L.*

Some things, by their affinity light's token—*Gunn*

Some time now past in the autumned tide—*Bradstreet*

Some times I dream bout u & me—*Sanchez*

Some where on his travels the strange Child—*Nemerov*

Some where, some when I've seen—*Gibson, Wilfred*

Some years ago you heard me sing—*Belloc*

Someday I'll go to Winnipeg—*Lee, Dennis*

Someone came knocking at my wee, small door—*De la Mare*

Someone had been walking in and out—*Patchen*

Someone's already—*Lifshin*

Something about standing—*Colbert*

Something all our own—*Fabio, Sarah Webster*

Something befell—*Untermeyer*

Something has ceased to come along with me—*Silkin*

Something in the wild cherry—*Ciardi*

Something inspires the only cow of late—*Frost, Robert*

Something is breaking loose—*Emanuel*

Something is taking place—*Gunn*

Something lies beyond the scene, the encre de chine—*Sitwell, Edith*

Something there is that doesn't love a wall—*Frost, Robert*

Something to live for—this the need—*Marshall, Helen Lowrie*

Something was marred in making at her birth —*Lewis, Janet*

Sometimes Billy rides in—*Hobbs*

Sometimes/ a night funeral—*Hughes, Langston*

Sometimes I feel like I will never stop—*Allen, Samuel*

Sometimes I go about the street—*Katzman*

Sometimes I have supposed seals—*Lowell, Robert*

Sometimes I think the hills—*Field, Rachel*

Sometimes, riding in a car, in Wisconsin—*Bly*

Sometimes seeds sown in seasons—*Marshall, Helen Lowrie*

Sometimes the foundering fury that directs—*Ciardi*

Sometimes you hear a question—*Giovanni*

Sometimes you know—*Gaver*

Sometyme the worlde was so stedfast and stable —*Chaucer*

somewhere i have never travelled, gladly beyond —*Cummings*

Somewhere in a turret in time—*Hacker*

Somewhere there was a piano playing—*Giovanni*

¡Somos islas! Islas verdes—*Lloréns Torres*

Son, braggart and thrasher—*Layton*

A son can make a father—*Brown, Otis*

Son forse un poeta? No, certo—*Palazzeschi*

Son las diez de la mañana—*Celaya*

Son, said my mother—*Millay*

Són tres fadrins que han vingut a la vila—*Sagarra*

A song in the valley of Nemea—*Durrell*

The song of canaries—*Nash*

A song of enchantment I sang me there—*De la Mare*

A song of the rolling earth and of words according —*Whitman*

Song!/ Rise as bright—*Chapin*

Die Sonne, wie sie mir zufällt—*Eich*

Die Sonne zeigt, vollendend gleich dem Helden —*Schiller*

Sonnez, sonnez toujours, clairons de la pensée —*Hugo, Victor*

Der sonnige Duft, Septemberluft—*Keller, Gottfried*

Sono una creatura/Come questa pietra—*Ungaretti*

The sons of the Prophet are brave men and bold —*Anonymous-English—Modern English*

Soon, Henry David, wind will fill the land—*Beecher*

Soon it will be showtime again—*Patchen*

The soote season, that bud and bloom forth bringes—*Surrey*

Sophie, mein Henkersmädel—*Morgenstern*

Sora sabbella.—Ée.—Ssora sabbella—*Belli*

Un sorbo de café a la madrugada—*Diego, Eliseo*

O sorella dell'ombra—*Ungaretti*

Soria fría, Soria pura—*Machado, Antonio*

Sorrowful dreams remembered after waking—*Millay*

A sort of beetle-bug is crawling—*Lee, Dennis*

The sort of girl I like to see—*Betjeman*

Sortosa la nissaga que té un baró perfet—*Liost*

Sosulek tonkii zvon—*Yevtushenko*

La sottise, l'erreur, le péché, la lésine—*Baudelaire*

Sotto la scure il disilluso ramo—*Ungaretti*

Soul ain't nothing but the blues—*Fabio, Sarah Webster*

The soul selects her own society—*Dickinson, Emily*

Souls of Poets dead and gone—*Keats*

The soul's Rialto hath its merchandise—*Browning, Elizabeth Barrett*

Sound no bells for ghostly glory—*Goldstein*

Sound the flute—*Blake*

Sound variegated through beneath lit—*Pritchard*

Sounds are heard too high for ears—*Bly*

Sounds sum and summon the remembering of summers—*Gardner*

Source délicieuse, en misères féconde—*Corneille*

Un souriceau tout jeune, et qui n'avait rien vu —*La Fontaine*

Sous le pont Mirabeau coule la Seine—*Apollinaire*

Sous les ifs noirs qui les abritent—*Baudelaire*

Sous une lumière blafarde—*Baudelaire*

South of the bridge on Seventeenth—*Stafford*

The South-wind brings—*Emerson*

Southern gentle lady—*Hughes, Langston*

Le souvenir avec le Crépuscule—*Verlaine*

Souvenir, souvenir, que me veux-tu?—*Verlaine*

Souvent, pour s'amuser, les hommes d'équipage —*Baudelaire*

Souvent sur la montagne, à l'ombre du vieux chêne—*Lamartine*

Soy como un niño distraído—*Jiménez*

Soyez la bienvenue—*Milosz*

Soyez tristes/ pleurez dans la hutte—*Lapointe*

Der soziologische Nenner—*Benn*

Spaces in darkness—*Plath*

The spacious firmament on high—*Addison*

Spades take up leaves—*Frost, Robert*

Spaghetti—*Merriam*

Spanish waters, Spanish waters you are ringing in my ears—*Masefield*

Spaparanze sti llastre é stu balcone—*Filippo*

A spark in the sun—*Gleason*

Sparrow dives from roof to ground—*Stryk*

The sparrows gleaning gutters—*Merwin*

Sparrows quarreled outside our window—*Levine*

Speak, earth, and bless me—*Lorde*

Speak roughly to your little boy—*Carroll*

Speak softly; sun going down—*Patchen*

Speak! speak! thou fearful guest—*Longfellow*

Speak to me child as I speak to myself—*Sobiloff*

Speak to me child as you fly your kite—*Sobiloff*

Speak to me child speak to me—*Sobiloff*

Speakin' in general, I 'ave tried 'em all—*Kipling*

Speaking of shocking things—*Marquis*

Speaking only that our words might bend grasses —*Patten*

The species is continued—*Rukeyser*

A speck that would have been beneath my sight —*Frost, Robert*

Speech after long silence; it is right—*Yeats*

Det spelar mjukt omkring mitt hjärta—*Asplund*
Spellbound held subtle Henry all his four—*Berryman*
Spenser's Ireland/has not altered—*Moore, Marianne*
Sphaire deute me porphyree—*Anacreon*
The spider glints—*Hall*
The spider holds a silver ball—*Dickinson, Emily*
Der Spiegel dieser treuen, braunen Augen—*Mörike*
Spirit going with me here—*Adams*
A spirit haunts the year's last hours—*Tennyson*
A spirit is coming across the valley—*Chapin*
Spirit of Alcohol—*Burke*
A spirit seems to pass—*Hardy*
Spit in my face, you Jewes, and pierce my side—*Donne*
To spiti gemise trizonia—*Seferis*
Ta spitia pou eikha mou ta peran—*Seferis*
The splendour falls on castle walls—*Tennyson*
Splinters of information, stones of information—*Redgrove*
Split the lark and you'll find the music—*Dickinson, Emily*
Splitting from Jack Delaney's Sheridan Square—*Walcott*
The spoiling daylight inched along the bar-top—*Wilbur*
The spontaneous man, the gifted assassin—*Goldman*
Sports and gallantries, the stage, the arts, the antics of dancers—*Jeffers, Robinson*
Sposa, è bbona la messa?—*Belli*
The spotted hawk swoops by and accuses me, he complains of my gab—*Whitman*
Sprang at my throat—*Emanuel*
Sprawled on our faces in the spring nights—*Kinnell*
Spread beneath me it lies—lean upland—*Gunn*
Spreading and low, unwatered, concentrate—*Winters*
Sprich aus der Ferne—*Brentano*
Spring. And in the vanquishing—*Antoninus*
The spring came round, and still he was not dead—*Day Lewis*
Spring drives them eagerly out into the street—*Souster*
The spring has darkened with activity—*Winters*
Spring is like a perhaps hand—*Cummings*
The spring is not so beautiful there—*Hughes, Langston*
Spring is your season. Where you are—*Marshall, Lenore G.*
Spring slipped in through the garden gate—*Marshall, Helen Lowrie*
Spring, the sweet spring—*Nashe*
Spring this year in Austria started off benign—*Auden*
Spring with its thrusting leaves—*Auden*
Springtide noon's low-watermark—*Hoffman*
Springtime, Summer and Fall: days to behold a world—*Auden*
Spute dich, Kronos—*Goethe*
A square sculled moonfaced—*Kavanagh*
Square sheets—they saw the marble into—*Crane, Hart*

Squatting at the rack in the store of the Salvation Army—*Kinnell*
A squeal of brakes—*Plath*
A squirrel to some is a squirrel—*Nash*
St' ortenzie ca tenite 'int 'a sta testa—*Di Giacomo*
Sta Federico imperatose in Como—*Carducci*
The stairway is not a thing of gleaming strands—*Levertov*
The stalks are thick—*Kumin*
Stand at attention—*Roseliep*
Stand back and take a good look—*Marshall, Helen Lowrie*
Stand from my shadow where it goes—*Merwin*
Stand on the highest pavement—*Eliot, Thomas Stearns*
Stand tall—reach high—*Marshall, Helen Lowrie*
Stand! the ground's your own, my braves—*Pierpont*
Stand with your lover on the ending earth—*Cummings*
Standing on top of the hay—*Hall*
A star hit in the hills behind our house—*Stafford*
Star light, star bright—*Children's Verses and Nursery Rhymes*
Star, star shining bright—*Derwood*
Staring at me, from across the room—*Eckels*
Starlight like intuition pierced the twelve—*Schwartz*
The stars are twinkling in the skies—*Field, Eugene*
The stars like stranded starfish pale and die—*Birney*
Stars over snow—*Teasdale*
Stars with fair and golden ray—*Heine*
Stars with golden feet are walking—*Heine*
The states when they black out and lie there rolling—*Dickey, James*
The Statue of Liberty's color—*Yevtushenko*
The statues do not—*Barker, George*
Stay on your outstretched wing O sweet, O lovely time—*Chapin*
Stchaste—bit—*Kirsanov*
Stealthily parting the small-hours silence—*Connor*
The steamfitter comes home in a pink cloud plainly—*Miles*
Steel barons, molten the next generation—*Byron*
Steep up in Lubitavish townland stands—*Jeffers, Robinson*
The steeps that onset—*Robson, Ernest M.*
Steer hither, steer your winged pines—*Browne, William*
Der Steinochs schuttelt stumm sein Haupt—*Morgenstern*
Stella, mia unica stella—*Ungaretti*
Le stelle che viaggiano sul mare—*Carducci*
The sterilizer's up for grabs—*Viorst*
Stern Daughter of the Voice of God—*Wordsworth*
The stethoscope tells what everyone fears—*Roethke*
Ein Stiefel wandern und sein Knecht—*Morgenstern*
Stiff both in passion and in pride—*Francis*
Still, citizen sparrow, this vulture which you call—*Wilbur*
Still faces on the wall—*Stafford*

Still falls the rain—*Sitwell, Edith*

Still grünt die Linde—*Bachmann*

Still let my tyrants know I am not doomed to wear —*Brontë, Emily*

Still missing it though—*Richards, I. A.*

Still to be neat, still to be drest—*Jonson*

Stimmen, ins Grün—*Celan*

Stirring porchpots up with green-fingered witch-craft—*Starbuck*

Sto menato ncopp' 'o lietto—*Di Giacomo*

Stoffel hackte mit dem Beile—*Busch*

Stomach of goat, crushed—*Levine*

The stomach pains—*Amini*

Stond whoso list upon the slipper toppe— *Wyatt, Sir Thomas*

Stone, bronze, stone, steel, stone, oakleaves, horses' heels—*Eliot, Thomas Stearns*

Stone/ cold/ daylight—*Sanchez*

Stone-cutters fighting time with marble, you foredefeated—*Jeffers, Robinson*

Stone gullets among—*Swenson*

The stone had skidded arc'd and bloomed into island—*Brathwaite*

Stone, steel, dominions pass—*Housman*

Stone walls are nothing—*Sherwin*

Stones that rolled in the sea for a thousand years —*Jeffers, Robinson*

Stonington: each morning boatloads of hands— *Lowell, Robert*

Stop bleeding said the knife—*Swenson*

Stop look &/ listen Venezia—*Cummings*

A stopwatch and an ordnance map—*Spender*

Storken er reist til fremmed land—*Andersen*

The storm-dances of gulls, the barking game of seals—*Jeffers, Robinson*

The storm is over, and the land has forgotten the storm—*Millay*

A storm rushed in his eye—*Arnez*

Storm. Storm in the trees—*Campbell, Alistair*

Stormen har slunyat den flygande—*Bergman, Bo*

A story, a story!/ Let it go—*Sexton*

The story of how she bowed to her brother—*Stein, Gertrude*

Stoyala zima—*Pasternak*

Stranded was written—*Brown, Otis*

Strange as it seems, the smallest mammal—*Nash*

Strange bird—*Wright, James*

Strange fits of passion have I known—*Wordsworth*

Strange how this smooth and supple point—*Untermeyer*

Strange, isn't it—of all the places—*Marshall, Helen Lowrie*

Strange now to think of you, gone without corsets and eyes—*Ginsberg*

Strange summer sun shines round our globe of circumstance— *Walker*

Strange walkers! See their processional—*Davie*

A stranger has come to share my room in the house not right in the head—*Thomas, Dylan*

The stranger within my gate—*Kipling*

Stranger, you who hide my love—*Spender*

Strangers were buying the house—*Cowley, Malcolm*

Streck deine Beine, mein hübscher Genoss—*Wedekind*

Strengthened to live, strengthened to die for—*Moore, Marianne*

Strew on her roses, roses—*Arnold*

Stripped of your matter—*Holland, Bill*

Der Strom der neben mir verrauschte, wo ist er nun?—*Platen-Hallermünde*

A strong man, a fair woman—*MacPherson*

The strong men keep coming on—*Sandburg*

Strong Son of God, immortal love—*Tennyson*

The struggler in the net—*MacPherson*

Student, do the simple purification—*Bly*

The student, lost in raucousness—*Weiss*

Studentu khotshetsya—*Yevtushenko*

Stupor of knowledge lacking inwardness—*Roethke*

Style is the perfection of a point of view—*Eberhart*

Su, figli d'Italia! su, in armi, coraggio—*Berchet*

Su luna de pergamino—*Garcia Lorca*

Su mano entre mis manos—*Becquer*

Su mano era la última embajada de su miseria —*Cuadra*

Sub luna amo—*Karlfeldt*

Sube a nacer conmigo, hermano—*Neruda*

Sube conmigo, amor americano—*Neruda*

Subir a otro país más abierto y más llano— *Vivanco*

The subject chosen for tonight's discussion—*Nabokov*

A subject thought: because he had a verb—*Spender*

Success is counted sweetest—*Dickinson, Emily*

Such a morning it is when love—*Lee, Laurie*

Such icy wounds the city people bear— *Williams, Tennessee*

Such jolly nights, my old friend, Jack Hammer —*Sherwin*

Such love is innocent, and may exist—*Byron*

Such perfect bliss, fair Cloris, we—*Rochester, Earl of*

Such were the tools; but a whole hydra more—*Dryden*

Sudan la al lawn—*Marvin X*

Sud'ba, kak raketa, letit po parabole—*Voznezensky*

A sudden blow: the great wings beating still—*Yeats*

The sudden death of Eugene Carman—*Masters, Edgar Lee*

Suddenly all the gold I ever wanted—*Francis*

Suddenly awake at two, and aware of the disintegration—*Plomer*

Suddenly, from the rocky spring—*Langland, Joseph*

Suddenly I saw the cold and rook-delighting heaven— *Yeats*

Suddenly, in my world of you—*MacCaig*

Suddenly in the dark wood—*Clarke*

Suddenly night crushed out the day and hurled —*Owen, Wilfred*

Suddenly out of its stale and drowsy lair, the lair of slaves— *Whitman*

Suffenus iste, Vare, quem probe nosti—*Catullus*

Sui-je, sui-je, sui-je belle—*Deschamps*

The sullen building up of pain—*Dowling*

Sumer is icumen in—*Anonymous–English–Middle English*

The summer before last I saw my vision—*Redgrove*

Summer ends now; now, barbarous in beauty, the stooks rise—*Hopkins*

Summer fading, winter comes—*Stevenson*

Summer grows old, cold-blooded mother—*Plath*

Summer is over, the old cow said—*Hillyer*

The summer is over, the trees are all bare—*Fyleman*

The summer that was ten—*Swenson*

Summer, the hay fever in the air—*Sherwin*

Summer, this is our flesh—*Tate, Allen*

Summon now the kings of the forest—*Brathwaite*

Summoning artists to participate—*Frost, Robert*

A sumptuous moss hoods the skull—*Fitzgerald*

Sun breaks over the eucalyptus—*Snyder*

The sun came, Miss Brooks—*Knight, Etheridge*

The sun comes in through shutters—*Bly*

The sun descending in the West—*Blake*

Sun dissolves to recreate—*Sitwell, Osbert*

The sun does arise—*Blake*

The sun has to solve—*Mac Low*

The sun is blue—*Lowell, Robert*

The sun is not a-bed, when I—*Stevenson*

The sun sets in the cold without friends—*Merwin*

The sun that brief December day—*Whittier*

The sun was shining on the sea—*Carroll*

A sunbeam on the well-waxed oak—*Graves*

The Sunday lamb cracks in its fat—*Plath*

Sundays too my father got up early—*Hayden*

Sundowning, the doctor calls it—*Kumin*

Sung sya wen tung dz—*Jya Dau*

Sunlight daubs my eye—*Moraes*

The sunlight on the garden—*MacNeice*

Sun's a settin'—*Hughes, Langston*

The sun's gone dim, and—*Parker*

Sunset and evening star—*Tennyson*

Sunt aliquid Manes: letum non omnia finit—*Propertius*

Super-cool/ ultrablack—*Lee, Don L.*

The supremes done gone/ and sold their soul—*Sanchez*

Suppose/ life is an old man—*Cummings*

Suppose those—*Lee, Don L.*

Suppose you stood just five feet two—*Masters, Edgar Lee*

Suppose we say that God is naked hope—*Bodenheim*

Sur la branche d'un arbre était en sentinelle—*La Fontaine*

Sur la côte du Texas—*Apollinaire*

Sur le bord d'un puits très profond—*La Fontaine*

Sur le haut mont, ça et là regardant—*Baïf*

Sur les ailes de l'oiseau-lyre je n'ai jamais rencontré—*Seghers*

Sur les bords du Mississippi—*Desnos*

Sur les Continents morts, les houles léthargiques—*Leconte de Lisle*

Sur l'océan/ nuit noire—*Damas*

Sur l'onde calme et noire où dorment les étoiles—*Rimbaud*

Sur mes cahiers d'écolier—*Éluard*

Sure, if we were all Sirens—*Ford, John*

Sure, it was so. Man in those early days—*Vaughan, Henry*

Surely this day—*Richards, I. A.*

Surely we hear thunder—*Blackmur*

The Surgeon General has determined—*Pietri*

Surgi de la croupe et du bond—*Mallarmé*

Surprised by joy impatient as the wind—*Wordsworth*

Susie's galoshes make splishes and sploshes—*Bacmeister*

Los suspiros son aire—*Becquer*

Süsse Luft und zartes Werden—*Hauptmann*

Suzy grew a moustache—*Lee, Dennis*

Svako svuche svoiu kozhu—*Popa*

Svisayu s vagonnoi ploshchadki—*Voznezensky*

Svite yasny, svite yasny—*Shevchenko*

Swallow, my sister, O sister swallow—*Swinburne*

The swan can swim while sitting down—*Nash*

A sweet, a delicate white mouse—*Kunitz*

Sweet Alice S. Morris, I am pleased of course—*Roethke*

Sweet and delicate and rare—*Stephens*

Sweet and low, sweet and low—*Tennyson*

Sweet Auburn! loveliest village of the plain—*Goldsmith*

Sweet Beast, I have gone prowling—*Snodgrass*

Sweet chimes! that in the loneliness of night—*Longfellow*

Sweet cyder is a great thing—*Hardy*

Sweet day, so cool, so calm, so bright—*Herbert*

The sweet desires blossom—*Heine*

A sweet disorder in the dresse—*Herrick*

Sweet dreams, form a shade—*Blake*

Sweet Echo, sweetest nymph that liv'st unseen—*Milton*

Sweet for a little even to fear, and sweet—*Swinburne*

Sweet heart, do not love too long—*Yeats*

Sweet honey-sucking bees—*Anonymous–English—Modern English*

Sweet Kate of late—*Anonymous–English—Modern English*

Sweet love, renew thy force: be it not said—*Shakespeare*

The sweet solid smell—*Clay*

Sweet songs, you said, were gonna come—*Fabio, Sarah Webster*

Sweet spring is your time—*Cummings*

Sweet was the song that youth sang once—*Landor*

Sweetest love, I do not goe—*Donne*

Sweetest Savior, if my soul—*Herbert*

Sweit Rois of Vertew and Gentilnes—*Dunbar, William*

Swift has sailed into his rest—*Yeats*

Swift little thought—*Hodges*

The swift red flesh, a winter king—*Crane, Hart*

Swift/ Signatures of the shore—*Rago*

Swift things are beautiful—*Coatsworth*

Swiftly walk o'er the western wave—*Shelley*

Swim so now million many worlds in each—*Cummings*

Swing, swing, sing, sing—*Allingham*

The swinging mill bell changed its rate—*Frost, Robert*

Swivelling flat-soled on the dirt but ready to bound in arches—*Wagoner*

Sye gung dzwei syan pyan lyan nyu—*Ywan Jen*

Sylvan meant savage in those primal woods—*Auden*

Syncopating rhythm, please echo home to me—
  Hodges
Syntaxe de l'éclair—*Perse*

T' he' levao ogni fogia—*Marin*
Ta vida és un desitg d'agilitat—*López Pico*
The table on which my earthenware rests its feet
  —*Jeffers, Lance*
Tacciono i boschi e i fiumi—*Tasso*
Taci. Su le soglie—*D'Annunzio, Gabriele*
Tag und Nacht hab' ich gedichtet—*Heine*
Der Tag, vor dem der grosse Christ—*Brecht*
Tage abziehen—*Heissenbüttel*
Taglang nachtlang stand mein Schiff befrachtet
  —*Goethe*
Täglich geh' ich heraus, und such' ein Anderes
  immer—*Hölderlin*
Täglich ging die wunderschöne Sultanstochter
  —*Heine*
Taj Mahal, where you come from—*Carter*
Take a note—*Giovanni*
Take all my loves, my love, yes, take them all—
  Shakespeare
Take it from me kiddo—*Cummings*
Take, now, the lone, immortal car—*Abbe*
Take of English earth as much—*Kipling*
Take somebody who—*Lifshin*
Take the cloak from his face, and at first—*Brown-
  ing, Robert*
Take the street where the cinders crunch—*Con-
  nor*
Take this kiss upon the brow—*Poe*
Take up the white man's burden—*Kipling*
Take whatever you've—*Lifshin*
Taking our time by the compass—*Aiken*
Taking the hands of someone you love—*Bly*
Takoradi was hot—*Brathwaite*
Tal vez en el amanecer—*Alurista*
A talented old gentleman painting a hedge—
  Smith, Stevie
Talk about beauty like a man—*Talen*
Talk about the grace of your bullfighters—*Souster*
The talk is of Johnson and a Congress—*Sward*
Talk of elegance—*Meltzer*
Tall heart, thin house—*Posner*
Tall nettles cover up, as they have done—
  Thomas, Edward
A tally of forces, consequent—*Creeley*
Tamed by Miltown, we lie on Mother's bed—
  Lowell, Robert
T'amo, o bove; e mite un sentimento—*Carducci*
Tan ta ra cries Mars—*Anonymous-English—
  Modern English*
Tan, tan, tan! canta el martillo—*Valle Inclan*
Tänd hoppets fackla i kvävande kväll—*Lagerk-
  vist*
Ein Tännlein grünet wo—*Mörike*
Tant que mes yeux—*Labé*
Tanto gentile e tanto onesta pare—*Dante Aligh-
  ieri*
Taped to the wall of my cell are 47 pictures—
  Knight, Etheridge
Tapetenblume bin ich fein—*Morgenstern*
The tarantula rattling at the lily's foot—*Crane,
  Hart*
Tarde lluviosa en gris—*Garcia Lorca*

La tarde respondía/ a las viñas doradas—*Ridruejo*
Tarry, delight; so seldom met—*Housman*
A tattering of rain and then the reign—*Schwartz*
Taubenflug über die Äcker hin—*Eich*
Taurus—*Olson*
Tawny are the leaves turned but they still hold
  —*Ransom*
Tax not the royal Saint with vain expense—
  Wordsworth
Te digo adiós y acaso te quiero todavía—*Buesa*
Te dormiste, niño mio?—*Hernández, Miguel*
Te han nacido los ojos con preguntas—*Garcia
  Nieto*
Te he dicho Platero, que el alma—*Jiménez*
Te odio. Lo digo con la unción enorme—*Monvel*
Te souviens-tu mon Lou de ce panier d'oranges
  —*Apollinaire*
Te veo mientras pasas—*Jiménez*
Te vi un punto—*Becquer*
Te voilà revenu, dans mes nuits étoilées—*Musset*
The teacher stands before the class—*Jong*
The teacher was a bad man—*Walker*
Tears/ hiding behind—*Kgositsile*
Tears, idle tears—*Tennyson*
Tearsplotches for my children will turn no muscle
  red—*Jeffers, Lance*
Ted Roethke was a tearing man—*Ciardi*
Teeth on the saw—*Cowley, Malcolm*
Tel, comme dit Merlin—*La Fontaine*
Tel qu'en lui-même enfin l'éternité le change—
  Mallarmé
Telegu obizhat' ne nado—*Yevtushenko*
A telephone line goes cold—*Stafford*
Tell all the truth but tell it slant—*Dickinson,
  Emily*
Tell brave deeds of war—*Crane, Stephen*
Tell her this, Dorkas—*Meleager*
Tell me all I want—*Sherwin*
Tell me, little spider—*Keeler*
Tell me no more how fair she is—*King*
Tell me no more of minds embracing minds—
  Cartwright
Tell me not here, it needs not saying—*Housman*
Tell me not, in mournful numbers—*Longfellow*
Tell me not (Sweet) I am unkinde—*Lovelace,
  Richard*
Tell me, O Octopus, I begs—*Nash*
Tell, tell our fortune, Mirabel—*Gregory, Horace*
Tell you what I like best—*Riley*
Telle est l'instance extrème où le poète a té-
  moigné—*Perse*
Telling lies to the young is wrong—*Yevtushenko*
Tem un leque de Plumas gloriosas—*Leal*
Le temps a laissé son manteau—*Charles d'Or-
  leans*
Tended by Faustine yes in a crazy house—*Bishop,
  Elizabeth*
Tender only to one—*Smith, Stevie*
Tendida en la madrugada—*Guillén, Nicolás*
Tengo el impuro amor de las ciudades—*Casal*
Tengo miedo a perder la maravilla—*Garcia
  Lorca*
Tengo mucho miedo / de las hojas muertas—
  Garcia Lorca
Tengo nemice? Faccio 'o paro e sparo—*Filippo*
Tenne mi amor anni vent'uno ardendo—*Petrarca*
Tenorino di grazia egli le strofe—*Saba*

Tenuous and precarious were my guardians—
Smith, Stevie

Terence, this is stupid stuff—*Housman*

Teresi, buono Natale—*Di Giacomo*

Terpsicore es Eolo—*Martinez Alonso*

A terra floresce—*Botto*

The terrace is said to be haunted—*Redgrove*

La terre, naguère glacée—*Desportes*

The terrified look—*Souster*

Tes beaux yeux sont las, pauvre amante—*Baudelaire*

Tes mains jonchant les draps étaient mes feuilles mortes—*Cocteau*

Tes pas, enfants de mon silence— *Valéry*

Tesserae commisure—*Olson*

Thá thaes rinces se ríca ongann—*Anonymous–English—Old English*

Thaet fram ham gefraegn Higelaces thegn—*Anonymous–English—Old English*

Thank heaven for the weather—*Marshall, Helen Lowrie*

Thank Heaven! the crisis—*Poe*

Thank you for sitting—*Dudek*

Thanks in old age—thanks ere I go— *Whitman*

That August the birds kept away from the village afraid—*Scott, Dennis*

That bull-necked blotch-faced farmer from Drumlore—*Reid*

That civilisation may not sink— *Yeats*

That cop was powerful mean—*Randall*

That crazed girl improvising her music— *Yeats*

That crazy wretch got up—*Blackmur*

That cry's from the first cuckoo of the year— *Bogan*

That day in the interpreter's house—*Redgrove*

That does not keep me from having a terrible need of, shall I say the word—*Sexton*

That God forbid that made me first your slave —*Shakespeare*

That God should love me is more wonderful— *Van Doren*

That hobnailed goblin, the bob-tailed Hob—*Sitwell, Edith*

That I am mortal I know and do confess—*Ptolemaios the Astronomer*

That I am yours—*Stephany*

That is no country for old men— *Yeats*

That light, that sight, that thought—*Traherne*

That lover of a night— *Yeats*

That March had a neck like an animal—*Abbe*

That melancholy—*Cummings*

That night your great guns, unawares—*Hardy*

That note you hold—*Larkin*

That pale face stretches across the centuries—*Smith, Stevie*

That part of the country— *Wellman*

That Stagolee was an all-right lad— *Walker*

That story which the bold Sir Bedivere—*Tennyson*

That strong creature / from before the flood—*MacPherson*

That Sunday morning, at half past ten—*Nabokov*

That the pear's boughs—*Hoffman*

That thou art blam'd shall not be thy defect—*Shakespeare*

That thou hast her, it is not all my grief—*Shakespeare*

That time of year thou may'st in me behold—*Shakespeare*

That war is an emotional release—*Dicker*

That was a place, when I was young—*Wright, James*

That was a shocking day—*Engle*

That was her beginning—*Lee, Laurie*

That was I, you heard last night—*Browning, Robert*

That was the best moment of the monk's life—*Stryk*

That was the fatal move—*Day Lewis*

That was the second year of the Third World War —*Benét, Stephen Vincent*

That which her slender waist confined— *Waller*

That which I have myself seen and the fighting —*MacLeish*

That winter love spoke and we raised no objection, at—*Day Lewis*

That with this bright believing band—*Hardy*

That you were once unkind befriends me now —*Shakespeare*

That's enough I said to the mourning dove—*Garrigue*

That's my last duchess painted on the wall— *Browning, Robert*

That's this moment—*Rukeyser*

Thay bozen bi bonkkez ther bozez ar bare— *Anonymous–English—Middle English*

The bigger the box the more it holds—*Sandburg*

The more you—*Lifshin*

Thee for my recitative— *Whitman*

Thee, God, I come from, to thee I go—*Hopkins*

Their belongings were buried side by side— *MacBeth*

Their madness can never be my God—*Jeffers, Lance*

Their prayers still swarm on me—*Merwin*

Their sense is with their senses all mixed in— *Meredith, George*

Their six-weeks-old daughter lies—*Spender*

Their time past, pulled down— *Williams, William Carlos*

Their voices heard, I stumble suddenly—*Spender*

Theirs is your house—*Crabbe*

Then call me traitor if you must—*Cullen*

Then came the cry of "Call all hands on deck" —*Masefield*

Then hate me when thou wilt; if ever, now— *Shakespeare*

Then hear, O son of David, virgin-born—*Milton*

Then I was sealed, and like the wintering tree —*Adams*

Then I'll be four-footed— *Van Doren*

Then it was dusk in Illinois, the small boy—*Kinnell*

Then let not winter's ragged hand deface— *Shakespeare*

Then out spake brave Horatius—*Macaulay*

Then spake King Arthur to Sir Bedivere—*Tennyson*

Then the knee of the wave—*Hall*

Then the time came for Quetzalcoatl too— *Anonymous–American Indian languages–Nahuatl*

Then those ill-favor'd Ones, whom none—*Crabbe*

Then to the west I look'd, and saw far off—*Keats*

A theory if you hold it hard enough—*Frost, Robert*

There all the golden codgers lay—*Yeats*

There are blk puritans among us—*Sanchez*

There are brightest apples on those trees—*Layton*

There are hermit souls that live withdrawn—*Foss*

There are holes in her walls—*Jimason*

There are in our existence spots of time—*Wordsworth*

There are lions and roaring tigers—*Milne*

There are more than a hundred Turkish poems—*Jong*

There are no bears among the roses—*Stevens, Wallace*

There are no girls among us now with small high breasts—*Scott, Winfield Townley*

There are no rooms here—*Patchen*

There are no stars to-night—*Crane, Hart*

There are no trenches dug in the park—*Benét, Stephen Vincent*

There are people so near nothing—*Sandburg*

There are poets—*Jimason*

There are portraits and still lives—*Tomlinson*

There are seven men in Moy Castle—*Anonymous-English—Modern English*

There are several people who I can claim I am glad I am not—*Nash*

There are so many things I have forgot—*Thomas, Edward*

There are some days the happy ocean lies—*Spender*

There are some heights in Wessex—*Hardy*

There are some qualities—some incorporate things—*Poe*

There are some words carry a curse with them—*Graves*

There are sounds—*Giovanni*

There are strange things done in the midnight sun—*Service*

There are two kinds of people who blow through life like a breeze—*Nash*

There are wolves in the next room waiting—*Tate, Allen*

There are words like Freedom—*Hughes, Langston*

There be none of beauty's daughters—*Byron*

There, by the flower vendor's stand—*Gregor*

There came a ghost to Margret's door—*Anonymous-English—Modern English*

There came a wind like a bugle—*Dickinson, Emily*

There fared a mother driven forth—*Chesterton, Gilbert Keith*

There in the sand grew a coconut face—*Sobiloff*

There is a brook I must hear—*Conkling*

There is a Cyprus Citrus surplus—*Nash*

There is a desperate loveliness to be seen—*Sandburg*

There is a garden in her face—*Campion*

There is a lady sweet and kind—*Anonymous-English—Modern English*

There is a legend—*Sklarew*

There is a magic melting pot—*Randall*

There is a part of me that looks—*Darr*

There is a perfect socket in the center—*Kavanagh*

There is a place—*Patchen, 1586*

There is a place that some men know—*Tate, Allen*

There is a place where love begins—*Sandburg*

There is a pleasure in the pathless woods—*Byron*

There is a scarlet sea that churns—*Goldstein*

There is a silence where hath been no sound—*Hood*

There is a singer everyone has heard—*Frost, Robert*

There is a star that runs very fast—*Conkling*

There is a tiny wind—*Kaufman, Shirley*

There is a tree that is growing alone on the hill—*Gallagher, F. O'Neill*

There is a wolf in me—*Sandburg*

There is a woman on Michigan Boulevard keeps a parrot—*Sandburg*

There is a yew-tree, pride of Lorton Vale—*Wordsworth*

There is always something—*Giovanni*

There is an arctic icefloe in the human soul—*Jeffers, Lance*

There is an inspiration—*Marshall, Helen Lowrie*

There is grey in your hair—*Yeats*

There is in my old picture-book—*Milne*

There is music in me—*Johnson, Fenton*

There is my country under glass—*Atwood*

There is no cafeteria in Hell—*Kramer*

There is no difference between being raped—*Piercy*

There is no frigate like a book to take us lands away—*Dickinson, Emily*

There is no laughter in the natural world—*Blunt*

There is no other time for us—*Heath*

There is no place to turn, she said—*Roethke*

There is no silence in the earth—*Dickinson, Emily*

There is no sorrow—*De la Mare*

There is not much that I can do—*Hardy*

There is nothing like it now—*Kresh*

There is nothing more perky—*Nash*

There is one form of life to which I unconditionally surrender—*Nash*

There is one source of marital discord—*Nash*

There is one story and one story only—*Graves*

There is one thing that ought to be taught in all colleges—*Nash*

There is our herd of cars stopped—*Swenson*

There is so much of darkness—*Marshall, Helen Lowrie*

There/is someone—*Moore, Marianne*

There is something—*Updike*

There is something about Death—*Masters, Edgar Lee*

There is sweet music here that softer falls—*Tennyson*

There is the line—*Swenson*

There is the star bloom of the moss—*Garrigue*

There is this black pauper's suit—*Mariah*

There is wisdom in this weather—*Sobiloff*

There it is, a block of leaping marble—*Eberhart*

There it was, word for word—*Stevens, Wallace*

There Jack-cock struts—*Howes*

There lived a wife at Usher's Well—*Anonymous-English—Modern English*

There mounts in squalls a sort of rusty mire—
Lowell, Robert

There once was a boy of Bagdad—*Anonymous-English—Modern English*

There once was a witch of Willoby—*Bennett, Rowena*

There once was an umpire whose vision—*Nash*

There sat down, once, a thing on Henry's heart—*Berryman*

There, spring—*Plath*

There the black river, boundary to hell—*Randall*

There they are, drooping over the breakfast plates—*Sexton*

There they stand together, like Moses standing with Aaron—*Walker*

There was a bird come recently—*Patten*

There was a boy was Oedipus—*Hughes, Ted*

There was a Boy whose name was Tim—*Belloc*

There was a Boy: ye knew him well, ye cliffs—*Wordsworth*

There was a child went forth—*Whitman*

There was a crooked man and he went a crooked mile—*Children's Verses and Nursery Rhymes*

There was a frog lived in a well—*Children's Verses and Nursery Rhymes*

There was a giant by the orchard wall—*Stephens*

There was a jolly miller once—*Bickerstaffe*

There was a little girl and she had a little curl—*Children's Verses and Nursery Rhymes*

There was a little green apple—*Conkling*

There was a little fire in the grate—*Stephens*

There was a little turtle—*Lindsay, Vachel*

There was a little woman—*Children's Verses and Nursery Rhymes*

There was a merry passenger—*Tolkien*

There was a naughty boy—*Keats*

There was a prince by the name of Tsing—*Field, Eugene*

There was a Queen of England—*Belloc*

There was a ram in Derbytown—*Children's Verses and Nursery Rhymes*

There was a rat who, whatever he did—*Starbuck*

There was a roaring in the wind all night—*Wordsworth*

There was a saviour rarer than radium—*Thomas, Dylan*

There was a sound of revelry by night—*Byron*

There was a time when meadow, grove, and stream—*Wordsworth*

There was a time when this poor frame was whole—*Thomas, Edward*

There was a town without roof tops—*Abbe*

There was a trampling of horses from Calvary—*Wheelock*

There was a weasel lived in the sun—*Thomas, Edward*

There was a whispering in my hearth—*Owen, Wilfred*

There was a woman loved a man—*Sandburg*

There was a wondeful bugaboo—*Field, Eugene*

There was a young boy of Quebec—*Kipling*

There was a young girl who said, Why—*Lear*

There was a young lady of Niger—*Monkhouse*

There was a young lady of Parma—*Lear*

There was a young lady of Sweden—*Lear*

There was a young lady of Wilts—*Monkhouse*

There was a young lady whose bonnet—*Lear*

There was a young lady whose chin—*Lear*

There was a young lady whose eyes—*Lear*

There was a young person of Smyrna—*Lear*

There was an old farmer in Sussex did dwell—*Anonymous-English—Modern English*

There was an old lady whose folly—*Lear*

There was an old man in a tree—*Lear*

There was an old man of Dunluce—*Lear*

There was an old man of the Nile—*Lear*

There was an old man of Thermopylae—*Lear*

There was an old man of Whitehaven—*Lear*

There was an old man on some rocks—*Lear*

There was an old man who said, Hush—*Lear*

There was an old man who said, Well—*Lear*

There was an old man with a gong—*Lear*

There was an old person of Bow—*Lear*

There was an old person of Crowle—*Lear*

There was an old person of Dutton—*Lear*

There was an old person of Sark—*Lear*

There was an old woman/and nothing she had—*Children's Verses and Nursery Rhymes*

There was an old woman, and what do you think—*Children's Verses and Nursery Rhymes*

There was an old woman tossed up in a basket—*Children's Verses and Nursery Rhymes*

There was an old woman who lived in a shoe—*Children's Verses and Nursery Rhymes*

There was never a sound beside the wood but one—*Frost, Robert*

There was once a king of York—*Anonymous-English—Modern English*

There was once an old sailor my grandfather knew—*Milne*

There was such speed in her little body—*Ransom*

There was that headland—*Thomas, Ronald Stuart*

There was this man and he was the strongest—*Hughes, Ted*

There was this road—*Graves*

There wasn't two—*Riley*

There were bizarre beginnings in old lands for the making of me—*Walker*

There were four crates of chickens—*Patchen*

There were four of us about that bed—*Morris, William*

There were ghosts that returned to earth to hear his phrases—*Stevens, Wallace*

There were no undesirables or girls in my set—*Lowell, Robert*

There were none of my blood in this battle—*MacLeish*

There were three gypsies a-come to the door—*Anonymous-English—Modern English*

There were three ravens sat on a tree—*Anonymous-English—Modern English*

There were twa sisters sat in a bower—*Anonymous-English—Modern English*

There were two little skeezucks who lived in the isle—*Field, Eugene*

There will be many other nights—*Blackburn, Paul*

There will be no Holyman crying out this year—*Hernton*

There will be the cough before the silence, then—*Merwin*

There ye gang, ye daft—*Smith, Sydney Goodsir*

There's a certain slant of light—*Dickinson, Emily*

There's a chirrupy cricket as guest in my room —*Thomas, Martha B.*

There's a combative artist named Whistler—*Rossetti, Dante Gabriel*

There's a four-pronged buck a-swinging in the shadow of my cabin—*Service*

There's a humming in the sky—*Green, Mary McBride*

There's a little cottage/ in a ring of hedge—*Conkling*

There's a lot of things I've done—*Johnston, Ellen Turlington*

There's a package, there's a package—*Fisher*

There's a Parthenon in Nashville large as life—*Shapiro, Karl*

There's a race of men that don't fit in—*Service*

There's a snake on the western wave—*Lindsay, Vachel*

There's a special little halo—*Marshall, Helen Lowrie*

There's a whisper down the line at 11:39—*Eliot, Thomas Stearns*

There's a wild promise—*Freivalds*

There's a woman in the earth, sitting on—*Swenson*

There's a youth in this city, it were a great pity —*Burns*

There's heaven above, and night, by night—*Browning, Robert*

There's many a strong farmer—*Yeats*

There's much afoot in heaven and earth this year —*Meynell*

There's my things—*Williams, William Carlos*

There's not a joy the world can give like that it takes away—*Byron*

There's nothing quite so beautiful—*Murphy*

There's nought but care on ev'ry han'—*Burns*

These are amazing—*Ashbery*

These are the blues—*Morris, James*

These are the days when birds come back—*Dickinson, Emily*

These are the gardens of the Desert, these—*Bryant, William Cullen*

These days the sunlight almost seems total—*Braun*

These golden heads, these common suns—*Nemerov*

These grand and fatal movements toward death —*Jeffers, Robinson*

These gray clouds, so thickly strewn—*Heine*

These hearts were woven human joys and cares

These here are words of radical advice for a young man—*Nash*

These, in the day when heaven was falling—*Housman*

These little limbs—*Traherne*

These market-dames, mid-aged with lips thin-drawn—*Hardy*

These new nights—*Kgositsile*

These nuts, that I keep in the back of the nest —*Stevenson*

These people with their illegible diplomas—*Nemerov*

These pools that, though in forests, still reflect —*Frost, Robert*

These spectres resting on plastic stools—*Ginsberg*

These stars and planets have no names—*Dickinson, Patric*

These trees stand very tall under the heavens—*Snodgrass*

These walls they knew those shadows—*Sandburg*

These were they whom the body could not please —*Merwin*

These wonderful things were planted on the surface—*Ashbery*

They all want to play Hamlet—*Sandburg*

They are all gone away—*Robinson, Edwin Arlington*

They are all gone into the world of light—*Vaughan, Henry*

They are and suffer; that is all they do—*Auden*

They are fighting, she—*Oppenheimer*

They are getting up from the table—*Lapalma*

They are murdering all the young men—*Rexroth*

They are not long, the weeping and the laughter —*Dowson*

They are rattling breakfast—*Eliot, Thomas Stearns*

They are ready for their party—*Nash*

They are the last romantics, these candles—*Plath*

They bide their time off serpentine—*Ormond*

They brought the mighty chief to town—*Service*

They brought thy body back to me quite dead —*Lee-Hamilton*

They built Bill Wagner's bones—*Polak*

They buried him at the crossroads—*Heine*

They call me and I go—*Williams, William Carlos*

They call me Uncle—*Brathwaite*

They came in with a bulldozer—*Robison*

They chose me from my brothers—*Aldis*

They chose pale green—*Robson, Jeremy*

They climbed on sketchy ladders towards God —*Ormond*

They come not back with steed—*Frost, Robert*

They come to him for subscriptions—*Brown, Sterling A.*

They could bend low—*Sandburg*

They dither softly at her bedroom door—*Kinsella*

They do not live in the world—*Muir*

They drag me raw on the gravel track—*Harnett*

They dream only of America—*Ashbery*

They drummed salvation in the darker districts —*Miles*

They dug ten streets from that there hole—*Nicholson*

They eat beans mostly, this old yellow pair—*Brooks, Gwendolyn*

They flee from me, that sometime did me seek —*Wyatt, Sir Thomas*

They got me into the Sunday-school—*Masters, Edgar Lee*

They hail you as their morning star—*Parker*

They hated me because I was short—*Sobiloff*

They have been burning leaves—*Young, Andrew*

They have been with us a long time—*Updike*

They have carried the mahogany chair and the cane rocker out under the lilac bush—*Rich*

They have not survived—*Mathias*

They have remained unaltered like nature—*Yevtushenko*

They have sed/ u will die in—*Sanchez*

They have slain you, Sean MacDermott—*O'Sullivan*

They hold a committee today—*Starbuck*

They laid their hands upon my head—*Parker*

They made a myth of you, professor—*Sandburg*

They made you complicated—*Gallagher, Tess*

They mark time, now, with blunt booms—*Fabio, Sarah Webster*

They more than we are what we are—*Raine*

They mouth love's language. Gnash—*Joyce*

They name this pain—*Hobbs*

They paddle with staccato feet—*Kell*

They pilled the dam—*Bruchac*

They put ma body in de ground—*Hughes, Langston*

They roused him with muffins—they roused him with ice—*Carroll*

They say: Black women are primitive—*Murphy*

They say La Jac Brite Pink Skin Bleach avails not—*Miles*

They say "Son"—*Emanuel*

They say that trees scream—*Piercy*

They say the clouds are men and women—*Williams, Hugo*

They say the first dream Adam our father had—*Muir*

They say the sea is cold, but the sea contains—*Lawrence*

They say there is a sweeter air—*Moore, Marianne*

They scoured the hill with steel—*Cowley, Malcolm*

They should not have left him there alone—*Scannell*

They shut the road through the wood—*Kipling*

They sit in a row outside the Kindergarten—*Sexton*

They stood, side by side, in an idle moment—*Sitwell, Osbert*

They take me aside—*Sereni*

They tell me—*Wilson*

They tell me of a distant zoo—*Nash*

They tell me that euphoria is the feeling of feeling wonderful—*Nash*

They tell me there are red birds—*Darr*

They that have power to hurt and will do none—*Shakespeare*

They told me you had been to her—*Carroll*

They took him out to die—*Rodgers*

They took me out—*Hughes, Langston*

They tore down my doll house—*Goldstein*

They used to tell him—*Wilson*

They warned Our Lady for the Child—*Belloc*

They wear air/ or water like a skin—*Swenson*

They went to sea in a sieve, they did—*Lear*

They went with axe and rifle—*Benét, Stephen Vincent*

They were—*Lee, Don L.*

They were all inaccurate—*Atwood*

They were alone, but not alone as they—*Byron*

They were human, they suffered, wore long black coat and gold watchchain—*Warren*

They were married—*Coward*

They will appear in the moist air—*Fabio, Sarah Webster*

They will seek you out, seducing you with words—*Robson, Jeremy*

They will soon be down to one—*Dickey, James*

They worked—*Pietri*

They would have lynched me—*Masters, Edgar Lee*

They're altogether otherworldly now—*Lowell, Robert*

They're changing the guard at Buckingham Palace—*Milne*

They're dancing—*Genser*

They're having a party this evening—*Heine*

They're twittering again, my day-starters and another—*Ciardi*

They've all gone away—*Sereni*

The thick lids of night closed upon me—*Hardy*

Thin, black javelin—*Emanuel*

Thin long bird—*Whalen*

Thine eyes I love, and they, as pitying me—*Shakespeare*

The thing about which I know the least—*Nash*

The thing could barely stand yet taken—*Layton*

A thing of beauty is a joy forever—*Keats*

The thing that arrests me is—*Rich*

The thing that eats the heart comes wild with years—*Kunitz*

The thing to do is to try for that sweet skin—*Garrigue*

Things are getting simpler—*Cavalieri*

Things die out—*Enslin*

Things I'd rather die—*Emanuel*

Things might be lazy—*Rossman*

Things of this world—*Eberhart*

Think about it at will: there is that—*Tate, Allen*

Thinker/ in the classic peristyle—*Whalen*

Thinking of something pretty—*Emanuel*

Thinkst thou to seduce me then—*Campion*

Thirteen's no age at all. Thirteen is nothing—*McGinley*

Thirty days hath September—*Children's Verses and Nursery Rhymes*

The thirty eighth year—*Clifton*

Thirty-seven today—*Souster*

Thirty-two years since—*Hardy*

This ae nighte, this ae nighte—*Anonymous-English—Modern English*

This age it is the same with less remembered—*Blackmur*

This amber sunstream, with an hour to live—*Van Doren*

This ancient hag—*Hughes, Langston*

This beast that rends me in the sight of all—*Millay*

This beauty makes me dream there was a time—*Thomas, Edward*

This being a time confused and with few clear stars—*Benét, Stephen Vincent*

This body, tapped of every drop of breath—*Kunitz*

This can't go on—*Yevtushenko*

This cat was bought upon the day—*Fuller, Roy*

This chair I trusted, lass, and I looted the heavens—*Hollander*

This coast's not/ easy in winter—*Reid*

This country might have/ been a—*Sanchez*

This darksome burn, horseback brown—*Hopkins*

This day winding down now—*Thomas, Dylan*

This death is timely—*Ansen*

This devils me: uneasy ease at my window—*Ciardi*

This dust was once the man—*Whitman*

This easy-gone world now—that one cloud—*Ciardi*

This Englishwoman is so refined—*Smith, Stevie*

This evening, motherly summer moves—*Hughes, Ted*

This face you got/ this here phizzog—*Sandburg*

This girl speaks five words—*Sandburg*

This having learnt, thou hast attained the summe—*Milton*

This heart that flutters near my heart—*Joyce*

This here's a tale of a sho-nuff man—*Walker*

This illumined wonder—*Chapin*

This is a day when good men die from windows—*Kizer*

This is a joy of a day—*Dodson*

This is a pig woman—*Sherwin*

This is a place/ where people live—*Sherwin*

This is a rocksaw seacoast—*Scott, Winfield Townley*

This is a rubbish of a human rind—*Cummings*

This is a song for the genius child—*Hughes, Langston*

This is a song to celebrate banks—*Nash*

This is a strange twilit country, but full of peace—*Pitter*

This is a theme for muted coronets—*Smith, A. J. M.*

This is a true story—*Pietri*

This is a well guarded place—*O'Gorman*

This is an African worm—*Danner*

This is before electricity—*Atwood*

This is enchanted country, lies under a spell—*Wheelock*

This is for reference purposes—*Shiva*

This is for you who are to come, with Time—*Benét, Stephen Vincent*

This is how the blind sees—*Zu-Bolton*

This is mint and here are three pinks—*Conkling*

This is my deck I unwrap—*Piercy*

This is my letter to the world—*Dickinson, Emily*

This is my nutcracker—*Colbert*

This is my play's last scene; here heavens appoint—*Donne*

This is my rock—*McCord*

This is no night to sleep, the dark—*Chapin*

This is not the man that women choose—*Scannell*

This is the Arsenal. From floor to ceiling—*Longfellow*

This is the black sea-brute bulling through wavewrack—*Merwin*

This is the children's playground—*Williams, Oscar*

This is the city where men are mended—*Plath*

This is the day His hour of life draws near—*Tate, Allen*

This is the debt I pay—*Dunbar, Paul Laurence*

This is the dragon's country, and these his own streams—*Warren*

This is the female form—*Whitman*

This is the forest primeval, the murmuring pines and the hemlocks—*Longfellow*

This is the hour that we must mourn—*Clarke*

This is the house of Bedlam—*Bishop, Elizabeth*

This is the house that Jack built—*Children's Verses and Nursery Rhymes*

This is the key of the kingdom—*Children's Verses and Nursery Rhymes*

This is the lair of the landlady—*Atwood*

This is the law of the Yukon, and ever she makes it plain—*Service*

This is The Making of America in five panels—*MacLeish*

This is the maneater's skull—*Hughes, Ted*

This is the midnight—let no star—*Kipling*

This is the month, and this the happy morn—*Milton*

This is the Night Mail crossing the Border—*Auden*

This is the pay-day up at the mines—*Service*

This is the plum season, the nights—*Atwood*

This is the road I have chosen—*Marshall, Helen Lowrie*

This is the road the Master took—*Marshall, Helen Lowrie*

This is the sea, then, this great abeyance—*Plath*

This is the ship of pearl, which, poets feign—*Holmes, Oliver Wendell*

This is the song of the parson's son—*Service*

This is the sort of face that sheep—*Engle*

This is the terminal: the light—*Winters*

This is the time lean woods shall spend—*Adams*

This is the time of day when we in the Men's Ward—*Betjeman*

This is the time of the whirlwind—*Randall*

This is the time, that special time—*Marshall, Helen Lowrie*

This is the weather the cuckoo likes—*Hardy*

This is thy hour O Soul, thy free flight into the wordless—*Whitman*

This is your elegy, the gray sea grieving—*Reeves*

This journey is exploring us. Where the child stood—*Rukeyser*

This (let's remember) day died again and—*Cummings*

This life, which seems so fair—*Drummond of Hawthornden*

This light is loss backward; delight by hurt and by bias gained—*Bogan*

This little boat you see, my friends, has not—*Blackmur*

This little bride and groom—*Cummings*

This little house is sugar—*Hughes, Langston*

This little piggy went to market—*Children's Verses and Nursery Rhymes*

This living hand, now warm and capable—*Keats*

This love of ours can only come—*Marshall, Helen Lowrie*

This love that joins today—*Troupe*

This lovely flower fell to seed—*Cullen*

This man brings me stones—*Ignatow*

This man kept courage when the map of fear—*Van Doren*

This man, this poet, said—*Kunitz*

This mind made war—*Cummings*

This moonlight lies—*Van Doren*

This morning being rather young and foolish—*Patten*

This morning, flew up the lane—*Ransom*

This moth caught in the room tonight—*Snodgrass*

This night shall thy soul be required of thee—
Smith, Stevie

This one/ a common—*Kumin*

This one's gone to straw—*Sklarew*

This pansy has a thinking face—*Conkling*

This pardoner hadde heer as yelow as wex—
Chaucer

This place, rumored to have been Sodom, might
have been—*Duncan*

This plot of ground—*Williams, William Carlos*

This poem gets locked up—*Rasul*

This poem is for my wife—*MacLeish*

This quiet dust was gentlemen and ladies— ··
Dickinson, Emily

This record played in the room has lost all the
music—*Hillyer*

This rock-bound river, ever flowing—*Scott, F. R.*

This room is breaking apart—*Cattonar*

This saying good-by on the edge of the dark—
Frost, Robert

This side of the truth you may not see—*Thomas,
Dylan*

This stringy lump—*Dodson-Letourneau, Gayle*

This thing is beautiful, I know—*Coffin*

This time of year a twelvemonth past—*Housman*

This tree outside my window here—*Day Lewis*

This twentieth-century mind—*Marshall, Lenore
G.*

This urge, wrestle, resurrection of dry sticks—
Roethke

This was a caustic bush—*O'Gorman*

This was a rough death—*Rodgers*

This was Mr. Bleaney's room. He stayed—*Larkin*

This was the first time—*Sobiloff*

This was the time in which enflam'd with hope
—*Wordsworth*

This was the Woman; what now of the Man—
Meredith, George

This will be answered—*MacLeish*

This wind brings all dead things to life—*Young,
Andrew*

This wisdom I learned from the motionless twig
—*Abbe*

This woman sandpapers—*Polak*

This year, maybe, do you think I can graduate
—*Hughes, Langston*

This year she has changed greatly—meaning you
—*Graves*

Thise ryotoures three, of which I telle—*Chaucer*

Tho' grief and fondness in my breast rebel—*Johnson, Samuel*

Tho' I'm no Catholic—*Williams, William Carlos*

Tho mastering me—*Hopkins*

Tho, when as chearlesse night ycovered had—
Spenser

Thomas Jefferson/ What do you say—*Benét, Stephen Vincent*

Thomas Lovell Beddoes inquired—*Nash*

Those blessed structures, plot and rhyme—*Lowell, Robert*

Those famous men of old, the Ogres—*Graves*

Those five or six young guys—*Walcott*

Those great sweeps of snow—*Bly*

Those hours, that with gentle work did frame—
Shakespeare

Those laden lilacs—*Wilbur*

Those lines that I before have writ, do lie—*Shakespeare*

Those lips that Love's own hand did make—
Shakespeare

Those lumbering horses in the steady plough—
Muir

Those parts of thee that the world's eye doth view
—*Shakespeare*

Those pretty wrongs that liberty commits—
Shakespeare

Those weddings in wartime!—*Yevtushenko*

Those who came short of love—*Graves*

Those who said God is praised—*Wilbur*

Those with few images, lyrics—*Bell*

Thou, America—*Whitman*

Thou art as tyrannous, so as thou art—*Shakespeare*

Thou art indeed just, Lord, if I contend—*Hopkins*

Thou art not fair, for all thy red and white—*Campion*

Thou art not lovelier than lilacs,—no—*Millay*

Thou blind fool, Love, what dost thou to mine
eyes—*Shakespeare*

Thou blind man's mark, thou fool's self-chosen
snare—*Sidney*

Thou blossom bright with autumn dew—*Bryant,
William Cullen*

Thou comest!—all is said without a word—*Browning, Elizabeth Barrett*

Thou hast left me ever, Jamie—*Burns*

Thou hast made me, and shall thy worke decay
—*Donne*

Thou hast thy calling to some palace-floor—
Browning, Elizabeth Barrett

Thou mighty Lord and master of the Lyre—*Herrick*

Thou shalt have one God only; who—*Clough*

Thou still unravish'd bride of quietness—*Keats*

Thou wast that all to me, love—*Poe*

Thou who hast slept all night upon the storm—
Whitman

Though he never played for faces—*Greenwald*

Though I do wonder—*Giovanni*

Though I'm not a woman—*Elmslie*

Though loath to grieve—*Emerson*

Though nurtured like the sailing moon—*Yeats*

Though the crocuses poke up their heads in the
usual places—*Roethke*

Though the world has slipped and gone—*Sitwell,
Edith*

Though three men dwell on Flannan Isle—*Gibson, Wilfred*

Though we are atoms and the self defined—*Marshall, Lenore G.*

Though you are in your shining days—*Yeats*

Though you are young and I am olde—*Campion*

Though your strangenesse frets my hart—*Campion*

The thought of what America would be like—
Pound

A thought went up my mind today—*Dickinson,
Emily*

Thou's welcome, wean, mishanter fa' me—*Burns*

A thousand doors ago—*Sexton*

A thousand times you've seen that scene—*Warren*

A thousand tymes have I herd men telle—*Chaucer*

Three blind mice, see how they run—*Children's Verses and Nursery Rhymes*

Three boulders like camel's humps—*Dodson-Letourneau, Gayle*

Three boys, American, in dungarees—*Updike*

Three children sliding on the ice—*Children's Verses and Nursery Rhymes*

Three faces . . ./ mirrored—*Walker*

Three hours chain-smoking words—*Rich*

Three jolly Farmers—*De la Mare*

Three Kings came riding from far away—*Longfellow*

Three large balloons in a dog-cart—*Sitwell, Osbert*

Three little kittens lost their mittens—*Follen*

The three men coming down the winter hill—*Berryman*

Three of us afloat in the meadow by the swing—*Stevenson*

Three things make earth unquiet—*Kipling*

Three wise men of Gotham—*Children's Verses and Nursery Rhymes*

Three woman have stepped at my books—*Durrell*

Three years she grew in sun and shower—*Wordsworth*

Three young Tennesseans—*Nash*

Thrice tosse these oaken ashes in the ayre—*Campion*

A thrifty soprano of Hingham—*Nash*

Thro the hush'd Air—*Thomson*

Through a great lion's head clouded by mange—*Walcott*

Through all the pleasant meadow-side—*Stevenson*

Through gilded trellises—*Sitwell, Edith*

Through his iron glades—*Sitwell, Osbert*

Through that window—all else being extinct—*Aiken*

Through the narrow street all day—*Lowbury*

Through the open porch window—*Aubert*

Through the revolving door—*Merriam*

Through the strait pass of suffering—*Dickinson, Emily*

Through the tall grass in your head—*Patten*

Through the windmills fairies weave—*Howard, Winifred*

Through throats where many rivers meet the curlews cry—*Thomas, Dylan*

Through water his own waterfall—*Starbuck*

Through woods, Mme Une Telle, a trifle ill—*Gunn*

Throwing away my youth—*Jong*

Thule, the period of cosmography—*Anonymous–English–Modern English*

Thunder: the flesh quails and the soul bows down—*Swinburne*

Thus Adam to himself lamented loud—*Milton*

Thus can my love excuse the slow offence—*Shakespeare*

Thus Eve with count'nance blithe her story told—*Milton*

Thus I/ Passe by—*Herrick*

Thus is his cheek the map of days outworn—*Shakespeare*

Thus piteously Love closed what he begat—*Meredith, George*

Thus reduced to few, the fresh spring surprised them—*Sereni*

Thus, some tall tree that long hath stood—*Freneau*

Thus spoke the lady underneath the tree—*Sitwell, Edith*

Thus systole addressed diastole—*Aiken*

Thus when with meats and drinks they had sufficed—*Milton*

Thy bosom is endeared with all hearts—*Shakespeare*

Thy forest, Windsor! and thy green retreats—*Pope, Alexander*

Thy gift, thy tables, are within my brain—*Shakespeare*

Thy glass will show thee how thy beauties wear—*Shakespeare*

Thy little brethren, which like Faery Sprights—*Donne*

Thy shadow, Earth, from Pole to Central Sea—*Hardy*

Thy soul shall find itself alone—*Poe*

Thy summer voice, Musketaquit—*Emerson*

Thy trivial harp will never please—*Emerson*

Thyme, thym' amekhanoisi kedesin kykomene—*Archilochos*

Thyrsis, or Meliboeus, or old Damoetas—*Heath-Stubbs*

Ti pomnish, Alyoshe, dorogi smolenshchini—*Simonov*

Ti-ri-ti-ri, Ay—*Garcia Lorca*

Tic-tic-tic—*Tippett*

Tiddle-de-dumpty, tiddle-de-dee—*Field, Eugene*

The tide rises, the tide falls—*Longfellow*

Tie the moccasin—*Guiterman*

Tief, tief im tiefsten Tannenwald—*Guggenmos*

Tiefab im Tobel liegt ein Haus—*Droste-Hülshoff*

Ein tiefes Märchen aus dem Morgenland—*Haushofer*

El tiempo había volado como las golondrinas—*Dávila, José Antonio*

El tiempo se ablandó—*Unamuno*

Tienen nombre, Señor; son los que sufren—*Rosales*

La tierra se hace madrasta—*Mistral*

Tierra seca/ tierra quieta—*Garcia Lorca*

Tiger, tiger, burning bright—*Blake*

Tight skin called face is drawn—*Scott, F. R.*

Till the blue grass turn yellow—*Pound*

Till they tangled and seemed to trip—*Hughes, Ted*

Till thinking had worn out my enterprise—*Eberhart*

Tillfällig som en vallmo, som vecket ien vandrandes kläder—*Lagerkvist*

The time come round again—*Winters*

Time, cruel Time, come and subdue that brow—*Daniel, Samuel*

Time for the wood, the day—*Bogan*

The time i dropped your almost body down—*Clifton*

Time is a harp—*Conkling*

The time I've lost in wooing—*Moore, Thomas*

Time like a lake breeze—*Stryk*

Time passing, and the memories of love—*Davie*

Time present and time past—*Eliot, Thomas Stearns*

Time swings her burning hands—*Kunitz*

Time to uproot again—*Patten*

Time to wipe away the slime—*Walker*

Time was away and somewhere else—*MacNeice*

Times were worse then—*Beecher*

Time will assuage—*Cunningham, James Vincent*

Time will say nothing but I told—*Auden*

The time you won your town the race—*Housman*

Timon, since you are dead—*Kallimachos*

Timothy Winters comes to school—*Causley*

A Tinker out of Bedford—*Kipling*

Tinkling treble/ Rolling bass—*Hughes, Langston*

Tirad ese anillo—*Garcia Lorca*

Tir'd with all these, for restful death I cry—*Shakespeare*

Tired of poultry, the experimental chemist—*Benedikt*

Tis better to be vile than vile esteemed—*Shakespeare*

'Tis Christmas weather, and a country house—*Meredith, George*

Tis de bios, ti de terpnon ater khryses Aphrodites—*Mimnermus of Colophon*

'Tis known, at least it should be, that throughout—*Byron*

'Tis like stirring living embers when, at eighty one remembers—*Holmes, Oliver Wendell*

'Tis said that some have died for love—*Wordsworth*

'Tis the middle of night by the castle clock—*Coleridge, Samuel Taylor*

'Tis the voice of the lobster: I heard him declare—*Carroll*

Tis the yeares midnight, and it is the dayes—*Donne*

'Tis time this heart should be unmoved—*Byron*

'Tis true, fair Celia, that by thee I live—*Anonymous-English—Modern English*

'Tis true, fellow citizens—*Masters, Edgar Lee*

A tisket, a tasket—*Children's Verses and Nursery Rhymes*

Title divine is mine—*Dickinson, Emily*

To a place of ruined stone we brought you, and sea-reaches—*Warren*

To all you ladies now at land—*Sackville*

To and fro—*Richards, I. A.*

To Apis the boxer—*Lucilius*

To ask the hard question is simple—*Auden*

To balance one hundred hats on my head—*Abse*

To be a Jew in the twentieth century—*Rukeyser*

To be black in America—*Arnez*

To be homeless is a pride—*Graves*

To be not jealous, give not love—*Stephens*

To be, or not to be: that is the question—*Shakespeare*

To be the father of the fatherless—*Byron*

To be the only woman alive in a vast hive of death—*Graves*

To begin at the beginning—*Thomas, Dylan*

To bring the dead to life—*Graves*

To brune Øine jeg nylig saae—*Andersen*

To burn is surely bad, to be—*Weiss*

To catch the meaning out of the air—*Eberhart*

To come to a Congress of books when thoughtless death—*Brinnin*

To conclude, I announce what comes after me—*Whitman*

To create the poem—*Gregor*

To-Day from each and all, a breath of prayer—*Whitman*

To-day we have naming of parts. Yesterday—*Reed, Henry*

To die with a forlorn hope, but soon to be raised—*Graves*

To drum-beat and heart-beat—*Finch, Francis*

To enter into their bodies—*Olson*

To every man—*Emanuel*

To exalt, enthrone, establish and defend—*Belloc*

To fair Fidele's grassy tomb—*Collins, William*

To feel and speak the astonishing beauty of things—earth, stone, and water—*Jeffers, Robinson*

To fight aloud is very brave—*Dickinson, Emily*

To fight history as it carries us—*Piercy*

To find the Western path—*Blake*

To fling my arms wide—*Hughes, Langston*

To get betimes in Boston town I rose this morning early—*Whitman*

To get off the ground has always been difficult—*Wheelock*

To go by the asters—*Levertov*

To go low, to be as nothing—*Nemerov*

To hasten night would be humane—*Abse*

To have no excuse—*Hannan*

To have stepped lightly among European marbles—*Eberhart*

To him who in the love of Nature holds—*Bryant, William Cullen*

To his house the bodiless—*Plath*

To know our destiny is to know the horror—*Graves*

To lie on these beaches for another summer—*Hollander*

To Lisa in a letter I once wrote—*Dowling*

To live/ believe in no one—*Sanchez*

To live in hell, and heaven to behold—*Constable*

To live, to lie awake—*Rich*

To love is to give—*Smith, William Jay*

To make a prairie it takes a clover and one bee—*Dickinson, Emily*

To me, fair friend, you never can be old—*Shakespeare*

To Mercy, Pity, Peace, and Love—*Blake*

To one who has been long in city pent—*Keats*

To own nothing, but to be—*Abse*

To put it all down I take—*Porter, Peter*

To save face we bomb—*Howes*

To see a world in a Grain of sand—*Blake*

To sleep I give my powers away—*Tennyson*

To So-Kin of Rakuyo, ancient friend—*Li Bai*

To start the world of gold—*Frost, Robert*

To the bob-white's call—*Williams, William Carlos*

To the field I carried my milking pail—*Anonymous-English—Modern English*

To the keen clamor of the Negro—*Diop*

To the legion of the lost ones, to the cohort of the damned—*Kipling*

To the Looking-Glass world—*Carroll*

To the lucky now who have lovers or friends—*Durrell*

To the man who has married an ugly wife—*Palladas*

To the ocean now I fly—*Milton*

To think of them—*Hollo*

To this generation I would say—*Masters, Edgar Lee*

To travel like a bird—*Day Lewis*

To travel Typhon, from the old holdings—*Olson*

To walk on hills is to employ legs—*Graves*

To wear the arctic fox—*Moore, Marianne*

To what purpose, April, do you return again—*Millay*

To whom are you talking you old fraud—*Goldstein*

To you, my purs, and to noon other wight—*Chaucer*

A toad can die of light—*Dickinson, Emily*

The toadstool towers infest the shore—*Nicholson*

Tobroken been the statuts hye in hevene—*Chaucer*

Toda esta noite o rouxinol chorou—*Espanca*

Todas las tardes en Granada—*Garcia Lorca*

To-day from each and all, a breath of prayer—*Whitman*

Today I am tired—*Sanchez*

Today I saw a picture of the cancer cells—*Eberhart*

Today, I want to speak of human agony—*Silkin*

Today, should you let fall a glass it would—*Tomlinson*

Today there is another marriage—*Eberhart*

Today was a ragamuffin day—*Marshall, Helen Lowrie*

To-day we have naming of parts. Yesterday—*Reed, Henry*

Todlich graute mir der Morgen—*Mörike*

Todo el astío, el polícrono sol—*Martinez Alonso*

Todo el barrio pobre—*Poveda*

Todo el jardín en una quietud de éxtasis—*Martinez Alonso*

Todo está como era entonces—*Andrade, Olegario Victor*

Todo lo puede el viento: va/ y viene—*Hierro*

Todo pasa y todo queda—*Machado, Antonio*

Todos estos señores estaban dentro—*Neruda*

Todos los días rezo esta oración—*Alonso*

Todos los ojos estaban abiertos—*Garcia Lorca*

Together in this grave lie Benjamin Pantier, attorney at law—*Masters, Edgar Lee*

Together, we looked down—*Emanuel*

Toi que j'ai recueilli sur sa bouche expirante—*Lamartine*

Toi qui, comme un coup de couteau—*Baudelaire*

The token woman gleams like a gold molar in a toothless mouth—*Piercy*

Toll for the brave—*Cowper*

Das Tollkirschendickicht—*Bobrowski*

Tom had a little pony Jack—*Belloc*

Tom, Tom, the piper's son—*Children's Verses and Nursery Rhymes*

The tombstone told when she died—*Thomas, Dylan*

Tomorrow I begin to cook—*Kizer*

Tomorrow I will not love you—*Vargas*

Tomorrow we'll find much to do—*Emanuel*

Ton o hapameibomenos prosephe polymetis Odysseus—*Homer*

Ton Passé! car tu as un Passé, toi aussi—*Geraldy*

Ton rire jaillissait, vif entre les eaux vives—*Mauriac*

Tone, des Schiffmanns Sohn, de er dienete noch bei dem Vater—*Mörike*

Tongue in the city—*Dlugos*

The tongue that mothered such a metaphor—*Francis*

A tongue's tickle is tickling inside me—*Sobiloff*

Tonight a blackout. Twenty years ago—*Lowell, Robert*

Tonight at noon—*Henri*

Tonight, Grave Sir, both my poor house and I—*Jonson*

Tonight in the pub I talked with Ernie Jones—*Scannell*

Tonight is the night when dead leaves fly—*Behn, Harry*

Tonight, then, is the night—*Scannell*

Tönte dir der liebliche Gesang—*Kuhn*

Too far for you to see—*Thomas, Ronald Stuart*

Too fierce the candlelight; your gentle voice—*Graves*

Too green the springing April grass—*McKay*

Too late to kiss my wife goodbye—*Kramer*

Too late, your sighs and smiles of promise—*Heine*

Too little has been said of the door—*Tomlinson*

Too many people on the earth—*Eastman*

Too many people scribbling—*Gioseffi*

Too many years, from a vague evening valley—*Engle*

Too proud to die, broken and blind he died—*Thomas, Dylan*

Too soon, too soon, a man will come—*Wright, James*

The top hat French poodle, the electric—*Gregor*

The tops of the spruces here have always done—*Hollander*

Tornami a mente il di che la battaglia—*Leopardi*

Torneramo le sere a intepidire—*Gatto*

Toro negro, toro bravo—*Garcia Lorca*

Torrigos, el general—*Garcia Lorca*

Une Tortue étoit, à la tête légère—*La Fontaine*

Ein Toter bin ich—*Bachmann*

Touch with your fingers—*Watkins*

Toughest gal I ever did see—*Walker*

Toujours ce souvenir m'attendrit et me touche—*Chénier*

Toujours il y eut cette clameur, toujours il y eut cette splendeur—*Perse*

A tourist came in from Orbitville—*Swenson*

Tournez tournez/ petite filles—*Prévert*

Les tours penchées les cieux obliques—*Tzara*

Tous les morts sont ivres—*Milosz*

Toussaint, the most unhappy man of men—*Wordsworth*

Tout a ce besoin d'évasion—*Damas*

Tout ce qu'ici la nature environne—*Du Bellay*

Tout est cru, tout est vert—*Queneau*

Le tout est de tout dire et je manque de mots—*Éluard*

Tout est mystère dans l'amour—*La Fontaine*

Tout là-haut, tout là-haut, loin de la route sûre—*Baudelaire*

Toute la ville est entrée dans ma chambre—*Soupault*

Toutes les choses au hasard—*Éluard*

Towards nightfall when the wind—*Tate, Allen*

Towmahss Mahnn: that's how you say it—*Lowell, Robert*

The town-hall clock seems to possess—*Bodenheim*

The town clock of Hiroshima was a usual sort of clock—*Goldstein*

Toy-maker Ptolemy/ made up a universe—*Ciardi*

Tra la la la—see me dance the polka—*Sitwell, Edith*

Tra le battaglie, Omero—*Carducci*

The trade-wind jingles the rings in the nets—*Stevens, Wallace*

Traffic, the lion, the sophisticate—*Williams, William Carlos*

The tragic, I would always shun—*Gregor*

Le train court on the sait où—*Queneau*

The train drives down the canyon walls—*Jeffers, Lance*

Translated furies sing—*Kgositsile*

Tras de un amoroso lance—*Juan de la Cruz*

Traveler take heed for journeys undertaken in the dark of the year—*Walker*

Traveler! Under this stone lies all that remains —*Heath-Stubbs*

Traveling through the dark I found a deer—*Stafford*

Die Trayeer die benkendicker oif mein vay—*Sutzkever*

Tre piccerille—*Filippo*

Tread out a marble hollow—*Richards, I. A.*

Treading afield I saw afar—*Baldwin, Michael*

Tree at my window, window tree—*Frost, Robert*

Tree-toad is a small gray person—*Conkling*

The trees along this city street—*Millay*

The trees are in their autumn beauty—*Yeats*

The trees crouch uphill towards the ridgecrest —*Griffiths*

La Treizième revient . . . C'est encore la première —*Nerval*

Trennen wollten wir uns? wähnten es gut und klug—*Hölderlin*

Le 31 du mois d'août 1914—*Apollinaire*

La très-chère était une, et, connaissant mon coeur —*Baudelaire*

Tres cosas me tienen preso—*Alcázar*

Tres moricas me enamoran—*Garcia Lorca*

Tres Morillas me enamoran—*Anonymous–Spanish*

Tri, tri, tri—*Palazzeschi*

A trick that everyone abhors—*Belloc*

Trigales del corazón—*Martinez Alonso*

Triple sphere of fox fire—*Wellman*

Triste está la casa nuestra—*Banchs*

Tristesse d'eau, Vierge qui pâme—*Jacob, Max*

La tristesse des illetrés dans les ténèbres des bouteilles—*Char*

Trocknet nicht, trocknet nicht—*Goethe*

Trois allumettes une à une allumées dans la nuit —*Prévert*

The trolley has stopped long since—*Hall*

Trop longtemps j'ai souffert de dénouer l'entreinte—*Mauriac*

Tropf, tropf, tau—*Zuckmayer*

A trouble—*Williams, William Carlos*

The trouble with a kitten is that—*Nash*

Trudge, body, and climb, trudge and climb—*Graves*

True Thomas lay o'er yon grassy bank—*Anonymous–English—Modern English*

Trueblood, he never heard of incest—*Ward*

El trueno horrendo que en fragor revienta—*Olmedo*

Truly, My Satan, thou art but a Dunce—*Blake*

Die trunkenen Fluten fallen—*Benn*

The truth I do not stretch or shove—*Nash*

The Truth is—*Viorst*

Truth is not the secret of a few—*Ferlinghetti*

Truth-loving Persians do not dwell upon—*Graves*

Tshernyi vetsher—*Blok*

Tu as eu tort! Tu as eu tort! je te répète—*Geraldy*

Tu demandes pourquoi je reste sans rien dire—*Geraldy*

Tu duorme, io te guardo—*Di Giacomo*

Tu eras el huracán—*Becquer*

Tu es malheureux? Ne pense pas—*Omar Khayyam*

Tu es mon amour depuis tant d'années—*Char*

Tu es seule mon coeur, mon sang et ma Déesse —*Ronsard*

Tu étais au bar—*Damas*

Tu forma se deshizo. Deshiciste tu forma—*Jiménez*

Tu glisses dans le lit—*Éluard*

Tu júbilo, en el vuelo—*Florit*

Tu m'as dit—*Damas*

Tú me levantas, tierras de Castilla—*Unamuno*

Tú me llevas, concienci a plena, deseante Dios —*Jiménez*

Tú me miraras llorando—*Jiménez*

Tú me quieres alba, me quieres de espuma—*Storni*

Tu ne quaesieris, scire nefas, quem mihi, quem tibi—*Horace*

Tu nombre viene lento como las músicas humildes—*Oquendo de Amat*

Tu non ricordi la casa dei doganieri—*Montale*

Tu pupila es azul—*Becquer*

Tú que callas, oh Cristo! para oírnos—*Unamuno*

Tu seras nue dans le salon aux vieilles choses—*Jammes*

Tu t'acharnes sur la beauté—*Apollinaire*

Tú venías vestida de guitarras y pájaros—*Fombona-Pachano*

Tu vi' che faccia allera tene ò muorto—*Bovio*

Tú y tu desnudo sueño. No lo sabes—*Diego, Gerardo*

Tuércele el cuello al cisne de engañoso plumaje —*González-Martínez*

Die Tugend will nicht immer passen—*Busch*

The tulip poplar is not a poplar—*Williams, Jonathan*

Tum pater Anchises: animae, quibus altera fato —*Virgil*

Tumannyi prigorod, kak turman—*Voznesensky*

Tumbling in twenty rings—*Hodgson*

A tumult of images insist—*Pols*

Tuot ûf. Wem? wer sît ir?—*Wolfram von Eschenbach*

The turf she strokes above his head—*Wilkinson*

Der Turmer, der schaut zu Mitten der Nacht—*Goethe*

Turn all thy thoughts to eyes—*Campion*

Turn right next corner—*Ginsberg*

Turn sideways now and let them see—*Vaughan, H. A.*

Turn to me in the darkness—*Heath-Stubbs*

Turncoat sleep is quick—*Marcus*

Turning and turning in the widening gyre—*Yeats*

Turning in the brain, to wake—*Hacker*

Turning it over, considering like a madman—*Berryman*

Les turques ont passé là—*Hugo, Victor*

Turquoise wings on Diamond Harbor road—*Williams, Hugo*

The turtle lives 'twixt plated decks—*Nash*

Tutt' 'e pulle d' 'o cumpare—*Mura*

Tutta la mia fiorita e verde etade—*Petrarca*

Tutti li forestieri, oggni nazzione—*Belli*

Tutti l'ingresi de Piazza de Spaggna—*Belli*

Tutto, tutto se scorda—*Di Giacomo*

Tuve en mi pago en un tiempo—*Hernández, José*

Tverdili pastyri, shto vreden—*Yevtushenko*

'Twas a balmy summer evening, and a goodly crowd was there—*D'Arcy*

'Twas at the royal feast, for Persia won—*Dryden*

'Twas brillig, and the slithy toves—*Carroll*

'Twas early in the month of May—*Anonymous–English—Modern English*

'Twas like a maelstrom with a notch—*Dickinson, Emily*

'Twas noontide of summer—*Poe*

'Twas on holy Thursday, their innocent faces clean—*Blake*

'Twas on a lofty vase's side—*Gray*

'Twas on the shores that round our coast—*Gilbert, Sir William Schwenck*

'Twas the night before Christmas, when all through the house—*Moore, Clement Clarke*

'Twas when the seas were roaring—*Gay, John*

Twelve hundred years—*Jones, David*

Twelve snails went walking after night—*Lindsay, Vachel*

The twentieth year is well-nigh past—*Cowper*

Twenty bridges from Tower to Kew—*Kipling*

Twenty-eight young men bathe by the shore—*Whitman*

Twenty years, every day—*Muir*

T' whom Satan turning boldly, thus: Ye Powers —*Milton*

Twice a week the winter thorough—*Housman*

Twice or thrice had I loved thee—*Donne*

Twice upon a time—*Abse*

Twilight. Red in the west—*Masefield*

Twin streaks twice higher than cumulus—*Snyder*

Twinkle, twinkle, little bat—*Carroll*

Twinkle, twinkle, little star—*Taylor, Ann and Jane*

Twirling your blue skirts travelling the sward—*Ransom*

Twitching in the cactus hospital gown—*Harper*

Twitching the leaves—*Thwaite*

Two athletes—*Wright, James*

Two bells six bells two bells six bells—*Sandburg*

Two boards with a token roof, backed—*Merwin*

Two boys are tossing a poem together uncoached —*Francis*

Two boys stand at the end of the full train—*Logan*

Two centuries—*Jones, David*

The two executioners stalk along over the knolls —*Hardy*

Two girls discover—*Levertov*

Two-Gun Buster was a railroad han'—*Walker*

Two hands lie still, the hairy and the white—*Shapiro, Karl*

Two loves I have, of comfort and despair—*Shakespeare*

Two nights in Manchester, nothing much to do —*Thwaite*

Two nudists of Dover—*Nash*

Two old bachelors were living in one house—*Lear*

Two old crows sat on a fence rail—*Lindsay, Vachel*

Two people in a room, speaking harshly—*Rich*

Two roads diverged in a yellow wood—*Frost, Robert*

Two things a man's built for, killing and you-know-what—*Warren*

Two things I remember about my grandfather —*Brock*

Two voices are there: one is of the sea—*Wordsworth*

Two years high by the world wide—*MacNeice*

Ty predo mnoyu—*Zhukovsky*

Ty raspugal moikh tovarok—*Pasternak*

Ty s tekoi zhivesh—*Voznesensky*

Ty znachil vso v moei sud'be—*Pasternak*

Tyger, Tyger, burning bright—*Blake*

Tyst står han vid stenen—*Martinson*

Tzwai yidden sitzen en zingen—*Tunkeler*

U beat them—*Lee, Don L.*

U feel that way some times—*Lee, Don L.*

U lyudei pred prazdnikom uborka—*Pasternak*

Über allen Gipfeln ist Ruh—*Goethe*

Über den Tod geht nichts—*Kaschnitz*

Über den weissen Weiher—*Trakl*

Über die Pferde hat der Herr die himmlische Satteldecke gebreitet—*Zuckmayer*

Über meines Liebchens Äugeln—*Goethe*

Ugliest little boy—*Brooks, Gwendolyn*

The ugly woman clutched her lover—*Williams, William Carlos*

Ugolino takes his rest—*Howes*

Újra és újra öket látom—*Pilinszky*

Ukazanie prishlo na zare—*Svetlov*

Ul-ul-ul-tra-tra—*Skellings*

Um Mitternacht, ich schlief, im Busen wachte —*Goethe*

Umer drug u menya vot kakaya beda—*Simonov*

Umom Rossiyu ne ponyat'—*Tyutchev*

Un dì, s'io non andrò sempre fuggendo—*Foscolo*

Un domingo sin ti, de ti perdido—*Carranza*

Un-ha tarde alá en Castilla—*Castro, Rosalía de*

Un jour—*Vian*

Un jour deux Pelerins sur le sable rencontrent —*La Fontaine*

Un jour la Terre ne sera—*Supervielle*

Un jour, maigre et sentant un royal appétit—*Hugo, Victor*

Un jour, quand nous dirons: c'était le temps du soleil—*Supervielle*

Un jour un coq détourna—*La Fontaine*

Un sueño soñaba anoche—*Anonymous–Spanish*

L'un t'éclaire avec son ardeur—*Baudelaire*

Una tarde, comenzamos a oír la melodía de un pájaro ideal—*Martinez Alonso*

Una tarde parda y fría—*Machado, Antonio*

Unaufhörlich begegnen sich—*Heissenbüttel*

Uncle Time is a ole, ole man—*Scott, Dennis*

Unconscious came a beauty wrist—*Swenson*

Und als der Krieg im vierten Lenz—*Brecht*

Und als der nächste Krieg begann—*Kästner*

Und bist du erst mein ehlich Weib—*Heine*

Und der Haifisch, der hat Zähne—*Brecht*

Und frische Nahrung, neues Blut—*Goethe*

Und Kinder wachsen auf mit tiefen Augen—*Hofmannsthal*

Und willst du wissen, warum—*Droste-Hülshoff*

Und wüsstens die Blumen, die kleinen—*Heine*

Undepilated beauty stands—*Conquest*

Under a sky the colour of pea soup—*Piercy*

Under a spreading chestnut-tree—*Longfellow*

Under a toadstool crept a wee Elf—*Herford*

Under bare Ben Bulben's head—*Yeats*

Under great yellow flags and banners of the ancient Cold—*Sitwell, Edith*

Under his helmet, up against his pack—*Owen, Wilfred*

Under my hat I custom you intricate, Ella—*Stafford*

Under my shell/ my pearly shell—*Marshall, Lenore G.*

Under my window-ledge the waters race—*Yeats*

Under the after-sunset sky—*Thomas, Edward*

Under the bronze crown—*Wilbur*

Under the burnt out green—*Brathwaite*

Under the dawn I wake to my two-wheel friend —*Yevtushenko*

Under the flag of this pneumatic moon—*Smith, A. J. M.*

Under the forest, where the day is dark—*Winters*

Under the Greenwood Tree—*Shakespeare*

Under the hive-like dome the stooping haunted readers—*MacNeice*

Under the palaces, the marble and granite—*Bergman, Alexander F.*

Under the parabola of a ball—*Douglas, Keith*

Under the sovereign crests of dead volcanoes—*Howes*

Under the thick beams of that swirly smoking light—*Snodgrass*

Under the veil—*Robson, Ernest M.*

Under the water tower at the edge of town—*Wright, James*

Under the wide and starry sky—*Stevenson*

Under the willow whose roots are shallow—*Heath-Stubbs*

Under the winter street lamps near the bus stop —*Amis*

Under yonder beech-tree single on the greensward—*Meredith, George*

Underneath the growing grass—*Rossetti, Christina*

Underneath this sable Herse—*Browne, William*

Understand that they were sitting just inside the door—*Patchen*

Understand what I have done—*Emanuel*

Underwater eyes, an eel's—*Hughes, Ted*

Une deux une deux—*Cendrars*

Une fois de plus l'exil—*Claudel*

Une fois, par malheur, si vous avez pris terre—*Vigny*

Une fois, une seule, aimable et douce femme—*Baudelaire*

The unheard, omnivorous—*Walcott*

Universes away from you—*Henri*

Unlike are we, unlike, O princely heart—*Browning, Elizabeth Barrett*

Unlove's the heavenless hell and homeless home —*Cummings*

Unmitigated England—*Betjeman*

The unmoving vault—*Tomlinson*

Unpacking the raw new rooms—*Gunn*

Uns hât der Winter geschât über al—*Walther von der Vogelweide*

Uns lockt die Morgenröte—*Hagedorn*

Unseen faces keep appearing—*Pietri*

Unter dem Gips meiner Gegenwart—*Goll*

Unter den Linden/ auf der Heide—*Walther von der Vogelweide*

Unter der Mövenschwinge des Morgens ist meine Zuflucht—*Piontek*

Unter Gelächter und Türenschlagen—*Krolow*

Untergangsstrassen zu überqueren—*Heissenbüttel*

Unthrifty loveliness, why dost thou spend—*Shakespeare*

Until the headlights darken—*Roethke*

Unto this process briefly compiled—*Skelton, John*

Unverständlich sind uns die Jungen—*Fontane*

Unwatch'd the garden bough shall sway—*Tennyson*

Up and down the small streets, in which—*Hall*

Up early, out of a dream—*Reid*

Up from the meadows rich with corn—*Whittier*

Up from the South, at break of day—*Read, Thomas Buchanan*

Up into the cherry tree / who should climb but little me—*Stevenson*

Up in the clouds, a blessed dot—*Clarke*

Up in the mountains, it's lonesome all the time —*Benét, Stephen Vincent*

Up the airy mountain—*Allingham*

Up the ash-tree climbs the ivy—*Betjeman*

Up the steps, along the porch—*Olson*

Up then, Melpomene, thou mournfulst Muse of mine—*Spenser*

Up there—*Williams, Hugo*

Up! up! my friend, and quit your books—*Wordsworth*

Up with me! Up with me into the clouds—*Wordsworth*

Up yonder hill—*Crabbe*

Uphill all the way—*Richards, I. A.*

Upon the eyes, the lips, the feet—*Dowson*

Upon what base was fixed the lath, wherein—*Taylor, Edward*

The upper slopes are busy with the cricket—*Gunn*

Uret slår med hammaren—*Karlfeldt*

The urgent letter that I try to write—*Kunitz*

L'usage seulement fait la possession—*La Fontaine*

V dni neslykhanno bolevyye—*Voznesensky*

V grade Khar'kove-grad—*Yevtushenko*

V Moskovskie osobnyaki—*Pasternak*

V sine more—*Shevchenko*
V starinny gody lyudi byli—*Lermontov*
V stranye perlona i dakrona—*Yevtushenko*
Va-t'en, chétif insecte, excrément de la terre—*La Fontaine*
Vacancies of Chirico Square repeated as far as Charon's River—*Scott, Winfield Townley*
Vaghe stelle dell' Orsa, io non credea—*Leopardi*
Vago augelletto, che cantando vai—*Petrarca*
Vago espaço de natal—*Lima*
The vague sea thuds against the marble cliffs—*Graves*
Vål formar den starke med svårdet sin värld—*Tegner*
Vale . . . do—*Melo Neto*
Valle che de' lamenti miei se' piena—*Petrarca*
Valle de Almería—*Ben Safar Al-Marini*
La vallée d'Alméria. La vallée d'Alméria—*Jammes*
Vallombrosa! I longed in thy shadiest wood—*Wordsworth*
Valmorbia, discorrevano il tuo fondo—*Montale*
Vamos dentrando recien—*Hernández, José*
Vamos llegando en el tren—*Jiménez*
Vanity, saith the preacher, vanity—*Browning, Robert*
Varför vaxa alla dessa blommor—*Hemmer*
El varón que tiene corazón de lis—*Darío*
Varus me meus ad suos amores—*Catullus*
Vas a venir, con que ilusión—*Mata*
Le vase où meurt cette verveine—*Sully-Prud-homme*
Vashu mysl'—*Mayakovsky*
Die Vaterschaft, wie find ich sie doch—*Brecht*
Vdali ot solntsa i prirody—*Tyutchev*
Ve voglio dì na cosa—*Filippo*
Ve voglio fa na lettera a ll'ingrese—*Di Giacomo*
Ved: sentado lo llevo—*Martí*
Vedlos pasar a través de los ensangrentados años—*Berger-Kiss*
Veggio nel tuo bel viso, Signor mio—*Michelangelo*
Veins that are extensible and expansible—*Antin*
Velloncito de mi carne—*Mistral*
Velox amoenum saepe Lucretilem—*Horace*
Vem gick förbi min barndoms Fönster—*Lagerkvist*
Vem kan inte räkna dem alla—*Ferlin*
Vem mötte du vid grinden—*Ferlin*
Vem rände dig på livet med sin treudd—*Lindegren*
Ven, acércate más, bebe en mi boca—*Laura*
Ven ich volt nit zein mit dere by nandt—*Sutzkever*
Ven, levántate hija, dijo mi viejo padre—*Godoy*
Venant du dedans—*Éluard*
Veniamos los dos, cargados—*Jiménez*
Venice at night, and I—*Gregor*
Venida es venida/ al mundo la vida—*Álvarez Gato*
Venisti tandem, tuaque exspectata parenti—*Virgil*
Venita, you have come to us—*Randall*
La venta de Cidones está en la carretera—*Machado, Antonio*
O vento varria as fôlhas—*Bandeira*
Venus, take my votive glass—*Prior*

The verbalist, with colours at his hand—*Eberhart*
Verde que te quiero verde—*Garcia Lorca*
Vergebt, dass alle meine Lieder klagen—*Platen-Hallermünde*
Vergine Madre, figlia del tuo Figlio—*Dante Alighieri*
Verhör ich Hauch und Klang—*Hauptmann*
La vérité fait notre joie écoute-moi—*Éluard*
The Vermont hills curve—*Conkling*
Verse, a breeze mid blossoms straying—*Coleridge, Samuel Taylor*
Verse is a turning—*Hillyer*
Verse is not written, it is bled—*Engle*
A very gross gentleman—*Edson*
Very old are the woods—*De la Mare*
Vesennei noch' yu dumai obo mne—*Yevtushenko*
Vespasien/ Empereur romain—*Obaldia*
Vestida con mantos negros—*Garcia Lorca*
Vezmolstvoval marmor—*Yevtushenko*
Vi kunde inte sova—*Gullberg*
Vi uppstäckte mer och mer—*Ferlin*
Vi vet allihop, hur det hände—*Ferlin*
Via arriva il poeta—*Ungaretti*
Il viaggio finisce qui—*Montale*
The vicious Winter finally yields—*Snodgrass*
Vides ut alta stet nive candidum—*Horace*
Vieil océan, ta forme harmonieuse—*Ducasse*
Un vieillard en or avec une montre en deuil—*Prévert*
Un vieillard hurle à la mort—*Prévert*
Un vieillard sur son Âne aperçut, en passant—*La Fontaine*
La vieille valise la chaussette et l'endive—*Péret*
Un viejo vive en mi fabricando mi muerte—*Carrera Andrade*
Viele versuchten umsonst das Freudigste freudig zu sagen—*Hölderlin*
Vielfach sind zum Hades die Pfade—*Mörike*
Viendo el Amor un día—*Melendez Valdes*
Viens sur mon coeur, âme cruelle et sourde—*Baudelaire*
Viens! une flûte invisible—*Hugo, Victor*
Viento contra viento—*Alberti*
Vier Elemente, innig gesellt—*Schiller*
La vierge, le vivace et le bel aujourd'hui—*Mallarmé*
Vierte, corazón, tu pena—*Martí*
Ein Vierviertelschwein und eine Auftakteule—*Morgenstern*
Vietnam: I need more than this crust of salt upon my eye—*Jeffers, Lance*
Un vieux Renard, mais des plus fins—*La Fontaine*
Views the phenomenal world as a congeries—*Aiken*
Vigil strange I kept on the field one night—*Whitman*
Vile, o natura, e grave ospite addetta—*Leopardi*
Le village à midi. La mouche d'or bourdonne—*Jammes*
The village life, and every care that reigns—*Crabbe*
Un villageois avoit à l'écart son logis—*La Fontaine*
Vino el que yo quería—*Alberti*
Vino, primero, pura—*Jiménez*
Vino, sentimiento, guitarra y poesía—*Machado, Manuel*

Vinte séculos de revoluçâo—*Lima*
Vinyes verdes vora el mar—*Sagarra*
Virgen hincada impieza—*Aridjis*
Vis, o människa, det blir du först—*Heidenstam*
Visages de la terre, quand j'aurai dit vos—*Pilon*
Visible, invisible—*Moore, Marianne*
A vision as of crowded city streets—*Longfellow*
Vision doesn't mean anything real—*Bell*
The vision of Christ that thou dost see—*Blake*
La vita fugge e non a'arresta un'ora—*Petrarca*
Vivamus, mea Lesbia, atque amemus—*Catullus*
Vive le 6 février/ grogne le jus—*Péret*
Vivement mes dix ans—*Obaldia*
Vivi entre os homens—*Mendes*
Vivía en una casa—*Fuertes*
Vivo sin vivir en mí . . . en mi yo no vivo ya—*Juan de la Cruz*
Vivo sin vivir en mí . . . vivo ya fuerade mí—*Teresa de Jesus*
Vnov, vnov, vnov—*Yevtushenko*
Vocca addurosa e fresca—*Di Giacomo*
Voces de muerte sonaron—*Garcia Lorca*
Vögel die um Futter kommen—*Eich*
Ein Vöglein singt so süsse—*Storm*
A voice by the cedar tree—*Tennyson*
A voice flew out of the river as morning flew—*Rukeyser*
The voice of the woodthrush played at half speed/ reveals to the halting ear—*Hoffman*
Voici la nuit qui m'éteint me traverse—*Fombeure*
Voici l'aire où le grain de froment céleste égrugé—*Claudel*
Voici le soir charmant, ami du criminel—*Baude-laire*
Voici les lieux charmants—*Boileau-Despréaux*
Voici pour toi, figure close—*Henault*
Voici venir les temps où vibrant sur sa tige—*Baudelaire*
Voilà les feuilles sans sève—*Lamartine*
Voll Harmonien ist der Flug der Vögel—*Trakl*
Volved, que os aseguro—*Castro, Rosalía de*
Volverán las oscuras golondrinas—*Becquer*
Volví al cabo de tres años—*Hernández, José*
Vom Bahnhof angeschwemmt—*Mehring*
Vom Himmel in die tiefsten Klüfte—*Storm*
Vom Lager stand ich mit dem Frühlicht auf—*Keller, Gottfried*
Vom Schatten eines Hauchs geboren—*Trakl*
Vom überhängenden Baum—*Bobrowski*
Von Fruchtomletts, da mag berichten—*Busch*
Von Kaffee und von Träumen lieg ich wach—*Eich*
Von Rôme Vogt, von Pülle Künec—*Walther von der Vogelweide*
Vor Kälte ist die Luft erstarrt—*Lenau*
Vor seinem Löwengarten—*Schiller*
Vor seiner Hütte ruhig im Schatten sitzt der Pflüger—*Hölderlin*
Voracities and verities sometimes are interacting—*Moore, Marianne*
Vorhergesagter Wind—*Eich*
Vorrei girar la Spagna—*Palazzeschi*
Vostra Eccellenza che mi sta in cagnesco—*Giusti*
Voto a Dios que me espanta esta grandeza—*Cervantes Saavedra*

Votre âme est un paysage choisi—*Verlaine*
Votre goût a servi de règle à mon ouvrage—*La Fontaine*
Votre nom?—*Prévert*
Voulentiers en ce moys isy—*Marot*
Vous aviez mon coeur—*Desbordes-Valmore*
Vous dont les ricanements—*Damas*
Vous êtes un beau ciel d'automne clair et rose—*Baudelaire*
Vous qui pillez l'émail de ces couleurs—*Aubigné*
Vous y dansiez petite fille—*Apollinaire*
Voy contra mi interés al confesarlo—*Becquer*
The voyage crossed, the firmament one star—*Gregory, Horace*
Vse moe, skazalo zlato—*Pushkin*
Vuestro nombre no sé—*Storni*
Vuie ccà—*Di Giacomo*
Vuie comm' a ll uva—*Di Giacomo*
Vurria c' uno, int' o' suonno—*Di Giacomo*
Vurria scrivere nu libbro—*Di Giacomo*
Vvie c'ancora tenite—*Di Giacomo*

Der Wächter auf dem Turme—*Guggenmos*
Wade in the water—*Lester*
Wade/through black jade—*Moore, Marianne*
Wagon Wheel Gap is a place I never saw—*Sandburg*
The waies, through which my weary steps I guyde—*Spenser*
Wait, Mister. Which way is home—*Sexton*
Waiting for the end, boys, waiting for the end—*Empson*
Waiting for when the sun an hour or less—*Gunn*
Waiting in front of the columnar high school—*Shapiro, Karl*
Wake! For the Sun, who scatter'd into flight—*Omar Khayyam*
Wake up, woman—*Anonymous–American Indian languages–Peruvian*
Wakened suddenly by my own voice—*Levine*
Waking alone in the multitude of loves—*Thomas, Dylan*
Waking has dangers where children—*Middleton, Christopher*
Waking then was like dreaming—*Yevtushenko*
Waking this morning—*Rukeyser*
Der Wald hinter den Gedanken—*Eich*
Walk carefully, walk prayerfully—*Marshall, Helen Lowrie*
Walk down Chinatown—*Chester*
Walker Evans, 65 years old—*Colbert*
Walking north toward the point, I came upon a dead seal—*Bly*
Walking swiftly with a dreadful duchess—*Smith, Stevie*
Walking the abandoned shade of childhood's habitations—*Lee, Laurie*
Walking to the museum over the outer drive—*Starbuck*
Walking toward the mountain—*Chapin*
Walking with a virgin heart—*Graves*
Wall, no! I can't tell whar he lives—*Hay, John*
Wallace for president—*Lee, Don L.*
Wallace Stevens, what's he done—*Roethke*
Wallowing in this bloody sty—*Lowell, Robert*
Walpole, traveling in the Alps—*Ciardi*
Walter Rodney going back—*Beaubien*

Wandelt sich rasch auch die Welt—*Rilke*

Wanderers outside the gates, in hollow—*Cowley, Malcolm*

Wandering lost upon the mountains of our choice —*Auden*

Wann treffen wir drei wieder zusamm?—*Fontane*

Wanna see a miracle—*Dupree*

Wanne mine eyhnen misten—*Anonymous–English—Middle English*

Wanting to cure—*Lifshin*

The wanton troopers riding by—*Marvell*

War ends, and he's returning—*Hardy*

The war is far away, sweet—*Hacker*

The warden said to me the other day—*Knight, Etheridge*

Warum bist du so kurz? liebst du, wie vormals denn—*Hölderlin*

Warum huligest du, heiliger Sokrates—*Hölderlin*

Warum ziehst du mich unwiderstehlich—*Goethe*

Was a man, was a twofaced man—*Booth*

Was dann nach jener Stunde—*Benn*

Was denkt die Maus am Donnerstag—*Guggenmos*

Was doch heut' nacht ein Sturm gewesen—*Mörike*

Was hör' ich draussen vor dem Tor—*Goethe*

Was ich am Tage stumm gedacht—*Morgenstern*

Was ist Traum? Was ist Tod—*Heine*

Was it an animal was it a bird—*Hughes, Ted*

Was it the proud full sail of his great verse—*Shakespeare*

Was it yesterday—*Sanchez*

Was machen wir immer und heuer—*Bergengruen*

Was meine Mutter mir sagte—*Brecht*

Was passt, das muss sich ründen—*Novalis*

Was reif in diesen Zeilen steht—*Brentano*

Was rennt das Volk, was wälzt sich dort—*Schiller*

Was sind wir Menschen doch—*Gryphius*

Was soll ich nun vom Wiedersehen hoffen—*Goethe*

Was tatest Du—*Goll*

Was the arrangement made between the two couples legal?—*Benedikt*

Was there ever a sound more brimming with cheer—*Marshall, Helen Lowrie*

Was wirst du tun, Gott, wenn ich sterbe—*Rilke*

Wash the dishes—*Porter, Bern*

Washed in the blood of the brave and the blooming—*Holmes, Oliver Wendell*

Wasn't it pleasant, O brother—*Riley*

Das Wasser rauscht', das Wasser schwoll—*Goethe*

Waste not, want not the quaint old Phrase—*Marshall, Helen Lowrie*

Watch him when he opens—*MacCaig*

Watch long enough, and you will see the leaf—*Aiken*

Watch, she said—*Gaver*

Watch the seagulls flying—*Lester*

A watched clock never moves—*MacNeice*

Watching my paralytic friend—*Shapiro, Karl*

Water is heavy silver over stone—*MacLeish*

The water turns—*Atwood*

Water turns back—*Williams, Hugo*

Water wanted to live—*Hughes, Ted*

Waterloo? We went once—*Garlick*

Waters and skies, hours and seas—*Goodman, Paul*

The wave withdrawing—*MacLeish*

Waving goodbye, from your banked hospital bed —*Hughes, Ted*

The way a crow—*Frost, Robert*

Way down South in Dixie—*Hughes, Langston*

Way down south where bananas grow—*Anonymous–English—Modern English*

The way I would look at the world the house—*Miles*

The way to the boiler was dark—*Roethke*

We all traveled into that big room—*Rukeyser*

We are—*Lifshin*

We are affrighted now to think we fear—*Williams, Oscar*

We are all imprisoned—*Giovanni*

We are approaching sleep: the chestnut blossoms in the mind—*Bly*

We are asleep under mirrors. What do I—*Hacker*

We are farmers—*Arnez*

We are going to do it—*Lee, Don L.*

We are hard on each other—*Atwood*

We are not come to wage a strife—*Bontemps*

We are not lovers—*Giovanni*

We are songs yet unsung—*Sanchez*

We are sorority—*Colbert*

We are the civil fathers, the poor necessary—*Van Doren*

We are the dead ones—*Sanchez*

We are the hollow men—*Eliot, Thomas Stearns*

We are the music makers—*O'Shaughnessy*

We are things of dry hours and the involuntary plan—*Brooks, Gwendolyn*

We are waiting—*Shiva*

We bear velvet cream—*Sitwell, Edith*

We built a ship upon the stairs—*Stevenson*

We can be anything we want—*Sanchez*

We can look into the stove tonight—*Rich*

We cannot be kept within the walls—*Bergman, Alexander F.*

We cannot celebrate with doleful music—*Hollander*

We cannot guess how long he'll wait—*Scott, Winfield Townley*

We cannot know our world—*Spencer*

We create the place—*Malanga*

We dance round in a ring and suppose—*Frost, Robert*

We dangled them upon the edge a week—*Beecher*

We draw our own dimensions; after all—*Hollander*

We drive between lakes just turning green—*Bly*

We enter the Roosevelt room—*Gaver*

We finished clearing the last section of trail—*Snyder*

We gave you food we did not want—*Arnez*

We go out together—*Patchen*

We gon be/ outa sight black/ men—*Sanchez*

We grow accustomed to the dark—*Dickinson, Emily*

We had a fine place to come—*Redgrove*

We had a picnic, we had buns—*Fisher*

We had always lived—*Howard, Lee*

We had expected everything but revolt—*Benét, Stephen Vincent*

We had this talent show—*Johnston, Ellen Turlington*

We handle our time—*Blackmur*

We have a good relationship, the elevator boy and I—*Swenson*

We have a secret, just we three—*Children's Verses and Nursery Rhymes*

We have been believers believing in the black gods of an old land—*Walker*

We have been here three days, and Rome is really —*Day Lewis*

We have climbed the mountain—*Justice*

We have fed our sea for a thousand years—*Kipling*

We have known such joy as a child knows—*Bell*

We have ridden out the waves—*Mackin*

We have tomorrow—*Hughes, Langston*

We hear the spring from far across the lake—*Ross, W. W. Eustace*

We is gathahed hyeah, my brothahs—*Dunbar, Paul Laurence*

We kissed at the barrier; and passing through—*Hardy*

We know of course the world will last—*Summers, Hollis*

We know others—*Lee, Don L.*

We lay on a grid of rock—*Sherwin*

We left our husbands sleeping—*Francis*

We lie here together—*Wellman*

We, like shades that were first conjured up—*Danner*

We listen, wind from where—*Adams*

We live in a third floor flat—*Porter, Peter*

We love the people, sir. You do?—*Vaughan, H. A.*

We make ourselves a place apart—*Frost, Robert*

We make up our faces—*Giovanni*

We may stop worrying—*Yorck*

We note the death, with small regret—*Fuller, Roy*

We ought not be alarmed if doubts—*Marshall, Helen Lowrie*

We ought to have a glory—*Marshall, Helen Lowrie*

We park and stare. A full sky of the stars—*Lowell, Robert*

We pattern our heaven—*Updike*

We prepare ourselves for mirrors—*Sukenick*

We programmed to death—*Sanchez*

We pulled for you when the wind was against us and the sails were low—*Kipling*

We real cool—*Brooks, Gwendolyn*

We rode into the fog—*Gleason*

We rose and then we slept—*Vogeler*

We run the dangercourse—*Lee, Don L.*

We sat across the table—*Piercy*

We sat there/ complaining a lot—*Johnston, Ellen Turlington*

We sat within the farm-house old—*Longfellow*

We saw a town by the track in Colorado—*Stafford*

We saw nothing but change in all the ways we went—*Eberhart*

We saw reindeer—*Moore, Marianne*

We saw the swallows gathering the sky—*Meredith, George*

We say the sea is lonely; better say—*Meredith, William*

We shall give this undeclared war—*Fremantle*

We shall have our little day—*Parker*

We shall not always plant while others reap—*Cullen*

We should have guessed—*Emanuel*

We sleep in the sleep of ages—*Service*

We slept that night in Delaware, Ohio—*Bly*

We spray the fields and scatter—*Betjeman*

We stand befo u—*Sanchez*

We started up—*Bly*

We stayed the night in the pathless gorge of Ventana Creek, up the east fork—*Jeffers, Robinson*

We stood together, side by side, rooted—*Graves*

We stood upon a corner, where—*Heine*

We strung our Wyandotte rooster dead on a post —*Langland, Joseph*

We tell beginnings—*Rukeyser*

We tend to fear old age—*Giovanni*

We, the judges, a literary lot—*Abse*

We, the symmetrians, seek justice here—*Derwood*

We three are on the cedar-shadowed lawn—*Meredith, George*

We too, we too, descending once again—*MacLeish*

We travel to Dublin's white streets—*Liddy*

We two elementals woman and man—*Graves*

We used to have a nice bell—*Johnston, Ellen Turlington*

We used to have a peach tree—*Marshall, Helen Lowrie*

We used to meet on this corner—*Jong*

We used to picnic where the thrift—*Betjeman*

We wake to double blue—*Swenson*

We walk on pebbled streets—*Alurista*

We walked in that green field—*Engle*

We walked where Victor Jove was shrined awhile —*Hardy*

We wanted Mars—*Joselow*

We watched a film one day—*Johnston, Ellen Turlington*

We watched the Condors winging towards the Moon—*Colum*

We wear the mask that grins and lies—*Dunbar, Paul Laurence*

We went to where the mountains—*Pietri*

We were apart; yet, day by day—*Arnold*

We were not ever of their feline race—*Graves*

We were sitting about taking coffee—*Yevtushenko*

We were taken from the ore-bed and the mine —*Kipling*

We were very tired, we were very merry—*Millay*

We were warned about frost, yet all day the summer—*Norris*

We were watching a movie in class—*Johnston, Ellen Turlington*

We were young, we were merry, we were very wise—*Coleridge, Mary Elizabeth*

We who must act as handmaidens—*Kizer*

We who play under the pines—*Coatsworth*

We, who remember Faith, the grey-headed ones —*Betjeman*

We will never die—*Dodson*

We will not whisper, we have found the place —*Belloc*

We will swing from giant cables—*Reed, Ishmael*
We work here together/ In blast and breeze—*Hardy*
Wearily, drearily—*Morris, William*
Weary with toil, I haste me to my bed—*Shakespeare*
The weather never changes—*Polak*
The weather was fine. They took away his teeth—*Berryman*
The weather wept, and all the trees bent down—*Roethke*
Webbed, yellow-billed and aquamarine—*O'Gorman*
Webster was much possessed by death—*Eliot, Thomas Stearns*
We'd found an old Boche dug-out and he knew—*Owen, Wilfred*
We'd liberated Naples and the Wops—*Beecher*
We'd rather have the iceberg—*Bishop, Elizabeth*
Wee, sleekit, cow'rin', tim'rous beastie—*Burns*
Wee Willie Winkie runs through the town—*Children's Verses and Nursery Rhymes*
Weep no more, woeful shepherds, weep no more—*Milton*
Weep not, weep not—*Johnson, James Weldon*
Weep you no more, sad fountains—*Anonymous-English—Modern English*
Weepe with me all you that read—*Jonson*
Weg welt! weg traurig-seyn! weg teuffel, fleisch und zagen—*Gryphius*
Weighing the steadfastness and state—*Vaughan, Henry*
Weird sister/ the Black witches—*Clifton*
Weisst du, was das Fischlein im Weiher macht—*Guggenmos*
Weisst du, wieviel Sternlein stehen—*Hey*
Die weite Bucht erfüllt der neue Hafen—*George*
Weland him be wearnum wraeces cunnode—*Anonymous-English—Old English*
Welcome, eccentric life—*Kunitz*
Welcome home, my Prince—*Sanchez*
Welcome Maids of Honour—*Herrick*
Well boss i had a/ great example—*Marquis*
Well, Catullus, so you knew—*Nims*
Well, Emily Sparks, your prayers were not wasted—*Masters, Edgar Lee*
Well I tell you—*Rossman*
Well! If the Bard was weather-wise, who made—*Coleridge, Samuel Taylor*
Well, life has been a baffled vehicle—*Brooks, Gwendolyn*
Well-meaning readers! you that come as friends—*Crashaw*
Well, Niggers, here we is—*Knight, Etheridge*
We'll see what we'll see—*Sandburg*
Well, son, I'll tell you—*Hughes, Langston*
Well, they are gone, and here must I remain—*Coleridge, Samuel Taylor*
Well, they rocked him with road-apples—*Hughes, Langston*
Well they'd made up their minds to be everywhere—*Merwin*
Well, though it seems—*Hardy*
We'll to the woods no more—*Housman*
Die Welt, aus der ich lange mich entwand—*Lasker-Schüler*
We 'as Leben leid ist—*Platen-Hallermünde*

Wen chung ji ye myan myan—*Bai Jyu Yi*
Wen hast du dir auserlesen—*Fontane*
Wendy put her black eyes on me—*Sandburg*
Wêne Herzen, wênent Ougen—*Anonymous-German*
Wenn alle untreu werden—*Novalis*
Wenn der Elstern Flug mich befragte—*Eich*
Wenn der Mensch aufrichtig bedächte—*Kästner*
Wenn der Schnee ans Fenster fällt—*Trakl*
Wenn der silberne Mond durch die Gesträuche blickt—*Hölty*
Wenn der uralte/ heilige Vater—*Goethe*
Wenn du zu mei'm Schatzel kommst—*Anonymous-German*
Wenn die Augen brechen—*Brentano*
Wenn die Tante Adelheide—*Busch*
Wenn du zur Arbeit gehst/ am frühen Morgen—*Tucholsky*
Wenn eena dot is kriste'n Schreck—*Tucholsky*
Wenn ein Gesicht, das man als Junges kannte—*Benn*
Wenn ein Verzweifeln—*Benn*
Wenn einer fort geht—*Bachmann*
Wenn er kommt, der Besucher—*Kaschnitz*
Wenn ich beseligt von schönen Küssen—*Heine*
Wenn ich das Wirkliche nicht—*Bobrowski*
Wenn ich ein Vöglein wär—*Anonymous-German*
Wenn ich ihn nur habe—*Novalis*
Wenn ich in deine Augen seh—*Heine*
Wenn ich sitze, will ich nicht—*Morgenstern*
Wenn ich, von deinem Anschaun—*Mörike*
Wenn ihre Freunde—*Hölderlin*
Wenn im Unendlichen dasselbe—*Goethe*
Wenn in bangen trüben Stunden—*Novalis*
Wenn man von Faltern liest, von Schilf und Immen—*Benn*
Wenn nicht mehr Zahlen und Figuren—*Novalis*
Wenn silbern Orpheus die Laute rührt—*Trakl*
Wenn zwei voneinander scheiden—*Heine*
Went into a shoestore to buy a pair of shoes—*Miles*
Wer allein ist, ist auch im Geheimnis—*Benn*
Wer baute das siebentorige Theben?—*Brecht*
Wer bist du, Fürst, dass ohne Scheu—*Bürger*
Wer einsam ist, der hat es gut—*Busch*
Wer immer seinen Schuh gespart—*Brecht*
Wer in den Blumen, Wäldern—*Tieck*
Wer in der Brust ein wachsendes Verlangen—*Platen-Hallermünde*
Wer möchte diesen Erdenball—*Busch*
Wer möchte leben—*Eich*
Wer möchte sich an Schattenbildern weiden—*Schiller*
Wer reitet so spät durch Nacht und Wind—*Goethe*
Wer Schönheit angeschaut mit Augen—*Platen-Hallermünde*
Wer wagt es, Rittersmann oder Knapp—*Schiller*
Wer wärmt mich, wer liebt mich noch?—*Nietzsche*
Wer weiss, ob diese Alten auf der Insel—*Kaschnitz*
Wer, wenn ich schriebe, hörte mich denn aus der Engel—*Rilke*
Wer wollte sich mit Grillen plagen—*Hölty*

Wer wusste je das Leben recht zu fassen—*Platen-Hallermünde*

Werdet nur nicht ungeduldig—*Heine*

We're foot-slog-slog-slog-sloggin' over Africa—*Kipling*

We're hoping to be arrested—*Walker*

Were I a king, I could command content—*Oxford*

Were't aught to me I bore the canopy—*Shakespeare*

Ein Werwolf eines Nachts entwich—*Morgenstern*

West of the sunset stands my house—*Blanding*

Westron winde, when will thou blow—*Anonymous-English—Modern English*

The wetness of that street, the light—*Creeley*

We've all known that special lift—*Marshall, Helen Lowrie*

We've fought with many men acrost the seas—*Kipling*

We've made a great mess of love—*Lawrence*

Whales have calves—*Nash*

Whan Phebus dwelled heere in this world adoun—*Chaucer*

Whan that Aprille with his shoures soote—*Chaucer*

What a battle it did make—*Moore, Rosalie*

What a grand old world we live in—*Marshall, Helen Lowrie*

What a proud dream horse pulling (smoothloomingly)—*Cummings*

What am I doing with a mid-life crisis—*Viorst*

What am I? Nosing here turning leaves over—*Hughes, Ted*

What are days for?—*Larkin*

What are little boys made of, made of—*Children's Verses and Nursery Rhymes*

What are little girls made of, made of—*Children's Verses and Nursery Rhymes*

What are the bugles blowin' for? said Files-on-Parade—*Kipling*

What are the light and wind to me?—*Watkins*

What are the negroes saying—*Emanuel*

What are we first? First, animals; and next—*Meredith, George*

What are we waiting for, all crowded in the forum—*Cavafy*

What are you able to build with your blocks?—*Stevenson*

What are you staring at, mariner-man—*Sitwell, Edith*

What artist's steady hand—*Derwood*

What beck'ning ghost along the moonlight shade—*Pope, Alexander*

What blood-red law—*Miller, Arthur*

What brings the sea wind so far ashore—*Reeves*

What can a young lassie—*Burns*

What can I do for you? she asked gently—*Graves*

What can I do to feel close to you—*Darr*

What can I give thee back, O liberal—*Browning, Elizabeth Barrett*

What can I say, because talk I must—*Williams, William Carlos*

What can it avayle—*Skelton, John*

What can purge my heart—*Hughes, Langston*

What can this careful lady think—*Francis*

What can we say of the night—*Sandburg*

What ceremony can we fit—*Jennings*

What color is the shadow of a tree—*Marshall, Lenore G.*

What common language to unravel—*Williams, William Carlos*

What continues to hold me—*Olson*

What could be dafter—*Graves*

What could be lovelier than to hear—*Coatsworth*

What desperate nightmare rapts me to this land—*Randall*

What did I dream? I do not know—*Graves*

What did my old song say?—*Davidson*

What dire offence from am'rous causes springs—*Pope, Alexander*

What do they think of—*Stryk*

What do you see in that time-touched stone—*Hardy*

What do you see now—*Masters, Edgar Lee*

What do you spin you ugly brute—*Borton*

What do you think endures?—*Whitman*

What do you think of us in fuzzy endeavor—*Brooks, Gwendolyn*

What do you want, Love—*Creeley*

What does he know, moving through the fields—*Thomas, Ronald Stuart*

What does it mean—*Sward*

What does it mean? Tired, angry, and ill at ease—*Thomas, Edward*

What drives you out in this night of Spring—*Heine*

What erratic wind from Andalusia—*Sitwell, Osbert*

What fascinated in childhood seems trivial—*Souster*

What feet are heard about these rocks—*Watkins*

What flecks the outer gray beyond—*Whittier*

What flocks of critics hover here today—*Dryden*

What freedom's not some under's mere above—*Cummings*

What glories would we—*Roethke*

What good's a baby sister—*Marshall, Helen Lowrie*

What got him was nothing—*Cummings*

What guile is this, that those her golden tresses—*Spenser*

What happens after—*Sanchez*

What happens afterwards, none need enquire—*Graves*

What happens to a dream deferred?—*Hughes, Langston*

What has the traveler to say about our dream—*Posner*

What has this Bugbear Death to frighten man—*Lucretius Carus*

What have I earned for all that work, I said—*Yeats*

What have you looked at, Moon—*Hardy*

What heart could have thought you—*Thompson, Francis*

What I assembled and dissembled—*Scott, Winfield Townley*

What I expected was/ Thunder—*Spender*

What I know—*Malanga*

What I like best's the lay of different farms—*Frost, Robert*

What I shall leave thee none can tell—*Corbet*

What I thought—*Whalen*

What I was would not work for them all—*Dickey, James*

What if a much of a which of a wind—*Cummings*
What if Prince Paris, after taking thought—*Graves*
What if this present were the worlds last night —*Donne*
What is Africa to me—*Cullen*
What is alive crawls—*Marcus*
What is it men in women do require—*Blake*
What is it to grow old—*Arnold*
What is life? Life is stepping down a step or sitting on a chair—*Nash*
What is man? the Psalmist cried—*Ciardi*
What is our innocence—*Moore, Marianne*
What is our life? A play of passion—*Raleigh*
What is pink? a rose is pink—*Rossetti, Christina*
What is poetry? Who knows?—*Farjeon*
What is reality—*Sexton*
What is required of us—*MacLeish*
What is she, while I live—*Roethke*
What is that island—*Blackmur*
What is the boy now, who has lost his ball—*Berryman*
What is the buzzing in my ears—*Browning, Robert*
What is the matter with Mary Jane—*Milne*
What is this—*Johnston, Ellen Turlington*
What is this life—*Dunbar, William*
What is this life if, full of care—*Davies, William Henry*
What is translation? On a platter—*Nabokov*
What is your substance, whereof are you made —*Shakespeare*
What it was, is—*Rasul*
What kind of notation is in my Time file for my life—*Shapiro, Karl*
What lewd, naked and revolting shape is this—*Williams, Oscar*
What lifts the heron leaning—*Ciardi*
What lively lad most pleasured me—*Yeats*
What lovely things thy hand hath made—*De la Mare*
What man that sees the ever-whirling wheele—*Spenser*
What mind has made that voyage—*Barker, George*
What need you, being come to sense—*Yeats*
What needs my Shakespeare for his honored bones—*Milton*
What of her glass without her—*Rossetti, Dante Gabriel*
What of the faith and fire within us—*Hardy*
What passing-bells for these who die as cattle—*Owen, Wilfred*
What potions have I drunk of Siren tears—*Shakespeare*
What rider spurs him from the darkening east —*Millay*
What sculptures here among God's works—*Traherne*
What seas what shores what grey rocks and what island—*Eliot, Thomas Stearns*
What shakes the eye but the invisible—*Roethke*
What shall be seen?—*Merwin*
What shall I give my children—*Brooks, Gwendolyn*
What shall Presto do for pretty prattle—*Schwartz*
What shall we do—what shall we think—*Aiken*

What should I saye—*Wyatt, Sir Thomas*
What should one wish a child—*Tomlinson*
What siren zooming is sounding our coming—*Auden*
What soft, cherubic creatures—*Dickinson, Emily*
What sound awakened me, I wonder—*Housman*
What stopped the ticking of the clock—*Arnez*
What the camera did—*Francis*
What the white ransoms did was to wipe away —*Norris*
What thing is love? for sure love is a thing—*Peele*
What though the first pure snowdrop wilt and die —*De la Mare*
What thoughts I have of you tonight—*Ginsberg*
What throws you out is what drags you in—*Swenson*
What wants thee, that thou art in this sad taking —*Anonymous–English–Modern English*
What was he doing, the great god Pan—*Browning, Elizabeth Barrett*
What was her beauty in our first estate—*Wilbur*
What was is . . . since 1930—*Lowell, Robert*
What was it—*Rukeyser*
What was the name you called me—*Sandburg*
What we know to be not possible—*Auden*
What were we playing? was it prisoner's base—*Wilbur*
What will you make of half a man—*Hughes, Ted*
What work is that—*Gregory, Horace*
What would happen to your lady wife—*Scannell*
What, you are stepping westward—*Wordsworth*
WhatCHU care—*Emanuel*
Whate'er we leave to God, God does—*Thoreau*
Whatever happened to Black America—*Braxton*
Whatever I have left unsaid—*Van Doren*
Whatever it was she had so fiercely fought—*Shapiro, Karl*
Whatever's merely wilful—*Cummings*
What's happening/ Mr. Jones—*Alurista*
What's happening to the westward—*Marshall, Helen Lowrie*
What's in the brain, that ink may character—*Shakespeare*
What's it like to be homeless—*Souster*
What's the monster of this week—*Nash*
What's this? A dish for fat lips—*Roethke*
What's up, today, with our lovers—*Snodgrass*
What's wrong with you-zie—*Smith, Stevie*
Wheesht, wheesht, my foolish hert—*MacDiarmid*
When a boat draws near—*Gregor*
When a city undergoes disaster, it moves as a mass —*Miles*
When a felon's not engaged—*Gilbert, Sir William Schwenck*
When a man has no freedom to fight for at home —*Byron*
When a master lived a king—*Jeffers, Lance*
When Abraham Lincoln was shoveled into the tomb—*Sandburg*
When Adam found his rib was gone—*Hollander*
When all around from out the ground—*Field, Eugene*
When all of them ran off—*Hollander*
When all our hopes are sown on stony ground —*Bontemps*
When all the over-work of life—*Rossetti, Christina*

When all the world is young, lad—*Kingsley*

When at home alone I sit—*Stevenson*

When awful darkness and silence reign—*Lear*

When both are strong with tenderness too wild —*Viereck*

When by thy scorne, O murdresse, I am dead—*Donne*

When cats run home and light is come—*Tennyson*

When chapman billies leave the street—*Burns*

When Chewed-ear Jankins got hitched up—*Service*

When children are playing alone on the green —*Stevenson*

When coltsfoot withers and begins to wear—*Young, Andrew*

When comes my second childhood—*Nash*

When Crow cried his mother's ear—*Hughes, Ted*

When Crow was white he decided the sun was too white—*Hughes, Ted*

When daisies pied and violets blue—*Shakespeare*

When Daniel Boone goes by, at night—*Benét, Stephen Vincent*

When David heard that Absolom was slain—*Bible and Pseudepigrapha*

When did you begin your quest—*Tate, James*

When/ Don/ Pasquito arrived at the seaside—*Sitwell, Edith*

When down I went to the rust-red quarry—*Graves*

When earth's last picture is painted and the tubes are twisted and dried—*Kipling*

When Egil Skallagrimsson/ Choked Grim's thralls —*MacBeth*

When everything but love was spent—*Cowley, Malcolm*

When eyeless fish meet her on—*Gunn*

When faces called flowers float out of the ground —*Cummings*

When Fall winds began to blow—*Coffin*

When fame arrives in a limousine—*Weber, Ron*

When fate from its plane stepped down—*Miles*

When first, descending from the moorlands—*Wordsworth*

When first my lines of heav'nly joyes made mention—*Herbert*

When first my way to fair I took—*Housman*

When first our Poet set himself to write—*Dryden*

When first the college rolls receive his name—*Johnson, Samuel*

When first we met, we did not guess—*Bridges*

When forty winters shall besiege thy brow—*Shakespeare*

When Francis preached love to the birds—*Heaney*

When Freedom from her mountain height—*Drake, Joseph Rodman*

When George's Grandmamma was told—*Belloc*

When God at first made man—*Herbert*

When hare heard of death, he started for his lodge —*Anonymous–American Indian languages– Winnebago*

When he brings home a whale—*Creeley*

When he came home / from her—*Sanchez*

When he lies in the night away from her—*Hall*

When he returned—*Moore, Merrill*

When he thought a love—*Sukenick*

When Hitler was the devil—*Simpson*

When I am dead—*Flint*

When I am dead, even then—*Rukeyser*

When I am dead, my dearest—*Rossetti, Christina*

When I am grown to man's estate—*Stevenson*

When I am living in the Midlands—*Belloc*

When I am old, and comforted—*Parker*

When I am playing by myself—*Roberts*

When i am woman, then i shall be wife of your eyes—*Sanchez*

When I bethinke me of that speech whyleare—*Spenser*

When I buy pictures/or what is closer to the truth —*Moore, Marianne*

When I can hold a stone within my hand—*Eberhart*

When I climb up to get a drink—*Chute*

When I come in f'om de co'n-fiel' aftah wo'kin' ha'd all day—*Dunbar, Paul Laurence*

When I consider everything that grows—*Shakespeare*

When I consider how my light is spent—*Milton*

When I did wake this morn from sleep—*Davies, William Henry*

When I do count the clock that tells the time—*Shakespeare*

When I dyed last, and, Deare, I dye—*Donne*

When I first became a teacher—*Johnston, Ellen Turlington*

When I gaze at the sun—*Allen, Samuel*

When I get to be a composer—*Hughes, Langston*

When I go downtown—*Kennedy, Marian*

When I go home—*Kizer*

When I have a house . . . as I sometime may—*Blanding*

When I have borne in memory what has tamed —*Wordsworth*

When I have fears that I may cease to be—*Keats*

When I have seen by Time's fell hand defaced —*Shakespeare*

When I heard the learn'd astronomer—*Whitman*

When I heard you were coming—*Lahui*

When I lay sick and like to die—*Blackmur*

When I left her, the roosters—*Lester*

When I lie down for comfort—*Heine*

When I lie where shades of darkness—*De la Mare*

When I lived down in Devonshire—*Amis*

When I look into my sons' eyes I see—*Bishop, John Peale*

When I play on my fiddle in Dooney—*Yeats*

When I reached his place—*Graves*

When I remember what I must forget—*Dowling*

When I saw that clumsy crow—*Roethke*

When I saw the Grapefruit drying—*Betjeman*

When I see birches bend to left and right—*Frost, Robert*

When I see the falling bombs—*Scott, F. R.*

When I see you, who were so wise and cool—*Brooke*

When I shall be without regret—*Cunningham, James Vincent*

When I sleepwalk into your room—*Kinnell*

When I think of my kindness which is tentative and quiet—*Miles*

When I turned to look back—*Stryk*

When I wake up—*Hodges*

When I was a beggarly boy—*Lowell, James Russell*

When I was a boy desiring the title of man—*Randall*

When I was a janitor's stepson among the wealthy whites—*Jeffers, Lance*

When I was a lad I served a term—*Gilbert, Sir William Schwenck*

When I was a little boy I lived by myself—*Children's Verses and Nursery Rhymes*

When I was a windy boy and a bit—*Thomas, Dylan*

When I was a young one—*Langland, Joseph*

When I was born at Nosey Bent—*Causley*

When I was born on Amman hill—*Watkins*

When I was but 13 or so—*Turner, Walter James*

When I was down beside the sea—*Stevenson*

When I was fair and young—*Elizabeth I*

When I was forty the stocktaker came—*Tripp*

When I was just a little girl—*Marshall, Helen Lowrie*

When I was once in Baltimore—*Davies, William Henry*

When I was one-and-twenty—*Housman*

When I was one/ I had just begun—*Milne*

When I was sick and lay abed—*Stevenson*

When I was sixteen and as smooth as a bee—*Beer*

When I was slated in a rocky cave—*Wordsworth*

When I was small and trees were high—*Coffin*

When I was small, I lived in a town—*Marshall, Helen Lowrie*

When I was young—*Winters*

When I was young and bold and strong—*Parker*

When I was young I dared to sing—*Stephens*

When I was young I used to wait—*Anonymous–English–Modern English*

When I was young I woke gladly in the morning—*Spender*

When I watch the living meet—*Housman*

When I went out to kill myself, I caught—*Wright, James*

When I went to the city, Mary McNeely—*Masters, Edgar Lee*

When I wrote of the women in their dances and wildness—*Rukeyser*

When icicles hang by the wall—*Shakespeare*

When, in disgrace with fortune and men's eyes—*Shakespeare*

When in the chronicle of wasted time—*Shakespeare*

When, in the dawn of love and my desire—*Dowling*

When in the festival of August heat—*Hollander*

When in the mirror of a permanent tear—*Derwood*

When it was finally ours, this freedom—*Hayden*

When Jesus hung upon the cross—*Dowling*

When Jesus walked into the wilderness—*Sexton*

When John Henry was nothin' but a baby—*Anonymous–English–Modern English*

When lads were home from labour—*Housman*

When Learning's triumph o'er her barb'rous foes—*Johnson, Samuel*

When leaves were the color of sun—*Randall*

When, like the early rose—*Griffin*

When lilacs last in the dooryard bloomed—*Whitman*

When little boys grown patient at last, weary—*Tate, Allen*

When love has changed to kindliness—*Brooke*

When love with unconfined wings—*Lovelace, Richard*

When lovely woman stoops to folly—*Goldsmith*

When Ma Rainey comes to town—*Brown, Sterling A.*

When Mary Price was five years old—*Davies, William Henry*

When melancholy Autumn comes to Wembley—*Betjeman*

When men are laid away—*Winters*

When men discovered freedom first—*Simpson*

When men shall find thy flower, thy glory, pass—*Daniel, Samuel*

When men were all asleep the snow came flying—*Bridges*

When Miriam Tazewell heard the tempest bursting—*Ransom*

When most I wink, then do mine eyes best see—*Shakespeare*

When music, Heavenly Maid, was young—*Collins, William*

When music sounds, gone is the earth I know—*De la Mare*

When my birthday was coming—*Mansfield*

When my body leaves me—*Levertov*

When my dears die—*Brooks, Gwendolyn*

When my dog came whimpering out of the hayfields—*Langland, Joseph*

When my grave is broke up againe—*Donne*

When my heart was young I wasted my body—*Heath-Stubbs*

When my love swears that she is made of truth—*Shakespeare*

When my mother died I was very young—*Blake*

When my moustache curled—*Masters, Edgar Lee*

When my young brother was killed—*Langland, Joseph*

When nothing is happening something is stacking up to happen—*Swenson*

When ocean-clouds over inland hills—*Melville*

When o'er the hill the eastern star—*Burns*

When old cars get retired they go to Maine—*Booth*

When 'Omer smote 'is blooming lyre—*Kipling*

When on the coral-red steps of old brownstones—*Updike*

When our brother Fire was having his dog's day—*MacNeice*

When our two souls stand up erect and strong—*Browning, Elizabeth Barrett*

When over the flowery, sharp pasture's—*Williams, William Carlos*

When plagued by the psychological—*Moore, Marianne*

When Queen Victoria died—*Coward*

When Reuben Pantier ran away and threw me—*Masters, Edgar Lee*

When Rome was rotten-ripe to her fall—*Kipling*

When Ruth was left half desolate—*Wordsworth*

When Sam goes back in memory—*De la Mare*

When Sarah Pierrepont let her spirit rage—*Ransom*

When serpents bargain for the right to squirm—*Cummings*

When she goeth out—*Skelton, John*

When she has gone you go into town—*Patten*

When she, laughing, plastered a snowball on me —*Hollander*

When/ Sir/ Beelzebub called for his syllabub—*Sitwell, Edith*

When smoke stood up from Ludlow—*Housman*

When snow like sheep lay in the fold—*Hill*

When Susanna Jones wears red—*Hughes, Langston*

When Thanksgiving came twice, who walked so proud—*Nash*

When the air was damp—*Hardy*

When the allegorical man came calling—*Spencer*

When the army of ecologists—*Porter, Peter*

When the babe in the cradle—*Barker, George*

When the boys came out of school—*Mitchell, Julian*

When the bright lamp is carried in—*Stevenson*

When the burnt black bodies of the homeless—*Beecher*

When the earth is turned in spring—*Bergengren*

When the exhibition opens—*Klappert*

When the far south glittered—*Clarke*

When the frost is on the punkin and the fodder's in the shock—*Riley*

When the golden day is done—*Stevenson*

When the goodwives knelt at the pump—*Sherwin*

When the gnats dance at evening—*Hughes, Ted*

When the grass was closely mown—*Stevenson*

When the green woods laugh with the voice of joy —*Blake*

When the Himalayan peasant meets the he-bear in his pride—*Kipling*

When the hounds of Spring are on winter's traces —*Swinburne*

When the intellect walks—*Barker, George*

When the lamp is shattered—*Shelley*

When the moon was new and the sun young—*Tolkien*

When the morning was waking over the war—*Thomas, Dylan*

When the new frogs in their exuberant arrivals —*Eberhart*

When the orchard that clings to the terrace is boxed for the winter—*Brinnin*

When the ox-horn sounds in the buried hills—*Merwin*

When the pale moon hides—*Durston*

When the present has latched its postern behind my tremulous stay—*Hardy*

When the serpent emerged, earth-bowel brown —*Hughes, Ted*

When the still-soft eyelid—*Hughes, Ted*

When the sun/ shines through the leaves of the apple tree—*Milne*

When the sun shouts and people abound—*Jeffers, Robinson*

When the tide was out/ and the sea was quiet —*Eberhart*

When the voices of children are heard on the green—*Blake*

When the wheel of light is turned—*MacLeish*

When the wind ends it is too much— *Van Doren*

When the wind is stirring in the evening—*Eberhart*

When the wind works against us in the dark—*Frost, Robert*

When the world takes over for us— *Williams, William Carlos*

When they brought on the sleeping child—*Durrell*

When they crack the sound barrier over us—*Sherwin*

When they had won the war—*Simpson*

When they hear/ these songs born of the travail —*Brown, Sterling A.*

When they rode up at first dark and called his name—*Brown, Sterling A.*

When they said the time to hide was mine—*Roberts*

When they're decent about women—*Rukeyser*

When they're shunting the cars on the Katy a mile off—*MacLeish*

When this perishable body ceases—*Dowling*

When thou must home to shades of underground —*Campion*

When thou, poor excommunicate—*Carew*

When thou shalt be dispos'd to set me light—*Shakespeare*

When three, he fished these lakes—*Emanuel*

When to her lute Corinna sings—*Campion*

When to the sessions of sweet silent thought—*Shakespeare*

When Tom Bailey wants to rest—*Coffin*

When true love broke my heart in half—*Roethke*

When two take gas—*Ignatow*

When we are in love, we love the grass—*Bly*

When we come riden our green horses—*Sanchez*

When we meet/ in the midnight hour—*Henri*

When we met first and loved I did not build—*Browning, Elizabeth Barrett*

When we stopped—*Gallagher, Tess*

When we two parted in silence and tears—*Byron*

When Westwall Downes I gan to tread—*Strode*

When, when, and whenever death—*Pound*

When will you ever, Peace, wild wooddove, shy wings shut—*Hopkins*

When you and I on the Palos Verdes cliff—*Jeffers, Robinson*

When you are old and grey and full of sleep—*Yeats*

When you are young/ you never notice—*Dickinson, Patric*

When you come, as you soon must, to the streets of our city— *Wilbur*

When you dream, may the dream be worthy—*Marshall, Helen Lowrie*

When you drive on the freeway, cars follow you —*Browne, Michael Dennis*

When you enter—*Marvin X*

When you go away the wind clicks—*Merwin*

When you got up in the morning—*Hodges*

When you receive this letter—*Pietri*

When you retired—*Schmitz*

When you see the traffic light—*Abbe*

When you shall see me in the toils of Time—*Hardy*

When you told of Paul—*Hodges*

When you watch for feather or fur—*Becker*

When you were here in wonderful Detroit—*Danner*

When you were there, and you, and you—*Brooke*

When young I scribbled, boasting, on my wall
—*Kunitz*

When young the Christians told me—*Cohen*

When your face—*Yevtushenko*

When your hair turns gray—*Souster*

When you're lying awake with a dismal headache
—*Gilbert, Sir William Schwenck*

Whenas in silks my Julia goes—*Herrick*

Whence and what art thou, execrable shape—
Milton

Whenever Auntie moves around—*Stevenson*

Whenever I am a shining knight—*Milne*

Whenever I behold an asp—*Nash*

Whenever I plunge my arm, like this—*Hardy*

Whenever I walk to Suffern along the Erie track
—*Kilmer, Joyce*

Whenever Richard Cory went to town—*Robinson, Edwin Arlington*

Whenever the moon and stars are set—*Stevenson*

Where am I going? I don't quite know—*Milne*

Where, and in the morning—*Merwin*

Where are Elmer, Herman, Bert, Tom and Charley—*Masters, Edgar Lee*

Where are the dear domestics, white and black
—*Hillyer*

Where are they now, the heroes—*Mitchell, Adrian*

Where are we—*Shiva*

Where are you going, child, so far away—*Farjeon*

Where are you going that I want to go—*Moss, Howard*

Where art thou, Muse, that thou forget'st so long
—*Shakespeare*

Where bees bowing from flower to flower—*Francis*

Where can the heart be hidden in the ground
—*Millay*

Where did you go—*Sherwin*

Where dips the rocky highland—*Yeats*

Where do the roots go—*Roethke*

Where have they fled—*Goldstein*

Where I came by torchlight there is dawn-song
—*Merwin*

Where I lectured, the platform was ankle-deep in water—*Abbe*

Where is all the bright company gone—*Sitwell, Edith*

Where is he now, in his soiled shirt reeking of garlic—*Millay*

Where is my boy, my boy—*Masters, Edgar Lee*

Where is my mother—*Ignatow*

Where is my Pegasus—*Braxton*

Where is the bell, the horn—*Van Doren*

Where is the Jim Crow Section—*Hughes, Langston*

Where, like a pillow on a bed—*Donne*

Where long the shadows of the wind had rolled
—*Robinson, Edwin Arlington*

Where marble stood and fell—*Corso*

Where might there be a refuge for me—*Moore, Marianne*

Where now he roves, by wood or swamp whatever—*Aiken*

Where once we danced, where once we sang—
Hardy

Where only flowers fret—*Simpson*

Where shall we go—*Williams, William Carlos*

Where should he seek, to go away—*Bogan*

Where the green airs seem fanning palms and the green psalms—*Sitwell, Edith*

Where the quiet-colored end of evening smiles
—*Browning, Robert*

Where the remote Bermudas ride—*Marvell*

Where the thistle lifts a purple crown—*Thompson, Francis*

Where the trails met—*Mitchell, Julian*

Where the water-lilies go to and fro—*Milne*

Where then is the nigger's home—*Brathwaite*

Where to go when—*Sanchez*

Where we made the fire—*Hardy*

Where we went in the boat was a long bay—*Tate, Allen*

Where were the greenhouses going—*Roethke*

Where will their names go down—*Emanuel*

Where will this end? Four times ten days I have passed—*Milton*

Where, without bloodshed, can there be—*Untermeyer*

Whereas the man who hits—*Creeley*

Whereat—the King unthroned, the God—
MacLeish

Wherein are words sublime or noble—*Cullen*

Where's Ruby, where has she gone this evening
—*Aiken*

Wherever a still apron—*Van Doren*

Wherever I am, there's always Pooh—*Milne*

Wherever I go (these—*Jordan, June*

Wherever the dead are—*Patchen*

Whether it was your way of walking—*Graves*

Whether it's just a gag or the old geezer's—*Souster*

Whether on Ida's shady brow—*Blake*

Whether to sally and see thee, girl of my dreams
—*Hardy*

Whether you sing or scream—*Bell*

Which, if with truth it correspond, and sink—
Wordsworth

Which is my little boy, which is he—*Williams, Tennessee*

While I sit at the door—*Rossetti, Christina*

While I slept, while I slept and the night grew colder—*Francis*

While I stood here, in the open, lost in myself
—*Wright, James*

While in the Convention they were nominating the next President—*Ozick*

While my mother ate her heart out—*Baldwin, Michael*

While people for what can satisfy their wants—
Derwood

While rain, with eve in partnership—*Hardy*

While the magician—*Ciardi*

While the other kids on the block were reading
—*Kresh*

While this America settles in the mould of its vulgarity, heavily thickening to empire—*Jeffers, Robinson*

While thus he spake, th' Angelic Squadron bright
—*Milton*

While troops moved in to Berlin last night—*Robson, Jeremy*

Whilom ther was dwellynge at Oxenford—*Chaucer*

Whilst I alone did call upon thy aid—*Shakespeare*

The whiskey book is round—*Den Boer*

The whiskey on your breath—*Roethke*

The whistling boy that holds the plough—*Crabbe*

White above the afterflare—*Hillyer*

White america is saying—*Sanchez*

White-arched in loops of silence, the bodega—*Lee, Laurie*

White blossom, white, white shell; the Nazarene—*Watkins*

The white cock's trail—*Stevens, Wallace*

White founts falling in the courts of the sun—*Chesterton, Gilbert Keith*

White globe of rain, we are caught—*Redgrove*

White in the Moon the long road lies—*Housman*

The white light is artificial, and hygienic as heaven—*Plath*

White man with hateless home to share—*Emanuel*

White-maned, wide-throated, the heavy-shouldered children of the wind—*Jeffers, Robinson*

The white mares of the moon rush along the sky—*Lowell, Amy*

White motha fucka—*Sanchez*

The white neighbor lady—*Aubert*

White sheep, white sheep—*Rossetti, Christina*

A white sheet on the tail-gate of a truck—*Shapiro, Karl*

The white stars laboring above the world—*Dowling*

The whites had taught him how to rip—*Brown, Sterling A.*

Whither, midst falling dew—*Bryant, William Cullen*

Whither, O splendid ship, thy white sails crowding—*Bridges*

Whitman animé par son peuple—*Éluard*

Within the city of the burning cloud—*Kunitz*

Who am I to speak up for the long dead—*Porter, Peter*

Who are the people who live in these huts—*Bly*

Who are these? Why sit they here in twilight—*Owen, Wilfred*

Who are you dusky woman, so ancient hardly human—*Whitman*

Who are you, sea lady—*Flecker*

Who calls her two-faced? Faces, she has three—*Graves*

Who can live in heart so glad—*Breton, Nicholas*

Who can pick up the weight of Britain—*Stevens, Wallace*

Who can tell how the lobster got—*Arden*

Who do you work for? Myself, he said—*Marshall, Helen Lowrie*

Who dreamed that beauty passes like a dream—*Yeats*

Who ever comes to shroud me, do not harme—*Donne*

Who ever guesses, thinks, or dreames he knowes—*Donne*

Who flung this world? What gangs proclaimed a truce—*Watkins*

Who goes there? hankering, gross, mystical, nude—*Whitman*

Who has seen the wind—*Rossetti, Christina*

Who hasn't heard of London Bridge—*Church*

Who have been lonely once—*Kunitz*

Who hears the humming/ of rocks at great height—*Levine*

Who, in the dark, has cast harbor-chain—*Bogan*

Who (is? are) who—*Cummings*

Who is Bernice—*Katzman*

Who is it that says most? which can say more—*Shakespeare*

Who is my shepherd—*Brinnin*

Who is Sylvia? what is she—*Shakespeare*

Who is that nude dude—*Aubert*

Who is this woman—*Braxton*

Who killed Cock Robin—*Children's Verses and Nursery Rhymes*

Who knows his will—*Cunningham, James Vincent*

Who live under the shadow of war—*Spender*

Who lived at the top end of our street—*Hughes, Ted*

Who loved more? William Carlos Williams—*Lowell, Robert*

Who loves the rain—*Shaw*

Who lyst his welthe eas retayne—*Wyatt, Sir Thomas*

Who murdered the minutes—*Treece*

Who now is watching—*Gitlin*

Who now remembers Almack's balls—*Hardy*

Who robbed the woods—*Dickinson, Emily*

Who said, Peacock Pie—*De la Mare*

Who (said the Moon)—*Francis*

Who said to the trout—*Thomas, Ronald Stuart*

Who sayes that fictions onely and false hair—*Herbert*

Who says I shall not straighten till I bend—*Wilbur*

Who shall have my fair lady—*Sitwell, Edith*

Who shall have my faire lady—*Anonymous–English—Modern English*

Who sharpens every dull—*Cummings*

Who that has sailed—*Blackmur*

Who, then, was Cestius/ and what is he to me—*Hardy*

Who wants my jellyfish—*Nash*

Who will believe my verse in time to come—*Shakespeare*

Who will buy my pretty wares—*Sitwell, Osbert*

Who will I be like—*Sobiloff*

Who will remember, passing through this gate—*Sassoon*

Who winds the clumsy flower-clock now, I wonder—*Brinnin*

Who would be/ a mermaid fair—*Tennyson*

Who you be—*Sanchez*

Whoe'er she be—*Crashaw*

Whoever despises the clitoris despises the penis—*Rukeyser*

Whoever has drowned and awhile entered—*Graves*

Whoever hath her wish, thou hast thy will—*Shakespeare*

Whoever loves, if he do not propose—*Donne*

Whoever you are, this poem is clearly about you—*Warren*

The whole day long, under the walking sun—*Hall*

Who's gonna make all—*Sanchez*

Who's that knocking on the window—*Causley*

Whose are these (wraith a clinging with a wraith—*Cummings*

Whose child is this they bring—*Hardy*

Whose minds like horse or ox—*MacLeish*

Whose tongues are twisted—*Williams, Miller*

Whose woods these are I think I know—*Frost, Robert*

Whoso list to hunt—*Wyatt, Sir Thomas*

Why are epics—*Garlick*

Why are the things that have no death—*Untermeyer*

Why are we here? This thing we call our soul—*Marshall, Helen Lowrie*

Why are you sighing—*Tessimond*

Why did Albert Schirding kill himself—*Masters, Edgar Lee*

Why did you give no hint that night—*Hardy*

Why didst thou promise such a beauteous day—*Shakespeare*

Why do I go on doing these things—*Hardy*

Why do they come—*Davidson*

Why do they pose—*Taylor, Rex*

Why does the sea burn? Why do the hills cry—*Levine*

Why does this lonely tear-drop—*Heine*

Why does your loneliness surge up—*Souster*

Why dois your brand sae drop wi' bluid—*Anonymous-English—Modern English*

Why has our poetry eschewed—*Untermeyer*

Why have such scores of lovely gifted girls—*Graves*

Why I don't dance—*Polak*

Why is it that a steering wheel—*Marshall, Helen Lowrie*

Why is it that the poets tell—*Morley*

Why is it that whenever I talk with the duchess—*Wilbur*

Why is my verse so barren of new pride—*Shakespeare*

Why is the sky—*Untermeyer*

Why must itself up every of a park—*Cummings*

Why say 'death'? Death is neither harsh nor kind—*Graves*

Why should I blame her that she filled my days—*Yeats*

Why should I have returned—*Merwin*

Why should I keep holiday—*Emerson*

Why should not old men be mad—*Yeats*

Why should this Negro insolently stride—*Wylie*

Why should you sweare I am forsworn—*Lovelace, Richard*

Why shouldn't I land my love—*Nash*

Why so pale and wan, fond lover—*Suckling*

Why then? Why there?—*Auden*

Why they closing down Alcatraz—*Sanchez*

Why was she lost? my darling said aloud—*Wain*

Why weep ye by the tide ladie—*Scott, Sir Walter*

Why, who makes much of a miracle—*Whitman*

Why, William on that old grey stone—*Wordsworth*

Why would a robin think that a sparrow—*Danner*

Wichita-ta, which which—*Rasof*

Wide though the interrupt be that divides us—*Auden*

A widow bird sate mourning—*Shelley*

Wie bald des Sommers holdes Fest verging—*Storm*

Wie hab ich das gefühlt was Abschied heisst—*Rilke*

Wie hässlich ist—*Kaschnitz*

Wie herrlich leuchtet/ mir die Natur—*Goethe*

Wie im Morgenglanze du rings mich anglühst—*Goethe*

Wie in der Hand ein Schwefelzündholz—*Rilke*

Wie in Gewölben von Smaragd—*Brentano*

Wie kam ich nur aus jenem Frieden—*Busch*

Wie kan ich, herr! dein lob vermehren—*Gryphius*

Wie kannst du ruhig schlafen—*Heine*

Wie konnt' ich das tun, wie konnt' ich das sagen—*Fontane*

Wie rafft ich mich auf in der Nacht—*Platen-Hallermünde*

Wie sank die Sonne glüh und schwer—*Droste-Hülshoff*

Wie schändlich du gehandelt—*Heine*

Wie selig ist der hohe Geist zu schätzen—*Gryphius*

Wie war das—*Borchers*

Wie wenn die alten Wasser, die/ in andern Zorn—*Hölderlin*

Ein Wiesel/ sass auf einem Kiesel—*Morgenstern*

Wieviel Herrliches auch die Natur, wie Grosses die edle—*Mörike*

The wild ass lounges, legs struck out—*Colum*

Wild birds fly over me—*Conkling*

The wild man that last night I dreamed—*Cuomo*

Wild white camel, camel wild—*Derwood*

Will define herself—*Lee, Don L.*

Will ich in mein Gärtlein wär—*Anonymous-German*

Will it sell—*Colbert*

Will there really be a morning—*Dickinson, Emily*

Will they castrate—*Robson, Ernest M.*

Will you walk a little faster? said a whiting to a snail—*Carroll*

Willie Wastle dwalt on Tweed—*Burns*

Willie works—*Eckels*

Willkommen, o silberner Mond—*Klopstock*

Willkommen süsse Nacht—*Gryphius*

Willkommen süsses Kind! der Mutter höchste Lust—*Gryphius*

Willst du dein Herz mir schenken—*Anonymous-German*

Willst du mich sogleich verlassen—*Goethe*

Wilt thou forgive that sinne where I begunne—*Donne*

Wilt thou go with me, sweet maid—*Clare*

Wind among prisons—*Durrell*

The wind comes from opposite poles—*Strand*

The wind doth blow to-day, my love—*Anonymous-English—Modern English*

The wind flapped loose, the wind was still—*Rossetti, Dante Gabriel*

The wind has picked up—*Hannan*

The wind has twisted the roof from an old house—*Wagoner*

Wind rocks the car—*Rich*

A wind sways the pines—*Meredith, George*

The wind-swept beach was empty but for three—*Hillyer*

Wind the season-climate mixer—*Frost, Robert*

The wind was a torrent of darkness among the gusty trees—*Noyes*

Wind whines and whines the shingle—*Joyce*

Windes Rauschen, Gottes Flügel—*Schlegel*

A winding Honolulu street—*Blanding*

The wind's bastinado—*Sitwell, Edith*

The winds brush pine against the pane—*Goldstein*

Winds changing their clothes—*Fry*

Winds on the stems make them creak like things of man—*Lowell, Robert*

The wind's on the wold—*Morris, William*

The winds out of the West land blow—*Housman*

A windy night was blowing on Rome—*Masefield*

Wine and oil—*Rukeyser*

Wine comes in at the month—*Yeats*

The winged bull trundles to the wired perimeter —*Day Lewis*

The wings of the nose—*Benedikt*

The winter deepening, the hay all in—*Wilbur*

The winter evening settles down—*Eliot, Thomas Stearns*

Winter for a moment takes the mind, the snow —*Aiken*

The winter is past and the summer comes at last —*Anonymous–English—Modern English*

A winter sun turned the mountains red—*Chapin*

Winter, that coils in the thickets now—*Kunitz*

The winters seem darker here—*Lifshin*

Winters when we set our traps offshore—*Booth*

Der Winterstrand ist leer—*Kaschnitz*

Wintertime—*Hardy*

Wir führen allein im dunkeln—*Heine*

Wir haben ein Bett, wir haben ein Kind—*Dehmel*

Wir haben so lange Krieg gesehen—*Bergengruen*

Wir haben viel füreinander gefühlt—*Heine*

Wir hatten kein Haus—*Goll*

Wir können bloss in Reih und Glied—*Kästner*

Wir schreiten auf und ab im reichen Flitter— *George*

Wir singen und sagen vom Grafen so gern—*Goethe*

Wirklich, er war unentbehrlich—*Busch*

Wirklich, ich lebe in finsteren Zeiten—*Brecht*

Wise men in their bad hours have envied—*Jeffers, Robinson*

The witch that came (the withered hag—*Frost, Robert*

With a bonfire throat—*Summers, Hal*

With a wall and a ditch between us, I watched the gate-legged dromedary—*Wagoner*

With all my will, but much against my heart— *Patmore*

With B. E. F. June 10. Dear Wife—*Owen, Wilfred*

With blackest moss the flower-plots—*Tennyson*

With deep affection and recollection—*Mahony*

With fingers weary and worn—*Hood*

With her latest roses happily encumbered—*Betjeman*

With how sad steps, O Moon, thou climb'st the skies—*Sidney*

With innocent wide penguin eyes, three—*Moore, Marianne*

With its cloud of skirmishers in advance—*Whitman*

With kisses my lips were wounded—*Heine*

With love exceeding a simple love of the things —*Meredith, George*

With luck and the slow hand—*De Frees*

With me, my lover makes/ the clock—*Day Lewis*

With one consuming roar along the shingle— *Betjeman*

With porcupine locks—*Reaney*

With prune-dark eyes, thick lips, jostling each other—*MacNeice*

With rope, knife, guns, brass knucks, and bloody laws—*Van Doren*

With rue my heart is laden—*Housman*

With sapphire for her crown—*Colum*

With secrets in her eyes, the blue-winged Hours —*Welles*

With the gulls' hysteria above me—*Barker, George*

With the last whippoorwill call of evening— *Walker*

With the same heart I said, I'll answer three— *Browning, Elizabeth Barrett*

With this rose I thee world—*Patchen*

With Usura/ with Usura hath no man—*Pound*

With visionary care/ the mind imagines Hell— *Winters*

With what amazing wand, oh night—*Kramer*

With you, my heart is quiet here—*Parker*

Withal a meagre man was Aaron Stark—*Robinson, Edwin Arlington*

Within this sober Frame expect—*Marvell*

Without you every morning would be like going back to work after a holiday—*Henri*

Wo aber werd ich sein im kunftigen Lenze?— *Eichendorff*

Wo bist du hingeflohn, geliebter Friede—*Rambler*

Wo bist du itzt—*Lenz*

Wo bist du? trunken dämmert die Seele mir— *Hölderlin*

A woeful silence, following in our wash—*Hollander*

Woefully arrayed—*Skelton, John*

Die Woge wogt, es wallt die Quelle—*Hesse*

Wohl unter der Linde erklingt die Musik—*Heine*

Woke up this morning—*Pietri*

Woken, I lay in the arms of my own warmth and listened—*Auden*

Der Wolf ist zum Huhn gekommen—*Brecht*

The wolf of winter—*Patchen*

Der Wolke Zickzackzunge spricht—*Morgenstern*

Wolves can outeat anyone—*Moore, Marianne*

The woman is perfected—*Plath*

Woman much missed, how you call to me, call to me—*Hardy*

The woman named To-morrow—*Sandburg*

A woman says you look young—*Sukenick*

Woman seen as a slender instrument—*Rukeyser*

Woman should gather roses ere—*Anonymous– French*

A woman waits for me—*Whitman*

Woman, when we left—*Lorde*

A woman who lived in Holland of old—*Howells*

Woman with her forest, moons, flowers, waters —*Graves*

A woman's body at auction, she too is not herself —*Whitman*

A woman's face with Nature's own hand painted —*Shakespeare*

Women are best when they are pressed—*Anonymous–English—Modern English*

The women gather—*Giovanni*

Women have no wilderness in them—*Bogan*

The women of the city where I was forgotten—*Sandburg*

The wood burns red on the hearth—*Goldstein*

The wood is full of shining eyes—*Treece*

The wood-weasel/emerges daintily, the skunk—*Moore, Marianne*

Wooden particle board—*Porter, Bern*

Woodlands are lost upon a haze—*Bishop, John Peale*

A woodman chanced to split the ax-haft—*Moore, Marianne*

Woodman, spare that tree—*Morris, George Pope*

The woods decay, the woods decay and fall—*Tennyson*

The woods of Arcady are dead—*Yeats*

The woodsmen blow their horns, and close the day—*Gunn*

Wool white horses and their heads sag and roll—*Sandburg*

The word bites like a fish—*Spender*

The word in the bread feeds me—*Rukeyser*

Word over all, beautiful as the shy—*Whitman*

A word sticks in the wind's throat—*Wilbur*

Words can be arrows—*Goldstein*

Words escape me, I face a loss—*Sward*

The words of love—*Khalil*

Words simple given—*Malanga*

The world below the brine—*Whitman*

The world is a beautiful place—*Ferlinghetti*

The world is charged with the grandeur of God—*Hopkins*

The world is not a pleasant place to be—*Giovanni*

The world is so full of a number of things—*Stevenson*

The world is too much with us; late and soon—*Wordsworth*

The world now has a grey look to it—*Davison, Peter*

The world of God has turned its two stone faces—*Davie*

World take good notice, silver stars fading—*Whitman*

The world turns softly—*Conkling*

The world was first a private park—*MacPherson*

Worldly designs, fears, hopes, farewell—*Cary*

A worldman/ with the careful eye—*Lee, Don L.*

The world's great age begins anew—*Shelley*

World's lopsided/ that's its trouble—*Swenson*

Worms would rather be worms—*Sandburg*

Would that the structure brave, the manifold music I build—*Browning, Robert*

Would—would that there were—*De la Mare*

Would you mind revealing to me exactly what is your symbol, a tendril—*Benedikt*

Wouldn't think—*Emanuel*

Would'st thou heare, what man can say—*Jonson*

Wraettlic is thes weall-stan—*Anonymous–English—Old English*

Wrap your sulky beauty up—*Durrell*

Wrapped in a cloak—*Cane*

Wrapped in a yielding air, beside—*Auden*

Wrapped in thick sweaters in the high cold room—*Hacker*

The wrecking-ball—*Souster*

Wrote my first poem—*Olson*

Wrote two letters while rain—*Piercy*

Wu yan du shang syi lou—*Li Yu*

Wunst upon a time—*Riley*

Wurzel, wir wollen nun an die See—*Fontane*

W'y, wunst they wuz—*Riley*

Wyatt resteth here, that quick could never rest—*Surrey*

Wynken, Blynken, and Nod one night—*Field, Eugene*

Y apenas la madrugada—*Hernández, José*

Y aserrín, aserrán—*Silva*

Y cuando en el palacio—*Neruda*

Y es que Andalucía es una Señora—*Pemán*

Y fue por este río de sueñera y de barro—*Borges*

Y la canción del agua/ es una cosa eterna—*Garcia Lorca*

Y podrás conocerte, recordando—*Machado, Antonio*

Y qué fuerza de Dios, qué ardiente y pura—*Vocos-Lescano*

Y qué me sirva—*Vargas*

Y que yo me la lleve a río—*Garcia Lorca*

Y te dí el olor de todos mis dalias—*Ibarbourou*

Y válgame Díos, el tesoro—*Lobo*

Y yo me iré. Y se quedarán los pájaros cantando—*Jiménez*

Ya cabalga Diego Ordóñez—*Anonymous–Spanish*

Ya dal raz'ekhat'sya domashnim—*Pasternak*

Ya-goiya—*Voznezensky*

Ya hay un español que quiere—*Machado, Antonio*

Ya, kak poezd—*Yevtushenko*

Ya konchilsya, a ty zhiva—*Pasternak*

Ya l' budu v rokovoe vremya—*Ryleyev*

Ya la rosada aurora comenzaba—*Ercilla*

Ya llegas, Oh dulce Primavera—*Martinez Alonso*

Ya lugami idu—veter svishchet v lugakh—*Nekrasov*

Ya pomnyu v vyazme starii dom—*Simonov*

Ya prokhadil na ulitse—*Turgenev*

Ya que el tiempo era llegado—*Juan de la Cruz*

Ya que era llegado al tiempo—*Juan de la Cruz*

Ya rasnyi—*Yevtushenko*

Ya sé lo que es el porvenir: la espera—*Unamuno*

Ya tozhe lyubil, i dykhan'e—*Pasternak*

Ya vas lyubil: lyubov ashche but' mizhet—*Pushkin*

Ya vas obyazan izvestit—*Simonov*

Ya veo que somos los dos—*Hernández, José*

Ya viene el cortejo—*Darío*

Ya viene la noche—*Garcia Lorca*

Ya yo me enteré, mulata—*Guillén, Nicolás*

The yachts contend in a sea which the land partly encloses—*Williams, William Carlos*

Yakbi vi znali panichi—*Shevchenko*

Yall out there looooken so cooooool—*Sanchez*

Yan lung han shwei ywe lung sha—*Du Mu*

Yawning, the girl in the Metepec tourist trap says 5 pesos—*Summers, Hollis*

Ye banks, and braes, and streams around—*Burns*

Ye banks and braes o' bonnie Doon—*Burns*

Ye distant spires, ye antique towers—*Gray*

Ye elves of hills, brooks, standing lakes, and groves—*Shakespeare*

Ye flowery banks o' bonnie Doon—*Burns*

Ye good men of the Commons, with loving hearts and true—*Macaulay*

Ye green-rob'd Dryads, oft at dusky eve—*Warton, Joseph*

Ye have been fresh and green—*Herrick*

Ye learned sisters, which have oftentimes—*Spenser*

Ye living lamps, by whose dear light—*Marvell*

Ye mu, splachno tou splachnou mu karthula tis karthias mu—*Ritsos*

Ye young debaters over the doctrine—*Masters, Edgar Lee*

Yeah/ my man got no place else to go—*Sanchez*

Yeah she said my man's gone too—*Giovanni*

Yeah, some folks tell me—*Lester*

Yeah/ they/ hang you up—*Sanchez*

Year that trembled and reel'd beneath me—*Whitman*

The years are turning toward home—*Levine*

The year's at the Spring—*Browning, Robert*

Years had elapsed; the long room was the same —*Winters*

Years later, I find the old grammar, yellowed—*Warren*

Years of the modern. Years of the unperform'd —*Whitman*

Yeats in brown-tone—*Lee, Don L.*

Yeh. Billie if someone—*Sanchez*

Yeh yeh yeh yeh yeh . . . taught them to wear big naturals—*Sanchez*

The yellow fog that rubs its back upon the window-panes—*Eliot, Thomas Stearns*

Yellow is for regret, the distal, the second hand —*Wright, Charles*

Yellow-lit Budweiser signs over oaken bars—*Ginsberg*

A yellow mote of sand dreams in the polyp's eye —*Brathwaite*

The yellow wallpaper and the polished floor—*Bishop, John Peale*

Yellow, yellow, yellow, yellow—*Williams, William Carlos*

Yes, call me by my pet name—*Browning, Elizabeth Barrett*

Yes, comin' home from the North Sea fishin'—*Brown, Thomas Edward*

Yes, I remember Adlestrop—*Thomas, Edward*

Yes, I was one of them. And what a cast—*Francis*

Yes it is there—*Rukeyser*

Yes, my ha't's ez ha'd ez stone—*Dunbar, Paul Laurence*

Yes, said the sister with a little pinched face—*Lindsay, Vachel*

Yes, she's quiet now—*Souster*

Yes, there are love poems—*Sherwin*

Yes, we were looking at each other—*Rukeyser*

Yes, yours, my love, is the right human face—*Muir*

Yesli bog nas svoim mogushchestvom—*Simonov*

Yesterday I wanted to—*Creeley*

Yesterday I went to Ms. B's room—*Johnston, Ellen Turlington*

Yesterday is my To-morrow—*Sitwell, Osbert*

Yesterday morning enormous the moon hung low on the ocean—*Jeffers, Robinson*

Yesterday read somethin new—*Emanuel*

Yesterday/ you brought to me—*Johnston, Ellen Turlington*

Yet Chloe sure was form'd without a spot—*Pope, Alexander*

Yet if his majesty, our Sovereign Lord—*Anonymous–English—Modern English*

Yet love, mere love, is beautiful indeed—*Browning, Elizabeth Barrett*

Yet Merlin thro' his craft—*Tennyson*

Yet once more, O ye laurels, and once more—*Milton*

Yin loong hrurn suy ye loong sa—*Du Mu*

Yo, americano de las tierras pobres—*Neruda*

Yo andaba solo y callado—*Lugones, Leopoldo*

Yo atravesé las hostiles—*Neruda*

Yo dije que me gustaba—*Jiménez*

Yo estoy cansando—*Alonso*

Yo fui cantando errante—*Neruda*

Yo las amo, yo las oigo—*Castro, Rosalía de*

Yo lo hrurn—*Wen Ting-Yueh*

Yo los llevaba dentro. Los tenía—*Alcántara*

Yo me lancé a la vida—*Fernandez Moreno*

Yo muero extrañamente . . . No me mata la vida —*Agustini*

Yo no puedo tener un verso dulce—*Camino Galicia*

Yo no quiero que a mi niña—*Mistral*

Yo no sé si te quise—*Toledo*

Yo no soy nadie—*Camino Galicia*

Yo no soy yo—*Jiménez*

Yo os prefiero maravillosas rosas rojas—*Martinez Alonso*

Yo, para todo viaje—*Machado, Antonio*

Yo, pecador, artista del pecado—*Otero*

Yo pienso cuando me alegro—*Martí*

Yo quiero salir del mundo—*Martí*

Yo sé que ver y oír a un—*Hernández, Miguel*

Yo sé un himno gigante—*Becquer*

Yo seguiré soñando mientras pasa la vida—*Buesa*

Yo siento por la luz un amor de salvaje—*Ibarbourou*

Yo soy aquel que ayer no más decía—*Darío*

Yo soy ardiente, yo soy morena—*Becquer*

Yo soy como el viajero—*Loynaz*

Yo soy como las gentes que a mi tierra vinieron —*Machado, Manuel*

Yo soy quien libre me vi—*Manrique*

Yo soy un hombre sincero—*Martí*

Yo sueño con los ojos—*Martí*

Yo te miré a los ojos—*Garcia Lorca*

Yo tengo en mi jardín aquel rosal—*Martinez Alonso*

Yo tengo una palabra en la garganta—*Mistral*

Yo voy soñando caminos—*Machado, Antonio*

You and me walked long—*Hegarty*

You and your bottle—*Pietri*

You are a cultured citizen—*Morgenstern*

You are a fat Jack Sprat—*Polak*

You are absolutely for the relative—*Hoffman*

You are already asleep—*Gunn*

You are always—*Creeley*

You are here now—*Bogan*

You are ill, Davies, ill in mind—*Thomas, Ronald Stuart*

You are, in 1925, my father—*Brinnin*

You are my Anchor and my Ship—*Williams, Gwyn*

You are not beautiful, exactly—*Bell*

You are old, Father William, the young man said —*Carroll*

You are only one of many—*Smith, Stevie*

You are the heroes—you—*Johnston, Ellen Turlington*

You are/ the kitchen sink—*Gilbert, Celia*

You are the priestess of a templed world—*Goldstein*

You are the Queen of Hair—*Garfinkel*

You are younger than I am, you are—*Atwood*

You beat a rock till it bleeds—*Alakoye*

You better not fool with a Bumblebee—*Riley*

You bid me try, blue eyes, to write—*Voiture*

You blow yourself to a handsome watch—*Nash*

You brave heroique minds—*Drayton*

You called her a raceless woman—*Goldstein*

You came to it through wild country—*Wheelock*

You cannot bear this silent heavenly sadness—*Viereck*

You cannot make remembrance grow—*Dickinson, Emily*

You can't have a slam offhand—*Sandburg*

You come to me quiet as rain not yet fallen—*Patten*

You could not stop the snow—*Watson*

You did not come—*Hardy*

You do not do, you do not do—*Plath*

You do not look like me. I'm glad—*Williams, Hugo*

You do not move about, but try—*Bell*

You earthly Souls that court a wanton flame—*Stanley*

You eyes, forever west of afternoon—*Van Doren*

You fill me up so much—*Shange*

You fit into me—*Atwood*

You, flat, yellow light—*Sherwin*

You give this man the sort of praise—*Engle*

You, going along the path—*Atwood*

You gotta be talked to, Anne—*Flanders*

You have, in a sense/ been through it all—*Weiss*

You have your hat and coat on and she says she will be right down—*Nash*

You head—*Wallace*

You hear my step—*Dickey, James*

You hip to herd runners?—*Dupree*

You know how it is with an April day—*Frost, Robert*

You know I almost forgot—*Douglas, Sharon*

You know, I must admit—*Stevens, Wendy*

You know Orion always comes up sideways—*Frost, Robert*

You know the bloom, unearthly white—*Parker*

You know w'at for ees school keep out—*Daly*

You know, we French stormed Ratisbon—*Browning, Robert*

You know what Bigger Thomas did—*Marvin X*

You know you're all nuts, boobs, scamps, frauds —*Patchen*

You lay so quiet at your end of the room—*Spender*

You left as you so often left before—*Scannell*

You lie there, Anna—*Smith, Stevie*

You like not that French novel? Tell me why—*Meredith, George*

You love us when we're heroes, home on leave —*Sassoon*

You may call, you may call—*Coatsworth*

You may have met a man—quite young—*Hardy*

You may never see rain, unless you see—*Bynner*

You may talk o' gin and beer—*Kipling*

You meaner beauties of the night—*Wotton*

You met at the crossroads—*Marshall, Helen Lowrie*

You must live through the time when everything hurts—*Spender*

You need not see what someone is doing—*Auden*

You need the untranslatable ice to watch—*Brooks, Gwendolyn*

You no/ tice—*Cummings*

You observe the carven hand—*Masters, Edgar Lee*

You open your mouth, I put my tongue in—*Bly*

You ought to have seen what I saw on my way —*Frost, Robert*

You ought to know Mr. Mistoffelees—*Eliot, Thomas Stearns*

You play the cop, and I'm the robber type—*Hall*

You refuse to own—*Atwood*

You say I o.k.ed/ long distance—*Hughes, Langston*

You say I'm as cold—*Giovanni*

You say that I've gone blind and pity me—*Marshall, Helen Lowrie*

You say you want to fight me?—*Lee, Dennis*

You see a man/ trying to think—*Rich*

You shall above all things be glad and young—*Cummings*

You shattered the many immense—*Ungaretti*

You sho' God bettah dig yo' task lessen—*Beecher*

You should have stopped them—*Aubert*

You show me the poems of some woman—*Rich*

You sleeping child asleep—*Durrell*

You stalk it patiently—*Weber, Ron*

You stand near the window as lights wink—*Patchen*

You strange, astonished looking, anglefaced—*Hunt*

You strop my anger, especially—*Piercy*

You sweet black semitic—*Braxton*

You tell me, for I—*Logan*

You that know the way—*Merwin*

You that love England, who have an ear for her music—*Day Lewis*

You that through all the dying summer—*Muir*

You, the women; I the man—*Patchen*

You there—I here—triangled with the mirror—*Scott, Winfield Townley*

You, too, seek beauty. Past the unlovely smells —*Vaughan, H. A.*

You turn yourself in—*Harkness*

You went to the verge, you say, and come back safely—*Aiken*

You were a God once—*Amini*

You were brushing your hair—*Bell*

You were only a grainy face in the newspaper —*Thomas, Lorenzo*

You were our first brave ones to defy their dissonance of hate—*Walker*

You will see this big-jawed man walking up and down—*Eberhart*

You will tire of many acceptances. Some of each day—*Ciardi*

You would not want too reserved a speaker—*Stafford*

You would think the fury of aerial bombardment—*Eberhart*

You wouldn't want to go there—*Booth*

You, you, you come on—*Brown, Otis*

You'd never have thought the queen was Helen's sister—*Jeffers, Robinson*

You'll wait a long, long time for anything much—*Frost, Robert*

Young Algernon, the Doctor's son—*Belloc*

The young are quick of speech—*Winters*

The young child, Christ, is straight and wise—*Sandburg*

Young Consuela—*Sanders*

The young Endymion sleeps Endymion's sleep—*Longfellow*

Young Jimmy Stone—*Gridley*

Young Juan now was sixteen years of age—*Byron*

Young man—/ Young man—/Your arm's too short to box with God—*Johnson, James Weldon*

The young pop-singers, newly mystical—*Patten*

Young women in their April moodiness—*Simpson*

Your attention please—*Porter, Peter*

Your beauty is more than beauty now—*Sobiloff*

Your eyen two wol slee me sodeinly—*Chaucer*

Your father's gone, my bald headmaster said—*Lucie-Smith*

Your fingers cruise—*Major*

Your ghost will walk, you lover of trees—*Browning, Robert*

Your hand in mine, we walk out—*Rexroth*

Your hands are envelopes—*Tropp, Steven*

Your hands lie open in the long fresh grass—*Rossetti, Dante Gabriel*

Your hands woke—*Randall*

Your letter wrecks my day—*Kizer*

Your lips pressed together—*Harriman*

Your love and pity doth th'impression fill—*Shakespeare*

Your love has lived in your long—*Sobiloff*

Your mother, whom the mirror-world has claimed—*Kunitz*

Your name is Parrot: a bird of Paradise—*Deutsch*

Your neighbor moves less and less, attempts less—*Hughes, Ted*

Your nurse could only speak Italian—*Lowell, Robert*

Your soul began to dance—*Bodenheim*

Your stillness here at evening, with the shade—*Van Doren*

Your tall French legs, my V for victory—*Scott, F. R.*

Your toothbrush won't remember—*Williams, Miller*

Your voice is coming trippingly—*Darr*

You're a brave man they tell me—*Yevtushenko*

Youre ugly tokyn—*Skelton, John*

Yours exasperate—*Sherwin*

Yousa yousa—*Gaver*

Youth, day, old age, and night—*Whitman*

Youth of delight! come hither—*Blake*

You've been away a long time—*Fox, Charles*

You've heard, no doubt, of the Dinosaur—*Cullen*

You've read of several kinds of cat—*Eliot, Thomas Stearns*

You've seen a strawberry—*Moore, Marianne*

Yr letter! How it spotted itself—*Olson*

Yusofe gom gaeshte baz ayaed be kaenahn—*Hafiz*

Yver, vous n'estes qu'un villain—*Charles d'Orleans*

Ywe hei yan fei gau—*Lu Lwun*

Ywe lwo wu ti shwang man tyan—*Jang Ji*

Za vse, za vse tebya blagodaryuya—*Lermontov*

Zabeeba—*Brown, Otis*

Zamani nikipendeza kamma ani la tambun—*Farahani*

Zasypet snet dorogi—*Pasternak*

Zavedi mne ladoni za plechi—*Voznesensky*

Zaviduyu ya—*Yevtushenko*

Zavorazhivaya, Manezha—*Voznesensky*

Zazhmuri se na iedno oko—*Popa*

Zdravstvui, v belom sarafane—*Vyazemsky*

Zebedee, the Zebra lived in a zoo—*Jeffries*

Zeichen/ Kreuz und Fische—*Bobrowski*

Die Zeit geht nicht, sie stehet still—*Keller, Gottfried*

Zeit ist zu gehen in das Haus des Freundes—*Kaschnitz*

Zeit. Vorzeit—*Heissenbüttel*

Zerstörungen—*Benn*

Zeus de heon pros doma theoi—*Homer*

Zeus lies in Ceres bosom—*Pound*

Zhdi menya, i ya vernus—*Simonov*

Zhivet u nas sosed bukhkin—*Voznezensky*

Zhizn vernulas' tak zhe besprichinno—*Pasternak*

Ziemlich viel Glück gehört dazu—*Krolow*

Zipping through concrete telarañas—*Alurista*

Zitto, Don Fabbio—*Belli*

Zrel li ty, pevets ty drevnii—*Derzhavin*

Zu Aachen im alten Dome liegt—*Heine*

Zu Dionys, dem Tyrannen, schlich—*Schiller*

Zu einem seltsamen Versuch—*Morgenstern*

Zu Potsdam unter den Eichen—*Brecht*

Die Züge deiner, die dem Blut verschworen—*Benn*

The Zulu King arrived at the new Basin—*Copeland*

Zum Kampf der Wangen und Gesänge—*Schiller*

Zvenela muzyka v zadu—*Akhmatova*

Zwei Tannenwurzeln gross und alt—*Morgenstern*

Der zweite Herr von links ist ausgetreten—*Kästner*

Der Zwölf-Elf hebt die linke Hand—*Morgenstern*

Zzzip—*Gaver*

Prefix "a/" signifies that poet is reading own works in this recording

Abbe, George. a/FOLKW 8, FOLKW 25
Abse, Dannie. a/ARGO 100, a/ARGO 140,
  a/JNP 9
Adams, Leonie. a/LIBC 25, a/LIBC 74,
  a/SPOA 96
Adrian, Max. ARGO 48, ARGO 66, ARGO 67,
  ARGO 88A, CAED 5, CAED 89, CAED 191,
  CAED 201, CAED 203
Agee, James. a/CAED 196
Agus, G. CETRA 50
Ai. a/WATSHD 9, a/WATSHD 46
Aiken, Conrad. a/CAED 31, a/CAED 183,
  a/CARIL 19, a/LIBC 23, a/LIBC 69,
  a/SPOA 93
Agajanian, Shah-Keh. FOLKW 77
Aksenov, V. MK 1
Alakoye, Adesanya. a/WATSHD 4
Albert, Eddie. CAED 185, CAED 195
Albertazzi, Giorgio. CETRA 1, CETRA 2,
  CETRA 3, CETRA 8, CETRA 9, CETRA 12,
  CETRA 14, CETRA 19, CETRA 20,
  CETRA 21, CETRA 22, CETRA 23,
  CETRA 24, CETRA 25, CETRA 27,
  CETRA 28, CETRA 46
Alberti, Rafael. a/APPL 5, INDA 1, POETAS 2
Alcántara, Manuel. a/AGUIL 3
Alcon, Alfredo. AGUIL 9
Aldan, Daisy. a/WATSHD 47
Aldini, Edmondo. CETRA 9, CETRA 12,
  CETRA 19, CETRA 20, CETRA 21,
  CETRA 22, CETRA 23, CETRA 24,
  CETRA 25, CETRA 27, CETRA 28,
  CETRA 46
Aleixandre, Vicente. a/AGUIL 3
Alfred, William. a/HARVOC 18
Allen, David. CAED 182, CMS 10A, CMS 11,
  CMS 12, CMS 13, CMS 14, CMS 20, EAV 14,
  EAV 22, EMC 2, POETRY 1, POETRY 2
Almquist. EAV 8
Alonson, Dámaso. a/AGUIL 3
Alurista. a/AUDIOT 6
Ameche, Jim. LION 1, LION 2
Amichai, Yehuda. a/WATSHD 48
Aminel, Georges. ADES 17
Amini, Johari. a/WATSHD 2
Amis, Kingsley. FOLKW 59A, a/SPOA 67
Amrouche, Jean. ADES 31
Anderson, Doug. a/WATSHD 1
Anderson, Judith. CAED 23, CAED 40,
  CAED 49, CAED 129, CAED 148
Anderson, Lee. a/CARIL 9, WESTNG 2
Andrews, Bruce. a/WATSHD 2
Angelou, Maya. a/TAPES 1
Antin, David. a/BLACKS 1, a/WATSHD 53
Antonicelli, Franco. CETRA 7
Antoninus, Brother. a/BIGSUR 4, a/CAED 119,
  a/SPOA 99
Aragon, Louis. a/GMS 4
Arden, John. a/ARGO 96
Arens, Peter. CHRIST 24, CHRIST 25
Aridjis, Homero. a/APPL 5
Arp, Hans. a/NESKE 2
Ashbery, John. a/JNP 10, a/SPOA 106

Ashcroft, Peggy. ARGO 15, ARGO 31,
  ARGO 35, ARGO 49, ARGO 60, ARGO 125,
  ARGO 135, CAED 63, LONDON 1
Asner, Edward. EAV 9
Attenborough, Richard. SPOA 67, SPOA 68
Atwood, Margaret. a/CAED 174
Aubert, Alvin. a/WATSHD 4
Auden, W. H. a/ARGO 80, a/ARGO 97,
  a/ARGO 98, a/ARGO 149, a/CAED 19,
  a/COLUMB 8, COLUMB 10, HARPV 4,
  a/HARVOC 11, a/JNP 11, a/LIBC 3,
  a/LIBC 6, a/NACTE 8, a/SPOA 85,
  a/SPOA 98, a/WESTNG 1
Audley, Maxine. SPOA 50, SPOA 66, SPOA 73,
  SPOA 74, SPOA 122
Aumont, Jean-Pierre. ADES 15, ADES 50
Avison, Margaret. a/FOLKW 50
Ayres, Harry Morgan, NACTE 2, NACTE 5

Bachmann, Ingeborg. a/NESKE 1
Baddeley, Angela. SPOA 67, SPOA 68
Baez, Joan. VAN 3
Bagg, Robert. a/JNP 12
Bahati, Amirh. a/FOLKW 47
Baker, Houston A., Jr. CASSC 12B
Baker, Howard. a/LIBC 25, a/LIBC 73
Balcon, Jill. ARGO 63, ARGO 89, ARGO 109,
  FOLKW 60, JUP 1, SPOA 35
Baldwin, Deirdra. a/WATSHD 9,
  a/WATSHD 54
Baldwin, Michael. a/ARGO 96
Bale. ARGO 120
Balser, Ewald. ATHENA 10
Barker, George. a/ARGO 100
Barras, Henri. FOLKW 84
Barrault, Jean-Louis. ADES 8, ADES 16,
  ADES 36, ADES 51, ADES 52, HACH 17,
  SPOA 32, SPOA 62
Barshay, Bernard. FOLKW 110
Barth, Diane. EAV 15
Bartolomei, Rafael. SMC 9
Barton, John. ARGO 9, ARGO 13, ARGO 88A
Basescu, Elinor. CMS 2, CMS 3, CMS 4
Bates, Alan. ARGO 54, ARGO 55, ARGO 56,
  ARGO 66, CAED 83
Bauer, Eric W. FOLKW 74
Baybars, Taner. a/ARGO 96
Bebb, Richard. ARGO 47, ARGO 50,
  ARGO 157
Becker, Maria. DEUTGR 11, DEUTGR 19
Beecher, John. a/BROADR 4, a/FOLKW 35
Beer, Patricia. a/ARGO 96
Begley, Ed. CAED 29, CAED 30, CAED 98,
  CAED 100, CAED 103, CAED 108,
  CAED 133, CAED 135, CAED 185,
  CAED 194, CAED 195
Begué, Armand. FOLKW 85
Belitt, Ben. a/JNP 69
Bell, Marvin. a/MICHM 14, a/WATSHD 10,
  a/WATSHD 22
Bellamy, Cecil. SPOA 65, SPOA 116, SPOA 117
Bellamy, Ralph. RCA 5, SINGER 4
Beloof, Robert. ARGO 11, ARGO 12

Benedikt, Michael. a/SCHOL 5
Benet, Stephen Vincent. a/CAED 141,
   a/LIBC 42, a/NACTE 10, a/SPOA 95
Benet, William Rose. a/NACTE 12, a/SPOA 92
Benn, Gottfried. a/DEUTGR 14,
   a/DEUTGR 18, a/DEUTGR 48
Bennet, Joseph. SPOA 15
Benson, Esther. CMS 15, LIST 18
Bentley, Eric. FOLKW 106
Bergengruen, Werner. a/CHRIST 2
Berger-Kiss, Andres. a/SMC 8
Bergman, Bo. a/GRAM 4
Bernardos, Carmen. FIDIAS 3
Bernstein, Charles. a/WATSHD 11
Berrigan, Daniel. a/CAED 158, a/SPOA 82
Berry, Wendell. a/JNP 70, a/MICHM 16
Berryman, John. a/APPL 2, a/HARPV 5,
   a/LIBC 17, a/LIBC 58, a/SPOA 101
Bertin, Pierre. ADES 46
Bessinger, J. B. Jr. CAED 81, CAED 87,
   CAED 91, CAED 104, CAED 105
Betjeman, John. a/ARGO 84, a/ARGO 86,
   a/ARGO 97, a/ARGO 121, a/CAED 178,
   FOLKW 65, a/SPOA 8
Bieneck, Horst. DEUTGR 40A
Bishop, Elizabeth. CAED 112, a/COLUMB 8,
   a/LIBC 19, a/LIBC 63, a/SPOA 99
Bishop, John Peale. a/LIBC 44
Blackburn, Thomas. a/ARGO 93, a/SPOA 68
Blackman, Gary. a/WATSHD 14
Blackmur, Richard P. a/CARIL 22, a/LIBC 19,
   a/LIBC 61
Blake, Edward. LIST 6, LIST 8, LIST 19
Blanchar, Pierre. HACH 20, POLYDR 2
Blanding, Don. a/TEMPO 1
Blin, Roger. ADES 47, ADES 52
Blomberg, Erik. a/GRAM 6
Bloom, Claire. CAED 5, CAED 56, CAED 89,
   CAED 164, CAED 169, CAED 186,
   CAED 201, CAED 202, CAED 203,
   HOUGHT 1, HOUGHT 2, POLYGL 2
Blunden, Edmund. a/ARGO 100
Bly, Robert. a/CASSC 4, a/JNP 71,
   a/MICHM 12, a/SCHOL 5, a/SPOA 105,
   a/WATSHD 3, a/WATSHD 15
Bobrowski, Johannes. a/WAGENB 1
Bodenheim, Maxwell. a/LIBC 44
Bogan, Louise. a/CARIL 7, a/LIBC 5,
   a/LIBC 10, a/LIST 13, a/LIST 14,
   a/LIST 15, a/SPOA 82, a/SPOA 95
Böhm, Karlheinz. DEUTGR 40
Bolo, Jean. ADES 29
Bond, Boyce. FOLKW 39
Bonnamy, Yvonne. ARGO 21, ARGO 30,
   ARGO 37, ARGO 58
Bontemps, Arna. a/FOLKW 6, FOLKW 41
Booth, Philip. a/JNP 72, a/SPOA 104
Borchert, Wilhelm. CHRIST 26
Borroff, Marie. CAED 91
Borton, Terry. a/ACTIV 1
Bosetti, Giulio. CETRA 9, CETRA 12,
   CETRA 19, CETRA 20, CETRA 21,
   CETRA 22, CETRA 23, CETRA 24,
   CETRA 25, CETRA 27, CETRA 28,
   CETRA 46
Bouquet, Michel. ADES 23, ADES 25,
   ADES 40, ADES 52, HACH 17, HACH 23

Brady, Leo. SPOA 10
Bragg, Robert. a/JNP 12
Brassens, George. PENN 2
Brasseur, Pierre. ADES 24, ADES 52
Brathwaite, Edward. a/ARGO 100,
   a/ARGO 104, a/ARGO 112, a/ARGO 113,
   a/CAED 153
Braxton, Jodi. a/WATSHD 4
Brenes, Maria. HOLT 1
Brett, Jeremy. CAED 132
Brewer, Derek. ARGO 27
Brignone, Lilla. CETRA 30, CETRA 45,
   CETRA 51
Brinnin, John Malcolm. a/HARVOC 14,
   a/JNP 73, a/LIBC 9, a/LIBC 20, a/SPOA 102
Broch, Hermann. a/SUHRK 1
Brogle, Peter. CHRIST 5, CHRIST 22,
   CHRIST 24
Bronk, William. a/WATSHD 40
Brook, Faith. CAED 191
Brookes, C. R. M. CAED 64
Brooks, Geraldine. RCA 10
Brooks, Gwendolyn. a/AUDIT 1, a/BROADV 5,
   a/CAED 114, FOLKW 1, a/NET 15,
   a/SPOA 102
Brophy, Robert. BIGSUR 3
Broumas, Olga. a/WATSHD 49
Brown, George Mackay. a/ARGO 96
Brown, Otis. a/WATSHD 10
Brown, Pamela. CAED 203
Brown, Sterling A. FOLKW 1, a/FOLKW 40,
   a/FOLKW 43, WATSHD 11
Brown, Thomas Edward. a/ARGO 127
Browne, Michael Dennis. a/JNP 74
Bruchac, Joseph. a/WATSHD 2
Brynner, Witter. a/LIBC 65
Bülow, Friedrich von. CHRIST 8, CHRIST 13,
   CHRIST 17, CHRIST 18, CHRIST 20
Bunting, Basil. a/ARGO 97
Burns, Robert. EAV 15
Burr, Robert. EAV 15
Burrows, Vinie. SPOA 88, SPOA 89
Burton, Richard. ARGO 5, ARGO 6, ARGO 21,
   ARGO 22, ARGO 58, ARGO 137,
   ARGO 158, CAED 77, CAED 78,
   POLYDR 1, WARNER 1
Busch, Ernst. DEUTGR 28
Bynner, Witter. a/LIBC 21, a/SPOA 91

Callan, Josephine. SPOA 10
Cambridge, Godfrey. DAV 1
Campbell, Alistair. a/KIWI 2
Campbell, Douglas. EMC 3, EMC 4
Campbell, Rex. BIGSUR 5
Cane, Melville. a/JNP 75
Carleton, Elaine K. CAED 128
Carlini, Paolo. CETRA 2, CETRA 5, CETRA 7,
   CETRA 9, CETRA 12, CETRA 13,
   CETRA 19, CETRA 20, CETRA 21,
   CETRA 22, CETRA 23, CETRA 24,
   CETRA 25, CETRA 27, CETRA 28,
   CETRA 41, CETRA 46
Carnovsky, Morris. CAED 107, CAED 193,
   SPOA 128, SPOA 129
Carradine, John. MINU 1, WORLDP 1
Carranza, Eduardo. a/LIBC 76
Carraro, Tino. CETRA 3

Carroll, Vinette. ARGO 17, ARGO 88
Carter, Ellen. WATSHD 14
Casares, Maria. ADES 10, ADES 45
Caspar, Horst. ATHENA 1
Casson, Christopher. SPOA 57, SPOA 64,
    SPOA 131, SPOA 132, SPOA 133,
    CHRIST 64, CHRIST 123, CHRIST 131,
    CHRIST 132, CHRIST 133
Casson, John. a/ARGO 143
Casson, Lewis. CAED 52
Castellani, M. CETRA 50
Cattonar, Joanna. a/WATSHD 11
Causley, Charles. a/ARGO 98, a/SPOA 67
Celan, Paul. a/SUHRK 6
Celaya, Gabriel. a/AGUIL 1, a/AGUIL 3
Cellor, B. FANT 1
Chapin, Katherine Garrison. a/LIBC 2,
    a/LIBC 3
Charters, Ann. BROADR 3
Chase, Ilka. RCA 6
Chaumette, François. ADES 55
Cheever, John. a/JNP 76
Chester, Laura. a/WATSHD 9, a/WATSHD 14
Childress, Alice. EAV 2
Church, Tony. ARGO 13, ARGO 15, ARGO 33,
    ARGO 36, ARGO 39, ARGO 40, ARGO 41,
    ARGO 42, ARGO 43, ARGO 44, ARGO 55,
    ARGO 56, ARGO 62, ARGO 64, ARGO 66,
    ARGO 90, ARGO 118
Ciardi, John. a/CASSC 12, FOLKW 3,
    a/FOLKW 36, a/JNP 77, a/LIBC 50,
    a/SPOA 71, a/SPOA 72, a/SPOA 102
Clark, China. a/FOLKW 47
Clark, Dane. COLUMB 15
Clark, Gillian. a/ARGO 152
Clark, John W. a/GRYPH 1
Clarke, Austin. a/ARGO 99, a/CLADD 1
Clay, Buriel. a/WATSHD 7
Cleverdon, Douglas. CAED 122
Clifton, Lucille. a/WATSHD 2, a/WATSHD 5,
    a/WATSHD 28
Clinton-Baddeley, V. C. BRITAM 2, BRITAM 3,
    FOLKW 67, SPOA 67, SPOA 68
Cocteau, Jean. a/CAED 54, a/GMS 10,
    a/PERIOD 3, PHIL 1
Codrescu, Andrei. a/WATSHD 55
Coffin, Robert P. Tristram. a/NACTE 16,
    a/SPOA 94
Coggio, Roger. ADES 43
Coghill, Nevill. ARGO 25, ARGO 26,
    BRITAM 4, SPOA 60, SPOA 61
Cohen, Leonard. a/FOLKW 49
Colbert, Alison. a/WATSHD 4
Collier, Tom. a/WATSHD 7
Collins, Allen F. CAED 182
Collymore, Frank. CAED 153
Colman, Ronald. AUDIBK 1, CROWN 1,
    LIST 9
Colomba, Sergio. CETRA 34, CETRA 35
Colum, Padraic. a/FOLKW 27, SPOA 6
Commons, Milt. FOLKW 57, FOLKW 58
Compton, Fay. CAED 191
Conkling, Hilda. a/CAED 154
Connor, Tony. a/ARGO 94
Coppola, August F. SCHOL 6
Corke, Hilary. a/ARGO 97
Cornell, Katherine. CAED 46, CAED 132

Corrado. CETRA 50
Corso, Gregory. a/APPL 2, a/UCALM 2
Cort, David. FOLKW 32
Corvalan, Octavio. FOLKW 80
Coward, Noel. a/CAED 61, COLUMB 9
Cowley, Malcolm. a/JNP 3, a/SPOA 95
Crast, Antonio. CETRA 3, CETRA 9,
    CETRA 12, CETRA 13, CETRA 19,
    CETRA 20, CETRA 21, CETRA 22,
    CETRA 23, CETRA 24, CETRA 25,
    CETRA 27, CETRA 28, CETRA 46
Creed, Robert P. FOLKW 54
Creeley, Robert. a/CASSC 9, a/JNP 78,
    a/NET 6, a/SPOA 105
Crespo, José. FOLKW 82
Crisp, Donald. DECCA 3
Crosby, Bing. DECCA 4
Crossley-Holland, Kevin. ARGO 75
Cucciolla, Riccardo. CETRA 51
Cuervo, Gemma. FIDIAS 3
Cullen, Countee. FOLKW 1, a/SPOA 97
Cummings. E. E. a/CAED 18, a/CAED 110,
    a/CAED 112, a/CAED 183, a/CAED 198,
    a/CAED 199, a/COLUMB 8, a/HARC 4,
    HOUGHT 5, a/LIBC 11, a/LIBC 33,
    a/SPOA 94
Cunningham, James Vincent. a/SPOA 99
Cuny, Alain. ADES 32, ADES 50, ADES 51
Curnow, Allen. a/KIWI 1
Curran, Chris. ARGO 74
Cusack, Cyril. CAED 53, CAED 68, CAED 143

Dahlberg, Edward. a/JNP 79
Dailey, Irene. FOLKW 21
Daitz, Stephen. JNP 95
Damas, Leon. a/FOLKW 78, a/WATSHD 11
Dammann, Anna. DEUTGR 5
D'Angelo, Carlo. CETRA 3, CETRA 5,
    CETRA 9, CETRA 12, CETRA 19,
    CETRA 20, CETRA 21, CETRA 22,
    CETRA 23, CETRA 24, CETRA 25,
    CETRA 26, CETRA 27, CETRA 28,
    CETRA 46
Danner, Margaret. a/BROADV 11
Dantes, Raúl. CAED 44
Darr, Ann. a/WATSHD 33
Darragh, Martina. a/WATSHD 2
Davidson, Donald. a/SPOA 94
Davie, Donald. a/MARV 1, a/STANFD 2
Davis, Norman. SPOA 60, SPOA 61
Davis, Ossie. CAED 120, CAED 156
Davis, Peter. WATSHD 2
Davis, Thulani Nkabinde. a/WATSHD 12
Davison, Peter. a/SPOA 106
Davy, Jean. HACH 2
Day Lewis, Cecil. a/ARGO 91, ARGO 107,
    a/ARGO 109, a/ARGO 144, a/CARIL 16,
    FOLKW 64, FOLKW 68, a/JNP 31,
    a/SPOA 67, a/SPOA 68
De Frees, Madeline. a/WATSHD 10,
    a/WATSHD 30
De la Mare, Walter. a/CAED 35
Dee, Ruby. CAED 120, CAED 155, CAED 156,
    CAED 176
Degischer, Vilma. SPOA 5
Demidov, Alexander. FOLKW 95
Den Boer, James. a/WATSHD 2

Denby, Edwin. a/LIST 15
Densh, Judi. ARGO 128
Derwood, Gene. a/SERIF 1
Desailly, Jean. ADES 3, ADES 37, SPOA 27
Deschamps, Jean. GMS 3, HACH 1, HACH 5,
    HACH 16, HACH 21, HACH 24
Deutsch, Babette. a/SPOA 95
Deutsch, Ernst. ATHENA 8
Devaul, Diane. a/WATSHD 7
Devaux, Alexis. a/WATSHD 10
Devlin, William. ARGO 21, ARGO 38,
    ARGO 46, ARGO 58
Dhiegh, Khigh. CMS 9, FOLKW 55
Dicenta, Manuel. FIDIAS 1, FIDIAS 3
Dickey, James. a/CAED 140, a/EBEC 3,
    a/SPOA 81, a/SPOA 104
Dickey, William. a/JNP 80
Dickinson, Patrick. a/ARGO 97
Dickson, Hugh. LONGM 1, SPOA 67, SPOA 68
Diego, Gerardo. a/AGUIL 3
Dinsmoor, Andy. WATSHD 9
Dodson, Owen. a/SPOA 101, a/WATSHD 42
Dodson-Letourneau, Gayle. a/WATSHD 5
Donat, Robert. ARGO 77, ARGO 82,
    SERAPH 1, SPOA 41
Donegan, Martin. CMS 1, CMS 10, CMS 16,
    FOLKW 21
Donley, Robert. LIST 16
Doolittle, Hilda (H. D.) a/SPOA 92
Dorado, Alcides. SMC 18
Dos Passos, John. a/JNP 96
Douglas, Helen Gahagan. CAED 185,
    CAED 195
Douglas, Maria. CAED 44
Dowie, Freda. ARGO 29, ARGO 63
Dowling, Allan. a/GRYPH 2
Drake, Alfred. CAED 22
Dreyer, Lynn. a/WATSHD 14
Duby, Jacques. ADES 4, ADES 22, ADES 38,
    ADES 50, SPOA 32
Dudek, Louis. a/FOLKW 49
Dugan, Alan. a/LIBC 54
Dullin, Charles. ADES 43, ADES 50
Dunbar, Maxwell John. FOLKW 59
Duncan, Frank. ARGO 48, ARGO 59,
    ARGO 64, ARGO 65, ARGO 66, ARGO 70A,
    ARGO 75, ARGO 76, ARGO 90
Duncan, Fred. ARGO 1A, ARGO 70A,
    ARGO 76
Duncan, Robert. a/NET 5
Dunn, Charles. FOLKW 53, SINGER 6
Dupree, Nacy Lorraine. a/FOLKW 38
Durán, Manuel. SPOA 39
Durán, Miguel. WATSHD 7
Durieux, Tilla. ATHENA 5
Durrell, Laurence. a/SPOA 34, a/VOIX 4

Eastman, Max. a/SPOA 91
Eban, Abba. SPOA 130
Eberhart, Richard. a/CAED 113, a/CAED 183,
    a/CARIL 11, a/LIBC 3, a/LIBC 8,
    a/SPOA 82, a/SPOA 97, a/TAPES 9
Eckels, Jon. a/BROADV 7
Eddison, Robert. SPOA 43, SPOA 47, SPOA 48,
    SPOA 121
Edson, Russel. a/WATSHD 14, a/WATSHD 36
Edwards, Hilton. SPOA 29

Eich, Günter. a/SUHRK 7
Eiseley, Loren. a/JNP 81
Eliot, T. S. a/ANGEL 2, a/ARGO 7,
    a/CAED 34, a/CAED 139, a/CAED 159,
    a/COLUMB 8, a/HARPV 1, a/HARVOC 2,
    a/HARVOC 15, a/HARVOC 16,
    a/HARVOC 17, a/HARVOC 17A, a/LIBC 7,
    a/LIBC 22, a/LIBC 24, a/LIBC 26,
    a/LIBC 28, a/LIBC 29, a/LIST 4, a/LIST 13,
    a/RCA 11, a/SPOA 25, a/SPOA 93,
    a/SPOA 183
Elliott, George P. a/JNP 82
Elmslie, Kenward. a/WATSHD 4,
    a/WATSHD 43
Eluard, Paul. a/GMS 5
Elvin, William. CAED 106
Emanuel, James A. a/BROADV 10,
    a/BROADV 16
Emmerson, George S. TENNY 1
Empson, William. a/ARGO 97, a/ARGO 183,
    a/LIBC 23, a/LIBC 70
Endrigo, Sergio. CETRA 34, CETRA 35
Engle, Paul. a/LIBC 5, a/LIBC 12, a/SPOA 99
Ennis, Julian. a/ARGO 93
Enright, D. J. a/SPOA 68
Enslin, Theodore. a/WATSHD 14,
    a/WATSHD 38
Enzensberger, Hans Magnus. a/SUHRK 2
Espert, Nuria. AGUIL 14, FIDIAS 3
Evans, Abbie Huston. a/SPOA 82
Evans, Edith. CAED 203, SERAPH 1

Fabio, Sarah Webster. a/FOLKW 16,
    a/FOLKW 17, a/FOLKW 18, a/WATSHD 5
Fabregues, Ricardo. SMC 14, SMC 15, SMC 16,
    SMC 17
Fagin, Larry. a/MICHM 17
Farrell, James T. a/JNP 83
Feldman, Irving. a/JNP 84
Feliciani, Mario. CETRA 9, CETRA 12,
    CETRA 19, CETRA 20, CETRA 21,
    CETRA 22, CETRA 23, CETRA 24,
    CETRA 25, CETRA 27, CETRA 28,
    CETRA 46
Felipe, Leon. AGUIL 10
Ferlin, Nils. a/GAZ 1, a/GAZ 2
Ferlinghetti, Lawrence. a/CASSC 11,
    a/FANT 2, a/NET 1, a/SPOA 103,
    a/UCALM 2, a/TAPES 10
Fernan Gomez, Fernando. AGUIL 5, AGUIL 6,
    AGUIL 7, AGUIL 11, AGUIL 12, AGUIL 13,
    AGUIL 15, AGUIL 16, AGUIL 17, AGUIL 18
Ferron, Marcelle. a/FOLKW 70
Field, Edward. a/MILLER 1
Figueroa, John. CAED 153
Filippo, Eduardo de. a/CETRA 4, CETRA 48,
    CETRA 49
Finkel, Donald. a/JNP 85
Fisher, Linette. PERIOD 2
Fitts, Dudley. a/CARIL 3
Fitzgerald, Robert. CMS 19, a/LIBC 21,
    a/LIBC 66
Fitzsimmons, Tom. a/WATSHD 12
Fleetwood, Harry. FOLKW 4, FOLKW 9,
    FOLKW 23
Fletcher, Bramwell. LIST 1, LIST 2, LIST 3,
    LIST 10

Fletcher, John Gould. a/LIBC 9, a/LIBC 18
Flint, Roland. a/WATSHD 8, a/WATSHD 35
Flon, Suzanne. ADES 55
Florit, Eugenio. DOVER 2, SPOA 37, SPOA 59
Florit, Ricardo. SPOA 37
Flye, Father James. CAED 196
Foa, Arnoldo. CETRA 1, CETRA 2, CETRA 3,
    CETRA 8, CETRA 9, CETRA 12, CETRA 13,
    CETRA 14, CETRA 18, CETRA 19,
    CETRA 20, CETRA 21, CETRA 22,
    CETRA 23, CETRA 24, CETRA 25,
    CETRA 26, CETRA 27, CETRA 28,
    CETRA 46
Fontanne, Lynn. RCA 7
Forster, E. M. a/ARGO 106
Foster, Gloria. SPOA 82
Fox, Charles. a/WATSHD 5
Fox, Siv Cedering. a/WATSHD 1
Francis, Robert. a/FOLKW 22
Franck, Walter. DEUTGR 15, TELEF 4,
    TELEF 5
Frankenberg, Lloyd. COLUMB 11
Franklyn, John. SPOA 57
Franks, David. a/WATSHD 10
Fraser, Kathleen. a/JNP 86, a/WATSHD 10
Fraser, Ronald. CAED 132
Freed, Edward. FREED 1
Fremantle, Anne. a/SPOA 82
Fresno, Maruchi. AGUIL 13
Friar, Kimon. JNP 13
Frost, Lesley. FOLKW 24
Frost, Robert. a/CAED 42, a/CAED 110,
    a/CAED 111, a/CAED 112, a/CAED 170,
    a/CAED 183, a/CAED 195, a/CARIL 17,
    a/DECCA 8, a/HARPV 3, HOUGHT 3,
    a/JNP 4, a/LIBC 13, a/LIBC 36, a/LIBC 47,
    a/LIBC 49, a/LIBC 51, a/LIBC 53,
    a/LIBC 55, a/MICHM 1, a/NACTE 1,
    a/NACTE 3, a/NACTE 4, a/NACTE 13,
    a/NBC 2, a/SPOA 90
Fuertes, Gloria. a/AGUIL 3
Fuller, John. a/ARGO 96
Fuller, Roy. a/ARGO 98, a/ARGO 155
Futterer, Agnes E. THEAL 1, THEAL 2,
    THEAL 3

Gallagher, Tess. a/WATSHD 11
García Nieto, José. a/AGUIL 3
García Pinto, Roberto. FOLKW 91
Gardner, Isabella Stewart. a/JNP 14, a/JNP 15
Garelick, Barry. a/WATSHD 14
Garlick, Raymond. a/ARGO 141
Garrigue, Jean. a/JNP 16, a/LIST 15, a/SPOA 101
Gassman, Vittorio. CETRA 2, CETRA 5,
    CETRA 8, CETRA 9, CETRA 10, CETRA 12,
    CETRA 13, CETRA 19, CETRA 20,
    CETRA 21, CETRA 22, CETRA 23,
    CETRA 24, CETRA 25, CETRA 27,
    CETRA 28, CETRA 30, CETRA 39,
    CETRA 43, CETRA 46
Gatto, Alfonso. a/APPL 4
Gaussens, Jean-Gabriel. SPOA 36
Gaver, Chasen. a/WATSHD 14, a/WATSHD 34
Gazzolo, Nando. CETRA 6
Gélin, Daniel. ADES 2, ADES 50
Geller, Richard. a/JNP 17
Gelli, C. CETRA 50

Genser, Cynthia. a/WATSHD 9,
    a/WATSHD 11
Géraldy, Paul. a/GMS 1, a/VOIX 1, a/VOIX 2,
    a/VOIX 2A
Ghose, Zulfikar. a/SPOA 68
Gibson, David. ARGO 13
Gibson, Margaret. a/WATSHD 5
Gide, André. a/ADES 31
Giehse, Therese. DEUTGR 37, DEUTGR 38
Gielgud, John. APPL 10, CAED 6, COLUMB 4,
    COLUMB 5, RCA 2
Giguere, Roland. a/FOLKW 70
Gilbert, Celia. a/WATSHD 7
Gill, John. a/WATSHD 2
Ginsberg, Allen. a/APPL 2, BIGSUR 1,
    a/CASSC 8, a/FANT 3, a/NET 1,
    a/SPOA 105, TAPES 2, a/UCAL 3,
    a/UCALM 2, a/UCALM 3, VERVE 3,
    a/WATSHD 11
Ginsberg, Ernst. DEUTGR 13, DEUTGR 19,
    DEUTGR 20, DEUTGR 30
Giorno, John. a/GIORNO 1
Gioseffi, Daniela. a/WATSHD 4
Giovanni, Nikki. a/FOLKW 108,
    a/FOLKW 109, a/NIKTOM 1
Gitlin, Todd. a/WATSHD 1
Glaze, Andrew. a/POSEID 1
Glover, Denis. a/KIWI 4
Glover, Julian. ARGO 53
Godfrey, Derek. ARGO 55, ARGO 56,
    ARGO 62
Godoy, Tamara. a/APPL 6
Gold, Edward. a/WATSHD 1
Gold, Kathe. ATHENA 14, DEUTGR 12
Goldman, Michael. a/JNP 18
Goldstein, Roberta. a/ASCH 1
Gonzalez, Agustin. AGUIL 5, AGUIL 7,
    AGUIL 11, AGUIL 12, AGUIL 16,
    AGUIL 17, AGUIL 18
Goodman, Paul. a/SPOA 82
Gordon, Alvin. a/IFB 1
Goulet, Robert. BANKST 1
Govey, Ronald. CAED 191
Graham, William Sydney. a/ARGO 100
Grandbois, Alain. a/FOLKW 70
Graves, Robert. a/ARGO 81, a/ARGO 97,
    a/ARGO 183, a/CAED 43, a/CAED 110,
    a/CAED 112, a/COLUMB 12, FOLKW 65A,
    SPOA 77, SPOA 86
Gregg, Hubert. ARGO 87
Gregor, Arthur. a/SPOWRD 2
Gregory, Horace. a/HARVOC 13, a/LIBC 17,
    a/LIBC 59
Grenfell, Joyce. CAED 65
Griffith, Hugh. CAED 122
Griffiths, Bryn. a/ARGO 145
Grigson, Geoffrey. a/ARGO 100
Grimshaw, James A. CASSC 1A
Grizzard, George. CAED 132
Guillen, Nicolas. a/WATSHD 41
Guilloton, Michel. CAED 204
Guinness, Alec. ARGO 114, FOLKW 69, RCA 1
Gunn, Thom. a/ARGO 95, a/ARGO 153
Gutiérrez Caba, Irene. AGUIL 4
Guy, Georges. PERIOD 2

Hacker, Marilyn. a/CAED 166

Hadas, Moses. FOLKW 102
Haines, John. a/CASSC 6
Hall, Donald. a/EMC 5, a/JNP 19,
  a/MICHM 8, SCHOL 8, SPOA 51, SPOA 53,
  SPOA 75, a/SPOA 106
Hall, Harvey. LONGM 1, SPOA 65, SPOA 116,
  SPOA 117
Halpern, Daniel. a/TAPES 11
Hamburger, Michael. a/JNP 20
Hampton, Richard. EAV 12
Hannan, Greg. a/WATSHD 9
Hardwick, Elizabeth. AUDIOT 3
Hardwicke, Cedric. AUDIOT 2, AUDIOT 3,
  CAED 25, CAED 38
Hardy, Robert. ARGO 5, ARGO 21, ARGO 58,
  ARGO 119
Harkness, Edward. a/WATSHD 12
Harnett, Michael. a/ARGO 96
Harper, Michael. a/WATSHD 9
Harris, Julie. CAED 69, CAED 82, CAED 85,
  CAED 98, CAED 102, CAED 109,
  CAED 110, CAED 111, CAED 112,
  CAED 130, CAED 185, CAED 190,
  CAED 195, HOUGHT 4, PYR 1, SINGER 5
Harrison, G. B. JNP 8
Hart, Joan. ARGO 49, SPOA 116, SPOA 117
Harteis, Richard. a/WATSHD 9
Hassall, Christopher. ARGO 2
Hasse, O. E. DEUTGR 26, DEUTGR 29
Hasso, Signe. GRAM 1
Hatfield, Hurd. CAED 20, CAED 21, SPOA 3,
  SPOA 87
Hayden, Robert. a/MICHM 19, a/TAPES 3
Hayes, Helen. RCA 4A, RCA 8, RCA 9
Hazo, Samuel. a/JNP 21
Heaney, Seamus. a/ARGO 99
Heath, Gordon. ARGO 17, ARGO 88
Heath-Stubbs, John. a/ARGO 93, a/SPOA 67
Hébert, Anne. a/FOLKW 70
Hecht, Anthony. a/SPOA 104
Hecht, Paul. SCHOL 7
Hedberg, Tor. a/GRAM 9
Held, Martin. DECCA 1, DEUTGR 31,
  TELEF 2
Hempton, Richard. EAV 12
Henault, Gilles. a/FOLKW 70
Henckels, Paul. ATHENA 3
Henderson, Hamish. a/ARGO 96
Henniger, Rolf. CHRIST 10, CHRIST 11,
  CHRIST 16
Henri, Adrian. a/ARGO 150
Herington, C. J. CAED 128
Herking, Ursula. DEUTGR 27
Hesse, Hermann. a/SUHRK 3, a/SUHRK 4
Hierro, José. a/AGUIL 3
Highet, Gilbert. JNP 87, JNP 88, JNP 89,
  JNP 90, JNP 91, JNP 92, JNP 93, JNP 94
Hill, Jason Geoffrey. a/ARGO 98
Hiller, Wendy. SPOA 113, SPOA 114
Hillyer, Robert Silliman. a/HARVOC 8,
  a/LIBC 46
Hine, Daryl. a/JNP 22
Hinz, Dinah. CHRIST 4, CHRIST 5, CHRIST 6,
  CHRIST 7
Hinz, Werner. CHRIST 14, CHRIST 16
Hitchcock, George. a/CASSC 1, WATSHD 2
Hobbs, Carleton. ARGO 111

Hobbs, Suzanne. a/WATSHD 12
Hodges, Frenchy Jolene. a/BROADV 2
Hoffman, Daniel G. a/LIBC 52
Hoffman, Elinor Gene. AUDIBT 1
Hoffman Llévano, Ernesto. SMC 1, SMC 2
Holbrook, David. a/ARGO 96
Holbrook, Hal. CAED 66, CAED 90,
  CAED 195
Holland, Bill. a/WATSHD 4
Hollander, John. a/CARIL 13, a/JNP 24,
  a/SPOA 107
Holloway, Stanley. CAED 50, CAED 65,
  CAED 76, HBCF 1
Holm, Celeste. CAED 58
Holm, Ian. ARGO 32, ARGO 52, ARGO 68,
  ARGO 71, ARGO 72
Holmes, John. a/SPOA 97
Holmes, Peter. ARGO 15
Holtzmann, Thomas. CHRIST 18, CHRIST 19
Hook, Lucyle. NACTE 7
Hooks, David. EAV 8, EAV 9, EAV 14, EAV 19
Hoppe, Marianne. DEUTGR 39
Hordern, Michael. ARGO 14, ARGO 55,
  ARGO 56, ARGO 65, ARGO 128
Horgan, Patrick. LIST 19
Howard, Alan. CAED 201, CAED 203
Howard, Lee. a/WATSHD 12
Howard, Richard. a/JNP 23
Howell, Peter. EAV 12
Howes, Barbara. a/JNP 25, a/SPOA 82,
  a/SPOA 100
Huff, Julie. WATSHD 26
Huff, Robert. a/JNP 26
Hughes, Langston. a/CAED 207, FOLKW 1,
  a/FOLKW 5, a/FOLKW 40, a/SPOA 96,
  a/SPOA 108
Hughes, Ted. a/ARGO 95, a/CAED 172,
  a/CAED 206, a/LIST 15, a/SPOA 67
Hugo, Richard. a/WATSHD 56
Huston, Walter. DECCA 4, DECCA 7
Huster, Francis. ADES 41
Hyde, Margaret F. ARGO 49
Hynd, James. CAED 128

Ignatow, David. a/WATSHD 37

Jackson, Anne. COLUMB 15
Jackson, Glenda. ARGO 116, ARGO 134
Jackson, Gordon. EAV 13
Jacob, Jere. FOLKW 57, FOLKW 58
Jacobs, Anthony. ARGO 13
Jacobs, Sumire Hasegawa. MUSENG 1,
  MUSENG 2
Jacobsen, Josephine. a/TAPES 4,
  a/WATSHD 25
Jacobson, Dan. a/JNP 27
Jarrell, Randall. a/CAED 150, a/HARPV 5,
  a/JNP 28, a/LIBC 15, a/LIBC 43,
  a/SPOA 101
Jeffers, Lance. a/BROADV 9, a/WATSHD 7
Jeffers, Robinson. a/HARPV 4, a/HARVOC 10,
  a/LIBC 11, a/LIBC 34, a/NET 4, a/SPOA 93
Jefford, Barbara. ARGO 70, ARGO 71,
  ARGO 72
Jeffrey, Peter. SPOA 83, SPOA 84, SPOA 113,
  SPOA 114
Jemma, Jean-Louis. ADES 20, HACH 22

Jennings, Elizabeth. a/ARGO 94
Jessel, Patricia. CAED 191
Jimason, Joanne. a/WATSHD 7
Jiménez, Juan Ramon. a/CAED 51
Johnson, B. S. a/ARGO 100
Johnson, James Weldon. a/EAV 2, a/SPOA 90
Johnson, Joe. a/WATSHD 4
Johnson, R. E. DECCA 10, DECCA 11,
    DECCA 12, DECCA 13, LIST 21, LIST 22,
    LIST 23
Johnson, Richard. ARGO 18, ARGO 19,
    ARGO 32, ARGO 34, ARGO 39, ARGO 40,
    ARGO 41, ARGO 42, ARGO 43, ARGO 44,
    ARGO 59, ARGO 60, ARGO 62, ARGO 73,
    ARGO 90
Johnston, Arnold. CMS 18
Johnston, Ellen Turlington. a/AGENTV 1,
    a/AGENTV 2, a/AGENTV 3, a/AGENTV 4,
    a/AGENTV 5
Jones, Basil. CAED 122
Jones, David. a/ARGO 91, a/ARGO 101,
    a/ARGO 142
Jones, James Earl. CAED 136, SPOA 119
Jong, Erica. a/SPOA 134, a/WATSHD 2
Jorda, José. SMC 11
Jordan, June. a/WATSHD 5, a/WATSHD 57,
    a/WATSHD 64
Joselow, Beth. a/WATSHD 11
Jostyn, Jay. DECCA 1, DECCA 13, LIST 22,
    LIST 23
Jourdan, Louis. CAED 27
Joyce, James. a/CAED 143, a/ORTH 1

Kaiser, Wolf. DEUTGR 34
Kallman, Chester. a/WATSHD 44
Karloff, Boris. CAED 48, CAED 58, CAED 92,
    CAED 132
Karlfeldt, Erik Axel. a/GRAM 10
Kasack, Hermann. a/SUHRK 8
Kaschnitz, Marie Luise. a/CHRIST 31,
    a/DEUTGR 43
Kästner, Erich. a/LITAR 1
Kaufman, Shirley. a/WATSHD 10,
    a/WATSHD 58, WATSHD 59
Kavanagh, P. J. a/APPL 3
Keach, Stacy. CAED 160
Keeley, Edmund. CAED 121
Kelly, Robert. a/SPOA 107
Kempson, Rachel. CAED 191
Kendrick, Delores. a/WATSHD 7
Kerouac, Jack. a/VERVE 1
Kgositsile, Keorapetse. a/BROADV 14
King, David. ARGO 30, ARGO 65, ARGO 67,
    ARGO 72, ARGO 75, ARGO 76, SPOA 83,
    SPOA 84, SPOA 113, SPOA 114, SPOA 117
Kinnell, Galway. a/BROADR 1, a/CAED 167,
    a/JNP 29, a/MICHM 9, a/POSEID 1,
    a/SCHOL 5, a/SPOA 82, a/SPOA 100
Kinsella, Thomas. a/ARGO 94
Kinski, Klaus. AMAD 1, DEUTGR 2,
    DEUTGR 3, FOLKW 73
Kitt, Eartha. CAED 195
Kizer, Carolyn. a/MICHM 11, a/WATSHD 16
Klappert, Peter. a/WATSHD 4
Klein, A. M. a/FOLKW 49
Klein, Arthur Luce. SPOA 127
Knight, Etheridge. a/BROADV 12, a/WATSHD 1

Knight, G. Wilson. JNP 5
Kökeritz, Helge. EAV 5, EAV 11
Kops, Bernard. a/SPOA 67, a/SPOA 68
Kovner, Abba. a/WATSHD 59
Kramer, Aaron. a/FOLKW 14
Krolow, Karl. a/SUHRK 9
Kumin, Maxine. a/WATSHD 19
Kunitz, Stanley. a/CARIL 2, a/LIBC 54,
    a/LIST 15, a/SPOA 82, a/SPOA 98,
    a/TAPES 12
Kurtz, Aaron. a/FOLKW 92
Kuzmany, Elfriede. CHRIST 11, CHRIST 12

Lagerkvist, Pär. a/GRAM 5
Laine, Cleo. ARGO 17, ARGO 88
Lally, Michael. a/WATSHD 2
Lang, Ian. ARGO 14
Lang, Robert. CAED 203
Langton, Basil. SPOA 2, SPOA 112
Lapalma, Marina. a/WATSHD 14
Lapointe, Paul-Marie. a/FOLKW 70
Lara, Mario de. HOLT 1
Larkin, Philip. a/ARGO 98
Lasnier, Rina. a/FOLKW 70
Last Poets. a/JUG 1
Laughton, Charles. CAPITOL 1
Lavin, Stuart. a/WATSHD 5
Laydu, Claude. ADES 9
Layton, Irving. a/FOLKW 49
Lee, Dennis. a/CAED 171
Lee, Don L. a/BROADV 4, a/BROADV 18
Lee, Laurie. a/ARGO 98, a/ARGO 133,
    a/FOLKW 66
Lee, Penelope. SPOA 78, SPOA 117, SPOA 123
Lefèvre, René. ADES 18, ADES 50
Le Gallienne, Eva. CAED 27
Lehmann, Lotte. CAED 47, CAED 75
Leighton, Margaret. CAED 61
Lenya, Lotte. COLUMB 15, DOVER 1
Leslie, Noel. LIST 7
Lester, Julius. a/WATSHD 6, a/WATSHD 21
Levendosky, Charles. a/WATSHD 10
Levertov, Denise. a/JNP 30, a/NET 18,
    'a/SPOA 104
Lévesque, Jacques Henri. FOLKW 2,
    FOLKW 13, FOLKW 87
Levine, Philip. a/CAED 168, a/WATSHD 12,
    a/WATSHD 24
Levinton, Catalina. FOLKW 79
Lewis, James. PERIOD 1
Lewis, Janet. a/LIBC 25, a/LIBC 60
Lewsen, Charles. ARGO 108
Liddy, James. a/ARGO 96
Lieberman, Laurence. a/JNP 32
Liewehr, Fred. AMAD 3
Lifshin, Lyn. a/SPOA 120, a/WOMAUD 1
Lillie, Beatrice. CAED 50
Lindfors, Viveca. COLUMB 15
Lindsay, Howard. SINGER 1
Lindsay, Nicholas Cave. CAED 102
Lindsay, Vachel. a/CAED 32, a/NACTE 6,
    a/NACTE 17
Linton, Mayne. REX 1
Lipsitz, Lou. a/WATSHD 60
Logan, John. a/SCHOL 5, a/WATSHD 14,
    a/WATSHD 31, a/WATSHD 32
Logue, Christopher. a/ARGO 100, a/FOLKW 66

Lo Kung-Yuan. FOLKW 76
Lo-Johansson, Ivar. a/GRAM 7
Lonsdale, Michel. ADES 55
Lorde, Audre. a/WATSHD 11
Lovelace, Earl. a/WATSHD 7
Lowbury, Edward. a/ARGO 92
Lowell, Robert. a/CAED 180, a/CARIL 20,
    a/HARPV 6, a/JNP 33, a/LIST 15,
    a/LIBC 23, a/LIBC 68, a/NET 7,
    a/SPOA 82, a/SPOA 102
Luce, Claire. FOLKW 56
Lucie-Smith, Edward. a/ARGO 100
Lüders, Günther. DEUTGR 8, DEUTGR 44,
    TELEF 3
Lühr, Peter. CHRIST 22, GMS 11
Luis, José. GMS 14
Lundkvist, Artur. a/GRAM 8
Lupo, Alberto. CETRA 1, CETRA 8, CETRA 9,
    CETRA 12, CETRA 13, CETRA 17,
    CETRA 19, CETRA 20, CETRA 21,
    CETRA 22, CETRA 23, CETRA 24,
    CETRA 25, CETRA 27, CETRA 28,
    CETRA 46
Lurie, Toby. a/WATSHD 4
Luzi, Mario. a/APPL 4
Lynn, Kenneth S. SPOA 40, SPOA 75

Macbeth, George. a/ARGO 96, a/JNP 34
MacCaig, Norman. a/ARGO 99
McCarthy, Denis. ARGO 45, ARGO 49,
    ARGO 64, ARGO 66
McCarthy, Eugene J. a/JNP 2
McCarthy, Neil. CAED 191
McCaughey, Barbara. SPOA 133
McClure, Michael. a/UCAL 3
McCord, David. PATHW 2
McCrimmon, Dan. a/WATSHD 1
MacDiarmid, Hugh. a/ARGO 99, a/JNP 35,
    a/JNP 36
McEwan, Geraldine. CAED 203
McGinley, Phyllis. a/LIBC 54
McGough, Roger. a/ARGO 146
McGregor, Ann. NAITV 1–6
McHugh, Heather. a/WATSHD 61
McIntyre, Duncan. ARGO 29
McKay, Claude. a/FOLKW 1
McKenna, Siobhan. CAED 53, CAED 151,
    CAED 152, SPOA 7, SPOA 16, SPOA 22
McKnight, Jo-Anne. a/FOLKW 47
MacLeish, Archibald. a/CAED 14, CAED 149,
    CAED 183, a/LIBC 23, a/LIBC 54,
    a/LIBC 71, a/NACTE 15, a/RCA 10,
    a/SPOA 94
MacLiammoir, Micheal. CAED 74, CAED 76,
    CAED 203, SPOA 20, SPOA 22
Mac Low, Jackson. a/WATSHD 2
MacNeice, Louis. ARGO 78, a/ARGO 83,
    a/ARGO 99, a/ARGO 183, a/CARIL 15
McNeill, Anthony. CAED 153
Macpherson, Jay. a/FOLKW 50
Mailer, Norman. a/PREST 1
Maistre, François. ADES 26, ADES 52
Major, Clarence. a/WATSHD 4
Malanga, Gerard. a/WATSHD 9
Malone, Kemp. ENGL 1
Manahan, Sheila. ARGO 74
Mandel, Ruth. GMS 6

Mankin, Paul. FOLKW 83, FOLKW 86,
    FOLKW 88
Manspeaker, Priscilla. UARIZ 1
Mant, Pamela. SPOA 133
Manuel, Denis. ADES 30, ADES 43, ADES 51,
    ADES 55
March, Frederic. DECCA 4, DECCA 10,
    LIST 21
Marchand, Nancy. EAV 6, EAV 7, EAV 10,
    EAV 14, EAV 22
Marcus, Adrianne. a/WATSHD 2
Marcuse, Theodore. EAV 18
Mariah, Paul. a/WATSHD 5
Markov, Vladimir. FOLKW 94
Marks, Eduard. CHRIST 11, CHRIST 16,
    CHRIST 18, TELEF 6
Marquand, Richard. ARGO 13, ARGO 27,
    ARGO 61
Marshall, Helen Lowrie. a/HELV 1, a/HELV 2,
    a/HELV 3, a/HELV 4, a/HELV 5,
    a/HELV 6, a/HELV 7, a/HELV 8,
    a/HELV 9
Marshall, Jack. a/JNP 37
Marshall, Lenore G. a/SPOA 18, a/SPOA 95
Marsillach, Adolfo. FIDIAS 3
Martin, John S. FOLKW 63
Marvin X. BROADV 1
Masefield, John. a/ARGO 8, a/ARGO 10,
    a/ARGO 85, a/CAED 79, a/FOLKW 52A,
    a/SPOA 23
Mason, Chris. a/WATSHD 12, a/WATSHD 14
Mason, James. CAED 37, CAED 96, CAED 97,
    CAED 132, CAED 162, CAED 179,
    CAED 205
Massey, Daniel. CAED 191
Massey, Raymond. SINGER 2, RCA 9
Masters, Edgar Lee. a/SPOA 90
Mattischent, Gisela. ATHENA 2
Maurois, André. a/SPOA 58
May, Gisela. DEUTGR 32, DEUTGR 33,
    DEUTGR 35
Mayer, Heidy. EAV 8, EAV 9
Medcalf, Stephen. CASSC 12C
Mehring, Walter. a/DEUTGR 9
Melato, Mariangela. CETRA 51
Meltzer, David. a/WATSHD 12
Melville, John. ARGO 45, ARGO 50
Menzel, Wilhelm. CHRIST 23
Mercure, Jean. ADES 6, SPOA 32
Meredith, Burgess. ISU 1
Meredith, William. a/LIBC 15, a/LIBC 39,
    a/SPOA 103
Merriam, Eve. a/BIGSUR 2, a/CAED 142
Merrill, Gary. NET 14
Merrill, James. a/SPOA 105
Mervin, W. S. a/CAED 127, a/MICHM 18,
    a/SPOWRD 3
Middleton, Christopher. a/ARGO 96
Miguéis, Jose Rodrigues. FOLKW 72
Millay, Edna St. Vincent. a/CAED 71
Miller, Arthur. a/SPOA 82
Miller, E. Ethelbert. a/WATSHD 5,
    WATSHD 11
Miller, Marvin. LIVLAN 1
Millo, Achille. CETRA 3, CETRA 32,
    CETRA 33, CETRA 51
Mistral, Gabriela. a/LIBC 77

Mistral, Nati. GMS 18
Mitchell, Adrian. ARGO 3, a/ARGO 96
Mitchell, Keith. ARGO 48
Mitchell, Norman. CAED 203
Mitchell, Thomas. RCA 9
Moffat, John. CAED 203
Mohyeddin, Zia. CAED 116
Moinot, Michel. DOVER 4
Mollica, Massimo. CETRA 31
Mon, Franz. a/LUCHT 1
Montale, Eugenio. a/CETRA 10
Montero, Germaine. VAN 2
Montoy, Enrique. SMC 10
Montreal Proscenium Studio. FOLKW 12
Moore, Honor. a/WATSHD 14
Moore, Marianne. a/CAED 24, a/CAED 183,
   a/CARIL 10, a/COLUMB 8, a/HARPV 2,
   a/JNP 1, a/LIBC 5, a/LIBC 14, a/LIST 13,
   a/SPOA 93
Moore, Merrill. a/SPOA 97
Moore, Rosalie. a/WATSHD 12
Moorehead, Agnes. DECCA 4, DECCA 10,
   LIST 21
Moraes, Dom. a/ARGO 98
Moray, Ann. SPOA 1
Morel, François. a/FOLKW 70
Morgen, Gareth. CAED 128
Morillo, Angel. SMC 12
Moritz, L. A. CMS 17
Morlacchi, Lucilla. CETRA 9, CETRA 12,
   CETRA 19, CETRA 20, CETRA 21,
   CETRA 22, CETRA 23, CETRA 24,
   CETRA 25, CETRA 27, CETRA 28,
   CETRA 46
Morris, Mervyn. CAED 153
Morrish, Ann. SPOA 83, SPOA 84, SPOA 117
Moss, Arnold. DECCA 10, DECCA 11,
   DECCA 12, LIBC 31, LIST 21, LIST 22,
   LIST 23
Moss, Howard. a/JNP 38, a/SPOA 103
Moss, Stanley. a/JNP 39
Moulinot, Jean-Paul. HACH 19
Mouloudji. ADES 21
Muir, Edwin. a/ARGO 100, a/LIBC 42
Murciano, Carlos. a/AGUIL 3
Murphy, Beatrice. a/BROADV 15

Nabokov, Vladimir. a/SPOA 52
Nägelen, Klaus. CHRIST 16, CHRIST 18
Naldi, Neda. CETRA 40
Nash, Ogden. a/CAED 3, a/CAED 16,
   a/CAED 123, a/CAED 134, CAED 137,
   a/CAED 138, a/COLUMB 8, a/DECCA 2,
   a/HARC 4, a/NET 10, a/RCA 3, SINGER 3,
   a/SPOA 97
Negri, Enrico de. FOLKW 103
Negroni, Jean. ADES 12, ADES 50, ADES 51
Nemerov, Howard. a/JNP 40, a/JNP 41,
   a/SPOA 103, a/TAPES 13
Neruda, Pablo. a/CAED 101, a/SPOA 109,
   a/TAPES 5
Nettleton, John. ARGO 49
Neville, John. ARGO 5, ARGO 21, ARGO 51,
   ARGO 58, ARGO 136, CAED 186
Newton, Robert. CAED 38
Nicholson, Norman. a/ARGO 92, a/ARGO 147
Nims, John Frederick. a/SPOA 100

Ninchi, Annibale. CETRA 2, CETRA 9,
   CETRA 12, CETRA 19, CETRA 20,
   CETRA 21, CETRA 22, CETRA 23,
   CETRA 24, CETRA 25, CETRA 27,
   CETRA 28, CETRA 46
Nissi, Otto. CHRIST 20
Noé, Ana Maria. AGUIL 5, AGUIL 8,
   AGUIL 13, AGUIL 15, AGUIL 16
Noll, Bink. a/SPOA 82
Nollier, Claude. ADES 13, ADES 19, ADES 32,
   ADES 51, SPOA 62
Norman, Howard. a/MICHM 20
Norton, Jim. ARGO 74
Nunes, Cassiano. a/FOLKW 71

O'Connor, Frank. FOLKW 52
Oden, G. D. a/MILLER 2
O'Gorman, Ned. a/LIBC 52, a/SPOA 82
O'Hara, Frank. a/NET 16
Olivier, Laurence. LONDON 2
Olmi, C. CETRA 50
Olmsted, Nelson. VAN 1
Olson, Charles. a/FOLKW 28, a/NET 18
O'Neal, Frederick. CAED 98, CAED 132,
   CAED 195
Oppen, George. a/JNP 42
Ornes, Maricusa. INSTPR 1
Orr, Gregory. a/MICHM 10
Orr, Peter. ARGO 14, ARGO 27, ARGO 55,
   ARGO 56, ARGO 57, ARGO 59, ARGO 75,
   ARGO 76, SPOA 55, SPOA 80, SPOA 83,
   SPOA 84, SPOA 113, SPOA 114, SPOA 117
O'Shaughnessy, Peter. SPOA 67, SPOA 68
Ostrowsky, Chaim. FOLKW 90
O'Sullivan, Arthur. ARGO 74
Ott, Maria. CHRIST 9, CHRIST 11,
   CHRIST 18, CHRIST 19, CHRIST 29
Owen, Guy. a/CASSC 2

Pack, Robert. a/SPOA 107
Pagis, Dan. a/WATSHD 62
Palazzeschi, Aldo. a/CETRA 11
Palladini, Mario. FOLKW 97
Panero, Leopoldo. a/AGUIL 3
Pardo García, German. a/LIBC 76
Parenti, Franco. CETRA 9, CETRA 12,
   CETRA 19, CETRA 20, CETRA 21,
   CETRA 22, CETRA 23, CETRA 24,
   CETRA 25, CETRA 27, CETRA 28,
   CETRA 46, CETRA 47
Parker, Dorothy. a/SPOA 11, a/SPOA 94
Pasco, Richard. ARGO 28, ARGO 70,
   ARGO 71, ARGO 72
Pastan, Linda. a/WATSHD 5
Pasternak, Boris. a/DISC 1
Patchen, Kenneth. a/FOLKW 19,
   a/FOLKW 20, a/FOLKW 107, a/SPOA 99
Patten, Brian. a/CAED 131, a/PENN 1
Paz, Octavio. a/APPL 6, a/FFHS 1
Pei, Mario. FOLKW 10, FOLKW 96
Peñalver Laserna, Juan. a/MIAMI 1, MIAMI 2,
   TROPIC 1
Penfold, Ann. EAV 12, EAV 13
Pennington, Earl. CBC 1
Périer, François. ADES 1, ADES 43, SPOA 27
Perrin, Marguerite. HACH 18

Peseroff, Joyce. a/MICHM 22
Peters, Brock. ARGO 17, ARGO 88, CAED 195
Philipe, Gérard. DES 52, GMS 8, GMS 9,
    SPOA 32
Piccioni, Leone. CETRA 17
Piercy, Marge. a/CASSC 13, a/WATSHD 1,
    a/WATSHD 17
Pietri, Pedro. a/FOLKW 112
Pilon, Jean-Guy. a/FOLKW 70
Pines, Paul. a/WATSHD 10
Pitöeff, Sacha. ADES 43, SPOA 27
Pitter, Ruth. a/ARGO 96
Plath, Sylvia. a/ARGO 95, a/CAED 177,
    a/HARPV 6, a/SPOA 107
Pleasants, Jeanne Varney. GMS 7
Plomer, William. a/ARGO 91
Plummer, Christopher. LIST 20
Pobers, T. SPOA 24
Poitier, Sidney. UA 2
Polak, Maralyn. a/WATSHD 4
Poli, Paolo. CETRA 9, CETRA 11, CETRA 12,
    CETRA 19, CETRA 20, CETRA 21,
    CETRA 22, CETRA 23, CETRA 24,
    CETRA 25, CETRA 27, CETRA 28,
    CETRA 46
Ponte, María Luisa. AGUIL 6, AGUIL 8
Ponto, Erich. DEUTGR 46
Poole, Roy. CAED 182
Pope, John C. EAV 5, EAV 23
Porter, Bern. a/WATSHD 4
Porter, Peter. a/ARGO 95
Portman, Eric. CAED 186, HBCF 1
Posner, David. a/SPOWRD 1
Pound, Ezra. a/APPL 1, a/BBC 2, a/CAED 70,
    a/CAED 84, a/CAED 183, a/HARPV 1,
    a/SPOA 92, SPOA 110
Power, Tyrone. CAED 33, COLUMB 2
Poyser, Brian. CAED 191
Prefontaine, Yves. a/FOLKW 70
Premice, Josephine. SPOA 119
Press, John. a/ARGO 93
Prévert, Jacques. a/ADES 44, a/GMS 12,
    a/VOIX 3
Price, Vincent. CAED 4, CAED 41,
    CAED 185, CAED 195, COLUMB 6, SPA 1
Prickett, Stephen. CASSC 12D, CASSC 12E,
    CASSC 12F, CASSC 12G
Prince, Michael. EAV 22
Probers, Tatiana. SPOA 24
Proud, Elizabeth. LONGM 1
Provost, Jeanne. SPOA 124, SPOA 125
Purcell, Roy. CAED 191
Purens, Ilmars. a/WATSHD 12
Putnam, Phelps. a/LIBC 17, a/LIBC 57
Pyatt, Richard. LIST 5, LIST 17

Quadflieg, Will. DEUTGR 4, DEUTGR 6,
    DEUTGR 7, DEUTGR 17, DEUTGR 20,
    DEUTGR 21, DEUTGR 22, DEUTGR 25,
    DEUTGR 41
Quayle, Anthony. CAED 43, CAED 46,
    CAED 60, CAED 94, CAED 118, CAED 124,
    CAED 125, CAED 163, CAED 184,
    CAED 191, CAED 192, CAED 197,
    CAED 200, CAED 202, CAED 203,
    POLYGL 2, SPOA 12
Queneau, Raymond. a/ADES 44

Raab, Lawrence. a/MICHM 21
Raffel, Burton. FOLKW 54
Raine, Stephen. a/ARGO 97
Rains, Claude. CAED 56
Randall, Dudley. a/BROADV 3,
    a/BROADV 11, a/WATSHD 2
Randolph, John. EAV 20, EAV 21
Randone, Salvo. CETRA 40
Ranganathan, S. R. FOLKW 75
Ransom, John Crowe. a/CARIL 6, a/NET 13,
    a/LIBC 11, a/LIBC 37, a/SPOA 93
Raper, Michele. a/SPOA 67, a/SPOA 68
Raps, Berrigan. CAED 158
Rasof, Henry. a/WATSHD 11
Rasul, Sha'ir. a/WATSHD 1
Rathbone, Basil. APPL 8, CAED 4, CAED 26,
    CAED 93, CAED 188, CAED 195
Rawlings, Margaret. ARGO 1
Ray, David. a/WATSHD 63
Ray, James. EAV 6, EAV 7
Ray, Shreela. a/JNP 43
Read, Herbert. a/ARGO 96, a/LIBC 17,
    a/LIBC 56
Read, Kathleen Danson. FOLKW 61,
    FOLKW 62
Reagon, Bernice. WATSHD 57
Reaney, James. a/FOLKW 50
Rebay, Luciano. DOVER 3
Rector, Liam. a/WATSHD 12
Redgrave, Colin. CAED 191
Redgrave, Michael. ARGO 39, ARGO 40,
    ARGO 41, ARGO 42, ARGO 43, ARGO 44,
    ARGO 70, CAED 88, CAED 191, HBCF 1,
    SPOA 63
Redgrave, Vanessa. CAED 203
Redgrove, Peter. a/ARGO 94, a/ARGO 154
Reed, Ishmael. a/WATSHD 2
Reed, Jared. FOLKW 29
Rees, Ennis. SPOA 38, SPOA 76
Reeve, F. D. a/JNP 44
Reeves, James. a/ARGO 91
Reggiani, Serge. PHIL 1
Reichmann, Wolfgang. CHRIST 25
Reid, Alastair. a/CMS 7
Reid, Sheila. CAED 203
Renaud, Madeleine. ADES 32, ADES 35,
    ADES 51, SPOA 62
Resnick, Seymour. CMS 5
Rexroth, Kenneth. a/SPOA 98,
    a/WATSHD 45
Reybaz, André. ADES 28, ADES 53
Riaza, Berta. AGUIL 7, AGUIL 8, AGUIL 11,
    AGUIL 12, AGUIL 17
Rich, Adrienne. a/JNP 45, a/SPOA 106,
    a/STANFD 1
Richards, I. A. a/LIBC 48
Richards, John F. C. FOLKW 98, FOLKW 99,
    FOLKW 100, FOLKW 101, FOLKW 104,
    FOLKW 105
Richardson, Ian. CAED 208
Richardson, Ralph. CAED 57, CAED 59,
    CAED 62, CAED 132, CAED 202
Richar, Janette. ARGO 49, ARGO 60
Riesen, Hans von. LUCHT 1
Riphahn, Marlene. CHRIST 22
Riquier, Georges. SPOA 49, SPOA 56
Risi, Nelo. a/APPL 4

Ritchard, Cyril. CAED 50, CAED 58, CAED 109, CAED 110, CAED 111, CAED 132, CAED 164, CAED 169
Riva, Emmanuèle. ADES 55
Roach, Eric. CAED 153
Robinson, Fred Norris. HARVOC 1
Robinson, Lennox. SPOA 21, SPOA 115
Robinson, Wanda. a/PERC 1
Robison, Margaret. a/WATSHD 12
Robson, Ernest M. a/UCALI 1
Robson, Flora. ARGO 69
Robson, Jeremy. ARGO 4
Roche, Paul. a/JNP 46, a/MERC 1, a/SPOWRD 4
Rochefort, Jean. ADES 56
Rodari, Gianni. a/CETRA 44
Rodero, José María. AGUIL 4
Rodgers, W. R. a/ARGO 92, a/ARGO 115
Rodriguez, Jorge Juan. FOLKW 11
Roethke, Theodore. a/CAED 146, a/FOLKW 26, a/HARPV 4, a/JNP 47, a/LIBC 21, a/LIBC 54, a/LIBC 64, a/SPOA 98, a/UCALM 1
Rosa, W. W. Eustage. a/FOLKW 50
Rosales, Luis. a/AGUIL 3
Rose, Clifford. ARGO 52
Rose, Norman. RCA 10
Ross, Robert. CAED 13, CAED 67
Rossman, Michael. a/WATSHD 1
Rosten, Norman. a/FOLKW 15
Roth, Eugen. a/DEUTGR 44
Rothenberg, Jerome. FOLKW 48, a/MICHM 15, a/WATSHD 1
Rothschild, Alfred. SPOA 126
Rouleau, Raymond. HACH 15
Rudnick, Raphael. a/JNP 48
Rudnigger, Wilhelm. a/AMAD 4
Ruggeri, Ruggero. CETRA 2, CETRA 9, CETRA 12, CETRA 19, CETRA 20, CETRA 21, CETRA 22, CETRA 23, CETRA 24, CETRA 25, CETRA 27, CETRA 28, CETRA 46
Rukeyser, Muriel. a/CAED 173, a/JNO 49, a/JNP 49, a/JNP 50, a/LIBC 25, a/LIBC 72, a/LIST 13, a/SPOA 100, a/WATSHD 6, a/WATSHD 18
Rylands, George. ARGO 13, ARGO 14, ARGO 48, ARGO 49, ARGO 50, ARGO 51, ARGO 75, ARGO 76

Saba, Umberto. a/CETRA 16
Sachs, Nelly. a/SUHRK 5
Sagarra, Josep Maria de. a/GMS 17
Saint-René, Martin. a/ACAD 1
Sakaki, Nanao. a/UCAL 4
Salerno, Maria. CETRA 51
Salinas, Pedro. a/LIBC 78
Sammataro, Piero. CETRA 9, CETRA 12, CETRA 19, CETRA 20, CETRA 21, CETRA 22, CETRA 23, CETRA 24, CETRA 25, CETRA 27, CETRA 28, CETRA 46
Sanchez, Sonia. a/BROADV 6, a/BROADV 17, a/FOLKW 42, a/WATSHD 3, a/WATSHD 20
Sandburg, Carl. CAED 72, a/CAED 80, a/CAED 109, a/CAED 110, a/CAED 111, a/CAED 117, a/CAED 189, a/CAED 195,

a/DECCA 5, a/DECCA 6, a/DECCA 9, a/SPOA 90
Sanders, Ed. a/NET 16
Sbragia, Giancarlo. CETRA 1, CETRA 7, CETRA 9, CETRA 12, CETRA 17, CETRA 19, CETRA 20, CETRA 21, CETRA 22, CETRA 23, CETRA 24, CETRA 25, CETRA 28, CETRA 38, CETRA 46
Scales, Prunella. ARGO 27, ARGO 39, ARGO 40, ARGO 41, ARGO 42, ARGO 43, ARGO 44, ARGO 49, ARGO 75, ARGO 76, ARGO 157
Scannell, Vernon. a/SPOA 67, a/SPOA 68
Scarpitta, Carmen. CETRA 44
Schatzdorfer, Hans. a/AMAD 2
Schildknecht-Wahlgren, Maria. GRAM 2
Schimmelpfennig, Heinz. ATHENA 7
Schmitz, Dennis. a/JNP 51, a/WATSHD 1
Schnaidnagl, Brigitt. FOLKW 74
Schneider, Siegmar. DEUTGR 15
Schnitzler, Heinrich. SPOA 5
Schradi, Manfred. CHRIST 17, CHRIST 20
Schuyler, Marcus. a/COLUMB 1
Schwartz, Delmore. a/LIBC 19, a/LIBC 75, a/SPOA 100
Scofield, Paul. CAED 73
Scott, Dennis. CAED 153
Scott, F. R. a/FOLKW 49
Scott, Harold. UA 1
Scott, Margaretta. ARGO 62, ARGO 64
Scott, Winfried Townley. a/CARIL 18, a/JNP 52, a/SPOA 99
Scourby, Alexander. AUDIA 1, AUDIA 2, DECCA 10, DECCA 11, LIST 1, LIST 2, LIST 3, LIST 11, LIST 12, DECCA 21, DECCA 22, SPOA 3, SPOA 31, SPOA 54, SPOA 69, SPOA 75
Searle, Humphrey. CAED 122
Seferis, George. a/CAED 121
Seldes, Marian. FOLKW 33, FOLKW 34, SPOA 82
Semple, Frank. REX 1
Senghor, Leopold Sedar. a/NET 12
Sereni, Vittorio. a/APPL 4
Servais. GMS 2
Sexton, Anne. a/CAED 161, a/JNP 53, a/NET 2, a/SPOA 106, a/TAPES 6
Shange, Ntozake. a/WATSHD 12
Shapiro, Karl. a/LIBC 15, a/LIBC 45, a/SPOA 100
Shatz, Marshall. CMS 6
Shaw, Maxine. WATSHD 7
Shelley, Norman. ARGO 130, ARGO 131
Shepherd, Jean. FOLKW 31
Sherwin, Judith Johnson. a/WATSHD 9, a/WATSHD 12, a/WATSHD 26, a/WATSHD 27
Shiva. a/WATSHD 2
Sidney, P. Jay. EAV 2
Silkin, Jon. a/ARGO 98
Silverna, Frank. CAED 20, CAED 21
Sim, Alastair. CAED 203
Simic, Charles. a/WATSHD 39
Simmons, Judy. a/WATSHD 1
Simonov, Konstantin. a/MONITR 1

Simpson, Louis. a/CARIL, a/MICHM 13,
    a/SPOA 104
Sitwell, Edith. a/ARGO 129, a/CAED 17,
    a/CAED 145, a/CAED 183, a/COLUMB 3,
    a/COLUMB 7, a/JNP 7
Sitwell, Osbert. a/CAED 15
Skellings, Edmund. a/WATSHD 1
Skinner, Cornelia Otis. RCA 4
Skratz, G. P. a/WATSHD 9
Smith, A. J. M. a/FOLKW 49
Smith, Eugene Osborn. a/BOS 1
Smith, Iain Crichton. a/ARGO 99
Smith, Jean Taylor. SCOT 2
Smith, Ken. a/ARGO 98
Smith, Stevie. a/ARGO 92, a/SPOA 67
Smith, Sydney Goodsir. a/ARGO 99
Smith, William Jay. a/JNP 54, a/LIBC 78,
    a/SPOA 102
Smolensky, Yakov. MELOD 1
Snodgrass, William DeWitt. a/LIBC 50,
    a/LIBC 54, a/SPOA 82, a/SPOA 104
Snyder, Gary. a/CENTCA 1, a/NET 9,
    a/UCAL 4
Sobiloff, Hy. a/GRYPH 3, a/SPOA 100
Somerset, Patricia. CAED 203
Sondé, Susan. a/WATSHD 5
Souster, Raymond. a/FOLKW 50
Sparer, Paul. EAV 6, EAV 7, EAV 10, EAV 20
Speaight, Robert. ARGO 102, ARGO 103,
    ARGO 105, HARVOC 3, HARVOC 4,
    HARVOC 5, HARVOC 6, HARVOC 7,
    SPOA 14, SPOA 28, SPOA 33, SPOA 35,
    SPOA 42, SPOA 43, SPOA 44, SPOA 45,
    SPOA 46, SPOA 47, SPOA 48, SPOA 50,
    SPOA 66, SPOA 73, SPOA 74, SPOA 77,
    SPOA 79, SPOA 111, SPOA 121, SPOA 122,
    SPOA 123, SPOA 124
Spencer, Theodore. a/HARVOC 9, a/LIBC 11,
    a/LIBC 35, a/SPOA 97
Spender, Stephen. a/APPL 3, a/ARGO 79,
    a/ARGO 97, a/ARGO 183, a/CAED 55,
    a/JNP 6, a/JNP 55, a/LIBC 19, a/LIBC 62,
    a/NET 3, a/SPOA 70
Spivack, Kathleen. a/WATSHD 51
Squire, William. ARGO 33, ARGO 38,
    ARGO 47, ARGO 50, ARGO 51, ARGO 57,
    ARGO 126
Stallworth, John. a/ARGO 98
Starbuck, George. a/APPL 9, a/CARIL 4,
    a/WATSHD 52
Stein, Gertrude. a/CAED 39, a/CAED 183,
    a/SPOA 90
Stephany. a/BROADV 8
Stephens, James. a/SPOA 17
Stevens, Dudley. CAED 191
Stevens, Wallace. a/CAED 45, a/CAED 183,
    a/HARPV 3, a/LIST 13, a/SPOA 91
Stone, Ruth. a/SPOA 101
Stoppa, Paolo. CETRA 9, CETRA 12,
    CETRA 19, CETRA 20, CETRA 21,
    CETRA 22, CETRA 23, CETRA 24,
    CETRA 25, CETRA 27, CETRA 28,
    CETRA 30, CETRA 46
Strand, Mark. a/SPOA 107
Strehler, Giorgi. SPOA 30
Stride, John. ARGO 37, ARGO 47
Stryk, Lucien. a/FOLKW 111

Stuart, Jesse. a/CASSC 7
Style, William. SPOA 57
Sukenick, Lynn. a/UCAL 2, a/WATSHD 11
Summers, Hollis. a/SPOA 101
Sutzkever, Abraham. a/FOLKW 91
Suze, Carl de. PATHW 1
Swann, Donald. CAED 106
Sward, Robert. a/WATSHD 2
Swenson, May. a/CAED 165, a/JNP 68,
    a/MILLER 3, a/SPOA 103

Talen, William. a/WATSHD 4
Tappert, Horst. CHRIST 22
Tarahata, Jessica. a/WATSHD 50
Taranto, Nino. CETRA 29
Tate, Allen. a/CARIL 1, a/JNP 56, a/JNP 57,
    a/LIBC 5, a/LIBC 16, a/LIBC 38,
    a/NACTE 11, a/SPOA 96
Tate, James. a/JNP 58, a/WATSHD 1
Taylor, William E. a/CASSC 10
Te Wiata, Inia. KIWI 3
Tennberg, Jean-Marc. CBS 1
Terzieff, Laurent. ADES 27, ADES 33,
    ADES 42, ADES 55
Teynac, Maurice. ADES 7
Thich Nhat Hanh. a/SPOA 82
Thomas, Dylan. a/CAED 2, a/CAED 7,
    a/CAED 8, a/CAED 9, a/CAED 10,
    a/CAED 11, CAED 86, a/CAED 112,
    a/CAED 122, CAED 126, a/CAED 144,
    CAED 145, CAED 147, a/CAED 182,
    a/CAED 183, a/CAED 187, a/COLUMB 8,
    a/SBARB 1
Thomas, Edward. a/ARGO 148
Thomas, Helen. ARGO 96
Thomas, R. S. a/ARGO 97
Thomas-Ellis, Aeronwy. a/ARGO 132
Thompson, Sada. CAED 182
Thorndike, Sybil. ARGO 143, CAED 52
Thwaite, Anthony. a/ARGO 96, a/SPOA 67,
    a/SPOA 68
Tolkien, Christopher. CAED 1
Tolkien, J. R. R. a/CAED 1, a/CAED 106
Toma, Vincenzo de. CETRA 9, CETRA 12,
    CETRA 19, CETRA 20, CETRA 21,
    CETRA 22, CETRA 23, CETRA 24,
    CETRA 25, CETRA 27, CETRA 28,
    CETRA 46
Tomlinson, Charles. a/APPL 3, a/ARGO 98
Tonks, Rosemary. a/ARGO 96
Topart, Jean. HACH 17
Torre, Emilio de. HOLT 1
Torrieri, Diana. CETRA 41
Toto'. a/CETRA 37
Towle, Tony. a/JNP 59
Treitel, Margot. a/WATSHD 14
Troupe, Quincy. a/WATSHD 5
Tullos, Rod. a/WATSHD 7
Turco, E. CETRA 50
Turner, Darwin. a/CASSC 5
Tutin, Dorothea. ARGO 88A
Tuwhare, Hone. a/KIWI 5

Ungaretti, Giuseppe. a/APPL 4, a/CETRA 17,
    a/CETRA 42
Untermeyer, Louis. a/JNP 60, a/SPOA 91
Updike, John. a/CMS 8, a/JNP 61, a/SPOA 107

Ustinov, Peter. ARGO 118, ARGO 123, SPOWRD 5
Uzhvy, Natalia. FOLKW 93

Valère, Simone. ADES 34
Valeri, Franca. CETRA 15
Valladovers, Francisco. FIDIAS 3
Valli, Romolo. CETRA 3
Van Doren, Mark. CAED 20, a/FOLKW 37, a/LIBC 3, a/LIBC 4, a/NACTE 9, a/SPOA 82, a/SPOA 94
Van Fleet, Jo. CAED 20, CAED 21
Vaneck, Pierre. ADES 11, ADES 32, ADES 51, HACH 6, HACH 17
Vargas, Roberto. a/UCAL, a/WATSHD 5, a/WATSHD 9
Vaughan, H. A. CAED 153
Veazie, Carol. SPOA 129
Vega, Janine Pommy. a/WATSHD 14
Vega, Oscar Fernandez de la. SMC 13
Velloso, Josep-Miquel. AGUIL 14
Vienne, Lucie de.FOLKW 12, FOLKW 84
Viereck, Peter. a/LIBC 54, a/SPOA 102
Vilar, Jean. ADES 5, ADES 14, ADES 42, ADES 46, SPOA 9, SPOA 27, SPOA 62
Villoresi, Pamela. CETRA 36
Violi, Paul. a/WATSHD 5
Viorst, Judith. a/CAED 181
Vitold, Michel. ADES 41
Vivanco, Luis Felipe. a/AGUIL 2, a/AGUIL 3
Vogeler, Sara. a/WATSHD 10
Voskovec, George. COLUMB 15
Voznesensky, Andrei. a/COLUMB 13, a/MONITR 2, a/TAPES 7, a/UCALM 2

Wager, Michael. COLUMB 15
Wagner, Linda. CASSC 12A
Wagoner, David. a/SPOA 105
Wain, John. a/JNP 62, a/JNP 63, a/SPOA 68
Wakoski, Diane. a/CASSC 3
Walcott, Derek. a/CAED 153
Waldman, Anne. GIORNO 1
Walker, Margaret, a/BROADV 3, a/BROADV 13, FOLKW 1, a/FOLKW 44, FOLKW 45, a/FOLKW 46
Wallace, Rudy. a/WATSHD 10
Walton, Ortiz. a/WATSHD 2
Ward, Jerry. a/WATSHD 5
Waring, Richard. FOLKW 51
Warren, Austin. IDIOM 1
Warren, Robert Penn. a/APPL 11, a/CARIL 21, a/HARVOC 12, a/LIBC 9, a/LIBC 32, a/LIBC 54, a/SPOA 98
Watkins, Vernon. a/APPL 12, a/ARGO 92, a/BBC 1, a/CARIL 14
Watson, Gary. ARGO 13, ARGO 27, ARGO 62, ARGO 63, ARGO 64, ARGO 67, ARGO 69, ARGO 75, ARGO 76, ARGO 119, LONGM 1
Wayne, David. CAED 85, CAED 109, CAED 110, CAED 111
Weber, Richard. a/JNP 64
Weigel, Helene. DEUTGR 23, DEUTGR 24
Weightman, Harold. SCOT 1
Weiss, Theodore Russell. a/CARIL 12, EAV 15
Welles, Orson. DANA 1
Wellman, John. a/WATSHD 10
Wenham, Jane. CAED 203

Werner, Oskar. DEUTGR 1, DEUTGR 10
Westphal, Gert. CHRIST 4, CHRIST 5, CHRIST 6, CHRIST 7, CHRIST 15, CHRIST 21, CHRIST 22, CHRIST 25, CHRIST 28, CHRIST 30, DEUTGR 42
Wevill, David. a/ARGO 96
Whalen, Philip. a/CENTCA 1, a/NET 9
Wheatley, Alan. LONGM 1
Wheelock, John Hall. a/FML 1, a/JNP 65, a/LIBC 46, a/SPOA 82, a/SPOA 92
Whistler, Laurence. a/ARGO 93
Whitaker, Cynthia L. LEARNS 1
White, Josh. SPOA 119
White, Tony. ARGO 13
Whittemore, Reed. a/WATSHD 29
Wiata, Iniate. KIWI 3
Wickwire, Nancy. CAED 56, CAED 182, LIST 1, LIST 2, LIST 3, SPOA 26, SPOA 31, SPOA 112
Wiemann, Mathias. ATHENA 4, ATHENA 6, ATHENA 9, ATHENA 11, ATHENA 12, ATHENA 13, DEUTGR 16, DEUTGR 45, DEUTGR 47, TELEF 1
Wieners, John. a/NET 5, a/JNP 66
Wilbur, Richard. a/CAED 115, a/CAED 183, a/LIBC 54, a/LIST 15, a/NET 7, a/NET 8, a/SPOA 19, a/SPOA 82, a/SPOA 103
Wildgans, Anton. a/AMAD 5
Wilkinson, Anne. a/FOLKW 50
Williams, Emlyn. ARGO 24, ARGO 117
Williams, Hugo. a/ARGO 150
Williams, Miller. a/JNP 67
Williams, Oscar. a/LIBC 48, a/SPOA 96
Williams, Tennessee. a/CAED 12, CAED 99
Williams, William Carlos. a/CAED 36, a/CAED 183, a/COLUMB 8, a/HARPV 2, a/LIBC 9, a/LIBC 30, a/LIST 13, a/SPOA 91
Wilson, Georges. ADES 39
Wilson, Pearl C. CAED 28
Winnick, R. H. TAPES 8
Winters, Yvor. a/CARIL 8, a/LIBC 15, a/LIBC 41, a/SPOA 96
Wiseman, Joseph. CAED 141, CAED 157
Woodward, Edward. ARGO 110
Woolf, Gabriel. ARGO 52, ARGO 109
Worlock, Frederick. CAED 64, CAED 202
Worth, Irene. ARGO 14, RCA 2
Wright, James. a/CAED 175, a/SPOA 106
Wussow, Klausjürgen. CHRIST 27, CHRIST 30
Wyatt, Andrea. a/WATSHD 1

Xirgu, Margarita. POETAS 1

Yeats, William Butler. a/CAED 183, a/SPOA 22
Yevtushenko, Yevgeny. a/CAED 83, CAED 107, CAED 193, a/COLUMB 14, a/MELOD 2, a/MONITR 2, a/NBC 1
Yonmar, Carola. SMC 3, SMC 4, SMC 5, SMC 6, SMC 7
Young, Andrew. a/ARGO 100
Young, Marguerite. a/SPOA 82

Zareschi, Elena. CETRA 9, CETRA 12, CETRA 19, CETRA 20, CETRA 21, CETRA 22, CETRA 23, CETRA 24, CETRA 25, CETRA 27, CETRA 28, CETRA 46

REGISTER OF POETS BY LANGUAGE OF COMPOSITION

The language of composition is usually the poet's native tongue.
*The symbol * means that, so far as can be determined, the works of the poet*
have been recorded in translation only.

ANGLO-SAXON
Bede
Caedmon

BASQUE
Eizmendi, Ignacio de

BENGALI
Tagore, Rabindranath

CATALAN
Alcover i Maspons, Joan
Arderiu, Clementina

Carner i Puig-Oriol, Josep
Costa i Llobera, Miguel

Espriu, Salvador

Foix, J. V.

Liost, Guerau de
Lopez Pico, Josep Maria

Manent, Maria
Maragall, Joan

Quart, Pere

Raimon
Riba Bracóns, Carles

Sagarra, Josep Maria de
Salvat-Papasseit, Joan

Verdaguer, Jacint

CHINESE
Bai Jyu Yi

Chen Dau

*Confucius

Du Fu
Du Mu

He Jr Jang

Jang Ji
Ju Ching Yu
Jya Dau
Jyang Jye

Li Bai (Li Po)
Li Ching Jau
Li Yu
Lu Lwun
Lyou Dzung Ywan
Lyou Yung

Meng Hau Ran

Su Shih

Tao-Chi (Tao-Yuan-Ming)

Wang Han
Wang Jyan
Wang Wei
Wei Jwang
Wen Ting-Yueh
*Whan Chei

Ywan Jen

CZECH
Holub, Miroslav
Novak, Ladislav

DANISH
Andersen, Hans Christian

ENGLISH
Abbe, George
Abrams, Robert
Abse, Dannie
Adams, Leonie
Addison, Joseph
Agee, James
Ai (Florence Anthony)
Aiken, Conrad Potter
Alakoye, Adesanya
Aldan, Daisy
Aldis, Dorothy
Alexander, Floyce
Alfred, William
Allen, Marie Louise
Allen, Samuel
Allingham, William
Alston, Gary
Alurista
Amini, Johari
Amis, Kingsley
Anderson, Beth
Anderson, Charles
Anderson, Doug
Anderson, Lee
Andrews, Bruce

Angelou, Maya
Ansen, Alan
Antin, David
Antoninus, Brother
Appleton, Peter
Arden, John
Arnez, Nancy Levi
Arnold, Matthew
Ashbery, John
Atwood, Margaret
Aubert, Alvin
Auden, Wystan Hugh
Austin, Mary
Austin, William
Averitt, Eleanor
Avison, Margaret

Bacmeister, Rhoda W.
Bacon, Josephine Daskam
Bagg, Robert
Bahati, Amirh
Baker, Howard
Baker, Karle Wilson
Baldwin, Deirdra
Baldwin, Michael
Balthasa, Martin
Bangs, John Kendrick
Baraka, Imamu Amiri
Barker, Eric Wilson
Barker, George
Barker, Richard
Barnes, Barnabe
Barnes, William
Barnfield, Richard
Barrows, Marjorie
Baruch, Dorothy Walter
Bashford, H. H.
Bass, George Houston
Bates, Katherine Lee
Baybars, Taner
Beasley, Joshua, Jr.
Beaubien, Michael
Becker, John
Beddoes, Thomas Lovell
Beecher, John
Beer, Patricia
Beerbohm, Max
Behn, Aphra
Behn, Harry
Belitt, Ben
Bell, Marvin
Bellamy, Francis
Belloc, Hilaire
Benedikt, Michael
Benét, Rosemary Carr
Benét, Stephen Vincent

ENGLISH (continued)
Benét, William Rose
Bennett, Bob
Bennett, Joseph
Bennett, Rowena
Berge, Carol
Bergengren, Ralph
Berger, Art
Bergman, Alexander F.
Berkeley, George
Bernhard, Thomas
Bernstein, Charles
Berrigan, Daniel
Berry, Wendell
Berryman, John
Betjeman, John
Bevington, Helen
Beyer, Evelyn
Bibbs, Hart Leroi
Bickerstaffe, Isaac
Binyon, Laurence
Birney, Earle
Bishop, Elizabeth
Bishop, John Peale
Bishop, Morris
Blackburn, Paul
Blackburn, Thomas
Blackman, Gary
Blackmur, Richard P.
Blair, Robert
Blake, William
Blanding, Don
Blunden, Edmund
Blunt, Wilfrid Scawen
Bly, Robert
Bodenheim, Maxwell
Bogan, Louise
Bolton, Edmund
Bond, Julian
Bontemps, Arna
Booth, Philip
Borton, Terry
Bourdillon, Francis William
Boyden, Polly Chase
Brackett, Kate
Bradstreet, Anne
Bragg, Robert
Braithwaite, William Stanley
Brathwaite, Edward
Braun, Henry
Braxton, Jodi
Breton, Nicholas
Bridges, Robert
Brinnin, John Malcolm
Brock, Edwin
Bronk, William
Brontë, Anne
Brontë, Charlotte
Brontë, Emily
Brooke, Rupert
Brooks, Gwendolyn
Brooks, Phillips
Broughton, James
Broumas, Olga
Brown, George Mackey
Brown, Hubert "Rap" Geroid
Brown, Otis

Brown, Sterling A.
Brown, Thomas Edward
Brown, William
Browne, Michael Dennis
Browne, William
Browning, Elizabeth Barrett
Browning, Robert
Bruchac, Joseph
Brukner, Ira
Bryant, F. J., Jr.
Bryant, William Cullen
Bulwer-Lytton, Edward Robert
Bunner, Henry Cuyler
Bunting, Basil
Bunyan, John
Burke, Kenneth
Burns, Robert
Burr, Amelia Josephine
Burr, Gray
Butcher, Grace
Butler, Celia
Butler, Samuel
Butler, William
Buxton, John
Bynner, Witter
Byron, George Gordon, Lord

Calverley, Charles Stewart
Campbell, Alistair
Campbell, Joseph
Campbell, Roy
Campbell, Thomas
Campion, Thomas
Cane, Melville
Carew, Thomas
Carey, Henry
Carroll, Lewis
Carryl, Charles Edward
Carryl, Guy Wetmore
Carter, Connie
Cartwright, William
Cary, Patrick
Casson, John
Cattonar, Joanna
Causley, Charles
Cavalieri, Grace
Caxton, William
Chapin, Katherine Garrison
Chapman, J. Alexander
Charles II, King of England
Chaucer, Geoffrey
Cheever, John
Chester, Laura
Chesterton, Frances
Chesterton, Gilbert Keith
Chettle, Henry
Child, Lydia Maria
Chopin, Henri
Church, Richard
Chute, Marchette
Ciardi, John
Clare, John
Clark, China
Clark, David Ridgley
Clark, Gillian
Clark, John W.
Clarke, Austin

Clay, Buriel
Clifton, Lucille
Clough, Arthur Hugh
Coakley, William Leo
Coatsworth, Elizabeth
Cobbing, Bob
Codrescu, Andrei
Coffin, Robert Peter Tristram
Cohen, Leonard
Colbert, Alison
Coleridge, Mary Elizabeth
Coleridge, Samuel Taylor
Collier, Tom
Collins, Leslie M.
Collins, William
Collymore, Frank
Colum, Padraic
Congreve, William
Conkling, Hilda
Connor, Tony
Conquest, Robert
Constable, Henry
Copeland, Josephine
Coplen, Grace Wilson
Corbet, Richard
Corke, Hilary
Corner, Philip
Corso, Gregory
Cotton, Charles
Coward, Noel
Cowley, Abraham
Cowley, Malcolm
Cowper, William
Cox, Kenyon
Crabbe, George
Crane, Hart
Crane, Stephen
Crashaw, Richard
Creeley, Robert
Crouch, Stanley
Cuestas, Katherine L.
Cullen, Countee
Cummings, E. E.
Cuney, Waring
Cunningham, Allan
Cunningham, James Vincent
Cuomo, George
Curnow, Allen
Curran, John P.
Curtwright, Wesley

Dahlberg, Edward
Daly, Thomas Augustine
Dana, Richard Henry
Daniel, Samuel
Danner, Margaret
D'Arcy, Hugh Antoine
Darr, Ann
Darragh, Martina
Davenant, Sir William
Davidson, Donald
Davie, Donald
Davies, John, of Hereford
Davies, Mary Carolyn
Davies, William Henry
Davis, Fannie Stearns
Davis, Gloria

Davis, Thomas
Davis, Thulami Nkabinde
Davison, Frances
Davison, Peter
Day Lewis, Cecil
De Frees, Madeline
Dehn, Paul
De la Mare, Walter
De Loach, Allen
DeRegniers, Beatrice Schenk
Dei-Anang, Michael
Dekker, Thomas
Delegall, Walter
Dempster, Roland Tombekai
Den Boer, James
Denby, Edwin
Derwood, Gene
Deutsch, Babette
Devaul, Diane
Deveaux, Alexis
Dibdin, Thomas
Dicker, Harold
Dickey, James
Dickey, William
Dickinson, Emily
Dickinson, Patric
Dlugos, Tim
Dobell, Sydney
Dobson, Henry Austin
Dodson, Owen
Dodson-Letourneau, Gayle
Domett, Alfred
Donaldson, June
Donne, John
Doolittle, Hilda (H. D.)
Dorn, Alfred
Dos Passos, John
Douglas, Keith
Douglas, Sharon
Douglas, William
Dowling, Allan
Dowson, Ernest
Dragonette, Ree
Drake, Joseph Rodman
Drake, Leah Bodine
Drayton, Michael
Dreyer, Lynn
Drinkwater, John
Drummond, William
Drummond of Hawthornden,
  William
Dryden, John
Dudek, Louis
Dugan, Alan
Dunbar, Paul Laurence
Dunbar, William
Duncan, Robert Edward
Dunlop, William
Dupree, Nancy Lorraine
Durem, Ray
D'Urfey, Thomas
Durrell, Lawrence
Durston, Georgia Roberta
Dwight, Timothy
Dyer, Sir Edward

Earley, Jackey

Eastman, Max
Eberhart, Richard
Eckels, Jon
Edman, Irwin
Edson, Russell
Edwardes, Richard
Edwards, Harry
Ehrmann, Max
Eiseley, Loren
Eliot, George (Mary Anne
  Evans)
Eliot, Thomas Stearns
Elizabeth I, Queen of England
Elliot, Ebenezer
Elliott, George P.
Elmslie, Kenward
Emanuel, James A.
Emerson, Ralph Waldo
Empson, William
Engle, Paul
Ennis, Julian
Enright, D. J.
Enslin, Theodore
Essex, Earl of (Robert
  Devereux)
Etherege, Sir George
Evans, Abbie Huston
Evans, Liz
Evans, Mari

Fabio, Cyril Leslie III
Fabio, Sarah Webster
Faerstein, Chana
Fagin, Larry
Farjeon, Eleanor
Farrar, John
Farrell, James T.
Farren, Robert
Fauset, Jessie R.
Feldman, Irving
Ferguson, Samuel
Ferlinghetti, Lawrence
Field, Edward
Field, Eugene
Field, Rachel
Fields, Julia
Figueroa, John
Finch, Anne, Countess of
  Winchelsea
Finch, Francis
Finkel, Donald
Fisher, Aileen
Fitts, Dudley
Fitzgerald, Robert
Fitzsimmons, Tom
Flanders, Jane
Flecker, James Elroy
Fletcher, John
Fletcher, John Gould
Fletcher, Phineas
Flint, Roland
Foleti, Adebayo
Follen, Eliza Lee
Ford, John
Ford, M. Lucille
Forster, Edward Morgan
Foss, Sam Walter

Fox, Charles
Fox, George
Fox, Siv Cedering
Francis, Robert
Franks, David
Fraser, G. S.
Fraser, Kathleen
Freeman, C.
Freivalds, Karl
Fremantle, Anne
Freneau, Philip
Frost, Frances M.
Frost, Richard
Frost, Robert
Fry, Harvey
Fuld, Nancy
Fuller, John
Fuller, Roy
Furse, Jill
Fyleman, Rose

Gale, Norman
Gallagher, F. O'Neill
Gallagher, Tess
Gardner, Isabella Stewart
Garelick, Barry
Garfinkel, Pat
Garland, Hamlin
Garlick, Raymond
Garrigue, Jean
Gascoigne, George
Gascoyne, David
Gaver, Chasen
Gay, John
Gay, Zhenya
Gee, Lethonia
Geller, Richard
Genser, Cynthia
Ghose, Zulfikar
Gibson, Margaret
Gibson, Wilfred
Gilbert, Celia
Gilbert, Dorothy
Gilbert, Sir William Schwenck
Gill, John
Ginsberg, Allen
Giorno, John
Gioseffi, Daniela
Giovanni, Nikki
Gitlin, Todd
Gittings, Robert
Glaze, Andrew
Gleason, Maud
Glover, Denis
Gogarty, Oliver St. John
Gold, Edward
Goldfarb, Sidney
Goldman, Michael
Goldsmith, Oliver
Goldstein, Roberta
Goodman, Godfrey
Goodman, Paul
Googe, Barnabe
Gordon, Alvin J.
Graham, D. L.
Graham, William Sydney
Grant, Carolyn Hart

ENGLISH (continued)
Graves, Robert
Gray, Thomas
Green, Kate
Green, Mary McBride
Greenaway, Kate
Greene, Robert
Greenham, Peter
Greenwald, Roger
Gregor, Arthur
Gregory, Carole
Gregory, Horace
Grenfell, Julian
Greville, Fulke
Gridley, Gordon
Griffin, Gerald
Griffiths, Bryn
Grigson, Geoffrey
Grimké, Angelina
Guest, Barbara
Guest, Edgar
Guiterman, Arthur
Gunderson, Keith Robert
Gunn, Thom

Hacker, Marilyn
Haines, John
Hale, Edward Everett
Hall, Donald
Halleck, Fitz-Greene
Halley, Anne
Halpern, Daniel
Hamburger, Michael
Handy, W. C.
Hannan, Greg
Hans, Marcie
Hardy, Thomas
Harkness, Edward
Harnett, Michael
Harper, Michael S.
Harriman, John
Hart, Howard
Harte, Bret
Harteis, Richard
Hawker, Stephen
Hay, John
Hay, Sara Henderson
Hayden, Robert E.
Hayes, Donald Jeffrey
Hazel, Robert
Hazo, Samuel
Heaney, Seamus
Heath, Gordon
Heath-Stubbs, John
Heber, Reginald
Hecht, Anthony
Hegarty, Teddy
Helton, Roy
Hemans, Felicia Dorothea
Henderson, David
Henderson, Hamish
Henley, William Ernest
Henri, Adrian
Henry VIII, King of England
Henryson, Robert
Herbert, George
Herford, Oliver

Hernández Cruz, Victor
Hernton, Calvin C.
Herrick, Robert
Herschberger, Ruth
Hershenson, Miriam
Heywood, Thomas
Hill, Geoffrey
Hill-Abu-Isak, Elton
Hillary, Richard
Hillyer, Robert Silliman
Hine, Daryl
Hines, Carl Wendell
Hinton, Robert
Hitchcock, George
Hobbs, Suzanne
Hodges, Frenchy Jolene
Hodgson, Ralph
Hoey, Edwin A.
Hoffenstein, Samuel
Hoffman, Daniel G.
Hogg, James
Holbrook, David
Holland, Bill
Holland, Josiah Gilbert
Hollander, John
Hollo, Anselm
Holman, Felice
Holman, M. Carl
Holmes, John
Holmes, Oliver Wendell
Honig, Edwin
Hood, Thomas
Hopkins, Gerald Manley
Hopkinson, Francis
Hopkinson, Joseph
Horne, Frank
Housman, Alfred Edward
Howard, Lee
Howard, Richard
Howard, Winifred
Howe, Julia Ward
Howells, Mildred
Howes, Barbara
Howitt, Mary
Hoyt, Helen
Huff, Barbara A.
Huff, Robert
Hughes, Langston
Hughes, Ted
Hugo, Richard F.
Humphreys, Emyr
Humphries, Rolfe
Hunt, (James Henry) Leigh

Ignatow, David
Inman, Will
Ipagongnaik, Nende

Jackson, Gerald
Jackson, Kathryn
Jacob, Violet
Jacobs, Leland B.
Jacobsen, Ethel
Jacobsen, Josephine
Jacobson, Dan
Jaffe, Dan
Jaffe, Ellen

James I, King of Scotland
Jarrell, Randall
Jaszi, Jean
Jeffers, Lance
Jeffers, Robinson
Jeffries, Christine F.
Jennings, Elizabeth
Jennison, Lucia
Jerome, Jerome K.
Jimason, Joanne
Joans, Ted
Johnson, B. S.
Johnson, Fenton
Johnson, Georgia Douglas
Johnson, Helene
Johnson, James Weldon
Johnson, Joe
Johnson, Lenore
Johnson, Lionel
Johnson, Robert
Johnson, Samuel
Johnson, Tom
Johnston, Ellen Turlington
Johnston, Percy E.
Jones, David
Jones, Gayl
Jones, Glyn
Jones, Ted
Jong, Erica
Jonson, Ben
Jordan, June
Jordan, Norman
Joselow, Beth
Joseph, Steven M.
Joyce, James
Justice, Donald

Kali
Kallman, Chester
Katzman, Allen
Kaufman, Bob
Kaufman, Shirley
Kavanagh, P. J.
Keats, John
Keble, John
Keeler, Charles Augustus
Kell, Richard
Keller, Helen
Kelly, Robert
Kendrick, Delores
Kennedy, Marian
Kennedy, X. J.
Kern, Bliem
Kerouac, Jack
Kersh, Gerald
Ketchum, Arthur
Key, Francis Scott
Keyes, Sidney
Kgositsile, Keorapetse
Khalil, Amma
Kilmer, Aline
Kilmer, Joyce
King, Henry
Kingsley, Charles
Kinnell, Galway
Kinsella, Thomas
Kipling, Rudyard

Kirkup, James
Kizer, Carolyn
Klappert, Peter
Klein, Abraham Moses
Knight, Etheridge
Knight, John
Komey, Ellis Ayitey
Kops, Bernard
Kostelanetz, Richard
Kramer, Aaron
Kresh, Dave
Krows, Jane W.
Kumin, Maxine
Kunitz, Stanley
Kyd, Thomas

La Farge, Peter
Laepa, L.
Lahui, Jack
Lair, Clara
Lally, Michael
Lamb, Charles
Lampman, Archibald
Landor, Walter Savage
Lang, Andrew
Langland, Joseph
Langland, William
Lanier, Sidney
Lanusse, Armand
Lapalma, Marina
Larkin, Philip
Last Poets, The
Laudon, Alice
Lavin, Stuart
Lawrence, D. H.
Layton, Irving
Lazarus, Emma
Le Gallienne, Richard
Leadbelly (Huddie Ledbetter)
Lear, Edward
Lechlitner, Ruth
Ledwidge, Francis
Lee, Dennis
Lee, Don L.
Lee, Laurie
Lee-Hamilton, Eugene
Leslie, Cy
Lester, Julius
Levendosky, Charles
Levertov, Denise
Levi, Peter
Levine, Philip
Lewis, Alun
Lewis, Janet
Lewis, Richard
Liddy, James
Lieberman, Elias
Lieberman, Laurence
Lifshin, Lynn
Lindsay, Lady Anne
Lindsay, Vachel
Link, Lenore M.
Lipsitz, Lou
Lipton, Lawrence
Lockwood, Annea
Lodge, Thomas
Logan, John

Logue, Christopher
Longfellow, Henry Wadsworth
Lorde, Audre
Lovelace, Earl
Lovelace, Richard
Loveman, Robert
Lover, Samuel
Lowbury, Edward
Lowell, Amy
Lowell, James Russell
Lowell, Robert
Lowenfels, Walter
Lucie-Smith, Edward
Lurie, Toby
Lyly, John

Macaulay, Thomas Babington
MacBeth, George
MacCaig, Norman
McCarthy, Agnes
McCarthy, Eugene J.
McClure, Michael
McCord, David
McCrae, John
McCrimmon, Dan
MacDiarmid, Hugh
    (Christopher Murray Grieve)
MacDonagh, Thomas
*McFarlane, Basil
McGahey, Jeanne
McGinley, Phyllis
McGough, Roger
McHugh, Heather
McKay, Claude
Mackin, Sharon
McKnight, Jo Anne
MacLeish, Archibald
McLeod, Irene Rutherford
Mac Low, Jackson
MacManus, Seumas
MacNeice, Louis
McNeill, Anthony
MacPherson, Jay
MacSweeney, Margaret Phyllis
Magee, John Gillespie, Jr.
Mahony, Francis
Mailer, Norman
Major, Clarence
Malam, Charles
Malanga, Gerard
Malcolm X (Malcolm Little)
Malory, Sir Thomas
Mandel, Oscar
Mangan, James Clarence
Mansfield, Katherine
Marcello, Joseph
Marcus, Adrianne
Mariah, Paul
Markham, Edwin Charles
Marlowe, Christopher
Marquis, Don
Marriott, Jack
Marshall, Helen Lowrie
Marshall, Jack
Marshall, Lenore G.
Marvell, Andrew

Marvin X
Masefield, John
Mason, Chris
Masters, Edgar Lee
Masters, Marcia
Mathias, Roland
Matiabe, Aruru
Mayer, Beatrice
Mayo, E. L.
Meigs, Mildred Plew
Meltzer, David
Melville, Herman
Meredith, George
Meredith, William
Merriam, Eve
Merrill, James
Merwin, W. S.
Meynell, Alice
Michie, James
Middleton, Christopher
Middleton, Thomas
Miles, Josephine
Millay, Edna St. Vincent
Miller, Arthur
Miller, E. Ethelbert
Miller, Joaquin
Miller, Mary Britton
Miller, May
Mills, Barriss
Milne, Alan Alexander
Milton, John
Mir, Marjorie
Mitchell, Adrian
Mitchell, Julian
Mitchell, Lucy Sprague
Mitchell, Ruth Comfort
Modisane, Bloke
Monkhouse, Cosmo
Monro, Harold
Montrose, 1st Marquess of
    (James Graham)
Moore, Amus
Moore, Clement Clarke
Moore, Honor
Moore, Marianne
Moore, Merrill
Moore, Rosalie
Moore, Thomas
Moraes, Dom
Mordaunt, Charles, Earl of
    Peterborough
Morgan, John
Morgan, Karen
Morgan, Robin
Morley, Christopher
Morris, George Pope
Morris, James
Morris, Mervyn
Morris, William
Morrow, Charles
Morton, David
Moss, Howard
Moss, Stanley
Mountzoures, H. L.
Muir, Edwin
Munday, Anthony
Munkittrick, Richard Kendall

ENGLISH (continued)
Murphy, Beatrice
Myers, Neil

Nabokov, Vladimir
Napier, Winston
Nash, Ogden
Nashe, Thomas
Nathan, R.
Neal, Larry
Nemerov, Howard
Nesbit, Edith
Newman, Cardinal John Henry
Newton, Mary Leslie
Nicholson, Norman
Nicol, Abioseh
Nims, John Frederick
Noll, Bink
Norman, Howard
Norris, Leslie
Nowlan, Alden
Noyes, Alfred

O'Connell, Richard
Oden, G. D.
O'Gorman, Ned
O'Hara, Frank
Oldmixon, John
Oldys, William
Olson, Charles
O'Neill, Catherine
O'Neill, Mary L.
Oppen, George
Oppenheimer, Joel
O'Reilly, John Boyle
Orlovsky, Peter
Ormond, John
Orr, Gregory
O'Shaughnessy, Arthur William
    Edgar
Ostroff, Anthony
O'Sullivan, Seumas
Overstreet, Bonaro W.
Owen, Guy
Owen, Wilfred
Oxford, Earl of (Edward de
    Vere)
Ozick, Cynthia

Pack, Robert
Page, William Tyler
Parker, Dorothy
Parkes, Francis Ernest Kobina
Pastan, Linda
Patchen, Kenneth
Patmore, Coventry
Paton, Alan
Patten, Bryan
Patterson, Raymond R.
Payne, John Howard
Peacock, Thomas Love
Peake, Mervyn
Pearse, Padraic H.
Peele, George
Peseroff, Joyce
Pestel, Thomas
Philips, Katherine
Picard, Barbara

Piercy, Marge
Pierpont, John
Pietri, Pedro
Pines, Paul
Pinkney, Edward Coote
Pitter, Ruth
Planz, Allen
Plath, Sylvia
Pleshette, Ann
Plomer, William
Poe, Edgar Allan
Polak, Maralyn
Pols, Edward
Pommy Vega, Janine
Pope, Alexander
Pope, Jessie
Porter, Bern
Porter, Peter
Porter, William N.
Posner, David
Poulsson, Anne Emilie
Pound, Ezra
Praed, Winthrop Mackworth
Press, John
Preston, George Nelson
Prince, F. T.
Prior, Matthew
Pritchard, Norman Henry
Prothro, Nancy
Purdy, Al
Purens, Ilmars
Putnam, Phelps
Pyle, Katherine

Quarles, Francis
Quasha, George
Quiller-Couch, Arthur Thomas

Raab, Lawrence
Rago, Henry
Railes, Vilota
Raine, Kathleen
Raine, Stephen
Raleigh, Sir Walter
Randall, Dudley
Rands, William Brightly
Ransom, John Crowe
Raper, Michele
Rashidd, Amir
Rasof, Henry
Rasul, Sha'ir
Ray, David
Ray, Shreela
Read, Herbert
Read, Thomas Buchanan
Reaney, James
Rector, Liam
Redgrove, Peter
Redmond, Eugene
Reecher, Edward
Reed, Henry
Reed, Ishmael
Reese, Lizette Woodworth
Reeve, F. D.
Reeves, James
Reid, Alastair
Rexroth, Kenneth

Reynolds, Malvina
Rich, Adrienne
Richards, Frank
Richards, I. A.
Richards, Laura E.
Riggs, Katherine Dixon
Riley, James Whitcomb
Rive, Richard
Roach, Eric
Roberts, Elizabeth Maddox
Robinson, Edwin Arlington
Robinson, Wanda
Robison, Margaret
Robson, Ernest M.
Robson, Jeremy
Roche, Paul
Rochester, Earl of (John
    Wilmot)
Rodgers, W. R.
Roethke, Theodore
Rogers, Samuel
Rook, Alan
Roscoe, William
Roseliep, Raymond
Rosenberg, Isaac
Rosenfeld, Morris
Ross, Muriel Sipe
Ross, W. W. Eustace
Rossetti, Christina Georgina
Rossetti, Dante Gabriel
Rossman, Michael
Rosten, Norman
Roth, Dan
Rothenberg, Jerome G.
Royde-Smith, Naomi Gwladys
Rubadiri, James D.
Rudnick, Raphael
Rukeyser, Muriel
Russell, Sidney King

Sackville, Charles, Earl of
    Dorset
Sakaki, Nanao
Sanchez, Sonia
Sandburg, Carl
Sanders, Ed
Santayana, George
Sarett, Lew
Sargent, William D.
Sassoon, Siegfried
Sawyer, Mark
Saxe, John G.
Scannell, Vernon
Schmitz, Dennis
Schuyler, James Marcus
Schwartz, Delmore
Schwerner, Armand
Scott, Dennis
Scott, F. R.
Scott, Sir Walter
Scott, Winfield Townley
Sedley, Sir Charles
Serraillier, Ian
Service, Robert William
Setoun, Gabriel
Sexton, Anne
Shakespeare, William

Shange, Ntozake
Shannon, Monica
Shapiro, Harvey
Shapiro, Karl
Shaw, Frances
Shelley, Percy Bysshe
Sheridan, Richard Brinsley
Sherman, Guy
Sherwin, Judith Johnson
Shirley, James
Shiva
Shpunt, Lori
Sidney, Sir Philip
Silkin, Jon
Sill, Edward Rowland
Sillitoe, Alan
Simic, Charles
Simmons, Judy
Simmons, James Stewart
  Alexander
Simpson, Louis
Sitwell, Edith
Sitwell, Osbert
Skellings, Edmund
Skelton, John
Skelton, Robin
Sklarew, Myra
Skratz, G. P.
Smart, Christopher
Smith, A. J. M.
Smith, Eugene Osborn
Smith, Iain Crichton
Smith, Ken
Smith, Samuel Francis
Smith, Stevie
Smith, Sydney Goodsir
Smith, Welton
Smith, William Jay
Snodgrass, W. DeWitt
Snyder, Gary
Sobecks, Elaine
Sobiloff, Hy
Solomon, Marvin
Somerville, Dora
Sondé, Susan
Sorley, Charles Hamilton
Souster, Raymond
Southey, Robert
Southwell, Robert
Spacks, Barry
Spatling, Neil
Spellman, A. B.
Spencer, Theodore
Spender, Stephen
Spenser, Edmund
Speyer, Leonora
Spicer, Jack
Spivack, Kathleen
Stafford, William E.
Stallworthy, Jon
Stanley, Thomas
Starbuck, George
Stefanile, Felix
Steffens, Lincoln
Stein, Charles
Stein, Gertrude
Stephany (Stephany Jean

Dawson Fuller)
Stephens, James
Sterns, Monroe
Stevens, Wallace
Stevens, Wendy
Stevenson, Robert Louis
Stirling, Earl of (William
  Alexander)
Stone, Ronald
Stone, Ruth
Stoneham, Gillian
Strand, Mark
Strode, William
Stryk, Lucien
Stuart, Jesse
Suckling, Sir John
Sukenick, Lynn
Summers, Hal
Summers, Hollis
Surrey, Earl of (Henry Howard)
Sutheim, Susan
Sward, Robert
Swenson, May
Swift, Jonathan
Swinburne, Algernon
Symons, Arthur

Tabb, John Bannister
Talbot, Ethel
Talen, William
Tarahata, Jessica
Tate, Allen
Tate, James
Taylor, Ann and Jane
Taylor, Edward
Taylor, Rex
Taylor, William E.
Teasdale, Sara
Tennyson, Alfred, Lord
Terry, Lucy
Tessimond, A. S. J.
Thackeray, William Makepeace
Thayer, Ernest L.
Thomas, Dylan
Thomas, Edward
*Thomas, H. Carey
Thomas, Jill
Thomas, Lorenzo
Thomas, Martha B.
Thomas, Ronald Stuart
Thomas-Ellis, Aeronwy
Thompson, Francis
Thompson, John
Thompson, W. H.
Thomson, James
Thoreau, Henry David
Thwaite, Anthony
Tichborne, Chidiock
Timrod, Henry
Tippett, James S.
Tobias, John
Toleau, Gwen
Tolkien, John Ronald Reuel
Tomlinson, Charles
Tonks, Rosemary
Toomer, Jean
Toure, Aski Mohammad

Tourneur, Cyril
Towle, Tony
Traherne, Thomas
Treece, Henry
Treitel, Margot
Tripp, John
Tropp, Gloria
Tropp, Steven
Troupe, Quincy
Trumbull, John
Tuckerman, Frederick Goddard
Tullos, Rod
Turco, Lewis
Turner, David
Turner, Nancy Byrd
Turner, Walter James
Tuwhare, Hone

Untermeyer, Louis
Updike, John
Uschold, Maud E.

Van Doren, Mark
Van Dyke, Henry
Vargas, Roberto
Vaughan, H. A.
Vaughan, Henry
Very, Jones
Victor, Florence
Viereck, Peter
Violi, Paul
Viorst, Judith
Vogeler, Sara

Wagoner, David
Wain, John
Wakoski, Diane
Walcott, Derek
Waldman, Anne
Walker, Margaret
Wallace, Rudy
Waller, Edmund
Walsh, William
Walters, Bryan
Wanley, Nathaniel
Ward, Jerry
Warren, Robert Penn
Warton, Joseph
Warton, Thomas (the Elder)
Warton, Thomas (the Younger)
Watkins, Vernon P.
Watson, Robert
Watts, Isaac
Watts-Dunton, Theodore
Webb, Harri
Weber, Richard
Weber, Ron
Webster, H.
Webster, John
Weiss, Theodore Russell
Welles, Winifred
Wellman, John
West, Graeme
Weston, Mildred
Wevill, David
Whalen, Philip
Wheatley, Phillis

ENGLISH (continued)
Wheelock, John Hall
Whistler, Laurence
Whitbread, Thomas
White, Elwyn B.
Whitman, Walt
Whittemore, Reed
Whittier, John Greenleaf
Widdemer, Margaret
Wieners, John
Wilbur, Richard
Wilde, Oscar
Wilkinson, Anne
Williams, Gwyn
Williams, Hugo
Williams, Jonathan
Williams, Miller
Williams, Oscar
Williams, Otis
Williams, Tennessee
Williams, William Carlos
Wills, Jesse
Wilson, Patrice
Winch, Terence
Winters, Yvor
Wither, George
Wolfe, Humbert
Wood, Marguerite
Woodworth, Samuel
Wordsworth, William
Work, Henry Clay
Wotton, Sir Henry
Wright, Charles
Wright, James
Wright, Judith
Wright, Richard
Wright, Robert
Wyatt, Andrea
Wyatt, Sir Thomas
Wycherley, William
Wylie, Elinor
Wynne, Annette

Yeats, William Butler
Yorck, Ruth Landshoff
Young, Andrew
Young, Bartholomew
Young, David
Young, Francis Brett
Young, Marguerite

Zaturenska, Marya
Zu-Bolton, Ahmos
Zukofsky, Louis

FLEMISH

Vree, Paul de

FRENCH

Apollinaire, Guillaume
Aragon, Louis
Arnault, Antoine Vincent
Arvers, Felix
Aubigné, Théodore-Agrippa d'

Baïf, Antoine de
Banville, Théodore de

Baudelaire, Charles
Bédier, Joseph
Belleau, Remi
Benserade, Isaac de
Béranger, Pierre Jean
Bernard, Roger
Bervoets, Marguerite
Boileau-Despréaux, Nicolas
Bonnefoy, Yves
Breton, André
Brierre, Jean-François

Cadou, René Guy
Carco, Francis
Cassou, Jean
Cayrol, Jean
Cendrars, Blaise
Césaire, Aimé
Char, René
Charles d' Orléans
Chartier, Alain
Chénier, André
Cherrier, Claude
Christine de Pisan
Claudel, Paul
Cocteau, Jean
Cohn, Marianne
Coppée, François
Corbière, "Tristan"
   (Édouard-Joachim)
Corneille, Pierre
Cros, Charles

Damas, Léon G.
Danton, Georges Jacques
Desangiers
Desbordes-Valmore, Marceline
Deschamps, Eustache
Desnos, Robert
Desportes, Philippe
Diop, David
Diouara, Bouna Boukary
Du Bellay, Joachim
Duchamps
Dufrêne, François

Éluard, Paul
Emmanuel, Pierre

Fargue, Léon Paul
Ferron, Marcelle
Fombeure, Maurice
Fondane, Benjamin
Fontaine, Pierre
Fort, Paul
Fourest, Georges
Frenaud, André
*Froissart, Jean

Garnier, Robert
*Gasztold, Carmen Bernos de
Gautier, Théophile
Geraldy, Paul
Gide, André
Giguere, Roland
Gilbert, Nicolas-Joseph
Gombauld, Jean Ogier de

Gourmont, Remy de
Grandbois, Alain
Guillevic, Eugène
Guyot de Dijon

Haraucourt, Edmond
Hébert, Anne
Henault, Gilles
Heredia, José-Maria de
Hugo, Victor

Jacob, Max
Jammes, Francis
Jarry, Alfred
Jodelle, Etienne

Klingsor, Tristan

La Fontaine, Jean de
Labé, Louise
Laforgue, Jules
Lamartine, Alphonse de
Lapointe, Paul-Marie
Larbaud, V.
Lasnier, Rina
Lautréamont
Leconte de Lisle, Charles
   Marie René
Lemaitre, Maurice
Lora-Totino, Arrigo

Machaut, Guillaume de
Maeterlinck, Maurice
Maison-Noire
Malherbe, François de
Mallarmé, Stéphane
Marguerite de Navarre
Marot, Clément
Masson, Loys
Mauriac, François
Maurois, André
Maynard, François
Michaux, Henri
Millevoye, Charles-Hubert
Milosz, Oscar
Molière (Jean-Baptiste
   Poquelin)
Moréas, Jean
   (Pappadiamantopoulos)
Morel, François
Musset, Alfred de

Nerval, Gerard de
Noailles, Comtesse Mathieu de
Noël, Marie

Obaldia, René de

Parny, Évariste-Désiré de
*Passerat, Jean
Péguy, Charles
Péret, Benjamin
Périn, René
Perse, Saint-John (Alexis
   Saint-Léger Léger)
Picabia, Francis
Pilon, Jean-Guy

Piron, Alexis
Prefontaine, Yves
Prévert, Jacques

Queneau, Raymond

Racan, Honorat de Bueil,
  Seigneur de
Racine, Jean
Régnier, Henri de
Reverdy, Paul
Rictus, Jehan
Rimbaud, Arthur
Rollinat, Maurice
Romains, Jules
Ronsard, Pierre de
Ruteboeuf

Saint-Amant, Marc-Antoine
  Girard de
*Saint-Exupéry, Antoine de
Saint-René, Martin
Sainte-Beuve, Charles Auguste
Samain, Albert
Scève, Maurice
Seghers, Pierre
Senghor, Léopolde Sedar
Soupault, Philippe
Sponde, Jean de
Sully-Prudhomme,
  René-François-Armand
Supervielle, Jules
Sylvain, André

Tardieu, Jean
Thibaut de Champagne
Tirolien, Guy
Toulet, Paul-Jean
Tristan l'Hermite (François
  l'Hermite)
Tyard, Pontus de
Tzara, Tristan

Valéry, Paul
Verhaeren, Émile
Verlaine, Paul-Marie
Vian, Boris
Viau, Théophile de
Vigny, Alfred de
Villon, François
Voiture, Vincent
Voltaire (François Marie
  Arouet)

GAELIC

*Merriman, Brian
Plunkett, Joseph Mary
Raftery, Antoine

GERMAN

Allmers, Hermann
Arp, Hans

Bachmann, Ingeborg
Balde, Jakob
Ben-Chorin, Schalom

Benn, Gottfried
Bergengruen, Werner
Bienek, Horst
Bobrowski, Johannes
Borchers, Elisabeth
Borchert, Wolfgang
Born, Nicolas
Brecht, Bertolt
Brentano, Clemens
Britting, Georg
Broch, Hermann
Brockes, Berthold Heinrich
Bürger, Gottfried August
Busch, Wilhelm

Carossa, Hans
Celan, Paul
Chamisso, Adelbert von
Claudius, Matthias

Dauthendey, Max
Dehmel, Richard
Droste-Hülshoff, Annette von

Eich, Günther
Eichendorff, Joseph von
Enzensberger, Hans Magnus

Fleming, Paul
Fontane, Theodor

Gan, Peter
Gellert, Christian Fürchtegott
Gemmingen, Eberhard
  Friedrich von
George, Stefan
Gerhardt, Paul
Gleim, Johann Wilhelm Ludwig
Göckingk, Leopold Friedrich
  Günther von
Goethe, Johann Wolfgang von
Goll, Yvan
Grass, Günter
Greif, Martin (Friedrich
  Hermann Frey)
Gryphius, Andreas
Guggenmos, Josef
Günther, Christian

Hagedorn, Friedrich von
Hagelstange, Rudolf
Hauptmann, Gerhart
Haushofer, Albrecht
Hausmann, Manfred
Hausmann, Raoul
Hebbel, Friedrich
Heine, Heinrich
Heissenbüttel, Helmut
Herburger, Günter
Herrmann-Neisse, Max
Hesse, Hermann
Hey, Wilhelm
Hoffmann, Heinrich
Hoffmannsthal, Hugo von
Hölderlin, Friedrich
Höllerer, Walter

Hölty, Ludwig Heinrich
  Christopher
Holz, Arno
Huch, Ricarda
Huchel, Peter

Jacobi, Johann Georg
Jandl, Ernst

Kasack, Hermann
Kaschnitz, Marie Luise
Kästner, Erich
Keller, Gottfried
Kirsch, Sarah
Klaj, Johann
Klopstock, Friedrich Gottlieb
Kraft, W.
Krolow, Karl
Krüger, Michael
Krüss, James
Kuhlmann, Quirinius
Kuhn, Friedrich Adolf
Kunert, Günter
Kunze, Reiner

La Motte-Fouqué, Friedrich,
  Freiherr de
Lasker-Schüler, Else
Lavant, Christine
Lehmann
Lenau, Nikolaus
Lenz, Jakob Michael Reinhold
Lessing, Gotthold Ephraim
Liliencron, Detlev von
Linde, Otto zur
Loerke, Oskar
Luther, Martin

Meckel, Christoph
Mehring, Walther
Melk, Heinrich von
Meyer, Conrad Ferdinand
Miegel, Agnes
Mon, Franz
Morgenstern, Christian
Mörike, Eduard
Mostar, Hermann
Müller, Wilhelm

Nietzsche, Friedrich Wilhelm
Novalis (Baron Friedrich von
  Hardenberg)

Opitz, Martin

Paulus, Helmut
Piontek, Heinz
Platen-Hallermünde, August
  Graf von

Rambler, Karl Wilhelm
Rilke, Rainer Maria
Roth, Eugen
Rückert, Friedrich
Rudnigger, Wilhelm
Rühm, Gerhard
Rühmkorf, Peter

GERMAN (continued)

*Sachs, Nelly
Santa Clara, Abraham a
Schaeffer, Albrecht
Scharpenberg, Margot
Schatzdorfer, Hans
Scheffel, Joseph Viktor von
Scheffler, Johann
Schiller, Friedrich von
Schlegel, Friedrich
Schröder, Rudolf Alexander
Schubart, Christian Friedrich
  Daniel
Schwitters, Kurt
Spee von Langenfeld, Friedrich
Stadler, Ernst
Stolberg, Friedrich Leopold
  von
Storm, Theodor

Thenior, Ralph
Theobaldy, Jürgen
Tieck, Ludwig
Tiedge, Christopher August
Trakl, Georg
Tucholsky, Kurt

Uhland, Ludwig

Vogel, Jakob
Vring, Georg von der

Walther von der Vogelweide
Weckherlin, Georg Rudolf
Wedekind, Frank
Weinheber, Josef
Weissenburg, Otto von
Werfel, Franz
Wildgans, Anton
Wolfram von Eschenbach

Zuckmayer, Carl

LOW GERMAN

Olfers-Batocki, Erminia von

GREEK, ANCIENT

*Agathias
 Alcaeus
 Alcman
*Ammianus
*Ammonides
 Anacreon
*Antipater of Sidon
 Archilochos

Cleanthes

*Diogenes Laertius

Homer

*Kallimachos

*Leonidas the Alexandrian
*Lucian of Samosata

Meleager (Meleagros)
Mimnermus of Colophon

*Nikarchos

*Palladas
*Paulus Silentiarius
*Philodemos the Epicurean
 Pindar
 Plato
*Ptolemaios the Astronomer

*Rufinus Domesticus

Sappho
Simonides

Tymnes

Xenophanes

GREEK, MODERN

*Cavafy, Constantine
Ritsos, Yannis
Seferis, George (Sepheriados)

HEBREW

Amichai, Yehuda
Kovner, Abba
Pagis, Dan

HINDI

Tul'si Das

HUNGARIAN

Pilinszky, Janos

ITALIAN

Achillini, Claudio
Addamo, Giuseppe
Agnello, Giuseppe
Alcamo, Ciullo d'
Aleardi, Count Aleardo
Alfieri, Count Vittorio
Andrea da Barberino
Angiolieri, Cecco
Ariosto, Lodovico
Artale, Giuseppe

Barbera, Renzino
Basso, Andrea del
Belli, Giuseppe Gioacchino
Bembo, Pietro
Berchet, Giovanni
Berni, Francesco
Betteloni, Vittorio
Bevilacqua, Alberto
Boccaccio, Giovanni
Boiardo, Matteo Maria, Count
  of Scandiano
Bosi, Carlo Alberto
Bovio, Libero
Bruni, Atilio
Burchiello (Domenico di
  Giovanni)

Buttitta, Ignazio
Buzzati, Dino

Camilleri, Andrea
Campana, Dino
Campanella, Tommaso
Campanile, Alfonso
Capurro, Giovanni
Cardarelli, Vincenzo
Carducci, Giosuè
Casa, Giovanni della
Cattafi, Bartolo
Cavalcanti, Guido
Celi, Maria Celeste
Cesarotti, Melchiorre
Chiabrera, Gabriello
Chiurazzi, Raffaele
Ciconi, Teobaldo
Cino Da Pistoia
Colonna, Vittoria
Corazzini, Sergio
Corsaro, Antonio
Cremona, Antonio
Crimi, Nino
Cultrera, Giuseppe

D'Annunzio, Gabriele
Dante Alighieri
Di Giacomo, Salvatore
Di Tarsia, Galeazzo
Donzella, La Compiuta
Dotti, Bartolomeo

Farinella, Mario
Filippo, Eduardo de
Fiore, Francesco
Folgòre da San Gimignano
Fontanella, Girolamo
Foscolo, Ugo
Francesco da Barberino
Francis of Assisi, Saint (San
  Francesco d'Assisi)
Freni, Melo
Frescobaldi, Dino
Frugoni, Francesco Fulvio
Fusinato, Arnaldo

Galdieri, Rocco
Gambara, Veronica
Gatto, Alfonso
Giàcomo da Lentini
Gianni degli Alfani
Giusti, Giuseppe
Giustiniàn, Leonardo
Gori, Mario
Govoni, Corrado
Gozzano, Guido
Gozzi, Count Carlo
Gramigna, Giuliano
Guido delle Colonne
Guinicelli, Guido

Isgrò, Emilio

Lapo Gianni
Leopardi, Giacomo
Lo Curzio, Guglielmo

Lombardi, Eliodoro
Lubrano, Giacomo
Lucini, Gian Pietro
Luzi, Mario

Mandarà, Emanuele
Manzoni, Alessandro
Marin, Biagio
Marino, Giambattista
Materdona, Gian Francesco
    Maia
Mazzini, Giuseppe
Medici, Lorenzo de'
Mercantini, Luigi
Metastasio (Pietro Antonio
    Domenico Bonaventura
    Trapassi)
Michelangelo Buonarroti
Montale, Eugenio
Monti, Vicenzo
Morra, Isabella de
Mura, Ettore de
Murolo, Ernesto

Nicolardi, Edoardo
Nina Siciliana

Palazzeschi, Aldo
Parini, Giuseppe
Pascarella, Cesare
Pascoli, Giovanni
Pavese, Cesare
Penna, Sandro
Pers, Ciro di
Petrarca, Francesco (Petrarch)
Piccolo, Lucio
Poliziano, Angelo
Porta, Carlo
Praga, Emilio
Pucci, Antonio
Pulci, Luigi

Quasimodo, Salvatore

Reale, Basilio
Rebora, Clemente
Redi, Francesco
Rinaldo d'Aquino
Risi, Nelo
Rodari, Gianni
Ronsisvalle, Vanni
Russo, Ferdinando

Saba, Umberto
Sacchetti, Franco
Saitta, Antonio
Sala, Alberto
Sbarbaro, Camillo
Sereni, Vittorio
Stampa, Gaspara

Tasso, Torquato
Tassoni, Alessandro
Todi, Jacopone de la
Tommaseo, Niccoló (Tomašić)
Torello, Barbara

Torrisi, Fiore
Totò

Uccello, Antonino
Ungaretti, Giuseppe

Vann'anto
Villaroel, Calogero
Villaroel, Giuseppe
Vittorelli, Iacopo
Vittorini, Elio
Viviani, Raffaele

Zogarrio, Giuseppe

JAPANESE

*Buson, Yosa

LATIN

Catullus, Gaius Valerius

Ennius

Hadrian
Horace (Quintus Horatius
    Flaccus)

*Juvenal (Decimus Junius
    Juvenalis)

Lucanus, Marcus Annaeus
Lucilius, Gaius
*Lucretius Carus, Titus

Manilius
Martial (Marcus Valerius
    Martialis)
Maximianus of Etruria
Messimanus

Namatianus, Rutilius Claudius

Ovid (Publius Ovidius Naso)

Persius (Aulus Persius Flaccus)
Phaedrus
Propertius, Sextus

Statius, Publius Papinius
Sulpicia
Sulpicius Severus

Tibullus, Albius

Valerius (Caius Valerius
    Flaccus)
Virgil (Publius Vergilius Maro)

PERSIAN

*Ferdovci (Abol Mansur)

Hafiz (Shams ad-Din
    Muhammad)

*Omar Khayyam

PORTUGUESE

Andrade, Mario de

Bandeira, Manuel
Bopp, Raul
Botto, António

Camões, Luis de
Castro, Eugénio de
Codax, Martin
Couto, Ribeiro

Drummond de Andrade, Carlos

Espanca, Florbela

Ferreira, Ascenso

Ivo, Ledo

Junqueiro, Guerra

Leal, Gomes
Lima, Jorge de
Lisboa, Henriqueta
Lisboa, Irene

Marques, Oswaldino
Meireles, Cecilia
Melo Neto, João Cabral de
Mendes, Murilo
Meyer, Augusto
Morais, Vinicius de

Nobre, António
Nunes, Cassiano

Palés Matos, Luís
Pascoaes, Teixeira de
Pessanha, Camilo
Pessoa, Fernando

Quental, Antero de
Quintana, Mário

Ricardo, Cassiano

Sá-Carneiro, Mario de
Sancho I, King of Portugal
Schmidt, Augusto Frederico

Verde, Cesário

PROVENÇAL

Bertrand de Born

Daniel, Arnaud

Raimbaut de Vaqueiras

RUSSIAN

Akhmatova, Anna

Blok, Aleksandr Aleksandrovich

Chlebnikov, Velemir

Derzhavin, G. R.

RUSSIAN (continued)

Fet, A. A.

Gogol, Nikolai Vasilyevich

Hippius, Zanaída

Karamzin, N. M.
Kirsanov, Simeon I.
Korolenko, V. G.

Lermontov, Mikhail

*Malevic, Kazimir
Martynov, Leonid N.
Mayakovsky, Vladimir
    Vladimirovich

Nekrasov, Nikolay Alekseyevich

Pasternak, Boris Leonidovich
Pushkin, Aleksandr Sergeevich

Ryleyev, K. F.

Shevchenko, Taras
Simonov, Konstantin M.
Slutsky, Boris A.
Svetlov, Mikhail A.

Turgenev, Ivan Sergeyevich
Tyutchev, Fedor Ivanovich
Tzvetaeva, Marina

Venevitinov, D. V.
Voznesensky, Andrei
Vyazemsky, P. A.

Yessenin, Sergei
Yevtushenko, Yevgeny

Zhukovsky, V. A.

SANSKRIT

*Bhartrihari
Valmiki

SERBIAN

Popa, Vasko

SPANISH

Abril, Xavier
Abu-l-Hasan al-Husri
Acosta, Agustín
Aguirre, Guillermo
Agustini, Delmira
Alberti, Rafael
Alcántara, Manuel
Alcázar, Baltasar del
Alegría, José S.
Aleixandre, Vicente
Alonso, Dámaso
Alurista
Álvarez Gato, Juan
Andrade, Olegario Victor
Arana, Felipe
Arboleda, Julio

Aridjis, Homero
*Arras-Caeta, Juan Julio
Arrieta, Rafael Alberto
Arriví, Francisco
Ascasubi, Hilario

Balbuena, Bernardo de
Ballagas, Emilio
Banchs, Enrique
Barba Jacob, Porfirio
Barbieri, Vicente
Becquer, Gustavo Adolfo
Bello, Andrés
Ben Safar Al-Marini
Benavente, Jacinto
Berger-Kiss, Andrés
Bernárdez, Francisco Luis
Blanco, Andrés Eloy
Borges, Jorge Luis
Botero, Juan José
Bousoño, Carlos
Brull, Mariano
Buesa, José Angel
Burgos, Julia de
Byrne, Bonifacio

Cabrisas, Hilarión
Cadilla, Carmen Alicia
Calderón de la Barca, Pedro
Camino Galicia, Léon Felipe
Campoamor, Ramon de
Capdevila, Arturo
Carranza, Eduardo
Carrasco, Benitez
Carrera Andrade, Jorge
Carvajal, Juan F.
Casal, Julian del
Casona, Alejandro
Castro, Rosalía de
Castro Saavedra, Carlos
Cavestany, Juan
Celaya, Gabriel
Cernuda, Luis
Cervantes Saavedra, Miguel de
Cetina, Gutierre de
Chamizo, Luis
Champourcin, Ernestina de
Conde, Carmen
Coronado, Carolina
Corretjer, Juan Antonio
Cremer, Victoriano
Cuadra, Pablo Antonio

Darío, Rubén
Dávila, José Antonio
Dávila, Virgilio
Dicenta, Joaquin
Diego, Eliseo
Diego, Gerardo
Diego, José de
Díez-Canedo, Enrique
Domínguez Alba, Bernardo

Ercilla, Alonso de
Escriva, Juan
Escudero, Gonzalo
Espada Rodriguez, José

Espina, Concha
Espronceda, José de

Fernandez Moreno, Baldomero
Figuera, Angela
Flores, Blanca
Flórez, Julio
Florit, Eugenio
Fombona-Pachano, Jacinto
Fuertes, Gloria

Gabriel y Galán, José María
Gaos, Vicente
Garcia Lorca, Federico
Garcia Nieto, José
García Tudurí, Mercedes
Girondo, Oliverio
Godoy, Tamara
Gómez de Avellaneda,
    Gertrudis
Góngora, Luis de Argote y
González, Ángel
González-Martínez, Enrique
Guillén, Jorge
Guillén, Nicolás
Güiraldes, Ricardo
Gutierrez, Juan Maria
Gutiérrez Nájera, Manuel

Heredia y Campuzano, José
    María de
Hernández, José
Hernández, José P. H.
Hernández, Miguel
Herrera y Reissig, Julio
Hickey Pellizzoni, Margarita
Hierro, José
Hoffman Llevano, Ernesto
Huidobro, Vincente
Hurtado de Mendoza, Diego

Ibarbourou, Juana de
Iriarte, Tomás de
Isaacs, Jorge

Jaimes Freyre, Ricardo
Jiménez, Juan Ramon
Joglar Cacho, Manuel
Juan de la Cruz
Juana Inés de la Cruz

Laura, Victoria
León, Fray Luis de
León, Rafael de
Lesto, Julio
Lezama Lima, José
Lloréns Torres, Luís
Lobo, Eugenio Gerardo
López, Luis Carlos
Lopez Silva
López Suria, Violeta
Loynaz, Dulce María
Lugones, Leopoldo
Lugones, Ricardo
Luis, Leopoldo de
Luna, José Carlos de

Machado, Antonio
Machado, Manuel
Macheral, Leopoldo
Manrique, Jorge
Mantero, Manuel
Mármol, José
Martí, José
Martinez Alonso, Isidoro
Martínez Capó, Juan
Martínez Estrada, Ezequiel
Martínez Sierra, Gregorio
Mata, Pedro
Matos Paoli, Francisco
Melendez Valdes, Juan
Mendive, Rafael María de
Mendoza, Esther Feliciano
Mendoza, Fray Iñigo
Menendez y Pelayo, Marcelino
Mesa, E. de
Milanés, José Jacinto
Mistral, Gabriela
Molinari, Ricardo E.
Monvel, Mario
Morales, Jorge L.
Moratin, Nicolas Fernandez de
Muñoz Marín, Luis
Muñoz Rivera, Luis
Murciano, Carlos
Muroti, Manuel

Nalé-Roxlo, Conrado
Neruda, Pablo
Nervo, Amado
Novo, Salvador
Nuñez, Rafael

Obligado, Pedro Miguel
Obligado, Rafael
Olmedo, José Joaquín de
Oquendo de Amat, Carlos
Otero, Blas de

Pacheco, José Emilio
Palma, Ricardo
Panero, Leopoldo
Pardo Garcia, German
Paz, Octavio
Pedroni, José
Pemán, José María
Peñalver, Juan
Péres Marchand, Lilianne
Pérez, Ana Maria
Pérez de Zambrana, Luisa
Piedra-Bueno, Andrés de
Pinar, Florencia
Pombo, Rafael
Portela, C.
Poveda, José Manuel
Prados, Emilio

Quevedo y Villegas, Francisco
  de
Quintana, Manuel José

Rega Molina, Horacio

Retamar, Roberto Fernández
Reyes, Alfonso
Reyes Fuentes, Maria de los
Ribera Chevremont, Evaristo
Ridruejo, Dionisio
Rosales, Luis
Ruiz, Juan, Archipreste de Hita

Saavedra, Angel de, Duque de
  Rivas
Sabat-Ercasty, Carlos
Salinas, Juan
Salinas, Pedro
Sansores, Rosario
Santillana, Marqués de
Santos Chocano, José
Semprit, José Dávila
Silva, José Asunción
Soynar, Dulce Maria
Storni, Alfonsina

Tejada, José Luis
Teresa de Avila, Saint (Teresa
  de Jesus)
Terrazas, Francisco de
Toledo, Lillian
Torres, César G.
Torres Bodet, Jaime
Torres y Villarroel, Diego

Uchoita, J. A.
Unamuno, Miguel de
Urrutia, Francisco A.

Valdés, Gabriel de la
  Concepción
Valencia, Guillermo
Valerio, Xandro
Valle Caviedes, Juán del
Valle Inclan, Ramón del
Vallejo, César
Valverde, José Maria
Vargas, Roberto
Vega, Garcilaso de la
Vega, Oscar Fernández de la
Vega Carpio, Lope de
Vicens, Nimia
Vicente, Gil
Victoria, Laura
Villaespesa, Francisco
Villalón, Fernando
Villegas, Esteban Manuel de
Vivanco, Luis Felipe
Vocos-Lescano, Jorge

Zardoya, Concha
Zenea, Juan Clemente
Zorilla de San Martin, Juan
Zorrilla, José

SWAHILI

Farahani
Nasibu

SWEDISH

Asplund, Karl

Bergman, Bo
Blomberg, Erik
Edfelt, Johannes
Edgardh, B.
Ekelöf, Gunnar
Elgström, Anna Lenah
Ferlin, Nils Johan Einar
Fröding, Gustaf
Geijer, Erik Gustaf
Gullberg, Hjalmar
Hallström, Per
Hasso, Signe
Hazze, Z.
Hedberg, Tor
Heidenstam, Verner von
Hemmer, Jarl
Karlfeldt, Erik Axel
Kefasdotter, M.
Kellgren, Johan Henrik
Lagerkvist, Pär
Lagerlöf, Selma
Lenngren, Anna Maria
Lindegren, Erik
Lindorm, Erik
Lindqvist, Ebba
Lo-Johansson, Ivar
Lundkvist, Artur
Malmberg, Bertil
Martinson, Harry
Nerman, Ture
Nordenflycht, Hedvig Charlotta
Ossiannilsson, K. G.
Österling, Anders
Runeberg, Johan Ludvig
Rydberg, Viktor
Selander, Sten
Siewertz, Sigfrid
Snoilsky, Carl
Södergran, E.
Stagnelius, Erik Johan
Tegner, Esaias
Ullman, Gustaf
Vennberg, Karl
Wallin, Johan Olaf

UKRAINIAN

Krucenych, Aleksei

VIETNAMESE

*Ho Chi Minh
Thich Nhat Hanh

XHOSA

*Jolobe, James J. R.

YIDDISH

Kurtz, Aaron
Lutzky, A.
Peretz, J. L.
Stein, Sholom
Sutzkever, Abraham
Tunkeler, Der